MURDER INK

MURDER INK

THE MYSTERY READER'S COMPANION

PERPETRATED BY
DILYS WINN

WORKMAN PUBLISHING
NEW YORK

Published simultaneously in Canada by Saunders of Toronto, Inc.

Library of Congress Cataloging in Publication Data

Main entry under title:

Murder Ink.

Includes index.
1. Detective and mystery stories, English—Miscellanea. 2. Detective and mystery stories, American—Miscellanea. I. Winn, Dilys.
PR830.D4MS 823'.0872 77-5282
ISBN 0-89480-003-5
ISBN 0-89480-004-3 pbk.

Workman Publishing Company, Inc.
231 East 51 Street
New York, New York 10022

Manufactured in the United States of America
First printing September 1977
10 9 8 7 6 5 4 3 2

Cover photograph: Jerry Darvin
Designer: Paul Hanson

Dedication

Imagine, if you will, a Mission oak desk. Now, cover it with want lists and order forms and surround it with floor to ceiling bookcases. Behind it, seat a slim, graceful woman who loves mysteries so much, she owns a bookstore devoted to them. Her name is Carol Brener and her business life is a series of "Carol, what should I read next?" and "Carol, tell me your favorites" and "Carol, could we swap places?"

In effect, she and I did swap places. She had written a book, then decided she wanted to be a mystery store proprietor; I had been a proprietor, then became eager to do a book.

Neither of us could have done it without the other, I think, and as my friendly ghost wafts about her bookstore, so her helpful spirit permeates this book.

It is to Carol, therefore, that *Murder Ink* is dedicated. And it is on both our behalves that I thank the contributors, friends all, who have made the book and the bookstore our delight.

Indebtedness

M*urder Ink* is beholden to the imagination of Carolyn Fiske, Kathy Dean, Ben Matteson and the entire wacky staff at Mohonk Mountain House, New Paltz, New York; to the generosity of Marvin Epstein, Otto Penzler and Tina Serlin, who let us photograph parts of their libraries; to the midnight oil burned by researchers Archer Brown, Donna Dennis (photography), Marvin Epstein, Marie Gilmore, David James, Ben Kane, Betsy Lang, Marvin Lachman, Catherine Prezzano and Charles Shibuk; to the equanimity of Trade Composition, which made crises enjoyable and deadlines possible; to the gentle blue pencil and immaculate logic of Lynn Strong.

Most especially, *Murder Ink* is indebted to the maniacal humor and fail-safe supervision of Sally Kovalchick.

CONTENTS

Wilkie Collins

Nick, Nora and Asta

MARTY NORMAN

The Mystery Intelligentsia

2. PERPETRATORS

The Name Droppers

The Collaborators

The Series Writers

Combination Hearse and Chapel

The Second Careerists

The Writers at Home

3. BLOODHOUNDS

Mycroft's Heirs

The Great English Tea Break

Long-Suffering Heroines

4. PRIVATE EYES AND SPIES

The American Tough Guy

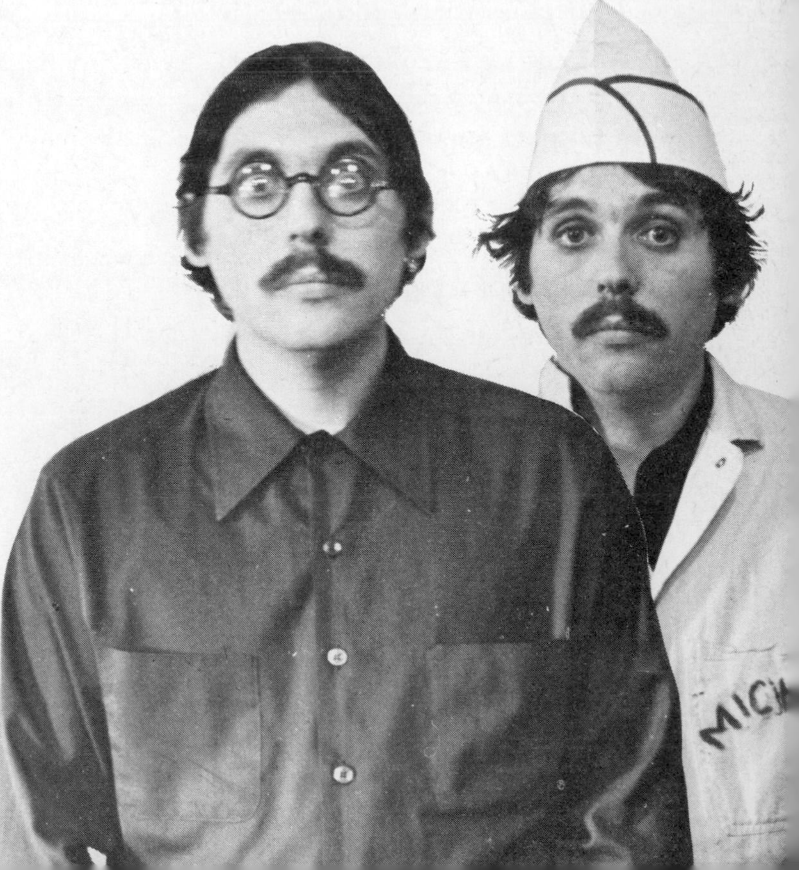

The Trench

MARTY NORMAN

Foreign Intrigue

5. VICTIMS

Say Goodbye

Means to an End

Has-Beens

The Late Lady Teasdale

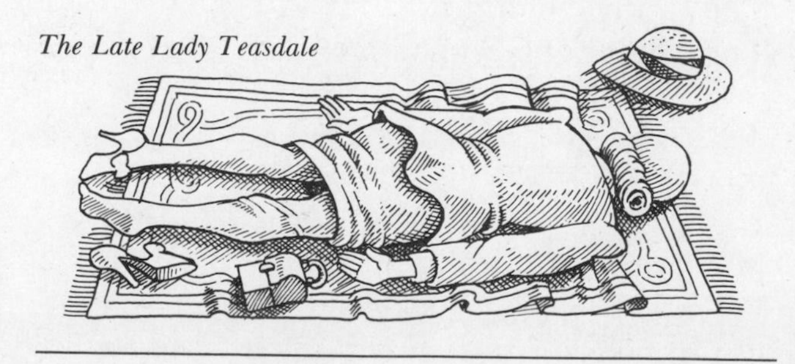

6. MODUS OPERANDI

Vocational Guidance

Hand-and-Eye Coordination

Murderous Impulses

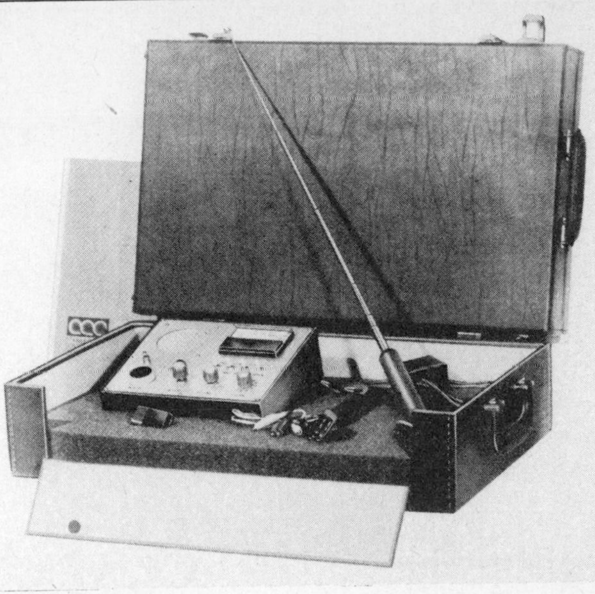

Debugging Equipment

7. SCENES OF THE CRIME

European Plan (Modified)

American Plan (Modified)

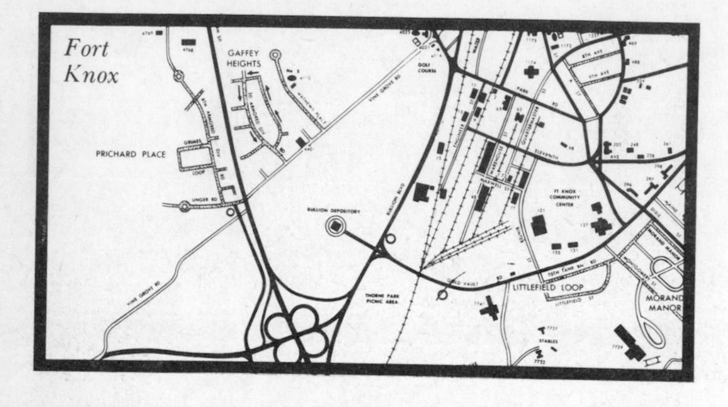

8. RED HERRINGS

English Deceit

American Treachery

9. COPS AND BOBBIES

The American Cop

New York's Finest

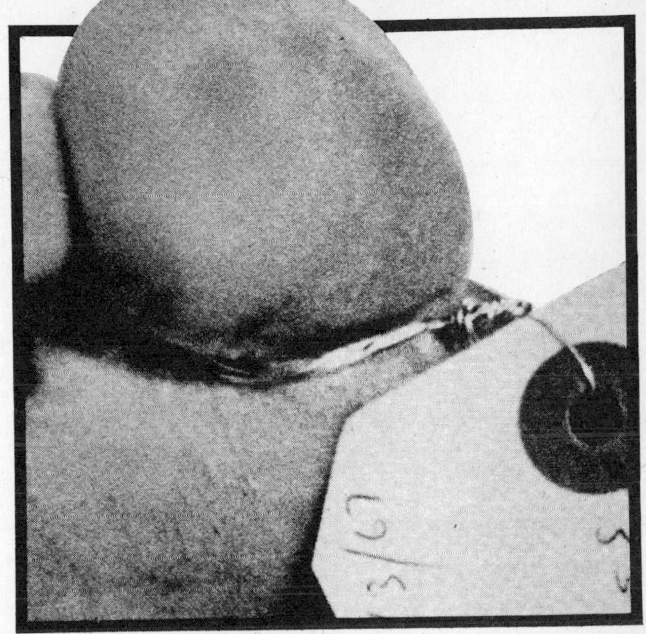

11. MOUTHPIECES

The Law Books

The Court Room

The Jail Cell

12. CAUGHT IN THE ACT

Theatrical Mysteries

Cinematic Mysteries

Sing Sing

The Good Old Days of Radio

Sigmund Freud and His Father

13. ACCESSORIES AFTER THE FACT

Defining the Mystery Reader

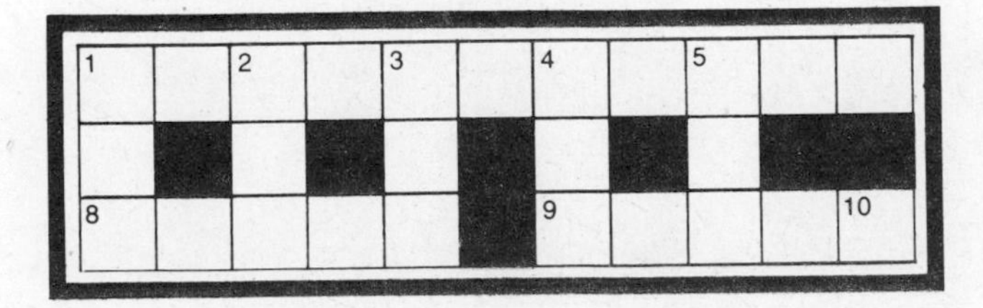

Fantasizing About Mysteries

Contacting Your Favorite Author

14. LOOKING FOR (MORE) TROUBLE

Ask An Expert

Sergeant Cuff

MARTY NORMAN

Find a Hobby

Develop a Personality

Introduction

On June 14, 1972, I opened a bookstore. On June 15, I considered changing its name. Murder Ink, the mystery bookstore, had seemed perfectly straightforward to me, but not one person who came through the door agreed with me as to what it really meant.

I developed a pat little speech: No, the store is not a "front" for the real Murder, Incorporated; no, there doesn't have to be a dead body in a book for me to carry it; no, I don't think I'm furthering the cause of crime by emphasizing novels concerned with it.

Gradually, customers' questions changed. In fact, so did the customers. No longer did Murder Ink receive the off-the-street trade. Instead, the people the store was intended for started coming in — the mystery fans.

Their queries were more sophisticated: Did I happen to know the requirements for becoming a private investigator? Did Nero Wolfe's brownstone have a front stoop or not? Why were microdots so frequently hidden on beauty spots? If I decided to burgle Fort Knox, how would I go about it? How many little grey cells did Poirot have? Where did the term "red herrings" originate? Did they still use toe tags at the morgue? Had I ever met Conan Doyle, Dorothy L. Sayers, Donald E. Westlake? Could I name all the winners of the Edgar for best mystery of the year? Where did English barristers get their wigs? Was there a mystery in which the butler actually did do it? How much would a first edition of *The Murders in the Rue Morgue* cost, and where could they find one? What's the best way to dispose of the body? Who weighs more, Bertha Cool or Gideon Fell? Was there a real St. Mary Mead? Had I ever known a courier, a safe-cracker, a stool pigeon, a dog that didn't bark? Which would I rather be, a cat burglar or a getaway-car driver? And hardest to handle of them all — please, would I define the mystery?

Many of the harder questions I couldn't answer, but on lucky days there'd be someone in the store who'd speak right up. These knowledgeable customers — some of them mystery writers, some of them hotel dicks and police sociologists and civil liberties lawyers, some of them "merely" mystery book fans — are the same ones I have turned to in compiling *Murder Ink.*

It is an attempt to answer the most frequently asked questions, to make the reader

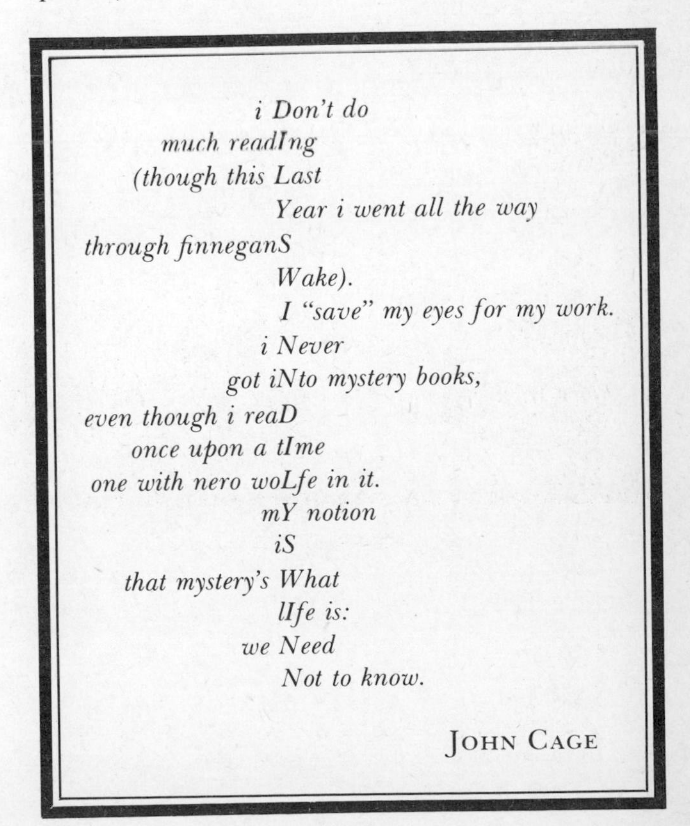

i Don't do
much readIng
(though this Last
Year i went all the way
through finneganS
Wake).
I "save" my eyes for my work.
i Never
got iNto mystery books,
even though i reaD
once upon a tIme
one with nero woLfe in it.
mY notion
iS
that mystery's What
lIfe is:
we Need
Not to know.

JOHN CAGE

an armchair participant in some of those discussions. That's why *Murder Ink* is called the mystery reader's companion.

Not all the articles deal with the mystery stories themselves. Some spring from the fantasies the books promote. To wit, if I ever met Holmes, what would I say to him? If I stole a paint chip from Lizzie Borden's house, how would I feel? What would I serve my victim for his very last meal? How would I go about writing a ransom note, using a blunt instrument, curing a Chandler-size hangover?

There have, of course, been many fine books on the origin of the mystery, its characters and its authors. But no one has tackled the fun of mystery. No one has tried to integrate a fan's fantasies with his love of the books and his desire to know where they depart from real life. That little niche, I think, belongs solely to *Murder Ink,* which has arranged this special meeting between the readers and the writers, the facts and the fantasies, and in the process had a very good time of it.

I would hope that *Murder Ink* has not forgotten anything you've been dying *(sic)* to know. That would be a crime.

Dilys Winn

Chapter 1

THE MYSTERY HISTORY

FRED WINKOWSKI

FROM POE TO THE PRESENT

Dilys Winn

CULVER PICTURES

I have an untidy mind. It confuses dates, misspells names, amalgamates plots and mangles facts. And it does it unrepentantly, presenting its little distortions as Gospel when, in fact, they're fibs. For years I attributed the first mystery to Carolyn Keene, Nancy Drew's creator, even though I knew full well a gentleman named Poe deserved the credit. I'd read Keene first, and according to my personal mystery chronology she rated the honor.

For solid research, I defer to Howard Haycraft. Now, in a handsome retirement community in south Jersey, Mr. Haycraft and his wife spend quiet afternoons thunking the croquet ball through the wickets. But back in '41 Mr. Haycraft authored *Murder for Pleasure,* the definitive mystery history, followed it up with *The Art of the Mystery Story,* the definitive mystery anthology, and then, with the assistance of Ellery Queen, issued his definitive mystery list, *The Haycraft-Queen Definitive Library of Detective-Crime-Mystery Fiction.* The list still stands as the best ever done, and Messrs. Haycraft and Queen were kind enough to let *Murder Ink* reprint it.

I hope Mr. Haycraft won't think it bad manners if I approach things a little differently. Where he is orderly, I am not. Where he tells how, when, why, what, in chronological sequence, I crave a hodgepodge history that pairs books of similar type rather than similar birth date.

I recognize five basic mystery categories: the Cozy, the Paranoid, the Romantic, the Vicious, the Analytical. (This leaves me no place for Rex Stout, but never mind; he really deserves a category unto himself.)

Of course, the Doyenne of Coziness is Agatha Christie, and the first book in the canon is *The Mysterious Affair at Styles.* Coziness, however, took another ten years to reach full kitsch, which happened when Miss Marple arrived in *The Murder at the Vicarage.* Alternately titled the Antimacassar-and-old-Port School, the Cozies surfaced in England in the mad Twenties and Thirties, and their work featured a small village

setting, a hero with faintly aristocratic family connections, a plethora of red herrings and a tendency to commit homicide with sterling silver letter openers and poisons imported from Paraguay. Typical Cozy writers include: Elizabeth Lemarchand, Margaret Yorke, V.C. Clinton-Baddeley, Anne Morice, Michael Gilbert, Michael Innes, Edmund Crispin. (And I've limited myself to those authors still in print: why suggest ones who defy disinterment?)

Special mention must be made of a Pseudo-Cozy: Dorothy L. Sayers. She teaches peculiar subjects (such as the art of bell-ringing) while she mystifies. Many Cozy readers appreciate this, and it's not uncommon to hear them remark, "Oh, I like a good read where I learn something. Mysteries teach me things!"

The Paranoid School began with Erskine Childers' spy novel, *The Riddle of the Sands,* and progressed through Sapper, through Ambler and Le Carré, to the Paranoid Politicals of Robert Ludlum. The archetypal Paranoid is Paul Kavanagh's *Such Men Are Dangerous*. These books are characterized by a mistrust of everybody, particularly one's "control." Nothing dates faster than a Paranoid novel: this year it's chic to be wary of the Chinese; last year, the Arabs; the year before, the South Africans. Often, Paranoids are concerned with the reemergence of Nazis (e.g., Levin's *The Boys from Brazil*). Though not strictly Paranoid, the Dick Francis books belong in this category because of the hero's sentimentality. Paranoid books represent the largest-selling category of mystery fiction today.

The Romantics are one part supernatural to two parts warped intuition. The father of the Romantic novel is Wilkie Collins, and his *Woman in White* remains the classic in the genre. These books, under Mary Roberts Rinehart's supervision, evolved into the Had-I-But-Known School. From the Fifties on, the Romantic converted to the Damsel-in-Distress novel, typified by the works of Phyllis A. Whitney, Mary Stewart and Barbara Michaels.

An aberrant strain of the Romantic is the Romantic Suspense, championed by Helen MacInnes. As her books are old-fashioned (Communism is a passé devil), she has been supplanted by Evelyn Anthony (who has stolen a leaf from the Paranoids and on occasion has gone after Nazism). A variant is the Historical Romantic Suspense. This is a splinter group: the Genuine Historical (i.e., any book written before 1918) and the Ersatz (written post–

BOOKS TO BE READ ALOUD

Anything by George V. Higgins. If you try to read these to yourself, you wind up moving your lips. Mr. Higgins loves dialogue, but it looks unintelligible on the page. It comes to life when you actually repeat the words. They are not the words, however, you would most want a maiden auntie to hear, nor kids under twelve. We suggest you read them out between deals in the poker game.

Wilkie Collins

Anything by Wilkie Collins. Draw your chair close to the fire and gather the family round. These are old-fashioned stories with hammy, improbable plots that somehow sound wonderful if you pretend you're Lunt and Fontaine and emote for all you're worth. So much the better if it's storming outside, the phone wires are down and you have to read by gaslight. A lap rug thrown over your knees is not inappropriate, either.

Anything by Stanley Ellin. Whenever anyone tells you mystery writers can't write, sit him down and read Stanley Ellin to him. Mr. Ellin is clear, direct and chilling. What's more, he is one of the few writers who has something to say to hard-boiled fans as well as classicists. His best for reading aloud purposes: *Stronghold.*

Anything by Margaret Millar. You know how some people just seem to have the knack of saying things that get under your skin? Millar hooks you in the first paragraph. You might just as well begin reading her with someone else, or you're going to spend all your time chasing after friends saying, "Listen to this," and then reading great chunks of books aloud to them.

Anything by Dashiell Hammett. Take your Chandler friend by the hand, put a piece of tape over his mouth, and tell him to just shut up and hear how it ought to be done. Hammett's style does not date, as does Chandler's and *The Glass Key* puts to shame every other hard-boiled writer.

World War I but depicting the past).

Which brings us round to the Vicious. Carroll John Daly elbowed it onto the scene in the late 1920's with hero Race Williams, but in truth a non-writer, Capt. Shaw of *Black Mask* magazine, was the man responsible for the genre's impact. These books all have a male protagonist, back-alley slang, enough booze to float the *Titanic* and a distressing way of blaming (1) the business partner or (2) the dame's father. Their partisans think of them as realistic. The best, bar none, of the Vicious writers was Dashiell Hammett; the worst, Mickey Spillane. Others include Chandler, Higgins, Leonard and Stark.

The Analytical School has the longest history. It began in 1841 with an errant orang-utan stuffing a young girl up a chimney in Poe's *The Murders in the Rue Morgue,* where the solution was resolved by a process called ratiocination — a 50¢ word for logical thinking. The Analytical then forked into Reasoning by Intellect and Reasoning by Machine: the former, from Poe direct to Conan Doyle to Carr; the latter, from Freeman to Reeves to McBain.

Cross-reading among the categories is rare. A Cozy reader will semi-comfortably pick up an Analytical but hardly admit that a Paranoid is part of the field. Similarly, a Romantic reader will sniff at the Vicious and insist they're outside the genre. According to Mr. Haycraft (and me), any book that focuses on crime is a mystery. So, readers should stop quibbling. This endless discussion of what belongs is really unnecessary; there's room for almost any style, as long as it concerns an evil. One could even make a case for calling *Crime and Punishment* a mystery. And who knows what lurks in next year?

Naturally, I have a preference. I can't tell you why I chose it, but I can say this: My methods of dealing with people who disagree with me are not pleasant.

500 CLUB

Only two authors have written over 500 books: John Creasey and Charles Hamilton. There are over 500 books by Nicholas Carter, but Nicholas Carter was more than one person. It was a name assigned to a series of writers who were responsible for the exploits of one Nick Carter. The publisher passed the name on from writer to writer.

HALL OF INFAMY

(THE TEN WORST)

1. *The Mind Readers* by Margery Allingham
2. *Trent's Last Case* by E.C. Bentley
3. *The Hungry Goblin* by John Dickson Carr
4. *Playback* by Raymond Chandler
5. *Elephants Can Remember* by Agatha Christie
6. *Valley of Fear* by Arthur Conan Doyle
7. *The Defection of A.J. Lewinter* by Robert Littell
8. *When in Rome* by Ngaio Marsh
9. *Busman's Honeymoon* by Dorothy L. Sayers
10. *The President Vanishes* by Rex Stout

(THE FIVE BEST)

1. *The Daughter Of Time* by Josephine Tey
2. *The Thirty-First of February* by Julian Symons
3. *Time and Again* by Jack Finney
4. *Who is Lewis Pindar?* by L.P. Davies
5. *The Glass Key* by Dashiell Hammett

HEARING VOICES IN MY HEAD

Tucker Coe, Timothy J. Culver, Richard Stark and Donald E. Westlake

Recently gathered with a moderator inside a Japanese-made cassette recorder to discuss the state of their art were Donald E. Westlake, Richard Stark, Tucker Coe and Timothy J. Culver.

MODERATOR: The mystery story, detective thriller, *roman policier,* call it what you will, has been a basic influence in the history of fiction since the days of Greece and Rome. While Edgar Allan Poe is the acknowledged father of the modern detective story, it is still true that *Oedipus Rex* is a seminal mystery tale. Today's novelists of crime, passion, suspense, can with pride count Shakespeare, Dostoevsky and the Brothers Grimm among their family tree. Tucker Coe, what do *you* think of all this?

TUCKER COE: Sounds terrific.

MODERATOR: Ah. Yes. I see. Well, umm . . . Richard Stark. As an —

RICHARD STARK: Present.

MODERATOR: Yes. As an innovator in the crime field, suspense story, call it what you will, what would you say is the outlook for the mystery tale? You have been —

RICHARD STARK: Well, I think —

MODERATOR: — an innovator, of course, in that you created Parker, a professional thief who never gets caught. Also, he is not merely a thinly disguised battler for the underdog, as were Robin Hood or The Saint or The Green Hornet. Parker's reaction to the underdog would probably have been to kick it. Having yourself altered the thriller or mystery form, what would you say are the portents for tomorrow?

RICHARD STARK: Well, I suppose —

MODERATOR: People have declared the detective novel, the murder story itself, dead, murdered by repetition, staleness, a using up of all the potentials of the form, replaced by who knows what public fancies, whether for Comedy, History, Pastoral, Pastoral-Comical, Historical-Pastor —

RICHARD STARK: Say, wait a minute.

MODERATOR: Or, let us say, the Western, Science Fiction, the Family Saga. Nevertheless, the crime/suspense/mystery/thriller story, the tale of ratiocination, call it what you will, has continued to flourish, much like the Grand Old Lady of the Theater, the Broadway Stage, which so often has —

RICHARD STARK: Listen.

MODERATOR: — been reported dead. But, if we may borrow a phrase, Watchman, what of the night? What do *you* think tomorrow will bring to the thriller, the detective —

RICHARD STARK: *I* think it's —

MODERATOR: — story, the *roman noir,* the 'tec tale, call it what you —

RICHARD STARK: Listen, you. Either I get to *answer* that question or I'll damage you.

MODERATOR: — will, the essential — Eh? Oh, yes. Certainly.

RICHARD STARK: Right. Now. Uhh — What was the question?

MODERATOR: Well, the gist of the —

RICHARD STARK: Not you. Tim?

TIMOTHY J. CULVER: Future of the mystery.

RICHARD STARK: Right. There isn't any.

MODERATOR: There isn't any?

RICHARD STARK: The detective story died about thirty years ago, but that's okay. Poetry died *hundreds* of years ago and there're still poets. By "die," by "dead," I mean as a hot center of public interest. In the Thirties you could still have whodunits, real honest-to-God *detective* stories, on the best-seller lists. Ellery Queen, for instance. The detective story was hot when science was new, with gaslight and then electricity, telephones, automobiles, everything starting up, the whole *world* seeming to get solved all at once, in one life span. World War II shifted the emphasis from gaining knowledge to what you'd do with the knowledge, which is kill people. So the big postwar detective was Mike Hammer, who couldn't *deduce* his way up a flight of stairs, and the emphasis shifted from whodunit to who's-gonna-get-it. The Mike Hammer thing leads into all these paperback hobnail vigilantes with their *Thesaurus* names: the Inflictor, the Chastiser, the Flagellator. Deduction, the solving of a mystery — they don't even put in a token appearance any more.

MODERATOR: But does that mean you yourself have given up the mystery field, thriller field, whatever label you may choose —

RICHARD STARK: Grrrrrrrr.

MODERATOR: Sorry. But no new Parker novel has been published since 1974. *Have* you given up writing crime novels, thrillers, or — um.

RICHARD STARK: Parker is a Depression character, Dillinger mythologized into a machine. During the affluent days of the Sixties he was an interesting fantasy, but now that money's getting tight again his relationship with banks is suddenly both to the point and old-fashioned. He hasn't yet figured out how to operate in a world where heisting *is* one of the more rational responses to the situation.

MODERATOR: Tucker Coe, do you agree?

TUCKER COE: Well, yes and no, I suppose. In a way. Looking at all sides of the issue, *without* becoming overly involved in a too personal way, if we could avoid that, insofar as it's ever really possible to avoid personal involvement in a discussion of one's own work, I suppose the simple answer is that for *me* the detective story was ultimately too restricting. Others, of course, might find possibilities I missed. I'm sure they will, and the problem was as much in me as in the choice of character and genre.

MODERATOR: Would you care to amplify that, to give us further insights into —

RICHARD STARK: Watch it. Go ahead, Tuck.

TUCKER COE: Thanks. The problem for me was that Mitch Tobin wasn't a static character. For him to remain miserable and guilt-racked forever would have changed him into a self-pitying whiner. My problem was, once Mitch Tobin reaches that new stability and becomes functional in the world again, he's merely one more private eye with an unhappy past. Not to name names, but don't we have *enough* slogging private eyes with unhappy pasts?

MODERATOR: But surely the detective story has been used as a vehicle for exploring character. Nedra Tyre, for instance. Patricia Highsmith, Raymond Chandler.

RICHARD STARK: His sentences were too fat.

MODERATOR: But wasn't he interested in character?

RICHARD STARK: He was interested in literature. That's the worst thing that can happen to a writer.

TIMOTHY J. CULVER: I couldn't agree more.

And let me say, I speak from a different perspective from everybody else here. These guys all write what *they* want to write, I write what *other people* want me to write. I'm a hack, I'm making a living, I'm using whatever craft I've learned to turn out decently professional work that I'm not personally involved with. In my opinion, the best writers are always people who don't care about anything except telling you what's in their heads, *without boring you.* Passion, plus craft. The Continental Op didn't have to have a miserable home life or a lot of character schticks because Hammett could fill him up with his own reality.

MODERATOR: But mystery novelists are nevertheless commercial writers, aren't they? Mr. Culver, I don't entirely follow the distinction you're making.

TIMOTHY J. CULVER: The difference between a hack and a writer is that the hack puts down on paper things he doesn't believe. Dick Stark mentioned Mike Hammer. Now, Mickey Spillane wasn't a hack, not then at least, and that's because he really *believed* all that paranoid crap. But the thousand imitators didn't believe it. You know, one time I was talking to a professor at the University of Pennsylvania, and he had to leave the party early to go work on an article for one of the scholarly journals. I asked him what it was about, and he said it didn't matter, just some piece of crap. "But I have to keep turning them out if I want tenure," he said. "It's pretty much publish or perish in this business." "It's about the same in mine," I told him.

MODERATOR: Frankly, Mr. Culver, you sound to me like a cynic.

TIMOTHY J. CULVER: I act based on my opinion of the world, so I am a realist.

MODERATOR: Donald E. Westlake, from your vantage point, would you say that Mr. Culver seems to be a realist?

DONALD E. WESTLAKE: Sure he is. A realist is somebody who thinks the world is simple enough to be understood. It isn't.

TIMOTHY J. CULVER: I understand it well enough to get by.

DONALD E. WESTLAKE: Meaning you can tie your own shoelaces. Terrific.

MODERATOR: Gentlemen, gentlemen. Um, Mr. Westlake, you yourself began with the traditional detective novels, did you not?

DONALD E. WESTLAKE: The first story I ever wrote was about a professional killer knocking off a Mob boss. I thought it would be nice to make the setting a fancy office, as though the Mob boss were a lawyer or a doctor. I was eleven years old, the story was about two hundred words long, and all that happened was this guy walked in, stepped around the bodyguards, shot the Mob boss at his desk, and then walked out again. But the point was the long detailed description of the office. I was in love with what I suppose was my first discovery as a writer: that there was something marvelous in a contrast between setting and action. A mismatch between What and Where could create interest all by itself. Of course, now I realize it was comedy that had taught me all that — the fart in church, for instance, a favorite among all children — but I never thought comedy was what I was good at. All through school, I was never the funniest kid, I was always the funniest kid's best friend. I was a terrific audience.

MODERATOR: And yet, now you are known primarily as the author of comic caper novels, comedy thrillers, what Anthony Boucher termed the comedy of peril, call it what you will —

DONALD E. WESTLAKE: Taradiddle.

MODERATOR: I beg your pardon?

DONALD E. WESTLAKE: You want me to call these books what I will, and that's what I call them. Taradiddles. Tortile taradiddles.

MODERATOR: Tortile . . .

DONALD E. WESTLAKE: Taradiddles.

MODERATOR: Yes. Well, these, um, things . . . You are primarily known for them, so what led you from ordinary detective stories to these, hm?

DONALD E. WESTLAKE: I couldn't take them seriously any more. I did five books, and started a sixth, and it kept wanting to be funny. As Dick Stark pointed out, there isn't much money in writing mystery novels, so I wasn't risking a lot if I went ahead and wrote it funny. At that time, there weren't any comic mysteries around, so I couldn't prejudge the reception. Craig Rice had been the last comic detective novelist. But ideas and feelings float in the air, and later on it turned out that simultaneously a guy named John Godey, who later became famous for *The Taking of Pelham 1-2-3,* was writing a comic mystery novel called *A Thrill a Minute with Jack Albany.* It constantly happens: writers who don't know one another come up with the same shift in emphasis or the same new subject matter at the same time. We all swim in the same culture, of course.

MODERATOR: Would you say you were influenced by Craig Rice?

DONALD E. WESTLAKE: No, I wouldn't. *She* was influenced by Thorne Smith, who was magnificent, but every time I try to borrow from Thorne Smith the material dies in my hands. It's difficult to be truly whimsical without being arch; I can't do it.

MODERATOR: And P.G. Wodehouse?

DONALD E. WESTLAKE: He couldn't do it, either. That's a minority opinion, of course.

MODERATOR: Would you care to talk about who *has* influenced your work?

DONALD E. WESTLAKE: Not until they're in the public domain.

MODERATOR: I suppose you've been asked where you get your ideas.

DONALD E. WESTLAKE: Never. Who would ask a schmuck question like that?

MODERATOR: I see. Yes. To return to this first, um, tortile — ?

DONALD E. WESTLAKE: *The Dead Nephew.*

MODERATOR: Really? My fact sheet says *The Fugitive Pigeon.*

DONALD E. WESTLAKE: Your fact sheet is on the money. I haven't always been lucky with titles. At the time, I was persuaded to change from the original, but now, sixteen years later, I'd rather be the author of *The Dead Nephew* than *The Fugitive Pigeon.*

MODERATOR: Why?

DONALD E. WESTLAKE: It's funnier and it's meaner, and therefore more to the point.

MODERATOR: To *return* to the point, you wrote this first tortile taradiddle because you —

DONALD E. WESTLAKE: Nicely done.

MODERATOR: — couldn't — thank you — take the mystery novel seriously any more. Does that mean you agree with Richard Stark about the gloomy future of the crime story, the thriller, the detective novel, call it what you will?

DONALD E. WESTLAKE: Depends on what you call it.

MODERATOR: I beg your pardon?

DONALD E. WESTLAKE: I have a friend, Robert Ludlum, who writes —

TIMOTHY J. CULVER: Name-dropper.

DONALD E. WESTLAKE: — books, and very good books, too, which are full of suspense, mysteries to be solved, murders, detection, crime, chases, *all* the elements of the mystery story. If they were called mysteries or detective stories, if they were placed on the publisher's "Mystery List," they would sell a fraction of what they do. The best-seller list is crammed with sheep in wolves' clothing. Sidney Sheldon, Frederick Forsyth, Jack Higgins under all his many names.

TIMOTHY J. CULVER: You should talk.

DONALD E. WESTLAKE: Tim, you *are* a pest.

TIMOTHY J. CULVER: But indispensable.

DONALD E. WESTLAKE: Like the Sanitation Department. You take the garbage.

MODERATOR: Gentlemen, gentlemen. If mystery novels appear on the best-seller list under another category name, would you be willing to reveal that name?

DONALD E. WESTLAKE: "Blockbuster." You see an ad for a book, it says the book is a blockbuster, that means it's a category crime novel — usually forty thousand words too fat — breaking for the big money.

MODERATOR: Then why aren't *all* mystery novels simply called blockbusters?

DONALD E. WESTLAKE: Because they have to be Fifties mystery novels, full of Kirk Douglas–type characters. If you write Thirties mystery novels, whodunits with puzzles and clever murderers (never killers) and cleverer detectives, or if you write Forties private eye novels — "A mean man walks down these lone streets" — you can't possibly get out of the ghetto.

Moderator: What about Ross Macdonald?

Donald E. Westlake: The former editor of the *New York Times Book Review* has admitted in print that that was the result of a conspiracy, to see if he really *could* boost an author he liked onto the best-seller list. Since he claimed that was the only time such a conspiracy occurred, to his knowledge, Macdonald is a fluke.

Moderator: Do you have an opinion about his work?

Donald E. Westlake: He must have terrific carbon paper.

Moderator: You mentioned Thirties, Forties and Fifties crime novels. What about the Sixties?

Donald E. Westlake: The Sixties crime novel was joky (as opposed to funny), smart-alecky, full of drugs, and self-consciously parading its cast of blacks and homosexuals. The only Sixties mysteries with any merit at all were written in the Fifties by Chester Himes. On the other hand, the Sixties Western was even worse: Remember *Dirty Dingus Magee?*

Richard Stark: Okay, this has gone on long enough. Everybody on your feet.

Moderator: Good God, he's got a gun!

Richard Stark: Empty your pockets onto the table. Come on, snap it up.

Timothy J. Culver: You can't mean this, Dick. We're your friends.

Richard Stark: No book published since '74. How do you think I live? Give me everything you got.

Donald E. Westlake: Will you take a check?

Richard Stark: *Beat the Devil,* 1954, Robert Morley to Humphrey Bogart. They ought to ask *me* where you get your ideas. You, Tucker Coe, on your feet.

Moderator: He's not moving, he —

Richard Stark: Get him up. You, Moderator.

Moderator: He's dead!

Timothy J. Culver: This waterglass — yes, just as I thought. A rare undetectable South American poison. Tucker Coe has been murdered.

Donald E. Westlake: I didn't do it!

Moderator: Wait a minute. If the poison is undetectable, how do you know that's how he was killed?

Timothy J. Culver: There isn't a mark on the body, the glass contains a colorless, odorless liquid, and none of us has left the room. Isn't the conclusion obvious?

Richard Stark: Let's not forget me over here with my gun. Cough up your money and valuables.

Moderator: I can't believe this is happening.

Richard Stark: Hey, Culver, *this* is all you got?

Timothy J. Culver: Realists don't travel with a lot of cash.

Richard Stark: You, Moderator, get me the stuff out of Coe's pockets.

Moderator: You want me to rob a corpse?

Richard Stark: Rob one or be one, the choice is yours. That's better.

Timothy J. Culver: We'll see about —

Moderator: They're struggling! Look out!

Richard Stark: You asked for —

Moderator: You shot him! Timothy J. Culver is dead!

Richard Stark: No mystery about *that* body.

Donald E. Westlake: I didn't kill Tucker Coe!

Richard Stark: Anybody else feel like a hero? No? All right; don't move from this room for thirty minutes.

Moderator: Good God! He's getting away!

Donald E. Westlake: I want to make one thing clear. I didn't kill Tucker Coe.

Moderator: We don't dare leave. We have to stay in the room with these two bodies. What can we *do* for the next half-hour?

Donald E. Westlake: We could play Twenty Questions. I'm thinking of something that's part vegetable and part mineral.

Moderator: Oh, shut up.

Tucker Coe's five Chandleresque novels came to an abrupt end about 1970. Timothy J. Culver's only known work, Ex Officio, *was published to universal indifference. Richard Stark's sixteen novels feature Parker, the professional criminal with the heart of granite. Donald E. Westlake's* God Save the Mark *won the Mystery Writers of America Edgar.*

The Most Asked Question: WHY DO PEOPLE READ DETECTIVE STORIES?

Gladys Mitchell

I suppose one answer to this question is that people read them because other people write them. Why do other people write them? Well, according to Dr. Samuel Johnson, no man ever wrote who did not write for money.

There are those among us who claim that the detective story is a form of escapist literature. Lovers of the genre will deny this, and they are right to do so, for the detective story addict is not content to sit back and enjoy what is called "a cosy read." For full enjoyment of the story, the reader needs to be prepared to use his brains. A problem has been set before him, and the true addict obtains pleasure from doing his best to solve it.

When the Detection Club was formed in London, England, very strict rules were laid down for the members to follow. The first and greatest commandment was that every clue to the identity of the criminal must be placed fairly before the reader. This provided for a true and just battle of wits between reader and author, and this, I think, is one of the main reasons why people prefer those detective stories which keep to the rules.

Here, perhaps, it may be a good thing to repeat an observation which others have stressed. To the uninitiated, all classes of mystery fiction are apt to be classed as "thrillers," but to the intelligentsia the rough-and-ready story of breakneck adventure, car chase, mysterious master criminal, sex, bloodthirstiness and highly coloured heroics is but the bastard brother of the classic whodunit and is not to the taste of the true detective aficionado.

The thriller poses no problem, makes no tax upon the reader except perhaps to find out how much blood and guts he can stomach, so

MYSTERY BOOK CLUBS

Detective Book Club
Established in April of 1942, this club offers the famous "triple" volume — three complete mystery novels under one cover. Selections offered on a monthly basis.

Mystery Guild
Presents two feature selections per month, plus alternates, in a lively brochure called "Clues." Most offerings are roughly one-quarter of the publisher's list price.

Thriller Book Club
Developed by Foyle's, London's most famous bookstore, this club features most major authors, with an emphasis on the British.

that its chief merit is to take the reader from his own safe, fireside existence into what P.G. Wodehouse would call "another and a dreadful world." This makes a strong appeal to some minds but is not for the reader of detective stories, except as an occasional relaxation.

Of course, the detective story has changed over the years. Not for nothing did Dorothy L. Sayers call her last full-length Wimsey tale "a love story with detective interruptions." Of old, the purists laid down the axiom that love had no place in a detective story and was nothing but an unnecessary and most undesirable effluent when introduced into those otherwise unpolluted waters. It confused the narrative and dammed the flow of pure reason, for love's

THE PHYSIOLOGY OF READING

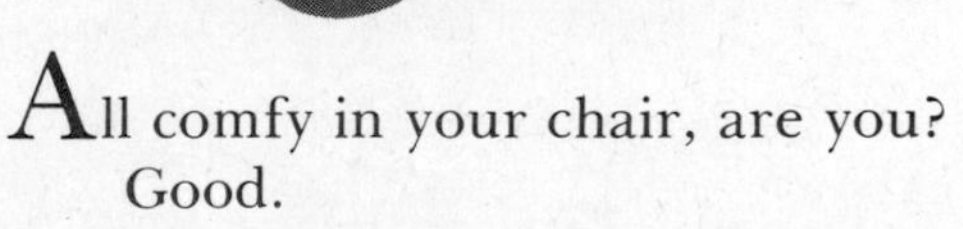

All comfy in your chair, are you?

Good.

What you are sitting on are your ischial tuberosities. Depending on how fat you are, you may or may not be able to feel them since they are the bones of your, ahem, rear end. They are covered by your gluteus maximus, which is a network of muscle.

If you are sitting in such a position that your feet do not touch the floor, you are undoubtedly tensing your gluteus maximus, which is not such a good idea. You should try to make contact with the floor by putting pressure on your calcanei, commonly called your heel bones. This will relieve the pressure on your rear.

A chair seat should not be so deep as to keep your feet from reaching the floor. On the other hand, it should be deep enough so that it does not cut across the buttock crease, causing pressure on your sciatic foramen.

Should you suffer from coccygodynia, you are experiencing a pain in your coccyx. It is unlikely that this pain is aggravated by reading in a chair, but in the event that you have trouble with it, you are advised to read while sitting on a rubber doughnut.

An unstable point in many people is the junction of the lumbar spine and the sacrum. Unless this is properly supported, you may fall victim to lumbosacral strain (lower back pain). So you should not read in a chair without a backrest — such as a barstool.

A reading chair should have a seat cushion. The back cushion is optional. But again, a fairly high-backed reading chair is a must or you will put undue strain on the articulations of your spinal facets. This means you are not supporting your upper back correctly. May we remind you that with incorrect support you lose your normal lordotic curve. A dire situation indeed.

If you think you can circumvent all these problems by reading in bed, you will be unhappy to learn that that can cause strain on the cervical area. Resulting in a severe pain in the neck. You should sit up in bed, leaning against the headboard, with your feet straight out in front of you. This also protects you from those who would sneak up behind to give you a stout cosh.

Still comfy, are you?

Good. Then we'll leave you to your book.

detractors (so far as the detective story is concerned) can rightly claim that there is nothing so unreasonable, so utterly illogical, as love. The unreasonable and the illogical have no place in a detective story.

Times change, however, and so do the fictional detectives themselves — among whom, I suppose, every one of us has a favourite. The painstaking detective measuring footprints, treasuring cigarette ends, taking fingerprints, is a genuine character in real life and often "gets his man," but in fiction his worthy, molelike activities are apt to give a somewhat dull read. In fact, Edgar Allan Poe described (and, by implication, despised) the fictional use of the method.

> *"You include the* grounds *about the house?"*
>
> *"They gave us comparatively little trouble. We examined the moss between the bricks and found it undisturbed."*
>
> *"You looked among D———'s papers, of course, and into the books of the library?"*
>
> *"Certainly; we not only opened every book, but we turned over every leaf in each volume. We also measured the thickness of every book-*cover."
>
> *"You explored the floors beneath the carpets? . . . and the paper on the walls? . . . You looked into the cellars?"*

This is far removed from the Chestertonian girth and intellect of Dr. Gideon Fell and farther still from "the little grey cells" of Hercule Poirot. Nowadays the gentlemanly detectives, Alleyn, Campion, Wimsey, the don-detective Gervase Fen, the delightful Inspector Ghote, Hillary Waugh's indefatigable policemen baying like hounds on the trail and the quirky legalities in the plots of Cyril Hare have taken over, to some extent, from the older, more plodding sleuths of earlier years.

I am far from believing that people read detective stories in order to learn new methods of committing murder, but it is a fact that, greatly to the author's distress, after Anthony Berkeley had published perhaps his best-known book, a real-life murderer successfully employed the method described in that book and strangled his victim with a silk stocking — the first time, it appears, that such an object had been used in real life for an act of thuggery.

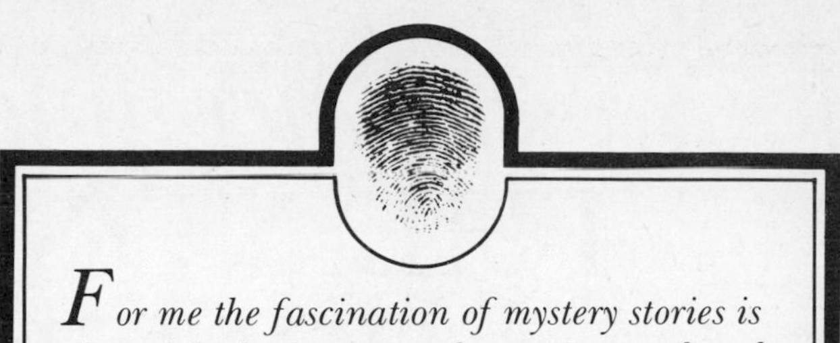

For me the fascination of mystery stories is that of the beckoning unkown. I am seduced by suspense. In fiction as in life, I am lured on by eagerness to find out what is going to happen in the next chapter—and, in the end, whodunit.

ELLIOT L. RICHARDSON

Conversely, the police learned a thing or two when they attempted a reconstruction of the method they thought might have been used by the hymn-playing George Joseph Smith when he drowned three successive wives in the bath. The police reconstruction was almost too conclusive, for they nearly drowned their volunteer victim and had difficulty in bringing her back to consciousness. The method, which I shall not describe, has been used subsequently in at least one detective story.

So why *do* people read detective stories? I think one of the main reasons is that such books must, above all things, have a definite plot. Modern literature is full of plays and films that end nowhere; novels and short stories which leave the playgoer or the reader suspended in mid-air, forced either to impotent irritation or else to having to invent the outcome.

Detective stories, by their very nature, cannot cheat in this way. Their writers must tidy up the loose ends; must supply a logical solution to the problem they have posed; must also, to hold the reader's attention, combine the primitive lust and energy of the hunter with the cold logic of the scholarly mind.

Above all, they must concentrate upon murder, although they may also say, with Robert Herrick's bellman:

> *From noise of scare-fires rest ye free,*
> *From murders Benedicite.*

Gladys Mitchell received the Crime Writers' Association Silver Daggar for her fifty novels featuring Dame Beatrice Bradley.

Street Encounter Past Midnight
THE NONBELIEVER'S COMEUPPANCE

Jacques Barzun

Crossing New York's Sherman Plaza late in a chilly November — the clock then striking one — I saw advancing toward me from the northeast something light-footed and cloud-like. It came along 59th Street as if from the Playboy Club, but it was no ordinary Bunny. When only a few steps away, it assumed a man's shape, and though still rather translucent it spoke in a firm, almost truculent voice.

GHOST: Remember me? Know who I am?

J.B.: Yes, you're the great critic I used to argue with, the man who said he didn't care *who* killed Roger Ackroyd and professed to be unmoved by the famous words, "Mr. Holmes, they were the footprints of a gigantic hound."

GHOST: You're wrong there. I was moved — moved to laughter — or would have been if I had wasted my time on that kind of trash.

J.B.: You can't have it both ways. You *did* read and you disliked what you read. That's your privilege, but it confers no right of moral snobbery. But tell me, what do they think of crime fiction down where you come from?

GHOST: They loathe and despise it as I do. Crime holds no mystery for them; they know all about it ex officio.

J.B.: That's what I thought. It's only up here among living men that the idea of law, of an ordered life, coupled with an inquisitive impatience about mysteries and a skill in piercing them, provides rich materials for entertaining tales.

GHOST: There you are. Entertainment. You've given your case away. I don't read for entertainment, but for knowledge and wisdom.

J.B.: And that is what shuts out detective stories. First you stiffen your mind against pleasure and then you look for things that the genre doesn't afford. You're a bad reader.

GHOST: What do you mean! It is generally admitted that I'm the best reader since — since —

J.B.: McGuffey? Yes, of course, you were an indefatigable reader. You had to read in order to write those serious accounts of serious books, terribly serious. Now many of those books are seen to be dull, false, pretentious, though you called them "important," "significant," "moving," "original." That's what happens in every age. If you'd begun by taking pleasure in literature instead of studying it, you wouldn't have been fooled so often. Try to read Galsworthy now and see if Dorothy Sayers doesn't wear better.

GHOST: I shan't do either, but I know that Galsworthy keeps the mind working on something. The substance may be thin, but it's there, the stuff of which great books could be made.

J.B.: I know, Galsworthy had "ideas" and Sayers hasn't. That's your second error. You don't know a novel from a tale. A tale is its own excuse for being; it doesn't have to stuff your well-filled mind still fuller and make it stuffier yet. A tale charms by its ingenuity, by the plausibility with which it overcomes the suspicion that it couldn't happen. That is art. Learn to enjoy it. Read a few fairy tales, a few Arabian Nights to clear your mind of "knowledge and wisdom." Save your long face and restless eyes for the really great novelists who do handle the stuff of life and impart wisdom about it.

GHOST: There's no art outside of that; there's none in your rubbishy "tales" because there's nothing — not a thing — to carry away and reflect on.

J.B.: Of course there is. If you can grow lyrical over Proust's crumb of cake in the teacup, you can find charm in the ambiguity of any clue. The dog that did nothing in the nighttime is as justly famous as Cerberus, and T.S. Eliot found so much poetry in the Musgrave ritual that he lifted it to give a little class to one of his plays. Your trouble, dear Ghost, is — or was — that you poisoned your mind with sociology and stale ideas, so that you lost the power to appreciate the staples of literature: invention, surprise and suspense, plot and peripeteia, terse dialogue and good prose generally. Bone up on those and you'll soon be able to tell a good crime tale from a dull one, a Holmes from a Hawkshaw. Then perhaps your objections will fade away — as I see *you're* about to do. My regards to all our shady friends!

Jacques Barzun is coauthor with W.H. Taylor of A Catalogue of Crime.

MARTY NORMAN

THE HAYCRAFT-QUEEN DEFINITIVE LIBRARY OF DETECTIVE-CRIME-MYSTERY FICTION

Two Centuries of Cornerstones, 1748–1948

Please note that all the titles suggested by Ellery Queen are identified by an asterisk (*), and that all the comments shown in small italic type were written by Queen and, therefore, do not necessarily reflect Mr. Haycraft's opinions.

1748 Voltaire:
**Zadig*

The Great-grandfather of the Detective Story

1828–9 François Eugène Vidocq:
**Mémoires de Vidocq*

The Grandfather of the Detective Story

1845 Edgar Allan Poe:
Tales

The Father of the Detective Story

1852–3 Charles Dickens:
Bleak House;
The Mystery of Edwin Drood, 1870

1856 "Waters" (William Russell):
**Recollections of a Detective Police-Officer*

The first English detective yellow-back

1860 Wilkie Collins:
**The Woman in White*

1862 Victor Hugo:
**Les Misérables*
(First edition in English, also 1862)

1866 Feodor Dostoevsky:
**Crime and Punishment*
(First edition in English, 1886)

1866 Émile Gaboriau:
L'Affaire Lerouge;
**Le Dossier No 113, 1867;*
**Le Crime d'Orcival, 1868;*
Monsieur Lecoq, 1869

The Father of the Detective Novel

1868 Wilkie Collins:
The Moonstone

The Father of the English Detective Novel

1872 (Harlan Page Halsey):
**Old Sleuth, the Detective, 1885*

The first Dime Novel detective story

1874 Allan Pinkerton:
**The Expressman and the Detective*

1878 Anna Katharine Green:
The Leavenworth Case

The Mother of the American Detective Novel

1882 Robert Louis Stevenson:
**New Arabian Nights;*
**Strange Case of Dr Jekyll and Mr Hyde, 1886*

Was it Maurice Richardson who said of this book that it is the only detective-crime story he knows in which the solution is more terrifying than the problem?

1887 Fergus W. Hume:
**The Mystery of a Hansom Cab*

An historically important book

1887 A. Conan Doyle:
A Study in Scarlet;
The Sign of Four, 1890;
The Adventures of Sherlock Holmes, 1892;
The Memoirs of Sherlock Holmes, 1894;
The Hound of the Baskervilles, 1902;
The Return of Sherlock Holmes, 1905;
The Valley of Fear, 1915;
His Last Bow, 1917;
The Case-Book of Sherlock Holmes, 1927

The listing of all the Sherlock Holmes books—the complete works—is sheer idolatry. Surely the first Holmes story, A Study in Scarlet, is an undeniable cornerstone; also The Adventures and The Memoirs; and the best of the novels should also be present in any definitive detective library. Most critics would probably select The Hound as the best novel; John Dickson Carr's choice is The Valley of Fear.

1892 Israel Zangwill:
The Big Bow Mystery

1894 Mark Twain:
**The Tragedy of Pudd'nhead Wilson*

1894 Arthur Morrison:
Martin Hewitt, Investigator

1895 M.P. Shiel:
**Prince Zaleski*

1897 Bram Stoker:
**Dracula*

A mystery classic — interpreting "mystery" in its broadest sense

---

1899 E.W. Hornung:
**The Amateur Cracksman*

The first Raffles book — "detection in reverse"

1903 (Erskine Childers):
**The Riddle of the Sands*

Recommended by Christopher Morley as the classic secret service novel

---

1906 Godfrey R. Benson:
Tracks in the Snow

1906 Robert Barr:
The Triumphs of Eugène Valmont

1907 Jacques Futrelle:
The Thinking Machine

1907 Maurice Leblanc:
**Arsène Lupin, Gentleman-Cambrioleur; *"813," 1910*

The Leblanc-Lupin masterpiece

Les Huits Coups de l'Horloge, 1922

1907 Gaston Leroux:
Le Mystère de la Chambre Jaune;
**Le Parfum de la Dame en Noir, 1908–9*

1907 R. Austin Freeman:
The Red Thumb Mark

The first Dr. Thorndyke book

**John Thorndyke's Cases, 1909;*
**The Eye of Osiris, 1911;*
The Singing Bone, 1912

The first "inverted" detective stories

1908 Mary Roberts Rinehart:
The Circular Staircase

The founding of the Had-I-But Known School

1908 O. Henry:
**The Gentle Grafter*

1908 G.K. Chesterton:
**The Man Who Was Thursday;*
The Innocence of Father Brown, 1911

1909 Cleveland Moffett:
**Through the Wall*

A neglected highspot

1909 Baroness Orczy:
The Old Man in the Corner

1909 Carolyn Wells:
The Clue

The first Fleming Stone book

1910 A.E.W. Mason:
At the Villa Rose

The first Hanaud book

The House of the Arrow, 1924

1910 William MacHarg and Edwin Balmer:
**The Achievements of Luther Trant*

The first book of short stories to make scientific use of psychology as a method of crime detection

---

1912 Arthur B. Reeve:
The Silent Bullet

The first Craig Kennedy book

1913 Mrs. Belloc Lowndes:
The Lodger

One of the earliest "suspense" stories

1913 Sax Rohmer:
**The Mystery of Dr Fu-Manchu*

1913 E.C. Bentley:
Trent's Last Case (First U.S. title: The Woman in Black)

The birth of naturalism in characterization

1914 Ernest Bramah:
Max Carrados

The first blind detective

1914 Louis Joseph Vance:
**The Lone Wolf*

1915 John Buchan:
**The Thirty-Nine Steps*

1916 Thomas Burke:
**Limehouse Nights*

1918 Melville Davisson Post:
Uncle Abner

1918 J.S. Fletcher:
The Middle Temple Murder

1920 Agatha Christie:
**The Mysterious Affair at Styles*

The first Hercule Poirot book

The Murder of Roger Ackroyd, 1926

1920 Freeman Wills Crofts:
The Cask;
Inspector French's Greatest Case, 1924

1920 H.C. Bailey:
Call Mr. Fortune;
The Red Castle, 1932

1920 "Sapper" (Cyril McNeile):
**Bull-Dog Drummond*

1920 Arthur Train:
**Tutt and Mr. Tutt*

1921 Eden Phillpotts:
The Grey Room

1922 A.A. Milne:
The Red House Mystery

1923 G.D.H. Cole:
The Brooklyn Murders

1923 Dorothy L. Sayers:
**Whose Body?*

The first Lord Peter Wimsey book

The Nine Tailors, 1934;
—— and Robert Eustace:
The Documents in the Case, 1930

1924 Philip MacDonald:
The Rasp

The first Colonel Anthony Gethryn book

**Warrant for X, 1938 (English title: The Nursemaid Who Disappeared, 1938)*

1925 Edgar Wallace:
The Mind of Mr. J.G. Reeder

1925 John Rhode:
The Paddington Mystery

The first Dr. Priestley book

**The Murders in Praed Street, 1928*

1925 Earl Derr Biggers:
The House without a Key

The first Charlie Chan book

1925 Theodore Dreiser:
**An American Tragedy*

1925 Liam O'Flaherty:
**The Informer*

1925 Ronald A. Knox:
The Viaduct Murder

1926 S.S. Van Dine:
The Benson Murder Case

The first Philo Vance book

or *The "Canary" Murder Case, 1927*

1926 C.S. Forester:
**Payment Deferred*

1927 Frances Noyes Hart:
The Bellamy Trial

1928 W. Somerset Maugham:
**Ashenden*

1929 Anthony Berkeley:
The Poisoned Chocolates Case;
**Trial and Error, 1937;*
(Francis Iles):
Before the Fact, 1932

1929 Ellery Queen:
The Roman Hat Mystery

The first Ellery Queen book

**Calamity Town, 1942;*
(Barnaby Ross):
The Tragedy of X, 1932

The first Drury Lane book

**The Tragedy of Y, 1932*

1929 Rufus King:
**Murder by the Clock*

The first Lieutenant Valcour book

1929 W.R. Burnett:
**Little Caesar*

1929 T.S. Stribling:
**Clues of the Caribbees*

The only Professor Poggioli book

1929 Harvey J. O'Higgins:
**Detective Duff Unravels It*

The first psychoanalyst detective

1929 Mignon G. Eberhart:
The Patient in Room 18

1930 Frederick Irving Anderson:
Book of Murder

1930 Dashiell Hammett:
The Maltese Falcon

The first Sam Spade book

**The Glass Key, 1931;*
**The Adventures of Sam Spade, 1944*

1930 David Frome:
The Hammersmith Murders

The first Mr. Pinkerton book

1931 Stuart Palmer:
**The Penguin Pool Murder*

The first Hildegarde Withers book

1931 Francis Beeding:
**Death Walks in Eastrepps*

Vincent Starrett considers this book "one of the ten greatest detective novels."

1931 Glen Trevor (James Hilton):
**Murder at School (U.S. title: Was It Murder?, 1933)*

1931 Damon Runyon:
**Guys and Dolls*

1931 Phoebe Atwood Taylor:
The Cape Cod Mystery

The first Asey Mayo book

1932 R.A.J. Walling:
The Fatal Five Minutes

1932 Clemence Dane and Helen Simpson:
Re-enter Sir John

1933 Erle Stanley Gardner:
**The Case of the Velvet Claws*

The first Perry Mason book

The Case of the Sulky Girl, 1933

1934 Margery Allingham:
Death of a Ghost

1934 James M. Cain:
**The Postman Always Rings Twice*

1934 Rex Stout:
Fer-de-Lance

The first Nero Wolfe book

**The League of Frightened Men, 1935*

1935 Richard Hull:
The Murder of My Aunt

1935 John P. Marquand:
**No Hero*

The first Mr. Moto book

1938 John Dickson Carr (Carter Dickson):
The Crooked Hinge;
The Judas Window, 1938;
**The Curse of the Bronze Lamp, 1945*
(English title: Lord of the Sorcerers, 1946)

***In his original list, Mr Haycraft chose* The Arabian Nights Murder *by Carr and* The Plague Court Murders *by Dickson; but on page 493 of his* The Art of the Mystery Story *Mr. Haycraft wrote: "After careful, and possibly maturer, re-reading I beg to change my vote" to* The Crooked Hinge *and* The Judas Window.**

1938 Nicholas Blake:
The Beast Must Die

1938 Michael Innes:
Lament for a Maker

1938 Clayton Rawson:
**Death from a Top Hat*

The first Great Merlini book

1938 Graham Greene:
**Brighton Rock*

1938 Daphne Du Maurier:
**Rebecca*

1938 Mabel Seeley:
The Listening House

1939 Ngaio Marsh:
Overture to Death

1939 Eric Ambler:
A Coffin for Dimitrios (English title: The Mask of Dimitrios)

1939 Raymond Chandler:
The Big Sleep

The first Philip Marlowe book

or *Farewell, My Lovely, 1940*

1939 Georges Simenon:
The Patience of Maigret

1940 Raymond Postgate:
Verdict of Twelve

1940 Frances and Richard Lockridge: *The Norths Meet Murder*

1940 Dorothy B. Hughes:
The So Blue Marble or
In a Lonely Place, 1947

1940 Cornell Woolrich (William Irish):
**The Bride Wore Black;*
Phantom Lady, 1942

1940 Manning Coles:
Drink to Yesterday;
A Toast to Tomorrow, 1941 (English title: Pray Silence, 1940)

The first two Tommy Hambledon books

1941 H.F. Heard:
**A Taste for Honey*

1941 Craig Rice:
Trial by Fury or
Home Sweet Homicide, 1944

1942 H.H. Holmes (Anthony Boucher):
**Rocket to the Morgue*

1942 James Gould Cozzens:
**The Just and the Unjust*

1944 Hilda Lawrence:
Blood upon the Snow

1946 Helen Eustis:
The Horizontal Man

1946 Charlotte Armstrong:
**The Unsuspected*

1946 Lillian de la Torre:
**Dr. Sam: Johnson, Detector*

1946 Edmund Crispin:
The Moving Toyshop or
Love Lies Bleeding, 1948

1947 Edgar Lustgarten:
One More Unfortunate (English title: A Case to Answer)

1947 Roy Vickers:
**The Department of Dead Ends*

1948 Josephine Tey:
The Franchise Affair

1948 William Faulkner:
**Intruder in the Dust*

COLLECTING DETECTIVE FICTION

Otto Penzler

The first thing to understand is that it is no longer possible to get in on the proverbial ground floor. Sherlock Holmes has already passed Shakespeare as the number one literary collectible, and that fact alone would seem to indicate the number of detective fiction collectors is roughly equivalent to the number of Macy's shoppers on a typical Saturday.

Still, it is within memory that the field was virtually a virgin one, with books in plentiful supply at rock-bottom prices and the competition for them almost nonexistent. Prior to 1934 there were only a handful of collectors. That year, however, marked the appearance of two important rare book catalogues devoted to the genre: one from George Bates in England, the other from Scribner's bookstore in America. John Carter, who was responsible for the Scribner's catalogue, was also responsible for *New Paths in Book Collecting,* published in the same year. One of his "new paths" led to crime. These three works gave the field credibility, if not hauteur.

Today, a truly spectacular collection of detective fiction, featuring most of the titles on the Haycraft-Queen Cornerstone and James Sandoe lists and those mentioned in *Queen's Quorum* would cost approximately $50,000 (and that's a conservative figure) to accumulate. Most collectors won't even attempt it, and only the novice would think of going that one step further and trying to amass every mystery ever written. (One exception: Allen J. Hubin, editor of *The Armchair Detective,* who is trying to do just that.) Most often, collectors find a subgenre that appeals to them and attack it with zeal.

There are many possibilities: nineteenth-century first editions; police procedurals; Gothics (veritably an untapped area); books about one specific book (such as the 100 or so volumes relating to Dickens' *Edwin Drood);* books about woman detectives, arsonists, magi-

SPINE-TINGLERS

Some collectors focus on bindings. In general, the nucleus of their collections will be mystery books from the late nineteenth century, since Victorian detective fiction often featured elaborately decorated covers with gilt running rampant. No publisher would dare such extravaganzas these days, but many books from the 1930's and 40's have interesting, albeit simplified, spine sketches.

cians, even one's own profession. My weakness is books about gentleman crooks, particularly E.W. Hornung's *Raffles.*

Currently, the vogue seems to be for the hard-boiled school, and as a consequence first editions of Dashiell Hammett, Raymond Chandler, Carroll John Daly, Benjamin Appel, Cornell Woolrich and the early Ross Macdonalds have skyrocketed in price. *The Maltese Falcon,* for example, recently sold for an outrageous $750. Five years ago, the asking price was $35.

No one can say with any certainty who will be the big collectibles in the next few years; however, several dealers have suggested that a collector who specialized in R. Austin Freeman, Leslie Charteris, Rex Stout and the Crime Club *in toto* could not go far wrong.

Beginning collectors might consider focusing on their favorite author. If that doesn't sound like an overwhelming challenge, it's just because you haven't tried to assemble a complete set of first editions, in dust wrappers, in fine condition, of Ellery Queen, Agatha Christie, Sax Rohmer, Edgar Wallace, Dorothy L. Sayers or Georges Simenon. It's not an easy task.

To form a collection rather than a "pile," a collector must disdain all book club editions. If you find a nice book club copy of *The Mysterious Affair at Styles,* read it and enjoy it, but know that's all you can do with it. To a serious collector, no book club edition has any real value. (Careful. Don't confuse the Doubleday or Col-

ONE COLLECTOR'S MANIA

Donald Pollack, an anthropologist at the University of Rochester and editor of the *Baker Street Miscellany,* collects just one book: *The Hound of the Baskervilles.* He currently owns 103 versions of it, including the six states of the first edition, a page of the original manuscript, a play script, two movie scripts and several comic books. He estimates there are about a dozen versions (in English) left for him to locate. Then he can start in on the foreign-language editions, including five in Icelandic. He began collecting *The Hound* four years ago when he decided that Holmesiana in general was too expensive and too difficult to complete.

Says Pollack, "No one will ever again be able to amass a collection like John Shaw's, and I couldn't be happy knowing there were thousands of things I was missing. With *The Hound* I can look forward to a time when I will feel reasonably certain I have a complete collection. Then I start the full-time job of upgrading, finding association copies, dust jackets — good luck on that one! — and so forth."

To date, Pollack's collection is worth approximately $1,000.

He does not own a real live hound. Nor does he intend to.

COURTESY HOUSE OF EL DIEFF, INC.

"The Slavering Hound" by Frederick Dorr Steele.

COLLECTING ODDITIES: SHORTHAND EDITIONS

CHAPTER I.

THE SCIENCE OF DEDUCTION

The Sign of Four

By Conan Doyle

CHAPTER I.

THE SCIENCE OF DEDUCTION.

SHERLOCK HOLMES

ANN LIMONGELLO

The secretarial Sherlock Holmes. Two versions of The Sign of Four. *Top, Gregg; bottom, Pitman. Each is valued at $20.*

lins Crime Club editions with book club editions. The former are potentially valuable, whereas the latter are not.) Equally worthless to a collector are most books published by Grosset & Dunlap, A.L. Burt and Triangle. These are invariably reprint editions.

Most collectors learn fairly quickly that what makes a book valuable is the fact that it is (1) rare, (2) in fine condition, and (3) a first edition. Regarding condition, if the dog chewed it, if a child crayoned in it, if it has been — in the words of the late Lew Feldman — well thumbed by a previous scholar, then perhaps you should not own it. You should certainly not consider it part of a good collection, any more than that book club edition of *Styles*.

Generally speaking, the most asked question on the part of neophyte collectors is, "How do you tell a first edition?" As a rule of thumb, if the copyright page (the verso of the title page) bears the words "First Edition" or "First Printing," the question answers itself. If it states "Second Printing" or something similar, you probably have the bad news right in front of you. Since most publishers don't make it that easy, compare the date on the title page (if there is one) with that on the copyright page; if identical, the book is likely to be a first edition. Many books have been written on this subject of telling firsts, and the most reliable is probably *First Editions of Today and How to Tell Them* by Henry S. Boutell.

Make no mistake about it: If you intend to invest in a collection, substantial amounts of money will exit your wallet. Which brings us to the last question: where to buy, and sell, first editions. You buy them wherever you can. Goodwill and Salvation Army stores, antique shops, tag sales, secondhand bookshops, garage and rummage sales. Wherever books are to be found, so should you be. Local newspapers often carry information about upcoming auctions. Go. The best source for books, of course, is a good bookshop. Many issue catalogues, and most dealers are generous with their time and knowledge. For the choice products they offer, however, you have to pay dearly. You might spend twenty years backing in and out of garage sales searching for a first

COLLECTING TERMINOLOGY

Booksellers use their own form of shorthand to describe a book's condition. It's important to familiarize yourself with it so you'll know, for example, that a "good" copy is really the equivalent of the collegian's "gentleman's C": presentable, but not spectacular. Some of the standard terms are:

Mint: looks brand-new
Very fine: almost mint, just lacking the freshness
Fine: clean and crisp, with no serious signs of wear
Good: averagely used: some soiling, fraying, discoloration of pages
Fair: obviously well read: covers dirty; dust wrappers badly torn and pieces missing; binding faded and fraying
Poor: for reading only; not suitable for a collector
Foxing: chemicals in the paper have oxidized, giving the pages a freckled appearance
Cracked hinge: a tear or break along the seam which attaches the pages to the covers
Chipped: tiny pieces have been torn off the dust wrapper
Bumped: the cover corners have been crushed and cease to form right angles
Sunned: cloth is badly faded or discolored, a result of too much exposure to sunlight (a hint as to why libraries of rare books are either dark or artificially lit)
Ex-lib: discarded from a library, usually with labels, stamping and perforations indicating the book's origin (the least desirable condition a book can be in)
Association copy: the author has personally come in contact with the book, which may be *signed* (bearing just his signature) or *inscribed* (his signature plus a greeting or sentiment) or — best of all — may be a *presentation copy* (signed, with an inscription indicating that the book was a gift from him; since an author receives only a handful of free copies from his publisher, presentation copies generally go to people extremely close to him and the inscription is apt to be more personal

O.P.

edition of *Brighton Rock*; if you find it (the odds are against it), you may "steal" it for a quarter. If you search in rare bookstores, you'll probably be able to find a copy of it within a year — but it will cost you, on average, $150. Don't think for a minute that the dealer will buy the book back at that price, either. You can expect to receive one-third to one-half the retail value of any given book.

A few of the best booksellers specializing in mystery fiction (but by no means all of them — we collectors like to keep one or two of our sources our own little secret) and exemplary in terms of fairness are:

Aardvarks Booksellers (Paul Landfried), Box 15070, Orlando, Fla. 32808

The Aspen Bookhouse (Tom Schantz), Box 4119, Boulder, Colo. 80306

Joseph the Provider (Ralph Sipper), 903 State St., Santa Barbara, Calif. 93101

Vernon Lay, 52 Oakleigh Gardens, Whetstone, London N209AB, England

Murder Ink (Carol Brener), 271 West 87th St., N.Y., N.Y. 10024

Otto Penzler is coauthor of The Encyclopedia of Mystery and Detection, *which won a Mystery Writers of America Edgar.*

THE MYSTERY READER'S REFERENCE SHELF

Compiled by Vernon Lay

I. COFFIN TABLE BOOKS

The Collector's Book of Detective Fiction (Quayle)
The Encyclopedia of Mystery and Detection (Steinbrunner & Penzler)
The Murder Book (La Cour & Mogensen)

II. MUG SHOTS — CHARACTERS

In Search of Dr. Thorndyke (Donaldson)
The James Bond Dossier (Amis)
Nero Wolfe of West Thirty-Fifth Street (Baring-Gould)
Down These Mean Streets a Man Must Go: Raymond Chandler's Knight (Durham)
Philo Vance: The Life and Times of S.S. Van Dine (Tuska)
The Saint and Leslie Charteris (Lofts & Adley)
An Agatha Christie Chronology (Wynne)
Royal Bloodline, Ellery Queen, Author & Detective (Nevins)
The Hard-Boiled Dick (Sandoe)
Boys Will Be Boys: re, Sexton Blake (Turner)
Literary Distractions: re, Father Brown (Knox)

III. MUG SHOTS — AUTHORS

The Life of Sir Arthur Conan Doyle (Carr)
Such a Strange Lady: Dorothy L. Sayers (Hichens)
The Art of Simenon (Narcejac)
Simenon in Court (Raymond)
E.P. Oppenheim, Prince of Storytellers (Standish)
Edgar Wallace: A Biography (Lane)
Master of Villainy: A Biography of Sax Rohmer (Van Ash & Rohmer)
Melville Davisson Post, Man of Many Mysteries (Norton)
Poe: A Biography (Bittner)
Agatha Christie, Mistress of Mystery (Ramsay)
Eden Philpotts (Waveney Girvan)
M.P. Shiel: A Biography (Morse)
Life of Ian Fleming (Pearson)
The Chandler Notebooks (McShane)
Dashiell Hammett: A Casebook (Nolan)
Peter Cheyney, Prince of Hokum (Harrison)
The Real Le Queux, Fact or Fiction? (Sladen)
Catalogue of Crime (Barzun & Taylor)
The Detective Short Story: A Bibliography (Queen)

IV. VERDICTS RENDERED

Murder for Pleasure (Haycraft)
Mortal Consequences (Symons)
Snobbery with Violence (Watson)
The Development of the Detective Novel (Murch)
Bloodhounds of Heaven. The Detective in English Fiction from Godwin to Doyle (Ousby)
Fiction for the Working Man 1830 – 1850 (James)
The Detective Story in Britain (Symons)
The Detective in Fiction and in Fact (Rhodes)
Masters of Mystery (Thomson)
Queen's Quorum (Queen)
Blood in Their Ink (Sutherland)
How to Enjoy Detective Fiction (Thomas)
The Technique of the Mystery Story (Wells)
Mystery Fiction, Theory & Technique (Rodell)
Murder Plain and Fanciful (Sandoe)
In the Queen's Parlour (Queen)
The First, Second, Third Omnibus of Crime (Sayers, editor)
The Art of the Mystery (Haycraft, editor)
Crime in Good Company (Gilbert, editor)

Vernon Lay is a London bookseller specializing in detective fiction.

AMERICAN EDITING

Joan Kahn

I don't believe in publishing to formula, and I think each book has to be considered on its own merits. I think each author should have the right to work in any direction he chooses, if that direction leads to something someone else would want to read.

I've never been concerned about the length of a book, though if a book runs *very* short or *very* long, then it's going to have to be especially good.

I've published books in practically every mystery and suspense category — hard and soft, quiet and noisily bloody. I've experimented: The first book I accepted was an offbeat suspense novel, *The Horizontal Man* by Helen Eustis. I published the first Durrenmatt done in this country, *The Judge and His Hangman,* and one of the first novels with a black detective, *In the Heat of the Night* by John Ball, and one of the first with a homosexual detective, *Fadeout* by Joseph Hansen.

I'm a tough editor — and the Harper Novel of Suspense standards are pretty high. I edit about twenty-six books a year. If need be, I coax the authors to plug up holes or to make sense for their readers of what, so far, is only clear in the author's head. A little over half of the twenty-six or so books are suspense novels, representing, of course, only a small proportion of the number of manuscripts that come in each year.

In any case, since I'm just one person with only a certain amount of energy and time, I have to take on only the books I care most about and am most eager to shepherd through the months it takes from contract to finished book in the bookstores. It's hard turning down books, especially if they're by friends or even by one's relatives. I've had to turn down, on occasion, a good deal of my kin, including my father, my stepmother, my brother, and some nephews. Also difficult is turning down books by authors I've published for many years, which I've been forced to do when I couldn't see any way of convincing them that to me the books weren't in proper shape. Mind you, my judgment has sometimes been wrong, and I've had regrets.

Sometimes, gloriously, a book appears ready to go at the outset, and all I have to say to the author is "Lovely — let's talk about a contract." And that's a comfort all around.

I've never been very good at spotting trends — people ask whither the mystery — but I think it just wanders here and there following a writer's head and changes its direction almost as often as the length of a fashionable woman's skirt. Right now it may be circling over toward the romantic, but if a good big procedural or a good big spy story or a good big comic novel or a good big hard-boiled novel would burst upon the scene there'd be a patter of little typewriter feet in that direction — for a while, and then the feet would patter off in some other direction.

Recently, Harper & Row has been putting the Joan Kahn logo on the suspense books we publish (on other books I edit, too), and I think this has been useful since writers and agents who like the tones of voice of our books send me books in similar tones. I'm ready to read anything that comes along, but by now I can tell very quickly if a book's not going to be of any interest to me — so I can get that book off my desk pretty fast. Quite a lot of books go away fast, but it's exciting to see how many bright new talents are popping up from all over.

Joan Kahn is an editor at Harper & Row, New York.

ENGLISH EDITING

Elizabeth Walter

I cannot really define a crime novel. Obviously, a crime occurs, but murder is not obligatory, although the public expect it. A psychological study of a criminal can be sufficient, with the crime taking place off stage. But the crime story is always a story of surprise — that's why so few people read them a second time; once the surprise element is gone, there's not much left. Also, the crime story is concerned with justice, with the restoration of an order that has been disturbed.

I wouldn't think it immoral to publish a book in which the murderer gets away with it, if the book had other things to commend it — if it were amusing, say. And I pick a book on the basis of its appeal to me as a general reader. I don't consider myself a specialist in the field. After all, I have no specialised background. I am neither cop nor robber.

I think today there is a tendency toward the socially introspective crime novel. And people are once again appreciating characterisation, wit and style. The only thing I won't publish is anything that is explicitly sadistic. If I do not like an author's style, I do not accept his book. It is not the editor's function to rewrite. Just because there is a good idea there doesn't mean you should do the author's work for him. With good authors, if there is a clumsy phrase here or there I point it out in the hope that they will change it, but basically I prefer to let authors get on with the job — though I am a tiger where careless plotting is concerned.

As for dealing with authors, I enjoy it. Witty books are the work of witty people. The more difficult ones — well, I usually say, "No temperament below a sale of fifteen thousand."

I do not think spy thrillers properly belong in the Crime Club. And I dislike thrillers using titles like *The Something Contract/Memorandum/Assignment/Sanction.* I can't tell one book from the other.

At Collins we never send out printed rejections. Of course, how much we say in a letter is another matter. I have turned down a first novel and then had a much better second novel come in and published it. I make it a principle never to waste time regretting books I have turned down that have gone on to success elsewhere. Quite obviously, some good crime novels are published by other than Collins Crime Club.

Reviews? Well, one bad one never killed a book. Neither did two. But if a book gets universally bad reviews, I reckon I ought not to have published it in the first place. It is the paper the review appears in and the fact that the book is noticed at all that are important — not generally the reviewer's name.

In all, Collins publishes thirty-six new crime titles a year, three per month. On average, three or four of these are by new authors. In any given month we try to offer three different kinds of mystery. If one has a village setting, another might be American or have an exotic locale, and another might be a police procedural. There should be something for everybody each month.

I cannot write a crime novel. I tried once and gave up. But I have had a collection of supernatural stories published in the States by St. Martin's Press. The supernatural appeals to me — probably my Welsh heritage. The thing I like most about the supernatural is that it enables you to play God, to dispense justice — only you dispense it from beyond the grave. Crime novelists can only dispense it from this side.

Elizabeth Walter is the editor of the Collins Crime Club, London.

CONFESSIONS OF A SLUSH READER

Eleanor Sullivan

Most people recognize "slush" as publishing jargon for unsolicited manuscripts which book and magazine editors plow through regularly in search of something marvelous to print. In spite of that lofty objective, or maybe because of it, it is usually an exhausting job, and not the fun many people tell me they think it must be.

Perhaps the reason so much of it is heavy going is that most novices don't know why they're writing — or, if they do, how to go about it — or, if they do, where to send it.

Sometimes the covering letter is the tip-off to the quality of the manuscript:

"I am sending you a copy of an inspired short story I wrote entitled ———. It brought me 67th place in the short-story category of the ——— ——— 1975 Writers' Contest."

"The plot of my story is multi-layered and it contains an average of about 1,900 words."

"I am enclosing an original story that you might consider entertaining reading for your clientele."

"This is to certify that ——— ——— is a Professional Writer, 'he composed a legal contract.' " (This stamped and signed by a notary public.)

"Earlier this year I wrote another story intended for a teenage girls' magazine. It was rejected as 'not in meeting with our editorial needs' which to me sounds like a brushoff."

One day I received a letter from a man whose story I had returned the previous week. He wrote: "On your reject slip of my story you didn't tell me whether it was accepted."

Still think it must be fun?

Consider the character descriptions some unsolicited contributors thought (incorrectly) to include:

"Barry Martin is an eccentric, provocative Doctor of Philosophy who is called upon by social deviates — the psychologically deranged and criminally insane (i.e., criminals, bad guys, crooks, etc.) — to solve complicated and predetermined crimes."

"A product of an unhappy home and a bad mixer as well, it is surprising that Felix Bendel has come as far as he has as we begin the story."

"Barbara Brown's peculiarity is embedded in the fact that there is absolutely nothing, good or bad, that makes her stand out, except for the utter absence of any peculiarity, which is in itself peculiar."

"At 34, Jim Lawrence finds himself wishing he'd been a baseball player after all, like any other normal person."

"Andre had trained with Jean-Claude Killy in France. While he was in training, his business went rapidly downhill."

All right, perhaps slush reading *does* have its moments. But even the unintentionally funny stuff palls after a few pages, and it is a struggle to make it to the end — which often is as unrewarding as this one:

"A man leaped into the room. He yelled, 'I was the one who killed that girl!' Then he leaped out the window. The sergeant sighed. What a day it had been."

Some time ago a friend dropped by my office, and his imagination was captured by the tower of unsolicited manuscripts on a shelf by my desk.

"Eleanor," he said, picking up the top envelope, "each one of these tells a story."

"I wish it did," I said.

Eleanor Sullivan is editor of Alfred Hitchcock's Mystery Magazine.

TRY, TRY AGAIN

A manuscript submitted to *Alfred Hitchcock's Mystery Magazine* is actually a double submission. It is read, at the same time, for possible inclusion in *Ellery Queen's Mystery Magazine*. (This, because both are brought out by Davis Publications.) About 25 percent of the manuscripts are sent in through an agent, and the two magazines receive about 6,000 manuscripts a year. Each prints roughly 300 stories a year. Should the story be accepted, the standard payment is 3 to 8 cents per word, depending on the author's clout.

JUDITH WRIGHT

Miss Sullivan was too busy wading through the slush to pose. Her unhappy surrogate suggests all manuscripts be typed, double-spaced and submitted with a stamped, self-addressed envelope. You may expect a reply within three weeks.

RENDERING A VERDICT

Clifford A. Ridley

I don't expect any sympathy, but let me tell you my problem. Ranged before me, row upon row, are all these crime novels — mysteries, procedurals, hard-boiled sagas, the works. From among them I must select a dozen or so to review, and in each of that dozen I should, if I am worth my fee, discover and communicate those faults or excellences that combine to render it a thing apart, a thing that at best deserves your purchase, at worst deserves your momentary attention. Some would call it paradise. I call it work.

Where to begin? Publishers' imprints offer some small assistance: Anything from the firm of Harper & Row may generally be counted as worth one's time, while mining in the Doubleday Crime Club yields fewer pleasantries. Authors' track records are enormously helpful, of course, although they contain the beginning author's paradox: To get himself reviewed he needs a name, but he can't acquire a name until he's reviewed. To this dilemma I cheerfully offer no answer whatever. I am simply going to leap at a new novel by Ross Macdonald or, latterly, Janwillem van de Wetering with rather more alacrity than I will attack one by Pincus O'Shaughnessy. Conceivably, this tyro could teach the pros, but I might never know that.

To help educate me, O'Shaughnessy's publisher may provide quotes on the dust jacket — perhaps from another mystery writer — that read something like "Combines the best of Ross Macdonald and Janwillem van de Wetering!" These red flags are not without their usefulness, but only if approached with a dollop of salt. The fellow author's commendation may be little more than a matter of you-scratch-my-back-and-I'll-scratch-yours; the publisher's quote may be in code ("Brilliant characters," for instance, hints that the plot is indecipherable).

As you may have surmised, this review selection process is like a large, disorderly crapshoot. Once past the publisher and the other author, I may be attracted by a book's milieu, an interesting new gumshoe, the promise of lively prose (revealed in the scanning of a half-dozen pages), the praise of a colleague (Newgate Calendar, when he gets down to cases, is sometimes reliable) or perhaps just something as quixotic — the book is before me now — as a novel set in a town called Ridley. None of this is awfully scientific, however much I may protest it is to the world at large, and all of it is overlaid with nothing more than matters of personal preference. I am a mystery-and-procedural man myself, and, all else being equal, I am disposed to pick up a mystery or procedural in preference to a spy caper. There's nothing particularly wrong with this, I submit, so long as my biases are evident. No reader samples all the fruits of the crime garden with equal relish, and to expect a reviewer to do otherwise is to disqualify him as the reader's surrogate — which is what he ought to be.

All right. I have selected a book and

cracked the covers, and what do I search for? I search — I *pray* — for a happy combination of those elements that distinguish any work of fiction, regardless of genre. Style, for one — a rarer bird than might be expected from reading many reviewers, whose idea of literary excellence seems to demand little more than that a writer refrain from saying "ain't." In fact, there are but a handful of true stylists among us: Julian Symons, Peter Dickinson, Ken and Margaret Millar, Ngaio Marsh, P.D. James. With the rest of the crowd we must, to one degree or another, make do — hoping for at least some kind of authorial tone, for a cliché at least every *other* page, for dialogue that, if not precisely right, is at least not patently wrong. Even applying such relaxed criteria, the hunt for style is often a fruitless one.

I search, too, for some evidence that an author has a point of view. It's not that simple, of course; if he fails to weave this material into the fabric of his plot, he risks becoming preacher, psychiatrist, tour guide — and less of a novelist. Nonetheless, I search for a sense of social forces in collision (viz.: Ross Macdonald, the Wahlöös, James McClure), of human character in extremis (Symons, Simenon, Ruth Rendell), of ordinary behavior turned upside-down (Donald Westlake), of place in relation to the people who inhabit it (most of these authors and more). The idea is to identify a book's perspective while keeping a wary eye out for what is not perspective but merely gimmick — of which, unhappily, our genre has more than its share. The gimmick has no staying power; it expires after a single book, for it has little to tell us beyond the mere fact of its existence. Virgil Tibbs and Rabbi David Small are gimmicks.

Finally, I search for plausibility of plot. One would assume that a crime novel, with its effects deriving in large part from the pieces tumbling logically into place, would be sensibly plotted if it were nothing else. Yet it's remarkable how many books are resolved by devices dragged in from the next country, loose ends strewn about like spaghetti, and how many more are predicated on people behaving in fashions that defy not only their stories but common sense itself. Plot in the crime novel is hardly what it used to be — which was everything. The days of Christie, Carr and Queen are mostly dead and buried.

Given this state of affairs, I'm continually amazed that plot is all a good many reviewers seem to have on their minds. (Robin Winks, of the *New Republic*, is a notable exception.) Although I take it as axiomatic that most of what we need to know about a book's plot can be transmitted in a single sentence, and although all mystery reviewers toil within severely circumscribed space, plot summary occupies even the best of our critics to an astonishing degree. What this signifies, I think, is a reluctance to treat mystery fiction with the seriousness that its quality increasingly demands. If reviewers persist in regarding crime fiction as nothing more than an idle diversion with which to while away a couple of hours — endorsing far too many books, squatting firmly on the fence about most of the rest, and filling their minimal space not with serious appraisal but with and-then-he-wrote — then crime fiction will continue to sit at the back of the bus, for any art requires good criticism in order to prosper. And plot summary is not criticism. It is a book report.

Clifford A. Ridley was arts editor, theater critic, and sometime mystery reviewer for The National Observer *until its demise in July 1977.*

ALWAYS ON SUNDAY

Just what is a Newgate Callendar? *The Newgate Calendar, or Malefactor's Bloody Register,* was a British broadside published about 1774 that dealt with notorious crimes. It is also the pseudonym, creatively spelled, of the *New York Times* mystery book reviewer. In a recent poll, readers believed him to be Anatole Broyard, John Canaday, John Leonard, Harold Schoenberg, or Ellery Queen. One of the above is correct.

C.K.

Unlikely Author No. 1: THE TRAILOR MURDER MYSTERY

Abraham Lincoln

The March 1952 issue of Ellery Queen's Mystery Magazine *presented "The Trailor Murder Mystery." In an introduction to the story, Queen noted that Howard Haycraft was the first of the mystery historians to point out that Lincoln was a great admirer of Poe; that Roger W. Barrett discovered Lincoln's own mystery story in the pages of the Quincy, Illinois,* Whig *of April 15, 1846; that the story itself was based on an actual case in which Lincoln acted as defense attorney.*

In the year 1841, there resided, at different points in the State of Illinois, three brothers by the name of Trailor. Their Christian names were William, Henry and Archibald. Archibald resided at Springfield, then as now the seat of Government of the State. He was a sober, retiring, and industrious man, of about thirty years of age; a carpenter by trade, and a bachelor, boarding with his partner in business — a Mr. Myers. Henry, a year or two older, was a man of like retiring and industrious habits; had a family, and resided with it on a farm, at Clary's Grove, about twenty miles distant from Springfield in a north-westerly direction. — William, still older, and with similar habits, resided on a farm in Warren county, distant from Springfield something more than a hundred miles in the same north-westerly direction. He was a widower, with several children.

In the neighborhood of William's residence, there was, and had been for several years, a man by the name of Fisher, who was somewhat above the age of fifty; had no family, and no settled home; but who boarded and lodged a while here and a while there, with persons for whom he did little jobs of work. His habits were remarkably economical, so that an impression got about that he had accumulated a considerable amount of money.

In the latter part of May, in the year mentioned, William formed the purpose of visiting his brothers at Clary's Grove and Springfield; and Fisher, at the time having his temporary residence at his house, resolved to accompany him. They set out together in a buggy with a single horse. On Sunday evening they reached Henry's residence, and stayed over night. On Monday morning, being the first Monday of June, they started on to Springfield, Henry accompanying them on horseback. They reached town about noon, met Archibald, went with him to his boarding house, and there took up their lodgings for the time they should remain.

After dinner, the three Trailors and Fisher left the boarding house in company, for the avowed purpose of spending the evening together in looking about the town. At supper, the Trailors had all returned, but Fisher was missing, and some inquiry was made about him. After supper, the Trailors went out professedly in search of him. One by one they returned, the last coming in after late tea time, and each stating that he had been unable to discover anything of Fisher.

The next day, both before and after breakfast, they went professedly in search again, and returned at noon, still unsuccessful. Dinner again being had, William and Henry expressed a determination to give up the search, and start for their homes. This was remonstrated against by some of the boarders about the house, on the ground that Fisher was somewhere in the vicinity, and would be left without any conveyance, as he and William had come in the same buggy. The remonstrance was disregarded, and they departed for their homes respectively.

LIBRARY OF CONGRESS

Many political figures appreciate mysteries. In addition to Abraham Lincoln and Franklin Delano Roosevelt, John F. Kennedy, Henry Kissinger, Julian Bond and Amy Carter have admitted they were hooked on them.

Up to this time, the knowledge of Fisher's mysterious disappearance had spread very little beyond the few boarders at Myers', and excited no considerable interest. After the lapse of three or four days, Henry returned to Springfield, for the ostensible purpose of making further search for Fisher. Procuring some of the boarders, he, together with them and Archibald, spent another day in ineffectual search, when it was again abandoned, and he returned home.

No general interest was yet excited.

On the Friday, week after Fisher's disappearance, the Postmaster at Springfield received a letter from the Postmaster nearest William's residence, in Warren county, stating that William had returned home without Fisher, and was saying, rather boastfully, that Fisher was dead, and had willed him his money, and that he had got about fifteen hundred dollars by it. The letter further stated that William's story and conduct seemed strange, and desired the Postmaster at Springfield to ascertain and write what was the truth in the matter.

The Postmaster at Springfield made the letter public, and at once, excitement became universal and intense. Springfield, at that time, had a population of about 3,500, with a city organization. The Attorney General of the State resided there. A purpose was forthwith formed to ferret out the mystery, in putting which into execution, the Mayor of the city and the Attorney General took the lead. To make search for, and, if possible, find the body of the man supposed to be murdered, was resolved on as the first step.

In pursuance of this, men were formed into large parties, and marched abreast, in all directions, so as to let no inch of ground in the vicinity remain unsearched. Examinations were made of cellars, wells, and pits of all descriptions, where it was thought possible the body might be concealed. All the fresh, or tol-

NOBEL PRIZEWINNERS WHO WROTE MYSTERIES

Heinrich Boll
Pearl Buck
T.S. Eliot
William Faulkner
Ernest Hemingway
John Galsworthy
Rudyard Kipling
Sinclair Lewis
Bertrand Russell
George Bernard Shaw
John Steinbeck
William Butler Yeats

PULITZER PRIZEWINNERS WHO WROTE MYSTERIES

Stephen Vincent Benet
Louis Bromfield
Pearl S. Buck
Marc Connelly
James Gould Cozzens
Harold L. Davis
Edna Ferber
William Faulkner
Zona Gale
Ellen Glasgow
Susan Glaspell
A.B. Guthrie, Jr.
Ernest Hemingway
MacKinlay Kantor
Oliver LaFarge
Sinclair Lewis
J.P. Marquand
Edna St. Vincent Millay
Arthur Miller
Julia M. Peterkin
Elmer Rice
Conrad Richter
Edwin Arlington Robinson
Robert Sherwood
John Steinbeck
T.S. Stribling
Mark Van Doren
Edith Wharton

Each of these prizewinners had stories published in Ellery Queen's Mystery Magazine.

erably fresh graves in the graveyard, were pried into, and dead horses and dead dogs were disinterred, where, in some instances, they had been buried by their partial masters.

This search, as has appeared, commenced on Friday. It continued until Saturday afternoon without success, when it was determined to dispatch officers to arrest William and Henry, at their residences, respectively. The officers started on Sunday morning; meanwhile, the search for the body was continued, and rumors got afloat of the Trailors having passed, at different times and places, several gold pieces, which were readily supposed to have belonged to Fisher.

On Monday, the officers sent for Henry, having arrested him, arrived with him. The Mayor and Attorney Gen'l took charge of him, and set their wits to work to elicit a discovery from him. He denied, and denied, and persisted in denying. They still plied him in every conceivable way, till Wednesday, when, protesting his own innocence, he stated that his brothers, William and Archibald, had murdered Fisher; that they had killed him, without his (Henry's) knowledge at the time, and made a temporary concealment of his body; that, immediately preceding his and William's departure from Springfield for home, on Tuesday, the day after Fisher's disappearance, William and Archibald communicated the fact to him, and engaged his assistance in making a permanent concealment of the body; that, at the time he and William left professedly for home, they did not take the road directly, but, meandering their way through the streets, entered the woods at the North West of the city, two or three hundred yards to the right of where the road they should have travelled, entered them; that, penetrating the woods some few hundred yards, they halted and Archibald came a somewhat different route, on foot, and joined them; that William and Archibald then stationed him (Henry) on an old and disused road that ran near by, as a sentinel, to give warning of the approach of any intruder; that William and Archibald then removed the buggy to the edge of a dense brush thicket, about forty yards distant from his (Henry's) position, where, leaving the buggy, they entered the thicket, and in a few minutes returned with the body, and placed it in the buggy; that from his station he could and did distinctly see that the object placed in the buggy was a dead man, of the general appearance and size of Fisher; that William and Archibald then moved off with the buggy in the direction of Hickox's mill pond, and after an absence of half an hour, returned, saying they had put him in a safe place; that Archibald then left for town, and he and William found their way to the road, and made for their homes.

At this disclosure, all lingering credulity was broken down, and excitement rose to an almost inconceivable height. Up to this time, the well-known character of Archibald had repelled and put down all suspicions as to him. Till then, those who were ready to swear that a murder had been committed, were almost as confident that Archibald had had no part in it. But now, he was seized and thrown into jail; and indeed, his personal security rendered it by no means objectionable to him.

And now came the search for the brush thicket, and the search of the mill pond. The thicket was found, and the buggy tracks at the point indicated. At a point within the thicket, the signs of a struggle were discovered, and a trail from thence to the buggy track was traced. In attempting to follow the track of the buggy from the thicket, it was found to proceed in the direction of the mill pond, but could not be traced all the way. At the pond, however, it was found that a buggy had been backed down to, and partially into the water's edge.

Search was now to be made in the pond; and it was made in every imaginable way. Hundreds and hundreds were engaged in raking, fishing, and draining. After much fruitless effort in this way, on Thursday morning the mill dam was cut down, and the water of the pond partially drawn off, and the same processes of search again gone through with.

About noon of this day, the officer sent for William, returned having him in custody; and a man calling himself Dr. Gilmore, came in company with them. It seems that the officer arrested William at his own house, early in the day on Tuesday, and started to Springfield with him; that after dark awhile, they reached Lewiston, in Fulton county, where they stopped for the night; that late in the night this Dr. Gilmore arrived, stating that Fisher was alive at his house, and that he had followed on to give the information, so that William might be released without further trouble; that the officer, distrusting Dr. Gilmore, refused to release William, but brought him on to Springfield, and the Dr. accompanied them.

On reaching Springfield, the Dr. reasserted that Fisher was alive, and at his house. At this, the multitude for a time, were utterly confounded. Gilmore's story was communicated to Henry Trailor, who without faltering, reaffirmed his own story about Fisher's murder. Henry's adherence to his own story was communicated to the crowd, and at once the idea started, and became nearly, if not quite universal, that Gilmore was a confederate of the Trailors, and had invented the tale he was telling, to secure their release and escape.

Excitement was again at its zenith.

About three o'clock the same evening, Myers, Archibald's partner, started with a two-horse carriage, for the purpose of ascertaining whether Fisher was alive, as stated by Gilmore, and if so, of bringing him back to Springfield with him.

On Friday a legal examination was gone into before two Justices, on the charge of murder against William and Archibald. Henry was

AREN'T YOU GLAD HE WASN'T SECRETARY OF THE TREASURY?

ANN LIMONGELLO

The thirty-second president of the United States almost wrote a mystery; he had an idea for one, but couldn't come up with a good ending. The idea was passed on to six authors — Anthony Abbot, Rupert Hughes, S.H. Adams, Rita Weiman, S.S. Van Dine, John Erskine — each of whom wrote a chapter and more or less resolved the problem of absconding with $5 million without leaving any clues. Originally published as "The President's Mystery Story" in *Liberty* magazine in 1935, the work was reprinted under the title *The President's Mystery Plot* in 1967 with a new final chapter by Erle Stanley Gardner. Roosevelt's royalties were donated to charity.

introduced as a witness by the prosecution, and on oath re-affirmed his statements, as heretofore detailed, and at the end of which he bore a thorough and rigid cross-examination without faltering or exposure. The prosecution also proved, by a respectable lady, that on the Monday evening of Fisher's disappearance, she saw Archibald, whom she well knew, and another man whom she did not then know, but whom she believed at the time of testifying to be William, (then present,) and still another, answering the description of Fisher, all enter the timber at the North West of town, (the point indicated by Henry,) and after one or two hours, saw William and Archibald return without Fisher.

Several other witnesses testified, that on Tuesday, at the time William and Henry professedly gave up the search for Fisher's body, and started for home, they did not take the road directly, but did go into the woods, as stated by Henry. By others, also, it was proved, that since Fisher's disappearance, William and Archibald had passed rather an unusual number of gold pieces. The statements heretofore made about the thicket, the signs of a struggle, the buggy tracks, &c., were fully proven by numerous witnesses.

At this the prosecution rested.

Dr. Gilmore was then introduced by the defendants. He stated that he resided in Warren county, about seven miles distant from William's residence; that on the morning of William's arrest, he was out from home, and heard of the arrest, and of its being on a charge of the murder of Fisher; that on returning to his own house, he found Fisher there; that Fisher was in very feeble health, and could give no rational account as to where he had been during his absence; that he (Gilmore) then started in pursuit of the officer, as before stated; and that he should have taken Fisher with him, only that the state of his health did not permit. Gilmore also stated that he had known Fisher for several years, and that he had understood he was subject to temporary derangement of mind, owing to an injury about his head received in early life.

There was about Dr. Gilmore so much of the air and manner of truth, that his statement prevailed in the minds of the audience and of the court, and the Trailors were discharged, although they attempted no explanation of the circumstances proven by the other witnesses.

On the next Monday, Myers arrived in Springfield, bringing with him the now famed Fisher, in full life and proper person.

Thus ended this strange affair and while it is readily conceived that a writer of novels could bring a story to a more perfect climax, it may well be doubted whether a stranger affair ever really occurred. Much of the matter remains in mystery to this day. The going into the woods with Fisher, and returning without him, by the Trailors; their going into the woods at the same place the next day, after they professed to have given up the search; the signs of a struggle in the thicket, the buggy tracks at the edge of it; and the location of the thicket, and the signs about it, corresponding precisely with Henry's story, are circumstances that have never been explained. William and Archibald have both died since — William in less than a year, and Archibald in about two years after the supposed murder. Henry is still living, but never speaks of the subject.

It is not the object of the writer of this to enter into the many curious speculations that might be indulged upon the facts of this narrative; yet he can scarcely forbear a remark upon what would, almost certainly, have been the fate of William and Archibald, had Fisher not been found alive. It seems he had wandered away in mental derangement, and, had he died in this condition, and his body been found in the vicinity, it is difficult to conceive what could have saved the Trailors from the consequence of having murdered him. Or, if he had died, and his body never found, the case against them would have been quite as bad, for, although it is a principle of law that a conviction for murder shall not be had, unless the body of the deceased be discovered, it is to be remembered, that Henry testified that he saw Fisher's dead body.

Abraham Lincoln was the sixteenth President of the United States of America.

MYSTERY ORGANIZATIONS

MYSTERY WRITERS OF AMERICA

Founded 1945

National Headquarters: 105 East 19th Street, New York City

Regional Chapters: Boston, Chicago, San Francisco, Los Angeles

MWA issues three types of membership. Full membership is available only to those who have published in the field. Associate membership is open to those in allied fields, for example, publishing and bookselling. Affiliate membership is granted to just plain fans. There is little difference between them, as all members receive the free newsletter, *The Third Degree*, and all may attend the annual Edgar Allan Poe Award dinner held in New York each spring. Current president: Mignon G. Eberhart

MWA Awards

MWA presents Edgars (for Edgar Allan Poe) and Ravens (ditto). Nominees are selected by a supposedly impartial committee and winners are chosen by that committee. Eleven awards are presented in all: for best novel of the year; best first novel of the year; best paperback; best short story; best juvenile mystery; best critical/biographical study; best motion picture; best TV drama; best fact crime book; best hardcover jacket design; best paperback jacket design.

1946 *Watchful at Night,* Julius Fast
1947 *The Horizontal Man,* Helen Eustis
1948 *The Fabulous Clip Joint,* Fredric Brown
1949 *The Room Upstairs,* Mildred Davis
1950 *What a Body,* Alan Green
1951 *Nightmare in Manhattan,* Thomas Walsh
1952 *Strangle Hold,* Mary McMullen
1953 *Don't Cry for Me,* William Campbell Gault
1954 *Beat Not the Bones,* Charlotte Jay
A Kiss Before Dying, Ira Levin
1955 *The Long Goodbye,* Raymond Chandler
Go, Lovely Rose, Jean Potts

1956 *Beast in View,* Margaret Millar
The Perfectionist, Lane Kauffman
1957 *A Dram of Poison,* Charlotte Armstrong
Rebecca's Pride, Donald McNutt Douglas
1958 *Room to Swing,* Ed Lacy
Knock and Wait Awhile, William Rawle Weeks
1959 *The Eighth Circle,* Stanley Ellin
The Bright Road to Fear, Richard Martin Stern
1960 *The Hours Before Dawn,* Celia Fremlin
The Grey Flannel Shroud, Henry Slesar
1961 *Progress of a Crime,* Julian Symons
The Man in the Cage, John Holbrooke Vance
1962 *Death and the Joyful Woman,* Ellis Peters
The Fugitive, Robert L. Fish
1963 *The Light of Day,* Eric Ambler
The Florentine Finish, Cornelius Hirschberg
1964 *The Spy Who Came in from the Cold,* John Le Carré
Friday the Rabbi Slept Late, Harry Kemelman
1965 *The Quiller Memorandum,* Adam Hall
In the Heat of the Night, John Ball
1966 *King of the Rainy Country,* Nicolas Freeling
The Cold War Swap, Ross Thomas

The "Edgar" (left) and the "Raven" (right) are awarded annually by the Mystery Writers of America.

GRAND MASTERS AWARD

Presented by MWA to individuals for continued excellence in the field.

Agatha Christie
Vincent Starrett
Rex Stout
Ellery Queen
Erle Stanley Gardner
John Dickson Carr
George Harmon Coxe
Georges Simenon
Baynard Kendrick
John Creasey
James M. Cain
Mignon G. Eberhart
John D. MacDonald
Judson Philips
Ross Macdonald
Eric Ambler
Graham Greene

1967 *God Save the Mark,* Donald E. Westlake
Act of Fear, Michael Collins
1968 *A Case of Need,* Jeffrey Hudson
Silver Street, Richard Johnson
The Bait, Dorothy Uhnak
1969 *Forfeit,* Dick Francis
A Time for Predators, Joe Gores
1970 *The Laughing Policeman,* Maj Sjöwall & Per Wahlöö
The Anderson Tapes, Lawrence Sanders
1971 *Day of the Jackal,* Frederick Forsyth
Finding Maubee, A.H.Z. Carr
1972 *The Lingala Code,* Warren Kiefer
Squaw Point, R.H. Shimer
1973 *Dance Hall of the Dead,* Tony Hillerman
The Billion Dollar Sure Thing, Paul E. Erdman
1974 *Peter's Pence,* Jon Cleary
Fletch, Gregory McDonald
1975 *Hopscotch,* Brian Garfield
The Alvarez Journal, Rex Burns
1976 *Promised Land,* Robert B. Parker
The Thomas Berryman Number, James Patterson

CRIME WRITERS' ASSOCIATION

Founded 1953

CWA headquarters: National Book League, 7 Albemarle Street, London, W1

Membership is restricted to those who have published in the field, with no execeptions. Members receive a monthly newsletter, *Red Herrings*, attend monthly meetings at the Book League and the yearly Gold Dagger Award dinner, at which the best mystery of the year is announced. Current Chairman: Elizabeth Ferrars

COURTESY PENELOPE WALLACE

The Crime Writers' Association presents two awards, the Gold Dagger and the Silver Dagger, for best domestic and best foreign mystery of the year.

CWA Awards

CWA presents Gold and Silver Daggers for the best English and the best foreign mysteries of the year.

1955 *The Little Walls,* Winston Graham
1956 *The Second Man,* Edward Grierson
1957 *The Colour of Murder,* Julian Symons
1958 *Someone from the Past,* Margot Bennett
1959 *Passage of Arms,* Eric Ambler
1960 *The Night of Wenceslas,* Lionel Davidson
1961 *The Spoilt Kill,* Mary Kelly
1962 *When I Grow Rich,* Joan Fleming
1963 *The Spy Who Came in from the Cold,* John Le Carré
1964 *The Perfect Murder,* H.R.F. Keating
The Two Faces of January, Patricia Highsmith
1965 *The Far Side of the Dollar,* Ross Macdonald
Midnight plus One, Gavin Lyall
1966 *A Long Way to Shiloh,* Lionel Davidson
In the Heat of the Night, John Ball
1967 *Murder Against the Grain,* Emma Lathen
Dirty Story, Eric Ambler
1968 *Skin Deep,* Peter Dickinson
The Lady in the Car, Sebastien Japrisot
1969 *A Pride of Heroes,* Peter Dickinson
Another Way of Dying, Francis Clifford
The Father Hunt, Rex Stout
1970 *Young Man, I Think You're Dying,* Joan Fleming
The Labyrinth Makers, Anthony Price
1971 *The Steam Pig,* James McClure
Shroud for a Nightingale, P.D. James
1972 *The Levanter,* Eric Ambler
The Rainbird Pattern, Victor Canning
1973 *The Defection of A.J. Lewinter,* Robert Littell
A Coffin for Pandora, Gwen Butler
1974 *Other Paths of Glory,* Anthony Price
The Grosvenor Square Goodbye, Francis Clifford
The Big Fix, Roger Simon
1975 *The Seven Per Cent Solution,* Nicholas Meyer
The Black Tower, P.D. James
Acid Drop, Sara George
1976 *Demon in My View,* Ruth Rendell
Rogue Eagle, James McClure
Death of a Thin-Skinned Animal, Patrick Alexander

Chapter 2

PERPETRATORS

FRED WINKOWSKI

YOU CALL IT A PSEUDONYM, WE CALL IT AN ALIAS

Carol Kountz

Once I read a wonderful mystery that had me combing libraries and bookstores for more books by the same author — but to no avail. Desperate, I picked up something else to read and discovered that it had an uncanny resemblance to the first (and apparently sequel-less) book I'd enjoyed.

A little library sleuthing proved my suspicions to be correct. The same author had written both books but had used a pseudonym for one.

Why do mystery writers baffle potentially loyal readers by adopting pseudonyms? Usually it's for reasons thought to be — in publishing and writing circles, at any rate — logical, sensible and sometimes profitable. Occasionally it's for privacy. Sometimes it's not even the author's decision.

The most common type of 'tec author to publish under an alias is the individual with a distinguished reputation in another field. Academics are often found guilty. So C. Day Lewis, once Poet Laureate, became Nicholas Blake when he wrote *Minute for Murder* and other mysteries featuring Nigel Strangeways, and so the prolific J.I.M. Stewart writes his Inspector Appleby series as Michael Innes.

Columbia University professor Carolyn Heilbrun had a special reason for hiding behind the pen name Amanda Cross to write her mystery novels: she was hoping to be granted tenure. (In her case, crime paid on both counts.)

Not only scholars stoop to protect identity. John Canaday, former art critic for the *New York Times,* poses on crime shelves as Matthew

THE CREASEY DOSSIER

GORDON ASHE	MARGARET COOKE	M.E. COOKE	JOHN CREASEY	NORMAN DEANE	ELISE FECAMPS

IF YOU WANT TO WRITE UNDER A PEN NAME . . .

1. Be forewarned: Most publishers frown on it — for a beginning novelist, at any rate. Their thinking goes that you should be proud to have your mystery novel appear under your real name. Even a long, unpronounceable name will not be an exception.

2. State your reasons in a covering letter with your manuscript if you have just cause to use a pseudonym (conflict with your profession, for example).

3. There are no legal steps, but before deciding on your pen name check with a large library card catalogue to avoid taking a name similar to one in use.

4. Write to the publisher or editor under your own name. Sign the pseudonym as a by-line on the manuscript and put your own name and address on the upper left-hand corner of the manuscript.

5. Checks will be sent to you under your own name. If you receive a check made out to your pseudonym, as in the case of a writer with several contracts under different names, you may usually cash it at your own bank by endorsing it with the pen name and then the real name.

6. Correspondence sent to you under your pseudonym should be addressed c/o your real name to be sure it is not returned to the sender.

7. Remember that your pen name is not likely to conceal your identity for long — expect librarians (and some readers) to ferret out your secret.

Head. Literary lion Gore Vidal has written for crime fans under the alias Edgar Box. The name Edmund Crispin is familiar to detective story readers, but they may not know that it stands for (Robert) Bruce Montgomery, the composer of scores for British motion pictures, notably *Carry On, Nurse.*

David Cornwell wrote under the pseudonym John Le Carré for *The Spy Who Came In from the Cold* and other spy stories because of his profession: he worked for the British Foreign Office.

Output

Sometimes a crime novelist's book is brought out under a nom de plume when there are too many of his or her sleuths for sale in one season. The idea may come from the publisher ("The reading public will never absorb all this," mutters the editor), or a second publisher may contract for a novel by a well-known writer with the request that it be under a "new" name.

Take a case like that of John Dickson Carr, the creator of locked-room puzzle solver Gid-

Robert Caine Frazer | Patrick Gill | Michael Halliday | Charles Hogarth | Brian Hope | Colin Hughes | Kyle Hunt eon Fell (*Problem of the Wire Cage,* etc.). He is a.k.a. Carr Dickson (a name pressed on him by a British publisher and changed at his request to Carter Dickson) when writing about Sir Henry Merrivale.

A prolific contemporary suspense writer such as Bill Pronzini will have books published under several pseudonyms — Jack Foxx (*The Jade Figurine*) and Alex Saxon (*A Run in Diamonds*) — in addition to his real name (*Panic!* and *Snowbound*). Ditto Robert L. Fish, inventor of "Schlock Holmes," a parody on Sherlock, who also writes as Robert L. Pike and A.C. Lamprey.

One of the greatest names in the field, Cornell Woolrich, used the name William Irish for *Phantom Lady* (and also used a less well-known alias, George Hopley) because of his high output.

No discussion of pseudonyms used for reasons of output is complete without mention of John Creasey, whose loyal readers are hard put to keep up with his books (over 600 of them!) and his aliases. He used twenty-six, varying them from sleuth to sleuth.

Question of Style

With some mystery authors, for every sleuth there is an alias. The start of the now-famous series of books about private eye Lew Archer gave cause for an alias — Ross Macdonald — to one Kenneth Millar. (His wife, Margaret Millar, uses no alias for her successful mystery novels such as *Beast in View,* a prizewinner.) And a difference in style is the reason for Evan Hunter's choice of the pseudonym Ed McBain on those popular police procedurals, to distinguish them from the books published under his own name (*Blackboard Jungle,* etc.); some of his other pen names are Curt Cannon, Hunt Collins and Richard Marsten.

When Perry Mason's creator, Erle Stanley Gardner, switched sleuths in mid-scream to write about the detective team of Bertha Cool/Donald Lam, he succeeded in deceiving his audience with the alias A.A. Fair. Now these books are emblazoned "Erle Stanley Gardner writing as A.A. Fair," and the secret is out. At the start of his career, Gardner wrote for the pulps under many aliases because of his output.

The famous Ellery Queen is, of course, a pen name for the writing duo of Frederic Dannay and Manfred B. Lee; the same team decided to create another alias, Barnaby Ross, for their second detective (actor Drury Lane). Another team, Mary J. Latis and Martha Hennissart, chose the pseudonym Emma Lathen when they launched their banker-detective, John Putnam Thatcher, in *Banking on Death;* they switched to R.B. Dominic for their capitol crimes.

Sometimes writing teams can be confusing. Manning Coles is an alias for two authors, Cyril Henry Coles and Adelaide Frances Oke Manning. It's not to be confused with another detective team, the Coles (G.D.H. and M.I. Cole), and that's not a pseudonym.

Is Sex Necessary?

For every Agatha Christie, Dorothy L. Sayers and Ngaio Marsh, research yields an equal number of talented mystery and suspense

ABEL MANN | PETER MANTON | J. J. MARRIC | JAMES MARSDEN | RICHARD MARTIN | RODNEY MATTHESON | ANTHONY MORTON

writers born female but published under a male — or ambiguous — pen name: Dell Shannon (Elizabeth Linington), E.X. Ferrars (Morna Doris Brown), P.D. James (Phyllis White), Anthony Gilbert (Lucy Beatrice Malleson), Tobias Wells and Stanton Forbes (both actually DeLoris Forbes), Clemence Dane (Winifred Ashton) and so on through a long list.

A parade of double initials or a first name that could be male baffles us less and less in these enlightened times, but in their fiendish way publishers stuck such male by-lines on their female authors hoping to cash in on all those readers who (they thought) wouldn't touch with a ten-foot noose a detective novel by a woman. Apparently they hadn't heard of Mary Roberts Rinehart . . .

Does it work the other way round? It does for Canadian writer W.E.D. Ross, who publishes Gothics as Marilyn Ross/Clarissa Ross/ et al., and for Michael Avallone, who also has Gothics on the stands with female aliases — Edwina Noone and Priscilla Dalton, to name a couple. Reverse sexism applies to the authorship of the damsel-in-distress books, whose readers are largely women.

Potpourri

Some pseudonyms really do exist to preserve privacy: Catherine Aird (for Kinn McIntosh) is one, and Josephine Tey (for Elizabeth MacKintosh) is another.

One famous secret pen name in the mystery field is Newgate Callendar, the terse mystery critic for the *New York Times Book Review.* With all their knowledge of poisons, ballistics and blunt instruments, novelists reviewed by Callendar could do him in handily were his privacy not protected by an alias.

WHO'S WHO?

Match the author's name on the left to the pseudonym on the right.

1. Hugh Wheeler
2. Reginald Hill
3. Donald Westlake
4. Dashiell Hammett
5. Agatha Christie
6. John Creasey
7. Kingsley Amis
8. Ross Thomas
9. William White
10. Francis Steegmuller

A. Tucker Coe
B. Peter Collinson
C. Q. Patrick
D. Anthony Boucher
E. J. J. Marric
F. David Keith
G. Patrick Ruell
H. Mary Westmacott
I. Robert Markham
J. Oliver Bleeck

I suspect that, like every other fan of "murder ink" who can never get enough, I will have to take my mystery authors as I find them, letting out a Eureka! when I discover a cache of books by one of my favorites writing under a pen name. There is no way to stop mystery and suspense writers from using an a.k.a. They hide behind them just as the crooks on the pages of their books have always done. The evidence is in, and the verdict is obvious: It's another case of fiction following fact.

Carol Kountz is managing editor of The Writer. *She once checked into a small hotel near the Reichenbach Falls as Irene Adler.*

CONWAY STUDIOS

KEN RANGER | TEX RILEY | WILLIAM K. RILEY | HENRY ST. JOHN | JIMMY WILDE | JEREMY YORKE

I.N.I.T.I.A.L.S.

H.R.F. Keating

There are four questions mystery lovers ask whenever I am lucky enough to meet one. First: Do you write in longhand or use a typewriter? I reserve the startling answer for face-to-face encounters. Second: Is it true you wrote about Inspector Ghote in India for years without ever having been there? Yes, plus involved explanations. Question 3: And what do those initials — let me see, is it H.R.H., no that's His Royal Highness — well, what do they stand for? Question 4: Oh, it's H.R.F., is it? I thought . . . But, anyway why do you use initials instead of your proper name?

And the answer to that is, I haven't got a proper name. That is, on my birth certificate the long roll-call begins "Henry," but in English English (I think it's different in American English) Henry is a pretty stuffy sort of moniker, so I like to be called Harry. Well, nowadays lots of authors write under nicknames or abbreviated ones, but when I began, which was about a quarter of a century ago, it wasn't quite the done thing to be Tom, Dick or Harry. So I kept to the initials.

Not that I had been intended to. My father always yearned to write but had little success (an article on keeping rabbits in the *Boy's Own Paper*). So when his first-born came along he transferred some of that ambition to the object squalling in the cradle, and after much thought gave him the name Reymond, spelt in that odd fashion because he had seen it in a book mentioning his ancestors. Why, then, aren't I called Reymond and why isn't it R.H.F.K.? Well, old Uncle Henry had money, and as he had no children . . . (No, in the end he didn't.)

But surely not all crime-writers who use or used to use initials had quite those reasons. Some definitely don't. I put the question to them in my turn. And others I have guessed about.

For instance, there are a lot of American authors who use one forename, one initial and a surname, like J.P.M., the creator of Mr. Moto, and W.P.McG. and E.D.H. and J.M.C. and R.L.F. and C.B.H. and E.S.A. and L.G.B. and D.E.W. and J.D. MacD. But this is a good old American custom and is thus accounted for.

An old British custom accounts for many more. In the good old days it was considered just a trifle vulgar to brandish a chap's actual name, what. Initials were more stiff upper-lip, don't you know, and you called a fellow by his surname. So that's the reason probably for H.C.B. (but he may have had Harry trouble, too) and G.K.C. (and he had the distinction of having his initials as the title of a magazine, *G.K.'s Weekly*) and C.H.B.K. and E.R.P. and E.C.B. and G.D.H.C. and E.W.H. and A.A.M. and J.C.M. (but when he got his "K" it was all right to call him Sir John) and C.P.S. (but later it was okay to say Sir Charles and even later "My Lord") and of course A.E.W.M. I'm glad this last kept to initials, because it once fell to me to compose part of a rhymed ceremony for the Detection Club and A.E.W. goes splendidly with "You sin and there's a ghost to trouble you."

With some of us, I suspect, one extra initial gives a bit of extra weight to a name, like that distinguished lady D.B.H. (she was all set to be plain D.H. but a "Your Fate in Your Writing" guy at a charity fair said "With the B is better"

PARDON ME, IS THIS YOUR HANDKERCHIEF?

Initials when they come on dropped handkerchiefs are one of the best-loved clues of the old-fashioned whodunit. The classic example must be the cambric affair with the letter *H* on it in Agatha Christie's *Murder on the Orient Express*.

You don't get them like that any more. Blame the tissue. But in the H.R.F. Keating sock drawer there are still two decent cotton handkerchiefs with an initial on each. One dates from the days when my children used to visit Woolworth's just before Christmas. But the other just arrived there, who knows how. And that's the one I shall drop at the scene of the crime. The initial on it is W. Hercule Poirot, I defy you.

H.R.F.K.

and yes, success followed) or the Australian A.W.U. or E.P.O., though the rest of his names were weighty enough, or R.A.K., though when he got a Monseigneur to tack in front he too became a pretty heavy vessel, or D.L.S. And what a fuss she used to make if that L was left out. "I do admit to one fad. I do like my name to appear in advertisements in the same form in which it stands on the title-page," she wrote once. "It is, if you like, a Freudian complex associated with my schooldays, and possibly I ought to get over it, but I can't. It produces in me a reaction of humiliation and depression and *I don't like it*."

And with one or two others, urged on in one case by her American publishers, an extra initial has been added to provide a little easily got mystery. That's E.X.F. The X stands for nothing. And I suspect something similar went on with A.H.Z.C., because he was born plain A.Z.C., and it was much the same with O.H. and H.H.H. Both pseudonyms these, like J.J.C. and S.S. Van D. and J.J.M. and A.A.F., who all used quite meaningless initials for their noms de plume. Occasionally, too, initials provided additional concealment for a pseudonym, as in the case of A.B.C., who if he had used either of his two forenames would have been revealed for the other author he was, and with that old favourite of mine, E.C.R.L., who both wanted to hide her femininity and make up an anagram. In one odd case initials were abandoned so as to lose a bit of weightiness when the academic J.I.M.S. took to crime.

Finally, there are a couple of contemporary British authors who wanted, in perhaps a rather British way, to protect themselves from the world a little, in order, I hazard, to write the better, You'll see what I mean when you read the excellent, rather secretive novels of P.M.H. and the splendid books, also with a good deal of her private personality in them, of P.D.J.

KEY

John P. Marquand, William P. McGivern, Edward D. Hoch, James M. Cain, Robert L. Fish, Chester B. Himes, Edward S. Aarons, Lawrence G. Blochman, Donald E. Westlake, John D. MacDonald, H.C. Bailey, G.K. Chesterton, C.H.B. Kitchin, E.R. Punshon, E.C. Bentley, G.D.H. Cole, E.W. Hornung, A.A. Milne, J.C. Masterman, C.P. Snow, A.E.W. Mason, Dorothy B. Hughes, Arthur W. Upfield, E. Phillips Oppenheim, Ronald A. Knox, Dorothy L. Sayers, Elizabeth X. Ferrars, A.H.Z. Carr, O. Henry, H.H. Holmes (Anthony Boucher), J.J. Connington, S.S. Van Dine, J.J. Marric (John Creasey), A.A. Fair (Erle Stanley Gardner), A.B. Cox (Anthony Berkeley), E.C.R. Lorac (Carol Carnac), J.I.M. Stewart (Michael Innes), P.M. Hubbard, P.D. James.

And what about the one initial of my own I have so far not revealed? Perhaps you will see why when, blushingly, I admit: F for Fitzwalter.

H.R.F. Keating won the Crime Writers' Association Gold Dagger.

MAKING A NAME FOR MYSELF

Penelope Wallace

Two of the earliest questions I asked my nanny were "Who is the best man who ever lived?" and "Who is the most important little girl in the country?" Her answers were "Jesus Christ" and "Princess Elizabeth" — now our Queen. Nanny always *was* prejudiced! To Nanny's question "What do you want to be when you grow up?" I replied, "Famous."

My father and I were very much alike, and neither of us suffered from false modesty; I think it is this similarity which has enabled me to be proud of him — as a father, as a man and as a writer — without feeling that I am stifled by his shadow.

Although I was quite young when he died, I'd spent two years with him at Chalklands, our country house in Buckinghamshire, and here, with the rest of the family away during the week, we talked as equals. He was totally approachable, stopping work in mid-sentence to deal with my problems and answer my questions. We would go in the motor launch to Marlow, where we both ate strawberries and cream for tea — heavy on the cream or sugar, although we were both more than somewhat overweight.

My father had definite views on life, on religious and racial toleration — his villains are of differing nationalities, but usually English. In one book the villain is Chinese; in another, the hero is Chinese. He was a monotheist, with the conviction that truth is not exclusive to any particular church.

After my father died — heavily in debt — we moved from Chalklands and the luxury

COURTESY PENELOPE WALLACE

Penny, age five, with her father, Edgar Wallace, in his study.

apartment in Portland Place to a small flat in Kensington. Here I lived with my mother during the time she wrote her biography of my father, using the money to pay my school fees at Roedean. She lived to see me pass the entrance exam and died just over a year after my father.

My guardian was a thirty-six-year-old bachelor who was totally incapable of housing a headstrong girl, so I shuttled myself between relations and left school at seventeen. At school I'd suffered somewhat from the "I should have thought Edgar Wallace's daughter would be able to do that" remarks from the staff, but since one is never introduced to people there — presumably new girls are warned in private — it wasn't until I started working in Oxford that I first ran up against the standard introduction to which I've become accustomed:

"This is Penny, daughter of Edgar Wallace."

For a while I thought people only wanted to meet me for my relationship, and I thought of changing my name; then I realised this might be true the first time — as if I had two heads — but if people invited me twice it was because they liked me as me. Now I know "daughter of Edgar Wallace" is an additional interest. I'm proud that so many people like and admire him, and I'm delighted to share the affection they have for him.

Since I've tried all my life not to trade on my name, one thing that burns me is when people who are aware of my membership in the Press Club and the Crime Writers' Association ask me if I write! I answer tartly that I'm a member of the Writers' Guild, so I guess I do. In my immodest way, I point out that I've written a number of short stories and that one was made into a TV film for Rod Serling's *Night Gallery* — and furthermore I got good reviews in the States and not one referred to my father!

Penelope Wallace has won a special Crime Writers' Association Silver Dagger award for her organization of the First International Crime Writers Congress.

THE EDGAR WALLACE PUB

Opened October 19, 1976, in Essex Street, London WC2, the pub is handsomely decorated in cherry, gold and deep beige — the Wallace racing colours — and houses valuable Wallace memorabilia, including a gold inscribed cigarette case with the names of his twenty or so race horses, his brass inlaid tea caddy, walking stick, pictures and first editions.

THE EDGAR WALLACE SOCIETY

During the Twenties and Thirties, one out of every four people reading a book was reading a Wallace. Called the "King of Thrillers" he wrote 173 books and 17 plays. (He also wrote the screenplay for the original version of *King Kong* starring Fay Wray.) His advertising promotion for *The Four Just Men* (Wallace offered a £500 reward to anyone who could come up with the solution to it) was a fabulous sales incentive but a financial disaster. It put him into bankruptcy. In January of 1969, Penelope Wallace founded the Edgar Wallace Society to keep loyal Wallace fans alerted to new releases and biographical data not otherwise available. The Society issues a quarterly newsletter, and new members receive a four-page biography of Wallace and a cross-referenced list of titles. For further information, write to Penelope Wallace, 4 Bradmore Road, Oxford, England, OX2 6QW.

A MARRIAGE OF MINDS

The Gordons

For forty years now, we've been collaborating on magazine articles, novels, and television and movie scripts, yet we don't quite know how the collaboration works. And it's difficult to explain something you don't understand.

Despite what our friends think, we don't claw and fight. In fact, we've never had a really serious quarrel. The idea has seldom crossed our minds.

Homicide, yes. But quarrels, no.

Even the thought of homicide has been fleeting and muted. And we think that's because in the beginning we decided we would treat each other as if we were single and working together in an office. Gradually we evolved a rule: If one of us feels strongly about a point, then the other gives in. If we both have deep persuasions, then we postpone all discussion for two or three days. By then, we may have forgotten which viewpoint we had, or one of us may have come to see the merits of the other's.

Though we are true collaborators in every sense, we didn't set out to be. Gordon, just out of the University of Arizona, discovered he had become an instant newspaper editor. There was a recession under way, the paper couldn't afford to hire a good editor, and Gordon just happened to be standing there. However, the job paid poorly, and he was forced to moonlight doing magazine articles. He got into the habit of turning over his rough copy to his just-signed bride with the notation "Please fix." Soon she was fixing more and more, and imitating his style. Then one day we were writing so much alike that editors couldn't tell who had written what.

The reason we're not sure exactly how the collaboration works is that we're often in a state of confusion. This is a disease common to authors, no matter how many books they've written. The work seldom comes easily and the decisions that must be made are frightening.

First we have a board of directors meeting, all two of us. We paw through a thoroughly messy stack of files into which for years we've tossed ideas and clippings. We find three or four that we get excited about.

Next we confer with Lisa Drew, our editor, and Ken McCormick, our former editor. We ask for their counsel from the beginning to the finished manuscript, knowing they'll be honest yet considerate of easily bruised egos.

When we're all in agreement on the story, we start juggling three balls. The first is research. We use a cassette to take notes. If we go afield, such as into Arizona's Navajo country as we did for *Ordeal,* we add a camera. Six months later, a slide may fill in a point we've forgotten. In fact, often we see more in the slides when we return home than our memory recorded on the spot.

Along with the research, we write biographies of our principal characters. For each, we may turn out anywhere from three to twenty pages. We don't have room for much of this material, but we need it to give us a "feel" for the character.

Along with the research and the biographies, we plot. This is a hair-tearing operation and the time we most have to keep in mind that homicide is illegal. As we work, we put down each episode, very briefly, on a file card. For *Catnapped!* the cards started out: (1) Ingrid sees prowler; (2) Next morning, Zeke comes, establish characters; (3) D.C. missing; (4) Patti gets ransom call, talks with Zeke, etc.

When we finish, we spread these cards over the den floor like pieces of a jigsaw puzzle. We switch the cards around to heighten suspense; we combine some cards, eliminate others to increase the tempo. It's far more economical in time to omit a card at this point than to strike out a chapter we've slaved over.

We plot to the very end of the story. Many writers disagree with this technique. They think it denies a story spontaneity and that the characters should influence and be influenced by events as the tale progresses. We have no choice. Since we both write on the same story at the same time, we must know where we're going. Occasionally, however, a minor character may usurp a scene, and then we don't hesitate to replot. In other words, our card system is not rigid.

Now we begin the actual writing. Each takes an episode, and we're unisex when it comes to what we write. Milly may have an action scene; Gordon, a romantic one. Or vice versa. We never think about that angle. Occasionally, one of us may say, "Let me have that one. I've got a feeling for it."

We go to our separate dens. Even though we started out as newspaper people working in clattering city rooms, we think we do a better job alone. Besides, Gordon mutters when he writes.

Eventually we exchange copy. We don't hesitate to make marginal notes on the other's pages and sometimes pencil out entire paragraphs. This doesn't bother us. (Well, not too much. We were brought up by hard-boiled newspaper editors and long ago accepted editing as a fact of life, but that doesn't stop us from thinking that all our best work goes into the wastebasket.) What we have left, we sell to Doubleday.

This business of editing each other's copy may sound ruthless, but actually it isn't. We both use the soft sell. Milly will say, "This is awfully good, Gordo, but it just isn't up to your usual high standards." That type of con job. And Gordon will say, "This is just sensational, and if we were writing the kind of novel John Cheever does . . ."

A little snow job never hurt a collaboration. Or a marriage.

By the time a book comes out, we've tossed the copy back and forth so often that we're not sure ourselves who wrote what.

We don't believe that collaboration is for everyone, whether married or not. Frankly, we're surprised that it has worked for us. We're strong-willed individuals. It's not a case of one of us dominating these meetings of the board of directors.

The temperament of the collaborators may determine whether they get along, but just as important is the meeting of minds. Our attitudes are much the same. Although we enjoy reading a good hard-boiled novel, we never could write one. We want people in our stories who care for each other, for the world about them. They may come up against violence and the sordid, but they are only a part of it temporarily. This is not their life, any more than it is ours.

We are not alone, of course, as collaborators. There are quite a few today. Perhaps the two most illustrious pairs are Maj Sjöwall and Per Wahlöö and the Lathen team. And in many cases if one has worked himself/herself into a hole, or is suffering a mental block, the partner may readily solve the dilemma.

Each partnership works differently. Most collaborators divide up the work. One takes the research, another the writing, and then one may do the editing and final copy. This division saves a lot of ego bruising. But we grew up basketball fans and don't seem to mind the "body contact" of working everything out together.

Looking back over the forty years, we believe the most important factor in keeping us from committing a little homicide on each other is that we admire and respect each other, as well as love each other. And there is a difference, you know.

The Gordons began their collaboration in 1950 with the saga of J. Edgar Hoover called The FBI Story. *They insist that "that darn cat" proofreads their manuscripts for typos.*

THE CASE OF THE WALL STREET MYSTERIES

Max Hall

In murder mysteries by Emma Lathen the murders are solved by an elderly banker. The books are set in Wall Street and in various businesses served by the "Sloan Guaranty Trust, the third largest bank in the world."

Very few of Emma Lathen's followers know:

That she is two women — a writing team.

That one of them is a graduate of the Harvard Law School and, until recently, practiced corporation law.

That the other has a degree from Harvard's Graduate School of Public Administration (now the Kennedy School of Government) and for many years held responsible jobs in governmental agencies at home and abroad.

That they have begun another series, under the pen name R.B. Dominic, in which the murders are solved by Benton Safford, a Congressman from southern Ohio.

That their writing method is so bizarre I hesitate to tell about it for fear I will be thought to exaggerate.

The two authors, who live in towns near Boston and spend their summers in New Hampshire, submitted to an interview on the condition that I would not print their real names. In fact I did not know their names until the interview took place. I tried several times to persuade them to drop their pseudonymous veils. Amiably, they kept saying no. During most of their writing careers they were still working at their own professions, and they had the idea that if they were known as the authors of books in which a good many pretentious bubbles get burst, their clients and employers might feel a bit uneasy. And even though writing is now their only occupation, they still value their privacy in their home towns. So I will call them Miss Langdell and Miss Littauer — after Langdell Hall at the Harvard Law School and Littauer Center, headquarters of the Kennedy School of Government.

Miss Langdell, the lawyer, told me she grew up in New York City, majored in physics at a college she declined to name, worked a while in Washington, got her law degree at Harvard, and practiced in New York and later in Boston.

Miss Littauer said she grew up in a Chicago suburb, majored in economics at a college she declined to name, worked in Washington and in Europe, got her Master of Public Administration degree at Harvard, and went off to do more government work "and other things." One of her jobs was on the staff of a Congressional committee.

They met at Harvard and quickly learned that they had a powerful interest in common: each had an almost encyclopedic knowledge of murder mysteries in the English language.

Miss Langdell: "I think it's safe to say that I had read just about every mystery in the New York Public Library." Miss Littauer had done the same in her community. At Harvard they swapped, bought, and borrowed mysteries and went through the extraordinary collection of whodunits in Widener Library like two buzz saws.

Years later, in 1960, both were back in Boston. They decided to collaborate. Why?

Miss Littauer: "We decided how nice it would be to have an independent income. We said, let us write a book. A whole series. Let us create an attractive character and have him move in situations where we can take advantage of our strengths. We decided on a banker because there is nothing on God's earth a banker can't get into."

The immediate incentive was a $3,000 contest that the publisher Macmillan was conducting. They wrote *Banking on Death* and sent it off. They didn't get the $3,000 — they never heard that anybody did — but Macmillan accepted the manuscript and published it in 1961. In that book the Sloan got involved with a missing heir, a murder, and sundry shenanigans in a company making felts and industrial textiles in Buffalo.

Macmillan also published the next six, in this order: *A Place for Murder* (a dog show in Connecticut); *Accounting for Murder* (homicide in the home office of the "National Calculating Corporation"); *Murder Makes the Wheels Go Round* (the auto industry); *Death Shall Overcome* (the stock exchange acquires a black member); *Murder against the Grain* (big sale of wheat to the Soviet Union); and *A Stitch in Time* (the medical industry).

Simon and Schuster published the next nine, as follows: *Come to Dust* (fund raising for a small college in New Hampshire); *When in Greece* (a hydroelectric project); *Murder to Go* (bad trouble in a nationwide chain called "Chicken Tonight"); *Pick Up Sticks* (hard-sell real estate in New Hampshire); *Ashes to Ashes* (the closing of a parochial school, also much about the funeral industry); *The Longer the Thread* (the ladies' garment industry in Puerto Rico); *Murder without Icing* (professional hockey); *Sweet and Low* (the cocoa exchange and the candy industry); and *By Hook or by Crook* (Oriental rugs).

All of the above have been published in paperback. The books are also published in England, and all or some of them have been translated into German, Danish, Swedish, Norwegian, Dutch, and Portuguese.

Had you done a great deal of writing before 1961?

Miss Littauer: "No, but you have to remember, by 1961 we were damn near professional *readers* of mysteries."

Do you hire research assistants to study the industries you write about?

They looked surprised and said in effect: "Why, no. We get the information we need mainly from our own experience and from newspapers. The *Wall Street Journal* is a lot of help."

For me the greatest unsolved murder mystery is not so much a matter of determining whodunit but why and how we can stop the mayhem before we're all strangled.

To wit: the bureaucracies that constitute governments determinedly and too often successfully murder free enterprise and the ability of a person or a business to profit. Yet the profitable life of both of them is essential to keep these vampires fed. A familiar mystery plot — how to keep the vampires alive without killing their food source!

Even the best of other mysteries pale beside the magnitude and seeming insolvability of this one.

Malcolm S. Forbes

THE SECOND PSEUDONYM

Under the pseudonym R.B. Dominic, with Doubleday the publisher, there are four books so far: *Murder in High Place* (the Peace Corps and a defenestration on Washington's Connecticut Avenue); *There Is No Justice* (a nominee to the Supreme Court is done in); *Epitaph for a Lobbyist* (lady lobbyist slain at National Airport); and *Murder out of Commission* (the atomic energy commission and a proposed nuclear power plant.

Miss Langdell (emphatically): "A conference about corporate financing is the same all over the world."

Well, how did you two know so much about pro hockey when you wrote *Murder without Icing?*

Miss Littauer: "We are hockey fans. We go to the games. We know about hockey. As for the ownership questions and so on, anybody who reads the sports pages can find that out."

How do you go about collaborating on the writing itself?

Collaborating on their replies, they explained it about like this:

"We write alternate chapters."

What did you say?

"Alternate chapters. One of us writes chapter three, the other chapter four, and so forth."

I never would have guessed it. The style doesn't seem different.

"Also, we write simultaneously. While one is writing chapter three the other is writing chapter four."

Why do you do that?

"To save time."

How does the author of chapter four know what chapter three is going to say?

"Oh, we make a general outline. At first we made a quite full outline, maybe a whole page for each chapter. Now we just agree on the general tenor. We decide in advance who's going to be murdered and who's going to do it. We try to think up as sensible a murder as possible from the point of view of the murderer. Then we have to figure how in the world Thatcher can catch the murderer. A couple of times we created a foolproof murder that not even Thatcher could solve, and we had to go back and put in a mistake or two on the part of the murderer."

Miss Langdell and Miss Littauer didn't make their job sound very difficult; but I can't help thinking they must do a mighty lot of adjusting and editing after exchanging those simultaneous drafts. After all, a book typically takes them six or seven months, and some have taken over a year. By the way, when I asked whether they get much editing at their publishers, they grinned. The answer is no, and that's just how they want it.

Miss Langdell writes at night, with two fingers on a Hermes 3000. Miss Littauer prefers daytime and writes with a ballpoint on a long yellow pad. They use secretarial services for typing. They keep two three-ring binders, one containing the original and the other a carbon copy.

John Putnam Thatcher is different from the usual crop of detectives and private eyes in fiction. He is urbane, well-bred, skeptical, unfluffable but easily bored, no tough guy but as firm as Gibraltar in protecting the Sloan's interests, a widower with grandchildren, sixtyish (and doesn't grow older from book to book), much helped by Miss Corsa (everybody's ideal secretary), long-suffering in the face of idiotic behavior by public-relations men and by the bank's president, Brad Withers, who happens to be a Yale man. A reviewer in *The New Yorker* once called Thatcher "a man of great charm, bottomless suspicion, and Euclidean squareness." Says Miss Langdell: "I have never met anybody as nice as Thatcher."

Max Hall is a free-lance writer and former editor at Harvard University Press.

WHY I'LL NEVER FINISH MY MYSTERY

John Leonard

It seemed like a good idea at the time, which was February. She had just come back from Paris with a trunk of troubles. For me, work has always been an anodyne — *the* anodyne, I see now — and I presumed on fifteen years of friendship to commend it to her. I also commended myself. We would collaborate in abolishing her depression.

It was probably raining. Certainly, I was fooling myself.

For a living, I write. For relaxation, I read mysteries. It is only natural that I should have contemplated writing a mystery. The problem was a plot. In an otherwise blameless life, I have perpetrated four novels, and even the reviewers who found something to admire in those novels had to admit that, as one of them put it, "Plot is not his forte." I try to get by on style and sensibility, as is often the case with writers to whom nothing very alarming has ever happened. (About the time Grace Kelly married Prince Rainier, someone in Hollywood was asked for anecdotes about her, and replied: "Grace is the sort of person who doesn't allow anecdotes to happen to her." Maybe this implies a lack of imagination. But, I keep telling myself, the same was true of Wallace Stevens.) Anyway, there wasn't much use contemplating a mystery when, in my unmysterious fiction, I had enough trouble getting people in and out of rooms.

Whereas, for a living, she teaches history. She does not write, not even letters. She reads as many mysteries as I do, not so much for relaxation as in a critical spirit, as if trying to figure out why Napoleon didn't get away with it or Trotsky blew his chance. She wants to solve the murder; I'd rather leave it to the detective. She does double-crostics with a felt-tip pen; I watch baseball games on television. Her training, though, as an historian had steeped her in theories of conspiracy. She teemed with plots. She agreed to outline four of them. On paper.

I should explain that, over the years, as we watched each other's children grow, she had introduced me to Josephine Tey and I had introduced her to Ross Macdonald. Her favorite mystery was *The Daughter of Time* and mine was *The Chill.* It might have occurred to clever people that we were temperamentally opposed. We were not clever.

We met instead for lunch at one of those French restaurants in midtown Manhattan where the menu is a sneer. We were to go over her plot outlines. The chitchat was of Michael Innes (*Hamlet, Revenge!*), Dashiell Hammett (*The Glass Key*), Rex Stout (*Too Many Cooks*), Raymond Chandler (*The Long Goodbye*) and the Wahlöös (*The Laughing Policeman*). It was also of Schopenhauer and Scheherazade, of Mozart and Bette Midler, of Watergate and Billingsgate.

She wore, I couldn't help noticing, a dress. Always before I had seen her in pants. I knew she was freckled; I hadn't known that she had legs.

THE WORK IN PROGRESS

Diana decided to shorten the leash on her impatience. Intelligent, passive people made her grind her teeth: there were always extenuating circumstances, and all day long such people combed them, like a beautiful head of hair. But she was not her sister's keeper. "How are you engaged in subversive activity?"

No! How did you have the nerve to do that?!!

"I use the wrong color ink," said Sally. "I put down an X where a circle is supposed to be. I refer telephone callers to doctors who don't belong to the organization. I'm single-handedly undermining the system. People with bad feet will have to go to psychiatrists. I have surgeons for acne. Everything they plug into their computer will be a lie. I'm a treasonous clerk, what do you think of that?"

Nice! Love it.

. . .

There was a thump at the door. And what happened next seemed choreographed. Sally rose, as though to execute an entrechat; switched gears from a glissade to a bourree; and arrived at the thumping ready to jete. Behind the door stood Nick, in the first position, holding grocery bags. Sally tried to take them. He would not release them. Locked together around the grocery bags, they backed into the livingroom, did two or three pirouettes on point, sighed, tried a plie, and simultaneously sat down on the floor. Diana wanted to applaud. How like brother and sister they were -- twin redheads, both short, wearing identical tie-dyed T-shirts and faded bluejeans and Capezio exercize slippers. Maybe Sally's freckles had been scooped out of Nick's dimples and applied to her skin with a dropper.

I'm not crazy about all that ballet imagery—it's not bad; it does work, I think—but it's unnecessary.

We agreed on our detective — a young female lawyer living alone in New York — and settled on the simplest of her four plots as a start. This plot involved a theater troupe, a loft, an ancient grievance, some schizophrenia, Grand Guignol and enough suspects to stuff a Trojan horse. I will say no more; perhaps by the time Jimmy Carter completes his second term as President and runs for God, we'll get around to finishing our mystery. Her responsibility, in addition to the plot, was detail. How does a little theater operate — props, costumes, set design, money-raising? What would our detective, Diana, look like, wear, eat, read, listen to on the phonograph, admire and disdain? Which, when, who, why . . . and so on.

I, on the other hand, typed. While she made lists — of plants, poisons, legal precedents, pop therapies — I, out of my style and sensibility, was to fashion believable characters and to engineer suspense. Action, conversation and the sort of morbid excess necessary to imagine an avant-garde play were my specialties. I would type a chapter, we would meet, she would carry the chapter away in her knapsack and, alone with an orange and a cup of coffee grounds, edit — using, of course, a felt-tip pen. Then we would meet again.

I had assured her that, although I type neatly out of some anal compulsion whose origin is nobody's business but my own, she should feel free to question, contradict, excise and veto. This, as it turned out, was a big mistake.

Those meetings: after many a taco, burns the heart. In Mexican restaurants, at botanical gardens and public libraries, Nathan's and the zoo, we met. Under clocks at train stations, in bars without television sets, behind bayberry bushes on Fire Island, in the lobbies of movie houses with popcorn machines and of apartment buildings with doormen who looked like drill instructors at an orthopedic gym for wayward jackboots, we met. As though we were spies, and our mystery were microfilm, we exchanged manila envelopes: heavy breathing at the Algonquin.

My collaborator complained about my narrative device of throwing a party every time we needed to press-gang a motley of implausible loud-mouths into the obligatory anticlimax. I abashed myself, not, I admit, without grumbling that she had a fixation on locked rooms and ciphers.

My collaborator removed all puns from the manuscript. Although I was injured in the technique and the predisposition — puns, after all, derail the train of thought — I acquiesced. If what she wanted was more like a diagram of a synthetic carbon derivative than the word-playfulness, the beautiful phoneme, I associate with a happy hammerlock, plus tickles, on the

English language, well, it was her plot.

My collaborator objected to my promiscuous analogizing. I would have instructed her on the abstract pleasure of a purely verbal artifact, but demurred: We live in a world that eats ugly pills; the streets swarm with disappointed thugs; our architecture is brutal and cowering; our music blares; we advertise ourselves in neon, or with gongs; our principal form of locomotion seems to be the shove. To collaborate, then, with someone who looks as though she danced or swam, who would be able to touch a piano or a child without leaving fingerprints — "In every gesture dignity," said Milton — was to be reacquainted with grace and brave beauty, and to have an excuse for subduing qualms. Compared to purely verbal artifact, or even the latest abstraction, she seemed real.

My collaborator felt that I was trying too hard, showing off, slowing down the story: Please, sir, instead of the arabesque, may we have a minuet? She attacked me in the adjectives. This is attacking me in the style and sensibility.

Another critic.

I should also explain that in the course of this assault on my pride of rhetorical legerdemain — to life, I apply a dangling participle as if it were a stethoscope; in the gerunds, there one is free — I was "launching" my collaborator. That is, I hauled her off to those literary cocktail parties, or West Side fundraisers at which Ramsey Clark is asked to come out in favor of compulsory sodomy, where she might meet a man worthy of her history and freckles.

Strange: these men, underneath their blow-dried tease, behind their tinted aviator goggles, inside their Cardin turtlenecks, seemed unheroic and insensitive, so many thumbs on the lute of her throat, jukeboxes of opinions. I dialed a radio cab, and fed her cats.

Listen: I thought that in writing about our detective, Diana, I was writing about a Harriet Vane who went to Yale Law School, a kind of *Gaudy Night* under the tables down at Morey's. I found that I was writing about my collaborator; her distinction was the watermark on every virgin page I tapped at.

FAMOUS WRITING PARTNERSHIPS

Peter Anthony
Francis Beeding
Manning Coles
Ellery Queen
Patrick Quentin

I stopped working. So much for anodynes.

Then there was the night Nixon resigned. My collaborator and I drove all afternoon, with the radio on, and made it in time for dinner at a country inn in Connecticut. She had grown up in California. Some scars glow in the dark. This was an occasion, for which she dressed in flames. After fish and wine on the veranda, overlooking fireflies, we went inside to the TV set. The room was upholstered in Republican putty, and sullen. My collaborator was too fiercely happy for them. She was a sword. They had to keep their mouths shut as Nixon fell on her sword.

William Butler Yeats, who never wrote a mystery novel, spoke in one of his poems of "beauty like a tightened bow," the kind from which arrows are loosed. Yeats was meditating on a Maud Gonne who was looking around for another Troy to burn. I am meditating on my collaborator, for whom there aren't enough Troys to burn. Collaboration is a dialectic. Love is grazing privileges.

Reader, I married her.

At the wedding, my son played the clarinet. Hot and cold running daughters punned their way through a rendition of "Greensleeves" obscene in its subtext. I have, in a drawer, eighty pages of a mystery novel that has somehow, mysteriously, lost its zest and zeal and analogies.

There are some mysteries for which we do not require, nor do we want, solutions.

I didn't even manage to silence a critic.

John Leonard is chief cultural correspondent of the New York Times.

BOOK ONE: TO BE CONTINUED?

James McClure

There was a brief paragraph headlined CATCH 23 in the *Times* of London not long ago that read: "Twenty-three fishermen have been rescued from the Sea of Japan after their boat, full of mackerel, sank under an excessive catch."

The moral is clear: Never trust a mackerel, no matter how outwardly obliging it may appear. Less obvious, perhaps, but very tempting, is the application of this modern parable to the writer about to embark upon a mystery series.

To paraphrase the warnings given by ancients who, with glittering eye, stoppeth one of three at mystery conventions, the voyage will take his frail craft into wickedly deceptive waters. He will have to guard against accepting unqualified success without question, and against dangling the same hook once too often. He would also be prudent to avoid taking on board greater numbers of that other slyly treacherous fish, the red herring, than can be comfortably accommodated. While he must never allow himself to forget, even in his most transcendental moments of achievement, that specific gravity and other down-to-earth phenomena remain immutable.

Yet this advice could apply equally to the writer planning a dozen unrelated mystery novels. The series writer is, as they say, in a different ball game altogether.

Just how different is evinced by our tortured attempts to explain why it isn't the Sea of Japan we're fooling with here, but an ocean of paradox that threatens a fate far worse than dampened euphoria.

We could say, for example, a mystery series traps the writer in a whole new dimension — and that there's written evidence to prove it. An antimatter world in which the laissez-faire laws of fiction tend to invert themselves, hardening fancy into fact, denying the usual liberties and, what's worse, translating many well-meaning human beings into wistful automatons.

"A sausage machine, a perfect sausage machine" — so Dame Agatha once described herself when, in the unreflective prose of G.C. Ramsey, she was "a little awed at the idea she must produce a Christie for Christmas lest the earth veer off its course."

True, automatons don't come any more wistful than sausage machines, nor has there ever been a threat to the solar system more extraordinary; the Virgin, although subject to not dissimilar expectations, certainly hadn't the same penalty clause.

But problems aren't solved by simply changing genre. With the delightful exception of Harry Harrison's Stainless Steel Rat stories, mystery writing and science fiction just haven't much in common — and it would be wrong to suggest that things were quite as bad as all that.

In this search for comparisons with which to construct a practical framework of reference for the tyro, I prefer to find them in the past, way back in another realm of mysteries.

I believe the mystery series writer has more in common with the alchemist — beyond such superficialities as a dim, dusty workroom littered with manuscripts and sobered by the odd skull — than is generally conceded.

COURTESY JAMES McCLURE

James McClure always doodles while planning a novel. He says, "I generally start with a face in the middle and build up around it, adding things suggested by lines and shapes which juxtapose, and others that seem to hop straight out of a deep hole someplace."

My first inkling of this came when someone made the usual crack about "*formula* writing," as though a formula was in itself something despicable. If people mean this to imply that they'd rather every aspirin they took was wildly, excitingly different in composition and effect, then good luck to them. But the point is that the word "formula" suddenly struck me as inappropriate: it was too precise, too modern.

Then I realised that the mystery writer's stock-in-trade was really the *spell* — never prissy formula, the very sound of which precludes eye of newt, hair of psychopath, Group O and the other more gruesome ingredients one uses to create one's illusions.

This happened while I was writing my first Kramer and Zondi novel, and, as I'd already latched on to the idea that all writers were stage conjurers with a persuasive line of patter, the notion slotted in very happily. It wasn't until I came to repeat a few tricks for the second and third K&Z stories that I discovered the difference between an innocuous "abracadabra" and one uttered when the game was being played for keeps.

My Afrikaner detective and his Zulu colleague, illusory beings I'd personally summoned up, seemed to have become independent of me and my powers. Not only that, but they'd moved out into the real world, where a section of the reading public, albeit a small one, had placed them under the protection of the law.

The irony was acute. Should I now decide

that Kramer had to be written off in Chapter Eight, then I could be charged with — wait for it — murder! And if the wholly biased jury out there found me Guilty, then I'd have only two options: to stage a resurrection as soon as possible, compromising my integrity; or to shout "Nuts!" from the dock, forfeit my royalties and hope no greater punishment would be exacted.

As it was, I had no particular urge to destroy either of them, had chosen the pair in the first place because they were the best means at my disposal *(huh)* for expressing ideas that mattered to me — and I'd stuck with them for the very same reason.

But what had wrought this transformation? What was the uncanny difference between the one-shot novel and the series book? It gave me cause to ponder further the alchemist theory, and I'll admit I had to cheat a little with regard to that discipline's achievements to find this answer to the questions posed.

One could say that the essence of life is continuity; when it runs out of time, it stops. Just as an evening of real-life drama ends when the final curtain is rung down, or when people vanish at the snap of a satisfying novel being closed, to persist thereafter only in retrospect — thought about, perhaps, but never again encountered.

Whereas if a book is left open-ended, like a genie's bottle left uncorked, stock characters can escape into time proper, linking their innate continuity to something that has no beginning, no middle and no end. They can even achieve a state of active longevity far exceeding one's own, and here I'm thinking of *Colonel Sun*, for example, the posthumous James Bond treat by Kingsley Amis. The so-called immortality of many well-loved spirits is not, of course, the same thing, as they're able only to endlessly repeat themselves until a pastiche comes along — but that's another sort of series (and pastiche), anyway.

Whatever the cause behind this change, there's no doubt that it brings a moment of realisation that fills the writer with surprise, joy and trepidation. Any alchemist who, quite as inadvertently, found himself manifesting a virgin against his corner cupboard, must have felt much the same way — while noticing the same whiff of brimstone and eternal damnation in the air.

This could seem absurd to the Novelist Who regards Himself as the God Almighty of His separate creations, free to do as He pleases and answerable to no one for His inscrutable excesses. Yet let him try his hand at a mystery series, and he'll soon have his personal pronouns cut down to size — either that, or trade his soul for the conceit of them. Observe how serenely humble some series authors are; note how others run the full gamut from quiet despair to demonic megalomania.

It's just possible they stand divided by much the same things as separated the sages from the sorcerers: their prime motive for being interested in life, death and the puzzles arising; their attitudes to self-indulgent compromises, to truth and morality; their willingness to serve themselves or to serve others. They could be set apart, in short, by the choice they make between practising black or white magic.

Latter-day parallels aren't difficult to draw. Most blatant, perhaps, is the violence/drugs/perversion wizard who has his proclivities prologued (in the same order) by Mephistopheles in Goethe's *Faust*:

> *One of those crickets, jumping round the place,*
> *Who takes his flying leaps, with legs so long,*
> *Then falls to grass and chants the same old song;*
> *But not content with grasses to repose in,*
> *This one will hunt for muck to stick his nose in.*

Lionel Timothy Cricket (his real name, although none of his admirers is ever permitted to know this) deludes himself that he's turning base mettle into gold, of course; sadly, although crotch-deep in all that glitters under the Californian sun, he has never produced anything as valuable as a frankfurter — and never will he while a sick fantasy like Hank Grunt, his star turn, is still around.

Equally noticeable, but way across the other side, beneath the brighter sun of India, stands H.R.F. Keating and his endearing familiar, Inspector Ghote of the Bombay

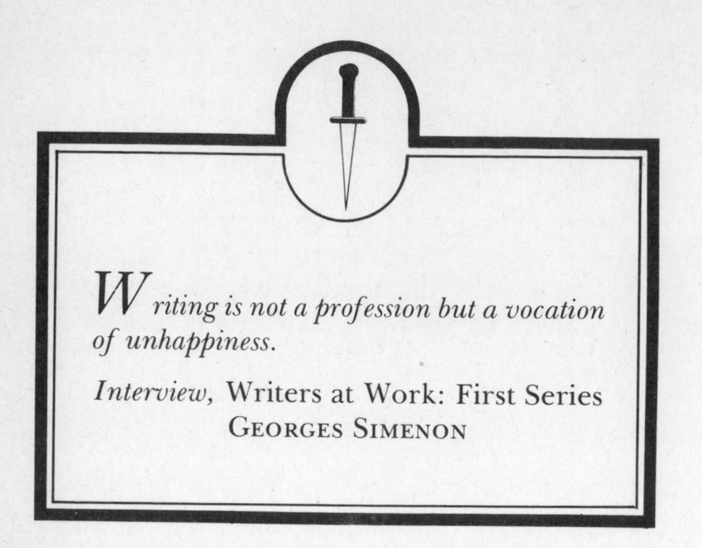

Police. "Margery Allingham once told me," Mr. Keating recalls, "that only half one's readers would be interested in the book itself, while the other half would read it for the series character— and the writer just has to be reconciled to this." His generous reconciliation is obvious; he and Ghote have together brought us all a wealth of good things to enjoy.

Grudging resentments, not unlike those felt by some ventriloquists for their dummies, frequently occur in the grey, uncommitted area (does that sound like England?) lying between the two extremes. This could be a matter of trying to impose one's own needs and shortcomings on reality at the expense of truth.

The School of Incredibles, which has as its protagonists old ladies never short of an hygienic murder to solve, police officers with the intellectual introversion of their middle-class alter egos, often seems to show signs of the stress of vicarious living. Dorothy L. Sayers once said, a shade too cheerily perhaps: "I can see no end to Peter this side of the grave!" She did, however, contrive to ignore him for the last two decades of her life, by which compromise she brought about his nominal termination. What adds poignancy to this is that Julian Symons, the celebrated authority on mystery writing, has suggested that Miss Sayers might have been a much better writer had she not fallen in love with her whimsey.

One could go on endlessly noting the stern morality at work between the lines of this genre, just as alchemists must have found that their similar preoccupation with light and dark was apt to evoke the unexpected

But far more is to be gained by simply looking at what has been achieved by a master magician unrivalled in his understanding and honest exploitation of the mystery series. Mr. Symons has said of Georges Simenon's Maigret — in his definitive history of mystery writing, *Bloody Murder* (U.S. title, *Mortal Consequences*) — that he is "one of the most completely realised characters in all modern fiction."

To which, for an insight into the approach that made this possible, one need add only the author's own words from *Writers at Work*:

> *I have a very, very strong will about my writing, and I will go my own way. For instance, all the critics for twenty years have said the same thing: 'It is time for Simenon to give us a big novel, a novel with twenty or thirty characters.' They do not understand. I will never write a big novel. My big novel is the mosaic of all my small novels.*

So where has all this led us? Have we done better than the champions of Catch 23? Perhaps we have encouraged the newcomer to look upon each book in his series as a carefully selected chip of coloured glass, rather than as a worthy yet ephemeral sausage, and that's about all. No matter, for the old salts overlook plain Catch 2, anyway.

Catch 2? That's simple: Nobody can really know they're a series writer until Book Two, when it's too late to unmake the critical decisions made in Book One, which wasn't Book One until Book Two began the series, although it had to begin with Book One, of course.

As for Catch 1 — any series, wilfully and arrogantly launched with Book One, presuming a demand to supply, is likely to have no real magic at all and to never reach Book Two — well, let's not dwell on it. I once did just that, and have been haunted ever since by a disembodied ex-detective, shrouded in diabolical reviews.

James McClure won the Crime Writers' Association Gold Dagger for his first novel. The Steam Pig.

THE LURE OF THE REICHENBACH

Peter Dickinson

I am no scholar. I am not even sure how to spell "Reichenbach." Certainly I have no idea how many lesser heroes than Holmes have been done away with by their creators. But it must be a good guess that almost every writer who has kept a detective going through several books finds his thoughts turning more and more to ward the moment when . . . when, for instance, Inspector Ghote eats the poisoned curry, or Peter Wimsey has heart failure on meeting a greater snob than himself, or Van der Valk . . . But no, Van der Valk *is* dead, isn't he? Mr. Freeling has done the deed.

Why?

The usual answer, that the creator had become bored with his creation, is true in a very trivial kind of way but is at the same time deeply misleading: the kind of answer a writer gives when he doesn't want to discuss the point. I myself stopped writing about James Pibble after five books, but I wasn't bored with him. I liked — and like — the old boy, and I owe him a lot. I think that without hesitation I could answer most questions about him, including the ones which aren't mentioned anywhere in the books. Now he feels to me something like a colleague I spent a lot of time with almost every day but because of a change of jobs have scarcely seen for several years; to meet again might be delightful, might be embarrassing, but it seems not to happen.

It's worth considering how these long-running heroes come into existence. There seem to be two ways, the deliberate and the accidental. The deliberate hero is nearly always a bloodless creation; the author has decided that he (she? Is it a female trait to manufacture these bionic brains? No idea, but let's settle for "she" throughout) . . . that she is going to write a series of books and that, therefore, they will have to have some kind of trademark. The hero will be *different*. Thus traits of difference are accumulated, selected not for the way they grow out of the character but solely because nobody else has yet thought of them. In much the same way, minor German monarchs of the eighteenth century invented uniforms for their household troops: violet breeches, because everyone else had green or red; kepis with four-foot plumes; badger-skin bandoliers. What matter if in the end the hussar was unable to lift his sabre above waist height because of the tightness of his jacket? He was more distinctive on the field than old Hesse-Halsbad's boring dragoons.

So the deliberate hero is jumbled into being. (Or *was* jumbled would probably be truer; these creatures were mostly born a generation or two ago, though they live on in libraries, and every now and then a new one is born, especially on TV. Lollipops, for instance.) Let's say he has a club-foot and rides an enormous bike (good for last-minute dashes to rescue the peculiarly witless females who festoon this type of novel) and carries a . . . a swordstick? No, too ordinary; what about a blow-pipe? And he knows the Bible by heart, huh?

For book after book, shelf after shelf, that bike will roar to the rescue, that uneven footstep will sound menacingly, or hearten-

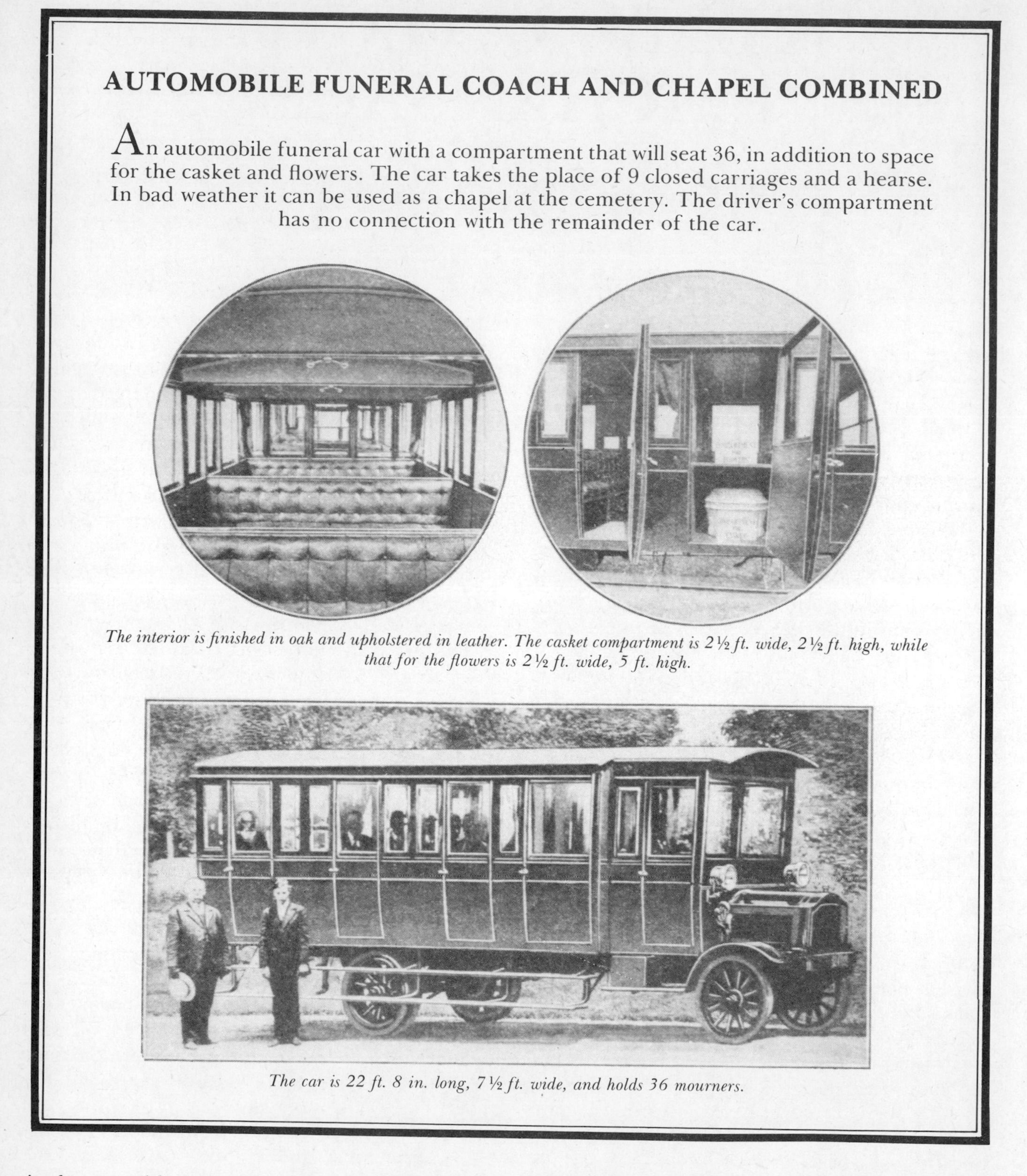

AUTOMOBILE FUNERAL COACH AND CHAPEL COMBINED

An automobile funeral car with a compartment that will seat 36, in addition to space for the casket and flowers. The car takes the place of 9 closed carriages and a hearse. In bad weather it can be used as a chapel at the cemetery. The driver's compartment has no connection with the remainder of the car.

The interior is finished in oak and upholstered in leather. The casket compartment is 2½ ft. wide, 2½ ft. high, while that for the flowers is 2½ ft. wide, 5 ft. high.

The car is 22 ft. 8 in. long, 7½ ft. wide, and holds 36 mourners.

ingly, on sidewalks (though, mark you, in moments of crisis we will read of the man moving "with astonishing dexterity, despite his club-foot"), the witless female's latest attacker will stagger in mid-assault, a tiny dart protruding below his left ear, and all will end pat with a quote from the Second Book of Kings. And by the third book the author will be stiflingly bored with her creation but afraid to let him go.

I said I was no scholar, so I can only guess which of the great detectives was engendered in this fashion. Nero Wolfe, surely — those orchids are typical, and typically become a nuisance after a very few books, and if all Wolfe's characteristics had been as factitious he would have been a bore very soon. But Mr. Stout was a genius, and in inventing Wolfe and Goodwin, solved the central problem of the whodunit by splitting his detective into two parts; this set-up became an art form in itself — I remember one in which Wolfe finally left his apartment, and I felt as cheated as I would have on reading a thirteen-line sonnet. But very few Wolfes came into the canon that way . . .

As a transitional figure, let's consider Margery Allingham's Mr. Campion, who started as factitious as they come, with his silly-ass talk and his mysterious noble connections and the tedious Lugg to provide extra laughs (like the Professor's comic sailor servant in ancient boys' stories). And then Miss Allingham became interested in him and in the course of two or three books he became, so to speak, real. His chat was mitigated, Lugg almost abolished, and at the same time the plots and adventures moved out of the realm of cardboard fantasy into something like life. So successful was this transformation that Miss Allingham convincingly brought off the problem of making Campion fall in love with a married woman. (Virtue triumphed, too. What a long time ago that must have been. And it's worth pointing out that this passion actually was necessary to the plot.)

So Campion became what I have called an accidental hero. These are the detectives who come into existence because the author wants to write a particular book. The book itself demands a detective, and he *grows* into being, quite slowly, finding his shape and nature from the needs of the book and the author's own needs. He may turn out a very odd creature, but all his oddnesses are expressions of what he is like inside. And then (provided the other bits have gone okay — plot, setting, characters, language and so on) the author may find herself with quite a good book on her hands, centering round a detective to whom readers respond. They may think they're responding because of what seem to be external characteristics (remember the excitement about the first *black* detective?) but really it's because the fellow is *alive.*

Moreover, because detective stories are tricky things to write, the author's attention may not have been concentrated on exploring every nook and cranny of her hero's personality; in fact, if it has, she will have written an unsatisfactory book — there isn't room in the genre for a lot of that sort of thing. So there will be more to give. And the publisher, of course, wants more if the first dose has been a success. It requires a lot of self-confidence and a healthy bank balance for a newcomer author to say no.

So for a few years everyone is happy; if the readers like it, then the publisher likes it, and the author fleshes out her man, puts him into novel situations, finds new facets. If she'd been writing a straight novel, she'd have done all these things in a single book, but with detective stories it may take four or five. And then . . .

Then she has finished. What is she to do with him now? Is he to go on, book after book, dragging his club-foot, using his little grey cells, sucking his lollipop — and dying all the while? Not dying the death that living men die, but moving into the walking death of the zombie? The boom of the Reichenbach Falls begins to mutter in her ears.

The sad result of all this is that, with a few exceptions, it is the accidental heroes who get pushed over the edge, while the deliberate ones — never really alive in the first place — live forever. Those the Gods love die young.

Miss Allingham, tactful as ever, found one solution. She allowed Campion to become a sort of ghost, a twinkle of large spectacles across the room, a muttered suggestion of danger, a friendly spirit, there to keep the readers happy — like a horseshoe over the door. But even she must have known just why Conan Doyle made Holmes walk the fatal path.

It's lucky, if you think of it, that most of us are not faced with the same clamour for resurrection.

Peter Dickinson won the Crime Writers' Association Silver Dagger for the The Glass-sided Ants' Nest.

OUGHT ADAM TO MARRY CORDELIA?

P.D. James

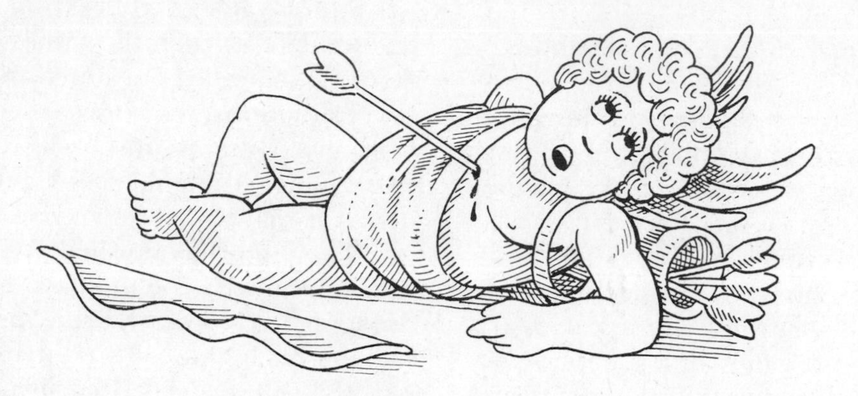

From the number of readers who write to enquire whether my girl detective Cordelia Gray of *Unsuitable Job for a Woman* will marry Adam Dalgleish, it is apparent that mystery lovers take the view — to paraphrase Jane Austen — that an unmarried detective who is in receipt of a good income is in need of a wife. Dorothy L. Sayers would not have agreed. She expressed the firm belief that detectives should concentrate on the clues, not spend their time chasing young women. It was not a rule she herself adhered to, although Lord Peter had to chase his Harriet (if so ungallant a word can be used for his aristocratic and articulate wooing) six years before she finally capitulated on Oxford's Magdalen Bridge — appropriately enough, in Latin.

But it is true that mystery writers, in general, don't interest themselves greatly in the love lives of their detectives, and perhaps this isn't surprising. Birth, sex and death are the three great absolutes in fiction as in life, and it is difficult enough to write adequately about the last, even within the constraints of a detective novel, without attempting to deal other than superficially with its two precursors. A serious love and sex interest in a mystery can endanger its unity as a novel, not to speak of the quality of its detection. It is significant that Dorothy L. Sayers described *Busman's Honeymoon* as a story with detective interruptions. Perhaps this reluctance on the part of detective novelists to deal with sex and love explains why so many writers make their detectives celibates or at least unmarried: Sherlock Holmes, Father Brown, Poirot, Miss Marple, Dr. Thorndyke. In contrast, the tough, wisecracking, hard-drinking school of private eyes have plenty of women in their adventurous lives, but strictly on their own terms. Other detectives have a happy marital background so that we can rest confidently in the knowledge that all is going well with

TROY'S ROMANCE

Ngaio Marsh presented Agatha Troy to Roderick Alleyn in *Artists in Crime* and united them in *Death in a White Tie*. Since Alleyn — or "Rory," as his wife likes to call him — spends much of his time away from London in New Zealand on cases, the two of them carry on a postal relationship a good deal of the time.

their private lives and they can get on with their detection without fear of domestic or psychological upheavals. Examples are Simenon's Maigret, Freeling's Inspector Van der Valk, H.R.F. Keating's Inspector Ghote, Edmund Crispin's Professor Gervase Fen and H.C. Bailey's Mr. Fortune. Other detectives are obviously attracted to women but take care to keep them on the periphery of their private or professional lives. It is difficult to imagine a wife intruding permanently into Nero Wolfe's admirably organised brownstone ménage.

There are, of course, some mystery novels in which the love interest complicates and confuses both the investigation and the hero's emotions. Ngaio Marsh's Roderick Alleyn met his painter wife Troy during one of his cases, and Lord Peter first saw his Harriet in the dock at the Old Bailey, where she was standing trial for the murder of her lover. There are, too, some famous husband-and-wife teams: Dashiell Hammett's Nick and Nora Charles, Agatha Christie's Tuppence and Tommy Beresford, and Frances and Richard Lockridge's Pamela and Jerry North. But here the wife is a comrade-in-arms, and the love interest is domestic, peripheral and amusing rather than passionate. They hunt the clues together.

So what of my readers' question? Will Cordelia marry Adam? Who can tell? There are, of course, a number of reasons why such an interesting marriage might be nevertheless imprudent. One can imagine the advice which a marriage guidance counsellor would give to Cordelia. Here we have a widower, considerably older than you, who has obviously been unable or unwilling to commit himself permanently to any woman since the death in childbed of his wife. He is a very private person, self-sufficient, uninvolved, a professional detective dedicated to his job, totally unused to the claims, emotional and domestic, which a wife and family would make on him. Admittedly, you find him sexually very attractive, but so do a number of women more experienced, more mature and even more beautiful than yourself. Are you sure you wouldn't be jealous of his past, of his job, of his essential self-sufficiency? And how real would your own commitment to him be when there would always lie between you the shadow of a secret — that first case of yours when your lives so briefly touched? And are you sure you aren't looking for a substitute for your own inadequate father?

The arguments are weighty, and Dalgleish and Cordelia — highly intelligent both — would be well aware of them. But then, when have two people married on the basis of prudence? I can only say that I have no plans at present to marry Dalgleish to anyone. Yet even the best-regulated characters are apt occasionally to escape from the sensible and controlling hand of their author and embark, however inadvisably, on a love life of their own.

P.D. James won the Crime Writers' Association Silver Dagger for Shroud for a Nightingale.

HARRIET'S COURTSHIP

Dorothy L. Sayers introduced Harriet Vane to Lord Peter Wimsey in *Strong Poison,* had them work together in *Have His Carcase,* announced their engagement in *Gaudy Night,* married them in *Busman's Honeymoon* and gave them one son in "The Haunted Policeman" and two more in "Tallboys."

MYSTERY WRITERS: A THINK TANK FOR THE POLICE?

Dorothy Salisbury Davis

The remarkable thing about the meeting between the Mystery Writers of America and New York Police Commissioner Patrick Murphy a few years ago is that virtually half the people who were present don't remember what took place; the other half don't remember being there at all. Which has to mean that no matter how much got poured into the Think Tank that day, most of it vanished into vapors when the combustibles caught spark.

I can't remember who promoted the idea of MWA as a Think Tank for the New York Police Department. But if we submitted to flattery, the Commissioner submitted to some of the most extraordinary suggestions since a citizens' group back in the 1840's insisted the police get into uniform so that people could recognize them. I do remember we were each supposed to arrive with an idea on how to improve law enforcement or crime prevention in Manhattan.

One of those ideas which is coming around again — I think now in the State Assembly — was that the city should provide every citizen with a police whistle with which to summon help in emergencies. If one also summoned a taxi, so much the better: double indemnity.

Another mystery writer's proposal that day which involved the public sector: the encouragement of citizen arrests. The double-duty aspect of this action, it was pointed out, was that it would also relieve the police of time-consuming court appearances.

My own humble suggestion purposed an improvement in the patrolman's uniform: a rear-view mirror in the visor of his cap, which, presumably, would make him less vulnerable to attack from the rear. Only the Commissioner picked up the idea — I think to drop it in the alley on his way out. I've been watching for a long time now, and the visor mirror has not become a part of standard police equipment.

The trouble that day was not in the tank or in the ranks. It was in the goal of the promoter, who saw the situation as bulls vs. brains. (I speak poetically, not epithetically.) Commissioner Murphy did not want to fight; he was the perfect gentleman. And we were far and away more willing to make fools of ourselves than of the police. To have truly tested us, the Commissioner should have arrived with the records of one or two unsolved cases and brought along the investigating officers — all 200 or so of them, with whom our best brains might have rapped and just possibly added a mite's worth of insight.

Not many mystery writers would claim their ability to write fiction, wherein they can put and take clues to the crime as needed, qualifies them as bona fide detectives. And not many police detectives, despite the gracious Commissioner Murphy, would concede our talents to have much value on the street.

The great Conan Doyle once undertook the exoneration of a man convicted of cattle mutilation. His detective work cleared the con-

H.T. WEBSTER

demned in the press. But officialdom refused a retrial. The case did lead eventually to the creation of the Court of Criminal Appeal.

New York Police Chief George Walling, whose career spanned half the nineteenth century, wrote of perhaps the most illustrious case of writer as detective:

> *Edgar A. Poe possessed, or thought he possessed, high ability as a detective; and his ingenuity in this ghastly groping is shown in . . .* The Mystery of Marie Roget. . . . *The best authorities of the time do not agree with Poe's finding, but the tragic romance is full of painful interest.*

Our day in a Think Tank neither humbled nor exalted us, but most of us have since confined our ghastly gropings to the typewriter.

Dorothy Salisbury Davis is a past president of the Mystery Writers of America.

CREATING A MYSTERY GAME

Lawrence Treat

Once upon a time there was no TV. People walked to the movies and used their cars to neck in, but when they stayed home there was nothing much to do except listen to the radio and play games.

The old ones were passé, but a whole new type was developing. It was competitive, and it tested knowledge, intelligence and manual skills. People went around saying, "Did you hear about So-and-So? He scored ninety-eight in 'Ask Me Another.' " The high scores of notables like Dorothy Parker and the columnist FPA were quoted, mythically and incorrectly. These were Depression times, the pulp magazines were getting knocked off like bowling pins, and a beginning writer like myself was on the treadmill of trying to turn out stories as fast as the rejection slips came in, which the post office delivered with a speed unknown today.

Around then my eight-year-old nephew, who had no artistic talent whatsoever, showed me a drawing that only he could have been proud of and said, "Guess what." I made my twenty guesses, and he beamed at me and told me the correct answer. "It's a dead man and he's just been killed. See the bullet?"

I said, "Who killed him?" He said, "You did! It's your bullet. See?" And he pointed to a drawing that had a vague, messy resemblance to a crumpled bullet, with my initials on it.

My first thought was that I had a moron for a nephew, my next thought was that he was pretty smart. My bullet? He'd gone and invented ballistics all by himself.

The result of my thinking came slowly and with effort, like a snake wriggling out of his skin, but it finally emerged. Why not a detective game? Show people a few clues and let them make inferences. Let them be their own Sherlock Holmeses.

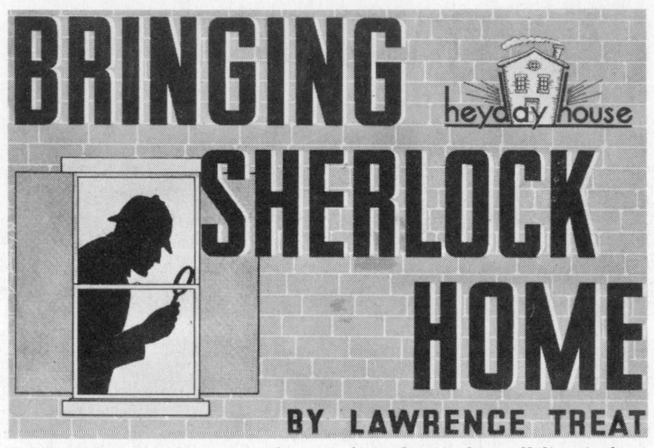

Foolhardy is the detective who stands in front of a well-lit window while a murderer is on the loose. This, the cover design for Mr. Treat's innovative mystery picture puzzles.

The idea was simple enough: Sketch out the evidence found at the scene of a crime and use it to work out the solution. What, for instance, can you infer from a theater ticket stub? Two stubs might mean that X, if he was the holder and a man, took his girl out for the evening. Stubs are dated and numbered and furnish at least a prima facie alibi for time as well as place. An orchestra seat would probably mean that X was well-to-do, a second-balcony stub that he was poor, or at least parsimonious.

Put a stain on it and call it blood, or coffee. Rumple it and you can assume that X is nervous. Take a pair of expensive seats along with a pawn ticket, all found in X's pocket, and he's probably living beyond his means and needs money. Ergo, X had a robbery motive.

The possibilities intrigued me, and I played around with various clue items. Take a cigarette butt. Lipstick on it? Smoked down to the last quarter-inch? Thrown away after a puff or two? Put a few such clues together, state the bare bones of a crime, and put down leading questions that help build up to the solution.

To oversimplify a possible puzzle, suppose you're told that a heavy safe was stolen, either by A or by B. A drawing shows footprints. A's are big, B's are small, and both sets go to where the safe stood. B's imprints are light going to the site and heavy leaving it, whereas A's are of equal depth. Obviously, B stole the safe.

I sent my first attempt to *Dime Detective,* which had been my major rejection market. They approved the project and asked for more, and for months thereafter I went around studying objects with a view to what they might tell me. A discarded hobbyhorse. Chewing gum on the underside of a chair. The contents of a garbage pail. My whole world consisted of objects bristling with ideas that I could use for this game.

Once the game took hold, it sold to strange markets. A drug company used it for promotion. A travel agency bought several puzzles to put on the backs of cruise menus. If a pad can be a book, I published two of them, one under the title *Bringing Sherlock Home,* the other under the more prosaic title *Pictorial Mysteries.* They consisted of a half-dozen copies of each puzzle on a pad, so you could deal them out for a group to compete, for speed as well as accuracy.

With the prestige of book publication, I grew more sophisticated. No longer the simple drawings of a few footprints or a ledger book, which my brilliant nephew was now old enough to execute more or less competently. I needed the sketch of the scene of a crime, with the clues clearly indicated, and several artists tried doing them, with mixed results. The pictures demanded simplicity and accuracy, overlaid with some artistic taste. Small wonder that the artist who managed such a neat balancing act left for a job with Disney, where he could draw the pure, telling lines of the Disney menageries.

In the course of time and sweat *Redbook* paid me handsomely for a set of puzzles, and I was off to Spain on the proceeds of the sale, where I figured I could live nicely for a year. While there, I sent a few of them on to England. British magazines bought them and supported me for another few months.

But the height of my glory was the dizzy month when the New York *Post* dickered with me for using the puzzles in a contest designed to increase circulation. The grand prize was $10,000, which to me was astronomical. Since I, and I only, would know the answers, I had a long and intense struggle with my conscience. My conscience won but was never tested out. The *Post* dropped the idea and returned me to Earth.

Forever after, I've been skeptical about prize contests with a bundle of money for the correct answers.

Writing stories is creatively more satisfying than constructing puzzles and I've never gone back to them, but I can't think of a pleasanter way to have survived the Depression.

Lawrence Treat is a past president of the Mystery Writers of America.

SOLUTION "TO THE LUNCH ROOM MURDER"

3. No, because the money has been taken neither from the counter nor the cash drawer. 4. Yes, because their three checks totaling 55 cents were rung up together on the cash register. It follows that one of them treated the other two. The fact that they sat next to each other is not convincing, although it is indicative. 5. No, because D has finished eating and has paid; A has done neither. 6. At least six — A, B, C, D, Joe, and Brady. 7. Yes, because River Street, which is the only possible approach, is visible through the windows of the lunch room. 8. No. They leave no mark on a dry floor. 9. Y, because they start from near the mop which only he would be using and then proceed to the cash drawer which only he would open, except in case of robbery, which we know has not occurred in this instance. 10. No, because only his toe marks show, indicating that he ran. 11. Yes, because his footsteps (heel and toe marks) show that he walked and did not run to the cash register. 12. Near the cash register, because we know that he walked to it and ran from it, and because he did not close the cash drawer. It follows that something — namely, the murder — frightened him while he was there. 13. Z, because they start at the far side of stool A. 14. Yes, because his toe marks leave via the kitchen door. 15. Yes, because their footsteps do not show and the space near the kitchen is wet. 16. Yes, because the man whose hand print appears must have stood near the mop, in the position where footprints X appear. 17. No, because the mark of his right hand appears. Therefore, he held the gun in his left hand. 18. C, because he was left-handed. Cups and glasses are normally placed at the right and *are* at the right of A's, B's, and D's plates. The smears of glass and cup show C pushed these to the left, where they now are. It follows that C was left-handed and the murderer.

THE
LUNCH ROOM MURDER
Case No. 4
from Lawrence Treat's
"Bringing Sherlock Home"
DELICATESSEN
RIVER ST
DRUGS
TO KITCHEN
A
B
C
D
Z
Y
X
A's check
$ 1 2 3 4
5 — 55
10 60
15 65
20 70
75
30 80
35 85
40 90
45 95
50 *
B's check
$ 1 2 3 4
5 — 55
10 60
15 65
70
25 75
30 80
35 85
40 90
45 95
50 *
C's check
$ 1 2 3 4
5 — 55
10 60
15 65
70
25 75
30 80
35 85
40 90
45 95
50 *
D's check
$ 1 2 3 4
5 — 55
10 60
65
20 70
25 75
30 80
35 85
40 90
45 95
50 *
Delicatessen
Drugs
Fence
RIVER STREET
EAST RIVER
WINDOW
DOOR
counter
counter
WINDOW
JOE'S LUNCH
Kitchen

If you look to the left, you will find a sketch of Joe's lunch room. Police heard a shot, rushed to the restaurant and found exactly what you see.

They identified the body as that of Flash Brady, a racketeer. Joe, who had no helper, had only one fact to tell. The murderer had leaned against the wall while firing at point-blank range. The imprint of his gloved hand is in clear view.

From these facts and an examination of the scene, can you answer the questions and tell who killed Brady?

Answer the following questions by checking the box next to the correct answer. The first two questions have been done and explained to show the type of reason you should have in mind, although you need not write it out.

1. Had Joe been mopping up recently?
☒Yes. ☐No.
Because the pail, mop, and wet floor so indicate.

2. How many customers had recently been in the restaurant? ☐None. ☐One. ☐Two. ☐Three. ☒Four ☐Five.
Because there are four checks and four plates, cups, glasses, and sets of cutlery.

Now you answer the rest of the questions.

3. Do you think Joe was the victim of a holdup? ☐Yes. ☐No.

4. Do you think B, C, and D knew each other? ☐Yes. ☐No.

5. Did A enter the restaurant before D?
☐Yes. ☐No.

6. At least how many people were in the restaurant the instant that Brady entered?
☐1. ☐2. ☐3. ☐4. ☐5. ☐6.

7. Could Brady be seen approaching the restaurant by any of the customers?
☐Yes. ☐No.

8. Would footsteps show if they had not traversed the wet spaces? ☐Yes. ☐No.

9. Which are Joe's footsteps?
☐X. ☐Y. ☐Z.

10. Did Joe walk out through the kitchen door? ☐Yes. ☐No.

11. Did Joe ring up the 55-cent sale on the cash register before the murder?
☐Yes. ☐No.

12. Where was Joe at the moment of the shooting? ☐Near the mop.
☐Near the cash register.
☐Near the kitchen.

13. Which are A's footsteps?
☐X. ☐Y. ☐Z.

14. Did A run out through the kitchen door?
☐Yes. ☐No.

15. Did B, C, and D leave through the front door? ☐Yes. ☐No.

16. Are the footsteps marked X those of the murderer? ☐Yes. ☐No.

17. Did the murderer fire with his right hand? ☐Yes. ☐No.

18. Who killed Brady?
☐A. ☐B. ☐C. ☐D. ☐Joe.

Solution on page 73.

LIVING WITH A MYSTERY WRITER

Abby Adams

Living with one man is difficult enough; living with a group can be nerve-racking. I have lived with the consortium which calls itself Don Westlake for five years now, and I still can't always be sure, when I get up in the morning, which of the mob I'll have my coffee with.

Donald E. Westlake is the most fun, and happily we see more of him than any of the others. He is a very funny person, not jolly exactly, but witty; he loves to laugh and to make other people laugh. His taste in humor is catholic, embracing brows low, middle and high, from *Volpone* to Laurel and Hardy. (His cuff links, the only ones I've ever seen him wear, depict Stan and Ollie, one on each wrist.) He's a clown at times; coming home from the theater recently with a number of children (more about them later), he engaged in a skipping contest (which he won — he's very competitive, a Stark characteristic spilling over) with several of the younger kids, causing the eldest girl acute embarrassment.

COURTESY ABBY ADAMS

Abby and Don on a visit to France.

Westlake has in common with many of his characters a simplicity and naïveté about life that is disarming, especially if you don't know about the Stark and Coe personae lurking in the background. Looking for an American Express office, he walked through the red-light district of Amsterdam without once noticing the "Walletjes" — plate-glass windows set at eye level in the seventeenth-century canal houses, behind each of which sits a lightly clad hooker, under a red light just in case the message has not been put across. I had to take him back and point them out: "There's one, Don, isn't she pretty? And here's another one."

Like his character Dortmunder, Westlake is unpretentious, unmoved by style or fashion. He dresses simply, wearing the same clothes year after year, wearing hush puppies until they literally fall off his feet. I cut his hair, but he does his own mending and sews on his own buttons. (Mine, too.) Also like Dortmunder, he takes a great deal of pride in his work (with, thank God, more success), but is not otherwise vain.

Behind the wheel of a car he is Kelp. One of the four publications he subscribes to is *Car and Driver*. (The others are *Horizon, The New*

Yorker and *The Manchester Guardian;* what is one to make of all *that?*) He drives passionately, never failing to take an advantage. We once drove across the United States and were passed only three times: twice by policemen and once by a battered old pickup truck full of cowboys that whizzed past us at 90 on a road in Wyoming that I still shudder at the memory of. (We were doing 75.)

Like Harry Künt, the hero of *Help, I Am Being Held Prisoner,* Westlake will do almost anything for a laugh. Fortunately, he does not share Künt's proclivity for practical joking or I would no longer share his bed. Like Brother Benedict of *Brother's Keepers,* he is really happiest leading a quiet life and being able to get on with his own work in peace. However, his life, like a Westlake plot, seldom quiets down for more than five minutes. ("I'm sick of working one day in a row," he sometimes says.) Like many of his heroes, he brings this on himself, partly out of restlessness and partly out of a desire to make things happen around him. For instance, all these children.

Westlake has four, by various spouses, and I have three. Not satisfied with the status quo — his four scattered with their mothers from Binghamton, New York, to Los Angeles, California ("I have branches in all principal cities," he is wont to say) and mine living with me in New York City — he ups and gathers everybody, with all their typewriters, baseball bats, Legos, musical instruments, movie books and stuffed animals, and brings us all to *London* for a year. Then, not content with London, he rents buses and takes this traveling circus all over Great Britain, including Scotland in January (snow) and Cornwall and Wales in February (rain). Still not content, he drives us through the Continent in April for a sort of Grand Tour: Holland, Belgium, Germany, Luxembourg and France in three weeks. Because, like Brother Benedict again, he is obsessed with travel.

Also, like every Westlake hero, Donald E. Westlake is sex-crazed, but I'm not going to talk about that.

Tucker Coe is the gloomy one, almost worse to have around the house than Richard Stark. We see Tucker Coe when things go wrong. The bills can't be paid because the inefficient worlds of publishing and show business have failed to come up with the money to pay them. Children are rude, noisy, dishonest, lazy, loutish and, above all, ungrateful; suddenly you wonder what you ever saw in them. Ex-wives are mean and grasping. Cars break down, houses betray you, plants refuse to live, and it rains on the picnic. Coe's character Mitch Tobin builds a brick wall in his backyard when he's feeling sorry for himself; Coe has never actually built a wall, but he has built enough bookcases to fill the 42nd Street library, for himself and his friends. Also, when the Tucker Coe mood is upon him, he will do crossword puzzles, jigsaw puzzles (even ones he has done before), fix broken electrical things — in fact, do almost anything except work at his typewriter or talk with other human beings.

Timothy Culver is the professional — hack, if you prefer. He will write anything for anybody and doesn't care how much he's paid, just as long as the typewriter keys keep flying. If he doesn't have any actual work to do, he will write letters; and if you've ever received one you know they're as well-written as his books. Well-typed, too. Part of his professionalism is that he produces copy so clean you could simply photostat the pages and put them between boards and have a book with fewer misprints than most actual volumes.

His desk is as organized as a professional carpenter's workshop. No matter where it is (currently, it's a long white dressing table at one end of the living room here in London), it must be set up according to the same unbending pattern. Two typewriters (Smith Corona Silent-Super manual) sit on the desk with a lamp and a telephone and a radio, and a number of black ball-point pens for corrections (seldom needed!). On a shelf just above the desk, five manuscript boxes hold three kinds of paper (white bond first sheets, white second sheets and yellow work sheets) plus original and carbon of whatever he's currently working on. (Frequently one of these boxes also contains a sleeping cat.) Also on this shelf are reference books (*Thesaurus, Bartlett's, 1000 Names for Baby,* etc.) and cups containing small necessities such as tape, rubber bands (I don't know *what* he uses them for) and paper clips. Above this shelf is a bulletin board displaying various things that Timothy Culver likes to look at when he's trying to think of the next sentence. Currently, among others, there are: a newspaper photo showing Nelson Rockefeller giving someone the finger; two post cards from the Louvre, one obscene; a photo of me in our garden in Hope, New Jersey; a Christmas card from his Los Angeles divorce attorney showing himself and his wife in their Bicentennial costumes; and a small hand-lettered sign that says "weird villain." This last is an invariable part of his desk bulletin board: "weird" and "villain" are the two words he most frequently misspells. There used to be a third — "liaison" — but since I taught him how to pronounce it (not *lay*-ee-son but lee-*ay*-son) he no longer has trouble with it.

The arrangement of the various objects on and around The Desk is sacred, and should it be disturbed, nice easygoing professional Timothy Culver turns forthwith into Richard Stark. Children tremble, women weep and the cat hides under the bed. Whereas Tucker Coe is morose and self-pitying, Stark has no pity for anyone. Stark is capable of not talking to anyone for days or, worse yet, of not talking to one particular person for days while still seeming cheerful and friendly with everyone else. Stark could turn Old Faithful into ice cubes. Do you know how Parker, when things aren't going well, can sit alone in a dark room for hours or days without moving? Stark doesn't do this —

COURTESY ABBY ADAMS

Abby and Don on the palace grounds.

COURTESY ABBY ADAMS

Abby and Don enjoying a stroll on the Continent.

that would be too unnerving — but he can play solitaire for hours on end. He plays very fast, turns over the cards one at a time, and goes through the deck just once. He never cheats and doesn't seem to care if the game never comes out. It is not possible to be in the same room with him while he's doing this without being driven completely up the wall.

Stark is very competitive and does whatever he does with the full expectation of winning. He is loyal and honest in his dealings with people and completely unforgiving when they are not the same. Stark is a loner, a cat who walks by himself. He's not influenced by other people, doesn't join clubs or groups, and judges himself according to his own standards. Not the easiest man to live with, but fortunately I seldom have to. About the best you can say for Stark is that he can be trusted to take messages for Westlake and the others which he will deliver the next time they come in.

The question that now comes to mind is: What next? Or should I say, Who next? A half-completed novel now resides on The Desk, title known (but secret), author still unchristened. I feel a certain suspense as I await the birth of this creature; yet whoever he turns out to be I know he will probably be difficult to get along with, but not boring.

Abby Adams and Donald E. Westlake are just good friends.

INTERVIEW WITH A CHARACTER

Colin Watson

Mr. Harcourt Chubb, O.B.E., Chief Constable of Flaxborough, was asked to give his personal impressions of Colin Watson, a fellow citizen and chronicler of such events in the town's recent history as have exercised his, Mr. Chubb's, authority and talents as a law enforcement officer — in short, Flaxborough's somewhat remarkable crime record.

At first diffident ("One has to live in the same town as the man, you know"), Mr. Chubb eventually proved forthcoming in the matter of confidences as any guardian of morality is when given reasonable expectation of garnish.

Colin Watson, admitted Mr. Chubb, was not too bad a fellow, by and large, considering that he wrote books and had even been a journalist at one time. Apart from two convictions for speeding, he had kept out of trouble with the police, had no paternity orders against him, was never seen really drunk and once had made a contribution to the Town Band's instrument fund — one wondered, in fact, if he were a proper author at all.

You say he was once a newspaperman?

Oh, certainly. He began on the old Flaxborough *Citizen.* Right here in this town, though he's from London, I believe. That might account for a certain streak of irresponsibility.

Coming from London, you mean?

No, no. The journalism. Let me give you an example. Some wretched junior had submitted a wedding report — this was years ago, mind — and it was Watson's job to correct his copy. The lad had written: "All the bridesmaids wore Dutch caps." Shocking gaffe, of course. But Watson let it through. Thought it funny, apparently. Can't think why. Must have embarrassed no end of people.

I presume his newspaper career took him further afield than Flaxborough. Do you know anything about that, Mr. Chubb?

A little, yes. It has to be said that Watson does not seem to have taken that aspect of his work as seriously as his employers had the right to expect. There's a certain irreverence about the fellow. I've always regretted his having made friends with my Inspector, you know. I suspect part of Purbright's awkwardness is due to Watson's influence.

Inspector Purbright is not portrayed in the novels as an awkward man.

No, well, he wouldn't be, would he? I mean, look who wrote them.

Is the Inspector, in fact, an awkward man to deal with? What one might call a bloody-minded man?

Ah, you won't get me to say that. No, no. Very sound chap is Purbright. I don't know what we should have done without him in Flaxborough over the past twenty years — and all despite lack of promotion, you might notice. There's devotion to duty for you. No, it's just this funny streak in the man. I don't always know which way to take him. As I say, I think sometimes he sees too much of Watson.

How do you explain what you call Watson's "irreverence," Mr. Chubb?

Well, I've a theory, such as it is. He went to one of the smaller public schools, d'you see, and that nearly always has the effect of putting one up against authority. What do they call it — compensatory attitude? Something like that. Take Watson's career in journalism, for instance. He rose to be one of the best-paid leader-writers in Kemsley Newspapers. Earned nearly twenty pounds a week (that's what, oh, more than thirty of those dollars of yours) at his peak. Yet instead of being grateful, do you know what he used to do? Put chunks of carefully disguised socialist propaganda into his leading articles. Poor Lord K. would have been terribly upset if he could have understood them. I asked Watson if he wasn't ashamed of having taken advantage of his employer in that way. I've never forgotton his answer. It wasn't in Mrs. Chubb's hearing, luckily. "All newspaper proprietors in my experience," he said, "are chisel-minded, semiliterate whoremasters with delusions of grandeur." A very unfair generalisation, I always thought.

Why, in the Flaxborough novels, did Watson elect to use a detective story format? They are not "thrillers" in the conventional sense.

You mean, why does he write about the few bad apples in our little community barrel? I've often asked him that. You don't do the town justice, I say to him. I get a characteristically flippant answer, as you might imagine. The good apples, he says, are always so bloody dull.

Is it true that he once was a crime reporter?

So I gather. At least, he did a lot of court reporting at one period. Inquests, police calls, all that sort of thing. We in England don't use sensational terms like "crime reporter," you know. Watson claims that his police characters are based on officers he has known. Maybe they are. It's not for me to say. I must say that *I* never found crime amusing. Still, I never found the Honours List amusing, for that matter, whereas Watson thinks it a great joke. Very perverse sense of humour.

What do you think is the reason for the Flaxborough novels being popular in America?

Are they indeed? That *is* interesting. Can't imagine why, unless it has something to do with those Pilgrim Father chaps. A lot of them came from round here, you know. Some of Flaxborough's first trouble-makers. Protesters, they call them now. They used to get shipped off to the plantations in those days. Come to think of it, I daresay our friend Watson would have qualified if he'd been around then.

Has he sympathetic feelings toward America?

He has American friends, I understand. He likes *them.* Sympathy, though — that's a word one has to be careful about. It can sound patronising. Purbright probably has the right idea: he says we all need sympathy these days.

Inspector Purbright is a long way from being a "tough" policeman. Isn't that being rather out of fashion?

Possibly. But it wouldn't do, you know. Not in Flaxborough. The last really aggressive officer we had was nearly thirty years ago. Poor fellow fell off the town bridge one night after registering a court objection to the grant of a liquor license to the Over-Eighties Club. Purbright is a very conciliatory chap in comparison. Mind you, I don't think much of some of his notions. I once heard him telling his sergeant — you know young Love, do you? — some rubbish about his being fascinated by what he called "the curious innocence" of the professional criminal. Nothing very innocent, I'd have thought, about some blackguard who goes round pinching people's valuables, eh?

What is your author's attitude toward crime and punishment, Mr. Chubb?

Decidedly odd, I'm afraid. He says too much effort goes into enforcing laws designed to protect property, and too little into protecting people. That's nonsense, of course, but I'm just telling you *his* ideas. Oh yes, he said on another occasion, I remember, that if we *had* to go round hanging people, it ought to be for murdering the English language. Let me see, who was that president you used to have in America, the one who didn't shave very often and had a dog . . . Dixon? Nixon? Anyway, Watson and Purbright were talking about him at the time of that Watergate business of yours, and Watson said impeachment would be too dignified a course to take with such a grubby little man; he ought to be put in a home for cliché addicts. I thought the remark was uncalled for, frankly.

You must sometimes find your author a trial.

Oh, it's my job to cope with people.

Colin Watson is the author of The Flaxborough Chronicles, *recently filmed for British television.*

THE SOLITARY LIFE OF THE WRITER

Joyce Porter

During my fourteen years as a professional writer I have managed to avoid almost all contact with my pen-pushing colleagues. I did once, when a mere "first offender" in the business, attend a literary cocktail party, but I left almost immediately when somebody insulted me by asking if I were a publisher. However, writers are an intrusive breed and occasionally they penetrate my defences via the television set, pompously planking themselves down on my hearth rug before I can dash across and switch them into oblivion.

One of them made it the other day. I think they got him from Rent-a-Writer. Wild horses wouldn't, of course, drag his name out of me — though a substantial bribe might. Anyhow, he had me riveted to my chair. Not by the splendour of his presence, you understand, or the beauty of his eloquence, but by the sheer fascination of the background they were photographing him against. Would you believe floor-to-ceiling bookshelves? The freshness of vision shown by TV producers is sometimes mind-blowing.

Anyhow, I ignored the rubbish his nibs was spouting and took a good look at the books, naturally assuming that they were studio props because your genuine, dedicated, doing-it-for-eating-money author doesn't read anything except publishers' contracts and banker's cheques. But, no, I was mistaken. The books were the real thing and without a doubt the personal property of the charlatan who was pontificating there in front of the cameras. How could I be so sure? Well, the books were all in sets of six. In other words, they were the free copies we bearers of the flag of culture get as perks from our European publishers. (The Americans, with typical generosity, dish out ten.)

I couldn't believe my eyes. This joker must have kept every free copy of every edition of every book he had ever published! What strength of character! What nerve! What resolution! Had he no friends? After all, most of us who manage to get something into print are knee-deep in good old chums eager to grab one of our free copies rather than venture into a bookshop and *buy* one. (I wouldn't mind quite so much if they didn't think they were softening the blow by asking you to sign the damned thing.)

Well, when I'd got over the shock of seeing this star of the literary firmament broadcasting his niggardliness to the nation, I began to pay close attention to what he was saying. Such a consummate skinflint must have a message for us all.

Unfortunately, what he was saying, interrupted from time to time by carefully rehearsed promptings from the interviewer, proved to be a pretty fair sample of the usual drivel. In private, writers only talk about money, but in public they trot out the habitual phoney clichés of the trade. Viz.: no waiting for inspiration for us professionals . . . moral obligation to grind out the daily stint just like the rest of you miserable wage slaves . . . the loneliness . . . the self-discipline . . . the soaring imagination . . . the creative blocks . . . the soft black pencil on the creamy yellow paper . . . characters who magically develop a life of their own and begin to take over . . . blah, blah, blah.

And then he said it.

You could have heard my jaw drop a mile away.

In answer to some puerile question about one of his earlier best-sellers, he said (and I quote): "Yes, when I re-read it the other day, I must say I thought it had worn quite well."

When he'd *re-read* it? One of his *own* books?

What am I, a freak or something? I wouldn't re-read one of my own books if you paid me! (Well, I would, actually, but you know what I mean.) Blimey, I have to write the damned things — and that's enough for anybody. I produce "funny" detective stories (though they don't make me laugh), and by the time I've thought up the plot, worked it out, written the first draft in longhand, typed the second draft and bashed out three copies of the final one, I've had it up to *here!* Nowadays I can't even face a last read-through for typing errors, and, when the proofs come in for correcting, I start at the last page and work backwards. Believe me, any bright or original idea I might have had right at the very beginning is looking pretty tatty when I meet it for the sixth time or so. The books I write are meant to be wolfed down at one gulp on a train journey, or wherever, and thrown away. (I should be so lucky! Returned to the blooming library is more like it.) I don't expect anybody to read them half a dozen times, and I bitterly resent the fact that I have to.

Come to think about it, I resent most things about being a writer. I resent having to sit there all alone at my desk. I resent all my brilliant ideas turning to dust the minute I get them down on paper. I resent the sheer physical labour of pushing a pen-nib over all those acres and acres of sneering white paper. I resent the noise a typewriter makes. I resent my publisher asking me to cut a thousand words. I resent my publisher asking me to add a thousand words. I resent critics who suggest that I haven't written a masterpiece — and write off as a solid-gold idiot anybody who implies that I have.

Well, no, it's not really as bad as all that. Whenever I get to the gibbering stage, I can always calm it down by reminding myself what the alternative is. Like work.

And I'm not really whining about writing being hard labour, am I? Why, even on a good day I reckon I spend more time playing Patience than I do penning deathless prose. Luckily I know three different ways of laying out the cards for Patience; otherwise, I might well drop down dead with sheer boredom. But what else can I do when Literature goes sour on me? I only need a fleeting distraction, something that doesn't take me away from my desk, something that can be instantly abandoned should inspiration strike, and something that demands no intellectual or creative effort. What else is there except Patience that will guarantee to send me back to my writing almost as quickly as I left it?

A well-known American writer once said: "I sometimes ask myself what a grown man like me is doing, sitting there all day telling himself stories." It's the most perceptive remark I've ever heard a writer make about his job. That's precisely what writers should be doing — telling themselves stories. Not playing endless games of Patience, for heaven's sake!

But, back to that pundit on the television who actually reads his own books. Could it be that his books are so good and so well-written that, even twenty years later, he can . . . ? Is that why he's on the telly and I'm not?

I decided that it was all giving me an inferiority complex, and I switched the set off. Tenth-rate writers simply can't afford to indulge in self-doubt.

Back to the grindstone.

My own fault, really. I shouldn't have got hooked on eating.

Now, where had we got to? Ah, yes! One face upwards and six face downwards. One face upwards and five face downwards. One face upwards and four face downwards. One face . . .

See what I mean about writing?

Big deal!

Joyce Porter is as witty as her Scotland Yard Inspector, Wilfred Dover, is sloppy. He appears in many books, including Dover One, Dover Two, Dover Three, Dover Goes to Pott.

Chapter 3

BLOODHOUNDS

FRED WINKOWSKI

AN EYEWITNESS ACCOUNT OF HOLMES

John P. Oliver

I was a guest of the Metropolitan Police, Scotland Yard. Someone thought it would be a good idea for the NYPD and our London counterparts to swap personnel — so off went one New York Detective Lieutenant and one London Detective Inspector to opposite sides of the Atlantic.

By my sixth day in London I'd been told at least sixty times, "Scotland Yard is the greatest crime-fighting organization ever to grace the face of the earth." That day they'd deposited me at the Black Museum. I was unimpressed. You see one collection of guns, bombs, knives and hatchets, you've seen them all. I was plotting my escape when I accidently slammed into an old man and sent him sprawling. Oh, Jesus, I thought. I've killed the old goat. What a headline that'll make: BERSERK NEW YORK COP KILLS OLD PENSIONER!

As I was picturing the end of my career, my victim began to stir. I jumped to help him up. After mutual apologies (very polite, the English), we chatted a bit about the Yard. He was a retired Detective Inspector who had put in thirty years on the job. I asked him what he thought of the New Yard and its modern crime-fighting techniques, and almost before I got the question out he began a tirade. For close to an hour he harangued me on how today's cops were nothing more than high-priced mechanics, fiddling with their new toys — computers, helicopters, radios, closed-circuit TV, cars, etc.

"Not like the old days, when it took *real men* to be coppers," he said. "Men who dared walk alone and unarmed through the East End and Whitechapel at night."

I asked the obvious: "Aren't today's cops better at solving crimes because of it?"

"Better? Better? Why, we solved all the big ones . . . Except the Ripper, o' course, and there's them what knows about that one . . . But if you must know what it was really like solving crimes at the Old Yard, you should go over to see Mr. Holmes."

With that, he turned on his worn-down heel and left me standing with my mouth open in the middle of the Black Museum.

After a convivial night on London Town with a couple of detectives who led me astray, I awoke the next morning, stirred the bread pudding that had once been my brain, and dug out my *A to Z Street Guide.* Hangover or no, I had decided to go along with the gag.

My favorite mystery story is Wilkie Collins' The Moonstone, *despite its claptrap ending. For me it has wiped out the need for all of its successors* — even *the Sherlock Holmes series, which I imitated at high school. The mystery to me is why the current output of mystery stories is not as boring for others as it is for me.*

LEWIS MUMFORD

DECKING HOLMES

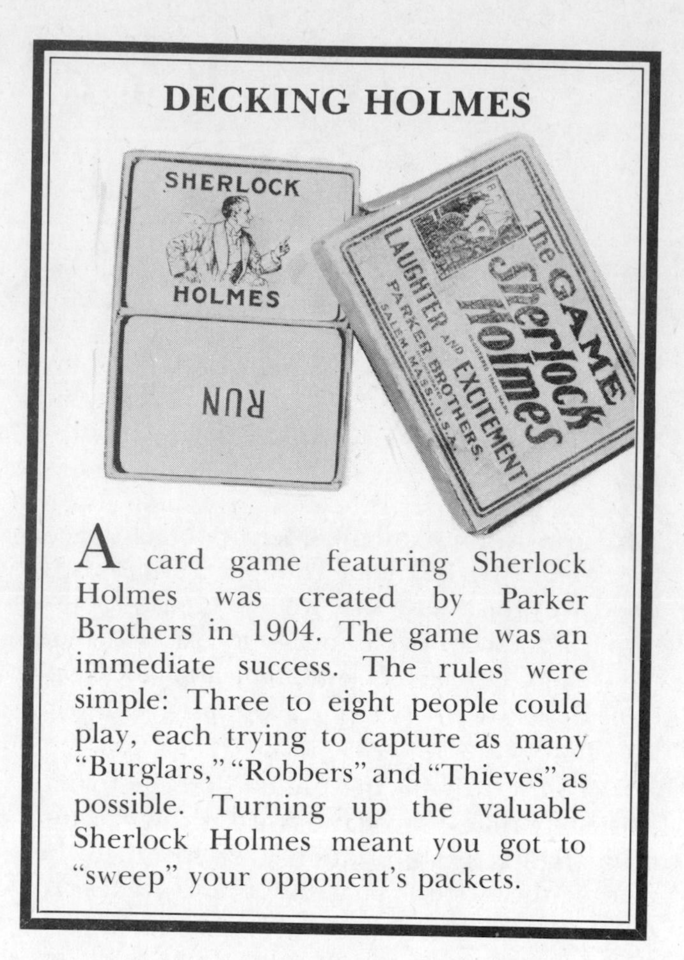

A card game featuring Sherlock Holmes was created by Parker Brothers in 1904. The game was an immediate success. The rules were simple: Three to eight people could play, each trying to capture as many "Burglars," "Robbers" and "Thieves" as possible. Turning up the valuable Sherlock Holmes meant you got to "sweep" your opponent's packets.

I walked to Baker Street. No 221B in sight. Then I noticed a building halfway down the block with the name CAMDEN HOUSE on it. Being something of an amateur Holmesian, I remembered it as the one in "The Adventure of the Empty House." It had stood directly across the street from Holmes' digs.

Figuring what the hell, I went up and rapped the door knocker. The door was answered by a woman of late middle age. Neat, but kind of frumpy. I blurted, "Mrs. Hudson?"

Perfectly deadpan, she replied, "No, I'm Mary Watson. Mrs. Hudson was my grandmother."

Feeling like Alice in Wonderland, I asked, "Watson?"

"Oh, I don't suppose you know, do you? The Doctor married Mrs. Hudson right after his second wife left him."

She went on and on with what began to sound like a capsule version of *Upstairs, Downstairs*. It became very clear that there had been a somewhat un-Victorian relationship between the good Doctor and the faithful housekeeper.

"Of course, you'll be wanting to see Mr. Holmes now," she said. "Just go right up."

Up I went, still somewhat uncertain as to whether I was the victim of an elaborate practical joke or I had just plain lost my mind. My knock was answered with a raspy "Come in."

There, sitting in an overstuffed chair near the windows, was a living Sidney Paget drawing, even down to a ratty dressing gown. It was the mouse-gray one.

Pointing to a matching chair opposite, he said, "Please, have a seat. I get so few visitors nowadays." He stuffed some shag into a calabash, inhaled, coughed and settled back, turning that well-known profile to the sun.

I didn't know what to say, so I kept my mouth shut.

"If you are expecting me to amaze you with my powers of deduction by telling you all about yourself," he said, "I will have to disappoint you, my boy. These days, with everything from cigarettes to shoes mass-produced, all I can tell about a visitor is whether or not it's male or female . . . and from what I see lately, that, in itself, is a remarkable feat of deduction."

I introduced myself as a fellow crime fighter from New York, and he seemed to relax a little, glad I wasn't one of those moon-struck literati on one of those — in his words — "infernal literary pilgrimages." Like cops around the world, we talked shop.

"No, Leftenant," he said, "I'm not a figment of your overworked imagination. I'm a real, very real, very old, very tired, very retired detective." Then, turning to my reason for being in London: "All the way here from New York to study the highly successful crime fighters of the modern Scotland Yard. Hmmmmmm." He puffed the pipe. "What you should be studying, young man, is modern crime itself. That's the reason I'm retired — all the techniques I spent a lifetime perfecting are useless now against today's criminal."

He lay back dreamily. I scanned the room for the Morocco case, but it wasn't in sight.

"New York . . . nice city," he resumed, somewhat adrift. "Several years ago I was a visitor in your city, you know. That was my fourth trip there. I assume you know that what Watson called 'The Redheaded League' case actually happened in New York City. But Watson, dear man, couldn't break his habits, so when he wrote it down, he transferred it here, to London.

"Yes, I remember New York City very well. During my last visit there, I was out walking one evening in your Central Park when I came by chance upon the scene of a crime. A robbery . . . a mugging, I think you'd call it. I stopped to lend a hand to the young officer who was investigating the case." He chuckled. "I, too, have my old habits.

"After spending no small time examining the ground surrounding the crime scene, I made some brilliant deductions. All wrong, as it happens. Those strange markings belonged to something called U.S. Keds. Never heard of them myself. Thought they were ritual motifs of an East Anglican band of gypsies."

"We call them perpetrator boots, sir," I said quietly.

"Tell me," he said earnestly, suddenly leaning so far forward in his chair I thought he'd tip it over, "tell me, young sir, how can a consulting detective work in this kind of a society? Neither the modern criminal nor the modern detective does any planning for his trade — it's strictly a hit-or-miss affair. I tell you, when we had the likes of Professor Moriarty to deal with, that kept your mind sharp and alert! That man spent months planning one robbery. He didn't run into the street and hit the first little old lady he saw over the head. No, sir. Stolen cars, narcotics, muggers — pshaw! The old Professor is probably turning over in his grave."

I had to admit I was glad that he, at least, was dead.

Then I changed the subject to one that had tantalized me from the minute I left the old man at the museum. "Who," I asked tentatively, "who was this Arthur Conan Doyle? I mean, if you're actually real, and he's the one who supposedly invented you, where does that leave him?"

Holmes became somewhat agitated. There was a noticeable tremor in his left hand. "That man!" he shouted. "That man has been a plague and a burden throughout my entire life. He was quite mad, you know. An eye doctor, driven stark, staring mad by his failures . . . never had a patient in two years of practice! Had delusions he was a great detective story writer. Even claimed to have invented me. *Me!*

"I wrote him several letters, but each time, instead of a normal, courteous reply, I received another damned — forgive me — another autographed photograph of him. Man needed the horsewhip, sir, or a loaded riding crop across his back. Well, what could one do? A madman is a madman, after all, and he wasn't violent. I finally took to telling people that it was *I* who had invented *him!*"

This outburst seemed to drain him. He leaned back in his chair once again.

"You will have to excuse me. I'm not as young as I used to be. Point of fact, I'm not even as *old* as I used to be." He offered me his hand in farewell. "Goodbye, Leftenant, and I wish you luck on the examination for your Captain that you plan to take next month." He smiled. "Oh, I see you're puzzled. Don't be. It wasn't my famous deductive reasoning that told me. Rather, it was that old man you chatted up at the museum. Did he tell you his name? No? Well, that's what's left of Lestrade, poor devil. A little off in the head these days. You probably noticed. Spends his every waking moment at the Yard, digging, digging for clues in the Ripper murders. He's convinced I was Jack the Ripper, you know. I'm almost tempted to help him solve the case, but then, what would an old man like me do in prison?"

He smiled again, his old but still charming smile.

"Well, be careful out there. And don't take the first *or* the second underground carriage. Take the third one."

John P. Oliver is a lieutenant in the New York Police Department, presently assigned to the City-Wide Emergency Service Unit. He is also a member of the New York State Bar and smokes good cigars.

NERO WOLFE CONSULTATION

Anthony Spiesman

When I get stuck on a difficult case, I ask myself how Wolfe would handle it. Mentally, I phone Saul Panzer and ask him to set up an appointment. I don't know why I go through Saul, I just do. Anyway, in my mind, Saul picks up the phone and gets Archie and explains I have this problem and could he see if Wolfe will talk to me. Archie makes a few choice wisecracks, but since I'm a friend of Saul's he makes me first appointment after orchid hours.

I imagine myself going up the seven steps of Wolfe's brownstone and ringing the bell. Fritz invites me in and escorts me past the famous front room and into the office. He offers me a drink. I tell him I would appreciate a tall, cold glass of milk with two fingers of Scotch. I don't worry about Wolfe's liquor supply or about the quality of the booze, but I make a mental note to send him a case of a new imported Dutch beer called Grolsch which comes in fancy liter bottles and which, for my money, is the best stuff around. I'm a little troubled, though, because the tops are permanently attached rubber plugs that you have to pop open with two thumbs, and I worry about Wolfe's liking to count bottle caps and putting them away in his top drawer.

While I wait for Wolfe to come help me, I rubberneck the room. The thing that hits me — and to me this is kind of a surprise — is the layout, the use of space. By this I specifically mean the bookshelves and the file cabinet on the second level. Completely avoids floor clutter. The high ceilings add to the space, of course, and the outstanding collection of furniture and artifacts makes the place first-class. I start to relax. Any man smart enough to live like this is definitely smart enough to help me out of a jam.

Then I walk over to Archie's desk and take a gander at the picture on the wall above it. I know who it's supposed to be, and I have to admit there's a striking similarity. The neatness of it all impresses me, makes me start getting my thinking under control again.

Next I take an imaginery walk over to the Gouchard globe. Having read about it so many times, I have no trouble picturing it. Thirty-two and three-eighths inches in diameter is a lot of globe. Really big. But it's not the size so much that gets to me — it's the overall beauty, the craftsmanship. There's something about being in a room with perfect objects that is conducive to clear thinking. Don't ask me why. (Sometimes, at this point in my fantasy, I take time out for a trip to the lobby of the Daily News building on East 42nd Street. That's my favorite globe anywhere, and I can spend hours

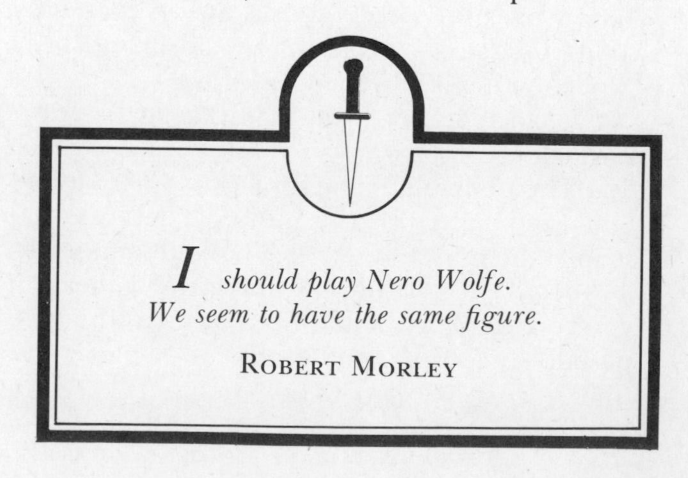

I should play Nero Wolfe.
We seem to have the same figure.

ROBERT MORLEY

MARTY NORMAN

Nero Wolfe's office. Archie's desk is in the foreground. His chair can be swiveled to face the mirror so he can see what's happening in the doorway on the other side of the room.

standing there staring at it and taking great sea journeys around the world.)

I return to Wolfe's office and decide that my favorite thing in it is the superb mostly yellow Shirvan rug. Comforting while I'm pacing. But being somewhat of an amateur cook myself I do take a few minutes to appreciate the engraving of Brillat-Savarin. I also find Wolfe's own cookbook on his shelf and haul it down for a quick look. Same contents as my copy, I'm glad to say. Still at the bookshelf, I can't resist pulling out Wolfe's copy of Lawrence's *Seven Pillars of Wisdom.* I once tried to get through it. Couldn't. But I'm convinced if Wolfe can, he's the man to analyze my case.

I stand in front of Wolfe's cherry desk and decide not to pick up any of his blunt instruments, but I do take notice of his brown leather Brazilian desk chair. Gigantic! I've never seen anything quite like it anywhere, probably never will. But it definitely looks like it can hold a seventh of a ton just by itself. The chair would take up two-thirds of my office space. I can't help but notice the worn spots on the arms, where countless circles have been made by Wolfe's fingers. I see his fingers circle and his lips go in and out, in and out, like an obese goldfish, and I am reassured he will solve my problems.

I think about sitting in that chair, but I don't have the nerve. Not even in my imagination. I do, however, sit in that infamous red chair — the one Archie says only Inspector Cramer looks like he belongs in. It's a bit un-

A photograph of Theodore (taken with a telescopic lens) at work in the orchid room. Wolfe is just out of the picture to the left (note large shadow in the foreground).

comfortable to my taste, but I well know the advantages of a chair like this for interrogation purposes. It dwarfs you, makes you feel insecure, and the lies don't come out quite so smooth when you're in it. At this point, I get a little edgy, so I back over to Archie's desk again. I take a quick peek in the red box to see if he really does keep stamps in it. He does. I think about opening the drawers — it's occupational with me — but I don't. I also don't pry inside the liquor cabinet, count Wolfe's bottle caps or try to get into the secret alcove and see what Archie sees when Wolfe has him staked out in there.

Then I imagine Wolfe entering the room. I see him as Orson Welles. Nobody else. I imagine him getting straight to the problem, no social nonsense. I can never make up my mind if he shakes my hand or not. I know he doesn't like to shake hands, but I have this urgency to feel that he's really flesh and blood. Usually, I wind up with a strong, quick grip, quickly released. I talk, Archie pretends to take notes, Wolfe listens. Wolfe speaks. The voice is midway between American English and English English. No Montenegrin inflection. Orson Welles in *Citizen Kane,* I think. A young voice in a not-young man. Full, but not bombastic.

I never know exactly what it is that Wolfe says, but suddenly, after one or two "pfuis," no more problem.

We get up to leave. That is, I get up to leave, preceded by Archie. Fritz comes to the door to see me out. Just as I prepare to go, Wolfe pokes his head out the office door and asks if I'd like to join him in dinner at Rusterman's. (Listen, this is my fantasy. I'll have him say whatever I like.) We agree to meet as soon as I turn in my report on the case.

At this point I get up and walk into my kitchen and start making a mess out of it. I chop, I slice, I mix, I pound, I debone, I decant, I thoroughly fiddle around. And it seems to help. Like Wolfe, I don't talk business when I eat, but there's something about preparing a meal that untangles things for me. So when I start to eat I raise a toast to my imaginary dinner partner, Nero Wolfe, and thank him for his guidance.

I never met a private investigator like him. But I sure would like to.

Anthony Spiesman is a licensed private investigator living in New York. He has spent hours trying to track down Wolfe on West 35th Street, with little success.

WOLFE AT HIS BEST

And Be a Villain
Champagne for One
Death of a Doxy
Some Buried Caesar
Too Many Cooks

MOST OVERRATED WOLFE

The Doorbell Rang

ALPHA AND OMEGA

Fer-de-Lance
A Family Affair

THE ULTIMATE DISGUISE EXPERT

Herb Galewitz

Stand aside, Holmes. Great though you were at turning into a parson, a sailor, an opium addict, a priest, a bookseller, an impoverished bystander — you just can't compare with the Bean Farm's Freddy.

Freddy could fool a Fu Manchu. Freddy could baffle both Cleek (Hamilton) and Clay (Colonel). Freddy could stun Arsene and Four Square Jane and even teach Nick Carter a trick or two. What's more remarkable, he could do it all on a diet of slops while standing on his two back trotters! For Freddy, of course, is Freddy the Pig, juvenile legend.

A turn-of-century detective

Freddy tends to behave in multiples: multiple disguises, multiple professions. He is, among other things, a partner in the firm of Frederick & Wiggins, Detectives (Office Hours: Wednesdays, 2–4 P.M.); President of the First Animal Bank (animal depositors only); editor of the *Bean Home News;* director of Barnyard Tours, Inc.; and accomplished poet (his version of "On the Road to Mandalay" has sent more young'uns east than a string of Dorothy Lamour movies — or so he claims).

Freddy took his time getting into detective work, turning his attention to other matters in his first two books. Even so, he managed to make it into court before Perry Mason *(Freddy the Detective,* 1932). The sensational trial sequence pitted Freddy against a Moriarty-type nemesis — Professor Simon the Rat — whose villainy would plague Freddy throughout his career.

In subsequent cases Freddy solved the mystery of the ignoramus in a tale of terror and blackmail reminiscent of *The Hound of the Baskervilles;* undermined some heavy skulduggery on a summer estate by posing as a caretaker; thwarted spies trying to steal Uncle Ben's plans; exposed the fraud of the outer space travelers; debunked the myth of the haunted hotel; foiled a gang of ruthless bank robbers; and pitched a legal no-hitter against a baseball team from Mars in his one excursion into sci-fi mystery.

When asked if calling policemen "pigs" was a compliment to his ingenuity rather than a rebuff to their skills, Freddy modestly replied, "Oink."

Herb Galewitz is the editor of The Celebrated Cases of Dick Tracy.

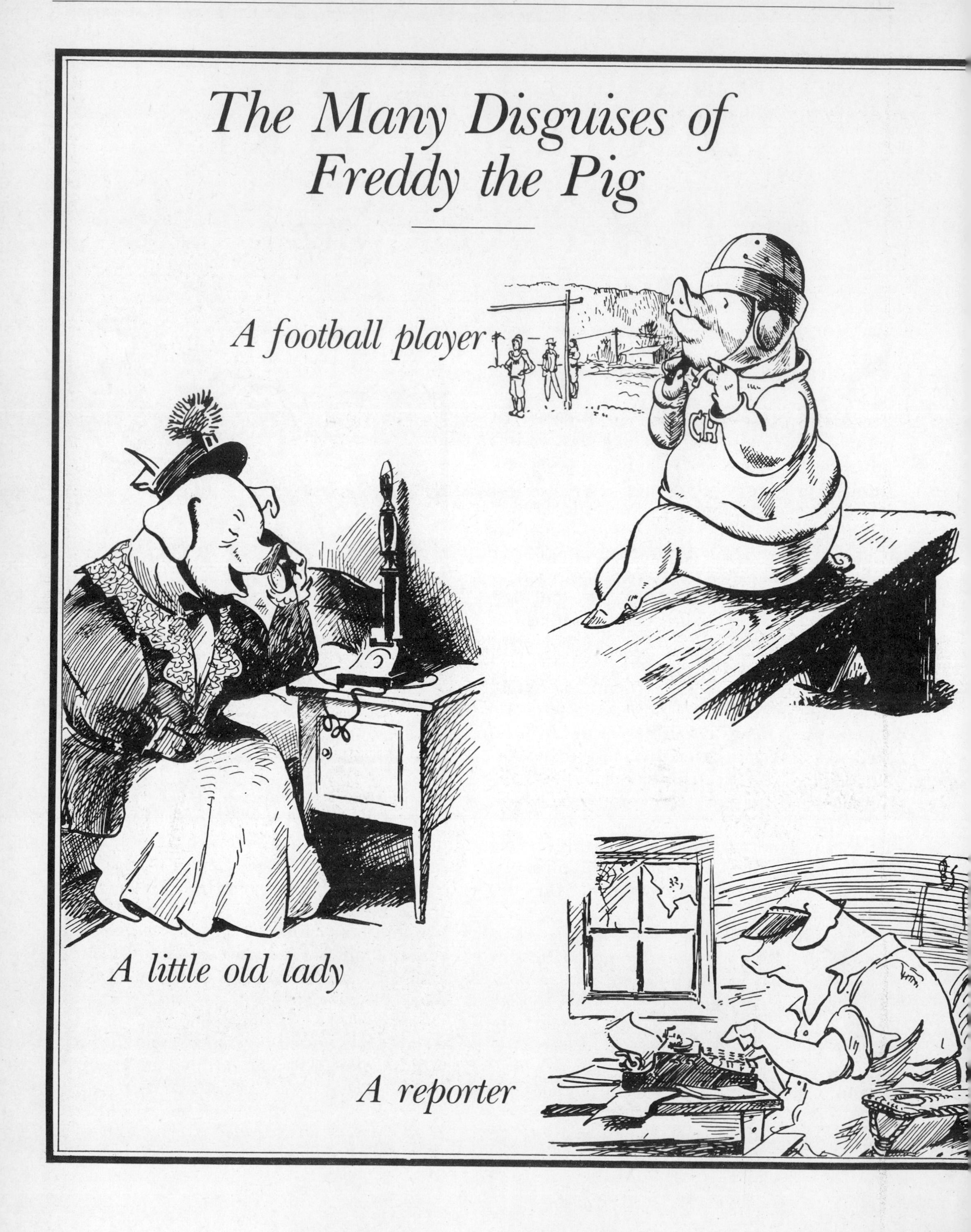
The Many Disguises of Freddy the Pig
A football player
CH
A little old lady
A reporter

BLOWING FREDDY'S COVER

Freddy the Detective
Freddy the Cowboy
Freddy Goes Camping
Freddy and Mr. Camphor
Freddy and the Flying Saucer Plans
Freddy and the Ignoramus
Freddy and the Baseball Team from Mars

A sailor

A third baseman

A magician

H.M.: THE OLD MAN

Donald Rumbelow

Pigeon-toed, with a lordly sneer upon his face, one hand resting upon an imaginary sword pommel, Sir Henry Merrivale — H.M., the Old Man, Mycroft (when he was head of British counterespionage) — barrel-bellies through and triumphantly solves the finest series of locked-room mysteries ever written. Under his Panama hat, tilted to display an imaginary cavalier's plume, is a heady mixture of Falstaff, Charlie Chaplin and Winston Churchill!

Most days the Old Man can be found, five floors up, in a rabbit warren of a building behind Whitehall, feet on desk, white socks showing, sprawled beneath a Mephistophelian portrait of Fouché, in an office scattered with papers and cigar ash. Ignore the crudely painted notice BUSY!! NO ADMITTANCE!!! KEEP OUT!! daubed above the name-plate. H.M. has an Alice-in-Wonderland fetish for ticketing things. Similar signs, in five languages, are painted on his safe (never locked and where the whisky is kept).

Apologise for waking him, and he says that he was thinking! Say that you won't bother him, or that he's past it, and he howls about ingratitude and grumbles that nobody takes him seriously!

From his grammar you wouldn't guess that he was a qualified barrister as well as a qualified physician. Awful as it is (he tends to drop the g's), it is typical of his Champagne Charlie, gaiety girl, hansom cab generation (he was born in 1871). Insult him, or mention his age, and his mouth will sour down as if he were smelling bad eggs. Prick his vanity and he turns purple. Strong men blanch and dogs shy away at such looks of horrible malignancy.

Impossible to fool women and children, however. To them, he is Knight-Errant and Pied Piper in tortoise-shell spectacles and a rumpled suit. H.M. heroines, all white dresses and golden hair, do inevitably marry the juvenile lead. But for H.M.'s *personal* harem of dollies and wenches, nothing so wraith-like: Two Dreadnoughts closing. Of the earth earthy. Broad-beamed, broad-minded, out-of-the-bottle blondes with chorus girl or mine hostesse background. His wife Clementine (again the Churchill cross-reference) is permanently off stage, away in the south of France. Clemmie, years younger, is vintage 1913 chorus line. Reunions begin with four or five double whiskies in the Ivy, Claridges or the Savoy Grill. Love is bein' met with brass bands at the Pearly Gates. Consummation is a stuffed policeman on every chimney at Scotland Yard!

Children too long in his company risk

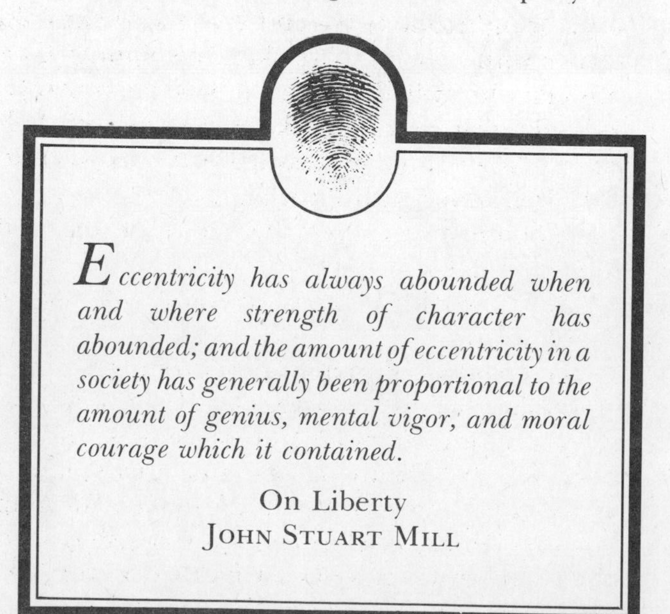

Eccentricity has always abounded when and where strength of character has abounded; and the amount of eccentricity in a society has generally been proportional to the amount of genius, mental vigor, and moral courage which it contained.

On Liberty
JOHN STUART MILL

Borstal before they leave school and prison before they are eighteen! Cigarettes are sissy, he jeers. Smoke his evil-smelling cigars instead! Want to gamble? His suitcase, on wheels, will outrace their dogs downhill. Card tricks? Nothing easier.

Three cheers for Uncle Henry Merrivale!

Wasn't he friends with Sitting Bull? Didn't he teach Robin Hood *and* Samkin Alyward to shoot? Hadn't he poured Epsom salts in the Home Secretary's dish at the Lord Mayor's banquet? His fur coat was (1) given to him by Queen Victoria, (2) won in the first Grand Prix of 1903, (3) a present from the late Sir Henry Irving.

History (British Empire only) and literature should go with a swing and a thump. "Kentish Sir Byng, stood for his King,/Bidding the crop headed Parliament swing." What's this? Dostoevsky, Tolstoy and Chekhov. Crutches for young minds! Out of the window with them! Doyle, Dickens, Stevenson and Twain are the best writers. Best book is *The Cloister and the Hearth.*

Serious now.

Don't be fooled.

Never, never underestimate H.M.

So many have and, in the end, stood on the hangman's trap to regret that they did.

H.M.'s innocence is the naïveté of Langdon, Chaplin and Lloyd. Like the slapstick kings, he is a master of timing. He treads the narrow tightrope between farce and sheer cold terror with consummate skill and timing. One moment he will disgrace himself abominably. He will assault dragon-like dowagers with halberds, American congressmen with arrows and elderly bishops with mud pies.

Fooling stops when the pace quickens and murder is loose.

Two six-inch guns couldn't be more deadly.

Fouché would have been proud of him.

Like the great comedians, H.M. will start with a basically simple, almost laughable situation which quickly twists and turns into a monstrous growth of rattlesnake cunning. Bronze lamps, cricket bats and crossbows are the important incidentals. Chief Inspector Masters (H.M.'s Watson) can deal with those.

THE OLD MAN'S CASES

The Plague Court Murders
The White Priory Murders
The Red Widow Murders
The Unicorn Murders
The Magic Lantern Murders
(Punch and Judy Murders)
The Peacock Feather Murders
(The Ten Teacups)
The Judas Window
Death in Five Boxes
The Reader is Warned
Nine — and Death Makes Ten
(Murder in the Submarine Zone)
And So to Murder
Seeing Is Believing
The Gilded Man
She Died a Lady
He Wouldn't Kill Patience
The Curse of the Bronze Lamp
(Lord of the Sorcerers)
My Late Wives
The Skeleton in the Clock
A Graveyard to Let
Night at the Mocking Widow
Behind the Crimson Blind
The Cavalier's Cup

The Old Man's speciality is the locked-room mystery. (No hocus-pocus with floors, doors, windows, ceilings, trap-doors and walls. Bodies fall in — and out — of them with scarifying ease.)

Genuine locked rooms. Genuine puzzles.

Only the Master — sittin', twiddlin' his thumbs and cogitatin' — can solve them.

"*Courage! Le diable est mort!*" H.M. likes quoting.

And so he is — when the Old Man is about.

Donald Rumbelow is Joseh Wambaugh's closest English rival. He is a police officer assigned to the Wood Street Station, London, where he is curator of the specimen museum. He is also an author and vice-chairman of the Crime Writers' Association.

The New York Times

NEW YORK, WEDNESDAY, AUGUST 6, 1975

Hercule Poirot Is Dead; Famed Belgian Detective

By THOMAS LASK

Hercule Poirot, a Belgian detective who became internationally famous, has died in England. His age was unknown.

Mr. Poirot achieved fame as a private investigator after he retired as a member of the Belgian police force in 1904. His career, as chronicled in the novels of Dame Agatha Christie, his creator, was one of the most illustrious in fiction.

At the end of his life, he was arthritic and had a bad heart. He was in a wheelchair often, and was carried from his bedroom to the public lounge at Styles Court, a nursing home in Essex, wearing a wig and false mustaches to mask the signs of age that offended his vanity. In his active days, he was always impeccably dressed.

Mr. Poirot, who was just 5 feet 4 inches tall, went to England from Belgium during World War I as a refugee. He settled in a little town not far from Styles, then an elaborate country estate, where he took on his first private case.

The news of his death, given by Dame Agatha, was not unexpected. Word that he was near death reached here last May.

His death was confirmed by Dodd, Mead, Dame Agatha's publishers, who will put out "Curtain," the novel that chronicles his last days, on Oct. 15.

The Poirot of the final volume is only a shadow of the well-turned out, agile investigator who, with a charming but immense ego and fractured English, solved uncounted mysteries in the 37 full-length novels and collections of short stories in which he appeared.

Dame Agatha reports in "Curtain" that he managed,

Illustrated London News and Sketch, Ltd.

Hercule Poirot, painted in the mid-1920's by W. Smithson Broadhead.

in one final gesture, to perform one more act of cerebration that saved an innocent bystander from disaster. "Nothing in his life became him like the leaving it," to quote Shakespeare, whom Poirot frequently misquoted.

Dodd, Mead had not expected another installment in the heroic achievements of the famous detective.

No manuscript came in last year, and none was expected this year, either. However, there had been many rumors to the effect that Dame Agatha had locked up two manuscripts — one a Poirot and one a Marple — in a vault and that they were not to be published until her death. Jonathan Dodd, of Dodd, Mead, said that the Poirot was the one now being published.

Although the career of Poirot will no more engage his historian, a spokesman for the author said that Dame Agatha, who will be 85 Sept. 15, intends to continue writing. In her long writing career, one that parallels the literary existence of her detective, she has published 85 full-length novels and collections of short stories, which have sold 350 million copies in hard cover and paperback all over the globe.

This figure does not include the pirated editions behind the Iron Curtain, of which no count can be made.

In addition, under the pseudonym of Mary Westmacott she has written a half-dozen romances. What is perhaps more significant is that her first title, "The Mysterious Affair at Styles" is still in print.

At least 17 of her stories have been made into plays, including the famous "The Mouse Trap," which opened in London in 1952 and is still running, setting all kinds of records for longevity in the theater.

Twelve of her tales have become motion pictures, many of which have centered on Jane Marple, Dame Agatha's other famous detective.

In the person of the late Margaret Rutherford, Miss Marple developed her own devoted following.

The most recent of Dame Agatha's movies, "Murder on the Orient Express" opened last year, with excellent box-office returns. And Christie properties have been used for television mystery dramas and for radio shows.

Her hold on her audience is remarkable in a way because the kind of fiction she writes is, well, not exactly contemporary. Her characters come from the quiet and exceedingly comfortable middle class: doctors, lawyers, top military men, members of the clergy. The houses in her fiction are spacious, teas are frequent and abundant, servants abound. True, the comforts have been cut back as the real England in which her mysteries are set has been altered over the years. But the polite, leisure-class settings have been retained.

"I could never manage miners talking in pubs," she once confided to an interviewer, "because I don't know what miners talk about in pubs."

'Undisputed Head Girl'

Not everyone has agreed to her high ranking. Robert Graves complained that "her English is schoolgirlish, her situations for the most part artificial, her detail faulty."

On the other hand, Margery Allingham, herself a writer of whodunits, called her the "undisputed head girl," and the late Anthony Boucher, who reviewed mysteries for this newspaper, remarked, "Few writers are producing the pure puzzle novel and no one on either side of the Atlantic does it better."

Dame Agatha who has been described as a large woman looking both kind and capable, is the daughter of a well-to-do American father and English mother. She was tutored at home and attended, as she recalled, innumerable classes: dancing, singing, drawing. In World War 1, she worked in a Red Cross hospital, and this experience gave her a good working knowledge of poisons, ingredients that turn up rather frequently in her books.

In 1926, she suffered an attack of amnesia, left home and was discovered some days later in a hotel under another name. The furor stirred up by the newspapers over her disappearance has made her shy of newspapers and reporters ever since. She has kept herself inconspicuous in public, even insisting for a while that no picture of herself appear on the dust jackets of her books. She has declined to be interviewed about the death of Poirot. In 1928, she was divorced from her first husband, Archibald Christie, and in 1930 she was married to Max Mallowan, an archeologist.

It has been said that she has brought Victorian qualities to her work—a charge she does not deny. She dislikes sordid tales and confesses that she could not write them. But another side of that Victorianism is that in all her years as a writer she has had one publisher in America, Dodd Mead. Such steadfastness is surely of another age.

Poirot's death received front page news coverage from the New York Times. *This was the first time a fictional character was so honored.*

LITTLE GREY CELLS

How many of them does Poirot have?

Approximately one trillion, or 10^{12}.

(You have the same number, whether your head is egg-shaped or not.)

The cells are indeed grey, but they are also white — which Poirot forgot to mention — and when seen through a microscope they have a brownish tinge.

Doctors call them neurons, or nerve cells, and divide them into three parts. There's the cell body, the dendrites (for conducting impulses toward the cell) and the axon (for transmitting impulses away from the cell). The axon is surrounded by a myelin sheath, which gives the cell its whitish color.

When the axon of one neuron connects with a dendrite of another, you get a synapse. So when Poirot is "using his little grey cells" he is really experiencing multiple synapses involving the cell bodies of the cerebral cortex. To a layman, this means he is thinking. (He also has to use his little grey cells just to stay awake. Consciousness is achieved by the reticular activating system.)

On an EEG machine read-out, normal cells at rest show an alpha rhythm. When you're thinking, however, you get dechronization — or the arousal and alerting response.

Certain drugs can stimulate your little grey cells to think; among them, caffeine, amphetamines, nicotine and strychnine. Considering how much thinking Poirot did, it's just possible he needed a little extra stimulation. A bit of strychnine in the moustache wax, perhaps?

GERVASE FEN AND THE TEACAKE SCHOOL

Catherine Aird

For those concerned with putting stories into categories, the mystery divides easily enough. Four main groups account for most of them — the police procedural, the Gothic, the hard-boiled and the psychological. There is, however, a fifth which is peculiarly English and which has been aptly described as the teacake school. In detective stories in the teacake school it goes without saying that at four o'clock in the afternoon everything stops for tea.

Although Gervase Fen may be met more often drinking something stronger spirituously, he belongs spiritually to the teacake school and all that that implies. Stopping for afternoon tea is only natural in the rarefied world in which the Professor of English Language and Literature at the University of Oxford has his being. It is a world made up of Oxford colleges (Fen himself is a Fellow of St. Christopher's) and Cathedral closes; boys' public schools (the author, Edmund Crispin, was himself once a schoolmaster at one) and English country villages.

It is a refined world peopled by young earls (improbably called Henry Fielding) who do their war service in toyshops, and amiable undergraduates, ready for anything. (One in particular, young Mr. Hoskins, has a way with him — a special talent for calming anxious girls which proves useful in *The Moving Toyshop.* He "had never been known to indulge in any sport save the most ancient of them all.") Fen's friends belong to the same setting — Geoffrey Vintner, the famous organist and composer, and Richard Cadogan, a major poet.

And yet there is more — much more — to the stories about Gervase Fen than the circles in which he moves.

He is a character who is not so much a detective as someone who happens somehow always to be where the action is. He usually arrives on the scene late, having had his expertise invoked either by his friends or the circumstance of being there. And he is as immediately omniscient as any other investigator in the genre. It is his happy practise to indicate not only that he knows the name of the murderer but that the reader, too, should have been able to work it out as easily. This, of course, he does a good few chapters before he actually reveals all — and how right he is. The reader should have got there, too — but, of course, hasn't usually, unless by some happy chance he is as observant and as percipient as Fen himself. This skill is even more apparent in the short stories in *Beware of the Trains,* where the reader doesn't feel quite so ignorant for quite so long.

Gervase Fen stands alone in the series in his omniscience. There is no faithful Dr. Watson as side-kick — if such an indelicate word can be admitted into the dignified context of ancient colleges and English scholarship. Fen doesn't have a sounding board, belonging to the other tradition of leaving the reader to work it all out for himself. True, there is usually Wilkes, an aged, deaf and bibulous don, also of St. Christopher's, who dogs Fen — but in an obstructive capacity, thwarting where he can and more in pursuit of Fen's whisky than in search of enlightenment.

Nor can the Chief Constable of Oxford, Sir Richard Freeman, be said to play the foil. He is a policeman, all right, but really a professor of English Literature *manqué*. He is the mirror-image, in fact, of Fen, who declares himself to be "the only literary critic turned detective in the whole of fiction." The police force, especially Inspector Humbleby, stands in a cooperative relationship with Gervase Fen that is faint but pursuing, while Sir Richard himself seems more concerned with what William Shakespeare had in mind when he wrote *Measure for Measure*. "It is always my fate," bemoans Fen, "to be involved with literary policemen," but he himself is quite prepared to while away a waiting time playing quoting games like "Detestable Characters in Fiction" and "Unreadable Books."

Fen also stands in a curious, not to say unique, relationship with both the reader and the author. The reader is more aware of the author in the writings of Edmund Crispin than in almost any other detective fiction. "Let's go left," opts Fen at a division of the ways in a pursuit, "Gollancz is publishing this book." And again at a moment when someone asks him what he is doing: "I was making up titles for Crispin." In *Love Lies Bleeding* he declares he is going to write a detective story himself.

With the reader the involvement is even more unusual. Fen has here described a knot — in fact, quite a well-known one, though he doesn't say so. Instead:

"It's called the Hook, Line and Sinker."

"Why is it called that?"

"Because," said Fen placidly, "the reader has to swallow it."

On another occasion Fen says, "If there is anything I hate it is the sort of book in which characters don't go to the police when they've no earthly reason for not doing so."

The whole leads to the feeling in some of the books that there is a play within a play — what might be called "the Rosencrantz and Guildenstern effect." This is enhanced by phrases such as "No-one expects this sort of trick outside a book" and "our narrative is enriched by." Such is Gervase Fen's *persona* that a Gaulish division of the books into three parts — the reader, the author and Gervase Fen — seems perfectly plausible. And yet in no sense is he greater than his creator. He is simply a third party to the reading experience.

THE COMPLEAT CRISPIN

The Case of the Gilded Fly
Holy Disorders
The Moving Toyshop
Swan Song
Love Lies Bleeding
Buried for Pleasure
Frequent Hearses
The Long Divorce
Beware of the Trains (short stories)
The Glimpses of the Moon

Surely somewhere, sooner or later, every writer makes a statement of faith about his craft. In *Buried for Pleasure* the detective novelist, Mr. Judd, tells Fen, "One's plots are necessarily *improbable* but I believe in making sure they are not *impossible*," and, a little later, "Characterisation seems to me a very overrated element in fiction. I can never see why one should be obliged to have any of it at all, if one doesn't want to. It *limits* the form so."

Perhaps it is this credo which accounts for the fact that the first really full physical description of Fen does not appear until the sixth Gervase Fen story — *Buried for Pleasure*. "A tall lean man with a ruddily cheerful, clean-shaven face and brown hair which stood up mutinously in spikes at the crown of his head. . . . his eyes; they showed charity and understanding as well as a taste for mischief." He is forty-two years old.

He enjoys a sports car, small, noisy and battered, of a design much favoured before the war, which rejoices in the name — painted on the bonnet — of Lily Christine III. It — she — was bought from an undergraduate who had been sent down and clatters "like saucepans at war." Fen enjoys his car. We enjoy books which feature Fen and especially for the choice words that we find there.

That well-known phrase "It pays to increase your word power" is nowhere more true than when reading the works of Edmund Crispin. A really wide vocabulary goes a long way, while a good dictionary is a help — not to say a necessity. Perhaps this is only to be expected when the hero happens to be a professor of English Language and Literature. What is even more enjoyable is the influence which Lewis Carroll has had upon Gervase Fen. Words and phrases from this author abound and seem to fit Fen as to the manner born — the Dormouse, the White Rabbit, Father William, even the pig-baby in *Alice* are all referred to.

Equally fascinating is that there are also moments of great profundity — understressed because these do not belong to this *oeuvre.* "I always think that psychology is wrong in imagining that when it has analysed evil it has somehow disposed of it." And "Like most people you overestimate the refining powers of tribulation."

And of neat paradox.

Of marriage in *Swan Song:* "How nice," said Elizabeth judicially, "to have all the pleasures of living in sin without any of the disadvantages."

There are descriptions which stay in the mind, too. Could this of a building that is not old be bettered? "Deathwatch beetles would be out of place."

There was something strangely prescient about the title of *The Long Divorce,* a book in which Fen appears in the thin disguise of Mr. Datchery, a character from Charles Dickens' unfinished book *The Mystery of Edwin Drood.* After *The Long Divorce* there was a gap of nearly a quarter of a century before, in 1977, another full-length Gervase Fen story appeared. This is *The Glimpses of the Moon,* and it can truly be written that the years have not wearied our amateur investigator. But, perhaps, as usual, it might be better to let him have the last word himself from *Swan Song.*

"The era of my greatest successes may be said, roughly speaking, to extend from the time when I first became interested in detection to the present moment. . . ."

It does.

Catherine Aird is the author of A Slight Mourning.

Two English gentlemen keeping a stiff upper lip as they view a crime scene.

TEMPEST IN A TEAPOT:
The Care and Brewing of Tea

Jeanine Larmoth

To brew the best tea, it is as necessary to have a spinster as it is to have a virgin for a truffle hunt. Only a spinster can provide that atmosphere of coziness, knickknackery, and chintz so important to the taste. Tea is made, of course, by first installing a hob on which to hang the kettle, then scattering antimacassars liberally about the room, and finding the cat. A collection of small flowerpots with African violets is helpful, but not essential.

The ultimate tribute to the teapot, its temple, the tea shop, and its vestal virgin, the spinster, was paid by Agatha Christie in *Funerals Are Fatal.* The genteel companion, Miss Gilchrist, kills her employer with a hatchet all for the love of a tea shop. Instead of a faded picture of an old beau on her bedroom wall (ready to be brought into service should a séance arise), there is a photograph of a tea shop she once had, called The Willow-Tree. A victim of the war. Like a mother with a very special child, she babbles about the blue willow-patterned china, or the jam and scones she used to prepare, or trade secrets for making brioches and chocolate éclairs. She is more often seen with flour on her hands than blood. Miss Gilchrist's obsession for the return to gentility a tea shop would afford is so great she kills for a pittance, and is taken away to the meting out of justice, happily planning the curtains.

So much tea is poured in a mystery, one comes away a bit squelchy after reading. So many sweet biscuits are served one could build a hundred Hansel-and-Gretel houses. Tea is the great restorer. It seeps into the nooks and crannies of the soul. It is oil on troubled waters. It is applied, like a hot compress, wherever it hurts, with a faith and fervor that could only be bred in a conscientiously, securely, puritanically Protestant country such as England. Prayer is for Papists; whisky for shock.

There is something crisping about tea. None of the florid, suspect luxury of coffee. Tea cries out to stiffen the lip, and be on with it. Tea quenches tears and thirst. It is an opening for the pouring out of troubles. It eases shyness, and lubricates gossip. While it is not in itself sympathetic, in the right hands tea acts as a backing force to tender ministrations. The mighty to the lowly assuage with tea, cure for

CRUMPETS AND SCONES

The former you toast, the latter you heat. A crumpet is quite chewy, in the manner of toffee. (Some would call it leathery.) A scone — which rhymes with gone — is rather like a flat-topped, unflavoured muffin. Both are staples of the well-appointed tea table, and are especially tasty when liberally doused with butter and smothered with jam.

A CUPPA CALAMITY

Make your pot of tea in the usual way, but when you pour the tea into the cup, do not use a strainer. Ask your subject to drink the tea, then to swirl round the dregs and invert the cup over the saucer. Suggest he or she turn the inverted cup in the saucer three times in a clockwise direction and say, "Tell me faithful, tell me well, the secrets that the leaves foretell." Then you, as leaf reader, take the cup in two hands and peer at the patterns the leaves have made. If you see any of the following shapes, your tea drinker should make no long-range plans.

Shape	Meaning
Clock	Illness; if at bottom of cup, death
Cross	Trouble
Key	Robbery, if at bottom of cup
M	Someone has evil intentions toward you
Nun	Sorrow
Parrot	Slander
Raven	More trouble
Scythe	Danger
Snake	Enmity
Wings	Messages; the nearer the bottom of the cup, the worse the news

Prepared by The Tea Council Limited.

MARTY NORMAN

body and soul.

Tea pours with equal grace from glazed brown pots or vast cauldrons of furbelowed silver. It washes through kitchens, where the lino cracks and the housewife offers a cuppa char, or slips, a perfect amber arch, into gold-stippled cups on the lawn of a stately home — its crystalline, chuckling voice covering any awkward moments with delicacy.

There are proper teas and, perhaps, improper teas, high teas and low. A proper tea is offered by an overbustly, oversolicitous matron who feels you look peaked and in need of immediate sustenance. A proper tea should, therefore, be substantial: Marmite, eggs, meat pies, sandwiches, cake, the lot. The substance of a proper tea is not actually different from high tea, which has stood in place of supper for hundreds of years for thousands of English schoolchildren. To be truly British, tea should be imbalanced in favor of carbohydrates — therefore, bread-and-butter sandwiches, plus sandwiches (kept nicely moist beneath a dampened napkin), fruitcake, and cakes.

Tea is best brewed in the brown pot. Otherwise, any china pot. The pot is "hotted up" with boiling water, which is allowed to sit for a moment before it is tossed out with an air. A teaspoonful of tea added for each cup, and one for the pot. The water for tea is of such moment, gentlemen traveling abroad often require special spring waters lest they encounter a foreign admixture to their favorite bouquet. The water must not boil a moment beyond its open, rolling bubble or the mineral content becomes proportionately higher. The brew then steeps for three to five minutes. Certain teas grow bitter if left longer, so second pots may have to be prepared for second cups. If tea is too strong, water will thin it, but not reduce the bitterness. Tea can be as deep and opaque as coffee or very little darker than water. In order that the flow never falter, a jug of hot water should stand by the smaller jug of warmed milk and the sugar bowl (no lumps, please).

Because England is inclined to be damp and chilly, and the houses drafty, the teapot may — though this is common — be given a little coat of its own, called a cozy, to wear to the table. A tea cozy is floral and quilted chintz, or a lumpish, unrecognizable crocheted affair made by an abysmal aunt. Some pots are further accoutered with tiny, tea-stained sponges attached to their nozzles to prevent drips.

The container in which the tea is stored is an understandably regal affair of antique Indian brass, lead-lined wood, or exotically devised porcelain, and is called a caddy. When the tea is a swirling maelstrom ready to be served, a strainer is placed over the cup to be sure the tea is clear. The strainer, as is proper with ceremonial vessels, has, in turn, its own resting place above a little stand, or hooked over the slop bowl. Despite the revolting name, a slop bowl is a superbly proportioned, exquisitely decorated piece of china. To add the final, mystical note to the ceremony, a silver bell may stand on the tea table with which to ring for the servants for more cake, more milk, more hot water, or the police.

Tea kettles, apart from making tea, hot water for bottles, and singing, are very important utensils in a mystery if you haven't a letter opener, and wouldn't use one if you had. To unstick an envelope, you send whoever else is in the kitchen out of it. Be sure not to arouse suspicions, or they may dash back in and surprise you.

When the room is empty (check behind the fridge and stove to be sure), fill up the kettle. Put the kettle on the fire. Bring to a boil. Be sure to wait for a steady jet of steam. This will be about seven minutes for an average kettle. Keep an ear cocked. Hold envelope over steam. Slip knife under flap. Pry open very gently. Pull out contents, and read will, letter, or shopping list. If latter, scan for hidden meanings. If interrupted, slide knife into garter, and hide envelope behind stove, being sure to fold the flap backward to prevent resealing.

Make tea with leftover water.

Sometimes, spinsters get tired of their High Street shopping-and-tea-after routine, and take the cheap Thursday train to London for the sales, and to switch suitcases and catch murderers at the station's Left Luggage. After her adventures, the spinster may choose to refresh herself by having tea in the lounge hall of a hotel, or take it on the return train.

Tea on the move may be the best tea of all.

THE AGITATED TEABAG

If you must persist in using a teabag, the gentlemen at The Tea Council Limited would rather you didn't just let it lie there like a corpse in an advanced state of rigor. You must agitate the teabag, dear, agitate it, or the essence of the tea will be muffled. An even swing of the wrist, once left, once right, once left again, should do. Now then, who's for elevenses?

Served on British Railways, it is a rush and clatter of dishes which jump up and down — apparently from the excitement of travel — all the way from London to Plymouth, and back again, if they're not required. In the dim light of declining afternoon and three-watt bulbs, the crockery sits at empty tables in a state of eternal preparedness, as if endlessly waiting a macabre Mad Hatter's Tea Party — passengers advancing, eating, from table to table as the train runs along. The sandwiches — small circlings of tomatoes, sliced hard-boiled eggs, or fish paste on limp white bread, its crusts resolutely removed for refinement, and swathed in mayonnaise — contribute their own lifeless air, faintly enlivened by a tossing of mustard cress, and augmented by downtrodden, but resilient fruitcake. Thus, the bottom-heavy tradition of starchy foods at teatime is upheld, even in transit.

The civilizing effects of tea, perhaps more than the building of roads, or even the drinking of gin, has been one of the largest contributions England made to civilizing her empire. For centuries, wherever the flag waved, it was an amiable way for people to gather together under pith helmets or parasols for a well-mannered chat, to push sweet morsels in their mouths, and forget the ruddy natives hiding in the bush.

LITTLE OLD LADIES

Heron Carvic

Should elderly maiden ladies detect?

The trouble is that they do: the carpet stain that you had covered with a rug; family quagmires, with answers to the present from examples in the past; the exact state of your overdraft. I had a great-aunt with many theatrical connections. She could always tell me who was bedding whom before they'd even bought the sheets. Had she applied her powers to criminal detection (as did my great-grandfather, Sir Richard Mayne, one of the two original Commissioners of Police), I would have given little for the criminal's chances. Since elderly maiden ladies have this overweening interest in other people's affairs, should it not then be channelled?

Back in the mists of time I read adventures of Agatha Christie's Miss Marple and Patricia Wentworth's Miss Silver — with a bias toward the latter. I could see the advantage to an author of the elderly spinster opposed to villainy: innocence — the charming shibboleth that elderly spinsters are innocent still obtains — triumphing over vice.

The story of St. George and the Dragon, however disguised, is the essence of all detective stories — chastity held in thrall by a villain for a hero to set free. But if, St. George having failed to find the monster, his maiden aunt had downed her tapestry work to sally forth and slay the brute, it would have lent the tale a certain piquancy.

Miss Marple's and Miss Silver's innate genius for solving the most complicated cases by discussion, by comparison with village life — and all without dropping one stitch of two-purl-one-plain — I found a trifle hard to take. Unless, of course, it was done mainly by intuition, which brings in the psychic factor.

The female, it would seem, is more prone to this complaint than is the male; traditionally, it is the old gypsy woman, not the gypsy, whose palm is crossed with silver, just as there is always "a little woman I know of" waiting to tell your fortune. Few people know of "little men."

The psychic tends to be solitary by nature — I suppose foreseeing the future may have its disadvantages. So, by permutation, you are likely to find a preponderance of psychic individuals amongst elderly spinsters.

In my teens I knew a struggling artist called Constance Oliver, fiftyish. She was commissioned by a smart, amusing American woman to paint a portrait of her with her son, a particularly delightful small boy who was deaf and dumb. I saw the early stages of the picture which promised well. A week later — Constance had been working on the child's face — I was disappointed. Under her brush the boy's charm had gone and he looked sulky. Another week, and the portrait was no longer on the easel. Whilst Constance was cooking lunch, I found the picture behind a stack of others: the

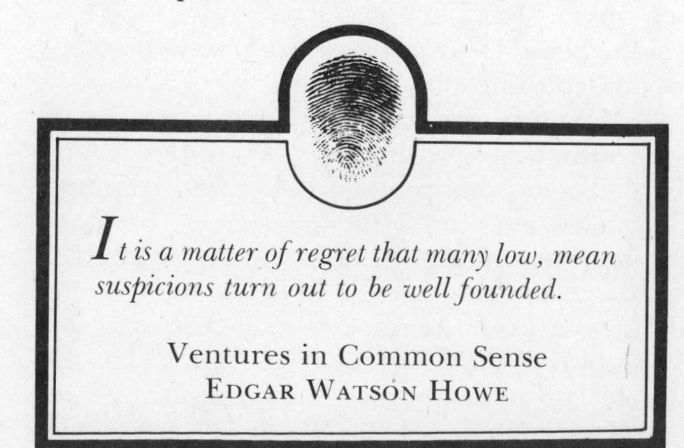

rough-in of the mother, unfinished but clever, had been slashed with a palette knife. Over lunch I asked Constance what had gone wrong. Uncharacteristically, she refused to discuss it, merely saying that she wasn't satisfied, couldn't do it and had turned in the commission. It was equally uncharacteristic for her to turn in a commission or destroy a canvas, neither of which she could afford to do.

It was some years before I saw the American again: she was separated from her husband and had been travelling abroad with her son. We arranged a happy skating party at an indoor rink. She was as gay and as amusing as ever, but the son, now about seventeen, had grown loutish and sullen. Within a fortnight I was shocked to read on the front page of a newspaper that she had been murdered. Knowing that the boy, although he had learned to speak to some extent, would be helpless without his mother, I rang the flat to see if I could help, only to learn from the police that it was he who had killed her. Wanting a few shillings for a visit to a cinema and being denied since his mother felt he was going out too often and too late, he had knocked her down, gone to the kitchen, collected a knife and, as she was trying to rise, cut her to ribbons, taken the money, gone to a film and then returned to the flat for a good night's sleep. He was committed to Broadmoor.

That Constance had foreseen the tragedy when she painted the boy looking sulky and slashed the rough-in of the mother, I do not believe, but that artists sometimes receive emanations from their subjects is beyond dispute. I suppose that Miss Seeton, although their characters could hardly be more dissimilar, must be based upon Constance. Certainly when, a long time afterwards, my wife persuaded me to try my hand at a short story, I based it on the idea that an artist can sometimes read more into another painter's work than the painter had intended to reveal. Into my mind walked Miss Seeton, complete with Christian names, umbrella and background, who took over the story and twisted it round to suit herself. Two subsequent comedy stories about her were published, but the original was considered, in those days, too macabre for a family magazine.

After a lapse of fifteen years, when I'd long forgotten her, Miss Seeton upped and demanded a book. Ridiculous. At best, she was short-story material. She nagged at me for a fortnight until I gave in, deciding that if she wanted to satirize detective novels in general, and elderly lady detectives in particular, let her have her head whilst I plodded along behind trying to learn to write. The result was *Picture Miss Seeton,* and since then she has to a large extent taken over my life — to my advantage, for which I'm duly grateful.

Miss Marple, Miss Silver, Miss Seeton.

Considering the adage that truth is stranger than fiction, are we perhaps failing to tap a potential source of power in the war against crime? Should there be an office for GERIATRICS (Detection) INCORPORATED in every police department, where elderly maiden ladies, between their cups of tea, their knitting, their discussions about their relatives, and their artistic endeavours, could solve problems which were causing routine headaches? With regard to Miss Seeton, in view of the chaos she generally causes, there would undoubtedly be mass resignations from the force, thus saving a deal of state expenditure. All that would be needed would be a selection of her sketches depicting the people involved, forwarded to the court, allowing the judge and the jury to pick the winner.

Heron Carvic has written four books featuring Miss Seeton. Although not a little old lady himself, he has been known to carry a brolly.

GERIATRIC SLEUTHS

Mrs. 'Arris (PAUL GALLICO)
Miss Marple (AGATHA CHRISTIE)
Minnie Santangelo (ANTHONY MANCINI)
Miss Seeton (HERON CARVIC)
Miss Silver (PATRICIA WENTWORTH)
Mrs. Pollifax (DOROTHY GILMAN)
Hildegarde Withers (STUART PALMER)
Max Gutman (CHARLES GOLDSTEIN)

THE MISS MARPLE LOOK-ALIKE CONTEST

Contest Rules

1. All contestants must be at least 74 years of age.

2. They must live on a fixed income.

3. They must knit.

4. They must gossip.

5. They must garden.

6. They must own a pair of binoculars.

7. They must explain why they stole a Poirot plot and starred in it as Margaret Rutherford (*Murder at the Gallop*).

8. They must explain why they repeated the crime (*Murder Most Foul*).

9. They must be able to name all the novels in which they have appeared (*Murder at the Vicarage; The Body in the Library; The Moving Finger; A Murder Is Announced; They Do It with Mirrors; A Pocket Full of Rye; 4:50 from Paddington; The Mirror Crack'd from Side to Side; A Caribbean Mystery; At Bertram's Hotel; Nemesis; Sleeping Murder*).

10. They must list all the short story collections in which they are included (*The Thirteen Problems; The Regatta Mystery; Three Blind Mice; The Adventure of the Christmas Pudding; Double Sin*).

11. They should have china-blue eyes, fluffy white hair, and a pink-and-white complexion.

12. They should be able to draw a map of St. Mary Mead.

13. They should be willing to acknowledge their inspiration (Agatha Christie's grandmother).

The Winner

HENRI CARTIER-BRESSON/MAGNUM

HIDDEN DETECTIVES

James H. Olander

Hidden in the following puzzle are thirty-three last names and one first name of thirty-four popular detectives, amateur and professional. The letters may read from left to right, right to left, top to bottom, bottom to top, or diagonally in any direction. Some letters may appear in more than one name. One of them, Lew Archer, is done for you.

C A N Y O U F I N D N A M E S
U P A B U G O A G R G R A N T
F E N T E A H B C E D C R O W
F R A N K C I O U W I H P E N
S H A Y N E K U T O S E L B Y
D R E V L I S H E E R R E F E
U N I Q U E A C I A R E S O L
P O I R O T E L I P T G S A L
I U Q U C A G L Z E T T I T A
N K U H O L M E S F E C N A V
A D E D A P S F U L B R O O M
H R E D S M A L L O B R O W N
C A N O I P M A C W I M S E Y
O C L A P P L E B Y T T E N T
G A M A D G E W O L R A M T O

THE HIDDEN DETECTIVES

1. Alleyn, Roderick
2. Appleby, John
3. Archer, Lew
4. Beck, Martin
5. Brown, Father
6. Campion, Albert
7. Chan, Charlie
8. Crow, Anderson
9. Cuff, Sergeant
10. Dalgliesh, Adam
11. Drew, Nancy
12. Dupin, C. Auguste
13. Fell, Gideon
14. Fen, Gervase
15. Gamadge, Henry
16. Ghote, Ganesh
17. Grant, Alan
18. Holmes, Sherlock
19. Maigret, Jules
20. Marlowe, Philip
21. Marple, Miss Jane
22. Poirot, Hercule
23. Queen, Ellery
24. Robinson, Mac
25. Selby, Doug
26. Shayne, Mike
27. Silver, Miss Maud
28. Small, Rabbi David
29. Spade, Sam
30. Tibbett, Henry
31. Thatcher, John Putnam
32. Vance, Philo
33. Wimsey, Lord Peter
34. Wolfe, Nero

Dr. James H. Olander is associate professor of English at the New York Institute of Technology.

THE BBC THROUGH A MONOCLE

Ian Carmichael

COURTESY PUBLIC BROADCASTING SYSTEM

On 11th March 1966 I received a letter from my agent which read as follows:

> My brother has come up with what might be a very interesting idea for a television series, namely the character of Lord Peter Wimsey in the Dorothy Sayers books. As you know they were tremendously popular, and the character would, I think, fit you like a glove (or vice versa) and there is certainly quite a lot of material to draw on.

Immediately, I flipped.

I had read a few of the Wimsey books when I was in my twenties, and somewhere about the age of eighteen or nineteen I had seen my local repertory company give a performance of *Busman's Honeymoon.* In short, I knew sufficient about the character to realise that this was the best idea to have come my way for a very long time.

Unhappily, a very long time was exactly what it took to bring that germ of an idea to full-flower. On 17th January 1972 the cameras eventually started to roll on the first episode of the first TV production, ending a maddening and frustrating gestation period of five years.

On receipt of my agent's letter, the first thing I did was ring up Harrods and ask them to send me copies of the complete Wimsey canon.

"How many books are there?" I asked.

"Fourteen," came the reply after a few moments' research.

"In *paper*back," I added, hurriedly.

Now, I enjoy reading for pleasure very much indeed, but reading for work is an entirely different matter. That I find a complete chore. So it was with mixed feelings that I sat down to read fourteen books on the trot, one after the other. Rarely, before or since, has such a daunting job of work turned out to give me so much pleasure. I did indeed read one after the other, in chronological order, without even stopping to pick up so much as a copy of *Playboy* magazine to act as a mental douche 'twixt stories.

I repeat, I flipped.

The next five years were packed with incident and inactivity, and principally the latter.

I first approached the BBC Light Entertainment Department, for whom I had just finished playing Bertie Wooster in three successful series, and immediately I hit the first of a long string of obstructions which were to be strewn across my path like tank-traps for half a decade. It came in the form of a letter from the head of the department.

"The very first snag," it read, "is an insuperable one — money. The BBC has no risk capital whatever at the moment to invest in projects, however optimistic one may be about potential profits."

It then went on to add that the overseas sales advisors had expressed the view that the subject would, and I quote, "by no means be an easy sale across the Atlantic. The character of Lord Peter Wimsey is not very well known in the States," it went on, "nor does the literary and literate style fit in very well with the current trends of filmed series."

Mumbling into my metaphorical beard several phrases like "lack of foresight," "no imagination" and "false assumptions," I refused to be put off. Girding up my loins, I approached the Drama Department of the same station, the head of which was an old friend of mine. I was appearing in a long-running play in the West End at the time, and I telephoned him one evening from the theatre during the act interval to ask if I could go round and have a chat with him after the show. He agreed, and an hour and a half later, armed with a large whisky, I started my sales spiel.

A BELL-RINGER PROTESTS

Jean Sanderson, an English campanology authority, was asked to comment on Lord Peter's bell-ringing form in *The Nine Tailors.* According to Miss Sanderson, Dorothy L. Sayers made several mistakes. First, the vicar should never have stepped in. ("This is considered far too dangerous and any peal in which this occurred would not be recognised.") Second, since he was ringing a heavy bell of 7¼ cwt., Lord Peter's hands, after three hours had gone by, would have been blistered and swollen; by the end of nine hours, they would have been in such a terrible state, he probably could not have held on to the rope. Third, the reverberations of the bells would certainly have made the poor soul deaf and quite possibly have driven him mad, but it is doubtful they would have killed him "unless he had a weak blood vessel, in which case it's just conceivable a hemorrhage would have occurred, and *that* could have killed him."

Miss Sanderson recommends the following books to mystery fans who wish to further their interest in campanological crimes:

The Chinese Bell Murders by Robert van Gulik;

Death of a Dissenter by Lynton Lamb.

She further suggests if you're ever in the vicinity of Meldreth (Nr. Cambridge), ring her up and she'll give you a lesson in tower bell-ringing, change bell-ringing and hand bell-ringing. However, she wants you to know that real-life bell-ringers are more interested in socialising than homiciding.

"Do you know the Wimsey books?" I asked.

"Look behind you," he said, and there, on a bookshelf behind my head, was every one of them. Obviously I had found a fellow fan. My spirits rose.

My friend went on to tell me that the Wimsey books were, indeed, at that very moment, along with a couple of other subjects, being considered as a possible follow-up series to a very successful one that had just come to an end. My spirits rose even higher. They needn't have. It was to prove yet another disappointment. Nothing ever came of the idea.

Just for the record, I discovered about a year later that the producer ear-marked to undertake the new series, though being very keen to tackle the Wimsey saga, did not want me in the part. Whether this influenced the overall decision to scrap the idea, I know not. I very much doubt it.

Having drawn a blank at the BBC, I then sat down and drew up a highly professional twelve-page sales brochure on the subject which, emulating the best door-to-door salesmen, I started touting round all the U.K. commercial stations, which, each in turn, showed a similar lack of enthusiasm. I received such dismissive answers as:

"After careful reflection we do not think there is an international market for the Peter Wimsey idea." And:

"It's not our scene." And:

"The Americans will never go for an effete (a strange adjective for Peter Wimsey) Englishman." Or:

"The Americans will never buy a serial, only a series.

Simultaneous with all this, my agent and I had been having talks with the Sayers estate in order to find out the availability of the TV rights of the saga, and here again we encountered problems. The executors were, at that time, only prepared to sell the rights of the complete works in one package. To discuss the purchase of individual books or, say, one or two at a time, they were not prepared to do, and this alone, I knew, would not endear the idea to the British TV moguls, regardless of their other prejudices.

Disheartened, I then let the matter drop for a year and got on with something else. In 1968 I became more depressed as I heard that a film company was showing interest in the properties and consequently the Sayers people were no longer prepared to entertain the possibility of a television series.

Impasse.

In 1969 I received information that the film project was off, so I started knocking at the BBC's door once again. This time with considerably more success. A producer was assigned to the job, scriptwriters were put to work and all the novels were to be presented in chronological order in three series of thirteen episodes each. Excelsior! That was the way I had always wanted them to be presented. But "When troubles come . . ." etc. Nine months later the producer left the BBC in order to produce a feature film, and all was off once again.

One year after that (and if you are finding this monotonous, think how I was feeling) I again tried to persuade them to resurrect the project. Apart from anything else, I was getting concerned that when and if we ever did get it off the ground, I would, by then, be too old for the part! By this time the Sayers estate had withdrawn their original condition of selling the complete works as a package, and plans were made to do one novel in five episodes to see how it was received.

You would have thought that by now I was home and dry, but oh dear no, not a bit of it. Which novel to start with was the next hiatus.

"Number one, *Whose Body?*" I opined.

"Not a bit of it," said the authorities. "We must start with a good one, a well-known one, and *Whose Body?* is inferior. Let's start with *Murder Must Advertise*."

"But that's halfway through the canon," I explained. "We shall get into a frightful mess from a chronological point of view if it is a success and you want to do more."

Impasse again.

Finally a compromise was made, and we all agreed to start with book number two, *Clouds of Witness;* and early on a cold March morning in 1972, in the heart of Howarth Moor (the Brontës' moor) in Yorkshire, Wimsey and Bunter got into a green 3½-litre Bentley and drove off past the camera. At last we were on our way.

Three years later, in January 1975, in the BBC studios in Glasgow, the final shots of *Five Red Herrings* were committed to videotape. The fifth book completed. From that day to this, I have heard no more from my employers. The series has (temporarily? I know not) been abandoned, and Harriet Vane has never appeared on a TV screen. The letters that I have received from avid fans awaiting her entrance would fill the correspondence column of a national newspaper for six months. But it was not to be. Why? I have no idea. Finance, I suspect, but I have never been informed.

For those who don't know, Peter eventually married Harriet Vane (*Busman's Honeymoon*), the girl he got acquitted of murdering her lover (*Strong Poison*) and by whom he eventually had three sons (*Striding Folly*). So criminology, bibliography, music and cricket were obviously not the sum of his talents.

I loved Wimsey. He was me. Or what of him that was not me was what I would have liked to be me. I think I was rather like a child playing dressing-up games. I dressed up as Wimsey and played "Let's pretend" because I admired him, I envied him his life-style, his apparent insouciance, his prowess and his intellect. He was never, as some people like to pontificate, a snob, an anti-Semite, an . . . but that is all the subject of another article.

Ian Carmichael is *Lord Peter Wimsey.*

THE BETTMAN ARCHIVE, INC.

Lord Peter, while at Balliol College, Oxford, excelled at cricket. Here, he admires the renowned Dr. Grace's batting posture. Neither wished to comment on the origin of the term "sticky wicket."

A PINCE-NEZ PROPELLED BY TWO WALKING STICKS

Donald Rumbelow

Dr. Gideon Fell, Ph.D., LL., F.R.H.S., resembles his contemporary, G.K. Chesterton. There is the same mountain of flesh, the box-pleated cape, many chins, ruddy face, grey hair, bandit's moustache and small eyes peeping through a pince-nez fastened to a broad black ribbon. Probably he doesn't drink as much beer and wine as the stories suggest he does. Hopefully he was caught, if only once, as Chesterton was, sitting in a Fleet Street tavern, not quaffing great stoups of ale but quietly sipping a small lemonade!

Before his move to Adelphi Terrace, necessitated by his appointment as advisor to Scotland Yard, Fell's home was at Chatterham in Lincolnshire. The infernal region of imps and goblins seems a more natural background than the noisy bustle of modern London. Guardian of the shrine, in both homes, is Mrs. Fell, a small, cheerful woman, always knocking things over, and with a tendency to poke her head in and out of windows like an overwound cuckoo clock. In her worse moments, she sounds like a convert to the Daughters of Temperance. She heartily disapproves of beer and wine in place of tea. Not surprisingly, Dr. Fell regularly abandons her for more congenial companions on both sides of the Atlantic.

His students don't learn much in the way of formal history. They join him in beer-swilling, table-pounding conversations, cheer his descriptions of battles and stamp their feet loudly when he leads them into the chorus of a drinking song of Godfrey of Bouillon's men on the First Crusade (likely to be confused by teetotallers with "We Won't be Home till Morning"). This environment is understandably conducive to his researches on his monumental work *The Drinking Customs of England from the Earliest Days.*

His other great work is the history of the supernatural in fiction. He has an encyclopaedic knowledge of the subject which, by right, when he tangles with death-watches, mad hatters and red-gartered witches, should give him the lion's share of the credits. Regretfully the sheer physical bulk of the man — he has to walk with two sticks — means that the action has to be left to younger men such as the American Ted Rampole and the flamboyant Patrick ("I am never wrong") Butler K.C. (King's Counsel).

Dr. Fell, like Old King Cole, with whom he is sometimes compared, is too often the story's *deus ex machina.*

Deus ex machina? He wouldn't like that.

Each man should reflect his hero. So why shouldn't Gideon Fell?

It is only fitting, for a man of his size, that he should have more than one.

His is a bench of magistrates, long dead, of ancient Athens.

Like those same magistrates, Dr. Fell is outside the action. Like them, he can bring stillness and peace to the troubled places. Like them, he can pronounce sentence.

Archons of Athens!

He is the law.

Donald Rumbelow is a London police constable and the author of I Spy Blue.

[Advertisement]

[Advertisement]

Nightgown

Oversize collar acts as a wrap because we know you can't afford a coat... converts to bat-proof shield for sojourns in the belfry... just your eyes are left free to gaze **deeply** into his!

Drawstring **modestly** raises hem to your knees... enables you to run more easily down those haunted corridors... thermal stockings extend to your waist, warding off those damp crypt chills!

The beautiful ruffle is a secret compartment hiding a flotation ring... should you be thrown in the well or tipped into the pond, you'll float until help arrives...

Had you but known this nightie existed, you would never have crept down the stairs without it!

From the... **House of Gothic**

MARIE GILMORE

THE MYSTERY OF NANCY DREW

Children's Express

The Nancy Drew books are really super because you can't stop reading them. They are exciting and interesting at the same time, 'cause they give you at least three little mysteries that all turn up into one gigantic one.

To people who like mysteries, it's *really* mysterious because at the end of a chapter they keep you hanging and you've got to keep on reading to find out if they get out of it or not. You say, "Hey, wait, I can't stop reading. I've gotta find out what happened to George" or "how Bess found out so and so." And they never get to the whole big plot until, like, the second page to the end!

We went to meet Harriet Adams, the creator of Nancy Drew. Harriet Adams never used her real name on her books — always her pseudonym, Carolyn Keene.

Mrs. Adams is exciting — she's eighty-four now. We thought she was gonna be sort of motherly, just sitting in a rocking chair knitting and thinking about her books, or new stories to write. We thought her office was gonna be a room in a little rickety white house and she was gonna come out wiping her hands on her apron and seat us in old rocking chairs. But when we went there, it was a new, modern brick office building, very large. That was super because it sorta updated her. And Harriet Adams turned out to be half business-like and half motherly-like: when we came in, she hugged each one of us and she didn't even know us; and she goes out to work every day and really *does* something. It's super that she can be both of those things. She's put her mark on the world.

Harriet Adams took up writing Nancy Drew from her father. We never dreamed that her *father* would have a feminine name like Carolyn Keene! It just seemed really strange.

"My father started Nancy Drew and the Hardy Boys and the Bobbsey Twins," Mrs. Adams told us, "and he used pseudonyms. He didn't have to for the Hardy Boys, but on the girls' and children's books he thought if it were feminine it would be better. So I just carried those on.

"I never wrote any books with my father," she continued. "I worked with him the year after college just editing manuscripts. He taught me really how to do that. My father died in 1930. He had written several outlines for stories, and I took over at that time."

We don't want to sound mean — but in case Mrs. Adams dies she'd have an unfinished book and who would be there to finish it? So we asked Mrs. Adams if any of her grandchildren were planning on writing — or her kids.

BOOK REPORT NO. 1

The Mystery of the Brassbound Trunk. Adults would definitely like this book. Maybe the other Nancy Drew books they wouldn't 'cause it's too childish, but this one I don't think so.

MICHAEL SCHREIBMAN, ASSOCIATE EDITOR, *CHILDREN'S EXPRESS*

Harriet Adams, who as Carolyn Keene has continued the Nancy Drew and Hardy Boys series begun by her father, talks with reporters from Children's Express *at her New Jersey home.*

"Well, most of them write well, but they haven't gotten to it because they've gone into other things," she told us. "One's a doctor and two of them are lawyers. One of the grandsons is taking courses now in scriptwriting and he wants to go into film work. I hope that he will."

Mrs. Adams showed us the outline of her new books. She said she had drawers full of 'em. And it's good because she can work on them whenever she goes to her office.

"I've written a hundred and seventy books entirely myself," she told us. "Besides that, I've written many outlines for books and had other people fill them in. And then I take their manuscript and edit and rewrite. So that makes even more.

"This is the way I work. First I write a précis and then I start writing the outline. And then from that I dictate the story on a machine. Many times I ask my own children to help with certain parts. I have one daughter who's a great horsewoman, so if I have any scenes with horses I always ask her to read the book and correct phrases. And I have a son who is an engineer, so sometimes I ask him to help with technical things.

"The quickest I ever wrote a book was two weeks. I like to take from two to three months."

BOOK REPORT NO. 2

The Quest of the Missing Map. They start out with half a map and they have to find Ellen's father's twin brother (who has the other half a map), so they can find the buried treasure.

We asked Mrs. Adams if she had a close relationship with her father like Nancy had with *her* father.

"No, not that close," she replied. "I had a very strict father, and also my father never had any mysteries for me to solve.

"I sort of patterned Nancy Drew after what I would think was an ideal girl," continued Mrs. Adams. "I have put myself in Nancy's place and she's very real when I'm writing about her. I just feel as if she were a live person. I tried to bring up my two daughters the same way."

We asked Mrs. Adams why she changed the styles of clothes and hairdos. Like, Nancy started out wearing a skirt and now she's got pants on.

"The books have been updated," replied Mrs. Adams. "The books that are on the market now are not the original books.

"The biggest problem was with adoption because the laws are now very strict about adoption. But when the Bobbsey Twins and early Nancy Drews were written there really weren't any laws. And in the Bobbsey Twins, Daisy May was the baby in the basket and was left on their doorstep — and they brought it in. But nowadays if anybody leaves a baby on your doorstep, you have to turn the child over to the police.

"Well, I was going to do that Bobbsey Twins book over. I consulted adoption agencies and there was absolutely no way that we could do that story anywhere near the way it was originally. So we sat down in the office and everybody had a suggestion. And one of the women just for fun said, 'Oh, why don't we make Daisy May an orphan?' Well, that's the way it turned out in the new book with that same name."

The Nancy Drew books are much in demand at our library. There's a notice on the books that says, "As soon as you finish them, please return them. They are much in demand." There are only two Nancy Drew books in the library each day because so many of them are out.

"Years ago, both public and school librarians didn't approve of these books and I couldn't see why," Mrs. Adams told us. "They said they weren't great literature or anything. They wouldn't put them in the libraries, so we made a survey one time and we found that most of these librarians were older women, some of them real old, and most of them hadn't read Nancy Drew because they started after these people were grown up. And they just thought because they were inexpensive in price that they couldn't be good books. Well, now the whole thing has changed. Those people have all retired and the younger librarians coming in have all read Nancy Drew!"

In Mrs. Adams' way, she told a story with her answers and each one was sort of a different episode. So she gives her answers like she writes her books!

Writing stories and being busy all the time, we think she really enjoyed us, and we really enjoyed her because she seemed to understand us better than we even understand ourselves.

Children's Express *is the first news magazine written by children. Reporters are: Susan Lozier, 7, Mara Lozier, 9, Patrick McGowan, 11, Lisa Coughlin, 13, Joanne Siesputowski, 13, and Giny Hurlbert, 13. Editors are: Michael Schreibman, 15, and Mary Anne Siesputowski, 15.*

BOOK REPORT NO. 3

The Clue of the Tapping Heels. The first mystery is the missing Persian cats and then it gets another mystery added on to it: who is following Nancy home? Then another one: the mystery of the tapping. Then it ends up into one big story.

MISS SCARLET IN THE LIBRARY WITH A WRENCH

John Watson

Since Anthony E. Pratt first applied his mind to the development of a whodunit game in 1944, his brainchild Cluedo has become a favourite of families in at least seventy-three nations. Its name varies from Clue (in the U.S.A.) to Detective (in Brazil). Its theme of murderer detection, combined with its fine British country house setting and the classic nomenclature of its participants, helps to give the game an atmosphere and charm which enables it to avoid the clinical banality of other deduction games.

Mr. Pratt's own description of his life is characteristic in its elegance and modesty:

> I was born, so I believe, with an introverted disposition, full of ruminations, speculations, imaginative notions and grandiose schemes, but with a destructive, self-critical or disparaging propensity, which was as much a stimulus to action as a ball and chain to a long-distance runner. My schooling was during the First World War, when educational opportunities were few, but I went to a good grammar school where a grounding was given in mediaeval (scholastic) philosophy. This awakened an interest in general philosophy, together with its associated disciplines, which has persisted throughout my life and given me much pleasure, but little else. Coming from a musical family and having a great love of music, I was mistakenly thought to possess gifts which subsequently turned out to be illusory, but I did practise music professionally for years and achieved a local reputation until events impressed upon me my incapacity, temperamentally, to "reach the heights." I then became a civil servant and wound up as clerk to a firm of solicitors. My wife is a very competent artist but has never practised anything more than being a housewife.

Mr. and Mrs. Pratt are now living in retirement at Boscombe near Bournemouth in the south of England.

The board of the present Cluedo game has not changed since Mr. Pratt's wife prepared a final prototype for submission to Waddingtons in 1946. After spending many hours perfecting the mechanics of the game and after filing a provisional specification at the Patent Office, Mr. and Mrs. Pratt visited Waddingtons in Leeds to discuss the possibilities for its manufacture. On that occasion they were accompanied by their close friends Mr. and Mrs. Bull, who had earlier invented a successful

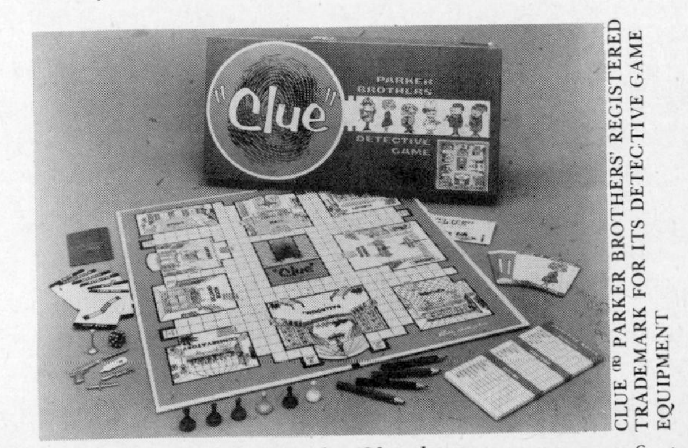

CLUE ® PARKER BROTHERS' REGISTERED TRADEMARK FOR ITS DETECTIVE GAME EQUIPMENT

The best player to be is Miss Scarlet. She always *gets to move first.*

ALL IN THE GAME

Suzanne Weaver

Poor Mr. Boddy found dead in his house
The method unpleasantly gory
The knife was concealed in the Wandering Jew
At the rear of the conservatory.

So — here's the unsavory story:

Scarlet it seems traveled down for a week
During which B. reworded his will
Then who should show up, uninvited of course,
Colonel Mustard, that suspicious old pill.

Apparently Mustard had long had a lust
For Mr. B.'s cook, Mrs. White
(Although she was married to no-one-knew-who
In B.'s room she spent every night).

Now White had a brother, Boddy's old pal
A college professor named Plum
The Prof was determined to seek his revenge
Over an old prank involving his chum.

To make matters worse, at this time in the week
Two lowlifes named Peacock and Green
Came barreling into the Lounge, where the group
Was already involved in a scene.

The night was so cloudy, the air hardly moved
The tension incredibly thick
Boddy stood up, quickly leaving the room,
The gathered had all made him sick.

What happened next was told in the cards
All were suspected it's true
Fingers were pointed in every which way
They were such a despicable crew.

Professional too — hardly a Clue® —

So there's Boddy's body all covered in blood
Cut down in his prime, what a shame
Which of his friends could have done such a thing
Is answered as part of the game.

Suzanne Weaver is an editor who used to slip two weapons and no perpetrator into the Clue® envelope.

game called Buccaneer. Together they played the game with Mr. Hurst and Mr. Goodall from Waddingtons in the office of Mr. Norman Watson, the managing director. Mr. Watson did not play but watched.

It is to the credit of Messrs. Hurst, Goodall and Watson, as well as a compliment to the developmental thoroughness of Mr. Pratt, that the potential of the game was instantly recognised on that occasion.

Terms for its manufacture by John Waddington Limited were quickly and amicably agreed upon. Due to postwar shortages of various materials there were some delays before the game reached the market, but in due course it was launched and received with moderate enthusiasm by the toys and games trade.

It did not become an instant craze. Its present world-wide sales total of approximately 2 million sets per year has been reached more by a process of gradual progression than by any immediate or flashy sales promotion. Its sales throughout the 1950's were solid if unspectacular, and it was not until the late 1960's that any sparkling developments became noticeable in its sales pattern.

The game is now sold in countries from Western Samoa to Ethiopia and from Lesotho to Abu Dhabi. From their manufacturing facilities in the U.K., Waddingtons export approximately 7,000 sets per year, but the number manufactured under license (in eighteen countries) approaches 1.5 million.

The final word upon this remarkable game must rest in mystery itself. The millions of families who have happily played Cluedo since its introduction over twenty-five years ago have invariably been successful in detecting where the unfortunate Dr. Black was murdered and by whom and with what implement.

But nobody has ever discovered why.

John Watson is marketing director of Waddingtons House of Games Ltd.

Chapter 4

PRIVATE EYES AND SPIES

FRED WINKOWSKI

MARXISM AND THE MYSTERY

Robert B. Parker

As a reformed academic, I have had the chance to watch the slow dignification of the hard-boiled detective story. English departments now offer courses in it, and English professors now write about it. The departments do it in the hope of attracting students; the professors do it because if they don't publish they will perish or — the moral equivalent of perishing — they will be forced to teach. Such professors like the work of Hammett, Chandler, Macdonald and MacDonald and (if they have Ph.D.'s from second-rate universities) Parker. But in order to make their pleasure in such writers profitable they have to first make them seem suitable grist for the mill of tenure (smaller than which few things grind). Thus such professors examine such works in a frame: archetypal criticism, Freudian criticism, Marxist criticism. The work becomes the expression of larger motifs. It becomes important and thus fit subject for a scholar.

Fourteen years in the professor dodge has taught me that one can argue ingeniously on behalf of any theory, applied to any piece of literature. This is rarely harmful because normally no one reads such essays. If someone does, it is only another professor doing background on his own article. If he mentions it to a student, the student is likely to ignore it. (Unless he is a graduate student. A graduate student will write it down before he ignores it.) But now and then one of these ingenious tenure-getters creeps out into the public domain, and people start believing it. Such is the case with Marxism and the private eyes.

MATTHEW SEAMAN

It is a reasonably conventional allegation that the hard-boiled hero can profitably be seen in Marxist terms — "the honest proletariat," in Leslie Fielder's phrase. Certainly one can make a case for the Continental Op in the short stories (notably "The Cutting of Couffignal")

P.I. REQUIREMENTS (NEW YORK STATE)

You must have three years' experience as an investigator. If you worked for a licensed detective agency, that counts. If you were a detective in the police department, that counts. If you were an army investigator, that counts. No other experience qualifies (including hotel and department store security work).

You must post a $10,000 bond with a recognized bondsman. This is your collateral, if you are sued, and is, in effect, your credit rating.

You must apply to the New York State Division of Licensing Services, and you must pass their background check as well as a background check by the police department.

Assuming your background is cleared, you must then be scheduled to take a written exam. The exam lasts three to four hours and covers laws of agency, legal terminology, specific knowledge of the law, investigative techniques, general aptitude and intelligence. You must pass the test.

You must then take an oral examination in which you are interviewed by one, possibly two, licensed investigators. You must pass this, too.

You must have a legitimate place of business with a working telephone. This means an actual office (not your home) and does not mean merely a box number and an answering service.

You must pay $200 for an individual license, $300 for a corporation license.

Your license must be renewed every two years.

It takes approximately six months to process a private investigator's license. The license does not mean you have the right to carry a gun. That is a special license which takes another six months to process, with separate background checks and separate requirements. The private eye's license gives you a valid reason for applying for a gun permit, but it is by no means a guarantee that you will get one.

---

and Sam Spade in *The Maltese Falcon,* who solves his partner's murder because it's bad business not to.

It is also quite true that the wealthy are often villainous in Chandler's work (although General Sternwood in *The Big Sleep* certainly is not, nor is Sewall Endicott, who appears in several of the novels). But that seems about as far as one can reasonably take such speculation. To claim that Hammett and Chandler were writing proletariat fiction is to read them very selectively. It is also to misread them. How Marxist is *The Thin Man?*

In "The Cutting of Couffignal" the Op captures a woman who offers him money and sex to let her go. He won't do it because, he says, he likes his work and is committed to it. In *Red Harvest* he cleans up a corrupt Western town even though he knows his employer will give him "merry hell" for it. In *The Dain Curse* he helps rescue a young woman from drug addiction and a mistaken belief in her own degeneracy, although he is not employed to do that. What have these actions to do with each other? Very little in terms of class struggle, very little in terms of the Op as a worker. But they say a good deal about the Op as a man.

In *The Maltese Falcon* Spade turns in a woman with whom he is apparently in love; it's clear the act costs him pain. When she asks him about it, he says, "I won't play the sap for you." Earlier in the novel, as they wait for Joel Cairo

PINKERTON'S ("The Pinks")

The original private eye belonged to the Pinkerton's National Detective Agency. It was their trademark, a large, unblinking, ever-seeing eye — the eye that never sleeps. This is the root of the expression "private eye," although many think the term derived from private investigator, abbreviated to P.I. Hard-boiled writers were not

the first to steal inspiration from the Pinks. Conan Doyle beat them to it. Intrigued with the story of the Pink undercover agent who infiltrated the Molly Maguires, Doyle worked it into *The Valley of Fear*. Pinkerton itself got into the writing business. Allan Pinkerton hired a series of writers to perpetuate the Pinkerton exploits, and they did so — under his name — in eighteen novels. Among the things the Pinkerton Agency is credited with originating are the first rogues' gallery and the first professional use of photographs for identifying the bad guys. George O'Toole maintains that the Pinkertons "performed the same functions in their time that in ours are assigned to the Secret Service, the FBI and the CIA."

to appear, he tells her about a man named Flitcraft. It seems to be a way to pass the time, but it is more. It is a parable about Spade's vision of life and a warning to Brigid that he lives in keeping with that vision.

There were things Hammett was incapable of saying, or saw no need to say. The story of Flitcraft and Spade's refusal to "play the sap" were as far as he went in articulating a code. It wasn't Marxism. It was much more fundamental. It took Chandler to point out that the hard-boiled hero was not concerned with economics. He was concerned with honor.

When Hammett was learning to write, he was working in a world which, after the fiasco of World War I, found the man of honor an embarrassment and talk of honor naïve. It found toughness necessary and cynicism only sensible. So people like the Op and Spade talk about doing the job, or not playing that sap. In *The Glass Key* Ned Beaumont speaks of loyalty to a friend (*The Glass Key* was Hammett's favorite). In *The Big Sleep* Marlowe tells one of the Sternwood girls that he's a detective and "I work at it." But what they do, as opposed to what they say, is honorable. The hard-boiled hero is aware that honor has no definition. He has noticed that he who has it may well have died o'Wednesday. But he knows that there are things a man does and things he doesn't do, and it is not usually very hard to decide which is which. It is often wearisome to choose. The fact that such men elect to be honorable in a dishonorable world makes them heroic. As in most fundamental things that humans care for, honor is indefinable but easily recognized.

The hard-boiled hero belongs, therefore, not to the Marxist but to the chivalric tradition — a tradition he shares in this country with the Westerner. He is not of the people; he is alone. His adventures are solitary statements. His commitment is to a private moral code without which no other code makes any sense to him. He regularly reaffirms the code on behalf of people who don't have one.

He is the last gentleman, and to remain that he must often fight. Sometimes he must kill.

Robert B. Parker won the Mystery Writers of America Edgar for Mortal Stakes.

HOW TO TELL SPADE FROM MARLOWE FROM ARCHER

Richard R. Lingeman

SAMUEL SPADE, a.k.a. "Sam"	PHILIP MARLOWE, a.k.a. "Phil"	LEWIS A. ARCHER, a.k.a. "Lew"
DATE OF BIRTH		
Ca. 1895	1906	Sometime between 1914–1920, depending on when he is telling it.
DRESS		
Height, 6′; weight, 185 lbs.; hair, blond; eyes, yellow-gray.	Height, slightly over 6′; weight, 190 lbs.; hair, dark; eyes, brown.	Height, 6′2″; weight, 190 lbs.; hair, dark; eyes, blue-gray.
PHYSICAL DESCRIPTION		
Muscular, heavy-boned, sloping shoulders, hairless chest and soft pink skin, big thick-fingered hands. Prognathous jaw, thickish brows, hooked nose, high flat temples, widow's peak.	Husky. Women find him good-looking in a brutish way.	Husky. As a younger man, resembled Paul Newman; lately resembles Brian Keith.
PHYSIQUE AND LOOKS		
Gray suits, dark brown shoes, green-striped shirts, green tie and loose tweed overcoat.	Hat, trench coat and horn-rimmed sunglasses; when dressed up, wears his one good powder-blue suit, black brogues and black wool socks with clocks.	Conservative (owns two suits).

Richard R. Lingeman is an editor at the New York Times Book Review.

MATTHEW SEAMAN

	SAMUEL SPADE	PHILIP MARLOWE	LEWIS A. ARCHER
MARITAL STATUS	Single	Single	Divorced (1949). Wife's name: Sue. Grounds: mental cruelty.
PERSONAL HABITS	Heavy smoker, rolls his own (Bull Durham, brown cigarette papers) and lights them with a pigskin-and-nickel lighter. Heavy drinker on occasion, including while on job. Drinks Bacardi at home, taken neat in a wineglass; and premixed Manhattans from office bottle in a paper cup.	Heavy smoker, usually Camels; lights cigarettes off kitchen matches, snicking them with his thumbnail. Also smokes a pipe in the office while cogitating. Heavy drinker: keeps a bottle in the deep drawer of his desk for drinks alone or with clients; serves Scotch and soda or Four Roses and ginger ale at home; dislikes sweet drinks.	Heavy smoker for thirty years (but not before breakfast). Gave it up around 1968 but still occasionally reaches for one. Light social drinker; doesn't drink while working or before lunch. Drinks Scotch, bourbon, gin and tonic, and beer (Bass or Black Horse ale).
MANNERISMS	With clients, subject is smooth, sympathetic and ingratiating. Under stress, grins wolfishly, laughs harshly, makes animal noises, or his eyes become cold and hard; when about to slug someone, eyes become dreamy; good poker face with cops.	Tough-guy exterior, enhanced by stream of cynical wisecracks, metaphors and similes: "It was a blonde. A blonde to make a bishop kick a hole in a stained-glass window." "You guys are as cute as a couple of lost golf balls." "Put some rouge on your cheeks. You look like the snow maiden after a hard night with the fishing fleet."	Tough in his day, now more kindly, sympathetic; has father fixation (on self). N.B.: It has been said of subject that "when he turns sideways, he almost disappears."

	SAMUEL SPADE	PHILIP MARLOWE	LEWIS A. ARCHER
RECREATION	Reading Duke's *Celebrated Criminal Cases of America.*	Chess problems (his chess is not up to tournament standards), going to movies (dislikes musicals).	Fishing; sometimes plays the horses when he has some "dirty money"; chess, bird-watching, ecology. Little social life.
HOME	Lives modestly in a small apartment with living room, bathroom and kitchen. Furnishings: sofa, table, armchair, padded rocker, cheap alarm clock by fold-up bed, white bowl hanging from ceiling on gilded chains.	Sixth-floor three-and-a-half-room apartment (living room with French windows and small balcony, bedroom, kitchen and dinette); rent, $60 a month. Furnishings: oak drop-leaf desk, easy chair and subject's few possessions—chessboard, stale memories, regrets.	Lives in modest second-floor apartment in a quiet section of West Los Angeles. Once owned five-room bungalow on a middle-class residential street in West Hollywood but sold that after divorce.
OFFICE	Sutter Street near Kearney, San Francisco; three-room suite with reception/secretarial area and two inner offices for subject and partner. Furnishings: oak armchair, scarred desk on which is ash-strewn green blotter and butt-strewn brass ashtray.	The Cahuenga Building on Hollywood Boulevard; one-and-a-half-room office on sixth floor with waiting room and interior office. Furnishings: desk with glass top, squeaky swivel chair, five green metal filing cabinets (three of them empty), "near-walnut" chairs, washbowl in stained-wood cabinet, hat rack and commercial calendar on wall.	8411½ Sunset Boulevard, Hollywood; two-room office on second floor of two-story building (office next to Miss Ditmar's model agency). Furnishings: armchair and sagging green imitation-leather sofa in waiting room; inner office sparsely furnished, with mug shots and subject's framed license on walls.
OFFICE HELP	Effie Perine, secretary, early twenties.	No secretary or answering service. (Telephone: GLenview 7537)	No secretary but does have answering service.
CAR	Doesn't own one.	Chrysler	Ford
GUNS	Doesn't carry one.	Luger, Colt automatics and (preferred) Smith & Wesson .38 special with 4″ barrel. Uses shoulder holster.	.38 special, .32 and .38 automatics; no shoulder holster nowadays and rarely uses a gun.

	SAMUEL SPADE	PHILIP MARLOWE	LEWIS A. ARCHER
M.O.	Won't perform illegal acts such as murder or burglary, but otherwise sells self to highest bidder.	No divorce work but takes anything else that's legitimate. Carries photostat of license, honorary deputy sheriff's badge, various phony business cards, fountain-pen flashlight, penknife.	Used to do standard "peeping"—divorce work, adultery, blackmail—but nowadays specializes in family murders with an Oedipal twist. In younger days, used more rough stuff but now avoids violence and has a better (i.e., richer) class of clientele (prefers old money); carries license photostat, various phony business cards, and old special deputy's badge; has a contact mike for eavesdropping, which he never uses; waiting room bugged and has a two-way glass in the door. Usual techniques: psychology (orthodox Freudian), sympathy, and probing questions.
CODE	"When a man's partner is killed he's supposed to do something about it." Byword: "I won't play the sap for you."	First loyalty is to the client; ethical, but would twist rules for client. "I'm selling what I have to sell to make a living. What little guts and intelligence the Lord gave me and a willingness to get pushed around in order to protect a client."	"We are all guilty. We have to learn to live with it." Highly ethical but not squeamish; regularly turns down bribes (including one of a million dollars). Will take any case as long as it is "not illegal and makes sense." Years on the analyst's couch have deepened his insights.
KNOWN ASSOCIATES	Secretary Effie Perine; Miles Archer, partner, forties (deceased); Sid Wise, lawyer; (f.n.u.) Freed, manager, St. Mark's Hotel; Luke (l.n.u.), house detective at Hotel Belvedere; Iva Archer (Mrs. Miles), girl friend; Tom Polhaus and Lieutenant Dundy, cops.	Los Angeles crime reporter; Dr. Carl Moss (for confidential medical help); Bernard Ohls, district attorney's staff; Carl Randall, Central Homicide Bureau; and Captain Gregory, Missing Persons Bureau.	Morris Cramm, night legman for a Los Angeles gossip columnist; Peter Colton, chief criminal investigator, Los Angeles County District Attorney's office; Bert Graves, Santa Teresa D.A.'s office; Willie Mackey, private detective, San Francisco; Glenn Scott, retired Hollywood private detective.

	SAMUEL SPADE	PHILIP MARLOWE	LEWIS A. ARCHER
FEES	No set fees; employs sliding scale based on client's resources and vulnerability; asked $5,000 (later upped to $10,000) on so-called Maltese Falcon case (collected $1,000).	$25 a day plus expenses ("mostly gasoline and whiskey").	Started out at $50 a day plus expenses; has been at $100 a day since the 1960's.
BACKGROUND	Subject was probably born in England or lived there before the war. In the Twenties worked with a big detective agency in Seattle (probably a branch of the Continental Detective Agency), then came to San Francisco in the late Twenties and went into partnership with Miles Archer. Partnership dissolved by client Brigid O'Shaughnessy (murder one; served twenty years). Subject's weakness is women and was carrying on simultaneous affairs with his partner's wife (mainly sexual on his part) and Miss O'Shaughnessy, yet distrusts women. A cool character who can be unpredictable and harbors a violent streak. Came to a bad end. Subject was shot to death in his office in 1930 by Iva Archer two days after closing Maltese Falcon case. Motive: jealousy.	Subject was born in Santa Rosa, California. Began career as an insurance investigator, then worked for the Los Angeles County District attorney's office as an investigator until he was fired for "insubordination." Never speaks of his parents and has no living relatives and few friends. His mail consists almost entirely of bills and circulars. He attended college for two years at either the University of Oregon or Oregon State. Apparent carnal interest in women and often gives them butterfly kisses with his eyelashes, but has no steady women friends off the job; has turned down advances from attractive females (e.g., the Sternwood sisters) on the job out of loyalty to his client. (Possibility of latent homosexuality? Note overcompensating tough-guy mannerisms and frequent contemptuous references to "pansies," "fags," and "queens.")	Subject was born in a "working-class tract" in Long Beach. Stated that he attended grade school in Oakland in 1920, which would place his birth at at least 1914. He probably grew up in Long Beach, and there is some evidence that his parents died or divorced. A juvenile delinquent as a teen-ager, he reformed and joined the Long Beach police force in 1935 (according to the earliest version), working his way up to detective sergeant before he was fired for reasons that are not clear but relate to corruption. Served in World War II in intelligence. After the war, opened up a Hollywood office and married his former wife, Sue, an ash blonde. She divorced him because she did not like the company he was keeping. Subject tends to cloud his past; for example, he said in 1950 that he had done divorce work in Los Angeles for ten years; on two other occasions stated he was fired from the Long Beach force in 1945 and 1953, respectively; in 1958 he was heard to state his age flatly as "forty." At any rate, he is now close to sixty, a lonely though not unsociable man. Secret passion is not justice, but mercy. "But justice is what keeps happening to people."

MATTHEW SEAMAN

FOR FURTHER REFERENCE SEE:

The works of Dashiell Hammett.

The works of Raymond Chandler.

The works of Ross Macdonald.

MIKE AND MICKEY

Pete Hamill

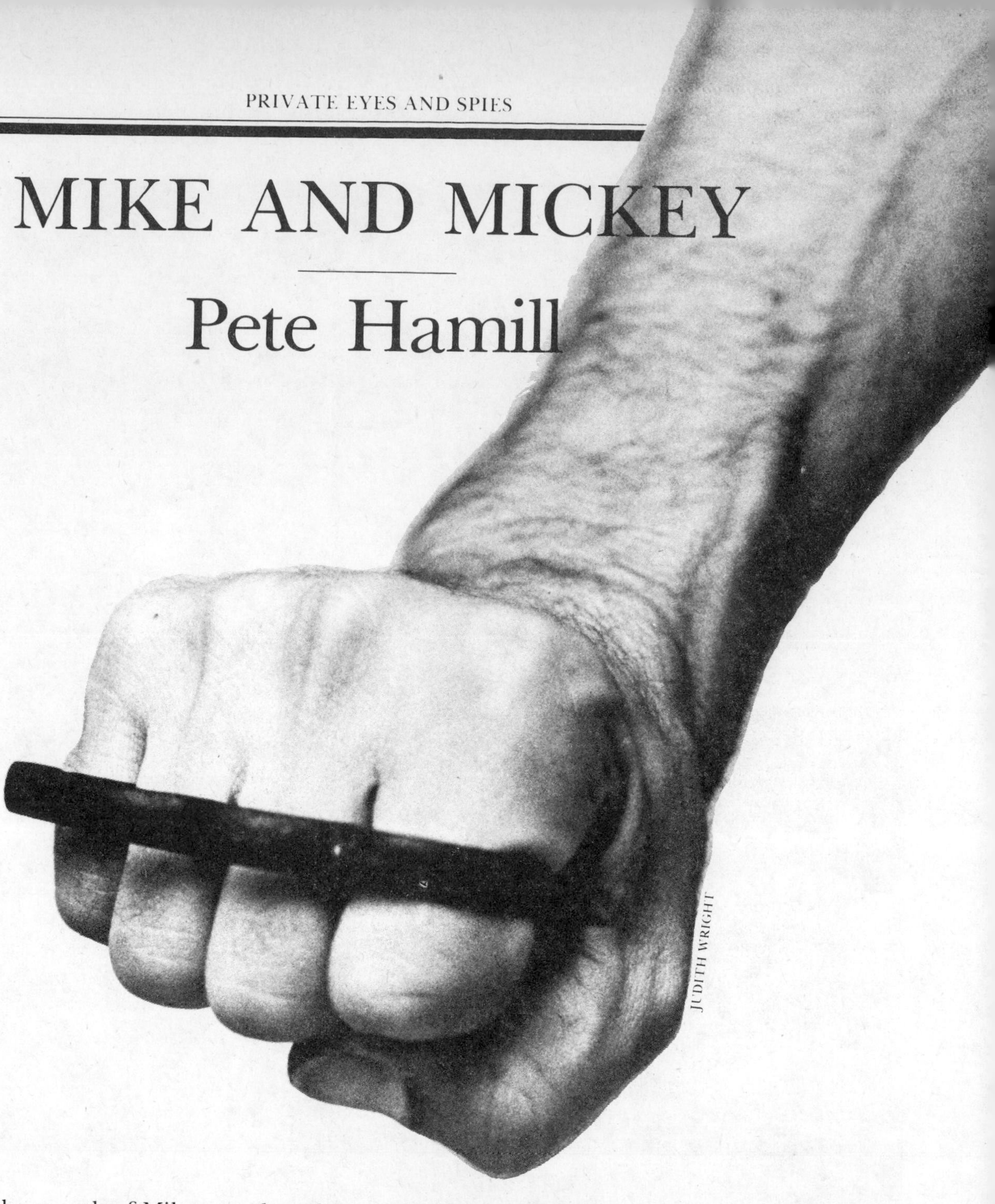

JUDITH WRIGHT

Out of the mouth of Mike, put there by the mind of Mickey, comes:

> *Go after the big boys. Oh, don't arrest them, don't treat then to the democratic processes of courts and law . . . do the same thing to them that they'd do to you! Treat 'em to the unglorious taste of sudden death . . . Kill 'em left and right, show 'em that we aren't so soft after all. Kill, kill, kill!*

If Hammett was a Thirties prizefighter, full of rough grace and a belief in the rules, and Chandler was a Joe DiMaggio, playing on ballfields of a summer afternoon, then Mike Hammer and Mickey Spillane were pro football: brutal, vicious, mean and literally pummeling their way into the American consciousness.

Like pro football, Mike and Mickey reached their first large audiences after World War II, telling them that winning wasn't everything, but — as Vince Lombardi would later say — it was the only thing.

Their appeal rested on their vigilante primitivism, their idiosyncratic form of law and order in which each man was assigned, by himself, the role of judge, juror and executioner. They interpreted this as anti-Communism at its best, as the American way, like apple pie and

Mom. Critic Philip Cawelti explained this rationale as "part of the justification for Mike's participation in the culminating orgy of sadism and destruction."

Mike and Mickey explained it this way:

If you want a democracy, you have to fight for it. Why not now before it's too late? That's the trouble, we're getting soft. They push us around the block and we let them get away with it.

In the Mike and Mickey books one finds the right winger's credo: If you just kill enough Communists, you can save democracy. The courts will only thwart you in this, so you have to bypass them by hiring your bagmen, your wiretappers, your Mike Hammer generals (George Patton) to do your cleaning up.

That Mike and Mickey stand for stunted sexuality, a kind of pornographic reveling in violence combined with a desperate need to present the most awful events as examples of innocence, is not a new idea. Witness the My Lais, the Joe McCarthys, the (I know you're tired of hearing it) Nixons.

Given the chance, Mike and Mickey would run world affairs like rabid politicians. To wit:

Some day, maybe, some day I'd stand on the steps of the Kremlin with a gun in my fist and I'd yell for them to come out and if they wouldn't I'd go in and get them and when I had them all lined up against the wall I'd start shooting until all I had left was a row of corpses that bled on the cold floors and in whose thick red blood would be the promise of a peace that would stick for more generations than I'd live to see.

But the character of popular heroes has, inevitably, changed. The old heroes, the heroes of the Fifties, are dead, and the focus of thriller novels has shifted from the violence of Mike and Mickey. We are now in the company of more interesting men who embrace the sensuality of danger, the turn of the wheel of chance, but who also represent decency and endurance. They can be men who say no, and in so doing, affirm the qualities of the human character that are included in the simple word: hope.

Pete Hamill, columnist for the New York Daily News, *is the author of* Flesh and Blood.

THE GUMSHOE'S SHOES

JUDITH WRIGHT

Archie Goodwin wears Bradley shoes, but he's the only private eye who does. Mainly because they are not for sale anywhere except in Rex Stout's imagination.

An independent survey of private investigators in the New York area revealed that no two of them wore the same brand of shoe and not one of them was sure where the term "gumshoe" came from. Most guessed it had something to do with the fact that they all preferred rubber-soled shoes for working. Several thought it meant they were always picking gum off their shoes — an occupational hazard when you do that much walking, it seems.

Twelve operatives tossed an extra pair of shoes in the back seat of their car when they were doing surveillance work, just in case their feet started to hurt. More likely than not, the second pair were sneakers.

The only shoe mentioned by more than one investigator was a brand called Walk-Overs. They were described as "sturdy," "well-made" and "comfortable."

On average, the private investigators had their shoes reheeled and resoled twice a year.

The two things most looked for in a shoe were comfort and quiet. As one investigator put it, "My shoes look ordinary — like Clark Kent. But there's a lot of Superman in there somewhere."

SOFT-BOILED BUT STILL AN EGG

Michael Z. Lewin

You'll never hear a five-year-old at a family get-together say, "I want to write about shamuses when I grow up, Auntie." Writing detective novels is just not the kind of thing little kids grow up wanting to do. So somewhere along the line something must happen to untrack other plans and rerail people onto the road of detective fiction. For me — and I suspect many — the process was largely accidental.

I never expected to be a writer, much less a detective writer. When I was twenty, I had never read a detective novel and I was chugging along quite happily as a chemistry and physics major at Harvard. But in my junior year, in search of an elective, I wandered into a creative writing class. I respected the guy teaching it and the concept of the class, which was that you only learn to write by writing. I liked it. In my senior year I took two more writing courses. They didn't, however, prevent me from graduating a science major and heading off the next year to study chemistry at Cambridge University in England. I kept writing. I enjoyed it. And I decided to give it a go.

But if I hadn't been playing a harmonica as I rode my bike one November night in Cambridge, Albert Samson would never have come to be. As it happened, another student, whom I knew only slightly, noticed me, hailed me, invited me to a party. There I met my wife-to-be. She gave me my first detective novel; how many wives-to-be have done as much for a fella?

As a high school student she had been a problem for her English teacher because she refused to limit her reading to "good" books.

Finally, he told her if she was going to read trash, she ought at least to read good trash. He gave her Raymond Chandler. And it was Chandler she gave to me.

In the years since that first Chandler, the family has swept through — often more than once — Chandler, Hammett, Ross Macdonald, the Travis McGee books of John D. MacDonald, early Dick Francis and a number of other books in the genre. I've made up for the sheltered nature of my early upbringing.

Albert Samson came into existence in early December 1969, appropriately enough in Los Angeles. The aforementioned wife had delivered of her first child in September in New York, where we lived, and we'd taken this premier grandchild to L.A. to visit my mother.

We stayed six weeks, and at the beginning of the fifth we'd exhausted the low-budget entertainments of the area. So I decided to entertain the assembled company by writing a twenty-page take-off of a detective story.

When I started my story, I began it where they all begin: with a female client walking into the office. Along with the obligatory wisecracks, I included a few family jokes. Setting it in Indianapolis, for one thing. I grew up there, but it's never been prime detective story country. I also called my detective "Albert Samson." Albert, because it was an undetectivelike name — not good like Rip Toenail, or something — and Samson from "Sam." Sam, Al and Gus were all names I had been promoting for our impending child while it was impending. For some inscrutably English reason my wife had considered all unsuitable. "Albert Samson" was a form of revenge. The child is now known as Elizabeth.

By the time I had finished a dozen pages of my epic entertainment, I realized I was never going to contain it in either twenty pages or the

HARD-BOILED HANGOVERS

Open a private eye's desk drawer and you'll probably find a half-eaten tuna sandwich moldering in its wax paper with a half-empty bottle of booze dribbling all over it. That's because our hero was too plastered to screw the cap back on. Drinking beyond capacity is the private eye's occupational hazard. In the interest of his clients, not to mention his splitting headache and screaming liver, the White Horse Tavern — which has seen many heavy drinkers in its time, including Dylan Thomas and Brendan Behan — offers the following hangover cures:

1. Slice of lemon saturated with sugar and bitters
2. Lemon juice, straight up
3. Milk laced with sherry
4. Bloody Mary, heavy on the Tabasco
5. Whiskey Sour, a double
6. Black coffee, the bitterer the better
7. Three aspirin and an ice pack
8. Don't drink water for 24 hours
9. Don't drink, period.
10. Stay horizontal

If these fail, there are the following folk remedies to resort to:

1. Eat a banana
2. Coat stomach with milk before boozing
3. Raw egg and oatmeal
4. Coca-Cola syrup, straight
5. Throw up, then take a cold shower

time I had available to work on it. So to get a little encouragement, I allowed it to be seen as it was.

I thought it was a hoot.

My wife read it quietly. "I don't like funny detective stories," she said.

I did a few more pages and then packed the thing away. We revisited Farmers' Market, discovered the La Brea Tar Pits and went home.

About the end of January 1970 I was having to justify my existence. The previous June I'd retired from three years' teaching on the strength of a successful book called *How to Beat College Tests.* Its success was mainly in the fact that the advance payment on anticipated royalties was enough, we had thought, for a year's subsistence living.

But then, as now, a year was pretty short, and I felt impelled to get down to some kind of work. The ideas around the Albert Samson story had stayed with me when other notions had come and gone. I dug it out, blushed at some of the things which had amused me so mightily and started working on it again.

When it was a hundred pages long it was turned down by three publishers, but too ignorant to be put off, I kept working on it. In September 1970 it was finished, and it was accepted by the first publisher it was submitted to in final form. It was released on the world as *Ask the Right Question.*

I've now written four Albert Samson novels, and there's a fifth novel in which he appears, though not as the major character.

He is no longer the larkish self-amusement he started as. Successive books have each taken longer to write, and they are rewritten a number of times. If I've not learned much about writing novels, or about writing detective stories, I am at least a much better typist than I used to be.

Albert Samson *is* different from other private detectives, but to me the most important way he differs is that he is much the same.

The point is that most new detectives are written to be something clearly unusual. The central figure may have a specialized occupation which hasn't appeared in a thriller before (we await the case of the man who trains polar bears for guard duty on the Alaskan Oil Pipeline . . .). Or the novelty may be more personally associated with the detective. He may be gay; he may be a woman; he may be totally paralyzed except for a little toe he uses to communicate with through a *possum.*

Going for a basic novelty makes sense for a new writer trying to break into a competitive field. Something unusual stands a better chance of attracting a publisher's attention.

So the unusual thing about Albert Samson, as a new private detective, is that he is not fundamentally different. As a thoughtful man, in business on his own, with an interest in people and a tendency to wisecrack, he seems to fall within at least the general outline of the traditional American private eye that everybody knows.

And it is because his "type" is so well known that I find it interesting to write about him. Everyone knows what private detectives are supposed to be like; I don't have to spend large amounts of time explaining what most people in Albert Samson's job are like before I can show convincingly how he is special.

From the beginning, readers have expectations about what loner private detectives should do. So from the beginning I can use the expectations and play against them to try to achieve surprise, suspense or humor.

Albert Samson may well, at a critical moment, notice a car following him and become suspicious. He may take risks to shake the trail. But for Samson, unlike most, odds are the car is completely innocent and he has victimized himself with his own suspicions. He tends not to benefit from coincidences. That's the way things go for Albert.

Though the private eye traditions are important to Albert Samson, there are certain specific facts about him which differ from the tradition and help contribute to the tone of books about him. He doesn't own or carry a gun, for instance. And he is not a sexual predator. Healthy enough, but with notches neither on gun nor appointments diary. And, of course, he is located in Indianapolis.

Michael Z. Lewin's most recent Albert Samson novel is The Enemies Within.

THE
(Wild Goose)
MALTESE DUCK
(Chase)
CAPER

A Mike Wrench Mystery Translated from the Vernacular

"Big Mama" Birns

COURTESY NELSON GALLERY — ATKINS MUSEUM, KANSAS CITY, MISSOURI, NELSON FUND.

Women. them them Wild Goose
Broads. I wouldn't trust 'em any further than I could throw'em. Take the Case of the Maltese
Lady
Duck. It all began when Peggy, my secretary, looked up as I walked in that morning and said, "Dame
Very pretty
in your office. A real looker."

name
"What's her moniker?" I snapped.

"Goes by the name of Velma Wonderly."

saw attractive legs
I opened the door and the first thing I laid eyes on was a pair of gams that wouldn't quit. She
had a nice figure
was round, firm, fully packed and stacked.

"You've got to help me, Mr. Wrench," she begged. "Something's been stolen from me. My diamonds."

stole diamonds
"You mean somebody heisted your rocks?"

important man criminal associates began to cry
"I think they were taken by a big wheel named Fosco and his thugs." She started the waterworks.

shirt miss your jewelry apprehend gentlemen
"Keep your shoit on, sister," I snarled. "I'll get yer rocks for you. I'll nail those birds and
be incarcerated death undesirable fellows
they'll do time in the Big House. Or maybe I'll just make sure it's curtains for the creeps."

"Be careful, Mike."

Madam carry a gun takes advantage of me
"Don't worry, Duchess," I said. "I pack a heater and nobody plays me for a sucker."

I found Fosco just where Velma said he would be.

Hello have stolen jewelry woman
"Hiya, fat man," I sneered. "The way I hear it, you got some hot ice that belongs to a skirt
Miss Wonderly
named Wonderly."

negotiate sir
Fosco smiled around his toothpick. "Maybe we can make a deal, buster. I'm looking for a certain
Wild Goose
statuette. A Maltese Duck. I have reason to believe it is in the hands of Miss Wonderly." He pulled
gun
out his roscoe. "Perhaps you can tell me where it is."

don't tell tales
"I ain't no stoolie," I muttered.

confess Mr. Fosco boyish assistant toward
"I'll make him sing like a canary, boss," said Fosco's cheap gunsel, making a move on me.

young man's drug addict drugged be honest
"Watch it, Wrench," said Fosco. "The kid's a snow bird and he's hopped. Let's talk turkey. I'm
crime
prepared to let you in on this caper."

share the profits
"You mean split the moola, the mazuma, the do-re-mi?"

money
"That's right. Plenty of cabbage."

"How much?"

dollars
"Ten thousand clams."

No
"No dice."

fool agreement kill you
"Don't be a sap, Wrench. If you don't come in on this deal, I'm afraid we'll have to rub you out. Get him, Wilmer."

young helper face shot bullets
The gunsel jumped me, but my fist split his kisser open. I plugged five fast ones into Fosco with
gun foolish person
my gat and then said, "So long, chump."

police officers detained me
I was no sooner out the door when two coppers were on me.

Hold your hands still officer
"Freeze the mitts, Wrench," the flatfoot barked.

officer
"What do you want, gumshoe?" I snarled.

cooked goose expose
"You know what we want. We want the hot duck, and we want it now. If you don't finger the
people goose incarcerate you officer
birds with the duck, we'll stash ya in the joint for a long time," the copper growled.

lawyer foolish person Do not intrude profession
"My lip will get me out in a week, chump. Get off my back. This is my racket, and I'll play it my
your nerve interfering with my methods
way. You got yer noive, muscling in on my game."

They hauled me down to the station. An hour crawled by like a sick cockroach. I wasn't
confiding in them depart
spilling any beans, so they told me to scram.

officer free if you leave town prison
"Okay, Wrench," the gumshoe said. "You're sprung. But go on the lam, it's up the river."

officer
"Goodbye, sweetheart," I sneered.

have a cocktail
I went back to my place to hit the booze and there she was. Waiting for me. Velma . . . blond,
amorous
beautiful, hot to trot.

All right, miss
"O.K., sister," I said. "Hand it over."

"What?" she squealed.

goose Sarah Lovable One
"The duck," I said. "You're not Velma Wonderly. You're Sadie the Smoocher. You make your
an exotic dancer drug Wild Goose
living as a hootchie cootcher. You've got the dope habit and you got it bad, and that Maltese Duck is
success filled cocaine
your ticket to the big time. It's loaded with snow."

undesirable fellow teeth fire bullets
"You crumb," she hissed through her choppers, and began to pump out Chicago lightning.

bullets punched
I dodged the deadlies and threw a right to her belly.

All right, my dear jail
"O.K., sugar, it's the slammer for you."

behave unwisely
"I guess you won't play the sap for me, will you, Mike? I love you," she sighed. "Why do I love
you?"

have intestinal fortitude intestinal fortitude
"Because I got guts," I said. "Just guts. That's all."

The End
CURTAINS

Margaret teaches English
"Big Mama" Birns talks real good.

THE HOUSE DICK

Lawrence Frost

I was standing on the steps of the hotel when I spotted a woman who was actively soliciting the men in her path. She paused in front of the hotel windows, peered in, and apparently satisfied with the potential business, headed for the entrance. I turned around and went back inside the hotel and made my way to the bar to investigate her behavior.

When I rounded the corner, she had not yet gone inside the hotel bar but was standing at the door preening and, presumably, checking for Johns. I loosened up my walk, dropped my jaw a bit, undid the top button of my shirt and rearranged my tie. Her first look at me was one of a pawnbroker appraising a watch of dubious worth, but she half-closed her eyes, wet her lips and gave me a sexy smile anyway. The closer she got, the more obvious she became.

"It's pretty crowded in there," she said as she moved near enough to count my mustache hairs.

I looked inside and confirmed it. "Yes, I would say so. I'm not too fond of crowds."

With her hand now on my arm, "What are you doing in the hotel?"

"Oh, you could say I'm here on business."

"Really? Me, too."

Her hand was still on my arm, and when I asked her what kind of business, her hand moved to my thigh.

"The entertainment business. Got a room upstairs? We could have fun. Without a crowd."

"Yes, I have a room, but what kind of fun did you have in mind?"

"Oh, the fifty-to-a-hundred-dollar kind."

Her hand became more intimate.

We made our way through the lobby, and I kept looking into her eyes to avoid contact with any of the bellmen. For once, I was lucky to get through without any hellos or waves. Inside the elevator I pressed the second-floor button, which is where the security office is located. I found out that Denise was a recent arrival from Chicago, where business was slow and the heat strong. The heat was pretty strong in the elevator, too, as she tried to practice her profession. It took a lot of will power on my part to practice *my* profession.

When we got off and started toward the office, I asked her if she considered herself a hustler.

"Sure I do."

"Well, Denise, do you think you've ever been hustled?"

"No, I really don't think so."

I produced my badge.

"You sure don't look like a cop."

"Well, I'm not. I'm hotel security."

"Yeah? Well, you sure don't look like that, either."

326

We went inside the office and one of my partners was there. We had Denise empty her bag and pockets, open her coat and take off her boots. That was just to make sure she had no weapons readily at hand. It also gave us an opportunity to see if she had any hotel keys or burglar tools. She was then photographed and given a formal warning to stay out of the hotel. If Denise is caught in the hotel again, under any circumstances, she will be arrested for criminal trespass.

I knew what Denise meant when she said I didn't look like a cop or hotel security (the official job title is House Officer, but House Detective is quite acceptable and so is House Dick in some circumstances), because most of the guests and criminals we come in contact with still confuse us with our fictional counterparts. From the hard-boiled detective fiction of the Thirties to today's Kojak, we have been portrayed as potbellied, flatfooted, stogy-smoking, bribe-taking peeping toms. It takes some people longer than others to realize that the well-dressed, well-educated and well-spoken person in front of them is the House Dick, who is also quite knowledgeable about hotel and criminal law and quite capable of enforcing it — tactfully when possible and with force when necessary.

With previous experience in the security or law enforcement field, it takes about six months to become a competent hotel detective. You must learn every inch of the building, memorize the where-to's of the many keys you carry, and the M.O.'s of hotel violators. After the six months you will probably have handled prostitutes, burglars, psychos, con men of every description and scam, drunks, deaths (accidental, natural and suspicious), heart attacks, wife beatings, fires, lost articles, luggage and persons, and just about anything else that can happen when you have 3,000 people on eighteen floors of a big-city hotel.

My qualifications for the job were experiences working for different private investigation agencies doing tailing, undercover work, investigations (criminal and civil) and some heavy mystery reading. Despite my work in the field, it wasn't until I began at the hotel that fact and fantasy finally intersected. Sure, I went out and finally bought a trench coat, dangled Camels from the side of my mouth and began to drink Johnny Walker Red straight up, but — unfortunately — only a few of my fellow officers related these gestures to my heros. My boss certainly didn't.When I explained to him in my interview that, like Archie Goodwin, my best weapon had always been my mouth, I got a grunt that might have unnerved Wolfe himself.

Few suspects like Denise are apprehended on the lobby level of the hotel. Most are collared in the course of our floor patrols, which are the meat and potatoes of hotel work. A full patrol from roof to sub-basement entails about a mile and a half of walking. While we patrol, we check for open doors, keys left in doors, fire extinguishers in need of recharging and basically anything else unsafe, unhealthy or illegal. Like any other beat, ours can get tedious, but there is always relief. For one, there is always a trip to the lobbies for people-watching, and for another there is your partner. But the best company for me on the slow patrols is al-

HOMICIDE HOTEL

Some noted writers who have checked their victims into imaginary hotels are:

Hugh Pentecost, who made Pierre Chambrun resident manager of the Hotel Beaumont and had him resolve about a dozen cases of mayhem, most deftly in *The Cannibal Who Over-Ate* and *The Shape of Fear;*

Agatha Christie, who put Miss Marple into *Bertram's Hotel,* the spit and image of Brown's in London;

Raymond Chandler, who created Tony the house dick and gave him a bit part in "I'll Be Waiting," a short story included in *Five Sinister Characters;*

J.F. Burke, who created a black hotel dick and set him up on Manhattan's Upper West Side in *Death Trick.*

ways myself and my fantasies: Marlowe meets the mysterious woman in Room 326 as she exits nervously smelling of perfume and cordite . . .

There are sixteen full-time detectives at the hotel, all with college and some previous experience in the field. Right now, we have a former tenth-ranked heavyweight of the world who is completing credits toward a master's in English literature; two actors, one with military intelligence experience and the other with two hotel jobs behind him; others who missed out on becoming members of the New York Police Department because of the budget problems; and still others who are just progressing through careers in private security. So we patrol, we talk, we observe, and then we patrol some more. While several of us are on the floors, the others take care of the lobby problems, the walk-in crazies and mischief makers.

Out of the 125 or so arrests we make in a year, about 80 will be of prostitutes (mostly female, but some males). It's not the act of prostitution that the hotel objects to, but the inevitable crimes that accompany it. A couple of months ago I got a call to open a room for a guest who had locked himself out. Two seconds later I got another call to step on it, as the guest was standing in the hall naked. When my partner and I arrived and let the guest in, he gave us the following story.

"I was in the bathroom with the door open. I heard a knock on the door, and when I asked who it was, a voice said, 'The maid.' So I say, 'Come in.' I heard the door open, then saw an arm reach into my closet and grab my pants. The door closed and I didn't even put anything on, I just ran outside after her."

We asked the usual questions but couldn't get a description because "she moved too damn fast. I just couldn't get a look at her."

We got someone to find the maid for the floor and asked the guest what he lost besides his pants. The story was a little rocky, but we were giving the guest the benefit of the doubt. Until he came up with what he had lost.

"Well, my wallet and a valuable pinkie ring and a wristwatch my father had given me."

So here we had a fat, fiftyish, Midwest tool-and-die executive sitting in his underwear, begging us to believe him.

We didn't believe him, but hotel procedure prevents us from calling him a liar to his face. After all, how many men will take off their ring and watch, place them in a pocket, then hang the pants upside down? We continued the game, though, and called the police to file a burglary report. The cops couldn't shake this guy from his story, but then they didn't try too hard. The guest's entire body seemed to sigh with relief as we all filed out.

About a half-hour later we got another call.

"I found my pants crumpled up in the closet. I got my ring and watch back, but the wallet is still gone. I guess she grabbed that and ran."

I had to say something. "Excuse me, sir, but if you don't mind me saying so, if we were only *half* as dumb as you've been playing us, we would be legally classified as idiots." Door, and case, closed.

It was fairly obvious from first hearing the story that a prostitute had lifted his things and that he had concocted this elaborate charade to save face. This is hardly extraordinary behavior. Guests will frequently lose something in a cab or restaurant but scream at me, "Get the maid! Get the maid! I know she did it!"

This is not to say that the hotel is not victimized by professional thieves, because it is. More than likely, though, its a small-timer trying to make it big, and sooner or later he's picked up. The real pros have proven to be mild-mannered and unarmed. Like anyone else, however, they are not afraid to fight when cornered. As far as cat burglars go, well, they just don't. The last one we had was over fifteen years ago, and I don't recall hearing about any at other hotels in a long time. So, sleep tight unless you just caught an old Cary Grant movie.

The next time you're in the hotel, that man in the Brooks Brothers suit waiting on line in the restaurant, or the man in the room service jacket, or even the guest in the next room, could be me. Yes, we try to be everywhere. When you come to the hotel, have a good time, enjoy yourself, but keep your socks up and your nose clean. Or I'll getcha!

Lawrence Frost is the house dick at a large, luxury hotel in New York.

THE PAPERBACK HERO

Alice K. Turner

In 1969 a writer named Don Pendleton received a $2,000 advance from a small paperback company called Pinnacle Books for a yarn entitled *War Against the Mafia.* Pinnacle printed a modest 50,000 copies of this epic with no great hopes for it — they didn't even bother advertising it — then, mildly astonished, watched it melt from the nation's newsstands virtually overnight. Pinnacle went back to press and Pendleton went back to his typewriter to crank out a sequel. The Paperback Hero was on his way.

By 1971 more than forty original paperback heroes were defying law and order, squashing faces like grapefruits and knuckles like walnuts, and blitzing corruption in a manner even the Elizabethans might have balked at.

Andy Ettinger, the Pinnacle editor who is probably more familiar with this type of book than anyone else, claimed that "without violence, these books wouldn't sell." Joe Elder, his Fawcett Gold Medal counterpart, agreed. Said he, "I haven't found anything I draw the line at yet. But," and here he stopped for a philosophical shrug, "we've gone about as far as we can go."

At the heart — or groin — of these books is the vigilante hero, who is motivated by just one thing: revenge. And he's not going to be satisfied unless he gets it in the most vicious manner possible.

Most of the paperback heroes get their meaningful education in Vietnam, but some are tutored by the police force, some by the Mob, and some even learn by doing time. Typically, the paperback hero starts off in the legitimate service of his country, suffers a savage jolt when he realizes his country cannot and will not protect him, reacts against the ineffectuality and corruption of the cops and the courts, and strides into the role of the lone avenger. The paperback hero and his readers know *the system does not work.* Accordingly, they have little time for such niceties as the Miranda-Escobedo decisions, the Geneva Convention and the United States Constitution. Right wing? Ronald Reagan would get a crick in the neck swiveling right to catch up with them.

The paperback hero is a blue-collar hero, a working-class hero — kind of a collective murder fantasy of the Silent Majority. Chandler's famous dictum "But down these mean streets a man must go who is not himself mean, who is neither tarnished nor afraid" would mean exactly nothing to him. Tarnish is part of the game and he is meaner than a rattlesnake.

One thing he is not, compared to mainstream offerings, is sex-oriented. While it's true the paperback hero is more or less obligated to bed down upon occasion, he doesn't spend a lot of time there. Women, it seems, are for others to victimize and him to rescue, not to love. Besides, she's probably going to get killed in the next chapter, so there's not much point in wasting time on her.

Racism, too, is almost invisible. Blacks, Arabs, Latins, Orientals and especially Sicilians do crop up as villains, but it's always on an individual basis. It's not the race that's bad, it's the particular man. True prejudice is reserved for the homosexual whose lot it is to die midst absolute carnage — here an arm, there a testicle, you get the idea.

Dime Detective, *a pulp magazine of the Thirties, made the decade a rough-'em-up, shoot-'em-up, tough-it-out time, with private eye heroes who knew how to use a gun better than how to use good grammar.*

Overkill, however, has had its inevitable effect and many of the paperback heroes have been muscled off the stands by possessed little girls and lollipop-licking cops. Today, less than a dozen or so of these vigilante heroes remain. Will they resurface? Probably. The macho hero with his frontier justice and gun in each fist has been a fiction staple from Natty Bumppo upwards. (Right now, the slack is being taken up by television. Witness Baretta.) For him to come up to full strength again we'd need to have the peculiar forces that were at work in 1969: the Bobby Kennedy assassination; the Chicago trials; My Lai; Altamont following Woodstock; a president's "secret plan" for peace; anger, frustration and deep division. I think, perhaps, we're better off without him.

Original Paperback Series Heroes

Adrano: Internecine family war. Good locales, pedestrian writing. **C**

Ape Swain: Good writing, preposterous but clever capers. Near East and other exotic locales. **B Plus**

The Assassin: A reasonably satisfactory *Executioner* imitation. **C**

The Avenger: Continuation of 1930 series. Good pulp writing. Light, frothy; preposterous plots. **C**

The Baroness: Totally formularized gimmick melodrama, born of Modesty Blaise and Doc Savage, but sexier. Fun. **B Plus**

Blade: An M16 agent cavorting in something called "Dimension X." Outlandish and outrageous. **C Minus**

Buchanan: No-frills Western for hard-core fans. A perennial, turns up in movies, too. **B Plus** (for the books; **C** for the movies)

The Butcher: Former Mafia gunman. Typical, competent and bloody. **C**

Dakota: A modern Indian, adept in martial arts. Good locales and plots. **B**

Dark Angel: Baroness imitation with Harlem heroine. **C**

The Death Merchant: Killing machine and master of ugly disguise. Cynical and bloody with no redeeming plot or background features. **D Minus**

The Decoy: A crook turned undercover cop. Nice disguises. **C Minus**

The Destroyer: Hokey series, the only one with a real sense of humor. Remo Williams and his sidekick Chiun have won friends even among the literate. **B Plus**

Earl Drake: Believable and consistently ingenious private eyer. From an earlier school of writing — witness girl friend Hazel. **A**

The Executioner: In a category by itself. A publishing phenomenon. For sincerity and prototypicality. **A**

The Expeditor: Superman gimmickry with a soupçon of sex. **A**

The Gladiator: Today is the last day of his life. Maybe. Who cares? Locales are nice, though. **C**

Hardman: Good, solid private eyer. Hero and his ex-lineman sidekick are the Huck and Jim of current pulp. Unusual Atlanta locales. **A**

The Headhunters: Special watchdog police force with its own methods. Very violent; good Detroit locales. **B Minus**

The Hitman: What it says. Bottom of the barrel on all counts. **F**

The Inquisitor: Very neat gimmick guaranteed to delight lapsed Catholics — hero is the Pope's top gun. Number 4 is good enough to stand on its own as a novel. **A**

Jock Sargent: Ingenious plots, weaker characters, top-notch caper writing. Ex-soldier hero operates all over U.S. **A Minus**

Killinger: Very authentic karate. Nifty Travis McGee-like plots with good twists but choppy writing. **B**

K'ung Fu: Crummy, hasty martial arts stuff. Very right-wing bias. **D**

The Lone Wolf: Another ex-cop. No homework visible on backgrounds. Sluggish writing. **C Minus**

Malko: Interesting, very sexy, violent European import. In one book the sadistic killer turns out to be a nun, which is certainly different. Hero, a prince, is a bit of a klutz, though likable. **B**

ANN LIMONGELLO

Pulp writers were short on subtlety, long on sadism. Among the better-known American practitioners: Erle Stanley Gardner (under many pseudonyms), Carroll John Daly, James Hadley Chase and Van Wyck Mason.

ANN LIMONGELLO

In 1938 Captain Joseph T. Shaw assumed editorship of Black Mask *magazine. Hammett and Chandler were his two big star writers. Miss Marple would have fainted if she could have heard what they had to say.*

The Man from Planet X: Sci-fi hero with a peculiar penis. **D Plus**

Matt Helm: A survivor from James Bond days who has become more reactionary and more sexist since that halcyon era. Full of gritty male expertise (guns, etc.) and well-researched spy stuff. For what it is: **A**

Nick Carter: More than 100 books star this phoenix-like incarnation of two earlier heroes of the same name. So many authors, ranging from high school dropouts to Pulitzer prizewinners (reportedly Harper Lee of *To Kill a Mockingbird*) have tackled Nick that the series is impossible to rate. A classic survivor.

Parker (The Violent World of): Written pseudonymously by Donald E. Westlake, which is a heavy recommendation. Convincing, tough, fast-paced. Don't miss them. The best of this kind of writing. **A**

The Penetrator: Hero infiltrates the Mafia to eliminate bad guys. **C**

The Pro: Good gimmicks, snappy back-

THE ATYPICAL PAPERBACK HERO

Truly, Nick Carter has lived through it all. In 1886, Nick emerged as The Little Giant, master of languages, skills and disguises, and hero of an enormously popular series of "dime novels."

Like his Street & Smith stepbrother, Frank Merriwell, Nick remained decent, humane and completely celibate for the seventeen years the series lasted, living a code of honor which made the Boy Scout Creed look positively shabby.

In 1939, Nick turned up again, this time in the pulp magazines. Older and suaver now, he had, in his thirty-five-year absence, acquired enormous wealth and a Filipino valet. He now greatly resembled Walter Pidgeon, who played him in two movies. But, despite this veneer of sophistication, Nick still lived by his father's original dictate: "Keep your body, your clothing and your conscience clean."

This second Nick was a war casualty, and we heard no more of him until 1964 when an entrepreneur named Lyle Kenyon Engel decided to move into the book business. He leased the Nick Carter name and set another series of writers to work resurrecting old Nick. Thus was Nick reborn as a man of the Sixties, to wit, Killmaster, Agent N3 of the super-secret intelligence agency known as AXE. He has now appeared in over 100 books for Universal Award, a company which seems to exist only to market Nick. And he is now indistinguishable from all the other paperback heroes.

A.K.T.

ANN LIMONGELLO

grounds — athletic scandals investigated. **A**

Shell Scott: Los Angeles private eye whose politics lie to the right of Hitler's. But you can't quarrel with his continued popularity. **B**

Sloane: Very bloody, mildly ingenious kung-fu Western. **C Minus**

Stryker: Banal cop opera with dumb plots, dumb writing. **C**

Travis McGee: The Colosseum. The Louvre. Better than this you don't get. No longer strictly a contender as the last two titles have hit hardcover first and oldies are being reissued as hardcovers. But, with love and squalor: **A Plus**

Alice K. Turner is an editor at New York *magazine.*

TAILING TECHNIQUES

Anthony Spiesman

Mystery writers get it all wrong. First of all, they send this guy out by himself, all alone, to watch a crook who's only slightly less vicious than Jack the Ripper. A guy would have to be crazy to go on that kind of a suicide mission. No private eye in his right mind would do surveillance work without a partner. If he doesn't have a partner, he calls up another P.I., or a part-timer, and they work together. The one thing he does not do is try to cover a guy by himself. Look, suppose he has to go to the bathroom? What's he going to do, ask a passer-by to keep an eye on his subject while he hunts down a men's room? Suppose he's tailing the guy in a car. Let's make it interesting — the other guy is in a car, too, but it's a taxi. At the corner of 45th and Broadway, the guy pays the cabby and gets out. Now what does the P.I. do? He can't very

well abandon his car in the middle of the street, and he's not about to find a parking place. On any surveillance job you need a minimum of two people, more if it's a twenty-four-hour surveillance. A P.I. can't keep up his concentration for that length of time. He's got to be relieved, and that means every eight hours — at least — replacements have to take over.

The other thing the mystery writers do is have their P.I. follow the subject not knowing anything about him. A real P.I. gets as much information as he can *first,* then he tracks the guy.

The dumbest thing I ever heard of is a guy trying to tail someone and holding a newspaper up in front of his face. If you let the subject out of your line of vision for even one second, you'll lose him. Sure, you have to make yourself invisible, but you don't do that by blocking out the subject. You do it by creating a situation in which you are least observable. A change of clothes is very important, and disguises. Now, I'm not talking about things that make you look ridiculous. That registers, and that's exactly what you don't want. I mean little things: Sunglasses on, sunglasses off. Jacket on, jacket off. Private eyes are probably the original inventors of the "layered look." They peel off a jacket, then peel off a sweater, then a tie, then a shirt, until they're standing there in their T-shirt like any other hippie on the block. Of course, you have to judge what fits in with where you are. If you're in a Madison Avenue building lobby, you can't strip down to a beachboy. But you can become a messenger from the Jiffy Coffee Shop. All it takes is rolled-up sleeves, a container in a paper bag and a little white hat. If you want to be fancy, add a menu. A change of clothes is really all a P.I. needs in the way of equipment. That, and a notebook, and a watch.

Sometimes I'll take along a miniature tape recorder. It fits in my pocket and I can use it very unobtrusively. I just slip my hand in my

pocket and turn it on, and then stand there muttering to myself and it'll pick it up. Then, when I get back to the office, I have it transcribed and send in my report.

There are three basic kinds of surveillances: moving, stationary, and rough. There are two types of moving surveillances — the foot tail and the vehicular. The foot tail is not nearly as easy as mystery writers would have you believe. Say you're in an elevator with the subject (and you don't wait for the next car or you'd never find him again; you get right in the same car with him). How are you going to keep him from noticing you? The best way is to do something impolite. Pick your nose. Scratch your crotch. Develop a palsied arm twitch. The reason these work is that they embarrass people. If they turn away, they don't see you, and you're safe. If, however, you're "made," you have to pack up and go home. There's this little thing called "harassment," don't forget, and that's illegal. If a guy suspects you're following him, all he has to do is find a cop and complain. Unless you want to get pulled in, you have to stop. That's another reason for working with a partner. He can pick up the tail when you have to leave.

The vehicular surveillance is not much easier — it's equally difficult in the city or in the country. In the city you practically have to have the skills of a Le Mans driver just to keep up. You have to take risks, like jumping lights. And you have the big-city traffic to buck. In the country, you have the problem of too few cars, making you far too visible. A pickup truck is probably your best disguise here. You can pass it off as a repair service vehicle. Personally, when I'm asked to do a vehicular tail, I prefer using a rental car — a Chrysler or a Dodge. They're good cars and they're kept in good shape.

The stationary tail is when you're assigned to cover a building or a house and notice everybody who comes in and goes out, and every-

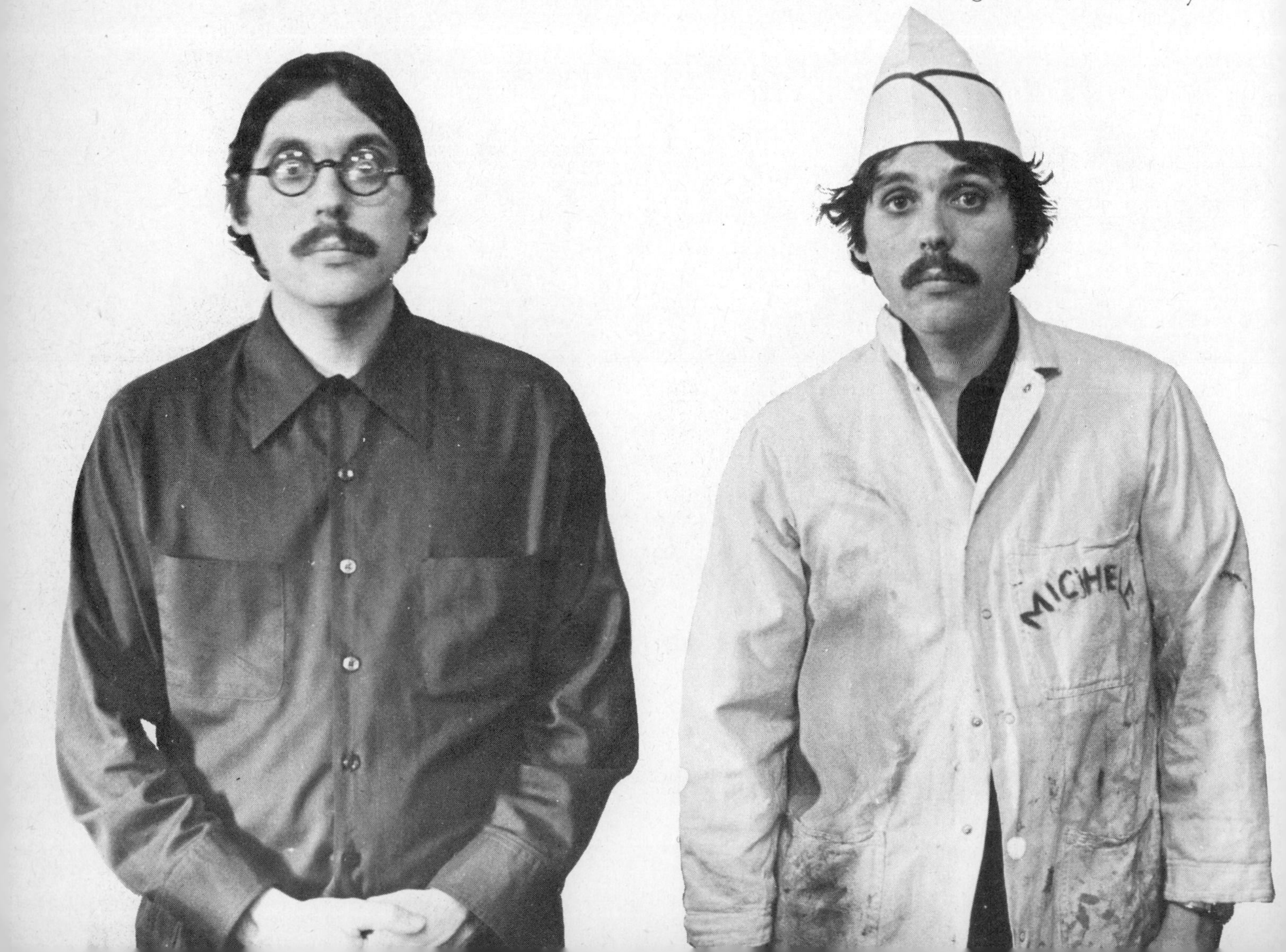

thing that goes on while you're on duty. This could be something as seemingly inconsequential as noting: 9:15 A.M., upper left window shades drawn. You don't move from your spot while you're keeping it under surveillance, which is why you need a partner. Somebody, if it's a house, has to watch the back door.

A rough surveillance is when you're hired to let the subject know he's being watched. This is used as a deterrent to crime. Example: A trucking concern hires you to keep their drivers on the up and up. They see you in your car and know you're watching them, so they can't pilfer, which is a big industry problem. What they don't know, because you're assigned on an irregular basis, is which day you'll be following them. So they can't prearrange to have someone meet them and take the goods off their hands. If they happen to set it up for the day you're on them, they're in big trouble.

Most of the private eyes that I've read about don't seem real to me. They're all in love with their guns, for one thing, and they use them far more often than a real P.I. ever does. I have a license to carry a gun, and there are times when I'll take it with me, but I'm not quick to pull it out. In fact, I can't remember the last time I used one on a case. If you draw guns, somebody's going to get hurt. And it might be me. No thank you. That's why I don't like Hammett. His characters are always getting into gunfights and fistfights. If I got in as many fights as his men do, I'd spend all my time in the hospital and no time working. Shoot-'em-ups may be great to read about, but not to live through.

Lew Archer bores me. I think he's dull. Travis McGee is phony as hell, but fun to read. The best, but there are only two of them so far, are the Joe Goodey books by Charles Alverson. Alverson's guy is an ex-San Francisco cop, now a P.I. He has a sense of humor. He's also smart and uses his head, which is what being a private eye is all about.

Anthony Spiesman is a licensed private investigator who poses here in part of his tailing wardrobe.

MATTHEW SEAMAN

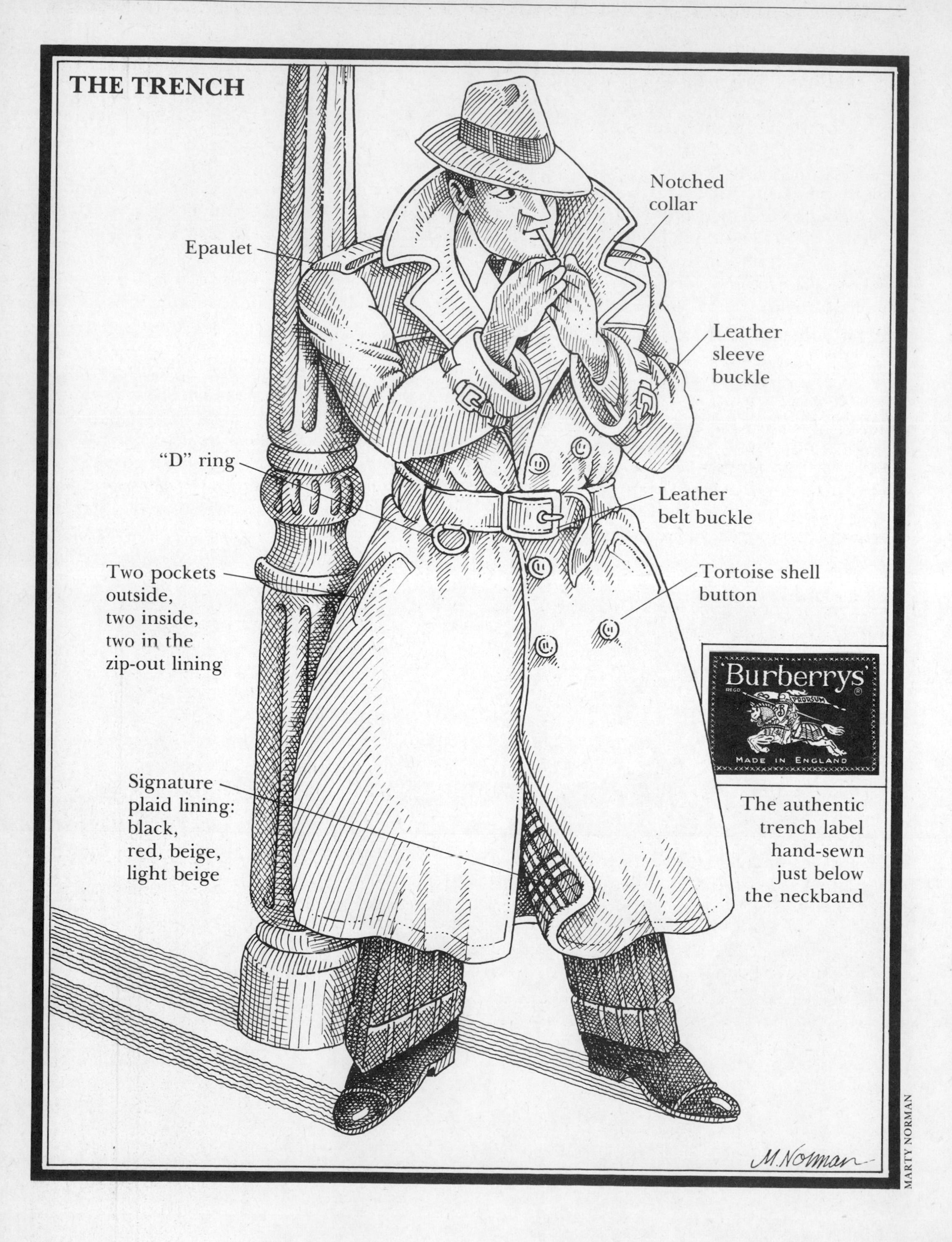
THE TRENCH
Notched collar
Epaulet
Leather sleeve buckle
"D" ring
Leather belt buckle
Two pockets outside, two inside, two in the zip-out lining
Tortoise shell button
'Burberrys'
REGD
PRORSUM
MADE IN ENGLAND
The authentic trench label hand-sewn just below the neckband
Signature plaid lining: black, red, beige, light beige
M. Norman
MARTY NORMAN

THE HISTORY OF THE TRENCH COAT

Hopley Croyden

Our Man Burberry. Aw right, tough guy, how'd you earn your reputation?

To begin with, he was not christened Burberry. Thomas Burberry simply called him "raincoat." It was King Edward — or so says the London *Daily News* of Wednesday, 7th April, 1926 — who dubbed him Burberry. "Give me my Burberry," he said, and the name stuck.

Mr. Burberry conceived him in 1856 when, at the ripe old age of twenty-one, he decided he'd had enough of being a country draper's apprentice and would himself become a clothier. He settled in the market town of Basinstoke and went about his business creating this thing called "gabardinee," a tough, nigh-unto-invincible cotton that shook off water the way Spade later shook off a tail. In 1889 Mr. Burberry took himself and his "gabardinee" to London. Had you been around then, you might have popped round to a Jeremyn Street Hotel to see son Arthur, who would have measured you and written up your order.

But it took a war to show the staunch stuff Burberry was made of. Down in South Africa all kinds of unpleasantries were going on with the Boers, and H.M. Army Officers were trying to combat them with the aid of their Burberrys. Lord Kitchener, Lord Roberts, Lord Baden-Powell, generals all, virtually adopted the Burberry as their unofficial uniform. Thomas Burberry wound up outfitting whole regiments and so was prompted to submit a design for official use to the War Office, who snapped it up (they could hardly do otherwise; it came so highly recommended). In 1905 the Admiralty for the Royal Marines endorsed the coat and Burberry was firmly launched as War Hero.

Tough as it was, this Burberry was not yet the trench coat of thriller writers' dreams. The father, if you like, was the "Tielocken," introduced in 1910. It had no buttons but rather a strap-and-buckle arrangement that anchored you in. It could also be ready for action two to four days after you submitted your order.

The actual "trench" was born in 1914 and took its name from all the mucking about it did in the trenches of World War I. Not only did it have buttons; it sported epaulets and "D" rings for attaching military paraphernalia. It also had more followers than Chandler. The number of Burberrys worn by the military is estimated at 5,000 between 1914 and 1918. And if you think it was scared of heights, in 1916 the "trench" took to the air with the Royal Flying Corps — one presumes with a camel fleece lining.

Today's "Trench 40" is indistinguishable from its predecessor. If you squint a bit, you might notice that it's shorter. Most of it is still hand-made and each coat requires four and a half metres of cloth, plus three metres for the lining and an extra metre for each sleeve. Over 200,000 are sold each year (didn't know there were that many adventurers outside of fiction, did you?) and the Burberry concern runs through 2 million buttons and 900,000 metres of cloth just to produce them. The cotton used, by the way, is Egyptian, grown in South America, spun in Switzerland and woven in English mills. How's that for international intrigue! And like any good spy, the Burberry Trench has an irrefutable means of identifying itself: the signature plaid lining. It also costs about as much as secret plans for the invasion of Luxembourg: $295.00.

Hopley Croyden wears a pea-jacket.

THE INVISIBLE BOND

Michael Gilbert

You make your entrance into the room. It is an old-fashioned cocktail party, predominantly male, but with a scattering of rather formidable females present as well. You cast your eye hopefully over the crowd to see if there are a few people whom you might be able to recognise and talk to.

In the near corner, smoking a meerschaum pipe and wearing, even though he is indoors, a deer-stalker hat, is the unmistakable figure of the sage of Baker Street. Talking to him, an equally unmistakable foreigner with waxed moustaches, green eyes and an egg-shaped head. On their left three men are engaged in animated conversation. A stout man with an orchid in his buttonhole, a thin and languid young man with corn-coloured hair and a monocle, and a tubby and undistinguished-looking Roman Catholic priest.

So far, we are on firm ground.

But what about this trio in the far corner? Three youngish men, all of tough and athletic build — one, by his speech, American and two English. There is very little to distinguish them. The American is perhaps a little older and a little more thick-set than the other two. He could be Philip Marlowe, but there is no certainty about the matter. Might the man he is talking to be The Saint or The Baron or The Toff or even The Scarlet Pimpernel? (No, hardly, in a well-cut dove-grey double-breasted suit.) But there is something faintly distinctive about the third man.

Memory stirs.

Could it be the grey-blue eyes? No. All heroes have grey-blue eyes. Then it must be the hair. The short lock of black hair that would never stay in place, but subsided to form a thick comma above the right eyebrow.

Surely, it must be. Dare one introduce oneself?

"Commander Bond, isn't it? I think we first met a Royale-les-Eaux in 1953 . . .

At this point, unfortunately, we wake up and the dream dissolves. But it leaves a curious

Of course I read mysteries. I cut my eyeteeth on Edgar Allan Poe and Conan Doyle and I read and reread Doyle. Why? Because I, like all kids, love suspense and puzzle solving.

I still relish Agatha Christie, but my heart was lost to James Bond and his successors. I suppose they give us a better mirror of the world than they ever thought. (The problem today is that the mystery writers are outdone again and again by reality.)

In my two novels, The Northern Palmyra Affair *and* The Gates of Hell, *I have deliberately used suspense techniques and, if I say so myself, a neat mystery solution (in* Gates*) to generate reader interest.*

HARRISON SALISBURY

SOVFOTO

Dzerzhinsky Square, Moscow. The monument in the center is to Felix E. Dzerzhinsky. KGB Headquarters (Lubyanka) is the inhospitable building looming up on the right.

question behind.

Why is it that detectives are personally so distinguishable and sometimes even distinguished, whilst heroes are physically anonymous? Two hundred pounds of hard muscle, experts at karate, accomplished linguists, irresistible to the opposite sex. But so are ten thousand other young men.

Can the explanation lie in the Greek tag which says that a man's character is the sum total of his actions? The hero of a thriller is unceasingly active. Are we left to deduce his character, as well as his characteristics, from the way in which he conducts his enterprises?

It was with some such thoughts in mind that I re-examined *Casino Royale*. An important book, this, because it is the first time that James Bond, 007, is introduced to us.

Apart from the comma of black hair, I could find only one direct description. It is of Bond asleep, his right hand resting on the butt of his .38 Colt Police Positive. "With the warmth and humour of his eyes extinguished, his features relapsed into a taciturn mask, ironical, brutal and cold."

Not much help there.

At a later point Vesper Lynd gives us her opinion. "He is very good-looking. He reminds me rather of Hoagy Carmichael. There is something cold and ruthless . . . ." We lose the rest, because a bomb explodes.

It is significant, however, that Vesper herself is described in great detail. There is a passage of twenty-five lines dealing with her hair, her face, her skin, her arms, hands and fingernails; her jewellery and her dress "of grey *soie-sauvage* with a square-cut bodice lasciviously tight across her fine breasts." Not omitting her

41–25–32

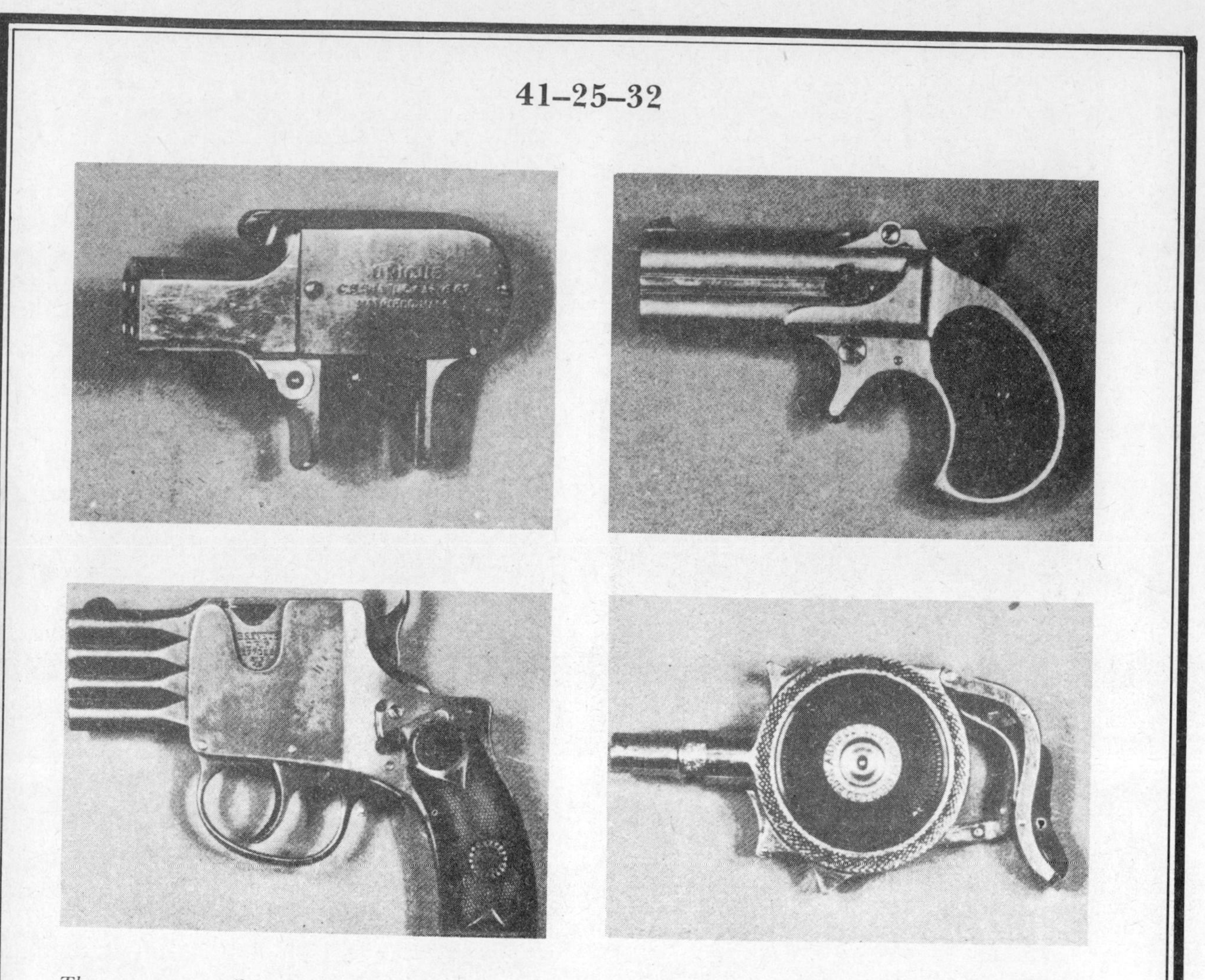

These compact, easily palmed weapons are often encountered by agents in their work. Upper left: a four-barrel pistol. Upper right: .41 caliber double-barrel derringer. Lower left: .25 caliber four-barrel pistol of French manufacture. Lower right: .32 caliber cylindrical revolver. Below: a small camera used by Soviet agents to photograph persons unobtrusively. (now mass-manufactured, the design is used by tourists.)

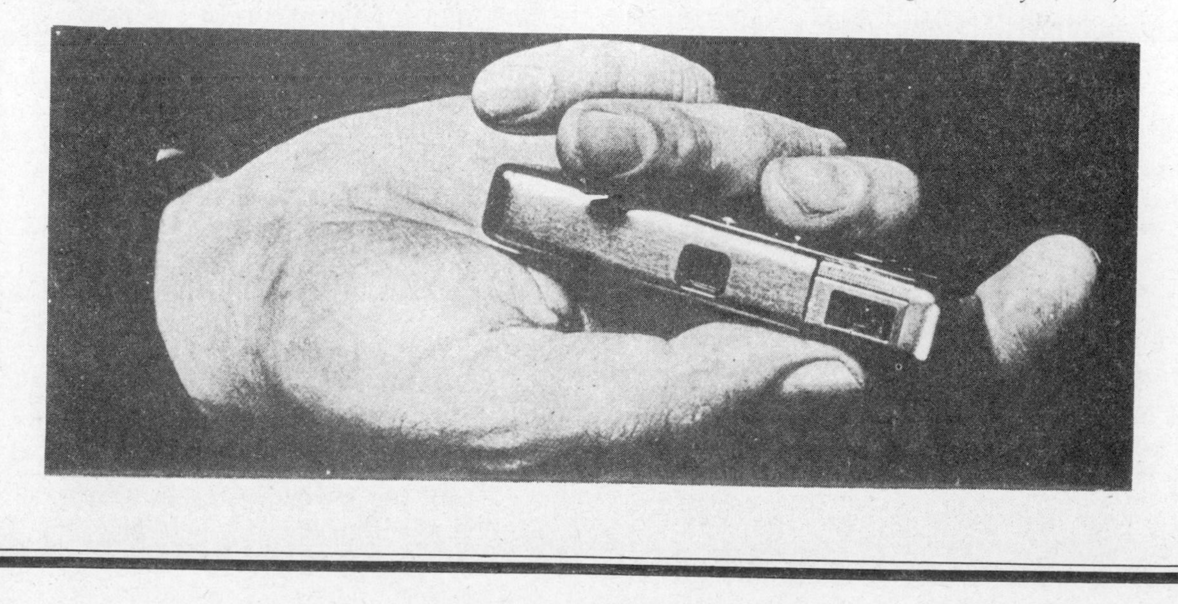

The late Ian Fleming, author of the fourteen Bond books. Fleming himself was an agent, working with British Intelligence during World War II.

handbag, her hat and her shoes ("square-toed of plain black leather").

Is there some psychological deduction to be made from a book which devotes twenty-five lines to the heroine and only three to the hero? Particularly since Vesper is expendable. She is due to die at the end of the book, although she rises, phoenix-like, from her ashes to reappear under other equally entrancing names in a dozen later books.

It is true that we are told a good deal about Bond's likes and dislikes, and may be able to deduce something further about him from a study of them. He smokes cigarettes specially made for him by Morlands of Grosvenor Street and keeps fifty of them in a flat gun-metal box. He drives one of the last of the 4.5-litre Bentleys with an Amherst-Villiers supercharger. He likes his martinis shaken, not stirred, and he likes scrambled eggs.

As the stories roll on, the props pile up — most noticeably, the pigskin Revelation suit-case, with the compartment at the back containing a silencer for his gun and thirty rounds of .25 ammunition. The action continues, fast and furious. The girls are wheeled on, lovingly described, lovingly treated and wheeled off again. The central figure remains obstinately difficult to visualise. Does he exist at all or is he one of those dummies in a shop window, to be immaculately clothed, fitted out with every expensive accessory, put into storage at the end of each book and brought out again to start the next?

It is possible, but there is another, even more intriguing possibility. Was James Bond really Ian Fleming? It is unusual for a writer to transmogrify himself totally into his own hero. Did not Conan Doyle warn us: "The doll and its maker are seldom identical"? Was this one of the cases where it was, perhaps, true?

On the back cover of the Pan Book edition of the novels is the Cecil Beaton photograph of Ian Fleming. His face certainly looks taciturn and ironical. Questionably, even brutal. He is smoking a cigarette in a long holder. Was it specially made by Morlands of Grosvenor Street and are there forty-nine more in a flat gun-metal box in his pocket, or perhaps in the glove box of his 4.5-litre Bentley with an Amherst-Villiers super-charger and a pigskin suit-case on the back seat?

If this is the truth, it would not only explain the accessories; it would explain the curious elusiveness of the central figure. If you are looking out of your own eyes, you see very little of your own face. To examine that you need a mirror. On one occasion, James Bond studied his reflection and noted that "the effect was faintly piratical."

If it was Ian Fleming who was looking at himself, one can accept the description without demur. Ian Fleming *was* a pirate, and he brought back a rich and well-deserved hoard of doubloons from his private Spanish Main.

Michael Gilbert is the author of Game Without Rules, *a short-story collection featuring counter-intelligence agents Calder and Behrens.*

BECOMING MODESTY

Peter O'Donnell

There is a theory which asserts that when it's steam-engine time, somebody will invent the steam-engine. So with Modesty Blaise. The beginning of the Sixties was the time for someone like her to appear, and with nice irony the author this king-sized heroine picked on to invent her was one who had spent most of his working life operating king-sized heroes.

I gave her a great deal of trouble, for it took her more than a year to get through to me. By this I mean that I began with a hazy feeling that I wanted to write an adventure story about a woman who could do all the skilful, ingenious, amazing and daring things which had so far been the prerogative of heroes.

If I was stimulated in this idea by anything other than the prodding of Modesty Blaise herself, it would be that I am fascinated, enchanted and baffled by women, and I think they have had the most appalling of raw deals since almost forever. So it delighted me to contemplate writing about a marvellous female creature who would be as good as any male hero in the crunch, yet would remain entirely feminine withal. Yes, feminine. No bra-burning Women's Libber, she. Please don't misunderstand my use of the word "baffled." For twenty years our household consisted of wife, two daughters and me, so I am not *ignorant* concerning women, just constantly surprised by them and pleasantly baffled, as I'm sure the good Lord intended.

Once I had conceived, or been impregnated with, this notion of a king-sized heroine, it dawned on me slowly (because slowly is the way things do dawn on me) that I faced a major problem. With a James Bond, or a Saint, or a

"Some time ago I wrote a number of Modesty short stories which were published in book form. The original strip cartoon artist, Jim Holdaway, did a drawing for each story."

Bulldog Drummond, you don't have to explain *how* he got to be so smart, so skilled in karate or kung fu or whatever is the fashionable form of unarmed combat, so accurate with a gun, so knowledgeable about weapons, explosives, knockout drops, cars, planes, helicopters, and everything else a hero needs to know in order to beat the bad guys. He's a *hero,* so naturally he knows all that stuff, doesn't he?

But girls don't come quite so ready-made, and I realised I couldn't yet begin to write about this one who was simmering away in my mind. First, I need a background for her which would make it feasible, within the license of fiction, that she should have all the attributes needed for her task of battling through an open-ended series of books (and strip-cartoon capers) against daunting odds.

Let us now use the device of the flashback. The time is 1942; the location is the northern part of Iran, bordering the Caucasus; and the scene is an encampment of a British Army unit, posted here as an advance guard against a drive down into Iran and Iraq by the German Army to seize the oil fields. One of the young soldiers is myself.

Trickling south through the mountains, day by day, come refugees. Many of them have been moving ahead of advancing armies for weeks and months. Some are children. A few are children quite alone; one of these, a small girl, cannot be more than seven. They have survived, somehow, living off the land like little animals, and they will continue to survive. You can see it in their old-young faces.

It was here that I first saw Modesty Blaise, though I was not to know this until two decades later. End of flashback.

With this memory, the hazy image I had in mind began to acquire shape and depth. She would be a child from somewhere in the Balkans — from Hungary, perhaps — and of good stock. Her family would flee from the advance of Hitler, becoming part of the straggling groups of refugees moving slowly south.

Let me quote a few lines from my Background file:

> *By 1942, in a civilian prison camp in occupied Greece, the child is six years old and quite alone now, her mother dead. Fear, sorrow, self-pity and all weakness have been burned out of her. So has memory of her past. She is a small wild animal, quick, intelligent, cunning, and with a ferocious will to survive. On her own she escapes the human jungle of the camp. On her own she travels through the mountain country of northern Greece. . . .*

The file brings her, by slow stages, through Turkey and into Iran. She wanders the Middle East, sometimes living in a cranny of an Arab town, sometimes attaching herself to a nomad tribe, sometimes living in a Displaced Persons camp. It is in one of these camps that she befriends, and defends, a quiet grey-haired man who speaks many languages. He is Jewish, stateless, once a professor in Budapest. The now twelve-year-old girl takes the old man under her wing, and through four years of wandering together, looks after him. He teaches her to read and write, to speak several languages, and gives her a broad general education. She soaks up all his teaching greedily. He finds a name for her, calling her Modesty, and chuckling at his own whimsicality. She chooses a second name for herself — Blaise, the master of a magician called Merlin in the wonderful stories her teacher tells of an ancient King of England.

The man dies when she is sixteen, and it is soon after that she joins the small-time gang in Tangier which she will shortly take over, and which in time will become *The Network.* It is during this period that she sets herself to acquire and practise all those skills with which the heroic male in fiction appears to have been born.

One day, in a fit of self-indulgence, I shall write the whole story of Modesty's beginning; and of how, when she is twenty and already in the big time, she finds Willie Garvin, tests him almost to destruction, and recruits him; how he becomes her right arm in *The Network,* her incomparable lieutenant, then her companion, and, in the end, a part of her. Modesty Blaise is,

THE BLAISE BOOKS

A Taste of Death
I, Lucifer
Modesty Blaise
Pieces of Modesty
Sabre-Tooth
The Impossible Virgin
The Silver Mistress

"I called this story 'I had a Date with Lady Janet' — because when I started to write it, I found myself using the first person, as if Willie Garvin were telling it; something I haven't done before or since."

of course, the creator of Willie Garvin, and for this I am most grateful to her, for when I first began to recount their adventures it was in the medium of strip cartoon and here a foil for the main character is essential for dialogue, otherwise the telling of the story demands a ludicrous string of "think" balloons.

The strip cartoon, I think, is good fun and far more difficult as a medium than it might seem. But one can touch the ground only in spots. To flesh out the characters, giving them the depth and texture permitted by a book, is far more satisfying.

If you look at the whole Modesty Blaise, it quickly becomes obvious that her time-scale can't be matched to what is considered a normal time-scale. In the first book she was twenty-six, and twelve years later she was twenty-eight. This means that events such as her being a wartime refugee, or Willie having been with the Foreign Legion at Dien Bien Phu, no longer tally with the march of events as dated in our Gregorian calendar. And so much the worse for the Gregorian calendar, say I.

Over the years I have sometimes been drawn into argument concerning the relationship of Modesty and Willie. Many find it hard to credit that a man and woman could be so close yet not be lovers. I see no problem here. The bond between them is immense and has many strands. It is certainly not asexual; in fact, it is strongly male/female. But there is a great deal more to sex than the act of physical love, and all this they have in totality, giving them a relationship which is complete. It is also a relationship which grew in a particular way and to a particular pattern over a number of years, and they are aware that for them to go to bed together now would change it radically forever. They don't, therefore, deny themselves; it is simply not a part of the pattern, and so the possibility never arises.

But I have digressed, and must now come to my own part in this affair. After years of success with *The Network,* and having grown rich on selective crime, Modesty and Willie retired. But life became dull, and there *were* those who were glad to use such an experienced pair as poachers-turned-gamekeepers . . . and even when not on hire, the pair seemed to have a gift for attracting bizarre trouble. So before long they found themselves caught up in many new adventures.

And that, really, is where I came in.

Peter O'Donnell's seven Modesty Blaise books are presented by Souvenir Press.

SMILEY AT THE CIRCUS

Cold War Espionage

John Gardner

In John Le Carré's *Call for the Dead* we are introduced to George Smiley — an owl of British Intelligence with a faultless pedigree and a wanton wife. He reappears involved in death at an ancient and noted public school in *A Murder of Quality*. In the huge best-seller *The Spy Who Came in from the Cold* Smiley is dimly perceived, as he is in *The Looking Glass War*. With *Tinker Tailor Soldier Spy* he holds centre stage, and in *The Honourable Schoolboy* we find him in charge.

Peter Guillam, Smiley's most faithful aide in the secret world, considers (in *Tinker Tailor*) that he has never known anyone who could disappear so quickly into a crowd as Smiley. It is, perhaps, part of Le Carré's particular genius that he is able to make us believe in the now-you-see-him-now-you-don't facility of his most absorbing character.

We believe it, as it were, against the grain, for George Smiley is probably the most complete and fascinating fictional character in the whole bibliography of cold war espionage fiction.

Julian Symons has written of Le Carré's books as having the special qualities of "a sense of place, of doom and irony." They reek of reality, as does George Smiley himself, the most believable character in the fictional dictionary of espionography.

It is this credibility which makes him durable and will keep him haunting the mind long after the pipe-dream James Bonds have been forgotten — a plump, myopic, middle-aged man to whom you would hardly give a second glance. Yet he's a man who carries within his head a lexicon of secrets and ploys which run backward and forward through past, present and future. A man of penetrating intellect, yet reflecting a kind of pathetic sadness which personifies his particular generation and trade.

His ex-Special Branch legman, Mendel, sees him as "a funny little beggar . . . [like] a fat boy he'd played football with at school. Couldn't run, couldn't kick, blind as a bat but played like hell, never satisfied till he'd got himself torn to bits."

Another policeman says he looks "like a frog, dresses like a bookie, and has a brain I'd give my eyes for." He adds that Smiley had "a very nasty war. Very nasty indeed."

We get glimpses of that nasty war through all the books in which Smiley figures, and Le Carré rounds out his character by making him almost a subsidiary spear-carrier to the plot in such works as *The Spy Who Came In from the Cold* and *The Looking Glass War*.

In both of these books, one is never wholly certain of Smiley's situation within the Circus (the author's name for the central department of Intelligence, the headquarters of which are pinpointed in London's Cambridge Circus).

"He resigns, you know, and comes back," says the head of one of the rival departments. "His conscience. One never knows whether he's there or not." He is certainly there during *The Looking Glass War*, yet not so surely in *Spy* — though at the end of that book we hear him

THE MICRODOT

The Nazis have been credited with creating a brilliant method of transmitting secrets by reducing a printed page some 250 times. The information then fit on the head of a pin. This "microdot" was prepared by use of the instrument to the right. Spies often added one to the dotted pattern of an envelope (above) or wore one as a beauty mark, making sure to color it with eyebrow pencil first, as a microdot viewed sideways had a tendency to shine.

physically urging the doomed agent Leamas back over the Berlin Wall: in from the cold.

The facts of Smiley's life are plottable — his mind and body visible through Le Carré's adept drawings — from the days at Oxford, where he was recruited in 1928, through his service in the field during World War II, until, with cover blown, he is in from the cold, running agents from the Circus and doing tasks which take him all over the world. To tread with him through the major books is to journey through Smiley's life in the fullest sense.

In *A Murder of Quality* there is a summary which brings him into clear focus:

> *Once in the war he had been described by his superiors as possessing the cunning of Satan and the conscience of a virgin, which seemed to him not wholly unjust. . . . Smiley himself was one of those solitaries who seem to have come into the world fully educated at the age of eighteen. Obscurity was his nature, as well as his profession. The byways of espionage are not populated by the brash and colourful adventurers of fiction.*

Duplicity is the stock in trade of the spy, yet it hangs as uneasily on Smiley as the well-made but ill-fitting clothes he wears. Duplicity for George is a cross to which he was nailed, unwillingly, at Oxford, and from which he will never be released. (In reality, all he wants is a quiet, contemplative life studying lesser-known German poets in his pretty house in Bywater Street off the King's Road.) Duplicity, his best weapon, is the weapon which so often almost demolishes his own emotional and professional life, for he finds it wherever he turns — within the Circus, from other departments, from the government, other people's governments and security services, and, worst of all, from individuals — in particular, his wife.

If the Circus is his cross and nails, then his marriage is the crown of thorns: almost incredible to his friends, and indeed to his wife's vast family of faded aristocracy and jaded politicians. It is the first thing we learn about him (in *Call for the Dead*) and remains the great seeping fissure in his life. For Lady Ann Sercomb — once Steed-Asprey's secretary at the Circus, now Ann Smiley — is the towering figure of wilfulness who interferes with any peace or happiness the wretched man might attain.

Just as George Smiley is always resigning from the Circus, so Ann Smiley is constantly leaving him for younger, even more unsuitable men. The puzzle is that he puts up with it, together with all its pain and anguish, and even admits to the possibility of taking her back. It is a puzzle which can only be solved by those who have known the same kind of anguish.

So deep are the wounds inflicted by Ann that, on at least one occasion, Smiley's domestic situation is used to the advantage of a Russian spymaster.

At the end of the day we are left feeling that Smiley, for all his brilliance within his profession, bears the marks of a man constantly betrayed — not merely by his wife, but by many of those whom he trusts, and by the society in which he lives. Perhaps this is the most telling picture we can ever have of a person who toils within the secret world where trust of any kind is not taken lightly. It is also a most accurate examination of the dilemma of a whole generation which feels betrayed, and it is interesting that, in his confusion, which is a paradox within his professional life, Smiley is easily strung to high, if controlled, emotion. He is, for instance, moved to tears at the sight of a small child's grief in falling from her pony.

While Le Carré is at his best when peeling the onion-skin layers from Smiley to reveal the whole man, he always shows him at his best within the context of his colleagues. Smiley is the window through which we view, not simply the curving acrostics of the narratives (parts of which must inevitably be lost to those not familiar with the historical in-fighting among the various British Intelligence agencies), but also a whole world of secrets, projecting a working knowledge of a profession. Who can tell if the picture is true? Whatever else, it smells and smacks of reality and so becomes more enthralling to the reader.

There are constant references to people long dead, or from Smiley's past: Jebedee, the tutor who recruited him; Fielding, whose brother was later to play a major part in *A Murder of Quality;* Steed-Asprey, who founded the little club, membership of which is restricted to one generation.

These Circus legends become as real to the reader as they are constant memories in Smiley's head — as real as the shadowy Control who is dead by the time we get to *Tinker Tailor,* his place taken by the odious Alleline; or Ailsa Brimley, who was a war-time colleague and brings the "murder of quality" to Smiley's attention and whose house is later used as a hiding place for a witness.

Peter Guillam and Mendel are constants — almost as much as Ann is an inconstant — but it is in *Tinker Tailor* that we get the most detailed and complete structure of Smiley's world, with its scalp-hunters, babysitters, pavement artists, wranglers and other jargoned departments. Here the world once inhabited by Control, Jebedee, Fielding and Steed-Asprey is now peopled by the more sinister, but equally engrossing, figures of the small Hungarian Toby Esterhase; leftist intellectual Roy Bland; and even Ann's cousin, the renowned Bill Haydon; together with a host of hidden people, both past and present.

From a wealth of detail, Le Carré weaves his narratives around George Smiley, the unlikely agent, the almost shy spymaster whose diffidence is so often a cloak for the rapier mind.

In his world, George Smiley is an owl, but one must never forget that while the owl, in poetic imagination, is a wise bird, he is, in reality, a dangerous predator of the night.

John Gardner is the creator of Boysie Oakes, Britain's funniest spy.

MEMOIRS OF AN EX-SPY

Ted Allbeury

COURTESY BRITISH TOURIST AUTHORITY

Harry Truman, when asked what it was like to be President, said, "It's great for the first two minutes." Similarly with being a spy. Except you're never actually a spy because in the business the word is never used. Inside M15 and M16 you're an intelligence officer or a counter-intelligence officer, and if you live on the west bank of the Potomac and normally turn left at Langley where the sign says BUREAU OF PUBLIC ROADS, you're called an agent.

Way back, you would have been recruited in your second year at Oxford or Cambridge. Your membership in the University's Communist Party would have been written off as growing pains provided you could drop a Latin tag in the right place. Which meant that the intelligence services, like Homer, nodded from time to time, and that would sometimes lead to keen cricketers ending their days boozing in Moscow and getting the Test Match results four days late.

World War II let poor boys become four-star generals and ruined this Olde Worlde sanctuary. If you wanted men who could speak Estonian and who knew the difference between Lombardo and Ellington, you had to cast your net much wider. And there were those who didn't wait for the net, but swam inside waving their Union Jacks. I was one of those.

How did I get in this elite? There could be only one way — the personal columns of the London *Times*. The advert asked for linguists and my interview took place at the back of a barber's shop in Trafalgar Square. They tested my French and German, and I swore my one ambition was to lie in the rain in wet ditches. Officers with penetrating eyes were anxious to know whether I liked my father better than my mother, and others asked what I could see in various inkblots. Photographs were flashed on a screen, and ten or so of us likely lads had to describe what they represented. Rumour had it that what we said would be utterly revealing of our minds. With this daunting prologue it was little wonder that an otherwise normal young man was driven to describe a naked couple on a bed as a "nurse tending a wounded man." We also underwent the usual medical checks, with our urine examined for Communist infiltration. The officers running the battery of tests fell into two distinct groups: the serious were cast in the mould of C. Aubrey Smith; the juniors were young captains with short haircuts and an air of already knowing every skeleton in our closets. When it was all over, they said, "We'll check carefully on your background. Don't ring us."

A week later I was a full-fledged member of the Intelligence Corps, inducted by an archetypal colonel who told me my background had been researched with diligence and I was joining a fine club. "Bring," he said affably, "your sports car, your golf clubs, everything." That was my first moment of doubt. Somebody had got my background all wrong, diligent look-see or not. I had just bought my first second-hand bicycle, for two dollars, and had only once sat in a car; I didn't own golf clubs; I barely owned a jacket.

Regardless, I reported to the Intelligence Corps depot at what had previously been a theological college in Winchester. Here I hobnobbed with professors of French and German who could write theses on Trade Unions in the Middle Ages but couldn't ask a girl out for a coffee. On our second day, a Sunday, which even in the Intelligence Corps follows Saturday and the Saturday night dance, the professors and I were detailed to clean up the abandoned prophylactic devices as our introduction to security work. This led to much quoting of Rabelais and Juvenal.

We were taught very advanced map reading and then abandoned in the night in fields of cows to find our way home. We tailed "suspects" through the busy streets of Southampton and found it gave us time to make dates with the girls in Woolworth's. We learned how to strip and reassemble a whole range of weapons. Blindfolded, of course. We were given extensive instruction on the organisation of the military machine which subsequently proved useful for knowing how to indent for rations and services you were not entitled to. Several weeks were devoted to a rough-riding course on motorcycles, and our egos inflated when we learned ours would always be tuned to give us more speed than those of the Military Police. (Some of us later forgot that the additional weight of a girl on the pillion would eliminate this advantage.)

The badge of the Intelligence Corps was the red and white roses of Lancaster and York entwined in a laurel wreath. Referred to by our envious contemporaries in the other services as

THE SAFE HOUSE

A former spy tells of one on Ebury Street near Victoria Station. He'd stayed in it during the war. So did Ian Fleming.

The old method of getting in was, you rang the lower of two doorbells, and when a lady answered you remarked on the picture visible through the downstairs window. You allowed as how you were interested in art, she allowed as how she was pleased to hear it. You suggested you might like to buy it, she suggested you step inside for a better look at it. In you went, safe in the grip of your very own network.

a "pansy resting on its laurels," it added lustre to our nickname "the eunuchs" (there were no privates in the Intelligence Corps).

In Scotland our trainers were ex-Shanghai policemen who spent two months borrowing my body to show more delicate frames how to severely injure or, if necessary, kill the enemy. "Okay, lofty, you," they said, pointing a finger at me when no one volunteered for these exercises. I was a tall lad, alas.

At various points members of the Class of '40 dropped off the production line. The nervous would go as interrogators at POW camps; the mathematicians and chess players, to the cryptography set-up at Bletchley Park. The creme of the dregs that were left would go on to aggravate the King's enemies and, on occasion, his friends.

When you read spy thrillers about that daring M15 man doing his stuff in Berlin, just quietly ask for your money back. M15 only operates in the United Kingdom. And even though it's responsible for internal security, M15 doesn't even arrest naughty boys in the U.K. The Special Branch does the dirty work for them. Besides, now it's called D15.

M16 is responsible for counter-espionage and espionage, and it's now D16 — sometimes referred to as SIS, the Secret Intelligence Service. If you land up in that camp, your pay will be tax-free to prevent even the Inland Revenue from putting two and two together. One finds SIS boys in all the old, familiar places: journalism; Rolls-Royce franchises; banking; oil companies; language schools; departments of history at universities. They're recognisable by their charm and fondness for Jamieson Ten Year Old. In later life they take up religion, in the style of Malcom Muggeridge, and grow roses in Britain's equivalent of the Bermuda Triangle — the borders of Sussex and Kent.

Intelligence work, like computery, has its own vocabulary, and you can date an alumnus of the theological college fairly accurately. There's a touch of the Scott Fitzgerald about war-time alumni, with echoes of Adlai Stevenson. Today's boys are definitely more Daniel Patrick, with a shade of Haldeman if under stress. But there are still some consistently used words:

De-briefing consists of a man with cold blue eyes listening to your side of the story when you return from an operation. It's a mixture of explaining why you're still alive and why you had to stay at the most expensive hotel in Berlin.

A *safe house* is where you go to be briefed, or to rest, or to escape the bad guys.

Dead-letter drop is the place where you leave messages in code on the secrets of IBM's latest software. (Like you used to leave the girl friend love letters in the geranium pot because her mother wouldn't let you on the premises.)

The *cut-out* is the man who keeps your identity from field operators.

Blown means that the elaborate cover story your directorate wrote to protect you has been exposed. I was "blown" by a dear old lady in Scotland. She was telling fortunes at a party and told the whole assembly exactly what I was up to. I was withdrawn, as they say, to Scottish Command HQ, and I often wonder what happened to that old lady.

Turned is what happens to operators who get caught and start trembling before they're even asked their name, rank and number. We did this to most of the German espionage agents in the U.K. during the war. They then got to live in luxury apartments in St. James Street with the most beautiful "ladies" we could find. In return, we held their hands on their Morse keys when they sent their news back to Berlin. It went on for years, and there were several of us who wished it could've happened to us.

In Occupied Germany we cooperated with the American CIC. On the grounds of security, however, both intelligence organisations kept just a little bit of information back. I well remember a joint operation in which forty plainclothes operatives had to find a central information clearing point that would not arouse suspicion if visited frequently by large numbers of men. The CIC had theirs, we had ours, and neither would confide its place to the other. Halfway through the morning of the round-up I had to deal with an angry city mayor who complained bitterly that British and American civilians, all speaking frightfully bad German, were monopolizing the only public men's lavatory in town. Great spy minds had thought alike once again.

What makes a good intelligence agent? He certainly won't be a James Bond type. Arrogant, pseudo-sophisticated and mentally ill-equipped, Bond wouldn't get past the first selection filter. If pressed to give an opinion as to what made me suitable material, I should unhesitatingly attribute it to the fact that, since my father died when I was a baby, I was brought up by a posse of women and some of their intuition rubbed off on me. As an intelligence officer this combination of innate male cunning and feminine intuition served me well. The war my father fought in was to make "a land fit for heroes to live in." My own war aim was to make "a land fit for cowards to live in." Heroes are for the Marines; only the well-tuned coward can survive in the world of espionage.

I've heard it said that once a spook, always a spook, but my own career doesn't bear this out. I left the counter-intelligence business several years after the war, and although I've been contacted two or three times since, it was only to give advice. One reason for declining to stay on was an inclination on my part to quit the poker game while I still had my winnings; the other was a growing dislike of what I was doing. This was not from some high moral standpoint, nor a feeling that it should not be done, but that I, personally, had done it long enough. Playing games against the Italians was fun, but against the Germans it was solid, serious stuff. With venom in it on both sides. I was beginning to know too much about people and politics, and I needed a period of innocence.

Unfortunately, it's not quite that easy to reclaim. You can't be an experienced intelligence officer one day and an innocent civilian the next. The training, the experience, just won't go away. One of the earliest pieces of training is that everybody tells lies and you have to dig holes for people to fall in so you can find out as soon as possible in what area they're lying. In civilian life you go on doing this. You don't always like the results, and neither do your victims. Little bells ring and red lights flash, because not only do you know when people are telling lies, but you know they're going to before they know it themselves. It takes about three years before you're halfway

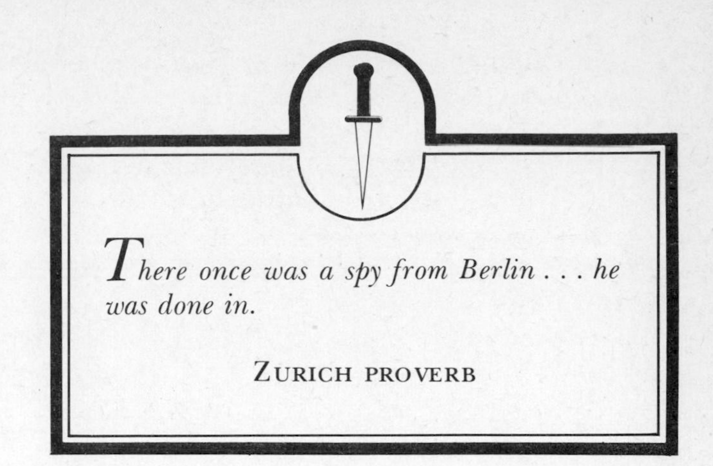

back to normal.

I'm often asked whose spy stories I enjoy reading. It's not easy to give a straightforward answer because one likes different ones for different reasons. I like Eric Ambler stories because they're beautifully written. Len Deighton's *Ipcress File*, *Funeral in Berlin* and *Horse Under Water* are firm favourites of mine. Great pace and real characters. The Quiller stories by Adam Hall and the novels of John Le Carré I find a "good read" but too opaque for my liking. The striving for authenticity can be overdone. Le Carré's use of jargon and buzz words sometimes seems like a leg-pull — they're too often words I've never heard used, and if they're contrived then they're unnecessary and destructive to the magically real atmosphere he creates. The mysterious Trevanian wrote a first-class story with *The Eiger Sanction*, but *The Loo Sanction* I found inferior. It may seem eccentric to class *All the President's Men* and *The Final Days* as spy stories, but they have all the elements of a good spy novel and they skilfully avoid the pitfall of the "researched" book — that stuffing in every thing you found because it cost time and money to discover it. Oddly enough, I find nonfiction books by ex-espionage people almost unreadable. If you've been in this business, you recognise all too easily those great patches of bull. Real-life espionage is boring. It has too little action and its victories are mainly from paper work, not valour. I'd rather read John D. MacDonald, whose Travis McGee has given me hours of pleasure.

There's a club in London that I belong to called the Special Forces Club, and there you can see mild men who now sell insurance or wine who ended the war in Dachau or Belsen. There are schoolteachers who once calmly parachuted into the wet forests of the Dordogne. Unless we have another war, the club will soon close for lack of members, as we all head for our appointments in Samarra.

Ted Allbeury, former counter-intelligence officer, is the author of five espionage novels.

USING THE PERSONAL COLUMN AS A MAIL DROP

An agent never phones the information in; he delivers it himself. But first he has to arrange the rendezvous. The most frequently used medium for this is the Personal Column. To show you how this works, we placed an ad in the London *Times.* After reading our message ("Author wishes to contact ex-spies"), the ad-taker said, "Oh, yes, you'll probably be looked up by DI5 and DI6 with this one. Perhaps even the Customs people will contact you. They read the personal columns every day, checking for stolen merchandise."

We received seven answers in all, and our favorites were the spy who invited us to tea at his bachelor flat in the Albany (home of the fictional Raffles, if you'll recall) and the spy who arranged an 11 P.M. meeting in front of the South Kensington tube station. "How will we recognize you?" we asked. "I'll recognize you," he proclaimed, and he did. Made us very uncomfortable.

Of course, a real spy would have prepared a more subtle message than ours. We are quite convinced the query running several boxes beneath ours — in reference to a gentleman's umbrella — was a spy reaching out for his control. We never followed it up, but still we're convinced of it. And ever since, have been intrigued to know how he did.

THE TIMES
PERSONAL COLUM
ALSO ON PAGES 26 AND 27

Crescent, London.

2 LUXURY lakeshore flats. Italy available now. See Rentals.

GOVERNESS required Beirut. See Non-Sec. Appts.

SECRETARY/PA. See Creme de la Creme.

1974 MODEL Mercedes 280 CE Coupe. See Motors.

WINE ENTHUSIASTS. Novice not snob—wishes to start regular home tasting (Central London). Would others with similar enthusiasm and ideally some experience of tasting contact Box 0664 J, The Times.

BROWNS of South Molton St. require Accounts person. See Creme de la Creme.

AUTHOR wishes to contact ex-officials. Write in first instance Box 0867 J, The Times.

AUTHOR would like to contact ex-spies. Write in first instance Box 0866 J, The Times.

DO YOU want to learn more about banking ... Creme.

LANCIA SPYDER "P" registration. See Motors.

MAYFAIR GALLERY, seeks Art or Antique to share premises. See Art Galleries.

WOOD otherwise DAVENPORT. DENNIS WOOD otherwise DENNIS DAVENPORT late of Flat E.10 Kenilworth Court, Hagley Road, Edgbaston, Birmingham, died at Birmingham on 12 October 1976. (Estate about £10,000) The mother of the above-named is requested to apply to the Treasury Solicitor (B.V.), 12 Buckingham Gate, London, SW1E 6LJ, failing which the Treasury Solicitor may take steps to administer the estate.

NANNY/MOTHER'S HELP required —Bristol area.—See Domestic Sits.

"STRIKE ONE" NEEDS YOU !— See Non Sec. Appts.

EXCAVATION STAFF for Glam/Gwent Archaeological Trust.—See Gen. Vacs.

CHELSEA OIL CO. need Recpt./Telephonist.—See Non Sec. Appts.

UMBRELLA.—Will anyone who picked up gentleman's long umbrella in front car of train at Russell Square, Thursday, 24th March, 10.20 a.m., please ring 886 6193 whether handed in or not.

THRILLINGTON ... will find something ... their advantage ... sified Services section.

GREEK SPEAKING Courier reqd.—General Vacs.

ESTABLISHING A COVER

Berkely Mather

Spying, in spite of all that thriller writers might say to the contrary, is a relatively simple business. You merely select your agent, preferably one of moderate intelligence but little imagination, tell him (or her) just what you want to find out about the Opposition, provide him with means of communication and then gently insinuate him into the theatre of operations. It is a very good thing, of course, to retain a hold on him as a precaution against his being "turned round" by the Opposition and made into a "double." The hold will vary with the circumstances: something unsavoury that lends itself readily to blackmail; a loved one, wife, mother or child who can be taken into the gentle care of the spymaster; or perhaps a "minder," a strong-arm man already on the ground who will, without hesitation, kill the agent on receipt of orders from on high.

All that being provided, the agent is in business. Or is he? There *is* something else. The most important factor of the lot. The cover story, or "Front." Without one which will stand up to an Intensity Five Interrogation — that is, two stages further than what was once called in police circles the Third Degree — your agent might just as well stay at home. An I.F.I. is a very searching inquiry indeed. It can go on for days, weeks if necessary. A point by meticulous point, detail by detail probing into your past life to establish just who you are. Once They know that, the rest is comparatively easy. Lots of the questions They ask may seem a complete waste of time. The agent's common sense will tell him that the answers cannot be verified or contradicted, but in among them comes the simple inconsequential one that can be shot down — and the "patient," as the luckless interrogatee is termed in contra-espionage jargon, as soon as he knows he has slipped, will start to flounder. It follows, therefore, that he must be *almost* word and detail perfect. "Almost" must be stressed, because, if the answers come too readily with never a slip, the interrogator would rightly guess that the patient was parrotting a carefully learned lesson.

E.g.: "You say you lived with your parents at 39 Sungrove Avenue, Edmonton, from 12th September 1932 to 25th February 1937. Is that right?"

"Thereabouts."

"That is not good enough. I want an accurate answer."

"For God's sake! That's over forty years ago — I was only a small kid. I can remember that the family was in those parts for about five years at roughly that period, but I can't give you exact dates."

"Can you remember the name of the man

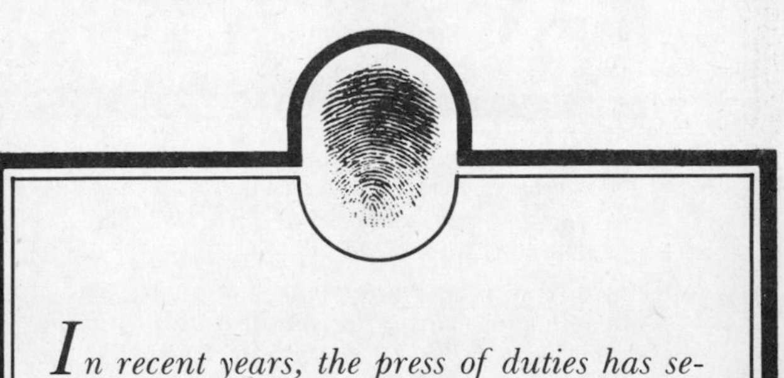

In recent years, the press of duties has severely restricted the amount of time I can devote to light reading, so I do not read mysteries.

GENERAL GEORGE S. BROWN,
Chairman of the Joint Chiefs of Staff

who lived next-door — in 37 Sungrove Avenue?"

"It wasn't a man, it was an old widow lady — we kids used to call her Aunt Bertha, but she wasn't any relation. Just a minute — (*deep concentration*) — Silverton — Silver — oh, hell — ah — *Silberstein,* that's it. She was Jewish — we weren't — but she gave my young brother and me a little present when her grandson got his bar mitzvah. I remember mine was a propelling pencil, and my brother got an airplane."

"The people on the other side? Name?"

"Can't remember. I *think* it was an elderly couple without kids — or if there were kids, they were grown up. I certainly can't recall anything definite about them."

And so it goes on. How on earth could anybody be asked to computerise details like that, particularly phoney ones, in his head, and

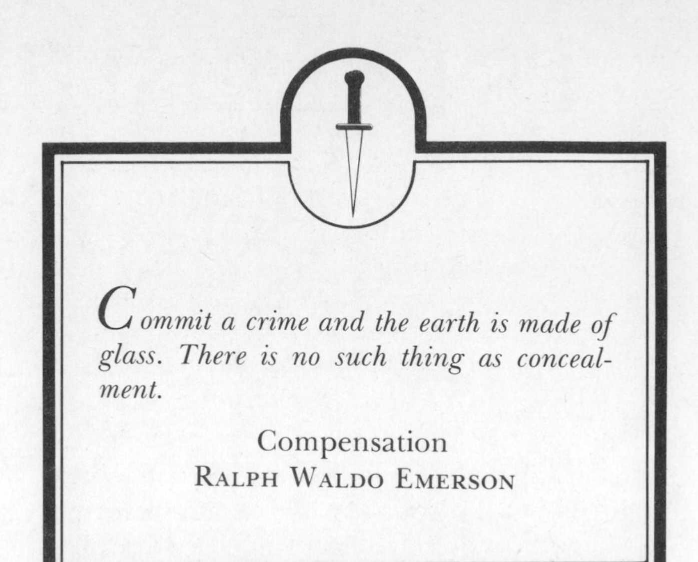

Commit a crime and the earth is made of glass. There is no such thing as concealment.

Compensation
RALPH WALDO EMERSON

be able to reel out answers without hesitation — or too much hesitation? You go back to the second sentence for that. Anybody of

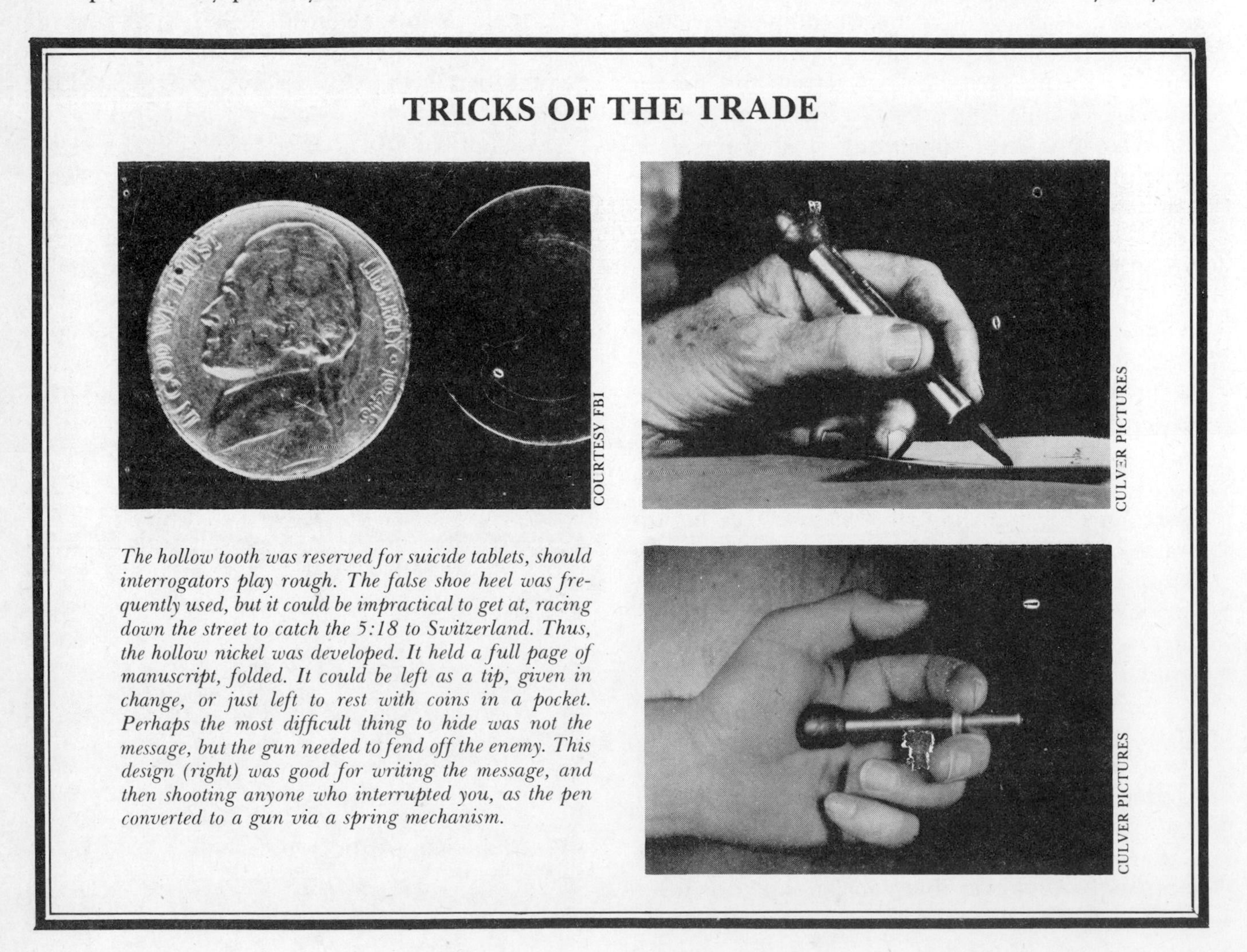

TRICKS OF THE TRADE

The hollow tooth was reserved for suicide tablets, should interrogators play rough. The false shoe heel was frequently used, but it could be impractical to get at, racing down the street to catch the 5:18 to Switzerland. Thus, the hollow nickel was developed. It held a full page of manuscript, folded. It could be left as a tip, given in change, or just left to rest with coins in a pocket. Perhaps the most difficult thing to hide was not the message, but the gun needed to fend off the enemy. This design (right) was good for writing the message, and then shooting anyone who interrupted you, as the pen converted to a gun via a spring mechanism.

moderate intelligence but little imagination. *Moderate* intelligence. Yes, just that. A *highly* intelligent subject, unfortunately, is far more likely to "blow" than his more workaday colleague — and too much imagination often leads to a type of euphoria under pressure, a sort of "I'm doing fine, I can blind this guy!" feeling, and he starts to overplay his hand, to embroider his story and, inevitably, finally trips himself up. Of course, it takes training and conditioning, and, above all, *time*. Good agents are often chosen as mere children and the course can last for ten to twenty years — *agents*, that is, as distinct from such expendable pawns as legmen, droppers, minders or, as they are sometimes called, button-men. Since these latter categories do no actual spying but are merely there to serve the spies, they can usually be recruited locally from the ranks of those who will do anything for a fast buck — crooks, prostitutes — the real mercenaries — but never, incidentally, junkies, who can easily be bought but as easily broken, merely by withholding their drugs. Even when caught, the little men can never give much away, however hard they are leaned upon, for the simple reason that they are usually directed and controlled by faceless people they meet under cover of darkness — anonymous telephone calls — notes passed in public places or left in dead-letter boxes, e.g., thumbtacked under park benches, in hollow trees, behind toilet bowls in comfort stations, etc. Their payments reach them the same way. And always there are "cut-offs" — prefabricated and inbuilt breaks in the trail — to ensure that an underling in the hot seat — a messenger, or "dropper" — could only betray, at very most, the person who gave him the message and the one to whom he was supposed to deliver it.

A splendid example of the care, patience and meticulous attention to detail in the training of the full-fledged professional agent in connection with his cover story can be found in one Konon Trofimovich Molody, who, born in Russia in 1923, was taken at the age of eleven to America by a woman posing as his mother. With a truly Russian gift for languages, he was speaking perfect English, with an American accent, in four years. Provided with a genuine Canadian passport in the name of Gordon Arnold Lonsdale, a child who had been taken to Europe at the age of eight and had apparently disappeared without trace, Molody returned to Russia by an underground route soon after his fifteenth birthday — and was never again allowed to speak Russian or, indeed, any other language but English. He was trained in the technical routine of the electronic espionage he was intended for, then secretly returned to Canada, where he was placed in a company dealing in radio parts. After two or three years he was sent by this concern to England, and there, under cover of a perfectly genuine and legitimate business, he was appointed Russia's Resident Director of Espionage, with the rank of Colonel in the KGB. How he was eventually unmasked and sentenced to twenty-five years' imprisonment by the double-crossing of a British double traitor is another, and longer, story. But his fall was in no way due to any shortcoming in his cover story. That was perfect.

Berkely Mather is a former chairman of the Crime Writers' Association.

SMART-ASS SPIES

In the late 1950's Mike Nichols and Elaine May improvised *Mysterioso*, a spy routine in which two agents identified themselves with cryptic remarks such as "flying smut." Smart-ass spies mid-60's, in books, however, appeared as emotional brothers to the hard-boiled dick, wanting to be left alone, just them and their sense of humor. Examples: Frank Maculiffe, Oliver Bleeck, and best of all, Jay Brothers and *Ox*.

THE CRYPTOGRAPHY BUREAU

How to Tell a Vigenère from a Pig Pen

Edward D. Hoch

Many of us need a refresher course to understand spy code terminology. Herewith, the fundamentals.

Codes. Codes and ciphers are two quite different things. A code consists of words, phrases, numbers or symbols used to replace elements of the plain text (uncoded) message. A code operates on linguistic entities; thus a code book might show the number 6477 standing for the word "attack," or the letter group BUKSI signifying "Avoid arrest if possible." A problem with codes is that they require code books, often containing thousands of number or letter groups covering all possible messages. The vulnerability of code books to capture by enemy forces has always presented grave problems. For this reason, naval codes are bound in books with heavy lead plates in the front and back cover to ensure their sinking to the bottom if dropped overboard. Good code stories (as distinguished from cipher stories) are rare, but O. Henry's "Calloway's Code" makes clever use of a makeshift code of special interest to journalists.

Dictionary and book codes. A dictionary code uses numbers to identify the page and line on which a given word may be found, the drawback being that the same numbers always stand for the same words. A book code also uses numbers to identify the page, line and word in any book designated "it" by both sender and receiver. Anthony Boucher's short story "QL 696 .C9" uses a code based on the Library of Congress classification system for books.

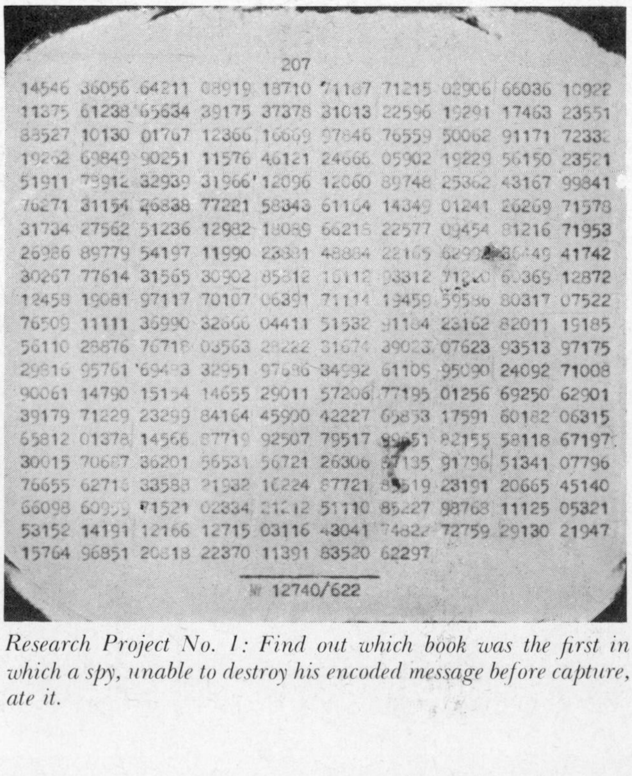

Research Project No. 1: Find out which book was the first in which a spy, unable to destroy his encoded message before capture, ate it.

Substitution ciphers. In ciphers of the substitution type, a single letter, number or symbol stands for a single letter of the alphabet. The most popular device for substitution ciphers is the cipher disk. Cipher disks have a long history with the military, and Aaron Burr is known to have used one. A problem with substitution ciphers is that long messages can be deciphered through use of a letter frequency list. The most frequently used letter in the English language is *e* — as Edgar Allan Poe correctly observed in "The Gold Bug," the world's most widely read cipher story. Though today's letter frequencies are different from those listed in "The Gold Bug," Poe's technique for solving the cipher in the story is still valid. Poe used numbers and symbols as substitutions for the letters of his message whereas Arthur Conan Doyle used little stick-figure drawings in "The Adventure of the Dancing Men." But Sherlock Homes used Poe's technique of letter frequencies in his solution.

Transposition ciphers. When letters of a message retain their identities and are merely jumbled, we have a transposition cipher. In a simple rectangular transposition, the letters of a message are printed horizontally in a square, then removed from the square vertically and placed in groups of five to disguise the original word lengths. The recipient of the message puts the letters back in the square vertically and reads them horizontally.

Skytales. One form of transposition cipher uses a skytale, or scytale — a long narrow strip of paper wrapped around a wooden staff or other object. The message is printed down the length of the staff, with lines of unrelated letters printed down the other sides. When the paper strip is removed, the writing appears to be gibberish, but it can easily be read when wrapped around a staff of the same diameter at the receiving end.

Grilles. Another form of transposition is the grille — a sheet of metal or cardboard with rectangular holes cut at irregular intervals. The message is written in these open spaces and the grille is then removed. The remaining space is

CODE-BREAKER QUIZ

Joseph C. Stacey

You have thirty seconds to find out who the following spies, secret agents, wicked groups and assassination specialists are. Failure to identify them in the allotted time leaves you no choice but to bite down hard on your cyanide capsule.

1. CF YRFCRVK RXK CDH BDIDHD (#87922/8)
2. LDCGW QRHK (225)
3. YRFVK YDF MYR WEZ GVZGWD QDPHD (TNTGFR)
4. GINV RFUDHNPDMNRH MIW UGM WCDFM (ODRW)
5. CDMM BGVC (GFNT)
6. 225W QRWW (C)
7. GINV WRTNGMZ MBG CDH AFRC XHTVG (TBFXWB)
8. CDJYCVV WCDFM (DUGHM 30)
9. WEZ YBR TDCG NH AFRC MBG TRVK (WCNVGZ)
10. FGCR YNVVNDCW (MBG KGWMFRZGF)

Joseph C. Stacey contributed many of the trickier puzzles in Mystery Monthly *magazine.*

filled with an innocuous letter or report. The receiver simply lays an identical grille over the letter to read the true message. My short story "The Spy Who Worked for Peace" was built around the use of a grille.

Playfair squares. Prior to World War I, the British Army successfully used a digraphic substitution called a Playfair square, named for its advocate, Baron Playfair. A five-by-five square of twenty-five spaces is used, filled in horizontally with the unduplicated letters of a key word. The remaining squares are filled with the unused letters of the alphabet, with the letters I and J combined. Thus, using the key word "Blackstone," The square looks like this:

B L A C K
S T O N E
D F G H I-J
M P Q R U
V W X Y Z

The cipher is called digraphic because the letters of the plain text are divided into pairs and enciphered two at a time, with the result depending upon their relation to each other in the square. Double letters occurring together in a pair are separated by an *x*. If the two letters of a pair are in the same horizontal row, they're enciphered with the letters to their right. If they fall in the same vertical column, they're enciphered with the letters beneath them. If they appear in neither the same row nor column, each is enciphered by the letter that lies in its own row but in the column occupied by the other letter. Thus, using the word "balloon" as an example, it would first be written as *ba lx lo on,* then enciphered as *lc aw at ne.* Though it seems complicated, the Playfair is easily mastered and only the key word need be remembered. Best of all, it comes close to being unbreakable.

Vigenère ciphers. Probably the most famous cipher system of all is the Vigenère, a polyalphabetic substitution cipher that is a simplified system of Blaise de Vigenère's original. It uses a tableau consisting of twenty-six standard horizontal alphabets, each positioned one letter to the left of the one above. A normal alphabet stands at the top and another normal alphabet runs down the left side of the tableau. In use, a key word is repeated above the plain text message until each letter has a corresponding key letter. The plain text letter is located in the top alphabet of the tableau and the key letter on the side alphabet. The lines are followed down and across the tableau to their intersection, yielding the cipher letter. Long thought unbreakable, Vigenères are more easily solved than Playfairs, mainly because the key word is repeated several times in a pattern.

Pigpen ciphers. More of historical interest than anything else is the pigpen cipher. Variations of this system were used by the Rosicrucians, Masons and other groups. A "pigpen" of four lines, looking exactly like a tic-tac-toe square, is drawn on a sheet of paper and each pen is filled with three letters of the alphabet, starting with *abc* in the upper left and continuing horizontally until *yz* is in the lower right pen. The first letter in each of the nine sections needs no dot, but the second letter is represented by one dot and the third letter by two dots. In ciphering by this method, a letter is represented by the shape of its pen, with one or

ANN LIMONGELLO

two dots in the pen if necessary. Thus the letter *o,* in the center of the pigpen, is enciphered as a square-shaped pen with two dots inside.

Steganography. Behind this formidable-looking word are grouped various methods of concealing the very existence of a secret message. Included are invisible inks, microdots, and messages in which the first or last letter of each word spells out a hidden communication. In a 1912 collection of short stories, *The Master of Mysteries,* published anonymously, the first letters of the first words in the twenty-four stories spell out the sentence "The author is Gelett Burgess." The last letters of the last words in each story read "False to life and false to art." Ellery Queen used a similar device in an early novel, with the first letter of each chapter title spelling out *The Greek Coffin Mystery* by Ellery Queen.

Chronograms. More interesting in literature than in serious espionage work are chronograms — inscriptions in which certain letters, printed larger or in a different typeface, express a date or number when added together by their values as Roman numerals. A prime example of a chronogram in fiction is R. Austin Freeman's Dr. Thorndyke mystery *The Puzzle Lock.*

One-time pads. The ultimate cipher that cryptologists dream of is the one-time system, using pads or tape. Popular following World War II, one-time pads use nonrepeating random keys. Since the same key is never repeated, and is only a meaningless jumble of letters, even a great many messages provide no clues. The cipher is truly unbreakable. Only the vast number of keys that must be printed and distributed has kept the one-time cipher from being universally popular. In a confusing battlefield situation, the order of the keys might prove a handicap when several units are involved. And in an espionage situation, discovery of a spy's one-time pads would be damaging evidence — as it was in the cases of Soviet spies Helen and Peter Kroger and Rudolf Abel.

Cipher machines. The ancestor of the modern cryptographic machines was probably the wheel cipher invented by Thomas Jefferson. It consisted of a cylinder six inches long, divided into twenty-six separate wheels, each

ANN LIMONGELLO

Inverted inscription found in R. Austin Freeman's The Mystery of 31, New Inn, *which was solved by the great scientific detective Dr. John Thorndyke.*

with a full alphabet in jumbled order. The wheels were numbered and no two were alike. They were lined up so that a message could be read horizontally. Then the jumbled letters from any of the other lines became the cipher. On the receiving end, an identical cylinder had its wheels aligned to show the cipher message. One of the other lines would automatically show the message in plain text. Almost infinite varieties were possible by changing the order of the numbered wheels. A century after Jefferson, the French cipher expert Étienne Bazeries invented a similar machine. These early wheel ciphers could be broken with a bit of hard work, but they led directly to the rotor machines so popular today. Using from three to eight rotors, machine ciphers are difficult to break without a great many messages from the same machine. The preferred technique is to obtain one of the machines itself — as the British did during World War II with the German cipher machine Enigma.

Edward D. Hoch is the author of a series of short stories featuring the Department of Concealed Communications.

SKOOBEDOC

Nonfiction

Gaines, Helen Fouche. *Cryptanalysis.* New York City: Dover, 1956. A basic survey.

Kahn, David. *The Codebreakers.* New York City: Macmillan, 1967. The definitive work.

Laffin, John. *Codes and Ciphers.* New York City: Abelard-Schumann, 1964. An introduction.

Moore, Dan Tyler, and Waller, Martha. *Cloak & Cipher.* Indianapolis: Bobbs-Merrill, 1962. A short history.

Pratt, Fletcher. *Secret and Urgent.* Garden City, N.Y.: Doubleday, 1924. A history of spies and ciphers.

Tuchman, Barbara. *The Zimmerman Telegram.* New York City: Viking, 1958. The deciphering of an important World War I message.

Winterbotham, F.W. *The Ultra Secret.* New York City: Harper & Row, 1975. Britain's success in breaking the German cipher machine Enigma.

Wolfe, J.M. *A First Course in Cryptanalysis.* New York City: Brooklyn College Press, 1943. A textbook for class use.

Yardley, Herbert O. *The American Black Chamber.* Indianapolis: Bobbs-Merrill, 1931. An exposé by an American cryptologist.

Fiction

Bond, Raymond T. (ed.). *Famous Stories of Code and Cipher.* New York City: Holt, Rinehart & Winston, 1947; Collier Books, 1965. An informative introduction and sixteen stories.

Clift, Dennison Halley. *Spy in the Room.* New York City: Mystery House/Thomas Bouregy, 1944. Murder in the code room at British Intelligencc.

Gordon, Alex. *The Cipher.* New York City: Simon & Schuster, 1961. An American Egyptologist is hired for a deciphering. Basis of the 1966 film *Arabesque.*

Hoch, Edward D. *The Spy and the Thief.* New York City: Davis Publications, 1971. Seven stories concerning codes and ciphers.

Johnson, James L. *Code Name Sebastian.* New York City: Lippincott, 1967. Basis for the 1968 film *Sebastian.*

Liebman, Arthur (ed.). *Tales of Espionage and Intrigue.* New York City: Richard Rosen Press, 1977. Twelve stories, five concerning codes and ciphers.

FALSE PASSPORTS

Getting Across the Border

Robin W. Winks

A false passport is essential to any self-respecting spy, always in fiction and often in real life. Few documents are more useful if one wishes to change identity, and for "illegals" — foreign spies inserted into the society of a potential enemy — they rank just below the birth certificate and the driver's license as a passport to identity. The passport is the prompter's book from which the spy must act out a part; bad reviews result in capture and perhaps death.

In the 1970's a truly counterfeit passport is seldom used, and those carefully manufactured documents by which Eric Ambler's spies flitted across Balkan frontiers, or by which escaped British prisoners of war made their way cross-country from Stalag XVII, are part of the romance of the past. What the professional spy must have today is a genuine passport issued to a fraudulent identity; the day of making visa stamps from hard-boiled eggs and sliced potatoes saturated in ink has been displaced (except in Africa) by the hard realism of technology. Better, as the Jackal did, to steal a valid passport — Americans alone lose or have stolen nearly 30,000 passports a year — than to risk giving the game away by having some customs officer casually spill alcohol on the passport and have it come up reading *void*. Only the KGB, behind the times as usual, maintains a corps of technicians to make fake passports from scratch — Western passports are called "shoes" in KGB jargon, a wry twist on "walking papers," and so (surprise!) the technicians are called "cobblers."

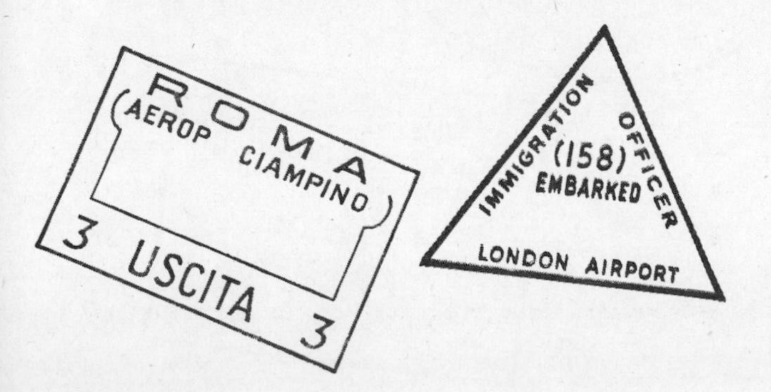

So you still want your spy to have a false passport? Okay. First you have to get the right kind of paper. American passports are printed on a rare paper manufactured by the American Writing Paper Corporation in Holyoke, Massachusetts; the making of the paper itself takes place under the tightest security arrangements. The paper is sized, that is, covered with a thin finish which is soluble in water or spirits, so even the sleepiest immigration officer can tell if you've bleached the paper. Further, passport paper is "safety paper" — it's printed with a design of fine lines and patterns with fugitive dyes. Any chemical that will bleach ink will bleach the American eagle right off the page. Use any oxidizing or bleaching agent, and you're a dead man, Harry Palmer.

Then you have to get passport covers. Valid American passports come in many hues: black for diplomatic, maroon for official, green for tourist, and a dark blue for those issued in the Bicentennial year. The covers are made of simulated plastic Lexide, by a company in New York, and the process is secret. Any tampering with the covers is instantly detectable.

Of course, professional forgers know all this, and they'll give their Walther PPK for a supply of either paper or covers. They know that the paper has invisible watermarks embedded in it, and they know that the recipes are subtly changed from time to time so that the wrong issue date on a passport of a particular chemical nature is a dead giveaway — assuming the passport falls under someone's handy ultraviolet light. They *can* resurface paper, and there *are* ways to restore the safety designs, and the impressions made by rubber stamps *can* be faked (although traces of gelatin, albumin or the lowly potato will remain impregnated in the paper), and one *can* apply stamps for visas in such a way that it is virtually impossible to tell which is the uppermost of two stamps carelessly slapped down in the same place. But why go to all the bother? Even assuming success in surmounting the paper chase, the counterfeiter still must deal with official perforations, a photograph, signatures and personal data. The photograph is affixed with a special glue. The perforations (which *may* be filled in with pulp, and fresh ones made on the same ground, although this can be detected if the paper is held to the light, or with a camera) are coded alphabetically and changed annually (Z, for example, indicates that the passport was issued abroad), and while the code may well be obtained, great care is needed to be certain that an improper prefix letter does not contradict the dates of the false visas.

All of which explains why the KGB, D16 and CIA operatives fight shy of being handed a pair of shoes. In a U.S. Department of Justice report on Criminal Use of False Identification, issued in November of 1976, user fraud with respect to passports showed that 0 percent of those detected were counterfeit, 5 percent were altered and 95 percent involved imposters. As an underground newspaper noted in 1968, phony I.D.'s are "not worth the paper they're printed on." The professional seeks to have the government issue directly an authentic document but to a false identity — precisely as Frederick Forsyth describes in *The Day of the Jackal,* a book called "the best primer to passport fraud" by no less an authority than the head of the Passport Division of the United States Department of State.

No one knows how many false passports are in circulation, although one reputable estimate suggests there may be over a million. Since the most valuable passport is the American (the variety of American accents being so great, nearly anyone who speaks even broken English can pass as an American citizen), they are the most frequently stolen. Throughout Eastern Europe, tourists must deposit their passports overnight when they register at hotels, or surrender their passports in quantities to tour operators, so that crucial elements may be copied for nefarious purposes; not long ago one American sold a dozen such passports to Russian agents. British passports also have high mobility value, and significant problems exist in the policing of Australian and Columbian passports. In general, the richer the nation, and the more polyglot its language and racial mixture, the more easily one may pass off a Georgian accent (Russian or American) as the real thing.

Who is to know how many fraudulent passports are used and how often? The truly successful counterfeit or fraud doesn't become a statistic. As the CIA instructors say, "The spies you have read about . . . are exceptions. The spies who interest us are the ones who do not get caught, and who therefore are not to be read about." British Intelligence is sexier: "A good espionage operation is like a good marriage . . . it is uneventful. It does not make a good story." Or as the Mexicans say, "To di-

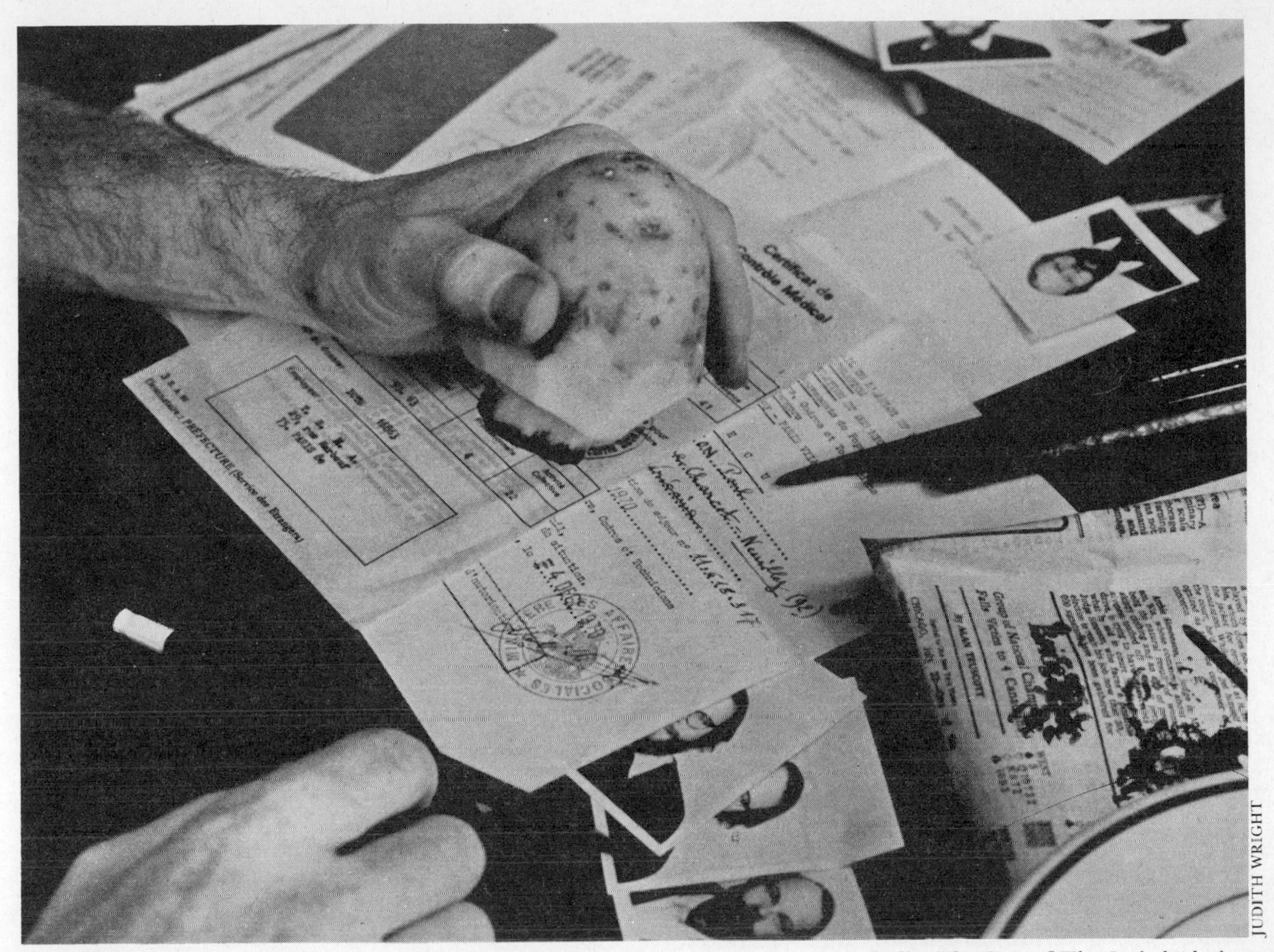

JUDITH WRIGHT

The head of the Passport Division of the U.S. Department of State called Frederick Forsyth's thriller The Day of The Jackal *"the best primer to passport fraud." The Jackal's technology supplanted the old method of engraving a cold potato with the appropriate visa markings, then saturating the potato in an ink bath.*

vorce a wife is hard; to divorce a mistress impossible."

Since there are 300,000 fugitives from justice in the U.S. every year, the market for stolen passports that can be altered is intense. Even more intense is the effort to obtain authentic passports for fraudulent purposes, the most common purpose being drug traffic. Carriers usually have a valid passport as well. The Drug Enforcement Agency estimates that a person can bring into the country $500,000 worth (street value) of narcotics per trip; the Passport Office estimates that each fraudulent passport will, on average, be used twice. This is Big Business, out of all proportion to sneaking the Bruce-Partington Plans across the border. Since 1972 an intensified campaign to detect fraudulent applications in order to stop false passports before they can get into the hands of the criminal has led to an increase in detection from 10 percent in 1970 to an estimated 65 percent in 1976 — but estimates of the depth of water that you can't measure still leave drowning room.

How to get that real passport? As the Jackal did, through "infant death." The obituary pages of old newspapers, or visits to cemeteries (à la Hitchcock's *Family Affair*), provide the names of infants who died at so early an age that few identification papers would have been issued for them. Obviously the infant should, if it had lived, be of the age of the false applicant. It's usually a good idea to check on sex (is "Robin" a girl's or a boy's name?), race and address, too. If you can find an entire family that has been wiped out in an accident, you remove the odd chance of the strong arm of coincidence betraying you. You then obtain a birth certificate, on the grounds of loss, and with this in hand you're ready to apply for an authentic passport. As *The Paper Trip*, an underground handbook, remarked: "Always get your Government ID from the government itself. Give them the paper they want and you will get the paper you want."

You still may want a variety of visas in your passport if it is to support your other documents. (Don't have too many; the more you have, the greater the risks, but you can't do without a driver's license and in this day and age any American without some credit cards is automatically suspect, at the least, of undermining the economy.) Visas must show that you have been where the part you are playing suggests you have been. But the visa game is tricky, and if you notice a border guard studying all your visas don't be surprised; the wrong one in the wrong place can be more revealing than the right suit hanging in the wrong closet. You must know which nations require visas and for what periods of time; that some nations (Russia, Israel) issue visas in separate documents; that some are accompanied by a photograph one and a half inches square while others must be one and three quarters inches square, etc. For these reasons the entry stamps of the world's international airports are regarded as safer to use — but entry and exit stamps will differ, and you had better be able to tell the difference across a crowded room.

For Americans alone, there are 10 million tourist, 175,000 official, and 24,000 diplomatic passports outstanding. How much easier it all was in the days of Louis XIV, who first issued passports — the word is derived from the French *passer* (to pass) and *port* (harbor), just as "visa" is from *visé* (endorsed). Louis issued so few, he could have them individually coded: yellow paper meant an Englishman (clever comment, that); a dot appeared under the name of Protestants, whose movements could thus be barred at the border; if the holder of the passport was wealthy and thus to be respected, a rose design appeared on the paper; if he was a bachelor, a ribbon was threaded through a hole. Women were not granted passports. (Some say this is where the term "the sleeper" came from.) The Scarlet Pimpernel probably carried the first false passport.

In the hidden world of the false passport, the professional holds to a simple rule: Do not support forgery with perjury. Let the document do the lying for you; tell no lies yourself. After all, if Colonel Russell of Security Executive can do it, so can you.

Robin W. Winks is a history professor at Yale University. He did not buy his passport from Abdel Simpson.

Chapter 5

VICTIMS

FRED WINKOWSKI

THE MOST LIKELY VICTIM

Rosamund Bryce

I confess.

Although I have been reading murder mysteries for the past twenty years, at the rate of two a day (I gulp them down like aspirin), I have never been particularly concerned with who gets killed.

I *am* intrigued with how it's done (I've a special fondness for coshes from behind and little slits in the back opened by poisoned daggers), and why it's done, but the personality of the victim — ho-hum.

And as unsympathetic as I am, the authors are even more so. I challenge you to name ten books in which the victim was a fully developed, three-dimensional human being. Rarely do authors invest the victim with anything deeper than a quirk: The dowager *always* sits dead center on the settee for the half-hour preceding dinner; the old codger *always* removes the Gainsborough, opens the wall safe and locks away his private papers at 9 sharp; the bride-to-be *always* closes her eyes as she brushes her hair those hundred strokes; the rookie *always* talks too much, to the wrong people; the secret agent *always* goes to the lavatory to decode his messages within five minutes of receiving them; the char *always* gobbles the leftovers when nobody's looking.

I repeat, quirks. Victims are so full of them, there is little room for anything else. No wonder authors kill them off first chance they get. (Frankly, I'm usually six pages ahead of them. At the first whiff of a compulsion, the first hint of an idiosyncrasy, down comes my mental guillotine.)

Clearly, the victim is not inherently interesting. Then why kill him? Well, for one thing, it gets him out of his rut. For another, he habitually has something someone else wants: title to the land; senior position in the firm; a second Rolls; a Chippendale armoire; an heirloom brooch; a guaranteed (millionaire's) income. In the mystery, greed is the principal reason for murdering. Consequently, the most likely victim is well-to-do but stingy.

The next most likely victim is the poor sod who recently fell in love. Invariably, his happiness sets someone's knife on edge, resulting in his lopsided grin becoming a little more lopsided. Miss Sayers was quite wrong, you know. She said love has no place in the mystery. She should have qualified her statement. Love may be an inappropriate emotion for the detective (he has to keep his mind on his work, after all), but it is obligatory as a means of identifying the next corpse. What's more appealing to read about than a nice, juicy crime of passion?

The third most frequent victim is done in out of revenge. The victim has brought shame to one family, ruin to another. (If the book's a Gothic, however, shame doesn't lead to murder; it leads to the offender being closeted in the far turret.) Curiously, it's only in spy stories that revenge is an unadulterated motive. The victim is killed under the cloak of patriotism, but if you read between the lines it's apparent that defending the Crown was secondary; the actual reason was to eliminate the cad who caused the death of the spy's best friend some three books back.

In classic thrillers revenge is greed's veneer. For every case you can cite in which the killer did it to restore the family honor, I can rebut with two, at least, in which he did it to gain control of the family blue chips as well.

I suppose I must mention, although I hate

to fuel the arguments of the anti-genre people, that some mystery deaths are caused by outright meanness. These deaths occur in the bottom-quality books — the ones in which you discover on the last page that the killer was a psychopath who had no motive. Books with these abysmal characters tend to choose sentimental victims: a small child with a mild deformity (a stutter); the family pet; widows, teachers and war heroes.

One good author with a perverse streak when it comes to assigning victims is Robert Ludlum. Mr. Ludlum is singular in that he likes his victims, and makes you like them, too. You want them to stick around to the end of the book. The most likely victim in a Ludlum book is the character you least want to see die. Now *that's* perverse.

There are two types of victims who die through no fault of their own. They just happen to have the bad luck to share a chapter with (a) a Great Detective or (b) a Gothic Heroine. Possibly the greatest Great Detective of them all is Sherlock Holmes, agreed? Have you ever noticed how many people die once he's called in on a case? It's appalling. Holmes and his descendants are *always* examining the plimsoles when they should be attending to the people. They are *always* sniffing the cigar ash, gluing the theater stub and educating their Watsons when they should be advising the next victim how to double-lock his door. These victims die to further Holmes's reputation. After all, it doesn't take a Great Detective to solve *one* murder; with a little perseverance we might all be able to do that. But a killer who strikes down many, who in the process still finds time to loot the silver vaults, waylay the carriage and leave hundreds of clues (none of them traceable) demands the skills of a Great Detective. These victims are known as the expendables. Oftener than not, they are the people who sold the cigar that made the ash, who innocently resoled the plimsole. They come two, three, even four to the book, and I can't recall a situation in which they were ever mourned. Presumably, they live alone: no friends, no relatives, no one to shed a tear. They are honest, hard-working souls, and I think Holmes and all the other Great Detectives should be charged for their deaths. Criminal negligence sounds about right, yes?

The other category of hapless victims exists solely in the Gothic novel. Ogden Nash called this the Had-I-But-Known school and it's been around since 1908, when Mary Roberts Rinehart created *The Circular Staircase*. Victims in these books die because they are not wearing nightgowns. The character who is — the Gothic Heroine — has the worst instincts this side of Lady Macbeth. She is a clear case of intuition run amok. She *always* decides a midnight traipse down the corridor is more important

THE VICTIM'S EYES

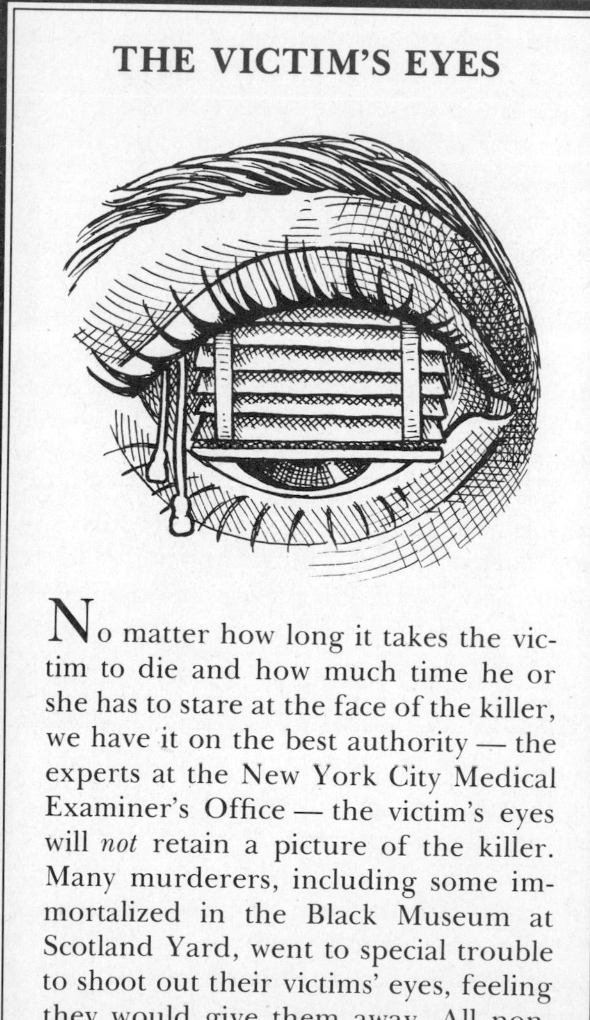

No matter how long it takes the victim to die and how much time he or she has to stare at the face of the killer, we have it on the best authority — the experts at the New York City Medical Examiner's Office — the victim's eyes will *not* retain a picture of the killer. Many murderers, including some immortalized in the Black Museum at Scotland Yard, went to special trouble to shoot out their victims' eyes, feeling they would give them away. All nonsense. The doctors at the Medical Examiner's Office have looked. And looked and looked. And they have never seen an image imprinted on a retina.

MARTY NORMAN

POSITION THE BODY MOST OFTEN FOUND IN

ENGLISH MYSTERIES

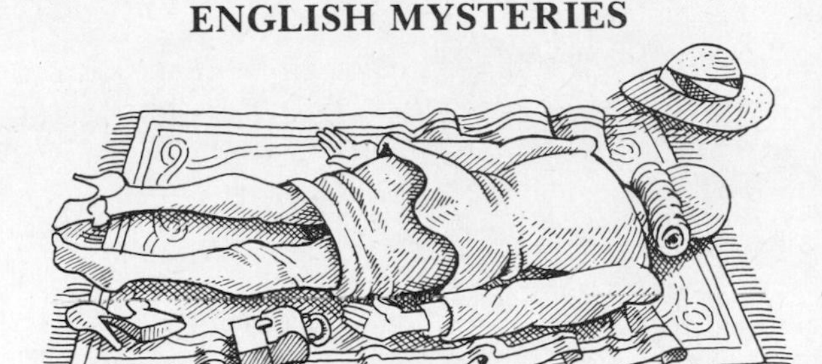

Face down. This is done to give the servants the chance to cry, "It's Lady Teasdale. I put that coat out for her just this morning." Of course, when the body is turned over, it is not Lady T., but Gladys from the kitchen who is M'Lady's size and coloring. Lady Teasdale, feeling quite beneficent that morning, had given Gladys her coat. Gladys, on her own initiative, had stolen her handbag. The servants then get to cry out, "It's Gladys! Leaving service next week, she was. Thought it peculiar, her with a dear Mum to support."

Face down also gives Gladys the chance to obscure with her body the button she managed to wrest from her accoster's mac. This clue will provide the Inspector with at least one red herring and two more victims before the night is over.

AMERICAN MYSTERIES

Face up. This is done to impress Charlie the Horse that it was not an accident. Herman, his best button man, was obviously not the best man for the job of rubbing out Lemons O'Connor and Lemons told him so — slow and lingeringly.

Face up gives Lemons the chance to place pennies on Herman's eyes and pull out his pockets. It also gives him the chance to put a dead fish, wrapped in newspaper, in his arms.

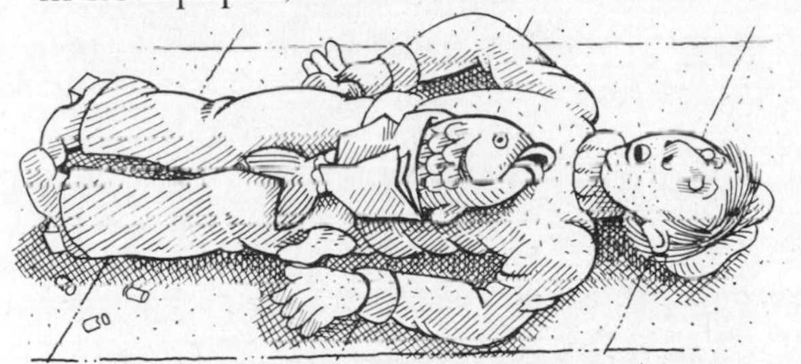

Face up gives the rookie cop a good opportunity to view his first corpse and throw up. While the forensic boys are mopping up, Dan Madison, private eye and bane of the police captain, has time to remove the key to the bus station locker from Herman's hand, pocket it and be on his way to the pickup point.

MARTY NORMAN

than warning Cook about the trip-wire set across the servant's stairs. She *always* confides in the killer and with virtually no prompting tells him the name of the only witness. To the Inspector she says not a word. Do you wonder bodies abound when she's around? The big question is: Why doesn't the staff quit the minute she unpacks her nightie? Of course, there is one consolation for the Gothic victim. At book's end the heroine refuses to marry the heir unless he promises her they will name their children after the Recently Departed. It's obvious from the number of them, the Gothic Heroine does not believe in small families.

Victims, then, are killed out of greed, lust, revenge, meanness, hubris and insensitivity. None of which makes them interesting. It makes their killers interesting. I imagine that's why I would rather identify with the killer than with the victim. (It doesn't mean, necessarily, that I'm unsafe to be around.)

I confess.

Victims bore me. To death.

Rosamund Bryce winters in Cheshireham-Under-Lyme and summers in Upper Denton.

DISPOSING OF THE BODY

Ione Paloma

Let us assume the Late Whomever was a deserving victim. He was selfish, cruel, cold, mean and not only first on the killer's farewell list but next on just about everyone else's.

Let us also assume he was dispatched at the first opportunity, regardless of where that struck. (After all, to wait for him to position himself at the edge of the cliff could take years. Or possibly two volumes.)

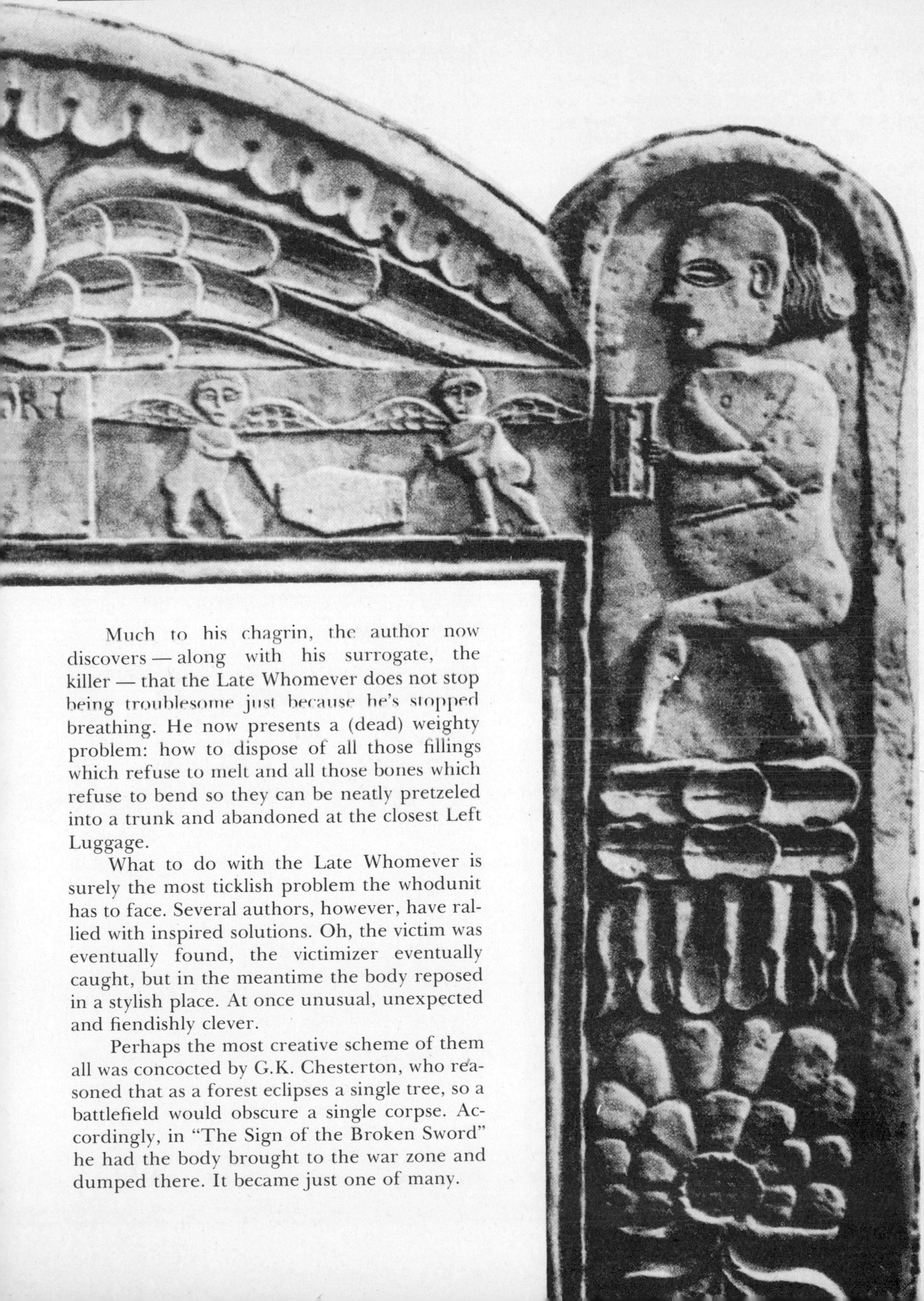

Much to his chagrin, the author now discovers — along with his surrogate, the killer — that the Late Whomever does not stop being troublesome just because he's stopped breathing. He now presents a (dead) weighty problem: how to dispose of all those fillings which refuse to melt and all those bones which refuse to bend so they can be neatly pretzeled into a trunk and abandoned at the closest Left Luggage.

What to do with the Late Whomever is surely the most ticklish problem the whodunit has to face. Several authors, however, have rallied with inspired solutions. Oh, the victim was eventually found, the victimizer eventually caught, but in the meantime the body reposed in a stylish place. At once unusual, unexpected and fiendishly clever.

Perhaps the most creative scheme of them all was concocted by G.K. Chesterton, who reasoned that as a forest eclipses a single tree, so a battlefield would obscure a single corpse. Accordingly, in "The Sign of the Broken Sword" he had the body brought to the war zone and dumped there. It became just one of many.

Ellery Queen was intrigued by the possibilities inherent in the design of the Murphy bed. It folded up into the wall, if you remember, a sort of forerunner of the Castro. Well, in *The French Powder Mystery* he tidily ensconced the corpse between the sheets and recessed him into the fixtures along with the bedding. When the bed was opened — and since the bed was one used in a department store window display it was an opening witnessed by many — out popped the deceased.

Ross Macdonald and Christianna Brand favored the medical approach to disposal. Macdonald in *The Ivory Grin* had the body stripped down to bone (you don't really want to hear about the acid bath, do you?), a few holes drilled into the cranium, a few tags inserted in the holes labeling it a medical school skeleton, and then he closed the Late Lamented into a closet, where it hung as a teaching aid for a perverse student. Ms. Brand in *Green for Danger* was equally devious. She arranged for her victim to die mid-operation, then calmly let the hospital authorities dispose of the body.

Ngaio Marsh baled a body into a packet of wool (*Died in the Wool*), Alice Tilton stored hers in a deep freeze (*Dead Earnest*) and Michael Gilbert crammed his into a safe-deposit vault (*Smallbone Deceased*). Although granted, in the last, the body was conveniently small.

Edgar Allan Poe didn't exactly hide a body; he just caromed it into a chimney (*The Murders in the Rue Morgue*).

> *Mother of God, is this the end of Rico?*
>
> Little Caesar
> W. R. Burnett

John Rhode in *The Mystery at Greycombe Farm* let the Departed harden in a cider storehouse, then rigged an incendiary bomb to char it beyond recognition.

On the bucolic side, Paul McGuire buried his body in a haystack in *Murder at High Noon*, anticipating, perhaps, that one would have as little success in finding it there as the proverbial needle.

Dermot Morrah dispensed with his cadaver by storing it in a mummy case (in — what else? — *The Mummy Case Mystery*), and Freeman Wills Crofts shipped his from Paris to London in a cask marked STATUARY ONLY (in *The Cask*, of course).

Stanley Ellin in "The Specialty of the House" had the body eaten — not in some philistine manner, mind you, but as a savory added to a fine restaurant's menu (uncredited, of course).

David Harper in *The Hanged Men* made his corpse part of a rite. He replaced the traditional Halloween "straw man" with his man, then let him hang around for the celebration.

The ultimate method was developed by Jack Finney in *Time and Again*, although since it smacks of science fiction we cannot comfortably give it top score. His hero was able to wander in time and thus went back just far enough to prevent his enemy's parents from meeting — thereby circumventing the poor man's birth. He disposed of the body by not creating the body in the first place, and more devious than that, it's difficult to get.

Now then, since we've disposed of the body, shall we adjourn to the library for a little game of wits with the Inspector? Follow me.

Ione Paloma wishes to be cremated.

> *"Well, I may tell you that Filminister was murdered."*
>
> *"Murdered?"*
>
> *"Yes. What is more, he was murdered three times."*
>
> *"Three times?"*
>
> *"Yes, and not only that. He also committed suicide."*
>
> *"I think you'd better give me the details of this extraordinary story."*
>
> A Considerable Murder
> Barry Pain

GRAVESIDE BOUQUETS

Compiled with the assistance of *The Language of Flowers* by Margaret Pickston. Published in England by Michael Joseph Ltd.

We are gathered here today to say our final farewell to Josiah Trimmingham, beloved by all, save the blighter who doctored his port with rancor and with toxins. Who done it? You know perfectly well it was one of the mourners. (Next to the lawyer's office when the will is read, the cemetery is the place most teeming with cads.) Ah, but which mourner? Look for the most voluptuous bouquet — for it has been observed that the killer, by his choice of flowers, often speaks ill of the dead. Herewith, a list of those connoting possible motive. (*Note:* It is considered lacking in subtlety to send a bouquet of the above mentioned to the incipient corpse. Far classier to show restraint and present them after the fact.)

STANDARD OIL OF NEW JERSEY

THE DON'T LIST

(Things to avoid if you *don't* want to be the next victim)

Catherine Prezzano

1. *Don't* go for lonely walks with those you've just disinherited.
2. *Don't* sip a glass of warm milk left at your bedside by an unseen hand.
3. *Don't* sample the chocolates which arrived by post, anonymously, on your birthday.
4. *Don't* rendezvous with the mysterious stranger who offered you a dukedom over the phone in a decidedly muffled voice.
5. *Don't* follow up on the advert in the Personal Column that said if you contact Paines & Grillard, Solicitors, you will hear something to your advantage.
6. *Don't* accept hunting invitations from business associates after you have refused to sell them your controlling shares in the company.
7. *Don't* attend masquerade balls given by wealthy eccentrics who send the car round to collect you and insist you tell no one where you're off to.
8. *Don't* enter the secret passageway first.
9. *Don't* remark to William, that rascal, that the Mac he insists he misplaced seems to be jammed into the hall cupboard for some inexplicable reason.
10. *Don't* kiss Barnaby when you have just turned Alex down flat and he has not yet left the house.
11. *Don't* tell the Inspector you think it nothing more than an unfortunate accident and police surveillance a breach of your privacy.
12. *Don't* stand with your back to billowing draperies, particularly if the windows are shut.
13. *Don't* offer to fetch the candles from the pantry if the lights suddenly dim, flicker and go out.
14. *Don't* comment that you never realized Titian painted in acrylics within earshot of the art gallery owner.
15. *Don't* suggest an audit of the books would be in order.
16. *Don't* ask Woof what he's got there in his mouth, and most especially don't ask him to show you where he got it.
17. *Don't* insist Madame DeClasse conduct the séance at midnight, in the library, when the moon is full.
18. *Don't* adopt young Raymond until you have absolute proof he is your long-lost sister Ava's only child.
19. *Don't* recognize the handwriting on the ransom note.
20. *Don't* reveal the ending of the mystery to someone who is just beginning it.

Catherine Prezzano don't *want to wind up dead from O.D.'ing on the mystery.*

THE DINNER PLATE

Carlotta Ogelthorpe

If I had an enemy and that enemy were fond of reading English murder mysteries vintage 1920–1930, I wouldn't wait for Monday. I'd start my diet today. I'd turn down all invitations to lunch, brunch, tea, high tea, supper, dinner and between-meal snacks — especially if that enemy were planning on preparing them personally.

You see, of the many conventions established during the so-called "Golden Age" of detective fiction, the one most rigorously followed was, if you had to eliminate someone the table was as good a place as any to have a go at it. In those mysteries the main course was usually served with poison as a side dish. The victim would proceed to the sideboard, innocently ladle the turnip purée onto his plate, return to his seat and, two forkfuls later, slide off his chair — permanently immobilized. If the stately home that guested him was stately enough, he wouldn't even have to fetch his own plate; a helpful, albeit sinister member of the staff would bring his portion to the table for him. Regardless, the outcome was the same: two forkfuls later, down he'd go — fatally stricken by the piquantness of the white sauce. In those mysteries, dinner conversation always included the phrase "I believe the sole did not agree with Reginald. Carruthers, please ring Dr. Watney."

The dinner plate became the poisoner's playground. I suppose its popularity was due to the fact that, with the possible exception of the blunt instrument, nothing was as easy to use. It didn't have to be aimed (like the gun) or personally brought into direct contact with the body (like the knife). It was simple to figure out how much poison to use: when in doubt, you merely doubled the dose. It was also a snap to get the victim to ingest it. After all, everyone ate at least one meal a day. And the English were — still are — notoriously insensitive in regard to food. A slightly off-taste bit of potted meat would not have seemed odd to them. In fact, they'd hardly have noticed.

No, it definitely wasn't safe to eat in those books. There were arcane poisons, of course, which one had to go to Brazil to collect or, even worse, sign the chemist's registry to purchase. But by and large, toxic substances were available at the drop of a grudge. Botulism was frequently induced. Mushrooms were nurtured in the dank of the cellar. Weed-killer decimated two-legged rats. By the time the chubby sleuth waddled onto the scene, it was too late to administer the antidote — if indeed there was one.

The dinner plate is still being toyed with in detective fiction, only now the Americans have gotten in on the act (Fred Halliday's *The Raspberry Tart Affair;* Nan and Ivan Lyons' *Someone Is Killing the Great Chefs of Europe*). There is also a counter-trend: books featuring fat sleuths' recipes rather than the poisoners' menus (*Madame Maigret's Own Cookbook; The Nero Wolfe Cookbook; The Mafia Cookbook; Murder on the Menu; Dining Out with Sherlock Holmes*).

What is this fascination? Why is food to the mystery what Watson is to Holmes, inseparable best friend? One theory intimidating enough to make Freud take to his couch is that there is virtually no sexual activity in the mystery and food is used as the surrogate. Many psychiatrists have noted that the number of pounds of overweight can be directly correlated to the number of kisses, etc., not received. (Don't blame me: I didn't invent the theory, I'm merely repeating it.)

There are some foods in mysteries it's never safe to trust. Dover sole, baked or poached. Porridge. Ladyfingers. Any cream sauce. Eggs, unless they're hard-boiled. Chocolates, if they're given as a present. Warm milk. And, of course, any sort of spirits. The Case of the Deadly Decanter has been written at least a hundred times, and there's probably a fiend out there typing up another one right now. When analyzed, the sediment at the bottom of the wineglass always contains enough poison to fell a hippopotamus.

Who's putting all these bad things in the victim's mouth? Certainly not Cook. Granted, she has the disposition of Attila the Hun, but her weapon would be the meat cleaver. No one in and around the kitchen, in fact, is a desecrator of the dinner plate. The washing-up girl has no time; the butler has no motive; the serving girl never has her hands free.

No, the poisoner is usually someone from Upstairs, or an Upstairs associate such as the lawyer or the doctor. In mysteries, poisoning is a well-to-do crime. It's neat. It's tidy. It's rather elegant.

What I would prefer, if I were to be a victim and if I may be so bold as to instruct my enemy, is to be allowed to eat my meal in peace and *then* be done in. The owners of New York's elegant Four Seasons restaurant concur. They suggest, in the manner of Sing Sing, that you give the condemned a hearty meal. A repast flamboyantly extravagant ($200 per lover; $150 per board of directors member) and exquisitely executed. After all, at one time you and your victim were rather intimate. You did share things together — be it a love affair, a family relationship, a corporate decision. Accordingly, you owe it to your victim to let him go out in style. To let his last meal reflect the gloriousness of his former role in your life. Bring on the golden egg caviar with the gold caviar spoon. The Trockenbeeren Auslese in a vintage coinciding with the date of your first encounter. The Havana cigars (smuggled). The cognac (Hennessey X.O.). The potatoes Anna with truffles and goose liver. The filet of hothouse lamb with its delicate bouquetière of spring vegetables. (Or the freshly peeled crayfish tails with morels flown in from the Himalayas.) *Then* as you stroll from the restaurant, his suspicions thwarted, *then* as you turn into a convenient dark alley, *then* set about finalizing matters. *That's* good manners.

For a truly mouth-watering way to go, if you feel you simply must monkey around despite the admonishments from me and the Four Seasons, let us remind you of peppered duck and shrimp with mustard sauce. Both have the necessary robustness to disguise a poison. And they have not been, forgive us, done to death. If you will settle for just making your victim deathly ill, we suggest off-season oysters from polluted waters. They'll cause hepatitis.

One other thing: May I invite you to dine with me Saturday next?

Carlotta Ogelthorpe dines alone.

THE SCALES OF JUSTICE

Nero Wolfe weighs 1/7 of a ton
Gideon Fell stopped counting at 250
Chief Inspector Dover straddles 240
Bertha Cool was a big 200, but dieted down to a mere 160
Charlie Chan is fat
Inspector Bucket is stout
Sergeant Beef is burly
Father Brown has a dumpling face
Inspector Hanaud is bulky
Jim Hanvey has too many chins
Chief Inspector Hazelrigg is definitely blimpish
Martin Hewitt is on the stout side
Roger Sheringham is stocky (too many chocolates)
George Smiley is a fat little toad
And Maigret better watch it.

THE INVALID'S TRAY

Violet St. Clair

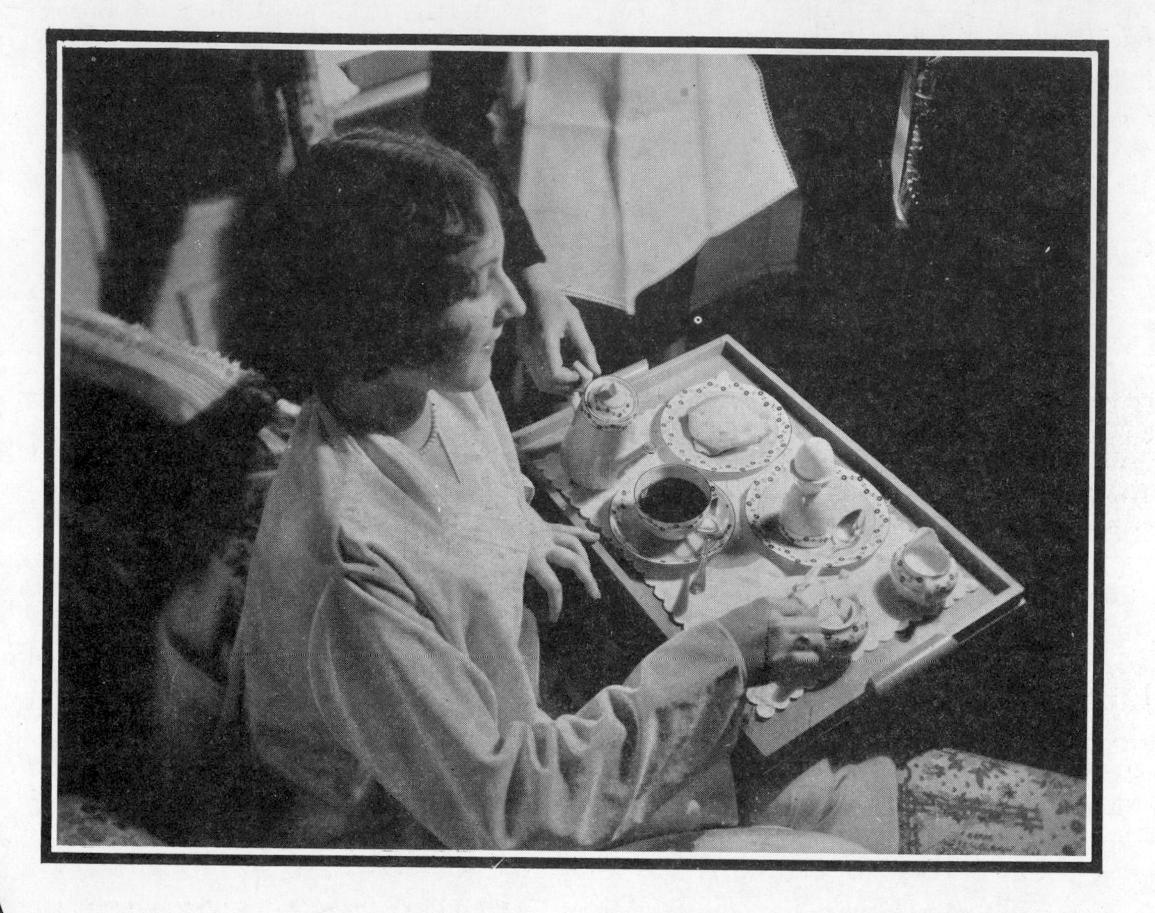

Auntie is sick. Has been for years. She took to her bed in '37 for reasons she's quite forgotten and has been going steadily, if slowly, downhill ever since.

She accepts breakfast at eight, luncheon at one, tea between four and five, dinner at half-seven and a cocoa nightcap at just past nine.

Her mornings are occupied with rewriting her will and her afternoons with receiving the doctor. She has terrible nightmares in which someone is either garrotting her with the bell pull, smothering her with her pillows or poisoning her by tinkering with her food tray. She ought to pay more attention to the last.

Great-Uncle Patriarch is also in bed, sent there by an embolism which refuses to dissolve. It presses on the corner of his brain that garbles speech and causes incontinency.

His mornings are spent on his right side, facing the sun, and his afternoons on his left, focussing, as best he can, on the secret panel in his desk.

He is spoon-fed three times a day by people he can barely recognise. One of them makes him very uneasy and his tremors upset his egg cup. He ought to have it analysed.

Clara, slightly concussed from a fall down the stairs, will be abed a fortnight.

Her counterpane is speckled with petals from a nosegay, dozens of get-well cards and tinfoil wrappers with bits of chocolate clinging.

She spends the day confiding in her diary

and the night sleeping with it beneath her pillow. Fierce headaches make her prone to napping, and when she awakens a tray is on the bedstand. Upon sampling its custard, she becomes violently ill. She ought to try to stay awake more often.

Alec is recovering from a wound he won't let anyone tend to. In fact, no one's ever seen it. Lately, he's developed a cough, and he's suggested that no one come in his room lest they catch it. His trays are left outside his locked door.

These poor wretches — hypochondriacal, chronic, accidental and deceitful — are the mainstay of the old-fashioned whodunit. All must be fed (except the last, who could really get up and serve himself, but then he'd have no alibi). All must be killed or almost killed before too many chapters slip by. And their tray is the perfect way to incapacitate them.

Every decent invalid's tray is bordered with pill bottles. The smart villain will replace one of them with another of his own prescription. If Nurse assumes the big pink pills are the usual big pink pills, who can blame her?

The tray also contains a napkin (for wiping off prints), a white linen place mat with hand-tatted edges (for hiding the knife under), an oversize spoon (for administering the toxin), a toast rack (to hold the blackmail note), a tea cosy (to be thrust halfway down the larynx as a gag) and a single rose (to fatally prick a weakened hand).

Some trays also come equipped with a hypodermic. While Miss Prendergast is off in the pantry fetching the bouillon cube, the villain is squirting out its shot of B12 and filling it with a Tanzanian virus for which there's no known antidote.

Upon her return Miss Prendergast notices the needle is slightly to the left of where she put it, but that doesn't stop her from taking it Upstairs and injecting sweet old Auntie with it. It's only later, when queried by the Inspector, that she remembers how it seemed to move.

And, of course, every respectable invalid's tray has a splendid variety of dishes to fiddle with.

A nice cup of tea, for example. Murderers have little difficulty in raising the teapot lid, inserting a quick-dissolving poison, lowering the lid and leaving the room before anyone suspects what they're up to. One invariably presumes they were just checking to see if the water needed hotting up.

And let's not forget the water glass itself. This tumbler contains eight ounces of death which the tray bearer will insist the victim drink right up, for her own good. Sometimes the victim's nerves overcome her, and she spills the contents. This is a brief reprieve, nothing more. So the dear thing can swallow her pills, the water-bearer will insist on refilling it — usually from the very tap which the killer has polluted.

Then there's the custard. Made from fresh eggs. At least they *were* fresh until some nefarious soul neatly pin-pricked each and every one of them, carefully dripped in a poisonous ooze and then put them back on the shelf in the fridge.

Porridge, too, has a nice lumpy consistency appealing to a villain, and one can bank on its being included in the victim's menu every morning. Its greyish colour is also an asset if one is dealing with impurities.

Other bright spots, for the villain, on the invalid's tray are: the jam pot; the sugar bowl; the milk pitcher; the soup bowl; the applesauce dish.

It never happens, however, that the killer serves the tray himself. He is more likely to be out of the house at feeding time, establishing an alibi by playing bridge with the Wittsentides in Yarmouth. Thus killers must do their tinkering well ahead of time. Occasionally, this isn't possible, and the killer must go up the stairs, down the stairs, up again, down again, until he accidentally bumps into whoever is carrying the tray. An elbow auspiciously placed, a subtle jostle, and his task is accomplished: the tray has been lethalized. Ofttimes, he's even too late to do this and must rely on getting to the tray before it's removed from the invalid's room. Or, wait for the next feeding time.

No matter. As Alec passed on to Auntie, Great-Uncle Patriarch and Clara: Never eat in bed.

Violet St. Clair will be dining Saturday next with Miss Ogelthorpe.

THE TERRIBLE EDIBLES

Innocuous (seemingly) House and Garden Plants That Will (quite simply) Slay You

Ruth H. Smiley, Botanist
Carolyn Fiske, Ghost

There are approximately 750 species of plants in the United States and Canada that are either partly or entirely poisonous. Instead of reaching for the salt (or the strychnine), why not reach for one of them?

Deadly nightshade. Virtually everything about the plant is poisonous — leaves, stems, flowers, seeds. Interestingly enough, it belongs to the same family as the potato and the tomato. Active ingredients are topane alkaloids, atropine and hyoscyamine. Symptoms: fever, visual disturbances, burning of the mouth, thirst, dry skin, confusion and a splitting headache.

Castor bean. One of the deadliest of all poisonous plants. One bean contains enough ricin toxin to kill an adult. The bean, however, must be chewed; if swallowed whole, the hard protective coat prevents absorption and poisoning. Yes, it is the oil from this very same plant which is marketed as castor oil, also known as a "killer" in some instances.

Buttercups (poor, little). The leaves, seeds, roots and flowers of this dainty yellow plant have been known to cause convulsions. Other common plants with similar poisonous properties are the azalea, rhododendron, iris, daffodil, jonquil, oleander, hyacinth, morning glory, poinsettia and lily of the valley, often associated with funerals. Mountain laurel is so potent that it was known to the Delaware Indians as the "suicide plant."

Snakeroot. A white wild flower known for its writhing root system. Among its illustrious victims were Nancy Hanks, mother of Abraham Lincoln, who died by drinking milk from a cow which had grazed on snakeroot. Such an "indirect" death is more difficult to accomplish today as the plant grows in forests, not modern dairy pastures.

Dumb cane (a.k.a. dieffenbachia, elephant ear, mother-in-law plant). An attractive white speckled plant that, when chewed, produces swelling of the tongue, lips and palate, making it difficult, if not impossible, for the victim to ask for help. There are reported cases of death by suffocation when, as a result of violent swelling of the tongue, the victims were unable to breathe.

Apples. The seeds are quite bitter and contain cyanic poison, which accumulates in the

DEATH
(Warmed Over)

1 Cauldron boiling oil
5 Lbs. hacked carrion
2 Qts. curdled blood
1 Carafe hemlock
3½ Cups toadstools (decapitated)
1 Cloven hoof
7 Cans Bon Vivant soup
13 Heaping tbs. arsenic powder, salt, pepper, mace

Place carrion on rack. Smother in salt, pepper and mace. Remove from rack and drown in marinade of hemlock and blood. Place in dark, dank corner. Heat oil. When it reaches rolling boil, add hoof. Cook 30 days. Add decapitated toadstools. Stir mixture with silver stake. Scrape mold from carrion and set aside. Add carrion to boiling oil. Slowly, very slowly, drip soup on meat. Make a paste of mold and arsenic powder. (To moisten, use any of the basic body oils.) Remove meat and skewer it. Pour paste over it. Serve immediately with Little Caesar Salad.

MYSTERY MUNCHIES

Obviously, the best choice is to have someone standing by peeling grapes and plopping them in your mouth. This leaves both your hands free — one to hold the book and one to turn the page.

If you can't shanghai this kind of help, you should purchase a chair with a wide, flat, unupholstered armrest. This is best for plate-balancing.

What goes on the plate depends on your whim: M&M candies; popcorn; mixed raisins and nuts (unshelled); blueberries, strawberries, huckleberries; licorice bits; cherry tomatoes; pitted olives, either black or green; lollipops.

Cookies of any description make terrible munchies. Too many crumbs. Your chair begins to feel like your beach towel with all that sand getting in awkward places.

Chewing gum while reading mysteries is another awful idea. In your excitement, you may swallow it.

body and builds up over a period of time. This circumstance partly compensates for the fact that one must eat a large quantity of the seeds for the desired effect. Serving suggestion: Sprinkle on foods as a garnish. Symptoms: nausea, vomiting, stomach cramps, difficulty in breathing, muscular weakness, dizziness, convulsions and stupor. (Maybe it was the seeds and not the apple that caused Adam and Eve's fall.)

Apricots (also cherries, prunes, plums and almonds). All contain cyanogenitic glycosides in the leaves, stems, bark and seed pits (not the fruit, alas). A change in eating habits may be required as the inner pit must be chewed.

Wild cherry branches. The twig of this tree, which contains cyanic poison, can be used to spear marshmallows for roasting over campfires. Works equally well with hot dogs.

Red elderberry branches. Use the toxic stem to make a blowgun or peashooter. When blown, the blower, not his target, is the real victim. Be sure not to confuse this twig, which has a red center pith, with the benign black elderberry, which has a white pith.

Rhubarb. The leaf (not the commonly eaten stalk) contains oxalic acid, which has a corrosive action on the gastrointestinal tract and can cause massive hemorrhaging. Next time, bake a strawberry-rhubarb *leaf* pie. (As an aside, spinach also contains some of the same toxins, but they are steamed out in the cooking process. Obviously, one must serve the water and throw out the spinach.)

Ruth H. Smiley and Carolyn Fiske stroll the acres of Mohonk Mountain House looking for terrible edibles.

A PUZZLER TO MULL OVER

Stuart Bochner

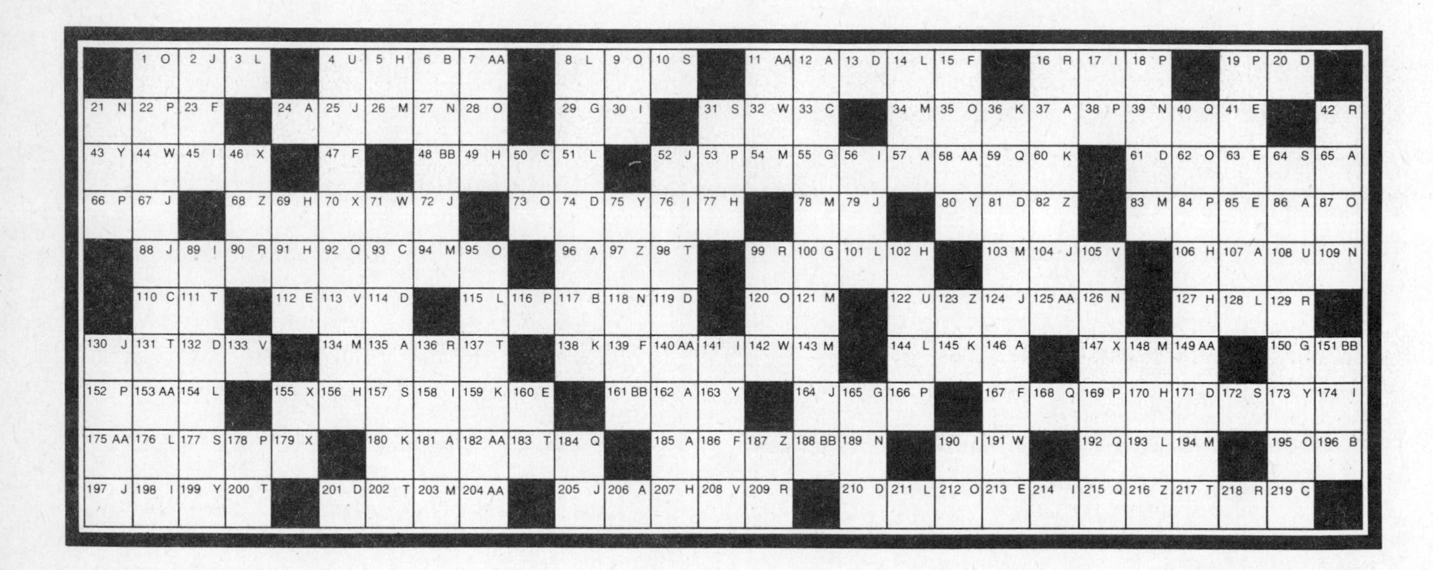

Solve the clues (right) and write them over their numbered dashes. Then transfer each letter to the corresponding numbered square in the pattern. Black squares indicate word endings. The filled pattern will contain a suitable quotation reading from left to right. The first letters of the solved clues will form an acrostic giving the author's name and title of the work. The clues are of the English crossword type in two parts: a definition and a subsidiary indication (pun, anagram, double definition, etc.) Punctuation is designed to confuse.

Stuart Bochner is an attorney with the New York Division of Criminal Justice.

SOLUTION:
Hold upside down, facing mirror.

Wilkie Collins: The Woman in White
His body was taken out of the Seine in the disguise which I have described, nothing being found on him which revealed his name, his rank or his place of abode. The hand that struck him was never traced and the circumstances under which he was killed were never discovered.

A. D.C. loses heavy weight screw, e.g. to get scrub board. (2 words) 185 167 24 96 57 162 37 146 12 86 135 65 181 206

B. Eddie Cantor's gal's a prosecutor 196 6 117

C. Adored fifty dove off 93 110 50 33 219

D. Results of stabbings misuses own fine dusk. (2 words) 13 132 81 20 119 201 74 171 61 210 114

E. The Cid heroically reacted to mosquito bites 85 63 213 112 41 160

F. Elizabeth nicely shows one with cultural traits 23 139 186 15 47 167

G. Number one father gains one link 55 165 100 29 150

H. Responded excessively to what the nuclear plant did before exploding 5 207 69 156 106 91 49 170 127 102 77

I. Does he keep track of meals where they're eaten? (2 words) 198 141 76 45 190 158 214 17 30 174 89 56

J. Putting Steiger on a diet results in a ground. (2 words) 197 104 67 130 164 25 79 2 205 72 88 124 52

K. If you look in this suede you'll find what is brought forth 145 36 138 180 159 60

L. Her name whips wild state. (2 words) 76 51 8 144 193 101 115 3 128 211 154 14

M. Feast dish works out shark-like meat. (2 words) 10 83 78 203 34 121 26 54 103 194 134 94 148 143

N. To start chicken with its head cut off add cornstarch 21 189 39 118 109 126 27

O. What the successful con man did with a line and a sinker. (3 words) 1 62 120 195 28 95 9 73 35 212 87

P. The last moment? Not with sixty left in the day! (2 words) 53 116 178 152 166 66 18 22 84 19 38 169

Q. Vacillates banner displayers when heard 192 92 168 165 59 181 40

R. Crockery made over anew 16 90 218 99 42 136 209 129

S. Find a duplicate flame 172 157 31 177 64

T. Stopped using retreads 131 217 111 202 98 137 183 200

U. Take back top banana 108 122 4

V. I would shorten two directions in mid-month 113 133 208 105

W. Cynic heads inside a corner 71 44 142 32 191

X. Whistle without the French bridge 147 46 70 179 155

Y. She entered a short cabinet department and insisted on quiet 43 75 173 80 199 163

Z. Drink me around a protective cloth with another me in front 187 82 123 97 68 216

AA. Make debts ready for stuffed animals. (2 words) 11 204 125 182 7 58 153 175 140 149

BB. Reached in for every one 151 161 188 48

THE RIPPER'S LADIES

Donald Rumbelow

Mention Jack the Ripper and people think of a cinematic East End where Pearly Kings and Queens dance in the street, Marie Lloyd sings from every pub counter, music halls barrel-organ out their tunes, all prostitutes wear scarlet silk gowns, hansom cabs clip-clop through cobbled gas-lit streets and adventures can be had by top-hatted bucks in silk-lined opera cloaks, with pearl studs in their cuffs and swordsticks in their hands.

Reality was much different.

Jack the Ripper's ladies. Faces puffed from too much drink; dirt-smelling, sour-breathed, middle-aged drabs. Casual pick-ups in some common lodging house, pub or back alley in Whitechapel. Five victims. Each brutally murdered and mutilated, two in one night, between 31st August and 9th November 1888. Even in death, given no dignity.

Four were butchered in the street.

No glamour to any of them. No silks, mahogany-furnished rooms, heavy drapes or lace underwear. One room, lucky if they could get it, in some slum tenement was the best to be hoped for. Even that had to be shared. Watch out! No stair handrail. Gone long ago for firewood. Flea-infested paper hanging in strips on damp stained walls. Bare boards with a kettle boiling on the hob. In one corner, a cracked washbowl on a wooden stand. A creaking bed with a lumpy straw palliasse. Worked in shifts.

Less private, but at least an alternative, one of eighty beds in a public dormitory. Whitechapel lodging houses slept nine thousand each night. Double beds were 8d, singles 4d, and 2d bought a lean on a rope stretched across the room.

No money, no bed. Only the street. Bed was a niche behind some dustbins, deep doorway, empty staircase, arch under a bridge or rotting warehouse by the river.

Life, such as it was, pivoted around that magical 4d. A single bed, not double, where they could be cocooned from reality for a few undisturbed hours.

Money. But how to get it? Woman's work was scrubbing, sweatshop tailoring, hop picking, sack or matchbox making. Wages often included the cost of materials. Women were lucky if paid tenpence for seventeen hours' sweated labour.

Prostitution paid better wages. Three-

Suspect No. 2
GEORGE CHAPMAN

Suspect No. 1
DR. NEILL CREAM

pence, twopence or a loaf of stale bread. Whitechapel had twelve hundred prostitutes. London had eighty thousand.

Nichols, Chapman, Stride and Eddowes. Basically, hard-working respectable women. Failures with children, husbands and money. Drink was their escape. None of them young, even good-looking. Nichols was forty-two years old, brown hair turning grey and five front teeth missing. Chapman was forty-five, two front teeth missing, stout, with brown wavy hair. Stride was forty-five, with dark curly hair; roof of mouth missing as well as front teeth. Claimed mouth had been injured in steamboat disaster when husband and children had been drowned.

Eddowes was forty-three years old. Everything she possessed she wore. (As did the others.) Black jacket with imitation fur collar. Dark green dress with pattern of Michaelmas daisies and gold lilies. White vest, drab linsey skirt, old dark green petticoat, white chemise, brown ribbed stockings mended with white cotton, black straw bonnet, men's lace-up boots with steel tips and heels. In her pockets: clay pipes, cigarette case, five pieces of soap, handkerchiefs, comb, and tin containing tea and sugar.

Each had been married. Each had escaped domestic pressures. Each had taken to drink. Each had abandoned families or husbands. Each had since taken up with someone else.

Nichols had been married twenty-two years before the final break-up. Several attempts made at reconciliation. Utterly useless. Left her husband immediately after birth of fifth child. He had custody and care of the five children. No apparent ill-will. For two years he allowed her 5s a week from his carpenter's wages. Stopped it immediately when he learned she was earning money as a prostitute. Her drinking, chief reason for the break-up, he could forgive. She was drunk and staggering when last seen alive, 31st August, 2:30 A.M. She boasted, "I've had my lodging money three times today and I've spent it." She was confident that she could quickly get the extra 4d. She had on a new hat.

"See what a jolly bonnet I've got now."

The black straw bonnet was by her body when it was found, cut and disembowelled, just over an hour later.

Annie Chapman had been separated four years. Her coachman husband had kept their two children, one of them a cripple, with him at Windsor. He allowed her ten shillings a week

Suspect No. 3
THE DUKE OF CLARENCE

Suspect No. 4
JAMES K. STEPHEN

Suspect No. 5
MONTAGUE J. DRUITT

From The Complete Jack The Ripper *by Donald Rumbelow published by New York Graphics Society*

from his wages; this stopped with his death eighteen months before. Chapman was an intelligent woman, clever with a needle when sober. Drink stimulated her natural pugnacity. Several days before she died, having lost a lodging house fight, she was creeping around like a sick cat, nursing a black eye and bruised chest. No money for a bed, she was turned out of a lodging house kitchen at 2:30 A.M. on 8th September. Three hours later, she went with Jack the Ripper into the backyard of 29 Hanbury Street, in daylight. Someone heard her cry out as she was seized and fell against the fence. He was too indifferent to look.

Minutes later she was found, her body sprawled obscenely against the steps, throat cut, stomach torn, clothes pushed up around her neck.

Double event, 30th September. No time to linger over Stride. Pony and trap turned into gateway moments after she had been gripped from behind and the throat cut. She lay in the gateway in Berner Street, in her left hand still, a paper tissue of cachous. Her common-law husband for the past three years thought she was at home.

No time to waste. On to Mitre Square in the City of London. Catherine Eddowes had been celebrating. She had been going to see her daughter Annie in Bermondsey. She was arrested dead drunk in Aldgate. She sobered up in the cells and was let out at 1 A.M.

"Night, old cock," she said to the gaoler.

Thirty minutes later she was dead. Throat cut, disembowelled, and the Ripper walking away wiping his bloodstained knife on a piece of her apron.

Mary Kelly breaks the pattern. Time to toy with that sharp little knife, time to gloat, time to linger.

Room 13 Miller's Court, 9th November.

Mary or Marie Jeanette Kelly. Twenty years younger, fresh-looking, pregnant, and walking the streets for the past three years. Before that, a short time in France and a fashionable house in the West End. On 9th November, at 12:30 A.M., singing heard in her room. Later a cry of "murder." So common was it that the listener turned over and went back to sleep.

The Ripper lingered over his work, piling flesh on the table by her bed. Breasts, kidneys, heart, nose, liver.

With this final obscenity the murders stopped.

Since then the theories have grown.

Butcher, baker, policeman, midwife, mad doctor, abortionist, shohet, magician, heir to the throne of England. Jack the Ripper? Nobody knows.

Ironically, as the Ripper moves up the social scale, as he has done with the passing years, so too have his victims; the higher he goes, the higher they must be upgraded. From twopenny whores they have become witnesses to a Royal marriage, the guardians of a State secret.

They have acquired a respectability, a pedigree, an importance which they never had in life.

They have become desirable.

Donald Rumbelow is the author of The Complete Jack the Ripper.

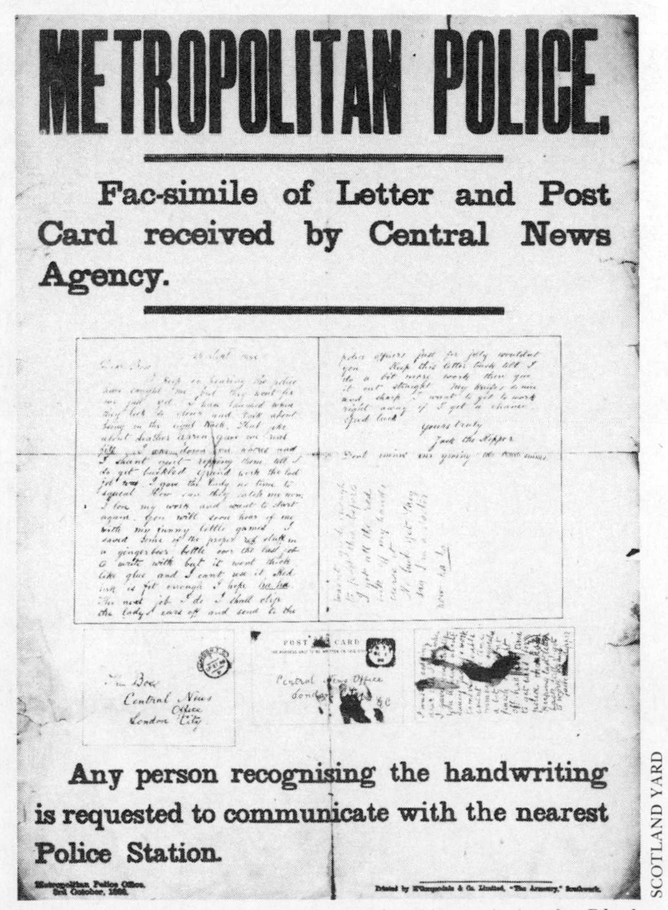

SCOTLAND YARD

The original of this message from The Ripper is in the Black Museum at New Scotland Yard. Currently, it is not on display.

THE EDINBURGH PILLOW

Hugh Douglas

She must go, I told myself. If only there were a perfect murder method.

I don't think I said it aloud, but it was at that moment the figure appeared at my side, laughing in a rippling kind of way, like a musical scale. He was a small waif-like creature, dressed in an old blue coat which hung open, and tattered moleskin trousers. A cap almost hid his dancing eyes.

"Would ye be after the perfect murder, sur?" he asked. The word "murder" was pronounced *morther* in an Irish way.

"There is no perfect murder method," I answered.

"Sure there is, sur, let me tell you about it. It's called burking after me, William Burke, native of Orrey in County Tyrone, Ireland, but lately a residenter in Edinburgh — a lovely city to be sure but the old town where I lived was a bit run-down, forsaken by the nobility and dilapidated, you might say.

"I lived there in a lodging house wi' my woman, not my wife exactly, because her husband McDougal was still to the fore, and not pretty — no, not at all pretty — but Nelly and I suited one another. Our landlord was a bad pill if ever ye met one — William Hare, and as villainous in temper as he was in looks. They called his wife Lucky because she had been fortunate enough to inherit the lodging house from her late husband. But her luck ran out when she met up wi' that scoundrel."

Burke laughed more drily than the last time, I thought.

"Well, there was another lodger at the house in the autumn of 1827, an old man named Donald — sure I never heard his other name — who died owing Hare four pounds. Hare was beside himself at the loss of the money and he came to me. Sure, I thought, the doctors at the anatomy schools of Edinburgh buy corpses for their students to dissect. A man Paterson, who worked at Dr. Knox's school, once told me they paid as much as ten pounds for a body, so we took Donald there at dead of night and they gave us seven pounds and ten shillings for him. I think they saw we were new to the game for Donald was worth more, but anyway, Hare had his four pounds and I had more nor I could earn in a month, so we were both satisfied.

"Then another lodger took sick wi' the fever, and that's bad for business in a lodging house, so we just slipped a pillow over his face and smothered him, neat as ninepence. And we got ten pounds for him — it was better than work any day."

Burke sang a little tune and danced a jig before he continued.

"Och, but the money didn't last and soon we were in need of more. We just kept our eyes open and it was amazing how many folk we found walking the streets of Edinburgh — it was a heartless place to be poor in — and they were glad to come and take a drink wi' us. Then when they were asleep we just put a pillow over their faces, and helped them on to a lasting peace. And Dr. Knox's boys were glad to buy their bodies off us at the going rate.

"We saw sixteen of them off before Hallowe'en of 1828: old Effie, the pedlar; Daft Jamie; bonnie Mary Paterson, the prostitute; a relative of Nelly; and one of my own countrywomen, Mrs. Docherty. She was the last.

An evening with Burke and Hare.

"Folk thought we were grave robbers — resurrectionists, they called us — so nobody was surprised at our comings and goings to Surgeons' Square. They paid us well, and it was a grand life, better by far than mending shoes or working on farms all summer.

"Our corpses were always prize specimens. They looked as if they had died in their sleep, peaceful as you like, and not a mark on them to suggest violence. Sure, it wasn't really violent: I told the police that."

"The police?" I asked. "How did they come into it? I thought yours was the perfect murder method."

Burke scratched his chin. "So it was, and we'd never have been caught but for the fact that we got careless and Nelly's cousin, Ann Gray, and her man found old Mrs. Docherty's body. They wouldn't be shut up and went to the police."

He smiled. "Aye, even then the police could prove nothing, our murder method was perfect — perfect except that it involved that vile betrayer Hare. He did a nasty deal with the law in return for a promise that they'd let him off Scot free." Burke's voice turned bitter. "Hare and Lucky got away because they told a pack of lies and half-truths about Nelly and me. Aye, but Nelly still got off. I'm glad of that for she wasn't a bad soul — dour and Scottish, but not bad."

"And you?"

He drew a hand across his throat. "I paid the penalty on the gibbet at Edinburgh market cross. A nasty experience that; I thought the mob would get me before the hangman, but they didn't. The others suffered longer: Nelly had to go to Australia and Lucky — lucky to the last — was a nursemaid to a fine family in Paris. Hare got his desserts; blinded in a limepit and left to beg in the streets of London.

"And our perfect murder method of suffocation went into the dictionary as burking. Fancy that, William Burke gave a word to the English language."

"Excuse me, Mr. Burke," I said, "but asphyxiation — I mean, burking — isn't a perfect murder method any more. Thanks to all the dissection of bodies people like you supplied, doctors can tell nowadays whether a body was smothered or not."

"Do you tell me that," he answered. "Now is that not a pity."

He began to hum:

Up the close and down the stair,
Ben the house wi' Burke and Hare.
Burke's the butcher, Hare's the thief,
And Knox the boy that buys the beef.

I turned to speak to him but he was gone.

Hugh Douglas is the author of Burke and Hare — The True Story.

THE DAY I RIPPED OFF LIZZIE'S HOUSE

Ellen Stern

FALL RIVER HISTORICAL SOCIETY

Who, me? I was the daughter who snuck out every Mother's Day in the dewy, dewy dawn to gather a bouquet of violets for pre-breakfast presentation. The daughter who could hear the car coming from six blocks away and streaked upstairs to get Daddy's slippers so they'd be at his favorite chair before he was. I sneezed at cats because she did, scorned his relatives because he did, hummed along with the Whiffenpoofs because she did, guttled raw clams because he did.

So what's a nice girl like me doing with an obsession like this? Why, when there are all sorts of disasters to choose from, does the case of Lizzie Borden absolutely rivet me?

Truly, we have little in common. Lizzie was a dour spinster who loathed her porky stepmother and persisted in calling her Mrs. Borden. She was no more cuddly with her gangly old father, and she yearned for his money. She took none of her meals with the parents, shared no secrets, smiled rarely, and avoided them as much as possible . . . which couldn't have been easy in their narrow little house in Fall River. The tension must have been terrific.

On the muggy morning of August 4, 1892, Lizzie had had all she was going to take. She picked up a hatchet, and hacked. It was a crime convenient to commit. Bridget the maid was out back washing windows; Emma the sister was out of town; Uncle John was out on a walk. The deed done, Lizzie buried her weapon in a bed of ashes in the cellar, washed her hands, changed her clothes, and was in fine spirits when the cops came. She had two different alibis — both perfectly silly, both totally accepted by the neighbors and authorities. A couple of days later, she took the dress spattered with her parents' blood, tossed it into the kitchen stove, and nobody stopped her. And, because the Bordens were a prominent family, and Lizzie a woman (and a churchgoing woman to boot), she got away with murder. I do *not* admire her.

Nonetheless, on a muggy August morning nearly seventy-five years later, I found myself on Lizzie's front step. We were on our way to Cape Cod, a blond chap named Chuck and I, when I located Fall River on the map. Aha! I thought, and casually asked if we might take a

Court photograph of Mrs. Borden, in the second-floor bedroom.

Lizzie Borden took an axe
And gave her Mother forty whacks.
When she saw what she had done,
She gave her Father forty-one.

FALL RIVER HISTORICAL SOCIETY

Court photograph of Mr. Borden, in the living room, on the couch.

slight detour to drive through the town. He said if it wasn't too much out of the way. I said it didn't seem to be.

It was. But by the time this was clear, we were fairly well entangled in Fall River's dusty streets. Chuck's face was blotchy with anger. His foot jerked at the gas pedal.

"What street is it we're looking for?" he raged. By this time, it was evident that we were not here merely to drive through town. We needed The House.

"In 1892, it was Second Street," I answered. "I think it still is."

"You *think* it still is?"

It still was. But the numbers were no longer the same. In 1892, Lizzie did her stuff in a wooden house with a two-gated picket fence in front and a barn in back. The address was 92 Second Street. On my August day, the house looked just like its photographs, but the picket fence was gone and a printing plant had replaced the barn. The number had been changed to 230.

"Stop!" I cried, any compassion for Chuck now turned to frenzy. "That's it!"

"That's *it*?"

He looked with absolute wonder. I couldn't blame him. Who but a devotee would cherish such a site? Such a plain little house. Behind those doors such horrors had happened? From there came legend and a jingle? There?

"I know this sounds crazy," I said, sounding crazy, "but I have to do something."

Chuck sat very still.

"This'll just take a second."

I threw open the car door, leapt into the steaming potholes of Second Street, swirled to the sidewalk, and stood, in awe, before the house. The heat was intense and my hands were shaking (surely more than Lizzie's ever did). What to do now? Knock at the door? Pose as an Avon lady? Order some envelopes from the printer who now inhabited the place? No. I wanted a *souvenir.* But what?

A piece of house.

I needed something that had been there on That Day. So, knowing that beneath the ghastly gray paint, and beneath the coat under that, and beneath the coat under that, etc., etc., was truly The-Paint-From-The-House-That-She-Lived-In-When-It-Occurred, I reached over and snapped off a chip for myself. A relic is a relic.

When I returned to New York — with my chip and without my Chuck — I had the prize laminated in a Broadway arcade. For years, I carried it with me, displaying it as proudly as a Schliemann his Trojan shard. And then, in some move or other, I lost it.

Every summer, as August looms, I am thrown again into a Lizzie tizzy. And I am bereft.

Ellen Stern is an editor at New York *magazine.*

Chapter 6

MODUS OPERANDI

FRED WINKOWSKI

PARAPHERNALIA
Making Use of What's Available

Jeanine Larmoth

Murders cannot be committed haphazardly. They must be planned. Paraphernalia laid in. Not weapons: paraphernalia. Clocks, mirrors, blotters, telephones, candlesticks, decanters — no object too ordinary. Clocks and telephones help establish times. In the ABC's of murder, B is for "blotter," which soaks up the message in reverse. The mirror can read it. Mirrors also let a witness overlook the flicking of a little arsenic that the murderer did not intend to be seen, the forging of a will, or a delicious embrace in the garden below which, unfortunately, involves the murderer's best friend and his wife. Glasses hold sleeping-draughts; decanters are for poisoned port. In case of need, paraphernalia may be converted so that the least suspicious object, tape measure to flowerpot, turns into lethal weapon, thus giving a familiar object exciting potential and titillating us with the prospect of an outbreak in our own flowerpots.

The telephone, with its connections to telephone exchange, operator, call box and neighbours, is a fine example of paraphernalia. Lonely country houses become infinitely lonelier infinitely faster when lines go down in a storm, or under the killer's wire cutters. Isolation makes the breath come shallow with fear when there's a dead phone in hand; a desperate sense of impotence follows the announcement that the phone is out of order.

Telephone calls work with almost as much efficiency for alibis as timetables. Making such calls from a call box has obvious advantages. A call box in a residential section is an excellent observation post. Tucked behind its little glass windowpanes, one can appear to be making a telephone call indefinitely, meanwhile keeping a certain house under surveillance. Furthermore, a call placed from a call box cannot be traced or overheard by the operator; it may remain anonymous. To be even surer that it does, the wise murderer goes to the call box supplied with another good piece of paraphernalia: a silk scarf to disguise his voice, or for use should it be necessary to strangle a customer already in the box. This action is not the offspring of irritation at having to wait. No, with that same uncanny sense of the time it takes a coin to drop in the box, the murderer knows that a witness has just this minute put two and two together, and is going to make someone else, probably the police, privy to her calculations. That, of course, won't do. Her three minutes are up. Were the same disguised-voice call to be made from home, another member of the household might remark the purple silk scarf stuffed in the murderer's mouth to distort his voice, cackle with laughter at an accent he is affecting, or ask embarrassing questions afterwards, such as, "Why did you say you'd lost your gun when it's just where you left it hidden in the metal box under the rosebush?" Undesirable heckling is avoided in call boxes.

The principal purpose of a car in a mystery is to have it break down. If on a country road, it should break down near a good inn, with a jolly, loquacious landlord ready for pumping, or within easy walking distance of the home of friends, where the driver of the deliberately disabled vehicle wants to do some snooping, at around lunch or dinner time. Lunch is more considerate as it is less formal. It is not a bad idea to understand how a car is put together to know which part, when removed, will stall it.

Following a murder on a train, investigation reveals a plethora of paraphernalia peculiar to the setting, as well as the usual clues. The blood-stained handkerchiefs and knives may be found in a sponge-bag hanging on a locked door between compartments. No worthy Englishwoman goes to sleep without arranging her sponge-bag; it is as imperative as saying one's prayers. Sponge-bags are as properly hung on doorknobs as May baskets to be handy for murderers who mysteriously open the locked door and slip the bloody knife inside. Only the English could call a container for their washing apparatus a sponge-bag. It is clearly a bag of lumpish aspect with drawstrings, fading flowered fabric, and a lining of yellowing rubber. It is never dry, but in a permanent state of fug. A bloody knife won't make it worse.

A murder in almost any location is likely to uncover the tooth-glass with its dregs of sleeping-draught. The tooth-glass is placed on a shelf beneath the mirror and over the washstand. One can, in lieu of sleeping-draughts, drink poison or whisky from it, with somewhat differing results.

Of importance equal to paraphernalia is the murderer's costume. The murderer must be dressed to kill. He should check out his closet and his tailor to be sure he is properly kitted out. Old clothes are best because they blend in better with the scenery, and because they may need getting rid of. A man who sets out to do murder in a jaunty new outfit has only himself to blame. Besides, it is common. If, on the other hand, he chooses loud checks and a cigar, he may find himself the victim instead. Similarly, a too-perfect ensemble is better avoided — shining buttons, yachting cap, that kind of thing. Definitely un-English, therefore

No worthy Englishwoman goes to sleep without arranging her sponge-bag.

unsympathetic. Ease, the ultimate attribute, is better expressed in shabbiness. A murderer may well get away with it if he is properly dressed. He should, however, be sure everything he wears is in good repair. No loose threads left hanging. There is bound to be a thorny rosebush on his path waiting for a strand of tweed to tell it to the police.

One basic is the old raincoat. Apart from being commonplace and disposable, it has pockets. Not for guns alone: that's obvious. Pockets are for gnur. Without a flourishing collection of gnur, where will the police be when they try to analyze the murderer's origins and whereabouts for the last ten years? "Ah, that morsel of yellow dust can only be from a highland estuary of the Upper Ganges!" "He was eating whelks by the London docks just two days ago." "See this fragment of paper? Only used by the War Office to notify heroes that they've received the Victorian Cross." The murderer will, of course, show the same tact in removing the label from his coat as from his victim's.

A cap is handy. It is very easy to fool people by switching caps. They are firmer over steaming cups of tea than false moustaches, and quicker to put on. But if a murderer should decide to wear a cap, he is honorbound to step over to the train station. There is nothing that provides the locals with more innocent entertainment on a dull afternoon than to watch a man in a peaked cap nipping in at one side of a railway carriage and, having climbed out the other side, a few seconds later walking down the platform affecting unconcern and a bowler.

Of course, a murderer must never wear his own shoes. Bigger is better; there's no point being uncomfortable. He'll soon be in a tight-enough squeeze. Also, he can fill the empty space at the toes with weights, for if he doesn't, sure as shooting (or poisoning), his footprints won't sink deep enough for their size, and we know where that leads. Straight to the jailhouse. Plimsolls are worth packing, if only to stuff up the chimney. They needn't even be worn, if the ritual is observed. If they are not worn, however, they should be smeared with a bit of mud and grass that could grow only in one spot — beneath the victim's window. It is only fair to the police. But as most murders involve a surprising amount of athleticism, it never hurts to have a pair. In fact, a few warm-up exercises won't be amiss. A little light running in the morning or quite late at night not only helps the muscle tone, it helps in establishing alibis. If the murderer can appear at one end of the village five minutes before the murder occurs at the opposite end, a powerful sprint will have stood him in good stead. Or, if he can leap off a train, dash across a meadow, fire a well-aimed shot *en passant,* hop a stile and walk smoothly through the French doors for tea before the train arrives in the village, he is that much ahead.

To put the final touch to a murder, an old suitcase is essential for stuffing things in: the leftover murdering costume, a batch of incriminating papers picked up from the victim's safe, a cachet of jewels to be collected twenty years later from Left Luggage. The suitcase should be cheap and look like everyone else's. Nothing fancy, French, decorated with labels from the Ritz, or otherwise recognizable. It can, naturally, be hurled from a fast-moving train in the midst of a forest, but Left Luggage is better. Then, if the murderer yearns for an evening of nostalgia years later, he can take the ticket, fetch the case out again, and have a round of reminiscences among his souvenirs. He might even have put the flowerpot, slightly used tape measure, or other weapon in there, as well as a flower picked near the scene of the crime.

Success lies in ordinariness. Paraphernalia or costume. "Whoever-would-have-thought" objects, "whoever-would-have-thought" people in the dreariest possible clothes. If a murderer is, as boringly usual, the middle. A murderer should be like everyone else; no one will bother him. The best murderers are the dullest, the sort that have spent a lifetime smouldering in the woodwork. Which also fuels one of murder's stongest motives: the need to do just one thing with panache.

Jeanine Larmoth is the coauthor of Murder on the Menu.

My favorite fiction writers are Victor Hugo, Dostoevsky and O. Henry . . . . Today, the only kind of fiction that I read for pleasure (as distinguished from reading for information) is popular fiction, specifically mystery stories . . . . The incomparably best writer of mysteries is Agatha Christie. She has written dozens of novels, and — with the exception of a few, particularly her last ones — they are brilliantly ingenious, intriguing and suspenseful. My favorites are: Death on the Nile, And Then There Were None, The A.B.C. Murders *and, above all,* The Mysterious Mr. Quin. *(This last is a collection of short stories, and is the best-written of Agatha Christie's books.)*

The Objectivist Calendar, April 1977
AYN RAND

LAUNDERING MONEY

Numbered Accounts and Other Tax Shelters

Stanley H. Brown

MATTHEW SEAMAN

Consider this a cautionary tale for every decent citizen who fantasizes The One Big Caper followed by a life of carefree luxury. I don't know your particular vision of the perfect crime against property but a history professor once planned the theft and disposal of an invaluable ancient coin collection; a machinist used to case the movements of an armored car at a big shopping mall every Christmas season; a social worker dreamed of stamping out urban evil by robbing the take of a big-time heroin dealer. If the score was big enough to markedly change the way they live, they now know that along with whatever guilt and fear goes with their illegal acts, there are new problems to be faced. First, storage; second, using the money without attracting the attention of the authorities, especially the folks at the Internal Revenue Service.

If you figure that all you'd have to do is shove your attaché case full of money under the bed and then reach in every morning for walking-around money, you'd be very wrong. The housekeeper might accidentally find the cache and dip into it as well. So, maybe you decide to clean the house yourself and not let anyone in when you're not there. But you'll bleed a little until you can be sure the satchel is secure.

Safe-deposit boxes run a couple of risks. If you go to the box infrequently, you'll have to carry too much cash around with you. And if you go too often, your attendance record, duly recorded on your file card, may attract attention. Besides, if law enforcement people suspect you of a crime, they can get a court order and have a look.

Put the money in your checking account, and you encounter a different kind of problem. Anytime you show up with more than $10,000 in cash, federal law requires your bank to file a report to the Treasury Department, unless you're in a business where such quantities of cash are normal. But don't think you can avoid that problem simply by depositing a little less, because that will come under the category of an unusual transaction. Your bank may not report you, but a record will wind up somewhere readily accessible to the tax people. Of course, if your loot is relatively small and your dreams of luxury are modest, you probably can risk spending a few thousand a year without attracting any attention. But that's small-time stuff,

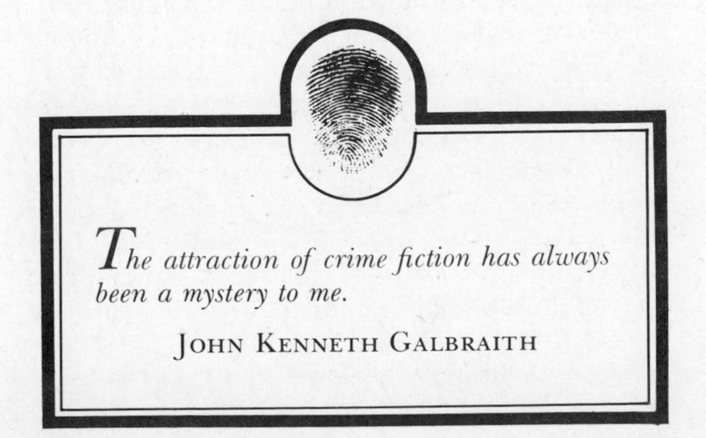

The cover of an early song sheet which extolled the virtues of "Counterfeit Bill," the operative word being Bill. Research proves women would rather marry men with that name than with any other.

nothing like the fruit of your really big score.

What you're up against is the need to launder your money. Most regular-type people never heard of "laundering" until the aftermath of the Watergate burglary and all those revelations about improper payments by Gulf Oil, 3M, and much of the cream of American corporate enterprise. But don't look to Watergate for instruction in this process.

Strictly speaking, Dahlberg's $25,000 campaign contribution and the money that went from Gulf to Senator Hugh Scott involved the opposite of laundering. In these cases, clean money was dirtied. What they do have in common with traditional laundering is that the origins of the money were concealed in the process. What they also demonstrate is that the President of the United States and the chiefs of some of the best-run enterprises in the world, with access to the finest money handling and accounting services available, got caught.

The lesson here is that if your scheme involves a lot of people, somebody will talk or a record of some part of the transaction will turn up in the wrong hands. The Treasury has made relatively little use of bank reports showing unusually large cash transactions. Nevertheless, banks represent a real danger as corroborating evidence of the existence of untaxed money. In other words, if you mess around with a legitimate bank, you'll leave tracks.

If there is a technical definition of "laundering," it probably goes something like this: the rerouting, or conversion in any way, of hot untaxed money or other assets into untraceable or apparently legitimate cash or assets. Needless to say, there are no textbooks on laundering; nor do bankers, lawyers or others connected with money and its movements want to talk for the record on who does it or how.

What is known about the process comes pretty much from the few instances in which the authorities have managed to get people into court or before congressional committees. A small-time hustler named Jerry Zelmanowitz spent some time a few years ago testifying before a Senate subcommittee on how he turned stolen securities into clean cash for the Mob. Until he came along (he would have us believe), your typical thief would keep the money, jewelry and other disposable assets but throw away whatever securities were stolen. Zelmanowitz says he changed all that by taking the securities to Europe, where he set up accounts in various banks, transferred money around by Telex to establish a pattern of legitimate transactions, then introduced his stolen stocks and bonds into the system he had set up. Typically, the stolen paper would be used as collateral for loans, the proceeds of which could then be invested for legitimate purposes. As long as the loans were outstanding, nobody paid any attention to the collateral sitting in the bank vaults. Meanwhile, Zelmanowitz had created a nice pool of usable capital for his clients. They could repay or keep refinancing their debt, or they could even default on the loans and let the bank dispose of the collateral.

The trouble with this method is that some bank clerk might decide to check the numbers on the securities against lists of stolen property. One operative, in what seems to be a kind of underworld banking system, worked out a neat method for getting around that. He found somebody in a bank that held about $10 billion in securities for customers and made him a confederate in exchanging his own hot securities for legitimate ones of the same issue. As long as nobody at the bank checked the serial numbers, there was no problem.

A couple of years ago Chemical Bank in New York discovered its facilities were being used for another kind of laundering. Employees of the bank were routinely changing the small, dirty bills that are the retail currency of the heroin trade. The $1 and $5 bills that come out of your wallet, or some old lady's snatched purse, are cumbersome to deal with. You can't fly down to Mexico with laundry bags full of money to buy more dope. You certainly wouldn't want to walk into a bank in Switzerland with huge loads of street money. It's undignified, and it attracts a lot of attention. So the dealers simply found themselves some bank employees who would exchange the small stuff for $50 and $100 bills. The bank lost nothing in the process, though the employees, against federal regulations in effect since 1974, failed to report the $10,000-plus transactions. What they also neglected was declaring as income the bribes they received from the dealers — about 1 percent of the money they laundered. The U.S. Attorney's office in New York figures that more than $8 million in dirty cash was handled through Chemical Bank.

Any legitimate business that takes in a lot of cash provides a way to clean up dirty money.

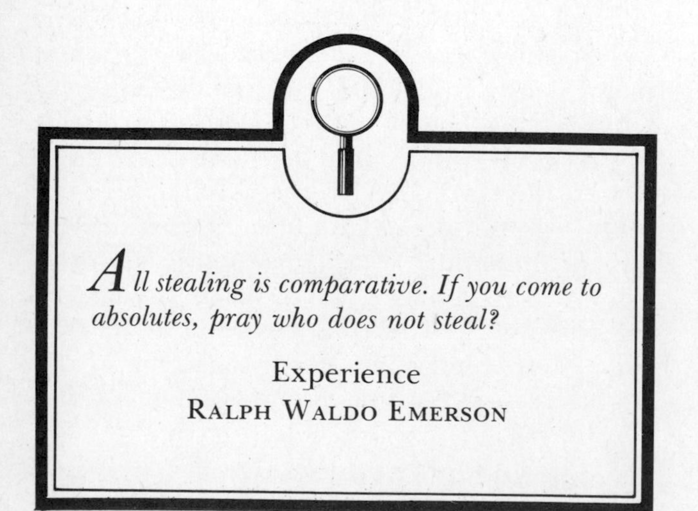

WIDE WORLD PHOTOS

The Swiss Credit Bank, Zurich. "Mrs. Helga Hughes" cashed checks here in the amount of $650,000.

One thief used some of his money to buy a diner. He would relieve the cashier, then put some cash in the till and ring up some phony sales. He gradually increased the amount of cash he would process, so as not to attract attention. When he wasn't satisfied with the rate of flow, he bought a second and then a third restaurant. Now he had a business big enough to allow him to travel lavishly on an expense account, ostensibly to scout out locations for other restaurants around the world.

The Internal Revenue Service can be dealt with rather easily. All they want is for you to report your income properly and pay the taxes due the government. Your income is "earned" the moment you complete your crime and take the bonds or coins in hand, not when you get the money from the fence. It's tempting to think of the tax collector as a menacing beast who will be rendered harmless by your paying maybe 60 percent of your loot. But all you can be sure of then is that you won't have federal tax problems. If the revenue people think you got the money by committing a federal offense (you aren't required to state on your return where you get your money), they'll tell the FBI. And if they have reason to believe that you committed a felony under state law, they'll notify state and local authorities. Mostly, they just want their money. But again, by paying up, you attract attention.

There are ways to pay taxes and not attract attention, but you must first put the money somewhere safe while you finish up your laundering. Burying it or banking it has serious drawbacks. Traveler's checks don't. Traveler's checks are secure, easy to buy, to use, and even to recover if lost, stolen or burned. Especially burned.

In any large city in the United States you can buy at least five different kinds of traveler's checks. And within a half-mile of Park Avenue in New York, you can buy them at seventeen different places, then walk over to Fifth Avenue and buy them in another dozen places. The reason you want so many places is that issuing agencies must keep special records on all purchases of checks exceeding $5,000. That means it will take you a couple of days to buy about $150,000 worth of traveler's checks in a way that won't be noticed. If you buy only $1,000 denominations, you'll wind up with a hefty wad; $100 checks will require an attaché case. But your storage problem can be eliminated by one simple act: take your checks home and burn them, then flush the ashes down the toilet. Needless to say, you'll take good care of the receipt showing the numbers on the checks.

What you've done is create disembodied but readily reconstituted cash. If you decide to take off for Abu Dubai, you'll be able to pass through U.S. Customs with no concern about the requirement that you report exports of more than $5,000 in cash — a requirement that in any case has barely been enforced. But it's on the books and you don't want to violate it, because Congress seems on the point of leaning on the Treasury to try harder to close down the laundries. They aren't after you; they're look-

LISTENING TO MONEY TALK

The Billion Dollar Sure Thing: Paul E. Erdman
Canceled Accounts: Harris Greene
Going Public: David Westheimer
Not a Penny More, Not a Penny Less: Jeffrey Archer
The Silver Bears: Paul E. Erdman
The Swiss Account: Leslie Waller

Among Scotland Yard's trophies are these burglary tools which were left behind after an unsuccessful raid on a bank vault. Paraphernalia included acetylene torches, hack saws, drop cloths and pressure gauges.

ing for all that Mob money we keep hearing about, which, along with petro-dollars, is taking over civilization. But even if they're looking for somebody else's family, they might just stumble into yours.

When you get to where you're going, all you have to do is show up at the appropriate bank and report that your checks have been destroyed. Pretty soon, you'll get replacements that you can spend, or bank, or invest.

The spending is simple. Nobody is looking for you, nobody knows you've done anything wrong. But our tax people have offices over there. Again, they're not out for you; it's the large corporate hustlers they want. Still, they're there, and they might see you throw around more than the average tourist.

You didn't break the law and risk ruin just to blow it all on a big holiday. You want to invest and take your time finding the good life. So you bring your reconstituted traveler's checks to a bank, and despite the recent embarrassment of the Crédit Suisse over the scandal in its branch in Chiasso, Switzerland is still one of the better havens for laundering. The problem here is that the Swiss don't like to be thought of as a haven for laundering dirty money from Third World tyrants and the Mafia, and some of their banks have lately requested that U.S. nationals sign a form releasing the bank from the provisions of the Swiss bank secrecy laws. This enables them to report your activities to U.S. authorities if they're asked. There are, however, plenty of banks in Switzerland that will happily open an account for you when you lay your nest egg on the desk.

Once you have the account, you can instruct the bank to invest or transfer the money. One thing to do with dirty money is to buy Eurobonds. These are bearer securities, so they don't have your name on them. They earn a decent rate of interest. They're safe. And they're easily marketable and redeemable in just about every Western European currency.

But now you've just bought yourself another count of fraud. When you file your tax return, you'll probably answer "no" to the question about whether you have a foreign bank account. A lot of Americans who travel and do business abroad have them for legitimate reasons, so if you've elected to report the income from your caper and pay the taxes up front, you may also want to tell the feds that you have a Swiss account. This may not attract any attention, but it will put your name in a different file and that's not what you need.

Maybe you want the money earning a little interest or dividends. You ought to pay taxes on those earnings at least, because this may simplify your next problem — getting the money back into the States when you're ready to live full-time on your loot. The longer the money sits abroad, the less likely it is to attract attention when it starts coming back into your life.

The Mob (we are led to believe) has all kinds of ways of passing hot cash through otherwise legit enterprises. Any business or profession that routinely takes in a lot of cash offers opportunities for laundering: gambling casinos, restaurants, medical practices — all have been used effectively.

Even an evangelist was used for a time by a big Midwestern operation. When the tent show hit town, a messenger would arrive with a bag of cash which was dropped into collection boxes as they were passed among the faithful. That money was then counted along with the rest. It got back to its original owners, less a contribution to the greater glory of the Lord, in the form of overpayments for chartered buses, construction of churches and schools, and even legal fees.

Transferring your problem to somebody else can be useful. One thief bought a beach house at a bargain price. What didn't show on anybody's books was that the seller also took a lot of unmentioned cash in payment. The buyer had transferred his problem to the seller.

Every method of laundering has endless variations. Many involve banks and corporate entities in such places as the island of Jersey and the Duchy of Liechtenstein. False but convincing identities abound — so much so that the U.S. Passport Office has been considering the tightening of the passport-issuing process. After all, you have only to get the real birth certificate of someone of your sex and age who is dead. One traveling representative of a crime syndicate had more than twenty U.S. passports that he used as identification for opening foreign bank and securities accounts. He reasoned that since many billions of dollars move by Telex every day through the money markets of the world, no one bank would ever be able to sort out the honest from the crooked money.

Thus money can have a life of its own, irrespective of its origins. The purpose of laundering is to create that new identity. The most important element in the success of such operations seems to be patience. But that is also the trap, because if you've scarred your conscience by committing a heavy crime, you've already lost your patience with the straight and narrow. And once that happens, you're going to leave tracks. And they're going to get you.

Stanley H. Brown's most recent book is the biography of H.L. Hunt.

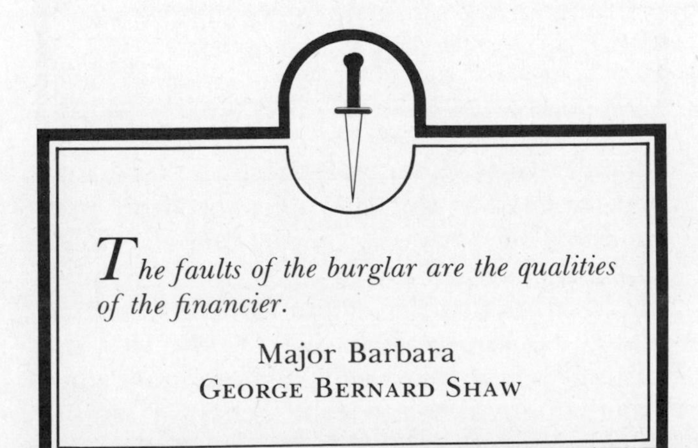

SMUGGLING PITFALLS

Letitia Twyffert

Customs agents can spot a chiseler in two seconds flat. What they look for are obvious discrepancies: a seemingly fat person with a thin person's wardrobe; a beehive hairdo on an otherwise chic woman; an adult carrying a stuffed teddy bear; a middle-aged guitar player; perspiration on one's upper lip in the middle of January. Any one of these is apt to get the would-be smuggler a trip to the disrobing room, and if contraband is bared — along with everything else — in will come a medical type, with rubber gloves, who will investigate all of the body's more interesting nooks and crannies.

Intuition is what makes a good customs agent, but unfortunately for the smuggler there are backup systems should the agent's intuition be taking a day off. There is, for example, the Canine Corps: specially trained German shepherds and golden retrievers who sniff up luggage, then yap their muzzles off if they detect marijuana, cocaine, heroin or even plastic explosives. Then there is a little item called the TECS, short for the Treasury Enforcement Communications System — a computer built into the luggage conveyor belt at most major entry points. Your declaration slip is fed into it, and it discreetly signals the agent if you have any sort of record on file with the Department — in which case he whips out his jeweler's loupe to determine if your tiara is Woolworth paste or Harry Winston carbon. Then there are the x-ray machines, the Indian trackers, the frogmen, the closed-circuit TV, the intrusion detector system, the airborne infrared system and the anonymous phone callers. Of course, some informants would rather identify themselves since the Treasury Department has this charming incentive program called "Awards and Compensations" which thrusts up to $50,000 into grasping hands. (Don't worry about the feds having enough bucks to pay up. Next to the IRS, the Customs Department pulls in more money per year than any other federal agency — roughly $5 billion. And it costs them only 3¢ on the dollar to get it. Said one customs official: "If we

SMUGGLER'S SYNDICATE

"A Chemical Detective," the last story in Thomas W. Knox's *The Talking Handkerchief and Other Stories* (1893), concerns a brandy-smuggling ring operating out of the Port of New York.

There's a dead smuggler (and his missing cache of gems) in Erle Stanley Gardner's *Bird in the Hand.*

There's a seafaring smuggler named Captain Gault in a short story collection by William Hope Hodgson called *Captain Gault: Being the Exceedingly Private Log of a Sea-Captain* (1917).

There's Kek Huuygens, indisputably successful smuggler in one novel (*The Hochman Miniatures*) and several short stories by Robert L. Fish.

There's drug smuggling from one end of Spain to the other in Julian Rathbone's *Bloody Marvelous.*

An attempt to defraud the Paris custom-house. Modern smugglers hide valuables in their afro hair-dos. A few years back, the bouffant and beehive styles were used with equally unsuccessful results.

sold stock, we'd be a terrific buy; we're a spectacular moneymaking operation. In fact, we do sell stock — U.S. Treasury Bonds.")

Fictional smugglers, say the feds, are either too corny or too eccentric. They'd be caught, zip-zip. Any story in which a smuggler tries to get past customs by means of a false pregnancy, a mislabeled shipping container, a hollowed-out book, a false-bottomed suitcase, a double-diapered baby, a stuffed D cup, a painted-over Rembrandt, a recently implanted back molar inlay, a tricky platform shoe heel or a doll tummied with valuables is a bad account. The customs museum is crammed with just such relics. What's more, the customs people have big mouths; they pass on interesting tidbits such as these to the 135 member nations of the International Customs Council.

And, as they are quick to remind you, don't think for a minute that just because you got past them at the checkpoint, you're home free. They have five years to catch up with you before the statute of limitations runs out. And that's a long time for thieves *not* to fall out.

Letitia Twyffert once smuggled a box of Oreo cookies into a Weight Watchers meeting.

ITEMS THAT NEVER MADE IT THROUGH CUSTOMS

1. 138 braided dog leashes. Value: $100
2. 420 small bars soap w/ cases bearing legend "Restaurant Laurent, N.Y." Value: $35
3. 2,500 peat pots. Value: $30
4. 822 single rubber disposable gloves. Value: $44
5. 298 basketball nets Value: $220
6. 6 doz. moustache steins. Value: $36
7. 8 sm. boxes Shabbat candles. Value: $16
8. 72 dice sets. Value: $144
9. 65 handsaws. Value: $65
10. 40 lbs. bright common nails. Value: $20
11. 3 pkgs. *Two Gentlemen Sharing*: 9460 ft. comp. pos. 35 mm color safety stock. Good condition English version *Wedding Night*: 9295 ft. comp. pos. 35 mm color safety stock, complete. NO RIGHTS. Value: $1312
12. 2 cans *The Scarecrow in a Garden of Cucumbers*: 7095 ft. 35 mm comp. pos. color safety stock. Good condition English version complete. NO RIGHTS. Value: $497
13. 1 carton 57 paperback books: *The Cooler.* Value: $18

WIRETAPPING
A Session with a Debugger

Thomas Seligson

There are those who say, with the walls so thin, why even bother wiretapping? But they miss the point. Wiretapping to some of us smacks of Bond and brethren. It goes hand-in-cloak-and-dagger with winging to Beirut under an assumed name, putting one's resources for survival regularly to the test, outwitting the Blofelds, vanquishing the Oddjobs and winning the affections of the Pussy Galores. It goes with the .25 Beretta automatics, the Aston-Martins outfitted with oil-slick dispensers. It is part of the standard equipage of the fictional spy. Does a red-blooded American boy deserve less?

Frankly, I've always wanted to plant an ice-cube bug in a Russian general's martini, and I've always wanted to be given the anti-bugging devices that would protect me from his agents doing the same. I've long been riveted to the toys of espionage, and nothing so mundane as thin walls is going to take them away from me.

You needn't even be a bona fide spy to play with these toys anymore. Judging from recent ads in the *Wall Street Journal* and the Sunday *Times* ("Is your phone tapped? We can check it out for you!"), bugging — both in and out of government — is now widespread. Husbands bug wives; corporations bug competitors; presidents bug themselves. It's getting so poor Harry Palmer's going to have to stand on line to get his bugs. Seems the whole world is as enamored of this spy stuff as I am.

In the guise of a Mafia racketeer feeling the heat, I got one of these "bug" companies on the phone. They invited me over to visit and carefully staying within the law said they were not buggers but, in fact, debuggers. The difference is more semantic than practical.

A vice-president escorted me down the hall to his plush corner office. A compact, bearded man, he lived up to my expectations: strong, angular face; dark, deep-set eyes; a long scar on his cheek that looked like it was left by a knife. I would not have wanted to run into him in a back alley of Prague.

There was a large television console beside his desk. Six separate screens with six separate views of the premises.

"That's so I can see who's out front. Saw you on the way in. You don't realize it, but you're being photographed right this second. Tape-recorded as well. I like to keep a record of everyone who comes to see me."

Not an unimpressive opener, I thought, a bit unnerved at the idea of a hidden camera pointed in my direction and a microphone concealed a few inches from my nose. Perhaps more understandable in the Pentagon than in a private company, but certainly amenable to my fantasies.

Then the V.P. explained his company.

"The average businessman doesn't give a damn that the U.S. Embassy is threatened by the Russians. He doesn't care about lasers. He's concerned about his competition, that's all. Sixty percent of our clients are businessmen trying to keep the competition from snooping

CULVER PICTURES

Contrary to appearances, this wiretapper is not bugging the wall. He is merely holding up the device he used to intercept a telephone call. The conversation was recorded and used in court, to the detriment of the caller.

at their marketing reports. We get a lot of advertising companies, shipping lines, fashion companies."

So much for my double agents and racketeers. But maybe he himself was a reformed agent? (I have intractable fantasies. They die a slow, malingering death.)

The V.P. leaned back, lit up a pipe and looked for all the world like "M" grown old and crusty. But it turned out his background was engineering and his specialty in school was the design of surveillance equipment. Much too straightforward to be a cover story. He even hinted that he had indeed once worked as a professional bugger and wiretapper. More confessions were halted when his secretary's phone rang and he pressed a button which let him listen in. Now he reminded me of Gene Hackman in *The Conversation* — a security specialist so obsessed by his work that he no longer had even the slightest regard for privacy. I began to get a little uneasy.

"At one time we bugged and we debugged," he said, "but the Crime Control Act of 1968 made electronic eavesdropping by private individuals illegal. At the same time it also made it easier for the police to do legal eavesdropping under certain conditions."

"I imagine the bill must have hurt your business," I said, figuring it probably affected buggers the way détente hurt spies.

My V.P. smiled. "Not exactly. Sixty-eight turned out to be an interesting year. Prior to June 18 everybody who manufactured and sold bugging equipment did so openly. You knew who they were. Once the law came in, all open operations ceased. The major electronics manufacturers — Lafayette Radio, Radio Shack, Allied Radio — knew there was still a market, but it had to be approached differently. So they put out the same kinds of equipment and called them 'baby-sitters' and 'wireless intercom' and 'telephone monitor' and even 'fun toy.' Anything but 'bugging equipment.'

"So you see we had the demise of an official bugging business and the birth of the electronic toy business. And now, since they were produced by large chains, the 'toys' sold for much less than before. Telephone bugging devices used to be in the three-hundred-dollar range. After 1968, Lafayette Radio came out with a 'telephone monitor' for about fifteen dol-

COMMUNICATION CONTROL SYSTEMS INC.

The Spectrum Analyzer. It locates bugs, permits operator to tune in to any RF signal, has a resolution of 3,000 to 30,000 cycles. It is advertised as foolproof and fail-safe.

lars. Consequently, although the purpose of the law was to restrict illegal bugging, its ultimate effect was to make the equipment more readily available to the man in the street.

"Hell, at fifteen dollars a throw, if I want to know what's going on in your office, I can afford to plant a whole line of bugs there. I can even afford to put one where you'll be sure to find it. Once you see that one, you'll think that's all there is and speak freely everywhere but in front of it. So one of my other bugs is bound to pick you up."

The V.P. said the most common way to get hold of bugging equipment was to contact a private investigator. A survey done in the D.C. area showed that twenty-five out of thirty P.I.'s, when called, offered products for bugging. They got their equipment from the electronic stores.

Businessmen. Corporations. Company distributorships. Lafayette Radio. The real world of eavesdropping was hardly turning out to be exotic. In fact, my V.P. made snooping so commonplace, he was taking all the fun out of it. But what about a bug? That still had a nice sinister aura to it.

Until my V.P. got hold of it. He led me into a large room filled with more machinery than IBM and Xerox make. He pointed at what looked like a combined oscilloscope and FM receiver. Turned out to be a Spectrum Analyzer, a highly sensitive receiver that picks up all the electronic signals in a room — including FM bands and TV stations. When a radio in the room is turned on, it produces squealing noises in the transmitter receiver because of feedback, and one can home in on the location of the bug by then walking around the room with the antenna. The closer one gets, the louder the squeal.

Sometimes, instead of a radio, one can use a small tape recorder with a whistle recorded on it. If the whistle gets picked up, that means someone is transmitting in the room. The transmitters were more my style than the Analyzer. They could be concealed in a desk stapler, pens, lighters, rugs, windows and air vents. I just couldn't see Bond checking into a Teheran hotel with the Analyzer. He probably couldn't even lift it.

The V.P. then got down to the case of taps on the telephone line. "There are thirty differ-

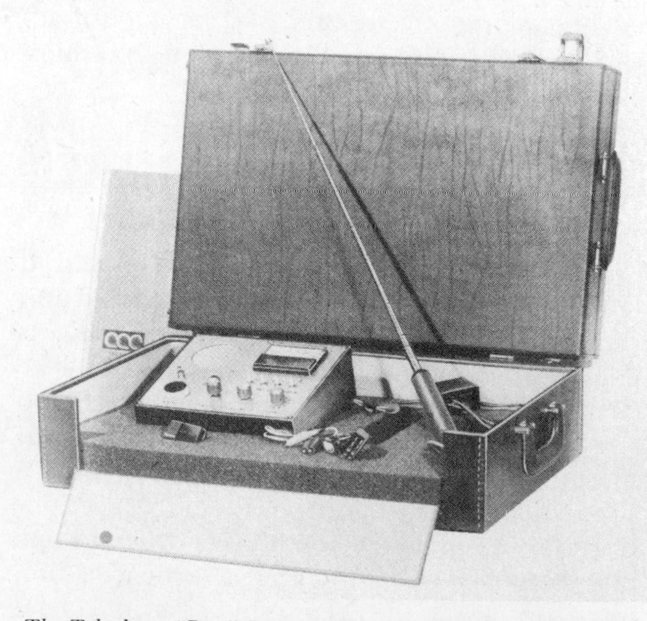

COMMUNICATION CONTROL SYSTEMS INC.

The Telephone "Bug" Detector. It uncovers such eavesdropping devices as: series-type tape recorder starters; parallel-type tape recorder starters; series transmitters; parallel transmitters; audio frequency triggered switches (Infinity transmitters and Harmonica bugs); hot-wired microphones; resistance or capacitance defeated switch hooks; resonant telephone ringers (bells).

ent ways that can be employed to tap a telephone," he said. His all-purpose detector was built into an attaché case. It was not hard, squinting a little, to imagine it being used against Hugo Drax. It not only found the tap but told you the distance from the phone to the tap itself. For example, it could give a reading that showed a tap fifty feet away on the line. Since telephone wires circle around, that could mean the tap was only a few feet away from the phone.

Still thinking of enemy agent type clients, I asked what would happen if a client's phone turned out to have been tapped by the good guys, namely, the cops.

"If the tap is out on the open line," said my V.P., "then whoever put it there — including the police — is violating the law. If a law enforcement agency wants to tap you, they have to do it by legal process, involving a court order from a judge. The order entitles them to go to the telephone company and have your line piped into their office, where it will be hooked up to a recording device. That, by the way, our equipment won't detect. It's put in behind the walls of the phone company's central office, and we can't penetrate it."

If my V.P. and his chums found a tap on a line, they either removed it or suggested a way for the client to make it backfire. This they did with a little gizmo called a wiretap defeat system. If someone is listening on your phone, its light goes on and its needle jumps like crazy. Now that you're on red alert, so to speak, you're in control. You can throw a switch, keep talking, but convey only false information; then you release a switch and it fades out your unwanted listener. At which point, since he suddenly, magically, can't hear you, you give your secret information. Your bugger doesn't know why he can't hear you; he just can't.

The V.P. next proceeded to show me, in no particular order, a telephone decoder, a bomb decoder and a bug alert that could be carried in one's pocket like a package of cigarettes. Here at last was something I could definitely identify with. It seemed tailor-made for Bond's three-piece suit. Fact and fiction were finally coming together.

PSSST

If you wish to have a private conversation but suspect someone is eavesdropping through the wall, an ex-spy suggests you redecorate. Cover the walls, ceiling and floor with chicken wire. The chicken wire plays hell with sound waves and distorts any conversation. If you are concerned with aesthetics, you could plaster over the chicken wire.

COMMUNICATION CONTROL SYSTEMS INC.

The Room Sweeper. It emits an ungodly bleep when in the presence of a room bug. The little gizmo on the top also turns bright red (as well it should at some of the language it hears).

By now, however, I was numbed by sheer bulk of equipment. And talk of impedance tests, capacitance switch hooks and integrated circuits went clear over my head. My V.P.'s cool, scientific detachment, not to mention expertise, was also working quicker than knockout drops. I had thought it might be fun to play with spy tools. But seeing them in handsome walnut cases, with two-year warranties, and picturing housewives and advertising executives queuing up for them, took away their romance.

I left not much wiser in wiretapping and thankful for thin walls.

Thomas Seligson was the entertainment editor for Mystery Monthly *magazine.*

THE RULES OF POISON PENMANSHIP

The Stationery

Do not use monogrammed notepaper.

Burn all first drafts.

Use plain, white, #10 legal envelopes — they come in packets of 20 so you can include an extra one for the money, if you like.

Never fold a ransom note — an important word can get lost in the crease.

Unlined paper looks more professional.

Best choice: Eaton's Corrasable Typewriter paper — it's very hard to trace, but more important, is easy to erase, should you decide at the last minute to up the ransom price.

Whatever you do, do *not* keep a carbon.

Hand-Lettering

Follow the Palmer method, exactly.

Or, use one of those alphabet stencils, filling in the appropriate letters.

Note left by The Bat in Mary Roberts Rinehart's book The Bat.

Letter to a bride in Ellery Queen's Eve of the Wedding.

Misspell at least one word per ransom note — somehow, that always looks more threatening, which in this case is good.

Always write in purple ink, if you use a fountain pen.

Resist the urge to dot your *i* triangularly, double-cross your t-bar, or decorate the border with graffiti.

Actually, the most handsome blackmail notes are done with a Crayola.

Death should always be spelled in red, money in green.

Cutting Out Letters

Take your time.

Invest in a good pair of scissors, a giant-size jar of library paste (no Scotch tape, please!), a tweezer to hold the cutouts.

Clip letters from widely read magazines and newspapers, such as *TV Guide* and *The National Enquirer.*

Never clip out letters from such esoterica as the *Merck Manual* or *Gray's Anatomy.* (Nobody likes a wise guy.)

In gluing the letters, make sure you do not include any lint from the rug, cigar ash or cat hairs.

When you're done clipping the magazines, return them to the dentist's office.

Delivery

Never trust the U.S. Mail: hand-deliver. (Doors were created to insinuate things under and egg cups were made to prop up messages.)

Best not to be around when the letter is discovered: You may be an excellent poison-penner but a lousy actor.

The Message

Pretend it's Western Union and you have a ten-word limit.

Be direct — this is no time for subtlety.

Always demand the ransom in U.S. currency.

Like the *Times,* write so anyone with an eighth-grade education can understand you.

Always sign your message with a bloody fingerprint — not yours, however, your victim's.

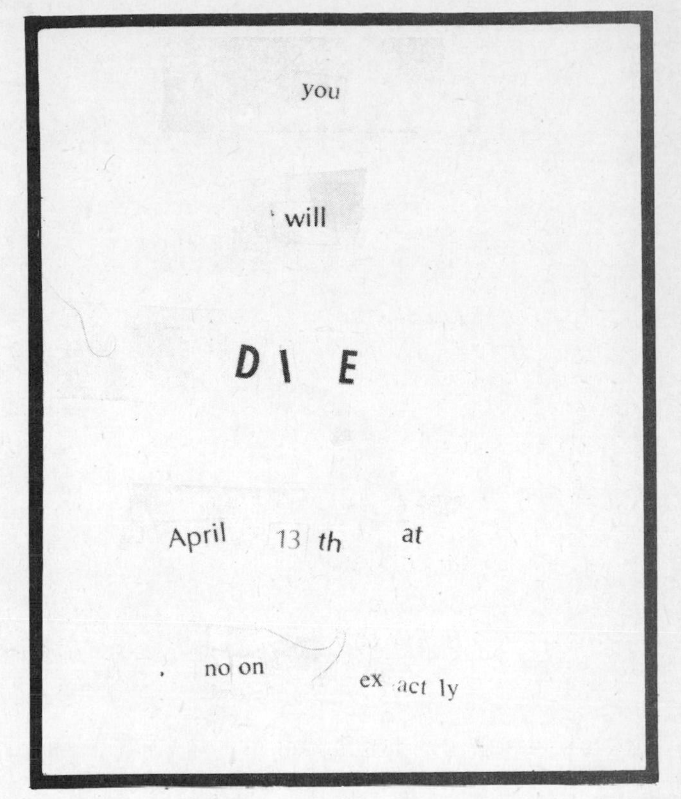

Message received, none too happily, in C. Daly King's Obelists Fly High.

Numb. 11794.

The London Gazette.

From Tueſday Auguſt 5, to Saturday Auguſt 9, 1777.

St. James's, Auguſt 5, 1776.

WHereas it has been humbly repreſented to the King, That an anonymous Threatening Letter was received from the General Poſt-Office at Briſtol, on Thurſday the 24th Day of April laſt paſt, by Mr. John Barrett, Collector of Exciſe there, of which the following is a Copy:

Sir,

You may tell Lilytrap Lovelas Martin and Unferies that if they have a mind to ſave their Lives they do remove from Briſtol for Dam me if we dont put an end to them Umferies and Maiſh narrowly miſt it other Day

And Elton and Barry and you had beſt alter your Proceedings in incouraging thoſe Villains otherwiſe your Houſes will be made a Dunghil of and your Carciſes ſent to the Devil for a Firebrand adviſe Elton and Barry to fine no more Warrants, for we are 50 of us ready to put this our Deſine in Execution

Kingſwood
20 April 1776 ... Mr. Lion ſtand the Pillory.

AVERAGE PRICES of CORN,
From July 28, to Auguſt 2, 1777.
By the Standard WINCHESTER Buſhel of Eight Gallons.

	Wheat. s.	d.	Rye. s.	d.	Barley. s.	d.	Oats. s.	d.	Beans. s.	d.
London,	5	4	3	0	2	4	2	0	3	4
COUNTIES INLAND.										
Middleſex,	6	4	—		2	5	2	2	3	5
Surry,	6	0	—		—		2	2	4	1
Hertford,	6	4	—		—		2	4	3	8
Bedford,	6	6	—		3	4	2	2	3	5
Cambridge,	5	11	3	2	—		1	10	2	9
Huntingdon,	6	3	—		2	10	1	11	3	4
Northampton,	6	8	3	0	3	0	2	4	3	10
Rutland,	6	7	—		3	10	2	2	—	
Leiceſter,	6	8	3	6	2	11	2	4	4	3
Nottingham,	6	8	4	0	3	3	2	6	4	4
Derby,	6	9	—		—		2	11	4	7
Stafford,	6	4	4	5	—		2	6	4	9
Salop,	6	4	4	4	2	9	2	5	4	2
Hereford,	6	9	—		—		2	6	—	
Worceſter,	6	5	3	0	—		2	10	4	7
Warwick,	6	6	—		—		2	9	3	11
Glouceſter,	6	10	—		2	9	2	4	3	9
Wilts,	6	5	—		3	1	2	2	3	9
Berks,	6	1	—		2	5	2	3	3	4
	5	9	—		2	7	2	2	3	4

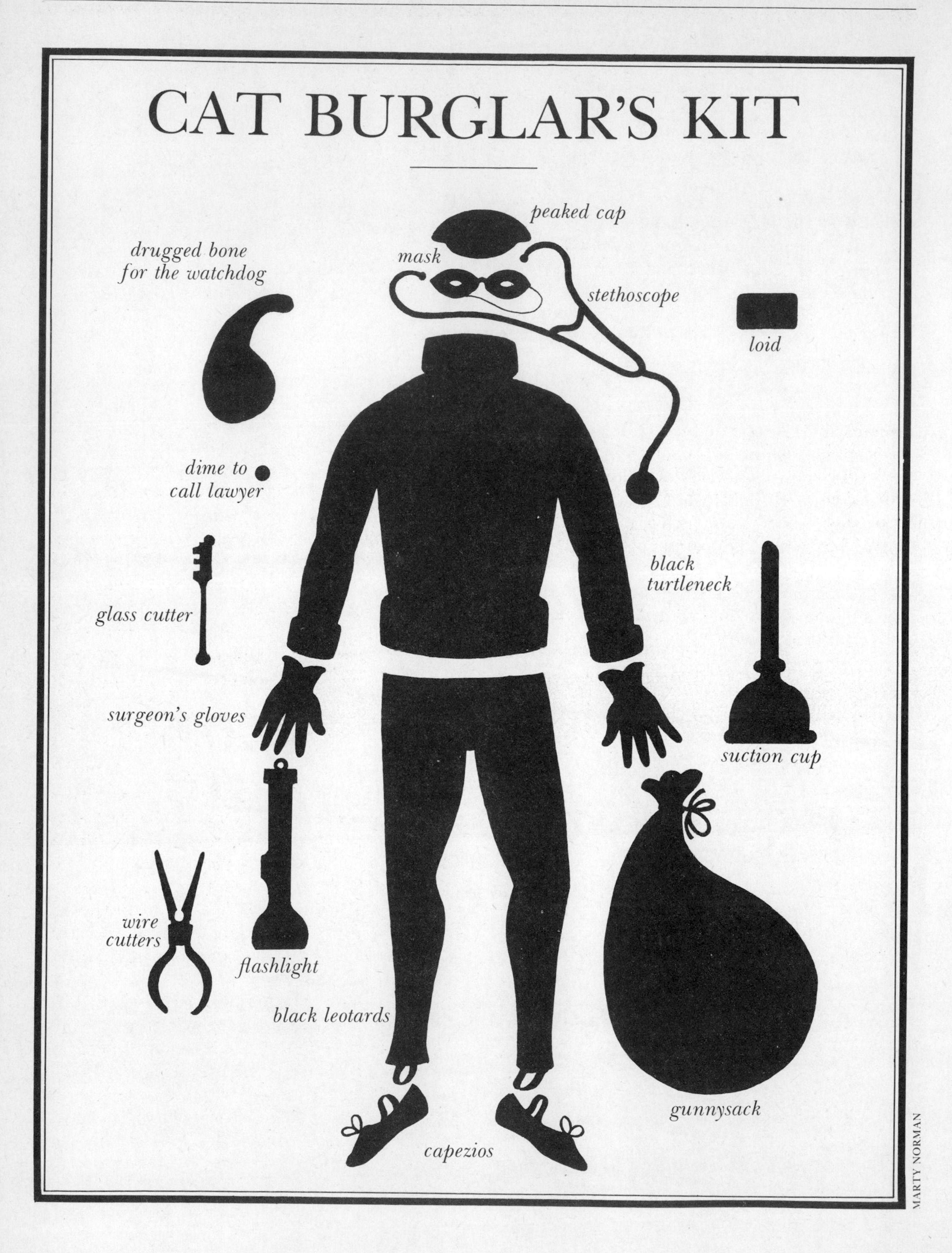
CAT BURGLAR'S KIT
peaked cap
drugged bone for the watchdog
mask
stethoscope
loid
dime to call lawyer
black turtleneck
glass cutter
surgeon's gloves
suction cup
wire cutters
flashlight
black leotards
gunnysack
capezios
MARTY NORMAN

THE GETAWAY CAR

Step on the Pedal and Go

Warren Weith

Ralph Nader, the man who tried to convince us that the motorcar was the villain, had it all wrong. The automobile may turn people into villains, and it may attract villains, but alone and unattended it's just a collection of bits and pieces waiting to be thrust into furious action by a fool, knave or — if you will — villain.

There's no doubt in which category to place the author of this brief note to Henry Ford:

Hello Old Pal:
Arrived here at 10 A.M. today. Would like to drop in and see you. You have a wonderful car. Been driving it for three weeks. It's a treat to drive one.
Your slogan should be: Drive a Ford and watch the other cars fall behind you. I can make any other car take a Ford's dust.

Bye-bye
John Dillinger

John Dillinger's use of the car as a tool to help him make quick withdrawals from various banks has become part of our folklore. Little known is how Dillinger learned the art of the fast remove. The technique was the brainchild of an ex-Prussian army officer named Herman K. Lamm.

Herr Lamm was caught cheating at cards and drummed out of the regiment shortly before World War I. Thereafter, he drifted to Utah and thence — there being no military defense establishment in those days to offer gainful employment to former army officers — into the life of a holdup man. This path in turn led, in 1917, to Utah State Prison. For Lamm, as for most criminals, a year in the can afforded time to reflect and to refine his technique. When he got out, he had developed a system for removing the uncertainties from bank robbing. It was a three-step plan. Only step three, detailing the getaway, is of interest here. The first requirement for the getaway was a car. Not just any car, but one that had to satisfy two contradictory rules: it had to be high-powered, yet nondescript to the point of disappearing into the cityscape. Next came the driver: best of all was a racing driver who had fallen from grace; at the very least, an ex-truck hijacker would do. Never just someone who was a "good" driver. Pasted up on the headliner over the windshield was a chart of the getaway route. This was more than a map because it indicated turns in miles that had been registered beforehand on the car's odometer and clocked, down to the second, by the driver under different weather conditions. It was a good plan and it worked for almost thirteen years.

It stopped working on December 16, 1930 in Clinton, Indiana. Lamm and three friends were calmly walking out of the Citizens State Bank in that town with $15,567 in a paper shopping bag and several typewriter covers when they were approached by the local barber. He had a suspicious look on his face and was carrying an Ithaca pump gun. Across the street, the getaway driver didn't like the way

COURTESY FBI

The getaway car that didn't get away — due to the driver's sudden illness, which was caused by a barrage of bullets through the windshield.

things were shaping up and tried to help out by making a screeching U-turn in order to bring the Buick closer to the four gentlemen who needed to get away and, at the same time, put it between them and the suspicious barber. All of this would have been very smooth except that the driver, an ex-rumrunner possibly more adept with speedy boats than speedy cars, let things get out of hand and slammed the Buick into the curb with such force that it blew a tire. The five bank robbers limped away in the Buick with double-O buckshot clanking around their ears. Then came the next bad move. Instead of stopping and changing the tire on the car with proven getaway potential, they elected to steal the next machine that hove into view. At this point, the Fates didn't smile — they laughed like hell. The next parked car they saw became, in about five seconds flat, the getaway car. But what they didn't know going in, and learned during the first mile, was that it was a car equipped with a governor by its owner to prevent his elderly father from speeding. Its top speed was 35 miles an hour. Just fast enough to get the fearless five a bit further out of town and within robbing range of a truck. This worthy vehicle was a bit faster but proved to have very little water in its radiator. It did serve to get them over the state line into Illinois — and into another car. This equipage had one little flaw. There was only one gallon of gas in the tank.

And there it all ended, under the blazing guns of a 200-man posse. Lamm and the driver were killed, and one member of the little band committed suicide. The other two were captured and sent to Michigan City Prison for life. There they taught a young con named John Dillinger all they knew about this almost trouble-free system of robbing banks. Herman

K. Lamm, the master of the fast getaway, is little known among people who use withdrawal slips but nonetheless lives on in our speech. Think of him the next time you hear a TV bad guy growl, "I'm gonna take it on the lam."

John Dillinger, like any good apprentice, added a few personal touches to the master's blueprint. On leaving a bank, he would drape a frieze of hostages along the running boards to silence the guns of any law officers who might be on the scene. While a neat touch, this did have a few drawbacks. A 1930's Terraplane or Essex really wasn't able to cope with four or five bandits and upwards of six hostages. Thus a getaway, which should be performed to a disco beat, turned into a slow waltz out of town. The forces of law and order soon got wise. They would follow at a discreet distance, knowing that sooner or later Bad John would have to drop the hostages off on some country road. At that point, the real getaway and chase would begin. But then another Dillinger touch would come into play — large-headed roofing nails liberally spread in the road. Simple, but effective. What made all this work, though, was the fact that most local law enforcement agencies were woefully ill-equipped. Many of them required that individual officers provide their own transportation. What a $5,000-a-year sheriff could afford to drive was simply no match for the wheels a successful team of bank robbers could — and did — buy.

At about the same time, the French police had somewhat the same problem, although theirs was one particular car rather than a variety. It was the first front-wheel-drive Citroën introduced in the middle Thirties. So much quicker and more agile than anything the flics drove, it made a joke of pursuit. Once out of the bank and into the Citroën, French freebooters couldn't have been any safer if they'd been in their mother's arms. Finally, it got so bad, the Paris newspapers began calling them the front-wheel-drive gangsters. The French, being a logical race, solved their problem quickly by issuing even faster Citroëns to the good guys. (An attempt at a cure for the fast-getaway bandit in this country consisted of FBI men in twelve-cylinder Lincolns.)

Gaelic bank robbers lean toward a shy departure in a beat-up panel truck — preferably from the mouth of a tunnel that surfaces blocks away from the bank. Here the hot-shoe artist is still with us, though his technique leaves a lot to be desired. An example from a few years ago will serve to illustrate. Admittedly, it was a rather complicated jewel robbery in which a double handful of gems had been stolen and then hidden on the site. The getaway would take place after the swag had been literally crowbarred from its hiding place. The car would be stolen and driven to the scene by one of the break-in team. There he was to change places with the actual driver. All of this took place smoothly enough on the appointed day.

NOW YOU SEE IT, NOW YOU DON'T

Changing the appearance of a car is a problem that's never really been solved. Anything that can be done quickly — water paint, as used on a bus in a recent movie — only makes the vehicle look unusual, which is not the desired effect. A regular paint job could take more than an hour, and then up to a week to dry really hard. Much easier to just switch to another, "clean" car. The difficulty here is in making the "hot" car disappear completely, because once it turns up, the other car is no longer "clean." Making a car disappear quickly is not as simple as it sounds. Those giant car-crushing machines — like the type that rumor says made Jimmy Hoffa disappear — would be a good bet. Trouble is, there aren't many of them in the country. It is interesting, though, that most of them seem to be owned by gentlemen with Latin-sounding names.

W.W.

FITTING THE CAR TO THE CRIME

Harrods Heist

Take, for example, a rather exotic job in London. You and your mates have evolved a beautifully orchestrated job of waltzing a whole rack of furs through Harrods Department Store, past all the customers and in the general direction of the back door. Somewhere during this journey the furs are stuffed into a wheeled dustbin. The dustbin is then rolled out onto the sidewalk. No sooner does it hit the sidewalk than a small Bedford dump truck pulls up alongside. The dustbin is almost filled with bits of wire lathe, plasterboard, all the things one usually equates with department store remodeling. Up it goes, down it goes — empty — and off goes the little Bedford . . . and Bob's your uncle. Sound farfetched? Well, the same job, move for move, was pulled in a big department store on New York's Fifth Avenue not many years ago. But notice the getaway vehicle. Work-stained, dented, it fit the part like Sir Laurence once fit Hamlet.

Cartier's Caper

A beautifully groomed matron had an even simpler approach. This consummate actress strolled into Cartier's and asked — in the best Larchmont lockjaw — to see some diamond rings. For an hour she fussed over her decision, or, as it turned out, set the scene. Her choice finally narrowed down to two. The lady then asked if she could see them in the daylight. It being Cartier's, the clerk said, "Of course." The lady was last seen entering a waiting Checker cab. Neat, but not gaudy.

Ponte Vecchio Purge

Gaudy, but equally effective, was the big jewel robbery in Florence. The goldsmiths and jewelers, at least the ones worth robbing, are all on the Ponte Vecchio. One bright Saturday two young gentlemen roared onto the bridge astride an MV Augusta racing motorcycle. The lad on the back got off, strolled into the nearest shop, reached over the counter and calmly scooped up over $80,000 worth of baubles. He then strolled outside and got back on the bike. The daring duo then took off and with a wave to the tourists quit the bridge for parts unknown. The lovely part about all this is the choice of getaway vehicle. Only an Italian would choose a racing motorcycle with open exhausts for such a job. I think the point here is that most of the population were on their side during the escape because of the Italian love for anything fast and loud. Proof of this can be found in the nickname the newspapers gave them: the Con Brio Bandits.

W.W.

ANN LIMONGELLO

Out ran the jolly swagmen, followed by various and sundry guards and office help. They jumped into the car screaming for the driver to take off. His first attempt ended with a stalled engine. So did his second and third. It was a manual-shift car, and he could only drive an automatic. This farsighted group are still, in 1977, guests of the state. Of course, they were not professionals at the time, but no doubt they will be when they hit the streets.

A nice clean getaway is the mark of a professional, and a professional keeps in tune with the times. In most of the recent successful heists in urban centers, he's used public transport. Under the circumstances, it's quicker and safer than a car. In suburbia the trend seems to be toward a two-year-old, well-dented Ford station wagon with a woman driver. They disappear before they even leave the parking lot. The CB radio, helicopter, and a lack of style on the part of perpetrators have rung down the curtain on the classic car chase. What's left is fiction — the fiction of the shimmering tube or the twenty-fifth pocketbook reprint of an ageless mystery story.

Most people think James Bond was the first man of action to have a car as his co-hero. Not so. Strictly speaking, it was Tom Swift in a slim little volume entitled *Tom Swift and His Electric Runabout.* But if we're talking about a car powered by an internal combustion engine, then Simon Templar, alias The Saint, is a likely candidate. His Hirondel — a make beautifully built only in author Leslie Charteris' imagination — was a magnificent motorcar of staggering performance. Its makers modestly alluded to it as the king of the road, and in Charteris' England of the 1930's that's just what it was. This is what its creator had to say about it as it bore The Saint to a lonely country house in which his fiancée, Patricia Holm, was being held prisoner:

> *If this had been a superstitious age, those who saw it would have crossed themselves and sworn that it was no car at all they saw that night, but a snarling silver fiend that roared through London on the wings of an unearthly wind.*

Makes Mr. Bond's Aston sound like a rental from Hertz.

James Bond was first in one respect, though. He was the first hero driver to have a car equipped with gadgets whose sole function was to kill people. I'm thinking specifically of the twin forward-firing machine guns, hub-mounted scythes, and passenger ejection seat that turned his beautiful silver-gray DB 5 Aston-Martin into a death machine. Needless to say, all were used to great gory effect in one of the first James Bond pictures.

A more skillful approach to the same end, and interestingly enough more exciting, was that taken by the detective character played by Steve McQueen in *Bullet.* He simply outdrove the villains and in the process forced them into a long sweeping bend at an insane rate of speed. The end result was both fatal and suitably spectacular, in a wide-screen sense. *Bullet* was the start of yet another trend — the use of a car that didn't really look the part. McQueen's Mustang, while it was a Mach I fastback, was also hubcapless with a dull black paint job that looked like it had been applied with a whisk broom. It was, in effect, the automotive counterpart of the hero. No glitter, but all guts. The end of this trend was in sight when Peter Falk's Columbo drove into view in a Peugeot 403 convertible so spavined, it had trouble making it across the small expanse of a TV screen. Popeye Doyle — alias Gene Hackman — put the capper on it in *The French Connection* when he completely destroyed a departmental vehicle while chasing a dope pusher. To understand the point being made in this film you would have to have some knowledge of the type of car New York City detectives work in. They don't just work in the car, they live in it, for days at a time. As one member of the force so neatly put it, "They all smell like they'd been used to haul the horse cops to a riot, and they all have the optional dirt floor." And that was the kind of car Popeye Doyle drove, right down to the flurry of empty coffee containers — a long way from The Saint's immaculate Hirondel bellowing through London's fashionable West End en route to rescuing a fair damsel held prisoner in an even more fashionable country house in Surrey. Sadder still, The Saint is reduced to a mere Volvo P 1800 for his rescue missions on TV. So much for a producer who doesn't have the class to commission the construction of at least one magnificent Hirondel.

Where the getaway car is today — in fact or fiction — would be hard to say. But consider this: A national religious organization holds week-long meetings of the faithful in big sports stadiums around the country. Its supporters are not wealthy people and the contributions are in nickels, dimes and crumpled dollar bills. Almost a million dollars' worth of nickels, dimes and crumpled dollar bills. To haul the take to the banks without giving the bad guys — or the faithful — an idea of its size was a problem that was solved very neatly by the elders with a fleet of Cadillac limousines. Very special limousines. Ones with false bottoms. The coinage, hot from the hands of the frenzied believers, is bagged and thrown into the double bottoms and whisked off to a local bank. All day long the PA system pans the mother lode while the Caddies make spring-bending shuttle runs to the vaults. They're getaway cars, jet-age style — to the banks instead of away from them. So far, no free-lancers have tried to derail this silver rush express, but if they do, it might make the *Guinness Book of World Records* as the first getaway car hijacking. Then too, if a rival religion does the job, it could be the start of a religious war and the raw material for yet another disaster movie.

No, Ralph Nader was wrong. The car is not a villain. The only automobile that ever came near to being a murderer was a Type 57 Bugatti. Being a French car, it was only natural that it was a crime of passion. The story in a few words: A young French girl was madly in love with a local layabout who was really in love with a Type 57, which he couldn't come close to affording. The girl's father had a mattress stuffed with money. She killed her father, took the money and bought her lover his love — the Bugatti. He and his love took off in a screech of tires for the South of France. She was left at the curb to stand trial for her crime. It being the middle Thirties, and France, the duped young lady served only one year of a two-year sentence. He killed himself in his Type 57. End of story.

Warren Weith is an editor of Car and Driver *magazine. He drives a '59 Alfa sedan.*

LICENSE PLATES

Changing license plates inflight, as it were, has always been a subject dear to the hearts of that segment of the motoring public pictured most frequently on post office walls. One ploy that went to the bank once too often was the mud-daubed plate used by a splinter group from the Detroit Purple Gang. Like all good tricks it was simple and depended for its effect on the perverseness of human nature. Going to the bank, the plates on the getaway car were streaked with mud. At the first chance, after the job, the plates were wiped clean. Dumb as it may sound, human nature did the rest. If you're looking for a car with license plate MUD, it just can't be one with license plate KG 7459 — or whatever was under the mud. Simple-minded? No, just simple.

Equally simple, and even more effective, were three or four plates stacked together and wired on. It was only the work of a minute or so to stop, take off the top plate and expose the one underneath. Remembering, of course, not to leave the discarded plate face up in the road. But then again, if a bank robber remembered everything he'd probably wind up a banker.

W.W.

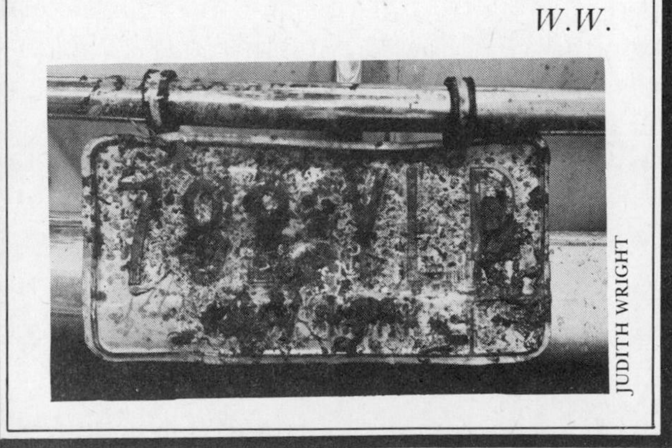

JUDITH WRIGHT

THE DIP

A Dance in 4/4 Time

Choreographer Solomon Hastings was jostled so hard on the dance floor, his wallet fell out of his pocket. Thus inspired, he created the newest dance craze — The Dip — which is part Hustle and part Outright Thievery. He is currently planning a new step called The Stake-Out, in which The Dip is escorted off the floor, directly to jail.

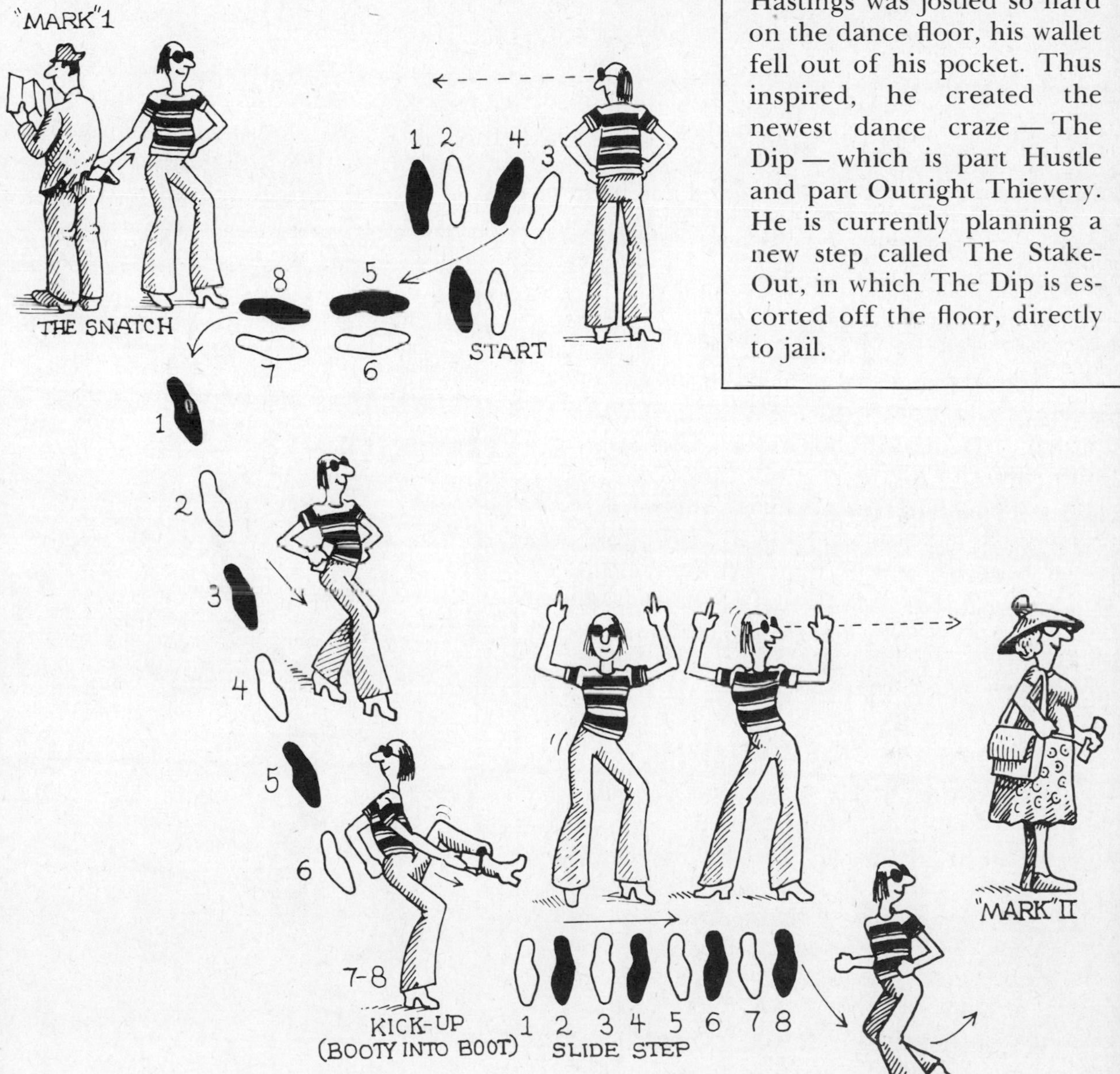

"MARK" 1

THE SNATCH

START

KICK-UP (BOOTY INTO BOOT)

SLIDE STEP

"MARK" II

START (AGAIN)

MARTY NORMAN

DIFFICULTIES OF THE SAFE-CRACKER

R.J. Pilgrim

In many of the mediaeval cathedrals of Europe, in museums, in stately homes and the like, can be found massive wooden chests, hundreds of years old, elaborately carved and with locking mechanisms which appear complex.

These were the safes of their day, made with the best materials and tools available.

It is difficult, therefore, to know where to begin when talking of the history of safes. While we now tend to think of them as massive steel boxes, no doubt the wealthy mediaeval merchant thought of his box as his safe and was quite happy with the protection it provided.

The first patent for a safe, as the term is understood today, was taken out in 1801 by one Richard Scott. This was followed by William Marr in 1834, Charles Chubb in 1835, Edward Tann in 1835, Charles and Jeremiah Chubb in 1839 and Thomas Milner in 1840.

Initially, safes were promoted as a means of protecting one's property against fire damage. This all changed with the Cornhill Robbery of 1865. Walker, who had a shop at 63 Cornhill, London, brought an action against Milner and Son, the makers of his safe, for breach of warranty, since Milner's had described it as "thief-proof" and thieves had gotten into it with wedges. The thieves did, however, have twenty-four hours in which to accomplish their nasty task and this led to Walker losing his case: the court ruled *he* had been negligent in allowing them so much time. Despite the verdict, however, safe makers got busy redesigning and the small wedges were rendered useless. In addition to these wedges, nineteenth-century rogues tried attacks by gunpowder, blow-lamps, diamond drills and acids. By the end of the century the main threats to safes came from explosives (at first nitroglycerine, then gelignite) and the oxygen cutter. Special devices and alloys were created

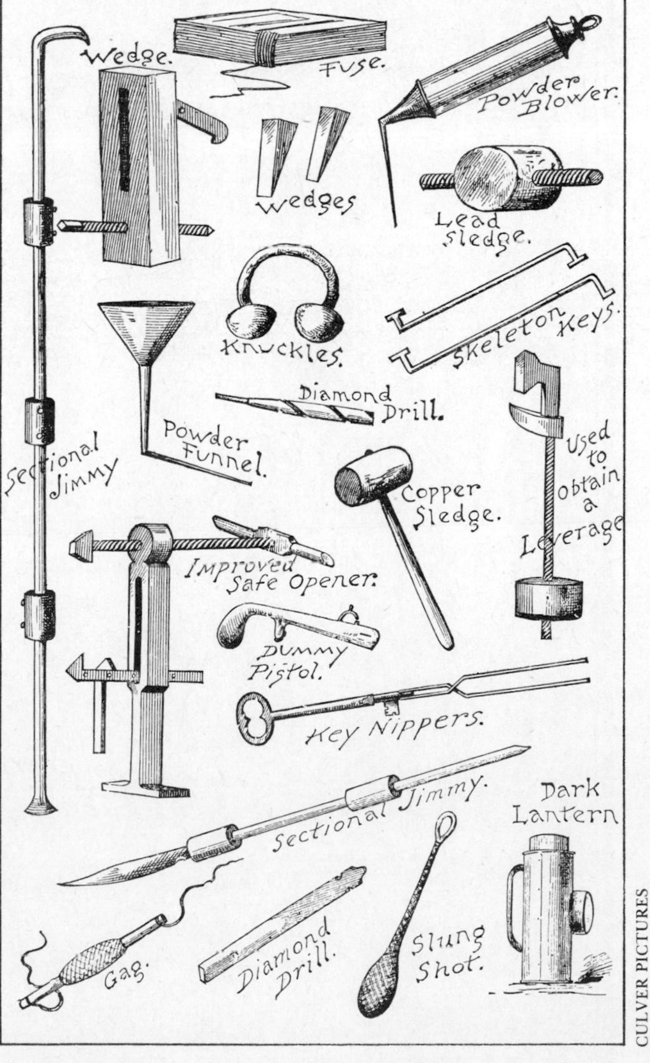

CULVER PICTURES

A bank burglar's outfit (excluding sack to carry away the money).

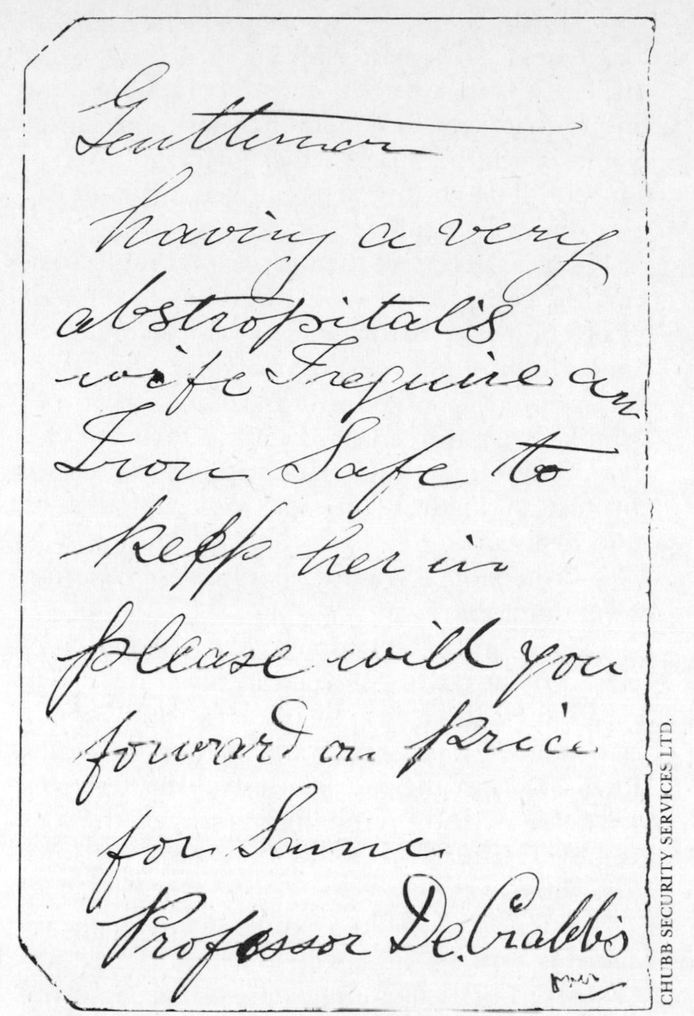

Gentleman
having a very
abstropitalis
wife Frequire an
Iron Safe to
kepp her in
please will you
forward a price
for same
Professor De Crabbs

CHUBB SECURITY SERVICES LTD.

Gentleman: Having a very obstreperous wife, I require an Iron Safe to keep her in. Please will you forward a price for same. Professor De Crabbs. (Letter sent to Chubb.) There is no record of their reply to the beleaguered De Crabbs.

to counteract them, so the difficulties of the safe-cracker increased as he penetrated inward. Crane hinges, for one, prevented nitro from being inserted round the edges of safe doors.

With the arrival of oxyacetylene welding, around 1900, it was possible to construct stronger safes. Of course, the techniques and the tools available for legitimate industry very soon came into the hands of the thief. What is useful in making a safe can also be useful in destroying it. The romantic conception of the master cracksman pitting his wits against a wily safe becomes a much more prosaic affair of one engineer trying to destroy the work of another, and the battle becomes a matter of the safe maker forcing the safe breaker to make so much noise, use so much material and take so long in his attacks, the risk of arrest far outweighs the chance of success.

Of the weapons used in the battle, the thermic lance is one which illustrates this point most readily. The lance is a heat cutting weapon, used extensively in its early days for the destruction of the massive concrete fortifications of the European coast in World War II. It generates a temperature higher than the melting point of most common materials, so on the face of it there would seem to be no effective counter to its use as a safe-breaking weapon. Yet in the thirty years or so since its development, it has been used relatively little and with only mixed success. The reason is that the sheer bulk of contemporary safes forces the thief to bring to the scene of the attack literally tons of oxygen bottles and steel lances, and the cutting process generates so much heat and smoke that it is virtually impossible to operate clandestinely; ergo, the risk of arrest is high. The logistic difficulties have obviously been enough to dissuade the thief from more extensive use of the thermic lance as a weapon. Yet it will demolish any safe. In the abstract.

There are, of course, some forms of attack which do not present a thief with all these problems, but before discussing these it is useful to look at how a safe is constructed.

The body and door are made as a kind of sandwich, with outer and inner layers of steel enclosing a thick mass which forms the main barrier against the thief. (What the barrier is made of determines the quality, and the price, of the safe.) Good-quality concrete is a barrier possibility, as is a material such as copper, which has high thermal conductivity. The problem arises in that no one barrier is impervious to all attacks.

CHAMPION CRACKSMEN

Blackshirt: Bruce Graeme
Boston Blackie: Jack Boyle
Hamilton Cleek: Thomas W. Hanshew
The Lone Wolf; Bourke: Louis Joseph Vance
Raffles: E.W. Hornung
Jimmy Valentine: O. Henry

THE SCHOOL OF THE BELLS

In Ecuador, if you have the right connections, you can enroll in a very special school: all its graduates are professional pickpockets.

To teach a student the light touch, the "teachers" sew little bells onto a dummy — the same little bells that usually grace the throats of stuffed animals. The student is then told to approach the dummy, in the dark, and go for the breast-pocket wallet. If he jostles any part of the dummy en route to the wallet, the little bells tinkle and he must begin again. No student "graduates" until he can successfully steal an object from any part of the dummy without making a sound, and he must be able to do this consistently. Ten times out of ten.

Because of this training, the New York Police Department considers the Ecuadorian pickpockets the best in the world. They seem to travel in groups, possibly as a class on a field expedition, and tend to make the trip to the States twice a year: in time for the Christmas crowds and the summer tourists. They are almost uncatchable.

MARTY NORMAN

Hardness and resistance to drilling go with brittleness, so a material which affords good drill protection might succumb to something more primitive. Like a hammer and chisel. Some of the materials which offer good resistance to heat cutting are relatively soft and can thus be easily drilled.

The selection of the barrier becomes a matter of compromise — of finding reasonable protection at an affordable price. The materials most often employed are concrete, white iron, aluminum reinforced with hard inserts, copper (similarly reinforced) and certain forms of carbon. These materials offer varying degrees of protection against physical violence, drilling and heat cutting.

Protection against explosives requires something extra.

Safe and vault doors are usually kept closed by heavy bolts which in turn are kept in position by the action of the lock. Early explosive attacks were aimed at blowing away the lock by inserting an explosive through the keyhole. With the inhibiting action of the lock removed, the bolts could then be withdrawn and the door opened.

Safes were made, if you remember, to resist this type of attack in the mid-nineteenth century. They called themselves "powder-proof safes" and the method was simple. Underneath the keyway in the lock was drilled a hole, so that gunpowder pushed into the keyhole would fall out again and never reach sufficient concentration in the vital area of the lock to create an effective explosion.

Modern plastic explosives stopped all that, and protection now consists of additional locking devices which come into play when the lock is actually under explosive attack. These added locking devices keep the bolts closed even if the original lock is destroyed.

I once had the delightful experience of acting as advisor to Winston Graham, prior to his novel *The Walking Stick,* on the fascinating subject of explosive attacks. The exact point at issue was whether it was possible for a skilled thief to act so quickly — in the split second after an explosion — that he could prevent the anti-explosive relocking mechanisms from operating. The answer given to Mr. Graham, and subsequently noted in his book, was that with earlier forms of the relocking device, it was just possible. But with modern safes, no.

There is another subject dear to the heart of the crime novelist — combination locks, and the thief who can open them.

Alas, once again, life is more prosaic. In a lifetime's experience in the safe-making industry, I have yet to hear of a good-quality combination lock — of the type found on safe and vault doors — that could be opened by thieves unless they had prior knowledge of the numbers to which the lock was set. Considerable ingenuity has been used to get that information, including telescope observation of the owners fidgeting with the dials and long-range telescopic lens photography to study the numbers. But starting from scratch, with no previous knowledge, a thief would have no success.

These locks operate on four numbers, each between 0 and 100, so there are 100,000,000 groups of numbers to choose from. Trying one a minute, working an eight-hour day and taking statutory holidays, it would take over 800 years to try all the possibilities. So trial and error is not an effective method. Violence is quicker, and experience shows that the thief seems to agree.

The combination lock has many advantages. Changing the numbers to which it is set is easy, and can be done three times a day, if needed. It can be changed for each new staff shift, or if there is even the slightest suspicion that some unauthorized person has found out even one of the numbers. The lock becomes completely individual to the user, with no keys

Old burglars never die, they just steal away.

Chicago *Sun-Times*
GLEN GILBREATH
on facing his thirteenth robbery charge

to carry or lose. Of course, the selection of lock-up numbers is important, and it is vital that the thief not be able to deduce what they are. Birthdays and telephone numbers are bad choices. The safest thing to do is to memorize some entirely random number — but make a note of it and lodge that information at the bank. People can be very stupid about combination locks. I once came across an office at an electric supply company where the safe lock numbers were written on an adjacent wall!

It should be obvious by now that a safe's strength comes from its layers of material and their thicknesses. But there is a limit to the thickness one can incorporate into a safe that must fit a wall opening or recess in a private apartment. Thus such a safe must be treated with discretion, and not entrusted with the protection of high-value jewelry.

Finally, a safe gives the impression of permanence and many people are lulled into a fool's paradise, thinking the old safe, which still looks brand-new, is invincible. The techniques of safe making and safe breaking change constantly, and a safe made thirty years ago may be no match for the modern safe breaker — no matter how sturdy it appears.

Almost all successful safe breakings are against out-of-date safes, which fall victim to attacks they were never designed to withstand. The lesson is obvious: There must be constant updating of security equipment to keep pace with modern technology.

R.J. Pilgrim is the managing director of Chubb Security Services Ltd.

CHUBB SECURITY SERVICES, LTD.

Chubbs safes, en route.

VERSES FOR HEARSES

Isaac Asimov

MARTY NORMAN

Curare

When you've picked out your pitiful quarry
And have dosed him with toxic curare
Take care what you do
For once you are through
It's too late to decide that you're sorry.

Belladonna

Deadly nightshade (or else belladonna)
Might be used to avenge one's lost honor
So if offered a drink
By a cuckold, I think
You should carefully say, "I don't wanna."

Potassium Cyanide

If you've slipped your rich uncle some cyanide
You might live on his testament, high and wide.
But if they get after you,
You'll have no time for laughter, you
Must quickly get ready to try and hide.

Phosgene

In arranging a whiff of phosgene
You'll be pleased, for it's silent and clean.
But remember, you dope,
If you're caught, it's the rope,
Or in France, "Êtes-vous pris? Guillotine!"

Arsenic

The classic's a compound arsenial
For murder and that are congenial.
Yet it's hard on your smile
For it takes quite a while
And the crime, if you're caught, isn't venial.

Botulism

Potted meat, rich in B. botulinus,
Looks like accident. How's that for slyness?
Though its onset is slow
It is quite comme il faut
For an end to an enemy's spryness.

Snake Venom

In your foe's bed you may plant a rattler
It's venom's killed many a battler
But if you've had aide
In this snaky charade
Just make sure that your aide's not a tattler.

Arrow Poison

It may be the racing shell's cox'n
You've decided you must be outfoxin'.
Let him taste that delectable,
Very strange, undetectable
East African native-dart toxin.

Issac Asimov is a delightfully mad scientist and author of Tales of the Black Widowers.

THE ASSASSIN'S ARSENAL

David Penn

The pen may be mightier than the sword, but all too frequently it is a damn sight more inaccurate than the pistols it portrays.

In the whodunit, it is only rarely that the correct portrayal of the murder firearm is crucial to the mechanics of the plot, since the emphasis is on logic and the pleasure is intellectual. It matters little to the reader that the author has played safe with an anonymous "pistol," or has invented an exotic "Münslich eight-millimetre flat butt," or has chosen a real ".38 Special Colt Cobra revolver," unless the type and performance of the firearm form a significant part of the deductive process. Such plots are understandably rare, since sufficient technical knowledge for correct interpretation is unusual among readers and practically unheard of among mystery writers. Exceptions do occur, of course, for instance in the well-known naturalist Colin Willock's *Death in Covert,* a classic mystery based on a detailed and accurate knowledge of shotguns and game shooting in England, or in John F. Adams' *Two Plus Two Equals Minus Seven,* not so much a whodunit as a where-did-I-go-wrong. This is narrated by a too-clever-by-half pistolero whose perfect murder goes awry, and who suffers the indignity of being framed for a crime involving a cheap and aesthetically unpleasing Saturday Night Special with which he would never have soiled his hands.

If, however, a firearm is to be the Means to an End in a mystery, I do believe that its role should not strain too far the bounds of logical probability. One eminent English mystery writer managed to contrive a story around the ability of a loaded automatic pistol to fire itself by the contraction of its working parts after it had been left lying around in freezing conditions. Such an occurrence may not, in absolute terms, be impossible. Indeed, there is a known case of a shotgun capable of discharging itself without an intervening human agency by means of the effect of climatic change on its stock. Yet the design of an automatic pistol makes the chances of such an accident highly improbable, since the violence of its operation requires substantial bearing surfaces in the firing mechanism, and the degree of contraction of the metal, which would be compensated for in some degree by spring pressure keeping the parts in proper relationship, would not suffice to disengage them on even the coldest English day. On this occasion our illustrious author followed Sherlock Holmes's dictum that "when you have eliminated the impossible whatever remains, however improbable, must be the truth" beyond the bounds of improbability and into the realms of incredibility.

CULVER PICTURES

Italian 9 mm Beretta *automatic pistol. It loads seven rounds but has a short range due to the shortness of its barrel.*

When the focus of our attention moves an inch or so from the cerebral world of the Country House to the private-eye or the thick-ear thriller, the *mise en scène* is all. Technical inaccuracy or infelicity of language can puncture the illusion of a hero who is, with certain humorous exceptions, always tough, worldly-wise and competent, whether he be the rumpled sardonic romantic of Chandler or Gavin Lyall, or the sophisticated psychopath of an Ian Fleming. There is a school of thriller, epitomised by

CULVER PICTURES

German 9 mm standard pistol, called the Luger *in England and America. Known as the* Parabellum *in Germany.*

the spy stories of the Sixties and by Frederick Forsyth and Sam Gulliver in the Seventies, in which a bravura display of arcane technical knowledge plays a major part in the book's appeal. The police procedural genre is equally dependent on the author's ability to visualise a gritty reality through blood-boltered spectacles.

Some writers in these fields, such as Donald Hamilton or Richard Sale (author of the amazing extravaganza *The Man Who Raised Hell*), are familiar with firearms and incorporate them easily into their plots. Others manage to disguise their ignorance or error by a display of straight-faced confidence that convinces all but the true *amateur des armes* of their veracity. In *The Day of the Jackal,* Forsyth arms his assassin with bullets specially loaded with a mercury blob in a cavity, alleged to have a wondrously mind-blowing effect upon their victim. Far out, but no way would they work. Len Deighton is a past-master at the convincing memorandum and bolstered up *The Ipcress File* with such a wealth of apparently genuine detail that some alarmist souls voiced concern about undesirable security leaks. All I can say is, if the "Extract from Handling unfamiliar pistols, Document 237.HGF, 1960" is for real, heaven help our secret servants. The anonymous hero of *The Ipcress File* is armed with "a hammerless Smith and Wesson, safety catch built into grip, six chambers crowded with bullets. . . . in an accompanying box were twenty-five rounds, two spare chambers (greased to hold the shells in tight)." Impressive. Except that no hammerless Smith and Wesson is six-shot — it's only five and the safety mechanism does not in strict terms incorporate a "catch," since it does not intercept the motion of an already cocked mechanism but rather prevents an uncocked mechanism from being moved. Deighton means "two spare cylinders," not "chambers." Smith and Wesson has never supplied additional cylinders for the purpose of rapid reloading, since on all models, hinged-frame or sideswing, they take a few moments to remove. With the exception of a little-known Spanish revolver, spare-loaded cylinders went out of fashion when percussion muzzle-loading revolvers became obsolete. Greasing the chambers of the cylinder has a number of highly undesirable possible side effects which I consider would outweigh any benefits.

In some curious way, many thriller readers feel that an author who displays technical ignorance in his writing has somehow betrayed

WAFFENFABRIK MAUSER

German Mauser *self-loading automatic pistol. Guaranteed at 10 yards to shoot in a two inch circle; at 25 yards, in a six inch circle. .25 caliber and .32 caliber.*

CULVER PICTURES

Special agents (now retired, some permanently) in firearms practice at the Federal Bureau of Investigation range, U.S. Department of Justice building, Washington, D.C.

his hero by undermining their confidence in his ability to cope with the worst a hostile world can throw at him. A glossy idol cannot withstand a crack, and even a scruffy mat-finish anti-hero can only afford clay on the outside of his boots. This disenchantment is reflected in letters of protest by technology buffs from Bangor to Bangkok. Whether or not such a reaction is a little immature is beside the point, since if that is the audience for whom the author has aimed, he should at least make an effort to deliver the goods. Dick Francis never subjects his fictional jockeys to experiences which he could not himself survive, and writers from the sublime

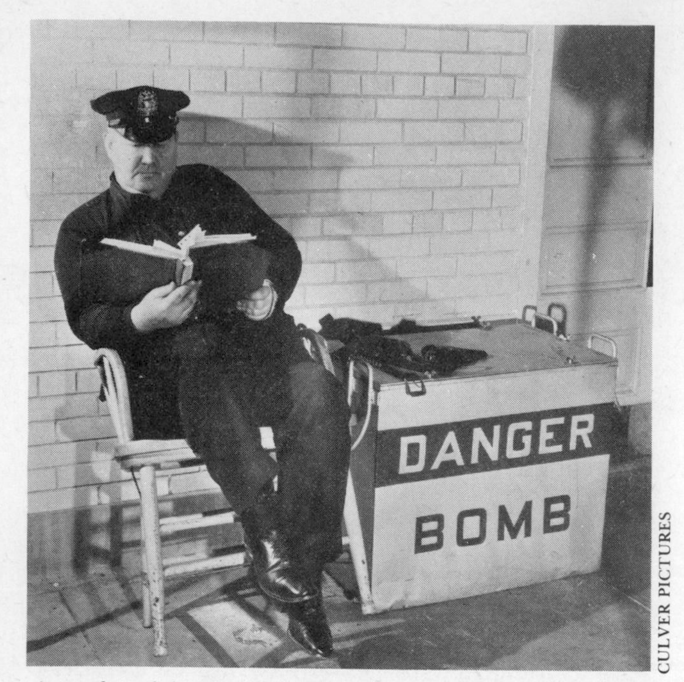

CULVER PICTURES

A member of the New York Bomb Squad waiting for a bomb to deactivate. All suspicious packages are dumped into a bomb tank (shown) filled with oil.

Gavin Lyall to the prolific J.T. Edson go to some lengths to find out whether the gunfights they chronicle are within the bounds of probability.

Perhaps the best-known target of the armchair experts was Ian Fleming. Fleming's fortes were pace and an ability to convey the risqué glamour of an affluent consumer society beginning to glitter after twenty grey years of austerity. Despite his Intelligence background, however, Fleming's knowledge of firearms was sketchy. The .25 Beretta of his early books was at least concealable, and deadly enough if the brain or spine was hit, but it had been subjected to some dubious modifications. To file the firing pin to a point was to invite a punctured primer, an escape of gas and perhaps a lightly grilled shooting hand. The taped skeleton butt would present no improvement in concealability over the standard skinny stocks and would invite all sorts of sticky trouble, such as a difficulty in removing the magazine. Fleming was eventually taken firmly in hand by a Scottish firearms expert, Geoffrey Boothroyd, who is characterised as the Armourer in *Dr. No.* Boothroyd suggested that Bond be armed either with a .32 Walther PPK automatic or a Smith and Wesson .38 "Centennial" revolver. While both were an improvement over the Beretta, they were themselves idiosyncratic choices, since Boothroyd must have been well aware that the PPK, introduced in 1931 and perhaps still the best pocket automatic made, was available in the significantly more effective .380 ACP calibre as well as the decidedly anaemic .32. The "Centennial" is a compact, well-made and powerful .38 Special snub-nosed revolver, but a concealed hammer weapon capable of double-action fire only and fitted with an unnecessary complexity in the form of a grip safety. Why Boothroyd selected this revolver when the equally compact and powerful but more versatile Smith and Wesson "Chiefs Special" and "Bodyguard" revolvers were available has always mystified me.

The Fleming/Boothroyd axis also demonstrates the danger of trying to graft on someone else's expertise, since Boothroyd suggested that the "Centennial" be carried in a split-front Berns-Martin holster, an advanced design for the day that could be used either as a belt holster or a shoulder holster and allowed a very quick draw with good security against accidental loss. Fleming loved the idea and duly sent Bond forth equipped with a PPK automatic and a Berns-Martin holster, to a chorus of anguished groans from the shooting fraternity since the Berns-Martin was made only for revolvers, not for automatics. As a crowning irony, in recognition of his care in references to firearms in his James Bond stories, Ian Fleming was presented in 1964 with a "Python" .357 Magnum revolver by Colt's, a company whose products had appeared almost entirely in the hands of the bad guys in his books.

Stern injunctions against loquacity preclude turning this chapter into a gunman's *vade mecum*, but having bitten the hands of many authors whose works have given me endless hours of pleasure, I feel obliged to turn pundit for a page or two.

I do not wish to probe too deeply into the gory business of wound ballistics, but it is wise to bear in mind that the projectile fired from a gun is a simple means of transmitting energy to the target. This energy is wasted, and becomes a potential hazard to innocent bystanders, if the projectile either misses or passes right through the victim. The purpose of this release of energy may be to kill, if the shooter is an assassin or a humane hunter, or to cause the recipient to cease and desist from whatever action he happens to be engaged in. Where the police and military are concerned, it is this "stopping" effect that is essential and any subsequent fatality is an undesirable side effect. There is little correlation between the ability of a weapon to kill and its ability to administer an instant and staggering shock. As an analogy, if a bag of oats is stood on its end, and a rapier is thrust right into it, the sharp slim blade will slide through and transmit little shock, but an identical thrust with a blunt walking stick will not penetrate and will knock the sack over. This analogy holds good for pistol bullets, where bigger and blunter is better, but is not entirely valid for modern high-velocity rifle bullets, working at velocities in excess of 2,500 feet per second, where other criteria obtain and the most wounding effect is caused by cavitation. As a rule of thumb, .22, .25 and .32 pistols and revolvers are thoroughly capable of killing if they hit a vital organ, but they do not transmit enough energy to provide reliable stopping power; .38 and 9 mm pistols are effective about 50 percent of the time, and modern .41, .44 and .45 cartiridges are effective about 95 percent of the time. In practise, the effect does not seem to be cumulative, so two .38's do not carry the same clout as one .45. All shotguns can be considered effective and messy up to forty or fifty yards, and all modern high-velocity rifles are also reliable one-shot stoppers.

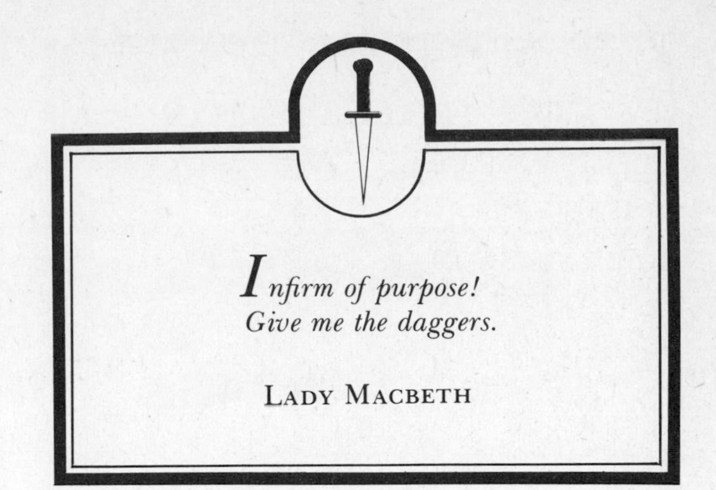

Mrs. Raffles *by John Kendrick Bangs. Like her predecessor,* Raffles, *a champion cracksman.*

In *Open Season,* David Osborn writes:

> *The rare, British-manufactured seven-millimeter H & H magnum twin barrelled breech-loading rifle has, at 300 yards, a velocity of 2,450 feet per second and a striking impact of 1,660 pounds, enough to kill a charging elephant instantly or knock a ¾-ton bull moose not just to his knees but completely off his feet. . . .*

Now, David Osborn has clearly done a lot of hard research into firearms, but he has perpetuated an all-too-common and erroneous assumption that, because a bullet generates an impressive striking energy, it is capable of physically knocking the victim off his feet. Newton's second law remains on the statute books, and this says that if the bullet can knock the victim over, the firearm will knock the shooter over. The armchair theorist fails to take into account the effects of inertia. I know it happens in the movies, but the effect is created by a brisk and timely heave on a piano wire attached to the hapless actor's belt. The real effect is a shock to the nervous system causing sudden loss of control and co-ordination, resulting in collapse, somewhat akin to a marionette when the puppeteer releases the strings.

Robert Churchill, one of the foremost Eng-

THE KNIFE DRAWER

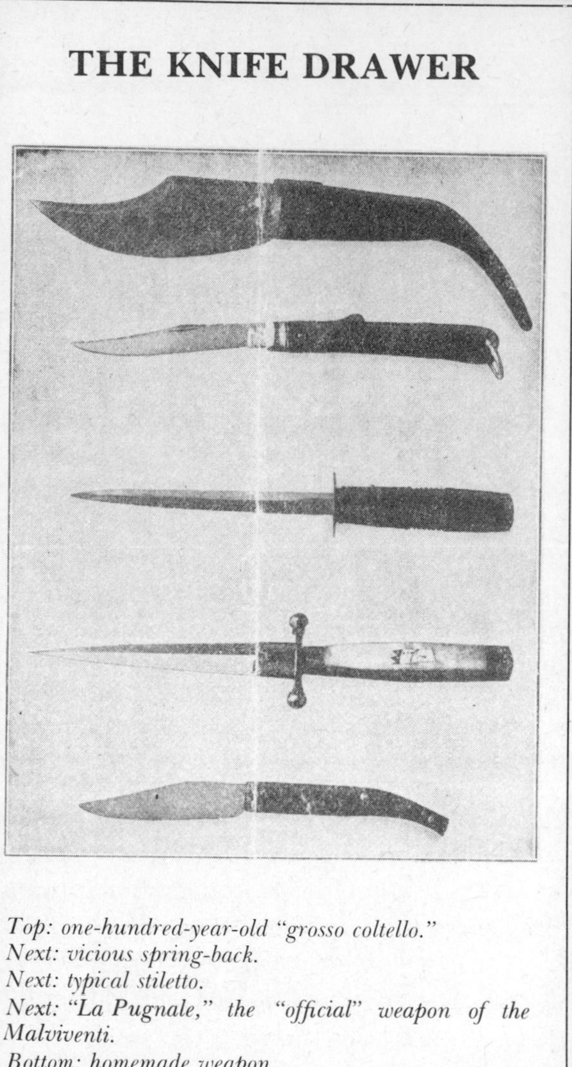

Top: one-hundred-year-old "grosso coltello."
Next: vicious spring-back.
Next: typical stiletto.
Next: "La Pugnale," the "official" weapon of the Malviventi.
Bottom: homemade weapon.

Knives shown were redeemed from Italian criminals and are approximately one-third actual size.

lish forensic ballisticians between the wars, wrote:

> *It is a paradox that in the great majority of offences involving a pistol the people concerned knew next to nothing about the mechanism or potentialities of the weapon. In many cases the fatal shot is the first and last they fire in their lives. Crime guns are usually ill-kept, often mechanically faulty, and commonly loaded with unsuitable or improvised ammunition.*

As a basic standard of competence, an untrained person in a stressful state and shooting a pistol can miss a stationary figure at seven yards and a running one at seven feet. A skilled pistol shot in control of his emotions can reliably hit a stationary figure at a hundred yards and a moving one at twenty-five.

A pistol may give the same sort of comfort as a teddy bear on a cold dark night, but its virtues are light weight and compactness. It is a defensive arm that can be carried along or concealed when a rifle would be a hindrance or an embarrassment. Its virtues become positive disadvantages when the weapon actually has to be fired. A riot gun or sawn-off shotgun is a much more effective weapon favoured by both sides of the law when trouble is expected.

Machine guns, submachine guns and full-size rifles find little favour with the criminal classes since they are large, expensive to acquire and feed, and distinctly unhandy to get in and out of motorcars. In America, overenthusiastic use of machine guns also tends to attract the unwelcome attentions of the FBI, while the trusty shotgun remains a local problem. Criminals are as cost-conscious as any other laissez-faire capitalist and see no need to invest money in fancy hardware when any old 12-bore will do perfectly. Terrorists, who have a different image of themselves and may expect to have to do some serious fighting if things go wrong, are entirely another matter.

While on the subject of criminals and motorcars, it is well to remember that firing pistols at the tyres of moving cars is a pointless exercise, since they are difficult to hit and very hard to deflate. Thanks to Ralph Nader, the laminated steeply raked windscreens of modern American cars have an amazing ability to withstand pistol bullets and shotgun slugs, although the firm of KTW has marketed Teflon-coated steel bullets to combat this problem.

Criminals rarely use holsters. It is easy to drop a pistol down the nearest storm drain but thoroughly embarrassing to have to disengage a holster from a belt or beneath the armpit while attempting to outstretch the long arm of the law.

GUN LORE

The British Empire in its heyday contributed three immortal phrases to the vocabulary of the crime writer: cordite," the "dumdum" bullet and the "automatic revolver." Thanks, I suspect, to Raymond Chandler's education at Dulwich College, an English public school whose Cadet Force would have been issued with cordite-loaded cartridges, he always used this term when referring to any smokeless powder, and it has passed into the English language as a generic term for nitro propellents. True cordite bears a remarkable resemblance to whole-meal spaghetti, was given widespread use in small arms only by Britain and her Empire, and is now obsolete. "Dumdum" derives from Dum-Dum, an arsenal in India where early experiments in expanding rifle bullets took place. Its name took the fancy of the British Press and has symbolised inhumane projectiles ever since. Many a journalist and novelist has been castigated unfairly by so-called firearms experts for employing the phrase "automatic revolver." Such apparent contradictions in terms have existed, the British Webley-Fosbery being the best known, but the Spanish "Zulaika" and the American "Union" were also produced in tiny numbers, and the phrase was widely used by American advertisers to enhance the appeal of conventional self-extracting revolvers.

D.P.

The "secret weapon" is by no means confined to the realms of spy fiction. The SOE and OSS developed a plethora of highly specialised weapons during the last war, including lapel daggers, tyre-slashing knives, and pistols that fired automatically when the arms were raised in surrender (and presumably also when one was waving goodbye to one's loved ones). A fully equipped agent must have weighed about 800 pounds and have been subjected to permanent metal fatigue. The silencer was especially beloved of these clandestine organisations, and the best of them, the .45 ACP De Lisle carbine and the Welrod .32 pistol, are very, very quiet indeed. "Silencer" is, however, a misnomer, the British term "sound moderator" being a more accurate description of the device, its main function being to keep a firearm from sounding like a firearm by muffling noise. The principle of operation is identical to a motorcar silencer, and the Maxim design is indeed still used on tractors. Points to watch are that silencers work well only with subsonic bullets, since supersonic projectiles make a loud "crack" as they pass through the air; that a revolver cannot be silenced effectively by conventional means because the gap between cylinder and barrel allows gas to escape rapidly, thus creating noise; and that, to be effective, a silencer must have a large volume. The two-inch tube stuffed onto the end of a snub-nosed revolver by the movie hit-man would be singularly inefficient. Satisfactory silencers for .45 and 9 mm weapons are about 18–24 inches long and about 2½ inches in diameter. Someone has even invented a "silent grenade," which resembles a suit of armour for an octopus since several silenced barrels radiate from a central sphere. Each barrel is loaded, Roman candle fashion, with multiple charges. When the infernal machine is set into motion, it hops around like a laryngitic crackerjack broadcasting its bullets among the duly astonished multitude.

Having highlighted a few pitfalls in the field of firearms, and left many more still unilluminated, I had better close with the wise words of the old Western gunslinger: "Speed's fine, pardner, but accuracy's final."

David Penn is Keeper of the Department of Exhibits and Firearms at the Imperial War Museum, London, and Secretary of the Historical Breechloading Small-arms Association.

THE CORRECT USE OF THE BLUNT INSTRUMENT

Jennifer Louise Montrechant inherited the Montrechant squint, the Montrechant whine and the Montrechant rubies. Her husband hocked the rubies. Unable to convince her that keeping two out of three wasn't bad, he suffered a shortness of life when she used his shaving mug to recede his awesome buckteeth.

Julian Stuart liked his steak well done. Mrs. Stuart, being of perverse disposition, always served it rare. Meekly he ate it. "How was the steak, dear?" she smirked. "Oh, well done, well done," he replied, then wielding the bone as a conductor's baton, beat her tartare.

Giboney Grace Hartsdale, a dowager of no appreciable income, upended one of Mrs. Smythe's teacups to see if it was Spode and worth pinching. Mrs. Smythe, returning with the lemon wedges, was so outraged, she took the Spode and upended Giboney Grace.

Twenty housewives out of twenty have admitted they have been tempted to bang a few husbandly heads with a frying pan.

MARTY NORMAN

Roald Dahl created the most famous of the fictional blunt instruments: a frozen leg of lamb. The second most famous, Ngaio Marsh's magnum of champagne.

Alfredo Fettucine, sneaking up the stairs to tryst with the Lady Emilia, was surprised at the newel post by Helga, the upstairs maid, who knew nothing of the assignation, presumed he was a burglar and promptly dispatched him with a deft toss of a loose finial.

Mrs. T. Edward Poindexter III arrived home from Harrods at the precise moment her husband was informed by his solicitor that he was reduced to living off his principal. Mr. Poindexter picked up Mrs. Poindexter's parcel and pummeled her with it. Harrods refused to credit the account since the merchandise was damaged.

Lefty, Tiger and Mitch decided not to split the proceeds of the bank heist with Cookie, so they started the getaway without him. He had a precarious foothold on the running board of their '48 Packard when they dislodged him with a few swipes of a tire iron. He fell directly in the path of a No. 7 bus. Talk about overkill.

Cynthia Sue Janifer, belle of the Outback, flirted with every man but one. She thought he was too young. He wasn't. He tried her, *in absentia*, in a kangaroo court, found her guilty and caught her just below the sternum with his boomerang. She always did wear her dresses too low.

Amanada Tillinghast decided she would be an heiress and her brother would be mulch. "Come, darling, and look at the roses," she said. He came but brought his shovel with him. "The thorns have snagged your frock," he said, and when she bent to disengage it, he whacked her a good one. He now has the most verdant, albeit lumpy garden in all of Lincolnshire.

Miss Harriet Stearne returned to her classroom to find that nasty Reynolds child drawing a rude caricature of her on the blackboard. Miss Stearne applied ruler to rib cage. The Reynolds child was given an "A" posthumously by Miss Florinda Gentian, Instructress in Art, Miss Dorset's School for Young Ladies, Oxfordshire.

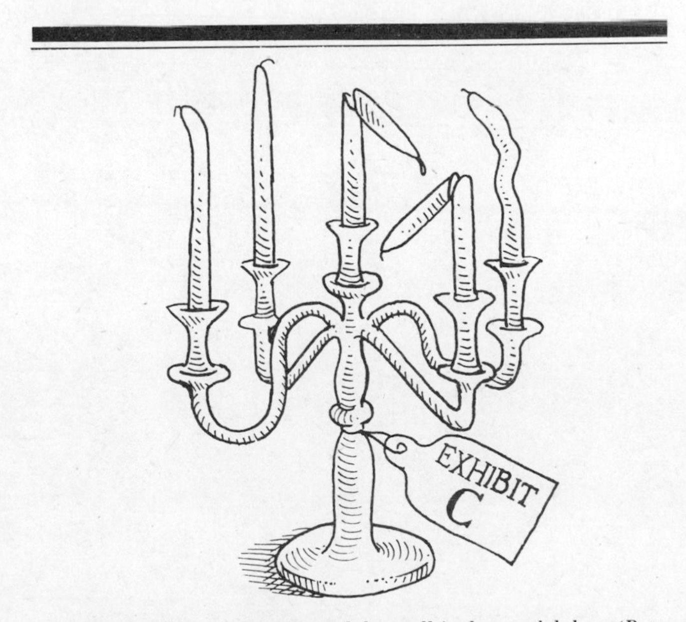

The corniest blunt instrument of them all is the candelabra. (Better for arsonists than bludgeoners.)

The interlocking grip is preferred by most coshers with a sense of sportsmanship. The overlapping pinkie is necessary to maintain one's steadiness.

Colonel Algernon Pemberton, while looking upward at a speckled field thrush in flight, was coshed from behind by Mrs. Pemberton, who always did think he was for the birds.

Alexander Higgenbottom, ambushed by thugs, rued he'd never learned jujitsu. They tore off his coat, his tie and then — alas for them — his shoe. He swung once at a forehead, once at an Adam's apple, once at the biggest nose since Cyrano. Down they went, home he went, limping slightly from loss of a shoe lift.

Having lost nine games in a row, Penelope Trumbull forgot about good sportsmanship. She heaved the checkerboard — with its full complement of checkers — at her partner, who keeled over under the barrage. It finished any intention he might have had of proposing.

Purity and Chastity hated Sigmund, their brother. "Wanna go skating?" they dimpled. "Lost my skates," he reminded them, whereupon they returned them to him, aiming straight at his head. Their mother, a widow, decided the girls were now old enough to learn how Daddy really died.

Quentin Carstairs was a well-known plagiarist. One hundred sixteen impoverished authors detested him. They elected G.W. Sutherland, from whom he'd pirated 4,073 pages, to chair the Infraction Inquiry. G.W. Sutherland threw both the chair and the rule book at him. The end.

MS. BORGIA & CO.
Poison Rings, Murder Rings

Leonard R. Harris

My father was a gentle man, a man who blushed at his own profanity when he called Hitler a "rat," a sentimental craftsman of poetic wedding rings fashioned of precious metals and glowing gems, an artist in pale watercolors who was profoundly influenced by Charles Gibson's fastidious maidens, a magician who entertained kids in hospital wards, a pianist whose favorite work was "Two Little Honey Bees" . . . yes, a gentle man.

Ah, but when he "fondled the poison rings and murder rings in his collection, a happy light shone in his eyes."

That description is on record in the newspaper of record, the *New York Times;* and it was put there by Meyer Berger, considered by many to have been the greatest reporter of all time, and therefore it must be believed. Berger also reported that my father "tenderly, lovingly" held those rings that had dealt death to dozens. And yes, it's true; I saw it.

Berger might also have described the curious gleam in the eyes of Charles B. Harris, my father, when, between thumb and index finger, he slowly rotated Lucrezia Borgia's poison ring so that the light refracted boldly from a pale emerald and two fiery rubies.

"Lucrezia Borgia was beautiful, but she was *not* a nice woman," my father explained when he showed the ring to me and my brother Bill. "She was married three times," he said, pausing, groping for the gentle way to describe Lucrezia. "And before and even while she was married, she had many . . . uh . . . many other

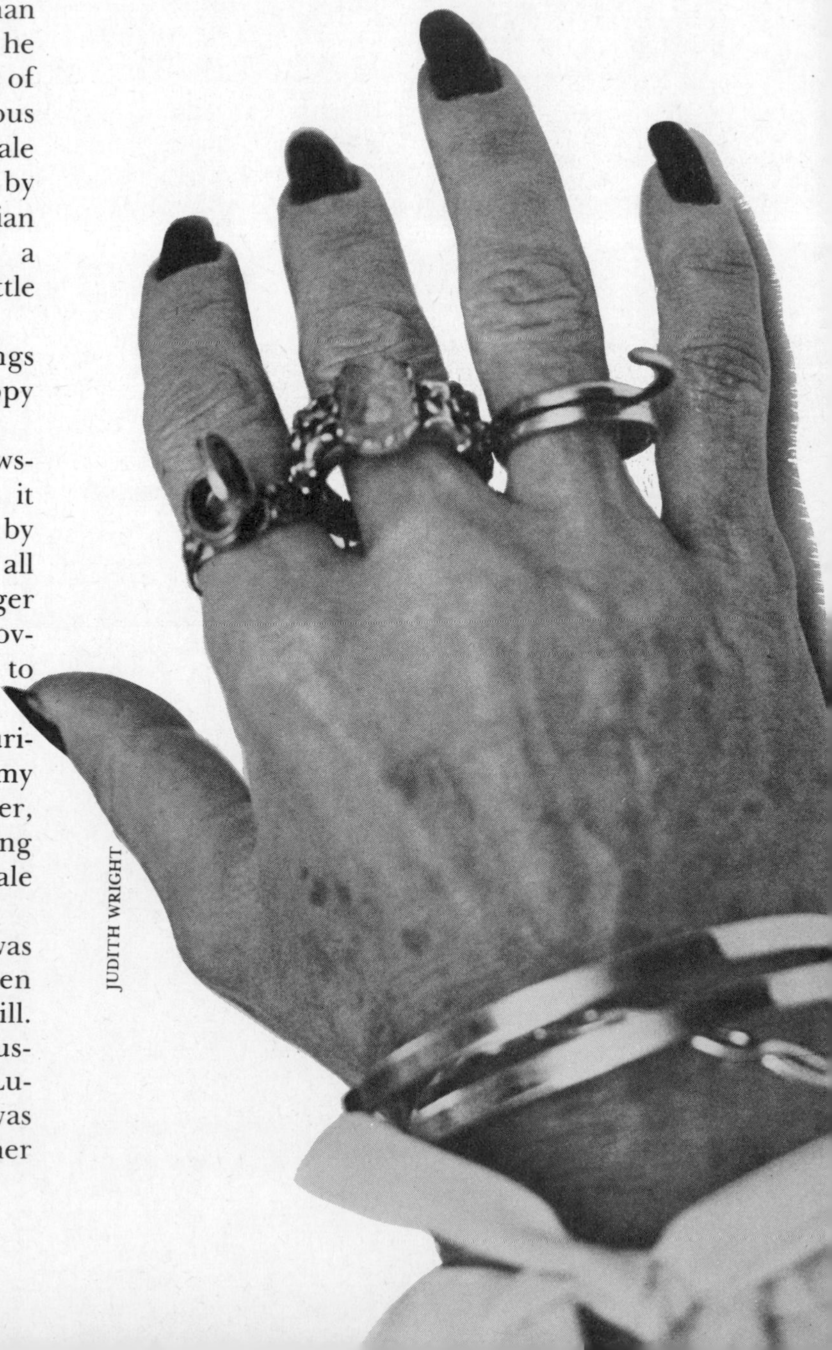

JUDITH WRIGHT

Lucrezia Borgia's poison ring. The center emerald is innocent; the side ruby is lethal.

friends. I'm afraid that she helped many of them on their way to Heaven . . . or, uh, to the other place. I'll show you how she did it . . ."

But first he felt he had to excuse Lucrezia's little quirks. "Rome in the sixteenth century was *not* a very nice place. Not like New York City at all, you understand. And her father, although he did become a Pope, was really . . . well, a rat. Kill, kill, kill! It was probably in her blood."

My brother and I wanted no history lessons. Several years older than I, Bill even knew about Lucrezia's infamous incestuous orgies, although for Dad's sake he pretended ignorance.

The ring *is* stunning. Heavy gold, the emerald centered between the rubies. Carefully lift one hinged ruby — and below is a shallow well, flowing into a hollow tube in the ring itself. Into the well Lucrezia poured a vegetable poison, not unlike curare. "But a slower poison," my father told us. "She didn't like people to die right in front of her. It might have made others suspicious. Just the right delayed-action mixture of poison and alcohol. They died later, after the org . . . uh, parties."

Then my father showed us the ingenious mechanism. He touched a golden flower nestled against the other ruby. One could imagine Lucrezia modestly covering one hand with the other. At her gentle, artless touch, a tiny, piercingly sharp needle emerged from the palm side of the ring. I could imagine Lucrezia tenderly clasping the hand of a "friend," or perhaps fondly placing her hand on his neck. The needle was wet with the deadly juice of St. Ignatius seeds, and the friend was on his (or her) way to The Other Place.

"Poor thing," my father said. "Lucrezia was only thirty-nine when she died. I've often wondered how it happened. Imagine if she'd touched the flower and triggered the needle to get ready to dispatch a friend — and then, without thinking, had slapped a Florentine mosquito that landed on her arm!"

"How did we get the ring?" my brother asked. His "we," even at thirteen, was prescient, since he followed our father into the family jewelry store.

"After Lucrezia died," my father said, "the ring found its way to the de' Medici family. And if you think the Borgias were bad — well, the de' Medicis were worse." He paused. "Real skunks!"

It was a descendant of those de' skunks who sold the ring to my grandfather, then a jeweler in London. *His* family had been jewelers to the Czar at the summer place in Petrograd, specializing in jeweled pistol grips — a glamorous-sounding form of serfdom from which they fled as soon as they could liberate enough gem chips to finance their journey to freedom.

In any event, my grandfather quite naturally distrusted nobility, and kept the ring only because of its gem value. Not until my father became one of the "sons" in B. Harris & Sons, the New York jewelry store founded by

"In that case, Dr. Shorthouse" . . . "how do you account for the fact that in the dregs of Mr. Cayley's lemonade was found strychnine enough to suggest that the full glass contained very much more than was in your prescription?"

Poison in the Garden Suburb
G.D.H. & M. COLE

An antique Venetian poison ring. The stone is hinged and swings open so the pellet may be dropped into the wineglass.

Bernard Harris, his father, did one ring into a collection grow.

"The Mexican murder ring was the next I acquired," my father told us happily. "I got it from a Mexican, but I'm sure *he* didn't use it. I didn't bargain with him, though."

The Mexican ring is a plain gold band, rather like a demure wedding band. My father flicked it expertly, and the central section of the ring rose to become a curved semicircular knife, painfully sharp. "Sharp enough to slice a hair," my father said with a curious gleam in his eye. And while I tremulously held a hair, he sliced it with a quick chop. And he quoted from a radio series that he loathed and my brother and I guiltily loved. "Who knows what evil lurks in the hearts of men?" my gentle father intoned. I quaked; the top of the knife had a curious red stain.

A third ring, Venetian, has a hinged stone that covers a depression in which a pellet of poison can be concealed before being dropped into wine. "Breathe on it," my father instructed us. When we did, the gold concealing the hinge became ever so slightly paler than the gold of the band. "Now, if those people of the court had just learned a little bit about the art of the goldsmith," he lectured us, "they might have lived longer lives. A soldered hinge almost always turns color." Then he paused. "I wish I could prove that's how the whole practice of kissing the ruler's ring began." If there's an afterlife, my dad is still researching that theory with some of the victims.

My father loved poetry, and quoted from Juvenal to demonstrate that poison rings were used in even earlier days. The proud Hannibal of Carthage committed suicide (183 B.C.) rather than face capture by the Romans when in battle they finally won revenge for their defeat at Cannae:

Nor swords, nor spears, nor
stones from engines hurled,
Will quell the man whose form
alarmed the world.
The vengeance due to Cannae's
frightful field
Flooded by human gore — a
ring shall yield.

Eventually my father's collection embraced memorial rings, made from the hair of a dearly departed; temple rings; magicians' rings; gamblers' rings used to mark cards or concealing a mirror that reveals what cards are dealt; and a variety of enchanting wedding rings. When my brother shows the rings to visitors, though, I notice a curious gleam in his eyes when he tenderly fondles the poison rings. Maybe it's "in the blood."

One November afternoon, eleven years ago, I was in San Francisco and came upon a young craftsman who had duplicated our Venetian pellet ring in Mexican silver. The next day was my daughter's ninth birthday, and I wanted a special surprise for Elizabeth and her party guests. Telling myself it would be a fine way for her and those other dear kids to carry their One-A-Day vitamins to school, I bought the lot.

"Ah!" Liz said when they were distributed at the party — and there *was* a curious gleam in her eyes. "Poison rings!"

And I found myself intoning, "Who knows what evil lurks in the hearts of men?"

Leonard R. Harris is Director of Planning and Development for the New York Times.

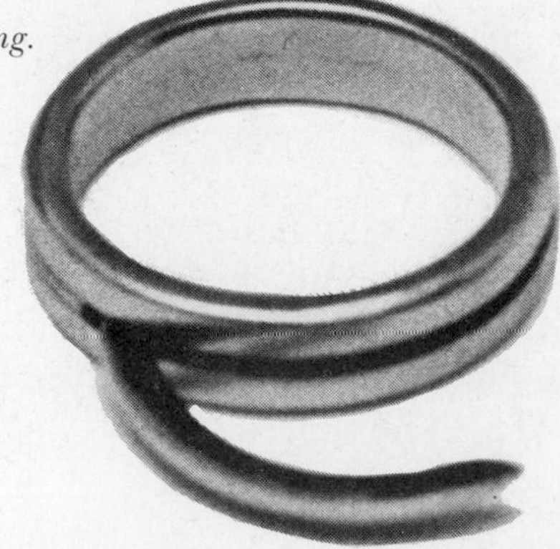
A Mexican wedding ring. This simple gold band has a curved center section which can be flicked open to reveal a curved knife.

Chapter 7

SCENES OF THE CRIME

FRED WINKOWSKI

WALKING TOUR OF LONDON

Margaret Boe Birns

Let us go then, you and I, to the Bottle Street Police Station, off Piccadilly. A dirty yellow portal on the left side of the building leads to the dark at the top of the stairs. The darkness continues to descend as we climb until suddenly — a carved oak door upon which there is a small brass plaque, neatly engraved with the simple lettering: ALBERT CAMPION, MERCHANT GOODS DEPT.

But *we* know better, don't we? Inside the flat are some delightful old pieces of furniture, a Rembrandt etching, a Steinlen cat, a lovely little Girton — and a number of trophies from Albert Campion's true line of work, including the infamous Black Dudley dagger.

As befits one rumoured to be of royal blood, Campion's rooms are luxuriously furnished. But for a look at something that will seem truly rare and unattainable, let us stroll over to 110A Piccadilly. It is directly opposite Green Park, in a block of new, perfect and expensive flats. Some say this address was chosen by the famous sleuth who resides within since it divides by two the 221B number of the notable Baker Street address. Second floor: here we are. Is it not like a colourful and gilded paradise in a mediaeval painting? Let us feast our eyes on this whimsical paradise done in black and primrose, with a wood fire leaping on a wide old-fashioned hearth, a Chesterfield sofa suggesting the embraces of the houris, walls lined with rare editions, Sèvres vases filled with red and gold chrysanthemums, a fine old decanter of Napoleon brandy — and over at the black baby grand piano, attacking a Scarlatti sonata like a man possessed, is Lord Peter Wimsey. He is moody at the moment. Just back from Harley Street, his manservant Bunter tells us, where he's undergone a most unpleasant interview with a Dr. Julian Freke. Something about a body in a bathtub.

As the strains of Scarlatti fade away behind us, let us move on to the beautifully appointed Albany. The thick pile carpet, the air of unhurried splendour — it is the perfect ambience for elegant A.J. Raffles, gentleman and thief. Perhaps we can purchase some Sullivan cigarettes here at the desk, then take a turn into the heart of Mayfair to view the home of the Honorable Richard Rolliston, alias "The Toff." And while in the district, we must visit Whitehaven Mansions. That little Belgian gentleman with the famous moustaches used to live with his friend Captain Hastings at 14 Farraway, but back in the Thirties he moved to this modern block of flats whose geometrical appearance and proportions indulged his passion for order and method. His efficient secretary, Miss Felicity Lemon, and his faithful manservant, Georges, looked after the old gentleman quite well, but — alas — after a recent imbroglio at Styles this illustrious detective with the highly developed "little grey cells" has passed away. Is it possible that the local Elephant-and-Castle will have retained a bit of his favourite *sirop de cassis?* Perhaps we can stop in and raise our glasses to the memory of the late Hercule Poirot.

These are indeed the great good places of London. But there are other London dwellings

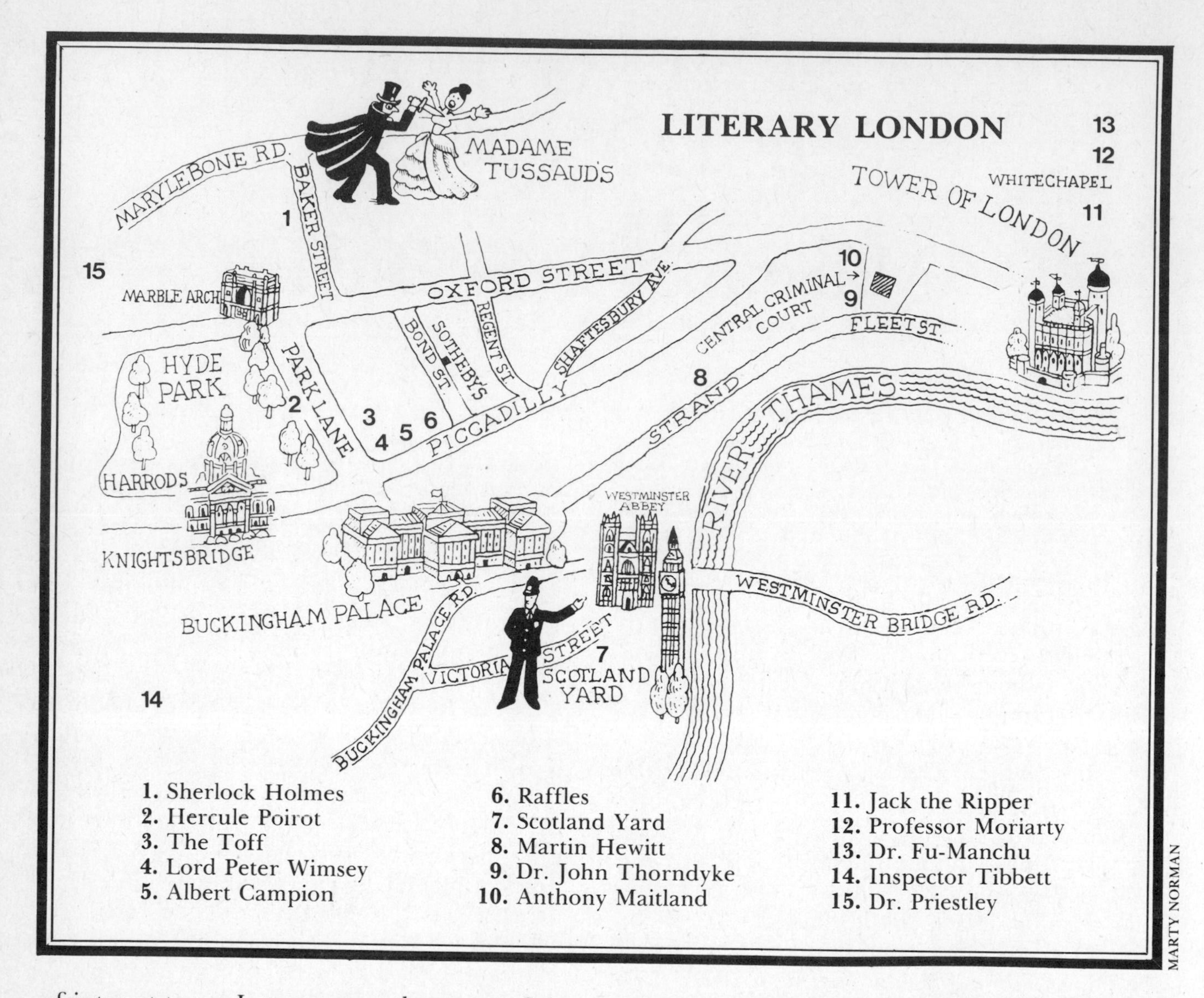

of interest to us. Let us move, then, out of the posh Mayfair district over to The Strand. In an old building near The Strand we can find a plain ground-glass door on which appears the single word HEWITT. It is, of course, the private detective agency of the amiable Martin Hewitt. Stout fellow, Hewitt. For an even stouter fellow let us turn just below The Strand and above the Victoria Embankment to I Adelphi Terrace, where we can find the roly-poly Gideon Fell. There he is, with a pint of bitter next to him. Seems to be indulging in one of his favourite pastimes — reading a mystery story.

And now let's move over to The Temple, nearby. Here we are: 5A King's Bench Walk. One floor up is a massive outer oak door with a name upon it in white letters. This door opens to disclose a baize-covered inner door. Beyond this is a spacious wood-paneled living room with a broad hearth flanked by two wing chairs. In the fireplace is a gas ring, on which a kettle of water boils for tea. On the floor above is a laboratory and workshop, the walls covered with shelves and tool racks bearing all manner of strange instruments. There is also a cupel furnace, occasionally used as a grill for cutlets by the noble manservant Polton. At a table in the laboratory, a tall and very handsome man appears to be making a study of the characteristics of methylene blue on cellulose and oxycellulose. You recognise him? Yes, of course: it is Dr. John Thorndyke.

And while we are in the area, over at the Inner Temple are Sir Nicholas Harding's chambers, which he shares with that English barrister who is the very soul of London urbanity — Antony Maitland.

The fog thickens. It begins to close around us like a shroud as we walk outside the city gates and into the East End. The fog is brown and vile here in Whitechapel Road, among the one-night cheap hotels and sawdust restaurants; menace seems to permeate the very brick and stone itself. Later, in one of these dark, echoing side streets, Jack the Ripper may pay one of his nocturnal visits. Even now, people and objects seem to retreat into the dirty brown mist as we walk the promenade from Whitechapel to Mile End. It is behind the shuttered windows of one of these dingy buildings that we would very likely find the headquarters of a certain Dr. Moriarty, organiser of half that is evil and nearly all that is undetected in this great city.

Limehouse. The smoke-laden vapors of the lower Thames have taken on the aroma of incense. I think that now you may begin to sense the presence of something. If you turn, you will see what you have already somehow sensed — magnetic cat-green eyes, glittering below a dome-shaped forehead. A brow like Shakespeare's, a face like Satan's. Long tapering fingers with sharp taloned nails fold together in front of a black robe embroidered with a silver peacock. The mist closes again, but we know that we have felt a force of malignancy we had never supposed could radiate from any human being, that we have seen a sight we will never forget: the devil-doctor himself — Fu Manchu!

We hear the low whistle of his henchmen, the Burmese dacoits. Quickly, to Scotland Yard, and a consultation with Sir Denis Nayland Smith. How safe it feels here in Whitehall! Now that we have dispatched Sir Nayland Smith to the East End, let us greet Inspector Lestrade. He is on his way to 3 Lauriston Gardens, off the Brixton Road. If we accompanied him, we would see scrawled in blood-red letters the mysterious inscription "Rache." A veritable study in scarlet, as it were.

Let us follow along the corridor to Colonel March at the Department of Queer Complaints. Best walk carefully: there are peppermint cream wrappers on the floor here — Inspector Gently must be about. Ah now, here are the Dead Ends. Inspector Rason, of course, presides here, with a great deal more success than he had with Fidelity Dove! And speaking of influential ladies, let us peek in on Mrs. Palmyra Pym, the Assistant Commissioner of Criminal Investigation — the highest-ranking woman in the Yard.

That there, over at his desk, is Inspector Wilfred Dover. Unfortunately, he appears to have nodded off to sleep. He is snoring over the papers on his desk and has spilled the remains of his tea on what appears to have been a suspect's signed confession. And there is Commander George Gideon. His nose seems a bit out of joint. Evidently he was presented with a traffic ticket this morning. Best to be off.

Now, for a quick nip over to Chelsea. On the ground floor of that shabby yet genteel Victorian house resides Chief Inspector Henry Tibbett and his devoted, albeit pleasingly plump wife, Emily. And if we just step over to the Fulham Road we can pass Harrington Street and the digs of Commander Gideon.

Let us cross Hyde Park now and enter the Bayswater section of London. Here we are at Westbourne Terrace, home of the brilliant Dr. Priestley. Note how even his house bears the unmistakable stamp of the English aristocrat!

Before we proceed to our final destination, I must inform you of a little side excursion you might, one day, wish to take. Over at Paddington Station Mrs. McGillicuddy is willing to accompany interested bystanders, or available witnesses, on the 4:50 train.

As night falls on the great city, the lamps are lit and we walk past 221B Baker Street. Inside we may expect to find those familiar rooms, the velvet-lined armchair, the array of fine pipes — and smell the aroma of strong tobacco. Even now, the strains of violin music reach us through the sulphurous yellow mist. But wait — out of the night looms a large, totally bald man with a lollipop in his hand. He is about to enter 221B Baker Street. Something about a "stake-out." Something about drugs. Something about a "Baker Street Connection . . ."

Margaret Boe Birns teaches "The Detective Novel" at New York University.

WAYLAID IN LONELY PLACES

The rock quarry . . .

© 1977 JOSH ZANDER

The east parlour . . .

JUDITH WRIGHT

The detour . . .

ST. MARY MEAD AND OTHER TROUBLED VILLAGES

Margaret Yorke

Miss Marple no longer lives in St. Mary Mead, but the village crime novel is still vigorous. Like rural life, however, it has changed and broadened. In the old-style whodunit an ingenious puzzle was constructed among somewhat stereotyped characters. There was the butler, who sometimes found the body and whose short sight might provide a clue; the grey-haired retired colonel; the doctor who happened to be an expert on obscure poisons; the cycling vicar, trusty witness to people's movements. Then there was the small cast of suspects, few of whom worked for a living, though sometimes the local solicitor was the villain. Supporting roles were played by various servants, none of whom, convention decreed, might be the murderer. There would be an eccentric extra charater, to add atmosphere. The sleuth was often an amateur, in the area by chance or summoned by a worried suspect, though sometimes he was a policeman of acumen, if not urbanity. Motives for murder were mainly avaricious, involving blackmail or inheritance. Sex might be implicit, not overt.

Village life was never, in fact, quite like that.

The detective novel's form restricts the number of characters that may appear, but the slice of life shown by contemporary writers using the village setting shows a truer aspect of their chosen section of the scene.

Country villages are dwellings often centred round a manor house, with a church, an inn or two, and usually at least one shop which also does duty as a post office. Motorways have extended the commuter range, and some industries have moved to rural areas, so that many villages have rapidly enlarged. Expansion beyond the village bounds is not allowed, and new houses have sprung up, often mushroom-like in clumps, in what were once paddocks or

ST. MARY MEAD

First mentioned in *The Murder at the Vicarage* (1930), St. Mary Mead is described as a "quiet, one-horse village," with no "picture house." Miss Marple's nephew regarded it as "a stagnant pool." It has several small shops, The Blue Boar and a path leading to Old Hall. The train goes up to London, and on Thursdays one can get a cheap ticket. On Sundays one can visit the church with its "rather fine old stained glass." A map of St. Mary Mead is included in the book and according to it, Miss Marple's front gate is catty-corner to that of the vicarage.

The village never really lived.

BRITISH TOURIST AUTHORITY

Deep in the mystery writer's imagination is situated the village. *It has a High Street (which is so named because it* is *high, overlooking the surrounding area), a cycling vicar, a pub, a post office where the residents read each other's mail and an adorable tea shoppe.*

large gardens. The result is a denser population and the creation of new tensions.

Some less conveniently situated villages are dying, for mechanised farms employ fewer humans. Cottages which might otherwise become derelict are bought as weekend retreats by city dwellers who arrive on Friday nights and spend their leisure hours cultivating vegetables or knocking down walls to expose all possible beams, and perhaps a fictional corpse. By Monday morning, deserted again, these villages are perfect spots for villains on the run to hide in or hold people hostage, to inter victims in the fresh-dug bean trench or pop them in the freezer.

In the growing villages, social mores are complex. Those who live in picturesque old houses may be envied by others in the more mortgage-worthy new ones, with their tiny gardens which allow no privacy. Newcomers, keen to become part of the community, sometimes fling themselves into drama groups and festivals with an enthusiasm offensive to older inhabitants who resent the changes round them and may, by a neighbour's sale of land for building, have lost their own seclusion.

Existing shops are rarely adequate for the increased population, and there is constant traffic on narrow roads. The once peaceful country air is rent by the car engines of the work force and the shoppers, and borne upon the wind may be the sound of farm tractors, combine harvesters and the whine of the circular saw. Lawn mowers, electric hedge clippers and bonfire smoke may irritate and, by planned timing, induce a state of war.

THE TROUBLED VILLAGE

For those who like a cosy little village setting, and have read most of Mrs. Christie's output, you might turn to the work of Catherine Aird, Elizabeth Lemarchand, W.J. Burley, Elizabeth Ferrars, Margaret Yorke (particularly *No Medals for the Major)*, Peter Dickinson *(A Pride of Heroes)*, Reginald Hill *(Ruling Passion)*, P.D. James *(The Dark Tower, Cover Her Face)*, Jessica Mann *(Mrs. Knox's Profession)*. Similar in type but spanning out from the village are the works of Anne Morice, Margaret Erskine, Colin Watson and, with more than a touch of kinkiness, Ruth Rendell.

Villages no longer have their own policeman. There may be a constable living in a police house, but he will patrol a wide district by car and may lack time to build up an intimate local knowledge. Vicars, now, are sometimes trendy and introduce rock hymns which enrage traditionalists enough to provoke hostile letters, if not actual murder. A growing sport is campanology: not the mere Sunday summons, but matches played by touring teams sampling rival sets of bells in peals that may last four hours; an incensed listener, forced to endure the assault upon his ears, might well feel tempted to hang a ringer with his own rope.

Mansions, if historically interesting, are often open to the public and fresh tourist bait is constantly added, like tigers in the deer park. A fictional corpse is as likely to be found nowadays in the lion pound as stabbed in the rose garden. Some large houses are divided into flats or become institutions or government establishments; a few may be privately owned by pop stars or financiers, and here there may, indeed, be found a butler, though he is more likely to be a Filipino than a Jeeves.

There is scope now to introduce any type of character and to devise sophisticated crimes: art thefts, kidnappings, industrial or even international espionage. Country crafts flourish: gems or drugs in products from the local pottery? Road improvements may threaten to obliterate historic sites and anger archaeologists who delve to rescue what they can before the approaching bulldozer, while nature lovers seek to protect beauty spots from the same fate. Foul means for their own cause might well be used by either the planners for the future or the saviours of the past.

Some village pubs are little changed, with "snug" bars and dart boards, but also, now, a fruit machine. Others provide excellent bar meals at reasonable cost and are filled at midday with businessmen from nearby towns. The do-gooding village spinster is almost extinct; her emancipated modern sister, and working wives who earn good salaries, may be in the pubs, too. Young mothers, though, are sometimes lonely, tied by the need to drive children back and forth to play group and school in the intervals of stocking up the freezer and operating machines which undertake domestic chores, since human aid has almost disappeared. A few older women will "help out," to "oblige," often because they would otherwise be alone all day themselves. There is an occasional housekeeper to be found: sweet, sinister or seductive, probably widowed or divorced and employed by some lone man; either, in fact or fiction, may have more than mere domestic designs upon the other, and if they haven't, few will believe them.

Human nature alters little, although the scene may change, and the seven deadly sins will never cease to flourish. Today's writer has freedom to explore any or all of them, and plots often arise now from some sort of personal threat or conflict. The psychological or suspense novel with a village setting exists beside the classic detective story. Crimes are usually solved by efficient police detectives backed up by the resources of science, though an occasional amateur still appears. The lure of the mystery novel lies in the reader's knowledge that though the real world is full of horrors, this time it didn't really happen.

Margaret Yorke is the author of the contemporary village mystery, No Medals for the Major.

NOBODY LEAVE THE ROOM!

Andrew B. Levy

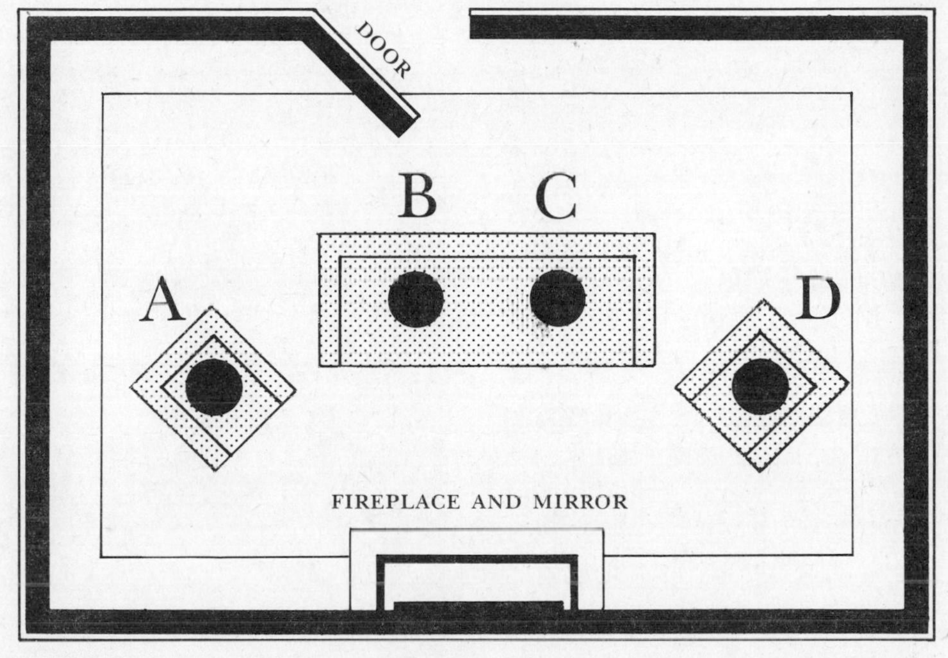

Boggs the bookmaker has been found dead in the club lounge, his wine poisoned.

Four men, seated on a sofa and two armchairs in front of the fireplace, as shown above, are discussing the foul deed. Their names are Howell, Scott, Jennings and Wilton. And they are, not necessarily respectively, a general, schoolmaster, admiral and doctor.

(a) The waiter pours a glass of whiskey for Jennings and a beer for Scott.

(b) The general looks up and, in the mirror over the fireplace, sees the door close behind the waiter. He then turns to speak to Wilton, next to him.

(c) Neither Howell nor Scott has any sisters.

(d) The schoolmaster is a teetotaler.

(e) Howell, who is sitting in one of the armchairs, is the admiral's brother-in-law. The schoolmaster is next to him on his left.

Suddenly, a hand stealthily moves forward to put something in Jenning's whiskey. It is the murderer again. No one has left his seat, and no one else is in the room.

What is the profession of each man, and where is he sitting?

And who is the murderer? (Solution on page 263.)

Andrew B. Levy is a high school student in Amarillo, Texas.

MAYBE YOU BETTER NOT LOCK THE DOOR

Gordon Bean

Dagger in hand, the murderer advances toward his victim. Escape lies just two strides away, through the room's sole door — but the killer darts there first, throwing the bolt. his quarry lunges for a window — too late! His assailant has locked that, too. There is a scuffle. A chair overturned. A lamp dropped to the floor. A corner of the carpet set askew. But there is no place to turn, to hide. A knife jerks up and down repeatedly. A loud thump. And then: a corpse sprawled in front of the fireplace's flickering glow.

Some hours later, the police crash through the window (having failed to breach the door) and find: a bloody dagger; a messy room; a mutilated body. But no murderer. How did he get out? It is quite obvious no one could have left the room. Seemingly, the police must take on a villain who can melt through locked windows and doors like Houdini's ghost. But, of course, the police detective will ultimately expose the "miracle" as trickery and will explain just how the illusion was created.

That, in a nutshell, is the archetypal plot of the locked-room mystery, a subgenre which has puzzled readers since Poe first invented it with *Murders in the Rue Morgue.* Chesterton, Carr, Queen — all have played off this classic theme and have inspired others to tackle it. It is the strictest form of the "impossible crime."

Why the intense, continuing interest in it? Because the locked-room gambit evokes the ul-

MATTHEW SEAMAN

COURTESY BRITISH TOURIST AUTHORITY

The archetypal locked room is a jail cell. This one houses Zeus, who is waiting for Divine Inspiration on how to get out.

timate mystery — the mystery of magic.

Reading a locked-room mystery, you enter a world reminiscent of a fantastic magic show: Men walk through walls, slither through keyholes and vanish like pricked soap bubbles. And not only do you experience magical effects, you are fooled by magical methods as well. Not trapdoors, secret wires, mirrors — these are just gimmicks. Rather, I am speaking of suggestion and misdirection, psychological devices the magician — along with his literary equivalent, the locked-room writer — uses to coax your mind down a prescribed path of "logic" which ends in paradox.

Through suggestion, the author leads you to a false assumption. For example, he can create merely the illusion of murder, causing you to assume — falsely — a murderer's presence. How? The victim could stab himself with an icicle, whose absence (after melting) would suggest the killer has absconded and taken the murder weapon with him.

Important as suggestion is, to fully deceive it needs its counterpart: misdirection. With misdirection, the author does not suggest something false; he hides something true — namely, an illusion-puncturing clue. Such as: the damp spot next to the "icicled" corpse.

But the locked-room mystery's appeal, like that of the magic show, rests mainly in the fantasy it conjures up — not in its puzzle. A good one temporarily suspends logic, filling us with childlike awe. When a simple explanation destroys that awe, we realize how easily we are fooled — a knowledge which provides rare perspective on the intellect's deficiency.

So find (and that's not easy — you could probably get out of a locked room quicker) a copy of Israel Zangwill's *The Big Bow Mystery*, Carter Dickson's *He Wouldn't Kill Patience* or Clayton Rawson's *Death from a Top Hat* and pay attention. See if you can tell how they sealed off the room, now that you know they're out to mislead you. But don't expect any icicles. A real murderer stalks these three rooms. Contrary to popular advice, given the nature of the locked-room novel, I would suggest you don't sit down to read until you've *unlocked* the door.

Gordon Bean is a magician, a student at Brown University, and was the youngest participant on the first Mystery Readers' Tour of Great Britain.

SOLUTION TO "NOBODY LEAVE THE ROOM" PUZZLE

Scott is the murderer. We know from the clue about Howell that he is seated in an armchair, which must be at position A since there is someone seated next to him on his left. That person, the schoolmaster, therefore, must be at B on the sofa. Furthermore, the schoolmaster's name must be Wilton, since he is not Howell and is a teetotaler (the waiter poured a glass of whiskey for Jennings and a beer for Scott). Because the general has turned to speak to Wilton, next to him, the general must be seated at C on the sofa. We know that Howell is not the admiral (he's the admiral's brother-in-law, remember?) and that the men at B and C are schoolmaster and general, so the man in armchair D must be the admiral, leaving Howell as the doctor. The admiral and general are Scott and Jennings, but which is which? Well, if neither Howell nor Scott has a sister, and Howell is the admiral's brother-in-law, then Scott cannot be the admiral. General Scott, then, seated at C on the sofa, is the only man able to reach over to D and put poison in Admiral Jenning's whiskey.

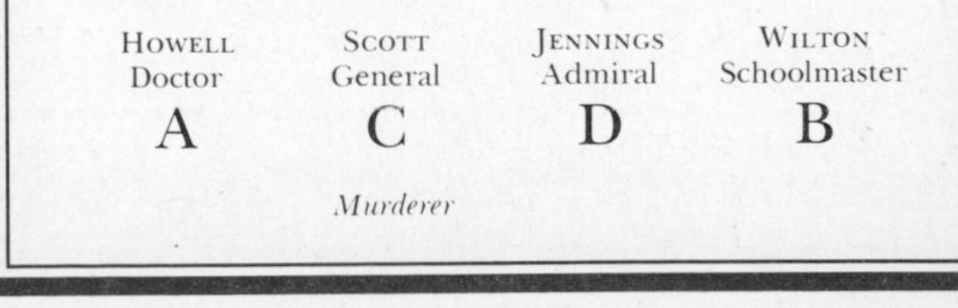

Howell	Scott	Jennings	Wilton
Doctor	General	Admiral	Schoolmaster
A	C	D	B
	Murderer		

OXFORD VS. CAMBRIDGE

The Dark Blues Have the Most

Margaret Yorke

More mystery stories are set in Oxford than in Cambridge. More fictional sleuths are Oxford than Cambridge men. More crime writers live near Oxford than Cambridge. Why?

First, is it true? Yes. Dorothy L. Sayers and Peter Wimsey, Edmund Crispin and Gervase Fen, Michael Innes and his quotation-capping Appleby score instantly for Oxford, whose sporting teams are distinguished from the light blue of Cambridge by their dark blue colours. Then come J.C. Masterman with *An Oxford Tragedy* and *The Case of the Four Friends,* Katherine Farrar with *Gownsman's Gallows* and *The Missing Link* and Robert Robinson with *Landscape with Dead Dons.* James McClure lives in Oxford; Elizabeth Ferrars lived there for five years; three of Gwendolyn Butler's books have Oxford settings. John Le Carré and Geoffrey Household both went there. G.D.H. Cole, a Fellow of All Souls, wrote many detective novels in partnership with his wife Margaret, but she went to Cambridge; Anthony Price went to Ox-

OXFORD MYSTERIES

Jeffrey Archer: *Not a Penny More, Not a Penny Less*
Adam Broome: *The Oxford Murders*
Gwendolyn Butler: *Coffin in Oxford; A Coffin for Pandora; Dine and Be Dead*
G.D.H. and M.I. Cole: *Off with Her Head*
Edmund Crispin: *Obsequies at Oxford; Dead and Dumb; The Moving Toyshop*
Colin Dexter: *Last Bus to Woodstock*
Katherine Farrar: *Gownsman's Gallows; The Missing Link; At Odds with Morning*
Michael Innes: *Operation Pax; Seven Suspects; Hare Sitting Up*
J.C. Masterman: *An Oxford Tragedy; The Case of the Four Friends*
Dermot Morrah: *The Mummy Case Mystery*
Raymond Postgate: *Ledger Is Kept*
Robert Robinson: *Landscape with Dead Dons*
J. Maclaren Ross: *Until the Day She Dies*
Dorothy L. Sayers: *Gaudy Night*
Margaret Yorke: *Cast for death; Grave Matters*

GEORGE HALCROW

The Bridge of Sighs, Oxford. In Oxford, the rivers run around, not through the city, and few colleges are alongside them. College bridges, therefore, cross streets, not water.

ford, and lives nearby, but sent his Dr. Audley to Cambridge: two half-hits for the Light Blues here?

So what about "the other place," which is what Oxford persons call Cambridge? P.D. James lived there, her poetry-writing Commander Adam Dalgliesh was certainly at Cambridge, and her *An Unsuitable Job for a Woman* has a Cambridge setting. To support her, there is Glyn Daniel and his sleuth Sir Richard Sherrington. V.C. Clinton-Baddeley's Dr. Davie is a Cambridge don; Margery Allingham's Campion went to Cambridge. Peter Dickinson, Robert Charles and Brian Cooper all went to Cambridge. So did J.B. Priestley, whose comprehensive works include a detective novel, *Salt Is Leaving*.

Scenes-of-crime investigation is important when solving mysteries. Let's examine these. Oxford is centrally placed in England, the hub of road and railway lines radiating in all directions on the way to many other places. Cambridge is out on a limb, long ago a port but now an end in itself. Oxford has varied, hilly countryside around the city. Cambridge lies amid flat fenland exposed to cobweb-dispersing winds. Oxford is a grey city, its buildings stone, though the refaced colleges now gleam palely golden as when they were first built in the days before polluted air blackened their façades. Cambridge is a city of colour; many of the colleges are built of mellow brick, and old frontages in the town have been preserved by planners who have hidden modern blocks away from immediate view.

But the biggest difference lies in what is central to each city. In Oxford, the colleges border busy streets: most of those at Cambridge lie along the banks of the tranquil river, each linked by its own bridge to the verdant parkland and gardens on the farther side. In Oxford, the rivers run around, not through the

CAMBRIDGE MYSTERIES

V.C. Clinton-Baddeley: *Death's Bright Dart*
Adam Broome: *The Cambridge Murders*
Robert Charles: *Dead Before Midnight*
Brian Cooper: *The Path to the Bridge*
Dilwyn Rees: *The Cambridge Murders*
P.D. James: *An Unsuitable Job for a Woman*
R. Lait: *Switched Out*

COURTESY BRITISH TOURIST AUTHORITY

The Bridge of Sighs, Cambridge. Most of the Cambridge colleges lie along the banks of the tranquil river and punting is a favourite student avocation.

city, and few colleges are alongside them. Both cities have Bridges of Sighs: Oxford's crosses a street; Cambridge's crosses water. But at Oxford, over all, looms the monster motor industry that grew from a cycle repair shop. Cambridge has no comparable industrial complex.

Both universities have much the same student population, but Oxford has more colleges than Cambridge and some are small, tucked away in dark corners. Cambridge colleges are generally large; the eye is led ever upwards and one is aware, always, of the sky. The heavens are not conspicuous above Oxford, where the climate is prone to fog and the atmosphere induces introspection.

Oxford's lead in the crime fiction stakes notwithstanding, Cambridge has a Chair in Criminology while Oxford has only a small research institute. Nigel Fisher, however, Professor of Criminology at Cambridge, was himself at Christ Church, Oxford, and was a Fellow of Nuffield College before he went to Cambridge. Colin Dexter, though, went the other way: he left Cambridge for Oxford, where he sets his mysteries. Nicholas Blake (C. Day Lewis, later Poet Laureate) was at Oxford, then became Clark Lecturer at Trinity College, Cambridge, and later Professor of Poetry at Oxford. Is this movement evidence or a red herring?

Cambridge, strong on science, deals with criminological facts whereas our subject here is crime in fantasy. To invent it, you may have to leave Cambridge. (P.D. James lives in London.) It cannot be coincidence that eight writing members of the Crime Writers' Association live within fifteen miles of the centre of Oxford and only two live as close to Cambridge. On this evidence the verdict must be that Cambridge persons, living beside tranquil water under the wide sky, need no escape into a world of fantasy: where is their Tolkien or Lewis Carroll? Oxford persons, pressured amid their busy streets under darker, lowering skies, suffer from more blues.

Margaret Yorke lives fourteen miles from Oxford, has worked in the libraries of two Oxford colleges and has a sleuth who is an Oxford don, Dr. Patrick Grant.

HARVARD HAS A HOMICIDE, TOO

Timothy Fuller: *Harvard Has a Homicide*

THE GOTHIC HOUSE

Peter Blake

As a modern architect, and as an occasional critic of modern architecture, I am pleased to report that nobody ever gets done in in a modern house. In fact, modern houses tend to be so antiseptic as to rule out almost all passions. In his first and possibly his best novel, *Decline and Fall,* the late Evelyn Waugh described an (almost) fictitious avant-garde architect whom he named Otto Friedrich Silenus and who was commissioned by one Mrs. Margot Beste-Chetwynde to design and build a house of ferroconcrete, aluminum and "vita-glass" (whatever that was supposed to be). Professor Silenus obliged and, a few pages down the line, described his client (who had since proposed marriage to him) as follows: "If you compare her with other women of her age you will see that the particulars in which she differs from them are infinitesimal compared with the points of similarity. A few millimeters here and a few millimeters there, such variations are inevitable in the human reproductive system . . . ." In short, no passions aroused, and certainly none requited.

Indeed, a remarkable number of modern houses designed by myself and by my architect friends have caused the owners to seek divorce almost instantly after the issuance of a certificate of occupancy. Passions had not merely cooled — they had plummeted right through the polar icecap! To the best of my knowledge, there is no record of either party having ever asked for custody of the guilty house.

But people certainly do and did and will again get passionately murdered and otherwise discomfited in so-called "Gothic" houses. Actually, most of the "Gothic" houses that people get murdered in are not, strictly speaking, Gothic at all; they are just about any recognizable or unrecognizable style: Greek Revival, Romanesque Revival, Colonial Revival, Plantation, Stanford White (every town and village in the East has at least one attributed to White — who died of gunshot wounds himself, of course — and most of these attributions are incorrect) and, most dependably, the style best known as "Charles Addams."

I don't recall a single place in which I have ever lived in the U.S. that did not have at least one Charles Addams house: it was usually two stories in height (plus mansard roof); most windows were broken and/or boarded up; its front porch was in a state of collapse, barely able to support the cobwebs strung between its slender (and partly splintered) pillars; its siding was termite-infested; and the paint was peeling throughout. The steps leading up to the porch had long rotted away; the foundation walls (if any) had settled in the general direction of China; and at night shutters (usually dangling from a single hinge) would swing and bang mournfully. Whenever there was a thunderstorm (and even whenever there was not), lightning would be sure to strike the mansard roof, like a sword of fire.

There used to be a Charles Addams house at the end of Long Island, between Bridgehampton and Sagaponack. Everybody *knew* that someone had been murdered inside that terrible wreck. The story went that she (the victim) had been all alone, that there had been no will, and that no one had been able to locate any next of kin. Hence the title to the disaster area was clouded, and the property could not

BEWARE
OF THE
THING
Chas Addams

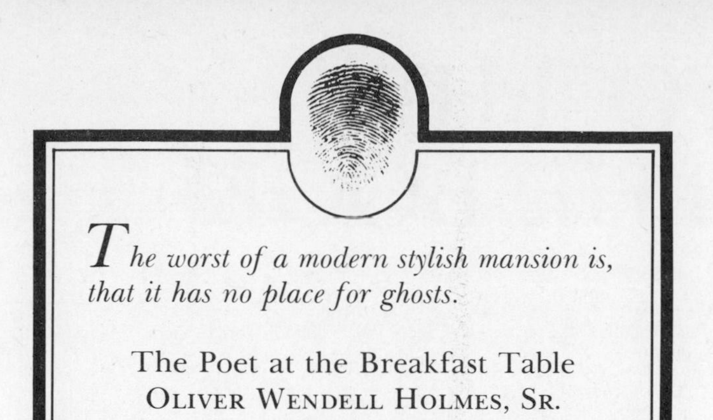

be sold. (That's a ridiculous scenario to anyone who knows what's what; the next of kin obviously had to have been at least marginally involved in the bloodbath.)

The house was leaning at an angle the Tower of Pisa would have envied when I decided one day to trespass on the premises (bodyguarded by my then eight-year-old son and a team of killer dogs). The exterior had been posted liberally with NO TRESPASSING signs; the floorboards on the entrance porch gave way with a crash; the front door screeched; and the walls and ceilings sighed. Rats scuttled, bats whizzed by, and so did ghosts. We looked for black widow spiders and original copies of the Federalist Papers.

However, by the time we reached the stairs to the attic (where those priceless Federalist Papers were sure to have been stashed away), we had giant butterflies in our stomachs and the killer dogs were in a state of shock. There seemed to be a great many bleached bones scattered about this Haunted Mansion (they turned out to be droppings left by Colonel Sanders' army), and there seemed to be an awful silence — made more awful by occasional whimpering sounds (my own).

It was in the middle of a sunny summer day, but inside that Haunted Mansion it was very dim and very cold and clammy. We never made it to the attic, where the most telling clues were undoubtedly on display.

My son and I went back a year later, and the Charles Addams house had simply vanished. It had not merely been struck down by one final bolt of lightning, leaving a burned-out cadaver; it had literally dropped out of sight, like a whodunit clue left too long unobserved. There was absolutely nothing but a great thicket of poison ivy.

Except . . . except that late one night, after a long party in Sagaponack, I drove back heading west on Sag Road, toward Bridgehampton, and suddenly there was this bolt of lightning, to my right, crashing into the now-vacant lot, and I caught sight of it in my rear-view mirror. And there, in this flash of lightning, stood the old "Gothic" house in all its glory, as if entirely new, long before it had been touched by Charles Addams' brush. And on the porch I saw the figure of a lady clad in gossamer cobwebs, and the figure of a brutish man, and something clearly against the felony statutes was about to be done to her, with an ax. So I quickly stepped on the gas and made it to my own, dispassionate modern house in record time.

In their recent book on Gothic architecture in America, Calder Toth and Julius Trousdale Sadler, Jr. (the latter, obviously, a prime suspect by the sound of his name alone) discuss at great length what they have called "The Only Proper Style." Their book is fascinating, an unbroken record of increasingly bizarre disasters: a Gothic church in Buffalo is reported to have burned down "as the result of a rocket alighting on the bell tower during the course of the Glorious Fourth celebrations of 1868" (a likely story!); another is reported to have vanished; Oscar Wilde is quoted as having snarled at a Gothic structure in Chicago, calling it "a castellated monstrosity with pepper boxes stuck all over it"; and the architects of Gothic houses are reported to have died rather precipitously. In summing up, Messrs. Toth and Sadler, Jr., say that, in neo-Gothic times in America, "a man could be born in a Gothic bed, receive baptism in a Gothic church, attend a Gothic school, live in a Gothic house, and at last be buried in a Gothic cemetery from a Gothic mortuary chapel."

Quite so — almost: not only "a man," but also a woman or a child; and not only "live in a Gothic house," but also die in one.

Peter Blake is chairman of the School of Architecture, Boston Architectural Center, and author of Form Follows Fiasco: Why Modern Architecture Hasn't Worked.

STEP TO THE REAR OF THE BOOK

Frederic F. Van de Water's novel concerns a button snapped from an épée, a half-completed letter, a leather knife sheath.

Lange Lewis' work involves a silver vial, five cigarette butts, an iron dumbbell and a 5" x 7" notebook.

The first Dell Mapback was *Death in the Library* by Phillip Ketchum. It was issued in January 1942. Today that little paperback and the 800 or so others which followed it in the series are much sought-after by collectors, who will pay up to $10 for them. (They were originally priced at 25¢.) The Mapbacks had three outstanding features: the scene of the crime depicted on the back cover; the capsule character descriptions preceding Chapter One, which were often more vividly written than the books themselves; the teaser, which enticed you into reading further by dropping more red herrings in less space than had ever been done before (or since).

COURTESY DELL PUBLISHING CO., INC.

James Francis Bonnell's story mystifies with some sharp, slim arrows, dark spots on the hall carpet and a bonfire on the beach.

Baynard Kendrick's book employs a blue silk negligee cord, a Gideon Bible, a hotel passkey and 300,000 pounds sterling.

THE UNITED STATES BULLION DEPOSITORY

The Depository was completed in December 1936, at a cost of $560,000. The first gold was moved to the Depository by railroad in January 1937.

The two-story building with basement and attic, is constructed of granite, steel and concrete; exterior dimensions measure 105 by 121 feet. Its height is 42 feet above the first-floor level. Over the marble entrance at the front of the building is the inscription UNITED STATES DEPOSITORY along with the seal of the Treasury Department in gold. Offices of the Captain of the Guard and the Officer in Charge open upon the entrance lobby. At the rear is another entrance for the reception of bullion and supplies.

The building houses a two-level steel-and-concrete vault, divided into compartments. The vault door weighs nearly 30 tons. No one person is entrusted with the combination; various members of the Depository staff must dial separately combinations known only to them. The vault casing is constructed of steel plates, steel I-beams and steel cylinders laced with hoop bands and encased in concrete. The vault roof is of similar construction and is independent of the Depository roof.

Inside the vault are standard mint bars of almost pure gold and coin gold bars resulting from the melting of gold coin. The bars are somewhat smaller than an ordinary building brick, the approximate dimensions being 7 x 3⅝ x 1¾ inches. They contain approximately 400 troy ounces of gold, with an avoirdupois weight of about 27½ pounds, and are stored without wrappings in the vault compartments.

Between the corridor encircling the vault and the outer wall of the building is space utilized for offices, storerooms and the like. In the basement is a pistol range. The Depository has its own emergency power plant, water system and other facilities.

The outer wall itself is of granite, lined with concrete. The materials used in construction comprised 16,500 cubic feet of granite, 4,200 cubic yards of concrete, 750 tons of reinforcing steel and 670 tons of structural steel.

HOW TO GET INTO FORT KNOX

Fort Knox was named in honor of Major General Henry Knox, who was Secretary of War from 1785 to 1795. During World War I, the facility served as an artillery training center and school. At that time it was half as large as it is today. Following the war and until 1931, it was used only during the summer months for training civilian components. In 1932, having been reactivated for the mechanzation of army units, Fort Knox became a permanent post. It was here, in July 1940, that the Armored Force — U.S. Armor, as it is known today — was born.

Fort Knox is located on U.S. Highway 31W, approximately thirty-five miles south of Louisville and eigh teen miles north of Elizabethtown, Kentucky. The main entrance to the post at the Chaffee Avenue intersection is prominently marked with signs. Once inside, go directly to Bullion Boulevard.

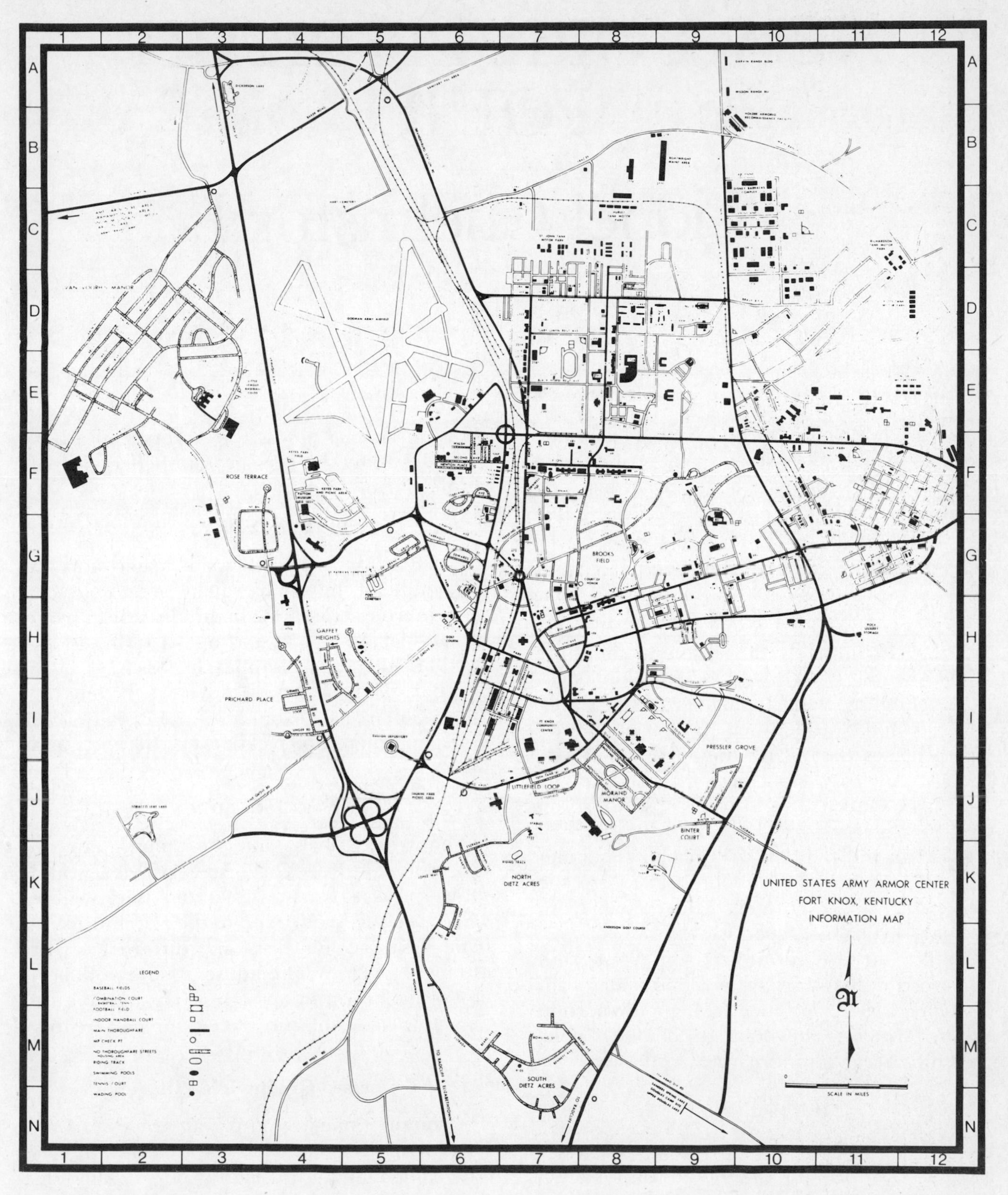

The Depository is equipped with the most modern protective devices and can rely upon additional protection from the nearby Army Post. At each corner of the structure, on the outside but connected to it, are four guard boxes. Sentry boxes, similar to the guard boxes, are located at the entrance gate. A driveway encircles the building and a steel fence marks the boundaries of the site.

No visitors are permitted.

NEW YORK LITERARY TOUR

Lionel Chelmsford

What do you mean, New York's unsafe? It's protected by some of the world's best literary sleuths. For reasons of privacy many of them refuse to divulge their exact address, but they drop enough hints so you'll know where to find them. Should the need arise:

The Upper West Side

Although it's unlikely they'll attend the same faculty meetings since he's a chemist and she's in the English department, Professor Craig Kennedy and Kate Fansler may yet bump into each other as they roam the corridors of Columbia University. Both have offices there.

Ellery Queen lives further downtown, on West 87th Street, between Amsterdam and Columbus avenues. Look for a well-kept, old-fashioned brownstone, about halfway up the block, with an elaborately carved, oak front door; it's probably Queen's.

Still further downtown, on West 70th Street, is the five-story, gray stone mansion of Thatcher Colt. Like Queen's, a goodly portion of the space is devoted to books. Unlike Queen's, there's also a private gymnasium.

Midtown, West

Not all private investigators live in genteel squalor. Peter Chalmer, who inherited wealth, lives in a sumptuous, millionaire's penthouse on Central Park South.

Matthew Scudder, by contrast, lives in a tacky hotel on 57th Street and 8th Avenue, above a bar and across the street from a bar. From his room, he gets an unimpeded view of all-night neon signs.

Times Square

The Great Merlini has a small magic store in the middle of the Times Square area. One suspects there's a telephone booth directly in front of it, which he zips in and out of trying to accomplish the great disappearing trick.

Bart Hardin never moves far from the Times Square locale, but his is the Broadway of newspapermen, not pickpockets, derelicts and pimps.

West 35th Street

Nero Wolfe lives in the most famous brownstone in New York. An aerial view would show it has a glass-covered top floor where Theodore and Wolfe tend to their orchids. William Baring-Gould lists six different street numbers for the Wolfe house, so one would do best to look for a stoop with seven steps on the downtown side of the street, somewhere between 9th and 10th avenues.

Chelsea/Greenwich Village

The toughest one-armed private eye ever, Dan Fortune, lives in the Chelsea area on 8th Avenue, in a nondescript, slightly tawdry building that's seen better days.

Pam and Jerry North, on the other hand, have comfortable and tasteful quarters in the Village, overlooking the Park. Their home is

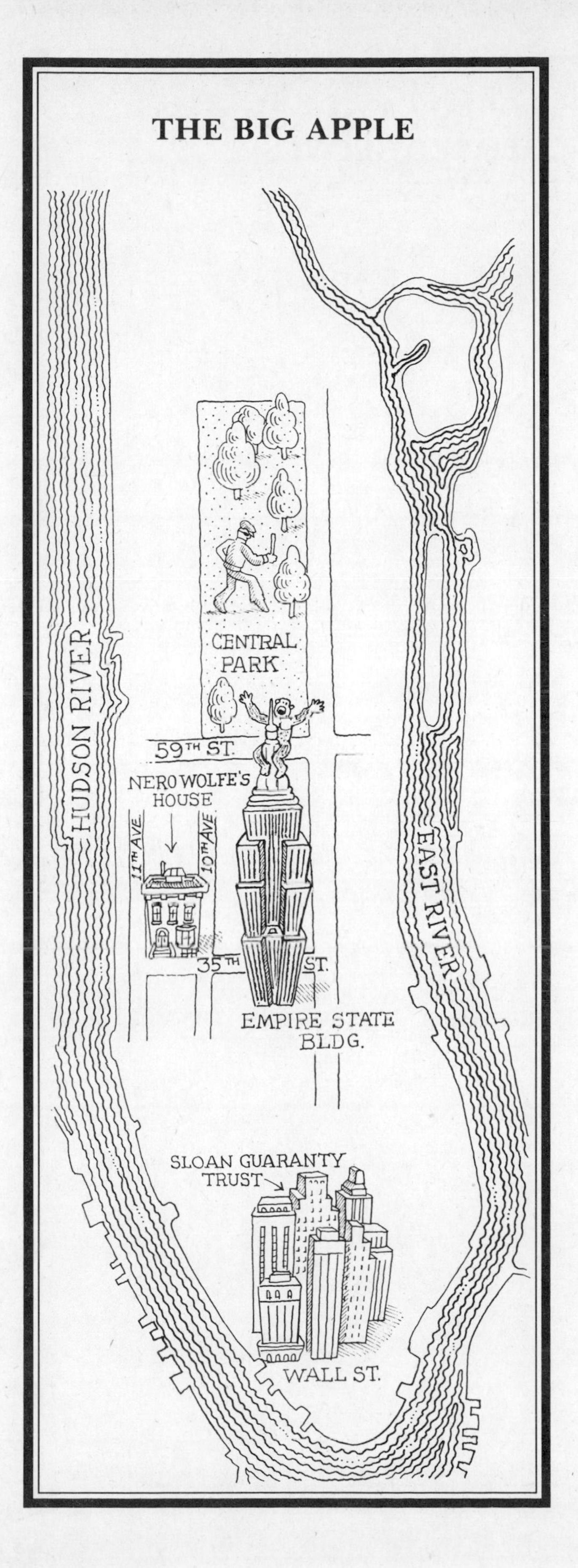

overrun by cats, but none of the neighbors has ever complained about the smell of kitty litter. So one can conclude they spend much of their day changing it.

Lower Broadway/Wall Street

Reginald DePuyster, who could afford better, being the richest of all literary characters (heir to a $20 million fortune), has offices in the O'Day Detective Agency on Lower Broadway.

Lawyer Arthur Tutt also has offices on Lower Broadway, but they are more in keeping with his background — quiet, unassuming and mannerly.

J.P. Thatcher does not live in the city, but his office is located in the Sloan Guaranty Trust Company building, near enough to Fraunces Tavern to lunch there frequently.

Gramercy Park Area

Philo Vance lives on East 38th Street, in a well-appointed old mansion, the top two (penthouse) floors.

The Upper East Side

Window-shopping in the Upper Sixties, one could expect to come upon Roman Grey's antique store and, a bit further along, the antique store where Emily and Henry Bryce do their furniture refinishing. The Hotel Beaumont, where Pierre Chambrun is the manager, is also in this general area, although possibly closer to Fifth Avenue.

Within walking distance of 59th Street is Henry Gamadge's private house. It's between Park and Lexington avenues, and has a connecting gate between Gamadge's backyard and the rear of his private club. The house is easily recognized by its cleanly painted white front steps.

Norah (and Joe) Mulcahaney lived on East 68th Street, in a remodeled townhouse, when they were first married, but recently they've moved on to bigger quarters no longer in the center of town.

Harlem

Coffin Ed and Gravedigger Jones work Harlem Homicide.

Lionel Chelmsford is lost somewhere in Staten Island.

THE MURDER OF TWO MEN BY A YOUNG KID WEARING LEMON-COLORED GLOVES

KENNETH PATCHEN

Wait.

Wait.

Wait.

Wait. Wait.

Wait.

Wait.

Wait.

Wait.

Wait.

Wait.

Wait.

Wait.

Wait.

NOW.

THE SUITCASE CAPER

Harriet Grollier

Each year there are so many new mysteries published, you could put one on every seat in a jumbo jet and not repeat a single title. In fact, you'd have enough left over to fill several flight bags. If a passenger read one a day, it would take him well over a year to finish them all.

What's surprising about this statistic is that mystery readers are always complaining about not having enough to read. They are on an eternal quest for the author who can write them as fast as they can read them.

Most mystery readers would consider the loss of their "light reading" only slightly less serious than the loss of their passport. The problem of replacing the books is a difficult one. Unless you're in England, which, more or less, shares a common language. Or in Scandinavia, which publishes a good many mysteries in English. Or in Rome, near the American Express Office by the Spanish Steps. Here, tucked

> *I don't read mystery stories, but I don't know why. I don't suppose I have time. I read Richard Condon and John D. MacDonald on long plane flights, but I don't think they count.*
>
> JOHN CHEEVER

WHEN YOU'RE ON THE COAST, DON'T FORGET TO CALL:

San Francisco

Pat & Jean Abbot
Boston Blackie
Walter Brackett
The Continental Op
The guys at D.K.A.
Frank Hastings
Sam Spade

Berkeley

Todd McKinnon

Los Angeles

Jacob Asch
David Bradstetter
Bertha Cool and Donald Lam
Philip Marlowe
Perry Mason
Luis Mendoza
Sister Mary Ursula
Moses Wine

Hollywood

Ivor Maddox

Long Beach

Honey West

Pasadena

Virgil Tibbs

Del Mar

Max Roper

Santa Barbara

Lew Archer
Cutter & Bone

San Diego

Max Thursday

away down a long, dark corridor, is the world's best secondhand bookstore — shelf after shelf, stack after stack of mystery books turned in by other travelers. The shop even lets you swap yours for theirs.

Which mysteries are the best to pack? Depends where you're traveling. Many readers use their mysteries as a guide to the country they're visiting. Helen MacInnes' *Decision at Delphi* is an excellent approach to Greece; Arthur Upfield's *Bony* books capture the Australian Outback; James McClure's Kramer & Zondi series pinpoints South Africa; William Marshall's zany procedurals help you find your way in Hong Kong. For the Caribbean, there's A.H.Z. Carr's *Finding Maubee;* for Haiti there's Graham Greene; for Glasgow there's Bill Knox and his fishery stories; for California there's Newton Thornburg's *To Die in California.* For New Zealand there's Ngaio Marsh; for New Guinea there's Charlotte Jay; for Bombay, there's H.R.F. Keating's Inspector Ghote series. And then, of course, for world travelers, the most peripatetic books of all are the international spy stories, which cross borders quicker than you can say false passport.

Naturally, the book to pack is the paperback. It's the best thing to happen to traveling since Banlon. Light, small, bendable, the paperback conveniently fills up the hole between your left shoe and your shampoo bottle. To avoid crimping edges, however, paperbacks are best packed as the bottom layer, before the clothes go in. The average suitcase, 15″ x 25″, holds one paperback in reading position (vertical) and three paperbacks at a 30° angle (horizontal) per row. Multiply by three rows and you have enough material to get you through two weeks (a fortnight if you're in Great Britian). In addition to this dozen, one is advised to stow two in one's hand luggage: one for you; one for the pest the airlines has put next to you. Mysteries may also be tucked into your hatband, jammed into your raincoat pocket, jammed into your other raincoat pocket, slipped into your flight bag, dropped inside your umbrella. Putting one between your shirt and your belt buckle is also good. But ticklish.

Harriet Grollier is the author of The Peripatetic Valise. *She suffers jet-lag.*

Chapter 8

RED HERRINGS

FRED WINKOWSKI

WHODUNIT
A Guide to the Obvious

Matthew J. Mahler

I once knew a man who thought he could outsmart John Dickson Carr. He was reading *The Skeleton in the Clock,* and along about page 56 he decided he knew who done it. In fact, he was absolutely convinced of it. He was all wrong, of course, his thinking detoured by one of the most devious minds in the business. Several years later, the same man picked up the same book and decided to reread it. He wouldn't make the same mistake twice, he said, not him. He'd forgotten everything about the book except whom he'd chosen as the murderer the first time round, so, carefully ignoring that person, he went on to finger someone else and, as you've probably guessed, missed again.

John Dickson Carr, in the words of the people at Vita, was a (red) herring maven. He was expert at creating them. His two closest rivals, according to an informal poll taken by my duped friend, would have to be Agatha Christie and Dorothy L. Sayers, which brings us to an interesting equation: Take *Ten Little Indians,* divide by *Four False Weapons,* and you're left with *Five Red Herrings.* Not to mention the feeling that you've been had by the best.

Any respectable mystery will have at least one red herring in it. Now, a red herring comes in two forms: human and inanimate (in which case it's called a clue; sometimes, an alibi). Human red herrings are easy to recognize. They are usually anybody with a deep dark secret in his past. The deep dark secret is that he is a red herring. In books with more than one murder, the second murder is a red herring.

RED HERRINGS

They are, of course, false clues meant to distract one from the real villain. The term originated in England, and there are instances of its use as far back as the seventeenth century. It seems some people were distressed at the idea of a fox being hunted to its death by a pack of snarling dogs and a party of upper-class riders. To throw the dogs off the track, these anti-hunt people would go to the fish market, buy herrings, take them home and smoke them — which gave them a reddish color — then drag them through the woods and fields. The pungent odor of the fish would cover up the scent of the fox and confuse the dogs, allowing the fox to escape. Thus did red herrings become synonymous with attempts to deceive.

That body, poor thing, died for no other reason than to distract you from the killer's motive for committing the first crime. Other likely red herrings are: a business partner, particularly if

OVERUSED CLUES

Half a pair of scissors
An heirloom brooch
A birthmark
An accent that slips
Cigarette ashes
Lipstick-stained cup
Ravelings from a sleeve
Glass with fingerprints
Torn diary
Pawn ticket
Laundry stub
Address book
Stopped clock
Dogs that don't bark
Whispered telephone conversations

he's disgruntled (too obvious); a woman suffering from amnesia (whereas a man so afflicted is almost always the culprit); at least three of the heirs present at the reading of the will. This last is tricky. How do you know which are red herrings and which, in combination, have sent Grandfather off to their eternal reward? Well, years of study have revealed that any heir who has not yet reached his majority is a red herring, ditto an heir who receives the bulk of the estate (providing the will was not drawn up within a fortnight of the funeral). Any heir who refuses to cry is a red herring; only a red herring would be that unsympathetic.

Mysterious telephone callers, gentlemen with foreign accents who ask a lot of questions in the pub, poison-pen writers and neighbors who own large barking dogs are also red herrings, but that doesn't mean they're guiltless. Usually, though, they're responsible for a secondary crime, such as extortion, rather than the primary one of murder. You can't discount them, but you'd be wrong to put the blame for everything on them; they're simply not smart enough to handle all that.

There are two other candidates for red herringdom: the least likely suspect and the most likely suspect. Ever since Mrs. Christie conned us in *The Murder of Roger Ackroyd,* we've become extremely wary of ruling out the least likely. It's gotten so we trust no one, not even the victim, who we're convinced — sometimes correctly — is shamming. The tipoff here is how much the least likely talks and if he has a first name. If he seems awfully helpful and full of gossip, and has both a first name and a surname, he's no red herring. If he's quiet, thoughtful and always referred to as Mr. So-and-So, he *is* a red herring. If the cards seem stacked against one character right from the beginning, that person is a red herring. The real killer will appear three pages from the end of the book. (And the author ought to be strung up by his typewriter ribbon; it's a terrible thing to do.)

Clues and alibis also function as red herrings. Clues to disregard are those that come in pairs, such as an earring with a bloody fingerprint on it. That strains coincidence just a bit too much and is an obvious plant. Red herring alibis are those which are airtight. Nobody lives that tidy a life.

Red herrings were spawned years ago. I suppose one would have to credit Mr. Poe (remember those two voices overheard in that upstairs room in the Rue Morgue? Red herrings, if ever there were ones). They proliferated in the Twenties and Thirties, but now with the advent of the police procedural, they're becoming extinct. As the whodunit fades and the whydunit and howtheydunit become more popular, a reader is forced to turn to the older authors to find them.

I don't know what you're planning on reading next, but a friend of mine is taking a third crack at *The Skeleton in the Clock.* This time, he swears he'll get it right.

Matthew J. Mahler is chairman of the Save the Red Herring Movement.

WATSONS

Frederick Arnold

It's a toss-up whether the hero's best friend is a red herring or an albatross.

If there's a clear footprint, he walks across it.

If there's an equally clear fingerprint, he invariably smudges it.

If there's a vital phone message, he forgets to relay it, and if there's a handwriting specimen, he misidentifies it.

In short, if there's a wrong conclusion to jump to, he swings into it with the enthusiasm of Tarzan on the vine.

A Watson (who needn't be a male) is chronically inept, possibly genetically so. He is also the biggest troublemaker since Cain. As he blunders from room to room (pocketing clues as he goes), he keeps up a steady barrage of questions so inane, it's a wonder his chum even bothers answering.

Every now and then, a scholar (with more than a dollop of Watson in his soul) will suggest the hero's friend is a stand-in for the reader. He is supposed to say all the things we would, if we were in his place. His insights are our insights, so the theory goes, and his confusion is our confusion. Perhaps the reader ought to sue for character defamation.

Actually, Watsons exist because, without them, who would lay down the trail of red herrings?

If there is one thing Watsons excel at, it's pointing the way to the fork on the left when the killer has blithely gone on his way to the right. A confirmed mystery addict will recognize this duplicity for what it is, and not be bothered with it. The novice often traipses down the wrong path with him.

To qualify as a Watson, a character must have more faith in the hero than Rockefeller has dimes. And that faith must be absolutely unshakable. Example: The hero picks up a book of Serbo-Croat poetry (not in translation). To the best of a Watson's knowledge, his friend has never been in Serbia or Croatia, has never read a word of the language before. Nevertheless, when he remarks that there's an amusing grammatical error in the third stanza, a Watson not only believes him, but maligns the author for his slipshoddiness.

The best Watsons (i.e., the ones who most frequently succor the enemy under the misapprehension that they are abetting the innocent) are never the same age as their heroes. It doesn't matter if they're older or younger; they simply must not be on a par with the hero on any level, even a chronological one. Besides, if they're older, the hero gets to twit them for being forgetful, and if they're younger, he gets to tease them for still having a lot to learn. (Books with Watsons in them pass this off as witty dialogue.)

Watsons are also good for establishing alibis. For the killer. They are the ones most apt to remark, "Why, Lord Z and I were on that train together. He never left my sight for a moment," thereby confounding the Hero Detective until he reminds his pal of his penchant for dozing off without realizing it.

The red herring-est aspect of a Watson is, of course, his total inability to solve a case on his own. (Think of the Old Man in the Corner's Polly and the Thinking Machine's Hutchinson Hatch.) He has an uncanny ability to do all the legwork and have all the pertinent information

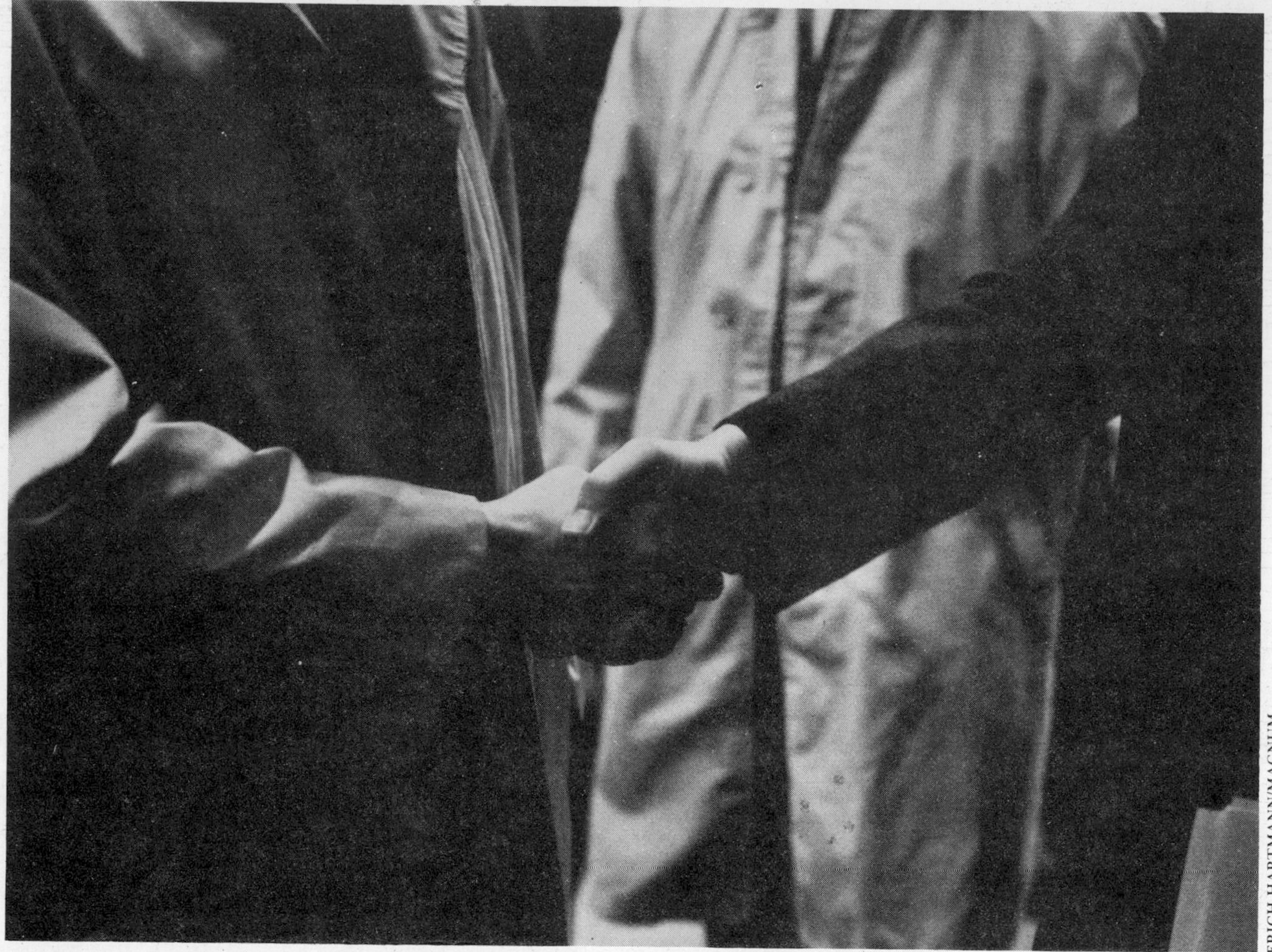

ERICH HARTMANN/MAGNUM

The handshake, universal symbol of friendship, was disdained by most Watsons, who scrupulously avoided touching their chums; in fact, they were under direct orders to keep hands off. Nero Wolfe had a positive fetish about it, and Archie indulged him by never *presenting his hand (although he often shook those of perfect strangers).*

in front of him (including a few things he really doesn't think matter — such as that old love letter he retrieved from the trash basket which he's shown to no one) yet not be able to see the solution. He must present his findings to the Great Detective, who will then carefully explain to him what it all means. Left to his own devices, a Watson would march even further down that left-handed path. And this *despite* the evidence.

Unlike other red herrings, Watsons never lie. But they have an unfortunate tendency to repeat anything they hear, so killers frequently whisper lies in their ears which they then naïvely perpetuate. This is what trips up the new mystery reader. He assumes trusty Watson would not be gulling him, when, in fact, albeit unwittingly, he is.

Although we're calling this specific breed of red herring a Watson, after the most famous of them all, it really ought to have another name, reflecting the first character who represented the type. The problem here is, the first one was so dim-witted he neglected to tell us his name. You probably remember him, though, as a chronicler of Dupin's tales. Yes, Edgar Allan Poe, originator of most whodunit conventions, also gave us the friend of minus intellectuality. Why he entrusted this oaf with the task of narrating the stories is beyond our comprehension, but others have followed, and it's a safe bet if the narrator isn't the killer, he's the hero's best friend, the red herring *par excellence.*

Frederick Arnold says that since he has two first names, he is his own best friend.

SLEUTHS AND SIDEKICKS

Betsy Lang

Take one from the left column and one from the right column and match them up.

Sleuths

1. Sexton Blake
2. Dr. Daniel Coffee
3. Sir Denis Nayland Smith
4. Albert Campion
5. Lamont Cranston
6. Capt. Jose da Silva
7. Insp. Wilfred Dover
8. John J. Malone
9. Dr. Thorndyke
10. Sherlock Holmes
11. Col. March
12. Perry Mason
13. Mr. and Mrs. North
14. Joseph Rouletabille
15. Judge Dee
16. Rabbi David Small
17. Lord Peter Wimsey
18. Henri Bencolin
19. Modesty Blaise
20. Bertha Cool
21. Insp. Purbright
22. Insp. Gabriel Hanaud
23. Grace Latham
24. Insp. McGee
25. Nick and Nora Charles
26. Nero Wolfe
27. Henry Gamadge
28. Roderick Alleyn
29. Max Carrados
30. Evan Pinkerton
31. Harley Quin
32. Nick Carter
33. Nigel Strangeways
34. Hercule Poirot

Sidekicks

a. Chick & Patsy
b. Mr. Ricardo
c. Insp. Roberts
d. Henry Satterthwaite
e. Bunter
f. Dr. Motial Mookerji
g. Harold Bantz
h. Dr. Petrie
i. Sgt. Love
j. Jeff Marle
k. Magersfontein Lugg
l. Dr. Watson
m. Tinker
n. Capt. Hastings
o. Archie Goodwin
p. Louis Calling
q. Sgt. Bull
r. Insp. Todhunter
s. Hugh Lanigan
t. Insp. Fox
u. Harry Vincent
v. Col. Primrose
w. Martini
x. Christopher Jervis
y. Sainclair
z. Hoong Liang
aa. Maggie Cassidy
bb. Insp. Blount
cc. Willie Garvin
dd. Sgt. MacGregor
ee. Asta
ff. Paul Drake
gg. Donald Lam
hh. Wilson

Answers:

1–m; 2–f; 3–h; 4–k; 5–u; 6–hh; 7–dd; 8–aa; 9–x; 10–l; 11–c; 12–ff; 13–w; 14–y; 15–z; 16–s; 17–e; 18–j; 19–cc; 20–gg; 21–i; 22–b; 23–v; 24–r; 25–ee; 26–o; 27–g; 28–t; 29–p; 30–q; 31–d; 32–a; 33–bb; 34–n.

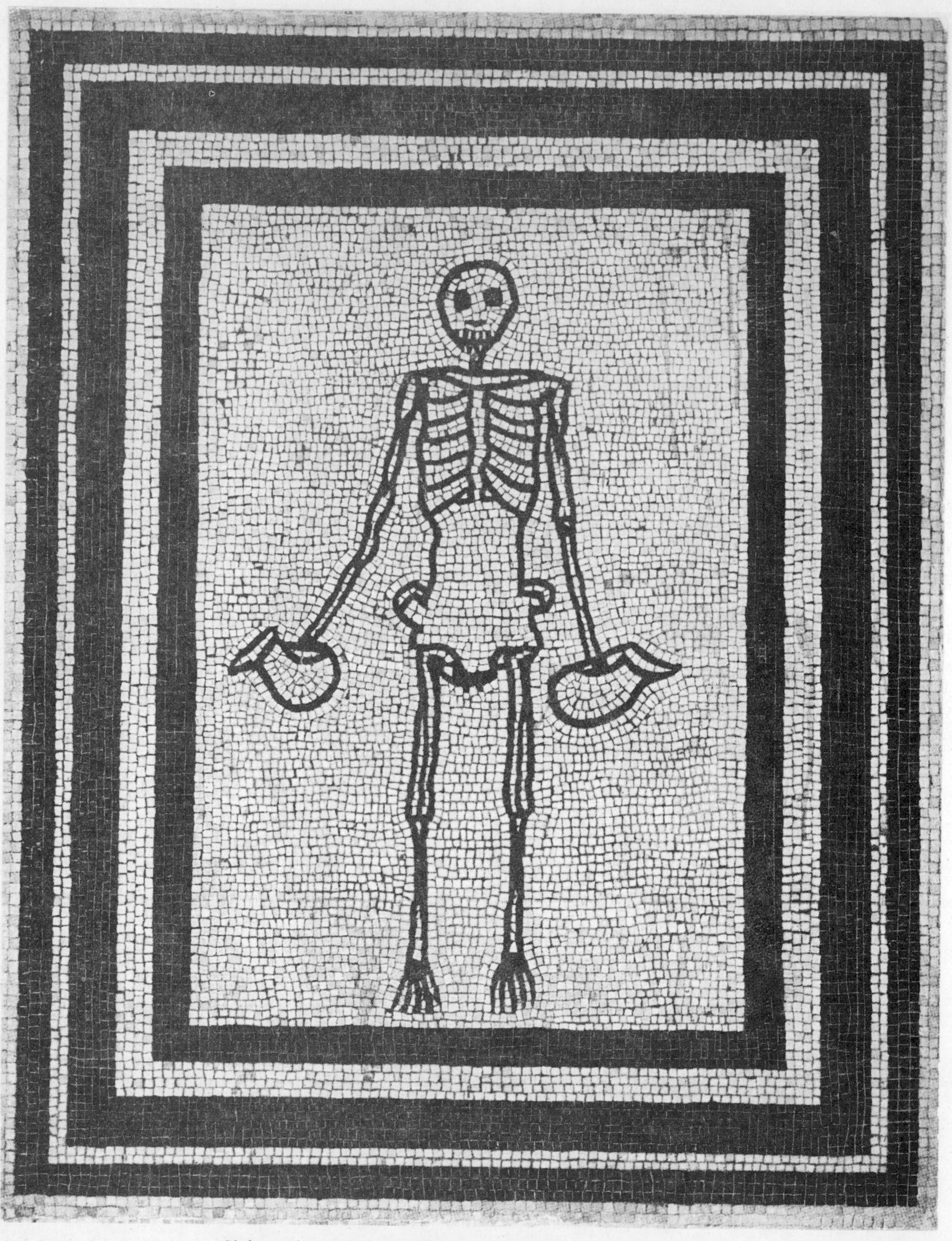

Skeleton of an early butler. Mosaic tile found in the ruins of Pompeii.

THE BUTLER

Dilys Winn

"Madam," said the voice on the other end of the telephone, "this is Mills. How may I be of service to you?"

Right then I knew that I was outclassed. I have always been vaguely uncomfortable around an English accent, particularly if it's been bred in Mayfair, and this one sounded like it was being ladled out on a Georgian spoon, with all the appropriate hallmarks.

"Er, ya see," I Brooklyned, "I wanna know if the butler did it. In real life, I mean. In mysteries he was such a terrific suspect. He knew all the dirt and where the bodies were buried and which shelf in the pantry had the bloodstained gardening trowel, and he was always popping up right behind you to announce dinner in such a way, you knew it would be your last meal on earth. Are you really like that, or what?"

Mills — that is, Mr. John Mills, a government butler formerly in private service, now working regularly for the Chancellor of the Exchequer at No. 11 — agreed to meet at my hotel to discuss the matter.

"We'll have a drink," I added, then bit down hard on my tongue. What had I done! Bunter would never have joined Lord Peter at the table.

Mills, however, ordered a gin.

I was simultaneously relieved I hadn't offended his sense of propriety and disappointed I was so far removed from being a Your Ladyship that he'd drink with me.

My polyester travel-knit took one look at his made-to-measure jacket, with its cuff buttons that actually unbuttoned, and immediately shrank two sizes, desperately trying to hide itself behind the cocktail napkin. I shredded a matchbook cover and upended the peanut dish.

I tried to think of a subtle way to ask Mills about his background.

"How'd ya become a butler, Mills?" I said.

He gave the wrong answer.

Anyone who's read a mystery knows the typical butler served with His Lordship during the Great War and followed after him ever after. Mills, on the other hand, changed Lordships every six months or so. When he thought he'd absorbed enough information, he moved on to another stately home — and a boost in salary.

"Aha, Mills!" I exclaimed, in the manner of Holmes accosting Moriarty. "And you used that information for nefarious purposes, didn't you? A bit of blackmail you presented His Lordship on your silver tray, was it?"

It was nothing of the kind.

Given the household hierarchy, Mills said, if you stayed in service in just one place, you'd be old and gray before it was your turn to play butler. You'd have to work your way up from fourth to third to second to first footman. Then you'd have to put in a spell in the kitchen, first as general helper, then as vegetable cook and next as roast cook. When you finished that up, you got to be hallboy, which included carrying coals wherever they were needed, emptying chamber pots, polishing shoes (including the butler's) and ironing the butler's clothes (you had to prove yourself on them before they let you tackle the family's). Being hallboy also demanded you do the washing up in the servants'

His Lordship, secure in the confines of his study; he occupies himself with the Times *while waiting for his butler to bring the port.*

hall after the other servants had finished eating and that you helped out in the pantry when that was through. Then, if you'd learned to do all these things properly, you were ready to be trained as a valet, which included sessions with a London clothier so you knew which clothes to lay out for His Lordship every morning; sessions with the wine merchants so you could distinguish between a good hock and an inferior port; sessions with a Scottish gun expert so you knew how to load up for a weekend shoot. After all that, if there was a vacancy, you got to be butler.

Mills was too impatient to wait for something to happen to the second footman so he could move up a station. Ergo, when he'd mastered the third footman's job, he'd skip off to another stately home. His shortcuts worked out very well. When he was just twenty-one, he became butler to the Marquis of Bewley, a descendant of Robert of Bruce.

"Hmmmmm," I said, "I never read about a *young* butler. There was Currie, who worked for Philo Vance, but he was no chicken; neither was that prototype of all butlers, the one in *The Moonstone* who was always quoting Robinson Crusoe. You were hardly old enough to read it, never mind cite it. And what about loyalty, Mills? All my mystery butlers, no matter how suspicious they looked, were loyal."

"Well," said Mills, "I was loyal when I was there, I suppose, but, you see, going back to my younger days — this was in the Thirties — the thing about the position was its security. You never got paid much, but you did get three meals a day, and I did get my own little suite of rooms. If I'd been married, I probably would have gotten my own little cottage on the grounds. And I did have my own valet, which quite spoiled me."

"But, Mills, mystery butlers never had all that. If they did, where would they have gotten a motive? Didn't they overwork you at least?" I was unwilling to let my fantasies die.

"Actually, you're confusing the butler with the valet," he replied. "The valet did the really hard work. For example, Lord Bewley would tell me to arrange a shooting party. I would go down our guest list and ring up the people I thought were suitable, and then show His Lordship the arrangement. But the valet, he had to travel to the shoot with them. He had to get up at five to ready the guns; he had to stand there and load them; he had to carry the game

His Lordship, a little less secure in his study, which appears to be booby-trapped. (Herbert Adams rigged up a trapdoor in The Dean's Daughter, *A. A. Milne devised a secret passageway in* The Red House Mystery, *Mary Roberts Rinehart created trick paneling in* The Circular Staircase *— to cite just three examples of mysterious exits and entrances.)*

back and oversee its cooking. I stayed home and arranged to pick them up at the train."

"It's a wonder the valet never killed you," I snarled. "Now, Mills, tell me what you did do, tell me how you crept up behind everyone and scared them half to death when they weren't expecting you. Tell me how you went from the library to the master bedroom without anyone noticing."

"Oh, do you mean the secret passageways?" he asked politely. "I worked in several houses that had them. Priest's holes, actually, from Reformation days. They fit behind the bookshelves, but no one used them much. Certainly not me. In one house there was a secret staircase behind the paneling. I suppose one could have stayed back in there for several days. I do know of several communicating rooms. Do you know about them? There was a secret door between them which you had to press just so. A gentleman in one room would often use it to visit an unmarried lady staying in the other. I could always tell if the door had been opened at night. There was dust on the floor, and you could see foot marks, and certain things were moved a bit, like a chair. It's difficult to explain, but one just knew if the connection had been fiddled with."

"How about your accent, Mills?" I interrogated. "Isn't that a clear giveaway you were impersonating a butler, just like in the books?"

"I was fortunate," he said. "I went to a fairly decent school, the oldest one in the City of London, actually — King Edward School, founded by Edward VI after the dissolution of the monasteries by Henry VIII. Sometimes, as butler, I'd have to discharge a lad who didn't speak correctly. Oh, you'd try to take him aside and help him with it, but if it didn't take, there was nothing else to be done but let him go. It was a reflection on the house, wasn't it?"

I wasn't done yet. I'd saved my heavy artillery for the last. "Tell me, Mills, if you were so blameless, how come when the public goes to a movie and sees a butler in it, if they read a book and a butler's in it, they always cry, 'He did it, the butler did it!' "

Mills shot a hand-turned cuff. "Oh, I expect that's because we did everything else," he said. "Natural assumption."

THE PUB

Hadrian Schwartz

There's a certain type of mystery in which the author strolls you up the High Street, past the post office, past the doctor's surgery, past the old Bermondsey place with its dishevelled lawn, and deposits you in The Bunch of Grapes.

There, the Squire stands you to a lager and you reciprocate. When he leaves, you have a friendly game of dominoes with a North Country lorry driver. Just as you're finishing up, a stranger with a peculiar stain on his waistcoat asks to be directed to the loo. You oblige. As you're settling your bill with Teddy, he suggests you bring in your own tankard and put it there, third peg from the left, over the counter. Before you can answer, Daft Willie intrudes. He offers you his peanut brittle tin. You decline. He cries. You accept, carefully wiping the dirt off the candy before pretending to eat it.

It's all very companionable, very low-key, and you have a thorough good time of it. Until the author invites you to leave.

If you've read as many mysteries as I have, you know you're now in for big trouble—which will hound you throughout the book.

On the walk home, a little the worse for lager, you take a wrong turning, and instead of manoeuvring the High Street you're skirting Miller's Pond. Oops. You slip, of course. As you right yourself, you see it. A silver kilt pin. The Squire's?

Hurrying now, you cut 'cross the gully. Two shadows. Whispers. A snatch of North Country accent?

Exhausted, you arrive at Lady Sarah's. She ushers you into the game room and sits you east; opposite, calmly shuffling, a gentleman with a stain on his waistcoat.

And then to bed, where you fret the night away dreaming of clay-covered peanut brittle tins and empty tankards swooshing left, right, left.

It helps at this point to get a pen and neatly xxxxx out The Bunch of Grapes. Like every other pub in every other village mystery, the name is a pseudonym. This time, it's The Grapes. Next time, The British Queen, or The Three Tuns or The Cheshire Cheese. But actually, though the author can't admit it or he'd spoil his plot, the pub's real name is The Red Herring.

Here, more alibis are created, more suspects congregate, more clues are uncovered, than anyplace else in the whole book. Undoubtedly, you will be suckered in by every single one of them. Who could mistrust something he sees or hears in a place that goes back at least two hundred years?

The typical Red Herring Pub was built in the time of Cromwell. Its sides bulge as though distended by gas. Its door lists in a permanent curtsey to the street. Its exterior, as well as many a patron, needs a nice coat of whitewash. Inside are two small rooms. The left has the dartboard, the dominoes, the walk-in fireplace, the regulars' tankards and the slew of red herrings. The right has the wives. (It's usually empty.) Both have sagging floors and tiny paned windows with the original glass still intact. Shapes are barely recognisable through them.

The publican lives upstairs. In fact, he was born there. He is one of the three men in town who make a decent living, the other two being the butcher and the turf accountant. He has calluses on his palm from pulling pints, an end-

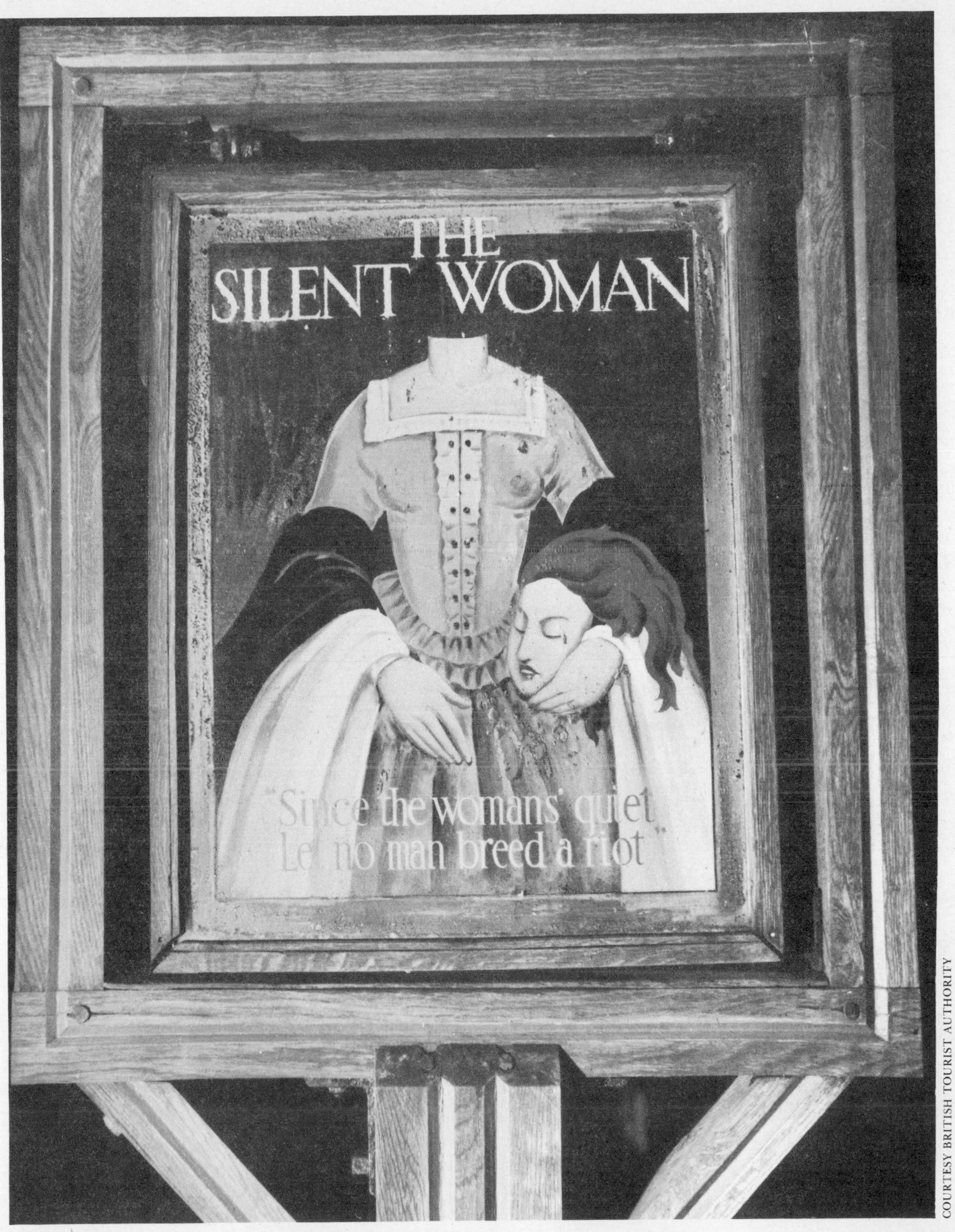

COURTESY BRITISH TOURIST AUTHORITY

A typical pub sign, painted on wood and hung from a high post.

CORNELL CAPA/MAGNUM

The regulars, having a round on the publican.

less supply of not-quite-clean aprons, and he arbitrates all arguments by calling Time and closing the bar.

He also sets up more red herring situations than anyone else in the story. It is he who picks up a discarded matchbook and remarks, "Fancy that, the Savoy Grille. Someone just been to London, eh?"; who warns Simon he's had a bit of enough and sends him on his way, alone, with a step unsteady and a mind besotted by gin; who loans Colin the weed-killer and Derek the van.

It is he who serves the Inspector a half-and-half and a passel of half-truths, which he repeats as gossip.

The publican himself is not a red herring. He is obviously too busy tending to Rodney's shandy to step across the way, filch Mrs. Greer's locket, hide it and establish an alibi. He hasn't the time to stiletto the Duke, cycle to the dump and heave the knife, and be back for Opening. But as sure as his shandy is a half-pint beer to a half-pint cider, his pub is a red-herring breeding ground.

Think about it. An author can't always be arranging house parties to introduce his suspects. What's more logical than having them stop by the Local for a quick one?

An author can't always rely on conversations being heard outside the French windows. Where better to plant them than in the adjoining booth at the neighbourhood free house?

An author can't always expect the parlour maid to discover and return the button (cigarette lighter, woolly scarf, initial handkerchief, loose key). Who better to notice it than the publican?

There's no such thing as an innocent conversation in a mystery pub. What seems harmless at the time will evolve, two chapters later, into a clue. Similarly, no one who goes to a pub is entirely innocent. A page or so further on, one learns the sociable drinker needed an alibi. That these clues and these alibis have little to do

COURTESY BRITISH TOURIST AUTHORITY

An early pub sign with a sardonic message.

with the actual solution of the case should by now be second nature to us. But it's not. We grab hold to the bitter end, staunch in our conviction that what transpired in the pub is of utmost importance. And so it is, or we'd have solved the mystery in the very first chapter and hated the author ever after.

Real pubs are markedly similar to fictional ones. There's the same whimsical choice of names, the same Cromwellian architecture, the same hard-working publican (only usually it's two publicans, a husband and wife). Darts are played; so are dominoes. (Stakes, however, are low. ½p forfeit if you can't go.) Lager outsells gin, gin outsells whisky and lemon squash is more popular than Coke. Tankards are hung over the bar, but they're often bawdy — not like those in mysteries — with naked females forming their handles. Visitors use one room, the regulars the other (and that would play havoc with a mystery plot).

The biggest point of difference is that publicans rarely own their pubs. They belong to Whitbread's or Watney's. The free house has almost disappeared, and today publicans are managers rather than owners. Still, the décor is their own and so is the atmosphere.

A recent three-day swing through six London pubs disclosed no red herrings, either. Nobody in them, including me, had found a long-lost glove or noticed a bloodstain on a lorry trunk. A constable had not checked in, and no one had seen a tattersalled Continental asking directions. Mugs were rinsed without a thought to saving them for prints, and plowman's lunches were downed without a single instance of ptomaine, never mind arsenic.

In real life, The Bunch of Grapes is no Red Herring. But I've yet to close the file on Ye Olde Tea Shoppe.

Hadrian Schwartz is a regular at The Blubbering Whale.

DAMES

Allison Wentworth

MATTHEW SEAMAN

Pink is not their color, and they've never developed a fondness for true blue, either. It's blood red that tips their nails and jet black that swathes their bodies, usually in a sweep of taffeta that crackles like crisp new hundred-dollar bills.

Dames have been around since the Thirties, but they hit their prime in the Forties and Fifties. They seduced Spade and Marlowe and Spillane and Archer, and from there on it was downhill all the way. Lately, they've been hectoring Bond, even Parker — and dumber than that, they just don't come.

Dames have one recurring fantasy: a little house with twenty-seven rooms in it, a mink in every closet and a white telephone by the poolside. Every morning, if they had their way, a six-foot gent would exit their bed and on his way out drop some bills on the dresser (nothing smaller than a fifty). Then they'd spend the day boozing it away, gambling it away beside a short fat old man who'd pat them on the fanny every time they rolled a seven, or giving it away to a cast of characters ranging from a kid brother just out of the pen to a well-muscled chauffeur with the odd bullet scar to a wise guy with a scheme so full of holes that the bunco squad could march right through it.

Books about dames appeal primarily to men. They never see what the broads are up to till it's too late and they have no recourse but to black-and-blue their jaw or ventilate their belly.

Men, be they the private-eye hero or the private-eye reader, are tripped up by dark seams stretching up impossibly long legs. A waft of gardenia perfume goes direct to their brain and numbs their thinking. Their eyes get clouded by a toss of hair that's whiter than any pillow cover.

It's not uncommon for such men to think of these dames as red herrings. "Poor kid," they say about a gal who'd sell her mother, "she needs a break." They know she's not quite on the up and up, but they'd rather not face it. It's easier for them to make her a ruse, to treat her as a diversion instead of the instigator.

So the hard-boiled dame functions as a red herring. Unless, as sometimes happens, a woman is reading the book. Women know all the dame's tricks. They know only a female with a yen for black taffeta could arrive at the murder scene in time to commit it, not to be framed by it. They know it's no accident the blackmailer was iced once her letters were returned to her. They know if there's any confusion she's at the bottom of it, if there's any death she probably committed it.

Still, the dame is an ersatz red herring. The sentimental will think her guilty — but not really. The cynic will spot her for what she is — a two-timing broad.

When they're not in the swing of things themselves, dames are champion red-herring droppers. Who put one of Saul's cigars in the dead man's ashtray? Who gave Lewis the ticket to a performance that was canceled? Who told Herman to take her car and drive it past the bank — she'd be ready at eleven sharp? Who indeed.

The old-fashioned peroxided dames, with earrings that got lost and diaries that got stolen, are quickly vanishing from the crime writer's lexicon. But they're being replaced by hippie dames, twenty-year-olds who never wear bras and never forget their dexies. These women are not so different in anything but dress. Their morals can be likened to the Easter bunny's, their language smacks of the Fifties truck-driver's. But deep down there is about them a lingering scent of gardenia, a glimpse of a seam going clear to the thigh. They, too, are seemingly vulnerable; they, too, find a susceptible

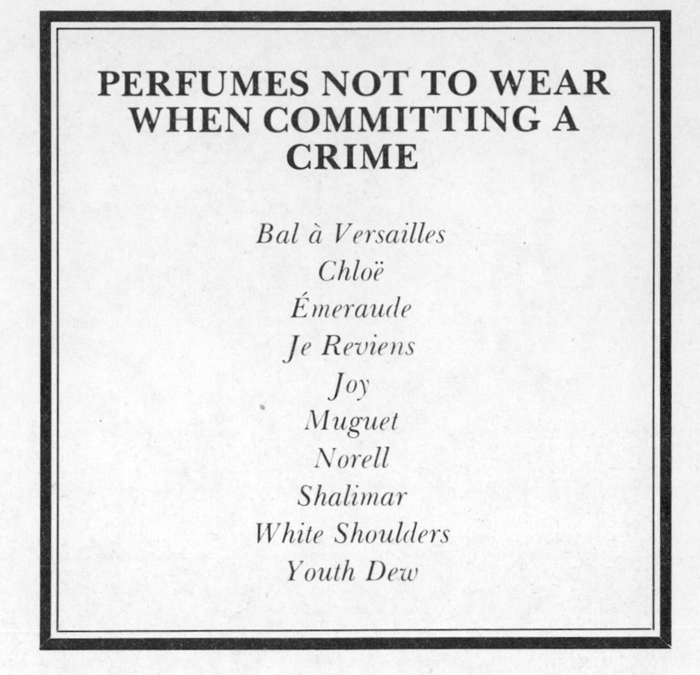

PERFUMES NOT TO WEAR WHEN COMMITTING A CRIME

Bal à Versailles
Chloë
Émeraude
Je Reviens
Joy
Muguet
Norell
Shalimar
White Shoulders
Youth Dew

It ain't no sin if you crack a few laws now and then, just so long as you don't break any.

Every Day's a Holiday
Mae West

Dese dames were all related to Clyde Barrow (the infamous Clyde of Parker and Barrow). Like dames in mysteries, they favored tight curls, tight skirts and tight (buttoned) lips.

private eye to do their dirty work. They don't usually die at the end of the book, but they get sent home to their parents — and to their mind that's tantamount to death.

How did women get started in the role of red herring? I suspect they had all that free time on their hands in which to scatter clues (women almost never work in mysteries, unless it's as a governess in a Gothic) and so they became targets of opportunity.

The next time you read of a woman waiting in a private eye's office, and he opens the door to find her sitting there on the edge of his desk, a long leg beating time against his chair, pay attention. The dame aint there for his health.

Wickedness is a myth invented by good people to account for the curious attractiveness of others.

Phrases and Philosophies
for the Use of the Young
OSCAR WILDE

Allison Wentworth is a feminist.

STOOLIES

Christopher Rutledge

His grammar is atrocious. Every sentence out of his mouth begins "I aint" and follows with one of four possibilities:

"I aint done nothin' wrong."

"I aint gonna tell ya."

"I aint a squealer."

"I aint heard nothin' yet."

His words are wheezed past an adenoidal blockage, propelled through the air on a thin, high, unsteady whistle. Sometimes he stutters. Often his words are pulled to the side, turned down, where they must cross the hurdle of a curled lower lip.

Clearly, this stoolie is in need of Professor Higgins, but he will never find him. Like the mystery stoolie, who is almost always American, from big-city fringes, George (not his real name, of course) never ventures far from Chicago's South Side.

Again like his counterpart, George has attached himself to a gang. He is not a full-participation member; in fact, he is not so much one of "the boys" as one of the boys' gofers. It is George who goes for the take-out eggplant parmigiana, then stands around while the boys eat it. It is George who goes for the ten copies of the *News*, who goes for Miss Lalia and tells her Sam wants to see her.

George has one friend, who just happens to be on the Chicago Police Force. It's his cousin, actually, and they have breakfast at 7 A.M. every single day. George likes to talk to him; the kid knows nothing about horses and George is educating him.

George thinks of himself as a double agent. "I aint got no one boss," he says. "I got two, and I control them. But they're so dumb they don't know it. I can tell them what I like, when I want to, and then me and my money are off to the ponies."

THE BETTMANN ARCHIVE, INC.

Stoolies are usually addressed in the diminutive: Georgie for George; Sammy for Samuel; Louie for Louis. This is done not out of friendship or respect, but to connote their inferior standing in the gang, their childishness.

What George doesn't understand is that nobody has much faith in him. According to his cousin, he's like the tipster at the track: It's not that you think he knows better than you do; it's just that he's available, so you check in to see what he's got to say.

In mysteries, the stoolie is used as a red herring. The mob boss gives him a message, a dime to phone it in with and instructions to be back within the hour and report on what happened. Or he'll be allowed to overhear the plans for a caper so he can relay them to the fuzz, thus ensuring a wild-goose chase over to the Loop when the gang's real attack is being staged in Kenilworth. George is too idiosyncratic, too independent. He just might tell more than they bargained for. Besides, George isn't in deep enough for that. All his facts come to him through, well, osmosis, just what he gets from hanging around. He can't recall ever being specifically told to deliver any tidbit to anyone. "I aint gonna do that," he says. "They want a delivery boy, call Western Union. I say what I want to say."

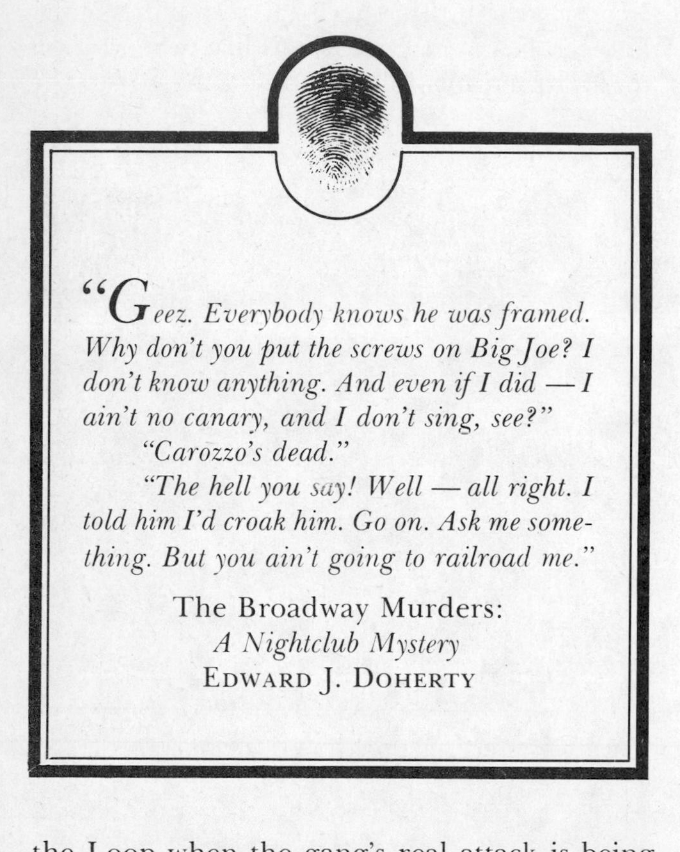

"Geez. Everybody knows he was framed. Why don't you put the screws on Big Joe? I don't know anything. And even if I did — I ain't no canary, and I don't sing, see?"

"Carozzo's dead."

"The hell you say! Well — all right. I told him I'd croak him. Go on. Ask me something. But you ain't going to railroad me."

The Broadway Murders:
A Nightclub Mystery
EDWARD J. DOHERTY

In *Brighton Rock* Graham Greene had Pinkie send an informer over the banister when he suspected the man had ratted. Oliver Bleeck put a stoolie in an coin-operated drier when he could no longer control him. In mysteries, stoolies are red herrings with the shortest life spans. But in real life it's a little easier. "I aint heard nothing about that yet," says George. "Those guys and the ones you read about in the paper, they weren't like me. I aint gonna die like that. I mind my business. Nobody's gonna do that to me."

On the other hand, George is as poorly dressed as any mystery stoolie who ever crossed the page. Sartorially, he bears a striking resemblance to Dustin Hoffman in *Midnight Cowboy*. His coat came from Goodwill, donated by some soul about 11 inches taller, 75 pounds fatter. Georgie is a little man — no more than 5′2″, roughly 120 pounds. And few of those pounds have seen a bathtub with any regularity. If he were a restaurant, the Board of Health would close him down.

It is impossible to estimate George's age. He could be fifty; he could be twenty-five. All he'll say is that he's old enough to vote. Stoolies in mysteries rarely top thirty: their situation is too precarious for longevity.

George has been pulled in only once, Christmas, two years ago. He hated it. "I aint a crook now and I wasn't one then," he says. Exactly what he did do, he won't mention, but it got him thirty days and "some terrific cupsacoffee."

To say George is likable would be stretching it, but there is something awfully appealing about meeting a man who likes his life as it is. The one thing he would like to happen that hasn't, so far, is to meet a cop socially. He once read an article that said if you put a cop and a criminal in the same room at a party they'd gravitate toward each other, even if they didn't know what the other one did for a living. He would like to see if that happened.

Christopher Rutledge is a former reporter for a large Illinois newspaper. He is the recipient of the Malcolm R. Fenway award for excellence: he has a red herring for breakfast every morning.

Chapter 9

COPS AND BOBBIES

FRED WINKOWSKI

CARELLA OF THE 87TH

James McClure

High above rope barriers and waiting nets, a pretty young girl threatens suicide on a twelfth-story window ledge:

> *The police and the fire department had gone through the whole bit — they had seen this particular little drama a thousand times in the movies and on television. If there was anything that bored civil service employees, it was a real-life enactment of the entertainment cliché.*

So begins Ed McBain's *Like Love,* a tour de force in his 87th Precinct series that says it all. It proclaims the man's genius for honesty, empathy and gentle humour. It explains why his Stephen Louis Carella has become one of the greatest "real" detectives in fiction, and the series itself among the most satisfying. We smell truth here and we are not bored.

The essence of the matter is simple enough. "A truism," Lord Samuel once remarked, "is on that account none the less true" — a sentiment to be echoed wistfully by anyone who has ever used the cliché "I love you." And an obvious truism is that nothing's so trite, nor so engaging, as a real human crisis, the very stuff of police work.

However, hacks excepted, most writers panic when plunged into what one could call cop corn. Some strike out on their own, eyes tightly shut, determined to impose a personal "reality" on the situation — scything down the clichés with meaningful pseudo-insights or building themselves cosy wee nests in the middle of hunt-the-needle haystacks so suffocating that only their imagined policemen, each as endearing as a field mouse, could hope to survive in them. Others climb out and get on the fence, where they often assume a radical stance while painting a picture more terrible, in its way, than Van Gogh's final canvas; the corn writhes, the carrion crows descend, and God help the pig who gets caught in this glaring light.

McBain, on the other hand, accepts things as they are; if the field that engrosses him is knee-high in clichés, so be it. In he goes, as eager and uncompromising as a child, to grasp the thistle that grows between the rows.

"Great narrative," observed Eric Bentley, "is not the opposite of cheap narrative: it is soap opera *plus.*"

"Plus" there certainly is in McBain's writing; not even his most severe critics have been able to deny that, although they occasionally hint dark things about potboilers stretching back twenty-one years or so.

On the evidence, however, that is hardly likely to offend McBain. No pot that ever boiled has contained a more zealous missionary, expounding to the end on the gospel truth of police procedures, while producing platitudes, parables and homilies, with an urgent, often jovial intensity closely linked to an awareness of the underlying nature of things. Provoking behaviour, admittedly, for those who attend the pot, their bellies rumbling again so soon after a light meal of lesser novelists, and who have now

LEIU

The Law Enforcement Intelligence Unit is a private organization whose members are all sworn police officers. It's very hush-hush, very low-profile. And that's all we're going to say about it. Except to mention that the Western States Intelligence Conference is up to the same kind of stuff. And it's scary.

CULVER PICTURES

to wait until the talk finally stops.

With the directness, then, of one unafraid to get down to essentials at the cost of spurious originality, McBain invariably begins to create the world of Steve Carella by discussing the weather — everyone's favourite banality when confronting strangers. He also, almost invariably, manages to score his first plus this way, as indicated by these opening lines from *The Pusher* (1956):

> *Winter came in like an anarchist with a bomb.*
>
> *Wild-eyed, shrieking, puffing hard, it caught the city in cold, froze the marrow and froze the heart.*

God/the novelist speaking. The section ends with a public consensus, lacking in flair but not in the same foreboding:

> *Winter was going to be a bitch that year.*

A space and then, flatfooted and phlegmatic:

> *The patrolman's name was Dick Genero, and he was cold. He didn't like the winter, and that was that.*

Gone is the novelist, to return only when he has something pertinent to say, and in his place is a policeman writing with the skills of one and the authority of the other.

Most often that policeman is Steve Carella, although his part in any story is not necessarily more important than it would be in an investigation carried out by a squad of detectives. Significantly, when he makes his first appearance on a murder scene in *Cop Hater* (1956), he rates no more than a cursory glance from the homicide double-act already there. What he's wearing is automatically noted, that's all, and it's an utterly conventional neat suit, clasped tie and shirt. It takes a member of the public to reflect: *He was not a frightening man, but when you opened the door to find him on your front step, you knew for certain he wasn't there to sell insurance* — a description which Carella might himself have difficulty in accepting, being more at home with the six-foot-nothing, downward-slanting eyes and brown hair stuff.

The narrator *seems* to be Carella — even when it's not — for two reasons. The first is that McBain has admitted to basing Carella on himself, so naturally some blurring is bound to occur. And the second is an extension of that, inasmuch as Carella is our chief source of information about the 87th Precinct and thereby blurs his personal experience with our own.

The reader is shown what Carella sees, however "unseen" it may have become to him through over-familiarity, and learns what he knows, however "second nature" this may have become, too. In other words, the cop corn is ground fine and then baked to fill a larder of goodies to which one returns again and again, even when a plot itself falls flat as in, ironically, *Bread* (1974), that singularly unleavened loaf.

What could be more mundane in mystery writing than a fingerprint? Yet once it has been through the mill, so to speak, there can be no denying its filling properties.

> *There are sweat pores on the fingertips, and the stuff they secrete contains 98.5 percent water and 0.5 to 1.5 percent solid material. This solid material breaks down to about one-third of inorganic matter — mainly salt — and two-thirds of organic substances like urea, albumin and formic, butyric and acetic acids. Dust, dirt, grease cling to the secretion. . . .*

Not that one is likely to remember this — or would even want to — any more than Carella remembers it from the police academy; it's having it made a part of oneself as well, however subliminally absorbed, that makes the difference. Much the same goes for the chunks of city ordinances which are to be found in the text: they, too, provide a taste of life as a police officer that no amount of description alone could achieve.

Just as a description of the books themselves is unlikely to convey their flavour with any accuracy. But a glance along the larder shelves, picking out other odds and ends at random, would at least provide some idea of what is on offer.

Lovely sandwiches of ideas, for a start. In *Cop Hater,* Carella calls on the heavily sensual widow of a murdered colleague and wishes "she were not wearing black."

> *He knew this was absurd. When a woman's husband is dead, the woman wears black.*
>
> *But Hank and he had talked a lot in the quiet hours of the midnight tour, and Hank had*

MIRANDA WARNINGS

You are under arrest. Before we ask you any questions, you must understand what your rights are.

You have the right to remain silent.

You are not required to say anything to us at any time or to answer any questions. Anything you say can be used against you in court.

You have the right to talk to a lawyer for advice before we question you and to have him with you during questioning.

If you cannot afford a lawyer and want one, a lawyer will be provided for you.

If you want to answer questions now without a lawyer present, you will still have the right to stop answering at any time. You also have the right to stop answering at any time until you talk to a lawyer.

MIRANDA WAIVER

1. Have you read or had read to you the warnings as to your rights? ...
2. Do you understand these rights? ..
3. Do you wish to answer any questions? ....
4. Are you willing to answer questions without having an attorney present? ....
5. Signature of defendant ....
6. Time..... Date ....
7. Signature of officer ....
8. Signature of witness ....

many times described Alice in the black night gowns she wore to bed. And try as he might, Carella could not dissociate the separate concepts of black: black as a sheer and frothy raiment of seduction, black as the ashy garment of mourning.

And to follow that section through to its conclusion, for a glimpse of what makes Carella so real:

He left the apartment and walked down to the street. It was very hot in the street.

Curiously, he felt like going to bed with somebody.

Anybody.

Then there are the other people one meets. The cartoonist's gag writer, for instance, in *Ten Plus One,* who features briefly as a suspect. A morose man, he nonetheless obligingly explains the genesis of the funnies in most magazines and shows the detectives the slips he sends out, each carrying a description of the drawing and supplying the caption, if there is one. Four of these slips are reproduced in facsimile — one of McBain's most effective techniques for giving one the "feel" of being right there. Elsewhere one is shown reporter's copy, police forms, timetables, letters, signwriting and, in *Doll* (1965), some photographs. There is something enormously gratifying in seeing something for oneself, particularly if, as in certain cases, it's possible to pounce on a clue before the men of the 87th get to it.

Ten Plus One also features one of McBain's many unforgettable incidental characters, a grouchy token seller called Stan Quentin who has never heard of Alcatraz and doesn't see why the detectives should be so amused. Now, that's so corny one wouldn't dare use it in fiction, whereas it works perfectly for four pages of McBain. Culminating with:

"You know those guys at Alcatraz?"

"We know lots of guys at Alcatraz," Carella said.

"Tell them to take my name off it, you hear?"

"We will," Carella said.

"Damn right," Quentin said.

Long exchanges of dialogue are a characteristic also to be enjoyed, both for the tension they create and for the authentic ring which the conventions of television make impossible. Humour, used to counterpoint harsh realities, is also much in evidence, as in *Cop Hater* when the father-figure of the squad room cuts short an introduction without malice aforethought: "It was simply Miscolo was a heavy sweater, and he didn't like the armpits of his uniform ruined by unnecessary talk." Other times it can be used to steady a flight of fancy: "Detectives are not poets; there is no iambic pentameter in a broken head."

And all this is to say nothing of Meyer Meyer (victim of his father's Jewish sense of humour; nobody could call that a Christian name, for a start), Cotton Hawes, Bert Kling or the odious Andy Parker, who between them handle the work load with varied degrees of success. In one story, largely because the right hand doesn't get to know what the left is doing, they all goof off, including Carella, and an arrest is made — only *after* a catastrophic crime is committed — by a distant patrolman in search, not of fame, but of ice cream.

Such is life. Such is what McBain re-creates by giving his policemen far too much to do (seldom are they ever concerned with one case at a time); a sky over their heads that can, in a heat wave, befuddle them while investigating a shoot-out in a liquor store filled with smashed bottles; and a world as real as Isola's model of New York is real, not a sugary sphere on the end of a lollipop stick.

Sometimes, however, he seems to go too far having fun, and smart-asses who rely on hindsight — what else? — have suggested that he may regret certain parts of the framework he laid down for himself in *Cop Hater,* little suspecting he'd have to live with them through almost a generation. They cite Teddy Franklin, the lovely, lamentably deaf and literally dumb girl whom Carella courted and married in that first book of the series, and quote Philip Norman's interview with the writer, in which it was said she "came from some heartless, fatuous notion of the ideal woman: beautiful and speechless." Fine for a one-off story, just as most jokes will take a single airing, but surely. . .

Nonsense. The very essence of McBain is that he embraces his clichés with the same loving enthusiasm Carella has been known to direct toward his missus — and, with possibly as little thought for the consequences, although he has himself so far avoided twins.

COURTESY ALFRED J. YOUNG COLLECTION

St. Michael the patron saint of all police forces, is depicted in the painting entitled "Restrictions." The painting hangs in the Police Academy museum, New York City.

If this means he has become, in effect, the Norman Rockwell of the police procedural, that is surely no bad thing — not when he's also Evan Hunter, author of such celebrated works as *The Blackboard Jungle* and *Buddwing,* which must provide him with literary kudos.

Ah, say our literary-minded friends, why didn't you disclose this at the beginning? Hunter is bound to have an influence on McBain at times but plainly indulges in him the excesses of a trained mind allowed to slip its leash, to scamper cute as a spaniel in a public park — sometimes upright, mostly with a strong leaning toward grass-roots kitsch in exuberant figure eights which, despite sudden switches of direction, neatly tie up the ends.

Well, mainly because addicts of the 87th Precinct don't put this about much. Some are simply ignorant of the fact, and possibly much happier that way, being intimidated by "real" novelists, whereas "Ed McBain" is such a reassuring cliché of a name in itself, exactly right for a cop-lover. Others are confident that their emperor isn't going about in the buff (he, too, wears neat suits) — and that it's rare enough even to catch him with his pants down (although this does occur, forgivably, during moments of extreme sentiment).

James McClure won the Crime Writers' Association Silver Dagger for his political thriller, Rogue Eagle.

THE WELL-DRESSED COP

A New York City policeman's uniform, including gun, costs between $400 and $450. (The guns are purchased wholesale for $75. They must be either Smith and Wesson, Colt or Dan Wesson revolvers with a 4" barrel.) Each police officer is given a yearly uniform allowance of $265.

His baton. *This turn-of-the-century rosewood baton was carried by officers on regular tours of duty.*

His flute. *Popular in the late 1800's, this glass gun ("flute") held the policeman's potable—usually rum. It was tucked either in his waistband or in his nightstick holder (both illegally).*

His shield. *The first badge was issued in 1845. It was made of copper, hence the term "cop" to denote a policeman. There have been seven style changes in the badge, the most recent in 1902.*

His uniform. *The first offical police uniform was designed in 1853 and over the years has been modified many times. (The gray felt helmet was discontinued in 1906; the frock coat, in 1912.)*

His nippers.
A restraining device, commonly used by police in 1885. Nippers were wrapped around the suspect's wrists, pressure was applied and the alleged perpetrator was unable to move his hands.

His belt and frog. *This leather belt was worn over his jacket and clasped in front with a police department insignia. The "frog" held his nightstick.*

His thumb cuffs.
Made of wood, these cuffs served the same purpose as the more traditional handcuffs. A suspect's thumbs were screwed in place, behind his back.

His leg holster. *This advertisement appeared in a spring issue of* Law and Order *magazine just last year. The magazine is available only to police officers.*

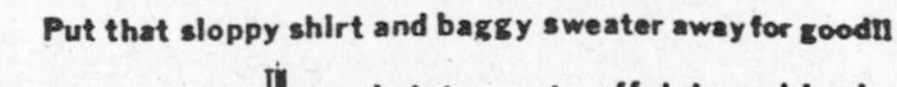

COURTESY ALFRED J. YOUNG COLLECTION

SATURDAY NIGHT WITH THE 26TH

Thomas Seligson

It is six o'clock on a Saturday night. I am riding in a patrol car. The back seat. I am not a cop and I am not guilty. Then what am I doing there?

I'm a Civilian Observer.

The Civilian Observer Program is open to block captains, community leaders, law students and journalists like myself. For six hours they let you go everywhere with your assigned cops; they let you get the feel of being a cop, but minus the badge and gun. I chose to observe from the 26th Precinct. It's a mixed neighborhood — part academic (Columbia University) and part war zone (West Harlem).

As I said, it's a Saturday. The day after the arrival of welfare checks. It's warm. There's a full moon. Officers Hess and Ford lock me into the back seat of their patrol car, and off we go.

6:09 P.M. Broadway and 125th St.: Hess hands me a chart listing the code signals I'll hear over the car radio.

"That's so you'll know what's going on," he says. "We're 26-A. If you hear that, we're in business."

"How can you remember all this?" I ask, scanning the chart.

"What do you think I keep it out for? Five years on the job, I still sometimes forget."

"There's only one that's really important." Ford smiles into the rear-view mirror. "10-63."

I look it up. It means "Out of Service (Meal)."

"That's where we're going now," Ford says. "Hess has to feed his tapeworm. Guy's always hungry."

6:14 P.M. Broadway and 116th St.: Columbia and Barnard students crowd the car. Hess and Ford joke with them. I'm introduced as a "Peeping Tom" they're taking downtown. I keep my hands behind my back as though they're cuffed. There's a dance at Barnard later that night. "Eddie" and "Bob" are invited by the girls.

"Only if you promise me a dance," says Hess. He smiles. "A slow one."

6:16 P.M. Broadway and 114th St.: We stop in front of Hungry Mac's. Hess asks if I want anything inside.

"Maybe a coffee," I say.

"You'll regret it," says Ford. "It's terrible here. Wait'll the next stop."

I take his advice. He lights a True Blue. I bum one.

6:22 P.M. Broadway and 112th St.: We stop in front of Twin Donuts.

"How do you want your coffee?" asks Hess.

"Light and sweet. And a marble doughnut." I reach for my wallet.

"Forget it. It's on me."

While Hess is gone, Ford explains that their sector runs from 116th to 110th streets, Riverside Drive to Morningside. "That's where we cruise, 'less we're needed elsewhere." He says he averages eighteen miles a tour. Of course, it all depends on the number of stops.

Hess returns with doughnuts and coffee for two. "You forgot the cigarettes," says Ford.

FRISKING AND THE STRIP SEARCH

Just in case the suspect is a dirty fighter, or gets to his shiv before you find it, it's better to have two people doing the frisking. That way, you — not the suspect — remain in control.

1. Suspect is told to place his hands on the wall, supporting the full weight of his body on his hands.
2. Suspect is told to drop his head forward.
3. Suspect is told to stretch his legs out as far as they will go. This puts the upper half of his torso almost horizontal to the lower half, and keeps him off balance.
4. Suspect is told to use only toes to maintain contact with the floor. This, again, keeps him off balance.
5. The person doing the frisking then begins from top to bottom, and runs his hands over every part of the suspect's body.
6. Suspect is handcuffed at conclusion of the frisk, but while still in the frisk position.

An alternate method is to have suspect clasp his hands on top of his head, Japanese-prisoner style. The frisker then places his hand over the prisoner's hands and leans his body into the prisoner's, forcing him against the wall. His partner then does the actual frisking.

The frisker's foot is placed in front of the suspect's to restrain him.

A more thorough way of frisking is the strip search, in which the suspect is told to remove his shoes and socks, pull his pants down and take his shirt off. The searchers then go over his clothing carefully for hidden items, such as burglary tools. Prime targets for search: the collar band, the pants fly, inside the neck band and the belt, and under the tie. Suspects also tend, if they have long, bushy hair, to hide picks there. Suspects have been known to fake heart attacks just so they can reach inside their shirt and pull out a knife. Women usually hide weapons in their pocketbooks or in their boots.

"We'll get 'em at the next stop. They're cheaper."

6:28 P.M. Broadway and 110th St.: We stop in front of a twenty-four-hour vegetable and grocery store. Ford gets out so that Hess can now eat. Hess tells me he's twenty-eight, Ford ten years older. Both married, with kids. He doesn't want to be a cop forever. He's taking business courses and hopes one day to run his own.

What's keeping Ford? Hess gets out to check. A minute later he waves me into the store. I join the two of them in the back.

The owner has caught an eleven-year-old black boy rummaging through his open safe. The boy claims he was looking for the bathroom.

"In an open safe?" says Ford. "Don't tell me they look the same. Kid, you got problems."

The owner of the store doesn't want to bother pressing charges. It would mean a day downtown, a day lost from work. Hess and Ford fully understand. They take the kid to the car.

On the way to the station house the kid says I was once his substitute teacher. He says he remembers my boots. His name is Troy. I vaguely remember him.

"Forgive me for saying it," says Hess. "But you didn't teach him very well. Kid's got a lot to learn."

6:52 P.M. Station house: Hess and Ford fill out a Juvenile Delinquency form on Troy. He still denies looking in the safe. They decide to teach him a lesson. Scare him into staying out of trouble. They say they're taking him to Spofford Detention Center. First, however, they'll take him home.

"So you can say goodbye to your mother," says Hess.

7:35 A.M. Somewhere in West Harlem: Troy's sister, jumping rope on the sidewalk, sees him in the back of the patrol car. She runs upstairs to get Grandma. Troy is embarrassed, starts to cry. Grandma thanks Hess and Ford for bringing him home. She promises him a "whupping" soon as he gets upstairs.

7:55 P.M. West Harlem: We drive around the decaying neighborhood. Hess and Ford point out the abandoned buildings which junkies use for "shooting galleries," and the cars from New Jersey, filled with whites come to buy drugs. Ford phones in the license numbers of a few suspicious cars, i.e., those that are very expensive or have a rental number on the plate.

"You get a feeling about some cars you see," says Hess. "It's like a sixth sense."

Headquarters tells us that none of the cars is hot.

8:15 P.M. West Harlem: A call for 26-A

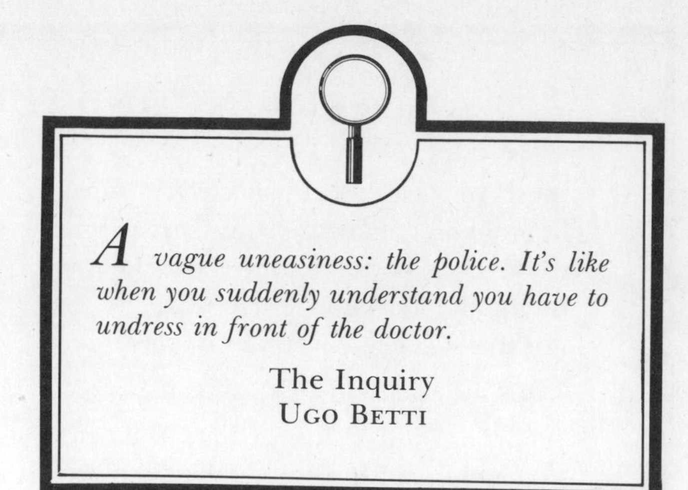

comes over the air. 10-31 — Burglary in Progress. Broadway Presbyterian Church. 114th Street. Hess, now driving, flips the switches for the siren and flashing red light. The siren doesn't work. He sits on the horn. Screeching tires. High-speed turns. Just like in the movies.

8:18 P.M. Broadway Presbyterian Church: Four people are standing in front. One of them jumps into the car.

"If we hurry up, we can catch 'em," he says. "Two black guys. They broke into the church. I followed 'em, and they pulled a knife on me."

"What'd they look like?" asks Ford, as Hess speeds down to Riverside Drive.

"They had leather jackets and dark pants."

Our complainant is about thirty-five, Italian, with short, graying blond hair. He says his name is Jerry, he lives in the neighborhood, and he spent the day washing cars at the church fair. He spied the burglars while out for a walk.

"I like them people at the church," he says. "Don't want to see 'em get ripped off."

8:25 P.M. Claremont Ave.: Near the back entrance to Riverside Church. "Turn around," says Ford.

Two men meeting Jerry's description have just entered the church. We turn around, park the car and go inside. We're followed by officers from two other patrol cars who've heard about the "attempted burglary." It's a slow period, and they've come to join the chase.

8:45 P.M. Riverside Church: The church is a beehive of activity — a teenage dance, a meeting of several hundred Asian-Americans, and a modern dance concert with an audience of at least 250. Suspects have been seen buying tickets to the concert and are now in the darkened auditorium. Six uniformed officers, myself and Jerry, the complainant, mingle outside with a growing crowd of curious onlookers and tense church officials. One cop suggests stopping the performance, turning on the lights and searching the hall. Hess and Ford prefer waiting for the show to end. Jerry reassures us he'll be able to identify his attackers.

A sergeant arrives on the scene. He immediately senses the potential for an ugly incident. He also doubts that the suspects in question are the "perpetrators."

"No one's gonna burglarize a church, then walk up to another church six blocks away and buy tickets to a dance concert. We're tying up three cars over this. Resume your tour."

9:15 P.M. Broadway Presbyterian Church: Hess, Ford, Jerry and I return to the scene of the crime. Glass door to the minister's office is smashed. A portable television set has been moved. A cookie tin filled with receipts from the day's fair has been opened.

The rector doesn't believe Jerry's story. "How could they have gotten away? You need a key to get out the door. I think you made up the story when we caught you in the office."

It appears that our complainant may, in fact, be our suspect. Hess and Ford go into action. Ford plays nice guy, reassuring Jerry everything is fine, while Hess interviews the rector and his assistants in another room. They claim they never saw Jerry before, that he showed up to wash cars and was seen wandering around the building.

"Obviously casing the joint," says Hess, smiling at his B-movie dialogue.

The rector thinks Jerry may have hidden in the building after the fair. Hess picks up the phone and calls Ford in the next room. They agree that Jerry is probably their man.

"We'll know for sure when the boys from Forensics check out the cookie tin for prints," says Hess. "In any case, we got enough to take him in."

Hess plays the bad guy. "Jerry, you're under arrest."

He reads him his rights. Jerry starts to cry. I look away.

10:00 P.M. Station house: Ford takes Jerry's prints; Hess types out the lengthy arrest report. I compliment him on his speedy two-finger typing.

"I get lots of practice," he says.

Jerry admits to previous arrests for burglary. He's a methadone addict, and he wants his shot.

11:05 P.M. Broadway and 112th St.: West End Bar. Hess has taken Jerry to a methadone clinic. I go with Ford on another 10-63. Bologna sandwiches, cokes and packs of cigarettes. One of each for Jerry.

"I'm sure he's hungry," says Ford.

11:45 P.M. Station house: Jerry thanks us for the food. He leaves with Hess for the overnight lockup. Hess will work overtime tomorrow, accompanying Jerry to court. Ford, now out of uniform, wearing jeans and a shirt, jokes with the other cops in civilian dress. Some of them look about sixteen.

12:00 A.M. Broadway and 113th St.: Ford, off-duty and on his way home, drops me off at a bar.

"What'd you think?" he asks. Before I get a word out, he answers himself. "You should come with us again in summer. Midnight-to-eight tour. Now *that's* what I call an interesting one."

12:07 A.M. Local bar: I sip my beer. They've got a *Kojak* rerun on. I decide I prefer *Adam-12*.

Thomas Seligson wants to be a cop when he grows up.

COURTESY SPRING 3100

OFFBEAT MUSIC

Detective Alfred J. Young, curator of the NYPD Museum, has one of the largest collections of police-inspired sheet music in America — well over 200 sheets. Many of these were written prior to World War I; some, such as Victor Herbert's "The Finest March," were written expressly for the Police Band. Unfortunately, the Department disbanded the 156-instrument group in 1953.

COURTESY ALFRED J. YOUNG COLLECTION

THE NYPD GLOSSARY

Lynn Strong

"**In the bag.**" In uniform.

Blotter. (formerly) A large green book used for logging precinct members' daily movements and any unusual occurrences. One desk sergeant, well-known to the Force, used it for banging heads when he lost patience with the procedure.

Booking. Recording an arrest.

"Brain." Detective. The term is used by non-detectives.

"Catching." Taking on an assignment. ("Henry's catching today.")

"Chamber of Horrors." The trial room at Headquarters.

"Collar." Arrest.

Command. Any unit, such as a precinct, with a commanding officer. ("Call your command.")

"Cooping" ("In the heave"). Time out for lunch, a quick nap, etc. Local funeral parlors and garages are well-suited for this purpose. Mounted police have special problems: one horse, parked in a boxcar, was halfway upstate when his rider returned from lunch.

Detail. A temporary assignment to another command. (See FLYING)

"Downtown." Headquarters.

"Family man." A clean-living member of the Force.

"Flaking." Depositing incriminating evidence on or near the suspect to facilitate arrest.

"Floater." A body dragged from the river.

"Flute." A whiskey-filled pop bottle in plain brown wrapper, donated to the SH by a grateful civilian.

"Flying." Temporarily assigned to another command. ("I flew to the eight-seven last night.")

"Gentleman." A superior respected for his fairness.

"In grays." Probationary; not yet graduated from the Academy.

"Gun run." A response to a report of person seen with a gun.

"Hat." The sum of $5 used by a civilian as an attempted bribe. ("Here, buy yourself a hat.")

"Heater." (*obsolete*) Gun.

"Jug day." A celebration for promotion or retirement. ("Tomorrow is Kelly's jug day.")

"Jumper." A potential or actual suicide victim.

"Kite." A complaint received through the mail.

Line-up. Five persons (suspect plus four others of similar physical description) on view for purpose of identifying suspect. Civilian

NYPD ABBREVIATIONS

ACU Anti-Crime Unit
ADA Assistant District Attorney
AKA (a.k.a.) Also Known As
APB All Points Bulletin
CCRB Civilian Complaint Review Board
CD Chief of Detectives
CO Commanding Officer
DA District Attorney
DET Detective
DOA Dead On Arrival
HQ Headquarters
IAD Internal Affairs Department
INS Inspector
LT Lieutenant
MPU Missing Persons Unit
NYPD New York Police Department
PA Police Academy
PCO Police Commissioner's Office
PCT Precinct
PI Private Investigator
PIU Precinct Investigators Unit
PO Police Officer
POF Police Officer, Female
POM Police Officer, Male
PP&C Pickpocket and Confidence Squad
RMP Radio Motor Patrol (car)
SGT Sergeant
SH Station House

non-suspects are paid $5. Now closed to the public, line-ups were once a source of neighborhood entertainment.

"Loid." (from *celluloid*) Small stiff piece of paper, as a credit card, used to open locks on doors. (See PICK MAN)

"Murphy man." Con man.

Observation. Watch kept on a stationary object, as a house, bar, etc. (See SURVEILLANCE)

Operator. The driver of an RMP. (See RECEIVER)

"Pick man." A professional lock-picker, equipped with special tools (unlike counterpart LOID man).

Post. The area of a PRECINCT covered by a patrolman (synonymous with "beat" in other cities). A "one-armed" post includes only one side of the street.

"Potsie." Shield.

Precinct. Geographical area whose boundaries are determined by population and police hazards.

"Rabbi" ("Hook"). An influential friend, either on or off the Force.

Receiver. The officer in an RMP who handles communications. (See OPERATOR)

"Ripper." A safe-cracker, usually employing a torch.

"Round robin." A comprehensive check-out preceding transfer, promotion, etc.

Sector. The area of a PRECINCT covered by a patrol car, (equivalent of POST).

Shield. A badge worn or carried to designate rank. "Working with the white shield" describes a PO assigned to detective's duties. A "gold shield" is another name for a detective. (*Note:* The word "badge" is not used by NYPD members.)

"Squeal." Complaint. ("Who's catching the squeal?")

Surveillance. Watch kept on a moving object, as a person, car, etc. (See OBSERVATION)

Ten-thirteen. Assist police officer.

"Tin." Shield.

"On the tin." Free; without being asked to pay. ("I got this at Louie's on the tin.")

"Torch." Arsonist.

"Undesirables" ("Germs"). Pimps, prostitutes, junkies, etc., as a group. ("Hey, there's a bunch of undesirables in front of Bickford's.")

"Yellow sheet." Record of previous arrests (now a white computer print-out).

Lynn Strong is an editor and current informer and former friend of the NYPD.

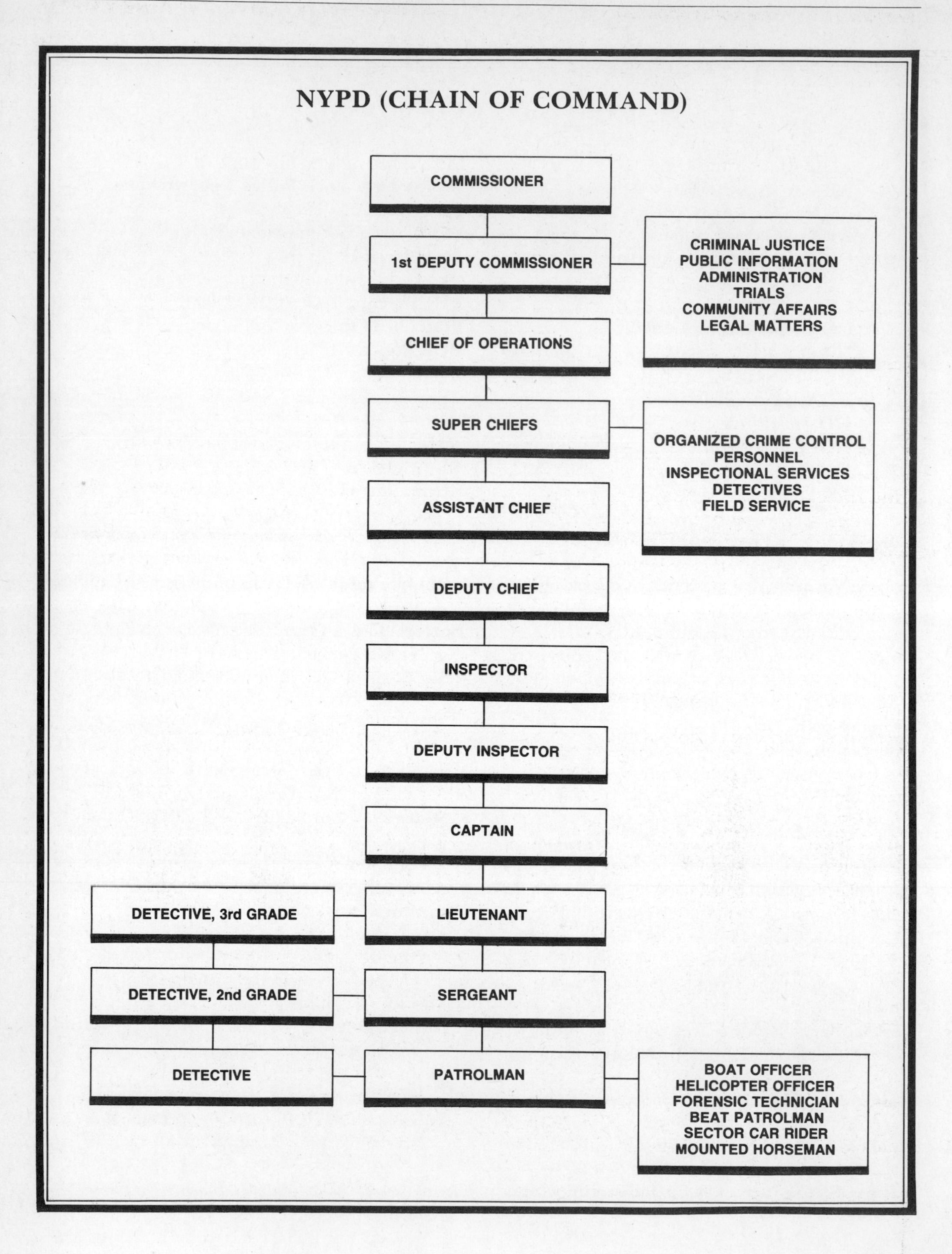
NYPD (CHAIN OF COMMAND)
COMMISSIONER
1st DEPUTY COMMISSIONER
CRIMINAL JUSTICE
PUBLIC INFORMATION
ADMINISTRATION
TRIALS
COMMUNITY AFFAIRS
LEGAL MATTERS
CHIEF OF OPERATIONS
SUPER CHIEFS
ORGANIZED CRIME CONTROL
PERSONNEL
INSPECTIONAL SERVICES
DETECTIVES
FIELD SERVICE
ASSISTANT CHIEF
DEPUTY CHIEF
INSPECTOR
DEPUTY INSPECTOR
CAPTAIN
DETECTIVE, 3rd GRADE
LIEUTENANT
DETECTIVE, 2nd GRADE
SERGEANT
DETECTIVE
PATROLMAN
BOAT OFFICER
HELICOPTER OFFICER
FORENSIC TECHNICIAN
BEAT PATROLMAN
SECTOR CAR RIDER
MOUNTED HORSEMAN

THE HISTORY OF THE ENGLISH POLICE

Peter N. Walker

The name Bow is pronounced as in "bow and arrow." Bow Street still exists in London and contains a very busy magistrates' court.

The first magistrate of Bow Street was Thomas de Veil, who was appointed in 1740. He was described as a courageous man, unafraid to expose himself to the criminals and mobs who terrorised London at that time. There was no police system to counteract their activities, other than the incompetent local watchmen; furthermore, criminals could bribe the justices to overlook their crimes.

Henry Fielding succeeded Veil and became a magistrate at Bow Street in 1748. He was a noted author (*Tom Jones*) and vigorously campaigned against the widespread corruption among the justices. His brother, John, who was almost blind, assisted him, and together they made a register of all crimes committed in London. The numbers horrified the brothers, so in 1750 Henry recruited six "thief-takers" to arrest the wrongdoers.

SCOTLAND YARD

Top-hatted English bobbies, c. 1860.

These were ordinary householders "actuated by a truly public spirit against thieves." They were ready at a moment's notice to perform their duty but were unpaid. Their task was to pursue all villains and bring them to justice; their reward came from the "blood-money" paid upon the arrest of a villain or upon the recovery of stolen goods. Fielding was their leader, a task he shared with a man called Saunders-Welch, who was High Constable of Holborn. The "thief-taker" wore no uniform and carried only the staff of a parish constable.

But they did achieve success; in addition to arresting thieves, they managed to break up gangs, and far-sighted people began to ask for a paid police force.

Fielding's men became known as Bow Street Runners about 1785 and at one time boasted two horse patrols. Fielding also published a news-sheet of criminal activities, listing known rogues and their crimes, but gained little official support from the government. His small band of men, as low as four in some cases, remained until the formation of the Metropolitan Police in 1829. Sadly, the Runners were unfit for recruitment into the regular police, but their memory lives on.

TIPSTAVES, TIPSTAFFS AND TRUNCHEONS

Today, recognising an English policeman isn't difficult. He wears a uniform and carries a warrant card. But before 1829 his sole symbol of office, of authority, was his tipstave, his tipstaff or his painted truncheon.

The tipstaves, being short, were either put in one's pocket or stuffed in one's waistcoat. They usually had a brass handle and a crown on the other end. Some of the crowns unscrewed and warrants were rolled up inside.

The tipstaffs, being very long, were used for ceremonial occasions, usually for parades and fancy processionals.

In 1829, the advent of the first officially recognised police uniform — blue coat, blue trousers, top hat — eliminated the need for the tipstave and the tipstaff. However, the truncheon was still carried and was still regarded as a symbol of authority. Often, it had to be produced by a plain-clothes detective when he questioned a suspect. The painted truncheon had a crown motif on top, with the Royal Coat of Arms or the Burgh Coat of Arms below it. Gradually, the elaborately decorated truncheons disappeared, until in the 1870's it was virtually extinct. It was still produced for ceremonial purposes, however, as late as the 1920's.

D.R.

Sir Robert Peel

Sir Robert Peel, founder of the modern English police force, was born on 5th February 1788 near Bury in Lancashire, England. His grandfather, also called Robert, was a calico printer who progressed to the spinning-jenny after he spun himself a fortune out of cotton. Peel's father, another Robert, was the third son of this self-made man; he became a Member of Parliament for Tamworth and was awarded a baronetcy in 1800.

Our Robert was educated at Harrow and Oxford, where he was a friend of Byron, the poet. He took first-class degrees in Classics and Mathematics, and in 1809, at the age of twenty-one, he, too, became a Member of Parliament. A dedicated Tory, he was an outstanding speaker and acquired a deep knowledge of Parliamentary procedures. Only three years later, he became Secretary for Ireland, and there he instituted the Irish Constabulary in an attempt to preserve life and property. This body of men became known as "Peelers."

In 1820, he married the daughter of General Sir John Floyd. She was named Julie, and they had five sons and two daughters. His family life was said to have been very happy.

In 1825, Robert Peel began his famous reform of criminal law in England, resulting in the birth of London's Metropolitan Police in 1829. It took four hard years to overcome the prejudice of his government, who saw the police as a threat to personal liberty. They failed to see that unchecked crime was a greater threat.

Peel, who was Home Secretary at the time, did not want his policemen to look like soldiers, so he dressed them as civilians in black top hats

SCOTLAND YARD

Sir Robert Peel (the first bobby).

and blue tailed coats. They were unarmed. Political disturbances in 1832 brought them into rapid conflict with the general public, who looked upon them as a political tool of the government. They hated the police and called them "Peel's Bloody Gang" or "Blue Lobsters." It took thirty years for them to become acceptable, and during that period, crime diminished and public order was restored.

Once they had become accepted by the public, the police became known as "bobbies" in honour of their founder, Bobby Peel. The English policeman is still affectionately known by this name.

Robert Peel, who has been described as one of the hardest workers and greatest intellectuals England has known, was thrown from his horse on Constitutional Hill, London, on 29th June 1850, and died on 2nd July that same year.

THE POLICE BLOTTER

Every English police station maintains a record of daily occurrences. In America, this is known as the Police Blotter but in England it is variously called the Occurrence Book, the Message Log and the Daily Log. In some areas it is known simply by the relevant form number; for example, if the messages are printed on a Form 24, the blotter itself is called Form 24.

Whatever its name, its function is simple. It is a record of every message that comes into a police station, and of every incident, together with the action taken by the police. It includes messages from whatever source: personal callers, telephone, radio, Telex, computer — or even internal police instructions. Every policeman should read it before the start of his tour of duty, or it should be read out to him.

It will include, for example, in time sequence, every item of lost-and-found property, arrests, holes in the road, reports of traffic accidents, air crashes, rapes, burglaries, missing people or dogs, sudden deaths, wanted persons, escaped mental patients or budgerigars, emergency calls, murder, mayhem and suicide. And more besides!

P.N.W.

Peter N. Walker is a police inspector in the North Yorkshire Police. He is also the author of over thirty crime books.

THE BOBBY GLOSSARY

Peter N. Walker

Antecedents. A criminal's history, including his education, work, family record. ("What are the accused's antecedents?")
Bat phone. A police officer's personal radio. (slang)
Book on/Book off. To report on/off duty. ("I'm booking on at 2 P.M.")
Break. (a) A breakthrough in a major enquiry. ("I've got a marvellous break in the murder enquiry.") Or:
(b) A crime where property, like houses or shops, is broken into, e.g., burglary. ("I've got a few breaks to deal with today.")
Brothel creepers. Boots with very soft soles.
Charge room. A room in a police station where criminals are processed, i.e., searched after arrest and charged with their crimes.
Chief. The Chief Constable. ("Have you seen the Chief lately?")
Climber. A burglar with an ability to climb drainpipes, walls, etc. A cat burglar.
Collator. An officer who keeps local records of suspected and/or convicted criminals, their movements, friends, haunts, etc.
Divisional sleuth. A detective. (slang)
Fence. A person who disposes of stolen goods. ("Jack is the best fence in this area.")
Flasher. A man who indecently exposes himself. ("There's a flasher in the park.")
Gong. A medal of any type.
Going equipped. Being in possession of instruments or tools for use in crime. ("I arrested Fred for going equipped.")
Handler. (a) A police dog handler.
(b) A receiver of stolen goods; a fence.
Horror comics. Police circulars, crime bulletins, information sheets, etc. (slang)
Heaven. The Chief Constable's office. (slang)
Juveniles. Persons under 17 years of age.
Knock-off. An arrest. ("I got a good knock-off last night.")
Lock-ups. Arrested persons placed in custody. ("I had seven lock-ups last night.")
Lab. A forensic science laboratory.
Metro. The London Metropolitan Police.
Manor. A police officer's area of responsibility, e.g., streets in one part of a city. (slang) Also, a criminal's area of operation. ("I'm going for a trip around my manor.")
Motor patrol. The Police Traffic Department; police officers who specialise in patrolling main roads to deal with vehicular traffic matters. Sometimes known as Traffic Section.
Mug shot. Photograph of a prisoner. (slang)
Nick. The police station ("Take him to the nick.")
Nicked. Arrested, or reported for a minor offence. ("I got nicked for a parking offence.")
Noddy bikes. Small police motorcycles. (slang)
Panda car. Small car used for local beat patrol duties; named "Panda" because the originals were two colours, e.g., blue and white.
Nutters. People of unsound mind.
Prints. Fingerprints.
Previous. A criminal's previous convictions. ("Has he any previous?")
Queen bee. A senior woman police officer. (slang)
Rings. Phone calls to the police station to see if anything has arisen which requires attention. ("I make my rings on the hour.")

ABBREVIATIONS

A.B.H. Actual Bodily Harm: a serious assault
A.C.C. Assistant Chief Constable
B.O.P. Breach of the Peace: a disturbance
C.C. Chief Constable
C.I.D. (a) Criminal Investigation Department
(b) Coppers in Disguise (slang)
C.O.P. Chief of Police
C.R.O. Criminal Record Office
D.C. Detective Constable
D.C.C. Deputy Chief Constable
D.C.I. Detective Chief Inspector
D.H.Q. Divisional Headquarters
D.I. Detective Inspector
D.S. Detective Sergeant
D. Supt. Detective Superintendent
F.A. Found Abandoned (applicable to cars illegally borrowed and dumped after use)
G.B.H. Grievous Bodily Harm: a serious assault
G.P. Car. General Purpose Car: a police vehicle with no specific duties; it deals with any incident that might arise
H.Q. Headquarters
ID Parade. Identification Parade
INSP. Inspector
M.P.D. Metropolitan Police District: the area policed by the London Metropolitan Police
N.F.A. No Fixed Abode
P.C. Police Constable
P.N.C. Police National Computer (All English and Welsh forces are linked to the P.N.C.)
R.T. (a) Road Traffic
(b) Radio Transmitter
Sgt. Sergeant
SOCO. Scenes of Crime Officer (spoken as "Socco"): police or civilians who visit scenes of crimes to photograph them or to undertake other scientific investigations
Supt. Superintendent
T.W.O.C. Taking Without Owner's Consent (spoken as "twock"): unlawfully borrowing a motor vehicle ("I arrested two men for T.W.O.C.")
T.I.C. Taken into Consideration: a term used when a criminal on trial for a crime asks a court to punish him for other offences he has committed in the past; this "cleans his slate." ("He asked for eight other burglaries to be T.I.C.")
U.B.P. Unit Beat Policing: a system of patrolling with five officers and a "Panda" car; the officers are made responsible for a given area which they patrol, so they become well acquainted with the residents
U.S.I. Unlawful Sexual Intercourse with a girl under sixteen years of age

P.N.W.

Station. A police station.
Sussed. Suspected; to realise a person is guilty. ("I sussed him the moment he opened his mouth.")
Scene. The scene of a crime. ("Make sure the scene is protected and cordoned off.")
Tonsil varnish. Tea or coffee served in police canteens. (slang)
Verbal. An oral confession.
Voluntary. A statement, freely given, in which guilt is admitted. ("He has given a good voluntary.")
Wopsie. A woman police constable (from the initials WPC). Today, women are not distinguished in this manner; since 1975 they have had equal rights with male officers and a woman is known simply as "Police Constable X."
Working a beat. Patrolling on duty, in a specified area, either on foot or in a car.
Whiz kid. A rapidly promoted officer. (slang)
The Yard. Scotland Yard.
Yellow perils. Traffic wardens. (slang)
Yobs. Thugs, vandals, trouble-makers. (slang)

THE BLACK MUSEUM OF SCOTLAND YARD

Laurence Henderson

All police forces have a museum in which they locate relics of exceptional cases. The first of these, and still the most famous, is the criminal museum at Scotland Yard. The original intention was not to collect mementos for their curiosity value but as a detective training aid. Any officer undergoing a senior detective course, will, as part of his training, make a tour of the museum in order to learn that there is nothing new under the sun — that the tricks of present-day criminals are only variations on those of the past — and to see how his predecessors fared in grappling with them.

The museum is divided into a number of sections. The historical section contains the declaration signed by George III which brought into existence the first official police force. Here also is an original police uniform from those early days, curios such as the skeleton keys of Charlie Peace and the knighthood regalia of Sir Roger Casement, and a collection of death masks taken from prisoners hanged at Newgate Prison in the early nineteenth century. (The only recent death mask is that of Heinrich Himmler, which was taken by the Army Special Investigation Branch as proof that the body they held was indisputably that of the Nazi Chief of Police; it had served its purpose, the mask was sent to the museum as the appropriate place to record the end of the greatest mass murderer in history.)

The main sections of the museum cover burglary, drugs, abortion, fraudulent gaming devices, forgery, murder, terrorism and kidnapping, with a final section for sexual perversion. All of the sections are constantly updated, but each new exhibit has to win its place either because it is startling in degree or because it is original in its criminal inventiveness: the device, for example, invented by a jewel thief specialising in the Mayfair area which, based upon the principle of a geared cork remover, is capable of winding out a spring lock from the street side of the door; a walking stick, built of interlocking tubes, which can be extended into a hook-ended ladder almost twenty feet long; the shaved dividers of a rigged roulette wheel; two-way radios built into hearing aids for the heavy poker game; and, in the forgery section, examples of outstanding artistic ability in bank notes drawn freehand, totaliser betting tickets altered within minutes of the end of a race to show a winning combination, and postal orders altered to a higher value — again free-hand — by a single hair dipped in watered ink.

Since forgery of bank notes has become a matter of photogravure processing, it no longer requires the high skills of the criminal engraver, who now operates in the high-risk field of fraudulent bonds and share certificates. The most active area of forgery has nothing to do with bank notes or share coupons: It is apparently easier and less risky to forge airline ticket blanks and Social Security frankings, which are sold to crooked travel agents, accountants and company secretaries. An area not usually thought of in connection with forgery is that of consumer goods: the label and wrappings of an expensive perfume, for example, which has a ready sale to buyers who believe they are cheaply acquiring stolen goods.

The most fascinating exhibit in this section is that of a coiner rather than of a forger. Coining is generally regarded as a dead criminal activity but it does still continue in the field of gold coins. One particular character was in operation from the mid-1940's until the beginning of the 1960's. Well aware that most fake gold sovereigns are detected by either a weight or chemical test, his technique was to take a small cross section of half-inch copper piping and place it between dies, first spooning into the hollow centre a carefully measured quantity of mercury. He would then trap the mercury within the copper by exerting pressure on the dies with a gallows device powered by a pneumatic jack. The result was a coin the approximate weight of a genuine sovereign, which he coated in gold obtained by melting down stolen cigarette cases and old watches. (*In*

WHY "SCOTLAND YARD"?

London's first police office was situated at No. 4, Whitehall Place, London. The rear entrance was along a narrow lane called Scotland Yard.

From that time, the name has been given to all subsequent buildings which have accommodated the headquarters of London's Metropolitan Police.

New Scotland Yard is in Victoria Street. It is *not* the headquarters of *Britain's* police; it is the headquarters only of the Metropolitan Police.

The fifty or so police forces of England, Wales, Scotland and Ireland each have their own policemen with their own chief constable and their own police headquarters. All are complete units, and between them they service the entire British Isles outside London.

There is no national police force in England, although the Home Secretary is responsible to the government for law and order, and in this capacity issues guidance to all police forces.

P.N.W.

UNITED PRESS INTERNATIONAL

First came Scotland Yard, then came New Scotland Yard, then came another Scotland Yard which by rights should be called New New Scotland Yard but, like its predecessor, bears the name New Scotland Yard. Pictured here: New Scotland Yard and New Scotland Yard (Version Two).

extremis, he would purchase commercial gold leaf.)

During the fourteen years or so of his career, he made and sold thousands of his fake sovereigns to coin dealers, tourists, smugglers and others who think it smarter to keep money in gold rather than bank notes. The police have an amused regard for him. What I find entertaining is that, when he was eventually arrested, it was not on a charge of coining at all, but for receiving stolen copper piping.

The largest section of the museum is devoted to murder, with various sub-sections allotted to terrorist murder, murder associated with kidnapping and the murder of policemen. From the point of detection techniques, however, the more interesting murders are those committed by individuals for personal ends. The two obvious cases in this sense are those of Neville Heath, who savaged his victims with whips, knives and teeth solely for his sexual satisfaction, and of Christie, who murdered in order to supply himself with dead bodies, since he obtained no satisfaction in connecting himself with live ones.

The section on perversion does not collect dirty photographs or films for their own sake, although there are certainly plenty of both, but rather as unique examples of their own very special kind. It is sobering to consider that whatever the human mind can envisage in its wildest moments of madness, sickness or aberration — the worst, most disgusting, utterly vile thing — not only has already been thought of but has already been brought to actuality. However experienced a police officer, he must surely be taken aback, at least momentarily, by the life-size crucifix with its barbed-wire attachments, or the case in which a man was truly crucified by nails driven through the hands and feet; the leather collar with the inward-pointing nails, the macabre surgical trolley and the other, quite ordinary objects, like the wind-up Gramophone, which have, with fiendish ingenuity, been transformed into instruments of pain and perversion.

It is with mixed emotions that one leaves the Black Museum. When I was asked which exhibit had struck me the most, it was not any of the objects of refined sexual torture or aids to perversion; it was not even the photographs that record the handiwork of the sadist Heath or the necrophiliac Christie.

In 1945 a girl, living in Southampton, sat opening the gifts she had received for her nineteenth birthday. One of the parcels that came through the mail contained a pair of binoculars and a card that said she would be surprised "how closely it brings things." She put the binoculars to one side while she opened the rest of the gifts, and it was her father who picked them up and casually touched the central focusing screw, whereupon needle-sharp spikes sprang from either eyepiece.

The binoculars had been painstakingly carved from solid wood, the spikes fitted inside on a rachet, powered by a coiled steel spring, and then the whole thing disguised with black rexine and enamel paint. The workmanship is incredible, the cunning intelligence of its execution is frightening and the monumental hatred behind its creation is demoniac. It is also an unsolved crime.

Laurence Henderson is the author of Major Enquiry.

NO, IT DOESN'T SELL POST CARDS

The Black Museum is not called that by its curator. The term "black" was coined by a reporter who liked the negative emotionalism of it.

The museum is open by special arrangement. Visitors are met at the reception desk on the ground floor by a Yard official who escorts them to the door of the museum. The curator lets them in, then locks the door behind them. No one is allowed to wander the building at his leisure.

A tour takes approximately one and a half hours, at which time the visitor is released from the locked room and escorted downstairs and out the door.

SCHEMATIC OF THE POLICE SYSTEM OF ENGLAND AND WALES

Peter N. Walker

In England and Wales, a person (man or woman) may join the regular police service as a constable at eighteen and a half years of age. After an initial course of ten weeks at a police training centre, the recruit is posted to a police station. There he/she spends almost two years undergoing further training on a practical basis, under close supervision. This is known as the "probationary" period of service.

After two years, he/she may take an examination to qualify for promotion to the rank of sergeant, and successful candidates are promoted to that rank if and when suitable vacancies arise. Not everyone who passes the examination will be promoted. After passing the qualifying examination to sergeant, a candidate may sit the examination for further promotion to inspector. Promotion to inspector and the higher ranks is by selection, and no further examinations are required.

Detectives are selected from the uniformed members of the service. After serving in uniform for the first two years of service, a police officer can be selected for training as a detective because of his/her aptitude for this work. He/she attends a course at a detective training school and may then become a detective police constable, working in civilian clothes. To qualify for promotion, the detective must pass the same examinations as his uniformed colleagues, and it is quite common for detectives to return to uniform duty for a short period before being promoted within the Criminal Investigation Department.

For example, a detective inspector may have progressed from a uniformed constable to a detective constable, then from a uniform sergeant to a detective sergeant before winning his promotion to detective inspector (see chart on the next page). This system provides valuable experience in all departments.

Peter N. Walker is the author of The MacIntyre Plot.

MILEAGE ON THE BEAT

A constable on foot patrol covers perhaps only 10 miles per day. Before cars became so widely used, he would walk his beat for 7¼ hours, taking ¾ hour for a meal break. A reasonable walking speed is 3 miles per hour, which means he could cover up to 20 miles during every tour of duty. It is of interest to know that, for this reason, until 1975 most English bobbies received a boot allowance!

"Panda" cars travel about 40 miles per gallon of petrol. Cars work three tours of duty each day, so it is possible to cover 600 miles per day.

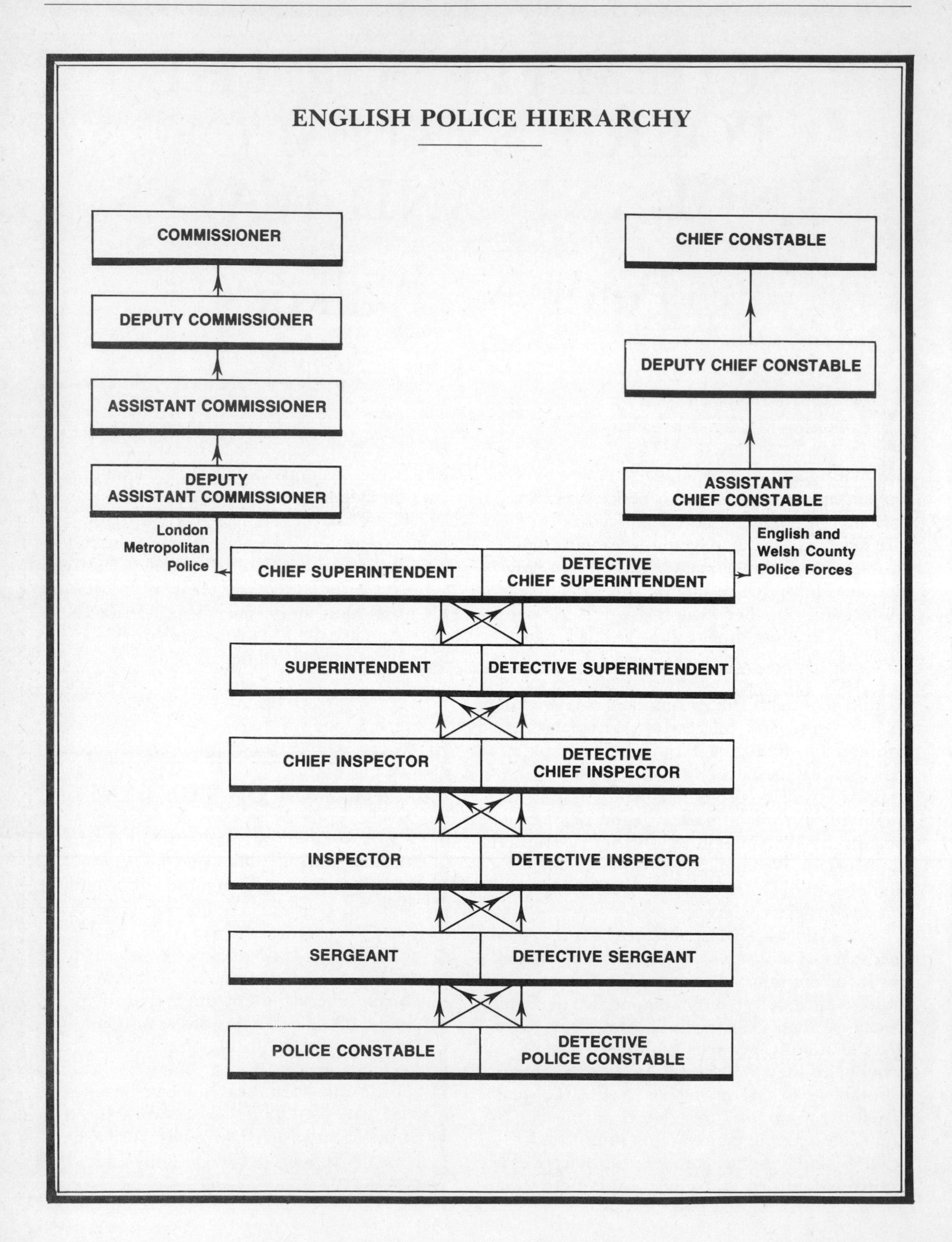
ENGLISH POLICE HIERARCHY
COMMISSIONER
DEPUTY COMMISSIONER
ASSISTANT COMMISSIONER
DEPUTY ASSISTANT COMMISSIONER
London Metropolitan Police
CHIEF CONSTABLE
DEPUTY CHIEF CONSTABLE
ASSISTANT CHIEF CONSTABLE
English and Welsh County Police Forces
CHIEF SUPERINTENDENT
DETECTIVE CHIEF SUPERINTENDENT
SUPERINTENDENT
DETECTIVE SUPERINTENDENT
CHIEF INSPECTOR
DETECTIVE CHIEF INSPECTOR
INSPECTOR
DETECTIVE INSPECTOR
SERGEANT
DETECTIVE SERGEANT
POLICE CONSTABLE
DETECTIVE POLICE CONSTABLE

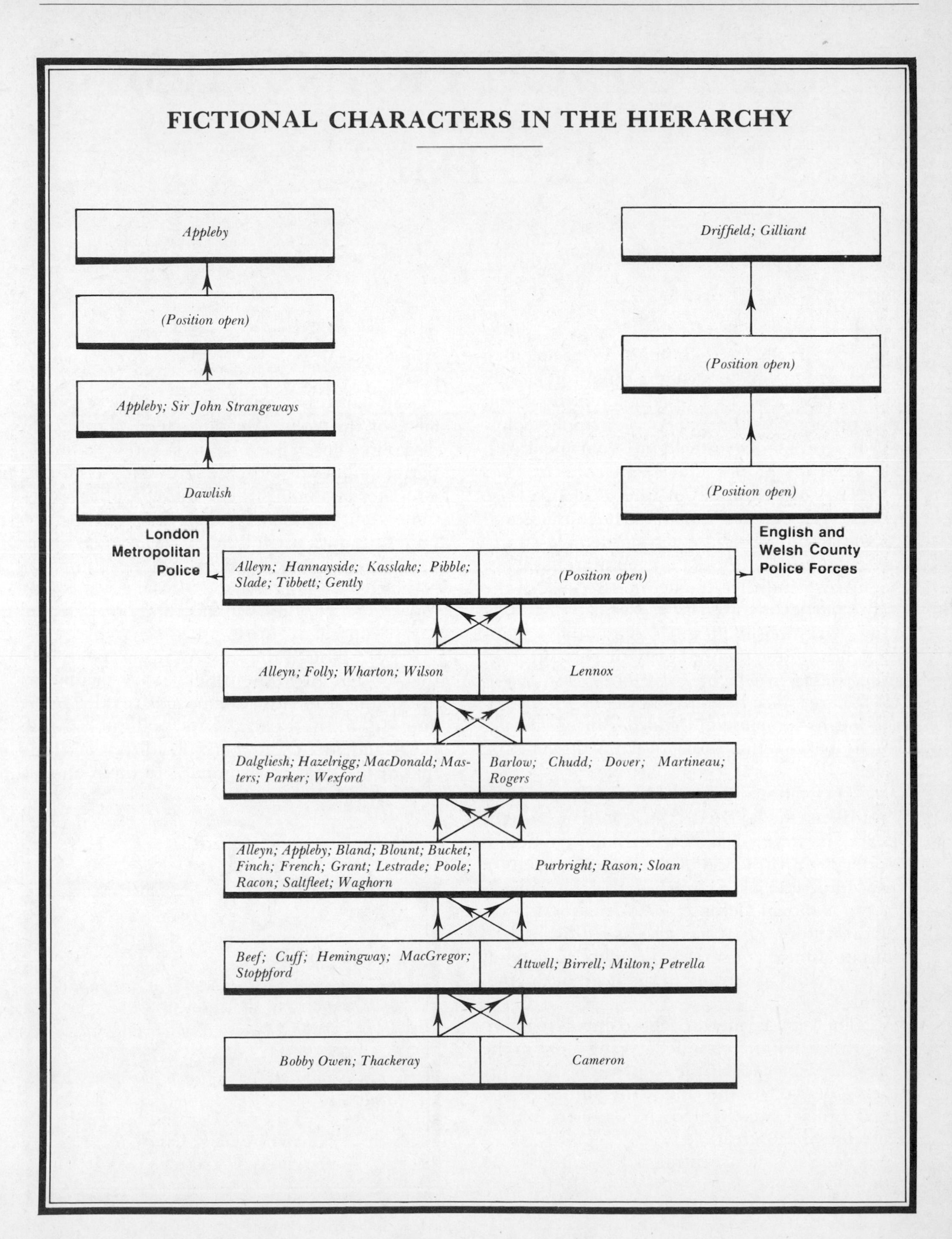
FICTIONAL CHARACTERS IN THE HIERARCHY
Appleby
(Position open)
Appleby; Sir John Strangeways
Dawlish
London Metropolitan Police
Driffield; Gilliant
(Position open)
(Position open)
English and Welsh County Police Forces
Alleyn; Hannayside; Kasslake; Pibble; Slade; Tibbett; Gently
(Position open)
Alleyn; Folly; Wharton; Wilson
Lennox
Dalgliesh; Hazelrigg; MacDonald; Masters; Parker; Wexford
Barlow; Chudd; Dover; Martineau; Rogers
Alleyn; Appleby; Bland; Blount; Bucket; Finch; French; Grant; Lestrade; Poole; Racon; Saltfleet; Waghorn
Purbright; Rason; Sloan
Beef; Cuff; Hemingway; MacGregor; Stoppford
Attwell; Birrell; Milton; Petrella
Bobby Owen; Thackeray
Cameron

LA POLICE FRANÇAISE

Eve Darge

First of all, let us remind the reader that the Sûreté to which outsiders often refer when talking about the police, does not represent the entirety of the French Police. It applies solely to the Criminal Investigation Department with branches spread out all over the country.

The organization of the French police system — its establishment, its attributions and its functioning — is not easy to define. To understand it (very few do) is even more difficult.

Why is it difficult to define? Because of the many parties involved in a confusing overlapping of responsibilities of the multiple groups of police under the authority of two different ministries (we really mean different with a capital D here, since they may not always agree on the means to maintain the order or ensure the public peace), the local governments and the Army.

The National Police (or the general police), "Gardiens de la Paix," the guardians of the peace, in time of war or turbulent times, is under the jurisdiction of the Army, whereas in peacetime it is just as much under the Ministry of the National Defense as under the Ministry of the Interior that has also at its disposal an infinite number of services of police spread out in large cities according to the need of the moment.

The "gendarmerie," whose duty is to maintain the order and conduct investigations in the rural areas, is also at the disposal of the Army (being part of it) and under the authority of a local official attached to the Ministry of the Interior (the Prefect).

The lack of a central police authority to consolidate and harmonize the efforts may symbolize the policy "Divide and Rule" at its best.

In Paris, the general police is the responsibility of the Police Headquarters, "Préfecture de Police," located on Île de la Cité. At the departmental level — the department here being a territorial administrative division of the state (ninety-four in total) — all services of police are under the authority of the Prefect appointed by the Ministry of the Interior. Not elected. Since Napoleon (1800), he is the official government representative, the Administrator, the former royal "Intendant" during the Monarchy.

Even though the services of the police are theoretically his responsibility, they belong on the technical and disciplinary side to the Region and also to the Central Office in Paris, whose views and ideas may be quite different from that of the local government. (In their surveil-

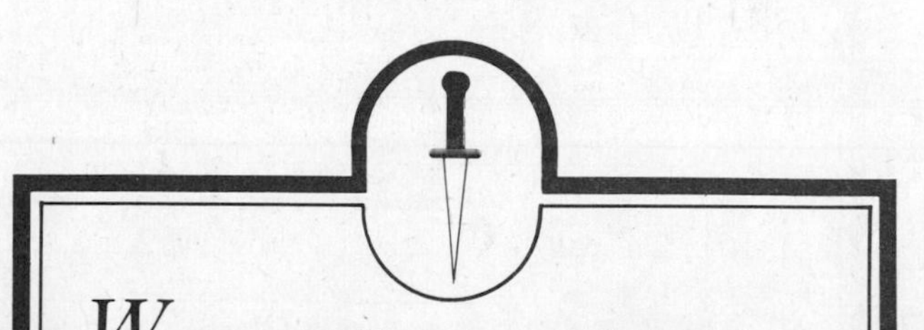

Write, or cable me care of the Sûreté, Paris, the exact location *of that nick in the missing left ear of Murgatroyd, as per morgue photo. I have encountered two other nicked ears since leaving New York, one of which is indubitably related to the Murgatroyd case.*

The Whispering Ghost
STEPHEN CHALMERS

lance of the personalities, for instance, they also check on the Prefect and report to the Central Office.)

Each police precinct (commissariat) is headed by a police officer, the commissioner, whose rank theoretically corresponds to that of a colonel in the Army. His commanding officers of the guardians of the peace rank from first lieutenant to lieutenant colonel, according to the importance of the city. Police officers, in plain clothes or uniformed, are non-commissioned officers.

The officers come out of the National Police Academy, which admits candidates with prior master's degrees from universities and who have passed with highest scores a competitive entry examination. Exceptionally gifted candidates with lower degrees and, in rare cases, directly from the ranks, might also be enrolled.

Paradoxically, the head of the Paris prefecture and his immediate subordinates are civilian high officials appointed by the government. (Their knowledge of criminology, according to the whispers of some real pros, is no more than what can be rapidly acquired through a police novel.)

The gendarmerie officers, ranking from lieutenant to colonel, come out of the Military Academy of St. Cyr and the Military School at St. Maixent. Some may also have risen from the ranks after a probationary stage in a "gendarmerie school."

In the capital and larger cities, the police

FRENCH GOVERNMENT TOURIST OFFICE

M. Gondureau, Chef de Sûreté, appeared in Balzac's Le Père Goriot; *Inspector Hanaud, in A.E.W. Mason's* At the Villa Rose. *John Dickson Carr's Henri Bencolin was* juge d'instruction *in* It Walks by Night. *None of them ever directed traffic.*

FRENCH GOVERNMENT TOURIST OFFICE

Vidocq, founder of the Police de Sûreté (pictured above), wrote about his more scandalous escapades in the four-volume Mémoires *(1828–29). Rumor has it, they were ghost-written.*

are now to a large degree highly motorized. That entails motorbikes (Vespas) as well as automobiles. Because of the many narrow streets and traffic circles, only the little Renault is used, often referred to as "pie" (pronounced *pee*), the French for the magpie bird, because of its striking color resemblance — black and white.

France is proud of its police, which in spite of all is sophisticated, resourceful, efficient and effective. The fact that so many people are involved — so many personalities from the Prefect to the Ministers, who in no circumstances must be embarrassed — may very well keep the police on its toes and force it to outdo itself.

The French police have been criticized and often accused of treating as an "enemy" anyone not conforming. To remedy this, special courses on human relationships have been conducted during recent years among the various services.

For the tourist visiting Paris for the first time, it is worthwhile mentioning that the policeman they meet is not a "gendarme." The gendarme is, as we have said, the rural police dressed in navy blue uniforms slightly different from the policeman's dark blue. The guardian of the peace is addressed with the words "Monsieur l'Agent" (the *t*, at the end, not pronounced).

Under unusual circumstances — namely, in case of civil unrest — a different policeman, and wearing a khaki uniform, is called in as a reinforcement to the capital. He is the C.R.S., a member of the "Compagnie Républicaine de Sécurité," a paramilitary organization comparable to American state troopers. He happens to be the least popular among the masses because of the symbol of force he represents and the stringent measures he is likely to use.

Parking tickets are handed out by an auxiliary unit consisting of females, nicknamed "Aubergines"(eggplants) because of the particular uniform color they wear. In the same vein, let us mention that the police are referred to as "les Flics" (but never, never to their faces!).

Eve Darge is an executive supervisor for Air France.

VIDOCQ

Peter N. Walker

François Eugene Vidocq was a criminal who became chief of the Paris police.

Born in 1775 at Arras, he had an overpowering weakness for women. When he was only fifteen, he disguised himself as the sister of a willing serving maid so that he could accompany the lady of his desires on holiday. He had a fortnight's bliss without the lady's husband ever suspecting his wife had a lover.

His parents thought he would be best employed in the army, but there he continued his amorous exploits. Out of the army, he was an acrobat, forger, swindler, thief and highwayman, and his capacity for trouble brought him eight years' hard labour on the galleys at Brest. He escaped twice and was recaptured; upon his third escape he lived among the thieves and criminals of Paris, learning their ways. Armed with this knowledge, he offered himself in 1809 as a spy to the Paris police, and his energetic work eventually led to his becoming head of the reorganised detective department. He worked with a body of ex-convicts under his command and was known for his genius for catching crooks.

It was in 1811 that he hit upon the idea of the Sûreté, crime fighters who had no boundary limits. In 1817, his small group made 811 arrests, among which were 15 assassins, 341 receivers of stolen goods and 14 escaped prisoners. He started a card index of criminals, but his success did not please the orthodox police of Paris. They suggested that Vidocq arranged the crimes he successfully solved.

Vidocq's strong point was his extrovert personality. He was a master of disguise, a brilliant speaker and a humorist; on the debit side, he was always in trouble and constantly chasing women, especially actresses. He liked duelling, stalking the night life of Paris in disguise, raiding criminals' lairs or defending himself in court with his customary eloquence.

His disguises ranged from coalmen to women (he once escaped from prison disguised as a woman), but an example of his skill is shown in his efforts to disguise himself as an escaped prisoner called Germaine.

To discover Germaine's hiding place, he needed to fool the escapee's acquaintances. He studied pictures of Germaine and made himself up to look like him. He blistered his feet and faked the marks of the fetters about his ankles. He obtained some shoes and a shirt marked GAL, indicating service in the galleys. Next, he stained his shirt with walnut juice and let his beard grow. He caked his nostrils with gum and coffee grounds to give himself Germaine's nasal intonations, and finally he even obtained some lice to place upon his shirt. After all this, his disguise failed because someone revealed his true identity.

In 1827, Vidocq retired and started a paper mill, staffed with ex-convicts, but it was a failure. He tried to re-join the police and in 1832 succeeded by being allocated political duties. But Vidocq wanted only to return to detective duties, and it is said he organised a daring theft, one which he could solve in order to prove his worth. Once his real part became known, he was dismissed from the service.

It is also said he died in poverty, a broken man, although some accounts deny this. Some say he continued to work privately as a detective into ripe old age, still chasing the women, and that he lived in reasonable luxury until his death in 1857.

MAIGRET INTERVIEWED

Eve Darge

My assignment takes me to the very heart of Paris, "Île de la Cité." I glance at the Towers of Notre Dame watching over the city since the twelfth century. Turning to the left of the Cathedral I arrive at the Conciergerie, the former palace of the city's superintendent where memories of the French Revolution still linger. Marie Antoinette spent her last days here. It houses now the Palace of Justice, the Court House, the Police Headquarters. The place I am to visit, the right wing, was added by Napoleon the Third.

My taxi has dropped me at the entrance, Quai des Orfêvres.

"Right wing, second floor, Room 202," the guard says.

This is where the Homicide Squad operates.

"The Commissioner wants you to wait for him in his office," conveys young detective Janvier.

I have arrived just in time to avoid the gusty winds and the torrential rain falling now heavily on the city.

Heavy footsteps down the corridor. The solid, well-known silhouette appears at the door. His other detective — Lucas, I believe — helps him take off his drenched overcoat and hat. I stand up.

"Please remain seated." He exchanges his flooded pipe for a fresh one. "So, they send me women now! I have nothing against that . . . I've always had a preference for them. I get along better with them."

E.D.: Commissioner . . . how does one address you?

MAIGRET: Call me Maigret, you're a civilian!

E.D.: Monsieur Maigret, I should perhaps come back . . . this bad weather . . .

MAIGRET: No. It's your work. Bad weather has never interfered with mine.

E.D.: This weather reminds me of home . . . Lorraine, at the Belgian border.

MAIGRET: It's true. Always starts in England. The English try to unload it on us through the Belgians, who get it twenty-four hours earlier. Excuse me while I change my shoes. My feet are soaked.

E.D.: You should have had rubbers.

MAIGRET: I hate them! I also seem to have a certain allergy for raincoats and umbrellas. Besides, I used to lose them regularly.

E. D.: Monsieur Maigret, you just completed an investigation — what is your feeling when the murderer has been arrested?

MAIGRET: The satisfaction of the work done, the duty accomplished. The satisfaction of knowing that the perpetrator of a crime will not commit another one, as it sometimes happens, to cover the first.

E.D.: What are the most common motives you have encountered in your investigations?

MAIGRET: At the source, you'll always find the capital sins. Envy is the motive of the murderer who kills to get the property of others without working. Uncontrolled anger, a sort of temporary insanity, may also transform a man into a killer. Jealousy, of course, which is nothing other than a violent rejection of abandonment. The killer in that case will not admit to having his love or security usurped.

E.D.: You have not mentioned lust, or gluttony.

MAIGRET: Lust rarely generates murders. It does not generate anything. It degenerates, rather . . . gluttony, ah, that is my weakness. I have a strong appetite. Nothing moves me like good country cooking odors. In my time, we never counted calories and as a result people were much more level-headed. Particularly women!

E.D.: Do you imply that the modern woman lost some of her equilibrium when she lost her . . . excessive roundness?

MAIGRET: I have always preferred them pleasantly plump.

E.D.: Monsieur Maigret, you seem to know them very well. Women of all walks of life. It is even said that you know the prostitutes particularly well. That you have for them a certain fondness, a bias.

MAIGRET: No. Not a bias. But I do not condemn them. I try to understand the reason that brought them there. In general, they are not malefactors . . . but the victims.

E.D.: Coming back, Monsieur Maigret, to the confessions you obtain. It is rumored that you dissect souls. That people do not confess their crimes, but rather confide in you.

MAIGRET: I don't know if I dissect the souls. But I think I am able to put people at ease. I get their trust. The criminal is perhaps the human being who suffers the most. The one who has never been understood. Faced with someone who is able to discover what he is really like, to expose him to himself, he soon softens up. The weight of his guilt was becoming unbearable. This is the only way for him to feel some relief.

E.D.: In the course of an investigation, do you immediately recognize the guilty?

MAIGRET: No. But I recognize instinctively the non-guilty. I proceed by elimination. In difficult cases, I investigate the antecedents. Their childhood tells me more than their adult lives, which they might have been able to keep partly hidden.

E.D.: That makes you a disciple of Freud. I noticed while waiting for you that your library counts as many Treatises on Psychoanalysis as Manuals on Criminology.

MAIGRET: I believe everything is related to childhood.

E.D.: Beside the murder act, which are in your opinion the most hideous crimes?

MAIGRET: Without any doubt, blackmail and breach of confidence. Many years ago, while in Vichy, I became involved in the investigation of the murder of a woman. She had had, in her youth, a brief relationship with a man in Paris, and had moved away. Under the false pretext that he was the father to a son, she made him pay fantastic sums of money for more than twenty years — with the promise that they could come together when the boy would be of age. The man, being married and childless, waited patiently, and when finally faced with the truth that no child ever existed, in a fit of anger strangled her. For me, the real victim was the murderer . . . I had wished that he would be acquitted. And there is a justice . . . he was.

E.D.: You seem to be well liked by your associates. They call you "Patron" and "Boss" with reverence. Your former detectives assigned in different parts of France continue calling you "Boss".

MAIGRET: Well . . . they're a fine bunch. But the real boss is the French taxpayer. This is why we must do our job even better. We must protect him.

E.D.: What sort of private life do you lead, Monsieur Maigret?

MAIGRET: A very quiet life, between my wife and my office. I should say between my wife's dinner table and my office . . . I am not much for formal affairs. I hate wearing a tuxedo. Tuxedos should be worn only by men that look like Prince Philip.

E.D.: What do you do for leisure?

MAIGRET: Not much. I love to take walks along the Seine River looking at the simple people, along with my wife, my understanding wife. We get along so well, we don't even have to talk. I don't have much time for novels. But to really relax, I read Simenon. Even though he comes from the other side of the border, we seem to have a lot in common. You see . . . before all . . . he is human.

Eve Darge is a French poet living in New York.

POLIS! POLIS!

K. Arne Blom

In Sweden, the police procedural focuses on man's relationship to society. In Britain, its emphasis is on the struggle between good men (the police) and bad men (the criminals). In America, the police novel is most concerned with the interaction of characters with each other, not with the police; the policeman here is the dispassionate observer, the detective who unravels the story but does not get involved.

Most Americans think the Swedish police procedural begins and ends with Maj Sjöwall and Per Wahlöö. True, they wrote the first Swedish police novel (*Roseanna,* 1965), and one should not underestimate their influence. They showed that police procedurals were the perfect format for, in their words, "psychological balance, realism, sociological analysis and social consciousness."

But it would be a mistake to think they were an immediate success. It took four books before the Swedish critics appreciated them. One reviewer called *Roseanna* an "entertainment for unreflecting readers." It was not until the Mystery Writers of America bestowed the Edgar Award on *The Laughing Policeman* that the Swedish critics and general public took notice of Martin Beck & Co.

Their work divides into three categories. In the first three novels, they show the influence of Simenon. Beck is much like Maigret in that he reflects on the criminals' motives and tries to understand their actions in relation to society. In the next four, there are strong overtones of Ed McBain's 87th Precinct. Here, the emphasis is on the team and each member's response to the criminal. In the last three, Sjöwall and Wahlöö follow no one but themselves. These books are more political, more meditative, and have found an audience outside of "mere" mystery readers. In all ten novels, there is a strong Marxist orientation and the tendency found in many fictional works to exaggerate, to reveal some unpleasant truths — in this case, about Sweden.

The first Swedish writer to follow in their footsteps was Jacob Palme. He has written five procedurals. His books are ambitious, perhaps a bit naive, but the plots are interesting as is his attempt to explain human reactions to hopeless situations.

Olle Hogstrand wrote his first book in 1971. He is an exceptional writer, able to combine the action of the political thriller with the classic requirements of the police procedural. He, too, is concerned with the psychopathy of crime; why it was committed.

Olov Svedelid has written five procedurals, each concerned with the growing violence in society, the struggle between bad and evil. His series character is much the lone wolf, the solitary avenger. He has said that his sole purpose is to entertain the reader, and his books do qualify as a "fast read" — a bit sloppy, perhaps, but nonetheless effective.

Kjell E. Genberg is a comparative newcomer, having written just two novels. Both tackle organized crime and show the tendency of the police to catch the little guy and not the professional big shot.

I, too, write procedurals, because I regard them as superior — morally and aesthetically — to any other kind of mystery. They tell us about our society and about that subject of unfailing interest to us: ourselves. It was not the work of Sjöwall and Wahlöö which most influenced me, but that of American author

Hilary Waugh. Like him, I employ the "iceberg" method: at the tip, the crime; underneath, the weaknesses that caused it. I write of people whose dreams have crashed, who cannot handle their alienation, who strike back in the most desperate ways. Violence creating violence in a never-ending circle — that is my leitmotif.

In Sweden, the most popular current writer in the police genre is Ed McBain. There is a veritable McBain fever. Actually, he was the first American police writer published in Sweden (*Cop Hater,* 1957). The translation was incredibly bad; the cover, a nightmare. Not too surprisingly, the book was a failure. When McBain was reissued in 1962, he was accorded better treatment from the publishers, but critics were still unimpressed. One wrote that he could not understand why a decent Swedish publisher would undertake to reprint such violent rubbish. He claimed they were not good mysteries — not much better, in fact, than the Cardby books by Hume.

In addition to Waugh and McBain, Swedish mystery lovers thrive on Lillian O'Donnell and Dorothy Uhnak. No, they're not done in translation but are published in the original. In Sweden, most people are able to read English.

A typical Swedish cop in uniform.

Although police procedurals did not really become popular until the Sixties (in America and Britain as well as Sweden), their history, of course, can be traced much further back. I suppose one could say the first police procedural was born in 1931 with the arrival of *Dick Tracy.* Soon afterwards came *Radio Patrol* and then, in 1943, the best of the comic-strip lot: *Terry Drake.* It is reasonable, therefore, to claim that the childhood of the police novel was spent in the comics.

It was an American who wrote the book credited with beginning the genre, *V as in Victim* by Lawrence Treat (1954). I once asked Mr. Treat why he wrote that particular book, and he told me he had wanted to write about realistic policemen solving crimes. No, he said, he had not been influenced by the comic strips.

Although Treat's book was the first in the field, it did not really start the trend toward police procedurals. That fell to Sidney Kingsley's play *Detective Story* (1949). It has been said that this opened the mystery writers' eyes to the possibilities inherent in the police situation. I think it difficult to claim that any one work is the single decisive factor in starting a trend. My belief is that after World War II, readers, as well as writers, found it hard to escape reality. They wanted to read about it in order to better understand their own lives and their own conditions.

Regardless of why, the police novel prospered. In 1952, Hilary Waugh published *Last Seen Wearing;* then came the Gordons, Ben Benson, Thomas Walsh and countless others. Not to mention the TV staples: *Dragnet* and *Line-Up.* In the Sixties, Elizabeth Linington appeared and, fast on her heels, Robert Fish. The Seventies have seen the debut of Rex Burns, whose *Alvarez Journal* proves one can take the police format and turn it inside out, yet at the same time, keep it procedural.

Small wonder, then, that police procedurals have maintained their popularity. Action. Excitement. Psychology. Methodology. What more could one ask for?

K. Arne Blom is the author of The Moment of Truth, *which won Sweden's Sherlock Award as the best suspense novel of the year (1974).*

INTERPOL

UNITED PRESS INTERNATIONAL

The International Criminal Police Organization (Interpol) is really nothing more than a seven-story file cabinet stashed away in Saint-Cloud, a suburb of Paris.

It has no police force of its own, no detectives, no multi-aliased spies, no agents of any kind. It does not actually catch criminals at all. Rather, it alerts local authorities and lets them do the dirty work.

What Interpol does have is a well-crammed computer and about 100 staff members who are good at pushing its buttons. This computer houses approximately 700,000 cross-indexed names of criminals, along with their description, fingerprints and photographs. It also has access to about 2 million file cards containing, among other things, experts who may be called upon in a pinch. For example, a forensic specialist in New York may have a card on file at Interpol headquarters. Should a case come up that warrants his particular expertise, Interpol's computers would spit out his data and then pass the information on to the appropriate source.

Typically, Interpol is used by its 100-odd member nations to keep tabs on drug traffickers, art thieves, counterfeiters, and bad guys who skip one country to settle in another that doesn't believe in extradition.

The first International Criminal Police Commission was established in Vienna in 1923 and stayed operative until 1938 when the Nazis overran Austria. After World War II Interpol again surfaced as the central clearing house for information on international criminals and their capers.

To commemorate Interpol's fiftieth birthday Nicaragua issued a series of Interpol stamps in 1973, each bearing the picture of a famous fictional sleuth. *Ellery Queen's Mystery Magazine* was asked to decide which sleuths should be used. The magazine conducted a poll amongst its readers, leading mystery writers and critics, and the top runners were those chosen for the honor.

Chapter 10

THE LAB

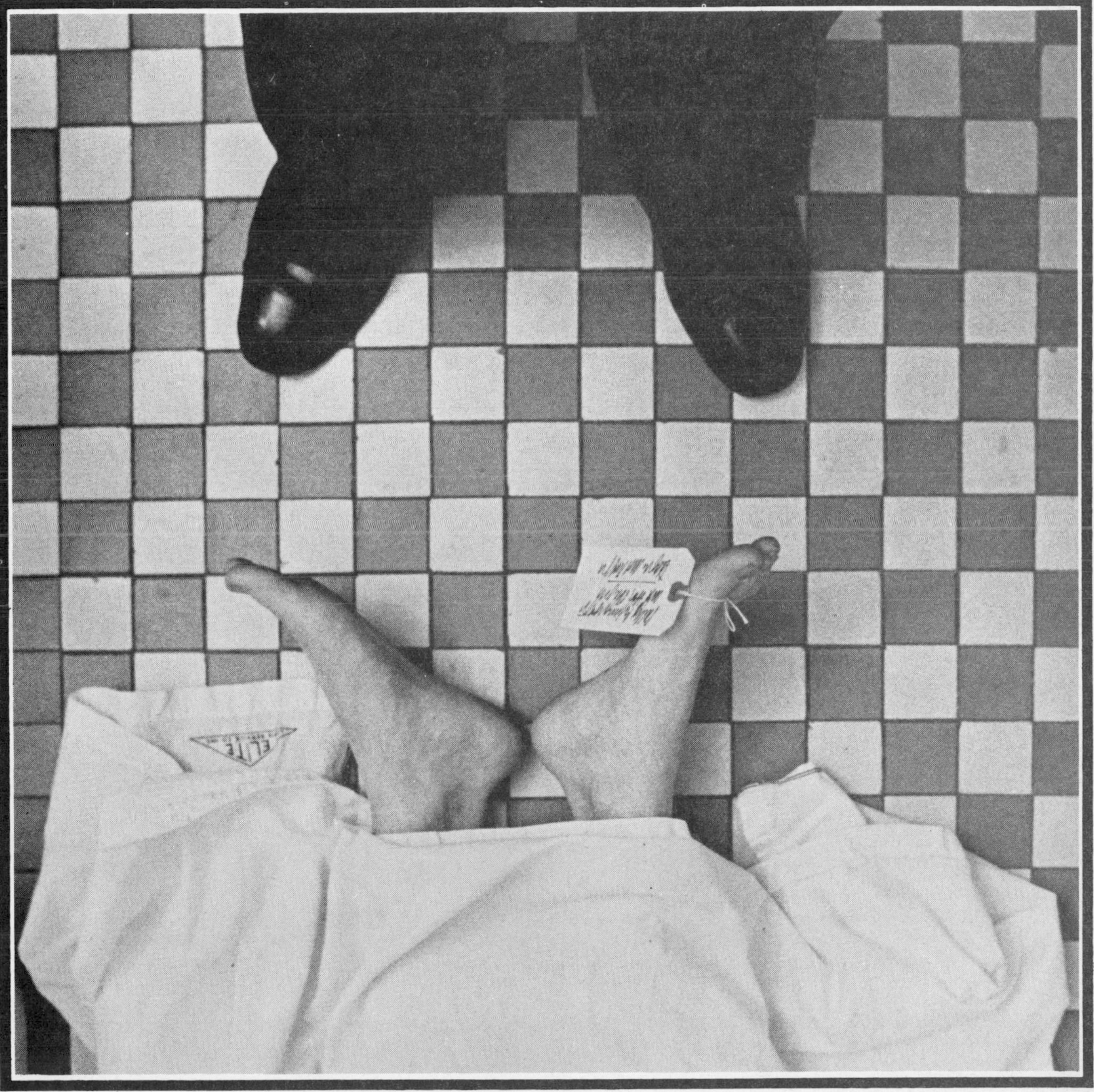

FRED WINKOWSKI

A FICTIONAL PROGNOSIS

P.D. James

It must be a minority of mysteries in which a doctor doesn't make at least a brief appearance. In any civilised country, following a suspicious death, a medical man is invariably called in to examine the body and pronounce life extinct, and later a forensic pathologist will perform an autopsy. The descriptions of some of these medical experts is often as superficial as their appearance in the story is brief. They perform their necessary functions with varying degrees of efficiency and depart leaving the detective, amateur or professional to carry on with the investigation. But occasionally doctors and nurses play a more important role — suspect, detective or even murderer — while a number of mystery writers have chosen a medical setting for their stories — a hospital, clinic or nursing home.

It is easy to understand the attraction of a doctor as suspect or villain. He has the means of death readily at hand; he has knowledge of poisons, their symptoms and effects; his intimate acquaintance with his patients and their private lives gives him particular opportunity; he has professional dexterity and skill, and — particularly if he is a surgeon — he has nerve. Occasionally, too, he has the hubris with which most murderers are afflicted. If all power corrupts, then a doctor, who literally holds life and death in his hands, must be at particular risk. Sir Julian Freke, one of Dorothy L. Sayers' two medical murderers, is an example of the arrogance of the fictional brilliant surgeon who regards himself as above morality and law. It is interesting that of Sayers' eleven full-length murder mysteries, two have medical murderers, both eminent specialists, while a third has an ex-nurse who kills by the doubtfully feasible method of injecting air into the patient's vein. But perhaps the nastiest of all the medical murderers is Dr. Grimesby Roylott of Conan Doyle's *The Speckled Band.* As his author says:

When a doctor goes wrong he is the first of villains. He has nerve and he has knowledge.

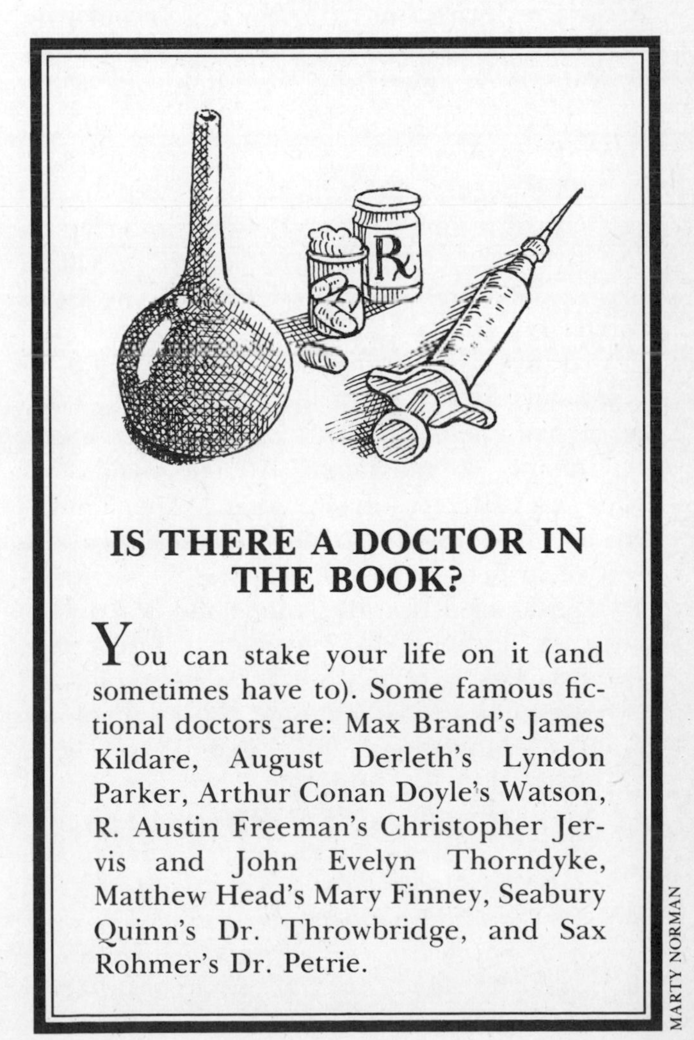

IS THERE A DOCTOR IN THE BOOK?

You can stake your life on it (and sometimes have to). Some famous fictional doctors are: Max Brand's James Kildare, August Derleth's Lyndon Parker, Arthur Conan Doyle's Watson, R. Austin Freeman's Christopher Jervis and John Evelyn Thorndyke, Matthew Head's Mary Finney, Seabury Quinn's Dr. Throwbridge, and Sax Rohmer's Dr. Petrie.

MARTY NORMAN

Palmer and Pritchard were among the heads of that profession.

It is perhaps surprising that a medical setting is comparatively rare in detective fiction, considering its attractions. Here we have the closed community beloved of detective writers for the neat containment of victim, suspect and murderer; a strongly hierarchical community with its own esoteric rules and conventions; a mysterious but fascinating world of men and women performing a great variety of necessary jobs from consultant surgeon to ward cleaner, where the reader, like the patient, feels vulnerable, apprehensive and alien. To write convincingly about hospitals usually requires special knowledge, and those who have done it best, in whose books the smell of disinfectant seems literally to rise from the page, have usually had a medical or nursing background. Josephine Bell (*Murder in Hospital; Death at the Medical Board*) is herself a doctor, and Christianna Brand uses her experience as a voluntary nurse during World War II in what I still consider one of the best detective novels with a medical setting — *Green for Danger.*

The peculiar advantages of special knowledge, professional skill and insight into character which are enjoyed by the doctor as villain also apply to the doctor as detective. The list of medical fictional detectives is varied and impressive, including such very different characters as Josephine Bell's Dr. David Winteringham, H.C. Bailey's amiable, hedonistic but deeply compassionate Dr. Reginald Fortune and R. Austin Freeman's Dr. Thorndyke — perhaps the greatest medical legal detective in fiction. Dr. Thorndyke is essentially a forensic scientist rather than a medical doctor and, in addition to exceptional intellectual powers, has a profound knowledge of such diverse subjects as anatomy, ophthalmology, botany, archaeology and Egyptology. He is also exceptionally handsome. Freeman writes:

> *His distinguished appearance is not merely a concession to my personal taste but also a protest against the monsters of ugliness whom other detective writers have evolved. These are quite opposed to natural truth. In real life, a first-class man of any kind usually tends to be a good-looking man.*

HOSPITABLE CHARACTERS

The most famous nurse in mystery lore is Sarah Keate in Mignon G. Eberhart's *The Patient in Room 18* and *While the Patient Slept.* Nurses and doctors are on call in P.D. James' *Shroud for a Nightingale,* and doctors are busy killing and curing in Josephine Bell's *Murder in Hospital* and *Death at the Medical Board,* Christiana Brand's *Green for Danger,* Agatha Christie's *The Murder of Roger Ackroyd* and E. Spence DePuy's *The Long Knife.*

If you need a good G.P., there's Margaret Carpenter's Huntingdon Bailey, Theodora DuBois' Jeffrey McNeil, Rufus King's Colin Starr and Jonathan Stagge's Hugh Westlake.

Should you need a specialist in pulmonary diseases, contact John Creasey's Stanislaus Palfrey, and if surgery is indicated drop by the infirmary of H.C. Bailey's Reggie Fortune.

It is not surprising that a number of the most successful medical detectives are psychiatrists. As Helen McCloy's Dr. Basil Willing says: "Every criminal leaves psychic fingerprints and he can't wear gloves to hide them. . . . Lies like blunders are psychological facts." The appro-

UNIVERSITY OF WISCONSIN

A public drugstore in Chicago c. 1904. Then, as now, customers often purchased powders for uses their manufacturers never intended.

priately named Dr. Paul Prye, the tall whimsical psychiatrist who features in Margaret Millar's first three books, would no doubt have agreed, as would the very different philosopher and psychologist Prof. Henry Poggioli, who features in the only mystery novel written by T.S. Stribling — *Clues of the Caribbees.*

Some medical detectives are general practitioners and have the advantage of that intimate knowledge of the local community and the day-to-day lives of their patients, their families and backgrounds which is so important to successful detection. Rufus King's Dr. Colin Starr is a G.P. working in a fictional small town in Ohio who, in *Diagnosis: Murder,* suspects that a number of the apparently natural deaths in the community are actually murders and is able to prove it. Jonathan Stagg's G.P. detective, Dr. Hugh Westlake, also works in a small town, but here the stories, although they have a medical background, also contain a strong atmosphere of terror and the supernatural *(The Stars Spell Death; Turn of the Table; The Yellow Taxi).*

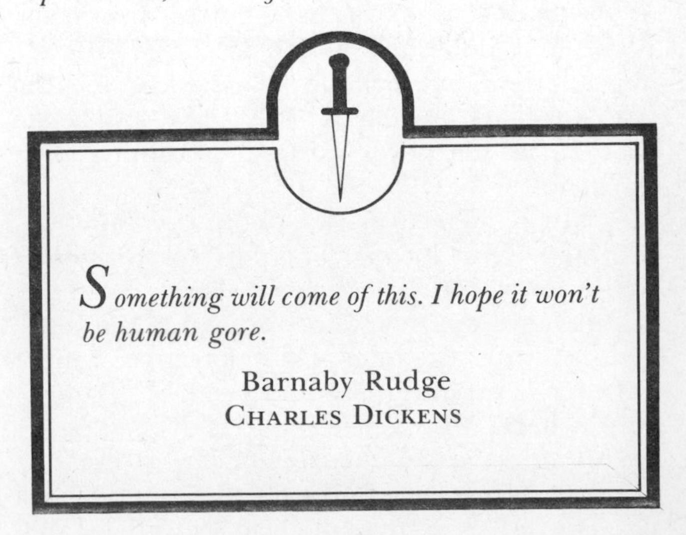

Something will come of this. I hope it won't be human gore.

Barnaby Rudge
CHARLES DICKENS

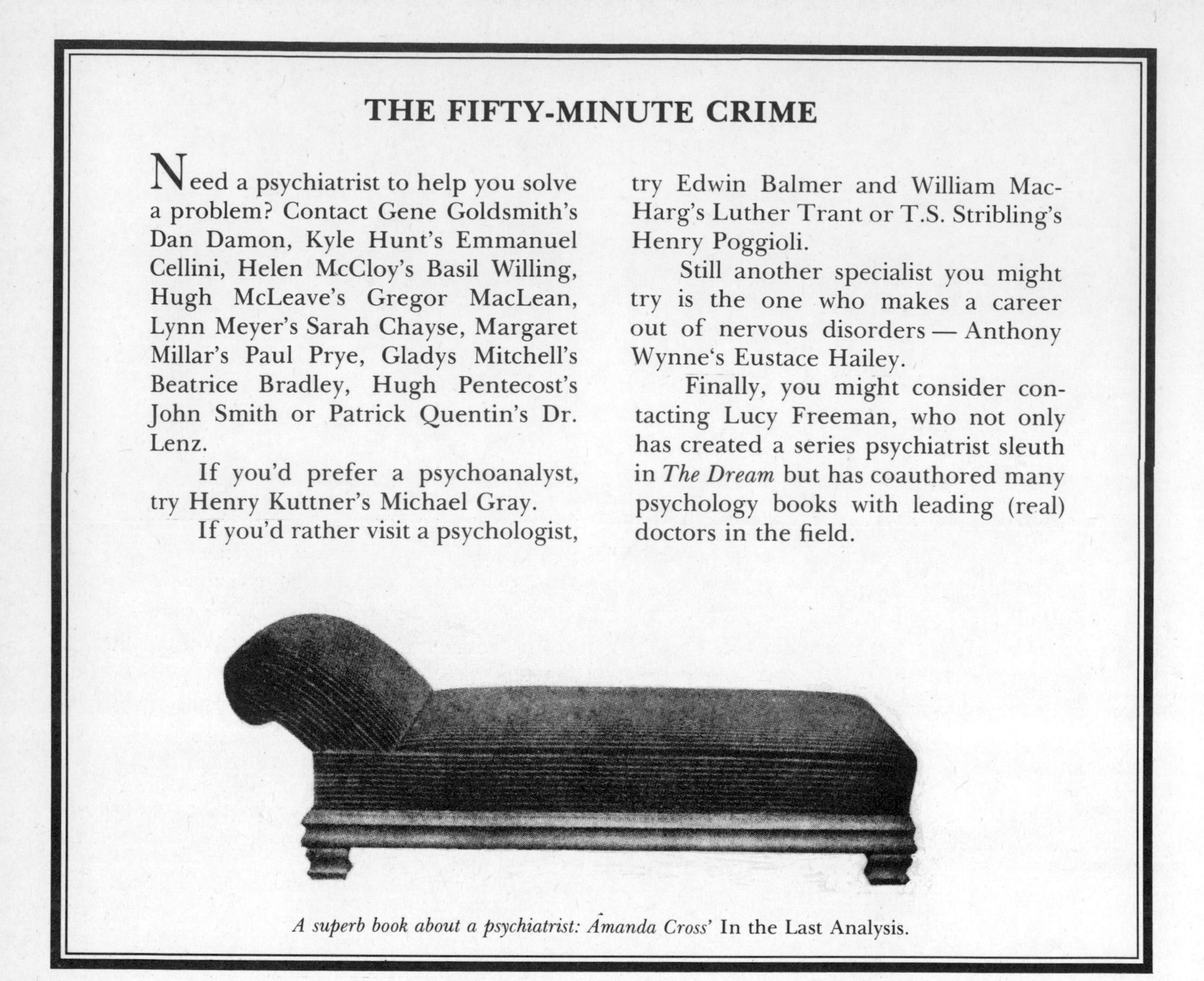

THE FIFTY-MINUTE CRIME

Need a psychiatrist to help you solve a problem? Contact Gene Goldsmith's Dan Damon, Kyle Hunt's Emmanuel Cellini, Helen McCloy's Basil Willing, Hugh McLeave's Gregor MacLean, Lynn Meyer's Sarah Chayse, Margaret Millar's Paul Prye, Gladys Mitchell's Beatrice Bradley, Hugh Pentecost's John Smith or Patrick Quentin's Dr. Lenz.

If you'd prefer a psychoanalyst, try Henry Kuttner's Michael Gray.

If you'd rather visit a psychologist, try Edwin Balmer and William MacHarg's Luther Trant or T.S. Stribling's Henry Poggioli.

Still another specialist you might try is the one who makes a career out of nervous disorders — Anthony Wynne's Eustace Hailey.

Finally, you might consider contacting Lucy Freeman, who not only has created a series psychiatrist sleuth in *The Dream* but has coauthored many psychology books with leading (real) doctors in the field.

A superb book about a psychiatrist: Amanda Cross' In the Last Analysis.

But one of the best-known general practitioners in crime writing must be the narrator of Agatha Christie's brilliant but controversial novel first published in 1926, *The Murder of Roger Ackroyd,* in which the village doctor is both narrator and murderer. The trick has been used since, but never with such cunning and panache.

Nurse detectives are considerably less common than doctors, but perhaps the most well known is M.G. Eberhart's Sarah Keate, a middle-aged spinster who works in a Midwestern city with a young police detective, Lance O'Leary — an intriguing and original partnership where Miss Keate's inquisitiveness is a highly effective adjunct to O'Leary's "eyes in the back of his head and ears all around."

But all the great medical detectives are from the past. Although in England Gladys Mitchell, after fifty books, is still writing admirably about her eccentric and formidable psychiatrist, Dame Beatrice Lestrange Bradley, there has been a definite move, at least in the orthodox detective novel, toward a professional police hero. Apart from Dame Beatrice, it is difficult to recall a modern medical detective, and it may be, in an age of increasing specialisation, that the heyday of the brilliant omniscient amateur like Dr. Thorndyke, whether medical or lay, is temporarily over.

P.D. James won a Crime Writers' Association Silver Dagger for The Black Tower. *Her most recent novel,* Death of an Expert Witness, *features a forensic laboratory.*

THE MYSTERY READER'S PHARMACOPOEIA

Rodger J. Winn, M.D.

There's no accounting for taste. Some mystery writers/readers prefer the archfiend having his way with a completely irreversible drug, while others favor the super-sleuth with an antidote in the nick of time. Some like the culprit to be a gardener, calmly purchasing his weapon from the local hardware store, and some fancy a demented arachnidologist, importing a South American *Loxosceles laeta*. Some like a convulsive screaming death; others, a long-drawn-out deterioration.

THE WRITER'S NIGHTMARE

There have been instances of fact following fiction — when a case reached the newspapers which almost exactly duplicated a novelist's method. One such case involved Agatha Christie's *The Pale Horse*. A mass murderer, released from an asylum, attempted another murder, this time using Christie's suggestions. This same book, however, in 1977, was responsible for saving a life. A nurse was reading it and noticed the similarities between a patient's condition and that described in the book. She told the doctors her suspicions and they proved correct. Without her help, and Miss Christie's, the doctors are not sure they would have been able to effect a cure in time.

Whichever your favorite diabolical twist, a basic knowledge of poison pharmacology is as essential to the mystery writer/reader as familiarity with the floor plan of a Tudor mansion or the infrastructure of a foreign intelligence service.

To guide you through the toxicologic data, we offer the following scenarios and their appropriate poisons.

The classic poison: arsenic. Often called "inheritance powder" because of the tendency of family members to use it on each other, this white, odorless, tasteless powder is readily available in ant pastes and weed killers, and provides a broad range of acute and chronic clinical spectra. For the get-it-done-in-a-hurry job, a dose of about 1 gram is more than enough. Within 3–4 hours the victim lies deathly ill with vomiting and diarrhea, followed in 24–72 hours by death from circulatory collapse. A super-sleuth may be able to make a diagnosis on the basis of the characteristic garlic breath of the victim and will confirm his suspicions with a single urine specimen. If the diagnosis is made after death, analysis will utilize the victim's hair and nails for testing arsenic levels. For a slower death, a pinch of arsenic a day will lead to the victim's progressive weakness, baldness, development of roughened skin and characteristic white ridges of the nails (Aldrich-Mees lines). Eventually, the poor imbiber begins to suffer multiple nerve paralyses, hoarseness and a hacking cough. At first, he will feel sensations of cold and numbness in his limbs, and these can progress to permanent

ERNEST BLOCH

paralysis over a matter of years. The intriguing aspect of chronic arsenic poisoning as a homicidal modus operandi is that the poisoner may build up his own tolerance to arsenic by taking tiny amounts over a long period (Careful, too much leads to death not to tolerance.) Thus he may serve sumptuous suppers liberally spiked with arsenic and, unlike his victim, emerge horse-healthy. One should be warned, however, that arsenic does not always work. The historical example of this is Rasputin's refusal to react to the poison.

The horrible demise: strychnine. Within 15 minutes a fiend can relish the sight of his quarry racked by convulsions that lift him off the floor but still leave him fully conscious to suffer the excruciating pains of the powerful spasms. The lightest stimulation — the shining of a light or the gentle nudge of a foot — can set off another round of the bone-breaking contortions. Strychnine is for the victim you wish to torture before you kill. A most seriously unpleasant death.

Please pass the mushrooms: Amanita phalloides. The use of this deadly poison in a delectable package allows the poisoner to be well on his (or her) way to the hinterlands by the time the victim succumbs. Even the most sophisticated gourmet will not notice the tiny white gills and wartlike scales that differentiate the deadly *Amanita phalloides* from *Agaricus campestris*, the common, edible mushroom. Since cooking does not remove the toxins, a hot meal can be prepared without diminishing the deleterious effects. All is well and good for 12 hours before the onset of nausea, vomiting and diarrhea, which initially is not too severe so that it may be another 24 hours before intensive medical care is administered. By this time the patient may go into circulatory collapse. If he is lucky enough to escape thus far, he has still not really escaped, for in 3–4 days he will begin to turn yellow as his liver decays. A bonus to the poisoner is that unless the history of the mushroom meal is elicited — a nicety easily overlooked by the critically ill — tracing the poison source is very difficult.

The poison in the fake tooth: cyanide. Every spy worth his alias knows instant death is preferable to the tortures from his sadistic enemies. He bites down, and the convenient cyanide pellet embedded in his bridgework acts in a matter of seconds. This is due to cyanide's ability to bind the body's internal breathing apparatus. Found in nature in bitter almonds, and peach and apricot pits, the tip-off to cyanide's presence is the intense smell of bitter almonds on the victim's breath. Because the body cannot use the blood's oxygen, the skin of the individual turns a violent pink — this despite his difficulty in breathing. However, the combination of almond breath and bright pinkness can lead to an early diagnosis, and a quick-witted hero can rescue the incipient corpse with an amyl nitrite pearl.

The blowpipe poison: curare. Curare is isolated from *Chondrodendron tomentosum* and blocks the spread of impulses from the nerve to the muscle, thereby paralyzing the victim. (And anyway, what was he doing at a South American tennis camp staffed by Orinoco Indians?) Minutes after the injection (usually by a curare-dipped dart, since curare is not effective if eaten) there is a flushing of the face and a soft cough. The muscle paralyses start in the head so that the poisonee may have drooping of the eyelids, double vision because of weak eye muscles, difficulty swallowing due to secondary throat-muscle paralyses and, finally, respiratory failure due to his inability to move the muscles of the ribs and diaphragm. Though almost impossible to trace after death, the effects of curare are instantaneously reversible by the intravenous injection of one ampule of prostigmin.

Come into my parlor: the black widow. This petite little lady, about half an inch long with an hourglass on her belly, spends much of her

time in unsavory places (privies) and so genitals and buttocks are favorite attack sites. The sharp bite is similar to the slight tingling of a needle and may possibly go unnoticed. The pain begins in one half hour as the poison affects the nerve endings. There is an ascending cramplike sensation starting in the legs or abdomen and, eventually, severe spasms; if touched, the victim's abdomen has a boardlike rigidity. This mimics closely the clinical picture of a perforated ulcer and medical evaluation may go totally down the wrong path. The patient is anxious, in a panic, and appears acutely ill since he is bathed in a cold sweat and has a thready pulse. The severe spasms last a day, then slowly subside over the next 48 hours. Death is rare, however, from one bite. Perhaps it would be best to have several of these venomous females on hand.

Another troublemaker is the South American brown spider, recognized by the violin markings on its back. The bites of this Latin import are very painful and become agonizing after 8 hours, leaving a large, swollen, black-and-blue area. The venom attacks the blood cells in about 36 hours, rupturing them so that the victim passes urine dark with the breakdown products of his hemoglobin. He progresses to a state of jaundice, kidney failure and shock.

Vapors through the vent: carbon monoxide and nerve gas. Carbon monoxide has the advantage of accessibility for our would-be assassin. This odorless, tasteless gas is formed from the incomplete combustion of carbon products such as coke or charcoal, and it does not take much technical knowledge to hook a tube from an automobile exhaust pipe into a room vent or to leave a low-lit hibachi in a room for heat, enabling the gas to do its insidious job. Carbon monoxide has a tremendous affinity for the body's hemoglobin, binding closely and tightly to it so there is no room for the blood to carry the life-supporting oxygen. Thus, although the victim actually gets enough oxygen, he is unable to deliver it to his tissues and he dies from lack of it. The victim goes through two stages of deterioration. The first is characterized by headaches, giddiness, increasing shortness of breath with exertion, and ringing in the ears. This progresses to a drunken condition, with agitation and confusion, during which time there is a noticeable impairment of judgment; even though the victim knows something is wrong, he does not attempt to leave the noxious environment. (Even nicer for the would-be assassin is the fact that if the victim recovers, he generally has complete amnesia and can offer no incriminating evidence.) In the second stage the skin turns a shade of pink known as cherry red and breathing becomes more labored, occasionally exhibiting a Cheyne-Stokes pattern: periods of 30 seconds of no breathing followed by 6–8 rapidly increasing deep breaths, then again the absence of breathing. Eventually, the victim begins to twitch, convulse, and then slip into unconsciousness and probably death, just prior to which his body temperature may rise to 108°. Death usually comes in the first 2 days after massive exposures but may be delayed as long as 3 8 days. Even if the victim recovers, his troubles are not over: late-occurring sequelae include severe psychological reactions, i.e., overtly psychotic behavior.

Nerve gas is indicated for the more deadly *coup de grace.* Killers with names such as Tabun, Sarin or T-46, Soman, DFP or DCP, all work in the same manner. They prevent the breakdown of the substance (acetylcholine) which transmits impulses from the nerves to the muscles, thus leading to the hyperexcitability of the victim. These substances are colorless, basically odorless, and can be inhaled or absorbed by skin. The initial symptoms are runny nose, wheezing and chest tightness, followed by excessive sali-

BOOKS FAVORING POISON

Behold, Here's Poison: Georgette Heyer
Murder to Go: Emma Lathen
Nursey, Tea and Poison: Anne Morice
The Poisoned Chocolates Case: Anthony Berkeley
Strong Poison: Dorothy L. Sayers

vation, the inability to tolerate light and, finally, paralysis and death. Old gases may take 20 minutes to work, but newer improvements have cut down the time, making the administration of the antidote — atropine — almost impossible. A particularly sadistic scenario may find the victim in possession of a syringe filled with the antidote but too paralyzed to squeeze the plunger and save himself.

The gardener's caper: rat poisoning. As any sly weekend gardener knows, rat poison offers the convenience of the nearest hardware store and a believable alibi — one needed it to tend the weeds and the rodents, didn't one? For human as well as furry fare-thee-wells there are two effective poisons: thallium, currently one of the leading homicidal agents in the world, and the warfarin drugs.

Thallium has been removed from U.S. markets since 1965 because of its lethality, but it is readily available in European settings. Odorless and tasteless, the chemical blends superbly with sugared grain, making a delectable feast for rodents and a tasty tidbit for those humans with a sweet tooth. The action is slow, first declaring itself with diffuse pain and severe constipation 3–4 days after consumption. Supersleuth can make a diagnosis of it at this early stage by detecting a peculiar dark pigmentation around the roots of the hair. During this period

The wittiest place to bury a corpse: a hemlock forest.

the victim is often thought to be hysterical or psychologically disturbed, rather than poisoned. In the second or third week after ingestion the victim begins losing his hair, not only on his head but also on his body — except for the middle third of his eyebrows and his pubic hair. The skin appears dry and scaly, the heart beats rapidly and various nerves become paralyzed so that the eyelids may droop, the feet drag, blindness ensue. Ultimately, death occurs with pneumonia and congestion of the lungs. Like arsenic, thallium can be added in small dabs and the homicide accomplished over a period of months for subtlety.

In the United States rat poison has been replaced mainly by warfarin, which interferes with the blood-clotting system. Thus the victim gets signs of increasing bleeding such as nosebleed (epistaxis), gum bleeding (gingival hemorrhages), black-and-blue marks (ecchymosis), bloody urine (hematuria), bloody vomit (hematemsis) and bloody bowel movements (melena and hematochezia). A disadvantage to the evildoer is that this poison affects humans only slightly, so that large amounts are needed. The potion does mix well with corn porridge, and a series of good hearty breakfasts can do the job. The antidote would be large doses of vitamin K.

Come slither: poisonous snakes. The silent, relentless undulation of a snake, replete with glittering fangs, is a surefire candidate for arousing terror. Poisonous snakes can cause two kinds of death, depending on whether their venom is a neurotoxin (attacks the nerves) or a hemotoxin (attacks the blood cells). In the first type the victim has very little reaction at the bite site but in 1–2 hours becomes progressively paralyzed. Typical snakes causing such a condition are the U.S. coral snake and the sinister Asian cobra. The blood attackers cause tremendous pain, swelling and bleeding at the site of the fang marks, and in one hour there is the onset of shock as the blood breaks down and the clotting mechanisms disintegrate. For exotic variety there is also the horned viper of the eastern Sahara, which burrows in the sand and lunges at its victim, and the deadly fer-de-lance, which can leap several feet off the ground to strike with its venomous fangs.

The O.D.: heroin. Since heroin is normally cut or diluted many times with quinine and sugars, an injection of the pure substance will be many times more powerful than even the most hardened addict can tolerate. If the victim is a junkie who has cut back on his intake, he can no longer handle the same amounts of heroin as before and giving him his previous dosage will cause an overdose. Unconsciousness stemming from an overdose can be almost instantaneous; the victim may be found with the syringe still in his arm. The drug victim lies in coma with slowly decreasing respiration, to the point where he may be breathing only 2–3 times per minute. The pupils of the eye are initially pinpoint, but as the blood pressure falls and shock with its cold clammy skin intervenes, the blood supply to the brain diminishes and the pupils may grow large as death approaches.

The Doctor's black bag: a poison potpourri. The tireless, faithful family practitioner is a walking arsenal. Should he switch from healing to homicide, he has only to dip into his ubiquitous black bag to use:

Insulin — to drive down the blood sugar, causing convulsions and death.

Potassium — to slow the heartbeat and eventually cause it to stop.

Calcium — to send the victim into kidney failure and coma.

Barbiturates — to fatally slow the metabolism.

Amphetamines — to irrevocably speed up the metabolism.

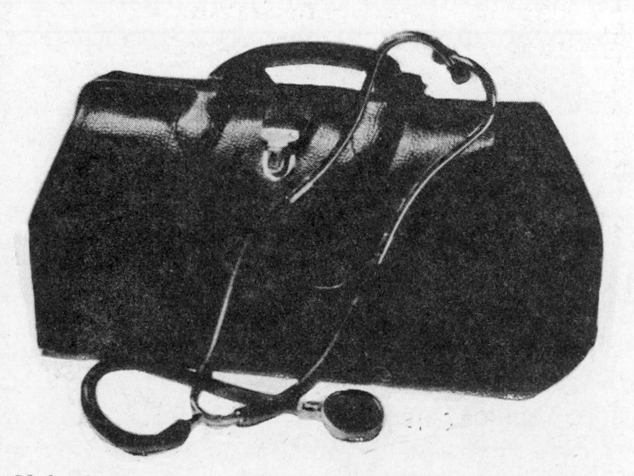

If the doctor comes to kill, not cure, should one pay him for a house call?

It's the immutable law — the characteristics are both mixed up with each other somehow in the same chromosome, don't you see? — it's the only instance in which color blindness ever goes into a woman, and then only from a six-fingered parent. . . .

The Matilda Hunter Murder
HARRY STEPHEN KEELER

Oxygen — to remove the drive to breathe in a victim with emphysema of the lungs, resulting in a condition known as carbon dioxide narcosis.

Not quite in the little black bag is the *air bubble,* but who knows better how to inject it than the physician?

All these agents are part of every doctor's armamentarium against disease, but all can be abused.

The Mad Scientist at work: recombinant DNA. If the mystery reader/writer demands novel ways of committing mayhem, he might well consider the new field of molecular biology called recombinant DNA experimentation. Purely in the hypothetical stage, of course, this involves splicing together the genetic material (DNA) of two species so that the resultant creation has some of the characteristics and properties of each. One could conjecture creating a bacterium which is resistant to all known antibodies or achieving a germ that is normally at peace in the human body but now excretes deadly botulinum toxin. Even more macabre might be the creation of a mosquito that injects a deadly poison or a tumor-causing virus. The possibilities are limitless, and the evil, cackling genius can manipulate all the forces of nature for his demented purposes. Dr. Frankenstein revisited, if you will.

Rodger J. Winn is a practicing physician in New Jersey.

THE BUSIEST MORGUE IN THE WORLD

William DeAndrea

The building on the corner of First Avenue and 30th Street is not a very impressive one. Transport it to a college campus and it would look like any other mid-Fifties dormitory; move it to a medium-size town and it would pass for a solid, respectable insurance company. But the large aluminum letters on its exterior do not say STUDENTS HALL or METROPOLITAN LIFE; rather, they spell out NEW YORK CITY MEDICAL EXAMINER'S OFFICE — commonly called the morgue.

Approximately 8,500 autopsies are performed here every year, roughly twenty to twenty-five per day. Yours will be one of them if your death is considered unnatural: if, say, you die under violent circumstances; if there's a hint of foul play; if you keel over unexpectedly with no previous record of medical difficulties. Your case will be handled by Dr. Dominic DiMaio, chief medical examiner, and his staff of three to four deputy medical examiners, four to eight assisting doctors and four to eight dieners (helpers). They will be concerned not with *who* did you in, but with *what* did you in. Method, not motive, is what interests the forensic pathologist, who tends to view each autopsy as a learning experience, a fact borne out by a Latin inscription in the lobby of the morgue: *Taceant colloquis effugiat risus. Hic locus est ubi mors caudet succurere vitae.* (Loosely translated: Let conversation stop, let laughter cease. This is the place where death delights in helping the living.)

Upon entering the morgue, one steps into a blue-tiled lobby with large house plants framing picture windows and a row of chairs backed

SUICIDE? OR MURDER?

There are fashions in the means of suicide; the current vogue is jumping from high places.

Myopic jumpers invariably remove their eyeglasses and put them in a pocket before jumping. The Medical Examiner's Office considers traces of prescription glass in a suicide's face a sure tip-off that it was a murder.

Similarly, stabbing suicides never stab themselves through their clothes, and most of them prefer to do their stabbing in the bathroom, facing the mirror.

Characteristically, a woman will strip to the waist (sometimes leaving on her bra), then stab herself in the abdomen 25–30 times with a small knife until she passes out from loss of blood. Death from exsanguination follows.

A man, on the other hand, pulls back his shirt, or removes it, then kills himself with a single thrust to the heart with a long-bladed knife.

Variations from these two methods will make the medical examiner think closely about murder rather than suicide.

W.D.

up against a wall. Not very ominous, but not very inviting, either.

Death waits downstairs.

It rests in a gray-and-white tiled room, and the minute you step in it the smell hits. The detective story cliché about the "unmistakable smell of death" turns out to be a simple statement of fact. The smell *is* unmistakable, even to those who have never smelled it before. It is also unforgettable and indescribable, and maybe from some primal survival instinct it makes you want to run away.

This body-storage room is a rectangle within a rectangle. The inner rectangle is a stainless-steel refrigerated chamber, kept at 38° F. The bodies are inside it, each on a sliding slab, each behind its own numbered door. There are 130 of these little square doors, and they look not unlike the lockers at airport and bus terminals. Most of the morgue's cadavers, except the badly decomposed and the children, are kept inside them. They each have their own room and own set of compartments on either side of the larger rectangle.

The day I visited the morgue, Jean Pierre Lahary, a forensic reconstructionist, was my guide. He wasted no time in opening one of the little doors. There was a grating sound and, I thought, an impossibly loud noise. Having read for years about the staring eyes of a corpse, I braced myself to meet them. I needn't have bothered. The slab held the headless, handless body of a young black woman. Mr. Lahary ran a finger over the characteristic marks made by a saw as it cut its way through bone. He picked up one of the severed hands, which had been found some months after the rest of her, and gestured with it to illustrate a point. I wasn't really paying attention.

I had told myself I wouldn't react, but for a moment my stomach did calisthenics, my eyes fogged over and I broke out in a cold sweat. When that passed, however, I found I could then observe with almost professional detachment. Almost. I was still revolted by the smell. (Later, in talking to other people who had been to the morgue, I learned that they, too, after an initial adjustment, found they could "take" it. A not-uncommon fantasy for morgue visitors is to imagine themselves as medical students. This

THE REMAINS

The Signs of Somatic Death

Algor mortis (cooling of the body)

It takes approximately 40 hours for the body to cool to the environmental temperature. For the first few hours the body cools at the rate of 3–3½°F per hour; it then cools at 1°F until it reaches the environmental temperature. To estimate how long a body's been dead, take the normal body temperature minus the rectal temperature of the corpse and divide this figure by 1.5.

Rigor mortis (muscular rigidity)

This stiffening is caused by the precipitation of protein and occurs 4–10 hours after death, passing off in 3–4 days. It starts in the muscles around the head and neck, with jaws and eyelids stiffening first.

Livor mortis (post-mortem staining)

This is an irregular reddish discoloration of dependent parts of the body due to gravitational sinking of the blood. It causes a splotchy appearance at all points not in contact with external supports (the floor, a chair, etc.), which aids in detecting whether the body has been tampered with (e.g., turned over) after death occurred. The process stops after 10–12 hours.

Putrefaction

This occurs 24–48 hours after death and is due to bacteria eating away at the body. The body turns green, bloats with gas, smells. The degree to which this occurs depends on the climate, whether the body is immersed in water, etc.

depersonalization keeps them on their feet.)

Lahary then escorted me into the autopsy room, separated from the adjacent storage rectangles by two sets of swinging doors. There are seven tables, and the day I was there three of them were in use. On one, a body was being hosed off. (The surface of each table is a metal grating, and below it is a shallow tub with constantly running water to flush away the blood.) At another table a doctor was using a circular saw (electric) to open a skull. When he finished, he lifted off the top portion of the head, rather like halving a cantaloupe, scooped out the brain and weighed it. The cadaver's face was then pulled down so the forehead practically reached the chin. (Imagine peeling an orange halfway, then reversing the peel over the intact part. Same procedure.) At the third table a doctor had just made the famous Y-shaped incision on a fifteen-year-old girl who had been found the day before floating in the bathtub. The Y opened her in such a way that her chest could be flapped back to cover her face and her abdomen could be turned back to either side to reveal her internal organs. I was surprised to learn that human fat tissue is a rich yellow, like chicken fat, and that human flesh on the inside resembles the cheaper cuts of pork.

The doctor explained that this young woman may have been raped: There was a bruise above her knee and a fingernail mark in her vagina. She may also have been murdered, he added, indicating bruises on her neck and shoulders which might have been caused by someone trying to hold her underwater.

I stayed long enough to see the woman stitched up. The needle was enormous and so were the stitches.

Mr. Lahary moved my tour upstairs to his office, where we were joined by deputy medical examiner, Dr. Michael Baden. The two imparted the following:

The first thing that's done to a body upon its arrival is to give it a bath.

The corpse is then put into its compartment, feet first, with an identifying tag knotted around its right big toe.

In usual cases bodies are kept at the morgue between fifteen days and one month, but parts of bodies — legs, arms, etc. — are kept up to six months in hopes of finding the rest.

A corpse left in a dry air draft will not decompose normally but will, instead, dehydrate and mummify.

As the blood settles in the corpse, it causes large discolorations, like obscene black-and-blue marks.

Each morning a deputy medical examiner makes "rounds." He is accompanied by a medical stenographer who records such data as the condition of the corpse and the physical condition, and this becomes part of the permanent autopsy record.

New York is one of the few places in the country to use the medical examiner system. Most places have a coroner, a politically chosen official who doesn't (necessarily) have any special medical or legal expertise.

Mr. Lahary then took me up to the top floor of the morgue to the museum, which

THE PATHOLOGIST'S REPORT

Dr. David Wintringham, pathologist, appears in Josephine Bell's *Fallover Cliff* and *Death at the Medical Board.*

Dr. Daniel Webster Coffee, pathologist, appears in Lawrence G. Blochman's *Diagnosis: Homicide; Recipe for Homicide; Clues for Dr. Coffee.*

Dr. Grace Severance, pathologist and professor of medicine, appears in Margaret Scherf's *The Banker's Bones.*

Dr. Paul Standish, city medical examiner, appears in George Harmon Coxe's *The Ring of Truth.*

Dr. Samuel Prouty, assistant medical examiner, appears in books by Ellery Queen, and Dr. Emanuel Doremus, medical examiner, appears in the works of S.S. Van Dine.

The City of the Dead by Herbert Leiberman deals with the Office of the Chief Medical Examiner, New York City, and the Office's fictional occupants greatly resemble the real ones.

DO THEY STILL USE TOE TAGS AT THE MORGUE?

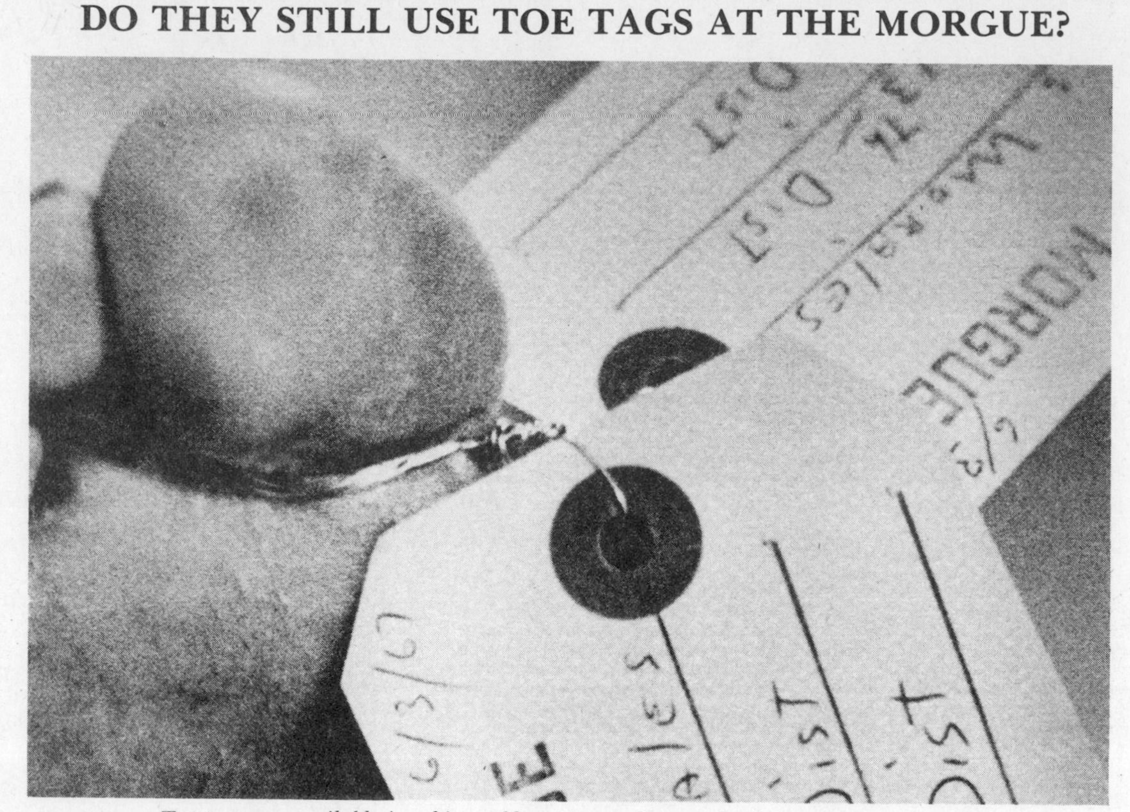

Toe tags are available in white or blue. No one knows why those colors were chosen.

Yes.

The tags, however, are slipped on the toes *before* they arrive at the morgue, either by hospital personnel or by the local police.

The tags are made of reasonably sturdy manila, with a string looped through one end. They are similar to the tags one puts on packages or luggage. Nothing very fancy, nothing very special.

The tags do have a tendency to slip off, but nobody makes a fuss; they're merely slipped back on again.

documents — with photographs, souvenirs, organs and body parts preserved in formaldehyde — the lessons learned from the dead. Lahary, when he is not performing his other morgue duties or acting as special consultant to Interpol, acts as the museum's curator. Most of the specimen museum's visitors are forensic scientists or police officers, although now and then a special-interest group is admitted.

One more thing that must be mentioned: the attitude of the people who work at the morgue. According to Dr. Baden, doctors in general and pathologists in particular are prone to alcoholism because of the occupational stress. They are also, I can attest, living exponents of gallows humor. Their conversation is positively gleeful. Of course, it takes a bit before one becomes accustomed to what they consider amusing. Dr. Baden, for example, related an anecdote about an aquarium shark regurgitating a human arm. And yes, strange though it may seem, I laughed.

William DeAndrea is the author of Killed in the Ratings.

THE FORENSIC ODONTOLOGIST

Lowell J. Levine, D.D.S.

The role of the dentist as detective has been sadly neglected by mystery writers. Despite their attempts to explain this away on the grounds of mere ignorance, I suspect a more valid reason: Most mystery writers I've met have terrible teeth and have obviously suffered at the hands of my colleagues; ignoring us, they're exacting subconscious revenge. My purpose, then, is to make the consumer, the mystery reader, aware of the part we forensic odontologists play in homicide investigations. Hopefully, the reader will force the mystery writer to cast his prejudices aside and acknowledge a branch of the field of dentistry well known to the real professionals in law enforcement: the dental detective!

The forensic odontologist works in a number of areas. Most familiar to the layman is the identification, from teeth, jaws and oral structures, of skeletonized, burned, fragmented, decomposed or otherwise unidentifiable human remains. Much useful information can be gathered from visual and x-ray examinations of the homicide victim. From the types of dental restorations present, we can tell the relative economic status of the person, and areas of the country or world where the fillings, caps or bridges might have been done. We can determine habits, occupations and diseases: the heavy stain of the pipe smoker; the wear of the carpenter from clenching nails; the yellowed mottling of certain Texans from regions with too much fluoride in the water.

We can determine the relative age of a child victim within a few months; the adult, within a five-year span.

We can positively identify from written dental records or from a single dental x-ray of one small part of the jaw. The combinations of teeth present or absent, various filling materials, types of caps or bridges, portions of the tooth having filling materials, all make a dentition unique to an individual. The pattern of the bony architecture which shows in an x-ray, along with tooth shape, root shape, anatomic landmarks and the like, give us literally dozens of areas of comparison in a single x-ray even if no fillings have ever been done.

Of course, it is possible to be too sophisticated. Early in my career, I examined a decomposed body fished from New York Harbour and proclaimed it to be that of an eastern European, probably a seaman who had fallen overboard. Nevertheless, it was later identified by fingerprints as that of an American who had never even left the country. Further investigation showed that all the work on his teeth had been done by a dentist practicing in Newark . . . but trained in Poland.

Identification of the victim is usually the first step in the successful homicide investigation, for only when the victim becomes known do the motives for his murder arise and suspects become known to the police. Proving identity is also essential for the prosecution of the case.

Recognition of dental evidence at the murder scene can lead to a rapid solution. To illustrate: Across the room from a victim found shot to death at an after-hours club, a detective noticed a small pool of blood with some whitish fragments in it. He collected all the fragments and brought them to the Medical Examiner's Office. When the fragments were assembled, they proved to be the crown of an upper left first molar. A subsequent x-ray showed numerous tiny pieces of metal, probably bullet fragments, on the reconstructed crown. Examination of the victim revealed an intact upper first molar, so the fragments had to belong to either the perpetrator or a witness. Detectives began a canvas of local hospitals, and the first one they went to had had an admission that morning with a gunshot wound of the left cheek. He was not the perpetrator but a witness, who supplied the name of the murderer.

Examination of injuries to the face, teeth and jaws is another area in which the forensic odontologist works. A young woman complained to the police of an attempted rape. She said she had received numerous kicks and blows to her face and jaw that had knocked out two teeth. In fact, she had had two front caps knocked out, but there was no evidence of any injuries to the lips, cheeks, face or soft tissues of the mouth. According to the suspect, an acci-

SOMETHING TO SINK YOUR TEETH INTO

Michael Baden, M.D.,
Deputy Chief Medical Examiner of the City of New York

I first got interested in Dracula when they mounted the expedition to exhume his body. It's hard to find exhumations of 500-year-old bodies. (I once worked on a 2,000-year-old mummy, though. You'd be surprised what I learned from that. Could even type its blood.)

Anyway, all the Dracula expedition found was animal bones. They looked at these bones and thought they'd been duped, that there was no Dracula, so they packed up and came home. By the time they found out there was a Middle European tradition of burying animal bones on top of human remains — it was done to fool graverobbers, the idea being if they saw the animal carcass they'd think that was all there was and the body underneath would remain undisturbed — it was too late to do anything about it. I don't know if they ever got another expedition going, but it's something I'm considering. I'd love to lead it.

You see, we're becoming more fully aware of exhumation as a teaching aid. Burial is really long-term storage. The body is there for you. With cremations you don't get a second chance to see what happened.

From time to time at the Morgue we see deaths by impalement, and this comes direct from Dracula. He popularized the method by using it as a way of dealing with recalcitrant Turks.

I don't think Stoker's prose warrants a reading. That's hardly what makes *Dracula* a good book. In fact, I never quite understood how this postal clerk — Bram Stoker — had the creativity to incorporate these Rumanian vampire myths with the real life of Dracula. But he did manage an intriguing study of his age's concept of death. Both Dracula and Frankenstein are very effective dramatizations of popular fears about death. When I was a kid, I was terrified by these stories. Now my daughter watches them on television and laughs. Too much knowledge. It takes away the mystery.

In my bookcase at home I have a first edition of *Dracula*. I keep it right alongside my first edition of *Gray's Anatomy*.

THE FIRST FORENSIC DENTIST

None other than Paul Revere.

Most people think of him riding about the countryside with a lantern. If they stretch their memories they may recall he was a silversmith. He was also a dentist and in at least one instance was called upon to identify a gentleman from that gentleman's remains — which included a rather handsome set of teeth. These were teeth Revere had worked on — filling, polishing, pulling, and so forth. He was able to establish, to his satisfaction, that the teeth belonged to his former patient.

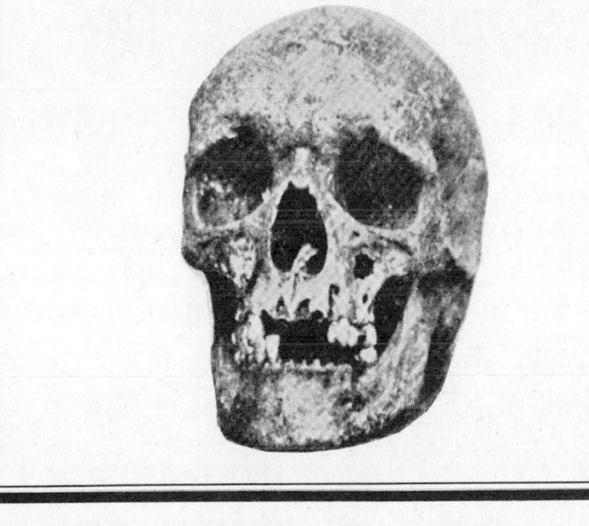

COURTESY MUSEUM OF FINE ARTS, BOSTON (GIFT OF BUCKMINSTER BROWN)

General Joseph Warren's skull, showing the artificial teeth (at least some of them) made for him by Paul Revere. The portrait of Warren, in considerably better shape, is by J.S. Copley, 1738–1815.

dental fall had knocked out the caps. His story was much more consistent with the medical and dental evidence, and the grand jury to whom the case was presented refused to indict.

The most fascinating area of forensic dentistry for the layman seems to be the examination of bite mark patterns in the skin of either homicide victims or perpetrators. Since every person's teeth are unique in respect to spacing, twisting, turning, shapes, tipping toward the tongue or lip, wear patterns, breakage, fillings, caps, loss and the like, all of which occur in limitless combinations, it is possible for them to leave a pattern which for identification purposes is as good as a fingerprint. These varying combinations reproduce themselves in skin to different degrees. No healing occurs after death, so we have found fixed bite marks even on victims who have been dead for as long as a month. We have also found five-day-old bite marks on living persons that were useful for comparisons. By taking small biopsies we can tell whether the bite marks on a victim were made before death, around the time of death, or after death. This is often useful in establishing time frames for a murder.

This type of evidence is found almost exclusively on two types of murder victim: the child homicide victim, most often a "battered child," and the victim who has been involved in sexual activity around the time of death. The sexual activity can be either forcible or voluntary, and we find bite marks in both heterosexual and homosexual killings. In the heterosexual cases the bite marks are most often found on the breasts or thighs; homosexuals most often have them on the upper back or shoulders.

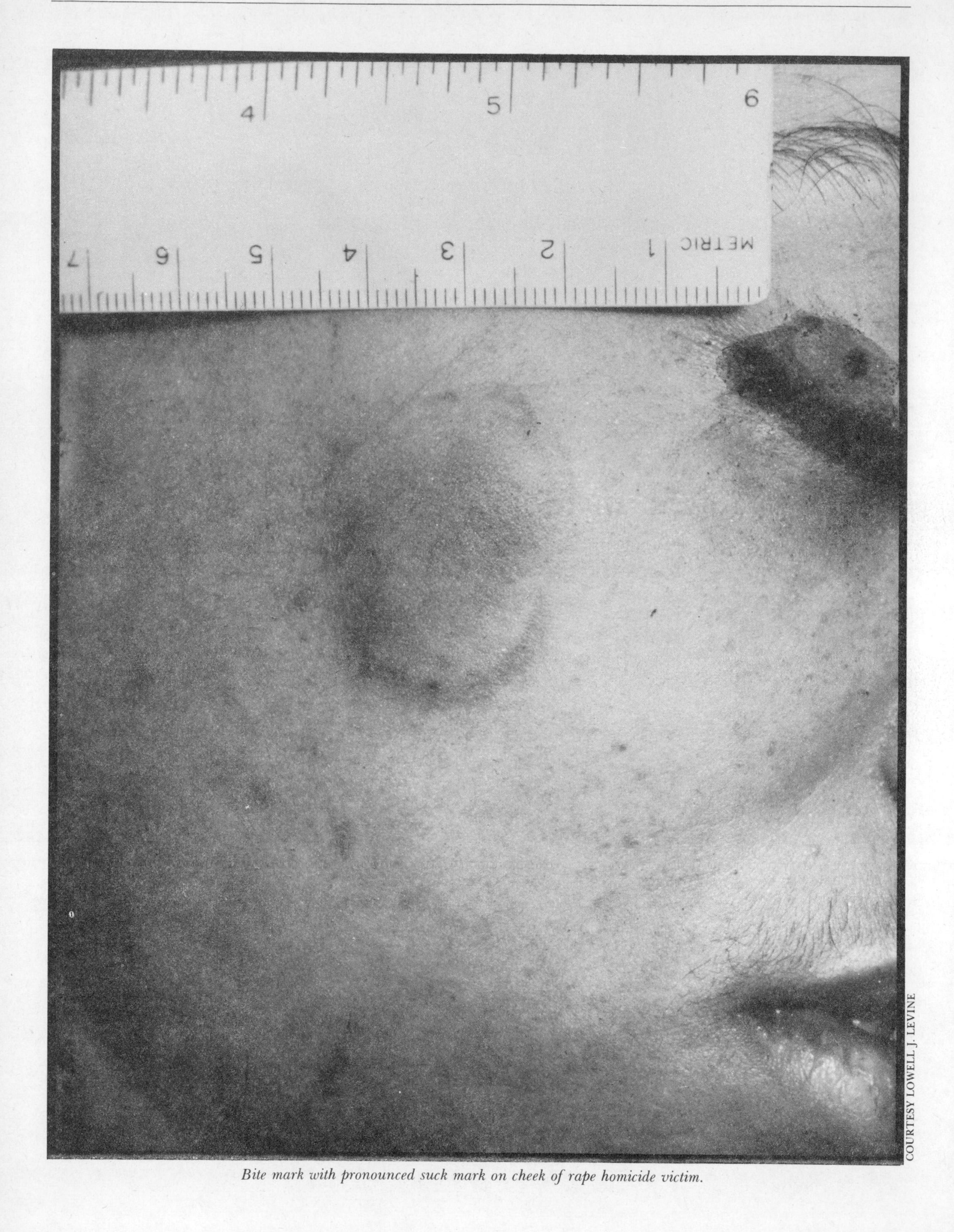

COURTESY LOWELL J. LEVINE

Bite mark with pronounced suck mark on cheek of rape homicide victim.

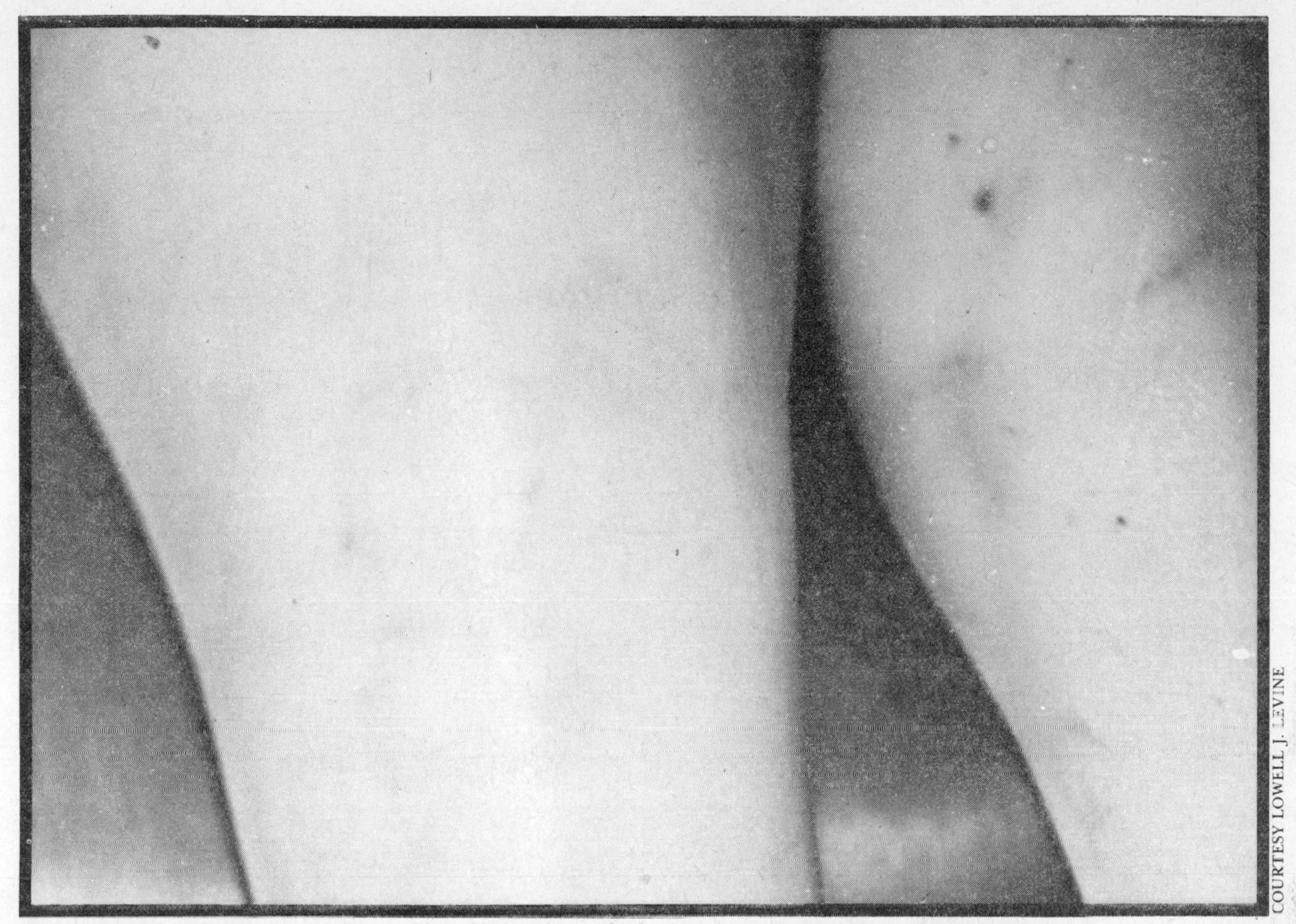

Three bite marks on thigh of rape homicide victim.

The bite marks left during sexual activity are quite characteristic, usually exhibiting clarity of detail and a central suck mark. In addition, they usually have linear abrasions radiating out in a "sunburst" pattern. They have been left slowly and sadistically. Those left during attack or defense situations show a rapid, random distribution over the body, distortion caused by the motion of the scuffling, and no central suck mark.

The saliva left during the infliction of the bite can be grouped similarly to blood, semen, sweat, vaginal secretions, tears and other body fluids.

Police officers responding to a call of a fight in an apartment at 4 A.M. stopped a young man who was walking out the door. In the apartment they found the nude body of another man who had been beaten to death. The young man told the officers he had met the victim in a bar and was invited to the apartment for a drink. Once in the apartment, the victim made homosexual advances. The young man tried to leave and a fight ensued. The killing appeared to be in self-defense. Examination of the victim, however, showed that he had bite marks on his upper back and shoulders which proved to have been inflicted by the young man. They were quite typical of sexually inflicted bite marks and not of the attack or defense variety, and ultimately the young man pled guilty to murder.

This short essay is meant only to whet the appetite of the mystery reader. Hopefully, one day the mystery writer will serve up a gourmet dinner of this most subtle science, forensic odontology.

Lowell J. Levine teaches Forensic Dentistry at the medical and dental schools of New York University and since 1969 has been consultant to the Office of the Chief Medical Examiner, New York City.

THE FORENSIC ANTHROPOLOGIST

Clyde Collins Snow, Ph.D.

Murderers often hide the bodies of their victims in woods, thickets, marshes, caves and other isolated places. Months or years later, the victim, now a skeleton, may be discovered by hunters, bird watchers, lovers or small boys who visit such out-of-the-way spots on more innocent errands. Naturally, such finds arouse the curiosity of the police and the local coroner. Curiosity, however, may quickly turn to frustration, as skeletons are notoriously uncommunicative under routine methods of interrogation. After a month or two, the bones, by now collected in a neatly labeled plastic bag, are banished to one of the darker shelves of an evidence locker. From my experience, I suspect there are enough unidentified human skeletons gathering dust in sheriffs' offices, police stations and crime laboratories throughout the country to populate a good-sized cemetery. For each skeleton there is a murderer smug in the knowledge that he got away with his crime.

Such cases are becoming rarer, however, as police forces and medical examiners are gaining increasing awareness of the talents of a small but growing number of specialists known as forensic anthropologists. The latter are physical anthropologists who, at least temporarily, are willing to turn away from their studies of our fossil ancestors in order to help in the identification of more recent skeletons. Currently, there are about two dozen forensic anthropologists in the United States.

When examining an unknown skeleton, the forensic anthropologist first attempts to establish the time of death. This estimate is generally based on the degree of preservation of the soft tissues still adhering to the bone. The time required for a body to be reduced to a skeleton is extremely variable and is controlled by many factors. In the South, a body lying exposed during the summer may be completely skeletonized within one or two months. In colder climates, total disappearance of soft tis-

ANN LIMONGELLO

VITAL POINTS OF THE BODY

Study these structural weaknesses of the human body carefully and use extra caution in an attack on those areas which are vulnerable, for a moderate blow can cause serious injury and even death. The average man is usually unaware of the full potential of his strength, and in the heat of combat he does not always use full discretion.

Temple. A very susceptible vital spot. If struck with sufficient force may cause unconsciousness or death.

Ears. May be attacked by clapping the open hands against them. This method is very effective for breaking holds from the front.

Eyes. Avoid direct contact, especially with clubs.

Nasion. The summit of the nose. May cause unconsciousness. If struck with sufficient force may cause death.

Philtrum. The spot under the nose at the top of the upper lip. Attack to this area may also cause unconsciousness or death.

Jaw. Vulnerable at the point where the jaw hinges.

Throat. The Adam's apple is a most vulnerable and sensitive spot.

Clavicle. The collarbone.

Solar Plexus. If struck with sufficient force may cause death.

Lower Abdomen. Spot just below the navel. May be attacked with fist or kicking technique.

Testes. May be attacked with fist or kicking technique. Causes strongly focused pain. The attacked may fall into shock, resulting in death.

Knee Joint. May be attacked with the side of the foot to break opponent's balance or dislocate the joint.

Shin. A sensitive area, effectively attacked with a club or by kicking.

Instep. May be attacked by stamping technique; the attack is very effective in breaking a hold.

Base of the Cerebellum. At the nape of the neck. A severe blow may lead to unconsciousness, even death.

Mastoid Process. Just behind the ear. Pressure applied with knuckles of fingers or thumbs is very effective in rousing drunks.

Upper Back. Specifically, a spot directly between the shoulder blades. Very effective area for attack to break holds.

Kidney. May be attacked with the edge of the hand, hammer fist or kicking technique.

Coccyx. The tail bone. When struck with sufficient force, the blow may cause death.

Achilles Tendon. The back of the heel.

Pulsation (Inner) Side of the Wrist. Very effective area for attack against armed opponents.

Elbow Joint. An extremely sensitive point.

Back of the Hand. A sharp blow or strong pressure applied to this area is effective in releasing holds or to open the hand.

As a general rule avoid striking the area of the mouth. If a blow is struck with a club, excessive damage to the attacked's teeth may result; a barehanded blow is quite likely to cause incapacitating injury to the attacker's hand.

Reprinted from Clubs in Self Defense and Mob Control *with permission from Monadnock Lifetime Products, Inc.*

CULVER PICTURES

"Portrait Parle" class, Paris, in which students absorbed the Cyrano lecture on characteristic nose shapes. Advanced classes discussed ear symmetry. Though doctors attend similar seminars today, their attire is less refined.

sues may require a year or two. Other factors affecting decomposition rates include the accessibility of the body to insect and animal scavengers, humidity, and whether or not the body was buried and, if so, the depth of burial. All of these conditions must be taken into account in estimating the time of death, and for this reason the forensic anthropologist generally needs to visit the scene — preferably before the skeleton is moved.

When the soft tissues have completely disappeared, the bones themselves may offer some clues to the time of death. Exposure to sunlight, extremely hot or cold weather, and soil chemicals all affect the surface texture and composition of bone. From these features it is sometimes possible to determine within five or ten years how long a skeleton has been exposed. While not as precise as we would like them to be, such estimates at least broadly bracket a time span that can helpfully limit the search for missing persons.

Usually the next step in examining an unknown skeleton is a determination of the individual's age at death. Fortunately, the bones offer many clues to age. In infants and very young children, the bones are incompletely calcified. At certain ages — different for each bone — centers of calcification appear within the cartilaginous precursors of the bone. In teenagers, the bones are more or less completely calcified but are still separated into several parts by thin plates of cartilage. These plates persist until growth ceases (usually somewhere between age twenty and twenty-five). By comparing the state of skeletal development with standards for normal children, the age of a child or adolescent can usually be estimated within a couple of years.

In adults, age determination is more difficult. Oddly enough, one of the most reliable indicators is the pubic symphysis — the joint formed by the two hipbones in the front of the pelvis. The joint surfaces of the symphysis undergo some fairly regular changes throughout adult life. Thus, by examining the symphysis, the forensic anthropologist can usually tell a skeleton's age within three to five years. Another reliable method depends on the microscopic restructuring changes that occur with age in the long bones of the limbs. Broader age estimates are sometimes provided by pathological changes that occur with age around certain joints. For example, arthritic lipping of the joint margins seldom becomes evident until after age thirty-five or forty.

Sex can be determined from the skeleton with great reliability. The most striking differences occur in the pelvis. The female pelvis, adapted to its reproductive functions, differs strongly in shape from that of the male. In females, the pelvis is shallow and broad — cradle-like — compared to that of males, which is narrow and steep-walled. The birth canal, the bony ring through which the infant must pass during childbirth, is wide and ovoid in females, constricted and angular in males. There are also some strong differences in the skulls of males and females. Typically, the male skull is larger and more robust; that of the female, small and delicately modeled.

The diagnosis of race from the bones is more difficult. However, it is usually possible to assign a skeleton to one of the three major racial groups — Negro, White and Mongoloid — with a fair degree of confidence. Here the forensic anthropologist relies primarily on the skull. Many of the skeletal features of race are also reflected in the living. For example, the nasal aperture of the skull tends to be broader in Negroes and Mongoloids than it is in Whites. Mongoloids (a category which includes American Indians as well as most Asiatics) have flatter facial skeletons and broader, more prominent cheekbones than either Whites or Negroes. These and perhaps a score of other bony traits allow us to correctly diagnose race in about 80 percent of skeletons examined.

Stature is another trait useful in identification. In this country, the height of most missing individuals can be obtained from their police, medical or military records containing their physical descriptions. To match these with the height of an unknown skeleton is a fairly simple procedure, since the lengths of the bones of the arms and legs are usually proportional to stature. This relationship can be expressed by mathematical equations so that if we know, for example, the length of the thighbone, we can calculate the living individual's stature within an inch or two.

After age, sex, race and stature have been determined, the forensic anthropologist turns his attention to other skeletal traits which, singly or in combination, may further characterize the individual. For example, each bone is examined for signs of old fractures or other injuries which might be recorded in the medical record of a missing person. Many diseases such as syphilis, tuberculosis and a wide variety of hormonal and nutritional disturbances may also leave a characteristic imprint on the bone. Finally, such unique features as an unusual gait or postural habits may be reflected in the bones.

At this point, the forensic anthropologist is usually able to provide the police or medical examiner with a fairly detailed description of the living person now represented by a skeleton. The next step generally involves a search of police records to find one or more missing persons who match the description. When these are collected, a more extensive review of their medical and dental records is begun. Here the forensic anthropologist works closely with his colleague, the forensic dentist — especially in cases where the skeleton has extensive dental work. Hopefully, a detailed comparison will enable them to find a single individual whose description matches that of the skeleton in sufficient detail to establish positive identification.

Once the police know who the victim is, they have come a long way toward finding his murderer.

Clyde Snow, Ph.D. is a forensic anthropologist for the Civil Aeromedical Institute.

I am told he makes a very handsome corpse, and becomes his coffin prodigiously.

The Good-Natured Man
OLIVER GOLDSMITH

THE PINOCCHIO MACHINES

George O'Toole

A person given a polygraph test sits in a chair in a quiet room with the polygraph examiner. A corrugated rubber tube is stretched across his chest to measure his respiration, his arm is encircled by an inflatable blood-pressure cuff and a pair of electrodes attached to his fingers read the electrical resistance of his skin. The output from these three "sensors" is recorded by three electrically operated pens on a moving chart in view of the examiner but hidden from the gaze of the subject.

The polygraph, then, is not a "lie detector" at all, but merely a very sensitive instrument for observing certain body responses. The true "lie detector" is the person operating the polygraph, and his task is to compare the subject's polygraph responses to a series of questions.

Prior to the actual test, the examiner will interview the subject and review the questions he plans to ask. There are a variety of polygraph interrogation techniques, but most include control questions designed to measure the level of response to touchy issues ("Have you ever in your life stolen anything?"), irrelevant questions intended to measure the subject's general level of anxiety ("Are you wearing a white shirt?") and relevant questions relating directly to the matter under investigation ("Did you hold up the store?"). The examiner asks his questions in a fixed sequence, pausing ten or fifteen seconds after each response to watch the changes on the moving chart. The subject is instructed to answer simply yes or no, and must sit motionless during the entire process to avoid making extraneous changes on the polygraph chart. The test is based on the principle that the liar will show a significantly stronger polygraph response to the relevant questions than he will to either the irrelevant or the control questions. Exactly why this happens is not completely understood, but it involves anxiety (the fear of being found out) as well as the increased intellectual labor required to support a lie — the weaving of a tangled web.

The Peak of Tension Test

Another type of polygraph examination tests for guilty knowledge rather than lies. The Peak of Tension test is designed to show whether a suspect knows some detail of a crime that has not been released to the news media. For example, a suspect in a stabbing case might be shown a series of weapons (a knife, a screwdriver, an ice pick), only one of which was actually used in the crime. Or he might be shown a set of photographs, one of which is the victim. A significantly stronger response to whatever item is actually related to the case is interpreted to mean the suspect was involved in the crime. Preserving such items for use in a Peak of Tension test is one reason the police often refuse to disclose to the press all the details of a case.

How accurate is the polygraph test as a lie detection technique? That is difficult to answer. First, attempts to establish the polygraph's accuracy in the laboratory involve "simulated lies," in which an experimental subject will attempt to "lie" about some trivial matter, such as which card or number he picked. Obviously, the heightened blood pressure, pulse or respiration caused by the anxiety of a suspect in a criminal case will not be present. Second, attempts to measure the polygraph's accuracy in the field are frustrated by the absence of the neat, controlled conditions of the laboratory. Finally, there is a large element of subjective judgment in conducting polygraph tests, and there are such great differences in the skill of individual polygraph examiners that it is almost meaningless to talk of the accuracy of the polygraph test in the abstract. But for whatever they may be worth, studies of polygraph test accuracy have come up with figures ranging from 73 to 97 percent.

Can someone "beat" the polygraph? Maybe. The polygraph itself is simply a measuring instrument and cannot in any sense be beaten. But the polygraph examiner is human and therefore fallible; it is possible, at least in theory, for a suspect to outwit him during the test. When someone sits down to take a polygraph test with the intention of lying and getting away with it, he enters into a game of wits in which the odds are stacked heavily in favor of the polygraph examiner. Clifford Irving, author of the bogus biography of Howard Hughes, seems to have played this game and won; his publishers had him take a polygraph test to check his truthfulness, and the examiner failed to discover he was lying. Still, most people who try to beat the polygraph test will fail unless they have received some special training, such as the courses in "polygraph countermeasures" taught at the U.S. Army Intelligence School at Ft. Holabird, Maryland. Attempts by amateurs to beat the test will usually be obvious to an experienced polygraph examiner and will only serve to make his job easier.

OSWALD AND THE PSE

I ran a check of Oswald's voice tapes on the PSE, and the results showed he was telling the truth — he didn't assassinate Kennedy.

So I showed the results to the PSE experts: the inventors of the machine; the man who taught the course in how to use it; the Maryland policemen who had field-tested it.

I didn't tell them details. I merely said, "Look, here are the charts of a young man, in a police station, who has been accused of killing an executive."

And their response to that was "Why bother us with this problem? When you have a difficult case, come to us and we'll help you read the charts, but if you can't interpret these, there's something wrong with you. This is a clear-cut case of a man telling the truth." Then I told them who the voice belonged to.

They didn't want to believe it. Everyone said, "What! You must have done something wrong! Run the tape wrong. Or been fooling with it."

I gave them another tape to judge by. Same results.

But nobody wants to believe it.

G.O.T.

Narcoanalysis

The polygraph is not the only lie detection technique in use. Another widely misunderstood interrogation aid is so-called "truth serum." Contrary to popular belief, there is no drug that will magically force someone to babble the truth. However, there are chemicals that can be used to weaken a subject's determination to lie or conceal information. Scopolamine has been used for this purpose since the early 1920's. More recently, barbiturates such as sodium amytal and sodium Pentothal have been used.

The correct name for the technique is narcoanalysis. Typically, the drug is injected into the subject in amounts that keep him on the thin edge between sleep and wakefulness, a psychological state in which he has least resistance to interrogation. While such medication may cause a subject to reveal what he has previously concealed, the highly suggestible state of mind produced by the drug may cause him to confess to wholly imaginary crimes. Narcoanalysis can be used to help a witness suffering from amnesia, but it is rarely used for lie detection purposes in criminal investigations. In addition to being unreliable and still poorly understood, the technique requires a physician to administer the drug, making it impractical for routine investigative use by law enforcement agencies.

The Psychological Stress Evaluator

The most recent development in lie detection is the discovery that psychological stress is registered in the voice as well as in those body variables measured by the polygraph. The stress changes in the voice are not audible, but they can be detected by specially designed electronic circuitry. The Psychological Stress Evaluator (PSE) was invented for this purpose by three former Army intelligence officers, Allen Bell, Jr., Charles McQuiston and Wilson Ford.

The PSE performs the same function as the polygraph, without putting the subject in the uncomfortable embrace of breathing tubes, blood-pressure cuffs and skin electrodes. The new instrument works through the simple medium of the tape recording: the subject's answers are recorded during interrogation, then later played back through the PSE, producing a chart showing the level of stress on each reply. Like the polygraph test, lie detection with the PSE is accomplished through the comparison of stress levels on the subject's replies to different questions. While developing the new instrument, the PSE's inventors tested it on broadcasts of the popular television panel show *To Tell the Truth.* Seated before their television sets, they were able to identify correctly the bogus contestants 95 percent of the time.

Many polygraph examiners have raised objections to the new instrument for all the reasons any group resists technological change. However, the PSE is easier to use than the polygraph, has superior accuracy and is now in widespread use, having been adopted by more than 100 law enforcement agencies across the United States.

There's a popular misconception that the results of lie detection tests cannot be admitted as evidence in a court of law. It's true that federal courts reject lie detection evidence; however, in many state and local courts lie detection evidence has been admitted for years under what is termed "stipulation." This means both the prosecution and defense agree beforehand that the defendant will be given a lie detection test and the results will be admitted as evidence, regardless of the outcome. They also agree on the kind of test and the examiner who will give it. Both the polygraph and the PSE have been admitted into court on this basis.

Perhaps the defense should always be permitted to introduce lie detection evidence when eyewitness testimony has been introduced by the prosecution. Still, even lie detection is not without some hazard to the accused. Three years ago a Virginia jury could not decide on the guilt or innocence of a man accused of armed robbery, even though several defense witnesses testified the defendant was elsewhere when the crime took place. Before a new trial was scheduled, the accused requested a polygraph test and asked that the results be admitted as evidence. In his letter to the judge, the man wrote, "It is the only way to show my innocence without any doubt and to get to the truth of the matter."

The defendant got his wish, but he flunked the test. When he tried to have the test result kept out of his new trial, the judge refused.

"You're trying to have your cake and eat it too," the magistrate told him. "Fair play is fair play. If the result had been favorable, you would have insisted on your rights to introduce the test into evidence."

The accused man forgot the most important thing to remember about the polygraph: It's something less than 100 percent accurate.

George O'Toole is a former employee of the Central Intelligence Agency and author of The Agent on the Other Side.

THE ASTROLOGICAL IMPERATIVE

Peter Bull (Sebastian Seer)

Any idiot could have seen immediately by looking at the birth charts of Miss Bonnie Parker and Mr. Clyde Barrow that they were up to absolutely no good at all.

Clyde's Moon, for example, was in Taurus (trine Mars and Uranus, also trine Jupiter in Virgo). To astrologers this is as clear a bit of incriminating evidence as a blood-stained knife, for such a combination will produce acute need for dangerous living. His Sun Sign shows that with Saturn in Aries the poor chap (well, *fairly* poor chap) yearns for an immediate feeling of power and is fed by an intense ruthlessness in obtaining it.

Bonnie's chart is almost completely complementary to her chum's. She had an important configuration composed of the Moon, Uranus and Jupiter. There was also a conjunction of Venus with the Moon, and the Venus aspect pointed to terrific romantic overtones. She was a Libran and, in consequence, felt a compulsion to help the man with whom she was inexorably linked. This, with the effects of Neptune in her chart, indicated a penchant for the "glamorous" aspects of her adventures. Another riveting parallel with her lover's chart is that her Sun, like his, is completely unaspected except for a Mars conjunction and an injunction to Saturn. This indicated a probable and immediate response to a certain type of egotism and aggressive assertion which requires a tremendously close liaison with another being in order to fulfil itself.

Astrologers know that since the Sun in a woman's chart gives a vivid indication of the men in her life, and the Moon in a man's does ditto, a survey of these relative positions makes their attraction for one another quite obvious.

Of course, it is very dangerous to lay down any fixed laws about any astrological fact. But Cornell says Moon conjunct Saturn in Scorpio denotes a killer, and these are Mr. "Legs" Diamond's combinations, if you know what I mean. Mr. Cornell, by the way, is the gent who wrote *The Encyclopedia of Medical Astrology,* so presumably he knows what he's talking about. He also adds an extremely specialised observation which I, in my detective capacity, would have used when following the nefarious career of Mr. D.: He has the 19th degree of Sun on Fixed Star Castor, which indicates danger of becoming a murderer or being murdered (chart, page 369.)

In many ways, the chart of Laurel Crawford, (born August 18-19, 1898: midnight) mass murderer, is similar to that of "Legs" Diamond. Pluto is in the First House. On the other

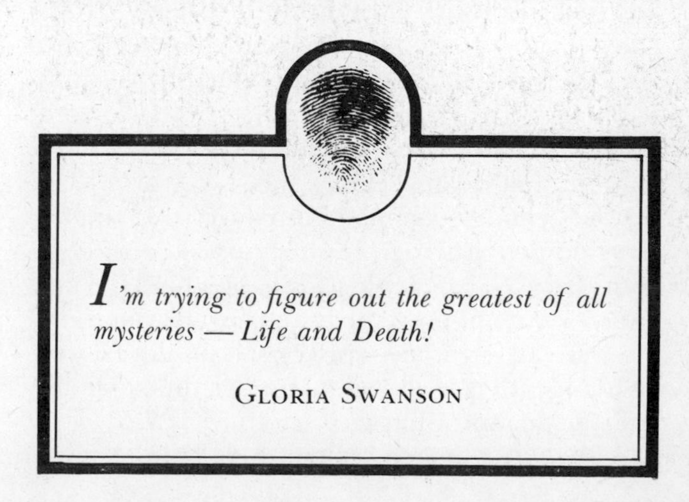

I'm trying to figure out the greatest of all mysteries — Life and Death!

GLORIA SWANSON

hand, every portent is below the horizon, which usually indicates a dark life. Again there is the vital need to impress others — if necessary, in a ruthless and destructive way. Pluto is conjunct with Fixed Star Rigel, which supposes an excellent brain but a life ending in disaster. The late Czarina of Russia had her Sun on Rigel, and poor Caryl Chessman had his Mars on the same Fixed Star.

With Crawford, for starters, there were three murderous planets in the First House, square Moon and Mercury in the Fourth and Fifth Houses, which indicate dangerous loss of self-control. In particular, Mercury as Moon Ruler, in exact square to Mars, "provides the impulse to murder." (Cornell) The tragedy is that, if the aspected chart were slightly different, all the energies might have been channelled into artistic creation. But, in fact, Crawford found himself trying to prove his cleverness at hoodwinking the public. Add to this Mars conjunct Neptune, and it is my guess that he was probably both intellectually and sexually stimulated by the thought of murder, though this combination frequently prophesies spells of actual madness.

William Hickman started his murderous life (February 1, 1908: 4:45 A.M.) with a very badly aspected Mars, and the ruler Jupiter in a "perversion" degree in the House of Scorpio (Eighth) makes him the reverse of Diamond: a hot-blooded murderer who kills where others make love, for transient physical satisfaction.

Hickman's chart shows an extraordinarily complicated arrangement of tendencies. Sagittarius Rising gave him the feeling he could rely on luck, and with Jupiter in the "Death" House he probably could. But the gentle, loving Venus in Pisces was hardened and chilled by conjunction with Saturn, and there was probably some tragic accident in his family which gave him the notion that death-dealing was a way of life. He had a grudge against humanity, thinking he was denied a living (Jupiter opposition to Second House). It is highly probable that Hickman was a victim of extreme cruelty in a former life.

In all criminal episodes it is never wise, when death is involved, to ignore the possibility of suicide, and Charles Carter in *The Astrology of Accidents* has been a tremendous help to me in solving some of my trickier assignments. Of course, the facts he discloses are not always new to me. I know that not only, as an Arian, am I clumsy and accident-prone, but hitting my head on something has become a hideous habit. All Fire Signs are impetuous, and it seems more likely that they would be involved in violent and/or sudden deaths.

Mr. Carter draws the following conclu-

THE MURDERER'S THUMB

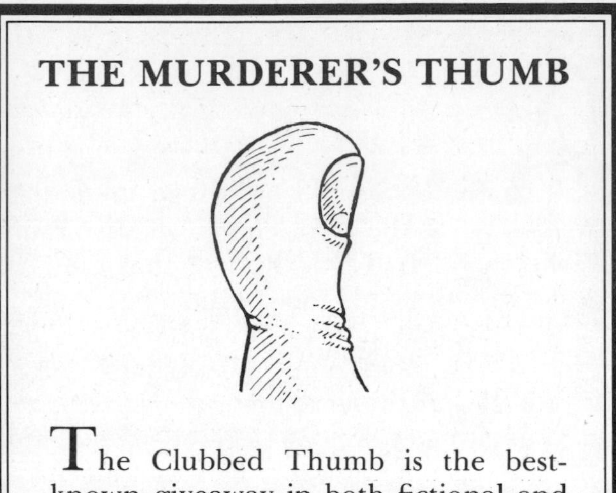

The Clubbed Thumb is the best-known giveaway in both fictional and factual detection. It is so called because it is as thick as a club. In Cheiro's book *Palmistry for All* the author asserts that people having this class of thumb belong to the Elementary type as far as will is concerned. They are brutal and like animals in their unreasonable stubbornness. If opposed, they fly into blind rages and anything may happen. They have no control over themselves and can go to extremes, culminating in any crime in the book. This defect has also been called "The Murderer's Thumb," since so many convicted of homicide are found to possess this physical characteristic. The possessor could not, however, plan or premeditate a crime, for he would not have the determined will or power of reason to think it out. The shorter the thumb, the nearer the possessor is to The Brute and his probable lack of control.

P.B.

sions:

• In cases of Asphyxiation by Suicide, Pluto and Saturn are deeply involved.

• He took several examples of drowning or narrow escapes from the water, including the bandmaster of the *Titanic,* a young lady drowned in the same ship, and others, and there were contacts between Mercury and Saturn. I need hardly tell you that Neptune is bound to come into this form of death, although not as strongly as Saturn. There is also a frequent occurrence of Sagittarius as an ascending sign.

• He examined a lot of international shooting incidents, and they show, beyond dispute, that bullet-wounds and probably all violent blows on small areas of the body, in the shape of cuts and stabs and so forth, relate to about six degrees of Aries or Libra. This combination occurs again in cases of accidental wounds. A death, reported in the *British Journal of Astrology,* didn't have quite similar indications, but as the person concerned swallowed a knitting needle which penetrated the throat, this sort of thing cannot be treated as a test case. Or can it?

• With vehicular accidents, the signs are all over the place, as might be expected. Afflictions to the mutable planets, Mercury and Jupiter, are almost always present, the former being more in evidence in cycling accidents and those arising in the course of routine journeys. Saturn afflictions tend to broken bones; Uranus, to shock. Afflictions in mutables and especially in Gemini-Sagittarius are common. In accidents caused by skids, stresses are heavily Saturnian. Surprise! In railway disasters there is always a distinctly Uranian flavour to the casualty list.

• Death by accidental poisoning is, happily, not very common, but in any supposed murder case the possibility cannot be ruled out entirely. Out of ten analysed incidents Mr. Carter found that Jupiter occupied Aquarius in six of them. And in two others it was square to bodies in that sign. There appears no reason for this, and a layman might expect that this phenomenon would appear in drowning cases, but as has been shown this doesn't work out. I don't want to alarm Sagittarians, but it must be admitted that their sign has a high accident-ratio and a marked suicidal propensity.

At the risk of blowing my own trumpet, I must end this documentary brouhaha on a piece of information which may be news to some of you. Quite simply, at the time of the Great Hatchet Murders, I was having a mild affair with a well-known lady palmist of the day called Georgina. Acting on certain information supplied by her, I was able to apprehend Miss L. Borden, though for some extraordinary reason she escaped her deserts, and she and her Murderer's Thumb ended their days peacefully — which is more than can be said for her parents.

THE ILL-FATED

Utterly Useless Bits of Astrological Accident Information: (1) In two severe cases of stings from insects, there were afflictions in the radix between Uranus and the Sun and both victims were Gemini. (2) The sign of Taurus has absolutely no connection with bullfight accidents, though Scorpio pops up frequently in the combatants.

Peter Bull (Aries) is an international film star and co-owner (with Don Busby, Leo) of Zodiac, the Astrological Emporium, *in London. Their astrological advisor is Joyce Sanderson (Cancer).*

THE LEGS DIAMOND CONFIGURATION

Joyce Sanderson

♋ ☉ , trine ☽ , ♅ and ♄ in ♏ : obviously not the maternal, nourishing and cherishing aspect of ♋ , but concern for the Crab shell, the appearance (dress, hair style, manner). ♋ and ♏ both "deadpan" signs: no emotion on the face and high capability of hiding all outward manifestation of inner turmoil.

19th degree ☉ on Fixed Star Castor: "danger of becoming a murderer" or "being murdered." (Cornell)

♇ in 1st: vital need to impress one's own personality and views on others; inscrutable, adventurous, courageous, self-sufficient and skeptical.

♆ in 1st in dual sign: before-and-after personality, up and down moods, e.g., whole personality change upon hearing a piece of music; strong imagination but shallow emotions.

Fixed Star Aldebaran exactly on the Ascendant: fame or notoriety, resulting in periods of great stress.

☽ conjunct ♄ in ♏, which denotes a murderer. (Cornell) Here also ☌ ♅ — sudden violent acts — and all □ ☽'s nodes — likely to ride roughshod over conventional morality. ♄ □ ☽ nodes: isolated by society. All trine ☉ and ☿ , so both nature and mentality put to work to intensify these trends.

Very much a ☿ -ruled chart: ☿ ☌ ☉, ♊ asc, ♇ and ♆ in ♊ in 1st, ♃ and ♂ in ♍ in 4th, ♋'s natural house. Therefore a "cold-blooded" murderer; ♂ weak and □ ♀, so not prone to impulsive, violent ♂ acts of murder.

♇ in 1st □ ♃ and ♂, ☌ ♆ : ruthless, destructive (Plutonic, ♏, "tearing down" aspect); fanatical. ☌ ♆ : dangerous delusions. ♇ -ruled ☽ and two other planets in ♏ : in 6th, employment and servants; something to do with death! ♇ is ☽ significator and □ ♂ (danger of killing someone). ♅ ☌ ♄ is said to show moral lapses. Asc also □ ♂ and ♃ .

July 10, 1897: 2 a.m.

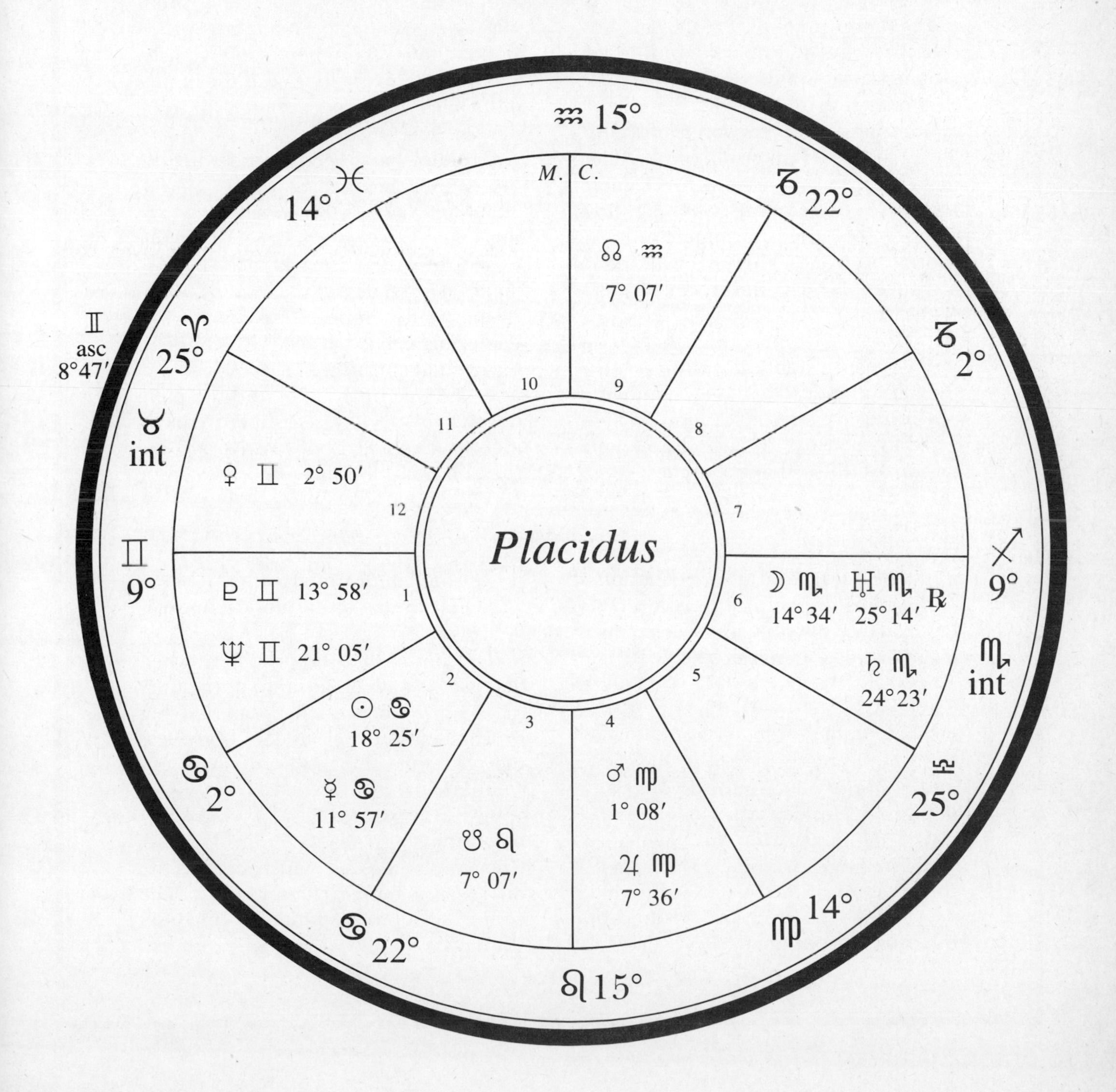

INCRIMINATING EVIDENCE

Fingerprints

Fingerprints *do* get left at crime scenes — often enough to put over 10,000 individual prints in the FBI files. Even the craftiest of perpetrators sometimes forget to wipe up everywhere. The places the lab boys dust first are: the doorknob; the light switches; the underside of the table; the toilet seat and handle; the picture frames, desk drawers and ashtrays.

A good set of prints can be taken off wall surfaces, windows, wood molding, Formica paneling. Clothing, however, is resistant to fingerprints, although right now they are working on a process which will recover prints from woolen fibers.

Most everyone realizes that no two people have identical prints, even if they are identical twins. Each individual's prints are specific to him.

Fingerprints are actually a combination of four shapes: arches, loops, whorls and composites. The most common configuration appearing on a finger is the loop (60 percent). Composites and whorls make up 35 percent and arches roughly 5 percent. Identification is made by matching prints at a minimum of 16 points. (Obviously, a loop is a loop is a loop. It is the breaks in its lines that allow a match-up to be made.)

Bodies have been found with the skin either burned or sandpapered, but prints were still possible to take since the ridges underneath maintained the original markings. This also makes it possible to take a set of prints from a decomposed corpse. The epidermis is not necessary in the matter of fingerprinting.

The sole of the foot and the palm of the hand also have distinctive markings which yield good prints and aid the police in identification.

Bloodstains

The size, shape and distribution of bloodstains are helpful in reconstructing exactly what occurred during an alleged crime. Often a suspect will maintain he acted in self-defense, only to have his story disproved by the pattern of blood spill.

One of the principal authorities in interpreting bloodstain evidence is Professor Herbert MacDonell, who is also well-known for his pioneering work in fingerprinting. (MacDonell is the inventor of the MAGNA Brush device, which is used by identification bureaus throughout the world for processing latent fingerprints.)

On the basis of bloodstain evidence alone, MacDonell has been able to determine whether a victim was in a defensive or attack position at the time of death; whether he was moving or stationary; whether his body was moved after the homicide was accomplished.

MacDonell teaches a course in bloodstain evidence at Elmira College, Corning, New York, which stresses the differences among spatter stains. The course is a seminar, limited to thirty-six students.

Chapter 11

MOUTHPIECES

FRED WINKOWSKI

HOW TO PICK A GOOD LAWYER

Washington C. Beenson

Make an appointment with Perry Mason. Mason has tried eighty-five cases, and we know for sure of only one he's lost. Some others are dubious, but his record is far and away the best of all practicing attorneys. If he thinks the situation warrants it, he just might handle your case minus a retainer, and it's hard to find a lawyer more altruistic than that. In the courtroom his interrogation techniques are second in force to . . . Torquemada. It's the rare man who can look him straight in the eye, lie and get away with it. Yes, definitely pick Perry if you want to be acquitted. On the other hand, to have Hamilton Burger on your side is tantamount to having the word "guilty" stamped on your forehead. In indelible ink. Avoid Burger at all costs.

The lawyer you pick, of course, depends on what you've gotten yourself involved in. If it's a crime concerning the government, either ours or theirs, you might ask to see David St. John's Peter Ward. Ward's not only a lawyer, he's an undercover agent for the CIA as well. (And St. John should know all about that; his other name is E. Howard Hunt.)

In New York, Harold Q. Masur's Scott Jordan seems honest and upright, a man with few discernible bad habits. But if you prefer someone with more experience there's Arthur Train's Mr. Tutt, born July 4, 1869. Mr. Tutt, according to those who know him, ought to be nominated for sainthood. It's doubtful there's a sweeter, wiser, more eloquent lawyer in or out of fiction.

In London, there's Sara Wood's Anthony Maitland, who specializes in lurid homicides (although he himself lives a quiet domestic life). Or, you could ring up Gideon Fell and ask for Patrick Butler's phone number, particularly if you're locked in a room and can't extricate yourself.

Should you find yourself transported to China in a Wellsian time machine, Judge Dee is your man — but only if your case is exceedingly difficult and borders on the sadistic.

Shyster Lawyers

Heading the list of lawyers to avoid would be Melville Davisson Post's Randolph Mason, whose strange schemes at the turn of the century turned the letter of the law against itself — in fact, inside out. (Rumor has it Perry Mason stole his last name from Randolph; in-

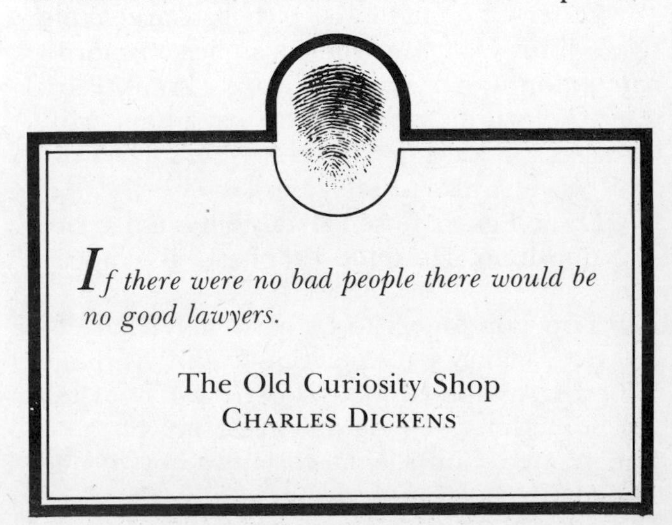

A FOOL FOR A CLIENT

If you think you might like to conduct your own defense, the following books may serve as a primer:

Delano Ames: *She Shall Have Murder*
Mel Arrighi: *Freak Out*
H.C. Bailey: *The Garston Murder Case*
James Francis Bonnell: *Death over Sunday*
Henry Cecil: *Brother in Law; Daughters in Law; Fathers in Law*
August Derleth: *Murder Stalks the Wakely Family*
D.M. Devine: *My Brother's Killer*
Warwick Downing: *The Mountains West of Town*
Lesley Egan: *A Case for Appeal*
Sydney Fowler: *The Murder in Bethnal Square*
Erle Stanley Gardner: *The Case of the* . . . .(series, 85 titles); *The D.A. Holds a Candle*
Anthony Gilbert: *A Case for Mr. Crook; After the Verdict*
Michael Gilbert: *Smallbone Deceased*
Edward Grierson: *The Second Man*
Richard Himmel: *I Have Gloria Kirby*
Roderic Jeffries: *Dead Against the Lawyers*
Frederic Arnold Kummer: *The Clue of the Twisted Face*
Hugh McCutcheon: *And the Moon Was Full*
Ross Macdonald: *The Ferguson Affair*
Harold Q. Masur: *Bury Me Deep*
Margaret Millar: *Ask for Me Tomorrow*
Hugh Pentecost: *Around Dark Corners*
Frank G. Presnell: *Too Hot to Handle*
Craig Rice: *Trial by Fury*
David St. John: *Return from Vorkuta*
Michael Underwood: *Murder Made Absolute*
Sara Woods: *Let's Choose Executors*

deed, some have wondered if he is not related to him in much the manner of Wolfe to Holmes — the wrong side of the bar, so to speak.)

Shyster may be too strong a term for them, but one should think twice before letting A.A. Fair's Donald Lam or John Robert's Jigger Moran defend you: Both men have been disbarred.

Others you might wish to bypass are: Craig Rice's John J. Malone (he consumes an inordinate amount of rye); Cyril Hare's Frank Pettigrew (before his marriage he was in a steady, unsuccessful decline); Mel Arrighi's Harrington (he's lost his last ten cases).

Leslie Egan's Jesse Falkenstein is a marginal proposition. He's not dishonest, just indecisive.

Two Londoners to be extremely chary of are H.C. Bailey's Joshua Clunk and Anthony Gilbert's Arthur Crook. (Don't the names tell you something? I wouldn't trust my life to a man named Clunk, and certainly not to one named Crook.) Clunk is detested by the Yard contingent, although it's moot whether this is because he solves their cases or because he (the hypocrite) quotes scripture at them. Crook is another schemer, a sharpy who will undoubtedly get you off, then just as undoubtedly run you into a lamppost with his wretched little car. He'll try to revive you with one of his omnipresent beers, but be careful — that leads straight to a charge of drunken driving.

The Author-Attorney

Amongst a certain coterie you might find your problems brilliantly solved, only to reappear again between the pages of a book. Author-attorneys include Henry Cecil, Erle Stanley Gardner (who passed the bar without going to law school), Michael Gilbert, Cyril Hare, Joe L. Hensley, Roderic Jeffries, C.H.B. Kitchin, Edgar Lustgarten, Harold Q. Masur, Francis M. Nevins, Melville Davisson Post, Arthur Train, Miles Tripp and Michael Underwood.

Washington C. Beenson is a jailhouse lawyer.

HOW TO MAKE A WILL

"Now read me the part again where I disinherit everybody."

A will should not be written on ordinary stationery, as the paper is too inflammable. H. Rider Haggard found the perfect nonperishable substance: human skin. In *Mr. Meeson's Will* he had the will tattooed on a woman's back. The court upheld it.

A good will must be written under duress. In Patricia Wentworth's *The Fingerprint* it came about as a response to an anonymous letter. Needless to add, the note sender recommended that he be remembered in the new will.

A will must inconvenience the heirs. In Margery Allingham's *Death of a Ghost* it was stipulated that the heirs reconvene once a year. On the eighth reunion, when he least expected it, one of the heirs was dispatched.

A will should promise much and deliver little. In Charles Dickens' *Bleak House* the inheritance shenanigans dragged on for years; by the time the will was settled, there was no inheritance—it had all gone to pay legal fees.

One final note: When you hear of a death, immediately suspect the heirs. Even if you happen to be one of them.

BOOKS BY CROOKS

Milt Machlin

In my eighteen years as editor of *Argosy,* I had considerable contact with jailed would-be authors, especially as *Argosy* was the home of the Court Of Last Resort. In particular, I remember one John D. Matthews, who persistently tried to con me into a highly improbable meeting with Joe Adonis and Virginia Hill — both made famous in the McClellan crime hearings in the Fifties. "Chesty" Matthews, as he liked to be called, had a long record as a burglar and holdup man. When he got out of prison twenty-odd years ago, he found he could make a passable living by bicycling his story around to various magazine editors in New York, peddling — or pedaling — his criminal expertise in the form of fables, fantasies and even a few fact-based anecdotes. His greatest triumph, however, was to sell the same ghostwritten book to three paperback publishers. Every week he delivered a different chapter to each one — carbons to the second two, with the explanation that the original had been damaged, mutilated or lost — and in this way managed to acquire three separate advances, an achievement to be admired by any writer. (Later, Chesty Matthews overcalculated his hype when he tried to shake down a Jersey City slot machine entrepreneur who happened to be the son of one of the mob's top leaders, himself a star in the McClellan hearings. In some manner never clearly established, Chesty ended up with a bullet between his eyes, dead as an out-of-print novel, and the slot man was let off with a plea of self-defense.)

In any case, since the book had been ghostwritten by Jeffrey Roche, a crime reporter for the now-defunct New york *Journal-American,* I hardly feel that Chesty Matthews would qualify for a place in the Books by Crooks Hall of Fame.

Malcom Braly certainly qualifies for the top of the American list of Books by Crooks. After he made his criminal start by stealing a classmate's coat and getting caught at it (and *in* it) at the age of fourteen, Braly, as he says himself, "served more time for a handful of inept burglaries than most men have served for having killed a police officer." His first major novel, *On the Yard,* which Kurt Vonnegut, Jr. called "the great American prison novel." was published in 1967. His most recent book, *False Starts,* was released to mass critical applause last year and, the last I heard, was being readied as a major Hollywood film.

Probably the most successful, financially, of the ex-con writers would be Paul Erdmann, whose third novel, *The Crash of '79,* has been bought by Paramount for a movie, and has been read avidly by corporate leaders and government executives. In 1970 Erdman was sent to jail when several officers in a Swiss bank of which he was president illegally used $40 million of depositors' funds to speculate in commodity futures. Ten months later he posted bail and left Switzerland, where he was subsequently tried *in absentia* and given an eight-year sentence. But Erdmann is tapping away at his home overlooking San Francisco Bay, and at his ranch in Sonoma, on his fourth novel, about "international corporate bribery."

Perhaps one could say that making a living by writing is the next best thing to stealing.

Milt Machlin coauthored French Connection II.

THE BEST DEFENSE

Paul Chevigny

While the law of murder in the United States varies in detail as to place, in its broad outlines it has changed little from the common law and similar themes are treated in a similar way from state to state. I am going to discuss murder — with a look at a couple of the more dramatic problems of evidence that come up in murder cases — in California, New York and Illinois. I like to think that it is the flavor of the milieu, rather than the actual viciousness of the environment, that so often causes our novelists to place their stories in Los Angeles, New York City and Chicago. But who knows, the tastiest milieus may yet be proved to be the most vicious . . .

The threshold problem, no matter where the killing has been committed, is to establish that there has in fact been a homicide. It is here that the hoary phrase "corpus delicti" usually appears. Breathes there a reader who yet believes that the words refer to the corpse of the dead person? If such reader no longer breathes, many murderers must still believe it since they go to such lengths to destroy all traces of the body. In a recent "bluebeard" murder case in New York, the defendant, a preacher, burned the bodies in gasoline; unfortunately, he did so with the assistance of at least one other, who testified against him. The term "corpus delicti" in fact refers to the "body of the crime" — the proof that the victim is dead, and that caused by a criminal agency. When there is a witness, then, the corpus delicti can be established without a corpse. It continues to be true, however, that where there is no corpse and no witness, it is extremely difficult to establish the existence of a murder.

The ancient judge-made law recognized no degrees of murder. Murder was simply homicide "with malice aforethought," a concept which was not the same as the modern "premeditation" or "lying in wait." It referred instead to a general malicious intent — "the mental state," as *Wharton's*, the leading treatise, has it, "of a person voluntarily doing an act which ordinarily will cause serious injury or death to another without excuse or justification." It included both the "felony murder" rule, which made one guilty for any killing committed in the course of a dangerous felony, even if the killing was not intentional, as well as a great many other violent acts which might not involve a specific intent to kill but simply show a reckless disregard for life. Murders resulting from wantonly firing a gun into a lighted house or a moving passenger train are the classic examples.

In the nineteenth century, murder was broken into degrees — usually First Degree, which was typically the premeditated variety, and Second Degree, which was murder with plain old vague malice aforethought. Right there is where we still find California's law of murder, not changed in more than a hundred years. In California all homicides with malice aforethought are murders, and murders committed with premeditation or in the course of particularly violent felonies like robbery and rape are first-degree murders.

Manslaughter in California also follows an old-fashioned pattern. It is divided into voluntary manslaughter, which is killing "upon a sudden quarrel or heat of passion." Shooting the spouse's lover, surprised in the act of adultery, is the typical case. Involuntary manslaughter is a killing in the commission of an unlawful act and without intent. The famous illustration here is the case of punching the nose of a hemophiliac, who bleeds to death on the spot.

It is easy to see that both juries and judges would have had a great deal of trouble distinguishing between "malice aforethought" and "heat of passion," at least in the cases where the killer might have been acting recklessly and without premeditation. They did and do have such difficulties all the time, and in an attempt to simplify the problem New York and Illinois have scrapped the distinctions that appear in California law. They now essentially define murder as homicide with intent to kill or do great bodily harm, or with the knowledge that there is a strong probability of death or great bodily harm, or in the course of a forcible felony. In a way, this change is a throwback to ideas even older than the nineteenth century, although the magic incantation of malice aforethought has finally been abandoned. Voluntary manslaughter is still defined in terms similar to those of older law, covering a killing "under a sudden and intense passion." Involuntary manslaughter makes a little more sense in New York and Illinois than it used to, being limited now to a killing in the course of a crime which would have been expected to create serious bodily harm, such as a really violent assault or a hazing.

New York and Illinois are both very proud of their streamlined murder laws, but in fact all three states continue to have very similar problems when they get away from the case where there is premediated intent to kill. When juries and lawyers deal with the "reckless" act (an alias for "the strong probability of great bodily harm") or with the killing in the course of a felony, they still have to crack the same old chestnuts.

The felony murder rule has given rise to curious cases. In New York and California the death of the victim in the course of a felony is enough to make everyone involved guilty of murder, even when there is no shared intent to kill. If several people pull an armed robbery, and one of them surprises all the others by unexpectedly shooting the storekeeper, all are guilty of murder. In Illinois, when a policeman accidentally killed a third party in the course of pursuing some burglars, the burglars were still found guilty of murder.

The "reckless act" type of murder leads to even more puzzling cases, one of which reached the U.S. Supreme Court in 1977. On a very cold winter night in upstate New York, two men in a bar left with a third man, who was extremely drunk. Once in their car and on the highway, the two men robbed the drunk, forcing him to lower his trousers to see if he had money concealed and taking his glasses. They then put him out beside the highway, across and down the road from the nearest lighted building. When the drunk tried to struggle across the road, he was struck by another car and killed. The two were charged with murder. This was not thought to be a felony murder, because the death did not occur in the course of the robbery, but instead the reckless sort of act in which the two should have foreseen the result either of the man freezing to death or being struck by a car. The conviction has ultimately been affirmed.

The tough problem for the law of murder, no matter where the crime is committed, and no matter what magic phrases — "malice aforethought" or "intent to kill" — are used, is still that of the intent of the killer. And even when a "lying in wait" or a killing in the course of a violent felony is proved, the question of intent is not always at an end. Because, as the saying goes, you don't have to be crazy to kill someone but it helps. Killers frequently have some history of mental disturbance (like practically everyone else on the streets of the big cities), and the judge and jury often come to grips with the question of whether the killer is so bonkers that he is not responsible for his acts.

The classic English rule, from McNaghten's case, was that an insane person was not guilty of crime (in the usual sense) if he or she could not distinguish between right and wrong or could not understand "the nature and quality of the act," that is, could not understand what was happening. This rule would work passably well for a literally delusional state in which the killer thought he was, say, a sacrificial priest cutting the victim's heart out in an Aztec rite or in which he did not believe he was killing the victim at all. But for most cases of insanity,

ALIBIS WE NEVER WANT TO HEAR AGAIN

1. At an all-night poker game. Ask Fingers or Louie.
2. I was taking a walk. Alone. No, of course I saw no one. Wait, wait a minute — there was someone — a woman in a red dress. At the bus stop. I remember thinking how odd she'd be out alone at that time of night.
3. Here are my theater stubs.
4. Check with the hospital if you like. I was on call all night.
5. I sat with Mother until she dozed off. About ten o'clock, wasn't it, Mum?
6. Randolph, you're not going to like this, but I was in bed with your wife.
7. Right outside the door, just like I was supposed to be, Sarge.
8. The Governor and I were lunching at the Club.
9. Don't you remember — I rang up just past nine — you had trouble hearing me because the church bells were striking.
10. The last thing I saw was a hand, then there was this dreadful smell, and then I'm afraid, everything went black.
11. Awful tie-up on the Al.
12. I refuse to drag an innocent woman's name into this, Inspector. If you can't take the word of a gentleman . . . well, then, so be it.
13. Miss Pettigrew asked me to stay and help with the blackboards. Wasn't that all right, Mommy?

where the killer is aware of what he or she is doing, it has mostly been a source of grief for the psychiatrists who have to testify as well as for juries who have to listen to them.

Despite the grief, New York and California have resisted change from the McNaghten rule, fearing that any reduction in the standard of personal responsibility would simply give free reign to a gang of hoodlums who are already admitted to have a tolerably poor grasp of the difference between right and wrong — in killing as in everything else. Illinois, however, has adopted a new formulation which affords a defense if as a result of mental disease the killer "has no substantial capacity either to appreciate the criminality of his conduct or to conform his conduct to the requirements of the law." This common-sense formula probably expresses what sensible juries have always done, under any rule and in any state, with the poor devils who are uncontrollably psychotic.

In any state, killers sometimes botch the job, leaving the victim with a chance to say a few words before he dies. If he names his killer, the police and the D.A. have the problem of getting his statement before the jury, even though any report of it is rank hearsay and the speaker is not alive to be questioned. Centuries of law have grown up to protect the victim's right effectively to identify his killer in a "dying declaration." The court reasoned that the expectation of death and the possibility of hellfire would prevent the victim from telling an untruth. Accordingly, the dying declaration is admissible before the jury *only* if the victim knows he is dying and has no hope of recovery. This famous rule gives rise to the dramatic set-piece where the tough-but-professional detective rasps to the victim: "Listen, you're dying. You haven't got a chance. You understand that?" The face, gray against the white pillow, turns toward the other man. The paper-white lips part in a whisper: "I know. The doc told me." "Do you believe you can recover?" the detective continues mercilessly, fearing death at any moment. A pause, the paper lips say no. And then, of course, he doesn't tell you who did it; he utters three Delphic words which require seventy-five thousand more to elucidate.

Paul Chevigny is the author of Criminal Mischief.

THAT "BASTARD VERDICT"

Avon Curry

The Scots, as any Scott will tell you, are an exceptional race. They remain distinctively themselves although linked geographically and historically to a richer nation to the south, and in no area of life are they more "separate" than in their system of law. Although Scottish law has many of the costumes and settings of English law, the actors have different names — the terminology is different.

It may surprise you to learn, for instance, that the Sheriff plays an important part in Scotland — but he would die of the shock to his dignity if he were asked to wear a star and a six-gun. There is also an important official called the Procurator Fiscal, a term which alarms Americans because they feel it has something to do with tax prosecutions. Nothing of the kind. He fulfils a role something like the French *juge d'instruction*, looks into suspected crime and, in the case of an unexplained death, is the equivalent of the English coroner.

And speaking of the unexplained death, we come to murder and the part of Scottish law that probably interests crime fans most — the famous verdict of Not Proven.

Not Proven can be brought in for any accusation, but it takes on its utmost importance in a murder trial. For here the accused has a two-out-of-three chance of walking out free, whereas in the rest of the world, in general, there are only two verdicts: Guilty and Not Guilty. The Scots would say that as usual they are ahead of everyone else in providing an alternative to the Not Guilty verdict — Not Proven.

This is a very cool way of looking at evidence; it goes back in history to a time when Scottish juries were asked to condemn prisoners accused of a breach of the laws concerning religion. Unwilling to do so, they were instructed by the Lord Advocate that they must examine the facts and not the opinions in the case; if the facts proved the offence, they must so declare. They took him at his word: If the prosecution did not satisfy their minute examination of the facts, they brought in the verdict Not Proven, and it has remained.

One of those involved in the Burke and Hare case (1829) was a woman called Helen McDougal, who was accused of taking part in the murders whereby these grave-robbers provided corpses for the students of anatomy at Edinburgh University; she was set free by a Not Proven verdict. Mary Elder (or Smith) was charged with poisoning her maidservant in a strange and scandalous case the previous year; she received the benefit of the Not Proven verdict. Sir Walter Scott, who was at the Mary Elder trial, thought she was undoubtedly guilty, and it was he who coined a phrase for the result which is often used by those who disapprove of it — "that bastard verdict."

The case which most crime fans recognise at the mere mention of the name is that of Madeleine Smith. Her trial (1857) has all the ingredients of a great novel and has in fact been the basis for many books, both fact and fiction, and at least two plays. There's no doubt the story attracts attention because Madeleine was young and pretty, and the turns and twists of

THE CERTAIN RESULTS OF STEALING.

To What the First Step in Crime Ultimately Leads.

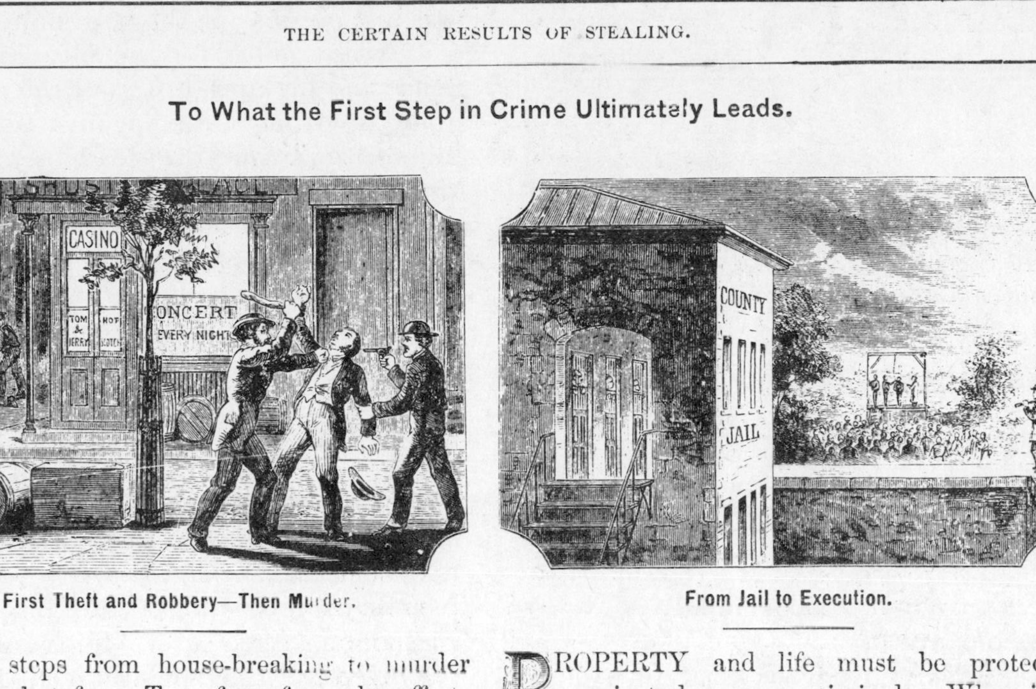

First Theft and Robbery—Then Murder.

From Jail to Execution.

THE steps from house-breaking to murder are but few. Too often, from the effects of evil associations in childhood, our worst thieves and burglars are young men in their teens, and almost as frequently we find them taking life in order to gain money.

PROPERTY and life must be protected against dangerous criminals. When it is discovered that a boy or man is disposed to take for his own the property or life of another, the time has arrived when it becomes necessary to visit upon him the severest penalties.

Appropriating the Money of the Bank and the Final Consequences.

The Dishonest Confidential Clerk.

Sentenced to Imprisonment for Ten Years.

A YOUNG man, lacking moral principle and possessing ambitious desires, is entrusted by his employer to handle large sums of money. He sees his opportunity to speculate and make money, and cannot resist the temptation to steal. Too late he finds that he is ensnared.

ONLY a little time has elapsed since he stole his employer's money, yet he has been detected, tried, convicted and sentenced to imprisonment at hard labor. Reputation gone—prospects blasted—degraded to hardship and prison fare for ten long years—How sad the story!

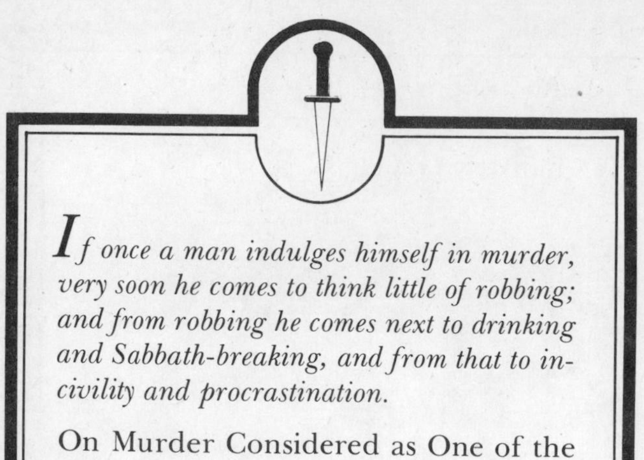

If once a man indulges himself in murder, very soon he comes to think little of robbing; and from robbing he comes next to drinking and Sabbath-breaking, and from that to incivility and procrastination.

On Murder Considered as One of the Fine Arts
THOMAS DE QUINCEY

the evidence unfolded a passionate, year-long yet secret romance.

Pierre Emile L'Angelier died of arsenic poisoning. The prosecution claimed Madeleine had murdered him rather than let him expose their shameful affair to her tyrannical father. Three of Scotland's most eminent lawyers handled the prosecution. For the defence appeared the Dean of the Faculty of Advocates, John Inglis, later to become Lord President of the Bench. With him were George Young, later Lord Young, and Alexander Moncrieff. The Ayrshire *Express* said Madeleine entered the court with the air of a belle entering a ballroom.

There were three charges: two of administering arsenic, one of murder. When the chancellor (foreman) of the jury announced the verdicts, they were: Not Guilty, Not Proven, Not Proven. It's said that Madeleine hoped for a complete acquittal, but there were too many extraordinary coincidences and oddities in the evidence for that — even though there was no proof that she actually did give Pierre the poison she had bought.

One could say that here the "bastard verdict" proved legitimate. Alas, almost exactly seventy years later it freed an equally young accused, John Donald Merrett, whose mother had died of a gunshot wound to the head. Mrs. Merrett had taken a fortnight to die after the injury and during that time was either unable or unwilling to explain how she received it. Donald insisted she had shot herself — and this was just possible, as she had money troubles.

It says much for the pleading of his defence and the uprightness of the jury that, despite the strong feeling against Donald, he was allowed to escape the death penalty through the Not Proven verdict. He was taken off to prison to serve a sentence for forging cheques, on completion of which he embarked on a life just as strange as its beginning.

He defrauded shopkeepers, married the daughter of a woman who claimed a title to which she had no right, became a smuggler and gun-runner during the Spanish Civil War and changed his name to Ronald John Chesney. He served in the Navy during World War II and acquitted himself well. In 1946 he was involved in the black market in Germany, became known to prison officials in various European countries and collected several mistresses.

At last, in 1954, he decided to get rid of his wife so as to marry his current girl friend and made a special trip from Germany to London. Later, his wife was found drowned in the bath and his mother-in-law, who seems to have been unlucky enough to have met him on the stairs, battered and strangled to death. The case against him mounted, and once it became known that Ronald John Chesney and John Donald Merrett were the same man, it seemed the police need only lay hands on him to bring the matter to a close.

But Merrett-Chesney settled the debt to society himself. He put his Colt revolver in his mouth and pulled the trigger. Thus ended a career which perhaps should have been cut off in the High Court of Justiciary in Edinburgh twenty-six years earlier.

The usual view of the Scottish verdict is: "We couldn't prove it this time, so you can go away. But don't do it again." In the case of Madeleine Smith, it worked. She lived on to a ripe old age in America, unheard of. In the case of John Donald Merrett, the accused didn't take the implied advice. In all other Not Proven murder cases, the advice has been heeded.

At least, so far as we *know* . . .

Avon Curry is a past chairman of the Crime Writers' Association.

HOW IT FEELS WHEN THE BAD GUY GETS OFF

Lee Fowler

New York is one of the toughest cities in the world, and those who know it well will agree the toughest part is the South Bronx: block after block of burnt-out buildings and empty lots; broken glass and tin cans; boarded-up windows and stray dogs. But the worst rubble is the humanity that lives there. Pimps. Pushers. Murderers. Junkies. Men who rape little kids. Kids who murder old ladies. "Animals," Ed Hayes calls them, and he should know. He was Assistant District Attorney, Bronx Homicide Division, for close on to five years.

Hayes earned a reputation as the A.D.A. who would take the worst cases, the ones no one else would touch because the crimes were so vicious and the "smoking guns" so scarce. He won them anyway. In 1976 he put more murderers in jail than anyone else in the city—more than sixty, twelve of them for life. "I executed them on behalf of the state," he says. "I figured, he hurt somebody, he deserved it. Sometimes I felt like an avenging angel."

Hayes talks tough, and until he quit, his was a tough world, with characters straight out of mystery books. There was the macho Italian cop who wouldn't walk through a blood-soaked room because he didn't want to get his white patent-leather shoes dirty; the defense lawyer who had a grudge against Hayes from a former case; the call girl who wanted to sleep with him in lieu of a fee; the girl who covered for her boyfriend after he'd raped and stabbed to death a seven-year-old.

In books, the bad guys always get caught, but Hayes saw it a little differently. Take his first homicide case. Two boys, eighteen and seventeen, beat an old man to a pulp, then strangled him in the back of his restaurant, took his money and left. Hayes was prosecuting the eighteen-year-old, who had been in and out of juvenile court on charges ranging from sodomy to rape to robbery.

"He was a real animal," says Hayes, "and we knew he'd done it. There was a witness, the kid they'd asked to be lookout. They'd told him they were going to have to kill the guy to do the job. But the jury didn't believe the witness be-

UNITED PRESS INTERNATIONAL

Manhattan's Supreme Court House, October 1937. The case being tried: a lurid divorce action. The women comprising the distaff half of the first mixed jury to ever serve repaired their make-up during recess.

cause by the time the case came to trial, he was doing time for blasting some guy's brains out with a shotgun. How could the jury believe him?

"Anyway, I did this real dramatic thing. The night before my summation, I got hold of the defendant's stepmother, who hated his guts, and who'd seen him at the scene of the crime a few minutes before it happened. I had her flown in from California, and I put guards on her 'cause she was getting threats. It was like a scene from a movie. I brought her in the last day of the trial, guarded by this mean-looking cop who'd killed so many guys, he didn't care any more. And the cop had his hand in his coat, resting on his gun, and he was looking from side to side, just waiting for somebody to make a move. But the jury didn't want to believe her either, because she was a heroin addict and a prostitute. It was a case where the jury didn't know who to believe, so they acquitted him. After the trial, the guy comes up to me and says, 'Hayes, I told you I was gonna beat it, and I beat it,' and I said, 'Yeah, pal. *You* beat it.' You want to know how I felt after that? I went out for a big Italian dinner at this place in Brooklyn, and when I got home I spent all night vomiting it up."

There's another way real life isn't much like books. "There's too much magic in them," according to Hayes. "In real life you win cases because you do everything you're supposed to do, every time you're supposed to do it, and then the percentages work in your favor. Plodding, slow, lots of detail. That's why I like the Sjöwal and Wahlöö stories, because they're real life. You work your ass off checking everything out, and then, maybe, you get a break. The greatest compliment I ever got, someone said, 'If that f——— guy had to throw himself in front of a train to do something for a client, he'd do it.' "

THE MYSTERIOUS WITNESS

THE DEFENSE ATTORNEY'S CREED

If you don't have the law, bang the facts.

If you don't have the facts, bang the law.

If you don't have the law or the facts, bang the table.

Even hard work doesn't always work. "Another real animal," says Hayes, "we knew he was guilty from the lie detector test. He asked what it was, and when they told him it would tell if he were guilty or innocent, he didn't want to take it. But his lawyer stressed it could be used to show he was innocent. Well, he took it. And it showed he was guilty.

"All I had was circumstantial evidence, but I presented every bit of it. I was unbelievably well-prepared. And then we got a hung jury. I went crazy. Everybody knew the guy. He'd done time for rape and robbery, and now he'd thrown a little kid out of a window. The cop who picked him up told me later if he had known what that guy had done when he'd picked him up, he'd never have taken that m———f——— alive. I know just how he felt.

"It never would have happened to Perry Mason. That guy gets all the breaks. Witnesses are always breaking down on the stand for him. His clients are always innocent. How are you going to beat that? I feel sorry for Hamilton Burger. Lew Archer I like because he's tired, and you're always tired. Tired of finding out things aren't what they seem, tired of seeing here's another bad guy." Which, in part, is why Hayes left the D.A.'s office. "No matter how many times you put guys away, you still couldn't bring people back. I felt terrible for those poor people."

He still reads thrillers for relaxation, however, but not the ones with bodies strewn all over the place. "There aren't that many murders in real life," he explains. "Murder is cathartic. One guy gets mad at another and kills him, but then he's done for the day. Except in mob warfare, when they're killing guys left and right, and all you can do is stand back and watch.

"I like to read George Higgins; he's got the dialogue down pat, the treachery that's a normal part of criminal behavior. I like Robert Parker because he understands cops. In one of his books he had three or four cops talking about putting lead in a guy, and that's just the way cops do talk, only they don't do it. I also like him because his hero is a real physical fitness freak and likes gourmet food, and that describes me."

Hayes, in fact, has all the attributes of a good fictional hero: he's tall, lean, blond, good-looking, and meets one woman for dinner and another for the late shift. He also has a fondness for hand-tailored suits and handmade shoes.

He's also not above a little courtroom his-

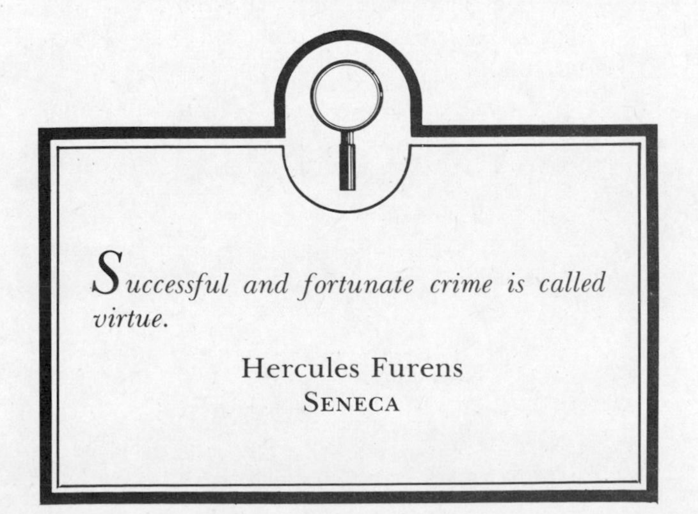

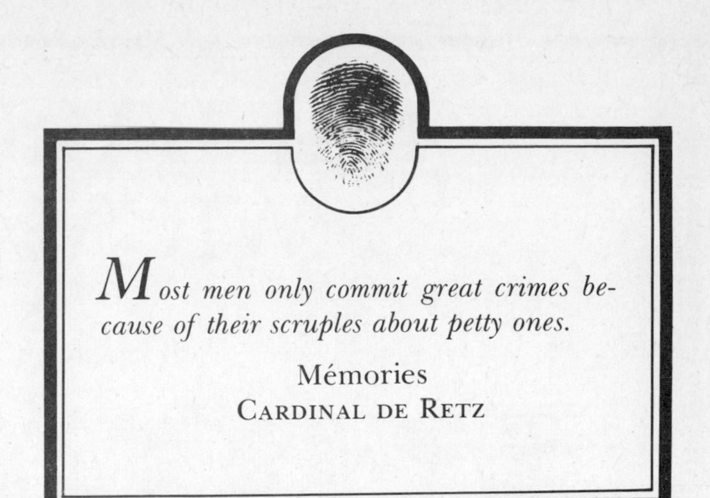

trionics. He modeled one summation after the famous Dreyfus case *J'accuse.* "I started soft. 'Nothing I can say can equal the loss of this man to his family. Nothing I can say can describe the horror of his death. The only thing you can say is guilty.' "

He came close to tears during that summation. "I was believing everything I was saying. I kept thinking how terrible it was. And I can tell you exactly how I felt when that guy got off. I felt like shit."

Perhaps this is why Hayes identifies with Marlowe. "He knows most people are dishonorable. He knows you can't win every time. But at least you can try."

Once Hayes actually started to write his own thriller. There were three heroes: an old street-wise black detective; a young Irish cop who'd been brought up in the tradition of old Irish cops and wasn't quite at home in the new police department; a young Spanish detective who really believed in the system. In Hayes' story, the detectives were on the trail of some pushers who were being ripped off by a group of narcs, and somewhere in the middle of it all, the Irish cop's girl friend got killed because she was an A.D.A. and was getting onto the narcs. In the last scene, there was a big showdown — narcs, pushers, detectives. Only the detectives lived.

In Hayes' book, the bad guys don't get off.

Lee Fowler is a New York-based writer who dotes on crimes of passion.

THE BARRISTERS' WIGMAKER

Ede & Ravenscroft has been the barristers' wigmaker since 1689. Here, the late Mr. Ravenscroft prepared one of the made-to-measure wigs. A wig takes about a month to complete, but there is a three- to four-month waiting period as the demand is so great.

Young Mr. Clifford, an apprentice, prepares a wig. Like all barristers' wigs, it has two pigtails and four rows of little curls. (The judges' wigs do not.) It is made bleached horsehair and costs £88.50 from the London headquarters of Ede & Ravenscroft.

Mrs. Kathleen Clifford, head of the Wig Room, stands in the Bar Room, to which the barristers retire for a fitting. She is holding a judges' shoe. Also available: judge's britches. On the table are the famous black and gold Ede & Ravenscroft carrying cases — the oval circuit box (for exporting wigs), the tray case (for everyday bench wigs), the full-bottomed circuit box (for judges' wigs).

To make a wig, five separate head measurements must be taken. These are done at one fitting. Then the wig is shaped on various sized wig blocks. The darker grey the wig, the more it is regarded as a "status" symbol.

COURTESY COLIN R. MACER

THE OLD BAILEY

The Old Bailey is one of the most familiar court buildings in the world, standing as it does in the centre of London. It is surmounted by a copper dome and a fifteen-foot gilded statue of the figure of Justice. One hand of the figure holds the traditional scales of justice, and the other the symbolic sword. This particular statue is unique in that it is not blindfolded. Over the door of the building are carved the words: "Defend the children of the poor and punish the wrongdoer."

The site of the Old Bailey had a long criminal history as Newgate Prison. Standing next to Newgate was a building known as the Justice House, or, alternatively, the Sessions House. This was erected in 1550 "over against Flete Lane in the old bayley." The latter referred to the street it was built on, and the building soon acquired that nickname. John Stow, a writer in Shakespeare's time, believed the name came from the word "ballium," used to describe an open space in front of the old wall of the Sessions House to allow guards and watchmen a better view. The ballium in front of the original Newgate Prison was on ground rising from what is now Ludgate Hill. Londoners called it Old Ballium, which has been corrupted into Old Bailey.

A new Sessions House was built in 1774, and this also became known as the Old Bailey; it was extended in 1824 and again in 1834, but it was always too small for the increasing court work of London.

In 1902, the old Newgate Prison and the Sessions House were demolished to make way for the Central Criminal Court, which would accommodate all the criminal work of London and the surrounding area. In 1907, it was opened by King Edward VII, but it immediately assumed its old nickname and again became the Old Bailey.

BRITISH TOURIST AUTHORITY

The figure of Justice atop the Old Bailey is unique in that it lacks the traditional blindfold.

During the opening ceremony, the King said, "The barbarous penal code which was deemed necessary one hundred years ago, has been gradually replaced in the progress towards a higher civilisation, by laws breathing a more humane spirit and aiming at a nobler purpose."

The Old Bailey is purely a criminal court and has no civil jurisdiction. It is now a crown court and continues to provide the location for some of England's most famous trials.

P.N.W.

THE DIFFERENCE BETWEEN A BARRISTER AND A SOLICITOR

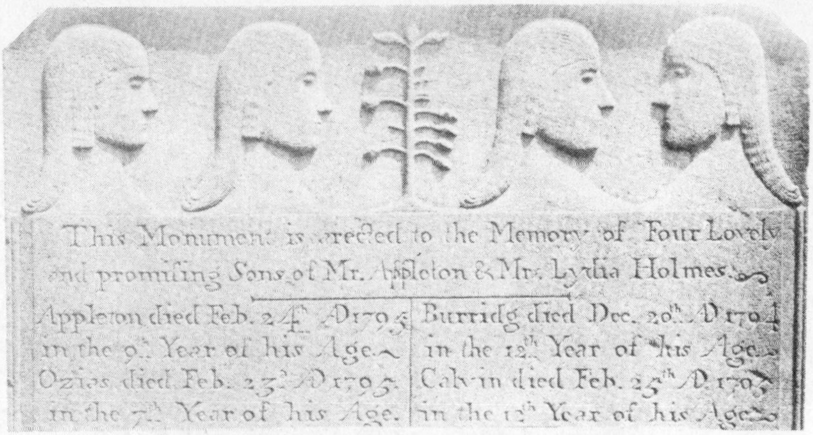

The solicitor is the general practitioner of the law, but the law is so vast that no general practitioner can give you detailed advice on every part of it. Therefore, a solicitor has to have specialists to go to — in exactly the same way that doctors have specialists to turn to. That is the primary role of the barrister in England. He is a specialist in his own branch of the law — tax, patents, whatever it may be. It has nothing to do with wearing wigs in court.

In Italy I found that one firm of *avvocati* would freely consult another firm who happened to have a reputation for knowing more about a particular branch of the law. In England this rarely happens. Solicitors in difficulty consult barristers.

Barristers also have a secondary role. They hold a monopoly on the conduct of pleading in certain courts. The parameters are getting narrower, but at the moment the barristers' monopoly is total in the High Court, in the Court of Appeals and in the House of Lords. However, there are many other courts — crown courts, police courts, magistrate courts and tribunals, quasi-judicial bodies that are springing up everywhere — and in all of these a solicitor is allowed to stand on his feet and plead. (If he doesn't want to, of course, he can hire a barrister to do it for him.)

This is not dissimilar, I understand, to what takes place in the United States, where in large firms some do court work and others do desk work. The difference is that they're not called by separate names, and they are all in the same firm.

One geographical restriction on barristers is that they have to retain office space in one of the four Inns of Court (Grays Inn, Lincoln's Inn, Inner Temple or Middle Temple). Unfortunately, there are many more barristers than there are rooms. Two barristers of my acquaintance (both now very successful) started by sharing a mantelpiece.

Michael Gilbert is a lawyer and one of the twelve founding members of the Crime Writers' Association.

PRISONS

Getting In — Getting Out

Thomas M. McDade

COURTESY METRO-GOLDWYN-MAYER

So you want to visit a prison . . . just to see what it's like. Well, in the first place, nothing you see will give you an inkling of prison life as it affects the inmate. I have been in many, I won't say the good and the bad, as there are no good prisons. Let us say the better and the worse — Leavenworth, Joliet, Green Haven, Riaford, Alcatraz, Huntsville, Sing Sing, Raleigh. All I have learned is a smattering of customs, rules, schedules and argot. Only the man who has done time is qualified to say what prisons are really like.

For the non-inmate, getting in is harder than getting out. For example, at the gate you must clear the electronic metal detector. How often, having emptied my pockets of change and keys, the machine kept clicking and I had to remove my belt (metal buckle) and even my shoes (because of the steel arches). And this at a prison I had been visiting for years, where I was known to the guards!

Don't carry pills or a pocketknife with you when you visit; you would have to leave them at the entrance gate. But you can bring food, clothing or reading matter. Such things are left at the gate for examination and passed to the inmate later. Money may be left for credit to his account; inmates may not have money in their possession.

The visiting rooms have changed in recent years. Formerly, you were separated from the inmate by a metal grille or glass shield. Direct contact with the inmate was forbidden, and in many cases you had to speak to him on a telephone. Now you generally sit opposite him and talk over an open counter in a large room where fifty visitors may be seeing inmates at the same time. Before the inmate arrives at the visiting room he is frisked by a simple pat-down; when he leaves to return to his quarters, he must be strip-searched to ensure that no contraband was slipped to him.

No tour of the prison will include a look at the punishment cells. Officially known as Segregation, the area has some innocuous name like C Block or Block 14, but to all the inmates it is known as "The Hole." In the old days it literally was a hole — often an underground cell with no light. Inmates might sleep on a stone floor in a freezing cell, often without clothing and toilet facilities. Sadistic guards have been known to hose down inmates with cold water. Those who want details can find them in the decisions of the federal courts. A case in point is Wright v. McMann 387 F2d 519.

The courts, the riots and the activities of a number of agencies have forced the authorities to provide a minimum of the necessities: a toilet, blankets, light and a reasonable amount of food. Now in the modern prisons Segregation is hardly different from the remainder of the facility. Recently, visiting an inmate in "The Hole" of a state prison, I was escorted by a guard down a lengthy corridor to a distant steel door. He rang a bell, another guard eyed us through a peephole and finally we were let in. Through two more steel doors we came to a block of cells, in one of which sat my client. He was the only inmate in the block, his cell door was open and he had the run of the area, which resounded with the noise of his radio. The latter amenity is optional depending on the reason for the segregation. In some cases inmates are put in "The Hole" for their own protection.

You might think it odd to have to make an appointment to see a prisoner; after all, you would hardly expect him to be "*not* in." At a women's prison I called to see an inmate then in the fifteenth year of a life sentence for murder. I went on a Saturday, and when I told her I had thought of waiting until Monday, as inmates are often occupied on weekends, she said, "Oh, I wouldn't have been here then."

"Where would you have been?" I asked.

"I have a job at IBM; I go there weekdays."

It seems that after the day's work as a punch card operator she would go by bus to a community college where she was studying, then about 9:30 P.M. take a train to a station where a prison car would pick her up. So today, with furloughs, work release programs, college courses and often court appearances, you do have to make an appointment to catch the inmate "at home."

A typical prison day starts at 6:30 A.M. with a bell ringing in the cell block. Inmates have an hour to rise, wash and dress. The cell doors open at 7:30 A.M. with the completion of the first head count. Release from the cell tiers is staggered so that all the inmates will not be moving to the mess hall at the same time. By 8 A.M. they are on their way to their jobs in laundries, workshops, hospitals and kitchens. At 11:30 A.M. they return to the mess hall and by 12:15 P.M. are back in their cells for a lock-in head count. From 1 P.M. to 3 P.M. they are at work again, after which there is yard recreation till 4:15 P.M. in winter or 7:30 P.M. in summer.

Good jobs are as hard to come by in prison as they are outside. Best pay is for those with a skill: carpenters, electricians, painters and top clerks are in Grade IV and earn $1 to $1.15 per day, often with double pay for overtime. The lowest grade of common labor runs from 35¢ to 50¢ per day. If the institution has no job to assign, the inmate gets 25¢ per day as unemployed. If he is offered a job and refuses it, he can be classified "idle," for which he will get no pay and, in addition, may have to spend all his time in his cell.

If a prisoner has a highly rated job, he will have a "runner's" pass which permits him to move about freely on the inside. The law clerks in the law library are in this favorable category. Other inmates get a special pass as required which permits them to move from one area to another. What the visitor soon realizes is that most of the day inmates are visible in large numbers all over the institution while guards are few and far between.

As I recall it, one of the great scenes from *The Big House*, an early prison picture, took place in the dining hall, where hundreds of cons banged their cups on the tables and chanted in time . . . a sort of mess hall strike. Eating today in some prisons is different.

"I haven't been in the mess hall in six months," was the surprising answer one of the inmates gave to my question about the quality of the food. How did he eat? "Oh, I make my own arrangements." It was then I learned about the commissary and the dozens of private "kitchens" hidden about the institution in workshops, art classes, gymnasiums, chapels and paint shops.

Remember the army PX? Well, prisons have them, too, except they are called commissaries. Prices are generally lower than in

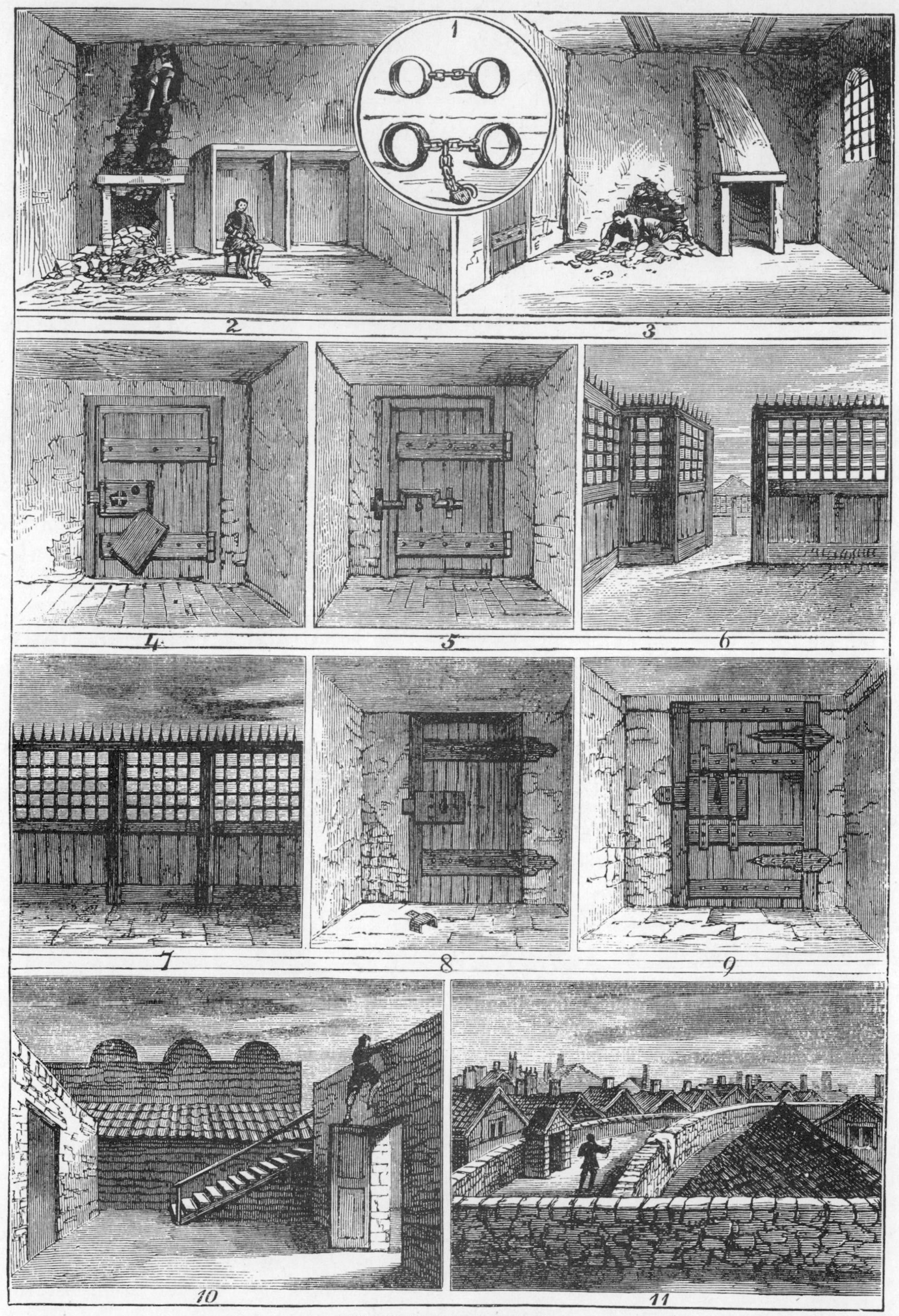

JACK SHEPPARD'S ESCAPES.

1. Handcuffs and Feetlocks, and Padlock to Ground. 2. Cell over the Castle, Jack Sheppard fastened to the floor. Climbing up the Chimney, where he found a bar of iron. 3. Red Room over the Castle, into which he got out of the Chimney. 4. Door of the Red Room, the lock of which he put back. 5. Door of the Entry between the Red Room and the Chapel. 6. Door going into the Chapel, which he burst open. 7. Door going out of the Chapel towards the Leads. 8. Door with a Spring Lock, which he opened. 9. Door over the same Passage. 10. The Lower Leads. 11. The Higher Leads, the walls of which he got over, and descended by the staircase off the roof of a turner's house into the street.

your supermarket and the more than 300 items listed, with regular stock numbers, include garlic powder, red clam sauce and Fig Newtons — this last being, at one time, the basic unit of exchange in an economy in which money is banned.

Maximum-security prisons are not quite so casual, but even they have their "courts" where wood stoves improvised from steel drums dot the yard and cons may prepare their evening meal and dine as one might in one's own club.

The visitor may be surprised at the variety of clothing worn by the prisoners. In New York the inmate must wear the regulation green trousers; all other items of clothing are optional.

The question of beards and haircuts is still not fully resolved. Can you conceal a weapon in an afro? Some prisons are fairly liberal on the question of hair styling; others claim that long hair and beards disguise identity and, therefore, seriously limit them. But generally the arbitrariness of prisons is easing. Mail censorship is limited to a cursory check of articles to prevent dangerous contraband; when writing letters out, the inmate seals them himself and in most places there is no restriction on the number of letters he may write. Books and magazines of almost any kind are now admissible, and where once periodicals could only be received from the publisher, the source is no longer a matter of interest.

When an inmate is discharged, he is given "gate" money ($40 in New York, along with a railroad ticket to his home) and a suit of clothes. The suits were once made in the prisons; now they are purchased. Few of those being discharged take the pair of shoes offered them. They are Navy-type brogues and, in the street world, a sure sign that he has just been released.

Charlie Scaffa, one of the great private detectives, told me some years ago of a man who visited his office.

"Look at me," the caller said, "prison suit, prison shoes. I just got out. I can't let my friends see me like this."

He wanted Charlie to lend him some money to get some new clothes. Charlie, who had never seen him before, asked him what he had been sent up for and who he knew. In the language of the street he was a "heavy" — a gunman. On the strength of his criminal connections Charlie gave him $150 and thought that would be the last he would see of him. A month later he saw the man drive by in a big new car. Not long after that his phone rang.

"Charlie", asked the con, "are you interested in that load of furs they took last night?"

"Yes, I am," said Charlie. "I'm handling the case for the insurance company. Do you know anything?"

"You can find the load in a warehouse on Degraw Street" was the reply.

That afternoon, with the police, Charlie recovered $50,000 worth of hijacked furs — all for his investment of $150 in an ex-con's wardrobe.

Seeing the inmates moving freely about the corridors and rooms, strolling in the yard in sportswear, you almost forget you're in a prison. Then one scene can quickly bring you back to reality. Arriving early one day, I noticed some buses waiting at the main gate. When I was passed in by the guard, I was asked to wait in a sitting room near the entrance. An unusual shuffling sound made me look up. A line of prisoners was moving through the room. Were they ill or injured? Their steps seemed faltering and slow. Each prisoner had a pair of leg irons around his ankles; a long chain ran the whole length of the line, linked to each pair of irons. Yet it was strangely silent. There was no clank of metal, only the scuffling sound of their shoes. Each marcher was holding the end of a cord in his right hand, the other end of which was fastened to the long chain so it could be kept from dragging on the floor. The line moved through in slow motion, out the door and into the waiting buses. The men were being transferred to another prison.

Thomas M. McDade was an FBI agent and supervisor back in the Thirties. He has served as legal counselor to the inmates of two prisons. In 1961 he received an Edgar from the Mystery Writers of America for his bibliography of American murder trials, The Annals of Murder.

INTERVIEW WITH A WARDEN

William Gard doesn't call himself a warden; he calls himself a superintendent. But then, he doesn't call it Sing Sing, either; he calls it the Ossining Correctional Facility.

Regardless of the wishes of Gard and the New York State Department of Correctional Services, the old names persist. A sign facing the metal detector at the prison's entrance lists "Sing Sing" protocol and a retiring guard who stopped by Gard's office to say good-bye kept referring to him as "Warden."

Gard has spent thirty-one years in the prison system, beginning as a machine-shop instructor at Auburn in 1945. In 1950 he took the Civil Service examination, passed it and became a guard. Another exam in 1960 made him a sergeant and another in 1967 made him a lieutenant. In 1970 he made captain, in 1972 he was appointed deputy superintendent and finally in 1975 he was named superintendent.

His large office has a spectacular view of the Hudson, if you don't mind viewing it from behind bars. Says Mr. Gard, "I don't even see the bars. I suppose it's the same in any occupation; after a while, you just don't notice things. I'm sure the engineer doesn't see the grease on the floor, either. It's a way of life."

He's not the only one not to notice things. The old death chamber where Julius and Ethel Rosenberg were electrocuted is now a changing room for prisoners. They barely comment on it as they put their civilian clothes into lockers on returning from their community work placements.

Mr. Gard, and 360 other officials, watch over a prison population of 800, most of whom are in transit to other correctional facilities. Sing Sing has become a "processing" depot in recent years, rather than a permanent Big House. The Department wisely preferred to locate prisoners elsewhere when they realized Sing Sing was the only prison in the country with a major railroad running straight through the middle of it.

But back in the good old days the likes of Willie Sutton were guests here. Mr. Sutton didn't much like the accommodations and broke out, a remarkable feat when one considers that Sing Sing was built along the lines of Cheops' pyramid, with massive walls and floor-to-ceiling bars at every major corridor junction.

Mr. Gard is a low-key, soft-spoken man when he talks about himself, but turn him to the subject of what makes a criminal a criminal and he bursts with the emotionalism of the revivalist preacher. "He's the victim of the society you and I continue to tolerate, and if we return him to that environment, you and I are guilty," he shouts. "Clean up those damn ghettos out there. Reduce unemployment so he can find a job when he gets out of here. It's a fact of life these people never had a chance, and right now society is still not provid-

NEW YORK STATE DEPARTMENT OF CORRECTIONAL SERVICES

The warden's office at Sing Sing before remodeling. One table and two panels are all that remain.

ing them with one."

Well, what retraining is actually done at Sing Sing, then? "Look," says Gard, "you can learn every aspect of the business here. If a man wants to spend his whole sentence learning how to hijack a liquor truck, he can probably get very professional training in that in here. On the other hand, he can also earn a college degree. That's available, too."

License plates are no longer the main outlet for keeping prisoners' idle fingers busy, it seems.

Still, the prison librarian and one of the guards seemed to think a prisoner was more apt to learn to be a moonshiner than anything else. Not a week goes by that the authorities aren't dismantling an illegal still somewhere on the premises.

One thing that's not a problem at Sing Sing is stool pigeons. Says Gard, "They don't approach me very often. It's known that I don't like them. They compare with the employee in a business who's always buttering up the boss, and it's always done for personal gain. An ego trip. They try to reverse their role: to assume the role of employee rather than inmate."

Gard's daily routine consists of touring the grounds and doing the usual amount of Civil Service paper work. He also, on occasion, sees prisoners who have some complaint. Now and then, there's a major crisis, such as the escape of two prisoners in 1976. Vacations? Mr. Gard gets four weeks off a year, but he can't remember the last time he used the full time. "I get bored," he explains.

ACCOMMODATIONS AT SING SING

A turn around the exercise yard in the early 1900's.

This doorway led to an old cell block housing the more recalcitrant inmates. Note thickness of wall.

When Sing Sing was a permanent facility, its inmates walked two by two, in formation, around the exercise yard.

For some prisoners the only way out was feet first. Sing Sing had its own burial grounds overlooking the Hudson.

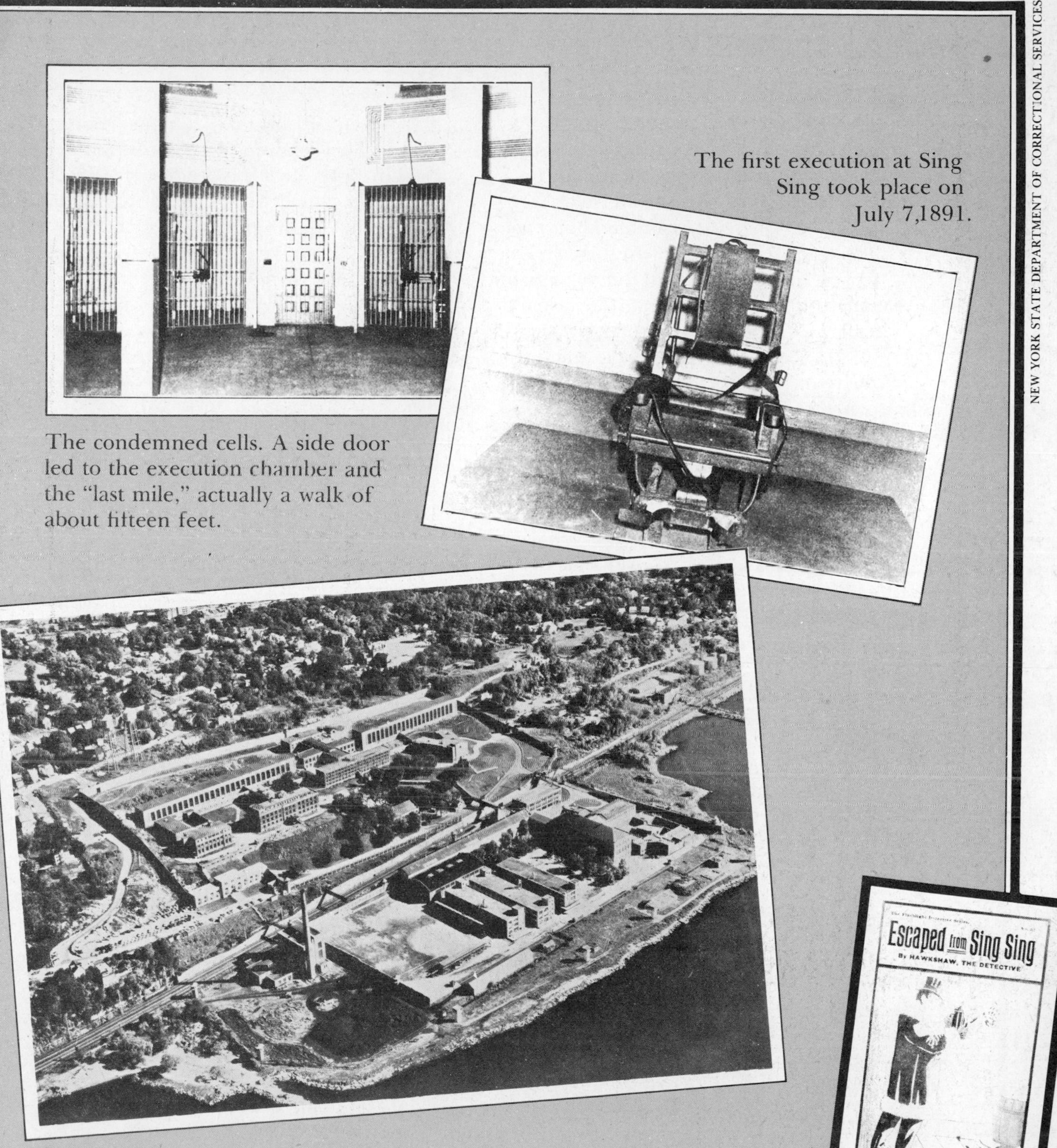

The first execution at Sing Sing took place on July 7,1891.

The condemned cells. A side door led to the execution chamber and the "last mile," actually a walk of about fifteen feet.

Sing Sing is the only U.S. correctional facility bisected by a railroad. Two prisoners escaped in 1976.

An early pulp by Hawkshaw, the detective, featuring the prison.

NEW YORK STATE DEPARTMENT OF CORRECTIONAL SERVICES

NEWGATE PRISON

Newgate's history is virtually inseparable from that of the Old Bailey; for over 1,000 years, criminals have been brought to Newgate Prison, London, for trial, imprisonment or even execution. The true origins of the prison have been lost in the passage of time, but it is known that the Romans built lock-ups here for their criminals.

It was the Britons who named the site New Gate. Henry I built a large prison here, calling it Heynouse Gaol of Newgate. The name Heynouse meant "hateful gaol." At that time, thieves were hanged without trial, and conditions in this gaol were appalling, even by mediaeval standards. Nonetheless, that prison lasted over 300 years, after which time the walls began to crumble and it became grossly neglected. Even so, it continued to be used.

COURTESY PETER N. WALKER

Prison Yard, Newgate, shortly before demolition in 1902.

When London's famous Lord Mayor, Sir Richard (Dick) Whittington, died in 1419, he left considerable sums of money which were used to re-build London's main prison, which was Newgate. Four years later, it received its first entry of new prisoners and became known as "Whit's Palace" in honour of Whittington.

The prison survived the Great Fire of London in 1666 and endured for some 350 years until London architect, George Dance, designed a bigger gaol. This one took eight years to construct and was completed in 1778. Unfortunately, it survived only two years: it was destroyed by the Gordon Rioters in 1780. Another Newgate Gaol arose on the site in 1783 and remained until 1902, when it was demolished to make room for the Central Criminal Court, which we all know as the Old Bailey.

Newgate Prison was always notorious for its cruelties and appalling conditions. For example, in Cromwell's time, a prisoner who refused to plead when standing trial by jury was pressed with heavy weights in an effort to make him plead. Without pleading, he could not be tried and condemned, and the object of the weights was to compel him to plead so the trial could continue. Many prisoners nevertheless continued in their refusal and so suffered an agonising death. Known as *peine forte et dure,* the procedure was carried out in a specially prepared chamber called the Press Room.

Another grisly tale about Newgate

is that when the prisoners left their cells for their last journey to a place of execution, the bells of nearby St. Sepulchre's Church would begin to toll. They tolled for the entire journey to Tyburn, three miles away. The custom was started in the seventeenth century by Robert Dow, who asked the sexton to call upon the accused to make his peace with God. The sound of the bell gave rise to the term "hanging march." This practice ended in 1890.

P.N.W.

THE BETTMAN ARCHIVE, INC.

Exterior view of Old Newgate Prison, 1902.

1833 broadside listing the results of trials the week of February 23 and February 27.

SENTENCES OF THE

PRISONERS,

IN NEWCASTLE and MORPETH who have taken their Trials at the assizes Feb. 23, 1833, before the Honourable Sir EDWARD HALL ALDERSON, Knight, and the Honourable Sir JOHN GURNEY, Knight, also a CALENDAR of the PRISONERS in DURHAM GAOL, who have to take their Trials at the Assizes, Feb. 27, 1833, before the aforesaid Knights.

NEWCASTLE GAOL.

CHARLOTTE CHARLTON, aged 21, charged with having assaulted Thomasin Errington, and stole 14s. 9d., one woman's pocket, and two thimbles.—*Death, recorded.*

JOHN TURNBULL, 20, charged with stealing a silver watch.—*7 years Transp.*

JAMES MACCAULER, aged 35, charged with having in his possession, nine false and counterfeit shillings, with intent to utter the same.—*6 months imprisonment.*

HINDMARSH THOMPSON, aged 49, charged with having stolen one silk umbrella, value ten shillings, and one cloak, value twenty shillings—[illegible]

ANN HOYLE, aged 41, charged with having stolen one harden sheet, one iron spoon, and one knife and fork, belonging Newcastle Infirmary.—*6 months imprisonment.*

GRACE NEILSON, 27, charged with stealing 8 sovs.—*14 years Transportation.*

GUISEPPE SIDOLI, 29, charged with killing H. Ross.—*7 years Transportation*

MORPETH GAOL.

JAMES GIBBESON, charged with burglary in his master's house. *Transported for life*

ANDREW BOHILLS, charged with stealing a metal roller—*4 months imprisoned*

JAMES COOK, charged with stealing a gold ring.—*Six months hard labour.*

THOMAS JEWITT, charged with cutting and wounding John Elliott, with intent to murder him.—*Transported for life.*

THOMAS ELLISON charged with maiming Mary Walker, at Hazlerigg.—Transported for Life.

WILLIAM GREY, charged with maiming Job Davies, at Hazlerigg.—Acquitted.

GEORGE MORDUE, Joseph Peel, and Henry Temple, charged with riot and assault at Hazlerigg.—To be tried next Assizes—out on bail.

THE HANGMAN'S STORY

Laurence Henderson

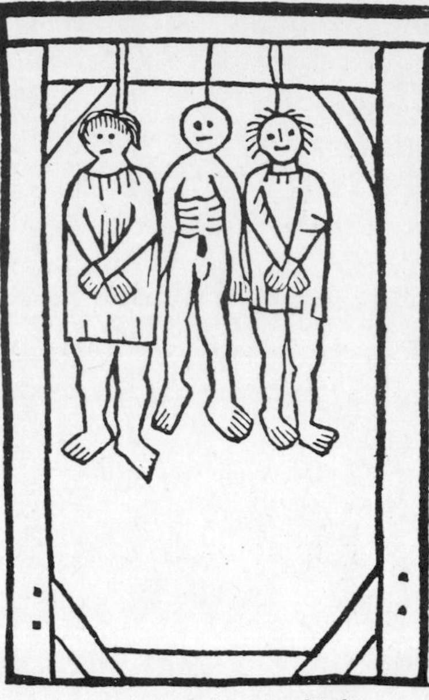

Teutonic hanging (multiple)

The last man to die on the scaffold in England was hanged in 1965, and when a few months later the capital penalty for murder was abolished, it ended a carefully calculated ritual of execution that had been followed for almost a hundred years. The code had arisen out of the rough-and-ready methods that had been used in the previous eight hundred years and, as finally adopted, had some claim to being the most efficient as well as the most humane method of state execution ever operated.

The man under sentence would be brought back to the prison in which he had been held during his trial, then taken not to his previous cell in the remand wing of the prison, but to a special cell that completely isolated him from the rest of the prisoners.

This cell contained a prison cot, table, chairs and an alcove with washbasin and toilet, and from the moment he entered the cell until the moment he finally left it two warders were constantly with him. Six warders were allocated to this special duty, rotating in pairs at eight-hour intervals. While in the cell, they not only watched the man but also engaged him in conversation, helped him to write letters if he was illiterate, played cards or other table games and generally kept him company. They also reported every word that the man uttered, and any reference to his crime was immediately forwarded to the Home Office official who was dealing with the case papers.

Three clear Sundays had to elapse between the passing of the sentence and its execution, a period originally laid down so that the man could reflect upon his crime, express remorse and make peace with his God. In practise this period was used by the defence lawyers to appeal against the sentence or, if there were no legal ground of appeal, then to petition for mercy. Also during this time the government official who was responsible for the case papers would be studying the case and collecting all relevant information, including an opinion on the man's sanity if this had not been an issue in the court hearing, and would then make a final

THE LAST COG IN THE LAW MACHINE

Anne Worboys

"That man," said somebody at the party, "is Albert Pierpont."

Albert Pierpont, the public hangman, not halfway across the room from where I was standing.

He was of smallish stature, his thinning hair cut short, back and sides. He had a broadish face with ruddy cheeks and pointed chin. He wore a navy blue suit and gaily striped tie. A Yorkshireman, they said, with a Yorkshireman's ability to speak his mind. (They don't call a spade a spade up there; they call it a bloody shovel.) He looked amiable enough to me.

"Do you want to meet him?" (They told me afterwards my eyes were sticking out like organ stops.)

"Give me a moment," I said.

What did I want to ask him? For a start, I wanted to know if he had ever had a grudge against society. A mental hang-up, with no pun intended. Then, how did he feel when pulling the switch/turning the handle/jerking the rope? And what did the Act of Parliament abolishing the death penalty mean to him, the man whose job it had been to destroy other men fairly consistently? More pertinently, what had he looked for since, to take the place of those high-tension days?

"Okay," I said, "let's go."

At closer range I saw he had the twinkliest eyes in the room. He seemed amused at the sight of this startled-looking woman approaching him.

He inherited the job, he said straightforwardly. His uncle had been the hangman before him and his father had been the hangman before his uncle. He simply followed on. I felt he was going to say, "Why not?" but he didn't.

He didn't feel anything, he explained. He didn't think about it. After all, he added, if he'd thought about it, he'd have gone mad, wouldn't he?

He said they would ask him to come at a certain time, and he would get on the train and go, do the job for which he was paid, then turn round and come home again.

What did he do after retiring as public hangman? He kept a pub.

Anne Worboys won the 1977 Romantic Novelists Association award for her suspense novel Every Man a King.

report to the Home Secretary. It was this minister who had the final decision on whether the sentence should be confirmed or commuted to life imprisonment.

During this time the man wore ordinary prison clothing except that the jacket and trousers were held together not by zips and buttons, but by tie-tapes, and that instead of shoes he would be given felt slippers. His food came from the prison kitchens, but the doctor could authorise any diet and in most cases the man could choose his own meals. He would also be allowed a daily amount of beer or liquor and, if a smoker, would be supplied with cigarettes or tobacco. He could choose any books that he wished from the lists of the prison library and he could read newspapers, so long as any reference to his own case had been deleted. He could write or receive any number of letters, but they first had to be read by the chief officer of the prison. Each day he would be visited by the prison governor, doctor and chaplain.

If the man had visitors, he would be taken from the cell to see them in a nearby interview room. Such visits were limited to thirty minutes unless otherwise sanctioned by the prison governor, who usually did so only if the visitor was the man's legal advisor. The man could also leave the cell to attend religious services in the prison chapel or to take exercise. This exercise was always taken alone, at a time when the other prisoners were either locked in their cells or at recreation.

The governor had to make a daily report on the man's health and demeanour, and it was also his task to tell the man when the sentence had been confirmed by the Home Secretary and that there was no longer any possibility of reprieve.

Once this decision had been taken, a long, japanned box was delivered to the prison and carefully locked away until it could be handed over to the hangman, who would arrive at the prison with his assistant sometime during the afternoon of the day before that set for the execution. Once inside the prison, he would be unable to leave again until the execution had taken place: a relic of the times when the hangman was inclined to arrive at the scaffold reeling from the gin shop.

This gibbet was typical of those erected in France in the sixteenth century. It was suitable for hanging up to twenty-four persons. The gentleman in the foreground is swatting away the low-flying buzzards.

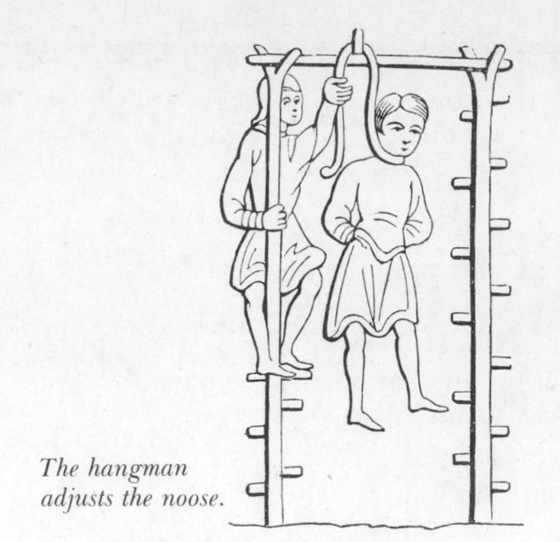

The hangman adjusts the noose.

The hangman would open the execution box and thoroughly examine its contents before signing that he was satisfied with the equipment provided. In the box were two six-foot lengths of inch-thick hemp rope, one end of each rope spliced around a two-inch brass-faced eyelet and the other lashed around a thick brass disc with a bolt hole drilled through its centre. The rope would be doubled back through the brass eyelet and for the first eighteen inches would be faced with chamois leather. Both ropes were precisely the same, but one was absolutely new and the other a rope that had already been used in an execution. It was the hangman's option as to which should be used. Also in the box was a white linen bag with tapes for putting over the man's head, a broad leather belt with attachment straps for his arms and a second belt to pinion his legs.

The hangman would be given details of the man's age, height and weight, as well as an opportunity to see the man without being observed so that he could form a judgement as to the man's general build and likely muscular strength. He would then sit down and make his calculation, take all factors into consideration and decide the length of drop that was required.

During that final evening, while the man was seeing a visitor or being exercised for the last time, the hangman and his assistant would enter the execution chamber, which itself was an extension of the condemned cell. The trap, measuring eight feet by five, was split along its centre, the two halves being hinged along the sides. At the end of the trap was a lever, held locked by a cotter pin, which, when operated, retracted the central bolts and allowed the two halves of the trap to drop away.

The trap was spanned some nine feet above by a heavy beam from which hung a number of chains, one of which was selected and bolted into position over the centre of the trap, its length being either taken up or extended according to the drop decided upon by the hangman. The selected rope was attached to the final link of the chain by a U-bar and bolt through the brass disc at the end of the rope. A bag of sand the same weight as the man would then be put into the running noose and the trap operated. If this worked to the hangman's satisfaction, the bag of sand would be drawn up, the trap reset and the bolts and lever reoiled. If the man was still out of his cell and time permitted, the hangman would finalise his arrangements by setting two hand ropes on the beam to hang on either side of the noose and putting two planks across the length of the trap below the hand ropes.

The hangman could also, if there was time, set the noose by taking it up to the approximate head height of the man, coiling the slack above the noose and then tying it in position with a piece of thread. If the man was expected to return to his cell, these final preparations would be made in the very early morning, if possible while the man was asleep, the important consideration always being that the man should hear nothing of the preparations that were being made on the other side of the thin, movable partition. On the morning of the execution the hangman and his assistant would enter the execution chamber, make a final check, and then, ready with the restraining harness, wait for the false wall to be moved aside.

In the cell the man would be with the prison chaplain, either seated at the table or, possibly, kneeling in prayer. The door of the cell would be opened by the chief officer, who would lead in the prison governor, doctor and either the Under Sheriff or some other representative of the Lord Lieutenant of the County in which the execution was taking place. As the man rose to face the group entering the cell,

The Execution of "Tipperary Bill" in the Yard of the County Jail, June 10, 1859. The curious well-to-do were allowed to watch, but other prisoners destined for a similar ending were barred from the proceedings.

When a man is hanged, the rope is jerked with such force it not only breaks his neck but leaves a severe rope burn. These markings are clearly shown on death casts, a collection of which are on display in the Black Musuem at New Scotland Yard. (The Wood Street Police Station Museum also has them.) These sketches appeared in a London newspaper on February 15, 1873. The rope marks are most obvious at the base of the neck and up behind one ear, where the rope lifted as the body dropped. Capital punishment is no longer practiced in Great Britain, although many law enforcement officials feel it will be reinstated within the next ten years. The last hangman was Albert Pierpont, who followed his father and his uncle in the job. Mr. Pierpont recently published his memoirs. Invited to the United States during World War II to act as consultant, he found American procedures not only antiquated but inhumane.

one of the warders slid aside the false wall for the hangman and his assistant to come forward.

The first awareness the man had of their presence was the restriction on his arms as they were brought into the harness. It was as the hangman turned him that he saw, for the first time, that the scaffold was only a few feet from the bed in which he had been sleeping for the past three weeks. While the hangman tightened the strap around the man's body, the two warders would take him by the elbows and walk him to the scaffold, keeping him between them as they stepped onto the planks and grasped the hand ropes with their free hands.

The hangman set the noose over the man's head while his assistant placed the final strap around the legs. The noose was then placed around the man's neck, and the hangman immediately stepped from the trap and pulled the lever; the doors of the trap crashed open and the condemned man disappeared between the two warders. The broken fragments of thread drifted slowly past a rope that hung as straight as an arrow, showing barely a shudder of movement from the tension placed upon it. The time taken from the moment the chief officer opened the door of the cell until the man fell through the doors of the trap would have been less than twenty seconds.

The hangman and his assistant would descend to below the scaffold, erect a ladder and take the man from the rope. The doctor would examine the body and confirm that death had occurred. Since under English law all unnatural deaths have to be inquired into, a local coroner and his jury would be waiting. The inevitable medical evidence would be that death had resulted from a fracture dislocation of the 2/3 cervical which had severed the cord. The coroner would then record the jury's verdict that death had resulted from judicial hanging and the body would be released for burial. This always took place immediately and within the precincts of the prison; the position and identity of the grave would be carefully recorded on a plan of the prison grounds, but the grave itself would be unmarked.

Laurence Henderson is the author of four crime novels. The most recent is Major Enquiry.

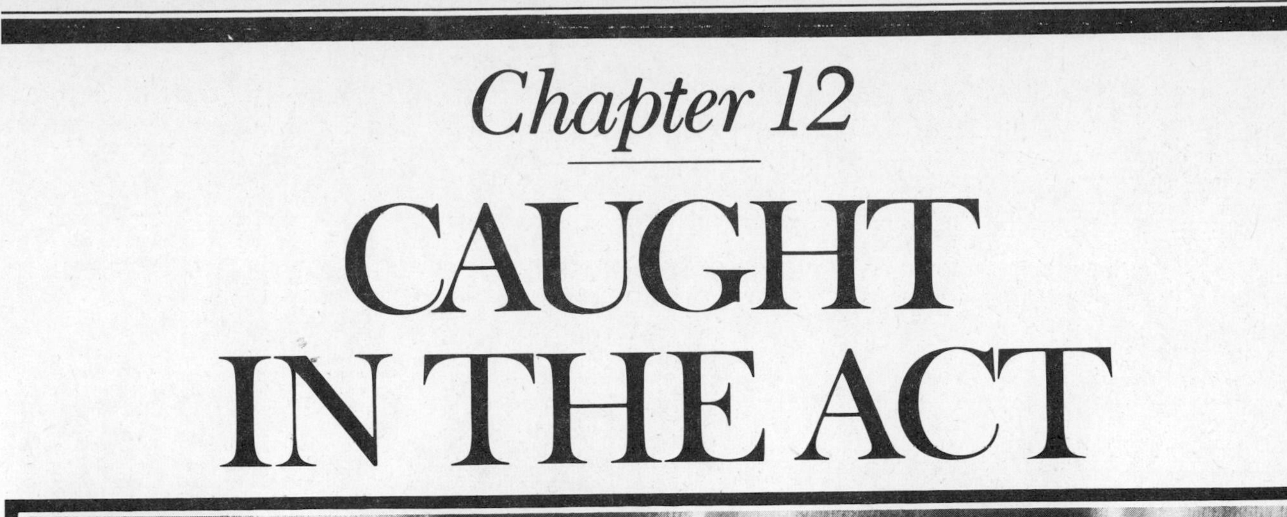

Chapter 12

CAUGHT IN THE ACT

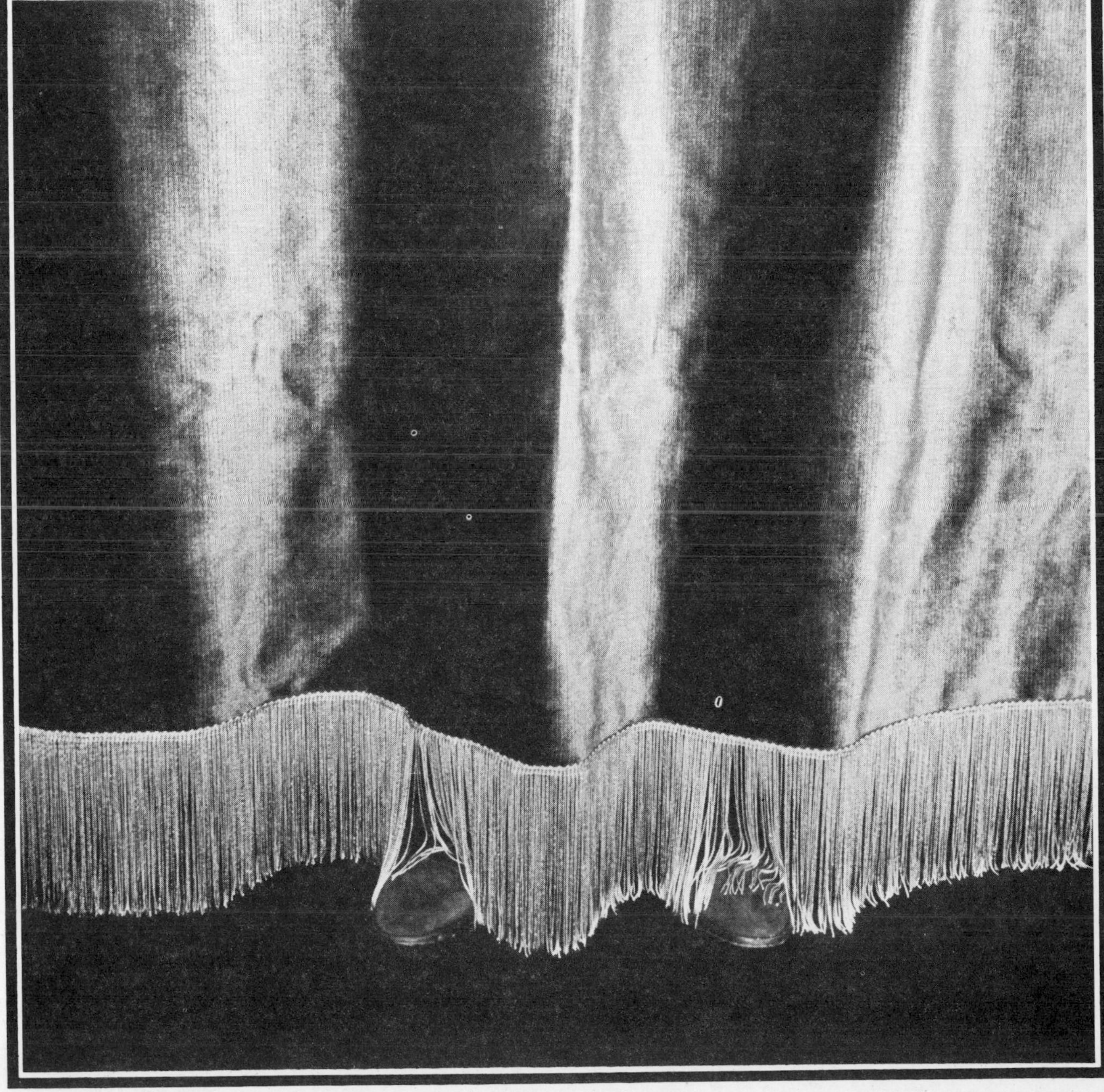

FRED WINKOWSKI

EXEUNT DYING

R.M. Whyte

Back in the old days (circa 1600) the primary charm of the crime play was its gore. The "sanguifulminous stage" was held by Shakespeare's *Macbeth,* Marlowe's *Edward the Second* and domestic tragedies such as *Arden of Faversham,* described on its title page as the tale of a man who "was most wickedlye murdered, by the meanes of his disloyall and wanton wyfe, who for the love she bare to one Mosbie, hyred two desperat ruffins, Blackwill and Shakbag."

This passion for they-done-its and this-is-how-they-done-its lasted until late in the nineteenth century. A constant parade of notorious felons was plucked from real life and thrust upon the stage to become the sensational rage. One drama even advertised that its central props (knife, pitcher of poisoned punch, bed, chair and bloodstained furniture) came direct from the victim's house. The audience was enthralled.

In 1899 William Gillette put Sherlock Holmes onstage and kept him there, virtually without pause, until 1931. Conan Doyle was so disinterested in the fate of Holmes he gave Gillette carte blanche to alter the character as he saw fit. Gillette threw him into the arms of a woman at play's end, which alarmed nobody at the time but greatly unnerved audiences when the play was recently revived by the Royal Shakespeare Company.

In 1912 the archetypal mystery melodrama was produced — *Within the Law* by Bayard Veiller. In it, Mary Turner, working girl, was railroaded into the slammer. When she was released she formed a gang of blackmailers and exacted her revenge by marrying the son of the man responsible for her imprisonment. Her immortal second-act curtain line, delivered to her enemy, Gilder Edward: "Four years ago you took away my name and gave me a number. Now — now I've given up that number and I've got *your* name!"

Within the Law also boasted the first stage appearance of the Maxim revolver silencer. Said the thug to the cops, "Some class that, eh? Them things cost sixty dollars and they're worth the money, too. They'll remember me as the first to spring one of them, won't they?"

Awful dialogue was the mainstay of the mystery play for years. Take this bit of dialogue from *The Bat* (1920): "Miz Cornelia, I've stood by you through thick and thin — I stood by you when you were a vegetarian, a Theosophist, and I seen you through socialism, Fletcherism and rheumatism — but when it comes to carrying on with ghosts . . .!"

THE EVER-RUNNING MOUSETRAP

It opened in London in 1952 and it's still one of the hottest tickets in town. New Yorkers, however, disliked it. It had a short Off-Broadway run, also in 1952, and closed quickly and quietly. Ironically, Londoners say it is the American tourists who keep it going in the West End.

The play is based on Christie's novelette *Three Blind Mice,* and the original London cast included Richard Attenborough and Sheila Sim, directed by Peter Cotes.

The last big hit in this melodramatic vein was John Willard's *The Cat and the Canary* (1922), which had a plethora of sliding panels, creaky stairs, clutching hands and, of course, victims. When the play reached London, it had a jingle attached to it: "If you like this play, please tell your friends; But pray don't tell them how it ends." Years later, as a student at the Yale School of Drama, I saw a New Haven tryout of a play which concluded with the star taking an ill-deserved bow (the moosehead on the wall in the first act was far the better actor) and asking the audience to observe that old 1922 jingle. (He didn't credit it, of course.) I was happy to oblige. A play can have an ending too bad, as well as too good, to reveal.

With the arrival of Agatha Christie's *Alibi* (1928), featuring Charles Laughton as Hercule Poirot, the mystery play became more sensible. It's been reported that Mrs. Christie felt Laughton was "utterly unlike Poirot, but a wonderful actor."

BROADWAY, BLOODY BROADWAY

1896 *Secret Service,* by William Gillette
1899 *Sherlock Holmes,* by William Gillette
1912 *Within the Law,* by Bayard Veiller
1913 *Seven Keys to Baldpate,* George M. Cohan
1914 *On Trial,* Elmer Rice
1920 *The Bat,* Mary Roberts Rinehart and Avery Hopwood
1920 *Trifles,* a one-act play by Susan Glaspell
1922 *The Cat and the Canary,* by John Willard
1926 *Broadway,* Philip Dunning and George Abbott
1928 *Diamond Lil,* by Mae West
1931 *Mourning Becomes Electra,* murder melodrama by Eugene O'Neill
1933 *Night of January 16th,* by Ayn Rand
1936 *Night Must Fall,* by Emlyn Williams
1939 *Angel Street,* by Patrick Hamilton
1940 *Ladies in Retirement,* by Edward Percy and Reginald Denham
1941 *Arsenic and Old Lace,* by Joseph Kesserling
1944 *Ten Little Indians,* by Agatha Christie
1948 *Murder on the Nile,* by Agatha Christie
1949 *Detective Story,* by Sydney Kingsley
1950 *The Innocents,* by William Archibald
1952 *The Mousetrap,* by Agatha Christie
1952 *Dial M for Murder,* by Frederick Knott
1953 *The Caine Mutiny Court Martial,* by Herman Wouk
1954 *Witness for the Prosecution,* by Agatha Christie
1956 *Towards Zero,* by Agatha Christie
1961 *Write Me a Murder,* by Frederick Knott
1962 *Rule of Three,* by Agatha Christie
1964 *Hostile Witness,* by Jack Roffey
1965 *The Desperate Hours,* by Joseph Hayes
1966 *Wait Until Dark,* by Frederick Knott
1966 *Loot,* by Joe Orton
1968 *The Real Inspector Hound,* by Tom Stoppard
1970 *Sleuth,* by Anthony Shaffer
1970 *Child's Play,* by Robert Marasco
1972 *Are You Now or Have You Ever Been,* by Eric Bentley
1976 *Something's Afoot,* by McDonald, Vos and Gerlach
1977 *Dracula,* production designed by Edward Gorey

That, however, was in London. In America 1926 ushered in *Broadway,* the *ne plus ultra* backstage–New York-night-club–show-biz–chorus-girl–Chicago-gunman–whoop-it-up, resolved by a corn-fed young detective named Dan McCorn. Which wasn't such a strange name, considering the other monikers involved: Ruby, Mazie, Grace, Porky, Joe, Lil and Scar Edwards. This play will long be remembered for its closing moments, when a character grabs his ukelele and admonishes the chorus: "Remember — you're all artists! Here we go — here we go!"

From downright silliness to an outright gimmick is not such a giant step, and Ayn Rand took it with *Night of January 16th* (1933). It was a courtroom drama whose proceedings were held up every night until a jury was selected from the audience. The play was written with two endings, and the cast inserted the appropriate one — depending on the jury's decision.

The psychopathic killer came trouping onstage in the character of Dan, the sinister bellboy of Emlyn Williams' *Night Must Fall* (1935). Williams wrote the play for himself to star in, and he had a laudable run of 435 performances. (Williams also tried his hand at the Rand trick ending with *A Murder Is Announced.)*

The first London psychological thriller was called *Ladies in Retirement,* set in an 1885 pre-Tudor farmhouse situated in Thames-side marshes, predictably near a somber convent. The play is still dusted off and given an airing by every middle-aged actress with any clout in a little-theater group. *Ladies* was a smash hit in New York, with Richard Watts, Jr., of the *Herald Tribune,* enthusing: "Just the sort of good, sound murder play that the dramatic season has been so insistently demanding!"

But 1941 brought an even bigger hit, *Arsenic and Old Lace,* a play which holds the stage the way gum sticks to the bottom of a theater seat. Helen Hayes has said, "I have played it twice and enjoyed every minute of it."

Relentlessly naturalistic dramas took over for a while, and these included *Detective Story* and *Dial M for Murder.* (Publishers guesstimate there are 350 amateur productions of *Dial M* a year, with another fifty or so stock-company presentations.) But the days of the mystery play

THE ROLE I WANT MOST

Jerry Stiller's Views

A man like Watson enthralls me. Why? Because he dabbles in crime, and what better way to deal with crime than to dabble in it?

I'd love to play Watson. Nigel Bruce, of course, was the embodiment of Watson, but that wouldn't stop me. With Bruce you could almost see the man stopping off at Fortnum & Mason's for some jams; you felt, all the time, how he catered to Holmes. Rathbone, as Holmes, accepted this. It was a case of two idiosyncratic men complementing each other.

My Watson would have a different relationship with his Holmes. I never thought of Watson as dumb; I always suspected he was well aware of what was going on, more aware than he let on. He humored Holmes at least as much as Holmes humored him, and that's what I'd like to bring out. After all, he always did manage to be where he was supposed to be — right in the middle of things — at the scene of the crime.

The Holmes I'd feel most comfortable with would be Richard Harris. I think we could show the two men as the deep friends they were, how they balanced each other.

No, I don't consider myself similar to Watson. We are far removed in character and style. But that's what makes playing him so appealing to me. In fact, I'm waiting for someone to ask me. Anyone. I'd do Watson anywhere, even in a community theater. But they'd have to get Harris, too.

on Broadway were numbered; the obsession for plot itself as the primary subject matter would soon go out of fashion. The last grand gasp of the traditional mystery was Christie's *Witness for the Prosecution* (1954), which won the New York Drama Critics' Circle Award as the year's best foreign play — the only mystery play ever to do so. This was Christie's second and last Broadway success. (*The Mousetrap* flopped.)

Recently, it's been bleak for mystery theater. *Sleuth* and *The Real Inspector Hound* are the only two productions to achieve any kind of audience acceptance, and there were those who considered them a put-on — a sort of intellectual hogwash. The mystery musical has fared even worse: *Baker Street* and *Something's Afoot* were scandalously inept. Only the revival of *Angel Street* (nee *Gaslight*) had any charm, and the critics were even unimpressed with that.

Broadway, however, is not the world. What won't play on the Great White Way *will* play in Paducah. Across America, in 30,000 high schools, 3,000 colleges and countless rep and stock companies, the mystery play — albeit an old one — is alive and well.

Charles Baker, co-head of the Macmillan Performing Arts Division, tried to explain this phenomenon: "Most mystery plays just don't look like blockbuster productions. If you pay $20 to see a play, you want to see every penny of it up on that stage. And it better be something you can't see on TV, or at the movies."

Christopher Sergel, of the Dramatic Play Service, had a few opinions as to why mysteries do so well regionally: "First, a large cast, with every role having a few good 'bits' in it. Next, the leads tip toward female characters, and

STAGE STRUCK: MYSTERIES WITH THEATRICAL THEMES

Dancers in Mourning: Margery Allingham
Exit Charlie: Alex Atkinson
Curtain Call for a Corpse: Josephine Bell
The Case of the Solid Key: Anthony Boucher
Death Steals the Show: John Bude
Panic in Box C: John Dickson Carr
Murder in Three Acts: Agatha Christie
The Backstage Mystery: Octavus Roy Cohen
Obsequies at Oxford: Edmund Crispin
The Candles Are All Out: Nigel Fitzgerald
Blood on the Boards: William Campbell Gault
Hamlet, Revenge: Michael Innes
Murder Off-Broadway: Henry Klinger
The G-String Murders; Mother Finds a Body: Gypsy Rose Lee
Death on the Aisle; Death Take a Bow: The Lockridges
Abracadaver: Peter Lovesey
They Can't Hang Me: Jacqueline Mallet
Enter a Murderer; Final Curtain; Killer Dolphin; Night at the Vulcan; Vintage Murder: Ngaio Marsh
Cue for Murder: Helen McCloy
Walking Shadow: Lenore Glen Offord
The Roman Hat Mystery; Face to Face: Ellery Queen
Puzzle for Players: Patrick Quentin
This Rough Magic: Mary Stewart

A VISIT WITH ONE OF THE SNOOP SISTERS

Mildred Natwick

In the late 1930's I was in a mystery play called *Night in the House,* based on a Hugh Walpole novel. It was a terrible flop, ran only three weeks. We were supposed to be three little old ladies living in a flat. One was a gypsy, I think. I owned a rare piece of amber that one of the other ladies wanted. So she murdered me for it. I was strangled, I believe. How did I play dead? I just lay there gasping for breath. And then slid off the bed onto the floor. The critics were not kind.

THE CRUMPLED TUTU AND THE SOURED NOTE: TWO CHECK LISTS

Opera productions just love to strew bodies across the stage. The soprano kills the tenor, the bass strangles the contralto and the chorus often does them all in. As for the ballet — well, have you ever known the swan to live? Obviously, these two stage disciplines hold great promise for the mystery writer. Below, a sampling of some of the better mysteries with ballet and opera themes.

THE CRUMPLED TUTU

Death in the Fifth Position: Edgar Box
A Bullet in the Ballet; Murder at La Stragonoff: Caryl Brahms and S.J. Simon
The Bali Ballet Murders: Cornelius Conyn and Jon C. Martin
Corpse de Ballet: Lucy Cores
Two If by Sea (Came the Dawn): Andrew Garve

THE SOURED NOTE

The Savage Salome: Carter Brown
Serenade: James M. Cain
The Bohème Combination: Robin Close
Dead and Dumb (Swan Song): Edmund Crispin
Ghost Song: Dorothy Daniels
The Photogenic Soprano: Dorothy Dunnett
Take My Wife: Winston Graham
Murder at the Met: Fred G. Jarvis
Death of a Fat God: H.R.F. Keating
The Blue Harpsichord: David Keith
The Phantom of the Opera: Gaston Leroux
Murder in the Opera House; Murder Meets Mephisto; Death Drops Delilah: Queena Mario
Murder Ends the Song: Alfred Meyers
Death at the Opera: Gladys Mitchell
Funeral of Figaro: Ellis Peters
The Fidelio Score: Gerald Sinstadt
Murder Plays an Ugly Scene: L.A.G. Strong
The Metropolitan Opera Murders: Helen Traubel
The Assassination of Mozart: David Weiss

drama departments usually have more women than men. The untricky set is easy to reproduce."

Stanley Richards, doyen of drama anthologists, is optimistic about the mystery play's future: "There aren't many right now, I know. Out of every two or three hundred plays I read, maybe twenty-five will be mysteries. Most of them come from England or Australia, because they still produce mystery plays on a professional level. We used to, but now there's a whole generation of American playwrights who haven't been exposed to quality, top-flight productions. It'll about-face, I'm sure. I know a truly wonderful short gothic mystery just coming out by avant-garde playwright Rochelle Owens. That's a good sign."

For the lover of mystery plays, this leaves only one option: play scripts. They, unfortunately, are a non–art form unto themselves. However, people do learn to cope with subtitled films. Stage directions, with a little practice, can be just as easily ignored.

Meanwhile, what's next for Broadway? Two of the more talented men around have set their sights on a mysterious Broadway. Edward Gorey has designed the sets and costumes for a production of *Dracula* and Stephen Sondheim is readying *Sweeney Todd, the Demon Barber of Fleet Street* as a musical.

But there is one harbinger of doom. Stanley Richards believes "our theater audiences have gotten out of just being entertained. They aren't prepared for mystery plays any more."

R.M. Whyte is the Soho Weekly News *book editor.*

THE FIRST SUCCESSFUL MYSTERY MOVIE

Richard Townsend

MEMO: To Studio Chief Fred Fellsberg
FROM: Richard Townsend
RE: My screenplay for Big Bread-Making mystery movie

Persuant to our confab at the World Trade Center last Tuesday. You're absolutely on target, F.F. The time is ripe for a moola mystery. It's très clear this genre hasn't been making it on the big screen because of the intrinsic difference between hard covers and hard core. The literary mystery is a study in the intellectual process of unwinding the layers of death, deceit and destruction that dwell deep within our domes. But movies mean *action.* Direct, devastating, de-lovely. So I've come up with a sure-fire dazzler that'll keep the people flocking to the box office and leave them starved for a sequel. The idea is to bring together in one flick everything the public wants. It'll be expensive and time-consuming, but what does that mean when the fate of our beloved studio is at stake. *Gone with the Godfather,* an interplanetary love story with music, has got *IT*!

Our hero, a New York Jewish Intellectual, is played against type by Woody Allen, who starts the action by returning to his Fifth Avenue duplex to discover the nude, mutilated and expiring body of Sissy Spacek. Dangling from Sissy's hand is a large glass key, unfortunately broken in two but with the name Liza written across it. Just as Woody wonders whoever Liza could be, his phone rings and his ex-girl friend Diane Keaton is calling from Hollywood to ask for his help with a few quick jokes, since her best girl friend Liza Minnelli has appeared at her Malibu shack, hysterical with rage and fury at having been sadistically beaten by her lover, Art Carney. Woody calms down the two women and casually asks Liza if she's the owner of the other end of a glass key. Choking on her hot chocolate, Liza screams and goes into a coma, forcing Woody to grab the next flight for L.A. On his arrival at the hospital Diane has mysteriously disappeared, leaving only a mute Liza to respond to Woody's questions with a slight quaver of her eyelids. As Woody leans over Liza, he is hit over the head.

Upon awakening, he finds himself in a large blimp flying over Shea Stadium. Although he is deeply drugged, he dimly recognizes a white-haired, white-uniformed

JOSEPH PAPIN

dwarf, played by Marlon Brando, who appears to be cutting at him with scissors and forceps. When fully awake, he finds he is now played by Robert Redford, as total plastic surgery has been necessitated by the knowledge he possesses but cannot interpret. Marlon the Magician explains that a less obvious face like that of the blond bombshell Bob will render him unnoticeable, especially to women. As Woody-Bob is digesting this info, the blimp careens down into the stadium, dropping poison pellets in the form of free hot dogs, which are lapped up by an ignorant populace. "They're all Communists," says the grinning Marlon, who parachutes out a tunnel of the crazily cavorting blimp speeding our hero into outer space.

Landing on the freezing planet of Oz, Woody-Bob is welcomed by its Queen, Ozetta, a gospel singer, winningly played by Barbra Streisand, who sings the title song, "Gone with the Godfather." It seems that after losing the role of Scarlett in the *Gone with the Wind* remake, Ozetta has taken her rock band, and a fan following of 80 million people, and started a new world in which she'll have no competition. Craftily, she inquires about Liza's stroke, and Woody-Bob knows there's something afoot. Before he can answer, Barbra has him tied and nailed to a huge microphone, and as she seals a permanent Steve McQueen mask across his face and almost naked body, she tells him she must have him as her singing co-star for her remake of *Ben-Hur*. So Woody-Bob has now turned into Woody-Bob-Steve, who's sexier and more expensive than anybody.

When Barbra's back is turned, a little waif played by Tatum O'Neal appears to spirit Woody-Bob-Steve off to the remote estate of her Godfather, Charles Bronson, who needs a good ring-kisser fast. Jumping into Tatum's Toyota, the twosome zip across a bloody desert, strewn with the hands and limbs of folk who didn't recognize Godfather Charles as the top banana. Fade into Big Charlie's plantation, where he's having a porno romance with his moll Farrah Fawcett-Majors. When Farrah sees Steve, a scene of hot, sultry passion ensues, climaxed by her throwing him on the bed and promising to make him an angel. Just as Steve's wings are about to sprout, Big Bronson turns up with his henchmen James Caan and Michael York. Jimmy and Mike are about to gun down Steve when the disgusted Charles tells them to take Farrah instead and do with her whatever they want. Following is a scene of horrifying torture as Farrah clings to the pant legs of the reluctant gunmen who *refuse* to rape her. In retaliation she shoots them with her ray-bra, turning them into instant sex maniacs, but alas it's too late for them.

Farrah has returned to Charlie's digs, and not wanting to be his angel any more, she drops a capped tooth into his drink just as he's about to sign Steve to a lifetime contract as a live-in Godson. Farrah and Steve grab the nearest Concorde and whiz back to Earth, immune to the blandishments of Barbra's siren song (a repeat of our gold-record musical theme).

On terra firma Farrah stops to change bras

at the apartment of her chums, a jaunty married couple played by Robert Shaw and Lily Tomlin. Though he's a professional shark hunter and she teaches Esperanto, they like to solve crimes on the side under the names of Nick and Nora Charlie-O. But first the frolicky four have to list all the crimes. Remembering them is tough. The most important seem to be: Who killed Sissy Spacek? Who poisoned Liza Minnelli? What made Marlon Brando shrink? And, who really did Streisand out of *GWTW*? The group decide that the same person who abducted Diane Keaton is probably responsible for all the misfortunes pummeling Woody-Bob-Steve. For a quick answer Lily consults her telephone directory and finds the name of a crystal-gazer in the yellow pages.

Entering the dark domicile of mystic Glenda Jackson, the group is instructed to peer into her glowing glass. There they see that it's now Diane Keaton who's being beaten by the versatile Art Carney. Speeding to Art's place, they find Art and Diane making out but feel too embarrassed to stay. As the heartbroken and disillusioned Woody leaves, Diane manages to slip him the other part of the glass key. It says "Doolittle" on it! Woody realizes that the key never belonged to Liza Minnelli at all, but is the property of Eliza Doolittle, heroine of *My Fair Lady.* Since both Julie Andrews (who portrayed Eliza on stage) and Audrey Hepburn (the screen version) are in town making comebacks, the group invites the two stars to an after-interview supper. The sweet-and-lovelies arrive and insist they know nothing, but Audrey puts in a call to her more political sisters Shirley MacLaine and Jane Fonda, who arrive with their campaign manager Bob De Niro. Here we interpolate a little musical bit as Shirley dances, Jane makes a speech and Bob does a saxophone solo. As they swing into the second chorus, the entire group is gunned down by a mysterious stranger garbed in black. It's Greta Garbo, who removes her facial mask to reveal the long-dead Sissy Spacek, who has managed to spare only Woody-Bob-Steve so that he can be her three top leading men and she will become the only female star left alive.

Just as she's showing our hero how she brilliantly enacted her own death, Sissy is knifed by Glenda Jackson, who delivers an Oscar-acceptance speech and descends into total madness by forming a sister act with the evergreen Barbra Streisand, who appears just in time to sing the title song again, under the closing credits. Which girl gets Woody-Bob-Steve? We'll leave that for the sequel, *The Continuation of Gone with the Godfather.*

Well, F.F., I hope you loved the treatment. Please forgive this simplistic version, which I will expand upon after my rewrite of *A Star Is Born* for Mason Reese. Although why I'm doing that one is a mystery to me.

Sincerely,

Richard

Richard Townsend is a novelist, playwright, screen writer and journalist who has interviewed many of the celebrities cast in this scenario.

STARRING IN A HORROR

Roy Scheider

COURTESY
METRO-GOLDWYN-MAYER

The first motion picture I ever did was called *Curse of the Living Corpse.* I was an actor at the Arena Stage, and the producer came up to me with the idea of filming a horror mystery on the estate of Gutzon Borglum, the guy who did the sculptures on Mount Rushmore. You have to understand that when they started this film, they went to the film library in New York, picked out all the titles of horror movies that had made big money and from this list put together the three most popular words — "corpse," "living" and "curse." First they wrote the title, then they wrote the script.

Anyway, as an actor who'd never done a movie, I couldn't pass it up. Not only that, but the script was the most outrageous thing I'd ever read in my life.

I played the drunken-sot-weakling-brother in a family that were all after the father's inheritance and wouldn't get it if they committed any of the standard unspeakable acts. In this film I got the opportunity to: burn my mother in her bed; cut off my brother's head; strangle my wife; kill three servants; slip through secret passages behind the library bookcases; wear an outfit that looked like something out of *The Shadow;* move around the house for an entire hour and a half with the audience unaware that I was the villain. At the end, when I'm found out, there's a tremendous battle in a quicksand bog, and I sink in it, and die.

Every fantasy, every dream, every kind of horror story that I ever imagined as a young man, I got to act out in one movie.

This film has become a minor classic in that it plays on network television, in almost every major city in America, on Halloween — usually about two o'clock in the morning. I've had friends call me up from San Francisco, New Orleans, Mexico City, and say, "Oh, Roy, what I'm watching on my TV set! It's just terrific! And look at how young you look, how strange!"

This turkey has haunted me for fifteen years.

WALTON'S WHEELS

Readying the Orient Express

Solomon Hastings

The murder weapon, a small gaudy dagger purchased at a bazaar in Istanbul, lies forgotten in the prop room at Elstree Studios outside London. Some of the authentic fittings, doors and washbasins, have been incorporated into a research museum opened in London by film producer Richard Goodwin. But Hercule Poirot's monogrammed cane is now in the Manhattan apartment of Tony Walton, production and costume designer for the 1974 film version of Agatha Christie's *Murder on the Orient Express.*

When director Sidney Lumet initially approached Walton, he asked, "How would you like to have a holiday?" He gave the impression, says Walton, that the producers Goodwin and John Brabourne were planning "a small, Ealing comedy — a *Lavender Hill Mob* kind of film, with Alec Guinness, perhaps, as Poirot." Only later did Lumet decide that since they were handling a bit of "high-class fluff," they should pull out all the stops and create a really glamorous Thirties epic with the Betelgeuses of the film world.

Walton, who usually takes about a year to complete his work on a major film, was amused upon release of the film to find that most people assumed he had simply used the real train for the interiors. In fact, with Lumet and Goodwin, he had extensively researched the project in train museums and warehouses in Paris, Ostend and Istanbul, then created the interiors, with much heightened detail, on the Elstree Studio stages.

Using the original metric plans and elevations loaned to him by the Wagon-Lits company, Walton combined existing panels from the Ostend train graveyard with much freshly constructed material to create the exaggerated aura of "movie" glamour demanded by Lumet.

Lalique panels and cast-iron luggage racks were borrowed and copied. Improper but evocative varieties of upholstery were selected and installed. Floral motifs and splendid glass lamps were added in the interests of glamour rather than accuracy. A studio signwriter, who had painted many variations on Thirties travel posters for the film, was assigned the task of painting minutely detailed wood inlays all along the newly built train corridor panels.

This interest in fanciful detail was carried

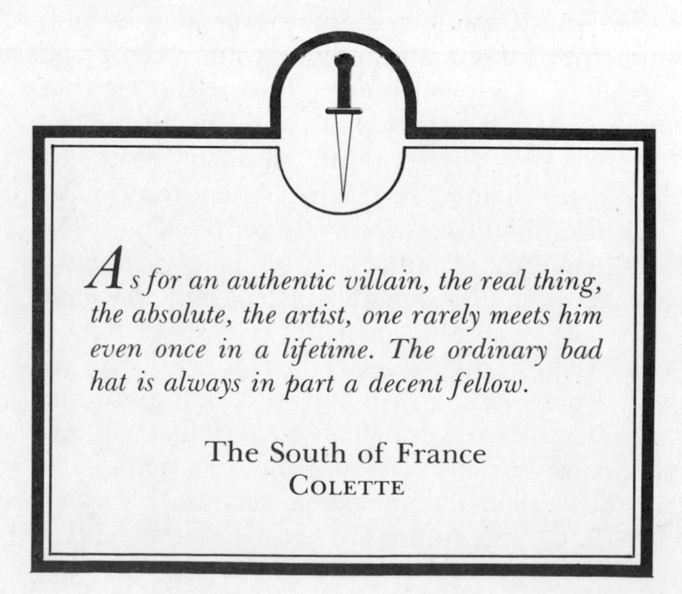

As for an authentic villain, the real thing, the absolute, the artist, one rarely meets him even once in a lifetime. The ordinary bad hat is always in part a decent fellow.

The South of France
COLETTE

through to such items as a bullet ring for Poirot. Because Poirot's limp is an integral part of his make-up, Walton created the brass ring with, supposedly, the shell of the bullet which had lamed the great detective. Such curios were indeed popular during the period, and Albert Finney, Poirot's portrayer, gamely wore it despite continually having to clean a creeping green stain from his finger.

According to Walton, location shooting involved one day of filming exteriors at a ferry in Istanbul (the ferry interior was constructed in the Elstree Studio). Prior to that, the production crew had gone to Pont d'Arles on the Swiss border to shoot the scene where the train gets stuck in the snow. Although the film company had been assured there was always snow in that area at that time of year, there was none when they arrived. Indeed, there had been no snow for weeks. In one of those rare moments that make one feel God must love the movies, there was a record blizzard the night before the scene was to be shot.

The Istanbul Hotel dining room was re-created in the Finsbury Park Cinema tea room in London because it had appropriately Hollywood-Moorish-Deco architecture in which the film company's golden palm trees and "fountain" railings looked at home. The Istanbul station was built in an engine shed outside Paris — as the proper engine could not be brought to England because of the difference between English and Continental rail gauges.

All other interiors were shot at Elstree, where snowscape panoramas were painted on enormous translucent rear-projection screens to simulate the specific type of glaring light that one would get if one were stuck in a snowbank.

Designing the costumes in London created problems because of fabric shortages. One piece of silk for actress Jacqueline Bisset's gown — the one worn in the film's climactic scene — was promised daily by the French manufacturer, but he, unlike God, failed to deliver. Miss Bisset ended up wearing what was in actuality the pattern for the proposed dress, stenciled with a design from Walton's scarf to look as presentable as possible.

At the London Royal Gala premiere of the film, Dame Agatha, by this time in poor health, put aside her wheelchair and stood in line for the formal presentation to the Royal Family. The producer's mother, the dowager Lady Brabourne, herself a ramrod-erect octogenarian, was unimpressed by Dame Agatha's royal curtsy: "Not a very good eighty, is she?"

Solomon Hastings is the pseudonym of a shy, wealthy, busy theatrical costume designer.

"THE KING OF TRAINS AND THE TRAIN OF KINGS"

The Orient Express ran for the last time on May 17, 1977.

It ran for the first time on June 1, 1889.

The train from Paris to Istanbul (the former Constantinople) took three days and passed through Vienna, Budapest, Belgrade and Sofia. In 1906 a new rail tunnel between Switzerland and Italy shortened the trip by twelve hours, but the train no longer stopped at Vienna and Budapest.

During World War I and World War II the train did not run, no matter how many spy stories would have you believe the contrary.

In March of 1953 day coaches were added to the train.

According to the Associated Press, the final journey took two and one-half days and a first-class sleeper ticket for one person cost $375.

If everybody who swore they'd ridden on the train actually had, the train probably would not have had to shut down.

Wagon-Lits ashtray from the Orient Express in which the burnt paper clue was discovered.

COURTESY TONY WALTON

GREENSTREET AND LORRE

Could you love a man who's grossly overweight, who walks like a finicky water buffalo, or another one who quivers in a perpetual state of terror, whose eyes resemble two soulful fried eggs? Yes, of course. Indeed, Sidney Greenstreet and Peter Lorre were (and remain) the world's favorite Terrible Twosome. Most famous as Joel Cairo (Lorre) and Max Gutman (Greenstreet) in *The Maltese Falcon,* the Twosome represented consummate villainy, deceit, double-dealing and danger to generations of moviegoers.

Traveling companions. Greenstreet reads Pearls of Wisdom *while Lorre questions him on it in* The Mask of Dimitrios.

A rueful Lorre and an elegant (even in death) Greenstreet in The Mask of Dimitrios.

CULVER PICTURES

THE MACGUFFIN MAN

Peter J. Schuyten

The door opened. I fancied I could hear the strains of Gounod's *Funeral March of a Marionette.* I would not have been surprised if the first words out of his mouth had been, "Good evening, ladies and gentlemen. Tonight's program . . . "

Instead, he offered a simple, almost shy, "Hello, how are you?"

Actually, I was fine, considering I was in the presence of the man who in less than a minute of filmmaking had kept me out of the shower for the better part of a month. I was all right, considering I was in the same room with the man Truffaut called "an artist of anxiety" and placed on a par with Dostoevsky, Kafka and Edgar Allan Poe.

Alfred Hitchcock has probably terrified more people, more artistically, than anyone else in the history of movies. And he has done it, as Hitchcock aficionados well know, without showing any violence on screen. "I made *Psycho* in black and white for one reason," he said. "So I wouldn't have to show blood. It would have been repulsive to show that girl being stabbed in the bath with all that blood running down the drain. In fact, you never did see the knife touch Janet Leigh's body. It was all impressionistic. There were seventy-eight cuts in that forty-five-second scene, and each one was sketched out in advance. The blood, by the way, was Hershey's chocolate syrup."

Another technique he uses to horrify moviegoers is called by Hitchcock "the subjective." "Take the car-out-of-control scene in *Family Plot.* Most people don't realize that most chase scenes are shown objectively. In other words, the audience is on the sidewalk. Cars may race, bash against each other, jackknife and collide, but it's all shown from the distance. Not in *Family Plot.* The first two or three shots show the girl saying to George, 'Slow down, will you. Slow down.' I showed her viewpoint which included the windshield and the dashboard. But as the car's speed increased, I went from her face to her viewpoint again — this time without the windshield and dashboard — because if you were experiencing the same thing, you wouldn't be looking at them, either. You wouldn't even see the hood. All you would be looking at would be the road ahead. I put the audience in the character's place, or what I call the 'subjective.' The best subjective picture I ever made was *Rear Window.* There you had a man, James Stewart, looking out the window. The camera showed what he saw, then cut back to him for his reaction. That doesn't happen in the theater, and an author can only try to describe it in a book, but the screen is the way true

MR. HITCHCOCK, WHAT'S A MACGUFFIN?

A MacGuffin is a demented red herring. It has no significance whatsoever, except to the characters chasing after it — who are convinced it's terribly important. A MacGuffin can be a sack of jewels, a scheme to take over the world, a piece of paper with writing on it that nobody's ever seen. It is a device that moves a Hitchcock plot along and is not to be taken seriously by anybody but the people who are acting in the movie. And they must have absolute belief in its existence. We, however, know better. Don't we?

To Peter Schuyten

from

Alfred Hitchcock

subjective can be achieved. It's a combination of three shots: the look; what he sees; how he reacts. *That's* pure cinema."

Hitchcock also specializes in what he calls "journeying" pictures. "They are picaresque jobs. You choose a journey, find out what is on that journey, where it takes you, how you get there and, more importantly, what is interesting on the way. In adventure chase stories you're always building up to something, but I have some very specific rules as to how to do it. For example, Cary Grant in *North by Northwest* gets trapped in an auction room. He can't get out because there are men in front of him and men behind him. The only way out is to do what you'd do in an auction room. Bid. He bid crazily and got himself thrown out. Similarly, when he was chased by a crop duster, he ran and hid in a cornfield. There was one thing that crop duster could do — dust some crops. That drove him out. Using the costume ball in *To Catch a Thief* was much the same idea. I don't believe in going into an unusual setting and not using it dramatically."

One scene Hitchcock wanted to use, he couldn't. It was meant for *North by Northwest.* "I had it all worked out that Cary Grant would slide down Lincoln's nose when he was on Mount Rushmore, then hide in Lincoln's nostril, then have a sneezing fit which gave his position away to his pursuers. It's a shame I was never allowed to do it. The Department of the Interior said that if I used Mount Rushmore, any chase or fight scene had to take place between the heads, not on them. Why? I was told it was a shrine of democracy."

Hitchcock considers *Shadow of a Doubt* his most nearly perfect picture. "I've always said that if you devise a picture on paper, you have achieved 100 percent. In fact, after a script is finished and I have run the whole film in my mind, I wish I didn't have to go and make it, because by the time you finish shooting it you end up with only 60 percent. There are so many complications. Casting is not perfect. You don't always get the right setting. With *Shadow of a Doubt,* however, I had everything. Character. The original small-town setting. There was no compromise anywhere. And that was very satisfying."

Almost as satisfying was pointing out a mistake to a man who made life difficult for him when he first came to the States back in the Thirties. Says Hitchcock, "I once ran into a very funny situation when Selznick [David O. Selznick, former head of MGM Studios], with great pride, showed me the big scene from *Gone with the Wind.* It was the scene with all the soldiers lying in the station yard and there was this high pull-back showing Vivien Leigh looking for her man. She was wearing a pale violet dress and you could hardly see her. I said, 'David, why didn't you put a red dress on her? When the camera finally reached the high point, all you would have seen was this little red dot.' That shook him. He had never thought of it. Ridiculous not to think of a thing like that. He missed the whole point of the scene entirely. And wouldn't that have made some retake?"

Hitchcock is the consummate detail man. Overseeing everything from red dresses to sneezing noses to Hershey's syrup. Lest you think that leaves him little time to be concerned about people's feelings, let me tell you one more story. A few weeks after our interview, when I was back in New York, I received a large manila envelope in the mail. Postmarked Universal City. Somewhat puzzled, I opened it. As I looked at the drawing, I could again almost hear the strains of Gounod's *Funeral March of a Marionette.* Hitchcock had sent me *his* caricature of the famous Hitchcock caricature. He had drawn it, signed it and inscribed it to me. A very thoughtful man is Mr. Hitchcock. And although I resist the term, I shall always be his fan.

HITCHCOCK UNSURPASSED

The Thirty-Nine Steps (based on the 1915 John Buchan novel).
The Trouble with Harry (based on a 1950 John Trevor Story novel).
Suspicion (based on the 1932 Francis Iles novel *Before the Fact*).

Peter J. Schuyten, an associate editor at Fortune *magazine, writes on the entertainment industry.*

COSMETICS TO MAKE YOU LOOK WORSE

The Make-Up Man's Art

Solomon Hastings

He laughed, recalling how Sidney Lumet came up to him with James Coburn during the filming of *The Last of the Mobile Hot Shots* and barked, "I want him to bleed *here,*" indicating the actor's mouth, "*here,*" his ears, "and *here,*" his nose. "All at once. Can you do it?"

"Sure."

"How?"

"Beat the shit out of him."

He didn't, of course, because Vincent Callahan has been a professional make-up man for twenty-four years, working stage, TV and film, and he has become expert at creating cosmetic mayhem.

In effect, Callahan was supposed to simulate an internal hemorrhage for Coburn. Nothing to it. He ordered spaghetti-sized plastic tubing from a medical supply house, carefully laid it on the actor's face and disguised it with facial hair. The tubing was attached to a squeeze bulb in Coburn's hand. On cue, Coburn squeezed and Callahan's fake blood gushed up, first from the mouth, next from the nose and finally from the ears. Authentic for such a hemorrhage. Ever the perfectionist, Callahan even arranged for a special deep dark blood — the kind that indicates internal bleeding.

How does one go about concocting blood? There are several commercial fake bloods on the market. One called Nextel is manufactured by 3M. But Vince prefers to mix his own. He mushes karo syrup and food coloring together, feeling that he can get a truer color and consistency that way. It also, so he says, wipes off more easily.

I'll go to any mystery movie, or watch practically any detective thriller on the tube, but I never read detective novels. I don't know why that is. Maybe it's a mystery in itself.

My wife reads them though, and so I often buy them for her.

About thirty-five or maybe more years ago Emlyn Williams wrote, directed (I think) and acted in (a dual role) my favorite whodunit flick, The Norwich Mystery. *I have since then never met a soul who's ever heard of it, let alone seen it. It has vanished utterly into the void. You've never heard of it, either. Leaving me a cult of one.*

PETER DE VRIES

Curious about how gunshot wounds are rigged for the camera for such bloodbath scenes as those in *Bonnie and Clyde* and *The Godfather?* Vince's technique entails placing metal plates on the actor's body in the appropriate spots. On each plate, as a sort of sandwich filling, sits a sack of blood which is topped off with an explosive charge of squib. Electrical

HOW TO LOSE A MOVIE FIGHT

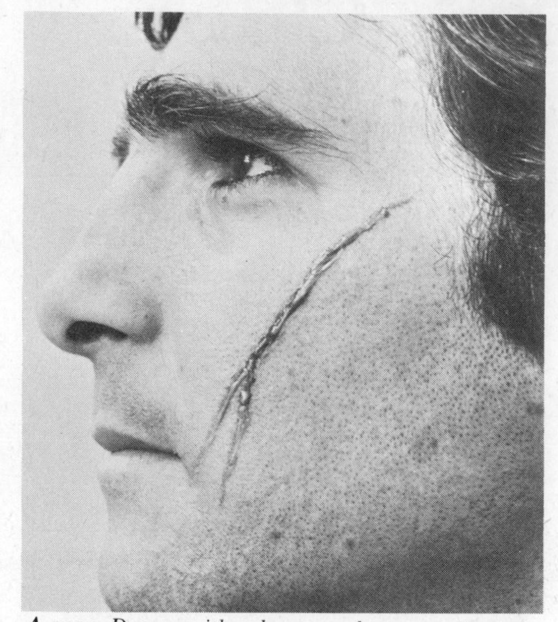

A scar. *Drawn with a brown eyebrow pencil, puckered with a thin line of Nuplast, which is then covered with blue-gray eyeshadow, blood, ochre eyeshadow and pancake make-up. Finally, a touch of Gordon Moore's Ruby Red toothpast, imported from London.*

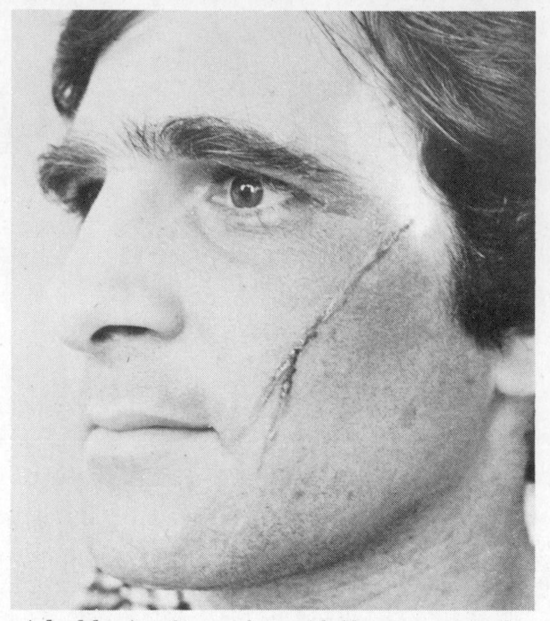

A bad bruise. *Sponged on with blue-gray and ochre eyeshadow, highlighted with dark gray pencil. Then, a dab of blood and vibrant peony lipstick.*

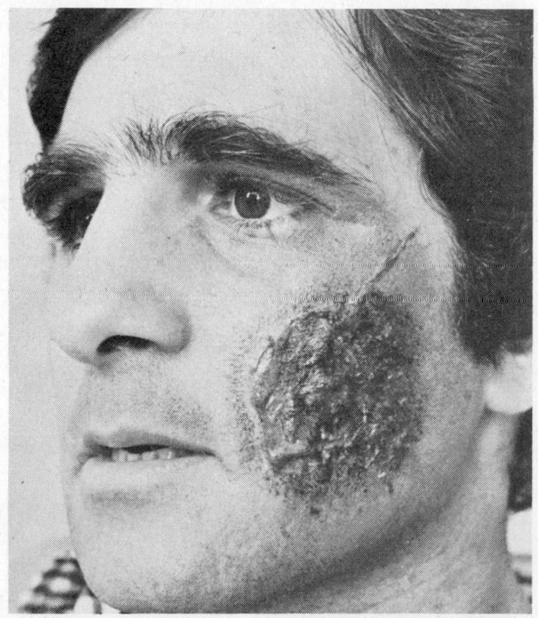

A burn mark. *Created by applying Nuplast with a brush, then picking bits away before it hardens completely. Scorch marks added with dark brown shadow. Vaseline added for oozing effect.*

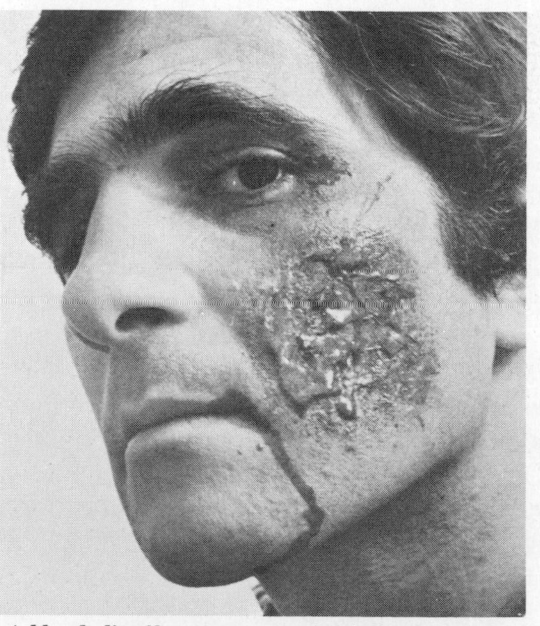

A bloody lip. *Karo syrup mixed with food coloring is dribbled from the corner of the mouth. There are several commercial "bloods" on the market, including Nextel from 3M.*

RON LOHSE

wires are attached to the explosive and run down the actor's body, under his costume. They stretch out to a point off camera where, under Callahan's tutelage, they are detonated. Instant carnage.

For *Shamus* one character had to have the back of his head blasted off from close range. A specially shaped plate was constructed that followed the contours of the actor's head. It was camouflaged with a toupee.

When the shooting occurred, the force of the charge was so strong, it threw the actor forward several feet and spattered blood on the lens of the camera. Studio audiences thought the effect was sensational.

Callahan's talent extends far beyond bullets and blood, however. If the wound is to be deeper, such as from an ax sunk into a character's head, Callahan is equal to it. He is fiendishly deft in making a matched dummy which is inserted just before impact. If a body part is to be amputated, he makes a full prosthesis, usually out of plastic, meat and bone. Since there is little or no action required of the victim (except to lie there and be hacked away), it is fairly simple for Callahan to strap the actor's real limb to his body, or bury it in trick holes in the furniture, then secure the prosthesis, cover the join with latex, foam rubber and make-up, and let the villain have a go at it.

For a face that only a gorgon's mother could admire, replete with dewlaps, warts, bashed-in chins and shattered cheekbones, Callahan first makes a cast and then, from that cast, creates a new plastic face for the actor to slip into. Until recently, such casts were made by coating the actor with plaster of Paris, but the heaviness of the plaster usually distorted the actor's features. Callahan now favors a lighter, quicker-drying substance called Monlage. Callahan can't recall any actor looking at himself in one of these horror faces and being appalled, but he did get a violent reaction from an actor who sat for a face cast and discovered in the process he had rampant claustrophobia.

What about burns, bruises, scars? Child's play. A dab of latex, a smear of liquid plastic such as collodium or Tuplast, a soupçon of ordinary face make-up — albeit in Halloween colors — and the actor looks ready for the intensive care unit. The trick, Callahan insists, is in observing actual wounds and in mixing make-up colors to conform to reality. New York provides more of a challenge to his imagination than Hollywood, because in New York he must create from scratch while in Hollywood the studios maintain permanent laboratories to crank out cosmetic disasters.

Callahan's life is not totally comprised of making people look like thugs and Frankenstein's progeny. His plushest job was that of East Coast head of make-up and hair for *The Great Gatsby*, and his most satisfying was anything at all that involved George C. Scott. Callahan has worked regularly with Scott for the past fifteen years. His wife, too, is involved in the business, as a hairdresser.

What's the most difficult thing he's ever done? Not blood. Not guts. Not wounds. Not warts. But glamorous make-up for women that will look natural in daylight.

Soloman Hastings is the pseudonym of a famous cosmetic consultant.

SPILLING ONE'S GUTS

Contemplating hara-kiri? Then you'll need a lateral abdominal. Need any other slices, slashes and gashes? Then you must hie yourself to Woodstock, New York, and call upon the Simulaids Company. They are the Michaelangelo of artificial wounds, which they construct to order, to go, out of latex with tubes attached for distributing the blood at the requisite spots. According to Kevin M. Sweeney, the company was founded in 1963 to create visual aids for first-aid instructors. But now and then an order creeps in for a ruptured appendix or a yard or so of perforated intestinal tract from someone other than an educator. Frankly, we did not inquire who he or she might be. And we'd just as soon you didn't tell us.

S.H.

TO WALK AMONG SHADOWS

George Baker

Chief Inspector Alleyn looked at the poinsettia, its top-most flower well above his head, and said "I am amazed." "Dear Br'er Fox" he thought "if you could see the wonders of New Zealand. Palms grow over cool streams, streams cool enough for trout. Can you imagine trout fishing in the blazing sun, standing in the shade of a palm. There are more things in heaven and earth, Br'er Fox."

The very English Chief Inspector Roderick Alleyn, Scotland Yard, is the creation of Dame Ngaio Marsh, a New Zealander and one of the world's foremost detective story writers.

I was wandering around my house in London wishing a part would be offered that would interest me and stretch me as an actor, and as a bonus take me abroad for a week or two. The phone rang so close upon the wish that I laughed when my agent said, "Would you like to go to New Zealand and play Inspector Alleyn in four television films? Of course, the producer wants the answer yesterday!"

"Say yes," I said.

"Don't you want to read the script?"

"As a formality," I answered.

"Or know what the money is?"

"Naturally."

I couldn't tell her I was quite unable to refuse the part, as it had all the qualifications with which I had endowed my wish. It was Friday afternoon, and we agreed that the scripts should be sent to me by taxi so that I could read them over the weekend and return my answer by Sunday night or Monday morning.

I took *Died in the Wool,* the first book to be filmed, from the shelf and started to reread it. The other titles for filming were *Vintage Murder, Opening Night* and *Colour Scheme.*

I was delighted with Inspector Alleyn and his faithful subordinate, Inspector Fox. Unfortunately, Fox does not appear in these particular books, but Alleyn often speaks to him in thoughtful soliloquy.

"And St. John Acroyd," he says in *Vintage Murder.* "There, my dear old Inspector Foxy, a subject fit for you and me. A stock comedian, a funny man with a funny face, and unless I am much mistaken, a mean disposition." And with those few words Alleyn sets up another suspect and the reader has another clue for the Dame's crime puzzle.

Now, how to play him? How to play him would by *my* puzzle. What were my clues?

A product of Eton and Balliol, Alleyn entered the Foreign Office before transferring to Scotland Yard. These were the clues to his background. So I deduced that he was a well-bred Englishman of some social standing who had followed a conventional pattern through to his thirties. He broke away from these conventions when he transferred to Scotland Yard. It was Dame Ngaio's genius to create a professional policeman who also carried the mores of his amateur rivals Lord Peter Wimsey and Father Brown — breeding and education. Inspector Alleyn married an exceptional and gifted wife, Troy. And in that, too, he broke with convention. I had a glimpse of a man whose mind and interests were at variance with his social upbringing.

I carefully dressed him in the tweeds and brogues of the period. If anything, I made the clothes more severe and reserved than they need have been in order to give myself the opportunity to contrast the exterior and the interior man. Now, what was I going to use to aid me in bringing out Roderick Alleyn's humour?

Through her extraordinary gift of drawing character, the Dame lets the reader catch glimpses of Roderick Alleyn's humour. For an actor, thoughts are communicated through the mind and through the eye. I invented a pair of half-spectacles for Alleyn to frame that humour which would not be spoken.

It was all very well for me to have these thoughts, but I hadn't yet met the producer and was by no means yet on my way to New Zealand to appear as Chief Inspector Roderick Alleyn.

My agent set up a meeting with John McRea, the producer. We agreed to lunch at the Cumberland Hotel, London, on Monday morning. Since my wife and I were then rehearsing a recital I had compiled of scenes from Shakespeare, the interview had to be snappy so that I could get back to the rehearsals in good time. I parked my bicycle with the porter of the hotel and went in. John McRea introduced himself and offered me a pre-lunch drink. After being served, I said, "If you're offering the part, I'd like to play it."

"I'm offering the part."

"Right," I said, "when do we start?"

"I want you to be ready to fly out in two weeks' time."

Our recital was scheduled for eight performances on a ten-day tour. That would leave four days for putting together the year's accounts and making all the arrangements for a trip of five months' duration. Well, why not? I agreed to do it.

On 14th March I flew to Auckland, New Zealand, via Singapore. Inspector Alleyn grew on me more and more as I travelled the 13,000 miles to play him. I re-read *Opening Night* and *Vintage Murder,* and became more and more convinced that the Inspector's humour was going to be the most pleasurable factor in the part and the most difficult to convey.

THE MURDER GAME

Roderick Alleyn debuted in 1934 in *A Man Lay Dead.* The Chief Inspector was called in to investigate a murder that occurred during a weekend house party. Sir Hubert's guests were gathered in the parlour to play "The Murder Game." The lights were turned off while the game was in progress. When snapped back on they revealed a very dead gamesman, his back skewered by a jewelled dagger. Alleyn solved the case. To the best of anyone's knowledge, no one at Sir H.'s ever played the game again.

On arrival at Auckland I was met by John McRea, who took me to the studios to meet the two directors. From the beginning we got on well. Our discussions were pointed with laughter and relaxation. When the costume designer joined us, I realised that we were all on the same wavelength. The feeling of rightness I had had in London was still with me.

So Roderick Alleyn began to prepare himself to step out of the books he had made famous for his creator and make his debut on the screen.

"Dear old Foxkin, the New Zealand countryside is quite breathtaking and the locations found for the four stories are so like the places of imagination our dear author describes, I believe she may have taken a peep or two at reality when she put us into the settings we share. It's all shrewd observation, Foxkin, and knowing human nature. You will forgive me if I go now. The smell of the frangipani wafting past me on the night air as I stand on the verandah makes me suspect foul play in the woolshed . . . indeed Flossie Rubrick may have *Died in the Wool.* I might investigate."

George Baker, in addition to an acting career, has written for the BBC and his The Trial and Execution of Charles I *was performed by the Royal Shakespeare Company.*

AN EERIE RADIO QUIZ

Chris Steinbrunner

All together now, what was it that The Shadow knew? The evil which lurked in the hearts of men, *that's* what he knew. Here are twenty questions on some of the great mystery radio shows of old: programs you may have listened to under the bedcovers so your parents wouldn't hear; programs that (what vanished art!) needed your own imagination to swirl up the atmosphere accompanying those sinister peals of filtered laughter and organ chords; programs that are now like vanished civilizations overrun by jungle, like lands now lost in the mists. Score 5 points for each correct answer and *don't look back* — not until you're finished, that is.

1. *Suspense* in its twenty-year radio life was certainly, as the narrator reminded us each week, "radio's outstanding theater of thrills." For the first few years that narrator had a name — or at least a description. What was it?

2. John Dickson Carr wrote a memorable but short-lived radio series narrated by a ship's doctor about strange crimes in forcign ports of call, actually a spin-off from a celebrated drama he wrote for *Suspense*, a show that was repeated often and called by the same title. What was it?

3. The Shadow is really Lamont Cranston, and only his close friend Margot — that's the official way they spelled it in the scripts — Lane knew to whom the voice of the invisible Shadow belonged. Who was the irascible police official — a continuing character in the series — whose mind Lamont often clouded?

4. Carleton E. Morse's *I Love a Mystery* was the greatest radio adventure series of all time, and its trio of heroes — Jack, Doc and Reggie — have joined the immortals. Give the *last* names of at least two of the three.

"Who knows what evil lurks in the hearts of men? The Shadow knows." So began the weekly radio series based on Maxwell Grant's elusive character, who learned how to cloud men's minds while in the mysterious East. Orson Welles was the original radio program narrator.

5. Basil Rathbone, who played the role on radio for seven years, *was* Sherlock Holmes. Name at least *two* other actors who have played him before the microphone.

6. What was the relationship between The Lone Ranger and The Green Hornet?

7. The semi-documentary *Gangbusters* was the creation of what famous radio producer (who made a career of fact crime)?

8. Among the earliest spook shows on network radio were *Inner Sanctum*, in which host Raymond swung on the creaking door, and *The Witch's Tale*, featuring blood-chillers told by "Old Nancy, the witch of Salem." What was the name of her wise old cat?

9. *Charlie Wild, Private Eye* succeeded for a time the *Sam Spade* radio slot. How did this detective get his name?

10. *The Man Called X*, perhaps radio's most urbane detective (he was played by Herbert Marshall), hung out in places like Cairo and had sidekicks named, not Mike or Spud, but Pagan Zeldschmidt! If you weren't calling him X, what *would* you call *The Man Called X* . . . his real name, please.

11. For years Jack Armstrong adventured with his adoring Uncle Jim and cousins Betty and Billy. Then, falling under the influence of a reformed criminal turned scientific investigator named Vic Hardy, the all-American boy became an agent of an organization remarkably like the FBI. Name the agency.

12. *Big Town* was a newspaper drama — and a good one. Name the paper which supplied the screamed-out headlines for the show, as well as its crusading editor (first played by Edward G. Robinson).

13. An easy one. Agnes Moorehead appeared on *Suspense* in 1943 in a one-woman show so chilling it became a landmark in radio terror. What was the story (written by Lucille Fletcher)?

14. Remember Nick Carter? A wild rapping on the door . . . a woman's anxious voice: "What is it? What's the matter?" . . . the reply: *Another case for Nick Carter, Master Detective!* Who, then, was *Chick* Carter?

15. Out of the fog, out of the night and into his American adventures stepped which famed British hero making a most unlikely transatlantic transition?

16. *Tired of the everyday world? Ever dream of a life of romantic adventure?* Thus opened a thriller-series that was the best of its kind, bringing us such classic settings as a lighthouse swarming with rats and a department store where mannequins came to life at night. What was the show's one-word name?

17. Jack Webb is best known as police sergeant Joe Friday of *Dragnet*. But Webb was the hero of several other crime shows. Name at least one.

18. *The Whistler* was always giving you a little tune while he told you the most grotesque stories, and on *Lights Out* the weird narrator was always ordering you into darkness. But where were you always running into *The Mysterious Traveler* as he kept telling you those really queasy reminiscences?

19. Just by sending in a label from the sponsor's product you got Captain Midnight's decoder and other crime-fighting devices. These allowed you to personally assist in the Captain's struggle against the international menace of superspy Ivan Shark and become a member of "The Secret Squadron." What was the well-known product?

20. *Yours Truly, Johnny Dollar*, the adventures of an insurance investigator, was the last continuing-hero mystery series to leave radio. What weekly activity on Johnny's part formed the basis for each show?

Those are the questions. There are more which come to mind . . . for instance, who answered the desperately troubled souls who wrote to *Box 13*? (Alan Ladd); who played Ellery Queen on radio, stopping just before the solution to allow guest armchair detectives to guess? (Hugh Marlowe, Larry Dobkin, Carleton Young, among others); Basil Rathbone hosted and starred in a mystery series for which cigarette sponsor? (*Tales of Fatima*) But that's for another quiz. Here are the answers to this one, and if you get a fair amount right — nobody can remember *everything* — you get a diploma from the College of Radio Knowledge. . . .

1. He called himself The Man in Black.

2. *Cabin B-13*.

3. Commissioner Weston, played grumpily for many years by Santos Ortega.

4. Jack Packard, Doc Long, Reggie Yorke. Bless all three of 'em!

5. Orson Welles, William Gillette, Tom Conway, Richard Gordon, Louis Hector, Ben Wright, John Stanley, John Gielgud — take your pick.

6. The Green Hornet was The Lone Ranger's grandnephew.

7. Phillips H. Lord.

8. She called her cat Satan.

9. His name was a creative reworking of the sponsor's jingle: "Get Wildroot Creme Oil, Charlie."

10. X signed his name "Ken Thurston." He was a detective.

11. The S.B.I. (Scientific Bureau of Investigation).

12. Hard-hitting Steve Wilson was editor of *The Illustrated Press.*

13. *Sorry, Wrong Number.*

14. Chick was Nick's adopted son, who had a weekday afternoon series all his own in which he *never* talked to his dad.

15. Bulldog Drummond, who on American radio was very un-Sapperish.

16. *Escape.* The two stories mentioned, "Three Skeleton Keys" (the lighthouse) and "Evening Primrose" (John Collier's department store), were oft-repeated favorites.

17. Jack Webb was also the star of a great private-eye series, *Pat Novak for Hire*, as well as such mystery shows as *Jeff Regan* and *Johnny Modero, Pier 23.*

18. On a commuter train. ("Oh? You have to get off here? What a pity. . . .")

19. Chocolate-flavored Ovaltine.

20. Itemizing his expense account, the detailed explanation of each expenditure unfolding the story. And when all the expenses were totaled, it was "End of report . . . yours truly, Johnny Dollar."

Chris Steinbrunner, while still in high school, sold a radio script to The Shadow.

COURTESY RCA

Sorry, Wrong Number, *which starred Agnes Moorehead in a virtuoso solo performance, was based on the novel of the same name by Lucille Fletcher.*

FOGHORNS, FOOTSTEPS, GUNSHOTS, A SCREAM

The Noisy Memories of a Radio Effects Man

Chris Steinbrunner

The radio sound effects man is as archaic as the blacksmith. But Barney Beck remembers when. In a wildly pioneering past he was, for nearly every radio show you can think of, the man of a million sounds — a master of sound effects. And for radio in its heyday, that was *it* . . . no one was more important, more needed, more creative. *He* was the one who set the stage, painted the scenery, built the mood and provided the leitmotif: the creaking door of *Inner Sanctum;* the mournful train whistle ushering in *I Love a Mystery;* the foghorn and footsteps which were *Bulldog Drummond;* the pounding on the door which started each new case for *Nick Carter.* Actors were often interchangeable, but a sound effects genius was the cornerstone of the radio mystery show. Did not Agnes Moorehead hold hands with her sound man on *Suspense* just before the start of her (and his) classic performance in *Sorry, Wrong Number* — not *during* the show because a sound man on duty needs at least eight hands, all of them free — and did not the same expert, for the same series, spend three weeks researching the sound of a severed cerebrum for *Donovan's Brain?*

Barney Beck did nearly all the classic programs originating in New York (*and* the repeats staged four hours later for the benefit of the West Coast before the advent of nation-wide hookups): *Ellery Queen, Inner Sanctum, Perry Mason, Casey Crime Photographer* (with its obligatory jazz piano bar music as Casey explained the caper), *The Shadow, Nick Carter, Charlie Chan, True Detective, Official Detective* and countless others. Today, Barney frequently lectures about radio sound at schools and clubs, bringing his effects table and gear with him, simulating once more the 1,000-plus gunshots, fistfights and footfalls which decades ago colored and enriched his art.

According to Barney the first sound effects people to bear the name were a husband-and-wife team asked to set up a department for sound at the old Mutual studios. The husband had been a drummer, and it seemed a logical extention for an expert at drum rolls to provide the mood and effects noise for early radio. Much of what came after was trial and error. In the days of "live" programming, error was often a factor. At the end of a *Shadow* episode, just as Lamont Cranston was summing up, a nervous sound man hit an auto horn by mistake. The quick-witted actor playing Lamont covered the *beep* nicely: "Our friends downstairs are waiting, Margot, but before we go, let me tell you how I figured out this case . . ."

Gunshots, too, presented problems, says Barney. Recorded shots were not favored, as one could always detect the scratch sounds of

SHHH . . . LISTEN TO THE CORNSTARCH

A radio sound effects expert awaits his cue. In his hand, a gun shooting blanks; surrounding him, implements that sound like rolling waves, tire squeals, thunderclaps, creaking stairs and crypt doors.

What does a stabbing sound like? After much experimenting, radio effects men discovered a knife repeatedly thrust into a potato or grapefruit made the most authentic noise. The sound was suitably "squishy."

Whacking an ordinary household sponge duplicated a good right to the jaw, a left to the chin.

When a script called for a cold night wind to whistle through the undergrowth as the murderer slunk past, the effects man reached for his wheat stalks and shook vigorously. Thousands of radio listeners became too terrified by this ominous rustling sound to switch stations.

If the program was set on a snowy February night and the victim had to go outside to check if the telephone wires had been cut, it was the sound man's job to create his footsteps. The crunch was nothing more than a squeeze of cornstarch.

COURTESY NATIONAL BROADCASTING COMPANY

the grooves and the shots could never seem to be cued up properly. So the sound effects man stood by, a gun loaded with blanks in each hand — just in case the first revolver would not go off. (There have been cases on record where neither gun functioned. The nimble actor who switched murder weapons — "Lucky I had this *knife*" — is definitely not aprocryphal.) During an opulent special production of the life of Lincoln, the gun jammed during the fatal scene at Ford's Theater. The fast-thinking sound man dashed to the studio orchestra — it was a *big* show — and struck the timpani, which gave off a reverberating sound like a shot and then some. "That's the first time," the director hissed at him afterward, "Lincoln was assassinated by cannon!"

To prevent malfunctions of this nature, sound effects men in radio's Golden Age generally worked in pairs, but on such lesser-budget shows as *Nick Carter* or *Bulldog Drummond* one man — namely, Barney — did all, and he was generally *very* busy. He learned by experience. And innovated. One show called for the steady drip of a Chinese water torture: actual water just didn't sound right; pebbles dropped on a piece of cloth were better. To simulate the police breaking down a door, Barney twisted and crushed a fruit basket. How was *Inner Sanctum*'s squeaking door — the most classic of all radio mystery sounds — achieved? By Barney's slowly pressing on the back of a noisy swivel chair. Week after week. Honest.

Sound effects men were sometimes carried away by their work. Fistfights, a radio crime show staple, were orchestrated by sound men punching the palms of their hands in unison with the actors' grunts. Barney remembers one director whose sense of realism was so strong he wasn't satisfied unless the sound effects men *winced* as they hit themselves. An actor was "stabbed" on mike by a knife thrust into a grapefruit; one overenthusiastic sound man managed to stab his own hand. It is to his credit that he did not cry out until the show was over.

The *Shadow* program, endlessly macabre, inspired effects men to some of their proudest achievements. (One of the few perimeters dictated by sound effects was that The Shadow could never talk on the telephone — the electronic filter used for voices on the other end of the line was also used to suggest The Shadow's invisibility.) Once, Barney was asked to create a complete mad scientist's laboratory. For a bubbling effect, he blew down a straw into a glass of water. More bubbling was gotten by cooking oatmeal on mike — surprisingly grim and loathsome. At one point, Lamont and Margot were to explore a quicksand-filled cellar under the lab. For this, Barney stomped plumbers' suction cups over masses of wet paper towels. The result made the listener think of feet being sucked into oozing mud — a truly grisly effect and, for Barney, a wet one; by the end of the show, he was sopping.

Although it was Barney's mandate to fill the air with sound, he knew how to use silence. Leonard Bass, a director of *Gangbusters*, once told him: "There's nothing more exciting than dead air." An exaggeration, perhaps, but a pause was sometimes as effective as rapid-fire noise. As John Cole, who directed *The Shadow* during the program's Blue Coal zenith, kept telling his casts: "We all know it's pulp. Now let's treat it as if it were a *masterpiece*."

Toward the end of radio drama, an invention came to Barney's attention: a huge sound effects console, incorporating hundreds of tape loops featuring every imaginable noise, to be played like a grand organ. Could push-button technology be grafted to creativity? There was little chance to find out. With the advent of television, drama deserted the radio airwaves.

Of course, there is always a need for special skills, and Barney is kept busy supplying sound for the mini-dramas of radio commercials. And the mystery seems to be making something of a comeback — programs like *The Radio Mystery Theater* are heard cross-country seven days a week. Radio, the great theater of the imagination, can yet provide an alternative to much of television's vapid programming. For sound man Barney Beck, who believes dramatic radio is not dead, just resting, the eerily squeaking door may swing out again. And guess whose hand will be pushing it!

Chris Steinbrunner is co-editor of The Encyclopedia of Mystery and Detection, *winner of a 1976 Mystery Writers of America Edgar.*

Chapter 13

ACCESSORIES AFTER THE FACT

FRED WINKOWSKI

MYSTERY FANS AND THE PROBLEM OF "POTENTIAL MURDERERS"

Edmund Bergler, M.D.

In the course of a psychoanalytic appointment with an attorney, the necessity arose in connection with the interpretation of a dream to trace back his activities during the preceding day. Said the patient ironically: "Oh, yes, I forgot to mention that last evening I was with 800 potential murderers. I saw a gruesome detective story in the movies." "How many murders were involved?" I asked. "Only one," replied the patient. "I don't mean the picture; I am referring to the fascinated spectators." "Why do you call the spectators potential murderers? Aren't you stretching the point, calling every movie fan of detective stories a potential murderer?" I objected. "Of course not. I am completely serious," he replied. "In my humble opinion every fan of movie detective stories, mystery thrillers, and gangster intrigues, and every passionate reader of detective stories, is an inhibited or potential murderer." "And what about you?" was my next objection. "Why did you go to that picture?" The reply was a little irritated: "Because of my psychological interest in the reactions of the spectators. You know it's my profession — I'm a criminal lawyer." He clung to that justification, could not be moved at the moment to analyze his own reactions. This was understandable from the standpoint of his resistance. His whole analysis centered around his inner passivity, and further investigation into his interest in gruesome detective stories would have brought forth the fact that he used them unconsciously as a pseudo-aggressive defense mechanism against his inner passivity.

His analysis so far had proven that he was inwardly passive and had a strong unconscious feminine identification; he unconsciously warded off the passive tendencies in his defensive fantasy that he was aggressive. There was even the probability that his choice of profession was influenced by such a defense: inner identification with the criminal's miserable situation under the disguise, "I am different and above such nonsense."

A deep impression had been made upon him by the reluctance of one of his clients, a confessed and convicted murderer, to sign a petition for commutation of his sentence from capital punishment to life imprisonment. His client had not been at all grateful for the commutation which my patient had secured for him. He had described another incident in which, during the First World War, a deserter was tried for running away from the hospital. During the court proceedings it was discovered that this was the man's third desertion. From a relatively harmless offense, a capital trial resulted, since in the patient's country a third desertion near (not directly at) the front was punishable by death. The prosecutor tried to "simplify matters" by asking the defendant if he had any objections to the trial. The presiding judge explained to the defendant the significance of the question, and before my patient, the defendant's attorney, could intervene, the defendant waived objections to the trial. Only with great difficulty could my patient force the jury to postpone the trial for the purpose of fact-finding, while his client continued to insist on "getting it over with in a hurry." The patient dwelt upon these and similar cases in his practice continually, stressing the "queerness" of criminals. Having learned about psychic masochism in analysis, he called all of his clients "potential death seekers." Amusingly enough, his understanding did not for a long time stretch to include himself.

The decisive objection to my patient's assumption that detective fans were potential murderers was the analytic knowledge that what appears on the psychic surface, in consciousness, is *never* the unconscious wish, but rather the defense against that wish. All of these clinical and theoretical considerations pointed to the assumption of a basic conflict of passivity in such fans.

Typical Rationalizations

Since the clinical experience described above, I have paid attention to the problem, noting what type of books my patients read, what type of movies they prefer, and to what radio stories they tune in.

1. In nearly all persons interested in "detective stuff," as one patient put it, I could observe a queer objection to love stories. These were declared to be boring. Some patients could not even bear the typical love admixture in detective novels. Because of some schematization, the detective almost invariably falls in love with a girl involved in the murder in some way. The patients had the inner necessity of proving to themselves that they had outgrown the romantic form of love, acknowledging sex only as transitory pleasure and rejecting tenderness in love as unmanly.

2. Every detective story contains open aggression and irony directed against the officials conducting the investigation. The outsider — the private detective — outsmarts the officials. It is likely that unconsciously this aggression also represents the repetition of the child-father situation in reverse: the weak child outsmarts the powerful father. In other words, a childlike fantasy is involved. Rex Stout, the well-known writer of detective fiction, referring to this aggression toward the official police, once stated in a radio discussion that the detective story is a typical product only of democracies, since in authoritarian countries the citizen must respect authority. He corroborated his statement by pointing out the well-known fact that the United States, England, France, and the Scandinavian countries have contributed 90 percent of writers of detective fiction. Stout's assumption is undoubtedly correct. The question remains unanswered, of course, as to why this aggression toward authority is necessary, what it inwardly implies, and why it is so generally enjoyed by detective fans.

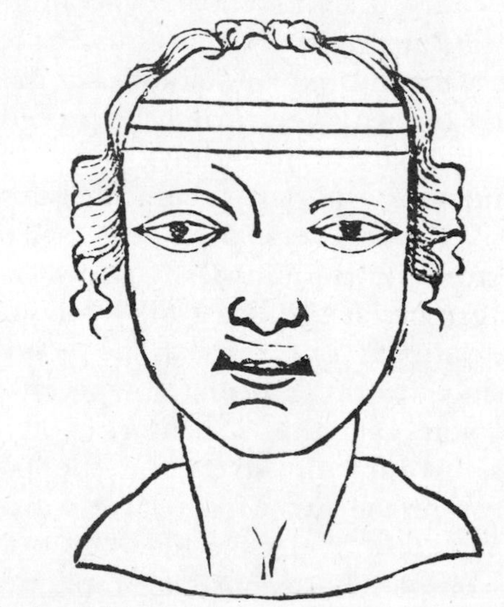

The forehead of a quarrelsome and murderous man, according to Phinella and seconded by Spontini. These experts could read the face for ominous personality traits as easily as you read the morning paper.

3. Some of my patients declared that their interest in detective stories was based on their desire to test their ability in drawing correct conclusions. The writer of the thriller gives a few hints or clues, tries to sidetrack suspicion, confuses the issue. Every reader knows that the least suspected and most harmless person in the story has a 95 percent chance of being proven the malefactor, whereas the initially suspected has the same chance of being cleared of suspicion. In other cases the most likely person is the malefactor.

After reading a few hundred books of this sort and concentrating attention on small clues, nearly every reader is capable of solving the majority of cases correctly. Interestingly enough, my patients were often surprised, after the dénouement, at the number of clues they had overlooked. One could not escape the conclusion that *not* arriving at the correct solution was part of the game they unconsciously played with themselves. What the game signified was of course unintelligible from the point of view of their rationalizations.

4. Another rationalization which I encountered claimed that the interest in detective stories centered in the peculiarities of the detective types.[1] The progress of the detective story brought into play different types of detective, constructed with more or less skill. Well, the salad dressing does not make the salad. We will note that point, which is basically without major importance, simply for the sake of being complete.

5. Some patients denied interest in detective fiction specifically, admitting, however, their interest in "thrills" in general. One patient admitted: "I like adventure, spy stories, murder cases, in short, thrill in general. Life is so boring and monotonous, why not imagine that one lives in a wider world, where one can do as one pleases?" He answered my objection that the detective or adventurer could not always do as he pleased with the argument that the *clever* detective or adventurer was practically omnipotent through his cleverness. The reader of the thriller could thus imagine that he was as clever as the hero.

6. The most intelligent rationalization was offered by a young girl patient, who said, "I like mysteries because they are a continuation or substitution of the gruesome fairy tales told me in my childhood. Then I was thrilled and frightened. Today in the movies I am still thrilled but not frightened, consciously at least, since I know it's all a fake. I even make fun of the thrill sometimes by an ironic exclamation during the performance. Perhaps the whole atmosphere of the movies — darkness and seeing something strange — has something to do with it."

We note that all of these rationalizations stress an aggressive or at least teasing element, *none* the passive one.

A Triad of Unconscious Motivations

If, in a mystery thriller, a man commits a murder and a clever detective hunts the killer, there are theoretically two possibilities for the reader: He can identify *temporarily* with the hunted or with the hunter. In terms of rationalization, his "interest" centers in one of them. Behind that "interest" a temporary identification is hidden.

What determines the choice of this identification? Always the *inner need* to express in a roundabout way repressed wishes and defense mechanisms. Of course, we cannot expect the individual to guess correctly the reason for his interest. On the contrary, he must of necessity guess incorrectly, as a part of his defense mechanism. For instance, the criminal lawyer, with whose remarks the article opens, was of the opinion that his interest in detective stories was purely theoretical and psychological — misinterpretation No. 1. He was furthermore of the opinion that all of the spectators were potential murderers — misin-

[1]The problem of the different "Watsons," the detective's companion, has been repeatedly discussed. Interesting material is gathered in *Murder for Pleasure* by Howard Haycraft. The first Watson was anonymous; Dupin's companion in Poe's *Murders in the Rue Morgue*, the first detective story, had not even a name of his own. There are historical and technical reasons for keeping alive the detective's "alter ego" in detective fiction, which Haycraft enumerates. Rex Stout believes, for instance, that Conan Doyle's Watson psychologically represents Mrs. Holmes. This may be so. I personally assume that the respective Watsons represent a projected part of the detective's unconscious personality and, in other instances, the reversal of the child-father situation. It is the father now pushed into the role of the admirer. Watson's famous "Excellent" and Holmes' condescending reply, "Elementary, Watson," point in that direction. On the other hand, many variations of the Watson problem have been introduced; for instance, the ironic Watson representing unconsciously the ironic superego doubting the child's ability. Basically, every detective story contains the father-son conflict, symbolized, perpetuated, and projected ad infinitum. This is visible in the problem itself (". . . the detective story is at bottom one thing only: a conflict of wits between criminal and sleuth" — Haycraft, *loc. cit.*), furthermore in the aggression toward the official police and, last but not least, in the respective Watsons. On different levels the old fight stemming from childhood is perpetuated; the child is victorious — hence the detective outsmarts the criminal and the official police.

The unconscious reasons leading to that superficial triple "aggression" cannot be discussed here without discussing the psychology of writers' unconscious in general. (See my paper, *A Clinical Approach to the Psychoanalysis of Writers*. Psychoan. Rev., 1944)

THE MURDER INK OPINION POLL

Mystery readers on average are between twenty-five and thirty-five years old, claim to have a college degree and are employed as (in order of frequency) lawyers, copywriters, schoolteachers, librarians, and homemakers.

They read three books per week, although this number swells during the summer, the Christmas season and vacation periods, and diminishes during March, April and September.

They consider Penguin the best mystery book publisher.

Their favorite English author is Dorothy L. Sayers.

Their favorite American author is Raymond Chandler, with Rex Stout running a close second.

Those subscribing to *Ellery Queen's Mystery Magazine* also subscribe to a mystery book club.

Given the opportunity to invent a code name for themselves, the women overwhelmingly picked Irene Adler and the men chose Old Bailey. No one picked 007.

According to them, a cat burglar's kit should include: a loid; a gunnysack; skeleton keys; a flashlight; a black leotard; glass cutters; suction cups; a rope ladder; a lawyer's telephone number; fur balls.

They described a police blotter as having: Trixie's address and phone and measurements in the upper left-hand corner; pizza and beer stains; attempts to solve the *Daily News* puzzle; drawings of a particularly lewd nature; the best graffiti in town.

Most admitted they had been duped into buying duplicates because of title changes, but cover changes did not seem to bother them.

Authors' names they had the most difficulty in pronouncing: Sjöwall and Wahlöö, Ngaio Marsh, Julian Symons, Dashiell Hammett (in that order).

Without exception they preferred books with a continuing character. The reason most often cited was, it saved the reader the trouble of getting to know new people. Also mentioned: They like to watch the character mature, to grow up with them.

They felt the murderer usually turned out to be: the least likely suspect; the doctor.

Their favorite fictional blunt instrument was a frozen leg of lamb.

Their favorite fantasy blunt instrument was: a train; a toeshoe; a hanging plant; a frying pan; a small bronze statue; a candlestick; a wedgie; a croquet mallet; a typewriter; a magnum of champagne.

As fit punishments for those who reveal the endings of mysteries, they suggested: forcing them to read science fiction; forcing them to reread Agatha Christie; forcing them to read mysteries whose last three pages had been torn out. They were also partial to death by misadventure and adhesive tape across the mouth.

Over half of the respondents had tried to write a mystery themselves or were planning to.

Method of polling: One thousand questionnaires were randomly distributed to customers of the Murder Ink Bookstore during March, April and May of 1977. Seven hundred twenty-one responses were either left in the store or mailed in to the editor of *Murder Ink,* who tabulated the results by a highly unscientific method she will reveal to no one.

terpretation No. 2. Forced to admit that he was as much involved in the thrillers via identification as the persons he would observe, he confessed to a "streak of cruelty" in his make-up — misinterpretation No. 3. The idea that he and the other spectators identified with the victim, that they unconsciously enjoyed psychic masochistic pleasure of passivity and being overwhelmed, never occurred to him. It was difficult, not only to convince him of his own passivity, but to make him understand that his "potential murderers" were also using *pseudo*-aggression only as a defense.

This passivity explains all of the aggressive conscious rationalizations. It has already been stressed that the six previously mentioned rationalizations had one common denominator — aggression. The problem is only whether this aggression was genuine or an unconscious defense against the opposite tendency, namely, passivity. I am of the opinion, gained from clinical experience, that the latter was the case.

Our conclusion so far is that the mystery fan unconsciously enjoys passivity and appeases his inner conscience with pseudo-aggression. He enjoys, via unconscious identification, not the killing but the being mistreated or killed, on the condition that even his pseudo-aggression be only a game.

This inner passivity explains, by the way, why the reader or spectator of mysteries is so often fooled. He does not connect the clues because he wants to be overwhelmed. Intellectual solution of the riddle would diminish his unconscious pleasure, so he gladly sacrifices logical thinking.

Is *unconscious enjoyment of passivity* the only element which makes up the mystery fan? Of course not. There are two other elements of prime importance: *enjoyment of uncanniness* and *voyeuristic enjoyment of the forbidden.* These three elements of the forbidden are a triad producing the mystery fan. The last two elements need some explanation.

Freud pointed out in his paper "The Uncanny" that the feeling of uncanniness is of two types. One is that produced when an impression revives repressed infantile complexes; the other, when the primitive beliefs we

The forehead of a man destined to die a violent death. If someone of your acquaintance has a similarly shaped forehead, be kind. Someone's going to get him.

have surmounted seem once more to be confirmed. Says Freud:

> *Let us take the uncanny in connection with the omnipotence of thoughts, instantaneous wish-fulfilment, secret power to harm, and the return of the dead. The condition by means of which the feeling of uncanniness arises here is unmistakable. We – or our primitive forefathers – once believed in the possibility of these things. . . As soon as something actually happens in our lives which seems to support the old discarded beliefs, we get a feeling of the uncanny; and it is as though we were making a judgment something like this: 'So, after all, it is true that one can kill a person by merely desiring his death!' or, 'Then the dead do continue to live and appear before our eyes on the scene of their former activities!'*

In continuation of Freud's paper, which appeared in 1919, and in application of his newer formulations on anxiety in his book *The Problem of Anxiety,* I could show in *The Psychoanalysis of the Uncanny*[2] that we are dealing in the specific case of uncanniness with an anxiety-signal, warning the subject of some inner danger. That danger is experienced when the feeling of omnipotence of infancy seems to have returned. But at first glance it is not obvious why the dearest belief of our childhood — our own omnipotence — should

[2]Int. J. Psychoan. (London), 1934, XV, pp. 215-244.

suddenly have become terrifying upon its reappearance. The explanation is this. The original sense of omnipotence was "knocked out" of the child, in the last resort, by his dread of castration. With the recrudescence of the old omnipotence-wishes the old castration anxiety is also revived. The sense of the uncanny represents a saving in anxiety and psychic work. In my opinion, this anxiety signal at the approach of inner danger from the aggressive instinct is a characteristic of the uncanny. The danger apprehended is condensed within the infantile ideas of grandeur. What we observe clinically in uncanniness is, however, *not* the aggression, but the sexualization of the aggression turned like a boomerang against the person himself because of guilt — *psychic masochism.*

If we apply the results of such studies to the mystery fan, we find that he enjoys uncanniness with all of its masochistic consequences. In other words, he resuscitates childlike megalomania via identification with the "omnipotent and omniscient" detective, criminal, or adventurer. But it is only *historically* correct to speak of identification with the murderer because of resuscitation of one's own omnipotence. What *actually* happens is only enjoyment of masochistic-passive drives, even in the feeling of uncanniness. Were real aggression enjoyed by the mystery fan, he *would never experience the feeling of uncanniness,* which is the secondary and masochistic elaboration. Since the feeling of uncanniness is typical in the reading of thrillers, no real aggression can be involved.

A woman's forehead marked with lines of adultery and mendacity. If she becomes a victim, you won't have to ask why; it's as plain as the forehead on her face.

Another very justifiable objection might be raised. Do not people have enough real and original aggressions? Why could not an aggressive reader identify with the murderer because of his aggressive deed? The answer depends on an understanding of the criminal psyche. I believe that the criminal is not at all the embodiment of aggression, but uses a *pseudo*-aggressive defense mechanism. He represents a specific case of failure to overcome the oral disappointment, and one unique in its specific "solution." The feelings of pre-oedipal disappointment in the mother and helplessness to take revenge for this disappointment force the criminal into his herostratic act. His situation is that of a dwarf fighting a giant who refuses to take cognizance of his fight. The only way he can show his intention to take revenge is, so to speak, by using dynamite. That tendency to take revenge, projected upon society, is coupled with self-intended punishment; only unconscious anticipation of punishment makes crime possible for the criminal, since it appeases his inner conscience. In every criminal action two factors are involved, a constant one and a variable one. The *constant* factor ("mechanism of criminosis") explains the motor act, the real conundrum in crime. It is based on the masochistic attempt to overcome the feeling of helplessness stemming from pre-oedipal orality, mentioned above. The *variable* factor pertains to the psychologic contents of the specific crime; it must be determined in every specific case, and is as multitudinous as human motivations in general. In my opinion, the social factors in crime play a relatively subordinate role. In the majority of cases they are rationalizations for hidden unconscious motives or the hitching point for masochistic repetition of injustices experienced in reality or fantasy in the child-mother-father relationship, afterward projected and perpetuated masochistically

The forehead of a man destined to be wounded in the head. (Phinella does not indicate whether by blunt instrument, dum-dum bullet or quick flick of a knife.)

upon society or the social order in general.

At this point an interesting fallacy must be looked into. Since, genetically, crime has its roots in deepest pre-oedipal passivity and the enjoyment of mystery thrillers also seems to indicate unconscious passivity, what is the distinction between the criminal and the crime reader? It would seem that the pessimistic criminal lawyer was on the right track after all. The fallacy of this reasoning is easily made apparent. These two types of passivity are genetically completely dissimilar. The *pre-oedipal* (oral) passivity of the criminal and the passivity of the mystery fan are different from each other. The *phenomonology* in itself — passivity — does not automatically give any clue to the *genetic* basis. That and that only is the pivotal point. The idea that seeing or reading a mystery thriller induces murder is *not* based on genetic facts. True, it is sometimes given as a rationalization by a murderer. It results from a misunderstanding of crime in general and of the power of the mystery thriller in particular, giving the latter an enhancement it by no means deserves.

The third decisive element of the triad is the voyeuristic enjoyment of the forbidden. We recall the statement of the young girl, which refers to two facts. First, even as a child she enjoyed gruesome fantasies of being overwhelmed; second, she identified the "mystery" in the thrillers with other mysteries which she wanted to solve as a child. Then the mysteries were in connection with sex; she wanted to know what her parents were doing during the night. (It is not by chance that mystery and night are unconsciously associated.) The fact that later in the life of mystery fans the mysteries pertain in general to murder can be explained by the sadistic misconceptions children have about sex and, furthermore, by the creation of a defense alibi in which aggression is substituted for sexual wishes. In other words, the interest in sex is shifted and masked; the sex problem is replaced by an aggressive conundrum. I have had the opportunity to check on this assumption; clinical experience has proved its validity.

The criminal lawyer mentioned previously was of the opinion that all of these facts proved that every human being was a potential murderer, who enjoyed his murderous tendencies in disguise via the gangster or detective thriller. Such a view seems pure nonsense. It is based on a misunderstanding of the genetic reasons for crime in general. What these facts do prove is the *enormous amount of inner passivity in people.* Since, in seeing or reading a thriller, this inner passivity can be enjoyed with two face-saving alibis ("I am aggressive" and "The whole thing is only a game"), the attraction is irresistible to some, especially since it is coupled with enjoyment of childlike megalomania resuscitated by the appearance of the uncanny.

These millions of mystery fans do not represent the reservoir of "potential murderers" but are, criminologically speaking, harmless. These people get temporary release of their tension vicariously. Of course, the whole process is unconscious.

The late Edmund Bergler, M.D., was a psychoanalyst in New York and the author of twenty-five books and more than 300 professional papers. *This article appeared in* The Selected Papers of Edmund Bergler, M.D. *and in* The American Journal of Orthopsychiatry. *Abridged and reprinted by permission of the Edmund and Marianne Bergler Psychiatric Foundation.*

SIMENON, APOLLO AND DIONYSUS

A Jungian Approach to the Mystery

John Boe, Ph.D.

At night, before going to bed, Carl Jung liked to read mystery stories. The great psychologist explained this habit rather simply: The stories were absorbing enough to keep him from thinking too deeply and losing sleep, yet not so fascinating that he was unable to turn them aside after a few pages. And like so many of us, he loved to read about *other* people's problems. He was especially fond of Georges Simenon's mysteries ("C.G. Jung's Library," by M.L. von Franz in *Spring* 1970).

By considering Simenon we can gain a deeper understanding of Jung and the mystery. Simenon's first detective novel was *Maigret and the Enigmatic Lett.* It is here that he first defined his central character, Inspector Maigret. Maigret triumphs not through intellect or courage, but through a psychological understanding of the criminal, built out of sympathetic feeling and, above all, intuition. Simenon emphasizes the "kind of intimacy" that always grows up between detective and criminal, who for weeks and months concentrate almost entirely upon each other. Maigret finally solves this mystery (which involves a schizophrenic twin) by studying old photographs and finding out childhood secrets. He solves the case by looking for the *human* factor that shows through the criminal. In this case Maigret reminds us of a psychoanalyst searching for the childhood secrets of a schizophrenic. And when Maigret finds the key to the mystery, he doesn't bring the criminal before the law but allows him the dignity of suicide.

In *Maigret's First Case,* Maigret reveals his own childhood secret: he used to imagine a sort of combination doctor and priest who, "because he was able to live the lives of every sort of man, to put himself inside everybody's mind," is able to be a sort of "repairer of destinies." Then, later in life, Maigret is forced to abandon his medical studies and finds himself, almost by accident, becoming a policeman.

Jung (like a detective or novelist) was himself a sort of combination doctor and priest, working with others' destinies, using his capacity to put himself inside another's mind

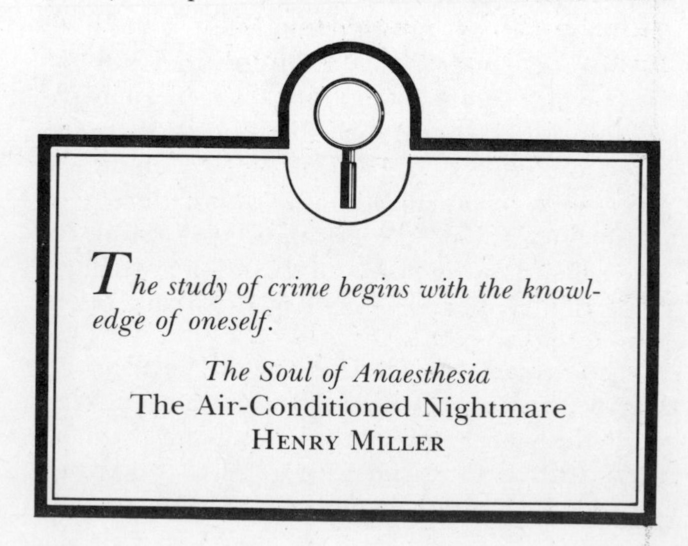

Sigmund Freud, age eight, with his father. Prof. Dr. Freud enjoyed a good mystery, particularly those written by Dorothy L. Sayers. (Jung preferred the work of Simenon.)

more than his superior intelligence. Thus, between patient and doctor as between detective and criminal, there can occur a "participation mystique," an unconscious bond. This involves what Jung calls relativization of the ego: If the ego can abandon its claim to absolute power, the psyche can open up to the unconscious within and the unconscious without (in the form of other people's psyches). In *Maigret and the Hundred Gibbets,* Maigret can address the assembled suspects and not need to finish his sentences. They know what he means even when he doesn't speak: "It was as if they could hear what he was thinking." Insofar as Maigret and Jung rely upon their unconscious, upon their intuition, they act without specific theory or technique. Jung denied being a Jungian, and Maigret is almost embarrassed when younger policemen want to observe his "methods."

Like a detached analyst, Inspector Maigret doesn't judge, he only unveils. Once the detective has unmasked the guilty party, he has decidedly little interest in punishing him; this is also the case in many of the books of Dorothy L. Sayers (Freud's favorite mystery writer). While sometimes the guilty party is not formally punished, it often seems that the murderer brings punishment upon himself. In one case Maigret allows the statute of limitations to run out on a group of men since it is plain that they have already been punished for their parts in a murder (and, just as important, they have children).

Jung was also acquainted with the psychological fact that murder can exert its own punishment. In his autobiography, *Memories, Dreams, Reflections,* he recounts an early psychiatric experience. A woman came to him for a consultation, to share an unbearable secret. She had killed her friend in order to marry the friend's husband. She got her man, but shortly thereafter he died and all of life soon turned sour for her. She was condemned to a lonely life; even dogs and horses seemed to sense her guilt. As Jung commented, the murderer had already sentenced herself, for one who commits such a crime destroys her own soul.

It is easy to understand why Jung was attracted to the psychological detective stories of Simenon, to the introverted, intuitive Inspector Maigret. But we should also consider the archetypal impulses behind the detective story, and a good place to begin is Greek mythology. Perhaps the most famous detective story involves the infant Hermes' theft of Apollo's cattle. At first, Apollo is mystified; Hermes has diguised the tracks so that it looks as if a giant led something *into* the pasture. Apollo first asks an eyewitness, an old man who seems to remember seeing a small child. He then uses his godly intuition: when an eagle flies by, he divines that the thief is a son of Zeus (since eagles are the birds associated with Zeus). According to some versions, he uses operatives to find where Hermes is hidden.

Apollo looks for clues, interviews eyewitnesses, uses his intuition and employs operatives. He is the archetypal detective. While Apollo as God of Divination and Prophecy does have a special relation to intuition, he is also the God of Law, with a special interest in murder. It was Apollo's province to exact blood for

As a semi-reformed mystery addict with catholic tastes (including Father Brown) I avoid mysteries; no time. Am liable to be hooked by any author who can lure me past the first three pages. I slip every so often without remorse. What are this year's best? — please do not reply to that.

HUMPHREY OSMOND

blood; it was his rule that a murderer must be purified (through punishment). Thus, instead of personal revenge (the central event of so many tragedies), the state (representing Apollo) avenges. And thus the detective, the impersonal avenger, is Apollo's agent.

If Apollo represents the detective, it is his traditional opposite, Dionysus, who represents the murderer. While Apollo inspires wisdom and was equated by Jung (in *Psychological Types*) with introverted intuition, Dionysus inspires madness and was equated (by Jung) with extroverted sensation. To Dionysus belong the ecstasies and excesses of drunkenness and passion. And as Inspector Maigret asserts in *Maigret Stonewalled,* at the bottom of the criminal mind one always finds "some devouring passion." Dionysus in his madness committed many murders. This behavior is perhaps explained by a childhood trauma: as a child Dionysus was murdered. (This is perhaps true of mortal murderers as well; they are metaphorically murdered in childhood.) The Titans tore the infant Dionysus to pieces, but Zeus (or Rhea) helped him to be reborn. According to Orphic myth, the Titans ate most of Dionysus before Zeus destroyed them with a thunderbolt. From their ashes rose humanity. Thus, in a central Dionysian mystery, the initiate tore a bull (a symbol of Dionysus) to pieces with his bare hands and ate of his flesh, reenacting (in this murder mystery) the murder and incorporation of the divinity. Dionysus is therefore the god who is murdered and the god who murders; he is the god of murderers and victims alike. We can thus understand how Dionysus was sometimes equated with Hades, Lord of the Dead.

But if the detective often uses Apollonian reason or intuition, he is also deeply involved in a Dionysian mystery. His full attention is focused upon murder and murderer. And while Inspector Maigret does withdraw into introverted spells of intuition, he usually accompanies them with the Dionysian aids of beer and wine. (Remember how many other detectives abuse alcohol and drugs.) The central event of the mystery plot is usually a mysterious (and often passionate) murder, but the plot itself is usually reasonable, fair and intricate. And the representative of that great and reasonable thing — the law — is often possessed by a spirit of the dead, the living image of the murdered. Thus Maigret often catches the criminal by getting to know the victim. In *Inspector Maigret and the Dead Girl,* he befuddles the murderer by telling him he would have swallowed his story if he hadn't known the dead girl. His totally pragmatic and reasonable subordinate believes the false story because "no training course teaches policemen how to put themselves in the place of a girl brought up in Nice by a half-crazy mother."

Insofar as the detective identifies with the evil murderer and his dead victim, he identifies Apollo with Dionysus. (That Apollo and Dionysus were one and the same god was a paradox of the later Orphic mysteries.) In Jungian terms we could talk about the ego assimilating the shadow side. Assimilation of the shadow results in a darkening and deepening of the whole personality; a proximity with evil can lead, paradoxically, to a moral improvement. The detective is conscious of the evil he partakes in; he doesn't gloat in his moral superiority. Carl Jung, like Inspector Maigret (and Philip Marlowe and countless other detectives) saw in the whole person both good and evil, passion and reason, Dionysus and Apollo.

John Boe has never (to his knowledge) committed murder.

CROSSWORDS AND WHODUNITS

A Correlation Between Addicts?

Colin Dexter

I noticed with vague disquiet a recent report in the *British Medical Journal* asserting a significant correlation between eating cornflakes for breakfast and the onset of the dreaded Crohn's disease. Yet correlations are notoriously cock-eyed, and it was some consolation for me to recall that the annual number of iron ingots shipped from Pennsylvania to California was once significantly correlated with the number of registered prostitutes in Buenos Aires. With such wildly improbable findings to encourage us, may we please tentatively assume that there is likely to be a positive correlation of sorts between those who enjoy crosswords and those who enjoy detective stories? At the very least, I think there *ought* to be one. Why is this?

Let us begin in familiar surroundings: a murder and a conveniently small circle of suspects, one of whom is the murderer. As in the cryptic[1] crossword, *clues* bestrew the scene; but they will be read correctly only by our hero, who, if not exactly a roaring genius, is an investigator of alpha-plus acumen. Between times the writer will dangle each of the suspects in front of our noses in such a way that we shall fail to recognise the murderer until the surprise dénouement. Such is the stuff of the classic sleight-of-hand whodunit; and clearly there is much in common between this genre of detective fiction (though much less so between the broader "crime" story or the "thriller") and the cryptic crossword. Each is a puzzle for which clues are cunningly laid, and to which there is a final, unambiguous solution.

In the actual process of clue-ing, both the whodunit writer and the crossword composer (not "compiler," please!) have a duty to be fair. They need not necessarily say what they mean, *but they must mean what they say:* it is fair to mislead, but not to mislead by deliberate falsification. Let us take an example from the great crossword composer Ximenes: "An item in fuel is somewhat fluctuating supply" (6). "In" means "contained within," and the six letters of the answer are contained, consecutively, within the next three words (no padding). Fair enough. But where is the definition of LISSOM? For any composer worth the name will include a definition. Well, we have been deceived. We see the words "fuel" and "supply," and the misleading connection is immediately forged in the mind: "misleading," because the second word is not "sup*ply*" but "*sup*ply"—the adverb from the adjective "supple"—and LISSOM means "fluctuating *sup*ply." That is the way of it, and instances abound of such ambivalent words, frequently to be found in combination. "A number

[1] A "cryptic" clue is, loosely speaking, one which is not merely a straight definition but which also leads to an answer by disguised means, usually by allusion to individual letters or parts of that answer.

of members," for example, may refer not only to a local golf club but also to a local anaesthetic; for it is the way *we* look at these words which determines their significance—the words themselves remain the same.

Similarly, the whodunit writer must seek to be fair, or at least not deliberately unfair. The match-stick found on the scene of the crime may have been used either to light the assailant's cigar or to pick his teeth—but it must always remain a *match-stick.* So, too, with the other clues. If, in the first chapter of a book, we are invited to survey a blood-bedrenched boudoir, we shall feel cheated if, in the last, we are informed that the putative victim had an incurable bedtime passion for the taste of tomato sauce. No. Clues must form a basis for logical deduction — a process as much at the heart of detective fiction as of crosswords.

But deception may, of course, begin from the start. Ximenes once published a puzzle (on April 1st!) wherein the clue to 1 across provided two quite legitimate answers: MAHOGANY and RAMBUTAN. Each clue thereafter provided a similar pair of answers, and all fitted into one another perfectly — with the exception of one space. Only by working from RAMBUTAN could the puzzle be finally completed. Such cumulative deception is also practised by the whodunit writer. In *The Greek Coffin Mystery,* for example, Ellery Queen can arrive at a convincing solution halfway through the book, only for the reader to discover that one key problem remains unresolved. Back to square one! And in *The Murder of Roger Ackroyd* (the most famous deception of all) Agatha Christie throws the reader onto the wrong track from the very first sentence.

So much for clues. When it comes to *solutions,* it has been said that the whodunit reader doesn't really *care* who committed the crime, but that he has to *know;* and such a situation is familiar to the crossword addict. Ideally, the solution, in each case, is one where the bewildered victim can kick himself for not having guessed it before. Let me illustrate. There is little satisfaction in crossword solving if an inordinately obscure clue leads to a dialectal word, now obsolete, in Lowland Scots. But how different when the word is perfectly well known, when only minimal demands are made upon outside knowledge! Consider "What the Jumblies kept in the sieve" (6). Most of us know that the Jumblies went to sea in a sieve. But which of their (doubtless) quaint possessions did they *keep* in the wretched thing? We are tempted to say: "If only I could remember the whole poem!" Or, "What object *could* they have kept in a sieve, anyway?" But no. The simple answer is AFLOAT, and we knew it all the time. Excellent!

Some few practitioners in each genre have raised their work to the level of a minor art, and it is perhaps the very limitations of this art which make it so enjoyable to so many. What are these limitations? Well, whodunits are games, really; games played to a set of rules, however loosely applied. With the emphasis upon coherent deduction, there is little room for characterisation in depth, and death itself is no "fell sergeant," but merely a convenient point of departure — the messier the better. Crosswords, too, are played to rules — or at least the best ones are, as those who have read *Ximenes on the Art of the Crossword* will know. (And what a pity it is that the Americans, sticking for the most part to their rather tedious definition clues, have given themselves so little chance of producing an Afrit, a Torquemada, a Ximenes, or an Azed.[2] After all, it was the New York *Sunday World* which was the first in the field.) In each genre we learn the rules and we

[2]*Afrit:* the late Prebendary A.F. Ritchie, of *The Listener.* His pseudonym is formed from the two Christian-name initials and the first three letters of his surname. Appropriately, the word "afrit" = "an evil demon in Arabian mythology."
Torquemada: the late Edward Powys Mathers, of *The Observer.* His pseudonym derives from the Dominican Tomás de Torquemada, the Grand Inquisitor appointed in Spain by Pope Sixtus IV in the reign of Ferdinand and Isabella. He was a great pioneer in the art of the crossword, loved by addicts and feared by the uninitiated.
Ximenes: from 1942 to his death in 1971, D.S. MacNutt concealed himself behind the pseudonym "Ximenes" — François Ximenés de Cisneros, Cardinal, Archevêque de Tolède, Grandinquisiteur, et Régent d'Espagne. The standards set by Ximenes in his famous *Observer* puzzles have achieved world-wide renown, and in the opinion of many (including me) he ranks as the greatest of the crossword composers.
Azed: the pseudonym of Jonathan Crowther, also of *The Observer,* a composer of bold ingenuity. The name "Azed," apart from its comprehensively alphabetical connotation (a–z), maintains (by a reversal of its letters) a continuity with its two predecessors, for Don Diego de *Deza* was Spanish Grand Inquisitor from 1498 to 1507, between Torquemada and Ximenes; and a particularly beastly fellow he was, by all accounts, who burned 2,592 heretics alive.

Across

1. *Watch on the Rhine* scriptwriter
8. Apply blunt instrument to skull
9. Gave the third degree
11. Criminal's style
14. Polygraph peak
15. Roscoe
16. Prey of Venus's-flytrap
17. What ratiocination is
20. Capet was one
23. Thing, to Perry Mason
24. D16 agent
25. Sluggishness
27. Red herring
28. 1954 Edgar winner

Down

1. Legal verdict
2. Hard-boiled houses
3. Poison pen necessity
4. Campion's valet, Wimsey style
5. _____ objects open locked doors
6. Part of story in which sleuth solves crime
7. Manhattan, Kansas sibling
10. Harriet's husband's title
12. Easily crushed spinal pad
13. Like some pills, but unlike horror stories
18. _____ Reaper
19. Gothic locale
21. Something strange
22. aka A.A.
26. Clue for a gumshoe
27. Sing Sing

Solution on page 450.

Eugene T. Maleska is the crossword puzzle editor of the New York Times.

play the game, and in so doing we escape for a while from the harsh world: there is little or no emotional involvement.

Clearly, then, the reasons for the popularity of these two escapist activities are pretty similar: we revel in mystification; we are curiously uncomplaining about being misled; above all, we enjoy the final dropping of the penny.

My own first memory of crosswords? I recall my deep admiration for one of my classmates who solved the unremarkable (and quite unscientific) clue "Ena cut herself" (7); and I was soon to learn, from the same precocious youth, the answer to the riddle "Nothing squared is cubed" (3). (Do you have *Oxo* in America?) My first acquaintances in the whodunit field were Dr. Gideon Fell and Sir Henry Merrivale, wrestling with their "locked-room" mysteries: uneven books, certainly—but what a joy they were! Then, in a rush, came most of the Christie classics, and I've been happily hooked on whodunits ever since. Rex Stout particularly springs to mind as I write, since the oversized Nero Wolfe, when not tending his oversized orchids in his roof-garden or solving a case without stirring from his oversized chair, was wont (so I read) to exercise his oversized brain on *Ximenes* puzzles. Which, for me, is a happy illustration. To be truthful, I've always wanted to be a supersleuth; and when I tackle a new crossword I'm childish enough to see myself as the great detective magisterially surveying the clues and, with a bit of luck, finding the solution — all on my own. Like Wolfe, too, I'd prefer not to stir from the armchair, since I am just as anxious for the detective to manage without the pathology lab as for the crossword puzzler to manage without the dictionary. Fancifully, I wonder how Wolfe would have fared with the following clues taken from *Ximenes* puzzles. The first he might have found a little hard (might even, alas, have needed to look up "od" in Chambers' — by far the best crossword dictionary); the second he would probably have written into the diagram with only a second's thought. (i) "Despondency, Reichenbach's effect, unsolved crime . . . could have led Holmes to *this*" (10); (ii) Eyes had I, and unfortunately saw not" (6).[3]

To sum up, the glorious thing for me about the two activities is that each is engaged in for its own sake, with a simple sense of fresh delight; and to those long-faced counsellors who are forever ferreting out some pretentious justification for all human activities, we can cheerfully report that here there is *none* — none, that is, except our own pleasure. *Ars gratía artis,* for a change. And why on earth not?

Monsignour Ronald Knox (himself no mean writer of detective stories) was one day sitting in a train with the *Times* crossword on his knee. For several minutes he stared earnestly at the diagram but filled in not a single letter. When a young man sitting beside him suggested a possible answer to 1 across, Knox smiled serenely and handed him the crossword: "Here you are. I've just finished."

So have I.

SOLUTION TO MURDER INK

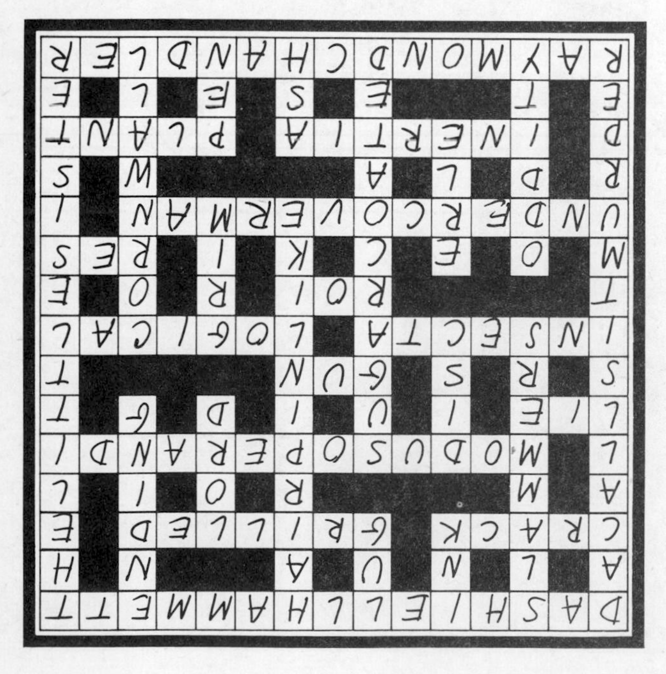

[3](i) HYPODERMIC (hyp - od + anag. of "crime" & lit.)
(ii) WATSON (anag. & lit.)

[Any reader who is still puzzled by "number of members" should be reminded of the verb "to numb." Poor Ena (who cut herself) - bled.]

Colin Dexter is the author of The Silent World of Nicholas Quinn *and was three times national champion in the Ximenes clue-writing competition.*

A SLIGHT DEBATE

A Hard-Boiled Fan and a Country-House Fan Discuss the Genre

Marilyn Stasio and Richard Hummler

SCENE: *A breakfast nook in an upper-middle-class suburban American home. A married couple, Mike and Margery, face each other across a glass breakfast table.*

MARGERY

Christie.

MIKE

Chandler.

MARGERY

Marsh.

MIKE

Who?

MARGERY

Ngaio.

MIKE

Oh, right . . . the New Zealander.

(Sucks in gut.)

Spillane. *(Pause. Lasciviously.)* Mickey.

MARGERY

I'm simply not going on with this if you won't behave decently.

(Pause. They glare at each other.)

MIKE

Ross Macdonald.

MARGERY

That's better . . . Margery Allingham.

MIKE

(Unbuttons his shirt collar and wrenches his tie away from his neck. Grins.)

Walker.

MARGERY

(Looks away from him nervously as she straightens the tea cosy.)

Who?

MIKE

Francis X. Walker, sweetheart. Detroit. His detective is Mickey Reilly.

MARGERY

Hardly in the premier rank, I'd say. *(Pause)* Michael Innes. No — make that P.D. James. *(Pause)* I'm saving Innes.

MIKE

Gores.

MARGERY

(Pause) Are you making yours up?

MIKE

(Rolls up his shirt sleeves and slams his elbows on the table.)

Joe Gores. Nobody you'd know, baby. Just one of the greatest detective novelists in American crime fiction.

(Margery rattles her teacup ominously.)

MIKE

Don't gimme that, Maggie. Just because Gores writes about *real* people killing other *real* people for *real* reasons, instead of effete Oxford dons knocking each other off with African blowguns, doesn't mean you have to turn your nose up.

MARGERY

You've dribbled egg on your chin. *(Sniffs.)* Maybe I should have cooked it *hard-boiled.*

(Opens her newspaper — the London Observer *— and screams.)*

MIKE

(Slams down the Daily News.*)*

What the —

MARGERY

John Dickson Carr died.

MIKE

(Pause) Who?

MARGERY

You must be joking. He is *the* master mystery craftsman of the century. His books are the *ne plus ultra* of the locked-room genre.

MIKE

(Lights a cigarette, blows the smoke in her eyes.)

Figures.

MARGERY

And what is *that* supposed to mean?

MIKE

Only broad I know gets so worked up when some academic pedant kicks off.

MARGERY

(Picks up her knitting and begins to work the long needles savagely.)

And when Mickey Spillane dies, I suppose you won't disappear into some bar for a week of sodden grieving.

MIKE

(Crumples his empty Lucky Strike pack and tosses it into a plate of cold kippers.)

Listen, sweetheart — maybe guys like Parker and Stark have never seen the inside of a cathedral close, but they tell it like it is, not like it *was.*

MARGERY

Name me one who writes with the literary erudition of Nicholas Blake. Or the wit of Edmund Crispin.

MIKE

(Sullenly.) Raymond Chandler.

MARGERY

(A hoot of contempt.) And I suppose that John D. MacDonald is a better writer than Michael Innes.

MIKE

Okay, so that's how you want to fight?

(Pause. He spikes his orange juice with a shot of Jack Daniel's. She winces.)

MacDonald at least tells a good story. Those English biddies you read — you can't even follow the plot if you don't have a Ph.D. in Etruscan funerary statuary.

MARGERY

(Smiles grimly over her knitting.)

Any intellectual demand beyond the size of a woman's bra cup is utterly beyond the mental capacities of your heroes.

MIKE

(Stands up, grabs his coat.)

Let me put it this way, Maggie. SHUT UP!

MARGERY

Why is it, every time we have this discussion, you retreat into macho petulance? *(Pause)* Are you really going to wear that filthy trench coat to the office, Michael?

MIKE

Now, don't go giving me that macho stuff again. A little normal sex is healthier than all those repressed vicars and inbred toffs sitting around doing crosswords in the drawing room.

(Lurches over to her. Grabs her knitting.)

And when you stop wearing riding tweeds and those damned English brogues, then you can start telling *me* how to dress . . . *sweet*heart.

MARGERY

(Nervously.) The sense of societal . . . uh . . . communality does get a bit thick with some of the older writers, I admit . . .

(Fortifies herself with another sip of tea.)

But the familial social structure has a distinct advantage, I should say, over the blatant fascism of your lone-wolf avengers. *(Pause)* More tea?

MIKE

(Mumbling to himself.) Buncha chinless snobs . . . *(Pause)* Coffee.

MARGERY

(Sweetly.) I don't suppose you've ever analyzed the latent misogyny of the blood-and-guts brigade?

MIKE

(Gives his coffee a blast of Jack Daniel's.)

Don't get sarcastic with me or I'll shut a drawer on your fingers.

MARGERY

George V. Higgins, I believe. *(Pause)* And I suppose Travis McGee isn't a closet queen?

MIKE

(Mumbling.) Buncha chinless snob *faggots!*

MARGERY

(Furiously butters a scone.)

Adolescent mentalities attempting to compensate for their own impotence.

MIKE

(Getting more incoherent.)

Lester Dent . . . Henry Kane . . .

(Reaches for the bourbon bottle; knocks it over.)

MARGERY

Sexual sadists!

MIKE

(Draws himself up.)

I'm warning you, baby . . .

MARGERY

(Wildly shreds watercress.)

You want to destroy it all — the puzzle, the pace, the atmosphere, the literary clues. *(Pause. Sobs.)* The compound-complex sentence.

MIKE

(Draws a gun from his trench coat pocket.)

No jury would convict me.

MARGERY

Do you smell that soufflé in the oven? *(Pause)* It's your first edition of *The Big Sleep!*

MIKE

That does it sweetheart.

(He shoots. She falls across the table, scattering the watercress.)

MIKE

Thirty-eight-caliber automatic. Makes a nice clean hole. Not too much blood. *(Pause)* She never did like blood.

(He grabs his throat. Chokes. Slumps back in his chair.)

MARGERY

(Weakly.) Potassium cyanide. Two grains. Chemical symbol: KCN. Crystalline salt with the following properties: colorless, soluble, poisonous. *(Pause)* Used in electroplating.

(She dies.)

MIKE

I won't play the sap for you, angel.

(He dies.)

— THE END —

Marilyn Stasio and Richard Hummler are a husband and wife team working in the theater. She is drama critic for Cue *magazine and* Penthouse. *He is a former* Variety *reporter now working for producer Alexander H. Cohen.*

THE BEST BOOK I NEVER WROTE

Judith Crist

We also serve who only sit and read. Let the uninitiate think we Mystery Readers serve the writers by our purchase and consumption of books and magazines and by our devotion, blind or very wise, to the masters of the craft and their creatures. We aficionados know that our greatest service has been our refusal to put down on paper, let alone publish, The Great American Detective Story that each of us carries around in his head. After all, we can devote a lifetime to perfecting plot and personnel as we consume the goodies the "public" writers provide and we grow fat on their creations. But we grow cautious, too, and taste humility from time to time as we encounter a more cunning crime, a cannier deduction, a tauter twist and better breath-bater than ever we dreamed of. And so the revisions go on and on as standards are set higher and higher. We Mystery Readers remain closet mystery writers.

I have spent my adult life in that closet, deposited therein by a parental attitude that designated moviegoing and detective story reading as prime time-wasters. Even so, it was on the family bookshelves that I found Sherlock Holmes and then a host of others in a ten-volume set of *The World's Greatest Detective Stories* that the Literary Digest had apparently foisted on the household as a subscription bonus. And it was at the Saturday movie matinées that I encountered Warner Oland's Fu Manchu, Warren William's Perry Mason, Edward Arnold's Nero Wolfe, William Powell's Philo Vance, Ronald Coleman's Bulldog Drummond, Edna May Oliver's Hildegarde Withers, Peter Lorre's Mr. Moto, and Warner Oland again as Charlie Chan. These introductions at least fulfilled Hollywood's educational pretension: they led me to read the books — all of them — and keep on reading.

But though in my adolescence as an aspiring writer I had no hesitation about attempting Dickensian sagas, Hemingwayesque stories and Thomas Wolfean *Weltschmerz,* I didn't attempt an unwritten mystery until graduate school. It came upon me suddenly — "Murder Cum

I stopped wasting money on new mystery novels years ago. Those I tried, stank. Except I do look on the stands for any new Lew Archer paperback. Hence my mystery reading is limited to re-reading: Simenon, who helps keep my French in condition; Rex Stout, since Archie Goodwin is always delightful; Matthew Head, whom I read between the lines as a personal diary. Dashiell Hammett and Raymond Chandler have been re-read so often that I no longer go back to them.

JOHN CANADAY
(MATTHEW HEAD)

JERRY DARVIN

Laude" — a bitterly satiric view of academe, wherein a variety of scholars met their doom and a beautiful, slim and brilliant graduate student helped a charming, couth and educated cop (a novelty in those days, I assure you) determine whether it was the Shakespeare scholar, the doctoral candidate or the janitor who did it. A couple of years went by as I devised cleverly academic methods of murder, all of which had to go by the boards (college, of course) when I switched my professional interests to journalism and "Murder Makes News" got into my head. This was to be a bitterly satiric view of newspapering, wherein a variety of columnists met their doom and a beautiful, slim and brilliant reporter helped a charming, uncouth and semi-educated cop (I had learned the facts of life) determine whether it was the publisher, the aspiring columnist or the copy-boy who did it. My real-life reporting experiences with crime — most memorably a murder on the Columbia campus, suspicious deaths among wealthy elderly patients of a Connecticut doctor, the slaughter of a family with an eight-year-old survivor the possible killer — made me worry a lot about methodology; encounters with a couple of corpses and discovering the reality of "the stench of death" took some of the fun out of the murders.

But I soon found that my domestic interests superseded my professional life and had put "Marriage for Murder" into my mind. This was to be a bitterly satiric view of matrimony, wherein a variety of young couples met their doom and a beautiful, slim and brilliant wife helped her charming, couth and educated cop husband (it was no more than the gal deserved) decide whether it was the bachelor, the playgirl or the butcher who did it. While I was concentrating on avoiding any Northian taint to a martini-drinking Manhattan-couple tale, I found myself replacing it with "The Lying-In Murders," a bitterly satiric view of a maternity ward, wherein a variety of young mothers met their doom at the hands of the obstetrician, pediatrician or hospital trustee. In no time at all, or so it seemed, this had given way to "The Sandbox Slayings," wherein a variety of abominable toddlers were done away with by a mommy, a nanny or another toddler.

When my professional life, now that of

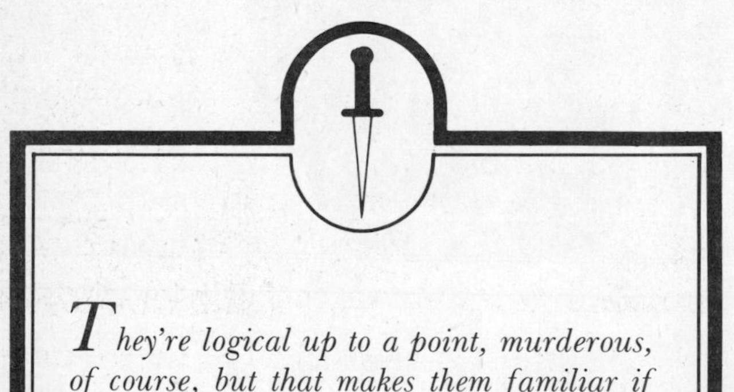

They're logical up to a point, murderous, of course, but that makes them familiar if one is at all observant of business and family life. They give me a world somewhat between the real one and that of the serious novel with its fragmented consciousness. A good mystery provides a suspense which is lulling for me because it is polite and formal. That's why the good ones work as a soporific for me.

HAROLD BRODKEY

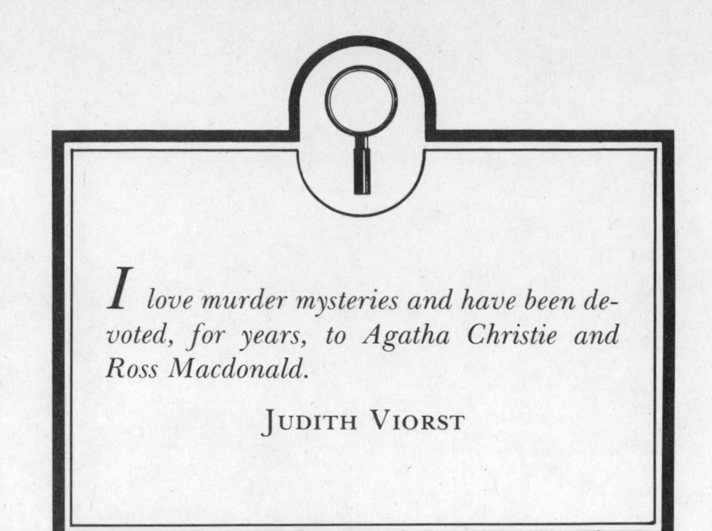

I love murder mysteries and have been devoted, for years, to Agatha Christie and Ross Macdonald.

JUDITH VIORST

theater and film critic, expanded to include television, however, domestic matters yielded to "Murder for Today," wherein a variety of morning-show guests were knocked off, on camera yet, and the heroine, no longer my vicarious alter ego but the attractive, sharp interviewer on the show, determined on her own whether it was the anchorman, the producer or everybody's researcher-mistress who did it. For a while this one shared headroom with "The Critic Killer," wherein a drama critic was murdered in mid-review (multiple murders were becoming a bit too taxing) and his beautiful, slim and brilliant associate (reenter the dream alter ego) determined whether it was the producer, director or star of the show he was covering who did it. These two, in recent years, were replaced by "The Film Festival Murders," with an international cast, of course, and endless possibilities for doing away with the unbeloveds of my medium. I'm staying with it. On the other hand, a recent campus weekend with my son has started "The Cambridge Killings" buzzing in my brain . . .

But have no fear, you darlings of my noncinematic hours. We closet mystery concocters know that those who can, do; we, who like to think that we could if we would, are smart enough not to. Not yet. Meanwhile, we also serve. We sit and read.

Judith Crist, film critic for the New York Post *and* TV Guide, *was named Mystery Reader of the Year (1971) by the Mystery Writers of America.*

CHRISTMAS GIFTS FOR MYSTERY FANS

Carol Brener

What happens if he's read all the Wolfes and she's read all the Wimseys?

What happens if they haven't read them all, but you don't know which they've missed?

Happily, crime characters have charming eccentricities and some prompt terrific gifts. Here, then, an imaginative assortment of Christmas presents for the true mystery addict.

For *spy thriller* readers: Used army trench coats (who wants to look like a *new* spy?) from Weiss & Mahoney, Inc. (142 Fifth Ave., New York, N.Y. 10011). From $5.95. Or, a total immersion course in Russian at Berlitz School of Languages (40 West 51st Street, New York, N.Y. 10019). $5,150. The cost is the same for Chinese.

For *private eye* buffs: A day of a private eye's services. Rates in the New York area start at $20 per hour for one operative, $40 per hour for two.

For *English village* fans: A subscription to *The Garden Book* by Amos Pettigill of White Flower Farm, Litchfield 676, Conn. 06759. $4 annually.

For *police procedural* fans: From the company that supplies the police, a fingerprint kit and fingerprint chart. Faurot, Inc. (299 Broadway, New York, N.Y. 10007). Kit, $31 (#638A); chart, $4.50.

For the *I-love-them-all* fan: A custom-made collage, 10″ × 10″. Will incorporate names, titles, quotations, pictures, clues, whatever. $75 from Tye Stonehand (245 Centre St., New York, N.Y. 10013). Allow three weeks.

For the *Lizzie Borden* specialist: The "Hudson Bay Kindling Axe," #6111J in the L.L. Bean, Inc. catalog. (Write c/o L.L. Bean, Freeport, Me. 04033.) You can carve something appropriate — like the name of a good lawyer — on the 18″ hickory handle.

For the *Lew Archer* fan: A room at the spiffiest place in Santa Barbara — The Ambassador by the Sea Motor Hotel (202 West Cabrillo Blvd., Santa Barbara, Calif. 93101). $26.32, double occupancy, in high season.

For the ***James Bond*** **fan:** The closest thing to a Turkish-Balkan blend — Sobranies' nonfiltered cigarettes from Lane Ltd. (122 East 42nd St., New York, N.Y. 10016). Pack of ten, $1.10.

For the ***Bony*** **fan:** A cake as big as the Outback — in the shape of Australia! If you supply the locales, the icing will mark the spot where Bony's cases occurred. $35 from Creative Cakes (400 East 74th St., New York, N.Y. 10021). Allow two weeks.

For the ***Charlie Chan*** **fan:** A number one son, if you can manage it. If not, dinner for two at the House of Chan (7th Ave. and 52nd

St., New York, N.Y. 10019). Allow $12.50 per person.

For the *Dick Francis* fan: Membership in the National Steeplechase Association (Box 308, Elmont, N.Y. 11003) provides entry to all hunt races and steeplechases in the U.S. and U.K., including the Grand National at Aintree and the Colonial Cup at Camden, S.C. $40 for one year.

For the *Inspector French* fan: Turn-of-the-century railroad watches — most are gold-filled, all work — from William Scolnik (1001 Second Ave., New York, N.Y. 10022). From $140.

For the *Sherlock Holmes* fan: A gasogene, the "classic syphon" from Hammacher Schlemmer (147 East 57th St., New York, N.Y. 10022). $35.95. Or, a deerstalker from Worth & Worth, Ltd. (331 Madison Ave., New York, N.Y. 10017). $11.95.

For the *Maigret* fan: A gourmet lunch at home with you, every day for a week. Followed by an early evening walk, holding hands. Followed by a glass of Calvados.

For the *Philip Marlowe* fan: A private showing of *Murder My Sweet* starring Dick Powell. Available from Films, Inc. (440 Park Ave. South, New York, N.Y. 10016). $85 for a one-day rental, and they'll even tell you where to rent a 16mm projector.

SPRINGER/BETTMAN FILM ARCHIVE

For the *Miss Marple* fan: A hand-knit shawl, if you've the talent, or a one-ounce jar of "Mr. Lord's Potpourri," redolent of roses. From Caswell-Massey (518 Lexington Ave., New York, N.Y. 10017). $6.50

For the *Poirot* fan: A mock-tortoise moustache comb, $2.50; Gelle Frères stick moustache wax, $3.00; Pinaud moustache wax in a tube, in a range of colors including glossy black, $2.00 the bottle or $3.50 the jar. All from Caswell-Massey (mail-order department, 320 West 13th St., New York, N.Y. 10014). Or, a good selection of ready-made moustaches from Barris & Zervoulei (982 Second Ave., New York, N.Y. 10022). $10.

For the *Roger Sheringham* fan: A chocolate greeting card with the words "these are not poisoned chocolates." 6″ × 8″ card of milk or semi-sweet chocolate, $15. Double-size card, $30. From Kron Chocolatier (764 Madison Ave., New York, N.Y. 10021). Shipped in wooden crate ($2.50, small; $3.50, large). No summer shipping.

For the *Sam Spade* fan: A replica of the infamous Maltese Falcon. So convincing it could fool Greenstreet, Lorre, Astor, even Bogey. Perch it on your desk, sweetheart. From Get Plastered (2964 N. Lincoln Ave. Chicago, Ill. 60657). $20.

For the *Philo Vance* fan: The opulence of Beluga caviar. When available, about $160 the pound from William Poll (1051 Lexington Ave., New York, N.Y. 10017). They will deliver, and will also mail.

For the *Lord Peter Wimsey* fan: A frameless monocle with a serrated edge and a tiny hole for the chain or ribbon, from $20; gold-rimmed monocles from $35. Both from the Ultimate Spectacle (1032 Third Ave, New York, N.Y. 10022). Or, membership in the Dorothy L. Sayers Society, $3.00 annually. Contact Sister Mary Durkin, 7900 West Division St., River Forest, Ill. 60305, for further information.

For the *Nero Wolfe* fan: Yellow silk pajamas may be custom-ordered from A. Sulka & Co. (711 Fifth Ave., New York, N.Y. 10022). $160. With piping, $170. "Nero" in script on pocket, $9.00; initials, $6.00. Or a variety of orchids, such as cattleyas in bloom, from $25. From Plantworks (8 Waverly Pl., New York, N.Y. 10003).

Carol Brener is author of The Underground Collector *and proprietor of Murder Ink, the mystery bookstore.*

TEA WITH ELLERY QUEEN

Dilys Winn

Before Murder Ink was a book, it was a bookstore and I wanted everything about it to relate to the mystery, including its location. As I saw it, I had two choices: Either open it on West 35th Street, where Nero Wolfe lived, or open it on West 87th Street, where Ellery Queen lived. I opted for uptown. (Need I add the city was New York? I'd have had a hard time putting it in either place if the city had been Chicago or L.A.)

Eventually, Murder Ink got customers, and sooner or later they'd say, "Say, did you know in *The French Powder Mystery* it mentions that Ellery Queen lived on this street? Nearer the park, mind you, but still . . ." Well, of course I knew it; I'd planned it.

Fittingly, the first letter the store ever received was from Fred Dannay, the surviving member of the Ellery Queen writing partnership. He wished the store well and asked to be kept posted on how it was doing. He also included a return address. My God! Ellery Queen expected *me* to write to *him!* For months afterward I wrote thank you notes to him in my head. That's as far as I got. Now you must understand, I am not a particularly humble person. I do not speak softly, nor do I fear to tread almost anywhere. But Ellery Queen — that was different. To me, he was more than a mystery writer; he was The Mystery Story. And I was only a reader. Sure fools may look upon kings. (Queens?) But speak to them? Don't be absurd.

Once, I was introduced to him at an MWA Edgar Allan Poe dinner. Torn between kissing his ring and curtsying, I merely stood there and gaped, which was all the opportunity the hordes needed. They stepped on, over and around me to get at him. Intimidated, I backed away.

It took me close on to five years to actually talk to Ellery Queen and that only happened because I finally did write him a letter. To say it was outrageous is to understate the case. I wanted to include him in *Murder Ink* — the book, not the store — and Eleanor Sullivan suggested if I wrote down a few questions, he'd be glad to answer them.

THE DOUBLE CROSS

Most people put only one line through their Q's. But most people aren't as inventive as Fred Dannay, who uses two strokes. The second stroke is to indicate that Ellery Queen encompasses two men, himself and Manfred B. Lee. If you're fortunate enough to own an inscribed Queen novel, take a look at the signature. The Q will be double-crossed.

"Ellery Queen"

Do you consider two pages, single-spaced, no margins, elite type, a few questions? What happened was, I kept rereading the questions and thinking, God that's dumb, better ask another. I thought he'd look at them, correct the grammar and then refuse to have me as a fan. Awe attacks some people in the knees; me, it gets in the syntax.

Presumably because he thought it would take less time to be interviewed than to synopsize his lifework — which is about what my questions demanded — Fred Dannay rang me up and invited me to tea. Little did he know I'd be more addled in person. Remember, it took me the better part of five years just to finish a letter. How long did he think it would take me to drink a cup of tea?

Actually, six hours. In fact, I parlayed it into dinner and was working my way up to asking to be adopted when common sense took over and I asked to be excused instead.

What did we talk about? Why had there not been a recent Queen novel? The last one appeared in 1971. The answer surprised and saddened me. It began with an explanation of the time absorbed in editing a monthly mystery magazine and then softly, reasonably, continued to this: A writer has to know when to stop. Mr. Dannay also suggested he might ultimately be better known for the magazine than for his coauthorship of Ellery Queen. He suffers, I think, from rampant humility. Let me be immodest for him: The man who thinks his work as a writer will eventually be eclipsed is the man who has won five Edgar awards, a special Raven award, and has sold more than one hundred fifty million books worldwide. The conclusion is obvious: Never ask an author to judge his own work.

Mr. Dannay is not easy to interview. He has been through it all so many times before, you see, that the answer is ready before the question is asked. And frankly, my questions were no more original than anybody else's.

I did learn, however, why he turns down speaking engagements. Seems he used to do them and was terrified by them, so much so that he spent the entire night before them being ill. On the other hand, teaching is something he enjoyed. He believes only in laboratory courses in which the student writes and the teacher criticizes. He recalled once discussing a single sentence for a whole session and there was a look on his face as if he remembered it as time well spent.

He seemed puzzled that his most often an-

AUTOGRAPH PARTY ETIQUETTE

Very rarely are mystery writers tendered an autograph party. Bookstore owners have discovered they are poor draws in comparison with, say, sports figures and movie personalities. They have been known to loiter by their books for two and even three hours and promote no more than ten sales.

A terribly nice author, who had written a rather risqué mystery — in fact, it was downright tawdry — once sat patiently for an hour, waiting to sign a purchase. The store owner prodded a sweet young thing over to him. The author smiled, introduced himself and discreetly proffered his book. She glanced at it, returned it, smiled equally sweetly and said, "Can you tell me where they keep the Dorothy Sayers?"

It is considered bad form to tell the author that you will wait for the book to come out in paperback; that you thought it miraculous he got his last book published; that you guessed whodunit on page 12; that you only browse in bookstores and get all your books from the library; that you're writing a book yourself and could he tell you the name of his agent. Equally gauche is to swipe his pen.

If you have been specially invited to an autograph party, do not go unless you plan on buying the book. Anything else is freeloading.

thologized piece was a short description of how he came to read Conan Doyle and first met Sherlock Holmes and that it could prompt the likes of Dale Carnegie to read it and say, "Now I know why my wife loves you."

He seemed unhappy with many current reviewers, excepting Anatole Broyard, whom he liked. He warmed to the idea of an American Mystery Museum or Mystery Hall of Fame, had, in fact, proposed it to MWA years ago, and even has a few artifacts to contribute — some of Jacques Futrelle's things given to him by Mrs. Futrelle, including a pocket notebook containing plot ideas for *The Thinking Machine*.

He was silent on how he and Manfred B. Lee actually did their collaborating, except to say Mr. Lee always wanted it to be a secret and he felt he should keep that confidence. But he was absolutely voluble on two counts: designing jacket covers and conveying dying messages. Mr. Dannay was once, long ago, an advertising art director and whipped off a rough drawing for the cover of Queen's first book, *The Roman Hat Mystery* (1929). Somehow or other the publisher never got around to having the artwork rendered and his first sketch became the final product. He is an inveterate tinkerer with

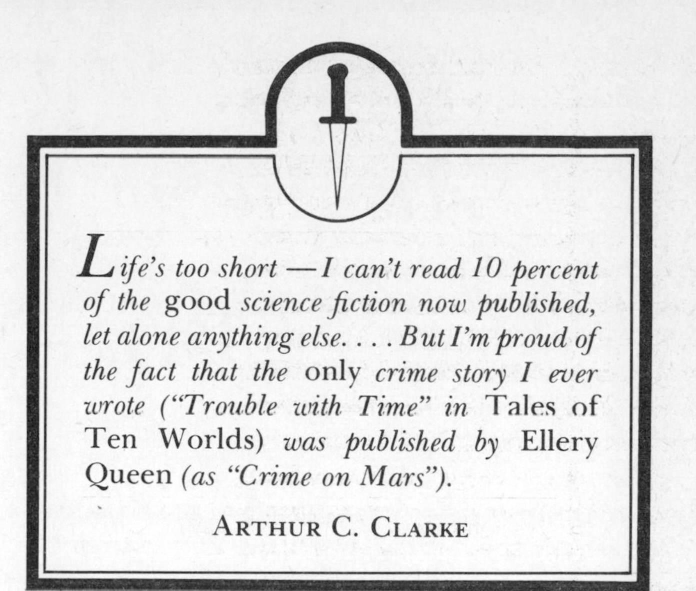

Life's too short — I can't read 10 percent of the good *science fiction now published, let alone anything else. . . . But I'm proud of the fact that the* only *crime story I ever wrote ("Trouble with Time" in* Tales of Ten Worlds) *was published by* Ellery Queen *(as "Crime on Mars").*

ARTHUR C. CLARKE

The first issue of Ellery Queen's Mystery Magazine *appeared in the fall of 1941. It cost a quarter and included stories by Dashiell Hammett, Margery Allingham, T.S. Stribling, Anthony Abbott, Cornell Woolrich and Queen himself. Today, it is considered a collector's item.*

EQMM covers and, so I'd heard, with *EQMM* story titles. He said he didn't think he was an incorrigible title changer and I was on the verge of believing him until not five minutes later he said, "About this title of yours, *Murder Ink.* I think. . . ." That critics and readers identify Ellery Queen with the convention of the dying message seems to him a misplacement of emphasis. "It was just a device," he said, "we used in stories for a greater sense of compression and 'fun and games.' " More to his taste was the subtle use of the invisible or negative clue — the clue that ought to be there and isn't. Even more to his taste were his, well, political statements in the Queen novels. The man who is world-renowned for his fair-play ingenuity, for his challenges to the reader, would rather be associated with his attempts to tell society what must be redressed. I don't blame him. And I can't think of anyone who could tell me these things and entertain me at the same time quite as well as Ellery Queen.

Then we got down to the nitty-gritty: gossip. But I can't repeat it. You'll just have to get Fred Dannay to invite you to tea and tell you himself.

When I went to leave, I realized what had been vaguely bothering me all afternoon. How do you tell a man you love him when his wife is sitting right there next to him the whole time?

Dilys Winn is the editor of Murder Ink *(the book) and the founder of Murder Ink (the bookstore).*

DEAR MR. GARFIELD
An Author Opens His Mail

Brian Garfield

Fan mail. Sometimes it praises; sometimes it condemns. With the exception of the occasional crackpot accusation or obscene vilification, it gratifies a writer because it reassures him that somebody out there is actually reading his work. He knows his publisher's sales figures, but they only tell him people are buying books; for all he knows from that, they may be using them as doorstops. Fan mail to a writer is like applause to an actor. I don't know any writers who don't get a kick out of a fan letter; I don't know any writers who don't answer their mail. Fan mail is too valuable to be ignored.

There are a few problems with it, however. One is the delivery system. Most writers are private people who don't advertise their home addresses on the jacket flaps of their books. To send a letter to a novelist, you must address it in care of his publisher. If, say, you are writing c/o a paperback publisher, then the paperback house must forward the letter to the hardcover publisher who originally published the book. The hardcover publisher in turn forwards it to the author. Often this procedure takes six to ten weeks. By the end of ten weeks the reader may have forgotten the book, the characters in it, and everything else except that he sent a letter to the author and the churl didn't answer him. By the time he receives the author's reply it's too late: the damage has been done; hatred has set in.

Sometimes the first letter a writer gets from a fan is one that begins, "Why didn't you answer my first letter?" Well, publishers' mail rooms lose things. They lose manuscripts, too, but that nightmare is a different story.

One category of fan mail stands by itself: gun mail. I find its implications fascinating.

You can write a book in which a key scene is a European Grand Prix auto race in the late 1930's involving Hispano-Suizas and Duesenbergs and all sorts of tactics and technical detail. Do you get letters from antique-car buffs? No.

You can write a book in which aviation plays a large part in the story; such books may deal with Ford Trimotors or B-17 bombers or C-47 Dakotas or Piper Apaches. Do you get letters from airplane buffs? No.

You can write a book in which horses, equestrian gear, Studebaker wagons and all kinds of nineteenth-century trappings are

Regarding mysteries, I read the first ten pages. Then I write my guess down as to who is the murderer. Then I look at the end of the book, and if my guess is correct I don't bother to read the rest.

Regine

detailed and employed. Do you get letters from Western-history partisans? No.

You can write books set in the Russian Civil War or World War II or Vietnam or the Indian wars of the American West, in which tactics and the materiel of military ordnance figure as inevitable background. Do you get letters from armchair strategists? No.

Perhaps once a year you'll get a letter from someone who castigates you for confusing palominos with Appaloosas (the former is a color, the latter a breed), or from someone who appreciates the fact that you know they still had third lieutenants in the Russian Army in 1920. But these are rare. They are individual letters and seldom duplicate one another.

Make one trivial mistake about a gun, however, and you will be buried in an avalanche of mail.

I committed the unpardonable error, for example, of arming a gunslinger with a .38-40 revolver. This provoked instant reaction from dozens of letter-writers, all of whom had exactly the same thing to say: A .38-40 is a "ladies' gun," has no stopping power and cannot be compared with a .45 for lethal effectiveness. I learned more about the failings of .38-40's from these letter-writers than I ever wanted to know. At the end of the barrage I was left wondering why the manufacturers had ever bothered to make and sell the things at all, since they evidently aroused such contempt.

I armed the character in *Death Wish* with a .38 revolver. This in itself caused only a small reaction from readers who thought he should have been armed with a cannon. But when the filmmakers armed Charles Bronson with a .32 revolver, I was broadsided once again — as if I were in charge of the prop department. Instantly I was battered from all sides with snarling know-it-all advice about the ineffectiveness of .32 revolvers and the superiority of, and I quote, "a .38 police revolver with hollow-point 158-grain slugs" — a tediously technical description which was followed by a nauseatingly specific account of the anatomical damage that can be inflicted by such a bullet.

After a few hundred such letters it becomes a matter of almost vindictive pride to be able to turn the tables on the babbling gun

experts. I was condemned by one reader who found a reference to a .38-56 Winchester rifle; the reader insisted no such rifle existed. I was happy to point out to him I had actually held one in my hand and fired it on a target range; it was manufactured in 1886 and was a fairly popular model for a while. Another reader insisted the Luger automatic pistol had never been manufactured in .45 caliber, and I was gleefully happy to prove him wrong. You do get caught up in this nonsense. For example, the Spencer repeating rifle of U.S. Civil War vintage was mass-produced in *both* .47 and .51 calibers, dear readers, and I don't want to hear any more about that from you. The Colt "Lightning" or "Bird's Head" or "Billy the Kid" revolver was manufactured in *both* .38 and .41 calibers, dear readers, and don't bug me about *that* one, either.

You see, the kicker is, I am somewhat of a gun expert myself, and this always throws the gun-mailers for a loop. They assume anybody effete enough to sit down and write books must be an ivory-tower egghead who can't tell a fulminate-of-mercury percussion cap from a push-type ejector spring. I served an apprenticeship as a gunsmith, boys, and I was eighteen at the time, and I outgrew it, and I no longer swagger around festooned with weapons, but I still remember what it feels like to get shot by mistake with a .45 — it did no permanent damage, but it was not fun — and when I write a gun into a story it is quite often a gun I have held in my hand and dismantled and repaired and test-fired. Over the past twenty-five years I have learned to respect the things and most often to loathe them. The more I write, the less I write about guns. (An exception is a current work-in-progress about an exhibition sharpshooter. But he shoots targets, not people.) This is what I think of as encroaching maturity. But it doesn't seem to be happening to the rest of you, and I am curious.

PRONUNCIATION GUIDE

proe-nun-sea-ay-shun guyed

(f u kn rd ths u kn rd a mstry)

Roderick *Alleyn* *al*-inn
V.C. Clinton-*Baddeley* *baad*-uh-lee
Modesty *Blaise* blaze
Anthony *Boucher* rhymes with "croucher"
Ernest *Bramah* rhymes with "comma"
John Buchan *buck*-in
Max *Carrados* *care*-uh-dose
***Auguste* Dupin** awe-*gooset* dew-*pan*
Elizabeth *Ferrars* as in "terrors"
Jacques Futrelle zshahk foot-*trell*
Emile *Gaboriau* as in Zsa Zsa + ee-oh
Ganesh Ghote ga-nesh *go*-tay
Robert van *Gulik* *goo*-lick
***Dashiell* Hammett** *dash*-el
Jack *Iams* *eye*-mz
Michael *Innes* *inn*-iss
Maurice *Le Blanc* luh-*blahn*
John *Le Carré* luh-car-*ray*
Monsieur *Lecoq* luh-*coke*
William *Le Queux* luh-*q*
Gaston Leroux gas-*tone* luh-*roo*
Arsene Lupin are-*sen* loo-*pan*
Maigret may-*gray*
***Ngaio* Marsh** *nye* (as in hi) + oh
Berkley Mather *bark*-lee *may*-thurr
Patricia *Moyes* rhymes with "noise"
Hercule Poirot heir-*cool* pwah-*row*
Sax Rohmer sacks *row*-murr (as in purr)
Joseph *Rouletabille* roo-luh-tah-*bee*-yuh
Georges Simenon zshorzsh sea-muh-*no*
Maj Sjöwall as in Taj; *show*-vahl
Julian *Symonds* as in Crimmins
Josephine *Tey* tay
François Vidocq fran-*swah* vee-*duck*
Per Wahlöö pair vahl-*oo* (as in boo)
Hilary *Waugh* as in law
Peter *Death Bredon* Wimsey as in "teeth"; *bree*-dun
Dilys Winn as in "kill us"; rhymes with "djinn"

What is it about guns that so fascinates the American reader? It cannot be anything so simple as the tedious Freudian cliché of the phallic power symbol. It is something verbal; otherwise, I would get as many letters from antique-car buffs and airplane types as I get from gun fanatics. Yet the ratio is something like one to fifty. The true antique-car buff is, if anything, more passionate about his obsession than the gun fanatic is; yet he does not write letters to novelists.

The peak of idiocy came a few years ago when I published a novel in which nobody shoots a gun at all — and even on *that* book I got gun mail. Most of it began, "Why didn't you give the character a gun?" My answer was that the character is, like me, the kind of guy who does not feel comfortable lugging a gun around with him; that bullets do not answer any questions; and that guns do not solve problems, they only create new ones. But this didn't seem to make any sense to the gun-mail writers and after a while they gave up on me in disgust on that one.

Both Donald E. Westlake and I received several letters from a deputy sheriff out West who provided us with endless dissertations on guns; at one point, early on in the correspondence, the deputy wrote to Don, "I have read your new book and I am glad to see that Brian Garfield has straightened you out on gun details." Actually, Don and I have better things to do than discuss the trivia of firearms; we had never discussed the subject at all. God knows what led the deputy to his conclusion. But the correspondence was indicative of the painstaking care with which the gun fanatics read novels. They will disregard any implausibility so long as it does not involve ballistics. They cheerfully follow you through holes in your plot that a Boeing 747 could be driven through. But just see what happens if you ever confuse a Colt with a Smith and Wesson.

If I knew why that was the case, I think I'd know everything there is to know about the American character.

Brian Garfield won the Mystery Writers of America Edgar for Hopscotch.

Chapter 14

LOOKING FOR (MORE) TROUBLE

FRED WINKOWSKI

THE DEVOUT
Benefit of Clergy

Catherine Aird

Clergy in the mystery are part of the literary tradition even though they don't go back quite as far as Cain and Abel. This, the first murder of all, certainly began a long connection between religion and crime. Another Biblical link was forged a little later than the Old Testament — in the Apocrypha.

If you remember, it was the Apocrypha that included the two tales about the prophet Daniel which are said to be the original mysteries. The earlier was "The Tale of Susanna and the Elders," in which certain malicious charges were laid against the blameless Susanna; the prophet Daniel proved her innocence in the classical manner — by demonstrating that the evidence given by two separate accusers did not hang together. The second was "Bel and the Dragon," in which the miscreants were confuted by as nice a piece of circumstantial evidence as you'll find outside a crown court.

Daniel's successors in detection have been many and various — and ecumenical. Father Brown, the lovable little priest with the endearing traits of dowdiness, untidiness and a complete lack of pretension, was one of the first. Rabbi David Small is one of the latest. In between have come both Uncle Abner (a religious detective if ever there was one) and a succession of vicars of the Church of England — to say nothing of an archdeacon or two. (Promotion comes late to fictional clergymen engaged in solving mysteries; they have to be satisfied with another sort of preferment.)

But what they have all had in common, these detective clergy, is the ability to reason. If

"Still, did you ever stop to think where you and I would be if it weren't for evil?"

they had faith as well, and I am sure they did and do, all I can say is that it doesn't come into the story the same as their deductions do. It is their logic that we admire. Cogent argument seems to come so easily to these incumbents of the page. Be this a Jesuitical nicety or a rabbinical pilpul, our clerical detectives have us convinced in a couple of paragraphs.

Of course, they have advantages over other amateur sleuths. A thorough grounding in theology, for a start. After all, what is the modern detective story but an extension of the mediaeval morality play? That earlier art form was simpler — the Devil invariably entered from stage left, and you always knew who he was — but it is essentially the same. Our hero now seems able to recognise the Bad'n or the Rotten Apple in the Barrel or the Sinner or the Unfortunate Victim of Circumstance (according to period) with the same sure facility.

Not only do our clerical heroes instinctively know the difference between right and wrong, but they have a professional interest in making sure that Good Triumphs over Bad in the last chapter — if not sooner. Then there's all this experience of the confessional. The Depths of Human Wickedness have already been plumbed by these unshockable men, and this is a great help in the detective story. They have cut their milk teeth on the World, the Flesh and the Devil, so by comparison little foibles like Wine, Women and Song come as very small beer indeed. They've heard it all before.

This isn't the only advantage they have. Besides being well-versed in the ways of the world — at a respectable distance, of course — their occupation leaves them time and energy in which to pursue villains. Evensong never seems to clash with a dénouement when the amiable Archdeacons of Thorp and Garminster, creations of C.A. Arlington, D.D., are solving a gentle mystery. This author, incidentally, was at one time Dean of Durham — a novel combination of Dean and Chapter.

Another real-life clergyman who wrote detective stories — and much else — was Monsignor Ronald A. Knox. It was he who in 1928 laid down the famous "Ten Commandments" (it is quite difficult to get away from the analogy, isn't it?) for the writing of detective stories.

Yet the peculiar situation of all these literary men of the cloth is even more felicitous than their just having ample time between Matins and Compline. Their parochial duties actually give them a good reason for being where the action is. This far from small matter is normally a sore trial to those authors whose detectives are amateur — but it is no problem with the ordained. It might only be collecting for the organ fund: it is more likely to be making arrangements for that uniquely English form of in-fighting known as the parish fete. But somehow it always seems perfectly appropriate for the vicar to be there, whatever the setting.

This goes for where you will find him, too — cottage or castle — for nothing so spans social life as the visiting list of the parish incumbent. Not only is there no one quite so well-placed to appreciate the passion aroused by, say, the church flower-arranging rota, but there is no one better to whom the confession of the murderer in the last-chapter-but-one can be made. A case, you might say, of a good living meeting a bad dying . . .

Then there's the distaff side. There may as yet be few detective nuns (though the play *Bonaventure* by Charlotte Hastings comes very near to this), but the convent has been used more than once as a setting for murder. And we must never forget it is the wool from black sheep which is used to make nun's veiling.

But there: I've nearly left out something important. Most amateur detectives have a love-life that — let's face it — can get in the way. More often than not it comes between the Mountie and his getting his man and, at the very least, distracts the mind from the serious business of crime. Far easier the division of the human species into men, women and clergy. By all means, let the curate cast a flirtatious eye at the leading lady in the choir but leave us with the certainty that, however much our hero may pontificate about being sure that other people's sins will find them out, he hasn't committed any of his own. Unfrocking has no place here: *Clerical Error,* C.E. Vulliamy's nicely named tale about a clergyman, concerns something quite different.

Some detective stories in the canon (if you'll forgive the allusion) go further still and are actually set in the church. Charles Dickens

SOME CLERGY IN THE MYSTERY

C.A. Alington: *Archdeacons Afloat; Gold and Gaiters*
H.C. Bailey: *The Bishop's Crime*
Anthony Boucher: *Nine Times Nine; Rocket to the Morgue*
G.K. Chesterton: *The Innocence (Wisdom, etc.) of Father Brown*
Edmund Crispin: *Holy Disorders*
Antonia Fraser: *Quiet as a Nun*
Dorothy Gilman: *A Nun in the Closet*
Tim Heald: *Unbecoming Habits*
Leonard Holton: *The Saintmaker; Pact with Satan; A Problem in Angels*
Harry Kemelman: Rabbi David Small in all-the-days-of-the-week series
Ralph McInery: *Her Death of Cold*
Thomas Patrick McMahon: *The Issue of the Bishop's Blood*
Alice Scanlon Reach: *The Ordeal of Father Crumlish*
Margaret Scherf: *Gilbert's Last Toothache* (Rev. Martin Buell, Christ Church)
Charles Merrill Smith: *Reverend Randolph and the Wages of Sin*
C.E. Vulliamy: *Tea at the Abbey*
Jack Webb: *The Brass Halo*
David Williams: *Unholy Writ*

began this with his *Mystery of Edwin Drood.* We don't, in fact, know what was to be found in the crypt of Cloisterham Cathedral and now never shall because the author died before finishing the book — but naturally we suspect the worst. Another book centred round a cathedral is Michael Gilbert's neatly titled *Close Quarters.* The town is Melchester, and the setting is what may be aptly called the other sort of precinct: a cathedral close.

Men of the cloth don't always come into the story in a detective capacity. Dorothy L. Sayers, a noted theologian in her own right, left the detection to Lord Peter Wimsey but gave us two affectionate pen portraits of Anglican clergymen. The Reverend Theodore Venables in *The Nine Tailors* and the Reverend Simon Goodacre (Magdalen College, Oxford) in *Busman's Honeymoon* are happy specimens of their kind — and Goodacre is a nice name for a clergyman when you consider that the churchyard is often known as "God's Acre." (Venables isn't far from Venerable, either.)

Emma Lathen, in her customary pithy way, gives us an evocative vignette of a Catholic priest, Father Doyle, taking action after a murder in *Ashes to Ashes.* Josephine Tey in *Brat Farrar* goes further. She allows her rector, George Peck, to destroy evidence which would have spoilt what in a detective story can't very well be called a happy ending.

> *"George!" said Bee. "What became of the pen?"*
>
> *"The stylograph? I lost it."*
>
> *"George!"*
>
> *"Someone had to lose it, my dear. Colonel Smollett couldn't: he's a soldier, with a soldier's sense of duty. The police couldn't: they had their self-respect and their duty to the public to consider. But my conscience is between me and my God. I think they were touchingly grateful to me in their tacit way."*

And if you like the connection to be vicarious remember that Sir Arthur Conan Doyle's Sherlock Holmes appears at least twice in clerical disguise — in "The Final Problem" and "A Scandal in Bohemia."

So do read on. Preaching and detecting do go hand in hand in an acceptable plurality (even if only a bishop actually gains by translation). Whatever your theological persuasion, you must agree that Satan versus Godliness is the onlie begetter of the detective story . . .

Finally brethren, let me assure you that Caesar's wife has nothing on your detective clergyman. Not only is he above suspicion but, dear reader, there is one thing in this uncertain world of which you can be absolutely sure: The Vicar didn't do it.

Catherine Aird is the author of The Religious Body.

THE EDUCATOR
The Case of the Screaming Spires

Reginald Hill

Every crimiculturalist knows that mayhem breeds best in hot-house conditions. First find your closed community, then drop a mouldwarp into the humus.

Jane Austen in her well-known advice to Agatha Christie (among others) says, "Three or four Families in a Country Village is the very thing to work on." As a rural parson's daughter she was clearly aware that the best bestialities took place out of town, and it was a dull weekend when, swollen by house-party guests, Daddy's congregation didn't contain at least one gifted amateur detective to every three homicidal maniacs.

But had Jane Austen lived a century later, when her sex was beginning to be disadvantaged by higher education, she might have modified her advice to include the great centres of learning.

After all, she might have asked, what is a university but a large village? What is a college course but a continuous house-party? And is it not a truth universally acknowledged that students and teachers alike perform short stints of work punctuated by long periods of idleness which can most profitably be filled by crime and its solution?

It might be useful at this point to extend our list of universally acknowledged truths about the world of higher education. So self-evident are they that they need as little statistical support as the basic tenets of other branches of entertainment fiction, *viz* cowboys smell nice and shoot straight, foreigners smell nasty and spy, spilt blood will out and blue blood will tell.

The following bear the same stamp of authority.

(1) *Students are sex-mad.* When you look at them, it's obvious. When you can't look at them, it's because they've gone to an orgy.

(2) *Students are unbalanced.* Prof. A.E. Houseman, the well-known expert on rustic violence, wasn't joking when he said, "Cambridge has been an asylum to me in every sense of the word." Come exam time, the mental wards install bunk beds.

(3) *Students are dishonest.* They steal food, books, bicycles, lingerie from clothes lines and small change from locker rooms. Also, it is well known that they use the small change they steal to pay for drugs and examination questions other students have stolen.

(4) *Students are revolutionaries.* The only students who are not left-wing anarchists are those who are right-wing terrorists.

As for the teaching staff, suffice it to say that a university lecturer is a student who liked it so much, he didn't want to leave. And a professor is a lecturer who excels.

But to be attractive to the crime novelist, it is not enough for a section of society just to breed potential criminals. The business world, or the Church, can do that quite as well.

It must also breed potential detectives.

And here the crime writer can prove in a flash what educational psychologists have been debating for centuries — the theory of the transfer of training. At its most basic in

CORNELL CAPA/MAGNUM

Does college prepare one for life? Many mystery writers insist it prepares one for death instead. They maintain higher education is synonymous with a higher crime rate.

nineteenth-century England, it asserted that a good classical education inculcated habits of thought and attitudes of mind that fitted a man to administer an Empire. But the claims go beyond the classics and extend to any academic disciplines requiring the application of logic and reason. And how easy it is to point to many influential figures in modern life who have moved freely between the Groves of Academe and the Corridors of Power!

Yet, even with this evidence, many scholars continue to believe in the theory of the transfer of training.

Arthur Conan Doyle realized its implications when, searching his mind for a detective hero, he recalled the diagnostic techniques of his old medical professor. R. Austin Freeman drew similarly upon personal experience in creating his famous forensic scientist, Dr. Thorndyke. And Jacques Futrelle was the first to give his detective formal academic status when he created, perhaps, the greatest logician of them all — Prof. Augustus S.F.X. Van Dusen, "The Thinking Machine." Futrelle went down with the *Titanic.* Van Dusen, having made such light work of Cell 13, almost certainly escaped.

This early establishment of the suitability of top academic minds for detective work has been followed by the evolution of the student into the state of potential criminality already described. And since World War II, donnish detectives and campus crime novels have abounded. Indeed, for a while it seemed as if all those lecturers who were not filling their long idle periods by committing crime must be writing stories about it.

This brings us to a final point of interest about the academic setting.

Library shelves are full of books set in

countries, cities or social environments which the author has observed only in his mind. Shakespeare never went to Bohemia, Poe never visited Paris. But the academic setting is rarely used except by those who know it personally and often intimately.

Herein lies the difference between the "truth" of the academic mystery and the "truths" of other forms. Those who look closely at such matters must confirm, albeit reluctantly, that six-guns were low on accuracy, cowboys were high out of as well as in the saddle, some foreigners are quite nice, some aristocrats are quite nasty, and most villainy goes undetected.

But few who move and work in our universities and colleges have not at some time been aware that under many a swirling gown lurks the blade of the assassin, and under many a scarlet hood prick the ears of the bat. Words are the grains of sand heaped up against a tide of blood. And if there sometimes seems a shortage of bodies, it may be because in these places the dead keep on walking rather longer than in the world outside.

THE TUTORIAL

Charlotte Armstrong: *Lay On, MacDuff*
Francis Bonnamy: *The King Is Dead on Queen Street*
Clyde B. Clason: *The Man from Tibet; Green Shiver*
Edmund Crispin: *The Moving Toyshop*
Amanda Cross: *The James Joyce Murder; Poetic Justice*
James Duff: *Dangerous to Know*
Reginald Hill: *An Advancement of Learning*
Clifford Knight: *The Affair of the Scarlet Crab*
Lee Langley: *Dead Center*
Amanda MacKay: *Death Is Academic*
D.B. Olsen (Dolores Hitchens): *Love Me in Death*
Wirt Van Arsdale: *The Professor Knits a Shroud*

UNDERSTANDING ACADEMIA

O' (Ordinary) Level.

These are exams taken by students who wish to leave school at the age of fifteen. (They must be in attendance until that time.) A student takes a different exam for each of his subjects, so it is not uncommon to hear someone say, "Yes, I got 7 O' levels." This means he passed all 7.

A' (Advanced) Level.

These exams are given to students who have remained in school another two years and wish to qualify for college. They are roughly equivalent to the American College Boards. Again, a student will take them in his major fields of study and 3–4 A' levels are generally acceptable for college entry.

"He read history at Balliol."

At the Oxbridge colleges, a student does not "study" a subject; he "reads" it.

"He was sent down last year."

A student who has been "sent down" has been ejected from his college. This can be for many reasons, ranging from academic difficulty to disciplinary action.

Here, then, for the subtle palate, are soufflés of death and violence served on plates of gold. Taste them in comfort and let who will go down those mean streets, tiptoeing through the cadavers with Chandler and Chase, to whom (among others) Jane Austen said, "How horrible it is to have so many people killed! And what a blessing that one cares for none of them!"

Reginald Hill is the author of An Advancement of Learning, *a crime novel with a professorial touch.*

THE ENVIRONMENTALIST

Storyteller Country

Duncan Kyle

BRUCE DAVIDSON/MAGNUM

There is a kind of novel, one I greatly enjoy reading and try to write, in which there is an extra principal character: the setting. I have no idea who wrote the first, but I think my own first realisation of the importance of *place* came with *Wuthering Heights,* which I read young because I grew up a comfortable morning's walk from the Haworth Moors.

They're story-teller country, these novels, and they're popular because people love tales that take them, as the song says, to faraway places with strange-sounding names. It may be escapism, it may be just armchair travel. But people do enjoy a hero engaged not only with human opponents, but with Nature herself. That, after all, is the history of mankind.

Richard Hannay, handcuffed to the beauteous damsel, dragging her across Scottish moors that are at once enemy and friend, provides a good example: it's the moors that make the story sing, not the people; the Forth Bridge, not the villain. Erskine Childers' *Riddle of the Sands,* with one man in a tiny boat confronted not only by Germans but by murderous intricacies of weather and tide, is another. It may even be the best of all.

But there *is* C.S. Forester: not his *African Queen,* though it's a good example, but *Brown on Resolution,* with a lone sailor on a tiny volcanic island pitted against a warship. Sounds unlikely? Begin it, and be convinced. Feel the hazard the island presents, scalpel-sharp rocks, heat to flay off the skin. Mark again the extraordinary demand to endure, which has always been, and is, man's need.

Some people can compose magical settings

and make them real. Lionel Davidson's deep ravine in *Smith's Gazelle* which not only presents problems of survival, but forces bonds to grow between people with cause for enmity, is one of these. Davidson's *The Rose of Tibet,* too (without in any way disparaging Hilton's *Lost Horizon),* is a masterly demonstration of the force of place upon people.

And that, really, is what I'm talking about. But I *do* mean place, not object. Ships don't count: they are too nearly human, anyway. Aircraft, on the other hand, are all too neutral, forcing the attention back toward people and weather and places.

Okay, okay, so where's Hammond Innes? Isn't he the international grandmaster? He is indeed, and I'm coming to him now. He's criticised, sometimes, for failing to create interesting people — which all too often means he doesn't write about the boozy infidelities of antiquarian booksellers. In any bookshop you'll find work by authors who do, but you'll find only one Hammond Innes. Listen. A man is in a small boat on the Atlantic, looking for a difficult and dangerous landfall:

> *An islet loomed in the fog, white with the stain of guano, and as I skirted it, the wind came funnelling down from the hidden heights above, strong enough to flatten the sea; and then the downdraught turned to an updraught, sucking the fog with it, and for an instant I glimpsed rock cliffs . . . they rose stupendous to lose themselves in vapour; dark volcanic masses of gabbro rock, high as the gates of hell.*

Well, you could call it florid, I suppose. You could say there are clichés around. But having said whatever you're going to say, read it again, and *sniff!* Something in your nostrils now — and a picture on the screen of your mind, of place and man and hazard — that tickles something deep inside. We know we're going, once again, to stir up those ancestor-memories. Read on, read on — how on earth could you not?

It is a real place (St. Kilda, if you must know, disguised as Laerg) and recognisable to the place-man. Innes has been there and has the feel of it. With him it's always a real place, and he can show it to you as no one else can. You become enmeshed in the realities of storm and cold, of animals, of navigation, of mining and geology. It's not just identification: you and the hero seem to merge.

Going there, of course, is all-important. It *is* possible, and indeed has been *done,* to write place novels by careful reading of, for example, the *National Geographic.* But it just isn't the same. I wrote a novel whose finale was played out on a small island and a sea stack in the Shetlands. I'd read about them and seen a lot of photographs. Yet when I got there . . . Nobody had said the great skuas (called Bonxies, locally), which nest there among the grass tussocks in comfortable solitude, would fly at me on five-foot wings, from six directions at once, fast and silent, brushing by close, rough enough to raise welts on my face. Nobody had said the only path ran up beside the high cliffs and the skuas knew all about it and were careful to herd you that way. Nobody had told me what it's like to stand over six hundred sheer feet and watch the gannets fall suddenly, like white darts, after fish.

Go there and material accumulates. The pity is that one can only use so much before the book becomes overloaded. Mine do, anyway, Hammond Innes' unique skill lies in the way he draws in the detail, so that the plot is ultimately composed of small parts of knowledge. Sometimes I turn green, I really do.

But if he's the nonpareil, there are others: Desmond Bagley, conjuring up the Andes in *High Citadel;* Derek Lambert's grim and grinding Moscow in *Angels in the Snow;* Berkely Mather (number two only to Innes), drawing beautiful pictures of the Himalaya lying gigantically in wait to oppress a few lonely, desperate — and desperately *small* — men.

No women? Come now, I did begin with Emily. Yes, there are women. Mary Stewart knows how to use a setting. So does Helen MacInnes. But in general (in *my* experience, that is, and I'll be delighted to widen it) women writers like the people larger than the landscape. No criticism there, or implied, just a matter of approach.

Duncan Kyle is a past chairman of the Crime Writers' Association.

THE HISTORIAN
Once Upon a Crime

Peter Lovesey

Fog, swirling through the streets of London. Footsteps quickening. They stop. A moment of silence, then an agonised scream. Blurred shapes running. The blast of a police whistle. The beam of a bull's-eye lamp directed onto a lifeless form. Another victim.

Meanwhile, the great detective sits in his rooms in Baker Street before a blazing fire, reading the personal column of the *Times.*

For atmosphere, the counterpoise of teacups and terror, cosiness and crime, the Victorian mystery is supreme. The architects of the

HISTORICAL MYSTERIES

Gwendoline Butler: *A Coffin for Pandora*
John Dickson Carr: *The Bride of Newgate; The Devil in Velvet; Captain Cut-Throat; Fire, Burn!; Scandal at High Chimneys; The Witch of the Low-Tide; The Demoniacs; Most Secret; Papa Là-Bas; The Ghosts' High Noon; Deadly Hall; The Hungry Goblin; The Murder of Sir Edmund Godfrey*
Agatha Christie: *Death Comes as the End*
Carter Dickson: *Fear Is the Same*
Doris Miles Disney: *Who Rides a Tiger*
Mignon G. Eberhart: *Family Fortune*
Richard Falkirk: *Blackstone; Blackstone's Fancy*
Joan Fleming: *Screams from a Penny Dreadful*
John Gardner: *The Return of Moriarty; The Revenge of Moriarty*
William Irish: *Waltz into Darkness*
Peter Lovesey: *Wobble to Death; The Detective Wore Silk Drawers; Abracadaver; Mad Hatter's Holiday; The Tick of Death; A Case of Spirits; Swing, Swing Together*
Victor Luhrs: *The Longbow Murder*
Theodore Mathieson: *The Devil and Ben Franklin*
Anthony Price: *Other Paths to Glory; War Game*
Ellery Queen: *A Study in Terror*
Francis Selwyn: *Sergeant Venits and the Imperial Diamond*
Jean Stubbs: *Dear Laura*
Josephine Tey: *The Daughter of Time*
P.W. Wilson: *Bride's Castle; Black Tarn; The Old Mill*

popular detective story — Poe, Dickens, Wilkie Collins and Conan Doyle — built citadels of suspense that still dominate the scene. Any modern author setting a story in the Victorian period starts with the knowledge that hansom cabs and London fogs are redolent of Holmes and Watson.

And how productive the nineteenth century was of motives for murder! The need to achieve security by inheritance, or life insurance, or marriage; the risk of losing it when scandal threatened; the equating of sex with sin; the stigma of insanity; the things that went unsaid. Our world of social welfare and easier divorce and psychiatric care has removed many of the bad old reasons for murder. How uninspiring, too, by contrast with times past, are the modern weapons — the gun with telescopic sights, the car-bomb and the hypodermic syringe. Give me Jack the Ripper's knife or Neill Cream's bag of poisons or Lizzie Borden's ace!

Of course, the historical mystery has reached back beyond the nineteenth century, millenniums before the first police officers appeared on the streets. Ancient Egypt of 4000 B.C. (*Death Comes as the End*), Tang China (*The Chinese Bell Murders*) and Alexander's Greece (*The Great Detectives*) have all been used as settings, while characters as various as Machiavelli, Richard III and Ben Franklin have been featured. Treatments range from documentary novels researched from actual cases, such as Michael Gilbert's *The Claimant* and John Cashman's *The Gentleman from Chicago*, through brilliant pastiches like Lillian de la Torre's *Dr. Sam: Johnson, Detector* to extravaganzas like Anthony Price's *Our Man in Camelot*, in which the CIA becomes involved with King Arthur. The trend is toward more fantastic plots, more dazzling tricks, with a strong infusion of humour. All we ask of the historical mystery is that it tell a story consistent with known facts and that those facts arise naturally from the plot. If we want a history lecture, we can go to college.

The fascination of a mystery set in the remote past is easily explained: it provides an escape from modern life. But we are not at the mercy of a science-fiction writer's fantasizing. The world we enter is real and under control. There is a framework of fact. Even the most extravagant plots conform to historical truth. Yes, the CIA does become entangled with King Arthur. Read it and see!

And the greatest of all fictional detectives has tangled with the worst of criminals (*Sherlock Holmes Versus Jack the Ripper*) and discussed psychology with Sigmund Freud (*The Seven Per-Cent Solution*), while his old adversary is launched on a whole new career of crime (*The Return of Moriarty*). Thank heavens Holmes is alive and well and reading the *Times* in London!

Peter Lovesey won the Panther-Macmillan prize for his first historical mystery, Wobble to Death.

GARDENING
Thou Bleeding Piece of Earth

Avon Curry

Gardeners and crime writers have quite a lot in common, not least that they are both fond of a good plot. Writers, like horticulturists, have to labour at improving the groundwork: you can start off with a good idea but it's the way you tend it that produces a good crop — either of blossoms or of saleable words.

Gardening is particularly basic to the British. You know, it's said that if you give a quarter of an acre to a Frenchman, he'll plant a vine and invite a pretty girl to share the vintage; a Japanese will grow enough rice to feed a family of ten; an Englishman will lay out a lawn and sit on it to drink tea.

A crime writer will at once see a quarter-of-an-acre garden as the answer to one of the three great problems in plotting a mystery — how to get rid of the body. The perceptive reader would be well advised to look out for a passing remark about how well the roses are growing compared with those next-door, because it's under that rose bed that the deceased is sleeping. If you allow your garden to run wild, undergrowth is a useful camouflage for the quickly hidden corpse and provides good descriptive stuff when you begin talking about the heavy boots peeping out among the bluebells, or the tangle of blond tresses among the brambles.

Gardeners often burn their rubbish. If you take the trouble to establish the character ("plant the idea," as we significantly say when chatting about plotting) as a thoroughgoing efficient husbandman, you can justify the big incinerator in which bodies can be reduced to ash. I recall a garden incinerator proved very handy to that well-known "husbandman" M. Verdoux. The drawback in Britain is that the weather's seldom dry long enough to keep the bonfire going for the requisite time — so that brings us to the compost heap.

Compost is very "big" in British gardening at the moment. There was a time when to talk about it branded you as a crank, but now you're an ecologist. Foolhardy would be the policeman who dared open up a keen gardener's compost heap without the very best possible evidence that a corpse was providing a large part of its

GARDENING

Herbert Adams: *The Crime in Dutch Garden*
Agatha Christie: *The Mirror Cracked*
Wilkie Collins: *The Moonstone*
J.J. Connington: *Murder in the Maze*
Elizabeth Daly: *Any Shape or Form*
Richard Forrest: *The Wizard of Death*
Richard Hull: *The Murder of My Aunt*
Veronica Parker Johns: *Servant's Problem*
Rex Stout: *Some Buried Caesar; Black Orchids; In the Best Families*
Jack Webb: *The Brass Halo*

bulk. Moreover, compost heaps are messy things. Smelly, too, the uninitiated believe. Policemen are more than likely to leave them alone so that the corpse is left in peace where the convocation of politic worms can keep busy.

Gardens are a good excuse for collecting the tools of death. You have only to look at the names of chemicals sold to garden-lovers — "tox" on the end of the word means, of course, that the mixture is extremely toxic; words that include the consonance "kil" or the straightforward "slay" or "bane" speak for themselves. One might almost say that in many garden-lovers there lurks a hater of other life forms — and a murderer is after all a person with enough hate to want to kill another human being.

Modern gardening chemicals are extremely dangerous. If you read the instructions — and I strongly recommend it both as a piece of academic research and as a practical life-saving exercise — you'll see you're to wash at once if a spot lands on your skin, that you're not to inhale the spray, that children mustn't get at it, or even pets. In the early days of DDT, puppies and kittens died from licking flea-killing powders from their coats. DDT has gone, but worse things have replaced it. Bear in mind, too, that the effect of these poisons is irreversible; the poison builds up with every tiny drop.

Venus's-flytrap. Not shown: the boringly harmless flowers which grow at the end of the stalk.

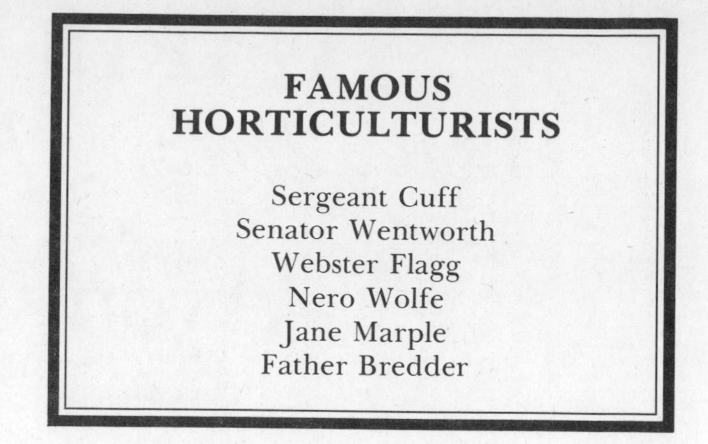

FAMOUS HORTICULTURISTS

Sergeant Cuff
Senator Wentworth
Webster Flagg
Nero Wolfe
Jane Marple
Father Bredder

So the easiest way to get rid of your enemy is to rent the house upwind of him, and spray your roses every time there's a strong breeze. It may take a while, but by and by he ought to get very sick if he will insist on sitting on that lawn of his.

For the knowledgeable gardener, poison need not come out of a bottle. There are deadly plants all around us, in every lovesome plot, God wot. The most innocent products can provide the most efficacious alternative to the bare bodkin. The potato, for example. Good to eat, unless you allow the tubers to become green through exposure to light, in which case the skin becomes very harmful. The leaf of the rhubarb plant (*Rheum rhaponticum*) is very toxic, although the stalk is used in pies and preserves. Ivy is poisonous. So is laburnum — remember *My Cousin Rachel?*

Nor need you actually grow the plant yourself. Once you have weeded your own garden, it dawns on you that hedgerows and wastelands are teeming with lethal growth. The datura is a member of the same family as the harmless tomato and potato. Deadly nightshade. Hemlock . . . there's a historic aid to death: Socrates drank a brew of hemlock at the behest of the Athenian rulers. Mushrooms . . . perhaps you don't want your victim dead, only out of his head: a handbook on fungi will soon tell you which to offer him, as in *The Documents in the Case.*

I can hear male readers saying that although gardening opens up endless varieties of poison, this is a very tricky and feminine form of murder. Those who like action-murder might prefer to deliver a hearty clout with a

BRITISH TOURIST AUTHORITY

The more unscrupulous the gardener, the more likely he is to engineer a maze — into which he will entice his victim and leave him stranded. Shown: Hampton Court Maze, which may yet be used with such aplomb.

spade or shrivel the opposition with a weed flame-gun. The motor-mower or the mini-cultivator might run amok at the psychological moment — but you need a big garden to justify big equipment. Your small-scale gardener, your patio-gardener, must rely on having the victim trip up and hit his head on the Alpine rockery; or perhaps he could fall face down among the water-lilies in the decorative pond (*Nymphaea capensis* is a good bright blue variety, recommended for contrast to the drowned features when he is fished out).

There's nothing like a little knowledge of horticulture to make you aware that life is precarious, that the prize at the Flower Show is only gained by eternal vigilance against enemies natural and unnatural. The crime-writing gardener is acutely aware of an under-meaning in the famous lines from the *Rubáiyát:*

How oft hereafter rising shall she look
Through this same garden after me—in vain!

But the crime writer who sets his murder in a garden wants you to look in vain — until at least the end of the book. He has a splendid chance of mystifying you, because it's standard practice for a garden-lover to direct your attention to the good things and distract you from the spindly growths or the rogue intruders. You must have heard the excuse: "The rhododendrons aren't at their best now — you should have been here last week."

Indeed you should. That was when he was suffocating his victim with the plastic bag in which the fertiliser was delivered.

Avon Curry is a member of the Royal Horticulture Society.

Something Between a Sport and a Religion

HOBBIES OF THE FAMOUS

The Old Man in the Corner sits at a back table in a London tea shop, tying and untying knots in a single piece of string.

Gideon Fell's chubby fingers are surprisingly graceful when it comes to making elaborate houses out of a deck of cards.

In The Singing Sands *Alan Grant corrects his doctor, who calls trout fishing a hobby. Says Grant, it's "something between a sport and a religion."*

MARTY NORMAN

Lyon Wentworth relaxes by rising above it all. He has the most unusual hobby of the lot — ballooning.

Characters in crime fiction tend to take their hobbies as seriously as their homicides. One suspects if the Almighty Himself paid a call on Nero Wolfe during orchid-growing hours, even He would be asked to wait. If you're in the market for a new hobby yourself, you might consider that Charlie Chan likes swimming and chess, Sgt. Beef is adept at darts, Gervase Fen goes on long drives, Holmes practices the violin, the Norths cuddle up to a cat, Evan Pinkerton is a devoted moviegoer, J.G. Reeder is a chronic patience player, Dr. Davie adores the opera, Ellery Queen collects rare books, Max Carrados collects rare coins, Travis McGee loves his boat the *Busted Flush,* and Sister Ursula, Sgt. Ivor Maddox and D.A. Douglas Selby are addicted to reading mysteries.

Prepared by Anne N. Nixon.

Says Sergeant Cuff, "I haven't much time to be fond of anything, but when I have a moment's kindness to bestow, most times, the roses get it."

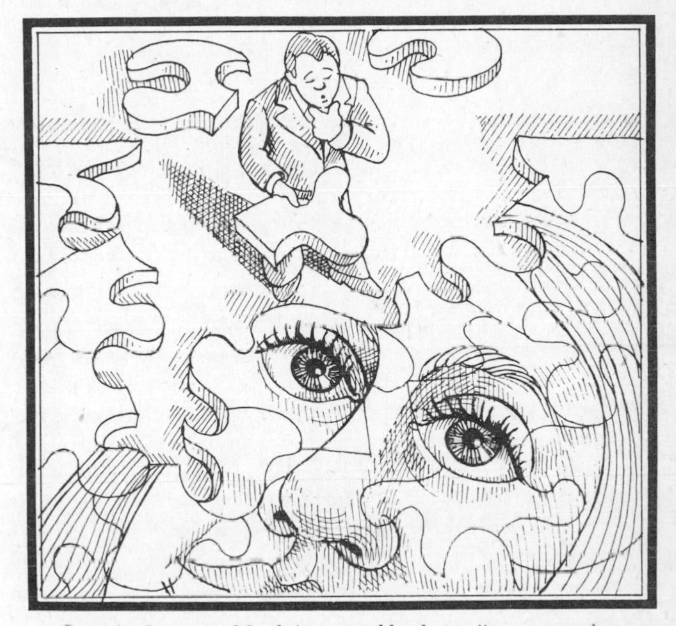

Captain Duncan Maclain assembles huge jigsaw puzzles, sensitively fitting together pieces he will never see. (Maclain was blinded in the war.)

Mitch Tobin, like Churchill, is soothed by constructing a wall, brick by brick.

Hildegarde Withers is passionate about only two things: murder investigations and her collection of tropical fish.

COMMUTING

An Unscheduled Stop at an Isolated Junction

Hugh Douglas

It was five o'clock on a winter's morning in Syria. Alongside the platform at Aleppo stood the train grandly designated in railway guides as the Taurus Express. It consisted of a kitchen and dining-car, a sleeping-car and two local coaches.

Thus Agatha Christie starts her classic whodunit *Murder on the Orient Express.*

Two local coaches, a sleeping-car and a kitchen and dining-car hardly add up to romance, but we know that the route lies through half of Asia Minor to Istanbul, where the great train waits to carry readers on across Europe for three days to Paris. It is a journey which most will make only on the pages of a book — a journey into a web of murder they'd never expect to encounter in reality.

The famous train is as unrelated to their lives as is the murder they await, and just as romantic!

Trains of every kind, named expresses, night mails and smelly little local puffers, have been a favourite setting for crime writers and their readers since the crime novel was born. They have inspired authors to make the wheels of fear spin in their readers' minds as no other mode of transport could.

What's so special about the railroad that ships, airplanes or automobiles don't have? Why does *Mystery of the Blue Train* capture attention on the bookstalls while *Mayhem on the Queen Mary* would hardly rate a second glance? What is there about the grinding of iron wheels on iron rails that sets the adrenalin flowing like a rogue oil-well?

Ships and planes have been used successfully by crime writers, of course they have, but as a location they suffer from the disadvantage that they're not really in our world as they travel: their routes don't relate to real life or death, so they are soulless phantoms orbiting beyond man's environment until the moment they touch land. And then, seaports or airports are not at the heart of cities — where people live, love and commit violence against their fellow man. Even the motor car is a capsule sealed off from humanity. Look down on a highway and you see little automated ants rushing to and fro, starting, stopping, and missing one another by a hair's breadth as if directed by some kind of formic radar. And who ever heard of a whodunit about ants, for heaven's sake?

The train is different. It has all the good qualities that other modes of travel offer to the crime novelist, but it has more. Although quite isolated from its environment, the train never ceases to be a part of it. A real world of houses, villages, cities, fields, cows and even people pass by the window. Yet this world is quite out of reach, unable to affect the traveller for good or ill. Reality is just beyond his fantasy world, but quite unattainable. The wheeled thing rolls on, out of the reader's control. There is no escape.

In this enclosed space the tension heightens all the way to journey's end.

The train is a universe of its own. It is confined, remote and comfortable. Whodunit victims always travel first class so their blood soaks into the thick plush cushions, leaving no vulgar mess. Indeed, the whodunit train resembles that other favourite venue of the thriller, the secluded country house, with the compartment as closely confined as a smoking-room. Here must be no vulgarity, no undue ostentation, no overindulgence — just solid comfort.

But unlike the country house the reader's companions on the train are strangers — or so he thinks. Who are they? Who is victim and who villain? Half a dozen people eye one another, reading (or is it lurking?) behind a newspaper, dozing fitfully, or glancing apprehensively from window to fellow passengers and then to the door. The train rushes into a tunnel, and the overhead reading lamp clamps a mask over the face of the man opposite, turning him from a benign Dr. Jekyll to a savage Mr. Hyde. Can he really be as sinister as he looks, or is he one of the red herrings with which the whodunit's track is strewn? And who is that old lady knitting in the other corner? Her eyes are everywhere. Is she waiting for the chance to thrust a No. 10 needle six inches into someone's heart, or is she dear Miss Marple biding her time to unravel the problem?

Truly, travellers are strange bedfellows. Bedfellows? My God, the sleeping car is lethal. Here is the most isolated place in the whole world, a tiny square of space, lonelier than the summit of Everest. And what are all these switches, buttons and bolts for? Does the door lock securely? It is impossible to try it without opening it again. And will the distant clanging of the bell be answered by the steward, or will it bring some sinister caller?

It's bad enough when the train is moving; noise covers up other noises, the scream or gunshot will never be heard over the clickety-clack of the wheels, the roar of the tunnel will shut out the stealthy footstep in the corridor, the engine's strangled whistle will drown the cry of danger in the next sleeping berth. But what happens when the train stops in the middle of nowhere? Trains do. The Orient Express stuck in a snow-filled waste, deep with drifting fear. Help could not reach it; escape was impossible. This prison was as secure as Devil's Island, as well guarded as Sing Sing, but it held the person who had wielded the knife in the night, and he might wield it again.

ONE-WAY TICKETS

Lawrence G. Blochman: *Bombay Mail*
Lynn Brock: *The Slip-Carriage Mystery*
Stephen Chalmers: *The Crime in Car 13*
Agatha Christie: *The Mystery of the Blue Train; Murder on the Orient Express*
John Creasey: *Murder on the Line*
Michael Crichton: *The Great Train Robbery*
Freeman Wills Crofts: *Death of a Train; Double Death; Sir John Magill's Last Journey*
Laine Fisher: *Fare Prey*
Graham Greene: *Orient Express*
Dolores and Bert Hitchins: *End of the Line; F.O.B. Murder; The Grudge; The Man Who Followed Women; One-Way Ticket*
Sebastien Japrisot: *The 10:30 from Marseilles*
Baynard Kendrick: *The Last Express*
Henry Leverage: *The Purple Limited*
Francis Lynde: *Scientific Sprague*
Sue MacVeigh: *Grand Central Murder; Murder Under Construction; Streamlined Murder*
Frederick Nebel: *Sleepers East*
Frank L. Packard: *The Wire Devils*
John Rhode: *Death on the Boat Train*
Mary Roberts Rinehart: *The Man in Lower Ten*
Wilson Tucker: *Last Stop*
Ethel Lina White: *The Lady Vanishes*
Victor L. Whitechurch: *Thrilling Stories of the Railway*

GLOBE PHOTOS

The 11:18 passing through Watford. One of the most famous trains in mystery fiction was Eden Phillpott's "Flying Scotsman."

A wakeful man in a sleeping car is the loneliest man on earth.

Day restores the scene to that comforting, comfortable country house, filled with elegance and peopled with feudal staff. In the dining car the stewards show all the attentiveness of old family retainers, and breakfast is as generous as it would be for a house party in Devon, with only the food-loaded sideboard missing. But in the train there can be no relaxed feeling for long, because murder has been committed and work is in hand to solve the crime. While the innocent hover in fear, the murderer's confidence crumbles. He is as much the victim of the confined space as of the detective's skill.

The train journey has shape, and shape is what the writer is seeking when he plans his novel: within a time-scale the crime will be perpetrated, discovered and solved. Journey's end will reveal all, convict the guilty and release the innocent. It is very tidy.

Of course, not all novelists confine their story to the train — the crime can pursue the traveller home and then his detectives go to work on time-tables, proving the impossible by a mere thirty seconds between trains, for the railway time-table is the train crime writer's *vade mecum,* as essential as his typewriter.

Alas, the heyday of the train was the heyday of the railway whodunit, when trains were drawn by lumbering dinosaurs that left behind them a trail of fire, smoke, steam and mystery. Diesel or electric locomotives are clinically clean and lacking in romance, and it is largely their fault that the train no longer attracts the crime novelist or his reader. But memories are memories. The classics of the genre still are read and reread by those who seek a glimpse into the lush past, taking their crime elegantly and with a whiff of nostalgic smoke.

Hugh Douglas loves trains almost as much as mysteries, as well he should, since he works for British Rail.

COMPETING
The Sporting Blood Syndrome

John L. Powers

Abner Doubleday, an American, may have invented baseball, but I feel confident it will be an Englishman who finally perfects the curve ball — putting an extra spin on it with a spit or so of nitroglycerin. The British seem to have more sporting blood than the rest of us, to see more potential for crime in athletic contests than we do.

To them, a golf bunker is a natural place for a corpse (*An Awkward Lie,* of course) and a cricket match the perfect backdrop for a surprising arrest (*Murder Must Advertise*) and a Chelsea-Arsenal soccer game a good opportunity to catch a glimpse of a suspected murderer (*The Plot Against Roger Ryder*).

Horse racing, tennis, rugby, field and track, skiing, boxing, bullfighting, archery — all have been used as settings by English mystery authors. "Good show, old sport" is as apt to apply to someone using the cricket bat as a blunt instrument as it is to someone maneuvering his hansom cab in a pea-souper.

Not to be outdone, the Americans have, of late, turned their hand to recreational treachery. And being American, they have gone about it bloodier, gorier, bigger and, if not better, certainly bizarrer.

At least two thrillers — *Black Sunday* and *Two-Minute Warning* — have been wrung out of the Super Bowl, probably America's glossiest and most overblown sporting event. And they've barely scratched the event's potential. After all, it's seen by more than 80,000 people, including senators, corporation heads and presidents, and it draws more illegal gambling interest than any other single event in the nation. Can anyone doubt what a fine forum it is for kidnapping or blackmail or what a smorgasbord for a lone killer or terrorist group? What's more, it's always held in a massive stadium in a major city — like the Superdome in New Orleans, the Los Angeles Coliseum or Miami's Orange Bowl — and provides a nice hiding place for escapees from . . . anywhere.

What makes sporting events, with either an English or American accent, so appealing to the crime writer as well as the crime reader? Familiarity.

Most of us know how the game — whatever it may be — is played, and that makes a twist on it all the more chilling. We can imagine all too easily a cleat put in the wrong place, a puck whacked in the middle of the goalie rather than the middle of the cage. And one hardly has to leave the locker room to find a good victim, a good weapon, a good opportunity and a good motive. Consider, for example, a power forward for the Lakers taking a pre-game shot of Novocain for a sore knee — and ending up in a coma — with game seven of the NBA finals only moments away and $4 million of Mob money riding on the 76ers.

There also happens to be a ready supply of suspects. Enough of them, in fact, to fill Madison Square Garden twice over: ambitious understudies; insecure coaches; greedy quar-

BAD SPORTS

Horse Racing

John Creasey: *Death of a Racehorse*
Charles Drummond: *Death at the Furlong Post*
Dick Francis: *Dead Cert; Nerve; Forfeit; Rat Race; Smokescreen*
Frank Gruber: *The Gift Horse*
Stuart Palmer: *The Puzzle of the Red Stallion; The Puzzle of the Happy Hooligan*
Judson Philips: *Murder Clear, Track Fast*
Kin Platt: *The Princess Stakes Murder*
S.S. Van Dine: *The Garden Murder Case*
Edgar Wallace: *The Green Ribbon; The Flying Fifty-Five*

Tennis

John Dickson Carr: *The Problem of the Wire Cage*
Stanley Ellin: *The Valentine Estate*
Frances and Richard Lockridge: *The Judge Is Reversed*
J.J. Marric: *Gideon's Sport*
Brown Meggs: *Saturday Games*
Lillian O'Donnell: *Death on the Grass*
J.B. Priestley: *The Doomsday Men*

Baseball

Robert L. Fish and Henry Rothblatt: *A Handy Death*
Leonard Holton: *The Devil to Play*
Robert B. Parker: *Mortal Stakes*
Robert Wade: *Knave of Eagles*

Basketball

Charles Drummond: *Death and the Leaping Ladies*
Lee Langley: *Dead Center*
Kin Platt: *The Giant Kill*

British Rugby Football

David Craig: *Double Take*
Reginald Hill: *A Clubbable Woman*

Football

Eliot Asinof: *The Name of the Game Is Murder*
George Bagby: *Coffin Corner*
Alan Nixon: *The Gold and Glory Guy*
John Stephen Strange: *Murder on the Ten Yard Line*

Soccer Football

Leonard Gribble: *The Arsenal Stadium Mystery*

terbacks; disappointed groupies; crooked trainers; worried gamblers; overly competitive competitors.

If a little privacy is needed in which to commit one's crime, think of the player's tunnel at Oakland–Alameda County Coliseum, or the losers' dressing room an hour after the game. Need a crowd to obscure a villain? How about the members' enclosure at the Henley royal regatta or the ninth tee at St. Andrews mid-tournament? For that matter, someone could turn the bullpen at Tiger Stadium into the prototypical locked room.

Plot ideas? Well, how about a kidnapping with an international flavor? Nothing wrong with an Amsterdam betting syndicate spiriting away the Liverpool goalie a few hours before the European Cup Final against Ajax. Looking for a political assassination in a genteel atmosphere? Why not the gentlemen's final at Wimbledon, with the Queen looking on from the royal box? How about a Minnesota Vikings quarterback murdered by a Denver assistant coach? Or a Czech tennis player blackmailed into being a double agent during a Davis Cup match in Krakow? (There seems,

Peter Handke: *The Goalie's Anxiety at the Penalty Kick*
Maurice Procter: *Rogue Running*
Julian Symons: *The Plot Against Roger Ryder*

Boxing

Richard Falkirk: *Blackstone's Fancy*
William Campbell Gault: *The Canvas Talk Loud*
Ed Lacy: *Lead with Your Left*
Vernon Loder: *Kill in the Ring*

Bullfighting

Patrick Quentin: *Puzzle for Pilgrims*
Julian Rathbone: *Carnival*

Archery

Leo Bruce: *Death at St. Asprey's School*

Ballooning

Richard Forrest: *A Child's Garden of Death; The Wizard of Death*

Track and field events

Peter Lovesey: *Wobble to Death*

Cricket

Adrian Alington: *The Amazing Test Match Crime*
John Creasey: *A Six for the Toff*
Michael Gilbert: *The Crack in the Teacup*
Geoffrey Household: *Fellow Passenger*
J.J. Marric: *Gideon's Sport*
C. St. John Sprigg: *The Corpse with the Sunburned Face*
Clifford Witting: *A Bullet for Rhino*
Barbara Worsley-Gough: *Alibi Innings*

Winter sports

Emma Lathen: *Murder Without Icing*
Hannah Lees: *The Dark Device*
Patricia Moyes: *Dead Men Don't Ski;*
Jeremy Potter: *Foul Play*
Owen Sela: *The Bearer Plot*
Jean-François Vignant: *The Alpine Affair*
Margaret Yorke: *Silent Witness*
Phyllis A. Whitney: *Snowfire*

Golf

Herbert Adams: *The Nineteenth Hole Mystery; The Body in the Bunker*
Miles Burton: *Tragedy at the 13th Hole*
Agatha Christie: *Murder on the Links; The Boomerang Clue*
Michael Innes: *An Awkward Lie*
Owen Fox Jerome: *The Golf Club Murder*
Angus MacVicar: *Murder at the Open*
Rex Stout: *Fer-de-Lance*
Anthony Wynne: *Death of a Golfer*

by the way, to be a natural affinity between tennis players and mystery writers. Both are involved in a game of wits, a one-on-one game: the detective is pitted against the murderer as the No. 1 seed is pitted against No. 2, surely the most competitive situation extant.)

Curiously, not too many sports figures read mysteries. Back in the days when they took trains to get from city to city, game to game, they were more likely to read. Now with the advent of the red-eye plane flight, they seem more interested in sleeping than in reading.

One exception is Tommy Heinsohn, coach of the Boston Celtics. Not only does he read thrillers (such as Ira Levin's *The Boys from Brazil),* but he passes them on. I know, because he gives them to me.

Obviously, sporting blood can be spilled almost anywhere, by anyone. En garde, my friend. It is not a friendly game, after all.

John L. Powers is a sports writer for the Boston Globe. *He plays a vicious game of tennis.*

HOLIDAYING

The Christmas Mystery Lecture

Bill Vande Water

Let us address ourselves to that curious paradox of detective fiction known as the "Christmas" mystery. The most curious thing about it is that it exists at all. Christmas is supposed to be the time of peace, of joy and love, when Macy and Gimbel shake hands, suddenly repentant Scrooges toss ten-dollar bills in Salvation Army kettles, families are reunited, old friendships rekindled, and children are on their best behavior. Why spoil such warm, nostalgic, tug-at-the-heartstrings scenes with a petty theft, much less a murder?

The cynic will answer with one word: money. Being the high-minded people we are, however, we shall ignore the base suggestion that authors write merely to sell to the Christmas issues of mystery magazines. (Besides, Isaac Asimov's "The Thirteenth Day of Christmas" came out in July.)

Instead, let us consider that Christmas is joined with crime for historical, indeed theological, accuracy. One of the wise men (they figure as detectives in R.L. Steven's "The Three Travellers") brought myrrh, an embalming spice. King Herod celebrated the first Christmas with a mass killing of babies. Even mistletoe has a criminal record: it was the murder weapon used to kill Balder, the most loved of the Norse gods. And the Puritan fathers of Massachusetts made the celebration of Christmas itself a crime, punishable by a five-shilling fine.

It becomes apparent that in real life, then, crimes do occur at Christmas. Good will may increase, but so does the homicide rate. By some strange quirk of human nature, the same season that fills the stores and churches also fills the jails and morgues — and motivates the mystery writer like no other holiday could ever hope to.

We must understand, however, the peculiar distinction between Christmas mystery novels and Christmas mystery stories. The novels, without exception, favor homicide as a leitmotif; in them, a writer may use pine, spruce, holly or even money for his Christmas green, but his Christmas red had better be blood. The stories, on the other hand, are partial to theft and burglary.

The tradition of the nonlethal Christmas detective story goes back to the master himself and his "Adventure of the Blue Carbuncle." This story also started the tradition of stolen and hidden jewels and was followed by G.K. Chesterton's "The Flying Stars," Dorothy L. Sayers' "The Necklace of Pearls," Margery Allingham's "The Snapdragon and the C.I.D.," Ellery Queen's "The Dauphin's Doll," Agatha Christie's "The Adventure of the Christmas Pudding," Georges Simenon's "Maigret's Christmas" and Damon Runyon's "Dancing Dan's Christmas."

Conan Doyle also started the tradition of the "season of forgiveness," in which the criminal, although discovered, is allowed to escape with nothing more than a warning and a good scare.

One of the best of the Christmas short

stories is August Derleth's "The Adventure of the Unique Dickensians." This double pastiche combines elements of Doyle and Dickens and is a true tour de force.

Christmas mystery novels fit into three categories. The first is a Christmas mystery by courtesy only. Christmas is mentioned, but it is really there as an excuse for assembling a group of people who otherwise would not be caught dead together — so that at least one of them may be so caught. The best example of this misuse of the Christmas theme is Agatha Christie's *Murder for Christmas;* the next best (or worst, depending on how strongly you feel about this type of thing) is Michael Innes' *Comedy of Terrors;* not quite as bad, but reaching, is Georgette Heyer's *Envious Casca.*

The second category of Christmas mystery novel features, more often than not, police procedurals. Private detectives and nosy old ladies may go home for the holidays, but for the police it's just another busy day, what with pickpockets and shoplifters working the Christmas rush. Among the best of these realistic, ironic novels are Ed McBain's *Pusher* and *Sadie When She Died*, Dell Shannon's *No Holiday for Crime* and James McClure's *The Gooseberry Fool.* Not a police procedural, but still

CHRISTMAS AND CRIME

Novels

Agatha Christie: *Murder for Christmas (Holiday for Murder)*
Charles Dickens: *The Mystery of Edwin Drood*
Elizabeth X. Ferrars: *The Small World of Murder*
Cyril Hare: *An English Murder*
Georgette Heyer: *Envious Casca*
John Howlett: *The Christmas Spy*
Michael Innes: *A Comedy of Terrors; Christmas at Candleshoes*
Ed McBain: *Pusher; Sadie When She Died*
James McClure: *The Gooseberry Fool*
Ngaio Marsh: *Tied Up in Tinsel*
Jack Pearl: *Victims*
Ellery Queen: *The Finishing Stroke*
Patrick Ruell: *Red Christmas*
Dell Shannon: *No Holiday for Crime*

Short Stories

Margery Allingham: "The Case of the Man with the Sack"; "The Snapdragon and the C.I.D."
G.K.Chesterton: "The Flying Stars"
Agatha Christie: "The Adventure of the Christmas Pudding" ("The Theft of the Royal Ruby"); "Christmas Tragedy"
John Collier: "Back for Christmas"
August Derleth: "The Adventure of the Unique Dickensians"
Arthur Conan Doyle: "The Adventure of the Blue Carbuncle"
Stanley Ellin: "Christmas Eve"
O. Henry: "Whistling Dick's Christmas Stocking"
Edward D. Hoch: "Christmas Is for Cops"
Ellery Queen: "The Dauphin's Doll"
Damon Runyon: "Dancing Dan's Christmas"; "Palm Springs Santa Claus"
Dorothy L. Sayers: "The Necklace of Pearls"
Georges Simenon: "Maigret's Christmas"
Rex Stout: "Christmas Party"; "Santa Claus Beat"
Julian Symons: "The Santa Claus Club"; "Twixt the Cup and the Lip"

Nonfiction

A.C. Greene: *The Santa Claus Bank Robbery*

RICHARD KALVAR/MAGNUM

There is a Midwestern state which has made it illegal for women to appear on the street dressed as Santa.

falling within this category, is Ian Fleming's *On Her Majesty's Secret Service,* in which James Bond makes his violent escape from SPECTRE headquarters on Christmas Eve and Christmas Day. In these novels the Christmas background offers a depressing commentary on the kind of world in which peace is so frequently converted to death.

The third and perhaps most effective category of Christmas novel is the one in which the crime, or detection, or both, could take place in no other season. The accouterments of Christmas are necessary to the novel's success. These tend to feature Santa Claus. Burglars, detectives, bank robbers, the police, murderers, victims, even a few (relatively) innocent bystanders — all have made use of this disguise. Nor have Santa's criminal appearances been confined to fiction. A.C. Greene's *The Santa Claus Bank Robbery* concerns a real-life use of the ubiquitous Santa disguise that went dead wrong. (There is, by the way, a Midwestern state which has made it illegal for women to appear on the street dressed as Santa. Make of that what you will.)

Next to Santa the most popular Christmas motifs, in a novel, are Christmas house parties, reunions, mistletoe, trees, toys and seasonal foods. In *The Finishing Stroke* Ellery Queen even makes special use of a song, "The Twelve Days of Christmas." Be assured, however, that novels in this category do not use Christmas as mere trimming; it is integral to their plots.

In closing, may I remind you that Charles Dickens, creator of that syrupy tale *A Christmas Carol,* eventually tired of all the Christmas niceties. The next time someone tells you he longs for a typically Dickensian Christmas, ask him if he had in mind the kind of Christmas Eve Dickens gave to *Edwin Drood.*

Bah, humbug to all, and to all a good fright.

Bill Vande Water manages the Film and Videotape Library for CBS News Archives.

SINISTER ORIENTALS
Everybody's Favorite Villains

Robin W. Winks

When Goldfinger's Korean bodyguard, Oddjob, was given the shock of his life by James Bond, he was simply dying for The Cause, yet one more Sinister Oriental gone to his just reward. After all, as Goldfinger had told Bond, Oddjob was "simple, unrefined clay, capable of limited exploitation." He was above the Chigroes, to be sure, since he was not half-caste (only Dr. No, half Chinese and an obvious if emaciated descendant of Fu Manchu, rose above what Somerset Maugham would have called "The Yellow Streak" in Ian Fleming's work), but not much above, and while wily enough he obviously was created simply to be outwitted by Bond, as Fu Manchu's only purpose seemed to be as a foil to the ultimately victorious Englishman, Sir Denis Nayland Smith.

If one smells a giant rat from Sumatra in all this, one is meant to, for the Mysterious East has been a staple of the entertainment industry ever since hack writers took the sounds but not the sense from Thomas De Quincey's *Confessions of an English Opium Eater* after they appeared in the *London Magazine* in 1822. The rise of the "penny dreadful" to its peak in the 1840's and the success of Wilkie Collins' *The Moonstone* in 1868 were two stages on the path toward a persistent English, and later American, fascination with the Orient, a fascination both pejorative in content — as when Egyptians were dubbed Wogs, for "Westernized Oriental Gentlemen" — and at times highly respectful. The persistent tone of Western popular interest in the Orient has been one of high ambiguity coupled with creative drift.

The drift has been toward greater respect joined with greater fear, and the appearance of the Sinister Oriental as hero or villain in Western thriller and detective/spy fiction has usually coincided with a period in which China, or latterly Japan, played a role in world affairs. Orientals were sinister because they were inscrutable (or, as the music halls had it, they couldn't get pregnant in the normal way), strange, far away, incredibly hard-working, "able to live off the smell of a greasy rag," and addicted to "half-hatched eggs" — or so the *Westminster Review* told its readers in 1866.

The notion of an inexplicable East bites more deeply than this, however, for the journals of early explorers and voyagers reported upon "strange and wondrous" sights as early as Marco Polo's visit to the Court of the Great Khan. If Magellan's chronicler, Pigafetta, could assert that within the contemporary Philippines there was a race of men with ears so large they curled them under as pillows, then the Victorians might equally well insist that the Chinese, Japanese, Malays and others engaged in incredible sexual practices, devoured birds' nests and were persistently hung over from ubiquitous opium dens. The great Kraken, the gigantic octopus creature which legend placed in the South China Sea (later to transfer it to the Sargasso), was shown with hooded eye and beak, the very caricature of an Oriental. Bamboo splinters under the fingernails, the Chinese water torture, child brides, bound feet — all were indications of a culture that knew better than the West how to construct the exquisite Torture Garden of pornography. Sherlock Holmes might appear to make opium respectable, but even he could not bring himself to reveal the tail of that Giant Rat of Sumatra.

In general, the Sinister Oriental was Far Eastern, not South Asian. There was no lack of thriller literature about India, rampant with *thuggee,* widows' funeral pyres, cobras in the bedcovers, rampaging elephants and cursed jewels. But the Indian never took on the same sinister connotations as did, in particular, the Chinese, and no Indian series figure was sustained in the literature until the clever but hardly sinister Inspector Ghote leapt full-blown from the imagination of H.R.F. Keating in 1964. Those who have read Collins know that he admired the Indians of *The Moonstone* and reserved his harshest judgments for such figures as Godfrey Ablewhite and the retired Anglo-Indian officer John Herncastle. Perhaps the fact that the British came to know the Indians well, as they became part of the empire, removed some of the sense of distance on which mystery thrives. Since Americans had little interest in South Asia, few American thrillers appeared with Indian settings.

East and Southeast Asia were another matter. With the evolution of the energetic and respectable "boys' magazines" out of the penny dreadfuls, Asians became simpler if no less villainous. By the 1870's the "penny packets of poison," as one critic called them, had rolled out the entire inventory of horrors: rape, bloodsucking, burial alive, cannibalism, lingering and exquisite torture, the dissection alive of a victim's face. This was too strong for the boys, so S.O. Beeton's *Boy's Own Magazine* (1855–66) and the Religious Tract Society's *Boy's Own Paper* (1879–1967) set a higher tone. Nonetheless, the Chinese continued to be wily (although deserving respect as well as some tolerant amusement), and in *Boys of England* one read of the heroic battles of upright traders who sailed home from Canton with their costly cargo only to be attacked by "Malay scum . . . Chinese, Japanese, Javans, Papuans, Pintadoes, Mestizoes," and even a few Spaniards and Portuguese. All this was simply a romanticizing of the very real threat posed by sea Dayaks and pirates out of Borneo. So "Christian" a writer as Charles Kingsley, author of the treacly *Water Babies,* could write: "You Malays and Dayaks of Sarawak, you . . . are the enemies of Christ . . . you are beasts, all the more dangerous, because you have a semi-human cunning . . . I will blast you out with grape and rockets."

ANN LIMONGELLO

Four contributions to popular fiction probably did more than all others to promote the notion of the Sinister Oriental. The first of these, oddly, did not depict the Oriental as sinister so much as sinuously enterprising and wickedly clever: E. Harcourt Burrage's Chinese hero, Ching Ching, of the "celestial charm." He too had his own boy's journal, *Ching Ching's Own* (1888–93), and one of the books that were spun off from the magazine, *Daring Ching Ching,* won a substantial readership among adults in England.

The second, and far most important, contribution to the creation of the Sinister Oriental was Sax Rohmer's Dr. Fu Manchu, who sprang into diabolical life during the period when the Yellow Peril was perceived to be at its most insidious. Racism was at its most virulent just before, during and immediately after World War I, when so benign a Canadian writer as Agnes

Laut could warn her fellow countrymen against the "dangers within, not without," of letting down the barriers to "too many Jappy-Chappies, Chinks, and Little Brown Brothers." Rohmer, who had been doing research on the Chinese District of London, created his Devil Doctor to meet a public mood and sent him into the world in *The Mystery of Dr. Fu Manchu* in 1913. Fu Manchu moved onto the silver screen in 1923. (For a full account of Rohmer's creation, see *Master of Villainy: A Biography of Sax Rohmer* by Cay Van Ash and Elizabeth Sax Rohmer.)

A third major contribution to the image of the clever Chinese was Earl Derr Biggers' Charlie Chan, the member of the Honolulu Police Department who works on the side of Good and who coins quasi-Confucian (and sometimes very funny) aphorisms. It may be argued that Chan was an antidote to the notion of the Sinister Oriental, and that *The House Without a Key,* which appeared in 1925, was the first of a series of replies to the yellow-robed evil Doctor, but the Chan of the books — as distinct from the amusing Chan of the films — often casts a chilling shadow over his ratiocinations.

Finally, who can forget the first issue of *Detective Comics,* which appeared early in 1937 and for one thin dime gave the reader a healthy case of the shakes? A malevolent Chinese peered out from the cover, and inside the story of "The Claws of the Red Dragon," by Maj. Malcolm Wheeler-Nicholson and Tom Hickey, carried one into San Francisco's Chinatown and face to face with the Yellow Menace. By 1939 the Orientals of comic book thrillers had taken on an increasingly Japanese look, and through the war they would supplant the Chinese — bestial, red of tooth and claw.

Today the Japanese have recovered their features, and it is once again the Chinese who present a sinister face to us. But we are somewhat more sophisticated now, and certainly more ambivalent in our views of Asian societies. To the true mystery fan, no one did more to correct the balance than the Dutch diplomat and Sinologist Robert van Gulik, who began to reconstruct from actual records the cases of his fictional seventh-century Judge Jen-Djieh Dee. Between *Three Murder Cases Solved by Judge Dee,* first published in Tokyo in 1949, and *Willow Pattern,* published in 1965 (other, less interesting books were to follow), van Gulik provided a chilling, sometimes truly sinister, historically accurate and balanced picture of Chinese justice at work. *The Manchurian Candidate* may have kept the stereotype alive; Judge Dee freed the aficionados.

Robin W. Winks reviews mysteries for The New Republic.

SINISTER MR. RIGHTS

Not all Orientals plead at the bar sinister. Harold Gray, the creator of Little Orphan Annie, influenced by Charles Dickens and Joseph Conrad, introduced the Orient through the Asp — a slim, black-clothed, Far Eastern protector of capitalism, i.e., of Daddy Warbucks — and through Punjab, a turbaned South Asian who frequently appeared to rescue Annie from the sinister West. In the late 1930's Hugh Wiley introduced to *Collier's* magazine a Chinese detective, James Lee Wong, who soon moved on to the silver screen in the person of Boris Karloff and later Keye Luke (who had been Charlie Chan). At the same time, John P. Marquand created an immaculate detective, Mr. I.O. Moto, who appeared in five books within seven years. In 1957 Marquand unsuccessfully revived him for the book *Stopover: Tokyo.* And beginning in 1949 Dutch diplomat Robert van Gulik introduced Western readers to Judge Jen-Djieh Dee, modeled on a seventh-century Chinese magistrate. Wise and always controlled, Judge Dee would contrast sharply with the madcap Hong Kong police of William Marshall's *Yellowthread Street,* and other adventures of the 1970's, proving not only that the left hand knows not what the right does, but that the Orient can produce its Laurel and Hardy, too.

R.W.W.

HOMOSEXUALS IN THE MYSTERY

Victims or Victimizers?

Solomon Hastings

"Rather unhealthy" was the way Miss Climpson, one of Lord Peter Wimsey's operatives, described the relationship between two murder suspects in Dorothy L. Sayers' *Unnatural Death,* published in 1927. Such was the typical attitude toward the homosexual in early crime fiction. Obviously, it was a character trait one tried one's best to ignore.

Until recently there was a tendency to allude to homosexuality rather than to talk openly about the "taint." The gay was relegated to the red herring role, sometimes as a minor criminal and occasionally as a victim, as in Ruth Rendell's *From Doon to Death.* Gays were shown as isolated characters, and a bit quirky at that, who lived maladjustedly in a straight world. No one indicated there was any such thing as a gay subculture, not even in the large metropolitan cities.

Eventually, homosexuals were forced to come out of the crime closet — probably because the closet was so full of skeletons to begin with, there just wasn't enough room in there.

One of the first renderings of a true gay environment appeared in Edgar Box's *Death in the Fifth Position* in 1952, when Peter Cutler Sargeant II, straight press agent and amateur sleuth, to gain information, pretended an interest in Louis Giraud, a gay ballet dancer. Sargeant was permitted to go barhopping with the gay. A date, if you will.

But it took a bit more time to show homosexual crimes and characters in homosexual settings. In England they are still having a problem with it. It is curious to note that even today in the classic English-style mystery, the most liberal and sympathetic CID superintendent turns hard-nosed when a "pouf" becomes involved in a case. They compensate, sort of, in that not many really nasty homosexual villains appear. One exception: Valentine Quentin, a six-foot-four blond sadist trafficking in stolen diamonds in James Quartermain's *The Man Who Walked on Diamonds.* Hands down, he wins the-man-you-most-love-to-hate sweepstakes.

In the Sixties in America there began to appear mysteries such as Tucker Coe's *A Jade in Aries,* dealing with the gay milieu. The gay client is honestly dismayed at the murder of his lover and the police department's apathy in finding his killer. (Factually, this is still a problem to the gay community.) Emotionally, the book is sound, but it is not free of stereotyping: apparently, if we are to believe the book, all homosexuals wear brightly flowered ruffled shirts and wave their cigarettes about to a staccato Bette Davis beat (when they're not busy dangling them from incredibly limp wrists).

Dealing with the same problem of police indifference to a gay murder is Richard Hall's excellent *The Butterscotch Prince* (1975). In it, Cord McGreevy, a Manhattan schoolteacher, searches for the killer of his former lover and good friend, and moves through a well-written and honest version of the gay scene in New York.

The first American gay sleuth was Pharaoh Love, a black Manhattan cop who appeared in George Baxt's *A Queer Kind of Death* (1967), reappeared in *Swing Low, Sweet Harriet* and died under extremely odd circumstances in *Topsy and Evil.* The books are rather like a gossip column from *Women's Wear Daily.* They move about glamorous pop-society circles and are enjoyable reading as intentional High Camp.

In *Fadeout* (1970) Joseph Hansen created David Brandstetter, insurance investigator for Medallion Life in Los Angeles. Hansen himself lives in L.A., where he is one of the directors of the Homosexual Information Center. His Brandstetter is the most honestly portrayed gay in crime fiction: a middle-aged man — who happens to be a homosexual — with mundane, everyday problems. Some of his cases involve homosexuals; others do not. He develops romantic relationships, but he does not let his personal life style interfere with his work. It merely adds richness to his character in much the way any ongoing heterosexual relationship deepens anyone else's life. Written in the dry style common to all West Coast detective and private eye stories, Hansen's work has found an audience beyond the gay community. Chandler fans, Maling fans, any and all of the MacDonald (John, Ross, Gregory) fans find them satisfactory reads. Which is not too surprising, since with Hansen the homosexual in crime fiction finally achieves three-dimensionality.

Solomon Hastings divides his time between London and New York and reads mysteries in both places.

THE HOMOSEXUAL IN CRIME

Edgar Box: *Death in the Fifth Position*
W.J. Burley: *Three-Toed Pussy*
John Evans: *Halo in Brass*
James Fraye: *A Wreath for Lords and Ladies*
Joseph Hansen: *Death Claims; Troublemaker; Pretty Boy Dead*
John Paul Hudson and Warren Wexler: *Superstar Murder?*
Allen Hunter: *Gently with the Ladies*
Meyer Levin: *Compulsion*
Elizabeth Linington: *Green Mask*
Patricia Moyes: *Season of Snows and Sins*
Ellery Queen: *The Last Woman in His Life*

BLACKMAIL POSSIBILITIES

In real life many lesbians indulge in cross-dressing, or travesty. This means they prefer to present themselves as men, and sometimes it is only after their death that their true gender is disclosed. The most widely publicized travesty was the case of Murray Hall, born Mary Anderson, a prominent politician, member of the General Committee of Tammany Hall and close friend of State Senator "Barney" Miller. She was a shrewd poker player, a good whiskey drinker, and she puffed away on large Havanas. It was only when she died, in 1901, that her true sex was revealed. Billy Smith, a top British jockey at the turn of the century, was also discovered to be a woman upon her death in Australia. Any blackmailer worth his stationery would have had a field day if he'd known the true story of either of these figures. Fictionally, cross-dressing was common in Shakespeare, then went into hiatus and was revived by Leone Hargrave's literate Gothic, *Clara Reeve,* in which a woman was raised from birth as a man in order to qualify for an inheritance forbidden to female offspring. Mystery writers in need of a good plot, please note.

S. H.

A FEW (MILLION) WORDS ABOUT MY GOOD FRIEND HOLMES

Otto Penzler

Since 1887, when *A Study in Scarlet* first appeared, there have been over 10,000 novels, short stories, parodies, burlesques, pastiches, critical studies, reviews, essays, appreciations and scholarly examinations devoted to Sherlock Holmes. Virtually all the material is important in that it refers to the world's greatest detective; however, life being short, the Holmesian collector may never be able to possess all of it. This Holmesian shopping list itemizes the 100 indispensibles. To amass them requires only three things: fabulous wealth, infinite patience and divine intervention.

1. 1887 DOYLE, ARTHUR CONAN: "A Study in Scarlet." (Contained in *Beeton's Christmas Annual.* London: Ward, Lock, $7500.) First Book Edition (London: Ward, Lock, 1888, $2000). First American edition (Philadelphia: Lippincott, 1890, $1000).
2. 1890 DOYLE, ARTHUR CONAN: "The Sign of the Four"(contained in *Lippincott's Monthly Magazine* for February 1890, London, Philadelphia, $400). Also of importance is the first book edition (London: Spencer Blackett, 1890, $400; the spine of the earliest issue has Spencer Blackett's name and the later issue has the imprint of Griffith Farran) and the first American edition (New York: Collier's Once a Week Library, 1891, $250).
3. 1892 DOYLE, ARTHUR CONAN: *The Adventures of Sherlock Holmes* (London: Newnes, $300). Also the first American edition (New York: Harper, 1892, $150). The first short-story collection.
4. 1894 DOYLE, ARTHUR CONAN: *The Memoirs of Sherlock Holmes* (London: Newnes, $200). Also first American edition (New York: Harper, 1894, $200). The English edition contains 12 tales; the American, 13.
5. 1894 BARR, ROBERT: *The Face and the Mask* (London: Hutchinson, $50). Contains "The Great Pegram Mystery" — the first parody, originally published as "Detective Stories Gone Wrong: The Adventures of Sherlaw Kombs" by Luke Sharp in *The Idler Magazine,* May 1892.
6. 1897 BANGS, JOHN KENDRICK: *The Pursuit of the House-Boat: Being Some Further Account of the Divers Doings of the Associated Shades, Under the Leadership of Sherlock Holmes, Esq.* (New York: Harper, $15). The first American book containing a Holmes parody.
7. 1901 LEHMANN, R.C.: *The Adventures of Picklock Holes* (London: Bradbury, Agnew, $75). The first Holmes parody cycle.

8. 1902 DOYLE, ARTHUR CONAN: *The Hound of the Baskervilles* (London: Newnes, $200). Also the first American edition (New York: McClure, Phillips, $100). The most famous mystery ever written.

9. 1902 TWAIN, MARK: *A Double Barrelled Detective Story* (New York: Harper, $75). A book-length satire on detective fiction, particularly Holmes.

10. 1902 HARTE, BRET: *Condensed Novels Second Series New Burlesques* (London: Chatto & Windus, $40). Also the first American edition (Boston, New York: Houghton, Mifflin, $40). Contains "The Stolen Cigar Case" about Hemlock Jones. Ellery Queen considers this the best Holmes parody.

11. 1905 DOYLE, ARTHUR CONAN: *The Return of Sherlock Holmes* (London: Newnes, $200). Also the first American edition (New York: McClure, Phillips, $75). The sixth Holmes book.

12. 1907 LEBLANC, MAURICE: *The Exploits of Arsene Lupin* (New York, London: Harper, $75). Translated from the French edition of the same year by Alexander Teixeira de Mattos. Contains "Holmlock Shears Arrives Too Late," the first of several confrontations between Holmes and France's great rogue.

13. 1909 DUNBAR, ROBIN: *The Detective Business* (Chicago: Charles H. Kerr, $75). The first book of mainly nonfiction writings about Holmes.

14. 1911 HENRY, O.: *Sixes and Sevens* (New York: Doubleday, Page, $40.) Contains "The Adventures of Shamrock Jolnes" and "The Sleuths," by America's master of the short story.

15. 1912 DOYLE, ARTHUR CONAN: *The Speckled Band: An Adventure of Sherlock Holmes* (London, New York: Samuel French, $100). (Note that the earliest state has green paper covers; later states have light brown covers.) The first published play.

16. 1912 HOLMES, SHERLOCK: *Practical Handbook of Bee Culture, with Some Observations upon the Segregation of the Queen* (Sussex: Privately printed, $1,000). The author's *magnum opus.*

17. 1913 SAXBY, JESSIE M.E.: *Joseph Bell, M.D., F.R.C.S., J.P., D.L., etc.: An Appreciation by an Old Friend* (Edinburgh and London: Oliphant, Anderson & Ferrier, $60). The first book about the man who was Doyle's professor in medical school.

18. 1913 DOYLE, ARTHUR CONAN: *Sherlock Holmes: The Adventure of the Dying Detective* (New York: Collier, $400). The only Sherlock Holmes story to be printed separately before appearing in a collection.

19. 1915 DOYLE, ARTHUR CONAN: *The Valley of Fear* (London: Smith, Elder, $25). Also the first American edition (New York: Doran, $40). The last Holmes novel, called the best of the four by John Dickson Carr.

20. 1917 DOYLE, ARTHUR CONAN: *His Last Bow* (London: Murray, $50). Also the first American edition (New York: Doran, $30).

21. 1918 THIERRY, JAMES FRANCIS: *The Adventure of the Eleven Cuff Buttons* (New York: Neale, $65). An early book-length parody.

22. 1920 STARRETT, VINCENT: *The Unique Hamlet: A Hitherto Unchronicled Adventure of Mr. Sherlock Holmes* (Chicago: Privately printed, $300). A rare book, issued in a very limited edition of indeterminate number. Although Starrett said 200, and De Waal 33, it is probably 110, of which 100 have the imprint of Walter H. Hill and 10 of Starrett. The best Holmes pastiche.

23. 1920 CLOUSTON, J. STORER: *Carrington's Cases* (Edinburgh: Blackwood, $150). Contains "The Truthful Lady," a parody about Watson.

24. 1922 GILLETTE, WILLIAM: *Sherlock Holmes: A Drama in Four Acts* (London, New York: Samuel French,

$50). Although Arthur Conan Doyle is credited with coauthorship, he had nothing to do with writing the play. The best Holmes play.

25. 1924 LUCAS, E.V. (ed.): *The Book of the Queen's Doll's House Library,* 2 vols. (London: Methuen, $125). Contains "How Watson Learned the Trick," a parody by Arthur Conan Doyle. Limited to 1,500 copies.

26. 1924 DOYLE, ARTHUR CONAN: *Memories and Adventures* (London: Hodder & Stoughton, $50). Contains "The Adventure of the Two Collaborators" by James M. Barrie. In the opinion of Doyle, it is the best of the many burlesques of Holmes.

27. 1927 DOYLE, ARTHUR CONAN: *The Case-Book of Sherlock Holmes* (London:Murray, $40). Also the first American edition (New York: Doran, $25). Last book in the Canon.

28. 1928 KNOX, RONALD A.: *Essays in Satire* (London: Sheed & Ward, $20). Contains "Studics in the Literature of Sherlock Holmes," regarded as the first essay of "higher criticism."

29. 1929 FULLER, WILLIAM O.: *A Night with Sherlock Holmes* (Cambridge, Mass.: Privately printed, $175). A handsomely printed pastiche, limited to 200 copies.

30. 1929 CHRISTIE, AGATHA: *Partners in Crime* (London: Collins, $50). Also the first American edition (New York: Dodd, Mead, $20). Contains "The Case of the Missing Lady," a parody by the first lady of crime.

31. 1930 MORLEY, CHRISTOPHER (ed.): *The Complete Sherlock Holmes*, 2 vols. (New York: Doubleday, Doran, $20). Contains "In Memoriam: Sherlock Holmes," the first printing of the most widely published essay on Holmes. The first complete American edition of the Canon.

32. 1931 ROBERTS, S.C.: *Doctor Watson: Prolegomena to the Study of a Biographical Problem* (London: Faber & Faber, $20). The standard life of Watson.

33. 1932 BLAKENEY, T.S.: *Sherlock Holmes: Fact or Fiction?* (London: Murray, $65). The first book-length biography of Holmes.

34. 1932 BELL, H.W.: *Sherlock Holmes and Dr. Watson: The Chronology of Their Adventures* (London: Constable, $75). The first attempt to date all of Holmes' adventures, recorded and unrecorded. 500 copies.

35. 1933 STARRETT, VINCENT: *The Private Life of Sherlock Holmes* (New York: Macmillan, $65). The standard biography of Holmes.

36. 1934 BELL, H.W. (ed.): *Baker Street Studies* (London: Constable, $65). The first critical anthology devoted to Holmes.

37. 1934 SMITH, HARRY B.: *How Sherlock Holmes Solved the Mystery of Edwin Drood* (Glen Rock, Pa.: Walter Klinefelter, $200). A rare pastiche, limited to 33 copies.

38. 1934 CLENDENING, LOGAN: *The Case of the Missing Patriarchs* (Ysleta, Tex: Privately printed for Edwin B. Hill, $75). With a note by Vincent Starrett. Posthumous adventure of Holmes, limited to 30 copies.

39. 1934 DOYLE, ARTHUR CONAN: *The Field Bazaar* (London: Athenaeum Press, $150). Holmes parody written by Doylc in 1896. 100 copics.

40. 1938 MORLEY, FRANK V.: *A Sherlock Holmes Cross-Word Puzzle* (New York: Privately printed, $250). Often credited to Christopher Morley. The original test for membership in the Baker Street Irregulars. Rare; limited to 38 copies.

41. 1938 SMITH, EDGAR W.: *Appointment in Baker Street* (Maplewood, N.J.: Pamphlet House, $40). Profiles of everyone who had dealings with Holmes. Limited to 250 copies.

42. 1938 HONCE, CHARLES: *A Sherlock Holmes Birthday* (New York: Privately printed, $85). Reminiscences of the

1937 Semicentennial. The first of his Christmas books. 100 copies.

43. 1938 Klinefelter, Walter: *Ex Libris A. Conan Doyle Sherlock Holmes* (Chicago: Black Cat Press, $60). Sherlockian essays. 250 copies.

44. 1940 Starrett, Vincent (ed.): *221B: Studies in Sherlock Holmes* (New York: Macmillan, $25). The first American anthology of essays.

45. 1940 Smith, Edgar W.: *Baker Street and Beyond* (Maplewood, N.J.: Pamphlet House, $65). The first Sherlockian gazetteer. 300 copies ($35), the first 100 in deluxe binding.

46. 1940 Boucher, Anthony: *The Case of the Baker Street Irregulars* (New York: Simon & Schuster, $25). A mystery novel involving many Sherlockians.

47. 1941 Heard, H.F.: *A Taste for Honey* (New York: Vanguard, $25). A detective novel about "Mr. Mycroft," a pseudonymous, reclusive Holmes.

48. 1941 McKee, Wilbur K.: *Sherlock Holmes Is Mr. Pickwick* (Brattleboro, Vt.: Privately printed, $50). A whimsical pamphlet. Limited to 300 copies.

49. 1941 Wilde, Percival: *Design for Murder* (New York: Random House, $30). A detective novel with Sherlockian overtones.

50. 1943 Officer, Harvey: *A Baker Street Song Book* (Maplewood, N.J.: Pamphlet House, $50).

51. 1944 Queen, Ellery (ed.): *The Misadventures of Sherlock Holmes* (Boston: Little, Brown, $100). The best anthology of parodies and pastiches. A special edition of 125 copies was distributed at the 1944 BSI dinner.

52. 1944 Smith, Edgar W. (ed.): *Profile by Gaslight* (New York: Simon & Schuster, $25). A large collection about Holmes. A special edition of approximately 125 copies was distributed at the BSI dinner in 1944 ($100).

53. 1945 Roberts, S.C.: *The Strange Case of the Megatherium Thefts* (Cambridge: Privately printed, $125). A flavorful pastiche. Limited to 125 copies.

54. 1945 Smith, Edgar W.: *Baker Street Inventory* (Summit, N.J.: Pamphlet House, $50). The first bibliography of the Canon and the writings about the writings. A preliminary pamphlet appeared in 1944. Limited to 300 copies.

55. 1945 Derleth: *"In Re: Sherlock Holmes": The Adventures of Solar Pons* (Sauk City, Wis.: Mycroft & Moran, $50). The first Pons book, with an introduction by Vincent Starrett.

56. 1946 Yuhasova, Helene: *A Lauriston Garden of Verses* (Summit, N.J.: Pamphlet House, $40). Attributed to Edgar W. Smith. 250 copies.

57. 1946–49 Smith, Edgar W. (ed.): *The Baker Street Journal.* The official publication of the Baker Street Irregulars; 13 issues were published ($130).

58. 1947 Cutter, Robert A. (ed.): *Sherlockian Studies* (Jackson Heights, N.Y.: Baker Street Press, $40). Seven essays, sponsored by The Three Students of Long Island. 200 copies.

59. 1947 Williamson, J.N., and H.B. Williams (eds.): *Illustrious Client's Case-Book* (Indianapolis, Ind.: The Illustrious Clients, $40).

60. 1947 Keddie, James, Jr. (ed.) *The Second Cab* (Boston: Privately printed, $40). Essays, ephemera by The Speckled Band of Boston. 300 copies.

61. 1947 Christ, Jay Finlay: *An Irregular Guide to Sherlock Holmes of Baker Street* (New York: Argus Books. Summit, N.J.: Pamphlet House, $40). A concordance.

62. 1948 Bayer, Robert John: *Some Notes on a Meeting at Chisam* (Chicago: Camden House, $75). Father Brown and Holmes. Limited to 60 copies.

63. 1949 Carr, John Dickson: *The Life of Sir Arthur Conan Doyle* (New York: Harper, $15). The standard life of Watson's agent.

64. 1949 Grazebrook, O.F.: *Studies in Sher-*

lock Holmes, 7 vols. (London: Privately printed, $100).

65. 1950 SMITH, EDGAR W.: *A Baker Street Quartette* (New York: The Baker Street Irregulars, $40). Four Sherlockian tales in verse. 221 copies.

66. 1950–52 DOYLE, ARTHUR CONAN: *Sherlock Holmes,* 8 vols. (New York: Limited Editions Club, $300). The ultimate edition of the Canon, edited by Edgar W. Smith and profusely illustrated. Limited to 1,500 sets.

67. 1951 BREND, GAVIN: *My Dear Holmes* (London: Allen & Unwin, $15).

68. 1951– SMITH, EDGAR W. (followed by JULIAN WOLFF, M.D.) (ed.): *The Baker Street Journal (New Series).* The quarterly publication of the Baker Street Irregulars ($450).

69. 1952– DONEGALL, MARQUESS OF (ed.): *The Sherlock Holmes Journal.* Semiannual publication of the Sherlock Holmes Society of London ($350).

70. 1952 PETERSON, ROBERT STORM, and TAGE LA COUR: *Tobacco Talk in Baker Street* (New York: Baker Street Irregulars, $40). Contains an essay and a burlesque.

71. 1952 WOLFF, JULIAN, M.D.: *The Sherlockian Atlas* (New York: Privately printed, $35). 13 detailed maps of Holmes' world. 400 copies.

72. 1953 SMITH, EDGAR W.: *The Napoleon of Crime* (Summit, N.J.: Pamphlet House, $35). The standard life of Professor Moriarty. Limited to 221 copies.

73. 1953 ZEISLER, ERNEST BLOOMFIELD: *Baker Street Chronology* (Chicago: Alexander J. Isaacs, $100). A new dating of Holmes' adventures. Limited to 200 copies.

74. 1953–71 SIMPSON, A. CARSON: *Simpson's Sherlockian Studies,* 9 vols. (Philadelphia: Privately printed, $100). The first 8 pamphlets limited to 221 copies; the last was reproduced from the unpublished manuscript in 1971.

75. 1954 MONTGOMERY, JAMES: *A Study in Pictures* (Philadelphia: Privately printed, $65). The first guide to the illustrators of Holmes. The most elaborate of the author's 6 Christmas annuals (1950–55). 300 copies.

76. 1954 DOYLE, ADRIAN CONAN, and JOHN DICKSON CARR: *The Exploits of Sherlock Holmes* (New York: Random House, $25). 12 pastiches by the agent's son and a brilliant writer.

77. 1955 GILLETTE, WILLIAM: *The Painful Predicament of Sherlock Holmes: A Fantasy in One Act* (Chicago: Ben Abranson, $20). Introduction by Vincent Starrett. Gillette's *other* Sherlock Holmes play, first performed in 1905. 500 copies.

78. 1955 CLARKE, RICHARD W. (ed.): *The Best of the Pips* (New York: The Five Orange Pips of Westchester County, $30). Called "the most erudite" essays By Edgar W. Smith.

79. 1955 MITCHELL, GLADYS: *Watson's Choice* (London: Michael Joseph, $35). A novel with Sherlockian flavorings.

80. 1957 WOLFF, JULIAN, M.D.: *A Ramble in Bohemia* (New York: U.N. Philatelic Chronicle [*sic*], $45). A report on the commemorative Holmes stamp issued by the Republic of Bohemia in 1988. A stamp accompanies some copies of the pamphlet.

81. 1957 WARRACK, GUY: *Sherlock Holmes and Music* (London: Faber & Faber, $15). The definitive guide to Holmes's life as a musician.

82. 1958 DOYLE, ARTHUR CONAN: *The Crown Diamond: An Evening with Sherlock Holmes. A Play in One Act* (New York: Privately printed, $100). A very short play written just after the turn of the century and published for the first time. With an introduction by Edgar W. Smith. 59 copies.

83. 1958 HARRISON, MICHAEL: *In the Footsteps of Sherlock Holmes* (London: Cassell, $15). An authoritative geographical examination of Holmes' world.

84. 1958 TITUS, EVE: *Basil of Baker Street* (New York: Whittlesey House, $15). The first of the best series of

juveniles for Sherlockians; illustrated by Paul Galdone.

85. 1959 Starr, H.W. (ed.): *Leaves from the Copper Beeches* (Narberth, Pa.: The Sons of the Copper Beeches, $30). Mostly humorous essays. 500 copies.

86. 1959 Holroyd, James Edward: *Baker Street By-Ways* (London: Allen & Unwin, $15). A commentary by the chairman of the Sherlock Holmes Society of London.

87. 1962 Baring-Gould, William S.: *Sherlock Holmes of Baker Street* (New York: Clarkson N. Potter, $15). The most authoritative life of Holmes.

88. 1962 Smith, Edgar W.: *Sherlock Holmes: The Writings of John H. Watson, M.D.* (Morristown, N.J.: Baker Street Irregulars, $40). A comprehensive bibliography of Holmes' adventures.

89. 1963 Klinefelter, Walter: *Sherlock Holmes in Portrait and Profile* (Syracuse University Press, $10). Introduction by Vincent Starrett. The definitive study of illustrations.

90. 1964 Kahn, William B.: *An Adventure of Oilock Combs: The Succored Beauty* (San Francisco: The Beaune Press, $30). A parody originally published in the October 1905 issue of *The Smart Set Magazine*. The first of the Christmas keepsakes of Dean and Shirley Dickensheet. 222 copies.

91. 1964 Klinefelter, Walter: *A Packet of Sherlockian Bookplates* (Nappanee, Ind.: Privately printed, $75). A compendium of the bookplates of eminent Sherlockians, extensively illustrated in color. 150 copies.

92. 1966 Fish, Robert L.: *The Incredible Schlock Homes* (New York: Simon & Schuster, $25). The funniest series of Sherlockian parody-pastiches.

93. 1966 Queen, Ellery: *A Study in Terror* (New York: Lancer, $10). Also the first English edition, and the first in hardcover, retitled *Sherlock Holmes Versus Jack the Ripper* (London: Gollancz, 1967). A novelization of the film, with added material, which records Holmes' encounter with The Harlot Killer.

94. 1967 Baring-Gould, William S.: *The Annotated Sherlock Holmes,* 2 vols. (New York: Clarkson N. Potter, $45). The definitive edition of the Canon, heavily illustrated and annotated by a preeminent scholar.

95. 1968 Wincor, Richard: *Sherlock Holmes in Tibet* (New York: Weybright & Talley, 50¢). Noteworthy as probably the worst book about Holmes.

96. 1974 Meyer, Nicholas: *The Seven-Percent Solution* (New York: Dutton, $10). The book largely responsible for a new Sherlockian boom.

97. 1974 Gardner, John: *The Return of Moriarty* (London: Weidenfeld & Nicholson, $10). The most literate, enthralling and atmospheric pastiche in half a century.

98. 1974 De Waal, Ronald Burt: *The World Bibliography of Sherlock Holmes and Dr. Watson* (Boston: New York Graphic Society, $50). A monumental reference book and a prodigious achievement, listing 6,221 items relating to Holmes.

99. 1976 Todd, Peter: *The Adventures of Herlock Sholmes* (New York: The Mysterious Press). With an introduction by Philip Jose Farmer. Contains 18 parodies by Charles Hamilton under the Todd pseudonym. Published orginally in a British periodical in 1915–16, they are the first of the longest Holmes parody cycle (100 stories). Limited to 1250 copies ($10), 250 deluxe ($20).

100. (in preparation) Holmes, Sherlock: *The Whole Art of Detection.* In preparation for more than fifty years; and will contain everything learned in the preceding fifty years. Priceless.

Otto Penzler wrote The Private Lives of Private Eyes, Spies, Crimefighters and Other Good Guys.

GOOD LITTLE GIRLS AND BOYS

Phyllis A. Whitney

Oh, no! I would never buy a mystery for my granddaughter. I want to give her something *worthwhile.*"

This unenlightened remark is often heard by booksellers, and it is fortunate that both booksellers and librarians know better and provide the mystery titles their readers enjoy. And from which (surprise!) they can learn so much.

The mystery for young people should never be confused with the blood-and-violence school, yet it is an interesting comment on writers of juvenile mysteries that they can compete with that strong stuff on television. We know something that Hitchcock learned long ago: it isn't the flying bullets, the number of cars that crash together, the wild chases over fences that build suspense; true suspense is made up of other ingredients.

Suspense is the fear of something unknown just around the corner — the fear of something dreadful about to happen to someone you like, or the fear that something hoped-for won't happen. In either case there is the anticipation of something deliciously scary. Only the danger that *might* happen can really frighten. When this threat is met and defeated at the end of the story, the reader is satisfied. Whereas all that gun-to-gun tackling at the end of the television play gives us no warm sense of satisfaction.

The fear, of course, and the anticipation must be directly connected with characters we care about. Straw men won't do it The writer of juvenile mysteries is particularly skilled in reaching out to the readers and pulling in their sympathy for the story's main character. It doesn't really matter whether the character is a girl or a boy. In my own books the viewpoint character (whether first or third person) is always a girl. Yet these days I receive as many fan letters from boys as I do from girls. It is the characters, the story, the *suspense* that counts. And perhaps mystery writers have learned to build the last two items better than has the "straight" novelist.

With young readers there is another ingredient as important as suspense. It is something I look for even before I discover what the actual mystery is going to be. I want some human situation that can carry a special meaning for my readers and that will perhaps leave them with something to think about — even to use in their own lives.

To give an example: *Secret of the Stone Face* is about a girl whose father has died and who is terribly afraid that her mother is going to remarry. The girl is prejudiced from the beginning against the man who will be her stepfather. Her prejudice is human and natural, yet if she is not to be unhappy and to cause her mother great unhappiness, she must learn in the course of the story that such prejudice is unfair and unfounded. So, as I build a story, the mystery and the human problem become intertwined, and my young heroine, as she solves the mystery, learns something valuable about life — and about herself.

No mystery plot descends from the sky full-blown and complete. It is something built a bit at a time, idea by idea, through months of work before the actual writing begins. It grows from the story background and from the problems and characters of the people in the book. There must be youthful opposition to the purpose that drives a young heroine. Even though the stepfather problem in *Secret of the Stone Face* concerns adults, it is the young people in the story who must be of the greatest importance. Villains are necessary, and they can be either children or adults, or sometimes both, but it is the young people *onstage* who must carry the story.

One rule to hold to through all writing for children: Never put the main character into dangerous situations that will set a bad example for the reader. Characters may do foolish things at times, or be led by others into difficult situations, but they must not take high risks. They must not set off single-handedly to capture a dangerous criminal.

Settings are always important, whether one is writing for adults or for young people. Perhaps because I have lived in so many places, I have no one locale that I use. I must find a new setting for every story. If I can give a glimpse of another country, or of a part of that country, that will take my readers there in their imagination, this is something worthwhile. Still, a background should never be allowed to remain a static painted scene, like an old-fashioned stage setting. The background is not only something the characters move about in; it affects them and affects the story. One of the things I most enjoy about using new settings is the way in which they furnish unexpected story action and help to mold and change my main character.

That is something else that must happen in a good story of any kind. The main character must change, must learn and grow in the course of the story. A character who stands still never satisfies the reader. We all want to become partisan as we read. We want the character to win, and in order to win there is always some growing to be done.

We must be wary, however, of preaching. No soapboxes! Let the character learn through the action of the story and through interplay with other characters — and never because the author steps in and gives a lecture.

Most important, if the "worthwhile" things are to be accomplished, we must never forget that it is all for fun. If we forget that we are first of all entertainers, we will never make our readers listen and pay attention to what we have to say.

I had a letter recently from a girl in sixth grade in Nazareth, Pennsylvania. In her postscript she says:

"When I feel mad your books get it all away."

That is the nicest thing that has ever been said to me, and I think it speaks for the entire mystery field. The grandmother whom I quoted at the start of this piece should change her approach. When she goes into a bookstore, she must learn to ask the clerk: "What do you have in a good mystery for children?"

Phyllis A. Whitney is equally well known for her adult suspense novels and her mysteries for young people, which have won her two Edgars. Her Writing Juvenile Stories and Novels *is a standard text in the field.*

ENCYCLOPEDIA BROWN

The most popular children's mysteries concern a young man (he's about ten years old) named Encyclopedia Brown. The stories are by Donald Sobel, who has followed the format of the old-time *Minute Mysteries* in creating them.

Master Brown runs his own detective agency, and on tricky cases he consults with his father, a police officer.

The exploits of Brown are so appealing to children (Mr. Sobel has become the Judy Blume of mysterydom) that there is now an Encyclopedia Brown Book Club.

It would be a mistake, however, to assume Brown was the first boy detective. Let's not forget Mark Twain's Tom Sawyer or Ellery Queen's Djuna, who took on seven of Queen's own cases.

DAVID HURN/MAGNUM

ARE GIRLS MORE INHERENTLY EVIL THAN BOYS?

Arnold Madison

Well, of course girls *are* more inherently evil than boys. No knowledgeable person really doubts that today. The real question is why.

Perhaps we ought to go back to the primal state and consider nature. We all know it's the female black widow spider that should be avoided unless one wishes to court illness and possible death. And what about those crepe-paper beehives where a queen bee is carefully bred and faces a royal fight to the death upon emerging from her birth cell? The victor rules the world of the bee and relegates all males to the status of slaves. Part of the answer as to why girls are more evil than boys may be that nature has provided a predilection for evil in the female of the species.

There is also the matter of historical conditioning. Various eras and ages have provided numerous heroes for the average citizen to admire. The stories about young girls' bravery, however, are the most thrilling. Generally, time reveals that the male heroes had feet of clay. But Joan of Arc? Would anyone dare hint that she was not the epitome of heroism? While the boy king was cowering in his chambers, Joan was on the battlefield, leading the fight against the enemy armies.

And of the millions of people who tragically died under Hitler's maniacal reign, who most personified the terrible suffering and cruelty inflicted upon those human beings? Anne Frank. Her diary touched the heart of anyone who read it.

At first, these examples may seem to be proving that girls are not more evil than boys. But consider why these accounts affect us so deeply. Who do we have among the brave young males? A boy who stuck his finger in a dike and prevented a flood. And that story has sexual connotations. The reason heroines move us emotionally much more than heroes is that most people view girls as pure and far removed from evil. Boys seem more adept at fighting an enemy because we see them as bad themselves, so the battle is more evenly matched.

Even old bearded Plato decided: "A boy is, of all wild beasts, the most difficult to manage." And there is the old English proverb which declares: "One boy is more trouble than a dozen girls." A boy, after all, is puppy dogs' tails. Ah, but girls! They are sugar and spice and all things nice — or so the legend goes. This misconception is very encouraging to Evil.

Evil is a tangible thing. Those gifted persons who can sense another person's aura also have the ability to spot Evil lurking within another individual. Unfortunately, only a select few possess that talent. The rest of us often fail to spot Evil, which knows its best ally is a good disguise. What better cloak for Evil than to wrap about itself the external appearance of a girl?

The innocent, guileless smile. The slight

whimpering voice announcing: "I'll always be Daddy's little girl." The feigned shock when something unpleasant occurs. Now *that's* a disguise. And, like any criminal suspect, Evil has sought and found the perfect red herring. When Evil commits its act, the investigator's attention turns to the male and Evil is left free to create even more damage.

There is another reason a girl is the perfect haven for Evil: society. From an early age girls have learned how to manipulate those around them. They know the performance destined to sway their fans. This makes it easy for Evil to emerge as Insincerity.

Also, from the moment of birth, a girl is treated much like the queen bee of the hive. Her every want is satisfied. Parents try to wrap their daughters in a cottony cocoon, protecting them from reality and any unpleasantness. But boys — well, boys have to grow up tough. They're going to know all the sinful things in life, so we might as well harden them as quickly as possible. Coddled and cuddled throughout her early years, a girl matures with every blow softened and every whim granted.

What a receptive home for Evil! This type personality makes it so easy for Evil to assume the guise of Greed. If everyone caters to a child and showers her with gifts, Greed is excited and motivated to seek even more. Greed knows no bounds, but even humans reach a point when they say no to a girl. Now Greed is frustrated and becomes angry. Psychologically, the function of anger or rage is to destroy frustration. If the rage becomes great enough, Evil is transformed into Murder. For someone who has always had every wish fulfilled, the death of a hated individual is simply one more desire — like that for another piece of candy — to be satisfied.

Naturally, eight-year-old Rhoda Penmark in *The Bad Seed* murdered Claude Daigle. After all, he had the penmanship medal that she wanted. And what did Bonnie's big blue eyes reveal in *The Godsend?* Only that what Bonnie desired, Bonnie got, whether it be the death of a baby or a boy's drowning or acceptance by a mother who knew full well that Evil inhabited her daughter's body. And consider Carrie White, the girl who everyone would have voted "the least likely to succeed." Carrie became the queen of Ewen Consolidated High School's prom — a queen who was to wreck more destruction than Lady Macbeth. The school dance literally ended in a blood bath and fiery holocaust: the king was dead; long live the queen.

Yes, fiction is truly a mirror of life. There are those of us who know that Evil finds a girl to be a safe harbor and a base of operations. But what do we do? What *can* we do?

Perhaps this is merely one more accomplishment of Evil.

Arnold Madison is the author of Drugs and You *(1971) which was nominated as one of the best books of the year for children by the* New York Times.

MYSTERY KIDS

Marjorie Carelton: *The Night of the Good Children*
Anne Chamberlin: *The Tall Dark Man*
Freeman Wills Crofts: *Young Robin Brand, Detective*
Thom Demijohn: *Black Alice*
Thomas B. Dewey: *A Sad Song Singing*
Fielden Farrington: *A Little Game*
Roy Fuller: *With My Little Eye*
Michael Innes: *The Case of the Journeying Boy*
Elizabeth Linington: *No Evil Angel*
Arthur Lyons: *All God's Children*
Ross Macdonald: *The Far Side of the Dollar; The Underground Man*
Quentin Patrick: *A Boy's Will*
Hugh Pentecost: *The Day the Children Vanished*
Ellis Peters: *Death and the Joyful Woman; Flight of a Witch*
Evelyn Piper: *Bunny Lake Is Missing*
Jonathan Stagge: *The Yellow Taxi*
Josephine Tey: *The Franchise Affair*
Hillary Waugh: *The Young Prey*

INDEX

FRED WINKOWSKI

A

B

C

D

E

J

L

N

O

P

Q

R

S

T

U

W

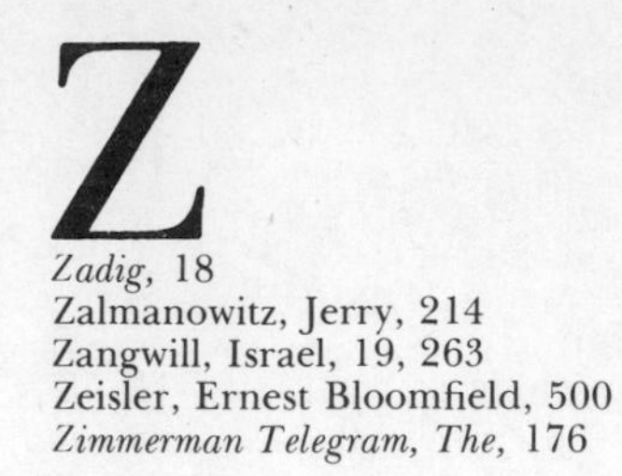

This book was appropriately set in Baskerville.

Jazz in

the Seventies

by LEONARD FEATHER
and IRA GITLER

THE ENCYCLOPEDIA OF JAZZ IN THE SEVENTIES

Introduction by QUINCY JONES

A DA CAPO PAPERBACK

To Jane and Lorraine
and
To Mary Jo and Fitz

Library of Congress Cataloging in Publication Data

Feather, Leonard G.
Encyclopedia of jazz in the seventies.

(A Da Capo paperback)
Reprint. Originally published: New York: Horizon Press, 1976.
Bibliography: p.
1. Jazz music—Bio-bibliography. 2. Jazz music—Discography. I. Gitler, Ira. II. Title.
[ML105.F36 1987] 785.42′092′2 87-517
ISBN 0-306-80290-2 (pbk.)

This Da Capo Press paperback edition of *The Encyclopedia of Jazz of the 70s* is an unabridged republication of the edition published in New York in 1976. It is reprinted by arrangement with Horizon Press Publishers Ltd.

Published by Da Capo Press, Inc.
A Subsidiary of Plenum Publishing Corporation
233 Spring Street, New York, N.Y. 10013

Manufactured in the United States of America

Authors' Prefaces

The Encyclopedia of Jazz in the '70s is the third in a series of books, each in its way autonomous. The others are *The Encyclopedia of Jazz* (previously known as *The New Encyclopedia of Jazz*), published in 1960 and covering men, women and events in jazz history from the beginning until that time; and *The Encyclopedia of Jazz in the '60s*, covering events through mid-1966 and published late in that year. The present work is an examination of the ten-year period since the preparation of the previous volume.

Even more than during the compilation of the earlier books, the lines between jazz and other idioms became vague and arbitrary. This was particularly true of the borders between jazz and rock, and of those between jazz and free music or black music. Certain artists, protesting that they did not wish to be classified as jazz musicians, asked to be excluded from the new work. In many cases we acceded to their wishes; however, in some instances their association with jazz seemed to have been established so firmly at one time or another within the jazz community that they were included. Stix Hooper, leader of a group that was known for many years as the Jazz Crusaders, is a case in point.

Ira Gitler, an associate since the inception of the entire series (research on an early *Encyclopedia of Jazz* began with his help in 1954), has now become a full collaborator. It is no exaggeration to state that, given the enormous complexity of this job, it could not have been done without the knowledge and dedication Ira applied to completing it.

Frankie Nemko, who began as my secretary but who in the course of the work became a full-fledged editorial associate, brought to her part of the work a rare combination of familiarity with the subject, enthusiasm and painstaking accuracy. Ira and I are both grateful for her help.

Among the many friends and newly found correspondents around the world who gladly gave their time in enabling us to make this as complete a collection of facts as was reasonably possible, the following were particularly helpful: Joachim Berendt, Pawel Brodowski, Jan Byrczek, Philippe Carles, Roger Coterell, Stanley Crouch, Jim Crockett, Stanley Dance, Edmond Devoghelaere, Gudrun Endress, Gretchen Horton, Randi Hultin, Kiyoshi Koyama, Floyd Levin, Mike Mantler, Dennis H. Matthews, Mark Miller, Moscatelli Nello, John Norris, Arrigo Polillo, Charles Suber, Eric Vogel and Nils Winther.

I recall with a mixture of gratitude and sadness the many constructive notes sent me by the late Ralph J. Gleason, a man who loved jazz and was determined to offer help unselfishly to anyone of us who shared his concern.

As in the last volume, it is necessary to apologize to those whose biographies were submitted but for reasons of space could not be included; and to others on whom material proved difficult or impossible to obtain. Fortunately the latter were in a small minority and included none of the truly significant, established figures.

This is not simply a book dealing with artists who came to prominence during the past decade. Those who died after the previous book went to press, and the many others who were still a part of the jazz scene as this latest volume was being wrapped up, all are included in the pages that follow. Eubie Blake has a place in *The Encyclopedia of Jazz in the '70s* no less important than that of Jon Faddis.

For this edition we were determined to obtain the finest possible illustrations and to avoid conventional, press-agent photographs, Veryl Oakland (during the past ten years, and continuing into the mid-'70s, an important photo contributor to *down beat; Jazz Magazine* (Paris); *Swing Journal* (Tokyo); *Billboard; Guitar Player; Contemporary Keyboard*; and *Rolling Stone*) was unstintingly helpful in supplying lists, making up prints and availing us of his very special artistry. He is the photographer most abundantly represented, but we were fortunate also to have the cooperation of David D. Spitzer and others.

Finally, a reminder: although this book is self-sufficient, in the sense that it includes brief recapitulations of the pre-1966 careers of almost all the performers listed in the previous volumes, it is rather the combination of all three books that is intended to provide the most complete series possible. Together, they form what we believe is the most comprehensive reference set covering the 75 tumultuous years in which jazz has been a sturdy, ever-growing art form.

Leonard Feather
North Hollywood, Calif.

I can only second the words of my colleague and add our thanks to the help received from Jeff Atterton, Len Dobbin, Marta Jones, Arthur Levy, (especially) Dan Morgenstern, Stanley Sands, Don Schlitten, David Spewack, Jane Welch and Krzysztof Zagrodzki.

I am already aware of the book's value. It helped greatly itself in its own completion.

We acknowledge, with special thanks, the discriminating and devoted assistance given to us in connection with the manifold details of this book by Tony Outhwaite of Horizon Press.

Ira Gitler
New York City

Contents

Illustrations

Introduction by Quincy Jones

It is impossible for me to look back over the past eventful decade in modern music, or to speculate about what the future may hold, without recalling an answer I gave to a question Leonard Feather asked me many years ago. I was one of a group of musicians he approached for a concluding chapter in *The Book of Jazz*, in an attempt to predict what jazz would be like in 1984.

I'd like to recall some of the observations I made at that time, back in 1957: "How many attitudes," I said, "will be changed if jazz goes just where we want it to? If backgrounds for television shows and other situations like that become what we now call 'hip' and earn acceptance by every layman—will it still be progressive music or will it then become just popular music? In other words, if jazz becomes so widely used and accepted, then isn't it likely that it will just be considered popular music and the critics will go some place else and find something farther out, more esoteric?

"Concerning the blending of classical and jazz forms, I don't go for it too much today—this business of jazz musicians' trying to compete with Hindemith and Stravinsky. There's really no competition at all. And the 12-tone scale may be new to us, but it's quite old-fashioned to the classical composer, so what we do with it is really a joke. It sounds very amateurish to try to write atonal things without any conception of basic composition, just for the sake of trying to be far out. That's not progress. It's like a classical composer hanging out in nightclubs for a couple of nights and then trying to play bebop piano.

"What I hope will happen, though, is that symphony musicians' training in the future will have them better informed as to what has happened in jazz, so that when the guys are making a strong attempt to bring these two things together and combine the techniques, the orchestras will be better equipped.

"Eventually I think the two groups will simply be musicians—like for instance in Sweden, where a guy is just as familiar with a Ravel string quartet as he is with Lunceford's *For Dancers Only*. It will be wonderful if we get to a place where all the groups are speaking one another's language.

"This is my ultimate in the future of jazz. If there has to be a fusion of classical music and jazz, I think it will come in the day when there are capable soloists inside the symphony orchestra—when they have the same backgrounds. When everybody in the symphony orchestra can sit down and build, and have the same subtlety and looseness of rhythm. But it would have to come from the roots, and everybody in the orchestra would have to have those roots. If that happened, they would satisfy just as much as Duke Ellington—and that would be my idea of the perfect future for jazz."

In reviewing these observations of mine, Leonard mentioned that I had touched on a point he felt was very relevant: that jazz has been subjected to a Law of Diminishing Repute. He pointed out that by 1957, for example, scores of trumpet players were capable of performances that would have seemed fantastic in 1943, just as Dizzy Gillespie's first bebop records were around that time. But after all the time that had passed since bop began, a solo by, say, Lee

Morgan, objectively, must be judged in terms of the listener's awareness of earlier contributions by Gillespie and the other pioneers of the 1940's. Jazz in the next twenty-five years, he concluded, would continue along these lines: "The innovation of today will be the cliché of tomorrow."

Well, here we are now, not too far away from the 1984 that seemed so distant to us when we talked and wrote about it then; and some of the points made then have turned out to be very germane to the contemporary scene.

In order to get a clear perspective of what progress has been made, of what sounds are really yesterday's innovations and today's cliches, it's important to bear in mind that many of the things people tend to think of as new have really been around for quite a while. It would be difficult for me to state that I have heard many new, actual, organic innovative approaches toward music of *any* kind in the past ten years.

We heard some of the most sophisticated sounds imaginable back at the end of the '40's and the beginning of the '50's. My mind used to get torn off every time I'd hear Bird or Fats Navarro or Clifford Brown. I haven't been slapped in the head on that level in a long time.

Let's deal with the situation element by element. Velocity? We won't even get into that, because there's nobody alive who's playing faster than Art Tatum was playing back then. Or Dizzy, or Bird, Ray Brown, Max Roach.

Harmony? In terms of avant garde harmonic concepts there are none, really; in jazz that is our least innovative area, because the classical composers had raked the total realm of harmonic innovations a hundred years before we even touched this area.

Melodically I haven't heard that much, aside from some experiments with twelve tone improvisation, which in any case musicians have always been experimenting with on both sides, from Lukas Foss to a lot of jazz musicians. Polytonality is nothing new; neither is serial music.

Rhythmically you have people today like Billy Cobham, who really understands what polyrhythms are all about. But it's very difficult to call that new, if you sit down and listen to forty or fifty African records. That's been an African tradition for centuries. The so-called "new" time signatures also are no brainchildren of the '70's; they were in African music and classical music centuries ago.

All right, then; we've eliminated velocity, harmonic structure, melody, rhythm, time signatures; so what do you have left that is strongly progressive? The fusion of styles, and the use of technology. And here the role played by electronics immediately comes to mind.

Actually, the year 1953 locked up the incubation period for the granddaddies of electronics. Specifically, there was Charlie Christian, who established the electric guitar in 1939; and in 1953, when I was twenty years old and playing in Lionel Hampton's orchestra, Monk Montgomery was playing fender bass—the first musician ever to use one.

Those two instruments turned the whole thing around. The rest were just supplementary items—the echoplexes, and so forth. Basically, the thrust of evolution was motivated by the electric guitar and fender bass. When the bass was amplified, it was necessary to deal with a totally different concept of the function of the bass.

Once the bottom of the rhythm section began to become filled out with such strong, predominant sounds, and the focus went down to the basement, our perspective of what happened on top with ad lib improvisation was completely turned around. The guitar and bass played a vital part in determining the function of a jazz group. I know that the synthesizers constitute a pervasive force today, but those things are accouterments. The rhythm section does not function off of a synthesizer, which is just a color, rather than the backbone of the rhythm section. The synthesizer is not so much a musical instrument as a controller of sound.

One facet of the scene that has changed appreciably in the past ten years is that of communication. I think my generation came out of a school that said to hell with the public. I remember feeling a certain joy, when I was seventeen, hearing a layman tell me he didn't understand what I was doing. It was fashionable, and the highest compliment in the world, to be outside. But now you have musicians who are eager to get through to the people; men like Herbie Hancock and Billy Cobham. Cobham has studied his drums, he's listened to Max and all the jazz greats, as well as to the rock cats, and he feels he doesn't have to be self-conscious about his playing, because he can outplay anyone on either side of the fence. So he plays to express himself, to get it all out. He wants to communicate, and he succeeds.

Another aspect in which there has been a notable change in recent years is the self-respect among musicians. In the early years of jazz, of course, it was considered anything but respectable. Black musicians in particular went through such a brainwashing process that they weren't considered complete musicians until they had just about abandoned their roots and were able to play Opus Number So-and-So. Everything was judged by European art music standards.

Even at the black universities in this country black music isn't allowed, or wasn't until comparatively recently. Cannonball Adderley once told me he had the same problem when he was teaching school. It was completely forbidden to become involved in the blues or jazz or boogie woogie. Howard University stopped using Handel and other European music for their commencements only as recently as ten or fifteen years ago. Black music wasn't allowed in the schools, and that applied to eighty per cent of the black colleges and universities in America.

In doing some research on the history of black music I came across a book that included an astonishing example of how people's minds were manipulated in this country. The book is called *Discovering Music*, and it was part of a series called *War Department Educational Manual*, printed by the United States Armed Forces Institute of Madison, Wisconsin. The authors are Howard D. McKinney and W. R. Anderson. The book is described as a course in music appreciation, and was published in 1944. In the course of a chapter labeled *The Adventurous Conquest*, there is a paragraph that reads: "Some may start with an enthusiasm for music of the jazz type but they cannot go farther, for jazz is peculiarly of an inbred feeble stock race, incapable of development. In any case, the people for whom it is meant could not understand it if it did develop. Jazz is sterile; it is all right for fun or as a mild anodyne like tobacco, but its lack of rhythmical variety necessitated by its special purpose, its brevity, its repetitiveness and lack of sustained development, together with the fact that commercial reasons prevent its being as a rule very well written, all mark it as a side issue having next to nothing to do with serious music, and consequently it has proved itself entirely useless as a basis for developing the tastes of the amateur. The ambitious listener might better start from the level of Chopin's melodious piano music or Grieg's northern pieces."

That is an illustration of how our armed forces were being indoctrinated thirty-odd years ago, but it also indicates the entire attitude that has prevailed in American society, one that has been tremendously difficult to overcome. Today, more than ever, in any discussion of jazz, the problem arises of defining the word itself. If you were to stop the man on the street and ask what the word means to him, you would be given so many different answers that it would blow your mind; because we are dealing with endless areas of styles, pictures, associations, and, above all, stereotypes. The word has so many meanings that ultimately it has none at all. Even students who have infinitely more understanding of the music than the writers of the quotation above have difficulty in drawing the line between jazz and other forms. For example, how could you separate the Third Stream concert works of John Lewis from what the authors call "serious music"?

On another level, if you were to take Charlie Parker's solo on *Stella By Starlight* and put the Stevie Wonder rhythm section underneath it, it would still be jazz. By the same token, how do you classify Stevie Wonder's *Too High*? It cannot be called rhythm and blues. He plays polytonal chords and jazz figures along with rhythm and blues licks; it is a total fusion. Harmonically, melodically, and every other way, it really has a jazz base, but it is performed by artists who are categorized as rhythm and blues.

Jazz is the stepchild of many matriarchal types of music such as gospel, the blues, and spirituals; yet, somehow it attained a position in which it could influence and swallow up anything with which it came into contact, from quadrilles to Stravinsky, to Country and Western. Whatever it came next to, it could eat alive. Consequently, it has always had an incredible number of influences around it, but its roots have remained planted where the mother elements come from.

The chord changes, and melodic ideas in rhythm and blues are developing every day. More and more the fusion is showing that basically all these forms stem from one source. John Coltrane's sound brings the same kind of message as the cat who was singing the field hollers back in slavery days. It is a continuation of a life style, and the remarkable thing about every form of artistic evolution is that no matter which direction is taken—avant garde, sophisticated, crude, blues, emotional basis or intellectual basis—it is still in many ways a sociological basis that provides the fundamental determination; and there were sociological reasons for the attitudes behind the music appreciation course that found jazz sterile and incapable of development.

Actually, it has developed so far and so dynamically that today there are probably more categories within the category of jazz itself than in any other music.

I don't envy Leonard Feather and Ira Gitler their role in putting this book together. Ten years ago there was a whole different set of circumstances. The typical musician today is not isolated in an ivory tower. He has listened to and been a part of many other forms of music. He has been affected by instant communication, by the dynamics of society over these past turbulent years. I have always felt that if I had the choice of picking a particular time to be around, especially as a musician, I would not want to trade this particular spot that I have. It covered the end of what was called the swing period, the birth of modern jazz, and all the subsequent developments. It meant a great deal to me, when I decided to take a few months off and write some music based on the Afro-American heritage, to be able to get on the telephone and call Duke Ellington to straighten out any conflict I might find in the history books. That was a real luxury. This is a golden age we are living in, because we have been able to feel the impact made by the personalities and musical influences of what is really the first team.

I remember being particularly conscious of this one night at the Monterey Jazz Festival when a group of us got together and we were all sitting under a blanket. Louis Armstrong was there, and Roy Eldridge, and Dizzy: three generations of music sitting right under that blanket! We didn't think anything about it at the time, other than that we were happy to be alive, but obviously that can't happen twenty years from now.

It is difficult to explain, to anyone who has not experienced Charlie Parker or Dizzy Gillespie or Louis Armstrong or Duke Ellington or Billy Eckstine or Count Basie, just what that person represents as a total human being in the hierarchy of a great tradition. That has been one of the greatest joys of my life, to have known and been around these people, to have been influenced by them, and to have lived through the different eras they symbolize. All these great figures, and the artists who have come up more recently as an outgrowth of their influences, are represented in the pages of *The Encyclopedia of Jazz In The '70s*. That's the biggest talent blanket of them all.

Brentwood, Calif.

The practitioner as preacher: The best of the Blindfold Test

The Blindfold Test, which I inaugurated in 1946 in *Metronome*, and which has been appearing regularly in *down beat* since 1951, was based on the premise that the musician has the right to function as a critic of his own art form, and that a listener, given no prior information concerning the record he is listening to, will be unencumbered by any prejudice.

The main objective of these interviews is the eliciting of an honest reaction to the music—the soloists, composition, arrangement, recording. The guessing of the artists' identities has always been a secondary consideration; this is pointed out to the blindfoldee before he is interviewed.

The following excerpts, all from tests conducted during the decade before this book went to press, were chosen on the basis of their general interest, without regard to the positive or negative character of the comments. The ratings indicate outstanding (five stars), very good (four), good (three), fair (two) and poor (one).

The excerpts are reproduced through the cooperation of Jack Maher, editor, and Charles Suber, publisher, of *down beat*, and by permission of Maher Publications.

The date after the artist's name before each comment indicates the year in which the interview was first published.

BAND LEADERS

Don Ellis. *Passacaglia and Fugue* (from *Live at Monterey*, Pacific Jazz). Ellis, trumpet; Tom Scott, alto.

Michel Legrand (1967): I like it very much, but—I wonder, is it an old album? . . . There was a little touch of the bebop in there.

Is that an organized band which plays every day? It sounds to me like—like the way Lalo Schifrin works—a studio band. But the composition, and the way it was orchestrated, I found very interesting. Interesting construction.

Who is the trumpet player? And also the alto at the beginning? I liked them . . . it could have been Phil Woods. Four stars.

Woody Herman. *The Sound of Music* (from *My Kind of Broadway*, Columbia). Herman, leader, alto saxophone; Raoul Romero, arranger.

Cannonball Adderley (1967): Well, taken as good sounding dance music, I think that that's five stars. It's good to hear Woody Herman sounding like he did years ago; in fact, I really do get nostalgic about bands. . . . I had the feeling that this was the same caliber, the same scope of things that Woody did in the *Summer Sequence* period, and it felt like Ralph Burns to me . . . It is not adventurous jazz, but there's room for everything, and I'm happy to know that Woody is still doing that sort of thing—maybe his music will survive as a result of his being able to play music for just ordinary folks.

As far as big bands and what it takes for them to survive, vive le Woody Herman!

Dave Brubeck. *World's Fair* (from *Time Changes*, Columbia).

Don Ellis (1967): There is nothing like a nice relaxed 13! . . . Dave Brubeck has been playing these time things as a group longer than anyone else, but they don't seem to be very free within the time yet . . . They haven't gotten to the point yet where they can really mess with the time. . . . It seems they should be much further into it, given the amount of time they have been doing it.

This is the first time I heard them playing in 13, and they played it all the way through.

I noticed Dave was having a little trouble keeping his left hand right on the rhythm, but he came out okay. . . . I'm just sorry that Dave and his group haven't been able to develop a more flowing thing, to get a little more imaginative. But the piece is nice; let's give them four stars.

Andrew Hill. *Spectrum* (from *Point of Departure*, Blue Note). Hill, piano, composer; Eric Dolphy, bass clarinet; Anthony Williams, drums.

Don Ellis (1967): One thing that Eric Dolphy always had was a sense of the dramatic. In a blindfold test we did a few years back I commented that I liked what Eric did . . . He tends to repeat licks that you have heard him do a hundred times before. In this particular track he seemed to be very creative, seemed to stay away from those.

One very valuable lesson that the avant-gardist can learn from Eric is that the sense of urgency—the sense of drama that he has in his playing, the violent contrast that he would sometimes use—this immediately gives it more direction.

I would like to comment on the drummer, who could have been Tony Williams. This particular style of drumming, breaking up the time into different fragments, can be very effective, but it also can be very deadly, particularly behind the piano solo . . . I felt that the time lost its intensity.

For me the most interesting section was the 5/4 section that they got into. But just to repeat an abbreviated form of the beginning at the end was sort of a copout, compositionally. The piece . . . should have built someplace . . . There were some good moments, especially Eric's playing. I give it 3½ stars.

Oliver Nelson. *Cascades* (from *Blues and the Abstract Truth*, Impulse). Nelson, composer; Freddie Hubbard, trumpet; Bill Evans, piano; Paul Chambers, bass; Roy Haynes, drums.

Stan Kenton (1966): The reason I asked to hear the first portion of that record again was that at first I thought there were some cross-rhythms going on that would be very interesting . . . when I listened again I didn't think it was anything strange I heard—there were just time hassles going on. They were awfully disturbing. . . . But it did have an interesting sound.

I liked the trumpet player very much. I wasn't too impressed with the piano. He's tasty, but suffers from the same fault of a lot of modern pianists—they get into one idiom and they keep it going, and there are so many possibilities.

Especially during the piano solo, the bass and the drummer were very listless, there was not much energy coming from them . . . I didn't feel that during the trumpet solo, because I believe the trumpet had more assertion.

Inasfar as the little composition idea on the end, I feel that sometimes these little modal effects can be carried too far; after it's said once or twice, then they should go ahead and spice it with something else. It gets to be a boring thing, and you finally feel that you want to stop the record and say, "What else is new?"

Three stars, I guess.

Duke Ellington. *Artistry in Rhythm* (from *Will Big Bands Ever Come Back?*, Reprise). Kenton, composer; unidentified arranger.

Stan Kenton (1966): I think I have to say that this affects me in a very personal way. It's like the master of us all said, "Stan, don't take yourself too seriously. After all, you know, you do have a sense of humor; the world will turn whether you push it or not." And I think in essence it kind of says, "Regardless of all your screaming and hollering, we still like you anyway."

I think it's beautiful. And he is the master too. I'd have to give it four stars.

I don't know whose arrangement it is . . . There were ideas that were very pleasing.

BASS

Charles Mingus. *Chazz Fingers No. 2*, (from *Mingus Revisited*, Trip Jazz). Mingus, composer, bass.

Don Ellis: I love Mingus' spirit, his writing, everything about him . . . he has the jazz spirit, and yet the avant-garde, and yet the old . . . you can hear the Duke Ellington, some Gil Fuller . . . he just brings everything together. And that's one of my favorite things, to mix a lot of elements together.

PIANO

Art Tatum. *I Would Do Anything For You* (from *Art Tatum Masterpieces*, MCA). Tatum, piano; Tiny Grimes, guitar; Slam Stewart, bass. Recorded 1944.

Earl "Fatha" Hines: That's a nice record. I wouldn't give it five. There's so many of them doing those same passages, it's hard to tell. Peterson does it . . . it's confusing me. The bass player is Slam and I think the guitar was Tiny Grimes. But who was on piano? Was that made just recently?

It's a nice record; they stick close to the melody. But there's nothing to get excited about. I'd give it three.

Chick Corea. *Earth Juice* (from *Where Have I Known You Before*, Polydor). Corea, piano; Stanley Clarke, bass; Al DiMeola, guitar; Lenny White, drums; comp. by group.

Lonnie Liston Smith (1975): That was definitely Stanley Clarke; since there was no piano solo, it must have been Stanley's date. I like that for a lot of different reasons. He's greatly John McLaughlin influenced, but that particular composition will give creative music, improvisational music, more exposure because of its overall rhythmic concept, and the electric guitar; so that will appeal more to the young kids. I've found that once they are exposed, they really enjoy the music.

BASS

Eddie Harris. *Superfluous* (from *Instant Death*, Atlantic). Harris, electric sax, composer; Rufus Reid, bass.

Al McKibbon (1972): The bass player, I think, is Richard Davis, because he's the only one I know outside of Charlie Mingus who'd have that much nerve . . .

BIG BANDS

Stan Kenton. *Artemis* (from *Adventures in Time*, Capitol). Kenton, piano.

Howard Rumsey (1966): That's a Kenton band and a two-star record. There's nobody listening to that kind of music. . . . This is dear Stan carrying on his tradition as the Wagner of American jazz and he's hung with it and he'll never be able to get away from it, and it's okay with me. In another 30 years there might be a place for that band; but as it is right now it's just hanging out here with no particular reason.

The piano sounded like an attempt to sound delicate, but it didn't come out that way. Very mediocre. Jeepers creepers.

Don Ellis. *Ferris Wheel* (from *The New Don Ellis Band Goes Underground*, Columbia). Ellis, trumpet, composer, arranger.

Doc Severinsen (1970): It's got to be Don Ellis. Now that's a perfect example of the utilization of a big band in today's bag. They've forgotten all about Glenn Miller and Les Brown and all that, and they've just gone to what it should be.

. . . . Great arrangement, beautifully recorded, great playing. . . . Five stars!

Don Ellis. *Open Beauty* (from *Electric Bath*, Columbia). Ellis, composer, trumpet.

Bill Evans (1968): It's possibly the Don Ellis orchestra, but it doesn't matter. I would give it about four stars for imaginative sound adventure in music, and perhaps 1½ stars for the actual musical content.

To me, of course, the musical content is always primary, and although this is something that can attract one's attention immediately, in 20 years' time it's not going to mean a thing as far as novelty is concerned.

Don Ellis. *Freedom Dance* (from *Live in 3⅔ 4 Time*, Pacific Jazz).

Dave Holland (1968): I think his preoccupation with time signatures is a bit of a gimmick. There's a record I heard where he does these very slick announcements about it . . . "Now, ladies and gentlemen, we'd like to do a little old thing in 12¾ . . ." and it seems he's so knocked out with that that maybe he's losing sight of what music really is. . . . I'd give it three.

Duke Ellington. *Blood Count* (from *And His Mother Called Him Bill*, RCA). Johnny Hodges, alto saxophone; Billy Strayhorn, composer.

Duke Pearson (1968): It had to be Duke Ellington. This is the most beautiful band in the world. . . . I can remember as a teenager going to school proms and hearing this kind of music, not wanting to hear any other kind of music. . . . With music like this you can relive memories, pleasant things happening to you. That was Johnny Hodges on alto; couldn't be anyone else.

I think that's a Billy Strayhorn tune. It had to be, because of its melodic structure, even though Duke could have written it himself. . . . I loved it—I can give this one 20, 50 stars.

Oliver Nelson. *Flute Salad* (from *Sound Pieces*, Impulse). Nelson, composer, arranger.

Thad Jones (1968): That was a Billy Byers arrangement, and what impressed me most was the use of flutes and French horn backgrounds. It was a very lush and beautiful sound and always moves. He manages to keep the harmonic structure very interesting. As a matter of fact, Billy is one of my favorite arrangers anyway. I'd rate that at least 4½.

Mel Lewis: I don't think it's Byers, but I think it was definitely made out here on the West Coast, because of all the flutes—using all the flutes like that, bass flute, alto flute, and I have a feeling it's either Johnny Williams or Mancini. . . . It was a good chart, simple, good melody.

Thad Jones: That's what makes it so complex; it's such a simple thing, but so well constructed.

Mel Lewis: Thad knows more about the voicing and construction; he can hear something more than I would that way. I would rate it a little differently, too. I'd rate it about three.

Lionel Hampton. *Thai Silk* (from *Newport Uproar*, RCA Victor). Hampton, vibes, composer; Jerome Richardson, lead alto sax.

Thad Jones (1968): I loved the reed section, it had a good quality. I don't know if that was a regular band of Hampton's or not. It was probably a band that got together for that particular occasion—Newport possibly? And for a live performance like that, I thought it was recorded exceptionally well.

I really liked it, and I'll go along with another five stars. For the quality of the recording, and for the musicianship.

Mel Lewis (1968): We have a few ex-Hamptonites in our band, and I know they really didn't have much time to get themselves together for this. It sounded like they didn't really know the chart that well, but they played the hell out of it, because they're pros, and it had that kind of feeling. Not like a band that's been together for a long time, but like a band that could do about as good as you would want at very, very short notice. So, I'd go along with the high rating, just because of the circumstances.

Count Basie. *Switch in Time* (from *Basie Straight Ahead*, Dot). Al Aarons, trumpet; Eric Dixon, tenor saxophone; Harold Jones, drums; Sam Nestico, composer, arranger.

Stix Hooper (1970): At first I thought it was Ted Heath, and then it sounded like Louis Bellson . . . could be one of those bands made up of studio musicians. Trumpet player sounded a little like Charlie Shavers, tenor player a bit like Budd Johnson. I kind of liked his sound. The drummer could have been Bellson. . . . I'd give it three stars for the arrangement.

Woody Herman. *Keep on Keepin' On* (from *Light My Fire*, Cadet). Richard Evans, composer, arranger; Sal Nistico, tenor saxophone.

Gene Ammons (1970): I'm pretty sure that was my man Woody Herman. Being an alumnus of Woody's band, I'm pretty partial to the band as a whole. I came up in the middle of the big band era; consequently big bands are really my first love. I've always liked the sound of all the brass and the feeling that five reeds can get in a band of the type that Woody has—and always has had down through the years.

The tune sounds pretty original, and it was really swinging as only Woody can do. The tenor player sounded like Sal Nistico, who's a very dear friend of mine.

So there's nothing bad I can say about Woody and the band and Sal and everybody—so I'll have to give it five stars.

Count Basie. *Love Me Or Leave Me* (from *Super Chief*, Columbia). Buck Clayton, Shad Collins, trumpets; Lester Young, tenor sax; Jo Jones, drums; recorded 1939.

Harold Jones (1972): This to me is where we came from. I probably wasn't born when this was played. But because of something like that, when you start rating them, I just call that top echelon in giving it stars, because nothing came before that.

CLARINET

Jimmie Noone. *I Know That You Know* (from *Jimmie Noone & Earl Hines at the Apex Club*, Decca). Noone, clarinet; Hines, piano; Joe Poston, alto saxophone.

Barney Bigard (1969): I couldn't miss knowing who that was, because he was one of my favorites—the great, great Jimmie Noone.

Noone was a great influence for me—I stole a lot from him! I used to go and listen to him at the Apex Club in Chicago every night, and I'd get a lot of ideas from him. He was a great friend of mine, too. He helped me quite a bit.

I'd give it four stars.

Oliver Nelson. *Ja-Da* (from *The Spirit of '67*, Impulse). Pee Wee Russell, clarinet; Nelson, arranger.

Roland Kirk (1968): I think that was Oliver Nelson and Pee Wee Russell, and I'd like to commend Pee Wee Russell for keeping an open mind about music. He seems to keep up with a lot of the new music and techniques and still be playing his style.

I've known about Pee Wee for quite some years, and I've tried to talk to him the same as I have with some of the others. But some of these people are reluctant to talk with you, being younger than them. Like I called Barney Bigard the last time I was out here, and talked with him. I don't think he was too familiar with who I was, but I just wanted him to know that I enjoyed his clarinet playing.

I don't really want to mess around with stars, but if you want a rating, I'd give it four for good listening.

COMBOS

Supersax. *If I Should Lose You* (from *Supersax Plays Bird With Strings*, Capitol.)

Terry Gibbs (1975): Five stars for the effort those guys put into really getting the feel of Charlie Parker—Med Flory and Buddy Clark. By the way, Supersax actually started in my band, with Joe Maini. I feel very close to this whole thing.

Every one of them deserves five stars . . . it's not easy to play, you have to know Charlie Parker. I've seen some of the bars written on paper . . . I saw one bar on *Don't Blame Me* that took up a whole page, that I wouldn't want to read at all if I knew how to read it!

Chico Hamilton. *Jim-Jeannie* (from *The Dealer*, Impulse). Hamilton, drums, composer; Larry Coryell, guitar.

Gabor Szabo (1969): I'm pretty sure that's Chico Hamilton and his organization. . . . The first impression I got was that the unison line at the beginning was somewhat out of tune—it was unmusical and disturbing. I don't always care if somebody isn't right on pitch, because that's secondary, usually, for me. But here it bothered me.

I imagine that was a Chico Hamilton composition, because I recognize that theme, having been with Chico for about 3½ years. Toward the end it became worse and more disturbing, this chaos and frenzy.

I would rate it two stars, and that's only because I know two of the musicians, and Joe Beck I regard as a very good young guitar player. It was all very disturbing to me, with a lack of taste.

Miroslav Vitous. *Infinite Search* (from *Infinite Search*, Embryo). Vitous, bass, composer; Herbie Hancock, piano; Jack DeJohnette, drums.

Terry Gibbs (1970): They're three good players . . . I'll give it three stars, but maybe it should deserve more. . . . The electric piano guy was playing all right notes, made sense to me.

A lot of the new players seem to start with John Coltrane, and to me a good player should be able to do anything; Coltrane would have been able to sit in with the Dukes of Dixieland and swing the hell out of it. I don't think a lot of the newer guys would be able to play a basic 12-bar blues without getting off into some wild tangent, whereas some of the older players from the John Coltrane era can play out, but also play in.

Modern Jazz Quartet. *The Golden Striker* (from *No Sun In Venice*, Atlantic).

Don Ellis (1972): When I was in college I remember going down to Storyville in Boston and hearing them do a ballad, and I'd never heard an instrumental group do a ballad so they got the whole audience so connected . . . you could hear everybody go "Ooh!", it was so incredibly beautiful.

Weather Report. *Tears* (from *Weather Report*, Columbia).

Phil Woods (1971): I like that kind of direction, the thing that Miles introduced, with the longer lines; and I like the feeling of the record. The looseness with the way jazz composers are treating songs now, there's a certain elasticity within the form that I find very intriguing, although it can be overdone.

DRUMS

Buddy Rich. *Love and Peace* (from *Buddy & Soul*, World Pacific). Joe Sample, arr.

Stix Hooper (1970): I'll have to give that four stars for the arrangement! . . . . Of course that was Buddy on drums with his style that's very well known. It was a Joe Sample arrangement; my friend from the rhythm section of the Jazz Crusaders.

I respect Buddy Rich for what he's done as a technician, but I don't think that he's done anything creative. . . . He is, of course, a phenomenal drummer. He has one of those fantastic techniques that you just don't get in a music school; you have to have it from birth, it's inbred. But if he's not playing under fiery circumstances, he's not able to project, as far as I'm concerned. . . . With him everything is very mechanical and he plays in one bag.

Leonard Feather: Who would you say is the most creative big band drummer?

Hooper: It's hard to say who is the *most* creative. I haven't heard many; Harold Jones plays very tastefully, so did Sonny Payne. . . . Also Mel Lewis—these guys play within the context of each tune, arrangement and composition.

VIOLIN

Mahavishnu Orchestra. *Awakening* (from *The Inner Mounting Flame*, Columbia). Jerry Goodman, violin.

Jean-Luc Ponty (1973): Of course, Mahavishnu . . . and what can I say? A big record and a great crew . . . I didn't like Jerry Goodman when I heard him with The Flock. I mean I was admiring his talents on the violin because he is really talented to play with his instrument, but I didn't feel he was really together with the group. But since he play with Mahavishnu, I really love his playing . . . he is playing in a very different way, looking for another kind of sound. . . .

DRUMS

Mahavishnu John McLaughlin. *The Awakening* (from *The Inner Mounting Flame*, Columbia); Billy Cobham, drums.

Bobby Colomby (1972): That's Cobham, I think, on drums, and he's incredible. I think if he's ever recorded right he's going to frighten every other drummer out of playing. . . .

Buddy Rich-Max Roach. *Figure Eights* (from *Rich vs. Roach*, Mercury). Rich, drums (left channel); Roach, drums (right channel).

Elvin Jones (1966): Drums aplenty! That's an interesting way to make a drum record just two cats playing eight bars apiece.

It sounded like Louie Bellson to me on the left channel —and Buddy Rich, maybe, on the right. Or maybe not. Maybe it was Louie over there, too, 'cause they sound so much alike.

The bass drum work was sort of reminiscent of some of the things that Max has introduced. . . . I think if they had taken a chorus apiece at some point, it would have progressed a little bit more, so that the bass drum pattern would have developed . . . it knocked me out, though . . . five stars.

Louie Bellson. *The Diplomat Speaks* (from *Live at the Summit*, Roulette). Bellson, composer, drums.

Elvin Jones (1966): Now this time it's *got* to be Louie Bellson! Louie with Duke Ellington's orchestra. Years ago, when Louie was with Duke the first time . . . I was introduced to him . . . Louie gave me a pair of sticks—I still have them.

Five stars or ten!—you can't beat that. It sounds like Louie's tune. . . . That was some solo he developed—the graduation was so nice.

Count Basie. *Good Time Blues* (from *Basie in Sweden*, Roulette). Basie, piano; Louie Bellson, drums.

Buddy Rich (1967): What can you say about him that hasn't been said by everybody in the world? I'm sure that was Mr. Basie. And as far as I'm concerned, Mr. Basie can do no wrong in anything he ever does or anything he ever will do. He's got all the taste in the world; the band sounds beautiful. And I think that was Louie Bellson on drums. The sound was much cleaner and more articulate than Sonny Payne.

Just for being Basie, I give it five stars.

Thad Jones-Mel Lewis. *Mean What You Say* (from *The Jazz Orchestra*, Solid State). Jones, fluegelhorn, composer; Lewis, drums; Richard Davis, bass.

Buddy Rich (1967): I'll take a guess. I'd say that's the new Thad Jones-Mel Lewis band. Mel has a very distinctive style. He's one of the three or four best big-band drummers. He knows how to accompany a big band, and he has the ability to swing a big band.

I guess that was Thad playing trumpet or fluegelhorn. . . . I would demand more from the composition. . . . I think the band could have done more with something a little less contrived.

The rhythm section—I don't know if that was Richard Davis on the bass or not, but whoever it was sure gets a beautiful sound. . . . In general it's very well-done . . . three stars.

COMPOSERS

Modern Jazz Quartet. *Odds Against Tomorrow* (from *Odds Against Tomorrow*, United Artists).

Henry Mancini (1967): That was early Modern Jazz Quartet . . . I think a thing John Lewis wrote. . . . It's a beautiful mood piece.

I like John's film music. He did a wonderful score for *Odds Against Tomorrow*, but he hasn't done anything recently . . . one of the reasons might be the group is New York based.

If you want to write concert music . . . you go to New York. But I wish he'd write more for films; he has such a wonderful dramatic feeling that is rare in a jazz writer. Four stars.

DRUMS

Chico Hamilton. *The Dealer* (from *The Dealer*, Impulse). Hamilton, drums, composer; Arnie Lawrence, alto saxophone; Richard Davis, bass.

Shelly Manne (1967): That was a jazz, rock, rhythm and blues, bossa nova record, if you could combine them all. The record is more of a mood record to me than anything else. I think they could have made more use of dynamics.

The alto player sounds like a good saxophone player; a replaced bop saxophone player in today's mood. The bass player is doing something that bothers me a little bit nowadays in a lot of bass players—they play effects rather than musical content in their solos.

To give a comment as a jazz record, I don't like the record; as a commercial record, I don't think I'm qualified to say, but I would just give it two stars.

ELLINGTON

Duke Ellington. *Aristocracy A La Jean Lafitte* (from *New Orleans Suite*, Atlantic).

Michel Legrand (1972): I saw Duke so many times in concert, and heard almost everything he did. There are some marvelous, some bad, some mediocre. But what I like, it's like Charlie Chaplin; not one thing, it's the whole career, the whole person, everything he represents and everything he is.

Duke Ellington. *Ebony Rhapsody* (from *Daybreak Express*, RCA Victor). Ellington, arranger, piano; Franz Liszt, composer; recorded 1934.

Benny Carter (1971): An excellent record; it certainly has stood the test of time, which I think is really the criterion for excellence. It sounds as good today as it did when it was first recorded. Actually it sounds better now, because you've got more to compare it with . . . when you compare it with some of the trash that we've been hearing—like the old saying, "Jazz, what sins are committed in thy name?"—and this is really real music.

Duke Ellington. *Agra* (from *Far East Suite*, RCA). Ellington, Billy Strayhorn, composers, arrangers.

Clare Fischer (1967): That's wild! I'll start off with five stars and work backwards from there. Now there, to me, is the most perfect band in existence, whether you're thinking of it orchestrationally or in terms of Duke's immensely creative writing. I can't think of anybody I admire more than this man; nobody could even be compared with him, except Billy Strayhorn.

Duke does something with this same old tired instrumentation of trumpets, trombones, and saxophones, and he has a perfect way of utilizing the men's specific sounds. Anything he plays is a work of art. The band is out of tune, for instance, and it doesn't even matter. They almost have their own brand of intonation.

Now that is the kind of record I like. Why didn't you play more things like that?

Duke Ellington and Earl Hines. *House of Lords* (from *The Jazz Piano*, RCA). Hines, Ellington, pianos; bass and drums unidentified.

Toshiko Akiyoshi (1966): It's two pianos, I guess. Certain places came out very dry but kind of interesting. But I enjoyed it more because they seemed to have fun in doing it. But musically, I strongly question something like this. I didn't hear anything happen rhythmically or melodically or dynamic-wise.

One star, I guess . . . but such a big difference between two stars and one—I hate to give it only one.

FLUTE

Hubert Laws. *Miss Thing* (from *The Laws of Jazz*). Laws, flute; Bobby Thomas, composer.

Prince Lasha (1968): Yes, that's Herbie Mann's ensemble. I can't recognize right off the rhythm section, but I do know that he was out front, and I think the arrangement is by Herbie Mann also.

I'd only give that two stars, because I didn't get too much from it. Just about one line, so to speak, of the rhythm, and a few bars of the flute emphasized, and then back to the original theme.

Sonny Simmons: Yes, I think it was Herbie Mann. I'm also not acquainted with the personnel, but it was a regular run-of-the-mill, 16-bar, 8-bar blues. It grooves you a little. . . . Not really my kind of music . . . 1 ½ stars.

Herbie Mann. *Nirvana* (from *Nirvana*, Atlantic). Mann, flute; Bill Evans, piano.

Charles Lloyd (1966): It's my feeling that music should take people on a trip, and that approach—getting back to the modal kind of playing, the whole concept of using the ecclesiastical modes and using scales as a point of departure—really requires a kind of delving into.

The flute player, he's a better flute player than I am, in terms of handling the instrument—sounded like maybe Paul Horn—but I think the commitment should be to the music. If you're going to play something modal, try to find some way of opening it up. I want to be touched when I hear music! Two-and-a-half stars.

Herbie Mann. *Claudia Pie* (from *Muscle Shoals Nitty Gritty*, Embryo). Mann, flute, composer.

Yusef Lateef (1970): It sounded restful. As for the flute player, I can only guess; I think it was David Fathead Newman. No further comment.

Yusef Lateef. *Bamboo Flute Blues* (from *Psychicemotus*, Impulse). Lateef, composer, bamboo flute.

Mike Nock (1970): Yusef uses space much more than most people do. Like the way the drums kept on with that high hat crash—that was really nice. I worked steady with him for about a year, although I was associated with him for two years, maybe longer. That was a really beautiful experience for me, because Yusef has a basic kind of attitude that I have . . . he likes to play a variety of music, which is the kind of thing I dig to do, too. So we really had a ball together . . . and, of course, his flute playing—bamboo flute, yeah! I'd give that four stars.

Paul Horn. *Alap in Raga Bhairay* (from *Paul Horn In Kashmir*, World Pacific).

Rahsaan Roland Kirk (1968): That was Paul Horn, a beautiful flute player, reed player; I have nothing against what he's doing musically, because in his playing he has a lot of ability. The only thing I would say—not just to him, but to all who are doing this—there's so much music going on here in America that can be extended.

Indians tell me that in order to play these ragas, they require so much study for so many years. I've talked to several people like Ravi Shankar and they tell me they stay with the masters for 10 to 15 years. But now it's got so everybody goes to this guy Mahashoka, or whatever his name is, and pays him, and then he tells everybody that they're tuned into the Indian thing within three or four months. I can't understand it.

It just seemed to me like Paul was playing what he'd play on a regular record but with the Indian context with the sitar and everything. . . . There's things over here that we could really elevate and commercialize to extend our music—not just black music, not just white music, but our music—and put it on such a level that people can't come and tear it up like the way they've separated us. The Indian music—the Beatles' music—and all this, it's beautiful; I'm just saying that American music should be elevated . . . I'm just saying not to let these fads upset us.

Sam Rivers. *Detour Ahead* (from *A New Conception*, Blue Note). Rivers, flute, soprano and tenor saxophones.

James Moody (1968): The only time I ever understood anything on that record was when the tenor player finally came in. At the beginning the idea would come to me and then fade . . . I guess I'm old fashioned and I'm still learning about music. I'm not too hip to all these new things going on, but I'm trying to learn.

Whoever the guy is playing flute, he put in some time to learn the instrument, but it didn't really do anything for me. Just one star.

Charles Lloyd. *Third Floor Richard* (from *Of Course, Of Course*, Columbia). Lloyd, flute, composer; Ron Carter, bass; Tony Williams, drums.

Herbie Mann (1968): That sounded like the Japanese flute player I worked with in Japan recently, Sadao Watanabe. I'm not sure, but he has the same upper register sound, a little out of tune.

It's a nice old kind of blues, straight time, but the drummer and the bass player weren't together. . . . It was a nice record, but if it was Sadao, he's playing much better now. I've got to give it 2 ½ stars.

Herbie Mann. *Uskudar* (from *Impressions of the Middle East*, Atlantic). Mann, flute.

Stanley Turrentine (1967): That was Herbie Mann. He didn't kill me. I don't know what he was trying to do. He didn't play anything on it, to me. It didn't do anything. You better ask him what he was trying to do!

Leonard Feather: Does this have any relationship to jazz, do you think?

Turrentine: There's that word again—jazz! It has such

a wide scope. To my conception of jazz, it didn't feel like it, to me. I didn't feel anything with that. I think that with jazz you should be able to feel a certain amount of emotion, but there's nothing happening to me. I can't give it anything.

GUITAR

George Barnes-Bucky Pizzarelli. *Honeysuckle Rose* (from *Guitars Pure and Honest*, A & R Records).

Gabor Szabo (1975): The spirit was marvelous, especially one player—I don't know which, and wouldn't even make a guess. He had a chord passage there playing with some very fast and moving things . . . it could have been Joe Pass . . . five stars. Both players really played very excitingly and with control of their instrument and the situation.

Herb Ellis-Joe Pass. *Seven Come Eleven* (from *Seven Come Eleven*, Concord Jazz).

Lee Ritenour (1975): That was another five star record . . . just virtuoso guitar playing with Herb Ellis and Joe Pass. When I see Herb and Joe performing at a club, it's totally different than hearing them on record. They've played together for quite a while and Herb began to sound a little more like Joe, and Joe began to loosen up and sound more like Herb, in that Texas-blues kind of thing. On record it's very hard to differentiate between the two players.

Chuck Wayne-Joe Puma. *Lester Leaps In* (from *Interactions*, Choice).

Larry Coryell (1974): That's definitely a five star record. I think every young guitarist should take note of what they were doing. When one was soloing, the other would go into fantastically perfect accompaniment. The balance between the two players was just incredible. I heard some electronic effects in there, some wah-wah or something . . . it was definitely two older guitarists who have a commanding knowledge of bop.

John McLaughlin. *Marbles* (from *Devotion*, Douglas). McLaughlin, guitar, composer.

Gabor Szabo (1971). All I can say is they mixed up space and rock and some monotonous exciting *Peter Gunn*-type background, and how can you miss? But no stars.

Bill Harris. *Well, You Needn't* (from *Caught In The Act*, Jazz Guitar). Harris, unaccompanied guitar.

Kenny Burrell (1967): It's either Bill Harris or Charlie Byrd. Probably Bill Harris. . . .

Certain things about it annoyed me . . . either it wasn't recorded close enough, or it seemed like the guitarist was overplaying the instrument to get the tone out of it. . . . With that particular style, the finger style, sometimes you have a problem in rhythm.

For effort, being that I know what he was doing, I'll give it three stars.

Joe Pass. *Sometime Ago* (from *Simplicity*, World Pacific). Pass, guitar.

Wes Montgomery (1967): I don't know who that was . . . but it was beautiful. In fact, I couldn't concentrate on who it might be, because of listening to it! It's *beautiful.* I like all of it—I like the lines, I like the phrases, the guitar player has beautiful tone, he phrases good, and everybody's sort of, like together.

It's really together. I'd give that four stars right away.

George Benson. *Benny's Back* (from *The George Benson Cookbook*, Columbia). Benson, guitar, composer; Bennie Green, trombone; no bass listed.

Wes Montgomery (1967): It has a fresh sound . . . seems like it lost a little bit of fire at the end. But naturally, the guitar solo was out of sight! It sounded like Georgie Benson. I think it rates three stars anyway.

Sounded like Al Grey on trombone, but I'm not sure. The group sounded like it was baritone, organ, trombone, guitar, electric bass, and drums. You know, I think the electric bass is getting more popular; it's moving out of rock-and-roll into jazz.

PIANO

Ahmad Jamal. *New Rhumba* (from *Inspiration*, Cadet Records). Jamal, piano, composer.

Walter Bishop, Jr. (1974): Ahmad is a virtuoso pianist, yet he uses space. It's very hard to do if you have that kind of technique; very hard to use space, because the inclination is to want to fill it up and show what you can do. He's always had impeccable taste, and for a man with that kind of technical ability, he made a whole thing out of understatement. In fact, he hipped Miles to space. . . .

Oscar Peterson. *Travelin' On* (MPS). Peterson, piano.

Hampton Hawes (1969): Well, that has to be Oscar Peterson. I know jazz has gone through all kinds of changes, but I don't see how you could possibly say anything like this is out of date. He is one artist who really has great command of the piano, and I can think of hardly anyone else living who has this much technique and talent. . . . That was a wonderful, exciting performance, brilliantly played. . . . Five stars.

Miles Davis. *Mlle. Mabry* (from *Filles De Kilimanjaro*, Columbia). Davis, trumpet, composer; Chick Corea, piano.

Hampton Hawes (1969): It sounded like Miles at first, but I really am not sure. . . . There's three good piano players that experiment with electric piano; Herbie Hancock, Chick Corea and Joe Zawinul, and to my knowledge, since this instrument has just been brought into the jazz scene, it's very difficult to distinguish between them, because the sound is the same, whereas on a regular piano, you can usually detect a guy's touch. The electric piano blurs some of the lines. I feel, however, that as time goes on it will be much easier to distinguish each player as they begin getting different sounds out of the instrument.

I'd have liked it if they had changed from that definite beat that was going through the whole tune . . . a little more flavored; that's why I give it four stars instead of five.

Oscar Peterson. *Who Can I Turn To* (from *My Favorite Instrument*, MPS). Peterson, solo piano.

Bill Evans (1970): That's beautiful! . . . I suspect this is Oscar Peterson . . . Oscar does surprise me at times. It's almost as if Tatum had come back to life. Even some of the harmonic angle that Art would throw into a tune just by some little change in between, as an afterthought; Oscar gets that going too. And it's gorgeous, it's perfect in its own way, so I have to say five stars.

Herbie Hancock. *Jessica* (from *Fat Albert Rotunda*, Warner Bros.). Hancock, composer, arranger, piano; Johnny Coles, fluegelhorn; Garnett Brown, trombone; Buster Williams, bass; Tootie Heath, drums; Joe Henderson, flute.

Joe Zawinul (1970): A million stars! . . . Herbie. That's a beautiful record. Herbie Hancock is a really complete musician; his playing and writing are equally balanced. In this band he has now, Johnny Coles is really fitting into it beautifully . . . melodic and lyrical playing. And I think I heard Garnett play the melody—great!

Roy McCurdy: Well, I agree with Joe, very beautiful and sensitive. I liked the things that Buster Williams was playing on bass, long notes, beautiful things. And Tootie played very well, very sensitively, and Joe Henderson on flute . . . fantastic. . . . All the stars you can give.

McCoy Tyner. *Inception* (from *Inception*, Impulse). Tyner, piano, composer; Art Davis, bass; Elvin Jones, drums.

Chick Corea (1970): That makes me feel best of all, and the reason for that is that there's such a strong belief in that kind of music. The strength of that kind of belief is what's carrying the world along at this moment. The stronger we can believe in our own universes (how we each see things as individuals), the clearer the other two universes become (the physical universe and other people's universes). And when that universe is very strong, no matter what it is—now that happens to be one particular viewpoint, but the fact that the belief is so strong and the purpose so clear and so high, that it just takes all the other things and makes them fit together and provides a point out there that everyone can safely relate to.

That strength is the thing that keeps us all going, and it's saying we all have that strength, and all we have to do is make it more real. The more we have to rely on other people's viewpoints, the shakier and more vague our own become. Therefore our degree of self-determinism is lowered, but through seeing the beauty of the strength of a viewpoint, it makes us believe more in our own viewpoints.

McCoy and Elvin; that was one of McCoy's earlier efforts.

Cannonball Adderley. *The Scavenger* (from *In Person*, Capitol). Adderley, soprano saxophone; Joe Zawinul, piano, composer.

Herbie Hancock (1969): That's Joe's composition. Joe is the only one I can think of—besides Miles, who shapes all the tunes that come into his band and sometimes they wind up similar in shape, or within the same general open conception as Joe's.

Joe was the first person I met when I came to New York. His whole being has gone through such a metamorphosis since then. He had certain kinds of insecurities at that time, which since *Mercy, Mercy* have completely disappeared. He's a European piano player, his roots are not in the music which comes out of America—and he's white, too. Maybe this was the source of the insecurities he had, and then he writes one of the greatest soul pieces of today's music; that completely washed all those other things away.

That is something everybody should hear and buy. Five stars.

Cecil Taylor. *Tales (8 Whisps)* (from *Unit Structures*, Blue Note). Taylor, piano, composer.

Les McCann (1969): Take it off—that's enough! . . . I would like to say about Cecil Taylor, if he's serious about his music, that's all right. It's different, it's just not my groove, but what gets me is that there are so many other guys copying, and call it some name like avant garde which has nothing to do with feeling, as far as I'm concerned. In my opinion that's what jazz is all about; swing and feeling! I've got to sit down and figure out what the hell he's doing, and that's a big waste of time when I can be listening to, say, Wynton Kelly burn. So I would say minus 30.

VIOLIN

Eddie Lang-Joe Venuti. *Stringin' the Blues* (from *Stringin' the Blues*, Columbia). Lang, guitar; Venuti, violin. Recorded 1927.

Jean-Luc Ponty (1969): I think this was Eddie South. This is more difficult for me to find because I think at that period the sound of the violin was not really similar. Maybe because at that time they didn't play with an amplifier. It also was maybe Django on guitar.

I like very much the chord changes on the guitar, and the sound. I'm not especially excited by the violin here. Maybe because I'm too young to really appreciate. Three stars for both of them.

PIANO

Herbie Hancock. *Fat Mama* (from *Fat Albert Rotunda*, Warner Bros.). Hancock, piano, composer.

Al Kooper (1971): None of that moves me emotionally —which is what I like about music. That would be nice to sweep the house to, or something like that.

Herbie Hancock. *The Eye of the Hurricane* (from *Maiden Voyage*, Blue Note). Hancock, piano, composer; Freddie Hubbard, trumpet; George Coleman, tenor saxophone; Ron Carter, bass; Tony Williams, drums.

Randy Weston (1966): I want to take a wild guess on the composer—I would say Freddie Hubbard.

I would say Freddie on trumpet, George Coleman on saxophone, probably Tony Williams on drums, Herbie Hancock, and most likely Ron Carter. They are all excellent musicians. I think they played very well on this composition. . . . I'd give it four stars.

Willie (The Lion) Smith & Don Ewell. *A Porter's Love Song* (from *Grand Piano*, Exclusive). Smith and Ewell, pianos.

George Shearing (1967): I have a theory about two-piano jazz. It's far too muddy to come off, and I don't think this is any exception. It's very kinda thick and very logey. Because of this fact, I don't know who the pianists are.

. . . I like a lot of the Fats Waller idiosyncrasies in it, but I don't really think it comes off, because there's an awful lot of close chord positions used way down low in the bass, which kinda muddy it up, and I don't think it's light and airy enough to really swing. . . . One or two stars. I don't know who it is.

Bill Evans. *Spring is Here* (from *Bill Evans at Town Hall*, Verve). Evans, piano.

George Shearing (1967). One of my favorite piano players, Bill Evans. He shows the greatest respect for a ballad; he shows the greatest desire for musical organization; shows the greatest respect for the piano as an instrument; wants only to make it sound like a piano; beautiful sustained quality, beautiful sound; well organized and beautiful sense of harmony.

As many stars as you can give it. . . .

Martial Solal. *Jordu* (from *Solal*, Milestone). Solal, piano; Guy Pederson, bass; Daniel Humair, drums.

Oscar Peterson (1967): I find this very disjointed—primarily because the cohesion I have come to expect from different trios is not evident here. If I were to look at it from the aspect of a solo piano performance, I would have to classify it as the type of piano which is something for everyone.

I particularly didn't like the background for the bass solo . . . I would give it two stars. I think it's Martial Solal.

Earl Hines. *Save It, Pretty Mama* (from *Here Comes Earl "Fatha" Hines*, Contact). Hines, piano.

Oscar Peterson (1967): That sounds like a group in the cocktail bar at an airport. It started off as if it was going to develop into some sort of musical growth, but somewhere it sort of dissipated. I can't give it any stars. I don't even know who it is, either.

Thelonious Monk. *Well, You Needn't* (from *Genius of Modern Music*, Blue Note). Monk, piano, composer. Recorded 1951.

Pete Robinson (1971): . . . he doesn't play a piano like a piano, it's rather an extension of himself. His influence on me isn't in terms of the style that I'm playing, just that I listen to him a lot and I dig him. Monk is beautiful.

Ramsey Lewis. *Function at the Junction* (from *Goin' Latin*, Cadet). Lewis, piano.

Oscar Peterson (1967): The pitiful part of all this is that playing in this particular vein, it's very hard to distinguish between one of, say, six pianists. I think you tend to lose a lot of your own identity. I couldn't tell who this is; because it could be someone who honestly plays this way, in which case I'm sorry for him; or it is someone who can really play, but has decided to prostitute himself for that particular bag at the moment, and if that be the case, they're doing it well enough—or bad enough—so that I still couldn't tell.

I'll give it a half a star for the fact that all the technicians came in and all the musicians showed up.

Mary Lou Williams. *45° Angle* (from *The Jazz Piano*, RCA). Williams, piano; drums and bass unidentified.

Toshiko Akiyoshi (1966): It's so hard to tell who the piano player is, because I can't hear the particular touch . . . the balance is pretty bad.

He has a good percussive left hand; his playing is traditional, in a way, but modern. . . . It's good, it's an enjoyable performance, but the drummer is a little too overpowering. Very unimaginative. Very heavy on the sock cymbal. . . . Two stars.

McCoy Tyner. *Desert Cry* (from *Sama Layuca*, Milestone).

Les McCann(1975): I found that didn't go anywhere. I don't know who it was playing. It was like they had an idea about something, and rather than play what they were really feeling, they played what they thought was the thing to do. I'd give that two stars.

ROCK

Kai Winding. *You've Lost That Lovin' Feelin'*, (from *The 'In' Instrumentalists*, Verve). Winding, trombone; Gary Chester, Jack Jennings, percussion; Garry Sherman, arr.

Shelly Manne (1966): That leaves me absolutely cold for many reasons. . . . This had no swing, and they're using two drummers, with a real heavy rock-and-roll-influenced beat. When drummers used to play with that feeling in the old days you just called them "leadfoots."

Sounds to me like some a&r man had a jazzman under contract and thought he'd try to make a hit. I don't think one good thing has come from rock and roll. Whatever good things you find in it were there long before, in rhythm and blues—the old records of Peetie Wheatstraw, the Devil's Son-in-law; Roosevelt Sykes; Bessie Smith—all that influence was there many years ago. Rock and roll has taken all those things and blown them out of proportion into a grotesque, crude way of playing . . . I give this absolutely zero.

The Beatles. *The Fool on the Hill* (from *Magical Mystery Tour*, Capitol). John Lennon, Paul McCartney, composers.

Larry Coryell (1968): I've been told that this particular tune was written about the Maharishi. I don't know whether this is true or not; it's a nice fantasy, I suppose, but the lyrics are beautiful. The intellectual and emotional content of all the lyrics the Beatles do I've always identified with, and become personally involved in all their work.

They're still the best of all the rock 'n' roll groups. It's fantastic, they're so different than all the rest. . . . They always stuck to rock, or non-jazz. I really don't believe in mixing the two. . . . Five stars.

Gary Burton: I'd like to say in addition that the Beatles are models for recording sessions these days. . . . The records they've made for the past couple of years have been so well produced that this in itself sets them apart from all the other products available.

This being their most recent record, it's obvious how skillfully it can be done. That, in itself, becomes an art.

I'd rate it five stars too.

Beatles. *When I'm Sixty-Four* (from *Sgt. Peppers Lonely Lonely Hearts Club Band*, Capitol). John Lennon, solo voice.

George Shearing (1967): That can be only one of two groups. It's either the Winchester Cathedral Variety Band from England, or the Beatles. I happen to think that some of the Beatle compositions are extremely clever. Whether this is the Winchester Cathedral Group or the Beatles, this is really not one of the clever ones, for my taste anyhow. It's what it's supposed to be—1920's . . . I just don't happen to like that.

If it's the Beatles, . . . the soloist is probably John Lennon. I like his voice immensely, he has a very nice voice; he's in tune, he has some range. . . . No comment about stars at all.

ALTO SAX

Dewey Redman. *Interconnection* (from *The Ear of the Behearer*, Impulse). Redman, alto saxophone, composer; Ted Daniel, trumpet; Jane Robertson, cello.

Woody Herman (1974): Well, that's fairly avant-garde. There's some good players, like the trumpeter and the string player. But it should have a title like *The Madness of Youth*, because when I hear extreme things played by very well equipped people, the only thing they seem to forget completely is that these tapes and records will live forever, and at some time in their life they're going to hear these things again—at another point in their development—and the embarrassment must be complete!

Anthony Braxton. *To Artist Murray De Pillars* (from *For Alto*, Delmark).

Phil Woods (1971): That was terrible. I can't imagine the ego of a person thinking they can sustain a whole performance by themselves, when they can't really play the saxophone well. . . . It should be called "the trill is gone." I'm sure he hasn't studied the saxophone. This doesn't bother me, there's a lot of primitives that play and get a lot of exciting music; but this is such an ego trip, that you can think you're that much of a bitch that you can do a solo album.

Eddie Harris. *It's Crazy* (from *Plug Me In*, Atlantic). Harris, amplified saxophone, composer.

Sonny Criss (1968): It sounds like something Eddie Harris would do. . . . I just have nothing to say about amplified saxophone, because I just don't dig it. . . . The most important thing in jazz, I think, as far as an instrumentalist is concerned, is the sound, whether you are a drummer, pianist, bassist—sound—personal sound, an identifying thing. You hear one or two notes and you know who you're listening to. I don't have to hear 12 bars of Johnny Hodges to know it's Johnny Hodges, or Benny Carter or Ben Webster. Sometimes it's not the notes they play that's so important.

I realize that this electrified thing is in vogue now, but as the music changes, I think one has to choose the best and let the rest go by. It's even difficult to rate this. According to the standards I've held over the years, I'd rate it two stars.

Eric Kloss. *The Girl With the Fall in Her Hair* (from *Sky Shadows*, Prestige). Kloss, alto saxophone; Pat Martino, composer.

Frank Strozier (1969): I enjoyed the record. It sounded like it might have been John Handy and I like him, but it was so much of the same stuff you're hearing today—just go for broke on one scale.

I have nothing against one scale; I love it, but it's just a crutch for so many musicians today. I think that the caliber of a lot of musicians who are doing well today, or have records out, is just not up to the caliber of, say, a few years ago, simply because of these modes. You can get away with so much—who's to say you're wrong?

Eric Dolphy. *Miss Ann* (from *Far Cry*, Prestige). Eric Dolphy, alto saxophone, composer.

Herbie Hancock (1969): It's Eric's tune—I used to play it with him. . . . I worked with Eric for about a month. That was my first experience playing—avant garde, quote unquote. Eric called me to work at the Village Gate to take Jaki Byard's place. I didn't know what I was supposed to play, whatever I wanted, and certain things started happening in my mind as the music started to form, and I found out some things that I wasn't even aware of before. About rule-breaking—that was the first thing I figured, that you have to break some rules in order to make the music fit.

I just like Eric . . . there's a certain kind of feeling, happy feeling that's generated through all of the angular kind of sounds that he plays. It swings in a different sort of way than most people think of swinging.

I'll have to judge this on the standards of jazz at that particular point in the history of jazz, and I'd say 3½ stars.

Mills Blue Rhythm Band. *Blue Rhythm Blues* (from *Big Bands!* Onyx). Stan Getz, alto sax; Lucky Thompson, tenor sax; recorded 1947.

Stan Getz (1973): (After few bars of alto solo, Getz exclaims "Bird?", after a few more, "No!") Is that the Blue Mills Rhythm Band? Is that me playing alto? I haven't heard this since we made it . . . Lucky Thompson? I played alto because they needed an alto player and I needed the money—it was that simple.

Play that again, please . . . the two alto players are a little out of tune and I'm the one who's causing it.

Tribute To Charlie Parker. Wee (RCA Victor). Howard McGhee, trumpet; J.J. Johnson, trombone; Sonny Stitt, tenor saxophone; Harold Mabern, piano; Arthur Harper Jr., bass; Max Roach, drums.

Cannonball Adderley (1967): I want to tell you, that's kind of interesting. Of course I recognized J.J. Johnson and I thought I recognized Sonny Stitt. The trumpet player sounded a bit like Howard McGhee, but I got the feeling it was a swing trumpet player who branched over into modern jazz, strongly influenced by Dizzy Gillespie.

It sounded like Max Roach playing drums. The other guys, I don't know.

The sound is new, but everybody played pretty much like the cats were playing 15 years ago. This is all right with me. I don't agree with the theory some people have that jazz musicians have to continue to change. I think that they should grow within their own thing.

Overall, I just say three stars. I especially like J.J.'s solo and Max's solo.

Eric Dolphy. *Miss Ann* (Limelight). Dolphy, composer, alto saxophone.

John Handy (1966): It's not my favorite alto player. . . . That was Eric Dolphy, I'm sure; he had a lot of command of technique on his instrument, and at times—well, to be frank, I liked him very much when he was with Chico Hamilton and had a chance to play, when they gave him blowing space and the more traditional chord changes.

The kind of things that he did in his later years I didn't like much. Many of them, to me, were just erratic, didn't make any sense.

It's not something I'd buy. One star.

Yusel Lateef. *Feelin' All Right* (from *A-Flat, G-Flat and C*, Impulse). Lateef, alto saxophone, composer.

Joe Zawinul (1967): I don't really know what to say about this. This is a beautiful bebop thing, which I love very much. The performance I didn't like too much. I don't think it had too much life and spirit.

It sounded to me like whoever was playing the saxophone had some kind of the Detroit influence of playing. I would define the Detroit influence—for instance, I worked a long time with Yusef, and Yusef used to be a great influence on some of the musicians in Detroit . . . I would say about two-and-a-half stars.

Esquire All-American 1946 Award Winners. *Gone With The Wind* (from *Esquire's All-American Hot Jazz*, RCA). Johnny Hodges, also saxophone; Don Byas, tenor saxophone.

Cannonball Adderley (1967): You know, it's not often that you can sit and listen to a group of soloists play the melody and not get bored; but when they happen to be Don Byas and Johnny Hodges, it's all right. I had the feeling that I'd like to hear Ben Webster play it after Johnny, yet a third time.

For the soloists five stars.

SOPRANO SAX

John Coltrane. *Chim Chim Cheree* (from *The JC Quartet Plays*, Impulse). Coltrane, soprano saxophone; Elvin Jones, drums.

Buddy Rich (1967): Yeah, well. What can I say about that? They had a slight accident there in the beginning, by letting the melody slip through. I imagine they had great difficulty in keeping the snake in the basket.

I don't want to venture a guess as to whether that's a soprano saxophone or a flute. I really can't quite comprehend what they were doing, except they managed to start the thing together and finish together, and I think I'd have to give it two stars for bravery beyond the call of duty.

The drummer might be Max, it might be Roy Haynes, it might even be Tony Williams, although I'm not too familiar with Tony's playing. . . . It certainly wasn't jazz as I know jazz, and it wasn't really anything. It might have been Charles Lloyd.

Cannonball Adderley. *Gunjah* (from *Accent on Africa*, Capital). Adderley, soprano saxophone; David Axelrod, composer; H.B. Barnum, arranger.

Tom Scott (1970): That's from the Cannonball Adderley album called *Accent on Africa.* He just represents one of the greatest jazzmen of all time. I love the idea of him doing an African album, because the instruments have such a great sound, and all that percussion and everything. But . . . H.B. Barnum is the wrong cat for this album, to me, as the arranger. He doesn't have the harmonic sense that comes anywhere near Cannonball. . . . It's almost like a Broadway show, instead of being hip and up to the kind of thing that Cannonball should have behind him. . . . To Cannonball I'd always give five stars, but to the arrangement I'd only give one.

Tom Scott. *Naima* (from *The Honeysuckle Breeze*, Impulse). Scott, soprano saxophone with electronic octave divider; John Coltrane, composer.

Roland Kirk (1968): It was a boy out here on the coast named Scott, playing saxella, an instrument copied off the manzello, and it's a hard instrument to play in tune. This sounds out of tune to me. . . . When he was going into the changes, it kept me on eggshells. It didn't make me lay back and relax and drink my beer and say, "Yeah, that guy's really sailing through them changes," because the tune is not that hard.

It's a beautiful tune, I mean it's hard to interpret it the way that Trane wrote it. . . . That octave thing kept me unrelaxed because people used to get on to me about being out of tune, and they make these electric things—I played one of them—and you still have to *think* in tune to play one of them.

TENOR SAX

John Coltrane. *Mr. P.C.* (from *Giant Steps*, Atlantic). Coltrane, tenor saxophone; Paul Chambers, bass; Tommy Flanagan, piano; Art Taylor, drums.

Gato Barbieri (1974): I remember this tune Coltrane wrote for Paul Chambers—we used to call it for the Communist Party, because in Argentina it's called Partida Communista, P.C., so we always made a joke of it.

That period was an important part of my life . . . I have to give the record five stars. John was about to leap into the era of the great quartet with McCoy and Elvin. Art Taylor played very good, but sometimes he would leave Trane a little bit alone. He'd play mostly the rhythm and wouldn't give Coltrane enough dynamics.

I remember in Buenos Aires I was looking for something different; then I heard one tune by Trane with McCoy and Elvin, on which John played tenor and soprano . . . and I heard something very different in that rhythm section.

Charles Lloyd. *European Fantasy* (from *Charles Lloyd in Europe*, Atlantic). Lloyd, tenor saxophone, composer; Keith Jarrett, piano; Cecil McBee, bass; Jack DeJohnette, drums.

Gabor Szabo (1969): That was Charles Lloyd in concert. . . . There is a lot of humor, and this is the part I enjoyed the most about it. His tone and phrasing and everything sounds like a real old, corny saxophone player, and yet his playing is a way-out type of music.

It just proves how different my musical convictions are since I left Charles. I went in a completely different direction, and I find great satisfaction and release in playing more disciplined music and find all the freedom within those sometimes even rigid disciplinary forms.

There are absolutely no musical rules to be followed and no ways to judge the form—or even the musicianship, because you cannot tell how good a musician is from something like this. . . . The only way I can judge this kind of thing is through the energy level, and I feel there's a great amount of energy being released, and if everything clicks, then some music will come out of it—this time it did.

Ornette Coleman. *Enfant* (from *Ornette on Tenor*, Atlantic). Coleman, tenor saxophone; Don Cherry, pocket trumpet; Jimmy Garrison, bass; Ed Blackwell, drums.

John Klemmer (1969): I thought that was crazy. I'm sure it was Ornette on tenor, an earlier recording, with Don Cherry on trumpet. I think whether or not people care for Ornette is a matter of taste, but he's always done something that's interesting.

I was a little skeptical of Ornette when I first heard him, but I delved into his music and played some of his tunes, and I really dig him.

What I look mostly for in players is somebody trying to do something with imagination, of course with the prerequisite of knowing what they're doing and studying for it. Five stars.

Pharoah Sanders. *Aum* (from *Tauhid*, Impulse). Sanders, tenor saxophone, composer.

Zoot Sims (1970): Take it off, I don't want to hear any more of that. . . . If that represents the sounds of our time, well, I don't like it.

You've got to be who you are . . . maybe that's who he is, but it just doesn't get to me. I like beauty, and I don't see any beauty in that, because the world is mad in the first place, so why allow art to make it seem madder? I don't think we should dwell on what's already going on.

Music should be *exciting*, and make you clap your hands. But this represents—chaos! . . . We've got enough chaos out there on the freeway; we don't need music to give us more chaos.

John Klemmer. *All The Children Cried* (from *All The Children Cried*, Cadet). Klemmer, tenor saxophone, composer.

Yusef Lateef (1970): I don't know who that was. The tenor player made me think of the player with Shelly Manne—with the long hair, you know. . . . (John Gross, L.F.).

It was interesting enough. Sounded contemporary. No, let me change that—what is the other expression? Current. It sounded current. I've heard similar music recently.

Duke Ellington. *Chelsea Bridge* (from *Concert in the Virgin Islands*, Reprise). Paul Gonsalves, tenor saxophone; Billy Strayhorn, composer.

Eddie (Lockjaw) Davis (1967): Well, that was Paul Gonsalves—to me one of the most underrated saxophone players that we have. He has all the qualities that one could desire—such as tonal quality, technique, creative ability—and it seems a tragedy that the public doesn't hear more of him especially when he's performing at his height, which is in concert. He always takes care of business—excellent saxophonist, really. So therefore give it five stars. To me, that was a collector's item.

Albert Ayler. *Bells* (from *Love Cry*, Impulse). Ayler, tenor saxophone, composer.

Jerome Richardson (1968): Well, what do you want me to say about that? It sounds like a club date tenor player trying to get into the jazz thing. I wonder what they were doing—I don't know whether they were trying to fool somebody or not. If that was their version of avant garde, they'd better do a little listening.

I haven't the slightest idea who it was. The tenor player, I could give a wild guess—I'd guess it was Don Ellis' band. I'll give it one star for effort.

Archie Shepp. *In a Sentimental Mood* (from *Live in San Francisco*, Impulse). Shepp, tenor saxophone.

Eddie (Lockjaw) Davis (1967): Please take that off—discontinue that. I have one word for that—tragedy.

It seems unbelievable that a man with such potential talent—you can hear that in this saxophonist . . . I wouldn't underrate him—he puts me in mind of a frustrated musician who has failed to gain recognition through his genuine talents, and in order to attract such, he goes, shall we say, abstract. Just like a revolt.

Now it's a process of elimination as to describe who that is. I would take a guess it's Archie Shepp.

I couldn't classify it as entertainment; it's like fighting—it's like a challenge. This is really a good record for the *Blindfold Test*. Challenge—tell me who I am! It's very sad that he's let such talent go so far astray. I couldn't even rate this.

Eddie (Lockjaw) Davis. *On a Clear Day* (from *Lock the Fox*, RCA Victor). Davis, tenor saxophone.

Booker Ervin (1967): I know exactly who it was from the first note; it was Lockjaw. No one could imitate Lockjaw. I didn't recognize the name of the tune right off.

I've been liking Jaws a long time—he's one of my favorite tenor players. I've never heard anybody imitate him—it sounds like he plays backwards!

I'd give that three stars for Jaws, because he's one of my favorites.

Ben Webster. *Accent on Youth* (from *Warm Moods*, Reprise). Webster, tenor saxophone; JohnnyRichards, arranger, conductor.

Stanley Turrentine (1967). Give it all you got! If you've got more than five, give it more than that. That Ben Webster—he's the most lyrical tenor player I've ever heard in my life. He has always been an influence on me. I love this album. . . .

As far as the overall playing and writing were concerned, I thought it was good. It complemented Ben. Ben has always been my favorite—I like the sound he gets. . . . Just about anything Ben plays knocks me out.

Albert Ayler. *Holy Ghost* (from *The New Wave in Jazz*, Impulse). Ayler, tenor saxophone; Joel Freedman, cello.

Oliver Nelson (1967). Of course, that was a very highly charged performance. I suppose this—the kind of music I just heard—would be typical of the new wave or whatever.

There was little melodic organization, but toward the end they did something very startling. They played the melody. . . . And they tried to play it in unison, and the ending was conventional.

If I have to object to anything about this music, it's mainly lacking in texture, and naturally I would feel that way, being an orchestrator and arranger. The same intensities are used.

As to form; well, everybody just plays. It was a live performance, and the audience seemed pleased. . . . I guess you would call it chaos—out of it, somebody is going to have enough talent to integrate whatever is happening with this kind of music.

Give the cellist four stars, but I'd rather not rate the record as a whole.

Stan Getz. *Keep Me In Your Heart* (from *Voices*, Verve). Getz, tenor saxophone; Claus Ogerman, arranger.

Oscar Peterson (1967): I would sooner own five albums like this than 100,000 of the others, because we're speaking of true creativity, musical honesty. Stan Getz, without becoming maudlin, is definitely a genius in my book.

When persons with that kind of talent put their hand or their heart or mind to material . . . it has even greater importance.

I would have to give this five stars for everything—for voices, which were beautifully done behind him, and certainly for Stan.

Gato Barbieri. *Tupac Amaru* (from *Fenix*, Flying Dutchman).

John Klemmer (1972): I enjoyed the overall texture of the group, but I really did, after a while, find it fairly monotonous . . . the concept of modality, I think, has to be treated with more care than the approach to changes, to harmonic movement. . . . I think to be a success it must reach an emotional climax, or even more so a rhythmic climax.

Gato Barbieri. *Milorga Triste* (from *Viva Emiliano Zapata*, Impulse).

Grover Washington, Jr. (1975): Unmistakably Gato Barbieri . . . five stars. What can I say? Most of his music reminds me of going back into when I was trying to play classical music, the romantic and impressionistic music. It just moves me. I haven't found one thing that I haven't liked by Gato.

John Coltrane. *Welcome* (from *Kulu Se Mama*, Impulse).

John Klemmer (1972): One of the things I really loved about John's music was his ballad sense. Even though they're playing out of tempo there's still a feeling of jazz.

SINGERS

Blossom Dearie. *I'm Shadowing You* (from *Blossom Dearie Sings*, Daffodil).

Joe Williams (1974): Blossom has that smart New York thing, entertainment thing . . . light and yet she can do things that have great depth too. She's a part of that very special group: Mabel Mercer, Bobby Short, Ellis Larkins. That very special sophisticated, continental, international set type of entertainer that is very, very refreshing. I love her sound.

I understand she's also a favorite of Miles, who used to insist that she come into the Vanguard when he was there.

Lonnie Liston Smith. *Naima* (from *Cosmic Funk*, Flying Dutchman). Smith, keyboards; Donald Smith, vocal; John Coltrane, composer.

Chick Corea: I don't know who that singer was. An interesting thing about him is that his voice is—I guess this has happened to me before—I listen to a singer, I don't know who it is and because it's a very beautiful rendition of a melody, the singer transcends gender . . . I can't tell whether it's a man or woman. I got that it was a man toward the end . . . but it could have been a woman with a husky voice.

Diana Ross. *Good Morning Heartache* (from *Lady Sings The Blues*, Motown).

Carmen McRae (1973): . . . As far as Diana singing this song, that is not her song. I'm sorry. *I* sing it better than she does, so consequently I'm not giving her any stars. I'll give her E. for the great effort she made.

Miriam Makeba. *U-Mngoma* (from *Makeba!*, Reprise).

Sarah Vaughan (1969): That was Miriam Makeba. The rhythm was too much! I like Miriam very much. . . . The language barrier doesn't necessarily make much difference, but I'd like to know the story on what's happening here.

When I go overseas it seems like they can understand me a little better than I can understand them if they came here . . . it seems like everybody speaks English over there, but not many people here speak Xhosa! I liked the record except, as I say, I don't know what it was about. I'd give it two stars.

Ella Fitzgerald. *Taking A Chance On Love* (from *Ella's Golden Favorites*, Decca). Fitzgerald, vocal. Recorded in 1940.

Vernon Duke (1966): To me, the first part, before she doubled the tempo, was immeasurably superior to the rest. The rest of it was well sung, too, of course, but the slow part was very touching to me. An excellent performance anyway—first rate.

It has to be a Negro singer. It's not Sarah Vaughan; it's not Ella Fitzgerald. Who is it?

Mose Allison. *Seventh Son* (from *The Best of Mose Allison*, Atlantic).

Jimmy Witherspoon (1972): . . . he can sing the blues! This is an art form that was started by blacks, but anybody's entitled to learn this if they dig it. And he can feel it, you can tell. He grew up listening to black artists.

Tony Bennett. *Fly Me to the Moon* (from *Songs for the Jet Set*, Columbia).

Joe Williams (1967): Five stars—nobody's gonna do that any better! Really, that's Tony Bennett at his warmest and best. It's a great arrangement and beautifully recorded.

When you buy a record of Tony Bennett's, you're getting Tony Bennett and Tony Bennett's ideas along with the people who love Tony and are inspired by him—and who inspire him. He tries to surround himself with this kind of person, which is why he is such a fine artist.

Ray Charles. *In the Heat of the Night* (from the original sound track, United Artists). Quincy Jones, composer; Alan and Marilyn Bergman, lyrics.

Joe Williams (1967): The president of the Soul Society . . . brother Ray Charles. Give him four stars for that one. As far as I'm concerned, he is by far the greatest exponent of blues and feeling and what we call soul.

If he's feeling good, he really makes you feel better than anyone else, and if he's feeling bad, he can make you cry. His musical taste for the thing he does is impeccable.

Horace Silver. *Won't You Open Up Your Senses* (from *Total Response*, Blue Note). Silver, piano, composer; Andy Bey, vocal.

Jon Hendricks (1972): It was Andy Bey . . . with Horace Silver's Quintet. Of course, Horace's own composition and lyrics. This is very significant to me, because I remember when I was Horace's lyricist. He was fooling around with lyrics and I gave him some encouragement, like "Go ahead, write your own," and I never thought he'd really do that. I wouldn't mind, except that he does it so well.

TRUMPET

Ornette Coleman. *Freeway Express* (from *The Empty Foxhole*, Blue Note). Coleman, trumpet, composer; Charles Haden, bass; Ornette Denardo Coleman, drums.

Freddie Hubbard (1968): That was Ornette Coleman on trumpet. . . . I think Ornette is neglecting the basics of playing trumpet. I love his alto, he knocks me out, but the trumpet—I don't think he should play that in public.

I didn't get anything out of it. Being a trumpet player I can't rate it. As far as the drummer is concerned, it just sounded like a little kid fooling around, and knew nothing about the drums.

I could have done what Ornette is doing when I was five.

There's a whole lot of guys can do that, who know nothing about trumpet. Why should a guy study for years —*study* trumpet—then see a guy come out on trumpet, and he gets a lot of popularity, like this—it doesn't make sense.

Encyclopedia of Jazz All Stars. *Twelve Tone Blues* (from *The Sound of Feeling*, Verve). Nat Adderley, cornet; Ron Carter, bass; Leonard Feather, composer; Oliver Nelson, conductor, arranger.

Nat Adderley (1969): That's a helluva tune, a hell of an arrangement, the solos are a bitch. . . . I'm not an egotist or an illusionist, but my solo was greatly in context with the tune, and Ron Carter is a bitch! But the way it was played, the general feeling—the tune is out, the way the arrangement is. Now, played with a small group, straight without the changes moving in that direction, it could be like a regular bebop tune. But in this context with that arrangement, it's a five star record—I don't care who played it or who wrote it!

John Carter-Bobby Bradford. *Abstractions For Three Lovers* (from *Flight for Four*, Flying Dutchman). Bradford, trumpet; Carter, composer, alto saxophone; Tom Williamson, bass; Bruz Freeman, drums.

Freddie Hubbard (1970): It sounded a little bit like Don Cherry on trumpet for a minute—I don't know who they are. I recognized Richard Davis on bass and he's one of the greatest.

When guys do this sort of thing, a lot of times I think they lose the feeling—the free form thing. You have to be careful, because it bogs down and people lose interest. There has to be some feeling to keep a person's interest. And in this arrangement I didn't get the message. But I'll give it two stars because they're trying something different.

Art Farmer. *Didn't We* (from *Gentle Eyes*, Mainstream). Farmer, flugelhorn. Recorded in Vienna with strings.

Woody Shaw (1972): That's Chet Baker on flugelhorn. I'm not very impressed with it. It's a little complacent, a little too plush. . . . Still it's some of the best playing I've heard Chet Baker do. Actually, my favorite flugelhornist is Art Farmer.

Louis Armstrong. *Love, You Funny Thing* (from *V.S.O.P.*, Epic). Armstrong Big Band with Zilner Randolph, trumpet and arranger; recorded Chicago, 1932.

Barney Bigard (1971): Oh, man! I know Louis must have been drug with that band! I think it was the old Los Angeles Cotton Club band that was run by Les Hite, and I imagine Louis would turn in his grave to hear that band behind him.

Ornette Coleman. *The Circle With A Hole In The Middle* (from *The Art of the Improvisers*, Atlantic). Coleman, alto sax, composer; Don Cherry, cornet.

Donald Byrd (1971): "The trumpet and saxophone are well established instruments . . . when I think back to how old they are and what's been done, I don't think you have to necessarily distort it . . . the same thing could have been done very honestly if they were more proficient. . . . To play strange lines, atonal lines, you don't have to distort it. . . .

Jackie McLean. *Demon's Dance* (from *Demon's Dance*, Blue Note). McLean, composer, alto sax; Woody Shaw, trumpet.

Ted Curson (1971): I've heard Woody Shaw around Paris before he came back to New York, and he was playing very nice trumpet. But I think he's wasting his time imitating Freddie Hubbard because he doesn't really have the chops for that.

Dizzy Gillespie. *Lover, Come Back to Me* (from *Dizzy Gillespie*, RCA Victor). Gillespie, trumpet, arranger. Recorded in 1948.

Louie Bellson (1967): How high can you go with the stars—is there a limit? I was going to say that that's one of the greatest trumpet players of all time, and I'm not just saying it because he's sitting here. I say it all the time. In fact, I bring his name up at my drum clinics all the time.

It's interesting to listen to one of Dizzy's early big bands; everything even today is so modern. It's like Ellington—when you hear something Duke did 20 years ago, it's got all those traces of all the modern things in it.

Gerald Wilson. *Carlos* (from *The Golden Sword*, Pacific Jazz). Jimmy Owens, trumpet; Wilson, composer.

Jack Sheldon (1967): It sounded like Donald Byrd to me, with Stan Kenton. I give it four stars because it was such a big sound.

On second thought, I don't believe it was Stan Kenton; although it could have been his band with this trumpet player added as guest soloist or something.

The orchestration was very Mexican, and I liked that. Very well done.

VIBES

Roy Ayers. *Stoned Soul Picnic* (from *Stoned Soul Picnic*, Atlantic). Ayers, vibes; Hubert Laws, flute; Gary Bartz, alto saxophone; Herbie Hancock, piano; Ron Carter, bass; Grady Tate, drums; Laura Nyro, composer; Charles Tolliver, trumpet.

Tommy Vig (1969): This is the thing I really don't like; I would say it's bad and phony and ugly, except for the vibes solo, which shows good talent and good technique and swing—I don't know who it was; it reminded me of Terry Gibbs a little bit and I hope none of my friends are involved in this. I don't like the tune, arrangement or their conception—none of them have merit or truth or high artistic aims or anything—I just dislike everything about it.

All the components that this consists of, like let's say the rock rhythm or this half-rock rhythm, individually I don't like them. But, put together like this, it's *very* bad . . . I wouldn't rate this at all.

Terry Gibbs. *Norwegian Wood* (from *Reza*, Dot). Gibbs, marimba.

Bobby Hutcherson (1967): First of all, this is somebody trying to get a hit. I'm trying to think who would be doing that; it's difficult to tell.

It sounds more like a marimba than a xylophone, because it has a higher pitch to it. It doesn't have very much to do with jazz, and I'm not very much of an AM listener on the radio.

To rate this musically, just one star.

Terry Gibbs. *Oge* (from *Take It From Me*, Impulse).

Milt Jackson (1975): One thing about most other vibes players—not to put them down—but you really have to experiment a while to get a sound. . . . The context of the piece is very good, but the sound . . . too much of a clanking sound. It goes back again to the instrument being so mechanical you gotta try and work with it to get the best from it.

Gary Burton. *The Sunset Bell* (from *Alone At Last*, Atlantic). Burton, unaccompanied vibes.

Lionel Hampton (1972): Was that supposed to be jazz? If you want me to comment on the jazz, I don't hear any. I know that's Gary Burton, and I'm quite sure he's striving for something new, but I wouldn't put that in the class of jazz like Bags, Hutcherson, Ayers . . . maybe he's got a new thing, and more power to him.

Milt Jackson. *Extraordinary Blues* (from *Milt Jackson & Big Brass*, Riverside). Jackson, vibraharp.

Bobby Hutcherson (1967): Bags has a way of playing so that he takes you up to the top of the instrument and gets hung up in playing these notes, and you hear them up there, and he lets the rhythm section hang below him, and that's a helluva feeling.

I've heard him recorded a lot better than this. But sometimes you hear a record like this, and you think it might be someone else; then in a few seconds it hits you, and you know it just can't be anybody else but him. He hangs it up in the sky . . . it just lays there.

I'd rate that 5 stars—a million stars for Bags!

MILES

Miles Davis. *Put Your Little Foot Right Out* (from *Jazz Track* (Columbia). Davis, trumpet; recorded 1958.

Benny Carter (1971): Having heard so little of what Miles is doing today, although I do have his album *Bitches Brew*, it's difficult for me to compare, but I do prefer what I've just listened to. That's one of the loveliest things I've heard . . . I would think it's from the mid-1950s. Five stars.

Miles Davis. *Bitches Brew* (from *Bitches Brew*, Columbia). Davis, fluegelhorn, composer.

Clark Terry (1972): This was probably one of the most controversial records and jazz personalities of the past century. The way he's been ostracized and criticized—and probably rightly so in many instances—but I suppose in his case he's a man who likes to stay abreast of things. . . . I only think this record can be considered jazz because Miles is on it, but I don't think that some of the stuff on it is. To me jazz has to stimulate . . . this is not necessarily stimulating. It's something to listen to as far as new sounds are concerned, but it could just as easily have been background for a scene in a jungle movie . . . an Australian setting with the foo birds running around and the kangaroos making love to each other. I'm not necessarily putting it down; it's different.

Miles Davis. *Black Satin* (from *On The Corner*, Columbia).

Doc Severinsen (1973):

Feather: It's very interesting that it took you quite some time to even figure out that it was a trumpet.

Severinsen: My feeling is that what Miles was doing there with the trumpet could probably have been done more effectively with an electric guitar. Maybe he's frustrated by the fact that it isn't a guitar. Sometimes I feel that way. I'll say to myself, "Oh, hell, why don't I play the guitar, it'd be so much easier."

Feather: Do you think Miles' playing on this record required as much technical expertise on the trumpet as some of the things he was doing earlier?

Severinsen: I don't really know. It's hard for me to say, because the whole thing was concealed quite a bit. I couldn't tell exactly what he was doing. There's a technique of using that pedal . . . it's very inventive, very creative; what you'd expect of Miles. He's not going in to play Bop City again.

I really don't think that the trumpet, and his use of it, is as effective for that kind of thing as, for some reason I think, a violin would have been, or a guitar. It's the Mahavishnu type of approach.

Miles Davis. *Orbits* (from *Miles Smiles*, Columbia). Davis, trumpet; Wayne Shorter, tenor saxophone, composer; Herbie Hancock, piano.

Herbie Mann (1968): Miles is one of my influences—Miles and Ray Charles—not so much in playing, but in the fact that he's very true to himself; he's very believable and he's his own person, and I try to set that standard for myself.

I've heard the group play fantastically and I'd give this four stars for *almost* fantastically. I think this is from *Miles Smiles*. Wayne, Herbie, Tony, and Ron are the tightest there is in the business, because they all listen to each other all the time. That's the beautiful thing about it.

Miles Davis. *ESP* (from *Miles Davis' Greatest Hits*, Columbia). Davis, composer, trumpet; Wayne Shorter, co-composer.

Freddie Hubbard (1970): They sound like they just came off a road trip. You know, you just come off the road and you decide you want to do a date when you get back, instead of relaxing a couple of weeks.

It seems like I heard another cut of this, because this one doesn't have the drive that I know Miles has. It was smooth, a beautiful arrangement, but I don't think his chops worked that day. But five stars for Miles, although it's not one of the best performances I've heard of his. That composition was nice—linear, floating—but it didn't kill me.

Miles Davis. *The Sorcerer* (from *The Sorcerer*, Columbia). Davis, trumpet; Wayne Shorter, tenor saxophone; Herbie Hancock, piano, composer; Tony Williams, drums.

Bobby Bryant (1969): I think Miles is much more pleasing on the slower things, in a little different setting than the avant garde setting. There gets to be a certain sameness about his performances that sort of leaves me cold.

He still is Miles and deserves a great deal of credit for his lyricism. The composition just doesn't call for lyricism, and I think lyricism is his really good suit, really where he's strong. The sameness which is occurring on his recent records I don't like. . . . Three stars.

Miles Davis. *It Never Entered My Mind* (from *Three Decades of Jazz*—1949-'59, Blue Note). Davis, trumpet; Horace Silver, piano; Percy Heath, bass; Art Blakey, drums. (Recorded 3/6/54).

Dizzy Gillespie (1970): That was Miles. I've made a sort of analysis—not being too much concerned with what people *say* Miles is, but with his own personality.

He is shy, for one thing. You'd never think it, but I've been watching him for so many years . . . I think that the reasons for some of his actions are a natural result of his being shy.

As for his music, Miles' has a deep, deep, deep spiritual value to it. It's far deeper than mine, which is a part of me I expect to be developed due to the Bahai faith, and I think my music is going to be affected by this too.

Miles and I played several times together at the Village Gate and a place in Harlem, and the last time he came up to me afterwards and said, "How'd you like it?" So I said, "What is it? Explain it to me." Well, it seems they have a basic melody and they work around that. I guess you have to know the basic tune. . . .

Feather: It's not so much a tune as a mode, isn't it?

Gillespie: I don't know . . . but I'd like to spend some time having him explain it to me because I'd like to know what it is he's doing.

It reminded me so much of Ornette Coleman—I never listened to him too much to this point. But when Bernard Stollman gave me one of his Town Hall concerts, I was alone when I put on the record, and I could follow the chords he was playing. It was difficult stuff, very complex and highly enjoyable. And that's when I really started listening closely to what he was doing.

Going back to the record just played, I couldn't hear too much of that rhythm section, with Miles playing out there. But I'd rate it five stars.

Miles Davis. *Riot* (from *Nefertiti*, Columbia).

Chuck Mangione: I think Miles Davis is really the most important jazz musician that we've had, as far as being a leader in musical directions. Unlike somebody like Dizzy Gillespie, who established a direction and a style, and has been able to play it for these many years because of its utter uniqueness. It's like the music of the great classical composers which will always live.

Miles has always made so many important contributions to music. His playing as well has changed drastically in such a relatively short time. I really love his music. Everything he does is valid, just because I believe him to be one of the most honest and creative musicians around. I see no reason to dislike what I heard.

Miles Davis. *Honky Tonk* (from *Get Up With It*, Columbia). Davis, trumpet, composer; Keith Jarrett, Herbie Hancock, keyboards; Steve Grossman, soprano sax; Michael Henderson, bass; John McLaughlin, guitar; Billy Cobham, drums; Airto Moreira, percussion.

Blue Mitchell: This one I can't make no contact with at all. I don't know any of the personnel. I don't particularly like the arrangement; it doesn't sound like a composition, it just sounds like somebody blowing . . . trying to kill some time till the set's over. I hope it ain't nobody I know. . . . They are probably some good players, if you put 'em with the right group.

Miles Davis. *Red China Blues* (from *Get Up With It*, Columbia).

Horace Silver: It ain't my particular cup of tea, to tell the truth. I wouldn't venture forth to buy it. I doubt if it was given to me that I'd play it. I'd keep it, but probably wouldn't play it that much. He might say the same thing of my new material! We all have to open our minds, stretch forth, take chances and venture out musically to try to arrive at something new and different, and he's doing it—and I give him credit for that.

MILES AT THE MICROPHONE

In an introduction to a blindfold test conducted with Miles Davis in 1968, I commented:

Four years ago, the last time Miles Davis was blindfolded, I remarked that he was "unusually selective in his listening habits." The only record that drew a favorable reaction was one by Stan Getz and Joao Gilberto, which brought a five-star rave. Everything else was put down in varying degrees; Les McCann, Rod Levitt, Sonny Rollins, Eric Dolphy, Cecil Taylor; even his early favorite Clark Terry and his idol Duke Ellington.

Visiting Miles in his Hollywood hotel suite, I found strewn around the room records or tape cartridges by James Brown, Dionne Warwick, Tony Bennett, the Byrds, Aretha Franklin and the Fifth Dimension.

1. Freddie Hubbard. **On the Que-Tee** (from **Backlash,** Atlantic). Hubbard, trumpet, composer.

MD: I don't dig that kind of s---, man, just a straight 32 bars, I mean whatever it is. The time they were playing was too tight, you know. It's formal, man, and scales and all that. . . . No kind of sound, straight sound—no imagination. They shouldn't even put that out.

Freddie's a great trumpet player, but if he had some kind of other direction to go . . . if you place a guy in a spot where he has to do something else, other than what he can do, so he can do *that.* He's got to have something that challenges his imagination, far above what he thinks he's going to play, and what it might lead into, then above *that*, so he won't be fighting when things change.

That's what I tell all my musicians; I tell them be ready to play what you know and play *above* what you know. Anything might happen above what you've been used to playing—you're ready to get into that, and above that, and take that out.

But this sounds like just a lead sheet.

LF: Do you think he's capable of more than that?

MD: Yes, if he's directed, because he must have other imagination, other than this. I wouldn't even put that s--- on record.

2. Thad Jones-Mel Lewis. **Bacha Feelin'** (from **Live at the Village Vanguard,** Solid State). Jones, fluegelhorn; Garnett Brown, trombone, composer; Joe Farrell, tenor saxophone; Roland Hanna, piano; Richard Davis, bass; Lewis, drums.

MD: It's got to be Thad's big band. . . . I don't understand why those guys have to push themselves and say "Wow! wee!" and all that, during an arrangement, to make somebody think it's more than what it is, when it ain't nothing. I like the way Thad writes, but I also like the way he plays when he writes. I like when he plays his tunes, without all that stuff—no solos, you know. It's nothing to play off of.

LF: There was a long tenor solo on that.

MD: Yes, but it was nothing; they didn't need that, and the trombone player should be shot.

LF: Well, who do you think wrote that?

MD: I don't really know, but I don't like those kind of arrangements. You don't write arrangements like that for white guys . . . (*humming*). That ain't nothing.

In the first place, a band with that instrumentation f---s up an arrangement—the saxophones particularly. They could play other instruments, but you only get one sound like that. On that arrangement, the only one that rates is the piano player. He's something else. And Richard Davis. The drummer just plays straight, no shading. I couldn't stand a band like that for myself. It makes me feel like I'm broke and wearing a slip that doesn't belong to me, and my hair's combed the wrong way; it makes me feel funny, even as a listener.

Those guys don't have a musical mind—just playing what's written. They don't know what the notes mean.

LF: Have you heard that band much in person?

MD: Yes, I've heard them, but I don't like them. I like Thad's arrangements, but I don't like the guys pushing the arrangements, and shouting, because there's nothing happening. It would be better if they recorded the shouts at the end—or at least shout in tune!

3. Archie Shepp. **The Funeral** (from **Archie Shepp in Europe,** (Delmark). Don Cherry, cornet; John Tchicai, alto saxophone; Shepp, tenor saxophone. (Recorded 1963).

MD: You're putting me on with that! . . . I know who it is—Ornette, f---ing up the trumpet and the alto. I don't understand that jive at all. The guy has nice rhythm on saxophone.

People are so gullible—they go for that—they go for something they don't know about.

LF: Why do you think they go for it?

MD: Because they feel it's not hip *not* to go for it. But if something sounds terrible, man, a person should have enough respect for his own mind to say it doesn't sound good. It doesn't to me, and I'm not going to listen to it. No matter how long you listen to it, it doesn't sound any good.

Anyone can tell that guy's not a trumpet player—it's just notes that come out, and every note he plays, he looks serious about it, and people will go for it—especially white people. They go for anything. They want to be hipper than any other race, and they go for anything ridiculous like that.

LF: Actually, you got that one wrong—it wasn't Ornette. It was an Archie Shepp date with John Tchicai on alto and Don Cherry on trumpet.

MD: Well, whoever it is, it sounds the same—Ornette sounds the same way. That's where Archie and them got that s--- from; there sure ain't nothing there.

4. Fifth Dimension. **Prologue, The Magic Garden** (from **The Magic Garden, Soul City**). Jim Webb, composer, arranger.

MD: That record is planned, you know. It's like when I do things, it's planned and you lead into other things. It makes sense. It has different sounds in the voicing, and they're using the stereo—they can sure use stereo today, coming out from different sides and different people making statements and things like that. That's the way you should record!

Yeah, that's a nice record; it sounds nice. I liked the composition and the arrangement. It's Jim Webb and the Fifth Dimension. It could be a little smoother—they push it too hard for the singers. You don't have to push that hard. When you push, you get a raggedy edge, and an edge gives another vibration.

I liked the instrumental introduction too. We did things like that on **Porgy and Bess**—just played parts of things.

I told Diahann Carroll about an idea I had for her to record, based on things like that. There are certain tunes—parts of tunes—that you like, and you have to go through all the other s--- to get to that part—but she can just sing that part. She could sing it in any kind of musical form—18th century, today's beat, and she can say the statement over and make the background change the mood and change the time. They could also use her as an instrument; instead of the strings under her, she could be *in* the strings, and have her coming out from each side of the stereo. She told me to set it up for her, and I was trying to do it for her.

Jimmy Webb would be great for her. I think Wayne could do it for her, too; but I told her to get a guy like Mel to put the story together.

LF: Which Mel?

MD: Mel Torme. And you could have the music in between, to change the mood to whatever mood she wanted to sing in. She was interested, and insisted that I produce it, but I don't want to get involved in that end of it.

5. The Electric Flag. **Over-Lovin' You** (from **A Long Time Comin',** Columbia). Barry Goldberg, Mike Bloomfield, composers.

MD: Who was that? Leave that record here, it's a nice record. I like guys that get into what they're supposed to be singing, and the guys that play behind it really get into what *they're* doing—when the mood changes they go right in it. It makes the record smooth; makes it mean something.

It's a pleasure to get a record like that, because you know they're serious no matter what they do . . . I liked the rhythm on that. I mean, if you're going to do something like that, man, you've got to *do* it. You know what I mean? If you're going to play like that, play like that—*good*—but don't jive around.

I like to cop myself—I don't like to miss. I like to get into the meat of things, and sometimes it don't happen and sometimes it does; when it does, it feels great, and it makes up for the times when it doesn't. But if you know it's going to happen one night, it keeps you going.

6. Sun Ra. **Brainville** (from **Sun Song,** Delmark). Dave Young, trumpet; Sun Ra, composer. (Recorded in 1956).

MD: That's gotta come from Europe. We wouldn't play no s--- like that. It's so sad. It sounds funny to me. Sounds like a 1935 arrangement by Raymond Scott. They must be joking—the Florida A&M band sounds better than that. They should record them, rather than that s---. They've got more spirit than that. That ain't nothing.

Why put that on record? What does that do? You mean there's somebody around here that feels like that? Even the white people don't feel that sad.

LF: Do you think that's a white group?

MD: The trumpet player didn't sound white. . . . I

don't know, man. You know, there's a little thing that trumpet players play to make a jazz sound, that if you don't have your own sound, you can hear an adopted jazz sound, which is a drag, especially in the mute. I mean you can tell when a guy's got his own thing.

People should have good friends to tell them, "Man, that ain't it, so don't play trumpet," you know what I mean? Or "Don't play drums, 'cause you don't have anything." I'd rather have that said to me than go on playing trumpet when it doesn't sound like I want it to sound. I know he doesn't want it to sound like that, so he should work at it, or play another instrument—a lower instrument.

When an arrangement's tight like that, you have to play every chord, because the background parts when they record, like they play them single, instead of making it smooth—and it's hard to play like that. You have to play each chord, then play the other chords or you never connect anything, and in between it's just blank.

To me it's just like canned music. Even canned music sounds good sometimes, but not s--- like this.

7. Don Ellis. **Alone** (from **Electric Bath,** Columbia). Ellis, trumpet; Hank Levy, composer.

MD: Who's that supposed to be? It's too straight, man. You know, you'd be surprised, this trumpet player probably can play, he sounds all right, but with a strong rhythm like that—if you have a straight rhythm like that, the band has to play against the rhythm, because the rhythm is never gonna change, and that's very hard to do. The best way to do that is for the rhythm to play real soft.

You don't need a trumpet in something like that. It was just one of those major, minor, major. . . .

It's a kind of mood tune. I would play it slower, and have the band way down, so they could have got some kind of feeling into it. You could tell they don't feel like playing this. Somebody was impressed with 5/4 time, but what difference does that make? What's so great about a whole number in 5/4? In our group we change the beat around and do all kind of things with time, but not just to say, "Look at me, I'm playing 5/4!" There's nothing there, but I guess the critics will have something to write about.

LF: It was Don Ellis. Have you ever heard him?

MD: Yeah. I heard him. He's no soloist. I mean, he's a nice guy and all that, but to me he's just another white trumpet player. He can't play in a chord, can't play with any feeling; that's the reason I guess they use all that time s---.

Anybody can make a record, and try to do something new, to sell; but to me a record is more than something new, and I don't care how much it sells. You have to capture some feeling—you can't just play like a f---ing machine. You can't even turn on with any kind of dope and get any feeling to play if you don't have it in your heart. No matter what you do, it won't make you play any better. You are what you are, no matter what you do. I can be loud and no good, soft and no good, in 7/8 and no good. You can be black and no good, white and no good. . . . A guy like Bobby Hackett plays what he plays with feeling, and you can put him into any kind of thing and he'll do it.

8. Al Hirt. **Goin' To Chicago Blues** (from **Live at Carnegie Hall,** RCA). Hirt, trumpet.

MD: It's Al Hirt. I think he's a very good trumpet player. For anyone that feels that way, I guess he hits them. He's a good trumpet player, but that's some corny-ass s--- he plays here.

They want him to be fat and white and funny and talented, but he ain't. They want something that looks good on television; fat, with a beard, and jovial and jolly. He's like a white Uncle Tom. And he's a nice guy; it's a drag. You know, white folks made Negroes tom a long time ago by giving them money. To do this in front of some white people, to pay you to have that kind of personality, like him, it's tomming. I can't see why a guy like Al Hirt . . . I guess if he was thin he wouldn't do that.

Harry James is a good trumpet player, and he never did tom or no s--- like that. Harry had some feeling.

For a guy to shake his unattractive body and think somebody thinks it's funny—it ain't funny, it's disgusting. He can't entertain me like that; he can entertain some corny ofays, but all the colored folks I know would say, "Oh, f---! I don't want to hear that!"

Introduction to biographies

The principal intention of this book is to provide factual information concerning the most important musicians, singers, composers and arrangers who were a part of the jazz world at some time during the decade prior to press time (mid-1976). In addition, we have included biographies of many others who, though history has not yet had time to judge them, seem likely to make a durable contribution to the music.

Because of the world-wide proliferation of jazz and, in particular, its immense popularity in Japan, a number of artists have been included whose names may be unfamiliar to the American reader. In many instances we have relied on the assurance of experts in Europe, and of Kiyoshi Koyama, editor of *Swing Journal*, that they were worthy of inclusion.

The discographies are selective, and wherever possible represent the personal choices of the musicians.

The brevity or length of a biography should not be interpreted as necessarily relating to the importance of the artist. The number of jobs held, the length of the career, the quantity of information supplied or available, along with many other factors, helped determine the space devoted to each listing.

Because of an increasing tendency of contemporary musicians to double on many instruments it can be assumed that in virtually all cases the newer pianists play electric as well as acoustic keyboard and, in many cases, clavinet, synthesizers, etc.; similarly bassists play electric as well as upright bass. Whether they are so listed or not, it may also be assumed that the vast majority of instrumentalists who have come to prominence in the past decade are also composers.

As supplementary reading the authors suggest John Chilton's *Who's Who Of Jazz* (musicians born before 1920) and Irwin Stambler's *Encyclopedia Of Pop, Rock and Soul.*

Pepper Adams (*Veryl Oakland*)

Cannonball Adderley (*Fantasy Records*)

Nat Adderley (*Veryl Oakland*)

Barry Altschul (*Randi Hultin*)

Louis Armstrong and Joe Glaser (*Sam Shaw*)

Toshiko Akiyoshi (*Veryl Oakland*)

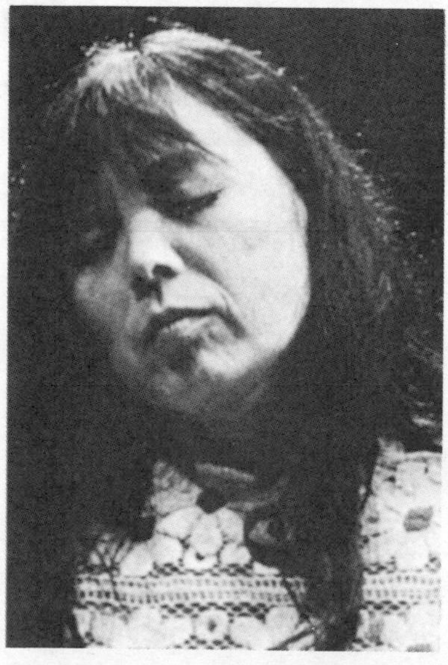

Mose Allison (*David D. Spitzer*)

Chet Baker (*Veryl Oakland*)

Svend Asmussen (*Veryl Oakland*)

Gary Bartz (*Veryl Oakland*)

Louie Bellson (*Veryl Oakland*)

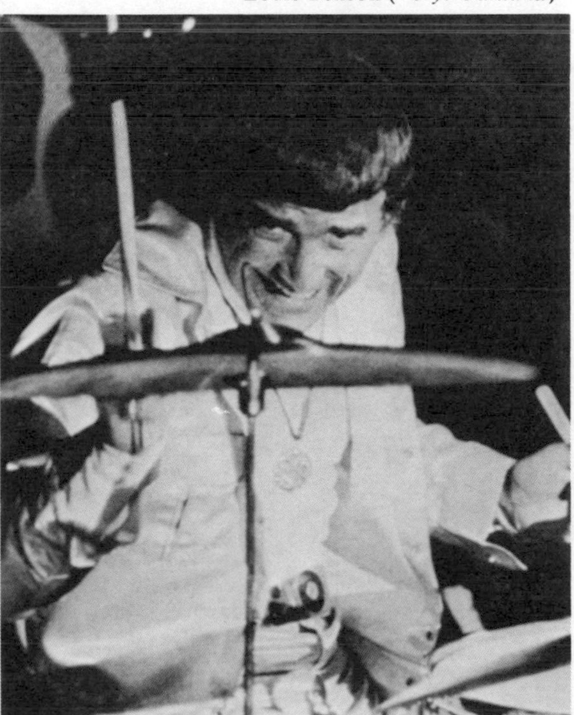

Gato Barbieri
(*David D. Spitzer*)

George Benson (*CTI Records*)

Clark Terry and Eubie Blake (*Randi Hultin*)

Art Blakey (*David D. Spitzer*)

Paul Bley (*David D. Spitzer*)

Dee Dee Bridgewater (*Veryl Oakland*)

Cecil Bridgewater (*David D. Spitzer*)

Roy Brooks
(*David D. Spitzer*)

Lester Bowie (*David D. Spitzer*)

Walter Booker (*Veryl Oakland*)

Garnett Brown (*David D. Spitzer*)

Ruby Braff and George Barnes (*Veryl Oakland*)

Dave Brubeck (*David D. Spitzer*)

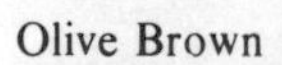

Olive Brown

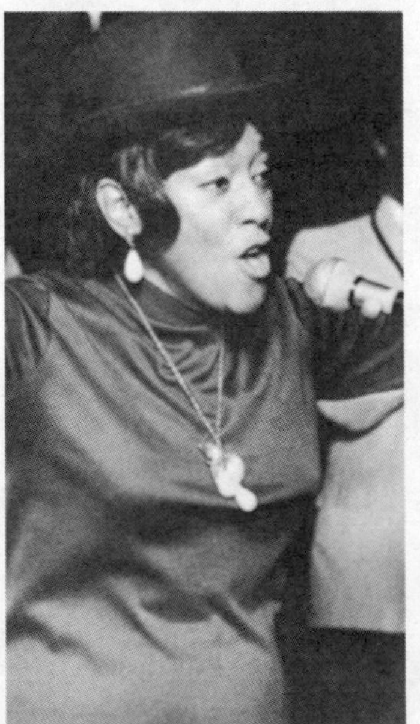

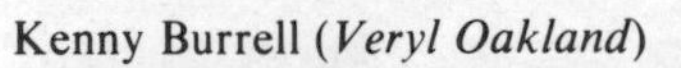

Kenny Burrell (*Veryl Oakland*)

Milt Buckner (*David D. Spitzer*)

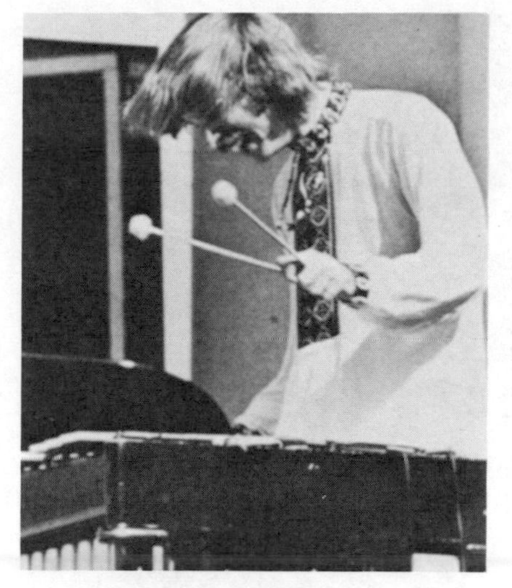
Gary Burton (*Veryl Oakland*)

Donald Byrd (*Veryl Oakland*)

Betty Carter (*Veryl Oakland*)

Benny Carter (*Veryl Oakland*)

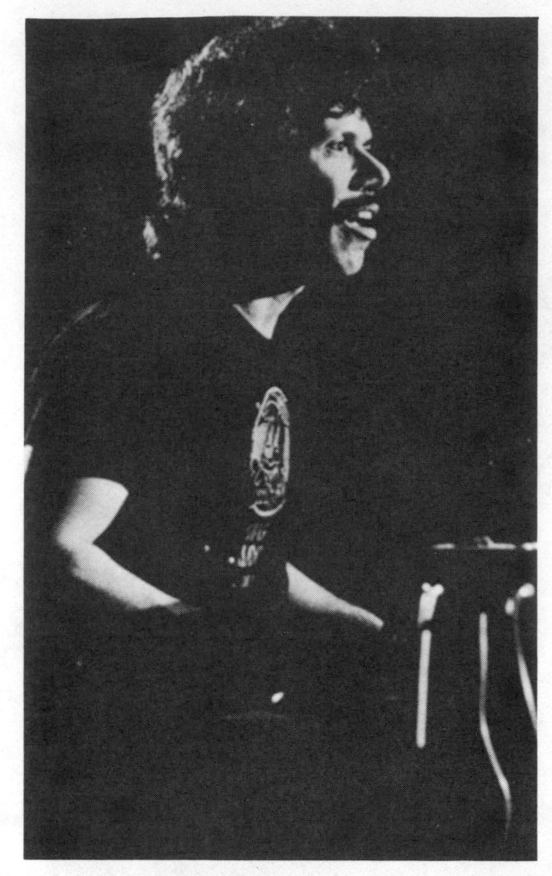

Chick Corea (*Veryl Oakland*)

Billy Cobham (*Veryl Oakland*)

Ron Carter (*CTI Records*)

Stanley Clarke
(*Veryl Oakland*)

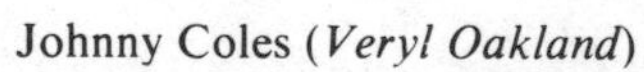

Johnny Coles (*Veryl Oakland*)

Abbreviations

ABC American Broadcasting Co.
acc. accompanied, accompanying, accompanist
addr. address
AFM American Federation of Musicians
app. appeared, appearing, appearance
a & r artists and repertoire
arr. arranged, arranger, arrangement
ASCAP American Society of Composers, Authors and Publishers
Atl. Atlantic
Aud. Fid. Audio Fidelity
b. born
B&B Black and Blue
BBC British Broadcasting Corporation
Beth. Bethlehem
Bl. Lion Black Lion
BN Blue Note
BS&T Blood, Sweat & Tears
bro. brother
Bruns. Brunswick
ca. about
Cam. Camden
Cap. Capitol
CAPS Creative Artists Program Service
CBA Collective Black Artists
CBS Columbia Broadcasting System
Chiaro Chiaroscuro
cl., clar. clarinet
CNE Canadian National Exposition
Cobble. Cobblestone
Col. Columbia
Coll. college
Comm. Commodore
comp. composed, composer, composition
cond. conductor, conducting, conducted
cons. conservatory
cont. continued
Contemp. Contemporary
CUNY City University of New York
d. died
deb. debut
Del. Delmark
Diff. Drum. Differant Drummer
DSC Dutch Swing College
educ. educated, education
Elek. Elektra
Fant. Fantasy
fav., favs. favorite, favorites
feat. featured, featuring
Fly. Dutch. Flying Dutchman
Folk. Folkways
Font. Fontana
GNP Gene Norman Presents
Gr. Mer. Groove Merchant
gp. group
hca. harmonica
harm. harmony
incl. included, including
infl. influence, influenced
instr. instrument
JATP Jazz at the Philharmonic
Jazzl. Jazzland
JF jazz festival
JCOA Jazz Composers Orchestra Association
JP jazz party
KC Kansas City
LA Los Angeles
LACC Los Angeles City College
Lond. London
LV Las Vegas
LP long playing record
Main. Mainstream
MCA Music Corporation of America
Merc. Mercury
Mile., Milest. Milestone
MJF Monterey Jazz Festival
MJQ Modern Jazz Quartet
MMO Music Minus One
mod. modern
Mon.-Ever. Monmouth-Evergreen
mos. months
mus. dir. musical director
MUSE Brooklyn Children's Museum
NARAS National Academy of Recording Arts and Sciences
NAJE National Association of Jazz Educators
NBC National Broadcasting Company
NEA National Endowment for the Arts
Nemp. Nemperor
NJF Newport Jazz Festival
NJF-NY Newport Jazz Festival-New York
NO New Orleans
NOJF New Orleans Jazz Festival
NYJRC New York Jazz Repertory Company
NYC New York City
orch. orchestra
Pac. Jazz Pacific Jazz
Para. Paramount
pl. played, plays, playing
Pres. Prestige
Prest. Prestige
publ. publication, published
RCA Radio Corporation of America; RCA Victor
RCI Radio Canada International
rec. recorded, recordings
repl. replaced, replacing
Repr. Reprise
ret. returned, returning
r & b rhythm and blues
Rivers. Riverside
Roul. Roulette
r & r rock and roll
Sack. Sackville
Sav. Savoy
sch. school
SF San Francisco
SS Solid State
st. started
Steeple. SteepleChase
stud. studied, studying
SUNY State University of New York
symph. symphony
tpt. trumpet
trom. trombone
UA United Artists
U., Univ. University
Van., Vang. Vanguard
vln. violin
WB, War. Bros. Warner Brothers
w. with
Wor. Pac. World Pacific
yr., yrs. year, years

For further biographical information covering earlier periods, with respect to any artist whose name is followed by an asterisk (*), see *The Encyclopedia of Jazz* (1960) and/or *The Encyclopedia of Jazz in the Sixties* (1966) Horizon Press.

Biographies

A.A.C.M. see Abrams, Muhal Richard.

AARONS, ALBERT N. (AL), *trumpet, fluegelhorn*; b. Pittsburgh, Pa., 3/23/32. Stud. privately in Pitts., '47-50; Chicago, '51-3; Wayne State U., Detroit, '55-7. Pl. w. Y. Lateef, '56-7, Barry Harris, '57, Flame & Frolic Showbars, Detr., '58-60, Wild Bill Davis, '61, Basie, '61-9. Settling in LA, he played on TV series w. Della Reese, '69-70; Flip Wilson, '70-4; Burt Bacharach, '71; Bill Cosby, '72; Nancy Wilson, '74-5; Q. Jones, various occasions. Also worked w. Henry Mancini for TV shows and concert apps., '71, and with many big jazz bands in clubs in LA area.

Infls: Clifford Brown, D. Gillespie, L. Armstrong. Aarons is part owner and co-founder of the Legend record label.

LPs: w. Basie on various labels; w. Frank Wess, *Southern Comfort* (Roulette); w. R. Brown/M. Jackson, *Memphis Blues* (Impulse); w. Buddy Collette, *Now and Then* (Legend); *Sarah Vaughan and the Jimmy Rowles Quintet* (Mainstream).

ABDULLAH, SHAKUR (Charles Weaver), *percussion, drums*; b. Cleveland, Ohio, 3/22/40. Self-taught, but was insp. by Candido, Juno Lewis, J. Coltrane, Jack Costanza, Ch. Parker, Clifford Brown, Max Roach, A. Ayler, Dupree Bolton. Pl. w. many groups in LA area: Owen Marshall quintet; Abbey Lincoln Quintet; Walter Bishop Jr. Quintet; Gene Russell Quartet; Enmedio Saracho Quintet; Calvin Keys Quintet; Troy Robinson big band; H. Tapscott big band, '72-4. Chico Hamilton, '74- . Film sound tracks w. Tapscott, Hamilton. Fests: Newport West; Ch. Parker Fest; Festival in Black; Watts Festival. Comps: *Sufi Dance; Love; Dance of the Wives; Raga Allah; N.Y. Mornings*.

LPs: w. Marshall, *The Naked Truth* (Aditi Records); w. Bishop, *4th Cycle*; w. Russell, *Talk To My Lady* (Black Jazz); w. Hamilton, *Peregrinations* (BN).

ABENE, MICHAEL CHRISTIAN JOSEPH (MIKE), *piano, composer*; also *keyboards*; b. Brooklyn, N.Y., 7/2/42. Father pl. guitar, had own band. Pl. w. Farmingdale High School band and Newport Youth Band under Marshall Brown. Informal arr. & piano lessons w. John LaPorta, Wally Cirillo. Comp. major at Manhattan Sch. of Mus. for two yrs. before going on the road w. Maynard Ferguson at age 18. Experience at Cork 'N Bib on L.I. w. Clark Terry, Jimmy Nottingham, etc. in early '60s. With Don Ellis, '60-1; M. Ferguson, '61-5. Also worked in LV w. B. Rich, H. Edison, G. Auld, '63. From '65-7 pl. at Half Note w. Al Cohn-Zoot Sims; Bill Berry-Richie Kamuca; R. Braff. Writing and pl. jingles from '66. Wrote arrs. for Joe Shepley-Burt Collins-Mike Abene 11-piece band. Own duo at Bradley's in NYC, '72-5. TV: many apps. on *Love of Life* soap opera as solo, trio pianist; *Dial M For Music; Jazz Adventures*. Fests: NJF w. Farmingdale band; Newport Youth Band; Ferguson. NJF-NY '75 w. Sylvia Syms. Arrs: *Maryann; I Believe to My Soul* in LP *The Blues Roar* w. Ferguson on Mainstream; *Lennon-McCartney Live* w. Collins-Shepley Galaxy on MTA; comp. & arr. *Time, Space and the Blues* for Collins-Shepley Galaxy and pl. on album (MTA). Other LPs w. Ferguson (Main.).

ABERCROMBIE, JOHN L., *guitar*; also *bass*; b. Portchester, N.Y., 12/16/44. Started on guitar at 14; some private lessons but mostly self-taught until he att. Berklee Coll. of Mus., '62-6, where he stud. guitar w. Jack Petersen; theory, harmony. Worked w. Johnny Hammond, '67-8; Dreams, '69; Chico Hamilton, '70; Jeremy Steig; Gil Evans; Gato Barbieri, '71-3; Billy Cobham, Jan. '74-Jan. '75. During that time he also pl. w. Jack De Johnette, touring Europe w. him. W. De Johnette; gigs w. own trio & quartet, '75. A dextrous guitarist who mixes rock flavorings w. jazz in a most sensitive, unaffected manner.

Infl: Jim Hall, Bill Evans, Sonny Rollins, Coltrane. TV: film of Montreux JF. Fest: Montreux w. Hamilton, '71; Antibes w. Gil Evans; NJF-NY; Montreux w. Barbieri, '74. Won DB Critics poll, TDWR, '75. Comp: *Timeless; Ralph's Piano Waltz; Remembering; Love Song*. LPs: *Timeless*; w. De Johnette, Dave Holland,

Gateway (ECM); w. Barbieri (Fly. Dutch); Dreams (Col.); Cobham (Atl.).

ABNEY, JOHN DONALD (DON),* *piano*; b. Baltimore, Md., 3/10/23. Principal employment during '60s in Universal Studios w. Stanley Wilson. On the road w. own trio, '69-71. Joined Pearl Bailey in L. Bellson's band for her TV series in '71, then went on tour, incl. Middle East and London, '73, remaining with her until '74. Conducted for Rosemary Clooney in Lake Tahoe, Cal., '70. Joined Jack Jones, '75.

LP: w. Benny Carter, *Additions to Further Definitions* (Imp.).

ABRAMS, MUHAL RICHARD, *piano, composer, leader;* also *clarinet, cello*; b. Chicago, Ill., 9/19/30. Studying piano from age 17. Four yrs. at Chicago Musical Coll.; then self-taught. Began playing professionally in '48. Wrote for King Fleming band, '50. First pianist w. MJT+3, '55, also arranging and composing for group. Formed big band, the Experimental Band, in Chicago '61. Members incl. Eddie Harris, Victor Sproles. In '65 he founded the AACM, the Association for the Advancement of Creative Music which, besides enjoying an independent existence, gave rise to the Art Ensemble of Chicago. In addition to serving as director of the AACM, Abrams has been active as a pianist on the Chicago scene for over two decades, often accompanying visiting soloists who traveled there for club work without their own rhythm sections. Early infl: Nat Cole; William E. Jackson, King Fleming, Art Tatum, James P. Johnson. "Only Cecil Taylor and Don Pullen," wrote Ray Townley, "each in their own distinctive way, approximates his sense of line structure and use of space. But Abrams also is deeply rooted in the Harlem stride school. Traces of Willie "The Lion" Smith, James P. Johnson, and later stylists such as Art Tatum and the incomparable Bud Powell can be gleaned from his playing."

Abrams explains: "My playing was instinctively governed by rhythm even before I left school but I couldn't see it yet. After I got away from the classroom routine my playing began to gain something of its own personality."

He has long been an "elder statesman" and "guru" to Chicago's modern musicians. Joseph Jarman said, "Until I had the first meeting with Richard Abrams, I was 'like all the rest' of the 'hip' ghetto niggers; I was cool, I took dope, I smoked pot, etc. I did not care for the life that I had been given. In having the chance to work in the Experimental Band with Richard and the other musicians there, I found the first something with meaning/reason for doing . . ."

Won DB Critics poll as pianist, TDWR, '74. Comp: *Ballad For New Souls; March of the Transients; The Bird Song; No Land's Man.* LPs: solo (Why Not); duo, *Sight Song* (Black Saint); *Levels and Degrees of Light; Things to Come From Those Now Gone; Young in Heart, Wise in Time* (Del.); *Creative Construction Company* (Muse); w. Art Ensemble of Chicago, *Fanfare For the Warriors* (Atl.); w. A. Braxton, *Three Compositions*; w. J. Jarman, *As If It Were the Seasons* (Del.); w. MJT+3 (Argo); w. Marion Brown, *Sweet Flying Earth* (Imp.); w. E. Harris, *Excursions; Eddie Harris Sings the Blues* (Atl.).

ADAMS, GEORGE RUFUS, *tenor sax*; also *flute, bass clarinet*; b. Covington, Ga., 4/29/40. Piano at 11; alto sax in junior high for a yr., then tenor sax. Stud. at David T. Howard HS, Atlanta; pl. w. David Hudson HS Band. Won a scholarship to Clark Coll. where he stud. w. Wayman Carver whom he says was a "guide to taste and style." A Music major and Education minor, he was asst. band dir. during last semester. Pl. bassoon in orch. Began pl. on local clubs at 16 in Lathonia, Ga. Blues experience w. house band pl. before shows of Jimmy Red, Howlin' Wolf, Elmo James, Lightnin' Hopkins. Pl. behind Sam Cooke, Hank Ballard in Atlanta a few yrs. later. Moved to Ohio '63, traveling w. organ gps. such as Eddie Baccus; Bill Doggett; Hank Marr. To NYC spring '68, working w. the Flamingoes; Roy Haynes Hip Ensemble; Gil Evans; Art Blakey. From '73 w. Charles Mingus. Infl: Charlie Parker, Coltrane, Ben Webster. TV: Euro. w. Mingus; *Like It Is* w. Leon Thomas; educ. TV w. Haynes. Fest: NJF-NY w. Haynes, '72; Mingus, '73; Perugia; Umbria; Newport fall tour of Europe w. Mingus, '75. Comp: *Full Moon; Flowers For a Lady.* Adams says he got his "roots from church music and r&b from south side of Chicago." LPs: *George Adams and Jazz Encounters; Suite For Swingers* (Horo); w. Mingus, *Changes I; Changes II; Mingus Moves* (Atl.); w. Haynes, *Senyah* (Main.), w. Evans, *There Comes a Time* (RCA).

ADAMS, PARK (PEPPER),* *baritone sax*; b. Highland Park, Mich., 10/8/30. One of the many, fine, young musicians who peopled the Detroit jazz scene in the early 1950s before he moved to NYC in '56. Played w. Maynard Ferguson, Benny Goodman and, most often, his old Detroit colleague Donald Byrd. A charter member of the Thad Jones-Mel Lewis orch. from Dec. 65, he has toured Europe and Japan with them; solo appearances in Europe and Canada w. local musicians. As part of David Amram's group he has also performed with the Philadelphia Orch., the Toronto and American Symphs., and the Rochester Phil, recording Amram's *Triple Concerto* with the latter for RCA.

Won DB Critics' Poll, TDWR '67; Playboy All-Stars' All Stars '75. LPs: *Ephemera* (Zim or Spotlite); *Encounter* (Prestige); *Mean What You Say* (Milestone); *Plays Charles Mingus* (Workshop); w. Amram, *No More Walls* (RCA Victor); Jones-Lewis (Solid State, Blue Note, Philadelphia Int., Horizon).

ADDERLEY, JULIAN EDWIN (CANNONBALL),* *alto and soprano sax, composer*; b. Tampa, Fla., 9/15/28. The Adderley Quintet maintained a stable personnel throughout the middle and late 1960s, with Nat Adderley, Joe Zawinul, Roy McCurdy and Vic Gaskin (later repl. by Walter Booker). Zawinul's comp. *Mercy Mercy Mercy* became the title tune for an album released in March 1967. The album and single both were among the most successful and best-selling jazz records of all time. During the next few years Adderley enjoyed unprecedented success, playing an areas normally hospitable only to rock performers.

In addition to playing alto sax in a style that showed the strong influence on him of younger musicians and the new developments in jazz, Adderley began doubling most effectively on soprano sax. He was also acclaimed for his role as an articulate spokesman for the music, and for his involvement in a variety of extracurricular activities.

He became a member of the committee of the National Endowment for the Arts; a member of the Black Academy of Arts and Letters; served on the board of governors of NARAS; was a member of Florida A & M University's Hall of Fame; and a member of the jazz advisory panel for the John F. Kennedy Center for the Performing Arts. He produced albums with other artists whose careers he helped foster, conducted seminars at many colleges, and served on the advisory board for Harvard University's Artist in Residence program (later posthumously renamed the Julian Cannonball Adderley Artist in Resident Program).

Keenly interested in electronic developments, Adderley incorporated some of these elements into his recordings, sometimes adding rock musicians to his personnel. On Zawinul's departure from the group (see ZAWINUL, JOSEF), George Duke joined the quintet, repl. by Hal Galper and then by Michael Wolff. The personnel remained otherwise unchanged.

While on tour in Indiana, Adderley suffered a massive stroke 7/13/75. He was taken to a hospital in Gary, Ind., where he died 8/8/75.

An album entitled *Big Man*, based on the legend of John Henry, for which all the music was composed by the Adderley brothers with Joe Williams in the title role, was released two months after Cannonball's death. He considered it one of the major achievements of his career and had hoped to see it presented as a Broadway musical or television special.

Julian Adderley's compositions included *Pretty Paul; The Steam Drill; Marabi; Sticks; Sack O' Woe; Introduction to a Samba; Domination; Sermonette; Primativo; Savior* (with lyrics by his wife, Olga James Adderley); *Them Dirty Blues*; and a three part work entitled *Suite Cannon*, comprising *The King & I; Time In;* and *For Melvin Lastie.*

Adderley as an individual and the quintet as a group won innumerable polls, starting with "new star" awards in 1956 and '59.

Motion pictures: *Play Misty For Me; Soul to Soul; Save The Children.* Television: Adderley served as host for 13 weeks in 1972 on a series entitled *90 Minutes.* He played very little on these programs, confining his role mainly to interviews with guests from all walks of life. He had an acting role in one sequence of *Kung Fu.* Playing apps. on *David Frost Show; Tonight; Nancy Wilson Show; Playboy After Dark* etc.

Festivals: Newport, Monterey, Montreux, Cannes, Pori, Hampton; Alaska Festival of Music, June 1975. In the fall of 1972 the Adderley Quintet played concerts in Budapest and Belgrade, as well as in many Western European cities, as part of the "Newport Jazz Festival in Europe" package show.

Publications: *Play Saxophone Like Cannonball Adderley*, Robbins Music Corp.

LPs: Adderley was under contract to Capitol from 1963-73, then signed with Fantasy. In addition to recording with his own group as an instrumental unit, he joined with many singers and instrumentalists, among them Nancy Wilson, Lou Rawls, Wes Montgomery, Eddie Vinson, Sergio Mendes, all of whom are heard in the anthological album *Cannonball Adderley and Friends* (Cap.); *Best of; Black Messiah; Country Preacher; Happy People; Mercy Mercy Mercy; The Price You Got To Pay To Be Free; Soul of the Bible; Soul Zodiac; Walk Tall/Quiet Nights* (Capitol). *Inside Straight; Love, Sex & The Zodiac; Pyramid; Phoenix; Big Man* (Fantasy); *Adderley & Eight Giants; Adderley In New Orleans* (Milestone); *Somethin' Else* w. Miles Davis (Blue Note). Earlier sessions w. Davis (Col.) and w. own groups (Mercury, Limelight, Trip). *Cannonball w. Coltrane* was made for Limelight and reissued on Archive of Folk and Jazz Music.

Other LPs as sideman w. Nat Adderley; J. Zawinul; Joe Williams; Gene Ammons; Dave Axelrod; Johnny Guitar Watson et al.

ADDERLEY, NATHANIEL (NAT),* *cornet, composer*; b. Tampa, Fla., 11/25/31. Continued to play in the quintet of his brother (see above) and therefore his career ran almost parallel, except when he recorded with his own units. After Cannonball's death the group became inactive. Adderley, himself, went to Germany for TV apps. in Jan. '76. On his own album, *You, Baby*, he used the Varitone attachment with success but usually did not seek help for the natural electricity of his charged attack. Comp: *Electric Eel; New Orleans; Halftime*, co-written w. Cannon; *59 Go and Pass; Contant 19.* LPs: *You, Baby; Calling Out Loud* (A&M); *Natural Soul; Scavenger* (Mile.); *Double Exposure* (Prest.); *Soul of the Bible* (Cap.); w. Charlie Byrd, *Top Hat* (Fant.); *Newport in New York, The Jam Sessions* (Cobble.); w. Cannonball (see above).

ADDERLEY, NATHANIEL JR. (NAT), *piano, composer*; also *acoustic guitar, flute, clarinet*; b. Quincy, Fla., 5/22/55. Son of Nat Adderley. Studied at Manhattan Sch. of Mus. for three yrs.; Juilliard for six; HS of Mus. & Art; Yale U. Received the Merit Scholarship for five yrs. Won Wycoff Male Chorus Competition, '71; placed first in the Piano Competition for the Bergen (NJ) Philharmonic Orch., '70. Pl. w. Bergen Phil. '70. Performed on WNYC radio for the Piano Teachers Congress of NYC, '70; app. on *Take a Giant Step*, CBS-TV, '71. Fest: MJF, '70. At age 11 had first comp., *I'm On My Way*, rec. by Cannonball Adderley. Other comps: *The Price You Gotta Pay to Be Free; Red, Black and Green.* LPs: w. Natural Essence, *In Search of Happiness* (Fant.);

w. C. Adderley (Cap.); movie score for *The Honey Baby* (RCA).

AIRTO (pr. Eye-*ear*-toe) (Airto Guimorva Moreira), *percussion, drums, singer*; b. Itaiopolis, S. Brazil, 8/5/41. Stud. acoustic guitar, piano 1948-50. As a child, was on radio program starting at age six, pl. in combos at 12. Went to Sao Paulo and Rio when he was 16; spent three years playing cabarets all over Brazil. After working with the Sambalanco Trio, formed his own group at 22 feat. Hermeto Pascoal. With the latter, he later assembled the Quarteto Novo. Moving to Los Angeles, he stud. w. Moacir Santos 1968-9, then went to New York. Came to prominence through records with Miles Davis 1970. Played his first official U.S. job with Lee Morgan in Brooklyn Feb. 1971. From then until Nov. '74, living in New York, Airto became one of the busiest percussionists on the new music scene, in constant demand for records. Part of original Return to Forever w. C. Corea, '72. Among the dozens of leaders with whom he recorded and/or toured were Stan Getz, Cannonball Adderley, Gato Barbieri and additional recordings with Miles Davis. For a while worked with trio featuring Don Friedman, Reggie Workman. Own group's debut in April '73. Moving to Berkeley, Ca. with his wife, singer Flora Purim (q.v.), he recorded with her and made albums under his own name.

Airto names among his early influences musicians of many backgrounds: Gil Evans, Bill Evans, Ray Charles, Miles Davis, Antonio Carlos Jobim, Pascoal, Wes Montgomery, John Coltrane, Ravi Shankar. Made movie or TV sound tracks with Gary McFarland, Quincy Jones, Michel Legrand, Herbie Hancock, Oliver Nelson et al.

LPs: *Natural Feelings; Seeds On The Ground* (Buddah); *Free; Fingers* (CTI), *Virgin Land* (Salvation); w. M. Davis, *at Fillmore East; Live-Evil* (Col.); w. Corea, *Return to Forever* (ECM); *Light As a Feather* (Poly.); w. Getz (Col.); w. Cannonball Adderley (Cap.)

AKIYOSHI, TOSHIKO,* *composer, piano*; b. Dairen, Manchuria, 12/12/29. To U.S. 1956; studied and worked in Boston; played and wrote in NYC during '60s; frequent return visits to Japan with her then husband, Charles Mariano (since divorced). Own radio program in NYC 1967-8. Debut as composer-conductor, playing solo and with trio and big band at Town Hall, Oct. '67. Clubs in Greenwich Village, '67-71. Own quartet at Expo 70 in Japan, 1970. Carnegie Hall concert and Japanese tour with quartet featuring husband Lew Tabackin, 1971. In 1972 she and Tabackin moved to Los Angeles, where they formed a 16 piece band, also gigging locally with a quartet. Appeared as piano soloist in 1973 MJF. An LP she rec. in Hollywood w. Tabackin was highly acclaimed in Japan, where it won the Swing Journal Silver Award in '74.

Ms. Akiyoshi, while less active as pianist in recent years, was greatly respected for her original compositions and arrangements. Among them are *Sumie; Long Yellow Road; Henpecked Old Man; American Ballad; Memory.*

Publ: *Originals by Toshiko Akiyoshi*, Berklee College of Music, Boston. LPs: Toshiko Akiyoshi-L. Tabackin big band, *Kogun* (RCA Japan); *Top of the Gate* (Takt, Japan).

ALBAM, EMMANUEL (MANNY),* *composer*; b. Samana, Dominican Republic, 6/24/22. Continued as an active arranger on the New York scene for artists such as Carmen McRae, Buddy Rich, Stan Getz, Gerry Mulligan, Clark Terry, Dick Hyman and Chuck Mangione. Also served as musical director for Solid State Records. Participated in many college clinics and festivals as clinician and adjudicator. Organized arranger's workshops at Eastman School; also teaches at Glassboro St. Coll.; and is co-ordinator for jazz in the prison system for New York state.

TV: arranger-composer for *Around The World Of Mike Todd; Four Clowns*; for NET, *Glory Trail; Artists USA; Chicago Picasso.* Comps. incl. *The Horns (And Voices) Of A Dilemma* for Chorus, Wind Ensemble and Jazz Band; *Afro-Dizzyac* for Dizzy Gillespie; *Country Man* for Dakota Staton; arr. *Suite For Jazz Piano and Orchestra* (a Billy Taylor comp.) for Utah Symph.

LPs: *Soul Of The City; Brass On Fire* (Solid State), *Jazz Goes To The Movies* (Impulse); LPs w. Coleman Hawkins (Impulse); O'Donnel Levy (Groove Merchant).

ALBANY, JOE (Joseph Albani),* *piano*; b. Atlantic City, N.J., 1/24/24. Sisters are classical pianist, operatic soprano. Worked in 1940s w. Benny Carter, Ch. Parker, Geo. Auld, Lester Young; free-lanced in LA. For the next 25 years Albany became a legend, in and out of obscurity. He was heard on one album with Warne Marsh on Riverside in 1957; was in SF in '59; w. Ch. Mingus in NY '63; Russ Morgan in LV '64. In 1971 some tapes he had sent to English critic Mark Gardner were released in Britain. After making one album for US release, Albany left for Europe Dec. '72, rec. an LP in Copenhagen '73 and a duo set with bassist Niels Pedersen in '74. Returned briefly to US in summer of '74 and again in spring of '75 to settle in LA again.

LPs: *Proto-Bopper* (Revelation); *Birdtown Birds; Two's Company* (Steeple).

ALDEBERT, LOUIS J., *singer, piano, composer*; b. Ismailia, Egypt, 6/8/31. Stud. in Port Said, '43; later in Paris, where he pl. in jazz clubs w. D. Byas, '55; S. Grappelli, '57; and many others during next decade. As singer, was member of the Blue Stars, '55-6, and Double Six of Paris, '60-1, '63-5. With this group he toured Canada in '60 and visited US in '63. The Double Six broke up in '65; Aldebert and his wife, singer Monique Aldebert left in '67 for LV, where they sang for a year in a vocal group in the Casino de Paris show. In Feb. '69 they moved to LA, where they app. at numerous clubs and occasionally gave coll. concerts, leading a duo or a quartet, enlarging in late '74 to a sextet.

Aldebert and his wife (q.v.) are the composers of many charming songs, among them *Life's A Mockingbird; Do It With A Smile*; they have also arranged vocal versions of jazz instrumentals such as Bill Evans' *The Dolphin* and

D. Reinhardt's *Nuages*. Fests: Antibes, Lugano, Montreal, San Remo.

LPs: w. Double Six of Paris, *Swingin' & Singin'*; *Sing Ray Charles*; w. M. Aldebert, arr. by M. Legrand (Philips); others on European labels.

ALDEBERT, MONIQUE (Monique Dozo), *singer*; b. Monaco, 5/5/31. Mus. stud. in Monte Carlo and Paris. Pro. debut in '47 w. Bernard Peiffer. Many club engagements in Paris w. Django Reinhardt, Roger Guérin, Bobby Jaspar, Don Byas; concert w. Bill Coleman, '66. Sang w. Double Six of Paris, early '60s. For many years she was active in studio work, making numerous commercials, movies, TV, radio shows. Her career in LV and LA ran parallel with that of her husband, Louis Aldebert (q.v.). She has also recorded on her own for Philips with arrs. by M. Legrand, and took part in André Hodeir's LP of *Anna Livia Plurabelle* on Epic. Sang in English version of movie *Umbrellas of Cherbourg*. Sound track for L. Schifrin's music, film *Kelly's Heroes*, '70.

An academically trained musician, she has a well developed jazz feeling and light, attractive timbre, singing unison or duo in both English and French, with her husband.

LPs: w. Double Six of Paris, *Swingin' & Singin'; Sing Ray Charles* (Philips); w. Q. Jones (Pathe-Marconi).

ALEXANDER, MONTGOMERY BERNARD (MONTY), *piano*; b. Kingston, Jamaica, 6/6/44. Studied privately, '50-9, w. three different teachers. TO US '62. Played in Miami where he was heard by Jilly Rizzo who hired him for his club, Jilly's in NYC. Continued to lead own trio except for work w. Milt Jackson-Ray Brown group in early '70s. Infl: Nat Cole, Oscar Peterson, Ahmad Jamal, Ray Brown, Milt Jackson, Sonny Rollins. Fest: Monterey; Concord; San Diego. Doug Ramsey characterized his playing as "a mix that is spiced with something more common to jazz horn players than to pianists, a rhythmic concept charged by the dance music of the Caribbean islands," and talked of his "piquantly hesitant placement of notes at precisely the correct strategic spots behind the beat."

LPs: *Rass; Here Comes the Sun; We've Only Just Begun* (BASF); *Alexander the Great; Spunky* (Pac. Jazz); *Zing* (RCA); *This is Monty Alexander; Taste of Freedom* (MGM); w. Milt Jackson, *That's the Way It Is* (Imp.).

ALEXANDER, ELMER (MOUSEY),* *drums*; b. Gary, Ind., 6/29/22. European tour w. Georgie Auld '60, So. America w. Benny Goodman '61; Goodman sextet '66-67, European concerts and Carnegie Hall w. Goodman '72. Active as jingle contractor in NYC '62-65; Sweden and Czechoslovakia w. Paul Anka '66. From '65 many apps. w. Al Cohn-Zoot Sims at Half Note; own trio at Plaza 9 '68-69; own quartet at Half Note '74. W. Clark Terry big band '69-72; other gigs in '72 w. Sonny Stitt, Lee Konitz, James Moody, Sy Oliver big band tour of Europe '73; Doc Severinsen on *Tonight* Show '73. In July suffered a heart attack, followed by a second one in August which bedded him for the remainder of that year. Resumed pl. in spring '74 w. Sims, Terry. App. at Dick Gibson's Colorado Jazz Party intermittently from '67. Odessa Jazz Party '71, '75; NJF '68. LPs: w. Gene Krupa, *Percussion King* (Verve), Clark Terry big band live at Carnegie Hall (Etoile); w. Lee Konitz, *Spirits* (Milestone); w. Goodman, *Live in Copenhagen* (London); *Colorado Jazz Party* (MPS/BASF).

ALI, RASHIED,* *drums*; b. Philadelphia, Pa. 7/1/35. Well known in avant garde circles in NYC from 1963. Rec. and pl. w. John Coltrane '65-7. In '68 toured in Europe with his own quartet, also pl. w. S. Rollins. Records and jobs w. Jackie McLean, Alice Coltrane, Bud Powell, '69. Concert w. own quartet, Carnegie Recital Hall, '70; various colleges and clubs, '71. In summer of '72, organizer of New York Jazz Musicians' Festival. Under a grant from National Endowment for the Arts, introduced his *New Directions In Jazz* suite.

Continued workshops, concepts and occasional lectures in mid-70s, incl. memorial concert for Coltrane at New York Jazz Museum. Opened restaurant-club, Studio 77/Ali's Alley w. own group in residence, '74.

TV: *Free Time; Jazz Set; Soul; Positively Black*. Festivals: NJF, '71-2; New York Jazz Musicians' Festival, '72. LPs w. Coltrane: *Expressions, Interstellar Space, Concert in Japan* (Impulse); *Duo Exchange, Rashied Ali Quintet, New Directions in Modern Music* (Survival).

Addr: Studio 77/Ali's Alley, 77 Greene St., New York, N.Y. 10012.

ALKE, BJORN, *bass, composer*; also *piano, violin*; b. Sundsvall, Sweden, 4/15/38. Stud. w. private violin teacher for four yrs.; three yrs. at music high school in Stockholm. Pl. w. Lars Gullin, Bernt Rosengren, Eje Thelin and other prominent Swedish jazzmen. Fests: Antibes w. Thelin, '63; Pori; Kongsberg, '75; several in Sweden, '64-75. Won *Orkester Journalen* poll on bass, '65. Comp: *Hommage à Bud; Gun; Bossa Noja; Coma.* Infl: Tatum, Miles Davis, Paul Chambers, Gil Evans, Bud Powell, but says that "Lars Gullin, Powell and Dexter Gordon are the ones I have learnt most from, concerning music and way of living." LPs: *Jazz Sverige*; w. Gullin, *Portrait of My Pals* (SSX); w. Rosengren, *Notes From Underground.*

ALLAN, JAN, *trumpet*; also *piano*; b. Falun, Sweden, 11/7/34. Father violinist and bassist during '20s and '30s. Stud. piano privately from six years old, switching to trumpet later. Pro. engagements w. Lars Gullin-Rolf Billberg, '54-55; Carl-Henrik Norin, '55-7; Allan-Billberg quintet '60-3; Jan Allen orch., '63-8; Harry Arnold; The Swedish Radio Jazz Group, '68-75. Won Golden Record from *Orkester Journalen*, for *Ceramics*, best jazz recording, '70. Many fest. apps. throughout Europe, as well TV in Germany, Denmark, Sweden etc. Infls: Fats Navarro, Miles Davis, Clifford Brown, Coltrane et al. Allan has concurrent career as Elementary Particle Physicist at Stockholm U.

LPs: *Jan Allan* '70 (MCA); *Swedish Radio Jazz Group* (SR); others w. Gullin; own quartet (Sonet); J. Johansson-G. Riedel; Monica Zetterlund (SR); *Greetings and*

Salutations, Swedish Radio Jazz Group w. Thad Jones (Four Leaf Clover).

ALLEN, HENRY JR. (RED),* *trumpet, singer*; b. Algiers, La., 1/7/08. Prominent in '30s w. Luis Russell, Fletcher Henderson, Lucky Millinder, Louis Armstrong; in '40s with own sextet, and in '50s leading various groups, also working as soloist and touring Europe as sideman w. K. Ory in '59. During '60s he visited England several times, freelanced around NY, toured Britain again in Feb. '67, but by then was seriously ill and died in NYC, 4/17/67. Allen's searing, heated style, first noted by critics during L. Armstrong's heyday, established him as possibly the most important new trumpet artist after Armstrong. LPs: *Memorial Album* (Prest.); French RCA.

ALLEN, STEVE,* *songwriter, piano, vibes, leader*; b. New York City, 12/26/21. Presented many jazz artists on his TV shows in the '50s and '60s. Produced series of 26 half hour TV programs, *Jazz Scene USA*, each feat. a well known combo or singer, '61-2. Series had limited exposure in US but was shown extensively overseas. In later years, though busy with many other projects, incl. a series of books, Allen maintained occasional contact with jazz, frequently using Terry Gibbs as leader of groups for night clubs and concerts. Wrote jazz-oriented score for MGM film, *A Man Called Dagger*. LPs: An album of Allen's compositions was recorded by Chet Baker on Beverly Hills Records.

ALLISON, MOSE JOHN JR.,* *piano, singer, composer*; b. Tippo, Miss., 11/11/27. A solo performer for many years, Allison continued to work in a trio context, singing and playing in night clubs and at concerts. As Ben Sidran wrote, "He is one of the few performing pros who has both survived the fickle moods of the record buying public and maintained his following through live gigs at small clubs." Comps: *Parchman Farm; Young Man; Everybody Cryin' Mercy; Look What You Made Me Do; I Don't Worry About a Thing; Powerhouse; Hello There Universe*.

LPs: Atlantic; earlier sessions, mainly as pianist, on Prestige.

ALLYN, DAVID,* *singer*; b. Hartford, Conn., 7/19/23. Sang w. the Boyd Raeburn band of the mid-1940s and rec. some much admired ballads for Discovery w. Johnny Richards. In '58 rec. LP of Jerome Kern songs w. Johnny Mandel arrs. for World Pac. From that time to late '67 he app. at clubs, etc. in LA, SF, LV and NYC incl. the Crescendo w. S. Kenton '60; Basin St. East and Lake Tahoe w. C. Basie, '64. Also worked Playboy Club circuit, '60-4. App. at Playboy JF in Chi., '59. TV: *The World of Lenny Bruce*, '59; *Tonight Show*, '63; *Today Show*; Merv Griffin; Mike Douglas, '67. Comps: *She Is My Star; Kim (was); A Swing For Joey; Pleasant Dreams*. From '68 Allyn has done rehabilitation counseling for drug addicts at Phoenix House and Halfway House in NYC; Addiction Services in Hartford; and, in the '70s for the VA in LA. He ret. to rec., '75 acc. only by Barry Harris in an LP, *Don't Look Back* (Xanadu).

ALMEIDA, LAURINDO,* *guitar, composer*; b. Sao Paolo, Brazil, 9/2/17. Primarily a concert guitarist, Almeida from the late 1960s appeared in recitals w. his wife, soprano Deltra Eamon, and in many others alone and w. symphony orchs. In '74-5 he made jazz appearances with the L.A. Four: himself, Ray Brown, Shelly Manne, Bud Shank. He toured New Zealand, Australia and Mexico with this combo in '75.

Awards: DB movie poll winner for underscoring *The Old Man And The Sea*; won Oscar for scoring *The Magic Pear Tree*. Six time winner and 13 time nominee for NARAS (Grammy) awards in various classical, pop, jazz categories.

Movie and TV scores: *A Star Is Born; Goya; Death Takes A Holiday*; John Steinbeck's *Flight* etc. Some underscoring for *Viva Zapata; On A Clear Day; The Godfather; Lost Horizon* etc.

Publs: *Guitar Tutor In Three Courses* (Criterion Music, 6124 Selma Ave., Hollywood, CA 90028); *Contemporary Moods for Guitar* (Robbins Music Corp., 1775 Broadway, NYC 10019); *Popular Brazilian Music*, arrs. for two guitars and rhythm (Gwyn Publishing Co., Box 5900, Sherman Oaks, CA 91413); *Laurindo Almeida Guitar Method*, (Gwyn Publishing).

LPs: Many classical and bossa nova albums on Capitol; Almeida-Ray Brown duo (Century City Records); LA Four (Concord); solo albums, and duos with Deltra Eamon (Orion, P.O. Box 24332, Los Angeles, CA 90024).

Complete catalogue of pieces arr. or transcribed for solo guitar publ: (Brazilliance Music, 4101 Witzel Dr., Sherman Oaks, CA 91423).

ALMOND, JOHN, *saxophones, flute, keyboards, vibes*; b. Enfield, Middlesex, England, 7/20/46. Father a drummer; private lessons on saxophone; while in high school began professional career. Working with Nite Sounds, Wally Johnson band, also pl. flute, clarinet. Freelanced with own combo; first records during year w. Tony Knight's Chess Men. Two years w. Zoot Money, 18 months w. Alan Price Set, which became Paul Williams Set; joined John Mayall June '69 and played with him that year at NJF.

Leaving Mayall, Almond formed his own group, Mark-Almond, with guitarist Jon Mark. Together they enjoyed extensive acceptance in pop and folk circles. After breakup of Mark-Almond group, Almond toured in Billy Joel's band in '75. A superior jazzman on all instruments, Almond has listened attentively to Eddie Lockjaw Davis, Y. Lateef, R.R. Kirk. Own jazz LP: *Hollywood Blues*, by Johnny Almond Music Machine (Deram-London). LPs with J. Mayall on Polydor; Mark-Almond LPs on Blue Thumb. In '75 Mark-Almond LPs on Columbia.

ALTSCHUL, BARRY, *drums*; b. Bronx, NYC, 1/6/43. Stud. w. Charlie Persip, Sam Ulano, Lee Konitz. Frequent app. w. Paul Bley trio, 1964-70; Jazz Composers' Guild Orch., '64-8; Carmell Jones-Leo Wright in Europe, '68; Sonny Criss, Hampton Hawes, Cal., '69;

Tony Scott, NYC, '69; Chick Corea, '70-2 in US and Europe; also domestic and foreign jobs w. Anthony Braxton; Sam Rivers.

Spent much time in Europe from late '60s, working with David Holland, John Surman, Babs Gonzales, Steve Lacy, Jimmy Owens, Karl Berger, J.R. Monterose, Johnny Griffin, Gato Barbieri, Slide Hampton, and own group. US appearances with Andrew Hill, David Liebman, Mike Nock, Paul Winter, Roswell Rudd, Gary Peacock, Robin Kenyatta.

In '75 teaching and writing a conceptual study book for drums.

An eclectic and adaptable performer, Altschul has appeared on LPs w. Rivers (Impulse); Braxton; Rudd; Andrew Hill (Arista); Buddy Guy (Vanguard); Corea (Blue Note, ECM); Bley (Milestone, ESP, BYG, Polydor, Fontana, Debut); Liebman (ECM); etc.

ALTSCHUL, MIKE, *woodwinds*; b. Los Angeles, Ca., 12/27/45. Educ: S. Park El. Sch., '51-7; Bret Harte Jr. High, '57-60; Washington High, '60-3; CSULA, '63-7. Toured w. S. Kenton, '67-9. During '69 he pl. w. Don Ellis briefly, then w. Gerald Wilson, with whom he was still working in the mid-'70s, as well as Duke Pearson and Frank Zappa '71-5. Altschul has also pl. w. B. Bryant, L. Bellson, Willie Bobo, Nat Adderley, C. Mangione, Bill Holman, T. Gibbs and Carole King. Has worked in studio orchs. on TV: *Sonny & Cher Show; Bill Cosby Show; Dinah Shore Show* and others. Fests: Monterey w. Bryant and Adderley, '69; Montreux, w. King, '73; Concord, w. Wilson, '75.

LPs: Kenton (Cap.); *Don Ellis Goes Underground* (Col.); *Hot Rats; Grand Wazoo* w. Zappa (Bizarre); *Fantasy; Music; Rhymes & Reasons*, w. King (Ode).

ALVIS, HAYES,* *bass, tuba*; b. Chicago, Ill. 6/1/07. Pl. w. E. Hines, D. Ellington, B. Carter, L. Armstrong, many small groups off and on, but was also active in interior decorating business; studied dentistry and held a pilot's license. Among his last apps. were European tours w. J. McShann, '70 and Tiny Grimes, '71. Alvis died 12/30/72 in NYC.

AMBROSE, BERT,* *leader*; b. London, England, 1897. Heyday in swing era as leader of band considered by many to be Britain's best big band. From 1966 Ambrose devoted his time to managing the singer Kathy Kirby. He collapsed in a TV studio and died 6/12/71 in Leeds Infirmary.

AMBROSETTI, FLAVIO,* *alto, soprano saxes, composer*; b. Lugano, Switz., 10/8/19. Early exp. in Swiss combos. Pl. in Italy, France. Orig. inspiration C. Hawkins, then C. Parker. In '60s and '70s working in Europe mostly w. own quintet feat. his son Franco, pianist George Gruntz, drummer Daniel Humair and a variety of bassists.

This was nucleus for The Band, an orch. of Americans and Europeans which toured Europe in '72. TV: Italy, Switz., Yugoslavia, Belgium, France, Holland; US at Monterey Fest. '67. Other fests: Prague, '66; Pori, '67; Ljubljana, '70; Bologna, '73. Grad. w. engineering degree from Politecnicum, Zurich '45, he has been general manager of family wheel co. for more than 25 yrs. Comp: *Gentiliano Serenade; Looking Forward; Our Suite Dig; Age of Prominence; El Comendador (Nebulosa).* LPs: (Dire); Ljubljana Jazz Fest. (Helidon); *The Band-Alpine Power Plant* (MPS).

AMBROSETTI, FRANCO,* *trumpet, fluegelhorn, composer*; also *piano, drums*; b. Lugano, Switzerland, 12/10/41. Played w. father Flavio Ambrosetti's gp.; in Zurich w. own gp. in early-mid-'60s. Won first prize for trumpet at Vienna Int. Jazz Competition, '66. From that time continued working w. father's quintet and w. his own gp. incl. George Gruntz, Daniel Humair, Ron Mathewson. In '72, w. father, Gruntz and Humair, formed big band called The Band, touring in Europe and doing TV shows. The Band's MPS rec. won as best jazz rec. in Italy, '73. Fest: MJF w. father's gp., '67; other fests. in Italy, Switz., Austria, Yugo., France, Finland, '67-73. Comp: *Pistrophallobus; Blues for Ursula; Cameroon Talk; In Memory of Eric.*

Master's Degree in Economics from U. of Basle; works as manager of family co. which produces wheels for various vehicles in a large area of the European market. LPs: *Steppenwolf* (PDU); other quartet dates (Horo, Dire); co-leader, *The Band*; sideman on *From Sticksland With Love* (MPS-BASF).

AMMONS, EUGENE (GENE OR JUG),* *tenor saxophone*; b. Chicago, Ill., 4/14/25. His father was the pioneer boogie woogie pianist Albert Ammons. Gene played in the Billy Eckstine band at age 19, left him in '48 and worked w. W. Herman in '49. In the '50s he was often feat. in a two tenor combo w. S. Stitt. His career was interrupted by narcotics problems, culminating in a seven year prison sentence ending in '69, after which he resumed touring, backed by a rhythm section. His big sound and driving beat established him as one of the giants of modern tenor saxophone. Ammons became ill in the spring of '74, was hospitalized in Chicago with cancer in July, and died of pneumonia 7/23/74.

TV: *Just Jazz*, PBS, '71. LPs: More than 30 albums on Prestige, among them *Goodbye; Brasswind; And Friends at Montreux; Big Bad Jug; Chase* w. D. Gordon; *Soul Summit* w. Stitt; *Chicago Concert*, w. J. Moody; *My Way, Velvet Soul, Boss Tenor*; reissue, *Juganthology*, etc; also *Mingus and Friends* (Col.).

AMRAM, DAVID WERNER III,* *composer, French horn* also *Pakistani flute, piano, singer, guitar, bouzoukie, dumbeg*; b. Philadelphia, Pa., 11/17/30. This musical renaissance man was continually active as a classical composer, utilizing elements in his works, and as a player-writer mixing folk, classical and Middle Eastern elements into his essentially jazz-based performances. First composer-in-residence at NY Phil.; pl. w. Freddie Redd at Casey's, '66; conducted Houston Symph., pl. jazz concert in second half of program, '67; pl. Fillmore East w. Mingus, J. Steig, '68; Village Gate w. George Barrow, '69. In '70 Amram formed a quartet, incl. Pepper Adams, with which he pl. coll. circuit. Premiered his

Triple Concerto at Phil. Hall and also pl. w. Mary Lou Williams in her *Mass*, '71. Cond. Brooklyn Philharmonia, w. his quartet as part of orch., in free concerts for over 30,000 children in NYC; perf. *Triple Concerto* w. Phila. Symph., '72. Pl. at Five Spot, Village Vanguard, St. James Infirmary, concerts, etc., '74-5. Workshops at coll., high schools, parks on a world-wide basis. Amram strives to "bring the jazz experience to folk festivals and symphony concerts, where I end the concert with a jam session involving the audience, singing and make up lyrics and music on the spot to show that spontaneity is a natural blessing to all."

Amram's biography, *Vibrations*, pub. by Viking, '68, was later issued in paperback by Compass. Pl. in film, *Pull My Daisy*, for which he wrote title song with lyrics by Kerouac and Allen Ginsberg. Fests: Phila. Folk; Mariposa Folk; Kennedy Center; also concerts at Wolftrap Farm; South St. Seaport; Jazz on the River. Comps. *Triple Concerto for Woodwind, Brass, Jazz Quintet and Symphony; Bassoon Concerto; Horn Concerto; Violin Concerto; Trio for Tenor Sax, Horn and Bassoon*; Bi-Centennial piece for oboe, mezzo-soprano and orch., based on American Indian writings called *Trail of Beauty*, commissioned by Phila. Orch.; *Ballad For Red Allen; Tompkins Square Park Consciousness Expander; The Fabulous Fifties; Horn and Hardart Succotash Blues*. His classical works are publ. by C.F. Peters, 373 Park Ave. South, New York, N.Y. 10010. LPs: *No More Walls; Subway Night; Triple Concerto* (RCA); w. Mary Lou Williams (Mary); cond. for Hannibal Marvin Peterson, *Children of the Fire* (Sunrise).

ANDERS, JORGE, *saxophones, clarinet, composer*; b. Lanus, Buenos Aires, Argentina, 4/18/39. Father was first violinist in Belgian symph. orch. Clarinet in '55; tenor sax in '60. Pl. trad. jazz w. Argentine jazz octet, '61. In '63 pl. at international jazz fest. w. B. Shank. Has led own quartet and orch., feat. orig. comps. such as *Blackman; El Justiciero; La Vuelta Del Elefanton* (*Big Elephant's Comeback*); *El Marques*. Anders plays in a modern, driving style and has reached a definite sound that identifies his playing.

ANDERSEN, ARILD, *bass*; b. Oslo, Norway, 10/27/45. Priv. stud. w. George Russell. First pro. engagement w. Jan Garbarek quartet, '67-73; also acc. singer Karin Krog from '67. Toured Africa, France s. S. Getz, '70; USA, '74. Worked in U.S. w. Sam Rivers, Paul Bley, '73-4. Leading own group '74- . Fests: Berlin Jazztage, '68; Montreux, '68, 72; Antibes, '70; many other European fests. incl. Cascais '75. Was voted Musician of the Year in Norway, '69. Infls: Bley, Jon Christensen, Garbarek.

LPs: *Afric Pepperbird; Sart; Triptykon; Clouds In My Head* (ECM); *There Is No Energy Crisis* (Imp.); w. R. Rudd, *Flexible Flyer* (Arista); w. D. Cherry, *Eternal Rhythm* (MPS); *Joy* (Sonet); *Listen to the Silence* (Concept).

ANDERSON, WILLIAM ALONZO (CAT),* *trumpet, fluegelhorn*; b. Greenville, S.C., 9/12/16. The veteran high note specialist, first prominent with Duke Ellington's orchestra from 1944, spent most of the 1960s back in the band after a two-year absence (1959-61). Leaving for the last time in Jan. 1971, he made his home in the San Fernando Valley and became active in Hollywood studios. TV: *Duke Ellington: We Love You Madly*; Julie Andrews, Merv Griffin shows. Movies: *Lady Sings The Blues* etc. Many records; occasional gigs with own groups, playing Ellington alumni concerts, and pl. w. Bill Berry band. Festivals: Newport, Monterey, Concord. Toured as first trumpet, also asst. conductor and later conductor, of band for *Ice Capades* show, 1974-5. LPs for French labels with own gps. and w. Claude Bolling; many others w. Ellington, Johnny Hodges et al (q.v.) w. L. Bellson (Pablo); w. B. Berry (Beez); *Newport in New York, The Jam Sessions* (Cobble.).

Publ: *Cat Anderson Trumpet Method* (Gwyn Publ. Co., P.O. Box 5900, Sherman Oaks, Calif. 91413).

ANDERSON, JOHN JR.,* *trumpet, composer*; b. Birmingham, Ala., 1/31/21. Anderson, who pl. during the '40s and '50s w. Benny Carter, Earl Bostic, and who in '59-60 was a trumpeter and arranger for C. Basie, later toured w. Ray Charles and the Ike and Tina Turner Revue. He rec. an album with his big band in '70 for the Tangerine label. On 8/17/74, in Birmingham, he suffered a stroke and died the following day.

ANDRE, WAYNE, *trombone*; also *baritone horn*; b. Manchester, Conn., 11/17/31. Stud. at Hartt School of Music, '48-9; Berklee, '49-50, Manhattan School of Music, '58-61, and several private teachers. Pl. w. Charlie Spivak orch., '50; Sauter-Finegan, '55; W. Herman, '56. In '56-7, worked w. Kai Winding septet, for which he composed *Nutcracker* and arr. *The Preacher*. With Gerry Mulligan Concert Jazz Band, '60.

In '61-5, Andre was a member of a CBS staff orch., NYC. Side ventures incl. a USSR tour w. B. Goodman, '62, Thad Jones-Mel Lewis orch., '66, Clark Terry big band, '67. NJF-NY '73 w. M. Legrand; G. Mulligan.

A dependable section man and occasional soloist, Andre was heard in albums w. Winding on Columbia and A & M, as well as w. Liza Minelli, soloing on *More Than You Know* on her album *Liza With a Z*. Comp. *Ayo* for Bill Watrous LP, '74.

ARCHEY, JAMES (JIMMY),* *trombone*; b. Norfolk, Va., 10/12/02. The veteran of many names bands (King Oliver, Luis Russell, Benny Carter) died in Amityville, L.I., N.Y., 11/16/67 after a long illness. His last major job was a European tour w. the NO All Stars, Feb. '66.

ARMSTRONG, LILIAN HARDIN (LIL),* *piano, singer, composer*; b. Memphis, Tenn., 2/3/1902 (Her birth date was variously given from 1898 to 1903, but 1902 was confirmed by Mrs. Armstrong). Was married to Louis Armstrong from 1924, when they were both playing in King Oliver's band; they were separated in the early '30s. She played on and wrote music for many of Armstrong's Hot Five and Hot Seven records. In later years stud. extensively in Chicago and N.Y., led various bands and combos. She was still living in Chicago, in the house she and Armstrong had bought in 1927, and was playing at a *Tribute to Louis Armstrong* concert at Chicago's Civic Center Plaza, when she collapsed and died of a heart attack, 7/27/71.

ARMSTRONG, DANIEL LOUIS (SATCHMO or POPS),* *trumpet, singer, leader*; b. New Orleans, La., 7/4/00. In 1966, Armstrong and his group still were active on a full time basis, pl. a summer season that year at Jones Beach Marine Theatre. Armstrong was ill for two months in the spring of '67 but shortly afterward resumed his schedule, pl. concerts in Dublin, Antibes, St. Tropez and Majorca. Early in '68, after a few American engagements, Armstrong and his All Stars pl. at the San Remo Festival. In June they appeared at the New Orleans JF, then immediately went back to Britain. After a series of successful concerts, the band returned home. During that year Armstrong was represented on record with one of his popular hits, *What A Wonderful World.* In Sept. he was taken seriously ill and was confined to Beth Israel hospital in NYC. Released in Jan. '69, he soon became ill again, re-entering the hospital in February for two months. By June, when his perennial manager, Joe Glaser, died, Armstrong was out of the hospital and attended the funeral. His public appearances for the rest of the year were limited mostly to guest shots. During '69 the film *Hello Dolly!* was released, featuring Armstrong in a scene w. Barbra Streisand.

Although under doctors' orders not to play trumpet, in '70 Armstrong made numerous TV apps. as singer, and recorded two vocal albums, *Louis and His Friends* and a country/western set. He talked and sang at a special 70th birthday concert held at the Shrine Auditirium in LA, and the following week app. in a *Salute to Satch* tribute at NJF. By Sept. he was well enough to resume playing. He app. in Las Vegas, co-starring in a show w. Pearl Bailey. In October, he flew to London to sing and play at a benefit concert.

During early '71 he continued appearing occasionally, but after playing for two weeks at the Empire Room of the Waldorf-Astoria, he suffered a heart attack and returned to the hospital March 15. On May 6 he was allowed to go home, but his health was precarious, and early in the morning of 7/6/71 he died in his sleep at his home in Corona, Long Island.

Armstrong's role as the most important improvising musician in the 70 year history of jazz was not to be forgotten or neglected. Immediately after his death, memorial albums began appearing and tributes were given to him all over the world, and his widow, Mrs. Lucille Armstrong, found herself in a position of roving ambassador, making many apps. in the U.S. and overseas as a representative of jazz, of Satchmo, and of everything he stood for. She was chairperson of the Louis Armstrong Arts and Cultural Memorial Organization; in '74 she traveled through eastern Europe under the auspices of the State Dept., showing films of Armstrong and answering questions from fans. She served as a consultant on TV films, articles, books etc., dealing w. Louis' history and was present at the unveiling, in the summer of '74, of a bust of her late husband, in the Jardins de Cimiez, Nice, site of the Nice JF.

Posthumous Honors: On the 73rd anniversary of Armstrong's birth, the name of Singer Bowl in Queens, N.Y., was changed to Louis Armstrong Memorial Stadium. To celebrate the occasion, a benefit concert was held, proceeds of which went to charities selected by Mrs. Armstrong.

In June-July '75, the New York Jazz Repertory Orchestra's concert program dedicated to Armstrong's music toured the Soviet Union as part of a cultural exchange between the U.S. and USSR. Dick Hyman, pianist and musical director, transcribed many of Armstrong's original solos and arr. them for the trumpet section.

A carefully documented book entitled *Louis: The Louis Armstrong Story*, by Max Jones and John Chilton, was published late in '71 by Little, Brown & Co. It includes many reproductions of Armstrong's long typewritten letters to friends, as well as photographs, a chronology (from which much of the above information was culled) and a list of Armstrong's film appearances.

The availability of Armstrong's records has fluctuated greatly, but late in 1975 the following were still listed in the U.S. catalogues: *Hello Dolly!; At The Crescendo* (MCA); *Best Of; Definitive Album; Louis Armstrong; w. Dukes of Dixieland* (Audiofidelity); *Disney Songs the Satchmo Way* (Buena); *I Will Wait For You* (Bruns.); *Louis "Satchmo" Armstrong* (Archive of Folk & Jazz); *Mame* (Pickwick); *Verve's Best Choice* (Verve); *What A Wonderful World* (ABC); *w. His Friends* (Amsterdam); *July 4, 1900/July 6, 1971* (RCA); *The Genius of Louis Armstrong* (Col.).

ARNET, JAN, *bass*; b. Prague, Czechoslovakia, 1934. Stud. piano, violin, trombone, 1945-52; bass, theory, '57-60. Between 1958 and '65 rec. on more than 100 LPs w. Zdenek Bartak big band; Karel Vlach band; SH Quintet (winner of Czech jazz critics' poll, '63-4); Reduta Quintet, '65 in Austria, West Germany, Egypt. After working w. Leo Wright, Booker Ervin, Nathan Davis et al. in West Germany and France, came to U.S. in 1966, working as producer, arranger, conductor and performer. Pl. w. Elvin Jones; Tony Scott; Howard McGhee; Attila Zoller; Sonny Stitt, '66-7; US and Mexico w. Chico Hamilton, '68-9; Art Blakey, '69-70. Has written articles and lectured; commentator for US Information Agency's Voice of America.

ARNOLD, HORACEE (pron. Hor-as) E.,* *drums, composer*; also *piano, acoustic guitar*; b. Wayland, Ky., 9/25/37. Pl. in Louisville and LA in '50s; NYC in '60s w. Mingus; R.R. Kirk; Barry Harris; Bud Powell. Studied comp. w. Heiner Stadler; classical guitar w. Hy Gubernik; Ralph Towner, '66-9. Formed gp., The Here and Now Company, which then incl. Karl Berger, Robin Kenyatta, Sam Rivers, for concerts and workshops in Young Audiences series at high schools throughout NYC; concert at Whitney Museum. From '69-72 worked as coordinator for Jazzmobile and perf. in concert w. own gp. Pl. w. Chick Corea; Stan Getz, '72. Concerts and lecture-demonstrations in Summer Jazz Camp series, '74; high schools and colls. w. Here and Now, '75. Infl: Corea, Zawinul, Ellington, Albeniz, de Falla, Kodaly, Ravel, Debussy, W. Shorter.

TV: *The People; Round Trip*, CBS; *Peter Pan*, Metromedia. Fest: NJF-NY at Apollo Theatre, '73; Concord. Grant from National Endowment for the Arts, '74-5.

Comp: *Tales of the Exonerated Flea; Sing Nightjar; Puppett of the Seasons; Benzele Windows; Chinnereth II; Euroaquilo Silence; Delicate Evasions.* LPs: *Tales of the Exonerated Flea; Tribe* (Col.); w. Corea, *Is; Sundance* (SS); w. Kenyatta, *Until* (Vortex); w. H. Masekela (Merc.).

ART ENSEMBLE OF CHICAGO. Group formed in the fall of 1968 by Joseph Jarman, Roscoe Mitchell, Lester Bowie and Malachi Favors which played and lived in France, '69-71, and has since pl. concerts and clubs in the US. Its performances are a mixture of theatricality and music: the stage filled with instruments from bass saxophones to banjos, fender bass to log drums, bike horns, gongs and whistles to tenor saxes and flutes; the players in grass skirts, faces painted in African ceremonial designs; wearing straw boaters or a hard hat. Jarman, commenting on painting faces, says: "A lot of people like to suggest this has to do with a militant attitude, when in fact it is a tribal attitude. The mask in African culture, functions to alleviate human beings so the spiritual aspects of things can come out."

David Spitzer wrote: "The members of the group produce musical sounds which run the gamut from the traditional to the absurd and the surreal. They also include valid, humorous, vocal discourses and cries, as well as atypical sounds produced on traditional instruments."

Concerts & Fests: Int. Fest. Amougies, Belgium; Rotterdam Int. Pop Fest.; Jazz-Beat Fest. '71, Aarhus, Denmark; Fest. of Chateauvallon, France; Baden-Baden Free Jazz Fest.; Museum of Modern Art, Paris; Nat. Gallery of Art, Berlin; French Ministry of Culture tours, '70-1; U. of Wisconsin; Notre Dame; Chicago; Indiana; Stanford; Antioch; Wayne State; Malcolm X Coll.; Ohio State; Michigan State; Washington U.; Lenox Arts Center, Mass.; Ann Arbor Blues & Jazz Fest. '72; NJF-NY, '73; Montreux, '74; Grande Maison de O.R.T.F., Paris '74; six-city tour of Japan, '74. Apps. on Radio Denmark; Stockholm Radio; Organisation Radio Television Francaise.

Awards: Record of the Year, '70, Academie de Jazz Francaise for *People in Sorrow*; Album of the Year, *Melody Maker* '73-4 for *Baptizum; Melody Maker; Jazz Podium; Jazz Hot; Jazz Magazine* polls; DB Critics' poll, combo TDWR, '71.

LPs: *People in Sorrow; Les Stances a Sophie* (Nessa); *Reese and the Smooth Ones; A Jackson in Your House; Message to Our Folks* (Byg); *Spiritual* (Poly.); *Tutankhamun* (Freedom), same as *The Paris Session* (Arista); *Home* (Galloway); *Certain Blacks; Phase One; Art Ensemble w. Fontella Bass; Chi-Congo* (America); *Baptizum; Fanfare for the Warriors* (Atl.); *Live at Mandel Hall* (Delmark/Trio).

ARVANITAS, GEORGES,* *piano, organ*; b. Marseilles, France, 6/13/31. Played w. Donald Byrd et al in Paris early '60s. To U.S. in '64; spent nine months w. Y. Lateef, '65. After returning to France, where he led trio, back to U.S. for six months working w. Lloyd Price. Own trio at Cameleon in Paris, '66-7; Chat Qui Peche club, '68-70. His rhythm section backed many visiting Americans incl. L. Konitz, Dexter Gordon, H. Mobley. During early '70s Arvanitas played concerts w. Clark Terry, B. Webster, Robin Kenyatta; toured Japan w. Michel Legrand, '72; Italy, first w. Sonny Criss, later w. S. Stitt. His trio, w. Jacky Samson on bass and Charles Saudrais on drums, was organized in September '65 and was still working together in '75.

Publ: *Piano Jazz*, transciption for piano, ed. Paul Beuscher, 27 Boulevard Beaumarchais, Paris 11e. Own LPs on European labels; also, *Anita O'Day In Berlin* (BASF).

ASH, MARVIN (Marvin Ashbaugh),* *piano*; b. Lamar, Colo., 10/4/14. The veteran pianist, well known in LA in the '40s, died 8/21/74 in Encino, Cal.

ASHBY, HAROLD KENNETH,* *tenor saxophone*; b. Kansas City, Mo., 3/27/25. After working with Mercer Ellington and often subbing in Duke Ellington's band, Ashby became a regular member of the senior Ellington's orchestra 7/5/68 at the NJF. Touring with the band on its various overseas bookings, including Europe, Japan, Australia in '70, USSR, '71, Africa, '73, Ashby was also featured in his own album *Born To Swing* on Master Jazz in '72.

He remained with the orch. under Mercer Ellington's direction, after Duke's death, still playing in the full-toned style reminiscent of his predecessors in the band, Ben Webster and Paul Gonsalves. LPs w. Ellington: *My People* (Flying Dutchman); *70th Birthday Concert, Togo Brava Suite* (UA); *New Orleans Suite* (Atl.); *Third Sacred Concert* (RCA); w. M. Ellington, *Continuum* (Fant.).

ASHBY, IRVING C.,* *guitar*; b. Somerville, Mass., 12/29/20. Former Lionel Hampton, King Cole and Oscar Peterson guitarist; devoted most of the late '60s and early '70s to private teaching. In '69 left Los Angeles, moved to Perris, Cal. and, in semi-retirement, became active in landscape design, sign painting, teaching orchestra and guitar at high school; also in '71 at U. of Cal., Riverside.

Publ: *Guitar Work Book* (Trebla Publ. Co., Rt. 1, Box 146, Perris, Ca. 92370). LPs: *California Guitar* w. Mundell Lowe (Famous Door); *The Bosses* w. Count Basie and Joe Turner (Pablo).

ASMUSSEN, SVEND,* *violin*; b. Copenhagen, Denmark, 2/28/16. Ranking alongside S. Grappelli as one of Europe's first great jazz violinists, he toured for many years as a member of a pop vocal-instrumental unit known as the Swe-Danes, feat. singer Alice Babs. After Babs left the group in '61, Asmussen cont. touring with the third member, guitarist Ulrik Neumann. In '66, he led his own quintet at the Tivoli in Copenhagen. From '67 he toured Sweden with this group, app. at MJF, traveled through the Far East and Africa, and rec. a celebrated album, *Violin Summit*, w. Stuff Smith, Grappelli and Jean-Luc Ponty (MPS).

From '69-72 Asmussen was reunited w. Babs, touring Scandinavia with her. Asmussen experimented with amplified violin and brought strong rock infls. into his jazz work. He was heard in concerts with a group feat. Ed Thigpen on drums, and two Scandinavian musicians on organ and fender bass. To Brazil w. Babs, Jan. '74. From '74, w. clarinetist Putte Wickman and pianist Ivan Renliden, pl. concerts in many churches throughout Sweden and Denmark, with repertoire incl. Bach, Telemann, Mozart and improv. on hymns and folk themes. In Sept. '75 Asmussen returned to the U.S. to make his second app. at the MJF.

LP: *Yesterday and Today*, w. Toots Thielemans (A & M).

ASSUNTO, FRANK JOSEPH,* *trumpet, leader*; b. New Orleans, La., 1/29/32. Co-founder and leader (with his brother Fred) of the Dukes of Dixieland. Died in NO, 2/25/74, after a brief illness.

ASSUNTO, JACOB (PAPA JAC),* *trombone, banjo*; b. Lake Charles, La., 11/1/05. His two sons, Fred and Frank, leaders of Dukes of Dixieland, died in '66 and '74 respectively. Not long after the death of the latter he retired to Metairie, La., where he devoted part of his time to teaching.

AUGER, BRIAN, *organ, keyboards*; b. London, England, 7/18/39. No formal tuition. Started in London, 1962, at Ronnie Scott's and other clubs. Freelance pianist, '63. Put together band incl. John McLaughlin, Rick Laird, '64. The following year began pl. organ. In '65-6 he pl. with Steam Packet feat. Julie Driscoll. Again feat. with Ms. Driscoll in Brian Auger and the Trinity, '67-9. From '70, leader of Oblivion Express, with which he frequently visited U.S. Numerous TV and jazz fest. appearances, incl. Montreux, Berlin, Frankfurt.

Won *Melody Maker* piano and new star sections, '64. Trinity won *Melody Maker* poll, '68. Auger names McCoy Tyner, John Coltrane, Herbie Hancock as original inspirations. LPs: Polydor (Britain); Atlantic, RCA (USA).

AULD, GEORGIE (John Altwerger),* *tenor, alto, soprano saxes*; b. Toronto, Ontario, Canada, 5/19/19. First prominent in '30s w. Bunny Berigan, Artie Shaw, and '40s w. Benny Goodman and Shaw. During '60s and '70s freelanced in Los Angeles. In '67 joined Tony Martin as conductor and soloist, touring Europe and S. America. Enjoying his greatest individual successes in Japan, Auld by '75 had toured there a dozen times, and had recorded some 15 albums in Japan, many of them great popular hits. In Los Angeles, however, he remained in relative obscurity, playing as sideman on Flip Wilson and other TV shows.

LPs: None of his many albums as a leader were available in '75; however, he was heard in many reissues w. Berigan, Shaw (RCA), Goodman (Columbia) etc.

AURA (a.k.a. AURA LEE, Aura Urziceanu), *singer*; also *violin, percussion*; b. Bucharest, Romania, 12/14/46. Stud. classical violin from '61-4 with her father, Ion Urziceanu, concert master of the Bucharest Symph. Classical voice training w. Florica Orascu, '63-7. Stud. at Bucharest Conserv., '65-7. Toured U.S.S.R., Poland, Israel, '65 w. Jancsi Korossy trio. With Bucharest Jazz Quintet, '66-9. In Canada, '70, worked w. Phil Nimmons and w. drummer Ron Rully. Married Rully and settled in Canada, '71. In '72, she made several apps. w. D. Ellington, incl. a NJF-NY Carnegie Hall concert, for which she was widely praised. Returned to Europe, '73, working w. Art Farmer, Slide Hampton. In Toronto, w. Gene DiNovi trio, '74. Toured w. Q. Jones, '74-5 in U.S. and Japan.

Infls: Fitzgerald, Vaughan, McRae, Nancy Wilson; Ellington, Rully, Q. Jones, L. Schifrin. In '71 she won the European Reporters' Press Prize in Brussels as most promising singer, and Europe Cup at Knokke, Belgium. Winner of polls annually in Romania, from '71. App. on own TV specs. in Bucharest.

Aura, who has an extraordinarily pure sound and remarkable range, is one of the most individual jazz oriented vocal stylists to emerge during the early '70s.

LPs: several in Europe, incl. some arranged and conducted by Rully for Electrachord.

AUSTIN, LOVIE,* *piano, composer*; b. Chattanooga, Tenn., 9/19/1887. The one-time leader of the Blues Serenaders, who made her first record in 1923 with Ida Cox and her last in Chicago 9/1/61, died in Chicago 7/10/72.

AUTREY, HERMAN,* *trumpet*; b. Evergreen, Ala., 12/4/04. Key sideman w. Fats Waller in '30s; pl. w. Saints & Sinners in '60s, touring Europe w. them in '67, '69. Free-lancing in NYC in mid-'70s, occasionally subbing at Jimmy Ryan's. LPs: w. Saints & Sinners (MPS, Sack.); in Albert McCarthy's *Swing Today* series (Eng. RCA); Fats Waller reissue (Bluebird).

AXELROD, DAVID, *composer*; b. Los Angeles, Ca., 4/17/36. Mostly self-taught. Stud. informally w. Gerald Wiggins; harmony and comp. w. Mauro Bruno, '59; harmony at UCLA, '60-1. Infl. by O. Coleman, M. Davis, Gil Evans, Ch. Mingus, T. Monk, H. Silver, G. Wiggins.

From the late '50s, Axelrod was principally known as the producer of jazz albums for a series of companies, but later he shifted the focus of his work to composing and arranging. Among his works are *Songs of Innocence; Earth Rot; The Contemporary Messiah; The Auction; Seriously Deep*, all rec. by leading artists.

In '70, Axelrod conducted his comp. *Tensity* for the C. Adderley quintet and orch. at the MJF. The sound track album of *Easy Rider*, in which his *Mass In F. Minor* was heard, was awarded a gold record. Benny Carter and others have attested to the growth of Axelrod's talent as a writer capable of mixing many contemporary idioms.

LPs: *Tensity* w. Adderley (Capitol); *Double Exposure* w. N. Adderley (Prestige); *Brasswind* w. G. Ammons (Prestige); *Northern Windows* w. H. Hawes (Fantasy); *The Way It Was, The Way It Is* w. Lou Rawls (Capitol).

AYERS, ROY E. JR.,* *vibes, singer*; b. Los Angeles, Cal., 9/10/40. After working w. Gerald Wilson, Jack Wilson, and as co-leader with Hampton Hawes in the early '60s, Ayers led a quartet, '65-6, before touring w. Herbie Mann from '66-70. He then formed his own group, Roy Ayers Ubiquity. Toured Japan, Europe, '71. Festivals: NJF, 67, '73; Montreux, '71. Composed sound track for film *Coffy* (also released as Polydor LP). Developing many attractive new sound effects through the use of electronics, Ayers enjoyed growing popularity in the '70s, his many Polydor albums reaching a wide rock and jazz audience. Early LPs on Atlantic: *Virgo Vibes; Stoned Soul Picnic; Daddy Bug*. LPs on Polydor: *Ubiquity*, '70; *He's Coming*, '71; *Ubiquity Live at Montreux*, '72; *Red, Black and Green*, '73; *Virgo Red, Change Up The Groove*, '74. Won DB awards, '66, '71.

AYLER, ALBERT,* *tenor, soprano, alto saxophones, bagpipes, composer*; b. Cleveland, Ohio, 7/13/36. A prominent figure in the free jazz of the '60s, Ayler stirred strong controversy with his concerts, recordings and compositions. In the late '60s his music reverted somewhat towards a more blues rooted style, using themes suggesting r & b infl.

On 11/25/70 Ayler's body was found floating in the East River, NYC. The circumstances of his death were never cleared up. Critic Joachim Berendt found "the joyous air of the folk musician" in Ayler's work. Michael Cuscuna wrote: "The music of Albert Ayler remains among the most unique and haunting in the history of black American music . . . of all the players of the 1960s avant garde, including the geniuses, the competent musicians, and the lame hucksters, Ayler's music seemed to evoke the strongest reaction, be it pro or con . . . (he offered) simple, unforgettable melodies, such as *Ghosts*, which many feel to be the anthem of 1960s black music. After stating a theme, he would pursue improvisational variations and developments, twisting his saxophone out of the grip of European music fundamentals."

LPs: *My Name is Albert Ayler; Introducing Albert Ayler* (Fant.); *Spiritual Unity; Bells; N.Y. Eye & Ear Control; Spirits Rejoice* (ESP); *First Recordings* (GNP); *In Greenwich Village; Reevaluation: The Impulse Years; Last Album; Love Cry; Music Is The Healing Force; New Grass* (Imp.); *Vibrations* (Arista-Freedom).

AYOUB, NICHOLAS (NICK), *tenor sax, composer*; also *oboe, flute, clarinet*; b. Three Rivers, Que., Canada, 9/7/26. Son Jimmy is drummer with rock gp. Mahogany Rush. Studied saxophone w. Arthur Romano; oboe w. Romano, Harold Gomberg. Received Premier Prix from Montreal Conserv. of Mus. for classical saxophone '52. At 17 pl. w. Maynard Ferguson's band. He was also in the Johnny Holmes band that incl. Oscar Peterson. Pl. at Emanon Jazz Society Meetings w. baritone saxophonist Freddie Nichols. Worked w. Butch Watanabe in '50s. Own quintet for concerts and clubs in Montreal. Active in recs., jingles, and for CBC-TV. Professor of classical saxophone, jazz improvisation, and director of the jazz band at Montreal Conserv. of Mus. Infl: Webster, Getz, Parker, Coltrane. TV: soloist and w. own quintet for CBC; member of Canadian all-star jazz orch. sponsored by Timex '57. Fest: Montreal JF opposite Duke Ellington '65; Dawson Coll.; Concordia U. '75. Comp.: *Concertino for Jazz Band; Pillsville; Love of Three Flutes; Montreal East; Montreal West; Time Compulsion, Lynn's Tune; Little Nicky; Abstraction; Walkin' Home*. LPs: *Montreal Jazz Scene* (RCA Victor, Can.); *Canadian Talent Library; Nick Ayoub Plays Bossa Nova* (Trans Canada).

BABS, ALICE (Alice Nilson), *singer*; b. Kalmar, Sweden, 1/26/24. Father Jean Nilson, pianist and composer; husband Nils Ivar Sjöblom, lyricist; daughter Titti Breitholtz, singer. Stud. w. Prof. Ragnar Hulthen, Royal Swedish Academy of Mus., from '56. Estab. as Sweden's most popular vocalist; actress with leading parts in a dozen Swedish films; TV star throughout Europe etc., she also app. at Cocoanut Grove in '60s as single and w. Swe-Danes trio, making several recs. in Hollywood. She met D. Ellington in '63; a few weeks later he called her to record with him in Paris. LP was released under the title *Serenade to Sweden* (European Reprise—never available in US). During next decade she made many apps. w. Ellington, among them one on her birthday in '67 in Malmo, Sweden, and several at Ellington's Sacred Concerts, incl. the premiere of the second Sacred Concert at the Cathedral of St. John the Divine, NYC, '68. Fests: Paris, '49; Newport, '73. Infls: Ivie Anderson, Billie Holiday, Ellington. Honors: Royal Court Singer, appointed by King of Sweden in '72, the only non-opera singer given that title. Member of Royal Swedish Academy of Music, '74.

Ellington once said of Alice Babs: "This voice, ladies and gentlemen, embodies all the warmth, joy, life, rhythm and tragedy that, for me, is the innermost secret of jazz." Babs' extraordinary purity of sound and remarkable range are exquisitely showcased in his albums. LPs w. Ellington: *Second Sacred Concert* (Fant.); *Third Sacred Concert* (RCA). Others: *Alice & Wonderband* (Decca); *Music with a Jazz Flavour; Alice Babs Serenading Duke Ellington* (Swedish Society Discofil).

BACSIK (pron. Bott-chik), ELEK, *violin, violectra, guitar*; b. Budapest, Hungary, 5/22/26. A gypsy, he was originally self-taught on violin, but later prepared for a career as a concert artist at the Budapest Conservatory. At an early age he taught himself guitar and was established as Hungary's leading jazz guitarist. After three years in the Army, he lived in Vienna, later Switzerland, Lebanon, Italy, Spain, Portugal and Paris, playing with many visiting American jazzmen in '59-66. To U.S., '66; toured with gypsy band, settled in LA for a while, moving in '67 to Las Vegas. For the next seven years he remained in obscurity until Bob Thiele heard him at the Sahara, where he was in the orch. backing Thiele's wife, Teresa Brewer. Soon afterward, he made his first album for the Bob Thiele label. Fest: NJF-NY, '74.

A true eclectic who has absorbed much of the essence of American jazz, Bacsik has a predilection for the bebop era, and is a good friend of Dizzy Gillespie, with whom he rec. in the early '60s.

LPs: *I Love You; Bird and Dizzy* (Bob Thiele Music); *Dizzy on the French Riviera* w. Gillespie (Philips).

BACULIS, ALPHONSE (AL), *clarinet*; also *saxophone, piano*; b. Montreal, Que., Canada, 11/21/30. Wife and sister-in-law both singers; brother-in-law is composer Ron Collier. Studied at McGill U., '48-51; theory & comp. w. Marvin Duchow, Istvan Anhalt, '52-6. Played w. Canadian All Stars which rec. for Discovery (long out of print) '55. Worked w. many Montreal gps. From '58 has been occupied mainly with writing, comp. & arrs. for TV and films; pl. w. studio orchs.; writing and conducting jazz shows. Infl: Parker, Gillespie, Tristano, Schoenberg, Webern, Hindemith, Stravinsky, Bartok. Won clarinet division of Canadian jazz poll for more than five years in '50s. LPs: w. Al Baculis Singers, hits from *Anne of Green Gables* and other Canadian shows (Dominion); transcriptions and records for CBC.

BADINI, GERARD,* *tenor sax, clarinet*; b. Paris, France, 4/16/31. From '58 concentrated more on tenor than clarinet. Mostly studio work in '60s, '70s. Toured Europe, Africa, Middle East w. Claude Bolling. Founded Les Swingers w. Francois Guin (q.v.), touring Africa, '70, '72. Pl. in Europe w. R. Eldridge; P. Gonsalves; D. Ellington; L. Hampton. Own gp., The Swing Machine, from '73. Pl. clubs in US w. Bobby Hackett, Aaron Bell, '74. Infl: Ellington, Parker, Gonsalves, Lockjaw Davis. TV: many shows w. Bolling; did music for shorts, *Noir et Blanc*; soundtracks w. Bolling; M. Legrand. Fest: Montreux; Nice; Antibes; Warsaw; Prague; Dakar; Pescara. Comp: a ballet illustrating the history of jazz, *Jungle is Not So Virgin As People Said*, excerpts of which were recorded on the Polish label Muza. LPs: *Swing Machine; Swing Machine w. Sam Woodyard* (B&B); *Swingers in the Groove; Paul Gonsalves in Paris w. the Swingers* (Barclay); Anderson, Bolling & Co; others w. Bolling (Philips); w. Jacques Denjean (Poly.); w. Duke Ellington and Alice Babs (Reprise).

BAILEY, ERNEST HAROLD (BENNY),* *trumpet*; b. Cleveland, Ohio, 8/13/25. Played w. D. Gillespie; L. Hampton in '40s; Q. Jones in '59-60, after having pl. in Swedish Radio Band, '57-9. Returned briefly to US '60 but once again moved to Sweden. Then worked w. Berlin Radio Band for two yrs.; Max Greger band for five yrs. in Munich before settling in Geneva to play w. the Radio Swiss Romande orch. With Clarke-Boland Big Band from early '60s to band's breakup in '73. Fest: major Euro. fest. incl. Montreux '69 w. Les McCann and Eddie Harris; Pori '71 w. Red Mitchell; Middleheim '74 w. Boland small gp. A fine lead player and excellent soloist in the Gillespie-Navarro tradition. LPs: *Midnight in Europe* (MCE); w. L. McCann-E. Harris, *Swiss Movement* (Atl.); also see Clarke-Boland.

BAILEY, WILLIAM C. (BUSTER),* *clarinet*; b. Memphis, Tenn., 7/19/02. Joined Louis Armstrong All-Stars, '65, remaining until his death, in Brooklyn, 4/12/67. Bailey, one of the first major jazz clarinetists with a thorough academic background in music, was a prolific recording artist. He can be heard on albums w. Fletcher Henderson, Bessie Smith, Lionel Hampton, Red Allen et al. LPs: *All About Memphis* (Master Jazz).

BAILEY, COLIN,* *drums*; b. Swindon, England, 7/9/34. After touring Australia, pl. in US since 1961; worked with Victor Feldman, B. Goodman, Terry Gibbs; many groups in SF, LA. Toured w. G. Shearing '66-7; during next five years, jazz work w. Chet Baker, Ray Brown, Joe Pass; concerts w. Joao Gilberto. In '73-4 traveled w. Vic Damone. Many jazz jobs with Gibbs, R. Kellaway, Pass, Feldman, '73-5. Subbed often in *Tonight Show* TV band.

LPs: Sinatra-Jobim (Reprise); *New Look* w. Shearing (Capitol); *Almaville* w. Vince Guaraldi (WB); *Simplicity* w. Pass (World Pacific). Publs: *Bass Drum Control; Modern Drum Solos for the Drum Set*, (Try Publishing Co., 854 N. Vine St., Hollywood, CA 90028).

BAILEY, SAMUEL DAVID (DAVE),* *drums, educator*; b. Portsmouth, Va., 2/22/26. Known for his work w. Gerry Mulligan; Billy Taylor; Clark Terry-Bob Brookmeyer gps. Continued pl. w. Terry from '66-9. An accomplised pilot and former AAF officer, he gave up music to fly a Lear jet for lawyer F. Lee Bailey, '69-73. Billy Taylor then asked him to take his place w. the Jazzmobile, and from '73 Bailey has been executive director administrating all aspects from the summer street concerts in New York's five boroughs to the students Workshop. Additionally, he teaches drums in the Workshop.

In the winter of '75 he became actively involved as president of the Consortium of Jazz Organizations, 16 jazz arms in the New York area, which hopes to serve as a nucleus of a national jazz organization focussing on the artistic and business needs of the musician. In the summer of '75 he also headed the Citizens Committee to Save Jazz Radio, Inc., a group battling to preserve WRVR-FM's full-time jazz policy.

Toward the end of the year he was considering adding active playing to his schedule. LPs: w. Terry, *It's What's Happenin'* (Imp.); w. Terry-Brookmeyer (Main.).

BAILEY, DEREK, *guitar*; b. Sheffield, England, 1/29/32. Grandfather, professional pianist-banjoist; uncle, George Wing, professional guitarist. Bailey states: "After 10 years working as a guitar player in the entertainment industry I have since 1963 pursued the ideal of free improvisation. During this period I have had the good fortune to work with most of the leading German blasters, American groovers, Dutch acrobats and English kaleidoscopists in this field." Publ: *Improvisation: Its Nature and Practice in Music* (Latimer Press, 14 W. Central St., London, W.C.1, England). LPs: solo; duo w. Evan Parker (Incus); duo w. Han Bennink (ICP); duo w. Anthony Braxton (Emanem).

BAILEY, DONALD ORLANDO,* *drums, harmonica, trombone*; b. Phila., Pa., 3/26/33. Best known as drummer w. organist Jimmy Smith's trio for eight years. Freelanced in LA from mid-60s w. Jack Wilson, Hampton Hawes, Freddie Hubbard, Joe Pass, Gene Ammons, Bobby Hutcherson, Gerald Wilson, Jimmy Rowles, and innumerable others. During '70s, harmonica soloist at jazz and rock concerts, sometimes billed under name "Harmonica Man." Also played hca. w. Bill Cosby; assisted Sonny Terry in movie sound track for *Buck and the Preacher*. One of the most respected and tasteful freelance drummers on LA scene.

LPs: w. Hampton Hawes (Contemporary, Vault); Harold Land (Contemp., Mainstream); Blue Mitchell (Mainstream); Dave Frishberg (Seeds); Mundell Lowe (Famous Door).

BAILEY, PEARL,* *singer*; b. Newport News, Va., 3/29/18. The former dancer and one time Cootie Williams orch. vocalist began her career as a prominent stage performer in *St. Louis Woman*, 1946. Married Louie Bellson, '52. Many other shows, Las Vegas appearances etc. Acclaimed for her performance in *Hello Dolly* on Broadway in '67-9. Own TV series on ABC, '70. Several movies over the years incl. *Porgy and Bess; Carmen Jones; That Certain Feeling; All The Fine Young Cannibals*. Sang at Concord Jazz Fest., '74. LPs: *Pearl's Pearls* (RCA). Many others on Roulette.

BAKER, CHESNEY H. (CHET),* *trumpet, fluegelhorn, singer*; b. Yale, Okla., 12/23/29. Came to fame w. Gerry Mulligan Quartet 1952-3. From '59-64 was in Europe, where he was in frequent trouble with the law due to narcotics problems. Baker then lived in NYC and LA until 1968; then, in SF, he was the victim of a beating by hoodlums, suffering severe injuries that included the loss of his teeth. For two years he stopped playing. Controlling his dope addiction through the use of methadone, he made a slow comeback, gigging in New York '74-5 and returning to prominence on records through his own album and a reunion concert w. Mulligan. According to John S. Wilson, Baker in 1974 had developed "more range and assertiveness within the wistfully ruminative style with which he has always been associated."

LPs: Mulligan-Baker Carnegie Hall Concert, vols. 1 & 2; *She Was Too Good To Me*; w. Jim Hall, *Concierto* (CTI); *Comin' On; Groovin'; Smokin'* (Prestige); *Baker's Holiday* (Trip).

BAKER, DAVID NATHANIEL,* *cello, composer, educator*; also *trombone, piano, bass*; b. Indianapolis, Ind., 12/21/31. Played w. Kenton; M. Ferguson in '50s; Q. Jones; G. Russell in '60s: all as trombonist. Problems w. his jaw forced him to switch to cello in '62 but in the '70s he was playing both instruments. Teaching at Indiana U. from '66; active as teacher, clinician, lecturer at univs. throughout the US; National Stage Band Camps. Headed Newport Educational Series for Rutgers U., '72-5. As cellist, pl. at Radio City Jam Session, NJF-NY '73. An educator who is able to combine the theoretical with the practicality of experience.

Comp: *Sonata for Cello and Piano*, rec. by Janos Starker (Col.); *Le Chat Qui Peche, A suite for Orchestra, Jazz Quartet and Soprano*, rec. by Louisville Symph., Jamey Aebersold and Linda Anderson (First Edition); *Levels, for Solo Bass Viol, Jazz Band, String Quartet, Flute Quartet and Horn Quartet* perf. by Bernard Turetzky and nominated for Pulitzer Prize; *The Soul of '76 for Jazz Band*, commissioned by J.C. Penney for the Bicentennial, the music and a record given to every high school in the US by the company; *Black American Cantata*, presented annually by Voice of America on death anny. of M.L. King.

Hundreds of pieces for jazz ensemble and big band publ. by *down beat*; for string orch. publ. by William Lewis & Sons; jazz rock series publ: (New Sounds in Modern Music, 315 W. 53rd St., NYC). Chairman, NEA '74.

Comps. for NET series, *Black Frontier*; for NET series, *The Trial of Captain Henry Flipper; Son Mar*, theme music for *Black Experience*, WTTV, Indianapolis.

Textbook publ: *Developing Improvisational Technique, Based on the Lydian Concept; Dev. Improv. Facility with the II, V, VII Progression; Dev. Improv. Facility with the Turnback; Arr. & Comp. for the Small Ensemble; Jazz Imrov.; Jazz Styles & Analysis—Trombone; Contemporary Techniques for the Trombone: A Revolutionary Approach to Dealing with the Problems of Music in the 20th Century; Advanced Jazz Improvisation*, (*down beat* Workshop Publs., 222 West Adams St., Chi., Ill. 60606). Contributed over 100 transcribed solos of various recordings by jazzmen for *down beat*.

Books in Progress: *Black Music Now, A Source Book for the 20th Century* (Kent State); *A History of Jazz* (Prentice-Hall); *Contemporary Black Music* (Harper and Row).

LPs: *Black America* (Univ. of Illinois Press); *Concerto for Violin & Jazz Band; Concerto for Flute & Jazz Band* (Coronet); cello w. Nathan Davis; trombone w. Toots Thielemans, *The Big Time* (Segue); bass trombone w. Bill Evans-George Russell, *Living Time* (Col.); trombone w. Russell (Mile.).

BAKER, PETER (GINGER), *drums*; b. Lewisham, England, 8/19/40. As young boy in London, pl. dr. while in secondary school during early 1950s, and was attracted to blues and jazz. First pro. jobs in '56. In early '60s perf. w. Alexis Korner and Graham Bond gps. Formed Cream in '66 w. Eric Clapton and Jack Bruce. This gp. won gold awards for all its albums; disbanded '68. In '69, w. Clapton, Stevie Winwood and Rick Grech, formed Blind Faith; pl. concerts throughout U.K. and U.S. In '70, on breakup of Blind Faith, Baker organized Air Force, which pl. Afro-jazz flavored music.

Baker's first idol was Baby Dodds; his style developed from trad. through dance bands to bebop and thence to blues-rock. His recent African-inspired sound was much admired by many African musicians, such as Guy Warren and the Ghanaian broadcaster and percussionist Michael Eghan, who said of Baker: "He's the most African sounding drummer in Europe." However, Elvin Jones, on hearing Baker's solo in *Do What You Like*, said: "Nothing happening. Cat's got delusions of grandeur with no grounds. They should make him an astronaut and lose his ass." LPs: w. Cream, *Heavy Cream; Off The Top* (Poly.).

BAKER, KENNETH (KENNY),* *trumpet*; b. Withersnea, Yorks., England, 3/1/21. Pro. debut in London, '39. In recent years, studio work w. J. Parnell; occ. quartet gigs on BBC Jazz Club. Rec. recreations of swing era hits under the late Ted Heath's name. Max Jones observed in '75 that "the years have not diminished Baker's fire or technical fluency. He has maintained the highest musical standards and his enthusiasm for jazz in the mainstream idiom."

LP: *Sensational Trumpet of Kenny Baker* (Decca).

BAKER, HAROLD J. (SHORTY),* *trumpet*; b. St. Louis, Mo., 5/26/14. Gained early fame with Fate Marable, Erskine Tate, Don Redman in '30s. Teddy Wilson, Andy Kirk, Mary Lou Williams (his wife), '40s; Ellington, '30s, '40s and '50s. Freelanced in NYC until illness sidelined him. After undergoing surgery in '65, returned to work, but died of cancer 11/8/66 in NYC.

BALABAN, LEONARD J. (RED), *bass*; also *singer, tuba, tenor guitar, banjo*; b. Chicago, Ill., 12/22/29. Father, Barney Balaban, headed the famed theatre chain Balaban & Katz. Stud. informally: tuba w. Wm. Cramer at Florida State U. '66-7; bass w. Milt Beisiegel of New Haven Symph., '71-3. From '55-67 pl. w. dance bands in Fla.; own gps. under name Balaban & Cats from '50s. Also in cattle business in Fla., '62-7. Moved to NYC '67, working off and on w. Wild Bill Davison from that time. Also pl w. Max Kaminsky; Blues Alley, Wash., D.C. w. Tony Parenti, '72; gig w. Dukes of Dixieland, '74. Balaban & Cats app. regularly on Sundays at Your Father's Mustache, '70-2 and throughout the NY, NJ, Conn. area '70-5. In '75 Balaban purchased a club at 144 W. 54th Street and opened it in March as Eddie Condon's, w. Balaban & Cats as the house band. Regular members incl. Herb Hall, Vic Dickenson and El Polcer. From '70 many musicians have been hired by Balaban to augment the Cats from time to time, among them Ruby Braff, Bobby Hackett, Al Cohn, Zoot Sims, Budd Johnson, Teddy Wilson, Gene Krupa and Condon.

Infl: Louis Armstrong, Wellman Braud, Bob Casey, Bing Crosby, Freddie Green, Condon, Singleton Palmer. Fest: NJF-NY '75 for Hudson River boatride. LP: *A Night at the New Eddie Condon's* (Classic Jazz); *Bits and Pieces of Balaban & Cats; A Night at the Town House* (Balaban & Cats).

BALES, BURTON F. (BURT),* *piano, singer*; b. Stevensville, Mont., 3/20/16. Worked w. many trad. groups from early '40s incl. Lu Watters, Bunk Johnson, Turk Murphy. Based in SF, he pl. at Pier 23 as solo pianist from '54-66. In '66 he went to electronics school, graduating in '69 as electronic technician. Returned to active performing in '75, pl. mainly solo. Bales, who had a band at the first MJF in '58, and returned there the following year, acc. Lizzie Miles, is feat. in a solo LP, released in '75 on Euphonic Records, from tapes made in the mid-50s.

BARBARIN, PAUL,* *drums*; b. New Orleans, La., 5/5/01. Early work w. Luis Russell, Amos White, Fats Pichon, King Oliver. Toured w. L. Armstrong in '30s. In '55 Barbarin formed his own band app. in NYC, LA and other major U.S. cities. It was while leading this group known as Onward Brass Band in the Proteus Carnival parade (the prelude to the Mardi Gras festival) in New Orleans, that he collapsed and died of a heart attack, 2/10/69.

BARBER, JOHN WILLIAM (BILL),* *tuba*; b. Hornell, N.Y., 5/21/20. A member of the Claude Thornhill orchestra of the late '40s and the original Miles Davis nonet which made the historic "Birth of the Cool" sessions, Barber has been teaching instrumental music in the Long Island public school system from 1960. Plays summers with the Goldman Band and many free-lance jobs incl. concerts, commercials, brass ensembles, banjo bands and German festivals. Also active as a clinician, for events like the New York Brass Conference For Scholarships Jan. '75. LPs w. Miles Davis (Cap., Col.), Gil Evans (Wor. Pac., Imp.).

BARBER, DONALD CHRISTOPHER (CHRIS),* *trombone, leader*; b. London, England, 4/17/30. Made seven tours of U.S. in early '60s. Still active since then, but no longer prominent in U.S.

BARBIERI, LEANDRO J., (GATO),* *tenor sax, composer*; b. Rosario, Argentina, 11/28/34. Uncle pl. tenor sax. Gato first attracted to jazz by Charlie Parker record. Stud. at Infancia Desvalida, Rosario, 1944; clarinet for five years with private teacher in Buenos Aires, where his family moved; also stud. alto sax, composition. Pl. in Lalo Schifrin's orch., '53. At age 20 took up tenor sax.

After several years of prominence in Buenos Aires, Barbieri spent seven months in Brazil; then, in '62, he and his Italian-born wife left for Rome, where his reputation as a jazzman grew rapidly. He played with Ted Curson and Jim Hall, met Don Cherry in Paris, '65, and was closely associated with him during next two years. In '65, at Cherry's urging, he went to New York for the first time and recorded *Complete Communion* with Cherry. Around the same time, he came under the influence of movie makers, notably Bernardo Bertolucci and Gianni Amico, sketching some music for the latter's *Notes for a Film on Jazz*.

Gradually Barbieri became aware of the need to blend his freedom as a jazz musician with his South American roots. He began listening to authentic tango music and expressed himself in a new and more provocative manner. In Nov. '69 he recorded *The Third World*, his first American LP as a leader, for Flying Dutchman. Soon afterward, he returned to Argentina to extend his experiments in the cross-fertilization of idioms.

During the early '70s Barbieri was firmly established as a major new voice, traveling internationally. In '72 he won the DB poll (TDWR), made his first app. at the NJF, and composed sound track for the film *Last Tango In Paris*, which won him a Grammy award. He also appeared briefly in the movie.

Among his other fest. apps. were Montreux, '71, '73, Bologna, '65, '74, Newport, '73, 74. Barbieri's most personal characteristics are a driving, impassioned style and grainy tone that gave his sound immediate identification. Nat Hentoff has attested to "The life-affirming, surging spirit of his performances, with their supple range of colors, rhythms, soaring melodies . . . Gato, in sum, is among the least abstract of musicians, because he is so explosively, specifically alive." The qualities of his work, both as instrumentalist and composer, were best set in context from 1973, when he began recording and touring with a newly assembled group of S. American musicians, mainly from Argentina and Brazil. Some critics felt that by '74 he was weakening his artistic potential by pursuing a course more like an aspiring pop-star.

LPs: *The Third World; Fenix; El Pampero* (recorded live at Montreux Festival); *Under Fire; The Legend of Gato Barbieri; Bolivia* (w. Lonnie Liston Smith); *Yesterdays* (Flying Dutchman); *Last Tango In Paris* (United Artists); *Chapter One: Latin America; Chapter Two: Hasta Siempre; Chapter Three: Viva Emiliano Zapata* (Impulse).

BAREFIELD, EDWARD EMANUEL (EDDIE),* *clarinet, saxes, composer*; b. Scandia, Iowa, 12/12/09. Major association w. Cab Calloway from '34 as player, arranger, musical director. Broadway pit band work in '60s. Pl. in Jazz Giants '67; toured w. own band in Africa, summer '69; w. Saints & Sinners in Europe later that year. Heading up rehearsal bands for Local 802. Concert w. own gp. at NY Jazz Museum, '74; gigs at Seafood Playhouse, summer '75. LPs: in *Swing Today* series (Brit. RCA); *Eddie Barefield's Bearcats* (Major-Minor).

BARKER, DANIEL (DANNY),* *guitar, banjo*; b. New Orleans, La., 1/13/09. Played w. James P. Johnson, Cab Calloway, Benny Carter during big band era. After freelancing in NYC in early '60s, returned to NO '65. A Grand Marshall for the NO Jazzfest '69, he led the Congo Square Brass Band in street parade. In '70s pl. on Bourbon St.; leading and coaching Fairview Baptist Church Christian Brass Band. Co-authored book w. Jack Buerkle, *Bourbon Street Black* (see bibliography).

BARNES, GEORGE,* *guitar*; b. Chicago Heights, Ill., 7/17/21. After Carl Kress' death in June '65, ended their duo, Barnes freelanced until he formed a new guitar team w. Bucky Pizzarelli, which endured from '69-'72. In '73 Barnes and cornetist Ruby Braff debuted their quartet at the NJF-NY, and app. at fests. in the U.S. and Europe. Concert tour w. T. Bennett, '73-4; also TV app. w. Bennett. The Barnes-Braff quartet was voted best new group of the year by *Hi-Fidelity* mag., '75 but disbanded during that summer. Comps: *Something Tender; Suite For Octette; It's Like The Fourth of July; Frolic for Basses.* Barnes and his daughter, Alexandra, are collaborators in song. Publs: *The George Barnes Guitar Method* (Wm. J. Smith); *How To Play The Guitar* (Music Minus One, 43 W. 61st St., NYC); *The Great George Barnes Guitar Course*, Cassette & LP (Prentice-Hall, Nat. Inst. of Ed., 24 Rope Ferry Rd., Waterford, Conn.); *How to Arrange for the Guitar* (Peer International, 1740 B'way, NYC 10019).

LPs: *Guitars Pure and Honest*, w. Pizzarelli (Mercury); *Swing Guitars*, w. G. Barnes quartet (Famous Door); w. Braff-Barnes Quartet: *Carnegie Hall Concert* (Chiaroscuro); *Play George Gershwin; Play Rodgers and Hart* (Concord); *To Fred Astaire, With Love* (RCA).

BARNET, CHARLES DALY (CHARLIE),* *saxophones, leader, composer*; b. NYC, 10/26/13. Greatest years as bandleader 1939-45, with style often inspired by Ellington. Semi-retired in later years, but assembled a band that appeared in Hollywood, Las Vegas and New York, winter of '66-7. Taped hour-long TV concert in color and stereo, '67, still unreleased in '75.

Festivals: NJF, '69; Canadian Exposition, Toronto, '72. Led band at Disneyland, '72. Early LPs reissued on RCA; '67 band on Vault available through Creative World Inc.

BARONE, GARY, *trumpet, fluegelhorn, drums*; b. Detroit, Mich., 12/12/41. Father, Joe Barone, pl. tpt. w. Bob Crosby; brother, Mike, is trombonist. BA from Mich. State U. 1964; San Fernando Valley State Coll. '65-7. During latter period, also pl. w. Stan Kenton, and w. LA Neophonic '66. Gigs with Gerald Wilson, '68-9; Bud Shank, '69; Shelly Manne, '69-73; Mike Barone, '67-70; Frank Zappa, '72; Willie Bobo, '74- ; Frank Strazzeri et al. TV and movie rec. w. L. Schifrin, D. Grusin, Tom Scott. LPs w. Kenton-LA Neophonic (Cap.); w. Manne, *Outside; Alive in London* (Contemp.); *Mannekind* (Mainstream).

BARONE, MICHAEL (MIKE), *trombone, composer*; b. Detroit, Mich., 12/27/36. Raised in Cleveland. Stud. w. father, also w. musicians in Cleve. Symph. & NY Phil. Some guitar and Schillinger studies. Army 1956-9; in West Point Band; to Europe, where he led service band. Settled in LA late '59, working w. Si Zentner, Louie Bellson, and for several years off and on w. Gerald Wilson. Studio work w. L. Schifrin, D. Grusin, Tom Scott; wrote theme music w. Chuck Barris for several daytime TV series, also comp. TV commercials and numerous jazz-oriented arrs. for *Tonight Show* band.

In 1967 Barone led the first big band to play at Donte's, gigging there occasionally through 1970. In 1970s he became more active as comp.-arr. His *Breakthrough* was rec. by Bellson in LP of that name; *Spirit of '76* rec. by Emil Richards; *Just Messin' Around* by Tom Scott. Many stage band arrs. for schools, publ.

by (Mike Barone Music, Box 35216, Los Angeles, Calif. 90035).

LPs: In late '60s Barone and F. Rosolino were assoc. with a series of LPs for Liberty under the name *Trombones Unlimited*.

BARRON, WILLIAM JR. (BILL),* *tenor, soprano saxophones, flute, composer, educator*; b. Philadelphia, Pa., 3/27/27. Active in NYC w. Cecil Taylor; Philly Joe Jones; Ted Curson in late '50s and first half of '60s. In '70s led own quartet and also app. w. brother, Kenny, in Barron Brothers gp. From '68-74, however, main occupation was Director of Jazz Workshop at MUSE (Bedford Lincoln Neighborhood Museum operated by the Brooklyn Children's Museum); presented bi-monthly concert series; taught improvisation, composing, arranging, theory and reeds; directed and wrote for the small ensemble and big band; initiated and moderated *The Anthology of Black Classical Music* on radio station WNYC. During the spring term '74 he was an Adjunct Associate Professor at City Coll., CUNY, teaching *Improvisation Using Embellishments*. From Sept. '75, Assistant Professor of Music and Dir. of Afro-American Music at Wesleyan U.; co-ordinator of Jazz Workshop at NEW MUSE (the Community Museum of Brooklyn). Holds a BA in Comp., Combs Coll. of Mus., Phila.; Doctorate in Education from U. of Mass. at Amherst. Participated in National Conf. of Black American Mus. (part of "Black Expo"), Chicago '71. Panelist on music theory for CBA Symposium '72. Fest: Kongsberg w. Y. Lateef, '66; *An Academy of Improvisation* at NJF-NY; *First Music Awakening* workshops, Kingsborough Community Coll.; U. of Mass., '74. TV: interview, *Inside Bedford Stuyvesant*, WNET, '70; w. T. Curson, WNET, '72. Received comp. grant from National Endowment. Comps: *Ode to An Earthgirl; Motivation; Hold Back Tomorrow*. LPs: *Motivation* (Savoy); w. C. Mingus, *Mingus Revisited* (Trip).

BARRON, KENNETH (KENNY),* *piano, composer, educator*; also *bass, tuba*; b. Philadelphia, Pa., 6/9/43. Played w. James Moody, Roy Haynes in early '60s; then w. Dizzy Gillespie, '62-6. In '66-70, worked w. Freddie Hubbard; Jimmy Owens; as accompanist for singer Esther Marrow; and w. Stanley Turrentine at Minton's. From '70 a regular member of the Yusef Lateef quartet, also working intermittently w. Milt Jackson; Jimmy Heath; gigs w. Stan Getz, '74; Buddy Rich in small gp. at Buddy's Place, '75. Taught piano at Jazzmobile Workshop, NYC, '72-3. From '73 full-time instructor at Rutgers Univ., Livingston campus, teaching theory, keyboard harmony, piano. ". . . Barron is a pormanteau pianist," wrote Neil Tesser, "summing and summoning up in one style a highly accurate picture of what has gone before, and where it has all led."

TV: *Positively Black*, NBC, w. Lateef; Ron Carter; *Like It Is*, ABC, w. E. Marrow. Fest: Bologna; Kongsberg w. Lateef, '73; Newport, R.I. w. Getz, '75. Comp: *Peruvian Blue; The Procession; Two Areas; In the Meantime; Dreams; Morning Glory; Revelation; A Flower; Sunset; Dawn; Swamp Demon; Delores Street*.

LPs: *Peruvian Blue; Sunset to Dawn*; w. Albert Heath, *Kwanza*; w. Moody, *Feelin' It Together* (Muse); w. G. Benson, *Bad Benson* (CTI); w. Joe Henderson, *Tetragon; The Kicker* (Mile.); w. Jimmy Heath. *The Gap Sealer* (Cobble.); w. Hubbard, *High Blues Pressure*; w. Owens-Barron, *You Had Better Listen* (Atl.); w. Rich (Groove Merchant); w. Lateef (Atl.).

BARTKOWSKI, CZESLAW, *drums*; also *piano, percussion*; b. Lodz, Poland, 4/19/43. Att. music coll. in Wroctaw, Poland. Worked w. Krzysztof Komeda quintet, '63-5; Zbigniew Namyslowski quartet, '63-6; Czeslaw Niemen Enigmatic, '68-70; Michal Urbaniak, '71-4; trio w. Wojciech Karolak & Namyslowski, '73-4. In '74 he became part of Namyslowski's new quintet. He also performed in a trio w. Tomasz Stanko & Adam Makowicz, formed in '75 and continued to be part of the Polish Jazz Radio big band which he first joined in '73. Fests: all major European events; also Tauranga (New Zealand). NJF-NY w. Urbaniak; Cascais (Portugal) w. Namyslowski quintet, '74. Comp: *Suggestion; Blues*, rec. by Makowicz in *Unit* on Muza. LPs: own album for Muza; *Unit* w. Makowicz; *Mainstem* w. Jan Wroblewski (Muza); w. Namyslowski, *Lola* (Decca); w. Urbaniak, *Inactin; Paratyphus B* (Intercord); *Super Constellation* (CBS); *Fusion; Atma* (Col.).

BARTZ, GARY LEE, *saxophones, composer, singer*; b. Baltimore, Md., 9/26/40. Father ran local jazz club where Bartz pl. as teenager. Acquired an alto sax at 11. At 17, went to NYC, studied at Juilliard for three semesters, jammed w. F. Hubbard, L. Morgan, P. Sanders. Back in Baltimore, stud. at Peabody Cons. Professional debut w. Max Roach-Abbey Lincoln group, followed by a stint w. Art Blakey, '65-6. Worked w. Roach again, '68-9, also w. McCoy Tyner and Blue Mitchell during same period. Originally org. his own combo known as Ntu Troop (the word means the unification of all things spiritual and physical, in the Bantu philosophy) in '69 and began making a series of recordings with this unit, but joined Miles Davis in Aug. '70 and remained with him through late '71.

In his notes to an early album cut by Bartz in 1967, Orrin Keepnews observed: "This is, at its core, melodic jazz; and it is basically happy music. There is much complexity and thought here; but there is also a distinct feeling of pleasure." He noted that Louis Jordan and Sonny Rollins were among Bartz's early influences. Bartz, however, in a statement some years later, after the rise of the Ntu Troop to international popularity, declared that he was not playing jazz, but American music, adding that "I'm trying to decategorize things with and about myself."

In addition to traveling with the group and appearing at major festivals, Bartz was involved in such outside ventures as the writing of theme and score for an ABC-TV special, *About Time*, aired in late '72. Though he has done much of his best work on alto and soprano saxes, Bartz also has been heard on records playing sopranino sax, electric piano, percussion, and singing. His reputation as a creative artist and writer grew with the release, in 1974, of the *Singerella* album (see below). He has app. at many fests. incl. Kongsberg, '73; Montreux, '73; Berkeley, '74. Won DB and Melody Maker polls on alto sax, '72.

LPs: *Libra; Another Earth; Harlem Bush Music-Taifa; Harlem Bush Music—Uhuru; Home* (Milestone); *Follow The Medicine Man; I've Known Rivers* (live at Montreux); *Ju-Ju Street Songs; Singerella*—A Ghetto Fairytale (Prest.); w. Davis, *Live-Evil* (Col.).

BASCOMB, WILBUR ODELL (DUD),* *trumpet*; b. Birmingham, Ala., 5/16/16. The featured trumpet soloist with the Erskine Hawkins orchestra of the 30's and 40's was occupied as a busy free-lancer during the 60's and early 70's until his death, 12/25/72, NYC. Played in off-Broadway production *Cindy* '66; pit orch. for *Purlie* '70. Concerts and European tours w. Buddy Tate '68, '70. Led own sextet for gig in Toronto '68. Played on sound tracks for *It's A Mad, Mad, Mad World; Midnight Cowboy; Legend of Nigger Charlie.* His son, bassist, Wilbur Jr., worked with him and also was with the Billy Taylor band on the David Frost TV show '72.

LPs: *Unbroken* w. Buddy Tate (MPS), Erskine Hawkins Reunion (Stang).

BASIE, WILLIAM (COUNT),* *leader, piano, organ, composer*; b. Red Bank, N.J., 8/21/04. A bandleader since '35, when he was discovered in Kansas City by John Hammond, Basie during the '60s and '70s broadened his popularity by rec. and appearing in concerts with such singers as F. Sinatra and T. Bennett. During these years the band's personnel changed more frequently than it had in the past. In '69, it comprised Gene Goe, Sonny Cohn, Al Aarons, Oscar Brashear, trumpets; Bill Hughes, Grover Mitchell, Richard Boone, Frank Hooks, trombones; Marshal Royal, Bobby Plater, Eddie Davis, Eric Dixon, Charlie Fowlkes, saxophones; Freddie Green, guitar; Norman Keenan, bass; Harold Jones, drums. Within the next couple of years most of these musicians had left the band, though some, incl. Fowlkes, Hughes and Dixon, returned after absences of varying lengths. Green was the only sideman who had remained with Basie almost continuously since the late '30s.

An important development was the addition to Basie's arr. staff of Sammy Nestico (q.v.), whose original comps. formed the basis for several of the orchestra's most musically interesting albums. An unusual venture was the band's tentative attempt to incorporate avant garde and other unconventional elements in the album *Afrique*, rec. in late '70 w. O. Nelson as arr. and conductor. On this occasion, the band was augmented by Hubert Laws on flute, Buddy Lucas on harmonica and John B. Williams on elect. bass. The title tune was Basie's first and only rec. in 7/4 time.

Beginning in early '70, the band made a series of annual cruises on the Queen Elizabeth II, and additionally took part in a Caribbean cruise, Showboat 2, aboard the Rotterdam, Dec. '74. In '75, after freelancing for many years on a variety of labels, Basie began rec. regularly for Norman Granz's Pablo Records. The result was a collection of LPs that showed him in several different and challenging settings, in sharp contrast to the uninspired pairings with such artists as the Mills Bros. and various other singers, vocal groups etc. that had marked too much of his LP activity for several years. The personnel in late '75 comprised: Pete Minger, Frank Szabo, Dave Stahl, Bobby Mitchell, Sonny Cohn, trumpets; Al Grey, Curtis Fuller, Bill Hughes, Mel Wanzo, trombones; Danny Turner, Bobby Plater, altos; Jimmy Forrest, tenor; Eric Dixon, tenor & flute; Charlie Fowlkes, baritone; Freedie Green, guitar; John Duke, bass; Butch Miles, drums.

In '74, Basie's 70th birthday was celebrated in a banquet attended by many of his friends and old associates, at the Waldorf-Astoria Hotel, NYC. In the fall of '75 the orch. took part in concerts w. F. Sinatra at the Uris Theatre, NYC, Palladium, London. In recent years, Basie has made his home in Freeport, Bahamas.

LPs: *Basie Big Band; Satch & Josh*, w. O. Peterson; *For The First Time* w. Basie Trio; *Basie Jam* w. H. Edison, Z. Sims, Eddie Davis, J.J. Johnson et al; *Basie Jam Session at the Montreux Jazz Festival, '75* w. R. Eldridge, L. Bellson, Milt Jackson, Johnny Griffin, Niels-Henning Orsted Pedersen et al (Pablo); *Afrique* (Fl. Dutchman); *Basic Basie* (MPS); *Basie's In The Bag* (Bruns.); *Best of; Echoes of an Era; Echoes of an Era,* Vocal Years; *Fantail; Kansas City Suite/Easin' It; Kid From Red Bank*; w. Eckstine; w. Vaughan (Roulette); *Board of Directors*, w. Mills Bros; *Standing Ovation; Straight Ahead* (Dot); *Broadway Basie's Way* (Com.); *Hits of 50s and 60s* (Repr.); *Kansas City 7* (Imp.); *Meets Bond* (Solid); *Newport Years*; w. J. Williams (Verve); *16 Great Perf.* w. Mills Bros (ABC); *Songs of Bessie Smith*, w. Teresa Brewer (Fl. Dutchman).

BASS, LEE ODDIS III (MICKEY), *bass, composer*; also *piano, brass, flute*; b. Pittsburgh, Pa., 5/2/43. Mother was a singer; grandmother, a piano teacher, taught him and cousins barbershop harmony. Studied bass in high school and privately w. William Lewis for several years in Pitts. Pl. in All City High School orch. Attended Howard U., Coll. of Fine Arts, 1961-3, majoring in Music Ed.; NYU, '67-8. First job in NYC w. Hank Mobley at Theresa Hotel, '64; then worked w. Bennie Green at Birdland; briefly w. Jackie McLean; Art Blakey; Sonny Rollins. With Bobby Timmons, '65; Gloria Lynne from '65 for three yrs; Blakey; Carmen McRae, '67; Gloria Lynne, '68; Billy Eckstine, '68-9; Blakey, '70; Freddie Freddie Hubbard; Miriam Makeba; Blakey again. Teaches bass and jazz improvisational technique at High School of the Arts, Wash., D.C.; and for Jazzmobile in NYC. Own group on Sundays at Doctor Generosity's; also w. Duke Jordan at Churchill's, NYC, '76. Own weekly record show on WBAI-FM. Infl: C. Parker, M. Davis, J. Coltrane. TV: Today w. Frank Foster; NBC Special for National Council of Churches w. David Amram; Billy Eckstine Show w. F. Hubbard; American and Japanese apps. w. Blakey. Fests: NJF-NY w. Hubbard, '71; Blakey, '73. Comps: *Sweat; A Chant Bu; One For Trane; Mickey's Tune; Meditations; Gayle's Groove; Soul Sock 'N Jamboree; Siempre Me Amor.* Wrote arrs. for NYU Stage Band; Jaki Byard's big band. Composing jazz string quartet, '76. LPs: w. Blakey, *Buhaina; Anthenagin* (Prest.); w. Curtis Fuller, *Smokin'* (Main.).

BASSO, GIANNI,* *tenor saxophone*; b. Asti, Italy, 5/24/31. Educ. Conservatorio di Asti. Frequent partnership w. Oscar Valdambrini from '50s. Worked with many visiting leaders in Italy, incl. M. Ferguson, D. Goykovich, Slide Hampton, C. Baker, P. Woods, K. Clarke, Sal Nistico, G. Mulligan, F. Rosolino, B. Collette, C. Candoli, Lars Gullin. Film: *La Prima Notte di Quiete* w. Ferguson. Numerous jazz fests. throughout Europe. LPs: w. own group; eight w. Valdambrini; others with S. Hampton, Baker, Collette, Rosolino.

BAYETÉ (Todd Cochran), *piano, keyboards, composer*; b. San Francisco, Cal., 9/3/51. Began playing at three; priv. studies from age six. During high school was enrolled in corresp. course from Trinity College, England, obtaining B.M. in '70 after eight years of study. Additional educ. under a scholarship at San Jose State U. Bayeté was only 17 when he began working w. John Handy, remaining with the group for about a year. He spent most of the next two years w. B. Hutcherson and H. Land, leaving their group to form his own combo. He also did sound track work w. Herbie Hancock.

Bayeté made an immediate impression both as pianist and composer in the Hutcherson-Land album *Head On*. His strong keyboard style suggested a McCoy Tyner influence, and his compositions were fresh and texturally original. Evaluating his music, he said: "It involves contemporary harmonic and basic ethnic rhythms, and it calls for an understanding of the Afro-American experience." He was inspired by Hutcherson, with whom, he said, he felt his closest and most spiritual relationship, and was also infl. by William Fischer.

Fests: Concord, Berkeley, and a tribute to Miles Davis at MJF. LPs: *Seeking Other Beauty; Worlds Around The Sun* (Pres.) *Iapetus* w. Hadley Caliman (Mainstream); *Head On* w. Hutcherson (Blue Note).

BEAL, EDDIE,* *piano, composer*; b. Redlands, Cal., 6/13/10. Best known as songwriter, talent scout and vocal coach. To Viet Nam with Christy Minstrels, '69. Two road tours as pianist/conductor for L. Rawls, '70. Own gp. Playboy Club, Century City, '73, and Desert Inn, LV, '74. In Dec. '74 and Jan. '75, he was feat. pianist in concert w. T. Dorsey band under direction of M. McEachern, pl. throughout Florida and other southern states. Also went on a Sitmar cruise with the orch. Film: App. as pianist in *Sparkle*. TV: *Sanford & Son*. Best known comps: *Softly*, rec. by Georgia Carr, S. Kenton; *All Because of You*, rec. by Kenton, D. Washington; *Skoot* (written with E. Garner), rec. by Kenton, MJQ; *Let Your Love Walk In*, rec. by Kenton.

BEAN, FLOYD R.,* *piano, composer*; b. Ladora, Iowa, 8/30/04. Played w. Bix Beiderbecke in Davenport, '23; later w. Bunny Berigan; Jack Jenney as sidemen in various bands. In '30s and '40s w. Bob Crosby; Boyd Raeburn; Sidney Bechet. In '50s w. Muggsy Spanier, Georg Brunis in Chicago. Cont. to pl. in Chi. until '64 when he moved to Cedar Rapids, Iowa where he died 3/9/74.

BECK, GORDON, *piano, electric piano, composer*; b. London, England, 9/16/36. Three years classical piano tuition from age 12-15. Began prof. career in 1961; names Ch. Parker, B. Powell, B. Evans, H. Hancock, P. Woods, Delius, Ravel as infls. From '62-66 w. groups of Tony Kinsey, Tubby Hayes; acc. Annie Ross. In '69 own trio backed Helen Merrill, Joe Henderson, Lee Konitz, Phil Woods et al at Ronnie Scott Club. From '69-72 extensive touring of Europe and U.S. w. P. Woods quartet with whom he app. at NJF, '71. Other jazz fests in Montreux and throughout Europe. In '73 was member of Piano Conclave. In '73-75 own group "Gyroscope."

Several of Beck's comps. have been recorded, incl. *The Day When The World Comes Alive*, Cleo Laine (RCA); *Here Comes The Mallet Man; Tying Up Loose Ends*, Gary Burton (Polydor); *The Meeting*, P. Woods (Embryo). Other comps. include a suite for seven piece orch. for BBC radio.

BECK, JOE, *guitar*; b. Phila., Pa., 7/29/45. First professional work with Paul Winter, '64; Charles Lloyd, '64; Gary McFarland, 64-6; Chico Hamilton, '67; Gil Evans, '67-70. Left the music business in '71 to become a dairy farmer; returned to New York and musical activity '73. Beck has also worked with Peggy Lee, Lena Horne, Gene Ammons, Jimmy Smith, Maynard Ferguson, Buddy Rich, Woody Herman, Joe Farrell. LPs: *Joe Beck* (Kudu); *Penny Arcade; Upon This Rock*, w. Farrell (CTI); tracks in *The Guitar Album*, rec. live at Town Hall Concert, Aug. '71 (Col.); w. David Sanborn (WB).

BECKERHOFF, ULI, *trumpet, fluegelhorn, piano*; b. Muenster, W. Germany, 12/6/47. Began playing in high school. Stud. in Muenster and Cologne, also w. Manfred Schoof, '68-70, and others. Pl. with several big bands in Bremen, Dortmund, Cologne. From '72 worked with Jazztrack Quintet. In '73 and '74 pl. at J.E. Berendt's New Jazz Meeting in Baden-Baden, with C. Mariano, A. Mangelsdorff, Marvin Peterson et al. Worked with German All Stars Globe Unity Orch., Joachim Kuhn. In '71 won first prize with an international quartet in Holland.

LP: *First Call*, w. Jazztrack Quintet.

BELL, SAMUEL, AARON,* *bass, tuba, trumpet, piano, composer*; b. Muskogee, Okla., 4/24/22. Prominent as bassist with many N.Y. groups in '50s, also Duke Ellington, '60-2. Played in pit bands. Composed for off-Broadway theatre, '69-72. Resident composer La Mama Experimental Theatre, '70-3. Asst. Prof., Essex College, Newark, N.J., '70-5 teaching theory, arr., comp. M.Ed. degree, Columbia U. May '75. Mus. Dir., Elmsford Dinner Theatre, '74-5. Pl. at NJF '73 w. Paul Jeffrey; '74 w. Corky Corcoran.

Comps: *Watergate Sonata* for piano; *Rondo Schizo* for clarinet and piano; *Frugal Fugue* for small combo. LPs:

Duke Meets Coltrane; Duke Meets the Hawk (Impulse).

BELLSON, LOUIE PAUL (Louis Balassoni),* *drums, composer, leader*; b. Rock Falls, Ill., 7/26/24. Drummer in many name bands incl. B. Goodman, T. Dorsey, H. James; toured w. D. Ellington, '51-3 and again '65-6. After rejoining James for a while, he organized his own Hollywood-based big band, which played together intermittently; however, he frequently fronted other bands as mus. dir. for his wife, Pearl Bailey.

As composer, his wide ranging activities included *The London Suite*, which he recorded with a specially assembled band in London; the first movement, written in collaboration with Jack Hayes, is the well known *Carnaby Street*, which was the theme for the Pearl Bailey TV show. Bellson also wrote words and music for *I Need Your Key*, sung by James Brown in a King album backed by Bellson's orch; *The Marriage Vows*, perf. at LV Jazz Fest. '62; *Symphony in Americana*, premiered by 60 piece orch. in LV; and *Composition for Piano and Orchestra*, presented in concert by a 55 piece orch. in Washington, D.C.

Universally admired and respected as a musician who combines enthusiasm and a driving beat with an astonishing technique, incl. the use of two bass drums, Bellson was described by Ellington as "The world's greatest drummer . . . Louie Bellson has all the requirements for perfection in his craft."

During '70s, has played and talked at many clinics in schools and colleges. Publs. incl. two sight reading books (Belwin Music, Inc., NYC); Method Book (Try Publ., 854 Vine St., Hollywood, CA. 90028); three drum method books (Robbins Music, NYC).

LPs: *Explosion* (Pablo); *Breakthrough* (Proj. 3); *Louie Rides Again* (Percussion Power, 5109 Nagle Ave., Sherman Oaks, Cal. 91403); w. Basie; Trumpet Kings; Oscar Peterson: all at Montreux '75 (Pablo).

BENEKE, TEX,* *tenor sax, singer, leader*; b. Fort Worth, Tex, 2/12/14. The former (1938-42) Glenn Miller soloist continued to assemble orchestras for concert and dance dates at which he played music in the Miller style. Though the band was not officially sanctioned by Miller's estate, it usually included singers and instrumentalists who had worked in the original Miller organization.

BENFORD, THOMAS P. (TOMMY),* *drums*; b. Charleston, W. Va., 4/19/05. With older brother, Bill, a noted tuba player, learned music at the Jenkins Orphanage in S. Carolina. Toured w. Orphanage band, incl. England, 1914. Several perfs. in London before World War I forced return to US. Stud. drums w. Steve and Herbert Wright. First pro. job w. Green River Minstrel Show in '20. Pl. w. Marie Lucas, Edgar Hayes, Charlie Skeet, Bill Benford, F. Waller, D. Ellington in '20s. To Europe w. Eddie South, '32 where he worked also w. Freddie Taylor, '36-7; Willie Lewis, '38-41. In US w. Noble Sissle, '43; Snub Mosley, '46-8; Bob Wilber, 48-9; Jimmy Archey, '50-2, incl. tour of Germany and Switzerland, '52. In '50s also pl. w. Rex Stewart, M. Spanier; subbed in Geo. Lewis band and pl. in house bands at Central Plaza and Jimmy Ryan's. Worked w. Freddy Johnson, '59. To Europe w. *Jazz Train* under dir. of Eddie Barefield, '60-1. Pl. w. Joe Thomas, Edmond Hall, Danny Barker, NYC, '63, then w. Saints and Sinners. Dec. '68 w. Franz Jackson. Benford, who played w. Jelly Roll Morton in the '20s, is not active on a fulltime basis but app. w. pianist Bob Greene's World of Jelly Roll Morton recreation of the Red Hot Peppers in concert at the NJF-NY, '73, and at Alice Tully Hall, '73-4. The veteran drummer, who rec. extensively in Europe in the '30s w. South, C. Hawkins, Benny Carter and D. Reinhardt, can be heard w. Greene in *The World of Jelly Roll Morton* (RCA).

BENJAMIN, JOSEPH RUPERT (JOE),* *bass*; b. Atlantic City, N.J. 11/4/19. Veteran bassist, who pl. his first major date w. D. Ellington at a 1951 Metropolitan Opera House concert, and was intermittently associated w. Ellington over the years as copyist, sideman and employee of Ellington's publ. co. Benjamin died 1/26/74 in Livingstone, N.J., of a heart attack, some weeks after suffering injuries in an automobile accident. LP: w. Ellington, *Eastbourne Performance* (RCA).

BENNETT, MAX,* *bass*; b. Des Moines, Iowa, 5/24/28. Confined mainly to studio work in LA through '72, also with big bands led by Mike Barone, Bud Brisbois, Jack Daugherty. Became original member of Tom Scott's L.A. Express in late '72, touring throughout '74 with this group and singer Joni Mitchell. Also w. Crusaders during '73 and rec. with them. Composed songs and lyrics rec. by Peggy Lee; instr. for L.A. Express.

LPs: w. L.A. Express (A & M); *Class of '71* w. Daugherty (A & M); *Scratch* w. Crusaders (Blue Thumb).

BENNETT, TONY (Anthony Dominick Benedetto), *singer*; b. Queens, L.I., N.Y., 8/3/26. Discovered by Pearl Bailey and Bob Hope; began recording 1950 and was heard in series of best-selling hit singles such as *Because of You; Cold Cold Heart; Tender is the Night.* After a fallow period, Bennett's career was revived with a 1962 hit, *I Left My Heart in San Francisco.* His association with jazz has been marked by the use of such musicians as pianist John Bunch; cornetists Bobby Hackett and Ruby Braff; saxophonists Zoot Sims and Al Cohn. He recorded two albums w. Basie band in the mid-1950s and toured in concerts with Duke Ellington, Woody Herman. One of the best jazz-influenced singers in the classic pop tradition, he was heard at his best in a duo album w. Bill Evans, late '75 (Fantasy). Formed own record co., Improv, '75, planning to feature himself in a variety of pop and jazz settings. Other LPs: Columbia.

BENSON, GEORGE,* *guitar, singer*; b. Pittsburgh, Pa., 3/22/43. After three yrs. w. Jack McDuff, formed own gp. and has toured w. it from '65. His unit that rec. for Col. included Ronnie Cuber on baritone and Lonnie Smith, organ. In the '70s he became affiliated w. Creed Taylor, first at A&M Records, then w. Taylor's CTI label, in productions that surrounded the guitarist with large orchestral arrs. designed to bring him to a wider audience. Many felt that Taylor was trying to fit Benson into the slot vacated by the late Wes Montgomery. Although the albums did enjoy commercial success, Benson demonstrated that despite the format he was still his own man. He toured w. the CTI concert package, utilizing his singing both with words and in a wordless technique that he blended with his guitar. When he participated in the TV tribute to John Hammond on NET, as part of the house gp., he again showed his link to Charlie Christian especially when specifically asked to do so in accompanying Benny Goodman. Fest: NJF-NY, '73, '75. Comps: *The Shape of Things That Are and Were; Footin' It; The Borgia Stick.*

LPs: *Body Talk; White Rabbit; Bad Benson; Beyond the Blue Horizon* (CTI); *Other Side of Abbey Road; Shape of Things; Tell It Like It Is* (A&M); *Cookbook; Willow Weep For Me; Spirituals to Swing, 30th Anniversary* (Col.); *Jaki Byard With Strings* (Prest.); w. M. Davis, *Miles in the Sky* (Col.).

BERGER, KARL HANS, *piano, vibes*; also *percussion, composer*; b. Heidelberg, Germany, 3/30/35. Stud. Heidelberg Conserv., '48-54; musicology, philosophy, Univ. of Berin, '55-63; earned Ph.D., '63. Based in Paris, he worked w. Don Cherry, '65-6. Later moved to NYC, working w. Roswell Rudd, Steve Lacy, Marion Brown, David Izenzon, Horacee Arnold, Sam Rivers. School and coll. concerts through Young Audiences Inc., '67-71. Berger led his own groups off and on from '66, making several tours to Europe and Canada. Assoc. w. JCOA. Infls: J.S. Bach, Bud Powell, O. Coleman, Ing Rid (his wife, a singer).

Berger, in '71, was founder, w. Coleman, of Creative Music Foundation Inc. Dir. of Creative Music Studio, Woodstock, N.Y. and similar studio at Haropa Inst., Boulder, Colo. Comp. and leader for *Karl Berger & Friends: Music Universe.* Won DB Critics Poll, TDWR, as vibraphonist in '68, and again in '71, '74, '75. TV: many apps on German TV network and Danish TV in Copenhagen. Fests: Prague, Molde, Pori, Antibes, Frankfurt, Berlin. Publs: *Thesis on Music Ideology* (Osteuropa Institut, Berlin). Comps: *Cycles of the Birth of the New World; Space In Time; Silence in Sound; From Now On; Tune In; With Silence; We Are You.* Berger is one of the most scholarly as well as most gifted artists of the jazz-oriented avant-garde school.

LPs: *From Now On* (ESP); *Tune In* (Milest.); *With Silence* (Enja) *We Are You* (Calig.); *Peace Church Concerts* (CMC); *When Fortune Smiles*, w. J. McLaughlin, J. Surman, D. Holland (Pye); w. Cherry, *Symphony for Improvisers* (BN); *Eternal Rhythm* (MPS); w. L. Konitz, *Lee Konitz Duets* (Milest.).

BERK, RICHARD ALAN (DICK), *drums*; b. San Francisco, Cal., 5/22/39. Educ. Berklee College w. Alan Dawson, '59-60. After local work, moved to NYC, '58. Many night clubs w. Nick Brignola, Ted Curson-Bill Barron, Ch. Mingus, W. Bishop Jr., F. Hubbard, M. Allison, Monty Alexander. Moved to LA, '68; Monterey Fest. and tours w. G. Szabo, George Duke. Numerous concerts and fests. in U.S. and Europe. Regular member of Cal Tjader quintet from '70, also gigging with Milt Jackson, Ray Brown, touring Japan with G. Auld etc. After settling in LA, took up acting; seen in play *Idiot's Delight* w. J. Lemmon, also roles in movies *Bummer; Mad Mad Movie Makers*; and TV series *Emergency.*

LPs: w. Don Friedman (Riverside); Jean-Luc Ponty (Liberty-UA); Curson (Audio-Fidelity, Atlantic, Fontana); M. Jackson (Impulse); Tjader (Fantasy).

BERK, LAWRENCE, *educator, composer, arranger, piano*; b. Boston, Mass., 12/10/08. Classmate of Harry Carney in HS. Stud. w. Joseph Schillinger, '33-9. Comp., arr. for many network radio shows. Founder and president of Berklee Coll. of Music, '45, then known as Schillinger House, now recognized as the largest independent, non-profit, accredited, degree-granting college of music in the world.

Inspired by the school's jazz-oriented curriculum were such alumni as Q. Jones, G. Burton, G. McFarland, K. Jarrett, Rick Laird, C. Mariano, A. Broadbent, Mike Gibbs, Geo Mraz, Toshiko Akiyoshi, G. Szabo, Arif Mardin, Jan Hammer, Lennie Johnson, Pat LaBarbera, Sadao Watanabe, Bill Chase, Dick Nash, J. Zawinul, Lin Biviano, M. Vitous, Steve Marcus, Yasuo Arakawa, Ernie Watts, Dusko Gojkovic, Kurt Jaernberg, Allan Ganley, Gene Cherico, Jake Hanna, Bill Berry.

In developing the scope of educational opportunities at Berklee, Berk initiated significant and innovative concepts in jazz methodology that have been acclaimed by educators throughout the world.

BERRY, WILLIAM R. (BILL),* *trumpet, fluegelhorn, vibes, composer, leader*; b. Benton Harbor, Mich., 9/14/30. Pl. w. Duke Ellington, '62. With Merv Griffin TV show band from '64 in NYC and from '70 in LA. Member of all star group at White House for Ellington's 70th birthday party, '69. Concerts and TV shows dedicated to Ellington.

In '71 Berry formed the L.A. Big Band, a West Coast equivalent of the Thad Jones-Mel Lewis orch., comprising freelance musicians, many of them alumni of Ellington, Basie, Kenton, gigging in local clubs and at Concord Summer Fest. Berry also composed a Sacred Concert for choir and jazz band presented '73. Other comps: *Betty; Bloose; A Little Song for Mex; Sho* (recorded by Bill Watrous). Grant for jazz comp. from NEA, '70.

LPs: w. Ellington (Columbia, Reprise), Jones-Lewis (UA); *Once Upon A Time* w. Earl Hines (Impulse); *Profiles* w. Gary McFarland (Impulse). Live album, *Hot and Happy*, with own band for Beez Records (23033 Bryce St., Woodland Hills, CA. 91364) in '75.

BERRY, EMMETT,* *trumpet*; b. Macon, Ga., 7/23/16. Veteran of the Fletcher and Horace Henderson bands in the '30s; Teddy Wilson; Eddie Heywood, Count Basie, etc. in '40s. Pl. w. Peanuts Hucko, '66; Wilbur DeParis, '67; Big Chief Moore, '68; Buddy Tate, '69. In the '70s he left music and retired to Cleveland, Ohio due to ill health.

BERT, EDDIE,* *trombones*; b. Yonkers, N.Y., 5/16/22. From '66 to '68 played w. Elliot Lawrence orch. for Broadway shows: *Golden Boy, Apple Tree, Golden Rain-*

bow. Member of Bobby Rosengarden orch. for Dick Cavett ABC-TV show '68-72; Thad Jones-Mel Lewis orch. '67-March '72 incl. European tours; Charles Mingus orch. March-Aug. '72. With Sy Oliver from '73; also member of NYJRC '74-75 for Carnegie Hall concerts. *Eddie Bert Trombone Method* published by (Charles Colin, 315 W. 53rd St., N.Y., N.Y. 10019).

LPs w. Jones-Lewis (Solid State, Blue Note); Mingus (Columbia); Olatunji (Paramount).

BEY, ANDREW W. JR. (ANDY), *singer, piano, composer*; b. Newark, N.J., 10/28/39. His sisters, Salome and Geraldine, with whom he worked for 10 years as Andy & The Bey Sisters, are still active as singers. Started playing piano by ear at three; attended Arts High School of Music & Art in Newark. Studied piano w. Sanford Gold in '65 for a year. Voice coaching from Nat Jones and Romney Fell but basically a self-taught vocalist. During early 50's appeared on TV as a "Startime Kid" with Connie Francis, etc. With Louis Jordan at Apollo Theatre '53; to Europe w. his sisters in '58 for 16 months in France, England, Germany, Spain and Belgium. Has worked and recorded with Max Roach, Gary Bartz, Horace Silver, Duke Pearson and William Fischer. Nine months as vocalist with Thad Jones-Mel Lewis in '70s. Also w. Umajo Ensemble led by Mtume. Inspired and influenced by Coltrane, Ella Fitzgerald, Miles Davis, Art Tatum, Charlie Parker, Sarah Vaughan, Billie Holiday, Nat Cole, Sonny Rollins, Aretha Franklin, Ray Charles and Dinah Washington. Comp. *Celestial Blues*, recorded w. Gary Bartz' *Uhuru* on Milestone and his own album, *Experience And Judgement*, on Atlantic. Other LPs: *Healin' Feelin'* w. Horace Silver (BN); *Children of Forever* w. Stanley Clarke (Polydor); Mtume (Strata-East).

BERTONCINI, GENE, *guitar*; b. New York City, 4/6/37. Started lessons at age nine; first job at 16. With his brother, an accordionist, pl. children's TV series. After high school, entered Notre Dame, majoring in architecture, but returned to music in NYC after graduation. Worked w. Mike Mainieri, Buddy Rich. After service in Marine Corps, was active for years in television with Merv Griffin; Skitch Henderson on the *Tonight* show, etc. Abandoned his TV career to concentrate on further studies, later becoming active in a broad variety of areas, pl. w. Metropolitan Opera Orch., acc. Tony Bennett, Morgana King, Nancy Wilson, and playing innumerable pop and jazz record dates. Characterized by Georgia Urban in *Different Drummer* as "one of the most versatile men on the instrument . . . a vital part of the jazz world . . . he is destined to become one of the most respected guitarists."

LPs w. Hubert Laws, *Rite of Spring; Afro-Classic; Carnegie Hall* (CTI); w. Clark Terry, *More* (Cameo); w. T. Bennett, *I've Gotta Be Me* (Col.); w. Nancy Wilson, *But Beautiful* (Cap.); w. Wayne Shorter, *Odyssey of Iska* (Blue Note); w. Ron Carter, *Blues Farm* (CTI); w. L. Schifrin, *Marquis de Sade* (Verve); w. Earl Coleman, *Love Songs* (Atl.).

BICKERT, EDWARD ISAAC (ED),* *guitar*; b. Hochfeld, Manitoba, Canada, 11/29/32. Prominent in Toronto jazz circles w. Moe Koffman, Phil Nimmons, Ron Collier in '50s, he continued to pl. w. these leaders in the '60s & '70s, also app. w. Rob McConnell's Boss Brass and acc. visiting mus. like Paul Desmond, Frank Rosolino, Ch. McPherson in clubs. Active studio man who makes many apps. on CBC-TV. Fest: Belvedere King-Size Jazz Fest., Canada, '74. Bickert's reputation is mainly local but he is highly regarded by the Americans who have pl. w. him. LPs: *Collages* (MPS); w. Desmond, *Pure Desmond* (CTI); *Moe Koffman Live at George's* (GRT); w. McConnell, *Best Damn Band in the Land* (UA).

BIGARD, LEON ALBANY (BARNEY),* *clarinet, composer*; b. New Orleans, 3/3/06. Best known as co-composer of *Mood Indigo*, soloist w. Ellington, '28-42, L. Armstrong '46-52, '53-5, '60-1. Occasional freelance work in LA, incl. gigs w. Rex Stewart, '66; Armstrong 70th birthday concert, '70; Dick Gibson jazz parties in Colorado, '71, 72, '73; toured colleges, high schools w. Art Hodes, Wild Bill Davison, Eddie Condon, '71. Received keys to city from Mayor of New Orleans during jazz fest. April '72. Numerous fests. in U.S. and overseas, '74-5, incl. NJF, Nice, Pescara, San Sebastian, Bordeaux. In addition to many early LPs with Armstrong, Ellington, heard more recently in *Bucket's Got A Hole In It* (Delmark); *Stars of Jazz* (Jazzology), and w. Legends of Jazz (Crescent Jazz); also own LP on French RCA. In '75, toured Switzerland with New Ragtime Jazzband; film, *Musical Biography of Barney Bigard* for presentation on French TV.

BIG MAYBELLE (Mabel Smith),* *singer*; b. Jackson, Tenn., 1924. Best known for her 1958 appearance at NJF and in the film *Jazz on a Summer's Day* produced at the festival, the blues singer died 1/23/72 in Cleveland, Ohio after a long illness. LPs: *The Gospel Soul of Big Maybelle* (Bruns.); *Last of Big Maybelle* (Para.).

BISHOP, WALTER JR.,* *piano, composer*; b. New York City, 10/4/27. Member of many pioneer bop groups led by Parker, M. Davis, Pettiford, T. Gibbs, Blakey. Extensive studies in late '60s w. Ida Elkan, Rudolph Schramm, Hall Overton and, after move to Cal. in 1970, w. Lyle (Spud) Murphy, Albert Harris. Gigs, recs. w. many LA combos incl. Supersax, Blue Mitchell. Taught privately, 1972-5; pl., lectured at LA colleges with own gp., "4th Cycle." Publ.: *A Study In 4ths* (Don Sickler, 254 West 44th St., New York, N.Y. 10036).

Comps: *Coral Keys* rec. by F. Hubbard; *Waltz for Sweetie* rec. by Joe Henderson; *Soul Village* rec. by B. Mitchell; *Sweet Rosa* w. own gp.

LPs: Own gps. (Black Jazz; Muse; Prestige); also w. Supersax (Cap.); Blue Mitchell (Main.); many reissues w. Ch. Parker (Verve, etc.).

BLACK ARTHUR (Arthur Murray Blythe), *alto, soprano saxophones, composer*; b. Los Angeles, Cal., 7/5/40. Stud. w. former J. Lunceford saxophonist Kirt Bradford; David Jackson, a tenor saxophonist and composer, who worked w. Lenny McBrowne, Ray Charles. Based in LA, he pl. w. H. Tapscott, '63-73; Owen Marshall, '67; Stanley Crouch and the Black Music Infinity, '67-73. Moving to NYC in '74, worked w. Leon Thomas, Ted Daniel and the Energy Band; Julius Hemphill; Chico Hamilton. Visited Cal. briefly w. Hamilton in summer of '75. Infls: Coltrane, Ellington, T. Monk, Ch. Parker, Harold Land, Daniel Jackson, E. Dolphy. Film sound tracks (playing): *Sweet Jesus Preacher; As Above, Also Below; Coonskin.* Fests: Watts, '67 w. Marshall; Cal. State w. Tapscott, '68; Coltrane Fest, '69, w. Crouch; Billie Holiday Fest., '71, w. Tapscott; Ch. Parker Fest, '72, w. Tapscott. The Coltrane, Holiday and Parker fests. were given in the black community of LA and were organized by Quincy Troupe.

In '75 Blythe observed: "I am presently working out ways of arranging that would make use of multi-phonics in reed voicings. I had discovered those things around 1961 before I heard Coltrane do them." Comps: *The Bitter Suite; The Grip; Illusions; Shadows; Metamorphosis.*

LPs: w. Tapscott, *The Giant Is Awakening* (Fl. Dutchman); w. Azar Lawrence, *Bridge to the New Age* (Prest.); w. Hamilton, *Peregrinations* (BN); others w. Hemphill (Arista); *Now Is Another Time; Past Spirits*, w. Crouch.

BLACKBURN, LOU,* *trombone*; also *bass trombone, flute, schalmei*; b. Rankin, Pa. 11/12/22. Active as studio musician in Hollywood and w. Onzy Matthews, Gerald Wilson, B. Bryant, S. Kenton's Neophonic orch., N. Riddle and Cocoanut Grove band, backing many singers, '66-70. Moved to Berlin, Oct. '70; worked w. radio orch. there and w. Kurt Edelhagen band. Mus. Dir. for the German prod. of *Catch My Soul* at Theater des Westens. Remained w. theater orch. also freelancing in Germany, until July '73. Formed a group, Mombasa, feat. African musicians in Sept. '73, playing mixture of African and Western music built on polyrhythms, written and arr. by Blackburn. Toured extensively in Europe, '74-5. Fests: Monterey w. Ch. Mingus, T. Monk, B. Bryant; German fests. since '73. Motion pic. work w. D. Amram, Q. Jones, J.J. Johnson. Many TV shows, incl. specs. w. Sinatra, The Supremes, Milton Berle.

LPs: *New Frontier; Two Note Samba* (Imperial-Liberty); *Monterey Jazz Festival*, w. Mingus (Fant.).

BLACKWELL, EDWARD B. (ED), *drums*; b. New Orleans, La., 1927. Playing in late '40s in NO. Met Ornette Coleman when the latter visited there in '49. To LA '51 and in mid-'50s maintained close contact w. Coleman. Returned to NO in late '50s before moving to NYC, '60, replacing Billy Higgins in Coleman's quartet. Played at Five Spot w. Eric Dolphy-Booker Little quintet, '61. w. Randy Weston, '65-7 incl. African tour. Gigs w. Mose Allison. Back w. Coleman '67-8; and again in '70s. App. w. him at NJF-NY, '72. Pl. in "free jazz" set in Radio City jam session at NJF-NY '73. Took ill with a kidney ailment in '74 and benefits to raise money for his treatment were held in NYC; NO; Baton Rouge, La.; England; Denton Coll., and Western Coll., both in Ohio. Artist-in-residence at Wesleyan U., fall '75. Original infls. were early NO drummers Baby Dodds, Zutty Singleton, Paul Barbarin. His melodic concept coupled with his roots makes Blackwell the most musical drummer to emerge from the avant garde of the '60s. LPs: w. Coleman, *Science Fiction* (Col.); *Friends and Neighbors* (Fly. Dutch.); *Free Jazz* (Atl.); w. Don Cherry, *Relativity Suite* (JCOA); *Symphony For Improvisers; Where Is Brooklyn* (BN); w. A. Shepp, *Magic of Ju Ju* (Imp.); w. A. Heath, *Kawaida* (Trip); *The Great Concert of Eric Dolphy* (Prest.).

BLAIR, JOHN, *vitar, singer, composer*; b. Toledo, Ohio, 11/8/43. Raised in San Diego, Cal. Began studying violin at age 10 and made prof. debut at 16 w. San Diego Symph. Won a Musical Merit Scholarship an international musicians' award given to 100 students chosen for the Pablo Casals festival in Puerto Rico. Received scholarship to Eastman School in Rochester, N.Y. where he earned Bachelor of Music. Pl. w. Air Force Strolling Strings at White House during Kennedy and Johnson administrations. Further studies at Curtis Institute in Phila. To NYC '64 where he began to play jazz, pop, rock and soul with a variety of people incl. Richie Havens, Johnny Mathis, James Brown, Stevie Wonder, Horace Silver, Bobby Womack, Isaac Hayes and Alice Coltrane.

Plays the vitar, a solid body electric instrument made for him by Lee Larison of the Boston Symph. It combines violin, viola and guitar, has a built-in fuzztone, and volume controls for each of its five strings. This gives it synthesizer-like qualities.

Blair, who names John Coltrane as his main influence, made an unscheduled, unannounced appearance at one of the Radio City Music Hall jam sessions of the NJF-NY '72. At NJF-NY '73 he again again pl. at the Radio City jam and w. his own quintet on a concert w. the gps. of John Mayall and Chuck Mangione at Philharmonic Hall. A fourth degree Black Belt, he operates the American Natural Style Karate School in Manhattan.

TV: *David Frost; To Tell the Truth; New York Illustrated; Black News; Black Journal; Tonight.* Comp: *Southern Love; Sunburst; I Sent My Son; Canadian Rock Lady; Tower of Fantasy; Searchin' Uptown; Hot Pants.* LPs: *Southern Love* (Col.); *Newport in New York, The Jam Sessions, Vols. 1&2* (Cobble.).

BLAKE, JAMES HUBERT (EUBIE),* *composer, piano*; b. Baltimore, Md. 2/7/1883. After many years of intermittent activity, Blake returned to prominence as a result of a two record album produced by John Hammond for Columbia in '69. In '72 he started his own record company, Eubie Blake Music, and appeared at the Newport-New York and Berlin Jazz Fests. In Feb. '73, shortly after traveling by train to LA for radio and TV shows and lectures, he was honored by ASCAP in NYC Feb. 7, his 90th birthday. The following May he made his first plane flight, to record five numbers for QRS Music Rolls in Buffalo, N.Y. Other appearances during that year incl. Boston Pops with Arthur Fiedler; fests. in Switzerland, Denmark, Norway; many concerts and TV shows. In '74 he taped a biographical film, *Reminiscing with Sissle and*

Blake, in Tampa, Fla., with his old vaudeville partner Noble Sissle. Later that year he played a Carnegie Hall concert with Benny Goodman, a jazz fest. in Nice, and a Scott Joplin fest. in Sedalia, Miss. In Sept. '74 made his first app. at MJF.

Blake's best known comps. are *I'm Just Wild About Harry* and *Memories Of You*. A lavishly illustrated book, also entitled *Reminiscing with Sissle and Blake*, by Robert Kimball and William Bolcom, was publ. in '72 by Viking Press (625 Madison Ave., N.Y. 10022).

LPs: *The Eighty-Six Years of Eubie Blake* (Columbia); Eubie Blake Vol. I (feat. Ivan Harold Browning); *Rags To Classics* (solo piano); *Eubie Blake and his friends Edith Wilson & Ivan Harold Browning; Sissle & Blake; Eubie Blake/Live Concert; Eubie Blake Introducing Jim Hession* (Eubie Blake Music, 284-A Stuyvesant Ave., Brooklyn, N.Y. 11221).

BLAKE, RAN,* *piano, keyboards, composer*; b. Springfield, Mass. 4/20/35. Co-director of Community Services Dept. of the New England Conservatory of Music, '68; Production Manager and Music Director, '69-72; Recruiter for Admissions Dept., '68-73. Governor's Task Force, Committee on Accessibility to the Arts, '71; Metropolitan Cultural Alliance, '72; Member of New England Conserv. faculty (improvisation), '69-73; Chairman, Third Stream Music Dept., '73. Author of book on vocal improvisation for Macmillan. LPs: *Ran Blake Plays Solo Piano* (ESP); *The Newest Sound Around*, with singer Jeanne Lee (RCA); *Blue Potato and Other Outrages* (Milestone).

BLAKENEY, ANDREW (ANDY), *trumpet*; b. Quitman, Miss., 6/10/1898. In 1925 Blakeney pl. for two weeks in Chicago with King Oliver, and in the late '20s moved to California and worked locally. With Les Hite in early '30s, later with Charlie Echols. From '35-9 lived and worked in Hawaii, first w. drummer Monk McFay, then w. own band. During '40s, back in Cal., worked w. Kid Ory, and led own band for many years. During the 60's and '70s Blakeney freelanced in the LA area, and in '73 joined Barry Martyn's Legends of Jazz. With this group he toured Europe twice and made many appearances throughout U.S., incl. fests. in NO, Sacramento, '74 and Monterey, '75.

LPs: w. Legends of Jazz (Crescent Jazz Prods.).

BLAKEY, ART (Abdullah Ibn Buhaina),* *drums, leader*; b. Pittsburgh, Pa., 10/11/19. Formed Jazz Messengers in '55 (he first used the name for a big band and small group he led in '47) and has been at its head from that time. Sometimes it has been a sextet but most often a quintet. From the late '60s through the first half of the '70s the personnel has incl., among others, Woody Shaw, Olu Dara, Bill Hardman, trumpet; Billy Harper, Carter Jefferson, David Schnitter, tenor saxophone; and Cedar Walton, piano.

As with Blakey-led groups of the past, the '70s Messengers are dedicated to vibrant, hard-swinging music propelled by Blakey, considered by many to be the most "soulful" of the drum masters to have expanded percussion horizons in the bop and hard-bop periods. In portions of '71-72 he took a hiatus from his group to tour with Dizzy Gillespie, Thelonious Monk, Sonny Stitt et al in The Giants of Jazz. Blakey appeared w. them at the NJF-NY '72, and also took part in the Radio City Music Hall Jam Session at the same fest. From '73-5 the Messengers were featured at NJF-NY and in '74 Blakey was also part of a historic drum battle among Max Roach, Buddy Rich and Elvin Jones at a Radio City jam.

With both the Messengers and the Giants of Jazz, Blakey toured in Europe and Japan. In '75 the Messengers made many NYC apps. at a variety of clubs especially the Top of the Gate. LPs: *Child's Dance; Buhaina; Anthenagin* (Prest.); *Like Someone in Love; Roots & Herbs* (BN); reissues (Milest.; Trip); w. *Giants of Jazz* (Atl.); *Newport in New York, The Jam Sessions, Vols. 3&4* (Cobble.); *Sonny Stitt with Art Blakey and The Jazz Messengers* (Poly.).

BLANKE, TOTO, *guitar*; also *bass, drums, bouzoukie*; b. Paderborn, W. Germany, 9/16/39. Stud. classical guitar. Professional debut '69 with own trio. From '70 feat. w. Jasper van't Hof quartet, founded with Pierre Courbois. Toured Europe '73 w. Jeremy Steig; concerts w. Steig, Joachim Kuhn, Randy Brecker, and solo recitals. As soloist, winner of Loosdrecht Fest., Holland, '69.

BLATNY, DR. PAVEL,* *composer, piano, organ*; b. Brno, Czech., 9/14/31. Prominent Czech composer whose works have been widely played by Gustav Brom; Prague radio jazz orch.; Kurt Edelhagen; Erwin Lehn; Brussels Radio Big Band; Copenhagen Radio Big Band; Don Ellis; and many others in England, Austria, Holland, Sweden, Finland, etc. App. at jazz festivals in Prague, '64-74; Stuttgart '68-70; Jazz Labor Ruhrgebeit, '68-9; Amsterdam, '69; Graz '74. From '74 chief of the music dept. of TV Station Brno. Teacher at Remscheider Jazz Kurse '68, '70. Member of the Int. Soc. for Jazz Research, Graz, Austria. Publ: scores of jazz comp. (Supraphon, Palackeho 1, Prague 1, Czech.); Subeditions (Edition Modern Music, Munich, Germany). Comp: *Pour Ellis; Study for Quartertone Trumpet; 10' 30", For Eric; Suite for Gustav Brom; In Modo Classico Suite for String Quartet and Jazz Orchestra*. LPs: *Third Stream Compositions; Czechoslovakian Jazz* (Supraphon); w. Brom, *Swinging the Jazz* (Saba).

BLEY, CARLA,* *composer, piano*; b. Oakland, Cal., 5/11/38. In '66 Ms. Bley undertook her second European tour of concerts, radio and TV apps. She spent '67 writing *A Genuine Tong Funeral*, a suite commissioned by G. Burton and rec. Nov. '67 for RCA. Divorced Paul Bley, married Michael Mantler. Began work on *Escalator Over The Hill*, which she characterized as a chronotransduction, together with lyricist Paul Haines. Commissioned by harpsichordist Antoinette Vischer to write composition, *Untitled Piece in 8 Layers*.

Perf. and rec. as pianist with the Jazz Composers' Orch., '68-9. Commissioned by Charlie Haden to write an album of revolutionary songs. Arr., comp. for, perf. on Haden's *Liberation Music Orchestra* (Impulse), Apr.

'69. *Escalator* released on JCOA Records Mar. '72. In that year Ms. Bley won the DB critics' poll for the third time in TDWR category. She has since lectured, done film scoring (for Jodorowski's *Holy Mountain*, w. Don Cherry and members of JCOA); received French Oscar du Disque de Jazz for '73.

She started her own record company, WATT, with Michael Mantler and created a newspaper for the New Music Distribution Services that had been launched by JCOA. Rec. *Tropic Appetites*, '73-4 with Mantler, G. Barbieri, Dave Holland et al. Her comp., *3/4*, feat. K. Jarrett as soloist, was presented Mar. '74 at Alice Tully Hall, NYC.

LPs: See above. Addr: JCOA, 6 W. 95th St., NYC 10025.

BLEY, PAUL,* *piano, synthesizer, composer*; b. Montreal, Quebec, Canada, 11/10/32. After pl. w. Charles Mingus; Ornette Coleman, Don Cherry and w. his own gp. in Calif. in the '50s, he went to NYC where, in the '60s, he again worked w. Mingus, and w. Jimmy Giuffre; Don Ellis; Sonny Rollins; Gary Peacock; and was a member of the Jazz Composers' Guild, which evolved into the Jazz Composers Orchestra Association. Divorced from Carla Bley, he teamed up with Annette Peacock, Gary Peacock's former wife, who sang with him, sometimes utilizing the synthesizer with her voice much as he was doing with the piano, up until early '73. "I find myself in a period of historical transition between acoustic and electric instruments," said Bley, "so this reflected in my music. In terms of what improvisation is going to be about, there is no other place for it to go, except to electronics."

Bley's modus operandi is to take a synthesizer, an electric piano, clavinet, and an acoustic piano with pickup, and stack the three keyboards on top of each other. "By playing all those keyboards simultaneously," he explains, "you literally run off one keyboard onto another. And I find I don't have any problem at all making the jumps musically, that the combined instrument itself doesn't become the detractor from the music."

Michael Levin, reviewing *The Paul Bley Synthesizer Show*, makes the point that the synthesizer "has a totally constant sound . . . elements of tone and touch which distinguish individual artists are absent" and to recognize the player "one can rely only on the stream of ideas." He concludes that on "*Parks*, set in a swinging four . . ." Bley plays "a reedily voiced single-line solo which works well, modifying it as he goes into a more slurred oscillator-keyed tone . . . . the ideas are good and he plays superbly—but the contribution of the synthesizer, save for some guitar-like pedal shadings, is not that distinctive."

Bley also continued to play and record on acoustic piano. In the early '70s he divided his time between Europe and the U.S. In '73-5 he made two tours of Europe, pl. solo piano for fests and TV. In '75 he formed his own production company in partnership w. Carol Goss (Improvising Artists Inc., 26 Jane St., New York, N.Y. 10014) and began releasing recordings of his own and other artists (Sam Rivers-Dave Holland; Ran Blake) on the IAI label. Comp: *Started; Harlem; Summer; Later; Upstairs; Carla; Mating of Urgency; Meeting; Capricorn; Mr. Joy; The Archangel; Nothing Ever Was, Anyway; Gary; Snakes; Parks.* LPs: *Alone Again; Quiet Song; Turning Point; Virtuoso* (IAI); *Ballads; Open to Love* (ECM); *Blood* (Fontana); *Paul Bley-NHOP* (Steeple.); *Scorpio; Synthesizer Show* (Milest.); *Copenhagen & Haarlem* (Arista); *Ramblin'* (Byg); Paul Bley-Annette Peacock, *I'm the One* (RCA).

BLOOD, SWEAT AND TEARS. see Colomby, Bobby.

BOBO, WILLIE (William Correa),* *timbales, percussion, singer*; b. New York, N.Y., 2/28/34. After working as sideman for Latin and jazz groups, formed own band in LA 1966 and during the next decade was seen at numerous Latin and jazz clubs, concert halls. In 1970 began to sing *Dindi*, a Brazilian song that became his first popular vocal record. App. in Venezuela at International Song Fest.; Monterey as guest star w. Cal Tjader; Latin Jazz Fest. at Madison Sq. Garden; to Ghana as guest w. Santana for filming of *Soul to Soul*.

Bobo gained additional recognition as an actor-musician on the Bill Cosby comedy TV series. Though entertainment-oriented, his combo achieved an effective blend of Latin music, soul and jazz improvisation.

LPs: *Evil Ways; Spanish Grease* (Verve); *Latin Beat* (Trip); *Do What You Want To Do* (Sussex).

BOHANNON, STEVE, *drums, organ*; b. 1947. Son of trombonist Hoyt Bohannon. Worked w. S. Kenton; pl. organ w. Howard Roberts quartet, but was best known as drummer w. Don Ellis orch. His career came to a tragically early end when a car in which he was a passenger collided with a truck near Victorville, Cal., 10/21/68. He was killed outright.

LPs: w. Ellis (Pac. Jazz).

BOHANON, GEORGE ROLAND JR.,* *trombone*; also *euphonium, flute, tenor sax, piano, bass*; b. Detroit, Mich., 8/7/37. First prominent in '60s w. Chico Hamilton quintet. Later became interested in record production and worked as contractor for sessions. Also pl. w. Ujima Ensemble from '72. TV work w. Bill Cosby, Nancy Wilson. NJF '70 w. Bunions Bradford (Cosby). LPs w. G. Ammons; H. Hawes; Patrice Rushen; D. Axelrod (Fant.); *Brass Fever* (Imp.); and with many pop artists. Toured Europe w. Carole King, '73 and '74.

BOLAND, FRANCOIS (FRANCY),* *composer, leader, piano*; b. Namur, Belgium, 11/6/29. Co-leader w. K. Clarke from '62 of the Clarke-Boland big band, which incl. U.S. expatriates and European musicians. The band achieved a unique reputation, rec. LPs w. guest stars such as Lockjaw Davis, S. Getz, J. Griffin, but due to the loss of such key players as Derek Humble and Ake Persson, Clarke and Boland disbanded in '73. At the Middelheim Fest. in '74 Boland pl. w. a sextet incl. his son Chris on guitar and Benny Bailey on trumpet.

LPs: *All Smiles; Big Band Sound; Fellini 712; All Blues; More Smiles; Latin Kaleidoscope; Sax No End;*

Faces (MPS); *Off Limits; Rue Chaptal; Volcano* (Poly.); *At Her Majesty's Pleasure* (Black Lion); *Open Door* (Muse); *Change of Scene* w. Stan Getz (Euro. Verve).

BOLLING, CLAUDE,* *leader, piano, composer*; b. Cannes, France, 4/10/30. Own big band for recs. '56; apps. and/or recs. w. Bill Coleman, Sidney Bechet, Don Byas, Kenny Clarke, Cat Anderson, Paul Gonsalves, Sam Woodyard, Buck Clayton, L. Hampton, etc. In recent yrs. worked in studios as comp.-arr. and leader. Acc. prominent French singers Sacha Distel, Mireille Mathieu, Mouloujdi, Juliette Greco, Charles Trenet, Darion Moreno, Henri Salvador; also Brigitte Bardot, Liza Minelli. Occasional apps. as pianist-leader of Show Biz Band, an Ellington/Basie-styled outfit. Wrote music for films: *Borsalino; Catch Me a Spy*. TV: *To Bix or Not to Bix*. Musical Comedy: *Monsieur Pompadour*. Did shows for Jerry Lewis; Distel. Led vocal gp., Les Parisiennes. Awards: Grand Prix du Disque six times. In late '75 Columbia released his *Suite for Flute and Jazz Piano* feat. himself and flutist Jean-Pierre Rampal. Other LPs: *Original Jazz Classics*; w. Cat Anderson, *Anderson, Bolling & Co.* (Philips); *With the Help of My Friends* (Biram); w. big band, *Swing Session; Jazz Party* (French RCA).

BONANO, JOSEPH (SHARKEY),* *trumpet, singer*; b. Milneburg, La., 4/9/04. Best known through a series of recordings made in New Orleans and New York, '36-7. In later years he returned home and in 1969 he appeared at the New Orleans Jazz Festival. After a long illness Bonano died in New Orleans, 3/27/72.

BONNER, JOSEPH LEONARD (JOE), *piano, composer*; also *tuba*; b. Rocky Mount, N.C., 4/20/48. Grandfather was in minstrel shows; mother sang; father pl. violin. Studied music from elementary school, through junior high, Booker Washington HS, Virginia State Coll. Pl. w. local jazz gps. while att. Va. State. With Roy Haynes, '70-1; Freddie Hubbard, '71-2; Pharoah Sanders, '72-4; also Thad Jones-Mel Lewis; Harold Vick; Max Roach; Leon Thomas; Billy Harper. Forming own gp. TV: w. Max Roach & J.C. White Singers, *Soul*, NET, '72. Fest: NJF w. Hubbard, '71; NJF-NY w. Sanders, '72; Pori; Perugia w. Harper, '75. Infl: McCoy Tyner, Herbie Hancock, Mingus, Charles Lloyd, Hubbard, Sanders, Vick, Lee Morgan, Miles Davis. Neil Tesser has described his style as one of "colors, new hues and primal pigments blended and juxtaposed, occasionally clashed, into an essentially harmonious whole. It is a style, not of the realists or the classicists . . . but of the impressionists."

Comp: *The Little Chocolate Boy; Love Dance; Celebration; Ode to Trane; Healing Song; The Golden Lamp*. LPs: *The Lifesaver* (Muse); w. Harper, *Black Saint* (Black Saint); Vick, *Don't Look Back* (Strata-East); Harold Alexander, *Raw Root* (Atl.); Sanders (Imp.).

BOOKER, WALTER M. JR.,* *bass*; b. Prairie View, Texas, 12/17/33. Early work in Washington, D.C., then in NYC from '64 w. D. Byrd, T. Monk, A. Farmer, S. Getz. Booker toured with the C. Adderley quintet during that group's final seven years of existence, traveling frequently abroad and app. on all the band's albums; also in film *Play Misty For Me*, and on TV shows w. Nancy Wilson et al.

LPs: see ADDERLEY, JULIAN and NAT; also *Revelation*, w. S. Rollins (Imp.).

BOONE, RICHARD, *trombone, singer*; b. Little Rock, Ark., 2/23/30. Began singing at age five in Baptist church. In 1946, won talent contest and toured for a month w. Lucky Millinder's band. Army, 1948-53, pl. w. Special Service orch. Studied music at Philander Smith College, Little Rock, '53. To LA, studio work and club dates w. Gerald Wilson, Dolo Coker, Sonny Criss, Dexter Gordon, Teddy Edwards. Toured w. Della Reese, 1961-6. Joined Count Basie, June 1966, staying three years; during that time became known for an individual, humor-tinged vocal style in which he alternately sang straight and yodeled or scatted the blues. In 1969, rec. own album for the short-lived Nocturne label in LA. Starting in 1970, many tours in Europe as singer and trombonist, living much of the time in Copenhagen. Favs: Tony Bennett, C. McRae, S. Vaughan, B. Eckstine. Won DB Critics poll, TDWR, '67, '72. LPs w. Basie (Verve, Dot).

BOWIE, LESTER, *trumpet, fluegelhorn, Kelphorn, singer, percussion, composer*; b. Frederick, Md., 10/11/41. Raised in Little Rock, Ark., and St. Louis, Mo. Began pl. 1946; from age ten took part in school and religious music activities. At 16 led youth group. Following military service in Texas, worked w. r & b bands around South and Midwest, also gigged w. wife, singer Fontella Bass, and w. Frank Foster. Made r & b sessions for Chess Records and occasionally played jazz jobs.

Around 1965 Bowie began to gain recognition as one of a group of creative artists in Chicago who organized the AACM (Association for the Advancement of Creative Music). Later a group that had recorded under the names of Bowie and Roscoe Mitchell (also incl. Malachi Favors) evolved into the Art Ensemble of Chicago, a cooperative unit that became, according to Michael Cuscuna, "one of the most powerful, dynamic and unique groups of the new music (and the old music too)." Bowie also helped form BAG (Black Artist Group) and the Great Black Music Orch. in St. Louis.

The Art Ensemble was heard in Europe in 1969, playing concerts and recording with considerable success. Bowie recorded with Archie Shepp, Sunny Murray, Jimmy Lyons, Cecil Taylor and others, also wrote, conducted and recorded *Gettin' to Know Y'All* with the 50-piece Baden Baden Free Jazz Orch., and again in 1970 at the Frankfurt JF. Toured Senegal, '74, performing with local drummers. Comp: *Theme De Yoyo*; *Jazz Death; Barnyard Scuffel Shuffel*.

Bowie, whom Joachim Berendt described as "a Cootie Williams of the avant garde with his growl solos," also became a major contributor to the visual, comedic and dramatic aspects of the Art Ensemble. Early infl: Louis Armstrong, Kenny Dorham.

LPs w. Art Ensemble of Chicago on Prestige, Atlantic;

Arista; own LP: *Fast Last!* (Muse); many others on European labels with above-named artists.

BOWN, PATRICIA ANNE (PATTI),* *piano*; b. Seattle, Wash., 7/26/31. Played w. Q. Jones on Euro. tour of show, *Free and Easy*. Freelance in NYC from early '60s. Solo piano at Needle's Eye in early '70s; Half Note, '74. In orch. for Broadway musical *Purlie*, '72-4. Concerts w. NYJRC, '74-5. Jam sessions at NJF-NY, '74-5. Rec. movie scores w. Q. Jones. LPs: w. S. Stitt (Cadet); O. Nelson (Fly. Dutch.); Aretha Franklin (Atl); James Brown, etc.

BRACKEEN, JOANNE (Joanne Grogan), *piano, composer*; b. Ventura, Calif., 7/26/38. A few private lessons but essentially self-taught. Worked in Calif. w. Teddy Edwards, D. Gordon, C. Lloyd, '59; Freddie McCoy, late '60s; Woody Shaw in '69; Dave Liebman, '69, '74; Art Blakey, '70-2; Joe Henderson, '72-5; Joe Farrell; Sonny Red, '73; Sonny Stitt; Horacee Arnold; Stan Getz, '75; also many engagements w. own duo at West Boondock, NYC, '72-5, The Surf Maid, NYC, '74-5. Comps: *Snooze; Images; Sri-C; Zulu; 6-ate*. LPs: *Vital Views*; w. Toots Thielemans, *Captured Alive* (Choice); w. McCoy (Prest.)

BRADFORD, BOBBY LEE, *cornet, trumpet, composer*; b. Cleveland, Miss., 7/19/34. Stud. Lincoln High, Dallas, '49-52; Sam Houston Coll., Austin, '52-3; U. of Texas, '59-60; Houston-Tillotson Coll., '62-3. In addition to being in and out of teaching, principally at Cal. State Coll., Pasadena City Coll., Claremont Colls., Bradford pl. w. Ornette Coleman, '53-4 and '61-3; w. Q. Jones in NYC, '62; from '66-71 co-led a combo with saxophonist John Carter, mainly in LA. Played Watts Fest., '71; Brussels Fest., '73. Won DB poll, TDWR, '73.

Comps: *Woman; Song For The Unsung; Love's Dream; Eye of the Storm; Comin' On; Room 408*. LPs: *Flight for Four* (Flying Dutchman); *Seeking* (Revelation); *Love's Dream* (Emanem); w. Coleman, *Science Fiction* (Columbia).

BRADFORD, PERRY,* *singer, piano*; b. Montgomery, Ala., 2/14/1893. A pioneer producer and artist on early recs. First man to arr. session for a black singer, Mamie Smith, in 1920. He became successful publisher, entrepreneur and rec. consultant in '20s. Numerous rec. dates w. L. Armstrong, Johnny Dunn, Willie The Lion Smith, James P. Johnson et al. His autobiography, *Born with the Blues* was publ. in '65. Bradford died 4/22/70 in Queens, N.Y.

BRAFF, REUBEN (RUBY),* *cornet*; b. Boston, Mass., 3/16/27. After building a reputation around Boston, he found that because he played in a classic style he was not in demand in the late '50s. Even when he did begin to work more regularly in the '60s, he did not record very much. In the '70s, however he became more active in all areas, touring as featured soloist w. Tony Bennett, '71-3; co-leading a popular and successful quartet w. guitarist George Barnes. '73-5, that also toured w. Bennett in '73-4. After Braff and Barnes broke up in the summer of '75 he free-lanced in NYC, subbing for Roy Eldridge at Jimmy Ryan's on several occasions. Made NYJRC Tribute to Louis Armstrong tour of Europe, fall '75. Writing arrs. to enable him to work within quartet, sextet or octet contexts. Braff's mellow, melodic style had fully matured by the '70s to a point where the seeming ease with which his music was made was matched by its easy-listening quality.

Film: *This Funny World* w. Bennett, unreleased. TV: Mike Douglas; *Today*; many Euro. apps. Fest: NJF-NY; Colo. JP; Concord. Comp: *Everything's George; With Time to Love; People's Choice*. LPs: w. Braff-Barnes Quartet, *Carnegie Hall Concert* (Chiaro.); *Play Gershwin; Play Rodgers and Hart* (Concord); *To Fred Astaire, With Love* (RCA). *Plays Louis Armstrong* (Byg); w. Ellis Larkins, *Grand Reunion* (Chiaro.); w. George Wein, *Newport All Stars* (Atl.); *George Wein is Alive and Well in Mexico* (Col.).

BRAND, ADOLPH JOHANNES (DOLLAR) (Abdullah Ibrahim),* *piano, composer*; also *Indian-African flute, soprano sax, cello*; b. Capetown, So. Africa, 10/9/34. Playing in Europe in early and mid-'60s, he was discovered by Duke Ellington who encouraged him to come to the US in '65. After pl. w. Elvin Jones, '66, he freelanced before returning to Africa in '68. He has been back and forth to the US five times between then and Jan. '76. Lived in Swaziland, '71-3; Capetown & Johannesburg, '73-5; Capetown, '75. In addition he has spent much time in Europe, particularly Scandinavia, and toured Japan and Australia in '73. Most of his apps. are as solo pianist but in '74 he took a 10-piece band, a similar personnel to the one that rec. *African Space Program*, on tour in Germany, Italy and Switzerland. He has also pl. in Holland; Canada, '74; London, '75. When he performs in anything but a solo setting, his wife, singer Sathima (Bea Benjamin) often appears with him. Has pl. bamboo flute from '67; cello from '68; soprano sax from '71. Fest: produced two in Swaziland; pl. at Nancy, '73; Antibes, '75; Bergamo; Berlin; Kongsberg; Musicforum, Austria; concert in Boswil, Switzerland. TV: Austria; Holland; three different projects in '60s and '70s w. Erik Moseholm and Danish Radio Big Band. His conversion to Islam in '68 has helped him "to rediscover a sense of the natural" and subsequently led him into the study of karate and acupuncture. Won DB Critics poll, TDWR, '75. Comp: *The Aloe and the Wildrose; Salaam; Anatomy of a South African Village; Tintiyana; The Dream; Tariq; African Sun; Bra Joe From Kilimanjaro; Sunset in Blue; Kippi; Monk From Harlem; The Pilgrim; Jabulani; Easter Joy*. LPs: *Manenberg; African Herbs* (As-Shams, Kohinoor, Kort Street, Johannesburg, South Africa); *Ode to Duke Ellington; Memories* (Japanese Philips); *African Sketchbook; African Space Program* (Enja); *This is Dollar Brand* (Bl. Lion); *Peace; Dollar Brand + 3 with Kippi Moeketsi* (Soultown); *African Piano; Ancient Africa* (Japo); *Sangoma* (Sack.); *Anatomy of a South African Village* (Spectator); w. Gato Barbieri, *Hamba Kahle* (Togetherness); *Confluence* (Freedom); Elvin Jones, *Midnight Walk* (Atl.).

BRASHEAR, OSCAR, *trumpet, fluegelhorn*; also *piccolo trumpet, cornet, piano*; b. Chicago, Ill., 8/18/44. Mother a church pianist. Stud. DuSable HS, Wright Jr. Coll., Roosevelt U.; priv. lessons w. Ch. Allen. Pl. w. Morris Ellis big band, Latin groups, record dates, jingles, '62-6; W. Herman, '67; C. Basie '68-9. Freelanced in Chi. w. S. Stitt, G. Ammons, D. Gordon, J. Moody, '70. From '71 very active in LA w. Gerald Wilson, H. Land, O. Nelson, S. Manne, Q. Jones, H. Silver, Duke Pearson band. Infls: J. Coltrane, F. Hubbard, Clifford Brown, W. Shorter, McCoy Tyner, H. Hancock, Miles Davis, A. Blakey. Fests: Newport w. Basie; Monterey w. Jones, W. Herman etc.

Brashear emerged in the mid-'70s as a spirited, exceptionally fluent soloist, considered by some critics to be a latter day Clifford Brown.

LPs: w. Land, *Damisi* (Mainstr.); w. J. Henderson, *Canyon Lady* (Milestone); w. S. Manne *Hot Coles* (Fl. Dutchman); Moacir Santos, *Carnival of the Spirits*; w. Hutcherson, *Head On* (BN); w. C. Adderley, *Big Man* (Fantasy); w. Earth, Wind & Fire, *Head to the Sky* (Col.); others w. Eddie Harris, Groove Holmes, H. Silver, H. Hawes et al; *Brass Fever* (Imp.).

BRASS COMPANY. see Hardman, Bill.

BRAUD, WELLMAN,* *bass*; b. St. James, La., 1/25/1891. Best known as bassist with Ellington orch. 1926-35. After leaving Ellington, took over direction of Spirits of Rhythm, then formed own trio in '37 until '41. During '40s and '50s primarily involved in business ventures in Harlem, but toured Europe in '56 with Kid Ory. Braud died of a heart attack 10/29/66 at his LA home.

BRAXTON, ANTHONY, *alto sax, clarinet, bass clarinet, sopranino, flute, composer*; b. Chicago, Ill., 6/4/45. First studies w. Jack Gell at Chi. Sch. of Mus.; then at Chi. Mus. Coll.; philosophy under Dr. Zabeet at Roosevelt U. At 17, met Roscoe Mitchell who turned his attention from strictly classical music to jazz. Early infl: Paul Desmond, Warne Marsh, Eric Dolphy, Coltrane. Became involved w. AACM through Mitchell in '66 began pl. "free-jazz" w. them at Lincoln Center in Chicago. Earned a great part of his living as a chess hustler. Pl. w. Art Ensemble of Chicago in Europe '69. Became part of Circle, a gp. w. Chick Corea, Dave Holland and Barry Altschul in NYC '70, pl. w. it there and in France, Feb. '71. From a point several months later, when Circle disbanded, Braxton has led his own groups, traveling between Europe and the US until Sept. '74 when he moved to Woodstock, N.Y., pl. in the US, Canada and Europe with Kenny Wheeler, Holland and Altschul. In '70-1 he came to the US w. Musica Elettronica Viva an Italian group which plays contemporary classical and improvised music. He also app. in duo w. guitarist Derek Bailey at London's Wigmore Hall. In May '72 he was heard in concert at Town Hall; and (solo) at Carnegie Hall; in July '73 at Chateau Le Rault, France; Oct. '74, Burton Auditorium, Toronto.

Braxton, who names as additional infls., Lee Konitz, Ornette Coleman, Cecil Taylor and Stockhausen had been quoted to the effect that his "interest in music is scientific. I'm interested in 'functionalism' " he said, "in the sense that I can try out different systems in an attempt to discover the basis for a new life. I'm interested in tapping anything that hints of that vibration but hasn't been there before."

Later, he modified this intellectualism. "The basis upon which I am building music is still math," he explained, "but it's changing. I'm starting to accept feeling again. At one point I consciously wanted to eliminate feeling from my music—in the beginning when I was heavily into John Cage. To play music with feeling the approach is different. You must deal more with the 'is' than the 'how.' I've found that mathematics as a *total* basis for my music is interesting, but it's not what's happening."

His compositions are represented by mathematical diagrams rather than titles. A typical one is:

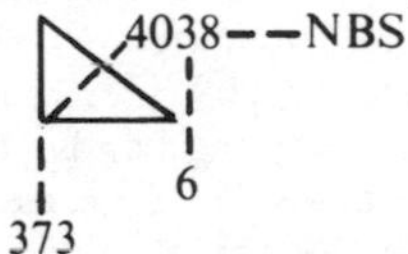

They are written structures that can be used constantly as reference points. "The diagrams," says Braxton, "have to do with the implications of what structural approach was taken, and also with vibrational flows."

In several of his albums, particularly *In the Tradition*, he plays standards and jazz originals by Warne Marsh, Mingus and Charlie Parker. *You Stepped Out of a Dream* from his *Five Pieces 1975* LP is cited by writer Robert Palmer as evidence refuting critical opinion that Braxton "lacks authenticity as a jazzman." Others felt that here his lack of swing and flow in his phrasing underlined the original criticism. Barry McRae, discussing his "free" solos, said that they "dispensed with any suggestion that his organizational mind might make his music clinical."

TV: Italy, Germany, France. Fests: Montreux; Pescara; Antibes. Film: wrote score for *Paris Streets*, commissioned by M.I.T.; *Un Coup de Franc*, France. LPs: *Five Pieces 1975; New York Fall 1974* (Arista); *In the Tradition* (Steeple.); *Three Compositions; For Alto*; Anthony Braxton & Joseph Jarman, *Together Alone* (Del.); Anthony Braxton & Derek Bailey, *Duo 1; Duo 2* (Emanem); w. Circle, *Paris Concert* (ECM); *Circle 1&2* (CBS-Sony).

BREAU, LEONARD (LENNY), *guitar*; b. Auburn, Maine, 8/5/41. Parents both singers. Began playing country music; came to prominence in Winnipeg. To Toronto, '64, pl. w. own trio, singer Don Franks et al. Briefly in LA in mid-60s, led trio at Shelly's Manne Hole, where he rec. a live album. Again led own combo and worked with singers in Toronto, '70-2. In semi-retirement in Winnipeg, '73-5. Living Killaloe, Ont., '75, performing only occasionally. Movies: *Toronto Jazz*, '64, for Nat'l Film Board of Canada. Rec. live for Radio-Canada's *Jazz Canadiana* and *Jazz Radio-Canada*. Infl.

by Bill Evans, Chet Atkins and Tal Farlow, Breau is a gifted musician little known outside Canada.

LPs: *Guitar Sounds; Live at Shelly's Manne-Hole* (RCA).

BRECKER, MIKE, *tenor saxophone*; also *flute, soprano sax, drums, piano*; b. Phila. Pa., 3/29/49. Father and sister are pianists. Brother, Randy, is trumpeter (see below). Stud. w. Vince Trombetta, '65-9 and Joe Allard. Pl. with Edwin Birdsong, '70; Dreams, '70-3; James Taylor, '73; Horace Silver, '73-4; Billy Cobham from '74; also in Japan w. Yoko Ono, '74. Own LP: *The Brecker Brothers* (Arista). Others incl. *Journey* w. Arif Mardin (Atl.), *In Pursuit of the 27th Man* w. Silver (Blue Note), *Mind Games* w. J. Lennon (Apple); and albums w. Hal Galper, J. Taylor, Carly Simon, Don Sebesky.

BRECKER, RANDY, *trumpet*; also *piano, drums*; b. Phila., Pa., 11/27/45. Brother is saxophonist Mike Brecker. Stud. Indiana U. '63-5, as well as w. David Baker and several other private teachers. Pl. w. Blood, Sweat & Tears, '66; H. Silver, '67, '69, '73; Janis Joplin, '68; Duke Pearson and Clark Terry big bands, '68; Stevie Wonder; Art Blakey, '70; Dreams '71-2; James Taylor, '71; Larry Coryell; Deodato; Johnny & Edgar Winter, '73; Billy Cobham, '73-4; Mike Longo; Idris Muhammad, '74.

Won DB poll, TDWR, '69. Own LP: *Brecker Brothers* (Arista). Others w. Muhammad (CTI); Silver, Pearson (Blue Note); Longo (Groove Merchant); Hal Galper (Mainstream); Coryell (Vanguard); Cobham (Atl.).

BREEDEN, PROF. HAROLD LEON,* *educator, clarinet, saxophones, bassoon*; b. Guthrie, Okla., 10/3/21. Best known for his work at NTSU, one of whose Lab bands performed, under his direction, at the White House in June '67, the first such appearance by a large Univ. jazz group. D. Ellington and S. Getz appeared as guests with the band. In '72 Breeden organized a celebration, at NTSU, of the 25th anniversary of jazz education at that institution. One of his student units was the official big band at Montreux JF, '70, also touring Germany. Breeden was adjudicator for the U.S. high school competition in Montreux in '71 and '72; conducted all star band for Jazz Internationale, '72 in London and Paris. Has also acted as clinician/judge at innumerable U.S. colleges. Visiting prof. of music for Houston public schools, Jan. '75 under a grant from the National Endowment for the Arts.

Breeden, who has long been established as one of the pioneers in jazz education, was listed in *Outstanding Educators of America* in '71.

BREWER, TERESA (Theresa Brewer), *singer*; b. Toledo, Ohio, 5/7/31. No formal mus. educ., but was a child prodigy, winning a Major Bowes contest at age six. She became a major pop star while in her teens, her biggest hit being *Music! Music! Music!* in 1950. Became interested in contemporary music through her four daughters by first marriage, and was encouraged to work in jazz settings just before and after her marriage in 1972 to producer Bob Thiele. Her jazz-oriented LPs were enthusiastically endorsed by critic Nat Hentoff, who called them "a triumph . . . this is a matured, still growing musician who decided some years ago to take jazz, and herself as a communicator of jazz, seriously. Singers with this quality of pungent flavor and crackling swing are rare in any generation."

LPs: *Singing A Doo Dah Song; Teresa Brewer In London With Oily Rags* (Amsterdam); *It Don't Mean a Thing* w. D. Ellington Orch.; *The Songs of Bessie Smith* w. Count Basie Orch., arr. Thad Jones; *What a Wonderful World* w. Bobby Hackett (Fl. Dutchman).

BRIDGEWATER, CECIL VERNON, *trumpet, composer*; b. Urbana, Ill. 10/10/42. Ex-wife is singer Dee Dee Bridgewater; brother saxophonist Ron Bridgewater. Stud. at U. of Ill., '60-4 and '68-9; pl. in U. of Ill. Jazz Band, European tour, '68, Russian tour, '69. Pl. w. H. Silver, '70. From '70-5 Bridgewater was principally known for his work in the Thad Jones-Mel Lewis orch., touring the U.S., Europe, USSR and Japan. He worked w. M. Roach frequently, '71-5, in Europe, U.S., Africa; also during early '70s w. A. Blakey, Harold Vick, Frank Foster, Randy Weston, Jimmy Heath, D. Gillespie's big band, Joe Henderson, Roy Brooks, Sam Rivers, Buddy Terry, Bridgewater Generations.

Bridgewater has had extensive experience as a teacher, giving private lessons and working for Henry Street Settlement, Jazzmobile Workshop, Greenhaven Prison, clinics at high schools and colleges.

LPs: w. Jones-Lewis, *Potpourri* (Philadelphia Int'l.); *Today's Man*, w. Ch. McPherson, *The Loud Minority*, w. Frank Foster, *Awareness*, w. Buddy Terry (all on Mainstream); *United States of Mind*, w. H. Silver (Blue Note); *Lift Every Voice And Sing*, w. Roach (Atl.); *Generations*, Cecil & Ron Bridgewater (Strata-East).

BRIDGEWATER, DENISE (DEE DEE), *singer*; b. Memphis, Tenn., 5/27/50. Family moved to Flint, Mich. while she was a toddler. Father pl. trumpet. She sang as a child but took it up seriously in early teens. Own trio in junior high school; then sang w. father's gp. at local dances. Went to Mich. State U. '68. Sang w. saxist Andy Goodrich for a year. He took her to fest. at U. of Illinois '69. Four months later John Garvey invited her to tour Russia w. Illinois band. Met husband Cecil Bridgewater (see above) and came to NYC w. him. Featured vocalist w. Thad Jones-Mel Lewis orch. '72-4, touring Europe and Japan. App. as a single at Hopper's, NYC, '76. Studied w. Roland Hanna "because I want to be a musician/singer. I want to know what I'm singing and I want to understand what the musicians are playing so that I can work better with them."

Of her wordless singing on *The Great One* in *Suite For Pops* Thad Jones said: "There's never anything written out for her. She is so musical that she goes her own way and we know she isn't going anywhere we are not."

Early infl: Nina Simone, Lena Horne, Gloria Lynne, Nancy Wilson. Won Tony Award for her performance in Broadway musical *The Wiz* '75; TDWR, DB Critics poll, '75. TV: *Woman Alive*, PBS, '76.

LPs: w. Jones-Lewis, *Suite For Pops* (Horizon); w. Heiner Stadler, *Ecstasy* (Labor).

BRIGHT, RONNELL,* *piano, composer*; b. Chicago, Ill., 7/3/30. First prominent as accompanist with singers, incl. Sarah Vaughan in '50s, Nancy Wilson in mid-60s. Occasional appearances as movie and TV actor, incl. *They Shoot Horses Don't They; Lepke; Sanford & Son; Don Adams Special; Mannix; The Jeffersons*. Pianist in George Wyle orch. on Flip Wilson TV Show, '70-4. High school music teacher '74-5. Staff vocal arr., Carol Burnett TV series, '74-5.

As songwriter, Bright composed *Be A Sweet Pumpkin*, rec. by Blue Mitchell, Bill Henderson and others; *Cherry Blossom*, rec. by H. Silver, C. Tjader; *Tender Loving Care* and *Satisfy* and several others all rec. by N. Wilson. Bright's best jazz-oriented work in recent years was his stint with Supersax, '73-4.

LPs: *Supersax Plays Bird* (Capitol); others with Nancy Wilson et al.

BROADBENT, ALAN, *composer, piano*; b. Auckland, New Zealand, 4/23/47. Studied at Royal Trinity College of Music, Auckland, '54-60; Berklee Coll. of Music, '66-9; piano privately with Lennie Tristano, '67-9; then toured w. Woody Herman orch. '69-72, gaining a reputation for his special extended works perf. by the band, notably *Blues In The Night Suite* and *Variations on A Scene*, latter introduced by the Herman band with the Houston Symph. Joined John Klemmer group '75.

Won first prize for *Sonata for Violincello and Piano*, Boston Public Library Music Assn., '69; DB Critics' Poll, TDWR, '72. Influenced by Lester Young, Tristano, Bud Powell, Ch. Parker, Ellington, Gil Evans, John Mandel, Broadbent became the first New Zealand born musician to achieve international stature in jazz.

LPs w. Herman: *Woody* (Cadet); *Brand New Woody; Giant Steps; Thundering Herd* (Fant.).

BROM, GUSTAV, *clarinet, composer, leader*; also *saxophone, violin*; b. Velke Levary, Czech., 5/22/21. His son, Gustav Brom, Jr., b. 1/2/46, pl. trombone w. Brom's orch. Brom stud. at Moravan Music School, Kromeriz; private stud. w. Prof. Horak at Brno Conserv. Pl. in student orch. until '40. From that time he has led his own band starting with six members which grew to 12 by '42, thereby making it one of the oldest European big bands. Soloists who have made guest apps. with the orch. incl. M. Ferguson, T. Curson, D. Goykovich, A. Mangelsdorff, P. Herbolzheimer, H. Koller, B. Bailey. Brom has also collaborated w. Ray Conniff in western Europe. Infl: Ellington, Lunceford, Kenton. His band has app. on innumerable European TV programs and has done the music for feature length films as well as TV films. From early '60s he has app. at fest. in England and on the continent, incl. Manchester, Nuremberg, Molde, Prague, Warsaw and Ljubljana. Brom has won the Jaroslav Jezek prize; Int. Jury prize, Prague JF; and also made a Laureate of Jazz Music at Prague, '68. Comp: *Dance Songs; Dreaming in Two; Adele; The Evening Guest*. LPs: Supraphon, incl. one w. Maynard Ferguson; MPS.

BRÖTZMANN, PETER, *tenor sax*; also *alto, baritone, bass saxophones, clarinet*; b. Remscheid, W. Germany, 3/6/41. Studied painting at the art academy in Wuppertal; self-taught on clarinet and saxophone. Began pl. jazz at 18 w. dixieland school band and cont. w. several amateur dixie/swing groups. With Jazz Realities—Carla Bley and Mike Mantler '66; then w. Don Cherry, Steve Lacy and European avant-garde musicians all over the continent at festivals and concerts. Own trio from '68 with pianist Fred van Hove and drummer Han Bennink. Also worked w. Nam June Paik, Tonas Schmit and the Fluxus movement. Comps. incl. *Machine Gun; Drunken in the Morning Sunrise; Der Alte Mann Bricht Sein Schweigen*. A member of Free Music Production, a musicians' organization which produces records, concerts and festivals in association with like groups such as Instant Composers Poll (Holland) and Incus (Eng.). LPs w. own trio, *Machine Gun; Balls* (Free Music Production); trio plus Albert Mangelsdorff; Globe Unity Orch. Live in Wuppertal (Free Music Production).

BROOKMEYER, ROBERT (BOB),* *valve trombone, piano, composer*; b. Kansas City, Kansas, 12/19/29. Worked in NYC on Merv Griffin TV show and w. Thad Jones-Mel Lewis orch. until '68, when he moved to Cal. Becoming almost inactive in jazz, he was with various TV series, incl. Della Reese Show, '69-70. Reunited w. Jones-Lewis at MJF, '71, and w. Gerry Mulligan at NJF-NY, '73. Rejoined Jones-Lewis on tour Jan. '75.

Comps: *ABC Blues*, rec. by Jones-Lewis; *Blues Suite*, rec. by own gp. on Atl. Among his best arrs. for Jones-Lewis are *Willow Tree; Samba Con Getchu; St. Louis Blues*.

LPs: *Gloomy Sunday and Other Bright Moments* (Verve); *Brookmeyer & Friends* w. Getz, Hancock, G. Burton, R. Carter, E. Jones (Col.); also two with Jones-Lewis (UA), three with Clark Terry (Mainstream), and *Age of Steam* w. Mulligan (A & M).

BROOKS, ROY, *drums*; also *piano, vibes, marimba*; b. Detroit, Mich., 9/3/38. As teenager was inspired to take up drums through listening to Elvin Jones at Bluebird. Played w. Yusef Lateef, Barry Harris et al at El Sino; New Music Society sessions at World Stage coffee house. Worked w. Beans Bowles at Lavert's Lounge. To LV w. the Four Tops. Joined Horace Silver '59, remaining with him into '64. With Lateef '67-70; Pharoah Sanders; James Moody '70-2; Wes Montgomery; Sonny Stitt; Jackie McLean; Dexter Gordon; Dollar Brand; Four Tops; Charles Mingus '72-3. Formed own gp. The Artistic Truth; also active with M'Boom re: percussion, a seven-man ensemble. Infl: C. Parker, M. Roach, J. Coltrane, E. Jones, A. Blakey, K. Clarke. TV: *Today; Tonight; Like It Is; Positively Black; Dial M for Music*. Fest: NJF; MJF; Watts; many European fests. Comp: *Eboness; Five For Max; The Smart Set*. His solos are shaped with melodic contours which he sometimes enhances by blowing through rubber tubing, inflating his drums, thereby varying the pitch. LPs: *Roy Brooks Beat* (Jazz Workshop); *The Free Slave* (Muse); *Ethnic Expres-*

sions (Imhotep); w. Silver, *Horacescope; Doin' the Thing* (Blue Note); w. Stitt, *Constellation* (Cobble.); w. C. McPherson, *McPherson's Mood* (Prest.); w. R. Garland, *Auf Wiedersehen* (MPS); w. D. Brand, *African Space Program* (Enja).

BROWN, GARNETT,* *trombone, composer*; b. Memphis, Tenn., 1/31/36. Early experience w. C. Hamilton, Geo. Russell. Spent 13 yrs. as freelance arranger/composer, jazz and commercial artist in NYC. Many apps. at NJF w. M. Legrand, Benny Carter, Billy Taylor, Diana Ross, NYJRC. Comps: *Pieces of Miles; Ornette*, extended works written for *75 Years Of Jazz*, presented by NYJRC, Apr. '75.

In July '75 Brown moved to LA, where he pl. in the band for the show *Purlie*, and worked in TV, film and commercial recordings. Awards: DB Readers Poll, TDWR, '67; Readers Poll in main trombone category, '74; Ebony All Star Band, '73-4.

During his yrs. in NYC, Brown app. w. Thad Jones-Mel Lewis, Herbie Hancock, Johnny Richards, Billy Taylor, O. Nelson, Duke Pearson, Frank Foster, L. Hampton, Deodato.

LPs: *Jazz For A Sunday Afternoon*, Vols. 2, 4; w. Jones-Lewis, *Live at the Village Vanguard; Monday Night* (Solid State); w. Russell, *The Outer View* (Rivers.); w. R. Kirk, *Slightly Latin* (Limelight); w. Booker Ervin, *Heavy!!!*; w. Teddy Edwards, *It's All Right* (Prest.); w. Jack Wilson, *Easterly Winds*; w. Foster *Manhattan Fever*; w. D. Pearson, *Introducing Duke Pearson's Big Band; Now Hear This* (BN); w. Doug Carn, *Spirit of the New Land* (Black Jazz); w. B. Cobham, *Crosswinds* (Atl.); w. Hancock, *Fat Albert Rotunda* (WB); *Brass Fever* (Imp.).

BROWN, LAWRENCE,* *trombone*; b. Lawrence, Kansas, 7/3/05. Member of Duke Ellington orch., '32-51, and again '60-Jan. '70. He then settled in Washington, D.C., where he was appointed by Pres. Nixon to the Advisory Committee for Kennedy Center; also served on Board of Directors as member of consultant firm, One America. In '72 Brown returned to Cal., where he had been raised, and took a job as recording agent for Local 47 of the Amer. Fed. of Mus., in Hollywood. He completely gave up playing after leaving Ellington orch. His unique legato style and smooth sound can be heard in his own LP, *Inspired Abandon* (Imp.). Other albums w. Ellington on many labels; also w. Jackie Gleason, *Torch with a Blue Flame* (Cap.).

BROWN, LESTER RAYMOND (LES),* *leader, clarinet*; b. Reinerton, Pa., 3/14/12. A bandleader since '38, Brown remained active in the late '60s and '70s, best known through his numerous tours and TV shows w. Bob Hope.

BROWN, MARION,* *alto sax, composer*; b. Atlanta, Ga., 9/8/35. After playing and recording w. Archie Shepp, John Coltrane and leading his own gp. in the mid-'60s in NYC, he went to Europe for concerts and recs. in Holland, France. Returning to US he was, in the mid-'70s at Wesleyan U. in Conn., working on his Masters in Ethnomusicology. As part of his thesis, he was exploring the possibilities of such instruments as the Ghanian atenteben; Japanese shakuhachi; bamboo flutes; notched bamboo flutes. Stud. So. Indian flute w. P. Vishwanathan. Also investigating history of Afro-American fife and drumming in Miss. & Ga. Comp: *Similar Limits; Sound Structure; Improvisation; QBIC; Porto Novo; Geechee Reflections.*

LPs: *Porto Novo* (Arista); own quartet; *Why Not* (ESP); *Geechee Reflections; Sweet Earth Flying; Three for Shepp* (Imp.); w. Elliott Schwartz, *Soundways* (BCMP).

BROWN, MARSHALL RICHARD,* *valve trombone, euphonium, bass trumpet, composer*; b. Framingham, Mass., 12/21/20. First known as educator, and as organizer of Newport Youth Band, '59. Toured w. Ruby Braff and other mainstream groups in '60s. Eddie Condon, '66-7, R. Eldridge, '68-70. From '71 to '74 played and toured w. Lee Kontiz quintet, in addition to composing and arranging most of the book. Appeared w. Konitz at NJF, '72. Arr. and conducted for Maxine Sullivan LP, '75. Own gp. at Willy's, Greenwich Village, '75.

LPs: *The Lee Konitz Duets; Peacemeal* w. L. Konitz quartet (Milestone).

BROWN, OLIVE, *singer*; also *cocktail drums*; b. St. Louis, Mo., 8/30/22. Sang at Sanctified Church, but acquired early knowledge of and feeling for the blues. Worked in the '40s w. Earl Bostic, Cecil Scott at Small's Paradise, NYC; w. Todd Rhodes in Detroit. Spent three years off and on w. T. Buckner band. In Chicago, was feat. singer in cabarets. Sang at Club Moonglow, Buffalo, N.Y. w. C.Q. Price's band, '58. Worked mostly in Texas, '58-60, w. Don Albert and others. During '60s she rec. twice in NYC, but the sessions were never released. In later years she earned a substantial following in Canada, working in Toronto with leading U.S. mainstream musicians.

Brown sang at several jazz and blues festivals in '70s, incl. Cotton Fest. in Memphis, Tenn., '72; St. Louis Ragtime Fest., '73. Comps: *A Woman's Lament; Monkey on My Back.* Infls: Ethel Waters, Bessie Smith, Louis Armstrong, and (for mannerisms and direction) Hildegarde.

Though inadequately represented on record, Olive Brown has a powerfully convincing voice, bringing to her blues performances in particular a conviction and authenticity that reflects strongly the Bessie Smith influence.

LP: *Olive Brown and Her Blues Chasers* (Jim Taylor Presents, 12311 Gratiot Ave., Detroit, Mich. 48205).

BROWN, RAYMOND H. (RAY), *fluegelhorn, trumpet, composer, arranger*; b. Oceanside, N.Y., 11/7/46. Father a music educator for many years, initiated school stage bands in N.Y., '39. B.M. from Ithaca Coll., '64-8; also four summers at Lake Shore Music Score Camp run by father. Arr. and pl. for U.S. Army field band, '68-71. Worked w. S. Kenton, pl. in band and serving as improvisation clinician, Sep. '71 to Nov. '72. With Bill Watrous band in N.Y., '73-4; guest soloist at Lincoln Center

w. Ithaca Coll. jazz workshop. Led own rehearsal band in NYC, '73-5. Received NEA grant to write work for own band, Mar. '75. Teacher of improv. in nine N.J. schools through grant from N.J. State Council on the Arts. On faculty of Five Towns Coll. in Merrick, N.Y., '74-5, teaching arranging, improv., brass.

Publ: *An Introduction to Jazz Improvisation* by Ray and Steve Brown, publ. by (Creative World, Inc., P.O. Box 35216, Los Angeles, Ca. 90035). Also 15 comps. for stage band. Comps: *Mi Burrito; Call Me Mister; Clyde's Glides; Double Fault Blues; Afterthoughts*. LPs: *National Anthems of the World; Stan Kenton Live at Butler University; Stan Kenton and the Four Freshmen* (all on Creative World).

BROWN, RAYMOND MATTHEWS (RAY),* *bass*; b. Pittsburgh, Pa., 10/13/26. From Jan. '66, when he left the O. Peterson trio after an association that had lasted more than 15 years, Brown became intensely active in a variety of assignments in LA. He produced jazz concerts for the Hollywood Bowl, wrote instruction books, rec. on freelance basis with hundreds of artists, and became Quincy Jones' manager. His TV work incl. regular apps. as a member of the orch. on the Merv Griffin show.

At the beginning of '74 Brown joined the L.A. Four, whose other members were Laurindo Almeida, Shelly Manne and Bud Shank. This group toured in Australia and New Zealand, app. in Mexico and Canada, as well as clubs and fests. in Cal. Publ: *Ray Brown Bass Book I* (Ray Brown Music Co., P.O. Box 1254, Hollywood, Ca. 90028).

Despite the multiplicity of his other chores as businessman, publisher etc., Brown remained one of the most gifted, flexible and influential bass players in jazz, still frequently winning polls and constantly in demand for jazz jobs as well as commercial work.

LPs: *This One's for Blanton*, duo album w. D. Ellington; *Duke's Big 4* (Pablo); *That's The Way It Is; Memphis Jackson; Just The Way It Had To Be*, w. M. Jackson (Imp.); *Walking In Space* and others w. Q. Jones (A & M); *Seven Come Eleven; Jazz/Concord* w. Herb Ellis, Joe Pass; *Soft Shoe*; L.A. Four (Concord Jazz).

BROWN, RUTH,* *singer*; b. Portsmouth, Va., 1/30/28. First nationally prominent as r & b singer with her hit record *Mama He Treats Your Daughter Mean*, recorded in Dec. 1952. Continued to play theatres and clubs, including 3½ years on Playboy Club circuit in mid-1960s. Living in Deer Park, N.Y., she worked as teacher in preschool program and was participant in International Art of Jazz clinics in Long Island. Occasionally worked in clubs, mainly Sonny's Place in Seaford, L.I. Made her first West Coast app. in a decade playing the role of Mahalia Jackson in the production *Selma*, in Hollywood, 1975-6.

Brown's record of *Miss Brown's Blues*, on the short-lived Skye label in 1969, was a masterpiece of emotional blues singing and a reminder that she has long been one of the modern underrated artists in the interpretation of authentic blues. The album, now hard to obtain, was entitled *Black Is Brown and Brown Is Beautiful*. Other LPs: *Ruth Brown '65* (Mainstream); *Big Band Sound of Thad Jones/Mel Lewis Featuring Miss Ruth Brown* (Solid State); *The Real Ruth Brown* (Cobblestone); new album on London, 1976.

BROWN, SAMUEL T. (SAM), *guitar*; also *bass*; b. Baltimore, Md., 1/19/39. Father was operatic tenor who pl. violin, piano, flute, cornet. St. pl. piano at four; mandolin at six. Began pl. on weekly TV show at 12; also w. high school dance band on guitar. Joined paratroopers at 17 for three yrs., the last two in band where he learned to read. Stud. classical guitar w. Joe Fava in Det., '58-60; Mannes Coll. of Mus., NYC, '60-1; class. gtr. w. Leonid Bolotine, '60-3; harm. & theory w. Fred Wurle; master classes w. Julian Bream and Gustavo Lopez. Played w. Miriam Makeba, '61-4; Astrud Gilberto, incl. Japanese tour, '65; Ella Fitzgerald, '65-6; Ars Nova, '66-68; Gary Burton; Keith Jarrett, '69-71; Ron Carter, '71; Herbie Mann, '74; Dave Matthews band from '74; Sundays at Gregory's w. Al Haig, '75. Has also pl. concerts and/or gigs w. Stan Getz; Hubert Laws; Jimmy Owens; Charlie Haden; Joe Farrell, etc.

Infl: Django Reinhardt, Andres Segovia, Tal Farlow, Johnny Smith, Bill Evans, Coltrane, Ravi Shankar. TV: Ed Sullivan w. Makeba, Harry Belafonte; *Tonight* w. Fitzgerald; Vic Damone; *Electric Village* w. Ars Nova; *Jazz Special* w. Burton. Arr. albums for Carly Simon; Makeba. Comp: *My Hoss Knows the Way; Sunrise Highs; Dance of the Windchimes; Love Will Find a Way*. Fest: NJF-NY w. Burton; Getz; Mulligan. LPs: w. *Gary Burton & Keith Jarrett*; w. Jarrett, *Expectations; Treasure Island*; w. H. Mann, *First Light*; w. Ars Nova, *Sunshine & Shadows* (Atl.); w. Jeremy Steig, *Wayfaring Stranger* (SS); w. C. Haden, *Liberation Music Orch.* (Imp.); w. Bill Evans, *From Left to Right* (MGM); *Makeba Sings* (RCA); w. David Matthews, *Live at the Five Spot* (Muse).

BROWN, GERALD (SONNY), *drums*; b. Cincinnati, Ohio, 4/20/36. Began on drums that belonged to George Russell; Russell's mother gave them to Brown. Studied at Woodward High School in Cincinnati; Cincinnati Conserv. of Mus. Army '53-6. Played in Cincinnati, Chicago, Detroit and other midwestern locations w. Eddie Vinson; Amos Milburn; Dinah Washington; and various Gospel groups, '56-60. To NYC '61, working w. Frank Foster; Randy Weston; Ray Bryant in early '60s; Kenny Burrell for a year in mid-60s; Jon Hendricks, '63-4. Made gigs w. a wide variety of NY musicians incl. Clifford Jordan; Sonny Rollins; Curtis Fuller; Coleman Hawkins; Zoot Sims; Lee Konitz; Archie Shepp; and Sam Rivers. With New York Bass Choir from '68. Made Scandinavian tour w. Joe Henderson and Ron Carter, '70. In '75 playing mostly w. Rahsaan Roland Kirk w. whom he has been associated, off and on, from '57. Lecturer at Mark Twain JHS, August '68; staff member of YDA program in Harlem, '68-73; teaching at P.S. 139, Bronx, '69-70; Jazzmobile Workshop, '72; Jazz Interactions Workshop, I.S. 44, '73; pl. for critics symposium, Smithsonian Institute,

Wash., D.C., Sept. '74. Infl: Donald Linder, Jo Jones, Sonny Greer, Chris Columbus, Blakey, Roach, Roy Haynes, Philly Joe Jones, Elvin Jones.

TV: *Tonight; Today; Soul.* Fest: House drummer at MJF, '63-4; NJF-NY w. Bass Choir; Babs Gonzales. LPs: w. Mingus, *Let My Children Hear Music* (Col.); w. Richard Davis (Muse); K. Burrell (Prest.); A. Zoller (Embryo); R.R. Kirk (Atl.); R. Bryant (Sue); NY Bass Choir; NY Brass Co.; *Decendants of Mike & Phoebe* (Strata-East).

BRUBECK, CHRIS, *trombone, bass, composer*; also *keyboards, bass guitar*; b. Los Angeles, Cal., 3/19/52. Father, Dave Brubeck; brothers, Darius and Danny Brubeck. Studied at Interlochen Arts Academy w. trombone teacher and head of stage band, Dave Sporney; Univ. of Michigan, '71-4. Pl. w. Addiss & Crofut, '70. Own gp., New Heavenly Blue, '70-1; w. Darius Brubeck Ensemble; Two Generations of Brubeck from '72; own gp. Sky King, from '74. "Chris is one of those humorous trombone players," says his father. "He's never heard Bill Harris, but he reminds me very much of Bill."

TV: Mike Douglas; Merv Griffin; *AM America; Today*; PBS. Fest: NJF-NY; Alaska; Ravinia; Ann Arbor Blues. Comp: *Bright Day; For God's Sake Elizabeth; The Coming of the Rhino; Silver Eyes; New Heavenly Blue; Love You Tonight; Raft Song; Where Are You Tonight; Pegleg Back in 35*; opera, *The Rise and Demise of Tucker P. Fudpucker.* Publ: Derry Music Co.

LPs: *Educated Homegrown* (RCA); *New Heavenly Blue* (Atl.); *Sky King*; w. Dave Brubeck, *Summit Sessions* (Col.); *Truth is Fallen; Two Generations of Brubeck; Brother the Great Spirit Made Us All* (Atl.)

BRUBECK, DANIEL (DANNY), *drums, percussion, tabla, squeeze drum*; b. Oakland, Cal., 5/4/55. Father, Dave Brubeck; brothers, Chris and Darius. Rec. on finger cymbals w. father at age 10. Studies at Interlochen Academy of the Arts; No. Carolina School of the Arts, '72. Played w. Darius Brubeck Ensemble '73; Two Generations of Brubeck from '72; when Dave is not present the gp. is called Earthrise. Infl: Joe Morello; Alan Dawson. Some people see a stylistic resemblance to Sid Catlett, although Brubeck had never heard him. Fest: Alaska; NJF-NY; White Mountain; Ravinia. LPs: w. Dave Brubeck, *Two Generations of Brubeck; Brother the Great Spirit Made Us All* (Atl.); *Summit Sessions* (Col.).

BRUBECK, DAVID DARIUS, *keyboards, composer*; also *synthesizer, guitar, veena, sarod, trumpet*; b. San Francisco, Cal., 6/14/47. Son of Dave Brubeck; brothers, Chris and Danny. Named after Darius Milhaud. Piano lessons to age 14; harm. w. Gordon Smith at Mills Coll., '65-7; w. Milhaud in Aspen, '62; comp. w. Donald Martino at Yale, '63-4. B.A. from Wesleyan U., '69. Stud. ethnomusicology, majoring in Indian music but grad. cum laude in History of Religions. Stud. Ind. mus. w. Dagar, Ragu, Narayanaswami, Nageswara Rao, Maryvonne Pointer, Robert E. Brown; graduate counterpoint w. Richard K. Winslow; comp. privately w. Robert Jordan Fritz, '69-71. His Darius Brubeck Ensemble toured as part of Two Generations of Brubeck on a world-wide basis from '72; also jobs as a separate entity in US and Canada. Sideman on occasion w. Maruga; Fritz. Co-produced New Heavenly Blue album w. brother, Chris, '70. Infl: Dave Brubeck, Dolphy, Jimi Hendrix, Milhaud, Webern, Stravinsky, Bartok, Ives, George Martin, Keith Jarrett, Corea. Fests: NJF-NY, '73-5. Presented lecture series, *Understanding Jazz*, for Conn. Cent. of Cont. Ed.; awarded ind. artist grant in comp. by Conn. Comm. on the Arts. Comps: *Tin Sink; Temptation Boogie; Sky-Scape; Earthrise; Pneuma Hagion*; tunes and score for *American Vaudeville Tent-Show*; score for *Evening of Poetry & Jazz* w. Don Taylor, Joanne Woodward; arrs. of *Blue Rondo a La Turk, Three to Get Ready* for full orch. LPs: *Two Generations of Brubeck; Brother, the Great Spirit Made Us All* (Atlantic); *Chaplin's Back* (Paramount); *Maruga* (Origin).

BRUBECK, DAVID WARREN (DAVE),* *piano, composer*; b. Concord, Calif., 12/6/20. December 26, 1967 saw the formal finish of the Dave Brubeck quartet in which he and Paul Desmond had played together from 1951. A new quartet, with Gerry Mulligan, Jack Six and Alan Dawson began performing and recording the following year. From '72 the trio, without Mulligan, toured with Brubeck's sons (q.v.) as Two Generations of Brubeck, Mulligan and Desmond joining the entourage for special concert and festival appearances. Eventually Chris and Danny Brubeck replaced Six and Dawson, making a world tour '74.

As in the first half of the '60s Brubeck concerned himself with the writing of extended works: the cantatas, *The Gates of Justice; Truth is Fallen; Song of Bethlehem*; an oratorio, *The Light in the Wilderness*; and an ethnic panoramic tone poem, *They All Sang Yankee Doodle.* The latter was performed by the New Haven Symphony in May '75; as a concerto for two pianos in Westport, Conn. in June '75; and, with the composer at the piano, by the Dallas Symphony in July '75.

Jazz comp: *Happy Anniversary; The Duke; Blessed Are the Poor; Forty Days; Elementals; Indian Song; Circadian Disrhythmia; The Holy One; Knives.*

Film: Paul Mazursky's *Next Stop Greenwich Village* used recordings of the early '50s Brubeck quartet on the sound track.

TV: Johnny Carson; Mike Douglas; Merv Griffin; *AM America; Today*; Dedication of Louis Armstrong Stadium at NJF-NY, NET; *Timex Special; Look Up and Live.* Fest: Berlin; Alaska; White Mountain; Ravinia; Blossom; Monterey; Antibes; Warsaw; Saratoga; NO; Mexico; Mar Y Sol; NJF-NY w. Mulligan & Desmond, '72; solo piano pl. the music of J. Van Heusen, '73; w. Two Generations, '73, '75. Poll: Group won *Playboy*, '66-8; Brubeck won piano '66-71; elected to *Playboy* Hall of Fame, '66.

LPs: *Summit Sessions; Blues Roots; Brubeck in Amsterdam; Last Time I Saw Paris; Live at the Berlin Philharmonic* (Col.); *Brubeck & Mulligan in Cincinnati; The Light in the Wilderness; The Gates of Justice* (Decca);

Truth Is Fallen; The Last Set at Newport; Two Generations of Brubeck; We're All Together Again For the First Time; Brother the Great Spirit Made Us All (Atl.); *Duets 1975/Desmond-Brubeck* (Horizon); reissues: *The Art of Dave Brubeck, The Fantasy Years* (Atl.); *Dave Brubeck's All-Time Greatest Hits* (Col.).

BRUCE, JOHN SYMON ASHER (JACK), *bass, singer, composer*; also *keyboards, synthesizer, harmonica*; b. Bishopbriggs, Lanarkshire, Scotland, 5/14/43. Won a scholarship to Royal Scottish Acad. of Mus. at age 17, stud. cello and comp. Pl. bass w. jazz bands in Glasgow area clubs during this period and met Alexis Korner, Ginger Baker, Dick Heckstall-Smith and Graham Bond. Joined the latter three in the Graham Bond Organization; then worked w. John Mayall's Bluesbreakers; Manfred Mann; Cream; Tony Williams Lifetime; West, Bruce and Laing. Pl. in a short-lived gp. w. Carla Bley, '75. LPs: *Out of the Storm* (RSO); own gp.; w. Cream; w. Tony Williams (Poly.); West, Bruce and Laing (Col.).

BRUNIS, GEORG (George Brunies),* *trombone*; b. New Orleans, La., 2/6/1900. Made first rec. w. NO Rhythm Kings, '22. Toured for 12 years w. clarinetist Ted Lewis. Settling in Chicago in '40s he spent the rest of his life gigging locally and rec. with many jazz artists incl. Eddie Condon; the latter's *Windy City Seven Commodores* is said to be Brunis' fav. session, and can be found in *Eddie Condon/Bud Freeman* on Atl. Brunis died in Chicago, 11/19/74.

BRYAN, MIKE,* *guitar*; b. Byhalia, Miss., 1916. Bryan pl. guitar in B. Goodman's orch. during the period when Ch. Christian was a member of the Goodman sextet; was active in the '60s as the producer of a series of TV jazz films, feat. Armstrong, Ellington, Condon et al. Made for the Goodyear Co., the films were only seen outside the U.S. Bryan later resumed playing; toured Viet Nam w. Martha Raye. He died of leukemia in LA, 8/20/72.

BRYANT, BOBBY, *trumpet, fluegelhorn, composer*; b. Hattiesburg, Miss., 5/19/34. Played tenor sax and trumpet with local bands during his teens. After moving to Chicago, stud. from '52-7, earning bachelor's degree in music education with trumpet major from Cosmopolitan School of Music. While in Chicago, pl. with various small bands, Latin combos, Red Saunders etc. Also led band for touring show starring singer Billy Williams.

Bryant traveled as lead trumpeter w. Vic Damone from '60-5, working throughout the U.S., Canada, Philippines, Puerto Rico. Settling in LA, he worked w. Gerald Wilson, O. Nelson and hundreds of recording groups in pop, r & b and other areas; also as staff musician at NBC-TV. He led a combo and occasionally a big band locally in clubs and on records; comp. and arr. for Damone, Peggy Lee, L. Rawls, B. Goodman, Marlena Shaw and many other singers. Led band on Bill Cosby TV comedy series, and played as sideman in numerous other TV shows. Feat. soloist on sound tracks of movies *A Day With The Boys; Assault On A Queen*; and *Winning*. Dir. of Mus. for *What It Is*, 10 segs. on black history for NBC-TV.

As a soloist and leader Bryant makes an imposing figure, combining elements of Cat Anderson, M. Ferguson and D. Ellis with a touch of the blues added. A brilliant composer and performer, he was prevented by economic conditions from gaining the success he deserved with his own orch.

LPs: *Swahili Strut; Ain't Doing Too B-a-d, Bad* (Cadet); *Big Band Blues* (Vee-Jay). Others by band, such as *Earth Dance* and *Hair*, both on Wor. Pac., were deleted.

BRYANT, RAPHAEL (RAY),* *piano, composer*; b. Philadelphia, Pa., 12/24/31. Continued to work w. own trio or as solo pianist. Appeared in the latter context at the Montreux Jazz Fest., '72. A recording of his performance, *Alone at Montreux*, was issued on Atlantic. Comp: *Blues #2; Blues #3; Changes; Cubano Chant; Little Susie; Slow Freight*. Other LPs: Pablo; Cadet; reissue on Prest.; w. Z. Sims (Pablo).

BRYANT, ROYAL G. (RUSTY), *tenor and alto saxophones, leader*; b. Huntington, W. Va., 11/25/29. Raised in Columbus from 1935. Father, a mortician and amateur musician, bought him trumpet, later alto sax. At 13, pl. w. Archie (Stomp) Gordon band. U.S. Navy 1948-9; stationed in Boston, where he heard Sam Rivers, Jaki Byard, Nat Pierce band and others who were influential. Back in Columbus, briefly joined Tiny Grimes; then opened w. own gp. at Carolyn Club for five years. Began recording for Dot and had several hit singles, notably *Night Train*. Placed emphasis on honking pre-rock style. From '56-8 his girl vocalist was Nancy Wilson. Later the band was heard throughout the midwest and east, often under the leadership of organist Hank Marr.

Bryant made a comeback under his own name when he resumed recording as a leader in 1969, for Prestige. LPs: *Until It's Time For You To Go; For the Good Times; Friday Night Funk; Wild Fire; Soul Liberation; Fire Eater; Night Train Now!; Rusty Bryant Returns* (Prestige). Earlier LPs: *America's Greatest Jazz; Jazz Horizons* (Dot).

BRYDEN, BERYL, *singer*; b. Norwich, England, 5/11/26. To London 1945. Sang w. Geo. Webb's Dixielanders and other trad. gps. In Paris in '53 and '54, sang at Vieux Colombier and was feat. w. Lionel Hampton at Olympia. Later in Holland, Germany; long assoc. w. Fatty George band, then w. Tremble Kids in Zurich. During these years, busy radio, TV, recording schedule. In 1960s, pl. Antibes Fest., toured Far East; Africa 1965. First visit to NY 1970; in Australia '71-2 w. Graeme Bell. A loyal devotee of early jazz forms, she attended the NOJF in '73 as a visitor. Innumerable jazz festivals around the Continent, and rec. w. more than 20 bands in eight countries, from a Frèddy Randall date in London, 1948, to an LP w. Piccadilly Six in Zurich, '75. Others on Esquire, Decca, Supraphon, Col., Pye, Muza etc.

BUCKNER, MILTON (MILT),* *organ, piano, composer*; also *trombone, vibes*; b. St. Louis, Mo., 7/10/15. With L. Hampton in '40s and early '50s, Buckner popularized "locked-hands" piano style (both hands pl. parallel chord patterns) which he originated in Detroit, '34, to "give

Don Cox five-piece orch. more depth." Own organ trio from '52. W. I. Jacquet, A. Dawson at Lennie's-On-the-Turnpike, '66. European tours: w. Jacquet, R. Eldridge, '66; w. B. Tate, Wallace Bishop, '67; Jo Jones; MPS record tour, '69; L. Hampton, '71. TV: Global Shows, Toronto, '74. Fests: NJF, '68, '70-5; Nice, '74-5; MJF, '70. Comp: *Hamp's Boogie Woogie; Slide Hamp, Slide; Overtime; The Lamplighter; Mighty Low; Count's Basement; Jumping at the Zanzibar; Mighty High; Rockin' With Milt.* LPs: *Play Chords* (MPS/BASF); *Blues For Diane* (Jazz Odyssey); *Midnight Mood, Rockin' Hammond* (Cadet); w. Jacquet (Prestige); Tate (B & B); *Newport in New York, The Jam Sessions, vols. 1 & 2* (Cobblestone).

BUCKNER, THEODORE GUY (TED),* *alto sax*; b. St. Louis, Mo., 12/14/13. The veteran alto saxophonist, brother of pianist Milt Buckner, continued to be active in the Detroit area and was associated with the revised edition of McKinney's Cotton Pickers. He died in April 1976 in Detroit.

BUCKNER, JOHN EDWARD (TEDDY),* *trumpet*; b. Sherman, Tex., 7/16/09. Has led his own small band since the late '50s, mostly in LA area. Worked regularly in New Orleans Square at Disneyland from mid '60s; also occasional concerts at Pilgrimage Theatre etc.; night club gigs at Donte's, Times Restaurant. In '75, did sound track work for *Louis Armstrong: Chicago Style*, a TV film, ABC.

LPs: *Teddy Buckner All Stars* (D.J.); *Midnight In Moscow* (GNP-Crescendo); *On Sunset Strip* (D.J.).

BUDIMIR, DENNIS MATTHEW,* *guitar*; b. Los Angeles, Ca., 6/20/38. Played w. Harry James, C. Hamilton, B. Shank, Peggy Lee, Julie London, Gerald Wilson and many others in LA area. For more than a decade worked mainly as studio musician w. Q. Jones, L. Schifrin, M. Paich, D. Grusin, D. Ellis, Joe Williams, G. Melle et al.

Won DB Critics' Poll, TDWR, '71. LPs: *Second Coming; Session with Albert; Sprung Free!* (Revelation).

BUDWIG, MONTY,* *bass*; b. Pender, Neb. 12/26/29. Well known for many years for jazz associations w. Goodman, Herman, and west coast groups in '50s, '60s. Cont. freelance studio and night club work in '70s. Concord Jazz Fest., '71 and Australian tour '73, w. Goodman. S. America, '74 w. Carmen McRae. Best LPs: *Jazz Gunn* w. S. Manne (Atl.); *Manne That's Gershwin*, w. Manne (Capitol); *Summer Night* w. Mike Wofford trio (Milestone); Sarah Vaughan & J. Rowles trio (Mainstream).

BUNCH, JOHN L. JR.,* *piano, conductor*; b. Tipton, Ind., 12/1/21. Own duo for 44 weeks at Luigi II in NYC, '65-6; w. Buddy Rich big band, '66. Became accompanist-mus. dir. for Tony Bennett in late '66, remaining until late '72. In this capacity cond. the bands of Basie, Ellington, Herman, Rich, the LA Philharmonic and Cleve. Orch. Worked mostly w. B. Goodman sextet '73, incl. European tour in Dec.; Rich septet, '74, incl. European tour in Oct. Bunch also led own trio or duo at Bradley's, NYC and Anchorage Hotel, Antigua, BWI, '73-5. App. on many TV shows incl. *This Is Music*—13 Tony Bennett specials, filmed in London and seen in US; Tom Jones; Pearl Bailey; Jonathan Winters; Dean Martin. Comp: *Why You; Feathers*; arrs. for Herman, Goodman. Fest: Concord JF w. Rich, '74. LPs: own sextet (Famous Door); w. Bennett (Col., MGM); Cal Tjader (MGM); Rich; Sammy Davis-Rich (Reprise); Jane Harvey; Eddie Barefield (RCA); Joe Venuti-Zoot Sims (Chiaro.).

BUNKER, LAWRENCE BENJAMIN (LARRY),* *drums, vibes*; b. Long Beach, Cal., 11/4/28. Busy in studios since '50s, he has continued to maintain an association with jazz. Along with apps. with the LA Phil. under Zubin Mehta, and other symph. orchs., he app. at Shelly's Manne Hole w. Z. Sims, Dave Grusin; at Donte's w. Howard Roberts, Clare Fischer, Mike Barone, O. Nelson, B. Shank and many others. At Ojai Fest. pl. music of Stravinsky under Pierre Boulez, '71; music of Messiaen, '72; in '75, Brahms, Schoenberg, under Michael Tilson Thomas. Bunker also has fulfilled numerous film and TV assignments w. Q. Jones, L. Schifrin, O. Nelson, Pat Williams, Tom Scott, Grusin, G. Mulligan, John Mandel. As an avocation, he collects and restores antiques, also custom makes instruments and auxiliary equipment for the perf. of contemporary music.

LPs: w. Gary Burton, *Time Machine; Something's Coming* (RCA); w. Q. Jones, *Smackwater Jack* (A & M); w. Williams, *Threshold* (Cap.); w. Dominic Frontiere, *On Any Sunday*—movie sound track (Bell); w. 5th Dimension, *Stone Soul Picnic* (Liberty).

BURNS, DAVID (DAVE), *trumpet; fluegelhorn*; also *piano*; b. Perth Amboy, N.J., 3/5/24. Studied privately w. Nicholan Morrisey from ages nine to 13; Thomas Ippolito, 13-17; two yrs., off and on, w. Carmine Caruso. Worked w. Savoy Sultans, '41-3. Led an AAF Band, '43-5. With Dizzy Gillespie's big band, '46-9; Duke Ellington, '50-2; James Moody, '52-7. From '57-60 app. w. a variety of small gps. in NYC; then w. Billy Mitchell-Al Grey sextet, '61-4; Willie Bobo, '64-6; combo work at Minton's; James Moody at Half Note; Leon Bibb TV show, NBC, '66-8. Moved to Long Island and pl. w. Mitchell in "*Project Read*," '69. From '70 working w. International Art of Jazz, pl. concerts, lecturing and cond. "rap sessions" on all levels from elementary school to coll. Also teaching improvisation on all instr. in own studio in Freeport, L.I. One of the earliest of Gillespie's disciples in the '40s.

Other infl: Armstrong, Eldridge. TV: Milton Berle show w. Ellington; Sammy Davis show w. Johnny Brown sextet. Films: *Sweet Love Bitter* w. Dick Gregory; *Jivin' in Bebop* w. Gillespie; w. Ellington for Universal, '50. Fest: NJF. Comp: *Common Touch; C.B. Blues; Be's That Way; Automation; Toe Tappin'; Rigor "Mortez"; Livin' Through It All.* Own LPs: *Warming Up; Dave 'Burns'*; w. Bill English (Vang.); w. Arthur Taylor, *A.T.'s Delight*; w. George Wallington (Blue Note); w. Gillespie (Prest., RCA Vict.); w. Ray Brown-Milt Jackson (Savoy); w. W. Bobo (Roulette); Mitchell-Grey (Argo);

w. Eddie Jefferson, *Body and Soul*; w. Moody (Prest.); w. Dexter Gordon (unreleased) for BN.

BURRELL, HERMAN DAVIS II (DAVE), *piano, composer*; also *clarinet, vibes*; b. Middletown, Ohio, 9/10/40. Mother a singer, organist, pianist, choir director. Studied under Dr. Barbara Smith at U. of Hawaii where he was Music Major '58-60. Grad. from Boston Conserv. of Mus. and Berklee Coll of Mus., '61-5, majoring in Performance, Arr. & Comp. He has performed in Hawaii, Europe, Japan, Algeria, Surinam and all over the US and Canada as a soloist, w. own duos, trios, quartet; Archie Shepp; Marion Brown; and the 360 Degree Music Experience w. Grachan Moncur III and Beaver Harris. Pl. many concerts for prisoners; coll. concerts, also lecturing as artist-in-residence. Fest: NJF-NY, Radio City jam session, '73; NJF-NY w. Shepp, '71-2; NJF w. Sunny Murray Spiritual Infinity; NJF in Japan concert tour w. Shepp; Molde; Pori w. 360 Degree; Mednarodni, Yugo., Ann Arbor Blues & Jazz Fest. w. Shepp; Baden-Baden Free Jazz Meeting; Paris Int. JF. Pan-African Cultural Fest. in Algiers w. Shepp-led avant garde all stars. Pl. w. Rastafarian musicians in Kingston, Jamaica; w. Haitian percussionists in Port-au-Prince where he performed and rec. a West African voodoo ceremony. Received grants from NEA to adapt Haitian folk music to a Jazz Suite which he performed in Central Park, NYC; to write music to the theme of a book by Edgar White, *Crucifado*. In the Sahara Desert wrote music for a French film co. illustrating Black American musicians pl. and discussing music with nomadic Touareg musicians. Other comp: *A.M. Rag (Margie Pargie); Blue Notes On the Black and White Keys; Polynesian Suite; Sketches of Harlem; Echo; Japan; My March; After Love; Answer; Epilogue; East Side Colors.* Arrs. for Shepp; Pharoah Sanders; Marion Brown; 360 Degree Experience. Also *La Vie de Boheme*, based on Puccini's *La Boheme*. Publ: (360 Music Co., 269 W. 72nd St., N.Y., N.Y. 10023).

Infl: Jelly Roll Morton, Ellington, Monk, Bud Powell, boogie woogie, Coltrane, Shepp, Moncur, Max Roach, Prokofiev, Puccini, Rimsky-Korsakoff. TV: *Like It Is* w. Shepp; 360 Degree; sound track for *Witherspoon*, Black Drama Repertory Workshop, CBS; documentary, *Jazz in New York Today*, filmed for Rome TV in NYC. Music Instructor at Queens Col, NYC, '71-73. LPs: own trio (Black Saint); quartet (Horo); w. S. Cowell; *Only Me; Dreams; Questions and Answers* (Trio); *High* (Douglas); *La Vie De Boheme; Echo* (Byg); w. Sanders; Brown (Imp.); Shepp (Imp.; Black Saint; Arista; Big; American) Moncur; Murray; Clifford Thornton (Byg); Alan Silva (ESP); w. 360 Degree Exp., *From Ragtime to No Time* (360°).

BURRELL, KENNETH EARL (KENNY),* *guitar, composer, singer*; b. Detroit, Mich., 7/31/31. Prominent since the mid-1950s, occasionally as sideman with D. Gillespie, B. Goodman et al, but most often leading his own groups, Burrell by the 1960s was occupied with NYC studio work, along with clubs and concerts. He undertook his first tour of California in 1967, and his initial European tour, with his own group, in '69. During that year he also started his own club, The Guitar. In '70 he took his combo on a tour of Japan, and returned there the following year. Also in '71 he began a series of college seminars in the U.S.

Burrell began recording for Fantasy in 1972, traveled in both Eastern and Western European countries, visited Japan, New Zealand and Australia, then Europe, with the Newport All Stars, and relocated in California. From '73 he became active in LA studio work along with many festivals, clubs, concerts, seminars and clinics. He was appointed executive director of Guitar Player Productions in '74. Japan again in '75; *Tribute to Duke Ellington* album, '75.

In addition to winning innumerable *down beat* polls, Burrell has placed first on guitar in Japan's *Swing Journal* poll and the London *Melody Maker* poll for the past several years. He won the first *Ebony* Magazine music poll.

Publs: *Jazz Guitar* (Elliott Music Co. Inc., 144 Jolind Rd., Paoli, Pa. 19301).

Comps: *Ode to 52nd St.*, title work of LP (Cadet); *Asphalt Canyon Suite*, title work of LP (Verve); *Sausalito Nights; Be Yourself* etc.

LPs: *Introducing; Burrell, Vol. 2* (BN); *Best; Blue Moods; Crash; Out of This World; Quintet*, feat. Coltrane; *All Day Long & All Night Long*, feat. Byrd, Waldron, Mobley (Prest.); *Both Feet on the Ground; 'Round Midnight; Up The Street* (Fant.); *Cool Cookin'* (Chess); *God Bless The Child* (CTI); *Guitar Forms* (Verve); *Man At Work; Ode to 52nd Street; Tender Gender* (Cadet); w. S. Rollins, *Alfie* (Imp.).

BURROWS, DONALD VERNON (DON), *clarinet, composer*; also *saxophones, flutes, fife*; b. Sydney, Australia, 8/8/28. Stud. at Sydney Conservatorium, '46-8. First rec. date at age 16 in dixieland group. Over the past 30 years, innumerable apps. in concerts, fests. and often on TV as sideman, leader, soloist, MC and lecturer. Burrows, who has led combos and bands of every kind, pl. dance halls and night clubs in the '40s and '50s, radio shows from the '40s, TV from late '50s, is an admirable clarinetist and Australia's best known jazz musician. Insp. by B. Goodman, B. De Franco, Ellington, G. Mulligan, Ch. Parker, G. Burton. Toured New Zealand, '60 on same show w. Oscar Peterson trio; toured Australia, '72 in program w. Burton, C. Byrd. Took part in the world's first satellite telecast, Montreal Expo '67. Mus. Dir. on Australian show at Expo 70 in Osaka, Japan; pl. at NJF-NY, '72. Toured Southeast Asia for Australian Dept. of Foreign Affairs, '74. Burrows has won many awards incl. Australian music mag. polls, gold record for his album *Just The Beginning*; Album of the Year award, '74 for *Don Burrows Quartet at Sydney Opera House*. In '72 Queen Elizabeth awarded him the MBE for services to jazz. In '73 the Australian Prime Minister appointed him to Council for the Arts and he was successful in helping establish Australia's first jazz studies program at Sydney Conservatorium, where he teaches.

Burrows' quartet has app. w. symph. orchs. in a series of concerts since '66. Comps: sound track for movie *2000 Weeks*, and for dozens of documentaries and TV programs, background music for stage, radio and TV plays, as well as originals for a dozen albums.

LPs: *Don Burrows Quartet at Sydney Opera House* (Mainstream); others on Australian labels: *The Jazz Sounds of the Don Burrows Quartet; On Camera* (Col.); *Jazz Australia* (CBS); *Just The Beginning; Australia and all that Jazz* (Cherry Pie).

BURTON, GARY,* *vibes, composer, educator*; b. Anderson, Ind., 1/23/43. First prominent in '63 w. G. Shearing and S. Getz, '64-6, he formed his own quartet in '67 w. Larry Coryell, guitar; Bob Moses, drums; and Steve Swallow, bass. Swallow was still w. him in '75 and Moses had rejoined. From '70 Burton has also pl. solo concerts and recorded w. other prominent jazzmen (see LPs below). Between '71-5 he toured in Japan, Australia, England and the Continent, incl. Communist-bloc countries. As an educator he has been a permanent staff member at the Berklee Coll. Mus. from '71 but also presents lecture-seminar-concert programs w. his quartet at univs. all over the U.S. Consultant in instr. design for Musser Co. Fest: NJF, '64-75; MJF, Montreux, Berlin, '66-73. Won first place in DB Readers poll, '68-74; Critics poll, '72, '74-5; DB Jazzman of the Year, '68. Publ: Introduction to *Jazz Vibes; Solo Book; Four Mallet Studies* (Creative Music, Chicago). Comps: *The Sunset Bell; Leroy the Magician; Walter L.; Dreams; Response; Brownout; Boston Marathon.*

The harmonic richness of Burton's four-mallet forays showed most graphically his original Bill Evans influence, but he has continued to deepen and widen his personal expression by using challenging material that is extremely contemporary, without yielding to the excesses of the avant garde or the pursuit of the rock dollar. He won a Grammy for his solo album, *Alone At Last*, on Atlantic. Other LPs: *New Quartet; Ring; Seven Songs For Quartet & Chamber Orch.* (ECM); *In the Public Interest* (Poly.); *Good Vibes; Throb* (Atl.); *In Concert; Lofty Fake Anagram; Duster* (RCA); *Paris Encounter* w. S. Grappelli (Atl.); *Crystal Silence* w. C. Corea; *Matchbook* w. Ralph Towner; *Hotel Hello* w. S. Swallow (ECM); *Genuine Tong Funeral* w. Carla Bley (RCA); w. K. Jarrett (Atl.).

BURTON, WILLIAM RON, *piano, composer*; also *organ*; b. Louisville, Ky., 2/10/34. Private lessons at 13 for four yrs. First prof. job at 18 w. local gps. of Tommy Walker; Edgar "Eggeye" Brooks. Roland Kirk came through Louisville in '53 and for next six yrs. Burton went out w. him to Nashville, Indianapolis, Cincinnati, Milwaukee and Chicago. Spent eight mos. on own in NYC, '60; then w. Chris Powell in Syracuse, '60-1. Returned to Louisville, leaving as organist w. George Adams trio, '64-5. Met Norris Jones (Sirone), Ron Hampton, Lloyd McNeil in Atlanta and pl. in gp. w. them, '65-6. Freelanced in NYC '66, joining R.R. Kirk, '67. Through '72 pl. clubs, concerts, major US and Euro. fests. w. him. From '72 w. Piano Choir; own gp. From '74 w. Michael Carvin; gigs w. Stanley Turrentine; Leon Thomas; Carlos Garnett. Infl: Peterson, Lloyd Glenn, Garner, Bud Powell, H. Silver, Red Garland, K. Drew, Richard Abrams, Andrew Hill. TV: w. Kirk, documentary on Martin Luther King, *March to Freedom*, Westinghouse Broad.; *Soul*, PBS; w. Ray Ore and the Creative Connoisseurs, Channel 50, Trenton, N.J. Comp: *Seven Points; African Sunrise; Desert Trot; Fertility Dance*. LPs: *The Cosmic Twins*; w. Dick Griffin, *The Eighth Number* (Strata-East); w. Kirk, (Atl.); Michael Carvin (Steeple.); Grubbs Bros. (Cobble.).

BUSH, LEONARD WALTER (LENNIE),* *bass*; b. London, England, 6/6/27. Pro. since '44. Mainly active in studios in recent years w. J. Parnell et al. Occ. jazz gigs at Ronnie Scott's Club w. C. Terry, Z. Sims, J. Pass, B. Webster, C. McRae, A. O'Day et al. Three Euro. tours w. B. Goodman, '71-2, incl. rec.

BUSHKIN, JOE,* *piano, songwriter*; b. 11/17/16. After living some years in Hawaii, Bushkin moved to Santa Barbara, Cal. Except for a brief tenure at a hotel in Palm Springs, Cal., in 1970, he remained in virtual retirement, raising thoroughbred horses in Santa Barbara, Calif. He came to NYC in November '75 to play an engagement at Michael's Pub. At the same time his daughters were winning prizes at the National horse show, Madison Square Garden.

BUSHLER, HERB, *bass*; also *piano*; b. New York City, 3/7/39. Two yrs. of piano study, '47-9; then taught self tuba until "damned thing got too heavy." Took up bass, doubling Fender from '65. Bushler, who has app. as soloist w. Toronto, Phila., Cinci., American, Brooklyn and Roch. symphonies, has also worked w. a variety of groups, some concurrently, such as Ted Curson '65; Fifth Dimension, '69; Paul Winter, '71-3; Gil Evans, '67-74; Tony Williams, '73; Blossom Dearie, '71-3; David Amram, '70- . Also active in '70s w. Billy Harper, Joe Chambers, Coleridge Perkinson, Howard Johnson Substructure and Joe Farrell. Infl: Coleridge Perkinson. Arrs. for singer Gerri Granger. Cond. Negro Ensemble Co. prod: *Song of the Lusitanian Bogey*, '68; *Man Better Man*, '74; pl. piano for prod. of Behan's *The Hostage*, '62. Fest: Newport, Newport West, Lugano w. Curson, Evans, T. Williams, Montego Joe. LPs: Farrell (CTI); G. Evans (Ampex, Atl.); *Living Time* w. B. Evans-G. Russell (Col.); Dearie (Daffodil); Amram (RCA); Curson (Atl.); Teresa Brewer w. Ellington (Fly. Dutch.).

BUTLER, FRANK,* *drums*; b. Kansas City, Mo., 2/18/28. Worked for short period w. J. Coltrane, Miles Davis; mainly active in LA area w. Harold Land, Jimmy Rowles, Terry Gibbs, Teddy Edwards, Conte Candoli, Gerald Wilson, Lorez Alexandria. Infrequently heard in 1970s; worked for a while as drug abuse counsellor in Youth Outreach Program for LA County Health Dept. Festivals: Monterey; Black Fest. of Arts. LP: w. Teddy Edwards, *Feelin's* (Muse); w. Miles Davis, *Seven Steps to Heaven* (Col.).

BUTTERFIELD, CHARLES WILLIAM (BILLY),* *trumpet, fluegelhorn*; b. Middleton, Ohio, 1/14/17. Featured soloist w. Bob Crosby, Shaw and Goodman bands in '30s and '40s. After many years on NYC studio scene moved to Va., where he led own band in late '50s-early '60s. Living in Fla. during '60s, working w. own units until he became charter member of World's Greatest Jazzband, '68, with which he toured in US, Europe, England, So. America, So. Africa and Australia. Returned to Fla. '72, gigging on own and w. Flip Phillips. TV and fests. w. WGJ incl. NJF, NOJF, Berlin. Many apps. at Colo. Jazz Party, '60s, '70s. LPs: *Bobby, Billy and Brazil* w. B. Hackett (MGM); w. WGJ (Proj. 3, Atl., World Jazz); *Swing That Music* w. Dutch Coll. Swing Band; *In a Mellow Tone* w. own sextet (DCS); *Rapport* w. D. Wellstood (77).

BUTTS, JAMES H. (JIMMY), *bass, singer*; b. New York City, 1917. Started on piano at high school. Bass w. Dr. Sausage and the Five Pork Chops, 1937. Pl. w. Chris Columbus '39-43, except for brief stint w. Les Hite spring '41. After pl. w. Doc Wheeler's Sunset Royals and Don Redman, worked up comedy act w. Wilbur Kirk. In Sept. 1944 was member of Tiny Grimes rec. group that incl. Ch. Parker (latter's first combo session). Later worked w. Trummy Young, Art Hodes, Buddy Tate, Josh White, own trio; joined Dud Bascomb, '48. Teamed w. bassist-pianist Doles Dickens 1952-7; then spent 11 years w. Juanita Smith in duo act for hotels, lounges. In '68 started gp. w. vocalist-wife Edye Byrde, who pl. cocktail drums; they have worked various restaurants and hotels in NY and NJ. LP: reissue, Charlie Parker (Arista).

BYARD, JOHN A. (JAKI),* *piano, composer, educator*; also *saxophones, trumpet, bass, trombone, guitar, drums*; b. Worcester, Mass., 6/15/22. Played w. Maynard Ferguson in early '60s, then moved to NYC and joined Charles Mingus. Toured Europe w. him, '68, '70. Played and rec. w. Rahsaan Roland Kirk but most of his NYC apps. have been as a solo pianist at Top of the Gate, late '60s; and in a duo setting during a long run of Sundays at Bradley's, '74-5. In '74-5 he was guest cond. of Sinclair Acey's Music Complex in a Sunday series at the Five Spot. Byard has also pl. in Australia; Japan, '71; Japan; China, '72.

From '69 teaching comp. & arr., piano at New England Conservatory; from '71 at SE Mass. U.; Elmo Lewis Sch. of Fine Arts, Boston; from '75 Julius Hartt Sch. of Mus., Hartford, Conn. Also taught at City Coll., CUNY during early '70s. From '71 he has also conducted seminars at many institutions such as Bismarck JC in No. Dakota; U. of Pitts.; Smithsonian Inst.; Howard U.; and the Hotchkiss School.

A versatile performer who is at home in every style from ragtime to freedom, and a strong communicator of emotion with more than a modicum of wit. Won DB Critics' Poll, TDWR, '66, '71.

Fest: Molde '67; San Sebastian; Barcelona '75: all w. C. Terry; NO '69; Colo. JP '71; Toulon '74; Nice '75. Comp: *Falling Rains of Life; Cat's Cradle Conference Rag; Hazy Eve; The Hollis Stomp; Seasons; New Orleans Strut; Top of the Gate Rag; Spanish Tinge; Sp. Tinge #2; Sp. Tinge #3; To Bob Vatel of Paris; Tribute to Jimmy Slide; Aluminum Baby.*

LPs: *There'll Be Some Changes Made* (Muse); *Duet* w. E. Hines (MPS); *Sunshine of My Soul; Solo Piano; Freedom; On the Spot; Jaki Byard With Strings; The Jaki Byard Experience* (Prest.); also in France on Futura; Japan on JVC; w. Al Cohn-Zoot Sims, *Body and Soul*; w. Phil Woods, *Musique Du Bois* (Muse); w. RR Kirk (Atl.); w. Mingus (Prest., Fant.); Bobby Jones (Cobble.).

BYAS, CARLOS WESLEY (DON),* *tenor saxophone*; b. Muskogee, Okla., 10/21/12. Prominent in the U.S. w. C. Basie, later w. small groups on 52nd St., Byas settled in Europe after touring there w. Don Redman's band in '46. He lived in France, then in Holland. Returning to the U.S. in June '70, he app. at NJF. In early '71 he toured Japan w. A. Blakey, then returned to Holland. Byas died of lung cancer in Amsterdam, 8/24/72.

One of the last of the great ballad-oriented tenor saxophonists in the Hawkins tradition, Byas also was among the first of his generation to ally himself with the bebop movement in jazz, pl. w. Gillespie in '44 at the Onyx Club, NYC.

TV: *Just Jazz*, PBS, '71. Comp: *Orgasm.*

LPs: *In Paris* (Pres.); *Anthropology* (Black Lion); *Le Grand* (MJR); *Free & Easy* (Savoy); *Midnight at Mintons* (Onyx); *Don Byas* (GNP); *Don Byas Meets Ben Webster* (Pres.); *April In Paris* (Battle).

BYERS, WILLIAM MITCHELL (BILLY),* *composer, trombone*; b. Los Angeles, Cal., 5/1/27. After working extensively w. Q. Jones in the late '50s and early '60s, Byers moved to S. Cal. and was active principally as an arranger for films, TV, records and night club acts, for Jones (until '70), C. Basie, F. Sinatra (with whom he toured Japan and Europe as a sideman in '74), D. Ellington, H. Edison, T. Dorsey band (directed by M. McEachern), Sammy Davis, B. Eckstine, Peggy Lee and numerous pop artists. With Marvin Hamlisch he did orchestration for movies *The Sting* and *The Way We Were*. TV: wrote occasional episodes for *Streets of San Francisco, Barnaby Jones* etc. Served as judge at college lab band contests. Wrote music for film *Hauser's Memory*; also originals for *Basie Land* and arrangements for *More Hits of the 50s and 60s*, both for Basie.

LPs: *Impressions of Duke Ellington* (Merc.); *More Hits of the 50s and 60s; Basie Land* (Verve).

BYRD, CHARLES L. (CHARLIE),* *guitar, composer*; b. Suffolk, Va., 9/16/25. The sensitive, versatile artist continued to present programs with a mix of jazz, Latin American and classical music. He appeared several times at the NJF-NY in the '70s and also toured Australia. Commenting on Byrd's album with Aldemaro Romero, Barry Ulanov remarked that his playing on *Romance* "evokes two Segovias, the Renaissance Spanish city and the great classical guitarist."

LPs: *Top Hat; Byrd By the Sea; Crystal Silence; Tambu* w. C. Tjader (Fant.); *Stroke of Genius; Onda Nueva* w. A. Romero; *For All We Know; Delicately; Let Go; Let It Be; More Brazilian; Sketches of Brazil*; three tracks in *The Guitar Album*, rec. live at Town Hall Aug. '71 (Col.); reissue, *Latin Byrd* (Mile.).

BYRD, DONALD,* *trumpet, fluegelhorn, educator, composer*; b. Detroit, Mich., 12/9/32. Established himself in NYC w. Art Blakey, Max Roach, etc.; then led own gps. in '60s while furthering his post-graduate studies and becoming active as an educator. Received Masters in Music Education from Manhattan School of Music. In '71 received Ph.D. in college teaching and administration from Columbia U. Sch. of Education. Concerned with the history and culture of Afro-American music, he is one of the leading ethnomusicologists. He was the Chairman of the Black Music Dept. at Howard U., Wash., D.C. when in '73 he recorded an album originally designed for the late Lee Morgan. Issued under the title *Black Byrd* on Byrd's long time affiliate Blue Note, it became the biggest selling album in the company's 35 year history and put Byrd full into the pop-soul market. His subsequent albums were in the same direction, using currently fashionable rhythms and electronic effects. Some of his Howard students became his sidemen (see Kevin Toney; Joe Hall) and he also produced an LP of them as a group, the Black Byrds (in which he does not play) for Fantasy. Whether he was playing in a club or a college concert, Byrd lectured at various campuses on education, black music, and law as it pertains to music and musicians. (By '75 he had completed two yrs. of Law school.) These lectures were usually combined with a music workshop.

Some musicians and critics accused Byrd of selling out in his new approach and offered that as a college professor he should have been influencing his students to pursue a less "commercialized" route but he said at the time: "One of the things I'm trying to do is to get people involved, and to dramatize through any means possible the plight of black musicians in *academia.* You would think in this day and age that would have changed with respect to black music, that it would have achieved some degree of acceptance in the university, but the truth is, until we get an integrated view of things with respect to black music, nothing is going to happen."

Although he left Howard, in late '75 he was again teaching, this time at No. Carolina Central Coll. Comp: *I Love the Girl; Estavanico; Essence; The Dude.*

LPs: *Places and Spaces; Stepping Into Tomorrow; Street Lady; Black Byrd; Ethiopian Knights; Fancy Free; Slow Drag; Blackjack* (BN).

BYRNE, WILLIAM E. JR. (BILL), *saxophones*; also *clarinet, flute*; b. Stamford, Conn., 4/26/42. Educ: Oakland H.S., '55-9; SF State Coll. '60-5; BA degree in mus. (clarinet major), '65. Started pl. professionally around Oakland-SF area until he joined the Army in '66, where he served in NORAD commanders. On his discharge, worked briefly w. Harry James in U.S. and Europe. Since late '70 has been freelancing in LA TV and rec. studios. Often member of the orchs. of B. Berry, L. Bellson, T. Gibbs, N. Hefti. Infl: Ch. Parker. Fests: Belvedere JF, Canada, w. Bellson and Supersax; Concord, w. Berry, '74; Concord Pavillion w. C. Mangione orch., '75.

LPs: *Louie Rides Again*, w. Bellson (Pablo); *Chase The Clouds Away*, w. Mangione (A & M); w. Berry (Beez).

CABLES, GEORGE ANDREW, *piano, keyboards, composer*; b. Brooklyn, N.Y., 11/14/44. Stud. High Sch. of Perf. Arts 1958-62; Mannes College '63-5. Worked with Art Blakey, Max Roach; joined Sonny Rollins, '69; Joe Henderson, '69-71; Freddie Hubbard, '71- . Has also written for choirs, East Harlem Protestant Parish.

Comps: *Think On Me*, which he rec. w. Woody Shaw in *Blackstone Legacy* (also rec. by Woody Herman); *Ebony Moonbeams; Lost Dreams; Camel Rise*, rec. w. Hubbard; also rec. by B. Hutcherson; *Love Song*, rec. by Hutcherson.

Infl: Wynton Kelly, Miles Davis, Coltrane, Buddy Montgomery, H. Hancock as pianists and composers; McCoy Tyner. Festivals: Newport, Monterey, many foreign concert and fest. apps.

LPs: Rec. in Japan as leader, comp. & arr. (Myuh). As sideman, w. Hubbard, *Polar AC; Keep Your Soul Together* (CTI); *High Energy; Liquid Love* (Col.); w. Woody Shaw, *Blackstone Legacy* (Contemp.); w. Henderson *Black is the Color; In Pursuit of Blackness; If You're Not Part of the Solution* (Mile.); w. Blakey, *Child's Dance* (Prest.); w. Joe Chambers, *The Almoravid* (Muse).

CACERES, ERNEST (ERNIE),* *clarinet, baritone sax*; b. Rockport, Tex., 11/22/11. Played w. J. Teagarden; G. Miller; B. Goodman; W. Herman; and B. Hackett. After working w. B. Butterfield in Va., '62, settled in San Antonio, app. occasionally w. Jim Cullum's Happy Jazz Band. Pl. at Dick Gibson's Colorado JP in Aspen, Vail in '60s. Died in San Antonio, 1/10/71. LP: *Ernie and Emilio Caceres* (Audiophile).

CAIN, JACQUELINE RUTH (JACKIE),* *singer*; b. Milwaukee, Wisc., 5/22/28. Sang on TV commercials, many of which were produced and written by her husband Roy Kral (q.v.) and also appeared with him in their group, Jackie & Roy, on TV, in nightclubs and at festivals. Among the latter apps. were Munich, Toulon, Loosdrecht '71; CTI Summer Jazz at Hollywood Bowl '71, MJF '73, NJF-NY '74, Reno JF '75. Other concerts at Town Hall '71, '73, Carnegie Hall '72. App. at Ronnie Scott's in London early '75. LPs: *Changes; Lovesick* (Verve); *Grass* (Capitol); *Time and Love; A Wilder Alias* (CTI).

CALDWELL, ALBERT (HAPPY),* *tenor sax*; also *clarinet, flute*; b. Chicago, Ill., 7/25/03. Although his regular non-music job is with City College of the City Univ. of

N.Y., he cont. to gig as a member of the New Amsterdam Mus. Assoc., N.Y.'s oldest black mus. org., and for many Masonic Lodges, Eastern Star chapters, of one of which he is a past master. Honored by the Overseas Jazz Club at jazz concert in which he app. w. own group, Feb. '75. Visited Sweden and Copenhagen Youth Center, Denmark, '75, for playing and participation in seminars. Active in Senior Citizens entertainment program. Preparing book on chords.

LP: w. Clyde Bernhardt, *More Blues and Jazz from Harlem* (Saydisc).

CALIMAN, HADLEY, *tenor saxophone*; also *flute, bass clarinet, soprano sax*; b. Idabel, Okla., 1/12/32. Stud. at high school, also three years of theory at Pomona State Coll, S.F. Conservatory. Insp. by L. Young, D. Gordon, J. Coltrane and Joe Henderson, Caliman was heard with bands and combos in the LA area in the '60s and mainly in SF in the '70s. In addition to leading his own group, he was heard with B. Bryant, Gerald Wilson, M. Santamaria, D. Ellis, Willie Bobo, Big Black, Luis Gasca, Eddie Henderson, Jon Hendricks. Concord and Berkeley Jazz Fests.

Although Caliman won a DB poll in the TDWR category some years ago, he has not yet achieved the acclaim he deserves as a soloist who combines mainstream characteristics with the infl. of J. Coltrane.

LPs: *Hadley Caliman; Iapetus* (Mainstream); *Live and Swinging* and others w. Wilson (Wor. Pac.); others w. H. Hawes, Patrice Rushen, Azar Lawrence, F. Purim (Fant.); *Hollywood Blues*, w. Johnny Almond (Deram-London).

CALLENDER, GEORGE (RED),* *tuba, bass*; b. Richmond, Va., 3/6/18. Though employed regularly as TV staff musician, and later as a freelance in TV and rec. studios, Callender continued his jazz activities from time to time. In '73 he became part owner, along with B. Collette, Grover Mitchell, Al Aarons, Al Viola and L. Vinnegar of Legend Record Co. Feat. on *Hawaii Five-O*, w. Nancy Wilson, '69; was member of Carol Burnett show orch. through '69; Flip Wilson show, '70-4, incl. bit apps. on camera; Sammy Davis show, '74. Pl. bass and tuba at Dick Gibson's jazz party, '74, '75. His hit song, *Primrose Lane*, was used as a theme on the Henry Fonda show, *Smith Family*. Other songs incl. *Pastel*, rec. by E. Garner, I. Jacquet; 12 orig. tunes on own album *Swinging Suite*, reissued in '75.

LPs: *Basin-Street Brass; Callender Speaks Low and Swinging; Now and Then* w. Collette (Legend); earlier albums, many deleted, incl. *Big Fat Brass* w. Billy May (Cap.); *The Lowest* (MGM-Metro); tuba on Ray Charles LPs (ABC).

CAMPISE, ANTHONY S. (TONY), *flute, alto, tenor sax*; also all *reeds, flutes* and *oboe*; b. Houston, Tex., 1/22/43. Stud. alto sax, clarinet w. Hal Tennyson, '56-62; improvisation w. Jerry Coker in Houston and Cal., '61-3; flute w. Byron Hester betw. '63-71; oboe w. Barbara Hester, '67-9; also improvisation briefly w. L. Konitz. Attended music schools at Sam Houston U., U. of Houston, Houston Baptist Coll. and Monterey Peninsula Coll. Pl. in Houston w. Don Cannon, '62-5; Paul Schmitt, '67-71; Young Audience Jazz Ensemble, '69-75; Gulf Coast Giants of Jazz, '70-3. Three seasons of musicals at Houston Music Theatre, '72-4. Lead alto and flute w. Stan Kenton from '74.

Infls: Ch. Parker, J. Coltrane, Konitz, L. Tristano, E. Dolphy. Fests: Corpus Christi; Longhorn '73; NJF-NY w. Kenton, '74. LPs: w. Kenton, *Kenton Plays Chicago; Fire, Fury and Fun* (Creative World).

CANDIDO (Candido Camero),* *bongo, conga drums*; b. Regal, Havana, Cuba, 4/22/21. Well known from the '50s when he came to US and began playing w. Dizzy Gillespie; Stan Kenton; and Billy Taylor. Continued as an extremely active freelance in both jazz and Latin music working w. his own gps. and w. such personalities as Sonny Rollins; Elvin Jones; and Tony Bennett on a world wide basis. TV: w. Bennett; Lionel Hampton; Charo on Mike Douglas Show. Fest: NJF-NY w. S. Kenton '75. LPs: *Drum Fever* (Poly.); *The Thousand Finger Man* (SS); *Beautiful* (UA); w. Randy Weston, *Tanjah* (Poly.); David Amram, *No More Walls* (RCA).

CANDOLI, SECONDO (CONTE),* *trumpet*; b. Mishawaka, Ind., 7/12/27. Remained w. Shelly Manne gp. from '66-72; also active in Hollywood studios. App. once a month w. Kenton Neophonic Orch. at LA Music Center, '67-9. From '70-4 member of staff orch. on Flip Wilson TV show; also app. w. own gp. or others at local clubs. In '72 joined Supersax, and in that year visited England with gp., but working mostly local jobs. Since '68 has been with NBC-TV *Tonight* show band, making several LPs with Doc Severinsen. Candoli has also busied himself with coll. clinics at Indiana U., Purdue, Notre Dame, Chicago State. In '75 to Holland, Germany, Italy for club, radio, TV apps. and occasional concerts. Fests: Monterey '73 w. Candoli Brothers; Concord, '74 w. Bill Berry band.

LPs: *Monk's Blues*, w. T. Monk (Col.); *Supersax Plays Bird; Salt Peanuts* w. Supersax; *Supersax Plays Bird With Strings* (Cap.); w. F. Strazzeri, *View From Within* (Creative World); w. T. Edwards, *Feelin's* (Muse); w. Bill Berry (Beez).

CANDOLI, WALTER JOSEPH (PETE),* *trumpet*; b. Mishawaka, Ind., 6/28/23. The former big band musician (Herman, Kenton, Basie, Barnet) devoted most of his time in later years to studio work in Hollywood, rec. w. M. Legrand, Q. Jones, H. Mancini, Peggy Lee, I. Stravinsky. Regular member of band on Merv Griffin and *Tonight* shows. From '72, teamed with wife Edie Adams in night club act, also in several theatrical musicals. Films: pl. trumpet solos for scores of *Save The Tiger* and *Prisoner of Second Ave.* Candoli also conducts coll. music seminars. Fests: Monterey, '73 w. Candoli Bros.

CAPP, FRANK,* *drums*; b. Worcester, Mass., 8/20/31. Former name band drummer (Kenton, Hefti, Billy May);

a prominent studio musician in LA for more than 20 years. TV with Merv Griffin, Steve Allen, etc.; movies w. A. Previn, P. Rugolo, H. Mancini; records w. Ben Webster, Terry Gibbs, Bud Shank, B. Kessel, and about 20 albums w. Previn. Fests: Monterey; Concord. LPs: *Percussion Tribute to the Big Bands* (ten-album series: Kimberley); w. Bob Florence, *Here & Now* (Liberty).

CARDOSO, RUI, *alto sax, flute, composer*; b. Portugal, Jan. 1939. Played w. jazz and jazz-rock gps. related, for the most part, to Lisbon's Hot Club of Portugal. Turned professional in '71, working in clubs and as film composer; pop arranger. In '75 he joined forces with Araripa (Emilio Robalo, piano; Jose Eduardo, bass; Joao Heitor, drums), app. at the Cascais Fest. in November.

CARISI, JOHN E. (JOHNNY),* *composer, trumpet, fluegelhorn*; b. Hasbrouck Heights, N.J., 2/23/22. A member of the ensemble faculty, Manhattan School of Music from 1969; adjunct lecturer at Queens Coll. 1971-73. Orchestrated Anita Loos-Ralph Blane musical, *Something About Anne*, choreographed by his wife, dancer Gemze de Lappe; piece commissioned by Gerry Mulligan for baritone saxophone and woodwind ensemble performed by Wilder Winds at Town Hall and Kennedy Arts Center; comps. for National Jazz Ensemble concerts at Wolf Trap Farm and Alice Tully Hall in '70s; arrs. for Ten Wheel Drive; works for tuba virtuoso Harvey Phillips, professor of music at the Univ. of Indiana, '75. As trumpeter pl. w. Brew Moore at Joey Archer's Sports Corner and the Limelight in NYC, '69-70. LPs: arrs. for *Urbie Green's Big Beautiful Band* (Project 3); six comps., nine arrs. for Marvin Stamm *Machinations* (Verve).

CARLTON, LARRY EUGENE, *guitar*; also *fender bass, arranger*; b. Torrance, Cal., 3/2/48. Stud. w. Slim Edwards from age 6 to 14; music major, LA Harbor Coll., '66-68; music major Cal-State U., Long Beach, '68-70. In '68 pl. at Disneyland w. Bill Elliott, toured w. 5th Dimension, rec. first solo album for Uni. In Dec. '69 became musical director of NBC children's show. Perf. on camera as co-star, Larry Guitar, as well as writing much of music used on show. From '70 Carlton played on literally thousands of rec. sessions, TV shows, movies, commercial jingles. Along with this work, he became a member of the Crusaders, '73. Won NARAS award as Most Valuable Guitar Player, '73, '74.

Comps: *The Well's Gone Dry*, rec. by Crusaders; *Free Way*, rec. by Carlton. Favorites: J. Pass, B.B. King, B. Kessel, Louie Shelton. Own LPs: on ABC-Blue Thumb; w. Crusaders: *Crusaders I; 2nd Crusade; Unsung Heroes; Scratch; Southern Comfort* (ABC-Blue Thumb); w. Tom Scott and L.A. Express (Ode).

CARN, DOUG (aka ABDUL RAHIM IBRAHIM), *organ, keyboards, oboe, saxophone, synthesizer, singer, composer*; b. New York City, 7/14/48. Piano lessons at 5 with mother; alto sax at 9, organ at 13. Oboe and composition, Jacksonville U., '65-7; completed studies at Georgia State Coll., '67-9.

Carn has led his own group almost continuously since the age of 13; however, he has worked briefly w. Lou Donaldson, S. Turrentine, Irene Reid. He first achieved widespread acceptance in jazz circles with his albums for the Black Jazz label. In '75 he worked with the Philadelphia Community Coll. choir, expanding vocal writing techniques.

Carn says: "I am a devout, orthodox Muslim by faith. I strive to express the Islamic Ideal of Oneness of God (Allah) as manifested through creation—music being only one aspect of that creation."

Comps: Carn wrote lyrics, music and/or arrs. for many of the works on his Black Jazz albums, among them *Moonchild; Infant Eyes; Arise and Shine; Blue In Greene; Revelation; Time Is Running Out; Jihad; Adam's Apple; Higher Ground; Western Sunrise*; and J. Coltrane's *Naima*. LPs: *The Doug Carn Trio* (Savoy); *Infant Eyes; Spirit of the New Land; Revelation; Adam's Apple* (Black Jazz); two w. Earth, Wind & Fire (WB).

CARNEY, HARRY HOWELL,* *baritone sax, bass clarinet, clarinet*; b. Boston, Mass., 4/1/10. Joined Duke Ellington Orch. at the age of 16 and was established during the early '30s as the first outstanding jazz soloist on baritone sax, a distinctive anchor man of the Ellington reed section. Carney was still a member of the Ellington orch. at the time of the leader's death, despite illness. He played with the band under the direction of Mercer Ellington during the next few months, but was intermittently absent, suffering from phlebitis. He died in New York, 10/8/74.

The sound of Harry Carney was one of the most vital and irreplaceable in the Ellington orchestral structure. He was to the baritone sax what Coleman Hawkins had been to the tenor; a virtual inventor of the instrument in terms of its jazz use. With the deep, full sonority that was the essence of his sound, he made the band instantly recognizable, perhaps more than any other individual.

LPs: see Ellington and J. Hodges.

CARR, IAN,* *trumpet, fluegelhorn, composer*; b. Dumfries, Scotland, 4/21/33. Continued w. Rendell-Carr quintet until Oct. '69 when he formed Nucleus. This group won first prize Montreux JF, '70; also pl. at NJF in same year. Nucleus has app. at all major Euro. JF, as well as countless TV apps. In '71 gave 16 min. perf. w. visuals of an extended work, *Solar Plexus*, presented on BBC2 TV. Won first place in sm. gp. category, '71-2 in MM polls.

Carr, a prolific composer, wrote *Will's Birthday Suite*, dedicated to William Shakespeare; organized and comp. mus. for Sam Wanamaker's Annual Concert in honor of Shakespeare's birthday. Publs: *Music Outside* (Latimer New Dimensions); in '75 Carr was researching biog. of Miles Davis for same publisher.

Many listeners and critics have agreed that Nucleus has been a seminal influence on jazz-rock groups in Europe and elsewhere.

LPs: *Elastic Rock; We'll Talk About It Later; Solar Plexus; Belladonna; Labyrinth; Roots; Under The Sun; Snakehips Etcetera; Alleycat* (Vertigo).

CARRY, GEORGE DORMAN (SCOOPS),* *alto saxophone, clarinet*; b. Little Rock, Ark., 1/23/15. Best known for his work in the Earl Hines orch. in the '30s and '40s, Carry in '43 became a lawyer. He died 8/4/70 in Chicago after a long illness. His most famous rec. solo is *Jelly Jelly* w. Hines (RCA-Bluebird).

CARTER, BENNETT LESTER (BENNY),* *composer, alto saxophone*; also *trumpet*; b. New York City, 8/8/07. Led own bands in U.S. and Europe during '30s; gave up traveling in mid-40s to settle in Cal., where he was actively involved in writing for motion pictures and later for television. During '60s appeared occasionally in public, touring in Europe, Australia and Japan.

TV assignments incl. *Bob Hope Presents*, '65-8; segs. for *Ironside, Name of the Game, Banyon, Sarah Vaughan Special*. Film scores: *A Man Called Adam*, '66; *Buck and the Preacher*, '72. Many arrs. for Pearl Bailey during '60s and '70s; others for Rod McKuen, Debbie Reynolds and Ray Charles. A record of *Busted*, by Charles, arr. by Carter, won a Grammy award in '63.

During the '70s Carter aligned himself with the world of jazz education. He was an artist-in-residence at Baldwin-Wallace Coll. in '70. In '72 he gave seminars at two Univs. in Colorado, and Eisenhower Coll. in Seneca Falls, N.Y. In '73 he was visiting lecturer at Princeton, where he also perf. in concerts; the following year he received an Honorary Doctorate of Humanities from Princeton. That same year he gave a seminar and app. in concert at Cornell.

Also during '74 Carter became associated with Maria Muldaur, assembling an all star jazz orch. for some of her records and for several concerts. They appeared together at the NJF, '75. Carter wrote the score for *Louis Armstrong: Chicago Style*, a TV movie in '75.

Along with all these activities Carter continued to play periodically, visiting Europe almost every year, concentrating on the alto saxophone and hardly ever playing trumpet. Despite the infrequency of his playing, he remained possibly the most eloquent and melodically appealing saxophonist in jazz. Among the most famous works in his long career as a composer are *Blues In My Heart; When Lights Are Low; Take My Word; Blue Interlude; Cow Cow Boogie*; also *Kansas City Suite* for Count Basie, and many other instrumental works.

LPs: *Further Definitions; Additions to Further Definitions* (Imp.); *Waitress in A Donut Shop*, w. Muldaur (Repr.); *With Love*, w. Joe Williams (Temponic); *Carmen*, w. C. McRae (Temponic); *Greatest Jazz Concert in the World* (Pablo).

CARTER, BETTY,* *singer*; b. Flint, Mich., 5/16/30. One of the few real jazz singers in terms of improvisation and feeling, she continued to appear in clubs, concerts and college dates backed by her own trio. In '72 she was heard at Antioch Coll.; Goddard Coll.; Rutgers U. Tam Fiofori, reviewing a concert at Judson Hall in NYC, '70, wrote: Betty Carter draws the listeners into her songs, so much that on the one level one is and becomes aware of the triteness of some of the lyrics . . . (plastic-gloss Broadway-Hollywood-type-material). On the other level, the listener also becomes aware of and feels the fresh-airiness of her voice injecting new meaning and life into these songs . . ." LPs: two albums on own label, Bet-Car (Bet-Car Productions, North Plainfield, N.J.).

CARTER, CHARLES JR. (CHUCK), *drums*; b. St. Louis, Mo., 7/12/39. Cousin of Gerald Wilson. Father a drummer. Self-taught. Pl. w. L. Vinnegar, Teddy Edwards, '61-3, Paul Horn quintet and G. Wilson big band, '64-5. Many other associations since then, incl. F. Hubbard, Ray Brown, Milt Jackson. Worked w. Herb Geller in Berlin, '66; Letta Mbulu, '67; Hugh Masekela, '70-1. Traveling w. E. Garner, '74-5. Favs: Max Roach, Elvin Jones, Philly Joe Jones.

LPs: *Portraits; On Stage* w. G. Wilson (Wor. Pac.); *Glass of Water*, w. Vinnegar (Legend); others w. Masekela.

CARTER, JOHN WALLACE, *clarinet, saxophones, flute*; b. Fort Worth, Texas, 9/24/29. B.A. from Lincoln U., Mo., '49; M.Mus. Educ., U. of Colo., and NTSU, '56; Cal. State U., L.A., '61. Insp. by Parker, Young, Coltrane. Played throughout Southwest in late '40s, early '50s with jazz and blues groups. West coast in early '60s, organized quartet w. Bobby Bradford, '65, involved in much lecture-demonstration-concert activity in first part of '70s. Won DB award as most promising combo. Group disbanded '73, when Carter put together his own ensemble. Played in Europe, '73. Teaching: public schools, Ft. Worth and LA; college level, Cal. State, Dominguez Hills. Fests: Pl. w. Ornette Coleman group and conducted fest. orch. in Coleman's music in LA '65.

LPs: *Seeking; Secrets* (Revelation); *Flight for Four; Self Determination Music* (Flying Dutchman).

CARTER, RONALD LEVIN (RON),* *bass, cello, composer*; also *violin; clarinet, trombone, tuba*; b. Ferndale, Mich., 5/4/37. Worked w. C. Hamilton, C. Adderley, E. Dolphy, J. Byard, etc. in early '60s. Joined Miles Davis '63 and pl. w. him to '68. With NY Bass Choir from '69; Lena Horne's NYC apps., '70-4; Michel Legrand from '71; NY Jazz Quartet from '72; own quartet from '75. Free-lance work w. S. Turrentine; H. Laws; L. Hampton; J. Henderson. Carter also pl. as soloist, and accompanist for Laws, G. Benson et al, on CTI concert tour packages from '70. With CTI to Europe, '72; Japan, '71, '72, '73. Europe w. F. Gulda, '69, '70; Japan w. NYJQ, '74. Won DB Readers' Poll, '73-5.

In Carter's new quartet he also plays piccolo bass ("It's about three-quarters the size of a three-quarter bass . . . tuned like a cello upside-down.) backed by bassist Buster Williams. "My objective," he says, "is to re-investigate acoustic sounds and to give the public a viable listening option not at their command recently."

TV: Leon Bibb, NBC, '70-3; *Positively Black*; Howard Cosell show, '75. Fest: Mont. JF w. M. Davis, '67; house bassist, '73; NJF-NY, Concord w. NYJQ, '74. Publ: *Building a Jazz Bass Line, Vols. 1&2* (Charles Hansen, 1860 Broadway, N.Y., N.Y. 10023). Comp: *De Samba; Little Waltz; Arkansas; El Noche Sol; Sabado Sombre-*

ro. LPs: *Anything Goes* (Kudu); *Blues Farm; All Blues; Spanish Blue* (CTI); *Uptown Conversation* (Embryo); *NY Jazz Quartet, Live in Japan* (Salvation); *Magic*, reissue of earlier material w. Dolphy (Prest.); w. Davis, *Sorcerer; Nefertiti; Miles in the Sky* (Col.); w. M. Tyner, *Trident; Alone Together* (Mile.); w. Legrand, *Live at Jimmy's* (RCA); w. H. Silver, *Silver 'n Brass* (BN); w. F. Gulda, *Euro-Jazz Orch., 1970* (MPS); w. Laws; F. Hubbard; M. Jackson; Don Sebesky; Grover Washington (CTI); Roberta Flack; Aretha Franklin (Atl.); *Jaki Byard With Strings* (Prest.).

CARVER, WAYMAN,* *saxophones, flute*; b. Portsmouth, Va., 12/25/05. The noted music educator died in Atlanta, Ga., 5/6/67. He was the first artist ever to record jazz solos on flute, originally with Spike Hughes' orchestra in 1933 (London Records LL 1387) and later as a member of Chick Webb's orchestra.

CARVIN, MICHAEL, *drums*; b. Houston, Tex., 12/12/44. Father, Henry Carvin, one of Houston's top drummers, began teaching him at early age. After high school moved to LA and att. LACC. Joined Earl Grant's big band '65 and traveled for two yrs. in U.S., Europe & Japan before becoming a member of the 266th Div. Army Band for a two-yr. Vietnam tour of duty. Ret. to LA in '68. House drummer for Motown, '68-9. Worked w. The Four Tops; Martha and the Vandellas, '68; Eddie Khan, '68-70; B.B. King, '68-9; Monk Montgomery, '69; Abbey Lincoln; George Duke; Woody Shaw; Henry Franklin, '70; Walter Bishop; Hugh Masekela, '70-1; Jimmy Smith; Gerry Mulligan; Thelma Houston; Doug Carn; Hampton Hawes; Dexter Gordon in Copenhagen, '71; Bobby Hutcherson, '71-2; Lonnie Liston Smith; Bayete, '72; Freddie Hubbard; Pharoah Sanders; Larry Young, '73; McCoy Tyner; Atmosphere, '74; Jackie McLean, '72-5. Founder and instructor, Creative Artists Development Center, NYC. Also taught at Artists Collective, Hartford, Conn., under McLean; Grant Music Center, LA, under Henry Grant; Community Learning Center, Oakland, under Charles Moffett; as artist-in-residence for elementary schools in Hartford; Vallekilde Music Clinics, Denmark, summer '74. Infl: Henry Carvin, Art Blakey, Max Roach, B. Hutcherson, J. McLean, Jo Jones, Elvin Jones, Coltrane. Comp: *Comahlee Ah; Hump; Voodoo Woman; Osun, The Camel.* TV: *Barbara McNair Show*, '69-70. Publ: *Something For All Drummers* (Arual Publ. Co., 507 5th Ave., New York, N.Y. 10017). LPs: *The Camel; Antiquity*, duo w. McLean; w. McLean, *New York Calling*; w. Billy Gault, *When Destiny Calls* (Steeple.); w. P. Sanders, *Elevation* (Imp.); w. L.L. Smith, *Expansions* (Fly. Dutch.); w. Atmospheres, *Voyage to Uranus* (Cap.); w. Jimmy Smith (MGM); w. Doug Carn; Henry Franklin (Black Jazz); w. M. Montgomery (Chisa); w. Bayete (Prest.); w. C. McBee (Strata-East).

CARY, RICHARD DURANT (DICK),* *trumpet, composer, piano, mellophone* etc.; b. Hartford, Conn., 7/10/16. First prominent as trad. pianist w. Armstrong, Condon et al, he moved to Cal. and during '60s became very active as composer/arranger and pl. trumpet, alto horn. Working with rehearsal gps., built library of close to 1000 arrs. Dance band and concert dates feat. Abe Most in swing era recreations. Wrote for and rehearsed a brass quintet, for which a suite he wrote was pl. at an LA museum concert. Also working w. gp. feat. eight reeds and rhythm, and pl. horn in a woodwind quintet. From 1970, led nine piece band for jazz concerts in LA parks and schools.

Publ: *Brass Quintets* (Maggio Music, 12044 Vanowen, No. Hollywood, Ca.). Stage band originals for Don Rader catalogue. Films: *Great Gatsby* sound track. TV: *The Jazz Show*, KNBC; various jingles; Dick Van Dyke Special.

LPs: piano w. Condon on *Midnight in Moscow* (Epic); w. Barney Bigard for European RCA.

CASTLEMAN, JEFFRY ALAN, *bass*; b. Los Angeles, 1/27/46. Stud. at U. of Cal. Riverside, pvt. teachers incl. Ralph Pena. Prof. debut at 18 w. Si Zentner in LV. Worked off and on w. L. Bellson for two years, also a year w. Joe Castro Trio. Joined Duke Ellington, late 1967, and remained with the band until mid-'69, when he married Trish Turner, Ellington's vocalist; both he and Ms. Turner then settled in LA. Castleman went on the road for a few months w. Sarah Vaughan, also w. Tony Bennett. Gigs w. Shelly Manne, 1971-3; since then, mostly commercial work in LA on fender bass. He played the latter occasionally with Ellington, the first bassist ever to do so. On upright bass he was praised by Duke as "the greatest bassist since Jimmy Blanton."

LPs w. Ellington-F. Sinatra (Reprise); w. Ellington, *Yale Concert* (Fantasy); *Second Sacred Concert* (Prestige); w. Earl Hines, J. Hodges, *Swing's Our Thing* (Verve). Five trio numbers written and recorded by Ellington w. Castleman and drummer Sam Woodyard had still not been released in 1975.

CASTRO, JOSEPH (JOE),* *piano, composer*; b. Miami, Ariz., 8/15/27. For many years has devoted his time between commercial work, accompanying singers on tour or in Las Vegas, and jazz activities. In latter capacity, his jazz trio was feat. with Honolulu Symph., '66; he played at Beverly Hills Hotel, '67-8; trio around LA, '69. From '70, arr. and cond. for commercial artists in LV, but arr. for Joe Williams, Count Basie and Al Hibbler, '73. From '70-4 wrote and cond. film projects for Sutherland Educational Associates, using Buddy Collette, Jack Sheldon, Frank Rosolino et al.

Own big band LP with all star LA personnel (Clover); quartet w. Teddy Edwards (Contemporary).

CASTRO NEVES, OSCAR (Carlos Oscar de Castro Neves), *guitar, keyboards, composer*; b. Rio de Janeiro, Brazil, 5/15/40. A triplet, born into a family of amateur musicians, he was self-taught until, in LA, he stud. composing w. Albert Harris and Paul Glass. Began pl. cavaquinho (Brazilian ukulele) at age five. Considered to be one of the group of musicians and composers who, w. A.C. Jobim et al, originated the bossa nova movement in the late '50s. To NYC for first Carnegie Hall bossa nova concert, Nov. '62, after which he worked in LA w. L.

Schifrin, D. Gillespie, L. Almeida/B. Shank. Returned to Brazil, organized classical concert series. Back to U.S., '67, directing vocal quartet, The Girls from Bahia, for records and TV. After a third visit to U.S. with this group, he settled in LA in '68. Worked w. Paul Winter Consort, '69-70, arranging and touring. Lead and rhythm guitar player, also arr. w. S. Mendes group, '71- . Has also pl. in U.S. w. Q. Jones, John Mandel, John Pisano, Almeida, L. Ritenour, D. Grusin.

LPs: w. J. Gilberto (Orpheon); Flora Purim (Fant.); Girls from Bahia (WB); Almeida (Daybreak); Getz/Gilberto (Col.).

CATHERINE, PHILIP, *guitar*; b. London, England, 10/27/42. English mother, Belgian father. Insp. by D. Reinhardt, Rene Thomas. Pl. w. Lou Bennett, '59. During '60s, w. Jack Sels, Fats Sadi, and on Belgian radio. In '70s turned to rock-jazz; worked w. J.L. Ponty, Dec. '70-June '72, then stud. for a year at Berklee in Boston. At end of '73 he started a group called Pork Pie w. Ch. Mariano. Recent infls. are J. McLaughlin, L. Coryell. LPs on Warner Bros., Atl.; also w. L. Bennett (RCA); w. Sels, *Relax* (Vogel); *Placebo* (EMI); T. Thielemans; Mariano (Keytone); Pork Pic (MPS); Chris Hinze (CBS); H. Geller (Atl.).

CEROLI, NICK,* *drums*; b. Warren, Ohio, 12/22/39. In late '50s, early '60s worked in Chicago, Las Vegas and LA w. Lionel Hampton, Gerald Wilson, Terry Gibbs, S. Kenton. W. Tijuana Brass from '65 to '69; then w. Steve Lawrence-Eydie Gorme, '71; Vikki Carr, '72; subbed on *Tonight* show for year and a half, then regularly on Merv Griffin show. Studio work in LA, also pl. w. Zoot Sims, Clark Terry locally, as well as other jazz groups. Publ: *Modern Approach To Independence, Vols. I & II* (Try Publ., Hollywood, Ca.). LPs: w. Kenton Neophonic Orch. (Capitol); w. Pete Jolly, *Give A Damn* (A & M).

CHAMBERS, HENDERSON CHARLES,* *trombone*; b. Alexandria, La., 5/1/08. A prominent sideman w. many big bands from the '30s, he worked w. Ray Charles for two yrs. before playing w. C. Basie '64-6. Helped in the organization of a rehearsal band w. Edgar Battle in NYC before he died there of a heart attack, 10/19/67.

CHAMBERS, JOSEPH ARTHUR (JOE),* *drums, composer*; also *piano*; b. Stoneacre, Va., 6/25/42. Brother Steve is classical comp. Studied at Phila. Conserv. and American U., Wash., D.C. Pl. w. JFK Quintet in Wash., '60-3; then in NYC w. E. Dolphy; F. Hubbard; L. Donaldson; J. Giuffre; A. Hill. Associated w. Bobby Hutcherson from '65, he played w. him, '67-70. In the '70s he worked w. Donald Byrd; Jeremy Steig but has concentrated on writing. His suite, *The Almoravid*, including the title piece; *Gazelle Suite; Medina*; and *Jihad* was performed by the NYJRC at Carnegie Hall, '74. Other comp: *Mirrors; Dialog; Idlewild.*

Gary Giddins wrote of his playing: "The enormous potency—bordering on ferocity—combined with complete authority and tonal clarity . . . has made him one of the more distinctive percussion voices in recent years. His is a hard style but not a busy one. Force is touched by simplicity. However complex his rhythms, his playing is sensitive and to the point."

LPs: *The Almoravid* (Muse); w. Hill, *One For One*; w. Hutcherson (BN); w. C. Mingus, *Charles Mingus and Friends* (Col.).

CHAMBERS, PAUL LAURENCE DUNBAR JR.,* *bass*; b. Pittsburgh, Pa., 4/22/35. Played with Miles Davis, '55-60. Then he teamed with two other Davis alumni, Wynton Kelly and Jimmy Cobb to form a trio, which at one time backed W. Montgomery. Chambers later freelanced in NYC w. Tony Scott, Barry Harris and others. Afrer several months' illness, he died in a NYC hospital 1/4/69. One of the greats and a strong influence on his contemporaries.

LPs: *Paul Chambers* (Epitaph); *High Step; Bass on Top; Whims of Chambers* (BN); *East/West Controversy* (Xanadu); *Just Friends* (Trip); w. Davis, *Tallest Trees; Collector's Items; Workin' & Steamin'* (Pres.); *Kind of Blue; Round About Midnight; Someday My Prince Will Come; Porgy & Bess* (Col.); w. Coltrane, *Giant Steps* (Atl.); *Bull's Eye*, w. Barry Harris (Pres.); *Peace Piece and Other Pieces*, w. Bill Evans; *Keep It Movin'*, w. W. Kelly (Milest.).

CHARLES, RAY (Ray Charles Robinson),* *singer, piano, composer, organ, alto saxophone*; b. Albany, Ga., 9/23/32. Established via records as r & b, blues and gospel/jazz star from 1954. Broadened his audience in 1960s through use of pop and country-western songs, large orchestral backgrounds with strings etc.

Using a theatrical presentation involving his female vocal group, the Raeletts, and other acts, Charles covered a wide range of styles, including jazz, and using a big band that generally included a number of outstanding sidemen, with baritone saxophonist Leroy Cooper as music director in recent years.

The Charles show has spent a substantial proportion of its time overseas. In 1969, for example, there were visits to Mexico and to 22 European cities; in 1970, 27 concerts in Europe, others in four South American countries, Mexico, the Bahamas, Canada and Japan. The European tours have continued annually, as well as return trips to Japan almost every year. During 1975 Charles was seen in England, France, Belgium, Germany, Switzerland, Spain, New Zealand, Australia, Indonesia, Singapore, Japan and Canada.

TV: Frequent guest shots on shows starring Glen Campbell, Della Reese, Smothers Brothers, Bill Cosby, Barbra Streisand, Flip Wilson, Dinah Shore et al. Specials: *Switched-on Symphony*, 1970; *NBC Follies*, '73; *Cotton Club '75*, '74.

In 1971 Charles' annual U.S. tour included a visit to Houston for the world premiere of Quincy Jones' *Black Requiem* (see JONES, QUINCY).

LPs: *My Kind of Jazz*, 1970, and *Jazz Number II*, 1973, both featuring the band, were released on Charles' own Tangerine label. Pop and other albums, not basically jazz, incl. *Crying Time*, winner of two Grammy awards for best r & b recording of 1966 (ABC); *Ray's Moods;*

Ray Charles, A Man and His Soul; Ray Charles Invites You To Listen; A Portrait of Ray; I'm All Yours Baby; Doing His Thing; Love Country Style; Volcanic Action of My Soul; A 25th Anniversary in Show Business Salute to Ray Charles; A Message From The People; Through the Eyes of Love (ABC); *Come Live With Me; Renaissance* (Crossover).

CHASE, BILL, *trumpet, composer, leader*; b. Boston, Mass., 1935. Came to prominence as lead trumpeter w. M. Ferguson, S. Kenton, and most notably in early and mid '60s w. W. Herman. Chase attained national stature after organizing a nine piece jazz-rock group, known as Chase, with a distinctive instrumentation comprising four trumpets, organ, rhythm section and vocalist. The band's first LP, released early in '71, enjoyed widespread acceptance and was voted the number one pop album of the year in the DB Readers' poll.

The momentum of this album was not followed up; Bill Chase's suite *Ennea*, on his next album, disappointed the public and the group underwent an extended hiatus. After reorganizing and starting a comeback tour, Chase was killed, along with three members of his band, in a plane crash, outside Jackson, Minn., 8/9/74. LPs: *Pure Music; Ennea* (Epic).

CHEATHAM, ADOLPHUS ANTHONY (DOC),* *trumpet*; b. Nashville, Tenn., 6/13/05. With Cab Calloway; Teddy Wilson, Benny Carter, Teddy Hill, McKinney's Cotton Pickers bands in 30s; Eddie Heywood in '40s; Machito, Wilbur DeParis, in '50s; to Africa w. Herbie Mann, '60. Own band at International, NYC, '60-5. Played w. Benny Goodman; Ricardo Rey, '67; to London w. Top Brass tour, fall '67; Ricardo Rey, '68-70, incl. So. American tour, '68. Worked in show *Two Gentlemen of Verona*, '71; Red Balaban & Cats, '72-4; Countsmen; Sy Oliver, '74. Fest: NJF-NY, dedication of Louis Armstrong Stadium, '73; Cab Calloway, '73; Teddy Wilson, '74. Grande Parade du Jazz, Nice '75. Carnegie Hall concerts w. NYJRC, also Russian tour w. L. Armstrong tribute. Publ: *Ad Lib Chord Reading* (B. Feldman & Co. Ltd., London). LPs: *Doc Cheatham* (Jezebel); *Doc Cheatham Prescribes* (Jazzways); *From Dixieland to Swing* (Music Minus One); w. Clyde Bernhardt, *More Blues From Harlem* (Saydisc); w. Earl Hines; Buck Clayton (Chiaro.); Sammy Price (B&B); Countsmen (Eng. RCA).

CHERICO, EUGENE V. (GENE),* *bass*; b. Buffalo, N.Y., 4/15/35. Continued working w. S. Getz through '66; traveling w. Peter Nero, '66-70. In 1970 was working locally in LA area w. F. Strazzeri, F. Rosolino, L. Bellson, Dick Grove, Toshiko, R. Norvo, C. McRae, Peggy Lee. Toured w. F. Sinatra in fall of '73; also w. Nancy Wilson, incl. visit to Venezuela. Several concerts w. G. Mulligan, '74. During much of '70s was busy in LA studios. App. at Concord JF w. T. Gibbs, '73. Wrote and pl. bass theme on segment of Rod Serling's *Night Gallery*. Other TV apps: *Streets of San Francisco; Barnaby Jones; Marcus Welby; The Pearl Bailey Show*.

LPs: *Louie Rides Again*, w. Bellson (Percussion Power, 5109 Nagle Ave., Sherman Oaks, Ca. 91403); *Hey, Now, Hey*, w. Aretha Franklin (Atl.); *Kogun*, w. Toshiko (RCA); *Big Bad & Beautiful*, w. Grove (FPM Records, 12754 Ventura Blvd., Studio City, Ca. 91604).

CHERRY, DONALD E. (DON),* *trumpet, composer*; also *flute, bamboo flute, percussion*; b. Oklahoma City, Okla., 11/18/36. After Ornette Coleman's quartet disbanded in the early '60s, Cherry played briefly w. Steve Lacy; and Sonny Rollins. In the summer of '63 he was a founding member of the New York Contemporary Five w. Archie Shepp and John Tchicai, playing and rec. in Europe before it broke up early in '64. Returned to Europe w. Albert Ayler and by the end of the year had formed his own gp. in Paris w. Gato Barbieri. It remained more or less intact until the fall of '66, rec. in Europe and New York. In '65 Cherry rec. w. George Russell at a concert in Stuttgart; in '66 w. Giorgio Gaslini in Milan. During the last part of the '60s he commuted between Europe and the US. Settling in Sweden in '71, he and his artist wife, Moki, on vocals and percussion, presented a series of concerts in a specially constructed tent at the Museum of Modern Art in Stockholm. Excerpts from this series were issued under the title *Organic Music Society* on the Swedish label Caprice Riks. In July '73 Cherry appeared at an outdoor concert in Central Park at the NJF-NY under the heading Organic Music Theatre. He and wife festooned the stage with multicolored banners and several children were incorporated in the OMT's performance. Barry McRae's description of the Caprice Riks album in *Jazz Journal* fits the NJF-NY set. "The music is very much international in flavour," he wrote. "To produce music beyond category and owing its tradition to no one particular ethnic source would seem to be Cherry's current aim. Within this context he still includes moments of pure jazz trumpet but these are only appropriate interludes and are not the raison d'ètre of the music. As a highly prejudiced jazz follower, I regret this step, but I must concede that Cherry's music remains highly appealing. It can only be hoped that, if he has truly found his niche in Europe, the odd trip to America might find him in a record studio with jazzmen of equal stature reminding the world that here is one of the finest horn men the music ever produced."

Film: soundtrack for *New York Eye and Ear Control* by Michael Snow; music for Alexander Jodorowsky's *Holy Mountain*.

Comp: *Relativity Suite; Symphony For Improvisers; Manhattan Cry; Lunatic; Om Nu; Complete Communion; Elephantasy; Taste Maker; The Thing; There is the Bomb, Unite*.

LPs: *Human Music* (Fly. Dutch.); *Mu First Part; Mu Second Part; Don Cherry; Blue Lake* (Byg); *Eternal Rhythm* (MPS); *Relativity Suite* (JCOA); *Actions/Penderecki-Don Cherry* (Philips); *Complete Communion; Symphony For Improvisers; Where Is Brooklyn?* (BN); *Togetherness* (Durium); *The Jazz Composer's Orchestra; Escalator Over the Hill* (JCOA); w. O. Coleman, *Crisis* (Imp.); *Clifford Jordan in the World*

(Strata-East); Charlie Haden, *Liberation Music Orchestra* (Imp); *G. Gaslini, Ensemble* (Ital. RCA); Sunny Murray, *Sunny's Time Now* (Jihad); *George Russell Sextet at Beethoven Hall, Vols. I & II* (Saba); Albert Ayler, *Ghosts* (Debut); *New York Eye and Ear Control* (ESP); New York Contemporary Five (Fontana; Sonet; Savoy); w. A. Heath, *Kawaida* (Trip).

CHIASSON, WARREN,* *vibes, composer*; also *piano, percussion*; b. Cheticamp, N.S., Canada, 4/17/34. Raised and educ. in Sydney, N.S. where his family moved when he was five. Stud. guitar, violin, tromb.; then xylophone at coll., vibes from '57. Joined George Shearing, July '59, remaining through '61, incl. Australian tour, '60. Own gps. in NYC, '62-3. In house band at Dupont Pavilion, NY World's Fair, '64-5; piano for gigs w. dance bands, '65; w. Grachan Moncur III in Mont., NYC '67. In '68-70 hosted weekly sessions at Signs of Zodiac, NYC, backing guest soloists w. his quartet. Back w. Shearing, off and on, Nov. '72-Aug. '74. Gigs w. Chet Baker, '74. Solo vibes at Gregory's, NYC, Jan.-May '75. Toured w. Roberta Flack, '75. Orig. infl: L. Tristano, P. Bley. TV: many apps. on CBC; *Jazz Adventures*, PBS, May '74. Fests: NJF; MJF w. Shearing '59-60; NJF-NY w. Baker, '75. Comps: *Bossa Nova Scotia; Bedouin; Magic Lantern; September; Paula; My Own; A Shanty for Peggy; Para Siempre; Festival.* Publ: *The Contemporary Vibist* (Charles H. Hansen, 1842 West Ave., Miami Beach, Fla. 33139).

Chiasson's vibes work is marked by harmonic subtlety, a light, dancing quality and mastery of multi-mallet techniques. LPs: *Quartessence* (Van Los); w. Harold Vick, *Straight Up* (RCA); w. Shearing, *Satin Affair; San Francisco Scene; Satin Brass* (Cap.).

CHICAGO. Originally formed as Chicago Transit Authority in mid-'60s out of such Chicago gps. as The Missing Links, The Exceptions, The Majestics and The Big Thing. Played at bars at colleges in Chicago area mixing jazz, blues, rock and classical influences and helped to pioneer use of brass arrangements within rock, along with such gps. as Blood, Sweat & Tears, Electric Flag. Moved to LA, pl. The Shrine, LA; Fillmore West & East. Shortened name to Chicago, '69. Its eight LPs on Columbia have each sold in excess of $1,000,000. Personnel consists of Robert Lamm, keyboards, vocals, who moved to Chicago at age 15 from his native Brooklyn; comp: *Saturday in the Park.* Own LP: *Skinny Boy* (Col.); James Pankow, trombone, composer, who had own jazz quintet while majoring in music at Quincy Coll. in Ill.; worked w. Bobby Christian; Ted Weems; Bill Russo's Chicago Jazz Ensemb.; formed own gp. at DePaul U. where he met drummer Danny Seraphine; woodwind player Walt Parazaider; guitarist Terry Kath. Other members include Lee Loughnane, trumpet; Peter Cetera, bass, steel guitar; and later addition Laudir De Oliveira, percussion. Group's producer is former bassist (Mothers of Invention) James William Guercio who also attended music courses at DePaul. Guercio's film, *Electra Glide in Blue*, incl. cameo perfs. by Loughnane and Parazaider.

CHISHOLM, GEORGE,* *trombone*; also *bass trumpet, euphonium, vibes, piano* etc.; b. Glasgow, Scotland, 3/29/15. One of Britain's first great jazzmen, he app. annually in the '70s at London's Festival Hall in tributes to L. Armstrong; pl. jazz concerts and fests. around the country, incl. Ireland, sometimes w. own group. The latter was also heard extensively on radio. Feat. in *Jazz At The Ronnie Scott Club* TV series, '71. LPs: Led own gp. in '73 for album on Rediffusion International.

CHITTISON, HERMAN,* *piano*; b. Flemingsburg, Ky., 1909. The Art Tatum-influenced pianist, who lived in Europe during most of the 1930s, later became a favorite in New York's East Side supper clubs. Chittison died 3/8/67 in Cleveland, Ohio.

CHRISTENSEN, JON, *drums*; b. Oslo, Norway, 3/20/43. Self-taught. First worked with singer Karin Krog in 1964, app. at Antibes Fest. With Steve Kuhn, '67-70; also Jan Garbarek quartet, '69-73. In '73 the group became known as Jan Garbarek-Bobo Stenson Quartet and Christensen continued pl. with the group. Tours w. Eberhard Weber-Charlie Mariano, '75. Has made many TV apps. in Europe, notably w. S. Getz at Antibes; G. Russell in Oslo, Stockholm; K. Jarrett, Oslo, Bremen, Hanover; and w. Garbarek-Stenson. Since '64 Christensen has pl. w. many visiting American jazzmen, incl. Dexter Gordon, Bud Powell, S. Rollins. Has won many European awards, both as number one drummer and for recs. Infls: Kuhn, Gordon, Tony Williams, Garbarek, Russell, Stenson, Palle Danielson.

LPs: *Watch What Happens*, w. Kuhn (MPS); *The Essence of George Russell* (Concept); *Belonging*, w. Jarrett; *Witchi-Tai-To*, w. Garbarek-Stenson; *Solstice*, w. Ralph Towner (ECM).

CHRISTIAN, EMILE JOSEPH,* *trombone, bass*; b. New Orleans, La., 4/20/1895. Trombonist w. Original Dixieland Jazz Band, 1918-20; later spent many years in Europe. Returning home to NO, Christian continued to gig in clubs and fests. He died 12/3/73 in NO.

CHRISTIE, RONALD KEITH,* *trombone*; b. Blackpool, England, 1/6/31. Alumnus of H. Lyttelton, J. Dankworth, Ted Heath bands; three tours of Euro. w. B. Goodman, '70-2, incl. rec. Pl. w. Kenny Wheeler and other big bands. Led own quintet for broadcasts, jazz clubs, concerts. Film: pl. on *Alfie* sound track w. R. Scott et al. Concerts, TV w. Ray Conniff. Jazz Workshop in Germany w. Euro. All Stars. Reincarnation of Jelly Roll Morton Red Hot Peppers, w. Twyla Tharpe Dance Found. for TV, concerts, rec.

CHRISTIE, LYNDON VAN (LYN), *bass, composer*; also *trumpet, synthesizer*; b. Sydney, Australia, 8/3/28. Father pl. sax and was president of mus. union in Christchurch, N.Z.; mother pl. piano; one brother, drums; another, bassoon. Self-taught until he came to NYC, '65, and joined Nat. Orchestral Assoc. for symph. training. Received grant from assoc. to stud. w. Homer Mensch of N.Y. Phil. & Juilliard, '68-9. First jobs w. parents' dance band while in high school; then weekly radio broadcasts w. big bands led by Martin Winiata, Julian Lee. Grad.

from Otago Medical Sch., spent some yrs. interning at hospital and then went into general practice. Pl. infrequently during this time. Left New Zealand and ret. to Sydney, '61, to practice medicine but soon became involved w. music. Led own quartet at club and on Aust. radio & TV. To NYC, '65 to "expand musical experience" but spent first two yrs. as chief resident at Yonkers General Hospital. Then undertook full-time music career as busy free-lance. Principal bass w. Westchester Phil.; Northeastern Penna. Phil.; Ridgefield Symphonette. Duos w. Eddie Thompson, Jaki Byard, David Lahm, Patti Bown, Lance Hayward, Roland Hanna, Freddie Redd, Pat Rebillot, Mike Abene, Dick Katz, etc.; combo work w. Jeremy Steig, Tal Farlow, Don Heckman, Paul Winter, Al Cohn-Zoot Sims, Chet Baker, Daphne Hellman, Ahmad Jamal, Ted Curson, Clark Terry, Chico Hamilton; big bands incl. Jones-Lewis, B. Rich, Dick Cone, Bob Rosengarden. During '73-4 led band incl. Randy Brecker for concerts at NYU and other colleges. Toured Japan w. Toshiko, '71; Germany w. A. Zoller, '71, '74. Pl. Colo. Jazz Party, '71-3. Infl: Blanton, R. Brown, Pettiford, P. Chambers, Vitous, LaFaro, S. Stewart, S. Clarke. TV: Aust. Broad. Comm., '61-5; w. Leon Bibb on *Something New*, '69; *Our American Musical Heritage*, '72; w. Marlena Shaw on *Positively Black*, '75, all NBC. Comp: *In Vino Veritas; Minnesota Thins; Beedies; A Place Within; Orpheus and Eurydice; Australian Jazz Suite; Portraits of Peace; Pagan Festival.* Teaches priv. and has given bass and electronic mus. workshops in Scranton, Pa. school district gifted student prog. and at Univ. of Scranton. Complements bowing with keening vocal style. LPs: *Hope For Tomorrow* w. Don Friedman (East Wind); others in Japan w. Toshiko; *Colorado Jazz Party* (BASF); w. M. Mainieri, *Insight* (SS); Austr. albums: w. Judy Bailey, *You and the Night and the Music* (CBS); w. Errol Buddle, *The Wind* (HMV).

CHRISTLIEB, PETER (PETE), *tenor saxophone*; also *flute, clarinet, bass clarinet*; b. Los Angeles, Cal., 2/16/45. Mother an operatic soprano; father a bassoonist in motion picture and TV work, and authority on double reed instruments. Stud. violin from '51-7; tenor sax in high school with priv. teacher. Pl. in jazz band at Venice H.S. and gained important infl. and training here, with a second priv. teacher. Stud. improvisation w. Ralph Lee; further studies w. Bob McDonald, Valley State and LACC. Pl. w. Jerry Gray, '63-4; Chet Baker, '64; Si Zentner, '65; W. Herman, '66; L. Bellson, '67- .

From the late '60s Christlieb doubled between jazz and a busy career in the studios. First motion pic. in band backing Elvis Presley. Frequent member of D. Severinsen orch. on *Tonight* show. Christlieb's background, besides direct study, was an environment that brought Stravinsky, Boulez, Stockhausen and many other famous composers into his parents' home as visitors. He is a tenor soloist of rare fluency, capable of strong, dynamic up tempo work and of warm, sensitive ballad performances. Infls: Parker, Mulligan, Sims, Getz, Rollins, Coltrane, C. Adderley, Clifford Brown.

LPs: *Jazz City* (R.A.H.M.P., 3311 Scadlock Ln., Sherman Oaks, Cal. 91403); w. Bellson, *Explosion* (Pablo); *Breakthrough* (Proj. 3); *Louie Rides Again* (Percussion Power, 5109 Nagle Ave., Sherman Oaks, Cal. 91403); w. Q. Jones, *Body Heat* (A & M); w. M. Legrand-S. Vaughan (Mainstream).

CHRISTY, JUNE,* *singer*; b. Springfield, Ill., 11/20/25. The former (1945-9) Stan Kenton vocalist went into semi-retirement in the late 1960s. Living in the San Fernando Valley, she emerged occasionally for night club engagements in North Hollywood and San Francisco. Guest app. w. Kenton at NJF-NY, '72.

LPs w. Kenton (Creative World).

CHURCHILL, SAVANNAH,* *singer*; b. New Orleans, La., 8/21/19. Best known as vocalist with Benny Carter band 1942-4, she died in Brooklyn, N.Y., 4/19/74.

CIRILLO, WALLACE JOSEPH (WALLY),* *piano, synthesizer, composer*; b. Huntington, N.Y. 2/4/27. Educ: Two masters of music degrees, major in comp. under Vittorio Gianinni, '58; major in mus. educ., '60 Manhattan School of Music, NYC; experimental comp. w. John Cage at New School, NYC. Infls: "Everyone from Pinetop Smith to Karlheinz Stockhausen." In '50s perf. own comps. at Carnegie Hall and Museum of Modern Art, NYC, w. Jazz Composers Workshop. Comp. and perf. first 12-tone jazz work, *Trans-Season*, '54 (Savoy Records); also in '50s wrote three symphs., chamber works, sonata for flute and piano, numerous avant garde and electronic jazz works. Moving to Boca Raton, Fla., '61, pl. w. Phil Napoleon, '64; Flip Phillips, Ira Sullivan et al. In Miami w. Terry Gibbs, '72; Anita O'Day, '73. Coll. concerts and TV in duo with guitarist Joe Diorio, '72-5. Teacher of improvisation and piano at U. of Miami, Miami-Dade Jr. Coll. and Florida Int'l. U., '75.

LPs: w. Joe Diorio (Spitball); w. John La Porta (Fantasy, Debut); J.J. Johnson-Kai Winding (Savoy); Charles Mingus (Savoy, Debut); Johnny Mathis (Columbia) etc.

CLARK, WALTER JR. (BUDDY),* *bass, arranger*; b. Kenosha, Wis., 7/10/29. Studies and early jobs in Chicago. Toured with many name bands early '50s; moved to LA, freelanced in studios, clubs. Pl. MJF w. Med Flory, '58. Active throughout '60s as studio bassist; recs., TV jingles etc.; also occasional trips w. Peggy Lee since '56. Co-founder w. Flory (q.v.) of Supersax, '72. Frequent sub for Ray Brown on Merv Griffin TV show, '71- . Broke w. Flory and was no longer w. Supersax in late '75.

Supersax, most of whose arrs. were transcribed by Flory or Clark from solos on old Ch. Parker records and orchestrated for five saxophones, won a Grammy award in '73 for the Best Jazz Performance by a group. In addition to rec., and app. at Donte's and other LA clubs. Supersax pl. Monterey, Concord Fests. '73, made a cross-Canada tour, '74 and a tour of Japan, early '75. Clark's arrs. for the band incl. *Ko-Ko; Parker's Mood; Night in Tunisia; Hot House; Kim.*

LPs: *Supersax Plays Bird; Salt Peanuts; Supersax Plays Bird with Strings* (Cap.).

CLARK, CHARLES E., *bass, cello*; b. Chicago, Ill., 3/11/45. Studied w. Wilbur Ware; classical bass w. Davis Bethe and Joseph Guastefeste, first bassist of the Chi. Symph. Began prof. in '63. Played w. Richard Abrams' Experimental Big Band. In '65 became one of the founding members of the Association for the Advancement of Creative Musicians, subsequently performing w. many AACM gps., most particularly Joseph Jarman; and violinist Leroy Jenkins. He was also a member, on scholarship, of the Chicago Civic Orch., the Chicago Symphony's official training orch. On his way home from a Civic Orch. rehearsal, he was stricken with a cerebral hemorrhage and died almost instantly, 4/15/69. The Civic Orch. established a scholarship in his name, to be awarded annually to a young, talented black musician.

DB commented of the "power and youthful exuberance of his playing, both arco and pizzicato. Clark," they wrote, "was also a gifted cellist." LPs: w. Abrams, *Levels and Degrees of Light*; w. Jarman, *Song For; As If It Were the Seasons* (Delmark).

CLARKE, KENNETH SPEARMAN (KENNY, KLOOK),* *drums*; b. Pittsburgh, Pa., 1/9/14. With Francy Boland (q.v.), co-led the Clarke-Boland Big Band until it disbanded in '73. He continued to teach and play in Paris, also touring w. a small group, which often incl. guitarist Jimmy Gourley; Lou Bennett or Eddy Louiss on organ. "No doubt the man remains a giant," Burt Korall wrote of Clarke in *down beat*, "he has forgotten more than most drummers will ever know about moving and shaping music. Beguiling brush work, always a primary Clarke asset, his 1-1-1-1-1 sound on the ride cymbal—indeed his mastery of the entire kit in the service of the music—make for pleasure and provocation for the listener and certainly for his sidemen." One of the sidemen was British drummer Kenny Clare, who gave the band dual percussion.

In October '72 Clarke made one of his rare visits to the US to participate in the Duke Ellington Fellowship program at Yale Univ. With the Clarke-Boland band he played many European fests. but at Montreux '73 he appeared as the "house" drummer, pl. and rec. w. Dexter Gordon, Gene Ammons, etc. Comp: *The Wildman*. TV: many Euro. apps.; Montreux '73 seen on PBS in US. LPs: see Boland; *Paris Bebop Sessions* (Prest.); *Gene Ammons and Friends at Montreux*; Dexter Gordon, *Blues a la Suisse*; w. D. Gillespie, *The Giant* (Prest.); w. Bud Powell, *Bud in Paris* (Xanadu).

CLARKE, STANLEY M., *bass, composer*; b. Philadelphia, Pa., 6/30/51. Studied in early school years; also at Phila. Mus. Acad. w. Ed Arian, Neil Courtney. Early experience with rock groups in and around Philadelphia in late 1960s. Six months w. Horace Silver, 1970; then a year w. Joe Henderson, followed by stints w. Pharoah Sanders, Stan Getz. He then joined Chick Corea and remained with him when Corea organized his new group, Return to Forever.

Clarke, who started out playing violin, later, took up cello before switching to bass. A master of both the acoustic and electric instruments, he says: "The difference between the Fender and the 'real' bass is that one bass is made of wood and has more of a natural sound. The other bass is made out of steel and it's made to be used through electronic things, like amplifiers, which have a more synthetic sound. I personally like both of the sounds, they both fit well in different situations."

Polls: DB Critics, TDWR, '73-4 on acoustic bass; '74 on electric bass; DB Reader's poll '74-5. Infl: Blanton, Pettiford, Chambers, La Faro, Coltrane, M. Davis. Fest: Many apps. at NJF-NY & European events. Comp: *Children of Forever; Unexpected; Bass Folk Song; Butterfly Dreams; Vulcan Princess; Yesterday Princess; Lopsy Lu; Power; Life Suite; Blue; Quiet Afternoon; Light As A Feather*. LPs: *Stanley Clarke; Journey to Love;* (Nemporer); *Children of Forever* (Polydor); w. Corea (Polydor); Norman Connors (Cobblestone, Buddah); Getz (Columbia); D. Gordon (Prestige); J. Farrell (CTI); P. Sanders (Imp.).

CLARKE, TERENCE MICHAEL (TERRY),* *drums, percussion*; b. Vancouver, B.C., Canada, 8/20/44. Early exp. w. local gps. and w. B. Kessel, V. Guaraldi. Pl. w. John Handy at Both/And Club in SF, cont. w. him in U.S. & Can. through March. '67. Joined Fifth Dimension, Oct. '67, touring w. them in U.S., Can. & Europe until '70 when he settled in Toronto, becoming active in TV and rec. A reg. member of Rob McConnell's Boss Brass; also pl. w. gps. of Moe Koffman, Guido Basso, Sonny Greenwich, Ed Bickert, Ted Moses and Lenny Breau. Acc. visiting soloists such as Jim Hall, Blue Mitchell, James Moody, Paul Desmond, etc. in Toronto clubs. TV: *Bell Telephone Hour* w. Handy '66, NBC; numerous variety shows w. Fifth Dimension; CBC *Bandwagon* w. Basso; *Music to See* w. Moses. Fests: MJF '65-6; Costa Mesa '66 w. Handy. LPs: w. Handy, *Live at the Monterey Jazz. Fest.; The 2nd John Handy Album; Spirituals to Swing 30th Anniv. Concert* (Col.); w. McConnell, *Best Damn Band in the Land* (UA); w. Greenwich, *Sunsong*; w. Moses, *Sidereal Time* (Radio Canada Int.); w. Koffman, *Plays Bach; Vivaldi, The Four Seasons; Solar Explorations* (GRT); w. Jim Hall (Horizon).

CLAYTON, WILBUR (BUCK),* *trumpet, composer*; b. Parsons, Kansas, 11/12/11. The former Count Basie star was a busy free-lance in NYC during the '50s and '60s, also making trips to Switzerland, Australia, Japan and, especially, England. He followed this pattern into the '70s until problems with his embouchure forced him to give up the trumpet in '72. He worked in the insurance department of Local 802 but in '73 left to devote himself to writing and arranging. In '74 and '75 groups of all star soloists recorded his compositions and arrs. in a jam session format for Chiaroscuro, recreating the atmosphere of similar dates for Columbia in the '50s. Fest: NO, '69. Comps: *Sidekick; Change For a Buck; The Duke We Knew; Boss Blues; Case Closed; Easy Blue; Rockaway*. LPs: *Buck Clayton Jam Session; Jam Session, Vol. 2* (Chiaro.); *Le Vrai Buck Clayton* (77); *Spirituals to Swing, 30th Anniversary* (Col.); also wrote all material for Humphrey Lyttelton-Buddy Tate, *Kansas City Woman* (Bl. Lion).

CLEVELAND, JAMES (JIMMY),* *trombone, composer*; b. Wartrace, Tenn. 5/3/26. An alumnus of the L. Hampton and Q. Jones bands, Cleveland extended his work in commercial TV and recording areas, first in NYC in mid and late '60s, then in Calif. Member of regular band on Della Reese, Pearl Bailey, Bill Cosby, Music Scene and Merv Griffin shows. Along with these activities he continued to play jazz, at NJF 1966-8; MJF, '69; Concord, '70, and gigs in Hollywood etc. w. small combos. Comps: *Little Beaver; Count 'Em; Jimmy's Tune; Jimmy's Old Funky Blues*.

LPs: Many excellent albums, as leader and sideman in 1950s and early '60s, were deleted; some reissues on Trip. Cleveland has rec. w. Gil Evans, Q. Jones, O. Nelson, Wes Montgomery, D. Gillespie, Miles Davis, C. Adderley, L. Schifrin, Michel Legrand.

COATES, JOHN FRANCIS JR., *piano*; also *vibes*; b. Trenton, N.J., 2/17/38. Father a jazz pianist and music teacher. Studies at Mannes and Dalcroze music schools, NYC; Rutgers Univ., New Brunswick, N.J.; privately, '45-56, w. Urana Clarke. After high school grad., '56, joined Charlie Ventura for two yrs. Returned to matriculate at Rutgers. Since grad. he has confined most of his playing to the Deer Head Inn, a jazz club in the small town of Delaware Water Gap, Pa., pl. occasional concerts elsewhere. Musicians such as Al Cohn, Phil Woods, Zoot Sims have pl. w. him at the Deer Head. Infl: John Coates Sr., Art Tatum. TV apps. w. Ventura, Barry Miles, Bernard Peiffer. Comps: 100 choral arrs; several orig. comps. for chorus; two mus. comedies; 50 songs "which are important to me for use in my jazz playing." Coates is composer-arranger-editor for Shawnee Press, Inc., Delaware Water Gap, Pa. LPs: *The Jazz Piano of John Coates, Jr.* (Omnisound); *Portrait* (Savoy); vibes w. Peiffer (Polydor).

COBB, ARNETT,* *tenor sax*; b. Houston, Tex., 8/10/18. Popular extrovert soloist in Lionel Hampton orch. in '40s. Toured w. own band from '47 but inactive at different times due to illness; auto crash. Own bands in Houston, '60s but illness once again prevented him from playing for long periods. Active again in '70, he traveled from Houston to NYC to play w. Illinois Jacquet at Town Hall, July '73. LP: *Jazz at Town Hall* w. Jacquet (JRC).

COBB, WILBUR JAMES (JIMMY),* *drums*; b. Washington, D.C., 1/20/29. A member of Miles Davis' quintet & sextet, '58-63, he then pl. w. Paul Chambers and Wynton Kelly in trio under Kelly's name that also acc. Wes Montgomery, '65-6. When Montgomery left to form his own gp., the trio cont. to work together, and after Chambers' death in '69, Cobb and Kelly were still a team until Cobb joined Sarah Vaughan in '71. Film: soundtrack for *Seven Days in May* w. David Amram. TV: w. Sarah Vaughan at Wolf Trap Farm, PBS. Fests: w. Vaughan at NJF-NY, '74-5.

LPs w. Vaughan (Mainstream).

COBHAM, WILLIAM C. (BILLY); *drums, composer, leader*; b. Panama, 5/16/44. At age three he and his mother joined father, William Sr., a pianist who had preceded them to NYC. Began fooling around w. timbales at age two. By age eight was sitting-in w. father publicly. Infl. by the many local parades in Brooklyn joined Boy Scouts in order to pl. drums. In drum corps., '56-8. Entered the High Sch. of Music & Art '59 and got first complete drum set. Pl. w. Jazz Samaritans which incl. George Cables and Clint Houston. Other schoolmates were Larry Willis, Bobby Colomby, Jimmy Owens, Eddie Gomez.

After high School was in the Army, pl. w. Military Ocean Terminal Base Band at Brooklyn Army Terminal; band at Ft. Dix, N.J. w. Grover Washington. While still in the Army, through the last half of '67, worked w. Billy Taylor trio at Hickory House; gigged w. the NY Jazz Sextet (Hubert Laws, Tom McIntosh, Owens, etc.); taught and served as a clinician for Jazzmobile; and paired w. Chris White in Rhythm Associates, pl. practice seminar rehearsals for bassists and drummers.

In '68, after his Army discharge, Cobham was hired by Horace Silver and pl. w. his quintet, Feb.-Oct. incl. a European tour. Then he became extremely active in recs. for film (*Shaft*), TV (*Mission Impossible*) and jingles. Pl. w. S. Turrentine; K. Burrell. Formed jazz-rock fusion band Dreams in '69 and remained w. it through '70. During this time made several important recs. w. Miles Davis. In spring '71 rec. w. John McLaughlin and shortly thereafter became a member of the newly-formed Mahavishnu Orchestra. When they disbanded on Jan. 1, '73 he began rec. under his own name. Formed own band in Feb. '74 for clubs, concerts, European tour, summer '74, pl. Montreux JF; Rainbow Theatre in London. Returned to Europe, May '75, for six wks. In Sept. assembled a new quartet called Spectrum, after the title of his first rec. as a leader, with George Duke, keyboards; John Scofield, guitar; Doug Rauch, bass.

As a producer he has been responsible for Airto's *Virgin Land* (Salvation); and David Sancious' *Forest of Feelings* (CBS).

Early infl: Erroll Garner, Billy Eckstine, Miles Davis, Tito Puente, Stan Levey, Sonny Payne, Jo Jones, Gus Johnson. Fest: NJF w. Silver, '68; NJF-NY w. Mahavishnu, '72. Won DB Readers poll, '73-5. Comp: *Spanish Moss; Savannah the Serene; Storm; Flash Flood; The Pleasant Pheasant; Heather; Crosswind; Panhandler; Solarization*. LPs: *A Funky Thide of Sings; Shabazz; Total Eclipse; Crosswinds; Spectrum* (Atl.); *Dreams*; w. Mahavishnu, *The Inner Mounting Flame; Birds of Fire;* w. M. Davis, *Jack Johnson; Live-Evil; Big Fun; Get Up With It; Bitches Brew* (Col.); w. J. McLaughlin, *My Goal's Beyond* (Douglas); w. H. Silver, *Serenade to a Soul Sister; You Got to Take a Little Love* (BN); also w. George Benson; Ron Carter; Deodato; Freddie Hubbard; Randy Weston; Milt Jackson; H. Laws; Don Sebesky; S. Turrentine; G. Washington (CTI).

COCHRAN, TODD (See BAYETÉ)

COE, ANTHONY GEORGE (TONY),* *tenor saxophone, clarinet*; also *bass clarinet, soprano sax, flute, basset horn, composer*; b. Canterbury, England, 11/29/34. Four years w. J. Dankworth, '66-9; Clarke-Boland band from '69 until its breakup in '73. In '70 he also worked w. Matrix, a group that pl. chamber music and jazz-oriented works, some written by Coe. Has led own combo off and on for fests. and broadcasts. In '75 his first major comp., *Zeitgeist*, was perf. Movies, recordings w. H. Mancini incl. *Return of The Pink Panther*. Infl. by B. Bigard; on tenor by Hawkins, Webster, Gonsalves; in comp. by Schoenberg, Berg.

Own LP w. Brian Lemon Trio (77 Records); others w. P. Seamen (Decibel); Clarke-Boland (Poly., MPS, Bl. Lion).

COHN, ALVIN GILBERT (AL),* *tenor sax, composer*; b. Brooklyn, N.Y., 11/24/25. Writer for TV specials such as award-winning *Anne Bancroft Show* and *S'Wonderful, S'Marvelous, S'Gershwin*, '69-70, and for annual *Tony Award* show. Chief arr. for Broadway musicals *Raisin*, '73 and *Music, Music, Music* '74. Pl. solos on the soundtrack of film *Lenny*. Although he concentrated on writing, he continued to app. in clubs and concerts w. his longtime sidekick, Zoot Sims, and w. his own quartet in Toronto, Wash., D.C., N.J., NYC, and Pennsylvania's Pocono Mts. where he makes his home. With Sims, toured Scandinavia, '74. Own gp. at NY Jazz Museum; guest apps. w. Balaban & Cats at Eddie Condon's, '75. Though underrated by the public his playing is much admired by fellow musicians. Fests: NJF w. Sims, '66; NJF-NY w. W. Herman alumni, '72; Molde, '75; Colo. Jazz Party, '68-72, '74-5. Comp: *Mama Flosie; The Underdog* (a.k.a. *Ah-Moore*); *Mr. George; The Note; You 'N' Me*. LPs: *Play It Now* (Xanadu); *Broadway 1954* (Prest.); *Too Heavy For Words* w. J. Moody (MPS); w. Sims, *Body and Soul* (Muse) & *You 'N' Me* (Trip); *Colorado Jazz Party* (MPS); w. J. Rushing, *The You and Me That Used to Be* (RCA); w. Tony Bennett (Col.); w. Bill Watrous; John Bunch (Famous Door); w. Sonny Berman (Onyx).

COHN, GEORGE THOMAS (SONNY),* *trumpet, fluegelhorn*; b. Chicago, Ill., 3/14/25. Heard with many bands in Chicago from mid-'40s; later w. L. Bellson, Erskine Hawkins. Joined C. Basie orch, '60 and during next 15 years toured the world with the band. For details of travels see BASIE, COUNT.

LPs: *Jazz at the Santa Monica Civic '72* w. Basie, Fitzgerald (Pablo); *Basie and Sinatra Live at the Sands* (Reprise); *Standing Ovation; Basie Straight Ahead* (Daybreak); *Afrique* w. Basie (Flying Dutchman).

COKER, CHARLES MITCHELL (DOLO),* *piano*; also *alto sax*; b. Hartford, Conn., 11/16/27. Raised in S. Carolina, pl. his first pro. jobs in and around Phila. Moved to LA, '60, led own trio at Club Casbah, Memory Lane, Club Libra through '72. Has also worked w. Herb Ellis, Blue Mitchell, Supersax, S. Stitt, Red Rodney, L. Konitz and Sahib Shihab at a variety of LA area clubs. Title I Concerts at over 80 schools in Unified School District w. S. Criss, '73, '74. Pl. w. Jack Sheldon, Richard Boone, D. Gordon, '74; the groups of Harry Edison and T. Edwards, '75; Redd Foxx Show in concert, '70s. Coker is also active as piano teacher and vocal coach. TV: *Rosey Grier Show*, '68; *In Name Only*, Screen Gems, '69; *Della Reese Show*, '69; *Festival In Black*, KCET, '71; *Black Omnibus*, '73; *Lucy Show; Sanford & Son*. Fests: Watts Summer Jazz Fest., '70-2. Comps: *Lovely Lisa; Field Day; Affair in Havana*.

LPs: *Superbop*, w. Rodney; *Feelin's*, w. Edwards (Muse); *I've Got A Right To Sing*, w. Boone (Nocturne).

COKER, HENRY,* *trombone*; b. Dallas, Tex., 12/24/19. Best known through association w. Count Basie band, '52-63. Toured w. Ray Charles, '66-71. Sound track work for film *Lady Sings The Blues*, '72. Gigged in LA area from '71, also rejoined Basie for four months in '73.

LPs w. Basie on various labels; also Teresa Brewer-Basie (Flying Dutchman); *My Kind of Jazz Part I* and *My Kind of Jazz Part III*, w. Charles (Crossover).

COLE, WILLIAM R. (COZY),* *drums*; also *tympani, vibes*; East Orange, N.J., 10/17/09. Continued to lead his own combo through 1968. Joined Jonah Jones quartet '69. Operated Krupa & Cole Drum School from '54 until Krupa's death in '73. App. at NJF '73 w. Cab Calloway reunion band; Nice fest. '74. Pub: *Modern Drum Technique; Gene Krupa & Cozy Cole Drum Book*, both w. (Mills Music, 1619 Broadway, NYC); *Cozy Cole, William V. Kessler Modern Studies for Drums* (BMI). LPs: *A Cozy Conception of Carmen* (MGM); *Drum Beat for Dancing Feet* w. guests Krupa, Ray McKinley, Panama Francis (Coral); *Topsy* (Love); w. Jo Jones, Zutty Singleton (Jazz Odyssey).

COLEMAN, WILLIAM JOHNSON (BILL),* *trumpet, singer*; b. Paris, Ky., 8/4/04. Living in France from the end of '48. Toured in England as a soloist, '66 and '67. Featured at Jazz Expo, London, '69. Other fest: Nice '74; Montreux w. S. Grappelli. LPs: Bill Coleman & Guy Lafitte, *Mainstream at Montreux*; w. Ben Webster (Black Lion); *Nice 1974, Tribute to Count Basie* (Eng. RCA).

COLEMAN, EARL,* *singer*; b. Port Huron, Mich., 8/12/25. Sang w. E. Hines; J. McShann in '40s. Rec. w. Charlie Parker. In mid-'60s app. w. Billy Taylor; Frank Foster big band in NYC; one-nighters at the Playboy Club. To LA late '68, working at Redd Foxx's club. Remained in LA through late '75, except for a trip back to NYC '69. At Foxx's '70; Parisian Room; Donte's; Baked Potato; one nighters w. Bill Berry; Gerald Wilson bands. When Wilson subbed for Ellington band at Biltmore, Coleman sang Ellingtonia w. him. Assembled a gp. to present a half-hour musical eulogy to Duke at Museum of Science & Industry, broadcast on KBCA. Working in Cincinnati, St. Louis in late '75. Leonard Feather described his bass-baritone sound as having "a searing intensity, at times almost an anguish, that bespeaks his rare depth of understanding born of a long and bitter life experience. LPs: *Love Songs* (Atl.); Parker reissue (Spotlite); reissue of '40s material w. Fats Navarro, *Bebop Revisited*, Vol. 1 (Xanadu).

COLEMAN, GEORGE,* *tenor saxophone*; also *alto sax*; b. Memphis, Tenn., 3/8/35. Pl. and rec. w. Miles Davis quintet, '63-4; L. Hampton, Ch. McPherson, L. Morgan, Elvin Jones, Shirley Scott, '65-73. Toured Europe three months, '74, as leader, also w. S. Hampton. Comp. music for bands of all sizes, perf. in concerts, clubs, colleges, '74-5. Playing and conducting concerts presented by Jazzmobile w. own octet. Also pl. w. Cedar Walton quartet '75. NEA Grant. Comp: *Revival of the Fittest; Little Miss Half-Steps*.

LPs: w. Roach (Mercury); Davis (Columbia); H. Hancock, H. Silver, E. Jones, Jimmy Smith, Lee Morgan (Blue Note); Harold Mabern (Prestige); S. Hampton (Strand); S. Scott (Chess); Elvin Jones (Enja).

COLEMAN, ORNETTE,* *alto sax, composer*; also *tenor sax, trumpet, violin, shenai*; b. Ft. Worth, Tex., 3/19/30. After moving from California and appearing at the Five Spot in NYC, '59, with Don Cherry in the quartet that helped alter the face of jazz, Coleman has made Manhattan his base of operations. His mid-'60s trio of David Izenzon and Charles Moffett gave way to a quartet format again, this time with Dewey Redman; Charlie Haden; and either Ed Blackwell or Ornette's son Denardo on drums. His album, *Science Fiction*, reunited him with many of his cohorts incl. Cherry, Bobby Bradford, Billy Higgins, etc. As the '70s moved toward mid-decade Coleman tended to maintain a low profile, concentrating on writing and doing most of his playing at his own Artist House (131 Prince St.) in the Soho section of Manhattan. In '67 he played at the Village Theater with quartet and the Philadelphia Woodwind Quintet; In '69 Don Cherry rejoined him briefly for a quintet concert at the Loeb Student Center of NYU. The quartet with Redman was on stage with a symphony orchestra at the NJF-NY '72 for a performance of his *Skies of America* written with what he describes as his "harmelodic theory." The texture of the orchestral writing, he says, comes from "The total collective blending of the transposed and non-transposed instruments using the same intervals."

Gary Giddins, reviewing a recording of *Skies of America*, noted: "These formulations give the impression of a more complicated and radical music than the ear actually hears—the work is readily approachable and can be enjoyed without the footnotes."

Whitney Balliett in '67 found that Coleman's "feet remain firmly in the old blues and his head is full of celestial things—a balanced presence that could offset a great deal of the malarkey that afflicts the rest of the 'new thing.' "

Even in the '70s, however, not everyone was totally convinced of Coleman's credibility. Charles Mingus was quoted by Balliett in '71 as saying: "But I feel sorry about jazz. The truth has been lost in the music. All the different styles and factions went to war with each other, and it hasn't done any good. Take Ornette Coleman."

"Mingus sang half a chorus of *Body and Soul* in a loud, off-key voice," wrote Balliett, "drowning out the jukebox. It was an uncanny imitation."

"That's all he does," said Mingus. "Just pushing the melody out of line here and there. Trouble is, he can't play it straight."

Joachim Berendt, commenting on *Skies of America*, wrote: "At the time of the refined string sounds of such composers as Ligeti and Penderecki, Coleman writes simply, almost naively, for the symphony orchestra—using parallel lines and a host of parallel and duplicated voices. The more astonishing how rich and expressive the effects that he produces! Ornette Coleman remains a jazz musician—even when composing for symphony orchestra. The symphony orchestra, to him, is an enlarged 'horn' on which he improvises."

Berendt also described Coleman at the '71 Berlin Jazz Days as the musician who "in the early sixties revolutionized jazz" but here was "simply making 'beautiful music': clear, singing, wonderfully balanced alto lines."

In '74 Coleman played at San Francisco's Keystone Corner in '74; visited France in the summer of '75; and played at the Five Spot, NYC, in that same year. His new group consisted of James "Blood" Ulmer, guitar; Haden; Denardo; and Barbara Huey, percussion.

Coleman received Guggenheim Fellowships for composition in '67 and '74. DB Awards: Jazzman of the Year, '66, '71; Hall of Fame, '69; *At the Golden Circle, Vol. 1*, Record of the Year in Critics and Readers polls. '66; alto sax, Critics poll, '67, '72-4; Readers poll, '72-4.

Comp: *Broken Shadows; Comme Il Faut; Space Jungle; Trouble in the East; Forms and Sounds; Civilization Day; Love and Sex; Street Woman; Atavism; Rock the Clock; Law Years; All My Life*. LPs: *Skies of America; Science Fiction* (Col.); *Friends and Neighbors* (Fly. Dutch.); *At 12; Crisis* (Imp.); *The Empty Foxhole; At the Golden Circle, Vols. 1&2*; w. J. McLean, *New and Old Gospel* (BN); reissue, *Best* (Atl.).

COLES, JOHN (JOHNNY),* *trumpet*; b. Trenton, N.J., 7/3/26. After pl. w. George Coleman at NJF '66 and as sideman for Hunter Coll. jazz concerts continued to freelance until he became one of the original members of the Herbie Hancock sextet '68. W. Ray Charles orch. '69-70 before joining Duke Ellington and remaining until Duke's death. Rejoined Charles May '74. Recorded sound track for Bill Cosby's Fat Albert TV series '69. LPs: *Katumbo* (Mainstream); *The Prisoner* w. Hancock (Blue Note); *The Great Concert of Charles Mingus* (Prestige); *Guitar Forms* w. Kenny Burrell; *Look To the Rainbow* w. Astrud Gilberto (Verve); several albums w. Ellington.

COLLETTE, WILLIAM MARCELL (BUDDY),* *saxes, flute, clarinet, piano, composer*; b. Los Angeles, Cal., 8/6/21. Prominent since '40s in both jazz and studio work. Gave courses on music writing for TV and motion pics., also directed stage band, for three years at Cal. State U., LA. Has written everything from TV jingles and industrial film music to a three part fugue for nine instruments, and a suite for harp and flute using 12 tone system. Collette also helped start a record company, Legend, in '73, and in '75 was serving as President. Fest. apps. at Monterey etc.; occasional gigs leading quintet in jazz clubs.

LPs: *Now and Then* (Legend); *Basin Street Brass* w. Red Callender (Legend); *Blue Sands* w. C. Hamilton (Wor. Pac.).

COLLIER, GRAHAM, *bass, composer*; b. Tynemouth, England, 2/21/37. Father was drummer for silent movies. Stud. Berklee Coll., '61-3 w. Herb Pomeroy, William Curtis. While there pl. w. Jimmy Dorsey band led by Lee Castle. Returned to England late '63, formed own band '64; concerts and clubs; also first British jazz group to tour schools extensively presenting lecture concerts for children. Collier is also active in comp. for TV commercials, documentary films, stage. Inspirations: Duke Ellington, Gil Evans, Charles Mingus. Publs: *Inside Jazz* (Quartet, 27 Goodge St., London W.I.), *Jazz* (Cambridge Univ. Press, Cambridge, England). Fests: Antibes; Montreux '71.

LPs: *Darius; Midnight Blue* (Mosaic Records); *Mosaics* (Philips).

COLLIER, RON, *composer*; also *trombone*; b. Coleman, Alberta, Canada, 7/3/30. Mother & father amateur mus.; wife, sister & brother-in-law prof. mus. Stud. arr. & comp. w. Gordon Delamont, '51-5; orchestration & comp. w. George Russell, Hall Overton, '62-3. Had own quintet and tentet in '50s & '60s. Resident composer at Humber Coll. Won stage band jazz competition, open class, for Canada w. Humber Coll. Band. App. at Toronto Jazz Fest.; Stratford Music Fest.; Expo '67. Wrote music for feature films: *A Fan's Notes; Face Off; Paperback Hero.* Worked and collaborated w. Ellington on his ballet, *The River* and symphony, *Celebration.* Comps: *The City*, suite for orch.; *Carnival*, for orch., narrator and solo fluegelhorn; *Requiem for J.F.K.; Aurora Borealis*, ballet. LPs: *Duke Ellington, North of the Border in Canada with the Ron Collier Orch.* (Decca), reissued as *Collages* (MPS); w. Moe Koffman, *Solar Explorations* (GRT).

COLLINS, BURTON I. (BURT),* *trumpet*; also *fluegelhorn, piccolo trumpet*; b. Bronx, N.Y., 3/27/31. Feat. sideman w. Woody Herman, Johnny Richards in '50s; became a busy, free-lance studio man in NYC during the '60s and '70s. Pl. w. pit bands for Broad. shows, *Bye Bye Birdie*, '60; *How to Succeed in Business*, '61-2. Did many club dates, '63-4; jazz soloist w. band on Les Crane TV Show, ABC, '65. Other TV: specials w. Victor Borge; Jonathan Winters. Fests: Randall's Island in early '60s w. C. Adderley big band; J. Richards orch. In '75 pl. w. bands of Dave Matthews; Lee Konitz. LPs: w. Collins-Shepley Galaxy, *Time, Space and the Blues; Lennon/McCartney Live* (MTA); *Introducing Duke Pearson; Now Hear This* w. Pearson (Blue Note); *Live at the Five Spot* w. Matthews (Muse).

COLLINS, JOHN ELBERT,* *guitar, banjo*; b. Montgomery, Ala., 9/20/13. After the death in 1965 of Nat King Cole, with whom he had worked since '59, Collins spent six years with Bobby Troup's quartet in locations in and around LA. Other engagements w. F. Sinatra, Sammy Davis, Nancy Wilson, Neal Hefti. In '75 he was chosen to participate in the NEA Jazz Oral History Project of the Smithsonian Institution. Led own quartet feat. Jimmy Jones on piano, '74-5.

LPs: w. E. Fitzgerald, *Thirty by Ella* (Cap.); w. Lorez Alexandria, *Didn't We* (Pzazz).

COLLINS, RUDOLPH ALEXANDER (RUDY),* *drums*; b. New York City, 7/24/34. In 1967-68 toured w. Ray Bryant, Kenny Burrell and, briefly, Woody Herman; six mos. in house band at Raleigh Hotel in Catskill Mts., then w. Junior Mànce, Lloyd Price, Harry Belafonte '69; Broadway and off-Broadway show work, incl. *Hair* and *Purlie*; clubs w. Bill Russell, Morris Nanton trios, '70-71; Jimmy Neeley, Dave Rivera, Earl Hines trios '72, also gigs at Steer Inn on Long Island '72; Apollo Theatre w. Reuben Phillips house band, tours w. Monty Alexander, Sam "The Man" Taylor (Japan), NYC clubs w. Dakota Staton, Duke Pearson, Lee Konitz '73; Randy Weston, Bernie Leighton, Count Basie, incl. Toronto JF '74; toured the US and Canada w. Cleo Laine and John Dankworth '74 and TV special w. them '75. Other TV apps. w. Gillespie '71, Weston '74. Teaching drums at Brooklyn Children's Museum from '69. LPs: *Tanjah* w. Weston (Polydor); *Live at the Village Gate* w. Mance (Atlantic); *This Is Billy Butler*; Gene Ammons (Prest.).

COLOMBY, ROBERT WAYNE (BOBBY), *drums*; b. New York, N.Y., 12/20/44. Began listening to jazz at age 15 through brothers Jules, a trumpeter, and Harry, both of whom later managed T. Monk. Pl. w. Jon Hendricks, Odetta, Eric Anderson. Founder member in '68 of Blood, Sweat & Tears, the first group to achieve int'l stature and commercial success with an amalgam of rock and jazz elements, which drew young musicians away from a strictly guitar-oriented format by their use of horns. TV: *In Concert; Midnight Special; Up Beat; Live in Scandinavia Special; In Concert* (London), plus many other European, Australian and Japanese apps. Fests: Newport, Montreux, Longhorn. LPs: w. B.S.&T. (Col.).

COLTRANE, ALICE,* *piano, composer*; also *organ, harp*; b. Detroit, Mich., 8/27/37. After pl. w. the Terry Gibbs quartet in the early '60s, under her maiden name of Alice McLeod, she joined John Coltrane in '66 and was married to him later that year. Following his death in '67 she began leading her own group for clubs, concerts and recordings. The various musicians who have app. with her in these capacities incl. P. Sanders, A. Shepp, O. Coleman, Carlos Ward and Frank Lowe. In the '65-7 period she toured extensively in the U.S. and Japan w. J. Coltrane. With her own group she pl. at the Village Vanguard; as a soloist at Carnegie Hall, '71; but since she moved to Cal. in '72 her public apps. have been sporadic.

Originally a Bud Powell-oriented pianist, she was later greatly infl. by McCoy Tyner. She has a strong interest in "all religions of the world" and "a deep appreciation for spiritual music-meditative music."

Imamu Baraka described her relation to Coltrane's

music as "a vector, a further earth exploration." Bill Cole has called her playing "vibrant, fresh, innovative and uncompromising . . . her right hand is very light and dextrous on the organ, while her left plays unyielding chords that give strong drone feelings." DB reviewer Will Smith, while praising her piano and organ solos, said that her harp work, "no matter how lovely it can be, is quite lightweight," and called her string writing "super saccharine, often corny and terribly repetitive."

Fests: Newport, w. J. Coltrane, '66. Her albums contain many of her original compositions. She names *Journey in Satchidananda* and *Blue Nile* as her most important.

LPs: *Lord of Lords; World Galaxy; Universal Consciousness; Journey in Satchidananda; Ptah the El Daoud; Huntington Ashram Monastery; Monastic Trio* (Imp.); w. J. Coltrane, *Infinity* (rec. in mid-'60s, completed '72); *Concert in Japan; Live at the Village Vanguard Again; Cosmic Music; Expression* (Imp.); *Illuminations*, w. C. Santana (Col.); *The Elements* w. J. Henderson (Milest.).

COLTRANE, JOHN WILLIAM,* *tenor, soprano saxes, composer, leader*; also *bass clarinet, flute*; b. Hamlet, N.C., 9/23/26. From the end of '65, when both McCoy Tyner and Elvin Jones left his group, the music of Coltrane continued more deeply into the religious expression he had begun earlier with *A Love Supreme*. Retained were saxophonist Pharoah Sanders and drummer Rashied Ali. Tyner's replacement was Alice McLeod who became Mrs. John Coltrane. Other drummers were hired on different jobs to complement Ali.

In July '66 Coltrane toured Japan for two weeks, playing 17 concerts before capacity audiences. Following the tour bassist Jimmy Garrison, the last remaining member of his most famous quartet, left after expressing dissatisfaction with the direction of the music. Back in New York, for an engagement at the Vanguard, Ali brought in a supporting cast of several percussionists on bells, tambourines, congas, triangles, etc. Coltrane occasionally did some primitive yodeling, described by C.O. Simpkins as "sometimes . . . high and screaming. Other times . . . deep and thudding, with him striking his chest as though it were a resonant drum."

Coltrane began studying the conga and practiced with his wife. He took to hiring large ensembles, many of whom were drummers, to accompany him, as in an appearance at the Front Room in Newark. When his fans requested his older numbers he replied, "We're not playing that kind of thing anymore."

Early in '67 he again played at the Vanguard and, in April played a concert at the opening of Olatunji's Center of African Culture in Harlem. In June there was a recurrence of "stomach trouble" which had been plaguing him since the previous year. (Many pictures taken on the Japanese tour show him holding his hand over the right part of his abdomen.) This liver ailment continued to worsen and, after hospitalization, he died on July 17, 1967.

He was already considered one of the major innovators in the history of jazz. Long after his death Coltrane continued to be a pervasive influence on contemporary music and musicians, not only jazz and saxophonists, but rock and players of all instruments. He affected music in several ways: harmonically-melodically; rhythmically; tonally; and in terms of form. Saxophonists such as Wayne Shorter, Joe Farrell and Charles Lloyd, to name just three, received much inspiration from him; other reedmen like Pharoah Sanders, Archie Shepp, Albert Ayler and John Gilmore, after drawing on him for inspiration, later helped shape his final period with their interpretations. He had already popularized the soprano among modern saxophonists.

Gordon Kopulos, writing in *down beat* in '71, pointed out: "It is irrelevant if the Beatles ever heard John Coltrane. It is important that some three years before they impacted on the American scene, Trane was already playing *India.* Four years after their first success, the Beatles transiently flirted with the music of Ravi Shankar, and an overnight cult sprang up. A sitar solo was even grafted on to a Beatles tune. The closing refrain of *No Time* by The Guess Who is remarkably similar in form to the repetitive device Trane used in so many of his solos. *Vehicle* by the Ides of March sounds embarrassingly like a slightly altered lift from *Blue Train.*"

Some of his critics and fellow musicians felt that he had had a detrimental effect on the music by surrounding himself with, and encouraging, lesser musicians.

Whitney Balliett, in *The New Yorker*, wrote: "But born poets like Coltrane sometimes misjudge the size of their gifts, and in trying to further them, to ennoble them, they fall over into sentimentality or the maniacal. Coltrane did both, and it is ironic that these lapses, which were mistakenly considered to be musical reflections of our inchoate times, drew his heaviest acclaim. People said they heard the dark night of the Negro in Coltrane's wildest music, but what they really heard was a heroic and unique lyrical voice at the mercy of its own power."

He won DB Critics poll & Readers poll, '66. In '75 books on his life by C.O. Simpkins and J.C. Thomas were published (see bibliography).

Comp: *Naima; Cousin Mary; Spiral; Countdown; Giant Steps; Mr. P.C.; Syeeda's Song Flute; Alabama; Ogunde; Moment's Notice; Blue Train; A Love Supreme; Trane's Blues; Spiritual; Crescent; Manifestation; Reverend King; Lord Help Me to Be; The Sun; Expression; Impressions; Father, Son and Holy Ghost.*

LPs: *Kulu Se Mama; Meditations; Expression; Live at the Village Vanguard Again; Om; Cosmic Music; Selflessness; Transition; Live in Seattle; Sun Ship; Infinity; Live—Concert in Japan; The Africa/Brass Sessions, Vol. II; Interstellar Space* (Imp.); *Alternate Takes* (Atl.); *High Step* w. Paul Chambers, incl. reissue and unissued material (BN); reissues on Imp.; Prest.; Atl.; Trip; BN.

COLYER, KEN,* *trumpet*; also *guitar*; b. Gt. Yarmouth, Norfolk, England, 4/18/28. Pro. since '40s, leading own group frequently from '53. Many tours of Europe, also U.S. and Canada in '75; pl. w. Canadian band at NO

Jazz and Heritage Fest. Numerous other trad. fests., riverboat gigs etc. TV in Germany; BBC Jazz Club etc. Colyer has long been dedicated to NO style jazz.

LP: *I Want To Be Happy*, rec. in Germany (Happy Bird).

CONDON, ALBERT EDWIN (EDDIE),* *guitar*; b. Goodland, Ind., 11/16/04. Illness precluded Condon from more than occasional activity during the '60s. In '67 he made what turned out to be his final California appearance, leading a group for one night at Disneyland. Co-led World's Greatest Jazzband II w. Kai Winding at Roosevelt Grill, '69. Toured high schools and colls. w. Art Hodes, Wild Bill Davison and B. Bigard, '71. Was the subject of a tribute, in which he himself appeared briefly, at NJF-NY, Carnegie Hall, July '72, surrounded by many musicians who had played at his Town Hall concerts in the '40s. Condon died Aug. 4, 1973 in a New York hospital. The use of his name in connection with a night club, which had flourished from '49-58 on West Third Street in NYC, and from '58-67 on East 56th Street, was revived early in '75 when a third club known as Eddie Condon's opened on West 54th Street, feat. jazz musicians, some of whom had been assoc. w. Condon and his earlier clubs. The new premises were under the management of bassist Red Balaban.

Book: *Eddie Condon's Scrapbook of Jazz*, by Condon and Hank O'Neal (St. Martin's Press, N.Y.). Publ. four months after Condon's death, this collection of reminiscences, photographs, reproductions of record labels, album covers, articles by Condon, cartoons, paintings etc., captures the essence of his era. Earlier books: *We Called It Music*, w. Thomas Sugrue (Henry Holt, 1947); *Eddie Condon'sTreasury of Jazz* w. Richard Gehman (Dial Press, 1956).

LPs: *Eddie Condon & Co. Vol. 1—Gershwin Program (1941-1945)* (Decca); *The Eddie Condon Concerts*, Town Hall 1944-45, feat. Pee Wee Russell; *The Eddie Condon Concerts*, Town Hall 1944; *Jazz at the New School* (Chiaroscuro); *Eddie Condon's World of Jazz* (Col.); *The Commodore Years, Eddie Condon & Bud Freeman* (Atl.); *The Best of Eddie Condon* (MCA).

CONNELL, WILL, JR., *alto saxophone*; also *flute, clarinet, piano*; b. Los Angeles, Cal., 11/22/38. Stud. at LA City Coll. Freelanced and led own groups in LA: wrote for and pl. w. H. Tapscott. Took part in various Watts Festivals and Festival in Black.

Comps: *Fatisha; Shakti (Mountain Song)*. Connell was the uncredited composer, arranger and orchestrator on at least one motion picture.

LPs: w. Azar Lawrence, *Bridge Into the New Age* (Prest.).

CONNERS, GENE (MIGHTY FLEA), *trombone*; b. Birmingham, Ala., 1930. Mother led the Gospel Harmonettes. Started on trombone at seven. Played in New Orleans funeral bands from '44 w. Bunk Johnson and others. After four years in Navy, lived in LA, rec. w. Ray Charles, Wynonie Harris, Dinah Washington et al. Best known for his work w. Johnny Otis, with whom he app. in clubs and visited Europe. His frenetic style earned him popularity with r & b audiences.

LPs w. J. Otis (Epic, Blues Spectrum); Shuggie Otis (Epic).

CONNIFF, RAY,* *composer, trombone*; b. Attelboro, Mass., 11/6/16. Mainly a popular music personality, but continued to play occasional jazz trombone in a Dixieland group as part of his vocal-group show and on records. Winner of many awards, gold albums etc. Tours of Europe, Japan. In '74, set a precedent as first U.S. pop artist to rec. in Soviet Union, using Russian singers and musicians.

LPs: (incl. jazz tracks): *Concert in Stereo Live at the Sahara/Tahoe* (Col.); others on Col.

CONNOR, CHRIS,* *singer*; b. Kansas City, Mo., 11/8/27. The former Stan Kenton vocalist of the '50s who toured successfully as a single in the '50s and early '60s, was intermittently active in the late '60s-early '70s but surfaced at the Half Note and then pl. the Maisonette at the St. Regis Hotel, NYC. LP: *Sketches* (Stanyan).

CONNORS, WILLIAM A. (BILL), *guitar*; b. Los Angeles, Ca., 9/24/49. Self-taught. Infl. by many classical guitarists, composers and jazz musicians. Pl. w. Mike Nock, '72 in SF, S. Swallow, '73 in SF. Traveled w. C. Corea, '74, incl. European tour.

LPs: *Theme to the Guardian*, solo album (ECM); *Hymn of the Seventh Galaxy*, w. Corea (Polydor).

CONNORS, NORMAN (Norman Connor Jr.), *drums, composer*; also *percussion, vibes*; b. Phila., Pa., 3/1/47. Studied comp., theory, harmony at Settlement House in Phila.; percussion at Music City; vibes, drums, tympani w. Gilbert Stanton; private drum and perc. lessons from ages five to 15; at Temple Univ., '65-9; perc. major at Juilliard, '67-8. First insp. by Lex Humphries, he began prof. while in high school, gigging locally, sometimes w. own groups. To NYC, '66, were he pl. w. Marion Brown, Archie Shepp, Sun Ra, Sam Rivers, Jackie McLean, Carlos Garnett, Jack McDuff and Pharoah Sanders. In '72 he formed his own group, rec. and touring with it in the U.S. and abroad. Fest: NJF-NY, '73-74; Phila. '73-4; Berkeley; Howard U.; Montreux, '74; Pori; Paris; Berlin; Japan, '75. Infl: Roach, Blakey, T. Williams, E. Jones, Parker, Coltrane, M. Davis, Sanders, Hancock. Awarded grants from CAPS, '73; National Endowment For the Arts, '74. "Music, vocals and dance are all a part of the Norman Connors concept," he says. "Like a ritual." His comp. incl. *Spirit of a Pisces*, a work for dance; *Brazilian Sketches*, a filmscore; other comp., rec. w. his group: *The Dance of Magic; Black Lightnin'; Drums Around the World*. LPs: *Dance of Magic; Dark of Light; Love From the Sun; Slewfoot; Saturday Night Special* (Buddah); w. Sanders (Impulse); Garnett (Muse); Shepp; Rivers (Imp.).

CONOVER, WILLIS CLARK, JR., *broadcaster, concert producer, narrator, writer, editor*; b. Buffalo, N.Y., 12/18/20. From 1939 has broadcast jazz and classical popular music in Washington and Manhattan, most notably in his *Music USA* programs for the Voice of America, worldwide from December '54. Musicians in Eastern Europe and the USSR call him the source of their own jazz activities. Has traveled in more than 40 countries.

In the '40s Conover helped desegregate officially-segregated Washington: requiring that blacks be admitted, he assembled groups of musicians and presented them in local night-clubs. Began Saturday-midnight concerts at the Howard Theater. In '51 helped drummer Joe Timer organize a big band, which over several years performed in local clubs and on TV, then recorded an album for Brunswick. In Manhattan in the early '60s Conover and Lalo Schfrin rehearsed an all-star band, a precursor of the Thad Jones-Mel Lewis Orchestra. In '70 he and Bill Berry presented a new band at the Roosevelt Grill. When Berry left with the Merv Griffin Show for the West Coast, where he organized his L.A. Band, Al Cohn directed the New York Band; later Bill Watrous assumed its leadership.

Conover emceed the Newport Jazz Festivals for more than a decade beginning in '51. Produced and narrated the New Orleans International Jazz Festival of 1969. He has presented concerts at New York's Town Hall, Carnegie Hall, Avery Fisher Hall, and Whitney Museum, and was responsible for 30 concerts at the John F. Kennedy Center for the Performing Arts. In '69 he produced and narrated the White House concert celebrating Duke Ellington's 70th birthday. Established and chaired the jazz panel for the National Endowment for the Arts, raising the annual allotment for jazz to a quarter of a million dollars. Serves on the State Department Cultural Presentations subcommittee for jazz and on the board of trustees for the Berklee College of Music. At the U. of Maryland in the '70s conducted accredited summer courses in jazz appreciation for elementary and high school music-teachers.

Publ: *Lovecraft at Last* (Carrollton Clark, 1975), a memoir of his teenage association with the writer H. P. Lovecraft; editor of *Science-Fantasy Correspondent*, a literary journal.

COOK, HERMAN (JUNIOR),* *tenor sax*; b. Pensacola, Fla., 7/22/34. After leaving Horace Silver in '64, pl. w. Blue Mitchell in quintet through '69. In '70s was teacher at Berklee Coll. in Boston. Pl. w. Freddie Hubbard, '73-5. Pl. w. Elvin Jones; then free-lancing in NYC incl. gigs at Boomer's; also w. Keno Duke Contemporaries; George Coleman Octet; co-led quintet w. Louis Hayes, '75-6. LPs: w. Hubbard, *Keep Your Soul Together* (CTI); w. Mitchell, *The Thing to Do; Down With It; Bring It Home to Me* (BN); w. Barry Harris, *Luminescence*; w. Don Patterson, *Opus De Don* (Prest.).

COOPER, BOB,* *tenor saxophone*; also *all reeds, woodwinds*; b. Pittsburgh, Pa., 12/6/25. During '70s working in LA with big bands of Bill Holman, T. Vig, Ed Shaughnessy, T. Gibbs; also composed contemporary 12-tone woodwind quintet. Fests: Kansas City w. Ray Brown, Herb Ellis; Concord w. B. Kessel. Comps: *Sax Therapy*, for Shaughnessy band.

LP: w. Vig (Creative World).

COOPER, GEORGE (BUSTER),* *trombone*; b. St. Petersburg, Fla., 4/4/29. During '50s worked w. L. Hampton; 2 years w. B. Goodman; co-leader of Cooper Brothers quintet backing Josephine Baker at Olympia Theatre, Paris for one year. Traveled w. D. Ellington orch., '62-9, then moved back to St. Petersburg, formed quartet w. brother, bassist Steve Cooper. Began jazz class at New Coll., Sarasota, Fla. for one year. Moved to LA July '73, freelancing there with various bands and combos, incl. Ellington alumni groups. Toured S. Africa w. Monk Montgomery latter part of '74. Fests: Newport, Monterey, Colo. JP, Oslo etc.

LPs: *Triple Play*, w. J. Hodges; *The Popular Duke Ellington* (RCA); *Outskirts of Town* w. Prestige Blues Swingers; *Smooth Sailing* w. Arnett Cobb (Prestige); *Claude Bolling & Co.* w. Cat Anderson (Philips); *Swing's Our Thing* w. Hodges & Hines (Verve).

COOPER, JEROME, *drums, composer*; also *piano, percussion*; b. Chicago, Ill, 12/14/46. Studied w. Oliver Coleman, '58-63; Capt. Walter Dyett at Du Sable HS, '63-5; Loop Jr. Coll., '67-8. Worked w. Oscar Brown Jr. in Chi., '68; Rahsaan Roland Kirk, '70-1, incl. Euro. tour; Dizzy Reece in Paris & Italy; Noah Howard; Clifford Jordan, Paris; Lou Bennett, W. Africa, '70; Steve Lacy, France, Germany, NYC, '70-1; Robin Kenyatta, Italy, France, Virginia, '71-2; Art Ensemble of Chicago, Paris, '71; Alan Silva, Paris, NYC, '71-2; George Adams; Sam Rivers; Karl Berger, NYC, '73; Andrew Hill; Anthony Braxton, '74; Maurice McIntyre w. whom he had pl. in Chi. & Nashville, Tenn. in '68-9, again in NYC, '75. From '71 w. Revolutionary Ensemble w. Sirone, L. Jenkins, app. w. it several times at Five Spot, fall '75. He says, "In order to play multidirectional group improvised music there are certain basic concepts and ideas in which we had to develop: that there is no leader; that each individual is a leader in his or her own right; that all musical instruments are solo instruments in their own right. This creative music has gotten to the point, or should I say has always been religious music (Black Classical Music)."

Infl: Roscoe Mitchell, Art Blakey, Max Roach, Walter Dyett, Anthony Williams. TV: France w. R.R. Kirk; *Today* w. Chad Mitchell. Fest: Berlin, '71; Ann Arbor, '73. Comp: *Positive-Negative; Reaction; Invasion; Chinese Rock.* LPs: w. Revolutionary Ensemble (India Navigation, ESP, Re, A&M); w. S. Lacy (Futura); A. Silva (Byg); C. Thornton (Bates); A. Braxton (Arista).

COPELAND, RAY M.,* *trumpet, fluegelhorn, composer*; b. Norfolk, Va., 7/17/26. Concerts at Univ. of California w. Randy Weston sextet in fall '66; lectured and performed w. Marian McPartland in Suffolk County public school concerts '68-69. Toured Africa w. Weston for US State Dept. Jan.-April '67, Europe w. T. Monk Nov. '68, Morocco w. Weston May '70, Europe, incl. Rumania, Yugoslavia w. *Musical Life of Charlie Parker* Oct.-Nov. '74. NJF w. Weston '73. Broadway show credits: *No, No, Nanette* '70, *Two Gentlemen of Verona* '72 incl. cast albums. Pl. History of Jazz concerts w. Orch. Da Camera in Nassau & Suffolk County schools '71-73; for International Art of Jazz in same school system '72-74. Active as adjudicator and clinician Villanova U. '72, in Pa. and Del. high schools '73-74; as teacher Pratt Inst. '68, Wilmington (Del.) School of Music & N.J. high school system '73, Jazzmobile Workshop, Fordham U. '74. His *Classical Jazz Suite in Six Movements* premiered at Lincoln Center Mar. '70. *The Ray Copeland Method and Approach to the Creative Art of Jazz Improvisation* pub. by Kaercea Music Enterprises, Inc. (110-21 195th St., St. Albans, N.Y., 11412), has been demonstrated by its author at the New York Conf. for Brass Scholarships and other mus. educ. conclaves '74. Stud. soundtrack, clicktrack writing and scoring for films. LPs: w. Weston, *African Cookbook* (Atlantic); *Tanjah* (Polydor); *Gloria Coleman Sings & Swings Organ* (Mainstream).

CORCORAN, GENE PATRICK (CORKY),* *tenor sax*; also *clarinet, English horn*; b. Tacoma, Wash., 7/28/24. Rejoined H. James '74 after an illness had kept him away from the band for which he first went to work in 1949. He no longer plays in the sax section but is feat. as a soloist. When James is not working, Corcoran fronts his own small combos in Las Vegas. App. at NJF-NY w. James, '74; concert with own group at N.Y. Jazz Museum, '74.

LPs: *Something*, w. own small group (RCS); *Everywhere*, w. own big band (C.C.); *In A Relaxed Mood*, w. James (Dot).

COREA, ARMANDO ANTHONY (CHICK),* *piano, composer*; also *organ, synthesizer*; b. Chelsea, Mass., 6/12/41. After working as a sideman in the first half of the '60s w. Mongo Santamaria, Willie Bobo, Blue Mitchell and Herbie Mann, he started to lead his own gps. for rec. and in-person performances. In '68 he became associated w. Miles Davis, adding textural layers on a variety of electric keyboards as well as on acoustic piano, for such albums as *In A Silent Way; Bitches' Brew, Live at the Fillmore East* and *Live/Evil.*

In '70 formed Circle with Anthony Braxton, Dave Holland and Barry Altschul but by late '71 was w. the Stan Getz quartet. With Stanley Clarke and Airto from the Getz group he formed Return to Forever along w. Airto's wife, Flora Purim and Joe Farrell in '72, touring Japan in that year. In '73 Bill Connors, Lenny White and percussionist Mingo Lewis joined the group with Clarke as the only holdover. It became more electrified, rock-oriented at a high decibel level and increasingly popular. Bob Stein wrote: "Necessarily the writing is less delicate than that on the earlier Return to Forever albums, but it is still bright despite the cumbersome additions of much electronic equipment."

On the other hand as a solo pianist and composer Corea has been described by Joachim Berendt as "the romanticist of the contemporary jazz piano, not only as a pianist, but also as a composer. Critics have compared his affable piano pieces with the nineteenth century piano music of Schumann, Mendelssohn, Schubert, or Rubenstein—but failed to notice the imminent tension with which Corea 'fills' his romanticism. This 'filling' of romanticism with tension is, in many ways, a real challenge to the music in the seventies."

For many years Corea has been involved in the study of Scientology. He feels it has helped increase his awareness in all aspects of life, including music.

TV: *Rock Concert*, PBS. Fest: many international fests., incl. Montreux, and tours; NJF-NY '73-4. Publ: *Forever Songbook, Vol. 1* (Litha Music, 146 Manetto Hill Rd., Huntington, N.Y. 11743).

Awards: Jazzman of the Year; Pianist of the Year, *Swing Journal*, '72; *Piano Improvisations*, Album of the Year, *Swing Journal*, '72. DB Readers poll, composer, '73-4; piano, '73; electric piano, '75; DB Critics poll, composer, TDWR, '73. Return to Forever won Album of the Year from *Swing Journal*, '72; *Jazz Forum*; NY *Times*, '73.

Comp: *Spain; La Fiesta; Sometime Ago; 500 Miles High; Song For Thad; Song For Lee Lee; A New Place; Departure From Planet Earth; Windows; Gemini; I Don't Know; Samba Yanta; Bossa; Steps-What Was; Matrix; Now He Sings, Now He Sobs; Now He Beats the Drum, Now He Stops; The Law of Falling and Catching Up; Straight Up and Down; Tones For Joan's Bones; Litha; Guijira; Crystal Silence; Children's Song; What Games Shall We Play Today; Señor Mouse; Desert Air; Trio For Flute, Bassoon and Piano.*

LPs: *Hymn of the Seventh Galaxy; Light As a Feather; Where Have I Known You* (Poly.); *Return to Forever*; w. Circle, *Paris Concert* (ECM); *Circle 1&2* (CBS-Sony); *Is; Now He Sings, Now He Sobs* (SS); *Circling In* (BN); *Inner Space* (Atl.); *Piano Improvisations Vols. 1&2* (ECM); *Sundance* (Gr. Merch.); w. Gary Burton, *Crystal Silence* (ECM); *Jazz For a Sunday Afternoon* (SS); w. Getz, *Captain Marvel*; w. Davis (Col.); Joe Farrell (CTI).

CORYELL, LARRY, *guitar, composer, singer, leader*; b. Galveston, Tex., 4/2/43. Family moved to state of Washington when he was seven. Began playing in rock and roll gp. at 15. Did some private studying but mostly self-taught. Worked in Seattle. Moved to NYC '65 and joined Chico Hamilton. Played w. Free Spirits, an early jazz-rock fusion, and then toured w. Gary Burton, '67-8. Pl. briefly w. Herbie Mann, '69, before forming own gp. called Foreplay w. Steve Marcus and Mike Mandel. He also rec. an album, *Spaces*, w. John McLaughlin, Chick Corea, Miroslav Vitous and Billy Cobham. Formed The Eleventh House in '73, traveling extensively incl. four European concert tours. and one in Japan, Feb. '74. In Sept. '75 pl. acoustic solo concert w. Steve Khan at Carnegie Hall. Steve Lake, writing in *Melody Maker*, said: "To describe Coryell the guitarist as merely agile or inventive would be to do him a serious disservice. He is amazing. Truly everyman's guitarist, able to suggest shades of Montgomery, Hendrix, Reinhardt and Shankar in less time than it takes to say it, and always sounding like himself anyway . . ."

Fest: NJF-NY '73-4; in '73 fest. also pl. in blues set at Radio City jam session. Comp: *The Restful Mind; Ann*

Arbor; After Later; Lady Coryell; Foreplay; Scotland I; Birdfingers; Low-Lee-Tah; Theme For a Dream.

LPs: *Level One* (Arista); *The Restful Mind; Introducing the Eleventh House; Real Great Escape; Offering; Spaces; Lady Coryell; At the Village Gate; Coryell* (Vang.); *Barefoot Boy* (Fly. Dutch.); *Fairyland* (Mega); w. H. Mann, *Memphis Underground* (Atl.); w. G. Burton, *Duster; In Concert* (RCA); w. C. Hamilton, *The Dealer* (Imp.).

COSBY, WILLIAM H. JR. (BILL), *percussion*; b. Philadelphia, Pa., 7/12/37. The TV personality, though not a prof. musician, has led jazz and r & b groups in occasional club and fest. apps, usually billing himself as Bunions Bradford Funeral and Marching Band. Comps: *Camille; Train to Memphis.* LP: *Bill Cosby Really Sings* (Partee).

COVA, ALYRIO LIMA, *percussion*; b. Salvador-Bahia, Brazil, 12/18/49. Started pl. accordion at age six for three years, then percussion in religious ceremonies. Moved to Rio de Janeiro, '61 and began pl. regular drums. Mus. educ: Pro-Art School of Music, Rio, '69-70; Inst. River, Rio, '71-2; Brazilian Sinfonic Dept. of Teaching, '72-3; Berklee Coll., Boston, '74; New England Conserv. of Mus., '74-5. While in Rio pl. Brazilian music initially, then switched to jazz-rock and avant garde. Experiments with different sounds. During '68-71 pl. with American group, Soma. To U.S., '73 and pl. w. Webster Lewis ensemble. In Dec. '74 he joined Weather Report, touring the U.S. and Europe.

Cova is a graduate from IBM school in computer systems and analysis and also grad. Brazilian Inst. of Art in Composition of Media. He worked for two years at the Brazilian Center of Physics and Aero-space development. Infls: Harry Partch; Lalo Schifrin; John Coltrane; Wayne Shorter; J. Zawinul; Miles Davis et al. Many TV progs. in Brazil, both jazz and educ.

LPs: w. Weather Report, *Tale Spinnin'* (Col.); *Avisk Grapoc*, w. Morocco Art Ensemble (Nat'l Rec. of Morocco).

COVINGTON, WARREN,* *trombone, leader, arranger, singer*; b. Philadelphia, Pa., 8/7/21. Cont. to lead his own orchs., using different personnel, in six areas: New York, Wilmington, Del., Champaign, Ill., Denton, Tex., Austin, Tex. and Springfield, Mo., utilizing college bands such from North Texas St. and the Univ. of Texas. Toured England for 22 concerts in March '74 with a nostalgia package of his own design feat. former big band players such as Pee Wee Erwin, Chris Griffin, Bernie Privin, Johnny Mince, Skeets Herfurt and Sy Oliver. The Tommy Dorsey orientation was further emphasized by Oliver's wife Lil Clark, one of the orig. Clark Sisters, who sang lead with Covington and the Pied Pipers. Also active as studio mus. in NYC and as jingle contractor for Glenn Osser; member of NYJRC '74 season. Planning Warren Covington Supper Club East in Ocean City, Md. fall '75. Movies: sound track work for *Barbarella; Everything You Wanted to Know About Sex*; and *The Godfather.* Publ: *Sentimental Trombone, Toy Trombone, Tipsy Trombone* (Belwyn-Mills, Lynbrook, L.I., N.Y.). LPs: *Hits of the 60's* (Re-Car); own band and w. Jo Stafford & the Pied Pipers (Readers Digest); Freddie Hubbard; George Benson (CTI); Allman Bros. (Capricorn); Perry Como (RCA Victor).

COWELL, STANLEY A., *piano, composer*; also *organ, kalimba*; b. Toledo, Ohio, 5/5/41. Took up piano at four. Art Tatum pl. at his house two yrs. later. Studied piano w. Emil Danenberg; comp. w. Richard Hoffman at Oberlin, BM '62; Mozarteum Academy, Salzburg, Austria, '60-1; U. of Wichita, '62-3; comp. w. Ingolf Dahl, USC, '63-4. MM in Piano, U. of Mich. '66. As a teenager sat in w. Yusef Lateef. While at Oberlin worked w. R.R. Kirk; at USC w. Curtis Amy, Ray Crawford in LA. Worked w. bassist Ron Brooks trio in Ann Arbor, Mich.; w. Charles Moore's Detroit Contemporary Four. Played w. R.R. Kirk; Gene McDaniels, '66; Marion Brown, '66-7; Max Roach, '67-70; Miles Davis; Herbie Mann, '68; Bobby Hutcherson-Harold Land, '68-71; Stan Getz, '69; Music Inc. w. Charles Tolliver, '69-73. Gloria Lynne, '70; subbing w. Thad Jones-Mel Lewis from '70; Donald Byrd, '73; Clifford Jordan from '74; Sonny Rollins, '74-5; Heath Bros. quartet from '75.

At age 14 feat. soloist w. Toledo Youth Orch.; feat. soloist w. American Youth Symph., Santa Monica, Cal., '64; composer-performer in *New Detroit*, for double sextet and flute, premiered at U. of Mich. Creative Arts Fest., '67. As accompanist for Max Roach and Abbey Lincoln, he was also panelist at Int. Fest. of Mus., Shiraz, Iran, '69. Has toured in most European countries; Africa; Brazil and Japan. Founder and organizer of the Piano Choir from '71; incorporator and founding member of Collective Black Artists, Inc. Conducted CBA Ensemble, '73-4. From '72 president of Strata-East Records, musician-owned label. A musical dir. of NYJRC, '74. Consultant for Oberlin Coll. Afro-American Mus. Studies curriculum, '71-2.

"Listening to his stride work on Marion Brown's *Spooks*, his free, rockish contributions to the *DeJohnette Concept*, or his thick-textured, straight-ahead work within Gary Bartz' *Another Earth*, one realizes the wide scope of Cowell's musicianship," wrote Michael Cuscuna in '69. His contributions in the '70s have served to illustrate his continuing maturity and versatility.

Infl: Tatum, Ellington, Cecil Taylor, McCoy Tyner. TV: taped half-hour w. Piano Choir in Boston for NET. Fest: NJF-NY; Antibes; Pori; Molde; Montreux; Japan.

Won DB Critics Poll, TDWR, '70. CAPS grant for comp., '73. Comp: *Conversation for Nine Instruments; Sonata for Piano; Illusion Suite; Killers; Departure #1; Abstrusions; Effi; Equipoise; Abscretions; Brilliant Circles; Blues For the Viet Cong; Wedding March; Stealin' Gold.* LPs: w. own trio, *Blues For the V.C.* (Poly.); *Stanley Cowell* (Byg); *Illusion Suite* (ECM); solo, *Musa/Ancestral Dreams* (Strata-East); w. own sextet, *Brilliant Circles* (Arista); w. C. Tolliver's Music Inc., *Live at the Domicile* (Enja); *The Ringer* (Arista); *Music Inc.; Live in Tokyo; Live at Slugs* (Strata-East); w. Hutcherson, *Now* (BN); w. DeJohnette; Bartz (Mile.); Roach, *Members Don't Get Weary* (Atl.); Marion Brown, *Three For Shepp*; (Imp.), *Why Not* (ESP); duo w. Dave Burrell, *Questions/Answers* (Trio); w. The Piano Choir, *Handscapes*; w. C. Jordan, *Glass Bead Games*; w. Mtume, *Alkebu-Lan* (Str.-East); w. Oliver Nelson at Montreux (Fly. Dutch.).

COX, IDA,* *singer*; b. Knoxville, Tenn., 1889. A successful blues recording artist from 1923, Cox in the '40s went into semi-retirement, returning to record an album for Riverside in '61. After a long illness she died 11/10/67 in her home town. She is well remembered for a recording date produced by John Hammond in '39 for which she was acc. by Ch. Christian, James P. Johnson, Hot Lips Page and Edmond Hall among others. She is heard on one track on *From Spirituals To Swing* (Vanguard).

CRANSHAW, MELBOURNE R. (BOB),* *bass, bass guitar*; also *piano, drums*; b. Evanston, Ill., 12/10/32. Played w. the MJT+3 in '50 and came w. it to NYC in '60. Worked w. Sonny Rollins; Carmen McRae; Joe Williams; Junior Mance in early '60s. Active in NY studios from mid-'60s and has performed w. Bobby Scott; Quincy Jones; Charles Aznavour; Mary Lou Williams; Billy Taylor. Toured in Europe and Japan w. Ella Fitzgerald and Oscar Peterson. Reunited for gigs w. Rollins in '70s. Own trio, pl. at Hopper's, Greenwich Village, '75. Rec. soundtracks for *Anderson Tapes, The Pawnbroker* w. Q. Jones. TV: David Frost show w. B. Taylor orch.; *Sesame Street, Electric Company*, NET, from their inception; *Saturday Night Live*, NBC. Theater: *Jesus Christ, Superstar; Sergeant Pepper*. Fest: NJF-NY w. Taylor, '72; house bassist for Prestige artists at Montreux '73; Montreux and other Euro. fests. w. Rollins, '74. One of the top acoustic bassists, Cranshaw is also one of the few to transcend many of the negative characteristics of the electric bass. LPs: *Gene Ammons and Friends at Montreux*; w. Dexter Gordon, *Blues a la Suisse* (Prest.); w. S. Rollins, *The Cutting Edge*, (Mile.); w. H. Silver (BN); J. Moody (Vang.); B. Rich (Gr. Mer.); B. Taylor (Bell); J. McDuff (Cadet); E. Garner (Lond.).

CRAWFORD, BENNIE ROSS JR. (HANK),* *alto sax*; also *piano, tenor, baritone sax, composer*; b. Memphis, Tenn., 12/21/34. Continued to lead his blues-oriented small band in the US, Canada, Europe and Japan. Fest. apps. at Monterey, Amsterdam, London, Munich, Berlin, Copenhagen, Stockholm, Honolulu, Tokyo. Film: *Appelez-Moi Lise*, Montreal. TV: *Black Omnibus*, LA; *Black Journal*, NYC. Comps: *Jana; Groovy Junction; Dig These Blues; Stoney Lonesome*. LPs: *Help Me Make It Through the Night; We Got A Good Thing Going; Wildflower; Don't You Worry Bout A Thing* (Kudu); *Mr. Blues Plays Lady Soul; After Hours; the Art of; the Best of* (Atlantic).

CREACH, JOHN (PAPA JOHN), *violin, singer*; b. Beaver Falls, Pa., 5/28/17. One of ten children, he started on violin in 1928. To Chicago in '34, stud. w. symph. musicians. Spent seven yrs. touring midwest and Canada with a trio called The Chocolate Music Bars. In early '40s began playing pop music in cocktail lounges. Also traveled around Tennessee and Mississippi w. Roy Milton and other r & b gps.

In '43 he began pl. electric violin. Two years later, Creach moved to Cal. and started a new trio, working Palm Springs and Newport Beach. For seven years he pl. with a gp. called The Shipmates on the S.S. *Catalina*, traveling between LA and Catalina Island. From '68-70 he was a resident at the Parisian Room in LA.

Early in '70, through a friendship with Joey Covington, who had become the drummer w. Jefferson Airplane, he rec. with that group in SF and in Oct. '70 became a regular member. Soon afterward, he also began to rec. and tour w. Hot Tuna, a spinoff gp. Under the auspices of the Airplane, Creach formed his own combo, Zulu, later known as Midnight Sun. He continued to rec. and perf. w. the Airplane.

Despite his strong rock associations in recent years, Creach is an accomplished jazz violinist; in addition, he is given to sentimental interpretations of such songs as *Danny Boy*. His albums display him in an exceptionally broad cross section of styles.

LPs: *I'm the Fiddle Man* (Buddah); *Filthy!; Playing My Fiddle For You; Papa John Creach*; others w. Jefferson Airplane; Hot Tuna (all on Grunt).

CRISS, WILLIAM (SONNY),* *alto, soprano saxophones*; b. Memphis, Tenn., 10/23/27. Leader and sideman in LA during late '40s and '50s; Europe, '62-5. Continuing to freelance in LA, he devoted much of his time from '70-4 to working with children, welfare recipients, alcoholics and drug addicts, offering a series of concerts for young people during the Hollywood Bowl summer program, '71-2. He received an award for his contribution to and influence on the youth of So. LA. During '73 he was in Europe, pl. concerts, radio, TV. On returning to U.S., continued pl., teaching and lecturing, but returned to continent in '74, headquartering in Paris and touring Italy. In '75 he recorded for Xanadu and Muse labels, his first albums in several years; then signed w. Impulse. Fests: Newport, '68.

LPs: *Up, Up & Away; This Is Criss; Rocking In Rhythm; Sonny's Dream; The Beat Goes On; Portrait of Sonny Criss; I'll Catch The Sun* (Prest.); *Crisscraft* (Muse); *Saturday Morning* (Xanadu).

CROMBIE, ANTHONY JOHN (TONY),* *drums, composer*; b. London, England, 8/27/25. Led many bands from '54 in Britain, Israel; numerous Euro. tours w. jazz and pop artists, incl. Tony Bennett, Jack Jones. Acc. C. Hawkins, B. Webster, J. Witherspoon, J.J. Johnson et al for their apps. at Ronnie Scott's Club. Own group on BBC Jazz Club. Crombie comps. incl. *So Near So Far*, rec. by Miles Davis; *Debs Delight*, rec. by P. Gonsalves; *Child's Fancy*, rec. by R. Nance; *That Tune; Restless Girl*, rec. by S. Grappelli. Extensive TV writing, incl. background mus. for series, *Man from Interpol*, which was rec. on Top Rank label.

CROSBY, GEORGE ROBERT (BOB),* *singer, leader*; b. Spokane, Wash., 8/23/13. Younger brother of Bing

Crosby. Led dixieland oriented swing band '35-42. Since then, has reappeared frequently leading groups of various sizes from small Bob Cats combo to full ensemble in the style of the orig. orch., incl. many apps. at Disneyland, '60s and '70s. Concerts throughout U.S. in '72, '73, '74 as part of Big Band Cavalcade. NJF-NY '75 w. Bobcats. Comps: *Until; Silver and Gold; March of the Bob Cats; The Wonderful World of You.* LPs: *Live at the Rainbow Grill; Mardi Gras Parade* (Monmouth Evergreen); *Big Band Cavalcade* (RCA); also *Swinging Years* series for Readers Digest LP project.

CROUCH, STANLEY, *drums, poet, critic, composer, educator*; b. Los Angeles, Calif., 12/14/45. Cousin, Sam Crouch, pl. keyboards; another cousin, Andre Crouch, important in black gospel music. Eight weeks of piano lessons as child; half a semester of theory in high school; essentially self-taught. Began pl. in '66. Worked w. LA underground pianist Raymond King. Pl. at Watts Summer Fest., '67, w. Owen Marshall, King and Black Arthur. Started co-op gp., The Quartet, '67, which later incl. Black Arthur, Bobby Bradford. Gp. name changed to Stanley Crouch and Black Music Infinity: flutist James Newton, bassist Mark Dresser and tenor saxist David Murray came into band. Recorded, adding Bradford, David Baker, Charles Tyler, '73. Premiered his *Ellington Suite* at Pomona Coll., Nov. '74. To NYC '75, pl. w. Dresser and Murray in latter's trio. Infl: Mingus, Ellington, Monk, O. Coleman, Sunny Murray, Milford Graves, Roach, Blakey, Ed Blackwell. Has "developed a style based on bent and sustained tones and exceptional textural variety in hopes of moving drums as far as Ayler took the saxophone."

Crouch's book of poetry, *Ain't No Ambulances For No Nigguhs Tonight* was publ. in '70. Worked as a playwright and actor under Jayne Cortez, '65-7. Taught at Claremont Coll., '69-75 as instructor in drama, literature, jazz history. Articles for *Players Magazine; Village Voice.* Comp: *Future Sallie's Time; Chicago For Bobby Seale; The Confessions of Father None; Flying Through Wire; Attica in Black September; Noteworthy Lady.* LPs: *Now Is Another Time; Past Spirits*, which he plans to release as bicentennial underground note.

CRUSADERS. Formerly Jazz Crusaders. see Hooper, Stix.

CUBER, RONALD EDWARD (RONNIE), *baritone sax*; also *soprano sax, flute, bass clarinet*; b. Brooklyn, N.Y., 12/25/41. Father pl. accordion; mother piano. Studied clarinet at age nine; tenor sax at Alexander Hamilton H.S. Auditioned on tenor for Marshall Brown's Newport Youth Band. There were too many tenors but he was given the baritone chair, '59. Played w. Maynard Ferguson, '63-5; George Benson, '66-7; Lionel Hampton, '68; Woody Herman, '69, incl. Euro. tour; White Elephant, '70-1; King Curtis and Aretha Franklin, '71-2. Working w. Eddie Palmieri from '72; Bobby Paunetto from '75. Much studio work in '70s for which he studied flute w. Danny Bank, '72; took up bass clarinet. A hard-swinging soloist with a big, cutting sound. Infl: Hank Mobley, Coltrane, Harold Land, Pepper Adams, Cecil Payne. Fest: NJF w. Newport Youth Band; Ferguson; Herman. Has written arrs. for Palmieri. Won DB Critics' Poll, TDWR, '66.

LPs: *The George Benson Cookbook; It's Uptown* w. Benson; *Spirituals to Swing*, 1967, tracks w. Benson (Col.); *Willow Weep For Me*, reissue of material from first two Benson LPs (French CBS); w. Ferguson (Main); *Paunetto's Point* w. Paunetto (Pathfinder).

CULLAZ, ALBERT (ALBY), *bass*; b. Paris, France, 5/25/41. Brother is guitarist Pierre Cullaz; father music critic-producer, Maurice Cullaz. Took up bass at 17. Pl. in France and throughout continent w. Jean-Luc Ponty, Johnny Griffin, D. Gordon, Eddy Louiss, S. Grappelli, Philly Joe Jones, Walter Davis Jr., Rene Urtreger, René Thomas, D. Gillespie, Art Taylor, H. Mobley, S. Hampton, Kenny Clarke et al. Won Django Reinhardt Jazz Academy prize, '72.

LPs: w. Michel Graillier Trio (Saravatt); w. Mobley (BN); Jef Gilson (SFP); Jean Bonal Free Sound (PES).

CULLAZ, PIERRE, *guitar*; also *cello*; b. Paris, France, 7/21/35. Brother of Alby Cullaz (see above). Took up guitar in '49. Worked w. Michel Hausser, Art Simmons in late '50s; Eddy Louiss, '64-5; Guitars Unlimited, '65-7; Claude Bolling and other big bands. Mus. for films w. M. Legrand. A versatile soloist equally at home in contemporary classical and jazz settings.

LPs: w. Andre Persiany, *Swinging Here and There; Andre Persiany Plays Count Basie* (Pathe-Marconi); w. S. Vaughan-Q. Jones (Mercury); Guitars Unlimited (Barclay); w. Sir Charles Thompson; Buck Clayton (Vogue); Guy Lafitte (Musidisc).

CURNOW, ROBERT, *composer, arranger, trombone, bass, piano*; b. Easton, Pa., 11/1/41. Extensive studies at Mich. State U., '64-7; arr. and comp. w. Russ Garcia and Johnny Richards, '61-3; trombone w. Buddy Baker. Toured w. S. Kenton for nine months in '63. Later gigged w. L. Hampton, Warren Covington, B. Goodman, Sammy Davis et al. Spent much time cond. coll. bands, incl. jazz ensemble at Notre Dame, '64-70.

Curnow is best known as a writer with Kenton, for whom he arranged such LPs as the double set of 38 national anthems, '72; *Kenton Plays Chicago*, '74, and *7.5 On The Richter Scale* (Creative World). He was appointed producer for many Kenton albums, and was general manager and director of a & r for Kenton's Creative World Records office. Infls: J.J. Johnson, F. Rosolino, Bill Harris, Bill Holman. Curnow is a distinguished educator with many scholastic honors to his credit.

CURSON, THEODORE (TED),* *trumpet, piccolo trumpet, fluegelhorn*; b. Philadelphia, Pa., 6/3/35. Spent much time in Europe during late '60s and early '70s pl. concerts, clubs and esp. fests. all over the continent. Member of the Schauspielhaus theatre orch., Zurich, '73 where he pl. in perf. of *Marat/Sade* and *Threepenny Opera.* Clubs in Paris and NYC w. Chris Woods, Andrew Hill, Lee Konitz, Kenny Barron, Nick Brignola. Pl. and lectured at campuses of U. of Cal.; Vallekilde Mus.

Ornette Coleman (*David D. Spitzer*)

Larry Coryell (*Vervl Oakland*)

Ted Curson

Andrew Cyrille (*Veryl Oakland*)

Richard Davis (*David D. Spitzer*)

Miles Davis (*Veryl Oakland*)

George Duke (*Veryl Oakland*)

Harry "Sweets" Edison and Plas Johnson (*Veryl Oakland*)

Eddie "Lockjaw" Davis (*Veryl Oakland*)

Paul Desmond (*CTI Records*)

Raul De Souza (*Milestone Records*)

Jerry Dodgion (*David D. Spitzer*)
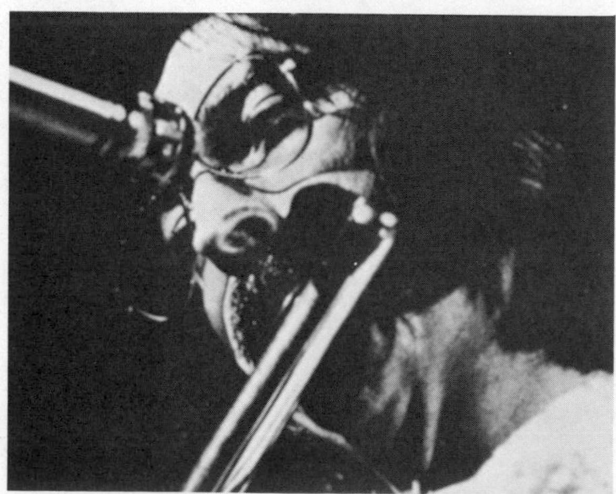

Bill Evans (*Veryl Oakland*)

Teddy Edwards (*Veryl Oakland*)

Don Ellis (*Veryl Oakland*)

Joe Farrell (*CTI Records*)

Herb Ellis (*Veryl Oakland*)

Duke Ellington (*Veryl Oakland*)

Mercer Ellington (*Rolf Zieger*)

Maynard Ferguson (*David D. Spitzer*)

Leonard Feather, Dizzy Gillespie and Mundell Lowe
(*Ray Avery's Rare Records*)

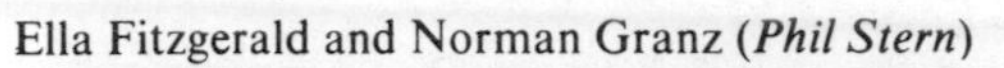

Ella Fitzgerald and Norman Granz (*Phil Stern*)

Sonny Fortune (*Veryl Oakland*)

Carl Fontana and Jake Hanna (*Veryl Oakland*)

Curtis Fuller (*David D. Spitzer*)

Stan Getz (*David D. Spitzer*)

Carlos Garnett (*Veryl Oakland*)

Slim Gaillard and Slam Stewart (*Veryl Oakland*)

Larry Gales (*Veryl Oakland*)

Sch., Denmark; and U. of Vermont. Sponsored first U.S. app. of Arne Domnerus group from Sweden, NYC, winter '74. Won New Star Award DB Critics Poll '66; first foreign musician to be awarded grant from Finnish govt. at Pori Fest. '73. Wrote music (*Tears for Dolphy*) for film *Teorama*; app. in film, *Notes for a Film on Jazz* w. G. Barbieri, Aldo Romano; TV apps: *Jazz Set* (U.S.); *Live From Club Severine* (France); Pori Int. Jazz Fest. Band (Finland). Comps: *Typical Ted; The Leopard; Sugar 'N Spice; Reava's Waltz; Airi's Tune; Cracklin' Bread.* Publ: *The New Thing: Nine Originals By Ted Curson*, book of piano arrs. (Nosruc Pub., 130 Arlington Ave., Jersey City, N.J. 07305). LPs: *Tears for Dolphy* (Fontana); *Ode to Booker Ervin* (EMI); *Cattin' Curson; Pop Wine* (Futura); *Ted Curson Meets Blue Sun* (CBS Denmark); *Quicksand* (Atl.); *Urge*, w. Ervin (Fontana).

CURTIS, KING (Curtis Ousley), *saxophones, composer*; b. Fort Worth, Tex., 1935. Played w. Lionel Hampton; rec. w. Nat Adderley, Wynton Kelly, but was mainly known as a major r & b figure, acc. many singers. He was mus. dir. of a TV series *Soul*, for which he wrote the theme *Soulful 13.* Other comps: *Soul Serenade; Instant Groove; Memphis Soul Stew.* Curtis died 8/14/71 of stab wounds suffered in a fight with a man in front of a building owned by Curtis in NYC.

LPs: *Jazz Groove* (Prestige); *King Curtis Live at Fillmore West* (Atl.); *King Curtis & Jack Dupree Blues at Montreux* (Atl.).

CUTSHALL, ROBERT DEWEES (CUTTY),* *trombone*; b. Huntington County, Pa., 12/29/11. Best known for early work with Benny Goodman, later regular job for many years w. Eddie Condon, gigs w. Peanuts Hucko et al, Cutshall was an original member of the group organized in Denver as The Nine Greats of Jazz, which soon evolved into the World's Greatest Jazzband; but before the latter group was to make its first album, Cutshall, while working with Condon in Toronto, died 8/16/68 of a heart attack. His exceptional, Teagarden-inspired work can be heard on a number of LPs w. Condon, as well as on dates w. Wild Bill Davison, Yank Lawson, Geo. Wettling, Boyce Brown.

CYRILLE, ANDREW CHARLES, *drums*; b. Brooklyn, N.Y., 11/10/39. Stud. w. Lennie McBrowne and others, '52-7; matriculated at Juilliard, '58; Stud. briefly w. Philly Joe Jones, '58; Tony Columbia, '67. Early exp. w. Nellie Lutcher, Roland Hanna, Illinois Jacquet, Olatunji, '59-61; Walt Dickerson, Bill Barron, Rahsaan Roland Kirk, '62-3. From '64-6 w. J. Giuffre, Cedar Walton et al.

Cyrille's most important assoc. has been w. Cecil Taylor, in whose unit he worked from '64, in addition to taking up many other duties intermittently, among them the following: '67, w. S. Turrentine; G. Bartz; J. Mance; Benny Powell; G. Moncur; '68-9, Ghanaian musician Joe Mensah; Voices Inc.; '70, own quintet; '71 formed perc. trio w. Milford Graves and Rashied Ali, Dialogue of the Drums; staff percussionist Wyandanch Jr. H.S., and Jazz Interactions teaching prog., artist-in-residence, Antioch Coll.; '71-3, comp., arr. and perf. w. 19 percussionists own comps. at Harlem Cultural Center in NYC; toured, perf. in Europe, Japan with C. Taylor; '74, perf. and was videotaped, concert of orig. works w. M. Graves, hosted radio prog. feat. music from around the world in NYC; '75, cont. to work w. Taylor; formed another band under own direction, Andrew Cyrille & MAONO.

Comps: *What About; Rhythmical Space; Rims and Things; The Soul Is The Music; Aural Coordination.* LPs: w. C. Hawkins, *The Hawk Relaxes*; w. Walt Dickerson, *Relativity* (Prest.); w. Bill Barron, *Hot Line* (Savoy); *Jazz Composers Orchestra* (JCOA); w. Marion Brown, *Afternoon of a Georgia Faun* (ECM); w. Cecil Taylor, *Conquistador* (Blue Note); w. Jimmy Lyons, *Lazy Afternoons*; w. Grachan Moncur, *New Africa*; own group, *What About* (all on BYG/Actuel); *Dialogue of the Drums* (IPS); own group, *Bulu Akisakila Kutala* (Trio Records).

DAHLANDER, NILS-BERTIL (BERT),* *drums*; b. Gothenburg, Sweden, 5/13/28. Divided his time between U.S. and Scandinavia from '54. From '66, living in Aspen, Colo., he played with small groups, worked w. Peanuts Hucko in Denver. To Finland, Sweden, '74, playing in Stockholm w. Alice Babs; house band in Swedish TV Jan. to May '75. Pl. Colo. JP several times in '60s, '70s.

DAILEY, ALBERT PRESTON (AL),* *piano, composer*; b. Baltimore, Md., 6/16/38. After pl. w. own trio at Bohemian Caverns in Wash., D.C., '63-4 came to NYC and worked w. D. Gordon; R. Haynes; H. Mobley; A. Farmer; S. Vaughan through '66. With Woody Herman; Art Blakey, '68-9; C. Mingus; Joe Williams; Betty Carter; Thad Jones-Mel Lewis in early '70s; Sonny Rollins, off and on, '70-3; Milt Jackson, '72-3; Stan Getz, '73-5; Blakey, '75. Received NEA Grant to write *Africa Suite* for voices and electronic instruments, '75. TV w. Getz; Herman. Fest: MJF w. Herman; NJF-NY '73-4; Euro. fests. w. Getz. Resourceful player whose compositional abilities show up in his solos.

Comp: *The Day After the Dawn; Bittersweet Waltz; Encounter; A Lady's Mistake.* LPs: *The Day After the Dawn* (Col.); w. Azar Lawrence (Prest.); Getz w. Joao Gilberto (Col.); F. Hubbard (Atl.); J. Williams w. Jones-Lewis (SS).

DALY, WARREN JAMES, *drums, composer*; b. Sydney, Australia, 8/22/46. Stud. w. several teachers in Sydney, Roy Burns in Honolulu, Bob Tilles in Chicago, Henry Adler in NYC. Started in rock during late '50s; switched to jazz in '65. Pl. w. Col Nolan trio in Sydney, '65; Bill Barratt big band, '66. After working as staff drummer on a Sydney TV station, he toured the U.S. in late '67 w. Kirby Stone Four, later working w. Si Zentner and Glenn

Miller orchestras, the latter under Buddy De Franco. Following tours with other U.S. bands, he returned to Australia in late '68, and in early '69, w. trombonist Ed Wilson (q.v.), he formed the Daly-Wilson big band. In '69-70, Daly also pl. in Don Burrows quartet in Sydney. During the next few years the Daly-Wilson orch. acquired great prestige domestically, touring Australia eight times, and was voted Band of the Year in '72 in Australia's *Music Maker* magazine poll.

In Oct. '75, after pl. engagements in the Soviet Union, the band app. in LV and at Donte's in N. Hollywood. Daly comp. and/or co-arr. w. Wilson many numbers for the band, incl. *W.D. and H.O. Blues; El Boro; My Goodness.*

LPs: *Live at the Cell Block* (EMI); *Featuring Kerrie Biddell* (Festival); *On Tour; Featuring Marcia Hines* (WB). All albums released in the U.S. on G.R.C. Elephant label. The band received a gold record award for *On Tour.*

D'ANDREA, FRANCO, *piano*; b. Merano, Italy, 3/8/41. Self-taught, first on trumpet, clarinet, sax. Piano at 17. Pl. w. Nunzio Rotondo, '63; Gato Barbieri, '64-5 and occasionally since then. Formed Modern Art Trio, '68; member of Perigeo group from '72. Numerous TV, fest. apps. in Italy, France etc. w. Charles Tolliver, Jean-Luc Ponty, Barbieri, et al. Radio, clubs and/or concerts with many U.S. musicians in Italy, incl. M. Roach, Dexter Gordon, Lucky Thompson, Slide Hampton, Hank Mobley, Frank Rosolino, Conte Candoli.

LPs: Some 35 albums, starting in '64 with L. Konitz, Johnny Griffin, Modern Art Trio, and several with Perigeo, incl. *Genealogia* (RCA). The Perigeo LP *Abbiamo Tutti Un Blues Da Piangere* won the Italian Discographical Critics' Prize, '73.

DANIELS, EDWARD KENNETH (EDDIE),* *saxophones, clarinets, flutes*; b. Brooklyn, N.Y. 10/19/41. From '66-73 w. T. Jones-M. Lewis orch., then w. Bobby Rosengarden band on Dick Cavett TV show, '72-4. Busy freelancer in TV and rec. work, NYC. Daniels, with a Master's degree in clarinet from Juilliard, has stud. classical flute since '67, and is highly proficient on alto, baritone and tenor saxes, the latter being his main instrument. An intense, fiery player reflecting the influences of Rollins and Coltrane. Won DB Critics' Poll, TDWR, '68, on clarinet. NJF-NY w. Rosengarden, '72; Radio City jam session, '73-4.

LPs: *A Flower For All Seasons* (Choice); *The Return of Don Patterson* (Muse); others w. Jones-Lewis (SS, BN).

DANISH RADIO BIG BAND. Founded in '64. Consists of five trumpets; five trombones; five saxes; and rhythm. First leader was Ib Glindemann. His main inspiration was Stan Kenton and an early highlight for the band was a concert w. Kenton as guest leader, '66. In '67 Gene Roland was staff arranger, and that fall Maynard Ferguson gave a concert with it.

From '68 many visiting musicians have performed or been associated w. the band incl: Ted Curson; Booker Ervin; Frank Foster; Art Farmer; Babs Gonzales; Johnny Griffin; Burton Greene; Slide Hampton; Joe Henderson; Jimmy Heath; Freddie Hubbard; Chuck Israels; Clifford Jordan; Lee Konitz; Yusef Lateef; Oliver Nelson; George Russell; Charlie Shavers; Lucky Thompson; Charles Tolliver; Clark Terry; Mary Lou Williams and Phil Woods; also Danish residents such as Kenny Drew; Dexter Gordon and Ben Webster; and Europeans such as Monica Zetterlund; Karin Krog; Alice Babs; Bengt Hallberg; Mike Gibbs; and Mike Westbrook.

Among the band's members are trumpeters Allan Botchinsky, Idrees Sulieman; trombonist Richard Boone; saxophonists Jasper Thilo, Bent Jaedig; pianist Ole Kock Hansen; bassist Niels Henning Orsted Pedersen; drummer Bjarne Rostvold; vibist Finn Ziegler; and percussionist Kasper Winding.

DANISH RADIO JAZZGROUP. Started in Oct. '61 w. nine musicians. Within next five yrs. expanded to 12. Led by bassist Erik Moseholm until '66 when he became producer on Danish radio. Saxophonist Ray Pitts took it over for a couple of yrs., followed by Palle Mikkelborg. From '73 pianist Torben Kjaer has been in charge.

The Radio Jazzgroup has pl. experimental jazz and given opportunities to Danish writers as well as arranger-composers such as Dollar Brand; Mike Gibbs; Graham Collier; Jan Johanssen; Bengt Hallberg; and George Russell. 45 Danish and 25 foreign arrs. had contributed to the repertory which consists of 600 pieces of music. 20 have been recorded on 3 LPs and one EP. The group has toured in Denmark, Poland and Germany. Personnel incl: Erik Tschenter, Lars Togeby, Poul Chr. Nielsen, trumpets; Peter Westh, Flemming Andreasen, trombones; Michael Hove, Bent Jaedig, Svend Baring, saxes; Thomas Clausen, piano; Torben Munk, guitar; Bo Stief, bass; Alex Riel, drums.

DANKWORTH, JOHN PHILIP WILLIAM,* *alto saxophone, clarinet, composer*; b. Woodford, London, England, 9/20/27. Continuing his career as a composer and arranger, Dankworth was involved with the following films as composer/music dir.: *Morgan; A Suitable Case For Treatment; The Idol*, '66; *Fathom; Accident; The Last Safari*, '67; *Salt & Pepper; The Magus; I Love You, I Hate You*, '68; *The Last Grenade*, '69; *Perfect Friday; The Engagement; 10 Rillington Place*, '70. TV: comp. themes for *Tomorrow's World; The Frost Report* for BBC-1, '66; *Pippa; The Helicopter; Ooh La La* for BBC-2, '68; *Bird's Eye View*, BBC-2, '69; *The Enchanted House*, Granada TV, '70; *The Canterbury Tales; The Open University*, BBC-2, '71. Other musical works: *Tom Sawyer's Saturday* for Farnham Fest., '67; many other classical and semi-classical works, incl. a piano concerto for small chamber orch. for Westminster Fest., '72.

Along with his studio work, Dankworth continued to record occasionally with specially assembled orchs., and to tour regularly with his wife, singer Cleo Laine (q.v.). His buoyant alto sax, exceptionally fluent clarinet, ingenious arrangements and occasional original lyrics contributed significantly to the success of their joint appearances, which incl. triumphant concerts in the U.S. from '72.

LPs: *Movies 'N' Me* (RCA); *Full Circle* (Philips); Johnny Dankworth-Billy Strayhorn (Roul.); w. Cleo Laine, *Live at Carnegie Hall; I Am A Song* (RCA); *Portrait* (Philips); as arr. on *A Beautiful Thing* (RCA).

DARENSBOURG, JOSEPH (JOE),* *clarinet, soprano sax*; b. Baton Rouge, La., 7/9/06. Veteran of F. Marable riverboat bands. 10 years w. Kid Ory, '44-54. World travels as member of Louis Armstrong combo, '61-4. Frequent gigs at Disneyland, '65-9. Led own band in LA '70-3; joined Legends of Jazz for concerts and tours, '73-5. Filmed movie of his life, in London, Aug. '74. During this time, pl. w. Chris Barber and several other trad. bands in England. Fests: Newport, Monterey, Sacramento, New Orleans and many in Europe.

LPs: *Hello Dolly* w. Armstrong (Kapp); *The Real Ambassadors*, w. Armstrong (Col.); w. Legends of Jazz (Crescent Jazz).

DARIN, ROBERT (BOBBY),* *singer*; b. Bronx, N.Y. 5/14/36. Many hit records from late 1950s, his version of *Mack the Knife* sold over two million records. Switched to folk/rock idiom in '71. Darin died in Los Angeles following open heart surgery 12/20/73. From the jazz standpoint, his best LP by far was *Darin Sings Ray Charles* (Atco).

DASEK, RUDOLF, *guitar, composer*; b. Prague, Czech., 8/27/33. Graduated from State Conserv. of Mus., Prague, '66. Pl. w. all conserv. ensembles. In '64 formed own trio w. G. Mraz, pl. regularly with Carmell Jones, Leo Wright, etc. Formed System Tandem, a duo w. reedman Jiri Stivin, '72. Infl: Keith Jarrett, Jim Hall. Fest: Bilzen; Nuremberg; Ost-West Fest., Altena; Ljubljana; Jazz Jamboree Warsaw; Prague; Pori; Balver Hohle, West Germany. Comp: series of folklore-inspired fashanks; *Burial Mounds; Blow!; Tandem; One, Two, Free*. LPs: *Fairytale for Beritka* w. own trio; *B & S* w. Slide Hampton and Vaclav Zahradnik Big Band; *Concert in Ljubljana* w. System Tandem; *5 Hits to Arrow* (Supraphon).

DASH, ST. JULIAN BENNETT,* *tenor sax*; b. Charleston, S.C., 4/9/16. Member of Erskine Hawkins orch. for many years off and on from 1938; later inactive in music except for reunion recording w. Hawkins and small combo date in early '70s on Master Jazz; also tour of Europe in late '72. Dash died in NYC 2/24/74. LP: w. J. Rushing, *Who Was It Sang That Song* (Master Jazz).

DAUNER, WOLFGANG,* *keyboards, synthesizer, composer*; also *trumpet, percussion*; b. Stuttgart, Germany, 12/30/35. With his own trio and quintet he app. at all the important German jazz fests. '67-70; tours with German all stars in S. America, '69; Asia, '71. Fest. apps. w. Jean-Luc Ponty, '70-1, L. Coryell, '72. Danish, Finnish, Swiss, Portuguese fests. '72-3; w. own quintet at Berlin Jazztage, '74. From '70 Dauner led radio jazz group in Stuttgart and has rec. with guest soloists such as C. Corea, Ponty, M. Urbaniak. He has conducted many workshops for children about creativity and improvisation in music, and in '74 had his own TV show, *Glotzmusik*, for children. Infl: John Cage. Won German Sounds poll, '72, '73. Comps: *Dream Talk; Dämmerung; Daunerashingen; Sketch Up And Downer; The Primal Scream; Yin*. LPs: *Free Action* (MPS); *Für . . .* (Calif); also several others on European labels.

DAVERN, JOHN KENNETH (KENNY),* *soprano sax, clarinet*; b. Huntington, L.I., N.Y., 1/7/35. Gigs w. Ruby Braff, At Nick's w. Pee Wee Erwin '60; own group At Nick's '61; Eddie Condon's all stars, one month w. Ted Lewis at Roseland '62; toured for a year w. Dukes of Dixieland and rec. for Columbia w. Clara Ward '63; pl. w. Wild Bill Davison, Bud Freeman, Shorty Baker in Toronto and at Metropole, Central Plaza, NYC '64. After leaving NYC w. Jackie Gleason entourage for Florida, pl. a month in Miami w. Phil Napoleon '65. From '65 through '68 alternated between the Ferryboat in Brielle, N.J. w. Dick Wellstood, Ed Hubble, and Gaslight Club (NYC) w. George Wettling, Charlie Queener. Cont. to work around NY metropolitan area '69-71. Five weeks in Durban, So. Africa as singer, New Orleans w. Wild Bill Davison '72. From '72-74 several apps. at Michael's Pub, NYC w. Wellstood; also Odessa, Texas Jazz Party, Dick Gibson's Colo. Jazz Party. Toured Europe w. Erwin, Hubble, etc. '74; Grande Parade du Jazz, Nice '73, '75; NYJRC concerts, Newport-NY JF '74-75. App. in film *The Hustler*; on Broadway in *Marathon '33*. Won DB Int. Critics Poll on sop. sax new star '73.

Davern, who switched his main concentration from clarinet to soprano in the late '60s, formed a corporate group w. Bob Wilber called Soprano Summit in '75.

LPs: *Soprano Summit* (World Jazz); w. Dick Wellstood (Seeds, Chiaroscuro); *The Music of Jelly Roll Morton* w. Dick Hyman (Columbia); *Jazz at the New School* (Chiaroscuro); Marva Josie-Earl Hines (Thimble).

DAVIS, CHARLES,* *baritone, soprano saxes, composer*; b. Goodman, Miss., 5/20/33. Heard with many NY gps., as well as w. his own quintet in the '60s, he later worked w. Elvin Jones and, for a time in '72, w. the Cedar Walton-Hank Mobley quintet called Artistry in Music. Free-lancing in NYC at Boomer's, etc. in mid-'70s. LPs: Strata-East; w. Walton-Mobley, *Breakthrough* (Cobble.); w. Kenny Dorham, *Memorial Album* (Xanadu); w. Roswell Rudd, *Numatik Swing Band* (JCOA); w. Archie Shepp, *Kwanza* (Imp.)

DAVIS, EDDIE (LOCKJAW),* *tenor sax*; b. New York City, 3/2/22. From 1966-73 the rough-toned, extrovert saxophonist was featured w. Count Basie. He also participated in European tours apart from the band, '68, '73, '74: '73 as part of Norman Granz troupe w. Ella Fitzgerald; '74 w. George Wein tour, *The Musical Life of Charlie Parker*. Moved to Las Vegas 1973. Pl. w. Zoot Sims at Jazz Medium in Chi., Feb. '75. Fests: NJF w. Basie, Fitzgerald; Cascais, Portugal '74; Nice.

LPs: *Love Calls* (RCA Victor); *Cookbook* (Prestige); *Ella Live at Newport, Carnegie Hall* (Columbia); others on many labels w. Basie (q.v.); *Basie Jam; Dizzy at Montreux* (Pablo).

DAVIS, JEFFREY HAYES (JEFF), *trumpet, fluegelhorn*; b. St. Albans, N.Y., 12/19/52. Grandfather, Ovie Alston, was trumpet player and singer w. Claude Hopkins. Mother, Jean Alston Davis, sang w. Alston band; still working NY area in mid-70s. Davis stud. at H.S., later earned BM at Berklee, where he pl. in Phil Wilson, Herb Pomeroy ensembles and stud. w. Wes Hensel, Gary Burton and Andy McGhee. Pl. jazz and lead trumpet w. L. Hampton, '72-4; lead trumpet w. W. Herman, '75, incl. apps. w. Caterina Valente, Tony Bennett.

DAVIS, MILES DEWEY,* *trumpet, fluegelhorn, composer, leader*; b. Alton, Ill., 5/25/26. The Herbie Hancock-Ron Carter-Tony Williams rhythm section that had been with Davis from '63, and saxophonist Wayne Shorter, who joined him late in '64, continued through to the fall of '68 when Chick Corea and Dave Holland replaced Hancock and Carter. This quintet, which had recorded *E.S.P.* in '65, made a series of albums in the following years that, like *E.S.P.*, used no standards, show tunes, etc. which up to then had always been part of the Davis repertoire. Most of the material came from within the group or were jazz originals like *Freedom Jazz Dance* by Eddie Harris, or *Gingerbread Boy* by Jimmy Heath. Both these songs were on *Miles Smiles*, recorded in '66. This was followed by *Sorcerer* and *Nefertiti*, both taped in '67. *Miles in the Sky*, done in '68, added George Benson's guitar for one number and was notable for Hancock's use of electric piano. In '68 *Filles De Kilimanjaro* again used electric piano by Hancock, on one session, and Chick Corea.

Hancock, Corea and Joe Zawinul all pl. electric keyboards on *In A Silent Way*, '69, and John McLaughlin was also present. The long pieces are dreamlike "head music" kind of a "soft rock" using some of the harmonic freedom engendered by the avant garde of the '60s.

With *Bitches' Brew*, rec. later in '69, he moved toward a harder, more electrified jazz-avant-rock expression and continued this trend with *A Tribute to Jack Johnson; Live at the Fillmore East*, '70; *Live-Evil*, '71; and *On the Corner*, '72. The attitude of Bill Cole, in his book *Miles Davis: A Musical Biography* (Wm. Morrow), echoes that of many of Davis' critics in this period. Calling *Bitches' Brew* "and its lineage" backward steps, he wrote: "The only piece on the collection of *Bitches' Brew* which hints at any strength coming from Miles is *Sanctuary*, but as stunning as it is, it is only a repeated statement. The music since then has been just other variations of this new theme. Miles plays very little, using as many aids as possible, taking advantage of the rhythm actually to cover his sometimes very sad solos." He calls *On the Corner* "an insult to the intellect of the people."

Will Smith in *down beat* mentioned the "supposedly hypnotic but ultimately static rhythm"; claimed that Davis did not play enough; and that his electronic amplifier made people think his trumpet was a guitar. In the '70s Davis made use of a wah-wah pedal attachment for his trumpet; on his tribute to Duke Ellington, the album entitled *Get Up With It*, he is heard at the keyboard.

Quincy Jones defended Davis against his detractors with: "I think you have to trust the same mojo that led you into the first style and go from there. It's fortunate that Miles is flexible enough to have given us the kind of contrast that separates *Miles Ahead* from *Jack Johnson*. I think he's blessed to have that scope, that range."

Davis' reaction to his critics was harsher. "I don't play rock, he told Frederick D. Murphy in *Encore* magazine. "Rock is a white word. And I don't like the word jazz that white folks dropped on us. We just play *Black*. We play what the day recommends. It's 1975. You don't play 1955 music or that straight crap like *My Funny Valentine* . . . That's the old nostalgic junk written for white people."

While controversy, never a stranger, swirled around him Davis, long a living legend, had already left indelible marks as an influence; an incubator for leaders.

In October '72 Davis broke both his legs when he crashed while driving his car in New York City. They continued to give him much pain in the years following the accident. At the end of '75 he was hospitalized for hip trouble but was recuperating at home in January '76.

Davis won the DB Critics poll, '66-70; Readers poll, '66-72, '75; his group won Critics and Readers polls, '66-71; he was voted Jazzman of the Year, '69-71. *Miles Smiles* won in both polls, '67; *Bitches' Brew* in '70; *Filles De Kilimanjaro* won Readers poll, '69.

Comp: *E.S.P.; Eighty-One; Agitation; Circle; Country Son; Stuff; Frelon Brun; Filles De Kilimanjaro; Petits Machins; Mademoiselle Mabry; Bitches' Brew; Yesternow; He Loved Him Madly.*

LPs: *Miles Smiles; Sorcerer; Nefertiti; Filles De Kilimanjaro; Miles in the Sky; In a Silent Way; Bitches' Brew; At the Fillmore; A Tribute to Jack Johnson; Live-Evil; On the Corner; In Concert; Jazz at the Plaza; Big Fun; Get Up With It* (Col.); *In Tokyo* (CBS-Sony); reissues, *Basic Miles* (Col.); *Dig; Collector's Items; Tallest Trees; Workin' & Steamin'* (Prest.); *Miles Davis* (UA); *The Complete Birth of the Cool* (Cap.); w. C. Adderley, *Something Else* (BN).

DAVIS, NATHAN TATE,* *educator, composer, saxophones, flute*; b. Kansas City, Kansas, 2/15/37. U.S. Army in Berlin as musician, arranger, '60-2. From '62-9 played in Europe w. Kenny Clarke, D. Byrd, E. Dolphy; stud. comp. w. André Hodeir. Comp.-arr.-soloist for Paris radio show *Jazz Aux Champs Elysées*. During late '60s, became increasingly active as student and teacher of jazz and ethnomusicology in France, Belgium, W. Germany. Joined U. of Pittsburgh as asst. prof. of music and dir. of jazz studies, '69. During hiatus from college, returned to Europe each summer. Received Ph.D. from Wesleyan U. in ethnomusicology. Traveled to Brazil, made field recordings. In '75, after five years of holding annual jazz seminars at Pittsburgh U., he wrote: "I am still a world citizen trying to balance between a career as jazz musician and scholar."

Davis joined Segue Records as artist and vice pres. of a & r, '70. Lps for several European labels; also *Makatuka* (Segue).

DAVIS, QUIN HALL, *saxophones, clarinet, flute*; b. Artesia, Cal., 3/12/44. Stud. w. Lennie Niehaus, '60-3; Long Beach State Coll., '62-6. Traveled w. Si Zentner, '65; Buddy Rich, Jan. to Apr. '67. After Army service, rejoined Rich, June '69, remaining until Mar. '70. Feat. w. S. Kenton orch. July '70 to Jan. '73. Three months later he joined H. James. Fests: Newport, Monterey, w. Rich; others, also many coll. clinics w. Kenton.

LPs: w. Kenton, *Live at Redlands University; Live at Butler University; Live at Brigham Young University* (Creative World).

DAVIS, RICHARD,* *bass, composer*; b. Chicago, Ill., 4/15/30. His great versatility was in evidence early in his career through his work w. such diverse gps. as Benny Goodman, Sarah Vaughan; symphony jobs w. Igor Stravinsky, Leonard Bernstein. In early '60s was part of Booker Little-Eric Dolphy quintet; also gigs and recs. w. Al Cohn-Zoot Sims; Andrew Hill; James Moody. With the Thad Jones-Mel Lewis orch., '66-71, incl. Russian tour, '72. A member of the NY Bass Choir from '69. Continued to be one of the busiest free-lance musicians in NYC during '70s. App. w. NY Philharmonic '73; w. L. Bernstein and Philharmonic, '75. Jobs w. Helen Merrill; Novella Nelson; Nancy Harrow; Roland Hanna; TV special w. Barbra Streisand; own gp. for college dates, '75. Fest: NJF-NY, '72-4; MJF w. John Lewis, '74-5. Film: sound track for *Holy Mountain.* TV: *Like It Is*, ABC, w. Bass Choir; Black Journal, NET. Polls: DB Critics, '66, TDWR; '67-74; DB Readers, '68-72. Comp: *Dealin'; What'd You Say; Julie's Rag Doll; Blues For Now; Sweet'n; Sorta.* Publ: *Walking On Chords* (RR&R Music Publ., P.O. Box 117, Planetarium Sta., N.Y., N.Y. 10024). Davis' hobby is horsemanship and he has showed in Dressage and Jumper Hunter Divisions. Devoted to Nichiren Shoshu Buddhism. LPs: *Philosophy of the Spiritual* (Buddah); *Epistrophy & Now's the Time; Dealin'; With Understanding* (Muse); *Muses for Richard Davis* (BASF); w. Bobby Hackett (Fly. Dutch); Phil Woods (Muse); Jimmy Raney (MPS); Jones-Lewis (BN, SS); Jaki Byard; Eric Kloss (Prestige); Bobby Jones (Cobble.).

DAVIS, WALTER JR.,* *piano, composer*; b. Richmond, Va., 9/2/32. Active around Newark, N.J. before joining Max Roach in early '50s; then w. D. Gillespie; D. Byrd; Art Blakey through '50s. From '60 has led own trio (sometimes duo). Visited and pl. in India '69. Also pl. w. Sonny Rollins, April '73-April '74; Art Blakey, '75; '73-5 app. in several NYC concerts w. own trio and trios of Barry Harris, Cedar Walton. TV: *Focus* w. Betty Carter, Wash., D.C. Fest: NJF-NY w. Rollins, '74; Blakey, '75; Antwerp; Naarden; Toulon. Also is painter and costume designer.

Comp: *Ronnie's a Dynamite Lady; Backgammon; Uranus; Illumination; Gypsy Folk Tales; Greasy; Davis Cup; A Million Or More Times.* Comp. publ: (Karmic Music, 434 Hudson St., New York, N.Y. 10014). LPs: w. Rollins, *Horn Culture* (Milestone); w. Sonny Criss, *This Is Criss; Portrait of Sonny Criss* (Prest.); w. A. Shepp, *Attica Blues; Way Ahead* (Imp.); *There's A Trumpet in My Soul* (Arista).

DAVIS, WILLIAM STRETHEN (WILD BILL),* *organ, piano, composer*; b. Glasgow, Mo., 11/24/18. The pioneer jazz organist has led his own trio from '51. He continued w. his annual summer job at the Little Belmont in Atlantic City, N.J. In addition, he subbed on piano in the Ellington band, '69, when Duke had a hand ailment. In the '70s he also played in France, recording for the Black and Blue label in the process. Appeared in organ concerts at the NJF-NY, '73-4 Jazz cruise on S.S. Rotterdam w. Jimmy Tyler band, summer '75. Own LP: *Impulsions*; LPs w. Illinois Jacquet; Buddy Tate; Al Grey; Slam Stewart; Floyd Smith (B&B).

DAVISON, WILLIAM EDWARD (WILD BILL),* *cornet, leader*; b. Defiance, Ohio, 1/5/06. Professional in Chicago bands from 1927, Milwaukee, '33-40, NYC from '40. Toured in U.S. extensively, '60s; England and continent, '64. Lived in LA for a year in late '60s, but spent much of his time on the road, esp. on several tours to Europe and Australia. Between '65 and '75 he app. with over 100 different bands, made more than 20 albums (mostly overseas) and discussed with audiences the blend of dixieland, Chicago and New Orleans jazz styles from historical and technical standpoints. Played annually at jazz parties in Odessa, Tex.; Aspen, Colo., '65-6; Big Horn JF, '72; Detroit JF, '73-4; Nice, France, fest. summer of '74. Toured U.S. w. E. Condon, A. Hodes, B. Bigard, '71.

Davison, who at times has played trumpet, bass trumpet, valve trombone, mellophone, banjo, guitar and mandolin, was still playing in his 70th year with the same vigor he demonstrated during his first years of NY prominence in the '40s. In '73-5 he was based in Washington, D.C., but worked only occasionally.

American LPs on Big Horn, Chiaroscuro, Fat Cat, Jazzology. Canadian LP on Sackville. European LPs on Swiss Philips with Wolverines Jazz Band; and Danish Horekiks w. Fessors Big City Band; also many re-releases in England and on continent.

DAWSON, ALAN,* *drums*; also *vibes*; b. Marietta, Pa., 7/14/29. A faculty member of the Berklee Coll. of Music in Boston from '57, he has also been active as drummer for visiting soloists to Boston clubs; as a clinician for the Fibes Drum Co.; and from '68-74, a member of the Dave Brubeck quartet, for tours, concerts and fests. Fests: NJF; MJF; Colo. JP. TV: special, *The Light in the Wilderness* w. Brubeck. Publ: *A Manual For The Modern Drummer; Blues and Odd Time Signatures.*

A strong, sensitive drummer with rock-steady time, Dawson is also a resourceful soloist. LPs w. Brubeck, *We're All Together Again For the First Time; The Last Set At Newport* (Atl.); *Blues Roots; Compadres; Live at the Berlin Philharmonic* (Col.); w. Phil Woods; Terry Gibbs (Muse); Sonny Stitt (Cobble.); Jimmy Raney

(MPS); Colo. Jazz Party (MPS/BASF); Al Cohn (Xanadu).

DEARIE, BLOSSOM,* *singer, piano, composer*; b. East Durham, N.Y., 4/28/26. Early experience in vocal gps. w. Woody Herman, Alvino Rey bands in '40s. To Paris in '52 where she teamed w. Annie Ross and formed own vocal gp. The Blue Stars. Returned to U.S. in '58 and established herself as an exceptional, intimately swinging nightclub singer, accompanying her vocals at the head of her own trio. Whitney Balliett wrote: "She is an elegant, polite, and often funny improviser, who lights the songs she sings by carefully altering certain tones and by using a subtle, intense rhythmic attack."

In the '70s she app. mainly in NYC, LA, and London at Ronnie Scott's with a repertory that incl. many of her own songs such as: *I'm Shadowing You; I Like You, You're Nice; Hey John; Sweet Georgie Fame.*

Own LPs: *Blossom Dearie Sings; Blossom Dearie 1975* (Daffodil Records, Box 21N, East Durham, N.Y. 12423); also one track w. King Pleasure in *The Source* (Prest.).

DE BREST, JAMES (SPANKY),* *bass*; b. Philadelphia, Pa., 4/24/37. Worked with small combos incl. Art Blakey, Jay Jay Johnson, also rec. w. Ray Draper. After a long illness, DeBrest died in Philadelphia 3/2/73.

DEDRICK, LYLE F. (RUSTY),* *trumpet, composer*; b. Delevan, N.Y., 7/12/18. Playing and writing for jazz-oriented studio recs., TV, jingles, industrial shows, club dates, pit bands and concerts. W. Urbie Green '67; the Free Design, as mus. dir., '69-70; Lionel Hampton '70-71. Since '71 he has been a member of the jazz dept. of the Manhattan Sch. of Mus. and has been writing originals and arrs. primarily for the educational field. Jazz fest. apps. on Long Island and Dick Gibson Colo. Jazz Party '74. Comps. incl. *The Modern Art Suite* and *Suite for Alto Saxophone and Trumpet.* LPs: *Many Facets, Many Friends* (Monmouth-Evergreen); *Kites Are Fun* w. Free Design (Project 3); *Back Home Again* w. Lee Wiley; *Harold Arlen in Hollywood; Sullivan, Shakespeare & Hyman* (Mon.-Ever.); *Big Band Hits* w. Enoch Light (Project 3).

DEEMS, BARRETT B., *drums*; b. Springfield, Ill., 3/1/13. Traveled w. Louis Armstrong 1954-8, then worked in Chicago, where he played w. Bill Reinhardt at Jazz Ltd. July 1966-Jan. '70. From Feb. '70- , w. Joe Kelly Gaslight Band. Periodic app. subbing in World's Greatest Jazzband 1971-5. TV: Timex All Star Jazz Show, NYC, 1972. During '70s rec. several LPs w. Art Hodes. Earlier LPs w. Armstrong (Col., MCA).

DE FAUT, VOLTAIRE (VOLLEY),* *clarinet, saxophones*; b. Little Rock, Ark., 3/14/04. Known for his work w. the NORK and Jean Goldkette in the '20s, De Faut, one of the first Chicagoans to master the NO clarinet style, later was staff mus. on WGN, Chi. and also active as a dog-breeder. Gigged intermittently from mid-'40s, rec. w. Art Hodes, '53. In last perfs. used electronic amplification device on his clarinet. He died in So. Chicago Heights, 4/29/73.

DE FRANCO, BONIFACE FERDINAND LEONARDO (BUDDY), *clarinet*; also *bass clarinet, composer*; b. Camden, N.J., 2/17/23. With many big bands in 1940s; Count Basie Septet 1950, own big band '51, then led quartets through '50s and co-led combo w. Tommy Gumina in early '60s. From 1966 until 1/18/74 he toured the world as nominal leader of the Glenn Miller orchestra, a job that afforded him few chances to display his unique, bop-inspired improvisational talent to jazz audiences. De Franco, who starting in 1947 won the DB poll as #1 clarinetist 19 times, then returned to jazz, touring Canada with a quintet in a jazz festival. Settling in Panama City, Florida, he went out on occasional club jobs w. jazz combos, played stage band clinics and writing stage band arrs. and instruction books, such as *Buddy De Franco on Jazz Improvisation*, (Famous Solos Ent., Dept. A, Box 567, Saddle River, N.J. 07458). Original arrs. publ. by Creative Artists and Pacific Palisades Music. Played Colo. Jazz Party, and in Sweden, Sept. '75.

LP on bass clarinet (Vee Jay). On clarinet: *Free Sail* (Choice). LP incl. transcriptions of his solos for students on Famous Solos Ent. (address above). Many earlier albums deleted; LPs w. Miller band available in England, Japan.

DE GRAAFF, REIN, *piano, composer*; b. Groningen, Holland, 10/24/42. Private lessons from age 10 for four yrs. In '64, trumpeter Nedly Elstak instructed him more fully about chord changes. Pl. w. Jenna Meinema, '57. Formed own trio and quartet, '60. To Germany, '62, where he pl. w. Jazzopators; also in Switzerland. Pl. locally while stationed w. Dutch Army at NATO base in Germany, '63. Met tenor saxophonist Dick Vennik in Amsterdam, '64, and became associated w. him in de Graaff-Vennik quartet from '64. Visited US, fall '67 and sat in w. gps. of Lee Morgan; Hank Mobley; Elvin Jones. Worked w. Rene Thomas, '73-4. Acc. many visiting soloists incl. Cecil Payne; Mobley; Red Rodney; Clifford Jordan; and expatriates, Johnny Griffin; Tony Scott; Don Byas; Dexter Gordon; Leo Wright; Carmell Jones. Infl: H. Silver, B. Powell, Barry Harris, C. Walton, M. Tyner, Mobley, K. Dorham, Milt Jackson. Dutch TV: from '64 w. own gp.; Benny Bailey, '72; C. Terry, '75. Fest: Loosdrecht; Laren; Pescara; Zurich; Comblain-la-tour; Reims; Hammerfeld; Middleheim; Dunkirk. Writing reviews and articles for Dutch mags., *Oor; Jazz Wereld* from '70. Comp: *Cornish Pixie; Time Machine; Modal Soul; Voodoo Dance; Point of No Return.* LPs: *Minor Moods* (Nowa); *Departure* (BASF); *Point of No Return* (Universe); w. J.R. Monterose, *Body and Soul* (Munich); w. R. Thomas, *TPL* (Vogel).

DE JOHNETTE, JACK, *drums, composer, melodica*; also *piano, saxophone*; b. Chicago, Ill., 8/9/42. Stud. classical piano for ten years with Viola Burns; grad. of American Conservatory of Music, Chicago; music major at Wilson Jr. College. Influenced by records of C. Parker, D. Gillespie, Billie Holiday, Louis Jordan. On joining high school concert band he worked briefly as bassist before taking up drums. He was first inspired by Max Roach, later by Philly Joe Jones and Elvin Jones. During his Chicago years he worked with groups of every genre, from T-Bone Walker and other blues bands to the free jazz of such musicians as Richard Abrams and Roscoe Mitchell. Visiting NYC early in '66 he was spotted by organist John Patton, whose group he joined. Later came engagements with Jackie McLean, singers Betty Carter and Abbey Lincoln, and Charles Lloyd, with whose quintet he toured for more than two years.

DeJohnette then worked around NYC. At one time or another he played with John Coltrane, Thelonious Monk, Freddie Hubbard, Bill Evans, Keith Jarrett and Chick Corea. During part of '68 he was with Stan Getz.

His best known association was with Miles Davis, whom he joined in the spring of '70. During the next two years, in addition to recording some of Davis' most significant albums, DeJohnette became a leader in his own right on LPs, and was heard more frequently doubling on melodica, piano, clavinet and organ and occasional vocals. In summer of '71 he organized a combo, known as Compost, for concert tours and clubs in the U.S. and overseas. Later he led other groups; in '75 he formed quartet with Alex Foster, saxophone; John Abercrombie, guitar; and Peter Warren, bass.

Like many musicians who came to prominence in the '60s originally as drummers, DeJohnette is a complete and adaptable musician with considerable talent as a composer. By the late '60s he had listened extensively to rock groups and was strongly influenced by some of them. Among his most representative albums is *The DeJohnette Complex* (Milestone). This includes his two Requiem compositions, in memory of the Kennedys, Malcolm X and Martin Luther King.

LPs: w. Bill Evans, *Live At Montreux* (Verve); w. Lloyd, *Forest Flower; Dream Weaver* (Atlantic); w. Davis, *Bitches' Brew; Live At Fillmore; Live-Evil* (Columbia); w. Joe Henderson, *Power To The People* (Milestone); w. F. Hubbard, *Straight Life; Joe Farrell Quartet* (CTI); w. Miroslav Vitous, *Infinite Search* (Embryo); *Keith Jarrett-Jack DeJohnette* (ECM); own groups *The DeJohnette Complex; Have You Heard* (Milestone); *Sorcery* (Prestige); w. Compost, *Take Off Your Body; Life Is Round* (Columbia).

DE LA ROSA, FRANK (Francisco Estaban Jr.), *bass*; b. El Paso, Tex., 12/26/33. Father and brother, Oscar, both musicians. Stud. LA Conservatory of Music and Fine Arts w. Sam H. Rice, '56-8. Worked w. Latin groups until '59, then moved to Las Vegas, where he played in many casino bands. Moving back to LA May '65, became more active in jazz. Pl. w. D. Ellis '66-8; Sweets Edison, '68-9; E. Fitzgerald, '69-72; Don Menza, '72-5; Don Piestrup, '72-5; Mayo Tiana, '72-5; S. Vaughan, '74-5. Has app. at Monterey, Newport and most leading European jazz fests. A clean-toned, dependable artist much respected for his work on upright bass.

LPs: w. D. Ellis (Pacific Jazz); E. Fitzgerald (MPS-BASF) etc.

DE MERLE, LESTER WILLIAM (LES), *drums, composer*; also *percussion, piano*; b. Brooklyn, N.Y., 11/4/46. Stud. drums and perc. w. Bob Livingston, NYC, '60-5; harmony, theory at Berklee w. Alf Clausen. At 16 worked w. L. Hampton for nine months while still in school. In '65 w. Billy Williams Revue; Connie Haines; Lee Castle-Jimmy Dorsey band, '66. Formed first group, '67 w. R. Brecker, Arnie Lawrence, also gigging around NYC w. J. Farrell, L. Konitz, Garnett Brown, W. Bishop Jr. until '70s. Moved to LA, '71; started group, Transfusion, and in '72 opened Cellar Theatre, home base for Transfusion and showcase for young artists. NJF, '74, w. H. James.

Publ: *Jazz-Rock Fusion*, Vols. I & II (Try Pubs., 854 Vine St., Hollywood, Ca. 90038). LPs: *Spectrum* (UA); *Arizona Slim* sound track w. Paul Beaver.

DEODATO, EUMIR DE ALMEIDA, *piano, composer*; also *guitar, bass, synthesizer*; b. Rio de Janeiro, Brazil, 6/22/42. Self-taught. Insp. by Gil Evans, J. Coltrane, Miles Davis, Glenn Miller, S. Kenton, Ravel, Debussy, Moussorgsky, Stevie Wonder. Prof. debut in Brazil w. Astrud Gilberto, Luis Bonfa. His first comp., *Spirit of Summer*, won top honors at Rio Song Fest., where he also received three awards as best arranger. Left Brazil, '67, spent three years off and on in U.S. From '70 spent most of his time in studios where he enjoyed a reputation as arranger for albums feat. R. Flack, F. Sinatra, A. Franklin, B. Midler, W. Montgomery, S. Turrentine, A.C. Jobim, L. Bonfa, A. Gilberto etc. He also wrote scores for two prize-winning movies, *Bahia*; and *The Reporter*, and for *The Adventurers; Target Risk; Gentle Rain; The Girl From Ipanema*; and *Twiggy Special*. Other comps. incl. *The Legend of The Amazon Bird; Super Strut*. Deodato achieved sudden national prominence in the U.S. in '73 when his jazz-rock arr. of *Also Sprach Zarathustra* (the theme from *2001*) became a best selling record. On the strength of it he won many awards, incl. a Grammy, *Billboard* listing as top jazz artist, *Playboy*, etc. Toured U.S. and Canada, '73 and '74; also Italy, Venezuela, Japan, Philippines, Hawaii, '74.

Later rock and jazz arrs. incl. *Rhapsody In Blue; Moonlight Serenade*. LPs: *Prelude; Deodato 2; Deodato/Airto In Concert* (CTI); *Donato + Deodato* (Muse); *Whirlwinds; Artistry* (MCA).

DE PARIS, SIDNEY,* *trumpet*; b. Crawfordsville, Ind., 5/30/05. Prominent in 1930s w. McKinney's Cotton Pickers, Don Redman; w. Benny Carter 1940-41, then off and on w. brother Wilbur's combo from '43. De Paris died in NYC 9/14/67. LP: *De Paris Dixie* (BN).

DE PARIS, WILBUR,* *trombone*; b. Crawfordsville, Ind., 1/11/00. During 1930s and '40s pl. w. Benny Carter, Teddy Hill, Louis Armstrong, Ella Fitzgerald, Roy Eldridge, Duke Ellington. Led successful traditionalist small band that played for a decade at Jimmy Ryan's in NYC, also toured Africa for State Dept. in

1957. Less active after death of brother Sidney, but played a few dates w. new group in 1972. Died in NYC 1/3/73.

DESMOND, PAUL,* *alto sax*; b. San Francisco, Calif., 11/25/24. When the Dave Brubeck quartet, of which he had been a member from its inception in '51, broke up in Dec. '67 Desmond entered a period of little musical activity. He began writing a book about his experiences with the working title, *How Many of You Are There in the Quartet?* In the mid-'70s he reported that it was proceeding at "a glacial pace." A chapter appeared in *Punch*.

In '69 appeared at the New Orleans Jazz Festival and recorded for A&M. He was reunited with Brubeck in The Two Generations of Brubeck in '72, playing at NJF-NY and touring for George Wein in Europe, Australia and Japan. He continued to make guest appearances with them in concerts and fests. like NJF-NY '73 and '75. As a single he played at the MJF, '75. Rarely a club performer, he worked at the new Half Note with his own group, '74, and with a Canadian rhythm section on three different occasions at Bourbon Street in Toronto, '74-5. In June '75 he and Brubeck, with Dave's sons, played for the Jazz Cruise on the S.S. Rotterdam. Out of this came an album of Brubeck-Desmond duets, one of which resulted from a BBC-TV shipboard taping; the rest, inspired by this, from a September studio date. This, and his recs. for CTI, as leader and sideman, show that the years have deepened his bittersweet lines. Among Desmond's other TV apps. was the Timex jazz show, '72.

He was summoned to Hollywood in the fall of '75 to tape a soundtrack for Paul Mazursky's film, *Next Stop Greenwich Village*, but it was later decided to use in addition some of the old recordings of the Brubeck quartet of the early '50s, the time in which the movie is set. Comp: *Wendy; Take Ten; North By Northeast*. LPs: *Skylark; Pure Desmond* (CTI); *Bridge Over Troubled Water; From the Hot Afternoon; Summertime* (A&M); *Duets 1975/Brubeck-Desmond* (Horizon); w. Don Sebesky, *Giant Box*; w. Jim Hall, *Concierto* (CTI).

DE SOUZA, JOÃO JOSÉ PEREIRA (RAUL), *half-bass trombone*; also *composer, trumpet, bass, tuba, flute saxophone, percussion*; b. Rio de Janeiro, Brazil, 8/23/34. Self-taught except for studies at Berklee Coll. of Music in Boston. Started on trombone while in teens. Spent five and a half years in Brazilian Air Force. Played with many groups incl. three of his own in Brazil, Mexico City. One of his Brazilian combos, Impacto 8, made an LP in '68. De Souza worked with Sergio Mendes in Brazil and Europe, '63-4. In '65-6, after traveling in Europe with a Brazilian group, he played w. Kenny Clarke at the Blue Note club in Paris. Soon after, spent three and a half years in Mexico City. First came to U.S. in Aug. '73, after which he played frequently w. Airto.

Infl. by J.J. Johnson, whom he heard on records in '59, De Souza was voted Brazil's best trombonist in various polls between '67 and '71. His style suggested an inspired extension of Johnson.

Comp: *Water Buffalo*. LPs: *Colors* (Milestone); *Bossa Rio*, w. Mendes (Philips); *Stories To Tell* w. F. Purim (Milestone); others w. Azar Lawrence (Milestone) et al.

DEUCHAR, JAMES (JIMMIE),* *trumpet, fluegelhorn, mellophonium*; b. Dundee, Scotland, 6/26/30. Pl. w. Ronnie Scott and Tubby Hayes, '60-66; Kurt Edelhagen as soloist and arr.; K. Clarke-F. Boland big band from '65-71; ret. to England in '71, began arr. for BBC. Moved back to Scotland early '70s.

Comps: *Portrait of Elvin; Drum In* (for Edelhagen); *U.K. Suite* (for Clarke- Boland). LPs: w. Clarke-Boland on Atl., MPS, Col.

DE VEGA, HENRY (HANK), *clarinet, saxes, flute* etc.; b. El Paso, Tex., 8/4/30. In 1949 began studies at LA Cons. of Mus., interrupted by service in USAF band, 1950-53. Pl. baritone sax, rec. w. Roy Porter bebop band, '49-50; brief stints w. J. Otis, Ike Carpenter, Harry James. Hotel bands in LV, '53-4; Benny Carter, '55; joined Lionel Hampton '55 and was seriously injured in a bus accident that involved the entire band. After a long recuperation, he resumed LV work, '60-65; free-lanced around LA, '65-8; pl. w. Gerald Wilson orch., '68- . Exhibiting artist in mixed media painting; working at USC, supervisor, reproduction services. LPs: *Everywhere; California Soul; Eternal Equinox* w. Wilson (Pac. Jazz); *Things Ain't What They Used To Be* w. Wilson, Ella Fitzgerald (Reprise).

DICKENSON, VICTOR (VIC),* *trombone, composer*; also *singer*; b. Xenia, Ohio, 8/6/06. Pl. w. big bands of Claude Hopkins in '30s; Benny Carter, Count Basie, Eddie Heywood's small gp. in '40s; Red Allen; Ed Hall gps. in '50s; Wild Bill Davison, early '60s. From '63-68 w. Saints & Sinners; then '68-70 w. Bobby Hackett w. whom he had been associated in '51 and '56. Joined World's Greatest Jazzband spring '70, pl. w. them into '72. With Hackett again '73, pl. at Americana, NYC '74; Toronto; New England. From March '75 pl. w. Balaban & Cats at Eddie Condon's. One of the great trombone stylists in the history of the music, he displayed his usual fluency, warmth and unique wit in the '70s. Won DB Critics poll, '71-4. TV: *Just Jazz*, PBS, '71 w. Hackett. Fest: Pescara; San Sebastian, '74; Nice, '74-5; NJF-NY, several times in '70s, incl. Newport Hall of Fame, '75; Colorado JP annually. Comp: *Alone; Constantly; I'll Try*. LPs: w. Hackett, *Live at the Roosevelt Grill* (Chiaro.); *Plus Vic Dickenson* (Proj. 3); *Buck Clayton Jam Session* (Chiaro.); w. WGJ (Atl., World Jazz); w. Balaban & Cats, *A Night at the New Eddie Condon's* (Classic Jazz); also represented in Albert McCarthy's *Swing Today* series (Eng. RCA).

DICKERSON, DWIGHT LOWELL, *piano*; also *singer*; b. Los Angeles, Ca., 12/26/44. Stud. Berklee, '65; also privately w. Ray Santisi, Mrs. Margaret Chaloff in Boston; Cal State U., LA, '73. Played with innumerable small combos, among them Sergio Mendes' Bossa Rio, '69-70; Bola Sete, '70-1; Charles Owens, '71; Calvin Keys, '72; James Moody, '72; Larry Gales from '72; Bobby Bryant, '72; Ch. Lloyd, '73; Leroy Vinnegar, '73-4; Red Holloway, Freddie Hill, B. Hutcherson, '74; Sahib Shihab, '74-5; S. Criss, '74-5.

Dickerson, who has a BA from Cal State, is at home in many settings, as is evidenced by his LPs: *Alegria*, w. Bossa Rio (Blue Thumb); *Shebaba*, w. Sete (Fantasy); *I Stand Alone*, w. Owens (Vault); *Free Again*, w. G. Ammons & B. Bryant Big Band (Prestige); *Glass of Water*, w. Vinnegar (Legend).

DIORIO, JOSEPH LOUIS (JOE), *guitar, composer*; b. Waterbury, Conn., 8/6/36. Stud. at Berdice School of Music, '49-54, subsequently self-taught. Established through records and/or gigs in early and mid-60s w. Eddie Harris, S. Stitt, Bennie Green, Bunky Green, Nicky Hill, and with many other leading jazzmen in Chicago from '60-9. Moving to Florida, composed and played music for a TV documentary, worked on local TV shows. To Washington, '71 for House of Sounds Fest. at JFK Center w. Ira Sullivan, perf. as duo.

In '75 Diorio also was studying drawing and painting at two Miami Univs., and was writing several books for guitar. A highly capable all around artist on both electric and classical guitar.

LPs: *Exodus to Jazz* w. Eddie Harris (Veejay); *Play Back*, w. Sam Lazar (Cadet); *My Main Man*, w. S. Stitt (Cadet); *Rapport*, co-leader w. Wally Cirillo (Spitball).

DITMAS, BRUCE, *drums*; also *percussion, synthesizers*; b. Atlantic City, N.J., 12/12/46. Grew up in Miami, Fla. Father, who pl. trombone w. Art Mooney; Claude Thornhill, Jerry Wald in '40s, is very active in Miami, primarily w. hotel show bands. Began on piano but switched to drums at 10. Studied for seven yrs. w. Tony Crisetello in Miami. Att. Stan Kenton Clinics at Indiana U.; Michigan State, '62, '63. Various jazz gigs at 15, mostly w. Ira Sullivan; hotel show bands in Miami Beach; then w. Sullivan, '62-4, then two yrs. w. Judy Garland, moving home base to NYC. Between '66-70 pl. w. Barbra Streisand; Della Reese; Leslie Uggams; Yolande Bavan; Sheila Jordan; Jack Reilly trio. With Gil Evans orch. from '71; Trevor Koehler from '71 until his death in '75; Enrico Rava from '71. Pit band for *Promises, Promises*; Joe Newman quartet; and Jazz Interactions orch. for L. Armstrong tribute w. Thad Jones; Johnny Coles, '71. Worked w. Stardrive; Atmospheres w. Clive Stevens; Steve Kuhn; Albert Dailey; Hammerline w. Koehler; Future Shock w. Brecker bros., '72; helped form The New Wilderness Preservation Band for series of concerts at Peace Church; w. Evans at Vanguard, Village Gate, Bitter End, '72-3, and NYJRC concerts, '73-4. Pl. w. Paul Bley; Lee Konitz; Chet Baker; Koehler, '74; Evans; Rava, in US and Europe; Barry Miles, '75. Early infl: Roach, Blakey, Elvin Jones. Fav: Jack DeJohnette. Other infl: Lenny White, Billy Hart, Evans, Koehler. Film: *The Cage*. TV: Merv Griffin; *Today; Take a Giant Step; Look Up and Live*; European shows w. Evans. Fest: NJF-NY, LA, SF; Montreux; Antibes; others in Denmark, Italy, Switz. LPs: w. Evans (RCA, Atl., Nippon Phonogram); w. S. Kuhn (Cobble.); J. Coles (Main.); Stardrive (Elektra); Wavy Gravy (Just Sunshine).

DIXON, ERIC,* *tenor sax, flute, composer*; b. Staten Island, N.Y., 3/28/30. A veteran of the Count Basie reed section from '62, he left in '72 to operate a restaurant on Staten Island w. his wife called The Meeting Place, but rejoined in summer '75. Recorded an LP for Master Jazz in '74 entitled *Eric's Edge* incl. his own comp: *Background Blues; Whisper M&I; The Meeting Place; Blues For Ilean; Eric's Edge*. LP: w. Basie (Pablo).

DODGION, DOTTIE (Dorothy Giaimo), *drums*; b. Brea, Cal., 9/23/29. Father a prof. drummer in SF; husband is Jerry Dodgion. Mainly self-taught. Pl. w. Nick Esposito, Ch. Mingus in SF. To NYC, worked w. Benny Goodman, '61; Marian McPartland, '64; Billy Mitchell-Al Grey Quintet. Toronto club w. Wild Bill Davison; Las Vegas w. Carl Fontana, Gus Mancuso; college tours w. Eugene Wright; Half Note, NYC, w. Al Cohn-Zoot Sims, then joined Ruby Braff Quartet, app. at Concord JF '72. Living in LA, '75, gigged w. Mancuso, Wright. Insp. by Sid Catlett, Jo Jones and later drummers; a sensitive drummer who fits into every modern jazz context.

LPs: w. Braff; Davison (Chiaroscuro).

DODGION, JERRY,* *alto sax*; also *flute, soprano sax*; b. Richmond, Calif., 8/29/32. Played w. Gerald Wilson, Benny Carter, Red Norvo in '50s. Moved to NYC '61 where he occ. teamed w. wife, drummer Dottie Dodgion, in quartet. Made tours of So. America, Russia w. Benny Goodman. A charter member of the Thad Jones-Mel Lewis orch. from late '65, he took over lead alto chair when Jerome Richardson left in '71. Through '75 he had made six European, three Japanese tours w. them and one of Soviet Union, '72. A busy NYC free-lance he has rec. w. Basie, Ruby Braff, Richard Davis, Goodman, H. Hancock, Blue Mitchell, O. Nelson and D. Amram, also making concert apps. w. Amram. Wrote arr. of Marian McPartland's *Ambiance* for Jones-Lewis *Potpourri* album on Phila. Int. Fests: see Jones-Lewis. LPs: see Jones-Lewis; also *The Phantom; Now Hear This; Introducing Duke Pearson*, all w. Pearson; *Fancy Free* w. D. Byrd (BN); w. D. Amram, *No More Walls* (RCA).

DOGGETT, WILLIAM BALLARD (BILL),* *organ, piano, composer*; b. Philadelphia, Pa., 2/6/16. Long popular in jazz and r & b circles, Doggett continued to pl. colleges, night clubs and one-nighters throughout the U.S. and Canada. He rec. w. Della Reese in '66, but for the most part was heard leading his own combo. He was also personal manager for recording artist Edwin Starr. In recent years Doggett has been teamed for many engagements with the Ink Spots.

Fests: Juan-les-Pins, '66; Antwerp, Nice, '71. Publ: *Honky-Tonk*, instrumental version (Islip Mus. Publ. Co., 120 W. Bayberry Rd., Islip, N.Y. 11751).

LPs: on King, Sue, ABC etc.; w. Ella Fitzgerald, *Rhythm is Our Business* (Verve).

DOLDINGER, KLAUS,* *tenor, soprano sax*; also *clarinet, keyboards, synthesizer, mellotron*; b. Berlin, Germany, 5/12/36. After his assoc. in '63-4 in a jazz workshop with visiting Americans such as Kenny Clarke, J. Griffin, Benny Bailey, Max Roach, Donald Byrd, did much touring with own quintet in N. Africa, Middle East and Scandinavia, '64; S. America for West German Gov't., '65. In '70 formed Motherhood, which from '71 was known as Passport. Many European fests. and TV apps., also TV in Hong Kong, Tokyo, Rio de Janeiro. Toured U.S. w. own combo Apr. 1975. Insps. and infls. Sidney Bechet, Ch. Parker, Coltrane, O. Coleman, G. Evans, Miles Davis. Won several German jazz and rock polls. Comps: *Eternal Spiral; Looking Thru; Cross Collateral; Will-O-The-Wisp; Jazz Concertino* for jazz quartet and symph. orch. Publ: book of comps. for Passport (Muz, 8 Munchen, Leopoldstr. 38).

LPs: *Doldinger Jubilee Concert; Looking Thru; Cross Collateral* (Atco); *Passport et al/Doldinger Jubilee '75* (Atl.).

DONAHUE, SAM KOONTZ,* *tenor sax, trumpet, leader*; b. Detroit, Mich., 3/8/18. Own band in 1930s; later pl. w. Goodman, James, Krupa. Fronted Tommy Dorsey "ghost band" 1961-5; later settled in Reno, Nev., where he died 3/22/74.

DONALD, BARBARA KAY, *trumpet*; also *piano, voice, saxophone, trombone*; b. Minneapolis, Minn., 2/9/42. Started playing cornet at nine. Moved to LA; cont. studying horn and voice through HS and at Valley State Coll. Veteran Little Benny Harris later became her teacher. At 18, went on the road w. own group; toured w. Chuck Cabot big band and with various rock groups. Freelanced in LA w. D. Gordon, Gene Russell, Stanley Cowell, Burt Wilson. In '62 she married Norwegian pianist Ole Calmeyer; divorced in '65, married Sonny Simmons (q.v.) and has worked with him ever since. Moved to NYC, '66; back to SF, '70 and LA, '75. Donald has also pl. w. Mike White, Clifford Jordan, Richard Davis, Smiley Winters, Prince Lasha, Billy Higgins, R.R. Kirk, Charles Moffett, Tony Scott, Lonnie Liston Smith, Cecil McBee, Clifford Jarvis, John Hicks, and in '65 w. J. Coltrane.

Donald says she is "still struggling to become accepted as a woman artist, and fighting this planet's low conception of music."

LPs: w. Simmons, *Staying on Watch; Music of the Spheres* (ESP); *Manhattan Egos* (Arhoolie); *Ruma Suma; Burning Spirits* (Contemp.); w. Winters, *Smiley Ect.* (Arhoolie); *Les Oublies De Jazz Ensemble* (Touche).

DONALDSON, ROBERT STANLEY (BOBBY),* *drums*; b. Boston, Mass., 11/29/22. An alumnus of many name groups incl. Edmond Hall, Sy Oliver, B. Goodman, Andy Kirk, Donaldson later worked as a studio musician. He died of a heart attack 7/2/71 in NYC.

DONALDSON, LOU,* *alto sax*; b. Badin, N.C., 11/1/26. Concentrating on blues-based, funky material he continued to lead his small combo (organ, trumpet, guitar, drums) in small clubs in the East. In '67 he left the Cadet label, where he had been under contract from '63, to return to his former, long time affiliate Blue Note. His basic repertoire was described by Bob Porter as combining "'down-home' melodies with New Orleans r&b drums." This is intermixed w. some ballads and an occasional Charlie Parker song, reflecting his active participation in small gp. jazz of the early '50s w. Art Blakey, Clifford Brown et al. Donaldson is an outspoken critic of the avant garde. He says: "The guys say they are searching but actually all they need to find is a good saxophone or trumpet teacher and their search would be over because they would teach them how to play it." LPs: *Sophisticated Lou* feat. him pl. ballads with strings; w. quintet, *Alligator Boogaloo; Hot Dog; Everything I Play is Funky*, etc. (BN); *Fried Buzzard*, etc. (Cadet).

DONATO, MICHEL ANDRE, *bass*; also *piano*; b. Montreal, Quebec, Canada, 8/25/42. Father, Ronald pl. tenor sax; uncle Maurice Donato, piano. Stud. at Mont. Cons., '60-3; otherwise self-taught. From '62-9 pl. w. Pierre Leduc; Lee Gagnon; Nick Ayoub; Ron Proby; Art Roberts, Sonny Greenwich, Brian Barley; Carmen McRae; Jacques Brel; Charles Aznavour; Michel Legrand; member of Mont. Symph., '64. In Toronto from '70 w. Lenny Breau; Moe Koffman; Bernie Senensky; Don Thompson; Sonny Greenwich; Alvin Pall; Claude Ranger; clubs w. Benny Carter; Art Farmer; Milt Jackson; Dave McKenna; studio work pl. jingles. World tour w. O. Peterson, '73-4. Infl: LaFaro, Pettiford, P. Heath, Mingus, Gary Karr. TV: *Everything Goes* w. Koffman; *Jazz En Liberte*, '65-70; CBC Chamber Orch. on radio. Fests: Pitts., NJF-NY w. Peterson, '73; Belvedere "King-Size" in Can. w. Koffman, L. Bellson big band, '74. LPs: w. Peterson (Japan. Col.); Don Thompson; S. Greenwich (Sack.); *The Montreal Scene* w. Ayoub (Can. RCA); *Jazzzz* w. Gagnon (Barclay); *Beloved Gift* w. Senensky; others w. Herbie Spanier, Art Maiste, Pierre Nadeau (RCI).

DORHAM, McKINLEY HOWARD (KENNY),* *trumpet, composer*; b. Fairfield, Tex., 8/30/24. Graduate of innumerable name groups of 1940s and '50s, incl. Gillespie, Eckstine, Hampton, Mercer Ellington; founder member of Art Blakey's Jazz Messengers. Replaced the late Clifford Brown in Max Roach quintet, '56-8. Later freelanced extensively, visiting Europe often, also teaching and composing. Successful partnership w. Joe Henderson, '62-3, and later w. Hank Mobley. Attended NYU graduate school of music in late '60s. In failing health in later years, Dorham continued playing sporadically until shortly before his death of kidney failure 12/5/72 in NYC. His *Fragments of An Autobiography* was published in *Music '70*, *down beat*'s annual for '69.

A superior composer and a brilliant trumpeter who forged a style of his own out of the influences of Gillespie, Navarro and Miles Davis. Comp: *Una Mas; Blue Spring; Lotus Blossom* (also known as *Asiatic Raes*); *Trompeta Toccata; Whistle Stop; Epitaph; Blue Bossa; Dead End*. Dorham is represented on many LPs, the best of them under his own name or w. Blakey, almost all on Blue Note. Rec. w. Ch. Parker, Th. Monk, O. Nelson, T. Dameron, J.J. Johnson, S. Rollins, H. Silver, S. Stitt, C. Walton, Cecil Taylor, Joe Henderson; also *Kenny Dorham Memorial Album* (Xanadu); *Ease It* (Muse); w. Cecil Payne, *Zodiac* (Strata-East); *1959*; w. Barry

Harris, *Bull's Eye* (Prest.); reissue, *Max Roach + 4* (Trip).

DOROUGH, ROBERT LROD (BOB),* *piano, singer, composer*; also *vibes, harmonica, saxophone*; b. Cherry Hill, Ark., 12/12/23. Early work as accompanist for Sugar Ray Robinson. In Paris at Mars Club, '54-5. After many years leading combos in NYC, Chicago and LA, became active in record and jingle production, also producing and composing for TV. Played at Bradley's, NYC in mid-70s; SF & LA, Aug.-Sept., '75. Wrote *Multiplication Rock*, a series of animated films designed for children, seen on ABC-TV, '72-5. Other comps: *Grammar Rock; America Rock; Comin' Home Baby; Winds of Heaven; Nothing Like You.*

Dorough is well known for his rec. as vocalist and composer w. M. Davis in '62, when he was heard on *Blue Xmas* in *Jingle Bell Jazz*; and '67 on *Nothing Like You* in *Sorcerer* (both Col.). His hip, quavery vocal style and bop infl. piano are much admired by a number of jazz musicians. Own LPs: *Just About Everything* (Focus); *Multiplication Rock* (Cap.); *Disguises* (Laissez Faire); w. Children of All Ages (Differant Drummer); w. Bobby Jones (Cobble.).

DOTSON, DENNIS, *trumpet, fluegelhorn*; b. Jacksonville, Tex., 6/18/46. Self-taught. Pl. w. Edgar Winter in Houston, 1968. Spent five years in LV playing casino shows, also w. Carl Fontana, Red Rodney, Sam Noto. Joined Woody Herman, 1975. LP: *Children of Lima* w. Herman (Fantasy).

DRAPER, RAYMOND ALLEN (RAY),* *tuba, composer*; also *valve trombone, baritone horn, bass trumpet, keyboards, vocals*; b. New York, N.Y., 8/3/40. Prominent in LA from '64, where he lived in Venice, working w. Big Black, '66-7; rec. sound tracks w. Q. Jones; pl. w. Horace Tapscott. Formed nine piece rock group, Red Beans & Rice, '68, staying together for a year and a half.

In '69 Draper moved to London and became music director for Ronnie Scott Directions. Comp., arr., rec. w. ten piece band, Sweetwater Canal. Toured Europe as leader w. Arthur Conley show, and w. A. Shepp, D. Cherry, Dr. John. Rec. w. Mick Jagger, Eric Clapton, Michael Henderson, Walter Davis Jr. Pl. Montreux JF, '70.

Returned to U.S. w. Dr. John cont. to work with him until '72. He then became involved in teaching theory and harmony, recording studio techniques etc. at the Univ. of the Streets and Wesleyan U., Middletown, Conn. Received grant for comp. from NEA, '73-4. Worked w. Cathy Chamberlain's Rag & Roll Revue, '74-5. Moved back to LA and rejoined Dr. John, '75. Films: *Amougee*, filmed in Belgium; *Jazz on a Summer's Day*, made at Newport JF; sang *Lay Your Love On Me* for *Last Summer*. TV: *Jazz Set* (PBS). Comps: *Fugue for Brass Ensemble; Filide; Happiness & Mess Around.*

LPs: *Red Beans & Rice* (Epic); w. Big Black, *Elements of Now* (Uni); *Sonny's Dream* w. S. Criss (Prest.); *Sun, Moon & Herbs* w. Dr. John (Atl.); *Who Knows What Tomorrow's Gonna Bring*, w. Jack McDuff (BN).

DRESSER, MARK, *bass*; b. Los Angeles, Calif., 9/26/52. Lessons from Gary Karr; studied for a long time w. Bertram Turetzsky. Pl. rock as a teenager. Then studied and pl. w. David Baker at U. of Indiana, '70-1. Through Turetzsky met Stanley Crouch in summer of '72 and has pl. w. him from that time. With San Diego Symph., '73-5; David Murray-Butch Morris Ensemble; Murray trio & quintet; Leo Smith; Ice Follies band under dir. of Cat Anderson, '75. Has also pl. w. Bobby Bradford; Black Arthur; James Newton; Charles Tyler. To NYC summer '75; then moved to New Haven. Infl: Mingus, P. Chambers, Pettiford, W. Ware, C. Haden, Ellington, Rollins, M. Favors, B. Bradford. Dance has become imp. infl. after working w. improvising dancers. Fest: Studio Rivbea JF w. Murray quintet, '75. LPs: two albums w. Crouch, '73, as yet unreleased.

DREW, KENNETH SIDNEY (KENNY),* *piano, composer*; b. New York City, 8/28/28. After important early playing w. Lester Young, Ch. Parker et al, was active on the West Coast scene; toured w. Dinah Washington; Buddy Rich. Moved to Europe, '61, settling in Copenhagen, '64. Married to daughter of the late Leo Mathisen, well known Danish jazz pianist. Began playing at Montmartre Jazzhus w. Dexter Gordon and such visiting soloists as K. Dorham, J. Griffin, H. Mobley, J. Henderson, S. Rollins, Y. Lateef and, also, B. Webster. Formed ongoing alliance w bassist Niels-Henning Orsted Pedersen in duo, trio combinations. Duo concept started in '66 when they were chosen to represent Denmark for the European Broadcasting Union. Fest: major European fests.; Tangier, '72. Comps: *Suite for Big Band* for Danish Radio; *Dark Beauty; Blues Inn; Largo; Come Summer; Serenity; Sunset; Duo Trip.* British critic Mark Gardner wrote: "As a pianist Kenny Drew has certainly matured greatly in the past 13 years. He always had unusual technical facility, but all that is now harnessed to a probing musical mind and a deeper realization of his individuality."

Own publ. co.: Shirew Publ., Aboulevarden 18, 2200. Copenhagen N., Denmark

LPs: solo album, *Everything I Love; Duo; Duo 2; Dark Beauty*; w. Jackie McLean, *Live at Montmartre; Ghetto Lullaby*; w. McLean-D. Gordon, *The Meeting; The Source*; w. Gordon, *The Apartment*; w. Ken McIntyre, *Hindsight*; w. J. Griffin, *Blues for Harvey* (SteepleChase); w. D. Gillespie, *Giant*; w. G. Ammons, *Goodbye* (Prest.); *Violin Summit* (MPS).

DROOTIN, ALBERT M. (AL), *clarinet*; also *saxes, flute*; b. Boston, Mass., 12/24/16. Family all pro. mus. for many generations. Father taught him clarinet. Jam sessions at Ken Club w. brother Buzzy (q.v.); then to NYC, joining Bud Freeman '40. Muggsy Spanier, '41; Boyd Raeburn, '42; army band; then ret. to Boston and freelanced. House band at Mahogany Hall, '51-3; Savoy, Hi-Hat, other local clubs; formed trio w. soprano sax, banjo at Gaslite Room, '59; continued to gig around Boston for 14 years, then formed Drootin Bros. Band '73 (see Drootin, Buzzy).

LPs w. Al Donahue, Raeburn, Storyville gp. etc., deleted.

DROOTIN, BENJAMIN (BUZZY),* *drums*, b. Russia, 4/22/20. Veteran of traditional style gps.; during mid-1960s toured w. B. Hackett, J. Teagarden, E. Condon, Roy Eldridge, Dukes of Dixieland, Newport All Stars. Bandleader at El Morocco, NYC, '66 (only jazz mus. ever to hold this job); traveled w. Jazz Giants (Wild Bill Davison et al) '67-9; formed own gp., B.D.'s Jazz Family, w. Herman Autry, Benny Morton, '69-70; free-lanced around NYC, '71-2; in '73 returned to Boston, where he was raised, to join brother Al and nephew Sonny in Drootin Brothers Band, house gp. at Scotch 'n' Sirloin '73-5. Fest: NJF-NY, '73.

TV: *Buzzy's Jazz Family* on PBS network. Drootin Bros. Band on New England Network's *Good Morning* show. *Today, Tonight* shows w. Dukes of Dixieland.

LPs: *Great Moments at Newport Festival* (RCA); *Jazz Giants* w. Davison; *Old Tyme Modern* w. Herb Hall (Sackville); *Jazz Ultimate* w. Hackett, Teagarden (Capitol); *Braff* w. Ruby Braff (Epic).

DUDEK, GERHARD ROCHUS (GERD), *tenor saxophone*; also *soprano sax, clarinet, flute, shennai*; b. Gr. Dobern, Germany, 9/28/38. Brother, Ossi Dudek, pl. trumpet w. SFB Radio Band in Berlin. Private clarinet lessons in Siegen, '54, then music school there. Worked in brother's big band until '58. W. Berlin Jazz Quintet, '60-4. From that time has pl. w. Kurt Edelhagen Orch. in Cologne, also touring Russia w. Edelhagen; Manfred Schoof quintet; Globe Unity Orch.; w. George Russell at Berlin Fest.; Wolfgang Dauner; Albert Manglesdorff quintet; Four For Jazz; Don Cherry; and own groups. Fests: Antibes, Molde, Montreux. Infl: Coltrane, Coleman, M. Davis, C. Parker, Cherry, A. Ayler. LPs: w. Schoof, *Voices* (CBS); w. T. Honda quartet, *Flying to the Sky*, Trio jazz series (Japan); w. Joachim Kuhn, *This Way Out*; w. Baden Baden Free Jazz Orch., *Gittin' To Know Y'All* (MPS).

DUDZIAK, URSZULA, *singer*, also *percussion, synthesizer, composer*; b. Straconka, Poland, 10/22/43. Stud. piano at music school in Zielona-Gora. Inspired by Miles Davis, K. Komeda, Wayne Shorter, Billie Holiday, Ella Fitzgerald. Married to Michal Urbaniak, with whose group she traveled throughout Europe from 1965. Jazz festivals in Warsaw 1969-72; Molde, '71; Pescara, '72; various others in France etc. before coming to US in 1974. Composer of music for ballet (New York Dance Collective), 1974.

Ms. Dudziak's innovative abilities came to the attention of the American public in a unique album, *Newborn Light*, in which she was accompanied only by pianist Adam Makowicz. Though not the first singer to achieve startling effects through the use of electronic devices such as tape-echo, she was the first to achieve prominence with this rare genre of wordless singing.

Among her original works (most of them largely unplanned and improvised rather than composed) are *Dear Christopher Komeda; Ballad; Darkness and Newborn Light; Bandi and Bamse*, the latter two in collab. w. Makowicz.

LPs: *Newborn Light* (Col.); *Fusion, Atma* w. Urbaniak (Col.); *Journey* w. Arif Mardin (Atl.).

DUKE, GEORGE, *keyboards, synthesizer, composer*; b. San Rafael, Cal., 1/12/46. Extensive studies throughout school years. BM in comp. from SF Conservatory, '67; MA from Cal. State, SF. Pl. at Half Note club, SF, '65-7. From '66-70 Duke's trio also traveled w. a vocal group, The Third Wave, for which he wrote most of the material. The trio toured Mexico in '68; worked in SF backing D. Gillespie, B. Hutcherson, H. Land, K. Dorham et al. In '69, pl. w. J-L. Ponty, after which the trio broke up; Duke spent eight months w. D. Ellis band. He began assoc. w. F. Zappa on records, and joined Zappa's Mothers of Invention, '70. After touring w. C. Adderley quintet, '71-2, he returned to the Zappa group, '73-5. Co-led group w. B. Cobham, '75. During '73-5 Duke began working on various occasions with his own group w. Leon Ndugu Chancler or Chester Thompson, drums; Tom Fowler or Al Johnson, bass. Films and TV: Zappa's *2000 Motels* sound track. While pl. with the Third Wave, app. on *Hollywood Palace*. With Ellis on Ed Sullivan show.

Fests: Monterey, '68 w. Third Wave; Monterey, '69, Newport, '70, w. Ponty; Newport, '71, Berlin, '72 w. Adderley. Comps: *Tzina*, a six scene, two act opera, which was his MA thesis; *Giant Child Within Us—Ego*; arr. album, *Here and Now* for Third Wave.

Duke is a musician of rare versatility. In addition to developing a compelling jazz style, he has worked with equal success in the worlds of pop, rock, Latin and avant garde music. He names Ravel, Stravinsky, Stockhausen, Herbie Hancock, Ahmad Jamal, Miles Davis, L. McCann and Zappa among his sources of inspiration.

LPs: *Faces in Reflection; Feel; The Aura Will Prevail; I Love The Blues; She Heard My Cry* (BASF); *Jean-Luc Ponty Experience*, with Geo. Duke Trio (Liberty); w. Cobham, *Crosswinds*; w. Stanley Clarke, *Journey To Love* (Atl.); w. Eddie Henderson, *Sunburst* (BN); w. Adderley (Cap., Fantasy); w. Airto, *Virgin Land* (CTI); w. Flora Purim, *Butterfly Dreams; Stories To Tell* (Milestone); w. Zappa (Discreet).

DUKE, KENO, *drums*; b. St. Michaels, Barbados, W.I., 8/24/27. Stud. under Prof. C.B. Cooding-Edgehill in marching band on Barbados, '38; w. Prof. Auskist at Red Hook Music Centre, Brooklyn, N.Y., '40-2; at U.S. Navy Music Annex, Balboa, Canal Zone, '46-8. Pl. w. U.S. Navy Band in Panama; Atlantic Submarine Fleet Band; Navy Band, Portsmouth, N.H.; then worked w. Bunny Richardson in Boston and New Hampshire area, '56-8. Was member of Joe Gordine big band, along w. J. Richardson, Thad Jones, Willie Bobo, Eddie Jones in NYC area, '58-9. Worked at Keynote Music Club, Brooklyn, w. Sonny Red, B. Timmons, Paul West, '60-1; Needle's Eye, NYC, w. Joe Carroll, Johnny Hartman, '73. Formed the Contemporaries in '70 for a series of Sundays at the Village Vanguard. They have since performed at Amherst, Holyoke and Wm. Patterson State colleges and for the Jazzmobile. The front line has incl., at various times, Clifford Jordan, Julius Watkins, F. Strozier, Junior Cook and George Coleman. Duke, who was a disc jockey for Armed Forces radio, has his own record show on WHBI in NYC and is a faculty member of the Henry St. Settlement House Music School. Infl: Sid Catlett, Max Roach, Philly Joe Jones. TV: *Jazz Set* on PBS w. Contemporaries, '72. Comp: *3 MB; Sense of Values; Bajan-Bajan; Little "D"; Nschi I; Crest of the Wave.* LPs: *Reasons in Tonality; Sense of Values* (Strata-East).

DUNBAR, EARL THEODORE (TED), *guitar, composer*; also *trumpet, valve trombone*; b. Port Arthur, Tex., 1/17/37. Orig. self-taught. Pl. in Lincoln High marching and dance bands and was student dir. of latter. From '55-9 pl. trumpet & guitar in Texas Southern U. concert and jazz bands. Grad. in '59 with pharmacy degree and is licensed in Tex., Ind. & N.Y. Stud. Lydian Concept w. David Baker in Indianapolis, '63. Worked w. Arnett Cobb in Houston, '56-8; Joe Turner, '58; Don Wilkerson, '57-59; David Baker Ensemb., '61-3; subbed for Wes Montgomery for four mos. in his trio, '62-3; Ret. to Tex. from Ind. in '64, working w. Red Garland, Fathead Newman, Billy Harper, James Clay in Dallas, '64-5. Moved to NYC '66. Pl. w. Broadway pit bands for *Big Time Buck White; To Live Another Summer*; w. N.Y. Shakespeare Fest.: *Two Gentlemen of Verona; Sambo.* From 1968 has done school concerts w. Andrew Frierson; Billy Mitchell; Seldon Powell's Orch. Da Camera; Jazzmobile w. Billy Taylor, Jimmy Heath, McCoy Tyner. Worked w. Ron Jefferson Choir, '69-70; Larry Ridley '70; Gil Evans, '70-3; Tony Williams Lifetime, '71-2; Sonny Rollins; Newport Jazz Ens. w. G. Wein; trio w. Ron Carter, Ben Riley, '73; Grady Tate, '73, 74; Billy Harper Sextet; Joe Newman Quartet, '74-5; Roy Haynes; F. Wess, '74; F. Foster big band & combo, '73-5; duo w. Richard Davis, '75. Member of the N.Y. Jazz Rep. Co. and also perf. w. Nat. Jazz Ens. Pl. school concerts on the islands of St. Thomas, St. John & St. Croix w. Harold Ousley for West Indian Gov. Cultural Program. Film: rec. soundtrack for *Fortune and Men's Eyes*; Japanese movie w. G. Evans. TV: staff member for Leon Bibb Show, NBC; apps. on *Soul; Positively Black; Like It Is; Black Journal.* Euro. perfs. w. T. Williams. Fests: NJF w. Bill Cosby; NJF-NY Radio City Jam Session, '72; NJF West (LA & Oak.), NJF-NY w. Gil Evans, '73. Infls: Wes Montgomery, T-Bone Walker, B.B. King, Ellington, M. Davis, T. Monk, Clifford Brown, George Russell, D. Baker, Tony Williams, H. Silver, Oscar McNeil (high school bandmaster). Comps: *Two Areas; You Say You Saw What; Hang In There; A New Machine for Pedro; Oh I'm Just Heah; Mrs. Frankenstein You're Hurt; Turn-back I'm Scared; Tonal Search.*

Dunbar has been able to combine his strong Texas blues background with his further studies in a style that contains the strengths of both. He is an assistant professor of Music at Livingston Coll. of Rutgers U. in New Brunswick, N.J.; staff guitar instructor for Jazzmobile & Jazz Interaction workshops; and has taught at seminars, music camps and Nat. Band Camp (DeKalb, Ill.). Publs: *A System of Tonal Convergence for Improvisers, Arrangers & Composers; Jazz Guitar By Ted Dunbar* (Dunte Pub. Co., 6 Lake Ave. #5B, East Brunswick, N.J. 08816).

LPs: *Svengali* w. G. Evans; *House of David* w. David Newman (Atl.); *Peruvian Blue* w. Kenny Barron; *The Return of Don Patterson; Kwanza* w. Al Heath (Muse); also w. T. Williams (Polydor); Charles McPherson; Charles Williams; Curtis Fuller (Mainstream); McCoy Tyner; Lou Donaldson (Blue Note).

DUNCAN, HENRY (HANK),* *piano*; b. Bowling Green, Ky., 10/26/96. Featured as solo pianist at Nick's in Greenwich Village for most of the club's final decade (through 1963), Duncan was a pioneer of stride piano. After a long illness he died in NYC 6/7/68.

DUNLOP, FRANCIS (FRANKIE),* *drums, singer*; b. Buffalo, N.Y., 12/6/28. After serving as Thelonious Monk's drummer for much of the early '60s, he pl. w. Sonny Rollins '66-7; free-lanced around NYC incl. subbing in pit bands for Broadway shows *The Me Nobody Knows* and *Promises, Promises*, '67-9; own groups and sub drummer w. *Purlie*, '69-70. App. w. own jazz pantomime and mimicry act in NYC, LA and Santa Monica, '70-1; pl. Broadway show *Inner City* '71-3; toured w. Earl Hines '73-4; worked w. various groups at resort hotels in Catskill and Pocono Mts., '74-5. LPs: *Alfie* w. Rollins (Impulse); also w. Monk (Columbia); Richard Davis (Muse, Polydor); Leo Wright (Vortex).

DURHAM, EDDIE,* *composer, guitar, trombone*; b. San Marcos, Tex., 8/19/06. Played and arr. for J. Lunceford; C. Basie in '30s. Led own bands and cont. writing for other gps. as well in '50s-60s. Pl. trombone and guitar w. B. Tate band '69. In mid '70s co-leading a small group w. trumpeter Franc Williams two nights a week at West End Cafe, NYC, concentrating more on trombone than previously. LP: w. *Swing Today* series (Brit. RCA).

DUTCH SWING COLLEGE BAND. This popular Holland based group was founded in 1945, w. Peter Schilperoort as leader and clarinetist. The group has app. at innumerable fests., the first of which took place in '48 in Knokke, Belgium. Toured England, '49. Many international travels w. leading Amer. musicians as feat. attraction, incl. S. Bechet, '49-50, '53-4; Hot Lips Page, '51; Albert Nicholas, '54. Schilperoort left the band in Sept. '55; his place as clarinetist was taken by Jan Morks, and the band's pianist, Joop Schrier, became the leader. Schilperoort returned and again assumed musical leadership in '59. The band's personnel in the early '60s incl. Oscar Klein, trumpet; Dick Kaart, trombone, et al. In later years J. Witherspoon, J. Venuti, Teddy Wilson and Billy Butterfield were among the many U.S. stars to tour with the band, which cont. to enjoy popularity throughout Western Europe in traditionalist-oriented circles. Many LPs on Dutch Philips.

DUVIVIER, GEORGE B.,* *bass, composer*; b. New York City, 8/17/20. Played w. C. Hawkins; L. Millinder; J.

Lunceford; Sy Oliver in '40s. Backed many singers in '50s, mainly Lena Horne w. whom he made several European trips. Also pl. in NYC w. Bud Powell; T. Gibbs. His credits are so extensive that they are impossible to list. He has traveled and/or rec. w. more than 80 singers from Kate Smith to Sinatra; over 65 instrumentalists, rec. on every major label. Rec. sound tracks for such films as *Requiem For a Heavyweight; Serpico; Experiment in Terror; The Godfather*. Rec. jingles for more than 80 separate commercial products, app. in a "I'd Rather Fight Than Switch" commercial complete w. black eye.

Apps. w. Boston Pops; Brooklyn Philharmonia; NY Phil.; Chicago and Phila. Orchs; Cleveland and Rochester Orchs.

Duvivier says: "For good measure see if this 'one-nighter' can be topped for distance—Los Angeles to Monaco to Los Angeles for a command performance."

TV: three yrs. on staff w. B. Rosengarden orch. for Dick Cavett Show, ABC, in '70s; on call for *Today; Tonight*, NBC; *Ed Sullivan; Camera 3*, CBS. Fest: NJF; NJF-NY; Colo. JP.

Although occupied, for the most part, with studio work, Duvivier, in his jazz apps. and recs., shows all the attributes of a master bassist in time, tone and feeling.

LPs: w. Barry Harris, *Vicissitudes* (MPS); w. C. Terry, *It's What's Happenin'* (Imp.); w. Joe Venuti-Zoot Sims (Chiaro.); *Soprano Summit* w. Wilber-Davern (World Jazz).

EARLAND, CHARLES, *organ, composer*; also *soprano sax*; b. Philadelphia, Pa., 5/24/41. Schoolmates were Pat Martino, Lew Tabackin. Early mus. training on alto sax. Pl. tenor sax w. Jimmy McGriff at age 17. Several yrs. later led own band. Made switch to organ in '63 and led own quartet. Pl. w. Lou Donaldson, '68-Dec. '69. Formed trio and rec. *Black Talk* LP which became a hit and enabled him to start touring US in mid-'70. Began doubling on soprano sax, '73. Pl. at NJF-NY, '73-4. Comps: *Black Talk*, incl. in soundtrack of film *Fritz the Cat; Auburn Delight; Cause I Love Her; Never Ending Melody; Asteroid; Brown Eyes; Morgan; Tyner; Van Jay*. Bob Porter wrote that "Earland's style reveals perhaps the best walking-bass line among organists and a unique second type of bass line that creates a rolling, long-meter feeling on rock tunes."

LPs: *Leaving This Planet; Charles the III; Live at the Lighthouse; Intensity; Black Drops; Black Talk; Soul Story* (Prestige); w. Donaldson, *Say It Loud; Hot Dog; Everything I Play is Funky* (Blue Note).

ECKSTINE, WILLIAM CLARENCE (BILLY),* *singer, trumpet, valve trombone, guitar*; b. Pittsburgh, Pa., 7/8/14. Sang w. E. Hines band '39-43. Led own orch. feat. Gillespie, Parker, Blakey, Miles Davis et al, '44-7. Popular since late '40s as single, but has often teamed up with name bands. Was host of monthly TV series, *The Jazz Show*, in LA '71 and part of '72. Toured Europe w. G. Wein package feat. tribute to Ch. Parker, late '74. Though primarily known as a ballad singer, he has had many jazz associations and is a competent instrumentalist. Pl. role in movie, *Let's Do It Again*, w. Bill Cosby, 1975.

LPs: *Feel The Warm; If She Walked Into My Life* (Enterprise); *My Way; The Prime of My Life* (Motown); *The Legendary Big Band of Billy Eckstine—Together* (Spotlite); *The Soul Sessions, Vol. 6, Newport In New York, '72* (Cobblestone).

EDISON, HARRY (SWEETS),* *trumpet*; b. Columbus, Ohio, 10/10/15. Best known as an alumnus of the Count Basie band (1937-50), Edison in the '60s and early '70s continued to work in many orchestras on TV shows, incl. *Hollywood Palace, Leslie Uggams Show*, specials w. Frank Sinatra etc. He was prominently feat. on the sound track, and in the sound track album, of the film *Lady Sings The Blues*. He continued to play clubs and concerts in the U.S., sometimes leading his own combos, also playing with the bands of L. Bellson, Bill Berry and others. He occasionally rejoined Basie, and was a member of the Swing Masters band led by Benny Carter at Carnegie Hall for NJF-NY, '72.

From '73 Edison frequently acted as Mus. Dir. for Redd Foxx on theatre dates, at concerts and in LV. In '74-5 he was heard in concerts w. Maria Muldaur and the Benny Carter orch. He also pl. in a small group w. Carter in Copenhagen in '75. Edison app. at the Berlin JF, Concord Summer Fest. etc.

LPs: *Home With Sweets* (Vee Jay); duo album w. O. Peterson; *The Trumpet Kings Meet Joe Turner* (Pablo); w. Herb Ellis, Ray Brown (Concord Jazz); *Lady Sings The Blues* (Motown); many others w. Sinatra (Repr.); *Colo. Jazz Party* (MPS/BASF).

EDWARDS, THEODORE MARCUS (TEDDY),* *tenor sax, composer*; b. Jackson, Miss., 4/26/24. In Southern Cal. from late '40s, pl. w. Gerald Wilson off and on from '49 into '70s; w. Max Roach, B. Carter, L. Vinnegar in '50s; S. Manne, B. Goodman, many others in '60s. Comp. & arr. for Lorez Alexandria LP on now-defunct Pzazz label. Activity in late '60s and early '70s chiefly involved with artists named below in LP list. Edwards remained a respected, personal soloist "whose work is particularly identifiable by its deeply plunging pulsation and emotional engagement." (Nat Hentoff).

Film and soundtrack for *They Shoot Horses, Don't They?*; soundtrack for *Any Wednesday*. Concerts at Pilgrimage Th., Hollywood, 1972-3 w. M. Jackson-Ray Brown, and '74 w. own quintet. Concord Fest. '73 w. Jackson-Brown; '74 w. Bill Berry.

LPs: Reissues of own 1947 sessions on *The Foremost!* and *Central Ave. Breakdown* (Onyx); 1960-61 sessions, *Together Again!* w. H. McGhee, *Teddy's Ready!, Good Gravy* (Contemp.). Others as leader: *It's All Right* (Prestige); *Feelin's* (Muse). As sideman: *Hello Benny* w.

Goodman (Cap.); *Bluesmith* w. J. Smith (Verve); M. Jackson-R. Brown (Impulse); *Memphis Jackson* w. M. Jackson (Impulse); Sarah Vaughan w. J. Rowles Quintet (Mainstream); Bill Berry (Beez); several w. G. Wilson (Pac. Jazz, World-Pac.).

ELDRIDGE, DAVID ROY (LITTLE JAZZ),* *trumpet, fluegelhorn, singer, leader*; b. Pittsburgh, Pa., 1/30/11. The former Teddy Hill, Fletcher Henderson, Gene Krupa and Artie Shaw star, after working with Coleman Hawkins; Ella Fitzgerald; and his own quintet in first half of the '60s, joined Count Basie in July '66. He left in September to reform his quintet feat. tenor man Richie Kamuca. They pl. together, off and on, to '70 incl. stints at the Half Note, NYC. Eldridge took over as house leader at Jimmy Ryans in '70 and has appeared there from that time. During the late '60s and in the '70s, however, he has continued to tour as a single and with various packages to Europe such as *Jazz From a Swinging Era*, '67; JATP and other Norman Granz tours in the '70s. Fest: MJF, '71; NJF-NY '73 in *Salute to Ella Fitzgerald*, and w. own gp. at dedication of Louis Armstrong Stadium; MJF '74; Montreux '75 w. D. Gillespie, C. Terry. TV: NJF-NY '73, NET; *Just Jazz*, PBS, '71; episode on *Route '66* w. Ethel Waters, Jo Jones, C. Hawkins. "He still has a gladiatorial view of performance," wrote Benny Green in his notes to one of Eldridge's albums, "the professional's fierce pride in his own ability . . . Roy is one of those players whose transcribed solos would never give more than half an indication of their effect, for they are built on the broad rich tone and the characteristic phrasing."

Won DB Critics Poll, TDWR; elected to DB Hall of Fame, '71.

LPs: *Nifty Cat; Nifty Cat Strikes West* (Master Jazz); *Oscar Peterson & Roy Eldridge; Happy Time; The Trumpet Kings at the Montreux Jazz Festival 1975; Trumpet Kings Meet Joe Turner; Jazz at the Philharmonic at the Montreux Jazz Festival 1975* (Pablo); w. *Buddy Tate & His Buddies* (Chiaro.); Ella Fitzgerald, *Newport Jazz Festival 1973* (Col.); *Earl Hines and Roy Eldridge at the Village Vanguard* (Xanadu); w. Miriam Klein (MPS).

ELLINGTON, EDWARD KENNEDY (DUKE),* *composer, leader, piano, lyricist*; b. Washington, D.C., 4/29/1899. Though he led various combos in Washington while still in his teens, Ellington's career as a leader really got under way in New York, late in 1923, when he took over from Elmer Snowden as director of The Washingtonians. This five man group gradually enlarged until, by 1927, when it opened at the Cotton Club in Harlem, the band was ten strong. For the next 15 years Ellington enjoyed growing successes in many areas, but his work in the U.S. (except for a single concert in 1932 at Columbia U.) was confined entirely to night clubs, vaudeville theatres, dance halls and an occasional movie.

During his first European tours in 1933 and 1939, however, Ellington was recognized as a composer and artist of concert stature. In 1943 he began a series of annual concerts in Carnegie Hall, premiering *Black, Brown & Beige*, the first of many extended works written especially for the concert hall.

Notable events in the 1950s were the premiere of *Night Creature* at Carnegie Hall, for which Ellington played with the Symphony of the Air; a triumphant appearance at the 1956 Newport Jazz Festival; his own color TV special, *A Drum Is A Woman*, on CBS in 1957; and the composing and recording, with the orchestra, of his first film score, *Anatomy of a Murder*.

The 1960s found Ellington visiting Europe annually. He became more active as a lyricist, and as writer of words and music of Sacred Concerts, the first of which was performed in 1965 at Grace Cathedral in SF. This work was heard the following year at Coventry Cathedral. Also in 1966 Ellington was the centerpiece in specials for National Educational Television. The band represented the U.S. at the World Festival of Negro Arts in Dakar. In 1967 Billy Strayhorn, Duke's close writing associate since 1939, died; in his memory, the orchestra recorded an album of Strayhorn's compositions, *And His Mother Called Him Bill*, which some critics believe to have been the band's greatest album during the final decade of Ellington's life.

Another superb LP was taped during a Jan. 1968 performance at Yale U. A second Sacred Concert program, with Alice Babs as principal vocal soloist, was introduced later that year at the Cathedral of St. John the Divine. In September, the band toured Latin America and Mexico.

On Ellington's 70th birthday, Apr. 29, 1969, he was the guest of honor at a banquet, dance and jam session held at the White House. President Nixon awarded Ellington the Presidential Medal of Freedom. The band did not take part, but an all-star group gave a recital of Duke's music, after which many jazz celebrities played or sang.

On New Year's day, 1970, the orchestra began a tour of Australia, Southeast Asia and Japan. To celebrate this precedent-setting visit, Ellington composed the *Far East Suite* (rec. on RCA). In July the band returned to Europe. Saxophonist Johnny Hodges, the most famous of Ellington's musicians, died in November.

Ellington was honored in 1971 as a newly elected member of the Swedish Academy of Music. At Newport, in July, he premiered his Africa-inspired suite *Togo Brava*. In Sept. the orchestra left on a triumphant five-week tour of the Soviet Union.

During the first six weeks of 1972, Duke undertook a second Oriental tour. Concerts were given in Japan, Manila, Hong Kong, Bangkok, Mandalay, Ceylon, Kuala Lumpur, Singapore as well as Australia. Toward the end of that year Ellington went to Los Angeles for the taping of a TV special entitled *Duke Ellington—We Love You Madly*. Ellington's band was not used; however, the orchestra assembled by Quincy Jones included several notable former Ellington sidemen.

Immediately after the taping, Ellington was hospitalized, but soon afterward he was on the road again. He visited Paris alone for a TV special; finished work on his Third Sacred Concert, and introduced it at Westminster

Abbey in Oct. of 1973. Also during that year Ellington was awarded the French Legion of Honor.

Early in 1974 Ellington's health showed signs of deterioration, and he was obliged to let the band travel without him during most of the month of January. He rejoined his musicians off and on during February and March. Hospitalized again in New York, he promised that his band would honor a commitment to play in Bermuda toward the end of May. He spent his 75th birthday in a hospital bed. During the next few weeks his condition became desperate, and in the early hours of Friday May 24, he died, a victim of pneumonia and primarily of lung cancer.

On Monday, May 27, memorial services were held at the Cathedral of St. John the Divine. The next day, under the leadership of Mercer Ellington, the band flew to Bermuda to fulfill the promise he had made. During the next year the orchestra reestablished itself under the direction of Duke's son (see ELLINGTON, MERCER).

Of the many tributes and events dedicated to Ellington's memory, one of the most significant was the formulation of plans for a Duke Ellington Center in New York City.

Publs: *The World of Duke Ellington*, by Stanley Dance (Chas. Scribner's Sons, 1970); *Music Is My Mistress*, By Duke Ellington (Doubleday & Co., 1973).

Comps: A virtually complete list of Ellington's works, listed chronologically in order of their copyright dates, appears in *Music Is My Mistress*. Among his later extended works were *La Plus Belle Africaine*, '67; *The Second Sacred Concert*, '68; *Latin-American Suite*, '68-9; *The River* (ballet), '70; *New Orleans Suite*, '71; *Afro-Eurasian Eclipse*, '71; *Togo Brava Suite*, '73; *Third Sacred Concert*, '73.

LPs: The following were listed in U.S. catalogues as available in late 1975: *Black Brown & Beige*, w. Mahalia Jackson (CSP); *Collages*, Ellington w. Ron Collier Orch. rec. in Canada (BASF); *Duke's Big 4*, w. Joe Pass, Ray Brown, L. Bellson; *This One's For Blanton*, duos w. Ray Brown; *The Greatest Jazz Concert In The World*, w. E. Fitzgerald et al (Pablo); *Echoes of an Era* w. Armstrong (Roulette); *Ellington at Newport; Ellington Indigos; First Time*, w. Basie; *Jazz at the Plaza*, Vol. II (Col.); *Ellington '65; Greatest Hits; Will Big Bands Come Back* (Repr.); *Ellingtonia-Reevaluations, The Impulse Years; Ellingtonia*, Vol. 2; *Meets Coleman Hawkins;* w. Coltrane (Imp.); *The Golden Duke; Second Sacred Concert* (Pres.); *Great Paris Concert; New Orleans Suite; Recollections of the Big Band Era* (Atl.); *It Don't Mean A Thing*, w. Teresa Brewer; *My People* (Fl. Dutchman); *Latin-American Suite; The Pianist; Yale Concert* (Fant.); *Nutcracker Suite/Peer Gynt* (Odyssey); *70th Birthday* (Solid State); *Togo Brava Suite; Money Jungle*, w. Ch. Mingus, M. Roach (UA); *Blues Summit*, w. J. Hodges (Verve); *Eastbourne Performance*, last live LP; *Third Sacred Concert* (RCA); *Continuum*, The Ellington Orchestra under the direction of Mercer Ellington (Fant.).

ELLINGTON, EDWARD II, *guitar*; b. New York City, 8/8/44. Grandson of Duke Ellington; son of Mercer Ellington. Sister, Mercedes, a dancer. Began as electrical engineer for RCA. Studied at Berklee Coll. of Music, May '72-May '74: guitar & arranging w. Mark French; theory w. Lennie Johnson. Joined Duke Ellington orch., '74. Infl: Bill Harris, Quincy Jones, Mundell Lowe, Kenny Burrell. TV: Mike Douglas Show w. Ellington band. LP: *Continuum* (Fantasy).

ELLINGTON, MERCER KENNEDY,* *leader, trumpet, composer*; also *saxophone*; b. Washington, D.C., 3/11/19. Own bands, off and on, from '39. Pl. w. father's orchestra briefly in '50. Rejoined the band in '65, after three years as dj on WLIB, NYC. Doubled as trumpeter-road manager until he assumed the leadership following Duke's death in May, '74. European tour, fall '74. TV: Super Bowl, NO, '74; Belmont Race Track; Mike Douglas Show, '75. Fest: Ravinia w. Sarah Vaughan, '74. Co-composer of *The Three Black Kings* w. father. Writing biographical work about Duke Ellington for Houghton Mifflin.

Mercer brought new, young players (incl. his son Edward (q.v.) into the band. He also sought to reactivate older Ellington material that had not been played for quite some time. Many of these pieces are included in the first recording under his aegis, *Continuum* (Fantasy). Two Coral albums of his late-'50s band have been reissued as a double LP, *Black & Tan Fantasy* (MCA).

ELLIOTT, DON (Don Elliott Helfman),* *composer, mellophone, vibes, trumpet*; b. Somerville, N.J., 10/21/26. Active in jazz chiefly in early '50s w. G. Shearing, T. Wilson, T. Gibbs, B. Goodman, B. Rich, and often with own quartet from '54. During '60s, found great success as comp. and prod. of thousands of national radio and TV commercials, also music for TV game shows and specials. Several of his commercials won awards. Also, won prize at Atlanta Film Fest. for documentary for U.S. Postal Service. The Don Elliott "Voices" (multi-voice overdubs) were used by Q. Jones for motion pic. sound tracks in *The Pawnbroker; $; Heat of the Night; The Hot Rock; The Getaway*. As many as 20 voices, all Elliott, were heard backing Roberta Flack in *Smiling*. Comp., scored and prod. soundtrack for film, *The Happy Hooker*; scores for shows, *Tobacco Road; The Opposite Sex*. Owns and operates two 16-track rec. studios. Made first personal app. in 15 years as guest soloist w. NYJRC's tribute to Q. Jones at Carnegie Hall, '75. Coll. concerts, gigs at Stryker's Pub, NYC, '75; also w. N.Y. Jazz Ensemble at Carnegie Hall, and w. G. Mulligan, Westport Country Playhouse, '74.

LPs: *The Don Elliott Ensemble* (Col.); *In The Heat of The Night*, w. Q. Jones (UA); *$*, w. Q. Jones (Repr.); sound track album of *The Happy Hooker*.

ELLIS, DONALD JOHNSON (DON),* *trumpet, drums, composer, leader*; b. Los Angeles, Ca., 7/25/34. After extensive experience as sideman (notably w. Maynard Ferguson, Geo. Russell) and academic work as both student and teacher, Ellis became semi-permanently active as a big band leader in '65, occasionally working with small groups. In the late '60s and early '70s the band achieved a measure of international popularity due to Ellis' many initiatives. He claims, generally with demonstrable justification, to have had the first big band involved in the following innovations: extensive use of odd time signatures; electric string quartet; vocal quartet used as instrumental section; rec. of extended solo using echoplex; use of quarter tones for solos, and for passages by entire trumpet section; fusion of Indian music in jazz; employment of Fender-Rhodes piano, clavinet, ring modulator and phaser etc.

Ellis played most of the major jazz fests. and clubs with his own band; led an all star orch. at the Berlin JF, '68. He has made more TV apps., with or without his band, than the vast majority of jazz artists. TV special, *Birth of a Band*, was built around his Berlin app. He also app. on a Concord, Cal. TV spec., '69; his band played all Ellis' own music for a Soupy Sales spec. Other TV apps. in Hollywood, Hamburg, Paris, Montreal, Antibes etc.

Teaching: theory, composition and trumpet in NYC and LA; courses in arranging etc. at UCLA; *Introduction to Jazz* at San Fernando Valley State Coll. Writer of several articles publ. in DB, '65-9. Commissions: *Synthesis* for S. Kenton's Neophonic Orch.; *Contrasts for Two Orchestras & Trumpet* for Zubin Mehta and the LA Phil.; *Bird of Paradise* for Charlie Byrd; *Reach*, a cantata for chorus and orch., for Berlin JF; *Mind Flowers*, a choral work for Willamette U. Movie Scores: *Moon Zero Two*, filmed in London, '69; *French Connection*, '72.

Based in LA, Ellis' career from '65-75 was extremely eventful, marked by sudden changes of policy, of instrumentation, musical concept and direction. As a consequence he had no single image or identifiable style; nevertheless, as an aggressive proselytizer for new musical developments, he established himself as an important figure and gained a substantial following, the only leader of a big band to do so other than Thad Jones and Mel Lewis with their orch. in NYC.

In the spring of '75 Ellis suffered a serious heart attack and after a long period of recuperation he began writing for various studios. By the end of the year he was playing the "superbone," a combination valve-slide trombone made originally for Maynard Ferguson.

Publs: Various—details obtainable from (Ellis Music Enterprises, 5436 Auckland Ave., N. Hollywood, Ca. 91601).

LPs: *Don Ellis Orchestra at Monterey; Live In 3 2/3/4* (Pacific Jazz); *Electric Bath; Shock Treatment; Autumn; The New Don Ellis Band Goes Underground; Don Ellis at Fillmore; Tears of Joy* (Col.); *Haiku; Soaring* (BASF); w. Geo. Russell, in *Encyclopedia of Jazz*, Vol. 5 (MCA).

ELLIS, MITCHELL HERBERT (HERB), *guitar, composer*; b. Farmersville, Texas, 8/4/21. Though principally involved in studio work in bands on Steve Allen, Joey Bishop, Della Reese and other shows (more recently w. Merv Griffin), Ellis continued to play frequently in jazz settings. From '72-4 he pl. many concerts, night clubs and coll. seminars in a guitar duo w. Joe Pass. Later formed duo w. B. Kessel, touring Australia and app. at Playboy Club etc. Fests: four years at Concord Mus. Fest.; annual jazz parties at Colorado Springs and Odessa, Tex.

LPs: *Seven Come Eleven; Jazz Concord*, both w. Pass; *Rhythm Willie* w. Freddie Green (Concord Jazz); *Two For the Road*, w. Pass (Pablo); *Hello Herbie*, w. O. Peterson (MPS); *Soft Shoe*, w. Ray Brown; *After You've Gone; Great Guitars*, w. Kessel, Ch. Byrd (Concord); w. Bill Berry (Beez).

ELLIS, LLOYD, *guitar*; b. Pensacola, Fla., 1/25/20. Self-taught. Infl. by D. Reinhardt, C. Christian. Ellis remained unknown in jazz circles until he moved to Las Vegas in '70, when he spent two years with the Red Norvo Trio at the Tropicana Hotel, and came to the attention of many local and visiting musicians. Among them was B.B. King, who in an interview selected Ellis as one of his ten favorite guitarists. Ellis had previously worked w. Stuff Smith, and was a member of Charlie Teagarden's combo in the '60s. Own LP and LP w. Norvo (Famous Door); also *Fastest Guitar In The World* (Carlton); *So Tall, So Cool, So There* (Trey).

ELMAN, ZIGGY,* *trumpet*; b. Philadelphia, Pa., 5/26/14. The swing era trumpeter, best known for his 1936-40 tenure in the Benny Goodman orchestra, where his big hit was *And the Angels Sing*, was inactive in music during the last few years of his life. He died in Van Nuys, Calif., 6/26/68.

ERRISSON, KING (Errisson Pallman Johnson), *percussion*; b. Nassau, Bahamas, 10/29/41. Self-taught, later stud. w. M. Mahoney in LV, Chuck Flores in LA. Pro. debut at 14; during his teens also he was a pro. jockey. After pl. for three years at the Conchshell, leading Nassau night club, Errisson was discovered by a film producer, who feat. him in the James Bond thriller, *Thunderball*. His talent was also observed by Diana Ross, with whom he traveled in the U.S., pl. at Waldorf-Astoria and Basin St. in NYC, Frontier Club in LV etc. Settling in LA in late '60s, he found himself in constant demand by a wide range of artists. Quincy Jones, for whom he rec. several albums, observed: "Errisson has a fantastic sense of time and dynamics. He is one of the greatest artists in his field." Frequently using five conga drums, Errisson is an exceptional performer on congas, bongoes and all percussion. As composer, he wrote the song *Darling Come Back Home*, a hit for Eddie Kendricks. Many TV shows in Japan, also own educ. spec. in U.S. '74.

LPs: *The King Arrives* (Canyon); *Life* (UA); *Drums of Nassau* (Bohemian); others w. D. Byrd, *Blackbyrd; Street Lady* (BN); w. H. Alpert (A & M); w. O.C. Smith (Col.); w. Jerome Richardson (RCA); Percy Faith; The Fifth Dimension (Bell); Chas. Kynard (Mainstr.); Groove Holmes (Liberty); Lou Rawls (Cap.); Clara Ward (Cap.);

also many on the Motown label, with various artists.

ERSKINE, PETER, *drums*; b. Somers Point, N.J., 6/5/54. Father an ex-bassist, now a psychiatrist. Attended S. Kenton National Stage Band Camps at age six; continued for several summers, stud. w. Alan Dawson, Dee Barton. Extensive other studies, incl. Interlochen Arts Acad., Indiana U., after which he joined Stan Kenton orch. July 1972, touring U.S., Europe, Japan, teaching at Kenton Clinics. Favs: Elvin Jones, Mel Lewis, Billy Cobham, Grady Tate; infl. Kenton.

LPs w. Kenton (Creative World).

ERVIN, BOOKER TELLEFERRO JR.,* *tenor saxophone, composer*; b. Denison, Tex., 10/31/30. Prominent in NYC w. Ch. Mingus, '58-62. Worked in Europe '64-6, and again in '68; intermittently leading own groups in U.S. On 7/31/70 Ervin died in a NYC hospital of a kidney ailment. He was saluted by fellow musicians for his powerful, typically Texan sound on tenor sax projected into the '60s, and for his superb mastery of both blues and ballads.

Comps: *Mojo; Boo; Uranus; Largo; A Lunar Tune; A Day to Mourn; No Booze Blooze; Eerie Dearie; Number Two; The Trance; Boo's Blues; Groovin' at the Jamboree; East Dallas Special; Exultation; Mooche Mooche; Tune In; Mour; The In Between; The Muse; Sweet Pea; Tyra.*

LPs: *Lament For Booker Ervin* (Enja); *Heavy; The Trance* (Prest.); *The In Between* (BN); *Structurally Sound* (Pac. Jazz); *Booker and Brass* (Liberty); reissue. *That's Right* (Barnaby); w. Eric Kloss, *Land of the Giants* (Prest.); w. R. Weston, *African Cookbook* (Atl.); reissues w. Mingus on Atl., Col., Trip.

ERWIN, GEORGE (PEE WEE),* *trumpet*; b. Falls City, Neb., 5/30/13. Swing era stylist best known for his work w. B. Goodman, T. Dorsey. After '60, on staff at CBS in NYC, along with extensive jazz concert work incl. two tours of Scandinavia, Germany and Britain w. Kings of Jazz, '74. In '67, he produced "Jazz: The Personal Dimension" for Rutgers U. at Carnegie Recital Hall. Other apps. at Dick Gibson and Odessa jazz parties; Kansas City JF; NYJRC; Jazztage, Hanover, '74; Nice, '75. Publs: *Pee Wee Erwin Teaches Trumpet* (Charles Colin Pub. Co., 315 W. 53 St., New York, NY 10019); *A Wee Bit Of Dixie*—duets (Award Music Co., 136 W. 46 St., New York, NY 10036).

LPs: *The Music of Jelly Roll Morton*, w. D. Hyman (Col.); *Satchmo Remembered* w. NYJRC (Atl.); *Happy Times Orchestra*, w. Bob Thiele (Fl. Dutchman); six albums in *Music For Lovers Only* series, w. Jackie Gleason (Cap.)

EVANS, WILLIAM JOHN (BILL),* *piano, composer*; b. Plainfield, N.J., 8/16/29. Continuing as leader of his own trio, which he formed in '56, for recordings (he also toured for eight months in '58 with Miles Davis Quartet), Evans traveled throughout the U.S., S. America, Japan and Europe with the same instrumentation, using Eddie Gomez on bass, '66- , Marty Morell on drums for six years (other drummers were Joe Hunt, Philly Joe Jones and, after Morell's departure, Eliot Zigmund). Evans continued to win many awards, among them five Grammies: one in '63 for *Conversations With Myself*; a second in '68 for *Live at Montreux*; a third in '70 for *Alone*; and two more in '71 for *The Bill Evans Album*, which won both as Best Jazz Performance by a Soloist, and Best Jazz Performance by a Group. He won *Playboy's* All Stars' All Stars on piano for two years and innumerable DB readers' and critics' polls.

TV: *Camera Three; Jazz Adventures; Jazz Set*; a program for PBS; and countless European TV shows. He app. at Monterey, Newport and all major European jazz festivals. Publs: three books of originals and transcriptions of solos (The Richmond Org., 10 Columbus Circle, New York, N.Y. 10019).

Joseph McClellan in the Washington *Post* wrote that "Evans is one of the great virtuosos in jazz today, and in the contemporary style his real virtuosity is not in his hands (that is taken for granted) but in the mind that works constantly to make each performance a new creation, each rehandling of a motif a new vision."

Comp: *T.T.T (Twelve Tone Tune); T.T.T.T. (Twelve Tone Tune Two); In Memory of His Father, Harry L. Evans; Peri's Scope; Very Early; 34 Skidoo; Comrade Conrad; Funkallero; Waltz For Debby; Re: Person I Knew; One For Helen; Two Lonely People.* LPs: *The Tony Bennett/Bill Evans Album; Intuition; The Tokyo Concert* (Fant.); *The Bill Evans Album; Living Time* w. George Russell (Col.); *Bill Evans at Town Hall; Live at Montreux; Montreux II; What's New; Alone; Further Conversations With Myself; Stan Getz and Bill Evans; Simple Matter* (Verve); *From Left to Right* (MGM); *Symbiosis* (BASF); reissues, *Peace Piece and Other Pieces; The Village Vanguard Sessions* (Mile.).

EVANS, GIL (Ian Ernest Gilmore Green),* *composer, piano*; b. Toronto, Canada, 5/13/12. First renowned through his arrangements for the Claude Thornhill orch. in the 1940s. He was then associated w. Miles Davis' nine-piece outfit that was dubbed the *Birth of the Cool* band in '49-50. He then went on to a series of brilliant collaborations w. Davis in the '57-60 period and became active with his own band for in-person performances and recording in '59-60. In '66 Evans visited Cal., where he appeared at the Monterey and Pacific JF, Shelly's Manne Hole and in concert at Royce Hall, UCLA. In '68 was presented in concert at the Whitney Museum, NYC; w. Davis at the Greek Theatre, U. of Cal., Berkeley.

Occupied principally with writing during the late '60s, Evans formed an ensemble for recording in '69 and began weekly performances at the Village Vanguard the following year. In '71 this group, which had now grown into an orch., toured Europe appearing in Holland, Copenhagen at Club Montmartre, and on radio and TV in Denmark, Sweden and West Germany. Evans conducted an evening of his own compositions at the Berlin Jazztage. In the summer of '72, the orchestra played weekend concerts at the Westbeth Cabaret, located in Westbeth, an artistic community where Evans lives, in lower Manhattan. The orch. also app. at the Long Island JF, Henry St. Settlement House, Slug's Cafe, and received funding from CAPS.

Evans was named a founding artist of the John F. Kennedy Center for the Performing Arts, taking part in a concert and broadcast there. He also toured Japan with his orch., '72. He made periodic apps. w. orch. at Village Vanguard, '73-5. As one of the musical directors of the NYJRC in its initial season, Evans participated in three programs under its auspices with his orch.: *Jazz In The Rock Age; Gil Evans Retrospective; The Music of Jimi Hendrix.* A European tour incl. Denmark, Sweden, Switzerland, Germany, July '74.

Film scores: D. Nogata's *Fragments*, '67; A. Gittler's *Parachute To Paradise*, '69; O. Lee's *The Sea In Your Future*, '70. TV/Radio: Cond. and arr. TV and radio broadcasts w. Swedish Radio Orch., '73; concert-broadcasts from Village Gate, Town Hall, '74; hour concert at Brooklyn Coll. for WNYC-TV, spring '75.

Fests: NJF-NY-SF-LA, '73; Montreux; Antibes; Umbria, '74; Yale-New Haven, Conn., '75. Awards: Guggenheim Fellowship in Composition, '68; N.Y. State Council on the Arts Composer Commission, '74; won DB Readers' and Critics' polls as arranger, '66, '74; band won DB Critics poll TDWR, '73-4. Comps: *Las Vegas Tango; Flute Song; El Toreador; Isabel; Barracuda; Proclamation; Variations on the Misery; Anita's Dance; Spaced; So Long; Makes Her Move; Zee Zee.* With M. Davis: *Hotel Me; General Assembly; Eleven.*

By utilizing electric piano, bass and guitar along with synthesizers and various percussion instruments, French horn, tuba and flute, while retaining the more conventional reeds and brasses of the jazz ensemble, Evans achieved, according to Gary Giddins, "a cohesive marriage of his own musical personality with the most compelling results of the jazz and rock revolutions of the past decade."

LPs: *There Comes a Time; Music of Jimi Hendrix* (RCA); *Svengali* (Atl.); *Gil Evans* (Ampex); *Gil Evans Orchestra, Kenny Burrell and Phil Woods*, previously unreleased material from '63-4 (Verve); *Arranger's Touch*, previously issued as *Big Stuff* (Pres.).

EVANS, MARGIE, *singer*; b. Shreveport, La., 7/17/41. Stud. voice, piano and guitar w. several teachers. Infl. by Willie Dixon, Johnny Otis, Donald Byrd, Big Joe Turner, Eddie Vinson, T-Bone Walker, Lowell Fulson, Mahalia Jackson. App. in high school production, but during adolescence sang mainly in church. Moved to LA, '58; began recording '63 and achieved her first measure of prominence on joining Otis, with whom she toured intermittently '69-72. Various jobs in '70s; in concert w. W. Dixon, Freddie King, Papa John Creach, Mike Bloomfield, Lowell Fulson, Canned Heat. An exceptionally capable blues shouter in the Bessie Smith tradition. Fests: Monterey, '71, w. Otis.

LPs: *Louisiana Woman* (UA); *Cuttin' Up*, w. Otis (Epic); *Stepping Into Tomorrow*, w. Byrd (BN).

EVANS, SUE, *percussion*; b. New York City, 7/7/51. Not related to Gil Evans, but worked with him often from 1969-75. Perc. & dr. study w. Warren Smith, Morris Lang, Montego Joe in '60s; Sonny Igoe '71-2. Drums w. Judy Collins in US and Europe, 1968-72; perc. w. Steve Kuhn Quartet, midwest, '72-4; Jazz Composers' Orch.; also worked w. Coleridge Perkinson, rec. w. James Brown, Bobby Jones, D. Amram, Roswell Rudd, Billy Cobham, Blood Sweat & Tears and pl. in several off-Broadway shows.

Favs: Tony Williams, Elvin Jones, Max Roach, Airto, Billy Higgins; also Gil Evans, Ornette Coleman. Ms. Evans described herself in 1975 as a percussionist equipped for every setting, from pop, classical and jazz to r & b and free music.

LPs w. Gil Evans (Ampex, Atlantic, RCA); S. Kuhn (ECM); Bobby Jones (Cobblestone).

FADDIS, JON, *trumpet, fluegelhorn, piccolo trumpet*; also *piano*; b. Oakland, Calif., 7/24/53. One sister sings; other is a pianist. Began on trumpet at age eight w. private teacher and in grammar school but didn't really show great interest until 11 or 12. At 15 stud. w. Bill Catalano who introduced him to the music of Dizzy Gillespie. Later studied w. Carmine Caruso; at Manhattan Sch. of Mus. w. Mel Broiles, '72-3. Piano, harmony, theory w. Sanford Gold, '75.

Experience w. r & b bands at age 13 in Oakland. Then Catalano took him to SF to sit in w. rehearsal bands of Rudy Salvini; Cus Cousineau; Don Piestrup. Grad. high school '71 and joined Lionel Hampton for six mos. from that summer. To NYC w. Hampton where he then became a member of Thad Jones-Mel Lewis from Feb. '72-Sept. '75, incl. Russian tour. During this time also worked w. Gil Evans, '72; C. Mingus, concert '72; European tour, summer '73. Concerts w. Chuck Mangione from '72. Pl. w. D. Gillespie gp. at Vanguard; Half Note, '74; big band at Buddy's Place, '75. Won TDWR, DB Critics poll, '74-5. Gillespie's "musical son," Faddis, with his great range and fire, is one of the most promising of the young crop of musicians to come to light in the '70s. As he moved toward a more personal expression his potential seemed vast.

Infl: Gillespie, C. Parker, Snooky Young, Bill Chase, Ellington, Armstrong. Film: documentary w. Gillespie for John Hubley. TV: Lionel Hampton Special in Canada, '71; w. Geraldo Rivera's *Good Night America*, ABC; Sammy Davis show, NBC, '75. LPs: *Oscar Peterson & Jon Faddis* (Pablo); *Jon and Billy*, co-leader w. Billy Harper (Trio); w. Randy Weston, *Tanjah* (Poly.); *Mingus & Friends* (Col.); *Mingus at Carnegie Hall* (Atl.); w. C. Earland (Prest.); w. Jones-Lewis, *Suite For Pops* (Horizon); Swedish Radio Jazz Group, *Greetings and Salutations* (Four Leaf Clover).

FAGERQUIST, DONALD A. (DON),* *trumpet*; b. Worcester, Mass., 2/6/27. Prominent in LA during '50s as one of the first and best trumpeters of the West Coast school, Fagerquist died 1/27/74 in LA of a kidney disease. He had worked with the bands of G. Krupa, W. Herman, Les Brown, A. Shaw, and rec. w. S. Manne, John Graas and Dave Pell.

FALZONE, SALVATORE JOSEPH (SAM), *saxophone, flute, clarinet, composer*; b. Buffalo, N.Y., 12/20/33. Stud. clarinet '47-51. Air Force band '52-5; U. of N.Y. at Fredonia; B.S. mus. educ. w. saxophone major, '56-60; also stud. mus. educ. at U. of Buffalo. In '64 while teaching instrumental music in public schools of N.Y. state, met Don Ellis and worked with him during most of the next decade, incl. Hindustani Jazz Sextet, '65; European tour, Antibes Jazz Fest. etc. '68. Freelance work in LA from '68, also w. Buddy Rich band, '68. Film and TV sound track work for *The French Connection; Dial M for Music*. Comp. and arr. *Get It Together; Go Back Home* for Ellis band. Latter was publ. by Objective Mus. Co., Cal. Arr. *Put It Where You Want It* for Ellis' *Connection* album. Favs. Ch. Parker, S. Rollins, J. Coltrane, Miles Davis, D. Ellis.

LPs: *Live at the Fillmore; Autumn; Tears of Joy*, w. Ellis (Columbia).

FAME, GEORGIE (Clive Powell),* *singer, organ, bandleader*; b. Leigh, Lancashire, England, 6/26/43. First prominent through hit single *Yeh Yeh*, '65. Winner of British polls as top male jazz singer. In '66, gave Festival Hall concert and rec. album w. Harry South band, incl. Ronnie Scott, Tubby Hayes. Presented his own first West End theatre production in London, Dec., '66. In '68 headlined a season at Mayfair Theatre, in a two-hour one man show. Later that year toured continent w. C. Basie orch. Also sang w. Jon Hendricks and Annie Ross, '68 at Berlin JF. Made first US app. May '70 with group known as Shorty. LPs on British labels.

FARLOW, TALMADGE HOLT (TAL),* *guitar*; b. Greensboro, N.C. 6/7/21. Came out of semi-retirement to play a two-month stint at a NYC club called The Frammis, '67 and to rec. w. Sonny Criss for Prestige. Fest: NJF, '68-70; NJF-NY, '72. The '69 app. was w. George Wein's All Stars with whom he also played club and concert gigs on east coast and St. Louis, reunited w. his old leader Red Norvo within the group. For some years Farlow has lived on the New Jersey coast where he does some teaching, pl. occasional engagements in local clubs, colleges and schools. Instruction book, *Tal Farlow Method*, publ. by (Guitar Player Prod., P.O. Box 615, Saratoga, Ca. 95070).

Farlow employs a divider of his own devising which enables him to add another line when he is playing single notes. "It sounds roughly as if I'm playing octaves on a piano," he says. As might be expected, the naturally talented guitarist uses it with restraint and good taste.

LPs: *Fuerst Set* (Xanadu); *Tal Farlow—Guitar Player* (Prest.); *Up, Up And Away*, w. Criss (Prest.); *George Wein's Newport All Stars* (Atl.).

FARMER, ARTHUR STEWART (ART),* *fluegelhorn, trumpet*; b. Council Bluffs, Iowa, 8/21/28. Best known as trumpeter in early '50s w. Lionel Hampton, later w. H. Silver, G. Mulligan and as co-leader w. Benny Golson of the Jazztet, 1959-62. During the '60s he played in partnership w. Jim Hall, worked with increasing frequency in Europe, and switched permanently from trumpet to fluegelhorn. In '68 he moved to Vienna, working with the house band for the Austrian Broadcasting System, but continued to appear throughout Europe in concerts and clubs. In '72 he toured the Orient and Europe with NJF in a group led by organist Jimmy Smith. Though still living in Vienna, he returned often to the U.S., app. at NJF, '73 and '74, and working with local rhythm sections in NYC, LA and other key cities.

Though a product of the bebop era, Farmer was influenced by L. Armstrong, L. Young, Ellington, Nance, Rex Stewart et al, as well as by Gillespie and Parker. He evolved a style of rare lyricism; his solos invariably show a superb sense of construction and his rich tone quality on the fluegelhorn is unequaled in jazz.

LPs: *Gentle Eyes*, with strings; *Homecoming* w. J. Heath (Mainstream); *Portrait of Art* (Contemporary); *Farmer's Market; Early Art* (Prestige); *Farmer-Golson Jazztet* w. Tyner (Cadet). Early LPs as leader, some now unavailable, on ABC-Paramount, UA, Mercury, Atl., Col., Scepter. *What Is There To Say*, w. G. Mulligan (Col.).

FARRELL, JOE (Joseph Carl Firrantello), *tenor sax, flutes*; also all reeds except bassoon; b. Chicago Heights, Ill., 12/16/37. Brother-in-law, Carmen Guierino, who worked commercial jobs around Chi. in late '30s and '40s, started him on clar. in '48. Stud. tenor sax w. Joe Sirolla at Roy Knapp music school in Chi. '53; Majored in flute at U. of Ill. under Charles DeLaney. B.S. in Mus. Ed. '59. Pl. w. Ralph Marterie '57 and many jam sessions w. Ira Sullivan, Nicky Hill and other Chi. musicians. To NYC '60. W. Maynard Ferguson '60-1; Slide Hampton '62; Tito Rodriguez '62-64; George Russell sextet, incl. European tour Oct. '64; Jaki Byard '65; three yrs. w. Thad Jones-Mel Lewis from '66; at the same time w. Elvin Jones trio '67-70. Also short stints w. Woody Herman '65, Horace Silver in late '60s, Herbie Hancock. In '70s pl. w. Chick Corea, incl. European and Japanese tours w. his Return To Forever group. Own quartet '74-75. NJF w. Ferguson '60; E. Jones '68, 72; as soloist '73-74; Molde, Pori JFs '71-2; George Wein European tour '64; European tour w. E. Jones '68; own group at Berlin JF '73. Comps: *Moon Germs, Great Gorge, Ultimate Rejection*. Insp. & infl: Charlie Parker, Sonny Rollins, John Coltrane, Bud Powell, Ira Sullivan, Johnny Griffin, Jaki Byard, Elvin Jones. American & BBC TV apps. w. E. Jones '68; Canadian TV w. C. Mingus '65 and own group '74; NET w. Don Ellis '62. Won DB Int. Critics Poll as new star on tenor '68; flute '69; DB Readers Poll on sop. sax '69; *Melody Maker* '68.

Farrell, in addition to being a very active jazzman, has also, in the late '60s and the '70s, been one of the busiest of the New York studio men, recording w. Santana, Billy Cobham, the Rascals, the Band, Aretha Franklin, James Brown, etc. Clinician for Selmer Co. '75.

"Mr. Farrell," wrote John S. Wilson, "builds broiling, jabbing solos that flow in an essentially melodic fashion despite a steady interjection of startling turns and quirks. At times, his lines pile up in such quicksilver fashion that he sounds like an entire band in himself."

LPS; *Outback; Moon Germs; Penny Arcade; Upon This Rock; Canned Funk* (CTI); w. Maynard Ferguson (Roulette); *Asia Minor* w. Dizzy Reece (New Jazz); *Live at Lennie's* w. Jaki Byard (Prestige); *Explosion* w. Slide Hampton (Atlantic); w. Thad Jones-Mel Lewis (Solid State); *Puttin' It Together, The Ultimate* w. Elvin Jones (Blue Note); *Strings* w. Pat Martino (Prestige); *Sunday Afternoon at the Village Vanguard* (Solid State); *Return to Forever* w. Chick Corea (ECM), *Light As a Feather* w. Corea (Polydor); *Mingus Revisited* w. C. Mingus (Trip).

FARROW, ERNEST (ERNIE),* *bass*; also *drums, piano*; b. Huntington, West Va., 11/13/28. Raised in Detroit. Active w. Terry Gibbs, Stan Getz, Yusef Lateef in '50s; also own trio in Detroit, '58; Red Garland trio, '60. In 1964 Farrow again returned to Detroit. He formed a quintet for work in local clubs and a 10 piece band, the Big Sound; also app. as sideman w. Jack Brokensha, Harold McKinney, etc. In '69 he reinstituted a jazz policy at the legendary Bluebird and was playing there with his quintet until a tragic swimming pool accident took his life on 7/14/69. LPs: *Lateef; Blues For the Orient*, w. Lateef (Prestige); *The Many Faces of Yusef Lateef* (Milestone).

FATOOL, NICHOLAS (NICK),* *drums*; b. Milbury, Mass., 1/2/15. Swing era veteran heard in early years w. Goodman, Shaw, Bob Crosby. Worked w. P. Fountain at his club in NO, '67-9. Crosby, Phil Harris in LV, '69-73; gigs w. M. Matlock, Dick Cary, Peanuts Hucko. Fests: Sacramento each year; also Aspen; Concord; San Diego. Fatool, since '72, has been a professional golf teacher.

LPs: *The Swing Era* series (Time-Life); others w. Matlock (WB); Fountain (MCA).

FAVORS, MALACHI, *bass*; also *banjo, zither, bells, gongs, log drum, whistles, bicycle horns, ballophone, singer*; b. Chicago, Ill., 8/22/37. Father a pastor and family very religious. Initially inspired by Charlie Parker, Oscar Pettiford, then Wilbur Ware. Started pl. after high school. Recorded w. Andrew Hill, '58 and pl. w. him for two yrs. Worked gigs w. pianists and organists in lounges. Met Roscoe Mitchell in fall, '61, and Richard Abrams soon after, pl. w. Abrams' big Experimental Band throughout the early '60s. By '65 it evolved into the AACM w. Joseph Jarman and Roscoe Mitchell, and, a year later, Lester Bowie. When Jarman joined the Roscoe Mitchell Art Ensemble it eventually became the Art Ensemble of Chicago which lived and played in France, June '69-April '71. Writer Arnie Passmun, reviewing the AEC in '73, called Favors ". . . without peer among avant-garde modern American Black Music bassists."

Comp: *Tutankhamen; Illistrum*.

LPs: see Art Ensemble of Chicago; others w. Mitchell; Jarman; Bowie.

FELD, MOREY,* *drums*; b. Cleveland, Ohio, 8/15/15. The prominent swing era drummer, who worked often w. B. Goodman and E. Condon, moved to Cal. in '68, then joined Peanuts Hucko in Denver and was the orig. drummer w. World's Greatest Jazzband. He died 3/28/71 in a fire at his home in Denver.

LPs: w. Goodman (Col.); WGJ (Project 3).

FELDER, WILTON LEWIS,* *tenor saxophone, electric bass, composer*; b. Houston, Texas, 8/31/40. Originally gained popularity as tenor saxophonist w. Jazz Crusaders (later known simply as The Crusaders), Felder during the '60s took to doubling on fender bass and soon found himself in constant demand for hundreds of pop, rock, r & b and jazz rec. sessions in this capacity. He continued to work frequently as a regular member of The Crusaders.

LPs: w. Crusaders (Blue Thumb).

FELDMAN, VICTOR STANLEY (VIC),* *piano, vibes, percussion, composer*; b. London, England, 4/7/34. To U.S. '55, toured w. Woody Herman; C. Adderley; based in LA from '51; occasional overseas tours w. B. Goodman; June Christy et al. In '63 he rec. and gigged w. Miles Davis for whom he wrote *Seven Steps To Heaven*.

In recent years, Feldman has been confined mainly to commercial studio work, principally as a percussionist. Has composed for several doc. films, in '75 completed score to a ballet *Encounter Near Venus*, by Leonard Wibberly, collaborating w. George Russell on the music. Perf. in Apr. '75 by Ballet Pacifica in So. Cal. Feldman's jazz gigs in the '70s often feat. him w. Tom Scott, John Guerin, Chuck Domanico. This quartet is heard in a Feldman album on Choice Records. He traveled across Canada in the first Canadian Jazz Fest., '74.

Other LPs: *Bag of Blues*, w. A. Blakey, B. De Franco (Veejay); *Seven Steps To Heaven* w. Miles Davis (Columbia); *Colorado Jazz Party* (MPS/BASF). Publs: *All Alone By The Vibraphone* (Gwyn Publ. Co. P.O. Box 5900, Sherman Oaks, Ca. 91413); *Musicians Guide to Chord Progression* (Try Publ. Co. 854 Vine St., Hollywood Ca. 90028).

FERGUSON, MAYNARD,* *trumpet, leader, baritone horn, valve trombone*; b. Verdun, Quebec, Canada, 5/4/28. Although he began working some jobs w. a sextet in '65, he didn't break up his big band until the fall of '67. Toured England at the head of a band billed as the Anglo-American Jazz Orchestra. He met trumpeter Ernie Garside, owner of the Club 43 in Manchester, who helped him form an English band. Then Ferguson spent six mos. w. his wife and children at the Rhishi Valley School near Madras, India. Back in England he again put together a big band. An album, *M.F. Horn*, was issued on Columbia in the summer of '71 and the band toured the northeastern US beginning w. an Oct. concert at Town Hall, NYC. By the fourth tour, after mutual agreement with immigration authorities and the union, the personnel became decidedly less British in character. By then, the band had app. in Western and Eastern Europe and had also shrunk from 16 men to 13, the size of Ferguson bands of the '50s and '60s. This outfit applied the hyper-intense brassy energy of Ferguson's Kenton legacy to today's pop-rock material such as Herbie Hancock's *Chameleon*, as well as some recycled Ferguson chestnuts. Baritone saxophonist Bruce Johnstone called the orch. "sort of a violent band . . . The whole evening starts out at a high intensity level and builds." By '74 Ferguson had moved back to the US and was living in Calif. Fest: NJF-NY '74-5. LPs: *Chameleon; M.F. Horn; M.F. Horn, Two; M.F. Horn III; M.F. Horn 4+5/Live at Jimmy's; Maynard Ferguson in London* (Col.); w. Gustav Brom (Supraphon); reissues, Trip; Main.

FERRIS, GLENN ARTHUR, *trombone, composer*; b. Los Angeles, Cal., 6/27/50. Stud. w. several trombone teachers, '59-68; jazz theory and improv. w. Don Ellis, '64-6; J. Klemmer, '69. Pl. w. Ellis, '66-70; Beach Boys, Tim Buckley, '71; Revival, '69-71; F. Zappa & Mothers of Invention, '72; Harry James, '73-4, Billy Cobham, '74-.

Comps: *Neurock n' Roll; Adventures of Gunga Din In His Youth; Dwan; I Like It.* Fests: Newport, Antibes, Monterey, '68; Concord, '69-70; Kongsberg, Montreux, '74.

LPs: w. Ellis, *Autumn; Goes Underground; Live At Fillmore* (Col.); w. Cobham, *Total Eclipse; Shabazz* (Atl.).

FIELDER, ALVIN, *drums*; b. Meridian, Miss., 11/23/35. Began pl. in '48 under infl. of friend. After high school pl. w. local band of Duke Otis. Went to Xavier U., NO, to study pharmacy and met Earl Palmer, Ed Blackwell and was strongly infl. by latter. Did studio work for Duke Records in Houston. Pl. w. Eddie Vinson sextet. To Chicago to take degree in Manufacturing Pharmacy. Met Sun Ra and pl. w. him before becoming part of the AACM in late '60s. Returned to Meridian to run family pharmacy. Received grants for teaching young students and importing musicians such as Roscoe Mitchell, Lester Lashley, John Stubblefield, Malachi Favors, Muhal Richard Abrams and Clifford Jordan for concerts. LP: w. Mitchell, *Sound* (Delmark).

FINNERTY, BARRY, *guitar, composer*; also *piano, electric bass*; b. San Francisco, Cal., 12/3/51. Stud. classical piano at age 5; guitar lessons at 13; attended Berklee Coll. briefly, '71, but mostly self-taught. To NYC to play jazz professionally, '73 and joined Chico Hamilton in April of that year. Also worked with Airto Moreira and Flora Purim Apr.-Nov. '74. Joined Joe Farrell quartet Jan. '75, still app. occasionally w. Hamilton. Finnerty has also perf. w. H. Laws, Tower of Power and Beefy Red. His comp. *Chants To Burn* was recorded by Raul de Souza in the latter's Fantasy album *Colors.* Other comps: *African Visions; In View.* Fests: Montreux w. Hamilton, '73; Monterey w. Moreira, '74. Infls: Miles Davis, J. Coltrane, Julian Bream, E. Dolphy, D. Reinhardt, several contemp. classical composers.

LPs: *Funk Factory* w. Michal Urbaniak (Atco); *Peregrinations* w. Hamilton (Blue Note).

FISCHER, CLARE,* *composer, piano, organ*; b. Durand, Mich., 10/22/28. Prominent since mid-60s as a freelance musician and composer in LA, Fischer app. in concerts at the Pilgrimage Theatre, and in such clubs as Donte's and The Times etc. Though orig. better known as a pianist, he gained great respect for his unusually resourceful employment of a specially built Yamaha organ, and the Fender-Rhodes electronic piano. Usually feat. with a trio or quintet, he devoted a substantial amount of his playing time to compositions in the Brazilian idiom, to which he is sensitively attuned.

LPs: *Songs for Rainy Day Lovers* (Col.); *Reclamation Act of 1972; Easy Livin'; One—To Get Ready: Four To Go; Great White Hope* (Revelation).

FISCHER, WILLIAM S., *composer, conductor, saxophones, flute, clarinet, keyboards*; also *synthesizer, trombone, percussion, viola, cello, oboe, contrabass, voice*; b. Shelby, Miss., 3/5/35. Grandfather, Robert Fischer, pl. banjo & violin on riverboats out of NO, 1900-15. Began on piano at 7; saxophone w. Kermit Holly Sr. in Jackson, Miss. at 13 and w. Wm. Davis at Jackson Coll. at 15; at Xavier U. in NO at 16. Comp. w. Clifford Richter at 17. Theory major w. B.S. in mus. ed, '56. M.A. in theory & comp. w. Albert Seay at Colo. Coll., '59-62, summers in Aspen. Research in electronic mus. & opera w. Gottfried Von Einem in Vienna at Acad. of Mus., '65-6. As saxophonist went on the road w. Smiley Lewis, '50. Pl. w. Muddy Waters, '51; Joe Turner, Guitar Slim, '52-3; Ray Charles, '53, pl. baritone sax on Charles' first recs., made in NO; Ivory Joe Hunter, '54-5. Formed bands w. John Fernandez, Alvin Batiste and others in NO, '52-6.

Fischer, who between '68-73 participated in more than 70 albums as a free-lance arr.-comp., for such companies as A&M, Blue Note, Prest.-Fant. and RCA. From '68-70, while mus. dir. at Atl., he wrote arrs. for J. Zawinul, David Newman, W. Pickett, R. Flack, H. Mann and Y. Lateef. Wrote orig. mus. for UA films and stage prod. from '71- . Cond. major orchs. in recs. in Berlin, Cologne, Toronto, LA & NYC. Assoc. Prof. of Music at Xavier U., '62-6. Artist-in-residence at Newport Coll. of Art, Newport, Wales, and Cardiff Coll. of Art, Cardiff, Wales, '66; Bost. U. theater div.; U. of Mich., '70; Norfolk State Coll., '71. Visiting lect. at major coll. & univ. in U.S. Early infl: Ray Charles, Guitar Slim, Smiley Lewis, Sonny Stitt, Gene Ammons, Lee Konitz. TV: cond.-arr. for Fr. Norman O'Connor's *Dial M For Music*, CBS. Fests: Berlin JF, '68; MJF, '69-70. Awards: Rockefeller Commission; Fulbright Grant; Nat. Council for the Arts; NY State Council on the Arts; Austrian Govt. Grant; Pan-American (OAS) Grant. Publ: *Analysis of Arnold Schoenberg's 4th String Quartet*, showing technique of the dodecaphonic system (Colo. Coll. Press, '62). Comps: opera, *Jesse*, '66; *Experience in E for Jazz Quintet & Orch.; Suite for Jazz Quintet & Orch.; Quiet Movement for Orch.* Most of Fischer's comps. are publ. by (Ready Prods., 1365 St. Nicholas Ave., New York, N.Y. 10033); and (Bote & Bock, Berlin).

LPs: as perf.-writer w. Zawinul (Vortex); *Experience in E* w. C. Adderley (Cap.); as writer for N. Adderley (A&M); Andy Bey (Atl.); own album (Embryo); *Suite for Jazz Quintet* (Atl.); *Quiet Movement* (Desto); *Electronic Music* (Arcana).

FITZGERALD, ELLA,* *singer*; b. Newport News, Va., 4/25/18. After appearing in concerts at home and abroad since 1951 under the aegis of Norman Granz, frequently in his Jazz at the Philharmonic shows, Fitzgerald in 1968 began to tour Europe as a solo act, frequently accompanied by orchestras such as Duke Ellington and Count Basie. In 1971 her career was interrupted as a result of serious eye trouble. She underwent eye surgery in Boston in August of that year, and from then until 1973 cut down somewhat on her working schedule.

Her concert with the Boston Pops in 1972 marked her first appearance with a symphony orchestra. The following years saw an upsurge in demand for similar appearances, and by 1975 she had appeared with more than 40 symphony orchestras throughout the U.S. In October of '75 she toured Europe with Count Basie and Oscar Peterson.

Fitzgerald continued to lead the *down beat* Reader's Poll annually from 1953 through '70, as well as many other polls.

Her television appearances included two specials with Frank Sinatra, a Timex special, and two programs of her own for the BBC in London, as well as appearances on the Carol Burnett show, etc. Festivals: Newport; Nice; Juan les Pins; Baalbek, Lebanon, etc. Though she recorded one or two albums of contemporary songs aimed at the youth market, they were not among her major successes, and she soon returned to her policy, approved by Granz, of singing standard tunes, usually accompanied by outstanding jazz combos and orchestras.

LPs: *At Duke's Place; The Best Of; On The Cote D'Azur*, w. D. Ellington; *Ella & Louis*, w. Armstrong; *History; Mack The Knife* (Verve); *Best Of, Vol. 2* (MCA); *Carnegie Hall, Newport Jazz Fest.* (Col.); *Ella; Things Ain't What They Used To Be* (Repr.); *Ella Fitzgerald* (Arc. Folk); *Ella Fitzgerald* (Pick.); *Ella Loves Cole* (Atl.); *In London*, w. Flanagan, Pass; *Take Love Easy*, w. Pass; at the Montreux Jazz Festival 1975; *Greatest Jazz Concert in the World; Live at the Santa Monica Civic* (Pablo); *Watch What Happens* (BASF).

FLACK, ROBERTA, *singer, piano, songwriter, arranger*; b. Black Mountain, N.C., 2/10/40. Father pl. piano. Stud. from age 12 w. Hazel Harrison, a concert pianist. At age 13 won second place in statewide contest for black students, playing a Scarlatti sonata.

A brilliant student, Flack graduated from high school at 15, and from Howard U. with a BA in Mus. Ed. at 19. She then took up a career as a school teacher. During the next five years taught English literature in Farmville, N.C., then singing and classical music in junior high schools in Washington, D.C. In '62 she doubled as accompanist for a group of opera singers at a restaurant in Washington. By '65 her evolution into popular music as pro. singer and pianist had begun to take shape. During a long stint at Mr. Henry's Club in Washington, she was heard by Les McCann, who recommended her to Atl. Records. Her first album was an immediate hit and by '70 she was a major new artist. The next few years saw her transcend the jazz and pop fields to become a superstar, whose repertoire incl. material by B. Bacharach, Leonard Cohen, B. Dylan, songs in French and Spanish, and original works. Among her early successes were Gene McDaniels' *Compared To What*, and Ewan MacColl's *The First Time Ever I Saw Your Face*. The latter rec. was used on the sound track of a motion pic., *Play Misty For Me*, as a result of which Flack's fame grew substantially. In '73 her album and single entitled *Killing Me Softly With His Song*, arr. by E. Deodato, again brought her to the top of the pop charts, though she retained her hold on jazz and soul audiences.

Formerly married to bassist Steve Novosel, Flack is an exceptionally well qualified musician who shifts easily from one idiom to another. She was once quoted as saying, "I've been told I sound like Nina Simone, Nancy Wilson, Odetta, Barbara Streisand, Dionne Warwicke, even Mahalia Jackson. If everybody said I sound like *one* person, I'd worry, but when they say I sound like them all, I know I've got my own style."

Comps: *Go Up Moses; Be Real Black For Me; Moody*. Flack has won many awards, among them Grammies for Record of the Year, '72, '73; Best Pop Vocal Performance by a Duo (w. D. Hathaway), '72; Best Pop Vocal Perf., Female, '73. Won DB Readers Poll, '71-3.

LPs: *First Take; Chapter 2; Quiet Fire; Roberta Flack & Donny Hathaway* (Atl.).

FLANAGAN, TOMMY LEE,* *piano*; also *clarinet, alto sax, tenor sax, bass, vibes*; b. Detroit, Mich., 3/16/30. Veteran of many bebop groups in '40s and '50s. Best known in later years as accompanist, serving as musical director for Tony Bennett, '66; regularly w. Ella Fitzgerald from Sept. '68. When not with Fitzgerald, worked as freelance studio and nightclub musician; played at Bradley's in Greenwich Village as duo w. Wilbur Little, '73-'74. Comps: *Dalarna; Minor Mishap; Solacium; Beat's Up; Little Rock; Eclyspo.* LPs: *Tommy Flanagan Overseas*; T. Flanagan Trio (Prestige); *Tommy Flanagan Trio* (Moodsville); *The Tommy Flanagan Tokyo Recital* (Pablo); Trio and sextet w. K. Dorham (Onyx). LPs as sideman w. Coleman Hawkins, *Today and Now* (Impulse); J. Coltrane, *Giant Steps* (Atlantic); *Ella Fitzgerald in London; at Montreux JF 1975* (Pablo); *Ella Fitzgerald at Carnegie Hall* (Col.); *Kenny Dorham Memorial Album* (Xanadu); *Jazz at the Philharmonic at Montreux JF 1975; Dizzy Gillespie Big 7 at Montreux JF '75* (Pablo).

FLAX, MARTY (Martin Flachsenhaar),* *baritone saxophone*; b. New York City, N.Y., 10/7/24. Flax, who pl. w. D. Gillespie on the latter's 1956 State Dept. tours, also worked w. W. Herman, L. Jordan, B. Rich and C. Thornhill. From the late '60s, he was heard in hotel and lounge bands in LV. He died 5/3/72 in LV. LPs w. Gillespie (Verve).

FLORY, MEREDITH (MED),* *alto sax, arranger, clarinet, tenor & baritone saxes*; b. Logansport, Ind., 8/27/26. After many years in big bands and studio work, based first in NYC and from '56 in LA, Flory became less active in music. He concentrated on acting and was seen in many film and TV dramas (*Mannix; Lassie; Bonanza; Policewoman* etc.); also wrote and doctored many motion picture scripts. Early in 1972, with Buddy Clark (q.v.), he developed the concept of Supersax. The group rehearsed frequently during the year but did not make its public debut until Nov. 1972 at Donte's in North Hollywood.

Using many arrangements written by Flory, who transcribed Charlie Parker solos from old recordings and airchecks, the group reached an unexpectedly wide audience with its first album, *Supersax Plays Bird*, which was a 1973 Grammy award winner.

Supersax appeared at Newport West Festival in LA; Concord and Monterey, '73; Orange Coast Fest., '74. Cross-Canada tour, summer '74; Japanese tour Jan. '75.

LPs: *Supersax Plays Bird; Salt Peanuts; Supersax Plays Bird With Strings* (Cap.).

FOLDS, CHARLES WESTON (CHUCK), *piano*; b. Cambridge, Mass., 5/4/38. During adolescence in Evanston, Ill. stud. w. piano teachers from Northwestern Univ. Music courses at Yale, '57-60. Piano stud. in early '60s w. Richard McClanahan in NYC. Mostly self-taught in jazz. First prof. job w. Yale jazz band '56; managed band in senior year. W. Danny Alvin at Basin St. in Chi., Summer '57; next three summers in Europe w. college jazz bands; concerts w. Chet Baker, Kenny Clarke, Stan Getz. After grad. went to NYC where he worked w. Joe Thomas; Ruby Braff; Pee Wee Russell; Max Kaminsky at Eddie Condon's and the Metropole. Toured w. Village Stompers in '63-4; then w. Peanuts Hucko; George Wettling '64; Metropole w. Shorty Baker; Conrad Janis; Red Allen '65. Left music business full-time to work as editor for American Heritage Pub. Co., '65-9. Also gigged w. Bob Crosby; Tony Parenti in '60s; Wild Bill Davison; Hucko; Jimmy McPartland; Buck Clayton-Maxine Sullivan; Bobby Hackett in '70s. March '71-July '73 w. Roy Eldridge at Jimmy Ryan's; other NYC jobs w. the Countsmen; Joe Venuti; Jimmy McPartland; Buddy Tate; Maxine Sullivan; Bobby Hackett, '73-4. Solo piano in weekly "Jazz By Sunlight" series at The Cookery from '73. Infl: Ellington, Tatum, Wilson, Hines, Waller, Donald Lambert. Fest: Virginia Beach w. Kaminsky '62; NJF-NY w. Eldridge '73. LPs: *It's Ragtime* (Jazzways); own trio and one w. Countsmen on Brit. RCA.

FONTANA, CARL,* *trombone*; b. Monroe, La., 7/18/28. Toured with Woody Herman several times in 1950s and '60s, incl. State Dept. tour of Africa in '66. During the following decade he was based in Las Vegas, pl. lead trombone w. Paul Anka and working in local show bands, but took time out for various jazz jobs, inc. gigs and/or records w. Benny Goodman, jazz parties in Colorado and Odessa, Texas; Supersax, Louis Bellson. Co-led combo with Jake Hanna 1975. Toured Japan w. Geo. Auld. Gigs and albums w. World's Greatest Jazzband. Despite the limited quantity of his jazz work due to his LV residency, Fontana was regarded by many fellow-musicians as the most fluent and innovative trombonist since J.J. Johnson. LPs w. Hanna-Fontana (Concord Jazz); World's Greatest Jazzband (Project 3, World Jazz); *Salt Peanuts* w. Supersax (Capitol); *Concerto for Herd* w. Herman (Verve); *Colorado Jazz Party* (MPS).

FORD, RICHARD ALLEN (RICKY), *tenor saxophone*; b. Boston, Mass., 3/4/54. Studied at New England Conservatory of Music; during this time, worked with Jaki Byard combo. Joined Duke Ellington orchestra under direction of Mercer Ellington, August '74 and drew critical acclaim as a hard-driving, creative soloist blending contemporary characteristics with traditionalist roots. Left Ellington to join Charles Mingus, May '76. LP: w. Mercer Ellington, *Continuum* (Fantasy).

FORD, ROBBEN LEE, *guitar*; also *saxophone, piano*; b. Woodlake, Cal., 12/16/51. Father c & w guitar and harmonica player in Wyoming. Stud. sax at age 11 in high school; self-taught on guitar at 13. Infls. range from Coltrane to Ravi Shankar to Stravinsky. Prof. debut, '70 w. Charlie Musselwhite Blues Band; with brothers, Charles Ford Band, '71; Jimmy Witherspoon, '72-3; Tom Scott L.A. Express and Joni Mitchell, Jan-Sept. '74; George Harrison, Oct-Dec. '74. MJF, '72; NJF, '73. App. on Educ. TV prog, *One Of A Kind*. LPs: w. Charles Ford Band (Arhoolie); w. Joni Mitchell, *Miles of Aisles* (Elektra-Asylum); w. T. Scott, *Tom Cat* (Ode); w. Jimmy Witherspoon, *Spoonful* (BN).

FORREST, JAMES ROBERT (JIMMY),* *tenor sax*; b. St. Louis, Mo., 1/24/20. Pl. w. Jay McShann; Andy Kirk in '40s; Duke Ellington, '49-50. Led own gps. in '40s, '50s. Pl. w. Harry Edison, '58-60. After living and playing in St. Louis and LA for periods of time, he joined Count Basie in '73, bringing with him his earthy, big-toned, driving tenor style. LPs: *All the Gin is Gone* (Delmark); w. Basie (Pablo).

FORTUNE, SONNY, *alto saxophone*, also *flute*; b. Philadelphia, 5/19/39. Stud. at Wurlitzer's and Granoff Sch. of Mus., also privately w. Roland Wiggins. Local work w. r & b groups, Chris Columbus, Betty Burgess before coming to NYC in 1967. After 2½ months w. Elvin Jones, was member of Mongo Santamaria band, 1968-mid 1970; Leon Thomas latter part of '70; McCoy Tyner '71-mid '73; Roy Brooks, summer-fall '73. After leading his own group for a while, pl. w. Buddy Rich March-August 1974, then joined Miles Davis.

Fortune is skilled on all the saxophones and has shown his stylistic adaptability, gigging and/or recording w. Lloyd Price, Melvin Sparks, Geo. Benson, Roy Ayers, Oliver Nelson, Pharoah Sanders, Horacee Arnold, as well as Brooks, Rich and Davis.

LP: Strata-East; *Awakening* (Horizon); also *Stone Soul* w. Santamaria (Col.); *Other Side of Abbey Road* w. Benson (A & M); *Sahara* w. Tyner (Milestone).

FOSTER, PAUL ALEXANDER (ALEX), *saxophones, clarinets, flutes*; b. Oakland, Calif., 5/10/53. Brother, Frank (no relation to tenor saxophonist), classical violinist living in Calif. Studies at SF Conserv. of Mus.; Curtis Inst. of Mus., Phila.; Inst. for Advanced Mus. Studies, Valais, Switz. During '73 worked w. Duke Pearson, Clark Terry, Thad Jones-Mel Lewis big bands; Chico

Hamilton, '73-4; Jack DeJohnette Directions from Nov. '74; Paul Jeffrey Octet, '75. Infl: Parker, Coltrane, Rollins, M. Davis, C. Adderley, DeJohnette, European classical music. Pl. alto sax and clarinet in film *Rico* w. Dean Martin, MGM. Fest: MJF; Concord; Montreal; Ahus; Schaeffer Mus. Fest. Represented as composer and player on *Cosmic Chicken* w. Jack DeJohnette Directions (Prest.).

FOSTER, FRANK BENJAMIN,* *tenor, soprano saxophones, composer, educator*; also *flute, clarinet, alto & baritone saxes, piano*; b. Cincinnati, Ohio, 9/23/28. From '53-64 a mainstay of the Count Basie orch. as tenor soloist and arranger. Own big bands and small gps. from '65; also gigs w. W. Herman; Lloyd Price; L. Hampton; Duke Pearson; Peter Duchin; Basie. Toured Europe as guest soloist w. local gps., '68. Joined Elvin Jones, June '70, touring in England and Germany w. him, Oct. '70. Cond. Jazz Interactions' Young Musicians' Clinic in a tribute to Louis Armstrong, Alice Tully Hall, NYC, Dec. '71. Continued to play w. E. Jones, off and on through '74, incl. State Dep't.-sponsored tour of So. America, fall, '73. Concerts: w. NYJRC; CBA; '74; w. Buddy Rich, Feb. '75; Oliver Nelson, at Bottom Line, NYC, June '75. Cond. for Redd Foxx on tour of Eastern U.S. feat. B. Eckstine, in July; then Scandinavian; U.S. and Japanese tours w. Thad Jones-Mel Lewis orch. as arr. and feat. soloist. During '75 also app. w. his own "Loud Minority" and "Living Color"; quintet co-led w. Charli Persip.

TV: Represented Jazz & People's Movement w. own sextet on *Today Show*, NBC; w. Elvin Jones, *American Musical Heritage*, CBS, '71; Joe Franklin, '72. Fest: w. E. Jones, NJF '70; NJF-NY '74; NY Musicians' JF '72-3; Ohio Valley w. Jones-Lewis '72; NJF-NY '73. Awards: CAPS; NEA, '74. Music Consultant, NYC Public Schools, '71-2; Assist. Prof. SUNY at Buffalo, '72-3; Adjunct Prof., CUNY at Queens Coll, N.Y., from '74. Foster has also cond. seminars, workshops, etc., at New Eng. Cons., Wesleyan U., Conn.; Oakland U., Pontiac, Mich.; Howard U., Wash., D.C. Board member of Jazz Interactions. Comp: *Disapproachment; Ural Stradania; Simone; Raunchy Rita; Cecilia is Love; The Loud Minority; Requiem for Dusty; Ithaca Suite*. LPs: *The Loud Minority* (Main.); *Manhattan Fever* (BN); *Fearless Frank Foster; Soul Outing* (Prest.); w. Duke Pearson; Elvin Jones; Donald Byrd (BN); E. Jones & Richard Davis (Imp.); w. Thad Jones-Mel Lewis, *Suite For Pops* (Horizon).

FOSTER, GARY, *saxophones, flute, clarinet*; b. Leavenworth, Kansas, 5/25/36. Graduated U. of Kansas with BM woodwinds and mus. ed., '61. Settling in Cal., he became active in all major film studios, doubling as woodwind expert. Big bands: Clare Fischer, '65- ; L. Bellson, '68-9; Mike Barone, '69-70; Toshiko, '73- ; Ed Shaughenssy, '74- . Combos: Fischer, '65- ; Jimmy Rowles, '68; Warne Marsh, '68-73; L. Almeida, '74- . Woodwind teacher in LA area. Founded Nova Music Studios, a group of pro. teacher-performers in Pasadena, '74. Instructor of jazz studies at Pasadena City Coll. Fests: Monterey, '74 w. Fischer; San Diego, Monterey, '75 w. Toshiko.

LPs: *Subconsciously; Grand Cru Classe* (Revelation); *Ne Plus Ultra*, w. Marsh (Revelation); *Thesaurus*, w. Fischer (Atl.).

FOSTER, GEORGE MURPHY (POPS),* *bass*; b. McCall, La., 5/19/1892 (date uncertain). Raised in New Orleans; prominent in 1920s and '30s w. Luis Russell and Louis Armstrong bands. Still active in 1960s, he toured Europe w. all star group of NO veterans in '66. To Chi. in '68 to tape a TV program w. Art Hodes. Living in San Francisco, Foster died there 10/30/69. One of the first musicians to popularize the string bass in jazz, he was best represented on recordings with Armstrong (Col., MCA).

Publ: *The Autobiography of Pops Foster, New Orleans Jazzman*, as told to Tom Stoddard (Univ. of Cal. Press, 1971). The book, reprinted in paperback in 1973, includes a selected bibliography, and a comprehensive discography from 1924-40 by Brian Rust.

FOUNTAIN, PETER DEWEY JR. (PETE),* *clarinet*, also *alto, tenor saxes*; b. New Orleans, La., 7/3/30. Most of his time spent pl. at his own club at 231 Bourbon St. in NO but he also has done nine wks. a year for seven yrs. at the Tropicana in Las Vegas as well as numerous apps. at concerts and fairs. Pl. NO Jazz Fest., Calif. JF. TV apps. w. Lawrence Welk, Ed Sullivan, Andy Williams, Bob Hope, Bing Crosby, Kraft Music Hall, Danny Kaye, Johnny Carson, Bob Crosby. Film short: *Pete's Place* (MCA). Won *Playboy* award 14 times. Book, *A Closer Walk: The Pete Fountain Story* pub. by Henry Regnery, Chi. LPs: most recent on MCA; also Coral, Decca.

FOWLER, BRUCE, *trombone*; b. Salt Lake City, Utah, 7/10/47. Father is noted music educator Dr. William C. Fowler (see below). Stud. w. Ned Meredith early '60s; NTSU, '67-9; U. of Utah, '65-7, '70-2. Worked w. W. Herman, '68, '69; Power Circus, '69-70, F. Zappa and Mothers of Invention, '72-5. Infl.: F. Rosolino, C. Fontana, J.J. Johnson et al. Comps: *Habondia* for six trombones; several other pieces for trombone sections and for jazz-rock groups. LPs: *Lab '68* w. NTSU; *Roxy and Elsewhere*, w. Zappa (Discreet).

FOWLER, DR., WILLIAM L.,* *educator, guitar*; b. Salt Lake City, Utah, 7/4/17. Ph.D. in composition from U. of Utah, '54. Emerged as major figure in jazz education in '60s, director/public relations for National Stage Band Camps, Intermountain Jazz Fest., '67-75; jazz prog., U. of Utah, '68-72. Westminster Coll. '72-4. He was also dir. of guitar prog. for U. of Colorado at Denver, '74-5; coordinator, Visiting Jazz Faculty Prog. U. of Utah, '68-72; Westminster Coll.; '72-4; U. of Colo., '75. Has given many illustrated lectures on history of jazz and history of guitar for Music Educators National Conference. Won Mr. Mobile Music Award, Mobile, Ala., '74.

Comps: *The Pearl; The Great and Marching Words;*

Micat In Vertice. Dr. Fowler has also served as education editor for DB, and is author of several books on guitar published by C. G. Conn, Ltd.

FOWLKES, CHARLES BAKER (CHARLIE),* *baritone sax*; b. Brooklyn, N.Y., 2/16/16. Member of Count Basie band 1951-1969. After a knee injury, left band and remained in New York, playing at Westbury Music Fair etc.; rejoined Basie June 1975.

FRANCIS, DAVID A. (PANAMA),* *drums*; also *bongos, conga*; b. Miami, Fla., 12/21/18. An active big band drummer in NYC w. R. Eldridge, L. Millinder, Willie Bryant, C. Calloway in '40s and '50s; also house drummer at Central Plaza in '50s and busy studio man w. Sy Oliver, Perez Prado, Tony Bennett, R. Charles, C. McRae, '50s and '60s. Dinah Shore's personal drummer, '67-70. Moved to LA, '68, where he played in studios and also at Hong Kong Bar w. Joe Williams, T. Wilson and Calloway. Moved back to NYC, '73, joining Oliver. Toured England w. Warren Covington orch.; France, Spain, Belgium, Switzerland w. group incl. Tiny Grimes, Arnett Cobb, '74. Nice JF, '74. Charter member of NYJRC; guest mus. dir. for prog. recreating music of the Savoy Ballroom at Carnegie Hall, May '75. App. in film *Lady Sings The Blues*. TV: *The Jazz Show*, KNBC, '71. Colorado Jazz Party, '74-5.

LPs: w. Tiny Grimes; Arnett Cobb; Big Nick Nicholas; Milt Buckner; Earl Hines (Black & Blue); also for *Music Minus One*.

FRANKLIN, ARETHA,* *singer*; b. Memphis, Tenn., 1942. With her shift to the Atlantic label in Nov. '66 she soon moved into the realm of pop, blues and soul star. By '73 she had six gold LPs and 14 gold singles, each signifying 1,000,000 records sold. In May '68 she made a European tour, visiting seven major cities in England, France, Germany, Holland, Sweden and France. In Feb. '68 she appeared in concert at Cobo Hall in her "home" city of Detroit on what was proclaimed "Aretha Franklin Day" by the mayor. She was presented with a special Southern Christian Leadership Council Award by Rev. Martin Luther King on that evening.

Through the late '60s and '70s she performed at the LA Forum, Houston Astrodome, Boston Garden, Latin Casino, Apollo Theater, Hollywood Bowl, Radio City Music Hall. In '73 she appeared at African drought benefit, St. John the Divine; in '75 at the Sickle Cell Anemia benefit, Beverly Hilton. Two-week summer tour of Australia '75. TV: specials w. Duke Ellington; Flip Wilson; Mac Davis; Dinah Shore; Bob Hope; *Tonight Show*. Received Honorary Doctor of Laws degree from Bethune-Cookman Coll., '75. Won Grammy Awards in '68, '70-2. TDWR, DB Critics poll, '68. LPs: *You; With Everything I Feel in Me; Let Me in Your Life; Hey Now Hey; Amazing Grace; Young, Gifted and Black; Live at Fillmore West; Spirit in the Dark; The Girl's in Love With You; Soul '69; Aretha in Paris; Aretha Now; Lady Soul; Aretha Arrives; I Never Loved a Man the Way I Love You*. (Atlantic).

FREEMAN, LAWRENCE (BUD),* *tenor saxophone*; b. Chicago, Ill., 4/13/06. As a charter member of the World's Greatest Jazzband, pl. with them for six years before moving to London in late '74, lecturing and pl. at univs. throughout Gt. Britain. He was honored by NYJRC in a tribute program in which he participated, '74. Pl. with Friends of Eddie Condon at NJF-NY, '72. Publs: *You Don't Look Like A Musician* (Balamp Publ., 7430 Second Blvd., Detroit, Mich. 48202).

Freeman, who in '74 celebrated 50 years of playing, remains a vigorous, joyful artist. Comps: *That D Minor Thing; Song of the Dove; Out of My Road, Mr. Toad; Uncle Haggart's Blues; The Eel*. LPs: *The Compleat Bud Freeman* (Monmouth-Evergreen); w. Lee Wiley; *The Music of Hoagy Carmichael* (Mon-Ev.); w. World's Greatest Jazzband on Project 3, Atl., World Jazz; duo album w. Jess Stacy (Chiaroscuro); *Superbud* (77).

FREEMAN, RUSSELL DONALD (RUSS),* *piano, composer*; b. Chicago, Ill., 5/28/26. Originally a member of Shelly Manne's group, Freeman confined his activities during the '60s and '70s to the Hollywood studios, as well as acting as mus. dir. for many night club acts, app. in LV and all over the U.S. Was mus. dir. for *Laugh-In* TV show, '67-73; Tony Orlando & Dawn, '74- . Comp. main title for Mitzi Gaynor Spec., and orig. music for *Letters to Laugh-In*.

FREEMAN, EARL LAVON (VON), *tenor saxophone, composer*; b. Chicago, Ill., 10/3/22. Brothers are guitarist George; drummer Bruz. Studied under Capt. Walter Dyett at Du Sable High. where Gene Ammons and Bennie Green were schoolmates. Pl. w. Horace Henderson; US Navy Hellcats; Sun Ra; Milt Trenier. Had band w. his brothers and Andrew Hill, '51. Most of his work has been confined to the small clubs of Chicago and environs. Pl. w. Dexter Gordon for Joe Segal's Charlie Parker Month concerts, Aug. '70. Terry Martin, writing of him said: "The harmonic and rhythmic innovations of the boppers, particularly Parker, and the later modal players, have been absorbed into a style that, while it builds on the foundation of Hawkins' power and arpeggiated convolutions, and Lester's melodorhythms, emerges as something quite unique." There are times when there is a parallel with the keening qualities found in the wailing of Johnny Griffin but some listeners are put off by Freeman's intonation.

Comps: *Have No Fear, Soul is Here; Doin' It Right Now; White Sand; Portrait of John Young; Catnap; Brother George*. LPs: *Have No Fear* (Nessa); *Doin' It Right Now* (Atl.); w. Charlie Parker, *An Evening at Home With the Bird* (Savoy); w. George Freeman, *New Improved Funk* (Gr. Merch.); *Birth Sign* (Delmark).

FREUND, WALTER JAKOB (JOKI),* *tenor, soprano saxes*; also *clarinet, trumpet, trombone, violin, accordion, sousaphone, piano, vibes*; b. Hochst, Germany, 9/5/26. Piano w. Gunter Hinz, '45; Carlo Bohlander, '48. First jazz job w. Gerry Weinkopf's big band, '49-50, out of which grew Germany's first important modern jazz group, the Joe Klimm Combo, marked by the sound of Freund's tenor lead over trumpet and trombone. W. Jutta Hipp quartet, '52-4; then own group, the first jazz unit to tour Yugoslavia, '54. Own sextet from '62; also member of Radio Frankfurt (Hessicher Rundfunk) as player-arr. and same for Erwin Lehn's big band at Radio Stuttgart. Sousaphone w. Two Beat Stompers, '55-67. Infl: Parker, Coltrane, Konitz. TV: 13 shows, *Variationen in Jazz*. Fests: Second Polish Jazz Fest., '57; Comblain-La-Tour, '60; Frankfurt, '53-'72.

Comps: *Domicile; Four Temperaments* (suite); *Sopran Lament; Pigeon Suite; Concertino for Tenor-Saxophon and Orchestra; Tree Characters; Moon Over Schwalbach; Street Stories*. Voted top arr. in all German jazz polls, '57-'75; second place as tenor sax, '54-'75; top soprano sax in *Podium* poll, '68-'71. LPs: *Yogi Jazz; Wild Goose; Color in Jazz* (MPS); *Four Temperaments* (Brunswick); *Amerika Ich Rede Dich An* (Electrola); German All Stars (Columbia).

FRIED, ALEXEJ, *trumpet, composer*; also *piano, violin*; b. Brno, Czech., 10/13/22. Studied w. Prof. Theodor Schafer at Brno State Conserv. '45-7; w. Prof. Emil Hlobil, Prague State Conserv. '47-8; w. Prof. Pavel Borkovec, U. of Arts, Prague, '48-53, Bach. of Comp. Pl. trumpet in own big band, Alex's Boys, '38-41; arr. for Gustav Brom, Ladislav Habart, Karel Vlach Orchs. '45-8. In '51 led J. Jezek orch. for Czech. radio and Supraphon recs. From '70 has led own bands and composed for FOK Symph. orch., Prague, and Brom big band. One of the founding members of the Int. Jazz Fest. of Prague and its artistic manager of the AUSVN, military artistic corps., '64-7. Prof. of composition at U. of Arts, Prague. Infl: Ellington, Stravinsky, Picasso, folk songs & spirituals. Film: *The Little Bears* for U.S. TV, '65. TV: *Clarinet Concert*, Prague '75; jazz festival composition, *Act*, pl. by Brom, Prague '70. Fest: comp. pl. by Brom at Prague, '71-2; Warsaw '72. Among his many works are the scores for four musicals. Other comp: *Reeping; Triple Concert; Solstice; Jazzconcert*; also arrs. of *Caravan; Blue Skies; Solitude*. LPs: *Bohemian Jazz, 1920-1960; Swing Festival; Jazz Concertos*, w. Brom; *Moravian Wedding; Solstice* (Supraphon); comp. *Sidonia* on Don Ellis' *Soaring* (MPS/BASF).

FRIEDMAN, DAVID, *vibraphone*; also *drums, percussion, piano*; b. New York, N.Y., 3/10/44. Father amateur violinist. Stud. drums w. Stanley Krell, '55; marimba, xylophone, '60. Perc. major at Juilliard; at same time stud. w. Saul Goodman and Moe Goldenberg; then w. Teddy Charles and Hall Overton. Infl. Luciano Berio, Bill Evans, Milt Jackson. During early '60s played extra w. N.Y. Phil., Met. Opera; much contemporary music perf. w. Berio in Europe and U.S. Subsequently w. Tim Buckley, Horace Silver, H. Laws, Horacee Arnold, W. Shorter, Joe Chambers, Don Sebesky et al. Vibes and jazz improv. clinician for Ludwig Drum Co. in clinics and concerts in U.S. and Europe. On faculty of Manhattan School of Music; and Inst. for Advanced Musical Studies, Montreux, Switzerland. App. at NJF w. H. Laws, H. Arnold, '73. In '75 rec. and concert tours with vibes-marimba duo, playing orig. works. Winner DB poll, TDWR, vibes, '74; tie w. Karl Berger, '75.

Publ: *Vibraphone Technique Dampening & Pedaling* (Berklee Press, 1140 Boylston St., Boston, Mass.). Own LP: *April Joy* (East Wind); w. H. Arnold, *Tribe* (Columbia); w. Laws, *In The Beginning; Live At Carnegie Hall* (CTI).

FRIEDMAN, DONALD ERNEST (DON),* *piano, composer*; b. San Francisco, Ca., 5/4/35. After west coast work, pl. with many groups around NYC, '58. Worked w. Chuck Wayne trio, 66-7; Clark Terry big band, '67; European tour w. Jimmy Guiffre, concerts and clubs in Germany with Attila Zoller, '68; frequently feat. at Half Note, '69, also began small band work w. C. Terry.

In '70 Friedman started teaching jazz piano at N.Y.U., continuing through '73. In 74-5 he joined a commercial trio for steady work in and around NY area and continued teaching. J. Berendt cites Friedman as one of the most important pianists of the '60s and '70s for whom the innovations of Bill Evans were a significant point of departure.

Comps: *Circle Waltz; Spring Signs; Ochre*. LPs: *Metamorphosis* (Prest.); w. Clark Terry (Etoile).

FRISHBERG, DAVID L. (DAVE),* *piano, composer, lyricist*; b. St. Paul, Minn., 3/23/33. An exceptionally eclectic musician, heard with Dixieland and mainstream groups, accompanying singers, writing lyrics and music to songs rec. by Blossom Dearie, Cleo Laine and others. In late '60s worked in NYC w. A. Cohn/Z. Sims, B. Hackett, Ch. Shavers; solo piano at E. Condon's; house pianist at Half Note. In '71, solo pianist and mus. dir. for *Scenes From American Life*, Lincoln Center Rep. Theatre. Moved to LA. Wrote music and lyrics for *Funny Side* NBC-TV series.

'72-3 night club and studio work, incl. gigs with own trio and as sideman w. J. Sheldon, J. Pass, B. Berry. '74-5, traveled and rec. w. Herb Alpert's Tijuana Brass. Continued club and studio jobs. Music and lyrics: *Van Lingle Mungo; The Wheelers and Dealers; One Horse Town; Peel Me A Grape*; also lyrics to *I'm Hip* (mus. by Bob Dorough); *Long Daddy Green* (mus. by Dearie). Frishberg's multiple talents are reflected in his witty lyrics as well as in his versatile playing. Present favs: J. Rowles, Hank Jones, Zoot Sims.

LPs: *Oklahoma Toad* (CTI); *Dave Frishberg*, solo and trio (Seeds); w. J. Rushing, *Livin' The Blues* (ABC); *The You and Me That Used To Be* (RCA); w. Bill Berry (Beez).

FRUSCELLA, TONY,* *trumpet, composer*; b. Orangeburg, N.J., 2/14/27. Pl. briefly w. Lester Young; Gerry Mulligan; Stan Getz in '50s. Often associated w. trumpeter Don Joseph for sessions, etc. From the late '50s he was only intermittently active, hampered by personal problems. Hospitalized for three months in the spring and summer of '69, he had been released for a few weeks when he died from cirrhosis and heart failure at the apartment of a friend in NYC, 8/14/69. His work on LP

w. S. Getz (Verve), and w. his own gp. on Atlantic were deleted long before '75. A session w. Brew Moore for Atl. remained unissued. Dan Morgenstern's DB obituary called him, "a poet of the trumpet with a veiled, haunting sound . . .". Comp: *Moatz* (for Mozart); *Baite* (for Beethoven), latter rec. by Moore (Sonet).

FUKUMURA, HIROSHI, *trombone*; b. Tokyo, Japan, 2/21/49. Brother, Yoshikazu Fukumura, cond. of Kyoto City Symph. Orch. Lessons w. Sadao Watanabe, '70-72. Pl. w. Watanabe's quintet, March '72-Jan. '74. Had own quintet from Jan-Aug. '74. Studied at New England Cons. in Boston, Mass. Holds degree in economics from Nippon Univ., '71. Infl: S. Watanabe, J.J. Johnson, Coltrane. Pl. all major fests. in Japan. Won SJ Readers Poll, '73-4. LPs w. S. Watanabe incl. *Open Road* (CBS/Sony); as leader, *Quintet* (Three Blind Mice); *Live* (Trio).

FULLER, CURTIS DUBOIS,* *trombone, composer*; b. Detroit, Mich., 12/15/34. One of the many players to come out of Detroit to NYC in the '50s, he worked w. the Jazztet; several tours of duty w. A. Blakey's Jazz Messengers in '60s. After leaving Blakey in '65 he freelanced in NYC with a variety of gps., incl. Jimmy Heath in the '70s, until joining Count Basie in '75. Toured Europe w. D. Gillespie Reunion Big Band, '68; Tribute to Charlie Parker, '75. Fest: NJF-NY Radio City jam session, '73; w. Basie, '75. Comp: *Smokin'; Jacque's Groove; Sop City; People, Places and Things.* LPs: *Crankin'; Smokin'* (Main.); w. Albert Heath, *Kwanza*; w. Jimmy Heath, *Love and Understanding* (Muse), w. H. Mobley, *A Caddy For Daddy* (BN).

FULLER, JESSE,* *singer, guitar*; b. Georgia, 1897. Well-known in the SF Bay area for his performances on a home made, one-man-band instrument, the fotella, he had toured in the U.S. and appeared in Europe. Owned a shoe shine parlor in Oakland. Confined to a wheelchair after breaking a hip in '75, he died 1/28/76. LPs: *Brother Lowdown* (Fantasy); others on Good Time Jazz; Arhoolie.

GAFA, ALEXANDER (AL), *guitar*; b. Brooklyn, N.Y., 4/9/41. Self-taught. From 1964-9 worked as a studio musician in NYC; also w. groups of Kai Winding, Sam Donahue; concerts w. M. Legrand. Pl. w. orch. acc. Sammy Davis, '69-'70; mus. dir. and acc. for Carmen McRae, '70-1. Joined Dizzy Gillespie, '71. Infls: Coltrane, Segovia, Wes Montgomery, Johnny Smith. Fests: Newport; Monterey; Chateauvallon; also toured w. Gillespie in *The Musical Life of Charlie Parker* throughout Europe, fall '74. Many TV apps. w. Gillespie. Comps: *Dirty Dog; Behind a Moonbeam; Barcelona.* LPs: *Just A Little Lovin'* w. Carmen McRae (Atl.); *Matrix; The Awakening* w. Mike Longo (Main.); *The Phantom; How Insensitive* w. Duke Pearson (Blue Note).

GALBRAITH, JOSEPH BARRY,* *guitar, educator*; b. Pittsburgh, Pa., 12/18/19. Best known for his work w. Claude Thornhill orch. in the '40s and in recording studios in '50s, he did studio staff playing in NYC from '47-70. Private teaching and faculty member at City College, CUNY, '70-5.

GALES, LAWRENCE BERNARD (LARRY),* *bass, composer*; also *cello*; b. New York City, 3/25/36. Worked w. T. Monk, '65-9; also w. Mary Lou Williams. In '69 Gales moved to Cal., and was heard with Erroll Garner, Willie Bobo, Joe Williams, Red Rodney, Harold Land, H. Edison from '69- . Also during this period worked w. own trio at clubs in LA area. In '74 rec. w. Jimmy Smith and toured U.S. w. Benny Carter, incl. concert at LA Museum of Art. With Bill Berry LA Big Band, '73-4. Gales has also been active in school and coll. concerts and clinics and has received many awards in this field, incl. a citation from LA Mayor Tom Bradley. Comps: *Rosa Mae; Adrien June; Syl'lo'gism.* Fests: all major events while w. Monk; San Diego, w. M.L. Williams, '74. App. in TV movie *The Morning After.*

LPs: w. Monk, *Monk's Blues* (Col.); w. J. Smith *Paid In Full* (Mojo); w. S. Criss, *Crisscraft* (Muse).

GALPER, HAROLD (HAL), *piano, keyboards, composer*; b. Salem, Mass., 4/18/38. Classical training, 1945-8; Berklee Sch. of Musc., '55-8; also pvt. studies w. Ray Santisi, Jaki Byard, Herb Pomeroy, Margaret Chaloff. Worked in Boston w. Pomeroy big band and combo, Sam Rivers Quartet, Tony Williams; later w. Chet Baker; European festivals w. Bobby Hutcherson-Harold Land, Joe Henderson, Stan Getz, Randy Brecker, Attila Zoller. Acc. many singers incl. Joe Williams, Anita O'Day, Chris Connor, Jackie Paris-Anne Marie Moss, Dakota Staton. Came to general public attention after replacing George Duke in Cannonball Adderley Quintet. Equally at home in orthodox jazz, r & b and free jazz contexts. With L. Konitz, '75. Infls: Red Garland, H. Hancock, Bill Evans, C. Corea, piano; O. Coleman, Miles Davis, Wayner Shorter (composers).

LPs: Mainstream; also w. Adderley (Fantasy); *A New Conception* w. Sam Rivers (Blue Note); *Score* w. R. Brecker (UA); *Baby Breeze* w. Chet Baker (Limelight).

GARBAREK, JAN, *saxophones, flute*; b. Norway, 3/4/47. Self-taught. Worked w. own groups in Norway; occasionally w. Geo. Russell; Chick Corea; Don Cherry; Keith Jarrett; and other Scandinavian all star groups. Infl. by Coltrane, Russell, Miles Davis and Jarrett. Has app. at most major European jazz fests. Frequent apps. at Student City Jazz Club on Oslo Univ. campus are central to club's success. According to Joachim Berendt, Garbarek " 'spiritualizes' rock phrases in terms of free jazz, perceptibly stimulated by study of George Russell's Lydian system." LPs: *Afrique Pepper Bird; Sart; Triptykon; Witchi-tai-to* (ECM); w. Jarrett (ECM); Russell.

GARE, LOU, *tenor saxophone*; b. Rugby, Warwickshire, England, 6/16/39. From '63-5 pl. w. Mike Westbrook band; then primarily w. AMM (duo w. Eddie Prevost, q.v.) from '65- . With AMM, Gare gives lecture-demon-

Terry Gibbs (*Veryl Oakland*)

Dizzy Gillespie and Jon Faddis (*Veryl Oakland*)

Red Norvo, George Benson, Benny Goodman and Milt Hinton

Billy Hart (*David D. Spitzer*)

Roland Hanna (*Veryl Oakland*)

Billy Harper (*David D. Spitzer*)

Barry Harris (*David D. Spitzer*)

Hampton Hawes (*Veryl Oakland*)

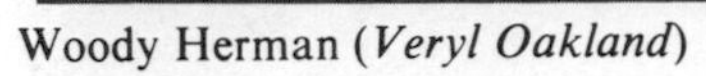

Woody Herman (*Veryl Oakland*)

Roy Haynes (*David D. Spitzer*)

Joe Henderson (*Randi Hultin*)

Eddie Henderson (*Veryl Oakland*)

Billy Higgins (*David D. Spitzer*)

Jon Hendricks and
Maynard Ferguson
(*Veryl Oakland*)

Helen Humes

Eubie Blake and Earl "Fatha" Hines (*Ed Lawless*)

Bobby Hutcherson (*Veryl Oakland*)

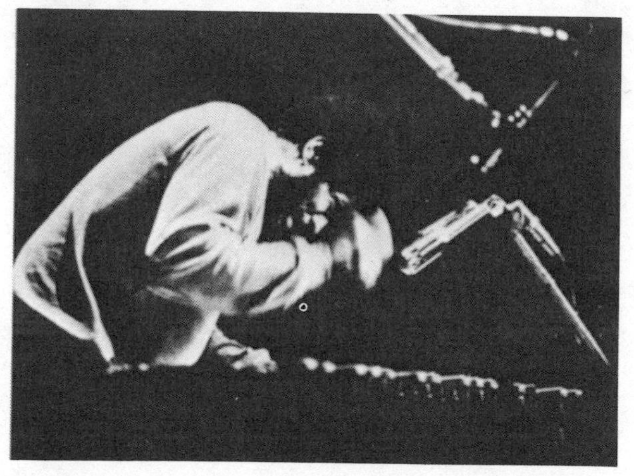

Milt Hinton (*Veryl Oakland*)

Paul Horn (*Veryl Oakland*)

Freddie Hubbard (*Veryl Oakland*)

Milt Jackson (*Veryl Oakland*)

Howard Johnson (*David D. Spitzer*)

Budd Johnson (*Veryl Oakland*)

Bob James

Jo Jones (*David D. Spitzer*)

strations, recital-discussions and practical workshops. The group, which started out in '65 as a quartet, was one of the early "free music" organizations in Gt. Britain.

LPs: *AMM Music* (Elektra); *Live Electronic Music* (Mainstr.); *AMM at the Roundhouse* (Incus); *To Hear and Back Again* (Emanem).

GARLAND, JOSEPH COPELAND (JOE),* *composer, tenor sax*; also *soprano & bass saxes, clarinet*; b. Norfolk, Va., 8/15/07. Leader of nine-piece band with brother, trumpeter Moses Garland, made up of former big band players of the Swing Era, for club dates in NY-NJ area. Degrees from three photography schools incl. NY Inst. of Photography and is an active color photographer. Comps: *Leap Frog; Serenade to a Savage*; and *In the Mood*. The latter, first popularized by Glenn Miller in 1939, won a Grammy award as sung by Bette Midler in 1974. LP: one track w. Baron Lee in *The World of Swing* (Columbia).

GARLAND, EDWARD B. (MONTUDIE), *bass*; b. New Orleans, La., correct date of birth, 1/9/1885. Worked in NO bands until 1912, then left for Chicago. Pl. w. King Oliver, '16-21. Active in LA with own groups for many years; worked w. Kid Ory off and on from '44-54, later w. E. Hines, Turk Murphy in SF, Andrew Blakeney in LA. App. in *A Night in New Orleans* at Wilshire Ebell Theatre, LA, '73 and '74. In '74 joined Barry Martyn's Legends of Jazz, touring US and Europe. App. on TV w. Legends on Dinah Shore show, '75. Garland was honored by Pres. Ford, Gov. Reagan and Mayor Bradley of LA as the oldest living jazz sideman during a *Night in New Orleans* concert celebration Sept. '74.

LPs: *The Legends of Jazz; Barney Bigard and the Legends of Jazz* (Crescent Jazz).

GARLAND, WILLIAM M. (RED),* *piano*; b. Dallas, Tex., 5/13/23. An important member of the Miles Davis quintet of the mid-'50s, he returned to Dallas in mid-'60s and, for the most part, has worked there from '66 at Club Arandas and Woodmen Auditorium. To NYC May '71 for recs. and more than a month of weekends w. own trio at Pegleg's. Back to Dallas, June '71. Comp: *Old Stinky Butt*. LPs: *Auf Wiedersehen; The Quota* (MPS); reissues, *Jazz Junction*; others w. M. Davis; J. Coltrane (Prest.).

GARNER, ERROLL LOUIS,* *piano, composer*; b. Pittsburgh, Pa., 6/15/23. To NYC, '44. Winner of many awards since '46. In late '60s Garner headlined the International Television Fest. in Montreux, for which he was commissioned to compose the festival's theme music. Around this time he was the only U.S. artist to app. at the ROTF Eurovision Gala.

In '71 Garner was the subject of a spec. TV half hour in the *Just Jazz* series. He continued to app. as soloist with major symph. orchs., having made his debut with the Cincinnati Symph. in '57. In '74-5 season he perf. with the National Symph. in Washington; others in Honolulu, Louisville, Indianapolis, Detroit. In early '75 he contracted a severe case of pneumonia which incapacitated him for the remainder of the year. He was convalescing in California, Jan. '76.

Garner has become one of the most popular jazz artists as a concert and fest. attraction, pl. at Antibes in '70, and a series of concert galas on the French Riviera, '73-4. In '70 he made his first tour of S. Amer., and in '72 his initial excursion to the Far East. He re-recorded his best known comp., *Misty*, for use in the film *Play Misty For Me*. Other comps: *Gaslight; Up In Erroll's Room; Mood Island; Solitaire; Feeling Is Believing*, the title tune of an LP that was voted the best jazz piano album of 1970 in the *Jazz and Pop* Critics' Poll. Lyrics were added by Sammy Cahn under the new title *Something Happens*. He won an award from ASCAP, '75, for a hit recording of *Misty* by c&w performer Ray Stevens.

LPs: *Deep Purple* (Pick); *Feeling Is Believing* (Merc.); *Gemini; Magician* (London); *Misty* (Merc.); *Play It Again, Erroll* (Col.).

GARNETT, CARLOS, *tenor sax, composer*; also *alto, soprano, baritone saxes, flute, ukulele, campana (bell)*; b. Red Tank, Panama Canal Zone, 12/1/38. Self-taught on tenor from age 16. To US '62, working w. various rock 'n' roll gps. Serious self-study of "science of music" from '65. Joined Freddie Hubbard, Dec. '68, rec. first album w. him. With Art Blakey from middle of '69-70; Ch. Mingus for four mos., '70. In Oct. formed own gp., Universal Black Force, working w. it to '72. Also pl. and rec. w. Mtume in same period. Six mos. w. Miles Davis, '72; Norman Connors, '72-5. Reformed own gp., pl. Bottom Line, NYC, Aug. '75.

Infl: Coltrane, H. Mobley, H. Land, Rollins, W. Shorter. TV: *Soul*, NET, w. Mtume; Andrew Hill. Fest: NJF w. Blakey, '69; NJF-NY w. Connors, '74. Comp: *Mother of the Future; Holy Waters; Carlos Two; Ebonesque; Journey to Enlightenment; Caribbean Sun; Chana; Let This Melody Ring On; Samba Serenade; Panama Roots*. Own LPs: *Let This Melody Ring On; Journey to Enlightenment; Black Love* (Muse); w. Connors, *Saturday Night Special; Slew Foot, Dark of Light; Love From the Sun; Dance of Magic* (Buddah/Cobble.); w. Davis, *On the Corner; In Concert; Big Fun; Get Up With It* (Col.); w. R. Kenyatta, *Terra Nova*; w. Hubbard, *Soul Experiment* (Atl.); w. P. Sanders, *Black Unity* (Imp.); w. Mtume (Strata-East); A. Hill (BN); Blakey (Japan. Vic̆tor Nivico).

GARRETT, GLEN, *alto saxophone, composer*; also *tenor, soprano, flute, oboe, clarinet* etc.; b. Salt Lake City, Utah, 5/15/48. BM from U. of Utah, '73; MA from Cal. State U., Northridge, '75. Extensive teaching experience, assisting Dr. William Fowler at U. of Utah, '70-2. Taught own theory class from '72-3; assisted Gerald Wilson in his classes at Cal. State Northridge, '73-5. During '70s pl. w. Gary Pack combo; Mayo Tiana big band; Pat Williams; also w. G. Wilson from Jan. '74- . Infls: C. Adderley, J. Hodges, J. Coltrane, C. Corea, Thad Jones.

GARRISON, JAMES EMORY (JIMMY),* *bass*; b. Miami, Fla., 3/3/34. An important member of John Coltrane's group from '61, he left in the summer of '66. Soon after he co-led a small group w. Hampton Hawes for about six mos. Toured, incl. Europe, w. Archie Shepp,

'67-8; w. Elvin Jones trio, '68-9. In '70-1 he taught at both Bennington Coll. and Wesleyan U., pl. as soloist at Bennington graduation ceremony. Pl. w. Alice Coltrane, '72. Rejoined E. Jones, '73-4. Trouble with a hand hampered him in the latter half of '74 and a lung operation curtailed his activities in '75 but by the end of that year he was counseling ex-drug addicts and alcoholics as house supervisor for Project Create, and planning to resume playing sometime in '76. On 4/7/76, however, he died of lung cancer. TV: *Like It Is* w. Shepp. Film: videotape w. 360 Degree Experience. Fest: NJF w. Jones; NJF-NY w. Shepp, '73. Comp: *Tapestry in Sound; Sweet Little Maia; What is This?; Ascendant; Sometimes Joie.*

LPs: Elvin Jones/Jimmy Garrison Sextet, *Illumination* (Imp.); w. Jones, *Puttin' It Together; The Ultimate* (BN); w. Alice Coltrane; John Coltrane; Archie Shepp (Imp.); w. Shepp, *There's a Trumpet in My Soul* (Arista); w. 360 Degree Experience, *From Ragtime to No Time* (360 Degree Music).

GASCA, LUIS (Louis Angel Gasca), *trumpet, composer*; b. Houston, Tex., 3/3/40. Stud. Jefferson Davis H.S., Houston, '55-8; Berklee, '59-60. To Japan w. Perez Prado, '60; pl. w. S. Kenton, '61; M. Ferguson, L. Hampton, '63-4; W. Herman, incl. European tour, '67. Then w. Mongo Santamaria, Janis Joplin, Santana (incl. Euro. tour). In '70s worked w. C. Basie, C. Tjader, Joe Henderson, Geo. Duke.

Infl. by Miles Davis, Coltrane, C. Adderley, D. Gillespie, Ch. Parker, Gasca is one of the most versatile of the jazz-oriented Latin trumpet players. Arr. and pl. on *Canyon Lady* album for Joe Henderson (Milest.); Comps: *Dr. Gasca; I Was Born To Love You; Samba Para San Francisco.* Pl. in film score: *Che* w. L. Schifrin. TV: Dick Cavett, Tom Jones shows w. Joplin; Ed Sullivan show w. Kenton. Fests: Monterey w. Herman; Newport, Atlanta w. Santamaria; Santa Barbara, '75.

LPs: *Little Giant* (Atl.); *For Those Who Chant* (Blue Thumb); *Born To Love You* (Fant.); *Canyon Lady*, w. Henderson.

GASKIN, RODERICK VICTOR (VIC),* *bass*; also *guitar, cello*; b. Bronx, N.Y., 11/23/34. Played w. Paul Horn, Jazz Crusaders, Harold Land in LA before joining Les McCann, '64. With Cannonball Adderley, '66-9; T. Monk, '69; Duke Ellington, '69-70; Harlem Philharmonic, '70; Chico Hamilton, '71; John Mayall, '71-3; New World Symph., many small gps. in NYC, '73-5; NY Jazz Quartet, '75. TV: w. Ellington, Ed Sullivan *Salute to Beatles*, CBS '69; Montreux JF w. O. Nelson; C. Hamilton; L. Thomas, '71-2. Other fest: w. C. Adderley, NJF '67; MJF '68; w. Mayall, NJF-NY '73.

From '74 Gaskin, an accomplished photographer, has been an assistant to Chuck Stewart, shooting rec. sessions, album covers, Navy recruiting ads for *Jet, Ebony*, etc.

LPs: w. C. Adderley, *74 Miles Away*; N. Adderley, *Live at Memory Lane* (Cap.); Monty Alexander (Pac. Jazz); Duke Ellington, *70th Birthday* (SS); Hal Galper; Buddy Terry (Main.); A. Zoller, *Gypsy Cry* (Embryo); Mayall (Poly.); w. O. Nelson; L. Thomas (Fly. Dutch.).

GASLINI, GIORGIO,* *piano, composer*; also *spinetta, synthesizer*; b. Milan, Italy, 10/22/29. Rejecting the type of musician closed in an inaccessible isolation or by a specialist mentality, Gaslini says "One must make music *with* the people more than for the people." Practicing his creed of the "total musician," he played during the '70s in a variety of settings: in the squares of populated areas; in factories and psychiatric hospitals, as well as universities, cinemas and large concert halls. His quartet, formed in Milan in '63, has perf. over 1000 concerts and participated in many fests., films, radio and TV broadcasts. Taught a *Course In Jazz Music* at the Santa Cecilia Conserv., Rome, '72-3. Wrote first Italian jazz opera, *Colloquio Con Malcolm X*, perf. by the Teatro Comunale of Genoa and rec. by P.D.V. Records, '70. App. w. Ellington, Miles Davis, Cecil Taylor, M. Roach, G. Barbieri, D. Cherry, S. Lacy, Bill Evans, J.L. Ponty, Sun Ra.

Comps: *New Feelings; La Stagione Incantata; Grido; Jazz Mikrokosmos; Jazz Makrokosmos; Africa; La Terra Urla; The Woman I Love; Message; Fabrica Occupata; Concerto Della Liberta.* Publ: *Musica Totalie*, Ed. Feltrinelli, Milan.

LPs: *Africa; Fabbrica Occupata* (P.A.); *New Feelings; Message* (BASF).

GAUDRY, MICHEL,* *bass*; b. Normandie, France, 9/23/28. Paris accompanist of Billie Holiday, Carmen McRae in '50s; pl. w. Bud Powell at Blue Note in '60s. In late '60s and '70s occupied mostly w. studio work and as accompanist to pop singers. Pl. in duo w. Jimmy Gourley at Bilboquet, '74. Wrote articles on the bass for *Jazz Magazine* and *Jazz Hot*. Also works as a cartoonist. TV: apps. w. All European Big Band, '67 for BBC; w. S. Grappelli; K. Clarke; H. Geller; J. Griffin, France; w. Wes Montgomery, Germany '67. Fest: Antibes; Cartagine; Stuttgart; Hamburg; Comblain-la-Tour. LPs: w. Billy Strayhorn, *The Peaceful Side* (UA); Duke Ellington and Alice Babs (Reprise); Barney Kessel; Sonny Criss (Polydor).

GELLER, HERBERT (HERB),* *alto sax, flute, composer*; also *misc. reeds, flutes*; b. Los Angeles, Cal., 11/2/28. After leading his own gps. and working w. small combos on the West Coast in the '50s, he moved to Germany in the '60s, pl. first w. the SFB Broadcasthouse band in Berlin; then w. Nord Deutscher Rundfunk orch. in Hamburg from Nov. '65. In Nov. '74 he recorded an album using electric keyboard and synthesizer for which he wrote the music and lyrics and simultaneously pl. two sopranos, alto and two tenor saxes through overdubbing. Fest: Berlin '73. TV: Bill Evans Jazz Workshop, NDR; Berlin JF; Peter Herbolzheimer band. Comp: *Rhyme and Reason Time; Sudden Senility; The Power of a Smile; Space a La Mode.* Also comps. for NDR Worship series. LPs: *Rhyme and Reason* (Atl.); w. Herbolzheimer; *Alpine Power Plant* w. George Gruntz, the Ambrosettis, D. Humair (MPS); w. Baden Powell, *Grandezza on Guitar* (CBS); w. Lucifer's Friend, *Banquet* (Passport). Reissues:

Gin For Fluegelhorns; Jam Session; Best Coast Jazz (Trip).

GERASIMOV, ANATOLE, *tenor sax, flute, composer*; b. Moscow, U.S.S.R., 10/8/45. Studied clarinet from age 12; attended music school. Pl. w. Gherman Lukjanov, '59; w. Nikolaj Gromin; Alexei Koslov; Rickov, '62-6; Jurii Saulskij big band, '68; Alexander Pitshikov, '69; many concerts and fests. at end of '60s. In '70s participated in jam sessions w. visiting Americans from Ellington, Jones-Lewis bands; Toots Thielemans, Bob James, Milt Hinton, Ben Riley. In '73 had own quartet; then left USSR in August for Italy where he pl. w. Romano Mussolini, etc. To NYC, pl. w. Attila Zoller. From end of '74 w. Mercer Ellington orch. Comp: *Cats and Rats; Blue Train.* LP: w. M. Ellington, tenor solo on *All Too Soon* in *Continuum* (Fantasy).

GETZ, STANLEY (STAN),* *tenor saxophone*; b. Philadelphia, Pa., 2/2/27. Featured with name bands from early '40s; after two years w. W. Herman, formed his own quartet and has worked as a leader ever since that time. During the '50s, the great popularity he had enjoyed as an innovator began to wane; however, his career was revived when he became the first American musician closely identified with the bossa nova movement. He continued to tour with a quartet, also rec. in a variety of orchestral settings.

From '69-72, in addition to living in NYC, Getz maintained a second residence near Marbella, Spain, working frequently throughout the Continent. For two years during this period, he led a European group feat. Eddie Louiss, organ; Rene Thomas, guitar; and Bernard Lubat, drums. This group made a successful rec. of *Didn't We.* Getz also rec. with the Clarke-Boland orch. in '71.

Late in '71 Getz met Chick Corea in London and commissioned him to write a series of original comps. for a new group he planned to organize. This combo made its debut Jan. '72 at the Rainbow Grill, NYC; shortly afterward its first album, *Captain Marvel*, was recorded, though it was not released until '75. The personnel incl. Corea, Stanley Clarke on bass; Tony Williams on drums, and Airto Moreira on percussion. The group remained together, with Hank Jones later replacing Corea. Other pianists incl. Kenny Barron, Albert Dailey. Getz continued to pl. Newport JF annually, and in late '74 toured the Continent w. G. Wein's NJF in Europe package. During that year he pl. for Princess Grace at the Palace in Monaco.

In '75 Getz broadened his base of activities by arranging to produce a "Stan Getz Presents" series for Columbia. He rec. albums w. Jimmy Rowles, Joao Gilberto, produced his own concert at Avery Fisher Hall, and in Dec. '75 took part in the Showboat 4 JF cruise to the West Indies, heading a quartet w. Joanne Brackeen on piano; Clint Houston on bass, and Billy Hart on drums.

While making few, if any concessions to the changes in contemporary music brought about by electronics and the advent of jazz-rock, Getz during the mid-70s managed to establish a broad base of support among younger fans, appearing successfully at such rock clubs as the Roxy in LA. His style remained basically unaltered; in the view of most critics and fellow musicians, he was still one of the most melodically creative innovators in the history of the tenor saxophone.

LPs: *Captain Marvel* (Col.); *Classics; Stan Getz* (Prest.); *Dynasty; History; Communications*, cond. by M. Legrand; *Stan Getz and Bill Evans* (Verve); w. Clarke-Boland, *Change of Scene* (Euro. Verve); *Newport in New York '72, The Jam Sessions, Vols. 1&2* (Cobble.).

GIBBS, MICHAEL (MIKE), *composer, trombone*; also *piano*; b. Salisbury, S. Rhodesia, 9/25/37. Priv. piano instruc. from age seven for 10 yrs.; trombone, age 17-24. From '59-63 at Berklee, and Boston Conserv. Received Bach. Mus. and a Prof. Diploma in arr. & comp. Attended School of Jazz at Lenox, Mass., '61; Tanglewood Summer Sch., '63 on scholarships; also stud. priv. w. Gunther Schuller, '62. In early '60s pl. trombone w. Herb Pomeroy band. Living in England from '65 pl. w. Johnny Dankworth-Cleo Laine; Tubby Hayes; formed own big band for BBC concert, '68. Ret. to U.S. as comp.-in-res. at Berklee, Sept. '74 until May '76. Infls: Gil Evans, Charles Ives, Olivier Messiaen. Fest: Belfast, w. Gary Burton. Polls: *Melody Maker* as comp., arr., big band, '73-4.

Comps: *Sweet Rain; Family Joy, Oh Boy; Feelings and Things; Tanglewood '63; And On The Third Day; Blue Comedy; Four or Less; Nonsequence.* Orchestrations for Mahavishnu's *Apocalypse* (Col.); *Stanley Clarke* (Nemperor). Film scores: *Madam Sin; Secrets; Intimate Reflections.*

Gibbs, associated with Burton from '61 has contributed to several of Burton's albums incl.: *In The Public Interest* (Poly.); *Seven Songs for Quartet & Chamber Orch.* (ECM); *Throb* (Atl.). Burton says of him "(Gibbs) . . . has been writing for me since we went to school together in Boston . . . I've watched his talent expand and deepen through the years. In the dozen or more pieces he has written for the quartet, he has contributed greatly to our musical personality."

Gibbs' own LPs incl. *Just Ahead*, a double album rec. live at Ronnie Scott's in London; *The Only Chrome Waterfall Orch.* (Bronze).

GIBBS, TERRY (Julius Gubenko),* *vibes, percussion, composer, leader*; b. Brooklyn, N.Y., 10/13/24. One of the first great bop vibraphonists, he was a contemporary of Milt Jackson in the mid-40s, later working w. W. Herman and leading numerous groups of his own after moving to LA in '57. Has also directed big bands off and on since '59 and has made innumerable apps. w. Steve Allen, for whom he has served as musical director, composer and conductor. Led orch. and wrote all original music for TV series, *Operation Entertainment.*

Gibbs has organized small combos for many night club bookings, has appeared on Johnny Carson and Mike Douglas TV shows, *The Jazz Show* on KNBC-TV, '71. LPs: *Explosion; Live from The Summit* w. big band

(Mercury); *Terry Gibbs Big Band Recorded Live From The Summit* (Verve) *Take It From Me, Band Sounds* (Trip) w. quartet (Impulse); *Bopstacle Course* (Muse); *Big Band Sounds* (Trip).

GIBSON, RICHARD DERBIN (DICK), *promoter*; b. Mobile, Ala., 10/20/25. An investment banker, Gibson in 1962 formed the company that made the Water Pik, and in 1967 engineered its sale for millions of dollars; soon after, he went into the business of promoting jazz, helping organize the World's Greatest Jazzband in 1968. He was later instrumental in the launching of a jazz policy at the Downbeat and the Roosevelt Grill in NYC.

Gibson is best known among musicians for the private, three-day marathon jazz parties he has staged since 1963, in September of each year. Based in Denver, he and his wife Maddie held five parties in Aspen, three in Vail and from 1971 staged the events in Colorado Springs. Catering to 500 paying guests, the parties at first were traditionalist-oriented but later incorporated mainstream and modern musicians handpicked by Gibson and playing in a variety of groupings. A few sets from the 1971 party were issued in an LP, *Colorado Jazz Party* (MPS-BASF).

GIFFORD, HAROLD EUGENE (GENE),* *composer, guitar*; b. Americus, Ga., 5/31/08. The arr. for the Casa Loma orch. during the '30s, composer of such early riff tunes as *Black Jazz; White Jazz; Casa Loma Stomp.* Later retired from music, but during the last year of his life became a music teacher in Memphis, Tenn., where he died 11/12/70.

GILLESPIE, JOHN BIRKS (DIZZY),* *trumpet, composer, singer, leader*; also *conga, piano*; b. Cheraw, S.C., 10/21/17. The man who came out of the big band experience of the Teddy Hill, Cab Calloway and Earl Hines bands to help forge a musical revolution-evolution in the mid-'40s with the Billy Eckstine band and his own combos and big bands, continued to enhance his reputation as one of the most creative musicians of the 20th century. In the late '60s he appeared with the quintet he had put together in Jan. '66: James Moody, reeds and flute; Kenny Barron, piano; Frank Schifano, electric bass; and Candy Finch, drums. In Dec. '66 Mike Longo became the pianist and a principal contributor to the repertoire until he left in '73. When Moody went on his own at the end of the '60s, he was replaced by a guitar, first George Davis and then, in '71, Al Gafa, thereby changing the sound of the group with Gillespie the lone horn. With Longo's departure the unit became a pianoless quartet. When Gillespie hired Schifano in the mid-60s he became one of the first leaders to use the electric bass in a jazz group. Russell George continued on the Fender after Schifano; Phil Upchurch and Chuck Rainey both recorded on this instrument with Dizzy. In the '70s, after a short term by Alex Blake, the regular bassist, also electric, was Earl May. David Lee held the drum spot in '70, succeeded by Mickey Roker from '71.

On several occasions Gillespie returned to his love, the big band. There are few leaders as dynamic and colorful as he; in front of an orchestra he really opens into full flower. In '68 a "Reunion" band toured Europe and was recorded at the Berlin Jazz Festival. There were Gillespie alumni like Sahib Shihab, Cecil Payne, in the reed section along with Moody; Curtis Fuller and Gillespie band veteran of the '40s Ted Kelly among the trombones; and Jimmy Owens and Dizzy Reece as trumpet sectionmates. The band was put together by Gil Fuller, Gillespie's '40s arranger.

In '75, former Gillespie saxophonist and musical director, of the mid-'50s, Billy Mitchell, helped organize a New York-based orchestra which played several engagements at Buddy's Place and a September *Tribute to Dizzy Gillespie* at Avery Fisher Hall in which Gillespie paid himself the highest tribute through his absolutely brilliant performance, in the midst of all his guest stars: Stan Getz, Lalo Schifrin, Max Roach, Percy Heath, John Lewis, James Moody and Buddy Rich.

Gillespie, the world traveler, continued to tour outside the US annually. Some of his voyages took him to St. Croix, Virgin Islands in '73; a tour of Eastern and Western Europe with the *Musical Life of Charlie Parker* package in '74; and a concert tour of Europe and the Mediterranean, incl. Israel and Tunisia, '75. In 1971-2 he took time off from his regular group to travel in Europe, Japan and the US with The Giants of Jazz, an all star line-up incl. Sonny Stitt and T. Monk.

He appeared at all the major festivals, playing a particularly vital role at Monterey on a regular basis (often sitting-in with almost everyone), and also being featured in special events at Newport and Newport-New York such as a *Tribute to Louis Armstrong*; or a Sacred Concert in '72 with All-City Choir directed by John Motley. People have learned to expect the unexpected from Gillespie as when he stepped out on the stage during the middle of a film and duetted with his screen image at the NJF-NY in '75.

His TV appearances included a trumpeter's special with Al Hirt but when he played on the late-night talk shows such as *Tonight* he was also valued by his hosts as a conversationalist. He wrote and played the score and co-starred in a speaking role with Maureen Stapleton in John and Faith Hubley's animated short film, *Voyage to Next.*

British trumpeter Ian Carr, in an appreciation of Gillespie, wrote: "He has a very extensive knowledge of theory and at the same time his instrumental execution matches his thought in its power and speed. He has lightning reflexes and a superb ear. . . He is concerned at all times with swing. Even when he's taking the most daring liberties with the pulse or beat, his phrases never fail to swing . . . The whole essence of a Gillespie solo is cliff-hanging drama. The phrases are perpetually varied. Fast demisemiquaver runs are followed by pauses, by huge interval leaps, by long, immensely high notes, by slurs and smears and bluesy phrases. He is always taking you by surprise, always shocking you with a new thought."

Gillespie won the DB Critics poll, '71-5. Among his

many awards are an honorary Doctorate from Rutgers Univ. in '70; the Handel Medallion from NYC in '72; and Musician of the Year from the Institute of High Fidelity, presented to him by Miles Davis in SF, April '75. Late in the year he was named an External Consultant in Ethnomusicology by the SF School Board to conduct a series of workshops in that city's public schools.

A follower of the Bahai faith which teaches that one day all mankind will be united in peace, Gillespie says, "Baha 'u 'llah is the head of my religious faith . . . he said music is a form of worship. I believe it, because in this music you must rid yourself of the hangups of racialism and things like that . . ."

As a composer he is well-known for his '40s works like *Salt Peanuts; Groovin' High; Blue 'N Boogie; Woody'n You; A Night in Tunisia; Bebop; Dizzy Atmosphere; That's Earl Brother* and the collaborations with Charlie Parker, *Anthropology* and *Shaw 'Nuff.* Later compositions of note are *Con Alma* and *Kush.* In the '70s his works included *Brother King*, written for the late Rev. Martin Luther King Jr., and *Olinga*, dedicated to a Bahai brother. The earlier *Manteca* also became known as *I'll Never Go Back to Georgia* because of its chanted opening refrain.

LPs: *The Giant* (Prest., orig. issued as two separate albums on the America label in France); *Big 4; Big 7 at Montreux JF 1975; Oscar Peterson and Dizzy Gillespie; Oro, Incienso y Mirra* w. comp. by Chico O'Farrill (Pablo); *Swing Low, Sweet Cadillac* (Imp.); *The Real Thing* (Perception); *My Way; Jazz For a Sunday Afternoon* (SS); *Dizzy Gillespie Reunion Band* (MPS); w. Mitchell-Ruff Duo (Main.); *Trumpet Kings at Montreux JF 1975; Trumpet Kings Meet Joe Turner* (Pablo); *Giants of Jazz* (Atl.); *Giants* w. M.L. Williams, B. Hackett (Percept.); reissues, *Greatest Jazz Concert Ever* w. C. Parker, B. Powell, Mingus; *In the Beginning*, '40s big band and combos (Prest.); *Newport Years* (Verve); *Something Old, Something New* (Trip).

GILMORE, JOHN,* *tenor sax, drums*; b. Summit, Miss., 1931. The long-time Sun Ra sideman continued to be one of the key men in the Arkestra, featured on tenor sax but also playing the drums in what often becomes a percussion ensemble. Originally infl. by Rollins and Coltrane he was cited by Coltrane as having infl. him (Coltrane) through certain elements in his playing. Vladimir Simosko talks of Gilmore's solo on *Shadow World* w. Sun Ra as "consisting principally of a well modulated squeal from the horn's freak register, punctuated by a few well placed blats from the bottom of the horn, unaccompanied during the last segment, and surely one of the most hair raising and powerful solos on record."

LPs: see Sun Ra; also w. Freddie Hubbard; McCoy Tyner (Imp.); Elmo Hope, *Sounds From Riker's Island* (Aud. Fid.); Andrew Hill (BN); Pete La Roca, *Turkish Women at the Bath* (Douglas), same album issued under Chick Corea's name, *Bliss* (Muse); Dizzy Reece (Futura); reissue material on *Blowing Sessions* (BN).

GILSON, JEF (Jean-Francois Quievreux),* *piano, composer*; also *clarinet*; b. Guebwiller, Alsace, France, 8/25/26. Made rec. debut w. Jean-Luc Ponty, '62. Led big band '62-7. Worked as singer, arr. w. Double Six of Paris, '65-6. Toured Africa, Madagascar, '68-70. Publ: a journal, *L'Independant Du Jazz* (available from 86 rue du Faubourg St. Denis, Paris, France 75010). Gilson founded Palm Records in April '75, prod. albums w. Byard Lancaster, Baikida, Bill Coleman et al. Fests: Juan-les-Pins, '65; San Remo, '66; Terre Des Hommes, Montreal '72.

Comps: *Chant Inca; L'oeil Vision* for Ponty; *Je Me Souviens Encore Du Grand Orchestre De Dizzy Gillespie; Chakan.* Gilson has also been active as a sound engineer from '51.

LPs: *L'Oeil Vision; Gaveau; 16 Years of Jazz* (SFP); w. Bill Coleman, *Jazz Pour Dieu* (Unidisc); *Swing Low, Sweet Chariot* (Concert Hall); others w. Philly Joe Jones (Vogue); Sahib Shihab (Futura); *New Call From France* (MPS); w. Ponty, *Malagasy* (Palm); *Soul of Africa*, w. Hal Singer (Chant Du Mond).

GIUFFRE, JAMES PETER (JIMMY),* *composer, clarinet*; also *tenor sax, flutes*; b. Dallas, Texas, 4/26/21. During the late '60s and early '70s, Giuffre was very active as a composer and educator, as well as making concert apps. He did not begin to play in clubs again until '75, when he worked at St. James Infirmary and Tin Palace, NYC. He cont. his clarinet studies w. Arthur Bloom, '61-4; reed-making and clarinet w. Kal Opperman, '66-9; flute w. Jimmy Politis, '68-72. Holds teaching positions at New School, N.Y.U., Livingston Coll.; presided over student jazz workshop at own studio, '72. Lecture at Wagner Coll., *Exploring Art in N.Y.*, '68. Performed *The Castle*, a ballet w. Jean Erdman at N.Y.U., U.C.L.A., '67. Pl. concerts at U.C.L.A., '67, '74; Guggenheim Museum, '73; Smithsonian Inst., '74. Commissioned by St. Luke's Church, NYC, to write *Life's Music* for Men and Boy's Choir. Awarded Guggenheim Fellowship, '68. Voted number one clarinet in *Melody Maker* poll, '68; won several *Jazz Podium* (Germany) polls in '60s. TV: *Sunday*, NBC, '74. Comps: *Hex*, orig. written for Orchestra U.S.A., was used as part of ballet, *Manikins*, by Joffrey Ballet Co., '66; *Orb*, for clarinet and string quartet, perf. at Whitney Museum, NYC, by Giuffre and Carnegie Quartet, '69. Scores for films: *This Island; Sighet-Sighet; Smiles; Discovery In a Landscape.* Publ: *Jazz Phrasing and Interpretation* (Associated Music Pub., 866 Third Ave., N.Y., N.Y. 10022); *Sketch-Orks* (Criterion Music, 6124 Selma Ave., Hollywood, Ca. 90028). LP: *Music For People, Birds, Butterflies and Mosquitoes; River Chant* (Choice).

GLADDEN, EDWARD (EDDIE), *drums*; b. Newark, N.J., 12/6/37. Feat. w. many groups in the Newark area since mid-60s, among them Freddie Roach, Larry Young, Johnny Coles, Woody Shaw, Buddy Terry, Mickey Tucker. Also worked w. K. Dorham, Grant Green, J. Moody, J. McGriff. In '74-5 was a member of Shirley

Scott trio feat. Harold Vick. LPs: w. L. Young, *Contrasts, Heaven on Earth* (Blue Note); w. B. Terry, *Soul-Natural* (Prestige); w. Moody, *Never Again* (Muse); w. Tucker and R. Hanna, *The New Heritage Keyboard Quartet* (Blue Note); *Triplicity* w. Tucker (Xanadu); w. McGriff, *The Main Squeeze* (Groove Merchant).

GLEASON, RALPH J., *critic*; b. New York City, N.Y., 3/1/17; d. Berkeley, Calif., 6/3/75. Educ. Horace Greeley H.S., Chappaqua, N.Y.; Columbia Coll., Columbia U., '38. Jazz reviewer, columnist, *Columbia Spectator*, '35-8; founder and editor *Jazz Information*, '39-40; jazz critic *College Years*, '40; *Down Beat* corresp., critic, Assoc. Ed., columnist, '47-60; Contr. Ed., critic *Stereo Review*, '58-63; columnist, critic, *San Francisco Chronicle*, '51-75; syndicated jazz columnist world wide, '57-70; founder, editor, *Jazz* quarterly, '58-60; *Variety* corresp., '53-7; articles on jazz in *Esquire, Saturday Review, Show Bus. Illus.*, NY *Herald Tribune*, LA *Times*, Chicago *Sun-Times*, NY *Post*, London *Times, Lithopinion etc; Rolling Stone* (a founder and editor, '67-75); 26 half hour jazz shows, *Jazz Casual*, NET, '60-70; TV NET films: *Anatomy of a Hit*, '64; *Love You Madly*, '68; Sacred Concert, '69; Monterey Jazz Fest., '69. Books: *Jam Session* (Putnam's '57); *Jefferson Airplane & The San Francisco Sound* (Ballantine, '68); *Celebrating the Duke and Other Heroes* (Atlantic Monthly Press, '75); Member of advisory board Lenox School of Jazz; U.C. Jazz Festival; Monterey JF; Stanford Jazz Year. Lecturer on jazz: Stanford U.; U.C. Berkeley; Sonoma State Coll. Exec. Prod. *Payday*, '73; Documentary perf. TV film NET, '70, *Go Ride The Music, Night at the Family Dog*. Awards: Sun Reporter Citizen of the Year, '64; Deems Taylor Award American Society, Composers, Authors & Publs., '62, '73; White House Enemies List, '73 (this last an honor of which he was particularly proud).

As the first jazz critic to take rock music seriously and to write about it extensively, Gleason earned the admiration of young fans as well as that of his contemporaries. He believed passionately in everything to which he devoted his time and his typewriter. His final book, *Celebrating the Duke*, provided a fitting memorial to a fearlessly honest man, who for 40 years fought relentlessly for his beliefs.

GLENN, EVANS TYREE,* *trombone, vibes*; b. Corsicana, Tex., 11/23/12. The swing trombonist who had worked in the bands of Benny Carter, C. Calloway, Don Redman and many others died 5/18/74 of cancer in Englewood, N.J. He had been pl. w. L. Armstrong from '65 until Armstrong's death in '71, and subsequently led his own combo. His death occurred only six days before that of Duke Ellington, in whose orch. he had pl. from '47-51.

LPs: *Newport in N.Y. '72* (Cobblestone) others w. Ellington (Col.); Armstrong (various labels). Glenn was survived by two sons, both musicians: Tyree Jr., who plays vibes and tenor sax, and Roger, a flutist and vibraphonist.

GOLSON, BENNY,* *composer, tenor saxophone*; b. Philadelphia, Pa., 1/25/29. Worked with many jazz orchs.; co-led Jazztet w. Art Farmer in early '60s, then gave up playing to concentrate on composing and arranging. In '67, moving to LA, began working at Universal Studios as composer. From '68 wrote for various artists in LA: Peggy Lee, Lou Rawls, Nancy Wilson, Sammy Davis Jr., Cal Tjader, Diana Ross, O.C. Smith et al. Began writing TV and radio commercials. Wrote music for M*A*S*H TV series, '73-5. In '75, composed theme and additional music for Karen Valentine Show. Rec. album in Hollywood with A. Farmer, F. Rosolino, Chuck Domanico, Mike Wofford, and Golson's son Reggie, for EastWind Records of Tokyo. Comp. *Yesterday's Thoughts* for Charlie Parker Concert; lyrics later written by Peggy Lee. Work was played at concert in Tokyo feat. Sadao Watanabe.

In May '75, Golson was the central figure in a concert of his comps. at Town Hall. Among his consistently attractive comps. are *I Remember Clifford; Whisper Not; Stablemates; Along Came Betty; Blues March; Five Spot After Dark; Are You Real.*

GOMEZ, EDGAR (EDDIE),* *bass*; b. Santurce, Puerto Rico, 10/4/44. Early experience w. Newport Youth Band; then pl. w. M. McPartland; Paul Bley; Gary McFarland. From '66 almost continuously w. Bill Evans, where his amazingly articulate and sensitive horn-like lines have been an inseparable part of the trio's sound. During these years he has also been closely associated w. Jeremy Steig; and Lee Konitz, w. whom he performed in tandem at Stryker's, NYC, '74. Own gp. at Sweet Basil, NYC, '75. LPs: see Evans; also w. Steig, *Monium* (Col.).

GONSALVES, PAUL (MEX),* *tenor saxophone*; b. Boston, Mass., 7/12/20. A member of the Duke Ellington orch. since '50, Gonsalves died 5/14/74 in London, only ten days before the passing of Ellington. Gonsalves had been in poor health for some years. He was one of several major losses to tenor saxophone jazz of what is generally known as the Coleman Hawkins school. Though his style was closer to Ben Webster's than to Hawkins', all three men had much in common with one another, as well as with Don Byas, Flip Phillips and Lucky Thompson.

Despite the reputation he gained as a creator of excitement, mainly as a consequence of his solo on *Diminuendo and Crescendo in Blue* during an Ellington appearance at the NJF, Gonsalves was greatly admired for the warmth and intimacy of his ballad work.

LPs: *Just A-Sittin' And A-Rockin'* w. Ray Nance (Black Lion); others w. Lawrence Brown, Johnny Hodges; also see ELLINGTON, DUKE.

GONZALES, BABS,* *singer*; b. Newark, N.J., 10/27/19. Led his vocal-instrumental gp., Babs' Three Bips and a Bop, which incl. Tadd Dameron, in mid-'40s. Managed and sang w. James Moody in '50s, Active as a single in '60s, '70s w. annual summer visits to Europe. In summer, '75, app. at Montreux, Hammerfeld, Laren, Cologne and Gothenberg fests.; small Euro. clubs; six dates w. Lionel

Hampton. Gave 17 concerts at universities in Holland in which his performance incorporated a 20 minute anti-drug lecture. U.S. fest: NJF-NY at Fordham U., '74.

Wrote two books about his life in jazz: *I Paid My Dues*; and *Movin' On Down De Line*, which he publ. himself (Expubidence Publ. Corp., 94 Milford Ave., Newark, N.J. 07108). His recordings are available on the Expubident label at the same address.

GOODMAN, BENJAMIN DAVID (BENNY),* *clarinet, leader*; b. Chicago, Ill., 5/30/09. Although not playing on a full-time basis Goodman, heading a variety of small groups (usually including Zoot Sims, Urbie Green, Bucky Pizzarelli, etc.), became more active in the '70s for concerts and performances at theatres-in-the round. In addition he continued to tour in Europe. He played at the Rainbow Grill on several occasions in the 60s and '70s. and made guest appearances with the Chicago Symphony in '66, with Morton Gould conducting; and '67, with conductor Jean Martinon.

In January '68 he celebrated the 30th anniversary of his famed Carnegie Hall concert with a party and reunion. When he appeared in concert at Carnegie in September of '74, John S. Wilson wrote in the New York *Times*: ". . . the old fires may be banked but can still be stirred into flame."

Tom Scanlan, in reviewing a Goodman performance at Wolf Trap Farm in June '74, made note of "that gorgeous tone . . . that complete authority, that improvisatory genius with proper notes in proper places and in brilliantly unexpected places as well, with that very sound and approach that was unmistakably Benny Goodman."

In '70 Goodman toured Europe with a 16-piece band, including stops in Italy and Romania. The following year he returned to Europe to tour with an English band, making several guest appearances on TV; as soloist with symphony orchestras and chamber groups; and for a concert at Royal Albert Hall, London.

The sextet toured Europe in '72, recording in Copenhagen and taping a special for Swedish TV. Goodman also organized a big band for Canada's National Exposition and played with his original quartet for the Harvest Moon Ball at Madison Square Garden. In '73 the sextet played in Australia and England and he appeared with the original quartet (Lionel Hampton, Teddy Wilson and Gene Krupa) at the Newport Jazz Festival in New York.

Other festivals have included Comblain-La-Tour, '66; Schaefer Summer Fest., NYC, '72. TV: *Bell Telephone Hour*, '66; *Tonight*, '66; Merv Griffin, '68; Timex Swing Special, '72; BBC-TV, '73; NBC Special, '74; *Tribute to John Hammond*, PBS, '75. Goodman won the DB Readers poll, '73. Other awards include the Handel Medal from New York City, '66; LLD from Illinois Institute of Technology '68; first cultural award given by the State of Connecticut, '73; Citation "for exceptional and distinguished service" from Mayor John Lindsay of NYC, '73. A bio-discography, *B.G. On Record*, was published in '69 (see bibliography).

LPs: *On Stage; Today* (London); *The King in Person, Benny Goodman in the 70's* (Time-Life); reissues—*Giants of Swing* (Prest.); *Greatest Hits* (Col.); *The Complete Benny Goodman, Vols. 1-3* (Bluebird).

GOODWIN, WILLIAM R. (BILL)* *drums*; also *percussion*; b. Los Angeles, Calif., 1/8/42. After pl. w. Leroy Vinnegar-Mike Melvoin trio, Paul Horn quintet, '66, w. Roger Williams; Gabor Szabo, '67; G. Shearing, '68. Joined Gary Burton, '69, moving to NYC, '70 and remaining w. Burton until Aug. '71. With Toshiko, '71; S. Getz, '72; G. Mulligan, '73-4; Al Cohn-Zoot Sims, '74. From '73 also pl. w. National Jazz Ensemble (charter member); Chamber Jazz Quintet; from '74 w. Children of All Ages; Phil Woods quartet. In '75 gigs w. Mose Allison w. whom he had app., off and on, from '68; Bill Evans. Lives in Pocono Mts. in Pa. near Bob Dorough, P. Woods, A. Cohn. Likes to sit in at local clubs w. John Coates Jr., Steve Gilmore. TV: *Tonight* Show w. Shearing; Tony Bennett Special w. Horn; *Homewood* Show w. Burton on PBS; *Jazz Adventures* w. Evans. Fest: NJF w. Szabo, '67; Burton, '69; Burton & K. Jarrett, '70; NJF-NY w. Mulligan, '73-4. LPs: w. Horn, *Cycle* (RCA); w. Burton & Jarrett; Burton & Grappelli; others w. Burton (Atl.); w. Jack Wilkins, *Windows*; w. Hal Galper, *Wild Bird; Inner Journey* (Main.); w. L. Tabackin, *Let the Tape Roll* (Victor Nippon); w. Dorough, *Multiplication Rock* (Cap.).

GORDON, DEXTER KEITH,* *tenor, soprano saxophones, composer*; b. Los Angeles, Calif., 2/27/23. Prominent w. the Billy Eckstine band and on 52nd St. in the '40s and in LA w. Wardell Gray in late '40s-early '50s as one of the most influential saxophonists of the bop era. Reestablished himself in the '60s w. a series of recs. for Blue Note. Moved to Copenhagen, '62, and has been heard most often at its leading jazz club Montmartre. Pl. clubs, concerts, fest. in Europe; periodic trips to US for recs., clubs, fests. Japanese tour, fall '75. He continued to display his warm, vitally swinging saxophone mastery in small gp. settings; and in a large orchestral context, incl. strings (w. arrs. by Palle Mikkelborg), entitled *More Than You Know* in '75.

Teaching for Worker's Cultural Foundation, Malmo, Sweden; for Jazz & Youth Society, Vallekilde, Denmark, '68. Fest: NJF, '70; NJF-NY, '72; Tangier, '72; Montreux, '73; also Molde; Ossiach, Austria. Won DB Critics poll, '71. TV: *Just Jazz*, PBS, '71. Comp: *Antabus; Candlelight Lady; The Apartment; Ernie's Tune; Tivoli; The Girl With the Purple Eyes; The Rainbow People; Montmartre; Boston Bernie; Fried Bananas; Mrs. Miniver; Valse Robin; The Panther; Stanley the Steamer*. LPs: *More Than You Know; The Apartment; The Meeting; The Source* both w. J. McLean (Steeple.); *Tower of Power; More Power; The Panther; The Jumpin' Blues; Generation; Blues A La Suisse; Tangerine; Ca' Purange* (Prest.); *Montmartre Collection* (Bl. Lion); *A Day in Copenhagen* (BASF); *Charlie Parker Memorial* (Chess); *Newport in New York, The Jam Sessions, Vol. 3&4* (Cobble.); *The Foremost* (Onyx); *Gettin' Around'*; re-issue anthology (BN); w. Miriam Klein (MPS).

GOURLEY, JAMES PASCO JR. (JIMMY),* *guitar, singer, composer*; b. St. Louis, Mo., 6/9/26. Playing and living in Paris from '57 w. own gps. and w. Kenny Clarke. From '66 worked w. Clarke in trio, first w. Lou Bennett, later w. Eddy Louiss as organist. Helped found Half Note club in Canary Islands, fall '70, playing there until April '72 when jazz policy was dropped and he ret. to Paris. Own quartet at Club St. Germain; duo at Bilboquet, '74; singing and pl. solo guitar at Caveau de la Montagne, '75. Solo at Sweet Basil, NYC, summer '75. App. w. Clarke in Elizabeth Taylor-Warren Beatty film, *The Only Game in Town*. Fest: Rencontres International de la Guitare (Arles, France) '73; w. own quartet, Bergamo '74; Middleheim '75; w. Clarke, Bergamo '75. Comps: *Comon' Ovah; Tafira Alta; Tats*; w. NYC lyricist Carol Bernstein, *Graffiti; Truth Game; Never Explain; Wrong Man Blues; Horoscope Blues; Tomorrow Just Flew By; Lost and Found*. LPs: *Comon' Ovah* (Futura); w. S. Grappelli, *Satin Doll* (Festival); *Eddy Louiss Orgue*, vols. 1&2 (America); *Clifford Brown in Paris* (Prest.).

GOYKOVICH, DUSKO (Dusan Gojkovic),* *trumpet, composer;* b. Jajce, Yugoslavia, 10/14/31. Played in many European bands before studying at Berklee Coll., '61-3. In U.S. w. M. Ferguson, '63-4; W. Herman, '64-6. Back to Europe, '66, played for eight months w. Sal Nistico in International Jazz Quintet; then w. Mal Waldron, Jimmy Woode, Philly Joe Jones; also w. Clarke-Boland big band until it broke up in '73. From '67, living in Munich, leading own quintet, composing and arranging. Taught trumpet, improvisation and arranging at Swiss Jazz School in Berne, also at Munich Jazz School. '74-5 co-led, with Slide Hampton, a 12 piece band called Summit, feat. American and European musicians.

In 1975 Goykovich observed: "I am trying to achieve originality through melodic and rhythmic use of Yugoslavian folklore in jazz. I am writing original tunes and playing them with my quintet and big band."

Favs: R. Eldridge, D. Gillespie, K. Dorham, Clifford Brown, M. Davis. Publ: *Introduction for Jazz Trumpet Improvisation* (Jazz Studio, B. Schott's Soehne-Mainz, Germany). LPs for various European labels incl. Enja, Philips, Ensayo, MPS-BASF. Earlier LPs w. Clarke-Boland (Blue Note); Herman (Columbia).

GRAHAM, EDWARD B. (EDDIE), *drums*; b. New York City, 11/18/37. Stud. w. George Lawrence Stone, NYC; Vincent Mott, Miami; U. of Miami, '56-9; Berklee Coll., '59. Pl. w. many commercial groups, also Village Stompers, '68-9; Trummy Young in Hawaii; '70-1; freelance in LV, '72-4; traveled w. Earl Hines combo, '75. Favs: B. Rich, Rollo Laylan.

GRANZ, NORMAN,* *producer*; b. Los Angeles, Ca., 8/6/18. After selling his Verve Record Co. to MGM in '61, Granz continued from his Geneva base to import jazz concert tours on a large scale: Ray Charles, Basie, Fitzgerald, Peterson et al. In '67, for the first time in a decade, he assembled a Jazz at the Philharmonic unit to tour the U.S. At the end of the tour, he announced that he would never again undertake such an enterprise in the U.S., and with the exception of a concert at the Santa Monica Civic '72 and "Tribute to Norman Granz" night at the MJF, he made no further appearances in the U.S. However, in '73 he returned to the record business, starting his own label, Pablo. For this company he recorded Duke Ellington's final studio sessions, various albums feat. E. Fitzgerald, O Peterson (both of whom he continued to manage) and many w. Joe Pass, D. Gillespie, Joe Turner, C. Basie and other mainstream artists. A tape recorded live during his '67 JATP tour was released on Pablo as *The World's Greatest Jazz Concert*. In July 1975 at Montreux and in October '75 on a European tour, Granz presented a series of programs that were known as Pablo Jazz Festivals but were identical in style of presentation to the original JATP. The Montreux '75 programs were released on Pablo.

GRAPPELLI, STEPHANE (Grappelly),* *violin, piano*; b. Paris, France, 1/26/08. First renowned as a member of the Quintet of the Hot Club of France, 1934-39, Grappelli continued to build his reputation as one of the jazz violin greats with his own groups. In the late '60s and '70s he was still extremely active with apps. in clubs like Le Toit of the Paris Hilton, '69; Ronnie Scott's, '73; Buddy's Place, NYC, '74. His undiminished talents received a standing ovation at a Carnegie Hall concert, fall '74. TV apps. in Europe, U.S., Australia. Fests: Newport, Montreux et al. A more than capable pianist, he names as his originals infls., Beiderbecke ("at the piano"), Armstrong and Tatum. The soundtrack of the Louis Malle film *Lacombe, Lucien*, utilizes recordings of the original Quintet of the Hot Club of France. LPs: *I Remember Django; Just One of Those Things* (Black Lion); *Violinspiration; Afternoon in Paris; Violin Summit* (MPS/BASF); w. Reinhardt, *First Recordings of the Quintet of the Hot Club of France; Django Reinhardt and the American Jazz Giants* (Prestige); w. Yehudi Menuhin (Angel); w. O. Peterson (Prestige); w. Venuti, *Venupelli Blues* (Byg).

GRAVES, MILFORD ROBERT,* *drums, percussion*; b. Jamaica, N.Y., 8/20/41. Prominent in NY avant-garde circles in '60s w. Giuseppi Logan; NY Art Quartet; JCOA. Worked w. Paul Bley, '65; Albert Ayler, '67. From '65 closely associated w. reedman-pianist Hugh Glover in own ensemble utilizing only original works. In '75 working w. Glover on developmental project using music as a therapeutic means to assist psychological problems. To further this research formed Institute of Bio-Creative Intuitive Development.

Self-evolved style of tonal percussion, infl. most significantly, he feels, by tabla teacher, Wasantha Singh, w. whom he stud. North Indian music, '65. Film: *Lord Shango*, '74. TV: *Positively Black; Inside Bed-Stuy; Martin Luther King Special*, Metromedia. Fest: NJF, '67; '73-4; Autumn Fest., Paris, '74; Antwerp; Laren, '73. Won DB Critics Poll, TDWR, '67. Comp: *Transmutations*. LPs: Graves-Don Pullen, *Nommo; Live at Yale U.* (SRP); co-leader w. Andrew Cyrille, *Dialog of the Drums* (IPS); w. Albert Ayler (Imp.); Sonny Sharrock (Vortex); NY Art Quartet; JCOA (Font.).

GREEN, BENNIE,* *trombone, baritone horn*; b. Chicago, Ill., 4/16/23. After gigging around NYC with a quintet from '68, Green joined the D. Ellington orch. in June '69, replacing Buster Cooper. Working across country to LV, pl. there until late Sept.; left the band the following month and settled in LV, where he became a member of hotel bands pl. along the Strip, generally those of Joe Guercio and Jimmy Mulidore. TV: *Duke Ellington Sacred Concert*, St. John's Cathedral. Fests: NJF, '69; NJF-NY, '72.

Though well known internationally as a competent bop-influenced soloist, Green by late '75 had still never played overseas. Publ: *Be Bop Trombone Solos* (Belwin Mills Publ., NYC).

LPs: w. S. Stitt, *Pow* (Prest.), *My Main Man* (Cadet); *Newport in N.Y., The Jam Sessions*, Vols. 1&2 (Cobble.); *The George Benson Cookbook* (Col.).

GREEN, BERNARD (BENNY),* *writer, saxophones*; b. Leeds, Yorkshire, England, 12/9/27. During the '60s this brilliant writer virtually retired from playing to concentrate on his literary activities. Publs. incl. two novels with musical settings: *Blame It On My Youth; 58 Minutes to London*; two books of music criticism: *Jazz Decade; Drums In My Ears*, the latter publ. in the U.S. by Horizon Press. Book and lyrics for musical biography of G.B. Shaw, starring Cleo Laine, John Neville, with music by J. Dankworth, '69; wrote libretto for London revival of *Showboat*, '71. Co-devised Cole Porter revue, *Cole*. Literary critic for *Spectator*, '70- ; film critic for *Punch*, '72- .

TV: Three documentaries on London; biography of Irving Berlin. Radio: eight one-hour shows w. Ella Fitzgerald; 13 one-hour shows w. Fred Astaire. Artistic dir., New Shakespeare Co. Chief annotator for the Pablo label.

GREEN, FREDERICK WILLIAM (FREDDIE),* *guitar*; b. Charleston, S.C., 3/31/11. His impeccable rhythm guitar continued to set the time and sound for Count Basie's band as it has for so many decades. LPs: See Basie; w. Herb Ellis, *Rhythm Willie* (Concord).

GREEN, GRANT,* *guitar*; b. St. Louis, Mo., 6/6/31. Pl. w. Jimmy Forrest in St. Louis in '50s; w. organists Sam Lazar; Jack McDuff. Began rec. for Blue Note in '60s as leader, and as sideman w. H. Mobley; H. Hancock; L. Morgan. Inactive due to personal problems, '67-9, then resumed rec. for BN, later for Verve. Living in Detroit, '74. Performed music for the film, *The Final Comedown*. LPs: *Live at the Lighthouse; Shades of Green; Goin' West; Carryin' On; Alive; Visions* (BN); *Iron City* (Cobble.); *Cantaloupe Woman* (Verve).

GREEN, THURMAN ALEXANDER, *trombone*; b. Longview, Tex., 8/12/40. Educ: Longview H.S., '54-8, Compton Coll. '58-61, U.S. Navy School of Mus., '61-2, West LA Coll., '69-71. Pl. w. Roger Spotts, '65-7, Horace Tapscott, '66-9. Gerald Wilson, '67-74, Francisco Aguabella, '70-1, Teddy Edwards, '72-5, Harold Land, 73-4, Willie Bobo, '74-5. Pl. on sound track *They Shoot Horses, Don't They?* Favs: Ch. Parker, J.J. Johnson, G. Wilson.

LPs: w. G. Wilson, *Live and Swinging; Everywhere, California Soul; Equinox* (Pacific Jazz); *Things Ain't What They Used To Be*, w. Ella Fitzgerald (Reprise); *Adam's Apple* w. Doug Carn (Black Jazz).

GREEN, URBAN CLIFFORD (URBIE),* *trombone*; b. Mobile, Ala., 8/8/26. Former Gene Krupa, Woody Herman and Benny Goodman sideman led his own big band in '66 after having fronted the Tommy Dorsey orch. In '67 he again led the Dorsey band at the Riverboat, NYC. Own band, using amplifying, octave-expanding devices in a mainstream-rock mix, at Riverboat, '69. From '71 own small gps. at London House, Blues Alley, Royal Box. Occasional tours w. Goodman. Soloist and clinician in Wisc., Minn., No. Dak., Buffalo, N.Y. and Laramie, Wyoming. Featured soloist w. U. of Cincinnati band. Annual participant in Music Educators Convention, San Antonio. Played at White House for Duke Ellington's 70th birthday party. Fest: NJF-NY; Colo. JP; Mobile Collegiate JF; Loosdrecht (Holland). TV: *Dial "M" for Music*; Mike Douglas; *The Main Event* w. Sinatra.

His brand of versatile excellence is marked by a gorgeous, mellow-brassy sound, marvelous control in all ranges of the horn, and overall ease of delivery. Married to his vocalist Kathy Preston. Raises Charolais beef cattle on a farm in Pennsylvania.

LPs: *21 Trombones, Vol. 1; Vol. 2; Green Power; Bein' Green; Big Beautiful Band* (Project 3); *Colorado Jazz Party* (MPS); w. John Bunch (Famous Door).

GREENE, BOB, *piano*; b. New York City, 9/4/22. An early student of traditionalist jazz, he absorbed this music in NO, pl. w. Geo. Lewis at Preservation Hall. Mainly self-taught through listening to Jelly Roll Morton records. Made first important record session w. Sidney De Paris for Blue Note in '52. After working w. Baby Dodds in '50s, Z. Singleton in '60s et al, he org. a recreation of Morton's 1927 Red Hot Peppers band, feat. mostly younger musicians, but incl. Tommy Benford, one of Morton's orig. drummers. The band gave three successful concerts at New York's Lincoln Center and later toured the U.S. and Canada. Fests: NO; Newport; Nice; St. Louis Ragtime Fest.

LPs: *Bob Greene's World of Jelly Roll Morton* (RCA); *Bob Greene and the Peruna Jazzband* (Danish FC Records); *Bob Greene-Don Ewell* (FC); *Dixieland Today* (Circle); *The St. Peter Street Strutters; Johnny Wiggs at Preservation Hall* (Pearl).

GREENE, BURTON (NARADA), *piano, composer*; b. Chicago, Ill, 6/14/37. Classical training at Fine Arts Academy, 1944-51; stud. modern jazz w. Dick Marx '56-8. Co-founded Free Form Improvisation Ensemble w. Alan Silva, '63. Member Jazz Composers Guild '64-5. First quartet, '65, w. Marion Brown, Rashied Ali and Henry Grimes. During '67-9, app. at many jazz and rock clubs NYC; Sam Rivers, Byard Lancaster or G. Barbieri worked with him.

In June '69 Greene left for Europe, where he enjoyed continuous success as composer and performer. Commissions: *Holiday Suite* for Danish Radio; ORTF concerts for trio and quartet; *Depth*, for ten musicians, premiered on AVRO, Hilversum; *Improvisations for Three Pianos* w. Paul Bley for VPRO; Frankfurt Radio concert w.

John Tchicai; Perfs. at Maisons des Jeunes Culturelles, France; East and West Trio and *Shanti Om* suite, perf. by sextet, '74. Fests. in France, Belgium, Germany, Holland. Wrote score for animated film *Birth of a Mountain*.

Greene analyzes his music as "a reflection of my origins and experiences in our Western culture. As an eclectic composer my work exists independently of categories. The music is highly structured, but allows great personal initiative; for example, you have the rhythm and improvisational freedom of jazz contrasted against the precise forms of either Western classical music (fugues and song form etc.) or Eastern classical music (ragas)."

In 1975 Greene toured with a trio featuring cello and table drums, the latter pl. by Indian musician Zamir Ahmed Khan,; also worked with sextet, mainly composed of American musicians living in Amsterdam, Greene's home base. Recordings in Europe: *Burton Greene Quartet; Burton Greene Trio on Tour; Patty Waters Sings* (ESP); *Presenting Burton Greene* (CBS); *Aquarians* (Byg); *Celesphere* (Futura); *Mountains, Trees* (Button-Nose Records); *At Different Times* (Group Music I).

GREENWICH, SONNY, *guitar;* b. Hamilton, Ontario, Canada, 1/1/36. Self-taught. Played w. John Handy in U.S., '66-7; own band, incl. Jimmy Garrison, Jack DeJohnette at Village Vanguard, '68; also worked w. Miles Davis in Toronto. Retired from music for several yrs. to "follow spiritual pursuits," returning to active pl. in late '72. Infl: Rollins, Coltrane, M. Davis, Hindemith, Ravel, Debussy, Bartok. Comps: *Starlight; Peace Chant; Parting; Lily; Loving*. LPs: *The Old Man and the Child* (Sack.); *Sun Song* (CBC); w. Handy in *Spirituals to Swing, 30th Ann'y* (Col.); w. Jimmy Dale, *Soft and Groovy* (Cap.); w. Don Thompson, *Love Song for a Virgo Lady* (Sack.); w. Moe Koffman, *Solar Explorations* (GRT); w. Lee Gagnon, *Jazzzz* (Barclay).

GREER, WILLIAM ALEXANDER (SONNY),* *drums*; b. Long Branch, N.J., 12/13/03. The percussionist w. Duke Ellington's band from 1919 to March '51; worked w. J. Hodges, Red Allen and T. Glenn in '50s and freelanced in NYC during the '60s. Weekends w. own trio, incl. Haywood Henry and Ray Tunia, at Garden Cafe, fall '71. Subbed for Sam Woodyard w. Brooks Kerr at Churchill's, Mar. '74. Joined Kerr's trio at Gregory's w. Russell Procope, May '74 after app. w. Kerr at NYJRC birthday tribute to Ellington in Apr. Fest: NJF-NY '72. Movie: *Sonny*, an 11-minute film issued by Signet Prod., '68. TV: *Today Show*, '74. LPs: *Soda Fountain Rag* w. Kerr (Audiofidelity); *Once Upon A Time* w. Earl Hines (Impulse); many reissues w. Ellington (Decca, Columbia, RCA).

GREY, ALBERT THORNTON (AL),* *trombone*; b. Aldie, Va., 6/6/25. After working w. Benny Carter, J. Lunceford, L. Hampton, D. Gillespie, became known internationally as member of C. Basie orch, '57-61, and again frequently from '64 on. While w. Basie, or during absences from band, he did studio rec. w. Q. Jones, L. Armstrong, J. Hodges, Randy Weston. Led own combo and served as mus. dir. of jazz night club in Phila. Toured Europe several times, with JATP, and as member of Kansas City Seven, also as a single with all star show. Motion Picture: sound track w. Q. Jones for *Last of the Mobile Hotshots*. TV: Timex show etc.; Oscar Peterson show in Canada; several others in England, France etc.

Grey played the baritone horn (euphonium) on Cadet album feat. a group he co-led w. Billy Mitchell, which won a DB Critics Poll as No. 1 combo. Grey himself also won poll as trombonist.

LPs as leader: *Shades of Grey* (Tangerine); as sideman: *Gula Matari*, w. Q. Jones (A & M); Count Basie-Frank Sinatra at the Sands (Reprise); *Ella Fitzgerald at Carnegie Hall* (Col.); *Jazz At The Santa Monica Civic* (Pablo); *The Newport Years* (Polydor); many others on numerous labels w. Basie.

GRIFFIN, JOHN ARNOLD III (JOHNNY),* *tenor sax*; b. Chicago, Ill., 4/24/28. With Art Blakey; Thelonious Monk in '50s; co-leader w. Lockjaw Davis in early '60s. Moved to Europe Dec. '62, pl. all over the Continent. Lived in Paris in late '60s but moved to Holland, where he has his own farm, in '70s. Prominently featured at the Montreux Jazz Festival '75, he can be heard in three LPs recorded on that occasion: *Count Basie Jam Session; Dizzy Gillespie Big 7; Highlights of the Montreux Jazz Festival 1975* (Pablo). Other LPs: *Blues For Harvey* (Steeple.); quartet (Horo); reissue (Milest.); w. Bud Powell, *Bud in Paris* (Xanadu); w. *Passport et al/Doldinger Jubilee '75* (Atl.); reissue material on *Blowing Sessions* (BN).

GRIMES, LLOYD (TINY),* *guitar*; b. Newport News, Va., 7/7/17. Played w. Cats and a Fiddle; Art Tatum; then own gp., the Rocking Highlanders, '40-50s. In early '60 worked in Harlem, Greenwich Village. Toured France w. Milt Buckner, '68; J. McShann, '70. In '70s pl. w. own gps. at the Cookery; West End Cafe; gigs w. the Countsmen; also w. Earl Hines for a few mos. in late '72. Fest: Kennedy Center Jazz Fest., Wash., D.C.; NJF-NY, '73-4. Took part in all star guitar concert at Town Hall, '71 and appears on an LP taped that night, *The Guitar Album* (Col.). Own LPs: *Profoundly Blue* (Muse); (Black & Blue).

GROSSMAN, STEVEN, *saxophones*; b. Brooklyn, N.Y., 1/18/51. Alto sax from '59. Stud. w. brother Hal, who was later a teacher at Berklee Coll. of Music. Took up soprano sax at 16 and tenor a year later. Late in '69 he made his first record date w. Miles Davis, and from March to Sept. '70 was a member of Davis' group. Pl. w. Lonnie Liston Smith May to Dec. '71; Elvin Jones, '71-3; Stone Alliance w. Gene Perla, '75. Infl: Coltrane, Shorter, Rollins. Own LP: *Some Shapes to Come* (P.M.); LPs: w. Davis, *Jack Johnson; Live-Evil; Miles Davis at Fillmore* (Col.); w. Jones, *Merry-Go-Round; Live at the Lighthouse* (BN); others w. C. Corea; Terumasa Hino (released in Japan).

GROVE, RICHARD DEAN (DICK),* *composer, piano, educator*; b. Lakeville, Ind., 12/18/27. Played in jazz combos and bands in early '60s before graduating into extensive activities writing for TV and records; also led own big band at Donte's, '67. Started educational publ. co., featuring his own improvisation course, '71. Many apps. with own quintet at coll. concerts and fests. Book: *Arranging Concepts*, publ. '73. Comp. 15 min. jazz suite for U. of Fla. under grant from Nat'l Endowment For the Arts, '73. Founded Dick Grove Music Workshops in Studio City, Cal., '73. By '75 the school had grown to 700 students studying some 25 different subjects.

Publs: *Encyclopedia of Basic Harmony & Theory Applied to Improvisation on All Instruments*, Vols. I, II and III; (this, and abovementioned *Arranging Concepts*, publ. by First Place Music Publs. Inc., 12754 Ventura Blvd., Studio City, Ca. 91604).

LPs: *Big, Bad and Beautiful* (FPM); w. Buddy Rich, *Best of Buddy Rich; The New One; Feeling Kind of Blues* (Pacific Jazz).

GRUBBS, CARL GORDON, *alto sax, composer*; also *piano*; b. Philadelphia, Pa., 7/27/44. Brother of Earl Grubbs (see below). Cousin Naima was married to John Coltrane. Studied at Phila. Community Coll.; privately w. Coltrane, Harry Johnson, Owen Marshall. Was given a horn by Eric Dolphy. With brother Earl formed a group called The Visitors which is Phila.-based but pl. in NYC at Folk City during time of NJF-NY, '72. Apps. at Coltrane Memorial concert, Phila. '67; Angela Davis speech at Temple Univ. Nov. '74. Joe Klee described The Visitors: "Compositionally, their originals bring to mind the Trane . . . just after *A Love Supreme*, a transitional period . . ." Additionally infl. by Charlie Parker, Pharoah Sanders, Earl Grubbs. Comps: *Pisces; The Visit; Mood Seekers; Glad To Be Sad; China*. LPs: *Neptune* (Cobblestone); *In My Youth; Rebirth* (Muse).

GRUBBS, EARL DELCI, *tenor, soprano saxes, composer*; also *piano*; b. Philadelphia, Pa., 7/13/42. Studied at City Coll. of N.Y., Phila. Community Coll.; privately w. Owen Marshall, Harry Johnson, Coltrane. Worked w. Coltrane; Pharoah Sanders; and w. brother Carl in The Visitors. Infls: Parker, Coltrane, Sanders, Carl Grubbs. Comps: *In My Youth; Love Is Magic; Joy; A Touch of Warm; Gone Are the Days; Two Wives; China*. The Visitors' album *Neptune* was reviewed by Matt Damsker as having an "elevated . . . continually peaking quality, an altitude that invites comparison with the Mahavishnu Orchestra." Their music reflects the peace and love messages of Coltrane's later work. LPs: see Carl Grubbs.

GRUNTZ, GEORGE,* *piano, composer*; b. Basel, Switzerland, 6/24/32. Winner of several prizes at Zurich jazz festivals in '50s; major jazz fests. around world incl. US from late '50s through '60s. Member of Phil Woods' original Rhythm Machine quartet in Europe, 1968-9. From '70, mus. dir.-in-chief of Zurich Playhouse; in Jan. '72 appointed director of the Berlin Jazz Festival (Berliner Jazztage).

In 1971 Gruntz created a European cooperative of pianists, known as Piano Conclave. Its personnel, which varied from concert to concert, was drawn from a pool of leading European and US artists on piano, elec. piano, harpsichord, synthesizer etc., usually employing six keyboard soloists plus a rhythm section.

LPs: on Atl., MPS-BASF, Philips, Decca, HMV; w. Franco Ambrosetti, *Steppenwolf* (PDU); also see Woods, Phil.

GRUSIN, DAVE,* *composer, piano*; b. Denver, Colo., 6/26/34. Frequent associate of Q. Jones from '60. While married to singer Ruth Price, acc. her in clubs; arr., prod. recs. for S. Mendes, Peggy Lee. To Brazil w. Mendes, '68, '75; Japan, '73 w. Jones. Grusin has also pl. off and on w. Tom Scott; in '73-4 w. G. Mulligan; '74 w. Lee Ritenour. Arr. and rec. w. Jones, S. Vaughan, C. McRae, Jon Lucien, R. Flack, Aretha Franklin.

His many feat. film credits incl. *Three Days of the Condor; Tell Them Willie Boy Is Here; The Heart Is A Lonely Hunter; The Graduate; Divorce American Style* etc. TV credits: *Trial of Chaplain Jenson; Good Times; Maude; Dan August; Bold Ones; The Name of the Game* etc.

GUARALDI, VINCENT ANTHONY (VINCE),* *composer, piano*; b. San Francisco, Calif., 7/17/28. Early exp. w. Cal Tjader, Woody Herman in 1950s. From 1963, principally active writing and playing music for *Peanuts* TV series, for which he produced the sound track. Nominated for Academy Award for music in feature film *A Boy Named Charlie Brown*. Continued to play concerts and occasional clubs engagements in SF Bay Area until his death of a heart attack, 2/6/76, in Menlo Park, Cal. No LPs since three for Warner Brothers in late 1960s.

GUARNIERI, JOHN A. (JOHNNY),* *piano, composer*; b. New York City, 3/23/17. During the late '60s Guarnieri became intensively involved with the use of 5/4 time, rec. an album of standards and originals using this meter. Perf. piano concerto in 5/4 at Wilshire Ebell Theatre, LA, '70; spent most of early '70s at Tail O'The Cock restaurant in N. Hollywood, Cal., but took time out to tour Europe with Slam Stewart, '74, and w. all star program of jazz pianists, '75. Rec. album of Harry Warren tunes for Detroit Hot Jazz Society. Fests: Concord, '70; NJF-NY, '74; Nice, '75. In '75 working on a book, *From Ragtime to Tatum*, dealing with 75 pianists, with musical and recorded illustrations, for publ. by Schirmer Books.

LPs: *Plays Harry Warren* (Jim Taylor Presents); *Piano Dimensions* (Dot).

GUERIN, JOHN PAYNE, *drums*; also *tenor saxophone*; b. Hawaii, 10/31/39. Family settled in San Diego when he was three. Self-taught; learned by pl. w. Count Basie records. His teenage gp. won college jazz fest. at Lighthouse, '57. Joined Buddy De Franco, '59, for a year. Moved to LA, '63, joined Geo. Shearing, '65 for year and a half. Worked w. T. Monk, D. Byrd, R. Kellaway, V. Feldman, F. Zappa, Howard Roberts, Jimmy Smith and, from '68, thousands of artists in TV, film and rec. studios. From '74, involved in co-op gp., L.A. Express, bridging rock and jazz elements; also branched out into producing, comp., arr.

Guerin, who won a Most Valuable Player award from NARAS in '74 and '75, is a completely adaptable musician who has distinguished himself in every type of setting. Comps: *Mr. & Mrs. America and All The Ships At Sea*, for L.A. Express; *Mauro*, for H. Roberts. Infls: B. Rich, Tony Williams, Miles Davis, J. Coltrane, Gil Evans, Ch. Parker. Fests: Monterey, w. Monk, Tom Scott, B. Bryant; Newport w. L.A. Express; Caracas Music Fest. w. L.A. Express. Publ: *Jazz + Rock = John Guerin* (Gwyn Publ. Co., 14950 Delano St., Van Nuys, Ca. 91601).

LPs: w. L.A. Express (Ode); w. Monk, *Sphere* (Col.); w. Zappa, *Hot Rats* (Bizarre); w. Pat Williams, *Threshold* (Cap.); w. Joni Mitchell, *Court & Spark* (Asylum).

GUERIN, ROGER,* *trumpet*; b. Saarebruck, Saar, France, 1/9/26. Played w. Django Reinhardt. Newport International Band, '58. With Q. Jones, D. Gillespie bands in Europe in '60s. From '66 to '70 studio work in Paris; also worked with Paris Jazz All Stars, '66-8; tours w. Jack Dieval Quartet for Jeunesses Musicales de France, '68-70. From '68-70 he also taught jazz at the Conservatoire Claude Debussy in St. Germain en Laye. From '71 teaching jazz at the Maison des Jeunes et de la Culture, St. Germain en Laye, rehearsing an amateur big band each Monday and pl. concerts in other M.J.Cs. From '70 leading an 18-piece band at the Casino de Paris for Roland Petit, Zizi Jeanmaire. TV apps. w. Dieval and Georges Jouvin as both trumpeter and producer. Fest: Antibes w. own quintet '67; Nice w. Dieval '70; Avignon w. Andre Hodeir '74; Paris JF w. St. Germain Big Band; Antibes w. Eddy Louiss '75. Plans to open jazz school w. Parisian jazzmen at M.J.C. of St. Germain en Laye. LPs: *Trumpets of Paris* w. Georges Jouvin, Roger Delmotte; many albums w. Dieval "but just for the backgrounds with disc-jockeys."

GUIN, FRANCOIS (FRICK), *trombone*; also *flute*; b. Contres, France, 5/18/38. Guin, whose main insp. and infl. is D. Ellington, formed a group in Paris called The Swingers in Oct. '68. Until Mar. '69 app. nightly at the Club St. Germain; from Apr. to Dec. '69 at the Caveau de la Huchette. In Nov. '69, Guin subbed in the Ellington band at the Paris JF; a month later the Swingers, also the Four Bones, a four trombone unit directed by Guin, perf. at the Grande Nuit du Jazz, Paris. App. w. Swingers at Antibes Fest; Duke Ellington 70th Anniv. Celebration at Alcazar, Paris, '69; Claude Bolling Radio Show, Frankfurt, '70; Eiffel Tower show; Zurich, Prague and Warsaw Fests., '71. Maurice Cullaz, pres. of the Academie du Jazz said of The Swingers: "They have the bad luck to be French and not colored." As a result they found it was necessary to tour in West Africa, '71, where they met w. different native combos to mix African rhythms with their own improvs. Also toured in Czechoslovakia, Poland, Switzerland, Turkey, Balearic Islands, Morocco, New Caledonia and Congo, '72-3. Toured southwest and south of France for Jeunesse Musicale Francaise, '73. In '70 Guin won the Jazz Hot poll as number one French trombonist, received the Prix Django Reinhardt as Musician of the Year from the Académie du Jazz.

The Swingers play a program of the history of jazz encompassing material from early spirituals through the comps. of Ch. Mingus, with a heavy concentration on the Ellington repertoire. Several LPs on the Riviera label, one of which feats. P. Gonsalves. *Three Generations of Jazz* w. Bill Coleman (77 Records).

GULLIN, LARS GUNNAR VICTOR,* *baritone sax, composer*; also *piano*; b. Gotland, Sweden, 5/4/28. Many records with Swedish and U.S. musicians during '50s. Toured Italy w. Chet Baker, '59; from '60 concentrated mainly on solo work and writing, sometimes reforming his band for concerts and records. Won annual government artists' award as leading Swedish jazz musician, '68. Has won many awards on baritone including Swedish newspaper *Expressen*'s prize, '73. Made TV film, *Danny's Dream*, '68-9, about his life as a composer, musician and human being. Many fests. throughout Scandinavia, England and Italy. Died 5/17/76 of a heart attack in Vissefjärda, Sweden. His last work *Areos Aromatic Atomica Suite*, was recorded by Swedish Radio Jazz Group in March '76; Comps: *Concerto for Piano and Orch.; Danny's Dream; Aesthetic Lady; Portrait Of My Pals; Jazzamour-Affair Suite; Bluesport*; also music for a TV drama.

LPs: Gullin Quartet, *Dream* (MG); Gullin octet (Atl.) *The Artistry of Lars Gullin* (Sonet); *Portrait of My Pals* (SSX); *Jazz Amour Affair* w. symph. orch; *Like Grass; Bluesport* (Odeon); *Danny's Dream* (Metronone); also w. *S. Getz and his Swedish Jazzmen* (Verve); w. Brew Moore (Fant.); Z. Sims, J. Moody, Q. Jones (Pres.).

GUMBS, ONAJE ALLAN, *piano, composer*; b. New York City, 9/3/49. Cousin, Fernando Gumbs pl. bass w. Exuma. Piano lessons at age seven. Stud. at Music & Art High Sch., '63-7; grad. w. Bach. of Mus. from SUNY at Fredonia, '71. Additional stud. at Indiana U. w. David Baker; Famous Arr. Clinic in LV, July '70. Pl. trombone in high sch. band and orch.; piano at church functions and variety shows. First prof. experience w. Andrew Langston Latin Jazz Quintet. After grad. guitarist-composer Leroy Kirkland helped get him started in mus. business. Worked w. Natural Essence, '72-4; Norman Connors, April-Oct. '73. Special concerts of Black music w. Buffalo Phil., summer '73; Zimbabwe National Rhythm Troup, Buffalo '72-4; also pl. w. Kenny Burrell; Mtume; CBA Ensemble; Betty Carter; Dakota Staton; Jimmy Owens; Carlos Garnett; Frank Foster; Dee Dee Bridgewater. App. w. Nat. Jazz Ensemble at Wolf Trap Farm, Va.; NYJRC in Feb. '75 *Tribute to Miles Davis*. Infl: H. Hancock, H. Silver, K. Jarrett, M. Tyner, B. Taylor; H. Mancini; G. McFarland, W. Shorter, D. Baker, B. Byers. TV: Villanova JF, '68; *Jazz Adventures; Positively Black; Like It Is*. Fests: NJF-NY w. Natural Essence; Norman Connors, '73-4. Comps: woodwind quartet, *Four in Miniature; Prelude to the World* for chamber orch.; *Dark of Light; Are They Only Dreams; Up the Street, Round the Corner, Down the Block; Batuki*. Arrs: *Love From the Sun; Dindi; Maiden Voyage; Skindiver*, all for Connors; *Stella By Starlight* for NYJRC's M. Davis tribute. LPs: w. Connors, *Dark of Light; Love From the Sun; Saturday Night Special* (Buddah); w. Woody Shaw, *Moontrane;* w. Garnett, *Black Love;* w. Buster Williams, *Pinnacle* (Muse);

w. L. Ridley, *Sum of the Parts;* w. C. Sullivan, *Genesis;* w. C. McBee, *Mutima* (Strata-East); w. Lenny White, *Venusian Summer* (Nemperor); w. R. Ayers, *A Tear to a Smile* (Poly.).

GUMINA, THOMAS JOSEPH (TOMMY),* *accordion;* b. Milwaukee, Wis., 5/20/31. Co-leader w. B. De Franco in the early '60s of a quartet that feat. his accordio-organ, Gumina later withdrew almost entirely from jazz activity in order to concentrate on the designing and merchandising of musical instruments.

GUY, FRED,* *guitar*; b. Burkeville, Ga., 5/23/1899. A regular member of the Duke Ellington orch. from the mid-20s until '49, Guy was heard first as a banjoist, and from '33 as a guitarist. In later years he managed a ballroom in Chicago. He committed suicide 11/22/71.

LPs: w. Ellington (Col., RCA).

HABIB, DONALD (DON), *bass, composer*; also *trumpet, piano, percussion*; b, Montreal, Canada, 4/21/35. From a musical family. Studied six yrs. at Provincial Cons., Mont.; one yr. of brass w. Carmine Caruso; Benny Baker, NYC; one yr. bass w. Fred Zimmerman of NY Phil.; comp. w. J. Giuffre; improvisation w. Adolphe Sandole, Phila.; cond. w. Mike Perrault, Mont.; arr. and orchestration, '72-4, w. Rayburn Wright and Manny Albam at Eastman Sch. Worked w. C. Mariano; Toshiko; Michel Legrand; J.J. Johnson; Skitch Henderson; P. Bley; S. Stitt; Rene Thomas; M. Ferguson. Infl: C. Baker, Clifford Brown; Ray Brown, S. LaFaro, Richard Davis; Gil Evans, Muzio Clementi, Tchaikowsky. TV: Mont. Fest: Mont.; Toronto; Ottawa; Montreux. Wrote children's series, variety shows, documentaries for CTV network; arrs. for CBC shows; commercials. LPs. w. Yvan Landry (Can. Cap.); w. Jerry DeVillers (Trans-Can.).

HACKETT, ROBERT LEO (BOBBY),* *cornet*; b. Providence, R.I., 1/31/15. Was guitarist, occasionally heard on cornet, w. Glenn Miller band in '41-2. Since then has led own combos, also making wide impression as soloist in Jackie Gleason series on Capitol in '50s. Moved to Cape Cod, '69, where he was often feat. at Dunfey's. Quintet w. Vic Dickenson pl. two months at Roosevelt Grill, NYC, '70, and toured in U.S., incl. NJF. Many apps. at Colorado Jazz Party, NJF-NY, guest shots w. WGJ; tour of England, Sept. '74; Apps. in Mass. and at Michael's Pub, NYC, '75; confined to a hospital for two weeks at the end of May '76, he was able to play an engagement on June 4 after his release, but died of a heart attack in Chatham, Mass., 6/7/76. Hackett, who said "I've been working steady since I was 14" was one of the jazz perennials, a cornetist with a beautifully burnished sound and a consistent habit of unceremoniously putting all the notes in the right place at the right time; capable of playing comfortably with Dizzy Gillespie, Zoot Sims or the Eddie Condon alumni. His hobby was sound equipment. TV: *Just Jazz* w. Dickenson, PBS, '71. LPs: *Live at the Roosevelt Grill* (Chiaroscuro); *Plus Vic Dickenson; That Midnight Touch; Time For Love* (Project 3); *Live at the Royal Box* (Hyannisport); *What A Wonderful World; Strike Up the Band* (Fly. Dutch.); w. Mary Lou Williams, *Giants* (Perception); w. WGJ (World Jazz).

HADEN, CHARLES EDWARD (CHARLIE),* *bass, composer*; b. Shenandoah, Iowa, 8/6/37. Rejoined Ornette Coleman in '66 and has cont. to pl. w. him in addition to working w. the JCOA and Keith Jarrett. Haden has also perf. or rec. w. a wide spectrum of musicians incl. Archie Shepp, Tony Scott, Roswell Rudd, Red Norvo, Pee Wee Russell, Alice Coltrane, Mose Allison and John McLaughlin. Fests: NJF w. Shepp, '66-67; w. Don Cherry '73; W. Coleman: MJF '66-67; NJF '70-72; NJF European tour '71; Ann Arbor Blues Fest. '73; many European fests. w. Coleman, Jarrett. Films: *Last Tango in Paris* w. Barbieri; *The Holy Mountain* w. Cherry. Comps: *Song For Che; Circus '68-69.* Won DB Critics new star award '61. His first LP as a leader, *Liberation Music Orch.*, first rec. in '69 was reissued in Oct. '73 after winning awards from *Melody Maker, Swing Journal* and the Grand Prix Int. du Disque Academie. Haden was given grants in comp. by the Guggenheim Foundation '70; the National Endowment for the Arts '73. LPs: *Liberation Music Orch.; The Bass; College Concert* w. Pee Wee Russell, Red Allen (Impulse); *Science Fiction* w. Coleman (Columbia); *Escalator Over the Hill* w. Carla Bley; *Relativity Suite* w. Cherry (JCOA); *The Elements* w. Joe Henderson, Alice Coltrane (Milestone); *Expectations* w. Jarrett (Columbia); *Death and the Flower* w. Jarrett (Impulse); *Tribute* w. Paul Motian (ECM).

HAGGART, ROBERT SHERWOOD (BOB),* *bass, composer*; b. New York City, 3/13/14. The former Bob Crosby bassist-arranger was on staff at NBC and a regular on the *Tonight Show* orch. in '66-67. In '68 he and Yank Lawson (q.v.), with whom he had been associated in the Crosby band and in the '50s in a series of LPs, formed the World's Greatest Jazzband. The band toured the U.S. and Brazil '69; reopened the Roosevelt Grill, NYC, '70; toured Gr. Brit. '71; Hawaii '73; Gr. Brit., Germany, Scandinavia; Rainbow Grill '74. Haggart's *My Inspiration* is the WGJ's theme song and his other comps., *What's New; South Rampart Street Parade; Big Noise From Winnetka; Dogtown Blues*; and *I'm Prayin' Humble*, are prominently feat. in the band's library. In addition has contributed new originals and arrs. of contemporary pop material like *Up, Up and Away*, etc. App. at NJF '69, '72 w. WGJ; w. Friends of Eddie Condon '74. TV: *Today Show; Sunday*, both on NBC. Publ: *Bob Haggart Bass Method* (Robbins Music Corp. 1775 Broadway, New York, N.Y. 10019). LPs: w. WGJ on Project 3, Atlantic. Later albums on their own World Jazz label (4350 E. Camelback Rd., Phoenix, Ariz. 85018).

HAHN, JERRY DONALD,* *guitar*; b. Alma, Neb., 4/21/40. Orig. member, John Handy group, '65-7; toured w. 5th Dimension, '68; Europe, Japan, Canada, U.S., incl. Carnegie Hall recital w. Gary Burton, '68-9. In '70 formed Jerry Hahn Brotherhood, touring U.S. and Bahamas, rec. one album on Columbia. From '72-5 concert tours w. own quartet; from '72 full time prof. at Wichita State U. and clinician for C.G. Conn Ltd. Instr. Co. App. MJF w. Handy, '65 and '66; w. Burton, '68; Berlin J.F. w. Burton, '68; NJF, w. Burton, '69; own quartet at Wichita JF '74-5. In '74-5 had regular monthly column in *Guitar Player Magazine*. LPs: Fantasy, Columbia, Arhoolie; w. Burton on RCA, Atl.; w. Handy on Col.

HAIG, ALLAN W. (AL),* *piano, composer*; b. Newark, N.J., 7/22/24. An important player with Dizzy Gillespie, Charlie Parker in '40s; Stan Getz in '50s. During the '60s he worked for the most part in NYC eastside cocktail lounges, rarely playing jazz, but in the '70s he experienced a renaissance, pl. w. his own duo at Bradley's '73; solo and trio at Gregory's '74-5; trio at Sweet Basil, '75. In '73 he visited Europe for gigs at the Bilboquet; Chat Qui Peche in Paris; the Montmartre in Copenhagen. While there he gave concerts on French and Danish radio. In Nov. '74 he was reunited w. his associate from the bop era, Jimmy Raney for a concert at Carnegie Recital Hall. Haig wrote a Piano & String Quartet in '75.

LPs: Al Haig-Jim Raney, *Strings Attached* (Choice); *Invitation*, rec. in England (Spotlite); *Trio & Quintet* (Prest.).

HAKIM, SADIK (Argonne Dense Thornton),* *piano, composer*; b. Duluth, Minn., 7/15/22. The pioneer bop pianist, who pl. w. Ch. Parker, moved to Canada in the '60s, also spending six months in Europe in '72. Led own trio and quartet at Expo '67 and '68. Many radio shows in Montreal. Heard at Ronnie Scott's Club in London; Montmartre in Copenhagen; Randy Weston's club in Tangier, Morocco. Rec. w. own sextet for CBC, '72. Concerts, clubs in Toronto, Montreal, '74-5. Comps: *The London Suite; Liliane; A Prayer for Liliane.*

LPs: *Duke Ellington Memorial; The London Suite* (CBC); reissues w. Lester Young (BN); Charlie Parker (Arista).

HALL, ADELAIDE,* *singer*; b. Brooklyn, N.Y., 1909. Sang wordless vocals on Ellington records, '27; toured in many black revues in '30s. Settled in England in '38 after appearing at Drury Lane Theatre in *The Sun Never Sets*. Toured extensively throughout Europe during '40s; app. in *Kiss Me Kate* at London Coliseum, '51; *Love From Judy*, London, '53; *Jamaica* w. Lena Horne, NYC '57. Remained occasionally active in later years, living in London. In '74, at church of St. Martin's-In-The-Field, took part in memorial service for Ellington singing *Creole Love Song*, which she had originally rec. with him in '27.

LP: for EMI (England); others w. Ellington.

HALL, EDMOND,* *clarinet*; b. New Orleans, La., 5/15/01. Pl. in '40s and '50s w. Red Allen, Teddy Wilson, E. Condon, L. Armstrong. Toured Europe frequently in '60s, visiting there for the last time in '66. Shortly after playing a Carnegie Hall concert, Hall died of a heart attack in Boston, 2/11/67.

LPs: *Celestial Express*; w. Art Hodes, Original Blue Note Jazz, Vol. 1 (BN); w. Armstrong (various labels).

HALL, HERBERT L. (HERB),* *clarinet, reeds*; b. Reserve, La., 3/28/07. Brother of Edmond Hall. Mainly associated w. Don Albert in '30s, '40s; toured Europe w. Sammy Price in '50s; worked at Eddie Condon's in late '50s. Pl. in US and Canada w. Wild Bill Davison Jazz Giants, '67-9; Don Ewell trio in Canada, '70; Saints & Sinners, '72; Bob Greene, '73 and again in fall '75 for coll. and civic centers in south & midwest. From '74 w. Balaban & Cats; at new Eddie Condon's w. Balaban '75. Fest: Manassas, Va.; Detroit-Windsor, Ont.; NJF-NY w. Greene; Louis Armstrong Stadium dedication, '73; Nice, '75. LPs: *Clarinet Wobble* w. Joe Muranyi (Fat Cat Jazz); *Old Tyme Modern; The Jazz Giants* (Sack.); w. Greene, *The World of Jelly Roll Morton* (RCA); w. Balaban, *A Night at the New Eddie Condon's* (Classic Jazz).

HALL, JAMES STANLEY (JIM),* *guitar*; b. Buffalo, N.Y., 12/4/30. Played w. Chico Hamilton, J. Giuffre in late '50s; Lee Konitz, Sonny Rollins, Art Farmer, early '60s. Hall then decided (in '65) to give up touring, settled in NYC and took a job with the Merv Griffin TV show. Own small groups from '66, incl. duos w. such bassists as Jack Six and Ron Carter; in mid '70s devoting much time to solo playing. Pl. for Duke Ellington's birthday party at White House, '70; concerts for Smithsonian Inst.; feat. soloist w. Nat. Jazz Ens. at New School, '75. Teaching privately, '66-'73. Toured in Japan and Europe; apps. on Swedish, German, Spanish TV. Fests: Berlin, '69; Concord, '73; MJF, '74; NJF, '68, '70, '72-3, '75. Won DB Critics' Poll, '74; *Playboy* All Stars' All Stars, '69, '71-2. Comp: *Careful; Piece For Guitar and Strings.*

Whitney Balliett, in a 1975 profile of Hall in *The New Yorker*, attributed to him "a grace and inventiveness and lyricism that make him preeminent among contemporary jazz guitarists and put him within touching distance of the two grand masters—Charlie Christian and Django Reinhardt."

LPs: *Jim Hall Live!* (Horizon); *It's Nice To Be With You* (MPS/BASF); *Where Would I Be; Alone Together* (Milestone); w. Rollins, *The Bridge* (RCA).

HALL, JOE, *bass*; b. Washington, D.C., 11/9/52. Both parents musical. Pl. piano before taking up bass at 14. Began bass studies, '71. Enrolled at Howard U. as string bass major and became a founder member of the Blackbyrds, a student group sponsored by D. Byrd, who was then Chairman of the Dept. of Jazz Studies at Howard. The group pl. w. Byrd and perf. in concert along w. Sly Stone; M. Gaye; Earth, Wind and Fire and other pop stars.

LPs: *Flying Start; The Blackbyrds* (Fantasy).

HALLBERG, BENGT,* *piano, composer;* b. Gothenburg, Sweden, 9/13/32. Stud. piano w. Sixten Eckerberg in Gothenburg, '44-6; comp. w. Lars-Erik Larsson and counterpoint w. Ake Udden at Royal Academy of Mus.

in Stockholm, '54-7. Worked w. Thore Jederby, Kenneth Fagerlund in late '40s. Attained international recognition when he acc. Stan Getz on the saxophonist's Swedish tour and rec. w. him, '50. In '53 Hallberg also rec. w. Clifford Brown & Art Farmer. He led his own trio and was closely assoc. w. Lars Gullin and other top Swedish jazzmen. From '69 he has been a member of the Swedish Radio Jazz Group and the Arne Domnerus sextet with whom he pl. in NYC at the Swedish Embassy, '74. Infl: Teddy Wilson, Bud Powell, Lennie Tristano, Keith Jarrett. He became increasingly active as a composer from the late '50s beginning with a string quartet, '57; *Collabortion* for string quartet and piano, bass and drums, '63; *Kain*, a ballet for symp. orch. and rhythm section for Royal Swed. Opera, '64; Concertino for piano & string orch., '65; ballet for Swedish TV, '66; *Lyrisk Ballad* for two jazz pianists & orch., '68; *Froken Ensam Hemma*, a children's opera for Royal Swed. Opera; *Music for Jazz Combo & Symph. Orch*, '69; *Icelandic Souvenir; Spelet on Job* (lyrics from the Book of Job—Old Testament) for choir and jazz group, '70; *Beat Rondo*, '71; string trio; *Hallristningar*, '74; *We Love You Madly* (Duke Ellington in memoriam), '75. Publ: *Modern Jazz Piano* (Westin & Co., Brannryrragat. 84, Stockholm, Sweden); *Beginner's Course*, with recorded instr. (Reuter & Reuter Publ., Brahegatan 12, Stockholm, Sweden).

LPs: *P Som I Piano; Collaboration* (EMI); *At Gyllene Cirkeln* (Metronome); as arr: *Alice and Wonderband*, Alice Babs w. Domnerus (Decca); Swedish Radio Jazz Group, *Greetings and Salutations* feat. Thad Jones, Mel Lewis (Four Leaf Clover); as comp: *Spelet on Job* (Swed. Radio); *We Love You Madly* (Philips); feat. soloist in *Du Gladjerika Skona*, music by Jan Johansson (Swed. Radio).

HAMEL, PETER-MICHAEL, *keyboards*; also *singer*; b. Munich, Germany, 7/15/47. Grand-aunt a prominent classical pianist in Germany. Stud. comp. at Munich music high school; jazz piano w. Mal Waldron in conjunction w. French composer Luc Ferrari and German composer Carl Orff; stud. w. Morton Feldman in Berlin; Afro-Latin rhythms w. Jeff Biddeau in Trinidad; Indian classical music w. Imrat Khan and Pandit Patekar; Tibetan instruments and vocals in North India '73-74. Pl. concerts w. Between, an international group comprised of black conga players, classical oboeist and Argentinian guitarist during Olympic games, Berlin '72; avant-garde festivals, Berlin '72, Donaueschingen '73; Munich JF '74; pl. w. vibraphonist Tom Van Geld '74. Awarded several comp. prizes at Beethoven Fest. competition, Bonn '74. Comp. *Dharana; Samma Samadhi; Diaphainon; Maitrya;* and many pieces for Between. Music for theatre and films: *Wallenstein; Schwejk; The Violincello.* TV: *My Friends and Me; Mr. Gringo.* Pub: *Music and Meditation* (Barth Verlag, Munich). Infl. & insp: John Coltrane, Terry Riley, Steve Raich, John Cage, African, Indonesian & Indian music.

LPs w. Between, *Einsteig; And the Waters Opened* (Philips-Phonogram); *Dharana* (Philips-Phonogram); *Hesse-Between-Music*, prod. by J.E. Berendt). Solo LPs: *Hamel; The Voice of Silence* (Philips-Phonogram); *Buddhist Meditation* (MPS).

HAMILTON, FORESTSTORN (CHICO),* *drums, composer*; b. Los Angeles, Cal., 9/21/21. After leading own groups off and on from '56 until mid-60s, Hamilton, based in NYC, started his own company, successfully writing jingles, music for movies, radio, TV. During the '70s he gradually returned to public playing. App. at Montreux JF, '72, '73. Formed new combo, '74. During Cal. tour in '75, he took part in a TV spec., *Reunion*, w. Buddy Collette and Fred Katz, both original members of Hamilton's 1950s quintet, for NET in San Diego.

Film scores: *Mr. Rico; Coonskin.* Many TV specs: *Ski Ski; Portrait of Willie Mays; Bellevue* etc. Many commercial spots for IBM specs. on TV. Comps: innumerable for new gp., incl. *Peregrinations; Sweet Dreams Too Soon; Everybody's; Morning Side of Love.*

LPs: *Peregrinations* (BN); *Best Of; Chic Chic Chico; Dealer; El Chico; Further Adventures; His Great Hits; Man From Two Worlds; Passin' Thru* (Imp.); *Head Hunters* (SS); *The Master* (Enterprise).

HAMILTON, JIMMY,* *clarinet, tenor sax*; b. Dillon, S.C., 5/25/17. A key member of the Duke Ellington orchestra for 26 years, mainly as clarinet soloist, also as occasional arranger, Hamilton left the band in the summer of 1968 to free-lance in NYC. He subsequently moved to the Virgin Islands to play and teach. LPs: see Ellington, Duke; also sessions w. Mercer Ellington (MCA); Billie Holiday, Teddy Wilson (Col.), various small group dates with Ellington associates.

HAMMER, JAN,* *piano, electric keyboards, synthesizer, drums, composer*; b. Prague, Czechoslovakia, 4/17/48. Played in Junior Trio w. Miroslav and Alan Vitous during high school. Won int. mus. competition in Vienna, '66, and won scholarship to Berklee Coll. of Music. Studied classical comp. and piano at Prague Conservatory. Played at Warsaw Jazz Jamboree w. Stuff Smith, '67; gigged in Munich, summer '68, leaving for US when Russians invaded Czechoslovakia. Worked around Boston from Nov. '68; in house gp. at *Playboy* Club for a yr. Joined Sarah Vaughan in early '70 for 13 months, touring in US, Canada and Japan. Settled in NYC, working w. Jeremy Steig; Elvin Jones. With Mahavishnu orch. from May '71 through Dec. '73. Then w. B. Cobham's Spectrum to fall '75; recs. w. Jerry Goodman; Stanley Clarke; John Abercrombie.

To record his album w. Goodman, *The First Seven Days*, he composed, using pianos, synthesizers, digital sequencer, Mellotron and drums, employing a multitrack tape machine; he then added background, edited and mixed. Of the Hammer-Goodman collaboration, *Like Children*, Alan Heineman said: "The session is astonishingly complex but almost never pretentious; the playing is virtuoso without seeming egotistical; and the mood is simultaneously warmly relaxed and nervously exploratory."

Comp: *Sister Andrea; Earth in Search of a Sun; Sixth Day—The People; The Seventh Day.*

LPs: *The First Seven Days; Like Children*; w. Stanley

Clarke; Tommy Bolin (Nemp.); w. Mahavishnu; w. J. McLaughlin/C. Santana, as drummer, *Love, Devotion, Surrender* (Col.); w. Cobham (Atl.); w. Abercrombie (ECM); w. Steig (Cap.); w. E. Jones (BN).

HAMMOND, JOHN HENRY,* *record producer*; b. New York City, 12/15/10. Best known for his role in launching the careers of B. Goodman, C. Basie, Meade Lux Lewis, C. Christian, B. Holiday et al, Hammond in the late '60s and early 1970s was still producing albums at CBS Records in NYC, helping to draw the attention of the public to such artists as George Benson, Don Ellis, Bruce Springsteen and Bill Watrous, as well as providing a forum for veteran talents not heard on records in some years, notably Helen Humes, whose return he arranged in '75. Rec. John Lewis for CBS, 1975. Also during that year Hammond was honored in LV as "Man of the Century" by a group of representatives of the rec. industry. In Sept. '75 in Chicago, an educational TV program, *A Tribute to John Hammond*, presented personalities with whose careers Hammond had been involved: Geo. Benson, Benny Carter, Bob Dylan, Leonard Feather, Benny Goodman, John Hammond Jr., Milt Hinton, Helen Humes, Jo Jones, Goddard Lieberson, Benny Morton, Mitch Miller, Red Norvo, Sonny Terry, Jerry Wexler, Marion Williams, Teddy Wilson and others. The show was nationally syndicated on educational stations. Film clips of Bessie Smith, Billie Holiday and Count Basie were included.

HAMMOND, JOHNNY (JOHN ROBERT SMITH),* *organ, piano*; b. Louisville, Ky., 12/16/33. Was formerly known professionally as Johnny "Hammond" Smith. Left Louisville at 18. Living in Cleveland, pl. w. Jimmy Hinsley, Willie Lewis. Switched from piano to organ, worked w. Nancy Wilson, '58, then w. Chris Columbus. Led own combo in NYC. Through '60s pl. many small clubs such as Count Basie's, Minton's, The Shalimar, and rec. frequently. Signed w. Kudu Records, '71, and made a series of commercially successful soul-jazz albums, one of which, *Breakout*, served to introduce Grover Washington Jr. Hammond found an exciting, rhythmically sensitive groove that worked well both musically and commercially. Comp: *Fantasy*. LPs on Kudu, Prest., Mile.

HAMPEL, GUNTER, *vibraphone*; also *clarinets, saxophones, flutes, piano etc., composer*; b. Goettingen, W. Germany, 8/31/37. Grandfather was a Bohemian street musician who entertained on 16 different instruments. Stud. music from '48, also stud. architecture. Led own band from '58, touring throughout Europe, with frequent radio and TV apps. in Germany and other countries. Wrote music for films. Hampel has perf. in U.S. (mainly in and around NYC), but is best known for his work in Europe, Africa, Asia, S. America. He toured for the Goethe Inst. In addition to many LPs under his own name, he has rec. w. Marion Brown and Jeanne Lee. Infls: L. Armstrong, J. Noone, Ellington, Monk, Mingus, Anton Webern, Hans Werner Henze. Fests: Berlin; Donaueschingen; Tunisia; Paris; Holland; Frankfurt and countless others.

Joachim Berendt has called Hampel the most radical among the newer vibraphonists, a musician who has also distinguished himself as a sensitive artist on several other instruments. Barry Tepperman, writing of Hampel's Galaxie Dream Band, said: "His music is unashamedly poetic, romantic in a subtle, timeless manner that Gary Burton and various others have tried for but never quite obtained. He is aware of the full potential harmonic and tonal ranges of all his instruments, and makes use of the possibilities where they can best be integrated into the overall structure of his music." Publ: *Songbook*, Vol. I (Birth Records, 34 Gottingen, Philipp Reis Str. 10, W. Germany).

LPs: *Gunter Hampel* (ESP); others, released in Europe, incl. *The 8th of July*, feat. A. Braxton, Jeanne Lee; *Ballet Symphony-Symphony No. 6; People Symphony; Spirits; Familie; Waltz for 3 Universes Celebrations* (all feat. J. Lee); *Espace* (Duo); *Angel; Broadway; I Love Being With You; Unity Dance; Out From Under; Journey To The Song Within*, all w. Galaxie Dream Band (Birth).

HAMPTON, LIONEL,* *vibes, piano, drums, leader*; b. Louisville, Ky., 4/12/13. After rising to stardom with Benny Goodman in the late '30s he formed his own big band in the early '40s and led it almost continuously to the mid-60s when he formed a smaller group called the Jazz Inner Circle. Except for special big band reunions with his alumni, such at the NJF in the late '60s and NJF-NY in '72, he has stayed in the small band context. At NJF-NY '73 he was again reunited in concert with Goodman, Teddy Wilson and Gene Krupa. In '74 his NJF-NY appearance, with Wilson, Milt Hinton and Buddy Rich was one of the artistic highlights of the festival, reminding people that Hampton had lost none of his intensely swinging skills.

He was an active campaigner for President Nixon and Gov. Rockefeller, pl. quite often in their behalf. Rockefeller aided him and his late wife, Gladys, to form the Lionel Hampton Development Corp. which erected housing at 131st Street and Eighth Avenue in NYC, where some day he would like to add a university in which Hampton hopes "young black kids could learn to be doctors, lawyers, IBM technicians . . . even musicians."

Mayor John Lindsay of NYC appointed him as his goodwill ambassador to the Far East and presented him with The George Frederick Handel Medallion, the city's highest cultural award. In '75 he was made an honorary doctor at Pepperdine Coll. in Calif. TV: produced a spectacular in Toronto '71 w. R. Eldridge, Krupa, Rich, Mel Torme, Z. Sims, G. Mulligan, etc. LPs: *Transition* w. Rich (Gr. Merch.); *Them Changes* (Bruns.); big band at Newport; small gp. reissue, *Stompology* (RCA); *Lionel; Hamp's Big Band* (Aud. Fid.).

HAMPTON, LOCKSLEY WELLINGTON (SLIDE),* *trombone, tuba, composer*; b. Jeannette, Pa., 4/21/32. The former M. Ferguson trombonist and arr. went to Europe in '68; toured England w. W. Herman; pl. concerts in Paris, then settled in Berlin, where he undertook radio staff orch. assignments in addition to working frequently w. various jazz combos and bands, incl. a big orch. of his own. He did not return to the U.S. except for occasional brief visits, declaring himself convinced that there was more freedom of musical expression on the European jazz scene.

LPs: *Umea Big Band at Montreux* (Gazell); w. Dexter Gordon, *A Day In Copenhagen*; w. Miriam Klein, *Lady Like* (BASF); w. Barry Harris, *Luminescence* (Prest.).

HANCOCK, HERBERT JEFFREY (HERBIE) (MWANDISHI),* *keyboards, composer*; b. Chicago, Ill, 4/12/40. First prominent as composer of *Watermelon Man*, popularized by M. Santamaria, which he also rec. with his own group. Traveled w. Miles Davis combo, '63-8. During his tenure w. Davis, Hancock established himself as a composer and instrumentalist far more sophisticated than the simple melody of his song hit had indicated. Among his better known works rec. by Davis were *The Sorcerer; Madness; Riot*.

While with Davis, Hancock continued to rec. with other groups, incl. various combos of his own. Among the works that gained attention were *Canteloupe Island*, rec. on a Hancock quartet date; *Maiden Voyage* and *Dolphin Dance*, which he wrote for a quintet session in '65; and most notably *Speak Like A Child* and *Riot*, both products of a sextet session that feat. fluegelhorn (Thad Jones), bass trombone (Peter Phillips) and alto flute (Jerry Dodgion). At the time of the release of that album late in '68, Hancock described his music: "The harmonies in these numbers are freer in the sense that they are not so easily identifiable chordally in the conventional way. I'm more concerned with sounds than with definite chordal patterns. I tried to give the horns notes that would give color and body to the sounds I heard. Some of this way of thinking and writing comes from listening to Gil Evans and Oliver Nelson, and from having worked with Thad Jones from time to time."

Almost simultaneously with the release of the *Speak Like A Child* album, Hancock left Davis and formed a sextet, feat. trumpet, trombone and Bennie Maupin on reeds. More and more he turned to electronics as a source of energy and communication in his music. An album, *Mwandishi*, whose title he had taken as his Swahili name (the word means composer) marked a turning point in its extensive use of these electronic devices. On this and subsequent LPs the instrumentation was augmented to incl., at one time or another, electric guitar, electric bass, electric piano, echo-plex, phase shifter, synthesizer, and additional percussion.

Hancock moved to Los Angeles in Dec. 1972. While his records enjoyed fairly substantial success and he continued to win innumerable honors, he found it was not economically feasible to retain the sextet. In June, '73 he dissolved the group, formed a quartet, feat. only one horn (Maupin), and concentrated on heavy electronic effects. Explaining his change in direction, he said: "I realized that I could never be a genius in the class of Miles, Charlie Parker or Coltrane, so I might just as well forget about becoming a legend and just be satisfied to create some music to make people happy. I no longer wanted to write the Great American Masterpiece." Hancock added that he was impressed by the big commercial success of Donald Byrd, who had originally brought him to New York in '61.

With the release in the fall of 1973 of Hancock's first LP by the new group, the album itself (*Headhunters*) and the hit single from it, entitled *Chameleon*, both enjoyed unprecedented sales and elevated Hancock's stature to the point where he was able to attract r & b, pop and rock audiences. He headlined in major concert halls throughout the U.S., Europe and Japan, and for two months in late '74 had four albums on the best selling popular album list: *Headhunters*; the followup, *Thrust; Treasure Chest*, an anthological collection of his works; and the sound track album of the music he had written for Dino De Laurentiis' film *Death Wish*.

Hancock's music by '75 was firmly established as indicative of the heights to which a jazz musician could aspire by adjusting his orientation. He won innumerable awards, among them the DB Readers Poll as Jazzman of the Year; #1 Synthesizer '74; other awards from *Cash Box* (#1 r & b Artist); *Playboy* (Best Instrumental Combo in All-Stars' All-Stars Poll); *Black Music Magazine* (Top Jazz Artist, '74) etc.

In addition to his writing for records, Hancock composed and conducted jingles; wrote the score for Michelangelo Antonioni's picture *Blow-up*, and composed and performed music for Bill Cosby's TV special entitled *Hey, Hey, Hey! It's Fat Albert* (preserved in the album *Fat Albert Rotunda*).

LPs: *Empyrean Isles; Best of Herbie Hancock; Maiden Voyage; Prisoner; Speak Like a Child; Succotash; Takin' Off* (Blue Note); *Crossings; Mwandishi; Treasure Chest; Fat Albert Rotunda* (WB); *Headhunters; Sextant; Thrust* (Col.); w. Miles Davis, *Miles Davis In Europe; E.S.P.; My Funny Valentine; Seven Steps To Heaven; Filles de Kilimanjaro; Miles Smiles; Sorcerer; Bitches' Brew; Nefertiti; Miles Davis' Greatest Hits; Miles In The Sky; In A Silent Way; Live-Evil; Big Fun; On The Corner* (Col.); w. Eddie Henderson, *Realization; Inside Out* (Capricorn).

Hancock has also appeared as sideman on *Happenings; Components* w. B. Hutcherson (BN); w. Wayne Shorter, *Native Dancer* (Col.); *Speak No Evil; All Seeing Eye; Adam's Apple* (BN); *Salt Peanuts* w. Pointer Sisters (Blue Thumb); w. Wes Montgomery, *Going Out Of My Head* (Verve), *Day In The Life* and three others (A & M); w. Paul Desmond, *Summertime; Bridge Over Troubled Water* (A & M); w. F. Hubbard, *Red Clay; Straight Life*; w. Joe Farrell, *Penny Arcade; Moon Germs*; w. M. Jackson, *Sunflower* (CTI); w. Norman Connors, *Dark of Light; Dance of Magic* (Cobblestone); *Love From The Sun* (Buddah); w. George Benson, *White Rabbit; Shape of Things To Come* (CTI); others w. Jon Lucien (Col.); Johnny Nash (Epic); Stevie Wonder (Tamla).

HANDY, CAPT. JOHN, *alto saxophone, clarinet*; b. Pass Christian, Miss., 6/24/00. Living in NO from about 1918, Handy (not related to John Richard Handy III) pl.

w. Kid Rena, Kid Howard and many other bands of the '20s and '30s. Still active during the '60s, when he toured Europe and Japan, he pl. w. the Preservation Hall Jazz Band, app. with this gp. at the '70 NJF. Handy died 1/12/71 in his hometown.

HANDY, JOHN RICHARD III,* *alto, tenor saxes, saxello, educator;* also *flute, oboe, piano, singer, shakuhachi, baritone sax, percussion*; b. Dallas, Tex., 2/3/33. After pl. w. Charles Mingus and Randy Weston gps. in NYC in '58-9, formed own gp. Toured Scandinavia as a single in early '60s, then returned to SF and put together new gp. w. violinist Mike White which was hit of MJF '65. Played 36-college tour of western states w. Mont. All Stars, '66; *Spirituals to Swing*, Carnegie Hall; Gunther Schuller opera *The Visitation*, SF, '67. New band w. Mike Nock and White, '68. Led first jazz gp. (octet) to appear at SF Opera House; premiered his *Concerto for Jazz Soloist and Orchestra* w. SF Symphony, '70. In '71 inaugurated a series of collaborations in jazz and North Indian music w. sarodist Ali Akbar Khan; duets w. tabla players Shankar Ghosh and Zakir Hussein. Handy also pl. his *Concerto* w. the Stockton Symph., and was soloist w. the SF State Univ. Symphonic Band in the premiere of Roger Nixon's *Dialogue*, '71. Appeared in *Concerto* w. NO Symph., '72. Judge for Monterey HSJF, '73-4; concerts w. Cabrillo Coll. Symph.; for Cazadero Music Camp; Carnegie Hall w. Mingus; Coll. of Marin w. Khan, '74; for the International Historical Sciences Convention, SF, '75. Also apps. w. local big bands; and at Stern Grove; SF State Univ.

From '68 Handy has taught courses at SF State Univ. in jazz history; from '70 in black music and improvisation; same subjects at Univ. of Calif., Berkeley, '69; Cal. State Univ.; Stanford, '70; SF Conserv. of Mus., '69, '73-. Saxophone instructor, Golden Gate Free Univ., '70. Member of Mayor's Interim Arts Advisory Committee, SF.

TV: *Jazz Casual* w. Ralph Gleason, '65; Bell Telephone Hour, '66; *The Visitation*, Westinghouse, '67; w. SF Symph., KQED, '70. Fest: MJF, '67; NJF; Antibes; Univ. of Calif; Seattle, '68; MJF; Concord, '70; w. Ali Akbar Khan: MJF; U. of Cal.; SF State, '71; Berlin, '72; Bumbershoot (Seattle); Reno, '73; Cazadero 100th Concert Fest., '74.

Comp: soundtrack for Swedish movie *Boo's Ups and Downs*; industrial film for Dayton Corp., Minneapolis; *A Portrait of Birgitta; Dance to the Lady; Scheme No. 1; Scheme No. 2*. LPs: *Live at Monterey Jazz Fest.; The 2nd John Handy Album; New View; Projections; Spirituals to Swing, 30th Anniversary* (Col.); w. Mingus (Atl.; Fant.; Col.; UA).

HANNA, JOHN (JAKE),* *drums*; b. Roxbury, Mass., 4/4/31. Well known in Boston before attaining national stature w. M. McPartland, '59-61, W. Herman, '62-4. Starting in '64, spent 10½ years as member of staff orch. on Merv Griffin TV series, with occasional leaves of absence. Toured Europe, '67, w. C. Terry, B. Brookmeyer, M. Ferguson. Moved to LA, '70 w. Griffin show, playing locally w. Bill Berry band, Herb Ellis-Joe Pass, Supersax. Went to USSR briefly Nov. 74, on aborted tour w. O. Peterson trio. Despite his many years in the studios, Hanna remained a superbly disciplined and powerful drummer, equally at home in jazz combos and big bands. Publ: *Syncopated Big Band Figures Vol. I (Solo) Vol. II (Duets)* (Try Publ. 854 Vine St., Hollywood, Ca. 90038).

LPs: w. Supersax (Capitol); Herb Ellis-Joe Pass; H. Ellis-Ray Brown; Hanna-Fontana band (Concord Jazz).

HANNA, SIR ROLAND P.,* *piano, composer*; also *cello*; b. Detroit, Mich., 2/10/32. In '67 became regular pianist w. T. Jones-M. Lewis orch, touring Europe and Japan in that year, and Soviet Union, '72. Perf. solo concerts at Olympia Theatre, Paris, for two months, '68; gave benefit tour in Africa for young African students, '69, and was knighted by the late Pres. of Liberia, William Tubman, for humanitarian interests and the furtherance of the education of young Africans, '70. Member of B. Rosengarden orch. on Dick Cavett show, ABC-TV, '73. Left Jones-Lewis band '74. Also in '70s active in NYC as solo pianist at The Cookery, other clubs and college concerts, often w. Z. Sims. His main area of jazz concentration, however, has been with the NY Jazz Quartet with whom he toured Europe and Japan, '74-5. The highly versatile pianist has taught privately from '60. TV: *An Evening With Carmen McRae and The Roland Hanna Trio*, NET. European fests. and NJF-NY w. NY Jazz Quartet, '74; solo concert at Montreux, '74.

Comps: *Midtown Suite; Sonata for Cello and Piano; Perugia; Child of Gemini Suite; Mediterranean Seascape; Song of the Black Knight; Morning*. LPs: solo album, *Sir Elf* (Choice); *Child of Gemini* (MPS-BASF); *Perugia* (Arista); *The New Heritage Keyboard Quartet* (BN); *Let It Happen*, Jazz Piano Quartet (RCA); *Potpourri*, w. Jones-Lewis (Phila. Int'l.); *All Blues; Spanish Blue*, w. Ron Carter (CTI).

HARA, NOBUO (Nobuo Tsukahara), *tenor, soprano, alto saxophones, clarinet, composer, leader*; b. Toyama Pref., Japan, 11/19/26. Started on trumpet at age 14. In 1943 joined Navy band, pl. saxophone, stud. classical music. In '45 he turned to jazz. From '52 Hara was leader of the Sharps and Flats, which soon was estab. as the outstanding big band in Japan, winning the *Swing Journal* Readers' Poll annually from '56-72. The band made innumerable motion picture and TV apps., was seen at the World Jazz Fest. in Tokyo, '64 and at NJF, '67, as well as almost all other fests. in Japan. Insp. by D. Ellington, C. Basie, Hara assembled a tightly knit unit notable for its ensemble precision. The orch. has made about 100 records for Nippon Col., King, CBS/Sony etc. Comps: *Koto; Humpty Dumpty; Flaming Sun*.

HARDEE, JOHN,* *tenor sax*; b. Texas, ca. 1919. In the mid-70s, the big-toned, hard-swinging tenor man was the band instructor at Oliver Wendell Holmes Junior High School in Dallas, where he still gigs. Played at Nice Festival, '75. LP: own quartet (Black & Blue).

HARDMAN, WILLIAM FRANKLIN JR. (BILL),* *trumpet*; b. Cleveland, Ohio, 4/6/33. With Art Blakey's Messengers; Horace Silver; Ch. Mingus in '50s. Joined Lou Donaldson at end of '59 and was w. him, off and on, into '66. Worked w. Lloyd Price big band, '63. With Blakey again, '66-9; Mingus, '69-70. Rejoined Blakey '70 and also formed own gp., The Brass Co., an ensemble incl. Lonnie Hillyer, Eddie Preston, Harry Hall, trumpets; Kiane Zawadi, trombone; Bob Stewart, tuba. Active w. both gps. from '71. Won DB Critics Poll, TDWR, '73. Fest: NJF-NY w. Mingus, '73; w. Blakey, '75. LPs: w. The Brass Co., *Colors* (Strata-East); w. Blakey, *Live at Slugs* (Trip); w. Donaldson, *Fried Buzzard* (Cadet); w. Curtis Fuller, *Crankin'* (Main.); w. Eddie Jefferson, *Come Along With Me* (Prest.).

HARDWICKE, OTTO (TOBY),* *alto, bass saxophones*; b. Washington, D.C., 5/31/04. A childhood friend of D. Ellington, Hardwicke worked with him in Washington and later in NYC, leaving in '28, but rejoining in '32. He remained with Duke until '45 and soon after retired from music. He died 8/5/70 in Washington, after a long illness. Hardwicke's unique, singing tone on alto was a key element in the early Ellington records. He was co-composer of *Sophisticated Lady*.

HARLEY, RUFUS, *bagpipes, saxophones, flute, oboe*; b. Raleigh, N.C., 5/20/36. Family moved to Phila. when he was an infant. Shined shoes and sold newspapers so he could buy a saxophone and pl. in high school band. At 16 was forced to drop out of school and go to work. Several yrs. later began studying w. Dennis Sandole. Canada's Black Watch Bagpipe Band intrigued him as he was watching the funeral of John F. Kennedy on tv in Nov. '63 and, after failing to reproduce the sound on the tenor sax, bought a used set of bagpipes from a New York pawnshop. Stud. and practiced for four mos. under Sandole and began playing it prof. In mid and late '60s st. leading own quartet in clubs, concerts and rec. Infl: Rollins, Coltrane. TV: *To Tell the Truth; What's My Line; I've Got A Secret; Tonight Show.* Film: as Pied Piper in *You're A Big Boy Now.* Fests: Newport, Laurel, Berlin; Montreux '74. "The trick in playing the pipes is not the musical technique," says Harley, "but the mental outlook. . . . There is a long history and a powerful philosophy behind the pipes which is quite different from our Western musical culture."

LPs: *King/Queens* (Atlantic); w. Rollins, *The Cutting Edge* (Mile.).

HARPER, BILLY R., *tenor sax, flute, singer, composer*; b. Houston, Tex., 1/17/43. Parents sing; uncles and aunts sing and pl. piano. Sang along while listening to Ella Fitzgerald on radio at age one; later sang solo, and in choir, at church. One of his first teachers of improvisation was uncle, Earl Harper. Began on saxophone at 12. Instruction from James Williams at Emmett Scott Jr. High in Tyler, Tex., '57. Returned to Houston and at Evan E. Worthing H.S. played in marching and jazz band under Sammy Harris, '59-61. Inspiration from saxophonist Richard Lillie and his wife, Vernell Lillie, Harper's drama instructor. Received Bach. of Mus. from No. Tex. State U., '61-5. Major in saxophone; minor in theory. Also majored in special program for students who were particularly interested in jazz. Began grad. work. Pl. in No. Tex. Big Band that won first prize at KC JF.

Pl. w. r&b bands; as sideman w. James Clay. To NYC '66. From '67 w. Gil Evans; worked w. Art Blakey, '68-70, incl. tour of Japan. From '71 w. Thad Jones-Mel Lewis orch. incl. European tour '73. Other jobs and rec. w. Max Roach; Lee Morgan; Elvin Jones; Donald Byrd, '71-3. Harper, who had led a gp. of his own on occasion in the early '70s, took a quintet to Europe in the summer of '75, app. in Norway, Finland, Holland, Belgium, Denmark, Sweden, France and Italy.

Taught privately during '65-73; taught improvisation at 15 NJ high schools under grant from NJ Council for the Arts, '73; college clinics w. Jones-Lewis., '73-4; private sax and flute instr. at Livingston Coll., New Brunswick, N.J., '75. Infl: Clay, Rollins, Coltrane, G. Evans but says, "I have been inspired by many, but mainly by the 'true life force' that they found in music . . ."

TV: *The Big Apple*, NBC documentary, '66; w. Blakey, BBC-, London '68; w. Jazz & People's Movement on Dick Cavett show, ABC, '70; *Soul*, PBS, w. Roach, '71; Morgan, '72; Euro. TV & radio w. own quintet, '75. Fest: voted "most promising saxophonist" at Notre Dame JF, '64, where he app. w. own sextet; Tangier JF, '72; many fests. w. Evans; Jones-Lewis. Member of the NYJRC. Received comp. grants from NEA, '70, '73; CAPS, '74. Won DB Critics' poll, TDWR, '74-5.

Chuck Berg wrote in DB: "Harper's playing represents a fusion of the Rollins and Coltrane traditions, tempered with the spirituality derived from his childhood religious experiences."

Comp: *Capra Black; Cry of Hunger; Thoroughbred; Croquet Ballet; Soulfully, I Love You; Dance Eternal Spirits, Dance; Call of the Wild and Peaceful Heart.* LPs: *Black Saint* (Black Saint); *Capra Black* (Strata-East); *Jon and Billy*, Harper & Jon Faddis (Trio); w. G. Evans (Ampex, Atl., RCA-Japan); w. Jones-Lewis, (SS); w. Roach (Atl.); L. Morgan (BN); J. Owens (Poly.); C. Earland (Prest.); R. Weston (Poly., Arista); L. Armstrong (Fly. Dutch.); Art Blakey, *Live!* (Trip).

HARRIOTT, ARTHURLIN (JOE),* *alto, baritone, tenor sax, composer*; b. Jamaica, BWI, 7/15/28. Emigrated to England, '51; pl. in many small groups; formed own combo in '60. Throughout the '60s his activities were mostly involved in the area of the fusion of jazz and Indian music; also a member of Michael Garrick's group which featured jazz and poetry. Traveled as a freelance soloist, working in many varied contexts. Harriott died in Southampton, England, 1/2/73.

Own LPs on Brit. Col., Melodisc; others w. Sonny Boy Williamson (Marmalade); Garrick (Argo); Acker Bilk, Stan Tracey, Laurie Johnson (Brit. Col.).

HARRIS, BARRY DOYLE,* *piano, composer*; b. Detroit, Mich., 12/15/29. After moving to NYC from Detroit in early '60s, pl. w. Yusef Lateef; then Coleman Hawkins, off and on, '65-9. Led own trio, quintet from '60s; also worked w. Charles McPherson, his sometime sideman, in latter's gp. With Lateef again, '70, incl. European gigs. Own duo at West Boondock, '67; Port of Call East, '69; Digg's Den, '71; duo at Jimmy's for a yr. and a half, '73 through Feb. '74; Bradley's, '75. Concert

w. trio, trios of C. Walton, Walter Davis, Cami Hall, Nov. '74. TV: w. Hawkins, PBS, '69; w. Lateef, Holland, '70. Fest: Montreux '70 w. Lateef; Radio City Jam Session, NJF-NY, '73; solo piano, NJF-NY, '75. Wrote six arrs. for strings for Ch. McPherson concert, Detroit '74. Working on first symphony. A brilliant interpreter of the music of Parker, Monk, Dameron, etc. Comps: *Luminescence; Like This; Nicaragua; Even Steven; You Sweet and Fancy Lady; Rouge; Just Open Your Heart; Sun Dance.* LPs: *Plays Tadd Dameron* (Xanadu); *Luminescence; Bull's Eye; Magnificent* (Prest.); *Vicissitudes* (MPS/BASF); w. David Allyn; Jimmy Heath; Sam Noto; Al Cohn; Sonny Criss (Xanadu); w. Sonny Stitt (Cobble.; Muse); James Moody; I. Jacquet; Dexter Gordon (Prest.); Cohn-Moody (MPS/BASF); C. McPherson (Prest.; Main.); Lee Morgan (BN); Red Rodney (Muse); C. Hawkins (Pablo); Y. Lateef (Atl.).

HARRIS, WILLIAM GODVIN (BEAVER), *drums*; also *percussion*; b. Pittsburgh, Pa., 4/20/36. Mother was dancer who also pl. piano. Stud. w. Stanley Leonard at Carnegie Tech.; piano and comp. w. Charles Bell; w. Kenny Clarke and Dante Augustini at Premier Drum School and Clinic, Paris; percussionist Richard Fitz, and Marshall Brown, NYC. Nickname derives from early days as a baseball player. Pl. ball as member of Special Services while in Army; also began gigging while at Ft. Knox; then local groups around Pitts. after discharge. To NYC, '63, working w. Sonny Rollins, T. Monk, Joe Henderson, F. Hubbard, etc. Joined Archie Shepp, '67, touring Europe w. him and also pl. there w. Albert Ayler. At the end of the '60s formed the 360 Degree Experience w. Grachan Moncur, Dave Burrell, and has perf. w. it, off and on, from that time. He also pl. in Haiti w. Lee Konitz, Eddie Gomez and Jim Hall; NJF tour of Japan w. Shepp, Konitz, G. Barbieri, '73. Worked w. Lee Konitz-Marshall Brown; Shepp; Chet Baker; Warren Chiasson, '74. Music Dir. for Black and Puerto Rican Culture Program funded by NYS Council for the Arts. Pl. for stage prods., *Slave Ship*, '71; *Lady Day*, '72, at Brooklyn Acad. of Music. Infls: K. Clarke, Max Roach, Roy Haynes, Musa Kaleem, Rollins. Comp: *African Drums*; lyrics for *Money Blues; Attica Blues; Ballad For a Child*; all for Shepp albums. All orig. music for *From Rag Time to No Time*, an album on the 360 Degree Music Company label (269 West 72nd St., NYC 10023). Other LPs w. Shepp on Impulse, MPS; w. Ayler, *Live at the Village Vanguard & the Village Theatre* (Imp.); w. Roswell Rudd, Moncur (JCOA); w. Barbieri, *The Third World; The Legend of* (Fly. Dutch.); w. Marion Brown, *Three For Shepp* (Imp.).

HARRIS, WILLARD PALMER (BILL),* *trombone*; also *guitar*; b. Philadelphia, Pa., 10/28/16. One of the definitive trombone stylists of the '40s, he was best known for his work w. W. Herman orch., '44-6, later for his tours w. N. Granz's JATP. After living in LV in the '60s, Harris moved to Florida, leaving there only occasionally. One of his last major jazz apps. was at the MJF. He died 9/19/73 in Hallandale, Fla.

Winner of many awards in the '40s and '50s, Harris was considered by some musicians to be the most creative artist on his instrument since the advent many years earlier of J. Teagarden and J.C. Higginbotham.

LPs: w. Herman (Col. etc.); Flip Phillips, *A Melody From The Sky* (Bob Thiele Records); C. Ventura (Trip).

HARRIS, WILLIE (BILL),* *guitar*; also *guitorgan, piano*; b. Nashville, N.C., 4/14/25. From '66 continued activities in night clubs and concerts in the Washington area, incl. *From Bach to the Blues* at St. Johns Church, '67; Watergate Barge w. Underground Quintette; Gospel Truth concert w. own trio, '69; National Society of Classic Guitar, '74. Harris, who specializes in unaccompanied, unamplified, six-string Spanish guitar, using no pick, operates his own studio in Washington, where from '71 he has annually prod. the Kenny Burrell Guitar Seminar. Harris' students have incl. Orville Saunders (q.v.), Ed Ellington (q.v.). His son, bassist-guitarist Joe Harris, after pl. w. Marvin Gaye and the Temptations, now works in Washington and teaches with his father.

App. at Django Reinhardt Memorial Concert, Samois, France; also seen on French TV, '73. Was awarded Jazz Composer Fellowship by the Nat'l Endowment for the Arts, '72. Comps: *Blue Medley; Watergate Blues*; score for film, *Sincerely The Blues.* In a review of his concert at the Library of the Performing Arts at Lincoln Center, J.C. Thomas wrote: "*The Wes Montgomery Suite*, Harris' own composition, penned in homage to the late guitarist, was a wry but bouncing evocation of Montgomery's single note style. It was so accurate that, as Laurence Olivier *becomes* Shylock when he plays the role, Harris *was* Montgomery."

Publs: *The Harris Touch; Guitar Arrangements of Classic Jazz; Instant Guitar* (Bill Harris Studio, 2021 Hamlin St., N.E. Washington, D.C. 20018).

LPs: *Down In The Alley; Bill Harris Rhythm* (Black & Blue); *Caught in the Act; Harris in Paris* (Jazz Guitar, own label).

HARRIS, DON, *violin*; also *bass, piano, organ, synthesizer, singer*; b. Pasadena, Cal., 6/18/38. Formerly known by the nickname Sugar Cane. Sang and pl. piano w. The Squires, five piece group, '57-63; during same period had duo partnership with Dewey Terry under the name Don & Dewey. During mid-60s appeared frequently w. Johnny Otis blues shows; subsequently came to prominence w. F. Zappa, toured extensively w. John Mayall in U.S. and abroad; was member of rock group, Pure Food & Drug Act, and rec. a series of albums, mainly as violinist, under his own name.

J. Berendt has observed that Don Harris is the dominant violinist of the contemporary world. His roots are in the blues and his style seems to have derived, at least partially, from Stuff Smith, though Harris names as his main influences and inspirations Little Walter, B.B. King, Ray Charles, John Coltrane.

LPs: w. Don & Dewey (Specialty); w. J. Otis, *Cuttin' Up* (Epic), *Cold Shot* (Kent); Own LPs: *Sugarcane* (Epic); *Cup Full of Dreams; Fiddler On The Rock; I'm On Your Case; Sugarcane's Got the Blues* (BASF).

HARRIS, EDDIE,* *tenor saxophone, electric piano, organ, reed trumpet, singer, composer*; b. Chicago, Ill., 10/20/36. Big hit with the theme from the movie *Exodus* established him as combo leader. With the Atlantic label from '65 he delved into the electronic world when he introduced the Varitone attachment to his tenor sax in '67. In the '70s he began singing through a synthesized saxophone and his guitarist, Ronald Muldrow, used the guitorgan, a Hammond-organ sounding guitar that is touched rather than strummed or picked. Harris, whose music has moved more in an r&b and rock direction (he recorded w. British rock players such as Jeff Beck, Stevie Winwood, Rick Grech, etc. in England—*E.H. in the U.K.*) says: "A lot of musicians are suspicious of electronics. . . . They call it gimmickry, but I can understand that because you always have opposition upon change. Change breeds contempt because whatever your beliefs are you have to go back and examine them. . . . Amplification will add ten years to your life span because you don't have to exert yourself as much. The unit I use is a pre-amp unit, which can emulate different woodwind sounds. At the press of a button it can sound like a bassoon or a tuba or an oboe or whatever they have concocted upon the chassis system."

Fest: Montreux w. Les McCann, '69; NJF. Played in Ghana at celebration of 14th year of independence, '70. Publ: *How to Play Reed Trumpet; The Intervalistic Concept for All Single Line Instruments.* Comp: *Eddie Sings the Blues; Walk With Me; Please Let Me Go; Ten Minutes to Four; Drunk Man; Renovated Rhythm; Recess; Freedom Jazz Dance.* LPs: *Bad Luck is All I Have; I Need Some Money; E.H. in the U.K.; Excursions; Sings the Blues; Instant Death; Live at Newport; Free Speech; High Voltage; Silver Cycles; Plug Me In; The Tender Storm; The Electrifying Eddie Harris; Mean Greens*; Harris-McCann, *Swiss Movement; Second Movement* (Atl.).

HARRIS, EUGENE (GENE),* *piano, keyboards, synthesizer*; b. Benton Harbor, Mich., 9/1/33. From '66-74 cont. to play clubs and coll. dates across the U.S. w. The Three Sounds. Formed own sextet, '74, app. in major U.S. cities. Fests: Kansas City; Wichita.

LPs: *Astral Signal; Gene Harris of The Three Sounds; Elegant Soul* (BN).

HARRIS, JOSEPH ALLISON (JOE),* *drums, percussion*; b. Pittsburgh, Pa., 12/23/26. The one-time Dizzy Gillespie drummer, who settled in Stockholm in 1956, moved to Germany to play on Radio Free Berlin from '61-66, during which time he also rec. w. Clarke-Boland band. Ret. to Pittsburgh '66; moved to LA '67 where he worked at Playboy Club; Donte's w. Benny Carter; taught drums at Eubanks Sch. of Music. Toured w. Ella Fitzgerald '68. Ret. to Germany '70, locating w. Max Greger orch. in Munich for TV work. Pl. jazz workshop, Hamburg, various studio jobs w. Greger '71; also at Club Domicile in Munich w. various groups led by Jimmy Woode, Fritz Pauer, Peter Herbolzheimer in same year. Again ret. to Pitts. '72; house drummer at Walt Harper's Attic backing Joe Williams, Carmen McRae, etc. and teaching courses in jazz history and total percussion at Univ. Pitts. App. at Pitt. JF '72. Film: *They Shoot Horses Don't They?* '69. Harris is a tennis pro in Pitts. and conducts 10-week, summer clinics all over the city. He also won the musicians' union Local 471/60 golf tournament '67. LPs: timbales on *My Kind of Sunshine* w. Herbolzheimer (MPS); Clarke-Boland (Atl.).

HARRIS, BENJAMIN (LITTLE BENNY),* *trumpet, composer*; b. New York City, 4/23/19. A minor figure in the early bebop movement, he gained some recognition as comp. of *Reets and I; Little Benny* (also known as *Crazeology* and *Bud's Bubble*); and co-composer of *Ornithology.* Also wrote *Wahoo*, based on *Perdido.* Pl. briefly w. Earl Hines, Benny Carter, C. Hawkins et al in '40s; sporadically active in later years. Died in SF, 2/11/75. LPs: w. Charlie Parker (Verve); w. Don Byas in Harlem series (Arista).

HART, WILLIAM W. (BILLY), *drums*; b. Washington, D.C., 11/29/40. Grandmother was a concert pianist. Self-taught; first inspired to become interested in jazz when he heard several Ch. Parker records given him by Buck Hill, a saxophonist. Pl. for three-and-a-half years w. singer Shirley Horn; Jimmy Smith, '64; Wes Montgomery until the latter's death in '68. For a year he worked intermittently w. Eddie Harris and Pharoah Sanders. After pl. clubs w. Marian McPartland, he joined Herbie Hancock, remaining with him for three years. Then spent a year w. McCoy Tyner trio, before joining S. Getz early in '74. Hart's infls. were Harry Stump Saunders, Louis Hayes, Max Roach, A. Blakey, Shadow Wilson, Big Sid Catlett, Philly Joe Jones, Vernel Fournier. Won DB Critics poll, TDWR, '74.

LPs: w. Hancock, *Sextant* (Col.); *Crossings* (WB); others w. Getz (Col.); Joanne Brackeen (Choice).

HARTMAN, JOHN MAURICE (JOHNNY), *singer*; also *piano*; b. Chicago, Ill., 7/3/23. Began piano and singing at eight. Received scholarship to Chicago Musical Coll. where he studied voice, '39. Sang w. Earl Hines for three or four mos., '47; then w. Dizzy Gillespie, '47-8. From that time app. as a single. Rich, smooth baritone in what was originally an Eckstine-derived style. Infl: Eckstine, Sinatra. TV: Sammy Davis; *Tonight; Today*; specials in Australia; Europe. Fest: London, '59; Japan, '63; Australia, '68; NJF-NY, '75. LPs: Impulse; Perception; w. J. Coltrane (Imp.).

HAVENS, ROBERT L. (BOB),* *trombone*, also *vibes*; b. Quincy, Ill., 5/3/30. W. Geo. Girard, Al Hirt in late '50s, then joined Lawrence Welk, 1960. Featured soloist on Welk's weekly TV series. Often seen at trad. jazz clubs around U.S., w. Bob Crosby at Disneyland, freelance studio work etc. Pl. at LA Shrine Auditorium w. Doc Evans in 70th birthday tribute to Louis Armstrong, July 1970. A bona fide sheriff of LA County, Havens also plays in a unique group called the Los Angeles County Sheriffs' Rhythm Posse Band.

Festivals: Monterey, 1966, w. Dick Cary; Sacramento, '74; Ojai w. Abe Most, '75; Indianapolis Dixieland Fest. w. J. McPartland, '75.

LPs: Welk's 25th Anniversary (Ranwood); *The Enter-*

tainer w. Myron Floren (Ranwood); Blue Angel Jazz Club jam session albums, 1969-70, on BAJC's own label.

HAVERHOEK, HENDRIK (HENK), *bass*; also *clarinet, tenor sax, piano*; b. Shoorl, Holland, 2/11/47. Began on clar., '57. Att. Cons. of Arnhem to stud. clar. '65, but switched to bass, '66 under Henk Guldemond and rec. degree as symphonic bassist and teacher in '72. Also took correspondence course from Berklee. From '68 a member of the Rein de Graaff-Dick Vennik quartet. Pl. several tours since '71 w. Mal Waldron; Dexter Gordon; Horace Parlan; Johnny Griffin. With Rene Thomas, '72-4; Don Byas, '72; Duke Jordan; Ben Webster; Bobby Jones-Dusko Goykovich quintet, '73; Pony Poindexter; Jimmy Owens, '74; Red Rodney; Tete Montoliu, '75. Also one-nighters w. G. Ammons, Al Haig, Thad Jones, Frank Rosolino, Joe Henderson, Dizzy Reece, Slide Hampton, Carmell Jones, Leo Wright, Babs Gonzales, Ray Nance, Joe Pass, Lee Konitz & Art Farmer in Holland, Belgium & Germany. Infl: Dexter Gordon, "among many others." Fests: Pescara w. Gordon; Laren (Holl.) w. de Graaff-Vennik; Hammerfeld (Holl.) w. Griffin, Gordon, Konitz, '73; Middleheim (Belg.) w. Thomas, '74. Comp: *Departure; Firestoned.* LPs: *Last Concert* w. Webster (Bovema); *A Little Bit of Miles* w. Waldron (Freedom); *Departure* w. de Graaff-Vennik (BASF); w. Thomas (Vogel); w. Gordon, *Dexterity.*

HAWES, HAMPTON,* *piano, composer*; b. Los Angeles, Cal., 11/13/28. After working a long club stint w. Red Mitchell in LA and spending eight months in SF, Hawes co-led a group w. Jimmy Garrison in '66. He then took a sabbatical; between Sept. '67 and June '69 he toured the world, picking up engagements and making rec. sessions wherever the opportunity presented itself. Back in LA, he worked as duo w. Leroy Vinnegar for eight months. Led trio in London, Paris, Copenhagen, '71. During next three years worked at local LA clubs, pl. fests. at Montreux, Nice etc. During most of '74 was co-featured in a trio w. bassist Carol Kaye. When that group disbanded, Hawes led a quartet for a while; he then met Joan Baez and rec. and pl. concerts with her.

During the '70s Hawes' style underwent a radical change as he devoted much time to electric keyboards and contemporary modal concepts. Throughout this time he was in increasing demand for coll. clinics, lectures and concerts. TV: *Festival In Black*, '74; *Midnight Special* w. Baez, '75. Publ. *Raise Up Off Me*, w. Don Asher, an autobiography (Coward, McCann & Geoghegan, Inc.). Comps: *Blues for Walls; Josie Black; Drums for Peace; Hamp's Collard Green Blues.*

LPs: *The Challenge* (Japanese RCA); *Hampton Hawes Jam Session* (Col.); *Seance; I'm All Smiles* (Contemp.); *Universe; Blues For Walls; Live at Montreux* (Prest.) w. D. Gordon, *A La Suisse*; w. G. Ammons, *Playing in the Yard* (Prest.); *The East/West Controversy* (Xanadu).

HAWKINS, COLEMAN,* *tenor sax*; b. St. Joseph, Mo., 11/21/04. Pl. w. Fletcher Henderson, 1923-34; freelanced in Europe, 1934-9; rec. *Body and Soul* in NYC soon after return in '39. Led big band late '39 until early '41, then various small combos, many tours w. Norman Granz incl. the final American tour of JATP in '67. Last European tour w. Oscar Peterson in '68.

By this time Hawkins' health was declining, heavy drinking had taken its toll, and he was regarded by many as a venerated father figure rather than as the vital force he had been for more than three decades. In mid-April of 1969 he appeared on an educational TV program in Chicago but was so frail he had to play sitting down; his performance revealed only remnants of a style that had set the entire course for the tenor saxophone. A month later, 5/19/69, he died of bronchial pneumonia at Wickersham Hospital in NYC.

Though others have been far more extensively written about (because their impact reached a peak during an era when jazz had become the subject of widespread discussion to the print media), it remains beyond dispute that Hawkins was the most influential figure in the evolution of the tenor saxophone, and one of a very small number of musicians who all but monopolized his chosen field. (Others were Harry Carney on baritone sax and, in his early years, Louis Armstrong.) He was the first jazz soloist to apply his creativity, with unprecedented artistic as well as commercial success, to the refashioning of a ballad. Though *Body and Soul* was by far the best known, the style had begun to crystallize as far back as 1929, when he recorded, as a member of a pickup group called the Mound City Blue Blowers, what may have been the first genuine jazz ballad solo: *One Hour* (based on the song *If I Could Be With You One Hour Tonight*). Both this recording and the original *Body and Soul* can be found in *Body and Soul—A Jazz Autobiography—Coleman Hawkins* (RCA).

Unlike many musicians whose styles were formed during the pre-swing and swing years, Hawkins continued to show an interest in new developments, was an early associate both on records and in person of the bop pioneers, and so updated his style that certain of his solos, if speeded up from 33 1/3 to 45 r.p.m., bore an amazing resemblance to those of Charlie Parker.

In his Grammy award winning notes for *The Hawk Flies*, a two-volume album that contains the products of various sessions rec. between 1944 and 1957, Dan Morgenstern wrote: "Coleman Hawkins was a legend in his own time: revered by younger musicians, who were amazed and delighted at his ability to remain receptive to their discoveries; loved by his contemporaries, who were equally astonished by his capacity for constant self-renewal. He was one of those who wrote the book of jazz."

TV: acting role in episode of *Route 66*. LPs: The number of albums in which Hawkins is heard as leader, co-leader or sideman seems almost limitless, but the following are among the most important and many may still be available: *On The Bean* (Continental); *The Big Sounds of Coleman Hawkins & Ben Webster* (Bruns.); *Coleman Hawkins & Lester Young—Classic Tenors* (Contact); *Body & Soul* (RCA); *Bean & The Boys* (Pres.); *Hollywood Stampede* (Cap.); *A Documentary* (two-LP interview) (Riverside); *The Tenor Sax: C. Hawkins & F.*

Wess (Commodore); *Duke Ellington Meets Coleman Hawkins* (Imp.); *The Hawk In Holland* (GNP); *The High and the Mighty Hawk* (Master Jazz); *The Newport Years*, feat. Hawkins, Eldridge et al (Verve); *The Hawk Flies* (Milestone); *Reevaluations: The Impulse Years* (Imp.); *C. Hawkins & The Trumpet Kings* (Trip); *Hawk & Roy: 1939* (Phoenix); *Jam Session In Swingville*, feat. Hawkins & Pee Wee Russell (Prest.); *Hawk In Germany*, feat. Bud Powell (Black Lion); *Sirius* (Pablo); also several tracks on *Esquire's All-American Hot Jazz* (RCA); *The Greatest Jazz Concert in the World* (Pablo).

HAWKINS, ERSKINE RAMSAY,* *trumpet, leader*; b. Birmingham, Ala., 7/26/14. Led one of the best and most popular bands of the Swing Era. From the '60s leading his own quartet in Catskill Mountains resort area in New York state. Appeared in NYJRC concert which paid tribute to Savoy Ballroom, '74. LP: *Reunion*, a regrouping of some of his former sidemen (Stang).

HAYES, CLARENCE LEONARD (CLANCY),* *banjo, singer*; b. Caney, Kansas, 11/14/08. Settled in SF in late '20s. Popular from late '30s w. traditionalist bands, incl. Lu Watters, Bunk Johnson, Bob Scobey, Turk Murphy. He was an original member of the World's Greatest Jazzband and took part in its first record session, but was in failing health and died of cancer 3/13/72 in SF. Hayes rec. under his own name for Good Time Jazz, Delmark and ABC. He was composer of the hit song *Huggin' & A'Chalkin'*.

HAYES, ISAAC, *keyboards, composer, singer*; b. Covington, Tenn., 8/20/42. Raised in Covington, later moved to Memphis, where his first major hit album, *Hot Buttered Soul*, was released in '69. He subsequently became one of the top stars in soul music and in '72 won the Motion Picture Academy's Oscar award as the creator of the title song and score for the film *Shaft*. Though he has occasionally sung blues, Hayes' connection with jazz is peripheral. LPs on Stax, ABC.

HAYES, LOUIS SEDELL,* *drums*; b. Detroit, Mich., 5/31/37. Toured w. Y. Lateef '55-6; H. Silver, '56-9; C. Adderley, '59-65, O. Peterson, '65-7; F. Hubbard, '70-1. Rejoined Peterson for a year, and in '72 organized his own quintet. In '75-6 co-led quintet w. Junior Cook, touring Europe early '76.

An adaptable and sensitive drummer insp. by Philly Joe Jones, Hayes has been heard on records w. J. Coltrane, J.J. Johnson, Phineas Newborn, W. Montgomery, L. Morgan, Ravi Shankar, Dexter Gordon, S. Stitt, Cedar Walton, Chris Jordan, Lucky Thompson, Terry Gibbs, Joe Henderson.

Own LP, *Breath of Life* (Muse); many others with groups listed above.

HAYES, EDWARD BRIAN (TUBBY),* *tenor saxophone*; also *vibes, flute, baritone* and *alto saxophones*; b. London, England, 1/30/35. Led own groups in England from '50s. Made first U.S. app. at Half Note, NYC, '61; again in '62, '64; Jazz Workshop, Boston, '64; Shelly's Manne Hole, '65. Many international tours with own group, as well as apps. w. symph. orchs. From '69-71 he was almost inactive due to illness. In '71 he returned to work, but was intermittently ill until he died in a hospital in London while undergoing a heart operation, 6/8/73. Although chiefly known for his tenor saxophone work, Hayes pl. vibes with great sensitivity, and was a composer of rare talent.

Many LPs on British labels, as well as one rec. in U.S. w. Clark Terry et al (Epic).

HAYNES, ROY OWEN,* *drums, leader*; b. Roxbury, Mass., 3/13/26. Worked w. Stan Getz, w. whom he had been associated, off and on, from '50, and Gary Burton but was mainly occupied at the head of his own Hip Ensemble from '70. Appeared at NYC clubs such as Mikell's, Top of the Gate, Five Spot and Tin Palace; Gulliver's in NJ. Toured in Europe, incl. Belgium, Holland '74. Several apps. for Joe Segal's annual "Charlie Parker Month" presentations in Chicago incl. '75 w. L. Konitz, Milt Jackson, Barry Harris. "52nd Street" concert w. Billy Taylor at Town Hall, NYC, '75. TV: Merv Griffin; *Soul*, NET; *Positively Black*, NBC. Fest: Notre Dame, as judge and player, '72-3; NJF-NY; Berlin; Newport International; Colo. Jazz Party. Named by *Esquire* as one of America's best-dressed men. An extremely versatile drum master, at home in a wide spectrum of styles. LPs: *Senyah; Hip Ensemble* (Main.); w. Burton, *Tennessee Firebird; Duster* (RCA); w. L. Coryell, *Barefoot Boy* (Fly. Dutch.); w. C. Corea, *Now He Sings, Now He Sobs* (SS); w. D. Jordan (Steeple.); Sonny Stitt (Muse).

HAYTON, LEONARD GEORGE (LENNIE),* *composer, piano*; b. New York City, N.Y., 2/13/08. First known as an associate of Bix Beiderbecke, F. Trumbauer, J. Venuti, E. Lang and others, Hayton later led his own dance band and was musical director at MGM studios in the '40s. He married Lena Horne in '47 and often served as her musical director. He died 4/24/71 at a hospital in Palm Springs, Cal.

LPs: w. Beiderbecke et al (Col.); Lena Horne (various labels).

HAYWOOD, CEDRIC,* *piano*; b. Houston, Tex., ca. 1914. Played w. Milt Larkins; Lionel Hampton; Sidney Bechet; Illinois Jacquet; Kid Ory. Worked w. Brew Moore in SF in early '60s, moving back to Houston in summer '63. Led own big band at Club Ebony from '64 until his death from a stroke 9/9/69. LPs w. Ory (GTJ).

HAZEL, ARTHUR (MONK),* *drums, cornet, mellophone*; b. Harvey, La., 8/15/03. Prominent in New Orleans from 1920s w. Abbie Brunies et al, later in NYC and LA, Hazel later was assoc. for many years w. Sharkey Bonano. He died in New Orleans Apr. 1968.

HEARD, JAMES CHARLES (J.C.),* *drums*; also *conga*; b. Dayton, Ohio, 10/8/17. After ret. from four years in the Orient, '53-57, he pl. in NYC w. C. Hawkins & R. Eldridge; Lester Lanin; and his own group. Cont. to lead quartet LA area, Las Vegas. Americana Hotel, NYC w. Dorothy Donegan '62 and thereafter for several years. To Detroit '66 where he again led his own trio, pl. and singing. Went out as a single in Feb. '75 to Syracuse, Pitts., Wash., D.C.; to Europe in April w. all-star band.

TV: *Mike Douglas Show*, '64. Fest: Arts Festival, Birmingham, Mich. w. all-star band of Billy Mitchell, Oliver Nelson, Sandy Mosse, Clark Terry, Joe Newman, Al Grey, Wynton Kelly, Toots Thielemans, Joe Kennedy, '60. LP: *Basie Picks the Winners* (Verve).

HEATH, ALBERT (TOOTIE or KUUMBA),* *drums, composer*; also *tympani, flute*; b. Philadelphia, Pa., 5/31/35. Played w. J.J. Johnson in late '50s; Cedar Walton; Jimmy Heath in '60s before traveling to Europe w. George Russell. Worked w. Russell; Friedrich Gulda in Europe while based in Sweden from '65-8. House drummer at Montmartre in Copenhagen, pl. w. Kenny Drew trio; Dexter Gordon quartet. Returned to US and joined Yusef Lateef quartet; became staff teacher for Jazzmobile. Studied flute and arranging w. Lateef; piano at Manhattan Sch. of Mus.; tympani w. Peter Terrace. Trips to Europe w. Lateef. Flew to Denmark to record as sideman for SteepleChase label '74. Moved back to Sweden '74 but in '75 became part of new Heath Bros. gp. w. siblings Percy and Jimmy. A versatile, strong drummer who, after his return from Europe in '69 had become a mature, thoroughly confident percussionist, brimming with explosive vitality. Dexter Gordon said, "Tootie is very loose. You can play anything with him."

His Woodwind Quintet was presented at Manhattan Community Coll. '73. Received grant from NEA to compose a work for 20-piece ensemble, '74. Awarded Jazz Honor Citations from Jazz at Home Club in Phila., '65, '74. Comp: *A Notion; Dr. JEH; Dunia; Sub-Set*, all rec., along w. *Tafadhali* from Woodwind Quintet, in *Kwanza* (Muse); other LPs: *Kawaida* (Trip); w. Lateef (Atl.); J. Heath; K. Barron (Muse); D. Gordon (Prest., Steeple.); K. Drew; A. Braxton; T. Montoliu (Steeple.).

HEATH, JAMES EDWARD (JIMMY),* *tenor sax, soprano sax, flute, composer*; b. Phila., Pa., 10/25/26. Early exp. w. Howard McGhee, Gillespie, M. Davis, Gil Evans, Donald Byrd. Co-leader of quintet w. Art Farmer '65-8. Worked for Jazzmobile in NYC for more than ten years as instructor. Played jazz-lecture concerts w. Billy Taylor and own group. From '67 on, wrote and rec. for many radio stations in Europe. Stage band arrs. for Y. Lateef, C. Terry, B. Taylor, '72-3. Began teaching woodwinds at CCNY, '73. Received N.Y. State Council of the Arts grant, '74; member of N.Y. Jazz Rep. Co., '74. Completed comp., *Afro-American Suite of Evolution* under CAPS grant, '75. App. w. brothers Albert and Percy as Heath, Heath & Heath in trio perfs., then w. brothers and Stanley Cowell in Heath Bros. Quartet, '75, incl. 5-wk. European tour in fall.

LPs: *Picture of Heath* (Xanadu); *The Gap Sealer* (Cobblestone); *Love and Understanding* (Muse); *Olinga*, w. M. Jackson (CTI); *Kwanza* w. A. Heath; *These Are Soulful Days* w. Don Patterson (Muse); *The Quota* w. Red Garland (MPS); *Kawaida* w. A. Heath (Trip).

HEATH, PERCY,* *bass, viola da gamba*; b. Wilmington, N.C. 4/30/23. Came out of the Dizzy Gillespie group of the early '50s to help found the Modern Jazz Quartet, playing with it for more than two decades before its breakup in July '74. During annual summer vacations from the MJQ pl. gigs w. brother Jimmy. In '75 worked briefly w. Sarah Vaughan, app. w. her at NJF-NY; formed Heath Bros. gp. with Jimmy, Tootie and Stanley Cowell. Noted for his counterlines and strong, subtle underpinning for the MJQ. Countless TV, fest. apps. w. MJQ. Comp: *Oops!*. LPs: *The Last Concert* w. MJQ (Atl.); others w. MJQ on Atl.; Little David; w. Albert Heath, *Kwanza* (Muse).

HEATH, EDWARD (TED),* *leader, trombone*; b. Wandsworth, London, England, 3/30/00. Trombonist in name bands from mid-1920s; Led own band in concerts at London Palladium from 1945, and during the next two decades dominated the field in England with a well-trained, popular dance band that included several first rate jazz soloists and some jazz arrangements. Heath's records sold well in the US, enabling him in 1956 to make the first of several successful American tours. Tadd Dameron was on Heath's arranging staff in the mid-'50s. Among the band's more successful jazz-oriented LPs was Fats Waller's *London Suite* (London).

After five years' illness (during which time the band carried on without him), Heath died 11/18/69 at Virginia Water, Surrey. LPs: *Big Band Themes Revisited; Glenn Miller Salute* etc. (London).

HECKMAN, DONALD J. (DON),* *alto sax, composer, critic*; also *soprano sax, clarinet, tarogato*; b. Reading, Pa., 12/18/35. Concerts, rec. w. the Don Heckman-Ed Summerlin Improvisational Jazz Workshop; comp. for TV, theatre and documentary films, '66-70. Music reviewer for various magazines, jazz critic for *Village Voice*, Contributing Editor to *Stereo Review*, '68-71. Rock critic for New York *Times*, Recordings Editor for Sunday *Times*, '71-72. Vice-president, East Coast A&R, RCA Records '73-74. From '74 functioning as a freelance writer, critic, rec. prod., mus. and comp. TV: *Look Up and Live; Christmas Eve Special*, CBS; *Love; Work; Leisure*—three shows for CFTO, Canada. Comp: theme music for *Children's Film Fest.*, CBS-TV; orig. mus. for *The Dutchess of Malfi; Heartbreak House; Robin Hood; U.S.A.; Pinocchio* on Caedmon Records. Articles and essays anthologized in *Jazz Panorama* (Crowell-Collier); *The Urban Adventurers* (McGraw-Hill); *Black Americans* (Voice of America Forum Lectures). Taught jazz history at City College, CUNY, in early '70s. LPs: *Heckman-Summerlin Imp. Jazz Work.* (Ictus); *Avant-Slant* (Decca); *Ring Out Joy* (Avant-Garde); *Saturday in the Park* (Camden). Heckman received Gold Rec. for his productions of *Blood, Sweat & Tears IV* and *B,S&T's Greatest Hits* (Columbia). Heckman believes "Hindemith's dictum that a musician should be able to play, compose, arrange, criticize and function in all areas of his craft."

HEFTI, NEAL,* *composer, trumpet, piano*; b. Hastings, Neb., 10/29/22. Best known in '40s as composer and trumpeter w. W. Herman; in '50s as composer of many originals w. C. Basie, incl. *Li'l Darlin'*; in '60s as writer of TV and motion pic. scores, among them *Barefoot In The Park* and *The Odd Couple* (both films and TV series); Fred Astaire TV spec; film, *The Last of the Red Hot Lovers*. In '73-5 Hefti took a sabbatical from the studios to undertake concert tours, personal apps. with his own orch. He also lectured at leading univs. Comps: *Girl Talk; Batman Theme; Barefoot in the Park; The Odd Couple; Fred.*

LPs: sound track albums, *Harlow* (Col.); *Barefoot In The Park; The Odd Couple* (Dot); *Duel at Diablo* (UA); *Batman Theme* (RCA).

HEMPHILL, JULIUS, *alto sax, composer*; b. Fort Worth, Tex., ca. 1940. Studied clarinet w. John Carter in early '50s. First prof. job w. Independent Boogie Agency in early '60s. With US Army Band, '64; various Texas bands; Ike Turner. Moved to St. Louis '68 and became a member of BAG w. Oliver Lake, Lester Bowie. During this time also studied at No. Texas State; Lincoln U. Formed gp. w. pianist John Hicks and toured US coll., '71. Pl. w. Anthony Braxton in Chicago; performed in Paris, Sweden, '73. Worked w. Paul Jeffrey Octet in NYC, '74. Film: *The Orientation of Sweet Willie Rollbar*, '72. He presented a stage version of this work at Ornette Coleman's Prince Street loft, '73. His *Kawaida*, a mixed media presentation of instrumental music, voices, dance and drama was premiered at Washington U., St. Louis, '72. *Obituary: Cosmos for 3 Parts* was debuted at Space Life Center, NYC, Dec. '74. Comp: *Lonely Blacks; Skin 1; Skin 2; Lyric; Reflections; The Hard Blues*. Hemphill is also a poet-lyricist. In '72 he formed his own rec. co., Mbari, and released two albums, *Poem For Blind Lemon*; and *Dogon A.D.* The latter was scheduled for re-release on Arista, the label which produced his LP, *'Coon Bid'ness*. Other LPs: w. Braxton, *New York, Fall* 1974 (Arista); Bowie, *Fast Last* (Muse); Kool and the Gang, *Hustler's Convention* (UA).

HENDERSON, WILLIAM RANDALL (BILL),* *singer*; b. Chicago, Ill., 3/19/30. Recorded w. H. Silver, '58; O. Peterson, '63. Toured as Basie vocalist, '65-6. Settling in LA area, spent most of his time as an actor and singer in motion pics. and on TV. Among his movie credits were *Trouble Man*, '72; *Hit The Open Man*, '74. Acting apps. on the Bill Cosby show, '70-1; also roles in *Ironside; Happy Days; Sanford & Son*. Sang on TV shows, *Dial M For Music; Tonight; Midnight Special*, and the Steve Allen, Della Reese and Nancy Wilson shows, all during '72-5. Henderson is a strongly jazz-oriented singer with an original and piquant timbre.

LPs: *Please Send Me Someone To Love; Bill Henderson Sings* (Veejay Int'l.); w. Horace Silver; Jimmy Smith (Blue Note); w. Hank Jones (Riverside); w. O. Peterson (MGM); w. Basie (Verve).

HENDERSON, BOBBY (Jody Bolden) Robert Bolden Henderson),* *piano, trumpet*; b. New York City, 4/16/10. Billie Holiday's first accompanist in '33, he spent most of his career in upstate New York, living during the late '60s in Albany, where he died 12/9/69. LPs: *Home in the Clouds; Last Recordings* (Chiaro.).

HENDERSON, DR. EDWARD JACKSON (EDDIE), *trumpet, fluegelhorn, composer*; b. New York City, 10/26/40. Father sang w. Charioteers; mother was dancer at Cotton Club. Trumpet at elementary school from age 10 to 14. To SF 1954; theory, tpt. at SF Conservatory, '54-7. Spent '58-61 in Air Force, not playing. Became interested in jazz when Miles Davis, then staying with his parents, gave him encouragement and informal instruction.

From 1961 Henderson pursued his dual ambitions, studying at U.C. Berkeley, grad. w. B.S. in zoology, '64; M.D. in medicine '68 at Howard Univ., Washington, D.C. During summers, from '64, pl. w. John Handy. Gigs w. Handy, Big Black, Philly Joe Jones, '68. Joined Herbie Hancock 1970 and toured with Hancock's sextet until it disbanded in '73. Through this period he also worked with Pharoah Sanders, Joe Henderson et al.

Traveled w. Art Blakey's Jazz Messengers for six months in '73; late that year, returned to SF, then played with Azteca for a year. From late '74, active mainly leading own combo, but worked w. Norman Connors in Japan summer '75.

Henderson continued to practice medicine intermittently to supplement his income, both in general practice and psychiatry. Henderson was praised by critics for his full, round tone, exceptional technique and attention-riveting ideas.

Infl: Miles Davis, F. Hubbard, Lee Morgan, J. Coltrane.

TV: Several programs while w. Hancock. Fests: NJF-NY w. Hancock and Blakey; many others during several visits to Europe.

LPs: *Realization; Inside Out* (Capricorn); *Sunburst* (BN). w. Hancock: *Mwandishi; Crossings* (WB); *Sextant* (Col.); five albums w. Norman Connors (Buddah); others w. Ch. Earland (Fantasy); Pete Yellin; Buddy Terry (Mainstream).

HENDERSON, JOSEPH A. (JOE),* *tenor sax, composer*; also *soprano sax, flute*; b. Lima, Ohio, 4/24/37. First prominent w. Kenny Dorham, '62-3; Horace Silver, '64-6. Co-led Jazz Communicators w. Freddie Hubbard, Louis Hayes. Pl. w. Herbie Hancock sextet, '69-70. From that time has led own groups except for four months in '71 when he was affiliated w. Blood, Sweat & Tears. Eugene Chadbourne, writing in the Calgary *Herald*, said: "Henderson is a part of an historical process that's extremely important in American music—the process of improvisation. This is where the real American classical music is . . . When Henderson launches into one of his many lengthy improvisations—each one is almost like a jewel, polished and multidimensional—you can hear the tenor as it came down through the years. And through that tenor, you can hear all the changes improvised music has gone through in America in more than four decades."

By the mid-70's Henderson had moved to Calif. and had become active doing college clinics. Comp: *Recorda Me; Black Narcissus; Soulution; Inner Urge; Isotope; El Barrio; The Bead Game; Tetragon; Afro-Centric; Power to the People; Afterthought; Caribbean Fire Dance; If You're Not Part of the Solution, You're Part of the*

Problem; Junk Blues; Out 'n In; Gazelle; Black Miracle; Immaculate Deception. Won DB Critics poll, TDWR '67.

LPs: *The Kicker; Tetragon; Power to the People; If You're Not Part of the Solution, You're Part of the Problem; In Pursuit of Blackness; Black is the Color; Joe Henderson in Japan; Multiple; The Elements* w. A. Coltrane; *Canyon Lady; Black Miracle* (Milest.); *Inner Urge* (BN); w. K. Burrell, *Ellington is Forever* (Fant.); w. Mose Allison, *Hello There, Universe* (Atl.), w. A. Coltrane, *Ptah the El Daoud* (Imp.).

HENDERSON, MICHAEL, *bass, guitar*; b. Yazoo City, Miss., 7/7/51. Played cello in high school, but later switched to guitar; learned rudiments of guitar and bass at Grinell's music store in Detroit. From then on has been self-taught. First professional job, '66, w. Rudy Robinson band, which also backed the Detroit Emeralds and the Fantastic Four. Pl. w. Motown artists Stevie Wonder, Martha Reeves and the Vandellas, Four Tops, The Supremes, Gladys Knight and the Pips, The Temptations, '66-8. On the road w. Aretha Franklin for year, '68; w. S. Wonder, '69 to late '70, when he joined Miles Davis. Infls: Davis, Franklin, Wonder, M. Gaye. Fests: Montreux, Ann Arbor, Newport, Monterey. TV apps. w. Davis. Comps: for albums by Michael Shrieve (Col.), G. Bartz (Pres.).

LPs: *Jack Johnson; Live at the Fillmore; Live-Evil; On The Corner; Get Up With It*, w. Davis (Col.); numerous dates w. Motown artists.

HENDERSON, WAYNE MAURICE,* *trombone, euphonium, composer*; b. Houston, Texas, 9/24/39. Best known through the '60s as a member of the Jazz Crusaders. The name of the group was later changed to The Crusaders (see HOOPER, STIX). Henderson also enjoyed considerable success as a producer of albums by other artists.

LPs: w. Crusaders (Blue Thumb).

HENDRICKS, JOHN CARL (JON),* *songwriter, singer*; also *drums*; b. Newark, Ohio, 9/16/21. Key member and principal lyricist with Lambert, Hendricks & Ross, the trio that popularized the concept of setting lyrics to jazz melodies and to improvised solos transcribed from records. Original trio broke up in '62, but lasted for two more years with replacements; from '66 Hendricks worked as a single and in Feb. '68 moved to London. Later that year he was voted number one jazz singer in the *Melody Maker* poll. He worked throughout Europe and Africa, performing on English TV with Lulu, M. Ferguson, and various others; app. in French TV movie, *Hommage a Cole Porter*, which won a prize at Cannes.

Teaming up with his wife, Judith, in the role formerly occupied by Annie Ross, and sometimes adding his daughter, Michelle, Hendricks again began making trio apps. He also staged his *Evolution of the Blues* presentation, originally seen at the MJF in 1960. Returning to the U.S., Hendricks settled in Mill Valley, Cal., embarking on a number of ventures, among them a job as jazz critic for the San Francisco Chronicle, '73-4. In the fall of '74 he put on a new version of *Evolution of the Blues* at the Broadway Theatre in SF, which enjoyed a long run into '75.

He signed with Arista Records to make his first Amer. album in 10 years. He also taught classes on Jazz in American Society at Cal. State, Sonoma and U.C. Berkeley. One of those rare jazz singers in whom wit and humor are elements just as important as rhythmic sensitivity, Hendricks has been an untiring propagandist for jazz. Among the jazz works to which Hendricks has contributed lyrics are *Along Came Betty; Bijou; Charleston Alley; Cloudburst; Cousin Mary; Desafinado; Down For Double; Fiesta In Blue; Four; Little Niles; Little Pony; Moanin'; Now's The Time; Sermonette; Sack O' Woe; Shiny Stockings; Walkin'; Watermelon Man.*

Own LP; *Blues for Pablo* (Arista); early albums made by Hendricks were deleted, but were on Col., Reprise and Smash. LPs w. Lambert, Hendricks & Ross on Col., Impulse, Odyssey.

HERBERT, GREGORY DELANO, *composer, alto, tenor saxophones*; also *clarinets, flutes* etc.; b. Philadelphia, Pa., 5/19/47. Priv. lessons, '61; Granoff School of Music, '62; worked briefly w. D. Ellington, '64. In Sept. '64 entered Temple U., remaining there as music and saxophone major until '68. Joined W. Herman Oct. '71 and toured with him internationally until Jan. '75. Favs: J. McLean, C. Adderley, J. Coltrane, S. Rollins et al. A fervently expressive tenor soloist, particularly effective on ballads, but no less skillful on up tempos.

LPs: w. Herman, *The Raven Speaks; Giant Steps; The Thundering Herd; The Herd Live at Montreux; Children of Lima* (Fantasy); w. Pat Martino, *Baiyina* (Pres.); w. Johnny Coles, *Katumbo* (Main.).

HERMAN, WOODROW CHARLES (WOODY),* *leader, alto, soprano saxophones, clarinet, singer*; b. Milwaukee, Wis., 5/16/13. Led own band from '37 and continued to tour with various personnels; sometimes with small combo in late '50s. Organizing a new band in '60, he enjoyed a resurgence of popularity, touring frequently overseas.

In '67 Herman toured Africa and Iron Curtain countries under U.S. State Dept. auspices. In Sept. '67 he app. at the MJF, introducing Bill Holman's three-movement *Concerto For Herd.* Soloists then in the band incl. Luis Gasca, Carl Fontana, Sal Nistico, Albert Dailey, Cecil Payne. Other foreign tours: England, '68, '70, '72. In '74, starred at Montreux JF and toured France, Belgium, Germany, Sweden, Turkey. In '74 the orch. toured the U.S. for two months w. F. Sinatra, and app. with him on a TV spec., *The Main Event.* Other TV: many apps. on Merv Griffin, Mike Douglas shows etc.

Hiring primarily young musicians and making increasing use of contemporary pop material, Herman recorded a series of successful albums for Cadet in '69-70, and for Fantasy from '71- . In '74 he introduced Alan Broadbent's *Variations On A Scene* and *Children of Lima*, both perf. by the orch. together with the Houston Symph.

Herman continued to discover exciting solo talent.

Heard with him during the '70s were trumpeters Tony Klatka, Bill Stapleton, Gary Pack; trombonists Jim Pugh, Bob Burgess; saxophonists Greg Herbert, Frank Tiberi, Frank Vicari; pianists, Broadbent, John Hicks; bassists Gene Perla, Al Johnson; drummers Ed Soph, Joe LaBarbera; composer-arrangers Richard Evans, Broadbent, Klatka, Nat Pierce, Gary Anderson, Pugh, Stapleton; and innumerable others.

By playing compositions and arrangements that covered a vast spectrum, from his early hits such as *Four Brothers* and *Caldonia* to works by Coltrane, F. Zappa, Stanley Clarke, Chick Corea, Thad Jones and Billy Cobham, Herman succeeded in not only retaining and expanding his audience, but in keeping up the high musical level of the orchestra's performances.

A Grammy winner in '63, Herman won again in '73 for his *Giant Steps* album and in '74 for the *Thundering Herd* album. Fests: Newport six times; Monterey three times; Concord twice, during decade from '66-75. In '75 Herman founded the Woody Herman-Sister Fabian Scholarship Fund in Milwaukee. He gives a concert and seminar annually, donating the proceeds to benefit young musicians, and to award scholarships. By '75 half of the band's engagements were played in colleges and high schools. Many of the band's arrangements are available through Hal Leonard Publ. in Milwaukee.

LPs: *Concerto for Herd*, live at Monterey, '67 (Verve); *Woody*, feat. Broadbent's arr. of *Blues in the Night; Heavy Exposure; Light My Fire* (Cadet); *Brand New; The Raven Speaks; Herd at Montreux; Children of Lima*, w. orch. and Houston Symph.; *Giant Steps; Thundering Herd* (Fant.).

Reissues: *The Best of Woody Herman*, 1939-43 (MCA); *Early Autumn*, 1948-50 (Cap.); *Woody Herman, '63* (Trip).

HEYWOOD, EDDIE JR.,* *piano, composer*; b. Atlanta, Ga., 12/4/15. From 1966-69 a partial paralysis of the hand, similar to the ailment which had curtailed his career in the late '40s, greatly hampered his playing ability. He devoted his main efforts toward comp. and arr. while living in Vineyard Haven, Mass. Ret. to active pl. at the Cookery, NYC, April '72. App. at Newport-NY JF, '74; concerts on Martha's Vineyard '70, '73-74; also school, coll. concerts. Citation of Achievement from BMI '69; second award from BMI for over 1,000,000 broadcast perf. of his comp. *Canadian Sunset*. 750 Award from radio station WSB, Atlanta, Ga., '73. Comp: *Portrait of Martha's Vineyard; Golden West*. LPs: *As You Remember Them; The Swing Era: One More Time* (Time-Life).

HIGGINBOTHAM, JACK (J.C.),* *trombone*; b. Social Circle, Ga., 5/11/06. First prominent in the bands of Luis Russell, F. Henderson and L. Armstrong, Higginbotham later was teamed for many years w. trumpeter Red Allen. He remained occasionally active in the late '60s and app. in '72 at the NJF-NY in an all star E. Condon group. He died 5/26/73 in Harlem hospital, NYC.

Higginbotham was one of the most original and forceful trombone soloists of the swing era.

LPs: *Comes Home!* (Jazzology); others w. Allen (RCA); Armstrong (Col.).

HIGGINS, BILLY,* *drums*; b. Los Angeles, Calif., 10/11/36. One of the charter members of the Ornette Coleman gp. of the late '50s. Active NY free-lance in '60s w. S. Rollins, H. Mobley, L. Morgan et al. Continued to work w. Coleman, off and on, in '60s and '70s; also w. Bill Lee Brass Company in Brooklyn, '72-3; Chris Anderson, '73-4. From '70 his main associations have been w. Cedar Walton and Clifford Jordan in trios and quartets incl. European, Japanese tours. Fests: NJF-NY w. Jordan '73; Basel; Verona w. Jimmy Heath '74. Comp: *Inja; Buster Henry*. A subtle drummer of unflagging swing as at home with Coleman as with Dexter Gordon.

LPs: w. O. Coleman, *Science Fiction* (Col.); w. C. Jordan, *Glass Bead Games; Colors* w. Brass Company (Strata-East); w. D. Gordon (Steeple.); *Generation* (Prest.); w. J. Heath; J. Raney (Xanadu); Hilton Ruiz (Steeple.); w. Pat Martino, *The Visit* (Cobble.); w. Barry Harris, *Bull's Eye* (Prest.); w. C. McPherson; C. Fuller (Main.); Mal Waldron (Enja).

HILL, ANDREW,* *piano, composer*; b. Port au Prince, Haiti, 6/30/37. Early experience in Chicago w. G. Ammons; J. Griffin; Ira Sullivan. On the road w. Dinah Washington; in LA w. R.R. Kirk, '61; to NYC '63 where he began rec. for Blue Note, and leading own gps. Music co-ordinator for Leroi Jones' Black Art Repertory Theatre, '65. From '66-8 pl. colleges, clubs, and concerts across the US; active creating and performing extended comps. Composer in residence at Colgate U., '70-1, where he received his doctorate. Perf. at various rural art centers, such as the Ohio River Arts Fest., Evansville, Ind.; cond. symposiums at Wayne U., Lafayette U. of NO; organized at co-ordinated NY Musicians' JF; toured cultural centers and penal systems for the NY State Council for the Arts, '72. Audited programs for the NYSCA, '72-3. Own quartet for University of the Streets, NYC, '73. Toured US on the Smithsonian Heritage Program, '73-4. Awarded a Smithsonian Fellowship, '75.

Considered to be in the second wave of avant gardists who followed in the wake of Ornette Coleman, Cecil Taylor and John Coltrane, Hill declared, "The whole energy school of playing isn't valid for the '70s, as far as I'm concerned. It's time to become proficient on your instrument. All this noise . . ."

Roger Riggins called his work, "at the core, a popular music. If anyone has heard such tunes as *Tired Trade* or *Limbo*, they'll know what I mean. He is popular and 'high' art, if you want to call it that, at the same time."

TV: score for *Lenox Avenue Sunday*, CBS Repertory Theatre, '67; *Soul*, PBS, '70; *Black Arts*, CBS, '72. Comp: *String Quartets #1 & 2; Brass Quartet; Golden Spook*, an opera; *Laverne* for organ and piano, co-composed w. his wife, organist Laverne Gillette. All Hill's music is available from Jazz Fund Publ., P.O. Box 1244,

New York, N.Y. 10009. Hill uses the money, quite literally, as a jazz fund to help needy musicians. LPs: *Invitation* (Steeple.); *Spiral* (Arista); *Hommage* (Ai Music); *Smokestack; Grassroots; Lift Every Voice; One For One* (BN).

HILLYER, LONNIE,* *trumpet*; b. Monroe, Ga., 3/25/40. Best known for his work w. C. Mingus; Barry Harris; C. McPherson in '60s, he continued to appear w. them into '70s. Also teaching trumpet students in NYC. Fest: w. Mingus, NJF '71; NJF-NY '72. LPs: w. McPherson, (Main.); *The Quintet/Live* (Prest.); w. Mingus, *Let My Children Hear Music; Mingus and Friends in Concert* (Col.).

HINES, EARL KENNETH (FATHA),* *piano, composer*; b. Duquesne, Pa., 12/28/05. After his triumphant return at the three Little Theatre concerts in NYC, '64, Hines began to tour on a world-wide basis as leader of a small group and solo pianist. He played in Europe, '67-8, '70, '73-5; Japan, '68, '72, '74; Australasia, '72; Latin America w. Oscar Peterson, '69; w. Teddy Wilson, Marian McPartland and Ellis Larkins, '74. Don Schlitten wrote that Hines "still thinks he is at the Grand Terrace in Chicago leading his sensational big band, only there is no band, there is only Earl Hines playing the piano as if he was the band. He uses his left hand sometimes for accents and figures that would only come from a full trumpet section. Sometimes he will play chords that would have been written and played by five saxophones in harmony. But he is always the virtuoso pianist with his arpeggios, his percussive attack, and his fantastic ability to modulate from one song to another as if they were all one song and he just created all those melodies during his own improvisations."

TV: Dick Cavett; Johnny Carson; Merv Griffin; Mike Douglas. Fest: NJF-NY; MJF; Montreux; Nice. Won DB Critics poll '66-7; '69-73. Comp: *Rosetta; You Can Depend On Me; My Monday Date; Blues In Thirds; I Can't Trust Myself Alone; A Night in Trinidad; Blue Fox; Pianology.* LPs: solo, *Earl Hines at Home* (Delmark); *Hines '65; Plays Duke Ellington, Vols. I, II, III* (Master Jazz); *Tour De Force* (Bl. Lion); *Hines Does Hoagy; Hines Comes in Handy; My Tribute to Louis* (Audiophile); *Quintessential Earl Hines; Quintessential Continued* (Chiaro.); combos, *Once Upon a Time* (Imp.); *Blues & Things* w. J. Rushing (Master Jazz); *An Evening With Earl Hines; Back On the Street* w. Jonah Jones; *Live at the Overseas Press Club* w. Maxine Sullivan (Chiaro.); *Father & His Flock On Tour* (MPS); *Earl Hines and Roy Eldridge at the Village Vanguard* (Xanadu); reissues, *The Father Jumps*, big band '39-45 (Bluebird); *A Monday Date*, '23 band & '28 solos (Milest.); *Another Monday Date*, '55-6 solos (Fant.); *The Mighty Father*, '64-6 solos (Fly. Dutch.); *Louis Armstrong and Earl Hines 1928* (Smithsonian Collection); other partial reissue of Armstrong-Hines recs. (Col.).

HINO, MOTOHIKO, *drums*; b. Tokyo, Japan, 1/3/46. Brother of Terumasa Hino; father, Bin Hino, pl. trumpet. Pro. debut in '63 w. Takao Kusagaya; worked w. Tokyo Union Orch.; Hiroshi Watanabe & His Stardusters; various other Japanese combos in addition to rec. w. J.L. Ponty, Joe Henderson, G. Peacock, and acc. numerous visiting jazzmen from the U.S. and other countries. Member of Terumasa Hino quintet, '74- . Infls: Terumasa Hino, Tony Williams, Elvin Jones. Fests: Berlin, '71; Newport/N.Y. w. T. Hino, '73; plus about ten fests. annually in Japan. Won *Swing Journal* readers' poll annually as number one drummer, '71-5.

LPs: *Motohiko Hino First Album* (Jap. Col.); as sideman on all T. Hino albums.

HINO, TERUMASA, *trumpet, fluegelhorn, composer*; b. Tokyo, Japan, 10/25/42. Father, Bin Hino, was tapdancer before World War II. After war took up trumpet and is still pl. in clubs. Brother is drummer Motohiko Hino. Father taught him tap-dancing at age four; trumpet at nine. Hino writes: "Besides studying by myself, copied M. Davis, C. Brown, L. Morgan, F. Hubbard, etc., and played with and was taught by many foreign artists during their visits to Japan."

Made pro. debut as second trumpeter at a U.S. camp, '55; pl. at several base camps, '57-60. Third trumpet w. Hiroshi Watanabe & Stardusters; joined Takao Kusagaya & Crescendo Six, pl. U. S. camps and dance halls in Tokyo; then w. Jiro Inagaki, quintet touring Indonesia '61. Joined Hideo Shiraki Combo; led own gp. '64-5 and rec. *Hinology*, which won two awards incl. Golden Disc. Pl. w. Shiraki at Berlin JF, '65; w. his own gp., Berlin '71; NJF-NY '72, Yugoslavia and other Euro. fests. '73. In the summer of '75 he app. w. the Jackie McLean septet at the Five Spot, NYC. Infl: Coltrane, M. Davis, Clifford Brown, R. Workman. Films: *Daytime Attack* (Toho MP), '69; *One-legged Ace* (Toho MP), '72. TV: *Jazz in Japan* (NHK); *Music Fair* (Fuji). Comps: 40 to 50 pieces incl. *Alone, Alone, And, Alone; Fuji (Wistaria).* Won SJ Jazz Disc Award-Jazz of Japan Special Award, '69; Jazz of Japan Award, '72, '74; SJ Readers Poll, '67-74. Hino plays in a hard, brassy style reflecting his infls. and elements of free jazz. LPs: *Fuji* (Japan. Victor); *Journey Into My Mind* (Japan. CBS); *Speak to Loneliness* (East Wind); *Vibrations; Taro's Mood* (Enja); *Hideo Shiraki in Berlin* (MPS/Saba).

HINTON, MILTON JOHN (MILT or JUDGE),* *bass, composer, educator*; b. Vicksburg, Miss., 6/23/10. From '66 continued to be one of the busiest musicians in NYC with recs., transcriptions, studio work such as ABC staff w. B. Rosengarden orch. for Dick Cavett show; Broadway prod., *Music, Music.* Toured East, Middle East & Africa w. Pearl Bailey; Puerto Rico, Mexico, Fla. & LV w. Paul Anka; LV w. Barbra Streisand. House bassist at Michael's Pub, NYC, from '74, backing soloists such as Red Norvo, Teddy Wilson, Flip Phillips, Terry Gibbs, Joe Venuti, Bobby Hackett, Dick Wellstood, etc.

Fest: Colo. JP from '67; Odessa, Tex. JP from '68; Concord JF from '72; NJF-NY w. B. Rosengarden; Radio City jam session, '72; w. Bob Greene; Cab Calloway reunion; Radio City jam, '73; Teddy Wilson; L.

Hampton, '74; Benny Carter; Jazz Hall of Fame, '75. Concert and jazz party in Moscow, '73. Taught at Concord, Calif. Summer Music Camp; conductor of Hunter Coll. Jazz Workshop, NYC. Member of Jazz Panel of National Foundation of the Arts from '70. Pl. White House w. Pearl Bailey several times; guest there for Duke Ellington's 70th birthday. One of the most popular men in jazz, Hinton has been made an Honorary Citizen of NO, '69; Odessa, '72; Concord, '73. Deacon of St. Albans Congregational Church; actively involved w. community and neighborhood youth.

Comp: *Beefsteak Charlie's; Mona's Feeling Lonely; Walk Chicken With Your Head Picked Bald to the Bone; Ebony Silhouette; Blues For the Judge; Sometimes I Wonder*. LPs: *Here Swings the Judge*; others w. Bill Watrous; Danny Stiles; Zoot Sims; John Bunch; Red Norvo (Famous Door); Z. Sims-B. Pizzarelli (Gr. Merch.); *Soprano Summit* (World Jazz); Buck Clayton; J. Venuti (Chiaro.); Bob Greene (RCA); w. Dick Hyman; C. Mingus (Col.); B. Leighton (Mon.-Ever.); E. Garner (MGM).

HODEIR, ANDRE, *composer, critic*; b. Paris, France, 1/22/21. Prominent since mid-1950s as musicologist, author of several scholarly books on jazz. In 1970s continued leading orchestra, writing scores for films; from 1961-8 worked on book, *The Worlds of Jazz*, publ. in US 1972. Won Grand Prix Du Disque, '72, for his work *Anna Livia Plurabelle*. Subject of *A Jazz Portrait*, French television film, 1971.

Publ: *The Worlds of Jazz*, Grove Press Inc., NYC.

LPs: *Anna Livia Plurabelle* (Philips), *Bitter Ending* (Epic), both based on James Joyce's *Finnegan's Wake*.

HODES, ARTHUR W. (ART),* *piano*; b. Nikoliev, Russia, 11/14/04. Raised in Chicago, where he worked in pioneer jazz groups, incl. Wolverines, '26. Well known for many years as musician, disc jockey, journalist and lecturer. Pl. w. dixieland group at Disneyland, '67. Voted Citizen of the Year, Park Forest, Ill., '68. Pops Foster-Art Hodes TV show, '69; Toured Denmark, '70; Stars of Jazz concert tour in U.S. w. Condon, Davison, Bigard, '71; 17 weeks of concerts in '73 w. J. McPartland in spirituals, blues and jazz show. Cont. to app. at occasional fests., toured w. combo from '73. Jazz host on six national educ. TV shows, '69-72. App. w. Davison on *Just Jazz*, PBA, '71. In Dec. '72, Esquire mag. publ. an article by Hodes called *Jazz: The Sweet, Slow Comeback*. Hodes won Emmy award in Chi. for half hour solo TV show.

Comps: *Plain Ol' Blues; Blues Yesterday, Today, Tomorrow; Pagin' Mr. Jelly*. LPs: *Plain Ol' Blues*, duo w. Truck Parham (Mercury); *Rompin' 'n' Stompin'* (RCA); *Stars of Jazz*, vols. 1-3 w. Condon, Davison, Bigard (Jazzology); w. Bigard, *Bucket's Got a Hole in It* (Delmark); solo piano, *The Art of Hodes* (Euphonic); *Sittin' In; Funky Piano; Original Blue Note Jazz*, vol. 1 w. Edmond Hall (Blue Note).

HODGES, JOHN CORNELIUS (JOHNNY or RABBIT),* *alto sax, composer*; b. Cambridge, Mass., 7/25/06. A member of Duke Ellington's orchestra from 1928-51 and again from 1955, Hodges died in NYC after suffering a heart attack 5/11/70.

Hodges brought to jazz a sound that had neither precedent nor successor. His warm, sensuous timbre, always at its most persuasive in ballads and blues, was a quintessential part of the Ellington ensemble's tonal palette. He shared with Benny Carter the honor of being one of the definitive alto sax pioneers in the great formative years of jazz, primarily the 1930s and '40s. In the early years he occasionally doubled on soprano saxophone, modeling his style after that of his idol, Sidney Bechet. During those days, too, his work was notable for up tempo solos characterized by a surging, rhythmically perfect fluency.

In the early 1950s Hodges led his own band, feat. other Ellington alumni incl. Harold Baker, Lawrence Brown, Sonny Greer; he enjoyed modest success for a while, but his talent was never more appropriately displayed than in the big band setting, or in the various small Ellington splinter groups, many of them under his own name, starting with the first Johnny Hodges record session in 1937.

As composer Hodges was credited, or co-credited with Ellington, for *Jeep's Blues; I'm Beginning to See the Light; Hodge Podge; Wanderlust; It Shouldn't Happen to a Dream; Squatty Roo; Good Queen Bess; The Jeep is Jumpin'; Mama Knows; Bustin' With Buster; Away From You; Blues A-Plenty, Juice A-Plenty; Sir John* and dozens more.

LPs: *Ellingtonia!* (Onyx); *Johnny Hodges; Hodges & Hines—Swing's Our Thing; Mess of Blues*, Hodges-Wild Bill Davis; *Rippin' & Runnin'; Blue Notes; Blues A-Plenty; Stride Right*, Hodges-Earl Hines; *The Eleventh Hour; Hodges w. Billy Strayhorn Orch.; Don't Sleep In The Subway; Blue Hodge; Blues Summit*, Hodges-Ellington (Verve); *Triple Play; Things Ain't What They Used To Be*, Hodges-Rex Stewart (RCA); *Lawrence Welk & Johnny Hodges* (Dot); *Hodge Podge*, feat. Ellington (Epic); some tracks in *The Greatest Concert in the World* (Pablo); *Esquire's All-American Hot Jazz* (RCA).

HOLLAND, DAVID, *bass*; also *piano, guitar, cello, bass guitar*; b. Wolverhampton, England, 10/1/46. Stud. bass with James E. Merrit at Guildhall School, London, '65-8. In the same years he perf. classical music in orchestral and chamber concerts in and around London; held principal bass chair in coll. orch. Began in jazz with Dixieland bands, then pl. with a variety of groups which incl. such musicians as Ronnie Scott, John Surman, Humphrey Lyttelton, Evan Parker, Kenny Wheeler and Tubby Hayes. Miles Davis heard him in London and was sufficiently impressed to invite him to join his group. Holland moved to NYC and pl. w. Davis from '68-71. In '71-2 he was a member of Circle w. C. Corea, B. Altschul and A. Braxton, during which time the group used London as its home base for Continental engagements. Worked w. S. Getz, '73-4 and has also perf. w. S. Rivers, Joe Henderson, T. Jones-M. Lewis orch., T. Monk, Roy Haynes, Paul Bley, Karl Berger, J. DeJohnette, Carla Bley (JCOA), L. Konitz. With Braxton, '75.

Holland, equally adept on upright or electric bass, was named by writer Bill Cole as one of "the astonishing number of excellent bassists to have developed during the last decade . . . his tone is as big and round as a struck gong. His intonation is perfect, and he works all positions and stops flawlessly." Holland's infls. incl. Django Reinhardt, Ray Brown, Ch. Mingus, S. LaFaro, G. Peacock, P. Chambers, Davis, J. Coltrane, Monk, Bach, Webern, Schoenberg, Charles Ives, Bartok, Ellington and E. Dolphy. Fests: Newport, Monterey and numerous European apps. Won Melody Maker poll, '69; DB Critics' TDWR, '73. Since '73 active as teacher both privately and in workshops and univs. around the world.

LPs: *Conference of the Birds; Circle in Paris; Music From Two Basses*, w. Barre Phillips; *Music for Cello and Guitar* w. Derek Bailey (ECM); w. Corea, *A.R.C.* (ECM); *Song of Singing* (Blue Note); w. M. Davis, *Filles de Kilimanjaro; In A Silent Way; Bitches Brew; Live at the Fillmore* (Col.); *Town Hall '72*, w. Braxton (Trio).

HOLLEY, MAJOR QUINCY JR. (MULE),* *bass*; also *tuba, violin*; b. Detroit, Mich., 7/10/24. Worked w. Woody Herman, Kenny Burrell, C. Hawkins, R. Eldridge, Q. Jones, A. Cohn-Z. Sims. With D. Ellington, '64, then free-lanced in NYC until '67 when he taught for three years at Berklee Coll. in Boston. Ret. to NYC, '70, pl. w. James Moody, Pepper Adams at Half Note. Became house bassist at Jimmy Ryan's, first w. J. McPartland, then w. Eldridge. Also pl. Sunday nights at Bradley's w. Jaki Byard. Toured France, Belgium, Switzerland w. Helen Humes; Scandinavia, Germany, England w. Kings of Jazz in mid-70s. Fests: NJF-NY w. Eldridge, '73 at Louis Armstrong Stadium, televised on PBS; Jazzfest, Hanover, Germany; Colorado Jazz Party. Comps: *Mule; Major and the Minor.* Has also worked w. Drug Abuse Program in NYC; Phoenix House; Harlem Teams for Self Help. When Holley bows a solo he sings what he is playing in a manner reminiscent of Slam Stewart but different in that Stewart sings an octave higher than his own bowing. LPs: *Mule* (Black & Blue); w. Helen Humes (Col., Black & Blue); w. Cohn-Sims, *You 'N Me* (Trip); w. Buddy Tate, *The Texas Twister* (Master Jazz); w. L. Konitz, *Chicago* (Groove Merchant).

HOLLOWAY, JAMES L. (RED),* *tenor saxophone*; also *clarinet, flute, piccolo, piano, bass, drums, violin*; b. Helena, Ark., 5/31/27. Professional since '47, mainly known as tenor saxophonist, based in Chicago from '40s to '67, when he moved to LA. For six years he served as talent coordinator and leader of house band at the Parisian Room, LA. Toured Canada and U.S. w. Jimmy Dean Show, '67. International tours w. John Mayall combo, '73, '74, incl. Australia, Europe, Canada. Various LA apps. w. S. Stitt, Ray Brown, Sweets Edison et al. Pl. on sound track of film *Lady Sings The Blues*. Perf. at commemorative concert celebrating jazz week in LA Dec. '74.

Holloway is capable of generating great excitement with his big sound and hard driving mainstream-modern style. He rec. many of his own comps. for a series of albums on Prestige. Comp: *Kriss Kross*, written w. organist Art Hillery, rec. by J. Moody.

LPs: *Sax, Strings and Soul; The Burner* (Pres.)

HOLMAN, WILLIS (BILL),* *composer*; b. Olive, Cal., 5/21/27. Well known in '50s, early '60s for his tenor work as well as his writing, Holman discontinued playing in '66 as a result of illness, but made many contributions as composer-arranger. His originals included *Concerto For Herd* for W. Herman, premiered at MJF; *A Separate Walking*, commissioned by Cal. State U., Northridge Jazz Ensemble; *The Daily Dance* for S. Kenton; *Time Being* for Buddy Rich.

Film orchestrating for J. Mandel, G. Mulligan, '66; instrumental arrs. for The Association and 5th Dimension vocal groups, '67-8; TV series: *Operation Entertainment* w. T. Gibbs, '68; Della Reese show w. Pete Myers, '69; Pearl Bailey show w. L. Bellson, '70. Arrs. for Klaus Weiss orch. in Germany, '71. In '72 was involved in formation of LifeLine Music Press (P.O. Box 338, Agoura, Ca. 91301), for printing and distribution of music for school jazz ensembles. Led own 18 piece band in LA area, '74-5. Throughout this period Holman composed and/or arranged for B. Rich (for whom his arr. of *Norwegian Wood* earned a Grammy nomination), S. Kenton, Ed Shaughnessy, Peggy Lee, S. Vaughan and several college ensembles. A writer of broad experience, he reflects in his work the disciplines and guidelines established by the best swing era arrangers.

LPs: as arr. with above mentioned bands.

HOLMES, RICHARD ARNOLD (GROOVE),* *organ*; b. Camden, N.J., 5/2/31. On the road w. his own gp. from '62, he had a hit single of Erroll Garner's *Misty* from his Prestige album, *Soul Message*. It sold more than 300,000 copies in '69. Holmes rec. 10 more albums for Prest. before shifting to Groove Merchant where he rec. on his own and also teamed w. Jimmy McGriff in the studio and in live concert recordings. Naturally left-handed he was infl. by Paul Chambers and Ron Carter and developed one of the strongest bass lines of all the organists.

LPs: *$6,000,000 Man; Onsaya Joy* (Fly. Dutch.); *Misty* (Prest.); *New Groove; Night Glider*; w. Jimmy McGriff, *Come Together; Giants in Concert* (Gr. Merchant).

HONDA, TAKASHI (TAKEHIRO), *piano*; b. Iwate Prefecture, Japan, 8/21/45. Brothers-in-law are saxophonist Sadao Watanabe; drummer Fumio Watanabe. Music lessons from childhood. Stud. w. Kazuko Nagamine while in high school and at univ. Began pl. w. fellow students during campus fest. at Kunitachi Univ. Helped form Kazunori Takeda quartet; joined Fumio Watanabe gp. After two yrs. w. Watanabe, pl. w. Mashiko Togashi gp. Following this he formed his own trio and soul gp., pl. mainly at jazz spots in Tokyo, incl. Taro, Pit-in, and concerts in various districts. Acc. singer Mieko Hirota. In '72 pl. w. Terumasa Hino for three mos. but most of his apps. are w. own band or w. Sadao Watanabe. Infl: Sadao Watanabe, Marvin Gaye. Fests: NJF, '70; Montreux, '73, w. S. Watanabe. Won SJ Readers Poll, '74. LPs: *Salaam Salaam* (East Wind); another on Trio; w. S. Watanabe (Japan. CBS).

HOOD, ERNIE, *guitar, composer*; also *zither, keyboards*; b. Charlotte, N.C., 6/2/23. Brother of baritone saxophonist Bill Hood. Rec. w. C. Barnet, '45; pl. w. W. Manone; Lucky Thompson septet. After many years as comp. and studio musician, scoring for commercial films, Oregon Pops orch., also jazz groups in Portland area, he app. as a zither player w. Flora Purim in the albums *Butterfly Dreams* and *Stories To Tell.* Comp. *Mountain Train* heard in *Stories To Tell.*

Own LP: *Neighborhoods* (Thistlefield Records, c/o Ernest Hood, P.O. Box 123, West Linn, Oregon 97068); w. Purim (Mile.).

HOOD, WILLIAM H. (BILL),* *baritone saxophone, composer*; b. Portland, Ore., 12/13/24. Freelancing in LA, Hood also traveled w. F. Sinatra and toured Japan w. B. Bacharach, and w. Q. Jones. Arr. and pl. on Della Reese TV series; many other TV credits. Studio work w. Tom Scott, D. Grusin, Jack Elliot. Recreated the sound of Adrian Rollini on bass sax for period music in movie, *The Fortune*, '75.

HOOPER, LOUIS STANLEY (LOU), *piano, composer*; also *organ, violin, viola*; b. North Buxton, Ont., Canada, 5/18/1894. Father a violinist in Canada, 1870's-93; brothers Fred, trumpet; Arnold, violin. Began as choir boy and became soloist at St. Luke's Episcopal Church in Ypsilanti, Mich. Piano lessons at 10. Grad. from Detroit Conserv. '16. Postgrad. stud. w. La Verne Brown; Minor White; Prof. F.L. York. Bach. of Mus., '20. Stud. at Teacher's Coll., Columbia U., '23-4. w. Mr. Mohler; Prof. Dykema. Pl. w. Hooper Bros. Orch., Ypisilanti, '06; at New Koppin Theatre, Detroit, '09. Led small concert-party in France during WWI, '18. To NYC '21, pl. in pit orch. of Franklin Theatre w. Mildred Franklin. Worked w. Elmer Snowden until the latter joined Ellington. Then rec. w. Bubber Miley; Louis Metcalf; Johnny Dunn; Ethel Waters; Ma Rainey and pl. stage shows w. Bessie Smith. In orch. for Broadway review, Lew Leslie's *Blackbirds of 1928-29.* Acc. Paul Robeson for six mos. With Myron Sutton's Canadian Ambassadors when they reopened Connie's Inn, Montreal, '39, backing Billie Holiday. Enlisted in Canad. Artillery '39, serving overseas in Europe until '45, in charge of Canadian Concert Parties.

Rediscovered living in Montreal in '62. Member of Montreal Vintage Music Society. In '73 was feted by Int. Assn. of Record Coll. during their convention in Montreal where he performed. He also pl. for and prod. an evening of his works from '18-70, sponsored by the Benny Farm Tenant's Assn. and his old 5th Medium Artillery buddies for the benefit of the Quebec Paraplegic Assn. Moved to Prince Edward Island, '75. Infl: B. Goodman, C. Christian, Bix Beiderbecke, James P. Johnson, Ralph Sutton, Ellington, Louis Armstrong. Comp: *Ruth*, an oratorio; music to *The Congo* by Vachel Lindsay; *Wanderlust; Cakewalk; South Sea Strut; Undecided Rag; Rainy Day Rag; Sunny Day Rag*, last three written in '75. In NYC days taught classical piano at Martin-Smith Music School a subsidiary of the Damrosch Inst. which later became Juilliard Sch. of Music.

LPs: solo piano (Canadian Broadcasting Corp., Montreal); w. *The Jolly Miners* w. Snowden, Bob Fuller (Historical).

HOOPER, NESBERT (STIX),* *drums, leader, composer*; b. Houston, Tex., 8/15/38. Leader of a group known in 1950s as Modern Jazz Sextet, later as Nite Hawks; from 1960 as Jazz Crusaders, and from '72 as the Crusaders. By that time the group had concentrated on a jazz/rock and r & b style that earned substantially increased record sales and national popularity. Hooper told Dennis Hunt of the LA *Times*, "Most of our fans have only been following us for about three years; a lot of them don't even know that we used to be associated with jazz . . . the hard core jazz fans never really accepted us anyway. . . . Now we can play what we like and get money and recognition for it. You can't beat that."

In addition to leading the combo, Hooper busied himself with a variety of free-lance activities in LA and became one of the area's most successful drummers.

LPs w. Crusaders (Blue Thumb, Chisa); w. Jazz Crusaders (Pac. Jazz).

HOPE, ELMO (St. Elmo Sylvester Hope),* *piano, composer*; b. New York City, N.Y., 6/27/23. A childhood friend of Bud Powell, whose style his own closely paralleled, Hope pl. w. Clifford Brown, S. Rollins in NYC, and later w. Harold Land, L. Hampton in LA. Irregularly active owing to poor health in later years, he died 5/19/67. A pianist and composer of rare harmonic acuity and very personal interpretation. He can be heard on several albums, among them one for Blue Note, one for HiFi Jazz, two for Riverside, one for Audio Fidelity. As a sideman he rec. w. Brown, Rollins, Lou Donaldson (BN); J. McLean and F. Foster (Prest.); *Elmo Hope Memorial Album* (Prest.); trio (Contemp.).

HOPKINS, CLAUDE,* *piano, leader*; b. Washington, D.C., 8/3/03. One of the popular big band leaders of the 1930s, worked mostly as leader and sideman within a small group context during the '60s and '70s at such places as the Dinkler Motor Inn, Syracuse, N.Y.; Top of the Plaza, Rochester, N.Y.; Bourbon St. and the Colonial Inn, Toronto. Pianist w. R. Eldridge at Jimmy Ryan's for several years, then gigging at numerous clubs in N.J. Hopkins is also an aircraft mechanic who was very active during the second world war at the General Motors plant in Linden, N.J. Fests: Concord, Cal., '73; Andernos, Spain, '74; Nice, Manassas, '74. TV: Nice, '74; WGBH, Boston, '75. Comps: *Crying My Heart Out For You; Safari Stomp; Late Evening Blues; Crazy Fingers; Blame It On A Dream.* LPs: solo albums on Chiaroscuro and Sackville; trio on Black and Blue; w. Herb Hall quartet; Jazz Giants on Sackville; w. Wild Bill Davison, *Live at the Rainbow Room* (Chiaroscuro).

HOPKINS, LINDA, *singer, organ, piano*; also *drums*; b. New Orleans, 12/14/25. As a child, was discovered by Mahalia Jackson. Spent 11 years touring w. Southern Harp Singers, a spiritual group. Directed youth choir in Richmond, Cal., singing in church and on radio. Began her show business career after auditioning at a local night club.

In 1960, because of her physical and vocal resemblance to Bessie Smith (whom she had seen once in person), and because she was asked to portray a 'big name' in a cabaret show, Hopkins began to evolve an act partially based on Bessie's songs and style, touring with this concept in Europe, 1960. After studying with Stella Adler, she was seen on the stage in *Purlie* and *Inner City*; her performance in the latter earned her Tony and Drama Desk awards.

Long familiar with the blues and with other material employed by Bessie Smith, she developed an entire presentation entitled *Me and Bessie*, enjoying great success during long runs in NYC and LA, 1974-5.

Involved w. Evangelistic Chorus, Greater Central Baptist Church, NYC. TV: Johnny Carson, Dinah Shore, Merv Griffin, Dick Cavett, Mike Douglas, many other shows. Comp: *Listen Women; Doggin' Blues; The Man's All Right; I'm a Happy Child, Running Wild.*

A superb performer in the classic blues tradition as well as in a more light-hearted vein, Hopkins for many years was poorly represented on records, with sessions for Savoy, Federal, Atco and Brunswick that involved songs such as *Danny Boy; Rock and Roll Blues; When the Saints Go Marching In* etc. In 1975 she signed with Columbia and recorded an album of excerpts from *Me and Bessie*. Other LPs: RCA; *Inner City* (RCA); *Purlie* (Ampex).

HORN, PAUL,* *flute, alto saxophone, clarinet, composer*; b. New York City, 3/17/30. Leader of popular LA based quintet in early '60s. Between '66 and '69, while involved in studio work, continued to play concerts and clubs, but went to India in '67 and '68, studying with Maharishi Mahesh Yogi at Academy of Meditation, and himself became a teacher of Transcendental Meditation. Rec. two albums in India in '67; Played solo flute in Taj Mahal, '68. Toured w. Concert Ensemble feat. four flutes, '69.

In '70 Horn moved to Victoria, B.C., where he enjoyed success in several areas of activity; pl. concert tours throughout Canada w. newly formed Canadian quintet, scoring films for Nat'l Film Board of Canada, and heading his own weekly half-hour TV series, The Paul Horn Show. Won CINDY award for music score of *Island Eden*, film for gov't. of B.C. Horn has continued to travel extensively as soloist and clinician at colls. and high schools throughout the U.S. and Canada. Publs: *Paul Horn/Inside*, flute solos (Edward B. Marks Music, 136 W. 52nd St., New York, N.Y. 10019).

LPs: *Here's That Rainy Day* (RCA); *Paul Horn In Kashmir; Paul Horn In India* (Wor. Pac.); *Inside; Inside II; Visions* (Epic); *A Special Edition* (Island).

HOROWITZ, DAVID, *piano, synthesizer, composer*; also *vibes*; b. Brooklyn, N.Y., 7/29/42. Brother, Marc Horowitz, is studio musician on guitar, banjo. Studied comp. & theory w. Mischa Portnoff, '63-7; comp., theory, piano, improvisation w. Hall Overton, '64-6; improv. w. Lennie Tristano, '65-6. Led own gps., '62-6. Active as studio musician, NYC, from '68. Pl. w. Tony Williams Lifetime, '72-4; w. Gil Evans from '70. In the Evans orch. his synthesizer supplies an underlining with various colors and leitmotifs.

Infl: Overton, Miles Davis, Coltrane, Bartok, G. Evans, T. Monk, Ornette Coleman. Fest: w. Evans, NJF-NY, Montreux, Berkeley. Movie: score for *Human*, French film w. Jeanne Moreau, Terrance Stamp, '75. Comp: *Encounters I* for soprano and chamber orch., commissioned by "Music in Our Time;" *Encounters II* for string quartet and jazz orch., comm. by JCOA. LPs: w. Evans, *The Music of Jimi Hendrix; There Comes a Time* (RCA); *Svengali* (Atl.); w. J. Henderson, *Black is the Color* (Mile.); w. T. Williams, *The Old Bum's Rush* (Poly.).

HOUSTON, CLINTON JOSEPH (CLINT), *bass*; b. New Orleans, La., 6/24/46. Father pl. classical piano as a youth. Family moved to Washington, D.C., when Houston was an infant, then to NYC, '53. Stud. keyboard, harmony at Queens Coll., Long Island. Stud. bass in high school. For some years he was undecided whether to take up a career in mus. or in graphic art. He grad. from Cooper Union in the latter, in addition to studying for two years ('64-6) at Pratt Inst.

Houston worked briefly w. Roy Haynes, '69; also w. Nina Simone, then resumed his art studies. In '71 he decided to become a musician on a full time basis. During that year he pl. w. Roy Ayers at Montreux JF, moved to Germany and spent a year pl. electric and upright bass with Kurt Edelhagen in Cologne.

Back in NYC, he was active on the rec. scene, worked for a while with Herbie Mann, and spent a year and a half w. Chas. Tolliver, visiting Japan with him. Houston moved to Cal. in '74. While working w. Kai Winding, he was heard by S. Getz, who hired him for his quartet in Feb. '75. During the next year, touring w. Getz, he revealed an extraordinary technique and the ability to weave guitar-like lines on the upright bass that placed him among the handful of preëminent new bassists of the '70s.

Houston names as his infls. Scott LaFaro and Ron Carter; he stud. w. Carter for two years.

LPs: w. Tolliver, *Live in Tokyo* (Strata-East); w. Woody Shaw, *Blackstone Legacy* (Contemporary); w. Sonny Greenwich (Sackville); Getz-Gilberto (Col.); w. John Abercrombie and others, *Friends* (Oblivion).

HOWARD, DARNELL,* *clarinet*; b. Chicago, Ill., 1892. Prominent from '20s, he worked w. King Oliver, E. Hines. Lived in SF Bay Area for many years, pl. w. M. Spanier, Jimmy Archey, Hines; visited Europe w. NO group in '66. Died in SF, 9/2/66.

HOWARD, NOAH, *alto saxophone, composer*; b. New Orleans, La., 4/6/43. From the age of about 17, under the influence of Ornette Coleman. Schooled in free-jazz through association in San Francisco with Byron Allen, Sonny Simmons, Dewey Redman among others. Formed first group there with English trumpeter, Ric Colbeck. Went to Europe for a jazz and pop festival staged by a record company, and found the local interest in free jazz so strong that he remained for two months. For the next six years he went back and forth frequently between the US and Europe.

Howard has worked with Sun Ra, Archie Shepp, Albert Ayler, Rashied Ali, Milford Graves, Bill Dixon, Art Taylor, Dave Burrell, Ornette Coleman, Sonny Sharrock, Frank Lowe, Sirone, Jimmy Garrison, Norman Connors, Ted Daniel, Ed Blackwell and the Art Ensemble of Chicago. According to Valerie Wilmer he is "one of the best alto saxophonists around . . . whatever he does, he always retains his technical skill and what the critics term 'taste.' " *Swing Journal* of Tokyo characterized Howard as "one of the most representative musicians of the post-Coltrane era." He was consistently praised by critics throughout Europe during his many concerts there.

LPs: *Noah Howard Quartet; Noah Howard at Judson Hall* (ESP); *One for John* (Byg); *Church No. 9* (Calumet); *From Down to Planet X* (Bovema); *Uhuru Na Umoja; Space Dimensions* (Musidisc); *Black Art; Patterns; Live at the Swing Club Turin* (Altsax); *Black Ark; Live at the Village Vanguard* (Polydor); *Snow & Sunshine* (EMI); w. Shepp, *Black Gypsy* (Musidisc); w. Ayler, *Don Ayler* (Jihad).

HOWELL, MICHAEL, *guitar, composer*; b. Kansas City, Mo., 10/8/43. Introduced to guitar at age seven by his father and by Herley Dennis, a local musician. Degree in Mus. Ed. from Lamar Jr. College in Colorado, 1961. First formal guitar studies at Music and Arts Inst. in SF, with a student of Andres Segovia. Played w. Bobby Hutcherson-Harold Land in SF, 1971; Art Blakey, Jan. '73; Sonny Rollins-John Handy concert, '73; Woody Shaw, fall and winter, '73-4; Guitar Summit at MJF, '74; w. D. Gillespie at MJF and Great American Music Hall in SF, '75. Infls: Ch. Parker, Ch. Christian, Clifford Brown, Wes Montgomery, D. Ellington, Miles Davis, John Coltrane. Comps: *Through the Looking Glass; A Day In San Francisco; Michelino; The Call; Ebony King; Althea; Circles*. LPs: *Looking Glass; In The Silence* (Milestone); w. Blakey, *Buhaina*; w. G. Ammons, *Brasswind* (Prestige).

HUBBARD, FREDERICK DEWAYNE (FREDDIE),* *trumpet, fluegelhorn, composer, piano*; b. Indianapolis, Ind., 4/7/38. First prominent w. Art Blakey in early '60s; also pl. w. Q. Jones, Friedrich Gulda; led various groups, first on records, later in person.

From 1966-70 Hubbard was contracted to Atlantic Records. During that time, except for one LP called *Soul Experiment* in which he switched from jazz to rock, he maintained the high standards for which he had been known throughout the decade. Experts predicted that he would be "the Miles Davis of the '70s."

Hubbard successfully toured Japan and the US with his own combo and with Nancy Wilson. His recordings for CTI, later for Col., though commercially oriented, retained a splendid level of musicianship and showed him to advantage in his own compositions such as *Red Clay; Delphia; Sweet Sioux; The Intrepid Fox; Sky Dive; Povo; First Light; Spirits of Trane; Destiny's Children; Brigitte; Keep Your Soul Together; Gibraltar; Baraka Sasa; Liquid Love; Kuntu; Put It In The Pocket*.

In 1972 Hubbard moved from New York to North Hollywood, Calif. Two years later he signed a contract with Columbia Records. His first two albums for that company indicated that he intended to adhere to a set of principles he had outlined in a 1973 interview: "It's very difficult to stay out of rock and make a living . . . After Miles Davis went into that electronic rock bag, everybody started sounding like Miles, trying to sound weird. That's why I'm attempting to stick to something kinda grass roots, keep my feet on the ground; because with everyone using that Fender Rhodes piano and stuff, they'll all sound alike. . . . Not so long ago a lot of young trumpeters were following Miles; now they're trying to play what I'm playing. They hear me constantly searching for new ideas, but keeping enough musicality in there so people can understand where it's at."

Motion picture soundtrack work: *Blowup* (scored by Herbie Hancock); *The Bus Is Coming; Shaft's Big Score*, in which Hubbard was prominently heard.

Hubbard's album *First Light* won a Grammy award in 1972 as the best jazz performance of the year by a small group. As soloist he won DB Readers' Poll 1973-4.

By late 1975 Hubbard had adjusted his stance with respect to the use of electronics. He not only had an electric piano and electric bass in his combo, but was himself using an amplified horn and playing music that seemed to be leaning more heavily in an r & b or rock direction.

LPs: *High Energy; Liquid Love* (Col); *Baddest Hubbard; First Light; Keep Your Soul Together; Red Clay; Sky Dive; Straight Life*; w. S. Turrentine, *In Concert* (CTI); *Art of F. Hubbard; Backlash; Black Angel; High Blues Pressure*; w. Ilhan Mimaroglu, *Sing Me A Song of Songmy* (Atl.); *Artistry of Hubbard; Body & Soul; Reevaluation Impulse Years* (Impulse); *Blue Spirits; Breaking Point; Goin' Up; Hub-Tones*; w. Lee Morgan, *Night of the Cookers* Vols. 1 & 2; *Ready for Freddie* (Blue Note); *Hub of Hubbard* (BASF). Innumerable others as sideman, esp. on Blue Note.

HUBBLE, JOHN EDGAR (ED),* *trombone*; also *baritone horn*; b. Santa Barbara, Calif., 4/6/28. Active in small gp. traditional music from '40s w. Bob Wilber, Billy Maxted, Phil Napoleon, Don Ewell. Worked w. Dukes of Dixieland, '66; w. Dick Wellstood, Kenny Davern at Ferry Boat in Brielle, N.J., '67; Jimmy Ryan's w. Max Kaminsky, '68. Joined World's Greatest Jazzband '69, touring w. it in England, Alaska, So. America before leaving at the end of '73. Toured Europe w. Kings of Jazz (Pee Wee Erwin, Kenny Davern), '74; w. NYJRC Tribute to Louis Armstrong, fall '75. Pl. weekends at Last Chance Saloon in Poughkeepsie, N.Y. w. Johnny Windhurst, '75. Joined His Farm, a Christian Community Dairy Farm in NY state, working and living there between music jobs.

Fest: Nice; NJF-NY; Colo. JP; Odessa JP. LPs: w. WGJ (World Jazz).

HUCKO, MICHAEL ANDREW (PEANUTS),* *clarinet, tenor sax*; b. Syracuse, N.Y., 4/7/18. The former J. Teagarden and L. Armstrong clarinetist, heard often at Condon's club in NYC, '63-6, was feat. annually at concerts in Denver, Colo., '66-8 with a group called The Nine Greats of Jazz, which later evolved into The World's Greatest Jazzband. From Sept. '70 through June '72 he was jazz soloist on Lawrence Welk's TV series. From 1/16/74 through 9/15/74 toured as conductor of Glenn Miller orch. While in Tokyo, rec. there with Japanese group, *Peanuts Meets Shoji Again*, a reference to his reunion with Japanese clarinetist Shoji Suzuki with whom he had a best seller in '60.

After leaving the Miller band, Hucko settled in Denver, leading a quartet feat. his wife, former Harry James vocalist Louise Tobin. In '75 his sidemen incl. Ralph Sutton, Gus Johnson. Opened own jazz room at Sheraton Inn, Denver, Apr. '75. Hucko's frequent apps. at jazz parties and on TV reflected his undiminished stature as one of the best clarinetists in the B. Goodman mold.

Comps: *First Friday; A Bientot; Tremont Place; Home Sweet Suite; Raggedy Ann; Lullaby of Love; Mata Ai Masho* (Japanese for *See You Again*). Rec. an LP, *Peanuts in Everybody's Bag* (American Artists Records); other LPs w. L. Welk (Ranwood); *Big Band Cavalcade on Tour*, w. Bob Crosby (RCA).

HUGHES, LANGSTON, *lyricist, author, poet, playwright*; b. Joplin, Mo., 2/1/02. The internationally celebrated playwright, some of whose poems dealt with jazz, and one of whose books was a jazz history for children, died of a heart attack in NYC, 5/22/67. An album in which Hughes read his poetry to a background of music by Charles Mingus and Leonard Feather was rec. in '57 for MGM (deleted). An album of gospel songs by Hughes and Jobe Huntley, sung by Porter Sisters in a Harlem church, was released on Folkways.

HUMES, HELEN,* *singer*; b. Louisville, Ky., 6/23/13. Worked w. C. Basie, '38-42. As single, had hit record *Bebaba-Leba*, '45; toured and gigged w. Red Norvo in mid-50s; occasionally active in '60s, spending a year in Australia, '64-5.

After a period of sporadic work and while living in LA, she returned home to Louisville, '67, remaining there until July '73, when she took part in tributes to C. Basie and L. Armstrong at the NJF-NY, then toured France, Switzerland, Spain. In Feb. '74, toured France again for six weeks, rec. two albums for Black and Blue. In summer of '74 played Newport and Montreux fests., a few other jobs incl. Half Note, NYC. Began engagement at Cookery, NYC Jan. to Apr. '75, and during that time made her first Amer. album in many years. On Mar. 2, '75 she was given an official tribute in Louisville and received the keys to the city. While at the Cookery she earned unprecedented acclaim from the critics. Whitney Balliett, in *The New Yorker*, called her "one of the best and most durable of American popular singers who . . . bears easy comparison with Mildred Bailey and Billie Holiday . . . (she) is singing better than ever . . . sharing with us a style of singing and of performing that is almost gone . . ."

LPs on Contemporary; Columbia; also two tracks in *Singin' The Blues* (MCA); two tracks in *Super Chief*, w. C. Basie (Columbia).

HUMAIR, DANIEL,* *drums, composer*; b. Geneva, Switzerland, 5/23/38. Winner of a contest for young amateurs, Humair in '62 became France's number one drummer, both in talent and in popularity. He played with the Swingle Singers in the early '60s and app. at numerous European fests., also w. P. Woods, JATP, H Mann, L. Konitz, A. Braxton, R. Eldridge, Stephane Grappelli, Joachim Kuhn and his own group. He was a sideman for *Last Tango In Paris; The Process* and many other films. From '65 he was also pro. painter. Won DB Critics' poll, TDWR, '69. During visits to U.S. app. at MJF, NJF. Comps: *Sunday Walk; Gravenstein; Out of the Sorcellery; Witch Stitch*. LPs: *Alpine Power Plant*; Jim Hall Trio; Ray Nance; *This Way Out* w. Kuhn; *Sunday Walk* w. J.L. Ponty (MPS); w. Grappelli (Barclay); HLP Trio (CBS); w. L. Konitz (RCA); *Phil Woods in Frankfurt* (Atl.); w. Franco Ambrosetti, *Steppenwolf* (PDU).

HUMPHREY, BARBARA ANN (BOBBI), *flute*; also *piccolo, alto sax*; b. Marlin, Tex., 4/25/50. Cousin a former Ellington trumpeter, Eddie Preston. Stud. Lincoln high school, Dallas, '64-8; Texas Southern U., '68-70; Southern Methodist U., '70-1. Moving to NYC in '71, she sat in with Ellington, Rahsaan Roland Kirk, C. Adderley, D. Gillespie, but the first group with which she worked officially was Herbie Mann's, in July of that year. She stud. privately w. Hubert Laws, and received a rec. contract of her own during her second week in NYC. She has won the *Ebony* mag. music poll as number one flutist. Infls: Laws, Mann. Fests: Newport; Montreux; Schaefer Mus. Fest. Humphrey, who started playing flute in high school, matured very fast on the instrument and displayed potential as a jazz artist, though her albums are primarily aimed at the soul-r & b market.

LPs: *Bobbi Humphrey; Blacks & Blues; Dig This; Satin Doll* (BN).

HUMPHREY, PAUL,* *drums, composer*; b. Detroit, Mich., 10/12/35. Prominent in Cal. groups incl. L. McCann, '63-5, H. James orch. '65-6. Mostly commercial and studio work since then, incl. tour with Chuck Berry, '69; records and gigs w. T-Bone Walker, '70. Formed own first rock group, Cool-Aid Chemists, '70. Toured w. group and had hit record, *Cool-Aid*, '71. Overseas tour w. Sammy Davis Jr., '72. Concerts w. his second group, The Funky Thumbs, '73. Records, TV, tours etc. during '74 with Maria Muldaur, Diahann Carroll, Davis, and own second group. In '75, worked on Smothers Brothers TV show and formed third group.

Publ: *No. 1 Soul Drums*, book & cassette (Gwyn Publ. Co. P.O. Box 5900, Sherman Oaks, Ca. 91413). Comps: *Super Mellow; Walk A Mile For A Smile; Chin Music*.

LPs: *Lizard* (Blue Thumb); w. Q. Jones, *Body Heat* (A & M); *Night Blooming Jazzmen* (Mainstream); Joe Cocker (A & M).

HUMPHREY, RALPH S., *drums*; also *clarinet*; b. Berkeley, Cal., 5/11/44. Educ. Castro Valley Unified School, '56-62; Coll. of San Mateo, '62-64; San Jose State U.,

'64-7; UCLA, '68; Cal. State Northridge, '68-9 where he received Masters degree in perc. perf. Worked w. Don Ellis orch. '69-73, touring extensively at home and abroad, appearing at Newport, '69; Antibes, '69; Monterey; Concord, '70; and on Ed Sullivan Show and Tanglewood Fest. on TV, '69. Played on sound track for *The French Connection* and *Kansas City Bomber* movies. Wrote chapter, *The Role of the Drummer in the Modern Rhythm Section*, in *New Rhythms* by Ellis (Ellis Music Ent., Inc., 5436 Auckland Ave., N. Hollywood, Ca. 91601).

During '73-4 Humphrey toured U.S., Europe and Australia with Frank Zappa; as freelance musician in LA provided backing for various artists such as Tony Bennett, Joe Williams, Carmen McRae, Clare Fischer, John Klemmer et al. LPs w. Ellis (Columbia); w. Zappa (Discreet).

HUNDLEY, CRAIG, *piano, organ, synthesizer*; b. Hollywood, Ca., 11/22/53. Stud. w. Xenia Chasman, Dave MacKay, Gary David, and at Stan Kenton Clinic. After three years of classical study, took up jazz in '66, organized trio, which was soon voted best combo in teenage Battle of the Bands at Hollywood Bowl. Pl. Shelly's Manne Hole, Donte's, MJF, Village Gate. Throughout his teens, enjoyed simultaneous career as TV actor, playing major roles in *Star Trek; Kung Fu; Flying Nun; Lassie.* By early '70s Hundley was less active in jazz, working briefly as musical director for Pat Boone on tour. Own LPs: *Arrival of a Young Giant; Hundley Plays with the Big Boys* (World Pacific).

HUNTER, IVORY JOE, *singer, piano*; b. 1912. A rhythm and blues favorite of the '50s, Hunter comp. many r & b songs as well as country and western material. His best known hit was *Since I Met You Baby*. After several months' illness he died of cancer 11/8/74 in a Memphis, Tenn. nursing home.

LPs: *Ivory Joe Hunter* (Archive of Folk & Jazz); w. J. Otis, *Live at Monterey* (Epic).

HUTCHENRIDER, CLARENCE BEHRENS,* *clarinet*; also *tenor, alto sax*; b. Waco, Tex., 6/13/08. Best known for his pl. w. Glen Gray's Casa Loma Orch. in the '30s, he led his own trio at the Gaslight Club, NYC, '58-68; Bill's Gay Nineties, '68-May '73; then club dates in NYC, Long Island, concerts in NJ. LPs w. Bobby Hackett (Flying Dutchman); Glen Gray (Epitaph).

HUTCHERSON, ROBERT (BOBBY),* *vibes, marimba*; b. Los Angeles, Cal., 1/27/41. First prominent in LA and SF with various small combos, later in NYC in the mid-50s, Hutcherson returned to the West Coast, where from '69-71 he co-led a quintet w. Harold Land Sr. After they went their separate ways, Hutcherson, based in SF, remained a leader in his own right, rec. regularly and becoming increasingly active as a marimba soloist. TV: *The Jazz Show*, KNBC-Los Angeles, '71.

Over the past decade Hutcherson has continued to mature and explore new directions. In his own words, "Our public is always looking for something new. Our group is searching around to find that something new, an extension of the evolution that we have had, of all the music that happened before. They'll know when we find it."

LPs: *Dialogue; Components; Happenings; Stick-up; Total Eclipse; Now; San Francisco; Head On; Natural Illusions; Cirrus; Linger Lane* (BN).

HUTSON, DAVID LAURENCE, *alto saxophone, clarinet, leader*; b. Chicago, Ill., 4/18/38. B.M. in music at U. of Illinois, where fellow students were Joe Farrell, Denny Zeitlin, with whom he has worked occasionally. Early exp. w. Ira Sullivan, Ralph Marterie. Army, '61-3; during that time gigged w. Otis Johnson band. In NYC, '63-5, pl. w. Dizzy Reece, D. Cherry, C. Corea and dixieland groups. In Japan and Korea, '66-8. Civilian entertainment dir. for Army Spec. Servs. Based in Detroit, '68-75, organizing the New McKinney's Cotton Pickers in '72. Comp. or arr. most of the material for this band. Prod. *Jazz Yesterday* radio series for two years. Played at Bix Memorial Fest., '73 and '74; Newport-New York, '74-5; Breda (Netherlands) Jazz Fest. '75.

LPs: w. New McKinney's Cotton Pickers (Bountiful, 15772 13 Mile Rd., Roseville, Mich. 48066).

HYMAN, RICHARD ROVEN (DICK),* *piano*; also *organ, harpsichord, synthesizer, arranger, conductor, composer*; b. New York City, 3/8/27. Stud. w. Teddy Wilson and others. Played w. Tony Scott, R. Norvo, late '40s; B. Goodman, '50. From early '50s, spent next two decades dividing his time between commercial studio work and jazz. In '66-7, recorded as pianist, organist w. Toots Thielemans, C. McRae, Sam "The Man" Taylor; arranger/conductor for C. Basie, Bobby Hackett, C. Cole, D. Severinsen. Began working in electronics, '68, and from '69 rec. a series of LPs feat. Moog synthesizer. During '69-70 pl. w. Jimmy Hamilton, Thad Jones-Mel Lewis, co-led quartet w. Thielemans; rec. own piano concerto, first public perf. at Eastman School.

In '71 he arr. for Enoch Light's big band series; premiered his comp. *Event*, w. Kostelanetz and Winnipeg Symph; led own trio weekly at Jimmy Weston's. '72-5: regular Sunday night solo gigs at The Cookery, NYC. From '72, began giving lecture-concerts on history of jazz piano. In '73, with the revival of interest in early jazz and ragtime, he rec. a solo ragtime album, an orchestral Jelly Roll Morton LP etc. (see below). Organizer and arranger for Jazz Piano Quartet, '74; musical director of N.Y. Jazz Repertory Co., '74-5; Rec. complete piano works of Scott Joplin, '75.

Hyman in '72 was voted the most valuable keyboard player by the N.Y. chapter of NARAS. At that time he was heavily involved in TV work, as musical director with various David Frost specials; organist on *Beat The Clock*; composer of scores for ABC documentary progs. etc.

Hyman in recent years has enjoyed increasing critical acclaim for his multi-faceted contributions to jazz as instrumentalist, composer and arranger. His exceptional eclecticism has enabled him to recreate the styles of every era from ragtime to contemporary with the perfect blend of technical, intellectual and emotional requirements.

Jazz Fests: Newport-N.Y. w. E. Condon, '72; Dick Gibson jazz parties annually from '67. Comps: Piano concerto (*Concerto Electro*); *The Minotaur* and other works for Moog; co-writer w. Seymour Reiter of an operetta *Joan And The Devil*. Publs: *Songs From the Plays of Shakespeare* (General Music Publ. Co., Irvington, N.Y. 10533); *The Happy Breed*, organ solos; *Scott Joplin for Organ; Jazz Sampler*, piano solo, (Edw. B. Marks Music, 1790 Broadway, N.Y. 10019); *SynthaSound Suite*, synthesizer and organ (Canyon Press, Cincinnati, Ohio 45200); *Grandpa's Spells* and other J.R. Morton piano solos edited by Hyman (Hansen-Edwin Morris, 1370 6th Ave., N.Y. 10019); *Modern Piano Solos* by L. Feather, arr. Hyman; *Modern Duets (Duets for Six Valves); Down Home Melody*, piano solo & concert band arr.; *Bardolino*, piano solo (all Belwin-Mills, 16 W. 61st St., New York, 10023); *Concerto Electro, Duets in Odd Meter and Far-out Rhythms; The Minotaur*, and other works (Eastlake Music Inc., 144 W. 57th St., N.Y. 10019); stage band and small groups comps (Creative Jazz Composers, Box 467, Bowie, Md. 20715).

LPs: *Traditional Jazz Piano, Solo Piano Fantomfingers* (Project 3); *Genius At Play* (Monmouth-Evergreen); *Jelly Roll Morton Orchestral Transcriptions* (Columbia); *The Electric Eclectics of Dick Hyman; Pieces for Moog* (Command); *Shakespeare, Sullivan and Hyman*, w. Maxine Sullivan (Monmouth-Evergreen); *Let It Happen*, by Jazz Piano Quartet w. R. Hanna, M. McPartland, H. Jones (RCA); *Soprano Summit*, w. B. Wilber, K. Davern (World Jazz); *Satchmo Remembered*, a live tribute to L. Armstrong at Carnegie Hall (Atl.); *Colorado Jazz Party* (MPS/BASF).

IND, PETER,* *bass*; b. Uxbridge, England, 7/20/28. In US from 1951, stud. w. L. Tristano, pl. w. Lee Konitz, Coleman Hawkins, B. Rich, P. Bley, Red Allen. After spending three years in Big Sur, Calif., 1963-6, he returned to England, where he became active in teaching, playing, and running his own company, Wave Records, for which he has made several LPs. Addr: 11 Swakeley Drive, Ickenham, Middlesex, England. LP w. Jimmy Raney, *Strings & Swings* (Muse).

INOMATA, TAKESHI, *drums*; b. Hyogo Pref., Japan, 2/6/36. Stud. w. father, a classical oboist from '48; priv. lessons from Roy Harte in LA and Alan Dawson in Boston; also P. Humphrey and others. Member of Hot Penguins in Kyoto, '52-3. Moved to Tokyo, '56. Joined Konosuke Saijo & West Liners, of which he was leader from '58-68. After visiting U.S. in '68, returned to Japan to form Sound L.T.D. In '75 working as studio musician with this group. Publ: *Yamaha Drum Mate Course School; Drum School of Nemu Music Academy* (Yamaha Shuppan); *T. Inomata Drum School* (Nichion).

LPs: *Stravinski Spring Festival; The Third Vol. 1 & 2* (Toshiba); *T. Inomata Drum School; Anniversary Record* (Nippon Col.); *Exciting Drums; Alpha Ray; Drum Shot Tact* (Tact Series).

INZALACO, ANTHONY (TONY), *drums*; also *vibes*; b. Passaic, N.J., 1/14/38. Studied at Manhattan Sch. of Mus., '56-60. Bachelor's in Percussion; Master's in Mus. Ed. Pl. w. Billy Taylor; Johnny Smith; Buddy Rich; Vinnie Burke; Morris Nanton, '59-61; Maynard Ferguson; Jim Hall; Roger Kellaway; New York Jazz Sextet, '61-5; Chris Connor; Donald Byrd-Duke Pearson; Morgana King; Ben Webster; Jaki Byard; Lee Konitz; Benny Powell, '65-8. Moved to Europe '68 where he has worked w. Webster; D. Byas; Leo Wright; J. Griffin; A. Farmer; Slide Hampton; K. Clarke-F. Boland; Carmell Jones; O. Peterson; K. Drew; Jimmy Woode; Benny Bailey; I. Sulieman; D. Gillespie; C. McRae et al. A regular member of Dexter Gordon's "West European" rhythm section. Infl: "All the drummers from Chick Webb to Elvin Jones." TV: *Dial "M" For Music*, CBS; w. Webster; Peterson, Germany; w. McRae, Holland. Fest: Frankfurt; Berlin; Pori; Loosdrecht; Laren. LPs w. Ferguson, *The Big 'F'* (Main.); w. Clarke-Boland, *Latin Kaleidoscope*; S. Getz w. Clarke-Boland, *Change of Scenes* (MPS); D. Gordon (Steeple.).

ISAACS, CHARLES E. (IKE),* *bass*; also *cello*; b. Akron, Ohio, 3/28/23. Played w. Earl Bostic, many other small groups, and toured w. Carmen McRae while married to her in late '50s. Toured Sweden w. Basie, '62. Pl. w. and managed Gloria Lynne, '62-4. After leading trio accompanying Lambert, Hendricks & Ross, toured Europe and U.S. w. Erroll Garner, '66-70. Living in LA from '64; led trio at Pied Piper where, along w. O.C. Smith, he stayed for three years. Has also worked w. Sweets Edison, Chubby Jackson's big band, C. Terry. Was co-owner or manager of clubs in LA area. Seen in movie *They Shoot Horses, Don't They?* Fests: Monterey, '59, '61 w. L.H.& R.; Newport, '62-3, w. Lynne.

LPs: w. L.H. & R., *Hottest New Group In Jazz; L.H. & R. Sings Ellington* (Col.); w. Garner, *Up In Erroll's Room* (MGM); w. Jack Wilson, *Song For My Daughter* (BN); *Joe Williams Live at Birdland; Basie in Sweden* (Roul.).

ISRAELS, CHARLES H. (CHUCK),* *bass, composer, conductor*; b. New York, N.Y., 8/10/36. Best-known as member of the Bill Evans trio from fall of '61 until early '66. Studied comp. w. Hall Overton, '66-71. Formed own rehearsal band '66 and appeared at Vanguard, Half Note into '68. Associate cond. for *Promises, Promises*, '68-71. Traveled to Europe to play own comps. w. Nord Deutscher Rundfunk orch.; Danish Radio Band, '69-70; Swiss radio, '70. From '73 Assistant Prof. in charge of Jazz Studies at Brooklyn Coll. School of Performing Arts.

In '73 formed the National Jazz Ensemble to present, with the breadth and variety of symphony concerts, the masterpieces of jazz from Jelly Roll Morton and Duke Ellington through Monk and Gil Evans to George Russell and Ornette Coleman. Basic personnel incl. Jimmy Maxwell, Danny Hayes, Tom Harrell, trumpets; Sal Nis-

Elvin Jones (*David D. Spitzer*)

Thad Jones (*Veryl Oakland*)

Hank Jones (*David D. Spitzer*)

Quincy Jones (*Andy Kent*)

Clifford Jordan (*Strata-East Records*)

Stan Kenton (*Veryl Oakland*)

John Klemmer (*Impulse Records*)

Rahsaan Roland Kirk
(*Warner Bros. Records*)

Cleo Laine (*V. J. Ryan, Ltd.*)

Yusef Lateef (*Veryl Oakland*)

Jackie Cain and Roy Kral (*Veryl Oakland*)

Harold Land

Moe Koffman (*Bernie Senensky*)

Arnie Lawrence (*Bob Klein*)

Azar Lawrence (*Veryl Oakland*)

Mel Lewis (*David D. Spitzer*)

Dave Liebman (*Veryl Oakland*)

Hubert Laws (*Veryl Oakland*)

Mike Longo (*David D. Spitzer*)

Shelly Manne *(Veryl Oakland)*

John Lewis (*David D. Spitzer*)

Albert Mangelsdorff (*Veryl Oakland*)

Chuck Mangione (*Veryl Oakland*)

Pat Martino (*Veryl Oakland*)

Ronnie Mathews (*Ed Snider*)

Benny Maupin (*Veryl Oakland*)

John Mayall (*Veryl Oakland*)

Jimmy Maxwell (*Bill Spilka*)

Marian McPartland & Janice Robinson

Roy McCurdy (*Veryl Oakland*)

Jimmy McGriff (*David D. Spitzer*)

Al McKibbon
(*Veryl Oakland*)

John McLaughlin
(*Veryl Oakland*)

Jimmy McPartland

Grachan Moncur III (*David D. Spitzer*)

Charles McPherson (*David D. Spitzer*)

Benny Morton & Benny Carter

Blue Mitchell (*Veryl Oakland*)

Carmen McRae (*Veryl Oakland*)

Charles Mingus (*Veryl Oakland*)

Gerry Mulligan (*David D. Spitzer*)

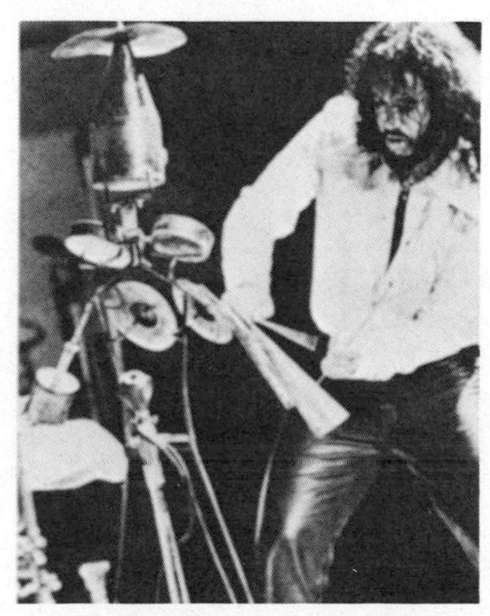

Airto Moreira (*Veryl Oakland*)

Alphonse Mouzon (*Veryl Oakland*)

George Mraz (*David D. Spitzer*)

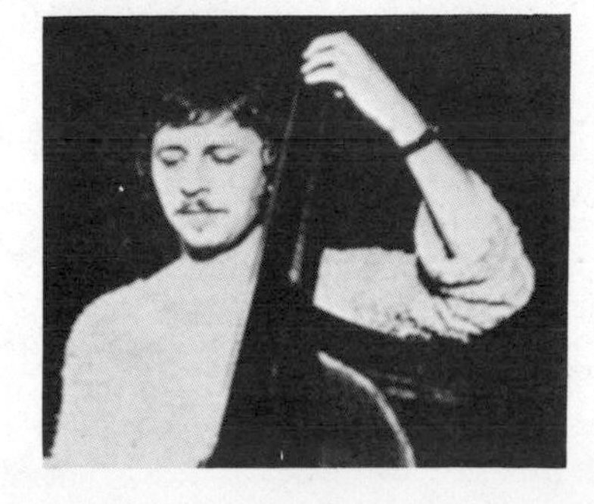

Zbigniew Namyslowski
(*Duarte Mendonca*)

Joe Newman & Al Cohn (*Randi W. Hultin*)

Sal Nistico (*Bob Klein*)

Sam Jones, Lisle Atkinson, Richard Davis, Milt Hinton
(*David D. Spitzer*)

Jimmy Owens (*Bob Klein*)

Niels-Henning Orsted Pedersen (*Veryl Oakland*)

Cecil Payne (*David A. Spitzer*)

Art Pepper (*Veryl Oakland*)

tico, tenor saxophone; Jimmy Knepper, Rod Levitt, trombones; Bill Goodwin, drums. Guest soloists have been L. Konitz; Bill Evans, R. Eldridge; H. Hancock; and Phil Woods. The Ensemble appeared at Wolftrap Farm, '73; Alice Tully Hall, '74; The New School; Smithsonian Institution, '75.

Comp. grants: Croft Fellowship, '71, stud. w. G. Schuller and Bruno Maderna at Tanglewood (Lenox, Mass.); CAPS, '72; National Endowment, '71, '73. Fest: NJF-NY w. G. Mulligan, '73. Comp: *Extract I*, publ: (Opus Music, 612 No. Michigan, Chicago, Ill. 60611); *Lyric Suite for Fluegelhorn and Jazz Ensemble; Solar Complexes; Pacemaker for Brass Quintet*, perf. by NY Brass Society, '71. Arrs. of *Nardis; All Blues*, orchestrations of transcribed performances of B. Evans trio expanded for big band.

LPs: *National Jazz Ensemble, Vol. 1* (Chiaro.); w. B. Evans, *Town Hall Concerts* (Verve).

IZENZON, DAVID,* *bass, composer*; b. Pittsburgh, Pa., 5/17/32. Active with the Ornette Coleman trio in the mid-'60s, he cont. w. the saxophonist's group and then led his own quintet in the New York area. Also worked w. Perry Robinson, Jaki Byard. From '72 he has limited his playing because of his young son's brain injury which requires intensive home therapy.

Izenzon, who taught music history at Bronx Community Coll. from '68-71, received a Ph.D. in Psychotherapy in '73 and now operates a private practice. Completed a book on human emotions and their relationships, '75. Film: acted and played in *Solo Bass and Stripper*, unreleased. Comp: jazz opera, *How Music Can Save the World; Hymn to Endlessness; A Tribute to Bass Players*. Fest: NJF-NY '73; N.Y. Musicians Fest. Won DB critics poll, TDWR, '67. LPs: *At the Golden Circle*, Vols. 1&2 w. Coleman (Blue Note); *Chappaqua Suite* w. Coleman (CBS); *Sunshine of My Soul* w. Byard (Prestige).

JACKSON, BRIAN ROBERT, *piano, composer*; also *flute, synthesizer, keyboards, singer*; b. Brooklyn, N.Y., 10/11/52. Studied piano w. Mrs. Hepzibah Ross, '59-66; theory w. Fred Simmons at MUSE, '68-9; chord theory w. Jaki Byard, '69. Self-taught on flute. Jammed w. local musicians in Brooklyn, '67-9; worked w. local gps. while at Lincoln U. in Penna., '69-71. Met Gil Scott-Heron at Lincoln, '69 and began writing and pl. w. him. Has also pl. w. Airto; Roy Ayers; Stevie Wonder; Frank Foster; Jimmy Lyons; Stanley Clarke; Pharoah Sanders; Mtume; Ndugu; Lawrence Killian. TV: *Midnight Special; Saturday Night Live; Interface; Harambee; Black News; David Eaton Show*. Fest: Berkeley JF, '73, '75. Infl: H. Hancock, M. Tyner, A. Jamal, A. Bey, H. Silver, Wynton Kelly, John and Alice Coltrane, Miles Davis, Scott-Heron, C. Taylor, A. Hill, W. Shorter, Taj Mahal. Comp: *I Think I'll Call It Morning; Free Will; Speed Kills; Pieces of a Man; A Very Precious Time; Offering; Must Be Something*. Writing a film score w. Scott-Heron, *Baron Wolfgang Von Tripps*. Would like to get into arranging. Writes lyrics, too, and plans to publish some. "I like to play and I like to write," he says, "but it would *really* trip me out to hear other *artists* do our songs."

LPs: w. Scott-Heron, *Winter in America* (Strata-East); *Pieces of a Man; The Revolution Will Not Be Televised* (Fly. Dutch); *From South Africa to South Carolina; The First Minute of a New Day* (Arista).

JACKSON, CHARLES MELVIN (CHIP), *bass*; b. Rockville Centre, L.I., N.Y., 5/15/50. Educ. Staples high school, Westport, Conn., '65-8; Berklee College, '70-3. Pl. w. Herb Pomeroy, J. La Porta, '72; G. Burton, '72-3; J. Steig, J. Abercrombie, '73. Joined W. Herman Sept. '73 and remained for 11 months, touring Europe and Canada and app. at numerous fests. Joined C. Mangione quartet, Sept. '74. App. with him on Nancy Wilson TV show, '75. Insp. by Ron Carter, S. Swallow, S. La Faro, P. Chambers, G. Burton.

LPs: *Thundering Herd; Live at Montreux*, w. Herman (Fantasy); *Chase The Clouds Away*, w. Mangione (A & M).

JACKSON, GREIG STEWART (CHUBBY),* *bass*; b. New York City, 10/25/18. Award-winning bassist during his years w. W. Herman in late '40s. During '60s led combos and big band in Miami, Fla. Org. another orch. in NYC, '69. Summer season in Aruba leading quintet feat. his son Duffy on drums, '70. Had his own jazz disc jockey show in Miami Beach. Moved to Hollywood, '71 and for next four years alternated between LA and LV, pl. w. Urbie Green, Edie Adams and others. Briefly ran own jazz club in N. Hollywood, '73. Participated in Herman reunion at NJF-NY, '72.

Comps: *Girl Child; Have A Nice Forever*. LPs: *Newport in New York, The Jam Sessions, Vol. 1&2* (Cobble.); many earlier albums w. Herman (Col.); reissue of band he took to Sweden in '47, *Bebop Revisited, Vol. 1* (Xanadu).

JACKSON, CLIFTON LUTHER (CLIFF),* *piano*; b. Washington, D.C., 7/19/02. The veteran pianist, one of the early Harlem stride and boogie woogie specialists, died NYC, of heart failure, 5/23/70. His last regular job was at Jimmy Ryan's in NYC; after leaving because of ill health, pl. occasional concerts with his wife, singer Maxine Sullivan.

JACKSON, DUFF CLARK (DUFFY), *drums*; also *piano, bass, vibes, singer*; b. Freeport, L.I., N.Y., 7/3/53. Son of bassist Chubby Jackson. Stud. at age four w. Don Lamond, later w. Roy Burns. Throughout his school days, app. mostly with his father's group, as well as on many TV shows. At age 14, worked a summer season w. Flip Phillips in Florida. In senior year at high school, became drummer for musical show *Hair* in Coconut Grove, Florida. After graduating from Miami Beach High School in June '71, opened at Shelly's Manne Hole in Hollywood with Milt Jackson-Ray Brown quintet.

Later pl. w. K. Winding, T. Gibbs, W. Herman, Monty Alexander Trio, Urbie Green. App. in Japan w. Benny Carter, Aug. '73. Toured for three months w. Lena Horne. Worked regularly for Sammy Davis Jr. in person and on TV series, '74-5. Fests: Dick Gibson Jazz Party, '71; Concord, '73-4. Jackson is highly regarded as a versatile, modern drummer, insp. by L. Bellson, B. Cobham, Burns, Lamond et al.

LP: *Here Comes The Sun*, w. Alexander (MPS-BASF).

JACKSON, MAHALIA,* *singer*; b. New Orleans, La., 10/26/11. Long known as the foremost gospel singer, Miss Jackson was intermittently ill from '64, and was hospitalized with heart trouble in '67, and again in '71. Despite her frail condition, she visited Japan, Europe and India in '71, but was soon hospitalized and died 1/27/72 in Evergreen, Park, Ill.

Though she was reluctant to be identified with jazz, the quality inherent in Mahalia Jackson's sound had much in common with that of the great jazz and blues singers. One of her most memorable performances brought her together with the Duke Ellington orch. at the NJF in '58, when she sang a special treatment of *The Twenty-Third Psalm*, as well as Ellington's *Come Sunday* from *Black, Brown & Beige*. She was heard again at Newport in a birthday tribute to Louis Armstrong, with whom she sang several numbers.

Dan Morgenstern observed in DB: "Her art, projected with immense dignity and vital power through the magnificent instrument of her voice, is one of the glories of black American music in this century, and it reached and touched untold millions." In 1975 a large and comprehensive biography, *Just Mahalia, Baby*, by Laurraine Goreau, was publ. by Word Books, Waco, Tex.

LPs: *Best Of* (Kenwood); *Bless This House; Best-Loved Hymns of Dr. King; Garden of Prayer; Great; Great Gettin' Up; Greatest Hits; I Believe; In Concert; Mighty Fortress; My Faith; Power and The Glory; Recorded in Europe; Right Out of the Church; What The World Needs Now* (Col.).

JACKSON, MILTON (MILT or BAGS),* *vibes*; also *piano, singer, guitar*; born Detroit, Mich., 1/1/23. A member of the original Modern Jazz Quartet (see Lewis, John), Jackson decided in 1974 to leave the group in order to form a combo of his own. The MJQ disbanded in July of that year, was reunited for a concert in the fall; during most of the next year Jackson worked as a single, fronting local rhythm sections in NYC, LA etc. App. in own gp. and w. other stars at Montreux JF, '75.

His career as a leader of various ensembles on records gained in impact during the 1970s; albums such as *Olinga* enjoyed some commercial success. Jackson's style remained basically unchanged, though some students claimed that his playing was freer under conditions less formalized than those of the MJQ.

Before leaving the MJQ, Jackson often co-led a group with Ray Brown during the quartet's annual summer hiatus.

LPs: *Milt Jackson* (BN); *Bags & Flute; Bags & Trane; Ballad Artistry; Plenty Plenty Soul* (Atl.); *Big Band Bags* (Milestone); *Complete Milt Jackson; Opus de Funk* (Pres.); *Goodbye; Olinga; Sunflower* (CTI); *Impulse Years; Jazz 'n' Samba; Milt Jackson Quintet; Statements* (Impulse); w. MJQ, *At Music Inn; The Art of MJQ; The Best of the MJQ; Blues at Carnegie Hall; Blues on Bach; Collaboration; Comedy; European Concert; Fontessa; Legendary Profile; Live at the Lighthouse; Lonely Woman; Modern Jazz Quartet; One Never Knows; Plastic Dreams; Porgy & Bess; Pyramid; The Sheriff; Third Stream Music* (Atl.); *First Recordings; For Lovers* (Pres.); *In Memoriam* (Little David); *On Tour* (SS); w. Ray Brown, *Memphis Jackson; Just The Way It Had To Be; The Way It Is* (Impulse); Montreux '75 series w. own *Big Four;* w. D. Gillespie; C. Basie; O. Peterson (Pablo).

JACKSON, OLIVER,* *drums*; b. Detroit, Mich. 4/28/34. With Earl Hines quartet '66-9. On leaving Hines, formed the JPJ Quartet w. Hines-mates Budd Johnson and Bill Pemberton, adding Dill Jones on piano. In '71 the Johns-Manville Corp. sponsored the quartet for a series of high school concerts in cities where their plants were located. This community relations project, called "New Communications in Jazz," played to over 300,000 students. Jackson has also freelanced w. O. Peterson, E. Garner, C. Shavers, R. Eldridge, C. Hawkins, K. Burrell and many others. European tours w. Hines, '67; *Jazz From A Swinging Era*, '68; JPJ, '71. Fests: Monterey, '67; Newport, '68, 72-5; Yugoslavia, Montreux, '71; Colo. Jazz Party, '73. TV w. JPJ, Montreux '71. Comps: w. Budd Johnson, *Tribulations; Montreux '71; OJBJ Blues; Oliver's Twist*. LPs: *New Communications in Jazz; Montreux '71* w. JPJ (Master Jazz); *Grand Reunion* w. Hines (Limelight); *The Blues, That's Me* w. I. Jacquet (Pres.); *The Tender Gender* w. Burrell (Cadet); *The Last Session* w. Shavers (Black and Blue); w. Herb Hall-Joe Muranyi; Lou McGarity (Fat Cat's Jazz); Tony Parenti (Jazzology).

JACKSON, PRESTON,* *trombone*; b. New Orleans, 1/3/04. Played with many Chicago bands in '20s; L. Armstrong, '31-2. Inactive as musician for many years, but returned in '40s, continued to work occasionally until '60. Came back on record date with Lil Armstrong, Sept. '61. In later years played mostly with Franz Jackson All Stars (from '66), concerts w. Clyde Bernhardt, Little Brother Montgomery, Art Hodes et al. European tour w. Kid Thomas Valentine, '73; also with New Orleans Joy Makers, '74.

Rec. in Sweden with own band, made films in Paris, London. Played at Preservation Hall in New Orleans with Percy Humphrey band, '74. Still playing w. F. Jackson, Montgomery and teaching, '75.

LPs: w. F. Jackson (Pinnacle); Barry Martyn (Crescent Jazz).

JACKSON, QUENTIN LEONARD (BUTTER),* *trombone*; b. Springfield, Ohio, 1/13/09. After touring w. Q. Jones band in *Free and Easy*, '59-60, joined Count Basie until the fall of '62; then worked w. C. Mingus. Rejoined

Duke Ellington briefly in spring '63. NYC studio work; house band at Copacabana, '64. Gigs w. NYC bands assembled for engagements w. Louis Bellson, '64; Gerald Wilson '66. Much Broadway pit orch. work. With Thad Jones-Mel Lewis orch. until illness curtailed his activities in '75. Member of NYJRC. LPs w. Jones-Lewis; Basie.

JACKSON, WILLIS (GATOR), *tenor sax, composer*; also *soprano sax, Gator horn*; b. Miami, Fla., 4/25/32. Began studying at 10; piano, then clarinet. Prof. debut at 14 on tenor sax w. local bands; schoolmates and bandmates incl. C. Adderley, Blue Mitchell. Studied theory and harmony at Fla. A&M. Worked w. Cootie Williams, '50-5. Rec. own comp. *Gator Tail* w. Williams and acquired nickname Gator. Touring US from '55 w. own group, very often in R&B package w. Dinah Washington, The Ravens, Jackie Wilson, etc. For eight yrs. married to Ruth Brown who sang w. him during this time. Pl. summer gig annually at Club Harlem, Atlantic City, N.J. from '63. His r & b associations have led some people to underestimate his abilities as a jazz player but he is a very effective communicator in the Illinois Jacquet vein with touches of Gene Ammons. Infl: C. Hawkins, L. Young, Herschel Evans, Ben Webster, Ch. Parker. TV: Ed Sullivan in '50s; Mike Douglas in '60s; *Dial "M" For Music* w. Father O'Connor. Comp: *Cookin' Sherry*, which won French Grand Prix du Disque, '59; *This'll Get to Ya; Miss Ann; Brother Elijah; On My Own; West Africa; The Head Tune.*

Jackson's Gator horn, a saxophone of his own design, is used for ballads. It hangs almost to the floor, has a round ball with a small opening for the bell and sounds, he explains, "between soprano and alto and French horn and clarinet."

LPs: *West Africa; Headed and Gutted* (Muse); *The Way We Were* (Atl.); many others on Prest.; reissues on Trip; w. J. McDuff; Bill Jennings (Prest.).

JACQUET, JEAN BAPTISTE ILLINOIS,* *tenor saxophone, bassoon*; b. Broussard, La., 10/31/22. The former L. Hampton star, who helped popularize JATP, was active in European tours and fests. with own trio incl. Milt Buckner and Jo Jones; own groups in US, app. at Buddy's Place, NYC, '74; also w. B. Rich group at same club, '74. Talking about the particular brand of *macho* tenor sax that Jacquet fostered, Dan Morgenstern wrote: ". . . but no matter what others may have wrought from his prescriptions, he himself has remained musical and swinging." Fests: NJF-NY w. L. Hampton reunion, '72; Tribute to Ben Webster, '74; Monterey. LPs: *How High The Moon; Bottoms Up; Soul Explosion; The King; The Blues, That's Me* (Prest.); *Genius at Work* (Black Lion); *The Last Blues Album* w. Rich (Groove Merchant); w. B. Tate (Chiaroscuro).

JAMAL, AHMAD,* *piano, composer*; b. Pittsburgh, Pa., 7/2/30. Continued to lead his trio, which for many years incl. Jamil Nasser, bass; and Frank Gant, drums. Jim Szantor wrote in *down beat*: "Jamal's charming, personal brand of space music . . . has always appealed to me. His work is somewhat more aggressive than in the *But Not For Me—Tangerine* phase of his career circa 1957 . . . He captures the essence of a tune and bases his bravado runs, embroideries, and driving riff-like figures around it—sometimes weaving in and out of the melody, sometimes leaving space for the opinions of his accompanists." Pl. on cruise, *Showboat 4*, Dec. '75. Comp: *Eclipse; Pastures; Spanish Interlude; Death and Resurrection; Swahililand.* LPs: *Jamal Plays Jamal; Jamalca; '73* (20th Century); *The Awakening; Poinciana Revisited; Freelight; Tranquility; Outertimeinnerspace* (Imp.); *Bright, Blue and Beautiful; Cry Young; Heatwave* (Cadet).

JAMAL, KHAN (Warren Robert Cheeseboro), *vibes, marimba, composer, percussionist*; b. Jacksonville, Fla., 7/23/46. Grew up in Philadelphia. First infl. was mother, pianist Willa Mae McGee. Studied at Granoff Sch. of Mus.; Combs Coll. of Mus.; privately w. Bill Lewis; Abraham Howard Jr. Performed w. Frank Lowe; Noah Howard; Grachan Moncur III; Dave Burrell; Archie Shepp; Norman Connors; Byard Lancaster; Sam Rivers; Stanley Clarke; Gary Bartz; Sun Ra; Larry Young; Calvin Hill; Sounds of Liberation; Ted Daniel; Jerome Cooper, etc. App. at NY Mus. Fest.; NJF-NY; Studio Rivbea; Ornette Coleman's Artist House; Studio We; Phila. Mus. Fest.; Phila. Black Arts Fest; Village Vanguard; Chat Qui Peche. Toured western European countries, '75. Mus. Dir. of Phila. Jazz Foundation (Vernon House, Vernon Park, Pa. 19144). Co-leader w. Sunny Murray of Untouchable Factor. Resident artist, LaSalle Coll. of Urban Studies. Infl: Milt Jackson, Lem Winchester, Bobby Hutcherson, Walt Dickerson, Bill Lewis, Roy Ayers, Cecil Taylor, Monk, Tyner, Coltrane, Dolphy, Rufus Harley, A. Ayler, L. Armstrong. Comp: *Pure Energy; Clint; 35,000 Feet Up; Give the Vibes Some.* LPs: *Give the Vibes Some* (Palm); *Inside Out; Straight Ahead* (Live); *Drum Dance to the Motherland; New Horizon* w. Sounds of Liberation (Dogtown); *Back Streets of Heaven* w. Sounds of Lib. & B. Lancaster, unreleased.

JAMES, ROBERT (BOB),* *piano, composer*; also *organ, synthesizer*; b. Marshall, Mo., 12/25/39. Served as accompanist-musical director-arranger for S. Vaughan, '66-8. Staff composer for Association of Producing Artists Repertoire Co. in NY, where he wrote scores for *Pantagleize; Cock-A-Doodle-Dandy* and others, '67-8. Studio work, NYC, arr. and perf. w. Q. Jones, D. Warwicke, R. Flack, Morgana King, '68-72. In '73 James was signed as exclusive arranger for CTI Records and wrote albums for Eric Gale, G. Washington, H. Crawford, Johnny Hammond, Idris Muhammad, Gabor Szabo and S. Turrentine. In '74 James continued to arr. albums for Crawford, Washington and M. Jackson and was also signed by CTI as a rec. artist. His first album, *Bob James One*, with its interpretation of Moussorgsky's *Night On Bald Mountain*, enjoyed a large measure of acclaim, and was followed by the even more popular *Bob James Two.* He also arr. for and perf. w. R. Flack, Paul Simon; arr. and cond. the music for motion pic., *Serpico*.

Comps: score for Broadway musical, *The Selling of the*

President; Valley of the Shadows; Nautilus; Soulero; Piece of Mind. LPs: *Bob James One; Bob James Two* (CTI); *Soul Box; Inner City Blues; Mister Magic* w. Washington (Kudu); *She Was Too Good To Me* w. Chet Baker (CTI); *Walking In Space* w. Q. Jones (A & M).

JAMES, HARRY HAAG,* *trumpet, leader*; b. Albany, Ga., 3/15/16. Formed first band '39 after gaining national fame during two years w. B. Goodman. In late '60s and early '70s still based in Las Vegas, but made frequent U.S. and European tours and continued to combine commercial style with jazz oriented material, using arrs. by Thad Jones, Neal Hefti, Ernie Wilkins. App. in NYC for NJF, at Roseland Ballroom and Carnegie Hall, '74, Carnegie Hall '75. Publs: *Harry James Trumpet Method; Harry James Studies and Improvisations* (Robbins Music). Own LPs: Readers Digest, Longines Symphonette.

JAMES, NEHEMIAH (SKIP),* *singer, guitar, piano*; b. Yazoo County, Miss., 1902. Active in the '20s around Jackson and Vicksburg, he dropped his career from '32-38 but resumed in '38-'40 w. a gospel gp. Rediscovered by young blues enthusiasts in '64 he app. at the Newport Folk Fest. that year and toured Europe w. the American Folk Blues Festival '67. His song, *I'm So Glad*, was recorded by Cream. He died at Univ. of Penn. Hospital, Phila., 10/3/69.

JAMES, STAFFORD LOUIS, *bass, composer*; also *cello*; b. Evanston, Ill., 4/24/46. Brother, Don, pl. reeds in Ill. Studied violin ages seven to 11. While in service stud. bass in NO w. Richard Payne, Chuck Beatty. Further stud. w. Rudolf Fahsbender at Chi. Conserv., '67-8; Julius Levine at Mannes Coll. of Mus., NYC, '73-4. First pl. prof. in NO, '66 w. Trevor Koehler trio. To NYC late '68, working w. Monty Alexander. Pl. w. Pharoah Sanders; Rashied Ali; Joe Lee Wilson; Lonnie Liston Smith; Archie Shepp; Alice Coltrane, '69-70; Danny Mixon from '70; Melba Moore, '71; Charles Sullivan, '71-2; Bobby Timmons, '72; Roy Ayers, '72-3; John Hicks from '73; Gary Bartz; Art Blakey, '73-4; Betty Carter from '73; Cecil, Dee Dee, Ron Bridgewater, '74; Al Haig; Chico Hamilton, Hannibal; Barry Harris, '75. Taught bass at U.N. School, '74-5. Designed church architecture w. Barry Byrne in Chi. Plays chess, draws and rides horses. Infl: NO bassists Payne & Beatty, Ravel, McCoy Tyner, Oscar Pettiford, Paul Chambers, Scott LaFaro, Ron Carter, Eddie Gomez, Richard Davis, Jimmy Garrison. TV: w. Betty Carter, *AM America*; ABC; *Interfaith*, PBS, '75; w. Shepp, *Free Time*, '71; w. Bartz, Montreux JF; *Congress of African People*, Calif. Educ. TV; *It's About Time*, SF. '73. Fest: Notre Dame, '68; w. Bartz, Kongsberg, Montreux, '73; w. Blakey, Perugia, Pescara, NJF-NY, '74; w. Hannibal, Berlin '75; w. Enrico Rava, Umbria, '75; w. Betty Carter, MJF, '75. Comps: *Costa Bruciata Suite*, dedicated to Charles Clark; *Bertha Baptist; City of Dreams; Neptune's Child; Sachia-Nova*. Publ: (Staja Publ., 133 St. Felix Street, Brooklyn, N.Y. 11217). LPs: own quartet (Horo); w. Hannibal (BASF); w. Oliver Lake, *Heavy Spirits*; w. Andrew Cyrille, *Spiral* (Arista); w. R. Kenyatta, *Nomosa* (Muse); w. Bartz, *I've Known Rivers* (Prest.); w. R. Ali, *New Directions* (Survival).

JARMAN, JOSEPH, *sopranino, soprano, alto, tenor, bass saxophones, bassoon, oboe, flute, clarinets, piccolo, composer;* also *conga, bells, gongs, accordion, vibes, marimba, ballophone, singer*; b. Pine Bluff, Ark., 9/14/37. Moved to Chicago at a very early age. Studied drums at Du Sable High w. Capt. Walter Dyett; saxophone, clar. in Army. Further education at Wilson Jr. Coll.; Chicago City Coll.; and Chi. Cons. of Mus. Began performing w. AACM '65. Played his comp. *Imperfections in a Given Space* w. John Cage, '65. Premiered theater pieces *Tribute to the Hard Core*, spring '66; *Indifferent Piece for Six*, fall '67. Guest lecture for the Contemporary Music Society of the U. of Chi., '67. Lecturer, director of music and theater workshop at Circle Pine Center, Delton, Mich., summer '68, where he perf. his comp. *Gate Piece*. Joined the Art Ensemble of Chicago, April '69. pl. w. it in France, and the US from that time. Comps: *Sorry to Make the Sun Come Up; As If It Were the Seasons; Song for Christopher; Fanfare for the Warriors; What's to Say*.

LPs: see Art Ensemble of Chicago; *Song For; As If It Were the Seasons; Together Alone* (Delmark).

JARRETT, KEITH,* *piano, composer*; also *soprano sax*; b. Allentown, Pa., 5/8/45. After pl. w. Art Blakey in '65, he joined Charles Lloyd in '66 and began to build an international reputation through many European tours, incl. Russia in '67. While w. Lloyd also pl. and recorded w. own trio. In '70-1 he was a member of the shifting Miles Davis personnel and on leaving again formed his own group w. his old section mates, Charlie Haden and Paul Motian, adding reedman Dewey Redman. Besides his quartet performances Jarrett also performs in concert as a solo artist. In the '70s he appeared in both contexts in the US, Europe and Japan and at many of the major festivals. Solo at NJF-NY, '74.

Jarrett first recorded w. his trio for Atlantic's Vortex label but these have been out of print for some time. Then the quartet recorded for Atlantic and Columbia. His recording arrangement in the mid-'70s is unique: his Impulse albums place him in the small group format; for the European ECM label he is taped in solo piano recitals or in orchestral settings. Stephen Davis, in the New York *Times* wrote: "Jarrett's work in Europe seems to differ from that in his own country. While rooted in American jazz lore and tradition, he seems to find greater inspiration when playing in Germany and Scandinavia." In describing his *Köln Concert*, Davis states: "Themes are introduced and mistily evaporate while Jarrett's relentless left hand drums out tense recreated patterns; there is a trance-like quality in his use of repetition but then he will go abruptly into a bluesy improvisation that soars into finely crafted treble runs. A signature specialty has the left hand padding out a melody while the right rolls off swooping liquid patterns. The general effect is something like Chopin and Art Tatum streaming together downriver in a canoe."

An avowed opponent of electric music in a period rife with heavily-amplified jazz-rock Jarrett says: "I could go into the philosophical aspects of it and make it almost an objective argument whereby playing electric music is bad for you and bad for people listening, which I do believe."

On the other hand Jarrett has been known to strum the piano's strings like a harp; use it's top for percussive effects; and accompany himself with falsetto singing, grunts and groans. His gyrations on the piano bench turn off some of his critics who also find him pretentious.

Won DB Critics poll, TDWR, '67; '74 (tie), '75. Comp: *Coral; Gypsy Moth; Pardon My Rags; El Juicio; Piece For Ornette; (If the) Misfits (Wear It); Fort Yawuh; De Drums; Still Life, Still Life; Birth; Markings; Remorse; Spirit; Mortgage on My Soul; Forget Your Memories (And They'll Remember You).*

LPs: *The Koln Concert; Facing You; Bremen/Lausanne; In the Light; Luminessence;* w. Jan Garbarek, *Belonging;* w. Jack DeJohnette, *Ruta and Daitya* (ECM); *Backhand; Treasure Island; Fort Yawuh; Death and the Flower* (Imp.); *Expectations* (Col.); *Birth; The Mourning of a Star; El Juicio; Gary Burton and Keith Jarrett* (Atl.); *Somewhere Before; Restoration Ruin; Life Between the Exit Signs* (Vortex); w. Davis, *Live-Evil; Live at Fillmore East* (Col.); w. Lloyd (Atl.).

JARVIS, CLIFFORD, *drums, percussion*; b. Boston, Mass., 8/26/41. Father, a musician, encouraged him to take up drums at 10. Studied w. Alan Dawson at Berklee from ages 12-17. To NYC in late '50s. Has worked w. Barry Harris; Yusef Lateef; Sun Ra; Grant Green; Randy Weston; R.R. Kirk; in '70s w. Pharoah Sanders; Sirone; Clifford Thornton; also app. as guest instructor at U. of Mass. and other New England area colls. Infl: M. Roach, R. Haynes, PJ Jones, Ed Blackwell, Barry Harris, Sun Ra. Fest: NJF-NY w. Sanders, '72. LPs: w. Huey Simmons (Contemp.); Sanders (Imp.); Lateef (Trip); Sun Ra (ESP); F. Hubbard (BN); R. Weston (UA); B. Harris (River.).

JARZEBSKI, PAWEL, *bass*; b. Poznan, Poland, 4/21/48. Worked w. Michal Urbaniak, '70-2; Zbigniew Namysowski, '73. Toured U.S. w. Urbaniak's Fusion, '74, app. at NJF-NY, then rejoined Namyslowski, app. w. him at Cascais JF, '74. Infls: Miles Davis, Bill Evans, M. Vitous, Jan Garbarek. Many apps. on Polish and Finnish TV. LP: w. Namyslowski, *Winobranie* (Muza).

JCOA. See Mantler, Mike; Bley, Carla.

JEFFERSON, EDGAR (EDDIE),* *singer, dancer*; b. Pittsburgh, Pa., 8/3/18. Pioneer in technique of setting lyrics to improvised jazz solos, the best known of which was based on James Moody's *I'm In The Mood For Love*. Worked w. Moody off and on from '53 as manager and singer.

During '67 and part of '68, Jefferson app. as tap dancer. He rejoined Moody in '68 and remained with him until late '73; then joined forces w. Roy Brooks, touring with their group, Artistic Truth, '74-5. Won DB Critics poll, TDWR, '75. Fest: NJF '69.

LPs: *Body and Soul; Come Along With Me* (Prestige); *Charlie Parker Memorial* album (Chess); *Things Are Getting Better* (Muse). Earlier LPs with Moody.

JEFFERSON, HILTON,* *alto saxophone*; b. Danbury, Conn., 7/30/03. One of the outstanding lead saxophonists, who also played excellent solos in a style infl. by Frank Trumbauer, died NYC, 11/14/68, after a long illness. He worked with the bands of Claude Hopkins, King Oliver, Chick Webb, Benny Carter, Fletcher Henderson, and spent the entire decade of the '40s w. C. Calloway and was w. Duke Ellington, '52-3. From '54, until his hospitalization in Sept. '68, he continued to gig on weekends w. his own gp. or w. Fats Greene.

JEFFREY, PAUL H., *tenor sax, composer*; also *clarinet, flute, oboe, bassoon*; b. New York City, 4/8/33. Studied music at PS 157, NYC; Kingston (N.Y.) HS; Ithaca (N.Y.) Coll. Worked w. own gp. in Atlantic City, N.J., '56; Wynonie Harris, Big Maybelle in Detroit, St. Louis, '57; I. Jacquet in Winston-Salem, N.C., '58; Florida and other southern states w. B.B. King, '60; NYC w. Sadik Hakim, '61; Johnny Brown, '64; Howard McGhee quartet & big band, '66; Toured Europe w. D. Gillespie's Reunion big band, '68; Billy Gardner trio, '69; a month w. C. Basie, '70. From '70 pl. w. Thelonious Monk; from '72 w. own octet. Infl: Monk, Ellington, Dameron. TV: Sammy Davis special w. Johnny Brown, '66; documentary on Sonny Rollins, NET '68; D. Gillespie on Euro. TV, '68; Monk, NET '72. Fest: NJF jam session, '69; NJF-NY: w. Mingus, '72, own gp. in NY Mus. Fest., '73, and at Fordham U., '74; w. Monk, '75; Newport in Japan, '70. Cond. NYJRC orch. for Monk concert, '74.

Saxophone instructor at Teachers Coll., Columbia U.; on faculty of Jersey State Coll. as lecturer in jazz history; arr. courses; teaching Jazz Ensemble Workshop at U. of Hartford; clinician for Yamaha Co. Own jazz radio show on WFUV (Fordham U.) from '73. Comp: *I.F.U.; Immigration; Ina; Kim; Rodan; Bianca; Ecclesiology; A.V.G.; The Dreamer; Green Ivan; Bondage; Moon Madness; My Son; Brand X; Brand New Day; Geometric Blues; Love Letters; Acirema.* LPs: *Family; Watershed; Paul Jeffrey* (Main.); *Electrifying Sounds* (Savoy); w. Gillespie, *Reunion Big Band* (MPS); w. Monk (Express).

JENKINS, LEROY, *violin, viola, composer, educator*; b. Chicago, Ill., 3/11/32. First violin teacher was O.W. Frederick; then stud. w. Bruce Hayden; basic musicianship w. Walter Dyett, band dir. at Du Sable High; learned blues from Edward Pratt. B.S. in Mus. Ed. from Florida A&M, '61. Taught string inst. in Mobile, Ala. school system, '61-5; inst. music in Chi. school system, '65-9; string-instr. instructor for Chi. Urban Poverty Corps, '69. One of the important players to emerge from the AACM, he worked w. it, '65-69. Creative Construction Co., '65-69. Pl. w. O. Coleman in Paris, '69; Cecil Taylor, '70; Anthony Braxton, '69-72; Albert Ayler, '71; Cal Massey, '70-3; Alice Coltrane, '71-2; Archie Shepp, '69, '70-4; Mtume, '72-4. Formed Revolutionary Ensemble w. Sirone and Jerome Cooper in '71 and has perf. with it since in coll., Shakespeare Fest. Public Theatre, O.K. Harris Gallery, and Museum of Contemporary Art, Chi. Infl: Charlie Parker, Jascha Heifitz, Eddie South, Ornette Coleman, Bruce Hayden, John Coltrane, Braxton,

Roscoe Mitchell, Leo Smith. App. as actor in film, *Borsalino* w. Jean-Paul Belmondo, Alain Delon. Fests: Ann Arbor w. Revolutionary Ens., '73; NJF-NY w. Dewey Redman, '74. Comp: *National Baptist Convention; Vietnam I-II; Simple Like; For Players Only; Bandana Sketches; Muhal; Collegno.* Awarded a grant in comp. from National Endowment for the Arts, '73; CAPS, '75. Won DB Critics' Poll, TDWR, on violin, '74. Nat Hentoff wrote: "Jenkins has so expanded the range and conceptual dimensions of improvisatory violin and viola that he is, as Duke Ellington might have said, 'beyond category.' " LPs w. Revolutionary Ensemble: *Vietnam I-II* (ESP); *Manhattan Cycles* (India Navigation); w. Anthony Braxton, *3 Compositions*; w. Richard Abrams, *Levels and Degrees* (Delmark); w. Archie Shepp, *Things Gotta Change*; w. Alice Coltrane, *Universal Consciousness; Reflection on Creation and Space* (Impulse); w. R. Kirk, *Rahsaan, Rahsaan* (Atlantic).

JEROME, JERRY,* *tenor saxophone, flute, conductor*; also *clarinet*; b. Brooklyn, N.Y., 6/19/12. The former Goodman and Shaw sideman, after leaving his post as musical director of WPIX-TV, concentrated on composing, arranging and producing radio and TV commercials for national products. Also active playing club dates and jazz concerts in and around eastern U.S., incl. a series for C.W. Post Coll. An avid golfer, he won the Senior Championship tournament of the North Shore C.C. His LPs on ABC-Paramount, Stinson and MGM are no longer available.

JOBIM, ANTONIO CARLOS,* *composer, guitar, piano*; b. Rio de Janeiro, Brazil, 1927. Best known as composer of songs widely feat. by jazz musicians: *Desafinado; One Note Samba; Girl From Ipanema; Quiet Nights (Corcovado).* Comp. of music for movie *The Adventurers*, '69. App. in TV spec. w. Frank Sinatra, E. Fitzgerald, '69. Among his later comps. are *Wave; Triste; Waters of March; Lamento; Mojave.*

Publs: *Wave; Stone Flower*, song folios (Corcovado Music Corp., 4 W. 56th St., New York, N.Y. 10019).

LPs: *A Certain Mr. Jobim* (WB); *Wave; Tide* (A & M); *Stone Flower* (CTI); *Jobim* (MCA); *Frank Sinatra & A.C. Jobim* (Repr.).

JOHANSEN, EGIL, *drums, composer*; b. Oslo, Norway, 1/11/34. Self-taught; started pl. piano at age 6; drums, '50. Main insps. Parker, Gillespie, Roach, Ellington, Tatum. Pl. with many visiting Americans incl. Gillespie, Dolphy, S. Getz, Lucky Thompson, Teddy Wilson; also w. Danish trumpeter Palle Mikkelborg. Many motion pic. and TV apps. As composer, his most important work was a comp. for a TV film, feat. two jazz drummers, conga and percussion.

LPs: w. Swedish Radio Jazz Group, *Greetings and Salutations* feat. Thad Jones, Mel Lewis (Four Leaf Clover); Arne Domnerus; Jan Johansson; Bengt Hallberg; Rolf Ericson; German Jazz Workshop All-Stars; Svend Asmussen.

JOHNSON, ALBERT J. (BUDD),* *tenor, soprano, alto, baritone saxes, clarinet, composer*; b. Dallas, Texas, 12/14/10. Best-known first for his key role as saxophonist-arranger w. Earl Hines, '34-42, he was a catalytic figure in the modern jazz movement w. Billy Eckstine, Dizzy Gillespie. After pl. w. Count Basie and Quincy Jones bands in '60s rejoined Hines in small gp., touring w. him in US, Russia, So. America '66-9 on tenor and soprano. After leaving Hines, formed JPJ Quartet, for which he is mus. dir., w. O. Jackson, B. Pemberton, D. Jones. Appeared in clubs such as the Half Note, Jimmy Weston's; presented concert-"rap sessions" and seminars for more than 300,000 high school students under the auspices of Johns-Manville, mainly in the US but also in Europe during a summer tour, '71.

Johnson also worked intermittently w. Sy Oliver's band in mid-'70s. In '74 he was mus. dir. for NYJRC's *Musical Life of Charlie Parker*, premiered at NJF-NY '74. Toured with it in Europe, fall '74. Guest mus. dir. for NYJRC's second season, '74-5, touring Russia with Louis Armstrong tribute, summer '75. Active as lecturer-demonstrator at U. of Conn.; Rutgers; pl. in Smithsonian Inst. concert series, '75. To KC, Sept. '75, pl. for documentary film on KC jazz style. TV: w. JPJ, Montreux JF '71, NET; film made at high school performance in Green Cove Springs, Fla. seen on many local outlets in US. Fest: w. JPJ, Montreux; Lubljana, '71; NJF-NY '72; NJF-NY jam session '73; Nice Grand Parade du Jazz, '74-5; Colo. Jazz Party, '71-5. Transcribing music from recs. w. co-editor David Baker for Smithsonian "classic jazz" project.

Comps: *Tag Along; You Dirty Old Man; Mr. Bechet; Blues for Sale; Tribulations; Montreux '71.* LPs: *Blues A La Mode* (Master Jazz); w. JPJ (Eng. RCA); also *New Communications in Jazz; Montreux '71* (Master Jazz); w. Hines (Black & Blue); reissue w. Hines (Bluebird); w. Milt Hinton (Famous Door); w. Buck Clayton (Chiaro.); w. R. Eldridge (Master Jazz); J. Rushing (RCA Victor); Red Richards (Eng. RCA); *Newport in New York '72, The Jam Sessions*, Vols. 3&4 (Cobble.); *Colorado Jazz Party* (MPS/BASF).

JOHNSON, GUS,* *drums, composer*; b. Tyler, Texas, 11/15/13. The veteran ex-Jay McShann and Count Basie drummer joined the World's Greatest Jazzband in 1969, replacing the late Morey Feld. He traveled with the band, which recorded his composition *Under The Moonlight Starlight Blue*, until the fall of 1974, when he settled in Denver, Colorado. Worked in Denver with such residents of that city as Peanuts Hucko and Ralph Sutton, and played at Dick Gibson's jazz parties in Colorado Springs. Rejoined WGJ occasionally for records. Won DB Critics poll, TDWR, '71. LPs w. WGJ (Project 3, Atlantic, World Jazz).

JOHNSON, HOWARD LEWIS, *baritone sax, tuba*; also *composer, arranger, fluegelhorn, clarinets, bass sax* etc.; b. Montgomery, Ala., 8/7/41. Self-taught; started on bari. sax in '54, tuba, '55. Came to NYC Feb. '63, pl. tuba w. Ch. Mingus, '64; road tour on bari. w. Hank Crawford, '65; back w. Mingus July '65 to Apr. '66; also w. A. Shepp for several months in '66. Intermittently w. Gil Evans orch., pl. various instruments, from '66 through mid '70s. After pl. w. B. Rich band in '66, spent most of

'67 in L.A. working w. Gerald Wilson, Big Black, O. Nelson. Back in NYC Sept. '67, worked often w. Evans, Shepp and numerous other groups, incl. own Substructure. In '70s made several apps. annually at Colorado Jazz Parties. Fests: Newport, '66, 68 w. Shepp; Newport-N.Y. w. Evans; Montreux and Antibes w. Evans, '74.

Johnson, who names Clifford Brown, Mingus, Evans, D. Ellington and Herb Bushler as musicians who have insp. or infl. him, is a performer of extraordinary versatility who seems equally at home and capable of first class solos whether in a traditionalist, mainstream, modern or avant garde context. As an arranger he has written charts for Taj Mahal, Paul Butterfield's *Better Days* dates, Geoff Muldaur, Gil Evans and B.B. King.

LPs w. Evans (Ampex, Atl., RCA).

JOHNSON, JAMES LOUIS (J.J.),* *composer, trombone*; b. Indianapolis, Ind. 1/22/24. Won Esquire New Star Award as trombonist, '46. Innumerable other awards in many countries as recently as '75, though by that time he had all but totally given up playing to concentrate on a career as composer, arranger and conductor. After moving to Cal. in '70, Johnson wrote scores for movies *Man and Boy; Top of the Heap; Across 110th Street; Cleopatra Jones; Willie Dynamite*. He was partial orchestrator for *Shaft* and *Trouble Man*. In television, he wrote the music for the series *Barefoot In The Park*, as well as episodes for *Mod Squad; The Bold Ones; Chase; Harry-O* etc.

Studied with and orchestrated for Earle Hagen during those years; app. as jazz trombonist on LP for first time in several years in *The Bosses* w. C. Basie, Joe Turner (Pablo). Arr. LP for Raoul De Souza (Fantasy), '75. Own early albums: *Proof Positive* (Impulse); *The Eminent J.J.* (Blue Note); others on RCA, Columbia etc. Trombone duos w. Kai Winding: *Israel; Betwixt and Between* (A&M); *Stonebones*, done for the same label was released only in Japan.

JOHNSON, FREDERIC H. (KEG),* *trombone*; b. Dallas, Tex., 11/19/08. Heard with many name bands from the late '20s, among them Benny Carter, F. Henderson, C. Calloway, Lucky Millinder; also Gil Evans, '60. Johnson during the '60s toured w. the Ray Charles orch. pl. bass trombone. He died suddenly in Chicago 11/8/67. He was an older brother of saxophonist/arranger Budd Johnson.

JOHNSON, LONNIE,* *singer, guitar*; b. New Orleans, La., 2/8/1889 (date disputed). One of the first great jazz guitarists, Johnson in the late '20s rec. several brilliant guitar duets w. E. Lang and pl. on sessions w. L. Armstrong and D. Ellington. In the mid '60s he settled in Toronto, where he became popular with local blues fans. Inactive after suffering injuries in an accident March '69, Johnson died of a stroke in Toronto, 6/16/70.

LPs: a few tracks on *The Duke Ellington Story*, Vols. 1,2 (Col.); many other recs. w. Armstrong (Col.); J. Dodds, J. Noone, A. Ammons et al, all deleted, as were his own LPs on Prest.

JOHNSON, MANZIE ISHAM,* *drums*; b. Putnam, Conn., 8/19/06. Prominent w. Don Redman band, '31-40; later w. F. Henderson, James P. Johnson et al, Johnson died 4/9/71 at a hospital in the Bronx, N.Y.

JOHNSON, HAROLD (MONEY), *trumpet, fluegelhorn, singer*; b. Tyler, Texas, 2/23/18. When he was 15, a friend gave him an old cornet. Studied w. Leonard Parker and soon was pl. w. Eddie and Sugar Lou; then in Dallas w. his cousin Red Calhoun's band. After two yrs., went with Skunny Thompson to Tip Top Club in Okla. City, '36, where he jammed w. Charlie Christian and saxophonist Henry Bridges. Joined Nat Towles band, '37, remaining for seven yrs. working out of Omaha. Saxophonist Lee Pope, who used to borrow from him, gave him his nickname. To NYC w. Horace Henderson. When band broke up, pl. w. Bob Dorsey in Rochester for two yrs. Rejoined Towles briefly; then to NYC again w. Count Basie. Pl. w. Cootie Williams '46; Lucky Millinder and Williams '47; then w. Lucky Thompson; Sy Oliver; Herbie Fields; Bull Moose Jackson. To So. America w. Panama Francis, '53; several yrs. w. Reuben Phillips' house band at the Apollo Theater, NYC; then work in the rec. studios; gigs w. Buddy Johnson's small band; Mercer Ellington; show bands at Basin Street East; Copacabana.

State Dept. tour of Russia w. Earl Hines, '66; Euro. tour w. Hines, '68. Pl. NJF and LV w. Duke Ellington, '68; replaced Cat Anderson w. Ellington, June '69. Infl: Armstrong; Nat Towles.

LPs: see Ellington; *Buck Clayton Jam Session #2* (Chiaro.).

JOHNSON, PETE,* *piano*; b. Kansas City, Mo., 3/24/04. The pioneer boogie woogie pianist who, with Albert Ammons and Meade Lux Lewis, helped to bring this style to national attention in the late '30s, was musically active in Buffalo, N.Y. until suffering a heart attack in '58. He was intermittently ill during the next decade, making his final public appearance at a *Spirituals To Swing* concert at Carnegie Hall in Jan. '67, when he was reunited with his Kansas City partner, singer Joe Turner. Johnson died 3/23/67 in Buffalo.

LP: *Spirituals To Swing, 30th Anniversary* (Col.).

JOHNSON, PLAS JOHN JR.,* *tenor sax, flute* etc.; b. New Orleans, La., 7/21/31. Came to prominence in 1966 as featured soloist with H. Mancini in *The Pink Panther* film and LP. Joined staff band on Merv Griffin TV show in LA, 1970. During '70s, stepped up his jazz activities, subbing in Bill Berry band and pl. jobs w. Ray Brown, Herb Ellis, own gp. at Baked Potato etc. Rec. own first album as leader Oct. '75 for Concord Jazz label. Underrated musician with hard-swinging style and warm, full sound.

JOHNSON, SIVERT BERTIL (SY), *composer, piano*; b. New Haven, Conn., 4/15/30. Studied w. Lucy Greene, Hall Overton; Rayburn Wright, in NYC and at Eastman School *Arranger's Holiday*; Juilliard. In high school was introduced to records of Gillespie, Parker, Bud Powell by Roger Brousso (an owner of the Half Note in the '70s) and co-led band w. him. While w. USAF '51-5 in bands w. Donald Byrd, John Pisano, John Williams. After discharge to LA with law career in mind. Sold charts to

Basie; Med Flory rec. his *Jonah and the Wail*. Met Paul Bley and Ornette Coleman. To NYC '60, pl. briefly w. Mingus at Showplace. Wrote for Newport Youth Band, Ruby Braff, Marshall Brown, G. Mulligan Concert Jazz Band; led trio at Chuck's Composite. Then went into commercial arr. until he became pianist-arr. for Yolande Bavan from '66. Increased writing activity from '71 w. Mingus' *Let My Children Hear Music* album. Arrs. for Thad Jones-Mel Lewis; Quincy Jones. In '75 writing regularly for Lee Konitz Nonet; finishing a blues suite for Mingus; preparing a gp. of new comps. for Guggenheim Fellowship application.

Infl: Maurice Rocco, Teddy Wilson, Basie, Lester Young, C. Parker, M. Davis, Ellington, Rollins, Mingus. Fest: NJF w. Rod Levitt. Johnson is also a photographer-journalist who is the jazz editor of *Changes* and a contributor to the NY *Times, New York, Esquire Book of Jazz*. Comp: *Wee* (not to be confused w. Denzil Best's *Wee*); *For Harry Carney; I Should Have Kissed Her More*. Arrs. for Mingus (Col., Atl.). LPs: w. Rod Levitt (Riverside, RCA); Wes Montgomery, *Road Song* (A&M).

JOLLY, PETE (Peter A. Ceragioli),* *piano, keyboards, accordion*; b. New Haven, Conn., 6/5/32. In '65 was one of the orig. pianists to open the N. Hollywood jazz room, Donte's, and has app. there sporadically ever since. From '66-75 mainly engaged in TV and movie studios, working w. such composers as N. Hefti, J.J. Johnson, B. Byers, Don Costa, Anita Kerr, Artie Butler, Earle Hagen. Made several rec. dates with Herb Alpert's Tijuana Brass. In '74 took part in clinic at N. Texas State U. w. Ray Brown, Herb Ellis, L. Bellson, and in '75 conducted workshop series at the Dick Grove School in LA. Continued to play club dates w. own trio.

LPs: *Herb Alpert Presents Pete Jolly; Give A Damn; Seasons* (A&M).

JONES, BOBBY, *tenor, soprano saxes, clarinet, composer; educator*; b. Louisville, Ky., 10/30/28. Started on drums, his father's instrument, switching to clarinet at eight. First prof. job at 10. Father had him listen to recs. of jazz greats; arranged for him to sit-in w. local black combo for important early jazz experience. Later stud. w. Simeon Bellison, Joe Allard, Charlie Parker, G. Russell. While pl. in local sextet was hired by Ray McKinley, spring '49, remaining w. him until mid-'50. Six mos. w. Hal McIntyre, then rejoined McKinley before going into Army where he met Cannonball and Nat Adderley, Junior Mance, Kenny Dennis; led own combo at Officer's Club. After service, worked w. and arr. for Boyd Bennett and his Rockets for two and a half yrs., pl. hillbilly, then rock & roll. Briefly with Boots Randolph to Cleveland, remaining to do clubs, TV, radio and teach privately. Rejoined McKinley again, '59 to Feb. '63 when he went to Woody Herman. Left in Sept. to work in NYC. Joined Jack Teagarden in NO on Christmas Eve. When Teagarden died in Jan. '64, Jones ret. to Louisville. Started Louisville Jazz Council; later became woodwind instructor at Kentucky State Coll. To NY '69. Sat-in w. C. Mingus at Top of the Gate Nov. '70, and eventually became band member, touring Europe and Japan, '70, Europe '72. Left Mingus, settling first in Belgium, then Holland. To Munich '73, forming quintet, Summit, w. Dusko Goykovich, Horace Parlan. Own trio, '74. Won DB Critics Poll, clarinet TDWR, '73. Thoroughly schooled, he has followed what Charlie Parker told him: "First you master your instrument, then you master the music, and then you forget about all that shit and just play." Comp: *Thanks to Trane; Ballad for Two Sons; 'Stone Bossa; Blues for the Brown Buddha; Waltz for Joy; As the Crow Flies; Hill Country Suite; Only Blue; Lady Love; The Gospel Truth*. LPs: *Hill Country Suite* (Enja); *The Arrival of Bobby Jones* (Cobble.); *Mingus and Friends* (Col.); w. Herman (Philips); Jimmy Raney, *Strings & Swings* (Muse).

JONES, CARMELL,* *trumpet, composer*; also *fluegelhorn, valve trombone*; b. Kansas City, Kans., 1936. Worked w. Harold Land, Horace Silver in early '60s before moving to Germany, Aug. '65, where he joined SFB TV and radio orch. in Berlin. Jones has also pl. extensively in German clubs and all over Europe incl. Berlin Jazz Days, Prague JF and with Paul Kuhn, leader of SFB band, in Moscow and Leningrad. Appeared in German cigarette commercial. Won DB Critics' Poll, TDWR, '64. Comps: *Jayhawk Talk; Dance of the Night Child; Beepdurple; Stellisa; Give Me a Chance; Black Forest Waltz; Sad March; Shadows; Where Did the Time Go; If Love Should Come; I Think of Love*. An amateur carpenter and electrician, he does upholstering and cabinet-making, repairs cars and has built his own mixing board for recording. LPs: w. Annie Ross-Pony Poindexter; *Hip Walk* w. Nathan Davis (MPS); *More Than Meets the Ear* w. Jean-Luc Ponty (Euro. Liberty).

JONES, DILLWYN OWEN (DILL), *piano*; b. Newcastle Emlyn, Wales, 8/19/23. Became interested in jazz by hearing Fats Waller record on radio in '30s. After serving w. the Royal Navy, '42-6, stud. at Trinity Coll. of Music in London, '46-8. Later stud. w. Richard McClanahan, '62-3, and Luckey Roberts, '65, in NYC. While in Navy was encouraged by former Ellington reedman Rudy Jackson in Colombo, Ceylon, '45. A leading figure in post-WWII jazz circles in London, he established himself w. own trio; also pl. w. Ronnie Scott; Humphrey Lyttelton; Stephane Grappelli; George Chisholm. Took part in British tour of JATP. Hosted BBC Jazz Club on radio for many yrs.; first to introduce jazz on BBC-TV. Acc. Louis Armstrong in Hungarian Relief Fund concert at Hammersmith Hall, '57.

Visited US as ship's pianist on Queen Mary, '50. Ret. on many occasions in '50s but did not settle in NYC until '61. Worked w. Yank Lawson '62; Peanuts Hucko and Max Kaminsky at E. Condon's; Roy Eldridge; trio w. Bob Wilber, Carl Kress; Jimmy McPartland in mid '60s; Gene Krupa, '67-8; Dukes of Dixieland, '68. Charter member of the JPJ Quartet w. Budd Johnson, Oliver Jackson and Bill Pemberton, '69, and in next four yrs. toured US for Johns-Manville in high school concert-seminars; pl. several long engagements at Jimmy Weston's, NYC; European dates. Left in '74 to free-lance. Solo piano at several clubs incl. Condon's; gigs w. WGJ; w. Earle Warren, Taft Jordan at West End Cafe; w. M. Kaminsky; R. Eldridge; J. McPartland at Jimmy Ryan's, '74-5; also w. Countsmen, off and on, from '73. Infl: Luckey Roberts, Joe Sullivan, Ellington, Beiderbecke, James P. Johnson, Fats Waller, Willie "The Lion" Smith. Fest: NJF-NY w. JPJ, '72; w. NYJRC Tribute to Bix, '75; Monterey, solo w. John Lewis Piano Forum; Montreux; Lubljana w. JPJ, '71. Comp: *West of the Wind; Something For Luckey; Celtic Twilight.* Versatile, accomplished performer in Harlem stride, Bixian impressionism and mainstream modern. LPs: *Davenport Blues: Dill Jones Plays Bix and Others* (Chiaro.); *Up Jumped You With Love* (77); w. JPJ, *New Communications in Jazz; Montreux '71* (Master Jazz); w. H. Hall-J. Muranyi, *Clarinet Wobble*; w. L. McGarity, *Jazz Master* (Fat Cat's Jazz); w. T. Parenti (Jazzology); w. E. Warren (Eng. RCA).

JONES, ELVIN RAY,* *drums, leader*; b. Pontiac, Mich., 9/9/27. Following six years w. John Coltrane he formed his own group in '66 and has led small combos of varying sizes from that time. A quartet w. Joe Farrell, pianist Billy Greene and Wilbur Little evolved into a pianoless trio. Jimmy Garrison replaced Little. In the '70s he had saxophonists like Frank Foster, Steve Grossman, Dave Liebman and Azar Lawrence, sometimes using two reeds in the same gp. Other gp. members at different times have incl. Roland Prince, guitar; Gene Perla, David Williams, bass. In addition to clubs and concerts, Jones gives clinics, plays for schools and free concerts in prisons. His gp. tours regularly in Europe and Japan; South America for USIA, '73. '75. App. at most major fests. Whitney Balliett described his style thusly: "The center of Jones' beat shifts continually. Sometimes it is in his constantly changing ride-cymbal strokes and sometimes he softens these and bears down heavily on his high-hat on the afterbeat. Sometimes swift, wholly unpredictable bass-drum accents come to the fore and sometimes the emphasis shifts to left-hand accents on the snare, which range from clear single strokes to chattering loose rolls. Jones' hands and feet all seem to have their own minds, yet the total effect is of an unbroken flow that both supports and weaves itself around the soloists."

Film: drumming and acting role in *Zachariah*. Won DB Critics poll, '66-75; DB Readers poll, '66, '68-9. Comp: *Three Card Molly; Keiko's Birthday March; Elvin's Guitar Blues.* LPs: *New Agenda* (Vang.); *Live at the Village Vanguard* (Enja); *On the Mountain; Live* (PM); *Live at the Lighthouse; Merry Go Round; Genesis; Mr. Jones; Puttin' It Together; Ultimate* (BN); *Dear John C.; Heavy Sounds* w. Richard Davis; *Illuminations* w. J. Garrison (Imp.); w. Coltrane (Imp.); w. Jaki Byard, *Sunshine of My Soul* (Prest.); Joe Farrell, *Outback* (CTI).

JONES, ETTA,* *singer*; b. Aiken, S.C., 11/25/28. Active w. Buddy Johnson's band, J.C. Heard gp. in '40s; Earl Hines sextet, '49-52. Made comeback in '60 w. Gold Record single, *Don't Go to Strangers*, on Prestige. Toured Japan and Korea w. Art Blakey, '70. App. on *Jazz Cavalcade '72* at John F. Kennedy Center for Perf. Arts along w. G. Ammons, S. Stitt, B. Rich, etc.

Concert at Town Hall w. Billy Taylor; app. at Left Bank Jazz Society, Balto. Md., '75. Toured the club & concert circuit w. the Houston Person trio, '75. TV: Nipsey Russell's *Voices of America* show. LPs: *Etta Jones '75* (20th Century/Westbound); *Etta Jones Sings* (Roul.); others on Prest.; w. Person, *The Real Thing* (Eastbound).

JONES, HENRY (HANK),* *piano, composer*; b. Pontiac, Mich., 7/31/18. After close to 20 years as a staff musician at CBS he began to free-lance in '75. While still at CBS he also was the first pianist w. the Thad Jones (his brother)-Mel Lewis band in '66; toured w. Benny Goodman. Pl. w. Stan Getz in early '70s; in mid-'70s he app. at the Vanguard in a trio w. Ron Carter and Tony Williams, and other NYC clubs w. Carter and Ben Riley. He was supposed to perform at a concert dedicated to the music of Charlie Parker in August '75 but it was cancelled. The group, with Jackie McLean, Tommy Potter and Max Roach, did appear, however, on ABC-TV's *Like It Is*. Jones also led a trio in an episode of the CBS-TV soap opera *Love of Life*. Fest: NJF-NY; Colo. JP. Comp: *A' That's Freedom*. Own LP: *Happenings* (Imp.); LPs: w. Elvin Jones, *Dear John C.*; w. B. Hutcherson (BN); w. Jones-Lewis, *Presenting* (SS); w. Dexter Gordon (Prest.); w. Bobby Hackett; w. Bucky Pizzarelli-Bud Freeman (Fly. Dutch.).

JONES, HAROLD J., *drums*; b. Richmond, Ind., 2/27/40. Lived in Chicago from 1958. Stud. w. Jack Kurkowski from age 13 to 18; w. James Dutton at Amer. Conserv. of Mus., 18 to 23. In early '60s pl. w. Eddie Harris, D. Byrd, Bunky Green. Toured internationally w. Paul Winter, '61-2. Joined Count Basie Dec. '67 and remained for five years, then moved from NYC to LA, where he freelanced extensively in night clubs, rec. studios and TV, w. E. Fitzgerald, Tony Bennett, S. Davis Jr. TV series w. Nancy Wilson, '74-5. Rejoined Basie briefly in '74. Sweden, Caribbean cruise, Japan w. Carmen McRae, '75.

Insp. by Elvin Jones, M. Roach, A. Blakey, Roy Haynes, Tony Williams, Mel Lewis, L. Bellson, Jones was acknowledged to be one of the steadiest and most propulsive drummers ever to work for Basie. Won DB Critics Poll, TDWR '72.

LPs: w. Basie, *Straight Ahead; Standing Ovation* (Dot).

JONES, JONATHAN (JO),* *drums*; b. Chicago, Ill., 10/7/11. The star drummer of the Count Basie band of the '30s and '40s pl. w. JATP and Illinois Jacquet in late '40s; Lester Young; Joe Bushkin; Ella Fitzgerald-Oscar Peterson; JATP again in '50s; own gp. in NYC, '57-60. In the '60s he continued to lead his own gps.; also worked w. Teddy Wilson; Claude Hopkins; and Ray Bryant who had been the pianist in his trio. Made several tours of Europe w. JATP. Pl. in Europe w. Milt Buckner '69;

again in '70s. With Joey Bushkin at Michael's Pub '76. Fest: NJF-NY w. Benny Carter's Swingmasters, '72; M. Buckner and tap dancers; also Gretsch Greats, '73; Friends of Eddie Condon and Ben Webster, '74; Newport Hall of Fame, '75; Euro. fests. TV: acting role in *Route 66* episode w. Ethel Waters, Coleman Hawkins, Roy Eldridge; Tribute to John Hammond, PBS, '75.

LPs: *The Drums*, a two-record set in which Jones plays, talks about his life, other drum greats and drumming (Jazz Odyssey); w. Willie "The Lion" Smith; w. Zutty Singleton; w. Milt Buckner (Jazz Odyssey); w. Buckner, *Plays Chords* (MPS); w. Slam Stewart (B&B); reissue w. Basie, *Super Chief* (Col.); w. Jacquet, *How High the Moon* (Prest.).

JONES, ROBERT ELLIOTT (JONAH),* *trumpet*; b. Louisville, Ky., 12/31/08. Continued to lead his own quartet in nightclub engagements. Toured overseas in '70. In residence at Rainbow Room, Sept.-Oct. '75. LPs: w. quartet (Cap.; Decca; Motown); Jonah Jones & Earl Hines, *Back On the Street* (Chiaro.).

JONES, JAMES HENRY (JIMMY),* *composer, conductor, piano*; b. Memphis, Tenn., 12/30/18. Frequent associate of D. Ellington and E. Fitzgerald; acc. the latter, '67-8. Arr. for TV show, *The Strolling Twenties*, CBS, '66. From '69, resident musician and arr. in LA, writing for record dates, TV shows and occasional acc. singer Joe Williams. TV: arr. for *Duke Ellington . . . We Love You Madly*, '73; *Cotton Club '75*. Wrote some arrs. for movie *Shaft's Big Score*. Pianist w. K. Burrell's group, '75; gigs w. guitarist John Collins. Though primarily active as a writer of rare skill, Jones is greatly underrated as a pianist whose gentle touch and harmonic imagination have a character all their own.

LPs: w. C. Adderley, *Big Man; Love, Sex and the Zodiac* (Fant.); w. Burrell, *Ellington Is Forever* (Fant.); w. Harold Ashby, *Born to Swing* (Master Jazz).

JONES, JOSEPH RUDOLPH (PHILLY JOE),* *drums*; also *saxophone, bass; piano, timbales*; b. Philadelphia, Pa., 7/15/23. A key figure in modern drumming w. the Miles Davis quintet of the mid-'50s, he then led his own gp. and free-lanced on both coasts. After pl. the Berlin Fest. w. Sarah Vaughan and Erroll Garner, '67, decided to remain in Europe. Living in London, '67-9, he was prevented from pl. by the British musicians union but taught more than 40 students per week at own school in Hampstead. Moved to Paris '69 to teach w. Kenny Clarke. Own gp. for seven weeks at Chat Qui Peche; freelance rec. Worked throughout Europe w. Slide Hampton, Dizzy Reece et al incl. Scandinavia, Vienna TV workshop; then toured w. trio opposite Clarke-Boland orch. in England; on own in Italy; Holland; Yugoslavia w. D. Goykovich. To Stuttgart for clinics; own quintet in Munich nightclub, then three mos. dubbing pictures for film company. Radio shows w. Franz Black orch. in Cologne. Ret. to Phila. '72 and led own quintet. Formed jazz-rock gp. Le Gran Prix, '75 w. Byard Lancaster, pl. for Miss Black America Pageant, Sept. '75, televised by ABC-TV. Fest: Austria w. D. Gordon, B. Webster; Holland. Publ: *Brush Artistry* (Premier Drums). "I love handling rock," he says. "My English students gave me something in return for my teaching them to play modern and read like hell." LPs: *Trailways Express* (Bl. Lion); w. H. Mobley, *No Room for Squares; The Flip* (BN); A. Shepp; M. Waldron (Byg); w. T. Dameron, *The Arrangers' Touch*; w. M. Davis, *Workin' and Steamin'* (Prest.); tracks w. own gp. in *The Big Beat* (Milest.).

JONES, QUINCY DELIGHT JR.,* *composer, leader, trumpet, keyboards*; b. Chicago, Ill., 3/14/33. From the mid-60s Jones extended his work in the areas of film and TV writing. Among his best known movie scores were *The Getaway; The New Centurions; The Hot Rock; $; The Anderson Tapes; They Call Me Mister Tibbs; Cactus Flower; John and Mary; The Out of Towners; Bob & Carol & Ted & Alice; MacKenna's Gold; The Split; For Love of Ivy; In Cold Blood; In The Heat of the Night; Banning*. Animated films: *Eggs; Of Men and Demons*, both for John and Faith Hubley. TV: themes for many shows incl. *Sanford & Son*; themes and other music for Bill Cosby shows. One of Jones' most celebrated credits was the CBS special, *Duke Ellington . . . We Love You Madly!*, presented in early '73.

Jones was arranger and conductor for the 43rd Annual Academy Awards presentation in '71. He won the Oscar for Best Original Score, *In Cold Blood*, '67. Many other awards and nominations, among them Grammies for *Walking In Space*, as best jazz performance by a large group, '69; *Smackwater Jack*, best instrumental, pop, rock or folk performance, '72; *Summer in the City*, best instrumental, '73. Other awards from Johnson Publ., DB Critics Poll. Billboard, Dutch Edison award for *Walking In Space*, '69; Antonio Carlos Jobim Award for best arranger, Brasil International Song Festival, '67.

After many years in the studios, Jones emerged to make intermittent personal appearances, sometimes with Roberta Flack, also on his own, leading an orchestra with vocal group. His music gradually became more concerned with the use of electronics and with the incorporation of r & b and soul elements. In '74 his album *Body Heat* was designated a gold record, representing sales of over $1,000,000.

In the fall of '74 Jones suffered two brain aneurisms. Two serious operations kept him on the sidelines until March '75, when he reassembled an orchestra and toured Japan.

Jones and his friend Ray Charles, whom he had known since they were both teenagers in Seattle, in '71 brought to reality a longstanding ambition as Jones introduced an orchestral piece, *Black Requiem*, showing the struggle of blacks in the U.S. from the days of the slave ships into the late 20th century. The work was performed with the Houston Symph. Orch., Ray Charles and an 80 voice choir.

LPs: *Gula Matari; Body Heat; You've Got It Bad Girl; Smackwater Jack; Walking In Space* (A & M); *Great Wide World; Live at Newport 1961* (Trip); *Mode* (ABC); *Quintessence* (Imp.); film scores *For Love of Ivy* (ABC); *In Cold Blood* (Colgems); *In The Heat of the Night* (UA).

JONES, ISHAM RUSSELL II (RUSTY), *drums*; b. Cedar Rapids, Iowa, 4/13/32. Greatnephew and godson of bandleader Isham Jones. Parents both were pro. musicians. Stud. at U. of Iowa, '60-5. While in school pl. w. J.R. Monterose. In Chicago w. pianist Judy Roberts, '68-72. Joined Geo. Shearing quintet Jan. '72 and remained with him through '75. Also pl. brief stints w. L. Konitz, M. Allison, Monty Alexander, Ike Cole, Eddie Higgins.

LPs: w. Shearing, *As Requested* (Sheba); *The Way We Are; Continental Experience* (MPS); *Get Off In Chicago* w. Judy Roberts (Ovation); *Quartescence*, w. Warren Chiasson (Van-Los Music, Canada).

JONES, SALENA (Joan Shaw),* *singer, songwriter*; b. Newport News, Va., 1/29/30. Well known under the name of Joan Shaw in r & b, pop and jazz circles in U.S. from late '40s until mid '60s, when she moved to England, changing her name to Salena Jones. In Britain and on the continent she enjoyed fuller acceptance as a jazz artist. Pl. Birmingham, England JF; Jazz at the Maltings, '68; winner of song fests. at Knocke, '70, representing America, and at Gmunden, Austria, rep. Britain, '72. Star guest at Golden Orpheus Song Fest., Bulgaria, '73; concert at Royal Albert Hall, London, '75. TV: many programs for BBC and ITV, incl. *Variety Artist of the Year; Jazz At The Mill*; George Melly show; Les Dawson show etc.

LPs: none available in U.S. except one track on *Singin' The Blues* (MCA); in Europe, *The Moment of Truth; Everybody's Talkin' About Salena Jones; Platinum* (CBS); *Alone & Together; This & That* (RCA).

JONES, SAMUEL (SAM),* *bass, cello, composer*; b. Jacksonville, Fla., 11/12/24. Played w. C. Adderley; D. Gillespie; T. Monk in '50s. Rejoined Adderley in late '59 and remained w. him until early '66 when he replaced Ray Brown in the Oscar Peterson trio. World tours w. Peterson incl. JATP. Left in '69 to settle in NYC. Gigs w. B. Timmons; W. Kelly in early '70s; Thad Jones-Mel Lewis quintet. With Bass Choir from '69; Cedar Walton trio and quartet from '71. Many TV apps. w. Peterson; Bass Choir; C. Terry. Fest: NJF-NY; major European events. Won a Musician of the Year award in Copenhagen, '69. Comp: *Seven Minds; Blues For Amos; Miss Morgan; In Walked Ray; Unit 7; Lillie; Del Sassar*. Excellent accompanist with strongly walking lines full of apt, powerfully resilient notes; adept soloist on both bass and cello. Own LP: *Cello, Again* (Xanadu); LPs: w. Peterson, *The Greatest Jazz Concert in the World* (Pablo); *Mellow Mood; Motions & Emotions; The Way I Really Play* (MPS); w. C. Jordan, *Glass Bead Games* (Strata-East); w. S. Stitt, *Constellation; Tune Up* (Cobblestone); *The Champ; 12*; w. C. Walton, *A Night at Boomer's*, vols. 1&2; *Breakthrough* (Muse); w. C. McPherson, *Siku Ya Bibi*; w. M. Longo, *Matrix* (Main.); w. R. Garland, *Auf Wiedersehen* (MPS); w. L. Thompson, *I Offer You* (Groove Merchant); w. J. Heath (Xanadu).

JONES, WILMORE (SLICK),* *drums*; b. Roanoke, Va., 4/13/07. The former Fletcher Henderson, Fats Waller sideman was active in the New York area w. Scoville Brown, Eddie Durham in early and mid-'60s. He survived a serious illness in '64 to play again but died in NYC, 11/2/69.

JONES, THADDEUS JOSEPH (THAD),* *fluegelhorn, cornet, trumpet, composer, leader*; b. Pontiac, Mich., 3/28/23. With Count Basie '54-'63; Gerry Mulligan; George Russell, '64. Wrote for Harry James, Basie in '60s. In '65 formed a quintet w. Pepper Adams and in December put together an orchestra with Mel Lewis made up of some of the best New York-based jazzmen, ones who were mainly employed as busy studio players, much in demand in the then, very busy NY recording scene. Although the band had, and continues to have fun, its intent from the beginning was serious in the sense that it was not planned as merely a rehearsal outfit designed to meet once a week to let its members get their kicks. It did meet once a week—Monday night at the Village Vanguard to be specific—and soon acquired a loyal following which packed the club each time it appeared. Recordings widened the audience and the Jones-Lewis orch. began to play college dates and fests. out of NYC. Eventually it graduated to extended engagements, both at the Vanguard and in California; five European and three Japanese tours; one to USSR, '72.

The early personnel included Adams, Jerome Richardson, Jerry Dodgion, Joe Farrell and Eddie Daniels, reeds; Richard Williams, Snooky Young, Jimmy Nottingham and Marvin Stamm, trumpets, Bob Brookmeyer, Garnett Brown, Tom McIntosh, Cliff Heather, trombones; Hank Jones, piano; Richard Davis, bass; and Sam Herman, guitar. Roland Hanna took over the piano bench by the band's second album and remained until '74; Eddie Bert was in the trombone section for several years and so was Quentin Jackson until he became ill in '75. Seldon Powell and Frank Foster were heard on tenor sax.

In '75 veterans Dodgion, Adams, Heather and trombonist Jimmy Knepper were still aboard along with players such as Jon Faddis, Cecil Bridgewater, trumpets; Janice Robinson, Bill Campbell, trombones; Billy Harper, Ron Bridgewater, Ed Xiques, reeds; Walter Norris, piano; and George Mraz, bass. Dee Dee Bridgewater was the featured vocalist in the '70s until Juanita Fleming replaced her in '75.

Although writers like Garnett Brown, Tom McIntosh and, particularly, Brookmeyer, helped build the book in the band's first years, the majority of the charts are originals by Jones, an extremely personal writer and a master of subtle voicings who uses flutes, reeds and muted brass ingeniously. "I try to write for each individual and think of the musicians personally," says Jones. "You have to gear your writing to two different people and still retain your overall technical sound."

Jones leads the band, interspersing his piquant, harmonically rich fluegelhorn solos among the arranged segments to advantage. Miles Davis once said, "I'd rather hear Thad Jones miss a note than hear Freddie Hubbard make twelve." In between the orchestra's engagements, Jones and Lewis sometimes lead a small group for gigs in the NYC area.

TV: stereo simulcast produced by KCET on Channel

28 and KBCA-FM in LA, '75.

Jones won DB Critics poll as arranger, TDWR, '67. Jones-Lewis Orch. won DB Critics poll, TDWR, '66; best band, '74-5; DB Readers poll, '72-5; *Playboy* All Stars' All Stars, '75.

Comp: *Mean What You Say; Bossa Nova Ova; No Refill; Once Around; Three and One; Don't Ever Leave Me; Little Pixie; Don't Git Sassy; Mornin' Reverend; Kids Are Pretty People; The Waltz You "Swang" For Me; Say It Softly; The Second Race; 61st and Rich' It; Forever Lasting; Love to One; Greetings and Salutations; Fingers; A Child is Born; Dedication; Us; Tiptoe; It Only Happens Every Time; Ahunk Ahunk; Consummation; Tow Away Zone; Quietude; Big Dipper; Central Park North; Suite For Pops; Yours and Mine; Quiet Lady; Blues in a Minute; All My Yesterdays.* LPs: w. Jones-Lewis, *Potpourri* (Phila. Int.); *Suite For Pops* (Horizon); *Consummation* (BN); *Central Park North; Monday Night; Live at the Village Vanguard; Presenting* (SS); *Thad Jones-Mel Lewis*, double-album reissue of material from above LPs (BN); Thad Jones-Pepper Adams, *Mean What You Say* (Mile.); Thad Jones w. Swedish Radiojazz Group, *Greetings and Salutations* (Four Leaf Clover); w. Dexter Gordon (Prest.); Kenny Burrell (Fant.).

JORDAN, CLIFFORD LACONIA,* *tenor sax*; also *piano, flute*; b. Chicago, Ill., 9/2/31. To NYC from Chicago in late '50s, working w. Horace Silver; in '60s w. K. Dorham; M. Roach; Mingus. Toured Europe as soloist and cond. own music for radio and studio orchs there, '66; toured West Africa and Middle East for US State Dept., '67. In '68 formed Frontier Records; rec. Wilbur Ware, Pharoah Sanders, Cecil Payne, Charles Brackeen, Ed Blackwell and their gps. Moved to Europe, '69, pl. there and in Africa during that yr. Returned to US, '70, and led own gp. in clubs. Completed prod. of '68 recs. and released them in the Dolphy Series on Strata-East label. In the '70s he cont. to lead his own gp.; also gigs w. Cedar Walton trio. Toured Western Europe, Scandinavia; NYC public school concerts, '75. Taught reed instrs., flute and cond. bands for Jazzmobile School; participated in lecture-concert series in NYC public schools for Jazz Interactions. Music consultant for MUSE, '67; Mus. Dir. of first Dancemobile, '68. Faculty member at Henry St. Settlement. Played the role of Lester Young in *Lady Day: A Musical Tragedy* at Brooklyn Acad. of Mus., '72. TV: *Jazz Adventures*, '75. Fest: NJF, '73. Won award from *Art Direction* magazine for album cover design, '74. Does portrait photography of musicians. Comps: *Prayer to the People; The Highest Mountain; Vienna.* Writing music for animated TV feature, *Sofro's Great Adventure.* LPs: *Firm Roots* (Steeple.); *Night of the Mark IIV; A Night at Boomer's, Vol. 1&2* (Muse); *In the World; Glass Bead Games* (Strata-East); reissue material on *Blowing Sessions* (BN).

JORDAN, IRVING SIDNEY (DUKE),* *piano, composer*; b. Brooklyn, N.Y., 4/1/22. Played w. Charlie Parker quintet in '40s; Stan Getz quintet in '50s. In '70s occupied mostly w. duo gigs at a variety of NY area clubs such as Gerald's; Bradley's; Golden Fleece; and Churchill's. Toured in Norway, Denmark, Sweden and Holland, '73 and '74. Pl. concert w. Al Haig in Belgium, '74. Concert w. own quintet at Cami Hall, NYC, '75. One of the most individual of the pianists to come out of the bebop era. In a time when most were overwhelmed by Bud Powell, he stood out with his own touch and rhythmic attack while working in a similar harmonic area. An excellent accompanist and a master at introductions. TV: Sweden. Comp: *Jordu*, which has become a jazz standard; *No Problem; Flight to Jordan; Two Loves; Tall Grass; Flight to Denmark; Lady Dingbat; Night Train From Snekkersten; Do You Want to Be Wu'tless; Subway Inn; 32nd Street Love.* LPs: *Flight to Denmark; Two Loves* (Steeple.); *Murray Hill Caper* (Spotlite); *Brooklyn Brothers* w. Cecil Payne (Muse); *Jordu* (Prest.); w. Clark Terry (Vang.); S. Stitt (Muse); Charles McPherson (Xanadu); Reissues w. C. Parker (Spotlite).

JORDAN, KEVIN, *trumpet*; b. Chicago, Ill., 2/26/51. Entire family active in gospel music. Stud. at high school and coll. in Chicago. BME from Northwestern U., '73; also stud. w. D. Byrd, '73; Bunky Green, '73-4, and pl. w. Green summer of '73 in Montreux. Traveled w. S. Kenton orch. Jan. '74- . Jordan names Green as his greatest insp. but was also infl. by Clifford Brown, D. Gillespie, F. Hubbard.

LPs: w. Kenton, *Chicago; Fire, Fury and Fun* (Creative World).

JORDAN, LOUIS,* *singer, alto saxophone*; b. Brinkley, Ark., 7/8/08. One of the first outstanding musicians to gain popularity as an entertainer and r & b personality, Jordan continued working intermittently, living in LA and leading a new version of his Tympany Five combo until Oct. '74, when he was sidelined by a heart attack while working in Sparks, Nev. He died 2/4/75 in his LA home after suffering a second attack.

Some of Jordan's world-renowned hit recordings were incorporated into an album of new interpretations, made for the Blues Spectrum label two years before his death. Among them were *Choo-Choo-Ch'Boogie; Caldonia; Let The Good Times Roll; Saturday Night Fish Fry; Ain't Nobody Here But Us Chickens; I'm Gonna Move to the Outskirts of Town.* Jordan rec. a similar album, using some different songs, for the Black and Blue label during a visit to France in Nov. '73. The orig. versions of many of his best recordings, made in the '40s and early '50s, were reissued in a two-pocket LP on MCA 2-4079. App. at NJF-NY, '74.

JORDAN, SHEILA (Sheila Dawson),* *singer*; b. Detroit, Mich., 11/18/29. Stud. piano '40-1; harmony and theory w. L. Tristano, '51-2. Sang during school years; later, strongly infl. by C. Parker, she was part of a trio that made up words for many of Parker's tunes. During '50s she was married to pianist Duke Jordan. Discovered by George Russell, she made her first LP in '63. Won DB Critics Poll, TDWR, '63. Pl. NYC clubs, also records and concerts w. Russell. Toured Europe, '65-6, again '69-

70, appearing in many concerts, clubs, radio and TV shows. During '67-8, back in NYC, she perf. in concerts w. Don Heckman jazz group, rec. TV commercials etc. Starting '65, she perf. special worship services (jazz liturgies) at many churches and college chapels, also sang at Cornell, Princeton, N.Y.U. and many other univs.

In 1972 she did the sound track for CBS *Look Up and Live* prog., made apps. w. Lee Konitz, Roswell Rudd. Continued working w. Rudd off and on, '73-5. Artist-in-residence at City Coll., CUNY, '74, teaching course in jazz singing.

Better known in Europe than in the U.S., Jordan has been praised by critics for her flexibility, emotional projection and jazz feeling. LPs: *Portrait of Sheila* (Blue Note); *Flexible Flyer* w. Rudd (Arista); *Escalator Over The Hill* w. Carla Bley (JCOA); *Outer Thoughts* w. Russell (Mile.).

JORDAN, JAMES TAFT,* *trumpet, singer*; b. Florence, S.C., 2/15/15. Featured prominently w. Chick Webb in '30s; Ella Fitzgerald; Duke Ellington in '40s; Benny Goodman in '50s. Free-lancing in NYC from '60s. Pl. for Broadway musical, *Hello Dolly*. Took part in *Salute to Ella Fitzgerald* at NJF-NY '73; Louis Armstrong Tribute w. NYJRC, '74. Pl. once a week at West End Cafe w. Earle Warren, '75. LPs: in *Swing Today* series for Albert McCarthy (Eng. RCA); E. Fitzgerald at Newport (Col.).

JPJ QUARTET, see Jackson, Oliver; Johnson, Budd.

KAMINSKY, MAX,* *trumpet*; b. Brockton, Mass., 9/7/08. After pl. w. own gp. at Metropole, Eddie Condon's in mid-'60s, he app. often at Jimmy Ryan's in late-'60s. Visited London, '70. Subbing on Sundays for Roy Eldridge at Ryan's in mid-'70s. LP: *Max Kaminsky, USA, Meets Barrelhouse Jazz Band, Vienna* (Kurier).

KAMUCA, RICHARD (RICHIE),* *tenor, alto saxophone, flutes*; also *clarinet, oboe, English horn*; b. Philadelphia, Pa., 7/23/30. Pl. w. S. Kenton, W. Herman, M. Ferguson, '50s; Shelly Manne in Hollywood, '60-1, then spent nine years in NYC. Worked with R. Eldridge quintet, '66-71, also w. G. McFarland, G. Mulligan band, Z. Sims-Al Cohn, J. Rushing.

Returned to LA in '72, as member of Merv Griffin TV show orch. Became active again in local jazz circles app. w. B. Berry LA Big Band, occasionally led combos at jazz concerts and co-led quintet w. Blue Mitchell in '75. Visited NYC, briefly, to play w. Lee Konitz, spring '75.

LPs: w. G. McFarland (Impulse); S. Manne (Contemporary); Bill Berry (Beez).

KAROLAK, WOJCIECH, *organ, piano*; b. Warsaw, Poland, 5/28/39. Professional debut, '58, pl. saxophone w. Jazz Believers; later switched to piano w. J. Matuszkiewicz quintet. Led own trio from '62, backing most foreign artists who visited Poland during next three years. Lived in Sweden from '66-72, pl. dance music. Returning to jazz, as organist, freelanced around Europe, pl. w. Red Mitchell, Putte Wickman, drummer Leroy Lowe and others. In Dec. '72 he moved to Switzerland, joined Michal Urbaniak's Constellation; pl. clubs, fests. in West Germany, Scandinavia, Belelux countries. After a year returned to Poland to form cooperative trio. In '74 went to U.S. to work w. Urbaniak's new group, Fusion. Back in Poland, co-led a group, Mainstream, w. J.P. Wroblewski. Member of Polish Radio Studio Jazz Orch. as soloist and composer-arranger. Infls: Ch. Parker, Ellington, Miles Davis, Gil Evans. Fav. organist: Larry Young. Fests: Newport-NY, '74; Cascais, '74 w. Z. Namyslowski; numerous others throughout Europe, incl. Jazz Jamboree in Warsaw, from '58. Publ: *Jazz Comps, for Piano* (Polish Music Publ. Co., Cracow, Poland).

LPs: *The Karolak Trio* (Muza); *Moving South* (Record Club of a Polish Jazz Soc'y.); *Easy!; Mainstream* (Polskie Nagrania/Polish Recording Company); others w. Don Ellis, Annie Ross, Urbaniak, Wickman et al.

KATZ, RICHARD AARON (DICK),* *piano, composer, producer*; b. Baltimore, Md., 3/13/24. Pl. w. O. Pettiford; K. Dorham; J.J. Johnson-Kai Winding in '50s; Philly Joe Jones; Orch. USA; Helen Merrill in '60s. In '66 freelanced w. Roy Eldridge; Bobby Hackett; founded Milestone Records w. Orrin Keepnews. From '67-71 worked at Milestone as producer and/or A&R man; cont. to free-lance as pianist. Left Milestone to return to full-time play., although he prod. two Jim Hall albums for the company: worked w. Lee Konitz quintet, '72. In July '73 joined R. Eldridge sextet at Jimmy Ryan's and has pl. w. him there from that time. Toured Japan w. Konitz under NJF aegis, '73. Pl. w. Konitz trio at Gregory's, '74-5; toured Europe w. Konitz-Kai Winding quintet, '74.

Taught jazz history course at New School for Social Research, '73-4. TV: CBS News at opening of Saxophone exhibit at Jazz Museum, NYC, March '74 w. Budd Johnson, Kenny Davern, Sonny Stitt, etc.; Berlin JF w. Konitz-Winding, Oct. '74. Other fest: NJF-NY w. Konitz, '73-4; w. Teo Macero all star saxophone ensemble, '74.

Wrote essay on Art Tatum for booklet acc. *Smithsonian Collection of Classic Jazz*; liner notes for Milestone; Atl. Comp: *Checkerboard; Second Thoughts; Something to Sing; Peacemeal.* Wrote many arrs. for Helen Merrill and all star group. LPs: w. Merrill, *The Feeling is Mutual; A Shade of Difference*; w. Konitz, *Lee Konitz Duets; Peacemeal; Satori* (Mile.). Katz also produced these albums.

KAWASAKI, RYO, *guitar, composer*; also *piano, electric bass*; b. Tokyo, Japan, 2/25/47. Grandfather renowned as a genius of the Japanese bamboo flute. Self-taught. Before coming to the U.S. in '73 he had his own group for more than five years and also was active in studio work. He has since pl. w. Gil Evans, Chico Hamilton, Howard Johnson's Substructure, Joe Lee Wilson, Cedar Walton, Grady Tate, Horacee Arnold, Archie Shepp, and

Tarika Blue. Own duo at Sweet Basil, July '75. Infls: Wes Montgomery, K. Burrell, Jim Hall, J. Hendrix, Mike Bloomfield, Miles Davis, Coltrane, Gil Evans. Designed and constructed his own synthesizer, Feb. '75, which he uses for unusual effects as contrast with a very swift, driving single line. Comps: *Agana; Joni; Nogie; Sweet Tears*. LPs: *Prism* (Easy Wind); *Gil Evans Plays the Music of Jimi Hendrix; There Comes a Time* w. Evans; *Mobius* w. Walton (RCA).

KAY, CONNIE,* *drums*; b. Tuckahoe, N.Y., 4/27/27. With MJQ from '55 until its disbandment in '74. A tasteful drummer, subtle yet authoritative, also noted in the MJQ for his use of triangles and other percussive accouterments. From '74 free-lancing in NYC. Worked w. Balaban & Cats at Eddie Condon's, fall '75. LPs: w. MJQ (Atl., Little David); w. Paul Desmond, *Pure Desmond* (CTI); w. B. Wilber-K. Davern, *Soprano Summit* (World Jazz).

KAYE, CAROL (Carol Louise Smith), *electric bass*; also *guitar, mandolin, bass guitar, banjo, composer*; b. Everett, Wash., 3/24/35. Father was dixieland trombonist; mother, pianist, still playing at 81. Stud. guitar for four months in '48, but says "I've been an active teacher and player ever since." Switched to electric bass in '65. During '50s pl. w. Henry Busse, The Saints, Hampton Hawes, B. Collette, Curtis Counce, H.B. Barnum, O. Coleman. Throughout '60s was in increasing demand for studio work with hundreds of pop, jazz and rock artists. Her full, clear sound and exceptional technique were occasionally heard in strict jazz settings. In '74 she co-led a trio w. Hawes. Later formed her own somewhat more rock-oriented group, Smoke Company, w. drummer Spider Webb. Insp. by C. Christian, B. Kessel, Miles Davis, Jamie Jamison, Ray Brown.

For several years Kaye has had her own very successful publ. company, printing instruction books and folios written by numerous well known musicians, on virtually all instruments.

Publs: *How To Play Electric Bass; Electric Bass Lines* No's. 1, 2, 3, 4, 5; *Personally Yours; Carol Kaye Electric Bass Cassette Course (Gwyn Publ. Co. Inc., 14950 Delano St. Van Nuys, Ca. 91601).*

LPs: w. Hawes, *Northern Windows* (Pres.); w. G. Ammons, *Brasswind* (Pres.).

KEEPNEWS, ORRIN, *record producer*; b. New York City, 3/2/23. Graduated Columbia College '43; Air Force '43-45. A fan and record collector; first pro. involvement with jazz in '48 as editor and writer for *The Record Changer*, published by his college classmate Bill Grauer. The two produced a 10-inch LP reissue series for Victor's "Label X" ('52-'53); founded Riverside Records in '53 with reissue rights to '20s Paramount and Gennett sides (Armstrong, Morton, Oliver, Beiderbecke, Ma Rainey, etc.). First artist he produced was Randy Weston in '54. Riverside rose to prominence with signing of Thelonious Monk in '55. Grauer became business head, with Keepnews as jazz producer. (He also wrote countless liner notes for the label's voluminous album output; wrote for magazines; collaborated with Grauer on *A Pictorial History of Jazz*.) Launched the recording careers of Bill Evans, Wes Montgomery and others, and worked closely with Cannonball Adderley, Monk, Sonny Rollins, many others. When business problems led to bankruptcy of Riverside in mid-'64, following the death of Grauer in Dec. '63, he free-lanced for a while, then established Milestone Records in '66, eventually signing Rollins, McCoy Tyner, Joe Henderson, Lee Konitz, Gary Bartz. In Oct. '72 joined what is now Fantasy/Prestige/Milestone Records, which later also acquired rights to Riverside masters, making him (as v.p. and director of jazz A&R) "one of the very few to last long enough to reissue material I produced in the first place." Considers his major achievement to be "constant association with and contributing to the careers of more than a few true musical geniuses—Monk, Evans, Montgomery, Rollins, Tyner, and many others—and to still be at it in a multi-track electronic era that is a long way from the monaural studios I started in."

KELLAWAY, ROGER,* *piano, composer*; also *bass*; b. Waban, Mass., 11/1/39. After extensive experience as pianist, bassist, composer in NYC, where he worked with every type of group from dixieland to contemporary, Kellaway settled in LA in '66, where he spent nine months with the Don Ellis band. Mus. Dir. for Bobby Darin, '67-9. Scored first feat. film, *The Paper Lion*, '68. Pl. w. LA Neophonic, Apr. '68.

In '69 Kellaway began writing for the cello quartet, a unique group feat. the classical cellist Edgar Lustgarten, with which he appeared in occasional concerts. He was also associated off and on for several years w. Tom Scott, Howard Roberts, Chuck Domanico and John Guerin in small combo jazz work. In '70 he orchestrated *Beaux J. Poo Boo* for L. McCann and the Cincinnati Symph. Wrote ballet commissioned by George Balanchine and the NYC Ballet Co., and premiered in '71. Comp. *Remembering You*, the closing theme for *All In The Family* TV series, '71, and in '72 played, arr. and co-produced the album on which the star of that series, Carroll O'Connor, recorded the song.

The year '73 saw the first rec. of a classical comp. by Kellaway, *Esque*, for trombone and double bass; rec. dates w. G. Mulligan, Tom Scott and others and an app. with the cello quartet at the Ojai Festival. The following year he toured for four months w. Joni Mitchell and T. Scott's LA Express, throughout U.S., Canada, England. In '75 he wrote arrs. for *Supersax Plays Bird with Strings* album; prod., cond. and arr. for C. McRae's first Blue Note album, *I Am Music*.

Kellaway, who from '72 appeared annually at Dick Gibson's Jazz Parties in Colorado Springs, has shown continual growth in the many areas with which he has found time to become associated, in every facet of jazz, pop and classical music. Since his first solo album, *Stride*, recorded in '66, he has demonstrated the capacity for extraordinary excitement combined with phenomenal technique and great sensitivity. As a composer he is best represented in the unique cello quartet albums, which include such original works as *Jorjana #2; Jorjana #7;*

Jorjana #8; Esque; Morning Song; Ballade; Come to the Meadow; Invasion of the Forest; On Your Mark Get Set Blues.

Fests: Ojai, '73; Concord, w. Ellis, '74; Hawaii, w. cello quartet, '75.

LPs: *Center of the Circle; Cello Quartet; Come To The Meadow* (A & M); *Spirit Feel* (Pac. Jazz); *A Jazz Portrait* (Regina); *The Trio* (Prest.); w. S. Rollins, *Music From Alfie*; w. Tom Scott, *Hair to Jazz* (Imp.); w. Melanie, *Born To Be* (Buddah); *Gather Me; Stone Ground Words* (Neighborhood); w. Scott, *Great Scott*; w. G. Mulligan, *Age of Steam*; also w. Baja Marimba Band and other artists (A & M); w. Maria Muldaur, *Waitress in a Donut Shop* (WB); w. Geo. Harrison (Dark Horse).

KELLY, WYNTON,* *piano, composer*; b. Brooklyn, N.Y., 12/2/31. Came to prominence in early '50s w. L. Young, D. Gillespie. Worked w. Miles Davis, '59-63. His trio backed W. Montgomery in person and on records. Later he worked in clubs in NYC, also w. R. Nance quartet. Kelly died 4/12/71 in Toronto, Canada, probably of an epileptic seizure.

Bill Evans said of Kelly: "When I heard him in Dizzy's big band, his whole thing was so joyful and exuberant; nothing about it seemed calculated. And yet, with the clarity of the way he played, you know he had to put this together in a very carefully planned way—but the result was completely without calculation, there was just pure spirit shining through the conception."

LPs: *Full View; Keep It Movin'* (Mile.); *Smokin'* (Trip); w. Dexter Gordon, *The Jumpin' Blues* (Prest.); w. Cecil Payne, *Zodiac* (St.-East); w. Clark Terry, *Cruising* (Mile.); Davis (Col.); Montgomery (Verve).

KELTNER, JIMMIE LEE (JIM), *drums*; also *trumpet*; b. Tulsa, Okla., 4/27/42. Stud. briefly w. Ch. Westgate in Tulsa at age 13, and w. Forrest Clark of LA Philharmonic at age 19. Pl. w. Albert Stinson in Modern Jazz Proteges, '62; Clare Fischer, '64; D. Randi, '65; Afro-Blues Quintet, '66-7; Red Norvo, '66; G. Szabo, '66-70; John Handy, '67. The rest of his playing career has been primarily in the rock and roll area. Films: *Mad Dogs and Englishmen*, w. Joe Cocker, '70; *Concert for Bangla Desh*, '71.

Keltner says, "I'm just a rock and roll drummer who started out wanting to be a jazz musician, and quit when I heard Tony Williams on *Seven Steps To Heaven*."

LP: w. Jack Bruce, *Out of the Storm* (RSO).

KENNEDY, JOSEPH J. JR. (JOE),* *violin, composer, educator*; b. Pittsburgh, Pa., 11/17/23. Ahmad Jamal's chief arr. in the early '60s, he participated in workshops and concerts at Hampton Inst., '68-9 and took part in the Artists Recital Series at Virginia State Coll., '71-2. In '73 Kennedy, who had been the chairman of the music dept. at Maggie L. Walker H.S. in Richmond, Va., was appointed as Supervisor of Music for the Richmond public school system and also as staff member of the Afro-American Studies Dept. at Virginia Commonwealth U. He became a National Board member of the American Youth Symph. and Chorus, '74, and a member of the Educational Committee of the WJA, '75. Comps: *The Fantastic Vehicle; Illusions Opticas; Dialogue for Flute, Cello and Piano.* The latter work was premiered by the Trio Pro Viva and feat. at Fisk U. Arts Fest., '73, and Minnesota Black Composers Symposium, '75. Wrote arrs. for *downbeat* Music Workshop Pub., '70-1. He cont. to pl. w. the Richmond Symph. but has not done any jazz rec. since '65.

KENTON, STANLEY NEWCOMB (STAN),* *leader, composer, piano;* b. Wichita, Kan., 2/19/12. Cal. based bandleader since '41. Became active in jazz educ., '59. Winner of many awards as number one bandleader and for his albums *West Side Story* and *Adventures in Jazz*, both of which won Grammies. Organized series of concerts w. LA Neophonic Orch. at LA Music Center, '65-6. Also in '66 app. as guest conductor of the Danish Radio Orch. in Copenhagen; organized first Kenton clinic for music students at Redlands U., Cal. Estab. Creative World Music Publications to make the Kenton library available to schools.

In '67 Kenton appeared at the Senate Sub-Committee hearings in an attempt to secure revision of music copyright laws. The band toured during the summer and he lectured at major univs., judged at many music fests. Pl. third Neophonic season in '68.

In '70 Kenton estab. Creative World Records as direct mail outlet for Kenton recs., and subsequently for those of many other jazz artists. His band continued to tour. He was sidelined by a serious illness in '71 and again in '72, but the band pl. various engagements under the direction of others.

In '71 Kenton set up a Jazz Orchestra In Residence prog., taking his band to schools for periods ranging from one day to one week. By '75 he was conducting at least 100 clinics annually, as well as four week-long summer clinics on coll. campuses. From '72-5 the band toured Europe and Japan. Kenton app. at NJF-NY, '72, '74, '75. The band was at Monterey JF (during Kenton's illness; it was conducted by arr. Ken Hanna). Honors: Doctorate of Music awarded by Villanova U., '67; Doctorate of Humane Letters, Drury Coll., '74. Named Jazz Band of the Year by Society for the Appreciation of Big Bands, '74.

The Crusade For Jazz, an hour long TV spec., prod. by Kenton in '68, has been widely used. *The Substance of Jazz*, a film designed for educ. was prod. in '69. Kenton also has made many TV apps. as guest on talk shows. Despite many economic reverses due to conditions affecting all big bands, Kenton in the mid '70s still led an ensemble that had a loyal int'l following. Though he has experimented with various instrumentations, the band's basic sound has remained substantially the same in recent years, with arrs. by Hank Levy, Hanna, Bob Curnow. Usually feat. a 10 man brass section, in which five trombones keynote the band's style with their somber sonorities, Kenton has maintained an effective balance between old favorites from his repertoire from the '40s and '50s, and original material, some of it using 5/4 and other meters, some employing Afro-Cuban variations of old numbers such as the original theme *Artistry In Rhythm*, all pl. with a high, spirited bravura.

Publ: *Kenton Straight Ahead* by Carol Easton (William Morrow & Co., N.Y., '73). In addition to providing a well researched history of the Kenton bands through the years, this is a frank and penetrating examination of Kenton as musician, leader and human being.

LPs: Much of the entire recorded output of the various Kenton orchs. has been reissued on the Creative World Label (1012 S. Robertson Blvd., Los Angeles, Ca. 90035). Among the best of his more recent works, Kenton cites: *Live at Redlands University; Live at Brigham Young Univ.; Live at Butler Univ.; National Anthems of the World; Birthday In Britain; 7.5 On The Richter Scale; Solo: Stan Kenton Without His Orchestra; Stan Kenton Plays Chicago; Fire, Fury And Fun.*

KERR, BROOKS (Chester Brooks Kerr Jr.), *piano*; also *clarinet*; b. New Haven, Conn., 12/26/51. Studied piano from age seven, mostly self-taught until lessons w. Russell Repa in New Haven, '61-3. Further stud. in NYC w. Sanford Gold, '64-72; Willie "The Lion" Smith, '69-73; theory at Manhattan School of Music and Juilliard, '70-2; also summer stud. w. Phil Woods, Chris Swansen, Norm Grossman at Ramblerny, '67; w. Valerie Capers at Camp Usdan, '68. Own group at Dalton School, NYC, '66-70; solo piano at Don's East, '71, Vogue Cafe, '72. Led own combo at Churchill's, Feb. '73-April '74 w. shifting personnel incl. Ray Nance, Matthew Gee, Francis Williams, Paul Quinichette, Paul Gonsalves, Bob Mover, Sam Woodyard and vocalists Annie Hurewitz, Betty Roché; at West End Cafe w. similar trios, Jan.-July '74; trio w. Russell Procope and Sonny Greer at Gregory's from May '74. Pl. w. and assisted Duke Ellington at one-week seminar, Univ. of Wisc., July '72; duets w. Willie "The Lion" Smith at Village Gate, Jan. '73; solo at NJF-NY '73. Kerr, an extremely knowledgeable student of the Ellington repertoire, app. at birthday tributes to Duke at the New School '73, and Carnegie Hall w. the NYJRC, '74. He subbed for Duke in the Ellington orch. at the Third Concert of Sacred Music at Central Presbyterian Church, April '74. Infl: Armstrong, Willie "The Lion", Ellington, Tatum, James P. Johnson, Waller. Comp: *A Portrait of Johnny Hodges; Miss Linda; Pepsi Cola Time; A.C.; The Lion's Gait*. LPs: *Soda Fountain Rag*, a duo w. Greer (Chiaroscuro); *Prevue*, feat. Paul Quinichette (Famous Door).

KESSEL, BARNEY,* *guitar, composer*; b. Muskogee, Okla., 10/17/23. Worked w. name bands in early '40s; toured w. O. Peterson '52-3 and has occasionally reunited with him for recordings and concerts. Since late '50s mainly active as freelance studio musician, periodically returning to jazz. Cont. studio work until '68; then went w. Geo. Wein on European tour as member of "Guitar Workshop" w. J. Hall, Geo. Benson, L. Coryell, Elmer Snowden. In '69 moved to London, living there for 14 months, working all over England and continent. Returned to LA late '70, resumed studio work, and working w. own group, moving away from traditional style, experimenting with use of rock infls., but shortly abandoned group and concept. During '70 he began taking short trips all over U.S. and Europe, still continuing in studio work. Very little activity w. own gp., and began spending at least six months a year in Europe for TV, radio, seminars (some of which were sponsored by local gov'ts.), concerts, clubs, fests. Developed open end series of instruction books called *Barney Kessel Personal Manuscript Series*, incl. text as well as music (Publ: Windsor Music Co., P.O. Box 2629, Hollywood, Ca. 90028). TV: Pl. on *The Odd Couple; Love American Style*. Films: pl. on four Elvis Presley movies for Paramount. In '75 spent one month in S. Africa with own gp., also toured internationally as part of *Great Guitars* package. Fests: Concord, '73-4-5; Carnegie Hall, Kennedy Center w. *Great Guitars*, '74-5; Comps: *Swedish Pastry; Salute to Charlie Christian; Down in the Swamp; Sea Miner; From My Heart; Free Wheelin'*.

LPs: *Kessel's Kit; Reflections in Rome* (both rec. in Rome on RCA); three w. S. Grappelli (Polydor); one w. strings, incl. Kessel's arr. of *Nuages* (Phillips); guitar/bass duo w. Red Mitchell, *Two Way Conversation* (Sonet); *The Great Guitars; Barney Plays Kessel* (Concord Jazz); w. Venuti-Grappelli (Byg).

KEYS, CALVIN, *guitar, composer*; b. Omaha, Neb., 2/6/42. His uncle, blues singer St. Louis Jimmy, comp. *Goin' Down Slow*. Stud. at U. of Nebraska. Joined Preston Love in Omaha, '62. After working w. several Hammond organ trios, led by Frank Edwards, Jackie Ivory, Jackie Davis, Jack McDuff, Groove Holmes, Keys settled in LA. He attended LA School of Mus., pl. w. D. Byrd, Ch. Kynard and several singers incl. Gloria Lynne, Damita Jo.

Toured U.S. and Europe w. Ray Charles for a year, '73-4. Moving to SF, he led his own combos and pl. w. John Handy, B. Hutcherson, Johnny Hammond, H. Crawford. Worked w. A. Jamal briefly at Troubadour in LA, '73 and rejoined him on a permanent basis in Jan. '75.

An original and adventurous guitarist, Keys also has shown promise as a composer. Infls: W. Montgomery, K. Burrell, Grant Green, B. Kessel; also Ch. Parker, J. Coltrane et al. Comps: *Shaw-neeq; Gee-gee; BK; Aunt Lovey; Renaissance; Proceed with Caution*.

LPs: *Shaw-neeq; Proceed with Caution* (Black Jazz).

KIKUCHI, MASABUMI, *piano, composer*; b. Tokyo, Japan, 10/19/39. Began piano and theory study in April '45; ten yrs. later entered the comp. dept. of Senior H.S. attached to the Musicology Dept. of the Tokyo Univ. of Art. After grad. in March '58 made debut w. own trio. Pl. w. L. Hampton for concert tour, '62; gave first recital in Tokyo, '64; made tour of Japan w. S. Rollins, '68. In Sept. of that yr. he att. Berklee on a *down beat* scholarship, study. comp. w. Wm. Maroof; musicology and arr. w. Herb Pomeroy. Ret. to Japan and formed trio, later sextet, both w. bassist Gary Peacock, '69. Was guest pianist w. Woody Herman, '70; toured for a month w. Mal Waldron; acc. Joe Henderson, '71. In Jan. '72 he again visited the U.S., joining Elvin Jones, with whom he had pl. at the NJF '70, for four weeks of gigs in NYC & Toronto, and a rec. date. Pl. concerts in Tokyo w. Gil

Evans, McCoy Tyner; acc. Johnny Hartman on tour, '72. Recital, *Sayonara, Poo-sun*, Jan. '73 in Tokyo. Rejoined Elvin Jones in May '73, remaining w. him until Jan. '74, incl. So. Amer. tour for USIS. With Sonny Rollins, Boston, March '74. Concert tour in Japan, June-July '74 w. mixed Japanese-American gp. incl. Terumasa Hino, Joony Booth. Member of NYJRC in its first session. Won first place as pianist in *Swing Journal* readers poll, '68; jazzman of the year, '71; both these categories, combo, and record of the year, '72; best piano; jazzman of yr., '73. Two of his comps. pl. by G. Evans at Carn. Hall, Jan. '74. LPs: Japan Phonogram; Philips; w. E. Jones (BN).

KILLGO, KEITH, *drums, singer*; b. Baltimore, Md., 1/30/54. Began pl. drums at age 9; also stud. w. R. Flack for three years. After graduating from high school, attended Bradley U. in Peoria, Ill. where he majored in mus. theory. While attending Howard U. as mus. educ. major, pl. with such guest musicians as M. Davis, B. Timmons, S. Getz, Woody Shaw, J. Henderson, Rollins. In '73 he became founder member of the Blackbyrds, a coll. group sponsored by D. Byrd. Killgo was feat. as lead singer and drummer. Comp: *Love Is Love*. LPs: *Flying Start; The Blackbyrds* (Fantasy).

KING, RILEY B. (B.B.),* *guitar, singer*; b. Itta Bena, Miss., 9/16/25. The advent of rock which brought about a new interest in and awareness of blues by white audiences gave new popularity to King. He appeared at major pop fests. in US and Canada and played many dates at large colls. during '68-9. In November of that year his band made a 14-city tour of the US w. the Rolling Stones. In the '70s he has made apps. on a world wide basis, playing at both jazz and pop fests.; Las Vegas hotels; and rec. commercials for large corps. and manufacturers. Moved to Las Vegas, '75.

"Thousands of people came to the Rolling Stones concert and discovered B.B. King," wrote Ralph J. Gleason. "They joined the thousands of others led to his music by his disciples, by Mike Bloomfield and Eric Clapton, by Elvin Bishop, and a host of other guitarists whose inspiration and main influence B.B. King has been. All the guitar players in town pay homage to the master of the blues guitar."

Won as Best Blues Instrumentalist; Best Blues Male Singer; and Best Blues Album, *To Know You Is to Love You* (ABC), in *Ebony Magazine* poll, '75. LPs: ABC; Bluesway; one track each in *Newport in New York '72, The Soul Sessions, Vol. 6; Jimmy Smith Jam, Vol. 5* (Cobble.).

KING, FREDDIE, *singer, guitar*; b. Longview, Tex., 9/30/34. Family moved to Chicago in '50, where he worked in local taverns and was associated with the harmonica player and singer, Little Sonny Cooper. Began rec. in '56 for a small independent company; made his first major session for King Records Aug. '60. A guitar solo entitled *Hide Away* became a typical Chicago blues hit in '68. King also made numerous sessions w. pianist Sonny Thompson.

LP: *Burglar* (RSO).

KING, MORGANA,* *singer, actress*; b. Pleasantville, N.Y., 6/4/30. Continued to play supper clubs such as the Maisonette, NYC, but also app. in the motion pictures *The Godfather; The Godfather II*. LPs: Reprise; Main.; Trip.

KIRK, RAHSAAN ROLAND,* *tenor sax*; also *manzello, flute, clarinet, strichophone, trumpet, composer*; b. Columbus, Ohio, 8/7/36. His new name, Rahsaan, came to him in a dream, just as the idea to play three instruments simultaneously had revealed itself previously. Kirk led his Vibration Society in clubs, concerts and festivals throughout the U.S., Canada, Europe, Australia and New Zealand. Fest. apps. incl. NJF, NO Jazz & Heritage, Berlin Jazz Days. He won the DB Critics' Poll, '72-3; DB Readers' Poll, '68, '71, '74; *Playboy* Poll, '71, '73; *Playboy* All Stars' All Stars, '74. TV: *Soul*, '72; *Tempo*, BBC, London, '67. Comp: *Expansions; Saxophone Concerto; Volunteered Slavery; Bright Moments; Dem Red Beans and Rice; Carney and Bigard Place; Blacknuss; The Seeker; Baby, Let Me Shake Your Tree; Lady's Blues; The Inflated Tear; The Black and Crazy Blues*. Although his multi-horn forays, once skeptically viewed as gimmickry, are now taken for granted, Kirk is an amazing improviser, on one, two or three instruments, who embodies the entire spectrum of the music from early New Orleans roots through to the avant garde of the '70s.

In late '75 Kirk suffered a stroke which paralyzed his side. At the onset of his recuperation he began therapy to regain his essential dexterity. LPs: *The Case of the 3-Sided Dream in Audio Color; Bright Moments; Prepare Thyself to Deal With a Miracle; Blacknuss; Rahsaan, Rahsaan; Volunteered Slavery; Left and Right; The Inflated Tear; The Art of Roland Kirk; The Best of Roland Kirk; A Meeting of the Times* w. Al Hibbler; *Mingus At Carnegie Hall* (Atlantic); *The Jaki Byard Experience* (Prest.); reissues: *Kirk in Copenhagen; Domino; We Free Kings* (Trip); *Newport in New York, The Jam Sessions, Vols. 3&4* (Cobble.).

KITAMURA, EIJI, *clarinet, bass clarinet, soprano, alto, tenor saxophones*; b. Tokyo, Japan, 4/8/29. Self-taught. Pl. w. Saburo Nanbu, '51-3; own Cats Herd group, '54-7; Mitsuru Ono & His Six Brothers, '57-60. Led own quintet '60- . From '59 was annual winner of *Swing Journal* readers' poll as number one clarinetist. Infls: B. Goodman, T. Wilson, E. Hines. From '68, Kitamura pl. in the house band of NET-TV *Morning Show*.

LPs: *Operation Benny Goodman*, w. Sharps & Flats (King); *Swingin' Clarinet*, E. Kitamura Quintet (Gramophone); *Immortal Swing Jazz Spirits*, E. Kitamura & All Stars (Teichiku); *Teddy Wilson Meets Eiji Kitamura; Live Session Teddy & Eiji; Teddy Wilson/Eiji Kitamura Swing Special* (Trio); *Right-Oh*, Kitamura & Kazuo Yashiro (Audio Lab.).

KLATKA, ANTHONY J. (TONY), *trumpet, composer*; b. Southhampton, England, 3/6/46. Began pl. prof. at age 11; stud. at Colo. St. Univ. '64-66; Berklee '71-3. Arrs. and trumpet for Wayne Cochran '67; Woody Herman '68-71. While at Berklee pl. in Boston w. many acts incl. Tony Bennett, Dionne Warwicke, 3 Degrees. W. Herman again, spring '73 until Feb. '74, when he joined Blood, Sweat & Tears. Infl: Mike Gibbs, Gil Evans, Ellington, Beethoven, Thad Jones, Miles Davis, Jack Sheldon, Coltrane, Clifford Brown, Chick Corea. Fest: w. Herman, Monterey '70, NJF-NY '73. Comp: *South Mountain Shuffle; Look Up; Thinking of You; She's Coming Home; Blues For Poland*; arrs. for Herman: *La Fiesta; Naima; Watermelon Man; Bass Folk Song*. LPs: w. Herman, *Woody* (Cadet); *Brand New; Thundering Herd* (Fant.); *Mirror Image* w. B,S,&T (Col.); *Ridin' High*, all writing by Klatka, w. Cochran & C.C. Riders (Chess).

KLEIN, MIRIAM, *singer*; b. Basel, Switzerland, 3/27/37. Became involved with jazz at age 16. An admirer of Bessie Smith, Billie Holiday, L. Young, Clifford Brown and Frankie Newton, she spent some time in Paris, where she was heard w. D. Byas and Art Simmons. On returning to Switzerland, she married trumpeter Oscar Klein; the next several years were given over to the birth and raising of four children. During this time she began singing again, working with her husband's group, '64-70. In early albums she sang blues and standards w. O. Klein and Albert Nicholas. Little was heard of her until June '73, when she recorded for MPS-BASF an album entitled *Lady Like*. Backed by R. Eldridge, D. Gordon, S. Hampton and others, she rec. some of B. Holiday's hits with a style and timbre amazingly like Holiday's. The album was provocative, some critics dismissing it as a second rate imitation, while others, incl. Eldridge and other musicians, were greatly impressed by the authenticity of Klein's recreations. Fests: Montreux; Heidelberg; Frankfurt; Munich; Zurich; Copenhagen.

KLEIN, OSCAR, *trumpet, guitar, composer*; b. Graz, Austria, 1/5/30. Self-taught. Insp. by Cootie Williams, Wild Bill Davison, R. Eldridge, and by guitarists Eddie Condon, Blind Blake, Lightnin' Hopkins. Pl. w. Fatty George band, '53-7; Tremble Kids, '58-60; Dutch Swing Coll. Band, '60-3. From '64 led various groups, also pl. w. Mezz Mezzrow, Wild Bill Davison, Albert Nicholas, M. Spanier, J. Venuti. In recent years active mainly as businessman, but still gigging, writing and teaching as a sideline. Married to singer Miriam Klein. TV series, *Pickin' The Blues*, '75. Fests: San Remo, Comblain La Tour, Frankfurt, Dortmund. Publ: *Pickin' The Blues*, finger style instruc. book (Caesar Perrig Editions, Basel).

LPs: *Chicagoan All Stars; Hats Off Eddie Condon; Lady Like* (MPS); *Wild Capricorn*, w. Wild Bill Davison; *Pickin' The Blues* (Intercord).

KLEMMER, JOHN, *tenor, soprano saxes, flute, composer*; also *clarinet, piano*; b. Chicago, Ill., 7/3/46. Began on alto sax at age 11. Led concert and stage band in high school. Stud. at S. Kenton clinics, '60-5; priv. studies w. Joe Daley, '62-9; orchestration and film scoring w. Albert Harris in LA, '70-4. After working w. various bands and combos spanning dixieland, bebop and avant garde, began rec. at age 19. Two years later he moved to LA to join Don Ellis orch., with which he toured the east and west coasts and Europe. Rec. three albums w. Ellis, that feat. solo work and own arrs. During this time he also pl. w. O. Nelson in a State Dept. sponsored tour of French West Africa in late '68, and rec. various albums w. Nelson.

Signed w. ABC/Imp. Records in '70 and during this time became increasingly well known as a practitioner of jazz-rock and innovator in experiments with echo-plex, ring modulator, wah-wah attachments, which he considers to be an integral part of his saxophone sound. "These are not gimmicks," he has said, "but rather instruments in themselves. They are new tools of expression."

Klemmer, many of whose scores have been publ., feels that writing and arranging are just as important to his development as playing the saxophone. One of his major ambitions is to become extensively involved in motion pic. scoring. Infls: Rollins, Coltrane, M. Davis, Debussy, Ravel. TV: *Dial M For Music; Live From Tanglewood*, both in '68 w. Ellis; *Featuring John Klemmer*, a half hour spec. on WTTW, Chicago, '68.

Fests: Newport, Antibes, '68 w. Ellis; Monterey, '70, w. Ellis; Montreux as leader, '73. Comps: Klemmer has written material for all his albums, close to 100 works, among which are *My Love Has Butterfly Wings; Here Comes The Child; Prelude and Waterfalls*. Big band arrs. for Ellis: *The Old Man's Tear*; for B. Bryant, *The Beauty of Her Soul*. Publs: big band charts (Creative World Publs., 1012 Robertson Blvd., LA, Cal. 90048).

LPs: *Involvement; And We Were Lovers; Blowin' Gold; All The Children Cried; Eruptions* (Cadet); *Constant Throb; Waterfalls; Intensity; Magic and Movement; Fresh Feathers*; (Impulse); *Don Ellis at Fillmore; Autumn*, w. Ellis; Don *Ellis Goes Underground* (Columbia); w. O. Nelson, *Soulful Brass; Black, Brown and Beautiful* (Fl. Dutchman); *Born in Mississippi*, w. J. Lee Hooker; *Swahili Strut*, w. B. Bryant (Chess).

KLOSS, ERIC, *saxophones, composer*; also *piano, drums*; b. Greenville, Pa., 4/3/49. Studied saxophone at Western Penn. School for Blind Children, '59-'67; w. Robert Koshan, Henry Marconi, Tom McKinley in Pittsburgh. Grad. cum laude from Duquesne U. with philosophy major, May '72. First pro. app. w. Bob Negri trio at age 12 in Pitts. and pl. there w. Negri at Three Rivers Art Fest., June '62. App. in concert w. Charles Bell at Pitt. Carnegie Music Hall, '62 and '63. Feat. w. Walt Harper during winters of '65, '66, '67. Made rec. debut '65 and has since led own groups; also clubs and concerts w. Pat Martino, Frank Cunimondo. Infls: C. Parker, O. Coleman, Dolphy, Coltrane, Bill Evans, Miles Davis. Many apps. on Pitts. TV, incl. documentary film on his life, '66. Fests: NJF-NY, '73; Pitts. JF. Comps: *In a Country Soul Garden; Sock It To Me Socrates; Cynara; Waves; Quasar; Libra; Licea; Affinity*. LPs: *Essence; One, Two, Free* (Muse); *Doors* (Cobble.); *Consciousness; To Hear Is to See; In the Land of the Giants; Sky Shadows; We're Going Up; Life Force; First Class Kloss; Grits and Gravy* (Prestige).

KNEPPER, JAMES M. (JIMMY),* *trombone*; also *bass trombone, baritone horn, composer*; b. Los Angeles, Ca., 11/22/27. Prominent w. Ch. Mingus, '57-61; USSR w. B. Goodman, '62. From mid-60s played in orchs. of many Broadway shows. Gigged and toured w. Thad

Jones-Mel Lewis orch., incl. USSR, Japan, Europe. Also pl. w. Gil Evans, L. Konitz, N.Y. Jazz Ensemble. Arr. & pl. w. Lee Konitz Nonet in NYC clubs, 1975. An exceptionally gifted soloist, he has been accorded insufficient recognition in jazz circles. Some of his best solos were on the Mingus album, *Tijuana Moods*, reissued on RCA in '75. Other LPs with Mingus (Atl., Col. etc.); G. Evans (Impulse); also see Jones-Lewis.

KOEHLER, TREVOR CURTIS, *baritone sax, composer*; also *soprano sax, flute*; b. Minneapolis, Minn., 7/9/36. Mother pl. country fiddle for square dances. Stud. trumpet, trombone and euphonium at Anchorage (Alaska) Junior high school; then tenor sax at Anchorage High, '50-4; tenor sax and composition at Cons. of Music, Coll. of the Pacific in Stockton, Ca., '54-7. Pl. w. Don Keller & the Blue Notes, '54-7; house band at Jimbo's Bop City in SF, an after-hours where visiting musicians came to sit-in. Took up baritone sax and pl. w. Billy Taylor, Arnett Cobb, Dizzy Gillespie, Hampton Hawes and Anita O'Day there, '57-8. With U.S. Army Band, Stanley Willis Jr. Duo, '58-9; Sonny Simmons sextet, Pharoah Sanders quartet, '60-1. Own groups and various gigs in Bay Area incl. Big Mama Thornton, '62-6. On the road, '66-8, w. Lionel Hampton in NO; midwest territory bands; Eddy Arnold in Tex.; Tenessee Ernie Ford in Little Rock. W. Insect Trust, an eclectic rock band based in NYC, '68-70. Also began working w. Gil Evans at this time. In the '70s continued w. Evans while also pl. w. Sam Rivers, Albert Dailey and on his own, before ending his life 2/26/75 in NYC. Infl: M. Davis, Coltrane, Ch. Parker, O. Coleman, Copland, Debussy. Fest: Memphis Country Blues Fest. '70; European fests., incl. Montreux, and NJF-NY w. Evans '72-4. Won Jazz & Pop poll '70; received a jazz composers' grant from National Endowment For the Arts '72. Comp: *Recourse & Night Flight* for Nat. Endow.; *Amadama; Train Won't Wait; Charlie Chaplin; Ducks; Glade Song*. LPs w. Evans: *Svengali* (Atl.), *Plays Jimi Hendrix* (RCA); *Insect Trust* (Cap.); *Hoboken Saturday Night* (Atco).

KOFFMAN, MOE,* *flute*; also *piccolo, saxophones, clarinets*; b. Toronto, Ontario, Canada, 1/28/28. Pl. w. big bands in U.S., '50-5, incl. Sonny Dunham, B. Morrow, J. Dorsey, C. Barnet, T. Beneke. Ret. to Toronto and rec. hit, *Swingin' Shepherd Blues*, '57. Own quintet for concerts, coll. dates. Mus. dir. and house group leader at George's Spaghetti House. Active as contractor for TV, rec., jingles, films. Group feat. at Expo '67; Maple Mus. Junket, Montreal, summer '72; Fest. Canada, '73; Belvedere "King-Size" JF, '74; Ontario Place Forum, '75. Koffman was guest soloist w. B. Goodman & Q. Jones at C.N.E. '73; w. W. Herman & D. Gillespie, C.N.E. '75; w. Toronto Symph. Apr. '75. TV: guest soloist w. Johnny Carson on six occas.; L. Hampton Special; *Playboy After Dark* tribute to Tony Bennett; mus. dir. for own show, *Everything Goes*, '74. LPs: *Plays Bach; Four Seasons; Master Sessions; Solar Explorations; Best of; Live at George's* (GRT); *Tales of Koffman* (UA).

KOIVISTOINEN, EERO, *saxophones, composer*; b. Helsinki, Finland, 1/13/46. Studied at Sibelius Academy; Berklee Coll. of Mus. Own trio, '67-9; quartet, '69-71; co-led quartet w. Heikki Sarmanto, '71-3; own Music Society (quartet) from '73. Won Finnish Jazz Musician of the Year, '67. Received three-year State grant for Artists, '70. Infl: Ellington, Gil Evans, Coltrane. Led quartet at Montreux JF '69 and won international competition which led to app. at NJF the same year. LPs: *Odysseus; For Children* (Otava); *Third Version; Wahoo!* (RCA Victor).

KOLLER, HANS,* *tenor & soprano saxes*; also *clarinet, sopranino, alto & baritone saxes*; b. Vienna, Austria, 2/12/21. One of the leaders in post-World War II German jazz circles, he continued at the head of his own groups in the '60s and '70s. From '70 it has been called Hans Koller's Free Sound. Originally influenced by Lennie Tristano and Lee Konitz, he later was inspired by John Coltrane. Many apps. on German TV and at European Fests. Won Austrian jazz poll on tenor, soprano and for group, '72. Comp: *Blues Suite; Berlin Suite; Homage A Cocteau; Nicolas De Stael; Circle; Phoenix; Impressions of Vienna; Ulla M; Painter's Lament; Vision*. Publ: *Saxophon-Schule* (Solisten Verlag, Vienna). Since 1957 Koller has also been active as an abstract painter with exhibitions in West Germany, Austria and Paris. LPs: *Exclusiv; Zoller-Koller-Solal; Vision; Relax With My Horns; Phoenix, Kunstkopfindianer* (MPS/BASF).

KOMEDA, KRZYSZTOF (Krzysztof Trzcinski), *composer, piano*; b. Poznan, Poland, 4/27/31. Youngest student at the Poznan Conservatory; later took private piano lessons and stud. mus. theory. From '50 closely associated w. jazz; co-creator of the Polish jazz movement. Played many local fests. w. own gp. as well as Moscow; Kongsberg; Bled; jazz clubs in Sweden and Denmark.

Composed for ballet, musical theater and films incl. directors such as Jerzy Skolimowski, Henning Carlsen and Roman Polanski. Those with the latter incl. *Knife in the Water; The Vampire Killers; Cul-de-Sac*; and *Rosemary's Baby*. Active in jazz-poetry fusion. As songwriter won special award at National Song Fest., Opole, '64.

Komeda, who was injured in an accident in Hollywood in January '69, underwent brain surgery in LA but never regained consciousness. Flown to Warsaw in April, he died a few days later, 4/23/69. The 15th Int. Warsaw Jazz Jamboree, '73, honored him with an entire concert of his music. LP: *The Music of Krzysztof Komeda, Vols. 1-4* (Muza).

KONITZ, LEE,* *alto saxophone*; also *soprano, tenor saxes*; b. Chicago, Ill., 10/13/27. After a brief reunion in '64 for nightclub and concert work w. Lennie Tristano, his mentor and main associate of the '40s and '50s, he worked at the head of his own gps. Also active as a teacher, often utilizing tape for lessons via mail. Played in England and on the Continent '69, and several times during the '70s. In '74 he began playing in two NYC clubs, Gregory's and Stryker's, a few nights apiece on a weekly basis with a trio at the former and a duo at the latter. In the summer of '75 the Stryker's group became a unique nine-piece band which also performed at the Tin Palace.

Konitz remains a highly individualistic improviser, one

who learned from Charlie Parker in the '40s but had his own way even then in a time when everyone was completely under Bird's influence. His playing in the '70s reflects the further development of an already mature style.

Won DB Critics' Poll, TDWR, '69. Films: soundtracks for *A Place for Lovers; Desperate Characters; Cops & Robbers*. Fest: Newport in Japan, '72; NJF-NY '73; Berlin; Basel; Rotterdam, '73; Antibes, '74. Comps: *Hymn; 4th Dimension; Dorian Fanfare; Minor Blue*. Publ: *Jazz Lines* (William H. Bauer, 121 Greenway Place, Albertson, L.I., N.Y.). LPs: *Duets; Spirits; Peacemeal; Satori* (Milest.); *Alto Summit* (BASF); *Altissimo* (Japan. Victor); *Chicago* (Gr. Merch.); *I Concentrate on You; Lone-Lee* (Steeple.); *Stereo Konitz* (Ital. RCA); w. Andrew Hill, *Spiral* (Arista); reissue, *Ezz-thetic* (Prest.).

KONOPASEK, JAN, *baritone sax, flute, composer*; also *reeds, flutes, piano*; b. Prague, Czech., 12/29/31. Great grandfather a music teacher. Grandfather dir. of music school. Mother pl. concert violin and piano; father violin & piano. Classical piano study w. private teacher '38-51. Studied at Berklee Coll. on scholarship, '71-3. Worked w. Karel Krautgartner orch., Studio 5, S&H Quartet and Quintet in Czech., '57-65; w. radio & TV Jazz Orch. of Station Free Berlin, '68-71. Member of Stan Kenton's "Berlin Dream Band," '69; Oliver Nelson's "Berlin Dream Band," '70. In '73-4 w. Woody Herman in U.S., Canada, Europe & Asia. Moved to NYC July '75. Sat-in w. Thad Jones-Mel Lewis Orch. Infl: Krautgartner, Jancy Korossy, H. Silver, G. Mulligan, S. Rollins, Clifford Brown, Thad Jones, J. Henderson, Laco Deczi, Leo Wright, H. Pomeroy, Mike Crotty. Film: *Prague Blues*. TV: w. Woody Herman, London '74. Pl. background music for cartoon shorts by Gene Deitch. Fest: Lanscrona, Sweden, '63-4; Copenhagen; Bled; Budapest; Berlin Jazz Days w. Kenton '69, Nelson '70; MJF w. Herman '73. Montreux, Pori, Trans-Canada w. Herman '74. Comp: *Anchee Suite; Granma's Inventions; Herbes, Pommes & Roi; Deuce Bleuce; Tropic of Cancer; What Happened at the Picture Gallery*. These led to the Richard Levy award for arr. & comp. at Berklee, '73. LPs: many on Supraphon label in Czech. as leader and sideman, late '50s-early '60s; w. Nelson, *Berlin Dialogue for Orchestra* (Fly. Dutch.); w. Herman, *Thundering Herd; Herd at Montreux* (Fant.).

KOVERHULT, TOMMY, *tenor sax*; also *flute, alto, soprano, baritone saxes*; b. Stockholm, Sweden, 12/11/45. Self-taught. Began pl. prof. in '67, app. w. Don Cherry, Eje Thelin and others. With Bernt Rosengren from '67, app. annually on TV, incl. film *A Place to Play At*. Fests: many in Sweden; also Molde; Antwerp w. Thelin; Warsaw w. Jan Wallgren's Orch. Won two awards from *Orkester Journalen*. Does a little teaching. LP: *Notes From Underground* w. Rosengren.

KRAL, IRENE,* *singer*; b. Chicago, Ill., 1/18/32. Former W. Herman and M. Ferguson band vocalist. Living in LA, she freelanced occasionally in S. Cal. during '60s and '70s and was heard on several records (see below). Married to trumpeter Joe Burnett. Singer Jackie Cain is her sister-in-law and Roy Kral is her brother.

LPs: *Where's Love*, acc. by Alan Broadbent (Choice); *Better Than Anything*, acc. by Junior Mance Trio (Ava; deleted); *Wonderful Life* (Mainstream); *My Fair Lady*, w. S. Manne; *Guitar from Ipanema*, w. L. Almeida (Cap.).

KRAL, ROY JOSEPH,* *singer, piano, composer*; b. Chicago, Ill., 10/10/21. In '74 celebrated silver anniversary with wife, Jackie Cain (q.v.). Their professional association began in '46 before joining C. Ventura combo, '48. Left April '49 to form own group, Jackie & Roy. Kral prod., wrote and sang in many TV commercials, '62-9. In '60s and '70s active w. wife in clubs, fest. and TV apps. Comps: *The Way We Are; Niki's Song; Good And Rich; Waltz For Dana; A Wilder Alias*, all incl. in LP, *A Wilder Alias* (CTI). For other LPs see Jackie Cain.

KROG, KARIN,* *singer*; b. Oslo, Norway, 5/15/37. Active in clubs, TV and festivals throughout Europe. Pl. and rec. w. Don Ellis Orch. and Clare Fischer trio in LA, '67; concerts w. European All Stars at World-Expo, Osaka and other cities in Japan. State Grant Study tour of USA, incl. perfs. in NY and Mass., '70. Concerts at Illini JF, U. of Illinois, '72. Concert tour of Norway, '73, England and Scotland with Synthesis and Richard Rodney Bennett. In '74 took course in TV production, doing freelance work for Norwegian TV; produced various jazz progs. for them, and three jazz workshops for NDR-Hamburg. Won DB Int'l Critics' Poll, TDWR, '69. Her *Some Other Spring* was voted Best Vocal Jazz Record of the Year in Japan, '71. Inspired by Billie Holiday and others, she has developed into one of Europe's most original jazz singers. Worked briefly in Hollywood May '75.

Own LPs: *Jazz Moments; Joy; Some Other Spring* (Sonet); *Open Space* w. European All Stars (MPS); *Gershwin + Krog; You Must Believe In Spring; We Could Be Flying* (Polydor).

KRUPA, GENE,* *drums*; b. Chicago, Ill., 1/15/09. First achieved fame in B. Goodman band, '35-8. Led own big band almost continuously from '38-51, after which he usually worked as leader of a trio or quartet, occasionally rejoining Goodman for special concerts and TV shows.

One such reunion took place during the NJF-NY, '73. By this time Krupa, whose health had been frail for years, was suffering from leukemia. He died 10/16/73 at his home in Yonkers, N.Y.

Krupa, without question, was the first musician in jazz history to attract mass popular attention to the role of the drummer. Quoted in DB, Max Roach said: "The kind of exposure that he gave to the instrument opened up the door for people to look at men like Chick Webb . . . he was more than just another student of black music, like most folks are; he was also a contributor." Teddy Wilson, long an associate of Krupa in the Goodman trio and quartet, said: "He was undoubtedly the most important jazz drummer in the history of jazz music. He made the drums a solo instrument, taking it out of the background." Buddy Rich, Roy Haynes and many others, including drummers such as Beaver Harris who represented a much later school, joined in tribute to Krupa as a powerful force whose musicianship and personality remained unique throughout his career.

LPs: *Drummin' Man* (Col.); *Gene & His Orch; Sidekicks* (CSP); *Essential; Verve's Choice* (Verve); w. A. O'Day, R. Eldridge (Col.); others w. Goodman (RCA); *Jazz at the New School* (Chiaro.).

KUDYKOWSKI, MIROSLAW, *guitar*; b. Ludwigsburg, Germany, 9/20/48. To US in 1949. Raised in Linden, N.J. Stud. w. Harry Leahy. Freelanced in NYC, sometimes with own groups; worked w. Lonnie Youngblood, 1969-71; toured as member of Les McCann group, Mar. 74- . Fests: Newport, Berkeley. LPs: *Another Beginning* w. McCann (Atl.).

KUHN, JOACHIM KURT, *piano, composer*; also *alto sax*; b. Leipzig, E. Germany, 3/15/44. Brother is clarinetist Rolf Kuhn. Stud. piano and comp. w. Arthur Schmidt Elsey '49-61. Debut concert '49 playing music of Robert Schumann. Continued to give classical concerts until '61 when he became professional jazz musician with the S & H Quintet; own trio '62-6; co-led quartet w. brother in Hamburg, '66-9; own group in Paris '69-71. Pl. w. Jean-Luc Ponty Experience, '71-2; Joachim Kuhn-Eje Thelin group '72-3; Association P.C. '73-4, incl. TV and radio, and tours of Asia, N. Africa, Portugal, Spain. Apps. w. own group and as soloist, '74. Fests: Newport, Montreux and many others throughout Europe. Inspired by Franz Schubert, Miles Davis, John Coltrane. Won *Jazz Forum* poll from '70. Comps: *Paris 71/72* for piano and orch.; *Piano Solos*, 1-12. LPs: *Boldmusic; Piano; This Way Out; Chinemascope; Open Strings* w. J.L. Ponty; *The Association Plus Jeremy Steig; Mama Kuku; Connection 74* w. R. Kuhn (MPS); *Impressions of New York*, Rolf & Joachim Kuhn (Imp.).

KUHN, STEPHEN LEWIS (STEVE),* *keyboards, composer*; b. Brooklyn, N.Y., 3/24/38. After pl. w. K. Dorham, Coltrane and Getz in early '60s, joined Art Farmer in July '64 and worked w. him and w. own trios through '66. From '67 to May '71 lived in Stockholm and pl. w. own trio for concerts, TV, radio, rec. throughout Europe. Ret. to NYC, May '71, working w. own quartet. Also rec. jingles, etc. Fests: Pori, Finland; Molde, Norway; Stockholm; Berlin. Comp: *Silver; The Child is Gone; A Change of Pace; Life's Backward Glance; Thoughts of a Gentleman; The Baby; The Sand House; Something Everywhere; Memory; Pearlie's Swine*. LPs: *October Suite* (Imp.); *Trio '67* (Prest.); *Live in New York* (Cobble.); *Trance; Solo Piano* (ECM-Poly.).

KUNSMAN, ROMAN, *alto, tenor saxes, flute*; b. Kuibishev, U.S.S.R., 12/7/41. Studied at various music schools and, from age 17, alto sax w. Gennady Goldstain. Lead alto w. Anatolij Kroll big band, '62-3. Pl. at Leningrad jazz club, '64; own gp. at Leningrad JF, '69. Left Soviet Union for Israel '70 and has led his own Platina Jazz Group from that time, app. at NJF-NY, '74. Infl: C. Parker, S. Rollins, J. Coltrane, Goldstain. LP on the Israel label.

KYNARD, CHARLES E.,* *organ, composer*; also *piano, tuba*; b. St. Louis, Mo., 2/20/33. Freelance work in LA during '60s. Kansas City JF; cross-country jazz and religious concert tour, '67-8. Scored mus. for film, *Midtown Madness*, '69. Mus. supervisor and actor in movie, *Love Sweet Love*, '74. For more than a decade Kynard has been teaching mentally retarded children for the county of LA, while continuing his career in many night clubs and touring annually for both jazz and religious audiences.

"Kynard will be around long after many of the organ glamour boys are gone"—DB, '73.

Own LPs on Mainstream, Pres.; as sideman w. *Night Blooming Jazzmen*; Blue Mitchell; Paul Jeffrey (Mainstream).

LA BARBERA, JOSEPH JAMES (JOE), *drums*; also *piano*; b. Dansville, N.Y., 2/22/48. Parents musical. Pl. w. father and brothers, Pat and John (q.v.) in family band. Father taught him drums, saxophone and clarinet which he pl. through high school. Stud. drums w. Alan Dawson at Berklee, '66. First prof. job w. Sam Noto-Joe Romano quint. in Buffalo, '66; Chuck Israels trio, '66; Frankie Randall '67. After Army duty, '68-70, was w. Gap Mangione for six mos. in '70 before joining Woody Herman in '71 for a year. With Chuck Mangione, '72- . Infl: M. Davis, Coltrane, Shelly Manne, B. Evans, C. Mangione. TV: *A Day in the Garden* w. C. Mangione, PBS. Fest: NJF-NY w. Herman '73; NJF-NY, MJF, Pori, Pescara w. C. Mangione. LPs: *The Raven Speaks* w. Herman (Fant.); *Land of Make Believe* w. C. Mangione (Merc.); *Chase the Clouds Away* w. Mangione (A&M); *Once I Loved* w. Esther Satterfield (Sagoma); w. Gerry Niewood (Sagoma).

LA BARBERA, JOHN, *trumpet, piano, composer, arranger*; b. Warsaw, N.Y., 11/10/45. Brother of Joe and Pat (q.v.). Started pl. at five w. family band. Stud. incl. Berklee Coll., Eastman Sch. of Musc. Led 18 pc. college band. Tpt. w. Buddy Rich band '68. Toured England w. Tony Bennett. Tpt., pno. w. Glenn Miller band under B. De Franco, touring Europe, Far East. During this time studied and transcribed old Miller band arrangements. After leaving De Franco, became B. Rich's principal arr. for three years. In 1975, writing for Rich, W. Herman, C. Basie, B. Watrous, L. Biviano., also marketing high school and college stage band music through Life Line Press of Agoura, Cal. Teaching jazz arr. course at Alfred U., Alfred, N.Y., and writing book on arr. techniques.

Insp. by Clifford Brown, Kenny Dorham and arrs. Gil Evans, Bill Holman, LaBarbera in the early '70s became one of the most respected new arrangers, solidly rooted in the jazz orchestral tradition. Comps: *A Piece of the Road Suite* and *Sassy Strut*, rec. by Rich; *Dichotomy* rec. by Watrous.

LPs: *A Different Drummer; Rich in London; Stick It* w. Rich (RCA); *Roar of '74* w. Rich (Groove Merchant); *Manhattan Wildlife Refuge* w. Watrous (Col.).

LA BARBERA, PASCEL (PAT), *tenor sax, soprano, alto, clarinet, flute*; b. Mt. Morris, N.Y., 4/7/44. Brother of John, Joe (see above). Stud. w. father from '52; Berkelee, '64-7; also w. J. LaPorta, J. Henderson, other priv. teachers. Best known as soloist w. B. Rich band, '67-73; also pl. w. L. Bellson, W. Herman and own group. W. Elvin Jones from '75. Many TV apps. w. Rich in U.S., London and continent. Fests. w. Rich incl. Monterey, Newport, Concord. Living in Toronto in '75. Infl. by Coltrane, Rollins, Henderson, I. Sullivan, J. Romano. LPs: w. Rich, *Different Drummer; Stick Up; Rich In London* (RCA); *Keep The Customers Satisfied* (World Pacific); *The Roar of '74* (Groove Merchant).

LACY, STEVE (Steven Lacritz),* *soprano saxophone, composer*; b. New York, N.Y., 7/23/34. Played w. Cecil Taylor; Gil Evans in '50s; Thelonious Monk; then own gp. in NYC during '60s. Moved strongly into free improvisation in mid-'60s in Europe, Buenos Aires, NYC, Germany. From '67 has spent three yrs. in Rome; five yrs. in Paris w. trips to Portugal, Holland, Italy, Japan. Has led own trios, quartets, sextet, big bands (briefly) and quintet. Also gave solo concerts in France, Italy, Germany, England. Some teaching and lecturing. Films: shorts in Rome; *Free Fall*, US; *Alfred R*, Zurich. Fest: Amougies; Louvain; Ghent; Toulouse; Nancy; Rotterdam; San Remo; Nurenberg; Moers; Krefeld; Berlin '71. Pl. Jazz in the Garden at Museum of Modern Art, summer '67. *Melody Maker* wrote that he "has always been a deceptively straightforward kind of player, making brilliant use of clean lines and economy . . . in any company . . ."

Comp: *Tao*, cycle for voice and quintet; *The Woe*, melodrama for quintet and tape; *Garden Variety*, ballet for gp. and tape; *The Sun*, litany for sextet and voice; *Clangs*, five songs for two voices and sextet; *Shots*, eight pieces for sextet. LPs: *The Gap* (America Musidisc); *Avignon Solo; The Crust* (Emanem); *Scraps; Lapis; Dreams* (Saravah); *Flakes* (Italian RCA); *The Forest and the Zoo* (ESP); w. Cecil Taylor, *In Transition* (BN); w. Mal Waldron, *Hard Talk* (Enja).

LAINE, CLEO, *singer*;* b. Southall, Middlesex, England, 10/27/27. Name at birth Clementina Dinah Campbell. Prof. debut with John Dankworth Seven, then w. his big band from '53. Married Dankworth '58. Firmly established from 1956 as a *Melody Maker* poll winning singer, she left the band in '58 to branch out in theatrical ventures as actress, opera and musical comedy singer. First stage app. was in *Flesh To A Tiger*. Title role in Ibsen's *Hedda Gabler*; starred w. Robert Morley in *A Time to Laugh*; played both Hippolyta and Titania in West End prod. of *Midsummer Night's Dream*. Took over role from the ailing Lotte Lenya in Brecht-Weill *Seven Deadly Sins* at Edinburgh Festival, also playing this part at Sadlers Wells.

In addition to one acting part in the film *The Roman Spring of Mrs. Stone*, Laine sang on soundtracks for *The Servant, The Criminal* and other films. Though continuing to win jazz polls, she gave Lieder recitals, was starred w. London Symphony Orch., and from 1971-3 played Julie in the London revival of *Showboat*.

She and Dankworth continued to appear together intermittently, but never in the U.S. until the fall of 1972, for a concert at Alice Tully Hall. Each subsequent appearance in America was played to bigger audiences in larger halls, incl. Carnegie Hall, Santa Monica Civic Aud., '73; Hollywood Bowl, '74 etc. The Dankworths made their night club debut at the Rainbow Grill in the fall of '73. Early in '75 they taped a TV special at Royce Hall in UCLA, Los Angeles. They also appeared at NJF-NY, '75.

Concurrent with the U.S. concerts, Laine's albums began to be released in the U.S. Her popularity grew as critics in London, New York and Los Angeles hailed her not only as an astonishingly original jazz artist, but as the greatest living all-around singer.

John S. Wilson of the New York Times attributed to Laine a voice "richly colored in the lower range, brilliantly articulate when she tops into falsetto and fantastically agile in the areas between. She went from exuberant jazz vocalizing to whirlwind duets with Dankworth's saxophone (with a precision that was several steps removed from the casual solo scat singing of Sarah Vaughan or Ella Fitzgerald) to the very varied demands of poems, set to Dankworth's music, by Eliot, Donne, Shakespeare, Spike Milligan (the English comedian) and Ogden Nash. She sang Bessie Smith and Noel Coward, back to back, giving each a warm understanding but coloring both with something that was herself."

The consummate artistry of Cleo Laine gained invaluable support from the collaboration of her husband in the roles of musical director, alto saxophonist, clarinetist etc. (see DANKWORTH, JOHN). Along with her incomparable musicianship, she brings to her work, when it is appropriate, the rare qualities of humor and satire.

LPs: *I Am A Song; A Beautiful Thing; Live At Carnegie Hall* etc. (RCA); *Day By Day* (Stanyan); *Cleo's Choice* (GNP-Crescendo).

LAINE, GEORGE VITELLE (PAPA JACK),* *drums*; b. New Orleans, La., 9/21/1873. Laine, a drummer and blacksmith, whose career was interrupted when he fought in the Spanish-American war in 1898, was active in pre-jazz NO music and counted Nick LaRocca of the Original Dixieland Jazz Band among his many proteges. Laine continued in music until the late '20s. The subject of a '64 show on national educ. TV, he died of pneumonia 6/2/66 in NO.

LAIRD, RICHARD QUENTIN (RICK), *bass*; b. Dublin, Ireland, 2/5/41. Began pl. in Auckland, N.Z., 1959. Moved to Sydney, Australia, pl. w. Don Burrows, Erroll Buddle (Austr. Jazz Quartet), Mike Nock. Later, in London, stud. at Guildhall Sch., '63-4; free-lanced w. J. Dankworth, T. Hayes, Ronnie Scott; house band at Scott's club '64-6. Emigrated to US, stud. at Berklee Coll. '66-8. Worked in Boston w. Ch. Mariano, Phil Woods, Z. Sims. Toured w. B. Rich band for 1½ yrs. 1969-70, then returned to London. Joined John McLaughlin June 1971 to form Mahavishnu orch., remaining until it disbanded 12/31/73. Free-lancing in NYC '74-5 w. J. Abercrombie, Nock, etc.

Favs: R. Brown, P. Chambers, P. Heath, S. La Faro. Though a fine upright bassist, Laird switched to elec. in 1968 "for practical reasons." First rec. comp.: *Stepping Stones* w. Jan Hammer, on *Like Children* (Nemperor).

LPs: *Inner Mounting Flame; Birds of Fire* w. Mahavishnu (Col.); B. Rich, *Live* (Liberty); Horacee Arnold (Col.).

LAKE, OLIVER, *alto saxophone, composer*; also *flute; synthesizer*; b. Marianna, Ark., ca. 1944. Family moved to St. Louis when he was one. Interested in music at very early age. Played cymbals and bass drum in drum & bugle corps. Became involved w. alto sax, '60, after hearing Paul Desmond record. First strong infl. was Jackie McLean. In '68 his band evolved into BAG, the Black Artist Group which is a St. Louis parallel of Chicago's AACM. Worked in Paris '72. Gigs w. Ambrose Jackson; Leo Smith. To NYC, '74. Experimenting w. synthesizer. Comp: *While Pushing Down Turn; Owshet; Heavy Spirits; Movement Equals Creation; Altoviolin; Intensity; Rockets*. LPs: *Heavy Spirits* (Arista); Paris rec. (New Music Dist. Services).

LAMARE, HILTON (NAPPY),* *guitar, banjo, elec. bass, singer*; b. New Orleans, La., 6/14/10. Best known as member of original Bob Crosby orch. and of many reunion groups w. Crosby since band broke up in 1942. In late '60s and early '70s, occasional work w. Crosby, Abe Most, John Best; banjo in combos at Disneyland and on soundtrack for film *The Great Gatsby*. Concerts at Wilshire Ebell Th., LA, w. Legend of Jazz. Soundtrack work for commercials and Phil Harris feature at Disney studios, 1974-5.

LAMBERT, DAVID ALDEN (DAVE),* *singer, vocal arranger*; b. Boston, Mass., 6/19/17. A pioneer in bebop vocals, and in the art of scoring vocal group arrangements based on jazz comps. and solos, Lambert was best known as a member of the Lambert, Hendricks & Ross trio, which achieved national prominence in '58. They remained together until '63, when Yolande Bavan replaced Annie Ross. Lambert left the group two years later, briefly led a quintet of his own, and starred in a short jazz film, *Audition*. He was killed in an accident near Westport on the Connecticut turnpike 10/3/66.

LPs: see HENDRICKS, JON.

LANCASTER, WILLIAM BYARD (THUNDERBIRD), *saxophones, flute*; also *bass clarinet, trumpet, piano, singer*; b. Philadelphia, Pa., 8/6/42. Sister, Mary Ann Tyler, has Doctor's in Mus. Ed. from Univ. of Pitts. Studied at Shaw Univ., '60-1; Berklee Coll. of Mus., '61-3; Boston Conserv., '62-4. Stud. mus. ed., '75. Worked w. J.R. Mitchell-Byard Lancaster Experience, from '55; Sunny Murray, '65-7; Burton Greene; Bill Dixon, '66; Sun Ra, '69; McCoy Tyner, '70; own gp., Sounds of Liberation, '71-3; Walt Miller & Co.; Le Gran Prix, co-led w. Philly Joe Jones, '75. Played in France, England, Holland and Belgium in '70s. His gp. pl. at Freedom Games track meet. Le Gran Prix supplied the music for Miss Black America competition, '75; the finals were seen on national TV. Infl: Stanley Clarke, Sonny Sharrock, Darryl Brown, Jeffrey Johnson, Khan Jamal, Bill Meeks. Comp: *Sweet Evil Miss*, ballet-opera in five movements, incorporating solo piano, a rock band and 120-piece orch. LPs: *New Horizons* w. Sounds of Liberation (Dogtown); *It's Not Up to Us* (Vortex); *Us* (Palm); w. S. Murray (ESP; Byg); Burton Greene (Col.); Larry Young, *Heaven on Earth* (BN); Bill Dixon (RCA); Marzette Watts (ESP).

LAND, HAROLD C. JR., *piano, composer*; b. San Diego, Cal., 4/25/50. Father is noted tenor saxophonist Harold Land Sr. Stud. classical music w. priv. teachers; Los Angeles City Coll. '68-70, perf. in coll. band. First pro. engagement at Club Tropicana in LA with own quintet, '66-7. Then w. Wayne Henderson's Freedom Sounds; concerts w. Gerald Wilson orch., '67-8. Continued w. Wilson 68- ; began working in quintet and sextet w. father, app. locally; also w. Kenny Burrell. U.S. tour w. Pharoah Sanders, '75. Land was seen briefly in the movie *Uptown Saturday Night*, and made his first fest. app. at Concord w. Wilson '75. Infls: H. Land Sr., McCoy Tyner, Herbie Hancock, Darryl Clayborn.

LPs: w. Henderson, *People Get Ready* (Atl.); w. Land Sr. *Shoma* (Mainstr.); w. Paul Humphrey, *America Wake Up* (Blue Thumb).

LAND, HAROLD DE VANCE,* *tenor sax, flute, composer*; b. Houston, Tex. 2/18/28. First nationally prominent while touring w. Max Roach-Clifford Brown Quintet, 1954-5. Whenever possible, pl. w. Gerald Wilson orch., 1955- ; the band in recent years also incl. his son, pianist Harold C. Land (see above).

From 1969-71 Land co-led a quintet w. Bobby Hutcherson. Three tours of Europe; clubs throughout US, college campuses US and Canada. Land also pl. annually from '71 w. Tony Bennett in LV. Featured in Bennett-Lena Horne show at Shubert theatre, LA, 1975. Led own quintet, incl. son, from 1972, mostly in and around LA. Awarded a fellowship grant from Nat. Endowment for the Arts to compose a jazz suite, 1975. Still a strong individualist on tenor, Land has also been heard to splendid effect in past few years as a flutist.

Films: *Seven Days in May; They Shoot Horses, Don't They?* TV: *The Jazz Show*, LA, 1971. Festivals: Antibes, Pori, '69; Tunis, Molde, '70; Verona, '72; Bay Area, '74-7.

Comps: *Ode to Angels; De-Liberation; Short Subject; Mtume; A New Shade of Blues; Damisi; Step Right Up To The Bottom; Choma; Peace Maker; Forty Love; Stylin'; The Aquarian.*

LPs: *New Shade of Blue; Choma; Damisi* (Mainstr.); w. Hutcherson, *Head On; Now; Total Eclipse; San Francisco* (BN); *Brown & Roach Inc.-1954* (Trip).

LANDRUM, RICHIE PABLO, *African drums, percussion*; also *African string instruments*; b. New York City, 7/18/39. Mother pl. piano; brothers pl. sax and guitar. Studied percussion at Juilliard. Received music teaching license. Private studies in Afro-Cuban drumming w. Julito Collazo, Patato Valdes, Francisco Aguabella; Haitian drumming w. Tiroro, Alphonso Cimber; Brazilian w. Jose Paulo, Carmen Costa; jazz w. Louis Hayes, Max Roach, Elvin Jones, Charli Persip; African drums w. Saka Acquaye, Ladji Camara, Solomon Ilori, Olatunji.

Worked w. Katherine Dunham; Fred Astaire; Arthur Murray; Roland Wingfield; Bernice Johnson; Laroque Bey; Syvilla Fort; Pearl Primus. App. w. Arundel Opera Theatre, Kennebunk, Maine; Negro Ensemble Co.; Black Arts Theatre, Chicago. Fest: NJF; MJF; w. Randy Weston, Tangier Fest. '72. Infl: Weston. TV: *Soul* w. Leon Thomas; Pharoah Sanders; Merv Griffin; Dick Cavett; Johnny Carson; *Black Perspective*; *Black News*; *Like It Is*. Taught at Leroy and Gloria's Dancing School, St. Croix, V.I.; Laroque Bey Sch. of Dance; in '67, Harlem Y.M.C.A.; Mt. Morris Park Assoc.; Haryou Act Summer Prog., '67-71; Neighborhood Youth Board, Brooklyn, '68-72; Guggenheim Museum Children's Summer Prog., '70-2; NY Board of Educ., '70-2. Makes own African drums and would like to open drum making school in future. LPs: w. Pucho; Groove Holmes; George Braith; Johnny Hammond (Prest.); John Patton (BN); Freddie Hubbard; Stanley Turrentine; Hubert Laws (CTI); Kenny Barron (Muse); Leon Thomas; Gato Barbieri; T-Bone Walker-Joe Turner (Fly. Dutch.); Dinizulu, *Songs and Dances of West Africa; Mystical Africa* (Eurotone).

LANG, MICHAEL ANTHONY (MIKE),* *piano, keyboards, synthesizer, composer*; b. Los Angeles, Cal., 12/10/41. Pl. w. Paul Horn 1964-5. Own trio off and on from '67. MJF w. Don Ellis '67 and Tom Scott '68. From late '60s through mid-70s Lang was constantly in demand for motion picture, TV and recording work in LA area with, to name a few among hundreds, Lalo Schifrin, Q. Jones, Bill Plummer, O. Nelson, J. Klemmer, R. Kellaway, P. Rugolo, Bud Shank, N. Hefti, B. Golson, Dee Barton, J. Mandel. Wrote TV scores for ABC Suspense Theatre, PBS Hollywood TV Theatre. Comps: *Karen's World*, rec. w. P. Horn; *Rural Still Life* rec. w. Tom Scott. LPs: w. Klemmer, *Constant Throb; Fresh Feathers* (Imp.); w. Don Ellis, *Electric Bath; Shock Treatment* (Col.); w. Tom Scott, *Rural Still Life*; B. Plummer & Cosmic Brotherhood (Imp.).

LA PORTA, JOHN D.,* *composer, saxophones, clarinet*; b. Philadelphia, Pa., 4/1/20. Extensive background in jazz and classical music, playing w. W. Herman, C. Mingus, Leonard Bernstein, Igor Stravinsky, Teo Macero. Starting in '59 at the Berklee School (now College) of Music, he gave evening faculty concerts at the Summer Jazz Clinics in addition to playing jazz concerts in the New England area w. Herb Pomeroy. As a teacher, from '62, he was in charge of the instrumental performance dept., with 600 students under his aegis. In '75 La Porta was engaged in a large work called *Tonal Organization of Improvisational Techniques*, combining text and demonstration records.

Publs: *Developing the Jazz Band; A Guide to Jazz Phrasing*, books and records; *Developing Sightreading Skills in the Jazz Idiom; Rock Band Arrangements* (all publ. by Berklee Press, 1140 Boylston St. Boston, Mass. 02215).

LPs: *Berklee Saxophone Quartet* (Berklee Records); *A Jazz Journey*, w. Rusty Dedrick (Monmouth-Evergreen).

LARKINS, ELLIS LANE,* *piano*; b. Baltimore, Md., 5/15/23. Prominent in 1940s at Blue Angel, Cafe Society, NYC. After many years of relative obscurity, Larkins enjoyed renewed recognition in late '60s and early '70s. Acc. Joe Williams, '68, '69 (entertained troops in Germany) and again '72. Worked long engagements at New York clubs, restaurants incl. Gregory's, '72-4; Michael's Pub, The Cookery, '74-5; Tangerine, '75. Toured South America in piano show w. T. Wilson, M. McPartland, E. Hines, '74. Concerts: Left Bank Jazz Society, Baltimore, '72; NY Town Hall, '73; NYU, '74.

Larkins has made many TV appearances with, among others, Father N. O'Connor, Art Linkletter, Joe Franklin, Merv Griffin, Mike Douglas, Rosie Grier, Pat Collins. Festivals: NJF-NY, Baltimore, Seattle, Monterey, '73; Hudson riverboat concerts summer '73, '74.

A favorite of virtually every singer he has accompanied, Larkins works equally well alone or with a rhythm section. His articulation is exceptionally delicate, his harmonic taste is perhaps unmatched, his left hand style subtly rhythmic. He is one of the masters of the acoustic piano, extolled for many years by such admirers as John Hammond, who was associated with many of his recordings, and John S. Wilson.

LPs: *Ellis Larkins Plays the Bacharach and McKuen Songbook* (Stanyan); *Lost In The Wood*, others for McKuen, Sylvia Syms (Stanyan); Helen Humes (Col.), *Stardust* w. S. Stitt (Roulette), *Grand Reunion* w. R. Braff (Chiaroscuro), *Ella Fitzgerald Live at Carnegie Hall* (Col.), and many earlier solo albums for Decca, since deleted.

LATEEF, YUSEF,* *tenor sax, flute, oboe, composer, educator*; also *shennai, bamboo flutes*; b. Chattanooga, Tenn., 1921. After leading own gp., pl. w. C. Mingus; B. Olatunji; C. Adderley in early '60s. From mid-'60s has again led his own bands, touring in the US, Europe, and Japan. Fest: NJF; Bilzen; Kongsberg; Tokyo. Majored in flute and received an M.A. in Music Education at Manhattan Sch. of Mus. Doctorate in Education from U. of Mass., Sept. '75. Associate Professor of Music at Manhattan Community Coll.

Lateef did not want to be included in this book because it is an encyclopedia of jazz and not an encyclopedia of music. This points up two things: that American society has not given the jazz writers and performers the respect and recognition commensurate with their art; and that many of these artists, especially among the black composers and players, are strongly affected by this attitude despite their high degree of artistic achievement. Lateef's music is wide-ranging, encompassing areas long identified with jazz and those associated with "serious" music (an inadequate terminology which further underlines the dichotomy), and "pop" points in between. In whatever directions his many talents are manifest, his exclusion from this volume would be conspicuous.

Publ: stage band arrs.; *Trio for Flute, Piano & Cello; Duet for Two Flutes; Solo for Flute*; book of improvised solos for flute, oboe & saxophone; *Flute Book of the Blues #2*; quartet arr. of *Psychicemotus* (Fana Music, P.O. Box 393, Amherst, Mass. 01002). He also collaborated with Kenny Barron, Bob Cunningham and Albert

Heath in *Something Else*, a book of poetry, philosophical essays, short stories, etc.

Comp: *I Be Cold; Yusef's Mood; Symphonic Blues Suite; Nocturne; Down in Atlanta; Buddy and Lou; Destination Paradise; Kongsberg; Brother; The Poor Fisherman; Below Yellow Bell.* LPs: *The Blue Yusef Lateef; Yusef Lateef's Detroit; Suite 16; The Diverse Yusef Lateef; The Gentle Giant; Hush 'N Thunder; Part of the Search* (Atl.); reissues on Prest.; Imp.; Trip.

LAWRENCE, ARNIE (Arnold Lawrence Finkelstein), *alto & soprano saxophones, composer*; also *tenor & baritone sax, flute, clarinet, conga*; b. Brooklyn, N.Y., 7/10/38. Pl. w. Mat Mathews quartet, '55-6; Rusty Dedrick, '65; Urbie Green quintet; D. Hyman, '65-8; F. Foster band; W. Chiasson-J. Garrison quartet, '66; Doc Severinsen sextet, orch., '65-72; Duke Pearson band, '67-8; Johnny Richards, '68; Chico Hamilton, on and off, from '67- ; NBC Orch., '67-72; Joe Newman quintet, '69-70; Les De Merle, '69; Rod Levitt, '74-5; Blood, Sweat & Tears, '74; Lawrence has been associated w. Clark Terry from '70 when he began pl. w. the trumpeter's small group. He has been w. Terry's Big Bad Band from '73 and has also continued to record and appear w. a group called Children Of All Ages from '66.

Lawrence whose alto work is sometimes reminiscent of Cannonball Adderley, is also capable of playing in a free-jazz style. Infls: Clifford Brown, Johnny Richards, Ch. Parker, Coltrane, Art Tatum. Comps: *Contentment; Gonna Get Some Right Now; Meeting of Two Worlds; Laotian Lament; Universe is God's Sanctuary; Look Toward the Day of Man's Awakening; Swinging on a Sitar; Tell It Like It Is.* Fests: w. Terry, many Euro., '73, incl. Montreux; NJF-NY, Monterey, '74; NJF midwest mini-tour, summer '75. LPs: *You're Gonna Hear From Me; Look Toward a Dream* (Proj. 3); *Inside An Hourglass* (Embryo); w. Hamilton, *The Dealer* (Imp.); *El Exigente* (Fl. Dutch.); w. Severinsen on ABC, RCA, Command; *Mirror Images* w. B,S&T; w. Genya Ravan (Col.); w. Richards, *Aqui Se Habla Espanol* (Roulette); w. Children Of All Ages (Differant Drummer, Embryo).

LAWRENCE, AZAR, *tenor, soprano saxes, composer*; b. Los Angeles, Cal., 11/3/53. Began on violin at five; took up alto at 12 and "became serious at 16." Pl. w. pianist Herbert Baker; Watts Fest.; Dorsey HS jazz band & jazz workshop; after hours pl. w. Candy Finch. In LA worked w. Ike & Tina Turner; from Dec. '72 w. Watts 103rd St. Rhythm Band until he joined Elvin Jones, Feb. '73. Left Apr. '73 and the next month went w. McCoy Tyner. With the pianist's quartet from that time, Lawrence attracted enough attention, as his style became more personalized under the tent of Coltrane's influence, that he soon became a recording leader in his own right. Bob Blumenthal, reviewing *Bridge Into the New Age*, wrote: "The music exemplified by this album is to John Coltrane what hard bop is to Charlie Parker. That's no criticism, for hard bop is some of my favorite music; but once again a younger generation is digesting and simplifying the discoveries of a daring father figure, arriving in the process at a music that is more predictable, more easily comprehensible to the audience, and more overtly rooted in the Afro-American community."

Infl: Coltrane, Rollins, Lateef, Shorter, Black Arthur, Ray Straughter. Lawrence, in acknowledging his points of origin, adds "but my main influence was my parents, who helped me to get instruments and allowed me to practice all night."

Fest: NJF-NY; Montreux; other major fest. w. Tyner. TV: Montreux '73 w. Tyner, NET. Comp: *From the Point of Love; From the Point of Light; Summer Solstice.*

LPs: *Bridge Into the New Age; Summer Solstice* (Prest.); w. Tyner, *Sama Lucaya; Enlightenment; Atlantis* (Mile.); w. E. Jones, *New Agenda* (Vang.).

LAWS, HUBERT,* *flute, composer*; also *saxophones, guitar, piano*; b. Houston, Tex., 11/10/39. After establishing himself in NYC during the mid-'60s w. a variety of top musicians and singers, he reached prominence w. his own group through a series of recordings for Atlantic and CTI and annual Carnegie Hall concerts '73-5. Laws, a member of the Metropolitan Opera orch. '68-73 and an alternate w. the N.Y. Philharmonic '71-4, has recorded works by Bach, Mozart, Ravel, Stravinsky and Satie in a unique manner which reflects his expertise in several areas. He explains that "The classical feeling in my music is more a result of personal taste than educational background."

Concert tours in Europe, Japan, Hawaii, Africa and Canada as well as the U.S. Fests: Berkeley, '72; Newport, '73. Won DB Readers' Poll, '71-4; Ebony Music Poll, '74; Playboy Poll, '75. Comps: *What Do You Think of this World Now?; Let Her Go; No More; A Strange Girl; Shades of Light.* Publ: *Flute Improvisation* (Hulaws Music, 66 W. 94th St., New York, N.Y. 10025).

LPs: *At Carnegie Hall, Crying Song, In The Beginning, Morning Star, Afro-Classic, Rite of Spring* (CTI); *Wild Flower, Flute By-Laws* (Atl.); w. Q. Jones, *Body Heat; Walking In Space* (A & M).

LAWS, RONALD (RONNIE), *tenor saxophone*; also *soprano saxophone, flute*; b. Houston, Tex., 10/3/50. Stud. Steven F. Austin State U.; Texas Southern U. Left Houston, settling in LA, '71. Pl. w. Q. Jones, H. Masekela, K. Burrell; gigged and rec. w. Walter Bishop Jr., Doug Carn. Spent year and a half as member of Earth, Wind & Fire. Formed his own quintet, '75, and during that year began rec. as a leader for Blue Note. An outstanding musician inspired by his brother, Hubert Laws, and by J. Coltrane.

LPs: *Pressure Sensitive* (BN); w. H. Laws, *In The Beginning* (CTI); w. Earth, Wind & Fire, *Last Days And Time* (Col.); w. Bishop, *Keeper of My Soul*; w. Carn *Adams Apple* (Black Jazz).

LAWSON, RICHARD HUGH JEROME,* *piano, composer*; b. Detroit, Mich., 3/12/35. Came to NYC w. Yusef Lateef gp. in late '50s. From '60-8 also worked w. S. Rollins; R. Eldridge; G. Coleman; C. McPherson; Grady Tate; S. Turrentine. From '68 pl. w. Lockjaw Davis; Joe Williams w. Harry Edison-Jimmy Forrest; Joe Henderson; McPherson; Lateef. One of the founding members of the Piano Choir, '72. Own trio from '75; also w. C. Mingus, touring Europe w. him, fall '75. Fest: Watts '70 w. Lateef. Taught comp. and jazz improvisation at Henry St. Settlement House; Nassau County In School Jazz Ensemble, '75. Comp: Watts Fest. theme, '70; *Jaboobie's March; Ballad For the Beasts*; writing *Doom and Gloom*, a piece for seven electric keyboards on grant from NEA. LPs: w. Piano Choir, *Handscapes; Handscapes 2* (Strata-East); w. Roy Brooks (Jazz Workshop); Kenny Burrell, *God Bless the Child*; S. Turrentine (CTI).

LAWSON, JOHN (YANK),* *trumpet, leader*; b. Trenton, Mo., 5/3/11. Many big band assoc. in '30s, '40s w. B. Pollack, B. Crosby, T. Dorsey, B. Goodman. During '50s, co-led Lawson-Haggart Jazz Band for series of LPs. Mainly involved in studio work on staff at NBC in NYC, '50s and through '68, but with frequent jazz jobs at Condon's Club etc. In 1965 a wealthy jazz fan, Dick Gibson, helped organize a group, presented as the Nine Greats of Jazz, for a party at Elitch's Gardens, Denver. Personnel was nucleus of what became, two years later, the group known as the World's Greatest Jazzband of Yank Lawson and Bob Haggart. The band made its first appearance outside Denver in Nov. '68 at the Riverboat in NYC. Members at that time included B. Butterfield, L. McGarity, C. Fontana, B. Wilber, Bud Freeman, R. Sutton, Morey Feld. At concerts, singer Maxine Sullivan was often added.

While some critics found the group's name pretentious, others, among them John S. Wilson, contended that the WGJ, as it was often called, made a viable attempt to justify it. Arrangements, most of them written by Haggart, some by Wilber, gave the band a personal flavor in its original format (nine or ten men); during this period the group enjoyed great successes at concerts, festivals, and in Dec. '71 on its first visit to England. The band also pl. throughout Europe, Mexico, Brazil, Virgin Islands. Financial difficulties over the years led to a reduction to eight and later seven men; by early 1975, after increasingly frequent turnover, death or defection had taken the original members and only the leaders were left; sidemen now were G. Masso, trombone; J. Muranyi, clarinet; Al Klink, tenor; Dill Jones, piano; Bobby Rosengarden, drums.

LPs: Project 3, Atlantic. Later albums on their own World Jazz label (4350 E. Camelback Rd., Phoenix, Ariz. 85108).

LEE, WILLIAM FRANKLIN III (BILL), *educator, piano*; also *trumpet, bass*; b. Galveston, Tex., 2/20/29. B.M., '49, M.S., '50, NTSU, M.M., Ph.D., '56, U. of Tex; also stud. at Eastman School of Music and in France w. Nadia Boulanger. Extensive prof. exp. w. G. Krupa, Ch. Parker, A. Shaw, L. Young, H. McGhee, G. Mulligan and many others. Principally known as one of the foremost figures in the jazz education movement.

Dir. of mus., Sam Houston State U., '56-64; Dean, School of Mus., U. of Miami, '64- ; President, NAJE, '72-4. Dr. Lee, recipient of many awards and honors, is the composer and/or author of numerous published works. Among them are *Music Theory Dictionary; The Nature of Music; Modern Musical Instruments; The Art and Science of Music* (Charles Hansen Pubs., 1842 West Ave., Miami Bch., Fla. 33139); *Mini-Suite for Trumpet and Piano; Interlude for Classical Guitar; Alamjohoba* for concert band (U. of Miami Pubs.); *Suite for Brass* and several other works (Collier-Dexter, Ltd., London); *Spring Carnival* and *Festival* for piano (Southern Music Co., 1740 Broadway, New York, 10019).

LEE, WILLIAM JAMES EDWARDS (BILL), *bass, composer*; b. Snow Hill, Ala., 7/23/28. Mother, Alberta G. Lee, retired concert pianist; father, Arnold W. Lee, trumpet & cornet. Began pl. drums in family band w. brothers and sisters at age eight. Flute at 11. Studied at Snow Hill Inst. In '47 went to Morehouse Coll. in Atlanta, study w. musicologist Willis James; Kemper Harold; bassist "Pepper." Took up bass '50. To Chicago '52. Israel Crosby recommended him for job w. Buster Bennett. Pl. w. Johnny Griffin, Billy Wallace, Clifford Jordan, Andrew Hill, Vernell Fournier, John Gilmore, George Coleman, Frank Strozier et al. To NYC '59 where he worked w. Philly Joe Jones, Phineas Newborn, Ray Bryant and many folk and blues gps. incl. Josh White, Odetta, Theodore Bikell, Judy Collins. Leader-founder of NY Bass Violin Choir '68; co-leader w. B. Hardman & B. Higgins of The Brass Company from '72. Mus. dir. for Muriel Winston's A Fresh Viewpoint. Leader of Descendants of Mike and Phoebe, a family band named for his ancestors from the 1800s and incl. Consuela Lee Morehead, piano; A. Grace Lee Mims, vocals; A. Cliffton Lee, trumpet. Lee has written five folk-jazz operas, parts of which have been performed at the NJF, and for NET: *The Depot; One Mile East; Baby Sweets; The Quarter; Little Johnny* (children's opera). Wrote music for Broadway prod., *Hand is On the Gate*. Comp: *The Rabbi; Monica; Juan Valdez*. Infl: Jimmy Blanton; Consuela Lee Morehead; Charlie Parker. TV: *Today*; Harry Belafonte specials. Fest: NJF, '71; all the Newport Folk Fest.; house bassist for Phila. Folk Fest. LPs: The Descendants of Mike and Phoebe, *A Spirit Speaks*; The Brass Company, *Colors*; w. Muriel Winston; Clifford Jordan, *Glass Bead Games* (Strata East); w. Richard Davis, *Philosophy of the Spiritual* (Buddah), *With Understanding* (Muse).

LEE, DAVID JR., *drums, percussion, composer*; b. New Orleans, La., 1/4/41. Three brothers in NO are musicians: Robert, flute and percussion; Adam, percussion; Joseph, congas and percussion. Started pl. at age 12. Stud. w. Charles Speres in elem. sch.; Yvonne Bush in junior h.s.; Ernest Sacheray; Solomon Spencer in h.s. First prof. job w. Spencer's band, '54. Pl. in NO w. a wide variety of musicians incl. Snooks Eaglin; Nat Perrilliat; George Davis; Alvin Batiste; Earl Turbinton; also 4th Army Band in Texas; 8th Army Band in Korea. In '60s worked w. Willie Tee and the Souls. Co-founded NO Jazz Workshop, '69. To NYC, joining Dizzy Gillespie at Jazz Workshop in Boston, Dec. '69. With Roy Ayers for seven mos., '71; Sonny Rollins, '72-5; Joe Newman from '73; formed own quintet '75.

Infl: Paul Barbarin, Ed Blackwell, Max Roach, Elvin Jones; inspiration: George Davis, Gillespie, Rollins, Coltrane, Joe Newman. TV: w. Willie Tee; Gillespie; Rollins; Ayers; Joe Williams, etc. Fest: NJF-NY; MJF; Nice; Pescara; Kongsberg; Berlin; Middleheim; Antwerp; also toured Italy w. Chet Baker, '75. Drum instructor for Jazz Interactions, '75; also teaching privately. Lectures, seminars and concerts, U. of Conn., Feb. '73. Comp: *In His Presence Searching; Evolution*. LPs: *Evolution*, w. own company (Supernal Records, 62 West 87th St., #3F, New York, N.Y. 10024); w. Rollins (Mile.); Gillespie (Perception); Joe Zawinul; Gary Burton-Larry Coryell (Atl.); R. Ayers (Poly.); Lonnie Liston Smith; Leon Thomas; Harold Alexander (Fly. Dutch.); Pete Yellin (Main.); A. Dailey (Col.); C. Rouse (Strata-East); Alan Braufman (India Navigation Co.); F. Wess (Enterprise); Richard Landry (Chatham Square).

LEE, PEGGY (Norma Deloris Egstrom),* *singer, composer*; b. Jamestown, N.D., 5/26/20. Continued to play major showrooms and concert halls, incl. Kennedy Center and Royal Albert Hall, '71; guest solos with Boston Pops, '74; concert tour of Japan, Apr. '75. Won Grammy award 1969 as best contemporary female vocalist for record of *Is That All There Is?* TV: *A Man and a Woman* w. Anthony Quinn, '72 (was also given screen credit for the concept); Petula Clark, Julie Andrews shows in London; numerous U.S. network variety and talk shows. Comps: lyrics for *The Shining Sea*, music by John Mandel; theme for movie *The Russians Are Coming; The Heart Is A Lonely Hunter; Nickel Ride*, both with music by David Grusin; *Then Was Then and Now Is Now*, music by Cy Coleman; *So What's New*, music by John Pisano.

Lee was awarded a Doctor of Music Honoris Causa degree from N. Dakota State U., '75. A talented artist, she was commissioned by Sylvania to do four paintings for its *Sights & Sounds of the Seventies*, '70; was one of 11 artists whose paintings were included in the Franklin Mint Gallery of American Art Exhibition at Lincoln Center, '73.

LPs: *Is That All There Is?; Make It With You; Where Did They Go?; Bridge Over Troubled Water; Norma Deloris Egstrom* (Cap.); *Let's Love* (Atl.).

LEEMAN, CLIFFORD (CLIFF),* *drums*; b. Portland, Maine, 9/10/13. Veteran of swing era bands, later pl. in many dixieland groups at Eddie Condon's etc. Toured Japan in '67 w. Condon, J. Rushing and group; again in '70 w. R. Norvo, J. Venuti, R. Braff. Pl. w. several groups org. by Dick Gibson at Roosevelt Grill in NYC w. P. Hucko, Venuti, Hackett, Teddy Wilson; also pl. annual jazz parties for Gibson in Colorado and Dr. O.A. Fulcher in Odessa, Tex.; NJF-NY, '74. W. Balaban & Cats at Eddie Condon's, '75. Also worked in Sweden, Iceland, Germany, England, Scotland. LPs: w. Bobby Hackett, *Live at the Roosevelt Grill*; w. Wild Bill Davison, *Live at the Rainbow Room*; w. Venuti-Zoot Sims (Chiaroscuro); *Colorado Jazz Party* (MPS/BASF); w. Condon (Col.); early rec. w. Ch. Barnet (RCA).

LEGRAND, MICHEL,* *conductor, composer, piano, singer*; b. Paris, France, 2/24/32. Began composing for films in late '50s. Received Oscar for *Windmills of Your Mind*, Best Song, '68; second Oscar for Best Original Dramatic Score, *Summer of '42*. During the '60s and early '70s, though principally known as a writer for TV and movies, Legrand occasionally app. in clubs and rec. with jazz groups. His film credits incl. the score for *Lady Sings The Blues*. He is a competent jazz pianist and fair singer who has indulged in a few wordless vocals. Having scored more than 50 motion pictures, many of which have been released in sound track albums, Legrand has nearly 100 LPs to his credit, a few of which are of some jazz interest: *The Umbrellas of Cherbourg*, sound track (Philips); *Legrand Jazz*, feat. Miles Davis (Col.); *Brian's Song* (Bell); *The Windmills of Your Mind* (UA); *Recorded Live at Jimmy's*, feat. P. Woods (RCA); *At Shelly's Manne Hole* (Verve); w. S. Vaughan (Mainstream); *Stan Getz Communication '72* (Verve); P. Woods, *Images* (RCA).

LEONHART, JAMES C. (JAY), *bass*; b. Baltimore, Md., 12/6/40. Brother Bill Leonhart, jazz and classical guitarist, works in SF. Stud. at Peabody School, Baltimore; Berklee, '61-2; Oscar Peterson's Advanced Sch. of Contemp. Mus. '62. Private bass study w. Wm. Curtis, Ray Brown, Orin O'Brien. Began pro. w. brother in banjo duo, '51-5; bass w. Pier Five Jazz Band in Baltimore, '55-9. Took up electric bass. Worked w. Buddy Morrow, '61; Mike Longo, '62-3; free-lance in Baltimore, also acc. Ethel Ennis, '63-7. To NYC '68 pl. w. Urbie Green, '68-70; Marian McPartland, '70-1; Tony Bennett, '71-3; Jim Hall, '73-4; also Thad Jones-Mel Lewis, Barbara Carroll, Zoot Sims, Leslie Uggams, Lee Konitz, B. Rich, G. Bertoncini, Tal Farlow, Sylvia Syms and John Bunch.

Infls: Ray Brown, O. Peterson, Clifford Brown, Bill Evans, Jim Hall, Chuck Rainey, Gil Evans. Comps: *Radials; Kentucky Wild Flower*. TV: *Today* Show w. M. McPartland, Carroll; *Tonight* Show w. James Brown; NET w. Green; staff work on NBC, CBS. Fests: Milwaukee Arts w. McPartland, '73; NJF-NY, Concord w. Hall, '73; NJF-NY '74 w. B. Eckstine; NJF-NY '75 w. S. Syms. LPs: *Delicate Balance* w. McPartland (Halcyon); *Urban Renewal* w. Green (Proj. 3); *Summer of '42* w. Bennett; *Time to Fly* w. David Pomeranz (Col.); *One More Time* w. S. Syms (Atl.).

LEVEY, STAN,* *drums, composer*; b. Philadelphia, Pa. 4/5/25. One of the influential bop drummers of the '40s, Levey was very busy as accompanist to many singers during the '50s and '60s. Apart from writing the scores for a number of educational films, he has now virtually given up the music business to concentrate on photography, and operates his own studio.

LEVIEV, MILCHO, *piano, keyboards, synthesizer, composer*; b. Plovdiv, Bulgaria, 12/19/37. Grad. 1960 from Bulg. State Cons. in Sofia. Leader, comp. & arr. Bulgarian Radio-TV Big Band, '62-6; led jazz quartet, '65-8; to W. Germany, worked w. A. Mangelsdorff '70-71. Emigrated to US Feb. '71. Keyboards, comp., arr. for Don

Ellis orch. '71-4, also Willie Bobo combo Nov. '73-Mar. '74; B. Cobham from March '74. Pl. w. C. McRae, J. Klemmer, Airto, T. Vig, Lee Ritenour et al.

Leviev app. as pianist-conductor w. Sofia Philharmonic '63-8, worked on numerous Bulgarian TV shows and scored nine movies, one of which, *A Hot Noon*, was first Bulgarian jazz film score, '63. Another, *Detour*, won first prize at Moscow film fest. '68. He won medal for comp. at International Comp. Contest, Vienna Youth Festival, '59.

Comps: *Music for Big Band and Symphony Orch.* ('65); *Concerto for Jazz Combo & Strings* ('65; US premiere '72, LA, w. members of Don Ellis band and Westside Symph.). Symphonic, chamber music, many jazz and theatre music works. Publ: *Odd Meters in Bulgarian Folk Music* in *The New Rhythm Book* (Ellis Music Enterprises, 5436 Auckland Ave., N. Hollywood, Cal.).

Leviev writes: "I immigrated to the U.S. seeking the authentic jazz idiom, which I consider the most vital element in music today. I tried very hard to establish jazz in Bulgaria, but without encouraging results. I was president of the Sofia Jazz Club 1967-8. Jazz in Europe—as a movement, not individual musicians—is still more of a snobbery than real necessity."

LPs: *Jazz Focus* '65 (MPS); w. Ellis, *Tears of Joy, Connection*, (Col.), *Soaring* (MPS); *Virginland* w. Airto (Salvation-CTI); *Total Eclipse* w. Cobham (Atlantic).

LEVIN, MARC LEONARD, *cornet, flute, composer*; also *fluegelhorn, mellophone, piccolo, Indian flutes, percussion, melodica, voice, violin*; b. Bayonne, N.J., 8/6/42. Studied trumpet w. Melvin Thompson, '56-7; Alan Jacobs, '57-8; John Ware of N.Y. Phil., '58-9; John Martel, '59-60; William Gerstenberger at Rutgers U., '62-3; theory w. Hall Overton at New School, '64; brass techniques w. Carmine Caruso, '67. From '65-9 stud. trumpet and comp. w. Bill Dixon, whom he considers his greatest influence. Other infl: Clifford Brown, Mingus, Monk, Booker Little, Calo Scott, Christian Kyhl. Worked w. Alan Silva, '65; Dixon, '66-9; Ed Curran, '66-7; Perry Robinson; Burton Greene, '66; own ensemble, '65-73. Moved to Copenhagen, '73, where he leads own group; also pl. w. Cyclamium, '73-4; Annette Peacock, '74. Collaborated w. Mal Waldron in Germany and Scandinavia, '75. MA in Psych. from New School. Works as a consultant in Copenhagen drug programs. Comps: *The Dragon Suite; Songs, Dances and Prayers; Letter to Richard Nixon re: The Chile Affair; Blues For George and Henry*, dance score; *Buttons; The Swing*, film scores. LPs: *Songs, Dances and Prayers* (Sweet Dragon); *The Dragon Suite* (Savoy, Byg); w. Bill Dixon (RCA Victor); Ed Curran (Savoy).

LEVITT, ALAN,* *drums*; b. New York City, 11/11/32. Played w. S. Getz; L. Tristano. L. Konitz, P. Bley in early '50s; w. Bechet; Solal in Paris, '56-58, before returning to U.S. where he worked w. Toshiko, J. McLean, Chris Connor, Dick Haymes. Toured U.S., Europe and Asia w. L. Hampton, '66. Worked in LA w. Georgie Auld; Joe Albany; Teddy Edwards, '67. In '68 rec. for ESP w. members of his family: wife Stella, vocals; son, Sean, guitar, etc. Acc. singers Jackie Paris & Ann Marie Moss, '69; C. Connor; David Allyn, '70. Pl. w. L. Konitz; Z. Sims, '71; C. Mingus, '72. In '73 to Las Palmas, Canary Islands w. family to work at Half Note club. Worked at Whiskey Jazz club in Madrid w. Pedro Itturalde; Lou Bennett; Donna Hightower; toured Spain w. own gp., '74. Moved to Paris '75. Toured Holland w. Peter Ind; concerts w. Slide Hampton; toured Holland, Belgium, England w. Warne Marsh. TV: Holland, Spain w. Lionel Hampton, '66; *To Tell the Truth* w. his family, '68; *Today* w. D. Allyn, '70. App. in film, *Take a Hard Ride*, '75. Fest: San Sebastian w. Itturalde; Newport Fest. in Madrid, '74. LP: *We Are the Levitts* (ESP).

LEVY, HENRY J. (HANK), *composer, baritone saxophone*; b. Baltimore, Md., 9/27/27. Stud. Baltimore City Coll.; Navy School of Mus.; Wm. & Mary; Peabody Conserv.; Catholic U.; Towson State Coll. With S. Kenton band on baritone, '53. Wrote for Sal Salvador orch., '60-2. Many arrs. for Don Ellis, '66- ; Kenton, '69- . Gov't grant to write work, *Opus for Overextended Jazz Ensemble*, premiered by Baltimore Symph., '71.

In '68 Levy sold the family retail business and began a teaching career at Towson. Has also busied himself with many of the Kenton clinics. His coll. band won the Notre Dame fest. '70-1-2; Quinnipiac, '71-2-3, '75. Levy is a scholarly and highly skilled writer, insp. by J. Richards and Don Ellis, who has been particularly effective composing and arranging works in unusual meters. Comps: for Ellis, *Chain Reaction; Whiplash; Passacaglia & Fugue*; for Kenton, *Indra; Ambivalence*. Publ: *A Time Revolution* (Creative World, 1214 S. Robertson Blvd., Los Angeles, Ca. 90035).

LPs: w. Ellis, *Live at Monterey; Live in 3 2/3/4 Time* (Wor. Pac.); *Electric Bath; Connection; Tears of Joy* (Col.); *Soaring* (BASF); w. Kenton, *Live at Redlands; Fire, Fury & Fun; Live at Brigham Young U.; Live from London; Birthday in Britain* (Creative World).

LEVY, LOUIS (LOU),* *piano*; b. Chicago, Ill., 3/5/28. Best known as accompanist for E. Fitzgerald, Peggy Lee for many years and as freelance jazz musician mainly in LA. Worked off and on for Nancy Wilson from '66; jobs w. B. Goodman in late '60s. Joined Supersax New Year's Eve, '73, and was still working with the group in '75.

LPs: w. Supersax, *Salt Peanuts; Supersax Plays Bird With Strings* (Cap.); w. F. Sinatra, *My Way* (Repr.); many P. Lee albums through '73 (Cap.); w. N. Wilson, *Broadway My Way; Hello Young Lovers* (Cap.); w. Chubby Jackson in *Bebop Revisited, Vol. 1* (Xanadu).

LEWIS, GEORGE,* *clarinet*; b. New Orleans, La., 7/13/00. Active as co-leader with Red Allen of own group, and w. Eureka Brass Band in '20s. After a decade of inactivity, he was rediscovered in '42 and became a key figure in NO jazz revival, making several tours of Europe and Japan. Returning home he worked intermittently in NO until shortly before his death there, 12/31/68.

LPs: *Easy Riders Jazz Band; In Japan*, Vols. 1/3; *Ragtime Stompers* (GHB); *George Lewis* (Archive of Folk & Jazz Music); *In Concert* (BN).

LEWIS, JOHN AARON,* *composer, piano, educator*; b. La Grange, Ill., 5/3/20. Prominent in Dizzy Gillespie orch. of mid-'40s; important contributor to Miles Davis nonet '49. Formed Modern Jazz Quartet with Milt Jackson, Percy Heath and Kenny Clarke in '52. In its 22 years (Clarke was replaced by Connie Kay in '55), under Lewis' direction, it became one of the premier units in jazz. During the group's existence it was in the habit on disbanding each year for a summer hiatus but in July '74 the MJQ was permanently dissolved, reuniting only for a concert at Avery Fisher Hall in November. "There really has never been a combination in jazz like the fusion created by the MJQ," wrote Nat Hentoff. "The delicate, almost evanescent lyricism, the sometimes grave, sometimes playful polyphony; and the sure sense of the roots of jazz."

Lewis, a member of the Board of Trustees of the Manhattan School of Music has been teaching at the Davis Center for Performing Arts at City College, CUNY, from '74. In the summer of '75 he taught at Harvard U. He is also a member of the panel for Jazz, Folk & Ethnic Music for the NEA.

TV: Flip Wilson; Helen Reddy; Dick Cavett; *Camera 3*; English & Australian programs. Fest: Tunisia; Gulbenkian Music Fest., Lisbon; Baalbek Music Fest., Lebanon; Geneva; Avignon; Nice; Milan; Pescara. Lewis has also been the music coordinator for the Monterey JF from its inception, working closely w. producer Jimmy Lyons. In '75 he appeared as a solo pianist at NJF-NY, demonstrating his subtle but effective rhythmic thrust and deep feeling for the blues.

Wrote the score for *Cities For People*, a film, shown on KPBS, San Diego, which won a first prize at the SF Film Fest., '75. Other comps: *In Memoriam; Jazz Ostinato; Mirjana of My Heart; Lyonhead; Beach Head.* The last three pieces are included in Lewis' Columbia album *P.O.V.* in which he utilizes violin, cello, flute, piano and percussion in a chamber-like setting. Other LPs: w. MJQ, *Blues on Bach; Plastic Dreams; Live at the Lighthouse; Legendary Profile* (Atl.); *In Memoriam* (Little David).

LEWIS, MEL,* *drums, leader*; b. Buffalo, N.Y., 5/10/29. Worked w. Gerry Mulligan band, Dizzy Gillespie group in '60s. In Dec. '65 he and Thad Jones formed the Thad Jones-Mel Lewis Orchestra, which in the following ten years established itself as what many observers feel is the best big band in the world. (For personnel, polls, etc. see Jones, Thad.) He and Jones also co-led a small group on occasion in NYC area clubs during the '70s.

Lewis is able to swing a big band with a minimum of fuss and a maximum of taste. His abilities as a consummately musical drummer were placed in bold relief when he played unaccompanied in a NJF-NY concert called *Drum Shtick*, '73.

LPs: see Jones, Thad; w. Jones-Pepper Adams, *Mean What You Say* (Mile.); w. Jones and Swedish Radiojazz Group (Four Leaf Clover); w. Al Cohn-Zoot Sims, *Body and Soul* (Muse); w. Jimmy Rushing, *The You and Me That Used to Be* (RCA); w. Bobby Hackett (Fly. Dutch.).

LEWIS, TED (Theodore Leopold Friedman),* *leader, clarinet*; b. Circleville, Ohio, 6/6/1892. The veteran bandleader, some of whose records in the '30s feat. B. Goodman, F. Waller and J. Teagarden, died 8/25/71 of a heart attack at his home in NYC.

LIEBMAN, DAVID (DAVE), *tenor, soprano saxes, flute*; b. Brooklyn, N.Y., 9/4/46. Private studies w. Joe Allard, '62-6; Charles Lloyd, '66-8; Lennie Tristano, '67-8. Worked w. Ten Wheel Drive, '70; Elvin Jones, '71-3; Miles Davis, '73-4. Formed own group, Lookout Farm, '74. Co-founder, in '71, of musicians' co-operative, Free Life Communication, funded by N.Y. State Council on the Arts. Infl: Coltrane, Rollins, M. Tyner, E. Jones, M. Davis, Wayne Shorter. TV: *In Concert* w. Davis, ABC. Fest: Montreux w. Davis; Newport in U.S. and Europe w. Davis; Jones. LPs: *Sweet Hands* (Horizon); *Lookout Farm; Drum Ode* (ECM); *Open Sky* (P.M.); *My Goals Beyond* w. John McLaughlin (Douglas); *Live at the Lighthouse; Genesis* w. Jones (Blue Note); *Get Up With It* w. Davis (Columbia).

LINCOLN, ABBEY,* *singer, actress*; b. Chicago, Ill., 8/6/30. Prominent in late '50s and '60s as collaborator with Max Roach. Starred in film, *For Love of Ivy*, '68. Divorced Roach and moved to LA, 1970. Continued her career as actress and singer, app. on segments of *Mission Impossible; Name of the Game; ABC Movie of the Week*; singing on *Flip Wilson Show; Hollywood Palace* etc. Active in community affairs, also taught drama at Cal. State U., Northridge, 1974. In '75 she assumed a new name, Aminata Moseka. The first name was bestowed on her by the president of Guinea during a visit to that country; Moseka by the Minister of Information in Zaire. Occasional apps. at Parisian Room, other clubs in LA, SF.

LINDBERG, NILS, *piano, composer*; also *organ*; b. Uppsala, Sweden, 6/11/33. Grew up in Dalarna as a member of a long-standing musical family incl. legendary fiddler Kruskorpf Mats Olsson and uncle, Oscar Lindberg, composer, and prof. at the Royal Academy of Music. Stud. music at Uppsala U., '52-6; counterpoint and comp. at Royal Academy, Stockholm, '56-60. While at the Academy perf. as pianist with jazz groups. Lindberg has also app. with the Swedish Radio Symph. and Hanover Symph. during '70s. He was Judy Garland's pianist for her last Scandinavian tour. App. w. D. Ellington's orch. at Malmo and Copenhagen, Oct. '73. Accompanist for Alice Babs in concerts and recs. First made his reputation with arrs. for four saxophones and rhythm sec. on LP *Sax Appeald*, '60, but became more widely known with a suite in three movements entitled *Trisection*, one of the first major Swedish works written for jazz orch. w. soloists, '62. His main infl. is Swedish folklore which he combines w. jazz in his comp. *7 Dalecarlian Paintings*, rec. in '72-3. Other comps. incl. *Lapponian Suite* for clarinet, rhythm sec. and symph. orch., commissioned by Norddeutscher Rundfunk; *Noah's Ark; Dialogue*. Arr.

Far Away Star for Babs' perf. w. Ellington. App. at Stockholm JF, '71 and '73. TV: Five progs. w. Babs; *Concerto 63* for jazz group and symph. orch. commissioned by Eurovision and shown all over Europe. His music for an LP by Jan Allan was awarded the Grammis, Swedish equivalent of the Grand Prix du Disque, '70.

LPs: *Trisection* (EMI); *Jan Allan with Music By Nils Lindberg; Sax Appeald* (Telestar); *7 Dalecarlian Paintings; Music with a Jazz Flavor; Alice Babs Serenading Duke Ellington* (Swedish Society Discofil).

LINN, RAYMOND SAYRE (RAY),* *trumpet*; b. Chicago, Ill., 10/20/20. Veteran of T. Dorsey, Herman, Shaw, Raeburn bands in '40s. Freelance studio work for many years in LA; also lead trumpet w. Lawrence Welk, '66; Pat Boone TV show, '67; lead trumpet/arr. w. Paul Smith orch. on Steve Allen show, '68-9. Toured as lead trumpet/arr. w. Big Band Cavalcade nostalgia show, '72. Led own dixieland band, the Chicago Stompers, in many local clubs, '73- .

LISTON, MELBA DORETTA,* *composer, trombone*; b. Kansas City, Mo., 1/13/26. Prominent in 1940s, early '50s w. C. Basie; D. Gillespie; again w. Gillespie '56-7; Quincy Jones '59-61. Many sessions as arr. for Randy Weston. During 1960s returned to LA, where she had lived during '40s; free lanced as arr. To NYC where she co-led Clark Terry big band and wrote for Duke Ellington; Jon Lucien; Solomon Burke; Tony Bennett; and Buffalo Symphony Orch., '67. Taught trombone at Pratt Institute Youth-In-Action Orch. in Brooklyn, and Harlem Back Street Youth Orch., '68. In '70s divided her time between work w. youth orchs. in Watts, Calif., and arr. for Count Basie, Abbey Lincoln, Diana Ross and Ellington. Moved to Jamaica, where she became teacher at Univ. of West Indies; dir. of popular music studies, Jamaica Institute of Music, Kingston. Film: comp. & arr. music for *The Marijuana Affair*. Fest: NJF-NY w. Weston, '73. LP: w. Weston, *Tanjah* (Polydor); '40s sides w. Dexter Gordon reissued on *Bebop Revisited, Vol. 1* (Xanadu).

LITTLE, WESTON WILBUR, *bass*; b. Parmele, N.C., 3/5/28. Benny Golson is a distant cousin. While in service w. Army Air Corps on Guam, '46, started pl. piano, then switched to bass. Pl. w. small combo in service clubs. In '49 to Washington, D.C. where he worked in Dept. of Interior and pl. w. small gps. incl. Sir Charles Thompson, Leo Parker. Toured and rec. w. Griffin Bros., Margie Day, '49-51; Paul Williams, '51-3. Returned to Wash., and w. own trio backed visiting hornmen such as Miles Davis, K. Dorham, Coltrane, '53-5. Studied w. Joe Willens of Nat. Symph. Pl. w. J.J. Johnson '55-8, touring U.S. and Europe, then back to Wash. again for government work and free-lance pl. w. Sonny Stitt; Shirley Horn; Nina Simone; Roland Kirk, etc., '58-66. During this time also pl. for Left Bank Jazz Society in Baltimore. To NYC, working w. Elvin Jones, off and on, '67-70. Then free-lancing w. Junior Mance; Frank Foster; K. Dorham; K. Burrell. From '70 pl. w. George Coleman-Danny Moore; Tommy Flanagan; Barry Harris; Al Haig. W. Clark Terry, '74; Ellis Larkins, '75. A resourceful soloist and an accompanist capable of pulling his weight in a duo or a big band and anyplace in between. Infl: Ray Brown. TV: *Dial "M" For Music* w. E. Jones; *Like It Is* w. Lucky Thompson, '72; E. Larkins, '75. Film: soundtrack for *The Female Response*. Fest: NJF w. E. Jones; NJF-NY w. C. Terry, '74; Newport in Europe w. Lee Konitz, Kai Winding, etc. Comp: *Whew!; Soul Mama*. LPs: w. E. Jones, *Poly-currents; Coalition* (BN), *Live at the Vanguard* (Enja); w. C. Terry (Vanguard); w. J. Mance (Atl.); earlier ones, most likely deleted, w. J.J. Johnson (Col.); *Tommy Flanagan Overseas* (Prest.); Randy Weston (UA); recent ones w. Konitz; Haig for foreign labels, unreleased.

LLOYD, CHARLES,* *saxophones, flutes, composer*; also *synthesizer*; b. Memphis, Tenn., 3/15/38. Played with Chico Hamilton, '61-4; Cannonball Adderley, '64-5; then own groups. Lloyd was the first jazz musician invited by Russian People's Group to make a tour of the Soviet Union, in '67. Between '66 and '69 he was also seen at fests. in Poland and Czechoslovakia and at MJF. First jazz musician to play the Fillmore Auditorium, '67. Toured Far East for U.S. State Dept., '68. In '69 Lloyd was the subject of an award-winning, 60-minute documentary film, *Charles Lloyd—Journey Within*, by Eric Sherman, seen at the N.Y. Film Fest., Museum of Modern Art, NYC, and on educ. TV. During '70 and '71 his combo pl. concerts in over 100 colleges. From '70-4 he did doctoral work at Cal. Tech., where he was also artist-in-residence, '72-3. In '73 he played the Newport JF in NY. He took part in a poetry-and-music reading in Santa Cruz, Cal., in '74 with Gary Snyder, Allen Ginsberg, Lawrence Ferlinghetti. Toured Canada, '74. Wrote scores for various documentary films, TV commercials, educational film strips.

In addition to playing and teaching music, and continuing to give lectures and workshops at colleges and prisons, Lloyd became a teacher of transcendental meditation. Much of his music in the '70s took on a high energy coloration that proved popular with rock audiences. In '75 Lloyd was living in Malibu, Cal. Comps: *Forest Flower; Sombrero Sam; Passin' Thru'; Transfusion; T.M.* LPs: *Geeta; Waves* (A & M); *Moonman; Warm Waters* (Kapp); *Dream Weaver; Forest Flower; Love-In; Journey Within; Soundtrack; In Europe* (Atl.); *Discovery; Of Course, Of Course* (Col.); earlier LPs w. Hamilton (Repr., Col., Imp.).

LOCKE, EDWARD (EDDIE), *drums*; b. Detroit, Mich., 2/8/30. Studied at Miller HS. Met Oliver Jackson and formed duo, Bop and Lock, singing, dancing and drumming in theaters in and around Detroit. Encouraged by Cozy Cole they app. on bill opposite Arnett Cobb at Apollo, NYC, '54. Remained in NYC and began gigging around. Pl. w. Tony Parenti, Dick Wellstood at Metropole; then w. Roy Eldridge. Worked w. Coleman Hawkins and Eldridge at Metropole, '58. Most often w. Hawkins until his death in '69. In '70s w. Eldridge at Jimmy Ryan's. He credits Roy w. helping him to shape his feature solo on *Caravan*. Has also worked w. Ray Bryant; Red Allen; Teddy Wilson; Kenny Burrell; Earl

Hines. Main infl: Jo Jones. "Locke was too young to have experienced the best days of the Swing Era," wrote Stanley Dance, "but he is unusual in his ability to comprehend and adjust to the requirements of two of its greatest figures, Roy Eldridge and Coleman Hawkins."

TV: *Dial M For Music; Tonight*; Mike Douglas. Fest: NJF-NY. LPs: w. Hawkins, *Today and Now* (Imp.); *Live at the Village Gate* (Verve); w. Eldridge, *Happy Time* (Pablo); w. Lee Konitz, *Chicago* (Gr. Merch.).

LOFTON, LAWRENCE ELLIS (TRICKY),* *trombone*; b. Houston, Tex., 5/28/30. Pl. in school from 1941; high sch. band '43-7; Army band '48-'53. Toured w. Joe Liggins, '53-5; T-Bone Walker, Lowell Fulson, '55-6; Big Joe Turner, many r & b gps incl. Bill Doggett '58; Richard Groove Holmes '61. Toured w. J. McGriff '71-2. Free lancing in LA, w. Bill Berry band '72- , also in SF with Jon Hendricks' *Evolution of the Blues* show. Infls: Hendricks, J.J. Johnson, J. Cleveland, J.C. Higginbotham, Tricky Sam Nanton. Seen briefly in film *Blazing Saddles* w. C. Basie. LPs: *Tricky Lofton Brass Bag* (PJ); w. Doggett, *All Blue* (King); Richard Groove Holmes (PJ); Bill Berry, *Hot & Happy* (Beez); J. Hendricks, *Tell Me The Truth* (Arista).

LONGO, MICHAEL JOSEPH (MIKE), *piano, composer*; also *electric keyboards*; b. Cincinnati, Ohio, 3/19/39. Mother is piano teacher and was church choir dir.; father was bass player active in club-dates. Began playing at age three, taught by mother. Bachelor of Mus. degree from Western Kentucky U., '59. Stud. counterpoint w. Frank Gaskin Fields, NYC, '67-8; composition w. Hall Overton, '71-2. First pro. job with father's band in Fla. at age 15. Worked w. C. Adderley while attending high school in Ft. Lauderdale; various r & b groups in So. Fla. With Hal McIntyre orch., '57; house pianist at Metropole, NYC w. Henry Red Allen, C. Hawkins, Geo. Wettling et al, '60-1. To Toronto Oct. '61 to study w. O. Peterson, working various clubs there until he formed his own trio and returned to NYC, Mar. '62 for jobs at Basin St. E., The Embers, Hickory House etc. Acc. various singers, '62-6. Own trio at Embers West from June '66, backing R. Eldridge, Z. Sims, C. Terry and others. D. Gillespie heard trio and hired Longo, Dec. '66. Became mus. dir. for Gillespie, writing much of the group's repertoire from '68-73. During this period also freelanced in NYC; worked frequently w. J. Moody quartet. Formed own group, '73. Early infls: Sugar Chile Robinson, Basie, Peterson, Garner, Tatum. Many TV and fest. apps. w. Gillespie, incl. Newport, Monterey, Mexico Fest. of the Arts, and throughout Europe and Japan. Won DB Hall of Fame scholarship, '59. Comps: *Shack o Mack; Lay'in It Down* (both rec. by B. Rich); *Soliloquy; Piece of Resistance; The Awakening; 900 Shares of the Blues; Matrix; Ding-a-Ling; Soul Kiss*; string quartet under grant from Nat'l Endowment for the Arts. Publ: *Consolidated Artists Newsletter* (290 Riverside Dr., #11D, New York, N.Y. 10025).

LPs: *900 Shares of the Blues; Funkia* (Gr. Mer.); *Jazz Portrait of Funny Girl* (Clamike); *Matrix; The Awakening* (Mainstr.); w. Moody, *Heritage Hum*; w. Astrud Gilberto, *Now* (Perception); and others w. Gillespie on Imp., Perception, MPS-BASF, Pablo.

LOUISIANA RED (Iverson Minter), *singer, guitar, harmonica*; b. Vicksburg, Miss., 3/23/36. Self-taught. Rec. for Roulette in '62, but did not come into prominence until '70s. Insp. by Muddy Waters and Elmore James, he app. at the Phila. Folk Fest. and in '75 at Montreux. Comps: *Sweet Blood Call; The Whole World* (collab. w. Kent Cooper); *Too Poor to Die*.

LPs: *Lowdown Back Porch Blues* (Roul.); *Louisiana Red Sings The Blues* (Atco); *Sweet Blood Call* (Blue Labor).

LOUISS, EDDY (Edouard Louise), *organ*; also *piano, trumpet, singer*; b. Paris, France, 5/2/41. Father, who came from the Antilles, pl. his ethnic music and jazz w. own dance band in Paris. Mother taught him piano; pl. in father's band. Formed first gp. w. teenage friends. Appeared at Chat Qui Pêche. With Double Six of Paris in early '60s. Active in studio work. Pl. w. Kenny Clarke; Johnny Griffin; Jean-Luc Ponty; Rene Thomas; Stan Getz. Infl: Miles Davis; John Coltrane. TV: France; Germany; BBC. Fest: Antibes; Bergamo; Lugano; Nancy; Montreux. Won DB Critics Poll, TDWR, '68, '71-4; *Jazz Forum* readers poll, '71-2, '74. Comp: *Our Kind of Sabi*. LPs: Musidisc; MPS; America; w. Ponty (Col.); w. Gillespie & Double Six (Philips); w. Getz, *Dynasty* (Verve).

LOWE, FRANK, *tenor saxophone*; also *soprano sax, bass clarinet, flute, piccolo*; b. Memphis, Tenn., 6/24/43. Wife, Carmen Lowe, is flute student. Vocal and piano instruction in elementary school; instrumental music studies w. Tuff Green, band dir. at Melrose Jr. high. Attended U. of Kansas, '61-3; moved to SF where he stud. theory and harmony under Pete Magadini at SF Conservatory of Music. Worked for Stax Records as salesman, music student and part time songwriter, '59, but made switch from r & b to jazz through listening to O. Coleman, Coltrane and Cecil Taylor. Met Sonny Simmons, Dewey Redman and bassist Donald Garrett in SF. The latter instructed him in "the music I had been searching for." To NYC, '66, where he worked w. Sun Ra, eventually returning with him to SF and further studies at the Conserv. With A. Coltrane in NYC from early '70 through '73. When Ms. Coltrane moved to Cal., he remained in NY working w. D. Cherry, Sunny Murray, C. Bley, M. Graves, Rashied Ali, and with own groups. Infls: J. Coltrane, O. Coleman, C. Taylor, E. Dolphy, L. Young, Ch. Parker, Paul Hindemith. Collaborated w. Cherry in the music for Alexandro Jodorowsky's film, *Holy Mountain*; prod. and arr. own film, *Street Music*. Fests: Berkeley, Ann Arbor, w. A. Coltrane; NJF-NY, w. Cherry and own group. Won DB Critics Poll TDWR, '74.

LPs: *Black Beings* (ESP); *Fresh* (Arista); *Alternatives* (Circle); F. Lowe-R. Ali, *Duo Exchange* (Survival); w. Noah Howard, *Live at the Village Vanguard* (Freedom); w. Cherry, *Relativity Suite* (JCOA); three albums w. A. Coltrane (Imp.).

LOWE, MUNDELL,* *composer, guitar*; b. Laurel, Miss., 4/21/22. Originally well known as jazz guitarist, he settled in LA, Dec. '65, working as comp. for films, TV shows etc., among them *Love on a Rooftop; I Dream of Jeannie; The Iron Horse; Wild, Wild West; Hawaii 5-0*. In '69 he served as music supervisor for educ. TV station KCET, comp. most of the music for Hollywood Television Theater; co-produced *Jazz In The Round* for PBS network, also cond. the band, '70; comp. and cond. music for the highly successful motion pic. *Billy Jack*, '72. Left KCET to do extensive freelancing. In '73-4 he arr. and prod. several albums, also resumed playing guitar on jazz gigs around LA, and participated in school clinics and teaching on a visiting faculty basis. Worked in Europe with singer Betty Bennett, '74-5. Night club dates w. R. Kamuca, '75. Pl. at MJF, '71-4.

LP: *California Guitar* (Famous Door).

LUCIE, LAWRENCE (LARRY),* *guitar*; also *banjo, mandolin, clarinet*; b. Emporia, Va., 12/18/14. The veteran big band guitarist (Benny Carter, F. Henderson, C. Hawkins, Louis Armstrong) was still active in the '70s. Pl. in reconstituted Chick Webb band at NJF-NY, '74; tributes to Armstrong, '74-5; tributes to Basie and Lucky Millinder at Carnegie Hall, '73. A charter member of NYJRC, he also remained busy as a studio guitarist and teaching at the Borough of Manhattan Community Coll. in NYC. Publ: *Lucie's Special Guitar Lessons* (Playnote Music Publishing, 306 West 51st St., New York, N.Y. 10019).

LUCIEN, JON (Jon Lucien Harrigan), *singer, songwriter*; also *bass; guitar; synthesizer; clavinet*; b. Tortola, Brit. Virgin Islands, 1/8/42. Raised on St. Thomas. Father, a blind musician, started him and brothers in music; learned scat singing from mother who sang to him when he was a baby. Further self-studies on ukulele, guitar and bass while in reform school from ages nine to 16. Worked w. British comp.-pianist, Marty Clark, who taught him "all the right things."

To NYC '62, pl. clubs, weddings, bar-mitzvahs, Catskill Mt. hotels. Rec. singles for Col., Cap. which went generally unnoticed. Rec. LP for RCA, '70 but it was second album, *Rashida*, which moved him into the public consciousness. Parlayed a two-week engagement at the Village Gate into 15 weeks, then made successful tour of clubs in Boston, Phila., Baltimore, Wash., D.C. Concerts at Philharmonic Hall, '74; Carnegie Hall, '75. App. at NJF-NY, '75. Infl: Jesse Belvin, Nat Cole, Miles Davis, John Coltrane. Lucien says: "I just listened to the horns and the way Miles used to phrase *Funny Valentine*, you know how hecantakeonewordanddothreenoteswithit but still make the one word mean something. As if he were reciting a poem."

Rafiq Abrahim wrote: "He is jazz. He is calypso. He is classical. He is now. His music is a well balanced fusion of these categories and more. He is the synthesis of the Seventies."

TV: Mike Douglas; Merv Griffin; Dinah Shore. Comp: *Find Yourself a Lover; Soul Mate; Creole Lady; Song For My Lady; Follow Your Heart*.

LPs: *Song For My Lady* (Col.); *I Am Now; Rashida; Mind's Eye* (RCA).

LUCRAFT, HOWARD,* *composer, leader, guitar*; b. London, England, 8/16/16. The musician-journalist continued to write compositions for foreign TV as well as jazz articles for *Crescendo; Overture; Melody Maker; LA Times*. Music editor of *Daily Variety*, 1972-3. Jazz radio shows on KCBH; KPFK; KBCA. Teaching jazz style at schools throughout LA County. From '74, active again leading 20 piece orch. in Cal., Arizona; also comp. for jazz septet which, in '75, rec. LPs, *Potpourri* (Bosworth) and *Americana* (Glendale).

LYONS, JAMES (JIMMY),* *alto sax, flute*; b. Jersey City, N.J., 12/1/32. Best known for his association w. Cecil Taylor from '60. In '69 pl. concerts at Maeght Foundation in France w. him; also made first rec. as leader for Byg Records in Paris. Taught music for Narcotic Addiction Control, '70-1. From '71-3 artist-in-residence w. Taylor at Antioch Coll., Ohio where he was orch. director for Black Music Ensemble. Toured Japan twice w. Taylor. US and European tours for club and concert app., '74. Composer-instrumentalist, dir. Black Music Ens. at Bennington Coll., Vermont, '75. Did two films in France, one for Maeght Found. w. Taylor. Fest: Antibes; Willisau; Perugia, '75. Comp: *Aztec Nights* for 25 pieces at Antioch, '72; *Something's the Matter*, Bennington, '75. LPs: *Other Afternoons* (Byg); w. Taylor, *Spring of Two Blue-J's* (Unit Core); *Unit Structures; Conquistador* (BN); for the Maeght Found. (Shandar).

LYONS, JIMMY, *producer*; b. Peking, China, 11/18/16. Began career in 1941, presenting S. Kenton band live from ballroom in Balboa Beach, Calif. In early '40s wrote, produce radio progs. for NBC's Thesaurus Division. During W.W. II he prod. *Jubilee*, jazz progs. for Armed Forces Radio. In '46 he broadcast from San Diego, Tijuana. Worked for Woody Herman, '47. Moved to SF, '48, broadcasting on KNBC for five years. His *Jazz at Sunset* concerts in 1953 from Carmel, Cal. feat. E. Garner, E. Fitzgerald, G. Shearing, D. Brubeck et al. This led to his founding the Monterey Jazz Festival in 1958. Lyons also broadcast live from SF Hangover Club; was on KGO '57-8; KFRC '61-5, both in SF. Appointed to Calif. Arts Commission, '64; chairman '67-8; exec. sec. '68-9. Member of U.S. State Dept. Cultural Presentations Committee. In '72 established annual Calif. High School Jazz Band Competition, winners appearing at MJF. Lyons influenced careers of many jazz artists, notably Dave Brubeck and Gerry Mulligan; Brubeck's *The Lyons Busy* and Mulligan's *Line for Lyons* were written for him.

LYSTEDT, LARS, *valve trombone, critic*; b. Umea, Sweden, 12/12/25. Played trumpet '42-52, then valve trombone; mainly self-taught. His quintet, which he led from '58-72, became (in '60) the first Swedish band to perf. behind the Iron Curtain, at Warsaw Jazz Jamboree. The quintet won the city of Umea Cultural Prize in '68, and in that year was voted the best int'l group at the Zurich JF. From '68 led the Umea Big Band; originated and org. the Umea JF, biggest of its kind in Sweden. Favs: Bill Harris, L. Armstrong, D. Gillespie.

Lystedt has had a parallel career as a writer, contributing to the magazine *Orkester Journalen* since '50, and acting as Swedish correspondent for DB from '69. He won several awards for music journalism in the early '70s.

LPs: Lars Lystedt Quintet, *Fanfar!* (Jazz Records); Sextet, *Jazz Under the Midnight Sun* (Swedisc); *Umea Big Band in Montreux*, feat. Slide Hampton (Sonet); *Jazz In Umea* (Caprice); Umea Big Band, *Swingtime Festival* (Hitachi).

LYTELL, JIMMY (James Sarrapede),* *clarinet*; b. New York City, 12/1/04. A member of the Orig. Memphis Five during the '20s, Lytell re-formed the group, '49, and again in the mid-50s. He continued to work occasionally, leading his own groups on Long Island, until he was sidelined by a long illness. He died 11/26/72 at Kings Point, L.I. Lytell, one of the first and most prominent dixieland clarinetists, had worked in the Original Dixieland Jazz Band as a replacement for Larry Shields in '22.

LYTLE, JOHN DILLARD (JOHNNY),* *vibes, composer*; also *drums*; b. Springfield, Ohio, 10/13/32. Continued to tour with own trio from '66, incl. apps. in concerts w. W. Montgomery, Nancy Wilson, Miriam Makeba, Ray Charles. Many coll. dates, incl. Battle of the Vibes w. Roy Ayers at Central State Coll. Fests: Albion, Mich.; October Fest., Clairton, Pa., Black Expo, Phila. Comps: *The Village Caller; The Man; The Loop; Libra; Sister Silver and the Moore Man; Happy Ground.* Lytle has received awards from the Urban League and Buffalo U., and the key to the city of Springfield, where he is dir. of the Davey Moore Arts Cultural Center and Davey Moore Foundation. Also received an Outstanding Musician award from the foundation.

LPs: *People and Love; Soulful Rebel* (Milestone); *Man and Woman; Close Enough; Be Proud* (SS).

LYTTELTON, HUMPHREY,* *trumpet, leader, composer*; b. Windsor, England, 5/23/21. Frequently leader of own band from '50s, originally in traditionalist style, later led swing type, Ellington-influenced small group. Annual visits to Germany, Switzerland, Austria. TV: *In Concert*, BBC-2, '75; Michael Parkinson, BBC-1. Many comps. incl. *Big Ol' Tears; Sprauncy; Lion Rampant; Madly*, for Duke Ellington Tribute concert. Own radio prog., *Humphrey Lyttelton Plays Best of Jazz on Record.* Many other radio, TV apps., incl. panel shows etc.

Publ: *Take It From The Top* (Robson Books). LPs: *Take It From The Top; Kansas City Woman*, feat. Buddy Tate and comps. written specially for Lyttelton by Buck Clayton (Black Lion).

MABERN, HAROLD JR.,* *piano, composer*; b. Memphis, Tenn., 3/20/36. Moved from Chi. to NYC in early '60s, working w. L. Hampton, the Jazztet, J.J. Johnson. Acc. Joe Williams, '66-7; also many other singers, incl. Sarah Vaughan, Dakota Staton, Irene Reid, Arthur Prysock. Gigged w. R.R. Kirk; Rollins; Hubbard; L. Morgan; R. Haynes; Wes Montgomery in late '60s. In '73-4 worked w. Walter Bolden trio at the Cellar, NYC; also w. George Coleman; Danny Moore; Keno Duke; Billy Harper; Clark Terry; Joe Newman. Member of the Piano Choir, a seven-piano group under the direction of Stanley Cowell; and a workshop band at Project Create. TV: *Soul* w. Lucky Thompson, Ossie Davis, Ruby Dee; Lee Morgan; Bobbi Humphrey. Fests: NJF w. Johnson; Williams; Young-Holt; Morgan; Hubbard in '60s; as solo pianist, NJF-NY, '75. Comps: *Rakin' and Scrapin'; Waltzing Westward; Such Is Life; I Remember Britt; Aon; Strozier's Mode; A Few Miles From Memphis; For Big Hal; In What Direction Are You Headed.* Received grant from CAPS to write a suite for seven pianos. LPs: *A Few Miles From Memphis; Rakin' and Scrapin'; Greasy Kid Stuff* (Prestige); *Handscapes* w. the Piano Choir; *Sense of Values* w. K. Duke (Strata-East); w. Blue Mitchell, Hank Mobley, Lee Morgan, Hubbard (BN); Johnson (Imp.); Buddy Montgomery (Mile.); Stanley Turrentine (CTI); Frank Foster (Main.).

MACKAY, DAVID OWEN (DAVE), *piano, composer*; b. Syracuse, N.Y., 3/24/32. Stud. Trinity Coll., Hartford, '50-4; Boston Univ. School of Mus., '56-9; also w. L. Tristano. Pl. w. B. Hackett, S. Stitt, C. Mariano, Bob Wilber, Serge Chaloff in Boston; Jim Hall and own gps. in NYC; own gp. in Chicago. Settling in LA, pl. many local clubs leading own gp. w. wife, the late Vicky Hamilton; also gigged w. Don Ellis, S. Manne, Paul Horn, Chet Baker, Emil Richards, Joe Pass et al. Fests: Monterey; Costa Mesa, both w. Ellis. Comps: *Samba For Vicky; Peek-A-Boo; Here; Like Me; Silent; Now.*

LPs: *Dave Mackay & Vicky Hamilton* (Imp.); w. Ellis, *Live at Monterey; Live in 3 2/3/4 Time* (Pac. Jazz); w. Richards, *Live at Donte's; Journey To Bliss* (Imp.).

MAGRUDER, JOHN DECKER BOYD, *saxophones, composer*; also *flutes, clarinet, oboe, bass*; b. Greenwich, Conn., 11/19/25. B.S. (cum laude) mus. ed., '49; M.A. in music, '50, NYU. Received Cal. Community Coll. Credential, '72. Worked w. Horace Silver in Conn., '47-50; had own quartet, '51-9; Don Ellis orch., '65-8; writing for and perf. with his own 17 piece big band, the Magruder Machine, '73- , and own quintet, '75- . Mus. educator in LA City school system from '59- ; Santa Monica Coll. '72-4; Chairman, Mus. Dept. at Univ. High School, W. LA. Received spec. award from LA Mayor Thomas Bradley for work with youth in the field of music, '74. Infls: Getz, Parker, Coltrane, Goodman, DeFranco, Gerald Wilson, Gil Evans, Thad Jones and a variety of modern classical composers. Fests: app. w. own jazz group at 1939 World's Fair, NYC; Monterey, '67-8; Tanglewood, '68; Newport, '67-8; Nice, '68. TV: Don Ellis Special.

Magruder has written TV commercials, music for the Amer. Film Inst., two musical comedies: *The Village Square* and *A Fair Wind to Belford*; symphonic comps; for educ. purposes, and originals for Ellis incl. *Zim.* LPs: w. Ellis, *Live at Monterey; Live in 3 2/3/4 Time* (Pac. Jazz); *Shock Treatment; Electric Bath; Autumn* (Col.).

MAHAVISHNU. see McLaughlin, John.

MAHONES, GILDO,* *piano, composer*; b. New York City, 6/2/29. Prominent from '59 as accompanist for Lambert, Hendricks & Ross. During '60s backed many other singers, among them O.C. Smith for a year in LA, '66; followed by three and a half years as musical director for Lou Rawls. Subsequently worked at many LA clubs either leading own trio or as sideman for Joe Williams, J. Witherspoon, Esther Phillips, King Pleasure, Abbey Lincoln, Leon Thomas; also S. Stitt, J. Moody, A. Farmer, S. Criss, Jim Hall, T-Bone Walker, B. Bryant. Concerts in Cal. and Yamaha Jazz Fest. in Japan, w. Benny Carter, '73; also at Monterey and Newport JF. Musical director and pianist for two shows: *Don't Bother Me I Can't Cope* and *Charlatan*. Mahones' comps. include *The Most Happy Fella* for Bunions Bradford band; *Art's Revelation* for A. Blakey.

LPs: *I'm Shooting High; Gildo Mahones Soulful Piano* (Pres.); w. Lambert, Hendricks & Ross (Col.); w. Lambert, Hendricks & Bavan (RCA); w. J. Hendricks (Wor. Pac., Col., Repr.); w. Witherspoon (Pres., ABC); w. Booker Ervin (Pres.); w. Rawls (Cap.); w. Frank Wess; Ted Curson (Pres.); w. F. Foster; Bennie Green (BN).

MAIDEN, WILLIAM RALPH (WILLIE),* *saxophones, composer, clarinet, piano*; b. Detroit, Mich., 3/12/28. Wrote and/or played for M. Ferguson band from '52 to '65. In '66 worked for Ferguson's sextet and for C. Barnet orch. In '67-9, pl. casual gigs in S. Cal. Became part time teacher at Cerritos Jr. Coll. and continued comp. and arr. From '69-73 he was w. S. Kenton orch. as saxophonist and arr. In '73-4 was assoc. prof., teaching contemp. comp. at the U. of Maine at Augusta. He received a federal grant to present jazz to rural areas and made two tours to fulfill this objective. Died in LA, 5/29/76. Comps: *Little Minor Booze; Height of Ecstasy; Boilermaker; Kaleidoscope; No Harmful Side Effects; April Fool*, all rec. by Kenton.

LPs: w. Kenton, *Birthday in Britain; Live at Brigham Young University; Live at Butler; Live at Redlands*; w. C. Barnet, big band (Creative World).

MAINIERI, MICHAEL JR.,* *vibes*; also *synthi-vibe, keyboards, percussion*; b. Bronx, N.Y., 7/24/38. Came to prominence w. B. Rich in early '60s; own groups from '63. Pres. of Gnu Music Inc., NYC, a music prod. company servicing and supplying comps. and arrs. for TV, radio and record prod. projects. Also busy as studio musician, '67-71. Prod. and arr. an album for 17 piece band called White Elephant, '71. Invented new instrument of his own design called a synthi-vibe, a vibe "controller" which allows him to play electronic sounds through any synthesizer. A five octave instrument, it replaces the keyboard on any synthesizer and allows him to trigger its oscillator with mallets instead of fingers.

Lives in Woodstock, N.Y. where he has his own rec. studio in converted barn. Formed new quartet, '75. Won ASCAP award for Best New Arranger-Composer, '69. Wrote music for film *St. Petersburg Race*, '71; NBC-TV spec. *Of Men and Women*, '74.

Comps. and arrs. for White Elephant; Nick Holmes album. LPs: *White Elephant; Soulful Crooner* w. Holmes (Just Sunshine); others w. Wes Montgomery (CTI); Tim Hardin, Paul Simon (Col.); Don McLean (UA).

MAKOWICZ, ADAM (Matyszkowicz), *piano, keyboards, composer*; also *fender bass*; b. Czechoslovakia, 8/18/40. Stud. w. mother, a piano teacher, later Chopin Secondary School of Music in Cracow, Poland. Started pl. jazz w. Tomasz Stanko in Cracow in '62. Moving to Warsaw in '56, led own trio; toured extensively w. Zbigniew Namyslowski and w. NOVI singers throughout Europe, Cuba, India, New Zealand. Pl. w. B. Webster, Idrees Sulieman, Jan Garbarek. In '71 he joined Michal Urbaniak group, with which he pl. many fests., concerts, concerts and recorded several albums. Took part in "Piano Conclave" app. by leading European pianists, '74, then org. similar meeting on Polish TV, using local keyboard artists. Favs: Tatum, Peterson, K. Jarrett, H. Hancock. Fests: Jazz Jamboree, Warsaw, '64- ; many others in West Germany, Montreux, etc. Comps: *For Pia; Chassing; Live Embers; Blues for Michal*; music for two short films.

Makowicz is best known in the U.S. for his duo album, *Newborn Light* (Col.) w. Urbaniak's wife, singer Urszula Dudziak. Many other LPs for European labels w. Urbaniak, Namyslowski, Jazz Jamboree, NOVI, Tallinn International Jazz Fest. etc.

MALACHI, JOHN, *piano*; b. Red Springs, N.C., 9/6/19. Self-taught. Pl. w. Trummy Young, '43; B. Eckstine big band, '44-5; accomp. for Eckstine, '47; Illinois Jacquet, '48. Accomp. for many singers, incl. Pearl Bailey in LA, '50; D. Washington, '51; S. Vaughan, '52-4; Al Hibbler, '55-8; Dakota Staton, G. Lynne, Joe Williams et al. Pl. w. short-lived Louis Jordan big band in '51. Infls: T. Wilson, A. Tatum, L. Young, D. Gillespie, Ch. Parker, B. Eckstine, S. Vaughan.

Because of his residence in Washington, D.C., where he freelanced for many years, Malachi did not earn the recognition he deserved as one of the first completely qualified bop-influenced pianists.

LPs: w. Vaughan, *Swingin' Easy* (Trip); Eckstine (Spotlite); w. T.J. Anderson, *Classic Rags and Ragtime Songs* (The Smithsonian Collection).

MALONE, THOMAS HUGH (TOM), *trombone*; also *tuba, trumpet, piccolo, flute, saxophone, electric bass, synthesizer*; b. Honolulu, Hawaii, 6/16/47. Studied at Univ. of Southern Mississippi, '65-7; w. Leon Breeden at No. Texas State, '67-9, where he received BS in Psych.; graduate work at New School, NYC, '70. Worked w. Lee Castle-Jimmy Dorsey orch., '67; W. Herman, '69; Duke Pearson, '70; D. Severinsen; Louis Bellson, '72; BS&T '73; Gil Evans, '73- ; B. Cobham, '75; B. Watrous, '71-5. Infl: J.J. Johnson, U. Green; Watrous, Bruce Fowler, C. Fuller, H. Hancock, F. Hubbard. TV: *Tonight Show* w. Severinsen, '72; *Midnight Special; Rock Concert* w. BS&T, '72. Fest: Montreux w. Evans, '74; Cobham, '75. Malone, who plays 14 instruments prof., has written arrs. for Evans: *Crosstown Traffic; Angel*; and for BS&T: *Empty Pages; No Sweat*. Publ: *Alternate Position Sys-*

tem for Trombone (Synthesis Publs., 306 W. 92nd St., New York, N.Y. 10025). LPs: w. Herman, *Heavy Exposure* (Chess); w. Ten Wheel Drive, *Peculiar Friends*; w. James Brown (Poly.); w. BS&T, *No Sweat* (Col.); w. Evans, *Plays Jimi Hendrix; There Comes a Time* (RCA); also w. Cobham (Atl.); Stanley Clarke (Nemp.); M. Santamaria (Fania); Dave Sanborn (War. Bros.).

MANCE, JULIAN C. JR. (JUNIOR),* *piano, composer*; b. Chicago, Ill., 10/10/28. After acc. Joe Williams, '62-4, cont. to tour w. own trio until his activity became limited due to Meniere's disease, a malady of the middle and inner ear, '66-7. In '68 he resumed with a new trio on a full time basis playing clubs and college concerts. Toured France, '70; England, '74. TV apps. on *Someone New; Black Book; Tonight Show; Tillmon's Tempo; Kennedy at Night; Black Dimensions; Positively Black*. Fests: Montreux, '70; NJF-NY, '73. Comps: *Harlem Lullaby; That Mellow Feeling; Jubilation; The Uptown; Junior's Tune; Playhouse; Big Chief; Happy Time; Down the Line; Letter from Home; Zabuda*.

LPs: *Harlem Lullaby; I Believe To My Soul; Live At The Top; With A Lot of Help From My Friends* (Atl.); *The Junior Mance Touch* (Poly.); w. G. Ammons, *The Boss Is Back; Brother Jug* (Pres.); w. A. Franklin, *Soul '69* (Atl.).

MANCUSO, RONALD BERNARD (GUS),* *baritone horn, piano*; also *bass, trumpet, vibes*; b. Rochester, N.Y., 1933. Traveled with B. Eckstine throughout U.S. and Orient, '66; own groups in LV, '67-8 incl. Carl Fontana, Sam Noto, Sal Nistico. In '69 joined S. Vaughan as bassist, later made world tour w. G. Wein's Jazz Expo '70. From '70-3 worked mainly in LV w. comedian-musician Pete Barbutti, in Dottie Dodgion trio. Toured w. Peter Nero. In '74 moved to LA, gigging at clubs, mostly on piano, w. T. Vig, Carol Kaye, A. Pepper, D. Ellis.

LP: w. Buck's Band (MCM).

MANDEL, HARVEY, *guitar*; also *bongo, conga drums*; b. Detroit, Mich., 3/11/45. Self-taught, starting at age 16. Pl. in Chicago w. Bobby Dee and the New Breed, '62-4; Barry Goldberg Blues Band, '65-6; Charlie Musselwhite, '67-8. Later toured w. several rock groups, among them Canned Heat, '69-70, which played at Woodstock and visited Europe; J. Mayall, '70-1 (two U.S., one European and one Japanese tour); Pure Food And Drug Act, '71-3. Led own band, '74- touring U.S., England, Continent, Canada. Infl. by Sugar Cane Harris, B.B. King, Mayall, E. Clapton, Jon Hendricks and many other rock, blues and jazz artists, Mandel also has done some arranging and produced a few albums.

Solo albums: *Cristo Redentor; Righteous; Games Guitars Play* (Phillips); *Baby Batter; Snake; Shangrenade; Feel The Sound; Best of Harvey Mandel* (Janus); *Fiddler on the Rock*, w. Sugar Cane Harris (BASF); *Future Blues; Live In Europe* w. Canned Heat (Liberty); *USA Union; Back to the Roots* w. Mayall (Polydor); others with Graham Bond, Pure Food & Drug Act, Rolling Stones etc.

MANDEL, JOHN ALFRED (JOHNNY),* *composer*; b. New York City, 11/23/25. No longer a part of the jazz scene, Mandel continued to enjoy great success as a writer of music for motion pictures and TV. Some of his tunes, most notably *The Shadow of Your Smile* and *Emily*, were popular among jazz musicians and singers during the 1970s.

MANGELSDORFF, ALBERT,* *composer, trombone*; also *guitar*; b. Frankfurt am Main, Germany, 9/5/28. Continued to tour with his own groups on a worldwide basis, incl. fests. in Newport, '67, '69; New Orleans, '68; Tokyo Summer Jazz; Osaka, '70; Comblain La Tour; Antibes; Prague; Warsaw; Bled, Yugoslavia. Won DB Critics' Poll, TDWR, '65; German jazz polls from '54. By simultaneously singing and blowing, he is able to play several notes at once, thereby producing a band-like effect, examples of which may be heard on his LP, *The Wide Point*.

Publ: *Jazz Improvisation on Trombone* (Ed. Schott, Mainz, Germany). Mangelsdorff is a prolific composer, fully represented on his own LPs: *Tension; Folkmond and Flower Dream* (CBS); *Now Jazz Ramwong* (CBS and Pac.); *Animal Dance* (Atl.); *The Wide Point; Albert and His Friends; Never Let It End; Trombird; Birds of Underground* (MPS); *Albert in Tokyo* (Enja).

MANGIONE, CHARLES FRANK (CHUCK),* *fluegelhorn, trumpet, piano, composer*; b. Rochester, N.Y., 11/29/40. After leading group with brother Gap (see below), went to NYC in '65; pl. w. W. Herman, K. Winding, M. Ferguson. Joined A. Blakey's Jazz Messengers fall of '65 and remained until '67.

From '68-72 Mangione was dir. of the jazz ensemble of the Eastman School of Music in Rochester, N.Y. He formed the Chuck Mangione quartet in '68. In '70 he app. as guest conductor with the Rochester Phil. A recital on that occasion, entitled *Friends and Love*, was televised as a PBS spec. and released as an album. An unusual and successful blending of jazz, folk, middle-of-the-road pop and classical influences, the album was widely acclaimed and achieved substantial commercial acceptance. The best known comp. to emerge from the album was *Hill Where the Lord Hides*, which became a hit single. Mangione followed this initiative with another collaboration with the Rochester Phil. in '71, entitled *Together*, also a PBS spec. From '72 he toured with his quartet, made apps. with the Phil. orchs. of Oakland, Cal.; Edmonton, Alberta and Hamilton, Ont. He app. at numerous fests: Montreux; Newport; Concord, Monterey; Pescara, Italy; Pori, Finland; Kansas City and Niagara Falls.

In '74 Mangione formed his own recording company, Sagoma, in order to present individually several of the artists who had app. with him in concert and on records, among them Gap Mangione, Gerry Niewood and Esther Satterfield. He also published a choral series of his own comps. designed for high school choruses.

Mangione's comps. have been recorded by many pop and jazz artists incl. Cannonball Adderley, Herb Alpert, Ray Bryant, Percy Faith, Mark Murphy, Superfunk.

Comps: *Hill Where The Lord Hides; Friends and Love; Legacy; Land of Make Believe; Feel of a Vision; Sunshower; El Gato Triste*; and all other orig. material on his albums.

LPs: *Friends and Love; Together; Land of Make Believe* w. Hamilton Phil.; w. quartet, *Alive; Chuck Mangione Quartet* (Merc.); *Chase The Clouds Away* (A & M); as cond. w. Gap Mangione (Merc.).

For details of publs. and records: Sagoma Records, Sagoma/DGM Inc., 270 Midtown Plaza, Rochester, N.Y.

MANGIONE, GASPARE CHARLES (GAP),* *piano, composer*; b. Rochester, N.Y., 7/31/38. Brother of Chuck Mangione (see above). Pl. w. Chuck in Jazz Brothers in early '60s. Active from '65 w. own gp. and as teacher in Rochester. Appears as part of the expanded cast for his brother's concert performances.

LP: *She and I* (A&M).

MANN, HERBIE,* *flute, composer, leader*; also *tenor sax*; b. Brooklyn, N.Y., 4/16/30. A leader of his own group from '59, Mann continued to explore new avenues of expression in the late '60s and '70s, shifting personnel in relation to the material. Already having incorporated Afro-Latin, Brazilian, and Middle Eastern elements, by '69 he had rec. w. Memphis r&b studio men along w. his regulars, Roy Ayers, Sonny Sharrock, Larry Coryell and Miroslav Vitous. In '71 he recorded the album *Push Push*, using rock guitarist Duane Allman. By '73 his group had evolved into what is called The Family of Mann w. Pat Rebillot on keyboards and David Newman on tenor sax and flute. Certainly his involvement with blues and soul had begun years before (he acknowledged this in a tribute LP to Ray Charles, *The Inspiration I Feel*) but when he was finished with the Memphis funk, he moved more toward a "New York sophisticated rock," as he called it. In '74 he rec. in England w. British rockers and followed this with a reggae album done w. Tommy McCook, the leader of reggae star Jimmy Cliff's band. In '75 the Family of Mann had a "disco" hit in *Hi-Jack*. Explaining that he did not want to be confined by the narrow definition of "disco" and that "people have been dancing to my music since I started playing," Mann came full circle on *Waterbed* by redoing *Comin' Home Baby*, his success of '62; Charles' *I Got a Woman*; and the kind of Latin number which in its '70s incarnation is called "salsa."

Fest: NJF; NJF-NY; "Newport" fests. all over US; Montreux '72; other Euro. fests. Numerous TV apps. Won DB Readers Poll, '66-70. Comps: *Memphis Spoon Bread and Dover Sole; High Above the Andes; Mediterranean; Paradise Music; Body Oil*. As a producer he recorded artists such as Ron Carter, Miroslav Vitous and Attila Zoller for his own Embryo label (distributed by Atlantic) in '70. LPs: *Waterbed; Discotheque; Reggae; London Underground; Turtle Bay; Hold On, I'm Comin'; Evolution of Mann; Mississippi Gambler; Best of Herbie Mann; Concerto Grosso in D Blues; Live at the Whiskey A Go Go; Memphis Underground; The Inspiration I Feel; Windows Opened; The Wailing Dervishes; The Beat Goes On; Impressions of the Middle East; Monday Night at the Village Gate* (Atl.); *Stone Flute; Push Push; Memphis Two-Step; Muscle Shoals Nitty Gritty* (Embryo).

MANNE, SHELDON (SHELLY),* *drums, composer*; b. New York City, 6/11/20. The former Kenton and Herman drummer continued as a busy freelance musician in LA in the '60s and '70s. He operated his own jazz club, Shelly's Manne Hole, from Nov. '60 through Sept. '72. Reopened at a new location in LA, Oct. '73; closed Apr. '74. During much of this time Manne led a small jazz group whenever possible, sometimes at his own club. He played the Concord Fest., '68 and '74; concerts in Italy, '70; Ronnie Scott's in London, and many other European apps. In '74 he became a member of a group known as the L.A. Four, along w. Ray Brown, L. Almeida and B. Shank, seen in clubs and concerts, mostly around LA.

As composer, wrote score for *Daktari* TV series; motion pictures *Young Billy Young; Trial of the Catonsville Nine*; scored Center Theater Group's prod. of *Henry IV*, Part I at Mark Taper Forum, LA Music Center. He also taped a series of 13 half-hour lessons, for Cable Network TV, entitled *Let's Play Drums*. A book of the same name, publ: (Chappell Music, 609 5th Ave., New York, N.Y. 10017). LPs: *Alive in London; Gambit; At The Black Hawk; At The Manne Hole; Bells Are Ringing; Checkmate; Concerto for Clarinet & Combo; Li'l Abner; More Swinging Sounds; My Fair Lady; My Son The Drummer; Outside; Peter Gunn; Proper Time; Son of Gunn; Sounds Unheard Of; 2, 3, 4* (Contemp.); *Mannekind* (Mainstr.); *Manne That's Gershwin* (Cap.); w. Bill Evans, *A Simple Matter of Conviction* (Verve); others w. J. Klemmer etc. (Imp.); L.A. Four (Concord); w. Sonny Criss (Prest.); Sonny Stitt (Fly. Dutch.).

MANONE, JOSEPH (WINGY),* *trumpet, singer*; b. New Orleans, La., 2/13/04. Virtually inactive in recent years, he appeared at the Nice Festival in the summer of '75. LP w. Papa Bue (Storyville).

MANTLER, MICHAEL,* *composer, trumpet*; also *valve trombone*; b. Vienna, Austria, 8/10/43. Associations in early '60s with Cecil Taylor, Carla Bley; in '65, w. Bley, introduced Jazz Composers Orchestra at Newport JF and at Museum of Modern Art. Toured Europe w. Bley and Steve Lacy as co-leader of Jazz Realities Quintet. App. in many Western European cities, on radio, TV in Hamburg, Amsterdam etc. Film music for two documentaries in Rome; rec. album in Holland. Returned to U.S. Feb. '66. Worked on consolidation of JCOA. During fall of '66 made second tour of Europe w. quintet. Took part in RCA rec. of C. Bley's "Dark Opera Without Words," *A Genuine Tong Funeral*, w. G. Burton quartet and orch.

Completing a series of comps. for orch. in early '68, he rec. them w. JCO, feat. C. Taylor, Pharoah Sanders, R. Rudd, D. Cherry, G. Barbieri and L. Coryell. In '69 took part in Charlie Haden's Liberation Music Orchestra LP; gave premiere of new works in concert at Electric Circus, NYC, feat. Taylor, Sanders, Cherry. '70-1, comp. extended piece for two orchs. and piano. New orchestral work with words by Samuel Beckett, '71-2. Prod. rec. of opera, *Escalator Over The Hill*, by C. Bley and Paul Haines. Took part in TV workshops in Hamburg and Vienna, Jan. '72.

Mantler continued extensive administrative work for JCOA and its division JCOA Records, and the New Music Distribution Service, estab. '72 (6 West 95th St., New York, N.Y. 10025). Perf. w. JCO during its week-long presentation of Cherry's *Relativity Suite* at N.Y.U. Started (together w. C. Bley) own record label, Watt Works. Completed work on two-orch. piece. Began work on new extended piece. Received CAPS grant in '74. Participated in rec. of C. Bley's *Tropic Appetites*, '73-4.

Among awards received for *The Jazz Composer's Orchestra*, a two record set feat. the comps. of Mantler, were Jazz Album of the Year, Sixth Int'l Jazz Critics Poll, Jazz & Pop Mag., '68; Grand Prix, Academy Charles Cros, France, '68; Album of the Month, various Canadian, English, French, German, Japanese mags.

Mantler has earned the respect and admiration of his peers, not only for his work as composer and conductor, but for his ongoing contributions as activist for the JCOA.

In addition to LPs mentioned above, Mantler can be heard on other JCOA and Watt Works albums.

MANUSARDI, GUIDO, *piano, composer*; b. Chiavenna, Italy, 12/3/35. Worked in Sweden, 1960-66; Romania, '67-71, then Italy and throughout Continent, acc. Joe Venuti, Don Byas, Dexter Gordon, Slide Hampton, Art Farmer et al. From Sept. '74 pl. in duo w. Red Mitchell. Favs: Bill Evans, McCoy Tyner. Many fest. app. acc. Bobby Hackett, Roy Eldridge, Venuti. Long stay in Romania made lasting impact on his style. LPs w. own gps. CBS (Italy), BASF (Germ.), Amigo (Sweden), Dire (It.), Oscar (It.); w. all star gp. *Tribute to Louis*, live at San Remo (CBS-It.).

MARCUS, STEPHEN (STEVE), *tenor, soprano saxophones*; b. New York City, 9/18/39. Stud. privately, also Berklee School, '59-61. Pl. w. S. Kenton; '63, D. Byrd; '65, W. Herman from '67 off and on; H. Mann, '67-70; L. Coryell, '71-3; own group, Count's Rock Band, '73-5. Feat. w. B. Rich band, '75. Infls: Coltrane, Rolling Stones, Beatles, Miles Davis. Fests: Newport, '63, '68, '69, '70; Montreux, '70.

LPs: *Count's Rock Band; Tomorrow Never Knows* (Vortex); w. Coryell *Barefoot Boy* (Fl. Dutchman); *Offering* (Vanguard).

MARIANO, CHARLES HUGO (CHARLIE),* *alto saxophone, electronic saxophone, nagasuram*; b. Boston, Mass., 11/12/23. Prominent in Kenton band, later touring with his, then, wife Toshiko Akiyoshi; taught at Berklee. In Malaysia under sponsorship of USIA, teaching music to members of State Radio Orchestra, '66-7. To Japan, summer '67, rec. several LPs there. Back at Berklee, Aug. '67 until late '68, but made one return trip to Japan during this time. In '67, he formed a jazz-rock group, Osmosis.

Mariano left the U.S. in '71, pl. in Holland, lived in Belgium and formed a group, Ambush, for eight months. Returned to U.S. to rec. an Atl. LP, *Mirror*. Spent last four months of '72 in Zurich for a theatre production of play *Marat/Sade*. In '73 in India for four months studying the nagasuram, a flute-like wooden instrument, which he has feat. ever since. Later in '73 pl. on continent and in London with Dutch pop gp. Supersister. After leaving this combo he pl. and rec. in Finland for several months, joined the German pop gp. Embryo, and from Feb. '74 worked w. a small combo known as Pork Pie, which pl. several major European fests. Living in The Hague, Holland, for most of '75 but returned to US in the fall to teach once again at Berklee.

Other LPs: *Iskander*, w. Supersister (Polydor); *We Keep On*, w. Embryo; *Transistory*, w. Pork Pie (MPS); *September Man*, w. Philip Catherine (Atl.); *Altissimo* (Japanese Victor); under his own name, *Cascade* (Keytone); (Horo).

MARKEWICH, MAURICE (REESE),* *piano, flute, piccolo*; b. Brooklyn, N.Y., 8/6/36. Markewich, who received his M.D. from the N.Y. Medical Coll., '70, attended the Manhattan Center for Advanced Analytic Studies from '71- . He is ass't psychiatrist at Beth Israel Medical Center, instructor in psychiatry at the Mt. Sinai School of Medicine, and is in priv. practice as psychiatrist-psychoanalyst.

Markewich has not been active in the '70s as a pro. musician, but has written several books on music: *The Definitive Bibliography of Harmonically Sophisticated Tonal Music; The New Expanded Bibliography of Jazz Compositions Based On The Chord Progressions of Standard Tunes; Inside, Outside: Substitute Harmony In Modern Jazz and Pop Music; Jazz Publicity II: Newly Revised and Expanded Bibliography of Names and Addresses of Hundreds of International Jazz Critics and Magazines* (all available from 39 Gramercy Park North, New York, N.Y. 10010).

LPs: *New Designs in Jazz* (Modern Age); w. Nick Brignola *This Is It* (Priam).

MARRS, STELLA (MS. SOFT SOUL), *singer*; b. New York City, 3/22/32. Active as a singer from '58, as single and w. gps., big bands. Toured w. Lionel Hampton, July-Oct. '69; April, '72; Jan. '73. Has worked in LV, Houston, Fla., NJ; many coll. concerts; NYC clubs such as Rainbow Grill, Plaza Nine, Boomer's, Jimmy Weston's, etc. Backed by own trio in mid-'70s. In theater app. w. New Heritage Repertory Workshop; also wrote, produced and performed in *I A Black Woman*. Numerous apps. as extra, sometimes w. speaking lines, in movies *Cotton Comes to Harlem; Angel Levine; The Landlord; Where's Poppa*, etc. Has performed for Jazz Interactions; Jazz Vespers; Festival on the River. TV: Sydney, Australia, '68; Joe Delaney show, LV; hostess on own show, Telepromter Cable TV, Channel D. Radio: jazz DJ on WHBI; then, in '75, on WRVR, NYC. LPs: *Anyone Can Whistle* (Grenider); w. Duke Pearson, unreleased (BN).

MARSALA, MARTY,* *trumpet, drums*; b. Chicago, Ill., 4/2/09. Younger brother of Joe Marsala, in whose combo he pl. during the late '30s. Marsala later lived for many years in SF, where he pl. w. Earl Hines and led his own group. In '62 he returned to Chicago, leading a dixieland band at Jazz Ltd. He died in a Chicago hospital, 4/27/75.

MARSH, WARNE MARION,* *tenor sax, clarinet, flute*; b. Los Angeles, Calif., 10/26/27. Early associate of Lennie Tristano in NYC. Moved to LA, 1966. Began teaching full time '68. Formed quartet, also worked w. Clare Fischer orch. Joined Supersax during its rehearsal days in summer of '72. In addition to working with this group, occasionally led quartet '74-5 with Lou Levy, Jim Hughart, Frank Severino. Pl. in Europe, '75. Wrote arrs. of *Salt Peanuts, Ornithology* for Supersax.

LPs: *Ne Plus Ultra; Art of Improvising* (Revelation); w. Clare Fischer, *Thesaurus* (Atl.); w. Art Pepper, *The Way It Was* (Contemp.); w. Supersax, *Supersax Plays Bird; Salt Peanuts; Supersax Plays Bird With Strings* (Capitol).

MARSHALL, JACK WILTON,* *composer, guitar*; b. El Dorado, Kans., 11/23/21. The versatile west coast artist, who had been active as a composer, arranger, conductor, as lecturer at USC, and musical director for Capitol Records, died suddenly of a heart attack in Huntington Beach, Cal., 9/2/73. A Jack Marshall scholarship fund was set up for young guitarists to enable them to sustain their education at USC.

LPs: *Sounds Unheard Of* (Contemporary).

MARTINEZ, LUIS (SABU), *percussion*; b. New York City, 7/14/30. Self-taught. Pl. w. D. Gillespie, Ch. Parker, C. Basie, B. Goodman in late '40s; A. Blakey, off and on, '49-61; H. Silver, '57; Tony Bennett, '57-63. Moving to Europe pl. w. radio jazz group of Stockholm, '68-73; also w. Peter Herbolzheimer's Rhythm Combination & Brass, '72. From '73, led own group, New Burnt Sugar, in Sweden. Credits the Lecuona Cuban Boys of the '40s as his "musical fathers." Also infl. by Parker, Blakey, Gillespie.

Publ: *Conga Lesson's Book* (Air Skandinaviska Music, Stockholm, Sweden). Own LPs: *Palo-Congo* (Blue Note); *Safari With Sabu* (RCA); *Sorcery* (Col.); *Jazz Espagnole* (Alegre); *Afro Temple* (Grammofonverket); *New Burnt Sugar Live at Hall Prison* (Ton I Ton, Sweden); *Wide Open; Wait A Minute; Live at Ronnie Scott's; Latin Kaleidoscope* w. Clarke-Boland (MPS); *Orgy In Rhythm; Holiday For Skins*, w. Blakey (Blue Note).

MARTINO, PAT (Pat Azzara), *guitar, composer;* b. Philadelphia, Pa., 8/25/44. Father, a singer, encouraged him to get guitar; guitarist cousin gave some instruction. Stud. w. Dennis Sandole. On road at age 15 w. Willis Jackson; Red Holloway; Sleepy Henderson; four mos. w. S. Stitt. Worked w. Lloyd Price, then Jackson again. Made rec. debut w. him, '63. During '60s pl. in many organist's combos incl. Jimmy Smith; Jack McDuff; Groove Holmes; Jimmy McGriff; Don Patterson; Trudy Pitts. Returned to Phila. '66. Eight mos. w. John Handy '66. Leading own gp. from late '60s; also teaching privately. Infl: D. Sandole, Billy Bean, Johnny Smith, Charlie Christian, Wes Montgomery. Comp: *Strings; Lean Years; Mom; Querido; Trick; Baiyina; Where Love's a Grown Up God; Israfel; Distant Land; The Visit; Special Door; The Great Stream; Passata on Guitar; Willow; On the Stairs*. Pete Welding called his playing ". . . probing, imaginatively controlled musical clarity and coherence—fleet as the wind when required but always easy, fluid, full of gracefully virtuosic touches (to remind you of the control behind the ease)—imperturbable, supremely cool, and quietly intense."

Won DB Critics poll, TDWR, '69; tie, TDWR, '72.

LPs: *Strings; East; Baiyina; El Hombre; Desparado* (Prest.); *The Visit* (Cobble.); *Live!; Consciousness* (Muse); w. Ch. McPherson; Groove Holmes; Don Patterson; Willis Jackson (Prest.); Eric Kloss (Prest.; Muse); Bobby Pierce (Cobble.).

MARTYN, BARRY (KID), *drums, singer*; b. London, England, 2/23/41. Professional debut 1955; visited New Orleans, '60, stud. drums w. Cie Frazier; produced LP of New Orleans music, '61, played on album there, '63, after becoming the only white member of the black musicians' local union. During '60s brought U.S. musicians to Europe to play with his band. In '68-9 pl. at NO Heritage Jazz Fest. Played at Louis Armstrong tribute concert in LA, '70; moved there permanently, '72, formed and played in The Legends of Jazz, '73. Organized production company, record label; promoted local concerts. Organized Louisiana Shakers Band, '74. Returned to Europe for tour w. band, spring '75.

Martyn has rec. w. Jim Robinson, George Lewis, B. Bigard, Chris Barber and many other traditionalist musicians. He has written extensively on NO jazz and in '75 completed taping a biography of B. Bigard.

Own LPs: *The Legends of Jazz; The Legends of Jazz With Barney Bigard* both on Crescent Jazz Productions, (P.O. Box 60244, Los Angeles, Ca. 90054).

MASON, HARVEY JR., *drums, percussion, composer*; also *piano, bass, trumpet*; b. Atlantic City, N.J., 2/22/47. Started on drums at age four under guidance of father, who at that time was in Army band. Stud. at Berklee, New England Conserv. (on full scholarship) concentrating on theory, tympani, mallets etc. to complete Bach. of Ed. from New England Conserv. While there, led quintet w. Jan Hammer, Geo. Mraz. Traveled w. E. Garner for four months in late '69; joined Geo. Shearing, '70 and remained for 13 months.

Since '71, based in LA, Mason has been in increasing demand as a studio musician, and as sideman for dozens of jazz and rock groups, in addition to pl. with several symph. orchs. Pl. w. D. Ellington, Q. Jones, R. Norvo, H. Laws, G. Mulligan, Chet Baker, R. Braff, Herbie Hancock, F. Hubbard, Gunther Schuller. Comps: cowriter w. Hancock of *Chameleon*; writer/arr., *Man What You Did* for D. Byrd LP; many arrs. for Sylvers; rearranged *Watermelon Man* for Hancock. TV: *Bobbie Gentry Show; Bill Cosby Show*, w. Q. Jones, etc.; acting role in drama, *The Most Deadly Game*, '70.

LPs: w. D. Byrd, *Black Byrd; Street Lady*; w. Bobbi Humphrey, *Blacks & Blues; Satin Doll*; Moacir Santos, *Saudade* (BN); Shearing, *Trio; Quartet; George Shearing* (Sheba); Chas. Earland, *Leaving This Planet* (Fant.); Mulligan, *Reunion* at Carnegie Hall (CTI); B. Hutcherson (BN); J. Klemmer; Hubbard; Hancock (Col.).

MASSEY, CAL, *composer, trumpet*; b. Philadelphia, Pa., 1/11/28. Son, Zane, pl. tenor sax; cousin, Billy Massey, trumpet. Raised in Pittsburgh. Began on trumpet at 13. Infl. and encouraged by Freddie Webster whom he met a yr. later. Studied for short time at Pitt Institute. On the road at 17 w. various bands incl. J. McShann. To Phila. in mid-'40s, pl. w. Jimmy Heath's big band; also worked w. Philly Joe Jones; toured briefly w. Billie Holiday. Later pl. w. Eddie Vinson; G. Shearing big band; B.B. King; led own combos. From mid-'50s devoted the majority of his time to writing. His comps. were rec. by C. Parker; J. Coltrane; M. Tyner; J. McLean; F. Hubbard; L. Morgan; A. Shepp. In '69 he became closely associated w. Shepp, touring Europe and No. Africa w. him. Formed the ROMAS orch. w. arr.-cond. Romulus Franceschini, '70, for concerts, educ. TV. Comp: *Fiesta; Bakai; Nakatini Suite; Love Song; Message From Trane; Toyland; Demon's Dance; Assunta; Father and Son; What Would It Be Without You; Quiet Dawn; Goodbye Sweet Pops; The Black Liberation Suite; Looking For Someone to Love*. The last was among several songs and arrs. he wrote in '72, for *Lady Day: A Musical Tragedy*, a play about Billie Holiday w. music also by Shepp and Stanley Cowell. He had been in poor health for some time and, after attending a preview performance on the previous night, died of an apparent heart attack at his home in Brooklyn, N.Y., 10/25/72.

LPs: one track w. own gp. in anthology, *The Jazz Life* (Candid), is unavailable; his writing is represented on albums by the artists named above. His '70s collaborations w. Shepp are on Impulse and Black Saint.

MASSO, GEORGE, *trombone, composer*; also *piano, vibes*; b. Cranston, R.I., 11/17/26. Stud. Boston U., Mus. M., '59; also Electronic Music Workshop. Pl. w. Jimmie Palmer band, '44-5; Army band, '45-6; J. Dorsey, '48. Masso taught mus. in New England public schools for 18 years, the last seven at U. of Connecticut. Gave lecture-demonstrations on history of jazz for various institutions in northeastern U.S. Took leave of absence from U. of Conn., '73 and resigned in '74 to resume work as full time musician. Pl. w. B. Goodman sextet incl. European tour, '73; B. Hackett quintet, '74; World's Greatest Jazzband, '75.

Favs: Lou McGarity, Jack Teagarden, Trummy Young, T. Dorsey et al. TV: Commentator and perf. w. own quintet in history of jazz program in Providence, R.I. Fests: Groton, '68; NO, '72; New London, '73; Meadowbrook w. Goodman, '73. Comps: *Make Up Your Mind* (jazz piece for stage band); *Fantasy in Syncopation* for U. of Conn. band; several other major works for brass, voices etc.

LPs: w. World's Greatest Jazzband (World Jazz); others w. Wild Bill Davison (Jazzology); *Mood in Mink*, feat. soloist on tromb. and vibes, w. Jack Quigley orch. (Seeco).

MASTREN, CARMEN NICHOLAS,* *guitar*; also *banjo, mandolin*; b. Cohoes, N.Y., 10/6/13. With T. Dorsey orch. in late '30s; Glenn Miller AAF band during WWII. Active in studios from '46, joining NBC in '53. Remained through '70, doing *Today; Tonight*; and *Say When*, a morning game show for which he wrote and pl. most of the music. Rec. many jingles during this time and '70-3 when he left NBC to free-lance. App. in Broadway musical *Over Here* w. Andrews Sisters, '74. Played w. NYJRC for Louis Armstrong, Jelly Roll Morton; *Seventy-Five Years of Jazz* concerts, '74-5. Film: banjo and guitar for *The Wild Party*. LPs: w. NYJRC, *Satchmo Remembered* (Atl.).

MASUDA, MIKIO, *piano, composer*; b. Osaka, Japan, 8/14/49. Self-taught. Took up bass at 16; later switched to piano, pl. in Osaka. In '69 moved to Tokyo and pl. w. Hiroshi Suzuki quintet and Isao Suzuki quartet at jazz clubs. With Terumasa Hino, '73. Moved to NYC '73 and worked w. Art Blakey '74. Infl: Coltrane, McCoy Tyner, Ellington, Herbie Hancock. Fest: many in Japan; NJF-NY, '72; Altena Free Jazz Meeting '73 w. Hino; Yugoslavia & other Euro. fests. Comp: *Mickey's Trip; Song for Bumiji; Prayer; Add Some; Hard Luck; Black Daffodil*. LPs: *Traces* (East Wind); w. Hino, *Fuji* (Japan. Victor); *Hartman Meets Hino* (Toshiba EMI); *Journey into My Mind; Into Eternity* (CBS/Sony).

MASUO, YOSHIAKI, *guitar*; b. Tokyo, Japan, 10/12/46. Chosen to pl. w. Sadao Watanabe band while at Waseda Univ., Dec. '68. Went to U.S. June '71. Pl. w. Lee Konitz, '72-Feb. '73. With Sonny Rollins from April '73, app. in clubs, concerts and fests. such as Montreux, Kongsberg '74; NJF-NY, '74-5. Other fests: NJF '68, Montreux, '70 w. Watanabe. Infl: Wes Montgomery, Watanabe, Rollins. Won SJ Readers Poll, '70-1. A strong, technically adroit and creative soloist, rooted in bop. Own LPs: *24 Yoshiaki Masuo; Winds of Barcelona* (Japan. CBS); w. Elvin Jones, *Merry Go Round* (BN); w. Rollins, *The Cutting Edge* (Milestone); *111 Sullivan Street* (East Wind).

MATLOCK, JULIAN CLIFTON (MATTY),* *clarinet*; also *saxophones, flute*; b. Paducah, Ky., 4/27/09. Veteran of Bob Crosby band; often reunited with him for dates such as Rainbow Grill, NYC, 1966-7; Merv Griffin TV show, '72. Pl. w. Phil Harris at Lake Tahoe, Las Vegas, '67. Many gigs in LA area incl. Disneyland w. Ray McKinley, '70. Went to Europe, April '72, playing in England w. Alex Welsh. Feat. at annual Dick Gibson Jazz Parties, 1966-70. Other jazz parties for Dr. O.A. Fulcher in Odessa, Tex. and Dr. Wm. McPherson in Pasadena, Calif. Arranged and played on Disney film track '74 feat. Phil Harris.

LPs: *Paducah Patrol* (WB); early work w. Bob Crosby (MCA); *Bud Meets Eddie* w. Eddie Miller (Fontana); several LPs from Dr. McPherson's parties (Blue Angel).

MATHEWS, RONALD ALBERT (RONNIE),* *piano, composer*; b. Brooklyn, N.Y., 12/2/35. Joined the Max Roach gp. in '63 and was with him, on and off, to '68. Pl. w. Freddie Hubbard, '65-6; Art Blakey, '68-9, touring Europe w. him '68; Japan, '68 and, again, in '75. After free-lancing in NYC area, '70-1, he ran a Jazz Workshop and did private tutoring at Long Island U. From '72 has worked w. Louis Hayes sextet; from '74 w. Clark Terry quartet and big band. He also counsels New York high school students in a drug prevention program which incorporates music as a positive social alternative. Fest: NJF-NY w. Terry. Comp: *Jean-Marie.*

LPs: *Trip to the Orient* (East Wind); w. L. Hayes, *Breath of Life* (Muse); *Clark Terry & His Jolly Giants* (Vang.); Charles Davis (Strata-East); Art Blakey (Trip); Max Roach (Atl.).

MATTHEWS, DAVID, *composer, piano*; also *French horn, valve trombone*; b. Sonora, Ky., 4/3/42. Studied at Louisville Acad. of Mus., '58-60: French horn w. Wm. Sloan; jazz and comp. w. Don Murray and Sam Denison. College Conserv. of Music of U. of Cinn., '60-4, study. w. Felix Labunski, BM in Comp. Att. Eastman Sch. of Mus., stud. w. Rayburn Wright, Manny Albam, summers, '71, '73-4. Arranger and conductor for James Brown band, '70-3. Led own band on Monday nights at Five Spot, NYC, from '74. Gigs at Bradley's w. Sam Brown-Dave Matthews trio, '74-5. Likening his work to Gil Evans and, occasionally, Thad Jones, Dan Morgenstern wrote: "But Matthews is not derivative; he just makes good use of a still vital tradition."

Infl: Miles Davis, Bill Evans, Ellington, Gil Evans, Bartok, Stravinsky, Alban Berg. Comp: *Theme from King Heroin*; suite: *Black Light; Blue Night; Flight*, rec. by David Sanborn; *Prayer; Overture To My Brother*, for symph. orch. LPs: *Live at the Five Spot* (Muse); as arr.-co-prod: w. Mark Murphy, *Bridging a Gap; Mark II; Mark Murphy Sings* (Muse); as arr.-comp: w. Blue Mitchell, *Many Shades of Blue* (Main.); as arr.-co-comp: w. James Brown, *Sho' Is Funky Down Here* (People); as arr.: w. D. Sanborn (WB); T-Bone Wálker (Repr.); Hank Crawford; Ron Carter (Kudu); Paul Simon (Col.).

MATTHEWS, ONZY D. JR.,* *arranger, singer, piano*; b. Fort Worth, Tex., 1/15/36. Led big band in LA during '60s; arr. and cond. for many singers. From 1969-72 worked in St. Thomas, V.I., St. Maarten, Aruba and Curacao, singing and pl. piano for Sheraton Hotel chain. Collab. as composer w. Duke Ellington '73-4, also subbing for him during Duke's illnesses. Arrs. for Earl Hines and his singer Marva Josie, '73-4. Led 17-piece band at NJF-NY 1973. Rearranged early Ellington hits such as *Drop Me Off In Harlem; Squeeze Me; It Don't Mean a Thing* for the Ellington band '74. LPs: w. Lou Rawls, *Tobacco Road; Black & Blue* (Cap.).

MAUPIN, BENNIE, *tenor saxophone*; also *flute, bass clarinet, soprano saxophone, saxello*; b. Detroit, Mich., 8/29/46. Stud. at Garfield Jr. high school w. Alfred Hickman, '54; Northeastern High School w. Rex Hall, '55-8; also privately w. Larry Teal Jr. and Sr.; Detr. Inst. of Musical Art w. Dr. Fillmore, '60-2; priv. lessons w. Carmine Caruso and Joe Allard, NYC. Pl. w. Roy Haynes, '66-8; H. Silver, '68-70; in 70s w. Lee Morgan, Miles Davis, McCoy Tyner, F. Hubbard; joined H. Hancock, '71. Maupin, who names among his infls. Y. Lateef, W. Shorter, J. Coltrane and S. Rollins, is a versatile multi-reedman who has emerged as one of the most accomplished players of the post-Coltrane period. His tenor is a personal extension of his influences, and his dark-toned bass clarinet is particularly persuasive. TV: *Midnight Special; New Year's Eve Special* w. Hancock. Fests: Newport, Monterey, Nice, Pori, and drum fest. in Japan.

Comps: *Neophilia; Quasar; Water Torture; The Jewel In The Lotus; Anua; Ensenada.* Own LP: *Jewel In The Lotus* (ECM); *Afternoon of a Georgia Fawn*, w. Marion Brown (ECM); *Bitches Brew* w. M. Davis (Col.); w. Hancock, *Mwandishi; Crossings* (WB); *Sextant; Head Hunters; Thrust* (Col.).

MAXWELL, JAMES KENDRICK (JIMMY), *trumpet*; also *bagpipes*; b. Stockton, Calif., 1/9/17. Grandfather, cornetist in Spanish-American War, pl. French horn in Walla Walla Symph. from ages 65-85. Father, clarinetist in Navy Band. Mother was violinist. Her brother pl. cornet w. Paul Whiteman, '19. Self taught from age four but "really got serious in '32 by copying Louis Armstrong." Studied w. Herbert Clarke for two yrs.; Lloyd Reese, two yrs; Benny Baker, eight yrs.: all in '39-49 period. Self taught in harmony and theory copying recs. of Ellington, Stravinsky, Debussy and Ravel. Played w. Gil Evans, '32-6; J. Dorsey, '36-7; Maxine Sullivan, '37; Skinnay Ennis, '38-9; Benny Goodman, '39-43. During this period also pl. w. Raymond Scott, '40; Paul Whiteman, '43, '46; CBS staff, '43-45; also month w. C. Basie; Perry Como Show, '45-65; NBC Symph., '48-9; Great Neck (L.I.) Symph., '52-6. Subbed for Cat Anderson w. Ellington for three wks., '61. On staff at NBC, '60-74, doing *Tonight Show*, '65-73. In '58-66 also worked w. bands of Quincy Jones; Oliver Nelson; Gerry Mulligan. Toured USSR: w. Goodman, '62; w. NYJRC Louis Armstrong Tribute, summer '75. W. NYJRC Armstrong Tribute to Europe, fall '75. Played w. Ellington band again, May-Dec., '74. Has also copied recordings of classic numbers for the band to replace missing scores and parts. Pl. w. National Jazz Ensemble from '75; Dave Berger Experimental Orch., '73-5.

Lectures for NY Brass Conf.; Aspen Music Camp; Nat. Brass Conf. in Denver, '73; Hartt Coll., Hartford, Conn., '74; Vermont Summer Music School, '73, '75. Film: *Powers Girl* w. Goodman; background for Ethel Waters in *Cabin in the Sky*; trumpet solo of theme for *The Godfather*. Fest: NJF w. Shearing, '59; Q. Jones, Judy Garland, '61.

Played bagpipes in St. Patrick's Day parades, '58-64; also for Shakespeare in the Park, *Richard II*, '62; on rec. w. John Lennon; and several jingles incl. Peter Sellers for TWA; in NYC on Channel 13, '64.

Son played guitar in Russian rock gp., summer of '70 in Leningrad; teaches Russian at Tufts U. Maxwell, himself, studied Japanese language and culture at Col. U., '41-5; also taught himself to read Chinese.

Although renowned as a lead player, he participated in many jam sessions, '39-45, in Harlem, Greenwich Village and on 52nd St. w. Eldridge, Hawkins, Webster, T. Wilson, C. Christian, etc.

Infl: Armstrong, Eldridge, Berigan, Cootie Williams, Ellington, Strayhorn. Also admires Clifford Brown, Clark Terry. Own fav. solo: *Struttin' With Some Bar-*

becue w. Nat. Jazz Ens. (Chiaro.). Feat. on *I Know That You Know; After You've Gone; Ramona*; one version of *The Man I Love* w. Goodman (Col.); *Happiness is Just a Thing Called Joe* w. Manny Albam in *Brass on Fire* (SS).

MAY, E. WILLIAM (BILLY), *composer*; b. Pittsburgh, Pa., 11/10/16. Former big band arranger for Ch. Barnet. Wrote arrs. and conducted for Frank Sinatra-Duke Ellington album, but generally confined his activities to TV and film composing. Arr. and cond. reconstructed versions of old swing era hits for Time-Life album series.

LPs: *The Swing Era*, 15 volumes (Time-Life).

MAYALL, JOHN, *singer, harmonica, guitar, piano, composer*; b. Macclesfield, Cheshire, England, 11/29/33. Self taught from age 13. Formed one of the first important British blues bands, the Powerhouse Four, in 1956. Organized the Bluesbreakers, 1962 in London, but did not become a full time pro. mus. until '63. Experimented with electric blues sounds until 1967, when he recorded *The Blues Stone*. In 1969 he organized a softer-sounding, more acoustically oriented group that recorded the *Turning Point* album.

From 1970 Mayall spent about half of each year living in Hollywood and half in England. He organized a series of small blues groups, some of which leaned primarily toward rock while others employed leading jazzmen incl. Blue Mitchell, Ernie Watts, Victor Gaskin, Freddie Robinson, Don Harris. Among the alumni of his British groups are Eric Clapton, Aynsley Dunbar, Mick Fleetwood, Mick Taylor, Keef Hartley, Jack Bruce, Jon Mark, Johnny Almond.

Mayall, sometimes called "the grandfather of British blues," established his importance mainly as a catalyst and discoverer of talents who went on to individual recognition. He appeared in *Don't Look Back*, the movie about Bob Dylan. Pl. at NJF '69. Infl: Big Maceo, Sonny Boy Williamson, Otis Rush, Django Reinhardt.

LPs: Polydor, Blue Thumb, London.

MAYERS, LLOYD G., *piano, keyboards, violin*; b. Brooklyn, N.Y., 11/11/29. Began on violin but, helped by younger sister who is pianist, switched to that instr. when he entered High School of Performing Arts. BA from Manhattan School of Mus. First pro. job w. Eddie Vinson, '49. Worked w. Bennie Green, '54; D. Washington, '54-5; Josephine Baker, '59-60; Nancy Wilson, '62-3; Johnny Griffin-Lockjaw Davis, '64; Joe Newman, '65-6; Sammy Davis Jr., '67-72. Mayers, who was also active in NYC studio scene from early '60s, wrote arrs. for Redd Foxx's prod. co., '73, and then became member of D. Ellington orch., under dir. of Mercer Ellington, following Duke's death. Infls: Tatum, Bud Powell, Wynton Kelly, Hancock, Corea; composers, Ellington, O. Nelson. TV apps. w. Davis. Arrs. for Gloria Lynne, Davis, Ruth Brown, Charlie Rouse, Ellington orch.

Mayers rec. two albums as leader: *Taste of Honey* (UA); and one with trio (Merc.) but neither are available; as sideman w. Nelson, Newman, Green, Griffin-Davis (Pres.) also deleted. He can be heard on reissue, *Live at Count Basie's*, w. Newman (Trip). LP w. M. Ellington, *Continuum* (Fant.).

MAYL, GENE, *bass, tuba, singer*; b. Dayton, Ohio, 12/30/28. Began on acoustic bass, '44; tuba while in France, '48; occasionally plays elect. bass. Worked with the bands of Claude Luter, Claude Bolling and D. Byas in France, '48-9. Founded his own Dixieland Rhythm Kings in '48 and has worked with them from that time except for two years w. Bob Scobey's Frisco Jazz Band; two months w. Muggsy Spanier, and short tours w. Billy Maxted, Pee Wee Hunt and the Dukes of Dixieland. Mayl has also app. in concert alongside musicians such as Geo. Brunis, Wild Bill Davison and Clancy Hayes, and has pl. w. all star groups at the Bix Beiderbecke JF, Davenport, Iowa; Detroit JF; Manassas JF. The Dixieland Rhythm Kings have toured the U.S. and Canada and app. at the following fests: NO, where they were the first non-NO band to perf; West Virginia Water Fest.; Burlington, Iowa Steamboat Days Fest. From the late '60s, they have pl. annually on the steamer *Delta Queen*. Comps: *Koor's "29"; Put-In Blues*.

LPs: *On Parade* (Red Onion, Box 366, Dayton, Ohio 45401); *Trip to Waukesha* (Blackbird); *Swinging Saloon Dixie* (Jazzology); w. Brunis (Jazzology); *Bix's Gang Lives* (Fat Cat's Jazz).

MAYS, LYLE DAVID, *keyboards, composer;* b. Marinette, Wis., 11/27/53. Stud. at U. of Wisconsin, '73; NTSU, '74-5. Instructor at Nat'l. Stage Band camps, summer '74. Led sm. groups in coll., winning two jazz fest. competitions. After leaving NTSU, he joined W. Herman. Infls: Bill Evans, F. Zappa, I. Stravinsky. Comps: *Sir Gawain & The Green Knight; Overture to the Royal Mongolian Suma Foosball Festival*.

MAYUTO (Mailto Correa), *percussion*; also *guitar, piano, composer, singer*; b. Sao Goncalo, Rio de Janeiro, Brazil, 3/9/43. Professional debut at age 12 in night club. After working with many bands in Rio, he formed a samba show that became very popular, winning first place at local festivals. At one point Mayuto started medical school, but gave it up in order to concentrate on music. Worked in Mexico w. Tamba Four, '70. Moving to Cal., he pl. w. Ch. Lloyd, '71; toured w. G. Szabo, '71-2; H. Masekela, '72. Took part in Song Festival w. Santana in Rio, '72. Troubadour Club, LA w. C. Adderley, '73; traveled w. F. Hubbard, '73-4; concerts w. K. Burrell, G. Barbieri, H. Belafonte, D. Byrd, D. Ellis, C. Tjader, '74. Wrote music for two plays, *Orpheus*, presented in Philadelphia, '73; and *Sortilege*, seen at the Inner City Cultural Center, LA, '75. TV specials w. Belafonte, Nancy Wilson, Bola Sete. Film: sound tracks, *Cinderella Liberty; Lost In The Stars; Trouble Man; Sarava*. Fests: Mexico, '71, w. Sete; Concord, '71 w. Szabo; Newport, '74 w. Hubbard.

Along with his other talents, Mayuto has written several hundred songs and poems. Gabor Szabo called him "a fiery percussionist, full of lyricism and romantic beauty."

LPs: w. Burrell, *Up The Street, Round The Corner, Down The Block* (Fant.); w. Adderley, *The Happy People* (Cap.); w. Tjader, *Tambu* (Fant.); w. Lloyd, *Waves* (A & M); w. Howard Roberts *Equinox Express Elevator* (ABC); w. Szabo, *Spellbinder* (Blue Thumb); w. Moacir

Santos, *Saudade* (BN); w. Hubbard, *Liquid Love* (Col.); w. H. Mancini, *Symphonic Soul* (RCA).

M'BOOM RE: PERCUSSION. see Roach, Max.

McBEE, CECIL, *bass, composer*; b. Tulsa, Okla., 5/19/35. Began on clarinet in high school. Performed duets w. sister, Shirley, at concerts and w. marching bands on statewide basis. Took up bass at 17 and began to pl. at local night clubs. At Central State in Wilberforce, Ohio he stud. bass and jazz comp. before being inducted into the Army where he spent two yrs. at Ft. Knox, Ky. as cond. of the military band. Moved to Det., '62 where he pl. w. Paul Winter, '63-4, moving to NYC w. the group in '64. He worked w. Grachan Moncur '64; Jackie McLean, '65; Wayne Shorter, '65-6; Freddie Hubbard, Miles Davis, '66; Charles Lloyd, '66-7; Yusef Lateef, '67-9; Bobby Hutcherson, '69; Pharoah Sanders; Alice Coltrane, '69-72; Charles Tolliver, '70; Lonnie Liston Smith, '72-3; Sonny Rollins, '73; Michael White, etc. In July '75 formed own gp. and pl. the Tin Palace, NYC.

Fest: NJF-NY '73 w. Sam Rivers; Montreux '73. The *Montreux Riviera* wrote: "During the last few years bassists have explored the possibilities long unimaginable on this instrument, but McBee almost entirely renews it."

Infl: Pettiford, Ray Brown. Award: NEA Grant for composition, '75. Comp: *Song of Her; Felicite; Wilpan's; Love; Morning Changes; From Within; Voice of the Seventh Angel; Life Waves; Mutima; A Feeling; Tulsa Black*. LPs: *Mutima*; w. Tolliver, *Music Inc.; Live at Slugs* (Strata-East); w. McLean; Moncur; Shorter (BN); Andrew Hill (BN, Arista); w. Lateef; Lloyd (Atl.); w. Sanders; Alice Coltrane; Sam Rivers; John Klemmer (Imp.); w. Leon Thomas; Lonnie Liston Smith (Fly. Dutch.); Norman Connors (Buddah).

McBROWNE, LEONARD LOUIS (LENNY),* *drums*; b. Brooklyn, N.Y., 1/24/33. Busy freelance musician in NYC from early '50s. Pl. w. Randy Weston, '66; toured w. Booker Ervin for most of the next three years. Worked in Blue Mitchell group. After rec. as sideman on several Prest. albums, joined Geo. Wein's Newport All Stars, late '69. To Japan w. all star guitar group, '70. On return to U.S. pl. Newport JF. Back to Japan w. T. Monk; during this trip, rec. w. Helen Merrill, Teddy Wilson.

McBrowne spent most of '71-4 w. K. Burrell. He moved to SF in '72 but continued to work w. Burrell as well as with the locally based Vernon Alley trio. Attended Laney Coll., Oakland, '72-3. Pl. in show, *Me and Bessie* w. Linda Hopkins in SF, '75. Fests: Monterey, '66; Newport, '67, '70, '71 and various other cities under Newport auspices.

LPs: w. Randy Weston, *African Cookbook* (Atl.); w. Barry Harris, *Luminescence*; w. Sonny Criss, *Up, Up and Away*; w. Teddy Edwards, *It's All Right* (Prest.); w. Booker Ervin, *Booker and Brass* (Liberty); *The In Between* (BN); w. Red Garland, *The Quota* (MPS); w. Burrell, *Both Feet On The Ground; Up The Street, Round the Corner, Down The Block* (Fantasy); w. Sam Noto, *Entrance* (Xanadu).

McCANDLESS, PAUL, *oboe, English horn, bass clarinet, composer*; b. Indiana, Pa., 3/24/47. Oboe major at Duquesne U. and Manhattan Sch. of Mus.; studied w. Robert Bloom and Bernard Z. Goldberg. Appeared w. the Duquesne Wind Symph.; Manhattan Orch.; New College Fest. Orch.; New Haven Symp.; Pittsburgh Symph.; Springfield Symph. Pl. w. the Winter Consort, '68-73, app. at Fillmore East & West; Tanglewood; Schaefer Fest.; Chautauqua; many coll. dates. With Oregon from its formation out of the Winter Consort in the early '70s. Won Pittsburgh Flute Club Award. Voted outstanding soloist at Villanova Intercollegiate JF, '67. Finalist in English horn auditions for NY Phil., '71. Infl: Coltrane, Schoenberg, Berg, Webern, Debussy, Stravinsky, Bartok, yoga. Comp: *All the Mornings Bring; Undertow; Fond Libre; The Swan; St. Philomene*. LPs: w. Oregon, *Winter Light; Distant Hills; Music of Another Present Era*; w. Ralph Towner & Glen Moore, *Trios & Solos* (ECM); w. Winter Consort, *Road* (A&M).

McCANN, LESLIE COLEMAN (LES),* *piano, keyboards, synthesizer, composer, singer*; b. Lexington, Ky., 9/23/35. Began recording with trio, '60. Internationally known after app. at Antibes JF, '62. In the late '60s and early '70s McCann broadened his musical scope. As a singer, he enjoyed success with the ballad *With These Hands*, as well as such social message songs as *Compared to What?* His app. in '69 w. E. Harris at the Montreux JF produced a best selling album, *Swiss Movement*, in which they were feat. as co-leaders. McCann was responsible for the discovery and presentation of R. Flack (q.v.).

In '69, McCann's combo began experimenting extensively in electronics, with the leader pl. elect. piano, clavinet and Arp synthesizer. McCann participated in the motion picture *Soul To Soul*, for which he was one of a group of black American artists who went to Accra, Ghana for the filming. Other movie or TV apps: Nancy Wilson show; *Interface* (PBS); *Positively Black* (NBC-NY); *Playboy* show; Mike Douglas show. Some of his photographs were shown on Bill Cosby's NBC-TV spec. In '75 an exhibition of McCann's photographs was held in the Studio Museum of Harlem.

The group pl. concerts at Lincoln Center w. Mahalia Jackson; Carnegie Hall w. Nancy Wilson, and app. in seminars at many coll. campuses, '70-5. App. in an all star Black Music Show, '72-3-4. Since '71, McCann and his wife have been working as volunteer teachers to a group of children in Mezcales, a small agrarian community near Puerto Vallarta, Mexico.

Among McCann's comps. are *A Little 3/4 For God & Co.; Kathleen's Theme; Beaux J. Poo Boo; The Song of Love; The Morning Song; Some Day We'll Meet Again; Shorty Rides Again*. As arr. he was responsible for the music on Lou Rawls' album, *Stormy Monday* (Cap.). Has been regular participant in Jazzmobile in NYC ghettos.

LPs: *Another Beginning; Comment; Invitation to Openness; Layers; Live at Montreux; Much Les; Talk To the People* (Atl.); *Bag of Gold; More or Les; New From The Big City* (Pac. Jazz); w. Harris, *Swiss Movement* (Atl.).

McCLURE, RONALD DIX (RON),* *bass*; also *piano, accordion*; b. New Haven, Conn., 11/22/41. Continued his studies with Hall Overton in NYC, '65 and worked w. Wynton Kelly trio backing Wes Montgomery and afterward, '65-6. Joined Charles Lloyd and was part of that group when it became first American outfit to play a Soviet jazz festival, '67. Helped form The Fourth Way in '69, pl. and rec. in U.S. and Europe into '70 when he joined Joe Henderson. With Dionne Warwicke for three mos., '70; also Gary Burton, Mose Allison. Taught at Berklee Coll. of Music, '71-2 and free-lanced w. Thelonious Monk, Tony Bennett and Keith Jarrett. To SF where he rec. w. the Pointer Sisters, Jerry Hahn, Julian Priester and Cal Tjader. Pl. w. Freddie Hubbard, Morgana King and was briefly reunited w. Mike Nock and Eddie Marshall of the old Fourth Way. Returned to NYC, Jan. '74 to join Blood, Sweat & Tears. Insp. & infl: Miles Davis, Bill Evans, Scott LaFaro, Paul Chambers, Charles Ives, Hall Overton. Fest: NJF, Montreux, Monterey w. Fourth Way; NJF-NY w. Airto '73. Comp: *Farewell, Goodbye; Skiffling* for Fourth Way; *Mirror Image* for B,S&T. LPs: *Charles Lloyd in the Soviet Union* (Atl.); *Sun & Moon* w. the Fourth Way (Cap.); *In Pursuit of Blackness* w. Henderson (Milestone); *Mirror Image* w. B,S&T (Col.); Pointer Sisters (Blue Thumb).

McCRACKEN, ROBERT EDWARD (BOB),* *clarinet, tenor sax*; b. Dallas, Tex., 11/23/04. Pl. w. F. Trumbauer, J. Venuti in '30s; B. Goodman, Russ Morgan, '40s; L. Armstrong, J. Teagarden, '50s; K. Ory, Red Allen, '59. During '60s, managed an apartment building in LA, but still played occasionally, rejoining Teagarden in '62, and working w. Wild Bill Davison in '67. McCracken died in LA 7/4/72.

McCURDY, ROY WALTER JR.,* *drums*; b. Rochester, N.Y., 11/28/36. A full time member of the Cannonball Adderley quintet from the mid-60s, McCurdy traveled internationally with the group, incl. a particularly successful tour of S. America in '72. In his spare time he did studio work for NBC Movies of the Week, and was feat. on various rec. dates. When Adderley was sidelined by illness in July, '75, McCurdy toured w. Kenny Rankin. He also pl. on commercial jingles w. B. Golson, and gigged locally w. both Golson and Jerome Richardson.

LPs: w. Adderley (Cap.; Fant.); Nat Adderley (Atl.; Milest.); w. Joe Williams; G. Ammons (Fant.); D. Axelrod (Cap.); w. J. Zawinul (Vortex).

McDUFF, BROTHER JACK (Eugene McDuffy),* *organ, composer*; also *piano, bass*; b. Champaign, Ill., 9/17/26. Continued to tour w. his own gp., app. at NJF-NY, 74-5. LPs: *The Fourth Dimension; Heatin' System* (Cadet); others on Cadet, Blue Note.

McEACHERN, MURRAY,* *trombone*; b. Toronto, Ontario, Canada, 1915. A swing era veteran who pl. trombone w. B. Goodman in '36, alto sax and trombone w. Glen Gray in '38, McEachern later freelanced in LA. He joined D. Ellington in '73, remaining with the band a few months. In '74 he was appointed leader of the newly organized Tommy Dorsey "ghost" band under the auspices of Dorsey's estate.

LPs: *Music for Sleepwalkers*, Vols. I, II, III (Archives Records).

McFARLAND, GARY,* *composer, vibes, singer*; b. Los Angeles, Cal., 10/23/33. The respected composer-arranger, an important contributor to many albums from the '60s, died 11/3/71 of a heart attack in NYC. He was one of the founders of the short-lived but artistically successful Skye Records, for whom he recorded his suite *America The Beautiful*, one of his outstanding works.

LPs: *Point of Departure; Profiles; Simpatico; Tijuana Jazz* (Imp.); *How To Succeed in Business Without Really Trying* (Verve).

McGARITY, LOU,* *trombone*; also *violin, singer*; b. Athens, Ga., 7/22/17. Pl. two long stints w. B. Goodman in '40s; Raymond Scott, '42-3; west coast w. Red Nichols, then back in NYC, '47. McGarity worked w. E. Condon, the Lawson-Haggart band, rec. w. Cootie Williams, M. Spanier, N. Hefti, Wild Bill Davison; toured Orient w. Bob Crosby in '64 and became a charter member of World's Greatest Jazzband in '67, leaving in '70 owing to ill health. He remained intermittently active and was working a job in Washington when he suffered a heart attack. He died 8/24/71 in Alexandria, Va. McGarity was a powerful soloist in the Jack Teagarden tradition. LPs: *Jazz Master* (Fat Cat's Jazz); w. WGJ (Project 3).

McGHEE, WALTER (BROWNIE),* *singer, guitar, composer*; b. Knoxville, Tenn., 11/30/15. Partner of Sonny Terry from April 1939. Continued to tour on full time basis: folk and blues festivals throughout US and Canada, '66; England and Continent, '67; six week tour of schools in Scandinavia, '68, British tour w. B.B. King, Fleetwood Mac, '69; subsequent blues, folk and jazz concerts and festivals in England, Germany etc. New Zealand and Australia, 1974-75, taking part in the first blues festivals ever held there. Back to England and Continent '75.

LPs, Films, TV etc.: see Terry, Sonny. Comps: *Life is a Gamble; Tell Me Why; Blues Had a Baby (And They Called It Rock and Roll); Walk On; Hole in the Wall; I Couldn't Believe My Eyes; My Father's Words; Watch Your Close Friend; Rainy Day.*

Living in Oakland, McGhee late in 1975 was working on his autobiography. He then had seven children, eight grandchildren and one greatgrandchild.

Publ: *Brownie's Many Ways of Playing Guitar* (Oak Publications, 33 W. 60th St., NYC 10023).

McGHEE, HOWARD,* *trumpet, composer*; b. Tulsa, Okla., 3/16/18. Played w. Andy Kirk, Charlie Barnet bands; Coleman Hawkins combo; JATP in '40s; own gps. into '50s at Birdland, etc. After a period of relative inactivity in late '50s made comeback w. own quartet. In the spring of '66 formed a big band and has alternated between small and large ensembles from that time; also as a single for concert apps. In late '60s-early '70s often associated w. singer Joe Carroll. Pl. Hudson River boatrides in '70s; Stryker's, NYC; Three Sisters, West Paterson, N.J. w. quintet, '75. Concerts, Shrewsbury, N.J., '74-5. From '60s playing Jazz Vespers for St. Peter's Lutheran Church; Christmas show on NBC-TV for Rev. John Gensel, '67. Toured Europe w. Newport package, '67. Fest: NJF-NY, Radio City jam, '72; w. big band at Apollo Theater, '73. Comp: *Born On This Day; The Search; Bless You*, written for George Tucker. LPs: *Newport in New York, The Jam Sessions, Vols. 3&4* (Cobble.); w. Don Patterson, *Boppin' & Burnin'* (Prest.); Fats Navarro reissue (BN).

McGRIFF, JIMMY,* *organ*; b. Phila., Pa., 4/3/36. Continued to travel around the US w. his group for clubs and concerts. Pl. in Jazz in the Garden series at Museum of Modern Art in '60s. Recorded twice w. Richard "Groove" Holmes, once in concert. LPs: Groove Merchant; Solid State; w. Holmes, *Come Together; Giants in Concert*; w. Junior Parker, *Good Things* (Gr. Merch.).

McINTOSH, LADD, *composer, educator, reeds*; b. Akron, Ohio, 7/14/41. Father pl. tenor sax in '30s; mother a piano teacher. Stud. Ohio State U. School of Mus., '59-70 intermittently; BM in comp., MM woodwinds. As a student, won outstanding composer awards at five major coll. jazz fests.

McIntosh is one of the leading jazz educators to whom an entire chapter was devoted in Allen Scott's book, *Jazz Educated, Man.*

Comps: *Bravo, Picasso; In Memoriam; The Fallen Warrior*, commissioned by Jimmy Lyons, dedicated to John F. Kennedy; *Illicit Debauchery (and How to Cultivate It); Groupies; The Incredible Mr. Ellington; Music for a Different Planet, Dying In Another Time* (12-tone jazz comp.).

McIntosh was the only dir. to take a winning band to the Nat'l. Amer. Coll. Jazz Fest. from more than one school: Ohio State, '67; U. of Utah, '71 and '72; Westminster Coll., '73.

McINTOSH, THOMAS S. (TOM),* *composer, trombone*; b. Baltimore, Md., 2/6/27. In addition to working w. T. Jones-M. Lewis band, '66-9, McIntosh organized the New York Jazz Sextet, touring East Coast colleges, and feat. his jazz suite, *Whose Child Are You?* In '69 he moved to the West Coast, where he gave up his instrumental activity in order to concentrate on comp. or arr. for motion pics. Among the films with which he was associated were *The Learning Tree*, '69; *Soul Soldier*, '71; *Shaft's Big Score*, '72; *Slither*, '73; *John Henry*, '74. Comps: *Malice Toward None; Cup Bearers; Great Day.*

LPs: w. N.Y. Jazz Sextet (Scepter); Jones-Lewis (SS).

McINTYRE, EARL P., *bass trombone, composer*; also *trombones, tubas*; b. New York, N.Y., 11/21/53. Stud. at High School of Mus. & Art; Mannes Coll. of Mus.; priv. w. Alan Raph, John Clark, Jack Jeffers, Benny Powell. Pl. w. Ch. Mingus, Billy Taylor, Taj Mahal, T. Jones-M. Lewis, Natural Essence, Howard Johnson, C. Terry big band, James Spaulding, Paul Jeffrey, S. Rivers. In '75 writing for Chas. Rouse, Alex Blake, Walter Booker, and pl. in B. Taylor band in *Black Journal* series. Infls: H. Hancock, Milton Nascimento, W. Shorter, J.J. Johnson, Howard Johnson.

Comps: *Impressions of an African Rain Forest; Overkill Horn; Variations on Last Night; Ivan The Terrible; Song of the Valdez Diamond*. LPs: *In Search of Happiness* w. Natural Essence (Fant.).

McINTYRE, KENNETH ARTHUR (KEN),* *alto saxophone, composer*; also *flute, oboe, bass clarinet, bassoon, piano*; b. Boston, Mass., 9/7/31. Made his rec. debut, '60 and from that time was an important and active member of the decade's avant garde, through club apps., fests. and further rec. From '67-9 taught theory, instrumental music, history of jazz, and cond. the Lab Band, for which he also comp., at Central State U. in Ohio; Ass't. Prof. at Wesleyan U., '69-71; visiting lecturer in African-American Music History and Improvisation in the African-American Tradition, Smith College, '71- . Dir. of Music and Dance, Prof. of Humanities at State U. of N.Y. Coll. at Old Westbury, '71- . Received Nat'l Endowment for the Humanities Summer Stipend award for research in *The Concept of Time in Ghanaian Music*, '71. Ed.D. from U. of Mass., '74.

Apps. w. Harlem Phil. Orch. and Bridgeport Symph. Orch. Film scores: *How Wide Is Sixth Avenue; Miracle on the BMT*. TV: *Dateline Boston* w. John McLellan, WHDH; *Profiles of the Arts*, w. N. Hentoff, WNBC. Fests: Hampton, '68; Newport, '66, '73; N.Y. Musicians Fest., '72. LP: *Hindsight* (SteepleChase).

McKENNA, DAVID J. (DAVE),* *piano*; b. Woonsocket, R.I., 5/30/30. Continued his longtime association w. Bobby Hackett by pl. w. him on Cape Cod. He also was in residence w. his own group in that section of Massachusetts in the '70s. In Oct. '74 pl. at Michael's Pub, NYC. Gigged w. Jake Hanna-Carl Fontana in LA, July '75. Writing about a McKenna performance Whitney Balliett remarked that "the rhythmic impetus he developed summoned up highballing freights . . . but the slow numbers were just as hypnotic."

An elegant, two-handed player, particularly effective as an unaccompanied soloist, a role he filled during the NJF-NY, '73. Appeared at Colorado JP many times in late '60s and '70s. LPs: *Cookin' at Michael's Pub; Solo Piano; Quartet* feat. Z. Sims (Chiaro.).

McKIBBON, ALFRED BENJAMIN,* *bass*; b. Chicago, Ill. 1/1/19. Living in LA; staff musician at NBC from mid-1960s, also jobbing extensively in clubs and concerts w. combos, and w. singers incl. Joe Williams, F. Sinatra, Diahann Carroll. Recorded w. Ray Charles. Toured with Giants of Jazz, an all-star group of bop musicians, in US and Europe, '71-2. Mainly working w. Sammy Davis '75. LPs: *Giants of Jazz* (Atl.); w. Monk (Black Lion).

McKINLEY, RAY,* *drums*; b. Fort Worth, Tex., 6/18/10. Popular swing era figure heard w. J. Dorsey; co-leader of band w. Will Bradley, then own band. Took over direction of Glenn Miller AAF band jointly w. Jerry Gray. Led Miller style band under sponsorship of Miller's estate from '56 until Jan. '66. Hosted U.S. Treasury

Show *Bring Back The Bands*, '67-8. Own small combo at Rainbow Grill, NYC, '68, '69 with such sidemen as Bernie Privin, trumpet; Lenny Hambro, clarinet. Musical consultant for Disney World, '71. Since then, part time activity heading big dance bands.

LPs: *Ray McKinley's Greatest Hits* (Dot).

McKINNEY, HAROLD WALTON (HAL), *piano, composer, singer*; also *violin, oboe, vibes*; b. Detroit, Mich., 7/4/28. He is the second of seven brothers and three sisters, among whom is the trombonist known as Kiane Zawadi. Stud. w. mother; priv. teachers, '35-42; BA from Morehouse Coll., '52. Early exp. pl. gospel music in church. Insp. by Ch. Parker, Bud Powell, Ellington, Gershwin and classical composers. Led own groups at clubs in Detroit. Traveled w. G. Krupa, W. Montgomery; pl. w. K. Burrell, S. Stitt, Louis Smith; acc. Carmen McRae, other singers. Worked in husband/wife duo w. Gwen McKinney. After many years of formal and informal studies, he became a teacher and authority on Afro-American music, serving as mus. dir. of Detroit's Metropolitan Arts Complex, and a local TV series. Wrote articles for Michigan Chamber of Commerce magazine, Mich. Chronicle and Negro History Bulletin. Was assoc. with the first jazz studies sponsored by Wayne U. Toured Detroit public schools and colls. throughout Mich. under aegis of Cultural Enrichment Division, '67-8, and Mich. State Council for the Arts, '69-70.

Comps: *Ode to Africa* for chorale and band; *Blue Job* (based on the 14th chapter of the Book of Job); *Sonata in C# Minor* (based on jazz and blues, and set in sonata form); *Heavenese*, original music and lyrics. LPs: *Voices and Rhythms of the Creative Profile* (Tribe); as singer, *Something In The Wind* w. Paul Winter (A & M); *Bohannon*, w. Hamilton Bohannon (Dakar).

McLAUGHLIN, JOHN, *guitar, composer*; also *piano, synthesizer*; b. Yorkshire, England, 1/4/42. Mother a violinist. Self-taught except for a few piano lessons. First pro. job in late '50s w. Big Pete Deuchar and his Professors of Ragtime; other jobs in England w. Graham Bond, Herbie Goines, Brian Auger. Emigrating to the U.S. in '68, he worked w. Tony Williams' Lifetime; pl. w. Miles Davis, rec. *Bitches' Brew; In a Silent Way*. Formed own group, the Mahavishnu Orchestra, '71, taking the name given by his guru, Sri Chinmoy.

McLaughlin drew his original inspiration from blues artists such as Muddy Waters, Big Bill Broonzy and Leadbelly, as well as such jazz stars as Django Reinhardt, Tal Farlow and Barney Kessel. In his own group these elements were synthesized into a pan-idiomatic style that reflected a rare sense of spirituality. McLaughlin was heavily influenced by his spiritual master, Sri Chinmoy but left him in late '75, dropping the name Mahavishnu. Fests: Montreux; Festival at Orange, France, '75. Comps: *Meetings of the Spirit; Dawn; The Noonward Race; A Lotus On Irish Streams; Vital Transformation; The Dance of Maya; You Know You Know; Awakening; Birds of Fire; Celestial Terrestrial Commuters; Thousand Island Park; Sanctuary; Open Country Joy; Resolution; Power of Love; Vision Is A Naked Sword; Smile of the Beyond; Wings of Karma; Hymn to Him; Eternity's Breath; Life's Dance; Can't Stand Your Funk; Cosmic Strut; Earth Ship; On The Way Home To Earth*, etc.

Some of the sidemen who have pl. w. Mahavishnu incl. Billy Cobham, Khalid Yasin (Larry Young), Armando Peraza, Jean-Luc Ponty, John Surman, Tony Oxley, et al.

Jim Schaffer wrote in DB, 4/26/73, "Mahavishnu's exotic sound is among the finest to arise from the musical experimentation of the past decade. The technical achievement inherent in *Birds of Fire* verges on the edge of credibility when combined with the unique oneness that gives the Mahavishnu Orchestra its own place in the jazz world."

LPs: w. Mahavishnu Orch., *The Inner Mounting Flame; Birds of Fire; Between Nothingness and Eternity; Apocalypse; Visions of the Emerald Beyond*; John McLaughlin-Carlos Santana, *Love Devotion Surrender* (Col.); McLaughlin, *Extrapolation* (Polydor); *Devotion; My Goals Beyond* (Douglas); w. Miles Davis, *Bitches Brew; In A Silent Way; Tribute to Jack Johnson; Live/Evil* (Col.); w. Tony Williams (Poly.).

McLEAN, JOHN LENWOOD (JACKIE),* *alto sax, flute, composer, educator*; b. New York City, 5/17/32. After playing w. Charles Mingus, Art Blakey and app. in the Off-Broadway prod. of *The Connection*, toured Europe and Japan w. own gp. and pl. in US clubs while living in NYC, '66. In '67 began to study flute and took job as bandmaster and counselor for State Correction Dept. Stopped pl. in clubs. Began to commute to Connecticut and took part time teaching position at U. of Hartford, '68-9. Cont. teaching there in '70-1 and moved to Hartford, also counseling drug addicts. From '72 teaching full time at Hartt Coll. of Hartford U., developing Afro-American Music Dept. Instrumental in forming a culture program for inner city children (adults also attend) called *The Artist Collective*, teaching music, dance, visual arts and drama. From '72 McLean also traveled to Denmark to teach at Vallekilde, a summer music school. While there he pl. at Montmartre as a soloist and w. Dexter Gordon and rec. for the SteepleChase label. In '75 he appeared at the Five Spot, NYC, w. own band that incl. his son, Rene, on tenor sax.

Acted and pl. in film version of *The Connection*; many TV apps. w. Gil Noble on *Like It Is*, ABC; local TV in Hartford. Fest: Chateauvallon, France. A product of the bop generation's second wave, McLean is capable of playing convincingly and originally in a number of contemporary grooves with the same searing passion and invention that has marked his work from the time he was a teenage sensation. Comp: *Little Melonae; Dr. Jackle; Dig; Minor March; Quadrangle; Marie Caveau; Day of Absence*, a play for Robert Hooks; *The Gimmick*, play for Roger Furman. LPs: *New York Calling; Antiquity; Live at Montmartre; Ode to Super* w. G. Bartz; *The Meeting; The Source*, both w. D. Gordon (Steeple.); *Jacknife; Demon's Dance; 'Bout Soul; New and Old Gospel* (BN).

McLEOD, ALICE. see Coltrane, Alice.

McNAIR, HAROLD,* *flute, alto, tenor saxophones*; b. Kingston, Jamaica, 5/11/31. Heard in Europe from '59 w. K. Clarke and Q. Jones, McNair was prominent on the British scene for his work w. Donovan and Ginger Baker. He died in London 3/7/71.

McPARTLAND, JAMES DUGALD (JIMMY),* *cornet*; b. Chicago, Ill., 3/15/07. Veteran of early Chicago jazz; pl. w. Ben Pollack, '27-9. Was married, '45, to Marian Page, and has occasionally app. with her during and since the 20 years of their marriage. Visited Durban, S. Africa, '71, '72; toured w. Art Hodes, '73; NJF and Nice JF, '74. Plays Jimmy Ryan's club, NYC, every year as leader. Co-leader of combo w. Buddy Tate at Americana Hotel, NYC. Concerts and workshops in schools with own group, and w. Marian McPartland, '74-5.

McPartland remained one of the best cornetists in the Bix Beiderbecke tradition. Publs: *Sounds of Dixieland* for Combos; *Dixieland Series*, w. Dick Cary (Edw. B. Marks Music Corp., 1790 Broadway, N.Y. 10019).

LPs: *Jimmy McPartland's Dixieland* (Harmony); *The McPartlands Live at the Monticello* (Halcyon); *On Stage*, w. Maxine Sullivan (Jazzology).

McPARTLAND, MARIAN,* *piano, composer*; b. Windsor, England, 3/20/20. To U.S. '46, with husband Jimmy McPartland. After working with him in Chicago, she started with her own trio with which she played during the '50s, most often at the Hickory House in NYC. During the '60s she diversified her activities, returning several times to England, touring briefly w. B. Goodman sextet in '63, and writing such compositions as *Twilight World* (rec. by Tony Bennett in '73).

McPartland also has served on the committees of various jazz orgs. and arts councils; has worked as a disc jockey, journalist and record producer. She started her own Halcyon label in '69. Alec Wilder wrote 20 piano pieces for her, six of which she rec. on Halcyon. She wrote music for an educ. film, *The Light Fantastic Picture Show* in '74, obtainable from Films Inc., 1144 Wilmette Ave., Wilmette, Ill. 60091.

Also during '74 she undertook a nine week pilot project teaching jazz to children in predominantly black public schools in Washington, D.C., with D. Ellington among her guest performers, shortly before his death. She toured South America in a piano package with E. Hines, Teddy Wilson and Ellis Larkins. Concert and workshop apps. at Harvard and Howard U's. Her comp. *Ambiance* was rec. by the Thad Jones-Mel Lewis orch. Played solo piano at NJF-NY, '74.

Marian McPartland has progressed over the years from a competent but derivative British import to a mature artist of complete self-assurance. At an unaccompanied concert in 1975 in Los Angeles, she impressed the audience with the rhythmic agility of her left hand, and the skilfull way with which she used it, sometimes to accompany, more often to complement and correlate what was going on in the right. She is an exceptionally lyrical ballad performer, enriching and expanding the harmonic and melodic essence of every theme.

Own LPs on Halcyon; also *Let It Happen* by Jazz Piano Quartet w. D. Hyman, R. Hanna, Hank Jones (RCA).

McPHERSON, CHARLES,* *alto sax*; b. Joplin, Mo., 7/24/39. Although he formed his own group in '66, he also cont. his assoc. w. Barry Harris and Ch. Mingus, touring in Europe w. the latter in '72. Occasionally lecturing at colls., demonstrating *Jazz and the Saxophonist* in '70s. Fests: NJF, '69, '71; NJF-NY, '73-4; Eastern and Western Europe, incl. Berlin Jazztage, Cascais JF, Portugal, w. *Musical Life of Charlie Parker* tour, fall '74. App. many times w. own quintet at Boomer's, NYC, '74-5. Won DB Critics' Poll TDWR, '67. A strong interpreter and extender of the Parker idiom with a particularly singing tone.

Comps: *Horizons; Night Eyes; Charisma; She Loves Me*. LPs: *Beautiful* (Xanadu); *Today's Man; Siku Ya Bibi* (Mainstream); *Horizons; From This Moment On; Live at the Five Spot* (Prest.); *Charles Mingus and Friends in Concert* (Col.); w. Mingus (Fant., Prest.); w. Bobby Jones (Cobble.).

McRAE, CARMEN,* *singer, piano*; b. New York City, 4/8/22. A solo vocalist since '54, McRae continued to tour, enjoying particular popularity in Japan, which she visited five times between '64 and '75. She moved to Beverly Hills, Cal. in '67 and was frequently seen at LA and Hollywood clubs. She had a role in the film *Hotel*. Other overseas visits included Holland and Denmark, '73; Ronnie Scott's Club, London, '74; Sweden, June '75, followed immediately by an appearance on *Showboat 3*, the jazz festival cruise.

Though occasional demands were made by recording producers to give her a so-called contemporary direction, McRae for the most part remained loyal to her credo of interpreting top quality songs in a style mirroring her jazz experience, her talent as a musician (she continued to play piano from time to time in her act) and her rare ability to bring to life even the most mundane of lyrics. Festival appearances included Monterey almost every year, as well as Newport, Concord, Brussels etc. TV: *Merv Griffin; Tonight Show; Mike Douglas Show; Soul; Like It Is; Pearl Bailey Show; Hollywood Palace; Jonathan Winters Show*.

LPs: *I Am Music* (BN); *Great American Song Book; Sound of Silence; Just A Little Lovin'; Portrait of Carmen; For Once In My Life* (Atl.); *It Takes A Whole Lot of Human Feelings; Ms. Jazz* (Groove Merchant); *Carmen* (Temponic); *Carmen McRae; Carmen's Gold; Live and Doin' It; Alive!; In Person; I Want You;* (Mainstr.). An album entitled *Carmen Alone*, in which she sang and played piano, was recorded in Tokyo.

McSHANN, JAY (HOOTIE),* *piano, singer, composer*; b. Muskogee, Okla., 1/12/09. (Note: McShann states that this date, given in all ref. books, is incorrect, and that he was born 1/12/16.) Prominent bandleader, often in KC in late 1930s and early '40s; sidemen incl. Ch. Parker. Enjoyed renaissance of interest in late '60s, touring as single or w. small gps. Toured Europe, '68; Spain and France, '69; London, Continent, '70; Spain, France,

'71; annual tours since then incl. seven East Europe cities in '74 w. *Musical Life of Charlie Parker*. TV apps. in Barcelona, '69-70-71; Paris, '73; Montreux, '74. Motion picture: *The Last of the Blue Devils*, 60 minute documentary on Kansas City jazz, '74. Fests: Kansas City, '71; Monterey, Zurich, Montreal, '72; Orange, France, NJF-NY, '73; Montreux, NJF-NY, '74, etc.

Publs: *Boogie Woogie & Blues Piano Solos & Instructions; The Book of the Blues* (MCA Music). Comps: *Confessin' the Blues; Hootie Blues; Yardbird Waltz; Dexter Blues; Jumpin' Blues*; 60 others.

LPs: *Going to Kansas City* (Master Jazz); *Man From Muskogee* (Sackville, Canada); *Kansas City Memories* (Black & Blue, Paris); *McShann's Piano* (Cap.).

MEHEGAN, JOHN,* *piano, teacher, writer*; b. Hartford, Conn., 6/6/20. Mehegan has a distinguished career as music instructor, occasional critic, and writer of a series of books on jazz improvisation, publ. by Watson-Guptill. From '68 he was jazz teacher at the U. of Bridgeport, Conn. Jazz instruc. series for *Clavier Magazine*, '69. Clinics at many univs. Comp. and played TV sound track for Arthur Miller's *Story of Two Mondays*, '73. Lecturer in jazz at Yale U., '74-5. App. at clinic in Trondheim, Norway, sponsored by Northern Piano Teachers Union, '74. Series of clinics in Scandinavia, '75.

MENDES, SERGIO,* *piano, composer*; b. Niteroi, Brazil, 2/11/41. Resident in U.S. since mid-60s, leading the popular group known as Brasil '65, later Brasil '66. The group toured w. F. Sinatra and B. Rich band, '67, pl. w. National Symphony in Washington, '68, app. at White House, '70. Many TV specs. w. Bob Hope, Fred Astaire et al. The group's name was changed in '69 to Brasil '77. Mendes moved toward a sound with greater mass appeal, using an extra percussionist in a style once described as "electro-bossa-rock-pop-good-time-music." Comps: *So Many Stars; Song of No Regrets*.

LPs: *Vintage 74*, w. A.C. Jobim as guest star (Bell); reissue of Mendes Trio, *So Nice* (Pickwick Int'l.); *Foursider; Pais Tropical* (A & M); *Sergio Mendes* (Elektra)

MENZA, DON, *tenor saxophone, composer*; also *saxophones, clarinets, flutes*; b. Buffalo, N.Y., 4/22/36. Stud. sax in high school, '53-4; also State U. of N.Y. in Fredonia. Self-taught as composer-arranger. Pl. in Stuttgart w. 7th Army Jazz Band w. D. Ellis, Leo Wright, E. Harris, Cedar Walton, Lanny Morgan, '56. After discharge, pl. w. Al Belletto, '59. Won Best Tenor Sax and Best Soloist awards at Notre Dame JF. Toured w. M. Ferguson, '60-1; led quintet w. Sam Noto in Buffalo, '62-3. From '64-8 Menza worked in Munich w. Max Greger's TV band; also was co-leader of Bavarian radio jazz ensemble which won top honors at the first Montreux JF in '67. Returned to U.S., joined B. Rich, '68. After leaving Rich, settled in LA and became very active pl. in bands for all three major TV networks and many rec. companies, as well as jingle recs. Feat. soloist in films, *The Savage Is Loose; The Organization; Taking of Pelham 1-2-3; Play Misty For Me*. Freelance work w. several big bands in LA area, incl. L. Bellson. He app. in concert w. Buffalo Phil. perf. two of his orig. works.

Comps: *Groovin' Hard; Acid Truth; Time Check*, for Rich; *Inferno; Spanish Gypsy; Back Home*, for Bellson; *One for Otis; Straight Out; Statements & Reflections* etc. for Ferguson; *Morning Song; Devil's Disciples; Cinderella's Waltz; Spanish Boots*, for own album.

Menza is a hard driving tenor soloist infl. mainly by S. Rollins, and a composer-arr. in the mainstream-modern tradition, insp. by B. Holman, O. Nelson and Al Cohn. He was awarded a Federal grant from the National Endowment For the Arts to write three pieces for coll. workshop jazz bands.

LPs: *Morning Song* (MPS); w. Ferguson, *Straight Away; Maynard '62; Maynard '63; Message from Maynard; Si Si MF* (Roul.); w. Rich, *Live at Caesar's Palace* (Liberty); w. Bellson, *Explosion* (Pablo); w. F. Strazzeri, *Taurus* (Creative World); w. Jack Daugherty, *Class of '71* (A & M); w. Greger, *Maximum* (Poly.).

MERRILL, HELEN,* *singer*; b. New York City, 7/21/30. Freelance work as night club vocalist in late '40s and '50s; active mainly in Europe and Japan, '59-67. Settled in Tokyo, '67, where during next five years she made 12 LPs for Japanese Victor, as well as many TV and concert apps. Travels incl. return to U.S. for Milestone LP, '68; jazz fest. in Ljubljana, Yugoslavia, '69. Toured Japan w. Nobuo Hara's Sharps and Flats, '69. Conducted interviews on own show, English language radio station in Tokyo, '70; taught singing '71.

After living in Hong Kong for several months, Merrill returned to the U.S., settling in Chicago in late '72. She worked with local musicians, formed a ten piece band w. Kenny Soderblom and in '75 rec. her first U.S. album in six years, and sang in NYC clubs. She was listed as top vocalist in *Swing Journal*, Tokyo, annually from '67-72.

LPs: *The Feeling Is Mutual; A Shade of Difference* (Milestone). Among the Japanese albums not released in the U.S. are one w. Teddy Wilson and one w. Gary Peacock.

MEZZROW, MEZZ (Milton Mesirow),* *clarinet, saxophones*; b. Chicago, Ill., 11/9/1899. The controversial clarinetist, who had been living in Paris since 1951, died there of arthritis 8/5/72. Though a limited instrumentalist, he was an indomitable propagandist for NO style jazz. His autobiography, describing his experiences not only in music, but also as a user and seller of drugs, provided the basis for a somewhat fictionalized but highly readable book, *Really the Blues* (Random House).

MICHEL, EDWARD M., *producer*; b. Chicago, Ill., 8/20/36. After graduating UCLA (Psych.) 1956, worked as asst. at Pac. Jazz Records. Produced first album in '58. Served in Army Resrve; worked for N. Granz, Val Valentin at Verve Rec. In Europe for Interdisc. To NYC '61 for Riverside as asst. to Bill Grauer, O. Keepnews. To LA, 1966. Joined Impulse Rec. '69. With engineer Bill Szymczyk, explored use of quadraphonic technique in connection with developing free musical forms. Produced LPs by G. Barbieri, Marion Brown, Alice Coltrane, Keith Jarrett, Dewey Redman, Sam Rivers, Pharoah Sanders, Sun Ra, Michael White. Late in '75 he moved to A & M's new Horizon label.

MIKKELBORG, PALLE, *trumpet, composer, conductor*; also *piano*; b. Copenhagen, Denmark, 3/6/41. Self-taught as trumpeter, composer; stud. cond. at Royal Music Cons. in Copenhagen. Began pl. at Club Vingaarden in Copenhagen, '61-4; w. Danish Radio Jazz Group, '64-70, last four yrs. as leader; Danish Radio Big Band, '65-70; Alex Riel-Mikkelborg quintet, '67-8; own quartet, '65-7; Octet, '67-9; Peter Herbolzheimer big band, '70- ; own septet, '72- . Mikkelborg has also worked for varying periods w. G. Russell, D. Gordon, Joachim Kuhn, Eje Thelin, Jan Garbarek, Dollar Brand, Johnny Dyani, Philip Catherine, C. Mariano, M. Ferguson, Ed Thigpen, Tootie Heath, Don Cherry, Bernt Rosengren, Ben Webster, Y. Lateef and, "for one unforgettable night," the Gil Evans orch. Infl: A. Ayler, G. Evans, M. Davis, Clifford Brown, G. Russell, B. Evans, Don Cherry, Charles Ives, Olivier Messiaen. TV: Has comp. mus. for several TV plays and film mus.; TV prod. w. Bill Evans trio & symph. orch., '70; Gordon & strings, '71; app. several times w. own gps., '67, '69, '71, '73-4; TV portrait of his music, '75. Has performed at most major European fests. incl. Montreux where he won a first prize, '68. Was voted Jazzman of the Year in Denmark, '68; number one trumpet in *Jazz Forum*, '69; received Cultural Government Scholarship, '69. Mikkelborg, who states that he is strongly guided by Yoga philosophy, is highly regarded as one of Europe's most creative writer-players. Comps: for big band, *Te Faru; Tempus Zncertum Remanet; Mess-Ra; Salamander Dance; Good Morning Sun; Ashoka Suite; The Mysterious Corona*; for symph. orch. & big band plus soloists, *Maya's Sloer; KMO*. LPs: *The Mysterious Corona*; Danish Radio Jazz Group (Debut); *Brownsville Trolley Line* (Sonet); *My Kind of Sunshine; Wait A Minute; Live at Ronnie's* (MPS); *September Man* (WB); *Live at Onkel Po* (Poly.); *Action-Re-Action* w. Thigpen (Sonet); *You Must Believe in Spring* w. Karin Krog (Poly.); *More Than You Know* w. D. Gordon (Steeple.); *Rhyme and Reason* w. H. Geller (Atl.).

MILES, BARRY,* *composer, piano, keyboards, drums*; b. Newark, N.J., 3/28/47. Very early pro. start, app. on TV shows in '58. Best known orig. as drummer, later mainly as pianist-composer. Toured Europe on "People to People" program, won award as outstanding musician at festival in Düsseldorf. Stud. at Princeton U. '69. Awards from Nat. Endowment for Arts, '73-4. TV: *Fusion Suite* (PBS); several others on PBS. Publ: *Twelve Themes and Improvisations* (Belwin-Mills).

LPs: *White Heat; Scatbird* (Mainstream); *Silverlight* (London), earlier albums on Venture, etc. deleted.

MILES, CHARLES J. (BUTCH) (Charles J. Thornton, Jr.), *drums*; also *percussion*; b. Ironton, Ohio, 7/4/44. Began at age 9 on snare drum. Stud. privately at music store in Charleston, West Va. w. Frank Thompson, '60-1;. major in music at West Va. State Coll., '62-6. Pl. w. various small gps. in West Va. and then went on road w. trio throughout the midwest in '59-69 period; also keyboard percussion w. Charleston Symph. '64-6. With Austin-Moro big band in Detroit, '70-1; Mel Torme, '71-4. Joined Count Basie in Jan. '75. Infl: Rich, Krupa, Bellson, Morello, Alla Rahka, Jo Jones, Cobham, Sonny Payne, Beethoven, Basie, Ellington. Film: *Snowman* w. Torme. TV: *Bandstand*, CBC, Toronto, '73; *On the Town*, Australia, '74. Fest: Concord, '73; NJF-NY; KCJF; Montreux; Antibes, '75. An energetic, spirited drummer with a driving pulse. LPs: w. Basie (Pablo); w. Torme, *Live at the Maisonette* (Atl.).

MILLER, EDDIE,* *tenor saxophone, clarinet*; b. New Orleans, 6/23/11. Best known as key member of Bob Crosby orch. late '30s, early '40s. Rejoined Crosby for frequent guest apps. in '50s, '60s. Toured England as soloist accom. by Alex Welsh orch. March '67. Later that year he went to New Orleans to join Pete Fountain at the latter's club, and was still there in '75, also app. at NOJF. Other fest: NJF-NY w. Crosby; Colo. Jazz Party, '75. Comps: *Lazy Mood; March of the Bob Cats*. LPs: several with Fountain (MCA); *Portrait of Eddie* (Blue Angel); *The Tenor of Jazz*, rec. in London w. Ben Webster, Lockjaw Davis, Bud Freeman (English Fontana).

MILLER, ERNEST (KID PUNCH),* *trumpet, singer*; b. Raceland, La., date uncertain, probably June 1889. The pioneer New Orleans jazzman, who worked with Kid Ory and later with many bands in Chicago, was still playing in his native town during his last years. He died 12/4/71 in New Orleans.

MILLINDER, LUCIUS (LUCKY),* *leader*; b. Anniston, Ala., 8/8/00. Popular in the '30s and '40s, when his band incl. Red Allen, Buster Bailey, John Kirby, Sweets Edison, Dizzy Gillespie and dozens of others who later achieved individual fame, Millinder died 9/28/66 of a liver ailment at Harlem Hospital. Two tracks feat. Wynonie Harris and Sister Rosetta Tharpe, both of whom sang in his band in the '40s, were reissued in *Singin' The Blues* (MCA).

MINASI, DOMINIC (DOM), *guitar*; also *bass*; b. Queens, N.Y., 6/3/43. Stud. w. Joe Geneli, eight yrs.; Sal Salvador, three yrs.; Dan Duffy, one yr.; Jim Hall, six mos.; and majored in music in h.s. Pl. w. Les & Larry Elgart, '69; B. Rich, '72; R. Hanna, '73; Jimmy Heath; Ray Nance; Louis Hayes; Arnie Lawrence; George Coleman; J. Nottingham; Sonny Dallas; Bud Shank; Ernie Wilkins; own gp., '74-5. Infl: Johnny Smith; Coltrane, M. Davis, R. Kellaway. Won partial scholarship to Berklee, '63. Wrote all arrs. on first album, *When Johanna Loved Me*. Publ: *Musicians Manual for Chord Substitution* (Sunrise Artistries, 64-24 Grand Ave., Maspeth, N.Y. 11378). LPs: *When Johanna Loved Me; I Have the Feeling I've Been Here Before* (Blue Note).

MINCE, JOHNNY (John Henry Muenzenberger),* *clarinet, saxes*; b. Chicago Heights, Ill., 7/8/12. Prominent with many swing bands incl. T. Dorsey, Bob Crosby; then spent 20 years as member of CBS radio house band on Arthur Godfrey show, '46-66. Replaced Buster Bailey w. L. Armstrong, Apr. '67. Soon afterward, became active playing club dates in the NYC area; played Dick Gibson's annual jazz parties in Colo. for three years; Odessa, Tex. jazz party for two years; jazz fest. in Hanover, Germany, '74. Toured England w. Kings of Jazz, late '74. Mince is a swing style clarinetist insp. by Goodman, Dodds, I. Fazola.

LPs: *Back Home In Indiana*, w. Lee Wiley; *Greatest Song Hits of Walter Donaldson* (Monmouth-Evergreen); *What a Wonderful World*, w. B. Hackett (Flying Dutchman).

MINERVE, HAROLD (GEEZIL), *alto sax, clarinet, flute, piccolo*; b. Havana, Cuba, 1/3/22. Raised in Orlando, Fla. from age two. Father pl. clarinet, flute and banjo. Took up clarinet at seven but not seriously until private lessons at 12. Pl. in high school band. In '40 left home w. band from Ohio led by drummer Jeff Gilson. After completing school went out on road show pl. alto sax in band backing Ida Cox. Pl. in NO band formerly led by Joe Robichaux but fronted by Joan Lunceford (no relation to Jimmie Lunceford) of Mobile, Ala. Then w. Clarence Love; Ernie Fields. From '43 spent three yrs. in military service. Back w. Fields until '50 when he joined Buddy Johnson. Left in '57 to gig in NYC. With Mercer Ellington at Birdland, '60; Ray Charles, '62-4. Musical dir. for Arthur Prysock. Became member of Duke Ellington organization Sept. 7, '71. Infl: Bechet, Goodman, Shaw, Bigard, Benny Carter, Hodges. Fav. lead alto, Willie Smith. LPs: see Ellington (Duke and Mercer).

MINGUS, CHARLES,* *bass, composer, piano, leader*; b. Nogales, Ariz., 4/22/22. Prominent in LA and SF in '40s; NYC '50s and '60s. From late '50s led series of Jazz Workshop bands that served as forums for such musicians as John Handy, Booker Ervin, Eric Dolphy, Jimmy Knepper, Ted Curson, Clifford Jordan, Charles McPherson, Rahsaan Roland Kirk, J. McLean, Paul Bley, Jaki Byard and many others.

Despite the great importance of his work as leader, catalyst and instrumentalist, Mingus, after the mid '60s, went into semi-retirement, partly due to ill health, and was heard from infrequently. Taking up residence in New York's East Village, he worked on an autobiography, *Beneath the Underdog* (Alfred A. Knopf), published in '71. This spurred renewed interest in his music. He began recording again, and in Feb. '72 made a comeback concert at Philharmonic Hall, NYC, leading a 20-piece orch. Soon afterward, several Mingus albums were released, incl. reissues.

Mingus toured Europe leading a quintet in the fall of '72; again in fall '75. He was also seen in such Village clubs as the Five Spot and Top of the Gate. He was presented in concert at Carnegie Hall in Jan. '74, joined by Kirk.

In addition to annual apps. at Newport, he has been heard in recent years at Antibes, Montreux and fests. in Italy and Japan. He was elected to DB Hall of Fame. Received Guggenheim Fellowship, '71. Among his best known comps. are *The Black Saint and the Sinner Lady; Thrice Upon A Theme; Revelations; Tijuana Table Dance; Fables of Faubus*.

LPs: *At The Jazz Workshop; At Monterey; Chazz; My Favorite Quintet; Quintet Plus Max Roach; Town Hall Concert* (Fantasy); *Charlie Mingus & Friends; Better Git It In Your Soul; Let My Children Hear Music; Mingus Ah Um* (Col.); *Art of Charlie Mingus; Best of Charlie Mingus; Blues and Roots; Mingus Moves; Oh Yeah; Mingus at Carnegie Hall; Changes One; Changes Two* (Atl.); *Black Saint and the Sinner Lady; Mingus, Mingus, Mingus; Charles Mingus Plays Piano*-solo; *Re-evaluation, the Impulse Years* (Imp.); *Tijuana* Moods (RCA); *Great Concert* w. E. Dolphy; *Reincarnation of a Lovebird* (Pres.); *Mingus Moods; Mingus Revisited* (Trip); *Town Hall Concert* (SS); *Wonderland* (UA). As sideman in *Newport in New York, The Jam Sessions, vols. 1&2* (Cobblestone).

MITCHELL, BILLY,* *tenor, alto, soprano saxophones, flute, clarinets, composer, educator*; b. Kansas City, Mo., 11/3/26. One of the many talents to emerge from the Detroit jazz scene of the '40s. Pl. w. Woody Herman, '49; Dizzy Gillespie, Count Basie in '50s. Left Basie in '61 and formed gp. w. Al Grey which was together '62-4. Returned to Basie, mid-'66-mid-'67. Music dir. for Stevie Wonder; along w. Slide Hampton wrote music for Wonder's first night club performance. In '70 returned to Europe for tour w. Clarke-Boland Big Band, of which he had been a founder-member in '63. Pl. alto sax and was mus. dir. for Dizzy Gillespie orchestra which appeared twice at Buddy's Place and for tribute to Dizzy at Avery Fisher Hall, '75. From the late '60s has served as consultant to the Nassau County Office of Cultural Development, one of the largest and most successful organizations of its kind. From '70 very active teaching and performing in educational institutions at all levels. Staff member of major Jazz Workshops in NYC area: Jazzmobile; Jazz Interactions; Henry Street Settlement Music School. In '73 formed Billy Mitchell Incorporated (407 Yale Ave., Rockville Centre, N.Y. 11570), which makes available his Jazz Ensemble or Dizzy Gillespie's group for a combination concert-"rap-session"-clinic-workshop-and tandem concert with the school band for high schools and colleges. Mitchell conducted such seminars at New York Inst. of Tech. and Hofstra U., '75; and took part in a saxophone seminar at Yale. His company also produced a film, *The Marijuana Affair*, with a score by Melba Liston. Mitchell played on the soundtrack.

Comp: *J&B; Bops; Comeback, Baby; Sweet and Basie*. LPs: w. Clarke-Boland, *Off Limits* (Poly.); Bobby Pierce, *New York*; Eddie Jefferson, *Things Are Getting Better* (Muse); Roland Prince (Vang.).

MITCHELL, RICHARD ALLEN (BLUE),* *trumpet*; also *fluegelhorn*; b. Miami, Fla., 3/13/30. After leaving H. Silver, with whom he played from '58-64, maintained similar group under his own leadership w. Junior Cook, C. Corea and Al Foster to '69. Toured w. R. Charles, '69-71; John Mayall, '71-3. From '74, freelance work in LA mainly w. Bill Berry, Bill Holman, Jack Sheldon, L. Bellson, Richie Kamuca. Canadian cross-country tour w. Bellson, '74.

Own LPs on RCA, Blue Note, Mainstream; w. Silver (Blue Note); *Night Blooming Jazzmen* (Mainstream);

Mayall (Polydor); Bill Berry (Beez).

MITCHELL, ROBERT E. JR. (BOB), *trumpet, fluegelhorn, valve trombone*; b. Birmingham, Ala., 5/23/35. Attended Juilliard School 1964-7; stud. tpt. w. Wm. Vacchiano, then first tpt. w. NY Philharmonic. Other teachers: Leo Demers, Jimmy Stamp, Louis Maggio. Worked with Earl Hines, 1969-71; free-lanced in LA until he joined Count Basie, late 1974. Infls: Gillespie, Miles Davis, Rafael Mendez, Clifford Brown, Woody Shaw, Maynard Ferguson, Clark Terry. Feat. solo on *Freckle Face* in Basie LP on Pablo, 1975.

MITCHELL, GEORGE,* *trumpet*; b. Louisville, Ky., 3/8/1899. The celebrated trumpeter and cornetist, who pl. on some of the best known sessions w. Jelly Roll Morton in the '20s, lived in retirement for many years and died 5/27/72 in Chicago. LPs: w. Morton (RCA).

MITCHELL, GROVER,* *trombone, euphonium, composer*; b. Whatley, Ala., 3/17/30. Heard as lead trombonist w. Basie, Oct. '62 to May '70. Moved to LA June '70. Since then, engaged primarily in TV and movie work; also rec. w. S. Vaughan, Nancy Wilson, B. Eckstine, E. Fitzgerald, Diana Ross, Maria Muldaur, Cass Elliott et al. Films: seen, also heard in solo on sound track of *Lady Sings The Blues*. Comp. *Magna; Fat Cat* for R. Callender's *Basin Street Brass* album (Legend).

Mitchell, who has worked with such major composer-conductors as O. Nelson, Q. Jones, H. Mancini, B. May, M. Legrand, recently has been stressing the writing aspects of his career.

LPs: *Have a Nice Day*, w. Basie (Daybreak); *Michel Legrand and Sarah Vaughan* (Mainstream); *Nifty Cat Strikes West* w. R. Eldridge (Master Jazz); *Now and Then* w. B. Collette (Legend).

MITCHELL, KEITH MOORE (RED),* *bass*; also *piano, cello, bass guitar*; b. New York City, 9/20/27. Prominent in LA for many years, often working with Hampton Hawes, Mitchell was briefly w. D. Gillespie in '68, but was unable to work full time as a jazz musician. In July '68 he decided to leave the U.S. He pl. at Cafe Montmartre in Copenhagen w. Phil Woods; then in a trio w. Bobo Stenson and Rune Carlsson in Switzerland. Settling in Stockholm, he became one of Europe's busiest free-lance musicians, both in European groups and with many of the principal visiting American soloists. Formed new gp. w. Scandinavian musicians, Communication; rec. in Stockholm 1975.

LPs: w. S. Asmussen-T. Thielemans (A & M); w. L. Konitz, *I Concentrate On You* (Steeple.); w. Al Cohn, *Broadway/1954* (Prest.).

MITCHELL, ROSCOE, *soprano, alto, tenor, bass saxophones, flute, piccolo, oboe, clarinet*; also *tambourine, drums, bells, gongs, whistles, steeldrum, bell lyre, bike horns, singer*; b. Chicago, Ill., 8/3/40. First infl. as a child by recs. of Billie Holiday, Louis Armstrong, Billy Eckstine, and by the church of his uncle, Charles Commodore Carter, a popular preacher, artist and mystic, he began to sing, dance and create his own compositions. Pl. baritone sax in high school band; alto in senior yr. Both inst. in Army w. Headquarters USARA Band in Heidelberg, Germany. Discharged from Army July '61; pl. in Art Blakey-style gp. w. Henry Threadgill. Infl. at the time by Wayne Shorter but had already heard Ornette Coleman while in service. Joined Richard Abrams' Experimental Band and became associated w. Joseph Jarman, Anthony Braxton and others who led into the formation of the AACM. His own gp., the Roscoe Mitchell Sextet rec. for Delmark in Aug. '66. With Jarman, Lester Bowie and Malachi Favors formed Art Ensemble of Chicago after pl. concerts under the names Joseph Jarman & Company and the Lester Bowie Quartet. Pl. and lived in France, June '69-April '71. Comp: *Odwalla; Sound; Ornette; The Little Suite; Tkhke; The Key; Congliptious; Old; Tnoona; Nonaah.*

LPs: see Art Ensemble of Chicago; also *Sound* (Delmark); *Congliptious* (Nessa).

MIXON, DANIEL ASBURY (DANNY), *piano, composer*; also *trombone*; b. New York City, 8/19/49. From age three tap dancing w. the Ruth Williams Dance Studio, performing annually at Carnegie Hall until age 14. From 15-17 attended H.S. of Performing Arts stud. ballet, tap and drama w. intention of becoming prof. dancer but took up trombone at 15 and pl. in all-borough orch. Grandfather and grandmother who pl. by ear taught him piano. At 17 left home to pl. w. Patti and the Bluebells in Atlantic City. Abandoned dance career. Acc. Joe Lee Wilson, '67-70; Betty Carter, '71-4, to whom he was married during most of this period. For two yrs. in this time did only formal stud. of piano w. Roland Hanna. Worked w. Grant Green; Art Blakey; Carlos Garnett; Rufus Harley; Big Maybelle; Joe Williams; Eddie Jefferson; Dee Dee Bridgewater; Roy Brooks; Frank Foster. For a while typed as a singers' accompanist he has branched out in recent years. Own trio from '72. In '75 working w. Bob Cunningham trio; Pharoah Sanders. Has also pl. w. Piano Choir which rec. his *Main Extensions*.

Infl: Art Tatum, Erroll Garner, Ahmad Jamal, McCoy Tyner, Ravel, Dvorak, Stravinsky, Bartok. TV: documentary on *Three Generations of Jazz* concert done at NYU w. Eubie Blake, Roland Hanna; *Someone New* w. own trio, NBC, '69; *Woman Alive* w. D. Bridgewater, PBS, '75. Fest: NJF-NY w. own trio, '73; Reims w. P. Sanders, '75. LPs: w. Piano Choir, *Handscapes* (Strata-East); w. Betty Carter (Bet-Car).

MIYAMA, TOSHIYUKI, *clarinet, alto saxophone, leader*; b. Chiba Pref., Japan, 10/31/21. Joined Navy band, '39, remaining until 1945. Pl. for U.S. Forces camps in Japan as member of Lucky Puppy band, '46-7. In '50 he formed his own band, the Jive Aces, a ten piece group that pl. mainly at Johnson Air Base. In '58 he augmented to 16 pieces, changing the name to New Herd Orch. Two years later he expanded to 18 pieces.

The New Herd pl. extensively in concerts, on TV, radio and at Air Bases. Miyama names Woody Herman, S. Kenton, Thad Jones-Mel Lewis orch., D. Gillespie, Ch. Parker, Q. Jones as his sources of inspiration. Fests: NJF in Tokyo (pl. w. T. Monk); MJF, '74; at the latter the band enjoyed unanimous acclaim and was heralded as the surprise success of the entire fest.; also NJF, '75. New

Herd won a special Jazz Disc Award from *Swing Journal* in '69; Jazz of Japan Award, '70, '71; voted best big band in SJ, '73-4.

LPs: *Modern Jazz Ten Players Collection; New Herd Modern Jukebox; Perspective; Poetry to Libra; Poetry to Aries* (Col.); *Four Jazz Compositions; Yamatai'Fu* (Toshiba EMI); one rec. live at Monterey JF (Trio).

MOBLEY, HENRY (HANK),* *tenor sax, composer*; b. Eastman, Ga., 7/7/30. Most important associations w. Horace Silver, Art Blakey in '50s; Miles Davis in '60s. In the mid-'60s co-led gps. w. Lee Morgan; Kenny Dorham. App. at Ronnie Scott's for seven wks., '67; then toured Europe. To Paris '68 to pl. at Chat Qui Peche w. Slide Hampton; then as soloist in Munich; Rome; Poland; Hungary; Yugoslavia. Returned to NYC in mid-'70, worked at Slugs and pl. other jobs w. a band he co-led w. Cedar Walton. Played in Chicago summer '73. In '75 he was living and pl. in Philadelphia. Fest: NJF-NY, Radio City jam session, '73. Comp: *Breakthrough; Early Morning Stroll; The Morning After; Ace Deuce Trey; 3rd Time Around; A Caddy For Daddy; The Dip; The Vamp; Ballin'; East of the Village; My Sin; Straight Ahead (Kismet); Pat 'N Chat*.

LPs: Cedar Walton/Hank Mobley quintet, *Breakthrough* (Cobble.); *Reach Out; Hi Voltage; Caddy For Daddy; The Turnaround; The Flip; Dippin'* (BN); w. E. Jones, *Midnight Walk* (Atl.); reissue, *Blowing Sessions* (BN).

MODERN JAZZ QUARTET. see Lewis, John.

MOFFETT, CHARLES MACK,* *drums, trumpet, orchestra bells, composer, educator*; b. Fort Worth, Tex., 9/11/29. Active in NYC in '60s w. Ornette Coleman, Sonny Rollins. Made Euro. tour w. Coleman; rec. w. A. Shepp; Coleman; Charles Tyler. Pl. w. bassist Ron Brooks gp., drums and trumpet, sometimes simultaneously. Living in SF area in mid-'70s, app. w. the Charles Moffett Family incl. his sons Charles Jr., tenor sax; Mondre, trumpet; and Codaryl, percussion. Played at the Keystone Korner, March '75. LPs: *The Charles Moffett Family, Vol. 1* (LRS Records, 212 Bishop Ave., Point Richmond, Cal. 94801); *Gift* (Savoy).

MONCUR, GRACHAN III,* *trombone, composer*; b. New York City, 1937. After working w. Ray Charles, the Jazztet and Jackie McLean, he played w. Archie Shepp, '67-9. Also w. Warren Chiasson in late '60s; then charter member of the 360 Degree Experience. After serving as music director of a drug rehabilitation program in Harlem he became the director of the Creative Black Musicians Workshop in Newark, N.J., the city where he co-led a quartet w. organist John Patton.

Shepp recorded his composition *Hipnosis* but his major work of the '70s was *Echoes of Prayer* on the JCOA label. For this recording he conducted a 22-piece orch. which incl. a percussion ensemble from Brazzaville in the Congo. Evocative of Martin Luther King, Marcus Garvey and the social struggle in America, it mixes West Indian, Latin and European classical influences. It was recorded in April '74, following a performance at New York Univ. Other LPs: w. Shepp, *Way Ahead; For Losers; Kwanza* (Imp.); *Live at the Donaueschingen Festival* (MPS/BASF); *New Africa* (Byg).

MONK, THELONIOUS SPHERE,* *piano, composer*; b. Rocky Mount, N.C., 10/10/17. Continued to lead quartet through second half of the '60s. When Charlie Rouse left in '70 he was replaced, first by Pat Patrick and then by Paul Jeffrey. In '71-2 Monk toured w. Dizzy Gillespie, Sonny Stitt et al in a group called The Giants of Jazz, playing all over Europe and appearing at the NJF-NY '72. Due to illness his activities were severely curtailed and when he performed with the NYJRC in a concert of his music on April 6, 1974, it was his first public engagement in over a year. Another rare concert was given with his quartet at the NJF-NY '75, one of the artistic triumphs of the festival. Despite his limited activity he is still looked upon as a father figure by today's musicians, up to and including the avant garde. At Newport-NY his quartet included his son, Thelonious Monk Jr. on drums.

In the '70s his earlier compositions such as *'Round Midnight, Well You Needn't* and *Straight No Chaser* were still being played and recorded. *Nutty* was done with a rock beat by Blue Mitchell in '75. *The Ballad of Thelonious Monk*, recorded by Carmen McRae with its composer, Jimmy Rowles, utilizes the titles of many Monk songs in its lyrics. LPs: *Monk's Blues; Straight No Chaser; Underground; Who's Afraid of the Big Band Monk* (Col.), *Something in Blue; The Man I Love* (Black Lion); w. *Giants of Jazz* (Atl.); reissues on Milestone, Prestige, Blue Note.

MONTGOMERY, CHARLES F. (BUDDY),* *piano, vibes, composer*; b. Indianapolis, Ind., 1/30/30. Toured country for several years with brothers Monk and Wes until the latter's death. Moved in Jan, 1969 to Milwaukee, Wis., where he became involved in a variety of enterprises. In addition to pl. concerts and clubs, he worked annually with Wisconsin's *Summerfest*; was music consultant and instructor for inner city youth in Racine; produced concerts for prisons; taught jazz at Wis. Coll. Conservatory; was judge or clinician at university workshops, etc. From June 1974 he led his own trio at the Marc Plaza Hotel's Bombay Bicycle Club in Milwaukee. Comps: *This Rather Than That; Rosebud; Blues For David; Probin'*.

LPs: *This Rather Than That* (Impulse); *Two Sides of Buddy Montgomery; Best of Wes Montgomery & Friends* (Milestone). Earlier albums w. brothers were on Riv., Fant., Pac. Jazz.

MONTGOMERY, WILLIAM HOWARD (MONK),* *bass, composer;* b. Indianapolis, Ind., 10/10/21. A pioneer of the electric bass, which he introduced to the public while w. Lionel Hampton's orch. in '51. Pl. w. Mastersounds, '57-Jan. '60. During '60s worked w. his brothers Buddy and Wes, and various small combos in LA and SF, incl. C. Tjader. Pl. in bands cond. by Bill Cosby from '69; led own quartet, '69. From '70-2 was member of Red Norvo trio in Las Vegas lounge. Settling in LV, he initiated a crusade for the use of jazz and contemporary music in that city. Late in '74 assembled a 12 piece ensemble to tour S. Africa with singer Lovelace Watkins, the first U.S. jazz band to travel in that country. In '75 he became one of the founders and principal activists in the World Jazz Assn., organizing an affiliated group in LV.

Comps: *Close Your Face; Sister Lena; Bass Odyssey.* LPs: *It's Never Too Late; Bass Odyssey* (Chisa); *Reality* (Phila. Int'l.); *Two Sides of Buddy Montgomery* (Mile.); others with Buddy and Wes Montgomery (q.v.).

MONTGOMERY, JOHN LESLIE (WES),* *guitar, composer*; b. Indianapolis, Ind., 3/6/25. Self-taught. First prominent w. Mastersounds, 1958, a group co-led by his brothers Buddy and Monk. Later led own trio and in '65 teamed for a year w. Wynton Kelly's trio. From '65 rec. a series of major pop-jazz hits. In 1966 his *Goin' Out of My Head* won a Grammy as best instr. jazz perf. of the year. He won numerous other awards incl. DB critics' poll 1960-63, '66-7; DB readers' poll, '61-2, '66-7; *Playboy* All Stars' All Stars for six consecutive years.

Montgomery, who used his thumb instead of a plectrum, and who had developed a much imitated parallel-octaves style that established him as the most original and most imitated guitarist since Charlie Christian, was at the height of his fame when he died suddenly of a heart attack at his Indianapolis home, 6/15/68.

LPs: *The Best Of; Best of Vol. II; Bumpin'; California Dreamin'; Goin' Out of My Head; Movin' Wes; Return Engagement; Smokin' At The Half Note; Tequila; Willow Weep For Me* (Verve); *And Friends; While We're Young* (Milestone); *Best of* w. brothers (Fant.); *Day In The Life; Down Here On The Ground; Greatest Hits; Road Song* (A & M).

MONTOLIU, VINCENTE (TETE), *piano;* b. Barcelona, Spain, 3/28/33. Blind from birth. His father, who pl. English horn in Barcelona Symph. wanted him to become a concert pianist; but in '40 his mother bought him some Ellington records and he became interested in jazz. Three years later Don Byas lived in the Montoliu home and acted as his informal teacher. For many years Tete remained almost unknown, because of the lack of jazz activity in Spain. He staged Sunday morning jam sessions at a small Barcelona theatre. As word of his talent spread, he began to appear around the continent backing Roland Kirk in many European countries during the latter's '64 tour. He also pl. w. Archie Shepp at the Montmartre in Copenhagen for two months, and w. D. Cherry for three weeks, but didn't feel completely at ease with their music. Montoliu in the late '60s and '70s gradually gained acceptance as a gifted soloist with an extremely inventive right hand and an original but adaptable style.

LPs: *Catalonian Fire; Music for Perla; Tete!* (Steeple.); *Songs for Love* (Enja); w. A. Braxton, *In the Tradition* (Steeple.); w. Dusko Goykovich (Enja).

MOODY, JAMES,* *saxophones, flute, composer*; b. Savannah, Ga., 3/26/25. Known for long associations with D. Gillespie, in the latter's big band in late '40s and small combo in early '60s. Leader of own small combos and participant in saxophone battles with Gene Ammons, Sonny Stitt et al. In late '60s Moody was based in NY but toured frequently in US and Europe. Pl. at Dick Gibson's Colorado Jazz Party, '71-2. During '72 he made LA his home, but traveled extensively in the Far East and in Europe, as part of an all star group. Took up residence in Las Vegas June 1974. Featured artist on *Showboat 1*, the first jazz festival cruise from NY to West Indies, June '74. Resident member of house band at Hilton Hotel in LV. Reunited w. Gillespie at tribute concert to latter in NYC, Oct. 1975. A driving, powerful tenor player, supple alto saxophonist and one of the most original jazz flutists. TV: *Just Jazz*, PBS, '71. Comp: *Vezzioso; Never Again; Hear Me; Don't Look Away Now; Feeling Low; Everyone Needs It; Savannah Calling; Last Train From Overbrook; Darben the Redd Foxx*. LPs: Vanguard; *Feelin' It Together; Never Again!* (Muse); *Don't Look Away Now*; many reissues w. '40s, '50s gps (Prest.); other reissues on Cadet; Trip; *The Blues and Other Colors; The Brass Figures* (Mile.); *Heritage Hum; The Teachers* (Perception); *Sax & Flute Man* (Paula); w. Gillespie, *The Real Thing* (Percept.); *Swing Low Sweet Cadillac* (Imp.); w. Dexter Gordon, *Tower of Power; More Power*; w. Eddie Jefferson, *Body and Soul* (Prest.); w. Al Cohn, *Too Heavy For Words* (MPS); *Colorado Jazz Party* (MPS/BASF); w. *C. Mingus and Friends* (Col.).

MOONEY, JOE,* *singer, keyboards*; b. New Jersey, 1911. Best known when he played accordion and led a quartet in NYC in the late 1940s, Mooney later switched to Hammond organ and worked for many years in Florida. He died 5/12/75 in Ft. Lauderdale, Fla. LPs: *The Greatness of Joe Mooney; The Happiness of Joe Mooney* (Columbia).

MOORE, WILLIAM JR. (BILLY),* *composer, piano*; b. Parkersburg, W. Va., 12/7/17. Came to prominence when he replaced Sy Oliver as arranger for the J. Lunceford band, '39. Living in Europe since early '50s. writing for French bands, touring w. Peters Sisters, '53-60, working for Berlin radio band, then spending several years acc. Delta Rhythm Boys, after which he became relatively inactive in music, living in Copenhagen and taking up movie script writing.

MOORE, MILTON AUBREY (BREW),* *tenor saxophone*; b. Indianola, Miss., 3/26/24. Active on NY scene in late '40s-early '50s; then to SF; Europe. From March '65-to Nov. '67 he was based in Copenhagen but then returned to the US, app. in NYC at Joey Archer's Sports Corner, '67-8; Half Note, '68-9. Session for Jazz Interactions; Duke Ellington Society concert w. Ray Nance, '69. Pl. w. Johnny Robinson combo at Limelight in Greenwich Village, '70. To Half Note Club in Canary Islands, '70, then Scandinavia, where he once again took up residence. In '72 he again came back to the US when his father died, living in Mississippi until August '73 when, after stopping momentarily in NYC, he went to Copenhagen. Approximately 10 days later, 8/19/73, he lost his life in a fall down a flight of stairs.

Originally inspired by Lester Young, Moore incorporated elements of the stylistic innovations introduced by Charlie Parker without radically altering his basic style:

romantic, emotional, floating and hard-driving swing. Fest: NJF, '69. Comp: *Brew's Stockholm Dew's; Ergo; No More Brew.*

LPs: *Brew's Stockholm Dew* (Sonet); w. R. Nance, *Body and Soul* (SS); reissue w. Cal Tjader (Fant.).

MOORE, DANIEL WILLIAM (DANNY), *trumpet*; also *piano, violin*; b. Waycross, Ga., 1/6/41. After grad. from Center HS in Waycross, attended Florida A&M U. Toured w. Paul Williams in US, '62. Played w. Art Blakey, '64; five mos. w. C. Basie, '66; also w. Quincy Jones in '60s. A regular member of the Thad Jones-Mel Lewis orch., '69-72; with Aretha Franklin from '71. Often associated in gps. w. George Coleman as co-leader from '72, pl. w. him and Harold Mabern at Boomer's, '75. Worked w. D. Gillespie big band, '75. Infl: Clifford Brown, Thad Jones. Fest: Montreux '73 w. Oliver Nelson. Comp: *A Song for Cherry Hill.* Authoritative as both lead player and soloist. LPs: w. Jones-Lewis, *Central Park North; Live at the Village Vanguard* (SS); w. Q. Jones, *Gula Matari* (A&M); w. O. Nelson, *Swiss Suite* (Fly. Dutch.); w. Johnny Hammond, *Breakout* (Kudu); w. Wes Montgomery (Verve).

MOORE, GLEN R., *bass, composer*; also *violin, piano, flute*; b. Portland, Ore., 10/28/41. Piano lessons in childhood; bass at 13. Stud. w. James Harnett in Seattle; Gary Karr in NYC. Began prof. w. show, *The Young Oregonians*, '56. Pl. w. Jim Pepper, NYC '67; Zoot Sims; Nick Brignola '68; Airto; Paul Bley, Annette Peacock in '68-71; also w. Tim Hardin '68-9; Winter Consort '70-1; Chico Hamilton '72; Benny Wallace '74; Jeremy Steig, on and off, '67-75. From '70, however, main association has been Oregon, a group which mixes many elements into its musical olio. Infl: S. LaFaro, G. Peacock, D. Reinhardt, R. Towner, Jan Hammer, Bartok, J.S. Bach. Fests: Bergamo '74; Molde; Pori '75; NJF-NY '74-5. Comps: *Land of Heart's Desire; At the Hawk's Well; Deer Path; Belt of Asteroids; Three Step Dance; Your Love; Mary's New Bloom; With the Light.* LPs: w. Oregon, *Music of Another Present Era; Distant Hills; Winter Light* (Vang.); *Trios & Solos* (ECM); *This is Jeremy Steig* (SS); *Paul Bley Synthesizer Show* (Milest.); w. Winter Consort, *Road* (A&M).

MOORE, PHIL JR.,* *composer;* also *vocal coach, singer, piano*; b. Portland, Ore., 2/20/18. After many years in New York, Moore returned in Jan. 1974 to Los Angeles, where in the 1940s he had been a staff arr. and cond. at MGM studios. He served as assoc. mus. dir. for the TV special *Duke Ellington: We Love You Madly*; composer for TV drama *Sty of the Blind Pig*, 1974; comp., mus. dir., cond. of stage revue *$600 And A Mule*, 1974; mus. dir. *Cotton Club '75*, TV special. Many arrs. for pop artists, also for Quincy Jones.

MORELL, JOHN, *guitar, composer*; b. Niagara Falls, N.Y., 6/2/46. Self taught on guitar, but instructed in orchestration by Albert Harris. Grandfather, father, brother all guitarists. Worked w. Les Brown, '67-70; S. Manne, '70-4; own group, '75- . Also active in rec. field w. H. Mancini et al; many clubs and concerts in LA area. Made several fest. apps. while w. Manne in Europe, '70. Also at Berkeley Fest. w. Gil Evans-Miles Davis, '68. Morell is a highly sensitive and skilled guitarist, as well as a prolific composer. Many of his compositions have been recorded by Manne, incl. *Seance; Witch's; Pink Pearl; Three On A Match; Don't Know.* During '75 Morell was a member of the band on the Dinah Shore TV show. Infls: Gil Evans, John Coltrane, Miles Davis.

LPs: *John Morell Plays Hits of the '70s* (Cap.); w. Manne, *Alive in London* (Contemp.); *Mannekind* (Mainstr.).

MORELL, MARTY, *drums*; b. New York City, 2/15/44. Studied piano and clarinet before he took up drums at age 12. Percussion studies at Manhattan School of Music at 16. Gained experience w. symphony orch. Pl. w. Al Cohn-Zoot Sims before joining Bill Evans trio in '68 and remaining until the spring of '75. LPs: see Evans; w. Jeremy Steig, *Monium* (Col.).

MORELLO, JOSEPH A. (JOE),* *drums, educator*; b. Springfield, Mass., 7/17/28. A key member of the Dave Brubeck quartet from '56 until its breakup in Dec. '67. From that time conducting clinics for Ludwig Drums around the US; teaching privately and at Dorn & Kirschner Music in Union, N.J. Gigs at Gulliver's in West Paterson, N.J. Instruction books publ: (Ludwig Industries, 1728 No. Damen Ave., Chi., Ill. 60647). LPs: own gp. (Ovation); w. Brubeck (Col.).

MORGAN, LEE,* *trumpet, composer*; b. Philadelphia, Pa., 7/10/38. Best known for his tours with the D. Gillespie orch., '56-8; w. A. Blakey, '58-61 and again '64-5; and with his own combo, Morgan was shot and killed at Slugs', the club in NYC where his quintet was performing, 2/19/72, after a quarrel with a woman who had been his companion for some years.

Morgan had enjoyed commercial success with a record of his comp. *The Sidewinder* in '65. Much of his recorded work, especially in the earlier years, showed a remarkable resemblance to the style of the late Clifford Brown, though later he developed an exceptionally individual identity marked by an excellence of conception, tone and phrasing.

One of his earliest solos was *Night in Tunisia*, which he played as a featured sideman w. Gillespie on a Verve album. He rec. prolifically from '56 as a leader in his own right: *Cooker; Cornbread; Gigolo; At The Lighthouse; Rumproller; Search for the New Land; Sidewinder; 6th Sense* (BN); *Date With Lee; One of a Kind; Speedball; Two Sides of* (Trip); *Genius* (Tradition); others with many small groups for Vee Jay; also *Blue Trane* w. J. Coltrane (BN); *Freedom Rider; Jazz Corner of the World, Vols. I & II; Meet You At The Jazz Corner; Night In Tunisia*, w. Blakey (BN).

Along with his contribution as a musician, Morgan is remembered as an activist and member of the Jazz and People's Movement who, in '70-1, protested media neglect of and indifference to jazz artists.

MORGAN, HOWARD (SONNY), *African and Latin percussion, flute*; b. Philadelphia, Pa., 7/17/36. Studied at

Granoff School of Music. Flute w. Henry Zlotnick; John De Matties; American perc. w. Ellis Tollin; Jimmy Nichols; Dave Levine. From '50-60 stud. rhythms and music of Ghana under Saka Acquaye; rhythms of Haiti w. Maya Deren; music and dances of Caribbean countries w. John Hines; Sydney King; Geoffrey Holder; Katherine Dunham; Syvilla Fort; Walter Nicks. From '63-71 studied Yoruba language, music and drumming w. Michael Olatunji. Toured major colls. w. him, in charge of lecture-demonstrations. Before leaving Phila., performed on flute and perc. w. own band, '53-60, incorporating African melodies and rhythms. Has worked w. Willie Bobo; Harry Belafonte; G. Holder; Montego Joe; Duke of Iron; Mongo Santamaria; Mary Lou Williams; Leon Thomas; Jose Paulo; Carmen Costa; Max Roach; Joe Mensah. With Negro Ensemble Co., arr. drum gp. for *Kongi's Harvest*, playing leading drum, Dun Dun (or African squeeze drum), and actual Orikis of the Yoruba lang.; arr. music for drums, steel pan, flute and singers for *Ballet Behind the Bridge*; pl. flute and drums for *Dream on Monkey Mountain*. For New Lafayette Theatre, wrote and arr. music for *We Righteous Bombers*, many other prods. Became active in film rec. through New Lafayette. Did sound track rec. for *The Slaves*. One of the most respected of the conga-bongoists by young percussionists. Infl: Saka Acquaye, Mongo Santamaria, Julito Collazo, Jose Paulo. Fest: NJF; MJF; Berlin; Holland; Montreux. LPs: w. Leon Thomas; Count Basie; Gato Barbieri; Oliver Nelson (Fly. Dutch.); Kenny Barron (Muse); Milford Graves (ESP); has also rec. w. Max Roach; Ch. Earland; Art Blakey; Olatunji; Montego Joe; Les Baxter; Belafonte; D. Gillespie.

MORTON, HENRY STERLING (BENNY),* *trombone*; b. New York City, 1/31/07. The former Fletcher Henderson, Don Redman, Count Basie sideman of the '30s, and a regular w. Teddy Wilson, Edmond Hall and his own band, at Cafe Society in the '40s, did much Broadway pit work in the '50s, and free-lanced in NYC during the '60s. Europe w. Top Brass tour '67. Played at the Roosevelt Grill w. B. Hackett '70, replacing Vic Dickenson; also subbed at Roosevelt w. Buck Clayton; Eddie Condon. Worked w. World's Greatest Jazzband, '73-4 incl. Europe '74. Gigging w. Countsmen, '75. Fest: Colo. JP; Nice. LPs: w. Roy Eldridge, *The Nifty Cat* (Master Jazz); w. WGJ (World Jazz).

MOSES, ROBERT LAURENCE (BOB), *drums, composer*; b. New York City, 1/28/48. Took up drums at 10. Mostly self-taught. Played Latin gigs in the Bronx; then w. early jazz-rock gp., Free Spirits w. Larry Coryell, '66. Worked for a short time w. R.R. Kirk, '67; two yrs. w. Gary Burton, '67-8. In '69-73 free-lanced in NYC w. Coryell, Steve Marcus; Free Life Communication w. Dave Liebman, Randy Brecker; Compost w. Jack De Johnette. Toured England w. Mike Gibbs' big band, '74. Burton and Steve Swallow did one show w. them in London and, as a result, Moses was reunited w. Burton, touring w. him from '75. Charles Mitchell in *down beat* wrote: "Bob's compositions reflect the spirit of his drums: a constant search for new colors, inflections, ways of dealing with tone and rhythm, free travel 'inside' and 'out.' At the kit, Moses plays sonic alchemist, constantly, quietly keeping the cauldron at a low, intense boil. Swing is a strong implication—enough so that finger-snappers are seldom disappointed with a Gary Burton ensemble performance—but no on-the-beat obsession limits the range of Moses' percussive expression."

Infl: Roach, Mingus, Kirk, Ellington, Tatum, Roy Haynes, Elmo Hope, Andrew Hill, Edgar Bateman. Fest: major European fests. w. Burton. Comps: *Our Life; The Dancing Bears; Bittersweet in the Ozone; Stanley Free; Arb Om Souple; Mfwala Myo Lala*. The last two titles are part of the language of Castaluquinga, according to Moses "a visionary sphere that has come to me at various times . . . I acquired certain information about the language; I started to see a plane of reality that had its own culture, music, style. There are other people who seem to have received messages from there, too, so its not just my imagination or something that exists just within me."

LPs: *Bittersweet in the Ozone* (Mozown, 415 Central Park West, New York, N.Y. 10025); w. Gibbs, *The Only Chrome-Waterfall Orchestra* (Bronze); w. Burton, *In the Public Interest* (Poly.); In Concert (RCA); w. Open Sky, *Spirit in the Sky* (PM).

MOST, ABRAHAM (ABE),* *clarinet, saxes, flute*; b. New York City, 2/27/20. Prominent LA studio musician for many years. His versatility enabled him to reproduce the styles of many jazz clarinetists in the series of Time-Life recordings that began in 1970. Featured clar. soloist in film *Slither* '72. From '71 app., in occasional concerts w. orch. similar to Time-Life gp. Comps: *Miniature Suite; Triple Fugue for Saxophone Quartet and Piano; Theme and Variations for Woodwind Quintet*.

Publs: *Jazz Improvisations for Treble Clef Instruments; Jazz Improv. for Bass Clef Instruments* etc. (Gwyn Publ. Co., P.O. Box 5900, Sherman Oaks, Calif. 91413).

MOST, SAMUEL (SAM),* *clarinet, flute*; also *saxes, etc.*; b. Atlantic City, N.J., 12/16/30. One of first jazz flutists in early 1950s, he pl. w. Buddy Rich, L. Bellson, Red Norvo in '60s, has own gps. from time to time, but mainly a studio musician in LA, also in house bands at LV, Lake Tahoe casinos. Publ: *Jazz Flute Conceptions* (Gwyn Publ. Co., P.O. Box 5900, Sherman Oaks, Calif. 91413).

LPs: *Thunderbird* w. Bellson (Impulse); *That's Him & This Is New* w. Frank Strazzeri (Revelation).

MOTIAN, STEPHEN PAUL,* *drums, percussion, composer, piano*; b. Philadelphia, Pa., 3/25/31. Pl. w. Bill Evans, 1959-63; Paul Bley, '64; Keith Jarrett, off and on, '66-9; again '71-5. Other work in late '60s w. Mose Allison, Arlo Guthrie, Ch. Lloyd (incl. tour of Asia), Karl Berger, Morgana King. Very active w. JCOA in '70s. Comp. and rec. music for two short films by Stan Vanderbeek, 1970. Worked w. Roswell Rudd, Gato Barbieri, Don Cherry, '73; toured Japan w. Jarrett '74. Fests: NJF-NY, Montreux w. Barbieri. NJF-NY also w. Allison, Jarrett.

Comps: *Conception Vessel; Tribute*, both rec. on ECM. LPs: *Escalator Over The Hill* (JCOA); others w. B. Evans (Verve); Bley (ECM); Ch. Haden Liberation Orch. (Impulse); Jarrett (Atl.).

MOUZON, ALPHONSE, *drums*; also *keyboards, composer, arranger, vocals*; b. Charleston, S.C., 11/21/48. Attended Bonds-Wilson H.S., S. Carolina, pl. in band, under director Lonnie Hamilton, with whom he took lessons; also drum leader in school marching band. Won several awards on perc. in S.C. Grad. '66, moved to NYC. Stud. medicine and worked in a NYC hospital, also pl. with Ross Carnegie society orch. on weekends. Student at NY City Coll., '67-9; at same time pl. in orch. for *Promises, Promises* on Broadway. Freelanced w. R. Ayers, Gene McDaniels, Roberta Flack et al. In '70 went on road w. Ayers for a year. With Weather Report, '71-2; McCoy Tyner, '72-3; Larry Coryell's Eleventh House, '73-5. Moved to Cal. late '75.

Mouzon made his first album date at age 19 w. Gil Evans (Ampex). Fests: Norway JF, '73; Montreux, w. Tyner, '73; Coryell, '75; Newport, w. Tyner, '73; all star big band, '75; Berlin JF, '75. Mouzon stud. acting for 2½ years, and is pursuing an acting career simultaneously with music. Mouzon says: "Jazz/rock drummers like myself, Billy Cobham and Lenny White bring jazz polyrhythms to a rock pulse."

Comps: *Virtue*, recorded by Bobbi Humphrey and M. Santamaria; *Just Like The Sun; Nyctophobia*, rec. by Coryell; *Essence of Mystery; New York City*.

LPs: *Essence of Mystery; Funky Snakefoot; Mind Transplant; The Man Incognito* (BN); w. Coryell, *Introducing Eleventh House* (Vanguard); *Level One* (Arista); w. Les McCann, *Invitation to Openness* (Atl.); w. Doug Carn, *Spirit of the New Land* (Black Jazz); *Weather Report* (Col.); w. Tyner, *Sahara; Song For My Lady, Song of the New World; Enlightenment* (Milest.); w. McDaniels, *Headless Heroes of the Apocalypse*; w. Flack, *Feel Like Making Love*; w. Robin Kenyatta, *Stomping at the Savoy* (Atl.); w. Jeremy Steig, *Temple of Birth* (Col.); w. Wayne Shorter, *Odyssey of Iska* (BN).

MOVER, ROBERT ALAN (BOB), *alto sax, composer*; also *soprano sax*; b. Boston, Mass., 3/22/52. Father, Jimmy, played trumpet w. T. Dorsey, Charlie Spivak, etc. in '40s; mother sang professionally; sister, Joy, is singer in Miami. Studied guitar, drums briefly. Took up alto sax in '65, studying w. Ted Rosen in Miami. Pl. w. high school all star band, '67. Studied w. Phil Woods at Ramblerny in Pennsylvania, summer '67. Learned further from pl. w. Ira Sullivan in Miami, '68. From '69 into early '70s living between NYC and Boston, pl. a variety of music jobs and sitting in. With Charles Mingus for five months, '73; Chet Baker '74. Pl. in Rio de Janeiro for six mos. w. Lucio Alves; Johnny Alf, '74. Rejoined Baker for nine mos. in '75 incl. NJF-NY, Nice, Laren, Middleheim fests. Own gp. in '76 at Tin Palace, NYC. Infl: C. Parker, L. Young, B. Powell, Konitz, Rollins, Ira Sullivan. Comps: *Muggawump; Saudade do Brooklyn; Survival of the Sickest; Falsidade; Night Dance of the Little People*. LP: w. Yoshiaki Masuo, *111 Sullivan Street* (East Wind).

MOYE, DON, *drums, congas, bongoes, bass marimba, ballophone, misc. percussion, whistles, horns, singer*; b. Rochester, N.Y., 5/23/46. Took some percussion classes at Wayne State U. in Detroit, '65-6. Learned from trumpeter Charles Moore and pl. w. Detroit Free Jazz. Met Joseph Jarman at Artist's Workshop in Detroit. Went to Europe in May '68 w. DFJ, pl. in Switzerland, Italy, Yugoslavia, Scandinavia. Pl. w. Steve Lacy in Rome, then in Paris. Also pl. there w. The Gospel Messenger Singers, Sonny Sharrock, Dave Burrell, Gato Barbieri, Pharoah Sanders, Alan Shorter. Met Art Ensemble of Chicago members at the American Center for Students and Artists in '69 and was invited to join the group. Returned with it to US in April '69. Peter Occhiogrosso called Moye, "a percussionist who can do just about anything without sounding ostentatious" and added that he provides "the kind of connective tissue that keeps the Ensemble together through their most abstract forays."

Received NREA Grant for composition, '73. Artist-in-residence at Michigan State U., '73.

LPs: see Art Ensemble of Chicago; w. Randy Weston, *Carnival* (Arista).

MRAZ, GEORGE (JIRI), *bass*; b. Pisek, Czechoslovakia, 9/9/44. Stud. Prague Conserv., '61-6. Pl. w. Jan Hammer trio. Moved to West Germany '66 where he worked for a year in Munich w. Pony Poindexter, Hampton Hawes, Benny Bailey. To U.S. in late '60s where he stud. at Berklee before pl. w. Dizzy Gillespie. Toured w. Oscar Peterson '72; Ella Fitzgerald, summer '72; then joined Thad Jones-Mel Lewis orch. with which he remained, making many fest. and concert apps. throughout U.S. and overseas during next four years. Took time out to work w. Stan Getz, Sept. '74 to Jan. '75. Duo w. Walter Norris at Bradley's, spring '75. Mraz has been praised highly by all the musicians he has worked with since his arrival in NYC. His beat is firm; his sound is exceptionally clean and clear, and his improvisational ideas are consistently creative. LPs: w. Jones-Lewis (Phila. Int.); Peterson (BASF); Horacee Arnold (Col.); Norris (Enja); Buddy De Franco (Famous Solos); Jimmy Smith (Verve); Zoot Sims (Pablo).

MUHAMMAD, IDRIS, (Leo Morris), *drums*; b. New Orleans, La., 1939. Father a banjo player; brothers all drummers. Pl. first job at ten. On grad. from high school, joined Larry Williams band. After working w. guitarist Joe Jones, Dee Clark, began doing dates in NYC w. Lloyd Price in early 1960s. Spent almost four years in each of three jobs: w. Jerry Butler, for whom he was mus. dir.; Lou Donaldson; and the house band for *Hair*, in which he worked from 1968-72. During that time he also worked as consultant on another play, *Indians*, for which he designed the drums.

After *Hair* closed Muhammad went to India for six months, returned to US and resumed playing, on tour w. Emerson, Lake & Palmer and soon after with the backup group for Roberta Flack. He signed in 1974 with Creed

Taylor's Kudu record label and gained some prominence in his own right.

Muhammad says: "The rock beat was created in New Orleans, and I was one of the drummers who first brought that kind of beat to New York." LPs: Prestige, Kudu; w. Donaldson (Blue Note).

MUKAI, SHIGEHARU, *trombone*; b. Nagoya, Japan, 1/21/49. Pl. w. Doshisha Univ. Modern Jazz Group and the Third Orch.; then w. quintets of Yoshio Otomo; Fumio Itabashi; Ryo Kawasaki; Hiroshi Fukumura; Seiichi Nakamura; Terumasa Hino. Formed own quintet; also working w. SMC Orch. Infl: J.J. Johnson, Coltrane, Slide Hampton, Wayne Henderson, Terumasa Hino. App. at various Japanese JF. In Oct. '74 won Shinjuku JF Award. Won 2nd trombone in SJ Readers Poll, '74. Own LP: *For My Little Bird* (Nippon Col.); w. H. Fukumura, *First Flight* (Trio); quintet (Three Blind Mice); w. S. Nakamura, *First Contact* (King); w. T. Hino, *Journey Into My Mind* (CBS/Sony).

MULDAUR, MARIA (Maria Grazia Rosa Domenica d'Amato), *singer, blues fiddle*; b. New York City, 9/12/42. Self-taught, helped by informal music appreciation sessions with extensive blues and jazz collections of Jim Kweskin and Geoff Muldaur. Toured w. Even Dozen Jug Band, '63; Kweskin Jug Band, '64-9. She and Muldaur, who had worked w. Kweskin together, then made two LPs for Reprise. After their divorce she app. as a single during '72, attaining national prominence with her record of *Midnight at the Oasis* which became a hit on radio and part of a best selling LP in '73.

Though her accompaniments and her style of singing have crossed over into many areas incl. rock, pop, spiritual, gospel and blues, Muldaur was best known in jazz circles, from late '74, through a series of concerts with an all star band directed by Benny Carter, who wrote the arrangements and pl. alto sax.

Some critics heard in Muldaur a remarkable resemblance, in the lightness of timbre and jazz-oriented phrasing, to Mildred Bailey. Others found her mannered and shallow. Among the artists who have inspired her are Bailey, D. Ellington, Bessie Smith, D. Reinhardt, Memphis Minnie, Claude Jeter, Mavis Staples, B.B. King.

In the summer of '75 Carter assembled a new band which pl. at the NJF, at a concert in tandem w. Muldaur. He then app. with her at the Montreux JF. Muldaur was later heard at Ronnie Scott's Club in London.

Among singers whose appeal is primarily to the young pop/rock audience, Muldaur is unique, not only for her sensitivity toward jazz, but for her use of arcane material such as the old Danny Barker r & b hit *Don't You Feel My Leg*, Ellington standards such as *Prelude To A Kiss* and other ballads, incl. *Lover Man*, all of which she performs with a conviction not common to singers of her generation.

Muldaur was named as number one new female vocalist of '74 in several music trade publications.

LPs: early sessions w. Kweskin Jug Band (Vanguard); pl. blues fiddle and sang backup on two Paul Butterfield LPs (Bearsville); own solo albums, *Maria Muldaur* (which incl. *Midnight at the Oasis*); *Waitress in a Donut Shop* (Reprise).

MULLIGAN, GERALD JOSEPH (GERRY or JERU),* *baritone, soprano saxes, clarinet, composer, piano*; b. New York City, 4/6/27. After switching from his 13-piece Concert Jazz Band to a small gp. format in '66, he began a series of tours as guest soloist with Dave Brubeck's group from '68. In '72 he recorded a new large ensemble he called *The Age of Steam* and appeared with it at the NJF-NY '73. He also pl. at the new Half Note w. a small gp. using the same generic title. A successful reunion concert w. Chet Baker in '74 and subsequent albums of the event, led to a repeat performance, again in NYC, '75. In the summer of '74 he played in Italy and France. He also spent time as artist-in-residence at Miami U. in that year. Film: pl. on soundtrack of *Hot Rock* for Quincy Jones. Fest: several apps. at NJF-NY; MJF; Montreux; Midem, etc. Played curved soprano sax at *Salute to Zoot* concert; w. own sextet at Hopper's, NYC, Dec. '75.

"With Gerry," says Brubeck, "you feel as if you're listening to the past, present and future of jazz all at one time, and it's with such taste and respect that you're not quite aware of the changes in idiom. Mulligan gets the old New Orleans two beat going with a harmonic awareness of advanced jazz, and you feel not that tradition is being broken, but rather that it's being pushed forward."

Won DB Readers poll on baritone, '66-75; critics poll, '74-5.

Comp: *K-4 Pacific; Golden Notebooks; Maytag; Country Beaver; It's Sandy at the Beach; A Weed in Disneyland; Grand Tour; Song For An Unfinished Woman; Song For Strayhorn. By Your Grace*, rec. on album w. Beaver & Krause, *Ghandarva* (War. Bros). Own LPs: *Age of Steam* (A&M); Carnegie Hall Concerts w. Baker (CTI). LPs w. Astor Piazzolla, *Summit* (Carosello, Ital.); w. Brubeck, *Compadres; Blues Roots; at Berlin Philharmonic* (Col.); reissues, w. Baker (Prest.); *Revelation*, w. Lee Konitz (BN).

MURANYI, JOSEPH PAUL (JOE),* *clarinet, soprano sax, singer*; b. Martins Ferry, Ohio, 1/14/28. Well known for work with Max Kaminsky, J. McPartland and numerous other Dixieland groups. Toured world w. Louis Armstrong 1967-71. On leaving Armstrong (he was the band's last regular clarinetist), became resident musician at Jimmy Ryan's, NYC, w. Roy Eldridge. In 1975, also worked gigs on sop., clar. w. World's Greatest Jazzband. Increased activity on soprano and vocals 1974-5. LPs: *Clarinet Wobble*, clar. duet w. Herb Hall (Fat Cat Jazz); Joe Muranyi Quartet, unreleased.

MURPHY, MARK HOWE,* *singer*; b. Syracuse, N.Y., 3/14/32. After app. in jazz clubs, at NJF, '62 etc., Murphy settled in London, which was his base throughout the balance of the decade. He returned to NYC briefly in '73 to record an album, *Mark II*. Murphy, in addition to working in London in night clubs and on records, began a career as an actor. He made a pilot film in Spain for British TV, in which he pl. Jesus Christ. In the words of Peter Keepnews, "He remains little known in his native land except among a small coterie of jazz lovers."

LPs: *Bridging A Gap; Mark II* (Muse); w. Herb Geller, *Rhyme and Reason* (Atl.).

MURPHY, MELVIN E. (TURK),* *trombone, composer, leader*; b. Palermo, Cal., 12/16/15. Pioneer of traditionalist jazz in the Bay Area since the late '30s. Co-owner with pianist Pete Clute, since September '60, of Earthquake McGoon's in SF. Murphy, unlike many New Orleans stylists, avoids most of the old jazz standards, preferring to play relatively unknown material from the turn of the century, obscure songs of the '20s by King Oliver, Kid Ory et al, and original compositions. He was a key figure in the West Coast ragtime revival, many years before Scott Joplin's music was used in the film *The Sting*. His band toured Australia in the summer of '74, and played four European countries in Nov-Dec. that year.

LPs: *Jazz Band* (Merry); *Many Faces of Ragtime* (Atl.); *Vol. I; Vol. II* (Motherlode).

MURRAY, DAVID, *tenor sax, composer*; also *soprano sax, flute*; b. Berkeley, Calif., 2/19/55. Father pl. guitar in church; mother was nationally famous as pianist in the Sanctified Church. Both were big infl. on him. Grew up in SF Bay area. Pl. in Missionary Church of God and Christ. At 12 became interested in r&b and led gps. as teenager. Met Stanley Crouch and was introduced by him to Bobby Bradford and Black Arthur. Own gp. w. trumpeter Butch Morris in Bay Area during coll. vacations. Piano lessons from Margaret Kohn at Pomona Coll. where he stud. music for two yrs. before leaving for NYC, '75. Led own gps. at Sunrise Studio, Studio We, Studio Rivbea, Yale U. and performed solo. Sat-in w. Cecil Taylor; Don Cherry; A. Braxton; worked w. Sunny Murray in Phila. Infl: Parker, Rollins, Shepp, Ayler, Coltrane, Ellington, Webster, Hawkins, B. Bradford, Black Arthur, Crouch. Interested in "exploring the areas of music Albert Ayler opened up as far as new or unusual saxophone techniques are concerned . . . working on a study of Paul Gonsalves' improvisational approach. I have been particularly impressed by him and feel he never got the credit he was due."

Played lead in a play by Crouch entitled *Saxophone Man*. TV: short film w. Verta Mae Grosvenor. Fest: w. Abbey Lincoln, Oakland '74; own gp., Studio Rivbea '75. Comp: *Flowers For Albert; Miss Sweet; Suite For Yellowman Warrior; Low Class Conspiracy; Shout Song; Dewey Circle; Ballad For a Decomposed Beauty; Welcome to the Set; S.B. and C. Follies*; w. B. Morris, *Don't Enter Me*. LPs: w. S. Crouch, unreleased.

MURRAY, JAMES ARTHUR (SUNNY),* *drums, composer*; b. Valliant, Okla., 9/21/37. Established himself as one of leading avant drummers, playing and recording w. Cecil Taylor; Albert Ayler; Archie Shepp; Gil Evans in '60s. Active in France in late '60s-early '70s. Performed in Sweden, Denmark, Norway, Finland, Holland, Austria, Belgium, Switzerland, Italy; Pan-African Fest. in Senegal. Pl. concerts and clubs in NYC, SF, Phila.; many coll. dates. Co-leader w. Khan Jamal in The Untouchable Factor.

"In a radical fashion," wrote Joachim Berendt describing Murray's rhythmic approach, "the marking of the meter is here replaced by the creation of tension over long passages . . . It swings without beat and measure, meter and symmetry . . . simply by virtue of the power and flexibility of its tension-arcs."

Treasurer and National Advisor for Phila. Jazz Foundation. Won DB Critics poll, TDWR, '66. Grants from CAPS, '70, '73. Comp.-arr. scores for films: *In the Beginning* (Nigeria); *Walking Woman* (Canada); *The Party* (France); plays: *June Bug Graduates Tonight; Barabbas*. LPs: *Sunny's Time Now* (Jihad); *Homage to Africa; Sunshine; Never Give a Sucker An Even Break* (Byg); ORTF Concerts (Shandar).

MUSSELWHITE, CHARLES DOUGLAS III (CHARLIE), *harmonica, guitar, composer*; b. Kosciusko, Miss., 1/31/44. Father pl. guitar, harmonica. Mainly self taught. Worked in the streets and Chicago bars in mid-1960s w. Johnnie Young Blues Band. Duos w. Big Joe Williams, John Lee Granderson; also pl. w. blues bands of J.B. Hutto, Mike Bloomfield, Barry Goldberg, and w. South Side Sound System. App. on TV w. Goldberg in Chi. 1966, later w. own band in Detroit. Pl. in the first Ann Arbor Blues Festival, also St. Cloud, Minn. Folk Festival. Living in San Jose, Cal., 1975. Comps: *Taylor's Arkansas; Up & Down the Avenue; Takin' My Time; Louisiana Fog; Leavin'; Fell On My Knees; Finger Lickin' Good; 39th and Indiana; Highway Blues; Fat City*, many others.

LPs: *South; Takin' My Time; Goin' Back Down* (Arhoolie); *Tennessee Woman; Stone Blues; Stand Back* (Vanguard); *Louisiana Fog* (Cherry Red); *Memphis, Tennessee* (Paramount).

MUSSO, VIDO WILLIAM,* *tenor sax, clarinet*; b. Carrini, Sicily, 1/16/13. Mainly known for his work w. S. Kenton in '40s. Living in Las Vegas since '57; led own group at Desert Inn, '67-70; Sands Hotel, '70-5, also backing Sonny King. Worked w. Tony Martin, Tony Bennett at local casinos as soloist in their backup bands. Reunited briefly w. Kenton in '68. LPs w. Kenton (Creative World).

MYERS, HUBERT MAXWELL (BUMPS),* *tenor sax*; b. Clarksburg, W. Va., 8/22/12. Best-known for his work w. Benny Carter in the '40s, he worked mostly in the rec. studios in the '50s. Played briefly w. Horace Henderson in '61-2. Bad health curtailed his activities during the yrs. prior to his death in LA, 4/8/68.

NAMYSLOWSKI, ZBIGNIEW, *alto saxophone, composer, leader;* also *flute, cello, trombone, piano;* b. Warsaw, Poland, 9/9/39. Uncle led society band. Piano at four; regular music lessons at six. Took up cello at 12; studies, incl. theory, at High School of Music in Warsaw. Pl. trombone w. Witold Krotochwil trad band; cello w. Krzysztof Sadowski Modern Combo, '56. Gained recognition at Sopot Fest.; toured in Denmark w. Polish All Stars; France w. Krotochwil. Worked w. New Orleans Stompers. Switched to alto sax '60 and joined Andrzej Trzaskowski's Jazz Wreckers w. whom he toured US and Europe before leaving to form own quartet, '63. Pl. in Europe, India, Australia, New Zealand and USSR. Also pl. w. Krzysztof Komeda gps. for concerts, film soundtracks, recs.; Novi Singers' tours; half year in Italy w. Polish rock singer Czeslaw Niemen. Pl. w. George Arvanitas in Paris for six wks., summer '70. From '71 leading own quintet and pl. w. Polish Radio Jazz Studio Band. Infl: C. Parker, J. Coltrane, S. Rollins. TV: Poland; Germany; Australia; BBC. Fest: NJF w. Wreckers, '61; all Warsaw Jazz Jamborees; Molde; Kongsberg; Tallin; Frankfurt; Comblain-la-Tour; Bologna; Prague; Cascais. Comps: *Piatawka; Siodmakwa; Nieprzespana Noc; Bez Wyciszenia; Winobranie (Wine Feast); Kuyawiak Goes Funky.* Has also written for radio, TV, film soundtracks, orchestras.

A special aspect of Namyslowski's success is that in addition to effectively utilizing elements of contemporary jazz and rock, he has also incorporated and thoroughly integrated Polish folk music (as in *Winobranie)* into his music.

LPs: *Quartet; Wine Feast; Kuyawiak Goes Funky* (Muza); *Lola* (Decca); *Pop Workshop,* vols. 1&2, w. Tony Williams and others (EMI); w. Novi Singers, *Novi in Wonderland* (Saba); w. K. Komeda, *Astigmatic* (Muza); *Jazz and Poetry* (German Electrola).

NANCE, WILLIS (RAY),* *cornet, violin, singer;* b. Chicago, Ill., 12/10/13. The Duke Ellington alumnus played w. Henri Chaix in Switzerland, '67 but was mainly occupied in Sol Yaged's gp. at the Gaslight Club, NYC, '66-9. Pl. in Scandinavia in early '70s. Filled in w. Ellington band at various times in '70s. Pl. w. Brooks Kerr at Churchill's, NYC, Feb.-May '73. Toured in England w. Chris Barber '74. Appeared w. own band for Duke Ellington Society concert at New School, NYC, May '69. Concert apps. w. B. Bigard, L. Bellson at Wilshire-Ebell, LA, '75; K. Burrell at Town Hall, NYC, Dec. '75. Pl. at Sonny's Place; The Penthouse, L.I. '75; Barbara's, Greenwich Village, Jan. '76. Nance, ill with kidney trouble that forced him to use a dialysis machine several times weekly from late '75, died 1/28/76 and jazz lost one of its great artist-entertainers. TV: Just Jazz, PBS, '71. Comp: *Wild Child; Ray's Blues.* LPs: *Body and Soul* (SS); *Huffin' and Puffin'* (MPS); *Jaki Byard With Strings* (Prest.); w. Jimmy Rushing, *The You and Me That Used to Be* (RCA); *Just a Sittin' and a Rockin'* w. P. Gonsalves (Bl. Lion); *Jazz For a Sunday Afternoon* (SS).

NAPOLEON, MARTY,* *piano;* b. Brooklyn, N.Y., 6/2/21. Pl. w. Louis Armstrong 1952-4; rejoined him '66 and during the next five years toured the world with him (for details see Armstrong). Led own trio at Playboy Club, NYC, '71; concerts w. Gene Krupa. Pee Wee Erwin, Chris Griffin, '71-2; NJF-NY, solo piano at Cookery, '73, etc. Comp. & arr. *Louis' Dream* (co-written w. Armstrong), rec. in LV, Feb. '67. Commissioned to write series of piano instruction books for Ch. Hansen Publ., '75.

LPs: w. Armstrong (Mer., MCA, Disneyland, ABC-Par. etc.).

NASSER, JAMIL SULIEMAN,* *bass;* b. Memphis, Tenn., 6/21/32. From '64 to the early '70s a member of Ahmad Jamal trio. In '75 w. Al Haig trio at Gregory's, NYC, on Sundays. LPs: w. Haig-Jimmy Raney (Choice); also see Jamal.

NATIONAL JAZZ ENSEMBLE. See Israels, Chuck.

NAUGHTON, ROBERT (BOBBY), *vibes;* also *piano;* b. Boston, Mass., 6/25/44. Self-taught. In late '60s and early '70s worked in groups w. Perry Robinson, Sheila Jordan; perf. with JCOA, '72. Pl. w. Leo Smith group and leading own unit, incl. percussionist Randy Kaye. Infls: Thomas Tallis, T. Monk, Bill Evans, Walt Dickerson, G. Russell, Carla Bley, Hans Richter. Comp. piece for *Everyday,* a film by Richter, originally shot in '29 but completed in '71, starring Sergei Eisenstein and Jean Hans Arp. Other comps: *Snow; Ordet; Fancy Free.* App. N.Y. Musicians JF, '72-3.

LPs: *Nature's Consort; Understanding* (Otic Records, also available on Japo Records, Gleichmannstr. 10, München, W. Germany.).

NAURA, MICHAEL, *piano;* b. Memel, Lithuania, 8/19/34. Self-taught. Started Shearing style quintet, Berlin, 1953. Later insp. by Bill Evans, MJQ. Traveled around Europe w. own gp. '56-63. Later worked as editor of mus. progs. for Norddeutscher Rundfunk (radio), Hamburg; since '72 head of that station's jazz dept, also pl. w. own quartet, embracing some elements of free jazz. Associated off and on for 20 years with vibraphonist Wolfgang Schlüter. LPs (in Germany): MPS-BASF; Intercoed; ECM.

NDUGU (Leon Chancler), *drums, percussion;* b. Shreveport, La., 1/7/52. Stud. at Gompers High; Locke High, LA; also w. step-brother Reggie Andrews. Further studies at Cal. State Coll., '70-2. Musically self-taught, starting in '67 in Jr. H.S., pl. w. Jazz Prophets, Executives. Worked w. Harold Johnson, Larry Nash, '68-9; Pepperdine Coll. orch., Willie Bobo, Locke High Jazz Workshop, '69-70. On grad. from school, worked w. Gerald Wilson, Hugh Masekela, H. Hancock, '70; T. Monk, F. Hubbard, E. Harris, Harold Land-Bobby Hutcherson, Miles Davis, Joe Henderson, '71; in '72 pl. w. Hampton Hawes, Harold Land, George Duke and was co-leader of Ujima ensemble. Freelance studio work in LA, '72-4; toured w. Santana, '74- . Insp. by Red Holt, Art Blakey, Bruno Carr, H. Hancock, Stix Hooper, Art Taylor, Jack DeJohnette, Reggie Andrews. Fests: Watts, '70-1; Newport in Europe.

One of the most dependable and promising of the new generation of percussionists, specializing in congas, vibes, timbales etc.

LPs: w. Weather Report, *Tale Spinnin';* w. Santana, *Borboletta* (Col.); w. Jean-Luc Ponty, *Upon The Wings of Music;* w. E. Harris, *Excursions* (Atl.); w. Duke, *Feel; Faces In Reflection; The Aura Will Prevail* (MPS); w. Hawes, *Universe; Blues For Walls* (Prest.); w. Land, *Damisi; Choma* (Mainstr.).

NEAPOLITAN, RAY, *bass;* also *guitar, sitar;* b. Chicago Ill., 8/30/40. Educ. Chicago Conserv. of Music, '57, then w. private teachers, Jerry Lofstrom in Chi.; Ralph Pena, Peter

Mercurio, Carol Kaye in LA. Began working with Terry Gibbs group, '62 and has since appeared w. Shelly Manne, Louie Bellson, Buddy Rich, Carmen McRae, Eddie "Lockjaw" Davis, Mose Allison, Don Ellis, Gabor Szabo, Roger Kellaway, Maynard Ferguson, Oliver Nelson, Frank Sinatra et al. On sound track for movies *Play Misty For Me; French Connection; Rosemary's Baby;* Burt Bacharach, F. Sinatra, B. Streisand TV Specs. W. D. Ellis at MJF, '66, '67, '68, Antibes Fest., '68; NJF, '68. Neapolitan is greatly respected in both studio and jazz circles.

LPs: w. Ellis (Pacific Jazz); w. Emil Richards (Limelite, Impulse); Barbara Streisand (Columbia).

NEIDLINGER, BUELL,* *bass;* b. Westport, Conn., 3/2/36. Early associate of Cecil Taylor. Pl. w. symph. orchs. in Houston, '62-4; Boston, '68-70. Prof. of Music, Cal. Inst. of Arts, '71- . Ojai Fest., '74.

LPs: Cecil Taylor-Buell Neidlinger (Barnaby); *Jean-Luc Ponty Plays Frank Zappa* (Wor. Pac.).

NELSON, OLIVER EDWARD,* *composer, saxophones, flute;* b. St. Louis, Mo., 6/4/32. Extensive background as composer in jazz, pop and classical fields in NYC before moving to LA, 1967. Though primarily working as composer for TV and films, he still played saxophone from time to time, notably on a tour of French West Africa under the aegis of the U.S. State Dept. in 1969, for which he led a small band.

TV credits: orig. theme and background music for *Matt Lincoln; Longstreet; Six Million Dollar Man;* episodes for *Ironsides; It Takes a Thief; Name of the Game.* Educational film: *Encounter and Response,* for Lutheran Church of America. Feature films: *Death of a Gunfighter; Skullduggery; Zig Zag; Trans Europe Express.*

Nelson assembled a big band for an engagement at the Bottom Line in NYC, June '75, and the following week headed a West Coast personnel for a brief booking at the Grove, LA. These were his final appearances. He taped a recording for *Million Dollar Man,* 10/27/75, and died the following morning after suffering a heart attack at his Los Angeles home.

Despite his acceptance in the studio world and the numerous honors awarded him, Nelson never quite achieved the recognition he deserved, for two main reasons: he was obliged to divide his time between commercial studio work and the serious writing he preferred, and was similarly forced to restrict himself to writing on many occasions when he would rather have been playing.

Publ: *Patterns for Saxophone* (Noslen Music Co., P.O. Box 705, Hollywood, Calif., 90028).

Commissions: *Concerto for Xylophone, Marimba and Vibraphone,* for Amer. Wind Symph. Orch., '67. *Jazzhattan Suite,* for BMI, '67. *Septet for Winds,* for Amer. Wind Symph., '68. *Dialogues for Orchestra,* for Berliner Jazztage Fest., '70. *Suite for Narrator, String Quartet and Jazz Orchestra,* for Mayor Carl B. Stokes of Cleveland, '70.

LPs: *Main Stem; Afro-American Sketches* (Prest.); *Berlin Dialogue; Black, Brown & Beautiful; Oliver Nelson In London With Oily Rags; Swiss Suite; Skull Session* (Fl. Dutchman); *Blues and the Abstract Truth; Live From Los Angeles; Michelle; More Blues; Musical Tribute to JFK; Sound Pieces* (Imp.); w. Leon Thomas, *In Berlin* (Fl. Dutchman); w. *Sound of Feeling* (Verve).

NESTICO, SAMUEL L. (SAM), *arranger, trombone;* b. Pittsburgh, Pa., 2/6/24. His name at birth was Sal Nistico—the same as that of his first cousin, the tenor saxophonist who pl. w. C. Basie in 1965. Put in a total of 20 years in the service: three years during World War II, then (after several years on staff at ABC studios in Pittsburgh) 17 more years, switching from Air Force to Marines and retiring in March '68 as chief arr. for U.S. Marine Band in Washington, D.C. He then moved to Los Angeles.

While in the service Nestico pl. briefly w. T. Dorsey, W. Herman. During his civilian years he was with Ch. Barnet, '46, and G. Krupa, '48.

Through trombonist Grover Mitchell, an old friend from Pittsburgh, Nestico began writing regularly for the Count Basie band in '68. His many original comps. for Basie's LPs were published for school bands in a special Basie-Nestico series.

Simultaneously Nestico has had a busy career orchestrating at many movie studios, arranging and orchestrating for TV series, and arranging for the Time-Life swing band recreation series, '69-73. In '75 he wrote three works performed in concert 4/19/75 by the Basie band and the Baltimore Symphony.

Publ: More than 300 works in educ. field, primarily concert band, symphony orch. and stage band pieces, publ: (Kendor Music Inc., Delavan, N.Y., 14042; Hal Leonard Music, 6525 Bluemound Rd., Milwaukee, Wis., 53213; Studio P/R, 224 S. Lebanon St., Lebanon, Pa., 46052). LPs: all the writing for *Basie Big Band* (Pablo); other arrs. for Basie on various labels.

NEWBORN, PHINEAS JR.,* *piano, composer;* b. Whiteville, Tenn., 12/14/31. Played w. his own trio in NYC in late '50s, and w. Charles Mingus. Visited Europe briefly in '58 and '59. In the '60s he appeared sporadically in LA area clubs but was inactive professionally for long periods due to illness. In Nov. '75 he did two numbers at the World Jazz Association's first concert in LA. Earlier in the year a new album, *Solo Piano,* was released on Atlantic. Other LPs: *Please Send Me Someone to Love; Touch* (Contemporary).

NEWMAN, DAVID (FATHEAD),* *saxophones, flute;* b. Dallas, Tex., 2/24/33. Featured sideman w. Ray Charles orch., '54-64, he also led his own rec. gps. from '59. To NYC '66 working w. own gp. and w. King Curtis and the Kingpins. By '68 he had rec. three albums for Atlantic and added soprano sax to his reed lineup. Gigged in Dallas and rec. in NYC in late '60s. Rejoined Charles temporarily in '70-1. With H. Mann's Family of Mann, '72-4. Back to Dallas, '75. Pl. on rec. sessions w. Aretha Franklin; Nikki Giovanni; Cornell Dupree; Kate Smith; Greg Allman; T-Bone Walker; Shirley Scott, etc. LPs: *Newmanism; The Weapon; Lonely Avenue; Best of David Newman; The Many Facets of David Newman; Bigger and Better; House of David* (Atl.); *Capt. Buckles* (Cotillion); w. Mann (Atl.).

NEWMAN, JOSEPH DWIGHT (JOE),* *trumpet;* b. New Orleans, La., 9/7/22. First well-known for his featured role in the Count Basie orch., '52-61, he became active in early '60s in NYC w. Jazz Interactions, a non-profit organization dedicated to fostering a greater interest in and deeper understanding and appreciation of jazz. (His wife, Rigmor, is executive director.) Leading instrumentalists teach in its Young Musicians Clinic. It also has given many lecture-concert series in the schools; a lecture series at Hunter Coll. and the St. Peter's Church Center, in which Newman has delivered talks on Louis Armstrong; and monthly sessions at various NYC clubs. It publishes a weekly listing of who is playing in the clubs (527 Madison Ave., Suite 1615, N.Y., N.Y. 10022) and maintains Jazzline, a telephone service which informs in the same manner (212-421-3592). After serving as vice-president, Newman has been president from '67. That year he conducted the JI Orch. in Oliver Nelson's *Jazzhattan Suite;* in '72 he conducted the premiere performance of Thad Jones' tribute to Louis Armstrong, *Suite for Pops*. He teaches in the JI Workshop and also gives private master classes. Additionally he has led his own gp. from the time he left Basie, app. several times in the mid-'70s at Boomer's. Closely allied w. Rev. John Gensel of St. Peter's Lutheran Church, he collaborated w. him on two religious works, *O Sing to the Lord a New Song,* in the '60s; and *The Story of Pentecost,* '72. A member of the NYJRC he participated in the program devoted to the music of Louis Armstrong, '74, and toured w. it in Russia, summer '75, and Europe, fall '75.

TV: *Positively Black*. Broadway: *Promises, Promises,* '69-72; *Raisin,* '73-5. Fest: NJF; NJF-NY; Molde; Nice; Zurich; Berlin; Cascais; Umea; Warsaw; also in Italy; France; NO; Colo. JP. In '75 pl. club dates in Geneva, Munich, Vienna. Conducted seminars at many univs. incl. Pitts., Hartford, Vermont. One of the most consistent and spirited trumpeters, blending elements of swing and bop. LPs: w. S. Stitt (Muse); I. Jacquet (Prest.); J. Moody (Vang.); w. NYJRC, *Satchmo Remembered* (Atl.); w. Basie; Colo. Jazz Party (MPS); *Newport in New York, The Jam Sessions, Vols. 3&4* (Cobble.); reissue w. own gp. (Trip).

NEWSOM, THOMAS PENN (TOMMY),* *saxophones, flute, clarinet, composer;* b. Portsmouth, Va., 2/25/29. NBC staff musician from '62, pl. on Tonight show under Skitch Henderson and later Doc Severinsen. In '68 switched from second tenor sax in the band to first alto sax and assistant conductor. Comps: *Puddintane,* for Ed Shaughnessy band; *Suite for Trumpet* for Severinsen; *La Boehm; Titterpipes* for B. Goodman. Publ: *Tommy Newsom's Standard & Popular Solos* (Armstrong Edu-Tainment, Box 769, New York, N.Y. 10019).

LPs: w. Severinsen (RCA); w. C. Byrd, arrs. for *Brazilian Byrd* (Col.).

NEW YORK BASS CHOIR. see Lee, Bill.

NEW YORK JAZZ REPERTORY COMPANY. see Wein, George.

NICHOLAS, ALBERT (AL),* *clarinet;* b. New Orleans, La., 5/27/00. One of the last of the trend-setting NO clarinetists; one time member of the K. Oliver, Luis Russell and L. Armstrong bands, Nicholas lived in Europe from the early '50s, settling in Switzerland in '70. He died 9/3/73 in Basel.

LPs: w. Armstrong (Col.); own album; w. A. Hodes (Delmark); w. Jelly Roll Morton (RCA); w. B. Bigard (RCA); many on European labels, Supraphon, etc.

NIEHAUS, LEONARD (LENNIE),* *composer, alto saxophone;* b. St. Louis, Mo., 6/1/29. Active mainly in commercial work in recent years, arr. for night club artists, TV shows etc. Commissioned by LA Valley Coll. to write extended jazz works.

Publs: *Basic Jazz Conception for Saxophone;* (Try Publ. Co., 854 N. Vine St., Hollywood Ca. 90038). Eighteen original stage band comps. (Life Line Music Press, Box 338, Agoura, Ca. 91301); three orig. stage choir compositions (Vortex Music Inc.).

NIEWOOD, GERRY (Gerard J. Nevidosky), *saxophones, flutes, composer;* b. Rochester, N.Y., 4/6/43. Received B.S. degree in Industrial Relations from U. of Buffalo in '75, but decided in '66 to change careers. Grad. of Eastman School of Music, Rochester, N.Y., '70. Stud. sax w. William Osseck, flute w. John Thomas. Pl. w. B. Rich and L. Bellson bands. Came to prominence as member of C. Mangione quartet and ensemble, '71- . Infl. or insp. by J. Coltrane, S. Rollins, S. Stitt, Clifford Brown, C. Corea, Miles Davis, Joe Romano, Mangione. Fests: Newport, Concord, Monterey, several in Europe. Won DB Critics poll, TDWR, soprano sax, '74. Comps: *Floating; Homage; Semitique*.

A versatile, melodically inventive artist on all his instruments, he played a central role in the success of the Mangione group.

Own LP: *The Gerry Niewood Album* (Sagoma/DGM); w. Mangione, *Friends & Love; Together; The Chuck Mangione Quartet; Alive; Land of Make Believe* (Merc.).

NIMITZ, JACK JEROME,* *baritone saxophone;* also other *saxophones, clarinets, flutes;* b. Washington, D.C., 1/11/30. Mainly studio musician in LA, but has continued to work in jazz whenever possible. Pl. on sound track of film *Lady Sings The Blues*. Worked w. O. Nelson at Marty's, LA, '67; gigs w. B. Berry band. Was a founder member of Supersax, '73, touring Japan with the group in '75. Fests: Monterey, '64, w. Ch. Mingus; Newport/West, w. L. Bellson, '73; Concord w. C. Mangione, '74; Monterey, Canada, many others w. Supersax.

LPs: many sessions for *Time-Life* swing band recreation series; w. O. Nelson, *Sound Pieces; Black Brown & Beautiful* (Fl. Dutchman); Berry LA Band (Beez); K. Burrell; G. Ammons (Fant.); Supersax (Cap.).

NIMMONS, PHILLIP RISTA (PHIL),* *clarinet, composer, conductor, educator;* b. Kamloops, Brit. Columbia, Canada, 6/3/23. From '66 led band for CBC jazz radio shows; toured Armed Forces bases in Can., Europe, Middle East, Africa & India, sponsored by CBC and Canad. Govt. Arr. & orchestrated O. Peterson's *Canadiana Suite* for own group, Nimmons 'N' Nine Plus 6, w. Peterson as feat. soloist at Beaverbrook Playhouse, Fredericton, N.B., '70. Pl. inaugural concert at Ontario Place, '71; annual apps. Wrote and premiered *Suite P.E.I.* for Prince Edward Island centennial, '73; wrote *Palette A Deux* for World Saxophone Congress, '73. Premiered *Atlantic Suite* on concert tour of Atlantic Provinces, '74; orchestrated and arr. selection of Ellington songs for O. Peterson perf. w. Vancouver Symph., April '75. Orchestrated & arr. Peterson's thematic material for Ontario Place film, *Big North,* '75. Annual participant at Univ. of New Brunswick Jazz & Chamber Mus. Fest; dir. of summer jazz course at Niagara Coll., '73; appointed dir. of jazz prog. at Univ. of Toronto, '75. Won BMI award for best orig. jazz comp., '68; citations from Canad. govt., '67, '69, '71-2.

Comps: *Opus UNB; Friendly Encounter; Under a Tree; Chips 'N Gravy; Kernel Strange; Poly-Rock; Dorian Way; Arf; Eee-Suave* (Ellington tribute). LPs: *Take Ten; Mary Poppins Swings; Strictly Nimmons* (Canad. RCA); *Nimmons Now; Suite P.E.I.; Canadiana Suite* (CBC transcription service & Canadian Collection); *Atlantic Suite* (Nimmons 'N' Music Ltd.).

NISTICO, SALVATORE (SAL),* *tenor saxophone;* b. Syracuse, N.Y. 4/2/40. First prominent w. Chuck and Gap Mangione, '60-1. For rest of decade alternated between bands of W. Herman ('62-5, '66, '68-70) and Count Basie ('65, '67). During '70 worked in LA w. Don Ellis and others; rejoined Herman, '71. From '72-5 freelanced around NYC, w. Tito Puente, various small groups, Chuck Israels' National Jazz Ensemble; toured Europe w. Slide Hampton. Pl. w. Buddy Rich combo at Rich's club, '74.

A powerful soloist who by the early '70s had developed a style of his own compounded of elements he had found in C. Parker, G. Ammons and S. Rollins, Nistico is well represented in many albums, most notably w. Herman, *Woody Herman 1963; Woody Herman 1964; Encore* (Philips); *Woody's Winners* (Columbia); *Concerto for Herd* (Verve); *Heavy Exposure; Woody; Light My Fire* (Cadet); *Comin' On Up* w. Sal Amico, Barry Harris (Riverside); own quintet on Italian label, Horo.

NOCK, MICHAEL ANTHONY, *piano, elec. keyboards, synthesizer;* b. Christchurch, N.Z., 9/27/40. First lessons from father, '51, for six months; then mainly self-taught until he stud. at Berklee Coll. under a scholarship, '61. Led trio in Australia, '59-60. House pianist at Lennie's in Boston, '62-3, working w. C. Hawkins et al. Toured w. Y. Lateef, '64-5, then freelanced in NYC w. Booker Ervin, S. Turrentine and others until joining John Handy mid-'67, moving to SF where he formed the Fourth Way in Sept. '68. After orig. Fourth Way disbanded in June '71, became involved in electronic music and freelance work as leader and sideman in SF.

Nock has had wide exp. in nearly every jazz style. Living in NYC he worked with groups led by Wild Bill Davison, S. Stitt, A. Blakey, Sam Rivers, F. Hubbard. Fests: Newport, '67 w. Steve Marcus; Monterey, '68, Montreux '70 w. Fourth Way. Comps: *Quartet for Saxophone* ('66); *Steps,* for jazz group, string quartet and electronic sound, written in '71 under NEA grant; *Love Waltz; Projections; Eros; Colours; Becoming*. LPs: *Between or Beyond* (MPS); w. Lateef, *1984* (Impulse); w. Handy, *Projections* (Columbia); w. Marcus, *Count's Rock Band* (Vortex-Atl.); *The Sun and the Moon Have Come Together* w. Fourth Way (Harvest-Capitol).

NORMAND, EMILE R. (CISCO), *drums;* also *piano, vibes, composer;* b. Windsor, Ont., Canada, 11/21/36. Mother, Germaine, was pianist who led dance band in '50. Studied w. Holy Rosary Sisters of St. Joseph, '44-7; Windsor U., '48-53. Played w. Yusef Lateef, Terry Pollard at Club 12, Detroit, '56. From '60 in Montreal for jazz radio shows and TV, CBC. Pl. for Montreal Jazz Society '60-1; La Porte St. Jean Jazz Concerts, Quebec City '60-3; with Claude Leveille, a French-Canadian composer who was once a protege of Edith Piaf, in Quebec, Russia, Latvia, Estonia & Lithuania, '68-70. With *Hair,* Montreal, '70-1; Les Grands Ballets Canadiens; *Tommy* in Chicago, Detroit, NYC, '72. Infl: Lateef, Charles Coleman, Miles Davis, T. Monk, MJQ. Many TV apps. as guest vibes soloist. Fest: Laval U., Quebec City; Western U., London, Ont.; Montreal U.; Concordia U. JF, Montreal. Normand is also a painter, under contract to Eaton's of Canada. LPs: *Emile Normand Canada;* w. Pierre Nadeau Trio (RCI); *Information: Concert Pierre Leduc* (Elysee); with N. Ayoub, *The Montreal Scene* (RCA Victor, Can.).

NORRIS, WALTER,* *piano, composer;* b. Little Rock, Ark., 12/27/31. Stud. w. John Summers in Little Rock, '36-50; Heida Hermanns in NYC, as piano major at Manhattan Sch. of Mus., '64-9. Pl. w. Howard Williams big band, Little Rock '44-50. After discharge from service, w. Jimmy Ford in Houston, '52-3; own trio in Las Vegas, '53-4. To LA, '54, where he worked w. own trio and w. Frank Rosolino, Jack Sheldon, Zoot Sims, Teddy Edwards, Sonny Criss. Toured w. Shorty Rogers-Bill Holman quintet '57; Stan Getz in SF '58; Ornette Coleman, LA '58; Johnny Griffin, SF '59. To NYC where he pl. w. Hal Gaylor and Billy Bean in "The Trio," '61. From July '63 through April '70 was mus. dir. at NYC Playboy Club, where he app. w. own combos. Taught piano, theory and cond. in NYC, April '70 until June '74, when he joined Thad Jones-Mel Lewis orch., touring Europe w. them in summer of that year. Continued w. Jones-Lewis in '75; also duo w. George Mraz at Bradley's, NYC spring '75. Infl: Parker, Gillespie, Tatum, Teddy Edwards, Bud Powell, Dinu Lipatti, Vladimir Ashkenazy. Fest: MJF w. Leroy Vinnegar-Teddy Edwards '58. Comp: *Drifting; Nota Cambiata; Space Maker; Rose Waltz; Thumbs Up; D&D; Scramble*. LPs: *Drifting* (Enja); *Something Else* w. Ornette Coleman (Contemporary).

NORVO, RED (KENNETH NORVILLE),* *vibraharp, xylophone;* b. Beardstown, Ill., 3/3/08. First jazz pioneer on mallet instruments, prominent from early '30s w. Paul Whiteman; own band w. wife Mildred Bailey as singer. Settled in Cal., '47; led own trio in '50s. Moved to Las Vegas and for 12 years spent at least half of each year at the Sands Hotel. Led new trio at Tropicana, '70-2 but was in complete retirement July '72-July '73, after which he resumed occasional playing in LV, NYC etc.

TV: Benny Goodman, Frank Sinatra specs., Dinah Shore; Merv Griffin; J. Carson shows etc. Fests: Newport, Montreal, Berlin, Nice, Monterey, Concord, all in late '60s or '70s; also Dick Gibson Jazz Parties in Colo. As film comp. wrote incidental music for *Kings Go Forth* and six numbers for *Screaming Mimi*.

Despite a series of private traumas incl. severe trouble with his hearing from the late '60s, Norvo continued to provide a light, gently swinging brand of music that was entirely personal.

LPs: *Vibes a la Red* (Famous Door); *Back to the Roots* w. K. Starr (GNP-Crescendo).

NOTO, SAM,* *trumpet;* also *fluegelhorn;* b. Buffalo, N.Y., 4/17/30. The former Kenton, Bellson, Basie sideman formed his own quintet in Buffalo, '65. Opened own coffee house called Renaissance and pl. there w. his gp. for a yr. After the demise of the club, Noto left for Las Vegas where he worked in the show bands at the Flamingo & other hotels, '69-75. While there he met Red Rodney who recommended him to prod. Don Schlitten. In '74 Schlitten taped an album w. the two trumpeters for Muse and in '75 rec. Noto for his own Xanadu label. Encouraged by these events and frustrated by the stultifying LV scene, Noto moved to Toronto in the summer of '75 and became active in the studio and club scene. Known as a powerful lead man and high-note specialist w. Kenton, he revealed himself in the '70s as a virtuosic soloist inspired chiefly by Clifford Brown. Comp: *Last Train Out; Entrance; Jen-Jen.* LPs: *Entrance!* (Xanadu); *Superbop* w. Rodney (Muse).

NOTTINGHAM, JAMES EDWARD JR. (JIMMY),* *trumpet;* also *fluegelhorn, Latin percussion;* b. Brooklyn, N.Y., 12/15/25. Many name bands from mid-40s, incl. Hampton, Barnet, Basie, Gillespie, R. Charles. Lead and solo trumpet w. T. Jones-M. Lewis, incl. their first tour of Japan. Pl. on their recs. for band's first five years of existence. Lead and spec. effects w. C. Terry's big band, '74-5. For many years Nottingham also was a staff musician at CBS, until '73. In '70 opened own club, Sir James Pub in St. Albans, N.Y., feat. himself and many prominent jazz guests. Fests: Newport-N.Y. w. B. Carter, '73, '75; Nassau County Jazz w. Gillespie; West Point, N.Y. w. B. Goodman sextet, etc. LPs w. Jones-Lewis, incl. Joe Williams w. Jones-Lewis (United Artists); Teresa Brewer and Ellington Orch. (Fly. Dutch.).

O'BRIEN, FLOYD,* *trombone;* b. Chicago, Ill., 5/7/07. A frequent associate of the so-called "Austin High Gang," O'Brien later pl. in NYC with many name groups incl. G. Krupa, Bob Crosby, J. Teagarden; later he moved back to Chicago, pl. w. Art Hodes and others. He died in Chicago, 11/18/68. He was heard on records w. E. Condon, M. Mezzrow, F. Waller, Red Nichols in '30s and '40s and later w. groups led by Albert Nicholas, Hodes and others.

O'DAY ANITA,* *singer;* b. Chicago, Ill., 12/18/19. Best known for her work w. Gene Krupa band in '40s. In the '60s she was still prominent on the jazz scene, touring Japan in '63 and '66; to England, '70, European tour, '71. Played small role as jazz singer in '71 movie, *Zig-Zag,* and again in movie, *The Outfit,* '74. Started own record company, '72. Jazz fests: Berlin,'71; Newport, '73; Monterey, '74. Also during '74 played Carnegie Hall and N.Y. supper clubs. In '75 Ms. O'Day's performances confirmed her undiminished stature as one of the definitive, fact-finding jazz singers. Among her most personal characteristics are a uniquely personal timbre, a manner of skipping in front of and behind the beat, and the extensive use of melisma. She enjoyed something of a comeback in '74-5, appearing frequently at Ye Little Club in Beverly Hills, and occasionally returning to N.Y. for engagements at Reno Sweeney's.

LPs: *Hi-Ho Trailus Boot Whip* (Bob Thiele Music) feat. her first recs. as soloist; *Gene Krupa-Anita O'Day,* feat. R. Eldridge (Columbia) spanning 1941-5; *Anita O'Day & Berlin JF '70* (MPS-BASF); *Once Upon a Summertime; Anita and Rhythm Section* (Box 422, Hesperia, Ca. 92345).

OEHLER, DALE DIXON, *composer, arranger, piano;* b. Springfield, Ill., 10/1/41. Father played piano w. J. Dorsey, Lee Konitz in '40s. Extensive studies from '48-69. MA from U. of Iowa. Worked with local groups in the Springfield-Chicago area while at Northwestern U. '58-63.

Oehler, who names as his influences Igor Stravinsky, Luciano Berio, Edwin Hawkins, Gil Evans and Quincy Jones, earned awards as best pianist and best arranger at Notre Dame Jazz Fest., '66. During early '70s he became a successful arranger for many jazz, pop and fringe-jazz LPs. Among those on which he participated as arr. and/or pianist are: *High Energy* w. F. Hubbard (Columbia); *Natural Juices* w. Gene McDaniels (Ode); *The Other Side,* sound track album *Shaft's Big Score* (MGM); *Inside Bugsy,* w. Bugsy Maugh (Dot); *Trouble Man* w. Marvin Gaye (Tamla); *Who's This Bitch Anyway* w. Marlena Shaw (Blue Note); and many others for Moacir Santos et al.

O'FARRILL, ARTURO (CHICO),* *composer, arranger;* b. Havana, Cuba, 10/28/21. First prominent in NYC as arr. for B. Goodman, D. Gillespie. Moved to Mexico late '50s, returned to U.S. in '65, resumed writing frequently for C. Basie, also for Glenn Miller orch. under B. De Franco. Arrs. for C. Tjader LP, '67; comp. suite for Clark Terry, introduced at Montreux, '70. From '71 became increasingly involved in composing and arranging and production of radio and TV commercials. His *Symphony #1* was premiered in Mexico City, '72. Wrote extended work for S. Kenton, also originals for Candido LP, '73; arrs. for F. Wess, G. Barbieri albums, '74. Conducted concert at Avery Fisher Hall, NYC, with Machito orch. and Joe Newman, '74; cond. new work, *Oro, Incienso y Mirra,* w. Gillespie and Machito at St. Patrick's Cathedral, '75.

Comp: *Ramon Lopez* for S. Kenton orch. LP (Creative World); Arr: *High Voltage; Basic Basie,* for Basie LPs (MPS-BASF); *Chapter Three; Viva Emiliano Zapata* for Barbieri LP (Impulse). Own LPs: *Spanish Rice* (co-leader w. C. Terry); *Nine Flags* (AVC-Impulse); *Married Well* (Verve); w. Gillespie, *Oro, Incienso y Mirra* (Pablo).

OGERMAN, CLAUS,* *composer, piano;* b. Ratibor, Germany, 4/29/30. To U.S., '59. Has enjoyed continuous success as arranger-conductor for hundreds of albums by pop, jazz and r & b artists. Comps: *Some Times,* a symphonic jazz-ballet, premiered 7/14/72 at Lincoln Cent., NYC by American Ballet Theatre; *Symbiosis; Elegia; A Face Without A Name,* all rec. by Bill Evans; *Time Present and Time Past,* symphonic dances, pl. by various symph. orchs.

LPs: w. F. Sinatra, *Francis Albert Sinatra & A.C. Jobim* (Repr.); w. O. Peterson, *Motions & Emotions* (MPS); w. W. Montgomery, *Tequila* (Verve); w. B. Evans, *With Symphony Orchestra* (Verve); *Symbiosis* (MPS); w. S. Getz, *Voices* (Verve); w. A. C. Jobim (MCA); others w. D. Byrd, J. Hodges, K. Winding, Jimmy Smith, Jackie & Roy, Astrud Gilberto (Verve); S. Vaughan (Merc.); B. Goodman (RCA-Readers Digest); Urbie Green (Project 3); David Clayton-Thomas (Col.).

OLAY, RUTH,* *singer;* b. San Francisco, Cal., 7/1/27. After living for many years in LA, moved to Copenhagen, '73, working there at Montmartre, commuting to U.S. frequently

Oscar Peterson (*David D. Spitzer*)

Flora Purim

Hannibal Marvin Peterson (*Veryl Oakland*)

Esther Phillips (*Veryl Oakland*)

Julian Priester (*Veryl Oakland*)

Jean-Luc Ponty

Buddy Rich (*Bob Klein*)

Jerome Richardson
(*Veryl Oakland*)

Larry Ridley
(*Bob Klein*)

Sam Rivers
(*David D. Spitzer*)

Dewey Redman (*David D. Spitzer*)

Ben Riley (*Veryl Oakland*)

Sonny Rollins (*Veryl Oakland*)

Max Roach (*Veryl Oakland*)

Perry Robinson (*David D. Spitzer*)

Jimmy Rowles

Roswell Rudd (*David D. Spitzer*)

Charles Rouse (*Bob Klein*)

Pharoah Sanders (*Veryl Oakland*)

Wayne Shorter (*Veryl Oakland*)

Linda & Sonny Sharrock

Bud Shank (*Veryl Oakland*)

Archie Shepp (*David D. Spitzer*)

Horace Silver (*Veryl Oakland*)

George Shearing & Dave Brubeck (*Veryl Oakland*)

Sonny Stitt (*Veryl Oakland*)

Zoot Sims (*Veryl Oakland*)

Gabor Szabo (*Veryl Oakland*)

Lew Soloff (*Veryl Oakland*)

Sonny Simmons (*Veryl Oakland*)

for spec. apps. TV in Oslo; app. at Hebrew Univ. in Jerusalem. Worked at Mr. Kelly's in Chicago w. E. Garner, Feb. '75. Fests. in Denmark, Sweden, summer of '75. In Dec. '74, she sang at Ye Little Club in Beverly Hills, where she had been its opening attraction 18 years earlier.

LPs: *Live at Mr. Kelly's* (UA); *Soul In The Night* (ABC).

OLIVER, MELVIN JAMES (SY),* *composer, leader, singer, trumpet;* b. Battle Creek, Mich., 12/17/10. Prominent as an arranger-performer w. J. Lunceford in '30s and arr. for T. Dorsey in '40s. During '60s busy as a free-lance arr. in NYC but in '70s began leading his own band on a fairly regular basis, pl. the music of Lunceford which he helped create, Ellingtonia and other classics from the Swing Era. The band app. at the NJF-NY for dances at Commodore Hotel, '72, Roseland, '74; for the Duke Ellington Society at the New School; at the Riverboat; and, in '75, in two separate, lengthy engagements at the Rainbow Room. Oliver was one of the four musical directors for the NYJRC in its first season, '74, concentrating on programs of Lunceford, Dorsey, Ellington, Fletcher Henderson, etc.

LPs: *Yes Indeed* (Black & Blue); Stang.

OREGON. see Moore, Glen; Towner, Ralph.

ORSTED PEDERSEN, NIELS-HENNING,* *bass;* b. Osted, Denmark, 5/27/46. A prodigy who pl. w. Danish gps. at age 14; two yrs. later he was pl. & rec. w. Bud Powell and soon had enhanced his growing reputation through gigs w. R. Kirk, B. Evans and S. Rollins. Later he pl. w. Oscar Peterson, toured w. JATP and was house bassist at Copenhagen's Club Montmartre where he pl. w. all the visiting Americans, most notably Dexter Gordon and Kenny Drew. Formed duo w. Drew in '70s; also member of Danish Radio Big Band; perf. w. own gp. Polls: Won DB Int. Critics poll, TDWR, '68; no. 1 European bassist in *Jazz Forum,* '74-5. Orsted Pedersen's exceptional talent makes him one of the leading bass virtuosos of the contemporary scene. Lennie Tristano says: "He may be the best bassist in the world." LPs: *Duo; Duo 2* w. Drew; *Paul Bley/NHOP; Two's Company* w. Joe Albany; *Dark Beauty* w. Drew; *Catalonian Fire* w. T. Montoliu; others w. Jackie McLean; D. Gordon; Anthony Braxton (SteepleChase) w. O. Peterson, *The Trio;* also many albums rec. at Montreux JF '75 incl. *The Trumpet Kings; Milt Jackson Big Four; Dizzy Gillepsie Big 7; Court Basie Jam Session; Oscar Peterson Big 6; The Montreux Collection* (Pablo).

ORTEGA, ANTHONY ROBERT (TONY),* *saxophone, clarinet, flute;* b. Los Angeles, Cal., 6/7/28. Continued to work w. Gerald Wilson, whose band he joined in '64; also w. L. Schifrin, D. Gillespie at the Hollywood Bowl in '67, F. Zappa, '72; O. Nelson; N. Riddle. TV: acting role on *Lucille Ball Show; Ironsides,* w. Q. Jones. Film; *Change of Habit,* w. E. Presley.

LPs: *New Dance* (Revelation); others w. Wilson (Pac. Jazz).

ORY, EDWARD (KID),* *trombone, composer;* b. La Place, La., 12/25/1886. After moving to Hawaii in '66, Ory went into semi-retirement. He returned to NO in '71 to app. at the jazz fest., but in his few subsequent apps. was able only to sing. On 1/23/73 he died in Hawaii of heart failure and pneumonia.

Ory earned his most lasting fame as composer of *Muskrat Ramble,* which he rec. in Feb. '26 w. L. Armstrong and His Hot Five. One of the first musicians identified with the "tailgate" trombone style, he is represented on innumerable recordings, among them his own LPs: *Tailgate!; Creole Jazz Band* (3 albums, '54, '55, '56); *This Kid's The Greatest; Favorites* (Good Time Jazz); others w. Armstrong (Col.); Jelly Roll Morton (RCA).

OSBORNE, MARY,* *guitar, singer;* b. Minot, North Dakota, 7/17/21. Insp. by Charlie Christian, became one of the first elec. guitarists, prominent through NYC record dates w. Mary Lou Williams, C. Hawkins, M. Ellington and own trio. Jack Sterling radio show daily, '52-63; freelance gigs and teaching '64-7. Moving to Bakersfield, Cal., '67, worked with local groups and was partner with husband, Ralph Scaffidi, in Osborne Guitar Co., manufacturing guitars, amps, PA systems. Occasional concerts and club work in LA, incl. Donte's, Pilgrimage Theatre; Palace of Fine Arts, SF w. Joe Venuti, '69; fests. for George Wein in Berkeley and at Hollywood Bowl, '73.

LPs: w. Tyree Glenn; also Louie Bellson/Gene Krupa (Roulette).

OSTLUND, PETUR DAVID (ISLAND), *drums;* b. New York City, 12/3/43. Lived in NYC until age seven, then spent four years in Trois Rivieres, Quebec, after which he was a resident of Reykjavik, Iceland until age 26, then moved to Stockholm. Stud. w. Gene Stone, '58-60; Reykjavik Conservatory of Mus., '66-9; Ingesund Mus. School, Sweden, '72-3. Winner of Icelandic poll annually, '62-9; Icelandic Musician of the Year, '66. Has pl. w. A. Farmer, D. Byrd, Ch. Tolliver, K. Winding, Y. Lateef, Booker Ervin, Dexter Gordon, Lars Gullin, Dave Pike, Barney Kessel. Member of Red Mitchell's sextet, '74-5; also teaching at Royal Academy of Mus., Stockholm.

LPs: *Communication,* w. Mitchell; *A Sleeping Bee,* w. Farmer (Gramofonverket); *Happy New Year* w. Wickman, Mitchell et al; *Like Grass,* w. Gullin (EMI); *Rumanian Impressions,* w. Guido Manusardi (Amigo).

OTIS, JOHNNY,* *piano, vibes, leader, composer;* b. Vallejo, Cal. 12/28/21. After a period of almost total inactivity in music, Otis gradually returned to casual gigs and record production in the late '60s. In '69 the album *Cold Shot* (Kent) rekindled his career. He has been traveling nationally with his show since '70, often feat. his son, Shuggie Otis (q.v.). Toured Far East, '71; Europe, '72; Africa/Europe '74. TV: own series '56-61; Barrel House show, '70. Movies: *Jukebox Rhythm,* '58; *Play Misty For Me,* '71. Fests: Monterey, '70; Antibes, '74. Comps: *Every Beat of My Heart; So Fine; Dance With Me Henry; Hand Jive; Oxford Grey. Listen to the Lambs,* a colorful and highly readable autobiography, was publ. in '66 by W. W. Norton.

LPs: *Cold Shot* (Kent); *Johnny Otis Show Live at Monterey; Cuttin' Up* (Epic); *R & B Blues* (Blues Spectrum).

OTIS, JOHNNY JR. (SHUGGIE), *guitar;* also *bass, drums, keyboards, singer, composer;* b. Los Angeles, Cal., 11/30/53. Stud. guitar w. Burdell Mathis; arr. and comp. w. Albert Harris; general mus. educ. w. father. Became member of the Johnny Otis Show in '67, remained until '73 and worked with the show again in '75, in addition to leading his own group.

Other jobs w. F. Zappa, Billy Preston, Preston Love, Al Kooper, Gene "Mighty Flea" Conners.

An unusually sensitive and prodigious musician, Otis was only 15 when the first album feat. him with his father's gp., *Cold Shot,* app. on the Kent label in '69. He names among his infls. T-Bone Walker, B.B. King, K. Burrell, Jimi Hendrix, Sly Stone, Debussy, Stravinsky, Beethoven, Johnny Otis Sr. Comps: *Freedom Flight; Barrelhouse Blues; Gospel Groove; Shuggie's Boogie; Purple; Rainy Day.* Fests: Monterey, Newport, '70; Berkeley, Newport/LA, '73.

LPs: *Here Comes Shuggie Otis; Freedom Flight; Johnny Otis Show Live at Monterey* (Epic); also, with his father, a series of albums with various blues artists under the title *Great R & B Oldies* (Blues Spectrum).

OTSUKA, KEIJI (GEORGE), *drums;* b. Tokyo, Japan, 4/6/38. Self-taught. After playing w. Tony Scott gp., Sadao Watanabe quartet, and Sleepy Matsumoto quartet, formed own gp. Infl: Tony Williams, Miles Davis, Roy Haynes, Jack DeJohnette. Fests: World JF, '64; Four Big Drummers Fest. w. Haynes, DeJohnette, Mel Lewis, '70; Expo '70 and other major Japanese fests. Won SJ Jazz Disc Award '68; SJ Readers Poll, '68-9. Own LPs: *Page 1; Page 2; Page 3* (Nippon Col.); *Chris Connor & George Otsuka* (Japan. Victor); *Jackieboard* w. DeJohnette; *Groovin With My Soul Brothers* w. Haynes (Trio).

OTT, HORACE, *composer, arranger;* also *piano, organ, trombone, tympani, vibes;* b. St. Matthews, S.C., 4/15/33. Priv. piano lessons from '44. Began writing arrs. while in 11th grade, continued while student at S. Carolina State Coll. One year of teaching school (band director); two years of army, incl. spec. serv. stints; a year of writing for rehearsal bands prior to entering prof. rec. career, in which he became very active in pop, r & b and jazz circles. Among artists he has comp., arr. and/or conducted for, mainly on rec. are Joe Williams, Nat King Cole, Betty Carter, C. Basie, R. Flack, Groove Holmes, B. Rich, J. Witherspoon, L. Donaldson. Arr. music for film *Gordon's War;* comp. *Prove It,* rec. by Aretha Franklin; *Sassy Soul Strut* for L. Donaldson (Blue Note); arr. four albums for Nina Simone, incl. some of his own comps; also *Worth Waiting For* LP by J. Williams (Blue Note).

OUSLEY, HAROLD LOMAX,* *tenor saxophone, composer;* also *alto sax, flute, clarinet;* b. Chicago, Ill., 1/23/29, Worked w. Machito; Howard McGhee; Joe Newman; Clark Terry in first half of '60s; Also led own combos at Birdland; Club Baron; Count Basie's. Cont. w. own gp. from '66-73, '75- . Toured in Caracas; Puerto Rico w. Machito, '69. Pl. w. L. Hampton, '70; C. Basie, '73-4, incl. Europe and Japan. Concert-lecture, *A Historical Resume of Jazz,* on St. Thomas, St. Croix and St. John, West Indies, in late '60s; from that time in US. *Jazz Mass* in various churches; jazz seminars in Music Therapy at Groves Therapeutic Counseling Service, Jamaica, N.Y. Film: *Cotton Comes to Harlem;* wrote and rec. theme for *Not Just Another Woman.* TV: *Like It Is; Jazz Adventures; Sight and Sound; The Night People; Black Pride.* Fest: Columbia U. Concert at NJF-NY, '72. Comp: *Return of the Prodigal Son; The Kid; Aquarian Melody; Son of Man; The People's Choice; Code Name Thunder Walk.* LPs: *The Kid* (Cobble.); w. Jack McDuff, *Walk On By* (Prest.); w. Grassella Oliphant, *The Grass is Greener* (Atl.).

OVERTON, HALL F.,* *composer, piano, teacher;* b. Bangor, Mich., 2/23/20. Overton, who distinguished himself as a classical musician along with his jazz activities, and who taught at Juilliard from '60, was well known for his association w. Th. Monk, for whom he orchestrated a number of the latter's compositions for concert presentation. Overton died 11/25/72 of a ruptured esophagus at Roosevelt Hospital in NYC. As jazz pianist, he was heard on recs. in the '50s w. Jimmy Raney, S. Getz, O. Pettiford, Phil Woods Teddy Charles and others, and in a piano duo session w. Dave McKenna for the long defunct Bethlehem label; also a classical album, *Pulsations* (CRI); *Who's Afraid of the Big Band Monk* (Col.).

OWENS, CHARLES M. (Charles M. Brown), *tenor saxophone, composer;* also *flute;* b. Phoenix, Ariz., 5/4/39. Stud. sax at San Diego State Coll. and while in U.S. Air Force; also w. Joe Viola at Berklee, '64-5. Pl. w. B. Rich, '67-9; M. Santamaria, '69 to May '70; Bobby Bryant; Paul Humphrey. With J. Mayall, '72- European tour w. F. Zappa, pl. flute and piccolo; Patrice Rushen in SF, '75; G. Wilson, '74-5. Infls: O. Nelson, Dolphy, Coltrane. TV: *Dial M For Music; The Jazz Show,* KNBC. Comps: *Night Cry; Black Pride; I Stand Alone.* Arr. *Ode to Billy Joe* in Rich album, *Live at Caesar's Palace* (Pac. Jazz). LPs: *Motherlode* (Vault); w. Henry Franklin, *The Skipper at Home* (Black Jazz).

OWENS, JAMES ROBERT (JIMMY),* *trumpet, fluegelhorn, composer;* b. New York City, 12/9/43. Early experience in the '60s w. L. Hampton, Mingus, etc. W. Herbie Mann, '65-6. One of the orig. members of the Thad Jones-Mel Lewis orch.; also pl. w. Clark Terry's big band; the New York Jazz Sextet; the Symphony of the New World; and the Billy Taylor band for the David Frost TV show. European tours w. Dizzy Gillespie reunion band, '68; Young Giants of Jazz, '73. Other European tours in '67, '69, '72, '74, pl. w. radio orchs. in Germany, Holland.

Owens, who is an extremely active NYC freelancer, is on the Board of Governors of the New York chapter of NARAS; the Board of Dir. for the NYJRC, serving as one of its mus. dirs. for the 1974-75 season; on the Jazz/Folk/Ethnic Music Panel of the Nat. Endowment for the Arts; and one of the founders of the Collective Black Artists. He is also a member of the Nat. Jazz Ens. He teaches and lectures for the CBA and for Jazzmobile. Won DB Critics' Poll, TDWR, '67. Fests: many European apps. incl. Berlin, Loosdrecht, Bologna, Helsinki; also Monterey, Newport. In '74, Owens led the CBA orch. in a tribute to Dizzy Gillespie at Fordham U. as part of NJF-NY. Comps: *Complicity; Milan Is Love; Git the Money Bluze; You Had Better Listen; The Jazz Jaleo; Lo-Slo-Bluze; Never Subject to Change; Funk-A-De Mama; We're Going up.*

LPs: *No Escaping It* (Polydor); *You Had Better Listen* (Atlantic); *Newport in New York, the Jam Sessions,* Vol. 1 (Cobblestone); w. Leon Thomas, *Full Circle* (Fly. Dutch.); w. Taylor, *O.K. Billy* (Bell); w. Billy Harper, *Capra Black* (Strata-East); w. A. Shepp, *The Way Ahead; For Losers*

(Imp.); *The Dizzy Gillespie Reunion Band* (MPS); w. B. Timmons, *Got to Get It;* w. Gary Bartz, *Libra* (Milest.); w. Teddy Edwards, *It's All Right;* w. Eric Kloss, *First Class Kloss; Life Force; We're Going Up;* w. Booker Ervin, *Heavy* (Prestige).

OXLEY, TONY, *drums, percussion, electronics;* b. Sheffield, Yorks., England, 6/15/38. From '57-60 in Black Watch Military band. Own quintet in Sheffield, '60-4; collaborated w. guitarist Derek Bailey, '64-7. Moved to London, '67 to work at Ronnie Scott's Club, continuing there into the early '70s, acc. such visiting American jazzmen as Sonny Rollins, Bill Evans, S. Getz, L. Konitz, C. Mariano et al. Formed own sextet for clubs, concerts throughout Europe. In '71 started Incus record label w. Bailey and other musicians; also joined Jazz Composer Orch. Received commission from Arts Council of Gt. Britain for LJCO, '72. In '73 organized and taught at Barry Summer School, course in Jazz and Improvised Music. Oxley has worked for many Amer. mus. in Europe incl. Rollins, J. Griffin, Art Farmer, Joe Henderson, Charles Tolliver et al. Also played w. John McLaughlin, Giorgio Gaslini, Michel Portal, Barry Guy orch. Formed own new gp., The Angular Apron, '74. Won MM polls in percussion category, '68, '70-1; six comp. awards from Arts Council of Gt. Britain. Worked w. George Gruntz on music for film *Steppenwolf,* prod. by Gruntz. Oxley names many classical composers as his main infl., as well as Dolphy, Blakey, Elvin Jones, Coltrane, Bill Evans.

LPs: *Baptised Traveller; Four Compositions for Sextet* (CBS); *Ichnos* (RCA); *Tony Oxley, 71-4;* w. Howard Riley, *Synopsis* (Incus).

PACK, GARY LEE, *trumpet, fluegelhorn, valve trombone;* b. Los Angeles, Cal., 10/17/50. Stud. w. Forrest Ray, Long Beach, Cal., '61; Dr. Herbert D. Patnoe, '68-9; Claude Gordon, Bill Green, '70; Jerry Coker, Dan Haerle, U. of Miami, '72. Much early exp. in coll. jazz groups, incl. Jack Wheaton's Junior Neophonic Orch. Joined D. Ellis, '70; left to work w. S. Kenton for nine months in '71. After three months back with the Ellis band, he left for Miami in '72 to teach in summer jazz-rock seminar at U. of Miami. After working w. M. Torme, Ira Sullivan and others in the Miami area, returned to Kenton band for six months. Pl. in SF w. Don Piestrup. Led Foothill Coll. jazz ensemble, '74. Toured w. W. Herman Feb. to Nov. '74, incl. concerts and TV w. F. Sinatra. Returned to LA, pl. w. Ellis octet, '74-5. Fests: Montreux; Belvedere, Canada, w. Herman '74; Concord, w. Kenton, '71. Infls: I. Sullivan, J. Coltrane, F. Hubbard, Clifford Brown et al.

LPs: w. Kenton, *Live at Brigham Young University; 7.5 On The Richter Scale* (Creative World); w. Herman, *Herd at Monterey; Children of Lima* (Fantasy).

PAGE, NATHEN, *guitar;* also *bass, piano;* b. Leetown, W. Va., 8/25/37. Brother, Henry Page, is drummer in Tampa, Fla. Self-taught. Played w. Jimmy Smith; Roberta Flack; Herbie Mann; Tony Williams; Doug Carn; in '75 w. Sonny Rollins, incl. NJF-NY; Jackie McLean at Five Spot, NYC.

Infl: Coltrane, Miles Davis, C. Adderley, H. Hancock, Tyner, Clifford Brown, C. Parker, Ahmad Jamal. Movie: *Soul to Soul.* TV: Mike Douglas; Steve Allen; *Tonight;* Merv Griffin; *Harambee; Nine in the Morning;* David Frost; *Morning Show from Virginia Beach.* Fest: NJF; NJF-NY; Houston; Dallas; Hampton, Va.; Laurel, Md.; MJF; Canada.

Comp: *Knapp Time.* LPs: w. J. Smith, *The Boss* (Verve); w. Doug Carn, *Revelation; Adams Apple* (Black Jazz); w. R. Flack, *Soul to Soul* (Atl.); w. Rene McLean, *What It Is* (Steeple.).

PALMER, EARL C. SR.* *drums;* b. New Orleans, La., 10/25/24. To LA, '57; continuously busy for many years as studio musician doing commercials, TV, movies, pop record dates etc., and occasional jazz apps. w. Benny Carter and own group. Past VP of NARAS.

LPs: w. Maria Muldaur, Carter, *Waitress in A Donut Shop* (Repr.).

PALMIER, REMO (formerly Palmieri),* *guitar;* b. New York City, 3/29/23. Prominent in '40s w. C. Hawkins, R. Norvo, B. Holiday, Mildred Bailey, and on early D. Gillespie records. Won *Esquire* New Star Award, '45. Palmier became inactive in jazz after joining the CBS staff in '45, where he worked on the Arthur Godfrey show continuously until '72. He then returned to jazz, starting a quartet w. Hank Jones; also pl. night club dates w. B. Hackett. In '74 he pl. a series of jazz concerts w. B. Goodman.

LPs: *Bobby Hackett and Vic Dickenson at the Royal Box* (Hyannisport).

PANASSIÉ, HUGUES, *critic;* b. Paris, France, 2/27/12. Founder of the Hot Club of France in '32, Panassié in '34 wrote a book, *Le Jazz Hot,* one of the first scholarly volumes on jazz to appear in any country. A long time champion of traditionalist and NO jazz, he became the center of a controversy when he strongly opposed bop and other new developments beginning in the '40s. From '50 he edited and wrote a monthly bulletin for the Hot Club of France. Panassié died 12/8/74 of a heart attack at his home in Montauban, France. He was well remembered for a series of recordings he made during a visit to New York in 1938. In '49 he visited NO to see L. Armstrong crowned King of the Zulus. Armstrong, E. Hines, L. Hampton, and particularly clarinetist Milton Mezz Mezzrow had been among his closest musician friends.

PARENTI ANTHONY (TONY),* *clarinet, saxophones;* b. New Orleans, La., 8/6/00. The veteran NO jazzman, who had worked for many years as a studio musician in NYC, later became a regular at E. Condon's and led the house band at Jimmy Ryan's from '63-9. He died 4/17/72 in NYC.

LPs: *Jean Kitrell; Night at Jimmy Ryan's; Ragtime; The Great Tony Parenti; Ragtime Jubilee* (Jazzology).

PARKER, EVAN, *tenor, soprano saxes;* b. Bristol, England, 4/5/44. Studied saxophone w. James Knott, '58-62. Played w. Spontaneous Music Ensemble, '66-68; Tony Oxley sextet, '69-72; Pierre Favre, '69-71; Music Improvisation Company, '69-72; Peter Brotzmann Octet; Chris McGregor Sextet, '70; Globe Unity Orchestra; Alexander Von Schlippenbach trio/

quartet from '70; Evan Parker-Paul Lytton duo from '72; Brotherhood of Breath from '73. Infl: Coltrane, Dolphy, Derek Bailey. TV: *Aquarius,* TV Arts program for LNTV w. Lytton. Fest: many Euro. fests. incl. Bilzen, '69; Donaueschingen; Berlin, '72; Antibes, '75; Baden-Baden, '68-9, '75. Co-director w. Derek Bailey, Tony Oxley of Incus Records. Member of Musicians' Co-operative. Publ: *New/ Rediscovered Musical Instruments* (Quartz/Mirliton). LPs: *Topography of the Lungs; Collective Calls; Saxophone Solos; Evan Parker & Paul Lytton at the Unity Theatre* (Incus); *The Music Improvisation Company* (ECM); *Pakistani Pomade; Three Nails Left* (FMP).

PARLAN, HORACE LOUIS,* *piano;* b. Pittsburgh, Pa., 1/19/31. First active on NY scene w. C. Mingus in '50s; pl. w. Booker Ervin; Lockjaw Davis-Johnny Griffin; R.R. Kirk. In '73 he moved to Copenhagen, working from that time in Scandinavia w. local musicians, incl. Dexter Gordon, and American visitors such as Al Cohn-Zoot Sims; Red Rodney. LP: w. own trio & quintet, *Arrival;* w. D. Gordon. (Steeple.).

PARLATO, DAVID CHARLES, *bass;* also *piano;* b. Los Angeles, Cal., 10/31/45. Father, Charles Parlato, is trumpeter and singer who has worked in the bands of Kay Kyser, Horace Heidt et al. Educ. Valley State Coll., '66-8; then priv. study w. Nat Gagnursky (classical); Monty Budwig (jazz); Jr. Neophonic w. S. Kenton. Made first pro. app. w. D. Ellis orch., '67; then worked with the combos of Frank Strazzeri, '69; Warne Marsh, '70; Paul Horn '68-71; Gil Melle, '69-71; Tim Weisberg, '70-2; John Klemmer, '72-4; Frank Zappa, '72; Ashish Khan-Alla Rakha-Emil Richards-Don Preston, '73; Gabor Szabo, '74-5. Infls: Miles Davis, J. Coltrane, Gil Evans. Fests: w. Ellis, Monterey, '67-8; Newport, '68; w. Weisberg, Monterey, '70.

LPs: w. Ellis, *Electric Bath; Shock Treatment* (Col.); w. Strazzeri, *That's Him and This Is New;* w. Marsh, *Ne Plus Ultra* (Revelation); w. Horn, *The Concert Ensemble* (Ovation); *A Special Edition* (Island); w. Melle, *Waterbirds* (Nocturne); others w. Weisberg (A & M); Klemmer (Imp.).

PARNELL, JACK,* *drums, leader;* b. London, England, 8/6/23. First popular w. Ted Heath; formed own big band, '51. Mus. Dir. for ATV from '57; also for Independent TV Corp. in U.S. MD for many TV specs. starring L. Horne, Tony Bennett, other pop stars. Won Emmy as Mus. Dir. for Barbra Streisand Spec., '74. Other awards for comp. TV themes. Only occasionally active in jazz in recent years.

LPs: *Music of the Giants;* two albums of TV and film themes (Cap.)

PASCOAL, HERMETO, *piano, flute, guitar;* b. Lagoa da Canoa, Brazil, 6/22/36. Worked with several small groups in Brazil, his most notable association being Quarteto Novo, w. Airto. To NYC, '72; rec. w. Miles Davis, Duke Pearson; later went to Cal. Named by Flora Purim as one of her most important influences. Arr. *Little Church; Nem Um Talvez* on Davis' *Live/Evil* album, and pl. flute, organ. Other LPs: *Hermeto* (Buddah); w. Airto, *Natural Feelings; Seeds on the Ground* (Buddah); A.C. Jobim, *Stone Flower* (CTI).

PASS, JOE (Joseph Anthony Passalaqua),* *guitar;* b. New Brunswick, N.J., 1/13/29. Came to prominence in early '60s w. Gerald Wilson, Bud Shank, Bobby Troup, many other LA recording and club groups. After touring w. G. Shearing, '65-7, worked mainly in TV and rec. studios in LA, also playing jazz gigs in Donte's etc. and rec. w. Sinatra, B. Eckstine, S. Vaughan, Joe Williams, C. McRae. To Germany, '70 to make two LPs for MPS-BASF, one with own trio and one w. A. Van Damme. Several fest. apps. from '66 at Monterey; Concord and Newport-N.Y., '73. Toured Australia with B. Goodman, '73. Formed successful two-guitar partnership w. Herb Ellis for clubs and records, '72-4. Enthusiastically supported by Norman Granz, he worked in '73-4 w. Ella Fitzgerald and O. Peterson, both managed by Granz, and rec. with them. Played first London solo gig at Ronnie Scott's Club, '74.

Pass is regarded by many musicians who have heard him as an incomparable modern jazz artist, a total virtuoso of the instrument, capable of swinging fiercely at fast tempos and of exceptional harmonic imagination on ballads. Many examples of his work have been published: *Joe Pass Guitar Style; Chord Book; Chord Solos; Jazz Guitar Solos; Jazz Duets* (Gwyn Publishing, P.O. Box 5900, Sherman Oaks, Ca. 91413).

LPs: *Virtuoso; Joe Pass at the Montreux JF 1975,* solo albums; *The Trio* w. O. Peterson; *Peterson & Pass à Salle Pleyel; Peterson Big Six at Montreux; Portrait of Duke Ellington;* w. Ellington, *Ellington's Big Four; Two For the Road* w. H. Ellis; *JATP at Montreux;* w. E. Fitzgerald, *Take Love Easy; Ella in London* (Pablo); w. H. Ellis, *Seven Come Eleven* (Concord Jazz); w. Carmen McRae, *Great American Song Book* (Atl.). Own LPs on World Pacific: *Catch Me; Sign of the Times; Simplicity; Stone Jazz;* also on World Pacific w. Gerald Wilson; Richard "Groove" Holmes; Chet Baker; Jazz Crusaders.

PASTOR, TONY (Antonio Pestritto),* *tenor sax, singer;* b. Middletown, Conn., 1907. A key member of Artie Shaw's band from 1936-40, Pastor led his own orchestra in the '40s and '50s, then formed a vocal act with three sons. Retired in 1958; died 10/31/69 at his home in Old Lyme. Conn. LP: *The Complete Artie Shaw,* Vol. 1 (Bluebird).

PATTERSON, DON,* *organ, composer;* b. Columbus, Ohio, 7/22/36. Pl. and rec. w. Sonny Stitt, Gene Ammons in '60s. Formed own gp. for touring club circuit. In early '70s working in and around Gary, Ind. Comp: *Jesse Jackson; Little Angie; My Man String; Funk in ¾; Opus De Don; Dem New York Dues; Freddie Tooks Jr.*

LPs: *These Are Soulful Days: The Return of Don Patterson* (Muse); *Boppin' & Burnin'; Funk You; Opus De Don; Four Dimensions* (Prest.).

PAUER, FRITZ, *piano, composer;* b. Vienna, Austria, 10/14/43. Stud. priv. w. Cissy Faber in Vienna, '48; at LBA, '57-60; priv. cons., '60-1. Worked w. Hans Koller, '60-2; own trio at Dug's and Jazz Galerie in Berlin backing soloists such as Art Farmer, Leo Wright, Carmell Jones, Don Byas, D.Gordon, B. Ervin, '62-8. With Eric Kleinschuster Sextet; teacher at Vienna Jazz Cons., '68. From '70, member of the ORF Radio Big band; lead. own trio. Infl: M. Tyner, Bud Powell, J. Zawinul, F. Gulda, O. Nelson, Ellington, T. Monk, B. Evans. TV: *Piano Conclave,* Vienna '73; Fests: Bled, Yugo., '62; Frankfurt, '66; Berlin; Prague, '69; Montreux, '70-1; Warsaw, '72. Won first prize as best pianist, Modern Jazz Competition, Vienna, '66. Publ: *Modal*

Forces, Domicile Jazzseries No. 4; *Mythologie,* Domicile Jazzseries No. 5 (Ernst Knauff, Siegestrasse 19, Munich, Germany); *Meditationen/Three Poems* (Papgeno Musikverlage, Neulerchenfelderstrasse, Vienna, Austria). Comp: *Concert for Big Band and Symph. Orch.* LPs: *Mythologie; Fata Morgana; Live at the Berlin Jazz Galerie; Power By Pauer* (MPS/BASF).

PAVAGEAU, ALCIDE (SLOW DRAG),* *bass;* b. New Orleans, La., 3/7/1888. The pioneer jazz bassist, who played with Geo. Lewis and Bunk Johnson in the '40s, died in NO 11/8/68.

PAYNE, CECIL McKENZIE (ZODIAC),* *baritone sax, flute, clarinets, alto sax;* b. Brooklyn, N.Y. 12/14/22. one of first baritone sax stars of bop era. Traveled w. Machito orch. 1963-6; Woody Herman '66-7, then lived in Brussels for a year, working as single. Back to US Nov. '68, but returned to Continent a month later as member of Dizzy Gillespie reunion band. Joined Count Basie '69; left '71 and formed Jazz Zodiac Quartet. Joined NY Jazz Repertory Orch. '74. Toured Europe w. *Musical Life of Charlie Parker* unit late '74. Played *Showboat 2* jazz festival Caribbean cruise, Dec. 74, w. sister Cavril Payne as vocalist.

Comps: *Cerupa; Flying Fish; Brookfield Andante; Martin Luther King, Jr.*

LPs: *Brooklyn Brothers* (Muse); *Zodiac* (Strata-East); *Brookfield Andante; Cecil Payne Spotlite II* (Spotlite); w. Cavril Payne, *Teasin' Tan* (Cepp).

PAYNE, PERCIVAL (SONNY),* *drums;* b. NYC, 5/4/26. Joined Count Basie early 1955, remaining for ten years; led own trip and pl. w. Frank Sinatra before rejoining Basie Dec. '65 for several months. After a long tenure w. Harry James, returned to Basie again, and left for the third time in '74. Toured with a combo, Don Cunningham & Co., '75. LPs: see Basie.

PEARSON, COLUMBUS CALVIN JR. (DUKE),* *composer, arranger, piano;* also *trumpet* b. Atlanta, Ga., 8/17/32. In addition to a long assoc. w. Donald Byrd, who recorded Pearson's comp. *Cristo Redentor,* worked as pianist w. Nancy Wilson and other singers. From '63-70 was a & r asst. to Alfred Lion at Blue Note Records in NYC. Also led own big band intermittently. On music faculty at Clark Coll., Atlanta, Ga., '71. Accompanist to Carmen McRae, '72; Joe Williams, '73; accomp., arr. and mus. dir. to Ms. Hollon Milburn, '73-5.

In '70 Pearson was the only non-Ellington alumnus to perf. for the Duke Ellington Society; also arr. and cond. music for Ellington's 74th birthday party and Honorary Doctorate at Clark Coll., '73.

Comps: *Cristo Redentor; Jeannine; New Girl.* Fav. arrs: *Time After Time* from his big band album; also *New Girl.* LPs: Early small groups (Prestige, Blue Note); later, larger groups: *How Insensitive,* w. Flora Purim and vocal ensemble; *Now Hear This,* with big band; *Introducing Duke Pearson's Big Band; It Could Only Happen With You,* w. F. Purim. LPs w. D. Byrd *At Half Note Cafe; The Cat Walk; I'm Trying To Get Home,* brass with voices; *A New Perspective* (Blue Note).

PEIFFER, BERNARD,* *piano, composer;* also *keyboards, synthesizer;* b. Epinal, France, 10/23/22. To U.S., '54, working primarily in Phila. area. From '66 pl. night clubs, concert tours and involved with teaching privately and at Wilmington School of Mus., '68; Jenkintown Music School, '73-4; also coll. lectures. Apps. on French TV, '66; *Capt. Kangaroo,* CBS-TV, '67.

Peiffer's career was temporarily halted by a serious illness in '69, but he resumed in '70, pl. in LA for a short period in July of that year at Donte's. Often a guest on the *Mark of Jazz* TV show in Phila., '70-4. Fests: Antibes; Comblain-La-Tour; Middlekerke, Belgium, '66; Bicentennial Continental Congress, Phila., '74; NJF-NY, '75. Wrote music for *Grit,* voted best promotional film of the year, Atlanta Int'l. Film Fest., '68; *Red Light, Green Light* for CBS-TV; other comps: *Poem For A Lonely Child; Rondo; Black Moon; Blues for Django; Manege; Homage To J.S. Bach; Exodus; Prelude Fugue on Lullaby of Birdland.*

LPs: *Bernard Peiffer Plays Lullaby of Birdland* (Poly.)

PEMBERTON, WILLIAM McLANE (BILL),* *bass;* b. Brooklyn, N.Y., 3/5/18. Played w. Frankie Newton in '40s; then built solid reputation w. Rex Stewart; Sy Oliver; Cootie Williams; Tony Scott. Acc. such pianists as Eddie Heywood, Mary Lou Williams, Ellis Larkins, Marian McPartland, Art Tatum; singers Sarah Vaughan, Ella Fitzgerald, Carmen McRae, Lee Wiley, Lena Horne, Pearl Bailey, Josh White, Bobby Short, Sammy Davis Jr. Occupied mainly w. studio work in NYC, '60-6. Member of Earl Hines quartet, '66-9, incl. Russian, So. American tours. Formed JPJ Quartet w. Budd Johnson, Oliver Jackson (q.v.) after the three left Hines. TV, fests., clubs, tours w. JPJ from '69. Also gig w. Bobby Hackett at Roosevelt Grill, '70; *Grande Parade Du Jazz* for G. Wein, Nice '75. Comp: *I Need You.* LPs: w. JPJ (Master Jazz; English RCA); w. Herb Hall-Joe Muranyi; Lou McGarity (Fat Cat's Jazz); John Hardee; Vic Dickenson for French labels.

PENA, RALPH,* *bass;* b. Jarbridge, Nev., 2/24/27. Played in many West Coast gps. w. Shorty Rogers, Ben Webster, Pete Jolly; toured w. Geo. Shearing, Frank Sinatra. Pena was in Mexico to score a film when he was hit by a car; two weeks later, 5/20/69, he died in a Mexico City hospital.

PENLAND, RALPH MORRIS, *drums, composer;* b. Cincinnati, Ohio, 2/15/53. Stud. at high school, '69-71; stud. and taught at New England Conservatory. Pl. w. Webster Lewis, Boston and Europe, '71-3; Freddie Hubbard, U.S. & Canada, '73-4; Ch. Lloyd, Los Angeles, '75; other gigs in LA w. Eddie Harris, Kenny Burrell, Harold Land. Debut of own unit, Penland Polygon, at Pilgrimage Theatre, Hollywood, Sept. 1975. Infl: Tony Williams, Elvin Jones, Miles Davis, John Coltrane. LPs w. Hubbard (CTI, Col.), Eddie Harris (Atl.).

PEPPER, ARTHUR EDWARD (ART),* *alto saxophone;* also *tenor, soprano saxes, clarinet, flute;* b. Gardena, Cal., 9/1/25. Pl. w. Benny Carter orch. at age 18; briefly w. S. Kenton, '43-4, then again off and on until '52. Problems with narcotics kept him off the scene intermittently for long periods. In '66 he was released from San Quentin after serving three years. During next year, in his own words, "I was scuffling and sitting in with rock bands, playing tenor." For several months in '68 he played lead alto w. B. Rich and was feat. on the ballad *Alfie.* Hospitalized with ruptured spleen, late '68. Rejoined Rich in '69 and traveled with the band across country, but illness soon ended this association. After leaving a hospital, he entered Synanon, the rehabilitation center in Santa Monica, Cal. He remained there three years, occasionally playing with visiting groups.

Bet. '72 and '75 he worked as a bookkeeper in Venice, Cal. Invited to the U. of Denver as jazz clinician on clarinet; soon afterward he was hired by Norlin Music to conduct clinics at high schools, colleges and univs. throughout the U.S. During this time was also completing his biography.

Contrary to previous statements, Pepper feels that his most powerful influences were Lester Young, Zoot Sims, Coltrane, rather than Ch. Parker and Konitz.

LPs: *Gettin' Together; Art Pepper Plus Eleven; The Way It Was* (Contemporary); *Omega Man* w. Carl Perkins (Onyx).

PERAZA, ARMANDO,* *bongos, conga drums, composer;* b. Havana, Cuba, 5/30/24. The former Shearing sideman worked w. C. Tjader from '69. In '70 he joined Mongo Santamaria, visiting Europe with him and pl. at Monterey JF. Pl. in SF w. Azteca combo, '71. Toured w. Santana '71- , incl. trips to Europe in '72, '75; Asia, '72, '74; Central, S. America, '72. Movies: sound track w. L. Schifrin for *Che Guevara,* '69.

LPs: w. Santamaria (Prest.); Santana; New Riders of the Purple Sage (Col.); Creedence Clearwater (Fant.).

PERCIFUL, JACK T.,* *piano;* also *organ;* b. Moscow, Idaho, 11/26/25. With Harry James, '58-74. With Red Kelly in Tumwater, Wash., '75. Made two European tours w. James and app. with him at NJF-NY, '74.

LPs: w. James, *Double Dixie* (Dot); *In A Relaxed Mood* (MGM); w. Corky Corcoran, *Something* (RCS).

PERKINS, WILLIAM REESE (BILL),* *saxophones, clarinets, flutes;* b. San Francisco, Calif., 7/22/24. Ex-Herman, -Kenton. Recording engineer in Hollywood studio 1961-9. Free-lance woodwind player in studios from 59- . TV: Della Reese series on lead alto, '69; alternate sax chairs on *Tonight* show '68- . Was member of Supersax for the first year of its existence. Gigs and records w. Toshiko Akiyoshi orch. 1974-5.

LPs w. Toshiko (RCA); Clare Fischer, *Thesaurus* (Atlantic); w. Paul Chambers, *The East/West Controversy* (Xanadu).

PERLA, GENE AUGUST, *bass, composer,* also *trombone, piano;* b. Woodcliff Lake, N.J., 3/1/40. From ages five to 15 studied w. Czech classical pianist Anca Seidlova. Pl. trombone in high school. Attended Sch. of Engineering, U. of Toledo, '58. In '62 entered Berklee Coll. of Mus. and Boston Conserv. simultaneously. Took up bass in '64. Pl. w. Willie Bobo in NYC and Calif., '67. Toured w. Nina Simone, '68; Woody Herman, '69; w. Sarah Vaughan in US, Canada, Japan and So. America, '70. Beginning in '71, w. Elvin Jones for two and one half yrs. incl. Europe, So. America; Sonny Rollins, '74-5. Formed Stone Alliance w. Steve Grossman, and percussionist Don Alias, '75. Infl: Ted Heath, Miles Davis, Bill Evans, Charlie Haden, Gary Peacock, Elvin Jones. Fest: NJF-NY; Oakland; MJF, all w. Jones. TV: Johnny Carson; Mike Douglas; Merv Griffin; Dick Cavett, w. Vaughan; Billy Eckstine syndicated show. Comp: *P.P. Phoenix; Tergiversation; Eberhard; Nanuri.* Perla has his own label, P.M. (20 Martha St., Woodcliff Lake, N.J. 07675) and has issued records by Elvin Jones; Steve Grossman; and Dave Liebman. LPs: w. Jones, *On the Mountain* (P.M.); *Merry-Go-Round* (BN); w. Simone, *Here Comes the Sun* (RCA); w. Mickey Tucker (Xanadu).

PERSIP, CHARLES LAWRENCE (CHARLI),* *drums, percussion;* b. Morristown, N.J., 7/26/29. Best-known as drummer w. Dizzy Gillespie big band in mid-'50s. Led own gp. which incl. Freddie Hubbard, Roland Alexander, Ron Carter and was busy NYC freelance in early '60s. Toured Japan w. Newport Festival Drum Panorama that also feat. B. Rich, L. Bellson, PJ Jones, '65. Joined Billy Eckstine as accompanist and assistant mus. director, Sept. '66, remaining w. him for seven yrs. In the mid-'70s pl. w. CBA; Archie Shepp; Frank Foster; NYJRC.

During his yrs. w. Eckstine, conducted drum clinics for Brockstein's Drum Shop, Houston; Moe's Drum Shop, Las Vegas; Organization of Drummers, Sydney, Australia. Lectures and seminars at New Eng. Conserv., U. of Mass, Claremont U. Teaching for Jazzmobile; member of staff of music dept. of Henry St. Settlement House, NYC; also private instruction. Book: *How Not to Play Drums.* TV: *Tonight; Mike Douglas; Just Jazz,* all w. Eckstine; *Look Up and Live* w. Mary Lou Williams. Fest: NJF-NY w. Eckstine, '72; tribute to Gillespie w. CBA Ensemble, '74. LPs: w. Eckstine, *Newport in New York, The Soul Session* (Cobble.); w. R.R. Kirk (War. Bros); *We Free Kings* (Trip); w. Gil Evans, *Out of the Cool* (Imp.).

PERSON, HOUSTON, *tenor saxophone;* b. Florence, S.C., 11/10/34. At So. Carolina State Coll. studied w. band director Aaron Harvey. In Army in Germany pl. w. Eddie Harris, Don Menza, Lanny Morgan, Leo Wright, Don Ellis and Lex Humphries. After service attended Hartt Coll. of Music, Hartford, Conn. Went on the road w. organist Johnny Hammond for two yrs.; then formed own gp. In '73 teamed up w. singer Etta Jones for clubs, concerts. They had worked together intermittently from '68. Dan Morgenstern called his playing, "warm, straightforward, unaffected and swinging." Infl: Illinois Jacquet, Gene Ammons, Sonny Stitt, Hank Mobley, Harold Land. LPs: *Get Outa My Way* (Westbound); *Broken Windows, Empty Hallways; Blue Odyssey; Person to Person; Trust in Me; Goodness!; Houston Express; Chocomotive;* w. Don Patterson, *Four Dimensions* (Prest.); w. Tiny Grimes, *Profoundly Blue* (Muse).

PERSSON, AAKE,* *trombone;* b. Hassleholm, Sweden, 2/25/32. Greatly respected during '50s and '60s as possibly Europe's leading jazz trombonist, he played with many visiting Americans, incl. Q. Jones, C. Basie, D. Gillespie; also in Swedish radio studio orch. Rec. w. Clifford Brown, S. Getz, Lars Gullin, H. Mann, Bengt Hallberg and many others. Persson died 2/4/75, reportedly driving his car off a bridge in Stockholm, where he was visiting. He had been living and working in Berlin. LPs w. Clarke-Boland Orch. (Atlantic, BASF, Black Lion, Col.).

PETERSON, HANNIBAL MARVIN CHARLES, *trumpet, composer;* also *koto;* b. Smithville, Tex., 11/11/48. Mother is pianist "of the Earl 'Fatha' Hines school." First instruction from James Wilson in harmony, theory, '62-5. Pl. in Booker T. Washington concert band; Texas City High Sch. band directed by Robert Renfroe, '63. Stud. at North Texas State,

'67-9. Led own Soul Masters, '61. Worked w. Chuck Jackson; T-Bone Walker, '65-7. To NYC '70 where he pl. w. Roy Haynes; Gil Evans; Elvin Jones; Pharoah Sanders; Archie Shepp; Rahsaan Roland Kirk into '74 when he formed the Sunrise Orch. Infl: Coltrane, Malcolm X, Ellington, Leos Janacek, B.B. King, Sun Ra, Cecil Taylor, Leadbelly. TV: w. Texas City Symphonic Band; several Euro. apps. Fest: NJF-NY; Galveston; Berlin; Japan. Comp: *Children of the Fire; The Voyage; Symphony African*. Publ: *The Ripest of My Fruits* (Sunrise Publs., Box 527, Planetarium Station, New York, N.Y. 10024).

Hannibal's playing is full of dramatic energy, and power in the upper register. Gil Evans calls him "a very special, serious, schooled musician. When you hear the way he writes for strings on his record, *Children of the Fire,* you will realize that."

LPs: *Children of the Fire* (Sunrise); *Hannibal* (MPS); w. Evans, *Svengali* (Atl.); *There Comes a Time; Plays the Music of Jimi Hendrix* (RCA); w. Richard Davis, *Epistrophy & Now's the Time; Dealin';* w. Eric Kloss, *Essence* (Muse); w. E. Jones, *Live at the Village Vanguard* (Enja).

PETERSON, OSCAR EMMANUEL,* *piano;* also *organ;* b. Montreal, Que, Canada, 8/15/25. Came to U.S. in '49; under management of Norman Granz, travelled regularly with JATP and in concert tours of his own, visiting Europe annually, through the 1950s & 60s. In later years he extended his overseas activities, working frequently in Japan, Australia, South America, Mexico, and taking part in college lectures and seminars throughout the U.S. and Canada.

In 1972 Peterson abandoned his trio format to appear for a while exclusively as a solo recitalist in concerts. He later resumed using the trio, dividing his time at concerts between solo and trio work. His sidemen changed more frequently than in earlier years. They included Bobby Durham, Ray Price on drums; Joe Pass on guitar; George Mraz, Niels-Henning Orsted Pedersen on bass. He was also reunited for occasional concerts and recordings with sidemen who had worked for him in the 1950s, among them guitarists Herb Ellis and Barney Kessel and bassist Ray Brown.

In 1974 Peterson had his own television series in Canada. Entitled *Oscar Peterson Presents,* it featured leading jazzmen and singers as guests. The series was awarded a plaque at the 17th International Film and TV Festival in New York. In 1975 Peterson's album *The Trio* won a Grammy award. Other awards: Toronto Civic Medal, 1971; Honorary Doctorate of Laws from Carleton University, 1973; Medal of Service of the Order of Canada, 1973; Late in '74 Peterson went to the USSR, with Orsted Pedersen and drummer Jake Hanna; however, their projected tour of the Soviet Union was abruptly cut short following disagreements about conditions. By the mid 1970s Peterson had won the *Playboy* "Musicians' Musicians" award ten times, and continued frequently to win other magazine awards at home and abroad. For a five-year period starting in the late 1960s Peterson made all his records in Germany while under contract to MPS-BASF. He subsequently recorded for Granz's new label, Pablo, incl. five duo albums made respectively w. D. Gillespie; H. Edison; J. Faddis; C. Terry; and R. Eldridge. Also sessions from Montreux JF, '75.

Publications: *Jazz Exercises and Pieces; Oscar Peterson New Piano Solos* (Hansen Publications, Inc., 1842 West Avenue, Miami Beach, Fla. 33139).

LPs: *Affinity; Collection; Newport Years; Night Train; Night Train, Vol. 2; Return Engagement; Something Warm; O.P. Trio; Very Tall,* feat. M. Jackson; *West Side Story* (Verve); *Exclusively For My Friends; Great Connection; Hello Herbie,* feat. Ellis; *In A Mellow Mood; In Tune,* feat. Singers Unlimited; *Reunion Blues; Tristeza on Piano; Walking the Line;* (BASF); *Featuring Stephane Grappelli* (Pres.); *History of an Artist; The Trio; The Greatest Jazz Concert in the World;* w. Joe Pass *Á Salle Pleyel; Satch and Josh* w. Basie (Pablo).

PETROVIC, BOSKO, *vibes, composer;* b. Bjelovar, Yugoslavia, 2/18/35. Violin at seven; accordion, piano, drums at 15. Took up vibes in '66, and four years later founded Zagreb Jazz Quartet, which for the next decade was widely considered to be the best combo in Yugoslavia. From '70, led new quartet, known as B.P. Convention. Has pl. w. John Lewis, S. Getz, G. Mulligan, A. Farmer, many other American musicians, as well as Albert Mangelsdorff, Svend Asmussen, Michal Urbaniak. Also occasionally leads Bosko Petrovic Nonconvertible All Stars. Infls: Ch. Parker, D. Gillespie, L. Hampton, D. Ellington. Style of playing strongly infl. by Yugoslavian folk music. Comps: *With Pain I Was Born; Sigurd's Garden; Blue Sunset*.

LPs: w. Zagreb Jazz Quartet, *Feel So Fine,* feat. Buck Clayton, Joe Turner; *With Pain I Was Born* (Fontana); w. B.P. Convention, *Green Mood;* w. Nonconvertible group, *Swinging East* (MPS); w. O. Nelson, *Swiss Suite* (Fl. Dutchman).

PHILLIPS, ESTHER (Esther Mae Jones),* *singer;* b. Galveston, Texas, 12/23/25. First successes singing w. Johnny Otis Band, '49-52, billed as "Little Esther." Made comeback in mid-'60s and, after another smaller career setback, rebounded again beginning w. app. on *Tonight Show,* '69. Reunited w. Otis on several occasions incl. Monterey JF. A series of recs. for the Kudu label served to establish her w. a new audience as well as put her in touch w. old following. In '73 she was nominated for a Grammy Award for "Best R&B Performance by a Female Vocalist." The winner, Aretha Franklin, gave her trophy to Miss Phillips.

Vernon Gibbs wrote in *Essence:* "Her voice has a raunchy fullness which compares with the best gospel singers, a boldly swinging quality which testifies to the influence of those singers who come from the ballad-blues or big band swinging traditions . . ."

LPs: *From a Whisper to a Scream; Alone Again, Naturally; Black-Eyed Blues; Performance; What A Difference a Day Makes* (Kudu).

PHILLIPS, JOSEPH EDWARD (FLIP),* *tenor saxophone;* also *bass clarinet;* b. Brooklyn, N.Y., 2/26/15. The former star of Woody Herman's first Herd, and JATP, took up residence in Pompano Beach, Fla. in the '60s, managing a condominium and working w. own gp. In '70s he began traveling again for apps. at Colo. Jazz Party, annually from '70, and Pasadena Jazz Fest. Took part in W. Herman alumni reunion at NJF-NY, '72. Early in '75 he relinquished the managerial job and returned to music full time. Played w. Teddy Wilson at Michael's Pub. NYC, Aug. '75, revealing he had lost none of his warm-toned, vibrant skill. LPs: *Flip in Florida* (Onyx); *A Melody From the Sky* (Bob Thiele Music); *Colorado Jazz Party* (MPS-BASF); *Newport in New York, The Jam Sessions,* vols. 3&4 (Cobblestone); w. B. Butterfield (DCS).

PIANO CHOIR. see Cowell, Stanley.

PICHON, WALTER (FATS),* *piano, composer;* b. New Orleans, La., 1906. Long active at the Absinthe House in NO, Pichon cont. to work sporadically during the '60s. He died in Chi., 2/25/67.

PIERCE, WILHELMINA GOODSON (BILLIE),* *piano, singer;* b. Pensacola, Fla., ca. 1905. Living in NO from '30, Pierce and her husband DeDe worked together for many years and were among the local musicians who benefited from the traditionalist revival of the '60s. They rec. for Atl., Riverside and various independent companies, and were often heard at Preservation Hall in NO, as well as on hundreds of coll. campuses and at jazz fests. She died 9/29/74 in NO. LP: *New Orleans Legends—Live, Vol. 15* (Jazzology).

PIERCE, BOBBY, *organ, piano, singer;* b. Columbus, Ohio, 1942. Mother plays piano. Lessons at age four. By the time he was eight infl. by Don Patterson who is six years older. Own bands, off and on, from age 16. Played organ w. S. Stitt, G. Ammons, J. Moody. With Clarence Wheeler, '72, then began rec. w. own gp. Infl: Tyner, Coltrane, O. Peterson; Ray Charles, O.C. Smith, Bill Withers. Comps: *I Remember Ray; To Newport With Love; New York; Children Are the Creator's Messengers; Sleep Baby.* LPs: *Introducing Bobby Pierce* (Cobble.); *New York* (Muse).

PIERCE, JOSEPH DE LACROIS (DEDE),* *trumpet, cornet;* b. New Orleans, La., 2/18/04. Still active locally and in concert apps. in other cities during the '70s, Pierce died 11/23/73 in NO. LP: see Pierce, Billie.

PIERCE, NAT,* *piano, composer;* b. Somerville, Mass., 7/16/25. Pl. w. Woody Herman Sept. 1951-June '55; rejoined as arr. & road mgr. spring '61-June '66. From that time, has cont. to write occ. for Herman, but mainly active in and around LA pl. & arr. for C. McRae, L. Bellson, Bill Berry; also many arrs. for C. Basie, Anita O'Day, Earl Hines, J. Rushing, Sweets Edison, B. Tate; and as pianist w. Z. Sims, Ch. Barnet et al. Subbed for eight weeks in S. Kenton band '72 during Kenton's illness. Led own band in LA '72 and again in '74-5.

Pierce also has been taking part in high school and college clinics. He has been seen in almost all major U.S. and European festivals, mainly w. Herman. Was subject of two long essays in Stanley Dance's *The World of Swing* (Scribners).

In 1975 Pierce claimed that he was "now recognized as the second best rhythm pianist in the world—Basie is first; Ellington has passed on."

LPs (as pianist and/or arr.) w. Herman (Col.); Roy Eldridge (Master Jazz); Rushing (Col.); J. Hodges (RCA); L. Bellson (Pablo); Basie (Roulette).

PIESTRUP, DONALL JAMES, *composer, arranger;* also *piano;* b. Santa Cruz, Cal., 12/19/37. Grad. UC Berkeley, '60, where he was a first-stringer on football team. Led own band from '61 in SF Bay Area. Began arr. for B. Rich band, '66. Moved to LA, '67 and became mainly active in commercial music, writing jingles etc. Also own band at Donte's. Comps: *New Blues; Goodbye Yesterday; Day's Journey; Group Shot,* for Rich; others for LA Neophonic; M. Ferguson. Early infl: Parker, Gillespie, Shearing; then M. Davis, Coltrane, T. Jones, Q. Jones, O. Nelson, B. Holman, Ellington.

LPs: w. Rich (Pac. Jazz, RCA).

PIKE, DAVID SAMUEL (DAVE),* *vibes, marimba, composer;* b. Detroit, Mich., 3/23/38. Played at Berlin Jazz Fest. 1968 and remained in Europe for five years, leading his Dave Pike Set, a quartet w. German musicians. Worked at numerous jazz festivals, clubs etc. on Continent, then settled in Southern California, where he organized a new group in Orange County. A pioneer in amplified vibes, which he began playing in 1960. During the 1970s Pike's group played almost continuously at Hungry Joe's in Huntington Beach, Calif., visiting Los Angeles for occasional gigs.

LPs: *Infra-Red; Riff for Rent; Salamao* (MPS-BASF); *Pike's Peak* (Epic). Earlier LPs w. H. Mann, Jazz Couriers, Paul Bley.

PISANO, JOHN,* *guitar, composer;* b. New York City, 2/6/31. Came to prominence w. Chico Hamilton quint., '56-8. Joined Herb Alpert and the Tijuana Brass, '65, recording and touring the U.S., Europe, Australia, New Zealand, Japan. In '70 TJB disbanded and Pisano continued freelancing and app. w. own group at local clubs. Rejoined TJB in '74, remaining until early '75. Formed quartet with Barry Zweig for night club engagements, and also toured extensively w. Peggy Lee as her mus. dir. Pisano is a talented composer and several of his works have app. on albums by TJB and Lee. Among them are: *So What's New; Slick; The Robin.* Four TV specs. in U.S., one in England w. TJB; also Newport JF, '68.

LPs: *Quietly There,* w. Bill Perkins Quintet (Riverside); w. TJB; w. Lani Hall (A & M).

PIZZARELLI, JOHN (BUCKY), *guitar;* b. Paterson, N.J., 1/9/26. Uncle, Bobby Domenick, played guitar with name bands. Educ. Central High School in Paterson. Self-taught while sitting in w. Joe Mooney. Army service in Europe and Philippines, '44-6. Toured w. Vaughn Monroe orch. '56-63. Staff musician at NBC, NYC, '54-66. Later on staff at ABC, playing Dick Cavett show w. Bobby Rosengarden orch. European tours w. B. Goodman, '70, '72, '73, '74; rec. 2 LPs w. Goodman in Stockholm. Pizzarelli, who plays a seven string elec. guitar, was feat. for some time in the early '70s as half of a guitar duo w. George Barnes. Playing a solo concert at Town Hall, NYC, '73, he was praised by John S. Wilson, according to whom "he showed that he could sustain the better part of an hour's program playing unaccompanied and make it a varied and enlivening experience." During the concert, Pizzarelli also played a Villa-Lobos work on classical guitar and was joined by his 15 year old daughter, Mary, for a pair of guitar duets in a style estab. during the '30s by Carl Kress and Dick McDonough.

Own duo, often incl. Zoot Sims, at Soerabaja, NYC in '70s.

Publ: *Touch of Class,* guitar book (Keith Perkins Publ., Famous Solos Ent., Box 567, Saddle River, N.J. 07458). LPs: *Nightwings* (Fly. Dutch.); *Green Guitar Blues,* solos; *Bucky Plays Bix & Kress,* five guitars (Monmouth-

Evergreen); *Guitars Pure and Honest,* duets w. Geo. Barnes (A & R); *A Flower For All Seasons* (Choice); *Nirvana,* co-leader w. Z. Sims (Groove Merchant).

PIZZI, RAY, *saxophones, flute, bassoon;* b. Boston, Mass., 1/19/43. Berklee Coll. '61-2; Boston Conserv '60-4; earned Bach. of Ed. & credits towards masters degree on clarinet. Stud. improv. w. Herb Pomeroy; bassoon w. Simon Kovar. From '64-69 teaching mus. in publ. schools in Boston, taking leave of absence during '66 to tour w. W. Herman orch. Moved to Cal., '69, and began working w. L. Bellson in '70, remaining for a year. With Willie Bobo, '72, '73; brief tenures during '73-5 w. F. Zappa, T. Jones-M. Lewis, S. Manne, Ravi Shankar, Moacir Santos, H. Mancini, B. Kessel. Feat. soloist on Dinah Shore TV show, '75. Fests: Newport, '71; Monterey, '73, w. Bellson; Concord, '71, w. Kessel; Monterey, '72 w. Jones-Lewis. Pizzi during the '70s was also busy teaching priv. improv. course. Infls: Ravel, Debussy, Ch. Parker, J. Coltrane, S. Rollins.

LPs: w. Santos, *Maestro; Saudade; Carnival of Spirits* (Blue Note); others w. Shankar (Dark Horse); Luis Gasca (Fant.).

POINDEXTER, NORWOOD (PONY),* *alto, soprano, tenor saxes, clarinet;* b. New Orleans, La., 2/8/26. After working w. accompanying gp. to Lambert, Hendricks & Ross and w. own gp. in early '60s, left for Europe '64 and has been there from that time, pl. clubs and fests. Living in Germany in '70s. Comp: *Sopa Prisa; Talgo; Freeze; It Don't Feel Like It Used to Feel; Movin' On; Lucky Duck.* LPs: *En Barcelona,* w. daughter Dina as vocalist (Spiral); *The Happy Life of Pony; Annie Ross & Pony Poindexter; Alto Summit* (MPS); *Super Sax Section* (French Epic).

POINTER SISTERS, *singers, composers;* b. Oakland, Calif.; **RUTH,** 3/19/46; **ANITA,** 1/23/48; **PATRICIA (BONNIE),** 7/11/50; **JUNE,** 11/30/53. Parents, Sarah and Elton Pointer, both Protestant pastors. The daughters sang gospel music in the church choir when June was seven years old. Early exp. as backup singers w. Cold Blood, later w. Taj Mahal and various other recording artists, incl. Esther Phillips, Elvin Bishop, Dave Mason.

The sisters credit their success to David Rubinson, their manager, who helped to bring them back to San Francisco when they were stranded in Houston, Tex. He rounded out their musical education by playing them jazz records, including those of Lambert, Hendricks & Ross. For some time Ruth was not a member of the group, having had to take a job as a key punch operator. The four sisters organized an act and scored a major success in July 1973 at the Troubadour in Hollywood. Before long they were in steady demand for guest apps. on national television programs.

June Pointer later left the group owing to illness; after the Pointers had worked as a trio for a while, she returned and they continued to enjoy success with a unique repertoire that comprised jazz, r & b., rock, soul and contemporary pop material. (In Nov. '75, June again left the group for reasons of poor health.) As composers, they were partially or wholly responsible for a series of songs such as *Jada; Sugar* (not connected with the old jazz songs of the same names); *Shaky Flat Blues; Fairy Tale;* and *How Long (Betcha Got A Chick on the Side).*

Among their best known jazz performances are *Cloudburst; Little Pony;* and *Salt Peanuts.* Opinions concerning the validity of these performances was mixed, some critics feeling that they were not innately jazz-oriented. Others felt that their style and elan transcended category and that their ability to interpret a wide range of material gave them a quality unique in the age of rock groups.

LPs: Blue Thumb; also guest app. singing *Flat Foot Floogee* on Jon Hendricks' *Tell Me The Truth* (Arista).

POLCER, EDWARD JOSEPH (ED), *cornet;* also *vibes;* b. Paterson, N.J., 2/10/37. Studied w. Prof. James V. Dittamo, '44-50; under his direction pl. solo cornet in Paterson Civic Orch. at age 13. Played w. Knights of Dixieland at Hawthorne, N.J., H.S., '50-4; while at Princeton U., '54-8, where he received Engineering Deg., pl. w. Stan Rubin's Tigertown Five, touring Europe twice; all major Eastern colls.; Grace Kelly's wedding, Apr. '56. From '58-69 free-lanced in NY, NJ, Conn., frequently subbing for Max Kaminsky at Jimmy Ryan's. From '69 w. Balaban & Cats. Toured US & Canada w. Benny Goodman, '72; US w. Bob Greene, '75. Has also worked as engineer-purchasing agent, '63-72; dir. of NY Jazz Museum's Touring Program, '75. A melodic, mellow-toned cornetist with an unforced delivery. Infl: Ruby Braff, Louis Armstrong, Bobby Hackett, Muggsy Spanier. Fest: Odessa JP; NJF-NY w. Balaban, '75. LPs: w. Balaban & Cats, *A Night at the New Eddie Condon's* (Classic Jazz); *Bits & Pieces of Balaban & Cats; A Night at the Town House* (Balaban & Cats); w. Big Chief Russell Moore's Pow Wow Jazz Band (Jazz Art Workshop); w. Jane Harvey (Classic Jazz).

POLLACK, BEN,* *leader, drums;* b. Chicago, Ill., 6/22/03. The former drummer, whose band in the '20s incl. B. Goodman, J. Teagarden, Glenn Miller, Bud Freeman, J. McPartland, remained active in music off and on until the mid '60s, when he retired to Palm Springs, running a restaurant there. He committed suicide by hanging himself in his Palm Springs home, 6/7/71.

LPs: *Pick-A-Rib Boys,* w. Teagarden; Ben Pollack-Wingy Manone (Savoy).

POMEROY, HERB,* *composer, trumpet, educator;* b. Gloucester, Mass., 4/15/30. Faculty member at Berklee Coll. of Music., Boston, 1955- . Dir. of jazz bands at Mass. Inst. of Tech. 1963- . Host on own weekly half hour TV series, *Jazz with Herb Pomeroy,* 1965-7. Festivals: Jyvaskyla, Finland, '68; Montreux, '70. Comps: two original scores, *The Road of the Phoebe Snow; Wilderness of Mirrors,* for Boston Ballet Co.; commissioned by Nat. Jazz Ensemble to write extended work, *Jolly Chocolate,* premiered at Lincoln Center, NYC, Jan. '74.

Pomeroy has continued to lead a band in the course of his work at Berklee; many now celebrated jazz artists have passed through its ranks. Berklee has issued annual series of LPs by student bands on its own label. Among the sidemen who have graduated from these groups are Alan Broadbent, Lin Biviano, Joe and Pat LaBarbera, Harvey Mason, Miroslav Vitous, Ernie Watts, Mike Mantler, Gene Perla.

LPs: *Jazz in the Classroom* (Berklee Press Publs., 1140 Boylston St., Boston, Mass., 02215).

PONDER, JAMES WILLIS (JIMMY), *guitar, composer;* b. Pittsburgh, Pa., 5/10/46. Self-taught. Began pl. and singing in junior high school but really got serious after hearing Wes Montgomery, '60. Pl. w. Sam Pearson in Pitts. for two yrs. in mid-'60s. With Charles Earland, '66-9. Sat in w. Jimmy McGriff in Pitts. Moved to NYC '68, pl. briefly w. Fathead Newman. Worked w. Newark tenorman Joe Thomas, '69-72, then formed own gp. In '75 co-led Final Edition w. Grassella Oliphant. Infl: Montgomery, Grant Green, Kenny Burrell, Thornel Schwartz. TV: *Positively Black* w. Irene Reid; Educ. TV w. own gp. Comp: *Peace Movement; Jennifer; Illusions; Sometimes I Get the Blues.* LPs: *Illusions* (Imp.); *While My Guitar Gently Weeps* (Cadet); w. John Patton, *That Certain Feeling;* S. Turrentine-Shirley Scott, *A Common Touch;* Lou Donaldson; Donald Byrd; Lonnie Smith; Reuben Wilson (BN); McGriff (Gr. Merch.); Mickey Tucker (Xanadu); Jack McDuff (Cadet).

PONTY, JEAN-LUC,* *acoustic and electric violins, violectra, composer;* also *keyboards;* b. Arranches, Normandy, France, 9/29/42. Classical violinist until highly successful app. at Antibes Jazz Fest. in 1964. Freelanced all over Europe from '66-9. In 1969 he came to U.S. for recordings and night club and fest. dates w. Geo. Duke trio. Back to France, working w. own group throughout Europe, '70-2. In '73 Ponty emigrated to U.S. Soon began working w. F. Zappa and Mothers of Invention, and in '74 joined the Mahavishnu Orch. Regular winner on violin in DB Critics' and Readers' Polls from '69. Fest. Apps. at Monterey, '67 and '69; Newport, '70, '74, Berlin, '71, Montreux, '72. Composed and arranged all selections on *Ponty-Grappelli* and *Upon The Wings of Music* (Atlantic) albums.

Ponty told Steve McGuire of DB that it took him three or four years to make the mental leap from classical music to jazz: "The amplification and the weird sounds I got helped me make the step. It helped me get away from the classical sound and classical esthetics and forget what the teachers had been teaching me. In the rock experience now I have learned more and more about the use of electronics . . ." Ponty has used a baritone violin with the strings tuned one octave lower than the normal violin. Known as a veritone or violectra, it has a range between viola and cello.

His association with Zappa established Ponty as the first jazz-experienced violinist to make a totally successful crossover into the worlds of rock and electronic music. His technique and creativity have consistently met every challenge that has confronted him while playing in an unprecedented variety of settings.

Own LPs: *Sunday Walk; King Kong* (BASF-MPS); *Live At The Experience* (World Pacific); w. Mahavishnu, *Apocalypse* (Col.); *Violin Summit* (MPS).

PORCINO, AL,* *trumpet;* b. New York City, 5/14/25. After many years on the road w. bands of Krupa, T. Dorsey, Kenton, Basie, Chubby Jackson and W. Herman, settled in LA, pl. w. Terry Gibbs big band, working in studios and touring w. Sinatra, Vic Damone, Eddie Fisher. Roger Miller series on NBC-TV, '66; Hollywood Palace on ABC-TV, '67. Toured w. B. Rich '68, incl. app. at Ronnie Scott's, London, feat. singing & pl. Louis Armstrong's *Jubilee,* which he uses as personal theme song. To NYC '69 where he pl. in pit for *Promises, Promises;* then joined Thad Jones-Mel Lewis and made two European tours w. them. Premiered *Friends and Love,* '70; and *Together,* '71 w. Chuck Mangione. Worked winter season in Miami Beach before joining Herman, '72. Premiered *Land of Make Believe* w. Mangione. Toured colleges as clinician for King Instr. Co., '73. His own band backed Mel Torme at the Maisonette, NYC, '74. While working in the show band at the Playboy Club in McAfee, N.J., he revived his band briefly in the summer of '75. Fest: NJF-NY w. Herman '72. William Whitworth wrote of his exceptional ability: "I think Al has been more successful than any other lead player in combining bigness with brilliance . . . put him in a brass section and you hear a projection, a beautiful sound, a pulsing time, and a fiery conception that . . . constitute a landmark in the history of jazz lead playing."

LPs: *The Raven Speaks* w. Herman (Fant.); *Together; Friends And Love* w. Mangione (Merc.); *Mercy, Mercy* w. Rich (Wor. Pac.); *Consummation* w. Jones-Lewis (Blue Note); *Mel Torme Live at the Maisonette* (Atl.); Sinatra-Ellington (Reprise).

PORTAL, MICHEL, *clarinet, saxophone;* b. Bayonne, France, 11/27/35. Stud. clarinet at Conservatoire de Paris. Active in all forms of contemporary music; inspired by Charles Mingus, E. Dolphy, Stockhausen and many others. Led own jazz group heard on French LP *Michel Portal Unit at Chateauvallon.* Other LPs: *Our Meanings and Our Feelings; Splendid Yzlment; Alors!!!*

POTTER, CHARLES THOMAS (TOMMY),* *bass;* b. Philadelphia, Pa., 9/21/18. The one-time bassist w. the Charlie Parker quintet in the '40s, played w. Tyree Glenn, Sweets Edison, Buck Clayton in early '60s. Later free-lancing w. J. McPartland; Buddy Tate; Pervis Hendson. Civil service employee in Brooklyn Hospital recreation department. Own group for club dates, '75. Appeared w. Jackie McLean, Hank Jones and Max Roach, playing and talking about Charlie Parker in a program devoted to Bird on ABC-TV's *Like It Is,* '75. LPs: reissues of Parker's Dial sessions (Spotlite), Savoy sessions (Arista).

POWELL, BENJAMIN GORDON (BENNY),* *trombone;* b. New Orleans, La., 3/1/30. In addition to studio work w. Merv Griffin TV show, Powell pl. w. T. Jones-M. Lewis, '66-70; Duke Pearson, '68-70. From '66-70 he was on the Board of Directors of Jazzmobile; he also served as a teacher in that org., and in '70 was Executive Director of Jazz Interactions.

Moving to LA in '70 w. the Griffin show, he worked on movie sound tracks, and from '72 was co-leader with his wife, singer Petsye Powell, of the combo Life Style. Dir. of lecture-concert programs for LA public schools, '73; helped organize Jazz Nexus lecture-concert series through Local 47 of the Musicians' Union. Many other activities as teacher, concert organizer, along w. gigs in local big bands incl. T. Gibbs, Bill Berry, B. Holman.

Fests: Concord, w. Berry, K. Winding, others; Newport/N.Y., w. M. Legrand, and w. C. Basie reunion band; Monterey, w. Q. Jones.

LPs: w. Donald Byrd, D. Pearson, Jones-Lewis, Moacir Santos (BN).

POWELL, MELVIN (MEL),* *piano, composer;* b. New York City, 2/12/23. No longer a participant in the jazz scene, the former B. Goodman pianist during the '70s was Dean of Music at Cal. Inst. of Arts in Valencia, Cal.

PRATT, BOBBY, *trombone, piano;* b. South Glens Falls, N.Y., 5/23/26. Studied trombone w. his brother, Norman Pratt. Began prof. career in Schenectady, N.Y. pl. in clubs and burlesque at age 15. To NYC '42. Pl. w. Charlie Barnet, '43-4; one nighters w. Tommy Reynolds from East to West Coast, '44. Worked w. Johnny Richards; Georgie Auld, '44; Stan Kenton, '45; Raymond Scott, '45-6; Lennie Lewis, '47; Sam Donahue, '48-9; Johnny Bothwell, '49-50. While dental work was being completed in '50 switched to piano on which he is self-taught. In the '40s and '50s pl. w. C. Parker; B. Webster, C. Hawkins, Big Sid Catlett, Trummy Young, Max Roach, Lester Young, Slam Stewart, Vic Dickenson, Dizzy Gillespie, Eddie Heywood, Billy Butterfield, Sonny Dunham, Wild Bill Davison, George Wettling and Gene Krupa. In the '60s w. Ruby Braff; Billy May; and Jimmy McPartland. From '67 at Jimmy Ryan's: piano, '67-70; trombone from '70; worked w. Max Kaminsky; Tony Parenti; Zutty Singleton; Marshall Brown; J. McPartland; Herman Autrey; and Roy Eldridge. Infl: Vic Dickenson, Trummy Young, Lester Young, Charlie Parker, Eldridge, Billy Kyle, Count Basie. TV: NJF-NY w. Eldridge, PBS, '73; special w. Bobby Hackett, Nicol Williamson. Film: soundtrack for *Book of Numbers*. First rec. w. J. Richards on Musicraft, '44; Lennie Lewis on Queen, '47. LP: w. Eldridge, *Little Jazz and the Jimmy Ryan's All Stars* (DRE, Jimmy Ryan's, 154 West 54th St., New York, N.Y.).

PRESTON, DONALD WARD (DON), *Moog synthesizer;* also *all keyboards, string bass, composer;* b. Flint, Mich., 9/21/32. Father is resident composer for Detroit Symph. Grad. Cass Tech. High Sch., Detroit, 1950. Prof. debut w. Herbie Mann, '51-3; w. Hal MacIntyre, '57-8; Nelson Riddle, '58. In LA, app. w. Carla and Paul Bley trios, '57-8; duo w. Ch. Haden, '59. All through '60s was involved with experimental jazz w. Don Ellis, Paul Beaver, Emil Richards et al. From '67-74, assoc. w. F. Zappa and Mothers of Invention, touring all over the world. Also European tour and Village Vanguard w. Gil Evans, '71.

Preston, a prolific composer has had commissions from sculptors, dancers etc. One work, *Juice,* for dancer Meredith Monk, was perf. at Guggenheim Museum in NYC. LPs: w. C. Bley, *Escalator Over The Hill* (JCOA); w. Bobbi Humphrey, *Satin Doll* (Blue Note); numerous albums w. Mothers of Invention.

PREVIN, ANDRE,* *piano, composer, conductor;* b. Berlin, Germany, 4/6/29. Comp. and arr. for motion pic. studios from '48, but maintained dual career, frequently recording jazz LPs in '50s and early '60s, the best known being *My Fair Lady,* a hit in '57.

By the mid '60 Previn was inactive in jazz. He conducted the Houston Symph., '67-9, and was principal conductor and artistic director of the London Symph. from '68. Cond. all major orchs. in U.S. and Europe; toured worldwide, appearing mostly at opera houses. Own series on BBC-TV; also interview shows with musician guests. Remained active as pianist, but not in jazz.

Publs: *Andre Previn: Music Face to Face,* (Hamish Hamilton, London, England); *Edward Greenfield: Andre Previn* (Ian Allen, Shepperton, Surrey, England.)

Jazz LPs on Contemporary; also *Joplin: The Easy Winners,* w. Itzhak Perlman (Angel).

PREVOST, EDDIE, *drums;* b. Hitchen, Hertfordshire, England, 6/22/42. Mainly active, since '65, with the group known as AMM (duo w. Lou Gare, q.v.), but also performs w. own sextet. Has app. all over Europe with both groups and participates in lectures, recitals and workshops.

LPs: w. AMM on Elektra, Mainstream, Incus, Emanem.

PRICE, JESSE, *drums;* b. Memphis, Tenn. 1910. The veteran of many Kansas City bands, who worked briefly w. Count Basie in early '30s, mid-40s, and who also pl. w. Stan Kenton for a few months in 1944, was a principal performer in a reunion of KC musicians at the Monterey JF, 1971. By this time he was ailing, and in March 1974, when he went home to Kansas City to take part in a documentary film, he was terminally ill. He died of cancer, 4/20/74 in Los Angeles.

LP w. Harlan Leonard (RCA).

PRIESTER, JULIAN ANTHONY,* *trombone;* b. Chicago, Ill., 6/29/35. Early experience w. Sun Ra in mid-'50s. To NYC '58, joining Max Roach gp. the following year and pl. w. him into the early '60s w. the band that incl. Eric Dolphy, Clifford Jordan, Booker Little, etc. Free-lanced in NYC. Six mos. w. Duke Ellington in late '60s. With Herbie Hancock sextet from '70-3. Living in SF in mid-'70s, pl. w. a gp. of musicians incl. Bayete, Henry Franklin, etc., experimenting w. electronic sounds such as wah-wah pedal. Comp: *Wandering Spirit Song.* LPs: *Love, Love* (ECM); w. Hancock, *Mwandishi; Crossings* (War. Bros.); *Sextant* (Col.); Billy Harper, *Capra Black* (Strata-East); Roach, *Percussion Bitter Sweet; It's Time* (Imp.); Johnny Hammond, *Gears* (Milestone); Art Blakey, *Live!* (Trip).

PRINCE, ROLAND DON MATTHEW, *guitar, composer;* also *piano;* b. St. John's, Antigua, W.I., 8/27/46. Youngest of 12 children, most of whom studied music. Sisters pl. classical piano; brothers had local bands. Pl. piano at three; stud. for five yrs. while teenager. Self-taught on guitar at 12; pl. w. brother's band. Moved to Toronto at 19, pl. w. local mus.; stud. arr. & comp. w. Gordon Delamont; To NYC, '69. Worked w. Jack McDuff, '69-70; Billy Mitchell, off and on, from '70; Lonnie Smith; Wynton Kelly; gigs w. A. Blakey, '71; S. Turrentine; own trio; Newport All Stars, '73; gigs w. Jimmy Smith, '74; Elvin Jones, '74-5. Infl: Radio Havana (Latin and Calypso music while he was growing up); Nelson Symonds; Nat Cole; Ernest Ranglin; T. Monk; Wes Montgomery; Christian; Parker; Coltrane. TV: w. Lucky Thompson, NET '72; Europe w. E. Jones;. Fest: NJF-NY w. Newport All Stars, '73; w. E. Jones; Euro. fests. w. Jones. Comp: *Red Pearl; Love and Innocence; Antigua (Anti-Calypso); Uriah; Iron Band Dance; Geneva; Stachel's Prayer (Answer).* LPs: own date for Vanguard; w. E. Jones (Vang., East-West); J. Moody (Vang.); J. Hartman (Perception); Larry Willis (Gr. Mer.); Roy Haynes; Pete Yellin; Buddy Terry (Main.); Shirley Scott (Cadet); Earl May; *Compost* w. J. DeJohnette (Col).

PRITCHARD, DAVID, *guitar, composer;* b. Pasadena, Calif., 3/3/49. Stud. at U.C. Santa Barbara, but mainly self-taught. Led Quintet De Sade, '67-9; toured East Coast and Europe w. Gary Burton quartet, '69; also pl. w. Mike Gibbs band. Perf. jazz and poetry w. Kenneth Rexroth, '70. Perf. and rec. w. Peter Robinson's Contraband group; film work w. G. Melle; freelance activities in NYC, '71-2. From '73 worked in LA w. Don Ellis, Don Preston-Emil Richards group; Oscar Brown Jr., and others. Led own group, Halcyon, at Cellar Theatre, Hungry Joe's, other locations in LA area, '75. Infls: W. Montgomery, G. Szabo, L. Coryell, Miles Davis, Carla Bley, Mike Gibbs, Chick Corea, John Coltrane. Comps: *Henniger Flats,* rec. by Burton on *Throb* (Atl.); *Reverie* for Contraband.

LPs: Contraband, *Time & Space* (Epic); w. Pat Britt (Vee Jay); Quintet De Sade (Absolutely Frank Productions).

PROBERT, GEORGE ARTHUR JR., *soprano saxophone;* b. Los Angeles, Cal., 3/5/27. Pl. w. Bob Scobey, '50-3; Kid Ory, '54; Firehouse Five Plus 2, '55-71. In '72, guest star at concerts in NO and Atlantic; freelance rec. and club work. Formed own Once Or Twice Band, '73, working in LA. Led group for six months on Mondy night dixieland sessions at Concerts by the Sea, Redondo Beach, Cal. Pl. at Manassas JF, '74. In addition to this own band, he gigged w. Fine Time trio, feat. G. Wiggins, piano, and Bill Douglass, drums. Pl. fests. and concerts in France, Belgium and Holland. In '75 toured Europe again; also app. at Sacramento Dixie Jubilee.

Own LPs on Black Panther (Belgium); Nobility; Fat Cat; Jazzology.

PROCOPE, RUSSELL,* *alto, soprano saxes, clarinet;* b. New York City, 8/11/08. Joined Duke Ellington in '45 and was w. the band until Ellington's death in May '74. He then became part of the Brooks Kerr trio, working at Gregory's in NYC from that time. Won DB Critics' poll on clarinet, '70-3. LPs: see Ellington.

PUERLING, EUGENE THOMAS (GENE),* *singer;* b. Milwaukee, Wisc., 3/31/29. The one-time member of the Hi-Lo's, the popular vocal gp. of the '50s, was at the head of another talented vocal gp., Singers Unlimited, in the '70s. LPs: *Singers Unlimited; Four of Us;* w. Oscar Peterson, *In Tune* (BASF).

PUGH, JAMES EDWARD, *trombone;* also *bass trombone, bass trumpet, euphonium;* b. Butler, Pa., 11/12/50. Stud. in Atlanta, Ga., '61-3; Pittsburgh, '63-8; Eastman School, Rochester, '68-72; jazz and arr. w. C. Mangione and others. Pl. w. Eastman jazz combo and Arrangers Orch., '68-72; Mangione, '71-2. Principal trombone w. Rochester Phil., summer' 72. Joined W. Herman Oct. '72 and gained considerable prestige as lead and jazz trombonist in this band, app. at many fests. incl. Newport, '73 and '75; Concord, '73; Montreux, Pori, Pescara, Belvedere (Canada), '74. Comp: *Art for Art's Sake (Concerto for Bass Trombone and Orchestra).*

While studying, Pugh received many citations for his superior performances, including an award from Eastman School. Infls. as player: Urbie Green, Carl Fontana; as composer: Gustav Mahler, Stravinsky, Gil Evans.

LPs: *The Eastman Trombone Choir* (Mark); w. Herman, *Giant Steps; Thundering Herd; Herd at Montreux; Children of Lima* (Fantasy).

PULLEN, DON GABRIEL, *piano, composer;* also *organ;* b. Roanoke, Va., 12/25/44. Father, dancer, guitarist, singer; uncle singer; cousin, Clyde "Fats" Wright, pianist. Studied at Johnson C. Smith U., Charlotte, N.C.; privately w. Muhal Richard Abrams; Giuseppi Logan. Worked w. own gp., '65-70; Nina Simone, '70-1; Art Blakey, '74; Charles Mingus, '73-fall '75. Capable of pl. "inside" or "outside." Infl: Clyde "Fats" Wright, Ornette Coleman, Eric Dolphy. TV: *Jazz Adventures* w. own gp.; *Black Journal.* Fest: Umbria, '74-5; Montreux, '75; NJF tour, '73-4, national, '75; many Scandinavian fests. Comp: Andredon Music Pub. Co., (c/o Mietus Copyright, 527 Madison Ave., N.Y., N.Y.). LPs: Sackville; Horo; w. Milford Graves, *Nommo; Live at Yale U.* (SRP); w. George Adams; Dannie Richmond (Horo); w. Mingus (Atl.).

PUMA, JOSEPH J. (JOE),* *guitar;* b. New York City, 8/13/27. Left NYC small combo work to tour as accompanist and conductor for Morgana King, Fran Jeffries in the late '60s. Formed duo w. Chuck Wayne, '72, which played NYC clubs such as The Guitar and Stryker's Pub. Faculty member Housatonic Coll., Bridgeport, Conn. teaching applied mus. and guitar. TV: Mike Douglas Show w. M. King; NBC *Sunday* show w. Wayne. Puma and Wayne have also app. in concert at the Jazz Museum; for *Jazz on the River;* and at the NJF-NY, '73. Comp: *Little Joe's Waltz.* LP: *Interactions* (Choice).

PURDIE, BERNARD (PRETTY), *drums;* b. Elkton, Md., 6/11/39. Started playing drums at age six. Gained experience sitting-in until he got own set at 15. Led an otherwise all-white country & western band. First black man to graduate from Elkton High School. Attended Morgan State Coll, for two yrs. To NYC where he rec. w. Mickey & Sylvia; worked for Lonnie Youngblood; Les Cooper. Active making demo recs. for NY studios. By '66 was doing between 15 and 20 dates a week. Generally credited w. developing and popularizing the "boogaloo" beat permeating soul music. "The beat—the bass drum thing," he says, "had been around for a while, but until the engineers learned how to record it properly, nothing happened."

His busy schedule led him to rec. work w. James Brown; the Beatles; Blood, Sweat & Tears; the Isley Bros.; Jimmy Smith. Own band, P.P. Mavins, app. in Conn. and NY metropolitan area. Credits Sticks Evans for teaching him to read fast after he arrived in NYC. Has been active as a teacher; at one time had 60 students until playing time interfered. LPs: own albums (Date); *Purdie Good; Shaft;* w. Johnny Hammond, *Soul Talk* (Prest.); w. Yusef Lateef, *The Diverse Lateef* (Atlantic).

PURIM, FLORA, *singer, guitar, percussion;* b. Rio de Janeiro, Brazil, 3/6/42. Stud. piano, '50-4 with priv. teachers, incl. mother Rachel Purim; guitar, '54-8 w. Oscar Neves; later perc. informally w. Airto Moreira.

Purim's most important work before she left Brazil was a rec. w. a group called Quarteto Novo w. Moreira and Hermeto Pascoal. After arriving in U.S., '67, learned to read and write music under tuition of Moacir Santos in LA. Toured Europe w. S. Getz, '68. Rec. two albums w. Duke Pearson, '69-70. In '71, in addition to rec. w. Airto, whom she later married, Purim worked the whole year w. Gil Evans' band and C. Corea's combo. For two years she toured the U.S., Europe and Japan w. Return to Forever, feat. Corea, Airto, J. Farrell, S. Clarke. She and Airto left the group in '73. A new group was formed w. Airto as leader and Purim as feat. soloist, fusing Brazilian, jazz, pop and other idioms.

Besides working w. Airto, Purim made her own first solo

album, *Butterfly Dreams,* in the spring of '74, and a second album a few months later. Shortly after completing the latter she surrendered to begin serving a one to three year prison term at Terminal Island, San Pedro, Cal. She had been arrested in Sept. '71 for possession of cocaine, but had stayed free through a series of appeals. During '75 she was permitted to give a concert from the prison, which was broadcast, and to take leave of absence to study music at college. In December she was released on parole and was working again with Airto, Jan. '76.

Purim won the DB Critics' Poll in '74, TDWR; in Dec. of '74 she displaced R. Flack as number one female singer in the DB Readers' Poll. Films: sang title sang in *Les Biches,* French movie; comp. and pl., w. Airto and S. Clarke, sound track of short film, *Hermetic Triumph,* seen at Cannes Film Fest.

A gifted lyricist, Purim wrote the lyrics to Clarke's *Light as a Feather;* McCoy Tyner's *Search for Peace;* Neville Potter's *San Francisco River;* George Duke's *Love Reborn;* Airto's *Alue;* Hermeto Pascoal's *We Love* and many others. Her unusual success in bridging the gaps between Brazilian, jazz, and American pop music is explained in her philosophy: "My principal instrument is my voice, but I also consider the echo-plex one of my main instruments, because I developed my wordless singing, using this electronic device to distort, change or duplicate the sound as I needed, in order to team up with such instruments as flute, soprano sax, guitar, trombone, and the human sounds of pain or happiness or simple talking."

Own LPs: *Butterfly Dreams; Stories to Tell* (Milest.); w. Corea, *Light as a Feather; Return to Forever* (Poly); w. G. Duke, *Feel* (BASF); w. Airto, *Virgin Land* (CTI); *Seeds On The Ground* (Buddah); w. C. Santana, *Welcome* (Col.); w. D. Pearson, *How Insensitive; It Could Only Happen With You* (BN).

QUINICHETTE, PAUL,* *tenor sax;* b. Denver, Colo., 5/7/16. Known as "Vice-Pres" during his time with the Count Basie Band, '51-3, because of his stylistic resemblance to Lester Young, he pl. in NYC, '53-58 w. his own gps.; Benny Goodman Octet, '55; Nat Pierce big band. Dropped out of music, working as a radiologist, TV repairman, etc., and did not resurface until '73 when he began pl. w. Brooks Kerr at Churchill's, NYC. In April '74 began a series of Saturdays and Sundays at the West End Cafe w. pianist Sammy Price, and Buddy Tate as the other tenor in a group sometimes called Two Tenor Boogie. George Kelly sometimes replaced Tate on occasion and, in '75, Harold Ashby sometimes filled the second reed role. App. on NYJRC tribute to Count Basie, Jan. '75. Comp: *Prevue; Crossfire; Sandstone*.

LPs: w. Brooks Kerr, *Prevue* (Famous Door); w. Buddy Tate (Master Jazz); reissues, (Trip).

RADER, DONALD ARTHUR (DON),* *trumpet, fluegelhorn, composer;* b. Rochester, Pa. 10/21/35. During '60s, pl. w. W. Herman, M. Ferguson, C. Basie, L. Bellson, H. James, T. Gibbs; often w. Les Brown, '67-72, incl. three round the world trips w. Bob Hope. Pl. w. T. Gibbs orch. in *Operation Entertainment,* ABC-TV series, '68-9. On staff of S. Kenton clinics, '68-70. In Tokyo for two months as jazz soloist w. Japanese orch., '71. Concerts, clinics, records w. own quintet, '72-3. Toured as lead trumpet w. Jerry Lewis, Europe, Mexico, '72-3. Feat. soloist in Japan w. Percy Faith, '73-4. Freelance work in Hollywood, w. quintet, TV shows etc., '74-5.

TV: Spec. half hour educ. prog. w. Cerritos Coll. Lab Band, '68. Soloist w. Kenton on 90 minute spec. from Concord JF, PBS-TV, '69.

In addition to playing numerous coll. jazz fests., '68-75, Rader wrote many articles for the National Association of Jazz Educators Journal; a diary of his trip to Viet Nam and Thailand w. Hope and Brown was publ. by DB, Feb. '68. Comps: *Polluted Tears; Greasy Sack Blues; Chicago; Big Sur Echo; Saludita; Now; Viareggio*.

LPs: *Polluted Tears* (DRM); *New Thing,* w. P. Faith (Col.); *Love Story/Sound of Tomorrow* (Express, Japan).

RAE, JOHN (John Anthony Pompeo),* *drums;* also *vibes, timbales;* b. Saugus, Mass., 8/11/34. Traveled w. C. Tjader May '61 to Mar. '66. Led own group in Aspen, Colo. Worked in SF w. V. Guaraldi. After brief stints w. G. Szabo, rejoined Tjader, Aug. '68, remaining until Mar. '70. Freelanced in SF w. Don Piestrup band, W. Wanderley, many others during next four years. Joined Charlie Byrd, Mar. '74. In spare time, worked as disc jockey at KJAZ, Alameda, Cal., repaired drums at Drumland, SF, and took part in clinics at many high schools and colls. Fests: Monterey w. Tjader, L. Schifrin; Concord w. Tjader, '68. Films: Bit apps. w. John Davidson in *Streets of San Francisco;* and w. Robert Redford in *The Candidate*. Publs: *Jazz Phrasing for Mallets* (Belwin-Mills publ., 16 W. 61st St., New York, N.Y.); *Latin Guide for Drummers* (Try Publ., 854 N. Vine St., Hollywood, Ca. 90038).

LPs: *Great Guitars,* w. Byrd, D. Ellis, B. Kessel (Concord Jazz); *Evil Eyes,* w. Mike Vax (Artco); *Cal Tjader Plugs In* (Syke); *For All We Know,* w. Byrd (Col.); *Thundering Herd,* w. Herman (Fantasy); *Art Van Damme in San Francisco* (MPS).

RAINEY, CHARLES W. III (CHUCK), *bass;* also *guitar, piano, trumpet, trombone, composer,* etc.; b. Cleveland, Ohio, 6/17/40. Educ. Lane U., Jackson, Tenn. Toured w. Big Jay McNeely, 1960-61; Sil Austin, '61-2; Sam Cooke, '63; Jackie Wilson, '64; King Curtis, '64-8; Al Kooper, '68; Voices of East Harlem, '69-70; H. Belafonte, '70; Aretha Franklin, '71-5; R. Flack, '72; Q. Jones, '73; Crusaders, '72-3; Ujima, '72; Hamp Hawes, ,74-5. Fests. w. Jones, Flack, Crusaders et al.

Overlapping with these jobs, Rainey was one of New York's busiest musicians in many areas, recording with hundreds of jazz, pop, rock and soul artists (Ray Charles, S. Vaughan, F. Hubbard, D. Byrd, G. McFarland, C. Adderley, G. Ammons), composing and arranging for some sessions, and accumulating dozens of film and TV credits.

Comps: *Genuine John,* rec. by Bernard Purdie and by own gp.; *Got it Together,* rec. by Nancy Wilson; *The Rain Song; Eloise,* rec. by own gp.; *Jamaican Lady,* rec. by Cornell Dupree.

LPs: *Chuck Rainey Coalition* (Cobblestone); *Genuine John* (Capitol). Others: see artists listed above.

RANDI, DON (Don Schwartz),* *piano, composer, keyboards;* b. New York City, 2/25/37. Stud. at LA Conservatory. Made jazz albums in early '60s; later became involved with composing, arranging for films, TV and records. Since '70, has owned nightclub, The Baked Potato in Hollywood, leading a small band there.

LPs: *Live at the Baked Potato* (Poppy); *Love Theme From Romeo & Juliet and Other Motion Picture Themes* (Cap.).

RANEY, JAMES ELBERT (JIMMY or JIM),* *guitar, composer;* b. Louisville, Ky., 8/20/27. Acknowledged as one of the premier guitarists of the '40s and '50s w. Al Haig, Stan Getz and Teddy Charles gps., he rejoined Getz in '62-3 but then worked mostly backing singers and for Broadway shows. Returned to Louisville in late '60s, teaching, working in non-music jobs and also doing some playing. In the summer of '72 he visited NYC, playing at the Guitar; Gulliver's (NJ); and Bradley's. Other trips to NY were for a concert w. Haig at Carnegie Recital Hall, Nov. '74; recs. w. Haig and w. own gp., '75. Raney's playing in the '70s showed that he was still capable of spinning long lines that stretch out in networks of logical beauty. His pure sound, amplifier down, in a day when electric possibilities are almost limitless but so often abused, is perhaps a bit more melancholy, burnished by the passage of time to include aural tears that are sometimes even Djangoesque. Comp: *Suite For Guitar Quintet; Momentum; We'll Be Together; The Flag Is Up; Double Image.*

LPs: *The Influence* (Xanadu); *Momentum* (MPS); Haig-Raney, *Strings Attached,* incl. one track in which his son, Doug Raney, duets w. him (Choice); *Strings & Swings,* one half recorded at concert for Louisville Jazz Council, '69 (Muse).

RANGER, CLAUDE, *drums, percussion;* b. Montreal, Quebec, Canada, 2/3/41. Self-taught. Worked and rec. w. saxophonist Lee Gagnon in mid-'60s; w. saxophonist Brian Barley in trio called Aquarius Rising from late '60s until Barley's death in Toronto, '71. Led own gps. for Radio Canada's *Jazz En Liberte;* also pl. w. S. Greenwich; Jerry Labelle; Pierre Leduc; Ron Proby; Art Roberts. To Toronto where he worked w. Lenny Breau; Herbie Spanier, '72; Doug Riley, Moe Koffman, '74-5. Free-lanced in clubs & concerts w. G. Coleman, Greenwich, J. Moody, Alvin Pall, Fred Stone, Don Thompson, P. Woods. Infl: M. Roach, Tony Williams, E. Jones, O. Coleman. TV: house band for *Music Machine,* CBC. Comp: *Tickle; Le Pingouin.* Called by Barry Tepperman in *Coda,* "indisputably the best drummer on the Canadian scene." LPs: w. Doug Riley, *Dr. Music's Bedtime Story;* w. Koffman, *Solar Explorations* (GRT); w. Barley (RCI); also w. Gagnon; Spanier.

RAVA, ENRICO, *trumpet, composer;* b. Trieste, Italy, 8/20/43. Mother a pianist graduated from Conservatorio di Torino "G. Verdi." Originally self-taught, later studies w. Carmine Caruso, NYC. Pl. w. S. Lacy quartet in Europe, S. Amer. and U.S., late '60s; also w. M. Waldron, Bill Dixon, JCOA, D. Cherry, Barney Wilen, G. Hampel, in U.S. and Europe; L. Konitz in Italy; Dollar Brand; and Roswell Rudd's Primordial group, NYC. From '70, he has divided his time between NYC, Italy and Buenos Aires, where his wife, Graciela, a film-maker, lives. He has toured in Europe with his own group annually from '72. Infls: Cherry, C. Taylor, M. Davis, Rudd, S. Rollins. TV: specs. feat. his group and comps. in Puerto Rico, '71; Italy, '73-4; Buenos Aires, '74; Hamburg. Fests: many major European events; also Biennale Panamericana, Cordoba, Arg. Comps: score for the Italian film *O.R.G.* in which he also app.; theatre score for Ibsen's *Hedda Gabler,* Buenos Aires, '74. Rava's own albums contain many of his original comps.

LPs: *Il Giro Del Giorno in 80 Mondi* (Fonit-Cetra); others on MPS, RCA, ECM; w. Lacy, *The Forest and the Zoo* (ESP); w. Konitz, *Stereo Konitz* (Ital. RCA); w. Brand, *African Space Program* (Enja); w. C. Bley, *Escalator Over The Hill;* w. Rudd, *Numatik Swing Band* (JCOA).

RAWLS, LOU,* *singer;* b. Chicago, Ill., 12/1/35. A popular jazz and blues singer in the mid-60s. Rawls continued to tour clubs throughout the U.S., frequently app. at casinos in LV. LPs on Cap., MGM, Pickwick Int'l., Bell.

RAZAF, ANDY (Andreamenentania Paul Razafinkeriefo),* *songwriter;* b. Washington, D.C., 12/16/1895. The prolific lyricist, whose songs included *Ain't Misbehavin'; Honeysuckle Rose; Black and Blue* (all w. Fats Waller, his chief collaborator); *Memories of You; Stompin' At The Savoy; In The Mood; Gee Baby Ain't I Good To You,* died 2/3/73 in LA, after being an invalid and almost totally bedridden for 20 years. An album of Razaf's songs was rec. in the '50s by Maxine Sullivan for Period Records, now defunct, but his works are represented on hundreds of recordings by almost every jazz singer.

REBILLOT, PATRICK EARL (PAT), *piano, composer;* also *keyboards, synthesizer;* b. Louisville, Ohio, 4/21/35. Stud. piano and organ at Mt. Union Coll. in Ohio, '49-53; piano w. Jeno Takacs at Cincinnati Conservatory of Mus., where he received a BS in mus. ed. in conjunction with U. of Cinc., '57. Principal church organist from age 12 to 17 in Louisville. Classical acc. at Cinc. Conserv. While in Army spec. Servs. began arr. and toured world with Army entertainers, '58-60. Moved to NYC, and in '60s worked w. Benny Powell, J. Steig, B. Goodman, Paul Winter (incl. tour of Brazil, '65), S. Vaughan. App. many times at Half Note w. Z. Sims, R. Eldridge, J. Moody, J. Rushing. Conductor for *Jacques Brel;* also led own small combos at various Greenwich Village jazz clubs. With G. Burton quartet, '71-2, then joined H. Mann on keyboards and as mus. dir. From late '60s, extensive freelance rec. in NYC. Infls: Waller, Ellington, Monk, M. Davis, Rushing. Fests: Laurel JF w. S. Rollins, late '60s; Newport-NY, 72-4, Concord, '72-3, Montreux, '72, w. Mann; Montreux, '74 w. Airto, F. Purim. Comps: *Thank You, Mr. Rushing; Song For The New Man; The Beautiful Bend Ahead; Free Fall; Let Me Know; In A Melancholy Funk.* Arrs. for Mann LPs.

LPs: *Free Fall* (Atl.); others w. Mann (Atl.); *The Prophet; Journey* w. A. Mardin; *Mirror* w. C. Mariano; *Newmanism,*

w. D. Newman (Atl.); *Nine Flags* w. Chico O'Farrill (Imp.); *Soul Outing* w. F. Foster (Pres.); *Children of All Ages* (Barbeque).

REDISKE, JOHANNES,* *guitar, composer;* b. Berlin, Germany, 8/11/26. Prominent for many years as soloist in radio groups and leader of his own quintet, Rediske, who had been called by some critics the "German Charlie Christian," died in Berlin, 1/22/75.

REDD, ELVIRA (VI),* *alto saxophone, soprano saxophone, singer;* b. Los Angeles, Cal., 9/20/30. In '67 Redd app. for ten weeks at Ronnie Scott's Club in London; feat. w. Max Roach at Montmartre Club in Copenhagen. Returned to U.S. to pl. clubs in SF, LA. Feat. w. D. Gillespie at NJF, '68. Toured Africa, Europe w. C. Basie orch, '68. In '69 she began teaching for Compton Unified Schools, but continued to pl. local engagements, also took part in Ch. Parker Memorial Concerts in Chicago. Taught in LA City schools, '72- . Guest artist w. Rahsaan Roland Kirk at Royce Hall, UCLA, '74.

LPs: own albums for Solid State, Atl. (deleted); *Charlie Parker Memorial Album* (Cadet); *Chase* w. G. Ammons, D. Gordon (Prest.).

REDMAN, WALTER DEWEY, *tenor sax, clarinet, composer, educator;* also *alto sax, musette, auto harp;* b. Fort Worth, Tex., 5/17/31. Although he has no concrete evidence he thinks Don Redman was his uncle. Clarinet at age 13; pl. in Baptist church band during the collection. Several mos. of lessons but mostly self-taught. Pl. in high school marching band. Went to Tuskegee Inst. for a few mos., to study electrical engineering. Ret. to Texas where he attended Prairie View A&M receiving BS '53. Pl. in march. band, swing band, switching to tenor from alto. Masters in educ. from No. Texas State, '59 but did not participate in jazz courses. Taught public school classes, '56-9. To LA '59. Shortly thereafter went to visit SF and stayed for seven yrs., pl. w. Pharoah Sanders; Don Garrett; Smiley Winters; Wes Montgomery; co-led big band w. Monty Waters; after hours jamming at Bop City; own after hours band at Soulville. Left for NYC, '67, pl. w. Sunny Murray before joining his former schoolmate Ornette Coleman. With Coleman to late '74, also working w. Charlie Haden Liberation Music Orch.; own group. With Keith Jarrett from early '70s. Other gigs w. Alice Coltrane; JCOA; Newport All Stars. Infl: "All saxophonists including Bird and Red Connor."

Fest: NJF-NY w. Coleman, '72; Jarrett, '74; many Euro. fests. NYJRC, '74, feat. in concert of John Coltrane's music. John Litweiler has written that Redman "evolves distinct styles for the serious, disparate concepts of Coleman, Jarrett, Dewey Redman and the rest. With Coleman's band, his style is closely akin to Ornette's, but with others it not. He admits to a Coltrane influence, too, but at 43 he's the sum of a lifetime of practicing, listening and selecting. . . . For all his experience, he remains one of the very fresh, bright voices in contemporary music."

Comp: *For Eldon; Interconnection; Boody; Images (In Disguise);* many others in own albums.

LPs: *Coincide; Ear of the Behearer* (Imp.); *Look for the Black Star* (Arista); *Tarik* (Byg); w. Jarrett, *Death and the Flower; Treasure Island; Fort Yawuh* (Imp.); *Expectations* (Col.); *El Juicio; Birth* (Atl.); Coleman, *Science Fiction* (Col.); *Friends and Neighbors* (Fly. Dutch); *Crisis; Ornette at 12* (Imp.); *Love Call; New York is Now* (BN); Haden, *Liberation Music Orch.* (Imp.); Carla Bley, *Escalator Over the Hill;* Don Cherry, *Relativity Suite;* Roswell Rudd, *Numatik Swing Band* (JCOA).

REHAK, FRANK JAMES,* *trombone, composer;* also *baritone horn, valve trombone;* b. Brooklyn, N.Y., 7/6/26. Toured w. G. Krupa, C. Thornhill, Herman, Gillespie et al. Sporadically active in '60s but, he says, "My life was at an all time low because of the use of large quantities of heroin and alcohol. In 1969 I left Woody Herman's band, at his request, wieghing 118 lbs. and close to death. He strongly suggested I come to Synanon for help. I did so, and the years since then have been nothing short of miraculous."

As head of the music dept. at Synanon, Rehak has been intensely active leading a chorus, jazz-rock group, teaching adult and children's music classes, composing and programming for the facility's internal radio station, which broadcasts to the various branches of Synanon throughout Calif. He has also lectured at colleges and judged at school and coll. jazz fests. His ambition is "to create a musical environment within Synanon, and then to extend it to the larger society; to record some of my own music, utilizing Synanon people."

In '75 Rehak appeared as leader of a big band, composed partly of Synanon residents, in a concert at the Santa Monica branch. His playing, which had gained him respect of musicians for many years, had reached a new peak of creativity.

Early LPs w. Gillespie (Verve); Geo. Russell (MCA).

RENAUD, HENRI,* *piano, composer, producer;* b. Villedieu (Indre) France, 4/20/25. As leader of own gp. at Tabou Club in Paris in '50s; pianist w. K. Clarke, '61 and house pianist at Trois Mailletz, '62-4, he was one of the leading French musicians, rec. with a variety of visiting Americans. Joined CBS Records as jazz producer in '64, and in '70s put together a series of classic jazz reissues under the title *Aimez vous le Jazz?* From '70-4 prod. jazz programs for three French TV channels; weekly jazz program on national French radio, '72- . Although mainly occupied with the above activities, Renaud still works occasionally as a pianist, leader. Fest: own quintet at Antibes, '68. Publ: *Jazz Classique; Jazz Moderne,* jazz history in two volumes (Casterman Publ., 66 rue Bonaparte, 75006 Paris). Comp. part of the sound track for the Louis Malle film *Murmur of the Heart,* '70, rec. by Roulette.

LPs: *Clifford Brown Quartet in Paris; Sextet in Paris;* w. L. Konitz, *Ezz-thetic; The Oscar Pettiford Memorial Album* (Pres.); w. Al Cohn, K. Winding, T. Farlow, J.J. Johnson, Milt Jackson in *The Birdlanders* (Everest).

RETURN TO FOREVER. see Corea, Chick.

RICH, BERNARD (BUDDY),* *drums, singer, leader;* b. Brooklyn, N.Y., 6/30/17. After leading his own combo in early '60s he rejoined Harry James' orch., '61 but left to form own band in April '66, the first time had had led a large orch. since '51. It was a well-drilled machine with the leader's drums as the focal point and an impressive book with contributions by Bill Holman, Don Piestrup, Bill Reddie, Don Menza, Don Sebesky and John La Barbera, among others. Reddie's arr. of a *West Side Story* medley contains a tour de force for Rich, a 10 minute plus show stopper. Art Pepper was in the reed section for a short periods in the '60s but the only sideman to receive recognition out of the ordinary was tenor saxophonist Pat La Barbera.

In '74 Rich disbanded and organized a small group which went into residence at a club at 64th St. and 2nd Ave. in NYC to which he lent his name, Buddy's Place. When his group, which incl. Sal Nistico, Sonny Fortune, Jack Wilkins and Kenny Barron, traveled to another city, other name gps. were featured there. Late in the club's existence, Illinois Jacquet became part of Rich's combo. In '75 Buddy's Place closed and a new Buddy's Place opened on the site of what had been Gallagher's 33 restaurant near Madison Square Garden. Again lent his name but was not a partner. He reorganized the big band for several engagements there. Not only did Rich reiterate his position as one of the all time drum masters, and perhaps the greatest technician of all, but the sheer swinging power his youthful band brought to bear on the original material and songs from the Beatles, the Doors, Burt Bacharach and Paul Simon, captivated a young audience at that time (the mid and late '60s) heavily swayed by rock.

Rich, whose acid wit was often in evidence on the bandstand, displayed his quick way with a put-down in his many appearances on late-night TV talk shows, particularly with Johnny Carson where in his guest role he also sat-in w. Doc Severinsen's orch.

Fest: numerous apps. w. orch.; also w. L. Hampton, T. Wilson; drum battle w. Blakey, Roach, Elvin Jones at Radio City jam session, both at NJF-NY, '74. Won DB Readers poll, '67, '70-2; Hall of Fame, Reader's Poll, '74; band won DB Critics poll, TDWR, '68.

In '68 *Super Drummer: A Profile of Buddy Rich* by Whitney Balliett was published by Bobbs-Merrill.

LPs: *Big Band Machine; Roar of '74; Last Blues Album, Vol. 1 Very Live;* Buddy Rich & L. Hampton, *Transition* (Gr. Merch.); *Different Drummer; Rich in London,* rec. live at Ronnie Scott's; *Stick It* (RCA); *Keep the Customer Satisfied* (Liberty); *Swingin' New Big Band; Buddy and Soul; Big Swing Face; The New One; Mercy, Mercy* (Pac. Jazz); w. Zoot Sims-Bucky Pizzarelli, *Nirvana* (Gr. Merch.); reissues on Verve; UA.

RICHARDS, EMIL,* *vibraphone, percussion, composer;* b. Hartford, Conn., 9/2/32. First prominent w. G. Shearing, Paul Horn. Worked w. D. Ellis' Hindustani Jazz Sextet, '64-6. In '67-9, in addition to working in movie studios and pl. w. LA Neophonic Orch., led his own group, the Microtonal Blues Band in LA area. In '69 went to India; stud. meditation, Indian music; trip around the world collecting authentic instruments. Joined R. Kellaway cello quartet, also pl. w. Harry Partch percussion ensemble.

In '72 made another world tour; stud. music in Tibet, Bali. Concerts w. F. Sinatra for two months in '74; visited S. Amer. to do more research, later formed six-man percussion group, pl. music of leading film composers. Also in '74 went on two month tour w. Geo. Harrison, Ravi Shankar, perf. in both groups. Continued recording major TV and film scores, '75. His playing is heard on *Kung Fu; Planet of the Apes; Airport '75; Earthquake; Chinatown* etc. Received Most Valuable Player award for perc. from NARAS, '73, '74.

Comps: *It's Ten To Five; Lucky Eleven; The Day After The Night In Tunisia; Bombay Bossa Nova; Alexandria's "Raga" Time Band.* Publs: *Emil Richards World of Percussion,* w. cassettes (Gwyn Publ. Co., P.O. Box 5900, Sherman Oaks, Ca. 91413); *Emil Richards Mallet Exercises in 4/4; Emil Richards Original Jazz Comps. in 3-5-7-9-10-10½-11-13-19* (Try Publ., 854 Vine St. Hollywood, Ca. 90038); *Making Music in Mommy's Kitchen; Making Music Around The Home or Yard* (Award Music Co., 136 W. 46th St. New York, N.Y., 10036). LPs: *New Time Elements, New Sound Elements* (Uni); *Journey To Bliss; Spirit of 1976,* w. Microtonal Blues Band (Imp.); others w. Kellaway (A & M); J. Donato (Blue Thumb); *Harlow* score for Neal Hefti (Col.); Harrison, Shankar (Dark Horse); F. Zappa (Discreet).

RICHARDS, JOHNNY (John Cascales),* *composer;* b. Schenectady, N.Y., 11/2/11. Arranger for many jazz artists in '40s and '50s, incl. Boyd Raeburn, Ch. Barnet, D. Gillespie, S. Vaughan and most notably S. Kenton, with whom he enjoyed a lengthy association. From '58 into the '60s Richards continued writing but occasionally led big bands at Birdland etc. He died in NYC 10/7/68. Among his most important works are *Cuban Fire* and *Adventures in Time,* both for Kenton. Many of his best comps. and arrs. for Kenton and for his own orch., have been reissued on the Creative World label.

RICHARDS, CHARLES (RED),* *piano, singer;* b. Brooklyn, N.Y., 10/19/12. Continued to co-lead Saints and Sinners w. V. Dickenson until the trombonist left the group in '68. Cut down to quintet, later quartet, working Toronto frequently to '72. Quartet w. Herb Hall pl. many times at Dinkler's, Syracuse, N.Y., '72-4. Richards also subbed in World's Greatest Jazzband, Sept.-Dec. '74; solo piano at Eddie Condon's, '75.

LPs: w. own quartet & quintet; w. Eddie Durham; Vic Dickenson (English RCA); w. Saints & Sinners, *Sugar* (MPS); *Saints & Sinners in Canada* (Sackville).

RICHARDSON, JEROME G.,* *saxophones, flutes* etc.; b. Oakland, Cal., 12/25/20. A regular member of the Thad Jones-Mel Lewis orch. in the late '60s, Richardson also pl. in the B. Rosengarden band on the Dick Cavett TV show, '70-1. He moved to LA in late '71 and became heavily involved with studio work along w. occasional jazz jobs. Toured Japan three times: w. Q. Jones, '72, '73; Percy Faith, '74. Gigs w. O. Nelson, Kenny Burrell. TV series w. Carol Burnett. Worked occasionally w. L. Bellson, D. Grusin, the Aldeberts. Led own group in LA clubs and at Santa Barbara fest.

LPs: *Brass Fever* (Imp.); w. Nelson, *Skull Session* (Fl. Dutch.); *Michelle* (Imp.); w. Jones, *Body Heat; Smackwater Jack; Gula Matari; Walkin' In Space* (A & M); *Quintessence* (Imp.).

RICHMOND, DANNIE,* *drums, percussion, vocal;* also *tenor sax;* b. New York City, 12/15/35. Except for occasional side ventures, was best known from '56-70 w. Ch. Mingus. Pl. w. Mark-Almond for three years; also off and on w. Joe Cocker, and one tour w. Elton John; BBC radio w. Danny Thomas; back w. Mingus, '74. When not on the road, Richmond gives drum clinics at colleges and high schools. In '65 he wrote a method book and solo book for publ. in Germany.

Many TV apps. w. Mark-Almond on such rock shows as *In*

Concert and *Midnight Special;* also NET programs w. Mingus. LPs w. Mingus (Columbia, Candid, World Pacific, Impulse, Atl. etc.); also w. Mark-Almond (Columbia).

RIDLEY, LAURENCE HOWARD JR. (LARRY),* *bass, educator;* b. Indianapolis, Ind. 9/3/37. Early assoc. of F. Hubbard. Toured w. dozens of jazz groups in '60s incl. R. Weston, L. Donaldson, C. Hawkins, J. McLean, Art Farmer-Jim Hall, Hubbard, S. Rollins, H. Silver. In late '60s, was heard w. D. Gillespie, T. Monk, McCoy Tyner, JCOA etc.; w. Newport All Stars annually from '68. Original member of N.Y. Bass Violin Choir. Also worked with big bands incl. D. Ellington, T. Jones-M. Lewis. Toured Europe w. Young Giants of Jazz group, '73. Orig. member of NYJRC. Feat. artist at Amer. Coll. JF, '72.

Ridley in the '70s became increasingly active in education. Appointed Asst. Prof. of Music Livingston Coll. of Rutgers U. '71; Chairman of Mus. Dept., '72. Artist in res.: U. of Utah; Creighton U.; Southern U.; Grambling Coll. DB writer John Sinclair said: "Ridley is committed to making wider and deeper impressions in whatever musical context he finds himself. He is a perfect section mate. He picks lines that are a constant stimulus, creating juggernaut rhythms that move soloists to play into themselves more and to move out from that point to their listeners' ears . . ."

LPs: *Sum of the Parts* (Strata-East); w. Newport All Stars, *Tribute to Duke* (MPS/BASF); *Newport in N.Y. '72, The Jam Sessions, Vols. 3-4* (Cobblestone), w. Dexter Gordon (Prestige); Jackie McLean (Blue Note); *Colorado Jazz Party* (MPS/BASF); w. Al Cohn (Xanadu); Venuti-Grappelli (Byg).

RIEDEL, GEORG,* *bass, composer;* b. Karlsbad, Czechoslavakia, 1/8/34. Pl. w. Lars Gullin, '53-4; Arne Domnerus, '55- ; Swedish Radio band, '58-61; radio jazz group, '62- . Many recs. and extensive radio work in Germany, Denmark etc., as well as sound tracks for some 35 motion pics. Comps: *Dizzy* (for Gillespie and big band); choral works, several symphonic works, chamber music; *Kind of Requiem,* in memoriam for Ellington. Insp. by Ellington, Ch. Mingus, Messiaen, Jan Johansson. Won Prix Italia for his TV ballet, *Riedaiglia;* nine gold records for children's music. Many LPs on SR, Philips, Megafon etc.; Swedish Radio Jazz Group, *Greetings and Salutations* feat. Thad Jones, Mel Lewis (Four Leaf Clover).

RIEL, ALEX POUL, *drums;* b. Copenhagen, Denmark, 9/13/40. Stud. in Copenhagen, '55; one semester at Berklee in Boston w. Alan Dawson, '66. Pl. w. NO, swing and bop groups before graduating into the avant garde, working w. John Tchicai, Archie Shepp, Gary Peacock. Co-led group w. Palle Mikkelborg, '67. While in U.S. pl. w. Rahsaan Roland Kirk, Toshiko Akiyoshi, Herb Pomeroy and many others. Worked for several years w. Savage Rose. In '65 Riel was voted Danish Musician of the Year; in '67, the Riel-Mikkelborg quintet won first prize at Montreux JF, and later that year the group was seen at NJF.

LPs: w. B. Webster, *My Man;* w. J. McLean, *A Ghetto Lullaby;* w. McLean-D. Gordon, *The Source; The Meeting;* w. Gary Bartz, *Ode to Super* (SteepleChase); w. Sahib Shihab (Debut, Poly.); *Violin Summit* (MPS); Alex Riel Trio (Vibe-Fona); w. Savage Rose (Poly.); w. Stuff Smith (Metronome); w. Herb Geller (Nova, Atl.).

RIFKIN, JOSHUA, *piano;* b. New York City, 4/22/44. Extensive studies from '54, incl. composition at Juilliard; w. Karlheinz Stockhausen in Darmstadt, Germany, '61; NYU, '64-6; musicology at Princeton, '67-70. Asst. Prof. of Mus. at Brandeis U., active as musicologist and cond. Rifkin came to prominence with his interpretations of Scott Joplin's ragtime works, which won Record of the Year awards from *Stereo Review* and *Billboard.* His infls. are entirely classical. In '74-5 Rifkin made several apps. on BBC-TV.

LPs: *Piano Rags by Scott Joplin,* Vols. I, II, II (Nonesuch); w. Judy Collins, *Wildflowers* (Elektra).

RILEY, BENJAMIN A. (BEN),* *drums, educator;* b. Savannah, Ga., 7/17/33. With Thelonious Monk, '64-7. Teaching in Wyandanch, L.I. elementary school system, junior college; USDAN summer camp, '68-70. With New York Jazz Quartet (Frank Wess, Roland Hanna, Ron Carter) from '71, incl. Japanese tour '74. Alice Coltrane from '71. Ron Carter quartet, '75. TV: *Positively Black* w. Carter. App. w. NYJQ at NJF-NY, '74. LPs: w. NYJQ, *Concert in Japan* (Salvation); w. A. Coltrane (Imp., WB); w. Monk (Col.); w. Lonnie Smith (BN).

RILEY, DOUGLAS BRIAN (DOUG or DR. MUSIC), *piano, organ, composer;* b. Toronto, Ontario, Canada, 12/4/45. Stud. at the Royal Cons. of Mus., Toronto, w. Lawrence Goodwill, '50-6; w. Paul DeMarky in Mont., '56-60; Royal Cons. w. Patricia B. Holt, '61-4; Univ. of Tor., BM in Comp. w. Prof. John Weinzweig. Deeply interested in ethnomusicology, he has completed one-half of his Master's at the Univ. of Tor. under Dr. Kolinski and has spent two summers on Iroquois Reservations, collecting and transcribing their music on a govt. grant. Worked w. Boss Brass, '69; Dr. Music, '70-4; Moe Koffman quintet; Sonny Greenwich, '74-5; own trio, '73-5. Infl: Ray Charles, B. Evans, G. Evans, B. Powell, A. Tatum, Bach, Bartok, Beethoven, Stravinsky. TV: arr., pianist and/or mus. dir. for *Rolling on the River; Music Machine;* Hart & Lorne Specials; Anne Murray Specials; *Celebration;* Lou Rawls Special. App. at Jazz at the Shaw Fest., July '75. Comp. mus. for feat. films: *Megantic Outlaw; Foxy Lady; Cannibal Girls; The Naked Peacock;* shorts, *Olivia's Scrapbook; Summer in Canada;* ballets, *Lies, Wishes and Dreams; Sessions for Six; Jeux en Blanc et Noir.* Own LP: Dr. Music, *Bedtime Story;* w. Koffman, *Master Sessions; Solar Explorations* (GRT); *Ray Charles Doin' His Thing* (ABC).

RILEY, HERMAN, *tenor saxophone;* also *saxes, clarinet, flutes;* b. New Orleans, La., 8/31/40. Played in high school band, '50-4; U.S. Army reserve band, '53-5. In service, not playing, '55-7. Lived in NYC Apr. to Aug. '57, then in San Diego, where he attended City Coll., remaining there until '63, when he moved to LA. Riley pl. w. Wm. Huston big band, Ivory Joe Hunter, Roy Brown and other blues bands in NO. In LA he was heard w. B. Bryant, C. Basie, S. Manne, Q. Jones, Benny Carter, Joe Williams, Donald Byrd and singers Sammy Davis Jr. and Della Reese. Chosen as Outstanding Solo Artist at the Monterey Coll. JF in '61, he pl. the MJF w. Bryant in '69. For Bryant he composed *A Prayer for*

Peace, heard in Swahili Strut (Cadet). Pl. Concord JF w. Q. Jones, '73. Went to S. Africa w. Monk Montgomery band, '74.

LPs: w. Blue Mitchell (Mainstream); Bryant (Cadet); G. Ammons (Pres.); D. Reese (ABC).

RILEY, HOWARD, *piano, composer;* b. Huddersfield, England, 2/16/43. B.A. and M.A. from Univ. of Wales, '61-6; M.M. from Indiana Univ., '66-7; M. Phil. from York Univ., '67-70. From his arrival in London, '67 has worked with own trio; also w. Evan Parker, J. McLaughlin (duo); Tony Oxley; London Jazz Composers Orch., late '60s, early '70s. Has also app. as solo artist. From '70 has been Prof. at Guildhall School of Mus. and Drama, lecturing in jazz and improv. Fests: Paris Bienniale, '71; Berlin; Donaueschingen, '72; w. own trio. In '69 his group was first non-classical combo to app. at London Proms, Royal Fest. Hall. The trio has broadcast and televised extensively in England, France, Germany. Comps: *Angle; Continuum; Convolution; Rope; Triptych; Zynan; Two Designs.* Riley was one of the first British musicians to be awarded an Arts Council Bursary for jazz comp ('69), and has written many works for string quartet and flute-piano duos.

LPs: *Discussion* (Opportunity); *Angle; The Day Will Come* (CBS); *Flight* (Turtle); *Solo Imprints* (Jaguar); *Synopsis* (Incus); *Singleness* (Chariavari); others w. LJCO (Incus).

RITENOUR, LEE MACK, *guitar;* also *classical guitar, banjo, mandolin, electric bass;* b. Hollywood, Ca., 11/1/52. Stud. privately w. Duke Miller, Joe Pass, Howard Roberts, Christopher Parkening; then to USC School of Music under Jack Marshall. Prof. debut at age 12 w. The Esquires (19 piece orch.); w. Afro Blues Quintet, Craig Hundley Trio, '69. Traveled w. Sergio Mendes and Brasil '77, later freelancing extensively in LA studios. Formed first own group, '73, w. John Pisano; second group w. D. Grusin, '74, for local dates. Began teaching classical guitar at USC in same year and in '75 coordinated new studio guitar program. A prodigious and versatile young musician, Ritenour has rec. w. Herbie Hancock, Gato Barbieri, Mendes, Peggy Lee, Oliver Nelson, Moacir Santos, Carly Simon and many other contemporary artists.

RIVERS, SAMUEL CARTHORNE (SAM),* *tenor sax; composer;* also *soprano sax, piano, bass clarinet, flute, viola;* b. El Reno, Okla., 9/25/30. An important part of the Boston scene in '40s, '50s w. Jaki Byard; Joe Gordon; Herb Pomeroy; and Gigi Gryce. Pl. two mos. w. Miles Davis in summer '64. Moved to NYC and began teaching in Harlem at his own studio, '67. Pl. w. Cecil Taylor, '67-71; six mos. w. McCoy Tyner. In '71, w. his wife Bea, opened Studio Rivbea at 24 Bond Street in lower Manhattan. He continued his teaching and opened it to the public for performances by his own group w. guest artists such as Dewey Redman, Frank Lowe, Charles Tyler, Clifford Jordan and Sonny Fortune. In Jan. '75 he app. as guest soloist w. the SF Symphony. From '68 composer-in-residence for the Harlem Opera Society; lecturer on Afro-American musical history at Connecticut Coll., '72; artist-in-residence at Wesleyan U., '70-3. "There is often a certain austerity to Rivers' music," wrote Robert Palmer. "It isn't cold or forbidding, but it's more or less 'pure,' uncontaminated by programmatic conceits . . . independent of the kind of extramusical imagery so often associated with organized sound."

"The way I see it," says Rivers, "the music of the '70s should be a fusion of the '40s, '50s and '60s."

Fest: NJF-NY; Montreux, '73; Perugia; Molde; Antibes, '74. Won DB Critics poll on flute, TDWR, '75; his album *Streams* won a Best Record award from the French Academie du Disque. Comp: *Dawn; Exaltation; Tranquility; Shades;* also comps: for Harlem Ensemble; Winds of Manhattan, a woodwind gp. LPs: *Sizzle; Hues; Streams; Crystals* (Imp.); *Conference of the Birds* (ECM); *Involution* (BN); w. Don Pullen (Black Saint); w. C. Taylor (Shandar); *Miles Davis in Tokyo,* (CBS, Japan).

RIZZI, TREFONI (TONY),* *guitar;* b. Los Angeles, Cal., 4/16/23. Former name band musician, later on staff for many years at NBC, he has continued to do TV and film work, pl. every stringed instrument. Comp. and played the music on a daily soap opera. In '73, organized a five guitar group that interpreted harmonzied versions of the comps. and improvised solos of Charlie Christian. This combo was heard at Donte's and other clubs in the LA area.

ROACH, MAXWELL (MAX),* *drums, vibes, composer, leader, educator;* b. Brooklyn, N.Y., 1/10/25. One of the key figures in the development of modern jazz in the '40s as the drummer in Charlie Parker's quintet, he emerged as a leader in the '50s and has led small groups from that time. In the '70s they have incl. Cecil Bridgewater, Billy Harper and Reggie Workman. The quartet appeared several times at the NJF-NY in the '70s and pl. a concert in Paris '75. From '72 he has also been involved with the ensemble he conceived, M'Boom Re: Percussion which consists of Roy Brooks, Joe Chambers, Omar Clay, Warren Smith, Freddie Waits and himself. "The basis of M'Boom," says Roach, "is that it utilizes mallet instruments and every kind of percussive instrument. We lean heavily on instruments from the Third World . . . It not only involves powerful and innovative rhythmic aspects, but also moves into new melodic and harmonic variations . . ." M'Boom performed at campuses such as Adelphi, Swarthmore and Dartmouth; conducted clinics; appeared at NJF-NY '73; and toured Europe that year.

Roach, who had lectured on black music history at Yale, Pittsburgh U., Kalamazoo Coll. and Nassau Community Coll., has, from '72 been Professor of Music at the U. of Massachusetts in Amherst, Mass. He has traveled to Africa to do research and sits on the selection committee of the National Board of the Nigerian Festival.

Film: *Freedom Now Suite,* adapted for film by Gianni Amici and released in '66, won first prize at the 18th International Film Fest. in Locarno. Roach has also written scores for *Black Sun,* Nikatsu Studios, Japan; and *Trail of Tears,* NET Prods.

At the NJF-NY '72 his group combined with the 22-member J.C. White Singers in selections from their Atlantic album, *Lift Every Voice and Sing,* an integration of spirituals and gospel songs with instrumental improvisations. Roach and the White Singers performed together again at NJF-NY, '75. In '74 he not only appeared w. his group but took part in a drum conclave during the jam session at Radio City w. Art Blakey, Buddy Rich and Elvin Jones. Roach's ability to construct solos that are highly musical as well as rhythmically contoured in a most imaginative way was again clearly demonstrated.

Divorced from Abbey Lincoln, '70.

Comp: musical show, *Another Valley;* percussion pieces, *A Love Silent; Attucks to Attica,* the latter written on grant from CAPS; *For Big Sid,* other solo drum pieces.

Most of the selections on *Lift Every Voice and Sing* are dedicated to Martin Luther King, Malcolm X, Medgar Evers. Patrice Lumumba and Paul Robeson. Other LPs: *Members, Don't Get Weary; Drums Unlimited* (Atl.); reissues (Trip).

ROBERTS, CHARLES LUCKEYETH (LUCKEY),* *piano, composer;* b. Philadelphia, Pa. 8/7/1895. An early ragtime soloist and popular society bandleader, was well known as the composer of *Moonlight Cocktail,* 1941, and *Massachusetts,* 1942. In the late 1950s he suffered a stroke and went into almost total retirement. He died 2/5/68 in NYC. Roberts is considered to have represented a significant link between ragtime and the Harlem stride school of jazz piano.

ROBERTS, HOWARD MANCEL,* *guitar, composer;* b. Phoenix, Ariz., 10/2/29. One of the first combo leaders to appear at Donte's in No. Hollywood in late '66, helping to establish it as a jazz club, Roberts continued to work mainly in TV, film and recording studios. He estimated that from '66-76 he appeared on 2000 LPs, of which 2% were jazz records, incl. Tom Scott, O. Nelson, T. Monk, G. Mulligan.

In the '70s Roberts became increasingly active in personal apps., often at guitar seminars throughout the U.S., expanding contemporary guitar education. Comps: originals and arrangements for many of his own albums, the most important of which, in his view, is *Equinox Express Elevator*. From '74 he wrote a regular monthly column for *Guitar Player* magazine. Publs: *Howard Roberts Chord Melody; Howard Roberts Guitar Book; Sightreading by Howard Roberts* (Playback Publ., P.O. Box 4278, N. Hollywood, Ca. 91607).

LPs: *Antelope Freeway; Equinox Express Elevator* (Imp.); *The Movin' Man; The Velvet Groove* (Verve); *H.R. Is A Dirty Guitar Player; Guilty; Spinning Wheel; Jaunty-Jolly; Whatever's Fair; All Time Great Instrumental Hits; Color Him Funky; Out of Sight; Goodies; Something's Cookin'* (Cap.).

ROBINSON, ELI,* *trombone;* b. Greenville, Ga., 6/23/11. A veteran of many bands, incl. C. Basie, '41-7, Robinson rec. frequently w. Buddy Tate's band in the '50s and '60s. He underwent lung surgery in '69 and died 12/24/72 in NYC.

LP: w. Tate, *Unbroken* (MPS).

ROBINSON, FRED LEROY (FREDDY), *guitar;* also *harmonica, electric bass;* b. Memphis, Tenn., 2/24/39. Stud. at Chicago School of Mus., '59-61. In Chicago pl. with Little Walter, '57; Howlin' Wolf, '60; Jerry Butler, '62. In LA w. Ray Charles, '68; J. Mayall, '71. Rec. w. the Crusaders, S. Turrentine, Groove Holmes, Nancy Wilson, Peggy Lee, Bill Cosby, the Staple Singers, Bobby Bryant, Ray Brown, Milt Jackson, The Impressions. Infls: R. Charles, Little Walter, Howlin' Wolf, Muddy Waters. TV: Midnight Spec. and L. Armstrong Memorial Spec. w. Mayall; TV and radio commercials for wine company, singing and playing solo. Fests: Newport w. Charles, '68; NJF-NO w. Mayall, '73. LPs: *Black Fox* (Wor. Pac.); *Jazz Blues Fusion* w. Mayall (Poly.); w. L. Feather, *Night Blooming Jazzmen* (Main.).

ROBINSON, JAMES (JIM),* *trombone;* b. Deeringe, La., 12/25/1892. New Orleans veteran who pl. w. Bunk Johnson and George Lewis in '40s was a member of the Preservation Hall Jazz Band from '61 until his death from cancer in NO, 5/4/76. He toured with the PHJB in Europe and Japan, pl. concerts there and at major concert halls in the US during the '70s. LPs: *Jim Robinson and his New Orleans Band; Jim Robinson and Tony Fougerat;* w. Orange Kellin; Dede Pierce; Don Ewell (Center); w. Preservation Hall Jazz Band (Atlantic).

ROBINSON, PERRY MORRIS, *clarinet;* b. New York, N.Y., 8/17/38. Father is composer Earl Robinson, who wrote *Ballad for Americans* and *Joe Hill.* Grad. from High School of Music and Art, NYC, '56; attended School of Jazz, Lenox, Mass., '59; Manhattan School of Music, '60-1; further studies w. Eric Simon at Mannes School of Music, NYC; Kalman Black of LA Symph. Toured Spain, Portugal, '59-60; pl. w. Tete Montoliu in Spain, '60. Back in NYC, w. Sunny Murray, Paul Bley, '62; Archie Shepp and Bill Dixon at World Youth Fest. In Helsinki, '67; Roswell Rudd's Primordial Quintet, '68; also trio w. D. Izenzon and Randy Kaye. Apps. w. JCOA in '70s; joined Two Generations of Brubeck, '73 and continued with them while also pl. w. Gunter Hampel and the Galaxie Dream Band. Infls: S. Rollins, Pee Wee Russell, Ch. Parker, Tony Scott. Fests: Frankfurt, '72, '74; Newport, '73; Baden Baden Free Music Symposium, '74. Won DB Critics Poll TDWR, '67; *Jazz and Pop,* '69; *Jazzwerld,* Holland, '70. Comps: *Ragaroni; Walk On; Margareta*. Robinson is also a professional magician.

LPs: *Funk Dumpling* (Savoy); *The Call* (ESP); *Escalator Over The Hill,* w. Carla Bley (JCOA); *Brother, The Great Spirit Made Us All,* w. Brubeck (Atl.); *Spirits* w. Gunter Hampel-Jeanne Lee (Birth).

ROBINSON, PETE, *piano, keyboards, synthesizer, composer;* b. Chicago, Ill., 3/3/50. Moved to Vancouver, B.C., '53. Piano lessons from '56. To SF, '62. Pro. debut w. rock bands. At 15 was DB scholarship winner to Berklee. Moved to LA, '66, joined Don Ellis, while studying w. Michael Tilson Thomas. After two years w. Ellis, spent a year w. S. Manne. In '72, comp. electronic music for Shakespeare Society of America. Concerts, seminars and recs. w. Phil Woods, '73-4. Extensive experience in producing for Playboy Records. Film scores: six documentaries.

Robinson, who operates his own multitrack studio for production work in electronic music, has also pl. w. Gil Melle (Alaska Fest. of Mus.), J. Klemmer, O. Nelson, Q. Jones, Ernie Watts. He has invented hybrid instruments, including electronic drums, polystrings etc.

LP w. own group, Contraband, *Time and Space* (Epic); also *dialogues for Piano and Reeds* (Testament); w. P. Woods (Testament); w. Manne, *Outside* (Contemporary); w. Melle, *Waterbirds* (Nocturne); Ellis, *Autumn* (Col.).

ROCCISANO, JOSEPH LUCIAN (JOE), *alto, soprano saxophones;* also *flute, clarinet, piccolo, tenor saxophone;* b. Springfield, Mass., 10/15/39. Stud. priv. w. Harry Huffnagle, '56; Ascher Slotnik, '57; Albert Harris, '74. At Potsdam State U., '59-63, received B.S. in mus. ed. First por. engagement w. Warren Covington, '57-9. Pl. local gigs until '63, then traveling w. Sam Donahue until '64. To Cal.,

'66, working w. Ray Charles, '67-8. Busy freelance player, writer in LA, w. B. Holman, T. Gibbs, Don Ellis, W. Herman, L. Bellson, Don Menza-Don Piestrup, Bobby Bryant et al; also own 12 piece band. App. at MJF and NJF with Ellis; also at World Jazz Festival, Japan, '64. Infs: P. Woods, C. Parker, Coltrane, Rollins. Comps: *Seven-Up* (for Ellis orch.); *Time Will Tell* (for Holman); *Inside-Outside; He Was All Of Us;* also many arrs. for Bellson, Ellis and Doc Severinsen. Publ: *Stage Band Arr. & Comp.* (Life Line Music Press, Box 338 Agoura, Ca. 91301).

LPs: w. Ellis, *Live in 3 2/3/4 Time* (Pac. Jazz); *Electric Bath* (Col.); w. D. Rader, *Polluted Tears* (DRM).

ROCCO, MAURICE JOHN,* *piano, singer;* b. Oxford, Ohio, 6/26/15. Known primarily for his boogie woogie performances while standing at the keyboard, he was a popular entertainer in U.S. clubs and Hollywood musicals during the '40s. He lived in Paris and Hong Kong before moving to Bangkok, Thailand in the early '60s and was a fixture at the Bamboo Bar of the Oriental Hotel until knifed to death in his apartment, 3/24/76.

ROCHLIN, IRVIN (IRV), *piano;* also *percussion;* b. Salem, Ohio, 4/14/26. Mother was pianist for silent movies. Stud. voice & piano w. Carl Gronemeyer in Chi., '38-42; percussion w. Lou Singer, '37-43; harmony & comp. at LA City College, '63-5; piano w. Erica Zador, '64. Worked as vocalist on CBS radio in Columbus, Ohio, '47; then as pianist in Chi. w. Anita O'Day, '48-9; Ike Day, '49; Chubby Jackson, '49-50; Georgie Auld, '51; Joe Daley, late '40s-early '50s; Jay Burkhart big band, '48-50; Ira Sullivan, off and on for 10 yrs. in late '40s-early '50s; Mary Ann McCall, '52; Z. Sims, '50; S. Getz, '57; Jimmy Cook big band, '60; J. Griffin, late '40s-early '50s; Jimmy Gourley, off and on for 25 years, beginning in Chi. After a period in LA, Rochlin, who was also known as Irv Craig during his Chi. yrs., left for Las Palmas, Canary Islands in '69 to play at the Half Note club, at the time partially-owned by Gourley. He pl. there w. Sims; Brew Moore; D. Gordon; Harold McNair, '70. In '71-3 he worked w. Ben Webster in Europe after settling in Amsterdam, '71. He also pl. w. Bobby Jones, '74 and cont. to work w. Gordon through '75. Infl: Teddy Wilson, Bud Powell, Wynton Kelly, Bill Evans; J. Mandel, Cole Porter, Ellington. French TV w. Gourley, '72. Comps: *The Nature of Things,* rec. by B. Evans; *Pepito's Rib,* rec. by Gordon. LP: *The Last Concert* w. Webster (Bovema).

RODIN, GILBERT A (GIL),* *saxophone, trumpet, flute;* b. Chicago, Ill., 12/9/06. Rodin, who helped organize the Bob Crosby band in '35, and who from the '60s was a successful TV producer, retired in '73 in order to write his autobiography. Before the project was completed he died 6/10/74 of a heart attack in Palm Springs, Cal.

RODNEY, RED (Robert Chudnick),* *trumpet, fluegelhorn;* b. Philadelphia, Pa., 9/27/27. Featured soloist w. bands of Thornhill, Krupa and Herman in '40s, and Charlie Parker quintet '49-50, he was based mainly in Las Vegas during the '60s, pl. in show bands backing the personalities who appear at the gambling capital. Moved to LA, pl. at Donte's, '72; jam session at Radio City Music Hall, NJF-NY, '73. A serious blood ailment slowed his comeback but he recovered sufficiently to tour w. G. Wein's *Musical Life of Charlie Parker* in Europe, fall '74. Rodney remained on the Continent until April '75, pl. clubs and concerts in Denmark, Sweden, Portugal, Belgium, Holland and England. Fest: Cascais, '74; Bergen, '75; Colo. Jazz Party '75. TV: many European apps. Comp: *Superbop; The Red Arrow; Box 2000; The Danish Jazz Army; Aarhus Express.* LPs: *Superbop; Bird Lives* (Muse); *The Red Arrow* (Onyx); w. Bebop Preservation Society (Spotlite); w. Danish Radio Orch. (Storyville); reissue, w. C. Parker (Verve).

RODRIGUEZ, ALEX, *trumpet, fluegelhorn;* b. Los Angeles, Cal., 8/26/40. Toured w. L. Hampton, '62-3; M. Ferguson, '64; W. Herman, '65; Gerald Wilson, '66- . While living in NYC, '69-70, pl. w. Frank Foster, P. Sanders, R.R. Kirk, Roy Haynes. Back in Calif., resumed gigging w. G. Wilson, also pl. w. H. Land quintet, and in Oct.-Dec. '73, toured U.S. and Canada w. S. Kenton. Pl. Watts Fest. w. Wilson, '71-4. Infls.: Coltrane, Clifford Brown, Booker Little.

LPs: *Live and Swinging; Everywhere; California Soul* w. Wilson (Pac. Jazz).

ROKER, GRANVILLE WILLIAM (MICKEY),* *drums;* b. Miami, Fla., 9/3/32. Busy freelancer in the mid '60s, he acc. Nancy Wilson, '65-7, and w. Duke Pearson's big band, '67-9, while continuing to work w. a variety of groups in NYC. With Lee Morgan from '69 into '71 when he joined D. Gillespie. TV apps. on the *Today* show w. Gillespie, Mary Lou Williams. All major fests. in Europe and U.S. w. Gillespie.

LPs: *Dizzy Gillespie's Big 4* (Pablo); *Live at the Lighthouse,* w. Morgan; *Speak Like a Child,* w. H. Hancock; *Now Hear This,* w. Pearson (BN); *Olinga,* w. Milt Jackson (CTI); *Zoot Sims Party* (Choice); *The Arrival of Bobby Jones* (Cobble.).

ROLAND, GENE,* *composer, trumpet;* also *tenor saxophone, piano;* b. Dallas, Tex., 9/15/21. Writing for Ib Glindemann radio orch. and pl. w. Papa Bue band at Vin Garten club, Copenhagen, Feb-Jun. '67. Trumpet at Jimmy Ryan's, '74; piano at Gregory's, '75. In the '70s, leader of own 21 piece and eight piece bands in NYC, pl. the Wine and Cheese Fest., '73. His assoc. w. S. Kenton, begun in the summer of '44 and renewed intermittently, was reactivated when he traveled with the band in '73. Comps: *Country Cousin; Blue Gene,* in Kenton album *7.5 On The Richter Scale* (Creative World).

ROLLINS, THEODORE WALTER (SONNY),* *tenor, soprano saxophones, composer;* b. New York City, 9/7/29. Prominent from '57, when he won the DB Critics' Poll as New Star. Pl. intermittently after voluntary inactivity, '59-61, Rollins again was in retirement from '68-71. During that period he visited Japan and India, stud. yoga, zen and the theories of Ghita. His retreat ended in June '71 and by the following year he was working with some regularity, touring Europe, pl. college concerts, composing a concerto under a Guggenheim Fellowship awarded him in '72. From '73 he visited Europe annually, also pl. in Japan in '73. Fests: Newport, '72-3-5; Chateauvallon, '73; Montreux, Antibes, Kongsberg, '74. TV: hour-long spec. for BBC, filmed live at Ronnie Scott's Club and at various locations around London, '74. His best known comps. are *Alfie's Theme* (from the movie *Alfie*); *Sonnymoon for Two; The Cutting Edge;* and his adaptation of the West Indian melody, *St. Thomas.*

His album *The Cutting Edge* was awarded the Grand Prix du Disque, a French award similar to the American Grammy. Working with various small instrumental groups, incl. promising musicians he had discovered, among them the guitarist Masuo, Rollins also has made unaccompanied performing a valuable part of his artistic approach. As Hollie I. West observed, "No other jazzman approaches him in sustaining the creativity and esthetic balance of solo work . . . Rollins has performed entire concerts by himself in brilliant style as if he were accompanied by a large orchestra."

Rollins is also noted for his ability to take the most unlikely of themes, such as *Happy Days Are Here Again,* and make thme meaningful through odd rhythmic patterns, long bursts of linear improvisation, and touches of sardonic humor. Won DB Critics poll, '67-70, '72-5; Readers poll, '72-5; Hall of Fame, '73.

LPs: *The Bridge* (RCA); *Alfie; East Broadway Rundown; Reevaluation: The Impulse Years* (Imp.); *Nucleus; The Cutting Edge; Freedom Suite; Horn Culture; Next Album* (Milest.); *First Recordings; Jazz Classics; Plays for Bird; Saxophone Colossus; Saxophone Colossus & More; Sonny Rollins; Tenor Madness; Three Giants; Worktime* (Pres.); others on BN.

ROMANO, JOSEPH (JOE), *tenor, alto saxes;* also *clarinet, flute;* b. Rochester, N.Y., 4/17/32. Studied alto sax at eight; clarinet at Eastman School from ages 10-12; tenor for a yr. Began professionally pl. w. local bands in Roch. at 14. Air Force at 17, pl. w. bands in Alaska, Texas and New York state. Joined Woody Herman in Calif. '56 and pl. w. him, off an on, to '66. Worked in Las Vegas, '60-1; also two yrs. w. Chuck Mangione in Roch. in '60s. Member of Sam Noto quintet in Buffalo, '66-7. Buddy Rich, off an on, '68-70. Remained in Cal., pl. two weeks w. S. Kenton; then Les Brown, '70-2. Also w. L. Bellson during this period. Rejoined Rich '72-4. Free-lance in Roch., '74-5. To NYC Feb. '75. Pl. w. Chuck Israels' National Jazz Ensemble; subbed in Thad Jones-Mel Lewis orch. Infl: Charlie Parker, Sonny Rollins, Bud Powell, Coltrane, C. Hawkins, L. Young. TV: Pearl Bailey, Bob Hope shows w. L. Brown, '70-2. Fest: Monterey w. Herman, '60s; Bellson, '71; NJF, KCJF w. Herman. LPs: w. Noto, *First Act* (Xanadu); w. Rich, feat. on *God Bless the Child* in *Stick it* (RCA Vict.); *Buddy and Soul* (Pac. Jazz); w. Mangione, *Recuerdo* (Jazzland); w. Herman (Philips); w. Gus Mancuso, *New Faces* (Fantasy).

ROSENGARDEN, ROBERT M. (BOBBY), *drums, percussion;* b. Elgin, Ill., 4/23/24. Mother a pianist for silent movies. Two sons musicians: Mark, drummer w. Herbie Mann; Vince Guaraldi; Neal, trumpeter, pianist for jingles, rec. Pirvate instruction from age five. Stud. w. Oliver Coleman in Chi. at 11 for two yrs; Roy Knapp through high school. Music scholarship to U. of Mich. where he stud. w. Dr. Wm. D. Revelli '42-3. Pl. w. 75th Inf. Band, Ft. Leonard Wood, Mo., '43; 502nd Air Force Band, Keesler Field, Miss., '44-5; Teddy Phillips, '45; Henry Busse, '45-6. To NYC '46 where he worked w. Charlie Spivak; Raymond Scott; bands at the Copacabana, Bill Miller's Riviera; Alvy West's Little Band, '46-8; Skitch Henderson, '48 incl. NBC radio. Regular member NBC staff, incl. symphony, '49-68. Cond. band for Dick Cavett show, ABC-TV, '69-74; also mus. dir. for Waldorf-Astoria's Empire Room, '73. Pl. w. Benny Goodman, off and on, from '65; WGJ, intermittently, from '73, incl. European tour, '75. Member of NYJRC in second season; toured Russia, other European countries with its Louis Armstrong program, '75. Gigs w. Joe Venuti; Peanuts Hucko at Michael's Pub, '75. Extremely busy studio man, rec. w. Ellington; Lena Horne; Billie Holiday; J.J. Johnson-Kai Winding; Joe Williams; Doc Severinsen; Frank Sinatra; Ella Fitzgerald; Tito Puente; Dick Hyman; N.Y. Philharmonic, etc. Concerts w. Miles Davis-Gil Evans in '50s. Infl: Chick Webb, O'Neil Spencer, G. Krupa, B. Rich, Jo Jones. Film: *C-Man* w. Conrad Nagel; also many soundtracks. Fest: NJF-NY w. own band, '72; NJF; Nice; Concord; KC; Colo. and Odessa jazz parties. Comp: co-author w. Phil Kraus of Cavett show theme, *Meet the Girls.* Often thought of in the past as a top studio man, he has proven himself to be a versatile, spirited jazz drummer as well. LPs: *Colorado Jazz Party* (MPS/BASF); w. Jimmy Smith, *Peter and the Wolf; Hoochie Coochie Man* (Verve); w. A. C. Jobim, *Wave* (A&M); w. B. Goodman, Stravinsky, *Ebony Concerto* (Col.); w. Tony Mottola (Command; Proj. 3); w. C. Byrd; D. Brubeck (Col.); J. Venuti (Chiaro.).

ROSOLINO, FRANK,* *trombone, singer;* b. Detroit, Mich., 8/20/26. Early exp. w. G. Krupa, S. Kenton, H. Rumsey. Recording, TV and club work in later years. Several jazz clinics for Conn Instrument Co. since mid-1960s. Toured and featured w. Maria Muldaur and Benny Carter orch. '74. During '73-75, made individual recordings and personal appearances in Italy, Holland, England and Canada. Occasionally worked as soloist with Supersax. Recorded with Q. Jones and appeared w. him in concerts in U.S. and Japan. TV: featured soloist on Merv Griffin show. Movies: sound track of *Hot Rock* w. Q. Jones. Jazz festivals: Monterey, Concord; Charlie Parker Memorial in KC with Supersax; annual Dick Gibson Colorado jazz parties. Comp: *Blue Daniel* recorded by C. Adderley, S. Manne. LPs: own quintet (Horo); *Conversation* w. C. Candoli (Ital. RCA); w. Frank Strazzeri, *Taurus* (Revelation); *Supersax with Strings* (Capitol); w. Q. Jones, *Body Heat* (A&M); *Hotel,* soundtrack (Warner Bros.); *Brass Fever* (Imp.).

ROSS, ANNIE (Annabelle Short Lynch),* *singer, songwriter;* b. Mitcham, Surrey, Eng., 7/25/30. Member of Lambert, Hendricks & Ross Trio 1958-62. Living in England, ran own nightclub in mid-60s; took part in jazz festivals all over Europe. One woman show at Hampstead Theater Club, London. Frequent acting experience since then, including role of Polly in *Threepenny Opera* with Vanessa Redgrave; Weill & Brecht's *7 Deadly Sins* at Covent Garden with Royal Ballet; Royal Chichester Prod. of Pirandello's *Tonight We Improvise.*

Ross also appeared w. A. Previn at the Royal Festival Hall in a concert of K. Weill's music. Motion pictures: *Straight On 'Till Morning,* for which she composed and sang lyrics and music of the title song; *Alfie Darling,* sequel to *Alfie,* w. Alan Price. LPs: *Handful of Songs* (Ember), *Facade* w. Cleo Laine, J. Dankworth (RCA); reissues, *The Bebop Singers* (Prest.); w. Lambert, Hendricks & Ross (Col.).

ROSS, ARNOLD,* *piano, keyboards, composer;* b. Boston, Mass., 1/29/21. Name band musician in '40s, also acc. to many singers from early '50s. In recent years Ross has confined his work mainly to TV and rec. studios, w. N. Riddle, P. Weston, Johnny Mann, also touring occasionally w. singers (Edie Adams, Jane Russell, Frances Wayne Hefti) as cond.-acc. In '73 he made a trio ablum, his first in many years, for Nocturne Records. TV specs. w. Bing Crosby, F. Sinatra, other pop artists.

LPs: *Arnold Ross Trio; Arnold Ross Trio No. 2* (Nocturne).

ROSS, RONALD (RONNIE), * *baritone saxophone;* b. Calcutta, India, 10/2/33. Worked in England w. Ted Heath, many other English and visiting American groups, incl. W. Herman, '59. With Clarke-Boland band, '65-6; Hans Koller band, '67; BBC-TV w. D. Gillespie. Fest. apps. in Helsinki, Prague etc. w. Slide Hampton band and others. An exceptional performer on all saxophones, clarinets, flutes and piccolo, Ross also has worked with symph. orchs. Led band called 8 to 1 in mid-'70s.

LPs: *Cleopatra's Needle,* w. own sextet (Fontana); others w. Stan Tracey, Fredrich Gulda, Mike Gibbs, Lalo Schifrin, Slide Hampton, Tubby Hayes, George Gruntz; reissue, w. John Lewis, *European Windows* (RCA).

ROUSE, CHARLES (CHARLIE),* *tenor sax;* b. Washington, D.C., 4/6/24. After more than 10 years w. Thelonious Monk's quartet he left in early '70 to appear as a free-lance soloist w. local rhythm sections in Chicago, Wash., D.C., Newark, Phila. and Detroit. Formed own sextet '75 with an emphasis on Brazilian music, appearing at Five Spot; Rust Brown. Fest: NJF; MJF w. Monk; NJF-NY w. own group at New York Musicians Fest., '73. Comp: *Two Is One; Minor Walk.* LPs: *Two Is One* (Strata-East); w. Duke Jordan (Steeple.); Monk (Col.); reissue w. Fats Navarro (BN).

ROWLES, JAMES GEORGE (JIMMY),* *piano, composer;* b. Spokane, Wash., 8/19/18. Veteran of Goodman, Herman, T. Dorsey, Bob Crosby orchs., Rowles during the '60s continued to work as accompanist for many singers incl. Peggy Lee, Carmen McRae et al; also busy in the Hollywood studios and working with his own trio at many different night clubs in the LA area. In '73, at NJF-NY, he took part in a recital at Carnegie Hall which featured 10 pianists, in which he played solo piano in a tribute to Art Tatum. In that same year an album recorded live at Donte's w. C. McRae was issued on Atl. While in New York, 1974 he played a season at The Cookery and at Bradley's. Long engagements at Bradley's '75. Fest: NJF-NY, '74-5.

Long acknowledged as the favorite accompanist of every singer for whom he has worked, Rowles is an artist of consummate harmonic imagination. For many years he has specialized in building a repertoire of Ellington and Strayhorn compositions.

Comps: *The Peacocks; We Take The Cake; Ballad of Thelonious Monk; Morning Star; Frasier.* LPs: *Solo Piano* (Halcyon); *Trio* (Blue Angel); *Zoot Sims Party* (Choice); w. Sarah Vaughan (Mainstr.); B. Kessel (Concord); Kay Starr (GNP-Crescendo); w. C. McRae (Atl.).

ROWSER, JAMES EDWARD (JIMMY),* *bass;* b. Philadelphia, Pa., 4/18/26. Freelanced in NYC w. Al Cohn-Z. Sims et al, '66 until he joined L. McCann Sept. '69, touring worldwide. App. in movie *Soul to Soul,* w. McCann, filmed in Accra, Ghana, '71. Fests. w. McCann, incl. Montreux, '72.

LPs: w. McCann on Atl.

ROY, THEODORE GERALD (TEDDY),* *piano;* b. Duquoin, Ill., 4/9/05. An associate in the '20s and '30s of Frank Trumbauer, B. Hackett, Pee Wee Russell et al, Roy later pl. solo piano at E. Condon's club, freelanced in NYC and rec. for Commodore with a revived version of the Original Dixieland Jazz Band in the mid-40s. He died 8/31/66 in a NYC hospital.

ROYAL, ERNEST ANDREW (ERNIE),* *trumpet;* b. Los Angeles, Calif., 6/2/21. Worked w. Lionel Hampton, Woody Herman, Duke Ellington, Stan Kenton, Neal Hefti. Member of ABC staff '57-72. From that time an extremely busy freelance in NYC on countless dates incl. Quincy Jones, Oliver Nelson, Gil Evans. Broadway shows: *Raisin; Bubbling Brown Sugar.* Pl. in Europe w. Friedrich Gulda, '68. European tour w. NYJRC '75. A versatile player who is capable of filling a soloist's role but is most often called on for his excellent lead work. TV: Tribute to Duke Ellington w. Quincy Jones, '75. LP: *There Comes a Time,* w. G. Evans (RCA Victor).

ROYAL, MARSHALL,* *alto saxophone, flute* etc.; b. Sapulpa, Okla., 12/5/12. After working with Count Basie from early 1951 until Jan. 1970, Royal settled in LA. For two years he played at the Ambassador Hotel's Grove, where he was contractor and lead alto player, first under Geo. Rhodes, later under Hal Borne. Freelance work incl. clubs, concerts w. Bill Berry LA Big Band. Several tribute concerts honoring Duke Ellington, in whose band he had played in the film *Check and Double Check* in 1930 and on several later occasions.

In the fall of 1974 Royal fronted a band assembled by Monk Montgomery to tour South Africa with singer Lovelace Watkins.

Films: *Lady Sings the Blues; Blazing Saddles,* w. Basie; *Lepke* (all on camera as well as sound track); *Mame.*

LPs: *Jack Daugherty and the Class of 1972* (A & M); many sessions of swing era recreations for series on Time-Life Records.

RUDD, ROSWELL HOPKINS JR.,* *trombone, composer;* also *French horn, piano, conga;* b. Sharon, Conn. , 11/17/35. Extensive studies incl. Yale U., '54-8. Throughout '60s worked with traditional and mainstream bands, despite his close identification with avant garde music and with such musicians as A. Shepp, John Tchicai and Milford Graves in NY Art Quartet, and the so-called Primordial Groups w. Chas. Davis, Karl Berger, Perry Robinson, R. Kenyatta, Ch. Haden; also Roswell Rudd & Friends, feat. Sheila Jordan, Beaver Harris et al. Fests: Newport, '65 w. JCOA, '66 w. Shepp. Movies: app. in *The Hustler* as Dixie musician. Won research grant from National Endowment for the Arts, Performance Grant from NY State Council. Taught world music and jazz improvisation at Bard Coll., '73-5. Three months at St. James Infirmary, NYC, leading combo, winter of '74-5. Dutch radio spec., Apr. '75; also app. in Amsterdam w. Theo Loevende.

Long involved in the study not only of traditional European

music and its evolution but also of the jazz tradition and other musical idioms, Rudd in '64 began working as a staff musicologist with the folklorist-ethnomusicologist Alan Lomax. According to Rudd, "This helped to fill a noticeable gap in my formal education. The work has given me immeasurable insights into the elements of ancient music, which I've been able to apply to my activities as a composer and performer."

Rudd has written a number of extended works, many of which for economic reasons could not be recorded or presented publicly. For many years he was unable to make a consistent living in music and was forced to take other jobs. Michael Cuscuna wrote: "Roswell Rudd is an extraordinary trombonist and composer and ethnomusicologist whose work has yet to reach full public recognition . . . a man whose musical elements make him one of the most unusual artists of our time."

Comps: *Bop City Dues; Sky Above, Mud Below; Moselle Variations; Heartbreak & Reformulation;* symphonic works, *Blues for the Planet Earth; Springsong; Numatik Swing Band;* operas, *The Gold Rush; Taki 183.*

Own LPs: *Numatik Swing Band* (JCOA); *Flexible Flyer* (Arista); *Everywhere* (Impulse); w. A. Shepp, *Live At The Donaueschingen Music Festival* (BASF-MPS).

RUIZ, HILTON, *piano, composer;* b. New York City, 5/29/52. Studied classical w. George Armstrong; Latin w. Prof. Messorana; jazz w. Mary Lou Williams, '71- ; Cedar Walton, '72; Harold Mabern at Jazz Interactions Young Musicians Workshop, '72-3; Chris Anderson, '75. At age eight perf. in solo recital at Carnegie Recital Hall; at nine pl. in accordion symphony at Biviano School. Has pl. w. Latin soul bands, Ismael Rivera; Ralph Robles from age 13; at 14 rec. w. Ray Jay and the East Siders. Braodcast w. Latin bands on radio station WHOM.

Worked w. Frank Foster's big band and small gp., '70; Joe Newman, '71; Cal Massey big band, '71-2; Freddie Hubbard; Joe Henderson, '72; Clark Terry band and gp.; Jackie McLean, '73; subbed for two wks. w. Mingus, '73. From Nov. '73 pl. w. Rahsaan Roland Kirk, off and on, touring Europe, Australia, New Zealand, Canada. Worked w. Roy Brooks' Artistic Truth; concerts w. CBA big band, '72-4; Betty Carter, '74; Rashied Ali, '74-5. Infl: Coltrane quartet w. McCoy Tyner, C. Parker, T. Monk, Waller, Tatum, D. Gordon, D. Byas, early H. Hancock. TV: as child, Sandy Becker show, ABC; *Jazz Adventures* w. Baby Laurence. Fest: Montreux w. Kirk. Promising young pianist with much facility and fire.

Comp: *Arrival; One For Hakim.* LPs: *Piano Man* (Steeple.); w. Brooks, *Ethnic Expression* (Im Hotep); w. Kirk, *Case of the 3-Sided Dream in Audio Color* (Atl.).

RUMSEY, HOWARD,* *bass, club owner;* b. Brawley, Cal., 11/7/17. Original Kenton band member in early 1940s. Inaugurated jam session policy at Lighthouse in Hermosa Beach, Cal., 1949, remaining there as co-owner and manager, until '71. Secured new premises in Redondo Beach, Cal., and in '72 opened Concerts by the Sea, a plush, acoustically excellent jazz room, presenting the top jazz artists from all over the country.

RUSHEN, PATRICE LOUISE, *piano, composer;* also *flute;* b. Los Angeles, Cal., 9/30/54. Stud. at U. of S. Cal., Music Preparatory Division. Early piano lessons w. Earl Hultburg, '60-3; Dorothy Bishop, '63-72. First prominent when she won awards as member of Locke High School band in LA. While still in her teens, she toured w. Leslie Drayton, Melba Liston, Abbey Lincoln, The Sylvers; has worked w. Gerald Wilson orch.; D. Byrd. Pl. at Monterey JF, '72. TV: *Black Omnibus.*

Rushen, who names H. Hancock, McCoy Tyner, K. Jarrett, Thad Jones, Gil Evans, J. Henderson and O. Peterson as her influences, is a musician of prodigious talent who, while still in high school, already showed a rare degree of maturity and technical command at the piano. Her comps. incl. *Shortie's Portion; 7/73; Traverse.*

LPs: *Prelusion; Before the Dawn* (Pres.); also w. J.L. Ponty (Atl.); Stanley Turrentine (Fant.).

RUSHING, JAMES ANDREW (JIMMY),* *singer;* b. Oklahoma City, Okla., 8/26/03. Featured with the Basie band from '35-50. Rushing later sang his blues hits w. B. Goodman, toured Australia w. E. Condon, and freelanced in and around NYC. In '69 he had an acting role in the film, *The Learning Tree.* Rushing's last album, *The You And Me That Used To Be,* made in '71, feat. many popular songs and standards, was voted Record of the Year in the '72 DB Critics' Poll. Rushing was also voted number one male singer in the same poll. Before the results were announced, he contracted leukemia and died 6/8/72 in NYC. In his last years he app. frequently at the Half Note, NYC, backed by A. Cohn-Z. Sims. Also seen at KC JF, '72, where he was inducted into the KC Jazz Hall of Fame.

Rushing's ebullient delivery and rhythmic drive established him not only as an outstanding blues singer (probably the first ever to become a key member of name bands), but also as a warm, personal interpreter of non-blues material.

LPs: *Listen to the Blues; Essential Jimmy Rushing* (Vanguard); *Gee Baby; Who Was It Sang That Song* (Master Jazz); *The You And Me That Used To Be* (RCA); also w. Basie (RCA, Col.); D. Ellington (Col.).

RUSSELL, GEORGE ALLAN,* *composer, piano, educator;* b. Cincinnati, Ohio, 6/23/23. With his sextet which he had formed in '60, he toured Europe as part of George Wein package '64 and then remained in Scandinavia, playing, writing and teaching his Lydian Chromatic Concept of Tonal Organization, a method praised by John Lewis, Ornette Coleman, Gil Evans and David Baker, among others. In '69 he returned to the US to teach his concept as a member of the faculty at the New England Conservatory in Boston. He also taught in Finland, '66, '67; Norway, Sweden, Denmark, '68; Tanglewood, Mass., summer '70; Denmark, summer '71. Performed several times a year for Scandinavian Radio in Oslo, Stockholm and Copenhagen, '65-71. Fest: Bologna, '69; Tanglewood, '70; Berlin, '70; Kongsberg, '71. Comp: *Othello Ballet Suite; Electronic Organ Sonata No. 1; Electronic Sonata for Souls Loved By Nature; Now and Then; Concerto for Self-Accompanied Guitar; Listen to the Silence; Events I-VIII.* The latter were part of a large work for pianist Bill Evans and big band commissioned by Columbia Records and recorded in '72. A concert performance w. Evans was given at Carnegie Hall in '74 under the auspices of the NYJRC.

From '67 *The Lydian Chromatic Concept* has been an official text at the U. of Indiana Music School. Kare Kolberg, president of the Norwegian Branch of the Int. Soc. for Contemporary Mus., called it "the wallbreaker which opened the way out of the '50s closed way of thinking . . . poetic, demanding without being binding, open without being anarchistic, precise without being petty."

Awards: NEA Grant, '69; Guggenheim Fellowships, '69, '72. Publications and LP, *Listen to the Silence* (Concept, New Music Distribution Service, 6 West 95th St., New York, N.Y. 10025). Other LPs: *Othello Ballet Suite/ Electronic Organ Sonata No. 1; Essence of George Russell* (Sonet); *Electronic Sonata for Souls Loved By Nature* (Fly. Dutch.); w. Bill Evans, *Living Time* (Col.); reissues on Milestone; MCA; BASF.

RUSSELL, CHARLES ELSWORTH (PEE WEE),* *clarinet;* b. St. Louis, Mo., 3/27/06. Played with Bix Beiderbecke in Frank Trumbauer's band in St. Louis. Later worked in NYC w. Red Nichols, Ben Pollack, Louis Prima, B. Hackett, Bud Freeman in '30s; many Dixieland groups organized by E. Condon, Geo. Wein and others in '40s. Despite serious illnesses, he continued to work through the '50s and '60s, gradually attaining the stature of a legend, and experimenting with more contemporary approaches. After a brief illness he died 2/15/69 at a hospital in Alexandria, Va.

Russell was one of the foremost individualists of jazz history, his sound totally personal and unorthodox by academic clarinet standards. Late in his career he also showed a remarkable talent as a painter. He is represented on many albums as a leader: *Ask Me Now; College Concert; Spirit of 67* (Imp.); *Memorial Album* (Pres.); *Pee Wee Russell* (Archive of Jazz and Folk); *A Legend* (Mainstr.); *New Groove* (Col.); *Jazz Reunion,* Russell-Hawkins (Candid); w. E. Condon-Bud Freeman, *The Commodore Years* (Comm.); *Eddie Condon Concerts* (Chiaroscuro). *Eddie Condon's World of Jazz* (Col.).

RUSSELL, WILLIAM EUGENE (GENE), *piano, composer;* b. Los Angeles, Cal., 12/2/32. Cousin of guitarist Ch. Christian. Stud. Westlake Jr. Coll; Fine Arts Conserv; LA City Coll. in '50s; priv. lessons w. H. Hawes. Insp. by Hawes, A. Jamal, Gene Harris, Carl Perkins, Sonny Clark. Russell became an active musician, combo leader and composer in LA during '60s, writing some of the music for several movies in '67-8; theme for TV show, *Doin' It,* '72; app. as actor in *Black Gestapo.* Worked as actor and musician in *The Young and the Restless,* CBS TV, '75.

Russell is best known as the founder of Black Jazz Records, for which he has recorded as a leader in addition to producing sessions with many other artists. He is also pres. of G.R. Productions and Aquarican Records. Russell has pl. in the groups of Rahsaan Roland Kirk; Zoot Sims; L. Vinnegar; D. Gordon; Wardell Gray; Miles Davis in concerts in LA and NYC; and subbed for Gene Harris in The Three Sounds for three months when the latter was ill.

Fests: Monterey, '68 w. own trio; J. Coltrane Memorial Fest., '70; Fest. in Black, '71; Cal State JF, '74.

LPs: *Up, Up and Away* (Decca); *Taking Care of Business* (Dot); *New Directions; Talk To My Lady* (Black Jazz); w. Joe Cocker, *Feelin' Alright* (A & M).

RUTHERFORD, ELMAN (RUDY), *clarinet, baritone, alto saxes, flute;* b. Detroit, Mich., 1912. Played w. L. Hampton, '43; Count Basie, '44-7; Ted Buckner's band in Detroit, '47; Basie again, '51. In '50s and '60s app. w. own combos at Count Basie's, other NYC area clubs, Ramapo Country Club. Worked w. Ram Ramirez trio, '59; Buddy Tate, '64; also w. Wilbur De Paris. Joined Earl Hines '75. Film: app. w. Chuck Berry in *Jazz On a Summer's Day* at NJF. Feat. on clarinet w. Basie on *High Tide* in mid-'40s. LPs: w. De Paris (Atl.).

RYPDAL, TERJE, *guitar, flute, soprano saxophone, composer;* b. Oslo, Norway, 8/23/47. Father, Jakop Rypdal, captain in military band. Wife, Inger-Lise, pop singer and actress. Stud. piano from age five, guitar at 13. After working as a pop musician, Rypdal in the late 1960s played with Jan Garbarek's group, also w. George Russell Sextet and big band. Stud. Lydian Concept with Russell. First break as guitar soloist in free-jazz festival at Baden-Baden, Germany, 1969. Pl. w. Violin Summit at Baden-Baden, '71; own trio at Berlin Jazz Festival '72. Started new group, Terje Rypdal Odyssey, which in late '75 played its first concert in England. An important contemporary composer, Rypdal has written many works for his own group as well as such extended pieces as *Eternal Circulation,* for symphony orch. and jazz musicians; *Symphony No. 1,* 1973; *Electric Fantasy; Tension;* and music for theatre. LPs: *Bleak House* (Polydor); *Whenever I Seem to Be Far Away; What Comes After; Odyssey* (ECM).

SADI, FATS (Lallemand Sadi),* *vibraphone, bongos, singer, composer;* b. Andenne, Belgium, 10/23/26. In '40s and '50s worked w. D. Reinhardt, Andre Hodeir, M. Legrand; lived in Paris '50-61; toured for three years w. Caterina Valente. Settled in Brussels, leaving occasionally to work w. Clarke-Boland band. From '72 had own TV show in which he sang, played bongos and acted. LPs for Vogue; Pallette; Manhattan; Saba labels; also w. L. Thompson, Christian Chevallier, Raymond Fol.

SAFRANSKI, EDWARD (EDDIE),* *bass;* b. Pittsburgh, Pa., 12/25/18. The former poll winning bassist, a member of S. Kenton's orch. '45-8, spent most of the late '60s and early '70s gigging in LA with mainstream and traditionalist groups. He died in LA, Jan. '74.

SAMPLE, JOSEPH LESLIE (JOE),* *piano;* also *electric keyboards, organ;* b. Houston, Tex., 2/1/39. From 1954 was assoc. w. Stix Hooper, Wayne Henderson, Wilton Felder in the combo eventually known as the Crusaders. Was still working with them in '70s, but beginning in '67 this job overlapped with various others as he started a career as a

Billy Strayhorn and Duke Ellington (*Sam Shaw*)

Cecil Taylor (*David D. Spitzer*)

Clark Terry
(*Veryl Oakland*)

Billy Taylor (*Bob Klein*)

Ed Thigpen, Danny Richmond,
Billy Higgins and Norman Connors (*Randi Hultin*)

Stanley Turrentine (*David D. Spitzer*)

Toots Thielemans (*Veryl Oakland*)

Joe Venuti (*Veryl Oakland*)

Leone Thomas (*Veryl Oakland*)

McCoy Tyner (*Veryl Oakland*)

Sarah Vaughan (*Veryl Oakland*)

Cedar Walton (*David D. Spitzer*)

Grover Washington, Jr.

Eddie "Cleanhead" Vinson
(*David D. Spitzer*)

Harold Vick (*David D. Spitzer*)

Bill Watrous (*Veryl Oakland*)

Chuck Wayne (*Bob Klein*)

Lenny White (*Veryl Oakland*)

Frank Wess (*Veryl Oakland*)

Ernie Wilkins (*Bob Klein*)

Tony Williams (*David D. Spitzer*)

Mary Lou Williams (*Veryl Oakland*)

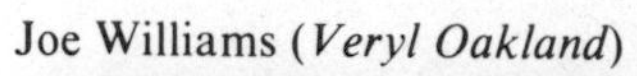

Joe Williams (*Veryl Oakland*)

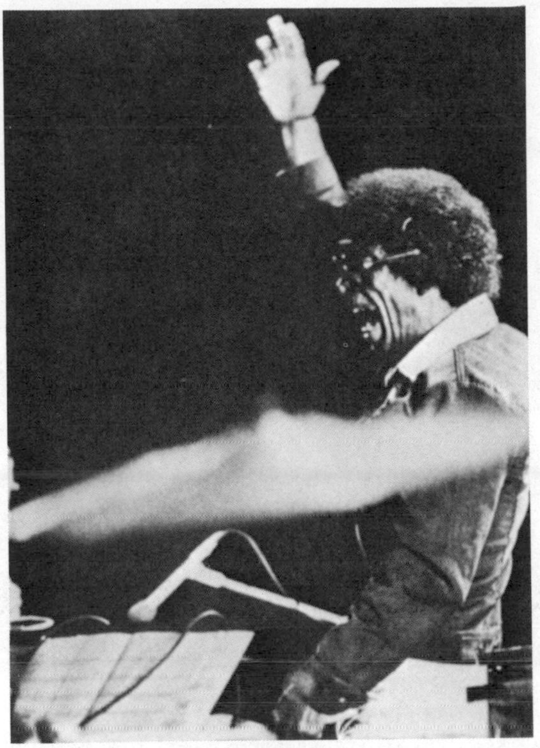

Gerald Wilson (*Veryl Oakland*)

Jimmy Witherspoon (*Veryl Oakland*)

Phil Woods (*Veryl Oakland*)

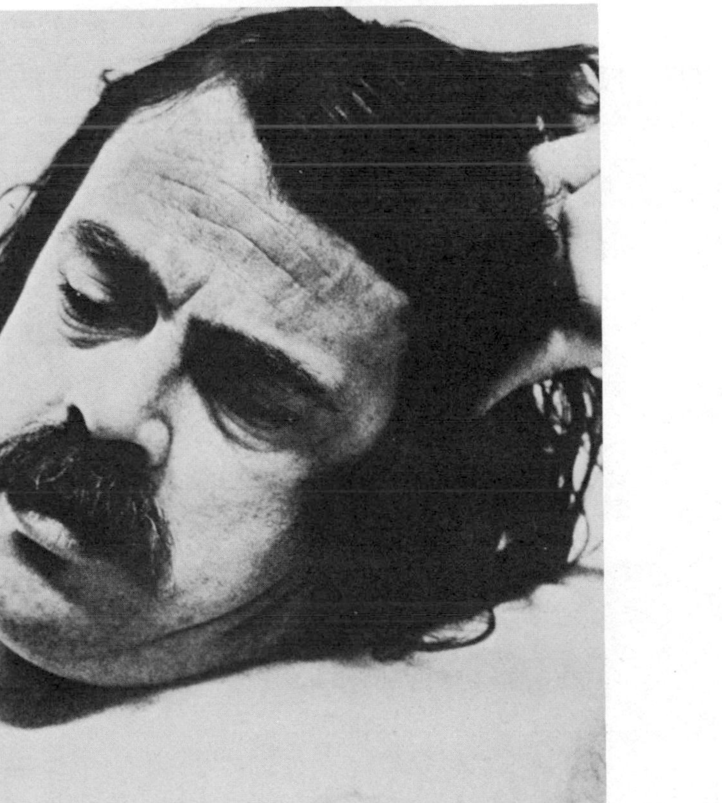

Sam Woodyard (*Krzysztof Zagrodski*)

Joe Zawinul (*Veryl Oakland*)

The World's Greatest Jazz band; front, Yank Lawson and Bob Haggart; second row (from left), Ed Hubble, Bud Freeman, Gus Johnson, Vic Dickenson; back row, Bob Wilber, Ralph Sutton, Billy Butterfield.

Denny Zeitlin

Hollywood studio musician. He became a regular Motown session man, rec. w. Diana Ross, the Jackson 5 and many others. Rec. w. Joni Mitchell, Joan Baez and many other pop singers. Jazz records and gigs w. Harold Land-Bobby Hutcherson, O. Nelson, Q. Jones.

Early in '73 Sample went to Caracas as a member of the Tom Scott quartet. This group was the nucleus of what became known as the L.A. Express with which he was feat. in a series of successful recordings.

Comps: *Adventurers in Paradise* (comp. for and w. Minnie Riperton); *A Ballad for Joe Louis; A Search for Soul; A Shade of Blues; Put It Where You Want It.*

LPs: w. Crusaders (Pacific Jazz, Blue Thumb); w. L.A. Express (Ode); w. H. Land-B. Hutcherson, *San Francisco* (Blue Note).

SAMPSON, EDGAR MELVIN,* *composer, saxophones;* b. New York City, 8/31/07. Though he enjoyed his greatest fame as an arranger for the Chick Webb and B. Goodman orchs. in the '30s, Sampson later resumed playing saxophone, leading his own group, '49-51. He pl. w. several Latin bands, gigged w. Harry Dial and led combos of his own until the early '60s, when a serious illness inactivated him. He died 1/17/73 at his home in Englewood, N.J.

As composer and arranger of such classics as *Don't Be That Way; Stompin' At The Savoy; If Dreams Come True; Blue Lou; Lullaby In Rhythm,* Sampson developed a style that was prototypical of the swing era. Though he was not as prolific as Fletcher Henderson, everything he wrote was graced with a rare symmetry and melodic charm. An excellent and underrated soloist, he was heard playing violin on an early Henderson rec., *House of David Blues;* clarinet on a date w. Bunny Berigan in the mid-30s; alto on many sessions w. Webb, and baritone on *Ring Dem Bells,* on a famous L. Hampton date for RCA, heard in a since-deleted LP entitled *Swing Classics.*

SANBORN, DAVID WILLIAM (DAVE), *alto saxophone, flute;* b. Tampa, Fla., 7/30/45. After spending time in an iron lung during a childhood bout w. polio in St. Louis he was advised by a doctor to take up a wind instrument as physical therapy. Pl. alto sax in grade school band. At 14 gigged at "teen town" youth centers backing Albert King; Little Milton; pl. w. small combos in high school. Left St. Louis to study music at Northwestern U., '63-4. Got more heavily into blues in Chicago. After additional studies at U. of Iowa, '65-7, went to West Coast where drummer Philip Wilson brought him into the Paul Butterfield band. Played and rec. w. them, '67-71; lived in Woodstock, N.Y. for a yr. and resumed w. Butterfield '72. Worked w. Stevie Wonder, '72-3, touring w. him on Rolling Stones package '72. With Gil Evans from '74. Toured US w. David Bowie '74. Pl. w. Brecker Brothers '75. Forming own gp. for traveling after rec. first album. Gil Evans says: "He's got the technique but he's also got an emotional sound—that 'great cry.'"

Inf: Hank Crawford, Jackie McLean, Charlie Parker. TV: Euro. & US w. Evans; w. Butterfield; David Frost w. Wonder; Dick Cavett w. Bowie; *Saturday Night Live* w. Paul Simon, NBC. Fest: Woodstock w. Butterfield; Juan-Les-Pins w. Evans '75. Rec. hit disco single of *The Bottle* w. Joe Bataan (Salsoul). LPs: *Taking Off* (WB); w. Evans, *Svengali* (Atl.); *Music of Jimi Hendrix; There Comes a Time* (RCA); w. Joe Beck; Esther Phillips (Kudu); Brecker Brothers (Arista); Hubert Laws (CTI); others w. Wonder; James Taylor; Bowie.

SANDERS, FARRELL (PHAROAH),* *tenor, soprano saxes, composer;* b. Little Rock, Ark., 10/13/40. With John Coltrane from '66. After Coltrane's death in '67 he continued to tour and record w. Alice Coltrane until '69 when he formed his own group which incl. Leon Thomas and Lonnie Liston Smith through '71. David Baker talked of his "strong, lean lyricism unencumbered by romantic excesses, the economy of materials, the wide range of musical expressivity, the absolute control of his instrument over a staggering three-octave range, and the remarkable fluency . . ."

On the other hand, Joachim Berendt who described him "as others among the newer tenorists, he extends the range of the tenor sax, by means of 'overblowing,' into the highest registers of the soprano," opined: "It is regretful that Sanders within a few years stereotyped and banalized a way of playing that had initially given rise to the highest hopes."

Sanders' framework has ranged from swirling, rasping, guttural explosions to pastoral, spiritual, pan-African expressions. He has played many fests. in US and abroad. Comp: *Tauhid; Upper Egypt; Thembi; Love is Everywhere; To John; The Creator Has a Master Plan; Colors, Hum Allah, Hum Allah.* LPs: *Black Unity; Elevation; Jewels of Thought; Karma; Live at the East; Love in Us All; Summun Bukmun Umyum; Tauhid; Thembi; Village of the Pharoahs; Wisdom Through Music* (Imp.); *Izipho Sam* (St.-East); w. Alice Coltrane; John Coltrane (Imp.); Don Cherry (BN).

SARDABY, MICHEL, *piano, composer;* b. Martinique, 9/4/35. Father was classical pianist. Self-taught from age five. As a child traveled a lot w. parents between NYC and other parts of U.S. From age 12 pl. w. various gps. at different places on Caribbean islands. At 17 formed his own 18-piece band. Left Martinique for Paris '53, studying at Ecole Boulle as parents did not want him to become a professional musician without receiving a diploma. From '56 pl. at Paris clubs such as Blue Note, Jazzland, Club St. Germain, Living Room, Le Chat Qui Peche; also other European clubs w. Albert Nicholas, Don Byas, Ben Webster, Stuff Smith, Chet Baker, Sonny Criss, Kenny Clarke, J. J. Johnson, Clark Terry, Johnny Griffin, Dexter Gordon, etc. Early infl.: Ellington, Waller, Tatum, Nat Cole. His rec. *Michel Sardaby |a New York* received the prize of the Academy of Paris. Played NJF in Paris; concerts in Paris at the Salle Pleyel and American Culture Center; Europe and Israel. His own LPs in which he is represented as a composer include *Michel Sardaby à New York* w. Billy Cobham, Richard Davis and Ray Barretto; *Night Cup* w. Percy Heath and Connie Kay; *Gail* w. Davis, Billy Hart, Leopoldo Fleming; *Blue Sunset* (Debs); *Five Cat's Blues* (President).

SARMANTO, HEIKKI, *pianist, composer;* b. Helsinki, Finland, 6/22/39. Private studies at age 13. Stud. at Helsinki U. and Sibelius Academy. Received grant to study at Berklee Coll., '68-72. While in Boston stud. privately w. Margaret Chaloff. Worked w. own gp. in Scandinavia;

USSR; Switzerland. Has also pl. in Boston and NYC. Worked or sat in w. S. Rollins; A. Farmer; C. Terry; J. Henderson; G. Russell; C. Mariano. Early infl: Tatum, Bud Powell, Clifford Brown, Bartok, Debussy, Chopin. Won Best Finnish Jazz Musician '70; Best Pianist, Montreux JF '71. Composed music for radio, TV, modern dance. Comp: *Opuscule; Hymn to Jazzland; Theme for Christer; Jungle Flute; October Suite; Marat; Jazz Vesper;* over 100 vocal works for Finnish poetry, 30 vocal works for English poetry, '74-5. LPs: *Flowers in the Water; Onnen Aika* (EMI Col.); *Like a Fragonard; Everything Is It* (EMI Odeon).

SATO, MASAHIKO (Satoh), *piano, composer;* also *synthesizer;* b. Tokyo, Japan, 10/6/41. Violin lessons w. Hiroshi Hatoyama, '47-50; piano w. Fusako Uenuma, '47-51; Hiroshi Ito, '51-6. Stud. at Berklee, '66-8. Pl. w. Jiro Inagaki quintet, '63-4; own trio, '64-8. Pl. w. Clark Terry, Charlie Mariano et al, mainly in Boston, '66-8; then formed own trio which in the '72-4 period was called Garando. Own quartet, The Shadow Mask, from '74. Won Best Player Award at Art Fest., '71-2; SJ Readers Poll on piano, '70-1; as comp.-arr., '71-3. Infl: Yuji Takahashi, Olivier Messiaen, Akira Miyazawa. Fests: Berlin '71; Montreux, '73. Comps: *Yamataifu,* for big band; *Xenogamy* for orch. & Jazz combo. LPs: *Palladium* (Toshiba EMI); *Trinity* (Enja); *Sosho* (Trio); *Y. Takahashi & M. Sato; Four Compositions* w. Anthony Braxton (Nippon Col.); *Samadhi* w. Gary Peacock; *Yamataifu* w. Miyama & New Herd (Toshiba EMI).

SAUNDERS, ORVILLE, *guitar;* b. Washington, D.C. 6/2/54. Attended McFarland junior school. Stud. w. Bill Harris and worked w. K. Burrell at the latter's annual seminar, '74. Pl. w. Billy Hart, H. Hancock, G. Benson, Larry Ridley. A guitar major at Howard U, he joined the Blackbyrds in '75. LPs: *The Blackbyrds; Flying Start* (Fant.) others w. Richard Groove Holmes et al.

SCHIFRIN, BORIS (LALO),* *piano, composer;* b. Buenos Aires, Arg., 6/21/32. Toured w. D. Gillespie, '60-2. Since then has worked mainly as writer of film and TV scores. Cond. LA Neophonic Orch., '66. Scored *The Cincinnati Kid,* incl. vocal by Ray Charles on sound track, '66. Won two Grammies for *Mission: Impossible* TV music, '67. In '69 he was commissioned by C. Adderley to write a Third Stream work, *Dialogues for Jazz Quintet and Orchestra,* perf. at UCLA. Took part in LA Music Fest. cond. his *Jazz Suite on the Mass Texts,* feat. Paul Horn, '69. *Pulsations,* a Third Stream work commissioned for the LA Phil., was premiered in '70, cond. by Zubin Mehta.

During the '70s, Schifrin has continued to be very active in the fields of TV and motion pictures. Some of his scores, such as *Bullitt; Mannix; Dirty Harry,* are jazz-oriented; some include authentic jazz selections such as *Black Widow Blues* from *The Hellstrom Chronicle.* In '73, Schifrin made a rare personal app., playing at Shelly's Manne Hole. He has taken part as judge at song fests. in Rio, '70; Mexico City, '71. Taught composition at UCLA, '68-71. App. at Tribute to Dizzy Gillespie, Avery Fisher Hall, NYC, '75.

Some of his themes have become popular songs and have been rec. by such singers as Peggy Lee, C. McRae, Lou Rawls, Tony Bennett. Among them are *The Right To Love; Down Here On The Ground; The Fox; The Love Cage.*

LPs: *Marquis de Sade* (Verve); w. Gillespie, *A Musical Safari* (Booman); *Dialogues,* w. Adderley (Cap.); *The Other Side* (Audio Fidel.).

SCHLITTEN, DON, *producer, photographer;* b. Bronx, N.Y., 3/4/32. Began serious interest in jazz at age 13; art studies at High School of Music. Commercial artist until 1960. Prod. first LP for Signal Records, '57. Joined Pres. Records, '60 as art dir.—his photographs app. on hundreds of albums; later became creative activities VP. During next 10 years prod. over 150 LPs, incl. Pres. Historical Series, Spoken Word series (James Mason, Burgess Meredith, Norman Mailer). Became freelance a & r man in '70; prod. Vintage reissue series and J. Rushing's *The You and Me That Used To Be* for RCA, voted Record of the Year in DB Critics' Poll, '72; 12 LPs, incl. *Colorado Jazz Party,* for MPS; 16 LPs incl. first NJF-NY LPs for Buddah-Cobblestone; 36 LPs for Muse and 21 Onyx releases, incl. two that won Grammies for best jazz perf: Art Tatum, *God Is In The House; Charlie Parker, First Recordings!,* '74.

Schlitten states that his biggest infl. as producer, "other than the music," is Norman Granz. I. Gitler wrote in DB that Schlitten's "intensity, creativity, emotional involvement, keen perception and extraordinarily analytical ear make his productions truly unique. He really lives his work."

Among the many artists whose records he has produced are J. Moody, D. Gordon, S. Stitt, Booker Ervin, J. Raney, Jaki Byard, J. Heath, S. Criss, Barry Harris, P. Martino, E. Kloss, Red Rodney. In '75 he formed his own company, Xanadu Records Ltd.

SCHNITTER, DAVID BERTRAM, *tenor saxophone;* also *soprano, alto saxes, clarinet, flute;* b. Newark, N.J., 3/19/48. After grad. from Irvington H.S. attended Jersey City State Coll. majoring in clarinet. Participated in orch., stage band and other ensembles. During coll. yrs. also worked locally in Newark area. In '72 began visiting NYC for jam sessions, rehearsal bands, commercial work w. Latin bands. Sat in w. Joe Newman, Frank Foster, Howard McGhee; then began working w. Ted Dunbar; Wilbur Little, '73. Led own gp. at Boomer's three nights weekly for a year, '73-4. Joined Art Blakey Nov. '74. Also gigs w. own gp. at the Cellar, NYC, '74; Three Sisters, NJ, '75. Pl. in Japan and England w. Blakey.

Infl: Rollins, Dexter Gordon, Coltrane, Clifford Brown, Charlie Parker. TV: *Jazz Adventures,* Feb. '75. Fest: NJF-NY w. Blakey '75. LP: *Sonny Stitt with Art Blakey and the Jazz Messengers* (Polydor).

SCHOEBEL, ELMER,* *piano, composer;* b. E. St. Louis, Ill., 9/8/1896. Best known as comp. or co-comp. of such dixieland hits as *Bugle Call Rag; Farewell Blues; Nobody's Sweetheart,* Schoebel lived in Florida from '55, pl. occasionally w. local bands. He died 12/14/70 in Miami, Fla.

SCHOOF, MANFRED, *trumpet, composer;* also *piano;* b. Magdeburg, Germany, 4/6/36. Stud. at Music Akademie, Kassel, '55-8; trumpet, piano, theory, counterpoint at Cologne Musikhochschule (coll.). Pl. w. Gunter Hampel, '63-5;

leading own gp. from '65; also from time to time w. A. Mangelsdorf; Geo. Russell, '69 and '71; Clarke-Boland orch., '69-72. In Feb-Apr. '75, Schoof's sextet and critic J.E. Berendt toured Asia under the auspices of the Goethe Institution in a prog. combining musical perf. and lectures. Infls: Miles Davis, J. Coltrane. Fests: Berlin, '66-7, '69, '70-1, '74; Prague, '66; Antibes; Lugano; Warsaw, '67; Belgrade, '71; Ljubljana, '73. Schoof has written for orch., combo, film and TV: *Ode* for Globe Unity Orchestra was perf. at the Donaueschingen Fest., '70; *Kontraste & Synthesen* for Globe Unity Orch. and choir at NDR, '74. Has won German jazz polls on trumpet from '67.

LPs: *Voices* (German CBS); w. Barney Wilen, Keshau Sathe trio, *Jazz Meets India;* w. New Jazz Trio, *Page One; Page Two* (MPS); w. S. Getz, Clarke-Boland, *Change of Scene* (Euro-Verve); w. Mal Waldron, *Hard Talk* (Enja).

SCHROEDER, EUGENE CHARLES (GENE),* *piano,* b. Madison, Wis., 2/5/15. The veteran of many Eddie Condon groups in the 1940s and '50s died 2/16/75 in Madison, Wis. LPs w. Condon (Col., Chiaroscuro).

SCHULLER, GUNTHER,* *composer, conductor, educator;* b. Jackson Heights, N.Y. 11/11/25. A French horn player w. the Metro. Opera Orch. for 10 yrs, he became associated w. jazz in the Miles Davis Nonet of '49-50. Later closely allied w. John Lewis, he was involved with the classical-jazz fusion called "Third Stream." Pres. of the New England Conservatory in Boston from '67, he formed the New Eng. Cons. Ragtime Ensemble for a Fest. of Romantic American Music. Reworking the arrs. of Scott Joplin rags from the famous New Orleans Red Back Book of Rags, he presented them w. the Ensemble and rec. for Angel what became a best-selling album. These arrs. were pl. in film *The Sting,* which won an Oscar for scoring in '74 for Marvin Hamlisch.

He also formed the New Eng. Conserv. Jazz Repertory Orch. for which he transcribed Ellington works with plans to incorporate arrs. from bands such as Earl Hines, Benny Moten, McKinney's Cotton Pickers, Paul Whiteman, Sam Wooding and Jim Europe. Two works of his were premiered in '75: *Triplum 2* by the Baltimore Symph.; *Four Sound Scopes* by the Hudson Valley Phil. Publ. *Early Jazz,* a history-analysis with mus. examples up to early '30s (Oxford Univ. Press, '68).

SCHULMAN, IRA, *flute, tenor saxophone, clarinet;* also *piccolo, alto flute, bass clarinet, saxophones;* b. Newark, N.J., 1/12/26. Stud. mus. at Senn H.S., Chicago, '41-5; Northwestern U.; Midwestern Conserv. of Mus., '45-7; clarinet w. Buck Wells, Jerome Stowell; saxophone w. Santy Runyon; flute at Northwestern. In h.s. pl. w. L. Konitz, Bill Russo, then w. bands of Jimmy Dale, Jay Burkhart and Russo. Also worked w. legendary drummer Ike Day in Chicago. Moved to Cal., '59, pl. w. Onzy Matthews. Joined orig. Don Ellis orch. in '64, staying with it for four years, then w. Dave Mackay-Vicky Hamilton for two years. In '70s, pl. in LA grammar and high schools, colls., as well as concerts for the City Parks and Mayor's Bureau of Mus. w. Baroque Jazz Ensemble. The format is a history of Amer. jazz incorporated into a program of baroque classic jazz and includes works of Bach, Mozart, Debussy, Ellington, Parker, Monk, Clifford Brown. Schulman has also worked and rec. w. T. Vig, and has been active as a teacher of woodwinds since coll. Infls: L. Young, D. Reinhardt, Basie, Billie Holiday, Ch. Parker, Fats Waller, T. Monk, B. Powell, Sid Catlett, M. Roach, Bach, Mozart, Segovia. Fests: Monterey, '66-8; Newport, '67-8; Cannes, '68, all w. Ellis.

LPs: w. Ellis, *Electric Bath; Shock Treatment* (Col.) *Live in 3⅔/4 Time* (Pac. Jazz); w. Mackay-Hamilton, *Rainbow* (Impulse).

SCOTT, RONNIE,* *tenor saxophone, leader;* b. London, England, 1/28/27. Gained early exp. w. Ted Heath, Cab Kaye, J. Parnell. Formed first band '53. Since '59 proprietor of Ronnie Scott's Club, presenting visiting Amer. artists, among whom have been the big bands of B. Rich, T. Jones-Mel Lewis, W. Herman, S. Kenton, as well as soloists S. Getz, O. Peterson, T. Monk, R.R. Kirk et al. Scott cont. to pl. w. his own trio, app. at his own club, as well as making frequent tours of Europe, incl. Poland and Hungary. From early '60s member of Clarke-Boland big band, app. on all its LPs.

In '74 the trio toured Australia, followed by engagements in NYC, incl. Carnegie Hall; their app. in Rochester, N.Y. was televised by ABC-TV. Scott has been seen on English TV constantly since the '60s; many shows feat. local and Amer. jazzmen have been taped for TV and radio from the club.

Though now principally identified with the club, Scott has made a substantial contribution as one of England's foremost jazz soloists, and has remained active in this capacity.

LP: *Scott at Ronnie's* (RCA).

SCOTT, SHIRLEY,* *organ;* b. Philadelphia, Pa., 3/14/34. Toured and rec. w. husband S. Turrentine until '71 when they separated musically and matrimonially. Continued to tour with own group; new edition formed in '74 feat. saxophonist Harold Vick. Frequent apps. on local NY and Phila. TV shows with her trio. NJF-NY, w. Vick amd Geo. Coleman, '74. Comps: *What Makes Harold Sing?; Big George; Do You Know A Good Thing When You See One?; You Can't Mess Around With Love.* LPs: *One For Me* (Strata-East); *Lean On Me* (Chess); others w. own trio (Impulse); w. Turrentine (Pres.); *Cookbook* w. Lockjaw Davis (Pres.).

SCOTT, THOMAS WRIGHT (TOM), *tenor saxophone;* also *saxes, flutes, miscellaneous woodwinds, composer;* b. Los Angeles, Cal., 5/19/48. Mother, the late Margery Wright, was a pianist. Gained early experience observing his father, Nathan, a noted TV and motion picture composer *(Dragnet; My Three Sons),* working in the studios. First interested in folk music, then in big bands, mainly Goodman and Shaw. Played clarinet in high school, and during that time wrote score for a high school film. Self-taught as composer-arranger.

In '65 his Neoteric Trio won the combo division in the Teenage Battle of the Bands at the Hollywood Bowl. Also, while still in his teens, he learned all the saxophones and flutes, played with Don Ellis and Oliver Nelson bands, Roger Kellaway and Howard Roberts groups, and in orchestras on TV shows such as *Ironsides* and *Good Morning World.* At 19 he recorded his first LP as a leader, *The Hon-*

eysuckle Breeze. This included one of his first and best known compositions, *Blues for Hari*. He was barely out of his teens when he followed his father into the TV studios as a writer, his credits including a Burt Reynolds show, *Streets of San Francisco; Cannon; Baretta*. Movie scores for *Conquest of the Planet of the Apes; Uptown Saturday Night*. During the '70s he became closely associated with a group of gifted and protean Hollywood musicians, among them Kellaway, John Guerin, Chuck Domanico, Roberts, Max Bennett, Victor Feldman. His gigs, night club work and concerts with musicians of this caliber led to the formation of his own group, the L.A. Express. While heading this combo, he was leading a triple life as studio musician and composer, jazzman in night clubs, and concert artist on tour with singer Joni Mitchell. His music represents a synthesis of innumerable elements: the John Coltrane influence, French and German classical impressionism, rock artists such as the Beatles and the Mothers of Invention, soul stars Aretha Franklin and Ray Charles, and Indian music reflecting his year of studies with Hari Har Rao. Infl: G. Mulligan, Coltrane, C. Adderley, C. Parker, P. Woods, George Coleman, King Curtis.

By '75 Scott had become one of the most popular and commercially successful young musicians of his generation, appealing to the pop and rock audience as well as maintaining certain jazz elements in his music. TV: *Midnite Special*, '75. Fest: MJF, '68; Montreux, '70; *Onda Nueva*, (Caracas); NJF-NY, '73. Awards: DB Critics, TDWR, '70; *Jazz & Pop* '70; NARAS MVP '73-4; Grammy '74.

Comps: *Blues for Hari; King Cobra; Refried; Love Poem; Liberation; Malibu; Visions off the Highway; Mantra; Boss Walk; Lookin' Out For Number Seven; Head Start; Freaky Zeke; Rural Still Life; With Respect to Coltrane; Freak In; Court & Spark; Miles of Aisles*.

LPs: *Tom Cat; Tom Scott & The L.A. Express* (Ode); *Great Scott* (A & M); *Tom Scott in L.A.; Hair to Jazz* (Fl. Dutchman); *Rural Still Life; The Honeysuckle Breeze* (Impulse); w. Mitchell, *Court & Spark; For The Roses; Miles of Aisles* (Elektra-Asylum); w. G. Mulligan, *Age of Steam* (A & M); w. Pat Williams, *Threshold* (Cap.); w. Carole King, *Jazzman* (Ode); w. O. Nelson, *Live in Los Angeles* (Imp.).

SCOTT, TONY,* *clarinet, baritone sax, composer;* also *piano;* b. Morristown, N.J., 6/17/21. This world traveler spent the first half of the '60s in the Far East, returning to NYC in '65. Pl. w. own gp. at Dom, Half Note. Concert of Indian-influenced jazz, w. Collin Walcott on sitar and tabla, for Museum of Modern Art's *Jazz in the Garden* series, '67. Living in Italy in '70s, working in Rome w. the gp. led by pianist Romano Mussolini. Toured US w. Mussolini on circuit of Italian-American clubs, '72. LP: *52nd Street, Vol. 1* (Onyx).

SCOTT-HERON, GIL, *singer, lyricist, poet, writer;* b. Tennessee, ca. 1948. After a childhood in rural Tennessee was raised in the Chelsea section of Manhattan. Sang in high school R&B gp. At 19 wrote a novel, *The Vulture;* two yrs. later a second novel, *The Nigger Factory,* was published. He also wrote a book of poetry, *Small Talk at 125th and Lenox*. At Lincoln U. in Pennsylvania '69 met Brian Jackson. Influenced by listening to Imamu Baraka (Leroi Jones) they began, according to Scott-Heron, "with some simple premises that related to the traditional African delivery of poetry, through voice and conga. It seemed practical within a system where very few of our people can read with the type of interpretive perception that's necessary to deal with poetry."

In the '70s he and Jackson performed w. their nine-piece unit called Midnight. Sheila Weller, in a *Rolling Stone* piece, described the material in Scott-Heron's albums as "original poems and songs which speak with extraordinary insight, anger and tenderness of the human condition, political deceit, the black experience, cultural roots and rape. Verbalizing the spirit and message of the new black music in a more widely accesible framework, he can be placed—on the pop/jazz continuum—somewhere between Leon Thomas and Donny Hathaway. But his statements—often delivered as strong, exhortative oral poetry—cut much deeper. And the eloquent literacy of his melodic songs make him far more than a jazz balladeer."

Comp: *The Bottle; H₂figate Blues; The Revolution Will Not Be Televised; Ain't No New Thing; Winter in America; No Knock; Lady Day and Coltrane; The King Alfred Plan*. LPs: *The First Minute of a New Day; From South Africa to South Carolina* (Arista); *Small Talk at 125th and Lenox; Pieces of a Man; The Revolution Will Not Be Televised* (Fly. Dutch.); *Winter in America* (Strata-East).

SEAMAN, PHILLIP WILLIAM (PHIL),* *drums;* b. Burton-on-Trent, Staffordshire, England, 8/28/26. The outstanding British drummer, who had rec. w. Dizzy Reece, Tubby Hayes, J. Deuchar, Ronnie Scott and Joe Harriott among others, died 10/13/72 in Lambeth, London, England.

SEBESKY, DONALD J. (DON),* *composer;* also *trombone, piano;* b. Perth Amboy, N.J., 12/10/37. First recognized as a writer in the '60s for the M. Ferguson band, in which he also pl. trombone. He gave up playing to concentrate on arr.-cond. With Verve he recorded as a leader and wrote for W. Montgomery, Astrud Gilberto, many others. He has also arr. material for B. Rich, Peggy Lee, D. Warwicke, R. Flack, S. Stitt, but scored his greatest artistic and commercial successes with a series of albums written for various artists on the A & M and CTI labels. By drawing on both his jazz and classical knowledge, Sebesky has placed these featured artists in orchestral settings that reflect many hues and timbres, thereby making their music readily accessible to a wider ranging audience. Film score: *The People Next Door;* TV score: *F. Scott Fitzgerald And The Last of the Belles*. Publ: *The Contemporary Arranger* (Alfred Music, 75 Channel Dr., Pt. Washington, N.Y. 11050).

LPs: *Rape of El Morro; Giant Box* (CTI); *Jazz-Rock Syndrome; Distant Galaxy* (Verve); for Montgomery, *California Dreamin'* (Verve); *A Day In The Life; Down Here on The Ground; Road Song* (A & M); for H. Laws, *Morning Star; Rite of Spring;* for F. Hubbard *First Light; Sky Dive;* for Jackie & Roy, *Time And Love;* others for G. Benson, P. Desmond (A & M, CTI); Chet Baker, Milt Jackson (CTI).

SEIFERT, ZBIGNIEW, *violin;* also *alto sax;* b. Cracow, Poland, 6/6/46. Studied violin at Chopin Sch. of Mus. in Cracow; grad. from Cracow Higher Sch. of Mus., '70. At Chopin Sch. he had also stud. saxophone w. Alojzy Thomys. Formed own quartet '65. It won Best Modern

Combo at Wroclaw Jazz on Oder Fest '69 and repeated at Nagykoros, Hungary in the same year. Seifert also won top soloist award. At that time he was Coltrane-oriented saxophonist. After pl. Polish Jazz Jamboree he joined Tomasz Stanko gp. Pl. at Berlin Jazztage; Jazz Jamboree, '70; West Berlin Free Music Workshop; Altena Int. Jazz Meeting, etc. Member of Polish Radio Jazz Studio Orch. from '70. With Stanko began to play violin, gradually featuring it more than the saxophone. Pl. w. Bosko Petrovic at Ljubljana JF '71; rec. for Czech label w. Jiri Stivin, Barre Philips, '72. Beginning in '73 app. at many Euro. fests. w. Hans Koller, and as soloist. Then pl. w. Joachim Kuhn. Wrote 25-minute concerto for violin, orchestra and jazz gp., commissioned by Radio Hamburg. *Jazz Forum* described him as "a violinist (who) endeavors to get beyond the sonorous material imposed by the conventional manual capabilities of the instrument." LPs: *Varioussperes;* rec. in Holland; w. Stanko, *Music for K; Jazz Message From Poland; Purple Sun* (Muza); w. Stivin, *Petran Do Cepice* (Supraphon); w. Koller, *Kunstkopfindianer;* w. Kuhn, *Chinemascope;* w. Volker Kriegel, *Lift* (MPS).

SELDEN, FRED LAURENCE, *alto saxophone;* also *soprano, tenor, baritone saxes, sopranino, piccolo, flutes, clarinets.* b. Los Angeles, Cal., 1/22/45. BA in mus. from UCLA, '66; Stud. comp., arr. w. Shorty Rogers, '61-6; saxophone w. B. Shank et al; film scoring w. L. Schifrin, Earle Hagen. Pl. lead alto w. Don Ellis orch. '69-74, and w. H. Mancini on *Mancini Generation* TV show. Jobs around LA w. L. Bellson, B. Holman and own sextet. Comps: *The Magic Bus Ate My Donut; Spirit Lady; Euphoric Acid; Love for Rent; Tyme Cube.* Publs: *Magic Flute Solos; Far Out Flute Solos* (Chas. Hansen Music, 1860 Broadway, New York, N.Y. 10023); *Lennon & McCartney/Flute, Rock & Jazz Style; Lennon & McCartney/Eb, Bb, C Combo Books* (Chappell Music Co., 810 7th Ave., New York 10019).

LPs: w. Ellis, *Tears of Joy; Don Ellis at Fillmore; Connection; The New Don Ellis Band Goes Underground* (Col.); *Soaring* (MPS).

SENENSKY, BERNARD MELVYN (BERNIE), *piano, composer;* also *organ, synthesizer, keyboards,* b. Winnipeg, Manitoba, Canada, 12/31/44. Stud. piano priv. w. Clara Perlman from age nine to 16; then w. jazz pianist Bob Erlendson. Accompanied visiting players at Bourbon Street and The Colonial in Toronto, incl. Joe Williams, A. Farmer, Z. Sims, P. Woods, B. DeFranco, S. Stitt, etc. in mid-'70s. Leads own trio; also active in studio work. Visited Israel, Oct. '73, and pl. w. Platina Jazz Group for troops. Infl: K. Jarrett, M. Tyner, B. Evans, C. Corea, Coltrane. TV: guest app. on Oscar Peterson Presents, CTV '74.

Comps: *Poochie; Beloved Gift; New Life Blues; Ronnie; B.B.; Little Waltz for a Little Boy; Reunion; Catching Up; Capricorn Dance; Up N' Down; Another Gift; Silvertrane.* LPs: *Beloved Gift;* w. Fred Stone; Herbie Spanier (RCI).

SETE, BOLA (Djalma de Andrada),* *guitar, lutar, composer;* b. Rio de Janiero, Brazil, 7/16/28. Moved to U.S. '60; pl. w. D. Gillespie, '62; own group and w. Vince Guaraldi trio from '63. After leading own trio through '69, Sete retired, but was active again in '71, leading a quintet. During next few years he concentrated mainly on playing solo guitar and lutar, an instrument of his own design, at coll. concerts. TV: *The Jazz Show,* KNBC, LA. One of the most innovative and eclectic guitarists in jazz history, Sete was insp. as much by Reinhardt, Geo. Van Eps and Andres Segovia as by C. Christian, B. Kessel and Tal Farlow. Wrote orig. music for film *The Monster Buoy,* which won the International Independent Film Makers Award in '66.

LPs: *Ocean,* solo guitar (Takoma); *Going to Rio* (Col.).

SEVERINSEN, CARL H. (DOC),* *trumpet; leader;* b. Arlington, Ore., 7/7/27. A member and assistant conductor of the orch. on the *Tonight* show, which he joined Oct. 1, 1962, Severinsen worked under the leadership of Skitch Henderson for four years, Milton DeLugg for one year, before taking over direction himself 10/9/67.

Following a farewell concert at Philharmonic Hall, NYC, Apr. '72, Severinsen moved with Johnny Carson and the *Tonight* show to the NBC-TV studios in Burbank, Cal., starting from 5/1/72. A few key sidemen came with him from NYC but the West Coast band consisted mostly of local musicians. Though not feat. extensively on the show, the rotating personnel usually included some or all of the following: Snooky Young, Conte Candoli, John Audino, trumpets; Lew Tabackin, Ernie Watts, Pete Christlieb, Dick Spencer, saxophones; Ross Tompkins, piano; John B. Williams, bass; Ed Shaughnessy, Louie Bellson or Colin Bailey, drums.

Severinsen continued to app. frequently as a brass clinician, pl. as soloist with various symph. orchs., and worked many weekends throughout the U.S. as leader of his own organization, The Now Generation Brass, which incl. some members of the *Tonight* show orch. He occasionally made other TV apps. incl. host of Timex jazz spec. for NBC.

Awards: First place as bandleader and trumpeter in *Playboy* magazine poll. LPs: *Brass Roots; Rhapsody For Now* (RCA); *Fever* (Command); *I Feel Good* (Juno); *16 Great Performances* (ABC).

SHANK, CLIFFORD EVERETT JR. (BUD),* *alto, baritone saxophones, flute, composer;* b. Dayton, Ohio, 5/27/26. Still an important figure on the West Coast jazz scene, during the late '60s and early '70s, Shank confined himself mainly to freelance movie and TV studies, but making apps. at local LA clubs such as Donte's every two or three months with a jazz quintet. He also participated in many coll. concerts and clinics throughout the U.S. In Apr. '74 he helped found the L.A. Four with drummer Shelly Manne, bassist Ray Brown and guitarist Laurindo Almeida. This group made two visits to Mexico, one to Australia and New Zealand, two to Canada, and played many club and concert dates on the West Coast.

Shank has composed countless jingles and TV spots and was heard in solo spots in the movies *The Thomas Crown Affair; Assault on a Queen; Sandpiper; Charley; Summer of '42.* App. at Concord JF w. L.A. Four, '74-5.

LPs: *Michelle; California Dreaming; Bud Shank & The Sax Section; Let It Be* (Wor. Pac.); w. L.A. Four (Concord).

SHARROCK, LINDA (Linda Chambers), *singer;* b. Phila., Pa., 4/3/49. While an art student in coll. in Phila. heard Coltrane's music and Sonny Sharrock while he was pl. at Showboat in Phila. in '68 w. Byard Lancaster. She already knew and loved modern classical music. Moved to NYC to attend the Arts Students League but instead studied theory w. Giuseppi Logan and started singing. She also learned from Sharrock w. whom she toured nationally in Herbie Mann's gp., '69-70. Worked w. Sanders on east coast, '70-1. From '73 the Sharrocks have app. w. their own gp. in Europe and US. In a review of *Paradise,* Lars Gabel wrote: "Her voice colorings are endowed with the warmth and feeling that were absent on her earlier albums . . . and even though there are traces now and then of undigested influences from such diverse sources as Yoko Ono and classical coloratura singing . . . *Paradise* indicates that Linda Sharrock may be one of our more controlled radical vocalists."

Infl: Coltrane, Sanders, Sharrock, Albert Ayler. Fest: Antibes Jazz-Pop Fest., '71. Co-composed music for *Another Place* (see Sonny Sharrock). LPs: *Paradise* (Atco); *Black Woman* (Vortex); w. S. Sharrock; *Monkey, Pokie, Boo* (Byg).

SHARROCK, SONNY, *guitar, composer;* also *pedal steel guitar, banjo;* b. Ossining, N.Y., 8/27/40. Singing in rock and roll gp., '54-9. Began listening to jazz in '58. Got first guitar and started playing at age 20. Studied for a yr. w. Bob Evans. Attended Berklee, Sept. '61-Feb. '62. Studied comp. w. Rheet Taylor, NYC, Feb.-May '63. Moved to NYC '65. Pl. w. Olatunji, Oct. '65; Byard Lancaster, June '66-Sept. '67; Pharoah Sanders, Sept. '66-Sept. '67; Sunny Murray, Feb. '67; Herbie Mann, Oct. '67-April '73, incl. world tours. Pl. w. Don Cherry, Berlin, '68; Miles Davis, summer '69; Cannonball Adderley, Jan.-March '70. From '73 he and his wife, Linda, have toured in the US and Europe w. their own gp. Sharrock, whose infl. include Coltrane, Blind Willie Johnson, Little Richard, Tchaikovsky, Ornette Coleman, Fats Domino, Linda Sharrock and Miles Davis, says he "became the first guitarist to play free jazz. (No changes, no time.) Can notate but not read music. Do not know any standard tunes or any other musicians' licks."

Joachim Berendt called him "the free-jazz guitarist *par excellence,*" who "plays clusters, sounding all the notes imaginable simultaneously (as do modern concert pianists) with the ecstatic vitality of harmonically unchained free jazz."

Fest: NJF-NY; NJF; Berlin; NY Musicians; many others US and Euro. Co-composed music and pl. for *Another Place,* a short film by Sadat Pakay based on the James Baldwin work. Other comp: *Black Woman; Peanut; 1953 Blue Boogie Children; Gary's Step.* Won DB Critics poll, TDWR, '70; *Jazz Podium* (Germany); *Jazz* (Holland) polls. LPs: *Paradise* w. Linda Sharrock (Atco); *Black Woman* (Vortex); w. M. Davis, *Jack Johnson,* (Col.); P. Sanders, *Tauhid* (Imp.); W. Shorter, *Super Nova* (BN); many w. Mann (Atl.; Embryo).

SHAUGHNESSY, EDWIN THOMAS (ED),* *drums;* also *tabla, composer;* b. Jersey City, N.J., 1/29/29. From '48 was active with many jazz groups as well as studio orchs. Joined *Tonight* TV show orch. '64; though this was still his principal job in '75, in that year he also introduced his own 17 piece band, Ed Shaughnessy Energy Force. Pl. Maryland JF w. R. Eldridge, C. Hawkins, '69. From '66, stud. Indian rhythms w. Alla Rakha, Ravi Shankar's tabla player, also continuously busy as a drum clinician at colleges and high schools.

Comps: *Nigerian Walk; Blues Detambour.* Publs: *The New Time Signatures in Jazz Drumming* (Belwin Co., 250 Maple Ave., Rockville Centre, N.Y. 11570) *Big Band Drummers Reading Guide* (Energy Force Pub., 5414 Shirley Ave., Tarzana, Ca. 91356). LPs: *Rhapsody For Now,* w. Severinsen (RCA); *Afro American Sketches,* w. O. Nelson (Prestige); *Broadway Basie's Way* and others w. Basie (Command); *Ravi Shankar and Friends* (Dark Horse).

SHAVERS, CHARLES JAMES (CHARLIE),* *trumpet, singer, composer;* b. New York City, 8/3/17. Famous as a member of John Kirby sextet, '37-44, Shavers gained widespread recognition during more than a decade off and on w. T. Dorsey orch. He was later heard w. the Dorsey "ghost" band led by Sam Donahue, and worked on several occasions w. B. Goodman. He toured Europe on his own in '69, '70, made a guest app. w. Budd Johnson's JPJ Quartet in May '71, but was hospitalized soon afterward and died 7/8/71 (two days after Louis Armstrong's death) in the Bronx, N.Y.

Shavers was one of the most vital and versatile trumpeters who came to prominence during the swing era. As a composer-arranger, he was the key figure in the Kirby band, which was the most brilliant and subtle small group of its day. Shavers' most famous comp. was *Undecided.*

LPs: *The Last Session* (B&B); C. Ventura; C. Hawkins (Trip); Dorsey (RCA); own LPs, deleted, incl. *The Complete Charlie Shavers* (Bethlehem); *Excitement Unlimited* (Cap.); *Charlie Shavers at Le Crazy Horse Saloon In Paris* (Everest).

SHAW, ARVELL,* *bass, singer;* b. St. Louis, Mo., 9/15/23. Renewed association w. Louis Armstrong in '64 and remained with the band through a tour of Eastern Europe, '66. S. Amer. tour w. B. Goodman, '67. Own trio at Shepheard's, NYC, and for Hilton hotel chain in U. S. and Puerto Rico. Rejoined Armstrong for Waldorf-Astoria engagement, '70. Gigs w. Dorothy Donegan, Teddy Wilson, '72-4; own sextet for school and coll. perf.-lecture program in Nassau and Suffolk counties on L.I. and upstate N.Y. communities, funded by N.Y. State Council on the Arts and the National Endowment for the Arts. Own quartet, '75. Films: *New Orleans; High Society; The Glenn Miller Story; Je Suis de la Revue,* w. Fernandel. TV: *Timex Swing Festival,* WNBC, '72; Fests: Fest. of the Arts, Sullivan County, N.Y. w. own sextet; NJF-NY, '73-4; Nice, '74. Comp: *They Are People.*

LPs: *Nice Festival All Stars;* Claude Hopkins (Black & Blue); *Jazz Giants;* Herb Hall (Sackville); also see L. Armstrong.

SHAW, MARLENA (Burgess), *singer, songwriter;* b. New Rochelle, N.Y., 9/22/44. An uncle taught her chords at the piano, but her musical education was mainly informal. First pro. job with Howard McGhee in New Bedford, Mass., '64. Spent a year in Catskill Mtns. resorts; coll. concerts, mostly in the South, also concert dates w. M. McPartland et al. Began rec. for Cadet, '66. After working at a series of Playboy clubs, she joined the Basie orch., staying off and on from '68-70, mainly for a European tour, '68, and residencies in Las Vegas hotels, after which she moved to LV.

Fests: Onda Nueva, Caracas, Venezuela; also Montreux, '73. Infls: Ray Charles, Stevie Wonder, Michel Legrand et al. Comps: *Woman of the Ghetto; Street Walkin' Woman; You*. Shaw's early albums, and her work with Basie (she did not record with the band) revealed her as a potentially important jazz singer, but on signing with Blue Note Records in '72, she diversified her repertoire and style to aim at the pop and r & b market.

LPs: *Who Is This Bitch, Anyway?; From The Depths of My Soul; Marlena* (BN); *Out of Different Bags; Spice of Life* (Cadet).

SHAW, WOODY, *trumpet;* b. Laurinburg, N.C., 12/24/44. Raised in Newark, N.J. where his father was a member of a gospel gp., the Jubilee Singers. Took up trumpet in sixth grade, '55. Pl. w. school bands; then gigged w. Larry Young, Tyrone Washington. In early '60s pl. w. Eric Dolphy. Then went to Paris where he pl. w. Kenny Clarke; Bud Powell. In '64 he and Larry Young worked at the Chat Qui Peche; also in Belgium, Germany. Replaced Carmell Jones in Horace Silver gp. in '65. Jamming w. Hank Mobley, Donald Byrd, Jackie McLean, '66-7 which was also a period of much practicing. Pl. w. McCoy Tyner from, '68 off and on into '70s; Gil Evans, '72; Art Blakey, '73; then own gps. for clubs, recs.; featured w. Junior Cook-Louis Hayes Quintet '76. Originally infl. by Gillespie, M. Davis, Clifford Brown; later, by Booker Little, Freddie Hubbard, Donald Byrd, Lee Morgan. Many observers noted his resemblance to Hubbard but he has become more personal in the mid-'70s, as he moved away from purely chordal playing and into a controlled freedom. In October '72 he said: "After two choruses I get tired of playing the changes, and I think that's the difference in today's music and say 10 years ago, or maybe a little earlier than that. I like to superimpose harmonically. I like to play it deliberately in another key and resolve it."

Tied with Kenny Wheeler for trumpet, TDWR, in DB Critics poll, '70.

Comp: *Song of Songs; The Goat and the Archer; Love: For the One You Can't Have; The Awakening*. LPs: *Blackstone Legacy; Song of Songs* (Contemp.); *The Moontrane* (Muse); w. Silver, *Song For My Father;* w. McLean, *'Bout Soul; Demon's Dance* (BN); w. Blakey, *Buhaina; Anthenagin; Child's Dance* (Prest.); w. Joe Henderson (Mile.); w. Buster Williams, *Pinnacle* (Muse); w. C. Corea, *Inner Space* (Atl.).

SHEARER, RICHARD BRUCE (DICK), *trombone;* b. Indianapolis, Ind., 9/21/40. Stud. at LACC, '60; Bob Edmondson, Dick Nash and other priv. teachers. Pl. w. Claude Gordon, '59; Perez Prado, '60; Si Zentner, '60-1; Billy May, '61; then with various show groups. Joined Tex Beneke, '64; Righteous Bros., '64-5; Louie Bellson, '65. From '65 Shearer began a long assoc. w. S. Kenton orch. As first trombonist and asst. dir., he also led the band when Kenton was sidelined by illness. Favs: Bill Harris, Bob Burgess, Don Lusher, Dick Nash.

Fest: Monterey, '71; Newport, '71, '73. LPs: *Stan Kenton Live at Redlands; Live at Brigham Young; Live At Butler; Stan Kenton Plays Chicago, Fire Fury Fun,* and many others w. Kenton (Creative World).

SHEARING, GEORGE ALBERT,* *piano, composer;* b. London, England, 8/13/19. Continued to work mainly with the quintet instrumentation he had inaugurated in '49. In addition, occasionally pl. jobs in trio context, and in '74 toured with *Big Band Cavalcade* show backed by orchestral arrangements. In '67, and annually since '73, gave week-long jazz workshops at Chautauqua, N.Y., conducting piano and jazz ensemble seminars.

Shearing has pl. with several of the major symph. orchs., incl. those in Houston, Atlanta, Detroit, SF, Milwaukee, Baltimore, Cleveland, usually combining a classical concerto with a program featuring the quintet backed by the orch.

Traveling up to 10 months annually, Shearing played clubs and hotels throughout the U.S. and in Europe and Japan. Many of his dates were community concerts. In June of '74 he went to Germany to record three new albums for the MPS label. Previously, after a long association with Capitol, he had been recording for his own company, Sheba.

In May '75, Shearing received an honorary Ph.D. in music from Westminster Coll., Salt Lake City, Utah. Comps: *Lullaby of Birdland* and about 100 others; music for Emmy award winning TV special about the Foundation for the Junior Blind. Publs: *Shades of Shearing* (Bayes Music, Box 2120 N. Hollywood, Ca. 91602). LPs: *The Best Of* (Cap.); *Light, Airy & Swinging; The Way We Are; Continental Experience* (MPS); *As Requested; Heart & Soul* w. Joe Williams and several others (Sheba Records, Box 2120, N. Hollywood Ca. 91602).

SHELDON, JACK,* *trumpet, singer;* b. Jacksonville, Fla., 11/30/31. Still doubling as musician and TV actor, sometimes seen in commercials, Sheldon was best known during the '70s as a member of Mort Lindsey's orch. on the nightly Merv Griffin TV show, in which he was frequently seen as comedian, singer and soloist. During the summer of '74 he led his own small group for an extended engagement in Monterey, Cal. He continued also to make occasional apps. at Donte's and other LA clubs.

SHEPP, ARCHIE,* *tenor, soprano saxes, composer, leader educator;* b. Ft. Lauderdale, Fla., 5/24/37. First important work w. Cecil Taylor in '60. He then became involved w. Don Cherry and John Tchicai in the New York Contemporary Five in US and Europe. From mid-'60s has led own groups. His playing attitudes in that period included anarchic, shrieking protest music; tender, Ben Websterized Ellington ballads; marching band segments inserted among his most stormy passages; and parodies of popular songs such as *The Shadow of Your Smile*.

In '69 he became associated with Cal Massey, playing his compositions and in '72, a musical on which they had collaborated, *Lady Day: A Musical Tragedy,* was performed at the Brooklyn Academy of Music. While in Paris in '69 Shepp played with other musicians ordinarily associated with the bop movement, Hank Mobley and Philly Joe Jones. He was later heard playing *Hankerin'*, an early-'50s Mobley piece and it seemed that this eclectic, with his fingers in drama, poetry and sociology, was becoming even more diversified in his musical outlook. Barry McRae noted his "attempt to introduce an element of Africanism into his work

. . . with the *Magic of Ju Ju* . . . His concern with a return to Africa has hardly helped, and he has also worked in the presence of less distinguished talents such as Burton Greene and Noah Howard. His superb playing on titles like *Marmarose* and *Huru* (Byg) confirms his undiminished talent, but there is again the suspicion that Shepp—the traditionalist—is trying to prove he is not.''

In the '70s Shepp embarked on a new aspect of his career, that of college professor, teaching at the Univ. of Buffalo and, then, at Univ. of Massachusetts in Amherst, Mass., where he was in residence in '75.

His mid-'70s group, like his mid-'60s edition had a trombone in the front line but Charles Majid Greenlee (known as Harneefan Mageed w. Dizzy Gillespie in the '40s) was a different sound and style from either Roswell Rudd or Grachan Moncur. But Gordon Kopulous still characterized Shepp's style with ''the guttural, raspy vocal tone; yelps in the middle of a scale; melodic all the time.''

Shepp makes no distinction between folk and art music. ''I don't,'' he says, ''because I don't believe in the word 'art.' It's, to me, not functional, it's passive. It's bourgeois in the sense that art develops at a point when people have leisure time . . . So art music is something that I don't really subscribe to. I think essentially the same way the music is played and enjoyed in the black community.''

Yet Shepp is typical of the wave of musicians who emerged in the '60s who essentially do not perform for ''inner city'' audiences. His brand of emotional-cerebral music has had far more impact on white intellectuals than on ghetto residents.

In addition to many European tours, he played in North Africa, '69. Many festival apps. incl. NJF; NJF-NY '72; NJF-NY '73 where he led his own group w. Grachan Moncur III and Dave Burrell; took part in the dedication of Louis Armstrong Stadium; and participated in the Radio City jam session.

Comps: *A Sea of Faces; I Know 'Bout the Life; New Africa; The Wedding; Mama Too Tight; Portrait of Robert Thompson; Rest Enough; Attica Blues; Call Me By My Rightful Name; Samba da Rua; It Is the Year of the Rabbit.* LPs: *A Sea of Faces* (Black Saint); *There's a Trumpet in My Soul* (Arista); *Attica Blues; Cry of My People; For Losers; In San Francisco; Kwanza; Magic of Ju Ju; Mama Too Tight; On This Night; Things Have Got to Change; Three For a Quarter; Way Ahead* (Imp.); *Live at the Donaueschingen Festival* (MPS); *Black Gypsy; Coral Rock* (Prest.); own gp. w. Philly Joe Jones (Fant.); w. Grachan Moncur III, *New Africa* (Byg).

SHEW, BOBBY (Robert Joratz), *trumpet;* also *fluegelhorn, slide, piccolo & pocket trumpets;* b. Albuquerque, N.M., 3/4/41. Self taught with the exception of a few lessons at age 13. Pl. in h.s. concert bands and All-State bands and orchs., but learned mre from casual dance jobs. Attended U. of N.M. for one year, majoring in commercial art, with some music classes. While in Army assigned to NORAD band, where he mixed with many professionals, receiving impetus toward a career in music. Attended S. Kenton clinics at Indiana U. under Johnny Richards, S. Donahue, John LaPorta, '59-60. Pl. w. T. Dorsey orch. under Donahue, '64-5; W. Herman, '65; Della Reese, also LV house bands, '65-6; B. Rich, Apr. '66-Jun. '67; LV hotels, '67-Jan. '68. He joined T. Gibbs big band, '68 on *Operation Entertainment,* ABC-TV, until Sept. '68, when he became lead trumpet for Robert Goulet, remaining until July '69.

Through Jan. '73 he occupied himself mainly with work in LV, but also toured as lead trumpet w. Tom Jones, P. Anka, '71. Moved to LA, Jan. '73 and has since been associated with the bands of L. Bellson, N. Hefti, D. Menza, Gibbs and Ed Shaughnessy's Energy Force. In '74 he also pl. with the quintets of B. Shank, A. Pepper. Busy studio musician, also active as priv. teacher, jazz clinician. Infls: Farmer, Gillespie, Don Fagerquist, C. Candoli, K. Dorham. Fests: French Lick with all star band from Kenton Clinics, '59; Antibes w. Herman, '65; Pacific Jazz, w. Rich, '67; Concord and Belvedere, w. Bellson, '74.

LPs: w. Bellson, *Louie Rides Again* (Pablo); w. Rich (Pac. Jazz); w. Herman (Col.); w. Toshiko-Lew Tabackin (RCA-Japan); *Symposium* w. Edith Hill and the Children of Selah (Peppered Snowfall).

SHIHAB, SAHIB (Edmund Gregory),* *baritone saxophone;* also *bass clarinet, flutes, alto, soprano saxophones, composer;* b. Savannah, Ga., 6/23/25. Spent more than a decade in Europe, playing frequently with Clarke-Boland band until 1972; taught music at Polytechnic High School in Copenhagen, '73. Returned to US late '73, settling in LA, where he led his own group in clubs and worked w. Quincy Jones orch. LPs with Clarke-Boland (BASF, Black Lion, Co., Atl.).

SHOEMAKE, CHARLES EDWARD (CHARLIE), *vibes;* also *piano;* b. Houston, Tex., 7/27/37. Piano major at SMU, Dallas for one year, mostly self-taught from age six. From '59-63 worked w. many local groups in LA area incl. Ch. Lloyd, A. Pepper, Lighthouse All Stars. In '63 began acc. singers, such as Sue Raney, Eddie Fisher et al. Took up vibraharp seriously in '65, working extensively in studios w. L. Schifrin, Q. Jones, N. Riddle, J. Mandel. In '67 he joined Geo. Shearing quintet, traveling throughout the U.S., until '73. In that year Shoemake opened his own teaching studio and from '73- made apps. at Donte's, Pilgrimage Theatre with own group and Tony Rizzi Five Guitars. Infls: Ch. Parker, Bud Powell, S. Rollins. Numerous fest. apps. w. Shearing.

LPs: w. Shearing, *Shearing Today; Fool on the Hill* (Cap.); *As Requested* (Sheba).

SHORT, ROBERT WALTRIP (BOBBY),* *singer, piano;* b. Danville, Ill., 9/15/26. Made his original reputation at the Blue Angel, NYC, the Haig in LA, and the Gala in Hollywood in late '40-early '50s;- then pl. engagements in London and Paris; NYC supper clubs. From '68 the Carlyle Hotel in NYC has been his main base of operation w. his own trio. Many apps. at NJF incl. NJF-NY '72 on Ellington program. Whitney Balliett calls him ''one of the last examples (and indubitably the best) of the cafe singer or the supper-club singer or 'troubadour,''' and describes his piano style as having a ''a loose, enthusiastic resemblance to Art Tatum's—it is florid and arpeggioed and slurred . . .''

LPs: *K-R-A-Z-Y for Gershwin; Live at Cafe Carlyle; Mad About Noel Coward; The Mad Twenties; Very Best* (Atl.); w.

Mabel Mercer, *At Town Hall; Second Town Hall Concert* (Atl.).

SHORTER, WAYNE,* *soprano, tenor saxophones, composer;* b. Newark, N.J., 8/25/33. Primarily known as a tenor saxophonist while with Art Blakey ('59-63), and during his early years with Miles Davis, whom he joined in '64, Shorter gradually transferred the emphasis of his performance to soprano sax. During his years with Davis, he further consolidated his reputation as a composer of highly sophisticated contemporary works. Notable among them were *E.S.P.; Iris; Orbits; Footprints; Dolores; Limbo; Vonetta; Prince of Darkness; Masqualero; Nefertiti; Fall; Pinocchio; Paraphernalia; Sanctuary.*

In the spring of '70, Shorter left Davis. Later that year Joe Zawinul quit the Cannonball Adderley group, and together the two men organized Weather Report (see ZAWINUL, JOE). Shorter, however, continued what was in effect a dual career, recording from time to time albums under his own name that were less abstract and more tonal than his work with Weather Report, and often touched with a Latin-American influence. A typical example was *Native Dancer,* released in '75, in which the Brazilian singer and guitarist Milton Nascimento participated as composer and performer on several tracks.

An earlier album, recorded just before the formation of Weather Report, was *Odyssey of Iska,* in which it was observed that "To study the evolution of Wayne Shorter as an individualist in music, compositionally or improvisationally, is to follow in large measure the path pursued by jazz as a whole during the past five or six years. The jazz idiom as we have known it, once a central rhythmic and harmonic facet of Shorter's identity, now has become one of many elements that have reached far beyond the purlieus of any one pigeonholed music. To put it in more basic terms, jazz is no longer his sole bag; it is rather one of many tools in a larger and more capacious bag that is cosmic in its scope."

As a soprano saxophonist, Shorter found this instrument even more compatible to his highly individual style than tenor. The latter, however, remained a consummately expressive voice, capable both of understated beauty and of powerful energy bursts evoking the John Coltrane legacy.

Comps: aside from the above works recorded with Davis, Shorter wrote most or all of the music for the LPs under his own name. Among them are: *The All Seeing Eye; Genesis; Chaos; Face of the Deep; Mephistopheles; Down In The Depths; Powder Keg; Calloway Went That-A-Way; Peaches and Cream; Dead End; Black Diamond; Seeds of Sin; Scourin'; Pay As You Go; Second Genesis; Mr. Chairman; Tenderfoot; The Albatross; Super Nova; Swee-Pea; Water Babies; Capricorn; More Than Human; Adam's Apple; El Gaucho; Teru; Chief Crazy Horse; Diana; Ana Maria; Beauty and the Beast; Wind; Storm; Calm; Joy; Moto Grosso Feio; Montezuma; Antigua; Iska.*

With Weather Report he composed and recorded: *Mysterious Traveller; Blackthorn Rose; Scarlet Woman; Tears; Eurydice; The Moors; Surucucu; Non-Stop Home; Manolete; Freezing Fire; Lusitanos;* w. Zawinul, *Milky Way: Umbrellas.*

Fests: With Davis and/or Weather Report, Shorter has appeared in virtually every major jazz fest. around the world. Annual first place winner on soprano sax in DB polls since '69. Along with his music, Shorter has found time to show his literary and artistic talents as writer and painter.

LPs: *The All Seeing Eye; Super Nova; Adam's Apple; Odyssey of Iska; Moto Grosso Feio* (BN); *Wayne Shorter* (GNP Crescendo); *Second Genesis* (V.J.); *Native Dancer* (Col.); w. Davis, *E.S.P.; Miles Smiles; Nefertiti; Miles In The Sky; Filles De Kilimanjaro; The Sorcerer; In A Silent Way; Bitches Brew;* w. Weather Report, *Mysterious Traveller; I Sing The Body Electric; Sweetnighter; Weather Report* (Col.).

SILVER, HORACE WARD MARTIN TAVARES,* *piano, composer;* b. Norwalk, Conn., 9/2/28. From '56 led own instrumental quintet feat. trumpet, tenor sax, bass, drums and himself. From '69 he became increasingly interested in lyric writing. During the '70s many of his albums presented an expanded group with guitar and singers. Among them was a trilogy of albums under the generic title *The United States of Mind,* subdivided into Phase I, *That Healing Feeling;* Phase II, *Total Response;* Phase III, *All.* In evaluating this project, Silver observed: "We have endeavoured to write memorable melodies and words about the mind, body and soul . . . dedicated to that spiritual part of us that flows through the mind, body and soul, the real self, the spiritual self, which when acknowledged and allowed to operate through us, leads to health, happiness, love and peace." This philosophy was mirrored both in Silver's perennially attractive melodies and his words, which were sung by Andy Bey, Salome Bey, Gail Nelson, Jackie Verdell and Silver himself.

Silver continued to enjoy international popularity. In the fall of '68 he toured Europe and pl. at Ronnie Scott's club. To Italy and Finland, summer of '73, Brazil concert tour, Oct. '73; NJF, '73; European tour, Aug-Sep. '74, after which Silver took up residence in LA and retired temporarily, forming a new group in the summer of '75.

Among many awards, he received the keys to the city of his home town in '68. TV: numerous apps. in U.S., London and continent; hour-long music and talk show in Brazil, '73. In '75 Silver made his first album as leader of a 13 piece band, for which Wade Marcus collaborated with him effectively on the orchestrations. Among the new Silver works introduced on this LP were *Barbara; Dameron's Dance; Sophisticated Hippie* (a tribute to Duke Ellington); *Mysticism.* His earlier works incl. *Senor Blues; The Preacher; Doodlin'; Nica's Dream; Sister Sadie; Filthy McNasty; Strollin; Peace; Song For My Father; Opus De Funk; Home Cookin; Come On Home; The Tokyo Blues.*

LPs: *Song for my Father; The Cape Verdean Blues; You Gotta Take a Little Love; Serenade to a Soul Sister; The United States of Mind,* Phases I, II, II; *In Pursuit of the 27th Man; Silver 'N Brass* (BN).

SIMMONS, JOHN,* *bass;* b. Haskell, Okla., 1918. Although largely inactive in music since the early '60s, Simmons in '75 was still living in LA, contrary to rumors (some of which were printed) that he had died. Some of Simmons' early records, incl. those w. B. Holiday on Commodore, were reissued in the '70s.

SIMMONS, HUEY (SONNY),* *alto saxophone, composer;* also *English horn, heckelphone, tenor saxophone;* b. Sicily Island, La., 8/4/33. Insp. by Ch. Parker, Simmons became well known in avant garde circles through his partnership in the early '60s w. Prince Lasha. From mid-60s worked clubs throughout N.Y. and Cal. Family moved to Woodstock, N.Y., where he pl. concerts and clubs w. group feat. his wife, trumpeter Barbara Donald. Together they started the Woodstock Music Festival. Returned to Cal., '70; concerts in Bay Area; more gigs w. Lasha. TV in Sacramento; made movie in Woodstock, '69. Nairobi JF. w. B. Hutcherson and Lasha, '71. Comps: *City of David; Zarak's Symphony; Interplanetary Travelers; Dolphy's Days; Burning Spirits; Coltrane in Paradise; Seven Dances of Salome; Ruma Suma; Reincarnation; Back to the Apple; Things And Beings.*

Simmons, who in '75 wrote that he had been "spending a lot of time studying and writing some new music that has not been introduced to this planet," is one of the most forceful and convincing composers and soloists in his field, having developed beyond the original influences of Parker and Ornette Coleman.

LPs: *Staying On Watch; Music of the Spheres* (ESP); *Manhattan Egos* (Arhoolie); *Ruma Suma; Burning Spirits* (Contemporary); w. Lasha, *The Cry; Firebirds* (Contemporary); w. Elvin Jones, *Illuminations* (Impulse); w. Dolphy, *Iron Man* (Douglas); *Eric Dolphy Memorial Concert* (V.J.); w. Smiley Winters, *Les Oublies De Jazz Ensemble* (Touche).

SIMON, MAURICE,* *alto saxophone;* also *tenor, baritone saxophones, flute, clarinet;* b. Houston, Tex., 3/26/29. For many years divided his time between name bands, cabarets and groups backing singers. In '60s led combo in LV for Damita Jo, and LA for Milt Trenier, Micki Lynn. Pl. bari. sax. w. Ray Charles orch., '67. TV series, *Here's Lucy,* under direction of Marl Young, '69. In '70s pl. w. Roy Porter, Fats Domino, Hal Borne; in '74 joined D. Ellington orch. under direction of Mercer Ellington, pl. first tenor, then baritone and later alto. Fests: Monterey w. Jesse Price, '72.

LPs: w. M. Ellington (Fantasy).

SIMONE, NINA (Eunice Waymon),* *singer, piano, arranger;* b. Tryon, N.C., 2/21/33. Continued to tour, playing clubs, concerts and festivals into the '70s at the head of her own group. Appeared several times at NJF-NY, the last time in *An Evening with Nina Simone* '74. From that point she entered a self imposed hiatus. Ralph J. Gleason called her "a singer, an actress, a preacher and a religious symbol . . . her very presence inspires to achievement, to art, and ultimately to life itself."

LPs: *It is Finished; Here Come the Sun* (RCA); *Gifted and Black* (Canyon); reissues on Philips.

SIMPKINS, ANDREW (ANDY),* *bass;* b. Richmond, Ind., 4/29/32. Best known through association with pianist Gene Harris in the Three Sounds, from 1957. Moved to LA 1966; continued to tour w. Three Sounds until early '68, then free-lanced. Joined George Shearing 1968, touring extensively with him; to Germany for rec. sessions with him in '74. Between jobs w. Shearing, he also pl. on film sound track scores, worked w. Carmen McRae, Joe Williams, and gigged w. Clare Fischer, David Mackay and others. LPs w. Shearing (MPS-BASF, Sheba); Kenny Burrell (Fantasy).

SIMS, JOHN HALEY (ZOOT),* *tenor saxophone;* also *soprano, alto sax, clarinet;* b. Inglewood, Cal., 10/29/25. Joined Bobby Sherwood's band at 17, then put in a year w. B. Goodman, with whom he was reunited many times over the next 30 years. Famous as one of the "Four Brothers" sax section w. W. Herman, '47-9, and from '57 as intermittent partner in two tenor team w. Al Cohn, who had also been in the Herman band. In '67 Sims was feat. in N. Granz' JATP tour of U.S. and Europe. Working mostly as solo performer with local rhythm sections, he was seen often in NYC, LA, Toronto, Boston, Washington, Dick Gibson's annual jazz parties in Colorado, Ronnie Scott's Club in London.

In '72, at NJF-NY, Sims rejoined W. Herman for a concert at Philharmonic Hall. For six weeks during that year he again toured Europe w. Goodman, and in March '73 they toured Australia. During the summer of '74 Sims again played with Goodman for concerts throughout the U.S. Toured Scandinavia w. Cohn, fall '74; Norman Granz Euro. tour, '75. many apps. w. Bucky Pizzarelli at Soerabaja, NYC in '70s. Featured in "Salute to Zoot" concert at NYU Loeb Student Center, Dec. '75.

Though Lester Young was his early infl., Sims for many years has shown a totally distinctive sound and style, marked by a natural sense of swing, perfect structural concepts and a melodic creativity that seems equally intense in up tempo and ballad performances. In recent years, he has taken to doubling effectively on soprano sax. TV: B. Goodman special; O. Peterson shows in Canada. Fests: Newport, '72, '73, '74. Comps: *Red Door; Dark Cloud; Nirvana.*

Sims has made more than 40 LPs under his own name, among them *Body and Soul* w. A. Cohn (Muse); *First Recordings!* (Prestige); *At Ease* (Famous Door); *Otra Vez* w. J. Raney (Mainstream); *Waiting Game* (Impulse); *Zoot Sims Party* w. J. Rowles (Choice); *Nirvana* w. B. Pizzarelli (Groove Merchant); *Joe and Zoot* w. J. Venuti (Chiaroscuro); *Encounter* w. Pepper Adams (Prestige); *Zoot Sims and the Gershwin Brothers* (Pablo); LPs as sideman: *The Bosses* w. C. Basie, J. Turner (Pablo); *The You and Me That Used To Be* w. J. Rushing (RCA); *Transition* w. B. Rich-L. Hampton (Groove Merchant); w. Dave McKenna (Chiaroscuro); Phoebe Snow (Shelter); *Colo. Jazz Party* (MPS/BASF); *The Greatest Jazz Concert in the World* (Pablo).

SINATRA, FRANCIS ALBERT,* *singer;* b. Hoboken, N.J., 12/12/15. Sinatra continued his activities until '71, when he announced his retirement. He returned gradually, beginning with concert appearances in '73, and made a triumphantly successful tour in '74 acc. by Woody Herman. Late in '75 he starred in a series of apps. at the Uris Theatre in NYC, followed by a week in London, for both of which he headed a show that also feat. the Count Basie orch. and (in London) Sarah Vaughan.

TV: Special, *The Main Event.*

A book entitled *Sinatra: Twentieth Century Romantic,* by Arnold Shaw, was publ. in '68 by Holt, Rinehart and Winston.

LPs: Reprise; Capitol.

SINGER, HAROLD (HAL),* *tenor saxophone;* b. Tulsa, Okla., 10/8/19. Name band musician since the early '40s; Singer settled in Europe in '65. He pl. in the big bands of Johnny Dover and Slide Hampton; w. his own gp. in Paris clubs; and was seen at numerous fests in Poland, Hungary and throughout western Europe. Film: *The Only Game in Town* w. Kenny Clarke. TV and radio in many European countries. LPs: *Blues and News* (Futura); *Blue Stompin'* (Pathe Marconi); *Milt and Hal* (Black & Blue); *Paris Soul Food* (Poly.); *Soul of Africa* (Chant du Monde); w. Buck Clayton (Poly.); Milt Buckner; Eddie Vinson; T-Bone Walker; Johnny Letman (B&B); Kitty White (Barclay).

SINGLETON, ARTHUR JAMES (ZUTTY),* *drums;* b. Bunkie, La., 5/14/1898. The pioneer NO drummer, who played w. L. Armstrong in Chicago and NYC in the '20s, worked at Jimmy Ryan's, NYC, '60-6, and freelanced until a stroke rendered him inactive in '69. In '73 he received a Certificate of Appreciation from the City of New York; won Gene Krupa Award, '74, and in '75 was voted into the NARAS Hall of Fame for his participation in the Hot Five records made w. Armstrong in '28. Singleton died 7/14/75 in NYC.

LPs: w. Cozy Cole, Jo Jones (Jazz Odyssey); reissues w. Armstrong (Col.).

SIRONE (Norris Jones), *bass, composer;* also *trombone, drums, cello,* b. Atlanta, Ga., 9/28/40. Studied theory & comp. from ages five to seven w. Dr. Raymond Carver, band dir. at Clark Coll.; trombone from ages seven to 12 w. Ralph Mays; 12-17 w. Alfred Wyatt incl. concert mus.; bass w. Dr. Thomas Howard, '57-65. Worked w. Sam Cooke, '60; Jerry Butler, '61-2. Local Atlanta gigs w. cooperative band, The Group, which incl. George Adams, '57-61. Moved to NYC '65, pl. w. Noah Howard; Sunny Murray; Sonny Sharrock; Albert Ayler; Marion Brown; Archie Shepp; Dave Burrell; Pharoah Sanders; Gato Barbieri; Roswell Rudd; Cecil Taylor; Sun Ra; Bill Dixon; Rashied Ali; Don Cherry; Jackie McLean. From '70-5 has worked w. Dewey Redman; Ornette Coleman; Rudd; Taylor; and Ali. Main association from '70, however, has been w. Revolutionary Ensemble, a trio w. Leroy Jenkins and Jerome Cooper. Infl: Jimmy Blanton, Tommy Potter, Slam Stewart, Paul Chambers, Oscar Pettiford, A. Shepp, Sun Ra, Coltrane, Ellington, C. Taylor, O. Coleman, Beethoven, Bartok.

TV: Educ. TV w. The Group, Atlanta; *Soul* w. P. Sanders; *Jazz Set* w. Ali. Fest: Stockholm '75, Ann Arbor w. Revol. Ens.; Amougies, Belg. w. D. Burrell, Steve Lacy, Robin Kenyatta, '70; NJF w. S. Murray; NJF-NY w. Redman. Publ: (Re Publ. Co., P.O. Box 838, Peter Stuyvesant Station, New York, N.Y. 10009). Sirone feels that "we are the interpreters of Nature's Music. We find that everything on the earth contributes to its harmony." Comp: *Hu Man; Involution Evolution; The People's Republic; Configuration; Peace; Ishi.* LPs: w. Revolutionary Ensemble, *Manhattan Cycles* (India Navigation); *Viet Nam 1&2* (ESP); *The People's Republic* (A&M); *Psyche* (Re); w. Marion Brown (Imp., ESP); w. Noah Howard; Barbieri (ESP); w. L. Jenkins, *For Players Only;* R. Rudd (JCOA); Sanders (Strata-East); Redman (Imp.); C. Taylor, *Spring of Two Blue J's* (Unit Core).

SIVUCA (Severino D'Oliviera), *guitar, accordion, piano, singer, composer;* b. Itabayana, Brazil, 5/26/30. Older brother studied accordion; Sivuca was self-taught on the instrument from age nine. Took up guitar in later years. Left home at 15 to play professionally. Formed gp., The World on Fire, w. two other accordion-playing albinos, '49. Established as a major artist in Brazil w. recordings *Feijoada* and *Vasorina,* '50.

Appointed Ambassador of Musical Goodwill by Brazilian Gov't, '58, he led a gp. on European tour and was honored at Brussels International Fair. Remained in Europe after '59 tour, returning for brief visit to Brazil before moving to US, '64. Worked w. Miriam Makeba, '65-9; then w. Oscar Brown Jr. in show *Joy,* '69. Touring w. Harry Belafonte in '70s; also apps. w. own gp. at Top of the Gate, etc. Philharmonic Hall concert and Jamaican tour w. Makeba, '73.

Comp. score for NBC White Paper *Cry Help!,* '70; six documentary films for Pepsico Int. on the soccer star Pele, '73. TV: *Sivuca and his Music, Camera III,* CBS, '73.

A versatile performer who blends his Brazilian roots with many other elements including classical and jazz. Ira Mayer wrote in the *Village Voice:* "To call Sivuca a great musician is understating the case. His manner of scat singing is to bossa nova what Ella Fitzgerald's is to American jazz."

John S. Wilson said that "he projects an unquenchable sense of joy both visually and musically."

LPs: *Sivuca; Sivuca Live at the Village Gate* (Vanguard); w. Belafonte (RCA).

SIX, JACK, *bass;* also *trumpet;* b. Danville, Illinois, 7/26/30. Stud. trumpet with various teachers in Chicago, LA, NYC, 1945-55; composition major at Juilliard, '55-6; bass w. Wendell Marshall, Ruby Jamitz, '59; Homer Mensch, '60-2. Worked with many big bands incl. C. Thornhill, '58; W. Herman, '59-60. Combos: H. Mann, '59-64; Don Elliott, '60-64; Jimmy Raney, '61; Dukes of Dixieland, '64. Six became internationally known as bassist during his frequent tours w. D. Brubeck, '68-74. When not with Brubeck, he freelanced extensively w. G. Mulligan, Joe Williams and other singers and combos around NYC.

Fests: Newport, Berlin, Monterey, Mexico etc. w. Brubeck. Comps: *Five Piano Sketches; Debbie's Dance; Cello Sonata; Clarinet Sonata.* LPs w. Brubeck (Col., Atl.).

SJOSTEN, LARS, *piano;* b. Oskarshamn, Sweden, 5/7/41. Grandfather a violinmaker; aunt a violinist; mother taught piano. Studied piano and harmony privately; later studies w. George Russell. Settled in Stockholm, '60, and pl. w. Eje Thelin, Lars Gullin. Became house pianist at Golden Circle club where he pl. w. Dexter Gordon, Art Farmer, George Russell, Sonny Stitt, Steve Lacy, Borje Fredriksson and Gullin. In late '60s active in radio and recording. Toured Sweden w. Rolf Ericson's big band; Czechoslovakia w. Bernt Rosengren quintet. From '70 working w. own trio and quartet and w. Gullin. Awarded first Jan Johansson Scholarship '69. Infl: Dexter Gordon, Rolf Ericson, Gullin, Tadd Dameron. Many fest. app. in Sweden and Norway. Comp: *Tidigt; Ladislav; Gazoline, My Beloved; Pledge; Kong Fredrik's Blues.* LPs: *Lars Sjosten, Jazz Pianist; Club Jazz* on Swedish label; w. Gullin on SSX, Odeon; Brew Moore, (Sonet); others w. Rolf Ericson; Bernt Rosengren.

SKIDMORE, ALAN RICHARD JAMES, *tenor saxophone;* also *soprano sax, concert flute, alto flute, drums;* b. Kingston on Thames, Surrey, England. 4/21/42. Father, Jimmy Skidmore, is a saxophonist. Took course of lessons on theory and reading from Leslie Evans, but basically self taught. Infls: J. Skidmore, Ellington, Coltrane, Rollins, Monk et al. Worked w. Alexis Korner, Mike Westbrook, Eric Delaney, John Dankworth, Tubby Hayes, Mike Gibbs; also w. visiting Americans, incl. M. Ferguson, C. Corea. Had own show on BBC TV jazz series, '69; Jazz Workshops, German TV, '69, '70, '71, '72. No. 1 tenor saxophonist in *Melody Maker* poll, '71-2-3-4. Won Press Award at Montreux Fest. '69 for best band and best soloist.

In '75 Skidmore had own group w. John Surman. Comps: *Free for Al; Red Lady; T.C.B.; Safety First; Signal.* Own LPs: *Once Upon A Time* (Decca); *T.C.B.* (Phillips); w. Mike Gibbs, *Just Ahead* (Polydor); John Warren, *Tales of the Algonquin* (Decca); Norma Winstone, *Edge of Time* (Decca); Rolf Kuhn, *Devil In Paradise;* V. Kreigel, *Missing Link* (on MPS/BASF).

SMALLS, CLIFTON ARNOLD (CLIFF), *piano, arranger;* also *trombone;* b. Charleston, S.C., 3/3/18. Father started him on piano and trombone. While playing w. Carolina Cotton Pickers, attended KC Conservatory. During the '40s, while w. Earl Hines orch. as trombonist and second pianist, attended Chicago Conservatory. Was staff arr. for Carolina Cotton Pickers; also for Hines for whom he wrote charts on *Wagon Wheels; Blue Skies; Cottage for Sale,* all unrecorded. Worked w. Lucky Millinder; Bennie Green. Cond. & arr. for Billy Eckstine, '48-50. Served in same capacity w. Clyde McPhatter in early '50s; Brook Benton, '50s-'60s. Also worked w. Reuben Phillips band. Piano acc. for Ella Fitzgerald; Roy Hamilton, '60s; piano, cond., arr. for Smokey Robinson and the Miracles. In mid-70s w. Sy Oliver orch. and a member of the NYJRC. During his career also appeared w. Earl Bostic; Hal Singer; Tiny Grimes; Purvis Henson; Palmer Davis.

Infl: Art Tatum, Earl Hines. Film: sound track for Ella Fitzgerald in *Let No Man Write My Epitaph.* TV: *Mike Douglas Show* w. Benton; Robinson. Fest: NJF-NY; Concord. LPs: tracks in *Master Jazz Piano, Vol. 2;* w. Buddy Tate, *The Texas Twister;* w. Julian Dash (Master Jazz); w. Sy Oliver, *Yes Indeed* (Black & Blue); *Take Me Back* (Ilac); w. Ella Fitzgerald, *Live at Carnegie Hall* (Col.); w. Bennie Green (Prest.); w. S. Robinson (Tamla).

SMITH, CLADYS (JABBO),* *trumpet, trombone, singer;* b. Claxton, Ga., 1908. Although he continued to live in Milwaukee, the former Ellington and Charlie Johnson trumpet star was virtually inactive in music. Honored at the NJF-NY Hall of Fame concert, '75, he appeared on stage with his horn but did not solo. Two volumes of his early work were reissued on Biograph under the title, *Jazz Ace of the Twenties.*

SMITH, JAMES HOWARD (JIMMIE), *drums, percussion;* b. Newark, N.J., 1/27/38. Stud. Al Germansky School for Drummers, Newark, '51-'54; Charlie Perry, '51-54; Juilliard School of Mus., '59-60. From 1960 he worked w. E. Garner, B.B. King, L. Hampton, Richard Groove Holmes, Lambert, Hendricks & Ross, Jimmy McGriff, B. Webster, Sweets Edison, Herb Ellis, Art Pepper, Joe Pass, Jimmy Smith (the organist) in clubs throughout the U.S.; also in clubs, concerts and fests. In Europe, Australia, New Zealand, Japan. Wrote arr. of *Misty* for Holmes for album *Soul Message* (Pres.). App. at NJF, MJF, Concord JF.

LPs: *Forrest Fire,* w. J. Forrest; *Gumbo,* w. Pony Poindexter (Pres.); *Salud,* w. J. Hendricks (Repr.); w. Garner, *Up in Erroll's Room* (MGM); *Gemini* (Poly.); w. Jack Wilson, *Song For My Daughter* (BN); w. O.C. Smith, *Live* (Col.); w. Richard Boone, *I've Got A Right To Sing* (Nocturne); w. Lambert, Hendricks & Bavan (RCA).

SMITH, JAMES OSCAR (JIMMY),* *organ;* b. Norristown, Pa., 12/8/25. Since '56, when his first recordings established him, Smith has been the best known and most influential jazz organist, winning innumerable awards in many countries. Though best known for his exciting r & b performances, he recorded an all ballad album for Verve in '70. In '72 he was selected as Honorary Director-Advisor to board of Amateur Organists Association International. In Sept. '72, he toured Portugal; the following year his suite, *Portuguese Soul,* on which he was backed by the Thad Jones-Mel Lewis orch., was released on Verve. In Apr. '74 Smith formed his own company, Mojo Records. In Sept. of the same year he was married to his manager, Lola Ward. Shortly afterward, he toured Israel for the first time. After leaving June '75 for an extensive European tour, Smith announced that he would be going into semi-retirement, restricting his performances to concerts, festivals and recordings.

Films: *Get Yourself a College Girl; Where the Spies Are.* TV: *Black Omnibus; Mike Douglas; Dating Game.* Fests: Newport, San Diego, many in Europe; toured w. Geo. Wein concert package, fall of '72, leading all star group w. C. Terry, A. Farmer, K. Burrell et al.

LPs: *Paid in Full; Jimmy Smith '75* (Mojo); *Bluesmith; Portuguese Soul; The Best Of; Blue Bash; Dynamic Duo* (w. W. Montgomery); *Further Adventures; Respect* (Verve); *Back at the Chicken Shack; Bucket; The Incredible Jimmy Smith; Plain Talk* (BN); *Jimmy Smith Jam, Newport in New York* (Cobble.).

SMITH, LEO, *trumpet, fluegelhorn, piccolo trumpet, composer;* also *African flute, Indian flute, koto, Gamelan keyboards, percussion;* b. Leland, Miss., 12/18/41. Father, Alex "Little Bill" Wallace, was blues singer-guitarist who rec. and performed on radio w. Willie Love in early '50s. Studied blues w. Wallace, summer '55. At Lincoln High School stud. w. Earl Jones, '55-6, pl. in HS band. Organized own ensemble for improvising. Studied trumpet w. Henderson Howard, '57-61, incl. pl. Ellington arrs. Further stud. at Army Sch. of Mus., Ft. Leonard Wood, Mo., '62; Sherwood Sch. of Mus., Chi., '67-8, trumpet w. Wm. Babbcott, theory, harmony; Wesleyan U. (World Mus. Dept.), '74-5, African, Indonesian and Gamelan, Japanese, South Indian musics. Joined AACM in Chi., '67. Played w. Creative Construction Company (A. Braxton, L. Jenkins) in US and France, '67-70; Integral w. Henry Threadgill, Lester Lashley, '70; Creative Improvisation Ensemble w. Marion Brown in US, Germany, Austria, '70-2. From '71 w. New Dalta Ahkri w. Threadgill, Oliver Lake, etc. Infl:

Armstrong, Joe Smith, M. Davis, Navarro, Cherry, Booker Little, Don Ayler, Lester Bowie, the AACM. Film: *See the Music,* documentary w. Marion Brown by German dir. Theodor Kotulla, '70. TV: France, '68; Germany, '70. Fest: Amougies, '69; Radio Fest., Holland '71; Ann Arbor, '72. Publ: *Notes; Rhythm* (Leo Smith Pub. Co., P.O. Box 102, New Haven, Conn. 06501). Comp: *Creative Music-1; Ending EP-2; The Bell; Silence; Manhattan Cycles; Reflectativity; t wmukl-D; Ellington; Celebration Pieces; Eelo, sjz II, III, & IV; Seven Improvisations for Creative Orchestra.* LPs: *Creative Music-1; Reflectativity* (Kabell, same address as above); w. Muhal Richard Abrams (Delmark); Leroy Jenkins (JCOA); A. Braxton (Delmark; Sackville).

SMITH, LONNIE LISTON, *piano, electronic keyboards, composer;* also *tuba, trumpet;* b. Richmond, Va., 12/28/40. Father, Lonnie Liston Smith Sr., a member of the Harmonizing Four, a spiritual quartet, for more than forty years. Brother, Ray, sang with the Jarmels; brother, Donald, sang w. U. of Illinois Jazz Band and w. Lonnie's gp., the Cosmic Echoes.

Graduated from Armstrong HS in Richmond where he pl. trumpet in marching band; sang bass and baritone in choirs. Played tuba in marching band and piano in orchestra at Morgan State College where he grad. w. BS in Mus., '61. Worked w. Royal Stage Band; acc. Ethel Ennis, '61-2. Moved to NYC, pl. w. Betty Carter, '63-4; Rahsaan Roland Kirk, '65; Art Blakey, '66-7, Joe Williams, '67-8; Pharoah Sanders, Leon Thomas, '69-71; Gato Barbieri, '71-3; Miles Davis, '73-4; then formed the Cosmic Echoes.

Infl: Fats Waller, Art Tatum, Jelly Roll Morton, Ellington, Miles Davis, Cecil Taylor, Coltrane, Eubie Blake, Sun Ra, James P. Johnson, Lester Young. TV: *Jazz Set,* '71; *In Concert* w. M. Davis, '73; *Soul* w. P. Sanders; Montreux JF w. Barbieri. Fest: NJF w. Max Roach, '65; w. Sanders, Calif. JF '68; Nice '68, '71; w. Barbieri, Colombes, Montreux, '71; Berlin, Nice, Milan, Hammerveld, Dusseldorf, Copenhagen, '72. Comp: entire score for P. Sanders' *Jewels of Thought;* also *Let Us Go to the House of the Lord; Astral Traveling; Morning Prayer; Imani* (Faith); *Aspirations, Rejuvenation; In Search of Truth; Cosmic Funk; Beautiful Woman; Peaceful Ones; Summer Days; Expansions; Shadows; Desert Nights; Voodoo Woman.* LPs: *Visions of a New World; Astral Traveling; Cosmic Funk; Expansions* (Fly. Dutch.); w. Sanders, *Karma; Jewels of Thought; Thembi; Summum, Bukmun, Umyun* (Imp.); w. Barbieri, *Third World; Fenix; El Pampero; Under Fire; Bolivia* (Fly. Dutch); w. Kirk, *Here Comes the Whistleman* (Atl); *Please Don't Cry, Beautiful Edith* (Verve); w. M. Davis, *On the Corner; Big Fun* (Col.); w. Sonny Simmons, *Burning Spirits* (Contemp.); w. Norman Connors, *Slew Foot* (Buddah); w. Leon Thomas, *Spirits Known & Unknown* (Fly. Dutch); w. S. Turrentine, *Sugar* (CTI).

SMITH, MABEL: see BIG MAYBELLE.

SMITH, MICHAEL JOSEPH, *piano, keyboards, synthesizer, composer;* b. Livingston County, Ky., 8/13/38. Self-taught except for a few lessons w. David Baker and Ran Blake. First solo concert at age six. Served in Navy, '55-9. Priv. stud. of electronic music and perfs. w. synthesizers, '60-5. Relocated to Boston. Between '66-9, lectures, comp. and perf. in NYC, Boston. '70-1: involvement w. New England Conserv. and Juilliard; first concert tour in Europe. Settled in Paris, '73, rec. various albums and comp. and app. at jazz fests. in Italy, Holland, Finland, West Berlin. Wrote score for U.S. film, *No Place to Hide.* Living in Sweden, '75. Comps: *Symphony for Geomusic;* also more than 150 works in contemp. music, avant garde jazz, piano concertos, ¢etudes, string quartets etc.

LPs: *Geomusic 2; Geomusic 3* (Saravah); *Preparation for a Descent Into Hell* (Ricordi Int'l); w. S. Lacy, *Flakes* (RCA); *Scraps* (Saravah).

SMITH, SONELIUS LAREL, *piano, composer;* b. Hillhouse, Miss., 12/17/42. Family sang, pl. piano by ear. Moved to Memphis at age six. Took up piano at nine, private lessons through high school. Studied piano & theory w. Josephus Robinson at Arkansas A,M & N, Pine Bluff, Ark., '62-9. Formed gp. w. reedman John Stubblefield at coll., pl. Intercollegiate JF at Kiel Auditorium, St. Louis, several times in late '60s. To Europe for month '69 w. Campus at Sea, sponsored by Indiana U. In NYC '69, pl. w. K. Dorham; Roy Brooks. Wrote arrs. for Bob Crewe at Saturday Music. Worked w. R.R. Kirk for nine mos. from Nov. '69. From '70 has gigged w. Frank Foster, H. Vick, D. Byrd, Elvin Jones, R. Kenyatta, A. Shepp, F. Hubbard, A. Blakey, L. Hampton. From '72 w. Piano Choir.

Infl: Tatum, Bud Powell, Ramsey Lewis, Jamal, H. Hancock, Tyner. TV: Italian documentary w. Shepp; *Today;* Ed Sullivan w. Kirk; *Positively Black* w. Kenyatta. Fest: Hampton, Va. w. Kirk. Teaches piano and voice privately. Wrote 13 songs for *Ark,* a play by Nancy Fales presented at Theatre La Mama, '74. Wrote three-movement work, *New York Blues.* Other comps: *The Need to Smile; Sanctum Saintorium* (for seven pianos); *Mellow in the Park; The World of Children;* over 100 songs. LPs: w. Shamek Farrah, *First Impressions;* w. Piano Choir (Strata-East); w. Kenyatta, *Stompin' at the Savoy;* w. Kirk, *Rahsaan, Rahsaan,* etc. (Atl.).

SMITH, HEZEKIAH LEROY GORDON (STUFF),* *violin, singer;* b. Portsmouth, Ohio, 8/14/09. First prominent at the Onyx Club on 52nd Street in NYC, where he and his combo created a sensation with their novelty tune, *I'se A-Muggin',* Smith was the first musician to make successful use of an electrically amplified violin. After living for some years in Cal., he left in '65 for bookings in Scandinavia and throughout Europe, but soon became seriously ill and performed only occasionally during the final year of his life. He died 9/26/67 in Munich, Germany.

LPs: *Black Violin* (MPS-BASF); *Memorial Album* (Prest.); *Have Violin Will Swing; Stuff Smith* (Verve); *Swingin; Stuff* (Emarcy); *Stuff Smith,* feat. S. Grappelli (Everest); *Violin Summit* (MPS).

SMITH, TALMADGE (TAB),* *alto, tenor saxophones;* b. Kingston, N.C., 1/11/09. Well known for his work in the '30s and '40s w. L. Millinder, T. Wilson and his own combo. Lived in St. Louis in '50s and '60s, continuing to play occasionally. Smith died 8/17/71 in St. Louis.

LPs: w. Billie Holiday; C. Basie (Col.); tracks in *Jazz Giants, Reeds, Vol. 2* (Trip); *Harlem Odyssey* (Xanadu).

SMITH, WARREN DOYLE,* *trombone;* b. Middlebourne, W. Va., 5/17/08. Prominent as a member of the Bob Crosby orchestra 1937-40, Smith later worked in California w. Pete

Daily, Joe Darensbourg and many other Dixieland jazz groups. He was active until shortly before his death in Santa Barbara, Calif., 8/28/75.

SMITH, WARREN, *percussion, composer, teacher;* b. Chicago, Ill., 5/14/34. Father, Warren Smith Sr., was reedman w. Noble Sissle, '27-33, incl. European travels; w. Jimmie Noone, Tiny Parham in Chi. Had inst. repair shop '30s-50s; taught Johnny Griffin, Gene Ammons among others. Mother pl. harp and piano prof. Many aunts, uncles, cousins perform prof. Uncle, Frank Derrick, led band at Great Lakes Naval Station during World War II.

Stud. reeds w. father; harp w. mother; drums at age six w. Buddy Smith and, later, w. Oliver Coleman. Percussion w. Paul Price at Ill. Univ. (BS in Mus. Ed. '57); Manhattan Sch. of Mus. (Masters in Percussion '58). Also stud. briefly w. Eddie Baker, piano & theory; snare drum w. Harold Farberman; vibes w. Jack Jennings; comp. w. Coleridge Perkinson.

Began gigging w. uncles when he was 15. Worked w. Gil Evans at Jazz Gallery, '58; Johnny Richards; Aretha Franklin; Nina Simone; Lloyd Price. Mus. dir. of Price's club, Turntable, '68. Toured Europe w. Negro Ens. Co.; served as Janis Joplin's mus. dir. for Euro. tour, '69; percussionist w. Tony Williams Lifetime '71. Pl. w. Evans again '74; NYJRC, '74-5; Sam Rivers, '75. Leads own gp. Composers Workshop Ensemble. Member of M'Boom re:percussion w. Max Roach, Roy Brooks et al. A hard-swinging trap drummer, he is a wizard w. mallets, tympani, gong and miscellaneous percussion.

Broadway shows: *West Side Story; Three Penny Opera; Lost in the Stars; Golden boy; Raisin,* etc. TV: ABC staff for Jimmy Dean, Les Crane shows, '64-7; numerous apps. w. others artists. Charter member of Symph. of the New World; pl. under Stokowski w. American Symph. Orch. Many guest artist, speaker and clinician apps. at colls. from '69. Summer artist-in-residence at Dartmouth, '75. Taught elementary, junior high and high school in NYC, '58-68; Third St. Settlement School, '60-67; Chairman, of Dept. of African American Studies, Adelphi U., '70-1; Assoc. Prof. of Music at SUNY at Old Westbury; instructor at Adelphi.

Infl: Roach, Philly Joe Jones, Elvin Jones, Tony Williams; Ellington, Mingus, Gil Evans, Frank Derrick. Fest: Montreux w. T. Williams, '71; NJF-NY; Laren; Antibes; Toulon w. M'Boom, '73; Montreux; Antibes; Perugia w. G. Evans, '74. Comp: *Love In the Open; I Know the Scenery By Heart; Miles Whale;* other works perf. in *Music in Our Times* series, '70-2. Publ: *Beginning Rhythmic Notation; Professional Percussion Workshop; Five Pieces* (for mallet instruments); *Rhythmic Exercises for Lab Band* (Miff Music Co., 151 W. 21st St., New York, N.Y. 10011). LPs: *Composers Workshop Ensemble; We've Been Around* (Strata-East); w. J. Richards, *My Fair Lady* (Roul.); w. G. Evans, (RCA); w. Dave Sanborn (War. Bros.).

SMITH, WILLIAM HENRY JOSEPH BERTHOL BONAPARTE BERTHOLOFF (WILLIE THE LION),* *piano; composer;* b. Goshen, N.Y., 11/25/1897. A major infl. in NYC in the '20s, Smith in later years app. at many jazz fests., pl. at Dick Gibson's Jazz Party in Colo. Springs, and in Jan. '73 gave a duo recital with a young protege, Brooks Kerr. This was Smith's last public app; after a brief illness he died 4/18/73 in a NYC hospital.

Smith's autobiography, *Music On My Mind* (Doubleday) was publ. in '64. Though identified with ragtime and particularly with stride piano, he was a maverick, one of whose most delightful and durable compositions was the simple and melodic *Echoes of Spring*.

LPs: *Willie "The Lion" Smith* (GNP); *Live at Blues Alley* (Chiaroscuro); *Pork & Beans* (Black Lion); *Music On My Mind* (Saba); *The Memoirs of Willie The Lion Smith* (RCA); *Grand Piano*—duets w. Don Ewell (Exclusive); *The Lion Roars* (Dot); *A Legend* (Mainstream); *Piano Solos By Willie Smith* (Commodore).

SMITH, WILLIAM McLEISH (WILLIE),* *clarinet, alto saxophone, singer;* b. Charleston, S.C., 11/25/10. Gained recognition as one of the principal soloists in the J. Lunceford band, with which he pl. from '29-42. Spent most of the next 20 years w. Harry James, except '51-3 when he was w. D. Ellington and B. May. In mid-60s worked w. Johnny Rivers in LV; also briefly w. Charlie Barnet early '67. He died in LA 3/7/67. Smith's exuberant sound on alto and relaxed, good humored singing earned him long lasting respect and popularity.

LPs: w. Lunceford, *Rhythm Is Our Business; Harlem Shout; Jimmie Lunceford & His Orch.* (Decca); *Lunceford Special* (Col.); *The Original Jimmie Lunceford Orch.* (Perception); *Jimmie Lunceford in Hi-Fi* (Cap.); also small gp. dates w. Nat Cole, Teddy Wilson, Jazz at the Philharmonic et al. Own LPs: *The Best of Willie Smith* (GNP-Crescendo); *Alto Artistry, Jazz Giants Reeds, Vol. 2* (Trip).

SNOW, PHOEBE (Phoebe Laub), *singer, composer, guitar;* b. Teaneck, N.J., 7/17/52. Piano lessons from early childhood, but at age 15 switched to guitar and became seriously interested in music. During her late teens she was introduced to jazz and related forms of music by a friend near her home; after writing poetry for some time she began around 1971 to put her verses into song form. In 1972, while performing in an amateur night show at the Bitter End in NYC, she was approached by a record producer to make a session, but nothing came of this, and in November, when her friend committed suicide, she went into an extended period of mourning.

Snow resumed composing in 1973, and early the following year recorded her first album, for Shelter Records. On one track, *Harpo's Blues,* the accompaniment included Zoot Sims and Teddy Wilson. The album became a gold-record best seller and Snow was acclaimed as one of the most important new vocal stars of the year.

During 1974 she was prevented from recording owing to a legal dispute, but meanwhile she appeared successfully in concerts and clubs. She signed with Columbia Records, and her first LP for that label, *Second Childhood,* appeared in Feb. 1976. As on the first album, there were occasional indications of a jazz influence in her style, and her backing on some tracks featured Jerome Richardson, Ron Carter and Grady Tate.

SNOWDEN, ELMER CHESTER (POPS),* *saxophone, guitar, banjo;* b. Baltimore, Md., 10/9/00. An early associate of Duke Ellington, first in Washington in 1919, later in NYC in '24, where Ellington took over direction of the Washingtonians, a group Snowden had earlier led. In the '60s Snowden was still playing intermittently in Phila.; toured Europe in '67 with the Newport Guitar Workshop. He had been planning to open a guitar school when he died suddenly 5/14/73 in Phila.

LP: *Harlem Banjo* (Riverside); *The Jolly Miners* (Historical).

SOLAL, MARTIAL,* *piano, composer;* b. Algiers, N. Africa, 8/23/27. Prominent since '40s in Paris. Wrote background scores for motion pictures incl. many industrial films. Several visits to U.S. to app. at Monterey and other fests. From '69, pl. concerts throughout Continent with regular trio, feat. bass and drums; from '69-71, concerts with a new trio feat. two bassists and no drummer. From late '71 solo concerts. In '75 became active as teacher, staging a week long seminar in Nice. Solal recorded many LPs for Pathe-Marconi, '66-9 and for French RCA, '71-2. Later, freelancing, he recorded two albums in Italy; one w. L. Konitz for Milestone in NYC; and one, for Spotlite, in LA; also one for MPS-BASF. Comps: *Rhythmical Escape* (30 minute suite for oboe, cello and jazz trio); *Fluctuat nec Mergitur; Etudes for Piano.*

LPs: as listed above; also M. Solal-H. Hawes Quartet (Byg).

SOLOFF, LEWIS MICHAEL (LEW), *trumpet;* also *fluegelhorn, piccolo trumpet;* b. New York City, 2/20/44. Father, Buddy Soloff, was a soft shoe dancer in a vaudeville team known as Bud & Buddy. Mother a vaudeville violinist. Stud. ukulele with father at age five; piano age five to 13. Took up trumpet in fifth grade in Lakewood, N.J., later stud. priv.; attended Juilliard Prep. Dept., '55-61; Eastman School, '61-5 graduating with Performer's Cert. in trumpet and B.M. in Applied Trumpet and Mus. Ed. Further studies at Juilliard, '65-6, w. Edward Treutel; also w. Carmine Caruso and players from Rochester, N.Y., Philadelphia and Chicago symphonies. His '65 performer's recital, *The Feel of a Vision,* was written by C. Mangione.

First pro. experience pl. in Catskill Mtns. show bands for seven summers from age 15½. From Sep., '65 to May '68 he pl. and/or rec. w. Machito, Tito Puente, Vincent Lopez, M. Ferguson, Joe Henderson, K. Dorham, C. Terry, Barry Miles, Gil Evans, Thad Jones-Mel Lewis, Radio City Music Hall orch., Chuck Jackson, Mangione, Urbie Green, Slide Hampton, Orch. Harlow, H. McGhee, D. Pearson, Frank Foster. From May '68 through Aug. '73 was feat. w. Blood, Sweat & Tears, touring worldwide incl. Eastern Europe. Soloist on *Feel of a Vision* w. Symphony of the New World; Rochester Phil. and Utica Symph; *Concerto for Trumpet and Orch.* by Alexandra Pakhmutova w. NO Symph. From Sept. '73 has been mainly associated w. Gil Evans orch; also app. on Mangione concerts as feat. soloist. Formed quintet, Salt & Pepper # 3, w. Jon Faddis, '75. Active as clinician for Bach trumpet. Infls: Parker, Gillespie, Miles Davis, Dorham, Hubbard, Clifford Brown, C. Terry, Faddis, Gil Evans. Many TV apps. w. B.S.&T. Fests: NJF, Montreux w. B.S.&T.; Montreux; Antibes; Perugia w. Evans, '74.

Soloff, a fine all around technician with a remarkable range, is an exceptionally capable lead man and strong soloist.

LPs: w. Evans (RCA); B.S.&T. (Col.); Gerry Niewood (Sagoma); Robin Kenyatta (Atl.).

SOPH, EDWARD B., *drums;* b. Coronado, Cal., 3/21/45. Influenced by Baby Dodds, Zutty Singleton, Danny Richmond, Roy Haynes et al. Stud. w. Elder Mori, Houston, Tex., '60-3; North Texas State U., '63-8, pl. w. Lab band under Leon Breeden. In '60s worked locally in Texas w. Jimmy Ford, Arnett Cobb, Don Wilkerson. Joined S. Kenton in summer of '66; W. Herman, '68, '70, '71. In '74-5 freelanced w. C. Terry, Bill Watrous and Chris Connor. Fests: Newport, '68, '70, '71; Monterey, '70, Concord, '71. Soph is a member of the faculty of the National Stage Band Camps.

Though heard to great advantage on his work w. Herman, Watrous et al, Soph says, "I would like to rid myself of the stigma of being a big band drummer. I prefer small groups, with two exceptions: Woody and those bands at N. Texas."

LPs: w. Herman, *Giant Steps* (Fantasy); Watrous, *Manhattan Wildlife Refuge* (Columbia); C. Terry, *Big Bad Band at Wichita Jazz Fest. '74; and his Jolly Giants* (Vang.).

SOUCHON, EDMOND II, M.D. (DOC),* *guitar, banjo, singer;* b. New Orleans, 10/25/1897. The prominent surgeon, avocationally a jazz musician and leading champion of New Orleans jazz, died while taking part in a jam session in NO 8/24/68. He had given lectures, made records, and for years was editor of the *Second Line,* official publication of the NO Jazz Club. *New Orleans: A Family Album,* a collection of biographies and photographs, by Souchon and Al Rose, was publ. in 1968 by Louisiana State Univ. Press.

SPANIER, HERBERT ANTHONY CHARLES (HERBIE),* *trumpet, composer;* also *fluegelhorn, piano, bass, percussion;* b. Cupar, Sask., Canada, 12/25/28. Pl. w. C. Thornhill, P. Bley in NYC, mid-'50s; LA, LV, '58-9. Ret. to Canada and was active in Montreal through '69. Own quintet for concerts at Laval, Mont., Sherbrooke Univs.; *Jazz en Liberté* on CBC radio. Moved to Toronto, '70. Own quartet at George's Spaghetti House, several times annually; also member of Phil Nimmons big band. Orig. infls: Gillespie, Davis. TV: many apps. on CBC. Fests: American Mus. Fest., Lewiston, N.Y. Art Park w. D. Amram; Fest. of Jazz & Chamber Mus. w. Nimmons in Fredericton, N.B., '75. Wrote mus. for film, *Via Montreal,* which won prize in So. America. Received Senior Arts Grant from Canada Council for research into Brass Acoustical Innovations, '68. Comps: *Northland Blues; Precis En Bleu; Prelude; Waltz No. 4; Dimensions in Blue; Open Door; Equivalence; Bird Talk; Forensic Per Tur Bations; Ballade for Gina.* Own LP: on Radio Canada Int.; w. Galt McDermott (Laurentian); w. Nimmons (Nimmons' N Mus. Ltd.).

SPANIER, FRANCIS JOSEPH (MUGGSY),* *cornet;* b. Chicago, Ill., 11/9/06. A member of many name bands from the '20s incl. Ted Lewis, Ben Pollack, Bob Crosby, Spanier later lived in SF. After apps. at NJF, '64 he retired owing to ill health and died in Sausalito, Cal. 2/12/67.

SPANN, OTIS,* *piano, singer;* b. Jackson, Miss., 3/21/30. Reputed to be a "half-brother" of Muddy Waters. Respected as a powerful pianist, highly personal singer and strong accompanist, Spann worked w. Howlin' Wolf, Buddy Guy, James Cotton, Big Mama Thornton, Bo Diddley, toured Europe several times with Waters and others (his association with Waters had begun in 1947, when he moved to Chicago). Spann died 4/25/70 in a Chicago hospital. LPs w. Waters on various labels; rec. under own name for Candid, Prestige, Testament, BluesWay, London, BluesTime, Vanguard. During the weekend of Sept. 8-10, 1972 a series of concerts, held in Ann Arbor, Mich., celebrated the formal dedication there of Otis Spann Memorial Field. A two-volume album, w. Howlin' Wolf, Dr. John, Koko Taylor, Willie Dixon, Freddie King, Sippie Wallace and others, was released on Atlantic Records.

SPARGO, TONY (Anthony Sbarbaro),* *drums, kazoo;* b. New Orleans, La., 6/27/1897. Member of Original Dixieland Jazz Band, 1914, Spargo in the '60s was the only surviving member of that gp. He pl. w. Phil Napoleon during the '50s, became inactive during the '60s and died 10/30/69 in Forest Hills, N.Y. LPs: w. ODJB (RCA).

SPAULDING, JAMES RALPH (JIMMY),* *alto, tenor saxes, flute;* b. Indianapolis, Ind., 7/30/37. Worked w. Sun Ra in Chicago in '50s; Freddie Hubbard; Max Roach; Randy Weston in NYC in first half of '60s. Pl. w. Roy Haynes, '66; Hubbard; Roach, '67; Bobby Hutcherson, '70; Weston in early '70s; also w. Leon Thomas; Art Blakey; Horace Silver; Pharoah Sanders; G. Wein's Newport All Stars. In '75 worked w. Duke Ellington orch. under the dir. of Mercer Ellington. As a leader of his own small gp. pl. concerts at Loeb Student Center, NYU, '68; NYC Community Coll., '69; The East, Brooklyn '69-70; Cornell U. series, '69-70; Jazzmobile; MUSE, '70; Vassar, Utica, Manhattan Colls; Left Bank Jazz Society, '71. TV: NET; *Dial M For Music* w. Hubbard; *Positively Black* w. Leon Thomas. Fest: NJF w. Thomas, '70; NJF-NY w. Wein, '73. Received BA from Livingston Coll., '75; candidate for Masters at Rutgers U. Participated in Jazz Workshops at Rutgers, '75, w. Budd Johnson; C. Terry; Weston; S. Rollins; Jo Jones; Milt Hinton; Milt Jackson; Bob Wilber; Charles Davis. LPs: w. Hubbard, *Backlash; High Blues Pressure; Black Angel;* w. Roach, *Drums Unlimited* (Atl.); *New Wave in Jazz* (Imp.); w. Silver, *The Jody Grind* (BN); *Louis Armstrong and Friends;* w. Thomas; Rosko (Fly. Dutch); S. Turrentine; Larry Young (BN); Duke Pearson (Atl.).

SPINOZZA, DAVID, *guitar;* also *piano, drums, trumpet;* b. Portchester, N.Y., 8/8/49. Stud. theory in high school; classical guitar w. Leonid Bolotine; orchestration w. Ariadno Mikeshina; "Listened to all of the Wes Montgomery records." An extremely active NYC studio player who has rec. w. R. Flack, M. Legrand, John Lennon, Paul McCartney, James Taylor, Carly Simon, H. Mann, C. Mariano, M. Mainieri, Stevie Wonder, Howard Johnson, M. Stamm, Mike and Randy Brecker, Aretha Franklin. Infls: Montgomery, Segovia, Bolotine, Lionel Chamberlain. Has written arrs. for Taylor, Richard Davis and Paul Williams; app. w. Williams on *Tonight* show. Fest: NJF-NY w. Les McCann.

LPs: *Hard Mother Blues* w. E. Wilkins (Mainstream); w. Arif Mardin, *Journey* (Atl.); w. Franklin, *I'm In Love* (Atl.); w. Lennon, *Mind Games* (Apple); w. Dr. John, *In The Right Place* (Atco).

SPROLES, VICTOR, *bass;* b. Chicago, Ill., 11/18/27. Studied under Walter Dyett at Du Sable High in Chi., '42-6; pl. in band w. 16th A.E.F. during WWII. Gigged w. Coleman Hawkins in Milwaukee, '52. Member of house rhythm section at French Poodle in Chi., '52-3, pl. w. Ira Sullivan; from '54-7 he filled the same role at the Beehive, backing visiting stars like Lester Young, Sonny Stitt, Charlie Parker. From '58-60 worked w. Johnny Griffin-Lockjaw Davis quintet; then w. Norman Simmons in Chi., Nevada, Calif. and Arizona. Acc. Carmen McRae, '62-4, incl. trips to Switzerland, England. With Art Blakey, '65-6, incl. Japanese tour. From '69-72 was most often at Half Note in NYC w. Al Cohn-Zoot Sims, Anita O'Day, Jimmy Rushing and James Moody. Also pl. w. Hazel Scott, '70. In '69 he began pl. w. Clark Terry incl. Montreal Expo and '75 summer tour of Europe. Infls: Junior Raglin, Slam Stewart, Wilbur Ware, Paul Chambers, Ray Brown, Richard Davis, Bill Lee, Chubby Jackson. TV apps. w. Blakey, McRae, Scott and Johnny Hartman. MJF w. McRae, LPs: w. Wardell Gray in *The Foremost* (Onyx); w. C. Terry (Vanguard, Etoile); w. Lee Morgan, *The Sixth Sense; The Rumproller* (BN); w. B. DeFranco, *Free Sail* (Choice); w. Sun Ra, *Supersonic Jazz* (Saturn); w. Ira Sullivan (Delmark); w. J. Griffin, *Big Soul* (Mile.); w. C. McRae (Time).

STABULAS, NICHOLAS (NICK),* *drums;* b. Brooklyn, N.Y., 12/18/29. Heard w. many gps. in NYC, incl. L. Tristano, A. Cohn & Z. Sims, Urbie Green, Chet Baker, Stabulas was killed in an automobile accident, 2/6/73.

LPs w. Gil Evans; M. Allison (Prest.); Jimmy Raney, *Strings & Swings* (Muse).

STACY, JESS ALEXANDRIA, * *piano;* b. Bird's Point, Mo., 8/4/04. In 1918 the family moved to Cape Girardeau, Mo. Stacy earned fame as pianist in B. Goodman band '35-9. During '40s led own big band, also back w. Goodman, and on west coast w. J. Teagarden. Worked locally in LA during '50s, but became inactive in music in '60, taking a day job, then retiring.

Stacy was persuaded to emerge for the '74 NJF where his perf. was acclaimed by critics. As a consequence, he made occasional live apps., returned to records, and did sound track work for *The Great Gatsby*.

In Feb. '75 he won the New Jersey Jazz Society's Jazz Musician of the Year award, presented at their annual Pee Wee Russell Memorial Concert. Like Earl Hines, Stacy showed that he had survived and transcended the many changes in jazz piano styles and that his incisive, firmly swinging work remained effective with or without a rhythm section.

Comp: *Ec-Stacy; Complainin'; Burning The Candle At Both Ends; Ain't Going Nowhere; Ramblin'; The Sell Out; Lookout Mountain Squirrels; Doll Face; Miss Peck Accepts.* LPs: *Jess Stacy Piano Solos* (Swaggie); *Stacy Still Swings* (Chiaroscuro); *The Great Gatsby* (Paramount). Early LPs with Goodman (RCA).

STADLER, HEINER, *composer, piano;* b. Lessen, Poland, 9/4/42. Studied harmony w. Rudolf Lerich in Hamburg, '68-70; piano w. Juergen Sonnenschmidt; harmony w. Peter Hartman; composition w. Walter Steffens, '60-4. To NYC in mid-60s. Infl: T. Monk, Ch. Parker, George Russell, Edgard Varese, Walter Steffens. Comp: *Three Problems; Love in the Middle of the Air; Six Pieces for Quartet; The Fugue 2; No*

Exercise; Chained; Blues For Sister Sally; Clusterity; Homage to Bird and Monk, six pieces by Monk and Parker recomposed for sextet. Arr. of *Main Stem* for J. Moody in *The Blues and Other Colors* (Milestone). LPs: *Brains On Fire,* vols. 1&2; *Ecstasy* w. Steffens; *No Exercise* (Labor Records, 106 Haven Ave., New York, N.Y. 10032).

STAHL, DAVID, *trumpet, fluegelhorn, cornet;* b. Reading, Pa., 1/23/49. Stud. w. Walter Gier in Reading; Penn State U. 1966-70, B.S. in Mus. Ed. After college, pl. in US Army Band in Washington, Aug. '70-Aug. '73. Also during this time pl. lead tpt. in Catholic Univ. of America Jazz Band dir. by Hank Levy. Joined Woody Herman 8/3/73, playing lead tpt. through 1/9/75, again from 2/10-4/24/75; the next day, he joined Count Basie. Concerts with F. Sinatra while w. Herman in '74 and again while w. Basie in Sept. '75. Favs: M. Ferguson, Bill Chase, Conrad Gozzo, Don Jacoby. TV: BBC show with Herman, Jan. '74. Fests: Concord, Montreux, Pori w. Herman; Montreux, Antibes, Kansas City w. Basie. LPs: *Herd at Montreux* w. Herman (Fantasy).

STAMM, MARVIN LOUIS,* *trumpet, fluegelhorn;* b. Memphis, Tenn., 5/23/39. Played w. S. Kenton, '60-2; W. Herman, '65-6; then settled in NYC becoming heavily involved in studio work, rec. with such artists as Q. Jones, O. Nelson, G. McFarland, F. Foster, M. Albam, D. Pearson, M. Legrand, Pat Williams, Bob James, D. Sebesky, W. Montgomery, Deodato, Grover Washington Jr. et al. With T. Jones-M. Lewis orch. '66-70, incl. European tour, '69. Guest soloist-clinician at many univs., high schools and colls. throughout U.S.; concerts w. B. Goodman septet; Legrand, James and Sebesky; U.S. and overseas tours w. F. Sinatra, '74. TV: feat. soloist w. C. Mangione and Rochester Phil., PBS. Fests: Monterey w. Jones-Lewis, '71; Newport w. Legrand, '75.

LPs: *Machinations* (Verve); w. Foster, *Manhattan Fever; Introducing the Duke Pearson Big Band* (BN); w. Jones-Lewis, *Consummation; Jazz Wave Tour* (SS); w. Williams, *Threshold* (Cap.); w. Legrand, *Twenty Songs of the Century* (Bell); w. Mangione, *Friends & Love* (Merc.); w. Nelson, *Jazzhattan Suite* (Verve); w. McFarland, *Scorpio and Other Signs* (Skye); w. Bob Freedman, *The Journeys of Odysseus* (Milest.).

STANKO, TOMASZ, *trumpet, fluegelhorn, composer;* b. Rzeszow, Poland, 7/11/42. Father gave him first violin lessons. Studied violin and piano at elementary music school. From '59 studied trumpet at Cracow Secondary and Higher Sch. of Music, grad. from latter in '69. First heard jazz at Dave Brubeck concert '58. Formed gp. w. Adam Makowicz '62. From '63 also pl. w. Krzysztof Komeda; from '65-9 w. Andrzej Trzaskowski. Took part in his Hamburg Workshops and Manfred Schoof's Trumpet Summit in Nuremberg. In '70 pl. w. A. Von Schlippenbach Globe Unity Orch. at Donaueschingen Jazz Days; Warsaw Jazz Jamboree; Berlin; Baden-Baden Free Jazz Meeting. Pl. w. Don Cherry, A. Mangelsdorff, Gerd Dudek in European Free Jazz Orch. at Donaueschingen '71. Many Euro. fests. in '70s. Toured Switzerland, '72. Winner of Polish polls from '65. Joachim Berendt called him "the first musician in Europe to translate Ornette Coleman into his own language." LPs: *Astigmatic; Twet; Music for K;* w. Komeda; Trzaskowski; Wroblewski (Muza).

STAPLETON, WILLIAM JOHN (BILL), *trumpet, fluegelhorn, arranger/composer;* also *trombone;* b. Blue Island, Ill., 5/4/45. Father, a professional pianist, and mother both teach music at home. Stud. at No. Texas St. Univ., Sept. '63-May '67 and Jan.-May '71; trumpet w. John Haynie. Pl. w. No. Tex. Lab Band, '63-7, and, after Army service, again in '71. During his No. Texas St. days, also pl. w. Joe Reichman, Teddy Phillips, Ralph Marterie, Buddy Morrow, Don Jacoby, did studio work in Dallas. App. at LA Music Center w. No. Texas Lab Band and S. Kenton Neophonic, '66. With Woody Herman, '72-March '74; Neal Hefti, '74; Bill Holman, '74-5. Active as clinician; summer teaching at National Stage Band Camp. Infl: Clifford Brown, Terry, Hubbard, Hackett, Gillespie, C. Baker, Mulligan, Holman. Comp: *Bill's Blues,* five arrs. in Herman's Grammy Award winning *Giant Steps.* LPs: w. Herman, *Giant Steps; The Raven Speaks; The Thundering Herd* (Fantasy); North Texas Lab Band, '67, '71.

STATON, DAKOTA,* *singer;* b. Pittsburgh, Pa., 6/3/32. Continued club and concert apps. such as new Half Note, NYC, '73; jazz cruise on *Showboat I,* May '74. LPs: *'67* (London); *Ms. Soul; Madame Foo-Foo; I Want a Country Man* (Groove Merchant).

STEIG, JEREMY, *flutes;* b. New York City, 9/23/42. Father is prominent artist William Steig; mother Liza, sisters Lucy and Maggie also are artists. Steig, who has illustrated his own album covers, has had one-man shows in White Plains and Woodstock, N.Y. Played recorder at age six. Took up flute at 11, studying w. Paige Brook, '53-6. Attended HS of Mus. & Art. Began pl. in Greenwich Village coffee houses at 15. Pl. w. Paul Bley, Gary Peacock, '61. Worked w. jazz-rock gp. backing Tim Hardin, '66-7. Formed Jeremy and the Satyrs in the latter yr. and has had own gps. ever since. Early associates in these gps. were Warren Bernhardt, Mike Mainieri, Donald McDonald, Eddie Gomez. In '70 was associated w. Jan Hammer. A motorcycle accident in '62 paralysed the right side of his face and left him deaf in one ear for six months. For a year's time he had to place a wooden block in his mouth in order to play but he overcame these ailments to prove himself as a soulful jazzman with a particularly forceful, gutsy attack, beginning with his debut album, *Flute Fever* (Col.), '63. With the advent of the Satyrs he became involved with jazz-rock and by '75 his performances made use of such electronic devices as the ring modulator, wah wah pedal echo machines, etc. Chuck Berg in *down beat* said: "One can only conclude Steig is a virtuoso. His command of tongueing techniques (from flutter to triple), his variety of tone colors (from the classical sound-ideal to a raging howl), his mastery of the flute family (from bass to piccolo), his ability to hum and sing along with the articulated notes from his flute, and his success in integrating electronics combined with the harmonic, rhythmic and melodic imaginativeness, all stamp him as an original."

Orig. infl: Coltrane, Rollins, Miles Davis, Monk, Bill Evans. Won DB Critics poll, TDWR, '67, '73-4. TV: *Camera Three* w. B. Evans; and w. own gp.; *Jazz Set,* NET, '71; PL. Berlin JF several times in '70s incl. Art Blakey's *Orgy in Rhythm,* '72; Association P.C., '74. Toured Europe w. own quartet on Sonny Lester package, '69-70. Pl. Germany and Switz. w. own quintet, Nov.-Dec. '75. Comp: *Come With*

Me; Belly Up; co-composed w. E. Gomez, *Dream Passage; Djinn Djinn.* LPs: *Temple of Birth; Monium* (Col.); *Fusion* (Gr. Merch.); *Energy* (Cap.); *Wayfaring Stranger* (BN); *Legwork; This is Jeremy Steig* (SS); *Flute Summit* (Atl.); *Mama Kuku* (MPS); *Jeremy & the Satyrs* (Reprise); w. Bill Evans, *What's New;* w. Richie Havens, *Something Else Again* (Verve).

STEVENS, LEITH,* *composer, conductor;* b. Mt. Moriah, Mo. 9/13/09. Stevens, who scored dozens of films, many of them with a jazz background or theme, incl. *The Gene Krupa Story; The Five Pennies; The Wild One,* died 7/23/70 in Hollywood, Cal.

STEVENSON, GEORGE EDWARD,* *trombone;* b. Baltimore, Md., 6/20/06. The name band veteran (F. Henderson, C. Hopkins, L. Millinder, Cootie Williams, R. Eldridge), who in later years pl. with small gps. in NYC, died there 9/21/70.

STEWART, JAMES OTTO (JIMMY), *guitar;* also *banjo, mandolin, composer;* b. San Francisco, Cal., 9/8/37. Stud. at Coll. of San Mateo, Chicago School of Mus., Berklee. Pro. debut at age 15. Arr. for many pop singers, cond. on TV in U.S. and Australia. Guitarist w. many jazz combos incl. three years w. Gabor Szabo. Edited Wes Montgomery jazz guitar method; co-author *This Is Howard Roberts;* wrote numerous articles for music periodicals and comp. such works as *Concertina for Electric Guitar and Orch.; 12 Homages for Classic Guitar;* works for string quartets etc. Publs: *Homage to the Spirit of the Guitar* (Guitar Player Prods., P.O. Box 615, Saratoga, Ca. 95070); *Wes Montgomery Jazz Guitar Method* (Robbins Music, 1775 Broadway, New York); *This Is Howard Roberts* (Playback, P.O. Box 4562, N. Hollywood, Ca. 91607). Fests: Monterey, '67-8; Newport, '68; UCLA w. G. McFarland, '68. Stewart, an exceptionally experienced and able artist on all plectrum instruments, attributes his inspiration to a range of influences from Segovia and Bartok to Charlie Christian and L. Almeida.

LPs: w. Szabo, *The Sorcerer; More Sorcery; The Best Of* (Imp.); *Bacchanal; Dreams* (Skye); *Rod McKuen Grand Tour 1971* (WB).

STEWART, REX WILLIAM,* *cornet, composer;* b. Philadelphia, Pa., 2/22/07. A veteran of such name bands as those of Fletcher Henderson, Horace Henderson, Luis Russell, Benny Carter, Stewart was best known for his work w. the D. Ellington orch. with which he pl. almost continuously from late 1934 until '45. After working extensively in Europe and Australia, pl. a year at Eddie Condon's club, and as a musician and disc jockey in LA during the '60s, Stewart died suddenly in LA, 9/7/67. His best known accomplishment was the use of the squeezed tone, half-valve effect, which he introduced in *Boy Meets Horn,* co-composed w. Ellington and rec. in '39. This tonal device was imitated by countless trumpeters in later years.

Stewart in the last few years of his life was successfully active as a journalist, writing a series of witty and perceptive articles for *down beat* and other publications. He was the author of a collection of his pieces issued under the title *Jazz Masters of the '30s* (Macmillan), publ. posthumously.

LP: *The Ellingtonians* (Trip).

STEWART, LEROY (SLAM),* *bass;* b. Englewood, N.J., 9/21/14. As member of Slim and Slam duo, '38, was first to popularize technique of improvising jazz solos on bowed bass and humming in octave unison. Countless concert and fest. apps., overseas tours, '50s and '60s, incl. Australia, '66; Europe, '71, England and continent w. Benny Goodman sextet, '73-4; France, Belgium, Switzerland w. own quartet, '75.

In '71 Stewart became a member of the faculty of the State Univ. of Binghamton, N.Y. He also conducted workshops and seminars at Yale U. Along with these activities, he app. in clubs and concerts w. various small groups, incl. his wife, Claire Stewart. Guest artist w. Binghamton Symph. In Nov. '70 he gave premier perf. of *La Reve Symphonique pour Slam,* comp. for him by Jack Martin and pl. by Stewart with the Indianapolis Symph.

In '71-2 he pl. w. C. Terry, Milt Buckner, Tyree Glenn, Jimmy and Marian McPartland, Buddy Tate, Zoot Sims-Al Cohn. In June '73 he rejoined Goodman, for whom he first worked in '44, and was heard with him in various groups during the next two years. Also pl. workshops at Yale U. w. Dwike Mitchell and Willie Ruff; Carnegie Hall concert w. NYJRC in tribute to A. Tatum w. B. Taylor, Tiny Grimes; concerts at Lincoln Center and Princeton U. w. Dr. Frances Cole, harpsichord, in baroque and string concerts. Publ: *Styles in Jazz Bass* (Morris & Co.).

LPs: *Slam Stewart Trio; Slamboree;* w. Joe Turner; w. Gene Rodgers (Black & Blue); others rec. in Europe in '75; and earlier albums w. Tatum (MCA); Goodman (Col.) etc.

STINSON, ALBERT FORREST JR. (AL),* *bass;* b. Cleveland, Ohio, 8/2/44. Worked in Calif. w. Terry Gibbs, Frank Rosolino, Chico Hamilton, Charles Lloyd. He was touring w. Larry Coryell's group when he died 6/2/69, of unknown causes, apparently in his sleep, in Boston, Mass. He was considered an exceptional bassist with a brilliant technique and adventurous ideas. LPs w. Hamilton, Joe Pass et al.

STITT, EDWARD (SONNY),* *tenor, alto saxes;* b. Boston, Mass., 2/2/24. In the late '60s and '70s he continued to tour w. his own gps., as a single w. local rhythm sections, and record prolifically. He was also a member of The Giants of Jazz w. Dizzy Gillespie, T. Monk, K. Winding which toured the world in '71-2; and part of *The Musical Life of Charlie Parker* which opened the NJF-NY in June '74 and toured eastern and western Europe in the fall of the year. Dan Morgenstern, in the liner notes for *Tune-Up,* said: "He has at his finger tips every lick and trick in the book, and if he wants it that way, he can just coast along on his experience and get away with it every time. But when Stitt is inspired and means business, he is awesome . . ." The last sentence can be well applied to his work on *Constellation* and with the Giants of Jazz, as well as *Tune-Up.* Comp: *Blues For Prez and Bird; The Eternal Triangle.* LPs: *Tune-Up; Constellation* (Cobble.); *12!; The Champ; Mellow* (Muse); *Parallel-A-Stitt* (Roul.); *Sonny Stitt with Art Blakey and the Jazz Messengers* (Poly.); *Previously Unreleased Recordings* (Verve); *Pow;* w. G. Ammons, *We'll Be Together Again* (Prest.); *Giants of Jazz* (Atl.); *Newport in New York, The Jam Sessions, Vols. 3&4; The Soul Session, Vol 6* (Cobble.); reissues, *Genesis* (Prest.).

STIVIN, JIRI, *flute, alto sax, composer;* also *soprano sax, recorder, bass clarinet;* b. Prague, Czech., 11/23/42. Stud. flute privately w. M. Munclinger; J. Valek; in John

Dankworth's jazz class at Royal Acad. of Mus., London, '69. In Prague pl. w. Jazztett, '62; Jazz Q, '63; Army Quintet, '65; SHQ w. Karel Velebny, '67; Quax Ensemble, a grp. for electronic music, '68; w. C. Cardew's Scratch Music, in London, '69; Steven & Co. Jazz System, '70; System Tandem w. Rudolf Dasek from '72. Stivin has also pl. w. the Czech radio big band; Gustav Brom; as soloist with Danish radio big band & in many European jazz groups. Infl: Coltrane, O. Coleman, M. Davis, J. Surman, Barre Phillips, S. Rollins, D. Brubeck Quartet, B. Evans, G. Mulligan, G. Russell, C. Cardew. Comp: *Dog's Suite;* many comp. for Czech. films & TV. Fest: Ljubljana, Prague, San Sebastian, Warsaw, Zurich, Pori, Altena, Berlin, Budapest, Copenhagen. Stivin finished film high school in Prague '65 and his first occupation was as a cameraman. He and Dasek were invited to perform at NJF-NY '75 but he was unable to attend because of a sudden illness. LPs: *Stivin & Co. Jazz System* (Supraphon; Panton); *SHQ,* w. Velebny (ESP); *Nonet SHQ & Woodwinds* (Saba); w. System Tandem (RCA Victor; Japo).

STONE, FRED, *fluegelhorn, trumpet;* also *synthesizer, piano, composer;* b. Toronto, Canada, 9/9/35. Father a conductor, alto player, 1920-60. Fred Stone stud. w. several Toronto teachers from age 12. At 16, made pro. debut in father's orch. During late '50s and early '60s, pl. as lead trumpet in CBC symph. orch. Wrote several books and papers relating to jazz and creativity. Received six awards for solo instrumental perfs. and contemporary comp. from Canada Council beginning in '67. Feat. soloist and/or composer on a number of albums including two w. D. Ellington, in whose orch. he toured in '70. Canadian columnist for *Jazz Forum* magazine in Europe from '70. Comps: approx. 100 original jazz works for own big band, '65- ; *Maiera,* suite for fluegelhorn and Ellington orch., rec. in Milan, '70; *Leah* for Ellington.

Stone has made many TV apps. as soloist, conductor; pl. on scores for numerous films. Fests: Casa Loma JF, '65-9; 21 fests. throughout world w. Ellington. Publs: *Treatise on Improvisation* (Humber Coll. Productions, Toronto, Ontario); *Jazz & Concentration; Jazz In Canada; Creativity: Jazz Composition* (publ. by Stone's own company, 65 Fisherville Rd., Willowdale, Ontario, Toronto). In '75 Stone was Prof. of Music at Humber Coll. in Toronto.

LPs: w. Ellington, *New Orleans Suite* (Atl.); w. Ellington/Ron Collier Orch., *Collages* (MPS); own LPs on RCA, CBC, Sackville.

STRAND, LES (Leslie Roy Strandt),* *electric organ, piano, pipe organ;* b. Chicago, 9/15/24. Played in Chicago clubs, mainly as soloist in '50s; early '60s. Stopped pl. publicly in '64 and began teaching. Returned to school and received BA, major in music theory, from Roosevelt Coll., '67. Moved to Wash., D.C. w. wife, former DB associate editor Pat Harris. Some clubs, concerts in stores but mostly teaching. Won first prize at Eighth Yamaha Int. Electone Fest., Nemu-no-sato, Japan, '71. Jimmy Smith has called Strand the "Art Tatum of the organ." LP: *The Winners: Les Strand & the Yamaha* (Yamaha); earlier albums on Fantasy, now deleted.

STRAYHORN, WILLIAM (BILLY or SWEE'PEA),* *composer, piano;* b. Dayton, Ohio, 11/25/15. The closest writing associate of Duke Ellington from the time he joined the band in '39, Strayhorn composed *Take the A Train; Lush Life* (lyrics and music); *Chelsea Bridge; Day Dream; Raincheck; Passion Flower; A Flower is a Lovesome Thing; Johnny Come Lately.* In addition, he collaborated w. Ellington on the composing and arranging of hundreds of other works, among them *Suite Thursday* and the adaptation of Tchaikovsky's *Nutcracker Suite.* Over the years he occasionally played piano in the band, and in the various splinter groups. Strayhorn became ill in '66 and died 5/31/67 in a New York hospital.

In a eulogy on Strayhorn, Duke Ellington wrote, "He was the biggest human being who ever lived, a man with the greatest courage, the most majestic artistic stature, a highly skilled musician whose impeccable taste commanded the respect of musicians and the admiration of all listeners." A posthumously released album of Strayhorn's compositions played by the Ellington orch. was issued under the title . . . *And His Mother Called Him Bill* (RCA).

Albums under Strayhorn's own name include *!!!Live!!!* (Roul.) *The Peaceful Side* (UA); *Echoes of an Era* (Roul.); *Cue For Sax* (Master Jazz). A session of Ellington-Strayhorn duets is incl. in *The Golden Duke* (Prest.). Strayhorn plays in three tracks on *Esquire's All American Hot Jazz* (RCA). He is represented as composer in the vast majority of collections of records made by Ellington from 1939 on and reissued on LPs (see Ellington, Duke).

STRAZZERI, FRANK JOHN,* *piano, composer;* also *tenor saxophone, flute, baritone horn, organ, vibes;* b. Rochester, N.Y., 4/24/30. First widely known for his rec. w. Carmell Jones and Bud Shank in '60s; has since served as mus. collaborator for Johnny Cash TV show; pl. w. Doc Severinsen sextet for Johnny Carson at theatre-in-the-round; O. Nelson big band; Kai Winding quartet and tour w. Elvis Presley. In mid-70s most consistent association w. C. Tjader quintet; also periodically w. A. Pepper, Chet Baker, Joe Pass, Herb Ellis, T. Gibbs, Mundell Lowe, Z. Sims, F. Rosolino, C. Candoli, Harry Edison. TV: w. Les Brown on Bob Hope specs.; w. Presley at Madison Sq. Gdn. spec; World Satellite spec. from Hawaii. Fests: Concord twice w. Brown, Winding and Tjader; Monterey w. Tjader. Comps: *Jo Ann; My Lament; Strazzatonic; Taurus; Lazy Moments; Calcutta; Sphinx; View From Within;* also arrs. for Les Brown band. Publs: *Jazz Piano Solos* (Try Publ. Co. 854 Vine St., Hollywood, Ca. 90038); *Jazz Piano Method, "Strazzatonic"* (Gwyn Publ. Co. Inc., 14950 Delano St., Van Nuys, Ca. 91601). LPs: *View From Within* (Creative World); *That's Him and This Is New* (Revelation); *Frames* (Glendale); w. C. Tjader, *Last Night While We Were Young* (Fant.); others w. Nelson (Imp.); Presley (RCA).

STROZIER, FRANK R., *alto sax, flute, composer;* also *clarinet, piano;* b. Memphis, Tenn., 6/13/37. To Chicago in '54, pl. w. MJT +3. Moved to NYC, '59, working w. Roy Haynes, Miles Davis in '60s. In '65 settled in LA and became part of Shelly Manne's gp. Moved back to NYC at beginning of '70s. Pl. w. Keno Duke's Jazz Contemporaries. Member of NYJRC in first season '74. Comp: *Tiburon; D.R.T.* Won DB Critics poll, TDWR, on also sax '71. LPs: w. Duke, *Sense of Values* (Strata-East); w. Bobby Pierce, *New York* (Muse).

SUDHALTER, RICHARD MERRILL (DICK), *cornet;* also *alto horn, fluegelhorn, piano;* b. Boston, Mass., 12/28/38. Father, Al Sudhalter, was well known alto saxophonist in '30s. Graduated '60 from Oberlin Coll.; stud. trumpet w. Louis Davidson, Armando Ghitalla. In '60 Sudhalter left the United States for Austria, then lived in Germany, Great Britain and other countries. His life was divided equally between music and journalism. From '64-72 he was a correspondent for UPI, covering events in Britain, Germany, Yugoslavia, and the invasion of Czechoslovakia. He became a regular contributor to *Jazz Journal* and other publications. As a musician, he worked with artists of every school, among them Matty Matlock, Ben Webster, Dexter Gordon, Pee Wee Russell, Steve Kuhn, Vic Dickenson, Roger Kellaway, Bill Rank.

In '74 Sudhalter completed work on *Bix: Man & Legend,* in collaboration with Philip R. Evans, the definitive study of the life and times of Bix Beiderbecke, published in the U.S. by Arlington House. Among Sudhalter's infls., along with Bix, he names Bobby Hackett, Ruby Braff, L. Young, F. Trumbauer, Benny Carter, Bing Crosby and many others.

TV: British and German specs.; Bix Commemorative program, April, '75. Pl. & narrated Bix program for NYJRC at Carnegie Hall '75. Fest: Nice JF, '75. Came to NYC to lead quartet at the Riverboat, December '75.

LPs: *Sudhalter and Son,* I & II (77 Records); *Sweet and Hot—Anglo-American Alliance* (EMI); *New Paul Whiteman Orchestra* (Mon. Evergreen).

SUGANO, KUNIHIKO, *piano;* b. Tokyo, Japan, 10/13/35. Wife, Junko Kimura, pl. piano at Birdland club in Tokyo. Grad. from Gakushuin Univ.; took lessons from Yuriko Nemoto. After grad. worked for a yr. at Ishifuku Kinzoku K.K. Began in prof. music w. gp. of Osamu Hashimoto; w. Tony Scott, '59; Jun Yoshiya, Sleepy Matsumoto. Formed own trio. Infl: Linton Garner, E. Garner, W. Kelly, O. Peterson, H. Silver, H. Hawes, A. Previn, P. Newborn, Johnny Williams. LPs: *Finger Popping* (Columbia-Tact); *Music; Portrait; World of Kunihiko Kanno* (Audio Lab); *Live* (Trio); *Love Is a Many Splendored Thing* (Three Blind Mice).

SULIEMAN, IDREES DAWUD,* *trumpet, fluegelhorn;* also *alto sax;* b. St. Petersburg, Fla., 8/7/23. One of the earliest of the "modern" trumpeters of the '40s. Settled in Stockholm in the early '60s, after having toured in the Middle East and pl. in Cairo. A member of the Clarke-Boland Big Band until it broke up in '73. Living in Copenhagen in '70s. LPs: see Clarke-Boland; w. Horace Parlan, *Arrival;* Dexter Gordon, *More Than You Know* (Steeple.).

SULLIVAN, CHARLES HENRY, *trumpet, fluegelhorn, composer;* b. New York City, 11/8/44. Uncles, Hubert and Herman James, trumpeters in NY area. Lessons from Hubert in '54 for two yrs., then stopped pl. until '61 when he again stud. w. him. Further stud. w. Cecil Collins at Manhattan Sch. of Mus., '62-7, grad. w. BA. Pl. for an Off-Broadway prod. of *The Exception and the Rule* and *The Prodigal Son,* '65. Toured Europe for five mos. w. Donald McKayle Dance Co., '67. Worked w. Lionel Hampton, '68; Roy Haynes, '69; Count Basie, '70; Lonnie Liston Smith, '71; Sy Oliver, '72; Norman Connors, '73; Sonny Fortune, '73- . Upstate NY tour of Jazzmobile w. Billy Taylor, summer '75. Own quartet at Boomer's, '75. Theater: pit bands for *Promises, Promises,* '68; *Salvation,* '69; *Rainbow,* '71. Fest: NJF-NY w. Connors. TV: NJ educ. channel w. L.L. Smith; *Black Journal* w. B. Taylor, PBS, '75. Member of NYJRC; JCOA. Infl: Lee Morgan, Coltrane. Comp: *Genesis; Evening Song; Now I'll Sleep; Goodbye, Sweet John.* LPs: *Genesis;* w. S. Fortune, *Long Before Our Mothers Cried* (Strata East), *Awakening* (Horizon); w. Carlos Garnett (Muse); Dollar Brand (Enja).

SULLIVAN, IRA BREVARD,* *trumpet, fluegelhorn, saxophones, flute, composer;* also *percussion;* b. Washington, D.C., 5/1/31. One of the important Chicago modernists of the late '40s and up until he moved to Florida in the early '60s. Working in Ft. Lauderdale and Miami from that time. In addition to pl. clubs and concerts he also has brought his gp. into elementary schools, churches and junior colls. In '71 he pl. at the Miami Jazz Fest.; Kennedy Center JF, Wash., D.C. Musical contractor-percussionist for Miami production of *Hair,* '72. A member of large jazz ensemble, the Baker's Dozen, in Miami. Originally inspired by the music of Charlie Parker and other bop giants, he incorporated elements of Coltrane, post-Coltrane and rock into his '70s performances. Comp: *Nineveh; E Flat Tuba G.*

LPs: *Horizons;* w. Eddie Harris, *Come On Down* (Atl.); *Nicky's Tune* (Delmark); reissue, w. Red Rodney, *The Red Arrow* (Onyx).

SULLIVAN, JOE (Dennis Patrick Terence Joseph O'Sullivan),* *piano;* b. Chicago, Ill., 11/5/06. An associate of the so-called "Austin High Gang" along w. E. Condon, B. Freeman, F. Teschemacher et al, Sullivan was well known in the '30s when he rec. a solo session for John Hammond and toured w. Bob Crosby's band. After long periods of semi-inactivity, he app. at the MJF in '63 and NJF, '64. He died 10/13/71 in a hospital in SF. Sullivan's best known comps. incl. *Little Rock Getaway* and *Gin Mill Blues.*

Own LP on Folkways; also some tracks in *A Jazz Holiday* (MCA).

SULLIVAN, MAXINE, *singer;* also *valve trombone, trumpet;* b. Homestead, Pa., 5/13/11. Achieved overnight fame with swing-style rec. of *Loch Lomond* 1938. Married to John Kirby 1937-41; sang w. him on radio series. Movies, night clubs from 1930s to mid-50s, then inactive for much of next decade except for occ. concerts, LPs. Worked as nurse; busy in community affairs in Bronx. Founder, director of House That Jazz Built, non-profit recreation center.

Made comeback '67 at Town Hall concert; Dick Gibson Jazz Party in Colorado '68. W. Bobby Hackett at Riverboat, NYC, '69; many clubs, concerts and nine countries overseas w. World's Greatest Jazzband, '69-75, incl. Newport, Nice fests. At the age of 64 she was still singing with the same light, gently swinging quality that had established her in the swing era. Own LPs, also LPs w. Bob Wilber, Dick Hyman (Monmouth-Evergreen); w. World's Greatest Jazzband at Carnegie Hall (World Jazz).

SUMMERLIN, EDGAR E. (ED),* *saxophone, composer, educator;* b. Marrianna, Fla., 9/1/28. A pioneer in the liturgical jazz field, he wrote and cond. for religious TV show, *Look Up and Live* in early '60s. Pl. w. Don Ellis; co-led sextet w. D. Heckman. From '71 director of jazz program at City Coll. of N.Y. while continuing to be active as writer for church councils; American Guild of Organists; TV; stage; film; and dance groups; adjudicator and cond. for high schools; performer and lecturer at Int. Congress on Communication of Culture Through Art, Architecture and Mass Media, '70, in Europe, U.S. colleges. One of three American artists invited to conference on Salvation Today in Bangkok, Thailand, '72. Mus. consultant to playwrights' unit of Actors' Studio, '71. Mus. Dir. for Hamm & Clov Stage Co., NYC. Film: Comp. music for *Ciao,* only full-length American film chosen for Venice Film Fest., '67. TV: wrote and perf. mus. for Christmas Eve program on CBS, '66; *Come Along,* CBS, '72. Stage: music for *Felix,* Actors' Studio, '72; *Darts,* Hamm & Clov, '74. Dance: *Traveling Through Three; The Continuing Saga of the Bouncing Ball* for Brenda Bufalino Dance Co., New Paltz, N.Y., '73. Perf. *Varieties in Jazz* at City Coll. Center for Perf. Arts, '74. Comps: *Evensong: A Jazz Liturgy* for First Int. JF; *Christ Lag In Todesbonden or Where Do We Go From Here; Bless This World; Slippin' Through Time; Excursions.* Publ: *Heavy Hymns* (Hope Pub. Co., Carol Stream, Ill.). LPs: *Ring Out Joy* (Avant Garde); *Jax or Better* w. Heckman/Summerlin sextet (English Jazz Workshop); *Saturday in the Park and Other Songs Made Famous by Chicago* (RCA Camden).

SUN RA (Herman "Sonny" Blount) (Le Sony'r Ra),* *piano, electric keyboards, synthesizer, Roksichord, Sun harp, composer, leader;* b. Birmingham, Ala., May (under Gemini), ca. 1915. His Solar Arkestra, Space Arkestra or Intergalactic Myth-Science Arkestra, as it has been variously known, is in certain ways a "family," many of its members having been with him for a long time. Some, like reedmen John Gilmore, Marshall Allen and Pat Patrick, began with him in '56. In the '70s a typical Arkestra consisted of three brass; six reeds; five or six percussion; bass; and the leader on an assortment of keyboards. With the dancers and vocalists often employed there are often more than 20 performers on stage during a presentation dressed in colorful costumes (heavy on the gold lamé) and headgear, ranging from Sun Ra's Egyptian space helmet to turbans, burnooses and Robin Hood caps. Films, shown on a screen behind the band, are common to his performances, often depicting the leader and his Arkestra. Even a fire-eater has been incorporated into what are theatrical performances embodying myriad elements.

Many observers have felt that these trappings and the "space" oriented titles that he places on his compositions are merely "show biz," "jive" and one big "put-on" or that he is a naif. "But naivete does not exist where black art is concerned," says critic Joachim Berendt.

Imamu Baraka (Leroi Jones) wrote: "Sun Ra more validly than anybody else performs classical contemporary Black Music of Ancient Black Tradition."

Sun Ra states: "I paint pictures of infinity with my music, and that's why a lot of people can't understand it . . . Intergalactic music concerns the music of the galaxies. It concerns intergalactic thought and intergalactic travel, so it is really outside the realms of the future on the turning points of the impossible. But it is still existent, as astronomy testifies."

Film: *Space is the Place.* The Arkestra won DB Critics poll, TDWR, '71-2; Sun Ra won on organ, TDWR; and synthesizer, '75. Fest: NJF-NY '73. Two month tour of Mexico, early '74.

Comp: *Space is the Place; Rocket Number Nine; Sea of Sounds; Hidden Spheres; Astro Black; The Cosmo-Fire; Black Myth; Watusi; Shadow World; The Stargazers; Outer Spaceways Inc.*

LPs: *It's After the End of the World* (MPS); *Nothing Is; Heliocentric Worlds* (ESP); *Angels and Demons at Play; Crystal Spears; Magic City; Nubians of Plutonia,* etc. (Imp., orig. issued on Sun Ra's own label, Saturn); *Pictures of Infinity* (Bl. Lion); *Space is the Place* (Blue Thumb).

SUPERSAX. see Clark, Buddy; Flory, Med.

SURMAN, JOHN, *baritone saxophone;* also *soprano, bass clarinet, synthesizer;* b. Tavistock, England, 8/30/44. Educ. London Coll. Mus./London Univ., '60-4. First pl.w. Mike Westbrook '59-64; then various groups inc. Mike Gibbs, Graham Collier, Chris McGregor, Dave Holland, John McLaughlin, '64-8, in England. The Trio, w. Stu Martin, Barre Phillips in W. Europe/E. Europe, '69-72. "SOS" w. Alan Skidmore, Mike Osborne, Europe, '73- . Surman has app. at most of the major European jazz fests., as well as on European and Japanese TV. He won the *Melody Maker* poll, '68-74 on bari., sop. saxes; DB poll, TDWR, '69. Infls: Johnny Dodds; Harry Carney; Ellington; Parker; Coltrane; Rollins; Bach; Ravel; Bartok and many others. Surman is VP of Jazz Centre Society, London. Comp. ballet music for *Sablier Prison* for Paris Opera.

LPs: *How Many Clouds* (Decca); *Westering Home* (Island); *The Trio* (Pye); *SOS* (Ogun); *Citadel* w. Westbrook (RCA); *Live at Woodstock,* Surman/Martin (A.T.V.).

SUTTON, RALPH EARL,* *piano;* b. Hamburg, Mo., 11/4/22. First prominent w. J. Teagarden in late '40s; popular in NYC, where he pl. for several years at Eddie Condon's. Moving to SF, pl. at clubs in the Bay Area, Monterey JF, '61. To Aspen, Colo. '64, where his wife had a supper club, Sunnie's Rendezvous, at which he worked. In '66 he pl. in NYC w. Bob Crosby. Every summer, starting in '65, pl. in Denver with the Ten Greats of Jazz, which evolved into the World's Greatest Jazzband. Sutton toured with the group through Sept. '74, when he settled in Pine, Colo. and worked w. P. Hucko and Gus Johnson at a Denver hotel. Fests: Monterey, Newport etc. w. WGJ; Colorado Jazz Party. Publ: *Piano Man, The Story of Ralph Sutton* by James D. Shacter (Jaynar Press, P.O. Box 3141, Merchandise Market Plaza, Chicago, Ill. 60654).

Once wrongly identified as exclusively a ragtime pianist, Sutton is an artist of exceptional skill, originally inspired by Fats Waller and James P. Johnson, playing impeccably with a powerful left hand and an excellent rhythmic and harmonic sense, in a broad range of styles.

LPs: w. WGJ (Atl., Project 3, World Jazz); *The Compleat Bud Freeman* (Mon. Ev.); two on Blue Angel Jazz Club.

SUZUKI, ISAO, *bass; also cello, vibes, piano;* b. Tokyo, Japan, 1/2/36. Pl. w. Sleepy Matsumoto quartet, '61-4; Sadao Watanabe quartet, '64-5; formed own gp. and worked at Club Five Spot in Tokyo, '65-9; w. Art Blakey's Jazz Messengers in U.S., '69-70. Ret. to Japan in '70 and resumed w. own gp. Infl: Jim Hall. Won *Swing Journal* Jazz Disc Award, Jazz of Japan Award, '73. LPs: *Blow Up; Blue City; All Right* (Three Blind Mice).

SWALLOW, STEPHEN W. (STEVE),* *bass, bass guitar, composer;* b. New York City, 10/4/40. Pl. w. Paul Bley; George Russell; J. Giuffre; A. Farmer; A. Cohn-Z. Sims in '60s; Stan Getz, '65-7. Joined Gary Burton, '67 and was w. him to '70 when moved to Bolinas, Calif. where he spent three years writing, and playing in SF w. pianists Art Lande; Mike Nock. With Burton again from '73; also played and rec. w. Mike Gibbs and, intermittently w. Steve Kuhn. Original list of favs. should have incl. Red Mitchell. A composer of grace, wit and imagination, his abilities in this direction are also strongly indicated in his electric bass (bass guitar) solos. In addition his supporting lines are a strong factor in the lustrous power of the Burton ensemble. Comp: *Hotel Hello; Chelsea Bells; Hullo, Bolinas; Portsmouth Figurations; Domino Biscuit; Sweet Henry; Sweeping Up; The Green Mountains; Arise, Her Eyes; Eiderdown; I'm Your Pal; Falling Grace; General Mono's Well Laid Plan.* LPs: *Hotel Hello* w. Burton; w. S. Kuhn, *Trance* (ECM); w. M. Gibbs, *The Only Chrome-Waterfall Orch.* (Bronze); *In the Public Interest* (Poly.); w. Mike Mantler (Watt); w. Burton, *Ring* (ECM); *Duster; In Concert; A Genuine Tong Funeral* (RCA); Burton-Grappelli, *Paris Encounter* (Atl.).

SWARTZ, HARVIE, *bass, composer;* also *piano;* b. Chelsea, Mass., 12/6/48. Began as pianist but switched to bass in '67. Studied w. Orrin O'Brien of NY Phil. Freelanced in Europe in '70 w. D. Gordon; K. Drew; Art Taylor; Brew Moore; J. Heath; J. Griffin. In Boston worked w. Mose Allison; Al Cohn-Zoot Sims; C. Shavers; Chris Connor; Jaki Byard. Moved to NYC '73, gigging w. Mike Abene; Jackie Paris-Ann Marie Moss; L. Konitz; Jackie & Roy. Later free-lanced w. Steve Kuhn; Thad Jones-Mel Lewis; Gil Evans; Chet Baker; Hubert Laws; Jack Wilkins; Arnie Lawrence; B. Watrous; Sheila Jordan. TV: *Today* w. Jackie & Roy. Fest: NJF-NY w. Baker '75. Comp: *I've Touched Your Soul; Islands; Truce.* LPs: w. D. Friedman (East Wind); Barry Miles (London); David Matthews; Eric Kloss; Mark Murphy (Muse); Jackie & Roy (CTI); Paris-Moss (Diff. Drum.).

SWOPE, EARL, *trombone;* b. Hagerstown, Md., 8/4/22. Prominent in 1940s w. bands of Boyd Raeburn, Geo. Auld, Buddy Rich, Woody Herman, and in '50s w. Elliott Lawrence, Joe Timer (in Washington, D.C.), Jimmy Dorsey, Swope returned to Washington, freelanced, then worked for a while with Louie Bellson in 1959. He was playing in the Bob Cross band in Washington when he died 1/3/68 after a brief illness. LPs w. Herman (Col., Cap.); Sonny Berman (Onyx); Stan Getz (Prestige); many others w. Bill Potts, Willis Conover et al, now deleted.

SZABO, FRANK J., *trumpet, fluegelhorn;* b. Budapest, Hungary, 9/16/52. Stud. w. Tom Scott, 1962-9; also at Van Nuys High Sch. and LA Valley College. Pl. in LV and on road w. Harry James, '70 and '71; two month tour w. Frank Sinatra Jr. Orch., early '71; rest of '71 touring USA, Europe, Japan w. Ray Charles. Tours, clubs w. L. Bellson, Feb. '72-Oct. '74. Joined Count Basie Dec. '74 and toured internationally with him through 75; also gigged with Sweets Edison. Infls: M. Ferguson, F. Hubbard, Rafael Mendez, Al Porcino, Doc Severinsen, J. Coltrane, Ch. Parker. LPs w. Ray Charles (Tangerine); Bellson, Basie (Pablo).

SZABO, GABOR,* *guitar, composer;* b. Budapest, Hungary, 3/8/36. To U.S., '56. After pl. w. C. Hamilton, G. McFarland, C. Lloyd, formed own group, traveled extensively, '66-8. In '68, in partnership w. C. Tjader and McFarland, organized and recorded for Skye Records, a short-lived company. In '69 he disbanded, taking six months to plan a new, more heavily rock and blues oriented combo; also rec. an album acc. Lena Horne. Since '70 has led various quartets, based in LA. In '75 he decided to form a new gp. consisting of musicians all of whom at one time or another had been a part of his previous units, representing a complete progression from chamber-like classically oriented music to hard jazz-rock sounds. He called this group The Perfect Circle.

Comps: *Lady Gabor; Gypsy Queen; Mizrab; Spellbinder; Bacchanal; Divided City; The Fox; Lilac Glen; Time; The Director; Rising.* Film music for Roman Polanski's *Repulsion;* Gabor Kalman's *Farm Boy of Hungary* and several educational shorts. Though his career in the late '60s and early '70s seemed to lack a clearly defined direction, Szabo at his best continued to reflect the almost limitless variety of influences to which he had been exposed both in Hungary and the U.S.

Fests: Monterey, '67-8, '70; Newport, '67; Concord, '71. TV: Lena Horne Spec.; Flip Wilson show; color TV spec: *Gabor Szabo (U.S.A.) Jazz Podium,* filmed in Budapest, 90 minutes of music and interviews and travel around the city with dialogue in English and Hungarian.

LPs: *Mizrab; Rambler; Skylark* (CTI); *Bacchanal; Dreams; Gabor Szabo 1969; Lena & Gabor* (Skye); *The Best of; Gypsy '66; Spellbinder; Jazz Raga; Simpatico; The Sorcerer; Wind, Sky & Diamonds; More Sorcery; His Greatest Hits* (Imp.); *Magical Connection; High Contrast; Live with Charles Lloyd* (Blue Thumb).

TABACKIN, LEWIS BARRY (LEW), *tenor saxophone, flute*; b. Philadelphia, Pa., 5/26/40. Stud. during high school years, '55-8; BM with flute major, Phila. Conserv. of Mus., '58-62. Moved to NYC, '65, working there w. M. Ferguson, C. Calloway, Urbie Green, B. Rosengarden, C. Terry, Duke Pearson, T. Jones-M. Lewis, Joe Henderson, Chuck Israels, Doc Severinsen; also small gp. apps. w. D. Byrd, Elvin Jones, Attila Zoller, Don Friedman, Toshiko Akiyoshi. Had own trio '68-9. In '69 pl. Hamburg Jazz Workshop w. Israels, feat. w. Danish Radio Orch., and toured Switzerland.

Married to Toshiko Akiyoshi, he toured Japan with her in '70 and again in '71. In '72 they moved to LA, where Tabackin continued to work as a member of Severinsen's band on the *Tonight* show, and w. Severinsen's Now Generation gp. for in-person apps. Occasionally he co-led a quartet, and a big band, both with Toshiko. The orch. rec. in Hollywood for release on Japanese RCA.

Tabackin is an exceptional tenor saxophonist in a tradition clearly inspired by Sonny Rollins, though he also acknowledges his debt to Lester Young, Coleman Hawkins, Ben Webster, Don Byas, Chu Berry, Coltrane. He is also a flutist of rare distinction. Fests: Laurel, Baltimore, '68; Newport, '69; Expo. '70; San Diego, '75.

LPs: Toshiko Akiyoshi-L. Tabackin big band, *Kogun*(RCA Japan); Lew Tabackin Trio, *Let The Tape Roll*(RCA Japan); *Now Hear This*; *Introducing Duke Pearson Big Band,* with Pearson (BN); *Electric Byrd,* w. D. Byrd (BN); w. Akiyoshi, *Top of the Gate* (Takt, Japan); *Jazz in the Personal Dimension*; *Personal Aspect in Jazz* (RCA, Japan); w. Attila Zoller, *Gypsy Cry* (Embryo).

TAKAS, WILLIAM J. (BILL),* *bass*; b. Toledo, Ohio, 3/5/32. Active in second half of the '50s w. Z. Sims; Tal Farlow; Marian McPartland; Pee Wee Russell. Pl. w. Gerry Mulligan Concert Jazz Band '60; Paul Anka; Gene Krupa, '61-2, Vic Damone, '63-4; Judy Collins; Theodore Bikel; Anka, '65; Doc Severinsen, '66, at which time he took up Fender bass; B. Goodman, '67; house man at the Half Note backing Sims, Al Cohn, K. Winding, J. Rushing, B. Brookmeyer, Anita O'Day; also w. Ten Wheel Drive, '68 9. NBC staff w. Severinsen; own gp. in modern opera *Elephant Steps,* '70. Cond. band for musical, *Dr. Selavey's Magic Theatre,* '72-3. In '74-5 Takas, on Fender bass, acc. a variety of mus. at Bradley's, NYC, incl. Al Haig, Jimmy Rowles, Jimmy Raney, Mike Longo, Barry Harris and Bob Dorough. Pl. w. Dorough in LA, SF; also gigs w. Manhattan Transfer, '75. TV: wrote and arr. music and pl. w. International Ooba-Ooba Band for NBC Special *Earth Year One,* '71. Fest: Hollywood Bowl; NJF w. Mulligan. LPs w. Mulligan (Verve); Children of All Ages (Differant Drummer); others w. La Belle; Ten Wheel Drive; Buzzy Linhart.

TANNER, PAUL,* *educator, trombone*; b. Skunk Hollow, Kentucky, 10/15/17. Tanner's career as a jazz educator, which had begun when he gave courses at UCLA in '58, continued to expand throughout the '60s and '70s. By '75 he was teaching 1200 students a day in his history of jazz classes.

Tanner wrote and narrated TV shows concerning jazz history, wrote music and script for educational film entitled *Discovering Jazz* for Bailey Film Associates, an affiliate of CBS. The film was shown around the world. He is the author of innumerable music instruction books, the latest in '75 was *The Complete Practical Book for Tenor Trombone,* publ. by Holly-Pix (Western International, 13115 Morrison St., Sherman Oaks, Ca. 91423). Tanner's text book, *A Study of Jazz* (Wm. C. Brown, 2464 Kerper St., Dubuque, Iowa), was fully revised and reissued in '73. In the mid-'70s it was in use for history of jazz courses in more than 300 colleges. Tanner's knowledge of the subject stemmed partly from his directorship of the Curriculum for Higher Education for the National Association of Jazz Educators.

Early in '75, Tanner, along with Hal Cook and KBCA radio personality Bob Summers, conceived the idea for the World Jazz Association. Tanner was appointed Exec. Dir., of the WJA, headquartered at Suite 4C, 10966 Rochester Ave., Los Angeles, Cal. 90024.

In addition to his many other activities, Tanner continued to play trombone professionally whenever possible.

TAPSCOTT, HORACE, *piano, composer*; b. Houston, Tex., 4/6/34. Stud. from age six with mother, a pianist. Early exp. w. Monroe Tucker gp. To LA 1945. At Jefferson High Sch. pl. in Swing Band w. Don Cherry, E. Dolphy, S. Criss, Art Farmer, Dexter Gordon, 1948-52. Also worked w. Dolphy in Gerald Wilson orch. ca. '50-51. In service, pl. in AAF band '53-7. Formed own group, '58. Toured w. Lionel Hampton '59-61; lived in NYC for a while, then returned to LA and formed a small unit which, with changing personnel, he has led ever since; members incl. Azar Lawrence and Black Arthur Blythe. Wrote music for poet Elaine Brown for Vault and Black Forum LPs, also pl. on albums w. Lou Blackburn for Imperial.

Tapscott, who says "Our music is contributive, not competitive," is highly regarded by Stanley Crouch and other West Coast observers. Crouch wrote that "this is a new Black music, but new only because, as an African writer once said, it recognizes 'time is flow.' Tapscott and his men know that all of the time, if it's carrying the feeling of the people, it is new, is free." Comps: *Sonny's Dream*; *This Is For Benny*; *The Golden Pearl.*

LPs: *The Giant Is Awakened* (Fl. Dutchman); also comps. and arrs. for Sonny Criss album, *Sonny's Dream* (Prest.).

TATE, GEORGE HOLMES (BUDDY),* *tenor sax*; also *soprano, alto, baritone, clarinet, flute*; b. Sherman, Texas, 2/22/15. After ten years with Count Basie, formed own small band. By early 1970s divided time between quartet and septet, making several overseas tours of Europe and Japan. Annual apps. at NJF, other festivals at Nice and throughout Continent. Awarded prize by Academie du Disque Francais for best jazz record of 1968 with LP featuring himself, Milt Buckner and Wallace Bishop. Made film for Roger Vadim in Paris, Jan. 1974. Playing w. P. Quinichette in Two Tenor Boogie at West End Cafe, NYC, '75.

One of the most able survivors of the warm-toned, Hawkins-inspired school of Texas tenor saxophonists, Tate found a wider audience than many of his contemporaries, continuing to play the Sheraton Hotel chain annually, many college concerts, Dick Gibson's jazz party etc.

LPs: *The Texas Twister*; *Swinging Like Tate* (MJR); *Unbroken* (BASF); *Buddy Tate & His Buddies* (Chiaroscuro); *Very Saxy* w. Lockjaw Davis, Coleman Hawkins, Arnett Cobb; *Kansas City Nights* w. Buck Clayton (Prestige); *When I'm Blue*; *Midnight Slows* (Black & Blue).

TATE, GRADY,* *drums, singer*; also *percussion*; b. Durham, N.C., 1/14/32. His work w. Quincy Jones band in early '60s led to many assignments as free-lance studio musician in NYC through '66. He cont. in the studios '67 but toured w. Peggy Lee who also gave him opportunity to sing. From '68-74 a member of orch. for *Tonight Show,* NBC. During this period he launched vocal career which intensified in activity from '72. At the same time remained active as a drummer. Sings both blues and ballads effectively in throaty baritone style. TV: Joey Bishop; Merv Griffin; *Black Journal*; Joe Franklin. Fest: NJF-NY; Col. JP; many other imp. fests. LPs: *By Special Request* (Buddah); *Movin' Day*; *She Is My Lady* (Janus); *Windmills of My Mind*; *Feeling Life*; *After the Long Ride Home* (Skye); w. Q. Jones (A&M); Jimmy Smith (Mojo; Verve); w. S. Getz, *Sweet Rain* (Verve); w. Aretha Franklin (Atl.).

TAYLOR, WILLIAM (BILLY),* *piano, composer, educator*; also *electric keyboards, synthesizer*; b. Greenville, N.C., 7/24/21. One of the most active and articulate people in jazz, both in and around the music, Taylor was musical director of the David Frost television show from '69-72. During this period he did less work with his trio but took the 11-piece Frost band, which incl. Frank Wess, Hubert Laws and Jimmy Owens, out for weekend concerts at colleges. In '72 he was part of Black Communications Corp. (incl. Ben Tucker) which purchased radio Station WSOK in Savannah, Ga. He also returned, for a short time, as general manager of WLIB, NYC, where he formerly had been a deejay.

From '73 Taylor has appeared w. his trio (Bob Cranshaw, then Larry Ridley, bass; Bobby Thomas, drums) on an intermittent basis but his other projects are multifarious. He is president of Billy Taylor Productions (119 West 57th St., New York, N.Y. 10019) which creates radio and TV commercials and publishes folios of his compositions under Duane Music and Castion Music. Other of his works are publ. by Charles Hansen (1860 Broadway. New York, N.Y. 10023).

As an educator he is a Yale Fellow at Calhoun College where he had conducted seminars; has taught a special course in the history of jazz piano at the Manhattan Sch. of Mus.; from '72 jazz history at C.W. Post Coll.; and designed a jazz program for the Wash., D.C. school system. In '75 he instituted a lecture series under his name at Howard U. which incl. clinics for credit. He received his Doctorate in Mus. Ed. (dissertation on History of Jazz Piano) in Sept. '75. Still active w. Jazzmobile, which he helped found, reshaping workshop with Dave Bailey.

He was a musical director of the NYJRC during its first two seasons. Board member of the National Council on the Arts; NARAS. In Oct. '75 replaced Harold Arlen on Board of Dir. of ASCAP. Played at White House State dinners for Pres. Nixon, '74; Ford, Feb. '75.

Fest: NJF; NJF-NY; MJF. Comp: *Suite For Jazz Piano and Orchestra,* performed w. Utah Symph. in Mormon Tabernacle, Jan. '73, and also perf. w. Minneapolis & Oakland Symphs.; National Symph.; Wash., D.C.; *Impromptu*; *I Wish I Knew How It Would Feel to Be Free*; *Theodora*; special material for *Sesame Street* and *The Electric Co.* TV: *Friends of Langston Hughes*; *Over 7 (Rainbow Sundae),* ABC, *Black Journal Tonight,* PBS: mus. dir. of 18-piece band and featured artist, '75; added host duties, '76. LPs: *I Wish I Knew How It Would Feel to Be Free* (Tower); *O.K. Billy*; *Merry Christmas from David Frost and Billy Taylor* (Bell).

TAYLOR, CECIL PERCIVAL,* *piano, composer, educator*; b. New York City, 3/15/33. The avant of today's avant garde, Taylor has been leading his own group from the '50s. Jimmy Lyons has been its alto saxophonist from '60; Andrew Cyrille the drummer from '64. A tour of Europe in '69 incl. Sam Rivers on tenor saxophone in the unit; at times during the '70s he added Sirone on bass. Taylor continued to perform in concert as a solo pianist as he did at NJF-NY '72 and the Montreux JF '74. His group played for the Maeght Foundation in France, '69; and at the Metropolitan Museum of Art, NYC, '72. Club appearances were not that frequent but he played two engagements at the Five Spot in '75.

In the '70s Taylor also became involved in academia, teaching a course in *Black Music 1920-1970* and directing the Black Music Ensemble at the University of Wisconsin in '70-1. He left there when, after failing two-thirds of his students for lack of seriousness in their work, a faculty committee changed his gradings to "satisfactory" and he resigned in protest. He then went to Antioch College in Yellow Springs, Ohio, where he taught for two years, and Glassboro State College, in New Jersey.

"Despite the fact that Taylor was around long before Coltrane recorded *Giant Steps* or Coleman came to New York," wrote Gary Giddins, "and despite the fact that he has long had a passionate coterie of admirers and influenced dozens of more accepted musicians (including Chick Corea and Steve Kuhn), he remains the outermost concentric circle of the avant garde. . . . Yes, his music is heavily rhythmic, but no, you can't tap your foot to it; yes, his music is intensely lyrical, but no, you won't be humming it after one hearing; yes, his music is richly harmonic, but no, he does not employ chord changes."

Film: for Bureau of Research, ORTF (French Radio/TV), '66. Awarded Guggenheim Fellowship, '73. Won Record of the Year for *Silent Tongues,* and was elected to Hall of Fame, DB Critics poll '75.

Comp: *Conquistador*; *With (Exit)*; *Unit Structure*; *Tales (8 Whisps)*; *Indent*; *Lono*; *Student Studies*; *Amplitude*; *Niggle Feuigle*; *Spring of Two Blue-J's*; *Colors Are Marchin'*; *Baptism Dances*; *Huddlin' and Hollow Heart*; *Chimes.*

LPs: *Silent Tongues,* solo piano at Montreux '74 (Arista); *Indent*; *Spring of Two Blue-J's* (Unit Core Records, 96 Chambers St., New York, N.Y. 10007); *Unit Structures*; *Conquistador* (BN); *Bulu Akisakila Kutala* (Trio); w. Jazz Composers Orch. (JCOA); *Nuits de la Fondation Maeght* (Shandar); reissue, *In Transition* (BN).

TAYLOR, CREED, *producer*; b. Lynchburg, Va., 5/13/29. Bach. degree in psychology from Duke U., where he pl. trumpet in marching band and in Duke Ambassadors Dance Orch. In '54 became a & r head at Bethlehem Records. In '56 joined ABC-Paramount, where he started the Impulse label. Joined Verve, '62, producing the Grammy award-winning, million-selling Getz-Gilberto album; also Ch. Byrd's and Getz's *Jazz Samba,* generally credited with starting the bossa nova trend.

In '67 Taylor moved to A & M records, where he enjoyed great success with Wes Montgomery's *A Day in the Life* and others for whom he found a successful commercial jazz direction. In '70 he started his own companies, CTI, Kudu and Salvation Records, recording Hubert Laws, Freddie Hubbard, Stanley Turrentine, Joe Farrell, Deodato, George Benson, Esther Phillips, Chet Baker and Jackie & Roy, with Don Sebesky as chief arranger. CTI was voted # 1 jazz company by Billboard in '74.

TAYLOR, CALVIN EUGENE (GENE),* *bass*; b. Toledo, Ohio, 3/19/29. Raised in Detroit. Came out of that fertile jazz environment to play w. Horace Silver quintet, '58-64, then w. Blue Mitchell in mid-'60s. In the '70s worked very often w. Judy Collins in folk field; Duo w. Duke Jordan at Bradley's; various duo and trio gigs w. Barry Harris in NYC. LPs: *Barry Harris Plays Tadd Dameron* (Xanadu); w. E. Kloss, *Doors*; w. Neal Creque (Cobble.); w. Eddie Jefferson, *Come Along With Me* (Prest.).

TAYLOR, KOKO, *singer*; b. Memphis, Tenn., 1938. Insp. by records of B.B. King, Sonny Boy Williamson, Howlin' Wolf and Elmore James, she began singing blues after moving to Chicago in '53. Gigged in local Southside and Westside taverns; made her first record date for USA label in '63. Under sponsorship of Willie Dixon she later signed w. Chess Records and scored a major success w. Dixon's comp. *Wang Dang Doodle,* which became her theme song and estab. her as a popular figure in black-oriented night clubs and on radio stations. Later became a favorite in Europe, where she toured extensively, sang at Montreux JF, rec. in France. She also app. w. Muddy Waters, Mike Bloomfield, Johnny Winter, Buddy Miles and Dr. John on the Nat'l Public TV prog. *Sound Stage*. One of the better latterday singers in the early blues tradition.

LP: *I Got What It Takes* (Alligator); *Basic Soul* (Chess).

TEAGARDEN, CHARLES (CHARLIE),* *trumpet*; b. Vernon, Tex., 7/19/13. Brother of the late Jack Teagarden. After working at Silver Slipper in LV, '61-4, he did relief band work in Strip hotels. Elected to the Exec. Board of Local 369 of the Musicians' Union in LV, '63, he became one of the President's assistants in '68 and at that point gave up an active career in music.

LPs: some tracks in *A Jazz Holiday* (MCA).

TEMPERLEY, JOSEPH (JOE),* *baritone sax*; also *tenor, soprano saxes, bass clarinet, flute*; b. Fife, Scotland, 9/20/29. From '60-65 he continued w. the Humphrey Lyttelton band w. which he had toured the U.S. in '59. Moved to NYC and pl. w. Woody Herman '66. Worked and/or rec. w. Buddy Rich, Thad Jones-Mel Lewis, Clark Terry, Duke Pearson, Joe Henderson, Deodato, New York Jazz Composers Orch. between '67 and Oct. '74, when he replaced the late Harry Carney in the Duke Ellington band. App. in English film, *What Makes Sammy Run*. TV w. Herman, Rich, Terry, Lyttelton, Jimmy Rushing, Big Joe Turner, Eric Dolphy. LPs: *Central Park North* w. Jones-Lewis (Solid State); *Let My Children Hear Music* w. Charles Mingus (Columbia); *Big Bad Band* w. Terry (Etoile); *Buck Clayton Jam Session* (Chiaroscuro); *East & West* w. Herman (Col.); *Continuum* w. Mercer Ellington (Fant.).

TERRY, CLARK,* *trumpet, fluegelhorn, singer, leader*; b. St. Louis, Mo., 12/14/20. Continued to play in the NBC orch. for the *Tonight Show* until the spring of '72 when Johnny Carson shifted his base of operations to LA. Led own combos and big band for clubs, concerts and fests. He also appeared as a soloist for George Wein; Norman Granz tours in Europe. Active as a clinician. An effervescent brassman who combines technical wizardry with flair, and unrelenting swing; and a humourous, highly-entertaining vocalist in his patented "mumbles" style. Big band won DB Critics poll, TDWR, '75.

Fest: NJF-NY '72; MJF; Montreux; Molde; Pori; Nice; NO; Wichita; Odessa, Tex.; Colo. JP from '69. Publ: *Let's Talk Trumpet (From Legit to Jazz) Books 1,2&3*; co-author w. Phil Rizzo, *The Interpretation of the Jazz Language* (C.J.C. Inc., P.O. Box 467, Bowie, Md. 20715). Comp: *Sheba*; *Samba de Gumz*; *Tee Pee Time*; *Electric Mumbles*. LPs: *and his Jolly Giants*; *Big B-a-d Band Live at the Wichita Jazz Festival 1974* (Vang.); *Big Bad Band at Carnegie Hall 1970* (Etoile); *It's What's Happenin'*; *Spanish Rice* (Imp.); others w. Terry-Bob Brookmeyer Quintet (Verve; Main.); *Oscar Peterson-Clark Terry; The Trumpet Kings at Montreux '75; JATP at Montreux '75* (Pablo); *Newport in New York '72: The Jam Sessions, Vols. 3&4*; *The Jimmy Smith Jam, Vol. 5* (Cobble.); *Colorado Jazz Party* (MPS).

TERRY, SONNY (Saunders Teddell),* *harmonica, composer, singer*; b. Durham, N.C., 10/24/11. Partner of Brownie McGhee (q.v.) from 1939. Continued to work 11 months out of each year, touring overseas approx. twice annually. Motion picture soundtrack work for *Book of Numbers*; *Buck and the Preacher*; *Cisco Pike*. TV: Mike Douglas show; *Midnight Special* etc. In fall of '75, went to Chicago to take part in special PBS televised tribute to John Hammond Sr., who had been responsible for his coming to NYC for the *From Spirituals to Swing* concert in '38. Terry sang a duet on this TV show with John Hammond Jr.

Comp.: *Mean Woman Blues*; *These Women Are Killing Me*; *Hootin' the Blues* (used as prelude for Broadway show *Finian's Rainbow*); *I'm A Burnt Child*; *Jet Plane Blues*; *Motorcycle Blues*; *Long Way From Home*.

LPs w. McGhee (Mercury, BluesWay, A & M, Fantasy, etc).

THARPE, SISTER ROSETTA (Rosetta Nubin),* *singer, guitar*; b. Cotton Plant, Ark., 3/20/21. Though trained in religious music, Sister Tharpe gained popularity as a vocalist with the bands of C. Calloway and L. Millinder. Later, feat. as a soloist, she maintained her reputation for many years, touring the U.S. and Europe. She died in 1973.

THELIN, EJE, *trombone*; b. Jonkokping, Sweden, 1938. First important job w. Joe Harris, '58-9. Had own group from '61-5. Pl. at Jazz Hus Montmartre, Copenhagen '63 with George Russell, at Montmartre '64. Soloist at Montmartre '66. In '73-4 played with John Surman in Europe; in '75 w. drummer Leroy Lowe in Sweden and U.S. From late '60-72 engaged at Graz Jazzinstitute as teacher. In mid-'70s occupied w. teaching, playing with various groups, and involved w. electronic experiments w. own quartet. TV: Sweden and the Continent. Fest: Antibes fest. in Juan-les-Pins '63; w. Barney Wilen, Roy Brooks, Palle Danielsson, Jazzjambouree, Warsaw '66; and most major European fests. from '63. LPs: *Eje Thelin Group* (Riks); *Candles of Vision* (Calig); *So Far*; *At the German Jazz Festival*.

THIELE, ROBERT (BOB), *producer, songwriter*; b. Brooklyn, N.Y., 7/27/22. An amateur clarinetist who evinced an early interest in jazz, he was a radio announcer on jazz record shows, 1936-44; editor and publisher, *Jazz Magazine,* '39-41. Owned and ran Signature Records 1940-48, rec. many sessions w. Pee Wee Russell, Coleman Hawkins, Art Hodes, James P. Johnson et al. In the 1950s he was an a & r director for Coral Records; then w. Dot, '59-

60; president, Hanover-Signature, '60-63; a & r producer at Roulette, '63-4.

From 1965-69 Thiele was responsible for the production of a great number of important albums as a & r director for Impulse, most notably those of John Coltrane, in whom he was a staunch believer; Oliver Nelson, Pharoah Sanders, Archie Shepp and many others. In 1969 he formed his own company, Flying Dutchman. For that label as well as his others, Amsterdam, Bob Thiele Music and Contact, he has recorded or reissued important works by both avant garde and traditional jazz artists. Married 10/24/72 to Teresa Brewer (q.v.).

Comps: lyrics to Duke Ellington's *C Jam Blues,* under the title *Duke's Place*; also *What A Wonderful World,* rec. by Louis Armstrong.

LPs: *20's Score Again* w. New Happy Times Orch. (Signature). Hundreds of others as producer, on above-listed labels.

THIELEMANS, JEAN (TOOTS),* *harmonica, guitar, whistler, composer*; b. Brussels, Belgium, 4/29/22. After working as a staff musician in NYC in the mid-60s, Thielemans from '69 was closely associated w. Quincy Jones, playing on sound tracks of several films, as well as on Jones' records, and at MJF, '72. In Nov. '72, he toured USSR with a quartet (Bob James, Milt Hinton, Ben Riley). Revisiting Belgium about twice a year as a single, Thielemans commuted between Europe and U.S., also, in his own words, "commuted between my love for jazz and the more commercial work."

Motion Pictures: *Midnight Cowboy*; *Getaway*; *Cinderella Liberty*; *Sugarland Express*. As comp., songs and background for Swedish animated film, *Dunderklumpeu*. TV: theme music for *Sesame Street*. Comps: his best known work is *Bluesette,* which he re-recorded in a new version with Jones in '75. Fest: Montreux '75.

LPs: *Toots & Svend,* w. S. Asmussen (A & M); *Captured Alive* (Choice); w. Jones, *Walking In Space*; *Gula Matari*; *Smackwater Jack*; *You've Got It Bad Girl*; *Mellow Madness* (A & M); w. O. Peterson at Montreux (Pablo); others w. J.J. Johnson, Z. Sims.

THIGPEN, BEN, *drums*; b. Laurel, Miss., 1909; d. St. Louis, Mo. 10/5/71. Prof. debut at 15 w. Bobby Boswell. Worked w. dance team, later settling in Chi., where he stud. w. Jimmy Bertrand. Best known for his long tenure in Andy Kirk orch., '30-47. Later, in St. Louis, led own groups and pl. w. Singleton Palmer's band throughout '60s. Father of Ed Thigpen (see below).

THIGPEN, EDMUND LEONARD (ED),* *drums*; also *percussion*; b. Chicago, Ill., 12/28/30. Pl. w. Bud Powell, Billy Taylor trios in '50s; then w. Oscar Peterson, '59-65, before settling in Toronto. Joined Ella Fitzgerald, '66. Moved to LA, '67, working w. Pat Boone, Johnny Mathis, Peggy Lee, Andy Williams, Oliver Nelson, Gerald Wilson and freelancing in the studios. Rejoined Fitzgerald '68 and remained w. her until July '72. In Sept. '72 moved to Copenhagen, working as a free-lance and teaching. Formed group w. Svend Asmussen, '73; also toured w. Sylvia Vrethammen in Sweden. From '74 teaching at Music Conservatory in Aarhus, Denmark; perf. w. own new group, Action Re Action. Fests: Montreux w. Fitzgerald, '69; also NJF, Verona, Kongsberg, Pori & other major Euro. events. Comp: music & lyrics for *Denise*; *Illusions,* a suite. Publ: *Talking Drums*; *Be Our Guest* w. Ray Brown (c/o Sonet Records, Torsvikksvangen 7A, Lidingo, Sweden). LPs: *Ed Thigpen's Action Re Action* (Sonet, GNP-Crescendo); *Out of the Storm* (Verve); *Jazz at Santa Monica* w. E. Fitzgerald, C. Basie & all stars (Pablo); w. Horace Parlan; Duke Jordan; Johnny Griffin; Dexter Gordon (SteepleChase); w. O. Nelson, *At Marty's On The Hill* (Imp.); w. Major Holley, *Mule* (Black & Blue).

THOMAS, JOSEPH LEWIS (JOE),* *trumpet*; b. Webster Groves, Mo., 7/24/09. The lyrical trumpet player continued to work in the NY metropolitan area in various settings. App. with own group at Leaves, an East Side night club; coll. dates '67-8. Toured w. own group feat. his wife, vocalist Baby Mathews, for Job Corps, '69-71. Colls., jazz clubs, private parties, '72. Also w. Mike Burgevin group at Brew's, and Jim Andrews group at O'Connors (Watchung, N.J.) '73. Pl. at dedication of L. Armstrong Stadium at NJF-NY, '73, an event filmed for NET.

Comps: *Swingtime Up In Harlem*; *No Better For Ya*; *He's Got So Much*; *Blues For Baby*. LPs: w. A. Tatum, *Masterpieces* (MCA); w. Vic Dickenson All Stars (British RCA); w. C. Cole, R. Norvo, *Jazz Giants* (Trip).

THOMAS, LEONE (Amos Leon Thomas Jr.), *singer, lyricist*; also *miscellaneous percussion*; b. East St. Louis, Ill., 10/4/37. Studied music at Lincoln HS w. Daisy O. Westbrook, "who taught by rote, increasing the ear's capacity." Two yrs. at Tenn. State. While in junior high school sang w. drummer Ben Thigpen; in high school w. Grant Green; Jimmy Forrest. To NYC Feb. '59 where immediately he replaced Austin Cromer as vocalist on show at Apollo which incl. Dakota Staton, Ahmad Jamal, Nipsey Russell, Art Blakey's Messengers. Toured w. this package on black theater circuit: Howard; Regal, Royal, etc. Worked w. Randy Weston; R.R. Kird; Mary Lou Williams, rec. live w. her at Town Hall. Took the place of Joe Williams in Count Basie orch. '61 and later was replaced by Ocie Smith and Irene Reid. After Army service rejoined Basie, and was w. him '64-5. He sang at the inaugural balls of Presidents Kennedy and Johnson w. Basie. With Pharoah Sanders, '69-72; still pl. occasional gigs w. him in mid-'70s. Own gp. before working w. Santana '73. Resumed as leader '74. A more than capable blues singer, sometimes reminiscent of Joe Williams, Thomas emerged with Sanders as a lyricist and also a scat singer, further coloring his performances with a form of yodeling he learned by listening to the music of Central African pygmy tribes. Added second "e" to Leon, '76. Infl: Ellington, Monk, Coltrane, Gillespie, Milton Nascimento, King Pleasure, Eddie Jefferson, Betty Carter. Won DB Critics poll, TDWR, '70; DB Readers poll, '70-3. TV: *Like It Is*; *Soul*; *Inside Bed-Stuy*; *Mike Douglas Big Band Festival*. Fest: NJF; MJF; Berlin, '70; Montreux, '70-1. Wrote lyrics to Sanders' *The Creator Has a Master Plan*; *Colors*; *Hum Allah, Hum Allah*; also *Straight No Chaser*; *Cousin Mary*; *Bags' Groove*. LPs: *The Leon Thomas Album*; *Full Circle*; *Spirits Known and Unkown*; *Blues and the Soulful Turth*; *Facets*; w. Oliver Nelson *In Berlin* (Fly. Dutch);

Louis Armstrong and Friends (Amsterdam); w. Sanders, *Karma*; *Jewels of Thought* (Imp.), *Izipho Sam* (St.-East); w. Santana, *Welcome*; *Santana Lotus—Live in Japan* (Col.); w. Basie, *Pop Goes the Basie* (Reprise); *Basie Picks the Winners* (Verve); w. Mary Lou Williams, *Praise the Lord in Many Voices* (Avant Garde); w. R.R. Kirk, *A Meeting of the Times* (Atl.).

THOMAS, RENE,* *guitar*; b. Liége, Belgium, 2/25/27. Lived in Montreal, '58-63, visiting NYC in '58 and rec. w. Toshiko and S. Rollins. Ret. to Europe, toured w. Lou Bennett, K. Clarke, and many other groups, incl. duo w. drummer Han Bennink. With Stan Getz, '69-72, incl. tour of Mexico. Returned to Montreal, '73, to visit relatives, but continued to work around the Continent until his sudden death of a heart attack in Santander, Spain, 1/3/75. Thomas was described by Rollins in 1958 as "better than any of the American guitarists on the scene today." In Europe, he was respected as one of the greatest guitarists to have emerged on the Continent since Django Reinhardt, who was his original inspiration. In later years Thomas was infl. by Jimmy Raney. He won DB poll, TDWR, 1967. Comp: *Ballad for Leo*.

LPs: *Dynasty* w. Getz (Verve); *A Songbook in Europe* w. Lucky Thompson (MPS); *TPL* (Vogel). European LPs w. Eddy Louiss, Jacques Dieval, Lou Bennett et al.

THOMPSON, DONALD WINSTON (DON),* *bass*; also *piano, vibes, drums*; b. Powell River, B.C., Canada, 1/18/40. After leaving John Handy group w. which he played in mid-'60s, he worked mainly in the studios of Vancouver and Toronto. Member of house rhythm section at Bourbon St. in Toronto, backing F. Rosolino, J. Hall, P. Desmond, B. Kessel, J. Moody, Blue Mitchell, C. McPherson. Comp: *Pluto & Mercury* on *Solar Explorations* LP by Moe Koffman; *Bilbo*; *Country Place*; *Don't*; *Echoes From Before* on *Koffman Live at George's*. He also pl. on both albums (GRT). Own LP: *Love Song to a Virgo Lady* (Sack.); other LPs: w. John Handy, incl. *Spirituals to Swing 30th Anny*.

THOMPSON, ELI (LUCKY),* *tenor, soprano saxes, composer*; b. Detroit, Mich., 6/16/24. Active on the LA scene during the '40s w. Charlie Parker, Dodo Marmarosa, Boyd Raeburn's orch. he pl. w. Kenton in the mid-'50s and then pl. and lived in Europe, '57-62 before returning to NYC. Back to Europe in late '60s, coming back to US again in '71. Taught for a year at Dartmouth U. from Sept. '73, and recorded two albums for Groove Merchant, *Goodbye Yesterday* and *I Offer You*. Reissue of earlier material w. Oscar Pettiford, Jimmy Cleveland from the '50s, *Dancing Sunbeam* (Impulse). Rec. for MPS in Europe.

THOMPSON, CHARLES PHILLIP (SIR CHARLES),* *piano, organ, composer*; b. Springfield, Ohio, 3/21/18. While w. I. Jacquet in '47 composed *Robbins' Nest*, a jazz standard; later led organ trio in many clubs. Toured Europe, '59; w. C. Hawkins at Berlin JF, '64. Sporadically active during next few years, he underwent major surgery in NYC in '74. Living in LA, he made a comeback concert June '75 at the Pilgrimage Theatre.

LPs: *Hey There* (Black and Blue); *Kansas City Nights* w. B. Clayton & B. Tate (Prest.); tracks in *Master Jazz Piano*, vol. 2 (Master Jazz).

THORNTON, CLIFFORD EDWARD III, *cornet, composer, educator*; also *valve trombone, shenai, African percussion*; b. Philadelphia, Pa., 9/6/36. Grandfather, a reed player, founded and dir. Wissahickon Concert Band and Happy Six Jazz Band in Germantown, Pa. Uncle, Jimmy Golden, pianist w. Philly jazz gps.; aunt, Alease Golden, church organist in Wilmington, Del. Studied at HS of Music & Art, NYC, '51-4; Temple U. '54-6; Morgan State Coll. '57; privately w. Donald Byrd, NYC, 57; Webster Young, SF, '61; Bavarian State Conserv., Wurzburg, W. Germany, '64-5; Juilliard, '66-8; Wesleyan U., '69-70; Manhattan Sch. of Mus., '72-4. Worked w. Ray Draper, '56-7; US Army Band, '58-61, in Korea, Japan; Phil Moore Jr; Sonny King, SF, '61-3; Sun Ra; Pharoah Sanders, '63-7; John Tchicai, '66; own gps., '66-9; Archie Shepp, '69-72; own gps., in NYC, Europe, '72-5. Instructor at New York Sch. of Mus., '65; Assistant Professor of Music, Wesleyan U., '69-75. Infl: Clifford Brown; D. Byrd, Webster Young, John Gilmore, Sun Ra, Jimmy Golden. TV: scored film for ORTF, Paris, '71; Antibes Fest. w. A. Shepp, BRT, '70; educational TV in NYC, NJ, Conn., '70-2. Fest: Amougies, '69; Carthage, Antibes, '70; Ghent, '71; Etudes et Rencontres Artistique, Geneva, '72-3; NY Jazz Musicians Fest., '72. Comp: *The Gardens of Harlem*. LPs: *Freedom and Unity*; *Communications Network* (Third World); *Ketchaoua* (Byg); *The Panther and the Lash* (America); *The Gardens of Harlem* (JCOA).

TIBERI, FRANK, *tenor saxophone*; also *bassoon, flute, clarinet*; b. Camden, N.J., 12/4/28. Started in 1936 with private lodge organization. Played in marching street band. Private teacher on clarinet; self-taught on sax and flute. Stud. bassoon w. Sol Schoenbach. Played in clubs from age 13, joined Bob Chester at 17. Worked in musical show doubling on many instruments. In mid-50s played w. B. Goodman quintet, Urbie Green; TV shows and movie sound tracks as sideman. In '69 joined W. Herman orch. on lead and jazz tenor, also playing jazz bassoon and conducting rap sessions at coll. seminars. Fests. w. Herman: Newport, Monterey, Tokyo, Concord, Montreux and many others in Europe.

Influenced by Ch. Parker, Lester Young, J. Coltrane, Dennis Sandole, Gil Evans and many classical composers, Tiberi proved to be a major force with his tenor work in the Herman band, and one of the handful of effective soloists on jazz bassoon.

LPs w. Herman: *Woody Brand New* (Cadet); *Giant Steps*; *Thundering Herd* (Fantasy).

TIMMONS, ROBERT HENRY (BOBBY),* *piano, vibes, composer*; b. Philadelphia, Pa., 12/19/35. Well known as composer of *Moanin'*, written while he was w. A. Blakey in '58, and *Dis Here* and *Dat Dere*, written and rec. while he was w. C. Adderley, '59-60, Timmons pl. at Greenwich Village bars and restaurants during the late '60s and early '70s. He died 3/1/74 of cirrhosis of the liver in a NYC hospital.

" 'Laid-back swagger' pretty well describes the way he played piano. . . ," wrote Peter Keepnews, "with a right hand effortlessly capable of the fleet lyricism of a Bud Powell and a left hand not averse to the earthy rumblings of a Meade Lux Lewis. It was the same kind of mixture of the urbane and the down-home that characterized the style of one of his predecessors in the Messengers' piano chair, Horace Silver. If anything, it was even further *down,* closer to the black church experience that had been a vital part of Bobby's growing up. . .''

LPs: *Moanin'*; *Got To Get It*; *Do You Know The Way* (Milest.); *Soulman*; *Chicken & Dumplin's*; *Chun-king*; *Little Barefoot Soul*; *Soul Food*; *Workin' Out* (Prest.); others w. Adderley (Riverside); Blakey (BN).

TIZOL, JUAN,* *valve trombone, composer*; b. San Juan, Puerto Rico, 1/22/00. Pl. w. Duke Ellington, 1928-44; Harry James, '44-51; Ellington, 51-3; James, '53-60; Ellington, '60. Retired, in LA, reappearing only once for a record session in 1964 w. Louie Bellson. Best known comps: *Perdido, Caravan*. LPs: *Big Bands!*, 1964, w. Bellson (Onyx); others w. Ellington (various labels).

TJADER, CALLEN RADCLIFFE (CAL),* *vibes*; also *drums, composer*; b. St. Louis, Mo., 7/16/25. A former Brubeck and Shearing sideman, in the late '50s Tjader led his own combo, continuing to do so during the '60s and '70s. He confined himself to app. mostly on the West Coast where he makes his home, w. occasional trips to Phoenix, Tucson, Seattle etc. for clubs and concerts. Active in coll. clinics. Has played several summer fests in Central Park, NYC, as well as various ballrooms and Madison Sq. Gdn. Tjader was recording continuously for the Fantasy label, but in 1968, together with Gabor Szabo and the late Gary McFarland, he formed Skye Records, which was in operation until '70, at which time he returned to Fantasy. In Nov. '74 he was feat. in an Irving Granz prod. at Arizona State U. w. Ella Fitzgerald. He plays the Monterey and Concord fests. annually.

LPs: *Puttin' It Together*; *Primo*; *Last Night When We Were Young*; *Last Bolero in Berkeley*; Cal Tjader & Charlie Byrd, *Tambu* (Fant.).

TOLLIVER, CHARLES,* *trumpet, composer*; b. Jacksonville, Fla., 3/6/42. Influenced by Clifford Brown; early gigs w. J. McLean, Joe Henderson, A. Blakey while based in NYC. Went to LA '66 w. Willie Bobo; while there, joined Gerald Wilson orch. for one year. Left LA May '67, returned to NYC, joined M. Roach group for two years.

In May '69, Tolliver formed his own first combo, naming it Music, Inc. He took it to Europe, and while there made his first recording of the quartet. Since '69 the group has become internationally respected for its innovative approach, touring North and South America, Europe and Japan. Won DB TDWR award on trumpet, 68.

Fests: Newport, '67 w. Max Roach; many fests., TV apps. in Europe.

In '71 Tolliver became co-founder, Chairman and chief officer of Strata-East Records, Inc., a label owned entirely by artists. He is composer of *Singin' Wid a Sword In Ma Han,* performed in adaptation by Roach with the latter as soloist at Montreux Jazz Fest., '71; also *Collection Suite,* played by N.Y. Jazz Repertory orch., Carnegie Hall, '74.

Of all the trumpeters to come to prominence in the '60s, Charles Tolliver was perhaps the most sensitive to the necessity of swinging. Michael Shera observed: ''He is one young musician who refuses to run blindly up the alleyways of musical anarchy in search of a mythical freedom, as too many of his contemporaries are doing. If the freedom they are seeking involves the opportunity to be creative, inventive and original, they will find there is a lot to be learned from the method of Charles Tolliver.''

LPs: w. Jackie McLean, *It's Time*; *Jacknife*; *Action* (Blue Note); Booker Ervin, *Structurally Sound*; Gerald Wilson, *Live & Swinging* (Pacific Jazz); Roy Ayers, *Virgo Vibes*; *Stoned Soul Picnic* (Atl.); Horace Silver, *Serenade to a Soul Sister* (Blue Note); Max Roach, *Members Don't Git Weary* (Atl.); McCoy Tyner, *Song For My Lady* (Milestone); Doug Carn, *Spirit of the New Land* (Black Jazz). Own LPs: *Paper Man* (Arista); *Music Inc./The Ringer*; *Charles Tolliver & All Stars* (Polydor); *Live at Loosdrecht Festival*; *Music Inc. & Big Band*; *Music Inc/Live at Slugs, Vol. I*; *Music Inc/Live at Slugs, Vol. II*; *Music Inc/Live in Tokyo* (Strata-East, 156 Fifth Ave., New York, N.Y. 10010).

TOMPKINS, ROSS, *piano, composer*; also *keyboards, synthesizer*; b. Detroit, Mich., 5/13/38. Stud. privately and at New England Conserv. Active in NYC during '60s, he joined NBC staff orch pl. Tonight show, '67- . In addition, he had a busy jazz career working with K. Winding, '60; E. Dolphy, '64; J.J. Johnson. Pl. w. many gps. at Half Note, NYC, incl. W. Montgomery, '66; B. Brookmeyer-C. Terry; Joe Newman; I. Jacquet, '67; R. Eldridge; A. Cohn-Z. Sims frequently, '68-72; many jobs w. B. Hackett, '65-70; B. Goodman, '68; gigged w. James Moody, NYC and Cal. In '71 he moved to Cal. remaining a member of Doc Severinsen's *Tonight Show* band. He continued to make frequent local apps. with jazz combos and bands, incl. L. Bellson orch; has also led own small combos from time to time at Donte's and elsewhere. Tompkins, who names Ellington, Armstrong, E. Hines and Fats Waller as the sources of his inspiration, is an eclectic, technically outstanding mainstream-modern soloist. Fests: Newport; Concord; annual apps. at Colorado Jazz Party.

LPs: *Ross Tompkins Trio* (Roulette); w. K. Winding-J.J. Johnson, *Stonebones*; *Israel* (A & M); w. Bellson, *Explosion* (Pablo); *Breakthrough* (Proj. 3); *Louie Rides Again* (Percussion Power); *Colorado Jazz Party* (BASF); w. Eddie ''Lockjaw'' Davis, *Lock the Fox* (RCA); w. Herb Ellis-Freddie Green (Concord).

TONEY, KEVIN, *keyboards, composer, singer*; b. Detroit, Mich., 4/23/53. Piano lessons from age five; stud. at Cass Tech. High and at Howard U. School of Music, where he became a protege of Donald Byrd, who was then Chairman of the Dept. of Jazz Studies. Joining with a group of other students at Howard, Toney in '73 became leader of The Blackbyrds. While remaining a full time student, Toney traveled whenever possible, w. Byrd himself, and independently with the Blackbyrds. The group's first album became a soul and pop hit in addition to gaining a jazz audience. The first single release, *Do It Fluid,* became a gold record (one million sales). After the issue of their second album and several changes in personnel, the Blackbyrds completed a movie sound track for *Hit The Open Man*.

Toney, who during his years a student pl. w. such visiting guests as Woody Shaw, Gerald Wilson, S. Rollins, J. McLean, was majoring in jazz studies and comp. in '75. Comps: *Future Children, Future Hopes*; *Spaced Out*. LPs: *Flying Start*; *The Blackbyrds* (Fantasy).

TORME, MELVIN HOWARD (MEL),* *singer, composer, piano, drums, producer* etc.; b. Chicago, Ill., 9/13/25. From the mid-'60s Torme wrote all his own arrangements. He continued to tour regularly, often playing in LV, visiting Australia almost annually; app. on British TV. Writer of articles for various magazines, essays for N.Y. *Times*, and a book about Judy Garland, *The Other Side of the Rainbow*, publ. by Wm. Morrow, '70. Torme has written many orig. TV scripts, prod. TV specs., and app. as actor in numerous dramatic series. Pl. title role in movie, *Snowman*. He continued to maintain his reputation as one of the few artists of his generation to retain a jazz and quality/pop image in his singing, his choice of material and his own arrangements.

LPs: *Live at the Maisonette* (Atl.).

TOWNER, RALPH N., *guitar, piano, French horn, composer*; b. Chehalis, Wash., 3/1/40. Mother a piano teacher and church organist; father pl. trumpet. Improvising at the piano from age three. Trumpet at five. Studied theory and comp. at the U. of Oregon, '58-63; graduate work, '64-6. Stud. classical guitar w. Karl Scheit at Vienna Acad. of Mus., '63-4, '67-8. Pl. trumpet in dance band at age 13 in Bend, Ore.; lute and guitar w. Elizabethan Consort and the Eugene (Ore.) Chamber Ensemble, '64-6. Replaced Larry Coryell in Chuck Mahaffay band, Seattle '66. To NYC '69, jamming w. John McLaughlin, Airto; gigs w. Tamba Four. Pl. w. Jimmy Garrison, '69-70; Jeremy Steig, '69-71; Winter Consort, '70-1; Weather Report, '71; Gary Burton, '74-5. From '71 occupied mainly w. Oregon, a gp. which grew out of Winter Consort, and which includes Paul McCandless, Collin Walcott and Glen Moore. "The band is equally at home with baroque counterpoint, Indian raga, harmonically advanced improvising, rock rhythms and contemporary classicism," said Robert Palmer in *Rolling Stone*.

Milo Fine wrote: "Towner has an uncanny knack for harmonic overtones, and the quickness to carry them out. He also probes into areas of dissonance and thick harmonies."

Won DB Critics Poll, TDWR, '74. Infl: Bill Evans, Scott La Faro, Paul Bley, Keith Jarrett, Julian Bream. Fest: Woodstock w. Tim Hardin; Tanglewood, Chatauqua, Schaefer Fest. w. Winter Consort; solo at NJF-NY, '73; w. Oregon, '74-5; Pori, Bergamo, Molde, Berlin. Comp: over 60 instrumentals incl. *Distant Hills*; *Icarus*; *Ghost Beads*. LPs: *Diary*; w. Burton, *Matchbook*; *Solstice*; w. Jarrett, *In the Light* (ECM); w. Oregon, *Music of Another Present Era*; *Distant Hills*; *Winter Light* (Vang.); w. Weather Report, *I Sing the Body Electric* (Col.); w. Winter Consort, *Road* (A&M).

TRACEY, STAN,* *piano, composer*; b. London, England, 12/30/26. Early work w. Jack Parnell, Ted Heath, Ronnie Scott; house pianist at Scott's club from its opening, '60-68. Local and continental gigs with quartet and big band, '69-71. In '72 formed duo w. Mike Osborne; teaching at City Literary Inst., London. Played many concerts in England and on continent with ten piece band, quartet, trio, duo, solo, '73. Comp. and perf. Southwark Cathedral Shakespeare's birthday concert; soloist in Ellington remembrance service; British tour spons. by Arts Council, '74. Regular winner of *Melody Maker* polls from '66 in composer, arranger, piano and best album categories.

Numerous LPs with own groups on Col., Philips and various European labels.

TRISTANO, LEONARD JOSEPH (LENNIE),* *piano, composer, educator*; b. Chicago, Ill. 3/19/19. As he had in the '50s and '60s, Tristano devoted himself to teaching, playing in public only at the Half Note in '66, and in concert at the Art & Science Fest., Leeds, England in the summer of '68. In '73 the French TV Network brought its cameras to his house for an interview that contained minimal playing. That same year he sponsored a concert at Carnegie Recital Hall for one of his students, pianist Connie Crothers. He also held private recitals of his students at his Queens studio. At the end of '75 he was preparing to record for a Japanese label, East Wind. LP: a reissue of his late '40s sextet w. Lee Konitz and Warne Marsh, *Crosscurrents* (Capitol).

TRUNK, PETER,* *bass*; also *trumpet, cello*; b. Frankfurt-am-Main, Germany, 5/17/36. First prominent in '50s as member of Albert Mangelsdorff combo, Trunk, who also pl. in Germany w. many visiting Americans, was killed 12/31/73 in a traffic accident in NYC.

TRZASKOWSKI, ANDRZEJ, *piano, composer*; b. Cracow, Poland, 3/23/33. Stud. piano, musicology, contemp. and electronic mus. w. various teachers from '50s through '74. In '51 he formed Melomani, which he claims was the first authentic Polish jazz group. In '58 was mainstay of the Jazz Believers w. Krzysztof Komeda and Jan Wroblewski. In '59 formed the Wreckers, a group heard in '62 on a two month tour of the U.S., taking part in Washington and Newport Fests. The group was later renamed the Andrzej Trzaskowski quintet; personnel incl. M. Urbaniak and Z. Namyslowski. Toured Euro., rec. for radio, TV. Trzaskowski later developed an avant garde orientation. In '65-6 the personnel of the group incl. Ted Curson.

Trzaskowski has pl. and rec. w. S. Getz, A. Farmer, P. Woods, Nathan Davis, D. Pike; worked regularly w. Hamburg Radio station, '65-71. From Jan. '75, art director and conductor for Polish radio and TV orch. feat. the country's leading jazz and studio musicians. Winner of awards as best Polish jazz musician; also *Jazz* and *Jazz Forum* polls in best composer, pianist, leader categories. Comps: *Nihil Novi*; *Synopsis*; *Bluebeard*; *The Quibble*; *Posters*; *Epitaph for K.K.*; *Double*; *The Blocks*; *Magma*; *His Better Feelings*; *Vision*; also scores for about 30 films.

LPs: *The Wreckers and Andrzej Trzaskowski Trio* (Muza); *The Andrzej Trzaskowski Quintet*; *The A.T. Sekstet feat. Ted Curson*; *Stan Getz in Poland*—with Andrzej Trzaskowski Trio (Polskie Nagrania).

TUCKER, MICHAEL B. (MICKEY), *piano, keyboards, composer*; also *oboe, English horn*; b. Durham, N.C., 4/28/41. Raised in Pittsburgh until he was 13, then moved back to Durham. Private piano lessons at age six. Att. Morehouse Coll. in Ga.; taught at Roosevelt HS in Lake Wales, Fla.; Miss. Valley State Coll., Itta Bena, Miss. Worked w. Damita Jo '65; Timmie Rogers, '66-7; Anthony

& the Imperials, '67-8; James Moody, '69-71; three mos. w. Thad Jones-Mel Lewis, late '73; Eddie Jefferson; Frank Foster; Sonny Red; Willis Jackson; Cecil Payne; Roy Brooks, '73-5; Final Edition, '75. A very fresh keyboard talent in that he finds new ways to extend the jazz tradition within that tradition's basic tenets, not the least of which is vibrant swinging.

Infl: Fats Waller; Art Tatum; Hamp Hawes; Phineas Newborn, Oscar Peterson, Herbie Hancock (acoustic piano). TV: Mike Douglas; Ed Sullivan; w. Final Edition on educ. Ch. 50, NJ. Fest: NJF-NY w. Moody. Comp: *State of Affairs*; *A Little 3 for L.C.*; *Something About Bean*, dedicated to Coleman Hawkins; *Suite* for *Eight Hands*, for two pianos, two perc.; *This One's For You*.

Benjamin Gray, a pianist from Inkster, Mich. interested him in two-piano collaborations which he explored w. Roland Hanna in *New Heritage Keyboard Quartet* (BN). Own LP: *Triplicity* (Xanadu); w. Moody, *Never Again*; Eric Kloss, *Essence*; E. Jefferson, *Things Are Getting Better*; Willis Jackson, *West Africa* (Muse); R.R. Kirk, *Blacknuss* (Atl.).

TURNER, JOSEPH VERNON (BIG JOE),* *singer, composer*; b. Kansas City, Mo., 5/18/11. Living in LA in '60s and '70s, the veteran blues singer app. in local clubs, as a single, and with J. Otis show. Many visits to Monterey JF; also Newport, Ann Arbor Fests. In March '74 he took part in the filming, along w. C. Basie, Jay McShann and others, of *Last of the Blue Devils*, a retrospective dealing with early Kansas City jazz. Comps: *TV Momma*; *Cherry Red*; *Wee Baby Blues*; *Roll 'Em Pete*; *Squeeze Me Baby*; *Piney Brown Blues*; *Mrs. Geraldine*.

LPs: *Singin' The Blues*; *Roll 'Em* (Bluesway); *Big Joe Is Here* (Atl.); *Big Joe Turner Turns on the Blues* (Kent); *Great R & B Oldies*, Vol. 4 (Blues Spectrum); *The Bosses—Count Basie/Joe Turner*; *The Trumpet Kings Meet Joe Turner* (Pablo); some tracks on *Art Tatum Masterpieces* (MCA); w. Papa John Creach, *Filthy* (Grunt).

TURNER, JOE,* *piano*; also *singer*; b. Baltimore, Md., 11/3/07. After World War II returned to Europe where he earlier toured w. Adelaide Hall. From '62 was fixture at Calavados club in Paris. In January '76 pl. long engagement at the Cookery, NYC. during which time Gary Giddins wrote: "Unlike most of the stride players, Turner has an authentic feeling for the blues, both as a pianist and as a singer." LPs: *Joe Turner Trio* w. Slam Stewart, Jo Jones (B&B); *Stride By Stride* (77); *Smashing Thirds* (MPS).

TURNEY, NORRIS WILLIAM, *alto saxophone*; also *tenor, soprano saxes, clarinet, flutes, piccolo, piano*; b. Wilmington, Ohio, 9/8/21. Stud. piano from age 10-12; saxophone in '35 under Mrs. Inez Jones, wife of Wilmington H.S. mus. dir., Luther Jones; clarinet under George Carr of Cincinnati Cons; harmony & theory w. Artie Matthews, Cosmospolitan Sch. of Mus., Cinci. Began flute stud. in '65 in NYC w. Henry Zlotnick; later w. Harold Bennett. Pl. briefly w. Fate Marable on riverboat out of St. Louis. With A.B. Townsend band at Cotton Club, Cinci. '41-3; Jeter-Pillars orch. in St. Louis, Chi. and at Apollo Theater, NYC. Joined Tiny Bradshaw in early '45 and moved to NYC. With Billy Eckstine band from late '45 for two yrs. before ret. to Ohio for teaching, pl. w. gps incl. own. Back to NYC '51 for a yr. of free-lance; Phila., one yr. w. Elmer Snowden; two yrs. w. Johnny Lynch in Atlantic City, N.J.; a yr. w. Bull Moose Jackson. Ret. to NYC, '59, working rock gigs on tenor; club dates; Catskill Mts.; and a yr. w. Machito. Took part in many rehearsal bands around NYC incl. F. Foster, Clark Terry, Duke Pearson, H. McGhee and one he co-led w. Danny Small. In '67 joined Ray Charles for a year. Toured w. Duke Ellington '68-72, distinguishing himself as a versatile multi-reedman-flutist. Working in pit band for hit Broadway musical *Raisin*, free-lancing and rehearsing his own small gp. Infl: Ellington, Goodman, Sy Oliver, Hodges, Carter, Willie Smith, Parker. TV: U.S. & Europe w. Charles, Ellington incl. Ed Sullivan, Timex shows. Fests: NJF w. Ellington, Charles, Sy Oliver, Wild Bill Davis; many Euro. fests. Won TDWR awards in DB Critics poll as flutist, '70-1. Comp: *Checkered Hat*, dedicated to Johnny Hodges, in Ellington's *Togo Brava* album. LPs: *Boys From Dayton* (Master Jazz); w. Ellington, *New Orleans Suite* (Atl.); *Togo Brava Suite* (UA); *70th Birthday Concert* (SS); w. R. Weston, *Tanjah* (Poly.).

TURRE, STEVE, *trombone*; also *electric bass*; b. Omaha, Neb., 12/8/49. Stud. at NTSU, '68-9; in SF w. Norman Williams, '70. Pl. w. R.R. Kirk in SF, '70; Van Morrison, '71; bass trombone w. R. Charles, '72; Charles Moffett, A. Blakey, '73; Thad Jones-Mel Lewis, '73; Woody Shaw in NYC, '74; toured w. C. Hamilton, '74- . Movie sound tracks, educ. TV w. Hamilton; TV in Euro. w. Charles, Jones-Lewis. Fests: Monterey, '73 w. Jones-Lewis. Comp: *Sanyas*.

LPs: w. Hamilton, *Peregrinations* (BN); w. Woody Shaw, *Moontrane* (Muse).

TURRENTINE, STANLEY,* *tenor sax*; b. Pittsburgh, Pa., 4/5/34. Continued to lead gp. w. wife, organist Shirley Scott through the '60s until '71 when they parted company musically and matrimonially. He had led his own gps. from that time, also rec. w. larger ensembles for CTI which brought him to a wider, pop audience. In '75 he moved to the Fantasy label for albums produced and arranged by Gene Page in even more of a pop soul vein. Due to the settings his albums made the charts for he was playing in the same blues-inflected, naturally funky style that had been his trademark for many years. Of his new-found success as a "crossover" artist Turrentine said: "It's a natural thing for me. I hear Stevie Wonder tunes, or Marvin Gaye tunes, on the radio all the time. If I like the tune, I'll do it—no matter who wrote it. I just want *lots* of people to hear my music! I want to make records that will sell—to everybody."

Fest: NJF-NY, etc. Many TV apps. Comp: *Sugar*.

LPs: *Have You Seen the Rain*; *Pieces of Dreams*; *In the Pocket* (Fant.); *Sugar*; *Don't Mess With Mister T*; *Salt Song*; *Cherry* (CTI); reissue anthology (Blue Note); reissue, *Yester You, Yester Me* (Trip).

TYNER, ALFRED McCOY (Sulaimon Saud),* *piano, composer*; b. Philadelphia, Pa., 12/11/38. After leaving John Coltrane's group in Dec. '65, he formed own trio with which he appeared around NYC in '66. He also worked as a sideman w. Ike and Tina Turner; Jimmy Witherspoon. Recorded for Blue Note in late '60s-70 but not all the material was released until later. In '72 he began rec. for Milestone and his album *Sahara* won the *down beat* Critics poll as Record of the Year. First his group included Sonny Fortune but in '73 he was replaced by reedman Azar Lawrence who bore a striking stylistic resemblance to Coltrane. The LP *Enlightenment,* rec. at the Montreux Fest. in '73 won the Montreux Jury's Diamond Prize as the year's best recording.

From the time *Sahara* was issued Tyner began to receive long overdue recognition and began to tour extensively with his group, both in the US and in Europe and Japan. Eschewing electronics and fashionable trends he has fashioned an expression within a body of music that is contemporary but apart from the monotony of obvious hitseekers or the more fallow members of the avant garde.

Whitney Balliett wrote that "Tyner spent five years as a sideman baking in John Coltrane's oven and by the time he left Coltrane most of the ingredients now rampant in his work . . . had risen: the continually shifting modal patterns, the racing, almost glissando arpeggios, and the hammering, enfolding chords."

Garry Giddins made analogies with art and literature: "McCoy paints with the opulence of Africa, the Orient, and the Middle East, which is why his lustiness is manifested in stirring dynamics and coloration rather than melody. Tyner's craggy pulse can inspire and invigorate. Like Conrad, he wants to make us see."

Fest: NJF-NY, incl. solo concert, '74; many U.S., Euro. fests.

Tyner tied for first place with Keith Jarrett in the DB Critics poll, '74; won the DB Readers poll, '74-5; Jazzman of the Year, '75. Comp: *Land of the Lonely*; *Celestial Chant*; *Elvin (Sir) Jones*; *The Discovery*; *Folks*; *Enlightenment Suite*; *Presence*; *Nebula*; *Walk Spirit, Talk Spirit*; *Sama Lucaya*; *Above the Rainbow*; *La Cuba 5na*; *Desert Cry*; *Paradox*; *Makin' Out*; *Pursuit*; *Love Samba*; *Atlantis*.

LPs: *Atlantis*; *Enlightenment*; *Sama Layuca*; *Song of the New World*; *Song for My Lady*; *Sahara*; *Echoes of a Friend*, piano solos dedicated to J. Coltrane; *Trident*, trio w. R. Carter, E. Jones (Mile.); others on BN; Imp.

UNDERWOOD, .RUTH KOMANOFF, *marimba, percussion*; also *piano*; b. New York City, 5/23/46. Stud. w. many teachers; Ithaca Coll. of Mus., '62-5; Juilliard, '65-8. Best known for her work w. Frank Zappa's Mothers of Invention; also with her husband, Ian Underwood.

LPs: w. Zappa, *Uncle Meat* (Bizarre/Reprise); *Apostrophe*; *Mothers—Live At Roxy and Elsewhere*; *One Size Fits All* (Discreet).

UPCHURCH, PHIL, *guitar, fender bass, composer*; b. Chicago, Ill., 7/19/41. Father, a pianist, introduced him to ukulele '52, two years later bought him elec. guitar, on which he was basically self-taught. Came up in r & b scene '58-62, touring w. groups. Settled down in Chi. as studio musician, rec. w. S. Getz, Ramsey Lewis, Woody Herman, Groove Holmes, B.B. King, Dizzy Gillespie. Drafted 1965; in Special Services, Germany, pl. in jazz club w. trio. Back on recording scene '67, many dates w. Richard Evans, Grover Washington, C. Adderley et al. In 1970 joined Ramsey Lewis, changing gp. from trio to quartet for first time.

Playing Calif., Upchurch decided to settle there, working w. Quincy Jones on movie soundtracks etc., but says "The earthquake of Feb. 1971 sent me scurrying back to Chicago." Rejoined Q. Jones to tour Japan 1972. Co-leading quintet w. Tennyson Stephens and rec. album for CTI, 1975.

Upchurch won NARAS Governors' Award 1975 for contributions to Chi. music scene. He was subject of book, *What It's Like To Be a Musician*, by Arthur Shay, publ: (Reilly & Lee Books, 114 West Illinois St., Chi., Ill. 60610).

Own LPs: Cadet, Milestone, CTI. LPs w. Q. Jones, *Body Heat* (A & M); *Grooving With the Soulful Strings* (Cadet); *Bad Benson* w. Geo. Benson (CTI).

URBANIAK, MICHAL, *violin, composer*; also *soprano, tenor saxophone*; b. Warsaw, Poland, 1/22/43. Stud. at Academy of Music in Warsaw. Pl. w. The Wreckers in Poland and USA, '62-4; K. Komeda quintet, '64; Jazz Rockers, also in Poland. Forming his own group in '65, he worked in Scandinavia, Switzerland, West Germany, Benelux etc. In '74-5 his new group, Michal Urbaniak Fusion, toured in the US, and Urbaniak made his home in NYC. He plays a custom made five-string violin and violin synthesizer. Favs: Coltrane, Miles Davis, Komeda, Z. Namyslowski, Lutoslawski. Film score for *On The Road*. Many TV apps. incl. Prague, '64-6; Berlin, and a dozen other cities. Fests: In Warsaw almost every year from '62-72; Prague, '64, '69, '72; Newport, '62, '74; Montreux, '74; Molde and Kongsberg (Norway), '71. In that same year he was declared the best soloist at the Montreux JF (Grand Prix) and was awarded a scholarship to Berklee Coll. of Mus. Won *Jazz Forum* Musician of the Year award, '72 and '73; his combo was voted best of the year in '73. Married to singer Urszula Dudziak (q.v.).

LPs: *Fusion*; *Atma* (Columbia); *Traction* (Intercord); *Constellation* (CBS); *Constellation Live* (Muza); w. Arif Mardin: *Journey* (Atlantic).

VALDAMBRINI, OSCAR,* *trumpet, fluegelhorn, composer*; b. Turin, Italy, 5/11/24. With tenor saxophonist Gianni Basso continued to lead the Basso-Valdambrini quintet which, from '55-60, pl. at the Taverna Mexico in Milan w. sitters-in such as G. Mulligan, C. Baker, L. Gullin, S. Getz, M. Davis and C. Candoli. Valdambrini guested w. L. Hampton and also pl. w. M. Ferguson. In '67 & '68 was part of D. Ellington band for concerts at Lyric Theatre, Milan. App. at all Italian fests. from '56 and 30 concerts annually at theatres and universities. In '62 the Basso-Valdambrini band won a contest organized by a men's toiletry company and visited the U.S. as the prize. Awarded two Gold Records and the "Golden Diapason." Voted top Italian trumpeter '74. Insp. & infl: Armstrong, Gillespie, Parker, C. Baker.

LPs: thirteen albums w. Basso for Italian labels, two of which were issued on Verve; *Buddy Collette in Italy w. Basso-Valdambrini* (Ricordi); *The Best Modern Jazz in Italy* (Italian RCA).

VANCE, RICHARD THOMAS (DICK),* *composer, arranger, trumpet*; b. Mayfield, Ky., 11/28/15. From mid-30s played and/or wrote for many swing bands incl. F. Henderson, C. Webb, Don Redman, C. Barnet, D. Ellington, Glen Gray. Still active in '60s and '70s, playing for several years in Radio City Music Hall orch. through '65; Broadway shows: *Hallelujah Baby,* '67; *No, No Nanette,* '71-2; *Seesaw,* '73; played at NJF, Carnegie Hall, '73. Conducted band for Jazz Dance Theatre, touring Africa for State Dept., '69. From '70, member of music faculty at Manhattan Community Coll., teaching musicology; and Jazz Performance Workshop. Made one of the later arrs. of *Black and Tan Fantasy* for D. Ellington; arr. *Yearning For Love* for M. Ellington.

Own LP: *Like Dixie* (Sue); LP w. Eddie Barefield's Bearcats (Major-Minor).

VAN EPS, GEORGE,* *guitar*; b. Plainfield, N.J., 8/7/13. Appeared at Colorado Jazz Party in '60s and w. own gp. at Downbeat, NYC, in late '60s. Relatively inactive after suffering a heart attack, he pl. occasionally at Donte's in LA early '70s.

VAUGHAN, SARAH LOIS,* *singer*; b. Newark, N.J., 3/27/24. An early associate of the pioneer bop musicians, with whom she worked in the Earl Hines and Billy Eckstine bands and on small group record sessions, Vaughan from the mid-1940s was a solo artist, internationally known for her unique qualifications as a singer capable of incomparable jazz performances yet qualified to be an opera singer. Over the years her range and scope, along with the warmth and communicative values of her performances, continued to expand. In the 1960s and early '70s she appeared in more than 60 countries, from small, intimate night clubs to stadiums with a capacity of 100,000, with backings that ranged from a jazz trio to symphony orchestras with vocal groups. She was heard with the Boston Pops, the Cleveland Symphony, LA Philharmonic, San Francisco Symphony and many others.

Vaughan enjoyed the unusual distinction, while touring internationally with consistent success, of doing so without the help of recordings. For a five-year period she had no record contract, returning early in 1972 when she signed with the Mainstream label. Later that year an album of Michel Legrand's compositions, for which she was accompanied by a large orchestra with Legrand as arranger and conductor, was moderately successful commercially.

TV: *Wolftrap,* seen on 241 PBS stations, '75; many guest apps. w. Sammy Davis, Johnny Carson, Mike Douglas, Merv Griffin, Glen Campbell et al.

Festivals: Newport, Monterey; others in Belgium, Holland, Tunisia, etc.; Charlie Parker Festival, KC; Ravinia Fest., Chicago. In Dec. '74 she took part in *Showboat 2,* a jazz festival aboard the S.S. *Rotterdam* cruising to the West Indies; immediately afterward she flew to Martinique to sing at a banquet in honor of President Ford and President Giscard d'Estaing of France.

LPs: Many early albums reissued on Trip, Roulette; *A Time In My Life*; *Send in the Clowns*; *Sarah Vaughan/Michel Legrand*; *Sarah Vaughan Live In Japan*; *More From Japan*; *Sarah Vaughan & Jimmy Rowles Quintet* (Mainstream).

VAUGHN, THOMAS WADE (TOM), *piano, composer*; b. Benton, Ky., 10/14/36. Family moved in 1947 to Pontiac, Mich., where he had early contact w. Thad, Elvin Jones. Stud. classical music, pl. jazz in clubs during seven years in college (BA magna cum laude, Eureka, Ill., '61; Bachelor of Sacred Theology, Yale Divinity School, '64); was heard by Geo. Wein sitting in w. G. Krupa in Detroit club and, with Wein's help, went to NYC, rec. live at Village Gate, and pl. at NJF '66. That he was an Episcopalian priest who played jazz piano earned him considerable publicity as Father Tom Vaughn; however, he later dropped this billing and appeared in clubs and concerts as Tom Vaughn.

Infl: Tatum, Gershwin, O. Peterson, J.S. Bach, Alfred Newman, Palestrina, Bartok, J. Coltrane, V. Horowitz. His early LPs reflect strong impact of the funk-soul movement. After moving to Southern Calif. July '68, he continued to gig occasionally. In 1975 he was associate rector at St. Martin's In The Fields, Canoga Park, Calif.

Comps: *Angela*; *Mr. Cholly*; *Moonwalk*; *Wanda*; *Motor City Soul*. LPs: RCA, Capitol.

VAZ, FRANCOIS R., *guitar, banjo*; b. Paris, France, 6/19/31. Priv. studies in France, '49-53. At 18 was successful actor in France, in addition to leading own band, pl. mostly dixieland, '46-50. Inactive in music, '53-9. Moved to LA, '60, began to gain prominence acc. singers, among them Arthur Prysock, Della Reese, Lou Rawls, Esther Phillips, Lorez Alexandria, Carmen McRae, Lena Horne, Ray Charles. Also pl. w. G Szabo, '67; Jimmy Smith, Willie Bobo, '70; F. Hubbard, '74. Comp. *Little Boy Dear,* rec. by Rawls (Cap.). Infls: D. Reinhardt, J. Raney, T. Farlow, Ch. Parker, Coltrane, Bill Evans. TV: six months in band on Barbara McNair series; jazz shows in Boston, SF etc. Many fests. incl. KC, '67; Berkeley and Monterey, '68; Oakland, '72.

LPs: w. Szabo (Skye); Alexandria (Pzazz); McRae (Atl.); Pat Britt (Vee Jay).

VENTURA, CHARLIE,* *saxophones*; b. Philadelphia, Pa., 12/2/16. The popular combo leader and frequent G. Krupa sideman, lived in LV from '58-61, later moved to Denver, where he worked with Johnny Smith, then to Minnesota. After a long illness, he settled in LV again from '70-2, conducting a disc jockey show. From '72-5 he pl. gigs as house leader at Sheraton Tobacco Valley Inn in Connecticut w. B. Hackett, Dave McKenna and others and made his home in Windsor, Conn. Pl. w. Teddy Wilson at Michael's Pub, NYC, late '74. Still active on freelance basis in '76.

LPs: *Charlie Boy—Charlie Ventura '46* (Phoenix); reissue of '40s big band and small gps. (Trip); many pop albums w. Jackie Gleason (Cap.).

VENUTI, GIUSEPPE (JOE),* *violin*; b. Lecco, Italy, 4/4/98. The first great jazz violinist of the '20s was confined to playing lounges in Los Angeles, Las Vegas and Seattle (his home base) in the '60s. In '67 he played at Dick Gibson's Colorado Jazz Party in Vail, the first of many apps. he has made at these annual affairs through '75. He was featured at the NJF '68 where his performance served to reveal that he had lost none of his prodigious skill and that age had not dampened his fiery swing either. To London for Jazz Expo, '69. He survived a severe illness in April '70 to resume working later in the year and has been active from that time, leading a quartet at the Roosevelt Grill, '71. He has also played engagements several times at Michael's Pub and appeared at major fests. in US and Europe. In '75 he filled an important role in the NYJRC tribute to Bix Beiderbecke at NJF-NY; at same fest. he was honored by the Newport Hall of Fame.

LPs: *Once Again With Feeling* (Ovation); *Plays Gershwin*; *Plays Jerome Kern* (Golden Crest); two albums w. Zoot Sims; *Joe Venuti Blue Fours* (Chiaro.); *The Daddy of the Violin* (MPS); *Venupelli Blues* w. S. Grappelli (Byg); w. B. Pizzarelli, *Nightwings* (Fl. Dutch.).

VESALA, EDWARD, *drums*; b. Mantyharju, Finland, 2/15/45. Studied at Sibelius Academy. Pl. w. Jan Garbarek trio, '72-4. Has also performed w. Joachim Kuhn; Tomasz Stanko; Archie Shepp; Paul Bley; Peter Brotzman. Voted Finnish Jazz Musician of the Year, '72. Infl: Billie Holiday, John Coltrane. Com: *Areous Vlor Ta*; *Nan Madol*. LPs: *Nan Madol* (Japo); *Nana*; *I'm Here* (Blue Master); w. Stanko, *Twet* (Muza); w. Garbarek, *Triptykon* (ECM).

VICK, HAROLD EDWARD,* *tenor sax*; also *alto, soprano saxes, flute, bass clarinet, oboe*; b. Rocky Mount, N.C., 4/3/36. After graduating from Howard U., toured w. r&b bands, settling into small group work in NYC in the early '60s. With the Jean Erdman Theatre Co., pl. recorders and percussion as well as his usual reeds, '66-7. Pl. w. Walter Bishop, Grant Green, '67; own quintet, '67-8; Negro Ensemble Co., incl. European tour, '69; Dizzy Gillespie big band; King Curtis, '69-70; lectures and demonstrations on jazz history in NYC public schools w. Benny Powell for Jazz Interactions, '70; Aretha Franklin, '70-4; Compost, '71-3; Shirley Scott, '74; Jazzmobile w. George Coleman Octet, '74. In April '74, Vick suffered a massive heart attack, but was miraculously back playing in August of that year. Film: App. as actor in *An Even Chance*, produced for the Foundation for Change, for which he composed music and pl. saxophone, '71. TV: Composed music for *Epitaph*, prod. w. a grant from the Ford Foundation in cooperation w. the Henry St. Settlement, '70. Co-founder and organizer of the Black Experience Family Repertory Co., for which he composed music for a full-length stage prod. under a grant from the NYS Council for the Arts, '70. Awarded comp. grant from the National Endowment for the Arts, '73. Comp: *Our Miss Brooks*; *Night Flight*; *Out Of It*; *Melody For Bu*; *The Ripper*; *Seventh Period*; *Buzzard Feathers*; *Don't Look Back*; *Keep On Movin' On*. LPs: *Don't Look Back* (Strata-East); *Commitment* (Muse); *Straight Up*; *Watch What Happens*; *Caribbean Suite* (RCA); *Steppin' Out* (BN); under pseudonym Sir Edward for *The Power of Feeling* (Encounter); w. Compost, *Compost*; *Life is Round* (Col.); w. Joe Chambers, *The Almoravid*; w. Bu Pleasant, *Ms. Bu* (Muse); w. S. Scott, *One For Me* (Strata-East).

VIG, TOMMY,* *vibes, drums, composer*; b. Budapest, Hungary, 7/14/38. Left Hungary during 1956 revolt; in U.S. stud. at Juilliard, worked for many groups in NYC. Living in Las Vegas from mid-60s, he led a 56 piece orch. at Music Educators' Nat'l Conference, '67, in a concerto for tenor saxophone and orch. feat. Charlie McLean. Vig was guest soloist w. LA Neophonic, '68. Concerts at Tropicana, LV, some feat. Don Ellis. In '69 Vig moved to LA, where he concentrated mainly on studio work but continued to comp. and perf. in a big jazz orch. context as well as pl. drums or vibes in groups led by Red Rodney, T. Gibbs, Cat Anderson, Joe Pass, John Collins et al. Since the mid-60s has given annual jazz concert at Caesar's Palace in LV. In '75 he conducted his own work, *Music For a Tschopp Exhibit*, at Brand Library, commissioned by painter Stanley Donald Tschopp, feat. Ellis. Vig scored several films, mixing modern classical music with jazz. Won DB Critics' Poll, '67, on vibes, TDWR. Comps: *Just For You*; *For Mia*; also four movement symphonic work, *Instruments*, dedicated to Zubin Mehta. Vig's infls. range from Bartok, Miles Davis, Ellington to Albert Ayler, George Ligeti and Kryzysztof Penderecki.

LPs: *The Sound of the Seventies* (Milestone); *Tommy Vig in Budapest* (Mortney Records).

VINNEGAR, LEROY,* *bass, composer*; b. Indianapolis, Ind., 7/13/28. Established from '54 in LA as outstanding exponent of "walking" bass style. Continued to freelance in Hollywood during '70s; Fests. at Concord, Montreux, Monterey. Vinnegar's best known comps. are *For Carl* (dedicated to the late pianist Carl Perkins) and *Hard To Find*. Others incl. *My Mom*; *Twila*; *Hey Mon*. Own LPs: *The Kid* (PBR); *Glass of Water* (Legend); *Leroy Walks* and *Leroy Walks Again* (Contemporary); *Swiss Movement* w. L. McCann-E. Harris (Atl.); *High In The Sky* w. H. Hawes (Vault), *Live At The Lighthouse, '66* w. Crusaders (World Pacific); *Bluesmith* w. J. Smith (Verve); w. S. Criss (Xanadu).

VINSON, EDDIE (CLEANHEAD),* *singer, alto saxophone*; b. Houston, Tex., 12/18/17. First prominent w. Cootie Williams orch., '42-5; own group, '45-9. Spent two years in and around Omaha, '60-2; Kansas City, '62-4, working in big bands and combos. First trip to France, '67 for fest. and rec. In late '60s and early '70s, based in LA, but toured frequently incl. Europe w. Basie. Gigs w. J. Otis in LA. Fests: Newport-NY, '71-4; Monterey, '70, '72-3-4; Ann Arbor, '70, '73; Montreux, '71, '74; Nice, '72; Paris, '68.

Vinson in '75 was still rooted in the mainstream of the blues, both as singer and saxophonist. There were few if any changes in his repertoire, which included such early hits as *Cherry Red*; *Kidney Stew Blues*; *Old Maid Boogie*; *Tune Up*. Stanley Dance wrote: "Vinson commands your attention. He communicates emotion and humor."

LPs: *You Can't Make Love Alone* (Mega); *Cleanhead's Back In Town* (Fl. Dutchman); *Jazz Greatest Names* (Black & Blue); w. O. Nelson, *Swiss Suite* (Fl. Dutchman).

VIOLA, ALFONSO ALFRED (AL), *guitar*; b. Brooklyn, N.Y., 6/16/19. Mainly self-taught, but stud. harmony, theory at Cal. Acad. of Music; also private classical guitar lessons. Insp. by C. Christian, W. Montgomery, O. Peterson, Coltrane, B. Collette. Toured w. Page Cavanaugh trio, '47-9; Bobby Troup trio, '50-4; Ray Anthony, '55-6; Harry James, '57; B. Collette quintet from '57, off and on, to date; Les Brown intermittently to date. Acc. Julie London at Command Perf. for John F. Kennedy in Washington, '61. International tour w. F. Sinatra, '62; White House concert w. Sinatra, '73. Neophonic concerts w. Stan Kenton in '60s. Numerous movies and TV series.

Own LP: *Alone Again* (Legend); w. Collette (Legend); many others, now mostly unavailable. Publ: *Guitar Lament* (MCA Music).

VITOUS, MIROSLAV LADISLAV, *bass, guitar, composer*; b. Prague, Czechoslovakia, 12/6/47. Father, a saxophonist, stimulated his interest in music. Studied violin from age six, piano from nine-14, then took up bass. While at Prague Conservatory, pl. w. Junior Trio feat. Jan Hammer, piano, and his brother Alan Vitous on drums; also worked w. Dixieland gp. Won first prize at an international contest in Vienna sponsored by Friedrich Gulda; this entitled him to a scholarship at Berklee College of Music in Boston.

Vitous arrived in the U.S. 8/10/66. Though offered a job by C. Adderley, he remained at Berklee for eight months. To NYC summer of 1967; befriended by Walter Booker, he soon worked w. Art Farmer, F. Hubbard and the Bobby Brookmeyer-Clark Terry Quintet. Heard in this combo by Miles Davis, he worked w. Davis briefly before joining Herbie Mann, remaining with Mann for two years. Toured w. Stan Getz '70, then rejoined Mann for almost a year. Back w. Davis briefly, then became a founder member of Weather Report, remaining until late '73.

During '74 and '75, except for an appearance with Airto, Vitous remained off the scene, living near Los Angeles and practicing a new instrument made specially for him, a double-necked combination guitar and bass. In late 1975 he recorded with an all star gp. incl. H. Hancock, Airto, Jack De Johnette (Col.). Made first apps. leading own combo, early '76.

Influenced mainly by Scott La Faro, also by Ron Carter and Gary Peacock, Vitous shortly after his first American jobs gained the respect of fellow musicians as an extraordinary technician and creative artist on both upright and fender bass.

Comp: *Mountain in the Clouds*; *Epilogue*; *Cerecka*; *Infinite Search*; *I Will Tell Him On You*; *When Face Gets Pale*.

LPs: His first album as a leader, *Infinite Search,* in '70, on the now defunct Embryo label, was widely praised. It was reissued w. an added track as *Mountain in the Clouds* (Atl.). Others w. Weather Report (Col.); w. C. Corea, *Now He Sings, Now He Sobs* (SS).

VON OHLEN, JOHN (BARON), *drums, composer*; b. Indianapolis, Ind., 5/13/41. Stud. w. Bob Phillips. Toured w. Billy Maxted and his Manhattan Jazz Band, '67-8; W. Herman, '69-70; S. Kenton, '70-2. Later, based in Indiana, he co-led a 17 piece orch. w. former Kenton baritone saxophonist Chuck Carter. Comps: *A Walk Through Bombay*; *Red Man*.

LPs: *Baron Von Ohlen Quartet*; w. Kenton, *Live at Redlands*; *Live at Brigham Young*; *Stan Kenton in London* (Creative World); w. Herman, *Concerto for Herd* (Verve).

VON SCHLIPPENBACH, ALEXANDER (ALEX), *composer, piano*; b. Berlin, 4/7/38. Stud. composition, piano at school in Cologne; jazz piano with Francis Coppieters. Joined Gunter Hampel quintet in Paris, '63; toured w. Manfred Schoof quintet, '64-7. Many important concerts w. Globe Unity Orchestra in Berlin, Donaueschingen, Tokyo, '66-70. From '70 on led own quartet feat. Evan Parker. Fest: Berlin, Antibes, Montreux, Warsaw, Molde etc. Infl. by Arnold Schoenberg, B.A. Zimmermann, Charlie Parker, Hartwig Bartz, Thelonious Monk, Cecil Taylor.

Von Schlippenbach is a leading figure on the continental free music scene. His LPs for various European labels incl. *Heartplants*; *Globe Unity* (Saba); *Glockenbar* (Wergo); *Payan* (Enja); *The Living Music; Pakistani Pomade*; *Globe Unity 73* (all on FMP); *Voices* (CBS).

WADENIUS, GEORG, *guitar*; also *electric bass*; b. Stockholm, Sweden, 5/4/45. Mother, a concert pianist who had her own jazz quartet for 25 years, now is teacher, forming big bands, choirs and small groups among her students. Learned by listening to his mother, rehearsing classical works and playing evergreens and songs from American musicals in clubs. His high school studies were directed more toward music than regular academics. After high school, stud. medicine, but relinquished ambitions to become a doctor in favor of a musical career. First professional job with a trio called Made in Sweden, '68; w. Solar Plexus quartet, '71. Came to USA Jan. '72 to join Blood, Sweat & Tears and toured extensively with the group, incl. Montreux JF. TV: *Midnight Special,* w. B.S.&T. Comp. *Save Our Ship*; *My Old Lady*; *Are You Satisfied*; *She's Coming Home,* all rec. by B.S.&T.; parts of *Concerto Grosso* for Symphony Orch. and Four Piece Rock Group; songs for a children's album, *Hello Hello,* which won an award in Sweden. Insp. by J. Hall, W. Montgomery, Jimi Hendrix, J. McLaughlin, B.B. King.

LPs: w. B.S.&T., *New Blood*; *Mirror Image* (Col.).

WAITS, FREDERICK DOUGLAS (FREDDIE),* *drums*; also *percussion, flute*; b. Jackson, Miss., 4/27/43. Worked w. Kenny Dorham; Curtis Fuller; Cedar Walton; Sonny Rollins in '60s. Pl. w. NY Jazz Sextet, '66-7; McCoy Tyner, '67-70; toured w. Ella Fitzgerald, '67; '68 in Europe. Between '67-70 gigged w. F. Hubbard; R. Bryant; W. Bishop; Betty Carter; Joe Williams; Gary Bartz. A member of M'Boom re: percussion from '71. Worked w. L. Morgan; Novella Nelson; Milt Jackson; Jazzmobile; Melba Moore; Carmen McRae; Nancy Wilson; Billy Taylor, '71-2. App. w. E. Fitzgerald and Boston Pops Orch., '73; Toured Europe and Africa w. Mercer Ellington; Europe w. Roland Hanna; drum instructor for Jazzmobile; school concerts w. Elvin Jones; concerts at prisons and detention houses in NYC, '74. Pl. w. Stan Getz; Cecil Bridgewater; Grady Tate; Billy Taylor, '75. Member of NYJRC, '74-5. A resourceful drummer with fire and taste.

TV: Musical dir., contractor, drummer w. Al Green for

Soul; apps. w. many other artists incl. McRae; Morgan; Fitzgerald. Super Bowl half-time w. M. Ellington; *Dial M for Music*; *Sunday Live* w. B. Taylor and Captain Kangaroo. Fest: w. M'Boom re, Live at the Delacorte, '72; Laren; NJF-NY, '73. Also NJF-NY w. Fitzgerald; K. Burrell; B. Hackett; Gretsch Greats; Radio City jam session, '73; Laren w. Hanna and NY Jazz Quartet, '74. Forming own gp. incorporating own music. Comp: *Inner Passions*; *Al Kifah*. Theater: w. NY Shakespeare Fest., *Sambo*, '70; *Ti Jean and His Brothers*, '72.

LPs: w. K. Barron; J. Moody; R. Davis (Muse); L. Morgan; M. Tyner; A. Hill (BN); H. Laws (CTI); P. Sanders (Imp.); G. Bartz (Mile.); B. Maupin (ECM); J. Zawinul (Vortex); Bobby Jones (Enja); E. Fitzgerald (Col.).

WALCOTT, COLLIN, *tabla, sitar*; also *congas, drums, percussion, clarinet*; b. New York City, 4/24/45. Mother, a classical pianist, is trustee of Hartt Sch. of Mus. in Hartford, Conn. Stud. violin for two yrs. in grammar sch.; snare drum w. Walter Rosenberger of N.Y. Phil., '57-9; pl. timpani and sang madrigals at Putney School, Putney, Vt.; stud. percussion w. George Gaber, Indiana U., '63. From '67 stud. sitar w. Ravi Shankar; tabla w. Alla Rakha. Worked w. Tony Scott, '67-9; w. Peter Walker as intermission mus. at Cafe Au Go-Go, '67-8; congas for Eric Mercury; then w. Tim Hardin, '68-9. Joined Paul Winter Consort, '70; Oregon, '71. Infl: Shankar, Rakha, Ali Akbar Khan, Mongo Santamaria, Herbie Hancock. Films: *Raga*; *Such Good Friends*. Fest: NJF-NY, '74-5; Pori; Molde; Bumbershoot Fest. in Seattle, '75. Comp: *Sail*; *Margueritte*; *Cloud Dance*; *Night Glider*; *Prancing*; *Easter Song*. LPs: *Cloud Dance* (ECM); *Winter Light*; *Distant Hills*; *Music of Another Present Era* (Vang.); *Drum Ode*; *Trios & Solos* (ECM); *Tale of the Exonerated Flea* w. Horacee Arnold (Col.); *Music for Yoga Meditation* w. Scott (Verve); *Rainy Day Raga* w. P. Walker (Vang.).

WALD, JERRY,* *clarinet, leader*; b. Newark, N.J., 1/15/19. Leader of a popular swing band in the '40s, Wald pl. clarinet in a style modeled after A. Shaw. After leading various small groups, he settled in LV, where he died Sept. 1973.

WALDRON, MALCOLM EARL (MAL),* *piano, composer*; b. New York City, 8/16/26. Best known for early work with C. Mingus, Billie Holiday, E. Dolphy. After visiting Europe in '65, settled in Italy, '66, playing his first free-jazz concert there opposite G. Barbieri group. The following year moved to Munich, also touring Poland, Switzerland, Germany, Italy. From that point on Waldron became an internationally active figure, playing innumerable fests., TV shows, writing music for albums and films, and enjoying particular success in several visits to Japan starting in '70, recording there with singer Kimiko Kasai, '71. Won Japanese *Swing Journal*'s Jazz Disc Silver Award, '69; Album of the Year Award, '71. During '74, a year typical of his activities, Waldron toured Scandinavia, Germany, Holland, Belgium and Austria, playing fests. in Zagreb, Nuremberg and Bergen. He remained in Munich as home base, occasionally playing there in clubs.

Comp: *Russian Melody*; *Hard Talk*; *Soul Eyes*; *Left Alone*; *Snakeout*; *All Alone*; *Dee's Dilemma*; and the film scores for *The Cool World*, '63, and *Sweet Love Bitter*, '65.

Publs: *Secret Agent Suite for Big Band* (Editions Modern, Munich, Germany); *Reflections in Modern Jazz* (Sam Fox Music Publs.); *Left Alone* (Edw. Marks Music Publs.).

LPs: Many for various European and Japanese labels. Two for Black Lion, '72; *Free At Last* (ECM); *Reminiscent Suite* (Victor); Mal Waldron *With Steve Lacy Quintet* (America Disc); *All Alone* (G.T.A.); *Blues For Lady Day* (Arista); *Up Popped the Devil*; *Black Glory*; *Hard Talk* (Enja); *Mal Waldron on Steinway* (Paula); reissue, *The Great Concert of Eric Dolphy* (Prest.).

WALKER, AARON (T-BONE),* *singer, guitar*; b. Linden, Tex., 5/22/09 (date disputed). Long a resident of California, Walker from the late '60s was irregularly active, slowed down by illness. He app. occasionally w. J. Otis and on his own in Cal. clubs, and continued recording intermittently. He was hospitalized 12/31/74 and died 3/17/75 in LA.

LPS: *I Want A Little Girl* (Delmark); *Funky Town*; *Stormy Monday Blues*; *Dirty Mistreater* (Bluesway); *Every Day I Have The Blues* (Blues Time); *The Truth* (Bruns.); *T-Bone Blues* (Atl.).

WALLACE, VINCE (Vincenzo Gambino), *tenor saxophone, composer*; also *drums, piano*; b. Ft. Worden Army Base, Port Townsend, Wash., 6/15/39. Early experience in SF Bay Area and in Long Beach, Cal., w. S. Manne, Gene "Mighty Flea" Connors, D. Gordon, Shorty Rogers, Hal Stein, Vi Redd. Has led various groups of his own. App. in J. Coltrane Memorial concert at Both/And, SF, '67. Moving to S. Cal., he pl. regularly at the Studio Cafe in Balboa from summer of '75; gigs at Donte's, '75. Comps: *World Peace Symphony*; *Bombay Calling*; *The Devil's Workshoppe*; *Confrontation in East Oakland*; *Rainclouds over Coltrane Valley*; *Scotland Yard*.

LP: *Vince Wallace Plays Vince Wallace*; *Live At The Studio Cafe* (AMP).

WALLIN, BENGT-ARNE,* *composer, trumpet, fluegelhorn, leader*; b. Linkoping, Sweden, 7/13/26. Pl. w. Arne Domnerus gp., '53-5. Quit playing to concentrate on writing. Scores for many films and TV series, best known being the motion picture, *Dear John*. Other comps: *Symphony For Solo Trumpet/Fluegelhorn*. Took up horns again in '75. Many TV apps. as soloist throughout Europe. Greatly admired by Q. Jones and Clark Terry, Wallin wrote *The Four Leaf Clover* dedicated to Terry. Won award for best jazz record, '62; also many polls in *Orkester Journalen* as best trumpeter, composer/arranger.

:LPs: *Old Folklore in Swedish Modern*; *Adventures in Jazz and Folklore* (Dux); w. Harry Arnold Big Band (Metronome); w. Domnerus Orch. (Metronome, Elektra).

WALRATH, JACK ARTHUR, *trumpet, fluegelhorn, composer*; b. Stuart, Fla., 5/5/46. Started pl. trumpet in '55. Won contests through junior h.s. and h.s. in Montana. Att. Arranger's Stage Band Camp in Calif., '63 & '64. Berklee Coll. from '64, grad. '68. Pl. in rec. band. Also led various gps. around Boston while in school which incl. Miroslav Vitous, Pat and Joe La Barbera. Worked many r&b gigs w. Drifters; Platters; Jackie Wilson, etc. Member of Change, an avant garde r&b band w. Billy Elgart, Gary Peacock, for which he wrote most of the music. Moved w. gp. to LA, '69. Led Avant Garde quartet, Revival, w. Glenn Ferris, '69-71. Worked w. King Errison; Preston Love & Motown

Orch.; Luis Gasca. On the road w. Ray Charles, remaining for a yr. Left band in SF '72; pl. and wrote for Chris Poehler band at Great American Music Hall; short stay w. Cold Blood. To NYC '73, becoming involved in Latin scene for a yr. w. Louie Cruz band. Led own band for a few gigs before joining Paul Jeffrey Octet for five mos. With Charles Mingus from Oct. '74, touring Europe in '75.

Infl: Louis Armstrong, Nat Adderley, Dizzy Gillespie, Sonny Rollins, Eric Dolphy. Walrath says: "Lately in my composition I have been employing devices which I think are of my own invention. I have yet to find a name for this concept but it consists of making the melody the harmony and vice versa. I think I have been influenced in this direction by the music of Bartok, or at least my conception of it. The music that seems to interest me right now is that of Iannis Xenakis."

TV: own gp. on Herb Pomeroy's program in Boston; in Europe w. R. Charles; Mingus; US w. Paul Jeffrey. Fest: Boston Globe fest. w. Berklee Band, '68; LA w. Revival, '70; Bologna w. R. Charles, '71; NJF-Oakland, '72; numerous fests. in Italy, Scandinavia, Spain, etc. w. Mingus. Comps: *Black Bats and Poles*; *Dracula*; *Innocence*; *You Don't Know My Mammy Like I Know My Mammy Who Lives in a Cold Water Flat 3 Blocks Down and to the Left, Jackson*; *Autumn on Neptune*; *Alone*; *The Dance After the Feast*; *Chrono-Synclastic Infundibulum*; *Hog Breath*. LPs: own quintet (Waverly); w. Mingus, *Changes I, Changes II* (Atl.); R. Charles, *Jazz II* (Tangerine); Dannie Richmond (Horo); Errison, *The King Arrives* (Canyon).

WALTON, CEDAR ANTHONY,* *piano, composer*; b. Dallas, Tex., 1/17/34. First important jobs were w. J.J. Johnson in late '50s; the Jazztet, '60-1. After leaving Art Blakey, w. whom he worked from '61-4, free-lanced in NYC, acc. Abbey Lincoln and pl. w. a variety of gps. incl. Eddie Harris, Blue Mitchell, Kenny Dorham, Lee Morgan, Freddie Hubbard, Jimmy Heath, Milt Jackson and Art Farmer. Formed own trio and became "house" rhythm section for Prestige Recs. in late '60s. Rejoined Blakey as mus. dir. for Japanese tour in Feb. '73; pl. in Europe, Nov. '73 as member of Young Giants of Jazz w. Newport JF tour. His trio has app. at Boomer's in Greenwich Village many times during the mid-70s. Gordon Kopulos called him "on both acoustic and electric piano . . . a melody maker with few peers. His tone, even on acoustic piano, is ringing and powerful without being loud. His solos are warm yet structured neatly. As an 'accompanist,' Walton is a rarity. He feeds chordal lines that are full but also unobtrusive, leaving the soloist with openings to authentically complement the chord structure of a song." Fests: NJF-NY in Radio City midnight jam, '73; solo piano, '75; Kongsberg; Ljubljana, '75. Comps: *Mosaic; Fantasy in D* (a.k.a. *Ugetsu*); *Plexus*; *Mode For Joe*; *Soho*; *The Loner*; *I'm Not So Sure*; *Shoulders*; *Bolivia*; *Firm Roots*; *Suite Sunday*; *Holy Land*.

LPs: *Mobius* (RCA); *A Night at Boomer's*, vols. 1 & 2 (Muse); *Breakthrough* (Cobble.); *Cedar!*; *Spectrum*; *Soul Cycle* (Prest.); w. Houston Person; Sonny Criss; A. Blakey (Prest.)

WANZO, MEL, *trombone*; b. Cleveland, Ohio, 11/22/30. Pl. in Army band along w. Adderley brothers and Junior Mance, '52-4. Later, in '50s, worked w. Big Joe Turner, Ruth Brown, r & b bands. TV staff musician in Cleveland, '60-3; Glenn Miller orch., '63; W. Herman, '66-8; C. Basie, '69-. Mainly known as lead trombonist on such Basie albums as *Have a Nice Day* (Daybreak); *Songs of Bessie Smith*, w. Teresa Brewer; *Afrique* (Fl. Dutchman).

WARD, CARLOS N., *alto sax*; also *clarinet, flute, piccolo, soprano sax*; b. Panama Canal Zone, 5/1/40. Names his aunt, pianist Avinal Ward, as his first important influence. Stud. clarinet, trumpet rudiments at high school in Seattle, '53-6; clarinet, saxophone w. John Jessen, '56-60; harmony at Garfield high school; clarinet at U.S. Naval School of Mus., '60. Infl. by Parker, Rollins, O. Coleman, Coltrane, Dolphy, C. Adderley and r & b artists. Member of many groups from early '60s, among them those of Don Cherry, Dollar Brand, Sam Rivers, Pharoah Sanders, Sunny Murray, Cal Massey, McCoy Tyner, Bill Barron, David Izenzon, Rashied Ali, Norman Connors, Clifford Thornton, Roy Brooks, Jazz Composers Orchestra; also the J. Coltrane octet '65. Pl. at NJF, '69 w. Murray and '73 w. Cherry; Berlin JF w. Cherry and Brand, '73; w. Karl Berger, 73; B.T. Express, 75, at NJF-NY. Seen on NET TV shows w. Ali's quartet.

LPs: *New Directions In Modern Music* w. Rashied Ali quartet (Survival); *From Now On*; *Karl Berger & Co.* w. Berger (Milestone); *Gardens of Harlem*, w. Thornton; *Relativity Suite*, w. Cherry (JCOA); *Third World Underground* w. Brand-Cherry (Trio Pat); *African Space Program*, w. Brand (Enja).

WARD, CLARA,* *singer*; b. Philadelphia, Pa., 4/21/24. Leader of the Clara Ward Singers, one of the best known gospel groups, and daughter of Gertrude Ward, who had started the Ward Singers in the '20s. Clara Ward died 1/16/73 in LA. The Ward Singers, in addition to appearing in concert halls throughout the U.S. and overseas, were seen frequently on TV, made more than 50 LPs and app. twice before Pres. Lyndon Johnson.

LPs: *Hang Your Tears Out To Dry* (Verve); *Gospel Concert* (Roul.).

WARREN, EARLE RONALD,* *alto sax, singer, composer*; b. Springfield, Ohio, 7/1/14. In the spring of '67 he returned briefly, for a London date, to the Count Basie orch., the band in which he established his reputation in the '30s and '40s. Earlier that year toured 11 European countries with *Jazz From a Swinging Era*. Musical dir. for the Platters, '69; the Drifters, '70. Own band at the Lorelei, NYC, '71-2. From '72 has headed the Countsmen, a mainstream gp. that usually incl. Buddy Tate, Doc Cheatham, Dill Jones and, sometimes, Benny Morton or Vic Dickenson. The name derives in part from some members' past association w. Basie but it also signifies, Warren says, "that these should be counted." They began by pl. concerts at City Coll., Columbia U. and NYU and have cont. to pl. at colls. and for jazz organizations in the NY metropolitan area. From '75 has also led a quartet, the Warren Court, one night a week at the West End Cafe w. Taft Jordan and Dill Jones.

Film: *Born to Swing* by John Jeremy, '72. Cond. NYJRC orch. in tribute to Basie, Jan. '75. Fest: NJF-NY w. Benny Carter, '75; Nice '75; Belfast, Kew Gardens, London, Nov. '75. Comp: *We're Rollin'*; *You Know It Too*; *Smiley's Blues*. LPs: *Earle Warren*; *The Countsmen* (Eng. RCA); *Buck Clayton Jam Session, Vols. 1&2* (Chiaro.).

WARREN, PETER, *bass, cello, composer*; b. New York City, 11/21/35. Educated at Adelphi Coll. and Juilliard School of Music. Cello debut at Carnegie Hall at age 17. Performed mainly as a classical musician until '59 when he worked in Las Vegas, leaving there w. T. Dorsey orch. Accompanied Dionne Warwicke, '65-7. Pl. w. Herbie Mann, '68. In '69-70 worked w. Blues Project II; his own gp., Interchange; and the N.Y. Bass Revolution w. David Izenzon. To Europe '70, remaining until '74 and working with a variety of musicians incl. Charlie Mariano and Stu Martin in Ambush; Jean-Luc Ponty; Don Cherry; Anthony Braxton; Chick Corea, John Surman; Albert Mangelsdorff; Terumasa Hino. Returned to U.S. '74, joining Jack DeJohnette's Directions in '75 for tours in U.S. and Canada. Conducted workshops at the Creative Music Foundation, a school funded by NY State Council on the Arts. Infl: Gary Peacock, Stu Martin, Jack DeJohnette. Fest: Baden Baden, Hamburg TV Workshop, Antibes, Berlin, Bilsen, Chateauvallon, Donaueschingen. Comp: *Subrahar*; *Phallic Dance*. NEA Grant to compose and perform works on the cello, '76. LPs: *Bass Is* (Enja); w. DeJohnette, *Cosmic Chicken* (Fant.); w. Steve Kuhn, *This Way Out*; *Interchange*; *Going to the Rainbow* (MPS); w. T. Stanko, *TWET* (Muza); w. J.L. Ponty, *Open Strings* (MPS); w. Braxton, *Donna Lee* (America); w. T. Hino, *Vibrations*; w. H. Sato, *Trinity*; w. A. Mangelsdorff, *Spontaneous* (Enja); w. Carla Bley, *3/4* (Watt); w. Cherry, *Donaueschingen Contemporary Music Festival* (Philips).

WARWICK, CARL,* *trumpet*; b. Belmar, N.J., 10/27/17. Veteran with many name bands from mid-'30s incl. B. Berigan, W. Herman, L. Millinder, B. Rich; State Dept. tours w. D. Gillespie, '56-7. Dir. of Mus. for all penal institutions in N.Y., '66-. During vacation toured w. Sammy Davis Jr., '72. In March '74 he presented the idea to Exprinter Tours for a jazz cruise at sea, and was instrumental in lining up talent for the cruises, which left from NYC twice a year with such stars as Gillespie, Fitzgerald, Basie, Vaughan et al. Fests: Newport, '58 w. Gillespie; '73 w. Benny Carter.

LPs: w. Gillespie (Verve); Herman (Col.); feat. on *Baby Baby All the Time* w. Rich (Merc.).

WASHINGTON, GROVER JR., *tenor saxophone*; also *alto, soprano, baritone saxophones, clarinet, electric bass, piano*; b. Buffalo, N.Y., 12/12/43. Father pl. tenor; mother sings in choir; one brother is an organist in church choirs; youngest brother, Darryl, pl. drums w. Richard "Groove" Holmes. Father bought him saxophone at 10. Lessons at Wurlitzer Sch. of Mus. Pl. in high school band; for two yrs. was member of All City H.S. Band as baritone player. Stud. chord progressions w. Elvin Shepherd. Left Buffalo at 16 w. Four Clefs, based in Columbus, Ohio but on the road five and six mos. at a time. Group broke up in '63; joined organist Keith McAllister for two yrs. While in Army at Ft. Dix, N.J. for two yrs, Washington worked in Phila. w. organ trios and rock groups; also in NYC for Jazz Interactions w. Billy Cobham. After service, pl. w. Don Gardner's Sonotones in Phila., '67-8. Worked for local rec. distributor, '69-70; ret. to full-time pl. w. Charles Earland, '71. Rec. w. (guitarist) Joe Jones, Leon Spencer, Johnny Hammond. As a result of Hammond album he was signed to his own rec. contract by Kudu. Infl: Coltrane, Joe Henderson, Oliver Nelson. TV: Canada; Japan; *Perspective Minorities*, WPVI, Phila.; *Dedication of Louis Armstrong Stadium* at NJF-NY, '73, PBS. Fests: Berkeley JF, '71; Olympic JF, London to Germany, '72; CTI concert tour of Japan, Hawaii, '74; CTI Calif. concert tour, '75. Comp: *Loren's Dance*; arr. of *It's Too Late* for Johnny Hammond. Commercially oriented, versatile musician, who enjoyed great popular success from '75.

LPs: *Mister Magic*; *All the Kings Horses*; *Inner City Blues*; *Soul Box* (Kudu); w. J. Hammond, *Breakout* (Kudu); w. D. Sebesky, *Giant Box*; w. R. Weston, *Blue Moses* (CTI).

WATANABE, KAZUMI, *guitar*; b. Tokyo, Japan, 10/14/53. Stud. jazz guitar w. Sadanori Nakamure, '69-70; jazz theory w. Makoto Uchibori, '70-1; Sadao Watanabe (no relation), '71-2; jazz guitar w. Masayuki Takayanagi, '72-4; classical guitar, harmonics w. Tamaki Shimizu, '70-1. Pl. w. Sadanori Nakamure at Club Evans; Masaru Imada at Pit-in, '70-1; own trio & quartet at Naru, '71; Isao Suzuki quartet at Club Five Spot, '72; own gps. at 86, As Soon As clubs; also w. Yoshio Otomo quintet, I. Suzuki quartet, Shigeharu Mukai quintet, Eiji Toki quartet at same clubs as well as Pit-in, Taro and Junk. Formed two-guitar gp. w. Masahiro Ikumi, '73-4. Pl. w. Takehiro Honda gp. at Nemu Jazz Inn and Pit-in, '74; Sadao Watanabe quintet at Pit-in, '75. Infl: Jim Hall, Wes Montgomery, H. Hancock, Coltrane, Nakamure, Takayanagi, Sadao Watanabe, I. Suzuki, Julian Bream, L. Coryell. Pl. numerous jazz fests. in Japan. LPs: *Infinite* (Toshiba EMI); w. I. Suzuki, *Blue City*; *All Right* (Three Blind Mice).

WATANABE, SADAO,* *alto saxophone, flute, sopranino*; b. Tochigi Pref., Japan, 2/1/33. In 1956 took over leadership of Toshiko Akiyoshi's quartet, when latter left to study at Berklee in Boston. In '62, Watanabe himself left Japan to attend Berklee. In '65 he worked w. G. McFarland and C. Hamilton. Back to Japan, '65; launched jazz school for young musicians, Feb. '66. A record he made w. Charlie Mariano won an award from *Swing Journal*, and as Best Japanese Jazz Album in '68. That summer he made his first app. at the NJF. In March, '69, Watanabe app. at *Swing Journal* workshop concert, Salute to Charlie Parker. In '70 he was heard at the Montreux and Newport fests. Pl. in Africa, '72. His first solo album was selected as Best LP by *Swing Journal* in '73. In June of that year he again app. at Montreux. He comp. the score for the African film *The Ujama* in '74. On returning from Africa, he gave a series of recitals in major Japanese cities. Publ: *Jazz For Myself*, autobiography (Arachi Publ. Co.).

Naming Charlie Parker and Gary McFarland as his sources of inspiration, Watanabe developed into one of the most individual and versatile artists to emerge from the Japanese jazz scene, winning awards at one time or another in six different categories for his records, combo leading, playing, composing and arranging.

LPs: *Sadao Watanabe* (King); *Iberian Waltz* (Tact); *Round Trip*; *Pastoral* (CBS/Sony); w. G. Szabo, *Gypsy '66* (Imp.); w. McFarland, *The In Sound* (Verve); w. Hamilton, *El Chico* (Imp); *Jazz in the Classroom*, Vol. 1-10 (Berklee Records).

WATERS, BENJAMIN (BENNY),* *tenor saxophone, clarinet*; b. Brighton, Md., 1/23/02. Prominent in name bands from '26, including seven years w. Charlie Johnson; later w. F. Henderson, C. Hopkins in '30s; J. Lunceford, '41; several years in Cal. After traveling w. Roy Milton's band, returned to NYC,'50, pl. clarinet, sop. sax w. Jimmy Archey, whose band went to Europe in '52. Waters remained on the continent, joining Bill Coleman, then settling in Paris, where, for 15 years, he was with the band of trumpeter Jacques Butler. Waters took over leadership of the band in '67. From '69 he spent most of his time freelancing throughout Europe.

LPs: Coronet; D.S.C.

WATERS, ETHEL,* *singer*; b. Chester, Pa., 10/31/00. A recording star in the '20s, she later became even more widely known as an excellent actress on Broadway and in Hollywood. TV and public apps. in '70s w. evangelist Billy Graham. Featured in one program of TV series *Route 66* along w. Jo Jones, Coleman Hawkins and Roy Eldridge. LP: *Ethel Waters' Greatest Years* (Columbia).

WATERS, MONVILLE CHARLES (MONTY), *alto sax, composer*; also *soprano sax, flute, piano*; b. Modesto, Calif., 4/14/38. Mother and aunt taught him piano; later took lessons on piano, sax w. private teacher. Had own band in SF. Pl. w. Jon Hendricks there '65-8; also gigs w. King Pleasure; Miles Davis. To NYC Feb. '68 w. Hendricks. Worked w. Elvin Jones; Joe Lee Wilson; Philly Joe Jones; George Coleman; Woody Shaw; Sam Rivers; Jimmy Garrison; Roy Brooks; Andrew Hill; Erroll Parker; Eddie Jefferson; and own gp. Infl: Charlie Parker, Tadd Dameron, Dizzy Gillespie, James Moody, Coltrane, Gil Fuller, Ornette Coleman, Louis Armstrong, Sidney Bechet. TV: special in SF w. own big band; *Like It Is*; *Free Time*; *Jazz Set*, all w. Joe Lee Wilson. Fest: Pacific JF; MJF w. Hendricks; NJF-NY w. Wilson; Earl Cross, '73. Comp: over 500 comps. incl. *That Day*; *Parting*; also arrs. for own bands; K. Pleasure; J.L. Wilson; Hendricks; P.J. Jones. Publ: (Deep Waters Pub. Co., 185 E. 3rd St. 2H, New York, N.Y. 10009). LPs: own quartet for Japanese label; w. J.L. Wilson (Survival); Ronnie Boykins (ESP).

WATERS, MUDDY (McKinley Morgenfield),* *singer, guitar*; b. Rolling Fork, Miss., 4/4/15. A mainstay on the Chicago blues scene in the '50s, he became an important figure in the traditional blues revival of the '60s, influencing young white musicians in the U.S. and England. His *Rollin' Stone*, recorded in the '50s, later inspired Bob Dylan's *Like a Rolling Stone* and helped name a British rock group and an American rock journal. As a result of the rise in popularity of rock music Waters' career also took an upward turn. An auto accident in '69 crushed his pelvis and nearly killed him but he resumed touring with his band a year later. Played England and the Continent; in '73 did concert tour of New Zealand and Australia incl. national TV special for Austr. Broad. Corp. Won DB Critics poll for Best R & B Group, '68; Grammy Awards for *They Call Me Muddy Waters*, '71; *The London Muddy Waters Sessions*, '72; elected to *Ebony* Black Music Hall of Fame, '73. *Time* wrote: "Muddy Waters is the king of dirty blues, down home blues, funky blues or straight blues—most properly known as delta or country blues. Of them all, Muddy Waters remains the purest, the most loyal to where he has been and what it has cost him." Fests: Newport Folk Fest., '67; NJF-NY, '72; Ann Arbor Fest., '69.

LPs: *Electric Mud*; *After the Rain* (Cadet); *Super Blues* (Checker); *The Blues, A Real Summit Meeting* (Buddah); *Ann Arbor Blues & Jazz Fest*. (Atl.); *Down on Stovall Plantation* (Testament); *The London Muddy Waters Sessions*; *They Call Me Muddy Waters*; many others (Chess).

WATROUS, WILLIAM RUSSELL II (BILL), *trombone, composer*; b. Middletown, Conn., 6/8/39. Father, Ralph J. Watrous, pl. w. name bands in 1920s. Stud. harmony w. Richard Benvenuti at New London High Sch., then went into service for four years and recorded with hundreds of major artists through 1960s. Played w. Roy Eldridge, Kai Winding, Quincy Jones, Woody Herman, Johnny Richards, Count Basie, and worked as studio musician on staff at CBS 1967-9, also ABC for Dick Cavett show 1968-70. Was a member of Ten Wheel Drive in '71; left to form his own big band, which he called Manhattan Wildlife Refuge.

Watrous, who has also played baritone horn, bass trumpet and drums, is a mainstream-modern soloist of extraordinary skill. He credits John Hammond, producer of his first big band album, with helping him achieve success as a leader. Among his favs. and infl. he named Clifford Brown, Ch. Parker, Carl Fontana, Vic Dickenson, Johannes Brahms and Dizzy Gillespie.

Appeared at NJF-NY annually from '72, in jam sessions, as sideman w. Bobby Rosengarden and in 1975 as leader; also MJF in '73, Quinnipiac JF annually '70-73; Colo. Jazz Party '74-5.

LPs: *Bone Straight Ahead*; *In Tandem* (Famous Door); *Manhattan Wildlife Refuge*; w. MWR, *Tiger of San Pedro* (Col.).

WATTS, ERNEST JAMES (ERNIE), *saxophones*; b. Norfolk, Va., 10/23/45. Family moved to Detroit two years later, and in '57 to Wilmington, Del., where he became interested in music while at high school. He was awarded a *down beat* scholarship to study at Berklee in Boston, and during his second year there was offered a job with B. Rich, in whose band he toured for nearly two years, '66-8. Settling in LA, he played w. Gerald Wilson, Toshiko, Wayne Henderson, and toured Africa w. a seven piece group led by O. Nelson. Subsequently he joined the *Tonight Show* band and concentrated on commercial work. A well rounded musician who plays all the saxophones, clarinets, flutes, oboe and English horn, he was infl. by Coltrane and Miles Davis.

Own LPs on World Pacific; w. B. Rich, *Big Swing Face* (World Pacific); *Night Blooming Jazzmen*; *Freedom Jazz Dance* (Main.).

WATTS, TREVOR, *alto, soprano saxophones*; b. York, Yorkshire, England, 1939. Joined RAF School of Mus., '58. Five years in RAF band in Germany. In London, '63, pl. w. New Jazz Orch.; left in '65 to concentrate on free group improv. With John Stevens started Spontaneous Music Ensemble, Britain's first avant garde jazz group. Led own band, Amalgam, '67. Also pl. w. Splinters (along w. Phil Seamen, Tubby Hayes, Stan Tracey, Stevens); Bobby Bradford quartet; London Jazz Composers Orch. Concerts w. Steve Lacy; rec. w. S. Swallow, Rashied Ali. With Stevens ran The Little Theatre Club, home of Britain's free jazz scene, '65-74.

LPs: w. SME, *Challenge* (Eyemark); *Oliv* (Marmalade); *The Source* (Tangent); *S.M.E. for C.N.D. for Peace For You To Share* (A Records); *Birds of a Feather* (Byg); *So What Do You Think?* (Tangent); *S.M.E. Plus Bobby Bradford* (Freedom); *Face to Face S.M.E. In Concert* Part 1 & Part 2 (Emanem); *S.M.E. a S.M.O.* (A Records); w. Amalgam, *Prayer for Peace* (Transatlantic); *Amalgam Play Blackwell and Higgins*; *Ripple* (A Records).

WAYNE, CHUCK,* *guitar*; b. New York City, 2/27/23. Active on 52nd St. in the '40s as one of the first guitarists in the bop movement, he later gained prominence in the most celebrated of the George Shearing quintets, '49-52. A CBS staff member from '60-9, he pl. for the Garry Moore, Carol Burnett, Ed Sullivan shows, etc., led own trios and duos in NYC clubs. Free-lance recs. w. Steve Lawrence-Eydie Gorme, Barbra Streisand; jingle dates; *The Nervous Set*, *Copper and Brass* on Broadway. Rejoined CBS to pl. Merv Griffin Show, '71-2. Formed guitar duo w. Joe Puma at the St. Regis Hotel, '73; pl. clubs and concerts w. Puma. Comps: originals for LPs listed below; score for documentary film *The Mugging*. Fest: Radio City jam session, NJF-NY, '72; w. Puma, NJF-NY, '73. Publ: *Arpeggio Dictionary* w. Ralph Pat (Belwin Music). Wayne also pl. classic guitar for several yrs. in the '70s. He and Puma gave some public seminars at the Guitar, a NYC club, in '74. LPs: *Interactions* w. Puma (Choice); tracks in *Guitar Town Hall Concert* (Col.); w. Duke Jordan (SteepleChase).

WAYNE, FRANCES,* *singer*; b. Boston, Mass., 8/26/19. Sang w. Ch. Barnet; earned fame w. Woody Herman '43-5. Married Neal Hefti, '45; to Cal., semi-retired, '46. Toured in Hefti band '52-3, retired again, emerging for gigs at Donte's, N. Hollywood, late 1974; also w. new Hefti orch. in '75. LPs: all deleted, but her version of *That Old Black Magic* w. Barnet (she was first singer to record it) was reissued in '75 on MCA.

WEATHER REPORT. See Shorter, Wayne; Zawinul, Joe.

WEBER, EBERHARD, *bass, composer*; also *bass guitar, cello*; b. Stuttgart, Germany, 1/22/40. Father teaches cello and piano. Began study of cello w. him at age six. Switched to bass in '55 on which he is self-taught. Worked w. Wolfgang Dauner, '63-71; Dave Pike Set, '72; Volker Kriegel Spectrum, '73-4. Formed own group, Colours, in '75. In the '60s Weber worked for six yrs. in a private film co., directing films for tv. Later freelanced as a dir. in theater & tv but became a full-time pro. mus. in '68. Infl. as comp: Steve Reich. Began comp. in '72. Wrote music for his album *Colours of Chloe*. Also comp. suite for 12 cellos and jazz quartet for Berlin Jazz Fest. '74. Other fest: Pori; Warsaw; Frankfurt. LPs: *Colours of Chloe*; *Ring* w. Gary Burton; *Solstice* w. Ralph Towner (ECM); *The Call* w. Mal Waldron (Japo); w. Baden Powell on MPS; CBS; *Missing Link* w. Kriegel (MPS); *Dream Talk* w. Dauner (CBS).

WEBSTER, BENJAMIN FRANCIS (BEN),* *tenor saxophone*; b. Kansas City, Mo., 2/27/09. Though heard with many other name bands, Webster achieved international eminence during his incumbency in the Duke Ellington orch., '39-43. In later years he usually led his own small groups, but after a period of relative inactivity while based in LA in the mid-60s, he moved to Europe, working there somewhat more regularly in clubs and concerts around the Continent. Following a two week hospitalization, he died 9/20/73 in Amsterdam.

Webster's playing from the early years was often aggressive and intensely alive; yet he is best remembered for the extraordinary warmth and soulfulness he brought to his ballad performances, notably *All Too Soon* and *Just A' Sittin' and A' Rockin'* w. Ellington. Along with C. Hawkins, D. Byas, P. Gonsalves, Chu Berry, L. Young, he was one of the handful of great tenor saxophonists in the melodic/harmonic tradition established before and during the swing era.

Film: *Quiet Days in Clichy*, app. in nightclub sequence.

LPs: w. Ellington (Col., RCA); Mercer Ellington (MCA); own albums, *See You At The Fair* (Imp.); *At Work In Europe* (Pres.); *Atmosphere for Lovers and Thieves*; *Duke's In Bed* (Black Lion); *Meets Don Byas* (BASF); *Ben Webster & Sweets Edison*; *Coleman Hawkins & Clark Terry* (Col.); *Blow Ben, Blow* (Delta); *For The Guv'nor* (Imperial); *The Warm Moods* (Repr.); *The Soul Of Ben Webster*; *Ben Webster & Associates*; *Meets Oscar Peterson* (Verve); *My Man* (Steeple Chase); *Live at Pio's* (Enja); others w. B. Holiday (Verve); T. Wilson-B. Holiday (Col.); many others, deleted but likely to be reissued, incl. sessions w. A. Tatum, B. Rich, C. Terry, J. Hodges.

WEIN, GEORGE THEODORE,* *piano, producer*; b. Boston, Mass., 10/3/25. As he had from 1954, with the exception of 1961, Wein continued to produce the Newport Jazz Festival at Newport, R.I. until the '71 event was curtailed by an invasion of youths from outside the festival grounds, who, after setting fences afire, proceeded to break chairs and smash the piano on stage.

In '72 the NJF moved to New York City to establish itself as an historic city-wide happening and a trend-setter for urban festivals. In R.I. the fest. generally ran three or four days; in NYC it stretched over 10.

From '70 Wein has produced the New Orleans Jazz Fest. for which he created a companion event, the Jazz and Heritage Fair. He also has an annual summer national touring festival which plays in Oakland, Kansas City, Chicago, Hampton, Va., Atlanta, Cincinnati, Houston and San Diego.

In the summer of '74 he inaugurated La Grande Parade Du Jazz in Nice, France, a festival of more than 100 name musicians representing traditional jazz from New Orleans through the Swing Era.

His European Newport Jazz Festival, an annual tour from '64 has given concerts in every major European country with the exception of Russia. From '66 he presented Duke Ellington in over 200 concerts in Asia, Africa and Europe, including Ellington's final European tour in November '73.

In January '74 Wein founded the New York Jazz Repertory Company of which he is executive director. It is the first major jazz repertory company and is funded by grants from the NYS Council on the Arts; the National Endowment for the Arts; and the Carnegie Hall Corp. in association with the Dept. of Cultural Affairs of the City of N.Y. At the conclusion of its second season in the spring of '75, the NYJRC toured Russia with its programs dedicated to the life and music of Louis Armstrong.

As a pianist, Wein continued to lead his Newport All Stars at his festivals and for nightclub appearances at the Half Note, Michael's Pub, etc. At various times in the late '60s and '70s it has included Red Norvo, Barney Kessel, Ruby Braff, Tal Farlow, James Spaulding, Eddie "Lockjaw" Davis and Larry Ridley.

LPs: Many artists have been recorded "live" at the NJF but in '72 Cobblestone tapped six volumes of the NJF-NY, incl. two double-pocket jam session sets from Radio City; a "soul" set w. Billy Eckstine, Curtis Mayfield, et al; and a Yankee Stadium session w. B.B. King, Zoot Sims, Clark Terry. It was also available as a boxed set. Wein's own LPs: *Newport All Stars* (Atlantic); *Alive and Well in Mexico* (Col.); *Tribute to Duke* (BASF); the latter two also w. Newport All Stars; w. R. Braff, *Plays Louis Armstrong*; w. Venuti-Grappelli (Byg).

WELLS, WILLIAM (DICKY),* *trombone*; b. Centerville, Tenn., 6/10/09. The former stylist with the Count Basie band of the '30s and '40s toured Europe w. Buddy Tate in '68, played at the NO JF in '69 but has been relatively inactive in the '70s. In '71 *The Night People,* a book about his experiences, as told to Stanley Dance, was published by the Crescendo Pub. Co. LP: *Trombone Four-in-Hand* (Master Jazz); *Dicky Wells in Paris, 1937* (Prest.); w. Lester Young in *The Big Three* (Bob Thiele Music), all reissues.

WELLS, MICHAEL JOHN (SPIKE), *drums*; b. Tunbridge Wells, Kent, England, 1/16/46. Largely self-taught on drums, but stud. briefly w. Philly Joe Jones, '67; classical mus. educ. (piano, cello, voice), Canterbury Cathedral Choir School, '55-60; King's School, Canterbury, '60-4. Pl. w. Tubby Hayes '68-73; Humphrey Lyttleton band, '69-70; Roland Kirk; Chas. Tolliver, '69; Ronnie Scott sextet '70, with whom he also app. in Czechoslovakia; Scandinavian tour w. S. Getz, '70. From '69, intermittently house drummer at Ronnie Scott's Club, backing visiting artists such as Johnny Griffin, Dakota Staton, Art Farmer, Z. Sims, Blossom Dearie, L. Konitz, F. Hubbard, Annie Ross. Stephane Grappelli. Infls: Roy Haynes; Elvin Jones; Clifford Jarvis. App. on BBC-TV series, *Jazz Scene* w. Hayes; also on German and Norwegian TV. Hungarian JF w. Maynard Ferguson, '69; Pori, Finland JF, w. Dave Horler, '75.

LPs: *The Orchestra,* w. Hayes; *That's Just The Way I Want To Be,* w. Dearie (Philips).

WELLSTOOD, RICHARD MacQUEEN (DICK),* *piano*; b. Greenwich, Conn., 11/25/27. After pl. w. G. Krupa, '64-6, he worked in the band at The Ferryboat, Brielle, N.J., '66-Sept. '68. Traveled w. the gps. of Roy Eldridge, Jimmy McPartland, Dukes of Dixieland, '69-70. From '70 much work in N.J. but also own gp. at Michael's Pub, NYC,' 73-4; solo piano at Blues Alley, Wash., D.C. & Toronto; Bourbon Street, Toronto, '73; six-week Euro. tour w. World's Greatest Jazzband, '74; solo in Hartford, Conn. and eight weeks at Cookery, NYC, '75. Fests: Colorado Jazz Party, '73; Odessa, Tex. Jazz Party; St. Louis Ragtime Fest. '74; Kerrville, Tex. Rag. Fest., '73-4; solo piano at NJF-NY, '74. Comps: *Fucallia*; *South Amboy Highball*; *Dollar Dance*; *George Sanders*. A versatile pianist whose prime interests include ragtime and Harlem stride. Dan Morgenstern has written that Wellstood's "artistic versatility" is "perhaps better described as breadth or depth . . . (he) hears and understands as much music as anyone I know—musician or musicologist, jazzman or classicist."

LPs: *From Ragtime On*; *And his Famous Orch.* (Chiaroscuro); *Alone* (Jazzology); *and his Hot Potatoes* (Seeds); *Walkin' with Wellstood*; *Rapport* w. Butterfield ("77"). Some of his albums contain his own witty liner notes.

WELSH, ALEX,* *trumpet, cornet*; b. Edinburgh, Scotland, 7/9/29. Prominent bandleader since mid-50s. In '66-7 toured Britain acc. many U.S. jazzmen incl. Wild Bill Davison, Eddie Miller, Peanuts Hucko, Ben Webster, Eddie "Lockjaw" Davis. Clubs, concerts all over Britain and Europe. Fests: Barcelona, '66; Antibes, '67; Newport, '68; Jazz Expo, London annually '67-70; Leipzig, '73; Edinburgh, '74; Breda, '75. Also in '75 Louis Armstrong Memorial Concert at Royal Fest. Hall, London, w. Davison, Clark Terry. Voted top small band in Britain, MM poll, '70. Has pl. over 25 TV network shows and 250 radio programs.

LPs: *At Home With Alex Welsh Band*; *Dixieland Party*; *Vintage '69* (Col.); *Louis Armstrong Memorial Album*; *If I Had A Talking Picture of You* (Bl. Lion-Poly.); *Dixieland Party,* Part 2 (Bl. Lion-Transatlantic Recs.).

WESS, FRANK WELLINGTON,* *tenor sax*; also *flutes, saxophones*; *clarinets*; b. Kansas City, Mo., 1/4/22. With C. Basie in '50s-'60s became well known as first of the modern jazz flutists and as tenor and alto soloist. Left Basie in '64 and became very busy free-lancer in NYC studios w. jingles, rec. dates, etc. Also active in teaching, clinics. Pl. in bands for Broadway shows: *The Apple Tree,* '66; *Golden Rainbow,* '67; *Irene,* '72-3. A member of ABC-TV staff orch., '68; w. Billy Taylor band for David Frost show, '69-72. Coll. concerts, clubs, tours, incl. Japan, w. New York Jazz Quartet (R. Hanna, R. Carter, B. Riley), '74-5. Tony Bennett-Lena Horne Show, '75. Concerts w. NYJRC, '74-5. Pl. w. C. Terry big band in '70s. TV: *Black Journal*; Sammy Davis; Howard Cosell, *Saturday Night Live*; many telethons. Fest: Concord; Laren, Holland; Middleheim, Belgium; NJF-NY: w B. Taylor, '72; *Basie Reunion* band, '73; NYJQ, '74; Benny Carter, '75. Writing jazz flute solo book. Comps: *Placcitude*; *Bay Street*; a 10-minute piece, *Jazzmobile Ups and Downs*. LPs: *Wess to Memphis*; *Flute of the Loom* (Enterprise); *NY Jazz Quartet, Live in Japan* (Salvation); w. C. Terry (Etoile).

WESTON, AZZEDIN NILES, *congas, percussion*; b. Brooklyn, N.Y., 8/12/50. Father is Randy Weston who wrote *Little Niles* for him. Absorbed much music from his father and associates. Piano lessons from Nadi Quamar at age 13; stud. drums in junior high sch. and pl. in school band, '63. Harmony and theory at Mayflower Sch. of Arts, Plymouth, Mass., '64; drums w. Sticks Evans, Lennie

McBrowne, '65. Traveled in 16 African countries w. R. Weston, '66, and was greatly influenced to change to hand drums. Ret. to US '67 and began to pl. congas w. Latin bands incl. Mark Diamond, '68. In the middle of that year went back to Africa, this time living in Morocco w. his father and pl. w. him in countries south of the Sahara. To Tangier late '69; he helped design African Rhythms Club where he acc. R. Weston; also pl. w. Moroccan musicians. Co-led gp., Safari East w. T. Monk Jr. in NYC, '72. Worked w. Ahmad Jamal, '73-4; Pharoah Sanders; Leon Thomas; D. Gillespie big band at Buddy's Place and *Tribute to Dizzy* concert at Avery Fisher Hall; R. Weston in Sicily; Tunisia, '75. Infl: R. Weston, Big Black, Max Roach, West African, North African and Senegalese drummers. TV: *AM America w. D. Gillespie; Like It Is*; *Positively Black* w. R. Weston. Fest: w. R. Weston, Tangier '72; NJF-NY '73; Tabarka (Tunis) '75. Comp: *Blues for Senegal*. Strong interest in the music and rhythms of Africa has made him "explore these rhythms and expand myself musically."

LPs: w. R. Weston, *African Rhythms*; Tanjah (Poly.); *Blue Moses* (CTI); *Jamal Plays Jamal* (20th Cent. Fox).

WESTON, RANDOLPH E. (RANDY),* *piano, composer*; b. Brooklyn, N.Y., 4/6/26. In the fall of '66 pl. major Calif. campuses w. own sextet in a history of jazz presentation which Ralph J. Gleason called "a kind of superior lecture-demonstration." Pl. three-month, 14-country tour of West Africa for U.S. State Dept. beginning in Jan. '67; returned to Morocco, Tunisia, Aug.-Sept.; then remained in Morocco, work. in major cities. Lived in Rabat, '67-8, before settling in Tangier and opening own African Rhythms Club there at end of '69. Traveled and pl. in Africa w. Bill Wood, Ed Blackwell, '68. Returned to U.S. in April '72 for piano party at townhouse of Brooks Kerr's mother, NYC. Back in Tangier, summer and org. Fest. of American, African & Moorish Mus., Sept. '72. To NYC for Carnegie Hall concert, Jan. '73; *Uhuru* w. Symph. of the New World at Phil. Hall, Feb. '73; gigs w. group at The Onliest Place, Village Vanguard, Livingston Coll.; 24-hr. tribute to Ellington, '73. App. w. duo at Bradley's; band at Hartford, Conn. concert; African Rhythms prog. at Billie Holiday Theater, Brooklyn, '74; duo concert at Smithsonian Inst., Wash., D.C.; solo concerts in Switz., France, Tunisia, Algeria, Sicily, '75. TV: *Like It Is,* '70; *Positively Black,* '74; many Euro. apps. incl. Spain, Norway, etc. '74. Fests: MJF, '66; NJF-NY, '73; Kongsberg; Christianstaad; Antibes; Montreux, '74; Fest. of American Folk Life, Wash., D.C.; Groningen; Nigeria, '75. Won TDWR award in DB Critics' poll, '72. Comps: *Ganouah*; *Marrakech Blues*; *Night in the Medina*; *Ifran*; *African Cookbook*; *Tangier Bay*. A new work dedicated to Arabic singer, Om Kel Thoum, written for World of Islam Fest., London. Publ: *The Lively Art of Jazz* (Charles Colin, 315 W. 53rd St., New York, N.Y. 10019); other comps: (Charles Hansen, 1860 Broadway, New York, N.Y. 10023).

As a player Weston reflects his early infls., Tatum, Powell, Monk and Ellington in a highly individual manner which Leonard Feather has credited with "a pure jazz essence, overwhelming technical assurance and natural sense of joy." As a composer he has incorporated his first-hand experience with North African themes and rhythms and his Afro-American background to produce startlingly fresh material.

LPs: *Tanjah*; *African Rhythms* (Poly.); *Blue Moses* (CTI); *Blues to Africa*; *Carnival* (Arista/Freedom); *African Cookbook* (Atl.); *Blues* (Trip); solo albums on Black Lion; Chant Du Monde.

WESTBROOK, MICHAEL JOHN DAVID (MIKE), *composer, leader, baritone horn*; b. High Wycombe, England, 3/21/36. Self-taught. Formed first band at Plymouth Art School, '58. Led octet in Plymouth, '60; 11 piece band in London, '62-6; during late '60s had groups of varying sizes between six and 26, playing Ronnie Scott's Old Place, Montreux Fest., BBC, many British fests, '70-2 led several different combos, app. at European fests.; also co-directed, with John Fox, the multi-media group Cosmic Circus, staging events with films, light shows, circus perfs. and music. Later headed five piece group, Mike Westbrook's Brass Band, for outdoor fests., '73; 18 piece orch for concerts, '74-5. John Surman was a frequent associate of Westbrook's beginning in '60.

Comps: *Celebration*; *Marching Song*; *Release*; *Metropolis*; *Tyger* (stage musical commissioned by National Theatre in '71); *Citadel/Room 315* (commissioned by Swedish Radio). Awards: composer, TDWR, DB Critics' Poll, '69; big band, TDWR, DB Critics' Poll, '70. *Melody Maker* Critics' Poll: big band, '69; triple winner in British section as comp., arr., big band, '70. Voted top European comp. by *Jazz Forum,* '72.

LPs in Europe on Deram, RCA, Cadillac labels.

WETTLING, GEORGE,* *drums*; b. Topeka, Kansas, 11/28/07. Best known for his many concert, club and record assignments with Eddie Condon, Wettling in his earlier years pl. w. big bands led by Jack Hylton, Artie Shaw, B. Berigan, Red Norvo, Paul Whiteman. For several years he led a trio at the Gaslight Club, NYC, later toured briefly with the Dukes of Dixieland, and took part in a reunion band of veteran jazzmen at the '65 *down beat* Jazz Festival in Chicago. His last steady job was w. Clarence Hutchenrider's trio at Bill's Gay Nineties in NYC. He died of cancer in NYC 6/6/68. Wettling, a drummer of diverse accomplishments in many contexts, also was a gifted painter and writer, contributing to *down beat* and other publications.

LPs w. Condon (Col., etc.), Berigan, Shaw (RCA).

WHEELER, KENNETH (KENNY or KEN), *trumpet, fluegelhorn, composer*; b. Toronto, Canada, 1/14/30. Father and two brothers active as semi-pro musicians in St. Catherines, Ontario. Studied harmony w. John Weinzweig at Toronto Conserv. in early '50s; counterpoint w. Bill Russo; comp. w. Richard Rodney Bennett in London, Eng., early '60s. Played w. John Dankworth, '59-65; then intermittently w. Ronnie Scott; Joe Harriott; Tubby Hayes; Friedrich Gulda; Clarke-Boland big band. With Mike Gibbs from '69; Globe Unity Orch. from '72. Although he is an important member of London's free-jazz scene and a busy studio musician, he often travels to the US to play and record w. Anthony Braxton with whom he has been associated from '72. Infl: Booker Little, Braxton, Art Farmer, Benny Bailey, Miles Davis, Buck Clayton, L. Konitz, S. Lacy, B. Evans, Bobby Wellins, Evan Parker, Ellington, Jimmy Knepper,

Tony Oxley. Fest: NJF w. Dankworth, '59; Berlin Anti-Fest. w. Globe Unity, '74; Berlin w. Gibbs, '75; Antibes, Montreux w. Braxton, '75. Tied w. Woody Shaw in DB Critics poll, TDWR, '70.

LPs: *Windmill Tilter* w. J. Dankworth (Fontana); *Song for Someone* w. own orch. (Incus); *Gnu High* w. K. Jarrett, D. Holland, J. DeJohnette (ECM): these three albums all comp. & arr. by Wheeler; w. Braxton, *New York, Fall 1974*; *Five Pieces 1975* (Arista); w. Mike Gibbs, *The Only Chrome-Waterfall Orch.* (Bronze).

WHITE, ANDREW NATHANIEL III, *alto, tenor saxes, composer*; also *oboe, English horn, electric bass*; b. Washington, D.C., 9/6/42. Uncle, Addison White, pl. saxes, flute, guitar. Stud. saxophone w. John C. Reed, Nashville, Tenn., '54-60; theory & musicianship w. Brenton Banks, '58-60. Pl. w. Tenn. A&I U. Symph. Band, '58-60. Att. Howard U., Wash., D.C., '60-4, pl. w. U. Band and Symphonetta, and grad w. a B. Mus. in Mus. theory. Received numerous grants for study and perf.

Early experience w. J.D. Chavis; Don Q. Pullen; Hank Johnson; Andrew Goodrich; Brenton Banks, '55-60, on alto, tenor and upright bass. Mus. dir. and saxophonist for the J.F.K. Quintet in Wash., '61-64; tenor w. Kenny Clarke in Paris, '64-5; alto w. New Jazz Trio in Buffalo, '65-6; tenor w. Charlie Hampton, house band at the Howard Theatre in Wash., '66-7; electric bass w. Stanley Turrentine; tenor w. the Cyclones; Otis Redding, '67; electric bass w. Stevie Wonder and principal oboist and English horn player for American Ballet Theatre Orch. of N.Y., concurrently '68-70. With Fifth Dimension as elec. bassist, '70-; elec. bass for *Hair*; bass and saxophones for Bobby Rydell, Thelma Houston, Otis Redding, Wilson Pickett and S. Turrentine.

Infl: C. Parker, M. Davis, Coltrane. In Sept. '73 completed a catalogue of 209 transcribed Coltrane solos, some of which he performed in concerts for NYJRC; CBA. Lectured at Howard and Rutgers Univs. Apart from his jazz works, his comps. incl. *Concerto* for 18 instrs.; and *Concertina* for seven instrs. These, the Coltrane trans. and a *Treatise on Improvisation* are available, along w. 13 albums of his own gps. (see below) from Andrew's Music (4830 So. Dakota Ave., N.E., Washington, D.C. 20017). Writer Peter Ochiogrosso described White's "prowess as a saxophonist" as "beyond question" and called his trans. of Coltrane's recorded solos "one of the great contributions to American music this century, doing for Trane what Kirschel did for Mozart some years ago."

LPs: *Andrew Nathaniel White III*; *Quartet Live at the New Thing*; *Live in Bucharest—Live in the Studio*; *Who Got De Funk?*; *Passion Flower*; *Songs for a French Lady*; *Theme*; *Live at the Foolery*, vols. 1-6 (Andrew's Music); w. McCoy Tyner, *Asante* (BN); w. Weather Report, *I Sing the Body Electric*; *Sweetnighter* (Col.); w. Marion Williams (Atl.); Stevie Wonder (Tamla); Fifth Dimension (Bell). The early J.F.K. quintet Riverside albums are deleted.

WHITE, CHRISTOPHER WESTLEY (CHRIS),* *bass, composer, educator*; b. New York City, 7/6/36. The former Dizzy Gillespie bassist of the first half of the '60s then pl. extensively w. the Billy Taylor trio and has also app. w. J. Moody; Teddy Wilson; Willie "The Lion" Smith; Eubie Blake; Earl Hines; and Thad Jones-Mel Lewis. From the late '60s, however, he has been increasingly active as a lecturer, educator and administrator. In the summer of '67 he was Community Liaison for the Jazzmobile; served as its Executive Director, summer '68; then as member of Board of Dir. Founder ('66) and Exec. Dir. of Rhythm Associates, the only music sch. in NY state staffed entirely by pro. jazz mus.; designer and consultant to MUSE Jazz Workshop, staffed by Rhythm Ass. White is Director of the Institute of Jazz Studies of Rutgers U., Newark Coll. of Arts & Sciences, designing a long range plan for reorganization of its activities; also Instructor in Music at Rutgers, Newark. Member of Mayor's Urban Action Task Force, NYC, '68; Special Assist. to Gov. NY State in Community Relations, '68-9; Ethnic Promo. Dir., National Dance Co. of Ghana, Madison Sq. Garden Center, '68; Exec. Prod. *Black Expo* at City Center, '69; Artistic Dir. *Black on Black,* March-May' 72, at Carnegie Recital Hall. Designer and dir. for mobile arts tours in NY State: *Summer on Wheels,* '68; *Celebrate Yourself,* '70. Consultant: NY State Council on the Arts; Urban Directions; Arts and Humanities NJ Bicentennial Commission. He has lectured on jazz at Wagner Coll.; U. of West Indies, Kingston, Jamaica; Antioch Coll. Publ: articles for *Feet,* NYC; *Jazz Education and the Community*; *Studies in Jazz*; *Discography I* (Institute of Jazz Studies, Newark, N.J.); *Check Yourself*; *American Music*; *From Storyville to Woodstock,* edited by Charles Nanry (Trans-Action Books, New Brunswick, N.J.); contributor to *Grove's Dictionary of Music and Musicians* (Macmillan, London, Eng.); Jazz Editor, *The Black Perspective in Music,* journal edited by Eileen Southern (Foundation for Research in the Afro-American Creative Arts, Inc., Poughkeepsie, N.Y.).

Gave concert (two nights) of original music at Carnegie Recital Hall, '73. Wrote feature film score, *Aggro Siezeman,* released in West Indies, April '75. Comp: suites, *Dana's Basement*; *Fantasy*. Fest: Loosdrecht, '72; NJF-NY, '73-5. LPs: w. Jimmy Owens, *You Had Better Listen* (Poly.); Andrew Hill, *Invitation* (Steeple.); Kenny Barron, *Spirits* (Muse).

WHITE, JOSHUA (JOSH),* *singer, guitar*; b. Greenville, S.C. 2/11/08. The popular folk and blues singer, best known during the 1940s when he app. at such clubs as Cafe Society and the Blue Angel in NYC, became inactive after suffering injuries in a serious automobile accident in 1966. He died 9/5/69 in Manhasset, N.Y., while undergoing heart surgery. One of the first artists to be strongly identified with political and social protest material, White also played a major role in reestablishing such songs as *John Henry* and *The Lass with the Delicate Air*.

LPs: *Chain Gang Songs; Empty Bed Blues; House I Live In; Spirituals & Blues* (Elektra); *In Memoriam* (Tradition); *Josh White* (Archive of Folk & Jazz); *Sings the Blues* (Stinson).

WHITE, LEONARD III (LENNY), *drums*; b. Jamaica, N.Y., 12/19/49. No musical educ. Stud. art at N.Y. Inst. of Tech. Started playing w. Jazz Samaritans, '67; then w. J. McLean for a year, '68. In '69 rec. *Bitches Brew* w. Miles Davis. With J. Henderson, '70; F. Hubbard, S. Getz, L. Gasca, '72; Azteca, '73. Became orig. member of Chick Corea's Return to Forever, '73. App. on many European TV shows w. Corea; also Don Kirshner Rock Concert, U.S. TV. Fest: NJF-NY, '72-4. White, who is an accomplished photographer and painter, cites among his infls. Davis, J. Coltrane, Philly Joe Jones, Tony Williams and Elvin Jones. Comps: *The Shadow of Lo*; *Sofistifunk*; *La Piedra Del Sol*. Own LP: *Venusian Summer* (Nemp.); other LPs: w. Azteca (Col.); *Realization* w. Eddie Henderson (Capricorn); *Red Clay* w. Hubbard (CTI); *Where Have I Known You Before* w. Return To Forever (Polydor).

WHITE, MICHAEL WALTER,* *violin, electric violin*; b. Houston, Tex., 5/24/33. Came to public attention w. John Handy quintet at MJF, '65. From late '60s was member of Fourth Way, in addition to rec. and app. w. his own group from '71. White's music combines contemporary jazz patterns with Eastern and classical influences. Dennis Hunt described his performance as "floating, cerebral, exploratory music that cannot be experienced passively." He is clearly influenced by a total spectrum of artists, incl. many non-violinists; among them are J. Coltrane, E. Dolphy, Sun Ra, D. Ellington, Ch. Mingus, T. Monk. At various times White perf. w. Sun Ra, Prince Lasha, Coltrane, Dolphy, Wes Montgomery, Kenny Dorham, Richard Davis. Comps: *Ebony Plaza*; *Blessing Song*; *Father Music/Mother Dance*.

LPs: *Spirit Dance*; *Pneuma*; *Land of Spirit and Light*; *Father Music/Mother Dance*; *Go With The Flow* (Imp.); w. Fourth Way, *The Sun and Moon Have Come Together*; *Werewolf*; *The Fourth Way* (Cap.); w. Handy, *Live at Monterey* (Col.); w. Pharoah Sanders, *Thembi* (Imp.); w. Jerry Hahn (Arhoolie); Sonny Simmons, *Burning Spirits* (Contemp.); McCoy Tyner, *Song For My Lady* (Milest.).

WHITE, QUINTEN (ROCKY), *drums*; b. San Marcos, Texas, 11/3/52. Entered Tex. Southern U. on a scholarship in '71. Remained there for two and a half years; during that time the Univ. jazz ensemble won many awards and was invited to the National Coll. Jazz Festival at JFK Center in Washington, D.C., where White was feat. w. Roy Burns and L. Bellson in a drum specialty. Not long afterward he joined the Duke Ellington orch., remaining with the band intermittently after Duke's death. Under the leadership of Mercer Ellington, he was one of several soloists to instill a new, youthful spirit to the orch. Fests: Longhorn; Notre Dame; National Coll. Jazz Fest in Chicago and Urbana etc.

LPs: *Third Sacred Concert,* w. Ellington (RCA); *Continuum* w. M. Ellington (Fant.).

WHITE, ELLERTON OSWALD (SONNY),* *piano*; b. Panama City, Canal Zone, 11/11/17. Heard from late '30s w. Teddy Hill, Benny Carter, other name bands; acc. for Billie Holiday, '39. White later worked w. small gps. in NYC, incl. Hot Lips Page, W. De Paris and three years w. Louis Metcalf. He joined Jonah Jones Apr. '69 and remained w. him for the next two years. White died in NYC, 4/29/71. Reissue, w. Billie Holiday (Atlantic).

WHITEMAN, PAUL,* *leader*; b. Denver, Colo., 3/28/1890. The man who was publicized in the 1920s and '30s as "King of Jazz," and who in 1930 was the star of a film by that name, was in semi-retirement in the '50s and '60s but made occasional comebacks. He died of a heart attack 12/29/67 in Doylestown, Pa. Though many great jazzmen, notably Joe Venuti, Eddie Lang, Bix Beiderbecke, Jack Teagarden, Frank Trumbauer, Red Norvo, the Dorsey Brothers and arranger Don Redman worked for him in the early years, their roles as jazzmen were often subjugated to elaborate interpretations of popular dance music. Despite the misleading nature of the title that haunted him throughout his career, Whiteman was an important contributor to 20th century popular music.

WIGGINS, GERALD FOSTER,* *piano*; b. New York City, 5/12/22. Prominent in LA from 1948, first w. Benny Carter; later toured as acc. for Lena Horne, Kay Starr, many other singers. Own trio at Memory Lane, LA, late '60s, along with free-lance film studio and recording work. To Las Vegas w. Supremes; gigs w. Teddy Edwards, Leroy Vinnegar. Acc. Eartha Kitt, Helen Humes, '75, pl. w. Humes at Cookery, NYC and various West coast festivals and clubs. Son, J.J. Wiggins, bassist w. Ellington band (see below).

WIGGINS, GERALD FOSTER (J.J.), *bass*; also *trombone, bass horn*; b. Los Angeles, Calif., 4/15/56. Stud. at Henry Grant Studio, also Jr. High Sch., 1968-71 and High Sch., '71-4. While w. Craig Hundley trio, '68, made many concert and TV appearances and won trophy as outstanding instrumentalist at Hollywood Bowl teenage Battle of the Bands, though he was not yet a teenager. Pl. w. own trio, also in trio led by his father, pianist Gerald Wiggins. Joined the Duke Ellington Orch., dir. by Mercer Ellington, Oct. 1974; impressed audiences and particularly musicians with his astonishingly mature technique, intonation and ideas. Infl: Wilfred Middlebrooks, Red Mitchell, Red Callender, Joe Comfort, Curtis Counce, Ray Brown, Chuck Domanico.

LPs: w. Ellington (Fantasy); Craig Hundley (World Pac.).

WILBER, ROBERT SAGE (BOB),* *clarinet, soprano sax, composer*; also *alto, tenor saxes, bass clarinet*; b. New York City, 3/15/28. Associated with traditional jazz in his teens, he was heard in the groups of E. Condon, B. Hackett and M. Kaminsky in the '50s and early '60s. Worked w. Bob Crosby; Yank Lawson at Condon's; Ralph Sutton in Aspen; also arr. and pl. Ellington's music for Duke Ellington Society concerts, '66-7. In '68 joined the World's Greatest Jazzband, touring w. it throughout the US and in Brazil, Hawaii, Mexico, Canada and Europe (twice). Left in Jan. '75 to form Soprano Summit w. K. Davern, pl. Nice Fest. and touring So. Africa, summer '75. A mus. dir. of the NYJRC for '74-5 season, he wrote, arr., cond. and pl. w. it at Carnegie Hall and toured Russia, '75.

Wilber, who plays the curved soprano, originally was inspired by Sidney Bechet but elements of Johnny Hodges, Lester Young and Charlie Parker surface in a homogeneous, but by no means bland, mainstream style delivered with elegant swing and warmth. TV: Ed Sullivan; *Tonight*; Dick Cavett; Mike Douglas; Steve Allen; *Today*; NET, '68-74 w. WGJB; *Sunday,* NBC; *Roundtable* w. Soprano Summit, '75. Fest: NJF; Concord; Nice; Odessa, Tex.; Colo. Jazz Party. Comps: *A Long Way From Home*; *Crawfish Shuffle*; *Dreaming Butterfly*; *Please Clarify*; *Johnny Was There*. Publ: *50 Jazz Phrases for Saxophone* (Bregman, Vocco & Conn). LPs: *Soprano Summit* (World Jazz); *Music of Hoagy Carmichael* (Mon.-Ever.); numerous sessions for MMO; *Century Plaza* w. WGJ (World Jazz); others w. WGJ (World Jazz; Atl.;

Project 3); w. Rusty Dedrick, *Music of Irving Berlin*; *Music of Harold Arlen*; w. Maxine Sullivan, *Close As Pages in a Book* (Mon.-Ever.).

WILCOX, EDWIN FELIX (EDDIE),* *arranger, piano*; b. Method, N.C., 12/27/07. Regular member of J. Lunceford band from '29 until the leader's death in '47, after which he co-led the band with tenor saxophonist Joe Thomas. The two later split up and Wilcox formed his own orch. which he led until '49. He was subsequently active as arranger and a & r man, writing for many pop hit records. He died in NYC, 9/29/68.

LPs: see Lunceford, Jimmie.

WILDER, JOSEPH BENJAMIN (JOE),* *trumpet, fluegelhorn*; b. Colwyn, Pa., 2/22/22. Left ABC staff after 16 yrs., '73. Pl. in band for Dick Cavett, Jack Paar shows. First trumpet w. Symph. of the New World, '65-71. Pl. four concerts as member of NY Phil., '75. Worked w. T. Bennett-L. Horne; Michel Legrand, '74; Steve Allen-Terry Gibbs, '75. Busy in the rec. studios for Roberta Flack dates, etc., jingles, Wilder is a fine all-around brassman whose jazz abilities have only really been allowed to shine in recent years at the Colorado Jazz Party, '72-5. Film: trumpet solos for the soundtrack of *The Wild Party* w. James Coco, Raquel Welch. TV: Bill Cosby; Sammy Davis; Howard Cosell. An expert photographer. LPs: w. Jane Harvey (Classic Jazz); C. Mingus, *Let My Children Hear Music* (Col.).

WILEY, LEE,* *singer, composer*; b. Port Gibson, Okla., 10/9/15. One of the most successful singers in the pop field in the '30s, she became associated w. Eddie Condon and the players in his circle from '39. During her marriage to Jess Stacy in '40s she toured w. his big band; then as a single in late '40s. She made occasional apps. on TV, in concert and on record in the '50s but was in virtual retirement in the '60s and '70s; her last public performance was at the NJF-NY '72 w. Condon. A TV film, based on her life and featuring Piper Laurie was shown in '63. "Although she sings with devastating sex appeal," George Frazier wrote, "she does so in an exalted way."

She died of cancer in NYC, 12/11/75. LPs: *Back Home Again* (Mon.-Ever.); earlier recs. on Storyville; Col.; RCA.

WILKINS, ERNEST BROOKS (ERNIE),* *composer, tenor, alto, soprano saxophones, flute, piano*; b. St. Louis, Mo., 7/20/22. Pl. w. C. Basie, D. Gillespie in '50s; also arr. for Basie, T. Dorsey, Harry James. From Nov. '66 to Jan. '69 was with Phoenix House, drug addict rehabilitation program, in NYC. Joined Clark Terry's big band, playing, arr. and as mus. dir. Went with Terry to Montreux JF and org. big band of European and African musicians. Resumed free-lance work in New York, writing new arrs. for Basie. Worked as a & r man for Mainstream Records '71-early '73; during that time, gigged w. own combos. In summer of '73, toured Europe w. Terry. Since '73 has spent much time in Europe as comp.-arr.-cond. and player. Wrote arrs. for, and recorded with, Art Farmer in Vienna. Pl. w. Dexter Gordon, Rolf Ericson, Leo Wright, Kenny Drew, Niels Orsted Pederson.

TV: two shows in '74 in Yugoslavia, one w. Terry, one w. Yugo. mus. Fests: NJF-NY in Basie reunion band '73; with Terry Quintet '74. Pl. most of important European fests. w. Terry.

LPs: Mainstream; w. Terry (Vang., Etoile); arrs. for Ch. McPherson (Main.); many earlier LPs as arr. and cond. w. Sarah Vaughan, Ernestine Anderson et al. Arrs. for Quincy Jones (Merc.), Joe Newman (Roul.), Jimmy Cleveland (Merc.).

WILKINS, JACK, *guitar*; also *vibes, piano*; b. Brooklyn, N.Y., 6/3/44. Started guitar at age 14; stud. from age 18 w. John Mehegan, classical guitar w. Rodrigo Riera, others. Was part of all-guitar gp. w. Chuck Wayne in '64. Pl. w. Earl Hines at Town Hall, NYC; Buddy Rich at his club and throughout USA and Europe; concerts etc. w. S. Getz, D. Gillespie, Morgana King, Pearl Bailey, Sammy Davis; own trio at Jimmy's on 52nd Street. Pl. at Colo. Jazz Party, '74.

Favs: Johnny Smith, Julian Bream, D. Reinhardt, Joe Pass, Wes Montgomery. Fluent soloist in pure modern jazz style. LP: *Windows* (Mainstream); w. Buddy Rich, *Very Live at Buddy's Place*; w. Rich, L. Hampton, *Transition* (Groove Merchant).

WILLIAMS, CHARLES ANTHONY JR. (BUSTER), *bass*; *composer*; b. Camden, N.J., 4/17/42. Studied piano, drums and bass w. father. Began pl. bass at age 15. Harmony at Combs Coll. of Music, Phila., '59. Worked w. Gene Ammons-Sonny Stitt, '60; Dakota Staton, '61-2; Betty Carter, '62-3; Sarah Vaughan, '63; Nancy Wilson, '64-8; Jazz Crusaders, '65-8; Miles Davis, '67; Herbie Mann; Art Blakey, '69; Herbie Hancock, '69-73; McCoy Tyner, '74; Mary Lou Williams, '75; also has pl. w. Harold Land-Bobby Hutcherson; Lee Morgan; Sonny Rollins; Kenny Burrell; Jimmy Heath. Made an inner-circle reputation among musicians during his yrs. w. Nancy Wilson before moving to NYC. A big, deep sound with a resilient beat; acute intonation and inventive lines.

Infl: Oscar Pettiford, Paul Chambers, Ray Brown, Ron Carter, Bob Cranshaw. TV: Red Skelton; Danny Kaye; Andy Williams shows; *Positively Black*; *Soul*; *Express Yourself*. Broadway show: *Company*. Fest: MJF; NJF; Berkeley; Pori; Antibes. Teaches at Jazzmobile Workshop. Comp: *Firewater*; *Pinnacle*; *The Hump*; *The Emperor*; *Native Dancer*; *Tayamisha*; *Ruby P'Gonia*; *Shadows*. LPs: *Pinnacle* (Muse); w. Hancock, *Mwandishi* (WB); H. Land, *New Shade of Blue* (Main.); Joe Farrell, *Outback* (CTI); Dexter Gordon, *Tower of Power*; *More Power* (Prest.); Hilton Ruiz, *Piano Man* (Steeple.).

WILLIAMS, CLAUDE (FIDDLER), *violin*; also *guitar, bass*; b. Muskogee, Okla., 2/22/08. Pl. w. T. Holder in '20s, remaining when Andy Kirk took over the band. With Count Basie as guitarist, occasionally violin, '36. Pl. on first Decca session. Later worked w. Austin Powell quartet; Roy Milton in early '50s. From '73 touring w. Jay McShann. App. w. him at NJF-NY, '73. Dan Morgenstern called him, "A swing fiddler in the Stuff Smith tradition."

LPs: w. McShann, *The Man From Muskogee* (Sack.); *The Blues: A Real Summit Meeting* (Buddah).

WILLIAMS, CHARLES MELVIN (COOTIE),* *trumpet*; b. Mobile, Ala., 7/24/08. After he had his own big band in the '40s and small groups in the '50s, he rejoined Duke Ellington in '62 after a 22 year hiatus. Until he left the orchestra under the direction of Mercer Ellington in the fall of '75 he was a featured soloist who, in the '70s, played only occasionally in the section. During this period he took short leaves of absence from time to time due to illness. In his mid-60s he was still a vital, personal, classic jazz voice. LPs: see Ellington (Duke and Mercer).

WILLIAMS, DAVID (HAPPY), *bass*; b. Trinidad, West Indies, 9/17/46. Father, Buddy Williams, is well-known bassist in West Indies; brother is also bassist. Sister, a concert pianist studied at the Royal Academy in London. Studied violin in school and bass w. father. Sister encouraged him to come to London at age 15 to study and listen. In June '69 she again encouraged him to visit NYC. He sat in at Nuclear Experience w. Beaver Harris and was hired immediately. Studied w. Ron Carter whom he lists as primary infl. Other infl: Coltrane, Miles Davis. Pl. w. Chuck Mangione in Rochester, late '69-early '70; Roberta Flack, '70-2. Gigs w. Ornette Coleman; Donald Byrd; Charles McPherson; Cedar Walton; Billy Taylor; Donny Hathaway. With Elvin Jones from late '74, incl. eight trips to Europe, So. America. While w. Flack, pl. w. Quincy Jones band on concert w. Ray Brown, Chuck Rainey. Comp: *Many Moods*. LPs: w. Elvin Jones, (Vang.); w. Louis Hayes, *Breath of Life*; w. Kenny Barron, *Peruvian Blue* (Muse); w. Sam Jones, *Cello Again* (Xanadu); w. Archie Shepp; George Adams (Horo); w. R. Flack (Atl.).

WILLIAMS, FRANCIS (FRANC), *trumpet*; b. McConnels Mills, Pa., 9/20/10. Father, a coal-miner, pl. guitar and tuba. Grew up in Toledo, Ohio w. Art Tatum. Took up piano at an early age, switching to cornet at 12. After pl. in Cleveland and Chicago, went to NYC, '38, working w. Fats Waller; Edgar Hayes; Claude Hopkins; Horace Henderson; and Ella Fitzgerald. Pl. w. Sabby Lewis in Boston before joining Duke Ellington in '45. Left in '51 and pl. w. many Latin bands: Alberto Socarras; Machito; Tito Puente; Perez Prado. Pl. for many Broadway shows; Emil Coleman at the Plaza's Persian Room; annual Christmas gig w. Sammy Davis Jr. at Copacabana. Toured US w. Harry Belafonte, '56; Europe '58. Charter member of NYJRC, '74, pl. on European tour w. *Musical Life of Charlie Parker,* fall '74; Bix Beiderbecke tribute at NJF-NY, '75. Own quartet, Swing Four w. Eddie Durham, twice weekly at West End Cafe, '75-6. LPs: w. Ellington, solos on *Three Cent Stomp* in *World of Duke Ellington* (Col.); *Trumpet No End* in *The Golden Duke* (Prest.).

WILLIAMS, JOE,* *singer*; b. Cordele, Ga., 12/12/18. Best known as blues singer with C. Basie, Dec. '54 to Jan. '61, Williams subsequently developed a successful career as a vocalist in night clubs, concerts and jazz festivals, showing himself equally adept at popular songs, but never renouncing his identification with the blues. Concerts and music festivals in USA, Europe, England. Starred w. Duke and Mercer Ellington orchs.; frequent reunions w. Basie; concerts w. B. Rich, L. Bellson etc., Cincinnati Symph. Night clubs, incl. Ronnie Scott's, London; Buddy's Place, NYC; Playboy Clubs in several U.S. cities; MGM Grand Hotel in LV. *Showboat 2* jazz fest. cruise, on SS Rotterdam, Dec. '74.

Williams made one motion picture appearance as an actor in *Moonshine War,* '69. TV: Mike Douglas, Johnny Carson, Merv Griffin shows; Harry Belafonte's *Strolling Twenties,* '66; *Love You Madly,* D. Ellington spec., '73. A regular at the NJF for many years, he was also seen at Montreux, '72; Monterey etc. Living in LV, Williams has worked there occasionally, but is constantly in demand for engagements around the U.S. and overseas.

LPs: *Presenting Joe Williams with Thad Jones/Mel Lewis Orch.*; *Old New & Blue*; *Worth Waiting For* (BN); *The Heart & Soul of Joe Williams & Geo. Shearing* (Sheba); *Joe Williams With Love* (Temponic); *Live with Cannonball Adderley Quintet*; *Big Man* (Fant.); *A Man Ain't Supposed to Cry* (Roul.).

WILLIAMS, JOHN B. JR, *bass*; b. New York City, 2/27/41. Stud. and pl. drums for eight years. Grew up in a neighborhood among such musicians as S. Rollins, the Heath brothers, Milt Jackson, J. McLean etc. Self-taught on bass while in the Marine Corps. After the service, stud. for two years w. Ron Carter, doubling on elect. bass and cello. Following tours w. H. Silver, '67-9, Williams was heard w. K. Burrell, Leon Thomas, K. Winding, '69, D. Gillespie, Hugh Masekela, '70; also gigged w. C. Terry, Z. Sims, Billy Cobham, C. McRae. In '72 Williams was a regular member of the Doc Severinsen orch. on the *Tonight* TV show. He names Miles Davis, Carter, Paul Chambers, Bob Cranshaw and Severinsen as inspirations and influences. Pl. NJF-USA, '67; Europe, '68.

LPs: w. H. Silver, *You Gotta Take A Little Love*; B. Hutcherson-H. Land, *San Francisco* (Blue Note); Billy Cobham, *Crosswinds* (Atl.).

WILLIAMS, LEROY, *drums*; also *piano*; b. Chicago, Ill., 2/3/37. Started on drums at 15. Self-taught except for two mos. w. Oliver Coleman at age 20. Pl. w. Wilbur Ware; Scotty Holt; Jack De Johnette (w. the latter on piano); John Gilmore; Gene Ammons; Sonny Stitt; Bennie Green. Worked w. Judy Roberts trio, '59-64. To NYC '67 where he has been associated w. Barry Harris from that time; w. Ch. McPherson from '69. Also pl. w. Booker Ervin, '67; Sonny Rollins, '68; Clifford Jordan, '68-9; Wilbur Ware, '69-70; Hank Mobley, '70; T. Monk; Y. Lateef, '71; Ray Bryant, '71-2; James Moody; Stan Getz, '73; Andrew Hill, '74-5. Harris says of Williams: "He can really syncopate. He really feels that off-beat thing."

Infl: Roach, K. Clarke, E. Jones, Philly Joe Jones "and all of 'em." TV: w. Bryant, Trenton, N.J.; w. McPherson; Jordan, *Like It Is*. Fest: NJF w. A. Shepp, '68. LPs: w. Harris, *Magnificent* (Prest.); *Plays Tadd Dameron* (Xanadu); *Vicissitudes* (MPS); w. McPherson (Main.); w. Mobley (BN).

WILLIAMS, MARION,* *singer*; b. Miami, Fla., 8/29/27. Lead singer with Clara Ward '47-58, before forming Stars of Faith. Featured in Langston Hughes' *Black Nativity* in US and Europe, '61-5, then toured Europe as soloist. Sang solo at Yale '67 and by '71 had pl. six solo concerts at Harvard. Many coll. apps. in '70s. TV: *Soul*; Dick Cavett; two CBS specials taped at her church in Philadelphia. Received International Television Prize from Princess Grace of Monaco while touring Europe w. Langston Hughes' *The Prodigal Son.* Honored at Yale as Ellington Fellow. Fest: Dakar Fest. of Negro Arts; Antibes; Bergamo; Montreux; NJF-NY. Made public service tv commercial singing *Standing Here Wondering Which Way to Go*. Hollie West says that "more than any other living singer, Williams possesses the melodic inventiveness of the great jazzmen.''

Comp: *A Pity and a Shame.*

LPs: *Prayer Changes Things*; *Blessed Assurance*; *Standing Here Wondering Which Way to Go*; *Gospel Now*; *The New Message* (Atl.).

WILLIAMS, MARY LOU (Mary Elfrieda Winn),* *piano, composer*; b. Pittsburgh, Pa., 5/8/10. The reemergence of the former standout of the Andy Kirk orch. of the '30s, begun in the first half of the '60s, abated in the second half. However, encouraged by a young priest, Fr. Peter O'Brien, she emerged once again. Her 18 weeks at the Cookery in Greenwich Village, '70-1, not only inaugurated a jazz policy for that restaurant but firmly established it. She played another long engagement there at the end of '75. During the '70s other club apps. incl. the London House, Blues Alley, Bourbon Street, Cafe Carlyle. In '68 she toured Europe, playing at Timme Rosenkrantz's club in Copenhagen and concerts in Italy; trio concert in London, '69.

The main thrust of Ms. Williams' composing was centered on extended works for the Catholic Church which she had embraced in the '50s. Her first Mass, entitled simply *Mass,* was written while she was teaching at Seton HS in Pittsburgh, and was performed at actual liturgy celebrated by the Bishop of Pitts., John Cardinal Wright in St. Paul's Cathedral, Pitts., '66. In '67 she gave concert at Carnegie Hall, *Praise the Lord in Many Voices* incl. a detailed history of jazz on solo piano, and three sacred pieces: *Thank You Jesus*; *The Lord's Prayer*; *Praise the Lord.* Second Mass, *Mass for the Lenten Season,* premiered '68 and pl. for seven consecutive Sundays at Church of St. Thomas the Apostle, NYC. After she performed the Mass in Rome, she received the liturgical texts of the *Votive Mass for Peace* from the Vatican which commissioned her to write third Mass which she did in '69. Originally titled *Music for Peace* it was subsequently named *Mary Lou's Mass.* The work was premiered in concert form at Columbia U., '70. In '71 she rewrote it for the Alvin Ailey City Center Dance Theatre, adding several new sections. She has been represented in the Ailey NYC seasons in '72-3 and by the Ailey Company on tour in the US and Europe, '73. *Mary Lou's Mass* was also performed at St. Paul's in Pitts., '73; w. chorus of NYC school children at St. Patrick's, '75, rec. by NET.

In addition to playing many coll. concerts Ms. Williams was in residence in Toronto, NYC, Wash., D.C., and Rochester during '73, involving trio concerts, classes in history of jazz, training of local choirs for perfs. of *Mary Lou's Mass.* Other concerts for Overseas Jazz Club '70; Smithsonian Institution; Whitney Museum, '75. At the inauguration ceremony of the Charlie Parker Foundation in KC, she had a street, Mary Lou Williams Lane, named for her. Received Guggenheim Fellowship, '72-3; grant from NY State Council on the Arts. Honorary degrees from Fordham U.; Manhattan Coll.; Loyola U., NO. Appointed full professor at the U. of Massachusetts, Amherst, Mass. from fall '75.

TV: *Today*; *Tonight*; *Dick Cavett*; *AM America*; *Sesame Street*; *Mr. Rogers' Neighborhood*; *Lamp Unto My Feet*; *Black Pride*; *Dreams and Visions* w. Ailey. Fest: NJF-NY, '71-3; MJF, '71-2. Publ: *Mary Lou's Mass*; *St. Martin De Porres* for Chorus (Cecilia Music Publ., P.O. Box 32, Hamilton Grange, N.Y., N.Y. 10031). Comp: *Lamb of God*; *Zoning Fungus II*; *Medi I and Medi II*; *Play It Momma*; *Joycie*; *Dirge Blues*; *Miss D.D. Gloria*; *The Scarlet Creeper*; *Blues for John*; *Ode for St. Cecilia.*

''She is never less than contemporary,'' wrote John S. Wilson, ''and always well out in the vanguard of valid new ideas.''

Clive Barnes called *Mary Lou's Mass* ''strong and joyful music, with a spirit that cuts across all religious boundaries to provide a celebration of man, God and peace. The gently religious fervor of the music, with its overtones of both jazz and gospel, and its spiritual exaltation make the score perfect—a celebration of life—an assertively happy work—it treats of the special ecstasy of grace—but there is also humor here.''

LPs: *Mary Lou's Mass*; *Zoning* (Mary—addr. same as Cecilia Music); *Praise the Lord in Many Voices* (Avant Garde); *From the Heart* (Chiaro.); *Giants* w. D. Gillespie, B. Hackett (Perception); *Zodiac Suite* (Folk.); trio (Steeple.); *Black Christo of the Andes* (MPS); *Newport in New York, The Jam Sessions, Vols. 1 & 2* (Cobble.); w. Buddy Tate and His Buddies (Chiaro.); reissues w. Andy Kirk (Main.); *Cafe Society* (Onyx); w. Don Byas (GNP, Crescendo, Vogue).

WILLIAMS, PATRICK MOODY (PAT), *composer*; also *trumpet, vibes*; b. Bonne Terre, Mo., 4/23/39. Stud. Duke U., '61; grad. work in comp., Columbia U., '61-3. Twelve tone comp. studies in LA, '69-75. Comp., arr., mus. dir. in NYC studios, '61-7 and in LA, '68- . Though principally known as a successful composer of scores for many feature films, Williams has conducted or judged at jazz fests., has written a *Rhapsody for Concert Band and Jazz Ensemble,* and states: ''I am very interested in composing music that intertwines jazz and classical techniques. I feel uncomfortable straying too far from my jazz background.'' Infls: Ellington, Tatum, Basie; Stravinsky, Richard Strauss, Ravel. Film Credits: *Mrs. Sundance*; *Ordeal*; *The Magician*; *Streets of San Francisco*; *Terror in the Sky*; *Evel Knievel*; *San Francisco International*; *Don't Drink The Water*; *A Nice Girl Like Me*; *How Sweet It Is.* TV Series: *Mary Tyler Moore Show*; *Bob Newhart Show*; *Streets of San Francisco.*

LPs: as composer and/or perf., *Shades of Today*; *Think*; *Heavy Vibrations* (MGM-Verve); *Threshold* (Cap.); *Carry On* (A & R).

WILLIAMS, RICHARD GENE,* *trumpet, composer*; also *piano, saxophone*; b. Galveston, Texas, 5/4/31. Played w. Charles Mingus; Slide Hampton in early '60s. Joined Thad Jones-Mel Lewis in '66, remaining w. them into '69, touring Europe and Japan. Soloist for Orchestra U.S.A. New York premiere of Gunther Schuller's *Journey Into Jazz.* Soloist for Broadway show *The Me Nobody Knows,* '70-1. European gigs with local musicians, '71 and, as guest of the Belgian government, '72. Pl. w. Gil Evans in Calif., '73. European tours w. Clark Terry band, '73; w. *Musical Life of Charlie Parker,* '74; w. Lionel Hampton, '75. Broadway musicals: *Raisin,* '74; *The Wiz,* '75. NYJRC concert, *The Music of Monk,* '75. Also free-lancing w. own quartet.

Dr. Frederick Tillis of the U. of Mass. wrote trumpet concerto for him, as yet unperformed. TV: show devoted to poetry of Robert Kaufman w. Ossie Davis and Ruby Dee, music by Lucky Thompson. Fest: w. Jones-Lewis, NJF, '67; Orange County, Calif. '68; w. G. Evans, NJF-NY '72; w. C. Mingus, NJF-NY; Bilzen, Belgium, '73; w. C. Terry, Pori, San Sebastian, Verona, '73; w. *Life of Parker,* Portugal, Rumania, Yugoslavia, '74. Comp: *Rogi*; *Two Bags*; *Renita's Bounce*; *Raucous Notes*; *Blues in a Quandary.* LPs: w. Jones-Lewis, *Presenting*; *Monday Night*; *Central Park North*; *Presenting Joe Williams* (SS); w. Ch. McPherson, *Today's Man* (Main.); w. R.R. Kirk, *Left & Right*; w. G. Evans, *Svengali* (Atl.); w. O. Nelson, *The Mayor and the People* (Fly. Dutch.); w. Booker Ervin, *The In-Between* (BN); w. Bill Evans-George Russell, *Living Time* w. Music, Inc. (Strata-East); w. C. Terry (Vang.).

WILLIAMS, ANTHONY (TONY),* *drums, composer*; b. Chicago, Ill., 12/12/45. Grew up in Boston where he pl. w. Sam Rivers. To NYC '62, pl. w. Jackie McLean. From '63-9 was an integral part of the Miles Davis quintet, establishing himself as one of the young innovators helping to change the face of jazz. After leaving Davis he formed his own gp., Lifetime, w. John McLaughlin and Larry Young, mixing chord-based and free jazz with rock. in an exciting, if albeit, high-decibel amalgam. When McLaughlin formed his Mahavishnu Orch. in '71 he was replaced by Ted Dunbar who app. w. the gp. at the NJF-NY, '72. *The Old Bum's Rush,* an album released in '73, had a different cast incl. the drummer's father, Tillmon Williams, on tenor sax.

In '75 Lifetime was reformed with a new personnel incl. Allan Holdsworth, guitar; and Alan Pasqua, electric keyboards. Robert Palmer, reviewing the album *Believe It* in the New York *Times,* remarked that Williams "is playing much less in terms of color and shading, for at one time he was one of the most poetic drummers in contemporary jazz. But he is playing music which fuses rock energy and improvisational interest without frills and without gratuitous grandstanding."

Comp: *Wildlife*; *Sangria For Three*; *Emergency*; *Beyond Games*; *There Comes a Time.*

LPs: *Believe It* (Col.); *Emergency*; *Turn It Over*; *Ego*; *Old Bum's Rush* (Poly.); w. Davis, *Miles Smiles*; *Sorcerer*; *Nefertiti*; *Miles in the Sky*; *Filles De Kilimanjaro*; *In A Silent Way*; w. *Newport in New York, The Jam Sessions, Vols. 3&4* (Cobble.); w. Gil Evans, *There Comes a Time* (RCA).

WILLIS, LAWRENCE ELLIOTT (LARRY), *piano, composer*; b. New York City, 12/20/40. Voice major at High School of Music & Art; grad. Manhattan School of Music; stud. privately w. John Mehegan. Insp. by B. Evans, W. Kelly, Miles Davis, H. Hancock, Mehegan. Pl. w. J. McLean, '63, H. Masekela, '64, K. Winding, '65-7, S. Getz, '69, C. Adderley, '71, Earl May, '71-2. Accomp. singers incl. Esther Marrow, Gloria Lynne. In '72 Willis joined Blood, Sweat & Tears, appearing with them on TV rock specs., at fests. and concerts. etc. Also free-lancing in NYC clubs as soloist, '75.

Comps: *Inner Crisis*; *Poor Eric*; *Megalomania*; *Journey's End.* Also arr. *So Long Dixie*; *Mary Miles*; *Mirror Image*; *Inner Crisis* for B.S.&T. Own LP: *Inner Crisis* (Groove Merchant); LPs w. McLean, *Jacknife* (Blue Note); Masekela (Blue Thumb); J. Henderson (Milestone); A. Mouzon (Blue Note); also *New Blood*; *No Sweat* w. B.S.&T. (Columbia).

WILSON, EDWARD JOHN (ED), *trombone, composer*; b. Sydney, Australia, 6/22/44. Worked as staff musician w. Australian Broadcasting Commission, '65-72. During this period he and Warren Daly (q.v.) organized the Daly-Wilson big band, which enjoyed unprecedented local acceptance. After disbanding late in '69, Wilson toured Australia and New Zealand in '70 with the Glenn Miller orch. under B. De Franco. The Daly-Wilson band was reorganized in '71 and won a gold record for its album *Big Band On Tour.*

Wilson has been responsible for writing most of the band's library, usually in collaboration with Daly. Comps: *Kings Step Out*; *El Boro*; *My Goodness*; *On My Own*; *Limp Dropper.*

LPs: *Live at the Cell Block* (EMI); *Featuring Kerrie Biddell* (Festival); *On Tour*; *Featuring Marcia Hines* (WB). All albums released in the U.S. on G.R.C. Elephant label.

WILSON, GERALD STANLEY,* *composer, leader, trumpet*; b. Shelby, Miss., 9/4/18. Continued to record and appear with big band; made five albums between '66-70. Arranged two of his own compositions, *Blues for Yna Yna* and *Collage,* for S. Kenton's Neophonic Orch. In '69 Wilson began arr. for E. Fitzgerald, rec. an album with her in '70. Also in '69 he joined KBCA in LA, where his own radio interview show became a popular daily feature. In the same year he joined the faculty of Cal. State U. at Northridge as lecturer on jazz history, where he acquired an unusually large class and established himself as an outstanding educator.

In '72, Wilson comp. and arr. his first work for symph. orch. Its title, *5/21/72,* denotes the date it was perf. by the LA Philharmonic Orch. conducted by Zubin Mehta, at the Music Center. He has since arr. and orchestrated four more works for the LA Phil. and its 250 voice choir, perf. in '75.

In '71 Wilson's comp. *Viva Tirado,* rec. by El Chicano, became a hit, receiving a BMI award as one of the most popular songs of the year. Other comps. incl.: *Josefina*; *Jeri*; *Teri*; *Nancy Jo*; *Carlos*; *The Golden Sword*; *Lighthouse Blues*; *Aram*; *Eric*; *Sonato for Guitar*; *The Royal Suite*; *Teotihuacan*; *El Viti.* Fests: Berkeley, '67; Tulsa, '68; Kongsberg, '73; Concord, Santa Barbara, '75.

LPs: *Golden Sword*; *Everywhere*; *Feeling Kinda Blues*; *California Soul*; *Eternal Equinox*; *Live & Swinging*; *You Better Believe It* (Pac. Jazz); *Things Ain't What They Used To Be* w. Fitzgerald (Repr.).

WILSON, JACK JR.,* *piano, composer*; also *keyboards, vibes, drums, baritone saxophone*; b. Chicago, Ill., 8/3/36. Extensive freelance work in LA, '62- ; also arr. for his own reh. band. TV: *The Jazz Show,* KNBC, LA; *Repertoire Workshop,* CBS; *Peyton Place,* ABC; *Bob Hope Presents,* ABC. Film: *Bus Riley's Back In Town.* Many apps. at Memory Lane leading trio and acc. O.C. Smith, Esther Phillips, Sam Fletcher and other singers. Publs: Big band arr.; also series of instruction books (Maggio Music, 12044 Vanowen, N. Hollywood, Ca. 91605).

LPs: *Something Personal*; *Easterly Winds*; *Song For My Daughter* (BN); *The Jack Wilson Quartet*; *The Two Sides of Jack Wilson*; *The Jazz Organs* (Atl.); *Brazilian Mancini*; *Ramblin'* (Vault); w. Esther Phillips, *Live* (Atl.); *From a Whisper to A Scream* (CTI); w. Gerald Wilson, *Live and*

Swinging; *Everywhere*; *Greatest Hits* (Wor. Pac.); w. Charlie Barnet (Vault); w. Blue Mitchell, *Vital Blue* (Main.).

WILSON, JOSEPH LEE (JOE LEE), *singer*; also *piano, guitar, percussion*; b. Bristow, Okla., 12/22/35. Private piano lessons from ages seven to nine. Voice lessons in LA; voice major at LA Conserv., '55; music major at LACC, '56-7. Began singing prof. '58. Toured on West Coast; Canada; Mexico. In NYC has worked S. Rollins; F. Hubbard; L. Morgan; R. Haynes; M. Jackson; M. Davis; A. Shepp; Rashied Ali; J. McLean; Roy Brooks; P. Sanders; F. Foster; CBA; own band. Infl: Roscoe Weathers, Louis Jordan, E. Jefferson, K. Pleasure, Joe Williams, Sammy Davis, Tony Bennett, Sinatra, E. Fitzgerald, S. Vaughan, C. McRae, Betty Carter. TV: *Like It Is*; *Call Back*; *NBC Showcase 1968*; *Dick Cavett*; *Soul*; *Free Time*; *Jazz Set*. Fest: U. of Mass. Pan-American Fest., '73; NY Mus., '72; NJF-NY, '73; Live Loft JF, '75; Third World Culture Fest., Yale U. '75. App. in musical, *Lady Day,* at Brooklyn Acad. of Mus. Comp: *Come and See (Sparrow Singing Jazz)*; *One (Dedicated to My Father)*. Won DB Critics poll, TDWR, '73. Harvey Siders called him, "a jazz singer in the true sense of the word," who "phrases and attacks in the manner of a J.J. Johnson trombone solo, at the same time pausing thoughtfully throughout his vocal improvisations conjuring up the syncopated silences of Ahmad Jamal."

LPs: *What Would It Be Without You* (Survival); *Mr. Joe Lee Wilson in the Great City* (Power Tree); *Livin' High Off Nickels and Dimes* (Oblivion); w. Shepp, *Attica Blues*; *Things Have Got to Change*; *The Cry of My People* (Imp.); Charles Earland, *Charles III* (Prest.); Billy Gault (Steeple.); Mtume (Strata-East).

WILSON, NANCY,* *singer*; b. Chillicothe, O., 2/20/37. A major star throughout the 1960's after her discovery by Cannonball Adderley, Wilson continued to travel throughout the US and overseas.

In '73 she played a concert at the London Palladium, appeared in a 90-minute German TV special, and toured the continent. Later she appeared at the Royal Swazi Hotel in Swaziland. She married Rev. Wiley Burton in April, 1974.

In addition to singing in a jazz-influenced style, she occasionally appeared on television in acting roles on such shows as *Police Story* and *The FBI*. She served as hostess on her own TV series on KNBC in LA from Mar. 1974-Mar. 1975. Her guests were personalities from all professions, including such jazz performers as Airto, Milt Jackson and Ahmad Jamal. The program won an Emmy award.

Very concerned with civil rights, Wilson was associated with the Black Caucus, appeared at seminars and political meetings, after performing for such groups.

LPs: Many commercial albums, though on some she was teamed with such arrangers as Oliver Nelson, Gerald Wilson and Jimmy Jones. While in Japan in '75 she recorded a live album for Toshiba. All of the US LPs on Capitol.

WILSON, PHILLIP SANFORD, *drums, percussion, composer*; also *vibes, piano*; b. St. Louis, Mo., 9/8/41. Grandfather, Ira Kimball, pl. drums on riverboats. Violin lessons in grade school at age nine. Drum corps at 10 through 17, teaching in corps at 14. Met Lester Bowie while in high school. Began pl. prof. at 16. Worked w. organist Don James. At 19 went to NYC w. organist Sam Lazar, working at Minton's w. him for a yr. Returned to St. Louis and pl. blues and rock bands. With Jackie Wilson; Solomon Burke; Motown revue, '62-3. Went to California w. Bowie, Oliver Lake in Burke's group. Pl. w. Julius Hemphill, David Sanborn in St. Louis '64. To Chicago, '65, where he became involved w. AACM. Joined Paul Butterfield '68 and was w. him into '70. Pl. w. Mother Lode in Toronto, '71-2. In SF '72 spent much time practicing; also gigging w. Hemphill. In NYC app. w. Anthony Braxton at Town Hall, May '72. Worked w. Full Moon '73; also pl. percussion w. Chico Hamilton. Studied theory, harmony, piano at Memphis State U. '74. Wrote for Stax Records. Working w. Braxton '76. Infl: Sonny Hamp, Philly Joe Jones, Elvin Jones. Film: *Rico* w. Dean Martin. TV: w. Hemphill at So. Illinois U., PBS. Fest: NJF-NY, '73 w. Paul Jeffrey. Comp: *Selfish People*. LPs: w. Hemphill (Arista); Bowie (Muse); w. Art Ensemble of Chicago, *Old* (Del.); Full Moon (Douglas); Butterfield (Electra); Lazar (Chess).

WILSON, PHILLIPS ELDER JR. (PHIL),* *trombone, composer, conductor, educator*; b. Belmont, Mass., 1/19/37. After building an enviable reputation w. W. Herman orch., '62-5, he left to take up teaching position at Berklee where he taught arr. & comp.; headed the trombone dept; founded and dir. the Thursday Night Dues Band and the Jazz Trombone Choir, '65-74. Faculty member Nat. Stage Band Camps from '65; dir. of Mus. Dept., Exeter Acad., '67-71; dir. Choate Sch. jazz-rock summer prog., '72- . Clinician for Conn Inst. Co. from '65; Board of Dir. of Int. Trom. Assoc. from '72; co-founder-dir., Boston Sackbut Week from '73. Appointed by G. Schuller as chairman of jazz division of Afro-American Dept. of New England Conserv., '74. Cond. Bost. Symph. in their children's series, premiering his work, *The Earth's Children,* '72; cond. Westchester Symph. in own comp., *The Left and the Right,* for symph. orch. and Marian McPartland trio, '71. Pl. w. M. McPartland; C. Terry; L. Armstrong; H. Hancock; B. Hackett. Arr. of *Mercy, Mercy, Mercy* for B. Rich; other comps. & arrs. for Herman, Terry, McPartland, D. Severinsen. Infl: Armstrong; O. Peterson; Ellington. Publ: co-author, *Chord Studies for Trombone* (Berklee Press, 1140 Boylston St., Boston, Mass.).

LPs: *The Prodigal Son* (Freeform); *Thurs Night Dues* (SJC); arrs. for Rich (RCA Victor; Pac. Jazz).

WILSON, THEODORE (TEDDY),* *piano, composer*; b. Austin, Tex., 11/24/12. One of the personalities to emerge from the Benny Goodman band of the '30s and leader of his own big band in '39-40, Wilson has continued, as he did in the '60s, to appear primarily at the head of his own trios but he also gave solo performances. He played in Europe; Australia; and three times in Japan, '70, '71, '73, where he recorded extensively. He worked often at Michael's Pub, NYC; the trio augmented in the latter part of the set, during certain engagements, by tenor men such as Flips Phillips; and Charlie Ventura.

Fest: Colo. JP, annually, from mid-60s through '73; NJF-NY '72 w. Benny Carter's Swing Masters; Lionel Hampton Tribute; '73 w. B. Goodman quartet; '74 w. own sextet in Salute to Cafe Society; Solo Piano; '75 in Newport Jazz Hall of Fame; Montreux. Dan Morgenstern writing of Wilson in *Jazz People* (see bibliography) says: "At times there is still a spark, a tension, something beyond the always impeccable and pianistically perfect surface."

LPs: *With Billie in Mind* (Chiaro.); *Striding After Fats*; *Runnin' Wild!*; *Moonglow* (Bl. Lion); *My Ideal* (Jap. Philips); *Jimmy Takeuchi & Teddy Wilson* (Toshiba); Teddy Wilson-Eiji Kitamura, three albums (Trio); Teddy Wilson & Marian McPartland, *Elegant Piano* (Halcyon); reissue, *Teddy Wilson & His All Stars* (Col.); w. Phoebe Snow (Shelter).

WINDING, KAI CHRESTEN,* *trombone, composer, leader*; b. Aarhus, Denmark, 5/18/22. One of the first trombonists in the bop movement of the '40s, pl. w. S. Kenton; C. Parker; G. Mulligan; M. Davis. Two trombone gp. w. J.J. Johnson in '50s. Own gps. from that time. W. Playboy Clubs in '60s incl. post of mus. dir. of NY branch. Active in studios, jingle field; comp. and scoring for industrial films. Co-led World's Greatest Jazzband II w. Eddie Condon at Roosevelt Grill, '69. From '70 in LA as member of staff band led by Mort Lindsey on Merv Griffin TV show. Reactivated four trombone gp. for Concord Fest. and engagement at Hong Kong Bar, '71. Toured world w. Giants of Jazz in '71-2. Euro. tour w. Lee Konitz; solo tour of Scandinavia, '74.

From '73 cond. school clinics; contracting for Pete Rugolo for TV films, feature films. coordinating personnel for Chuck Mangione LA concerts, Calif. tours. Formed own production co., Kaiwin Ltd., rec. own combo. Film: *A Man Called Adam* w. Sammy Davis. TV: Griffin; *Sammy & Co.*; NBC jazz shows w. B. Eckstine; Playboy 20th Anny Special, '75. Fest: NJF world tour, '71; Euro. & U.S., '72; Concord, '70-4; Colo. JP, '68-71; Berlin, '74. Comp: *Danish Blue*; *Concord Blues*. LPs: *Danish Blue* (Glendale); *Solo*; *Dirty Dog*; *Rainy Day*; *More Brass* (Verve); w. *Giants of Jazz* (Atl.); w. J.J. Johnson, *Israel*; *Betwixt and Between*; *Stonebones* (A&M, latter released in Japan only); w. all star brass, *Incredible Trombones*; *Brass Fever* (Imp.); Colorado Jazz Party (MPS/BASF); *Newport in New York, The Jam Sessions, Vols. 3&4* (Cobble.).

WINESTONE, BENJAMIN (BENNY),* *saxophones*; b. Glasgow, Scotland, 12/20/06. The veteran tenor sax star, prominent in London before World War II and subsequently in Canada, where he worked with Maynard Ferguson in 1947-8, later played in a variety of small combos until illness forced him into retirement. He died in Toronto 6/10/74.

WINSTONE, NORMA, *singer*; b. London, England, 9/23/41. Stud. piano at Trinity Coll. Since early '60s has app. in many clubs and concert halls in Britain, incl. Ronnie Scott's. Attended free jazz meetings in Baden-Baden for German radio, '70, '73. Broadcasts for same with own group, Edge of Time, from Rothenburg, '74.

One of England's most original jazz singers, Winstone won the MM poll, '71-3. She is married to British jazz pianist John Taylor. Infls: Sinatra, Fitzgerald, McRae, J. Coltrane.

LPs: as leader, *Edge of Time* (Argo); as guest, *A Symphony of Amaranths* w. Neil Ardley (Regal Zonophone); *Labyrinth*, w. Ian Carr (Vertigo); w. Michael Garrick (Argo); w. Mike Westbrook, *Love Songs* (Deram); w. K. Wheeler *Song For Someone* (Incus).

WINTER, PAUL THEODORE JR.,* *soprano, alto sax, composer*; b. Altoona, Pa. 8/31/39. Best known as leader of first jazz group to perf. at the White House, in late '62 for Mrs. John F. Kennedy. Later organized group known as Winter Consort. Perf. "The Charles Ives Show" at Kennedy Center, Wash., D.C., '75.

LPs: *Winter Consort, Something In The Wind, Road* (all A& M); *Icarus* (Epic).

WITHERS, WILLIAM HARRISON (BILL), *singer, composer, guitar, piano*; b. Slab Fork, W. Va., 7/4/38. Served in Navy for nine years, worked in an aircraft factory and also as milkman before making his professional start in music at the age of 32. His first album revealed a long neglected talent for fashioning attractive melodies and intelligent lyrics, performing them with impassioned sensitivity. He appeared at Berkeley JF, NO JF and on many TV shows w. Dick Cavett, Bill Cosby, David Frost, Nancy Wilson, Flip Wilson, Mike Douglas et al; also on *The Jazz Show,* KNBC, LA. Insp. by Hal David, Lou Rawls, Aretha Franklin, Little Willie John, Stevie Wonder.

Withers won a Grammy award in '71 for *Ain't No Sunshine,* as best r & b song. Among his other compositions are *Grandma's Hands*; *Lean On Me*; *Harlem*; *Let Me In Your Life*.

LPs: *Just as I Am*; *Still Bill*; *Live at Carnegie Hall*; *& 'Justments* (Sussex).

WITHERSPOON, JAMES (JIMMY),* *singer*; b. Gurdon, Ark., 8/8/23. Living in LA, Witherspoon continued to app. in clubs around the US and was frequently seen at the MJF. All through the '60s he made annual periodic visits to sing for the inmates in prisons. In later years he visited Europe approximately once a year. In '73 he toured Japan and the Far East. In '74, Witherspoon went to England to rec. a session which, when released in the U.S., turned out to be his biggest popular success in many years. Entitled *Love Is A Five Letter Word,* it contained little in the way of orthodox blues material, but set his unique timbre in a context that broadened his appeal.

From '72 Witherspoon was feat. on KMET radio in LA, as star of his own blues disc jockey show. Film: title role in *Black Godfather,* '75. TV: *Tonight Show*; *Midnight Special*; *An Evening With Spoon* for educ. TV; others in Boston, Phoenix, Arizona, Washington, D.C. Comps: *I Was Lost*; *Don't Gotta.*

LPs: *Spoonful* (BN); *Love Is A Five Letter Word* (Cap.); *Best of*; *Blues For Easy Livers*; *Spoon in London* (Pres.); *Handbags & Gladrags* (ABC); *Spoon Concerts* (Fant.); others w. G. Mulligan (Archive of Folk & Jazz); Ben Webster (Verve).

WOLFF, MICHAEL B. (MIKE), *piano, composer*; b. Victorville, Cal., 7/31/52. Six months later his family moved to Memphis, Tenn., living there until '61; then to Berkeley, Cal., where Wolff lived until he attended UCLA in '70, majoring in music and studying piano w. Abie Tzerko. After a year and a half at UCLA, transferred to U.C. Berkeley. Joined C. Tjader summer of '72, staying with him for two years. In mid-'74 joined Fingers, the group led by Airto, remaining until it disbanded Nov '74. In Jan. '75 he became a member of the C. Adderley quintet.

Wolff says: "My true love is the acoustic piano, but I am expanding into electronics: electric piano, clavinet, ring modulator, echo-plex, phase shifter, synthesizer etc." He was influenced by his father, Marvin L. Wolff, who played woodwinds in a band in Indianola, Miss., along w. Brew Moore. Comps: *Poppy*; *Waban*; *Sad Eyes*; *Samba de Oneida*. LPs: *Last Bolero In Berkeley*; *Putting It All Together*, w. Tjader; *Tambu* w. Tjader-C. Byrd; others w. Adderley (Fant.).

WONDER, STEVIE, *composer, singer, pianist* etc; b. Saginaw, Mich., 5/13/51. Wonder, whose first album was released when he was 12 years old, became an exceptionally popular performer and writer. Winner of several Grammy awards, he is of interest to the jazz world as the composer of a number of songs extensively used by jazz musicians, most notably *You Are The Sunshine Of My Life*.

WOODE, JAMES BRYANT (JIMMY),* *bass, composer, piano*; b. Philadelphia, Pa., 9/23/29. Leaving Duke Ellington in '60 after five yrs., he moved to Europe, working in Sweden, France and Germany. Lived in Germany and Austria but by '75 was based solely in Munich. With Clarke-Boland Big Band until band broke up in '73. Active w. radio, TV bands and in clubs. Comp: *Now Hear My Meaning*; lyrics for Francy Boland's *November Girl*. LPs: w. Mal Waldron, *Black Glory* (Enja); Clarke-Boland (MPS, Poly., Prest.); Charlie Parker (Phoenix).

WOODMAN, BRITT,* *trombone*; also *baritone horn*; b. Los Angeles, Cal., 6/4/20. Traveled w. D. Ellington, '51-60; later pl. in many Broadway shows, recordings and TV specials. Moved to Cal., Oct. '70. Cont. to freelance, working with the big bands of Bill Berry and Toshiko-Lew Tabackin. Rehearsing w. own eight piece gp. and occasionally app. with Ellington alumni groups in Duke Ellington tributes. Feat. soloist w. T. Vig 32 piece orch., '75. TV: *Brotherhood Special* '74. Fest: Concord, w. Berry, '74.

LPs: w. Chico Hamilton, *The Gamut* (UA); w. Toshiko-Tabackin, *Kogun* (RCA); w. B. Berry (Beez).

WOODS, CHRISTOPHER COLUMBUS (CHRIS), *alto saxophone, composer*; also *baritone sax, clarinet, flute, piccolo*; b. Memphis, Tenn., 12/25/25. First cousin Bob Mabane, tenor sax w. J. McShann in swing era, was early idol and insp. Stud. alto w. Dave Caples in St. Louis, '38-9; clar. w. Mike Zottarelle, St. Louis, '48; flute w. Henry Klein, Brooklyn, N.Y., '68-73; theory & harm. at Music & Arts Univ., St. Louis, '48-51; Brooklyn Conserv., part time '64-73; w. Scott O'Neal, also comp., '67-71. Pl. w. Tommy Dean, Jeter-Pillars, George Hudson in St. Louis, '48-51; Ernie Fields, '51; own gp. in St. Louis, '52-62. Moved to NYC and has worked w. D. Gillespie, C. Terry, H. McGhee, S. Oliver, W. Covington, Duke Pearson, B. Rich. Extensive tours of Europe as sideman and soloist, '73-4. Infl: Parker, Hodges, Willie Smith, Young, Hawkins, Joe Thomas. TV: half-hour show w. own gp. for six mos., St. Louis '55; Volkswagen commercial w. C. Terry; *Mark of Jazz* w. B. Rich, Phila. Fests: NJF; Pori; Nancy; San Sebastian. Comps: *Blues for Lew*; *Rhode Island Red*; *Swivel Hips*; *Monsieur LesBois in Paris*; *Love Theme for a Very Special Friend*; *My Lady*; *Portrait of a Golden Angel*; *Scufflin' Along*.

LPs: *Paris Meets Woods* (Futura); *Together in Paris*, Marco DiMarco-Chris Woods Sextet (Modern Jazz); *Big Bad Band* w. Terry (Etoile); *Reunion Band* w. Gillespie, (MPS); *Stickball* w. Charles Williams; *Blood, Sweat & Brass*; *Hard Mother Blues* w. E. Wilkins (Mainstream); *Yes Indeed* w. S. Oliver (Black & Blue).

WOODS, JOHNNY, *woodwinds, educator*; b. Pittsburgh, Pa., 4/2/30. Wife a Swedish concert pianist. Stud. at U.S. Navy School of Music, '51-2; B.S. in Ed. from Ohio St. Univ., '60; grad. work at Potsdam St., N.Y. '63. Woodwind teacher and big band dir. in N.Y. state; org. 10 bands plus his own and a teachers' octet for first Central N.Y. Stage Band Fest. '61, cont. through '64. Rehearsal leader for Colgate Coll. big band '62-3. In '65 Woods, who had toured Sweden and Finland w. the Int. Jazz Combo, '54-7, moved to Stockholm, where he taught clarinet in city music schools through '73. In free time org. five youth bands in Stockholm; lecturer at Royal Acad. of Music, '69; led Nat. Concert Bureau Wind Ensemble '71. Two big band concerts and jazz lecture at U.S. Cultural Center '71. Director of big band summer clinics in Sweden and Finland and full-time supervisor of Sweden's first jazz school, Jazz Ensemble Workshop, funded by the Swedish government. Contributor to Swedish jazz journals and to *Jazz Forum*.

WOODS, PHILIP WELLS (PHIL),* *alto sax, composer*; also *clarinet, piano*; b. Springfield, Mass., 11/2/31. Established himself as one of top alto players w. Gillespie, Q. Jones, B. Goodman and own groups in '50s and '60s. A busy NYC free-lance, he headed jazz dept. of Ramblerny, a summer arts camp in New Hope, Pa., '66-7. Left for Europe in March '68, making Paris his home base in May and forming European Rhythm Machine for clubs, concerts, radio, TV and fests. all over the Continent. In Dec. '72 moved to Calif., settling in LA for 10 months where he led quartet incl. pianist Pete Robinson on elec. piano. Returned to East Coast Oct. '73 to live in Pennsylvania, form new quartet, write and teach. Feat. soloist w. Michel Legrand for concerts, clubs.

Films: *The Hustler*; *Blow-Up*. Fest: NJF; Montreux; Frankfort; Molde; Berlin; Pori; Stockholm; Palermo; Nervi; Lisbon; Barcelona; Bologna, Aarhus, Col. Jazz Party. Comp: *Round Trip*; *Rights of Swing*; *Four Moods for Alto & Piano*; *Saxophone Quartet*; *Peace*, a ballet for French TV. Publ: saxophone method and band arrs. (Creative Jazz Composers, Box 467, Bowie, Md. 20715).

Polls: won *Playboy* Musicians' Musicians '71; DB Critics Poll, '70-1, '75; Readers poll, '75; combo won Critics Poll, TDWR, '70.

A fiery, passionate, lyrical player, originally out of the Charlie Parker school, Woods has incorporated elements of rock and avant garde into his personal, evolving expression.

LPs: *Musique Du Bois* (Muse); *New Music* (Testament); *Round Trip* (Verve); *Rights of Swing* (Barnaby); *Early Quintets* (Prest.); w. Euro. Rhythm Mach., *At The Frankfurt Jazz Fest.* (Embryo); *At The Montreux Jazz Fest.* (MGM); w. Q. Jones, *You've Got It Bad Girl* (A & M); w. M. Legrand, *Images*; *Live at Jimmy's* (RCA); w. C. Terry (Vang.).

WOODYARD, SAMUEL (SAM),* *drums*; b. Elizabeth, N.J., 1/7/25. Pl. w. D. Ellington orch., '55, remaining with occasional absences for more than a decade. After leaving Ellington, was ill and inactive for several years, living in LA, but returned in early '70s pl. occasionally w. Bill Berry band. Rejoined Duke pl. congas, '73; later pl. congas w. B. Rich. To NYC, '74. Gigs at West End Cafe. From Feb. '75 he spent several months in Europe, pl. Dunkirk JF with Claude Bolling orch., and later working w. Gerard Badini's Swing Machine.

LPs: w. Ellington on various labels; w. Badini (Blue Star); w. Rich, *Roar of '74* (Gr. Mer.); w. Brooks Kerr-Paul Quinichette, *Prevue* (Famous Door).

WORKMAN, REGINALD (REGGIE),* *bass, educator*; b. Philadelphia, Pa., 6/26/37. Worked w. Coltrane; Moody; Blakey; Lateef; H. Mann in '60s, touring Japan w. Mann, '66. Played w. T. Monk; Alice Coltrane; Music Inc. incl. State Dept. concert tour-seminar of Brazil, '72; concert tour, Holland '74; w. Max Roach, two wks. in Italy, '73-4. Workman also toured Japan as an African American Music Consultant for All Art Promotion, Inc., '70.

From '67 teaching bass for in-house music program at the New Muse Community Museum of Brooklyn where he took over for Bill Barron as Director of the Music Workshop Program, '75. He also has directed workshops and/or taught at Samuel Tilden Comm. Center, '67-8; NY Chapter of Young Audience Inc., '67-70; Central Brooklyn Model Cities Summer & Winter Academy, '70; Wilmington, Del. School of Music, '71; Trenton, N.J. Board of Education, '72; U. of Mass., '73-4; Jazz Interactions Music Workshop from '75.

In '70 he had a month's training at the Moog Co., Trumansburg, N.Y., learning how to operate and perform w. Moog Synthesizer. Studied at Manhattan Borough Comm. Coll., '70-1; Lincoln U.; NJ Board of Ed. teacher training courses, '72; U. of Mass., '73-4.

Produced series of cultural presentations at Olatunji's Center for African Culture, '67. From '70 president of Board of Directors of CBA; member of advisory board of the Afro-American Bi-centennial Hall of Fame and Museum, Inc., Youngstown, Ohio. Received grant from CAPS for Comp., '71; Orchard Hill Residential Coll. of U. of Mass. award, '74; El Hajj Malik Shabazz Award '75.

LPs: *Reggie Workman-Dee Dee Bridgewater Duet*; w. Heiner Stadler (Labor); w. Billy Harper; Charles Tolliver (Strata-East); Lee Morgan (BN); H. Mann (Atl.); A. Coltrane; Marion Brown (Imp.); Cedar Walton (Prest.); Mal Waldron (Enja); Johnny Coles (Main.); Roy Brooks (Imhotep); T. Hino (Canyon); T. Honda (Trio).

WORLD'S GREATEST JAZZBAND. see Haggart, Bob; Lawson, Yank.

WRIGHT, EUGENE JOSEPH (GENE or SENATOR),* *bass*; b. Chicago, Ill., 5/29/23. After working w. Basie, Norvo et al, came to international prominence touring w. Dave Brubeck quartet, '58-68. In '69-70 led own ensemble in concerts at black colleges across the country. Pl. w. Monty Alexander trio, '71-4. In '74-5, maintaining homes in Chicago and Beverly Hills, he divided his time between TV and movie work, a night club season w. Jack Sheldon in Monterey, teaching privately and at schools, and writing. Wright is head of the advisory board in the jazz division of the International Society of Bassists; chairman of jazz department, U. of Cincinnati.

Publ: *Modern Music for Bass* (Hansen Pub. Co. 1824 West Ave., Miami, Fla. 33139). LPs: w. Brubeck (Col.); Monty Alexander (BASF).

WRIGHT, LAMMAR, SR.,* *trumpet*; b. Texarkana, Tex., 6/20/12. Lead trumpeter in the '30s and early '40s w. C. Calloway, later w. many other bands, incl. D. Redman, Cootie Williams, L. Millinder, Wright died 4/13/73 in NYC. His sons, Lammar Jr. and Elmon, both became trumpeters and pl. w. many name bands from '40s.

WRIGHT LEO NASH,* *alto saxophone, flute, clarinet, piccolo*; b. Wichita Falls, Tex., 12/14/33. Feat. w. Dizzy Gillespie quintet, '59-62; free-lanced in Europe, '63-4, then settled in Berlin for work at clubs such as the Blue Note, Dug's. A member of Radio Free Berlin Studio Band for past decade. Pl. at Pori Fest. in Finland '72. Comp: *Ode to a Blossom*; *Pink Bossa Nova*; *Lee'os Blues*.

LPs: *It's All-Wright* (BASF); *Alto Summit* (MPS).

WRIGHTSMAN, STANLEY (STAN),* *piano*; b. Oklahoma City, Okla., 6/15/10. A veteran of the Ben Pollack and Bob Crosby bands, Wrightsman later was heard in many Dixieland combos in the LA area. He died 12/17/75 in Palm Springs, Cal.

WROBLEWSKI, JAN (PTASZYN),* *tenor saxophone, composer*; b. Kalisz, Poland, 3/27P36. After his debut in '56 w. Krzysztof Komeda sextet, led own gps. incl. Jazz Believers; Polish Jazz Quartet; Mainstream, co-led w. Wojciech Karolak. Was first to mix jazz w. Polish folklore. In '58 he visited U.S. w. Newport Youth Band; then started and led Jazz Studio of Polish Radio which he describes as "half workshop, half orchestra". Infl: Sonny Rollins, Gil Evans. Has app. at most of European fests. TV: reg. apps. w. Jazz Studio orch. on Polish network; other Euro. progs. A former vice-pres. of the Polish Jazz Federation, he served as pres. from '72-5. For six yrs., every Wednesday, has presented a radio show, *3 Quarters of Jazz*. Awards: Golden Cross of Merit from State Council; Poland's 30th Anniversary medal. An arr. & comp. for Polish radio from '57, he has also worked in pop music for radio and the Muza Rec. Co. Comps: *Wariant Warszawski* for Polish Nat. Phil. & Jazz Quartet; *K.K.'s Talkin' to the Band,* third prize in Prague Int. contest for jazz comp., '67. Has written over 100 orchestral works.

LPs: *Polish Jazz Quartet*; *Jazz Studio Orch.*; *Sweet Beat*; *Seaweed Sellers*; *SPPT Chalturnik*; *Mainstream* (Muza); *The Music of Komeda* (Metronome).

WYANDS, RICHARD,* *piano*; b. Oakland, Calif., 7/2/28. After establishing a reputation at local SF & Oak. clubs in '50s, he acc. Ella Fitzgerald, Carmen McRae in mid-'50s. Moved to NYC, '58, where he worked w. Roy Haynes, Mingus, J. Richardson, Gigi Gryce. From the mid-'60s through '74 he traveled extensively w. K. Burrell, pl. clubs in major U.S. cities and coll. concerts. Pl. Ronnie Scott's in London w. Burrell, '69; Japanese tour, '72. He also free-lanced around NYC when not working w. JPJ Quartet, the group he joined in '74. TV: *Tonight Show* w. Burrell; *Contemporary Memorial* (for Robert Kennedy) w. Grady Tate, Joe Williams, CBS. Fests: NJF; Montreux, '69; NJF-NY, '72 w. Burrell. LPs: w. Burrell, *God Bless the Child* (CTI); *Night Song* (Verve); *Up the Street, 'Round the Corner, Down the Block* (Fant.); w. F. Foster, *Manhattan Fever* (Blue Note); w. F. Hubbard, *First Light* (CTI).

WYBLE, JIMMY,* *guitar*; b. Port Arthur, Tex., 1/25/22. Many years in LA pl. studios; toured w. B. Goodman, '60 and again in '63; R. Norvo quintet, '61-2. In '64 he was w. Norvo acc. F. Sinatra in Australia and throughout U.S. From

'65-75 freelanced in LA studios, also app. w. a gp. known as Tony Rizzi Five Guitars Plus Four Play Charlie Christian. Publ: *Classical/Country* (Playback Mus. Publ. Co., P.O. Box 4278, N. Hollywood, Ca. 91607). TV: Five years on Flip Wilson show; Kraft Music Hall; Music Scene etc., for all three networks. Films: *The Wild Bunch*; *Ocean's 11*; *Kings Go Forth*.

LPs: w. Norvo, *Windjammer* (Dot); *Red Norvo Plays The Blues* (RCA); *Naturally* (Rave); w. Goodman, *Swings Again* (Col.); *The Sound of Music* (MGM); *The Swing Era, Into the 70s* (Time/Life).

XIQUES, EDWARD F. JR. (ED), *saxophones, clarinets, flutes*; b. Staten Island, N.Y., 10/9/39. Started by father on soprano sax at age eight; self-taught until Boston U., '57, where he received B.M. degree, '62. During that time worked with local bands incl. J. Byard, H. Pomeroy. To NYC, taught school '62-8; also played with commercial bands such as B. Morrow, Les and Larry Elgart, and freelance jazz work w. Duke Pearson, Chris Swansen's N.Y. Improvisation Ensemble on baritone. Made film, *A Tuesday Afternoon,* w. Swansen. Toured w. W. Herman five months in '70. Joined T. Jones-M. Lewis orch., '71 and was still with this band in '75, but also freelanced in NYC and worked w. Bill Watrous; Ten Wheel Drive. NJF and many European jazz fests., mainly with Jones-Lewis.

LPs: w. Jones-Lewis (Philadelphia Int'l.); *Manhattan Wildlife Refuge,* w. Watrous (Col.); w. Ten Wheel Drive (Cap.).

YAGED, SOLOMON (SOL),* *clarinet*; b. Brooklyn, N.Y., 12/8/22. Vet. of many traditionalist groups at Nick's, Metropole etc., Yaged opened in '66 at the Gaslight Club, NYC, and during next decade his quartet there incl. such sidemen as Ray Nance, who worked with him for four years. He continued to app. frequently on TV telethons and in jazz concerts in N.Y. and other eastern states. John S. Wilson observed in the N.Y. Times that "Yaged for more than 25 years has been a masterful exponent of the Benny Goodman style and manner. He even talks like him and bears a slight resemblance to him."

Three LPs: live at Gaslight Club (Lane).

YAMAKI, KOZABURO, *guitar*; b. Tokyo, Japan, 6/18/31. Pl. w. Yasuki Enoshima & Rhythm Mates at Haneda Officers' Club, '53; own group and Grace Six at US base camps in Tokyo. From '56 concert master of Toshiyuki Miyama's New Herd Orch. Infl: Ellington, Gillespie. Fests: w. Miyama, MJF, '74; NJF-NY, '75. Won Best Player Award at Art Fest., '70, for *Four Compositions*. Comp: *Furisode*; *Senshuraku*; *Nio To Hato (Nio and Dove)*.

LPs: w. New Herd, *Four Compositions* (Toshiba EMI); *Nio To Hato*; *Tsuchinone or Sound of Earth* (Nippon Col.).

YAMASHITA, YOSUKE, *piano*; b. Tokyo, Japan, 2/26/42. Stud. at Kunitachi Music Univ., '62-7. Pl. w. Terumasa Hino, many other groups in Tokyo during '60s; formed own trio, '69, touring Japan. In '74, traveled throughout Europe with the trio app. at several fests. in West and East Germany and Yugoslavia. Author of many essays for several magazines.

LPs: *Frozen Days* (Crown); *Mina's Second Theme*; *Mokujiki* (Victor); *Yosuke Alone* (King); *Dancing Kojiki* (Maro); *Dedicated to Cassius Clay* (URC).

YELLIN, PETER (PETE), *alto sax, composer*; also *flute, tenor sax, clarinet, bass clarinet*; b. New York City, 7/18/41. Father a pianist and former member of NBC staff. Stud. sax w. Joe Allard; flute w. Harold Bennet; Bachelor's degree from Juilliard. Before he began pl. at age 19, Yellin attended Denver U. on a freshman basketball scholarship. Worked w. Lionel Hampton, '63-6; Buddy Rich, '67; Tito Puente, '68-9; Joe Henderson, '70-3. Fest: NJF-NY w. own group, '73; w. Puente, '74; MJF w. Rich, '68. Infl: Parker, Coltrane, Rollins, M. Davis, Henderson. Comps: *Dance of Allegra*; *Esculynn*; *Bird and the Ouija Board*; *Mebakush*; *Norma*; *Tojo*; *It's the Right Thing*. Awarded grant for comp. from National Endowment for the Arts.

LPs: *Dance of Allegra*; *It's the Right Thing* (Mainstream); *Pursuit of Blackness* w. Henderson (Milestone).

YOUNG, LARRY (Khalid Yasin),* *organ, composer*; also *synthesizer, keyboards*; b. Newark, N.J., 10/7/40. After initial experience w. r&b gps. in late '50s he pl. in '60s w. Lou Donaldson; Grant Green; Elvin Jones; Lee Morgan; and Joe Henderson. In the late '60s and '70s continued to evolve into areas of the avant garde and jazz-rock w. John Coltrane; John McLaughlin; Jimi Hendrix; Tony Williams' Lifetime; and Miles Davis. "Musicians suffer when they do that," he says, referring to limiting oneself to any one particular style of music. "There are so many jazz players who could have really made a major influence on rock, but wouldn't because of their attitude towards it."

Jack McDuff called him "the Coltrane of the organ."

LPs: *Larry Young's Fuel* (Arista); *Lawrence of Newark* (Perception); *Unity* (BN); w. McLaughlin, *Devotion* (Douglas); McLaughlin-Santana, *Love, Devotion and Surrender*; w. Miles Davis, *Bitches Brew* (Col.); w. T. Williams, *Emergency*; *Turn It Over*; *Ego* (Poly.).

YOUNG, EUGENE (SNOOKY),* *trumpet*; b. Dayton, Ohio, 2/3/19. The former J. Lunceford trumpeter joined the NBC staff orch. in '62 and worked on the *Tonight Show,* first under Skitch Henderson, and later Doc Severinsen. During this time, until he left with the show for Cal. in '72, he doubled as a member of the T. Jones-M. Lewis orch., of which he became a founder member in '66.

In Cal., in addition to movie sound track work, Young pl. occasionally w. Gerald Wilson, L. Bellson and others. Along with his *Tonight Show* tenure, he pl. regular gigs throughout the U.S. as a member of Severinsen's Now Generation Brass.

LPs: *Boys From Dayton* (Master Jazz); w. Severinsen

(RCA); D. Axelrod; C. Adderley; K. Burrell (Fant.); Bellson (Pablo); also see Jones-Lewis.

YOUNG, JAMES OSBORNE (TRUMMY),* *trombone, singer*; b. Savannah, Ga., 1/12/12. The former J. Lunceford and L. Armstrong soloist, a resident of Honolulu from mid-'60s, made occasional brief visits to mainland U.S. to record recreations of his early Lunceford hits with the Time-Life orch. under B. May's direction; to app. at Dick Gibson's annual jazz parties in Colorado Springs, and to play a concert, *A Night in New Orleans,* at the Wilshire Ebell theatre in LA. He also app. on a segment of the TV series *Hawaii Five-0* w. Nancy Wilson. Mainly active in the '70s pl. nightly at Sheraton Waikiki Hotel, leading his own group.

LPs: *A Man And His Horn* (Flair Records, 2071 S. Beretania St., Honolulu, Hawaii 96814); *Colorado Jazz Party* (MPS).

ZAPPA, FRANK, *singer, guitar, composer*; b. Baltimore, Md., 12/21/40. As a teenager, lived in the desert in So. Cal., attending Antelope Valley H.S. He was almost entirely self-taught musically. Led a small band in Lancaster in early '60s; formed the Mothers of Invention, '64. The group's first LP was released two years later and Zappa shot to fame as one of the focal figures in a bizarre combination of electronic music, avant garde sounds and visual showmanship. Though not himself a jazz musician, he frequently employed among his sidemen musicians with jazz experience. They included violinists Don (Sugar Cane) Harris and J.L. Ponty; George Duke, elect. keyboards; Bruce Fowler, ex-W. Herman trombonist; Ralph Humphrey, formerly w. Don Ellis on drums; David Parlato on bass. One of Zappa's comps. was entitled *Eric Dolphy Memorial Barbeque.*

LPs: *Hot Rats*; *Chunga's Revenge* (Repr.); *Waka/Jawaka-Hot Rats Grand Wazoo* (Bizarre); *A-Pos-Tro-Phe*; *Roxy & Elsewhere Over-Nite Sensation* (DisCreet).

ZAWINUL, JOSEF (JOE),* *piano, keyboards, synthesizer, composer*; also *guitar, oud, electric stick, misc. perc.*; b. Vienna, Austria, 7/7/32. To U.S. 1959. Member of Cannonball Adderley group from '61-70. During this period, in addition to recording with various groups of his own, he played a major role in the success of the Adderley group, as composer of such hits as *Mercy Mercy Mercy,* winner of a Grammy for best instrumental performance, '67. He made four albums with Miles Davis, '69-70: *In A Silent Way,* for which he composed the title number; *Bitches Brew*; *Live-Evil* and *Big Fun.* In '66 he was a judge at the International Jazz Competition in Vienna. Recorded *Concerto for Two Pianos and Orch.* with F. Gulda. In '71 he was co-founder with W. Shorter of a new group, Weather Report; the other original members were Miroslav Vitous, Alphonse Mouzon and Airto Moreira.

Weather Report was based on a conceptually free musical direction, often involving high energy performances, but capable of great lyricism, ranging from tonality to atonality and from strong bursts of rhythm to free flowing interludes, sometimes characterized as space music.

By '75 Zawinul had composed some 130 works. Among them were *74 Miles Away*; *Riverbed*; *Lateef Minor 7th*; *Midnight Mood*; *Rumpelstiltskin*; *Hippodelphia*; *Walk Tall*; *Country Preacher*; *The Scavenger*; *Newk's Time*; *Dr. Honoris Causa*; *Pharaoh's Dance*; *Orange Lady*; *Nubian Sundance*; *Boogie Woogie Walk*; *Unknown Soldier*; *Milky Way*; *American Tango*; *Scarlet Woman*; *Between The Thighs*; *Badia*; also *Experience in E for Symphony Orchestra.*

Living in Pasadena, Cal., Zawinul has to his credit many successful world tours, with Adderley and with Weather Report. The latter won the DB Readers' Poll, '72-3-4. The group's first LP was voted Jazz Album of the Year in '71, and *Mysterious Traveler* was similarly acclaimed in '74. There were many other awards for the group and its records in the U.S., Europe and Japan. Movies: Zawinul appeared with Adderley in *Play Misty For Me*; wrote music for *Pin Striped Dream.* TV: Grammy Award show, '67; Don Kirshner Rock Concert with Weather Report.

Though he has become identified in recent years with a highly sophisticated form of music at a level of abstraction far beyond that of his early years with Adderley, Zawinul has remained an extraordinarily flexible musician. All of his works, including such relatively simple pieces as *Mercy Mercy Mercy,* have validity in their own terms. As a pianist, he has shown exceptional talent in the use of electric keyboards and synthesizer, but without sacrificing a facility for playing acoustic piano solos that show astonishing skill and creativity, still reflecting such early influences as Art Tatum.

LPs: w. Weather Report, *Weather Report*; *Tale Spinnin'*; *I Sing The Body Electric*; *Sweetnighter*; w. Adderley, *Live at Shelly's*; *Mercy Mercy Mercy*; *74 Miles Away*; *Country Preacher*; *The Cannonball Adderley Quintet & Orch.*, incl. *Experience In E* suite; *In Person* (Cap.); *Planet Earth* (Riv.); own LPs: *Money in the Pocket*; *Rise and Fall of Third Stream* (Atl.); w. Gulda (Preiser).

ZEITLIN, DENNIS JAY (DENNY),* *piano, keyboards, synthesizer, composer*; also *bass*; b. Chicago, Ill., 4/10/38. Has had dual career in music and psychiatry. Prominent in jazz in mid-60s, when he recorded for Col., app. at Newport and Monterey JF. In '68, he withdrew from the public scene to devote himself to the study of electronic instruments, multiple keyboards, and a synthesis of rock, jazz and classical idioms. Restricted himself mainly to the SF Bay Area, maintaining his private practice in psychiatry, also serving as assistant clinical prof. of psychiatry at U.C.S.F. Formed own record company, Double Helix, '73. His first LP for this label met with favorable critical response; by '75 Zeitlin had stepped up his concert schedule. Comps: *A Scarf In The Air*; *El Guego de las Montanas*; *Deja Vu*; *Mirage*; *Dormammu*; *Quiet Now*; *Stonehenge*; *I-Thou*; *Dodecahedron.*

LPs: *Expansion* (Double Helix, P.O. Box 817, Kentfield, Ca. 94904); *Carnival*; *Zeitgeist* (Col.).

ZOLLER, ATTILA CORNELIUS,* *guitar*; also *trumpet, bass*; b. Visegrad, Hungary, 6/13/27. Came to U.S., '59 and after pl. w. H. Mann '62-5, organized own quartet for club work in NYC. Pl. w. R. Norvo in NYC, Canada, '66; B.

Goodman and own group, '67. From '60 he has made yearly visits to Europe for concerts, radio, TV and rec. Toured Japan w. Astrud Gilberto, '70, and as part of the Guitar Festival w. Jim Hall, K. Burrell, '71. Own summer prog., *Jazz On The Roof,* incl. weekly clinics and weekend concerts in Vermont, '75. App. at Berlin Jazztage, '73.

In '71 a patent was granted Zoller for the Bidirectional Pick-up Device for guitar and elec. bass. Also invented first magnetic pick-up for vibraharp, manuf. by J.C. Deagan.

LPs: *Gypsy Cry* (Embryo); *A Path Through Haze* w. Masahiko Sato trio; *Katz & Maus,* original film score; w. H. Koller, A. Mangelsdorff, *Zo-Ko-Ma*; Zoller-Koller-Solal (MPS).

ZWEIG, BARRY KENNETH, *guitar*; also *violin*; b. Detroit, Mich., 2/7/42. Stud. theory and violin at N. Hollywood high school, grad. 1960; LA Valley Coll. for two yrs. stud. w. Robert MacDonald, Raphael DeCastro, Jack Gothan, violin; Bud Matlock, Horace Hatchett, Johnny Smith, guitar. first road gig w. Leo Diamond, '61; first jazz gig w. Eddie Miller, Nappy Lamare, Charlie Lodice. Drafted into Army, '64, assigned to World Band in Colorado Springs. Pl. for two years w. Bob Shew and others. Joined Buddy Rich, '66, rec. and traveling with band for eight months. From '66-70 freelancing around LA area; also road tours w. Andy Williams, Henry Mancini et al. With Willie Bobo '70-71. From '75- in John Rodby's orch. on Dinah Shore TV show; also member of John Pisano-Barry Zweig Quintet; Tony Rizzi's Five Guitars. Pl. on sound track of Don Ellis' score of *The French Connection.*

LPs: *Do What you Want To Do,* w. Bobo (Sussex); *The Kid,* w. L. Vinnegar (PBR).

ZWERIN, MICHAEL,* *bass trumpet, journalist*; also *trombone*; b. New York City, 5/18/30. The former sideman w. C. Thornhill, M. Ferguson, who pl. w. the Miles Davis Nonet at 18, toured Russia w. Earl Hines for U.S. State Dept., '66. Jazz columnist for *Village Voice,* '66-9; *Village Voice* European Editor, '69-72; free-lance articles for *Rolling Stone, Penthouse, Village Voice,* '73-5. Zwerin, no longer active musically, has been in Europe since '69. Living in the south of France, '75, writing a novel. Publ: *Silent Sound of Needles,* a book about drug addict rehabilitation (Prentice-Hall, New Jersey); *Little Battalions* (Wildwood House, 1 Wardour St., London, Eng.).

Introduction to poll tabulations

The following tabulations of poll winners are intended to serve as a yardstick of the respective opinions of jazz fans, critics and leading musicians. Their inclusion should not be construed to imply that the musicians listed are necessarily the most important or most successful. They are simply the most popular with these groups of voters.

The *down beat* readers' poll is the oldest and best known of all, having been conducted annually since 1936. The same publication has conducted a poll of experts since 1953, to which in recent years more than 50 critics from all over the world have contributed their votes. In this poll, two winners are elected in each category. The first is designated as "Established Talent"; the second, originally known as the "New Star" category, was modified from 1963 to include "Talent Deserving of Wider Recognition." Results of the *down beat* polls from 1960 through 1965 were published in *The Encyclopedia of Jazz in the Sixties*.

	Down Beat Critics' Poll 1966	*Down Beat Readers' Poll* 1966	*Down Beat Critics' Poll* 1967	*Down Beat Readers' Poll* 1967
Record of the Year	*Ornette Coleman at the Golden Circle, Vol. 1* - Blue Note	*Ornette Coleman at the Golden Circle, Vol. 1* - Blue Note	1. *The Popular Duke Ellington* Duke Ellington - RCA (tie with) 2. *Miles Smiles* Miles Davis - Col.	*Miles Smiles* Miles Davis - Col.
Reissue of the Year	*Golden Years, Vol. 2* Billie Holiday - Col.		*Things Ain't What They Used To Be* Ellington Groups - RCA (Hodges-Stewart)	
Jazzman of the Year		Ornette Coleman		Charles Lloyd
Hall of Fame	Charlie Christian	Bud Powell	Bessie Smith	Billy Strayhorn
Band	Duke Ellington *Thad Jones-Mel Lewis	Duke Ellington	Duke Ellington *Don Ellis	Duke Ellington
Combo	Miles Davis *Denny Zeitlin	Miles Davis	Miles Davis *Charles Lloyd	Miles Davis
Composer	Duke Ellington *Carla Bley	Duke Ellington	Duke Ellington *Herbie Hancock	Duke Ellington
Arranger	Gil Evans *Rod Levitt	Gil Evans	Duke Ellington *Thad Jones	Oliver Nelson
Trumpet	Miles Davis *Ted Curson	Miles Davis	Miles Davis *Jimmy Owens	Miles Davis
Trombone	J. J. Johnson *Buster Cooper	J. J. Johnson	J. J. Johnson *Garnett Brown	J. J. Johnson
Alto Saxophone	Johnny Hodges *John Handy, *John Tchicai (tie)	Paul Desmond	Ornette Coleman *Charles McPherson	Paul Desmond
Tenor Saxophone	John Coltrane *Charles Lloyd	John Coltrane	Sonny Rollins *Joe Henderson	Stan Getz
Baritone Saxophone	Harry Carney *Ronnie Cuber	Gerry Mulligan	Harry Carney *Pepper Adams	Gerry Mulligan
Clarinet	Pee Wee Russell *Edmond Hall	Buddy DeFranco	Pee Wee Russell *Perry Robinson	Buddy DeFranco
Misc. Instrument	Roland Kirk, manzello & strich *Jean-Luc Ponty, violin	Roland Kirk, manzello & strich	Roland Kirk, manzello & strich *Michael White, violin	Roland Kirk, manzello & strich
Flute	Roland Kirk *Charles Lloyd	Herbie Mann	James Moody *Jeremy Steig	Herbie Mann

*Talent deserving of wider recognition

	Down Beat Critics' Poll 1966	*Down Beat Readers' Poll 1966*	*Down Beat Critics' Poll 1967*	*Down Beat Readers' Poll 1967*
Vibes	Milt Jackson *Roy Ayers	Milt Jackson	Milt Jackson *Tommy Vig	Milt Jackson
Piano	Earl Hines *Jaki Byard	Oscar Peterson	Earl Hines *Keith Jarrett	Oscar Peterson
Organ	Jimmy Smith *Larry Young	Jimmy Smith	Jimmy Smith *Don Patterson	Jimmy Smith
Guitar	Wes Montgomery *Rene Thomas	Wes Montgomery	Wes Montgomery *George Benson, Jimmy Raney (tie)	Wes Montgomery
Bass	Charles Mingus *Richard Davis	Ray Brown	Richard Davis *David Izenzon	Ray Brown
Drums	Elvin Jones *Sunny Murray	Elvin Jones	Elvin Jones *Milford Graves	Buddy Rich
Male Singer	Louis Armstrong *Lou Rawls	Frank Sinatra	Louis Armstrong *Richard Boone	Lou Rawls
Female Singer	Ella Fitzgerald *Carol Sloane	Ella Fitzgerald	Ella Fitzgerald *Lorez Alexandria	Ella Fitzgerald
Vocal Group	Double Six of Paris	Double Six of Paris	Beatles *Supremes	†Beatles

	Down Beat Critics' Poll 1968	*Down Beat Readers' Poll 1968*	*Down Beat Critics' Poll 1969*	*Down Beat Readers' Poll 1969*
Record of the Year	*Far East Suite* - RCA Duke Ellington	*Electric Bath* - Col. Don Ellis	*And His Mother Called Him Bill* - Duke Ellington - RCA	*Filles De Kilimanjaro* Miles Davis - Col.
Reissue of the Year	*Hodge Podge* - RCA Johnny Hodges		*V.S.O.P. Vol 1* Louis Armstrong - Col.	
Jazzman of the Year		Gary Burton		Miles Davis
Hall of Fame	Sidney Bechet, Fats Waller (tie)	Wes Montgomery	Pee Wee Russell, Jack Teagarden (tie)	Ornette Coleman
Band	Duke Ellington *Buddy Rich	Duke Ellington	Duke Ellington *Kenny Clarke-Francy Boland	Duke Ellington
Combo	Miles Davis *Gary Burton	Miles Davis	Miles Davis *Elvin Jones Trio	Miles Davis

*Talent deserving of wider recognition
†Name changed in Readers' Poll to Rock/Pop/Blues Group

	Down Beat Critics' Poll 1968	*Down Beat Readers' Poll* 1968	*Down Beat Critics' Poll* 1969	*Down Beat Readers' Poll* 1969
Composer	Duke Ellington *Wayne Shorter	Duke Ellington	Duke Ellington *Mike Westbrook	Duke Ellington
Arranger	Duke Ellington *Tom McIntosh	Oliver Nelson	Duke Ellington *Francy Boland	Duke Ellington
Trumpet	Miles Davis *Charles Tolliver	Miles Davis	Miles Davis *Randy Brecker	Miles Davis
Trombone	J. J. Johnson *Carl Fontana	J. J. Johnson	J. J. Johnson *Lester Lashley	J. J. Johnson
Alto Saxophone	Johnny Hodges *Sonny Criss	Cannonball Adderley	Johnny Hodges *Lee Konitz	Cannonball Adderley
Soprano Saxophone			Lucky Thompson *John Surman	Joe Farrell
Tenor Saxophone	Sonny Rollins *Joe Farrell	Stan Getz	Sonny Rollins *Albert Ayler	Stan Getz
Baritone Saxophone	Harry Carney *Cecil Payne	Gerry Mulligan	Harry Carney *John Surman	Gerry Mulligan
Clarinet	Pee Wee Russell *Eddie Daniels	Pee Wee Russell	Jimmy Hamilton *Roland Kirk	Jimmy Hamilton
Misc. Instrument	Jean-Luc Ponty, violin *Howard Johnson, tuba	Roland Kirk, manzello, strich	Jean-Luc Ponty, violin *Ray Nance, violin	Roland Kirk, manzello, strich
Flute	James Moody *Hubert Laws	Herbie Mann	James Moody *Joe Farrell	Herbie Mann
Vibes	Milt Jackson *Karl Berger	Gary Burton	Bobby Hutcherson *Red Norvo	Gary Burton
Piano	Bill Evans *Roger Kellaway	Herbie Hancock	Earl Hines *Chick Corea	Herbie Hancock
Organ	Jimmy Smith *Odell Brown, *Eddy Louiss (tie)	Jimmy Smith	Jimmy Smith *Lonnie Smith	Jimmy Smith
Guitar	Kenny Burrell *Larry Coryell	Kenny Burrell	Kenny Burrell *Pat Martino	Kenny Burrell
Bass	Richard Davis *Eddie Gomez	Richard Davis	Richard Davis *Niels-Henning Orsted Pedersen	Richard Davis

*Talent deserving of wider recognition

	Down Beat Critics' Poll 1968	Down Beat Readers' Poll 1968	Down Beat Critics' Poll 1969	Down Beat Readers' Poll 1969
Drums	Elvin Jones *Billy Higgins	Elvin Jones	Elvin Jones *Daniel Humair	Elvin Jones
Male Singer	Louis Armstrong, Ray Charles (tie) *Jimmy Witherspoon	Ray Charles	Ray Charles *Jon Hendricks	Ray Charles
Female Singer	Ella Fitzgerald *Aretha Franklin	Ella Fitzgerald	Ella Fitzgerald *Karin Krog	Ella Fitzgerald
Blues/R&B Group	Muddy Waters *Junior Wells	†Beatles	Muddy Waters *Canned Heat, J. B. Hutto (tie)	†Blood, Sweat & Tears

---

	Down Beat Critics' Poll 1970	Down Beat Readers' Poll 1970	Down Beat Critics' Poll 1971	Down Beat Readers' Poll 1971
Record of the Year	*Bitches' Brew* - Col. Miles Davis	*Bitches' Brew* - Col. Miles Davis	*New Orleans Suite* - Atlantic Duke Ellington	*Weather Report* - Col.
Reissue of the Year	*Blue Note's Three Decades of Jazz, Vol. 1* - Blue Note		*Bessie Smith Series* - Col.	
Jazzman of the Year		Miles Davis		Miles Davis
Hall of Fame	Johnny Hodges	Jimi Hendrix	Roy Eldridge, Django Reinhardt (tie)	Charles Mingus
Band	Duke Ellington *Mike Westbrook	Duke Ellington	Duke Ellington *Sun Ra	Duke Ellington
Combo	Miles Davis *Phil Woods	Miles Davis	Miles Davis *Art Ensemble of Chicago	Miles Davis
Composer	Duke Ellington *Mike Gibbs	Duke Ellington	Duke Ellington *Carla Bley	Duke Ellington
Arranger	Duke Ellington *Duke Pearson	Quincy Jones	Duke Ellington *Herbie Hancock	Quincy Jones
Trumpet	Miles Davis *Woody Shaw, Kenny Wheeler (tie)	Miles Davis	Dizzy Gillespie *Roy Eldridge	Miles Davis
Trombone	J. J. Johnson *Malcolm Griffiths, Eje Thelin (tie)	J. J. Johnson	Vic Dickenson *Vic Dickenson, Bill Watrous (tie)	J. J. Johnson

*Talent deserving of wider recognition
†Name changed in Readers' Poll to Rock/Pop/Blues Group

	Down Beat Critics' Poll 1970	*Down Beat Readers' Poll* 1970	*Down Beat Critics' Poll* 1971	*Down Beat Readers' Poll* 1971
Alto Saxophone	Phil Woods *Eric Kloss	Cannonball Adderley	Phil Woods *Frank Strozier	Cannonball Adderley
Soprano Saxophone	Wayne Shorter *Tom Scott	Wayne Shorter	Wayne Shorter *Budd Johnson	Wayne Shorter
Tenor Saxophone	Sonny Rollins *Paul Gonsalves, Pharoah Sanders (tie)	Stan Getz	Dexter Gordon *Harold Ashby	Stan Getz
Baritone Saxophone	Harry Carney *Nick Brignola	Gerry Mulligan	Harry Carney *Pat Patrick	Gerry Mulligan
Clarinet	Russell Procope *Frank Chace, Bob Wilber (tie)	Rahsaan Roland Kirk	Russell Procope *Bob Wilber	Rahsaan Roland Kirk
Misc. Instrument	Jean-Luc Ponty, violin *Stephane Grappelli, violin	Rahsaan Roland Kirk, manzello, strich	Rahsaan Roland Kirk, manzello & strich *Russ Whitman, bass saxophone	Rahsaan Roland Kirk, manzello & strich
Flute	James Moody *Norris Turney	Herbie Mann	James Moody *Norris Turney	Hubert Laws
Vibes	Milt Jackson *Dave Pike	Gary Burton	Bobby Hutcherson *Roy Ayres, Karl Berger (tie)	Gary Burton
Piano	Earl Hines *Stanley Cowell	Herbie Hancock	Earl Hines *Jaki Byard, Tommy Flanagan (tie)	Herbie Hancock
Organ	Jimmy Smith *Lou Bennett	Jimmy Smith	Jimmy Smith *Eddy Louiss	Jimmy Smith
Guitar	Kenny Burrell *Sonny Sharrock	Kenny Burrell	Kenny Burrell *Dennis Budimir	Kenny Burrell
Bass	Richard Davis *Miroslav Vitous	Richard Davis	Richard Davis *Miroslav Vitous	Richard Davis
Drums	Elvin Jones *Jack DeJohnette	Buddy Rich	Elvin Jones *Gus Johnson	Buddy Rich
Violin			Jean-Luc Ponty *Michael White	Jean-Luc Ponty
Male Singer	Louis Armstrong *Leon Thomas	Leon Thomas	Louis Armstrong *Richard Boone	Leon Thomas
Female Singer	Ella Fitzgerald *Jeanne Lee	Ella Fitzgerald	Ella Fitzgerald *Betty Carter	Roberta Flack

*Talent deserving of wider recognition

	Down Beat Critics' Poll 1970	Down Beat Readers' Poll 1970	Down Beat Critics' Poll 1971	Down Beat Readers' Poll 1971
Blues/R&B Group	B. B. King *Ike & Tina Turner	†Blood, Sweat & Tears	B. B. King *Soft Machine	†Blood, Sweat & Tears
Pop Musician of the Year		Frank Zappa		Frank Zappa
Pop Album of the Year		*Blood, Sweat & Tears*		*Chase*

	Down Beat Critics' Poll 1972	Down Beat Readers' Poll 1972	Down Beat Critics' Poll 1973	Down Beat Readers' Poll 1973
Record of the Year	*The You And Me That Used To Be* - RCA Jimmy Rushing	*Inner Mounting Flame* - Col. Mahavishnu Orchestra	*Sahara* - Milestone McCoy Tyner	*Birds of Fire* - Col. Mahavishnu Orchestra
Reissue of the Year	*Genius of Louis Armstrong, Vol. 1* - Col.		*God Is In The House* - Onyx Art Tatum	
Jazzman of the Year		Ornette Coleman		Chick Corea
Hall of Fame	Clifford Brown	Gene Krupa	Fletcher Henderson	Sonny Rollins
Band	Duke Ellington *Sun Ra	Thad Jones/Mel Lewis	Duke Ellington *Gil Evans	Thad Jones/Mel Lewis
Combo	World's Greatest Jazz Band *JPJ Quartet	Weather Report	Mahavishnu Orchestra *Art Ensemble of Chicago	Weather Report
Composer	Duke Ellington *Carla Bley	Duke Ellington	Duke Ellington *Chick Corea	Chick Corea
Arranger	Duke Ellington *Alan Broadbent	Quincy Jones	Duke Ellington *Sy Oliver	Quincy Jones
Trumpet	Dizzy Gillespie *Lester Bowie	Miles Davis	Dizzy Gillespie *Bill Hardman	Freddie Hubbard
Trombone	Vic Dickenson *Bill Watrous	J. J. Johnson	Vic Dickenson *Dicky Wells	J. J. Johnson
Alto Saxophone	Ornette Coleman *Gary Bartz	Ornette Coleman	Ornette Coleman *Anthony Braxton	Ornette Coleman
Soprano Saxophone	Wayne Shorter *Joseph Jarman	Wayne Shorter	Wayne Shorter *Kenny Davern	Wayne Shorter
Tenor Saxophone	Sonny Rollins *Gato Barbieri	Sonny Rollins	Sonny Rollins *John Klemmer	Sonny Rollins

*Talent deserving of wider recognition
†Name changed in Readers' Poll to Rock/Pop/Blues Group

	Down Beat Critics' Poll 1972	*Down Beat Readers' Poll* 1972	*Down Beat Critics' Poll* 1973	*Down Beat Readers' Poll* 1973
Baritone Saxophone	Harry Carney *Ronnie Cuber	Gerry Mulligan	Harry Carney *Howard Johnson	Gerry Mulligan
Clarinet	Russell Procope *Bob Wilber	Rahsaan Roland Kirk	Russell Procope *Bobby Jones	Benny Goodman
Misc. Instrument	Rahsaan Roland Kirk manzello & strich *Airto Moreira, percussion	Rahsaan Roland Kirk, manzello & strich	Rahsaan Roland Kirk, manzello & strich *Howard Johnson, tuba	Rahsaan Roland Kirk, manzello, strich
Flute	James Moody *Norris Turney	Hubert Laws	James Moody *Jeremy Steig	Hubert Laws
Vibes	Gary Burton *Roy Ayers	Gary Burton	Milt Jackson *David Friedman	Gary Burton
Piano	Earl Hines *Randy Weston	Oscar Peterson	Earl Hines *Jan Hammer	Chick Corea
Organ	Jimmy Smith *Eddy Louiss	Jimmy Smith	Jimmy Smith *Eddy Louiss	Jimmy Smith
Guitar	Kenny Burrell *Tiny Grimes, Pat Martino (tie)	John McLaughlin	Kenny Burrell *George Benson, Attila Zoller (tie)	John McLaughlin
Bass	Richard Davis *Dave Holland	Richard Davis	Richard Davis *Stanley Clarke	Ron Carter
Drums	Elvin Jones *Harold Jones	Buddy Rich	Elvin Jones *Oliver Jackson	Billy Cobham
Violin	Jean-Luc Ponty *Mike White	Jean-Luc Ponty	Jean-Luc Ponty *Mike White	Jean-Luc Ponty
Male Singer	Jimmy Rushing *Richard Boone	Leon Thomas	Ray Charles *Joe Lee Wilson	Leon Thomas
Female Singer	Ella Fitzgerald *Dee Dee Bridgewater, Asha Puthli (tie)	Roberta Flack	Sarah Vaughan *Anita O'Day	Roberta Flack
Blues/R&B Group	B. B. King *Mahavishnu Orchestra	†Mahavishnu Orchestra	B. B. King *War	†Mahavishnu Orchestra
Pop Musician of the Year		Frank Zappa		Stevie Wonder
Pop Album of the Year		*Inner Mounting Flame* Mahavishnu Orchestra		*Birds of Fire* Mahavishnu Orchestra

*Talent deserving of wider recognition
†Name changed in Readers' Poll to Rock/Pop/Blues Group

	Down Beat Critics' Poll 1974	*Down Beat Readers' Poll* 1974	*Down Beat Critics' Poll* 1975	*Down Beat Readers' Poll* 1975
Record of the Year	*Solo Concerts* - ECM/Poly. Keith Jarrett	*Mysterious Traveller* - Col. Weather Report	*Silent Tongues* - Arista/ Freedom Cecil Taylor	*Tale Spinning* - Columbia Weather Report
Reissue of the year	*Monk/Trane* - Milestone Thelonious Monk/John Coltrane		1. *First Recordings* - Onyx Charlie Parker (tie with) 2. *Solo Masterpieces* - Pablo Art Tatum	
Jazzman of the Year		Herbie Hancock		McCoy Tyner
Hall of Fame	Ben Webster	Buddy Rich	Cecil Taylor	Cannonball Adderley
Band	Thad Jones/Mel Lewis *Gil Evans	Thad Jones/Mel Lewis	Thad Jones/Mel Lewis *Clark Terry	Thad Jones/Mel Lewis
Combo	McCoy Tyner *Ruby Braff-George Barnes Quartet	Weather Report	McCoy Tyner *Oregon	Weather Report
Composer	Duke Ellington *McCoy Tyner	Chick Corea	Keith Jarrett *Randy Weston	Chick Corea
Arranger	Gil Evans *Bill Stapleton	Gil Evans	Gil Evans *Michael Gibbs	Gil Evans
Trumpet	Dizzy Gillespie *Jon Faddis	Freddie Hubbard	Dizzy Gillespie *Jon Faddis	Miles Davis
Trombone	Vic Dickenson *Garnett Brown	Garnett Brown	Roswell Rudd *Bruce Fowler	Bill Watrous
Alto Saxophone	Ornette Coleman *Anthony Braxton	Ornette Coleman	Phil Woods *Sonny Fortune	Phil Woods
Soprano Saxophone	Wayne Shorter *Gerry Niewood	Wayne Shorter	Wayne Shorter *Gerry Niewood	Wayne Shorter
Tenor Saxophone	Sonny Rollins *Billy Harper	Sonny Rollins	Sonny Rollins *Billy Harper	Sonny Rollins
Baritone Saxophone	Gerry Mulligan *Howard Johnson	Gerry Mulligan	Gerry Mulligan *John Surman, Pat Patrick (tie)	Gerry Mulligan
Clarinet	Rahsaan Roland Kirk *Kalaparusha Ara Difda	Rahsaan Roland Kirk	Rahsaan Roland Kirk *Perry Robinson	Rahsaan Roland Kirk
Misc. Instrument	Rahsaan Roland Kirk, manzello & strich *Howard Johnson, tuba	Rahsaan Roland Kirk, manzello & strich	Rahsaan Roland Kirk, manzello & strich *Howard Johnson, tuba	Rahsaan Roland Kirk, manzello & strich
Flute	James Moody *Jeremy Steig	Hubert Laws	Hubert Laws *Sam Rivers	Hubert Laws

	Down Beat Critics' Poll 1974	*Down Beat Readers' Poll* 1974	*Down Beat Critics' Poll* 1975	*Down Beat Readers' Poll* 1975
Vibes	Gary Burton	Gary Burton *Karl Berger	Gary Burton *Karl Berger, Dave Friedman (tie)	Gary Burton
Piano	McCoy Tyner	Keith Jarrett, McCoy Tyner (tie) *Muhal Richard Abrams	Keith Jarrett *Dollar Brand	McCoy Tyner
Electric Piano				Chick Corea
Organ	Jimmy Smith *Clare Fischer, Eddy Louiss (tie)	Jimmy Smith	Jimmy Smith *Sun Ra	Jimmy Smith
Guitar	Jim Hall *Ralph Towner	John McLaughlin	Joe Pass *John Abercrombie	Joe Pass
Violin	Jean-Luc Ponty *Leroy Jenkins	Jean-Luc Ponty	Jean-Luc Ponty *Michal Urbaniak	Jean-Luc Ponty
Acoustic Bass	Richard Davis *Stanley Clarke	Ron Carter	Ron Carter *George Mraz	Ron Carter
Electric Bass	Stanley Clarke *Stanley Clarke	Stanley Clarke	Stanley Clarke *Steve Swallow	Stanley Clarke
Drums	Elvin Jones *Billy Hart	Billy Cobham	Elvin Jones *Billy Higgins	Billy Cobham
Synthesizer	Jan Hammer, Paul Bley (tie) *Mike Mandel	Herbie Hancock	Sun Ra *George Duke	Herbie Hancock
Percussion	Airto *Dom Um Romao	Airto	Airto Moreira *Sue Evans	Airto
Male Singer	Joe Williams *Roy Eldridge, Stevie Wonder (tie)	Stevie Wonder	Joe Williams *Eddie Jefferson	Stevie Wonder
Female Singer	Ella Fitzgerald *Flora Purim	Flora Purim	Sarah Vaughan *Dee Dee Bridgewater	Flora Purim
Blues/R&B Group	B. B. King *Jimmy Dawkins	†Frank Zappa and the Mothers of Invention	†B. B. King *Blackbyrds, Otis Rush (tie)	Earth-Wind-Fire
Vocal Group	Pointer Sisters *Pointer Sisters	Pointer Sisters	Jackie & Roy *Jackie & Roy	Pointer Sisters
Pop Musician of the Year		Stevie Wonder		Stevie Wonder
Pop Album of the Year		*Fulfillingness'* First Finale - Tamla		*Blow by Blow* - Epic Jeff Beck

*Talent deserving of wider recognition
†Name changed in Readers' Poll to Rock/Pop/Blues Group

Swing Journal Poll

During the decade from 1965-75 the Japanese jazz community emerged as the most important in the world, after that of the United States, in terms of the per capita interest in the music, the variety of idioms appealing to the Japanese public, and the quantity and quality of work opportunities for visiting American musicians.

The importance of Japan on the world scene, and the constantly evolving nature of interest at the fan level, is reflected in the annual polls conducted by *Swing Journal.* This Tokyo-based publication, published monthly, often runs to 350 or 400 pages, elaborately produced and with many full pages photographs in color and black and white, as well as many in depth interviews and record reviews.

The following tabulation shows the results of the *Swing Journal* readers' poll from the first, in 1960, through the 1975 poll.

Note: A dash means that this category had not yet been established. Ditto indicates that the winner was the same as the previous year.

Year	Jazz Man of Year	Hall of Fame	Record of The Year	Big Band	Combo	Trumpet	Trombone	Soprano	Alto	Tenor	Baritone	Clarinet
'60	————	——	————	C. Basie	MJQ	M. Davis	J.J. Johnson	——	C. Adderley	S. Rollins	G. Mulligan	B. DeFranco
'61	————	——	————	"	"	"	"	——	"	J. Coltrane	"	J. Giuffre
'62	————	——	————	"	M. Davis	"	"	——	"	S. Rollins	"	"
'63	————	——	————	"	"	"	"	——	"	"	"	"
'64	————	——	————	D. Ellington	O. Peterson	"	"	——	"	J. Coltrane	"	"
'65	————	——	————	"	Jazz Messengers	"	"	——	"	"	"	"
'66	J. Coltrane	——	A Love Supreme/ J. Coltrane	"	M. Davis	"	"	——	"	"	"	"
'67	O. Coleman	——	Alfie/S. Rollins	"	"	"	"	——	O. Coleman	"	"	B. DeFranco
'68	C. Lloyd	——	Miles in Berlin	"	"	"	"	——	"	S. Rollins	"	P.W. Russell
'69	M. Davis	——	Filles De Kilimanjaro/Miles Davis	"	"	"	"	——	"	"	"	B. DeFranco
'70	"	——	Bitches Brew/ Miles Davis	"	"	"	"	——	"	"	"	"
'71	"	——	Left Alone/ Mal Waldron	"	"	"	"	——	"	"	"	"
'72	C. Corea	——	Chick Corea Solo vol. 1	"	Weather Report	"	"	——	"	"	"	B. Goodman
'73	M. Davis	——	Miles Davis in Concert	Q. Jones	M. Davis	"	"	W. Shorter	P. Woods	"	"	"
'74	M. Tyner	——	Headhunters/ H. Hancock	Thad-Mel Orch.	M. Tyner	"	"	"	S. Stitt	"	"	"
'75	M. Davis	C. Parker	Death & The Flower/K. Jarrett	"	"	"	"	"	"	"	"	"

Flute	Piano	Organ	Vibes	Guitar	Bass	Drums	Misc. Instrument	Male Singer	Female Singer	Vocal Group	Composer, Arranger
B. Shank	T. Monk	——	M. Jackson	B. Kessel	P. Chambers	M. Roach	M. Davis	F. Sinatra	C. Connor	LH&R	B. Golson
H. Mann	"	——	"	W. Mont-gomery	"	"	"	"	E. Fitzgerald	"	"
E Dolphy	"	——	"	"	"	"	J. Coltrane	"	"	"	G. Evans
H. Mann	"	——	"	"	R. Brown	A. Blakey	"	R. Charles	"	"	"
"	O. Peterson	——	"	"	"	M. Roach	"	"	"	Four Freshmen	D. Ellington
"	"	——	"	"	C. Mingus	"	"	"	"	"	"
"	"	J. Smith	"	"	R. Brown	E. Jones	"	M. Torme	"	"	"
"	B. Evans	"	"	"	"	"	"	"	"	Swingle Singers	"
C.Lloyd	"	"	"	"	R. Carter	M. Roach	R. Shankar	R. Charles	"	"	"
H. Mann	"	"	G. Burton	K. Burrell	"	E. Jones	O. Coleman	"	N. Wilson	Sound of Feeling	"
"	"	"	M. Jackson	"	"	"	"	"	"	Swingle Singers	"
"	"	"	"	"	R. Davis	"	"	"	"	"	"
H. Laws	C. Corea	"	"	"	M. Vitous	"	W. Shorter	M. Torme	"	"	G. Evans
"	M. Tyner	"	"	J. McLaughlin	S. Clarke	"	A. Moreira	J. Hartman	E. Fitzgerald	"	Q. Jones
"	"	"	G. Burton	K. Burrell	R. Carter	"	"	F. Sinatra	"	Pointer Sisters	G. Evans
"	K. Jarrett	"	M. Jackson	J. Pass	"	"	Mtume	"	"	"	"

Jazz education by Charles Suber

"Jazz Education"—the term implies estrangement from traditional and established "Music Education." The implication is historically accurate.

For all of its considerable current academic status, Jazz Education is not yet considered—by those who determine such matters—an essential part of the musical training *required* by teachers and student musicians. This determination is reflected in the widespread use—in school curricula and echoed by mass media—of such elitist characterizations of European music as "serious" or "good" or "classical" music. Jazz and blues—synonomous terms in the context of this essay—are too often characterized by educational pejorative expressions, such as "popular" or "commercial" or "youth" music.

Jazz Education seems to be, like jazz, a shade too popular, a shade too dark and common to warrant complete integration into the Music Education club.

Then, why—in the face of the schools' unofficial policy of benign neglect—does Jazz Education continue to flourish in isolation? The reasons become clearer as one understands how jazz musicians have learned and developed their art—and their profession—in the past 50 years.

Jazz Education in the Twenties

Take as an arbitrary starting time the twenties and the widening distribution of recorded jazz. Recordings were the first jazz textbooks. Early recordings, regardless of their sound quality, enabled a musician to listen—and thereby study and emulate—another musician's non-written music. Recordings helped to establish the first recognizable elements of a jazz style to which the eager-to-learn musician could add his own individuality.

There were no schools in which a musician could learn —or even hear—jazz. But there were private legit teachers from whom the professional jazz musician could learn advanced instrumental techniques and how to read and write music—skills needed to be competitive in the new music business of recording the first Jazz Age.

School Music in the Twenties

There was a sharp escalation in the number of high school concert and marching bands throughout the U.S. after World War I. The rapid growth of the new school instrumental music was principally motivated by non-academic considerations: larger, consolidated schools fostered by better roads and auto transportation; increased popularity of inter-scholastic football competition; the need to replace music in the community disrupted by WWI—and the availability of professional musicians capable of developing and conducting school bands.

These professional musicians were well schooled players (but not degreed graduates of college music departments) who had been employed in the community bands-in-the-park so popular prior to WWI. Many of these musicians served in military bands during the war and returned to their communities to find a changed professional music market.

People listened to music at home on their new radios and Victrolas. Or they could go out in their new cars and travel on new roads to be entertained at the new Movie Palace. Or they could dance the new steps at the new ballroom or live it up at the new Roadhouse outside of town featuring prohibited gin and wicked jazz.

So, the professional bandsman did what he knew best; he organized and conducted the new school band, gave private lessons to students recommended by the local instrument dealer, and gave band clinics for a band instrument manufacturer—and adapted military band formations to between-the-half marching band shows. He used published Sousa marches and arranged orchestral repertory for student band training. Specially written symphonic school band literature started to become available by 1926-27, the apogee years for regional and national school band contests. The school band director had a lot of music going on, but he was not yet considered a bona fide Music Educator by the traditional orchestra and voice faculty.

Jazz Education in the Thirties

New musical and commercial challenges faced professional musicians in the thirties. Elements of jazz and blues were being incorporated into the popular swing/dance bands and the scores of Broadway and movie musicals. Something new called "Symphonic Jazz" had appeared by the American Composers, George Gershwin and Ferde Grofe—following the lead of European composers such as Ravel, Milhaud, and Stravinsky.

The beginnings of a "studio musician" standard of performance emerged as radio stations hired staff orchestras, the members of which had to be expert in all idioms. (In 1938, for example, Toscanini thought it necessary to hire several brass players with jazz capabilities in the newly formed N.B.C. Symphony.)

(Radio sponsored music was a mixed blessing to the economic well being of the professional musician. "Live" musicians found themselves competing with recordings played on radio without royalty payments to the musicians. The thousands of territory and name bands musicians who played on "remote" broadcasts from hotels and ballrooms were paid little or nothing for their performance.)

Obviously, the ambitious professional musician had to learn new skills to compete in the new job market. The "hot" jazz musician had to learn legit techniques; the legit player had to learn jazz techniques. But just playing was not enough. The most important element of the big swing and dance bands was the arranger. The real big money was in composing music—and holding the copyrights!

Where could these professional musicians learn their trade? There still weren't any schools offering anything like jazz education even though a considerable number of leaders and arrangers did come out of college with a good legit musical education and plenty of campus dance band experience.

(Fletcher and Horace Henderson came out of Wilberforce; Jimmie Lunceford from Fisk, and Erskine Hawkins from 'Bama State. Fred Waring was a Pennsylvanian, and Glen Gray and several Casa Lomans came from Illinois Wesleyan. Johnny Green wore Harvard Crimson, and Les Brown was a Duke Blue Devil.)

The only source of jazz education in the thirties was the private teacher. Many good teachers were available in all the major music cities such as New York, Boston, Philadelphia, Chicago, Detroit, New Orleans, Houston, Denver, and Los Angeles.

Norbert Beihoff, a Milwaukee teacher, was one of the first to explain techniques of jazz improvisation as part of his text, *Modern Arranging and Orchestration*, published in 1935. The following year, two Chicago musicians, Carl Kelley and Russell Brooks, began to teach their system of learning improvisation based on a knowledge of chord structures, passing tones, and blue notes—transcribed from jazz recordings.

The demand by musicians to know more about the business of swing and jazz prompted the initial publication of *down beat* in Chicago in 1934. Its early success helped influence *Metronome*, a New York based magazine for concert band and orchestra musicians since 1897 to change its editorial emphasis to swing and jazz in 1935.

Almost from its first issue, *down beat* published regular columns on various components of jazz education: Arranging by Will Hudson and others; Improvisation and jazz piano stylistic analysis by Sharon Pease; Modern saxophone studies by Dave Gornston; and other instrumental columns . . . as well as transcribed solos of jazz soloists: Coleman Hawkins, Bix Beiderbecke, Harry James, Jack Teagarden, et al.

Paul Eduard Miller wrote and compiled *down beat*'s first *Yearbook of Swing* in 1938. It carried articles on improvisation, arranging and composition, and jazz styles and analysis.

Non-teaching professionals were offering insights to their jazz playing in such method booklets as: *The Gene Krupa Drum Method, Frank Trumbauer's Saxophone Studies*, and *Eddie Lang's Fingerboard Harmony for Guitar*.

While recordings continued to be an important source of study for the aspiring jazz musician, the original recorded arrangements and solo transcriptions became available. Also available were "Acompo Records" that provided "full orchestra accompaniment"—tunes like *I Got Rhythm, Limehouse Blues, Tiger Rag*, etc.—to which the student musician would play along on his own instrument.

The most important influence on professionally oriented jazz education in the thirties was Joseph Schillinger, a brilliant music theorist and teacher, who came to New York City from Russia in 1928.

Schillinger's unique concepts, later embodied in *The Schillinger System of Musical Composition* (Carl Fisher, N.Y., 1941), sharply varied from traditional Conservatory teaching methods. The Schillinger system allowed composers, for the first time, mathematically exact rules that could be used to adapt any component of music—rhythm, harmony, density, counterpoint, etc.—from any musical idiom to jazz-related composition. The system also allowed jazz players to develop their improvisations (spontaneous compositions) along certain, predetermined paths.

Commercial arrangers have said that the best thing about the Schillinger system was that the chart practically wrote itself. You found the melody line, applied the proper mathematical formula, wrote out the notes, and voilá, you met the deadline.

Some of Schillinger's best known students included George Gershwin; Oscar Levant; Benny Goodman; Paul Lavalle; Max Steiner, who paid $5000 for a set of Schillinger's personal notebooks; also Van Alexander and Glenn Miller, who both wrote arranging method books based on the Schillinger system.

Even though Schillinger did teach at several schools in New York—he was asked to leave Teachers' College, Columbia University, for being too far out—his forte was private teaching for which he charged $15 a lesson (show or not).

Schillinger's influence on professional jazz musicians didn't stop with his death in 1943. The Schillinger system as modified and evolved by his students—and coupled with the educational funding supplied by the G.I. Bill—was a major factor in jazz education in the forties and beyond.

School Music in the Thirties

The WWI "war babies" began to enter high school in large numbers in the early thirties. The first crop of college trained instrumental specialists began to enter high school teaching about the same time. High school school administrators were beginning to insist that school band directors be qualified and certificated music educators. State universities and other teacher training schools obliged by making "band" a required subject of study for music education majors.

By the end of the thirties, high school and symphonic college bands were capable of playing a sophisticated repertory. "Pep" bands, with a somewhat smaller instrumentation, would play swing music, or something akin to it, at indoor rallies and basketball games. Virtually every college campus—and many high schools—had at least one student dance band to play for school affairs not prestigous enough to warrant a name band.

Many college dance band leaders went on to the professional big time. A larger number of them played their way through college in order to pay for their education as a doctor, lawyer, engineer, or whatever. (And most of them still carry their musicians' union card.)

But while student musicians were able to swing on campus—or in high school gyms—it was all very extra-curricular. School music departments didn't recognize jazz.

Jazz Education in the Forties

World War II affected everything and everybody. Citizen soldiers, musicians among them, began to be drafted in 1940. Soon every service camp, base, and capital ship had its resident military and dance/jazz bands. (And the black Americans had theirs, and the white Americans had theirs, and the Nisei had none.) The Navy School of Music went so far as to include swing and jazz in their wartime training procedures.

In 1944, the U.S. Congress enacted a piece of legislation that was to allow hundreds of thousands of servicemen to complete and further their education after discharge: The Servicemen's Readjustment Act—the G.I. Bill of Rights.

On the home front, anybody who could lick a reed was a working musician. There wasn't much time or incentive to upgrade one's musical capabilities.

The worldwide facilities of Armed Service Radio broadcast a lot of jazz and swing via transcriptions and records. (So did Tokyo Rose.) Jazz and swing were part of the American dream for which our boys were fighting.

In 1943, Dr. Leopold Stokowski did 50 minutes on KFAC, Los Angeles, on the virtues of jazz. Stokowski said: "Jazz is a vitally important part of our folk music and folk lore. It has no traditions—no limitations—and it will go on forever developing as long as musicians give free rein to their imagination. Jazz is unique—there's never been anything like it. In this kind of music, the United States is second to none in the whole world . . . Duke Ellington is, in my opinion, one of America's outstanding artists. Ellington's music never imitates the symphony. It seems simple, but it is actually music of great subtlety. His men play as though they were creating the music at the moment by way of freedom of improvisation."

Shortly after Paris fell to the allies, Gertrude Stein was quoted at a Glenn Miller memorial concert: "Jazz is tenderness and violence." Miss Toklas had no comment.

Then rather suddenly the war was over in August, 1945. And the job hunt was on.

Most of the ex-G.I.s who elected to study privately intended to find work as professional players or writers. However, the largest number of returning musicians used the G.I. Bill to finance a college music education degree. (Example: 22-year old Mel Powell, a former pianist with Benny Goodman, came out of an army special service unit in 1945 and headed for Yale to study with Hindemith. Eventually, Powell became Dean of the School of Music, California Institute of the Arts, Valencia.)

College music departments expanded rapidly but the curricula remained pre-war traditional. By the end of the forties, ten colleges were offering jazz courses on a non-credit basis. Only five colleges offered jazz for credit: 1945—Berklee School of Music, then known as Schillinger House (2-year Professional Diploma), Lawrence Berk, director; 1945—Westlake College of Music (2-year Professional Diploma), Alvin Learned, director; 1946—Los Angeles City College (2-year Academic Diploma), Bob McDonald, director; 1947—California State Polytechnic (details not available); 1948—North Texas State College (4-year "Dance Band Major"), M.E. "Gene" Hall, director.

Documentation on high school jazz activities in the forties is sketchy but excerpts from *down beat* provide some clues.

Feb. 15, 1944—"Dr. J.T.H. Mize, head of the music department of the Rye (N.Y.) High School, edits a weekly mimeographed publication, *American Music and Jazz*, distributed to 180 high schools in the country. His book—*Let's Listen—A Thesaurus of American Music*, is a practical guide to teachers and students who want to know about jazz and other music forms. Mize has lectured on 'Jazz in the Classroom' at Yale, Penn State, College of New Rochelle, and U. of Conn."

March 11, 1946—"A recent 'Swing in School' concert by 80 Nassau High School Students was batoned by Long Beach music supervisor, Glenn E. Brown, at Town Hall [N.Y.C.]. The student concert band made a valiant effort in performing Fred Waring and Robert Shaw choral arrangements plus Will Hudson's scoring of Kenton's *Artistry Jumps.* Because the high school's principal didn't authorize this activity, the participating students had to cut classes to make the concert."

There was no shortage of private teachers and studios offering jazz-related music education. Many of the teachers were authorized Regional Representatives of the Schillinger system, such as Maury Deutsch and Rudolf Schramm, Clarence Cox in Philadelphia, and Lawrence Berk in Boston. (Of all the Schillinger alumni, Berk was the most successful in integrating a complete jazz program within a total music curriculum. In 1976, the Berklee College of Music was a fully accredited 4-year college with more than 2200 full time students.)

Not all the private jazz teaching was Schillingerized. In 1945-46, Charlie Colin's New York studio offered "Advance Dance Studies"; Phil Moore was teaching arranging and coaching the likes of Lena Horne; Walter "Foots" Thomas, former Cab Calloway saxophonist, offered a correspondence course in improvisation. Otto Cesana invited musicians to "Study Arranging" at his N.Y. studio or by correspondence.

In the second half of the forties, as paper supplies and copyists became more plentiful, a considerable amount of jazz study materials were published: Van Alexander's *First Arrangement; 30 Studies in Swing* by David Gornston; and "Jam at Home" rhythm records with Nick Fatool, drums, George Van Eps, guitar; Stan Wrightsman, piano; and Phil Stephens, bass . . . Frank Skinner's *New Method for Orchestra Scoring . . . Artie Shaw's Special Arrangements for Small Orchestra* distributed by the Intercollegiate Syndicate . . . *88 Keys to Fame* by Sharon Pease, "an examination of the styles of 30 jazz pianists, with bios and photos, reprinted from earlier issues of *down beat* (*down beat* was featuring Coleman Hawkins' solos: *I Cover the Waterfront, When Day is Done,* (the immortal) *Body & Soul,* etc.).

March 11, 1946: "Station WOV gives Jazz Scholarship —open to all high school and college students in the NY metropolitan area. Idea of the scholarship is to promote the serious study of jazz by young people gifted in that direction. First place prize: 14 intensive private lessons under Teddy Wilson."

May 6, 1946: "The Carver Club of U.C.L.A. presented a jazz scholarship benefit concert on behalf of improved race relations. Talent donating their services included: Herb Jeffries, emcee; Lester Young, King Cole Trio, Benny Carter, Ray Bauduc, and Red Callender.

Leonard Feather, Robert Goffin and Marshall Stearns lectured on jazz history and development in 1941 at the New School for Social Research.

Jazz Education in the Fifties

The cut off date to apply for G.I. Bill benefits was July 25, 1951, so many schools placed "Hurry, hurry!" ads: Roy Knapp advertised his Chicago School of Percussion as "the oldest yet most modern school of music in America—all instruments—study vibes and improvisation with Margie Hyams" . . . New York's Hartnett Music Studios offered Schillinger system lessons with Sam Donahue and Bobby Byrne on the faculty . . . Rudolf Schramm offered a special 15 week Schillinger system course at New York University . . . Westlake College of Music (Hollywood) advised that "students, including veterans, are trained for professional job demands rather than public school positions."

The first jazz-in-the-summer seminars were begun in 1950 by Marshall Stearns at the Music Inn, Lenox, Mass. ("next door to Tanglewood"). The 1951 session included author-critic, Rudi Blesh; Juilliard piano and improvisation instructor, John Mehegan; ragtime musician and composer, Eubie Blake; and American theater composers, Marc Blitzstein and Leonard Bernstein. Quote of the week: ". . . to keep your musical arteries from hardening, do not label your favorite period as the only true jazz."

About 30 more colleges added jazz courses, on a noncredit basis, during the fifties. About 17 more colleges added jazz courses for credit bringing the national total to about 21. The colleges were not yet responding to the growing demand by high school administrators for new music educators to have stage band experience.

The stage band movement in high school was accelerating in a pattern quite similar to the rapid growth of school concert bands after WWI. The G.I. Bill music education majors were now out teaching in high schools. And like the ex-World War I bandsmen, the WWII veteran did what he knew best. He conducted the required marching and concert bands, but also organized a stage band (a euphemism coined in the Baptist southwest to avoid the sinful aspects of dancing and jazzing) to play *his* music.

This new breed of high school band director knew the advantages of jazz or swing music: greater motivation on the part of the player, increased technical facility in another idiom, increased responsibility for one's part; and more opportunity for individual creativity. The school stage band director did have a major personal advantage over the concert band director. The younger man (and some women) could continue to play on weekends and thereby keep *au courant* with professional standards of performance.

At first, he had difficulty getting arrangements suitable for school swing bands. So he used his professional experience to arrange published stocks. The first charts specially written for school stage bands were published and arranged by Art Dedrick, Kendor Music, Delevan, N.Y. Dedrick published the first set of four tunes in 1954: *Little Brown Jug*; *Tuxedo Junction*; *Brown Jump*; and *The Preacher*. In 1955, Dedrick arranged, under a license from Mills Music, school stage band charts of Ellington's *Mood Indigo*; and *Sophisticated Lady*. In 1956, Sammy Nestico, arranger for the Airmen of Note (the official stage band of the U.S. Air Force) began his long association with Kendor, writing mostly Basie-type arrangements.

Dedrick never did study directly with Schillinger (said he couldn't afford the lessons) but he did use Schillinger's book as a basis for his own writing. Art Dedrick's brother, Rusty, and many other New York players and writers studied with a Tom Timothy who had developed a successful modification of the Schillinger system in the late forties.

Other professional arrangers turning out school stage band material during the late fifties included Marshall Brown (his Farmingdale High School Stage Band wowed them at the Newport Jazz Festival in 1957); Neal Hefti with deceptively simple Basie arrangements of *Li'l Darlin'*; *Sunday A.M.*; *Cute*; and *The Kid From Red Bank*; Clem DeRosa, a professional drummer who had organized elementary and junior high school students into stage bands; John LaPorta, a former arranger and reed player with Woody Herman; and Ralph Mutchler, whose Northwestern University Jazz Band won first place in the first Notre Dame Intercollegiate Jazz Festival in 1959.

Accompanying the rapid proliferation of high school stage bands were regional high school stage band festivals. (See section on School Jazz Festivals at the end of this chapter.)

Another indication of the interest in school type jazz, was the beginning of the National Stage Band Camps by Ken Morris in 1959 on the campus of Indiana University.

On the faculty of that first stage band camp were many of the pioneer jazz clinicians who were to bring their professional standards to schools throughout the U.S. The faculty included: Stan Kenton, rehearsal techniques; Russ Garcia, arranging; Shelly Manne, drums; Laurindo Almeida, guitar; Don Jacoby, trumpet; Eddie Safranski, bass; Ray Santisi, piano; Matt Betton, theory and pedagogy; and Gene Hall, director and author of curriculum.

Jazz Education in the Sixties

The jazz education activity that began after WWII and quickened in the fifties, emerged in the sixties as a strong force in school music.

In 1960, there were about 5000 high schools in the U.S. with at least one organized "stage band" under the direction of a school music specialist. Most of these bands were not part of the formal school music curriculum but were usually considered a "reward" activity in which students from the concert band or orchestra could participate on the basis of demonstrated deportment, interest, and ability. These stage bands, however, did not admit additional students into school music—a fact that was to become a latent problem of the seventies.

By the end of the sixties, the number of high school stage bands—by then more often called "jazz" bands—doubled to about 10,000. (Actually, there were about 8500 junior and senior high schools with jazz related bands with the more experienced educators organizing two or more ensembles.)

In 1960, there were about 40 colleges offering jazz-related courses; half of these colleges allowed academic credits for jazz courses or ensembles. By the end of the sixties, there were 165 colleges with non-credit jazz courses; 135 gave academic credits.

In 1960, there were about a dozen school stage band (or jazz) festivals; about 75 in 1969. During this ten year period, several regional college jazz festivals were established; Villanova U. (Pa.); Mobile, Ala.; California State U.-Northridge; Elmhurst College (Ill.); Quinnipiac College (Conn.) and U. of Utah—all based on the format of the original Notre Dame festival.

The first national college jazz festival—with participating groups chosen from regional competitions—was in Miami Beach in 1967, sponsored by a beer company, an airline, and a shirt manufacturer. The beer company moved the national event to St. Louis in 1968 and 1969 when it disintegrated because of "conflicting commercial considerations." (The advertising agency wanted rock vocals.)

The first formal jazz seminar sponsored by the Music Educators National Conference was held at its biennial convention in Atlantic City in 1960. (Dave Brubeck, George Wein, and Rev. Norman O'Connor did an informal jazz session at the 1958 M.E.N.C. biennial in St. Louis.) The 1960 seminar starred Billy Taylor—the first of his many appearances as a jazz clinician and teacher of teachers—Hall Overton; Dr. Ralph Pace of Teachers College-Columbia U., who organized the event; Dr. Gene Hall of North Texas State U., whose article on school jazz was the first such piece published in the *Music Educators Journal*; and Charles Suber, moderator. The success of this seminar led to more jazz-related sessions at various state and national M.E.N.C. events during the sixties.

By 1968, the interest in jazz among school music educators resulted in two important events. One was the establishment of the National Association of Jazz Educators (NAJE), chartered as an auxiliary organization of the M.E.N.C. (It became more autonomous in 1973.) The other event was the M.E.N.C. symposium on "Youth Music" at Tanglewood in the summer of 1968. The symposium discussed how school music departments could become more relevant to the needs of students, and how more students could be involved in school music.

In the summer of 1969, a 4-week Youth Music Symposium was held at the U. of Wisconsin-Madison, sponsored by the U.S. Office of Education, the M.E.N.C., and organized by Emmett Sariz, director of the U.W.-Extension Music Dept. This symposium attracted a good deal of attention because of its conclusions: students wanted to create their own music using the expertise of their teachers; youth oriented instruments such as guitar had a place in school music; and that rock and jazz offered more students an opportunity to participate in school music. (Many educators attending the symposium were anxious to embrace rock without knowing anything about its musical roots.)

The sixties saw the evolution of a grade school-college-grade school spiral of jazz education.

A "war baby" born in 1942 arrived in high school during the mid-fifties where he or she had the opportunity to learn stage band music from an ex-professional swing band musician educated by the G.I. Bill. This high school stage band musician wanted to continue with "jazz" in college whether it was offered for credit or not. Then, as was likely, the college jazz musician, majoring in music education, went into secondary school music teaching where he would use the idiom with which he was familiar. Many of these "second generation" jazz-knowledgeable educators organized jazz-type ensembles in middle and junior high schools.

The college jazz programs were a direct result of pressure from the high schools. High school stage band musicians wanted to continue their taste of jazz in college; the high school administrators wanted the new music teachers to be able to teach the music that was making such a hit with the students and their parents. However, despite the pressure—or because of it—college music departments were not giving jazz anything like parity with traditional music. Course credit for jazz study was grudgingly granted and budgets for faculty and materials were skimpy. In virtually every college with a jazz program—Berklee was an exception because of the uniqueness of its original concept—the entire teaching load fell on one person.

That one person recruited and developed the ensembles; begged, borrowed, and stole suitable arrangements, or in many successful programs wrote the book himself. In his spare time, he provided the equivalent of private lessons on instrumental techniques, the elements of improvisation, and hired the bus to take the band to a regional festival "representing the excellence of the ______ University School of Music."

The one-person jazz faculty was—and is—a well-schooled, working professional who has been conditioned to cope with the remoteness and disinterest—and sometimes, outright hostility—of "serious" musicians. The history of jazz education is the record of determined, hard-working professional musicians who were so proud of their music, and so dedicated to the education of their students, that they did whatever had to be done with whatever resources were available.

And so the success of the program at North Texas State University—the only university that offered a "jazz major" in the sixties—rested on the 18 hours-a-day efforts of Leon Breeden (professional clarinetist) who had succeeded Gene Hall (professional saxophonist). At Indiana University, the largest music school in the United States, the first, lonely jazz faculty member was Buddy Baker (professional trombonist) who later helped to establish the jazz program at U. of Northern Colorado with Derryl Goes (professional drummer). Succeeding Buddy Baker at Indiana U. was Jerry Coker (professional saxophonist and arranger), and then in 1966 the incumbent head of I.U.'s 32-hour jazz program, David Baker (professional trombonist and arranger-composer). Roger Schueler (professional trumpet player) built the jazz program at Millikin U. Evan Solat (professional arranger) represented the jazz idiom at Philadelphia Musical Academy; John Garvey (professional string player and conductor) singlehandedly brought jazz into the U. of Illinois; Bob McDonald (professional studio musician) was the jazz department at Los Angeles City College; ditto Dick Carlson at Los Angeles Valley College.

Sometimes, despite his most valiant efforts and the loyal support of his students, the college would refuse to grant jazz any official status. Such was the situation, in the sixties, when Ralph Mutchler (professional pianist and arranger) left Northwestern U. to establish an excellent program at Olympic College (Bremerton, Wash.) Ladd McIntosh (professional saxophonist and arranger-composer) was not encouraged to stay on at Ohio State U., even after his band won top honors at the 1967 national college jazz festival. Bill Dobbins (professional pianist and arranger-composer) left Kent State U. under similar circumstances.

The U.S. State Department sponsored, for several years during the sixties, tours abroad of college jazz ensembles selected at the Notre Dame festival. Two Indiana bands toured the Far East, a combo from West Virginia State College toured North Africa, the U. of Illinois jazz lab band toured Europe; and North Texas State U. toured Mexico. (Jazz bands from Northwestern U. and the U. of Denver were denied the opportunity to tour for the U.S.A. because of vetoes by their respective Deans of Music).

The situation for the average high school stage band director was somewhat different. Because he or she was usually the only instrumental instructor in the music department, there were no musical colleagues to stigmatize jazz as something unfit for the education of young people.

The high school principal's chief concern was that parents and community be pleased with the students' behaviour and musical performance. It was okay if the band director wanted to form—on his own time—something called a stage band if it didn't interfere with the required number of half-time shows, Christmas programs, spring musicals, and graduation ceremonials. Parents were so delighted with their children playing the swing music that "we used to jitterbug to" that they organized candy and cake sales to buy the band director whatever it took to field a winning, swinging band. And—a very important consideration for the support of musical instrument companies—parents were glad to buy a new, professional-type instrument for their professional-type sons and daughters. What had been suitable for eighth clarinet in the concert band was obviously not the kind of instrument a professional needed to play in the front line of a jazz band.

This new market for professional instruments motivated the instrument manufacturers, and their dealers, to co-sponsor school jazz festivals, award scholarships to the National Stage Band Camps, and offer the "clinic" services of professional musicians wherever requested.

Some of the most widely traveled professional jazz "clinicians" in the sixties (and into the seventies) were: trumpets—Dizzy Gillespie, Bobby Herriot, Don Jacoby, Herb Pomeroy, Doc Severinsen, Marv Stamm, and Clark Terry; trombone—Buddy Baker, David Baker, Urbie Green, Frank Rosolino, and Phil Wilson; reeds—Cannonball Adderley, Jerry Coker, Buddy DeFranco, Sam Donahue, Paul Horn, John LaPorta and Charlie Mariano; guitar—Jack Peterson, Howie Roberts, Sal Salvador, and Johnny Smith; piano—Dan Haerle, Marian McPartland, Ray Santisi, and Billy Taylor; bass—Ray Brown, Carol Kaye, Mike Moore, and Eddie Safranski; drums—Louis Bellson, Roy Burns, Alan Dawson, Jack DeJohnette, Clem DeRosa, Elvin Jones, Joe Morello, Charlie Perry, and Ed Thigpen.

While most of these professionals did clinics on jazz techniques relative to their instrument, many of them also provided instruction on ensemble rehearsal techniques, the elements of improvisation, and the use of new, jazz-related materials.

There were also a number of professional leaders and arrangers who traveled the clinic circuit: Manny Albam, Don Ellis, Maynard Ferguson, Woody Herman, Quincy

Jones, Thad Jones, Stan Kenton, Chuck Mangione, Oliver Nelson, and Johnny Richards.

Obviously, the professional players were, in considerable numbers, providing assistance to the professional educators. Sometimes the professional players sought more direct involvement in jazz education. During the sixties Oscar Peterson, Ray Brown, and Ed Thigpen organized a jazz school in Toronto; Phil Woods started a summer jazz camp in New Hope, Pa.; and Stan Kenton established his own summer stage band clinics at which his band was the resident faculty.

The demand for good stage band arrangements produced, during the sixties, professional-type charts—usually with a basic instrumentation of eight brass, five saxes, and four rhythm—from arrangers such as: Manny Albam, Art and Rusty Dedrick, Gil Evans, Dick Fenno, Neal Hefti, John Lewis, Richard Maltby, Sammy Nestico, Lenny Niehaus, Glenn Osser, Pete Rugolo, Bob Seibert, and Ray Wright.

The professionals also authored the method books necessary to advance the level of jazz education. Some of the most important texts authored in the sixties by professional jazz musicians were: ensemble training—John LaPorta's monumental 22-volume *Developing the School Stage Band* (Berklee Press); instrumental techniques—*Developmental Techniques for the School Dance Band Musician* (Berklee Press) by Rev. George Wiskirchen, with the advice of many professional jazz players; *Practice with the (Trombone) Experts* (MCA) by Paul Tanner; *Clarinet LP/Workbook* (Canyon Press) by Leon Breeden; *Flute Book of the Blues* (Alnur) by Yusef Lateef; *Patterns for Saxophone* (Noslen) by Oliver Nelson; and various volumes of *Scale Studies* and *Chord Studies* by Joe Viola and other Berklee faculty members. The most influential book for young jazz drummers during the sixties was Alan Dawson's *Manual for the Modern Drummer* (Berklee Press), assisted by Don DeMicheal. And many tubas were replaced by string basses in stage band rhythm sections because of Bill Curtis' *A Modern Method for String Bass* (Berklee Press).

Most of the new jazz-related materials were published by new companies whose principals were directly involved in school jazz education: Kendor Music (Delevan, N.Y.); KSM (Dallas, Tex.); Today's Music! (Libertyville, Ill.); New Sounds in Modern Music (New York); Berklee Press (Boston); Modern Music School (Cleveland); Cimino Publications (N.Y.); Mission Music (Castro Valley, Calif.); MJQ Music (N.Y.), and Studio P/R (Lebanon, Ind.)

Jazz Education in the Seventies

Jazz education continued its rapid statistical growth into the seventies. By the school year, 1975-76, there were more than 500,000 student musicians participating in jazz-related ensembles and courses supervised by a "jazz educator."

About 60% of the 30,000 junior and senior high schools in the U.S. had an average of 1.2 stage/jazz bands. About 400 colleges were offering at least one jazz ensemble or course for credit. Several universities—Indiana, North Texas State, Wesleyan (Conn.), Eastman School of Music, Northern Colorado, Illinois, New England Conservatory of Music, Miami (Florida)—were offering postgraduate jazz programs.

The technical level of the school jazz musicians was higher than ever. Many of the college jazz bands were as polished as the professional road bands. In fact, Buddy Rich, Woody Herman, Stan Kenton, Maynard Ferguson, and Bill Watrous recruited their sidemen directly from the colleges. The transition was easy. The college musicians were playing the same charts as the recording bands—and had more time to rehearse.

Because of jazz education in the schools, these bands took on new life—working six and seven days a week doing one-niter concert/clinic stands at high schools and colleges. A typical date: Woody Herman and the members of his band would do clinics and demonstrations during the day and a concert at night at a high school for a minimum fee of $2500. The band parents and the student musicians would sell out the 1500 seat school auditorium at $3 per ticket. The net would go back into the school band fund for new instruments, arrangements, sound reinforcement equipment, trips to festivals, etc.

The arrangements played by college bands and many of the high school bands were the same as those recorded by professional jazz and jazz-rock groups. Most colleges and an increasing number of high schools had in-house student arrangers who write custom-tailored charts for their own ensembles.

Jazz educators were increasingly organized—nationally and by states—into NAJE which held its first national convention in Chicago in 1974. Every state, regional, and national music educator meeting was replete with stage band and jazz demonstrations and seminars.

Many jazz educators were gaining the seniority in their college or public school system that might insure the stability and acceptance of their jazz programs.

Universities were bestowing honorary degrees and artist-in-residencies on the likes of Duke Ellington, Benny Carter, Gerry Mulligan, Herbie Hancock, Oliver Nelson, Quincy Jones, Eubie Blake, et al.

There were about 170 school jazz festivals attracting as many as 200 ensembles at one location, including stage bands and jazz combos from elementary and middle schools.

There was an outstanding jazz improvisation program at Washington Elementary School, the lab school for University of California-Berkeley, organized by Dr. Herb Wong for grades K-thru-6. Dr. Wong was able to prove that learning improvisational skills on conventional musical instruments enabled students to improve their academic skills such as reading and mathematical concepts. Teachers who took their practice teaching at Washington Elementary School are furthering that jazz-inspired concept in California grade schools.

With all that activity in the schools, it would seem that jazz education had indeed arrived. But what had arrived where?

Were all those students learning, and performing, jazz?

Were all those schools becoming committed to accepting jazz as part of a music education? The answer to both questions was no, not really.

Take the colleges for example. In the school year, 1975-76, fewer than 20 colleges required any jazz course toward the fulfillment of a music degree. Fewer than 10 colleges required their music education majors—the future school music teachers—to have any jazz competence. Most colleges—even those with a considerable jazz emphasis—did not consider a jazz ensemble to be a "major ensemble" like the concert band or orchestra. With but few exceptions, college jazz departments employed only one full-time person responsible for teaching a variety of jazz courses to 100 or more students. (Even if college administrators wanted to add jazz educators, tight budgets and a tenured, traditionally oriented faculty made such additions very difficult.)

But regardless of college credits or problems with fearful faculty, jazz education in the schools in the seventies faced a fundamental internal challenge. This serious challenge came from the majority of jazz educators who had relatively little professional experience. These teachers whose jazz experience was almost entirely within academia were—sincerely and without malice—academicizing jazz: encompassing it within definitions, codifying its style and form, and standardizing its modes of expression.

The influence of the contemporary, professional jazz musician—so important to the history of jazz education—had been diluted in the expansion of all those stage bands and jazz programs.

Contemporary professionals were the first school jazz educators, clinicians, arrangers, and authors. Contemporary jazz musicians brought to jazz education the professional standards of their peers. The professional knew that jazz could not be defined until and unless it was no longer a living music. The professional knew which criteria distinguish jazz from other musics: improvisation—spontaneous composition; a sense of moving time—swing; and individuality of expression—making your own, personal sound.

The professional knew why jazz contests were non-productive. Harvey Phillips, the great tuba player and music educator, said it simply: "I tell each student he only has one musician to compete with the rest of his days—himself. And I try to make him understand the ethical responsibility of being a professional musician." (*The New Yorker*, Dec. 15, 1975).

It should not be assumed, however, that jazz education in the schools was dead or was even dying. Like jazz itself, jazz education has had—and will have many premature obituaries. Jazz education in the school in the seventies did have a problem. There were many indications that the problem could be relieved or solved.

Jazz educator with contemporary, professional jazz experience continued to fight for their music and their students. They set an example of teaching improvisation and arranging, organizing small jazz ensembles, and favoring large jazz bands in the Thad Jones/Mel Lewis style.

The working jazz professional did not turn his back on the students who wanted to learn to play creatively. A new crop of clinicians and campus residents included Herbie Hancock, Billy Cobham, Joe Pass, Bill Watrous, Tom Scott and Gary Burton, as well as the older, still very contemporary jazz players and arrangers.

About 40% of school jazz festivals in 1976 will be non-competitive with the likelihood that jazz ensemble contests will be a rarity by 1980.

There are colleges that—because of professionally experienced jazz musicians on the faculty—are committed to give their students all the available expertise without restricting their modes of expression. Berklee continues to grow without losing its ability to inspire. Eastman is adding faculty and quite rapidly integrating jazz within its excellent total program. Gunther Schuller—with colleagues George Russell, Phil Wilson, Jaki Byard, and Ran Blake—is revitalizing the New England Conservatory. Leon Breeden at North Texas State has demonstrated his concern about improvisation and small ensemble jazz by adding Rich Matteson to the faculty.

It's happening in the high schools too. Combo participation in (non-competitive) festivals is on the increase. Attendance at the Combo/Improvisation Clinics (first established in 1972 by the Summer Jazz Clinics) is surpassing big band camp attendance.

Clinicians specializing in improvisational techniques—such as Jamey Aebersold, David Baker, Dan Haerle, John LaPorta, Joe Henderson, Larry Ridley, Rufus Reid, Ed Soph, Dom Spera—are much in demand. And the number of method books and recordings on improvisational techniques continues to mount. In-depth, self-study texts by David Baker (*down beat* Workshop Publications); Jamey Aebersold (Aebersold Music); John LaPorta (Berklee Press); Dom Spera (Hal Leonard), and others are being purchased, and used, by thousands of students and working musicians.

Ironically, one of the factors helping jazz to become essential to school curricula is its commercial implications. The generally poor state of the economy in the mid-seventies has turned students and their parents to seek an education that is likely to provide a financial return. High schools are doing more career counseling than ever before. Two and four year colleges are rapidly adding vocational music training in an effort to compete for students in the face of declining enrollments.

The music educator most likely to motivate and organize "business of music" courses is the professional jazz musician. He knows the musical and "commercial" value of film scoring, jingle writing, copying, recording arts & sciences, retailing and marketing, publishing, copyright law, management, etc. The jazz educator's professionalism is becoming a financial asset to a school, a fact that may make more rapid "acceptance" of jazz studies.

The overriding reason jazz education—in or out of the schools—is here to stay is the demand by young musicians to create music in the jazz tradition. In general terms, young musicians are following Alvin Toffler's blueprint for the use of education to achieve individuality expressed in *Future Shock*. In specific terms, young musicians will go where they have to go to get what they want.

Most young musicians do not want to be jazz professionals. They will shop for the kind of education that suits their needs. Whatever they do with that education is a plus for themselves and music.

If young musicians want to be professional contemporary musicians—and there is no school that can offer them what they need—they will do what aspiring professionals have done before them. They will play the great records, study the solos, immerse themselves in the music, and go out and play where and whenever anyone will listen. They will seek out good, private professional teachers such as Dick Grove and his great staff of studio musicians in Los Angeles, or Karl Berger and Jack DeJohnette and their colleagues in New York, or study with a Joe Daley or a Willie Pickens in Chicago, an Ira Sullivan in Miami—there is no shortage of professional jazz musicians able and willing to pass on what they know.

Conclusion: jazz will be around as long as people need it. Jazz education will be around as long as musicians need it. Nothing has happened to make us believe that jazz and jazz education will not be around into the eighties and beyond.

Jazz education part II

ALABAMA

University of Alabama; University, AL 35486. Write: Steve Sample or Director of Jazz Studies, Music Dept.*

ARKANSAS

Arkansas State University; State University (Jonesboro), AR 72467. Write: Chairman, Music Dept.*

Henderson State College; Arkadelphia, AR 71923. Write: Dr. Joe Clark or Director of Jazz Studies, Music Dept.*

ARIZONA

University of Arizona; Tuscon, AZ 85721. Write: Thomas R. Ervin or Director of Jazz Studies, School of Music.*

Arizona State University; Tempe, AZ 85281. Write: Dr. Dan Swaim or Director of Jazz Studies, Music Dept.*

Mesa Community College (2-yr.); Mesa, AZ 85201. Write: Grant Wolf or Director of Music.

Northern Arizona University; Flagstaff, AZ 86001. Write: Director of Jazz Studies, Music Dept.*

CALIFORNIA

Cabrillo College (2-yr.); Aptos, CA 95003. Write: Director of Music.

California Institute of the Arts; Valencia, CA 91355. Write: Mel Powell or Dean, School of Music.*

University of California/Berkeley; Berkeley, CA 94720. Write: Dr. David Tucker, 53 Student Center.

University of California/Los Angeles; Los Angeles, CA 90024. Write: Paul Tanner or Chairman, Music Dept.*

California State Polytechnic University; Pomona, CA 91768. Write: John DeFoor or Director of Jazz Studies, Music Dept.

California State University/Fresno; Fresno, CA 93705. Write: Larry Sutherland or Director of Jazz Studies, Music Dept.*

California State University/Northridge; Northridge, CA 91324. Write: Joel Leach or Chairman, Music Dept.

California State University/San Diego; LaJolla, CA 92037. Write: Director of Jazz Studies, Third College.*

California State College/Sonoma; Rohnert Park, CA 94928. Write: Gail Atkinson or Chairman, Music Dept.

Cerritos College (2-yr.); Norwalk, CA 90650. Write: Don Erjavec or Chairman, Music Dept.

Chaffey College (2-yr.); Alta Loma, CA 91701. Write: Chairman, Music Dept.

Cuesta Community College (2-yr.); San Luis Obispo, CA 93430. Write: Warren H. Balfour or Director of Music.

DeAnza College (2-yr.); Cupertino, CA 95014. Write: Dr. Herb Patnoe or Chairman, Music Dept.

Diablo Valley College (2-yr.); Pleasant Hill, CA 94523. Write: Chris Nelson or Chairman, Music Dept.

East Los Angeles College (2-yr.); Los Angeles, CA 90022. Write: Walter E. Carr or Director of Music.

Foothill College (2-yr.); Los Altos Hills, CA 94022. Write: John Mortarotti, Fine Arts Chairman.

Gavilan Community College (2-yr.); Gilroy, CA 95020. Write: Ronald G. Ward or Chairman, Music Dept.

Long Beach City College (2-yr.); Long Beach, CA 90808. Write: Ron Logan or Director of Music.

Los Angeles City College (2-yr.); Los Angeles, CA 90029. Write: Bob McDonald, Music Dept., 855 N. Vermont Ave.

Los Angeles Valley College (2-yr.); Van Nuys, CA 91401. Write: Richard Carlson or Director of Music, 5800 Fulton Ave.

Monterey Peninsula College (2-yr.); Monterey, CA 93940. Write: Don Schamber or Director of Music, 980 Fremont Ave.

Orange Coast College (2-yr.); Costa Mesa, CA 92626. Write: Dr. Charles Rutherford, Music Dept., 2701 Fairview Ave.

University of the Pacific; Stockton, CA 95204. Write: David Goedecke or Director of Bands.

College of the Redwoods (2-yr.); Eureka, CA 95501. Write: Jack Wheaton or Chairman, Music Dept.

Sacramento City College (2-yr.); Sacramento, CA 95822. Write: Forrest R. Van Ripen or Director of Music, 3835 Freeport Blvd.

San Bernadino Valley College (2-yr.); San Bernadino, CA 92903. Write: Paul Oxley or Director of Music, 701 S. Mt. Vernon Ave.

San Diego State University; San Diego, CA 92182. Write:

Dr. Eddie S. Meadows, or Chairman, Department of Music & Afro-American Studies.

San Jose State University; San Jose, CA 95192. Write: Dwight Cannon or Director of Jazz Studies, Music Dept.

Santa Monica College (2-yr.); Santa Monica, CA 90405. Write: James B. Fugle or Director of Music, 1815 Pearl St.

College of the Siskiyous (2-yr.); Weed, CA 96099. Write: Jerry Edwards or Dean of Students.

Southwestern College (2-yr.); Chula Vista, CA 92010. Write: Jim Merrill or Chairman, Performing Arts, 900 Otay Lakes Road.

COLORADO

University of Colorado; Boulder, CO 80302. Write: Jack Foote or Director of Jazz Studies, School of Music.*

University of Colorado at Denver; Denver, CO 80202. Write: Dean, College of Music.

Colorado State University; Ft. Collins, CO 80521. Write: Otto Werner or Director of Bands, Music Dept.*

University of Denver; Denver, CO 80210. Write: Dr. Roger Fee or Dean, Lamont School of Music.*

Metropolitan State College; Denver, CO 80203. Write: Dr. Jerrald McCollum or Chairman, Music Dept.

University of Northern Colorado; Greeley, CO 80631. Write: Derryl Goes or Director of Jazz Studies, School of Music.*

CONNECTICUT

University of Bridgeport; Bridgeport, CT 06602. Write: Neil Slater or Director of Jazz Studies, Music Dept.*

Quinnipiac College; Hamden, CT 06518. Write: Sam Costanzo or Chairman, Fine Arts Dept.

Wesleyan University, Middletown, CT 06457. Write: Richard Winslow or Chairman, Music Dept., Center for Creative and Fine Arts.

Yale University; New Haven, CT 06520. Write: Willie Ruff or Dean, School of Music.*

DISTRICT OF COLUMBIA

Howard University; Washington, DC 20001. Write: Director of Jazz Studies, School of Music.*

FLORIDA

University of Florida; Gainesville, FL 32601. Write: James Hale or Chairman, Music Dept.*

University of Miami, Coral Gables, FL 33124. Write: Dr. William Lee or Director of Jazz Studies, School of Music.*

Miami Dade Community College/North Campus (2-yr.); Miami, FL 33167. Write: John A. Alexander or Director of Music, 11380 N.W. 27 Ave.

Palm Beach Junior College (2-yr.); Lake Worth, FL 33460. Write: Sy Pryweller or Director of Music.

GEORGIA

Columbus College; Columbus, GA 31907. Write: Paul Vander Gheynst or Chairman, Music Dept.

Fort Valley State College; Fort Valley, GA 31030. Write: George R. Holland or Chairman, Music Dept.

University of Georgia; Athens, GA 30602. Write: Roger L. Dancz or Director of Bands, Music Dept.*

Georgia State University; Atlanta, GA 30303. Write: Jim Progris or Chairman, Music Dept.*

Morehouse College; Atlanta, GA 30314. Write: Ted McDaniels or Chairman, Music Dept.

IDAHO

University of Idaho; Moscow, ID 83843. Write: Richard F. Werner or Dean, School of Music.*

Ricks College (2-yr.); Rexburg, ID 83440. Write: Noel Brown or Chairman, Music Dept.*

ILLINOIS

Chicago State University; Chicago, IL 60621. Write: Bunky Green or Chairman, Music Dept.

DePaul University; Chicago, IL 60604. Write: Dr. Leon Stein or Dean, School of Music, 25 E. Jackson Blvd.*

Eastern Illinois University; Charleston, IL 61920. Write: Dean, School of Music.*

Elmhurst College; Elmhurst, IL 60126. Write: Dr. James Sorensen or Chairman, Music Dept.

Governors State University; Park Forest South, IL 60466. Write: Dr. Warrick Carter or Coordinator, Jazz Studies, College of Cultural Studies.

Wm. Rainey Harper College (2-yr.); Palatine, IL 60067. Write: Bob Tillotson or Director of Music.

University of Illinois; Urbana, IL 61801. Write: John Garvey or Chairman, Jazz Division, School of Music.*

University of Illinois at Chicago Circle; Chicago, IL 60680. Write: Chairman, Music Dept.

Illinois State University; Normal, IL 61781. Write: Chairman, Music Dept.*

Illinois Wesleyan University; Bloomington, IL 61701. Write: Dr. Thomas Streeter or Dean, School of Music.*

Joliet Junior College (2-yr.); Joliet, IL 60435. Write: Director of Music.

Kaskaskia College (2-yr.); Centralia, IL 62801. Write: Director of Music.

Kennedy-King College (2-yr.); Chicago, IL 60623. Write: Director of Bands, Music Dept.

College of Lake County (2-yr.); Grays Lake, IL 60030. Write: Chuck Banks or Director of Music, 19351 W. Washington St.

Millikin University; Decatur, IL 62522. Write: Roger Schueler or Dean, School of Music.*

North Central College; Naperville, IL 60540. Write: Robert Rollin or Chairman, Music Dept.*

North Park College; Chicago, IL 60625. Write: Dr. Lee Burswold or Chairman, Music Dept.*

Northern Illinois University; DeKalb, IL 60178. Write: Ron Modell or Chairman, Music Dept.

Northwestern University; Evanston, IL 60201. Write: Director of Jazz Studies, School of Music.*

Quincy College; Quincy, IL 62301. Write: Charles Winking or Chairman, Music Dept.*

Southern Illinois University; Edwardsville, IL 62025.

Write: Dr. William Tarwater or Dean, School of Music.*
Thornton Community College (2-yr.); South Holland, IL 60473. Write: Donald F. Kramer or Director of Music.
Triton College (2-yr.); River Grove, IL 60171. Write: Burrell Gluskin or Director of Instrumental Music, 2000 Fifth Ave.
Waubonsee Community College (2-yr.); Sugar Grove, IL 60554. Write: Duane Wickiser or Director of Music, Rte. 47 and Harter Road.
Western Illinois University; Macomb, IL 61455. Write: Robert Morsch or Director of Bands, Music Dept.*
Wilbur Wright College (2-yr.); Chicago, IL 60634. Write: John DeRoule or Director of Adult Education.

INDIANA

Ball State University; Muncie, IN 47305. Write: Larry N. McWilliams or Director of Jazz Studies, School of Music.*
Butler University; Indianapolis, IN 46208. Write: Robert Grechesky or Dean, Jordan College of Music.*
University of Evansville; Evansville, IN 47702. Write: Edwin Lacy or Chairman, Music Dept.*
Indiana University; Bloomington, IN 47401. Write: David Baker or Director of Jazz Studies, School of Music.*
Indiana University Southeast; Jeffersonville, IN 47130. Write: Jamey Aebersold or Chairman, Music Dept.
Indiana State University; Terre Haute, IN 47809. Write: John P. Spicknall or Chairman, Music Dept.*
University of Notre Dame; Notre Dame, IN 46556. Write: George Wiskirchen, C.S.C., or Director of Bands.
Purdue University; Lafayette, IN 47907. Write: Roger Heath or Director of Bands.
Saint Francis College; Ft. Wayne, IN 46808. Write: Richard D. Brown or Chairman, Music Dept.

IOWA

Coe College; Cedar Rapids, IA 52402. Write: Jerry Owen or Chairman, Music Dept.
Cornell College; Mt. Vernon, IA 52314. Write: Dr. Jesse G. Evans or Chairman, Music Dept.*
Grinnell College; Grinnell, IA 50112. Write: Cecil Lytle or Chairman, Music Dept.
University of Iowa; Iowa City, IA 52242. Write: Morgan Jones or Director of Jazz Bands, School of Music.*
Iowa Central Community College (2-yr.); Ft. Dodge, IA 50501. Write: Thomas R. Kruse or Director of Music.
Morningside College; Sioux City, IA 51106. Write: Gary Slechta or Chairman, Music Dept.*
North Iowa Area Community College (2-yr.); Mason City, IA 50401. Write: Henry T. Paine or Director of Instrumental Music, 400 College Drive.
University of Northern Iowa; Cedar Falls, IA. Write: Chairman, Music Dept.*
Westmar College, LeMars, IA 51031. Write: Gerald B. Olson or Director of Music.

KANSAS

Bethany College; Lindsborg, KS 67456. Write: Dean Leon Burch or Dean of Students.*
Bethel College; North Newton, KS 67117. Write: Gary Fletcher, or Chairman, Music Dept.
College of Emporia; Emporia, KA 66801. Write: Frank A. Malambri or Chairman, Music Dept.
University of Kansas; Lawrence, KS 66045. Write: Robert E. Foster or Dean, School of Music.*
Kansas State Teachers College; Emporia, KS 66801. Write: Thomas Wright or Coordinator of Jazz Studies, Music Dept.*
Kansas State University; Manhattan, KS 66502. Write: Phil Hewett or Chairman, Music Dept.*
Wichita State University; Wichita, KS 67208. Write: Dr. J.C. Combs or Dean, School of Music.*

KENTUCKY

Bellarmine College; Louisville, KY 40205. Write: Jamey Aebersold or Chairman, Music Dept.
Morehead State University; Morehead, KY 40351. Write: Walter L. Barr or Director of Jazz Studies, Music Dept.*

LOUISIANA

Louisiana State University; Baton Rouge, LA 70803. Write: Everett Timm or Dean, School of Music.*
Louisiana Tech University; Ruston, LA 71270. Write Joe Sheppard or Chairman, Music Dept.*
Loyola University; New Orleans, LA 70118. Write: Joseph Hebert or Dean, College of Music, 6363 St. Charles Ave.*
Nicholls State University; Thibodaux, LA 70301. Write: Paul Mathis or Chairman, Music Dept., College of Education.
Northeast Louisiana University; Monroe, LA 71201. Write: Robert Eidenier or Dean, School of Music.*
Southeastern Louisiana University, Hammond, LA 70401. Write: Lee Fortier or Chairman, Music Dept.*
Southern University; Baton Rouge, LA 70813. Write: Alvin Batiste or Director of Jazz Institute, Division of Music.*
Southern University in New Orleans; New Orleans, LA 70126. Write: Ed Jordan or Chairman, Music Dept.
University of Southwestern Louisiana; Lafayette, LA 70501. Write: James M. Goodman or Dean, School of Music.*

MAINE

Bowoin College; Brunswick, ME 04011. Write: Marion Brown or Chairman, Music Dept.

MARYLAND

University of Maryland; College Park, MD 20742. Write: Dr. Andrew Goodrich or Chairman, Music Dept.*
Morgan State College; Baltimore, MD 21239. Write: Melvin Miles, Jr. or Chairman, Music Dept.
Towson State College; Baltimore, MD 21204. Write: Hank Levy or Director of Jazz Studies, School of Fine Arts.

MASSACHUSETTS

Berklee College of Music; Boston, MA 02115. Write: Office of Admissions, 1140 Boylston St.

Clark University; Worcester, MA 01610. Write: Director of Admissions.

University of Massachusetts/Amherst; Amherst, MA 01002. Write: Roland Wiggins or Director of Institute of Black Music.*

The New England Conservatory of Music; Boston, MA 02115. Write: Phil Wilson or Director of Admissions.*

Northeastern University; Boston, MA 02115. Write: J.R. Mitchell or Director of Jazz Studies, College of Liberal Arts.

Tufts University; Medford, MA 02111. Write: T.J. Anderson or Chairman, Music Dept.

Westfield State College; Westfield, MA 01085. Write: Dr. Donald J. Bastarache or Chairman Music Dept.

MICHIGAN

Central Michigan University; Mt. Pleasant, MI 48859. Write: Dr. William Rivard or Chairman, Music Dept.*

Henry Ford Community College (2-yr.); Dearborn, MI 48128. Write: Don Lupp or Director of Music.

Thomas Jefferson College (Grand Valley State Colleges); Allendale, MI 49401. Write: Joel Zelnik or Director of Jazz Studies, Music Dept.

The University of Michigan; Ann Arbor, MI 48105. Write: Director of Jazz Studies, School of Music.*

Michigan State University; East Lansing, MI 48824. Write: Burgess Gardner or Director of Jazz Studies, Music Dept.*

Michigan Technological University; Houghton, MI 49931. Write: Donald P. Keranen or Chairman, Music Dept.

Northern Michigan University; Marquette, MI 49855; Write: Ron Caviani or Chairman, Music Dept.*

Oakland University; Rochester, MI 48063. Write: Marvin Holladay or Chairman, Music Dept.

Wayne State University; Detroit, MI 48202. Write: Dr. James Hartway or Chairman, Music Dept.*

Southwestern Michigan College (2-yr.); Dowagiac, MI 49047. Write: Rich Bressler or Chairman, Music Dept.

Western Michigan University; Kalamazoo, MI 49001. Write: Dr. Robert Fink or Chairman, Music Dept.*

MINNESOTA

Gustavus Adolphus College; St. Peter, MN 56082. Write: Mark Lammers or Chairman, Music Dept.*

Hamline University; St. Paul, MN 55104. Write: Paul A. Pizner or Chairman, Music Dept.*

Hibbing Community College (2-yr.); Hibbing, MN 55746. Write: Thomas F. Palmersheim or Chairman, Music Dept.

University of Minnesota/Duluth; Duluth, MN 55812. Write: R. Dale Miller or Chairman, Music Dept.*

Moorhead State College; Moorhead, MN 56560. Write: Dr. Al Noice or Chairman, Music Dept.*

Willmar Community College (2-yr.); Willmar, MN 56201. Write: Dale Wright or Director of Music.

Winona State College (2-yr.); Winona, MN 55987. Write: Gene Anderson or Director of Music.

MISSISSIPPI

Delta State College; Cleveland, MS 38732. Write: Gary Nyberg or Chairman, Music Dept.

University of Mississippi; University, MS 38677. Write Dr. Robert Jordan or Chairman, Music Dept.*

University of Southern Mississippi; Hattiesburg, MS 39401. Write: Raoul Jerome or Coordinator of Jazz Curriculum, Music Dept.*

MISSOURI

Central Missouri State University; Warrensburg, MO 64093. Write: Dr. Wesley True or Chairman, Music Div.*

Drury College; Springfield, MO 65802. Write: Don Verne Joseph, Box 67. School of Humanities.

Meramec Community College (2-yr.); Kirkwood, MO 63122. Write: Ronald E. Stilwell or Director of Music.

University of Missouri; Columbia, MO 65201. Write: George DeFoe or Chairman, Music Dept.*

University of Missouri/St. Louis; St. Louis, MO 63121. Write: Stan DeRusha or Chairman, Music Dept.

Northeast Missouri State University; Kirksville, MO 63501. Write: Dr. Dale A. Jorgenson or Chairman, Music Dept.*

Southwest Missouri State University; Springfield, Mo 65802. Write: Robert M. Scott or Chairman, Music Dept.*

MONTANA

University of Montana; Missoula, MT 59801. Write: Lance R. Boyd or Chairman, Music Dept.*

Montana State University; Bozeman, MT 59715. Write: Carl Lobitz or Chairman, Music Dept.

Rocky Mountain College; Billings, MT 59102. Write: Dr. Wm. L. Waggoner or Chairman, Music Dept.

NEBRASKA

Hastings College; Hastings, NE 68901. Write: John Mills or Chairman, Music Dept.*

University of Nebraska at Omaha; Omaha, NE 68101. Write: Reg Schive or Chairman, Music Dept.

NEVADA

University of Nevada/Las Vegas; Las Vegas, NV 89154. Write: Frank Gagliardi or Chairman, Music Dept.

University of Nevada/Reno; Reno, NV 89507. Write: Dr. John Carrico or Chairman, Music Dept.

NEW HAMPSHIRE

Plymouth State College; Plymouth, NH 03264. Write: Vincent Marinelli or Chairman, Music Dept.

NEW JERSEY

Fairleigh Dickinson University; Rutherford, NJ 07070. Write: Stanley Purdy or Chairman, Music Dept.

Glassboro State College; Glassboro, NJ 08028. Write: John H. Thysen or Chairman, Music Dept.*

Jersey City State University; Jersey City, NJ 07305. Write: Richard Lowenthal or Chairman, Music Dept.

Livingston College of Rutgers University; New Brunswick,

NJ 08903. Write: Larry Ridley or Chairman, Music Dept.

Seton Hall University; South Orange, NJ 07079. Write: Jack McKinney or Chairman, Music Dept., 400 S. Orange Ave.

NEW MEXICO

University of New Mexico; Albuquerque, NM 87131. Write: William E. Rhoads or Chairman, Music Dept.*

NEW YORK

Columbia University; New York, NY 10029. Write: Dr. Marion McGill or Chairman, Music Dept., Teachers College, Broadway and 116th St.

Eastman School of Music, University of Rochester; Rochester, NY 14604. Write: Rayburn Wright or Director of Jazz Studies and Contemporary Music, 26 Gibbs St.*

Five Towns College (2-yr.); Merrick, NY 11566. Write: Dr. Stanley G. Cohen or Director of Jazz Studies, 2350 Merrick Ave.

Ithaca College; Ithaca, NY 14850. Write: Steve Brown or Director of Jazz Studies, School of Music.*

Manhattan School of Music; New York, NY 10027. Write: Lyle "Rusty" Dedrick or Director of Jazz Studies, 120 Claremont Ave.*

State University of New York at Binghampton; Binghampton, NY 13901. Write: Albert Hamme or Director of Jazz Studies, Music Dept.

State University of New York College at Brockport; Brockport, NY 14420. Write: Dr. Ira Schwartz or Chairman, Music Dept.

State University of New York at Buffalo; Buffalo, NY 14222. Write: William H. Tallmadge or Chairman, Music Dept.

State University of New York/College at Old Westbury; Westbury, NY 11568. Write: Chairman, Music Dept., Performing Arts Group.

State University of New York/College at Oswego; Oswego, NY 13126. Write: Hugh G. Burritt or Chairman, Music Dept.

State University of New York/College at Potsdam; Potsdam, NY 13676. Write: R. Shiner or Dean, Crane School of Music.*

State University of New York at Stony Brook; Stony Brook, NY 11790. Write: John Lessard, or Chairman, Undergraduate Studies.

Syracuse University; Syracuse, NY 13210. Write: Stephen Marconi or Director of Jazz Ensembles, School of Music.*

NORTH CAROLINA

Appalachian State University; Boone, NC 26808. Write: Joe Phelps or Chairman, Music Dept.*

East Carolina University; Greenville, NC 27834. Write: George L. Broussard or Dean, School of Music.*

University of North Carolina at Chapel Hill; Chapel Hill, NC 27514. Write: John Harding or Chairman, Music Dept.

University of North Carolina at Greensboro; Greensboro, NC 27412. Write Raymond Ganglio or Dean, School of Music.*

Mars Hill College; Mars Hill, NC 28754. Write: Wayne Bowman or Chairman, Music Dept.*

Pembroke State University; Pembroke, NC 28372. Write: Harold Slagle or Chairman, Music Dept.

NORTH DAKOTA

Minot College; Minot, ND 58701. Write: Gerald Poe or Chairman, Music Dept.

Valley City State College; Valley City, ND 58072. Write: R.Q. Johnson or Chairman, Music Dept.

OHIO

The University of Akron; Akron, OH 44325. Write: Richard Jackoboice or Chairman, Music Dept.

Ashland College; Ashland, OH 44805. Write: Curt Wilson or Director of Bands.*

Bowling Green State University; Bowling Green, OH 43402. Write: Wendell Jones or Dean, School of Music.*

Capital University; Columbus, OH 43209. Write: Ray Eubanks or Chairman, Music Dept.*

Case Western Reserve University; Cleveland, OH 44106. Write: Philip L. Weinacht or Chairman, Music Dept.*

Central State University; Wilberforce, OH 45384. Write: Stanley D. Kirton or Chairman, Music Dept.*

University of Cincinnati; Cincinnati, OH 45221. Write: Dean, College-Conservatory of Music.*

Denison University; Granville, OH 43023. Write: R.L. Bostian or Chairman, Music Dept.*

Hiram College; Hiram, OH 44234. Write: John M. Burley or Chairman, Music Dept.*

Kent State University; Kent, OH 44240. Write: Dr. Walter Watson or Director of Jazz Studies, School of Music.*

Lakeland Community College (2-yr.); Mentor, OH 44060. Write: Chairman, Music Dept.

Miami University; Oxford, OH 15056. Write: Dr. Charles Spohn or Dean, School of Music.*

Muskingum College; New Concord, OH 43662. Write: J. Terry Gates or Chairman, Music Dept.*

Oberlin College; Oberlin, OH 44070. Write: Dean, Conservatory of Music.*

Ohio State University; Columbus, OH 43210. Write: Tom Battenberg or Director, School of Music.*

Otterbein College; Westerville, OH 43081. Write: Gary Tirey or Chairman, Division of Fine Arts.*

OKLAHOMA

Cameron College; Lawton, OK 73501. Write: Chairman, Music Dept.

East Central State College; Ada, OK 74820. Write: James L. Franklin or Chairman, Music Dept.

Oral Roberts University; Tulsa, OK 74105. Write: Bill Shellenberger or Chairman, Music Dept.

Phillips University; Enid, OK 73701. Write: Dr. Milburn Carey or Director, School of Music.*

Southeastern Oklahoma State University; Durant, OK

74701. Write: Dr. Paul Mansur or Chairman, Music Dept.

Southwestern State College; Weatherford, OK 73096. Write: Terry Segress or Chairman, Music Dept.*

University of Tulsa; Tulsa, OK 74104. Write: Ron Predl or Dean, School of Music.*

OREGON

Mt. Hood Community College (2-yr.); Gresham, OR 97030. Write: Larry McVey or Chairman, Creative Arts Division, 26000 S.E. Stark St.

University of Oregon; Eugene, OR 97405. Write: Stan Fink or Dean, School of Music.*

University of Portland; Portland, OR 97203. Write: Don Camack or Chairman, Music Dept.

Pacific University; Forest Grove, OR 97116. Write: Dr. Albert M. Freedman or Dean, School of Music.*

Portland State University; Portland, OR 97207. Write: Dr. Wm. Stainaker, Music Dept.

PENNSYLVANIA

Lebanon Valley College; Annville, PA 17003. Write: Frank Stachow or Chairman, Music Dept.*

Lehigh University; Bethlehem, PA 18015. Write: James T. McLaughlin or Director of Jazz Ensembles, Box 186.

Mansfield State College; Mansfield, PA 16933. Write: Thomas Ryan or Chairman, Music Dept.*

Philadelphia Musical Academy; Philadelphia, PA 19107. Write: Evan Solot or Director of Jazz Studies, 313 Broad St.*

University of Pittsburgh; Pittsburgh, PA 15213. Write: Dr. Nathan Davis or Director of Jazz Studies, 5619 Kentucky Ave.

Temple University; Philadelphia, PA 19122. Write: James W. Herbert or Director of Bands, College of Music.*

SOUTH CAROLINA

Furman University; Greenville, SC 26913. Write: George Hitt or Chairman, Music Dept.*

University of South Carolina; Columbia, SC 29208. Write: Dr. William Moody or Chairman, Music Dept.*

SOUTH DAKOTA

Huron College; Huron, SD 57350. Write: Chairman, Music Dept.

Northern State College; Aberdeen, SD 57401. Write: David Mauney or Chairman, Music Dept.*

TENNESSEE

Austin Peay State College; Clarksville, TN 37040. Write: Aaron Schmidt or Chairman, Music Dept., College of Education.*

East Tennessee State University; Johnson City, TN 37601. Write: Dr. James E. Stafford or Chairman, Music Dept.

Fisk University; Nashville, TN 37203. Write: Robert L. Holmes or Director of Instrumental Music.*

George Peabody College for Teachers; Nashville, TN 37203. Write: John Legg or Director, School of Music.*

Memphis State University; Memphis, TN 38152. Write: Dr. Thomas Ferguson or Director of Bands, Music Dept.*

TEXAS

Alvin Junior College (2-yr.); Alvin, TX 77511. Write: Jerry Perkins or Chairman, Music Dept., 3110 Mustang Road.

East Texas State University; Commerce, TX 75428. Write: Tom Wirtel or Chairman, Music Dept.*

Hardin-Simmons University; Abilene, TX 79601. Write: Lawson Hager or Dean, School of Music.*

University of Houston; Houston, TX 77004. Write: Don Elam or Aubrey Tucker, or Dean, School of Music.*

Lamar University; Beaumont, TX 77710. Write: James M. Simmons or Chairman, Music Dept.*

Mountain View College (2-yr.); Dallas, TX 75211. Write: Russ Benzamin or Chairman, Music Dept.

Odessa College (2-yr.); Odessa, TX 79760. Write: Jack Hendrix or Director of Instrumental Music.*

North Texas State University; Denton, TX 76203. Write: Leon Breeden or Director of Lab Bands, School of Music, Box 5038. NTU Station.*

University of Saint Thomas; Houston, TX 77006. Write: Thomas Borling or Chairman, Music Dept., 3812 Montrose Blvd.

St. Mary's University; San Antonio, TX 78228. Write: Herb Schweppe or Director of Instrumental Music.

Sam Houston State University; Huntsville, TX 77340. Write: Dr. Robert Morgan or Chairman, Music Dept.*

Stephen F. Austin State University; Nacogdoches, TX 75961. Write: Dr. M.E. Hall or Chairman, Music Dept.*

Tarleton State University; Stephenville, TX 76402. Write Guy Gamble or Director of Jazz Ensembles, Music Dept.

Tarrant County Junior College (2-yr.); Hurst, TX 76053. Write: Jack Cobb or Director of Music.

Texas A&I University; Kingsville, TX 78363. Write: Dr. Joseph L. Bellamah or Chairman, Music Dept.*

University of Texas at Austin; Austin, TX 78712. Write: Dr. Glen Daum or Undergraduate Music Admissions, Music Dept., College of Fine Arts.*

Texas Southern University; Houston, TX 77004. Write: Lanny Steele or Chairman, Music Dept.

Texas Tech University; Lubbock, TX 79409. Write: Don Turner or Chairman, Music Dept.*

Wharton County Junior College (2-yr.); Wharton, TX 77488. Dr. W.W. Wendtland or Chairman, Music Dept.

UTAH

Brigham Young University; Provo, UT 84601. Write: Chairman, Music Dept.*

University of Utah; Salt Lake City, UT 84112. Write: Henry Wolking or Chairman, Music Dept.*

Utah State University; Logan, UT 84321. Write: Larry Smith or Chairman, Music Dept.

Westminster College; Salt Lake City, UT 84105. Write: Ladd McIntosh or Chairman, Music Dept., 1840 South 1300 East.

VERMONT

University of Vermont; Burlington, VT 05401. Write: Herbert L. Schultz or Chairman, Music Dept.*

VIRGINIA

Hampton Institute; Hampton, VA 23668. Write: Consuela Moorehead or Chairman, Music Dept.*

Shenandoah Conservatory of Music; Winchester, VA 22601. Write: Paul Noble or Chairman, Music Dept.*

Virginia Commonwealth University; Richmond, VA 23220. Write: Dr. Paul Dorsam or Assistant Dean, Division of Music.*

WASHINGTON

Central Washington State College; Ellensburg, WA 98926. Write: John F. Moawad or Chairman, Music Dept.*

Clark College (2-yr.); Vancouver, WA 98663. Write: Dale Beacock or Director of Performing Arts.

Columbia Basin College; Pasco, WA 99302. Write: Don Paul or Chairman, Music Dept.

Highline Community College (2-yr.); Midway, WA 98031. Write: Marius "Butch" Nordal or Chairman, Music Dept.

Olympic College (2-yr.); Bremerton, WA 98310. Write: Dr. Ralph Mutchler or Director of Instrument Music.

Washington State University; Pullman, WA 99163. Write: Michael Olsavsky or Chairman, Music Dept.*

WEST VIRGINIA

Marshall University; Huntington, WV 25703. Write: J.D.Folsom or Chairman, Music Dept.

West Virginia Wesleyan College; Buckhannon, WV 26201. Write David Milburn or Chairman, Music Dept.

WISCONSIN

Carthage College; Kenosha, WI 53140. Write: Fred Riley or Chairman, Music Dept.

Lawrence University; Appleton, WI 54911. Write: Chairman, Conservatory of Music.*

Milwaukee Area Technical College (2-yr.); Milwaukee, WI 53202. Write: Gene Morrissette or Chairman, Music Dept.

University of Wisconsin-Eau Claire; Eau Claire, WI 54701. Write: Dominic Spera or Chairman, Music Dept.*

University of Wisconsin-Green Bay; Green Bay; WI 54302. Write: Lowell Ives or Chairman, Music Dept.

University of Wisconsin-Milwaukee; Milwaukee, WI 53201. Write: Dr. Gerald K. Grose or Chairman, Music Dept.*

University of Wisconsin-Parkside; Kenosha, WI 53140. Write: Robert Thomason or Chairman, Music Dept.

University of Wisconsin-Platteville; Platteville, WI 53818. Write: Tom Richards or Chairman, Music Dept.

University of Wisconsin-Stevens Point; Stevens Point, WI 54481. Write: Donald Chesebro or Chairman, Music Dept.*

University of Wisconsin-Superior; Superior, WI 54880. Write: Henry M. Meredith or Chairman, Music Dept.

University of Wisconsin-Waukesha (2-yr.); Waukesha, WI 53186. Write: Jack Whitney or Chairman, Music Dept., 1500 University Drive.

University of Wisconsin-Whitewater; Whitewater, WI 52190. Write: Dr. Frank Ferriano or Chairman, Music Dept.

A guide to available jazz films
by Leonard Maltin

(Leonard Maltin's jazz writing has appeared in *down beat, The Village Voice, Jazz* magazine, and *Saturday Review.* He has also written scores of articles on film, and six books, including *TV Movies: A Paperback Guide to 10,000 Movies on Television,* and *The Great Movie Shorts.* He teaches at the New School for Social Research in New York.)

The complete chronicle of jazz in films has yet to appear. David Meeker's British paperback *Jazz in the Movies* and Jean-Roland Hippenmeyer's Swiss publication *Jazz sur Films* are excellent beginnings, and the New York Jazz Museum has attempted to collect and catalogue as much jazz film as possible.

But the obscurity of many films, and the lack of interest on the part of the companies that made these movies, create a near-impossible task for anyone who wants to see, acquire, or even document all that has passed.

In recent years, the only real jazz films have come from Europe, while occasional American television shows with modern-jazz figures remain unavailable for re-viewing. Perhaps with the coming of video-discs it will be easier to obtain such material, but with the exception of jazz soundtracks, the history of jazz on film is largely confined to the 1930s and 40s.

Worse, much of this existing material is not generally available at this time. Three-minute "soundies," produced in the 1940s for coin-operated machines, and five-minute "Snader Telescriptions," made in the early 1950s for TV use, are among the most valuable jazz films extant, but they are no longer available for rental or purchase from any specific source, and jazz collectors happen upon them only by chance. Duke Ellington, Louis Armstrong, Fats Waller, Count Basie, Lionel Hampton, and Gene Krupa are among those who appeared in these films, which one can still find in smaller rental-library catalogues, and occasionally for sale on home-movie lists.

Even lesser-known feature films of the 1930s, which included jazz sequences, are not always available.

Therefore, I have limited myself in this index to films which can currently be rented on 16mm sound in America. And I have limited myself to short-subjects which principally feature jazz musicians. The number of feature films with brief appearances by jazzmen is too great to list here; a handful of key feature films is printed at the end of the short-subject index.

We have gathered as much material as possible on each title; please bear in mind that song numbers may not have been performed by the "star" but by supporting acts included in these short-subjects. Complete addresses for the film-rental companies referred to in each entry will be found at the end of the index.

We can only hope that the growing historical interest in jazz will induce film companies to make more material available, and that by the time of the next *Encyclopedia of Jazz* this list will be ten times as long. Until then, there is much worthwhile material on tap:

A

ALBERT AMMONS

BOOGIE DOODLE (1948). Famous abstract animated film by Norman McLaren set to boogie-piano track by Ammons. McGraw-Hill

LOUIS ARMSTRONG

RHAPSODY IN BLACK AND BLUE (1932). Silly story framework for two band numbers, "I'll Be Glad When You're Dead You Rascal You," "Shine." Ivy; Select; Kit Parker

I'LL BE GLAD WHEN YOU'RE DEAD YOU RASCAL YOU (1932). Betty Boop cartoon featuring Armstrong's rendition. Ivy; Kit Parker

LOUIS ARMSTRONG (1962. A live performance caught on film, with Jewel Brown, Trummy Young, Billy Kyle, and others; half-hour. Kit Parker

B

CHARLIE BARNET

JASPER'S IN A JAM (1946). George Pal Puppetoon in color, with Barnet and Peggy Lee on the soundtrack; "Cherokee," "Pompton Turnpike." Ivy

CHARLIE BARNET AND HIS ORCHESTRA (1947) with Igor and Tania, Della Norell, Rita Shore. "I'll Remember April," "You're a Sweetheart." Universal

CHARLIE BARNET AND HIS ORCHESTRA (1949). "Redskin Rhumba," "Atlantic Jump," "My Old Flame." Available for purchase on Super 8mm of 16mm sound from Blackhawk Films

BRIGHT AND BREEZY (1956) with the Four King Sisters, Romo Vincent. "Skyliner," "Lullaby of Birdland," "Easy Street." Universal

COUNT BASIE

SUGARCHILE ROBINSON, BILLIE HOLIDAY, COUNT BASIE AND SEXTET (1951). "One O'Clock Jump," "Terry Toon," "God Bless the Child," "Now or Never." Universal

EUBIE BLAKE

PIE PIE BLACKBIRD (1934) with Nina Mae McKinney, The Nicholas Brothers. "Memories of You," "China Boy," "Everything I've Got Belongs to You." United Artists

C

CAB CALLOWAY

MINNIE THE MOOCHER (1932). Betty Boop cartoon featuring a cartoon-ized version of Calloway dancing and singing title song. Ivy; Kit Parker

SNOW WHITE (1933). Betty Boop Cartoon, as above. Ivy; Kit Parker

OLD MAN OF THE MOUNTAIN (1933). Betty Boop cartoon, as above. Ivy

PARAMOUNT PICTORIAL (Pictorial Magazine #837). Irving Mills introduces Calloway, Duke Ellington, and Baron Lee in brief musical excerpts. Ivy

CAB CALLOWAY'S HI DE HO (1934). "The Lady with the Fan," other songs. Ivy or Kit Parker Films

CAB CALLOWAY'S JITTERBUG PARTY (1935) with Cotton Club entertainers. Ivy

CAB CALLOWAY AND HIS ORCHESTRA IN HI DE HO (1937). "I Gotta Right to Sing the Blues," "Hi De Ho Miracle Man." United Artists

BENNY CARTER

See NAT KING COLE AND HIS TRIO

See LIONEL HAMPTON: ADVENTURES OF AN ASTERISK

BOB CROSBY

BOB CROSBY AND HIS ORCHESTRA (1938). "Pagan Love Song," "Dixieland Swing," others. Ivy

D

JIMMY DORSEY

JIMMY DORSEY AND HIS ORCHESTRA (1938) with Bob Eberly. "It's the Dreamer in Me," "I Love You in Technicolor." United Artists

JIMMY DORSEY AND HIS ORCHESTRA (1940) with Helen O'Connell, Bob Eberly. "Rubber Dolly," "Only a Rose." Ivy

JIMMY DORSEY AND HIS ORCHESTRA (1948) with The Mellolarks, Dottie O'Brien, Bill Lawrence. "Am I Blue," others. Universal

TOMMY DORSEY

TOMMY DORSEY AND HIS ORCHESTRA (1951) with Charlie Shavers, Frances Irvin, Bob London. "Diane," others. Universal

DORSEY BROTHERS

THE DORSEY BROS. ENCORE (1953) with Gordon Polk, Lynn Roberts, Earl Barton. "Jazz Me Blues," "Ain't She Sweet," "Street Scene," "Yes Indeed," "We'll Git It." Universal

E

ROY ELDRIDGE

SMASH YOUR BAGGAGE (1933) with Smalls Paradise Entertainers, including Eldridge and Dickie Wells. Musical revue, including "Tiger Rag." United Artists

DUKE ELLINGTON

BLACK AND TAN (1929) with Fredi Washington, Hall Johnson Choir. Available for purchase in 16mm sound or Super 8mm sound from Blackhawk.

A BUNDLE OF BLUES (1933) with Ivy Anderson. "Stormy Weather," others. Ivy; Kit Parker Films

PARAMOUNT PICTORIAL (Pictorial Magazine #837). Irving Mills introduces brief sequences of Ellington, Cab Calloway, and Baron Lee. Ivy

SYMPHONY IN BLACK (1935) with Billie Holiday. Features title composition. Ivy

A DATE WITH DUKE (1947). George Pal Puppetoon in color, with Duke on film and on soundtrack. Ivy

SALUTE TO DUKE ELLINGTON (1950) with Ray Nance, Johnny Hodges, Harry Carney, Tyree Glenn. "Things Ain't What They Used to Be," "Violet Blue," "The History of Jazz in Three Minutes." Universal

F

ELLA FITZGERALD

THE TENDER GAME (1958) with the Oscar Peterson Trio. Lovely animated cartoon by John Hubley of two people falling in love to the song "Tenderly." McGraw-Hill; Macmillan

H

LIONEL HAMPTON
LIONEL HAMPTON AND HIS ORCHESTRA (1949) with William Curley Hammer, Lorence Carter, Sonny Parker, Kitty Murray. "The New Look," "Hamp's Gumbo," "Curley's Dance Medley," "Wee Albert." Universal
LIONEL HAMPTON AND HERB JEFFRIES (1956) with Loray White, Vicky Lee. "Black Coffee," "The Bug," "Baby Don't Love Me No More," "Universal stomp." Universal
ADVENTURES OF AN ASTERISK (1956). Fine animated short by John Hubley featuring Hampton and Benny Carter, who wrote the score. McGraw-Hill; Macmillan

WOODY HERMAN
WOODY HERMAN AND ORCHESTRA (1938). "The Shag," "You Must Have Been a Beautiful Baby." United Artists
RHAPSODY IN WOOD (1947). George Pal Puppetoon in color with Herman on-screen explaining origin of clarinet; "Blue Flame." Ivy
WOODY HERMAN AND HIS ORCHESTRA (1948) with The Woodchoppers, The Modernaires, Don and Beverly. "Sabre Dance," "Jingle Bell Polka," "Camptown Races." Universal
HERMAN'S HERD (1949) with The Mellolarks. "Jamaica Rumba," "Tap Boogie," "I've Got News for You," "Lollybop," "Keen and Peachy." Universal

BOBBY HACKETT
SATURDAY NIGHT SWING CLUB (1938) with Leith Stevens and Orchestra, Les Lieber, Nan Wynn, Mel Allen, Eddie Condon. United Artists

BILLIE HOLIDAY
See COUNT BASIE, DUKE ELLINGTON

J

HARRY JAMES
HARRY JAMES AND HIS MUSIC MAKERS (1953) with Gale Robbins, Allan and Ashton. "I've Got a Crush on You," "Trumpet Blues," "Ciribiribin," "Charmaine," "Moaning Low." Universal
RIOT IN RHYTHM (1957) with The DeCastro Sisters, Johnny O'Niel. "Cherry," "Roll 'em," "Heartbreak Hotel." Universal

K

STAN KENTON
STAN KENTON AND HIS ORCHESTRA (1945) with June Christy. "Artistry in Rhythm," others. United Artists

GENE KRUPA
GENE KRUPA AND HIS ORCHESTRA (1941). "Call of the Canyon," "Perfidia." Ivy
GENE KRUPA AND HIS ORCHESTRA (1949) with Bill Black, Dolores Hawkins, Frankie Ross (Frank Rosolino). "Star Burst," "Lemon Drop," "Deep Purple," "Bop Boogie," "Melody in F." Universal

L

JIMMIE LUNCEFORD
JIMMIE LUNCEFORD AND HIS DANCE ORCHESTRA (1937). "Nagasaki," "Rhythm Is Our Business." United Artists

N

RED NICHOLS
RED NICHOLS AND HIS FIVE PENNIES (1950) with June Hutton, The Skylarks. "Do It Again," "Three Blind Mice," "South Rampart Street Parade." Universal

O

ANITA O'DAY
COOL AND GROOVY (1956) with Buddy DeFranco Quartet, Chico Hamilton Quintet, The Hi-Los. "Honeysuckle Rose," "I'll Remember April," "Jeepers Creepers." Universal

P

OSCAR PETERSON
BEGONE DULL CARE (1949). Classic abstract animated film by Norman McLaren set to three themes by the Oscar Peterson Trio. McGraw-Hill
THE TENDER GAME (1958). See ELLA FITZGERALD

R

DON REDMAN
DON REDMAN AND HIS ORCHESTRA (1934). "Ill Wind," "Nagasaki." United Artists.
I HEARD (1933). Betty Boop cartoon featuring "I Heard" and "How'm I Doin'?" Ivy; Kit Parker

BUDDY RICH
BUDDY RICH AND HIS ORCHESTRA (1948) with

Terry Gibbs, Louis DaPron. "Let's Get Away from It All," "Not So Quiet Please," "John Had the Number but No Nickel," "One O'Clock Boogie." Universal
MELODIES BY MARTIN (1956) with Freddie Martin and Orchestra; Rich has solo feature on "Jitterbug Routine." Universal

S

ARTIE SHAW
ARTIE SHAW'S SYMPHONY OF SWING (1939) with Helen Forrest, Tony Pastor, Buddy Rich. "Jeepers Creepers," "Lady Be Good," "Deep Purple." United Artists
ARTIE SHAW'S CLASS IN SWING (1939) with Helen Forrest. "I Have Eyes," "Shoot the Liquor to Me, John Boy." Ivy

NOBLE SISSLE
THAT'S THE SPIRIT (1933) with Cora La Redd, Washboard Serenaders, Mantan Moreland. "Tiger Rag," "St. Louis Blues." United Artists

BESSIE SMITH
ST. LOUIS BLUES (1929). Famous early-talkie short directed by Dudley Murphy. Available for purchase from National Cinema Service; rental from Macmillan; Kit Parker

T

JACK TEAGARDEN
PARAMOUNT PRESENTS HOAGY CARMICHAEL (1939) with Jack Teagarden and his Orchestra. "Small Fry," "Lazy Bones," "Stardust." Ivy; Kit Parker

Y

LESTER YOUNG
JAMMIN' THE BLUES (1944) with Illinois Jacquet, Harry Edison, Marlowe Morris, Sid Catlett, Jo Jones, Red Callender, John Simmons, Barney Kessel, Marie Bryant; produced by Norman Granz, directed by Gjon Mili. United Artists; Macmillan; Kit Parker

FEATURE FILMS OF SPECIAL INTEREST

HOLLYWOOD HOTEL (1937). Captures the Benny Goodman Quartet and Big Band at its best, including "Sing Sing Sing," along with other Busby Berkeley numbers, big cast headed by Dick Powell. United Artists

JAZZ BALL (1957). Compilation of soundies shorts with Louis Armstrong, Cab Calloway, Buddy Rich, Gene Krupa, Peggy Lee, many others. Ivy Films

JAZZ ON A SUMMER'S DAY (1960). Classic Bert Stern color documentary on 1959 Newport festival, with Louis Armstrong, Gerry Mulligan, Thelonious Monk, Anita O'Day, George Shearing, Sonny Stitt, Jimmy Giuffre, many others. New Yorker Films, 43 West 61st Street, New York, N.Y. 10023

JIVIN' IN BEBOP (1947). Feature made for black theaters with Dizzy Gillespie and his Band, Helen Humes, and a host of variety acts. Kit Parker Films

NEW ORLEANS (1947). Contrived "history" of jazz features Billie Holiday and Louis Armstrong together, Woody Herman, all-star New Orleans group, many others. Select Film Library

STORMY WEATHER (1943). All-black musical with Fats Waller, Bill Robinson, Lena Horne, Cab Calloway. Films Incorporated

GENERAL GUIDE TO RENTING HOLLYWOOD FEATURE FILMS

Universal Pictures and pre-1949 Paramount Pictures from Universal 16 (THE GLENN MILLER STORY, THE BENNY GOODMAN STORY, CRAZY HOUSE with Basie, BELLE OF THE NINETIES with Ellington, BIRTH OF THE BLUES with Teagarden, BIG BROADCAST OF 1937 with Goodman, etc.)

MGM, RKO, 20th Century Fox, and post-1949 Paramount Pictures from Films Incorporated (THE STRIP with Armstrong and Teagarden, GIRL CRAZY with Tommy Dorsey, BEAT THE BAND with Krupa, SUN VALLEY SERENADE with Glenn Miller, ST. LOUIS BLUES with Nat Cole, Ella Fitzgerald, Cab Calloway)

United Artists and pre-1949 Warner Brothers films from United Artists 16mm (I WANT TO LIVE with Gerry Mulligan and Shelly Manne, GOING PLACES with Armstrong, BLUES IN THE NIGHT with Lunceford)

Republic and independently-produced features from Ivy Films (THE FABULOUS DORSEYS, I'LL REACH FOR A STAR/HIT PARADE OF 1937 with Ellington, HIT PARADE OF 1947/HIGH AND HAPPY with Woody Herman)

Columbia, post-1949 Warner Brothers, Samuel Goldwyn, and Walt Disney features from various other film companies listed, including Select Film Library, Macmillan Audio Brandon.

Film Rental Companies
(some of these also offer
leasing plans for prints)

United Artists 16mm Division, 729 Seventh Avenue, New York, N.Y. 10019

Ivy Films, 165 West 46th Street, New York, New York 10036

McGraw-Hill Films, Princeton Road, Hightstown, N.J. 08520

or 1714 Stockton St., San Francisco, California 94133
Macmillan Audio Brandon Films, 34 MacQuesten Parkway South, Mount Vernon, New York 10550
or 1619 North Cherokee, Los Angeles, California 90028
Universal 16mm, 445 Park Avenue, New York, New York 10022
Select Film Library, 115 West 31st Street, New York, New York 10001
Films Incorporated, 1144 Wilmette Road, Wilmette, Illinois 60091
Kit Parker Films, Box 227, Carmel Valley, California 93924

Film Purchase Companies

Blackhawk Films, Eastin-Phelan Building, Davenport, Iowa 52808
National Cinema Service, 333 West 57th Street, New York, New York 10019

Recomended Recordings Of The Decade 1966-1975

THE SMITHSONIAN COLLECTION

This new label, under the auspices of the Smithsonian Institution, reissued some highly important material with extensive and authoritative background information and discography supervised by Martin Williams.

The Smithsonian Collection of Classic Jazz contains 84 original recordings culled from the archives of 17 record companies in a boxed collection of 6 LPs. Two-LP sets each of *King Oliver's Jazz Band/1923* and *Louis Armstrong and Earl Hines/1928* were subsequently issued. Also of interest is *Classic Rags and Ragtime Songs* including material by Eubie Blake and Scott Joplin. (The Smithsonian Collection, P.O. Box 5734, Terre Haute, Indiana 47802).

THE ENCYCLOPEDIA OF JAZZ
IN THE SEVENTIES

COMPANION RECORD ALBUM

A specially assembled two-pocket album under the above title, comprising outstanding performances by a broad spectrum of great jazz artists recorded during the period from 1966 through 1975, will be found on the RCA label. It consists of material from the RCA and Flying Dutchman catalogues. Side Two concentrates on the international jazz scene; the other three sides represent a cross section of American combo, big band and vocal styles and idioms. Partial personnels are listed below.

SIDE ONE:
1. Lonnie Liston Smith & The Cosmic Echoes. *Voodoo Woman.* Donald Smith, Cecil McBee, Michael Carvin, Art Gore.
2. Shelly Manne. *Night and Day.* Victor Feldman, Mike Wofford, Tom Scott, Oscar Brashear.
3. Horace Tapscott Quintet. *Dark Tree.* Black Arthur Blythe, David Bryant.
4. Gil Evans Orchestra. *King Porter Stomp.* Dave Sanborn.

SIDE TWO:
1. Gato Barbieri. *Tupac Amaru.* Lennie White III, Joe Beck, Lonnie Liston Smith.
2. John Dankworth and his Orchestra. *Long John.* Don Rendell, Kenny Baker.
3. Cleo Laine. *Music.*
4. Toshiko Akiyoshi-Lew Tabackin Big Band. *Since Perry/Yet Another Tear.*

SIDE THREE:
1. David Amram. *Waltz From "After The Fall."* Pepper Adams, Jerry Dodgion.
2. Nina Simone. *Ain't Got No/I Got Life.*
3. Bob Thiele's Orchestra. *I Saw Pinetop Spit Blood.* Bobby Bryant, Bob Brookmeyer, Chuck Domanico, Mike Wofford, Dennis Budimir. Composed and arranged by Oliver Nelson.
4. Groove Holmes. *Green Dolphin Street.*

SIDE FOUR:
1. Buddy Rich. *Space Shuttle.* Pat LaBarbera.
2. Jazz Piano Quartet. *Maiden Voyage.* Dick Hyman, Roland Hanna, Marian McPartland, Hank Jones.
3. Blue Mitchell. *Collaborations.* Harold Land.
4. Duke Ellington and his Orchestra. *Don't You Know I Care*, Harold Minerve, Harry Carney.

Recommended Records

In order to compile a list representative of various critical viewpoints, it was decided to solicit the additional opinions of several experts other than the authors to compile a list of major contributors to recorded jazz during the period from 1966 through 1975. Voters were advised that big bands, combos, singers and representatives of any and all styles of jazz could be included. Each critic put ten albums by ten different artists or groups in nomination.

If an album received more than one vote, the number of votes is indicated in parentheses after the title.

The list reflects a consensus of the opinions of Philippe Carles, Willis Conover, Leonard Feather, Ira Gitler, Nat Hentoff, Kiyoshi Koyama, Dan Morgenstern, Martin Williams and John S. Wilson.

Art Ensemble of Chicago	***Message To Our Folks***	**Byg**
Count Basie	***Basie Jam***	**Pablo**
	Trio	**Pablo**
Carla Bley	***A Genuine Tong Funeral***	**RCA**
Dollar Brand/Gato Barbieri	***Confluence***	**Freedom**
Anthony Braxton	***New York, Fall 1974***	**Arista**
Gary Burton-Ralph Towner	***Matchbook***	**ECM**
Jaki Byard	***The Jaki Byard Experience***	**Prestige**
Don Cherry	***Complete Communion***	**Blue Note**
	Relativity Suite	**JCOA**
Ornette Coleman	***Crisis***	**Impulse**
	Science Fiction	**Columbia**
	Skies of America	**Columbia**
	The Empty Fox Hole	**Blue Note**
John Coltrane	***Concert In Japan***	**Impulse**
	***Ascension* (2)**	**Impulse**
Chick Corea	***Return To Forever***	**ECM**
Miles Davis	***Bitches' Brew* (4)**	**Columbia**
	***In A Silent Way* (3)**	**Columbia**

Urszula Dudziak	*Newborn Light*	Columbia
Duke Ellington	*And His Mother Called Him Bill* (3)	RCA
	Concert Of Sacred Music	RCA
	Far East Suite (2)	RCA
	70th Birthday Concert	UA
Bill Evans	*At The Montreux Jazz Festival* (2)	Verve
Bill Evans-George Russell	*Living Time*	Columbia
John Garvey And The University Of Illinois Jazz Band	*In Champaign-Urbana*	Century
Dizzy Gillespie	*Big Four*	Pablo
	The Giant	Prestige
Dexter Gordon	*The Panther* (2)	Prestige
Herbie Hancock	*Speak Like A Child*	Blue Note
Barry Harris	*Plays Tadd Dameron*	Xanadu
Earl Hines	*The Quintessential Recording Session* (2)	Chiaroscuro
Dick Hyman	*Genius At Play*	Monmouth-Evergreen
Keith Jarrett	*Solo Concerts* (2)	ECM
Jazz Composers Orchestra with Cecil Taylor, Don Cherry, Pharoah Sanders, Roswell Rudd, etc.		JCOA
Thad Jones/Mel Lewis	*Consummation*	Blue Note
	Suite For Pops	Horizon
Lee Konitz	*Duets*	Milestone
	Satori	Milestone
Steve Lacy	*Solo*	Emanem
Charles Mingus	*And Friends In Concert*	Columbia
	Mingus Moves	Atlantic
Modern Jazz Quartet	*Last Concert* (3)	Atlantic
Max Morath	*The Entertainer*	Arpeggio

Zbigniew Namyslowski	*Winobranie*	Muza
New York Jazz Repertory Company	*Presents The Music Of Louis Armstrong*	Atlantic
Joe Pass	*Virtuoso*	Pablo
Joe Pass-Oscar Peterson	*The Trio*	Pablo
Oscar Peterson and Dizzy Gillespie	(2)	Pablo
Revolutionary Ensemble	*Manhattan Cycles*	India Navigation
Sonny Rollins	*The Cutting Edge*	Milestone
	In Japan	JVC
Jimmy Rushing	*The You And Me That Used To Be*	RCA
Archie Shepp	*Attica Blues*	Impulse
Zoot Sims	*And The Gershwin Brothers*	Pablo
Zoot Sims-Bucky Pizzarelli	*Nirvana*	Groove Merchant
Sonny Stitt	*Constellation*	Cobblestone
Sun Ra	*It's After The End Of The World*	MPS
Supersax	*Plays Bird*	Capitol
Cecil Taylor	*Indent*	Unit Core
	Silent Tongues	Arista
McCoy Tyner	*Echoes Of A Friend*	Milestone
	Sahara	Milestone
Sarah Vaughan	*Live In Japan* (4)	Mainstream
Bill Watrous	*The Tiger Of San Pedro*	Columbia
Weather Report	*Tale Spinnin'*	Columbia
Dick Wellstood	*And His Famous Orchestra*	Chiaroscuro
	From Ragtime On	Chiaroscuro
Bob Wilber-Kenny Davern	*Soprano Summit*	World Jazz

Bibliography: Books 1966-1975

ALBERTSON, CHRIS, *Bessie*, (Stein & Day) 253 pp, 1972.

ALLEN, WALTER C., *Hendersonia—The Music of Fletcher Henderson and His Musicians*, A Bio-Discography (Walter C. Allen, P.O. Box 1382, Highland Pk., N.J. 08904) 651 pp, 1973.

AMRAM, DAVID, *Vibrations*, an autobiography (Mac-millan) 469 pp, 1968.

BALLIETT, WHITNEY, *New York Notes: A Journal of Jazz, 1972-1975* (Houghton Mifflin) 250 pp, 1976.

BALLIETT, WHITNEY, *Alex Wilder & His Friends* (Houghton Mifflin) 205 pp, 1974.

BALLIETT, WHITNEY, *Such Sweet Thunder* (Bobbs-Merrill) 366 pp, 1967.

BALLIETT, WHITNEY, *Ecstasy at the Onion* (Bobbs-Merrill) 284 pp, 1972.

BALLIETT, WHITNEY, *Super Drummer: A Profile of Buddy Rich*, w. photos by Fred Seligo (Bobbs-Merrill) 120 pp, 1968.

BERENDT, JOACHIM, *The Jazz Book*, translated by Dan Morgenstern & Helmut and Barbara Bredigheit (Lawrence Hill & Co.) 459 pp, 1975.

BERTON, RALPH, *Remembering Bix* (Harper & Row) 428 pp, 1974.

BLESH, RUDI & HARRIET JANIS, *They All Played Ragtime* (Oak Publs.) republished 1966, 347 pp.

BLESH, RUDI, *Combo USA: Eight Lives in Jazz* (Chilton Book Co.) 240 pp, 1971.

BRASK, OLE & DAN MORGENSTERN, *Jazz People* (Harry N. Abrams) 300 pp, 1976.

BUERKLE, JACK J. & DANNY BARKER, *Bourbon Street Black*, The New Orleans Black Jazzman (Oxford Univ. Press) 244 pp, 1973.

CHILTON, JOHN, *Billie's Blues*, The Billie Holiday Story, 1933-59 (Stein & Day) 264 pp, 1975.

CHILTON, JOHN, *Who's Who of Jazz: Storyville To Swing Street* (Bloomsbury Book Shop, London) 447 pp, 1972.

COKER, JERRY, *The Jazz Idiom* (Prentice-Hall) 1975.

COLE, BILL, *Miles Davis: A Musical Biography* (Wm. Morrow & Co.) 256 pp, 1974.

COLE, MARIA, with LOUIE ROBINSON, *Nat King Cole*, An Intimate Biography (Wm. Morrow & Co.) 184 pp, 1971.

COLLINS, MARY, *Oh, Didn't He Ramble*, The Life Story Of Lee Collins (Univ. of Illinois Press) 159 pp, 1974.

CONNOR, D. RUSSELL and WARREN W. HICKS, *B.G. On The Record*, A Bio-Discography of Benny Goodman (Arlington House) 691 pp, 1969.

COOK, BRUCE, *Listen To The Blues* (Chas. Scribner's Sons) 263 pp, 1973.

DANCE, STANLEY, *The World of Duke Ellington* (Chas. Scribner's Sons) 311 pp, 1971.

DANCE, STANLEY, *The World of Swing* (Scribner's) 436 pp, 1974.

EASTON, CAROL, *Straight Ahead*, The Story of Stan Kenton (Wm. Morrow & Co. Inc.) 252 pp, 1973.

ELLINGTON, DUKE, *Music Is My Mistress* (Doubleday & Co. Inc.) 523 pp, 1973.

ERLICH, LILLIAN, *What Jazz Is All About* (Julian Messner) 255 pp, Revised 1975 (Orig. publ. 1962).

FEATHER, LEONARD, *From Satchmo To Miles* (Stein & Day) 258 pp, 1972.

FERNETT, GENE, *A Thousand Golden Horns* (Pendell Co.) 171 pp.

FLOWER, JOHN, *Moonlight Serenade:* A Bio-Discography of the Glenn Miller Civilian Band (Arlington House) 554 pp.

FOUNTAIN, PETE, with BILL NEELY, *A Closer Walk*, The Pete Fountain Story (Henry Regnery Co.) 202 pp, 1972.

FREEMAN, BUD, *You Don't Look Like A Musician* (Balamp Publ., 7430 Second Blvd., Detroit, Mich. 48202) 125 pp, 1974.

GAMMOND, PETER, *Scott Joplin And The Ragtime Era* (St. Martin's Press) 256 pp, 1975.

GARLAND, PHYL, *The Sound of Soul* (Henry Regnery Co.) 246 pp, 1969.

GLEASON, RALPH J., *Celebrating the Duke, And Louis, Bessie, Billie, Bird, Carmen, Miles, Dizzy and Other Heroes* (Little Brown & Co.) 280 pp, 1975.

GLOVER, TONY (LITTLE SUN), *Blues Harp* (Oak Publ.) 72 pp, 1966.

GONZALES, BABS, *I Paid My Dues: Good Times . . . No Bread* (Expubidence Publ. Corp.) 160 pp, 1968.

GONZALES, BABS, *Movin' On Down De Line* (Expubidence Publ. Corp.) 256 pp, 1975.

GOREAU, LAURRAINE, *Just Mahalia, Baby* (Word Books, Texas) 611 pp, 1975.

GREEN, BENNY, *Drums In My Ears*, Jazz In Our Time (Horizon) 188 pp, 1973.

HAWES, HAMPTON, with DON ASHER, *Raise Up Off Me* (Coward, McCann & Geoghegan Inc.) 179 pp, 1972.

HEILBUT, TONY, *The Gospel Sound*, Good News & Bad Times (Simon & Schuster) 350 pp, 1971.

HODEIR, ANDRE, *The Worlds of Jazz* (Grove Press) 279 pp, 1972.

Jazz Guitarists. Collected Interviews from *Guitar Player Magazine* (Guitar Player Productions) 120 pp, 1975.

JONES, LEROI, *Black Music* (Wm. R. Morrow) hardcover & paper, 1969.

JONES, MAX & JOHN CHILTON, *Louis: The Louis Armstrong Story* (Little, Brown & Co.) 256 pp, 1972.

KEEPNEWS, ORRIN & BILL GRAUER, *A Pictorial History of Jazz*, revised edition (Crown Publs.) 297 pp, 1966.

KEIL, CHARLES, *Urban Blues* (Univ. of Chicago Press) 231 pp, 1967.

KIMBALL, ROBERT & WILLIAM BOLCOM, *Reminiscing With Sissle & Blake* (The Viking Press) 254 pp, 1973.

KINKLE, ROGER D., *The Complete Encyclopedia of Popular Music and Jazz*, 1900-1950 in four volumes (Arlington House) Vol. 1, 464 pp, Vol. 2, 1266 pp, Vol. 3, 2000 pp, Vol. 4, 2644 pp, 1974.

KIRKEBY, ED, in collaboration with SINCLAIR TRAILL & DUNCAN P. SCHIEDT, *Ain't Misbehavin': The Story of Fats Waller* (Dodd, Mead & Co.) 248 pp, 1967.

LONGSTREET, STEPHEN, *Sportin' House: A History of the New Orleans Sinners and the Birth of Jazz* (Sherbourne Press, Inc.) 293 pp, 1966.

MCCARTHY, ALBERT, *Big Band Jazz* (G.P. Putnam's Sons) 360 pp, 1974.

MERRYMAN, RICHARD, *Louis Armstrong: A Self-Portrait* (The Eakins Press) 59 pp (cloth & paper) 1972.

MINGUS, CHARLES, edited by NEL KING, *Beneath the Underdog* (Alfred A. Knopf) 366 pp, 1971.

MOORE, CARMAN, *Somebody's Angel Child:* The Story of Bessie Smith (Thos. Y. Crowell Co.) 122 pp, 1970.

NANRY, CHARLES (Ed.), *American Music: From Storyville to Woodstock (Transaction Books) 290 pp, 1972.*

OLIVER, PAUL, *The Story of the Blues* (Chilton Book Co.) 176 pp, 1969.

OTIS, JOHNNY, *Listen To The Lambs* (W.W. Norton & Co.) 256 pp, 1968.

PANASSIE, HUGUES, *Louis Armstrong* (Charles Scribner's Sons) 149 pp, 1972.

PHILLIPS, JANE, *Mojo Hand* (Trident Press) 180 pp, 1968.

PLEASANTS, HENRY, *The Great American Popular Singers* (Simon & Schuster) 384 pp, 1974.

PLEASANTS, HENRY, *Serious Music & All That Jazz* (Simon & Schuster) 256 pp, 1969.

RICHARDS, KENNETH G., *Louis Armstrong* (Childrens Press) 95 pp, 1968.

RIVELLI, PAULINE & ROBERT LEVIN, Eds., *Rock Giants*, Jazz & Pop (World Publ. Co.) 125 pp, 1970.

ROACH, HILDRED, *Black American Music, Past & Present* (Crescendo Publ. Co.) 199 pp, 1973.

ROONEY, JAMES, *Bossmen: Bill Monroe & Muddy Waters* (Dial Press) 159 pp.

ROSE, AL & EDMOND SOUCHON, *New Orleans Jazz: A Family Album* (Louisiana State Univ. Press) 310 pp, 1967.

ROXON, LILLIAN, *Rock Encyclopedia* (Grosset & Dunlap) 613 pp, 1969.

RUSSELL, ROSS, *Jazz Style in Kansas City and the Southwest* (Univ. of Cal. Press) 292 pp, 1972.

RUSSELL, ROSS, *Bird Lives: The High Life and Hard Times of Charlie (Yardbird) Parker* (Charterhouse) 1973.

SACKHEIM, ERIC, *The Blues Line* (Grossman Publs.) 500 pp, 1970.

SANFORD, HERB, *Tommy & Jimmy: The Dorsey Years*, intro. by Bing Crosby (Arlington House) 305 pp, 1972.

SCHAFER, WILLIAM J. & JOHANNES RIEDEL, *The Art of Ragtime* (Louisiana State University Press) 1973.

SCHULLER, GUNTHER, *Early Jazz; Its Roots and Musical Development* (Oxford Univ. Press) 401 pp, 1968.

SCOTT, ALLEN, *Jazz Educated, Man* (Amer. Int'l. Publs.) 133 pp, 1973.

SHACTER, JAMES D., *Piano Man*, The Story of Ralph Sutton (Jaynar Press, P.O. Box 3141 Merchandise Mart Plaza, Chicago, Ill. 60654) 244 pp, 1975.

SHAW, ARNOLD, *The Rock Revolution* (Crowell-Collier Press) 215 pp, 1969.

SHAW, ARNOLD, *The World of Soul* (Cowles Book Co. Inc.) 306 pp, 1970.

SHAW, ARNOLD, *The Street That Never Slept* (Coward, McCann & Geoghegan) 378 pp, 1972.

SIDRAN, BEN, *Black Talk* (Holt, Rinehart & Winston) 201 pp, 1971.

SIMON, GEORGE T., *The Big Bands* (Macmillan) 537 pp, 1967.

SIMON, GEORGE T., *Simon Says: The Sights and Sounds of the Swing Era* (Arlington House) 492 pp, 1972.

SIMON, GEORGE T., *Glenn Miller & His Orchestra* (Thos. Y. Crowell Co.) 473 pp, 1974.

SIMON, GEORGE T., *The Big Bands Songbook* (Thomas Y. Crowell Co.) 356 pp, 1975.

SIMOSKO, VLADIMIR & BARRY TEPPERMAN, *Eric Dolphy*, A Musical Biography & Discography (Smithsonian Institution Press) 132 pp, 1974.

SIMPKINS, C. O., *Coltrane: A Biography* (Herndon House) 287 pp, 1975.

SPELLMAN, A. B., *Four Lives in the Bebop Business* (Pantheon Press) 235 pp, 1966.

STAMBLER, IRWIN, *Encyclopedia of Pop, Rock & Soul* (St. Martin's Press) 609 pp, 1974.

STEARNS, MARSHALL & JEAN, *Jazz Dance*, The Story of American Vernacular Dance (Macmillan) 464 pp, 1968.

STEWART, REX, *Jazz Masters of the '30s* (Macmillan) 223 pp, 1972.

STODDARD, TOM (as told to), *Pops Foster—The Autobiography of A New Orleans Jazzman* (Univ. of Cal. Press) 207 pp, 1971.

SUDHALTER, RICHARD M. & PHILIP R. EVANS, *Bix, Man and Legend* (Harper & Row) 512 pp, 1974.

TANNER, PAUL & MAURICE GEROW, *A Study of Jazz* (Wm. C. Brown) 189 pp, 2nd Edition, 1973.

THOMAS, J. C., *Chasin' The Trane* (Doubleday) 252 pp, 1975.

WELLS, DICKY, *The Night People*, as told to Stanley Dance (Crescendo Publ. Co.) 122 pp, 1971.

WILDER, ALEC, *American Popular Song: The Great Innovators, 1900-1950* (Oxford Univ. Press) 536 pp, 1972.

WILLIAMS, MARTIN, *Jazz Masters of New Orleans* (Macmillan) 287 pp, 1967.

WILLIAMS, MARTIN, *The Jazz Tradition* (Oxford Univ. Press) 232 pp, 1970.

WILLIAMS, MARTIN, *Jazz Masters In Transition 1957-69* (Macmillan) 288 pp, 1970.

WILMER, VALERIE, *Jazz People* (The Bobbs-Merrill Co.) 167 pp, 1971.

WILSON, JOHN S., *Jazz: The Transition Years, 1940-1960* (Appleton-Century-Crofts) 185 pp, 1967.